Denver Regional

street guide

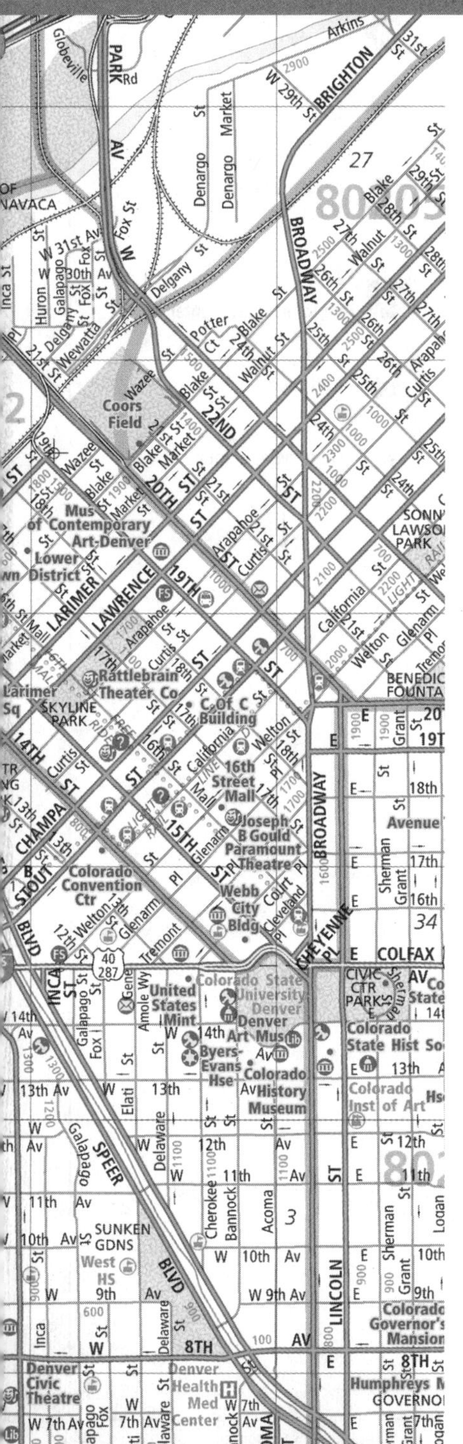

Contents

Introduction

Using Your Street Guide	A
PageFinder™ Map	B
Legend	D
We've Got You Covered	E

Maps

Downtown Map	F
Street Guide Detail Maps	1269-2955
Vicinity Map	Inside back cover

Lists and Indexes

Cities & Communities Index	1
List of Abbreviations	3
Street Index and Points of Interest Index	4
Comment Card	Last page

PageFinder™ Map U.S. Patent No. 5,419,586
Canadian Patent No. 2,116,425
Patente Mexicana No. 188186

RAND McNALLY
Rand McNally Consumer Affairs
P.O. Box 7600
Chicago, IL 60680-9915
randmcnally.com

For comments or suggestions, please call (800) 777-MAPS (-6277)
or email us at:
consumeraffairs@randmcnally.com

Legend

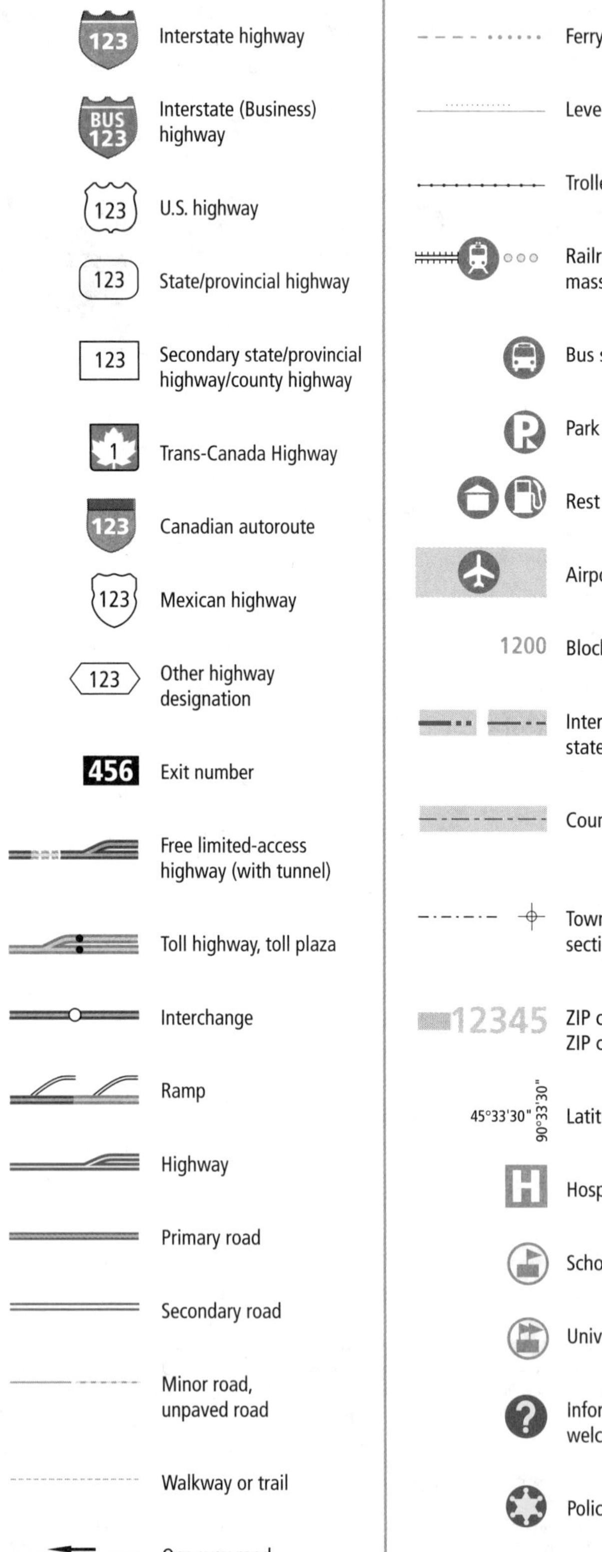
123
Interstate highway
BUS 123
Interstate (Business) highway
123
U.S. highway
123
State/provincial highway
123
Secondary state/provincial highway/county highway
1
Trans-Canada Highway
123
Canadian autoroute
123
Mexican highway
123
Other highway designation
456
Exit number
Free limited-access highway (with tunnel)
Toll highway, toll plaza
Interchange
Ramp
Highway
Primary road
Secondary road
Minor road, unpaved road
Walkway or trail
One-way road
Ferry, waterway
Levee
Trolley
Railroad, station, mass transit line
Bus station
Park and ride
Rest area, service area
Airport
1200
Block number
International boundary, state boundary
County boundary
Township/range boundary, section corner
12345
ZIP code boundary, ZIP code
45°33'30"
90°33'30"
Latitude, longitude
Hospital
School
University or college
Information/visitor center/ welcome center
Police/sheriff, etc.
FS
Fire station

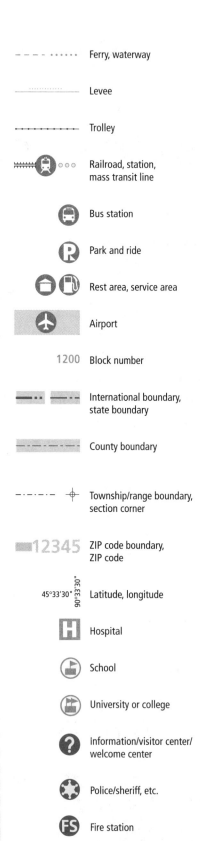

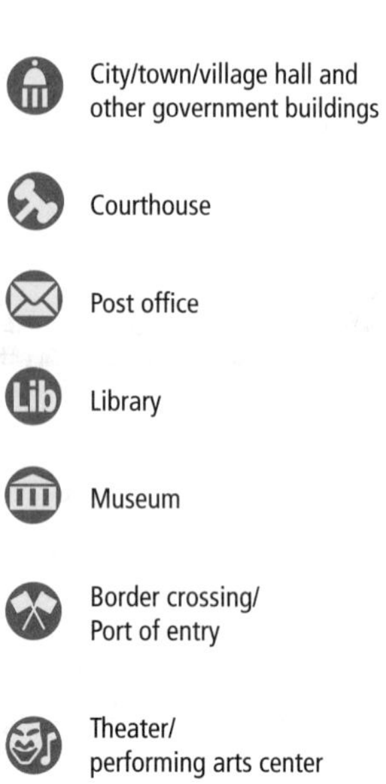
City/town/village hall and other government buildings
Courthouse
Post office
Lib
Library
Museum
Border crossing/ Port of entry
Theater/ performing arts center
Golf course
Other point of interest

we've got you COVERED

Rand McNally's broad selection of products is perfect for your every need. Whether you're looking for the convenience of write-on wipe-off laminated maps, extra maps for every car, or a Road Atlas to plan your next vacation or to use as a reference, Rand McNally has you covered.

Street Guides

Colorado Springs
Denver Metro
Denver Regional
Northern Colorado

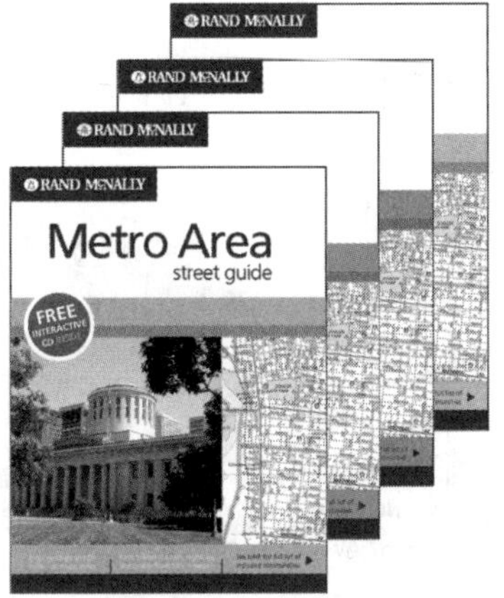

Folded Maps

EasyFinder® Laminated Maps

Boulder
Colorado Springs
Denver
Denver Front Range & Vicinity
Fort Collins

Paper Maps

Boulder/ Longmont
Colorado Springs
Denver
Denver Front Range & Vicinity
Fort Collins/ Loveland/ Greeley
Pueblo

Road Atlases

Road Atlas
Road Atlas & Travel Guide
Large Scale Road Atlas
Midsize Road Atlas
Deluxe Midsize Road Atlas
Pocket Road Atlas

Wherever Rand McNally products are sold or at
www.randmcnally.com

Downtown Denver

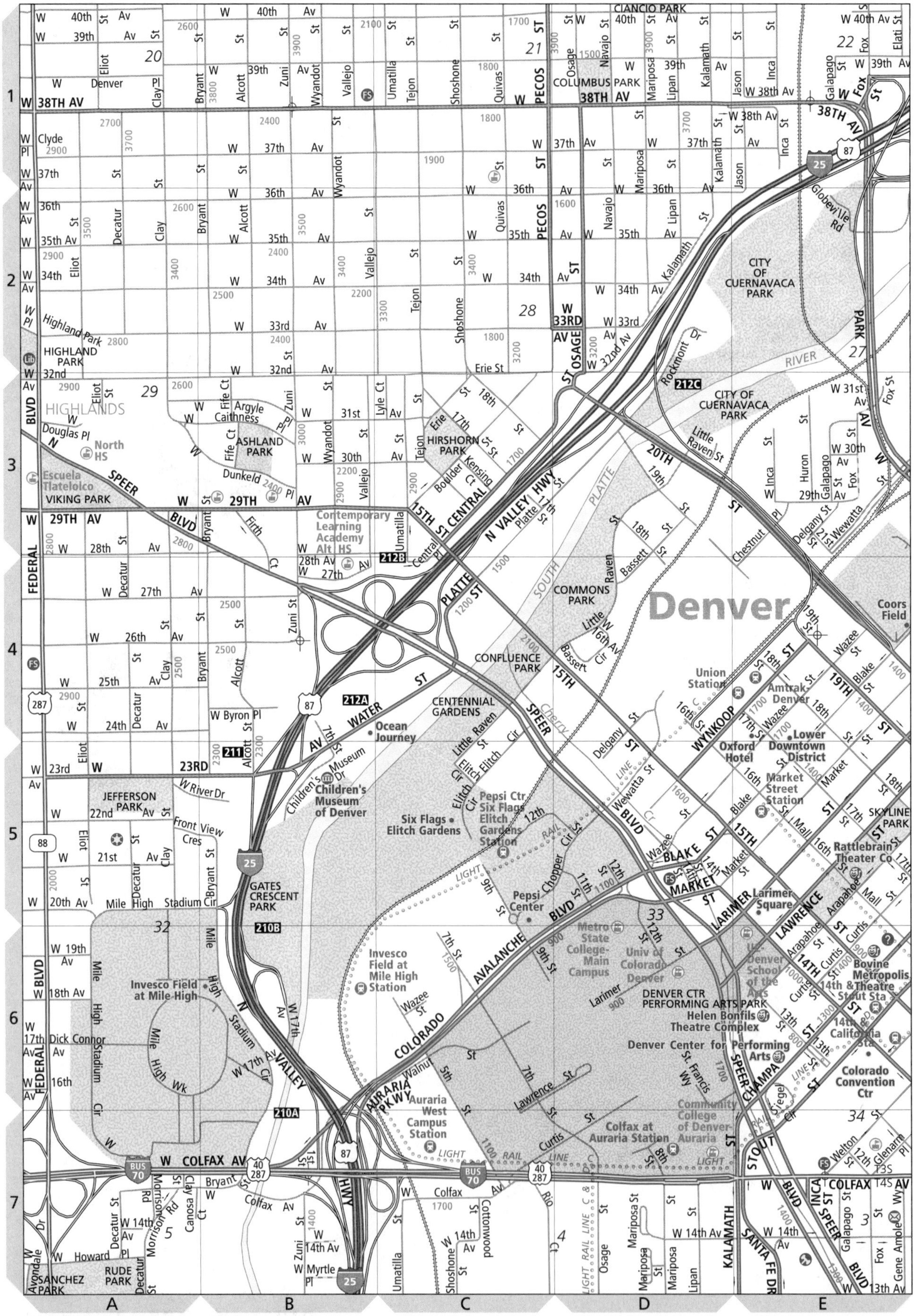

W 38TH AV

W 29TH AV

FEDERAL BLVD

N SPEER BLVD

N VALLEY HWY

W COLFAX AV

HIGHLAND PARK

HIGHLANDS

North HS

Escuela Tlatelolco

VIKING PARK

ASHLAND PARK

HIRSHORN PARK

COLUMBUS PARK

CIANCIO PARK

CITY OF CUERNAVACA PARK

Contemporary Learning Academy Alt. HS

COMMONS PARK

CONFLUENCE PARK

CENTENNIAL GARDENS

Ocean Journey

Children's Museum of Denver

Six Flags Elitch Gardens

Pepsi Ctr Six Flags Elitch Gardens Station

Pepsi Center

JEFFERSON PARK

GATES CRESCENT PARK

Invesco Field at Mile High

Invesco Field at Mile High Station

Denver

Coors Field

Union Station

Amtrak Denver

Oxford Hotel

Lower Downtown District

Market Street Station

SKYLINE PARK

Rattlebrain Theater Co.

Larimer Square

Metro State College-Main Campus

Univ of Colorado Denver

DENVER CTR PERFORMING ARTS PARK

Helen Bonfils Theatre Complex

Denver Center for Performing Arts

Denver School of the Arts

Bovine Metropolis Theatre

14th & Stout Sta

14th & California Sta

Colorado Convention Ctr

Auraria West Campus Station

Colfax at Auraria Station

Community College of Denver-Auraria

SANCHEZ PARK

RUDE PARK

A B C D E

1 2 3 4 5 6 7

Note: This grid references this map only

RAND McNALLY

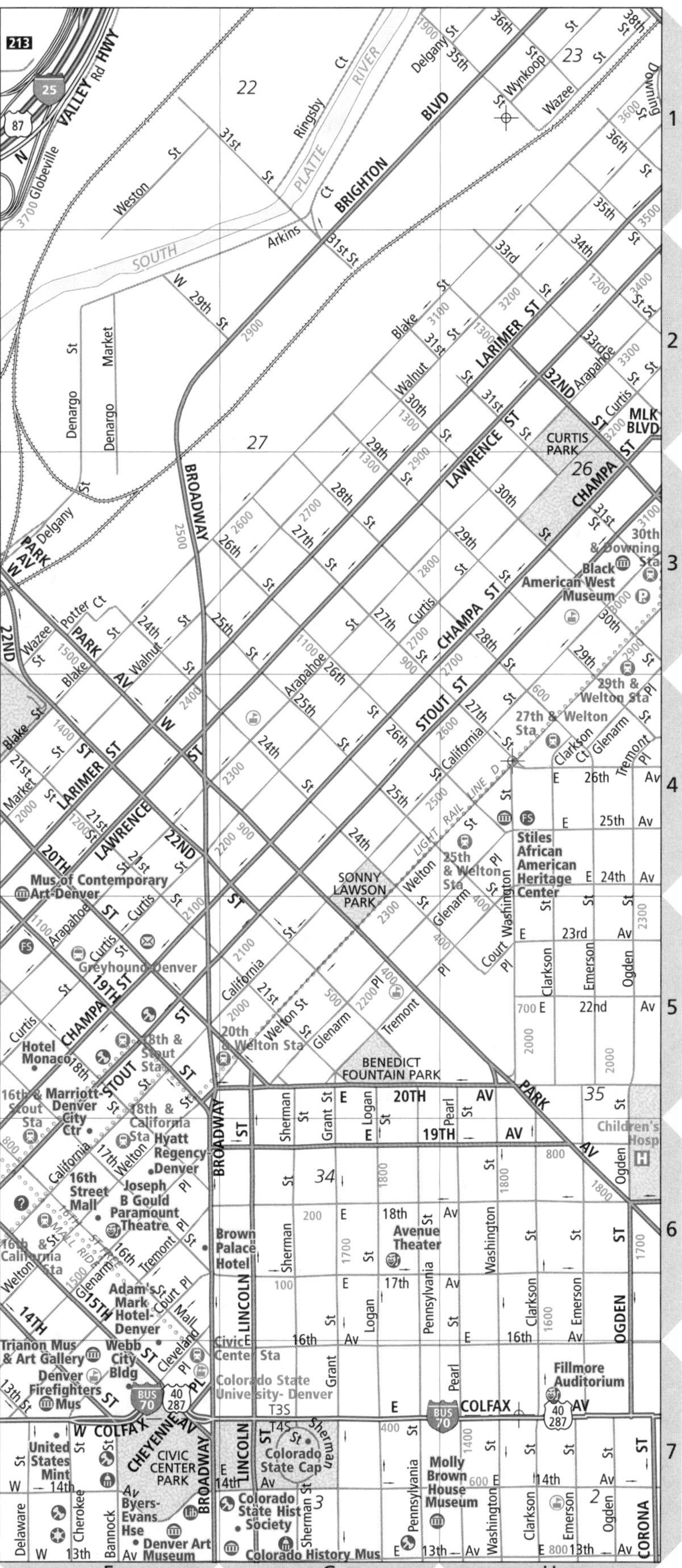

Points of Interest

14th & California Station	E6
14th & Stout Station	E6
16th & California Station	F6
16th & Stout Station	F5
18th & California Station	F6
18th & Stout Station	F5
20th & Welton Station	G5
25th & Welton Station	H4
27th & Welton Station	H4
29th & Welton Station	H4
30th & Downing Station	H3
Adam's Mark Hotel-Denver	F6
Amtrak-Denver	E4
Ashland Park	B3
Auraria West Campus Station	C6
Benedict Fountain Park	G5
Black American West Museum	H3
Brown Palace Hotel	G6
Byers-Evans House	F7
Centennial Gardens	C4
Children's Hospital	H6
Children's Museum of Denver	B5
Civic Center Park	F7
Civic Center Station	G7
Colfax at Auraria Station	D7
Colorado Convention Center	E6
Colorado History Museum	G7
Colorado State Capitol	G7
Colorado State Historical Society	G7
Colorado State University-Denver	G7
Commons Park	D4
Community College of Denver-Auraria	D6
Confluence Park	C4
Coors Field	E4
Denver Administrative Office	G7
Denver Art Museum	F7
Denver Center for Performing Arts	E6
Denver Center Performing Arts Park	D6
Denver City Hall	F7
Denver County Court	F7
Denver County Supreme Court	G7
Denver Firefighters Museum	F7
Denver Library-Central	F7
Denver Metro Convention & Visitors Bureau	F6
Denver Police Department-Headquarters	F7
Downtown Station Post Office	F5
Gates Crescent Park	B5
Greyhound-Denver	F5
Helen Bonfils Theatre Complex	D6
Hirshorn Park	C3
Hotel Monaco	F5
Invesco Field at Mile High	A6
Invesco Field at Mile High Station	B6
Joseph B Gould Paramount Theatre	F6
Larimer Square	E5
Lower Downtown District	E4
Market Street Station	E5
Metro State College-Main Campus	D6
Mile High Station Post Office	E7
Molly Brown House Museum	G7
Museum of Contemporary Art-Denver	F4
Ocean Journey	C4
Oxford Hotel	D5
Pepsi Center	C5
Pepsi Center Six Flags Elitch Gardens Station	C5
Six Flags Elitch Gardens	C5
Skyline Park	E5
Trianon Museum & Art Gallery	F7
Union Station	D4
United States Court of Appeals	F5
United States District Court	F5
United States Mint	F7
University of Colorado-Denver	D6
Viking Park	A3
Webb City Building	F7

1 in. = 1400 ft.

0 0.25 0.5

miles

1:24,000
1 in. = 2000 ft.
0 0.25 0.5
miles

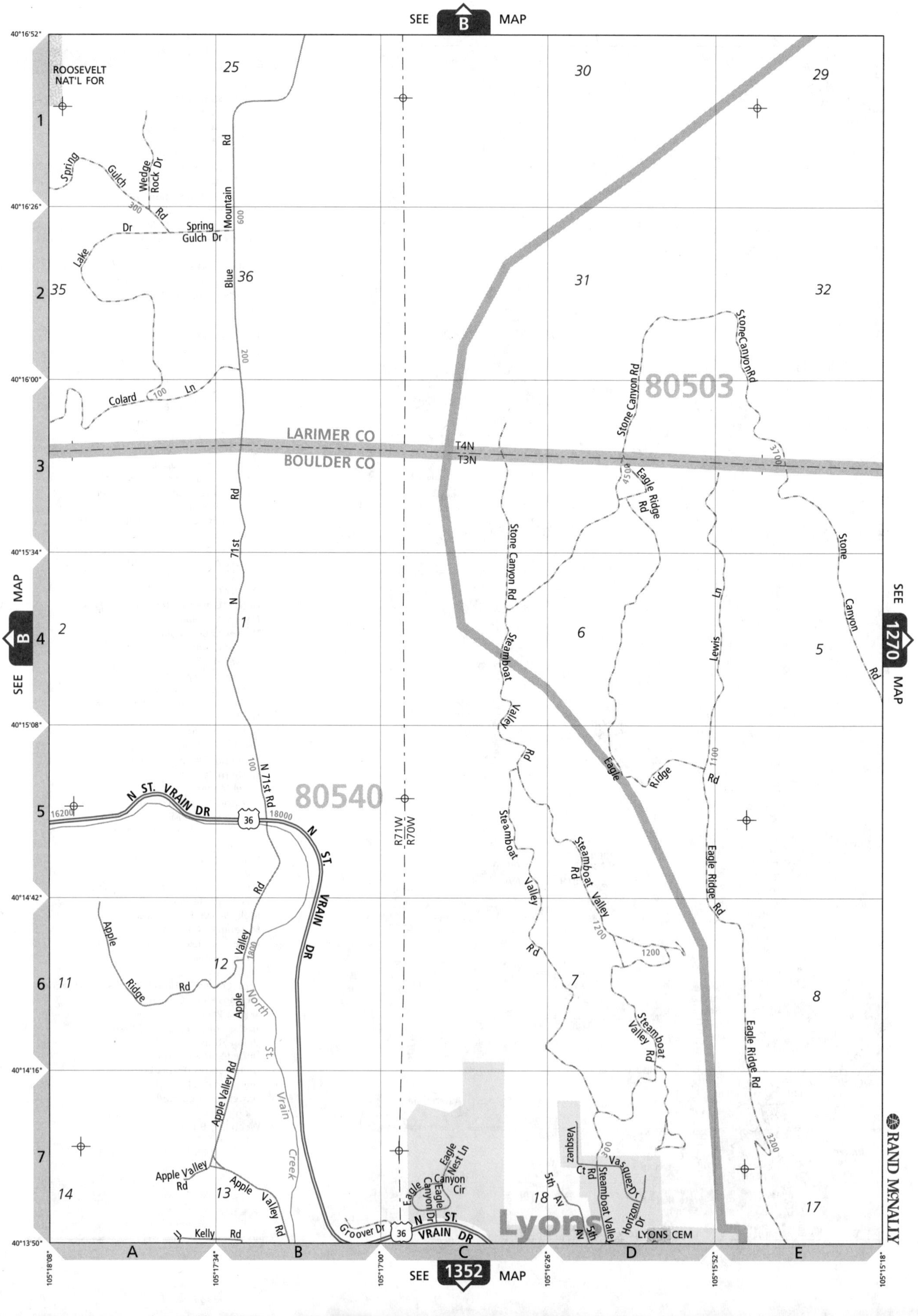

SEE B MAP
SEE B MAP
SEE 1270 MAP
SEE 1352 MAP

RAND McNALLY

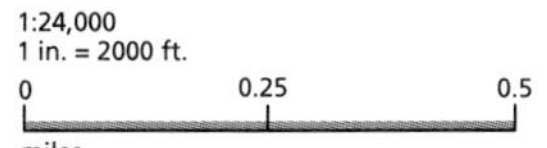

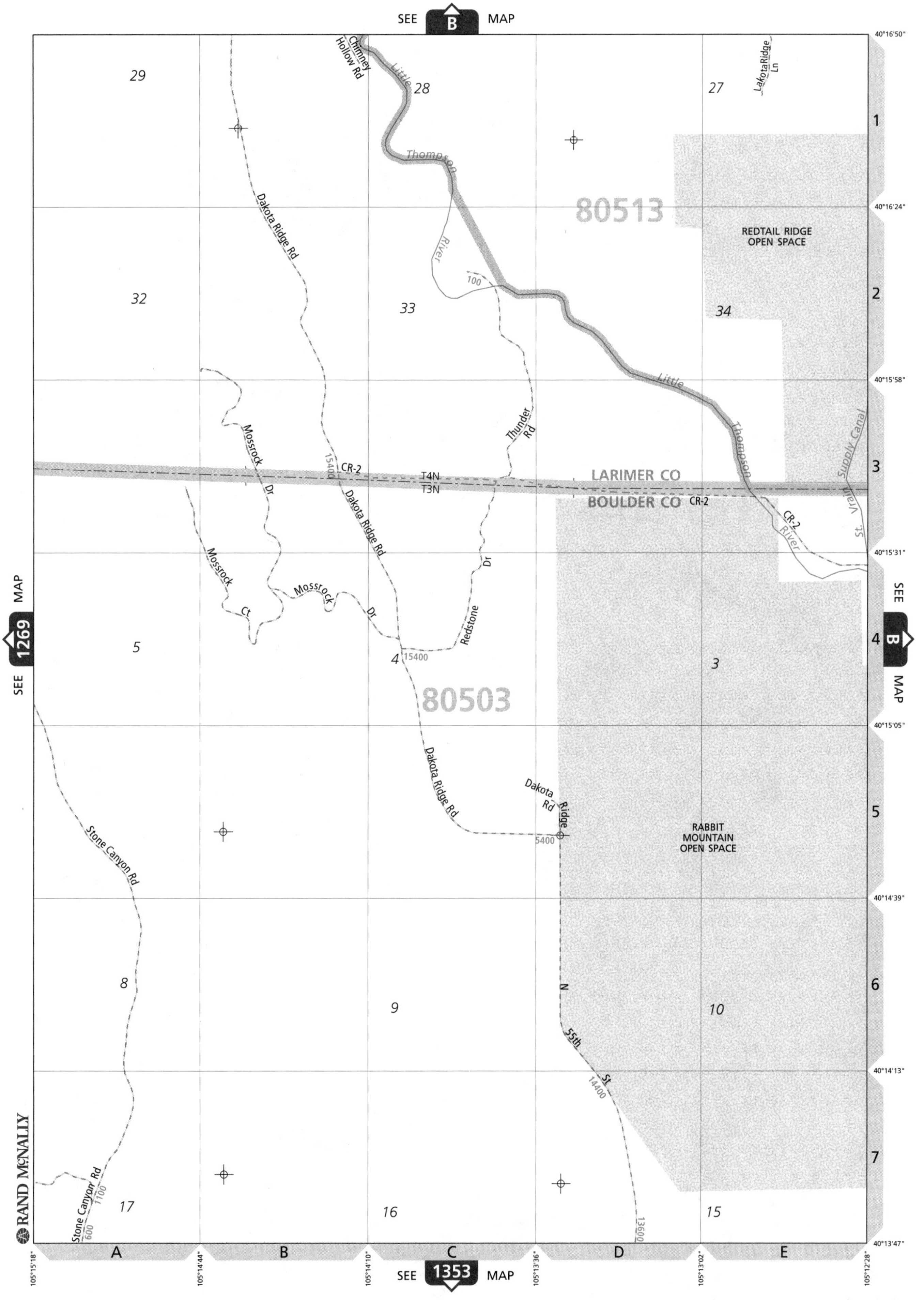

SEE B MAP

SEE 1269 MAP

SEE B MAP

SEE 1353 MAP

1:24,000
1 in. = 2000 ft.
0 0.25 0.5
miles

SEE 1269 MAP

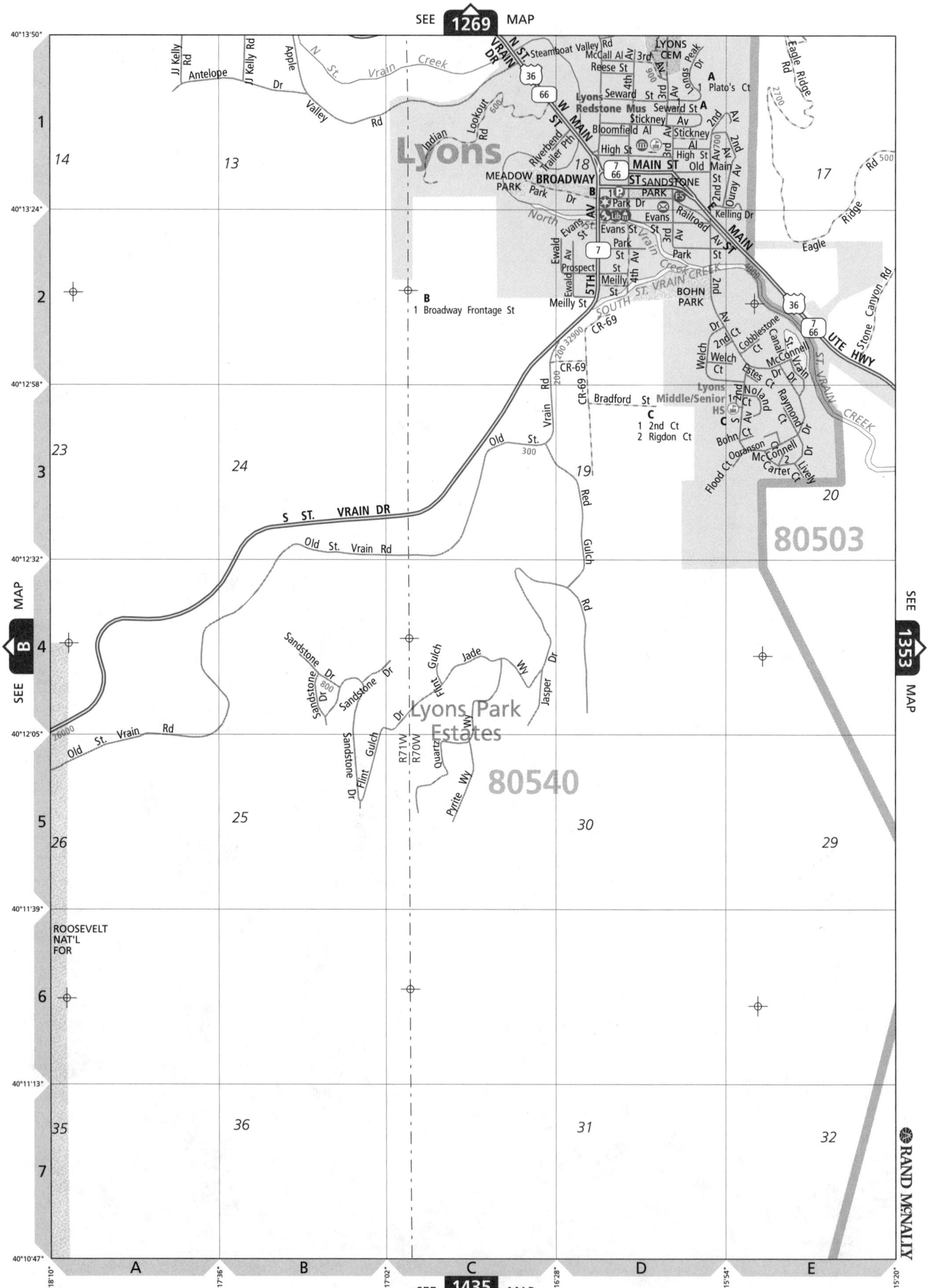

Lyons
MEADOW PARK
BOHN PARK
LYONS CEM
Lyons Redstone Mus
Lyons Middle/Senior HS
Lyons Park Estates
80503
80540
ROOSEVELT NAT'L FOR
S ST. VRAIN DR
Old St. Vrain Rd
UTE HWY
MAIN ST
BROADWAY
W MAIN ST
E MAIN ST
VRAIN DR
N ST.
5TH AV
Steamboat Valley Rd
McCall Al
Reese St
Seward St
Stickney Av
Stickney Al
Bloomfield Al
High St
Sandstone Park
Park Dr
Evans St
Railroad Av
Kelling Dr
Prospect St
Meilly St
Ewald Av
Antelope Dr
Apple Valley Rd
JJ Kelly Rd
Indian Lookout Rd
Riverbend Trailer Pth
North St. Vrain Creek
South St. Vrain Creek
Red Gulch Rd
Bradford St
CR-69
Eagle Ridge Rd
Stone Canyon Rd
Sandstone Dr
Flint Gulch Dr
Jade Wy
Jasper Dr
Quartz Wy
Pyrite Wy
Welch Ct
Cobblestone Ct
Canal Dr
McConnell Dr
Estes Ct
Noland Ct
Raymond Ct
Bohn Ct
Ooranson Ct
Flood Ct
Carter Ct
Lively Dr
Longs Peak Dr
Ouray Av
R71W R70W

A
1 Plato's Ct

B
1 Broadway Frontage St

C
1 2nd Ct
2 Rigdon Ct

13 14 17 18 19 20 23 24 25 26 29 30 31 32 35 36

40°13'50" 40°13'24" 40°12'58" 40°12'32" 40°12'05" 40°11'39" 40°11'13" 40°10'47"
105°18'10" 105°17'36" 105°17'02" 105°16'28" 105°15'54" 105°15'20"

SEE B MAP
SEE 1353 MAP
SEE 1435 MAP

RAND McNALLY

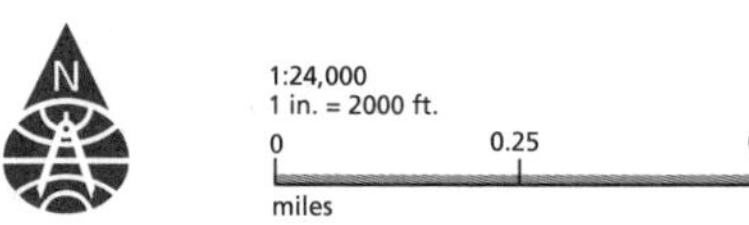

SEE 1270 MAP

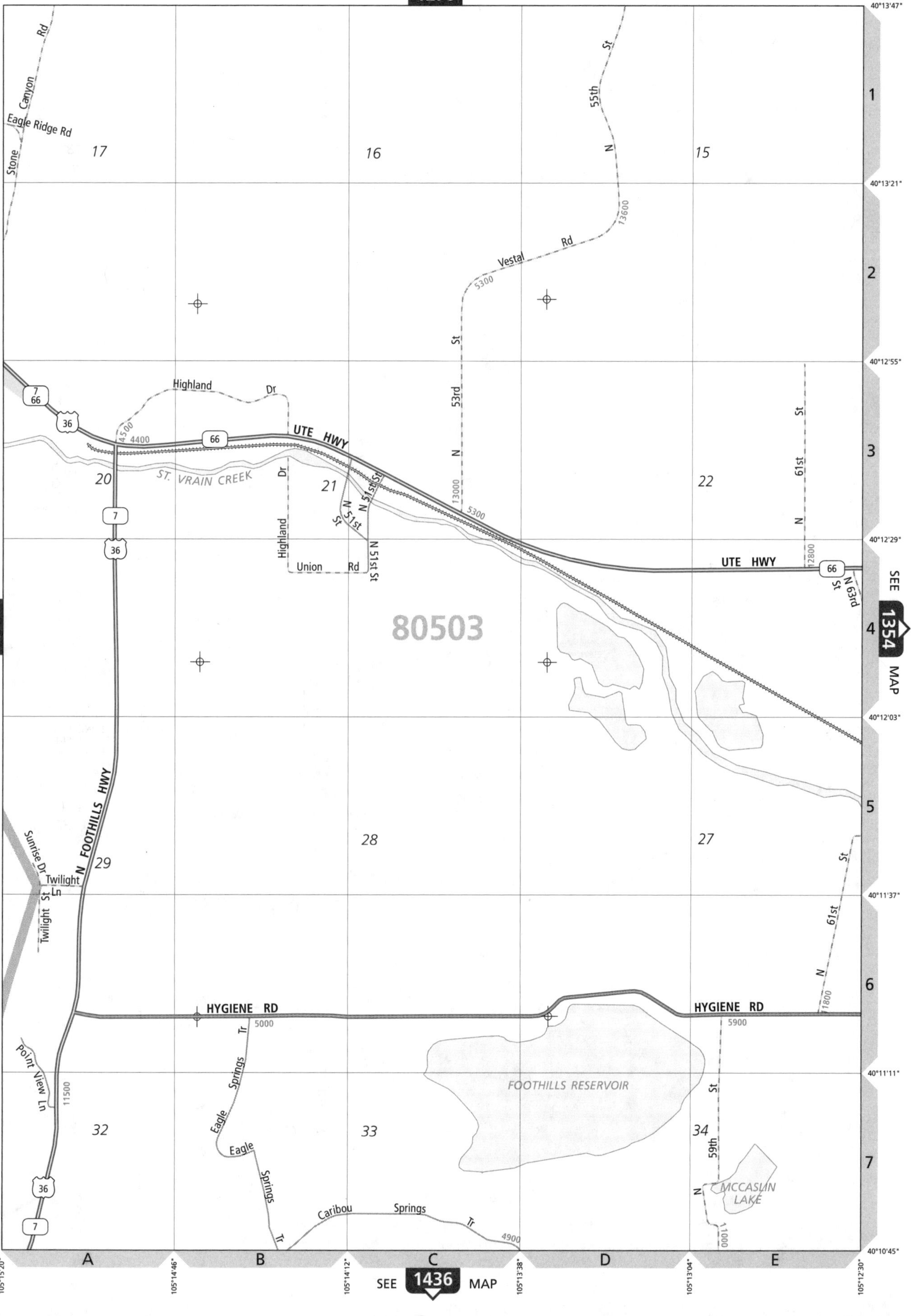

SEE 1352 MAP

SEE 1354 MAP

SEE 1436 MAP

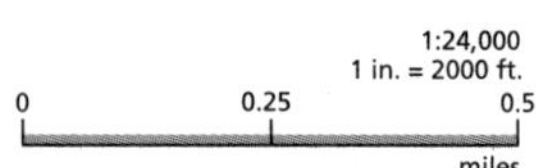

SEE B MAP

SEE 1353 MAP

SEE 1355 MAP

SEE 1437 MAP

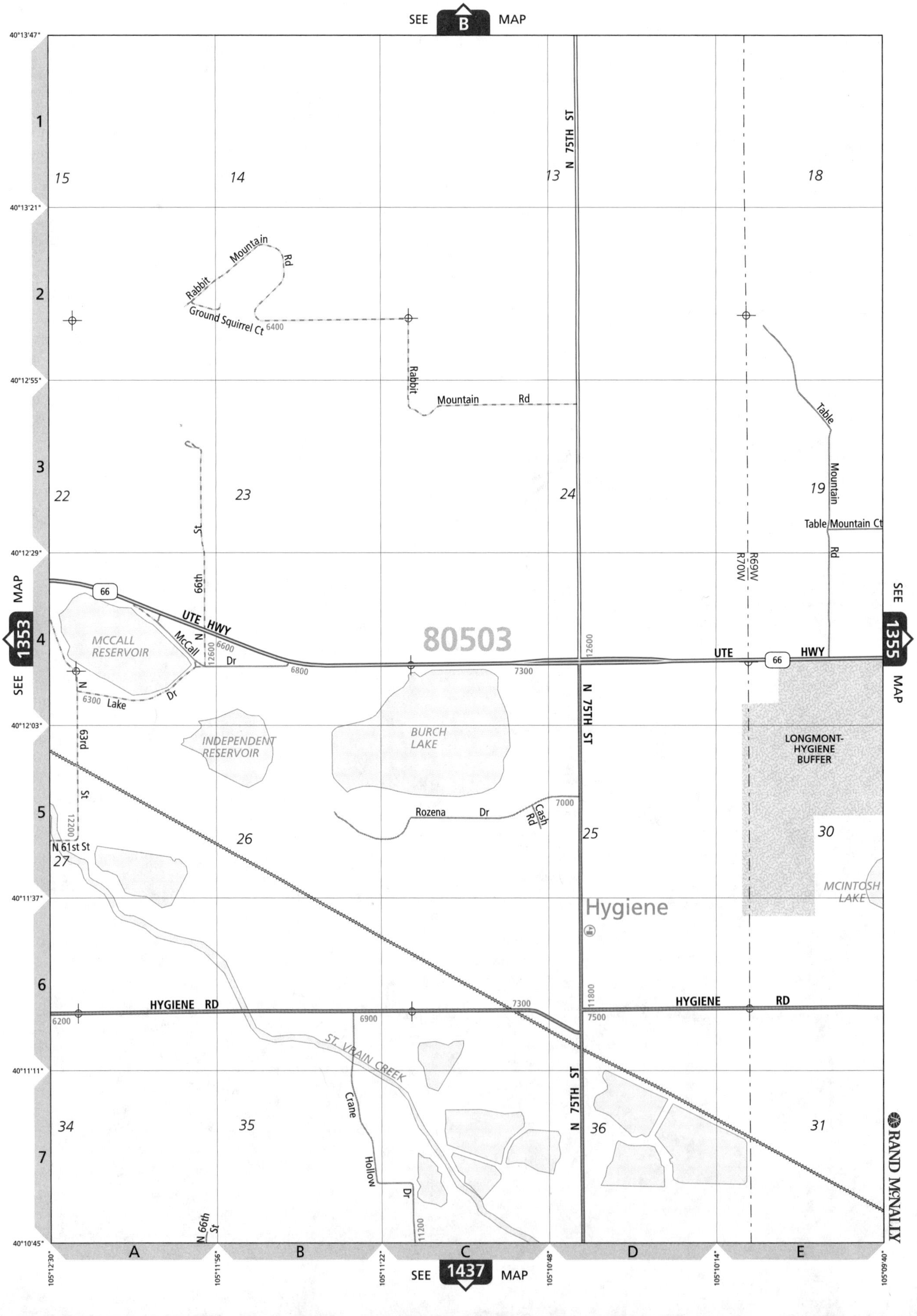

1:24,000
1 in. = 2000 ft.
0 0.25 0.5
miles

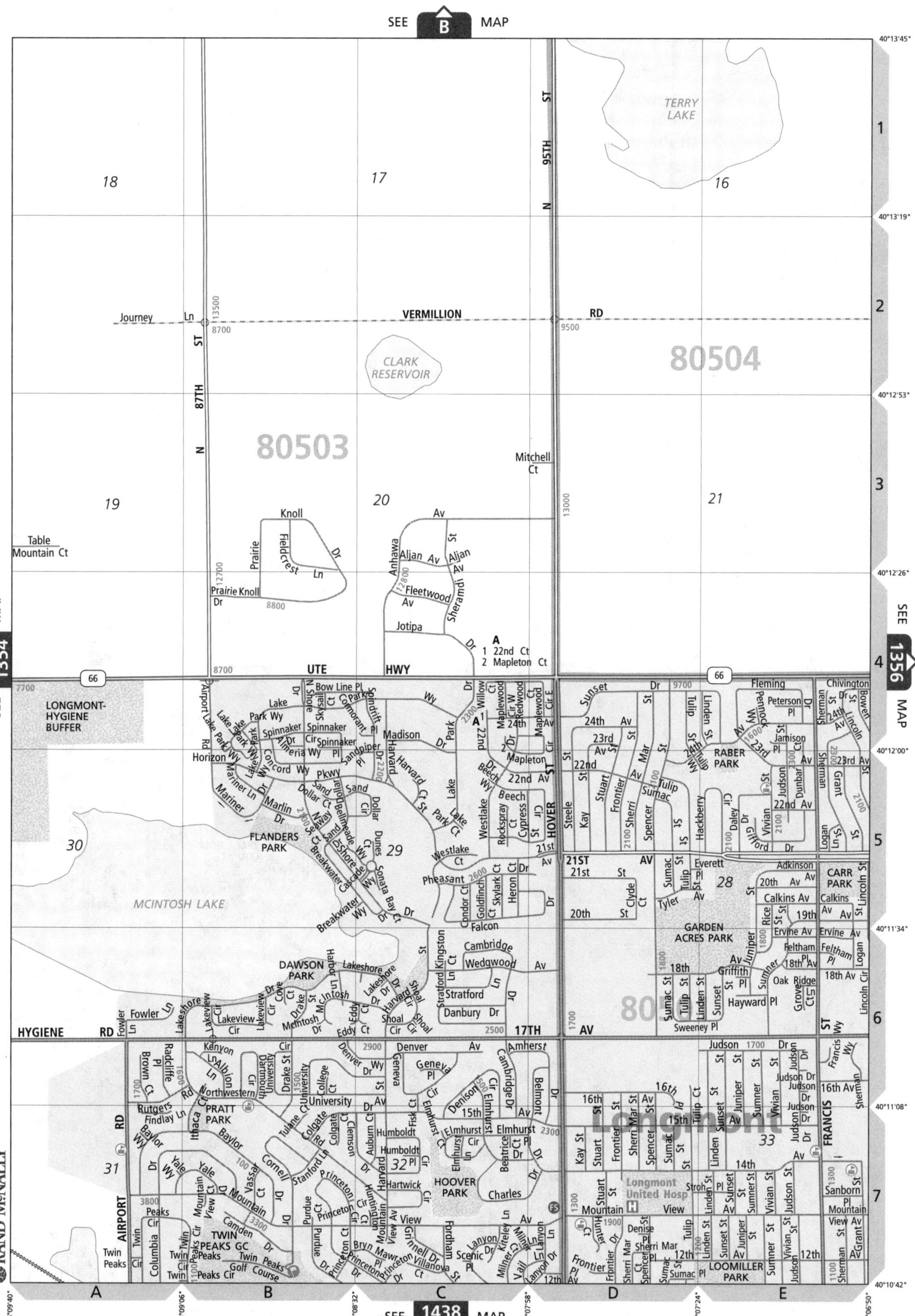

1:24,000
1 in. = 2000 ft.
0 0.25 0.5
miles

SEE B MAP

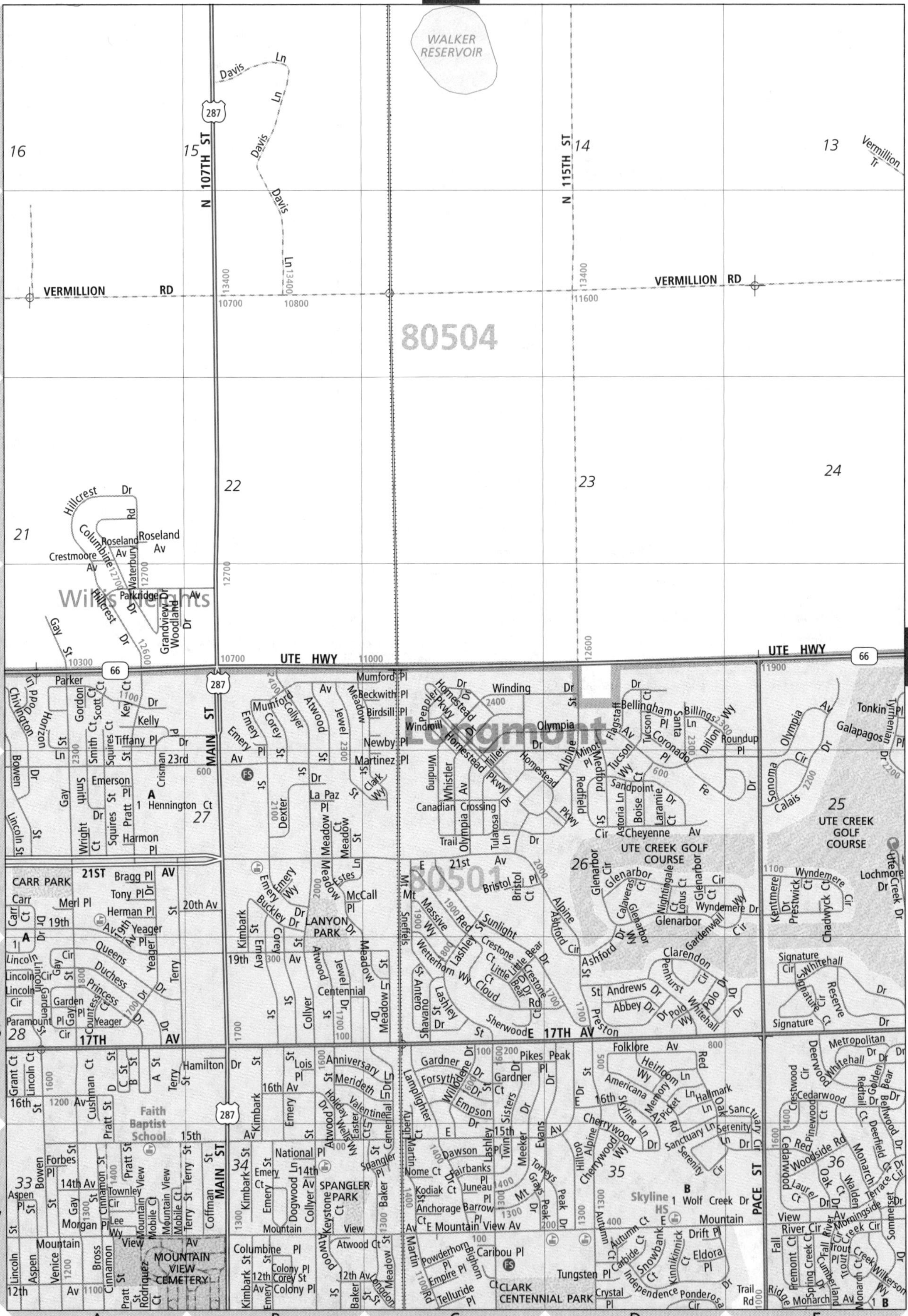

WALKER RESERVOIR

VERMILLION RD

N 107TH ST

N 115TH ST

UTE HWY

MAIN ST

PACE ST

17TH AV

21ST AV

80504

80501

Longmont

Wills Heights

UTE CREEK GOLF COURSE

CARR PARK

LANYON PARK

SPANGLER PARK

MOUNTAIN VIEW CEMETERY

CLARK CENTENNIAL PARK

Faith Baptist School

Skyline HS

SEE MAP 1355

SEE MAP 1357

SEE 1439 MAP

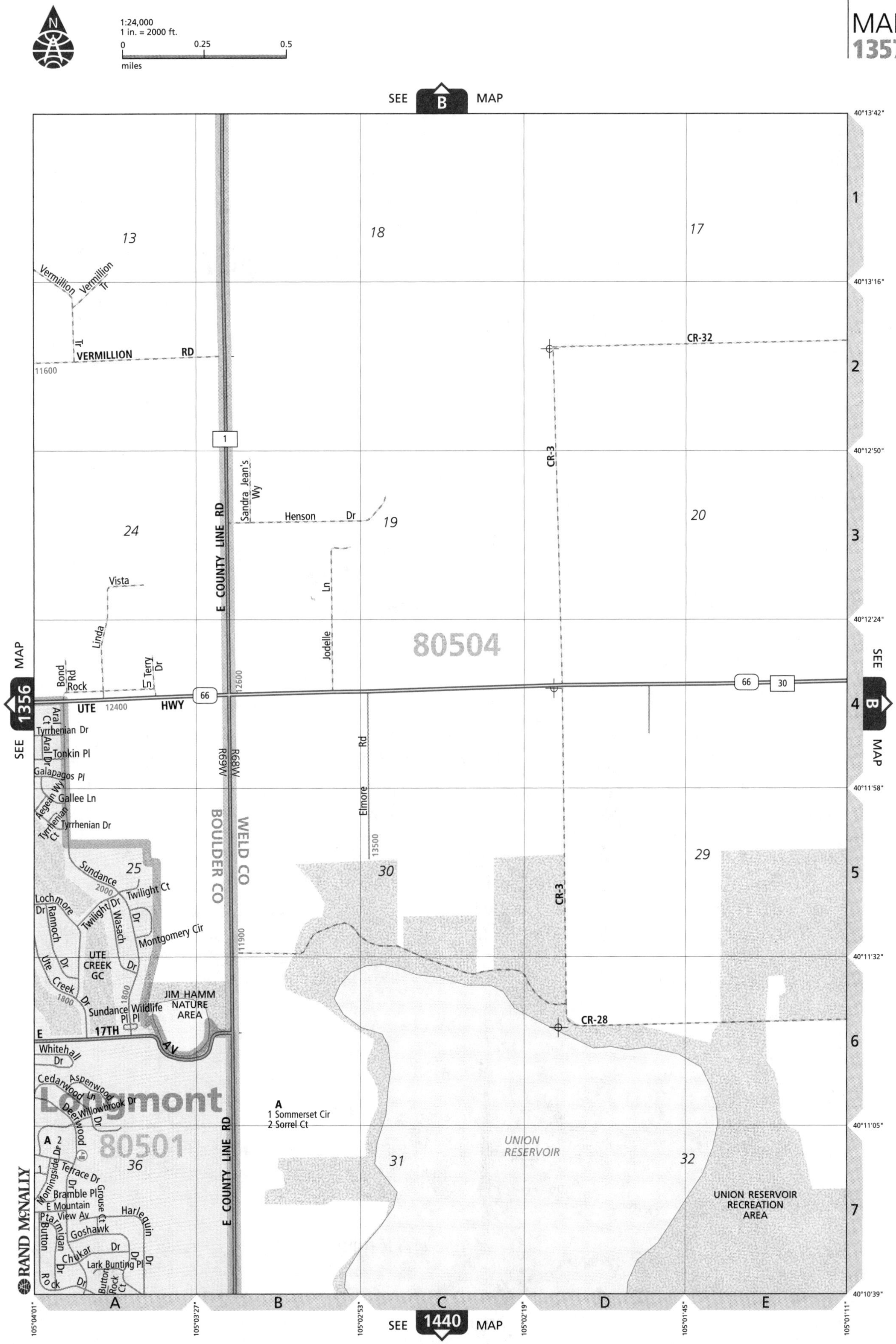

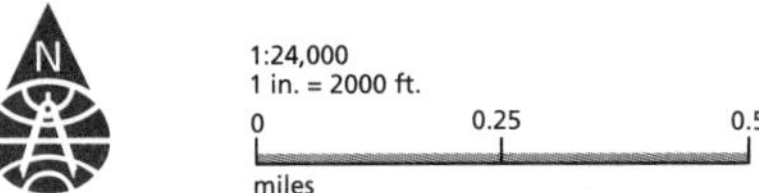

SEE B MAP
SEE 1356 MAP
SEE B MAP
SEE 1440 MAP

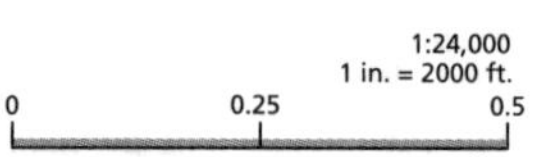

SEE 1352 MAP

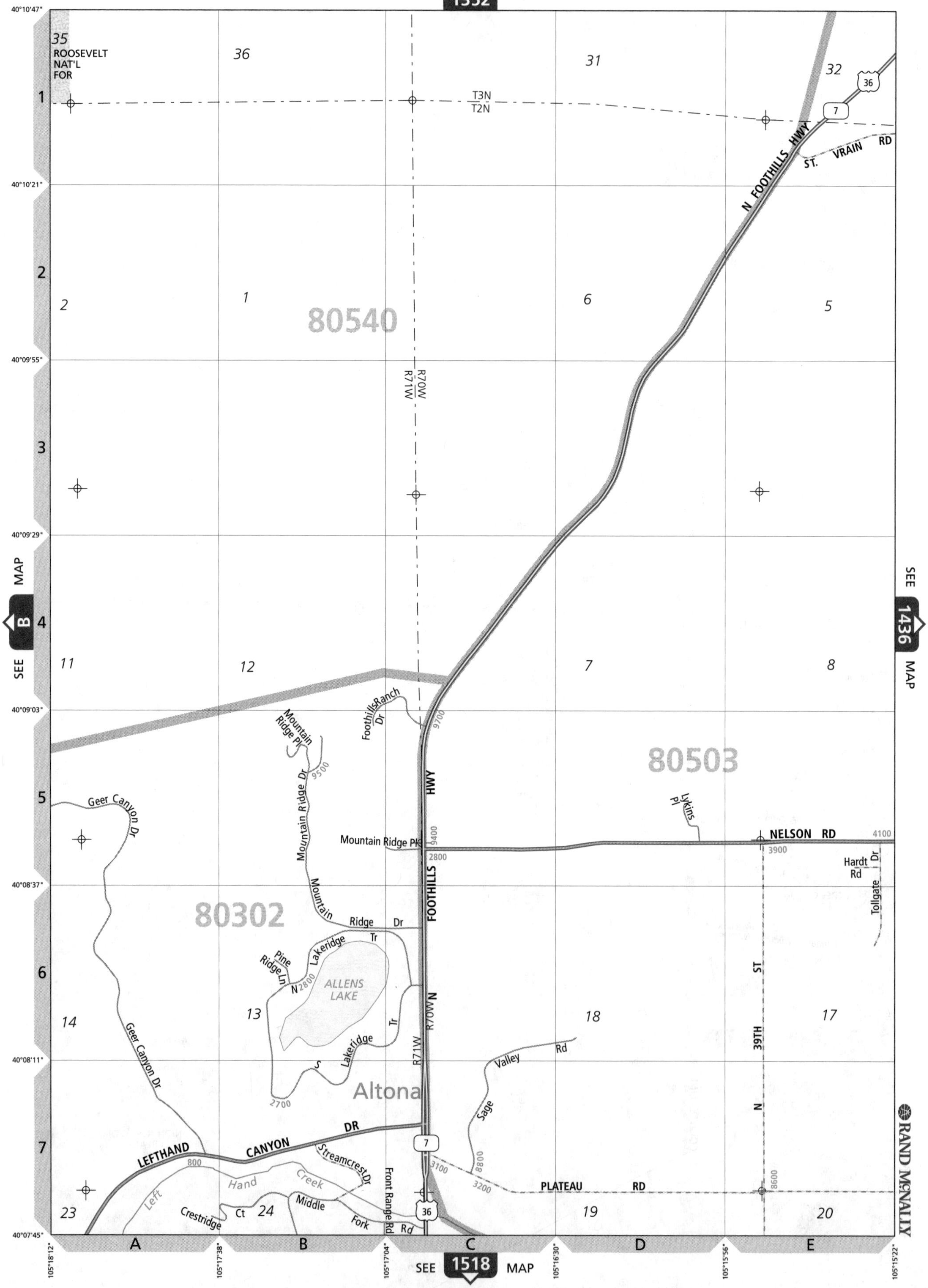

SEE B MAP

SEE 1436 MAP

SEE 1518 MAP

1:24,000
1 in. = 2000 ft.
0 0.25 0.5
miles

SEE 1353 MAP

SEE 1435 MAP

SEE 1437 MAP

SEE 1519 MAP

1:24,000
1 in. = 2000 ft.
0 0.25 0.5
miles

SEE 1354 MAP

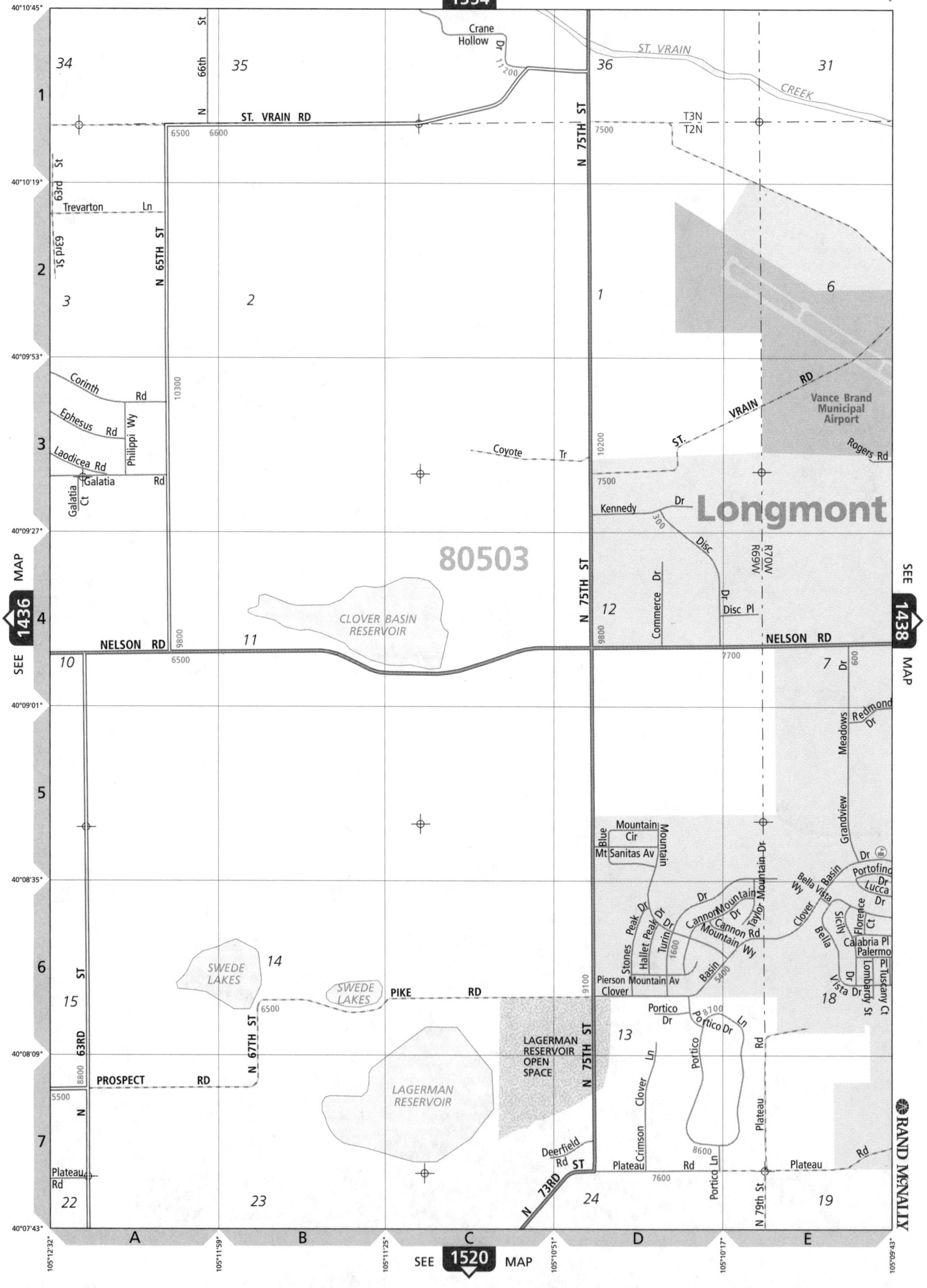

40°10'45"
40°10'19"
40°09'53"
40°09'27"
40°09'01"
40°08'35"
40°08'09"
40°07'43"

1 2 3 4 5 6 7

A B C D E

105°12'32" 105°11'59" 105°11'25" 105°10'51" 105°10'17" 105°09'43"

SEE 1436 MAP

SEE 1438 MAP

SEE 1520 MAP

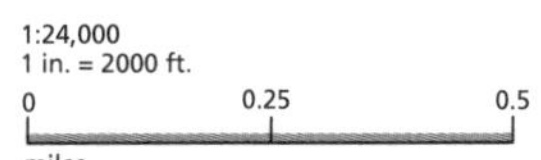

SEE 1355 MAP

SEE 1437 MAP

SEE 1439 MAP

Longmont

80501

80503

80504

Dominion

TWIN PEAKS GOLF COURSE

GOLDEN PONDS PARK & NATURE AREA

Vance Brand Mun Arpt

Boulder County Fairgrounds Park

Twin Peaks Mall

ISAAK WALTON PARK

WILLOW CREEK PARK

LEFTHAND CREEK PARK

AFFOLTER PARK

SUNSET PARK

VALLEY PARK

LOOMILLER PARK

Longmont HS

SUNSET GC

A
1 Thornwood Wy
2 Honeysuckle Wy
3 Sandcherry Pl
4 E Buckthorn Dr

B
1 Emerald Dr

SEE 1521 MAP

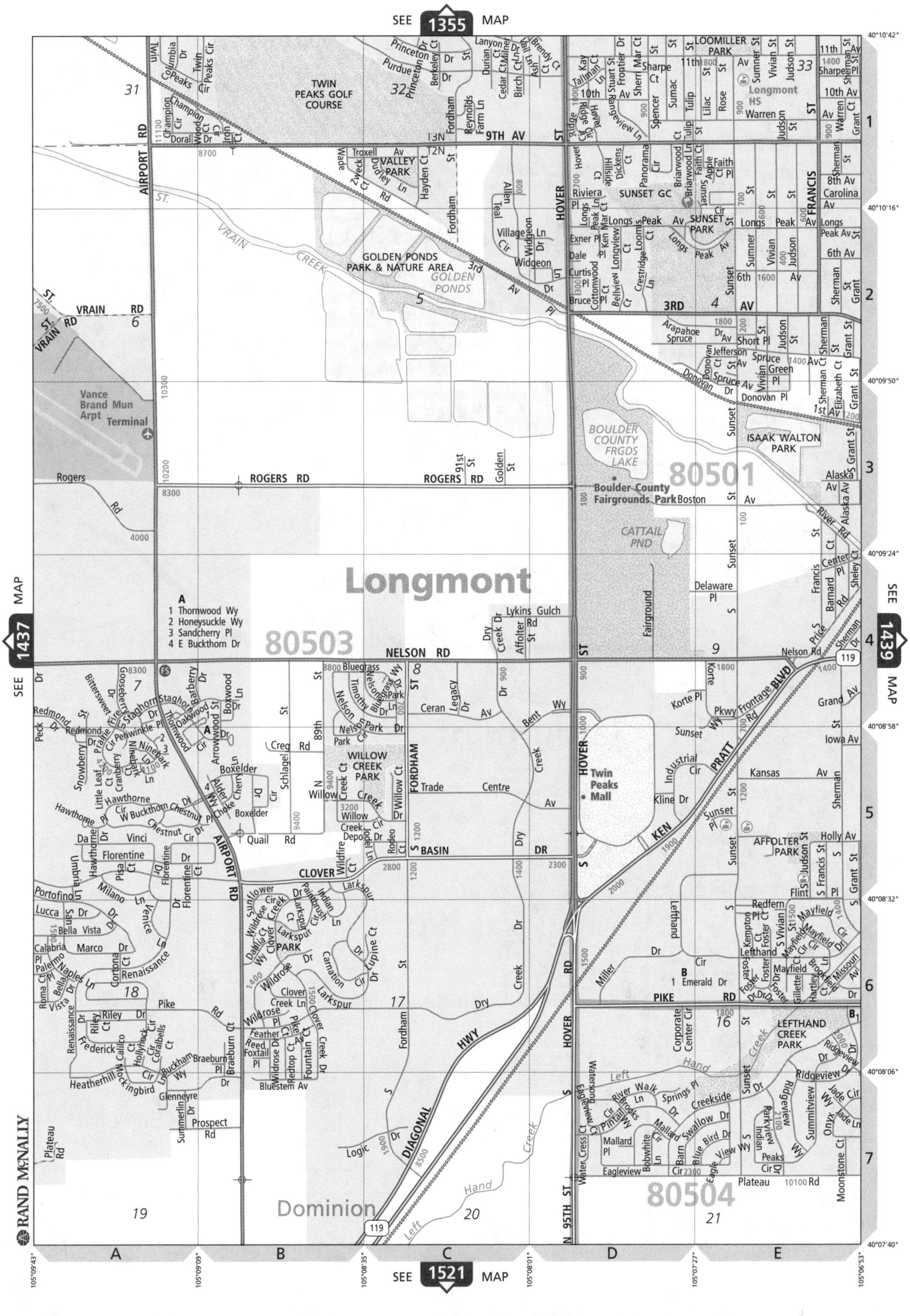

1:24,000
1 in. = 2000 ft.
0 0.25 0.5
miles

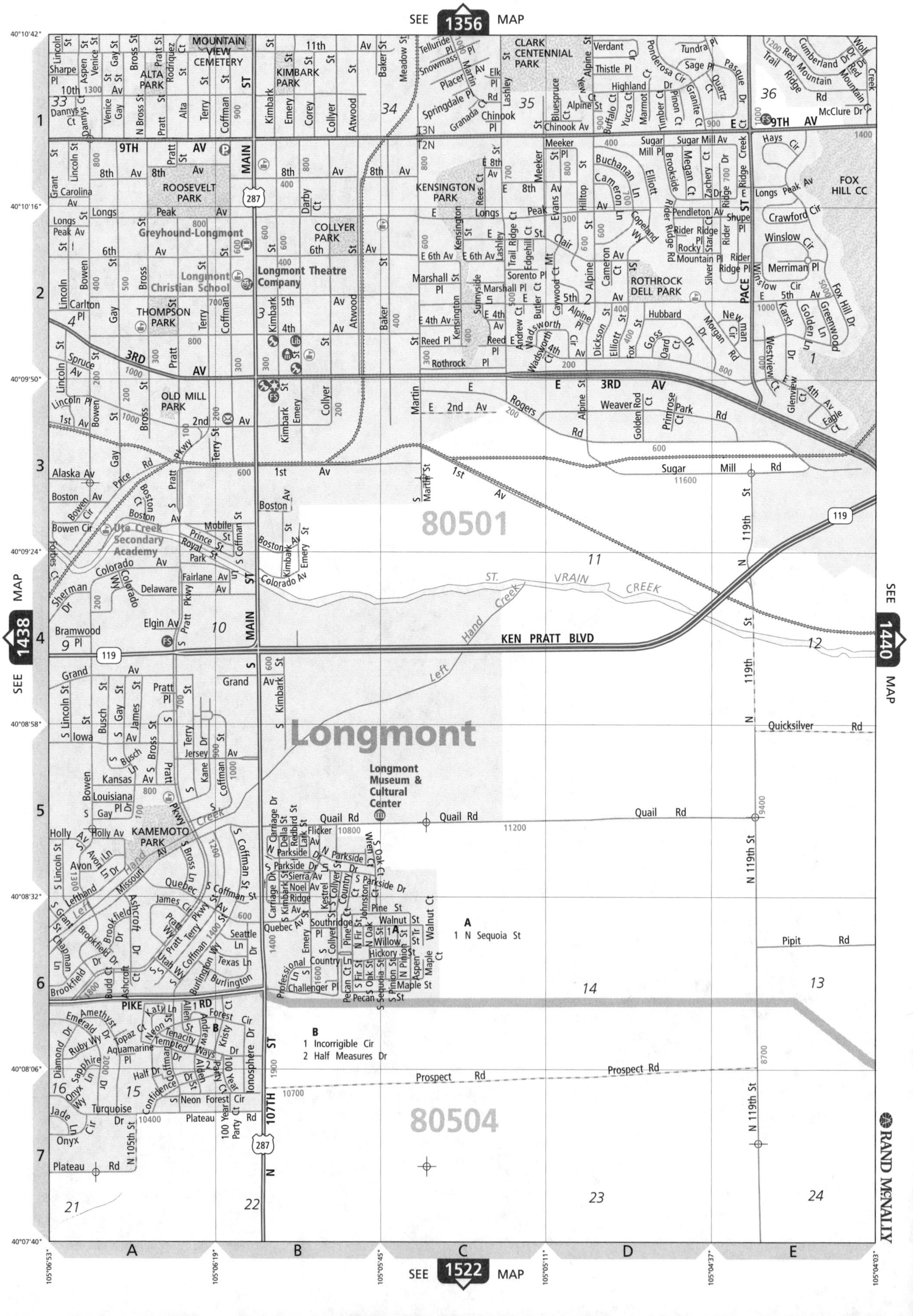

SEE 1356 MAP

Longmont

80501

80504

SEE 1438 MAP

SEE 1440 MAP

A
1 N Sequoia St

B
1 Incorrigible Cir
2 Half Measures Dr

RAND McNALLY

SEE 1522 MAP

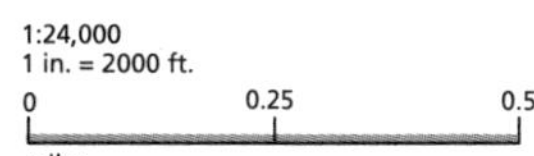

SEE 1357 MAP

Longmont

A
1 Button Rock Ct

B
1 Shoshone
2 W Longview Blvd
3 E Longview Blvd
4 S Longview Blvd

UNION RESERVOIR

UNION RESERVOIR RECREATION AREA

FOX HILL COUNTRY CLUB

SANDSTONE RANCH COMMUNITY PARK

SANDSTONE RANCH DISTRICT PARK

80501

80504

E COUNTY LINE RD

BOULDER CO

WELD CO

KEN PRATT BLVD

E 9TH AV

E 3RD AV

CR-26

CR-3.5

CR-20

CO-119

ST. VRAIN CREEK

Quicksilver Rd

Pipit Rd

Pike Rd

Vista View Dr

Skyway Dr

Fairview Dr

Peak Av

Colorful Av

Blue Mountain Rd

T3N

T2N

R69W

R68W

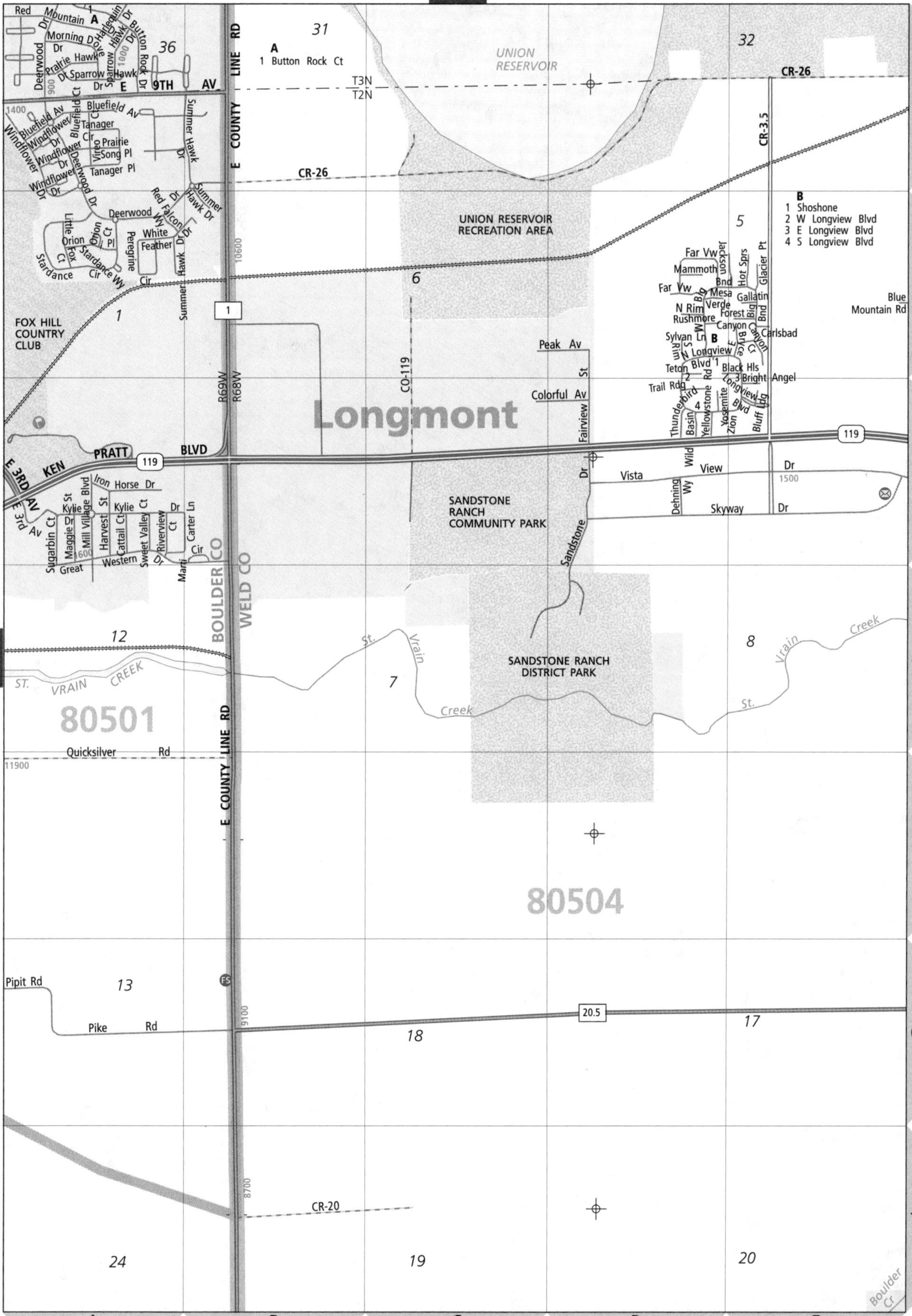

SEE 1439 MAP

SEE B MAP

SEE 1523 MAP

1:24,000
1 in. = 2000 ft.
0 0.25 0.5
miles

SEE B MAP

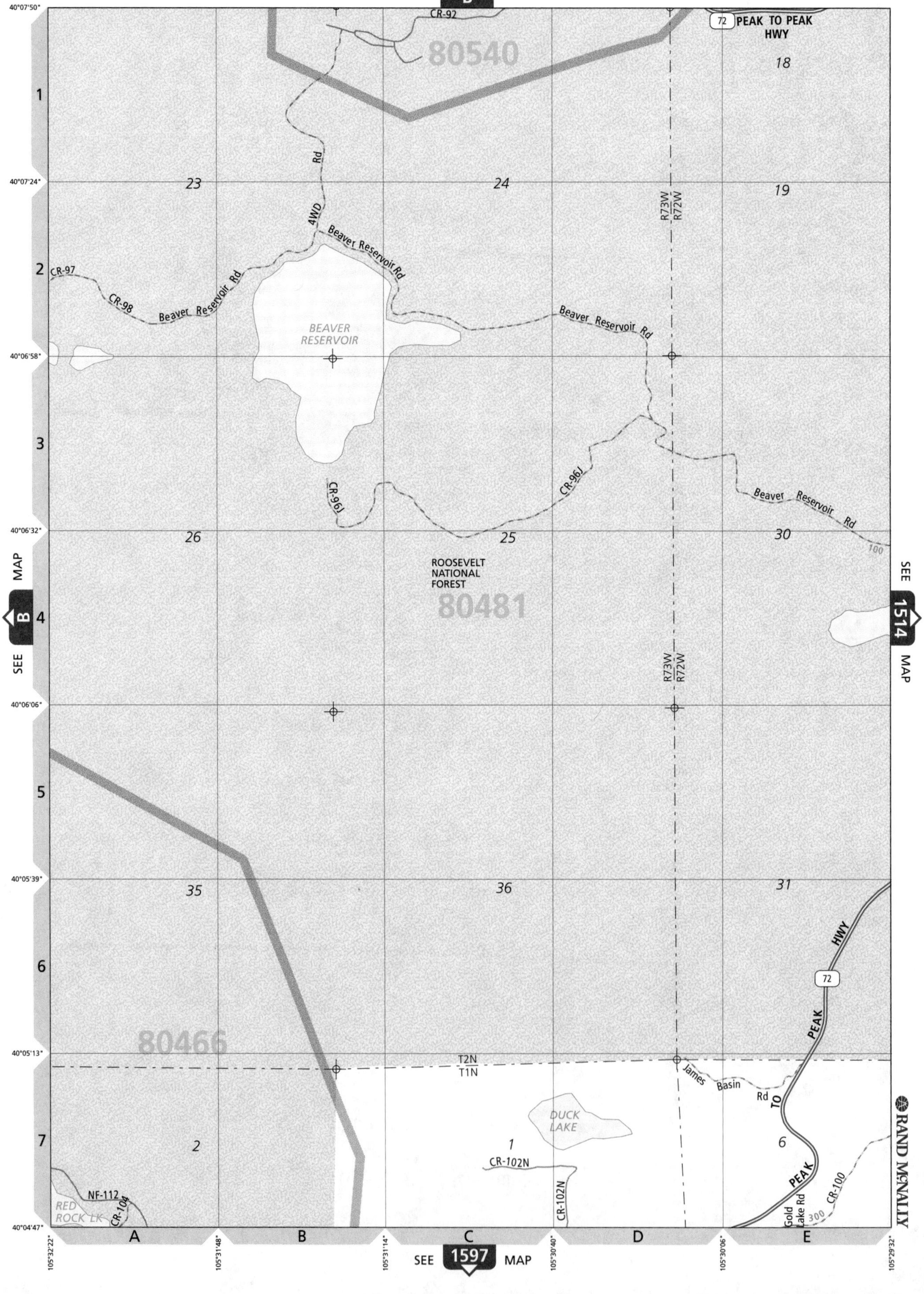

SEE B MAP

SEE 1514 MAP

SEE 1597 MAP

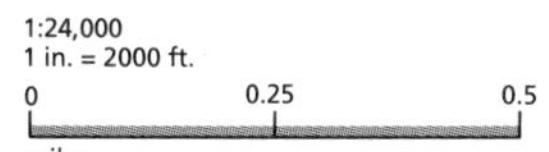

SEE B MAP

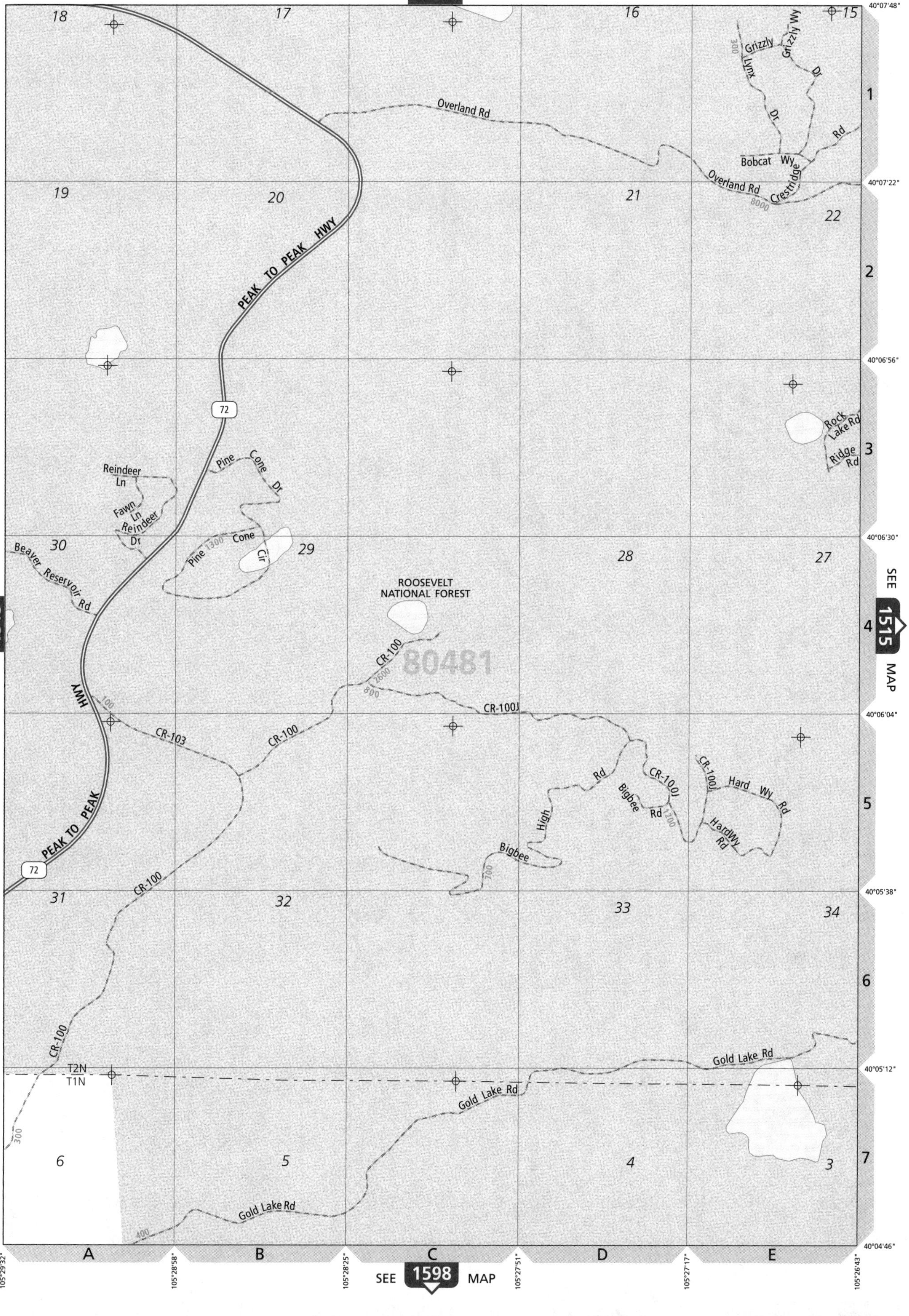

SEE 1513 MAP

SEE 1515 MAP

SEE 1598 MAP

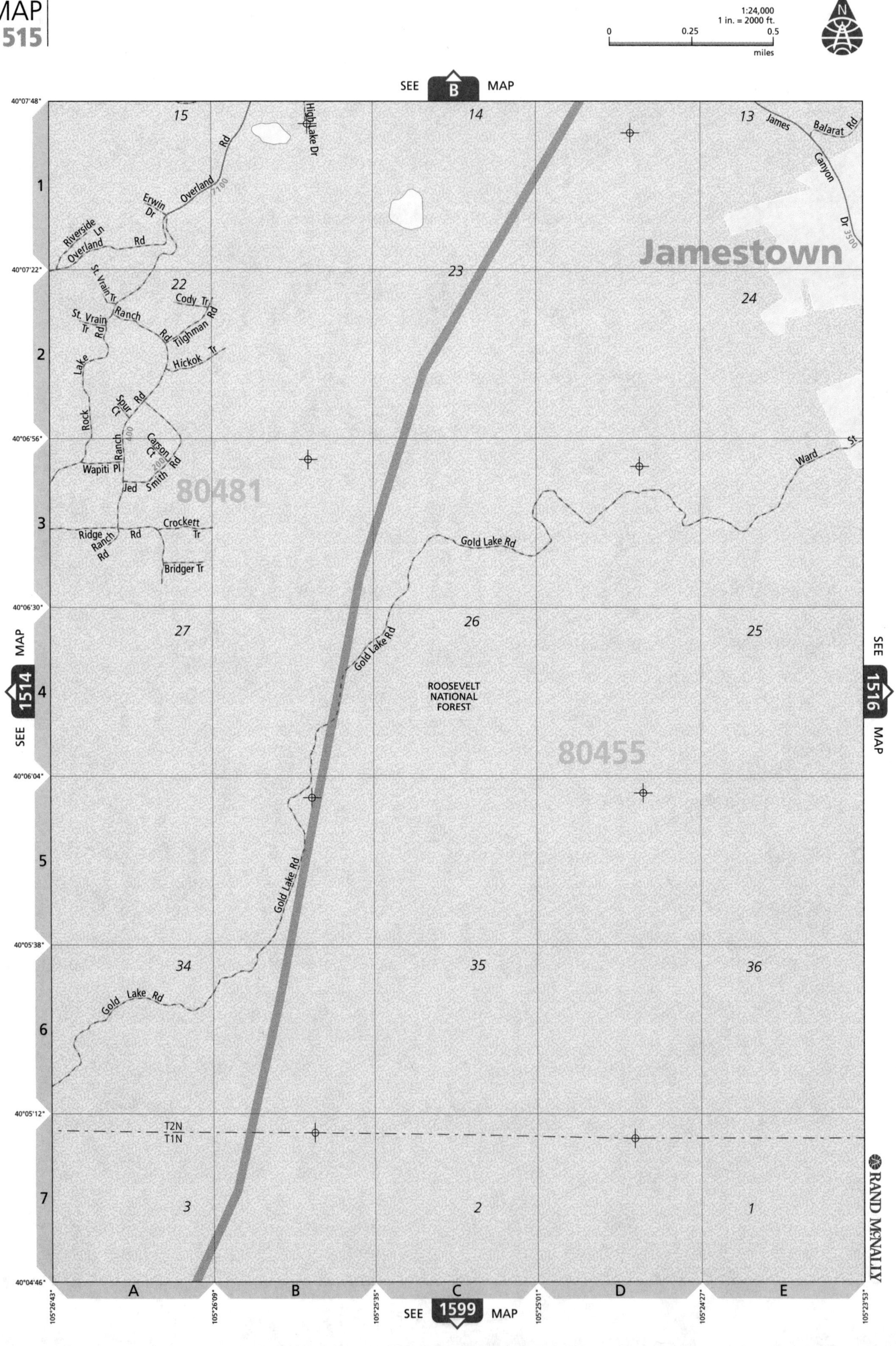

1:24,000
1 in. = 2000 ft.
0 0.25 0.5
miles

SEE B MAP

SEE 1514 MAP

SEE 1516 MAP

SEE 1599 MAP

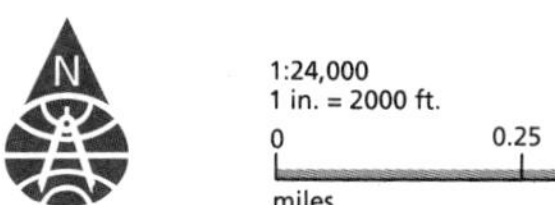

SEE B MAP

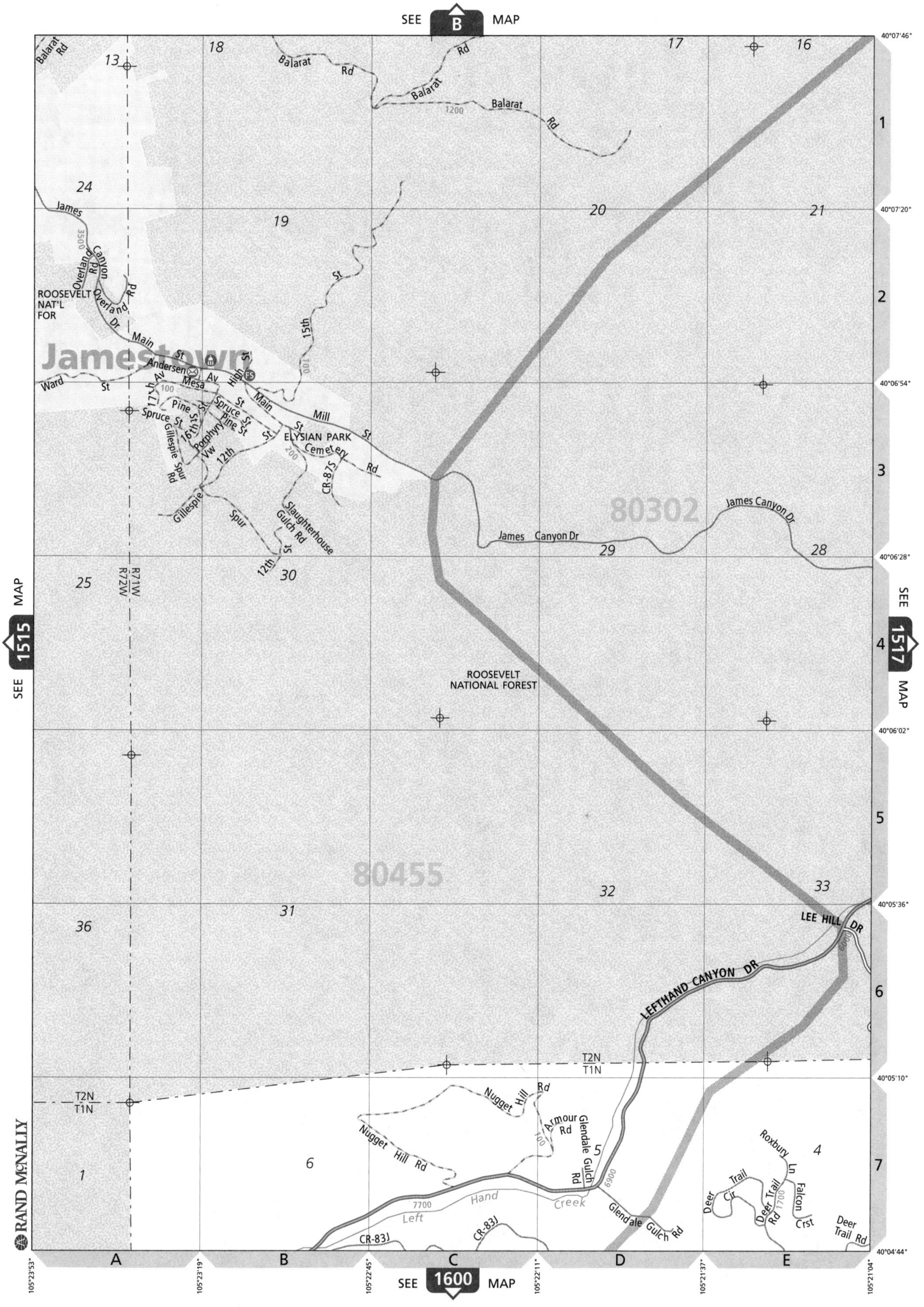

SEE 1515 MAP
SEE 1517 MAP
SEE 1600 MAP

1:24,000
1 in. = 2000 ft.
0
0.25
0.5
miles
N
SEE B MAP
SEE 1516 MAP
SEE 1518 MAP
SEE 1601 MAP
40°07'46"
40°07'20"
40°06'54"
40°06'28"
40°06'02"
40°05'36"
40°05'10"
40°04'44"
105°21'04"
105°20'30"
105°19'56"
105°19'22"
105°18'48"
105°18'14"
1
2
3
4
5
6
7
A
B
C
D
E
21
22
23
26
27
28
33
34
35
2
3
4
80302
ROOSEVELT NATIONAL FOREST
BUCKINGHAM PARK
Boulder Heights
LEFTHAND CANYON DR
Left Hand Creek
James Canyon Dr
Olde Stage Rd
Rembrandt Rd
Valley Ln
Red Hill Rd
Peakview Cir
Peakview Dr
Antler Dr
Peakview Rd
Ranch Rd
Reed
Nugget Dr
Crooked Spur
Elk Ridge Ln
LEE HILL DR
Pineview Ln
T2N
T1N
Forrest Ln
Deer Trail Rd
Sentinel Rock
Valley Vista Ln
Green Meadow Ln
Silver Cloud Ln
Hillside Ct
Tall Pine Ln
Deer Trail Rd
Brook Rd
Cliffhanger Dr
High View Ln
Brook
Ridgeview Ln
Brook Cir
Spring Ln
Cutter Ln
1500
3500
4000
4700
7000
400
1800
6000
RAND McNALLY

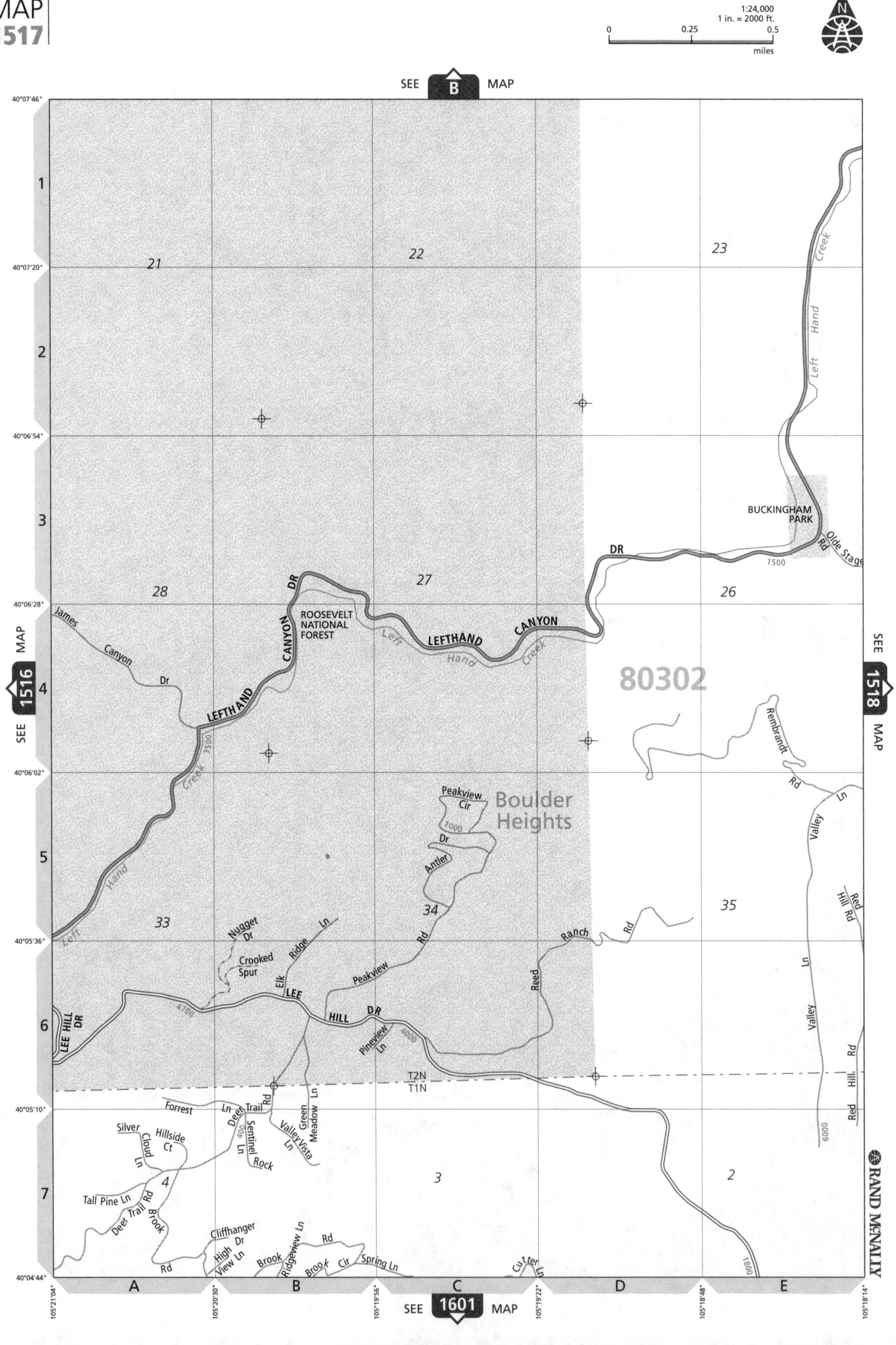

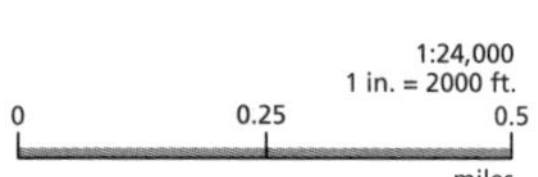

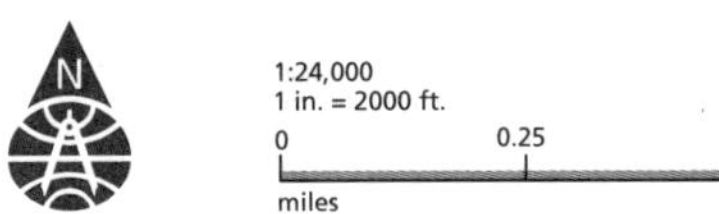

SEE 1435 MAP

SEE 1517 MAP

SEE 1519 MAP

SEE 1602 MAP

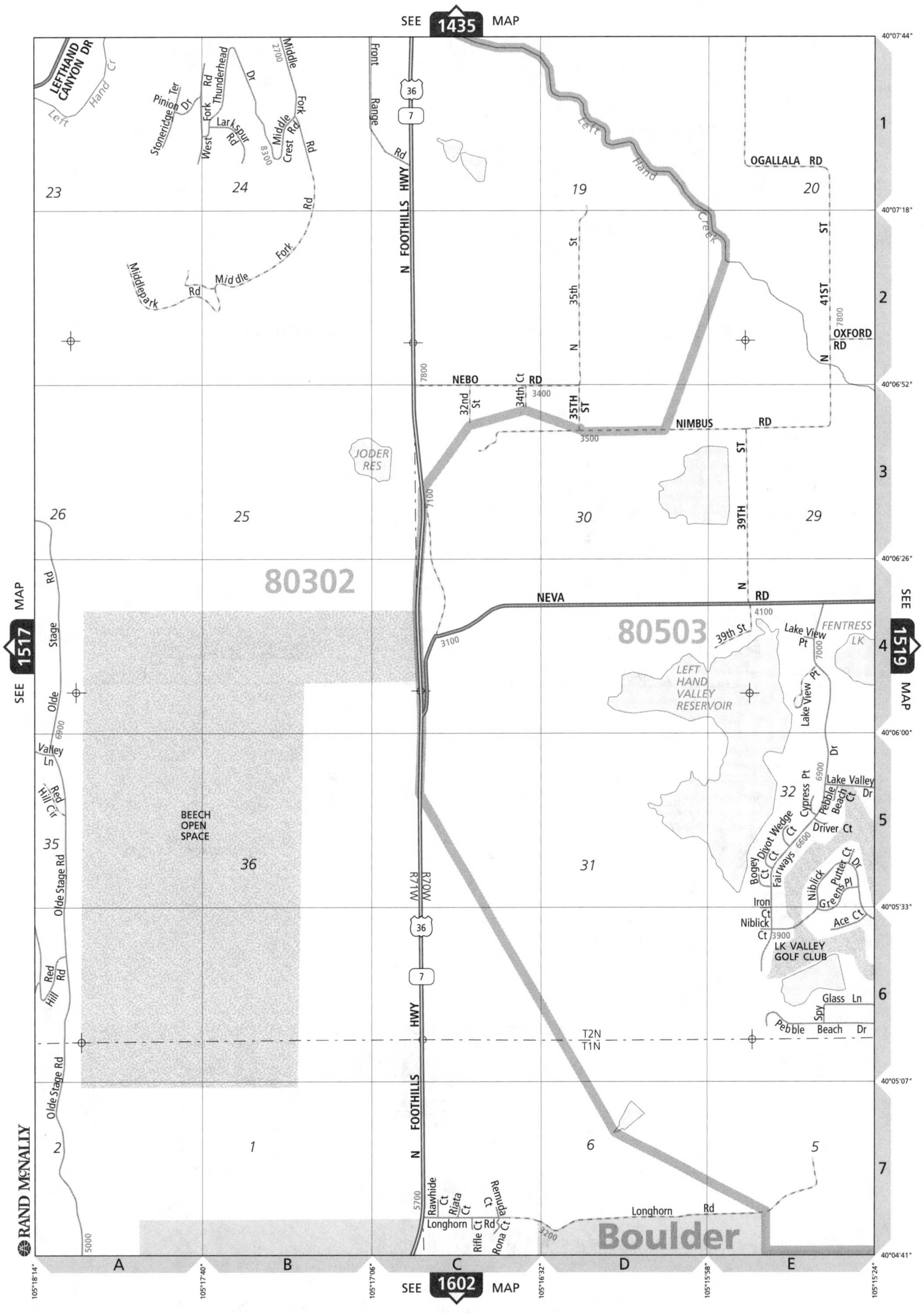

1:24,000
1 in. = 2000 ft.
0 0.25 0.5
miles

SEE 1436 MAP

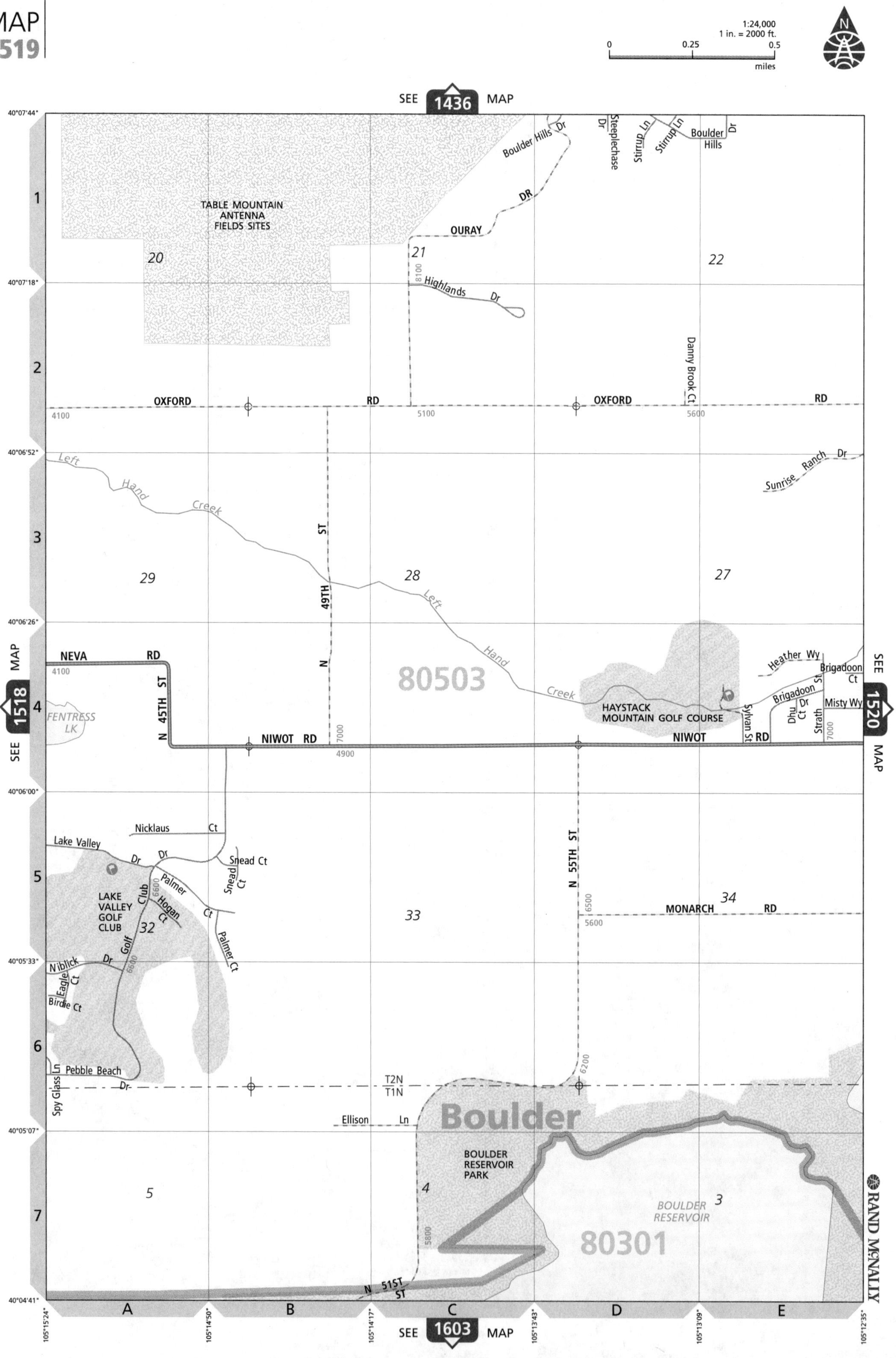

SEE 1518 MAP

SEE 1520 MAP

SEE 1603 MAP

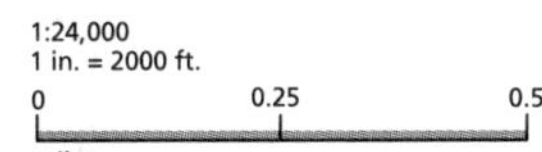

SEE 1437 MAP

SEE 1519 MAP

SEE 1521 MAP

SEE 1604 MAP

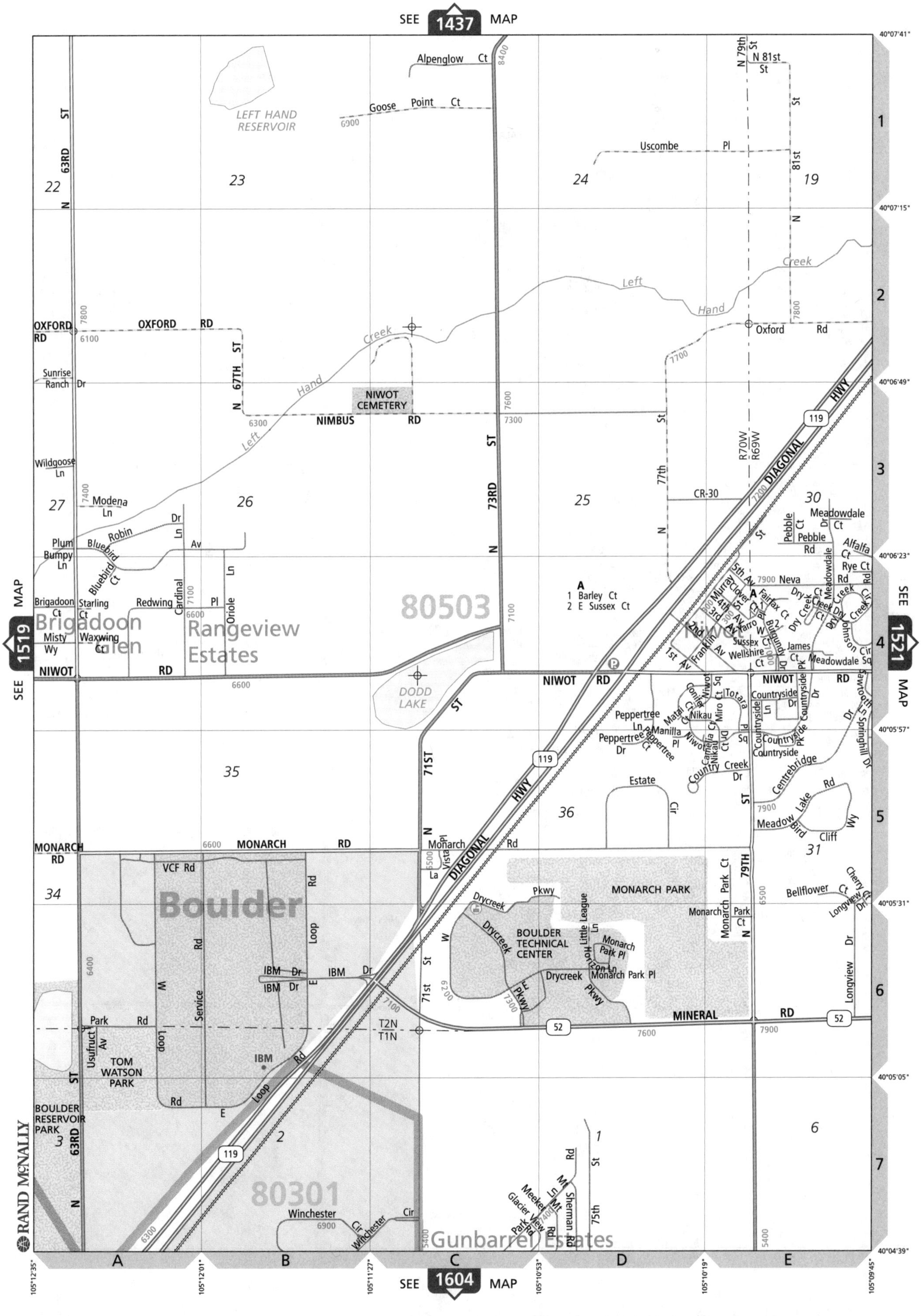

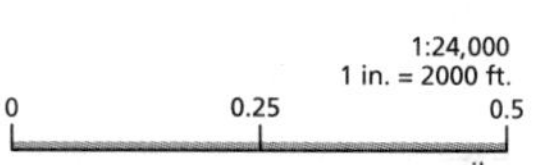

SEE 1438 MAP

Longmont

GAYNOR LAKES

LONGMONT-NIWOT BUFFER

A
1 Oxford Rd

B
1 Christopher Ct
2 Johnson Cir

80503

80504

80026

Niwot HS

LEFT HAND VALLEY GRANGE PARK

SEE 1520 MAP

SEE 1522 MAP

SEE 1605 MAP

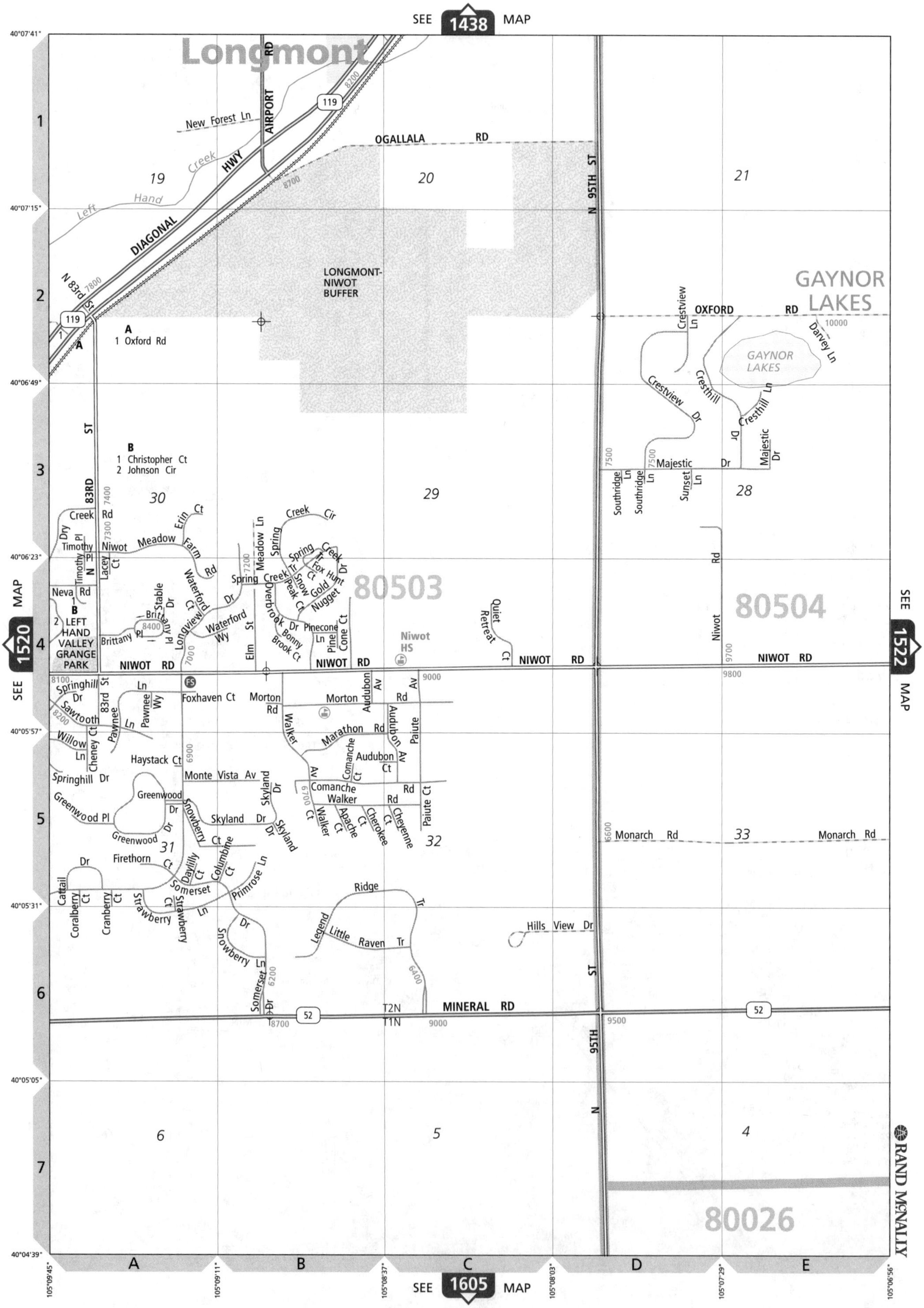

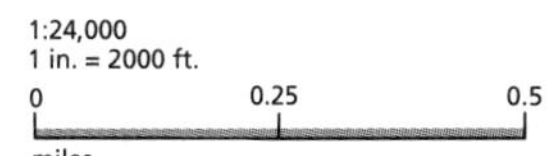

SEE 1439 MAP

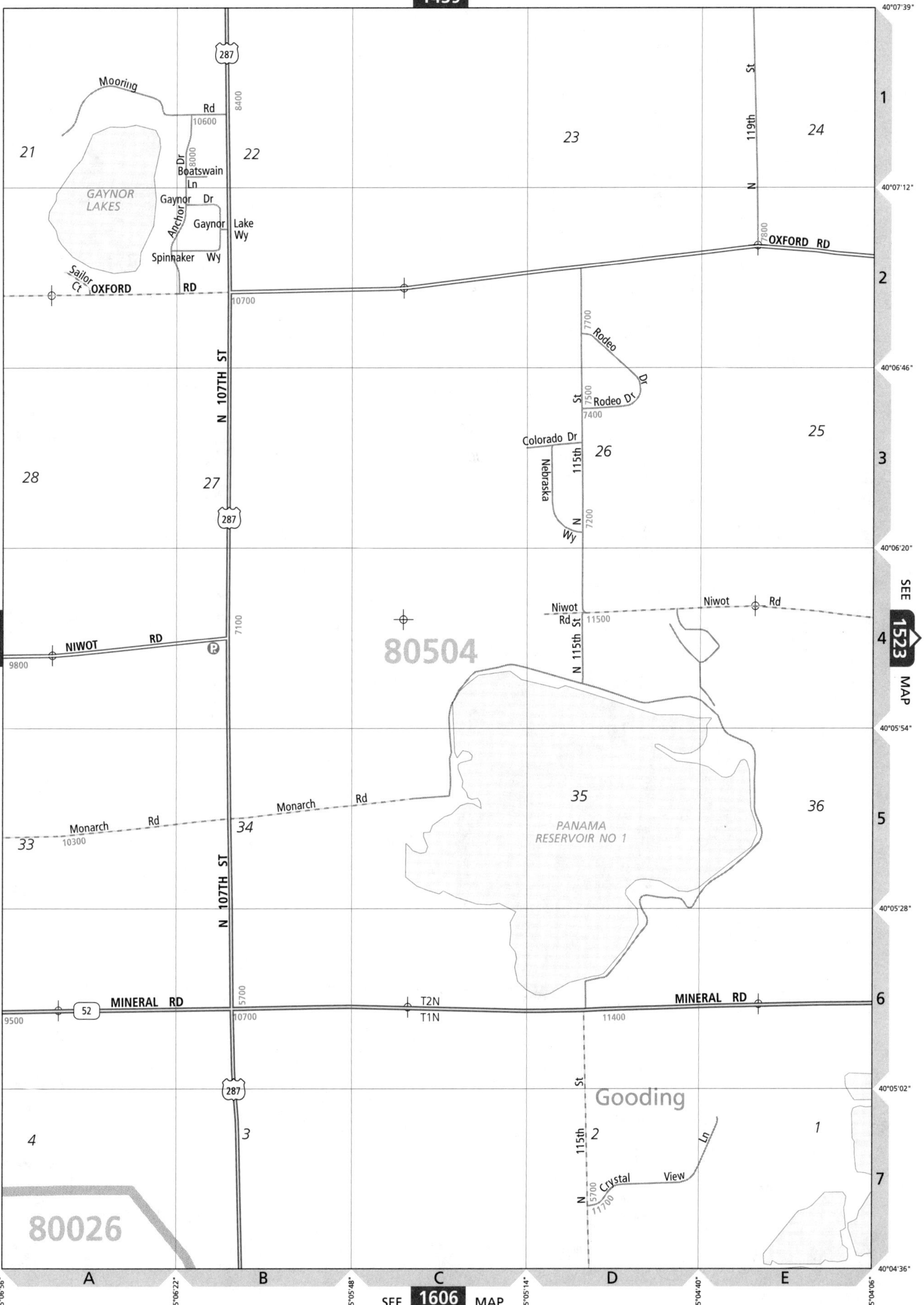

SEE 1521 MAP

SEE 1523 MAP

SEE 1606 MAP

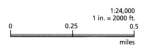

1:24,000
1 in. = 2000 ft.
0 0.25 0.5
miles

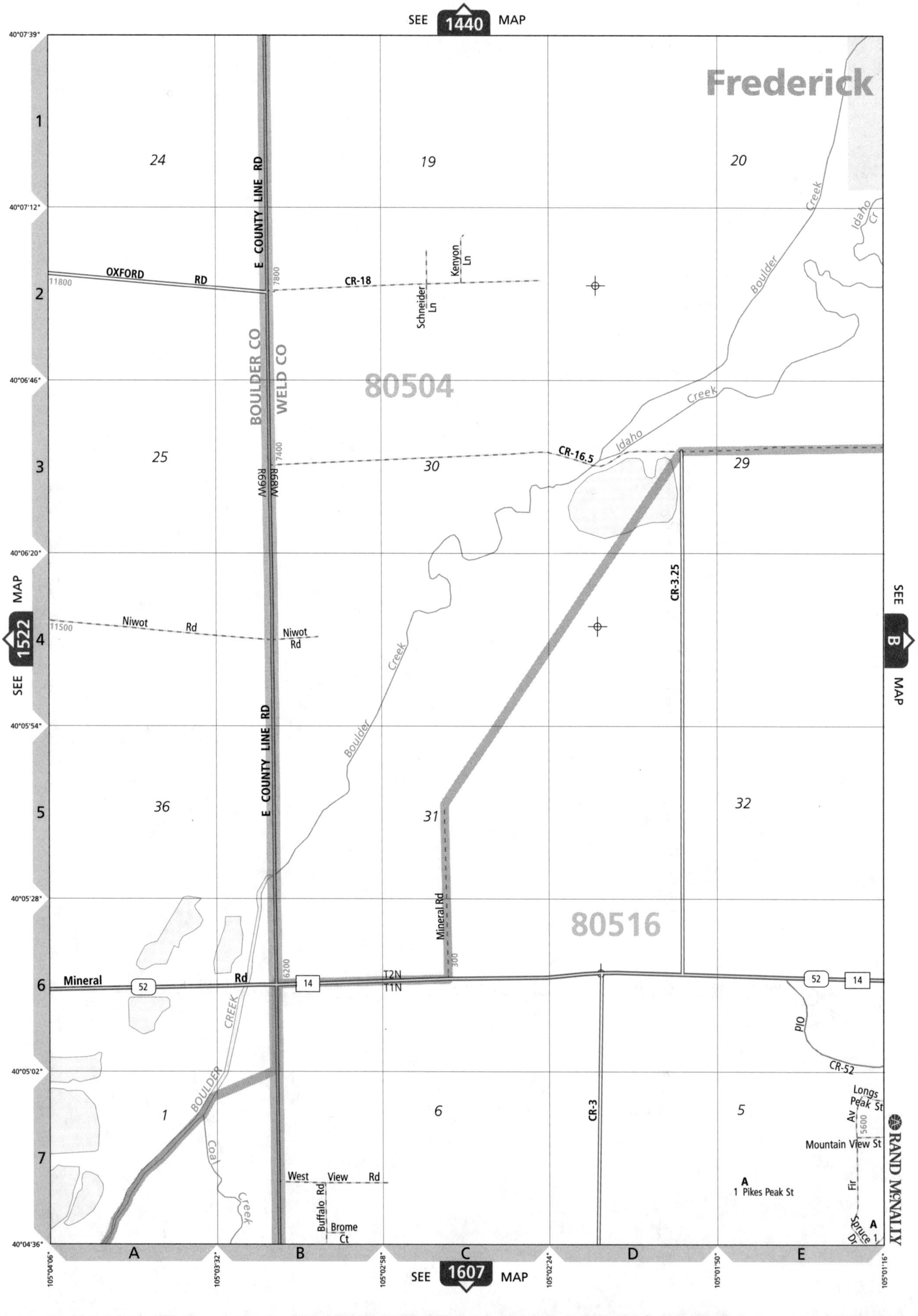

SEE 1522 MAP

SEE B MAP

SEE 1607 MAP

1:24,000
1 in. = 2000 ft.
0 0.25 0.5
miles

SEE 1513 MAP

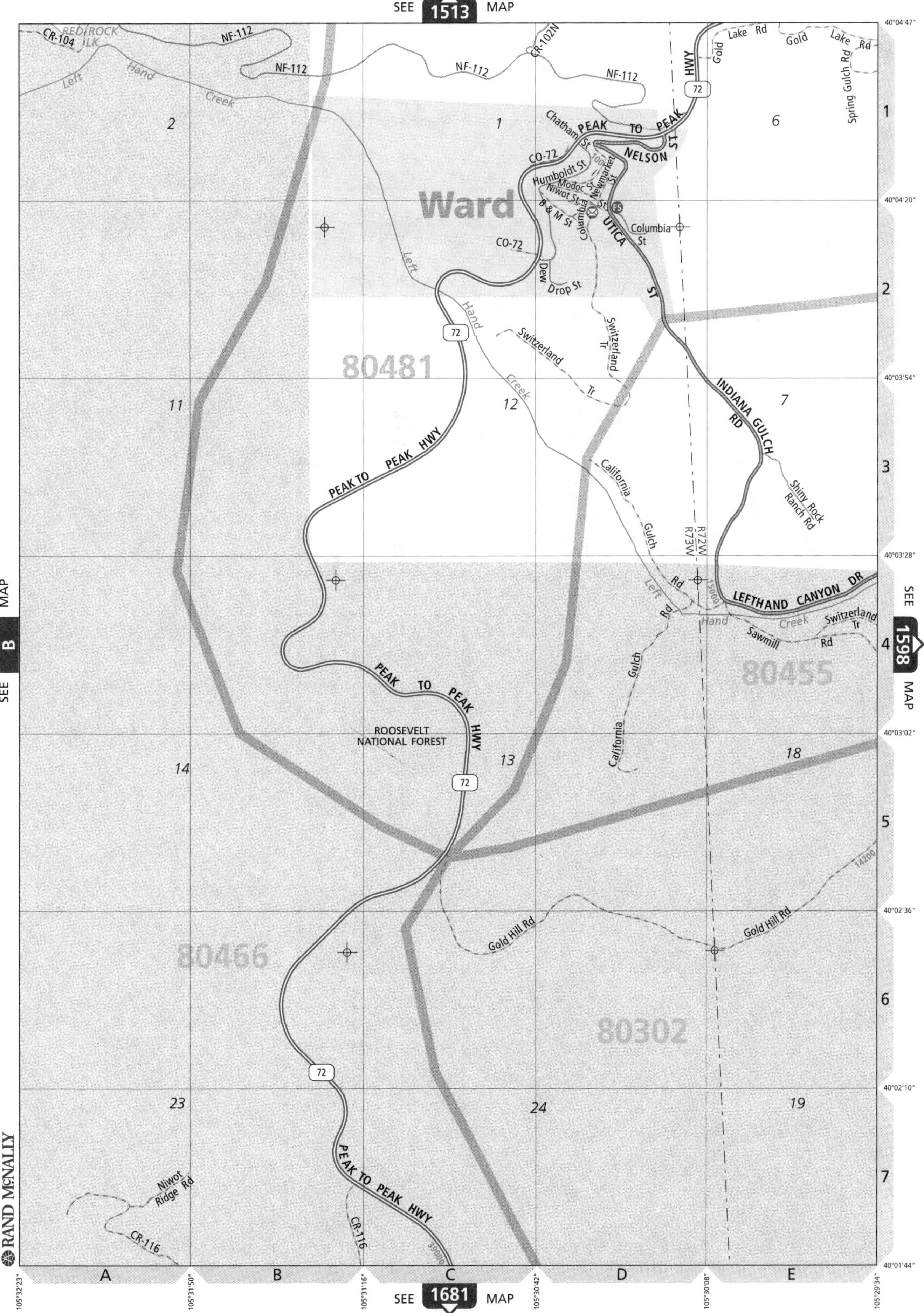

SEE B MAP

SEE 1598 MAP

SEE 1681 MAP

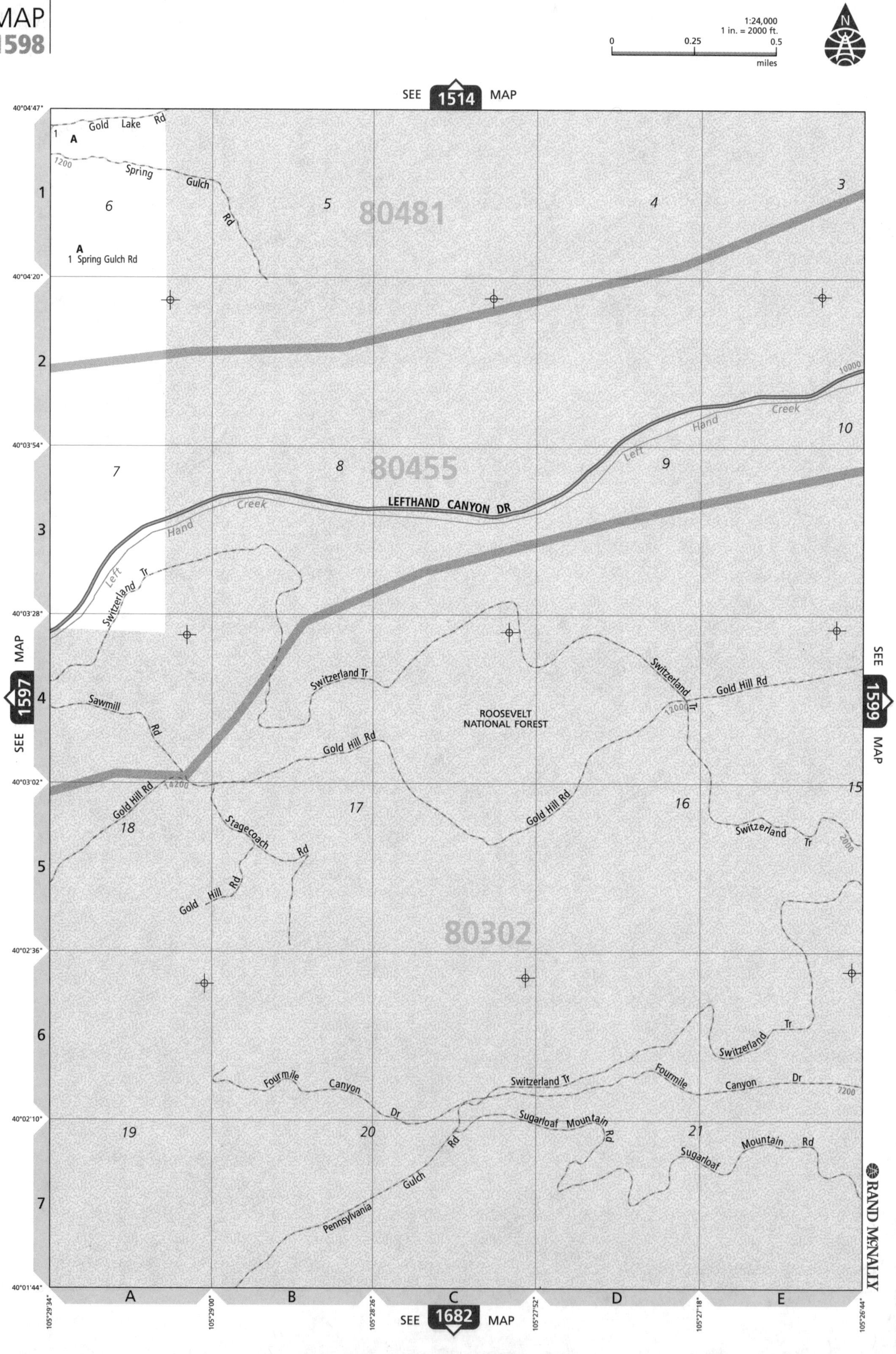

1:24,000
1 in. = 2000 ft.
0
0.25
0.5
miles
N
SEE 1514 MAP
SEE 1597 MAP
SEE 1599 MAP
SEE 1682 MAP
40°04'47"
40°04'20"
40°03'54"
40°03'28"
40°03'02"
40°02'36"
40°02'10"
40°01'44"
105°29'34"
105°29'00"
105°28'26"
105°27'52"
105°27'18"
105°26'44"
1
2
3
4
5
6
7
A
B
C
D
E
Gold Lake Rd
Spring Gulch Rd
A
1 Spring Gulch Rd
80481
80455
80302
LEFTHAND CANYON DR
Left Hand Creek
Switzerland Tr
Sawmill Rd
Gold Hill Rd
ROOSEVELT
NATIONAL FOREST
Stagecoach Rd
Fourmile Canyon Dr
Sugarloaf Mountain Rd
Pennsylvania Gulch Rd
3
4
5
6
7
8
9
10
15
16
17
18
19
20
21
RAND McNALLY

1:24,000
1 in. = 2000 ft.
0 0.25 0.5
miles

SEE 1515 MAP

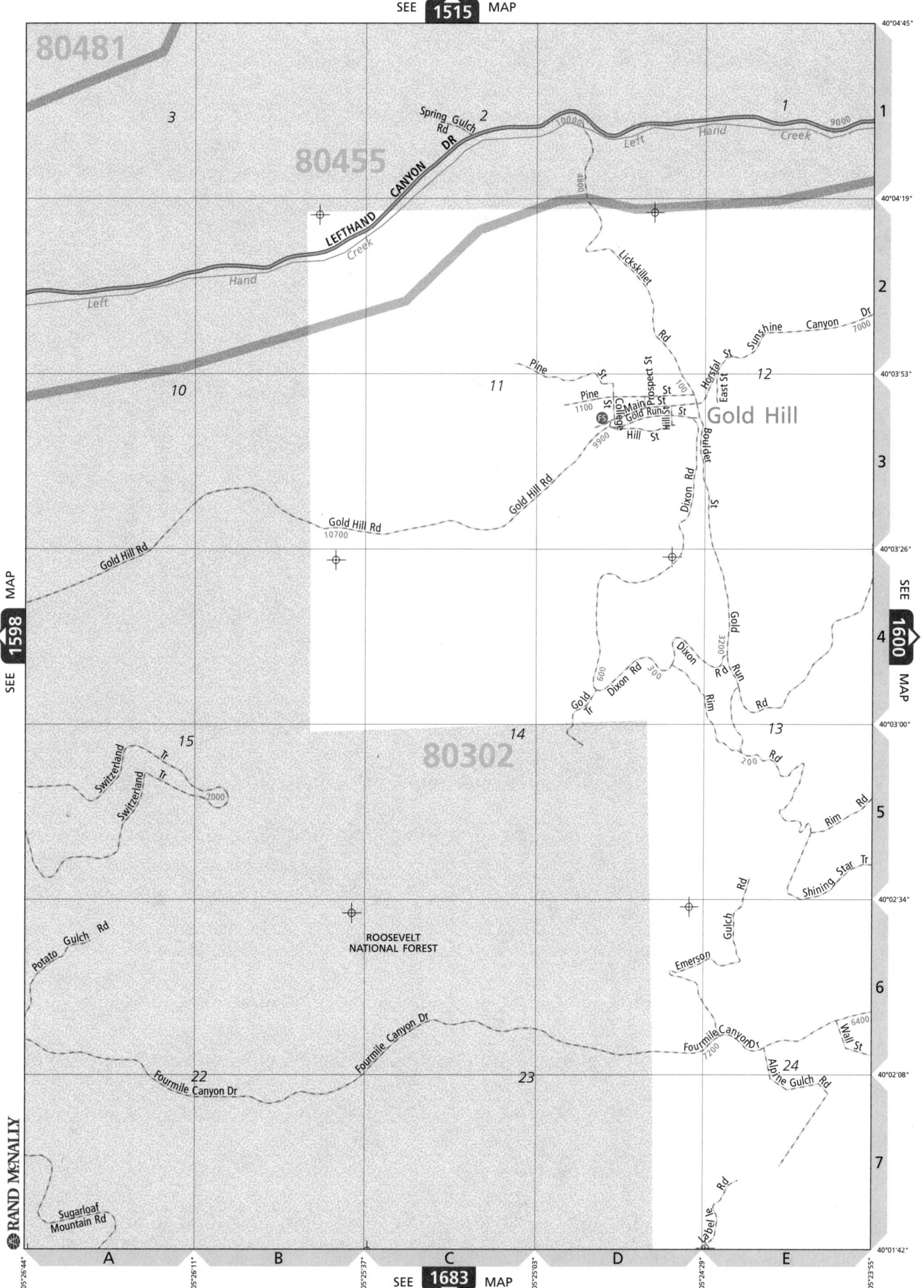

SEE 1598 MAP

SEE 1600 MAP

SEE 1683 MAP

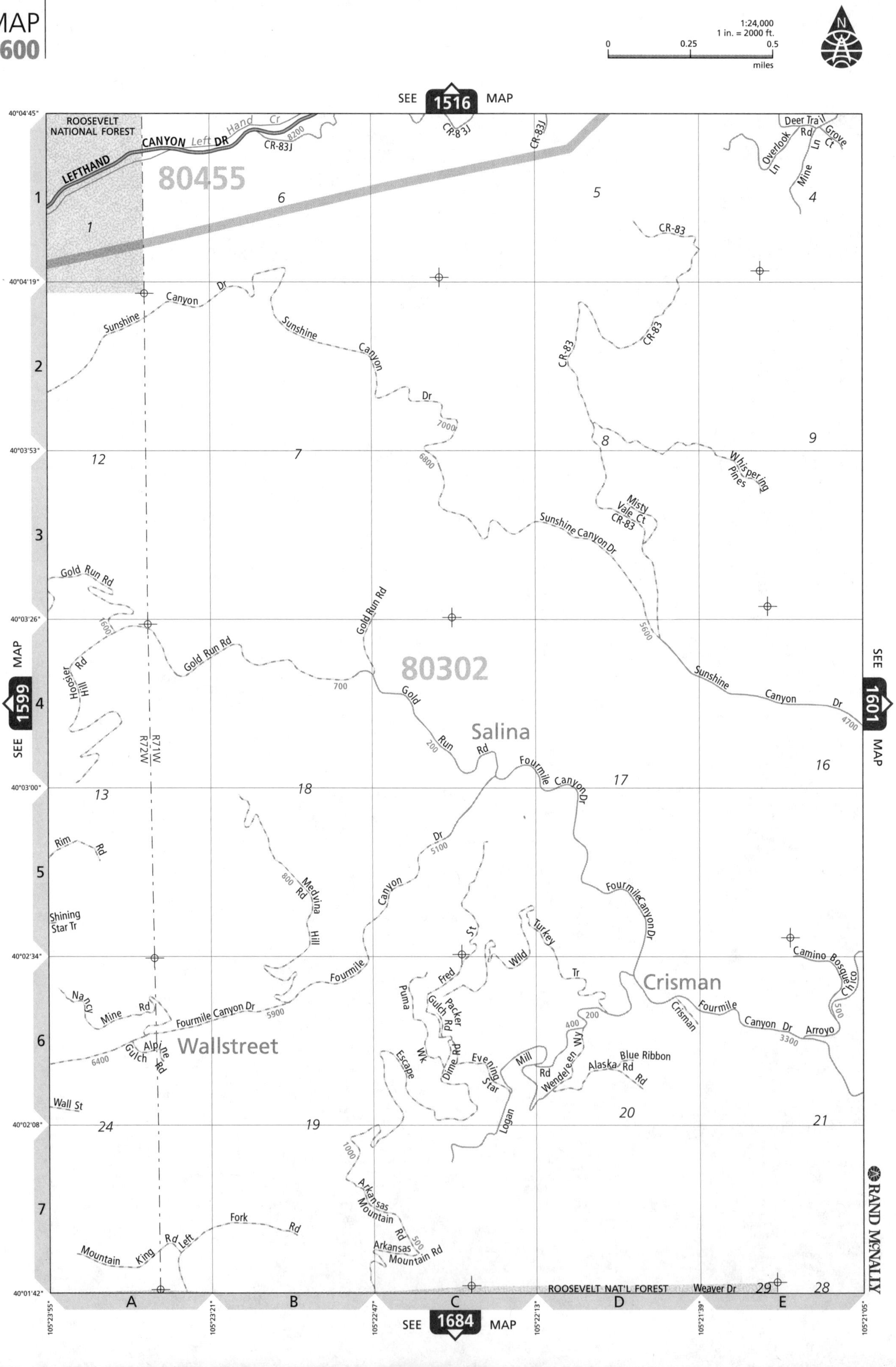

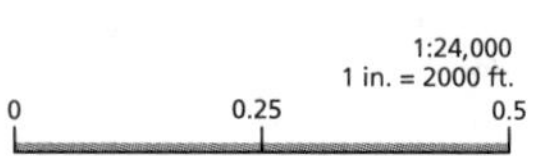

SEE 1516 MAP

40°04'45"
ROOSEVELT NATIONAL FOREST
LEFTHAND CANYON DR
Left Hand Cr
8200
CR-83J
80455
1
6
5
4
Deer Trail Rd
Grove Ct
Overlook Ln
Mine Ln
CR-83
40°04'19"
Sunshine Canyon Dr
Sunshine Canyon Dr
CR-83
CR-83
2
Dr
7000
8
9
40°03'53"
12
7
6800
Whispering Pines
Misty Vale Ct
CR-83
Sunshine Canyon Dr
3
Gold Run Rd
Gold Run Rd
40°03'26"
1600
5600
Hoosier Hill Rd
Gold Run Rd
700
80302
Sunshine Canyon Dr
Gold Run Rd
4700
4
R71W
R72W
200
Salina
Fourmile Canyon Dr
17
16
40°03'00"
13
18
Rim Rd
Dr
5100
5
800
Medvina Hill Rd
Canyon
Fourmile Canyon Dr
Shining Star Tr
St
Turkey
40°02'34"
Fred
Wild
Camino Bosque Chico
Fourmile
Tr
Crisman
Nancy Mine Rd
Fourmile Canyon Dr
5900
Puma
Gulch Rd
Packer
400
Wy
200
Crisman
Fourmile Canyon Dr
Arroyo
500
3300
6
6400
Alpine Gulch Rd
Wallstreet
Escape Wk
Dime Rd
Evening Star
Mill Rd
Wendeleen
Alaska Rd
Blue Ribbon Rd
Wall St
Logan
40°02'08"
24
19
20
21
1000
Arkansas Mountain Rd
7
Fork Rd
500
Arkansas Mountain Rd
Mountain King Rd
Left
40°01'42"
ROOSEVELT NAT'L FOREST
Weaver Dr
29
28
A
B
C
D
E
105°23'55"
105°23'21"
105°22'47"
105°22'13"
105°21'39"
105°21'05"

SEE 1599 MAP

SEE 1601 MAP

SEE 1684 MAP

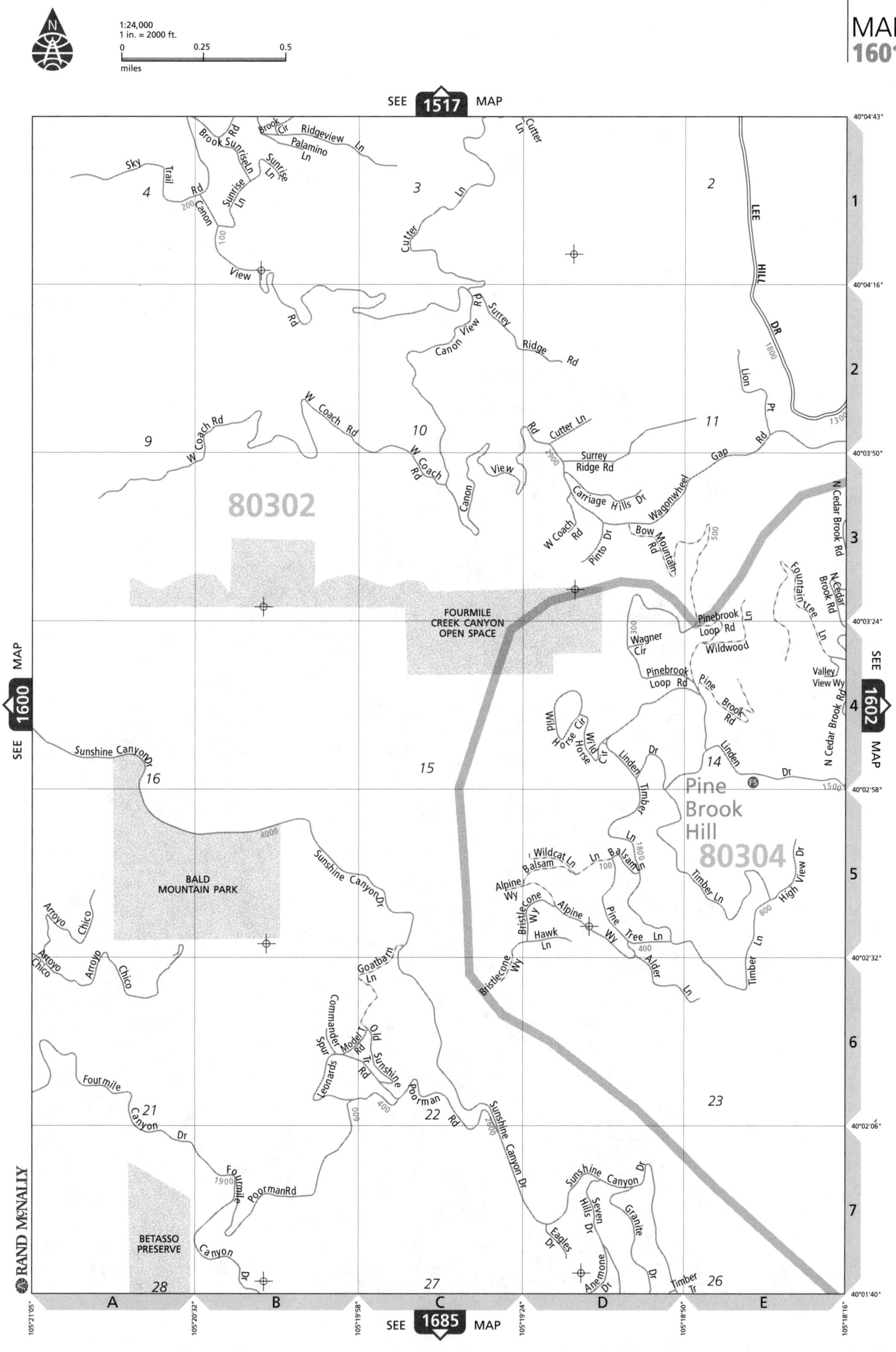

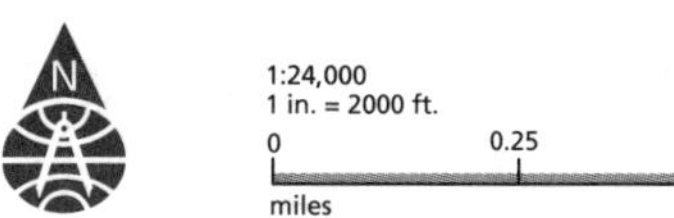

SEE 1517 MAP

Sky Trail Rd
Brook Rd
Sunrise Ln
Brook Cir
Ridgeview Ln
Palamino Ln
Sunrise Ln
Canon View Rd
Cutter Ln
Surrey Ridge Rd
LEE HILL DR
Lion Pt
Gap Rd
W Coach Rd
Cutter Ln
Surrey Ridge Rd
Canon View
Carriage Hills Dr
Wagonwheel
Bow Mountain Rd
Pinto Dr
N Cedar Brook Rd
Fountain Tree Ln
Pinebrook Ln
Loop Rd
Wildwood
Wagner Cir
Pinebrook Loop Rd
Pine Brook Rd
Valley View Wy
80302
FOURMILE CREEK CANYON OPEN SPACE
Wild Horse Cir
Linden Dr
Timber Ln
Pine Brook Hill
80304
Sunshine Canyon Dr
BALD MOUNTAIN PARK
Wildcat Ln
Balsam Ln
Alpine Wy
Bristlecone Wy
Hawk Ln
Pine Tree Ln
Alder Ln
High View Dr
Timber Ln
Arroyo Chico
Goatbarn Ln
Commander Spur
Model T Rd
Old Sunshine Tr
Leonards Rd
Poorman Rd
Fourmile Canyon Dr
BETASSO PRESERVE
Sunshine Canyon Dr
Seven Hills Dr
Granite Dr
Eagles Dr
Anemone Dr
Timber Tr

4 3 2 9 10 11 16 15 14 21 22 23 28 27 26

1 2 3 4 5 6 7
A B C D E

40°04'43" 40°04'16" 40°03'50" 40°03'24" 40°02'58" 40°02'32" 40°02'06" 40°01'40"
105°21'05" 105°20'32" 105°19'58" 105°19'24" 105°18'50" 105°18'16"

SEE 1600 MAP

SEE 1602 MAP

SEE 1685 MAP

1:24,000
1 in. = 2000 ft.
0 0.25 0.5
miles

SEE 1518 MAP

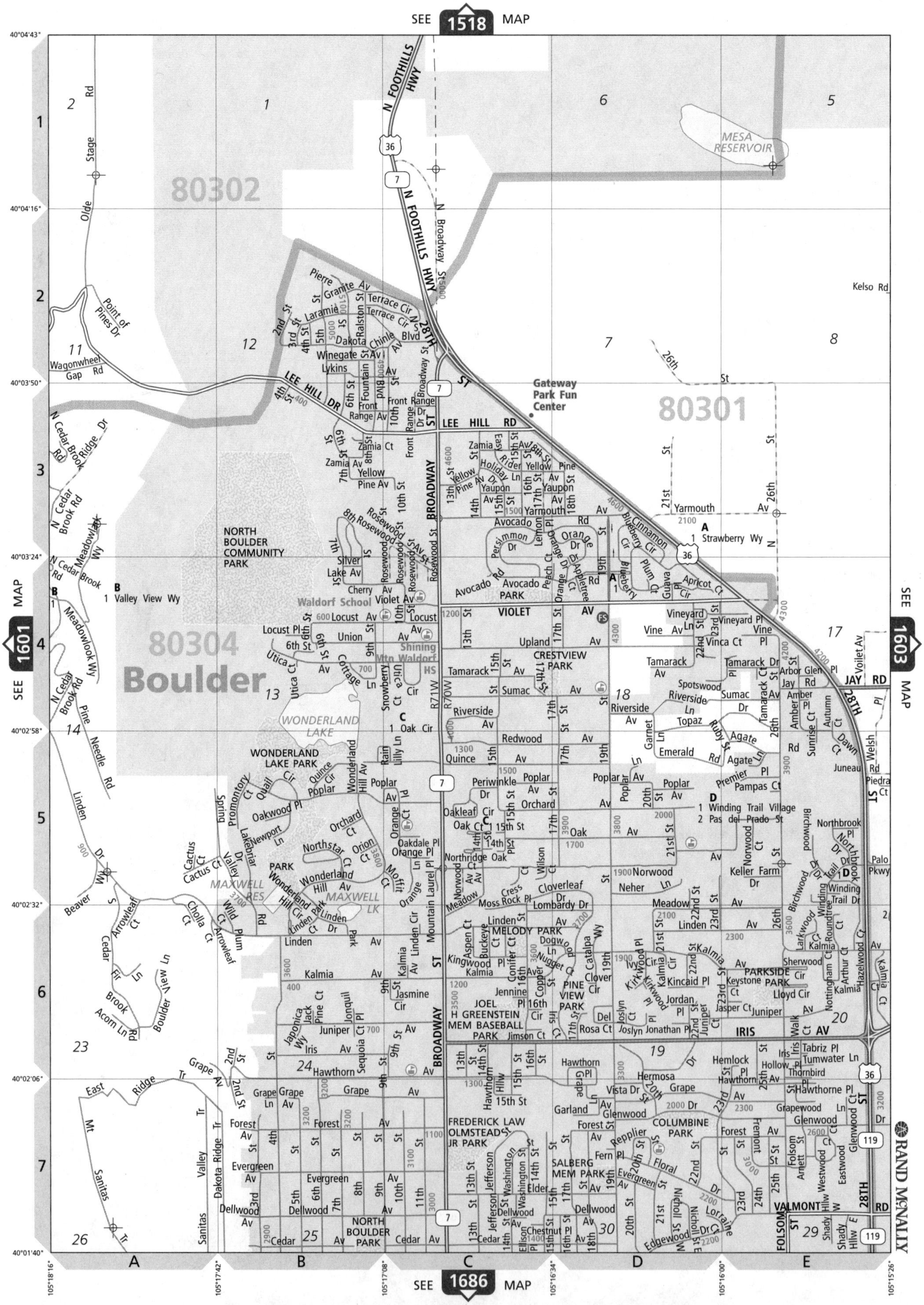

SEE 1601 MAP

SEE 1603 MAP

Boulder

80302

80301

80304

NORTH BOULDER COMMUNITY PARK

WONDERLAND LAKE PARK

WONDERLAND LAKE

MAXWELL LK

MAXWELL RES

MESA RESERVOIR

Gateway Park Fun Center

Waldorf School

Shining Mtn Waldorf HS

CRESTVIEW PARK

AVOCADO PARK

MELODY PARK

PINE VIEW PARK

JOEL H GREENSTEIN MEM BASEBALL PARK

FREDERICK LAW OLMSTEAD JR PARK

SALBERG MEM PARK

COLUMBINE PARK

PARKSIDE PARK

NORTH BOULDER PARK

A
1 Strawberry Wy

B
1 Valley View Wy

C
1 Oak Cir

D
1 Winding Trail Village
2 Pas del Prado St

N FOOTHILLS HWY

BROADWAY

28TH ST

LEE HILL DR

LEE HILL RD

VIOLET AV

JAY RD

IRIS AV

VALMONT RD

FOLSOM ST

40°04'43"
40°04'16"
40°03'50"
40°03'24"
40°02'58"
40°02'32"
40°02'06"
40°01'40"

105°18'16"
105°17'42"
105°17'08"
105°16'34"
105°16'00"
105°15'26"

A B C D E

1 2 3 4 5 6 7

RAND McNALLY

SEE 1686 MAP

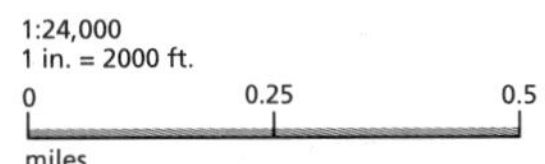

SEE 1519 MAP

BOULDER RESERVOIR PARK
5
4
N 51ST ST
BOULDER RESERVOIR
3
1
Odin
Valhalla Av
Dr
4900
Thor Av
Reservoir Rd
119
Kelso Rd
MESA RESERVOIR PARK
Loki Av
Valkyrie Dr
Boulder Reservoir Marina
SIXMILE RESERVOIR
Spine
Lookout Rd
2
Kelso Rd
4700
Kelso Rd
5000
9
10
8
Leanin' Tree Mus of Western Art
Longbow Dr
Gunbarrel Business Park
6000
Longbow Dr
Longbow Ct
Westridge Dr
Meadowcross Ln
Westridge Dr
5300
Boulder
Gunbarrel Av
Longbow
4700
Habitat Dr
Pleasant Ridge Rd
4700
55th St
Waterstone Dr
Zinger St
Spine Rd
Willow Ln
Sleepytime Dr
Indigo Ct
Almond Ln
47th St
N 55th St
4600
4500
Sleepytime Dr
White Rock Cir
3
DIAGONAL HWY
Orchard Creek Ln
Cloud Ct
Brandywine Ct
Robinson Ct
Robinson Pl
80301
Pioneer Rd
Clay St
Pussy Willow Ct
Maple Creek Ct
Scotswood Ct
Old Brompton Rd
Orchard Cir
Orchard Creek Cir
Wellington Rd
Chelsea Manor Ct
Applewood Ct
4400
ORCHARD PARK
16
S Orchard Creek Cir
Mulberry Ct
Pembroke Gdns
JUHLS LAKE
N 55th St
30th St
30th Pl
Plum Ct
Macoun Wy
Peach Ct
Apple Ct
Apple Wy
Peach
4500
Wy
Black
Cherry Ct
3500
JAY RD
4200
4200
Juhls Dr
JAY RD
Spine
4
5000
5700
15
5900
Sumac Ct
Cayman
St. Croix
17
Redwood Ct
Barbados
Martinique
St. Lucia St
Eleuthera Ct
Redwood
Nevis
Guadeloupe
Bimini Ct
St. Vincent Pl
Kingstown
Nassau Pl
New Haven Ct
Scarsdale Pl
Stone
Quince Ct
PARK
Juneau Rd
A
1
2
St. Petersburg St
St. Johns
3
Old Westbury Ct
3900
Piedra Ct
Ponderosa
Culebra
Piedra Pl
Arbol Ct
Bosque
Corriente
Campo
Dehesa Ct
Escuela Ct
Savannah Pl
Dr
Savannah Pl
Hampton Cir
Corriente
Hoya Ct
3000
Abeyta Ct
Angelovic Ct
Fredericks Ct
Hauptman Ct
Howe Ct
Prado
Pas del
Monterey
Nebrina
Palo Pkwy
Nogales Ct
Maya Pl
Madera Ct
Loma Pl
A
1 Dominica Pl
2 Mustique Ct
3 Montclair Ln
119
57th St
Cairn Ct
Woodbourne Hollow Rd
5
N
ANDRUS RD
Links Dr
Island
Dr
SALE LK
20
3100 Kalmia Av
Kalmia Av
PKWY
DIAGONAL
HWY
47th St
Rustic Knolls Dr
Knoll Crest Ct
3600
Independence Rd
5400
4800
Kalmia Av
MOUNTAIN VIEW CEMETERY
3600
Boulder Municipal Airport
Creek
61ST ST
6
119
HAYDEN LAKE
21
Terminal
Airport Rd
Airport Rd
Airport Rd
Blvd
22
Penrose Av
Pl
St
Chisholm Tr
Iris Tr
Greyhound Boulder
Bridger Tr
34th St
34th St
Talisman Pl
Talisman Dr
Mitchell Ln
Sentinel Dr
Hopkins Pl
Independence Dr
Independence
Airport
5400
Pheasant Ln
Sparrow Ln
Boulder
SAW HILL PND
Corona Tr
Hickok Pl
Spring Creek
Macintosh Pl
Bridger Ln
Ute
Kenosha Dr
O'Neal Cir
O'Neal Pkwy
O'Neal Pl
Hayden Pl
Hayden Pl
Baldwin Pl
Kings
Ridge
Sentinel Dr
Wright
Tesla
Wright
B
1 Gatling Ln
Valley Ln
Lark Ln
Swallow Dr
Bob-O-Link Ct
Valmont
Rd
Glenwood Dr
Glenwood Dr
HOWARD H HEUSTON PARK
Gibbs
Franklin
Bell
Edison
Gamow Ln
Galileo Ln
Blvd
Circle
Monarch Dr
Santa Anna
Vail St
Ashley Ct
Pass St
Cir W
Sterling Cir
Robin Ct
Robin Ct
Cline Av
Flamingo
Falcon
Boulder
Boulder
Cr
Indian
3100
3200
Eagle Wy
Eagle
3100
St
30TH
St
Center Green Dr
FOOTHILLS
47th
Edison Ln
Fulton Cir
Darwin Ct
Curie Ct
Kings Ridge
Packer Ln
Butte St
Carlson Ln
Cody Ln
CHRISTENSEN PARK
Noble Park Pl
Airport Rd
Boulder
Sterling Cir
Minshal Dr
Butte
Mill Rd
6200
7
29th St
3000
34th
157
VALMONT RD
PEARL PKWY
Valmont Dr
2900
29th St
Bluff St
32nd St
33rd St
29
Wilderness Pl
Center Green Ct
47th St
Sterling Ct
5100
28
Sterling Dr
Pearl St
55TH ST
N 57th St
27
Stazio Dr
STAZIO RECREATIONAL FIELDS
63rd St
61ST
N
ST

A B C D E
1 2 3 4 5 6 7

40°04'40" 40°04'14" 40°03'48" 40°03'22" 40°02'56" 40°02'30" 40°02'04" 40°01'38"
105°15'27" 105°14'53" 105°14'19" 105°13'45" 105°13'11" 105°12'37"

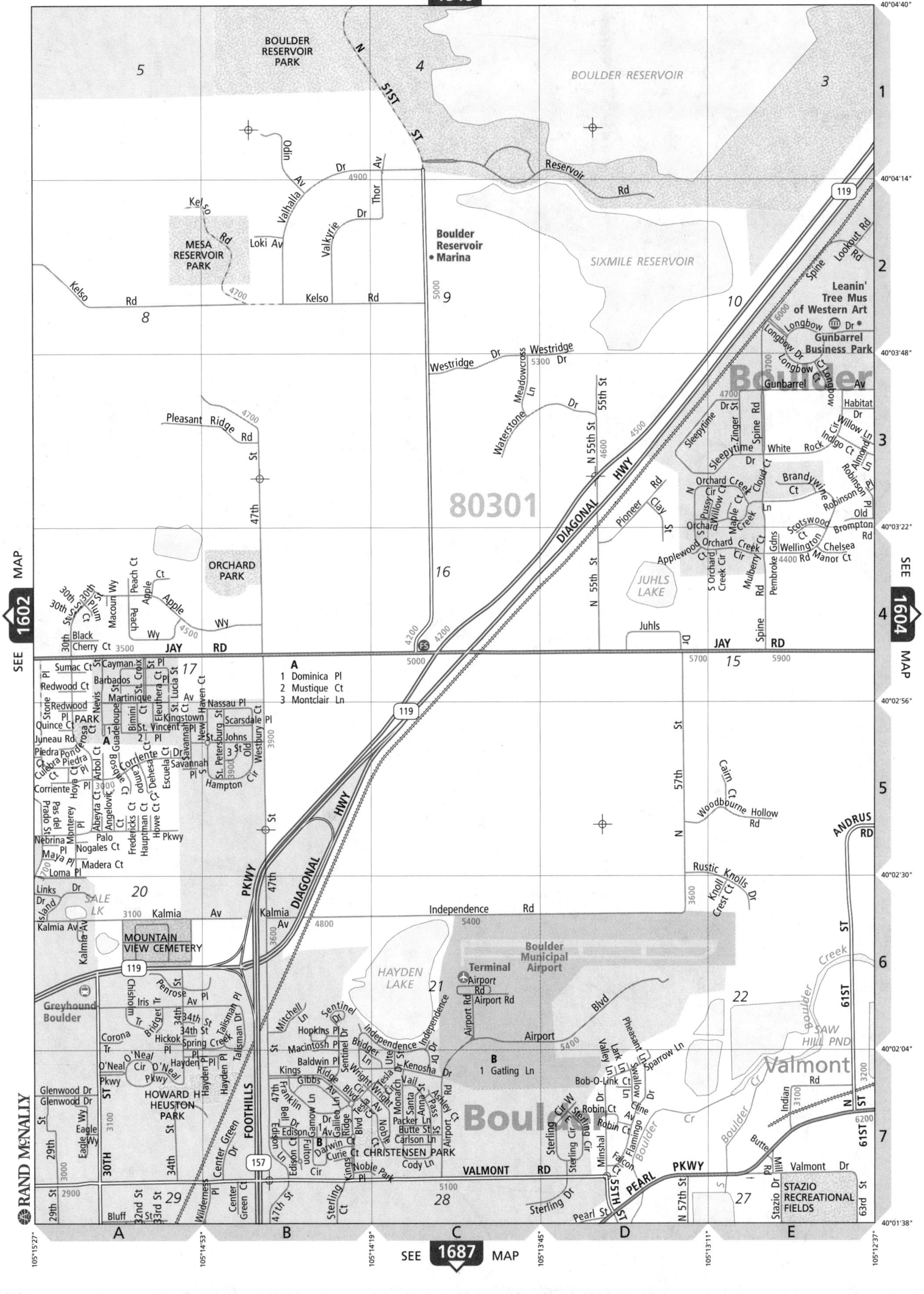

SEE 1602 MAP
SEE 1604 MAP
SEE 1687 MAP

1:24,000
1 in. = 2000 ft.
0 0.25 0.5
miles

SEE 1520 MAP

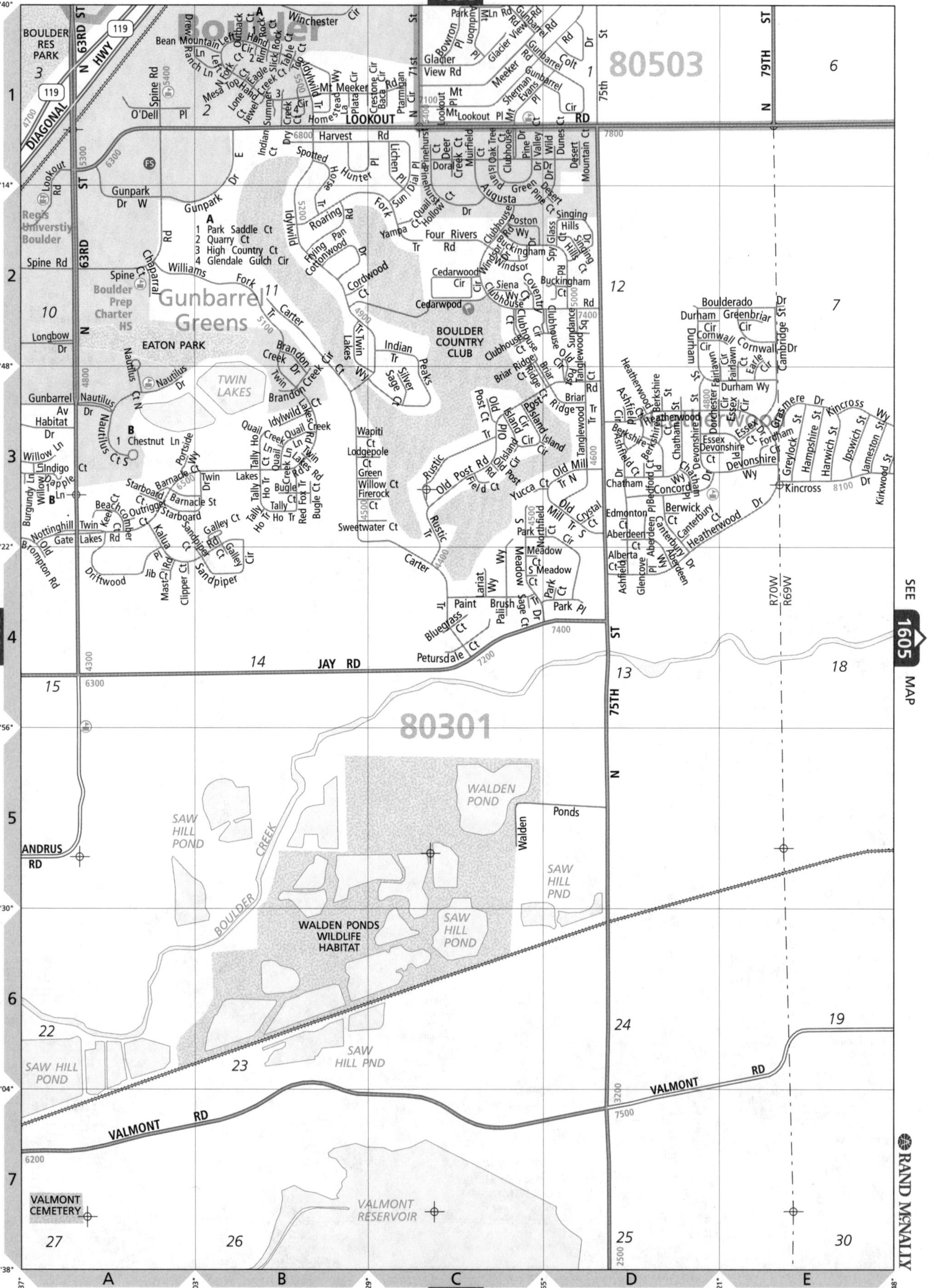

BOULDER RES PARK

Boulder

80503

80301

Gunbarrel Greens

EATON PARK

BOULDER COUNTRY CLUB

Regis Universtiy Boulder

Boulder Prep Charter HS

TWIN LAKES

Heatherwood

WALDEN POND

SAW HILL POND

WALDEN PONDS WILDLIFE HABITAT

SAW HILL PND

VALMONT RESERVOIR

VALMONT CEMETERY

BOULDER CREEK

N 63RD ST

DIAGONAL HWY

119

LOOKOUT RD

Gunpark Dr

Spine Rd

Williams Fork Tr

Carter Tr

Longbow Dr

Gunbarrel Av

Habitat Dr

Nautilus Dr

JAY RD

N 75TH ST

N 79TH ST

ANDRUS RD

VALMONT RD

Ponds

Walden

Kincross Dr

Heatherwood Dr

Durham Wy

Boulderado Dr

Cambridge St

Winchester Cir

Harvest Rd

Four Rivers Rd

Cedarwood Cir

Indian Peaks Tr

Old Post Rd

Old Mill Tr N

Twin Lakes Rd

Spotted Horse Tr

Yampa Ct

Brandon Creek Dr

Idylwild Creek Ct

Quail Creek Ln

Rustic Tr

Petursdale Ct

Bluegrass Ct

Paint Brush Dr

Park Pl

Starboard Dr

Galley Ct

Sandpiper Cir

Driftwood Pl

Nottinghill Gate Rd

Brompton Rd

Old Post Ct

Island Cir

Tanglewood Tr

Tanglewood Sq

Singing Hills Ct

Glacier View Rd

Gunbarrel Rd

Meeker Dr

Mesa Top Ct

Bean Mountain Ct

Drew Ranch Ln

O'Dell Pl

Wapiti Ct

Lodgepole Ct

Green Ct

Willow Ct

Firerock Ct

Sweetwater Ct

Edmonton Ct

Aberdeen Ct

Alberta Ct

Glencove Pl

Berwick Ct

Canterbury Ct

Concord Wy

Chatham Ct

Devonshire Wy

Essex Ct

Fordham Ct

Greylock St

Hampshire St

Harwich St

Ipswich St

Jameston St

Kirkwood St

Grasmere Dr

A
1 Park Saddle Ct
2 Quarry Ct
3 High Country Ct
4 Glendale Gulch Cir

B
1 Chestnut Ln

Yucca Ct

Crystal Ct

Meadow Ct

S Meadow Ct

Lariat Wy

Sage Ct

Feild Ct

Silver Sage Ct

Twin Lakes Wy

Cordwood Ct

Flying Pan Ct

Cottonwood Dr

Roaring Fork Rd

Lichen Pl

Hunter Pl

Sun Dial Pl

Pinehurst Ct

Doral Ct

Deer Creek Ct

Muirfield Ct

Augusta Dr

Poston Dr

Buckingham Rd

Windsor Dr

Siena Wy

Coventry Ct

Clubhouse Cir

Briar Ridge Ct

Old Post Ct

1 2 3 4 5 6 7

A B C D E

10 11 12 13 14 15 18 19 22 23 24 25 26 27 30

R70W R69W

40°04'40" 40°04'14" 40°03'48" 40°03'22" 40°02'56" 40°02'30" 40°02'04" 40°01'38"

105°12'37" 105°12'03" 105°11'29" 105°10'55" 105°10'21" 105°09'48"

SEE 1603 MAP

SEE 1605 MAP

SEE 1688 MAP

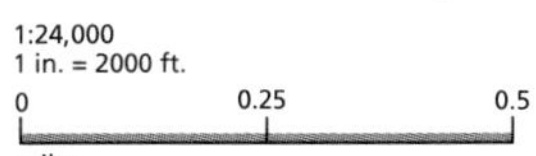

SEE 1521 MAP

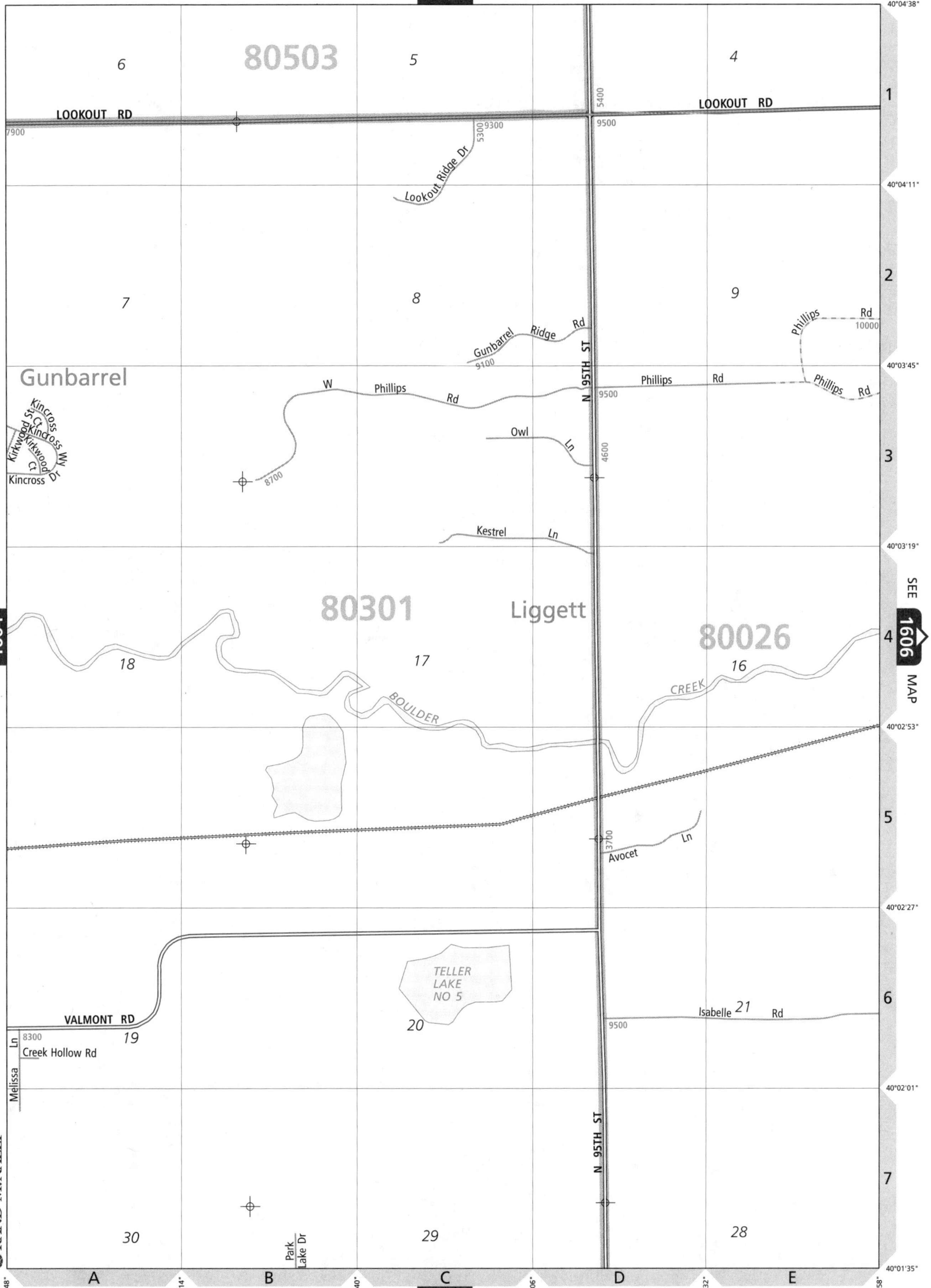

SEE 1604 MAP

SEE 1606 MAP

SEE 1689 MAP

1:24,000
1 in. = 2000 ft.
0 0.25 0.5
miles

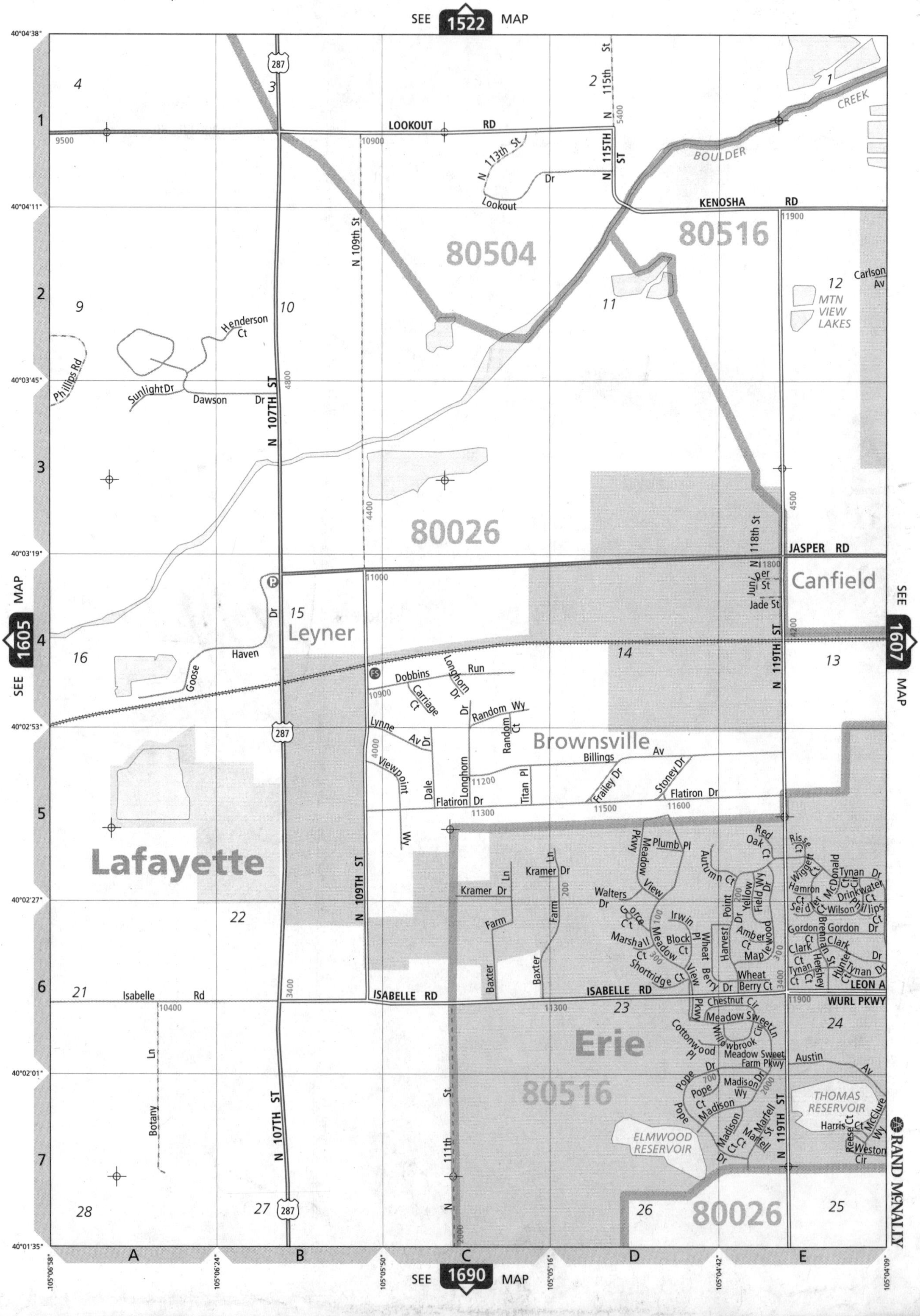

SEE 1522 MAP

LOOKOUT RD
KENOSHA RD
JASPER RD
ISABELLE RD
WURL PKWY
N 107TH ST
N 109TH ST
N 115TH ST
N 119TH ST
80504
80516
80026
Leyner
Canfield
Brownsville
Lafayette
Erie
BOULDER CREEK
MTN VIEW LAKES
THOMAS RESERVOIR
ELMWOOD RESERVOIR

SEE 1605 MAP

SEE 1607 MAP

A B C D E

SEE 1690 MAP

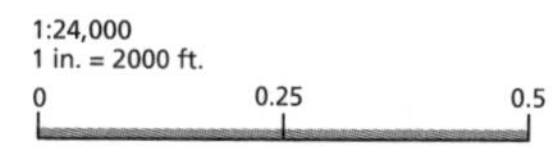

SEE 1523 MAP

KENOSHA RD
E COUNTY LINE RD
JASPER RD
JAY RD
CHEESMAN ST
BOULDER CO
WELD CO
LEON A WURL PKWY
CR-10.5
CR-12
CR-10
CR-3
CR-1.5
CR-6
Erie
80516
80026
COAL CREEK PARK
Erie Middle & HS

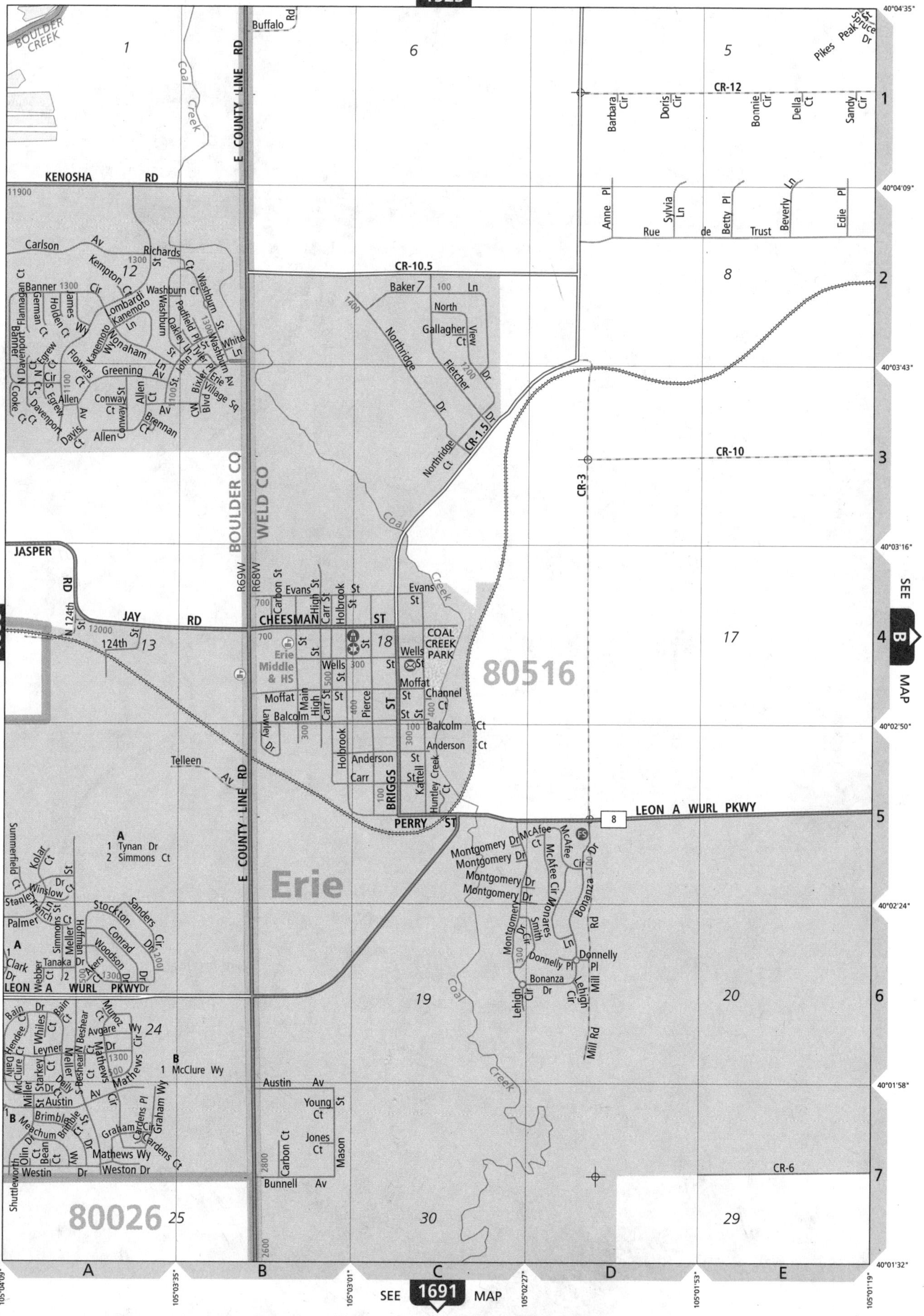

SEE 1606 MAP

SEE B MAP

SEE 1691 MAP

1:24,000
1 in. = 2000 ft.
0 0.25 0.5
miles

SEE 1597 MAP

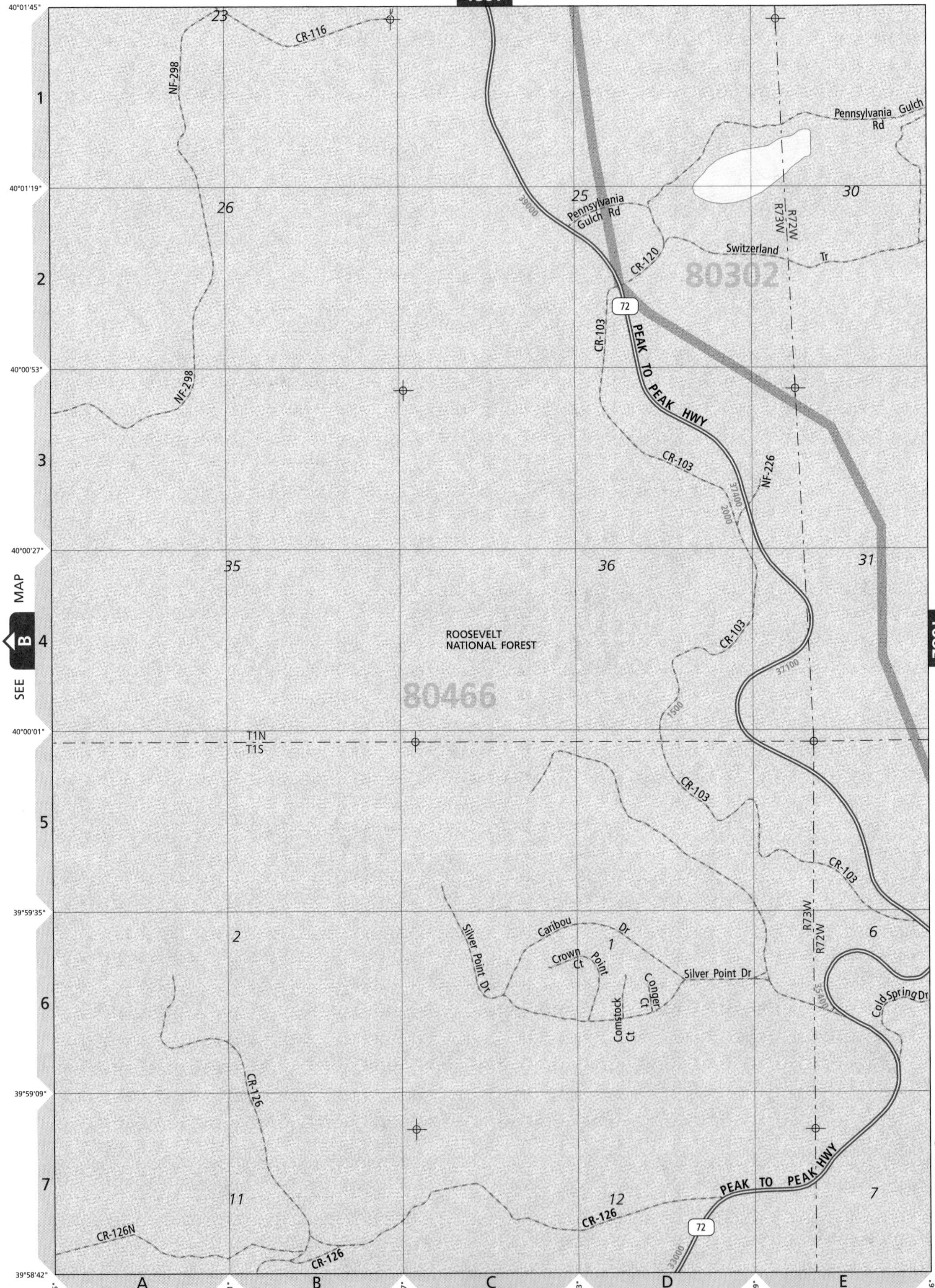

SEE B MAP

SEE 1682 MAP

SEE 1765 MAP

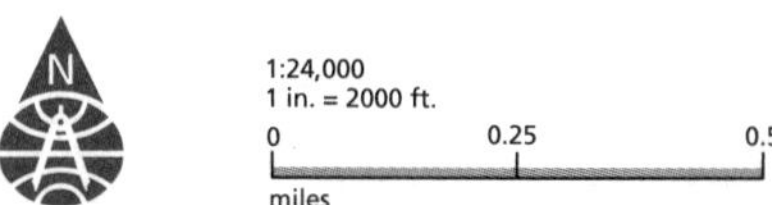

SEE 1598 MAP

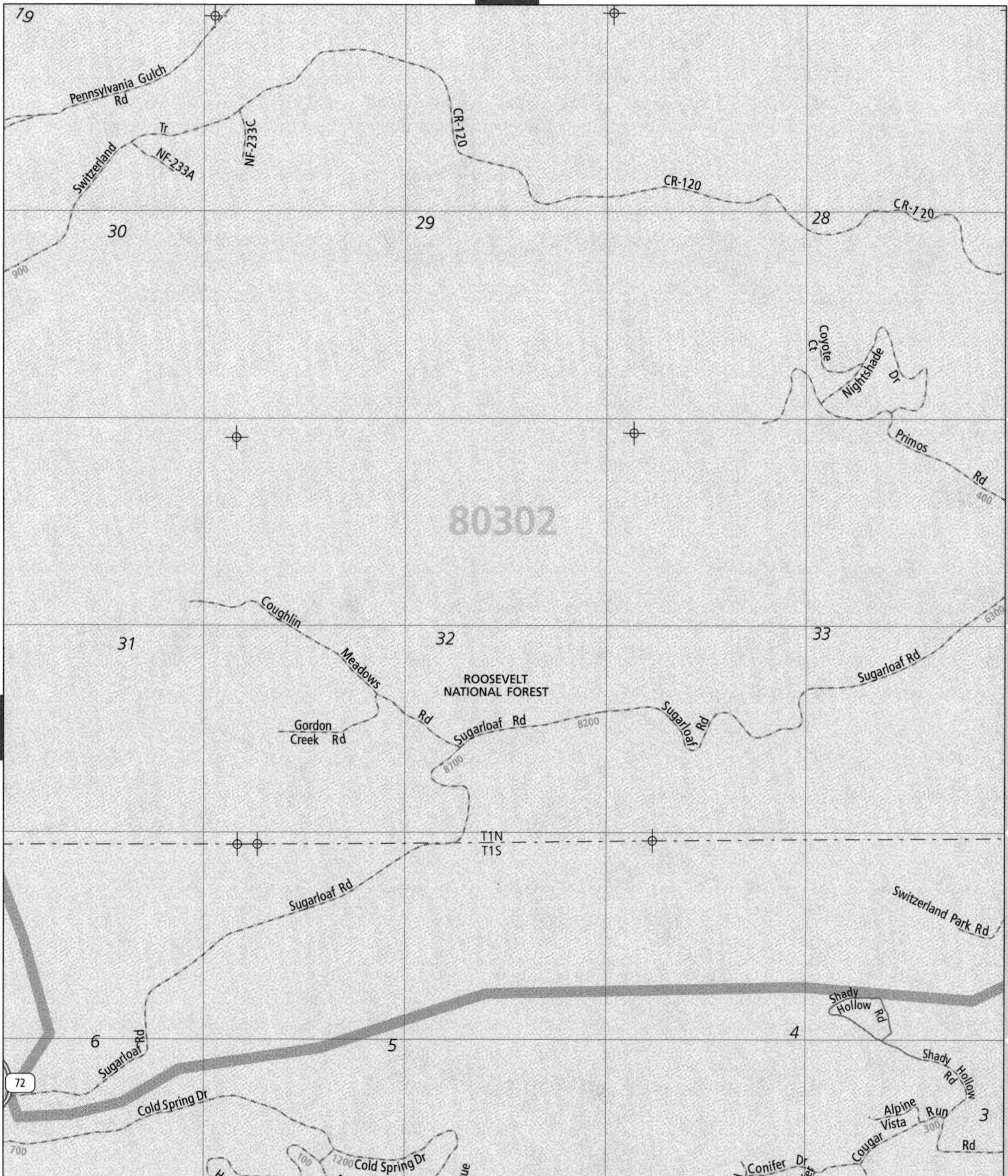

SEE 1681 MAP

SEE 1683 MAP

SEE 1766 MAP

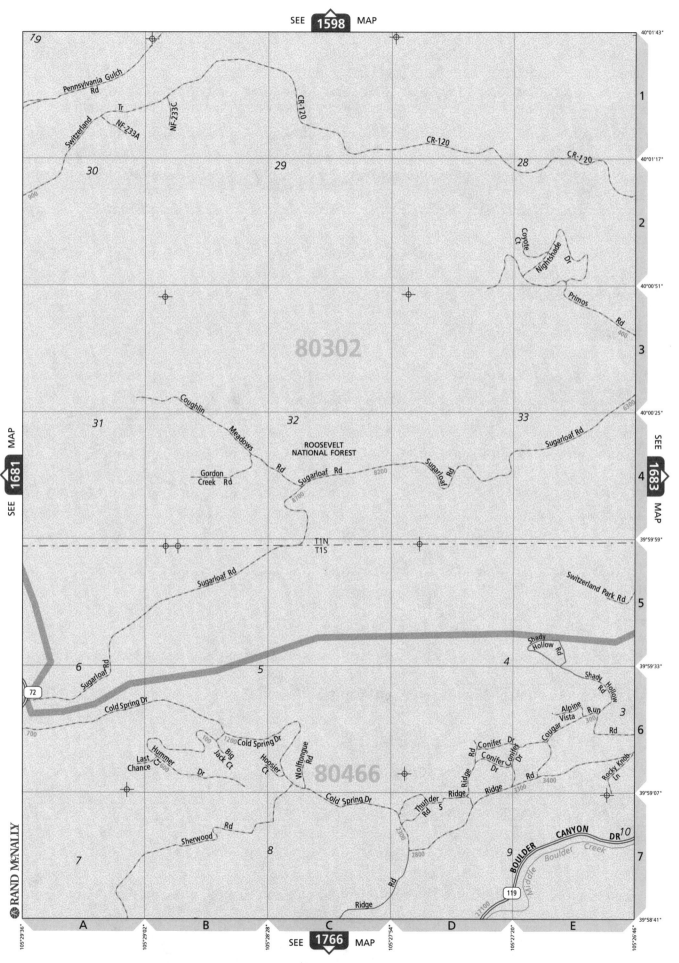

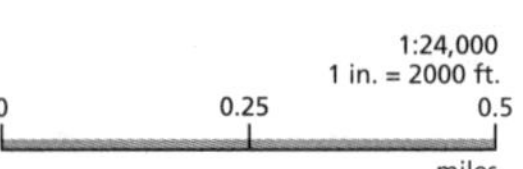

SEE 1599 MAP

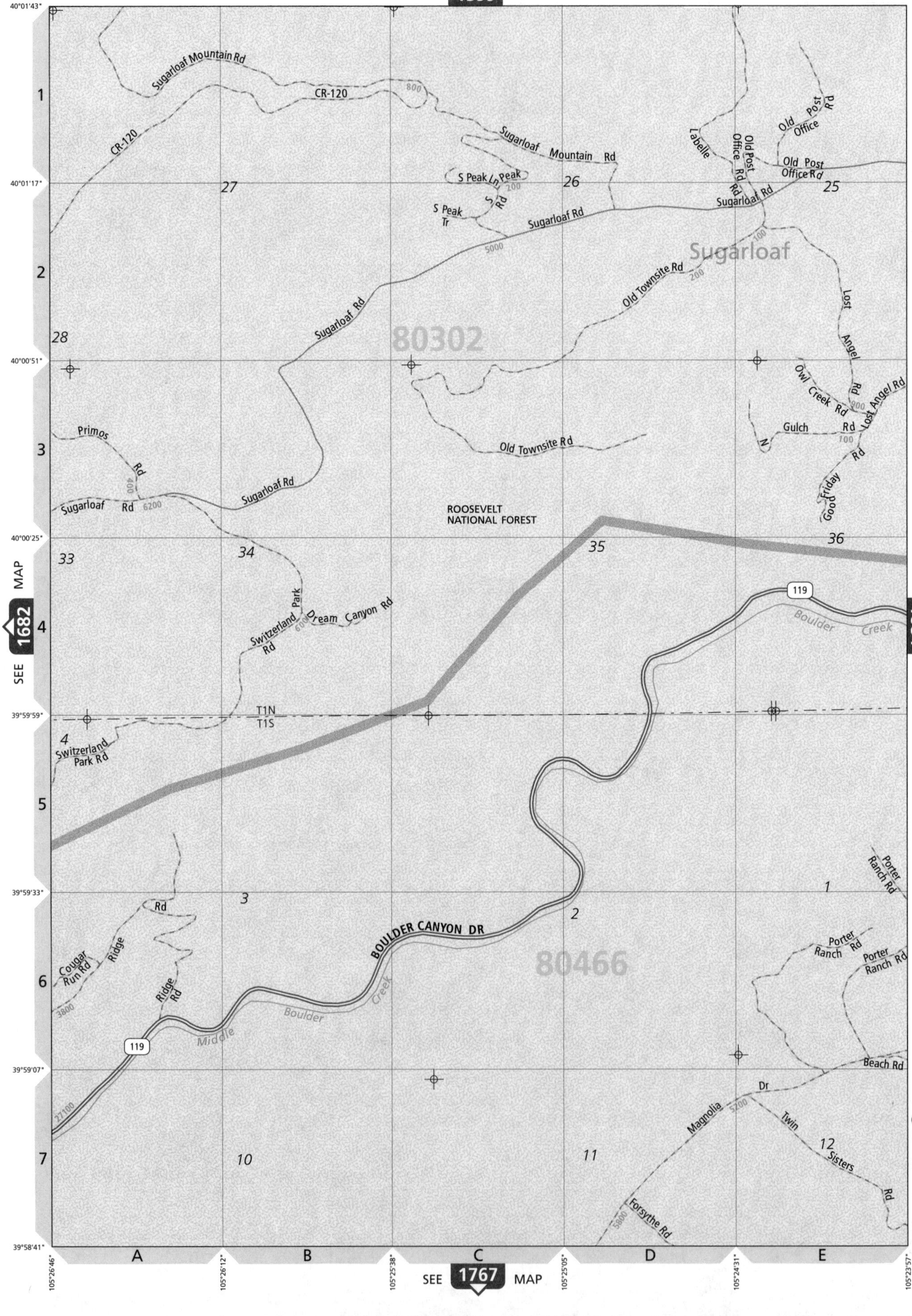

SEE 1682 MAP

SEE 1684 MAP

Sugarloaf Mountain Rd
CR-120
Sugarloaf Mountain Rd
S Peak Ln
Peak
S Rd
S Peak Tr
Sugarloaf Rd
Labelle
Old Post Office Rd
Old Post Office Rd
Old Post Office Rd
Sugarloaf Rd
Sugarloaf
80302
Old Townsite Rd
Lost Angel Rd
Owl Creek Rd
Gulch Rd
Lost Angel Rd
Good Friday Rd
Primos Rd
Sugarloaf Rd
Old Townsite Rd
ROOSEVELT NATIONAL FOREST
Switzerland Park Rd
Dream Canyon Rd
T1N
T1S
119
Boulder Creek
Porter Ranch Rd
BOULDER CANYON DR
Middle Boulder Creek
Cougar Run Rd
Ridge Rd
80466
Porter Ranch Rd
Beach Rd
Magnolia Dr
Twin Sisters Rd
Forsythe Rd

SEE 1767 MAP

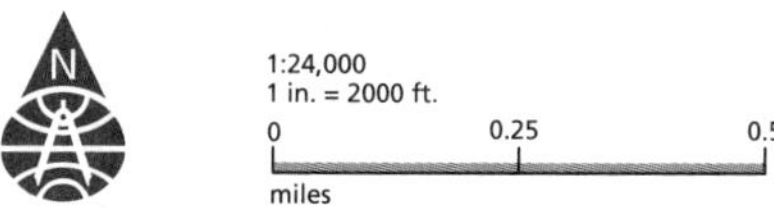

SEE 1600 MAP

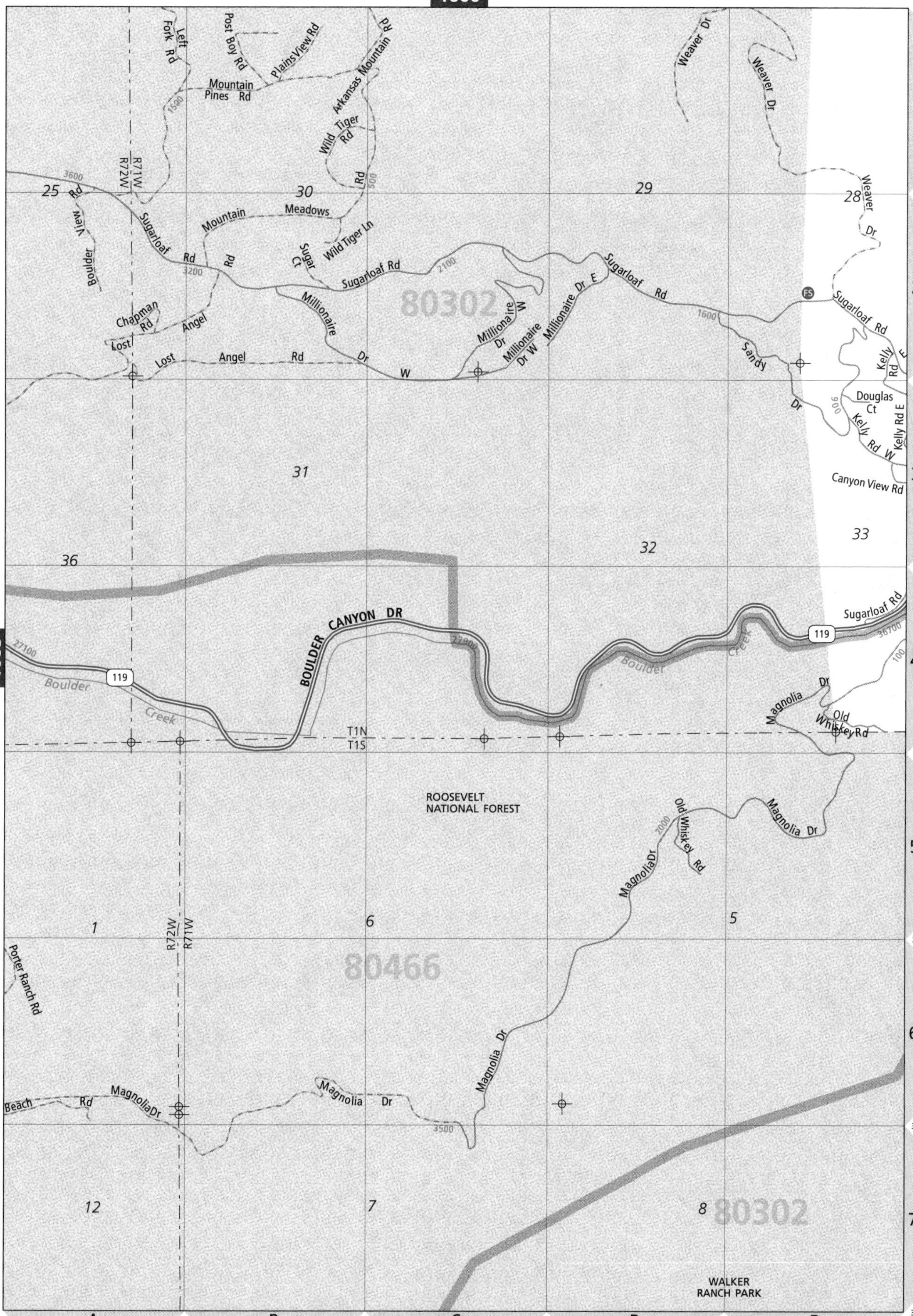

SEE 1683 MAP

SEE 1685 MAP

Left Fork Rd
Post Boy Rd
Plains View Rd
Arkansas Mountain Rd
Mountain Pines Rd
Wild Tiger Rd
Weaver Dr
Boulder View Rd
Sugarloaf Rd
Mountain Meadows Rd
Sugar Ct
Wild Tiger Ln
Chapman Rd
Lost Angel Rd
Millionaire Dr W
Millionaire Dr E
Sandy Dr
Kelly Rd E
Kelly Rd W
Douglas Ct
Canyon View Rd
80302
BOULDER CANYON DR
119
Boulder Creek
Magnolia Dr
Old Whiskey Rd
T1N
T1S
R71W
R72W
ROOSEVELT NATIONAL FOREST
80466
Porter Ranch Rd
Beach Rd
WALKER RANCH PARK

SEE 1768 MAP

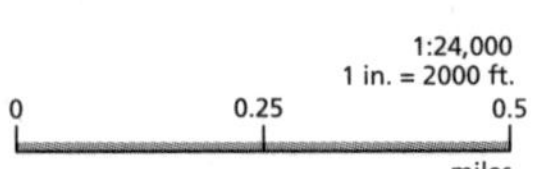

SEE 1601 MAP

Orodell
Fourmile Canyon Dr
Sunshine Canyon Dr
Granite Dr
Timber Tr
Seven Hills Dr
Anemone Dr
Seven Hills Dr
BETASSO PRESERVE
Broken Fence Rd
Betasso Rd
Kelly Rd E
Canyon View Rd
Sugarloaf Rd
Turnagain Ct
Canyonside Dr
Boulder Creek
BOULDER CANYON DR
119
Chapman Dr
BOULDER CANYON DR
Silver Spruce
El Vado
Red Lion Rd
Magnolia Dr
80302
80466
T1N
T1S
Flagstaff Summit Rd
Flagstaff Rd
ROOSEVELT NATIONAL FOREST
BOULDER MOUNTAIN PARK
WALKER RANCH PARK
KOSSLER LAKE
Bison Dr
BOULDER MOUNTAIN PARK
RAND McNALLY

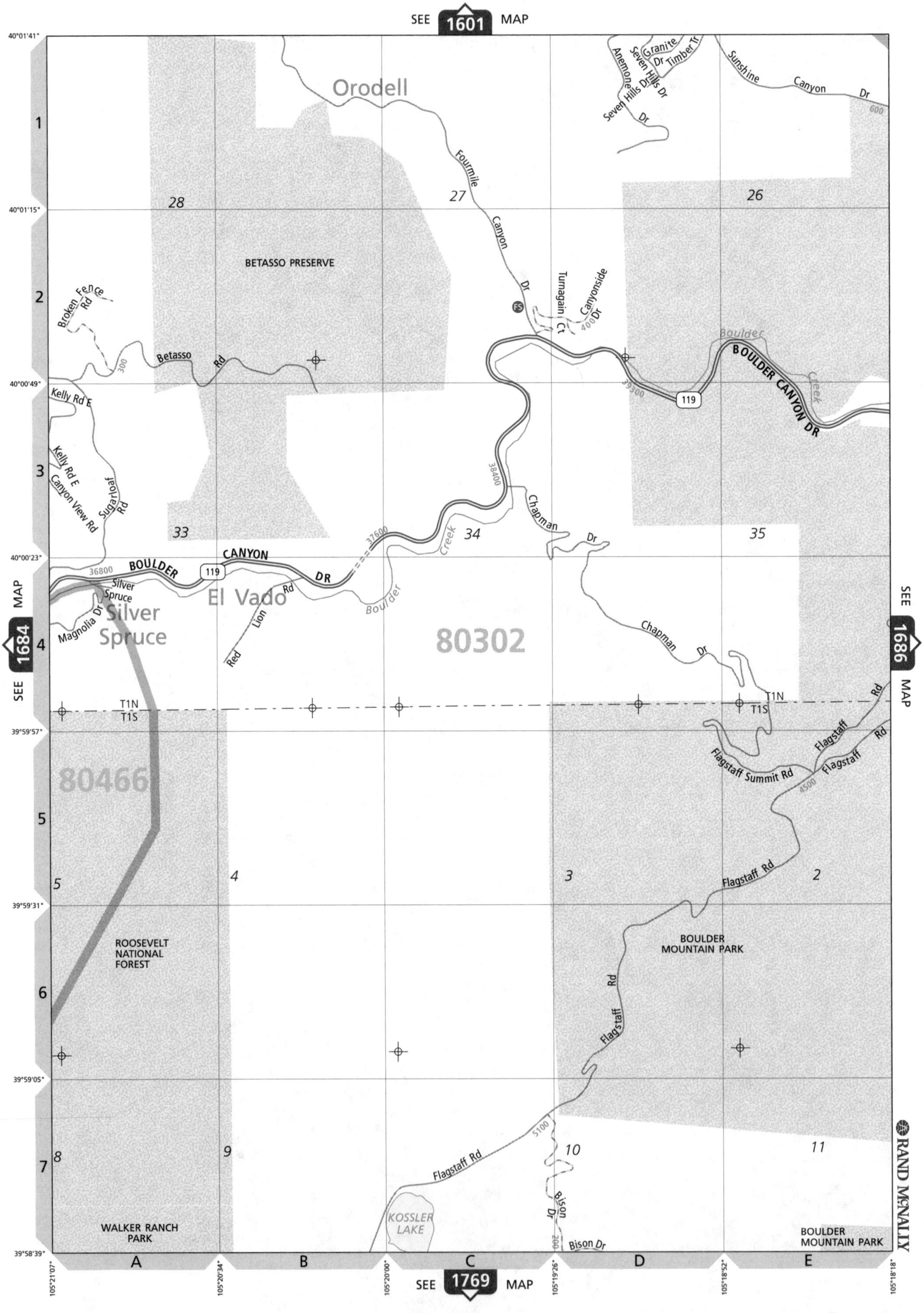

SEE 1684 MAP

SEE 1686 MAP

SEE 1769 MAP

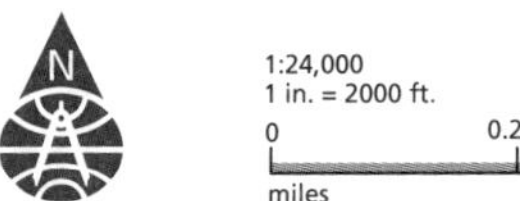

SEE 1602 MAP

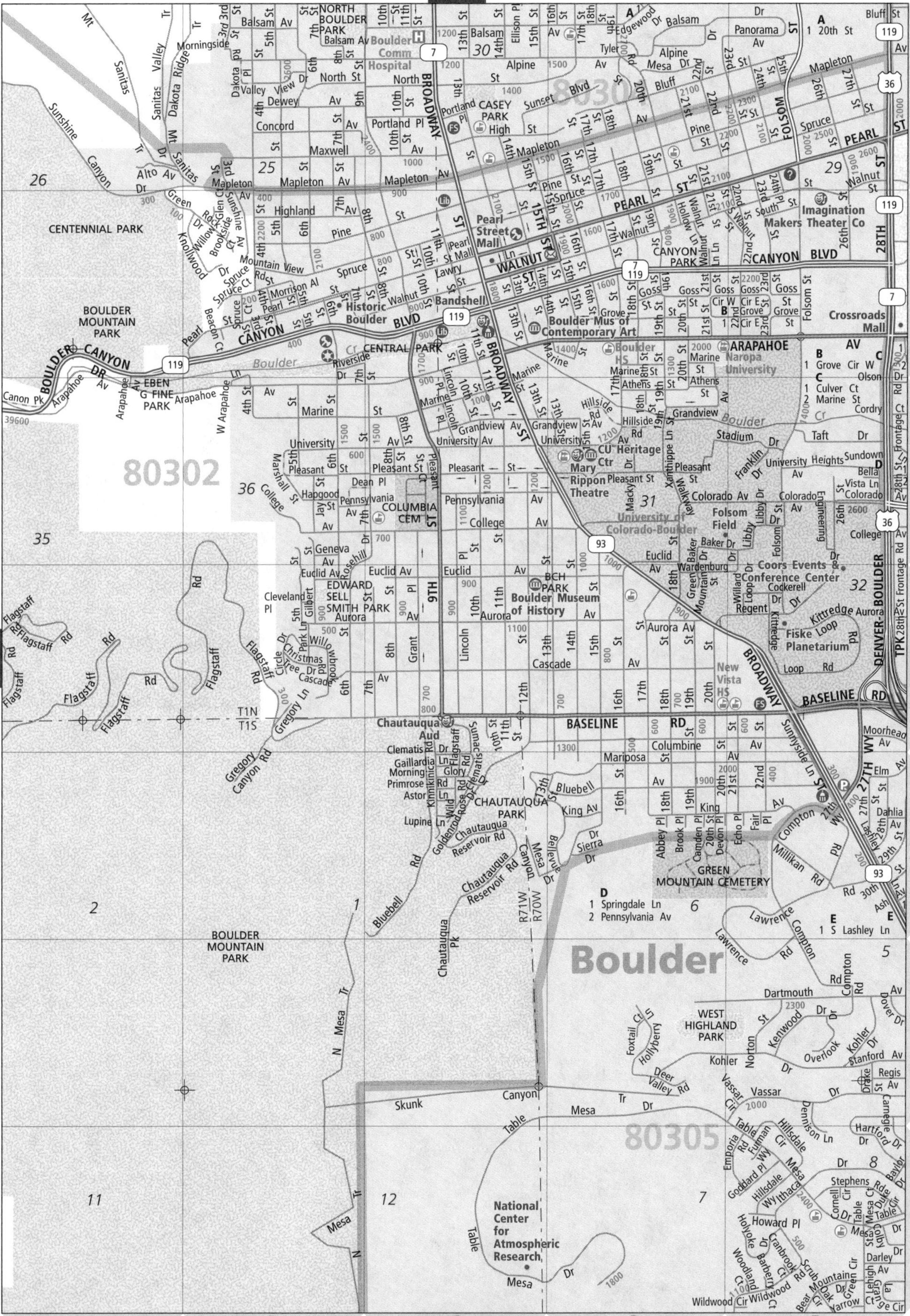

SEE 1685 MAP

SEE 1687 MAP

SEE 1770 MAP

Boulder

80302

80304

80305

CENTENNIAL PARK

BOULDER MOUNTAIN PARK

EBEN G FINE PARK

NORTH BOULDER PARK

Boulder Comm Hospital

CASEY PARK

Pearl Street Mall

Historic Boulder

Bandshell

CENTRAL PARK

Boulder Mus of Contemporary Art

Boulder HS

Naropa University

Crossroads Mall

Imagination Makers Theater Co

CU Heritage Ctr

Mary Rippon Theatre

University of Colorado-Boulder

Folsom Field

Coors Events & Conference Center

Fiske Planetarium

COLUMBIA CEM

EDWARD SELL SMITH PARK

BCH PARK

Boulder Museum of History

New Vista HS

Chautauqua Aud

CHAUTAUQUA PARK

GREEN MOUNTAIN CEMETERY

WEST HIGHLAND PARK

National Center for Atmospheric Research

A
1 20th St

B
1 Grove Cir W

C
1 Culver Ct
2 Marine St

D
1 Springdale Ln
2 Pennsylvania Av

E
1 S Lashley Ln

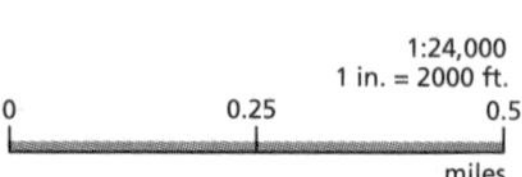

SEE 1603 MAP

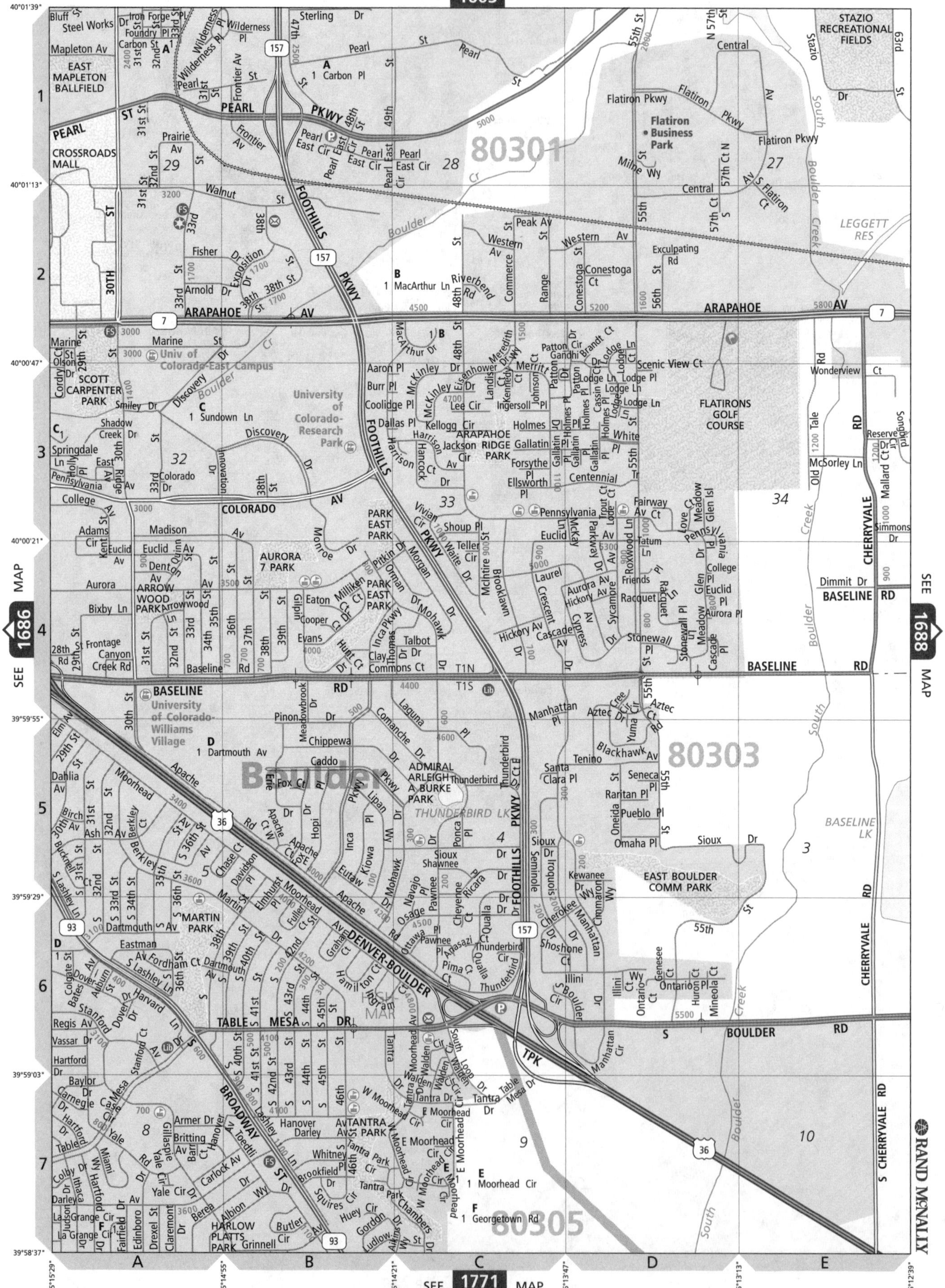

SEE 1686 MAP

SEE 1688 MAP

SEE 1771 MAP

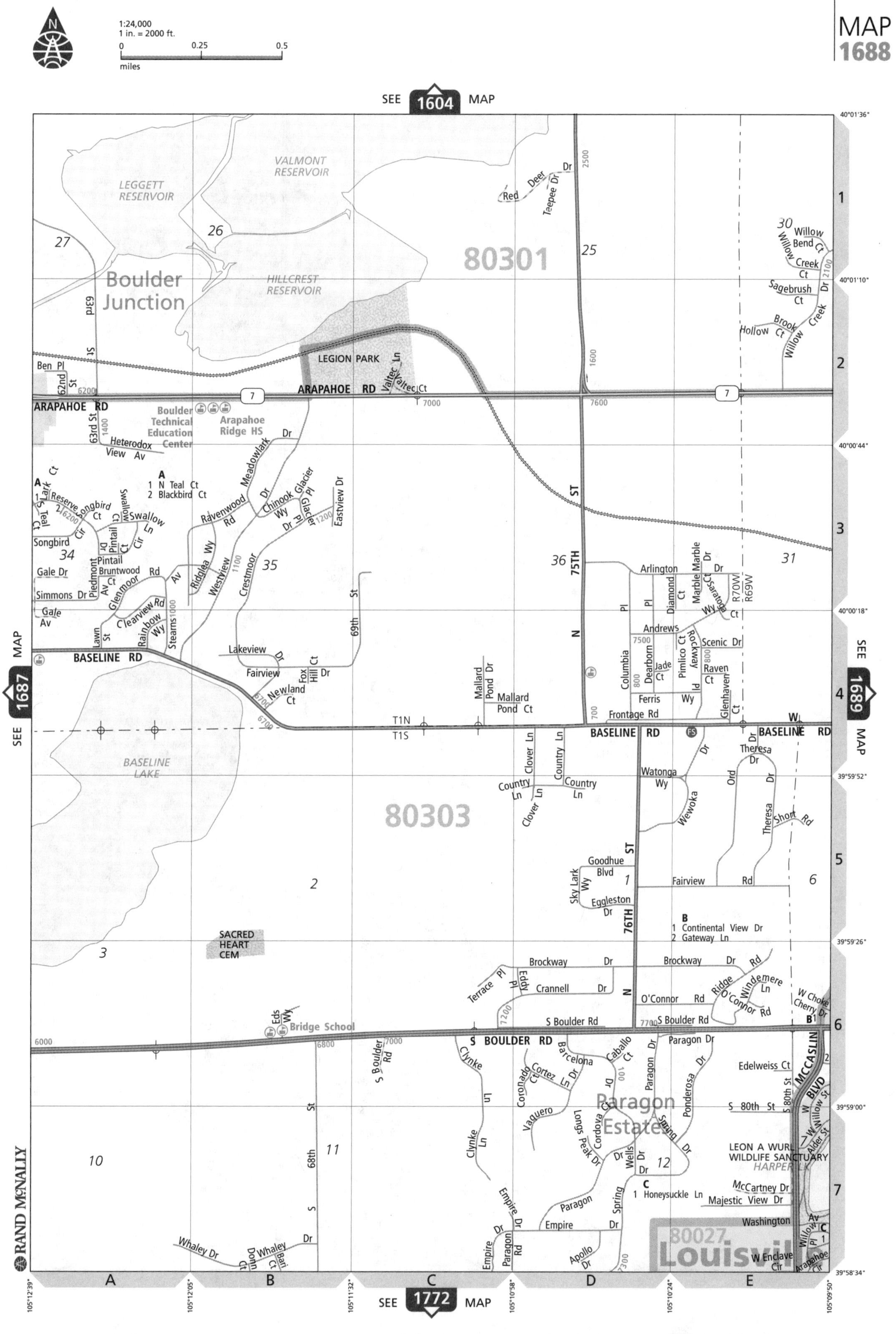

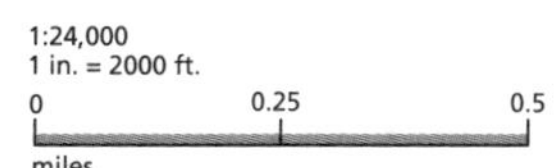

SEE 1604 MAP

SEE 1687 MAP

SEE 1689 MAP

SEE 1772 MAP

1:24,000
1 in. = 2000 ft.
0 0.25 0.5
miles

SEE 1605 MAP

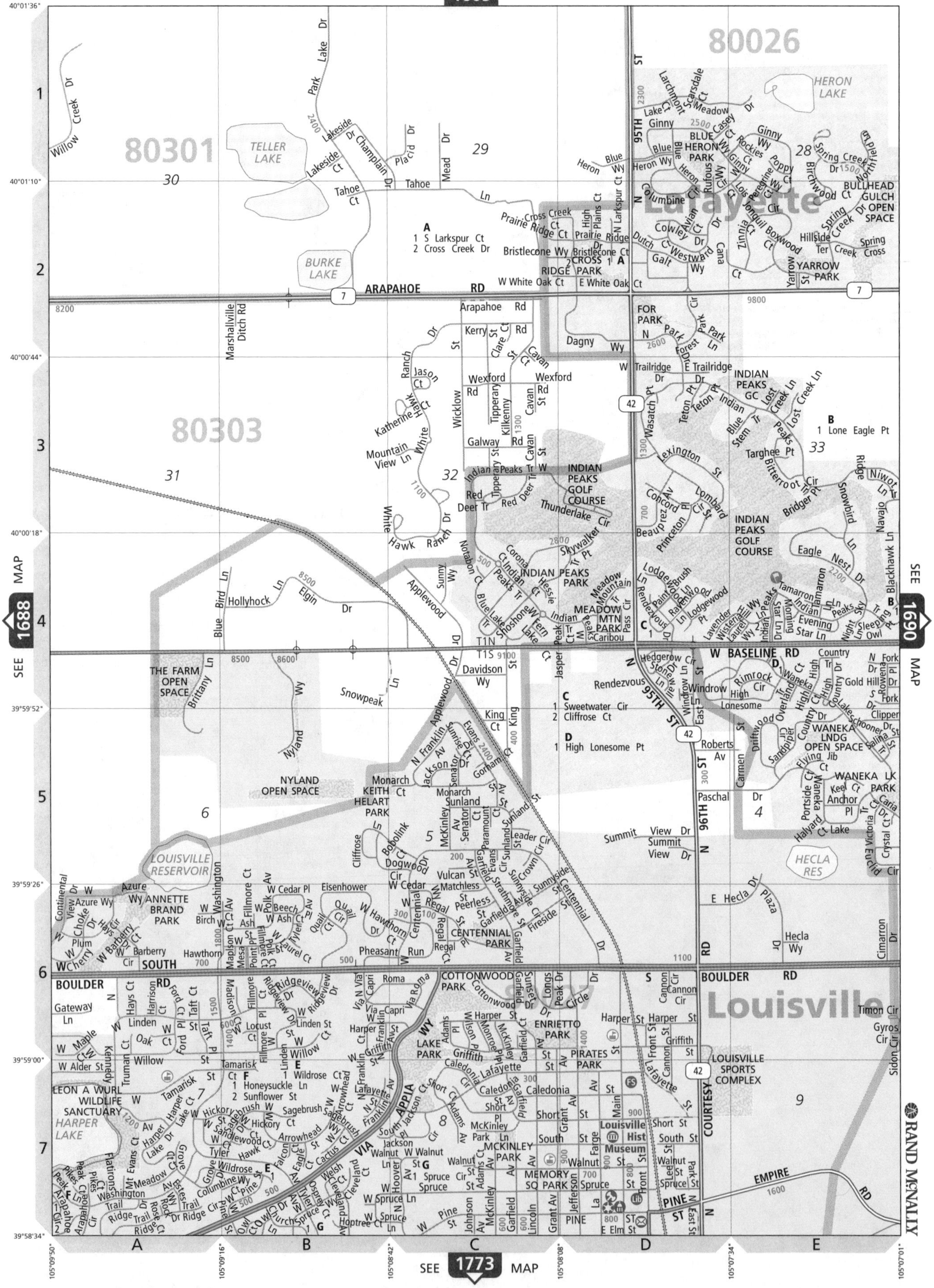

SEE 1688 MAP

SEE 1690 MAP

SEE 1773 MAP

80026
80301
80303
Lafayette
Louisville

A
1 S Larkspur Ct
2 Cross Creek Dr

B
1 Lone Eagle Pt

C
1 Sweetwater Cir
2 Cliffrose Ct

D
1 High Lonesome Pt

E
1 Wildrose Ct

F
1 Honeysuckle Ln
2 Sunflower St

TELLER LAKE
BURKE LAKE
HERON LAKE
HECLA RES
LOUISVILLE RESERVOIR
HARPER LAKE
BLUE HERON PARK
BULLHEAD GULCH OPEN SPACE
CROSS RIDGE PARK
YARROW PARK
FOR PARK
INDIAN PEAKS GC
INDIAN PEAKS GOLF COURSE
INDIAN PEAKS PARK
MEADOW MTN PARK
THE FARM OPEN SPACE
NYLAND OPEN SPACE
KEITH HELART PARK
WANEKA LNDG OPEN SPACE
WANEKA LK PARK
ANNETTE BRAND PARK
CENTENNIAL PARK
COTTONWOOD PARK
ENRIETTO PARK
PIRATES PARK
LAKE PARK
LEON A WURL WILDLIFE SANCTUARY
MCKINLEY PARK
MEMORY SQ PARK
LOUISVILLE SPORTS COMPLEX
Louisville Hist Museum

ARAPAHOE RD
W BASELINE RD
SOUTH BOULDER RD
N 95TH ST
N 96TH ST
COURTESY RD
EMPIRE RD
VIA APPIA WY
PINE ST

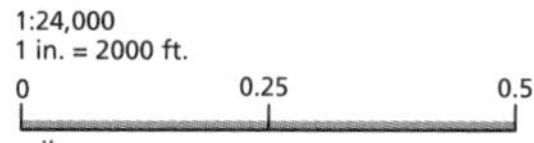

SEE 1606 MAP

Erie
80516
Lafayette
80026
Ninemile Corner
Louisville

PRINCE LAKE
ERIE LAKE
MARFELL LAKES
PRINCE RESERVOIR
GREENLEE RES
WANEKA RESERVOIR
WANEKA LAKE PARK
AUTUMN ASH PARK
LINDENWOOD PARK
GREAT PARK
CITY PARK
LAFAYETTE CEM
SUNSET MAPLE PARK
MILLER GDNS
BARBERRY PARK
LAMONT DOES MEM PARK
WHISPERING MEADOWS PARK
COTTONWOOD PARK
RED OAK PARK
CORAL CREEK CORRIDOR
COAL CREEK CORRIDOR
COAL CREEK AT AVALON OPEN SPACE
WAREMBOURG OPEN SPACE
WOW Children's Mus
Miners Mus
Centaurus HS
Peak to Peak Middle/High Charter School

ARAPAHOE RD
N 107TH ST
N 111th St
N 119TH ST
N 120TH ST
S 120TH ST
W BASELINE RD
E BASELINE RD
N PUBLIC RD
S PUBLIC RD
SOUTH BOULDER RD
EMPIRE RD
S 112TH ST
FLAGG DR

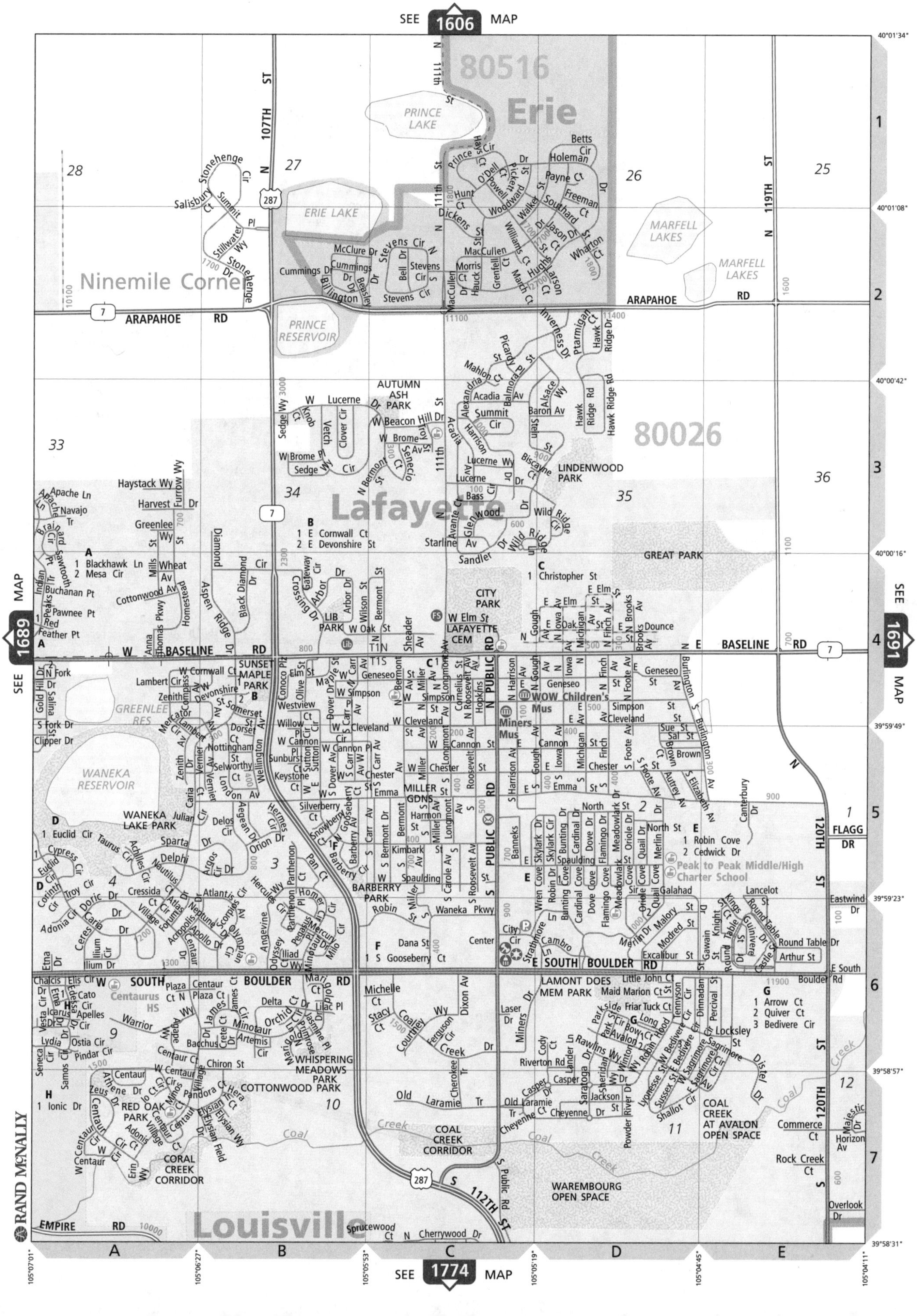

A
1 Blackhawk Ln
2 Mesa Cir

B
1 E Cornwall Ct
2 E Devonshire St

C
1 Christopher St

D
1 Euclid Cir

E
1 Robin Cove
2 Cedwick Dr

F
1 S Gooseberry Ct

G
1 Arrow Ct
2 Quiver Ct
3 Bedivere Cir

H
1 Ionic Dr

SEE 1689 MAP
SEE 1691 MAP
SEE 1774 MAP

1:24,000
1 in. = 2000 ft.
0 0.25 0.5
miles

SEE 1607 MAP

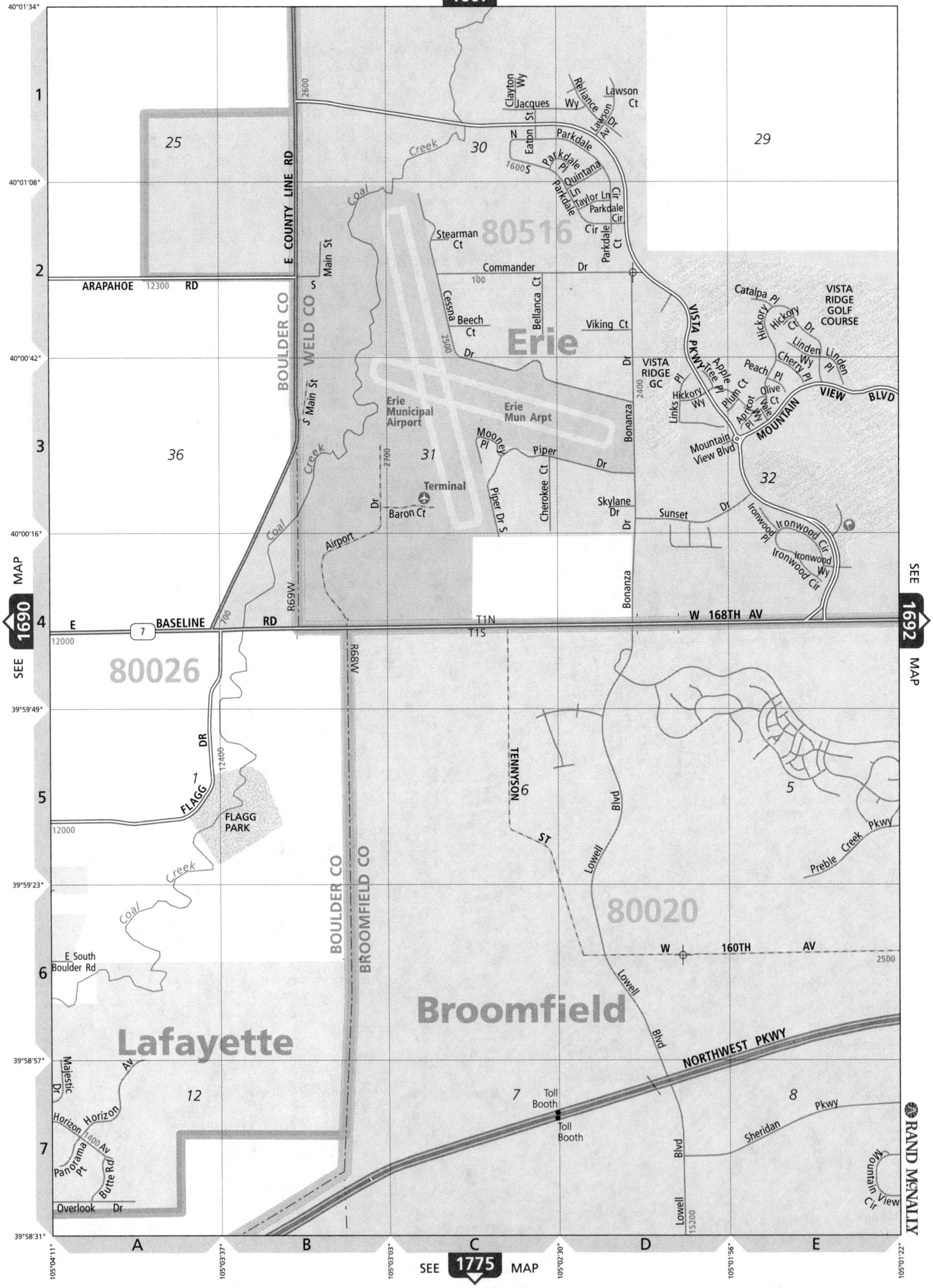

SEE 1690 MAP

SEE 1692 MAP

SEE 1775 MAP

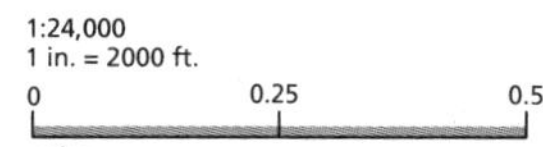

SEE B MAP

SEE 1691 MAP

SEE 1693 MAP

SEE 1776 MAP

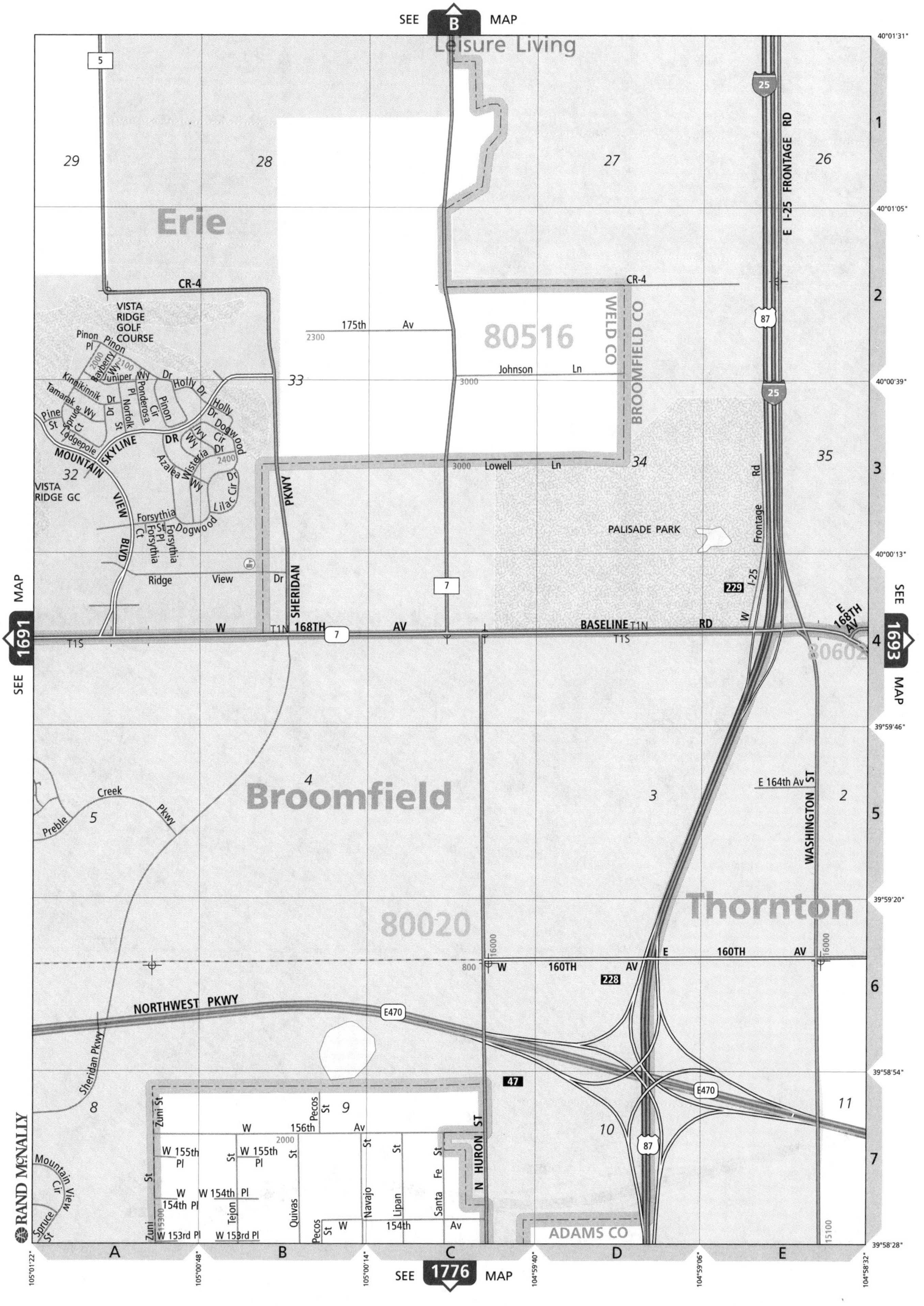

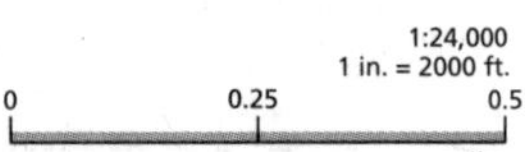
1:24,000
1 in. = 2000 ft.
0
0.25
0.5
miles

N

SEE B MAP
Broomfield
80516
80603
CR-11
CR-13
CR-4
BROOMFIELD CO
WELD CO
ADAMS CO
Thornton
E 168TH AV
T1N
T1S
R68W
R67W
Gilpin
Franklin
Humboldt
Lafayette
Marion
E 166th
E 165th
E 164th Av
E 164th Pl
Race St
High Pl
York St
Josephine
Columbine
Elizabeth
Clayton
Fillmore
Milwaukee
Paul St.
Steele
E 166th Av
E 164th Av
E 162nd Av
7
80020
80602
GERMAN RESERVOIR NO 1
Big Dry Creek
E 160TH AV
Jackson St
COLORADO BLVD
E 156th Av
E470
Toll Booth
45
43
26
25
30
35
36
31
2
1
6
11
12
7
SEE 1692 MAP
SEE 1694 MAP 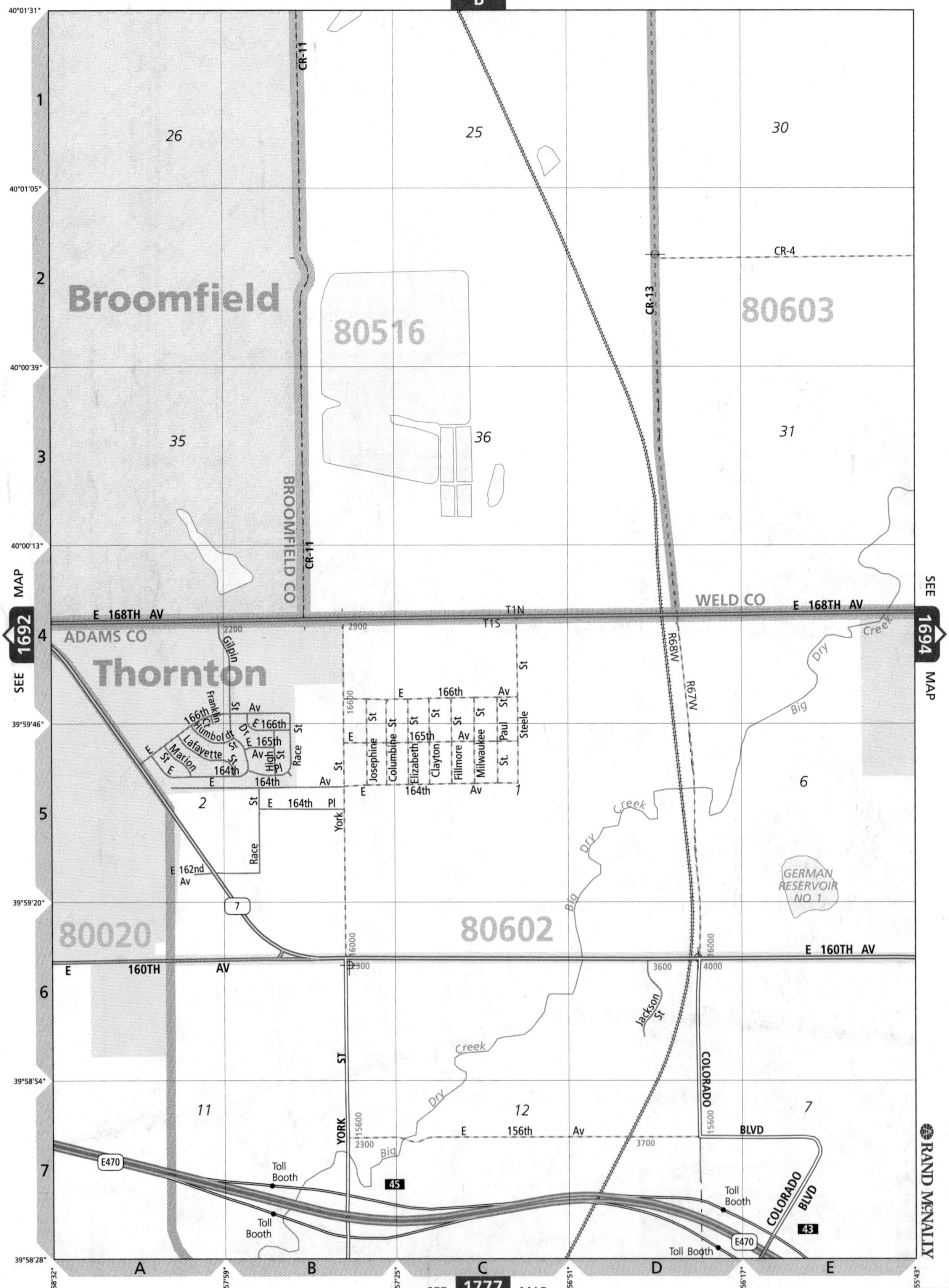
SEE 1777 MAP
A B C D E
1 2 3 4 5 6 7
RAND McNALLY

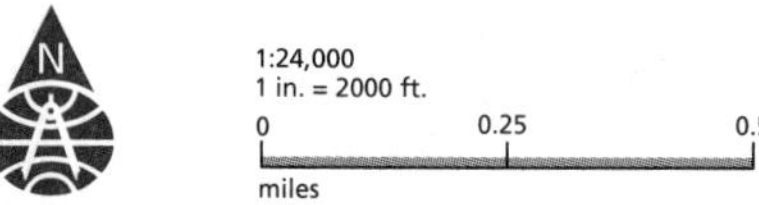

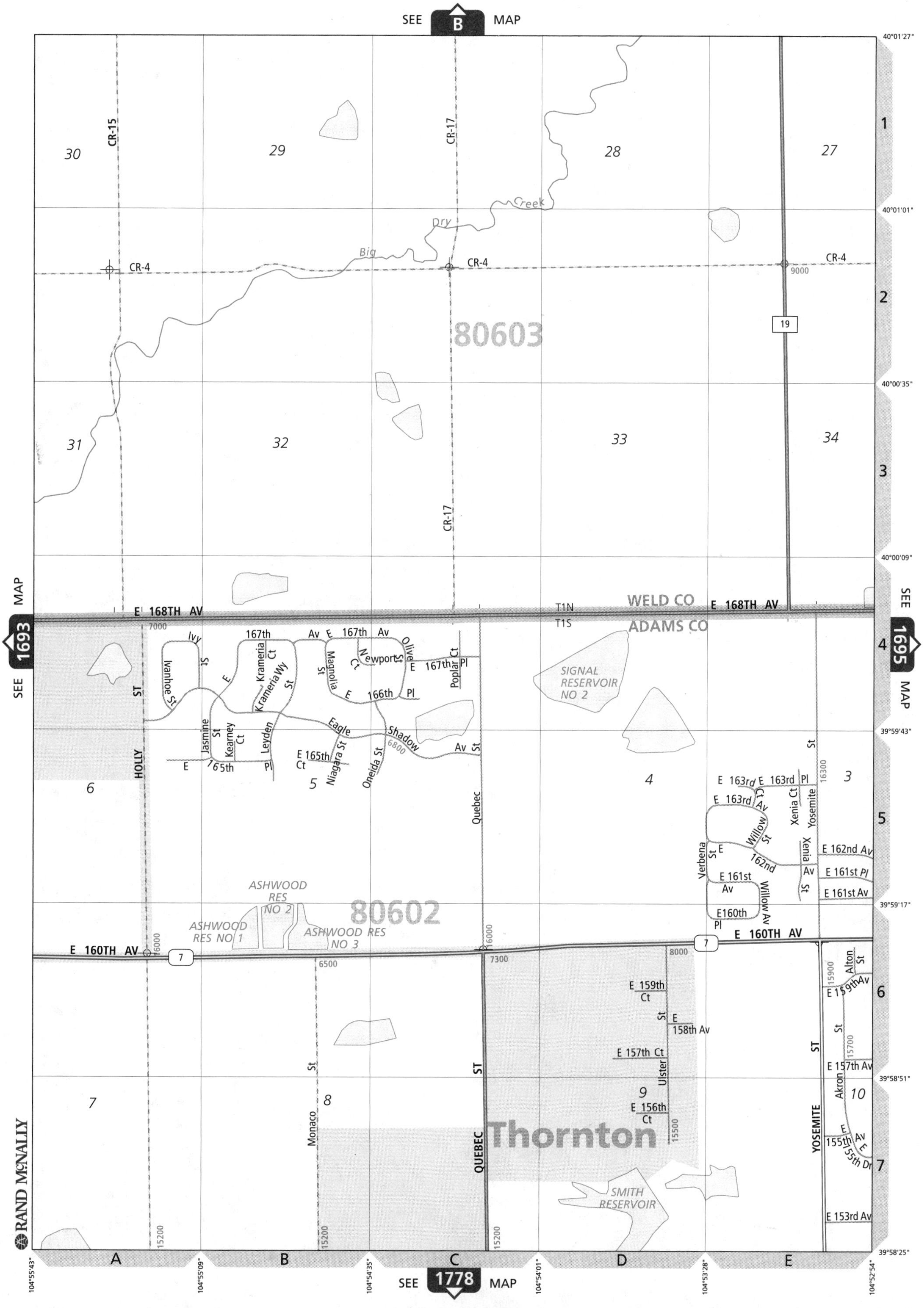

SEE B MAP

SEE 1693 MAP

SEE 1695 MAP

SEE 1778 MAP

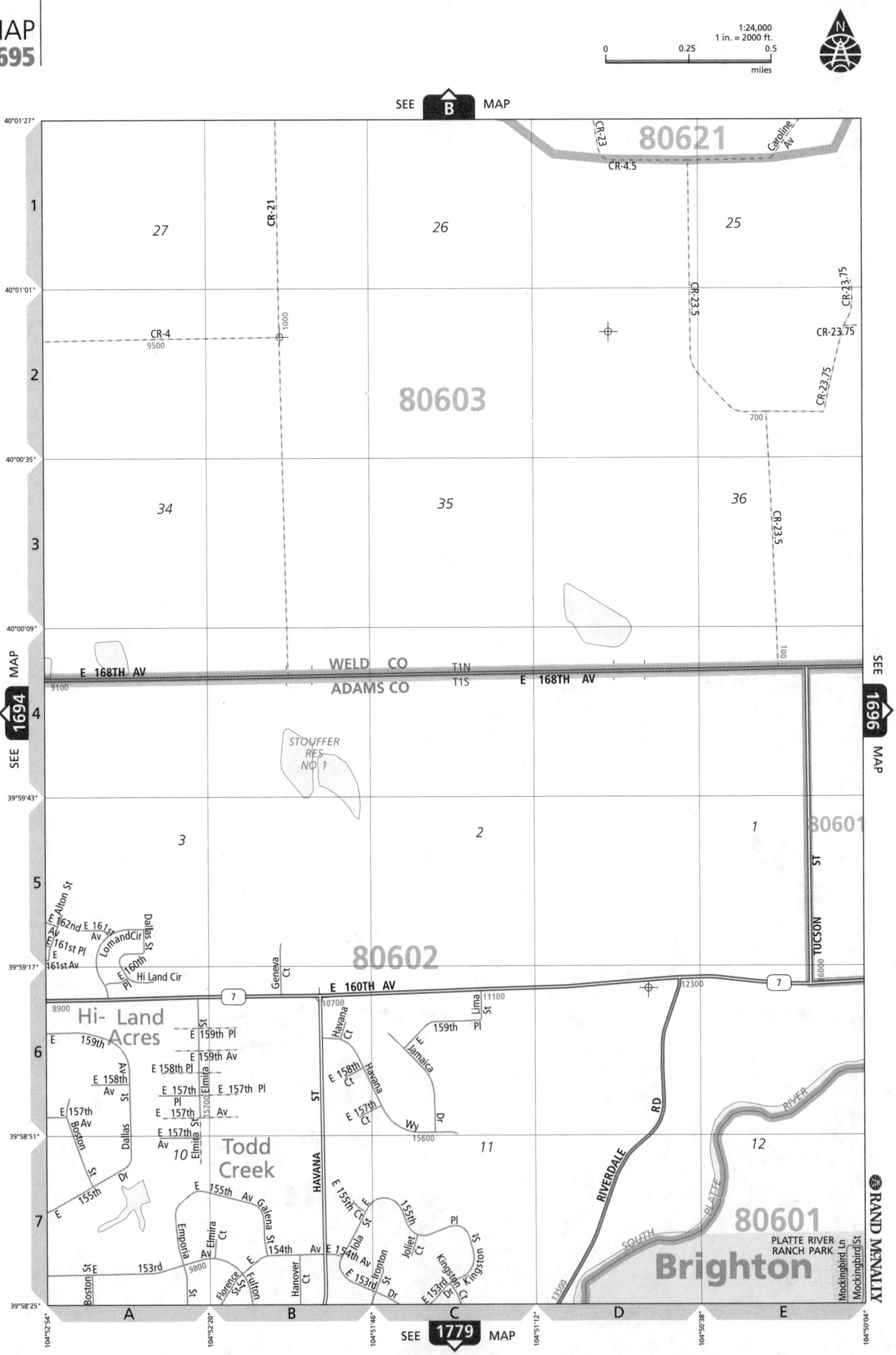

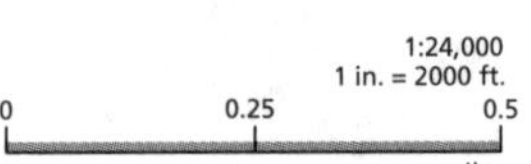

SEE B MAP

SEE 1694 MAP
SEE 1696 MAP
SEE 1779 MAP

1:24,000
1 in. = 2000 ft.
0 0.25 0.5
miles

SEE B MAP

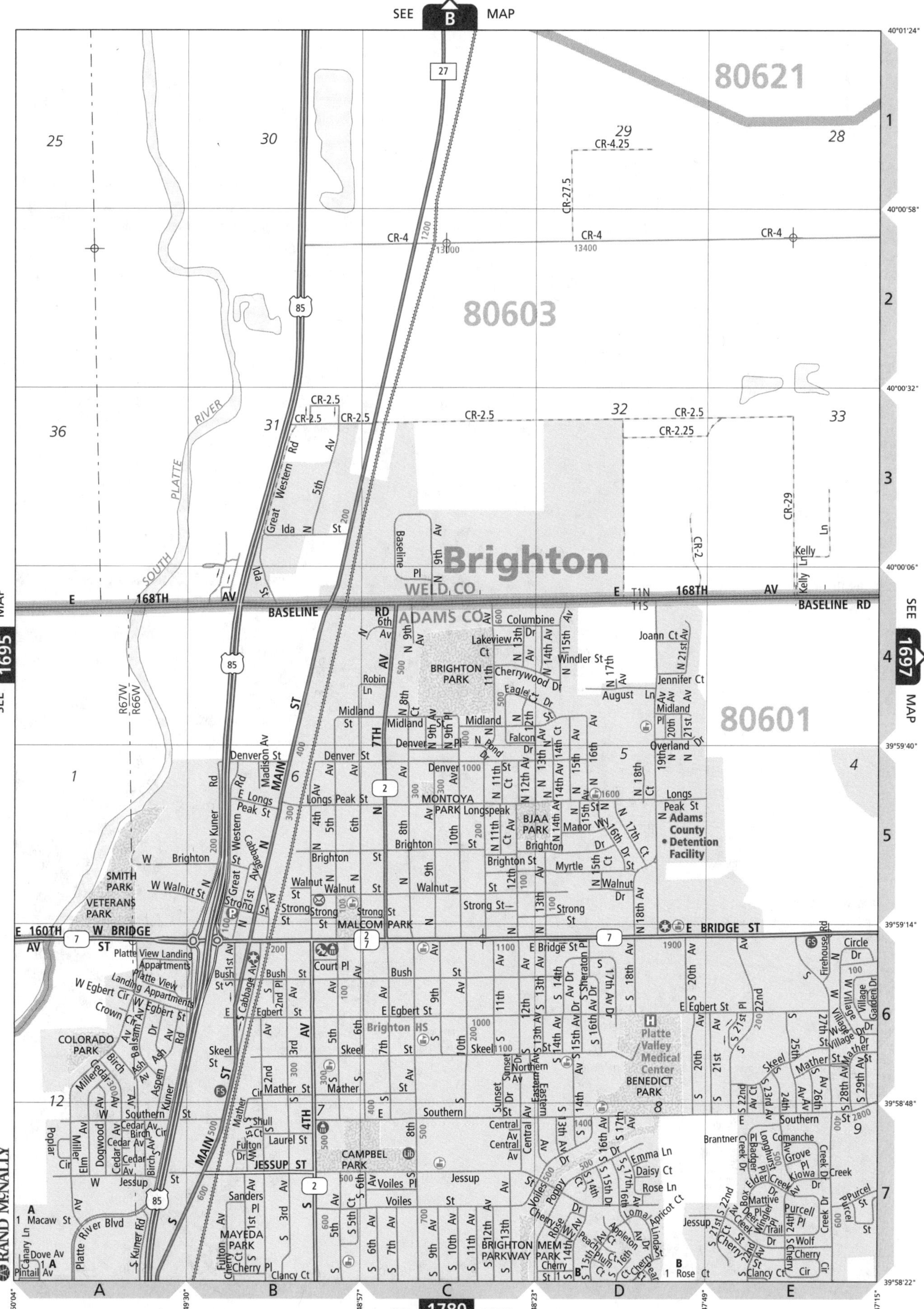

A B C D E
1 2 3 4 5 6 7

40°01'24"
40°00'58"
40°00'32"
40°00'06"
39°59'40"
39°59'14"
39°58'48"
39°58'22"
104°50'04"
104°49'30"
104°48'57"
104°48'23"
104°47'49"
104°47'15"

SEE 1695 MAP
SEE 1697 MAP
SEE 1780 MAP

1:24,000
1 in. = 2000 ft.
0 0.25 0.5
miles

SEE B MAP

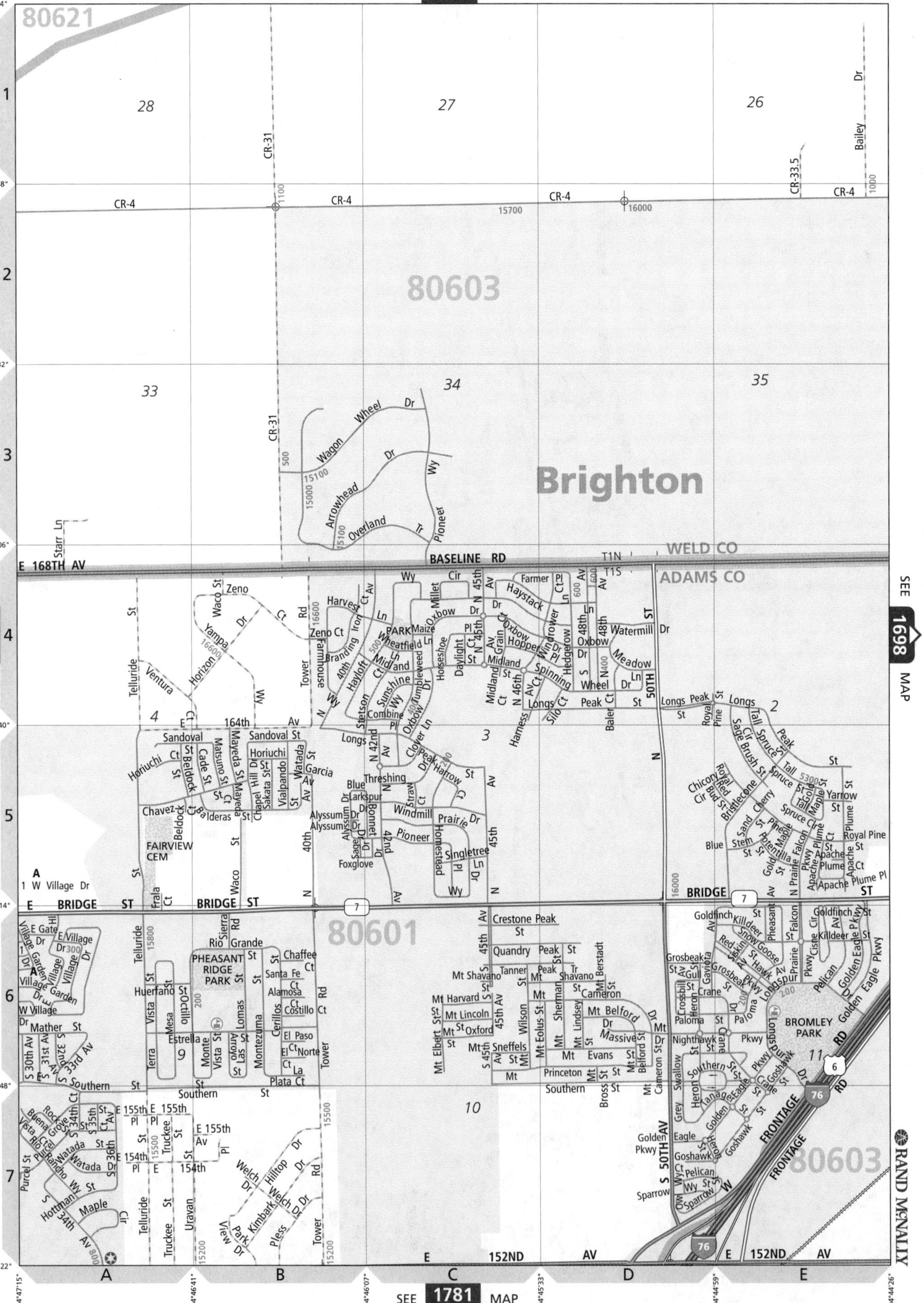

80621
80603
Brighton
80601
80603

WELD CO
ADAMS CO
T1N
T1S

E 168TH AV
BASELINE RD
E BRIDGE ST
BRIDGE ST
E 152ND AV
FRONTAGE RD
CR-4
CR-31
CR-33.5

28 27 26
33 34 35
4 3 2
9 10 11

FAIRVIEW CEM
PHEASANT RIDGE PARK
BROMLEY PARK

SEE 1696 MAP
SEE 1698 MAP
SEE 1781 MAP

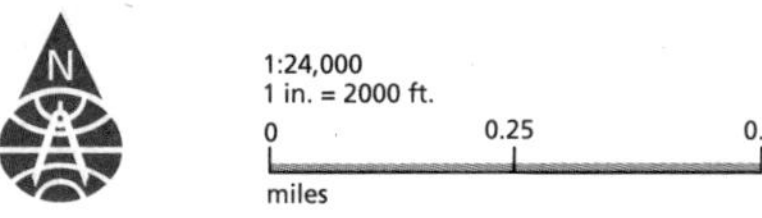

SEE B MAP

CR-33.75
26
25
37
30
CR-39
I-76
FRONTAGE RD
29
CR-4
80642
1100
CR-4
16900
CR-4
4
76
6
FRONTAGE RD
Cedar Cir
Zante Wy
400
Zante
Pinyon Cir
Yakima Ct
Av
700
Valdai
Spruce Pl
Wy
BLVD
Lilac Dr
Zante Ct
1100
Lilac
Plum
Av
Dr
St
Lilac Cir W
Laredo Wy
Ravine Wy
Bonanza Blvd
36
35
31
32
Jordan Wy
500
Locust
Av
E Locust Av
Winnipeg
Zante
STEELE
Willow Pl
Willow Ct
Elm
Cherry
Dr
CR-39
400
Fox Haven Ct
18500
Stampede Dr
Cherokee Pl
Apache Pl
Valdai St
St
St
Spruce St
Winnipeg St
Versailles
Wenatchee
Yakima St
Cherokee Ct
Stampede Av
200
100
Poplar St
Willow
700
Lochbuie
700
Prairie
Laredo Pl
Ravine Pl
Frontier Pl
Willow Dr
FRANCES ST
Canyon Ln
Canyon Ct
Ravine Ct
Meadowlark Cir
Meadowlark Ln
25
T1N
T1S
WELD CO
ADAMS CO
2
BASELINE RD
E 168TH AV
18900

SEE 1697 MAP

SEE 1699 MAP

BOWLES RES NO 1
R65W
R66W
CALHOUN RES
CALHOUN RES
Harvest Rd
80601
2
Brighton
1
6
5
80603
76
6
FRONTAGE RD
BOWLES RES NO 2
BOWLES RESERVOIR NO 2
16000
E 160th Av
E 160th Av
BRIDGE ST
7
E 160th Av
W FRONTAGE RD
E 160th Av
23400
22400
Delta Ct
Fortune Ct
100
Bromley Business Pkwy
MEEKS RESERVOIR NO 1
Duquesne Cir
15800
E 157th Av
Degaulle Cir
Harvest Ct
Club Rd
15600
E 156th Av
24100
Elk Cir
Av
15600
Harvest Rd
8
11
12
7
Gun Club Rd
E 155th Wy
23000
Edna Dr
Green Dr
Harvest
E 154th Cir
E 153rd Cir
MEEKS RESERVOIR NO 2
PICADILLY RD
21800
E 152ND AV
24100
E 152ND AV
18
17

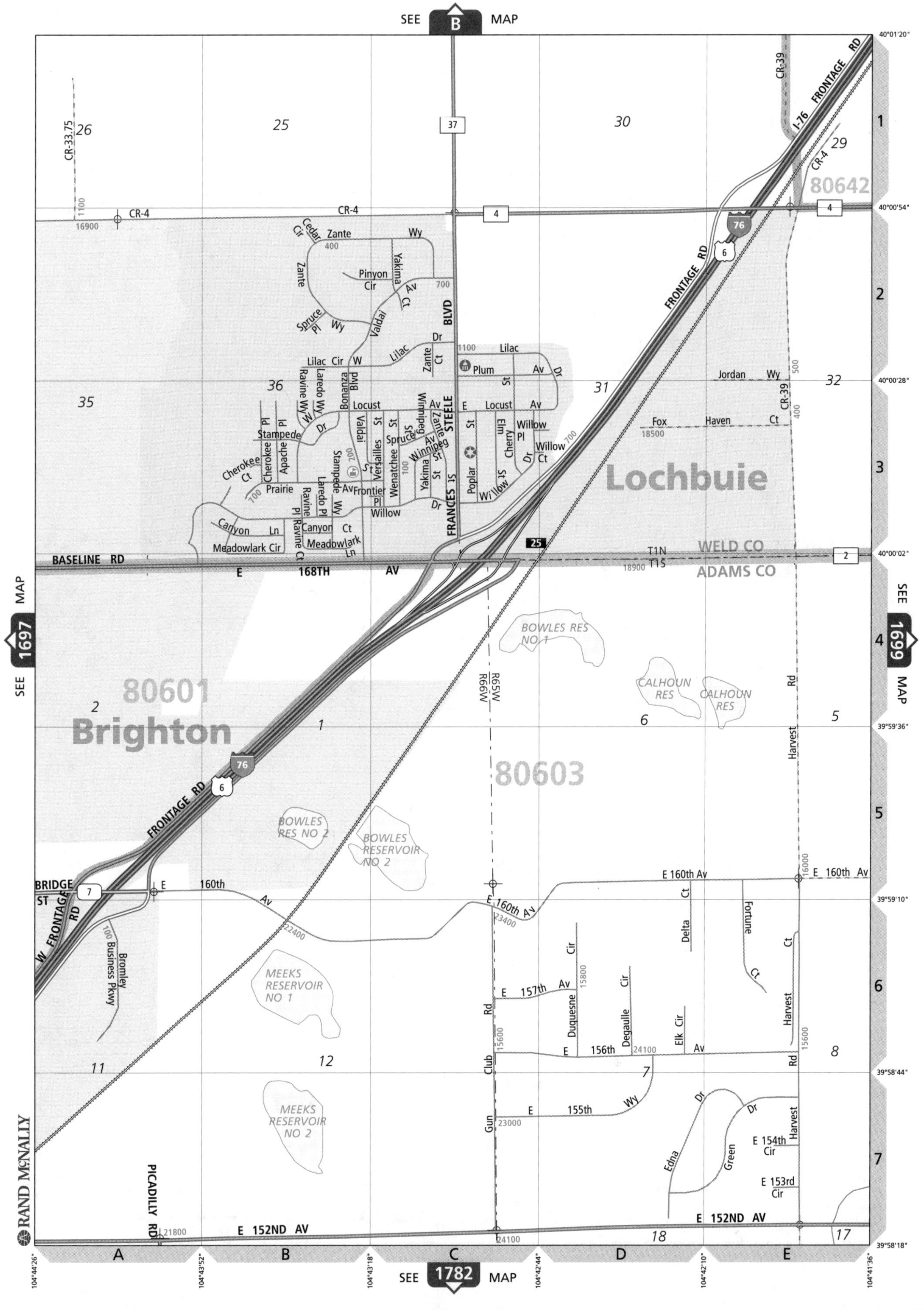

40°01'20"
40°00'54"
40°00'28"
40°00'02"
39°59'36"
39°59'10"
39°58'44"
39°58'18"
1
2
3
4
5
6
7
A B C D E
104°44'26"
104°43'52"
104°43'18"
104°42'44"
104°42'10"
104°41'36"

SEE 1782 MAP

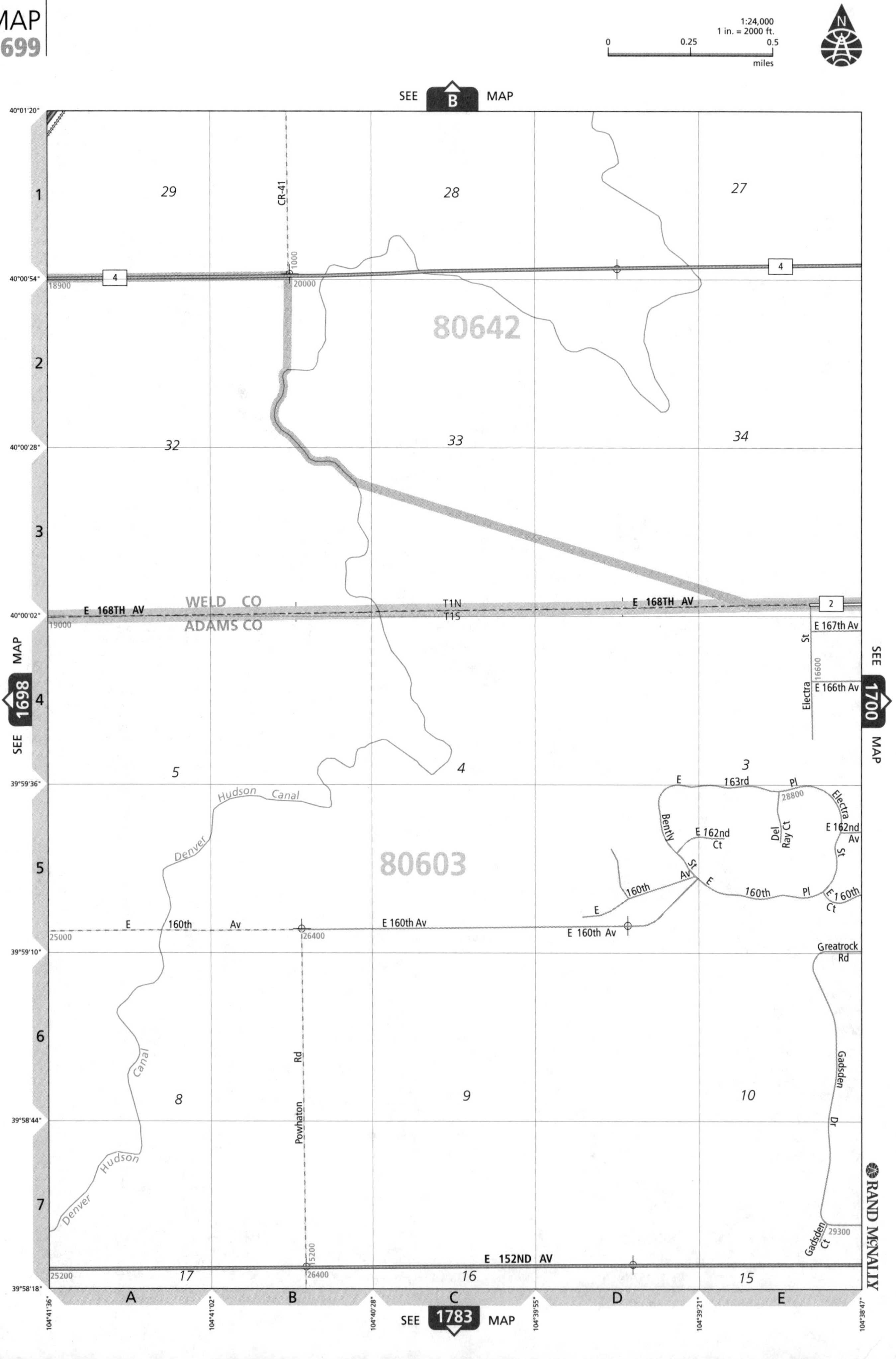

1:24,000
1 in. = 2000 ft.
0 0.25 0.5
miles

SEE B MAP

SEE 1698 MAP

SEE 1700 MAP

SEE 1783 MAP

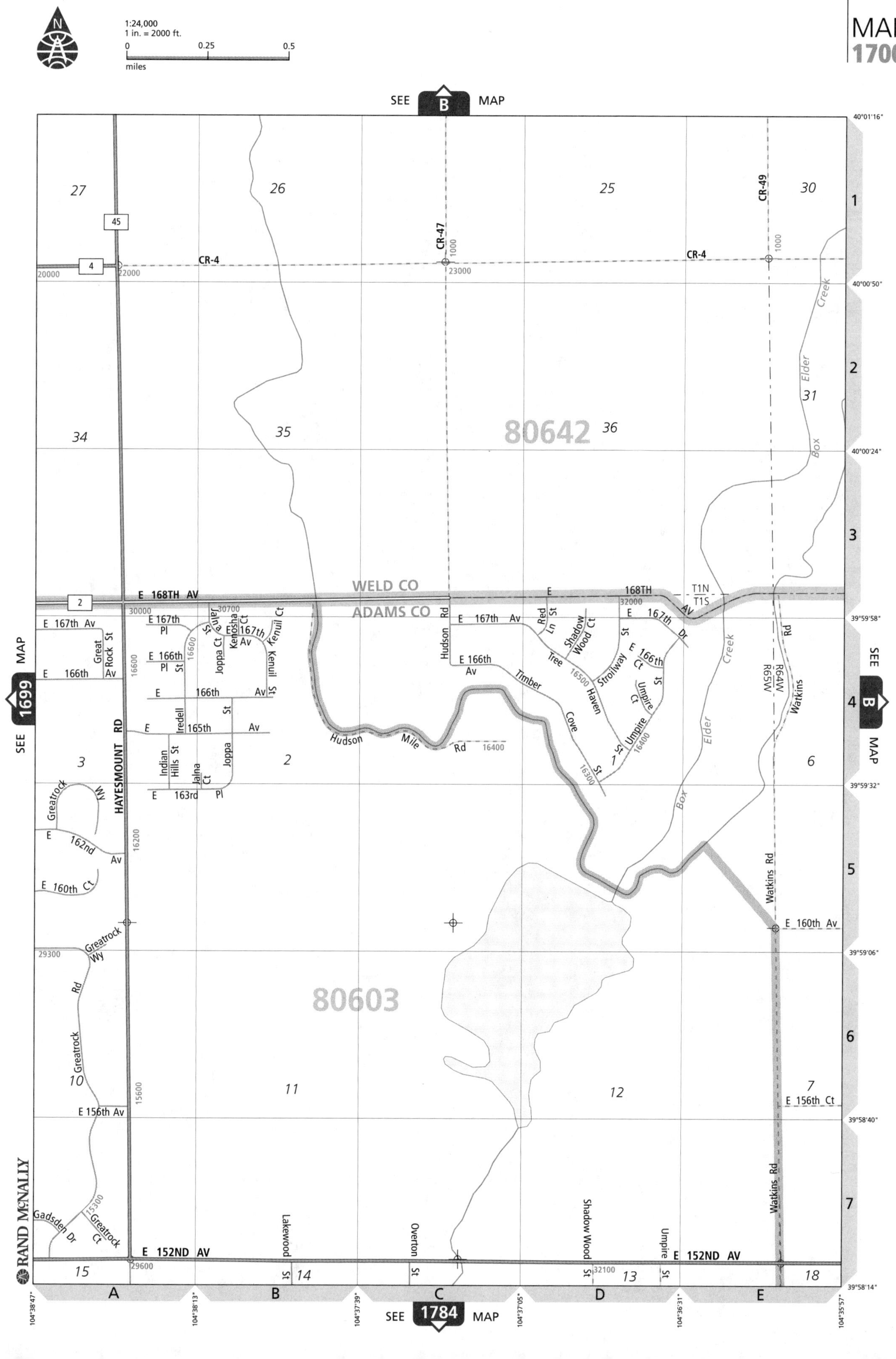

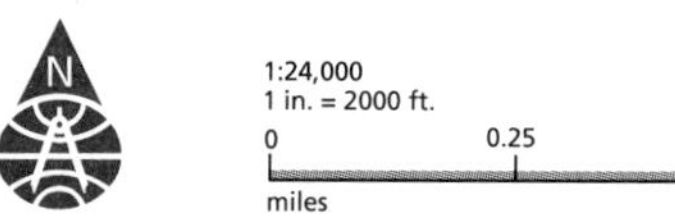

1:24,000
1 in. = 2000 ft.
0
0.25
0.5
miles
SEE B MAP
SEE 1699 MAP
SEE B MAP
SEE 1784 MAP
80642
80603
WELD CO
ADAMS CO
CR-4
CR-47
CR-49
45
4
2
E 168TH AV
168TH
E 167th Av
E 166th Av
E 167th Pl
E 166th Pl
E 166th Av
E 165th Av
E 163rd Pl
E 167th Av
E 167th Dr
E 166th Ct
E 166th Av
E 162nd Av
E 160th Ct
E 160th Av
E 156th Av
E 156th Ct
E 152ND AV
Great Rock St
Joppa Ct
Jalna St
Kenosha Ct
Kenuil Ct
Kenuil St
Iredell St
Indian Hills St
Jalna Ct
Joppa St
Red Ln St
Shadow Wood Ct
Stroilway St
Umpire Ct
Umpire St
Tree Haven
Timber Cove St
Hudson Rd
Hudson Mile Rd
HAYESMOUNT RD
Greatrock Wy
Greatrock Rd
Greatrock Ct
Gadsden Dr
Watkins Rd
Lakewood St
Overton St
Shadow Wood St
Umpire St
Box Elder Creek
T1N
T1S
R64W
R65W
27
26
25
30
34
35
36
31
3
2
1
6
10
11
12
7
15
14
13
18
20000
22000
23000
1000
30000
30700
32000
16600
16500
16400
16300
16200
15600
15300
29300
29600
32100
A
B
C
D
E
1
2
3
4
5
6
7
40°01'16"
40°00'50"
40°00'24"
39°59'58"
39°59'32"
39°59'06"
39°58'40"
39°58'14"
104°38'47"
104°38'13"
104°37'39"
104°37'05"
104°36'31"
104°35'57"
RAND McNALLY

1:24,000
1 in. = 2000 ft.
0 0.25 0.5
miles

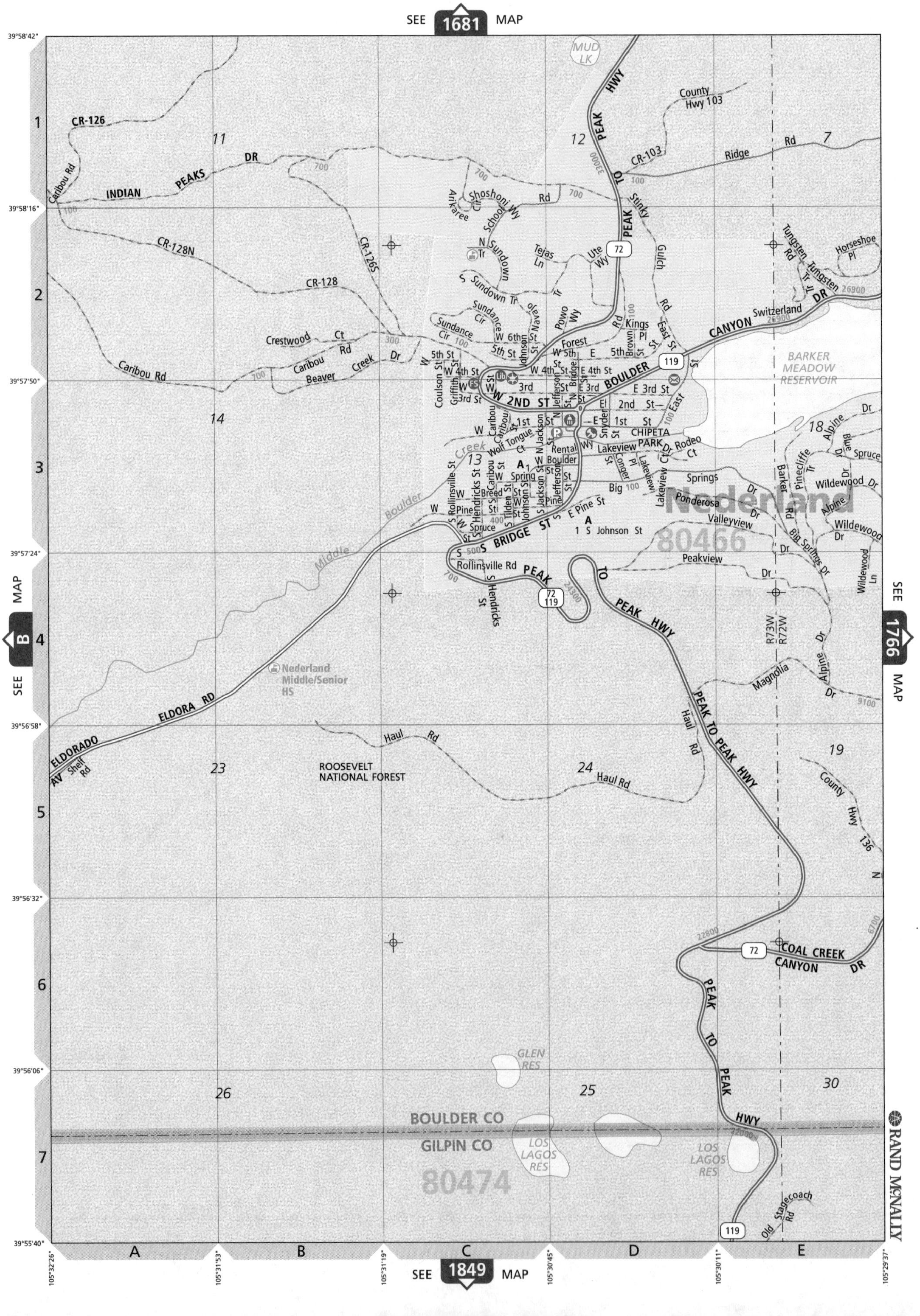

SEE 1681 MAP

SEE B MAP

SEE 1766 MAP

SEE 1849 MAP

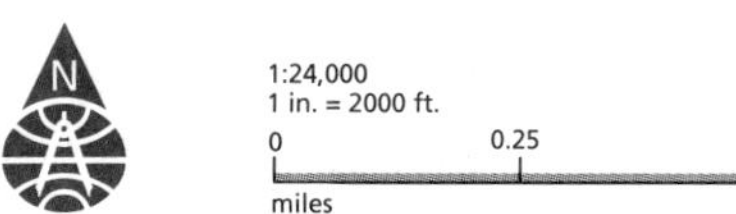

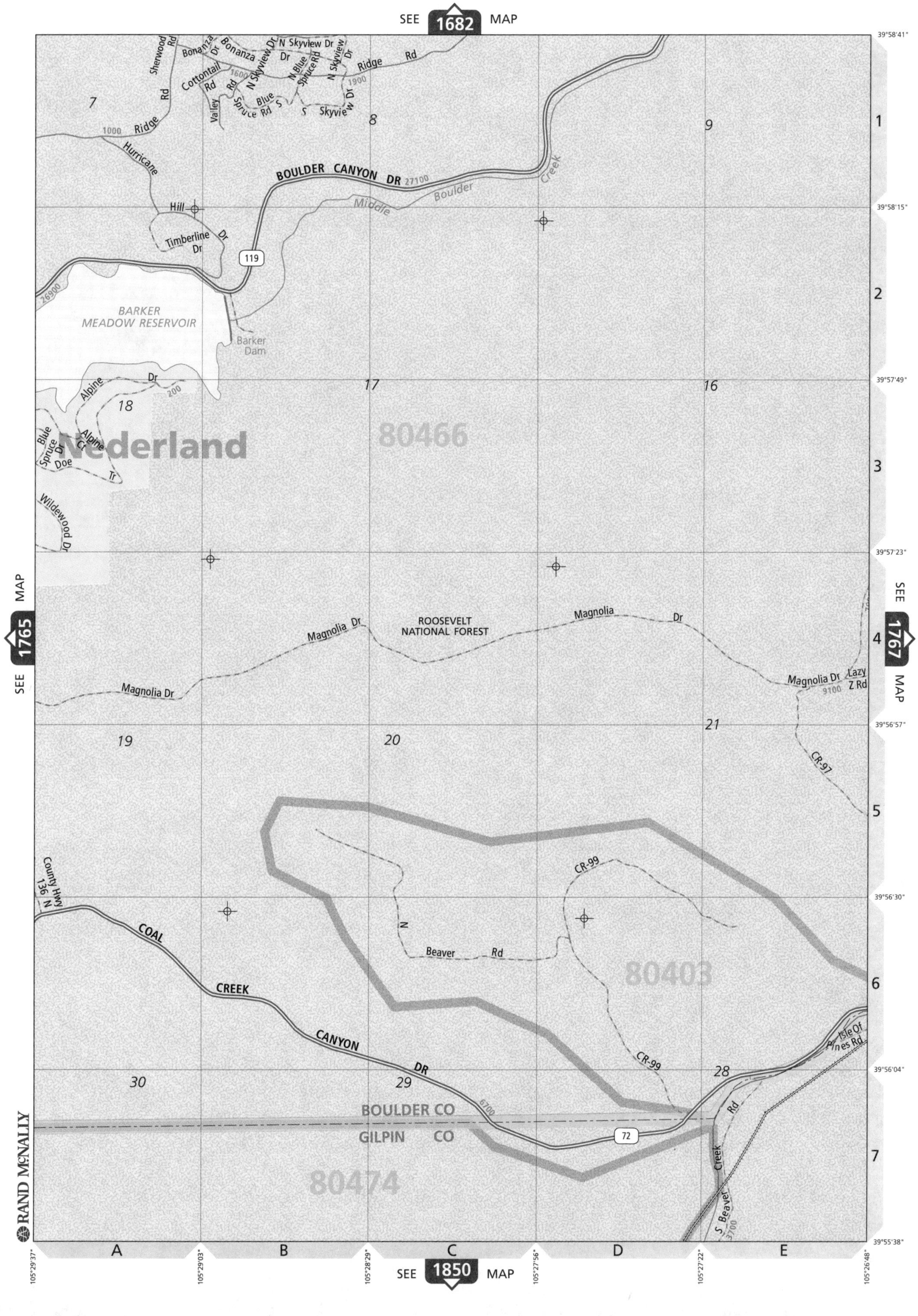

SEE 1682 MAP

SEE 1765 MAP

SEE 1767 MAP

SEE 1850 MAP

1:24,000
1 in. = 2000 ft.
0 0.25 0.5
miles

SEE 1683 MAP

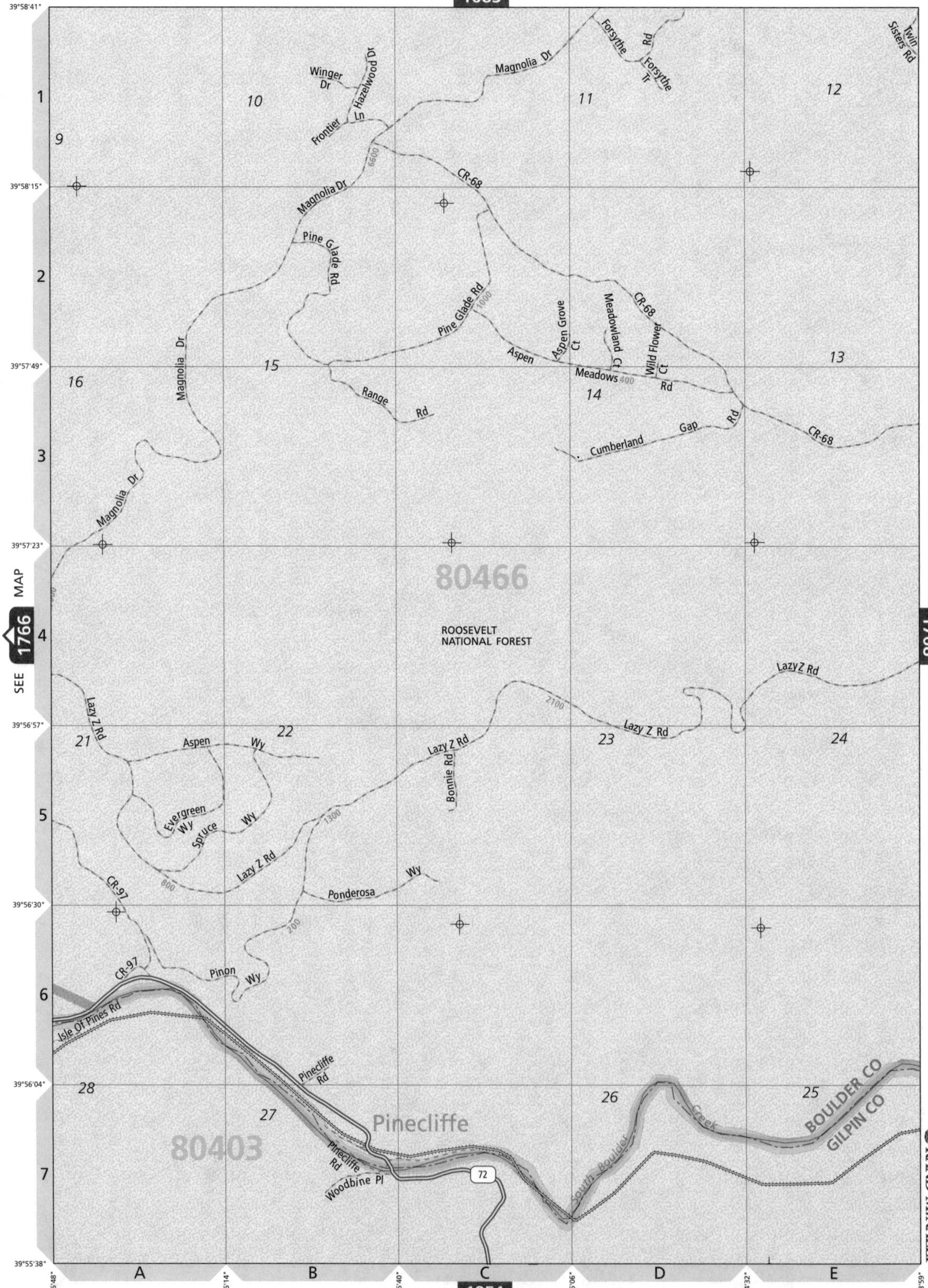

SEE 1766 MAP

SEE 1768 MAP

SEE 1851 MAP

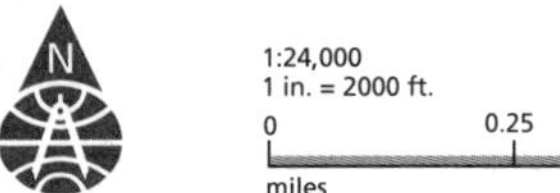

SEE 1684 MAP

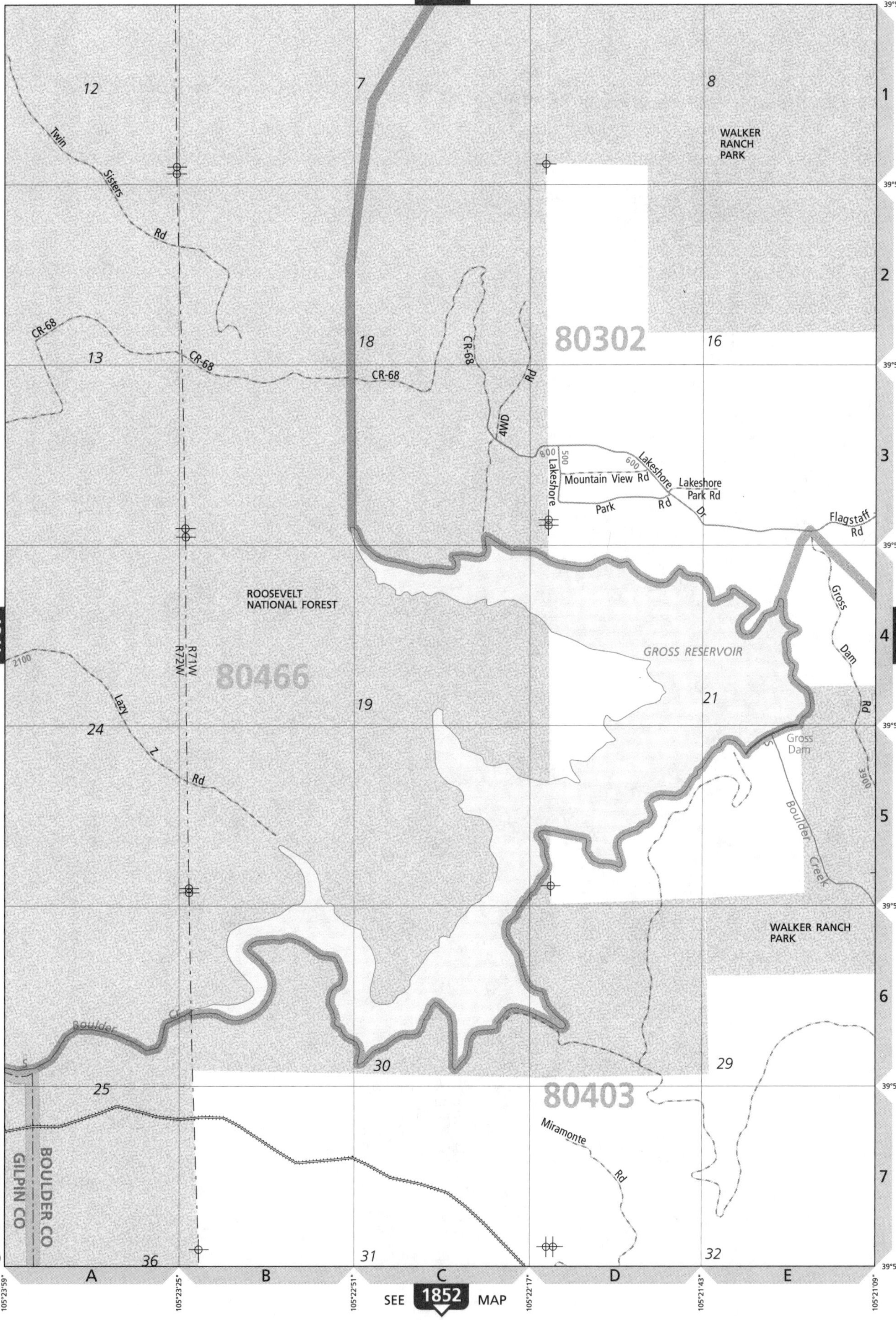

SEE 1767 MAP

SEE 1769 MAP

SEE 1852 MAP

MAP
1769

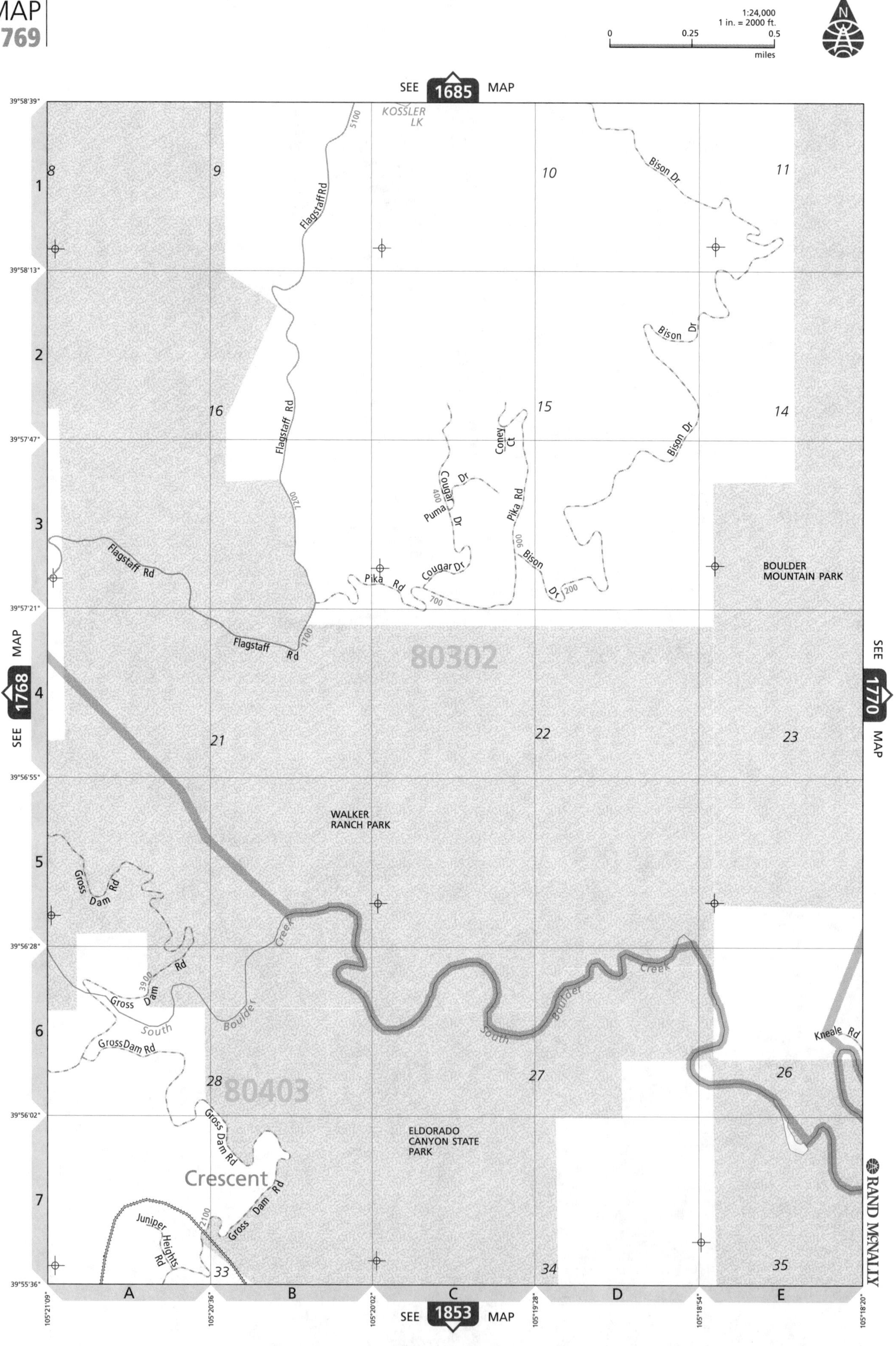

1:24,000
1 in. = 2000 ft.
0 0.25 0.5
miles
N
SEE 1685 MAP
SEE 1768 MAP
SEE 1770 MAP
SEE 1853 MAP
KOSSLER LK
5100
Flagstaff Rd
Bison Dr
Coney Ct
Cougar Dr
Puma Dr
Pika Rd
400
900
700
200
1700
Bison Dr
BOULDER MOUNTAIN PARK
80302
WALKER RANCH PARK
Gross Dam Rd
3900
South Boulder Creek
Kneale Rd
80403
ELDORADO CANYON STATE PARK
Crescent
2100
Juniper Heights Rd
8
9
10
11
16
15
14
21
22
23
28
27
26
33
34
35
1
2
3
4
5
6
7
A
B
C
D
E
39°58'39"
39°58'13"
39°57'47"
39°57'21"
39°56'55"
39°56'28"
39°56'02"
39°55'36"
105°21'09"
105°20'36"
105°20'02"
105°19'28"
105°18'54"
105°18'20"
RAND McNALLY

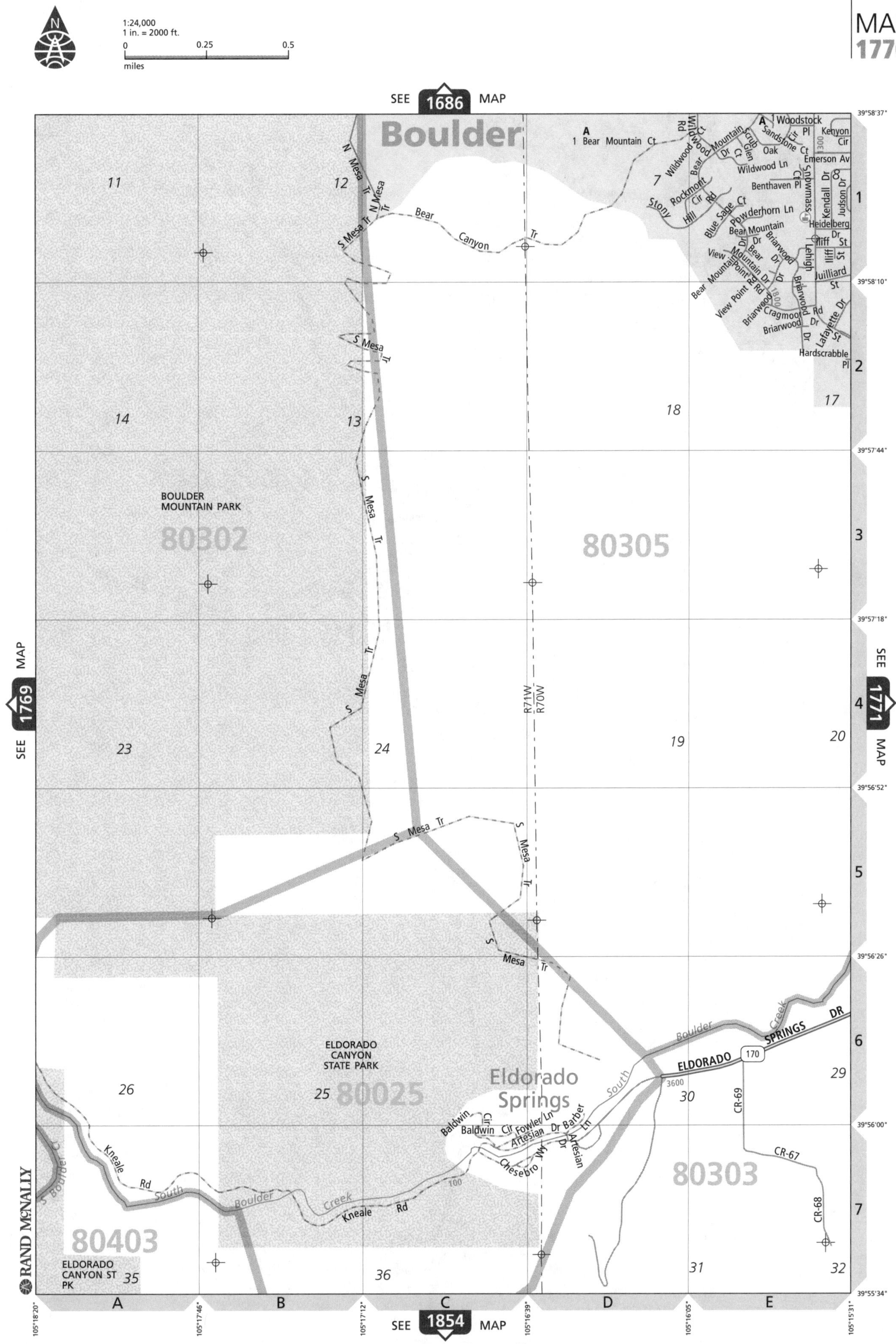

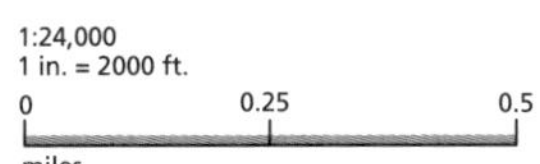

1:24,000
1 in. = 2000 ft.
0
0.25
0.5
miles
SEE 1686 MAP
SEE 1769 MAP
SEE 1771 MAP
SEE 1854 MAP
Boulder
1 Bear Mountain Ct
Woodstock
Kenyon Cir
Sandstone Ct
Cir Pl
Oak
Emerson Av
Wildwood Ln
Benthaven Pl
Snowmass Ct
Kendall Dr
Judson Dr
Powderhorn Ln
Heidelberg
Iliff St
Lehigh
Juilliard St
Briarwood Dr
Cragmoor Rd
Lafayette Dr
Hardscrabble Pl
Bear Mountain Dr
View Point Rd
Blue Sage Ct
Rockmont Cir
Stony Hill Rd
Wildwood Ct
Scrub Oak Ct
Glen
N Mesa Tr
S Mesa Tr
Bear Canyon Tr
BOULDER MOUNTAIN PARK
80302
80305
R71W
R70W
ELDORADO CANYON STATE PARK
80025
Eldorado Springs
Baldwin Cir
Fowler Ln
Artesian Dr
Barber Ln
Chesebro Wy
Boulder Creek
South Boulder Creek
ELDORADO SPRINGS DR
170
3600
CR-69
CR-67
CR-68
80303
Kneale Rd
S Boulder Ct
80403
ELDORADO CANYON ST PK
11
12
7
13
14
17
18
19
20
23
24
25
26
29
30
31
32
35
36
1
2
3
4
5
6
7
A
B
C
D
E
39°58'37"
39°58'10"
39°57'44"
39°57'18"
39°56'52"
39°56'26"
39°56'00"
39°55'34"
105°18'20"
105°17'46"
105°17'12"
105°16'39"
105°16'05"
105°15'31"

1:24,000
1 in. = 2000 ft.
0 0.25 0.5
miles

SEE 1687 MAP

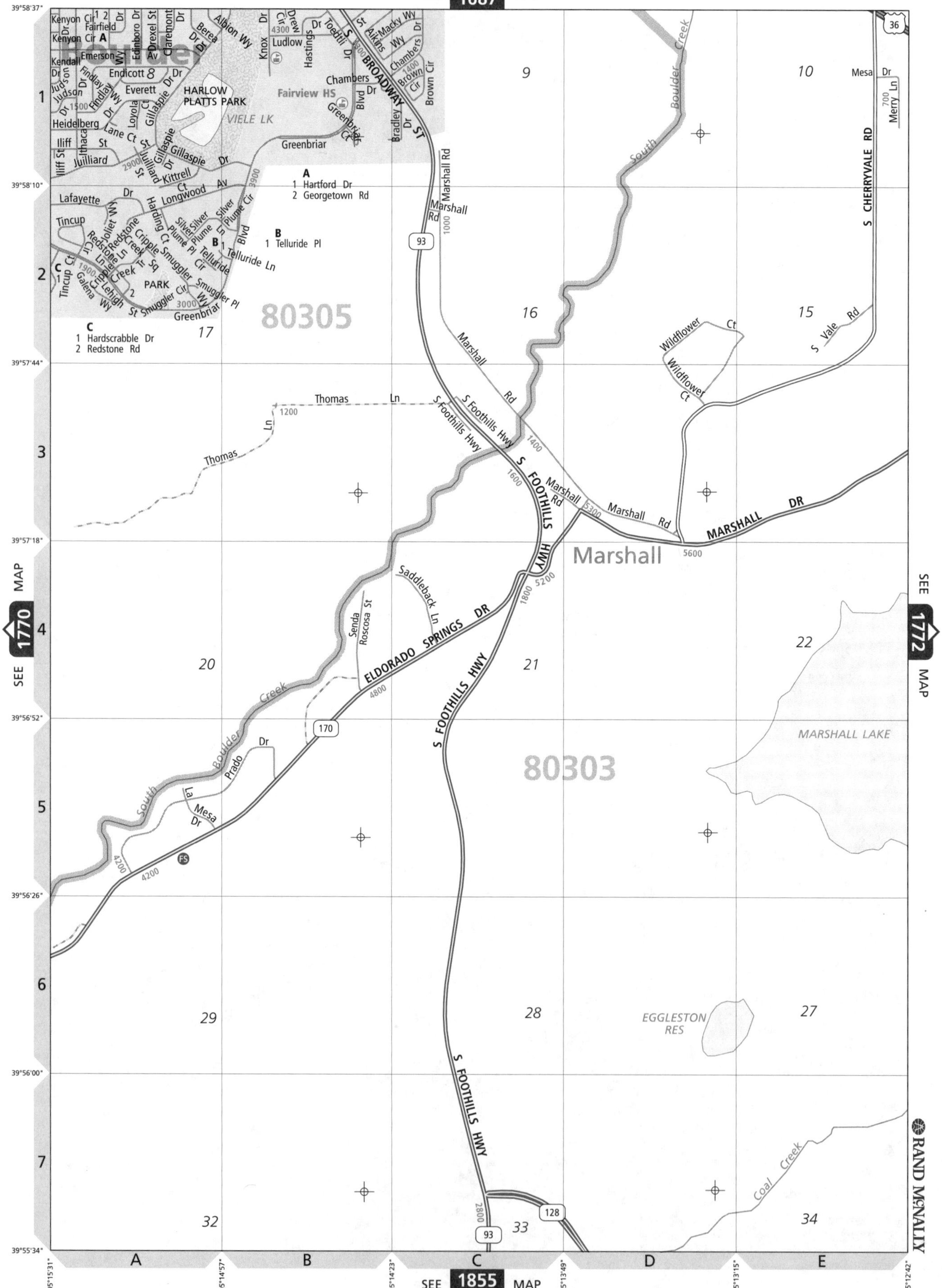

SEE 1770 MAP

SEE 1772 MAP

SEE 1855 MAP

A
1 Hartford Dr
2 Georgetown Rd

B
1 Telluride Pl

C
1 Hardscrabble Dr
2 Redstone Rd

Boulder
HARLOW PLATTS PARK
VIELE LK
Fairview HS
S BROADWAY ST
S FOOTHILLS HWY
S CHERRYVALE RD
MARSHALL DR
ELDORADO SPRINGS DR
Marshall Rd
Thomas Ln
Greenbriar Blvd
South Boulder Creek
Marshall
80305
80303
MARSHALL LAKE
EGGLESTON RES
Coal Creek
Wildflower Ct
S Vale Rd
Saddleback Ln
Senda Roscosa St
Prado Dr
La Mesa Dr
Mesa Dr
Merry Ln
PARK

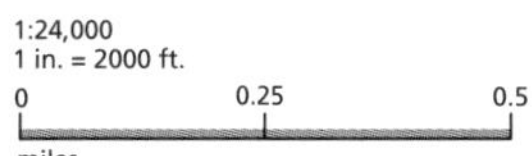

SEE 1688 MAP

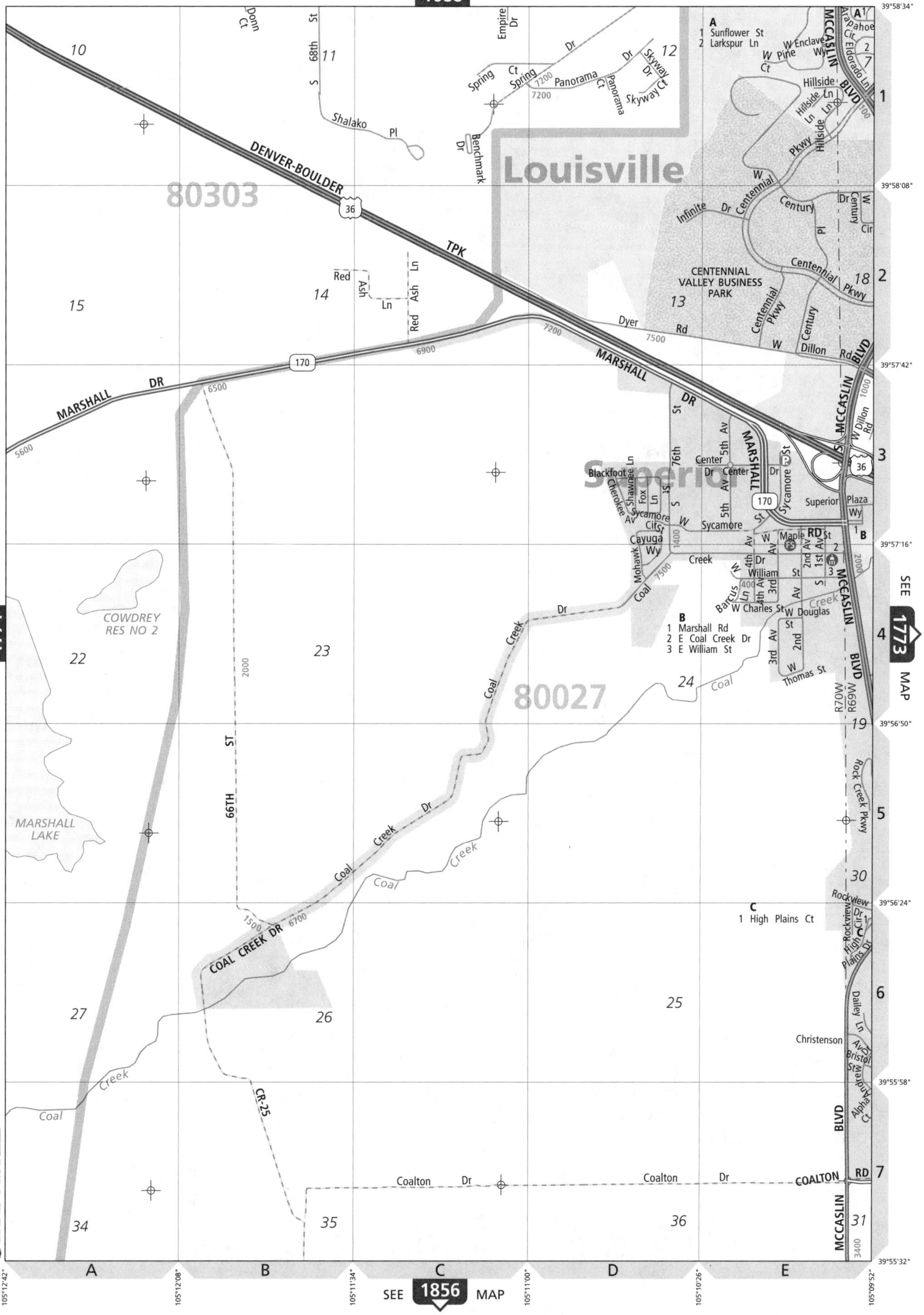

SEE 1771 MAP

SEE 1773 MAP

Louisville
Superior
80303
80027
DENVER-BOULDER TPK
MARSHALL DR
MCCASLIN BLVD
COAL CREEK DR
COALTON RD
CR-25
66TH ST
CENTENNIAL VALLEY BUSINESS PARK
COWDREY RES NO 2
MARSHALL LAKE

A
1 Sunflower St
2 Larkspur Ln

B
1 Marshall Rd
2 E Coal Creek Dr
3 E William St

C
1 High Plains Ct

SEE 1856 MAP

1:24,000
1 in. = 2000 ft.
0 0.25 0.5
miles

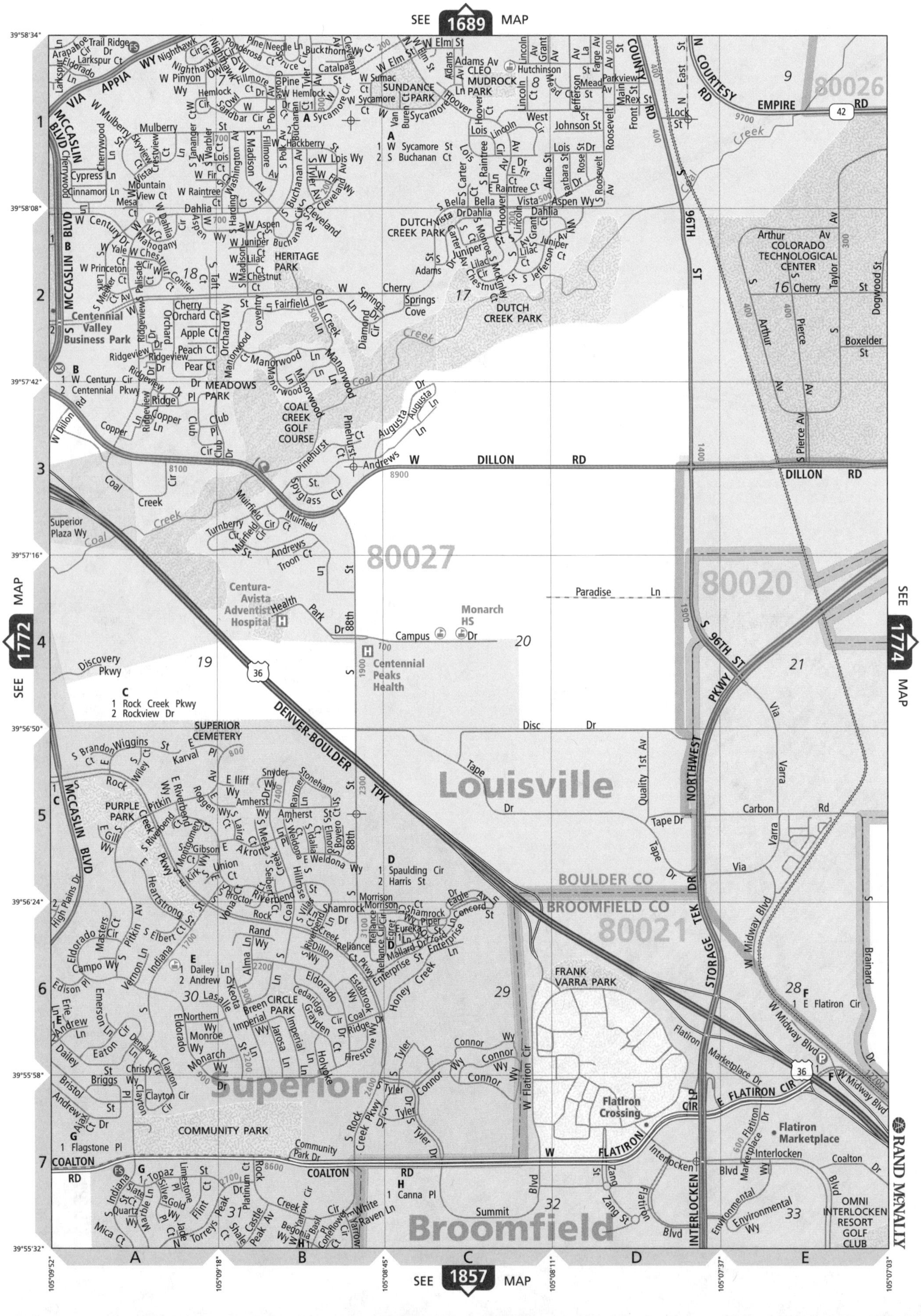

SEE 1689 MAP

SEE 1772 MAP

SEE 1774 MAP

A
1 W Sycamore St
2 S Buchanan Ct

B
1 W Century Cir
2 Centennial Pkwy

C
1 Rock Creek Pkwy
2 Rockview Dr

D
1 Spaulding Cir
2 Harris St

E
1 Dailey Ln
2 Andrew Dr

F
1 E Flatiron Cir

G
1 Flagstone Pl

H
1 Canna Pl

CLEO MUDROCK PARK

SUNDANCE PARK

HERITAGE PARK

DUTCH CREEK PARK

COLORADO TECHNOLOGICAL CENTER

Centennial Valley Business Park

MEADOWS PARK

COAL CREEK GOLF COURSE

Centura-Avista Adventist Hospital

Monarch HS

Centennial Peaks Health

SUPERIOR CEMETERY

PURPLE PARK

Louisville

BOULDER CO

BROOMFIELD CO

FRANK VARRA PARK

CIRCLE PARK

Superior

COMMUNITY PARK

FlatIron Crossing

Flatiron Marketplace

OMNI INTERLOCKEN RESORT GOLF CLUB

Broomfield

80026

80027

80020

80021

W DILLON RD

DILLON RD

EMPIRE RD

DENVER-BOULDER TPK

MCCASLIN BLVD

NORTHWEST PKWY

STORAGE TEK DR

INTERLOCKEN LP

W FLATIRON CIR

COALTON RD

S 96TH ST

A B C D E

SEE 1857 MAP

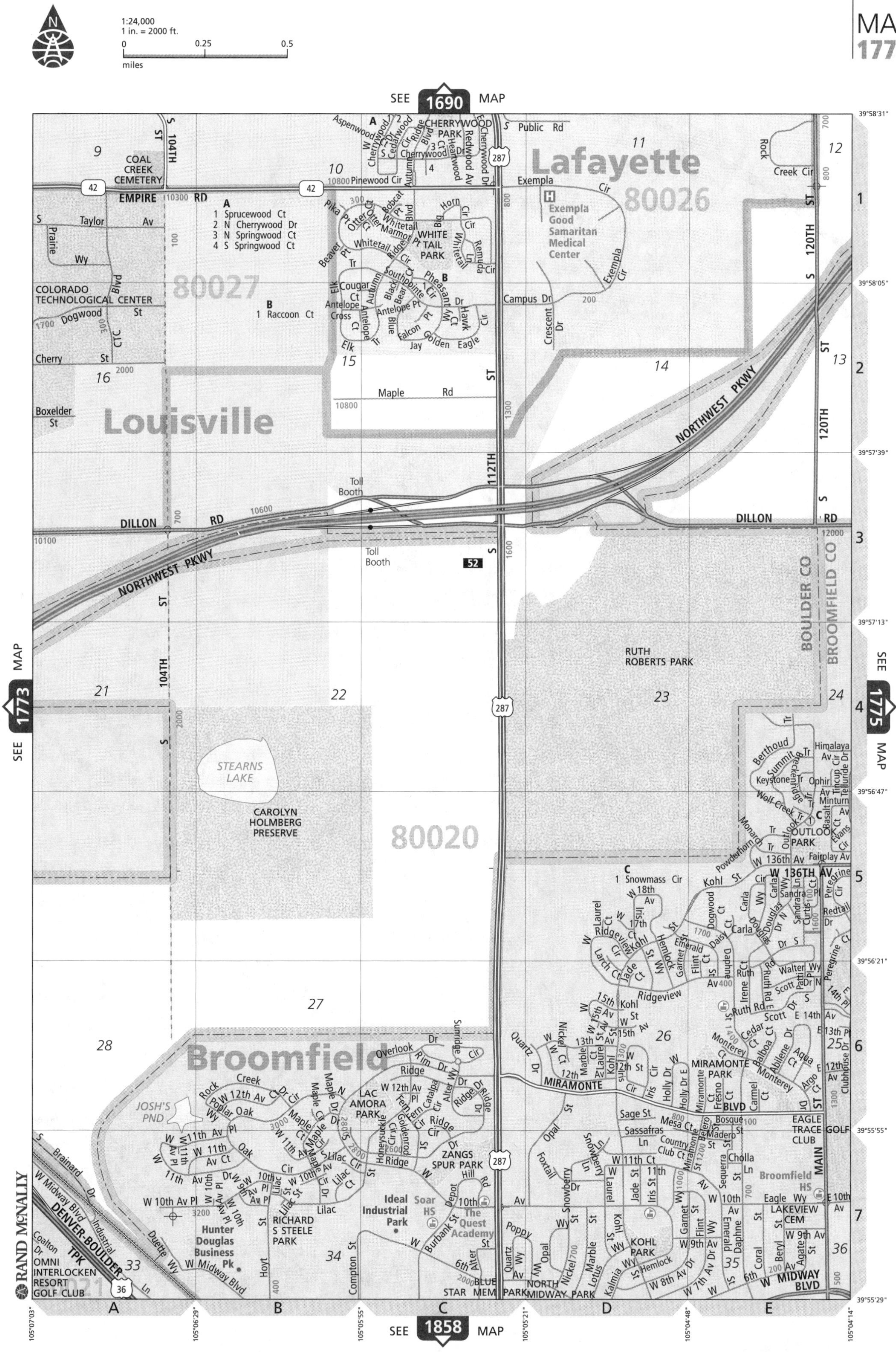

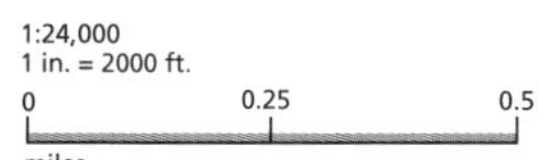

SEE 1690 MAP

Lafayette
80026
Exempla Good Samaritan Medical Center
COAL CREEK CEMETERY
EMPIRE RD
80027
COLORADO TECHNOLOGICAL CENTER
WHITE TAIL PARK
CHERRYWOOD PARK
Louisville
NORTHWEST PKWY
DILLON RD
Toll Booth
112TH ST
104TH ST
120TH ST
RUTH ROBERTS PARK
BOULDER CO
BROOMFIELD CO
STEARNS LAKE
CAROLYN HOLMBERG PRESERVE
80020
OUTLOOK PARK
W 136TH AV
MIRAMONTE PARK
MIRAMONTE BLVD
Broomfield
LAC AMORA PARK
ZANGS SPUR PARK
JOSH'S PND
EAGLE TRACE GOLF CLUB
Broomfield HS
LAKEVIEW CEM
KOHL PARK
RICHARD S STEELE PARK
Hunter Douglas Business Pk
Ideal Industrial Park
Soar HS
The Quest Academy
BLUE STAR MEM PARK
NORTH MIDWAY PARK
W MIDWAY BLVD
DENVER-BOULDER TPK
OMNI INTERLOCKEN RESORT GOLF CLUB

A
1 Sprucewood Ct
2 N Cherrywood Dr
3 N Springwood Ct
4 S Springwood Ct

B
1 Raccoon Ct

C
1 Snowmass Cir

SEE 1773 MAP

SEE 1775 MAP

SEE 1858 MAP

RAND McNALLY

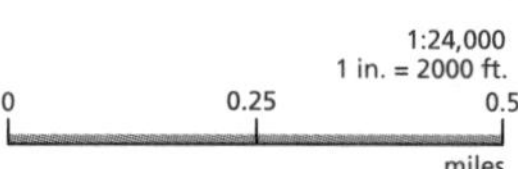

SEE 1691 MAP

SEE 1774 MAP

SEE 1776 MAP

A
1 Hillside Ct
2 Spruce Meadows Dr

B
1 Spring Harbor Wy

C
1 Westhampton Pt

D
1 Quail Creek Dr
2 Creekside Dr

E
1 Bayberry Ct

F
1 Evans Cir

G
1 W 134th Av
2 Federal Pl
3 W 134th Pl
4 W 134th Ct
5 W 132nd Ct

H
1 W 126th Pl
2 James Cir
3 Hazel Ct

J
1 Pronghorn St
2 Newton Wy
3 Forest View St
4 Tammywood St

K
1 Aspen Ct
2 Bellaire Ct
3 Cottonwood Ct
4 Dover Ct

80020

Broomfield

RAND McNALLY

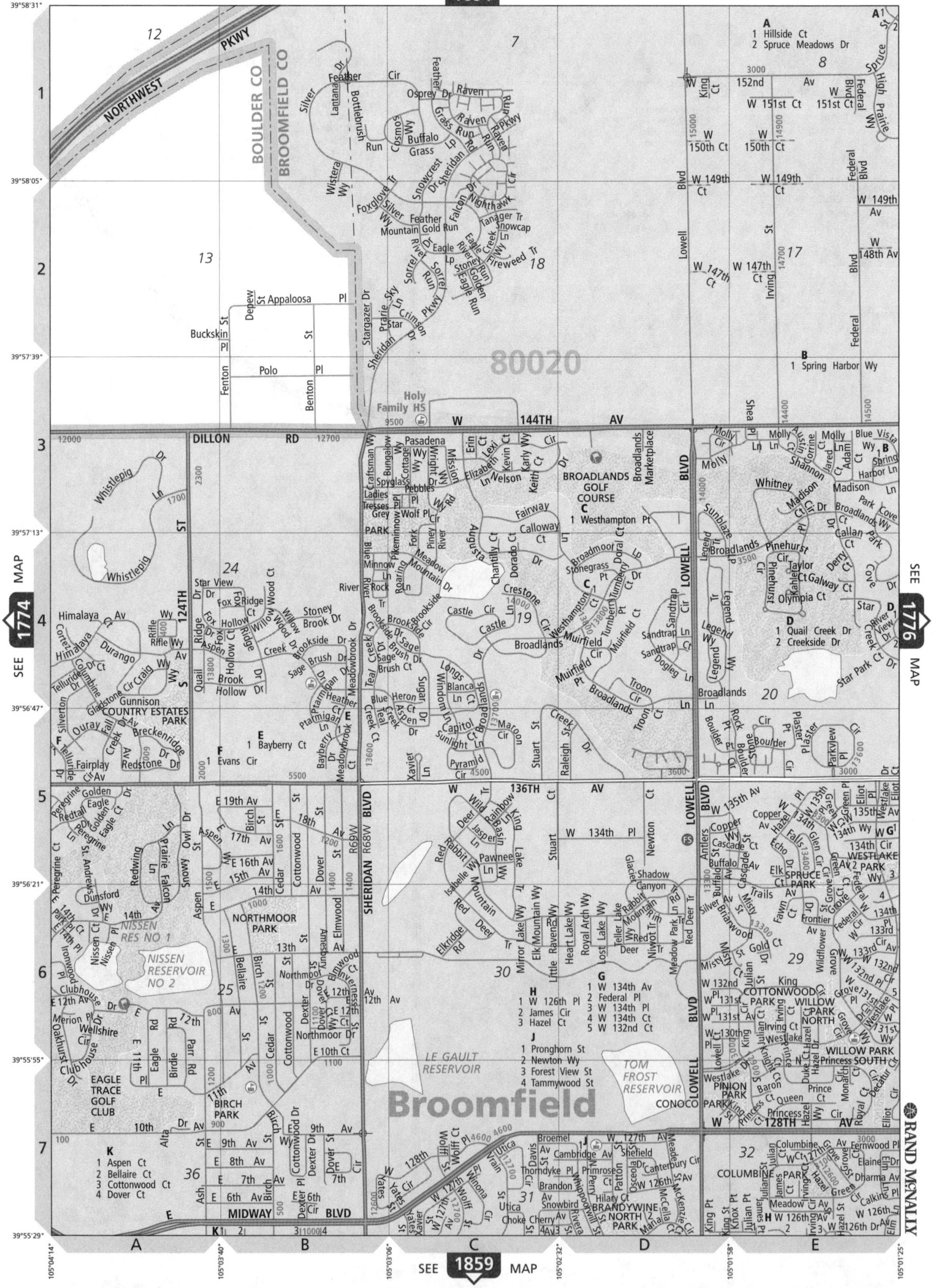

SEE 1859 MAP

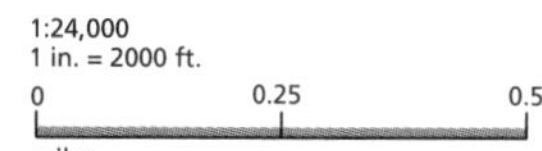

SEE 1692 MAP

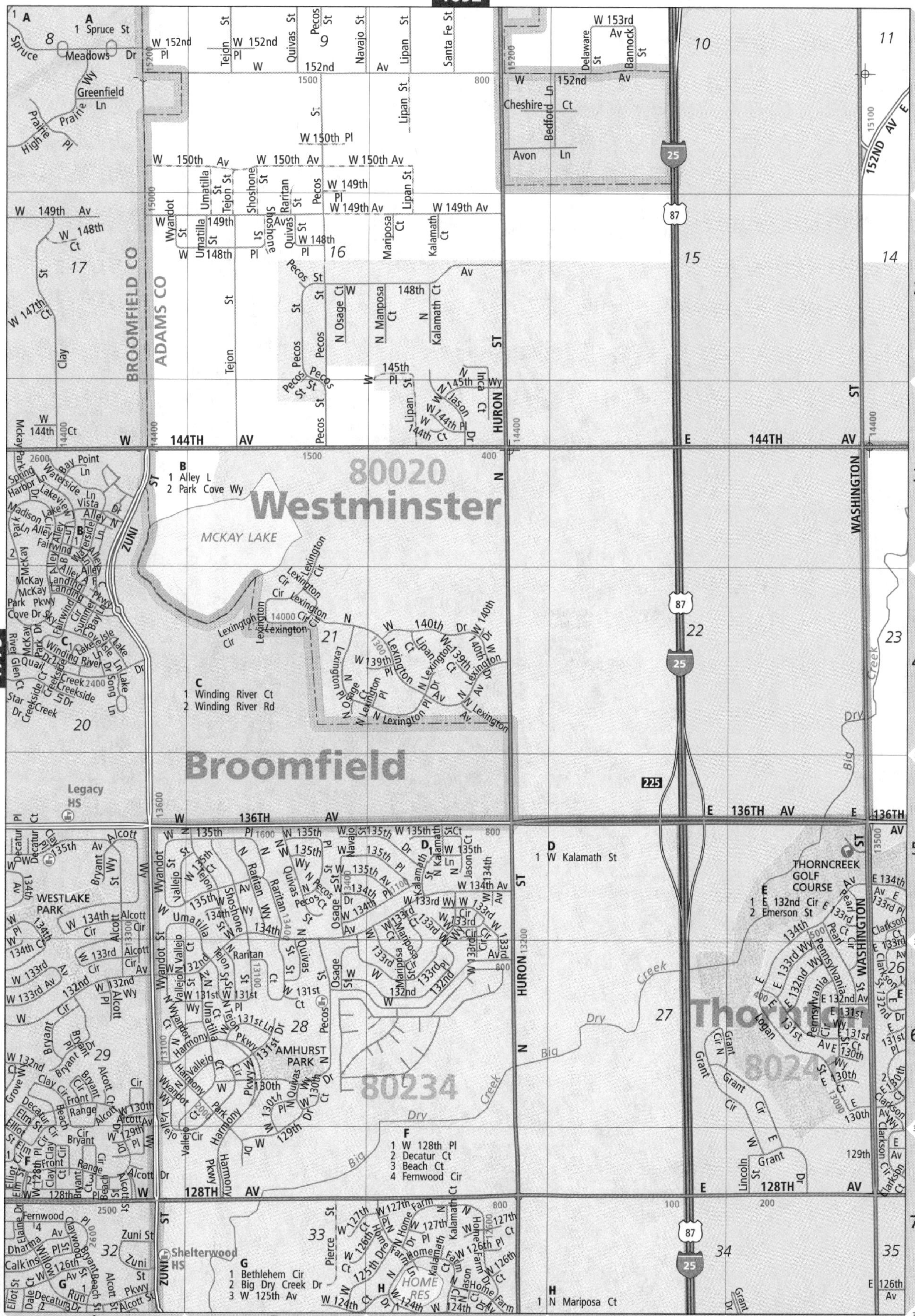

SEE 1775 MAP

SEE 1777 MAP

80020
Westminster
Broomfield
Thornton
80241
80234

BROOMFIELD CO
ADAMS CO
MCKAY LAKE
Legacy HS
WESTLAKE PARK
AMHURST PARK
THORNCREEK GOLF COURSE
Shelterwood HS
HOME RES

W 144TH AV
E 144TH AV
W 136TH AV
E 136TH AV
W 128TH AV
E 128TH AV
ZUNI ST
HURON ST
WASHINGTON ST
152ND AV E

A
1 Spruce St

B
1 Alley L
2 Park Cove Wy

C
1 Winding River Ct
2 Winding River Rd

D
1 W Kalamath St

E
1 E 132nd Cir
2 Emerson St

F
1 W 128th Pl
2 Decatur Ct
3 Beach Ct
4 Fernwood Cir

G
1 Bethlehem Cir
2 Big Dry Creek Dr
3 W 125th Av

H
1 N Mariposa Ct

SEE 1860 MAP

1:24,000
1 in. = 2000 ft.
0 0.25 0.5
miles

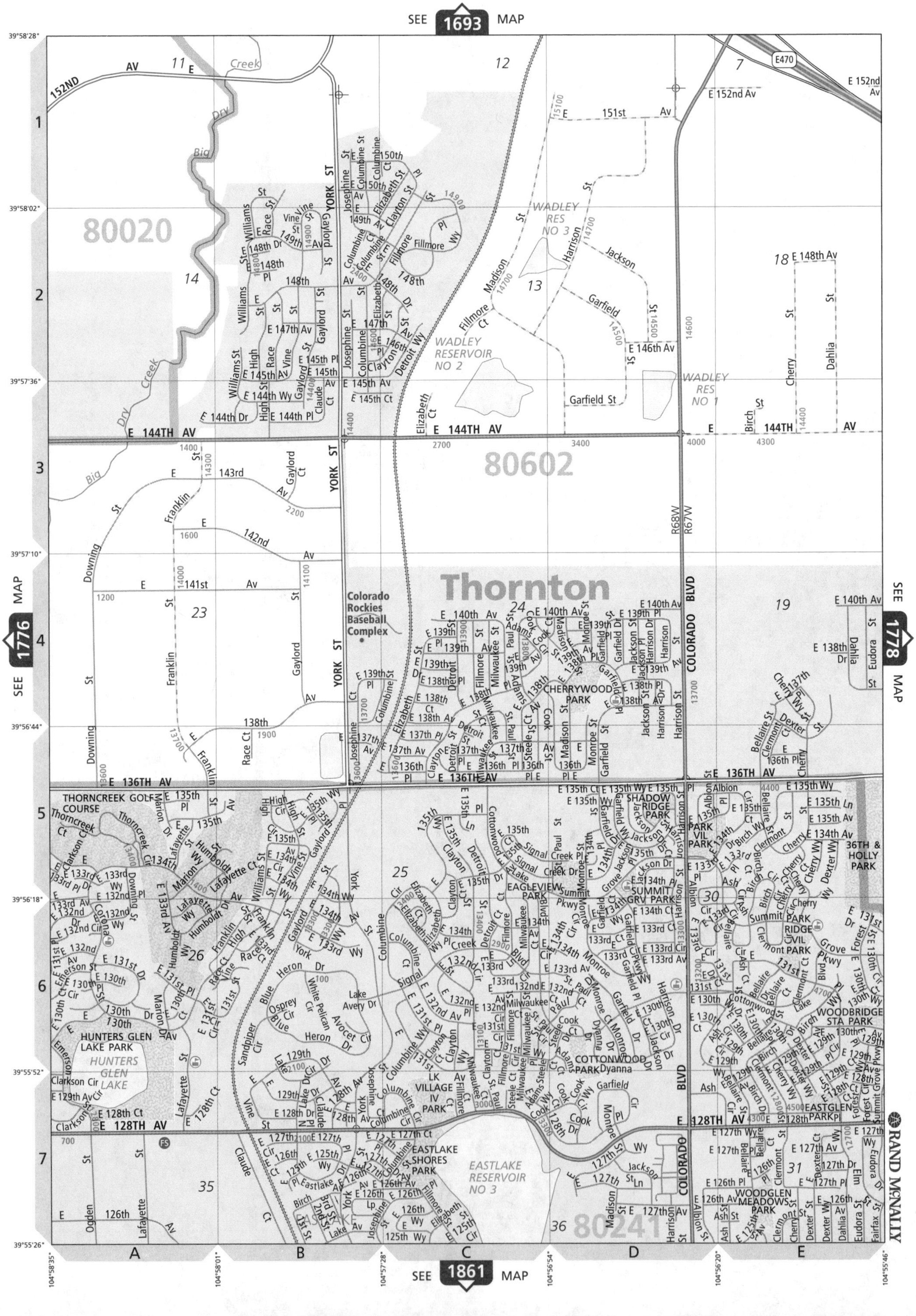

SEE 1693 MAP

SEE 1776 MAP

SEE 1778 MAP

Thornton

80020

80602

80241

E 152ND AV
E 144TH AV
E 136TH AV
E 128TH AV
YORK ST
COLORADO BLVD
E470
E 152nd Av
E 151st Av
Big Dry Creek

Colorado Rockies Baseball Complex

WADLEY RES NO 3

WADLEY RESERVOIR NO 2

WADLEY RES NO 1

THORNCREEK GOLF COURSE

HUNTERS GLEN LAKE PARK

HUNTERS GLEN LAKE

LK VILLAGE IV PARK

EASTLAKE SHORES PARK

EASTLAKE RESERVOIR NO 3

CHERRYWOOD PARK

SHADOW RIDGE PARK

PARK VIL PARK

EAGLEVIEW PARK

SUMMIT GRV PARK

36TH & HOLLY PARK

RIDGE VIL PARK

WOODBRIDGE STA PARK

COTTONWOOD PARK

EASTGLEN PARK

WOODGLEN MEADOWS PARK

R68W R67W

A B C D E

1 2 3 4 5 6 7

39°58'28" 39°58'02" 39°57'36" 39°57'10" 39°56'44" 39°56'18" 39°55'52" 39°55'26"

104°58'35" 104°58'01" 104°57'28" 104°56'54" 104°56'20" 104°55'46"

SEE 1861 MAP

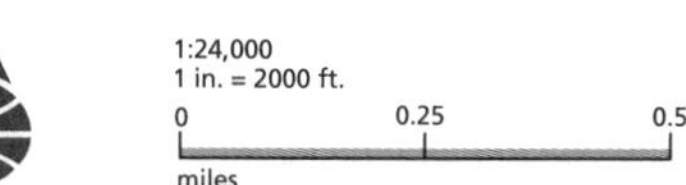

SEE 1694 MAP

SEE 1777 MAP

SEE 1779 MAP

Thornton

80602

80241

SMITH RES

E 152nd Av

E 144TH AV

E 136TH AV

128TH AV

QUEBEC ST

HOLLY ST

YOSEMITE ST

RIVERDALE RD

HENDERSON RD

EHLER PKWY

E470

Horizon Senior HS

SPRINGVALE PARK

36TH & HOLLY PARK

WOODBRIDGE STA PARK

PARK

RIVERDALE GC

ADAMS COUNTY REG PARK

Bachman

E 140th Av

E 139th Av

E 138th Av

E 137th Av

E 132nd Av

E 131st Av

E 130th Av

E 129th Av

E 128th Wy

E 127th Dr

E 146th Av

E 145th Pl

Akron St

Uinta St

Verbena Ct

Wabash Wy

Dahlia St

Elm St

Fairfax St

Forest St

Glencoe St

Grape St

Hudson St

Ivanhoe St

Jersey St

Jasmine St

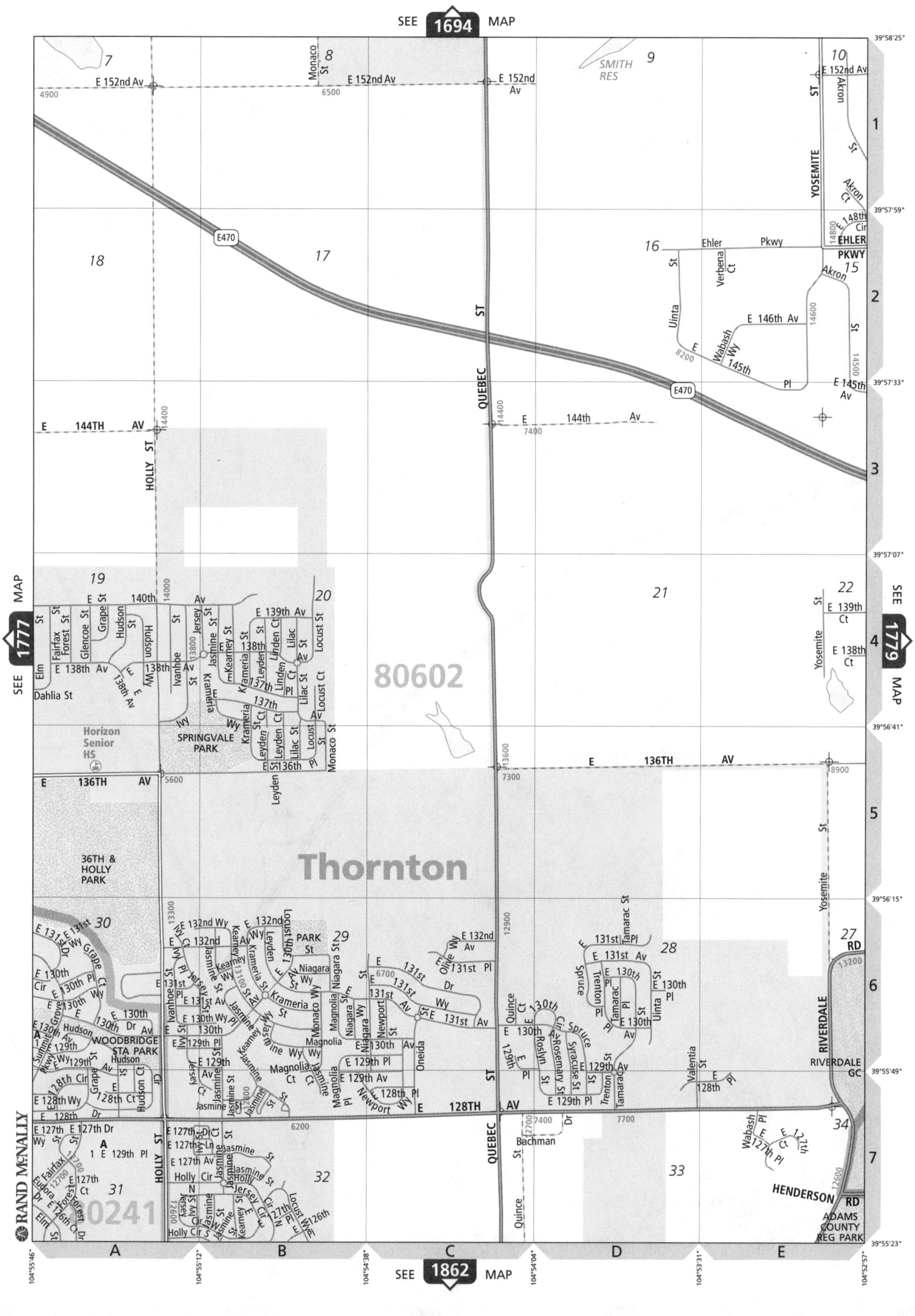

Kearney St

Krameria St

Leyden St

Linden Ct

Lilac St

Locust St

Monaco St

Niagara St

Magnolia St

Newport St

Oneida St

Olive Wy

Quince St

Roslyn St

Rosemary St

Spruce St

Syracuse St

Trenton St

Tamarac St

Valentia St

SEE 1862 MAP

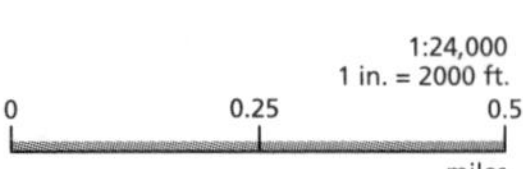

SEE 1695 MAP

Brighton

PLATTE RIVER RANCH PARK

A
1 Mockingbird Ln
2 Canary Ct
3 Mockingbird St

80602

80601

80640

RIVERDALE RD

BRIGHTON RD

E 136TH AV

E 144TH AV

E 132ND AV

EHLER PKWY

HAVANA ST

HENDERSON RD

SOUTH PLATTE RIVER

Toll Booth

Elmwood Baptist Academy

RIVERDALE GOLF COURSE

DEBETZ LAKE

ADAMS COUNTY REGIONAL PARK

MANN-NYHOLT LAKE

Adams County Museum Complex

Adams County Fairgrounds

SEE 1778 MAP

SEE 1780 MAP

SEE 1863 MAP

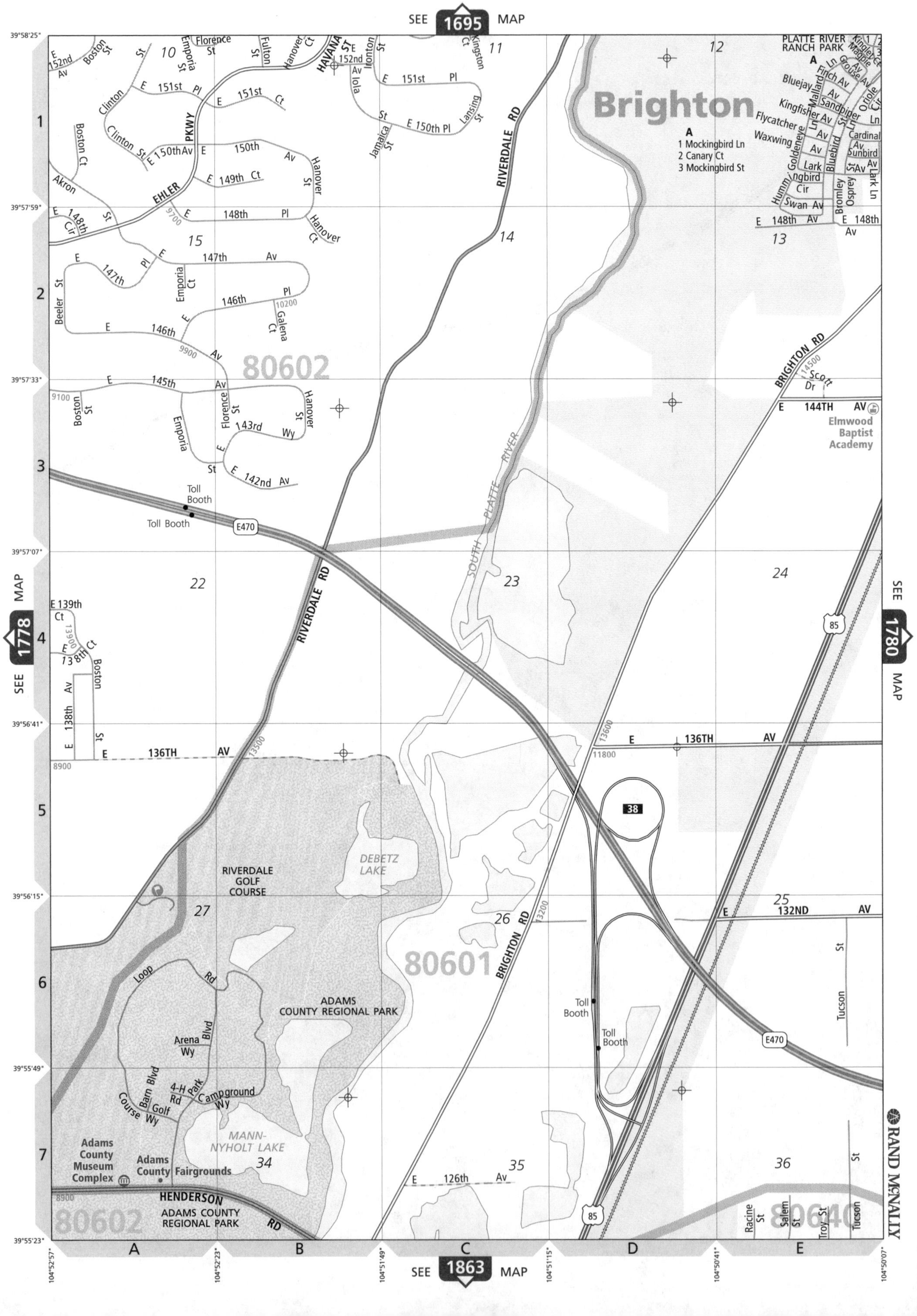

1:24,000
1 in. = 2000 ft.
0 0.25 0.5
miles

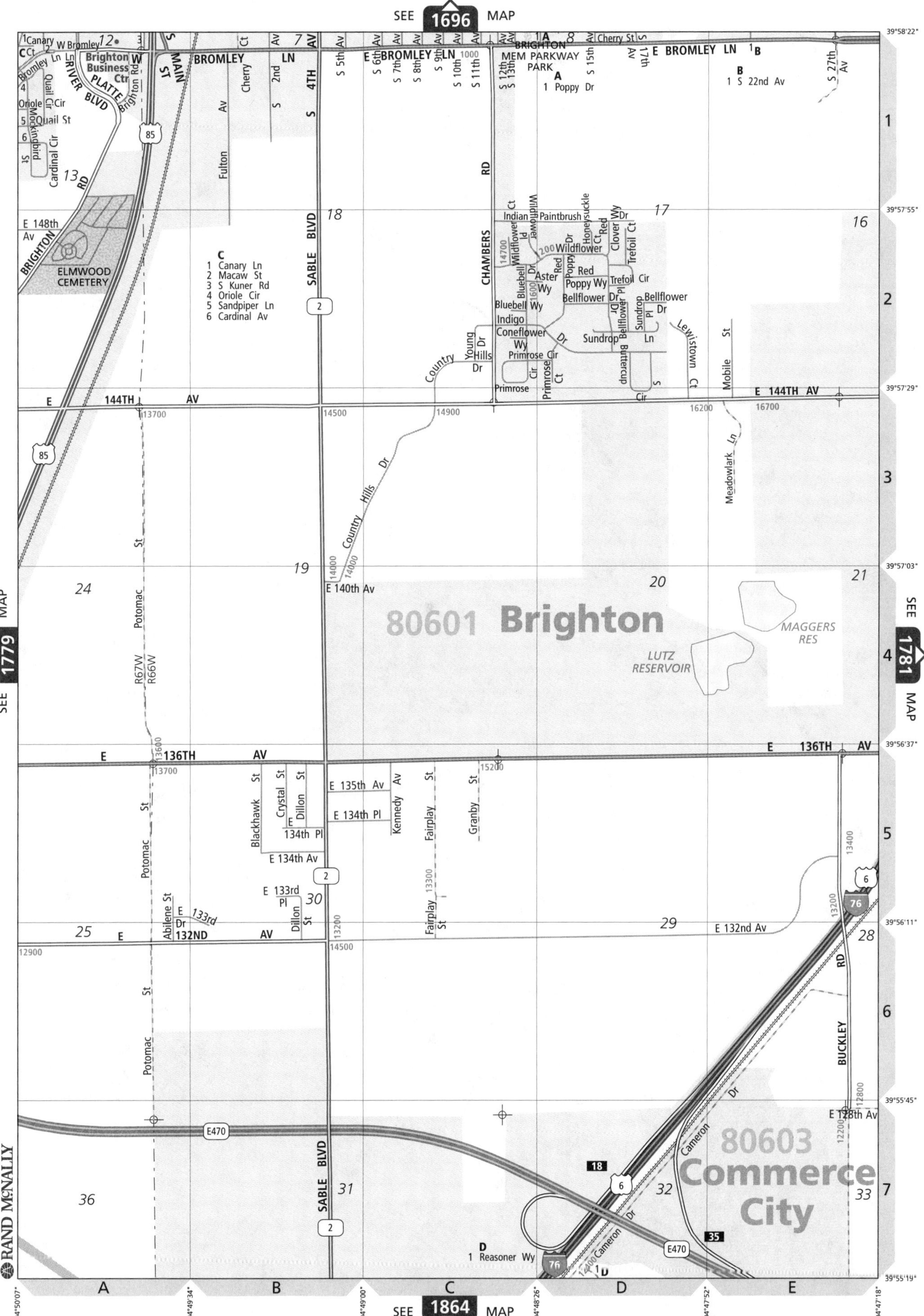

1:24,000
1 in. = 2000 ft.
0 0.25 0.5
miles

SEE 1697 MAP

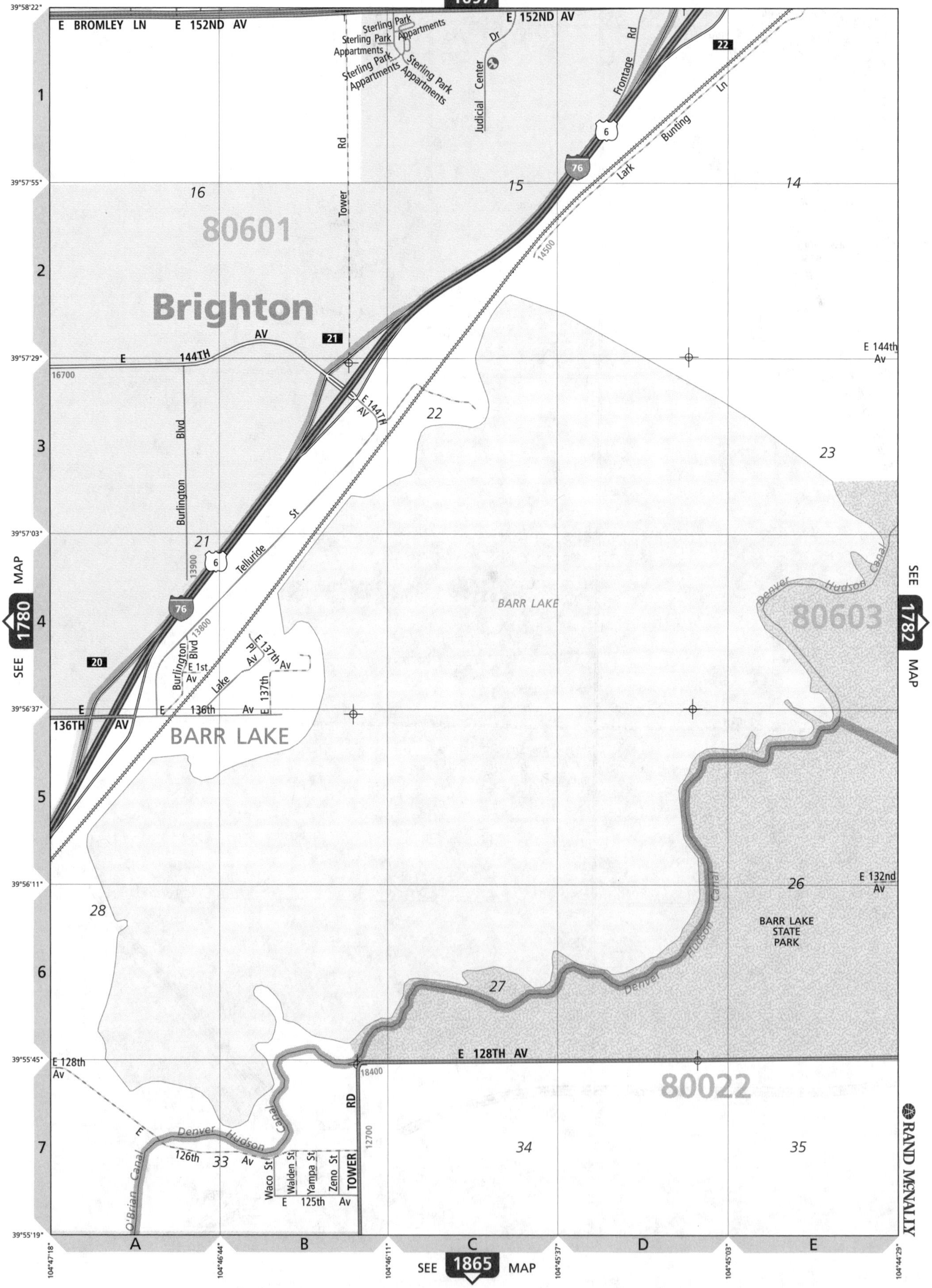

SEE 1780 MAP

SEE 1782 MAP

SEE 1865 MAP

1:24,000
1 in. = 2000 ft.
0 0.25 0.5
miles

SEE 1698 MAP

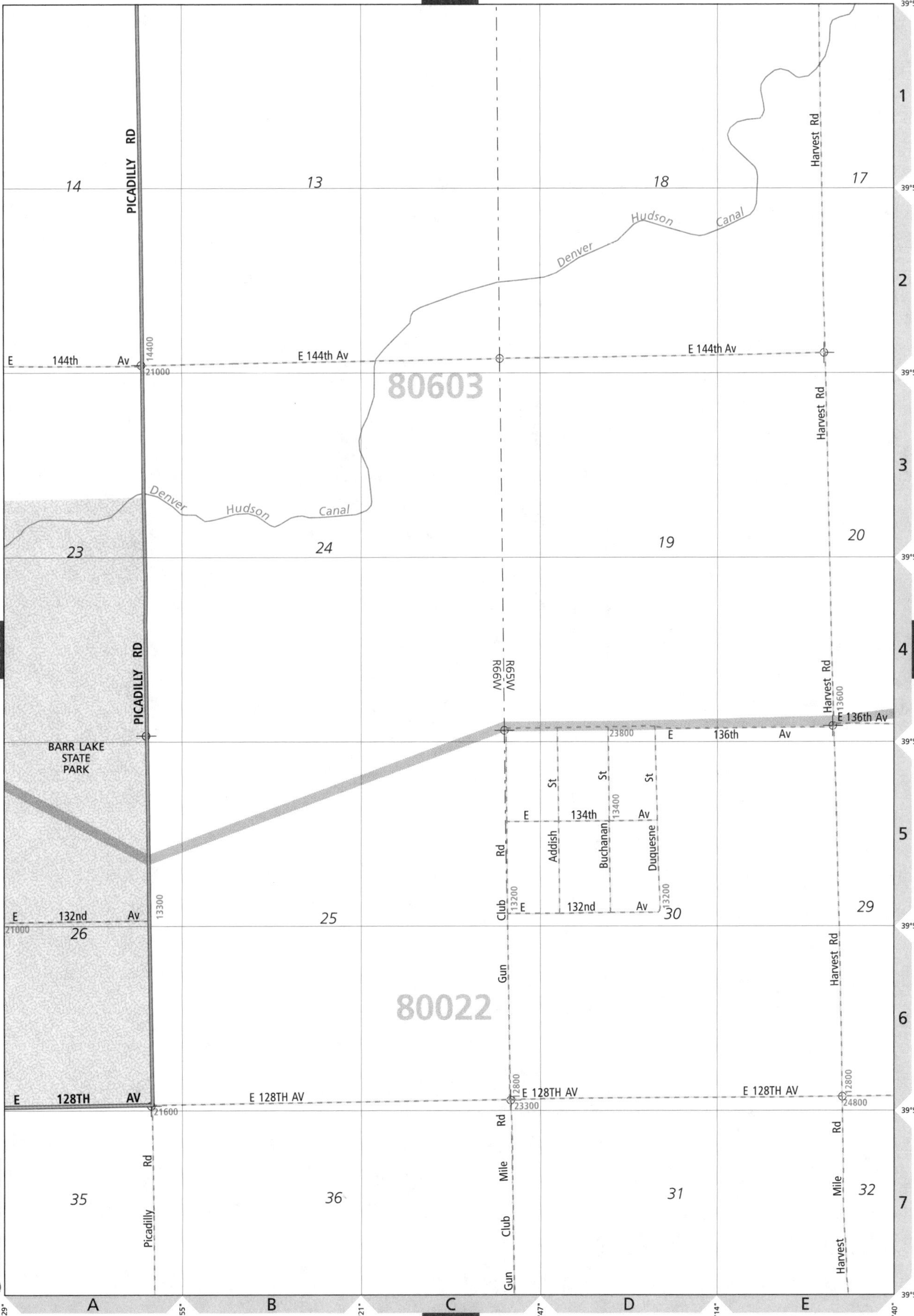

SEE 1781 MAP

SEE 1783 MAP

SEE 1866 MAP

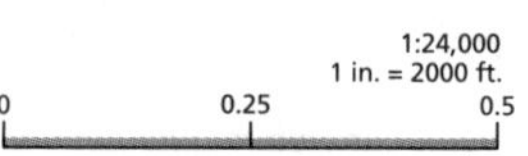

SEE 1699 MAP

SEE 1782 MAP

SEE 1784 MAP

Powhaton Rd
E 148th Av
17
16
15
80603
E 144th Av
20
21
22
Powhaton Rd
13700
E 136th Av
E 133rd Cir
13400
25900
E
133rd Cir
29
28
27
80022
E 128th Av
24800
26400
E 128th Av
E 128th Av
Powhaton Rd
32
33
34

39°58'18"
39°57'52"
39°57'26"
39°57'00"
39°56'34"
39°56'07"
39°55'41"
39°55'15"

104°41'40"
104°41'06"
104°40'32"
104°39'58"
104°39'24"
104°38'50"

1 2 3 4 5 6 7
A B C D E

RAND McNALLY

SEE 1867 MAP

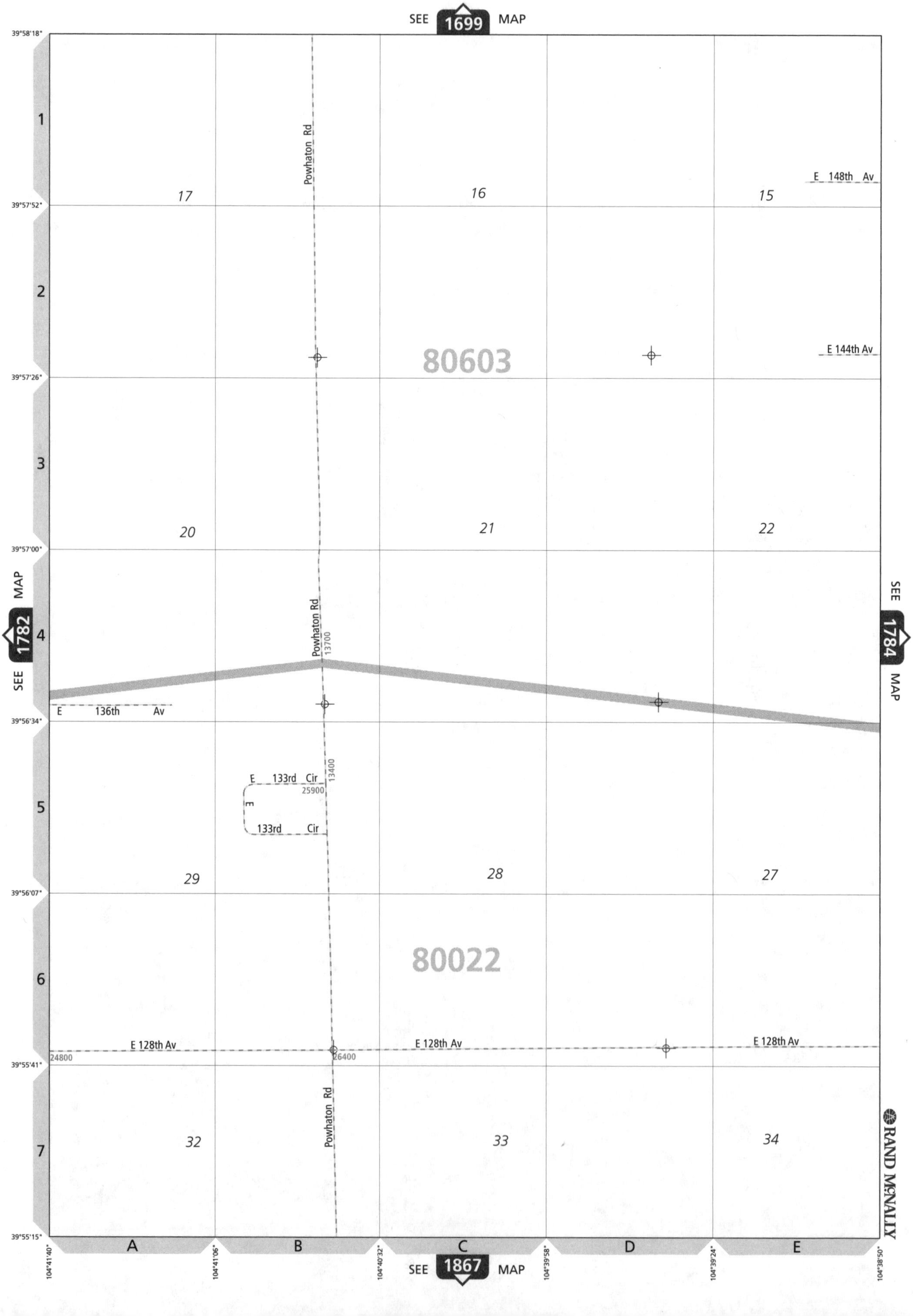

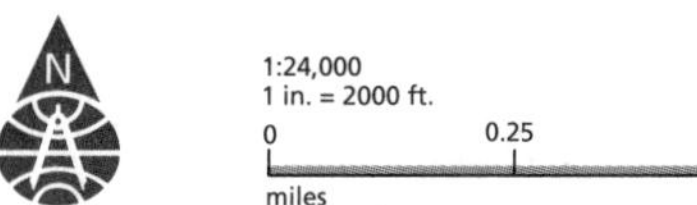

SEE 1700 MAP

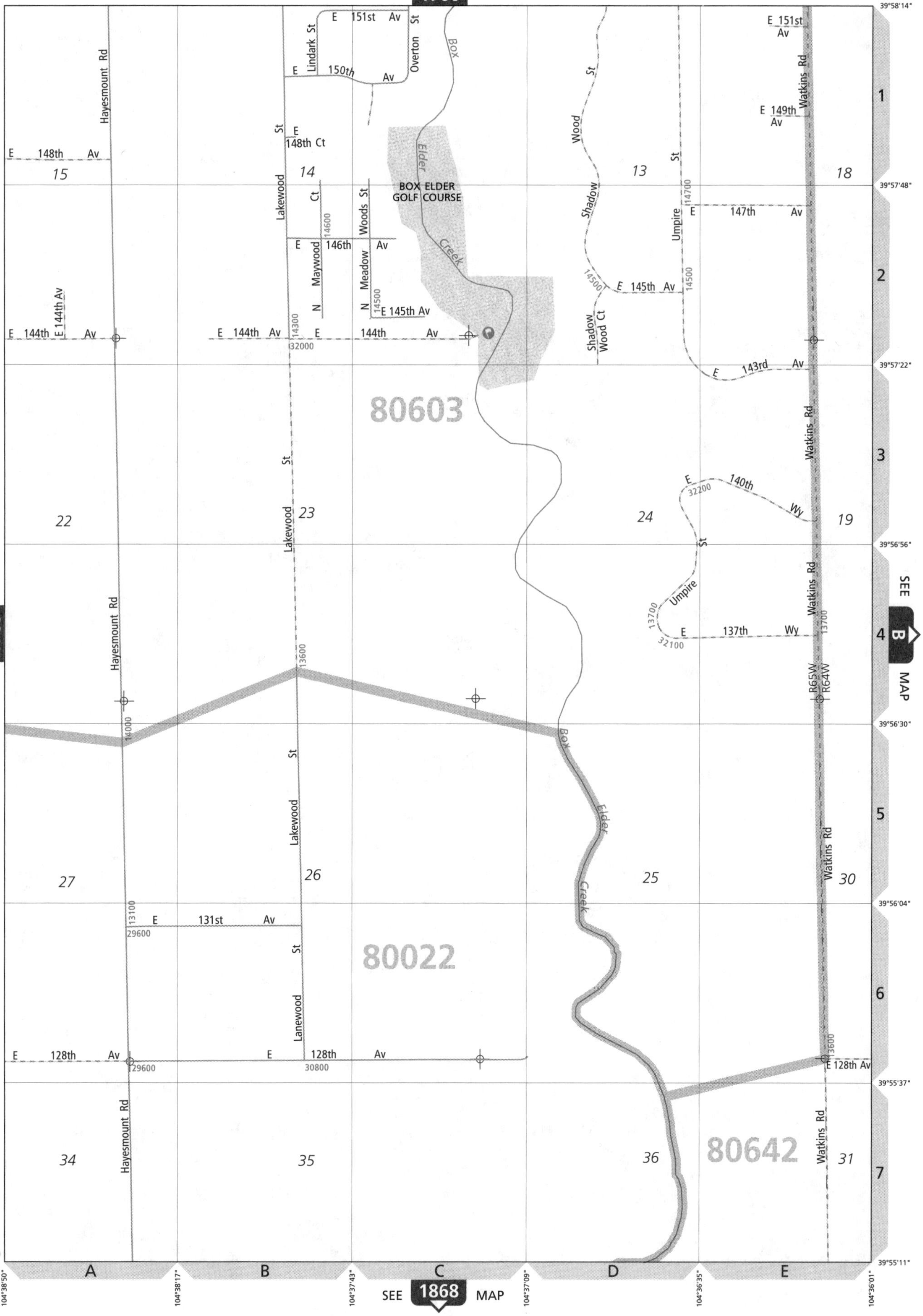

SEE 1783 MAP

SEE B MAP

SEE 1868 MAP

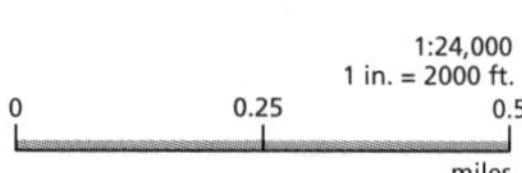

SEE 1765 MAP

Rollinsville
MANCHESTER LAKE
Old Stagecoach Rd
Shoshoni Rd
Old Stagecoach Trail
County Rd
Willie's Ln
Owl Dr
Owl Dr
High St
Vera Marie Ln
Patricia
Albert
Dude's Dr
Art's Ln
Patricia Rd
Colorado Av
Rollins Pass Rd
Main St
Rd
NF-105
119
South Boulder Creek
Rollins Pass Rd
80474
Moon Gulch Rd
Upper Moon Gulch Rd
Lower Gulch Rd
T1S
T2S
Moon Gulch Rd
CR-14
CR-14
CR-14
Travis Gulch Rd
Gamble Gulch Rd
Geneva's Wy
GILPIN RD
ROOSEVELT NATIONAL FOREST
Upper Moon Gulch Rd
CR-14
Gamble Gulch Rd
Gamble Gulch Rd
R73W
R72W
Harry St
Ward St
Diane Av
Paula Av
Newman St
Laura
Irene Av
Ward
Lake St
Lake St
Av
Av
Donald St
CR-12
Gilpin Rd
GILPIN RD
CR-13
SNOWLINE LK
Cindy Ln
View Dr
Independent Dr
Mountain
Gamble Gulch Rd
80403

26 25 30 35 36 31 2 1 6 11 12 7 14 13 18

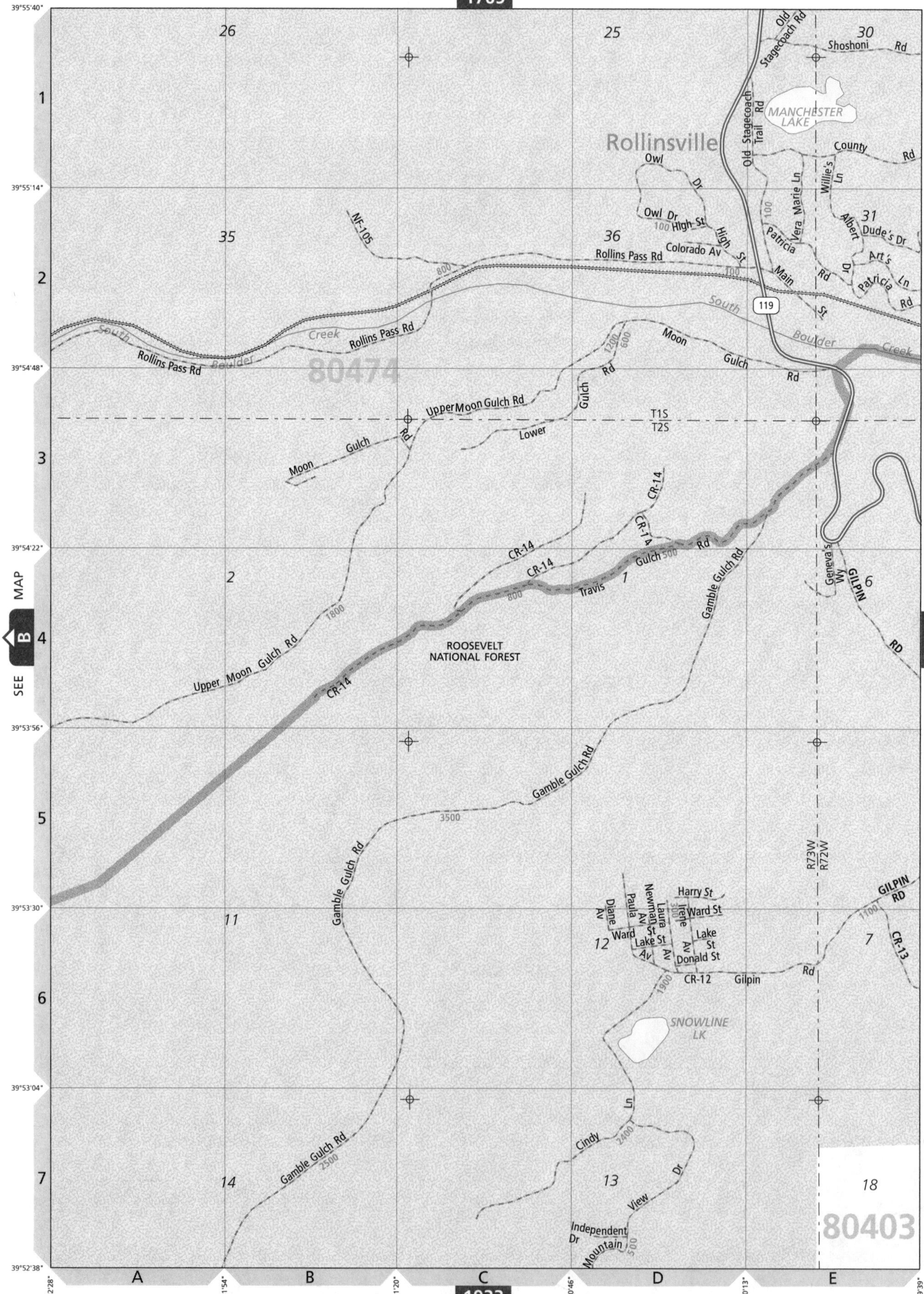

SEE B MAP

SEE 1850 MAP

SEE 1933 MAP

A B C D E
1 2 3 4 5 6 7

39°55'40" 39°55'14" 39°54'48" 39°54'22" 39°53'56" 39°53'30" 39°53'04" 39°52'38"

105°32'28" 105°31'54" 105°31'20" 105°30'46" 105°30'13" 105°29'50"

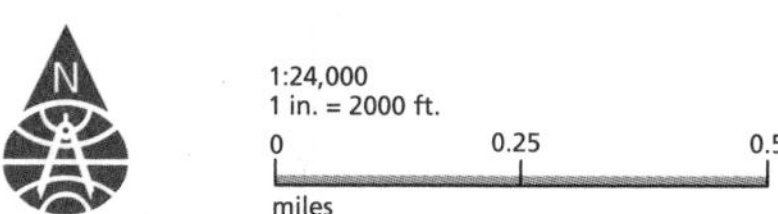

SEE 1766 MAP

Pactolus
80474
80403
ROOSEVELT NATIONAL FOREST
GOLDEN GATE CANYON STATE PARK
THORN LAKE

Shoshoni Rd
County Rd
Dude's Dr
Art's Ln
Patricia Rd
South Boulder Creek
Pactolus Lake Rd
Farrell Dr
S Beaver Creek Rd
La Chula Rd
Wedgwood Rd
Road 11B
Road 11C
Road 11A
Bowles Ranch Rd
Severance Lodge Rd
119
GILPIN RD
Glen Mawr Dr
S Mountain Meadows Dr
Aspen Cir
Midway Dr
Meadow Wy
Ridge Wy
Pine Hillcrest Dr
Aspen Ln
CR-13
Paint Brush Rd
Paint Brush Dr
Columbine Ln
Oak Terrace Rd
CO-119
Potato Gulch Rd
Old Gold Rd
Mica Rd
Feldspar Rd
Quartz Rd
Pyrite Rd
Silver Rd
Blue Spruce Rd
Spruce Rd
Scenic Rd
Easy St
Gap Rd
Willow Ln
Meadowlake Dr
Pine Glade Dr
Apex Rd
Thorne Cir
Trinity Mountain Ranch Rd
Damascus Rd
State Park Rd
T1S
T2S

39°55'38"
39°55'12"
39°54'46"
39°54'20"
39°53'54"
39°53'28"
39°53'02"
39°52'36"
105°29'39"
105°29'05"
105°28'31"
105°27'57"
105°27'23"
105°26'50"

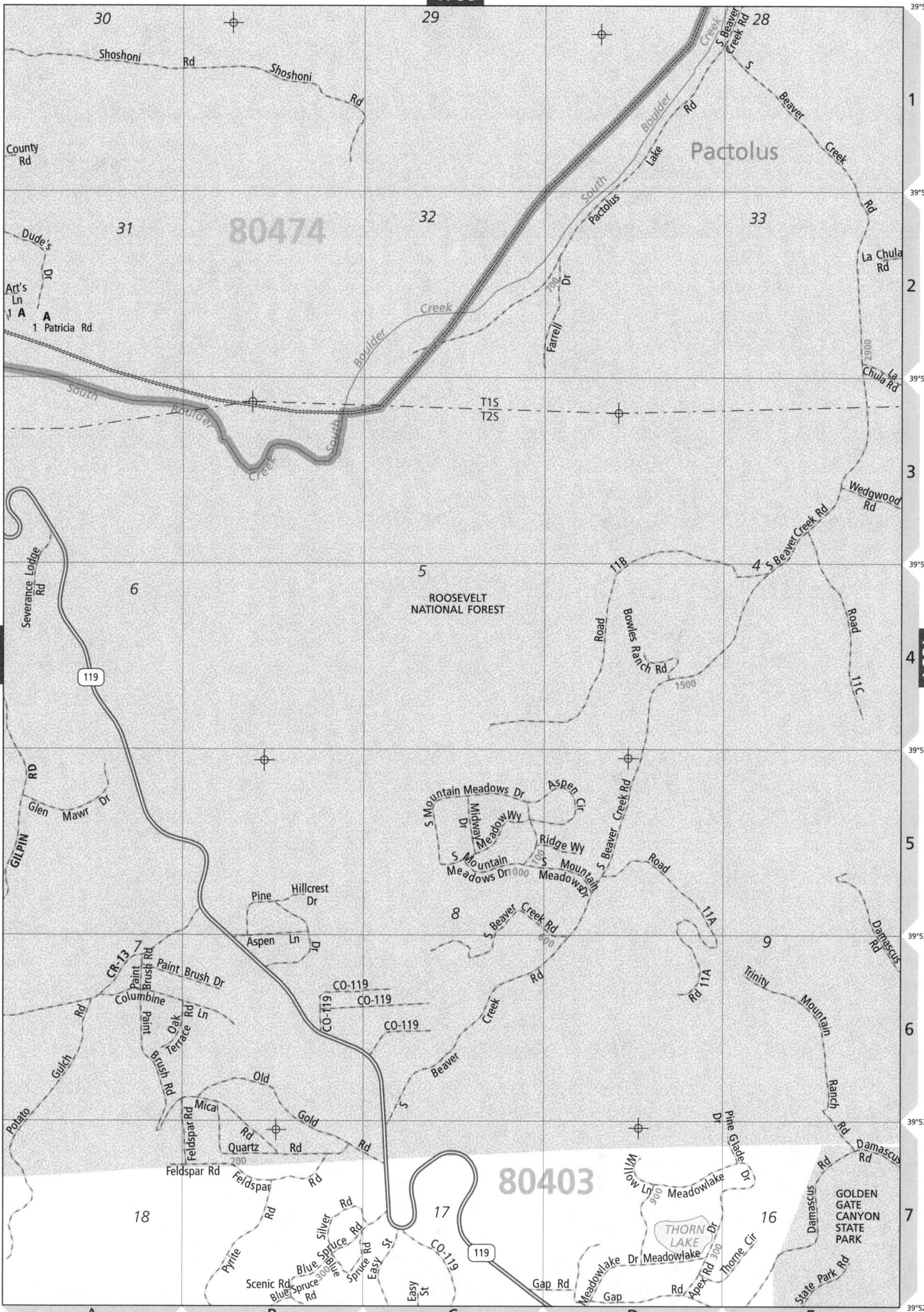

SEE 1849 MAP

SEE 1851 MAP

SEE 1934 MAP

1:24,000
1 in. = 2000 ft.
0 0.25 0.5
miles

SEE 1767 MAP

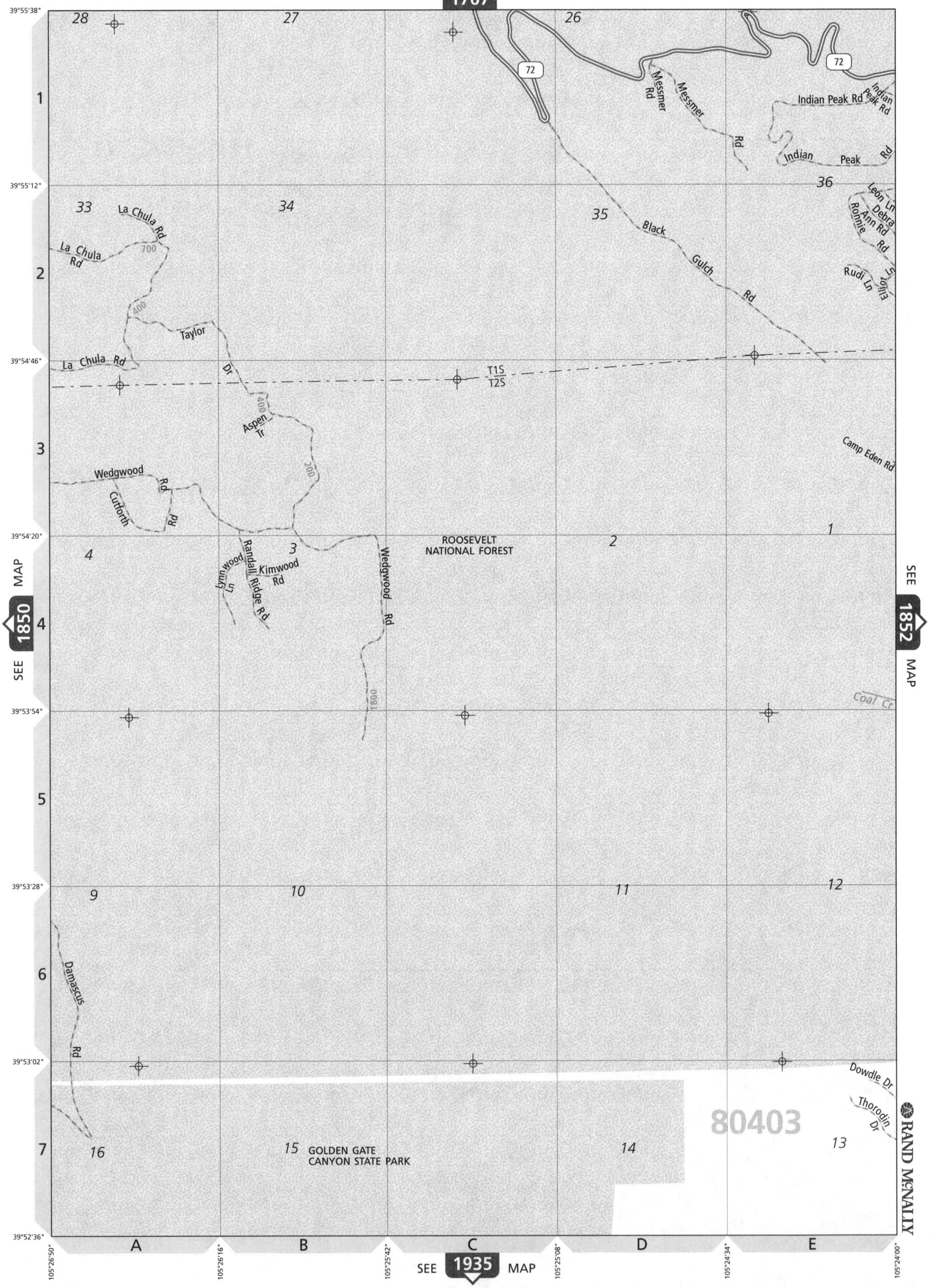

SEE 1850 MAP

SEE 1852 MAP

SEE 1935 MAP

1:24,000
1 in. = 2000 ft.
0 0.25 0.5
miles

SEE 1768 MAP

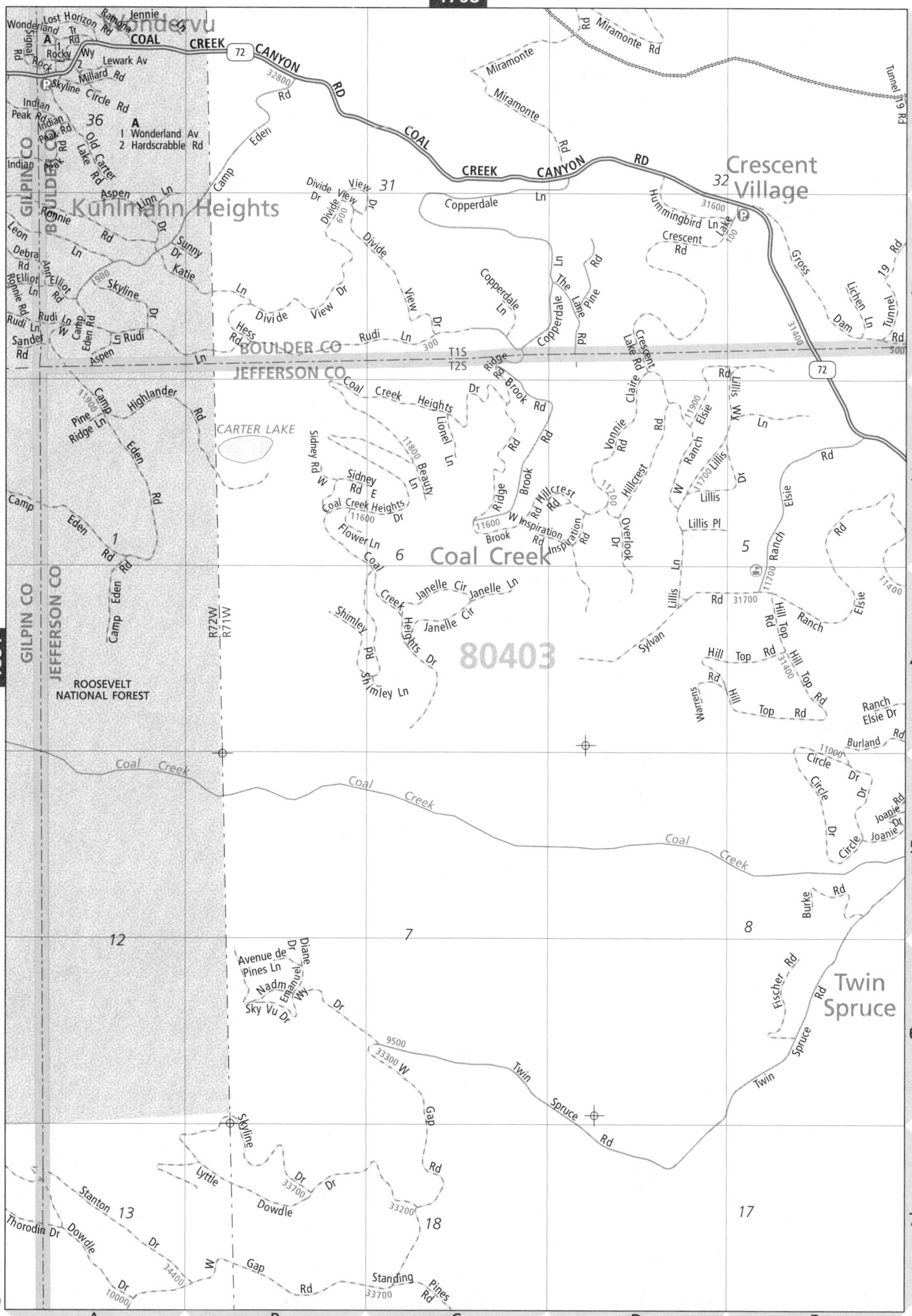

SEE 1851 MAP

SEE 1853 MAP

SEE 1936 MAP

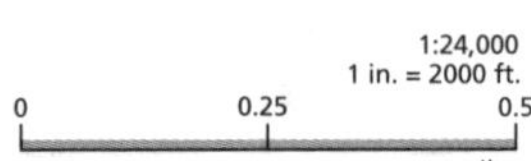

SEE 1769 MAP

Copperdale
ELDORADO CANYON STATE PARK
ELDORADO CANYON STATE PARK
BOULDER CO
JEFFERSON CO
T1S
T2S
80403
ASEL OPEN SPACE
GOLDEN GATE CANYON STATE PARK
COAL CREEK CANYON RD
72
Chute Rd
Gross Dam Rd
Tunnel 19 Rd
Hollings Wy
Seaver Dr
Spruce Canyon Dr
Nob Wy
Begole Canyon Cir
Canyon Dr
Crescent Park Cir
Park Dr
Crescent Park
Butte Dr
Granite Peak Ln
Loomis Wy
Georgian Cir
Ranch Elsie Rd
Skyline Dr
Ranch Elsie Dr
Blue Mountain Rd
Burland Rd
Burland Dr
Joanie Rd
Joanie Dr
Twin Spruce Rd
Cattle Trail Dr
Coal Creek

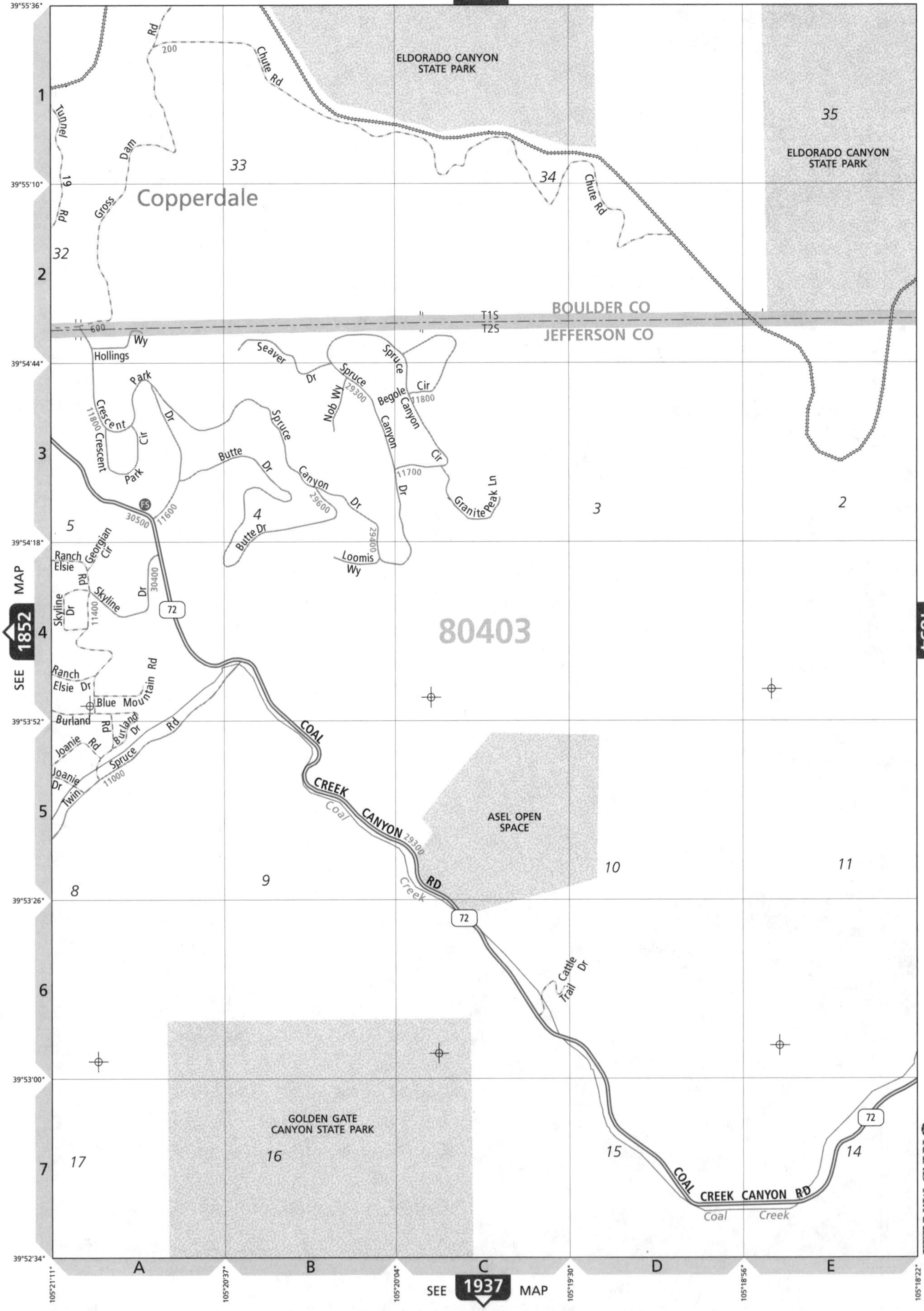

SEE 1852 MAP

SEE 1854 MAP

SEE 1937 MAP

1:24,000
1 in. = 2000 ft.
0 0.25 0.5
miles

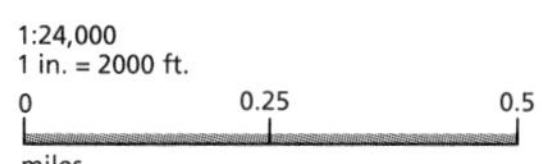

SEE 1770 MAP

ELDORADO CANYON STATE PARK
80025
80303
80403
35
36
31
32
2
1
6
5
11
12
7
8
14
13
18
17
BOULDER CO
JEFFERSON CO
T1S
T2S
R70W
R71W
Plainview Rd
A
1 Blue Mountain Dr
Coal Creek
26800
COAL CREEK CANYON RD
72
Arvada
23800
10000
A
1
2
3
4
5
6
7
A
B
C
D
E
39°55'34"
39°55'08"
39°54'42"
39°54'16"
39°53'50"
39°53'24"
39°52'58"
39°52'32"
105°18'22"
105°17'48"
105°17'14"
105°16'41"
105°16'07"
105°15'33"

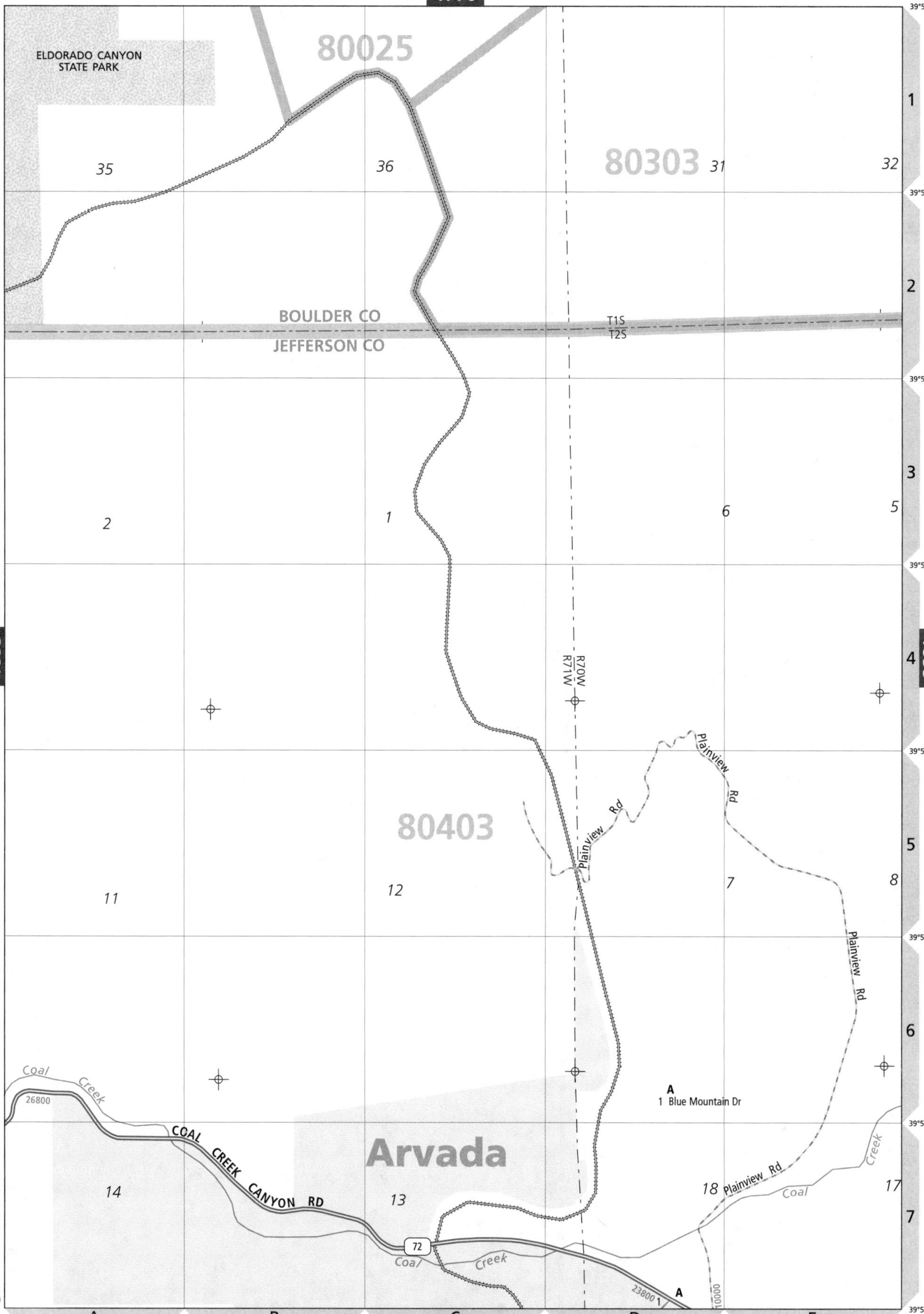

SEE 1853 MAP
SEE 1855 MAP
SEE 1938 MAP

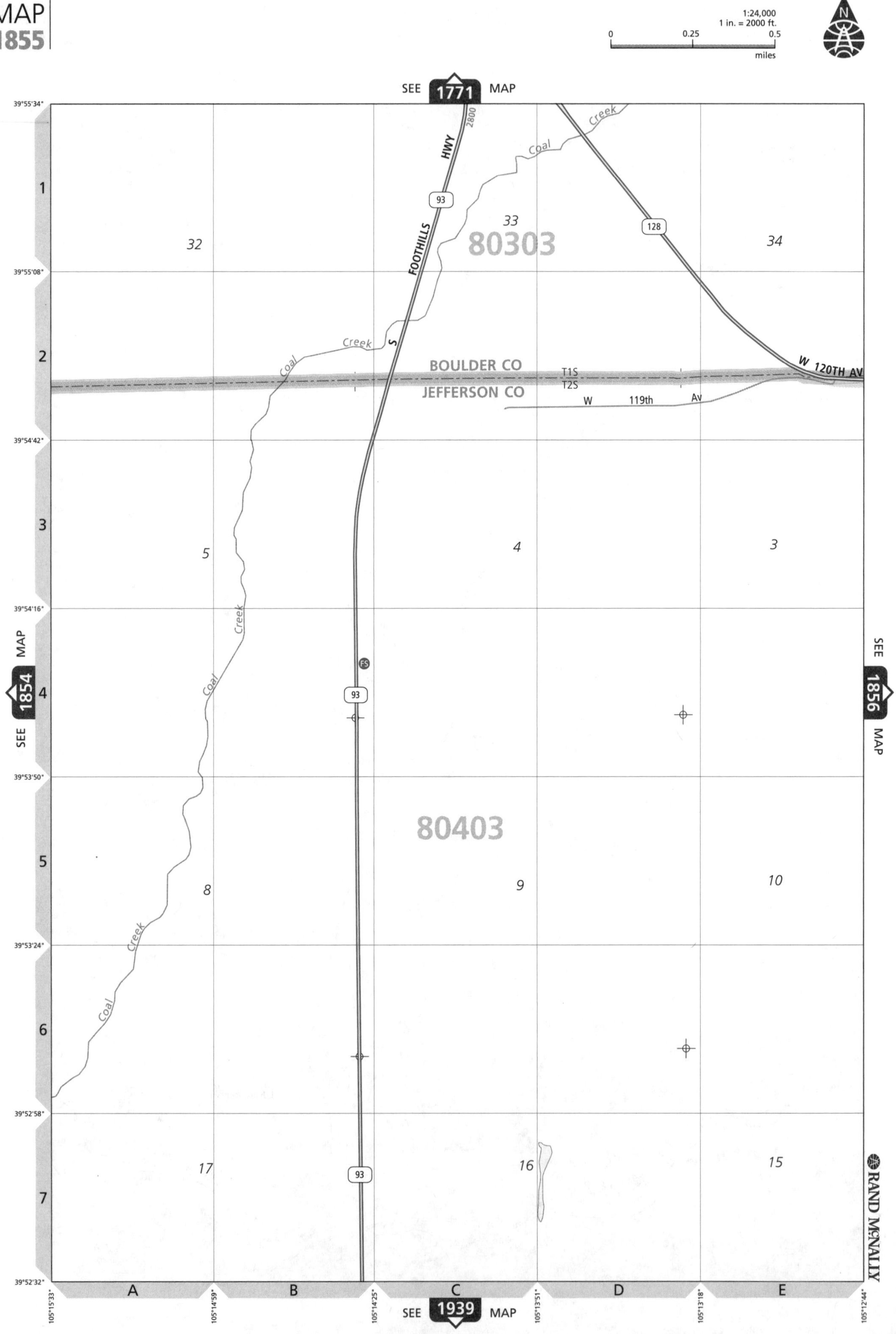

1:24,000
1 in. = 2000 ft.
0 0.25 0.5
miles

SEE 1771 MAP

SEE 1854 MAP

SEE 1856 MAP

SEE 1939 MAP

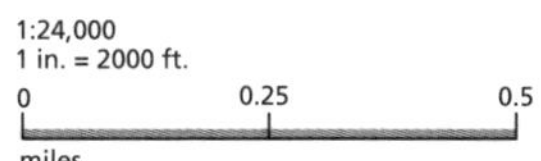

SEE 1772 MAP

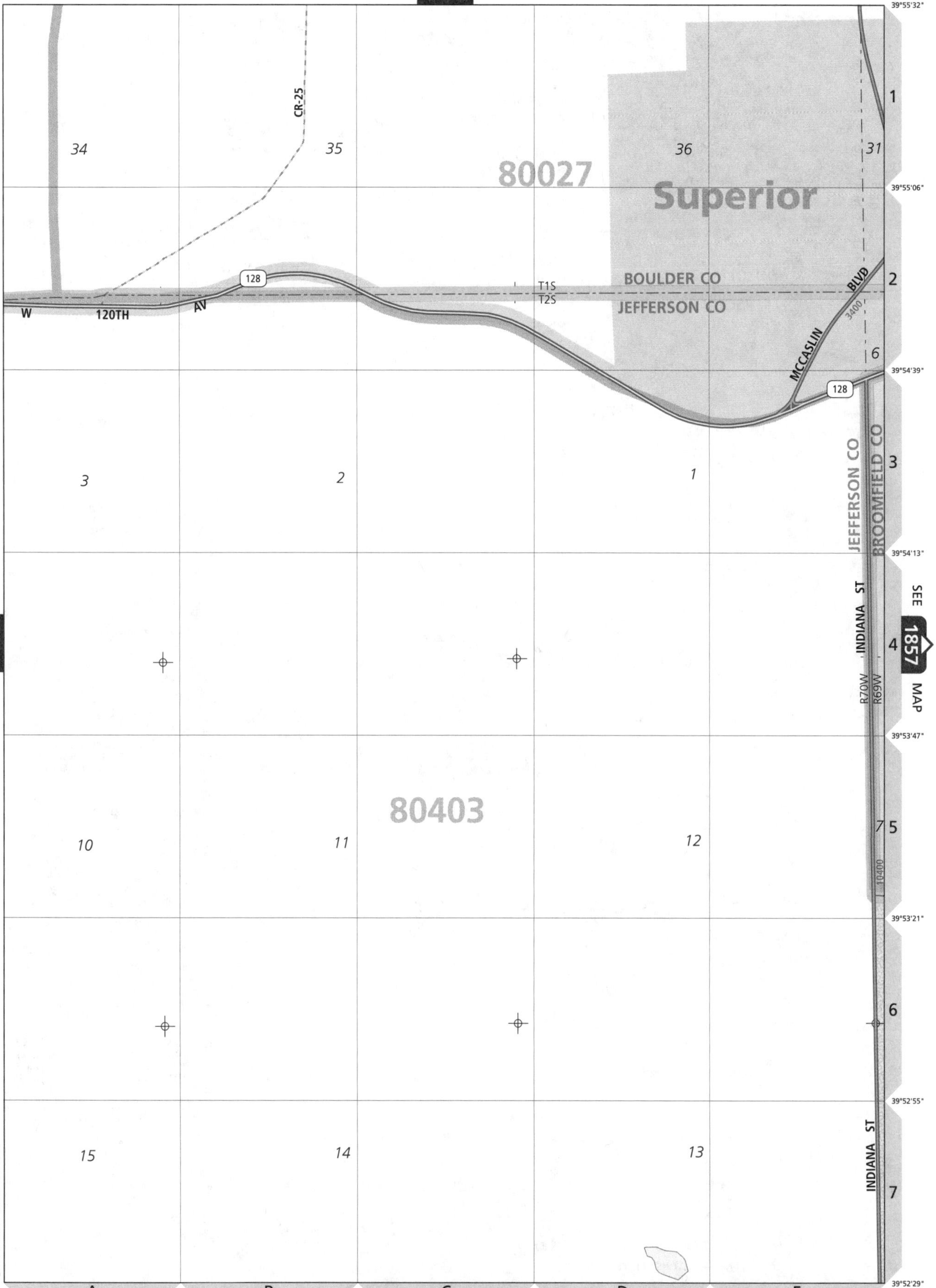

SEE 1855 MAP

SEE 1857 MAP

SEE 1940 MAP

1:24,000
1 in. = 2000 ft.
0 0.25 0.5
miles

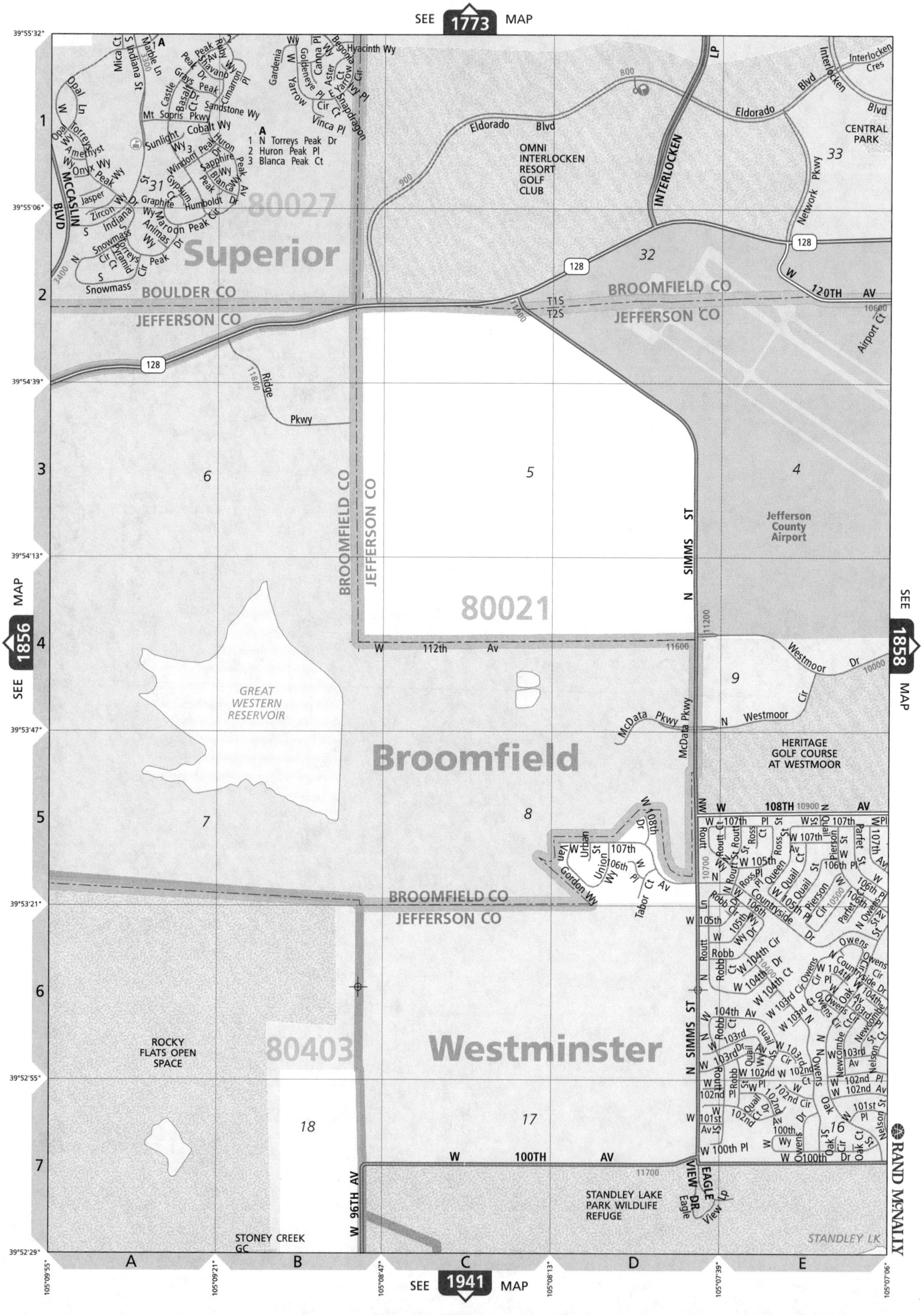

SEE 1773 MAP

SEE 1856 MAP

SEE 1858 MAP

Superior
Broomfield
Westminster
80027
80021
80403
BOULDER CO
JEFFERSON CO
BROOMFIELD CO
OMNI INTERLOCKEN RESORT GOLF CLUB
CENTRAL PARK
Jefferson County Airport
GREAT WESTERN RESERVOIR
HERITAGE GOLF COURSE AT WESTMOOR
ROCKY FLATS OPEN SPACE
STANDLEY LAKE PARK WILDLIFE REFUGE
STONEY CREEK GC
STANDLEY LK
MCCASLIN BLVD
INTERLOCKEN LP
N SIMMS ST
W 120TH AV
W 112th Av
W 108TH AV
W 100TH AV
W 96TH AV
EAGLE VIEW DR
Eldorado Blvd
Ridge Pkwy
Westmoor Dr
McData Pkwy

A
1 N Torreys Peak Dr
2 Huron Peak Pl
3 Blanca Peak Ct

SEE 1941 MAP

RAND McNALLY

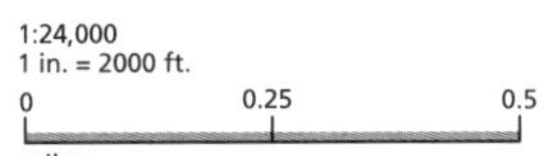

SEE 1774 MAP

SEE 1857 MAP

SEE 1859 MAP

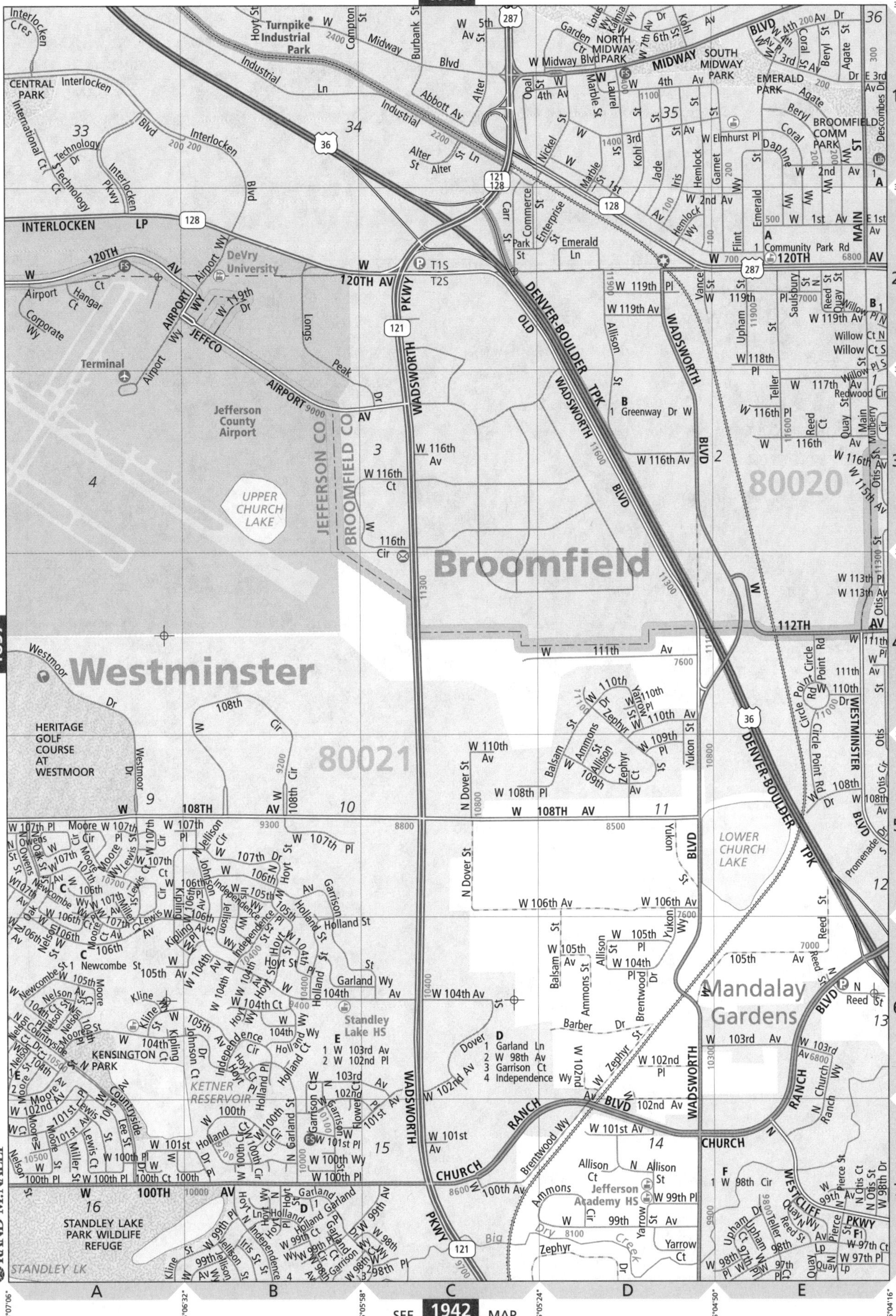

Turnpike Industrial Park

CENTRAL PARK

NORTH MIDWAY PARK

SOUTH MIDWAY PARK

EMERALD PARK

BROOMFIELD COMM PARK

DeVry University

Terminal

Jefferson County Airport

UPPER CHURCH LAKE

JEFFERSON CO

BROOMFIELD CO

Broomfield

80020

Westminster

80021

HERITAGE GOLF COURSE AT WESTMOOR

LOWER CHURCH LAKE

Mandalay Gardens

KENSINGTON PARK

KETNER RESERVOIR

Standley Lake HS

Jefferson Academy HS

STANDLEY LAKE PARK WILDLIFE REFUGE

STANDLEY LK

A
1 Community Park Rd

B
1 Greenway Dr W

C
1 Newcombe St

D
1 Garland Ln
2 W 98th Av
3 Garrison Ct
4 Independence Wy

E
1 W 103rd Av
2 W 102nd Pl

F
1 W 98th Cir

39°55'29"
39°55'03"
39°54'37"
39°54'11"
39°53'45"
39°53'19"
39°52'52"
39°52'26"

105°07'06"
105°06'32"
105°05'58"
105°05'24"
105°04'50"
105°04'16"

A B C D E

1 2 3 4 5 6 7

SEE 1942 MAP

1:24,000
1 in. = 2000 ft.
0 0.25 0.5
miles

SEE 1775 MAP

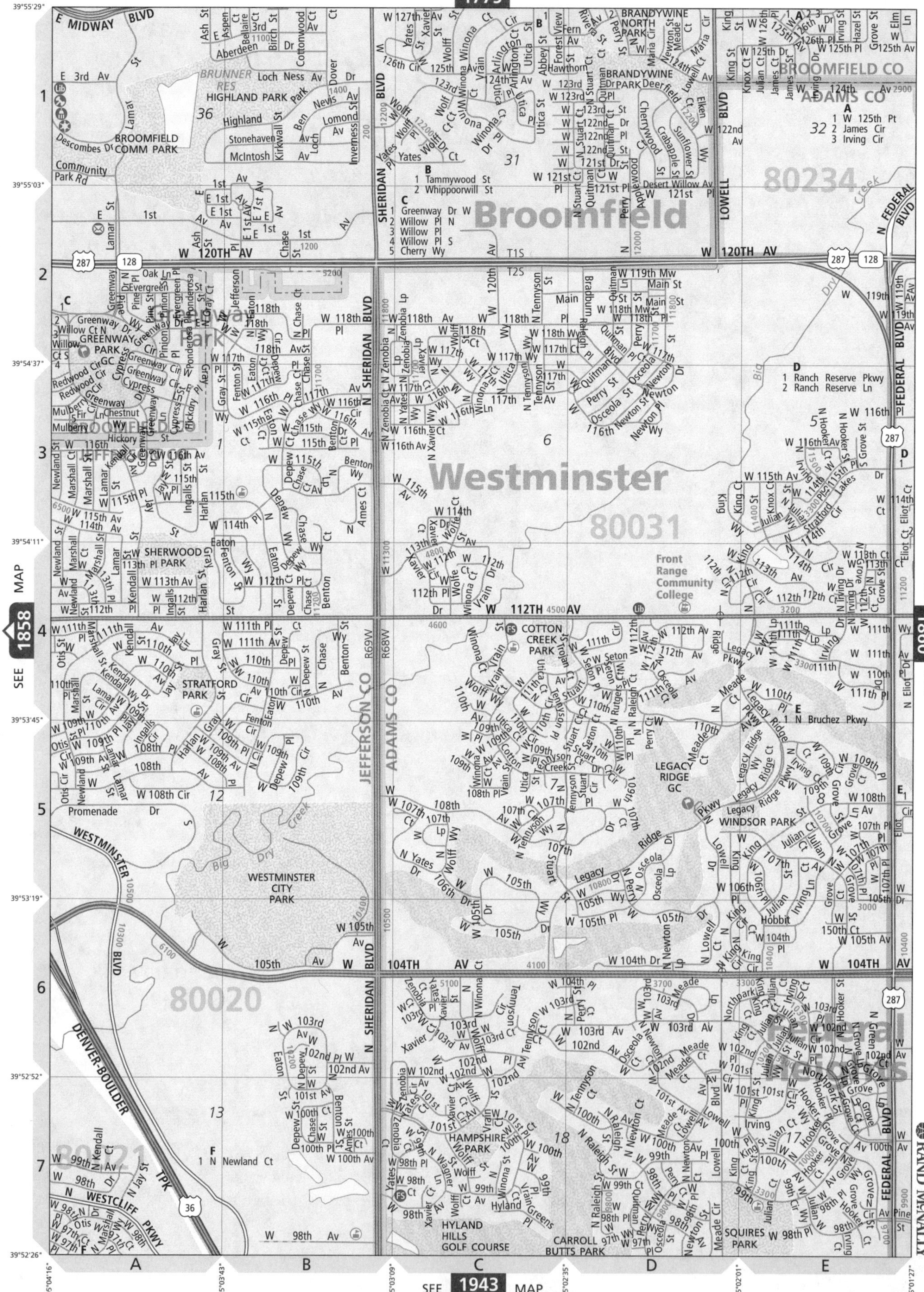

Broomfield

Westminster

BROOMFIELD CO
ADAMS CO

80234

80031

80020

80021

HIGHLAND PARK

BROOMFIELD COMM PARK

BRUNNER RES

GREENWAY PARK

Greenway Park

BROOMFIELD JEFFERSON

SHERWOOD PARK

STRATFORD PARK

WESTMINSTER CITY PARK

BRANDYWINE NORTH PARK

BRANDYWINE PARK

COTTON CREEK PARK

Front Range Community College

LEGACY RIDGE GC

WINDSOR PARK

HAMPSHIRE PARK

HYLAND HILLS GOLF COURSE

CARROLL BUTTS PARK

SQUIRES PARK

Federal Heights

JEFFERSON CO

ADAMS CO

E MIDWAY BLVD

W 120TH AV

W 112TH AV

W 104TH AV

N SHERIDAN BLVD

N FEDERAL BLVD

LOWELL BLVD

WESTMINSTER BLVD

DENVER-BOULDER TPK

WESTCLIFF PKWY

287

128

36

A
1 W 125th Pt
2 James Cir
3 Irving Cir

B
1 Tammywood St
2 Whippoorwill St

C
1 Greenway Dr W
2 Willow Pl N
3 Willow Pl
4 Willow Pl S
5 Cherry Wy

D
1 Ranch Reserve Pkwy
2 Ranch Reserve Ln

E
1 N Bruchez Pkwy

F
1 N Newland Ct

SEE 1858 MAP

SEE 1860 MAP

39°55'29"
39°55'03"
39°54'37"
39°54'11"
39°53'45"
39°53'19"
39°52'52"
39°52'26"

105°04'16"
105°03'43"
105°03'09"
105°02'35"
105°02'01"
105°01'27"

1 2 3 4 5 6 7

A B C D E

SEE 1943 MAP

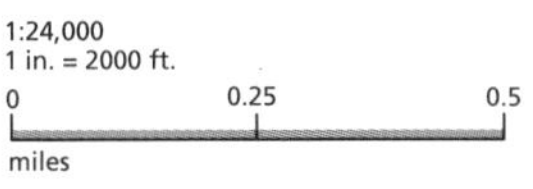

SEE 1776 MAP

SEE 1859 MAP

SEE 1861 MAP

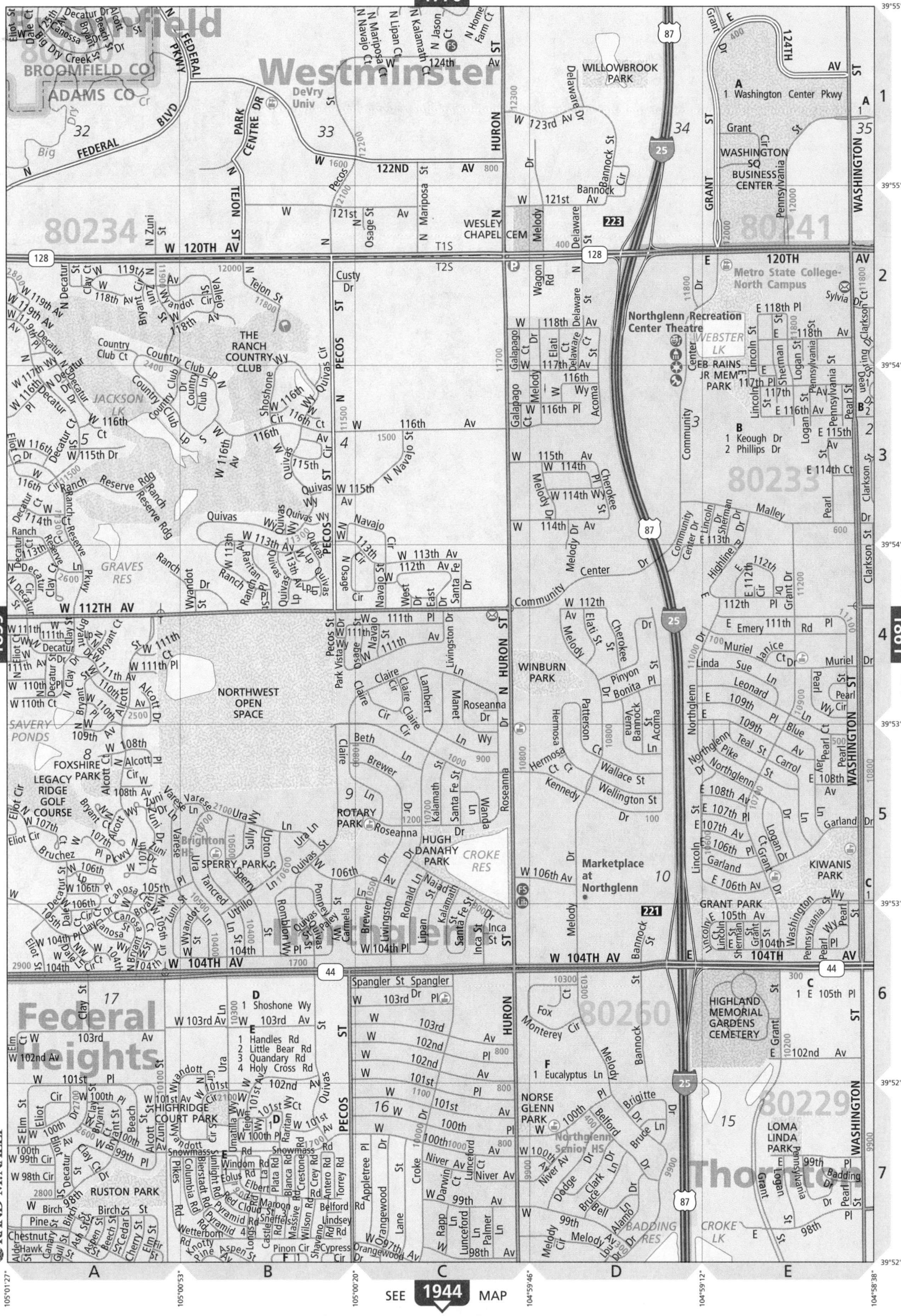

Broomfield
BROOMFIELD CO
ADAMS CO
Westminster
Northglenn
Federal Heights
Thornton

80234
80241
80233
80260
80229

WILLOWBROOK PARK
DeVry Univ
WESLEY CHAPEL CEM
WASHINGTON SQ BUSINESS CENTER
Metro State College-North Campus
Northglenn Recreation Center Theatre
WEBSTER LK
E.B. RAINS JR MEM PARK
THE RANCH COUNTRY CLUB
JACKSON LK
GRAVES RES
NORTHWEST OPEN SPACE
SAVERY PONDS
FOXSHIRE PARK
LEGACY RIDGE GOLF COURSE
WINBURN PARK
ROTARY PARK
HUGH DANAHY PARK
CROKE RES
SPERRY PARK
Brighton HS
Marketplace at Northglenn
KIWANIS PARK
GRANT PARK
HIGHLAND MEMORIAL GARDENS CEMETERY
HIGHRIDGE COURT PARK
RUSTON PARK
NORSE GLENN PARK
Northglenn Senior HS
LOMA LINDA PARK
BADDING RES
CROKE LK

A
1 Washington Center Pkwy

B
1 Keough Dr
2 Phillips Dr

C
1 E 105th Pl

D
1 Shoshone Wy

E
1 Handles Rd
2 Little Bear Rd
3 Quandary Rd
4 Holy Cross Rd

F
1 Eucalyptus Ln

W 120TH AV
W 112TH AV
W 104TH AV
N FEDERAL PKWY
FEDERAL BLVD
PECOS ST
HURON ST
WASHINGTON ST
GRANT ST
122ND AV
124TH AV

39°55'26"
39°55'00"
39°54'34"
39°54'08"
39°53'42"
39°53'16"
39°52'49"
39°52'23"

105°01'27"
105°00'53"
105°00'20"
104°59'46"
104°59'12"
104°58'38"

A B C D E

1 2 3 4 5 6 7

SEE 1944 MAP

1:24,000
1 in. = 2000 ft.

0 0.25 0.5
miles

SEE 1777 MAP

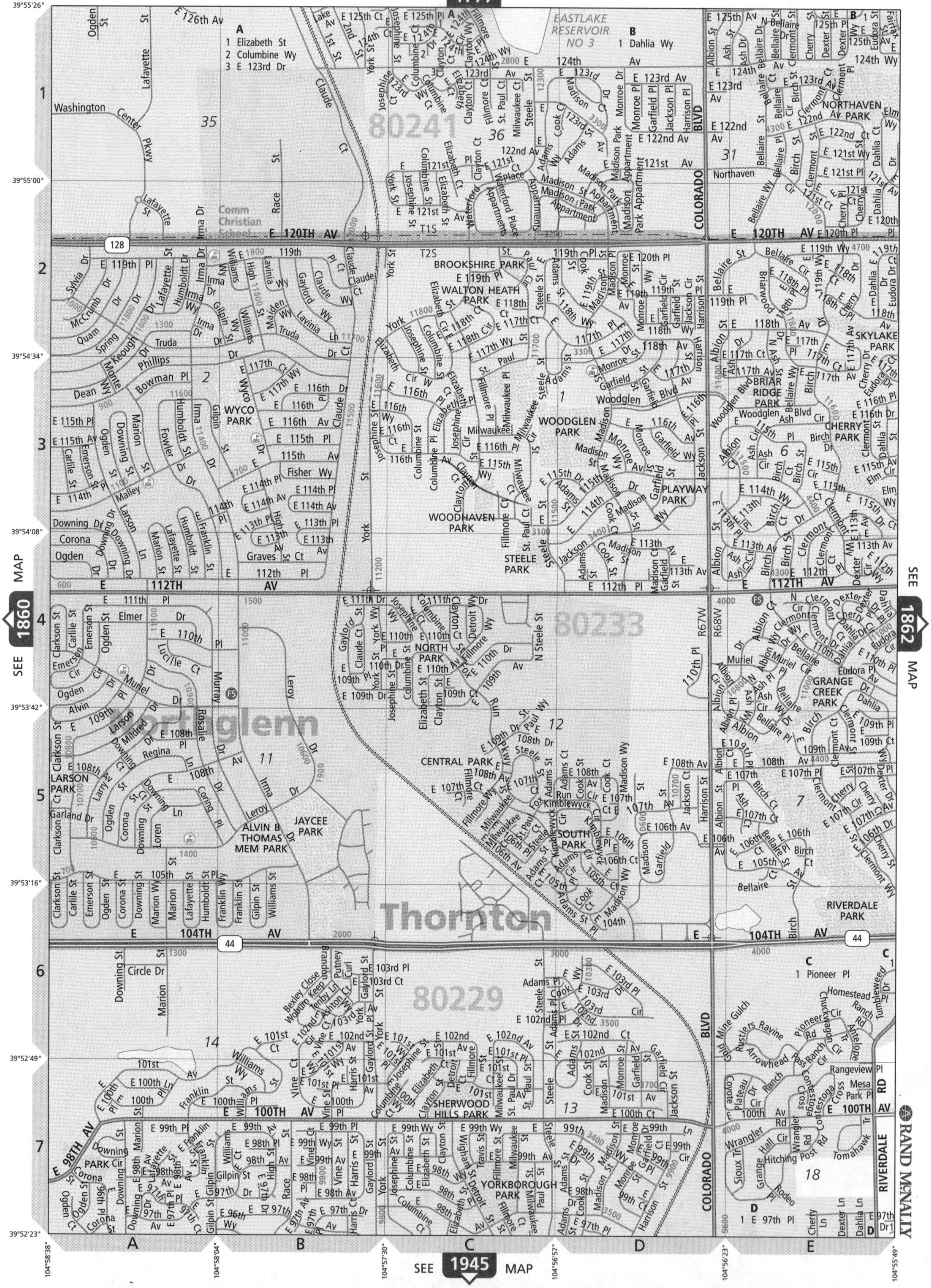

A
1 Elizabeth St
2 Columbine Wy
3 E 123rd Dr

B
1 Dahlia Wy

C
1 Pioneer Pl

D
1 E 97th Pl

EASTLAKE RESERVOIR NO 3

80241

80233

80229

Northglenn

Thornton

BROOKSHIRE PARK

WALTON HEATH PARK

WYCO PARK

WOODGLEN PARK

PLAYWAY PARK

WOODHAVEN PARK

STEELE PARK

NORTHAVEN PARK

SKYLAKE PARK

BRIAR RIDGE PARK

CHERRY PARK

NORTH PARK

GRANGE CREEK PARK

CENTRAL PARK

SOUTH PARK

LARSON PARK

JAYCEE PARK

ALVIN B THOMAS MEM PARK

RIVERDALE PARK

SHERWOOD HILLS PARK

YORKBOROUGH PARK

Comm Christian School

E 120TH AV

E 112TH AV

E 104TH AV

E 100TH AV

E 98TH AV

COLORADO BLVD

RIVERDALE RD

SEE 1860 MAP

SEE 1862 MAP

SEE 1945 MAP

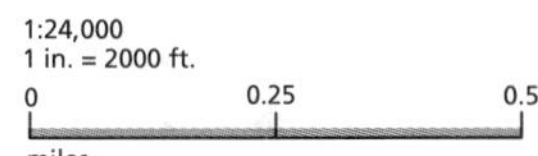

SEE 1778 MAP

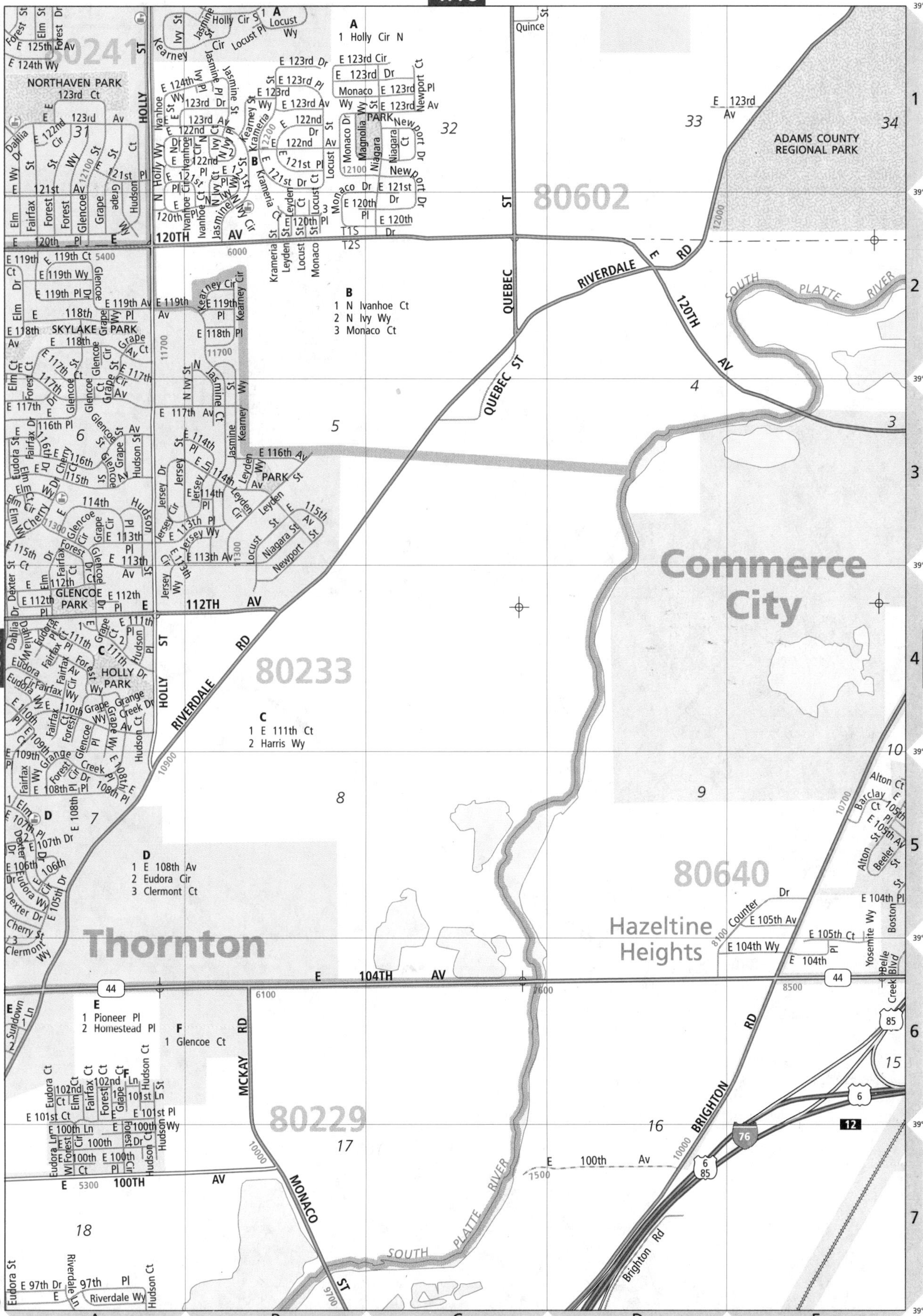

SEE 1861 MAP

SEE 1863 MAP

A
1 Holly Cir N

B
1 N Ivanhoe Ct
2 N Ivy Wy
3 Monaco Ct

C
1 E 111th Ct
2 Harris Wy

D
1 E 108th Av
2 Eudora Cir
3 Clermont Ct

E
1 Pioneer Pl
2 Homestead Pl

F
1 Glencoe Ct

NORTHAVEN PARK
SKYLAKE PARK
GLENCOE PARK
HOLLY PARK
ADAMS COUNTY REGIONAL PARK

Commerce City

Thornton

Hazeltine Heights

80241
80602
80233
80640
80229

120TH AV
112TH AV
E 104TH AV
100TH AV
HOLLY ST
QUEBEC ST
RIVERDALE RD
MCKAY RD
MONACO ST
BRIGHTON RD
SOUTH PLATTE RIVER

39°55'23"
39°54'57"
39°54'30"
39°54'04"
39°53'38"
39°53'12"
39°52'46"
39°52'20"

104°55'49"
104°55'15"
104°54'41"
104°54'07"
104°53'34"
104°53'00"

A B C D E

1 2 3 4 5 6 7

SEE 1946 MAP

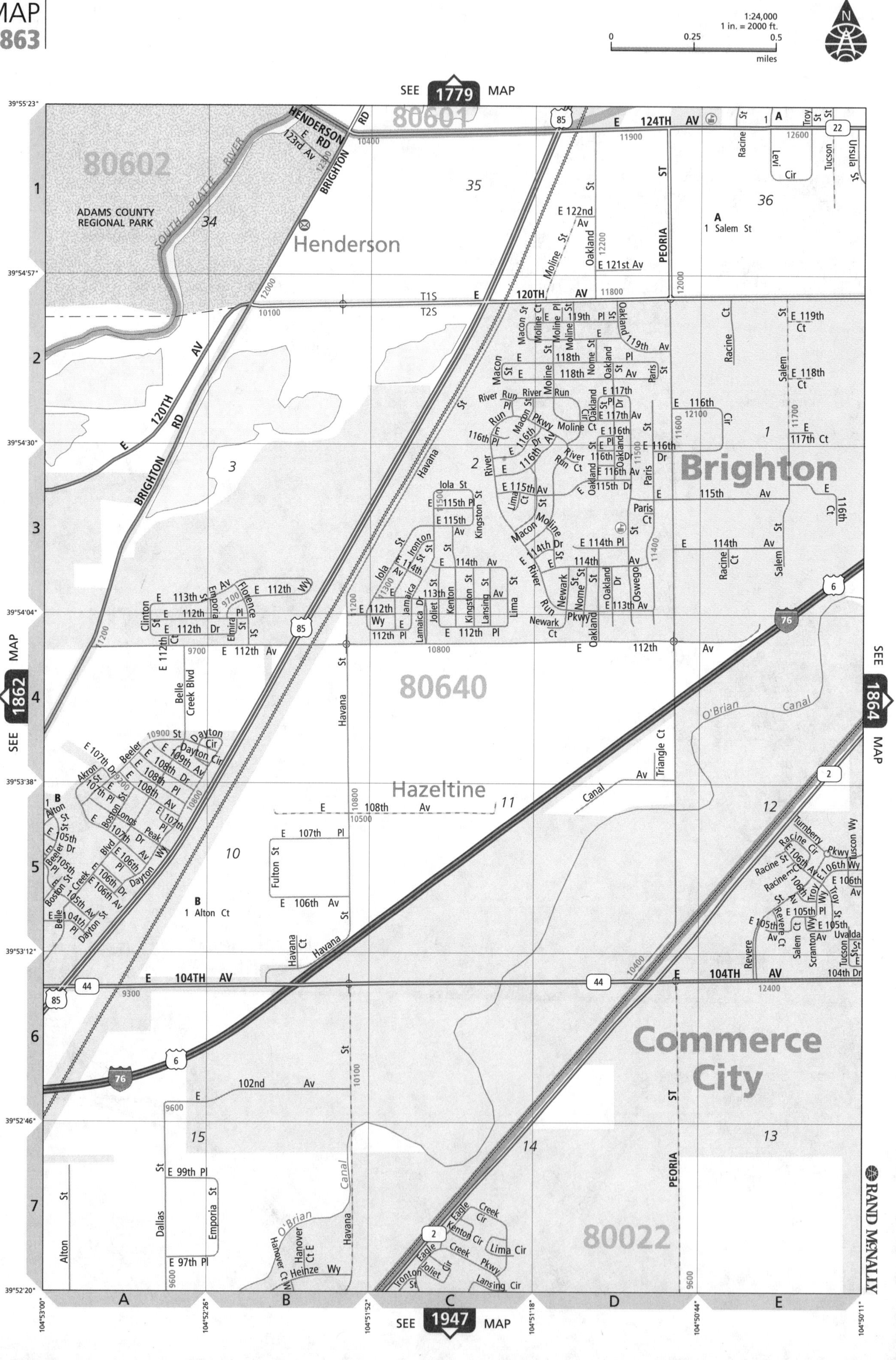

1:24,000
1 in. = 2000 ft.
0 0.25 0.5
miles
SEE 1779 MAP
SEE 1862 MAP
SEE 1864 MAP
SEE 1947 MAP
80601
80602
80640
80022
ADAMS COUNTY REGIONAL PARK
SOUTH PLATTE RIVER
Henderson
Hazeltine
Brighton
Commerce City
E 124TH AV
E 120TH AV
E 120TH RD
BRIGHTON RD
HENDERSON RD
E 123rd Av
E 104TH AV
PEORIA ST
Havana St
E 112th Av
E 115th Av
E 114th Av
E 116th Dr
E 108th Av
E 107th Pl
E 106th Av
E 102nd Av
E 99th Pl
E 97th Pl
Belle Creek Blvd
Dayton St
Fulton St
Dallas St
Emporia St
Alton St
Oakland St
Moline St
Macon St
Nome St
Paris St
Oswego St
Racine St
Salem St
Tucson St
Ursula St
Levi Cir
Triangle Ct
O'Brian Canal
Eagle Creek Cir
Kenton Cir
Lima Cir
Lansing Cir
Tronton St
Joliet Cir
Heinze Wy
Hanover Ct
Turnberry Pkwy
A
1 Salem St
B
1 Alton Ct
T1S
T2S
1
2
3
10
11
12
13
14
15
34
35
36
A
B
C
D
E
1
2
3
4
5
6
7
RAND McNALLY

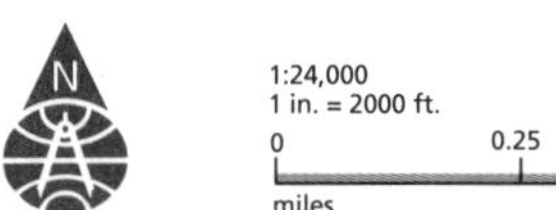

SEE 1780 MAP

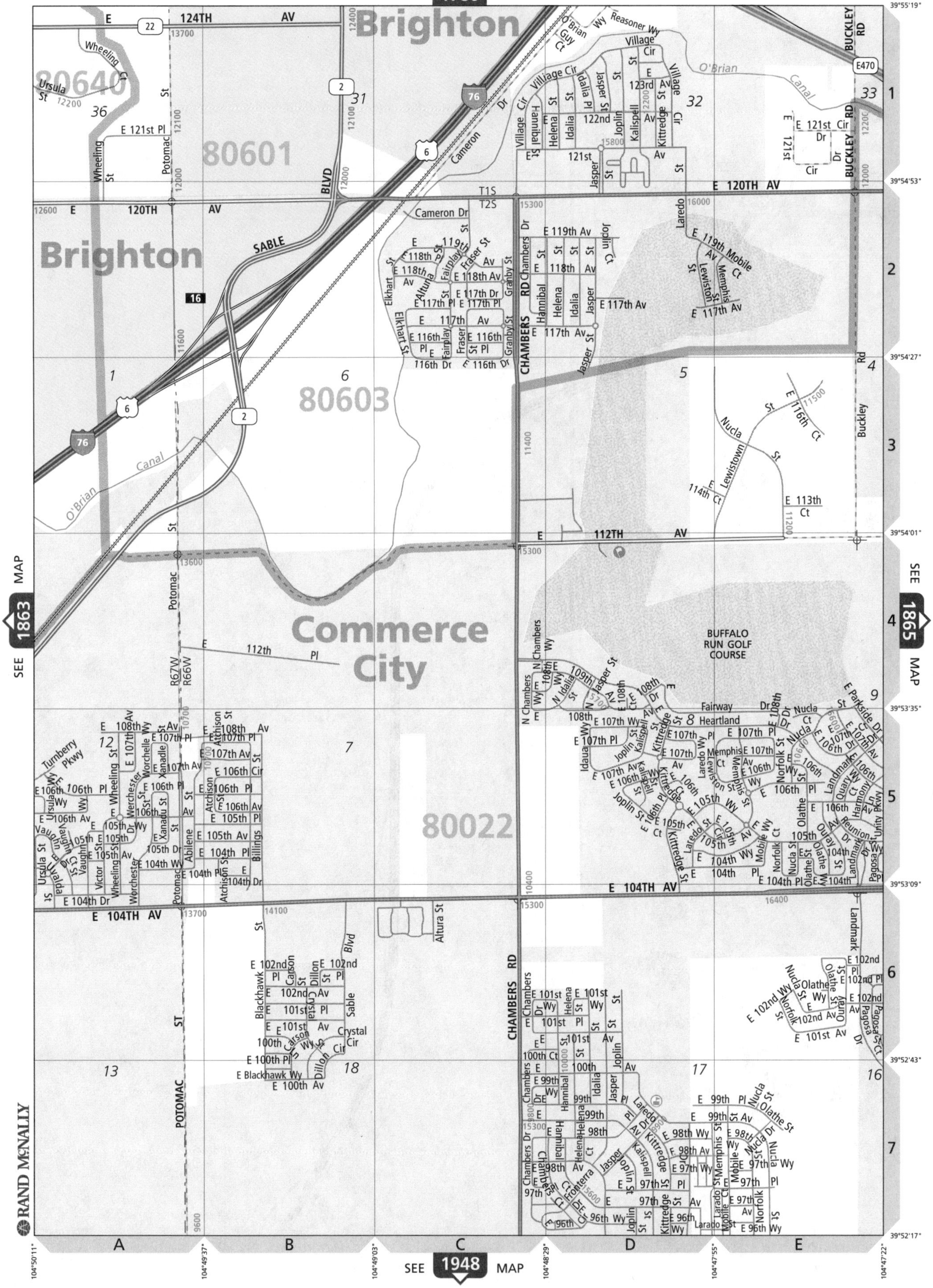

SEE 1863 MAP

SEE 1865 MAP

Brighton

80640

80601

Brighton

80603

Commerce City

80022

BUFFALO RUN GOLF COURSE

E 124TH AV
E 120TH AV
E 112TH AV
E 104TH AV
SABLE BLVD
CHAMBERS RD
POTOMAC ST
BUCKLEY RD
O'Brian Canal
Cameron Dr
Reasoner Wy
Village Cir
E 121st Pl
E 112th Pl
Nucla St
Lewistown St
E 113th Ct
E 116th Ct
Fairway Dr
Heartland
E Parkside Dr
Turnberry Pkwy
Landmark
Altura St
Blackhawk St
Crystal Cir

T1S
T2S
R67W
R66W

A B C D E

1 2 3 4 5 6 7

39°55'19"
39°54'53"
39°54'27"
39°54'01"
39°53'35"
39°53'09"
39°52'43"
39°52'17"

104°50'11"
104°49'37"
104°49'03"
104°48'29"
104°47'55"
104°47'22"

RAND McNALLY

SEE 1948 MAP

1:24,000
1 in. = 2000 ft.
0 0.25 0.5
miles

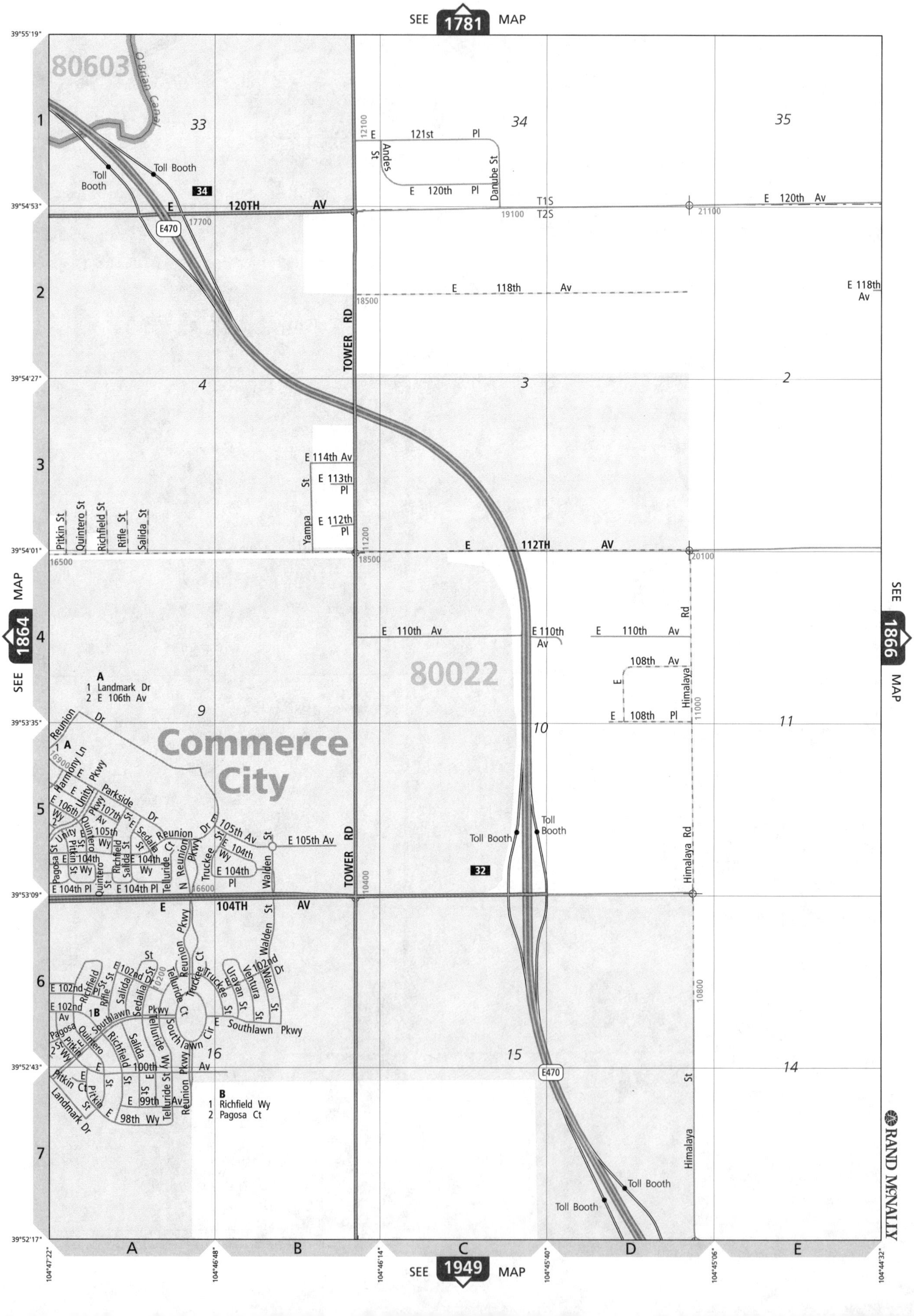

SEE 1781 MAP

80603
O'Brian Canal
Toll Booth
Toll Booth
E 120TH AV
E470
17700
E 121st Pl
Andes St
Danube St
E 120th Pl
T1S
T2S
19100
21100
E 120th Av
E 118th Av
18500
E 118th Av
TOWER RD
E 114th Av
E 113th Pl
E 112th Pl
Yampa St
Pitkin St
Quintero St
Richfield St
Rifle St
Salida St
11200
16500
18500
E 112TH AV
20100
E 110th Av
E 110th Av
E 110th Av
E 108th Av
E 108th Pl
Himalaya Rd
11000
80022
Commerce City
A
1 Landmark Dr
2 E 106th Av
Reunion Dr
Harmony Ln
Unity Pkwy
Parkside Dr
E 106th Wy
E 107th Av
E 105th Wy
Sedalia St
Reunion Pkwy
E 105th Av
E 104th Wy
E 104th Pl
Walden St
E 105th Av
Truckee St
N Reunion Pkwy
Telluride Ct
Pagosa St
E 104th Pl
E 104th Pl
16600
10400
Toll Booth
Toll Booth
Himalaya Rd
E 104TH AV
E 102nd Av
E 102nd Dr
Richfield St
Rifle St
Salida St
Sedalia St
Telluride Ct
Truckee Ct
Uravan St
Ventura St
Waco St
E 102nd Dr
Southlawn Pkwy
Southlawn Cir
Telluride Wy
E 100th Av
E 99th Av
E 98th Wy
Pitkin Ct
Landmark Dr
Reunion Pkwy
10200
10800
B
1 Richfield Wy
2 Pagosa Ct
E470
Himalaya St
Toll Booth
Toll Booth
33 34 35 4 3 2 9 10 11 16 15 14
32 34
1 2 3 4 5 6 7
A B C D E
39°55'19" 39°54'53" 39°54'27" 39°54'01" 39°53'35" 39°53'09" 39°52'43" 39°52'17"
104°47'22" 104°46'48" 104°46'14" 104°45'40" 104°45'06" 104°44'32"

SEE 1864 MAP
SEE 1866 MAP
SEE 1949 MAP

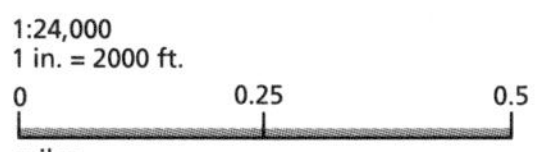

SEE 1782 MAP

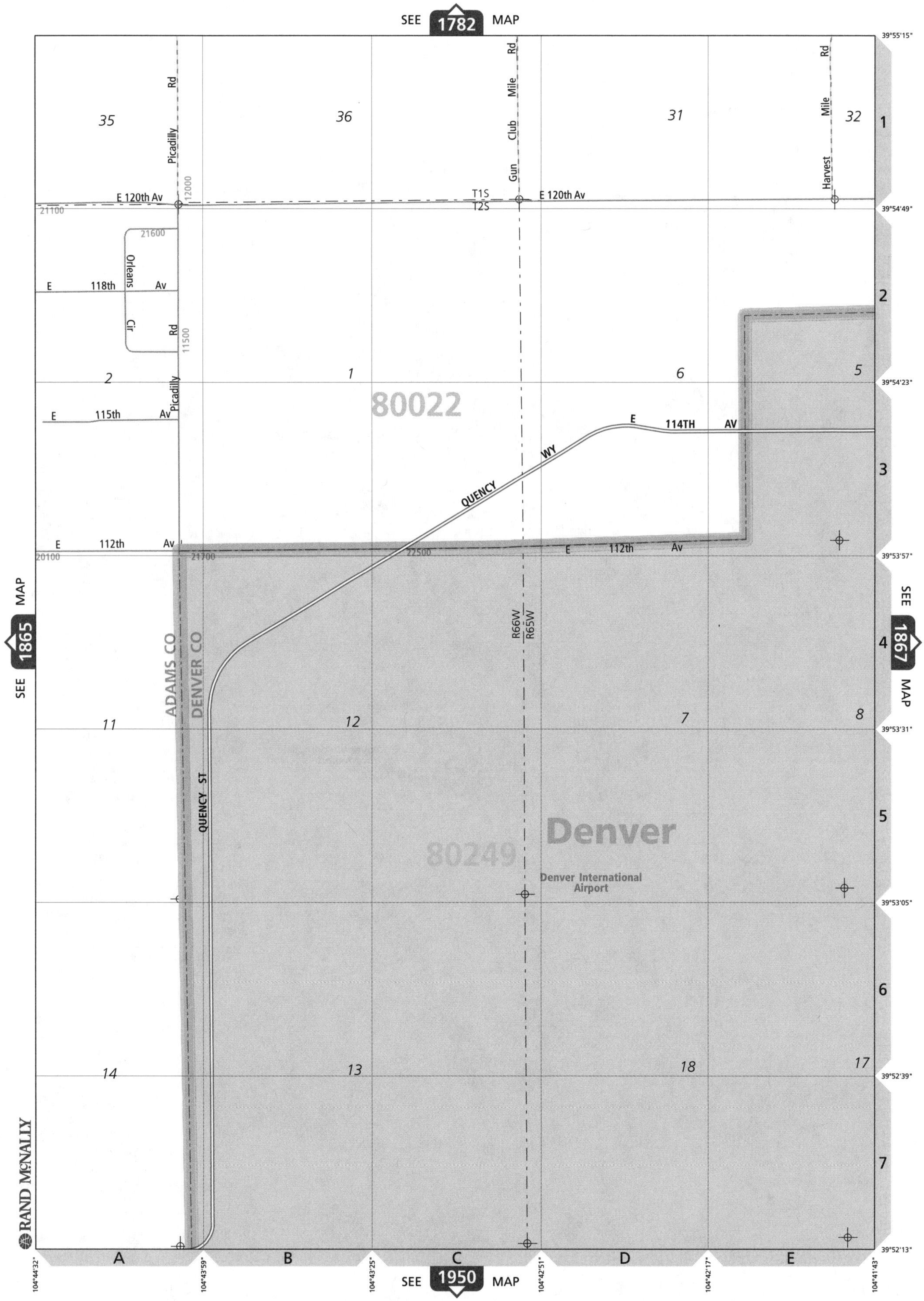

SEE 1865 MAP

SEE 1867 MAP

SEE 1950 MAP

1:24,000
1 in. = 2000 ft.
0 0.25 0.5
miles

SEE 1783 MAP

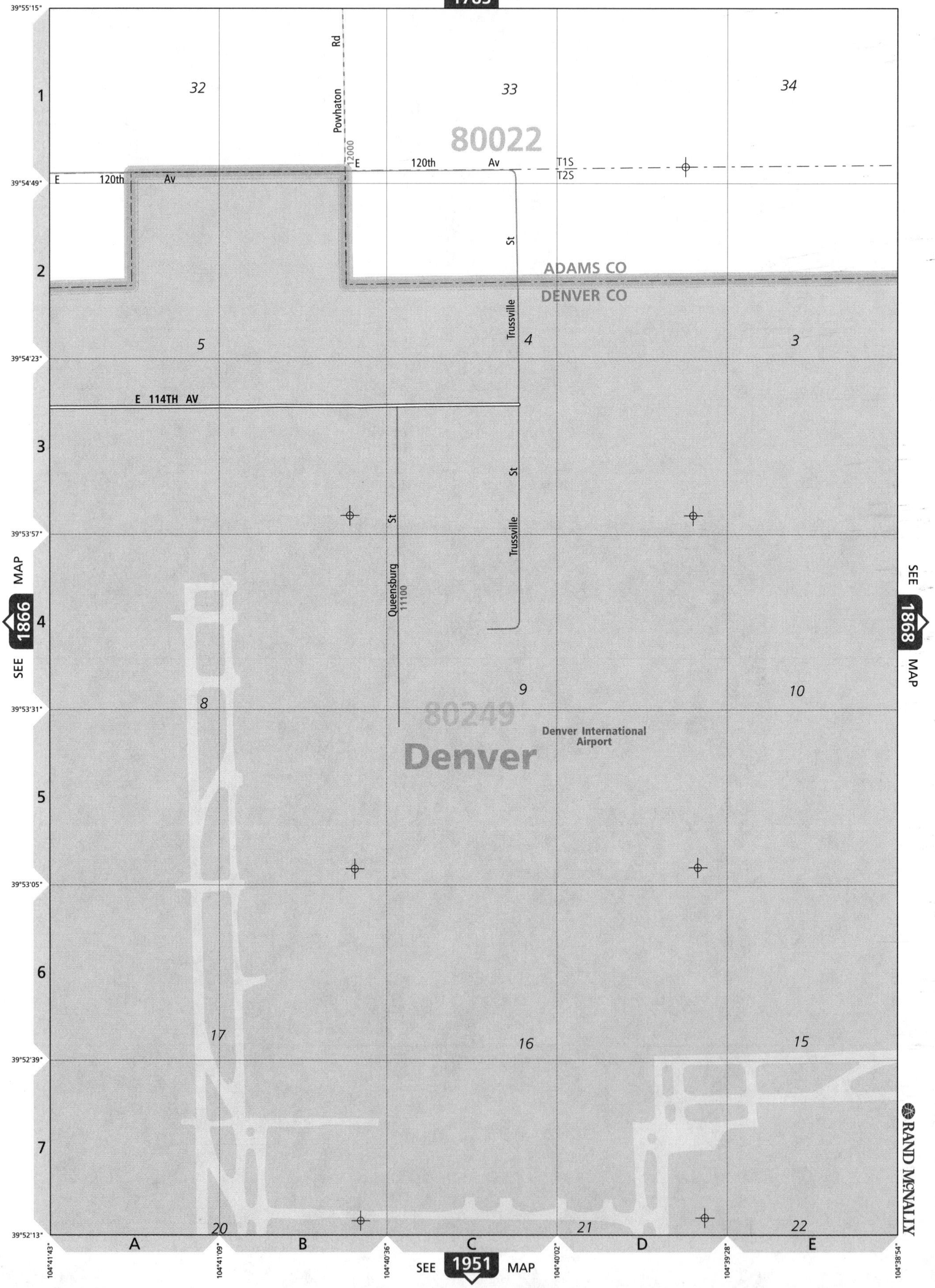

39°55'15"

1

32 33 34

Powhaton Rd
12000

80022

E 120th Av
T1S
T2S

39°54'49"

E 120th Av

Trussville St

2

ADAMS CO
DENVER CO

5 4 3

39°54'23"

E 114TH AV

3

Trussville St

Queensburg St
11100

39°53'57"

SEE 1866 MAP

SEE 1868 MAP

4

8 9 10

39°53'31"

80249

Denver

Denver International Airport

5

39°53'05"

6

17 16 15

39°52'39"

7

20 21 22

39°52'13"

A B C D E

104°41'43" 104°41'09" 104°40'36" 104°40'02" 104°39'28" 104°38'54"

SEE 1951 MAP

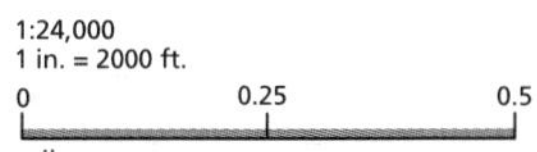

SEE 1784 MAP

34
35
36
31
Hayesmount Rd
Watkins Rd
E 120th Av
T1S
T2S
29700
12000
33200
80022
Box
Mile Rd
Watkins
11200
3
2
1
6
Elder
Creek
Hayesmount Rd
DENVER CO
ADAMS CO
80642
R65W
R64W
10
Denver International Airport
11
12
7
Hudson Mile Rd
11000
10400
29600
E 104th Av
E 104th Av
38200
Denver
80249
Box
Elder
Creek
Umpire St
15
14
13
18
80102
Hudson Mile Rd
E 96th Av
E 96th Av
31300
32100
22
23
24
19

39°55'11"
39°54'45"
39°54'19"
39°53'53"
39°53'27"
39°53'01"
39°52'35"
39°52'09"

104°38'54"
104°38'20"
104°37'46"
104°37'13"
104°36'39"
104°36'05"

A B C D E

1 2 3 4 5 6 7

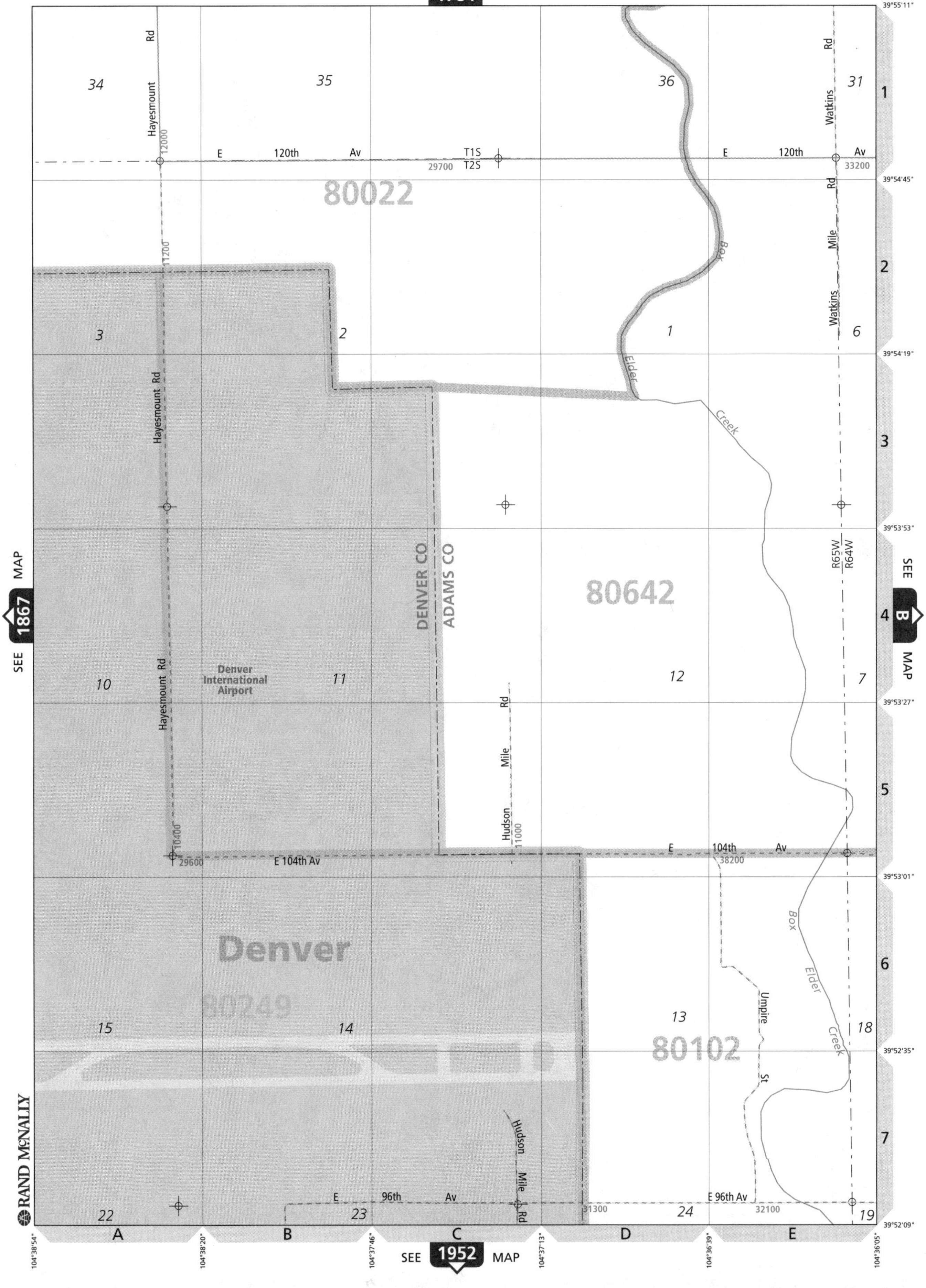

SEE 1867 MAP

SEE B MAP

SEE 1952 MAP

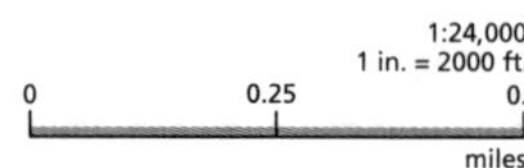

1:24,000
1 in. = 2000 ft.
0 0.25 0.5
miles

SEE 1849 MAP

Gamble Gulch Rd
1700
14
13
18
ROOSEVELT
NATIONAL FOREST
23
24
19
Missouri Gulch Rd
R73W
R72W
ARAPAHO
NATIONAL FOREST
26
25
30
Cold Springs Campground Rd
Upper Hughesville Rd
119
80403
Crest View Dr
Evans View Dr
Elk Place Rd
Lake View Dr
Lake Front Dr
Lake
View
Juniper Rd
Lodgepole Ln
Hawk Wy
Foxtail Dr
Bristlecone Wy
Badger Rd
Fox Tail Cir
Cedar Wy
35
36
31
Coyote Cir
100
Triumph
HS
Spruce Wy
Aspen Rd
Pinon Ln
Pinon Cir
Evergreen
200
Forest
Hills
Hughesville Rd
1200
Apex Valley Rd
T2S
T3S
2
1
6
Old Hughesville Rd
39°52'38"
39°52'12"
39°51'45"
39°51'19"
39°50'53"
39°50'27"
39°50'01"
39°49'35"
105°32'29"
105°31'56"
105°31'22"
105°30'48"
105°30'14"
105°29'40"
1
2
3
4
5
6
7
A
B
C
D
E

SEE B MAP

SEE 1934 MAP

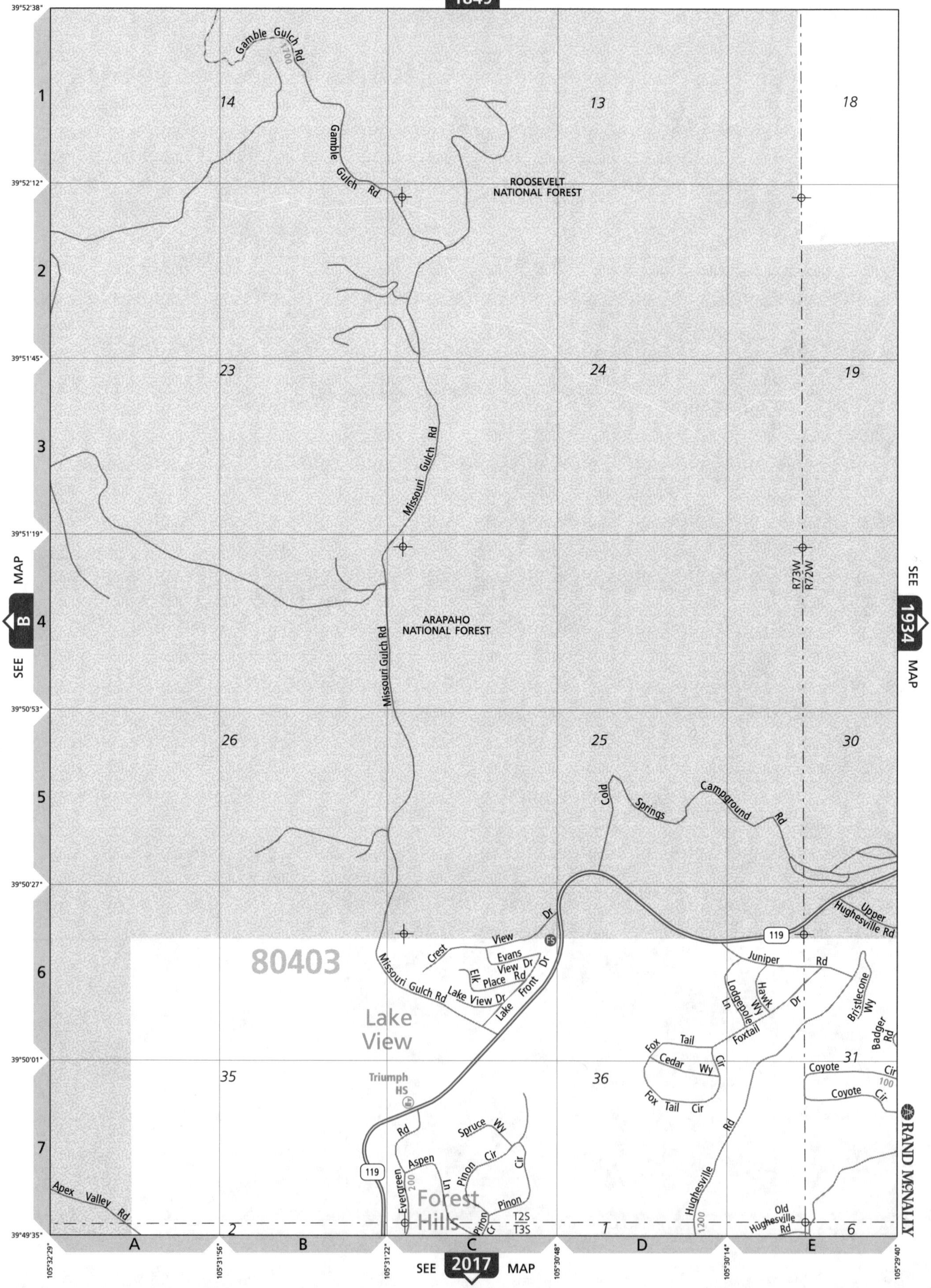

SEE 2017 MAP

1:24,000
1 in. = 2000 ft.
0 0.25 0.5
miles

SEE 1850 MAP

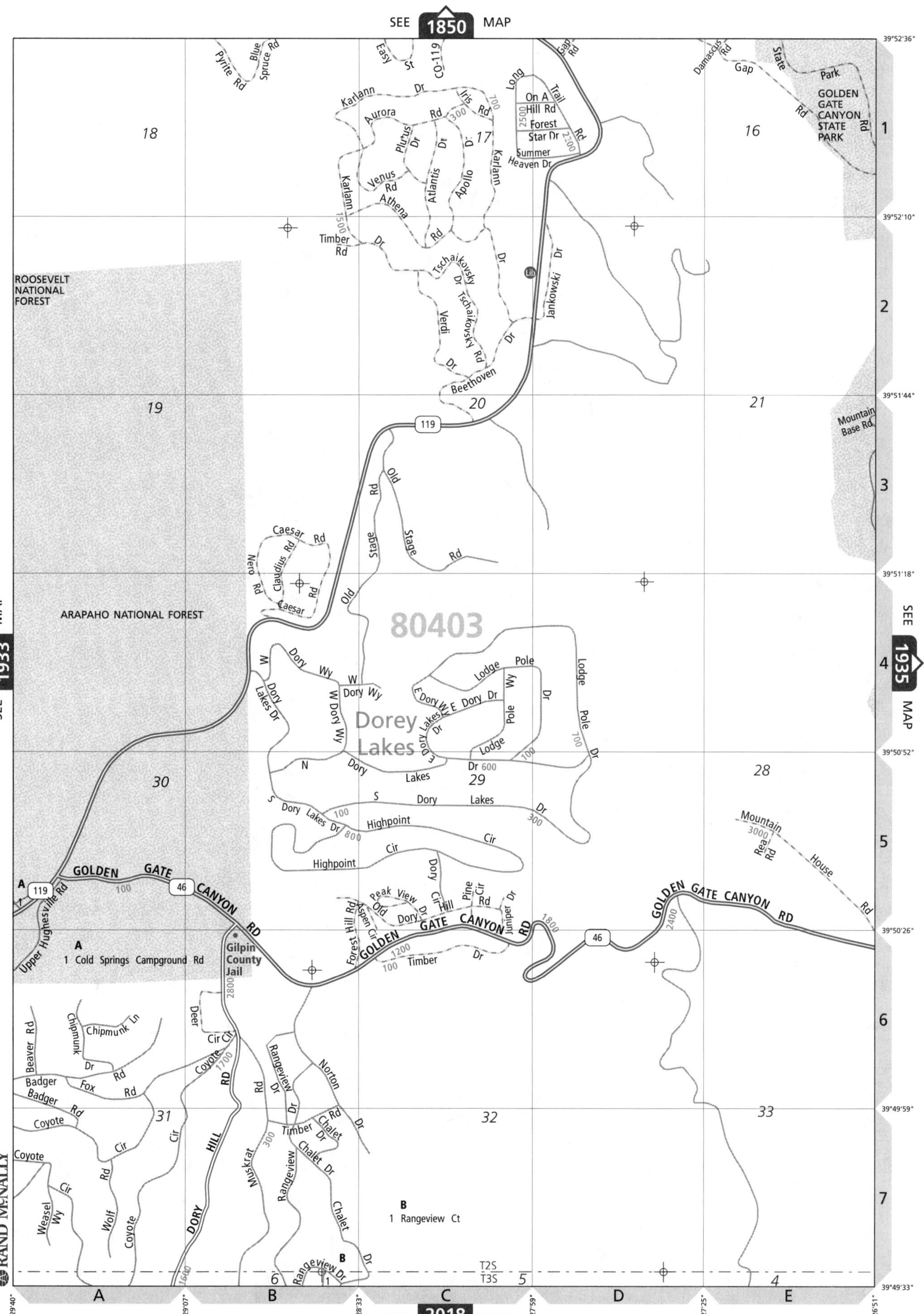

SEE 1933 MAP

SEE 1935 MAP

SEE 2018 MAP

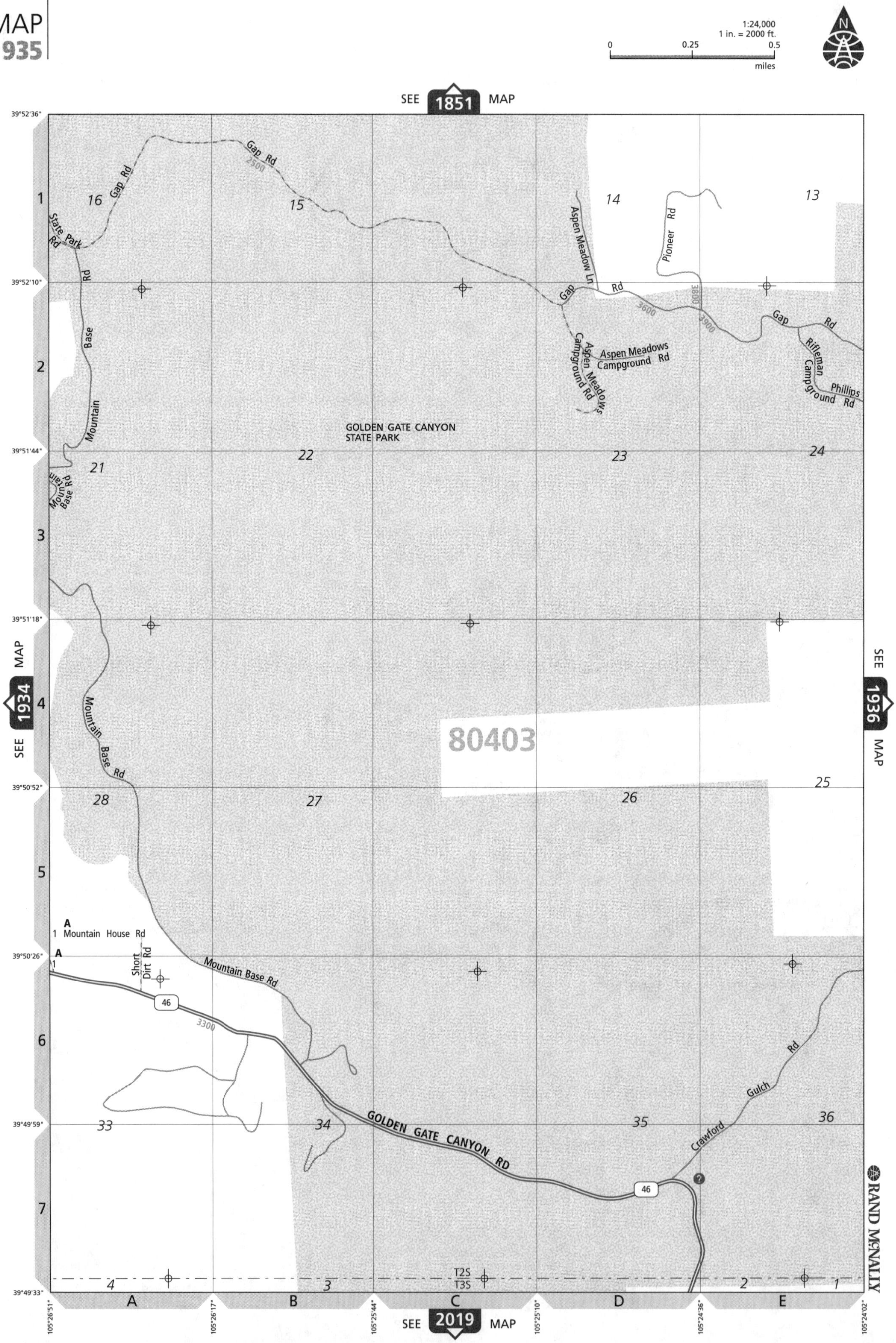

1:24,000
1 in. = 2000 ft.
0 0.25 0.5
miles

SEE 1851 MAP

SEE 1934 MAP

SEE 1936 MAP

GOLDEN GATE CANYON STATE PARK

80403

Gap Rd
State Park Rd
Mountain Base Rd
Aspen Meadow Ln
Pioneer Rd
Aspen Meadows Campground Rd
Rifleman Phillips Campground Rd
Mountain House Rd
Short Dirt Rd
Golden Gate Canyon Rd
Crawford Gulch Rd
46
T2S
T3S

A
1 Mountain House Rd

SEE 2019 MAP

RAND McNALLY

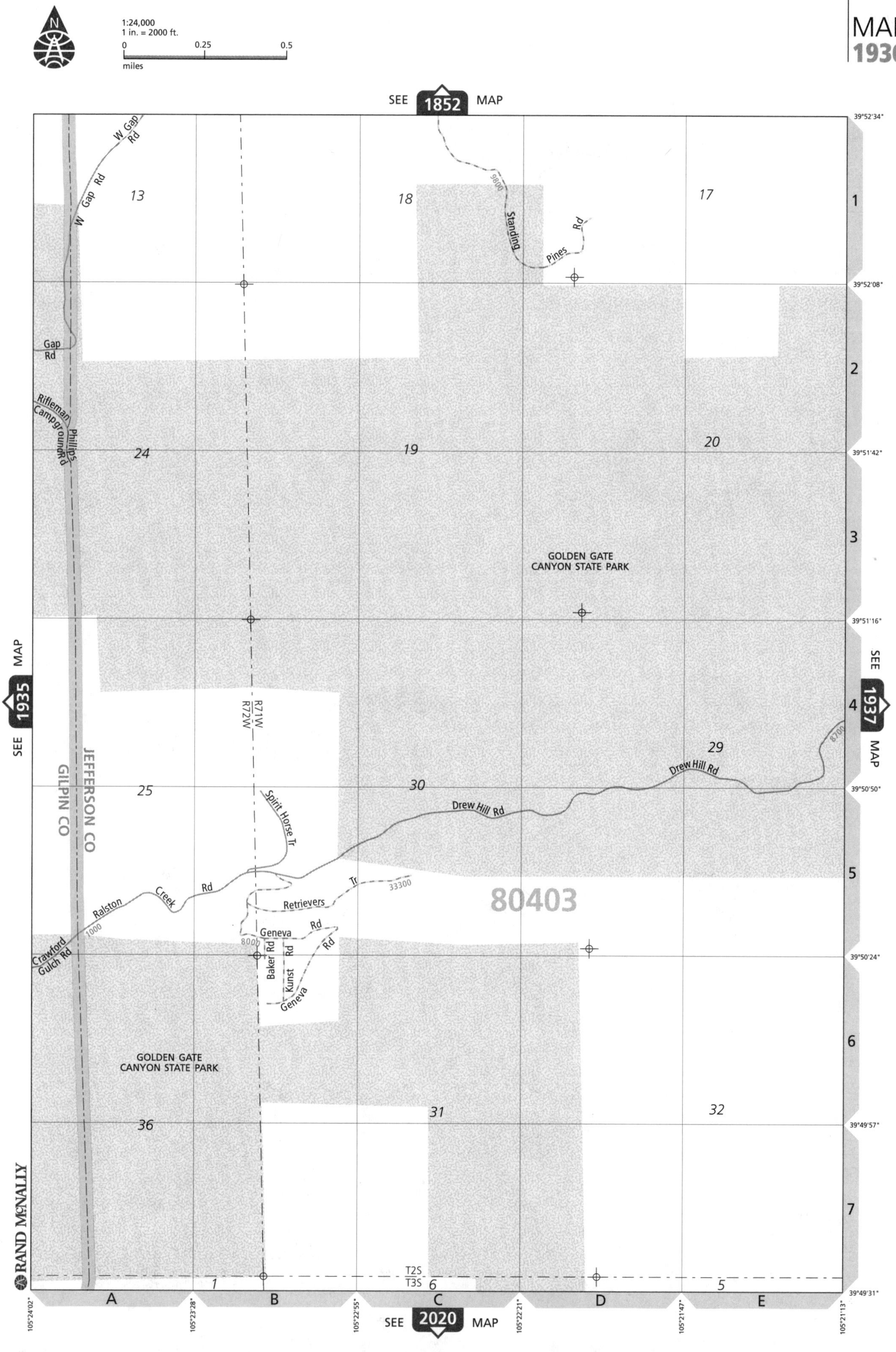

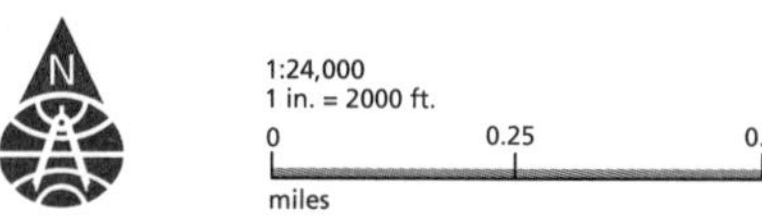

N
1:24,000
1 in. = 2000 ft.
0
0.25
0.5
miles
SEE 1852 MAP
SEE 1935 MAP
SEE 1937 MAP
SEE 2020 MAP
W Gap Rd
Gap Rd
Rifleman Campground Rd
Phillips
Standing Pines Rd
9800
13
18
17
24
19
20
25
30
29
36
31
32
1
6
5
GOLDEN GATE
CANYON STATE PARK
R71W
R72W
JEFFERSON CO
GILPIN CO
Drew Hill Rd
8700
Spirit Horse Tr
Ralston Creek Rd
1000
Retrievers Tr
33300
80403
Crawford Gulch Rd
Geneva Rd
8000
Baker Rd
Kunst Rd
Geneva
T2S
T3S
39°52'34"
39°52'08"
39°51'42"
39°51'16"
39°50'50"
39°50'24"
39°49'57"
39°49'31"
105°24'02"
105°23'28"
105°22'55"
105°22'21"
105°21'47"
105°21'13"
A
B
C
D
E
1
2
3
4
5
6
7
RAND McNALLY

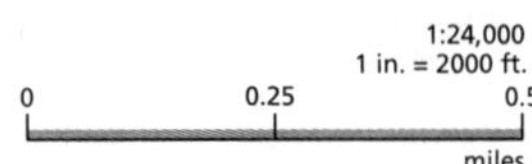

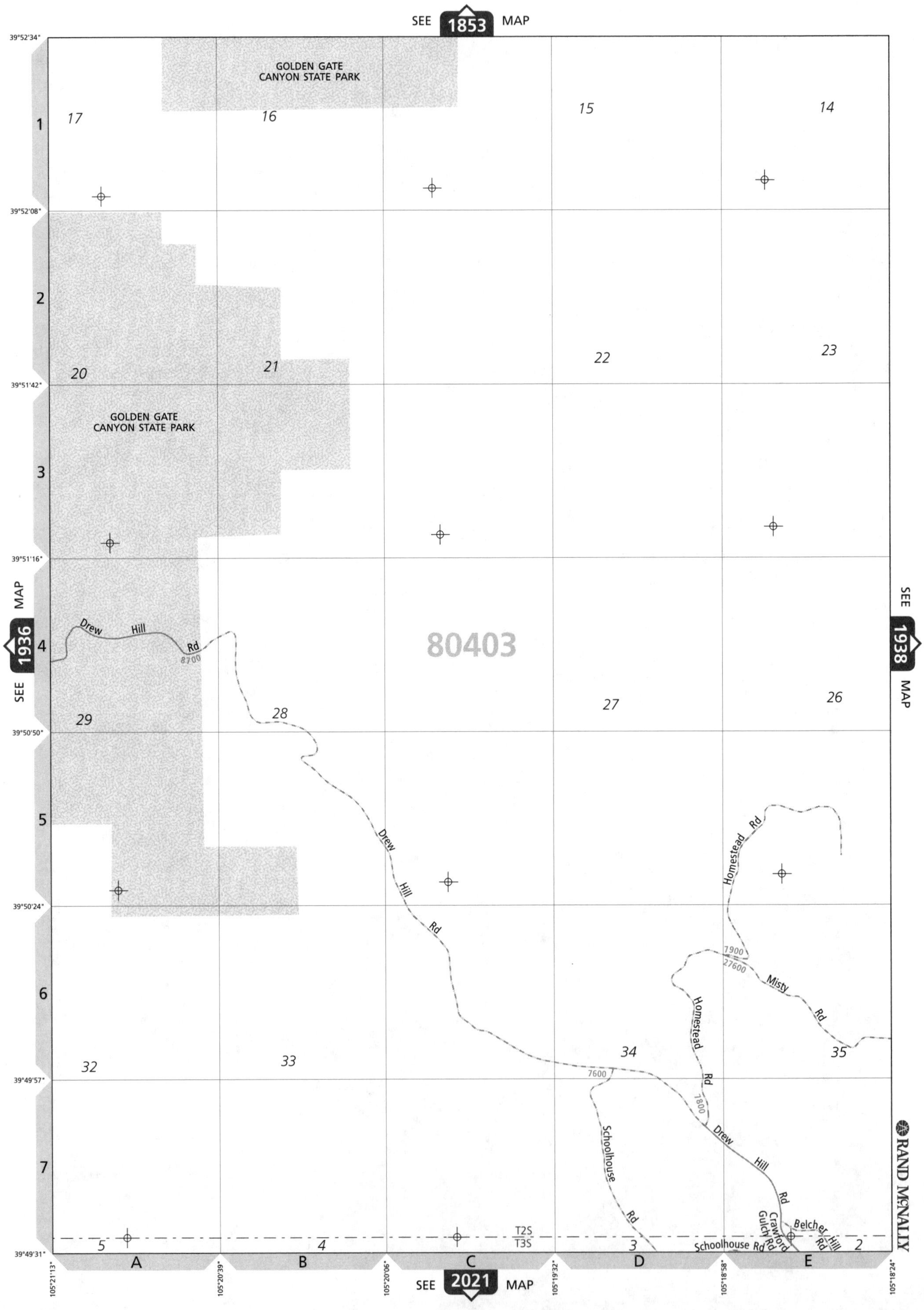

1:24,000
1 in. = 2000 ft.
0
0.25
0.5
miles
N
SEE 1853 MAP
GOLDEN GATE CANYON STATE PARK
17
16
15
14
20
21
22
23
GOLDEN GATE CANYON STATE PARK
Drew Hill Rd
8700
80403
28
29
27
26
Drew Hill Rd
Homestead Rd
7900
27600
Misty Rd
Homestead Rd
32
33
34
35
7600
7800
Drew Hill Rd
Schoolhouse Rd
Crawford Gulch Rd
Belcher Hill Rd
Schoolhouse Rd
T2S
T3S
5
4
3
2
1
2
3
4
5
6
7
A
B
C
D
E
39°52'34"
39°52'08"
39°51'42"
39°51'16"
39°50'50"
39°50'24"
39°49'57"
39°49'31"
105°21'13"
105°20'39"
105°20'06"
105°19'32"
105°18'58"
105°18'24"
SEE 1936 MAP
SEE 1938 MAP
SEE 2021 MAP
RAND McNALLY

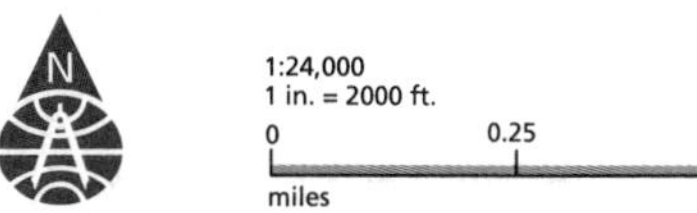

SEE 1854 MAP

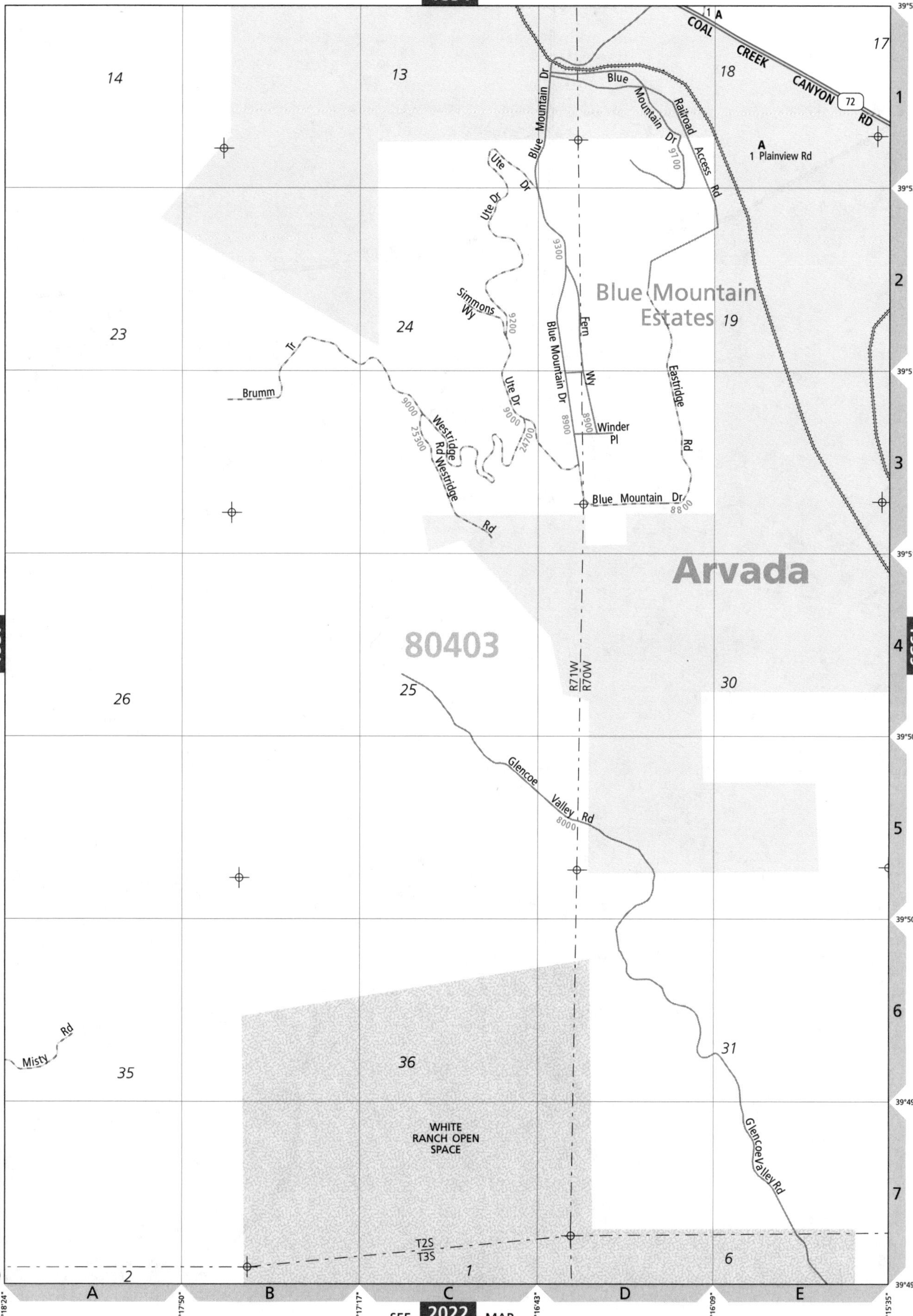

SEE 1937 MAP

SEE 1939 MAP

Blue Mountain Estates

Arvada

80403

COAL CREEK CANYON RD
72
1 A
A
1 Plainview Rd
Blue Mountain Dr
Railroad Access Rd
Ute Dr
Simmons Wy
Fern Wy
Winder Pl
Eastridge Rd
Brumm Tr
Westridge Rd
Glencoe Valley Rd
Misty Rd
WHITE RANCH OPEN SPACE
R71W
R70W
T2S
T3S

14 13 18 17 23 24 19 26 25 30 35 36 31 2 1 6

39°52'32" 39°52'06" 39°51'39" 39°51'13" 39°50'47" 39°50'21" 39°49'55" 39°49'29"

105°18'24" 105°17'50" 105°17'17" 105°16'43" 105°16'09" 105°15'35"

A B C D E
1 2 3 4 5 6 7

SEE 2022 MAP

1:24,000
1 in. = 2000 ft.
0 0.25 0.5
miles

SEE 1855 MAP

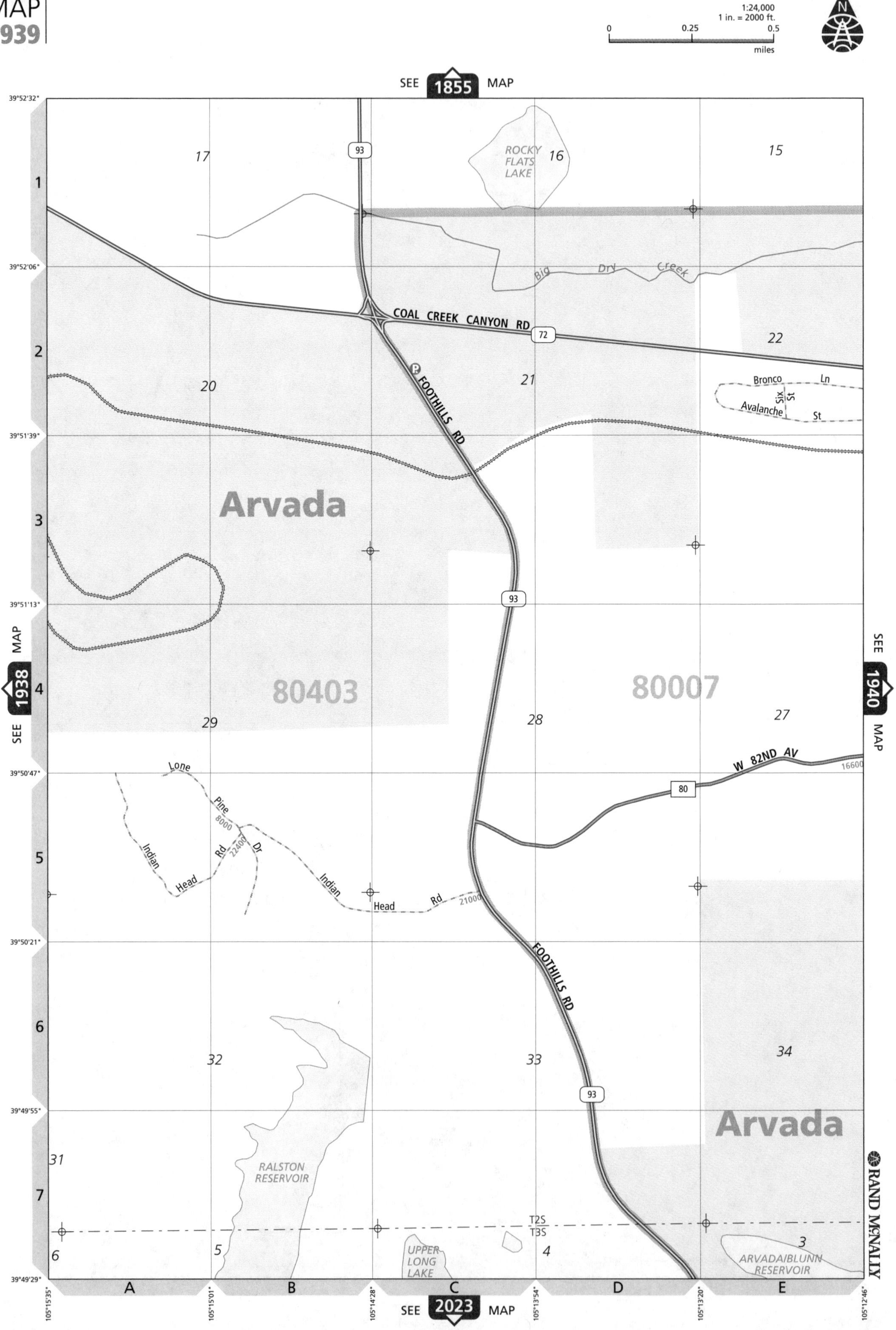

SEE 1938 MAP

SEE 1940 MAP

SEE 2023 MAP

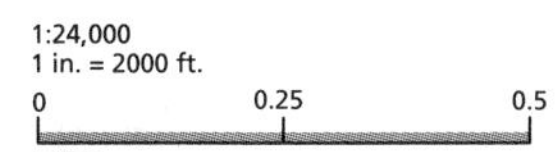

SEE 1856 MAP

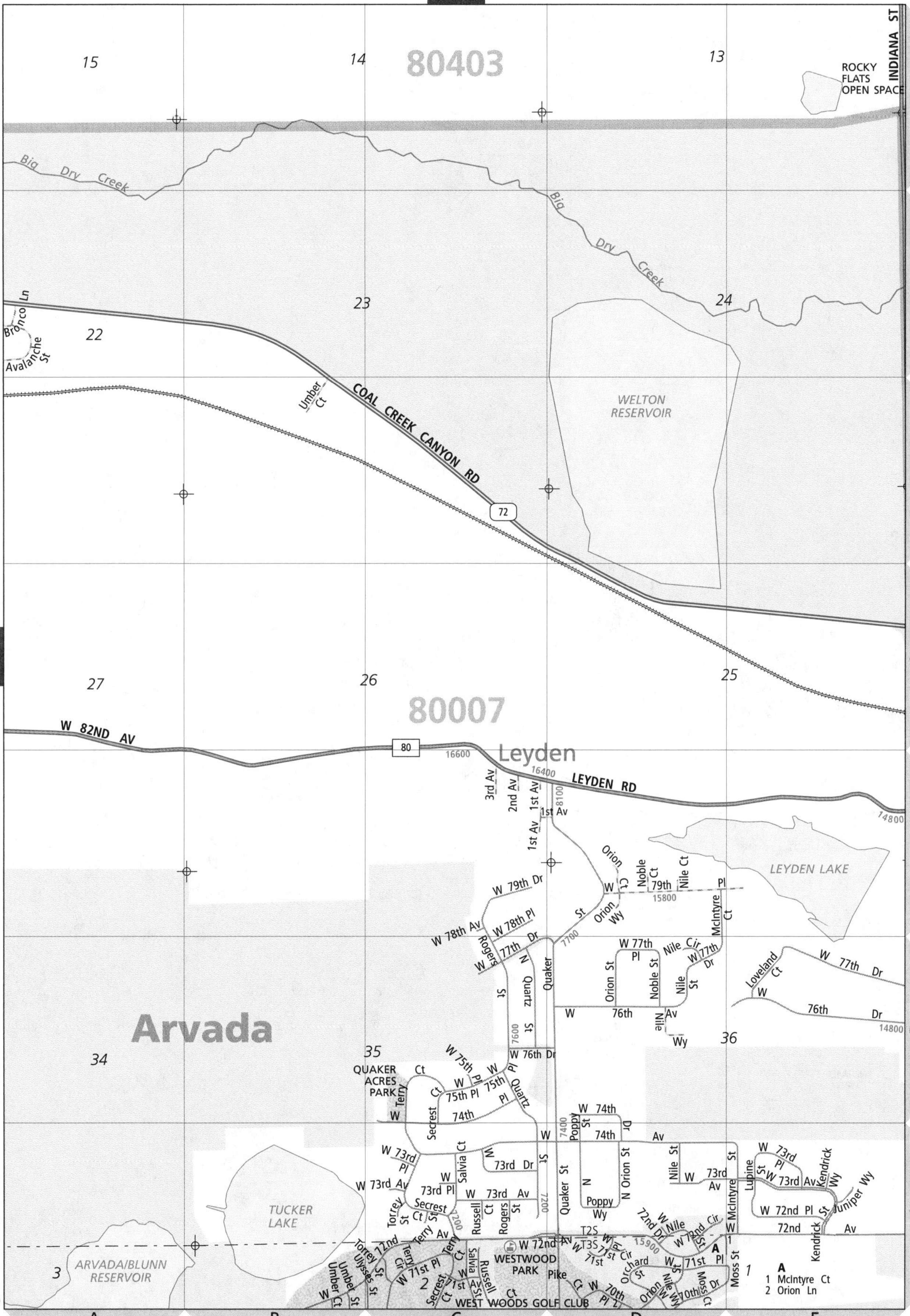

SEE 1939 MAP

SEE 1941 MAP

SEE 2024 MAP

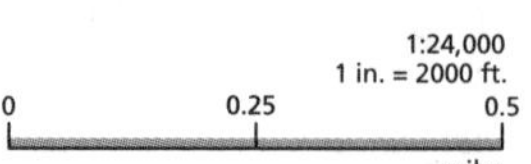

SEE 1857 MAP

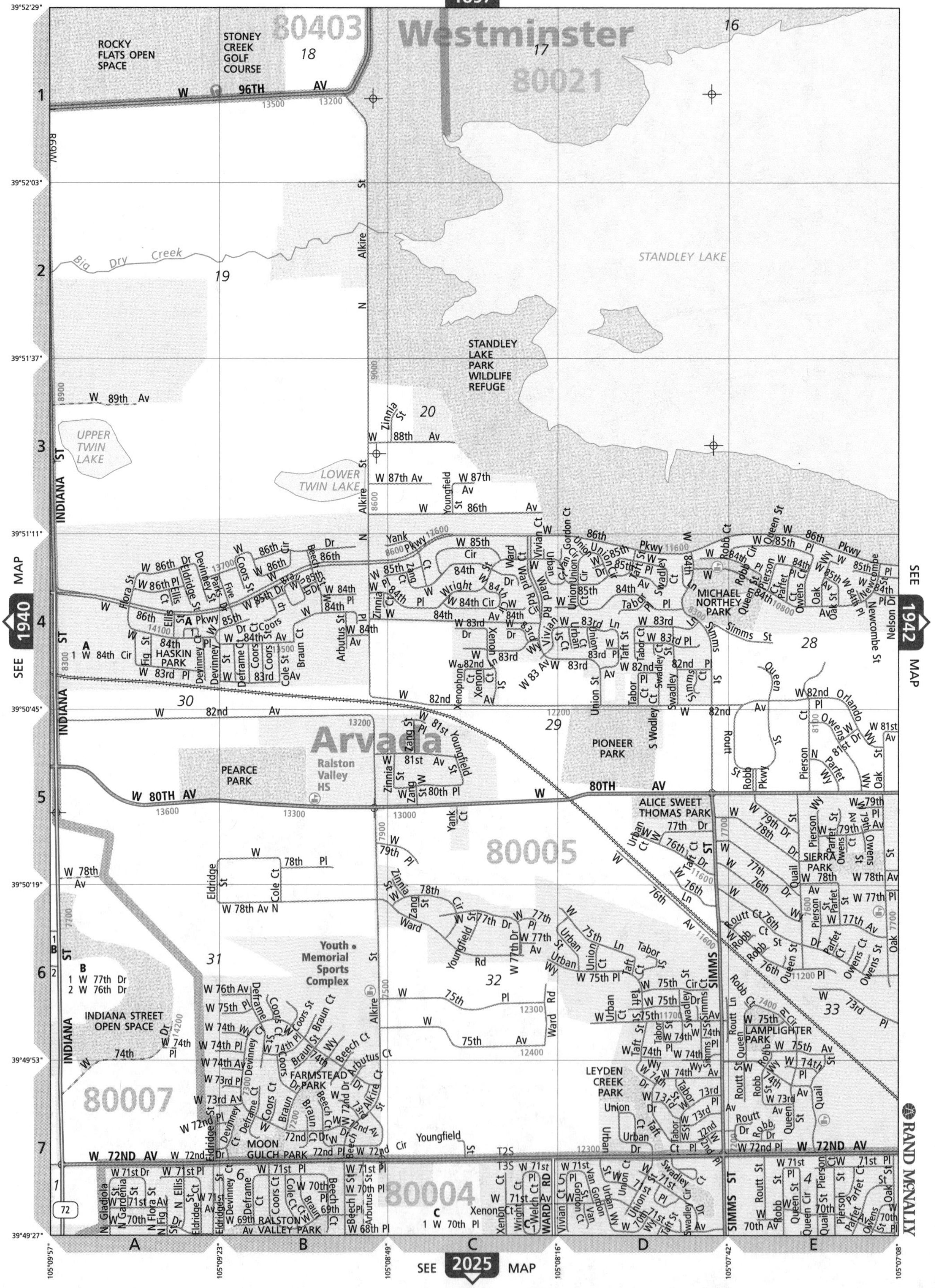

SEE 1940 MAP

SEE 1942 MAP

Westminster
80403
80021
ROCKY FLATS OPEN SPACE
STONEY CREEK GOLF COURSE
W 96TH AV
STANDLEY LAKE
STANDLEY LAKE PARK WILDLIFE REFUGE
UPPER TWIN LAKE
LOWER TWIN LAKE
Big Dry Creek
INDIANA ST
N Alkire St
Arvada
80005
80007
80004
MICHAEL NORTHEY PARK
HASKIN PARK
PEARCE PARK
Ralston Valley HS
PIONEER PARK
ALICE SWEET THOMAS PARK
SIERRA PARK
W 80TH AV
W 82nd Av
W 86th Pkwy
Simms St
SIMMS ST
Youth Memorial Sports Complex
INDIANA STREET OPEN SPACE
FARMSTEAD PARK
LEYDEN CREEK PARK
LAMPLIGHTER PARK
MOON GULCH PARK
RALSTON VALLEY PARK
W 72ND AV
WARD RD
A
1 W 84th Cir
B
1 W 77th Dr
2 W 76th Dr
C
1 W 70th Pl

SEE 2025 MAP

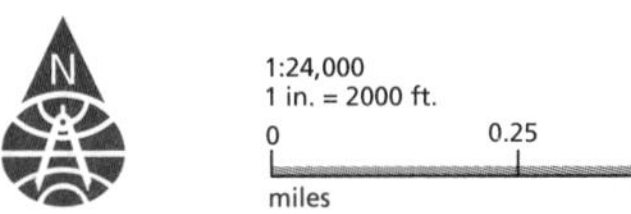

SEE 1858 MAP

16 A
1 W 99th Av
2 Independence Wy
3 Holland Cir

B
1 W 96th Dr
2 N Pierce St
3 W 94th Pl

C
1 W 81st Cir

D
1 Barnes Ln

E
1 W 79th Wy

Westminster

Arvada

STANDLEY LAKE

STANDLEY LAKE PARK WILDLIFE REFUGE

OAKHURST PARK

KING MILL PARK

DOVER SQ PARK

LAKE ARBOR GOLF CLUB

LK ARBOR GOLF CLUB

WESTREE PARK

Pomona HS

POND LAKE

VOLUNTEER FIRE FIGHTERS PARK

LAKECREST PARK

WOODRUN PARK

POMONA LAKE

TWO PONDS NATIONAL WILDLIFE REFUGE

LITTLE DRY CREEK PARK

CLUB CREST NORTH PARK

CLUB CREST SOUTH PARK

ROBBI FARRIFINO PARK

HACKBERRY PARK

INDIAN TREE GOLF COURSE

THUNDERCLOUD PARK

EMIL SCHNEIDER PARK

MAJESTIC VIEW PARK

OBERON RES LK

Maranatha Christian Ctr School

WADSWORTH PKWY

WADSWORTH BLVD

W 92ND AV

W 88TH AV

W 86TH PKWY

80TH AV

W 72ND AV

KIPLING ST

80021

80005

80004

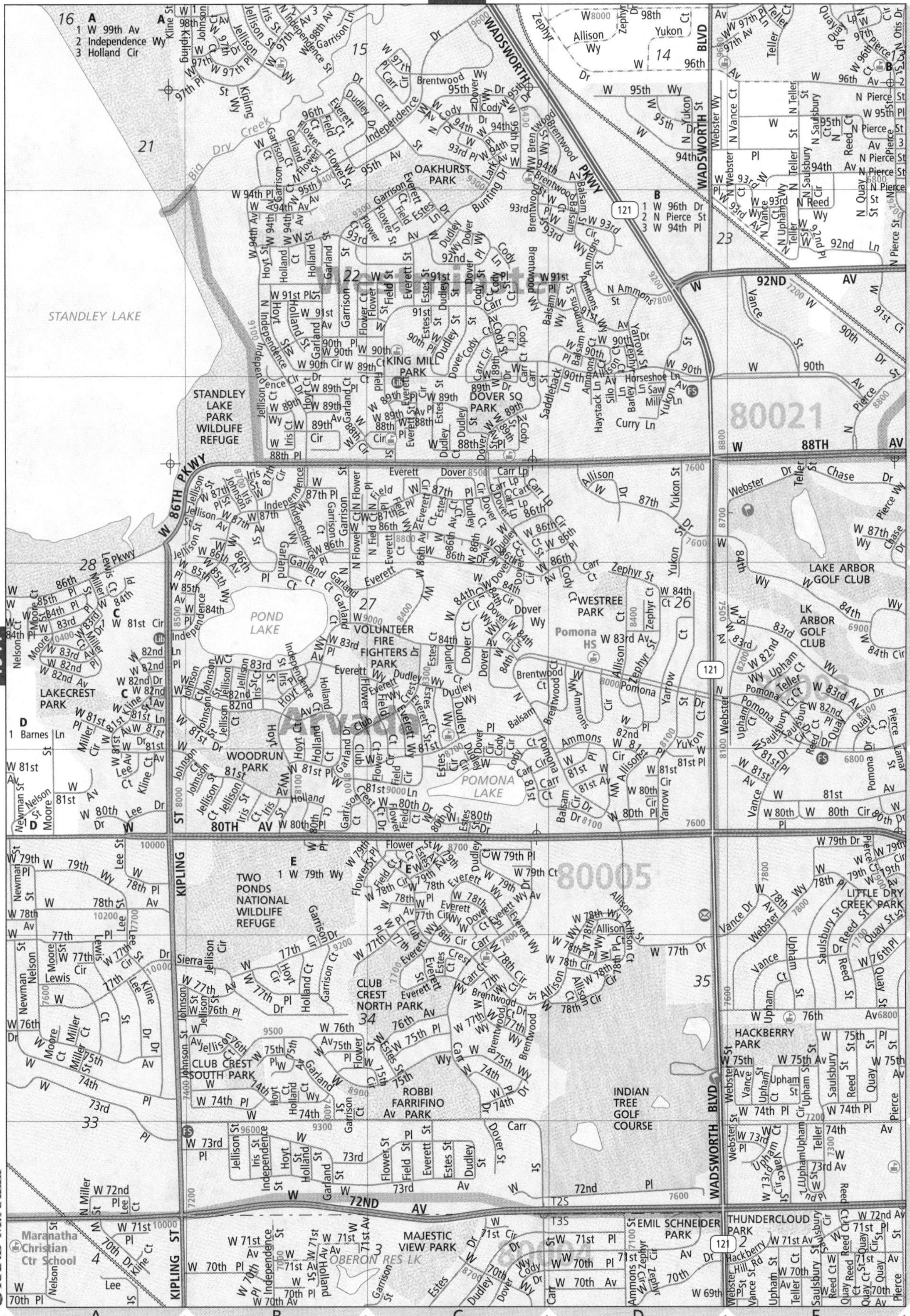

SEE 1941 MAP

SEE 1943 MAP

A B C D E

1 2 3 4 5 6 7

39°52'26" 39°52'00" 39°51'34" 39°51'08" 39°50'42" 39°50'16" 39°49'50" 39°49'24"

105°07'08" 105°06'34" 105°06'00" 105°05'27" 105°04'53" 105°04'19"

SEE 2026 MAP

1:24,000
1 in. = 2000 ft.
0 0.25 0.5
miles

SEE 1859 MAP

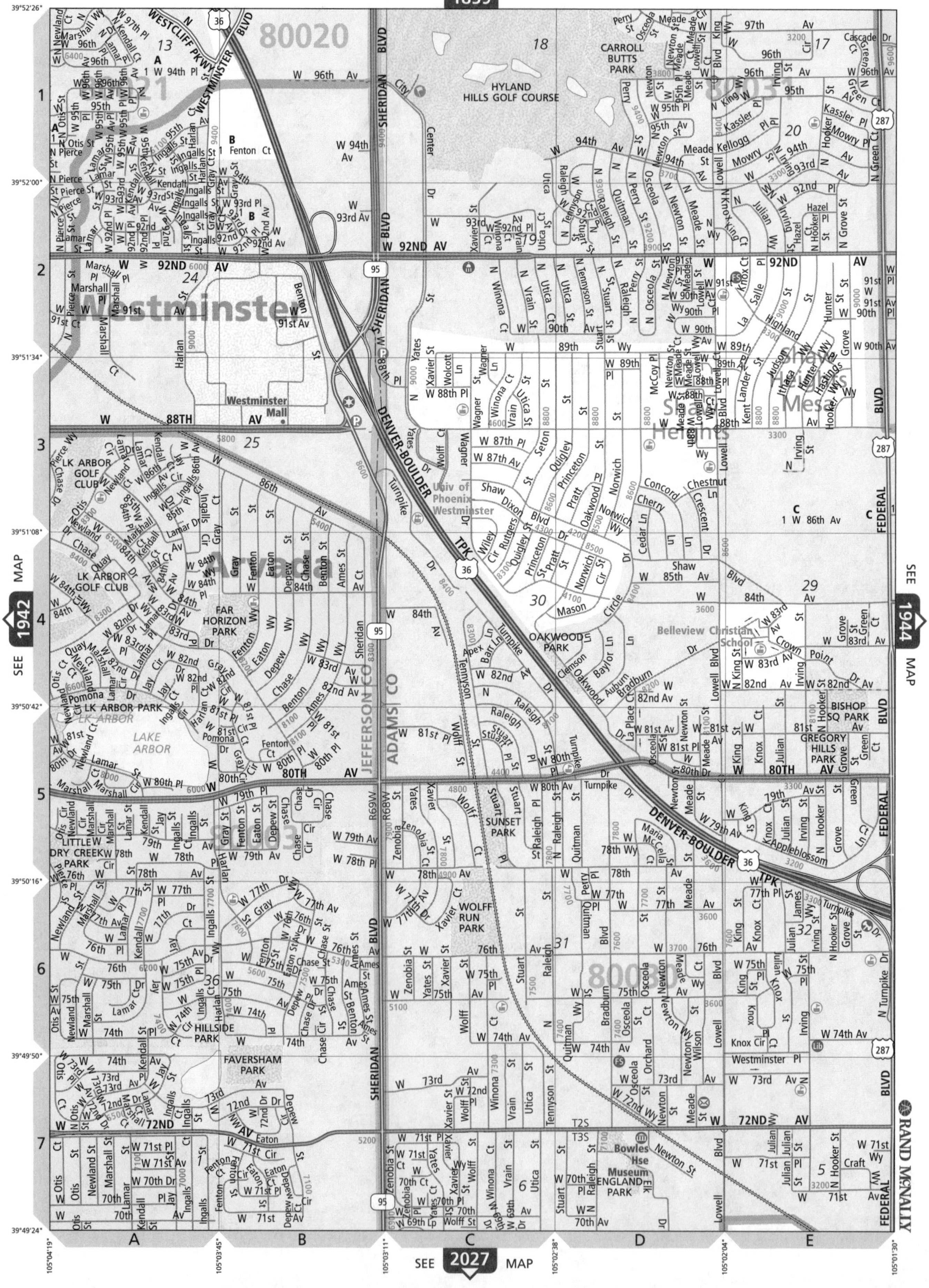

SEE 1942 MAP

SEE 1944 MAP

39°52'26"
39°52'00"
39°51'34"
39°51'08"
39°50'42"
39°50'16"
39°49'50"
39°49'24"

1
2
3
4
5
6
7

Westminster
80020
80031
80030
80003

WESTCLIFF PKWY
WESTMINSTER BLVD
SHERIDAN BLVD
DENVER-BOULDER TPK
FEDERAL BLVD
W 92ND AV
W 88TH AV
80TH AV
72ND AV
JEFFERSON CO
ADAMS CO

HYLAND HILLS GOLF COURSE
CARROLL BUTTS PARK
Westminster Mall
Univ of Phoenix-Westminster
LK ARBOR GOLF CLUB
LK ARBOR PARK
LAKE ARBOR
FAR HORIZON PARK
OAKWOOD PARK
Belleview Christian School
BISHOP SQ PARK
GREGORY HILLS PARK
LITTLE DRY CREEK PARK
SUNSET PARK
WOLFF RUN PARK
HILLSIDE PARK
FAVERSHAM PARK
Shaw Heights
Arvada
Bowles Hse Museum
ENGLAND PARK

A
B
C
D
E

105°04'19"
105°03'45"
105°03'11"
105°02'38"
105°02'04"
105°01'30"

SEE 2027 MAP

1:24,000
1 in. = 2000 ft.
0 0.25 0.5
miles

SEE 1860 MAP

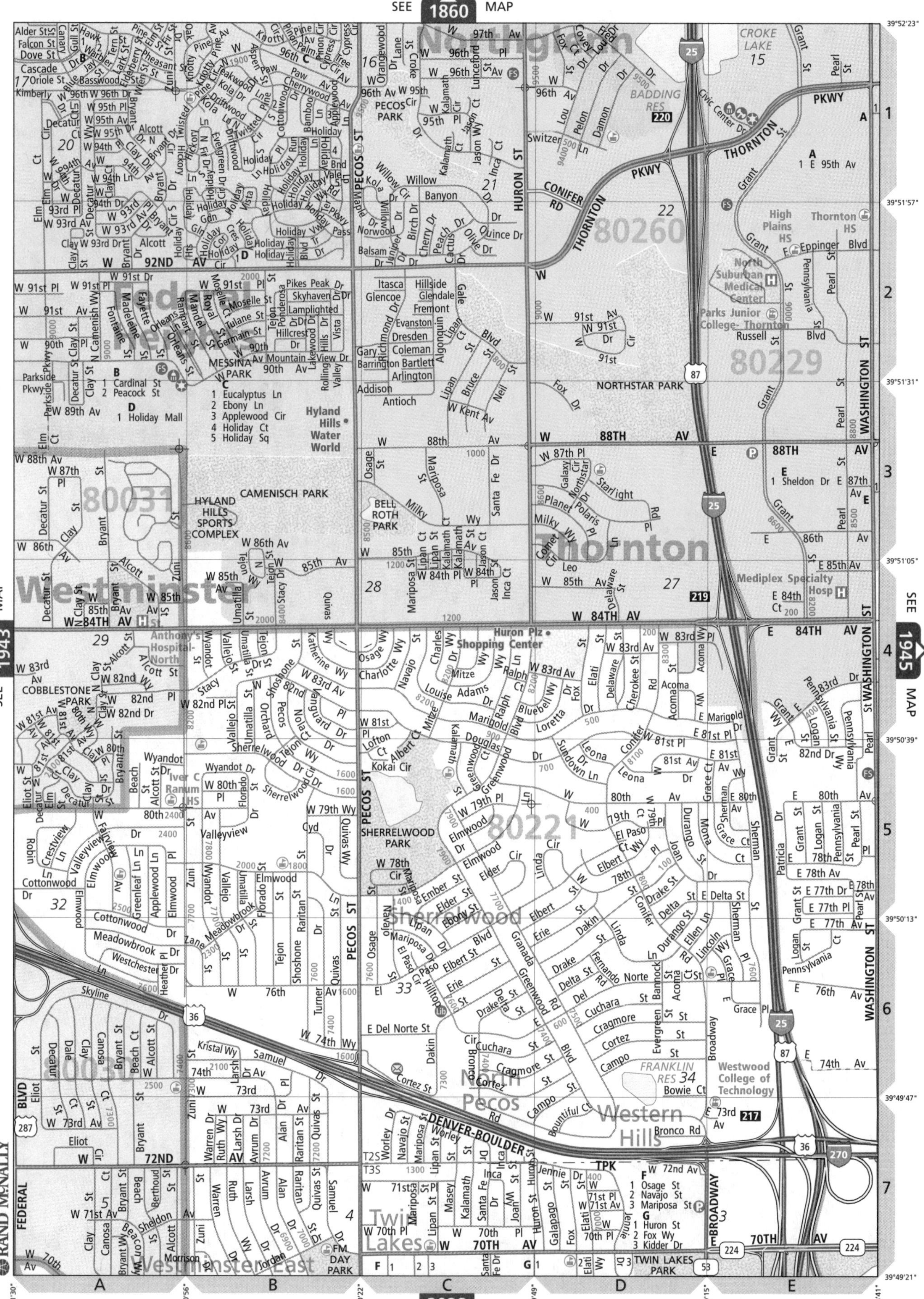

SEE 1943 MAP

SEE 1945 MAP

SEE 2028 MAP

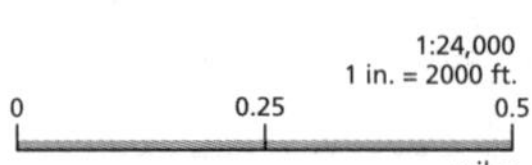

SEE 1861 MAP

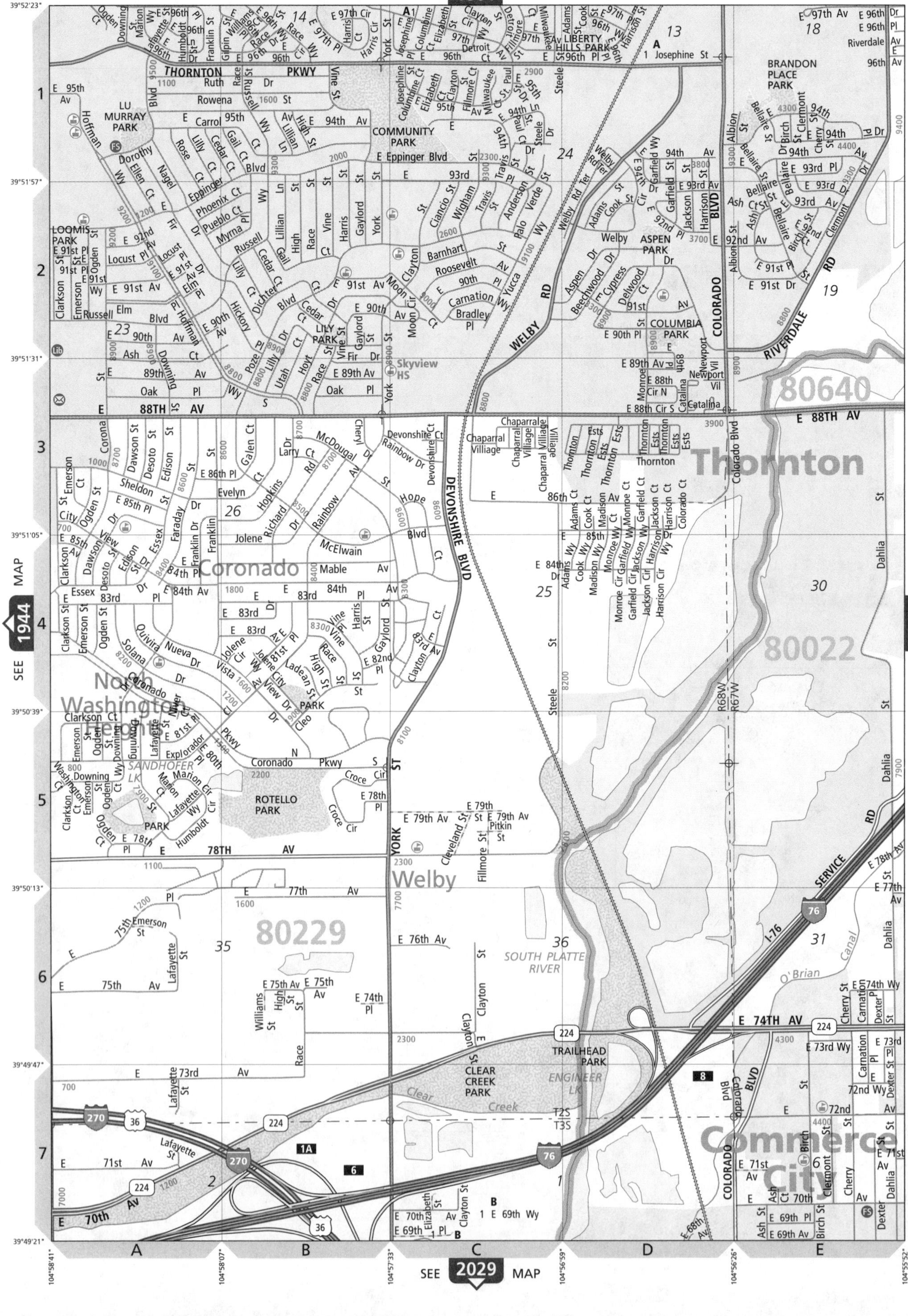

SEE 1944 MAP

SEE 1946 MAP

SEE 2029 MAP

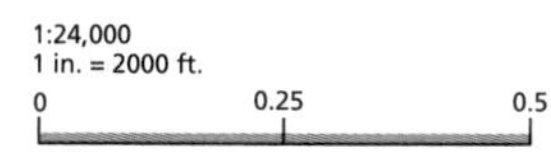

SEE 1862 MAP

Rolla

Commerce City

80229

80640

80022

Derby

Dupont

Irondale

SOUTH PLATTE RIVER

O'Brian Canal

E 96TH AV

E 88TH AV

E 72ND AV

E 74TH AV

MONACO ST

BRIGHTON RD

BRIGHTON BLVD

I-76 FRONTAGE RD

I-76 SERVICE RD

QUEBEC ST

Quince St

Holly St

Fish Hatchery Rd

E 91st Av

E 90th Av

E 89th Av

E 92nd Av

E 87th Av

E 86th Av

E 85th Av

E 84th Av

E 83rd Av

E 82nd Pl

E 82nd Av

E 81st Av

E 80th Av

E 79th Pl

E 78th Av

E 77th Av

E 76th Av

E 75th Av

E 73rd Av

E 72nd Av

E 71st Av

E 70th Av

E 69th Av

Rosemary St

Roslyn St

Syracuse St

Ulster St

Uinta St

Valentia St

Tamarac St

Verbena St

Wabash St

Willow St

Xanthia St

Xenia St

Yosemite St

B St

Ivanhoe St

Ivy St

Jasmine St

Kearney St

Krameria St

Leyden St

Locust St

Magnolia St

Niagara St

Newport St

Oneida St

Olive St

Pontiac St

Poplar St

Lester R Arnold HS

ROCKY MOUNTAIN ARSENAL
NATIONAL WILDLIFE REFUGE

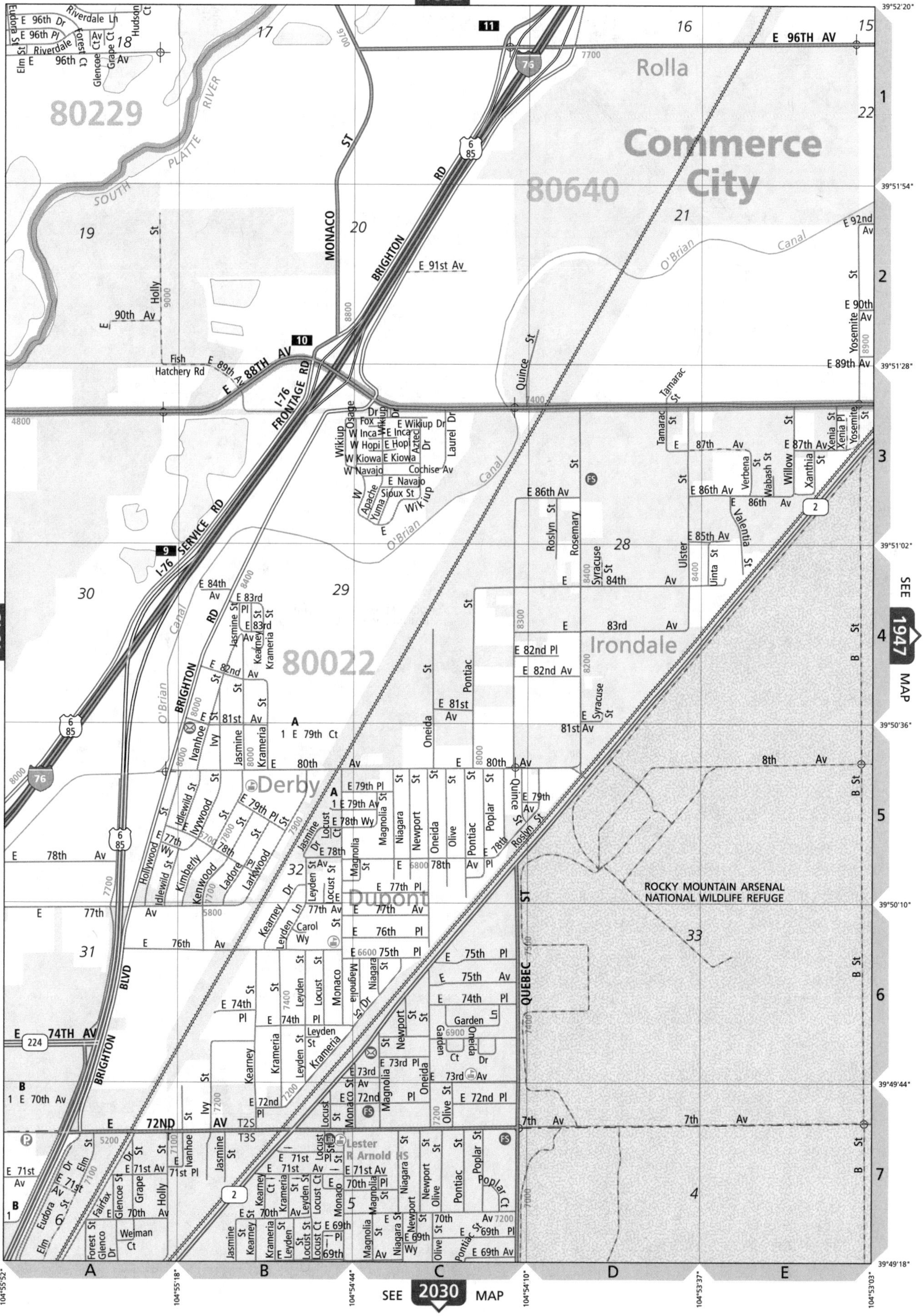

SEE 1945 MAP

SEE 1947 MAP

SEE 2030 MAP

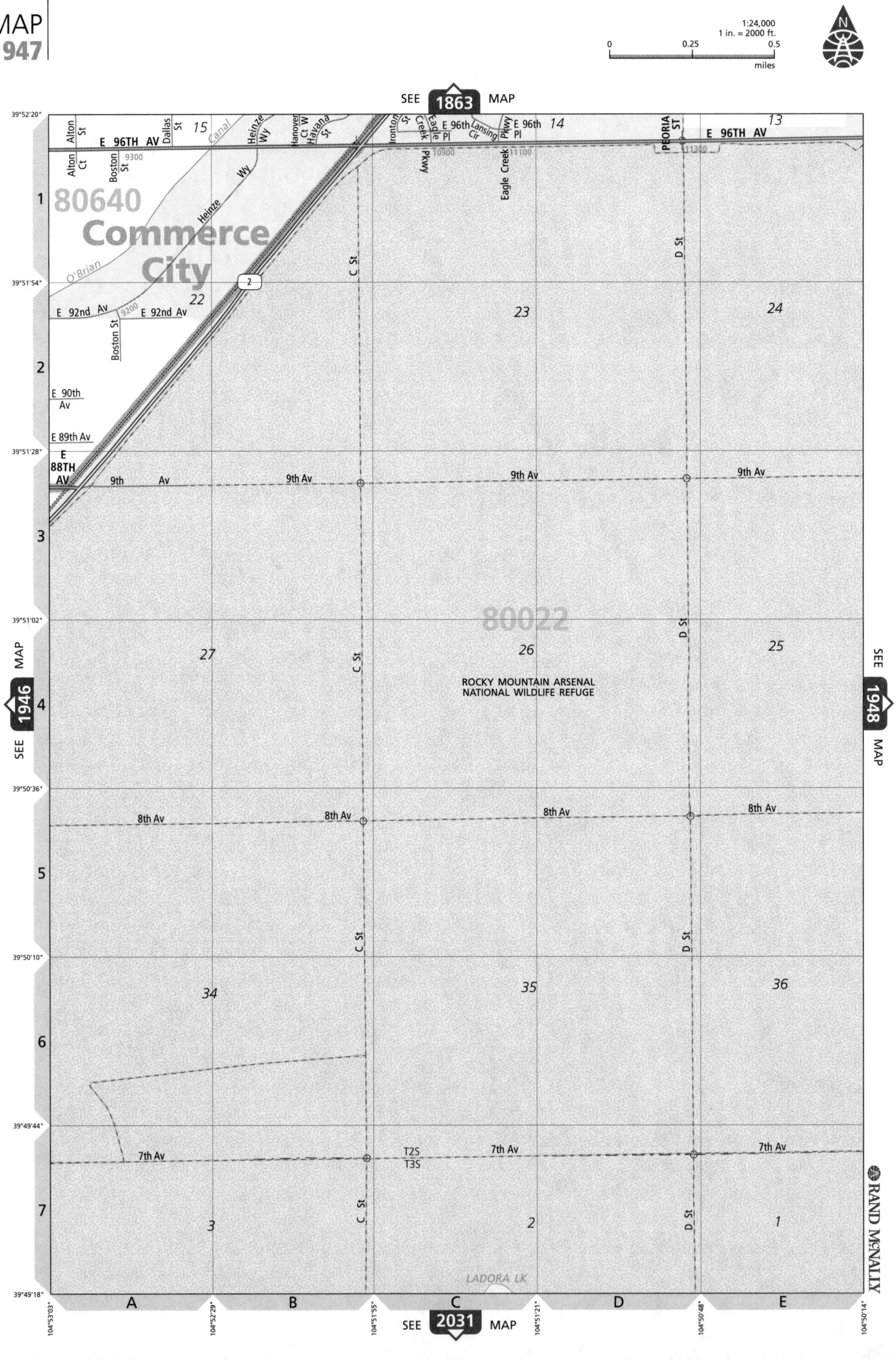

1:24,000
1 in. = 2000 ft.
0 0.25 0.5
miles

SEE 1863 MAP

E 96TH AV
Alton St
Alton Ct
Boston St
Dallas St
Heinze Wy
Hanover Ct W
Havana St
Ironton St
Eagle Creek Pkwy
Eagle Pl
E 96th Pl
Lansing Cir
Pkwy
E 96th Pl
Eagle Creek
PEORIA ST
9300
10900
11100
11300
80640
Commerce City
O'Brian
Canal
Heinze Wy
2
E 92nd Av
E 92nd Av
9200
Boston St
E 90th Av
E 89th Av
E 88TH AV
9th Av
9th Av
9th Av
9th Av
C St
D St
80022
ROCKY MOUNTAIN ARSENAL NATIONAL WILDLIFE REFUGE
8th Av
8th Av
8th Av
8th Av
7th Av
7th Av
7th Av
T2S
T3S
LADORA LK
15 14 13 22 23 24 27 26 25 34 35 36 3 2 1

39°52'20" 39°51'54" 39°51'28" 39°51'02" 39°50'36" 39°50'10" 39°49'44" 39°49'18"
104°53'03" 104°52'29" 104°51'55" 104°51'21" 104°50'48" 104°50'14"
1 2 3 4 5 6 7
A B C D E

SEE 1946 MAP

SEE 1948 MAP

SEE 2031 MAP

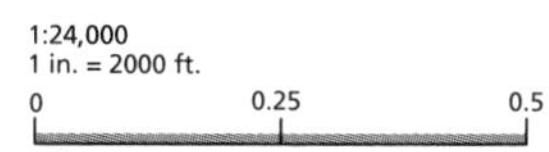

SEE 1864 MAP

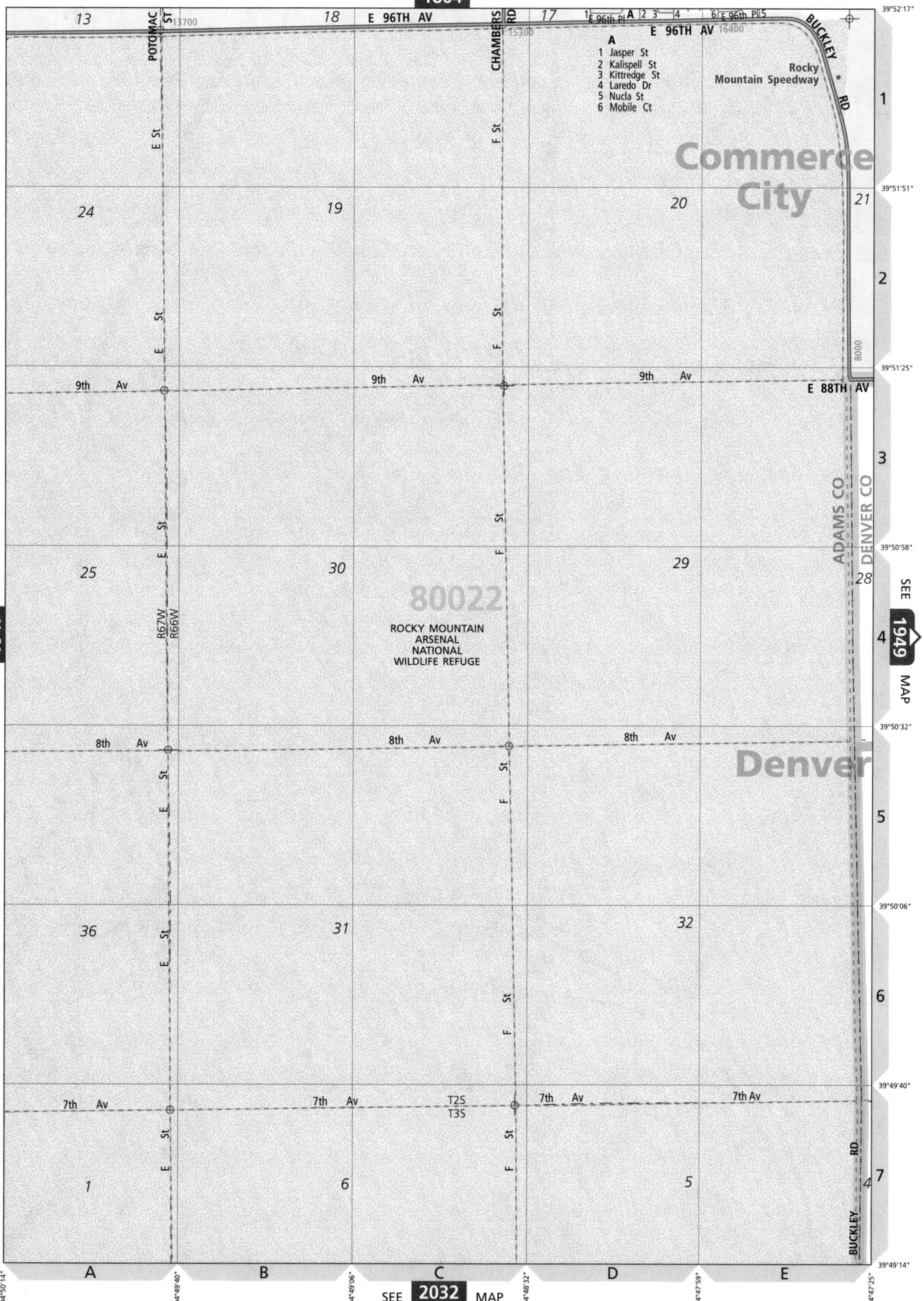

SEE 1947 MAP

SEE 1949 MAP

SEE 2032 MAP

1:24,000
1 in. = 2000 ft.
0 0.25 0.5
miles

SEE 1865 MAP

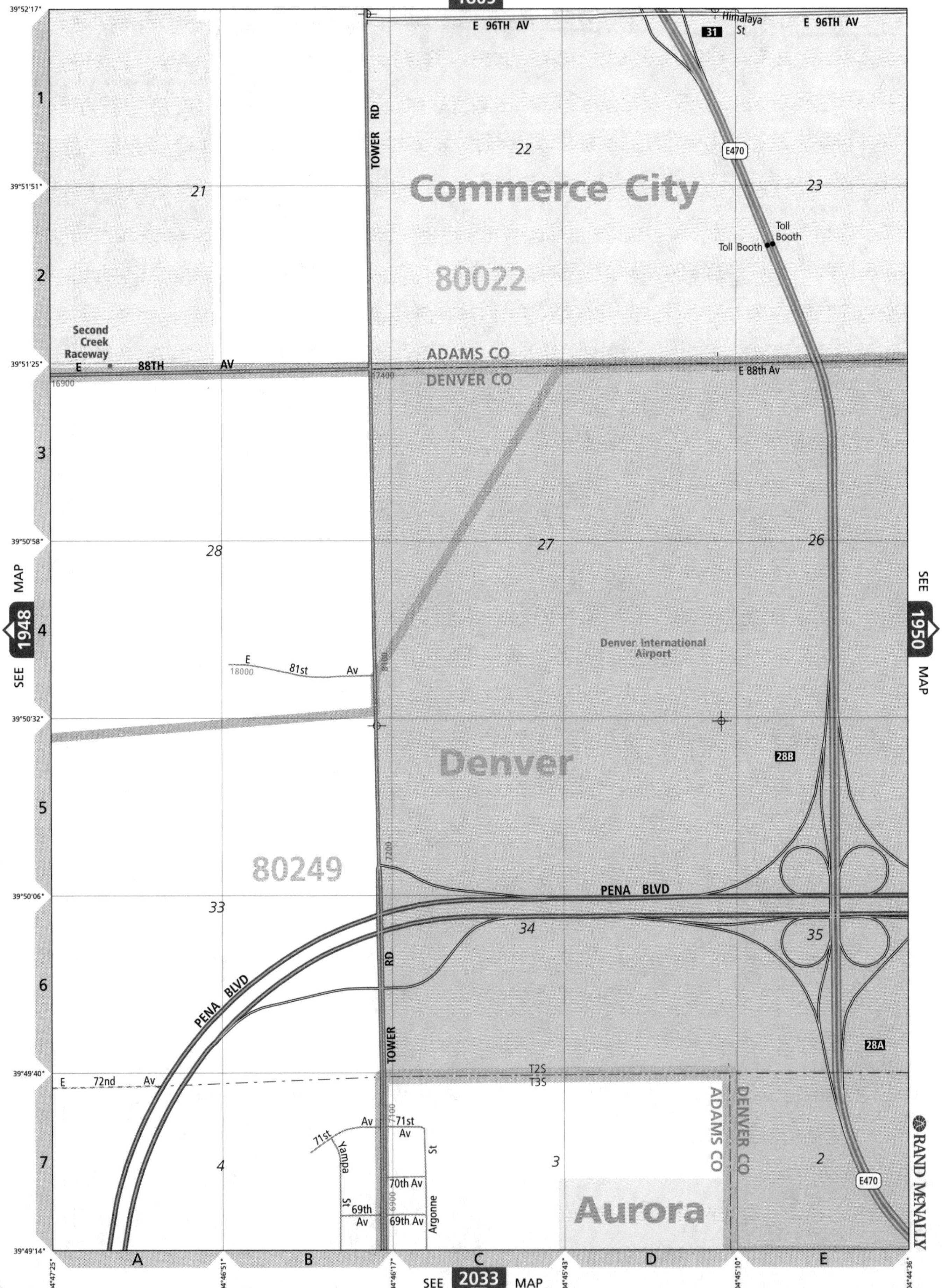

SEE 1948 MAP

SEE 1950 MAP

SEE 2033 MAP

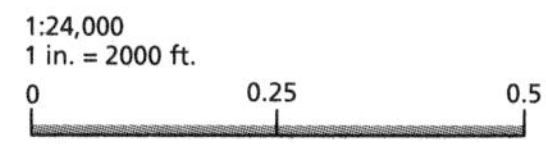

SEE 1866 MAP

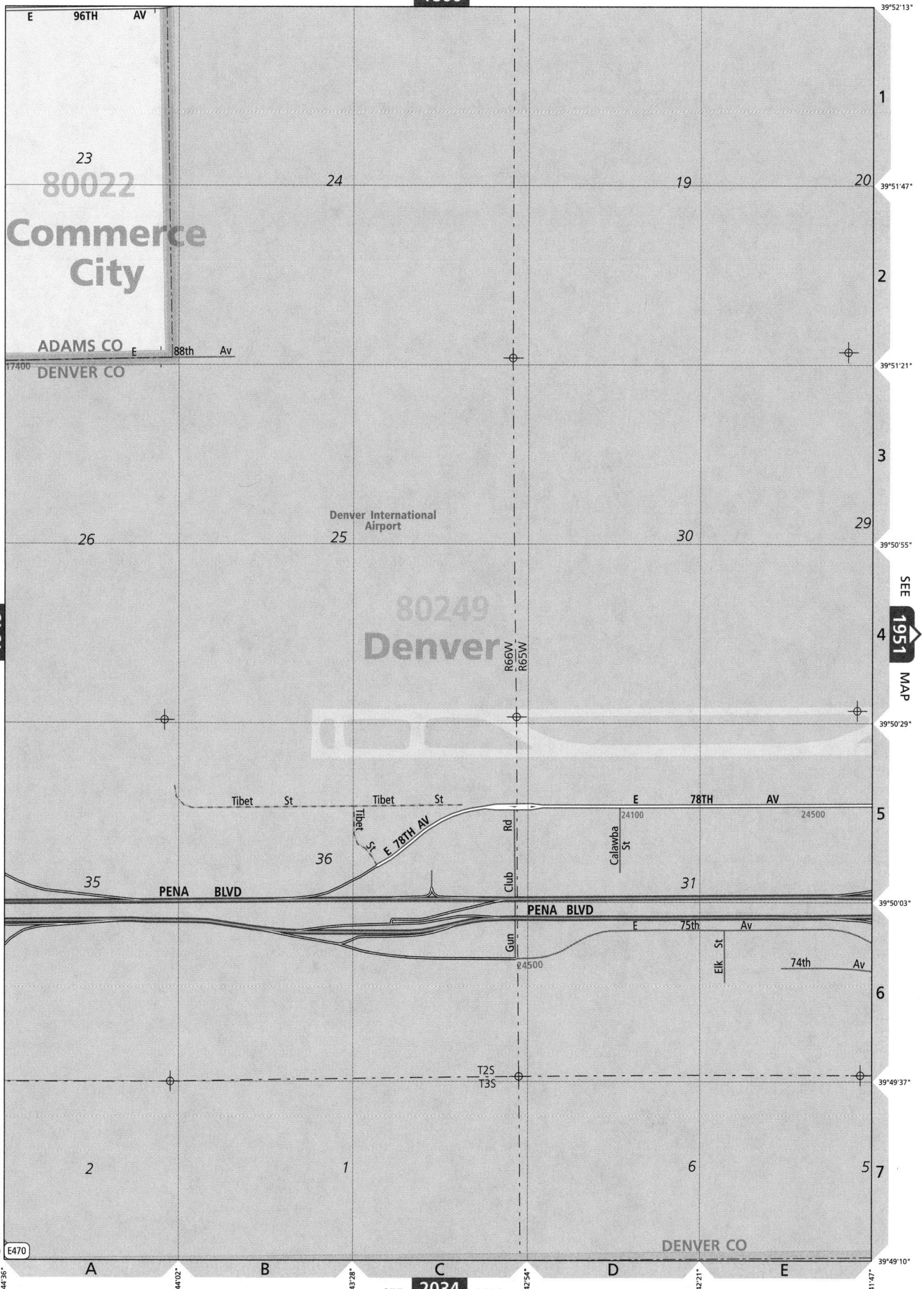

SEE 1949 MAP

SEE 1951 MAP

SEE 2034 MAP

1:24,000
1 in. = 2000 ft.
0 0.25 0.5
miles

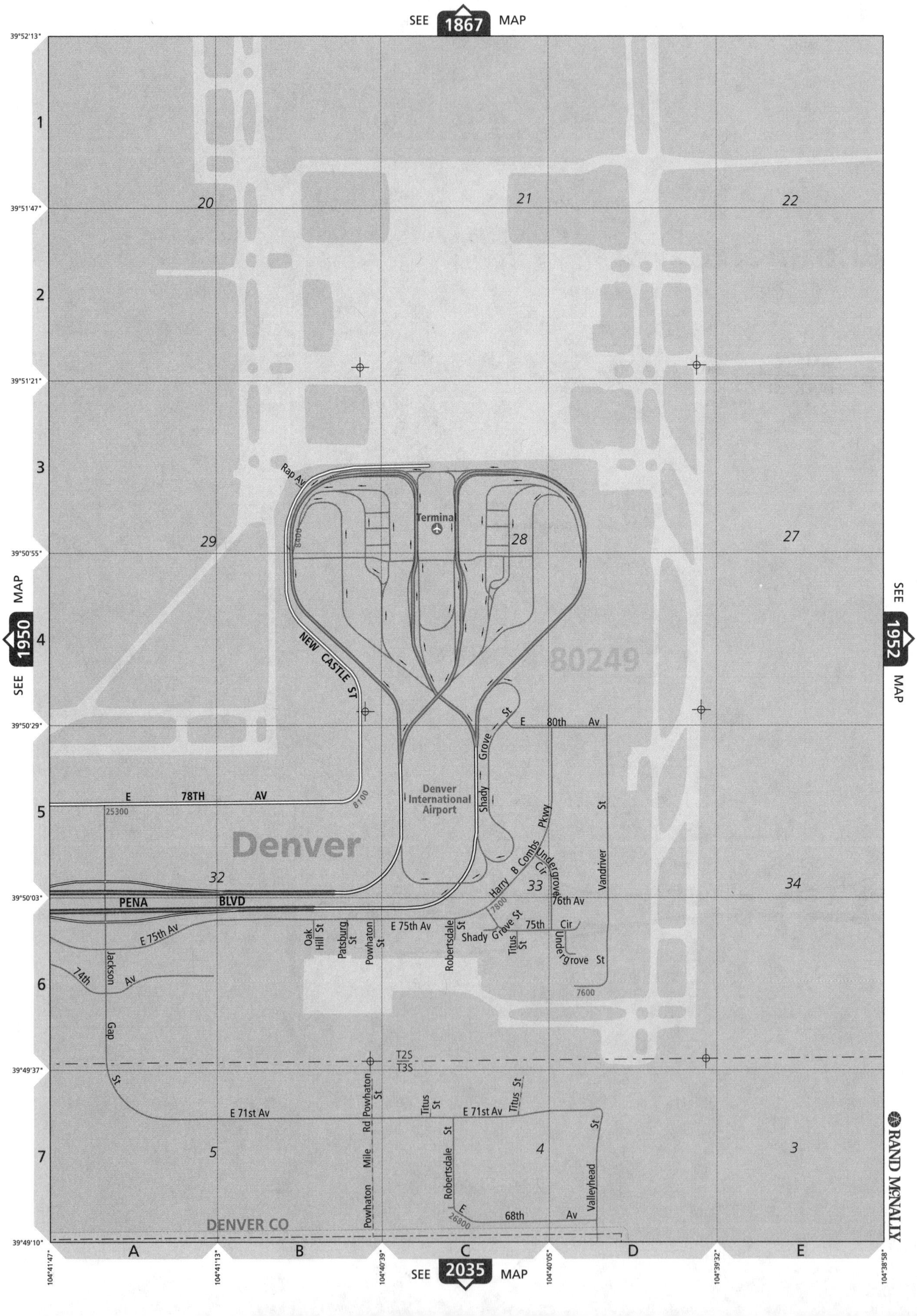

SEE 1867 MAP

SEE 1950 MAP

SEE 1952 MAP

1 2 3 4 5 6 7
A B C D E

39°52'13"
39°51'47"
39°51'21"
39°50'55"
39°50'29"
39°50'03"
39°49'37"
39°49'10"

104°41'47"
104°41'13"
104°40'39"
104°40'05"
104°39'32"
104°38'58"

SEE 2035 MAP

1:24,000
1 in. = 2000 ft.
0 0.25 0.5
miles

SEE 1868 MAP

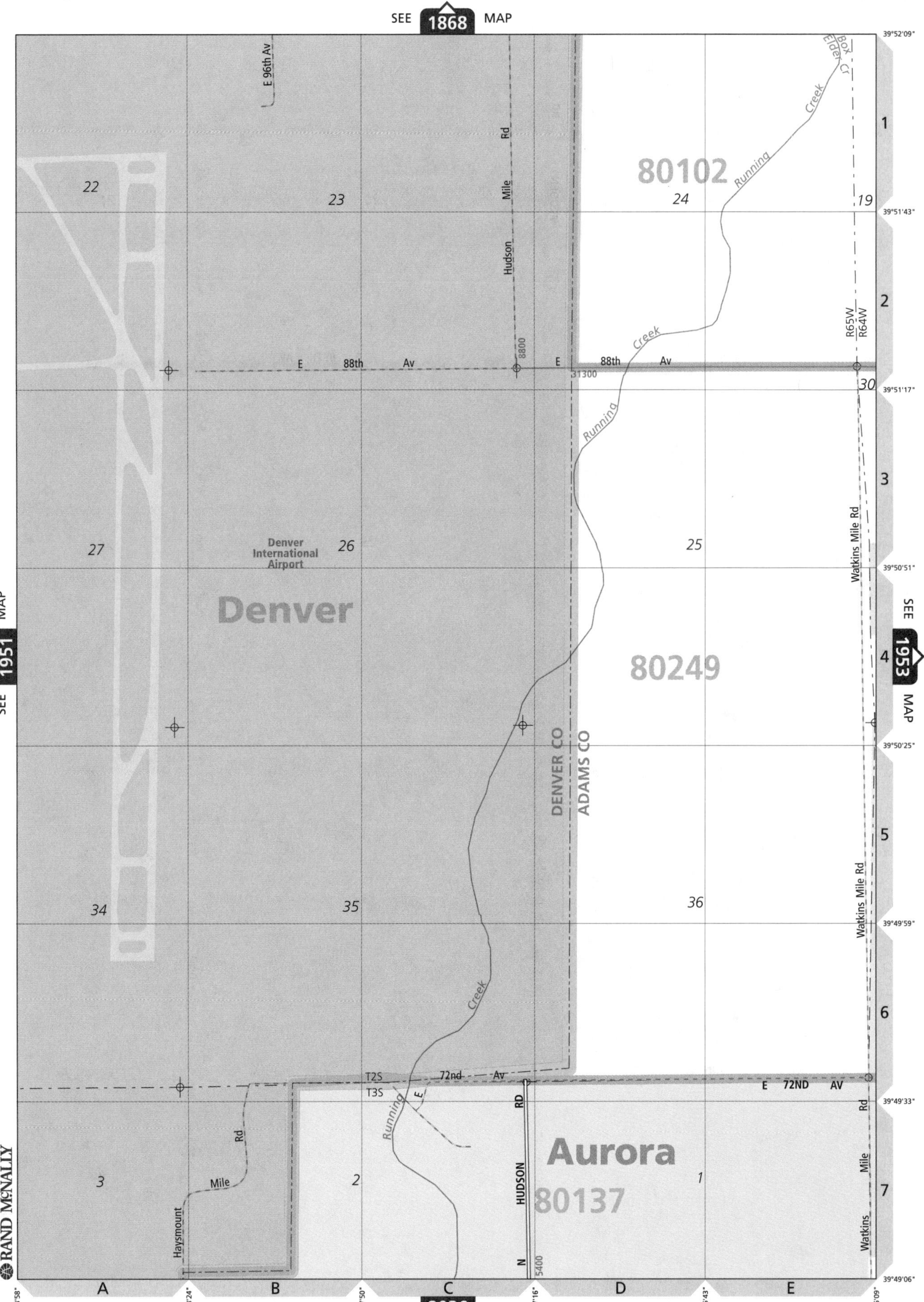

SEE 1951 MAP

SEE 1953 MAP

SEE 2036 MAP

1:24,000
1 in. = 2000 ft.
0 0.25 0.5
miles

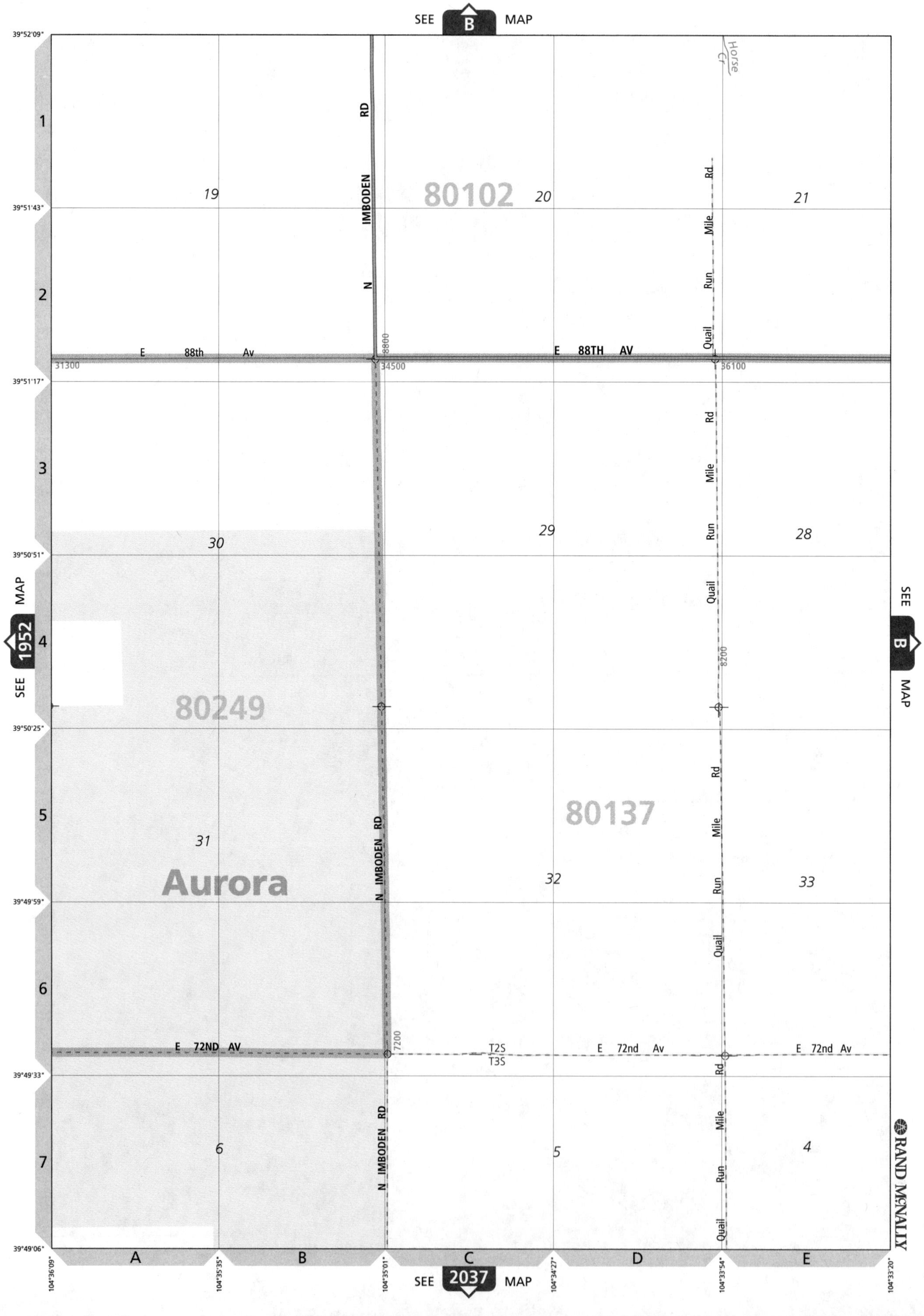

SEE B MAP

SEE 1952 MAP

SEE B MAP

SEE 2037 MAP

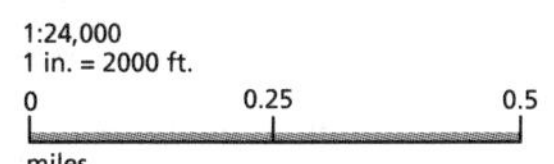

SEE 1933 MAP

Apex Valley Rd
Evergreen Rd
Aspen Ln
Hughesville Rd
Old Hughesville Rd
119
Upper Apex Rd
Columbine Campground Rd
Chase Gulch Rd
Quartz Valley Rd
80403
Flats Rd
King
Eureka
Barrett St
G St
North St
Dump Rd
Old Tram Rd
Prosser St
Gilpin History Mus
Historical Society & Museum
Central City Opera Hse
Teller Hse
Harrah's Casino
Bullwhackers Casino
GREGORY ST
CLEAR CREEK ST
Central City
Black Hawk
ARAPAHO NATIONAL FOREST
Nevada St
Academy
Prize St
Mine Rd
Nevadaville
Kings Rd
Letcher St
Kenogha St
Mammoth View Ln
Powder Run Dr
Mountain Dr
Gold Mountain Rd
Bobtail Cir
VIRGINA CANYON RD
Central City Pkwy
Lake Gulch Rd
Powder Run Dr
CR-6
Hidee Mine Rd
Russell Gulch Rd
Roy Smith Rd
Ray Smith Rd
Harris Rd
OH MY GOD RD
Lower Russell Gulch Rd
Creek Bed
Main St
Front St
Neck Mine Rd
Druid Mine Rd
R73W
R72W

A
1 St. James St
2 Main St
3 Bourion St
4 Nevada St
5 Dostal Al

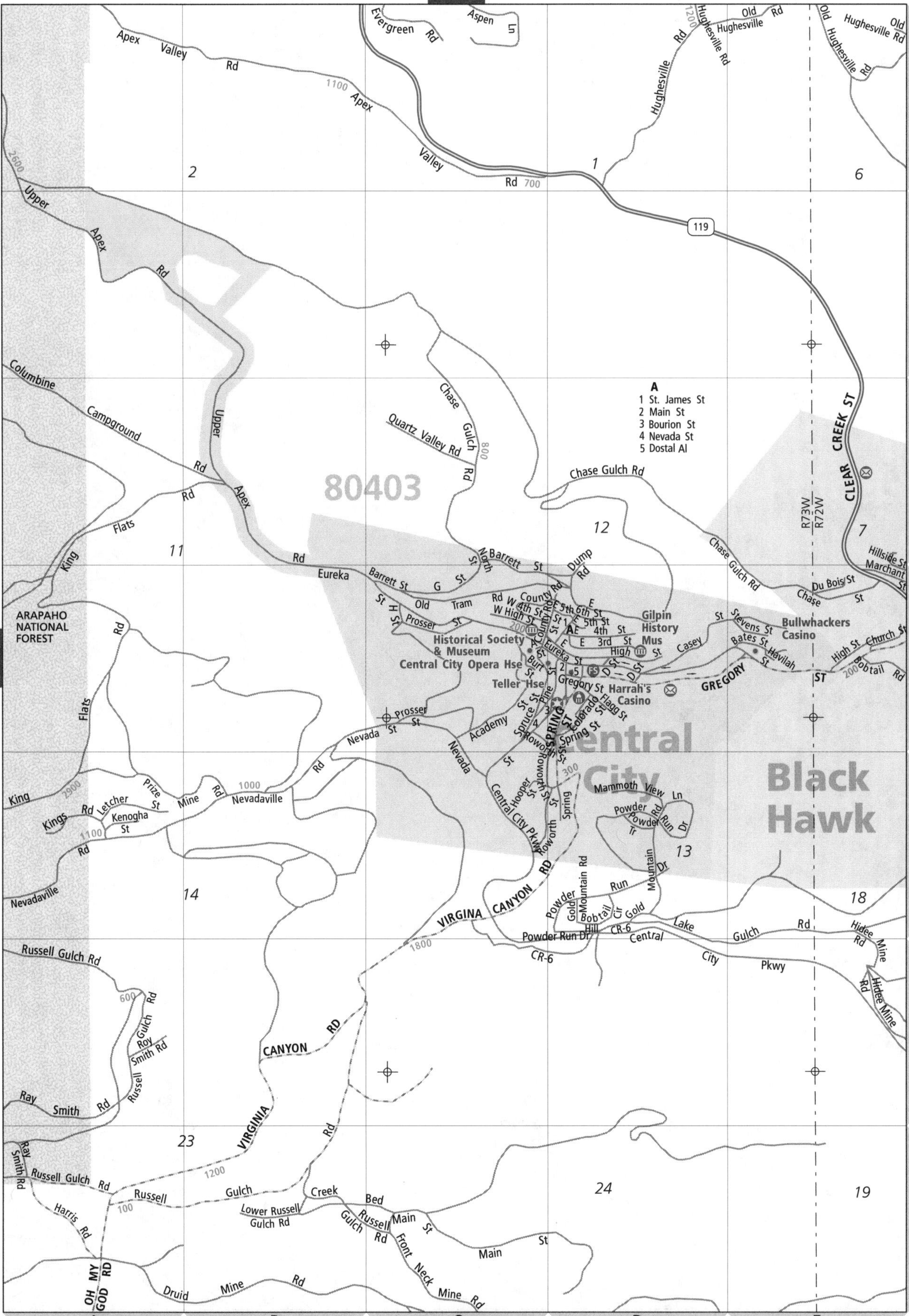

SEE B MAP
SEE 2018 MAP
SEE 2101 MAP

1:24,000
1 in. = 2000 ft.
0 0.25 0.5
miles

SEE 1934 MAP

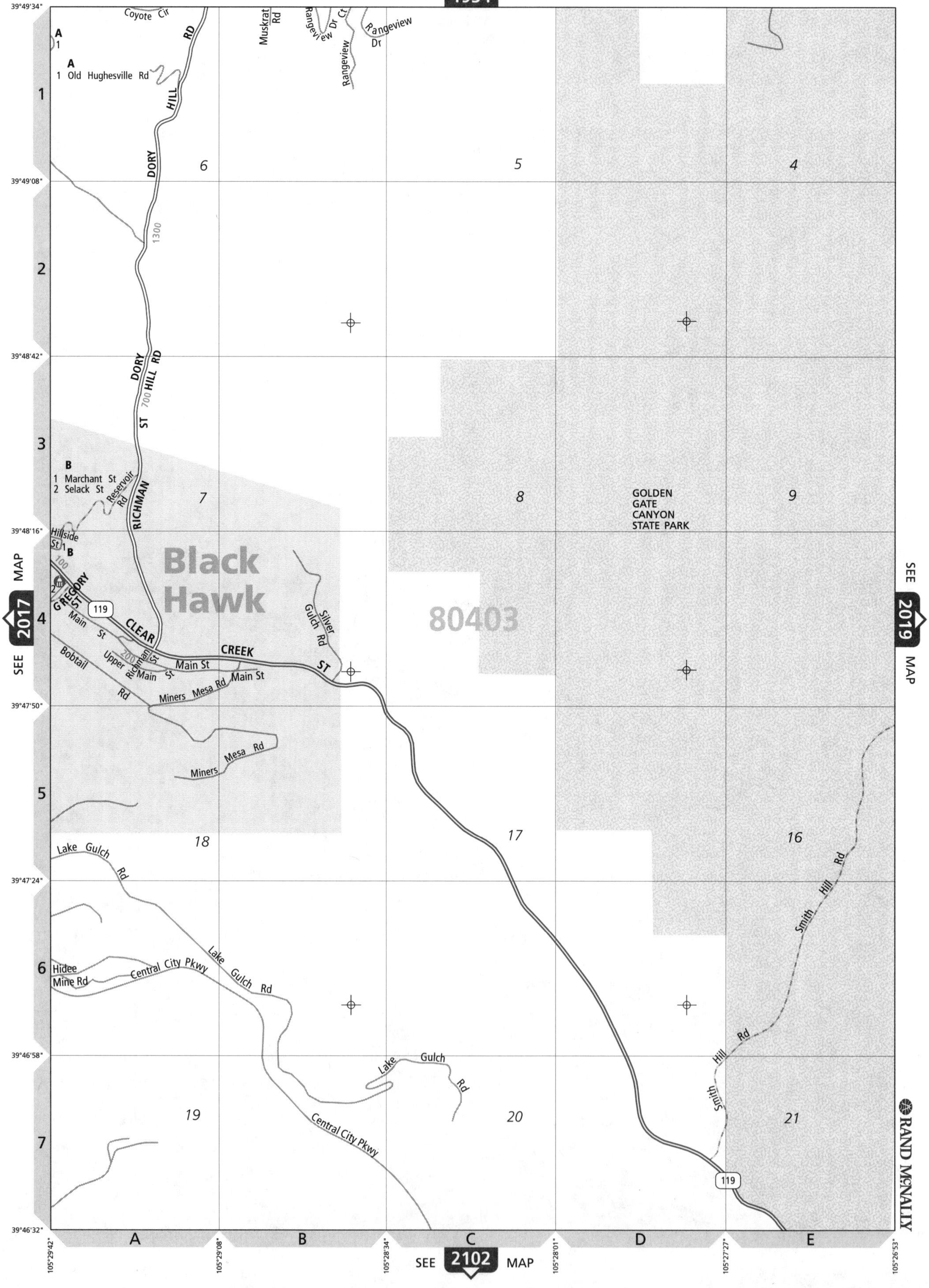

SEE 2017 MAP

SEE 2019 MAP

SEE 2102 MAP

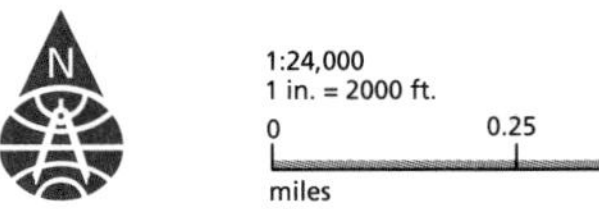

SEE 1935 MAP

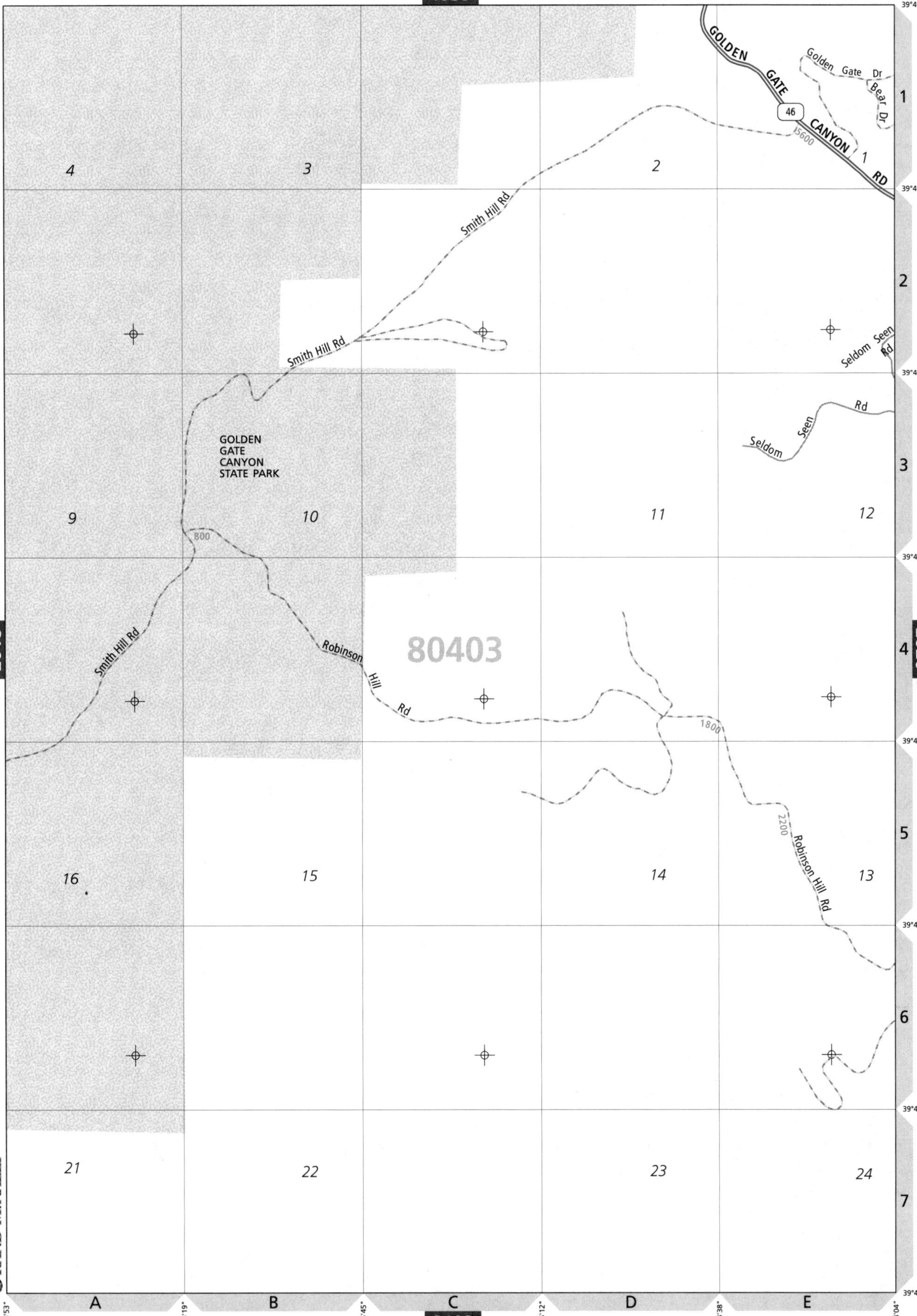

SEE 2018 MAP

SEE 2020 MAP

SEE 2103 MAP

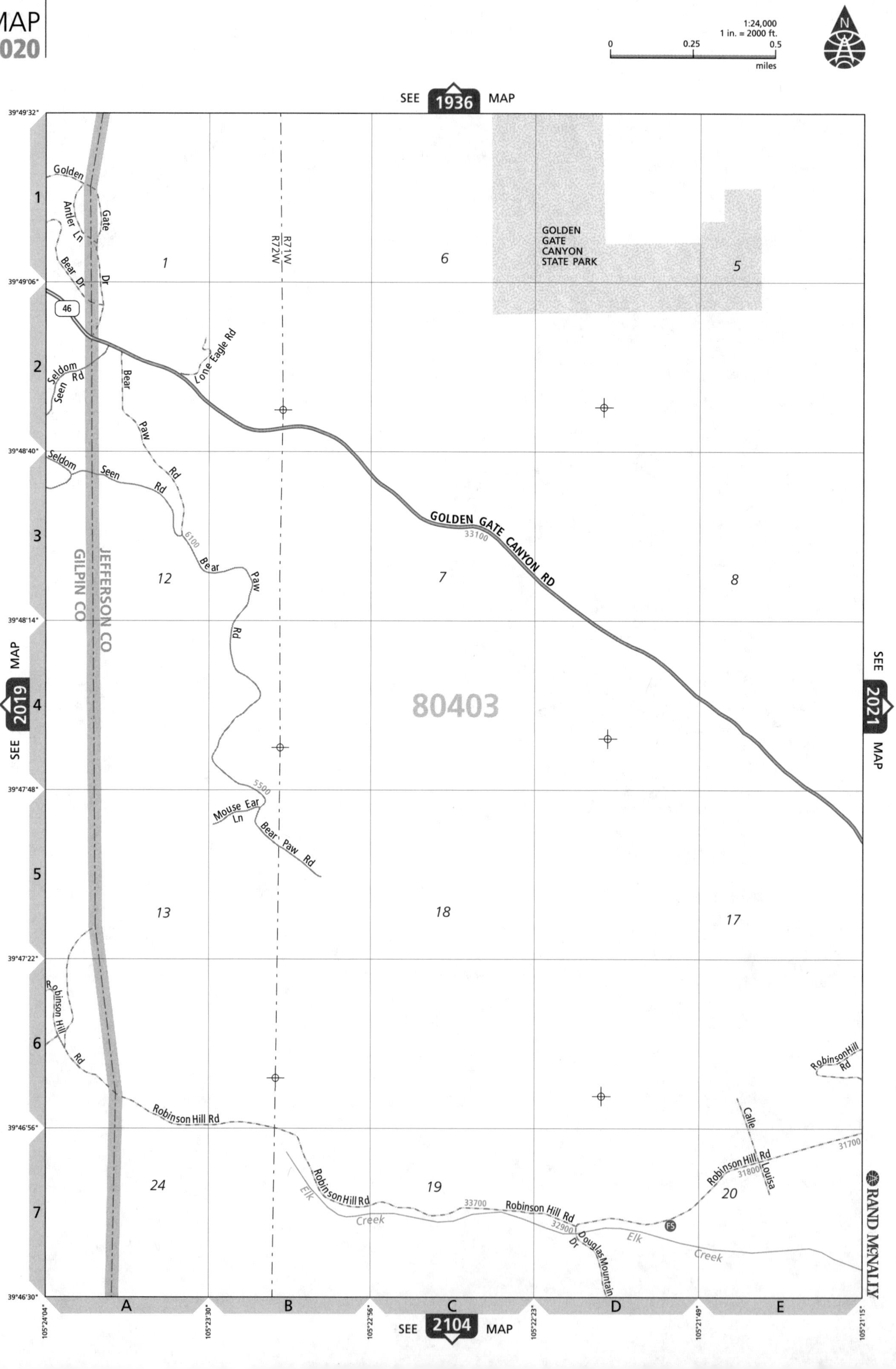

1:24,000
1 in. = 2000 ft.
0
0.25
0.5
miles
N
SEE 1936 MAP
SEE 2019 MAP
SEE 2021 MAP
SEE 2104 MAP
GOLDEN GATE CANYON STATE PARK
GOLDEN GATE CANYON RD
33100
80403
JEFFERSON CO
GILPIN CO
R71W
R72W
46
Golden Gate Dr
Antler Ln
Bear Dr
Seldom Seen Rd
Lone Eagle Rd
Bear Paw Rd
6100
5500
Mouse Ear Ln
Robinson Hill Rd
Elk Creek
33700
32900
31800
31700
Douglas Mountain Dr
Calle Louisa
FS
1
6
5
12
7
8
13
18
17
24
19
20
A
B
C
D
E
39°49'32"
39°49'06"
39°48'40"
39°48'14"
39°47'48"
39°47'22"
39°46'56"
39°46'30"
105°24'04"
105°23'30"
105°22'56"
105°22'23"
105°21'49"
105°21'15"
RAND McNALLY

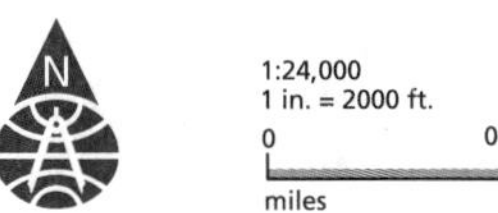

SEE 1937 MAP

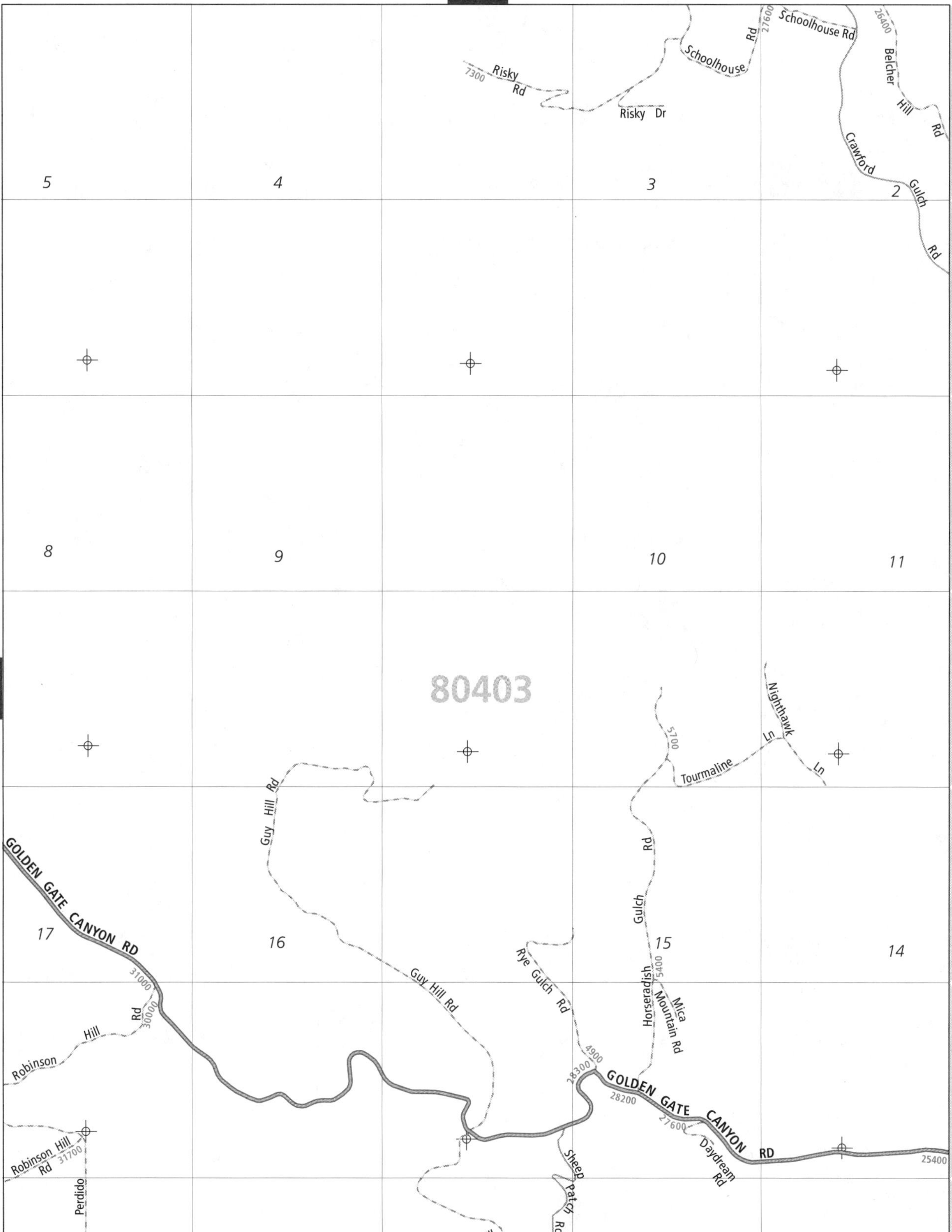

SEE 2020 MAP

SEE 2022 MAP

80403

GOLDEN GATE CANYON RD
Schoolhouse Rd
Risky Rd
Risky Dr
Belcher Hill Rd
Crawford Gulch Rd
Nighthawk Ln
Tourmaline Ln
Guy Hill Rd
Horseradish Gulch Rd
Mica Mountain Rd
Rye Gulch Rd
Robinson Hill Rd
Sheep Patch Rd
Daydream Rd
Camino Perdido
Elk Cr

1 2 3 4 5 6 7
A B C D E

39°49'30" 39°49'04" 39°48'38" 39°48'12" 39°47'46" 39°47'20" 39°46'54" 39°46'28"
105°21'15" 105°20'41" 105°20'08" 105°19'34" 105°19'00" 105°18'26"

RAND McNALLY

SEE 2105 MAP

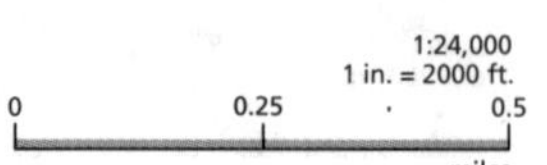

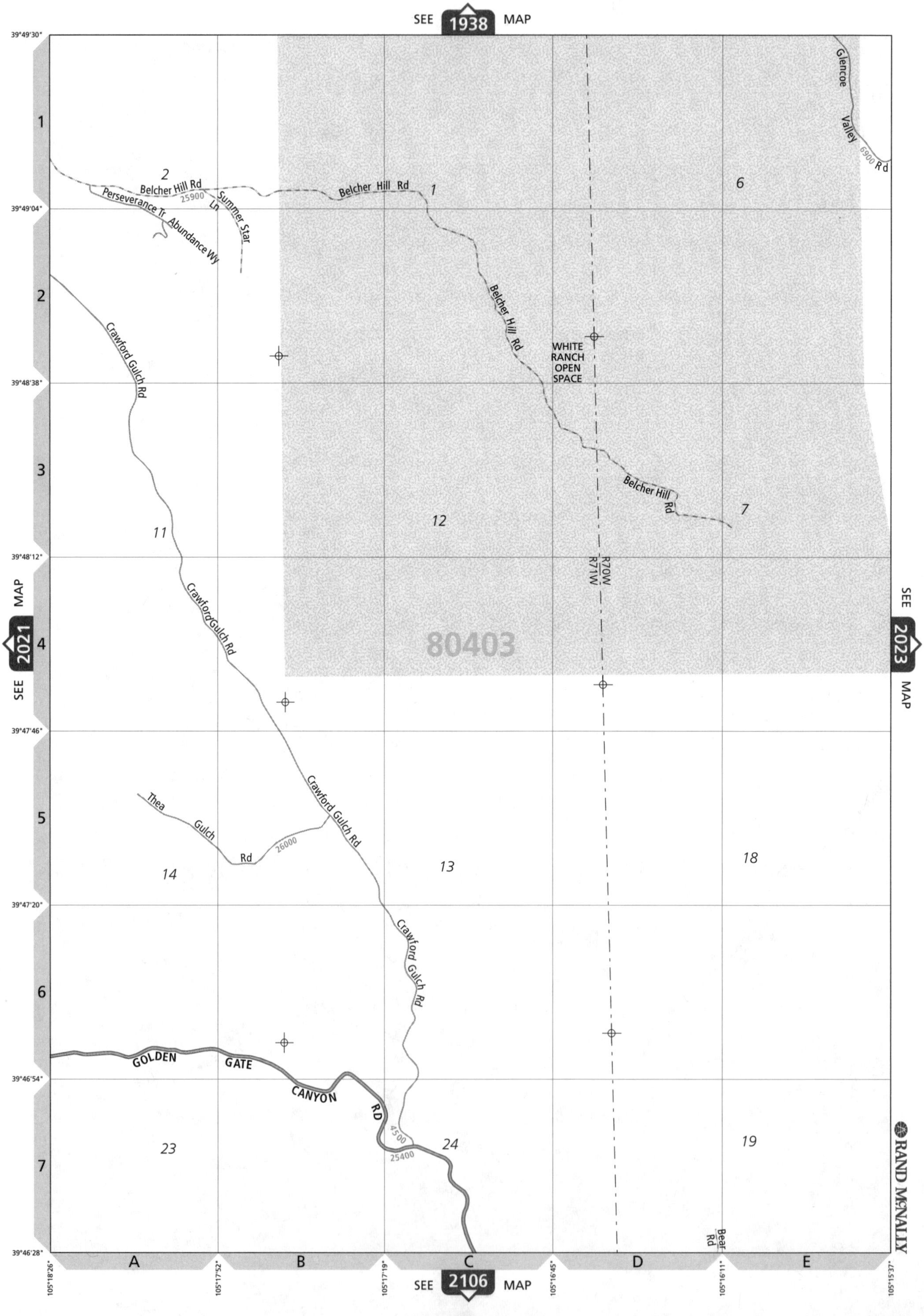

1:24,000
1 in. = 2000 ft.
0
0.25
0.5
miles
N
SEE 1938 MAP
SEE 2021 MAP
SEE 2023 MAP
SEE 2106 MAP
39°49'30"
39°49'04"
39°48'38"
39°48'12"
39°47'46"
39°47'20"
39°46'54"
39°46'28"
105°18'26"
105°17'52"
105°17'19"
105°16'45"
105°16'11"
105°15'37"
1
2
3
4
5
6
7
A
B
C
D
E
Belcher Hill Rd
25900
Summer Star Ln
Perseverance Tr
Abundance Wy
Belcher Hill Rd
Belcher Hill Rd
Belcher Hill Rd
Glencoe Valley Rd
6900
WHITE RANCH OPEN SPACE
R70W
R71W
80403
Crawford Gulch Rd
Crawford Gulch Rd
Crawford Gulch Rd
Crawford Gulch Rd
Thea Gulch Rd
26000
GOLDEN GATE CANYON RD
4500
25400
Bear Rd
1
2
6
7
11
12
13
14
18
19
23
24

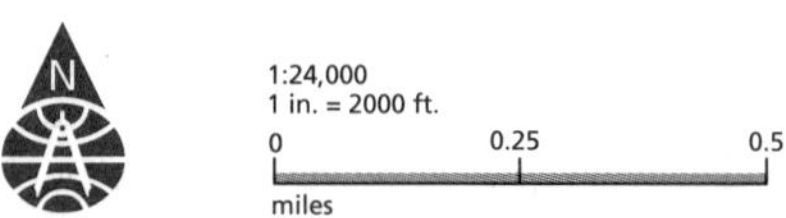

SEE 1939 MAP

Grid: 1–7; A–E
Sections: 3, 4, 5, 6, 7, 8, 9, 10, 15, 16, 17, 18, 19, 20, 21, 22

39°49'28" 39°49'02" 39°48'36" 39°48'10" 39°47'44" 39°47'18" 39°46'52" 39°46'25"
105°15'37" 105°15'03" 105°14'30" 105°13'56" 105°13'22" 105°12'48"

SEE 2022 MAP

SEE 2024 MAP

SEE 2107 MAP

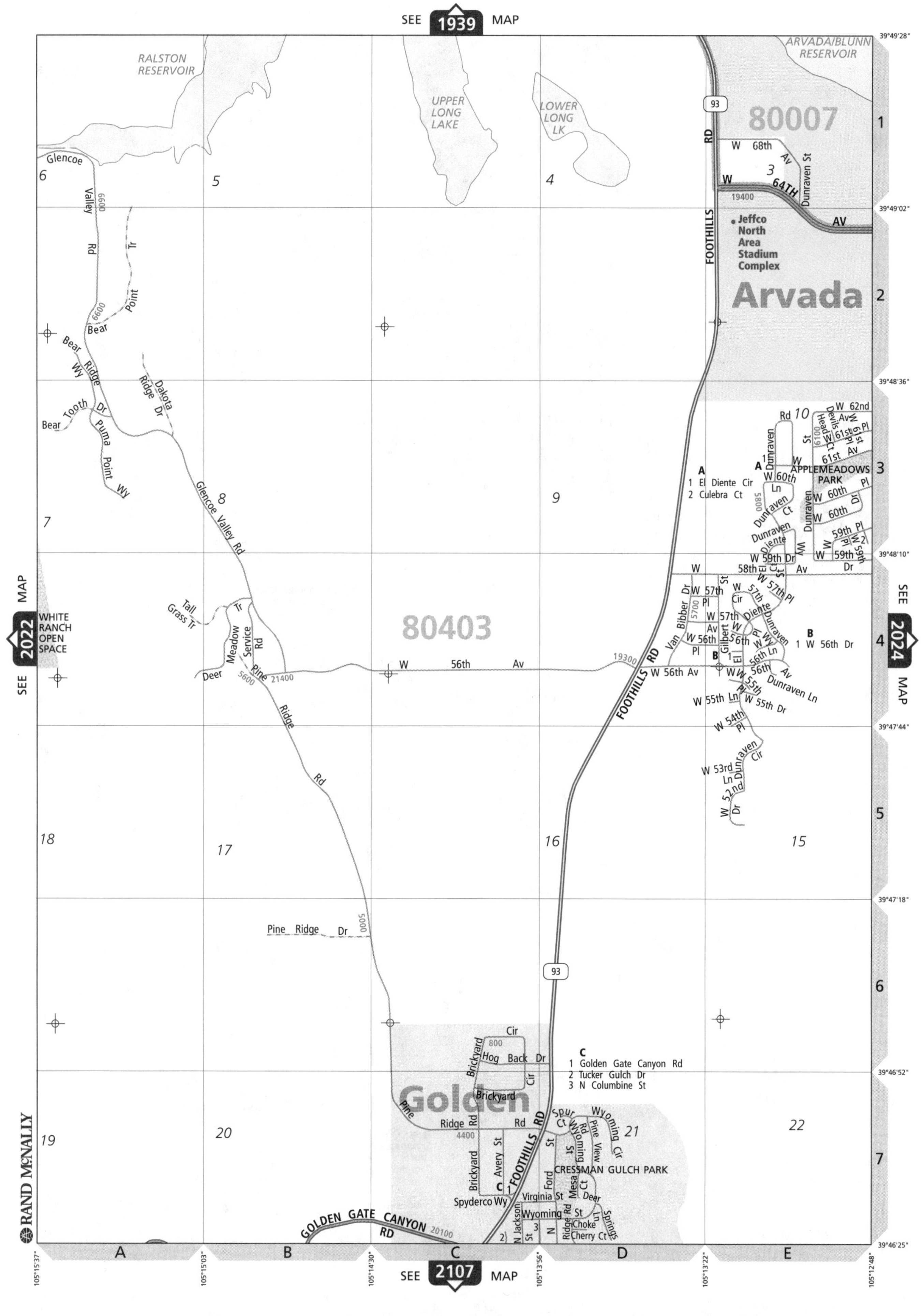

1:24,000
1 in. = 2000 ft.
0 0.25 0.5
miles

SEE 1940 MAP

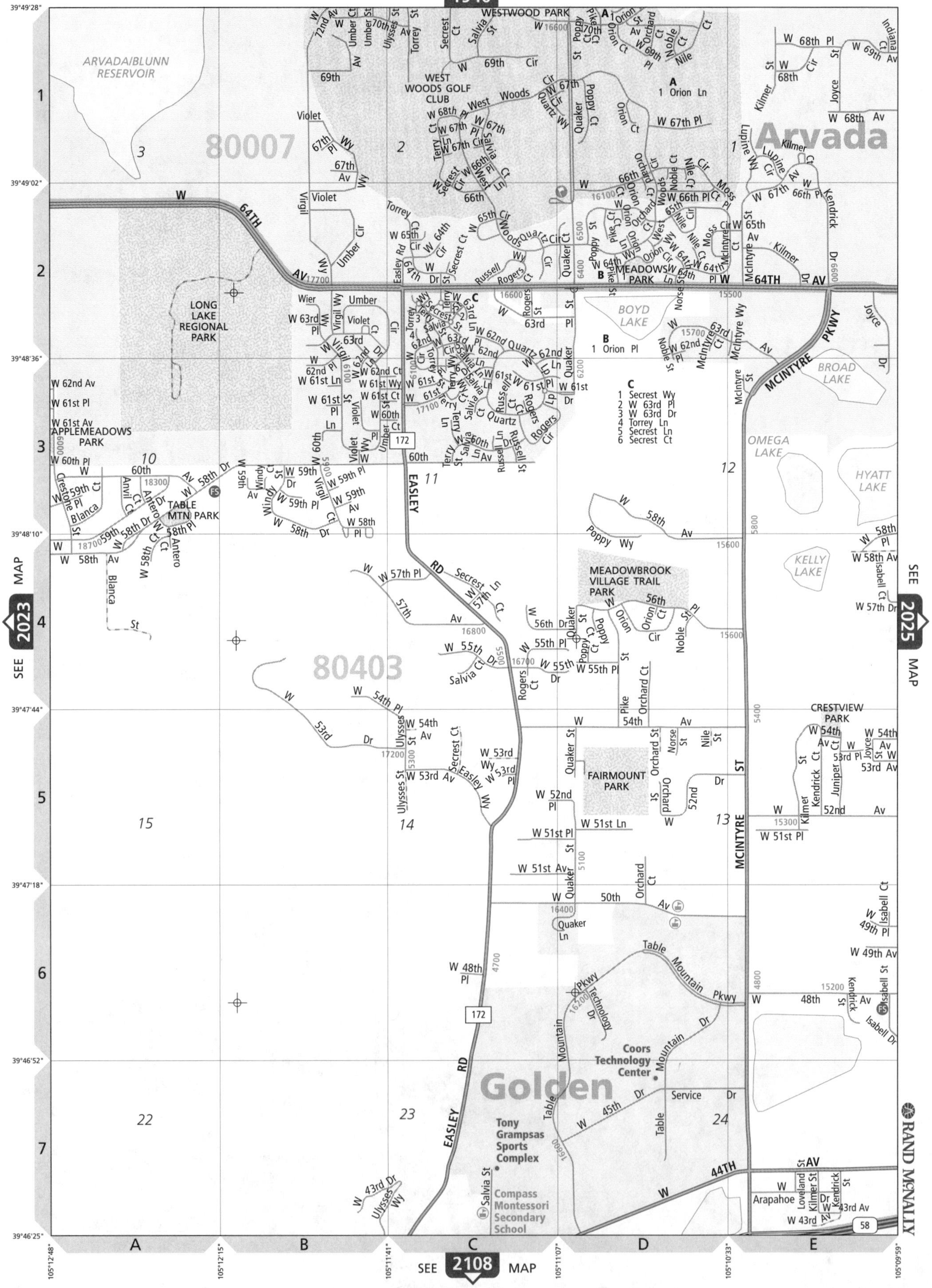

SEE 2023 MAP

SEE 2025 MAP

SEE 2108 MAP

A
1 Orion Ln

B
1 Orion Pl

C
1 Secrest Wy
2 W 63rd Pl
3 W 63rd Dr
4 Torrey Ln
5 Secrest Ln
6 Secrest Ct

Arvada

Golden

80007

80403

ARVADA/BLUNN RESERVOIR

LONG LAKE REGIONAL PARK

WEST WOODS GOLF CLUB

WESTWOOD PARK

MEADOWS PARK

BOYD LAKE

BROAD LAKE

OMEGA LAKE

HYATT LAKE

KELLY LAKE

APPLEMEADOWS PARK

TABLE MTN PARK

MEADOWBROOK VILLAGE TRAIL PARK

CRESTVIEW PARK

FAIRMOUNT PARK

Coors Technology Center

Tony Grampsas Sports Complex

Compass Montessori Secondary School

W 64TH AV

MCINTYRE PKWY

MCINTYRE ST

EASLEY RD

W 44TH AV

Table Mountain Pkwy

A B C D E

1 2 3 4 5 6 7

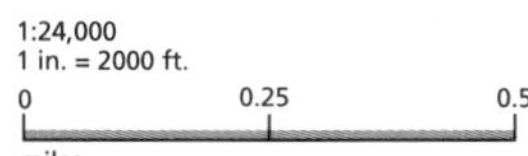

SEE 1941 MAP

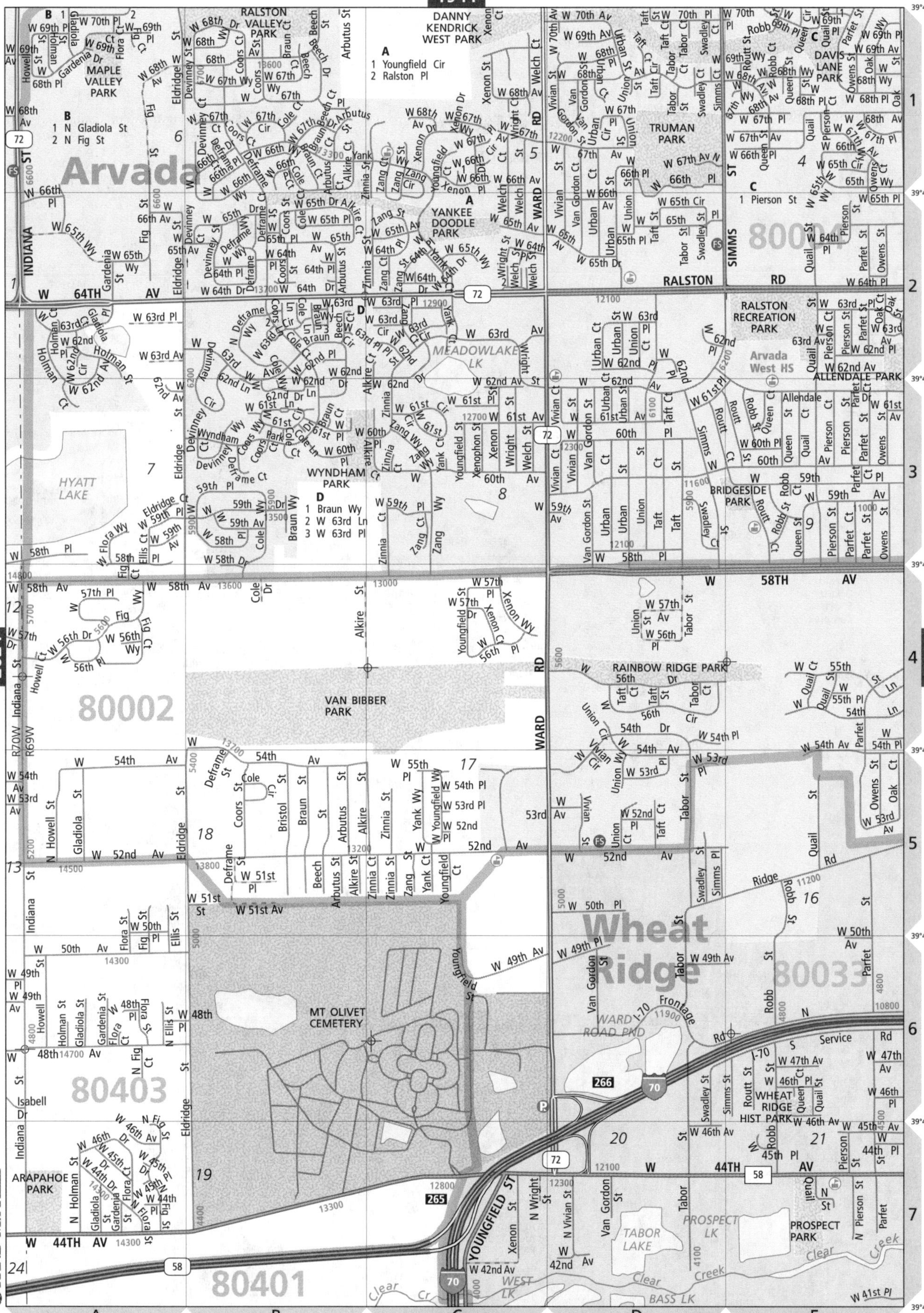

SEE 2024 MAP

SEE 2026 MAP

SEE 2109 MAP

A B C D E

1 2 3 4 5 6 7

Arvada

Wheat Ridge

80002 80004 80033 80403 80401

RALSTON VALLEY PARK

DANNY KENDRICK WEST PARK

MAPLE VALLEY PARK

TRUMAN PARK

DAVIS LANE PARK

YANKEE DOODLE PARK

RALSTON RECREATION PARK

Arvada West HS

ALLENDALE PARK

MEADOWLAKE LK

HYATT LAKE

WYNDHAM PARK

BRIDGESIDE PARK

VAN BIBBER PARK

RAINBOW RIDGE PARK

MT OLIVET CEMETERY

WARD ROAD PND

WHEAT RIDGE HIST PARK

ARAPAHOE PARK

TABOR LAKE

PROSPECT LK

PROSPECT PARK

WEST LK

BASS LK

Clear Creek

INDIANA ST

WARD RD

SIMMS ST

YOUNGFIELD ST

W 64TH AV

RALSTON RD

W 58TH AV

W 44TH AV

I-70 Frontage Rd

A
1 Youngfield Cir
2 Ralston Pl

B
1 N Gladiola St
2 N Fig St

C
1 Pierson St

D
1 Braun Wy
2 W 63rd Ln
3 W 63rd Pl

R70W R69W

39°49'25" 39°48'59" 39°48'33" 39°48'07" 39°47'41" 39°47'15" 39°46'49" 39°46'23"

105°09'59" 105°09'26" 105°08'52" 105°08'18" 105°07'44" 105°07'10"

1:24,000
1 in. = 2000 ft.
0 0.25 0.5
miles

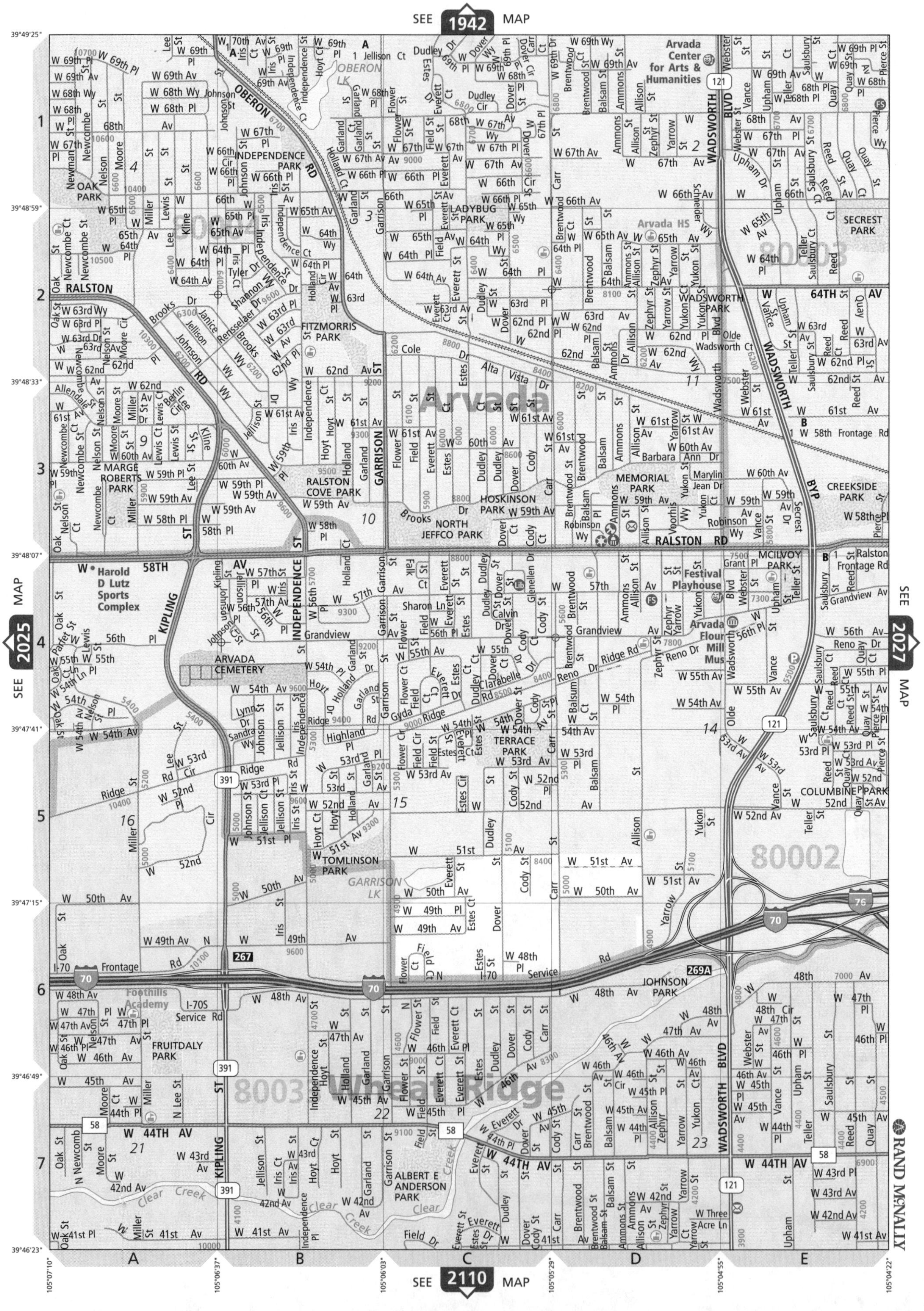

SEE 1942 MAP

SEE 2025 MAP

SEE 2027 MAP

Arvada

Wheat Ridge

Arvada Center for Arts & Humanities

Arvada HS

Harold D Lutz Sports Complex

Arvada Cemetery

Festival Playhouse

Arvada Flour Mill Mus

Foothills Academy

Oak Park, Independence Park, Ladybug Park, Secrest Park, Fitzmorris Park, Wadsworth Park, Marge Roberts Park, Ralston Cove Park, Hoskinson Park, North Jeffco Park, Memorial Park, Creekside Park, McIlvoy Park, Terrace Park, Columbine Park, Tomlinson Park, Johnson Park, Fruitdaly Park, Albert E Anderson Park

Oberon Lk, Garrison Lk, Clear Creek

80004, 80003, 80002

SEE 2110 MAP

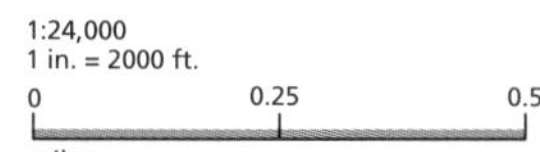

SEE 1943 MAP

Westminster
Arvada
Wheat Ridge
Lakeside
Mountain View
Denver

HIDDEN LAKE
Westminster HS
LAKE SANGRACO
HOMESTEAD PARK
TENNYSON KNOLLS PARK
CREEKSIDE PARK
LEW WALSH PARK
TRAILHEAD PARK
COLUMBINE PARK
JEFFERSON CO
ADAMS CO
DENVER CO
WILLIS CASE GOLF COURSE
INSPIRATION POINT PARK
Regis University-Denver
BERKELEY LAKE
BERKELEY LAKE PARK
ROCKY MOUNTAIN LAKE
ROCKY MOUNTAIN LAKE PARK
Lakeside Amusement Park
LAKE RHONDA
Lakeside Center
Historic Oriental Theater
Arrupe Jesuit HS
TENNYSON PARK
HORACE E RANDALL PARK

RALSTON RD
SHERIDAN BLVD
FEDERAL BLVD
LOWELL BLVD
HARLAN ST
I-70 SERVICE RD
W 44TH AV
W 48TH AV
W 64TH AV

80003
80002
80221
80033
80212
80211

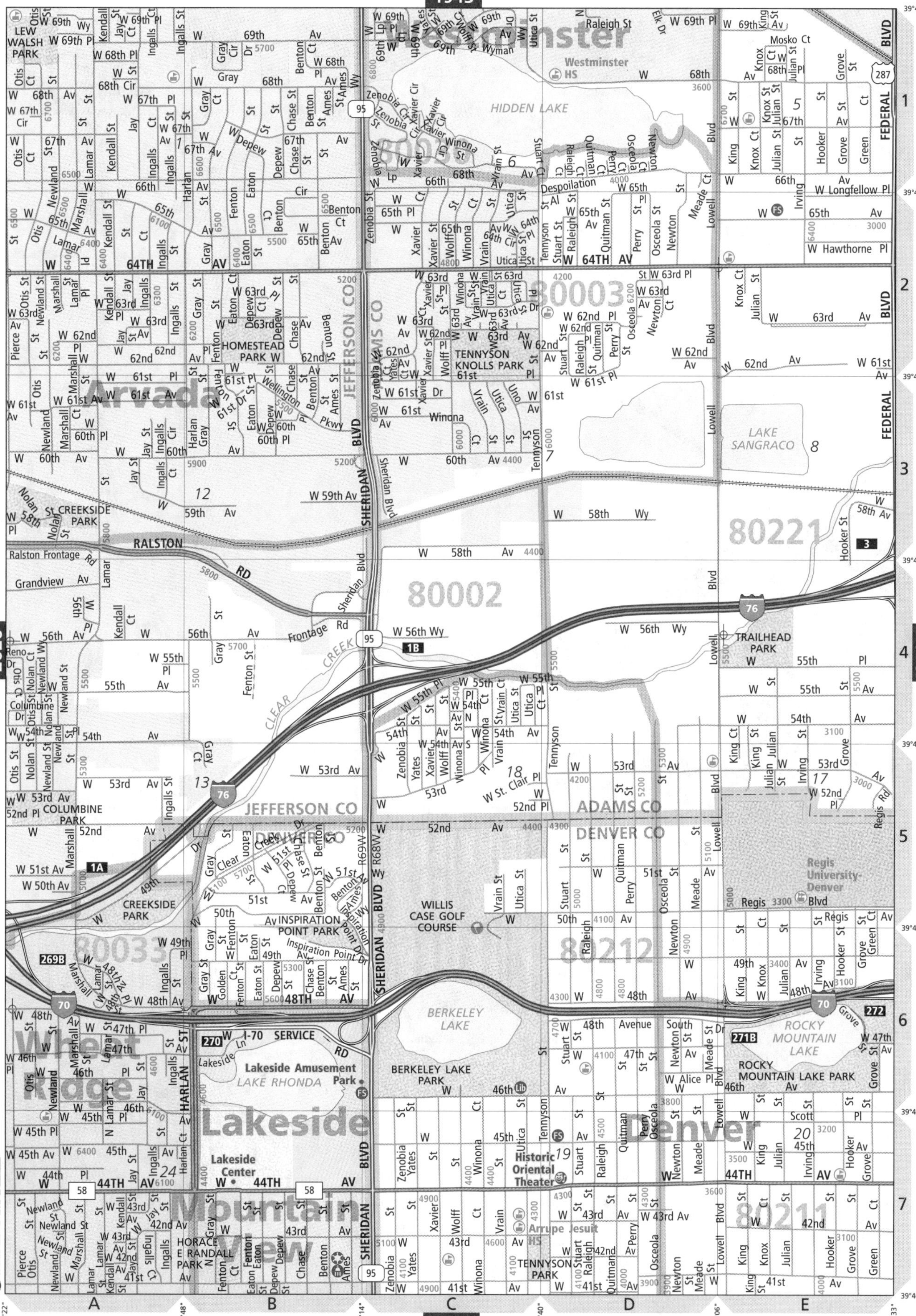

SEE 2026 MAP
SEE 2028 MAP
SEE 2111 MAP

1:24,000
1 in. = 2000 ft.
0 0.25 0.5
miles

SEE 1944 MAP

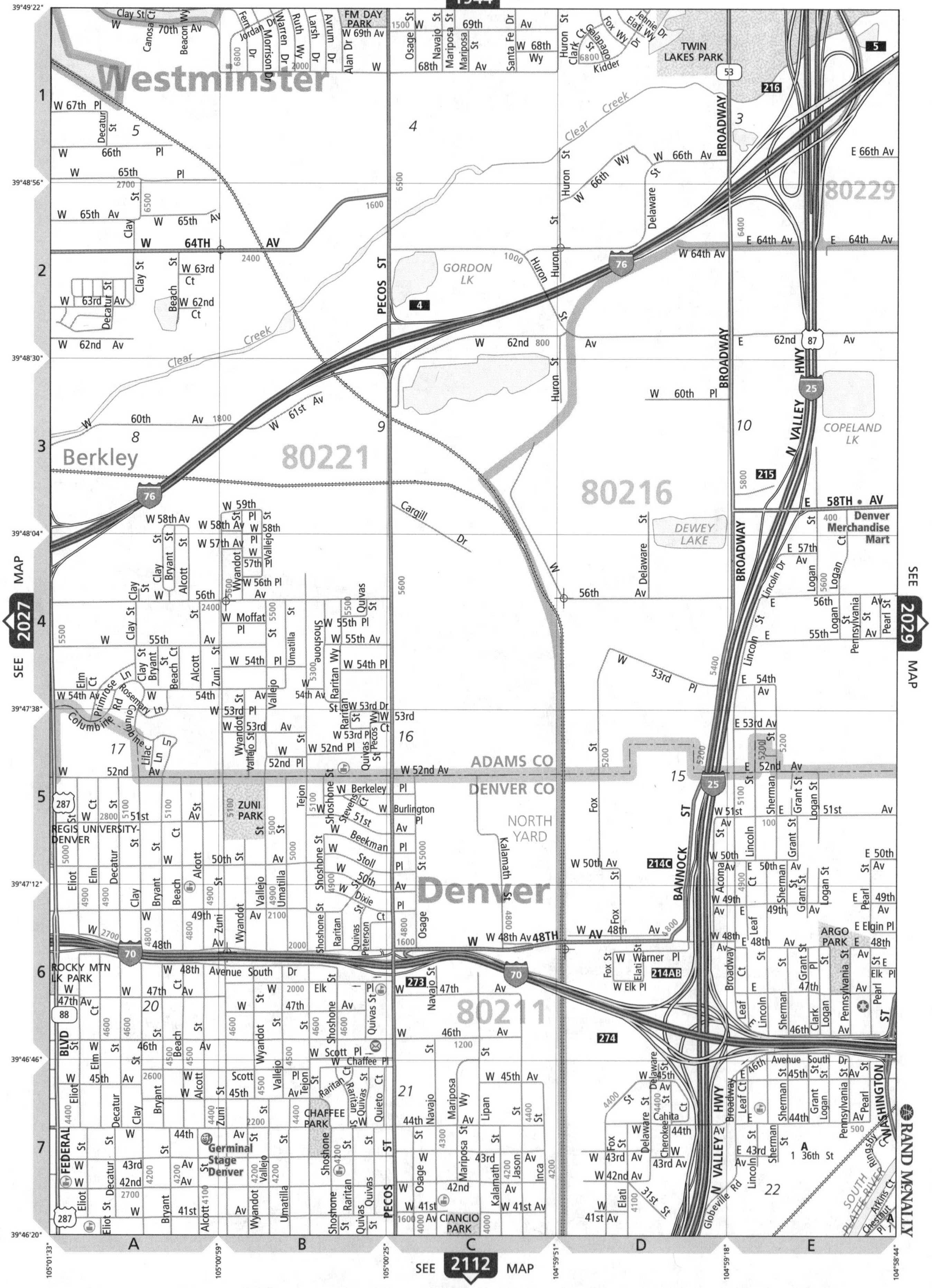

Westminster

Berkley

80221

80216

80229

80211

Denver

TWIN LAKES PARK

GORDON LK

COPELAND LK

DEWEY LAKE

Denver Merchandise Mart

ADAMS CO
DENVER CO

NORTH YARD

REGIS UNIVERSITY-DENVER

ZUNI PARK

ROCKY MTN LK PARK

CHAFFEE PARK

Germinal Stage Denver

CIANCIO PARK

ARGO PARK

FM DAY PARK

PECOS ST

BROADWAY

N VALLEY HWY

BANNOCK ST

FEDERAL BLVD

WASHINGTON ST

W 64TH AV

E 58TH AV

W 48TH AV

SOUTH PLATTE RIVER

Clear Creek

SEE 2027 MAP

SEE 2029 MAP

SEE 2112 MAP

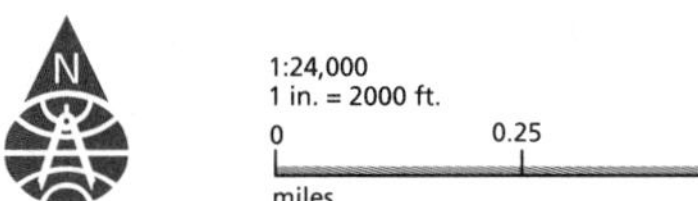

SEE 1945 MAP

SEE MAP 2028

SEE MAP 2030

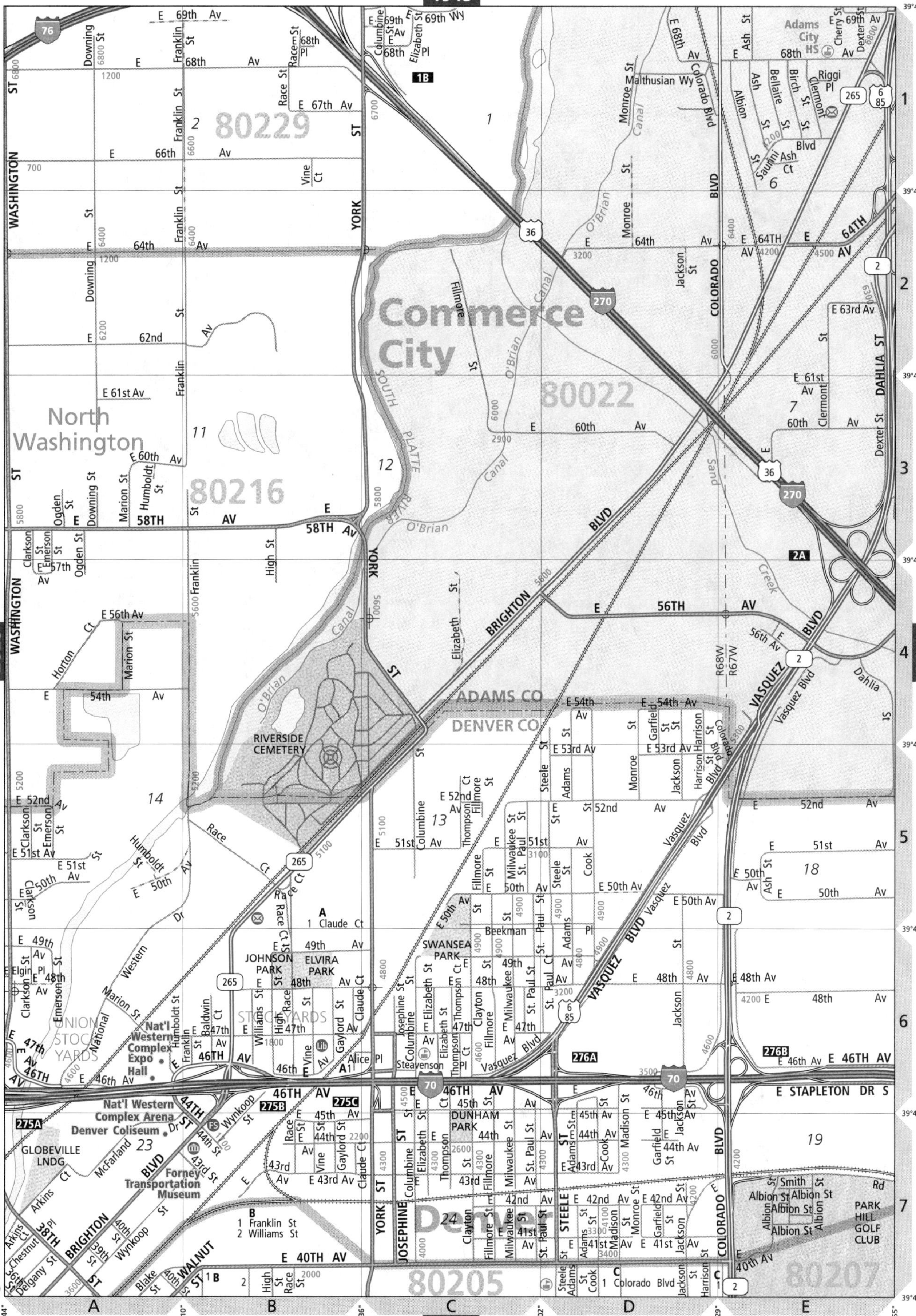

Commerce City

North Washington

Denver

80229 80022 80216 80205 80207

ADAMS CO
DENVER CO

RIVERSIDE CEMETERY

JOHNSON PARK

ELVIRA PARK

SWANSEA PARK

DUNHAM PARK

UNION STOCK YARDS

Nat'l Western Complex Expo Hall

Nat'l Western Complex Arena

Denver Coliseum

Forney Transportation Museum

GLOBEVILLE LNDG

PARK HILL GOLF CLUB

A
1 Claude Ct

B
1 Franklin St
2 Williams St

A B C D E

1 2 3 4 5 6 7

SEE 2113 MAP

1:24,000
1 in. = 2000 ft.
0 0.25 0.5
miles

SEE 1946 MAP

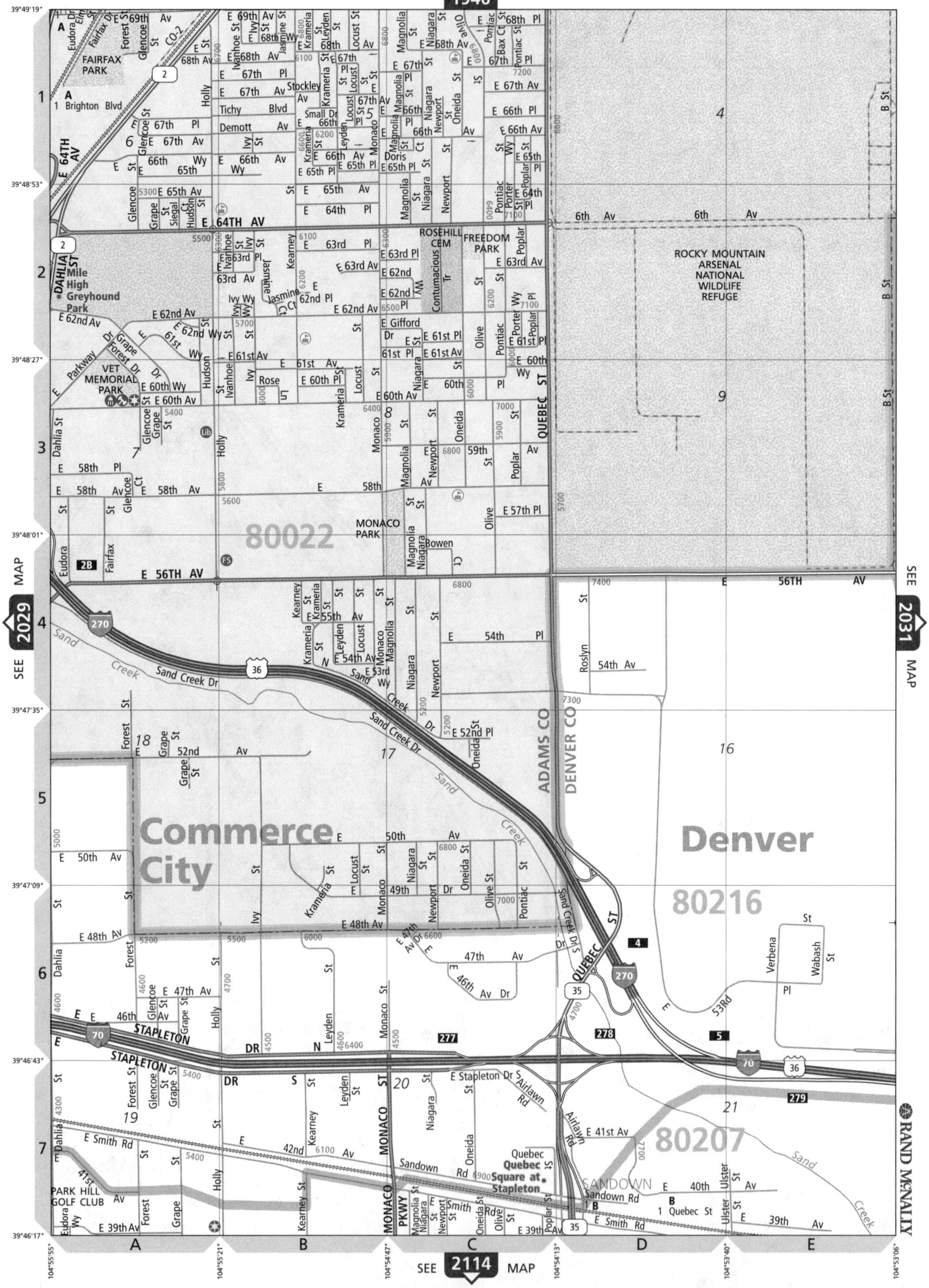

FAIRFAX PARK

Mile High Greyhound Park

VET MEMORIAL PARK

ROSEHILL CEM

FREEDOM PARK

MONACO PARK

ROCKY MOUNTAIN ARSENAL NATIONAL WILDLIFE REFUGE

80022

Commerce City

Denver

80216

80207

ADAMS CO

DENVER CO

PARK HILL GOLF CLUB

Quebec Square at Stapleton

SANDOWN

E 64TH AV

E 56TH AV

E STAPLETON DR

QUEBEC ST

MONACO PKWY

DAHLIA ST

SEE 2029 MAP

SEE 2031 MAP

SEE 2114 MAP

RAND McNALLY

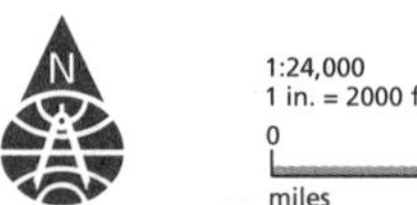

1:24,000
1 in. = 2000 ft.
0 0.25 0.5
miles

SEE 1947 MAP

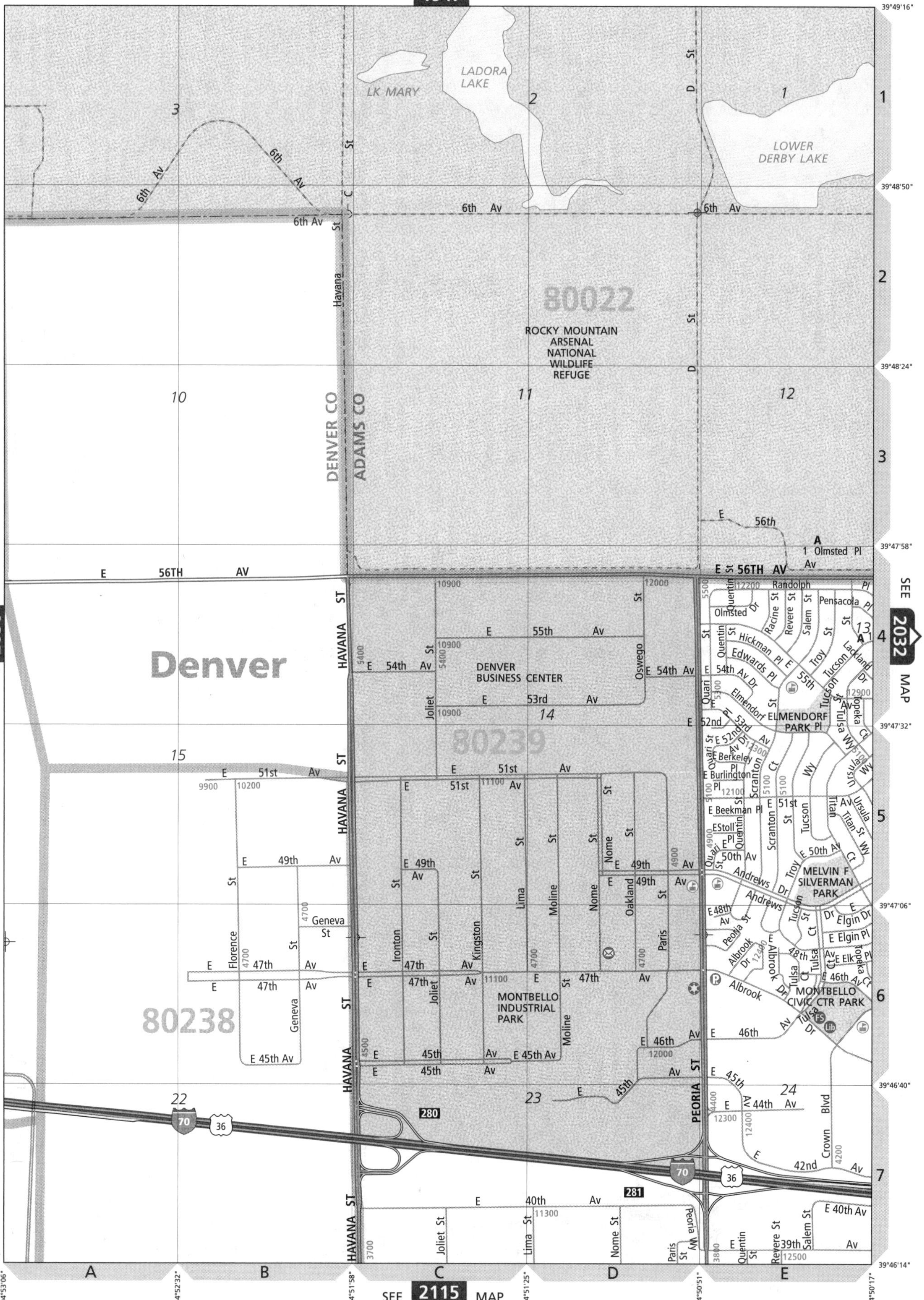

SEE 2030 MAP

SEE 2032 MAP

SEE 2115 MAP

A B C D E

1 2 3 4 5 6 7

1:24,000
1 in. = 2000 ft.
0 0.25 0.5
miles

SEE 1948 MAP

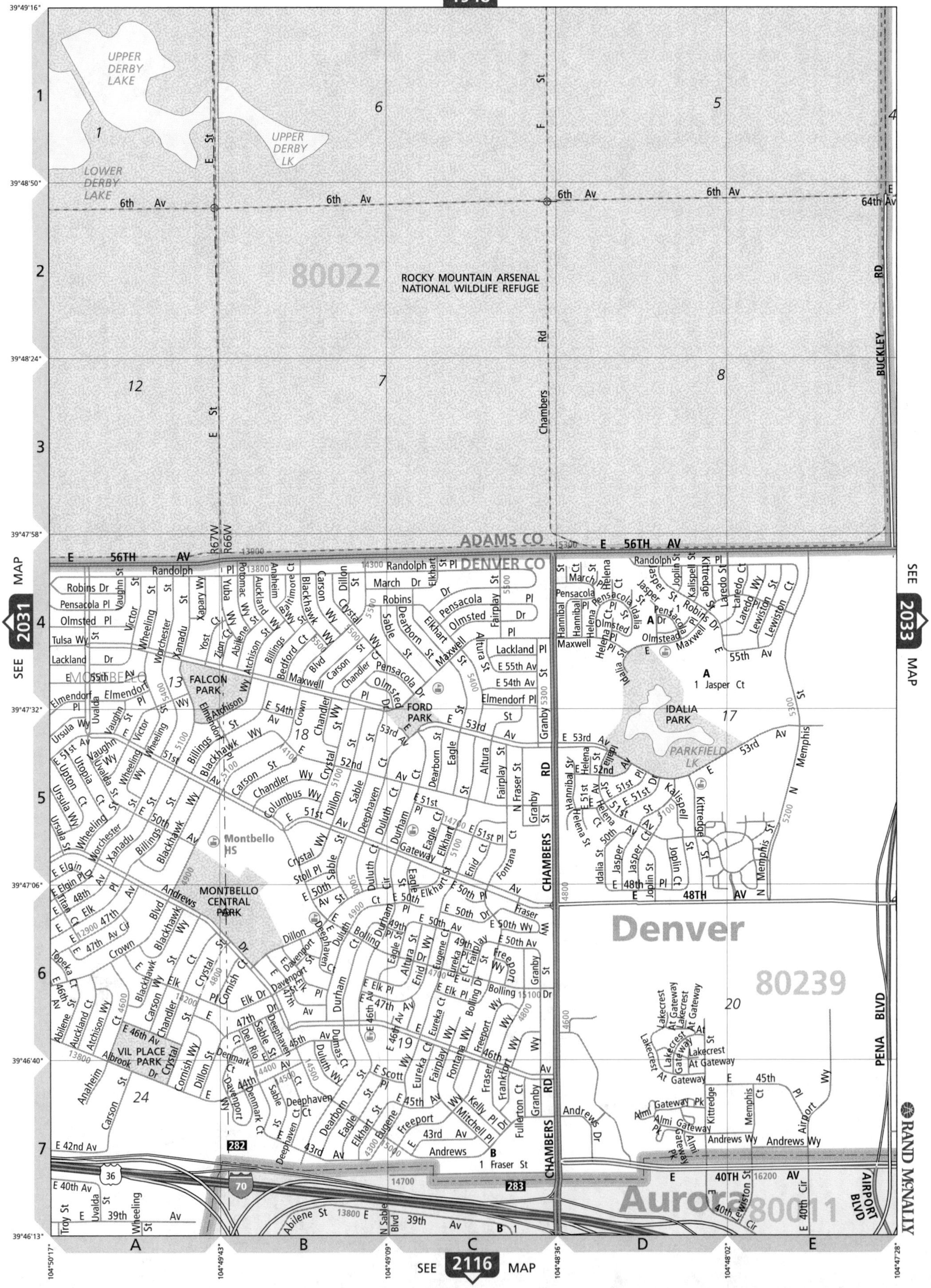

SEE 2031 MAP

SEE 2033 MAP

SEE 2116 MAP

UPPER DERBY LAKE
UPPER DERBY LK
LOWER DERBY LAKE
ROCKY MOUNTAIN ARSENAL NATIONAL WILDLIFE REFUGE
80022
ADAMS CO
DENVER CO
E 56TH AV
6th Av
E St
F St
Chambers Rd
BUCKLEY RD
64th Av
R67W R66W
FALCON PARK
FORD PARK
IDALIA PARK
PARKFIELD LK
Montbello HS
MONTBELLO CENTRAL PARK
VIL PLACE PARK
MONTBELLO
CHAMBERS RD
48TH AV
Denver
80239
PENA BLVD
Aurora
80011
40TH AV
AIRPORT BLVD
E 40th Av
39th Av
36
70
282
283

1 2 3 4 5 6 7
A B C D E

39°49'16" 39°48'50" 39°48'24" 39°47'58" 39°47'32" 39°47'06" 39°46'40" 39°46'13"
104°50'17" 104°49'43" 104°49'09" 104°48'36" 104°48'02" 104°47'28"

1:24,000
1 in. = 2000 ft.
0 0.25 0.5
miles

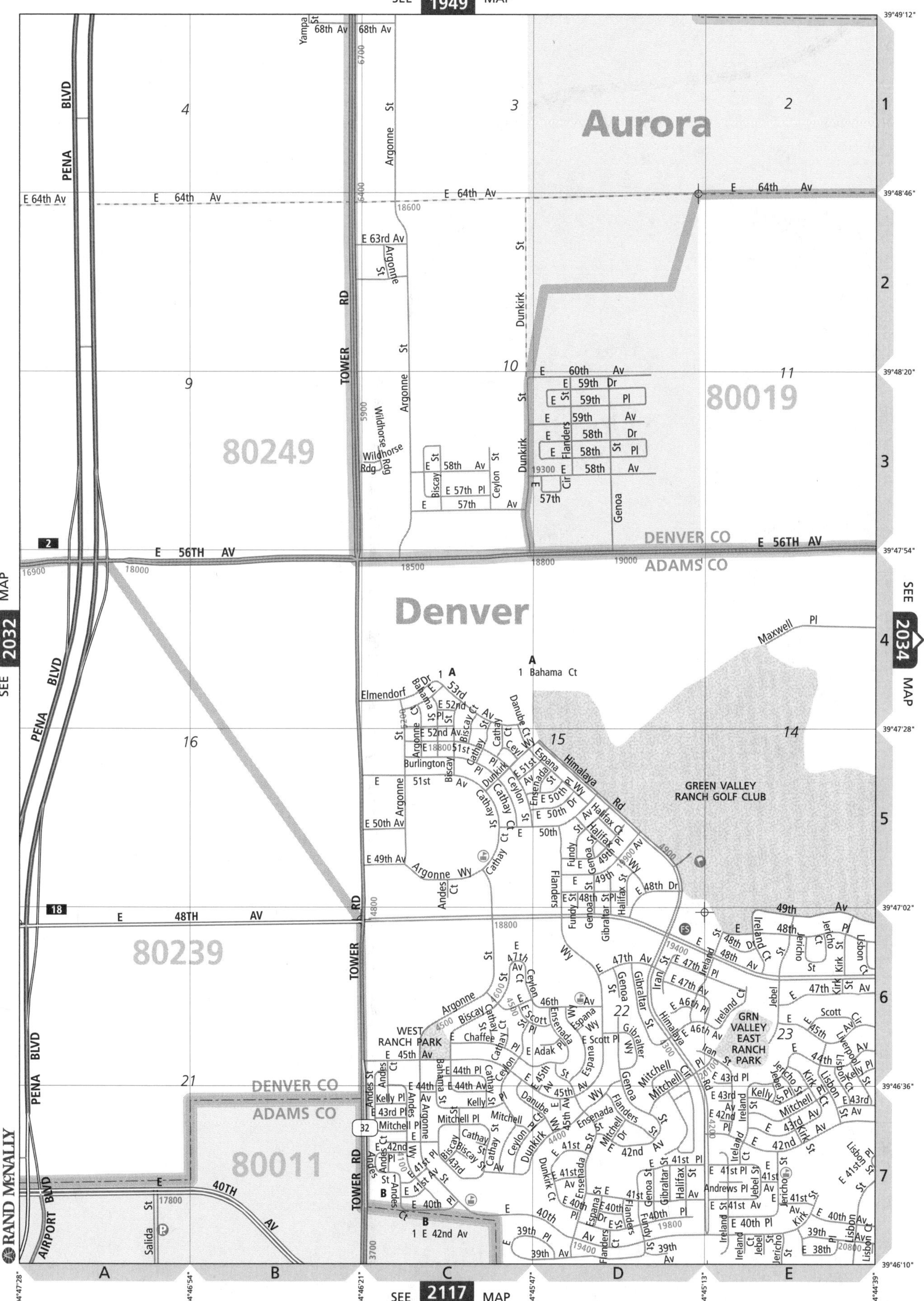

1:24,000
1 in. = 2000 ft.
0 0.25 0.5
miles

SEE 1950 MAP

SEE 2033 MAP

SEE 2035 MAP

SEE 2118 MAP

1:24,000
1 in. = 2000 ft.
0 0.25 0.5
miles

SEE 1951 MAP

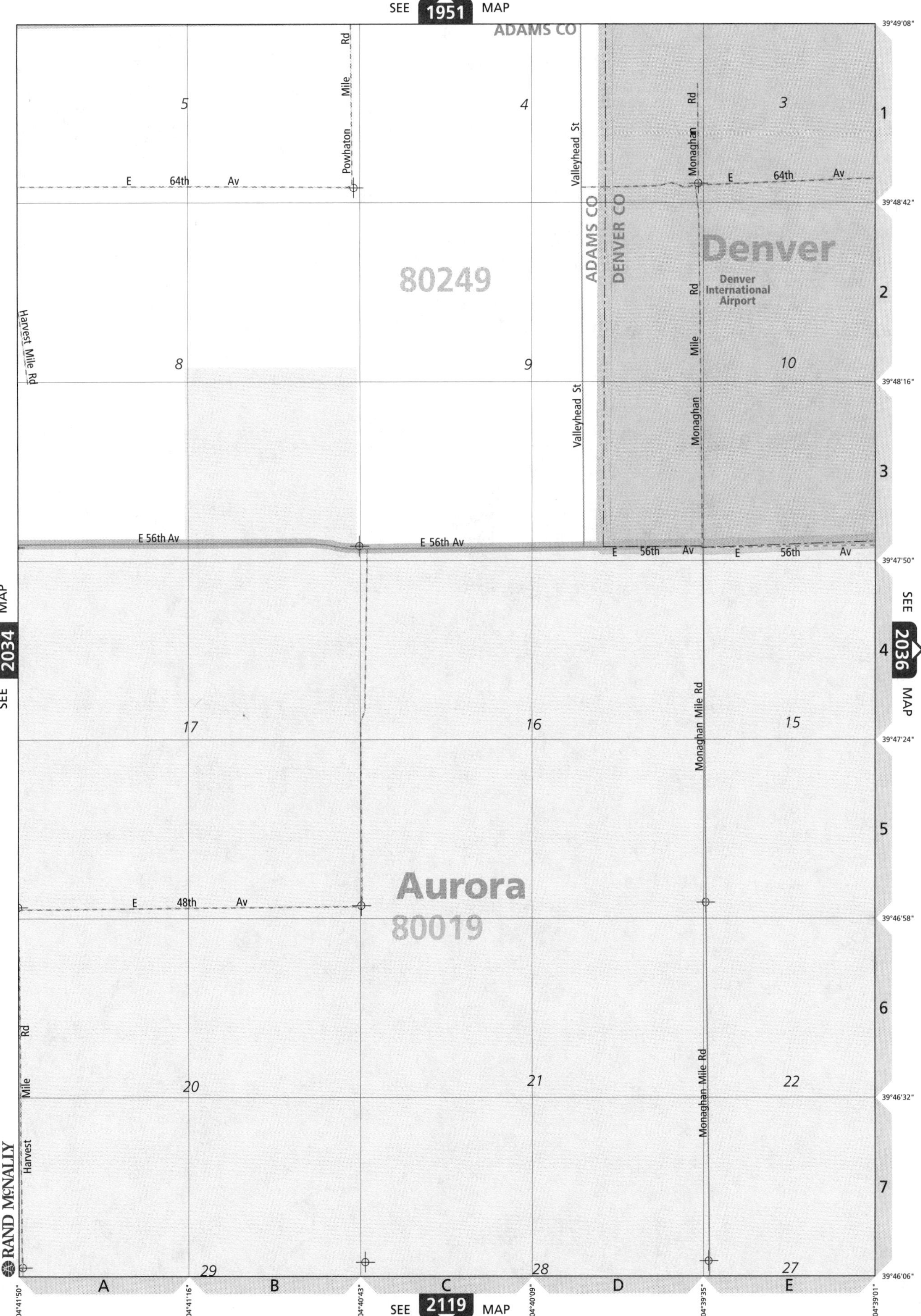

SEE 2034 MAP

SEE 2036 MAP

SEE 2119 MAP

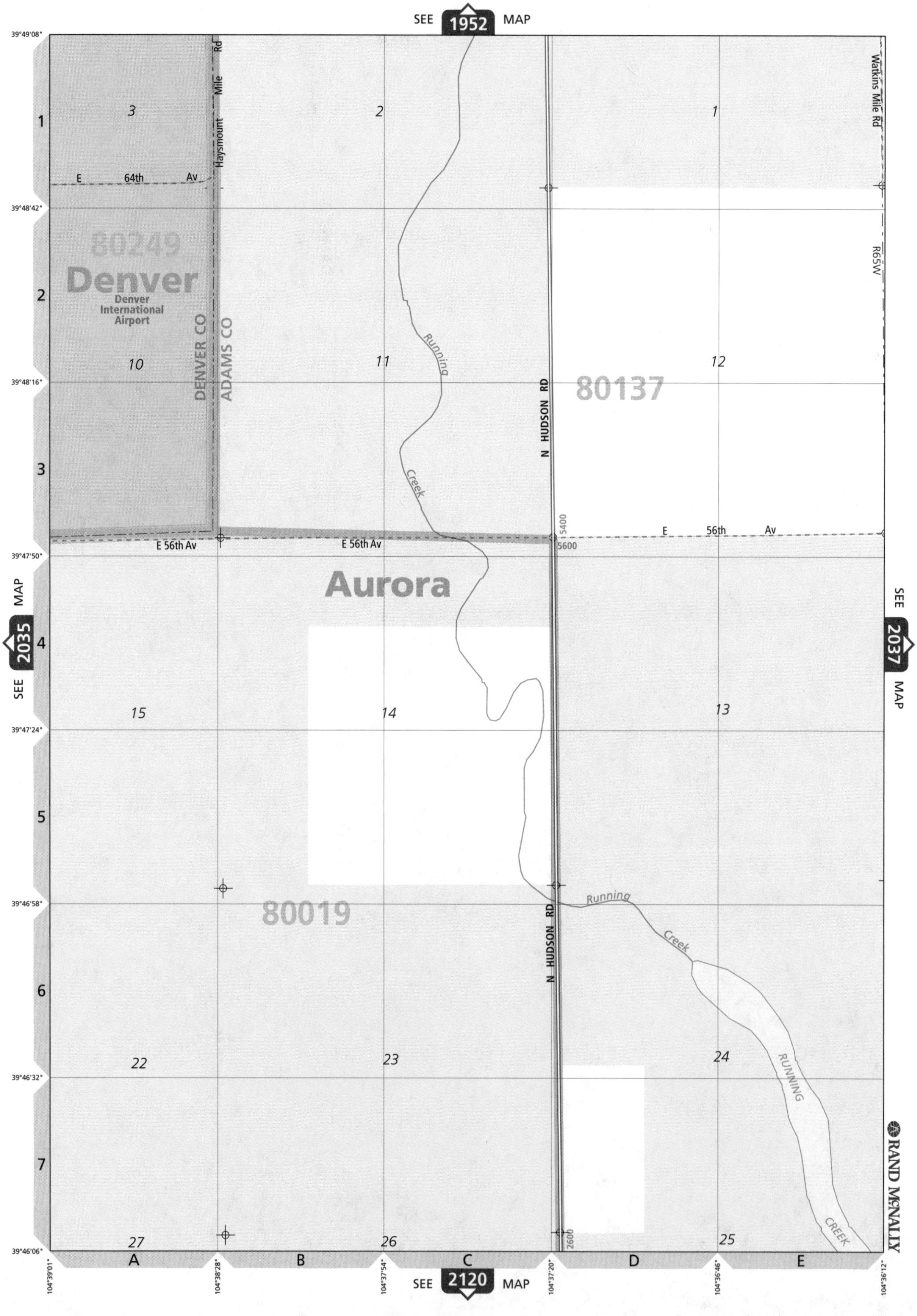

1:24,000
1 in. = 2000 ft.
0 0.25 0.5
miles

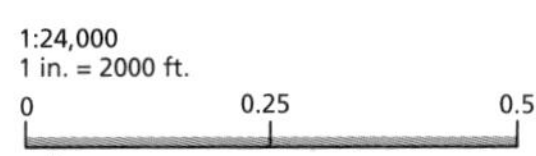

SEE 1953 MAP

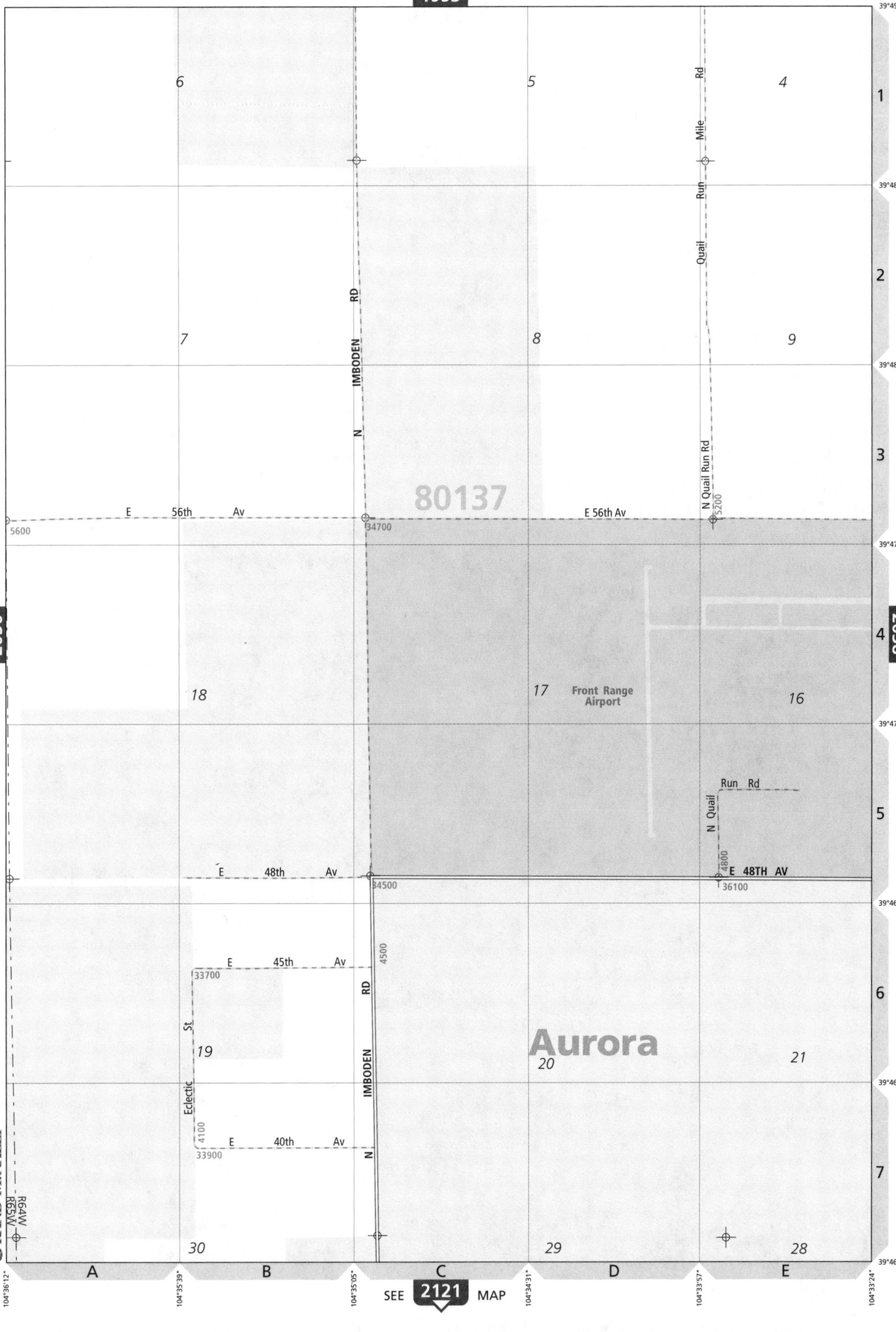

SEE 2036 MAP

SEE 2038 MAP

SEE 2121 MAP

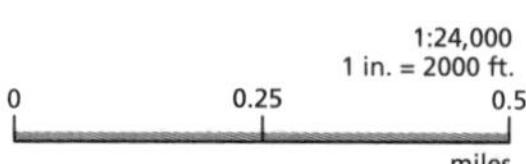

SEE B MAP

SEE MAP 2037

SEE MAP 2039

SEE 2122 MAP

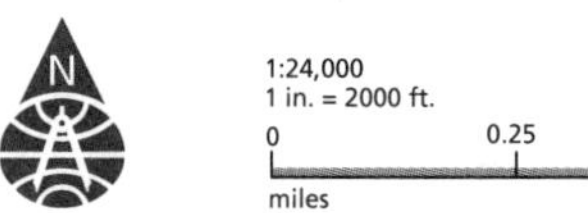

SEE B MAP

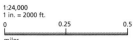

N Peterson Rd
N Schumaker Rd
E 64th Av
42500
1
6
5
12
7
8
11
E 56th Av
R64W
R63W
80102
14
13
18
17
E 48th Av
41000
42000
44000
N Harback Rd
23
24
Aurora
19
20
2600
4000
E 38th Av
42500
44000
26
25
30
29
A B C D E
1 2 3 4 5 6 7
39°49'00" 39°48'34" 39°48'08" 39°47'42" 39°47'16" 39°46'50" 39°46'24" 39°45'58"
104°30'35" 104°30'01" 104°29'27" 104°28'53" 104°28'20" 104°27'46"

SEE 2038 MAP

SEE 2040 MAP

SEE 2123 MAP

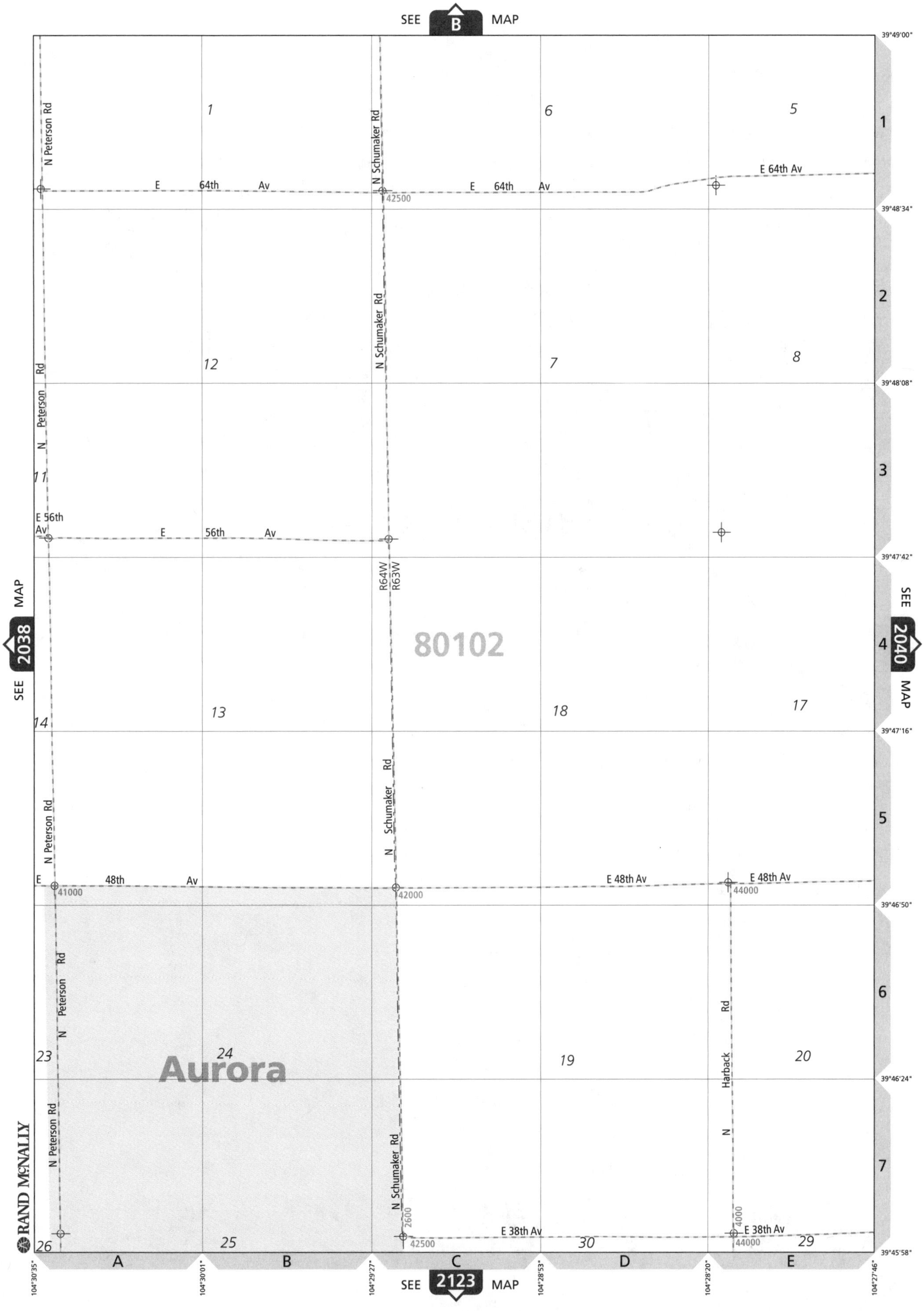

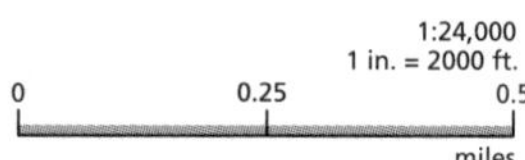

SEE B MAP

39°49'00"
39°48'34"
39°48'08"
39°47'42"
39°47'16"
39°46'50"
39°46'24"
39°45'58"

1
2
3
4
5
6
7

5
4
3
Converse Rd
E 64th Av
E 64th Av
45700
8
9
10
Penrith Rd
Converse Rd
5600
E 56th Av
E 56th Av
45700
47300
80102
17
16
15
Rd
Penrith
E 48th Av
44000
20
21
22
Penrith Rd
Converse Rd
4100
E 38th Av
E 38th Av
E 38th Av
47300
48000
Darco Dr
29
28
27
Bennett

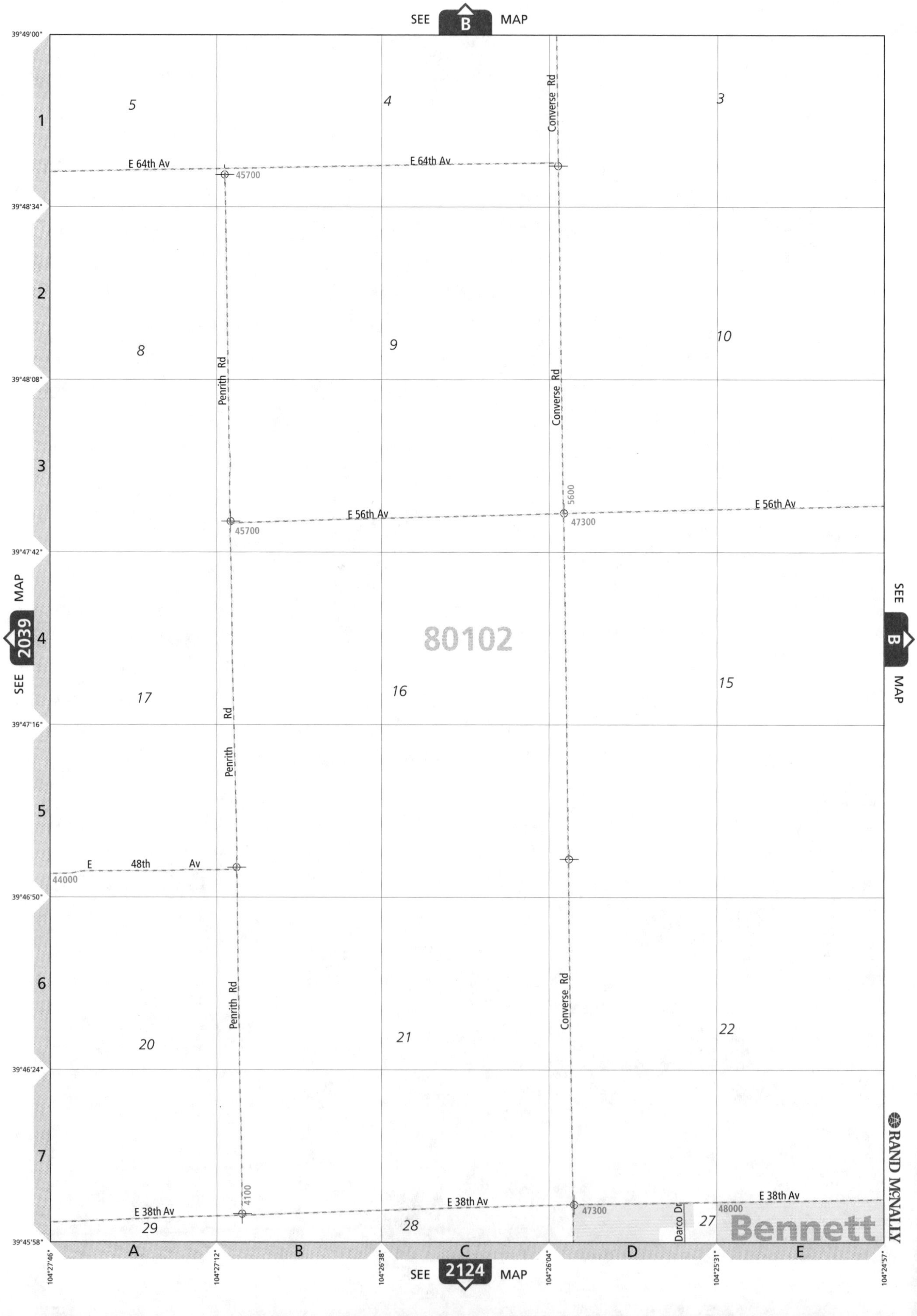

SEE 2039 MAP

SEE B MAP

A
B
C
D
E

104°27'46"
104°27'12"
104°26'38"
104°26'04"
104°25'31"
104°24'57"

SEE 2124 MAP

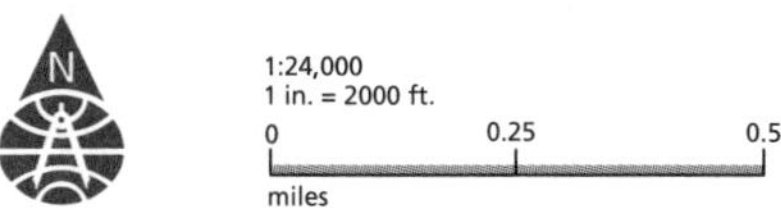

SEE 2017 MAP

SEE B MAP

SEE 2102 MAP

39°46'32"
39°46'06"
39°45'40"
39°45'14"
39°44'48"
39°44'21"
39°43'55"
39°43'29"

1
2
3
4
5
6
7

23
24
19
OH MY GOD RD
CR-281
Front Neck Mine Rd
VIRGINIA CANYON RD
GILPIN CO
CLEAR CREEK CO
80403
Elkhorn Gulch Rd
26
25
30
4600
TWO BROTHERS RD
Virginia Canyon Rd
35
36
31
R73W
R72W
80452
70
6
40
239
BUS 70
Stanley Rd
Clear Creek
High St
900
8th Av
Virginia
Wall St
Blair Dr
Illinois St
19th Av
2000
1st Av
2nd Av
3rd Av
4th Av
5th Av
6th Av
7th Av
Miner St
COLORADO BLVD
Idaho St
8th Av
9th Av
10th Av
11th Av
12th Av
13TH AV
Center
Underhill Mus
4th Av
15th Av
16th Av
17th Av
PLACER ST
Center
Mall
Water St
Idaho St
20th Av
22nd Av
23rd Av
Riverside Dr
Miner St
Water St
Argo Gold Mill & Mine Museum
Gilson Av
Riverside Dr
Riverside Dr
Clear Cr
COLORADO BLVD
BUS 70
Edwards St
25th Av
26th Av
27th Pl
Lane A
Lane B
Lane C
Lane D
Spruce
T3S
T4S
Idaho Springs Heritage Mus
Waldorf Pl
Lamertine Pl
Montane Dr
Freeland Dr
240
100
Idaho Springs
Spring Gulch Rd
Pine Slope Rd
Soda Creek Rd
300
RD
103
IDAHO SPRINGS CEM
2
CHICAGO CREEK
800
Skyline Dr
1000
1
Hidden Wilderness Rd
6
ARAPAHO NATIONAL FOREST
1300
Hidden Wilderness Rd
Soda Creek Rd
11
1100
Little Bear Creek Rd
Van Eden Rd
Van Eden Rd
1500
12
7

A
B
C
D
E

105°32'32"
105°31'59"
105°31'25"
105°30'51"
105°30'17"
105°29'44"

SEE 2185 MAP

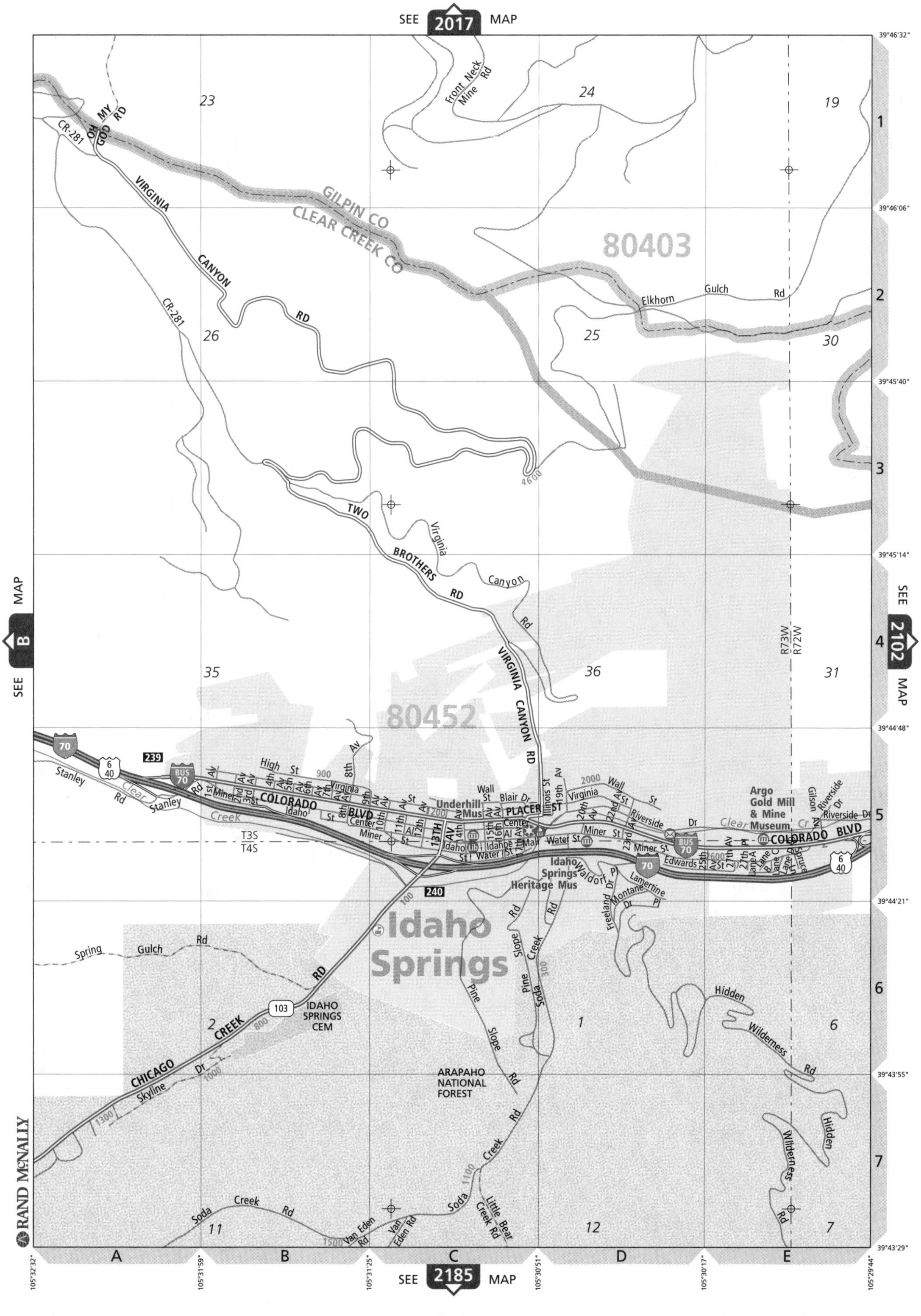

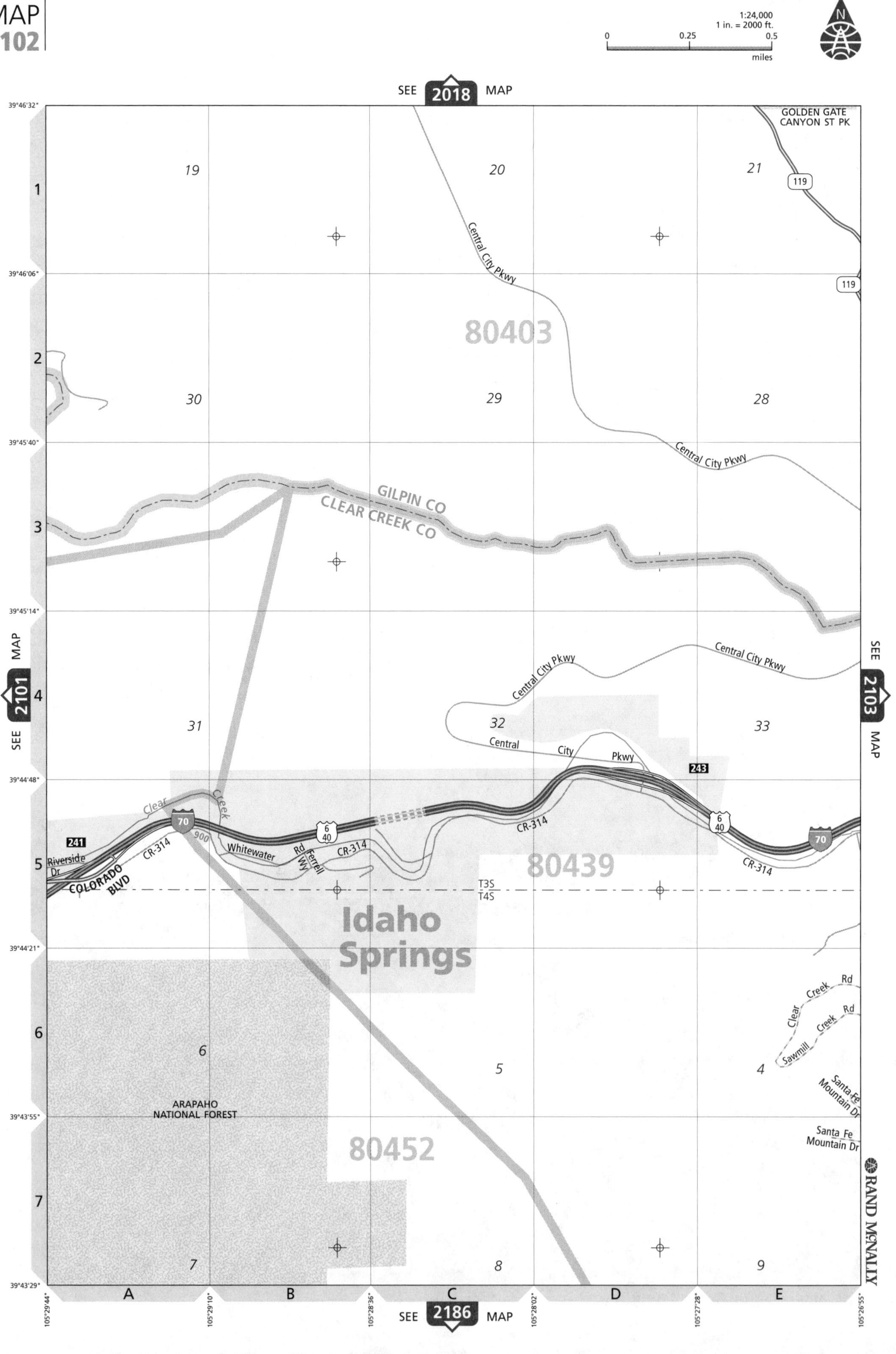

1:24,000
1 in. = 2000 ft.
0 0.25 0.5
miles

SEE 2018 MAP

SEE 2101 MAP

SEE 2103 MAP

SEE 2186 MAP

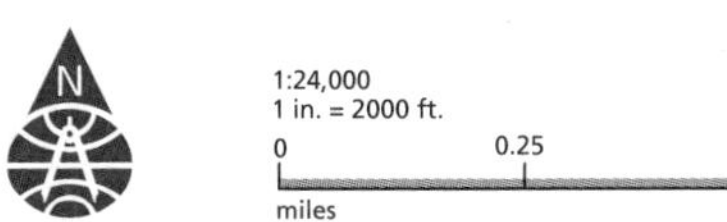

SEE 2019 MAP

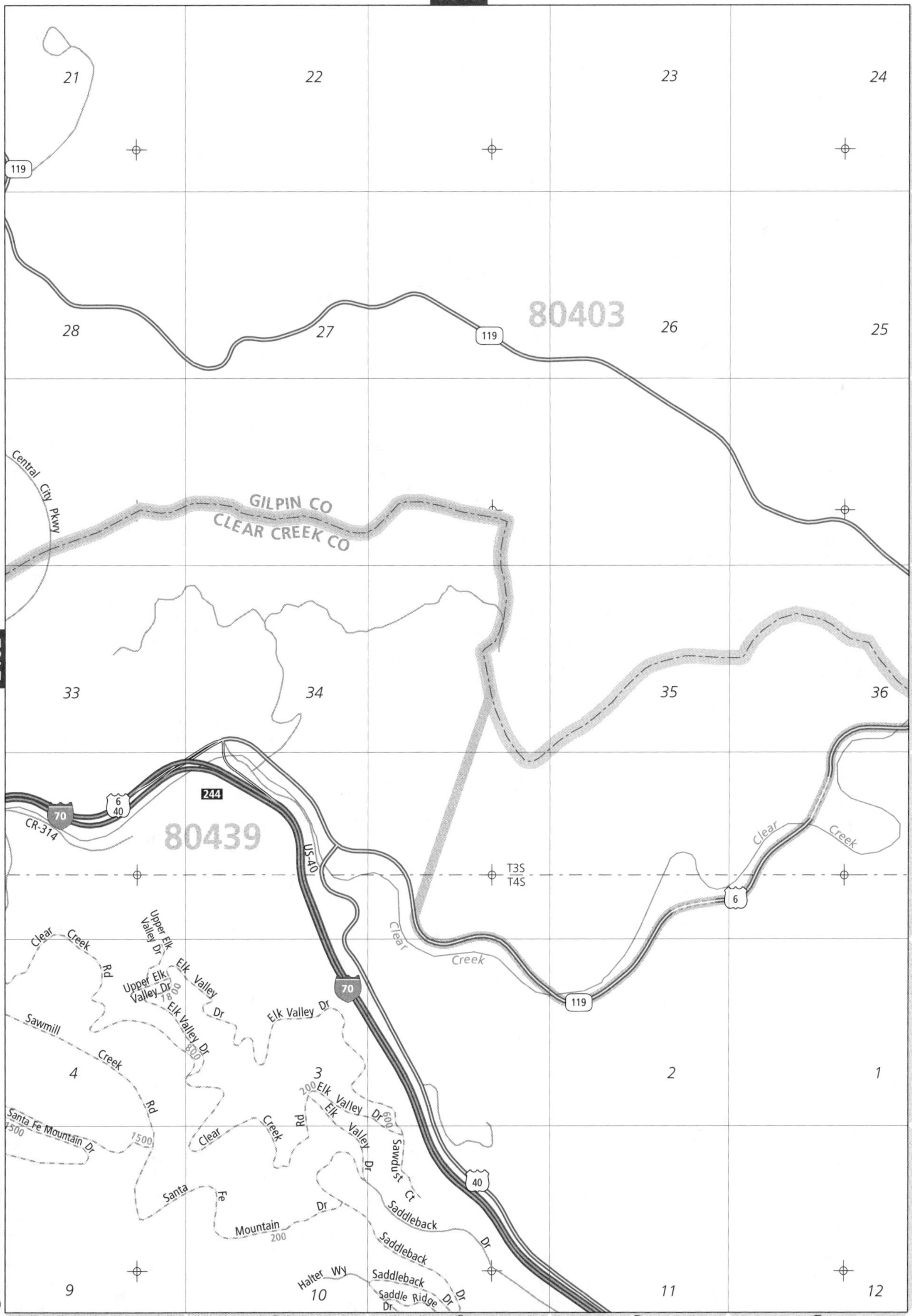

SEE 2102 MAP

SEE 2104 MAP

SEE 2187 MAP

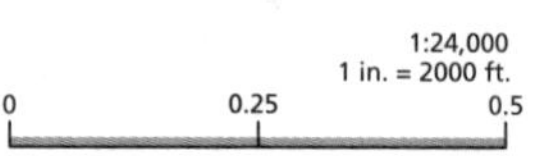

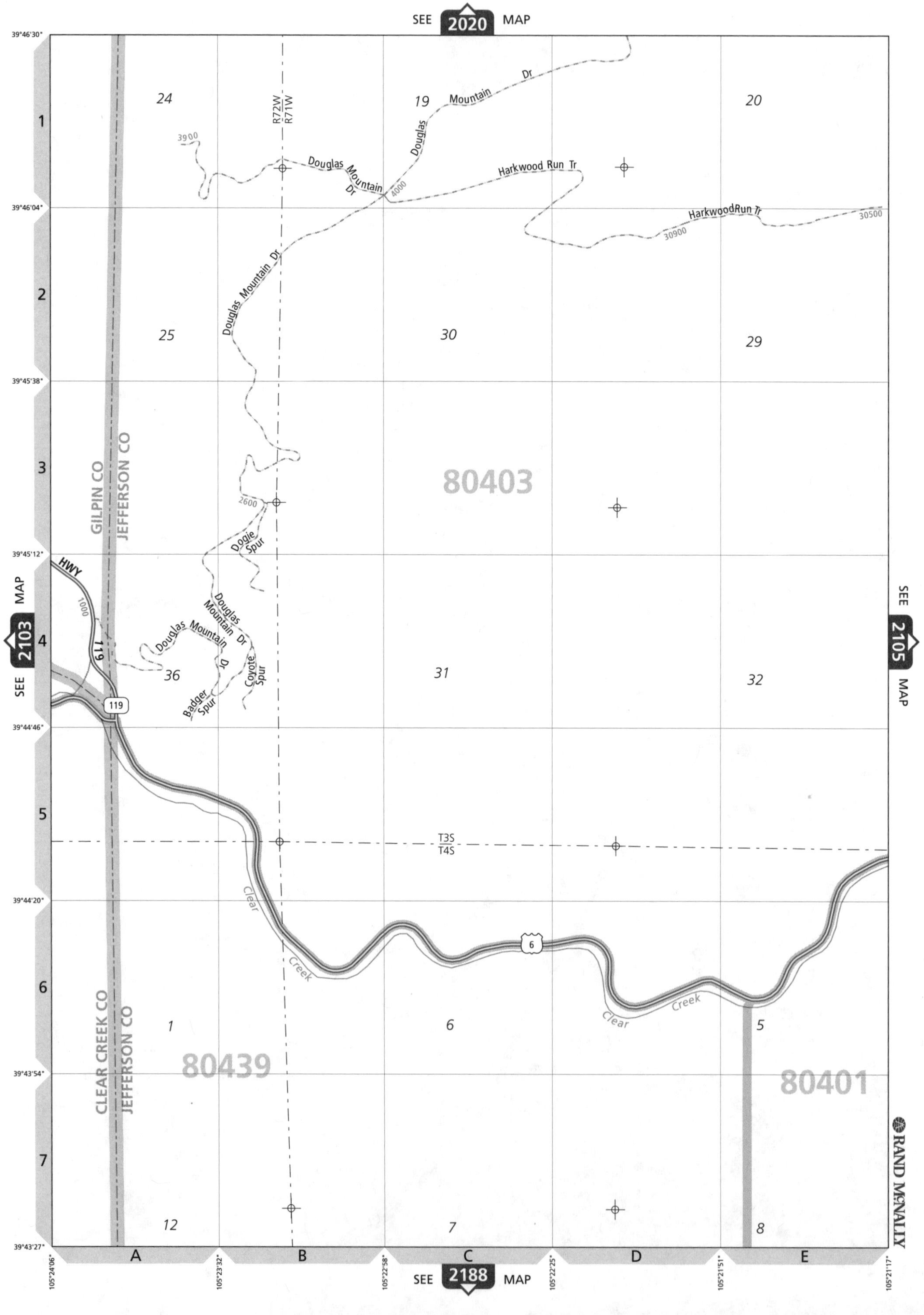

1:24,000
1 in. = 2000 ft.
0
0.25
0.5
miles
N
SEE 2020 MAP
SEE 2188 MAP
SEE 2103 MAP
SEE 2105 MAP
39°46'30"
39°46'04"
39°45'38"
39°45'12"
39°44'46"
39°44'20"
39°43'54"
39°43'27"
105°24'06"
105°23'32"
105°22'58"
105°22'25"
105°21'51"
105°21'17"
1
2
3
4
5
6
7
A
B
C
D
E
24
19
20
25
30
29
36
31
32
1
6
5
12
7
8
R72W
R71W
T3S
T4S
Douglas Mountain Dr
Douglas Mountain Dr
Douglas Mountain Dr
Douglas Mountain Dr
Douglas Mountain Dr
Douglas Mountain
Harkwood Run Tr
HarkwoodRun Tr
3900
4000
30900
30500
2600
1000
Dogie Spur
Coyote Spur
Badger Spur
HWY
119
119
6
Clear Creek
Clear Creek
GILPIN CO
JEFFERSON CO
CLEAR CREEK CO
JEFFERSON CO
80403
80439
80401
RAND McNALLY

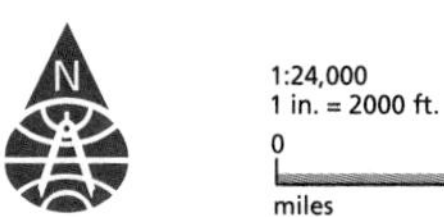

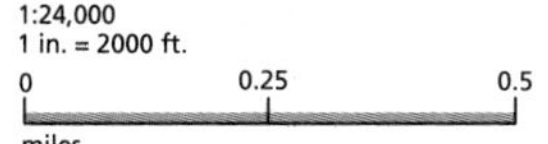

SEE 2021 MAP

SEE 2104 MAP

SEE 2106 MAP

SEE 2189 MAP

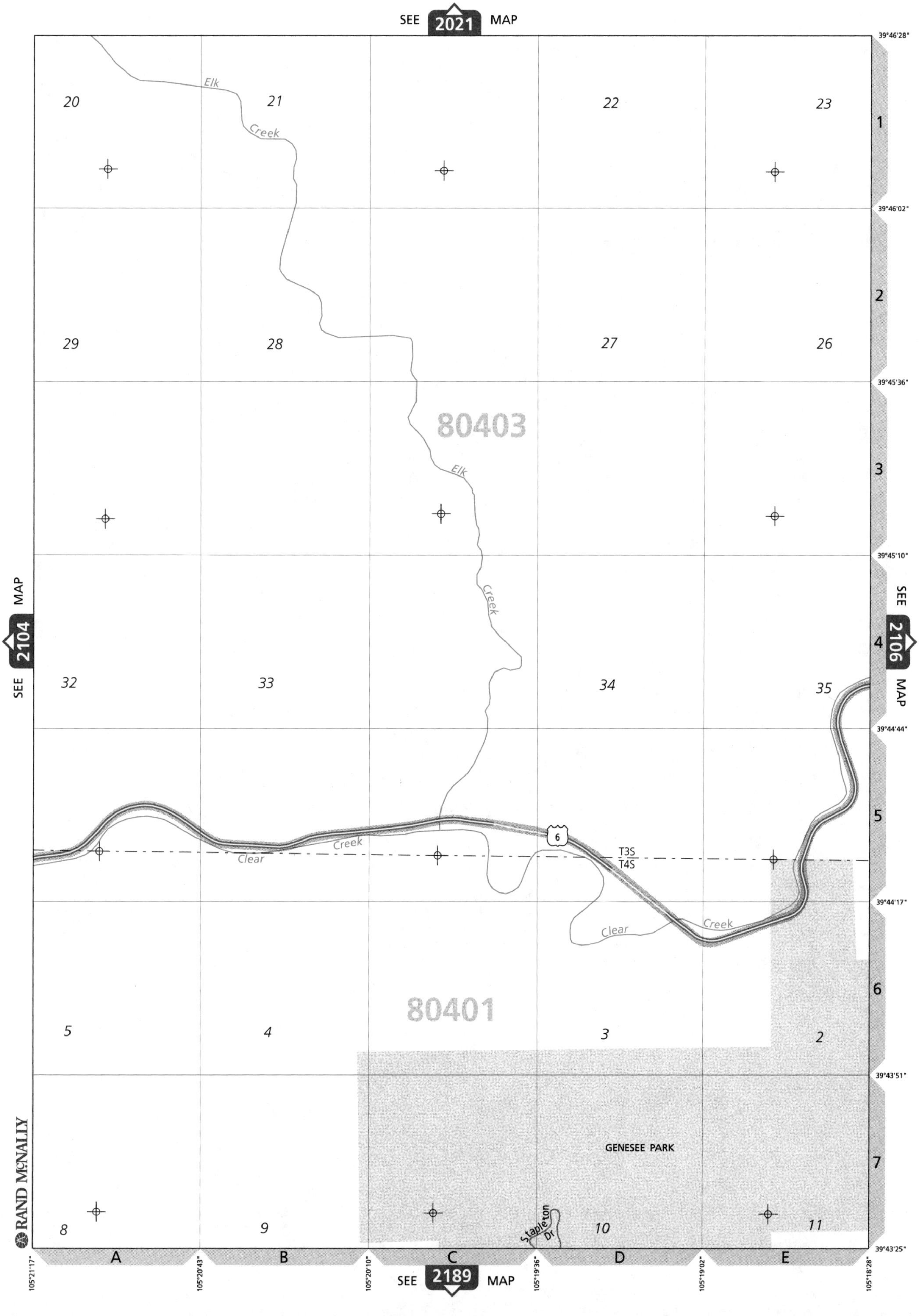

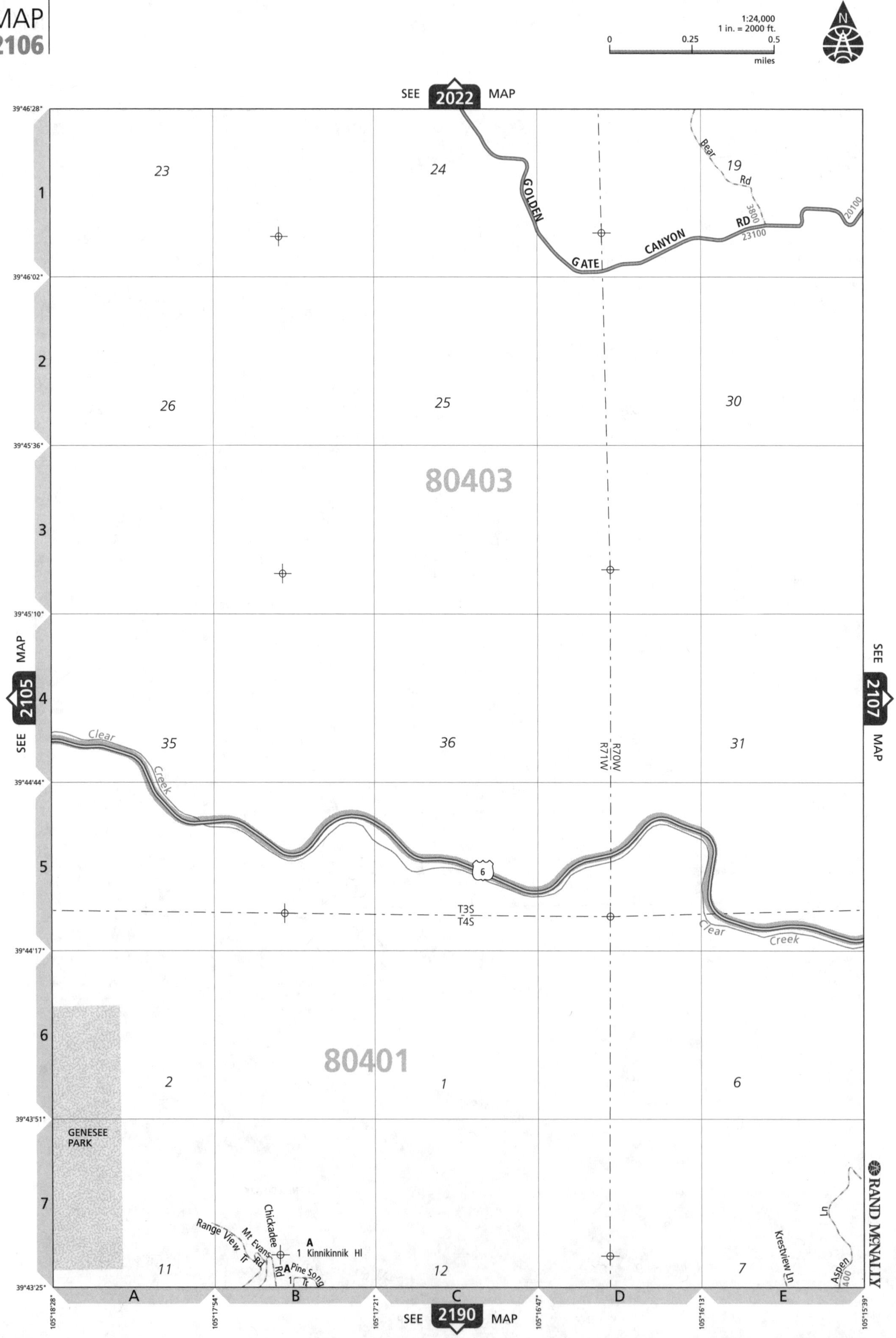

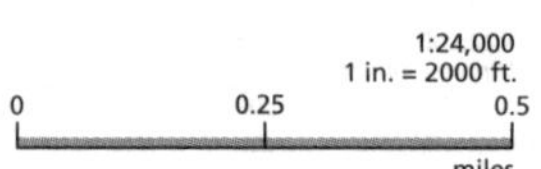

1:24,000
1 in. = 2000 ft.
0
0.25
0.5
miles
N
SEE 2022 MAP
SEE 2105 MAP
SEE 2107 MAP
SEE 2190 MAP
GOLDEN GATE CANYON RD
Bear Rd
3800
23100
20100
80403
80401
Clear Creek
6
R70W
R71W
T3S
T4S
GENESEE PARK
Range View Tr
Mt Evans Rd
Chickadee
Pine Song Tr
1 Kinnikinnik Hl
Krestview Ln
Aspen Ln
400
23
24
19
26
25
30
35
36
31
2
1
6
11
12
7
A
B
C
D
E
1
2
3
4
5
6
7
39°46'28"
39°46'02"
39°45'36"
39°45'10"
39°44'44"
39°44'17"
39°43'51"
39°43'25"
105°18'28"
105°17'54"
105°17'21"
105°16'47"
105°16'13"
105°15'39"
RAND McNALLY

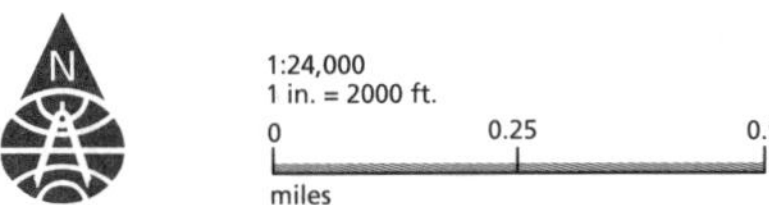

SEE 2023 MAP

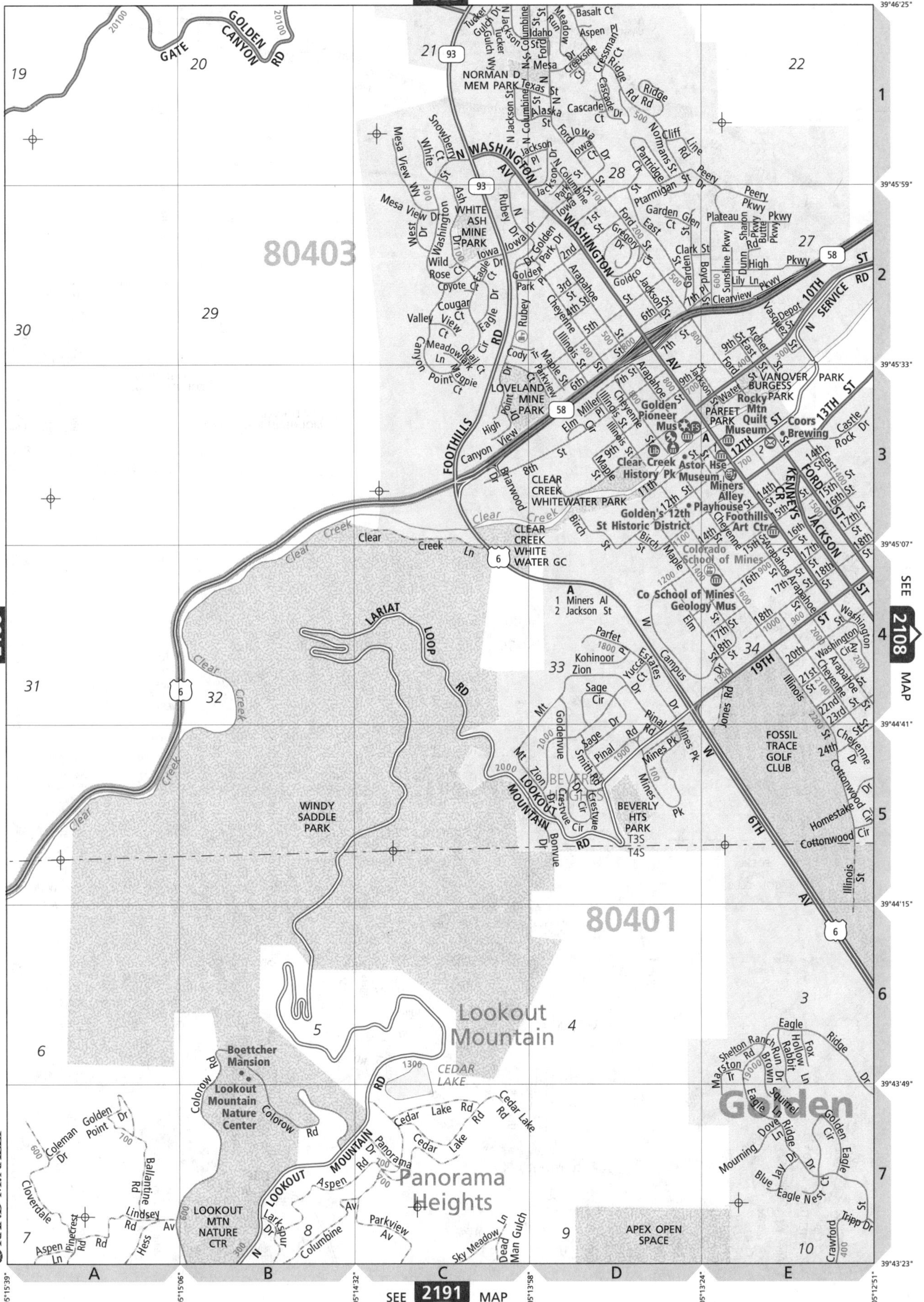

SEE 2106 MAP

SEE 2108 MAP

80403

80401

GOLDEN GATE CANYON RD

NORMAN D MEM PARK

N WASHINGTON AV

WHITE ASH MINE PARK

LOVELAND MINE PARK

FOOTHILLS RD

Golden Pioneer Mus

PARFET PARK

Rocky Mtn Quilt Museum

VANOVER BURGESS PARK

Coors Brewing

Clear Creek History Pk

Astor Hse Museum

Miners Alley Playhouse

Foothills Art Ctr

CLEAR CREEK WHITEWATER PARK

Golden's 12th St Historic District

CLEAR CREEK WHITE WATER GC

Colorado School of Mines

Co School of Mines Geology Mus

A
1 Miners Al
2 Jackson St

LARIAT LOOP RD

WINDY SADDLE PARK

BEVERLY HTS PARK

FOSSIL TRACE GOLF CLUB

T3S
T4S

Lookout Mountain

Boettcher Mansion

Lookout Mountain Nature Center

CEDAR LAKE

LOOKOUT MOUNTAIN RD

Panorama Heights

LOOKOUT MTN NATURE CTR

APEX OPEN SPACE

Golden

A B C D E

1 2 3 4 5 6 7

SEE 2191 MAP

1:24,000
1 in. = 2000 ft.
0 0.25 0.5
miles

SEE 2024 MAP

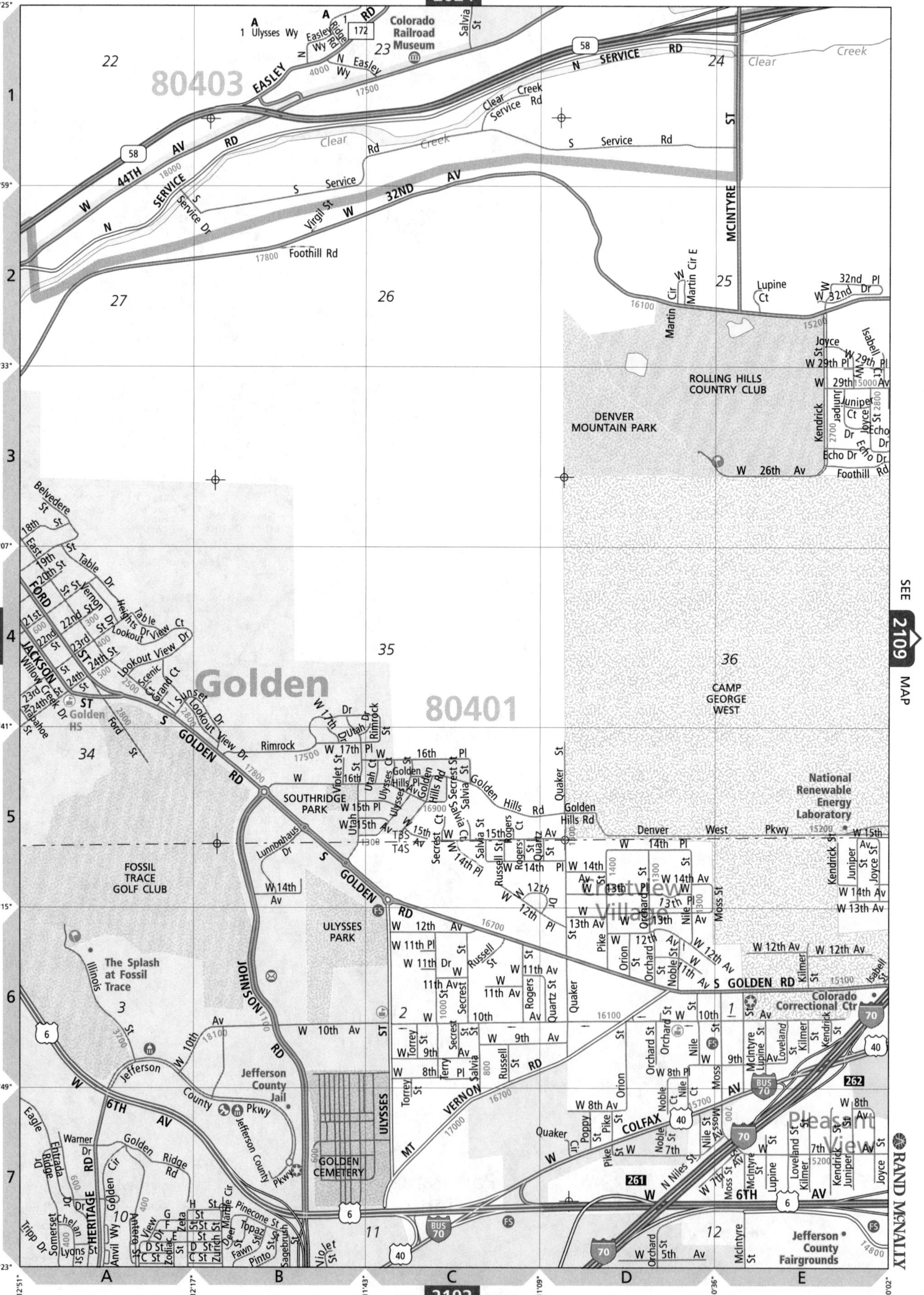

SEE 2107 MAP

SEE 2109 MAP

Colorado Railroad Museum
80403
80401
Golden
ROLLING HILLS COUNTRY CLUB
DENVER MOUNTAIN PARK
CAMP GEORGE WEST
National Renewable Energy Laboratory
SOUTHRIDGE PARK
FOSSIL TRACE GOLF CLUB
ULYSSES PARK
The Splash at Fossil Trace
Jefferson County Jail
GOLDEN CEMETERY
Colorado Correctional Ctr
Pleasant View
Jefferson County Fairgrounds
Golden HS

W 44TH AV
N SERVICE RD
W 32ND AV
MCINTYRE ST
S GOLDEN RD
JOHNSON RD
ULYSSES ST
MT VERNON RD
COLFAX AV
W 6TH AV
HERITAGE RD
FORD ST
JACKSON ST
EASLEY RD
W 6TH AV
Clear Creek

SEE 2192 MAP

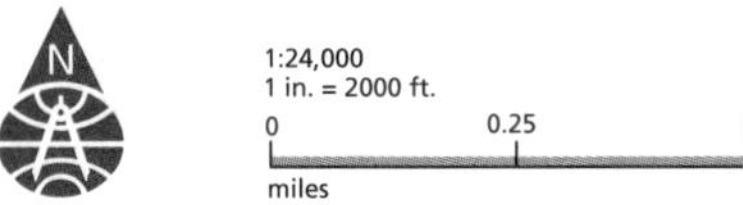

SEE 2025 MAP

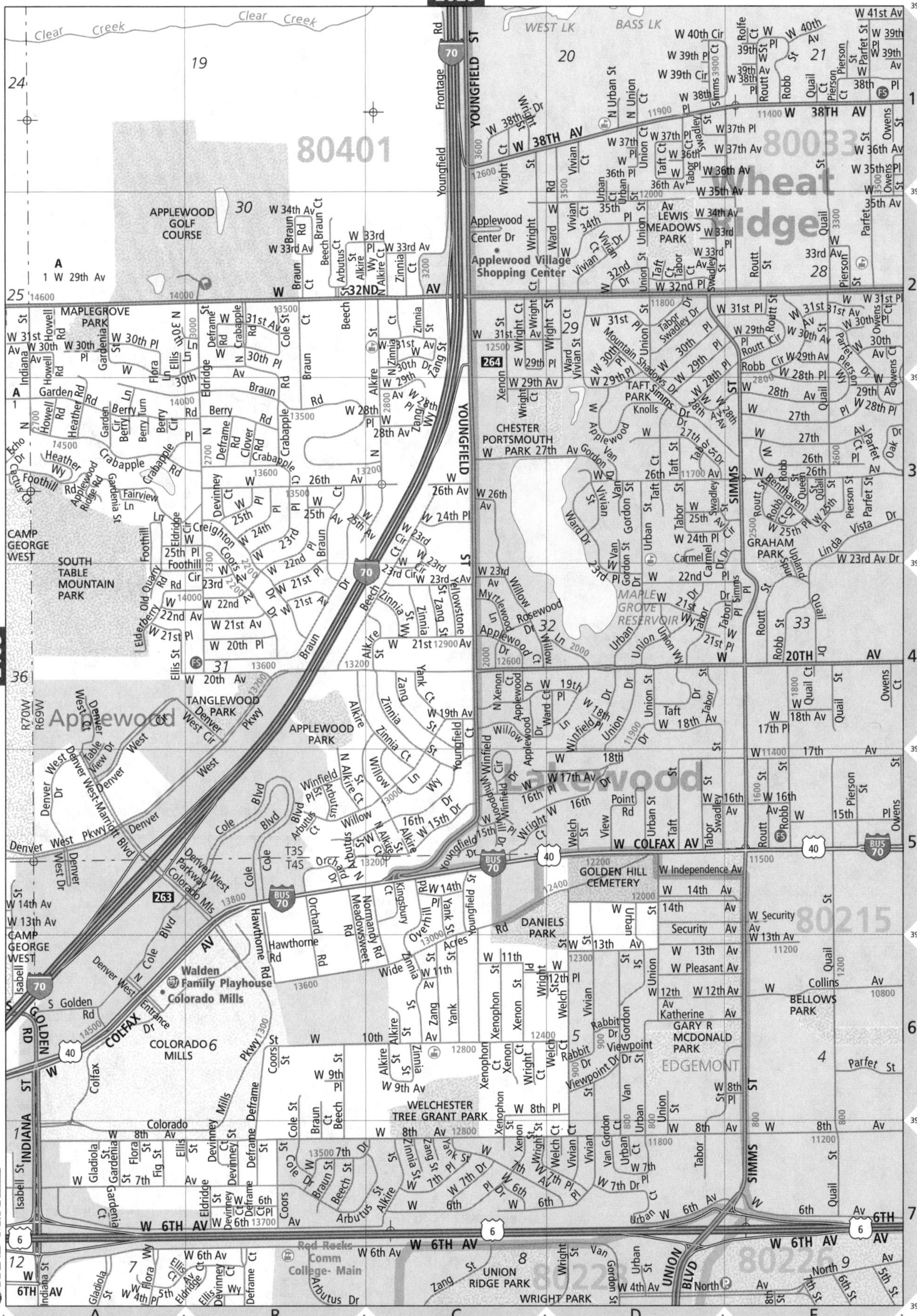

SEE 2108 MAP

SEE 2110 MAP

Applewood

Wheat Ridge

Lakewood

EDGEMONT

80401

80033

80215

80228

80226

APPLEWOOD GOLF COURSE

MAPLEGROVE PARK

CAMP GEORGE WEST

SOUTH TABLE MOUNTAIN PARK

TANGLEWOOD PARK

APPLEWOOD PARK

Applewood Village Shopping Center

LEWIS MEADOWS PARK

TAFT PARK

CHESTER PORTSMOUTH PARK

GRAHAM PARK

MAPLE GROVE RESERVOIR

GOLDEN HILL CEMETERY

DANIELS PARK

BELLOWS PARK

GARY R MCDONALD PARK

Walden Family Playhouse

Colorado Mills

COLORADO MILLS

WELCHESTER TREE GRANT PARK

Red Rocks Comm College - Main

UNION RIDGE PARK

WRIGHT PARK

Clear Creek

WEST LK

BASS LK

YOUNGFIELD ST

W 38TH AV

W 32ND AV

W 20TH AV

W COLFAX AV

W 6TH AV

SIMMS ST

INDIANA ST

UNION BLVD

A B C D E

1 2 3 4 5 6 7

SEE 2193 MAP

1:24,000
1 in. = 2000 ft.
0 0.25 0.5
miles

SEE 2026 MAP

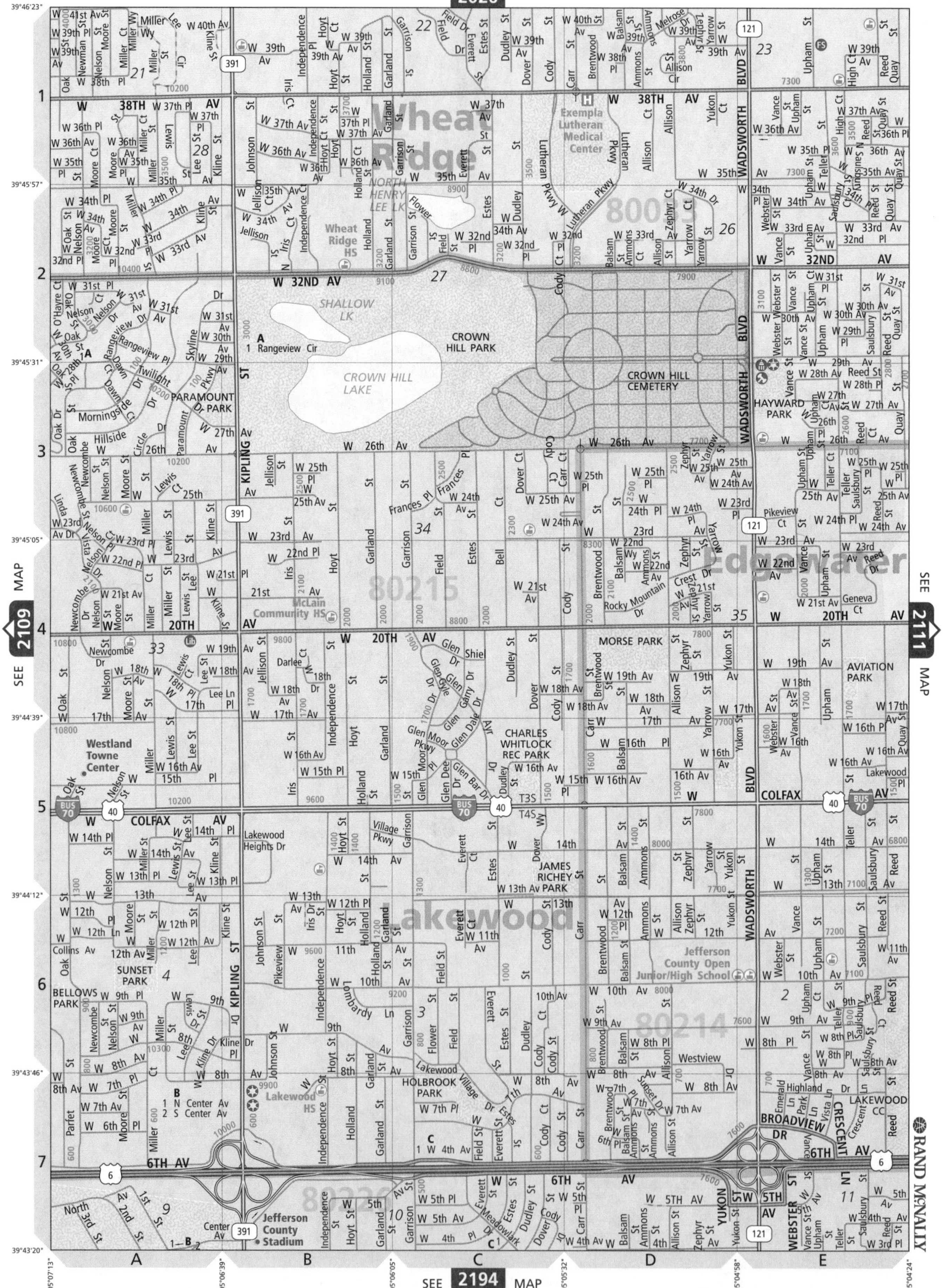

SEE 2109 MAP

SEE 2111 MAP

Wheat Ridge

Edgewater

Lakewood

Exempla Lutheran Medical Center

Wheat Ridge HS

NORTH HENRY LEE LK

SHALLOW LK

CROWN HILL PARK

CROWN HILL LAKE

CROWN HILL CEMETERY

PARAMOUNT PARK

HAYWARD PARK

McLain Community HS

MORSE PARK

AVIATION PARK

CHARLES WHITLOCK REC PARK

Westland Towne Center

JAMES RICHEY PARK

SUNSET PARK

BELLOWS PARK

Jefferson County Open Junior/High School

HOLBROOK PARK

Lakewood HS

LAKEWOOD CC

Jefferson County Stadium

W 38TH AV

W 32ND AV

W 26th Av

W 20TH AV

W COLFAX AV

6TH AV

KIPLING ST

WADSWORTH BLVD

80033 80215 80214 80226

A 1 Rangeview Cir

B 1 N Center Av 2 S Center Av

C 1 W 4th Av

39°46'23" 39°45'57" 39°45'31" 39°45'05" 39°44'39" 39°44'12" 39°43'46" 39°43'20"

105°07'13" 105°06'39" 105°06'05" 105°05'32" 105°04'58" 105°04'24"

1 2 3 4 5 6 7

A B C D E

SEE 2194 MAP

1:24,000
1 in. = 2000 ft.
0 0.25 0.5
miles

SEE 2027 MAP

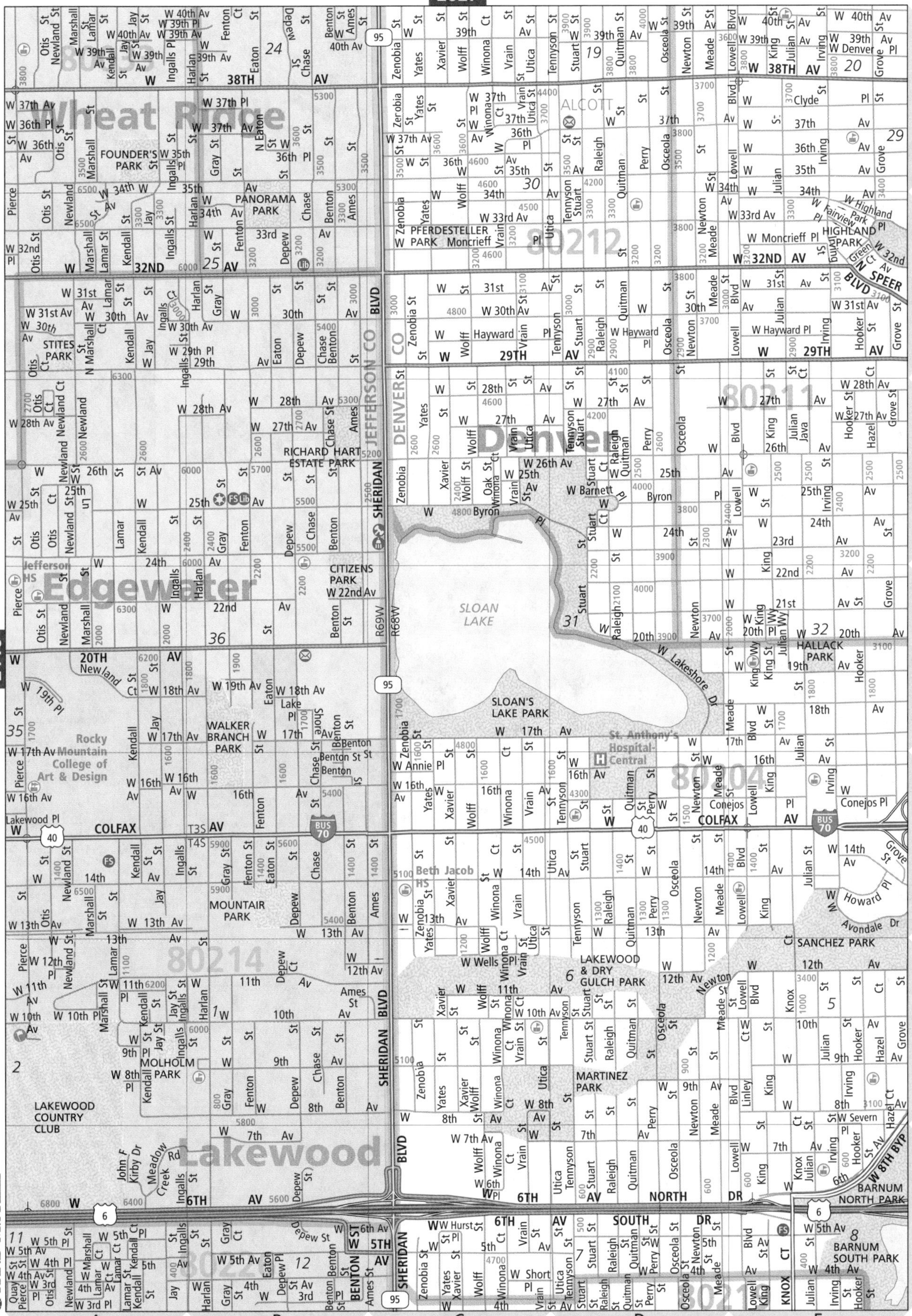

SEE 2110 MAP

SEE 2112 MAP

SEE 2195 MAP

Wheat Ridge
Edgewater
Lakewood
Denver
ALCOTT
SLOAN LAKE
SLOAN'S LAKE PARK
FOUNDER'S PARK
PANORAMA PARK
STITES PARK
RICHARD HART ESTATE PARK
CITIZENS PARK
Jefferson HS
PFERDESTELLER PARK
HIGHLAND PARK
HALLACK PARK
WALKER BRANCH PARK
Rocky Mountain College of Art & Design
St. Anthony's Hospital-Central
MOUNTAIN PARK
Beth Jacob HS
SANCHEZ PARK
LAKEWOOD & DRY GULCH PARK
MOLHOLM PARK
MARTINEZ PARK
LAKEWOOD COUNTRY CLUB
BARNUM NORTH PARK
BARNUM SOUTH PARK
JEFFERSON CO
DENVER CO
80033 80212 80211 80204 80214 80226 80219

39°46'20" 39°45'54" 39°45'28" 39°45'02" 39°44'36" 39°44'10" 39°43'44" 39°43'17"
105°04'24" 105°03'50" 105°03'17" 105°02'43" 105°02'09" 105°01'35"

A B C D E
1 2 3 4 5 6 7

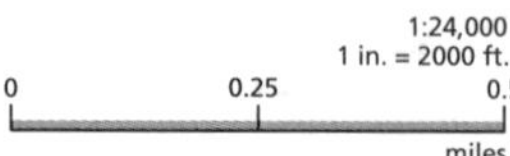

SEE 2028 MAP

SEE 2111 MAP

SEE 2113 MAP

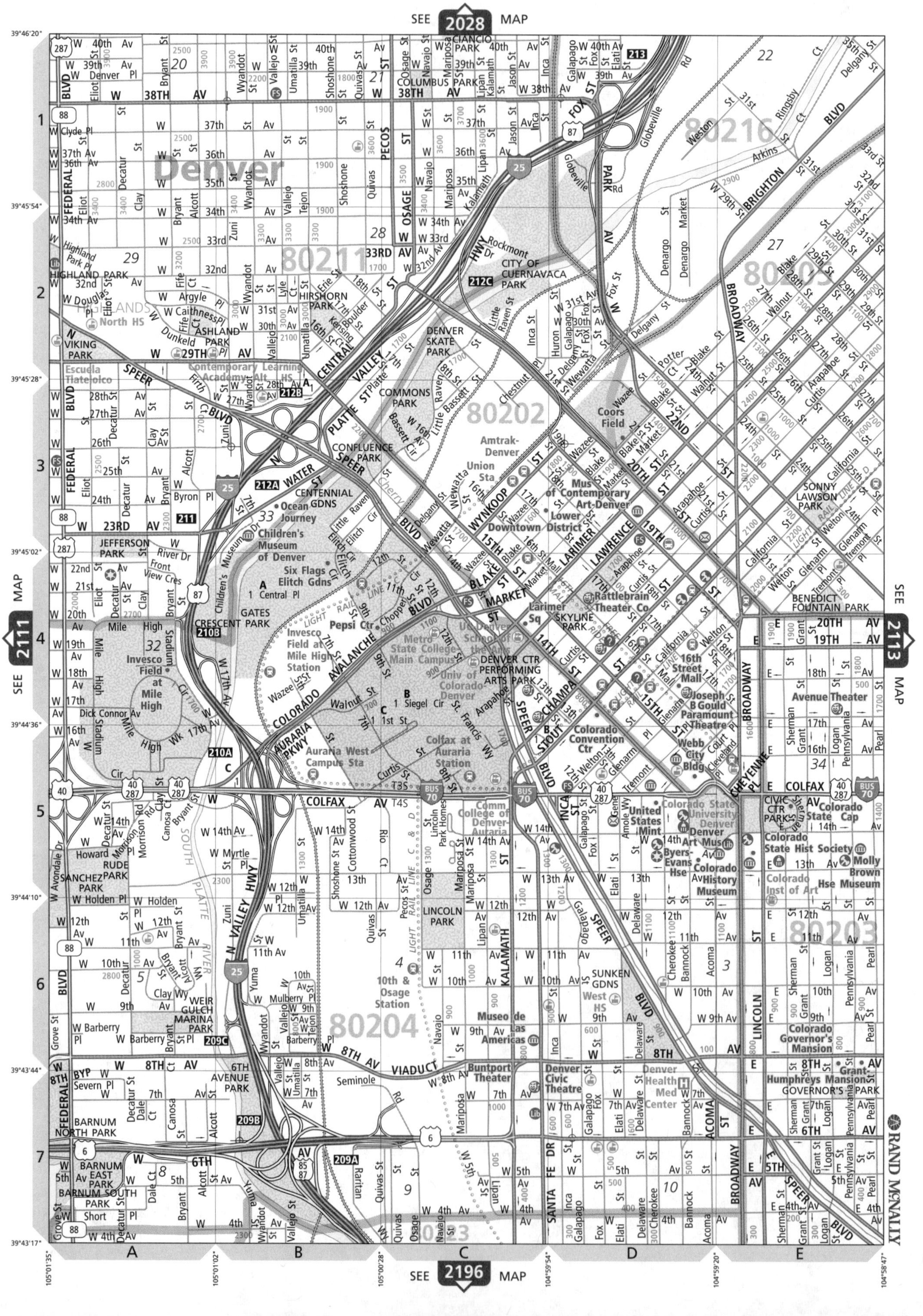

SEE 2196 MAP

1:24,000
1 in. = 2000 ft.
0 0.25 0.5
miles

SEE 2029 MAP

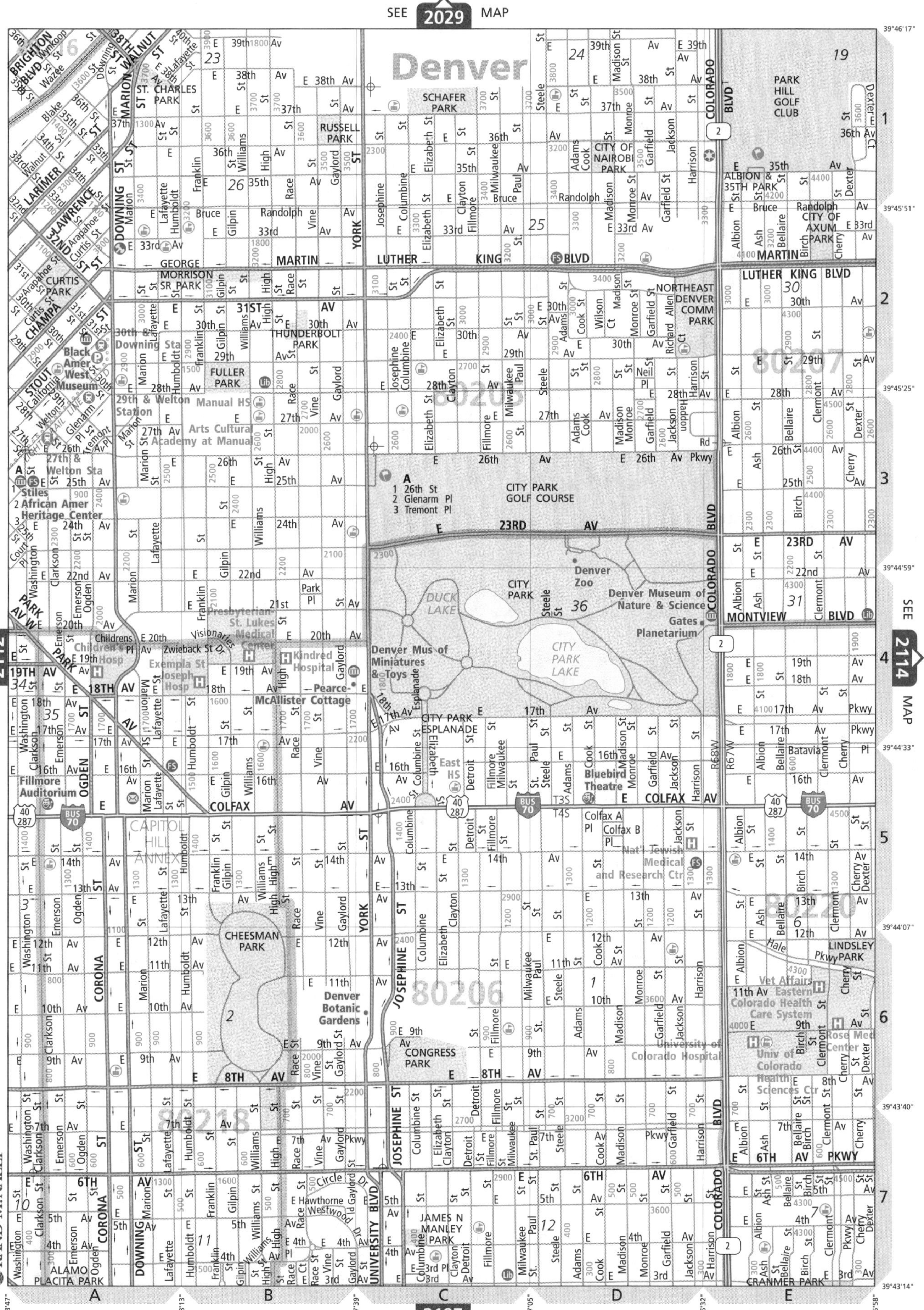

SEE 2112 MAP

SEE 2114 MAP

SEE 2197 MAP

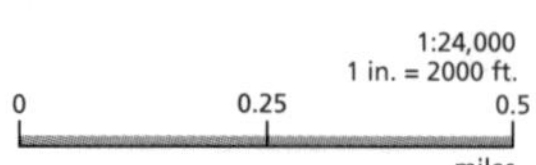

SEE 2030 MAP

Denver

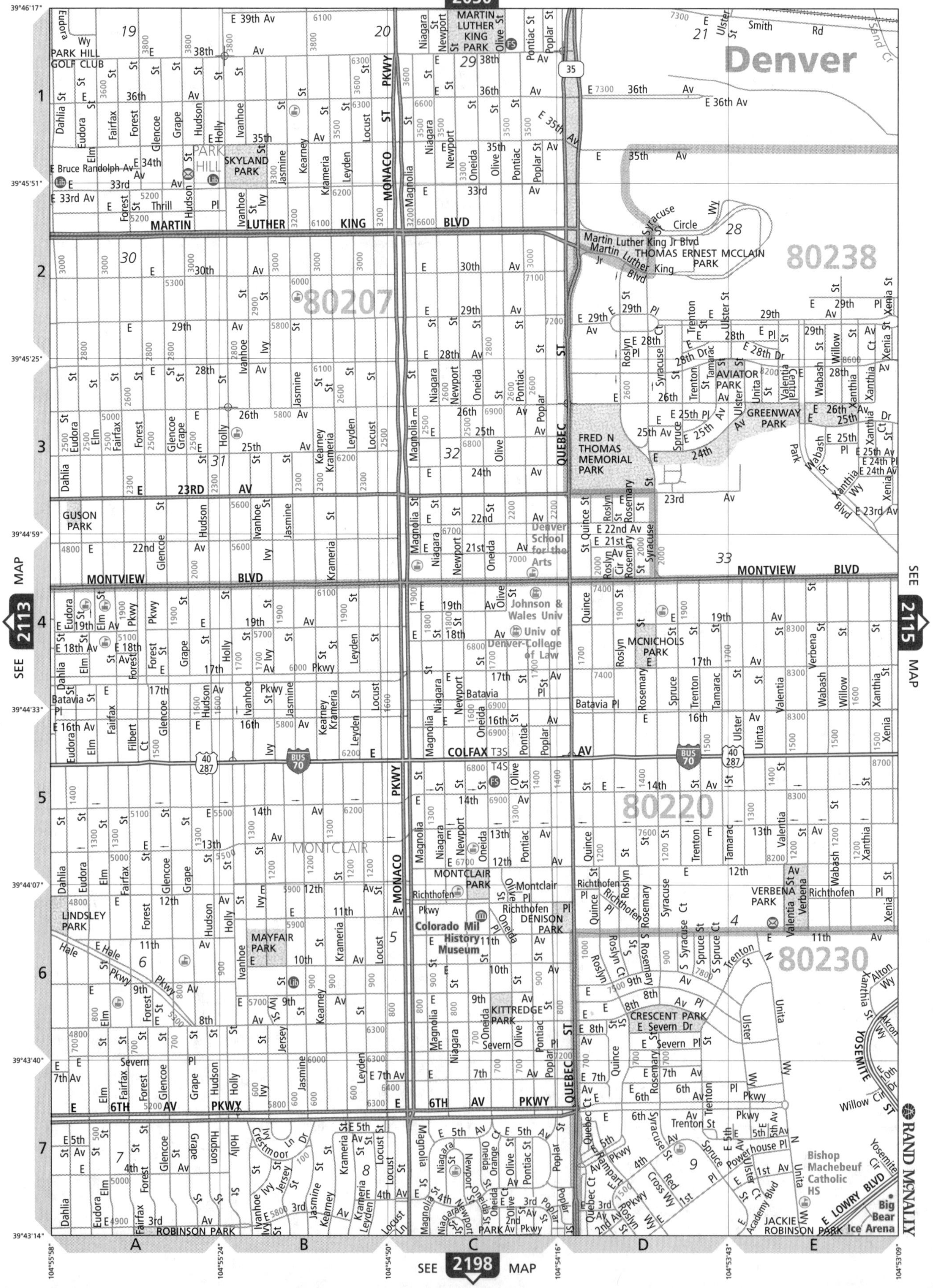

SEE 2113 MAP

SEE 2115 MAP

SEE 2198 MAP

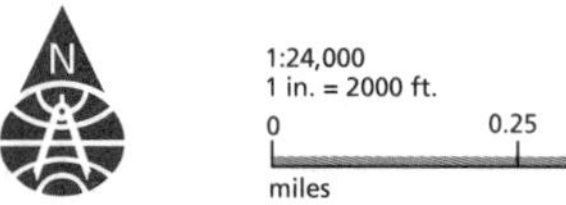

SEE 2031 MAP

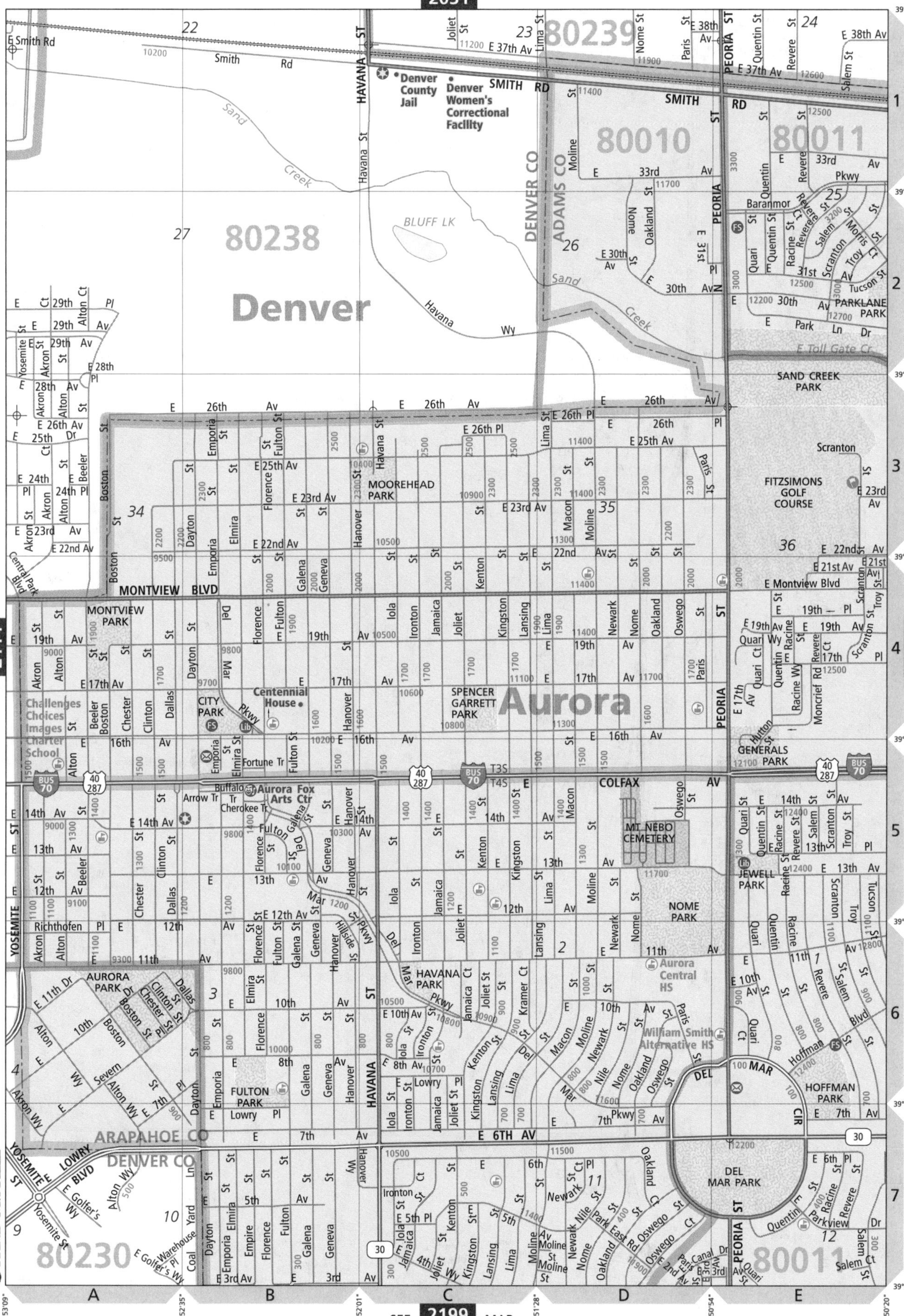

SEE 2114 MAP

SEE 2116 MAP

Denver

Aurora

SEE 2199 MAP

1:24,000
1 in. = 2000 ft.
0 0.25 0.5
miles

SEE 2032 MAP

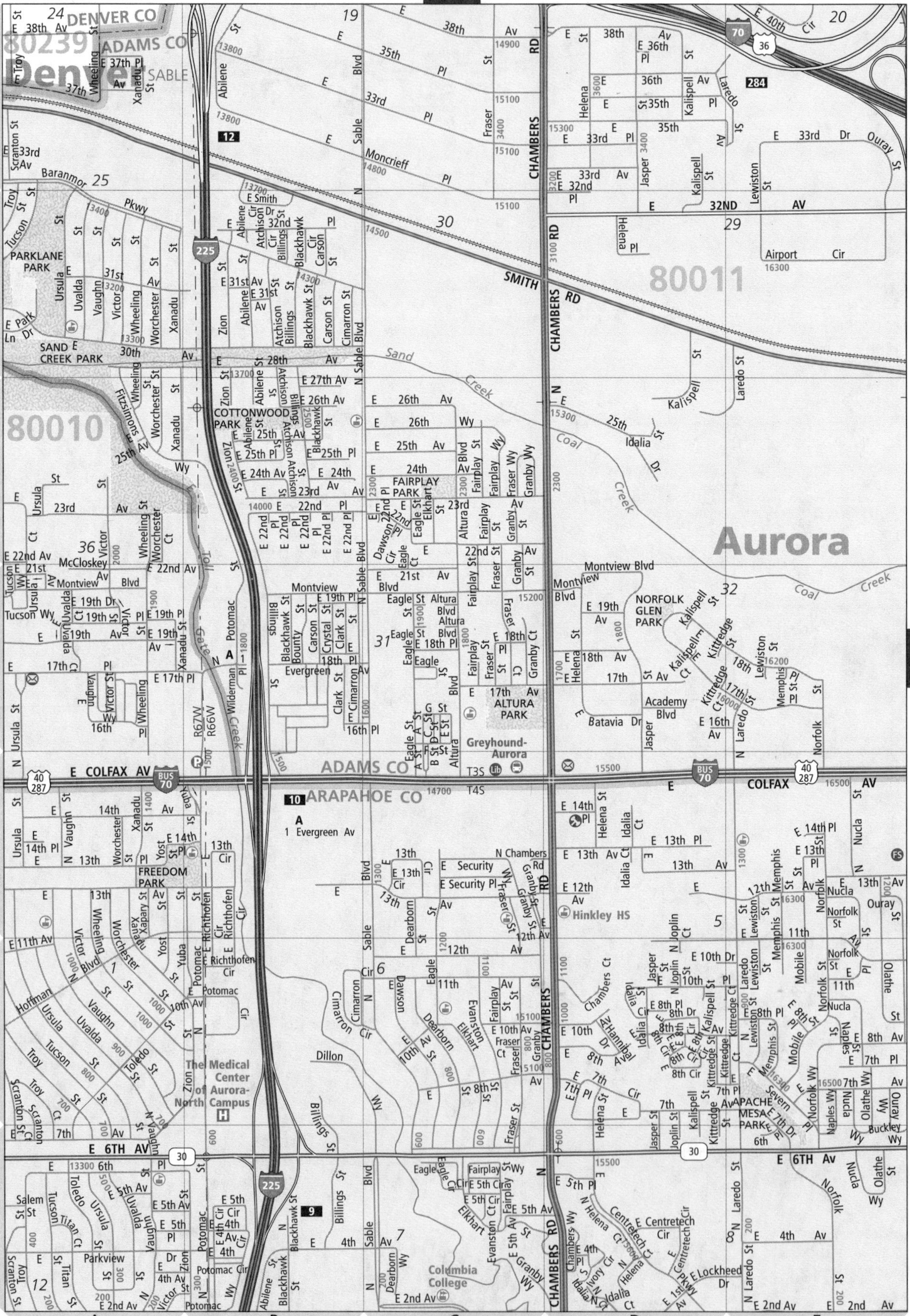

Denver
Aurora
DENVER CO
ADAMS CO
ARAPAHOE CO
80239
80011
80010

PARKLANE PARK
SAND CREEK PARK
COTTONWOOD PARK
FAIRPLAY PARK
McCloskey
NORFOLK GLEN PARK
ALTURA PARK
Greyhound-Aurora
FREEDOM PARK
The Medical Center of Aurora-North Campus
Hinkley HS
APACHE MESA PARK
Columbia College

E COLFAX AV
E 6TH AV
E 32ND AV
CHAMBERS RD
SMITH RD
Montview Blvd
Sand Creek
Coal Creek
Toll Gate Creek

SEE 2115 MAP

SEE 2117 MAP

39°46'13"
39°45'47"
39°45'21"
39°44'55"
39°44'29"
39°44'03"
39°43'37"
39°43'11"

1
2
3
4
5
6
7

104°50'20"
104°49'46"
104°49'13"
104°48'39"
104°48'05"
104°47'31"

A B C D E

SEE 2200 MAP

1:24,000
1 in. = 2000 ft.
0 0.25 0.5
miles

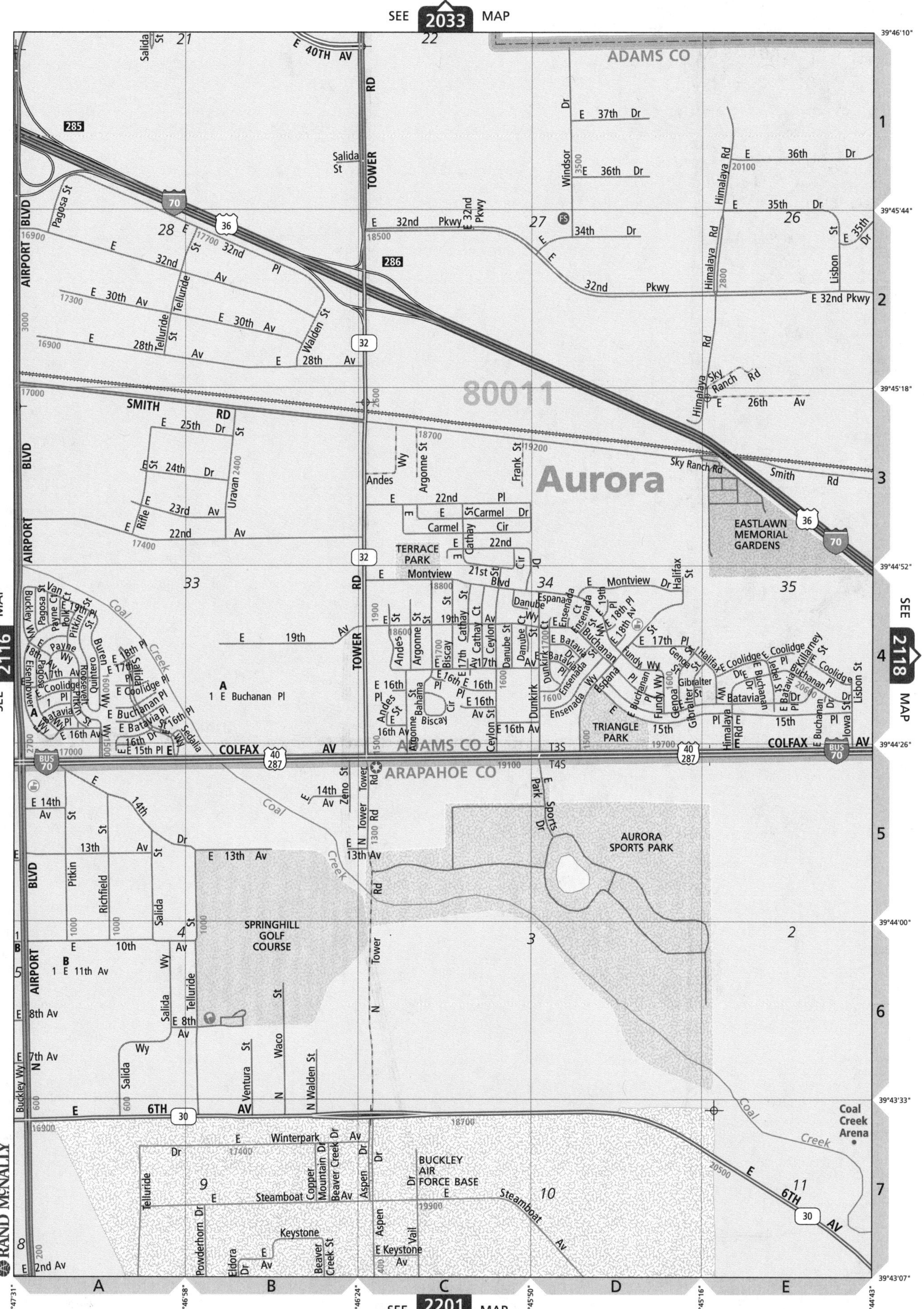

1:24,000
1 in. = 2000 ft.
0 0.25 0.5
miles

SEE 2034 MAP

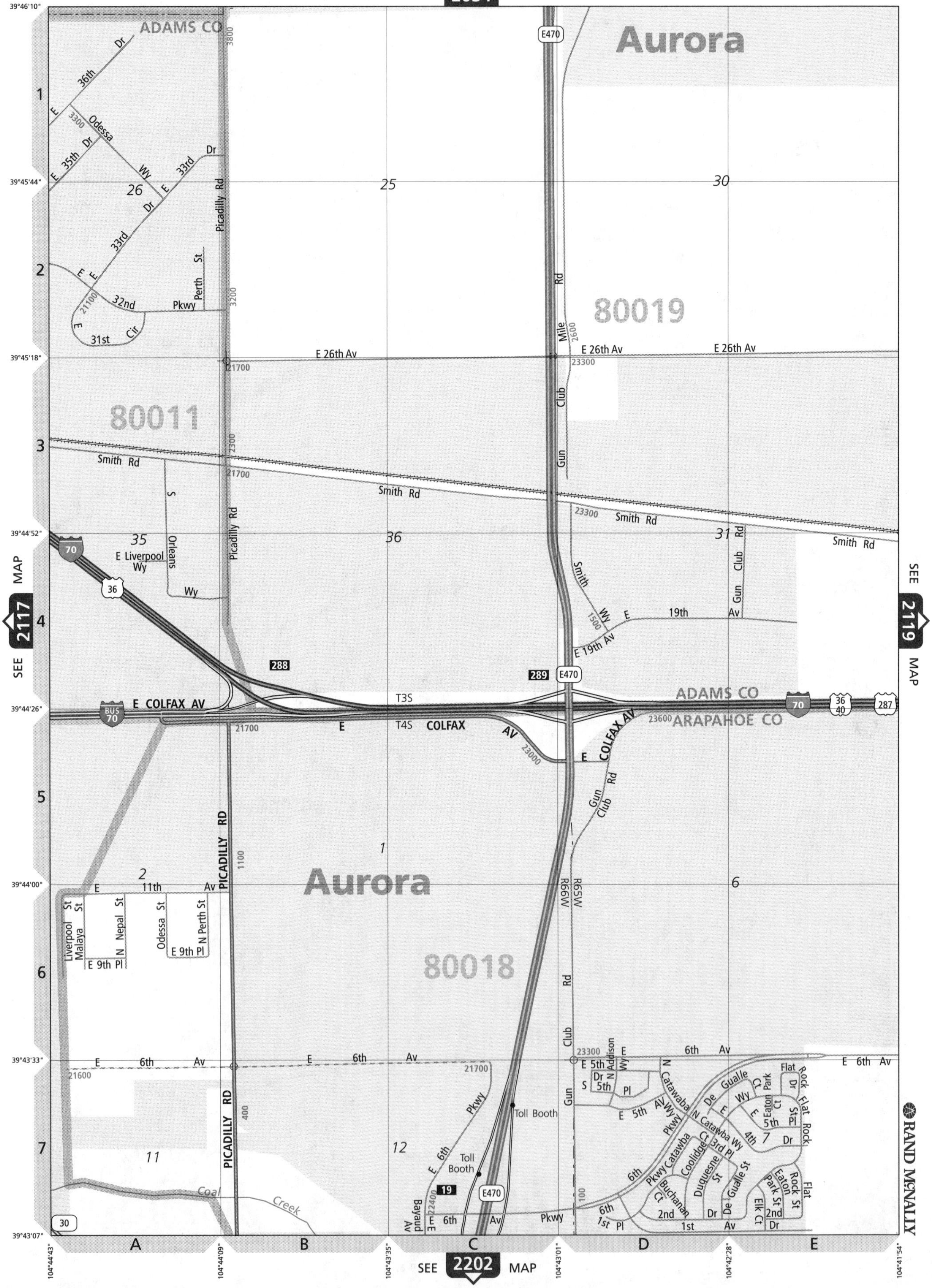

SEE 2117 MAP

SEE 2119 MAP

SEE 2202 MAP

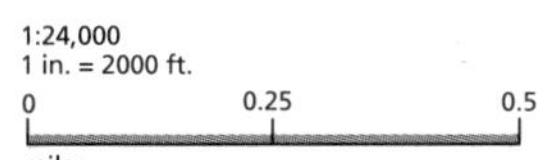

SEE 2035 MAP

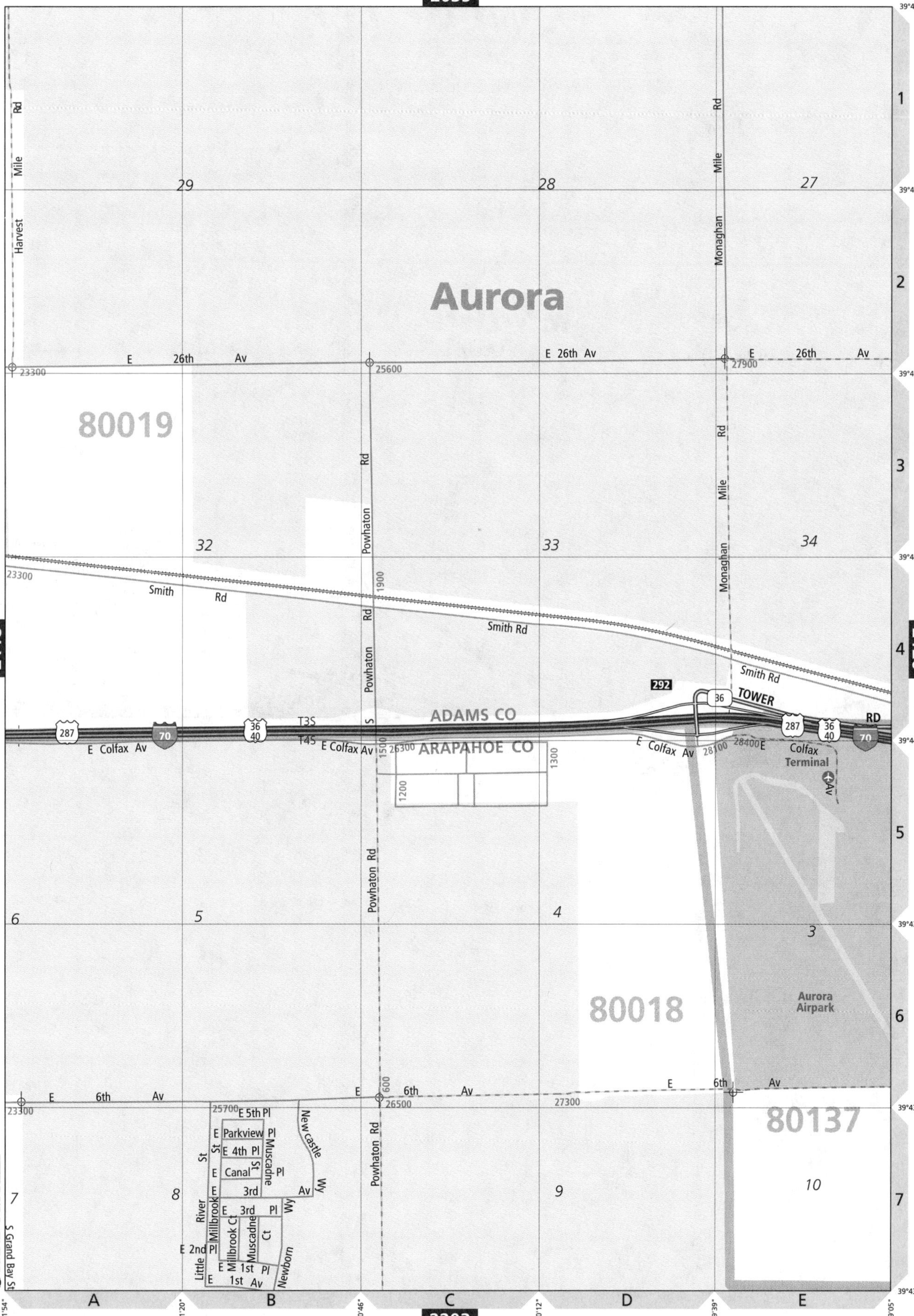

SEE 2118 MAP
SEE 2120 MAP
SEE 2203 MAP

1:24,000
1 in. = 2000 ft.
0 0.25 0.5
miles

SEE 2036 MAP

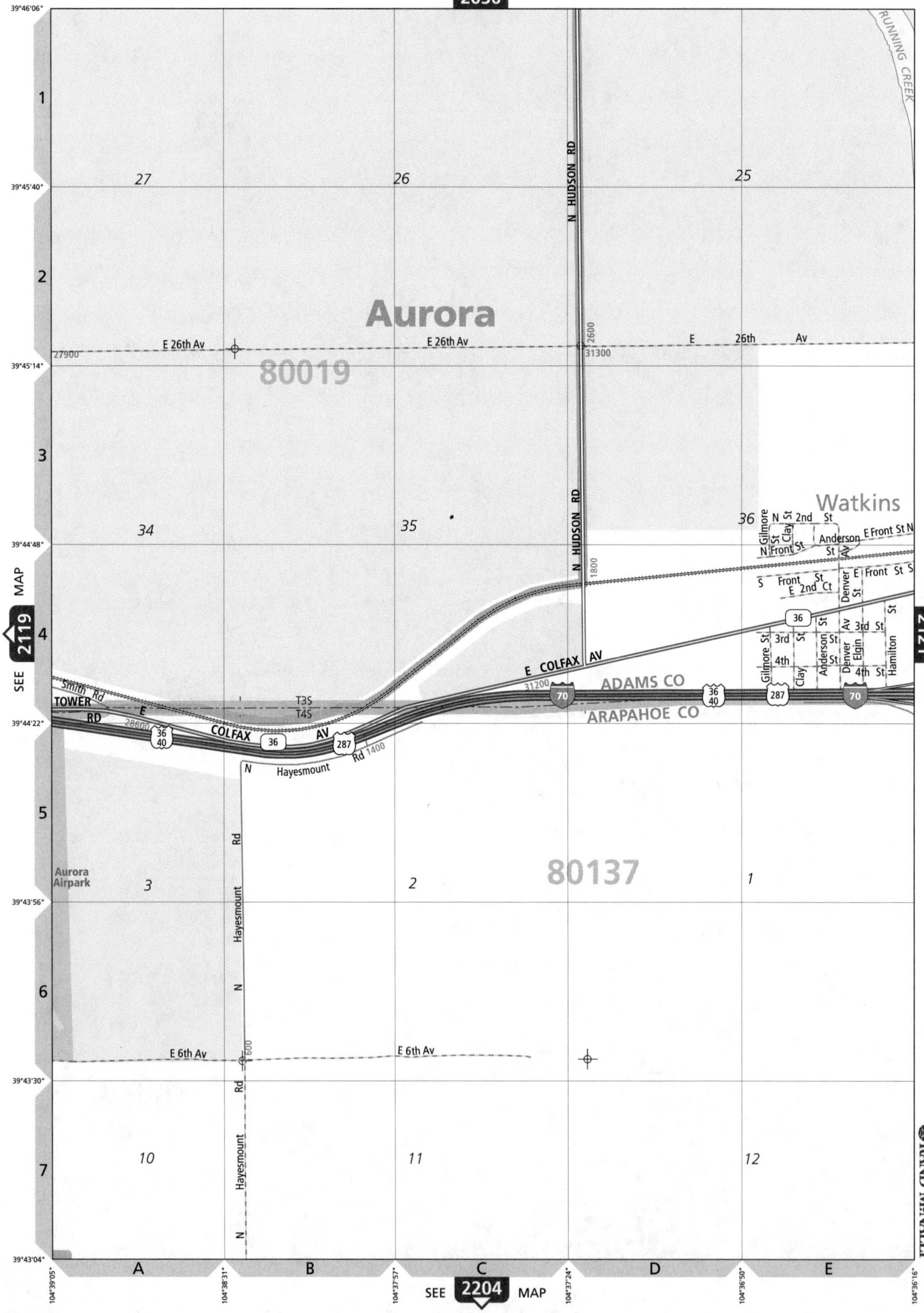

SEE 2119 MAP

SEE 2121 MAP

SEE 2204 MAP

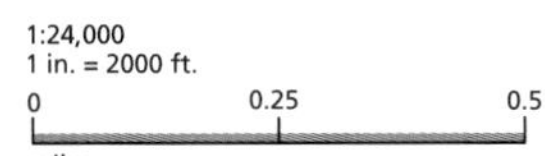

SEE 2037 MAP

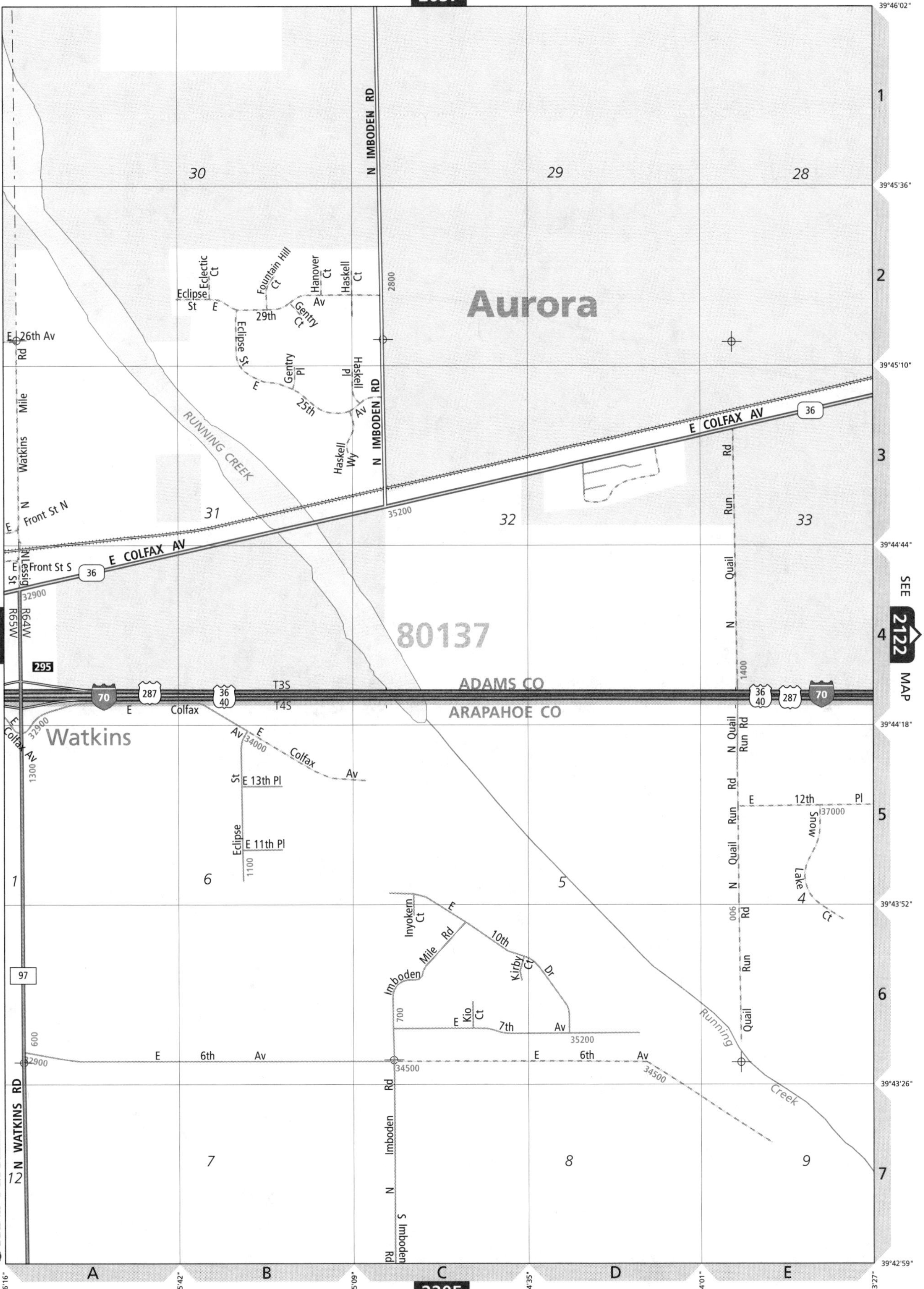

SEE 2120 MAP

SEE 2122 MAP

SEE 2205 MAP

1:24,000
1 in. = 2000 ft.
0 0.25 0.5
miles

SEE 2038 MAP

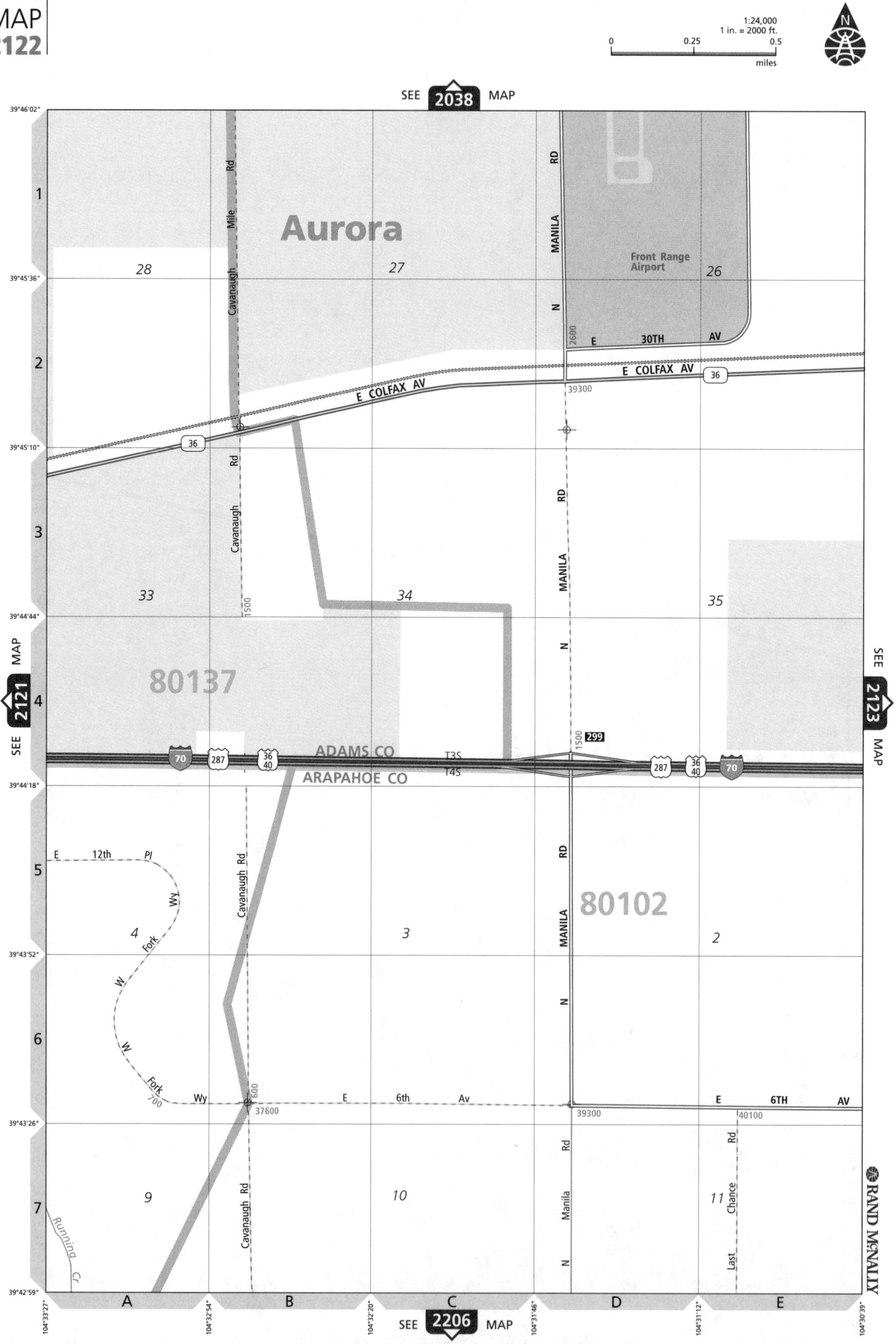

SEE 2121 MAP

SEE 2123 MAP

SEE 2206 MAP

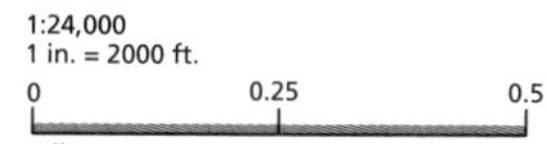

SEE 2039 MAP

SEE 2122 MAP

SEE 2124 MAP

SEE 2207 MAP

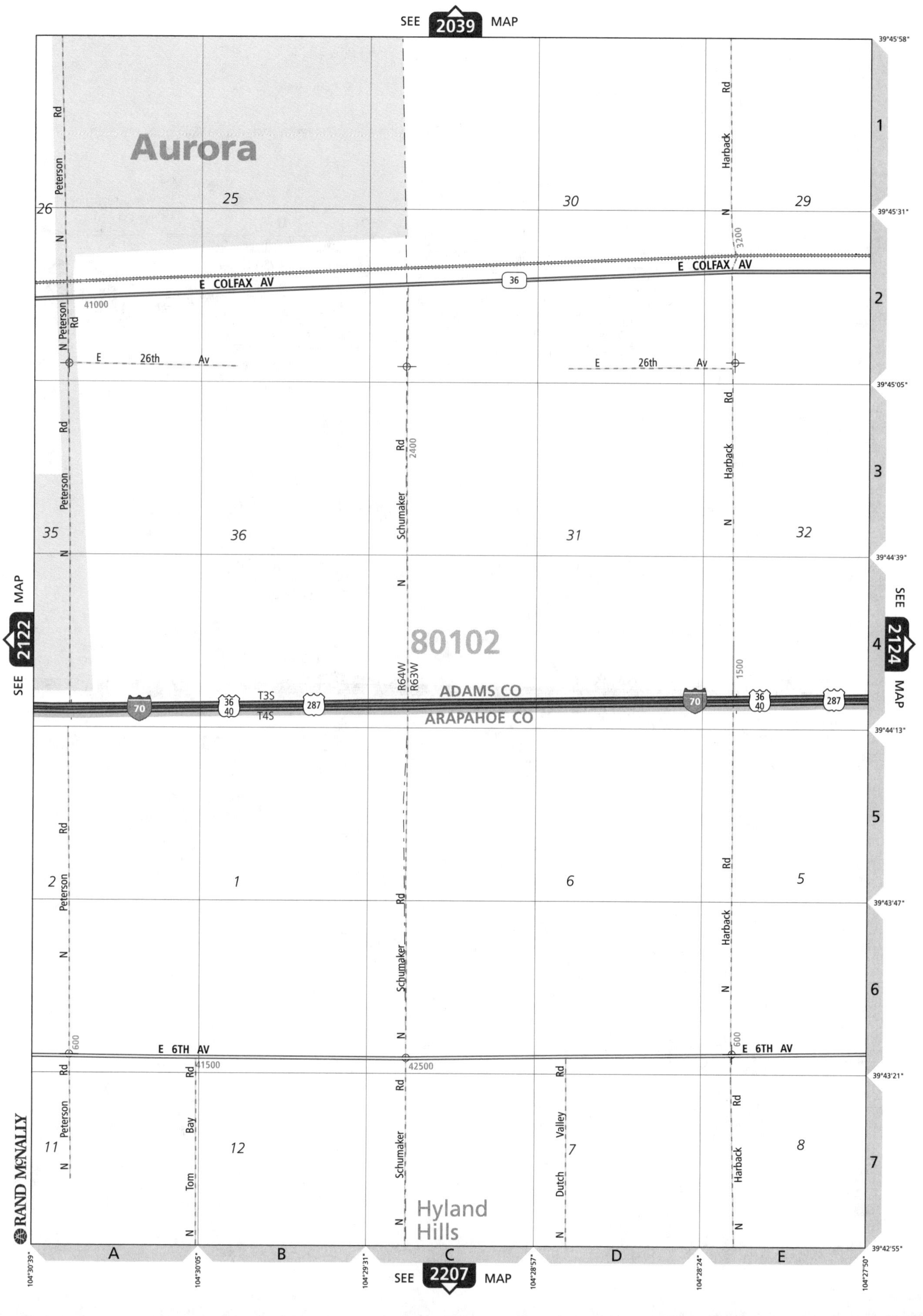

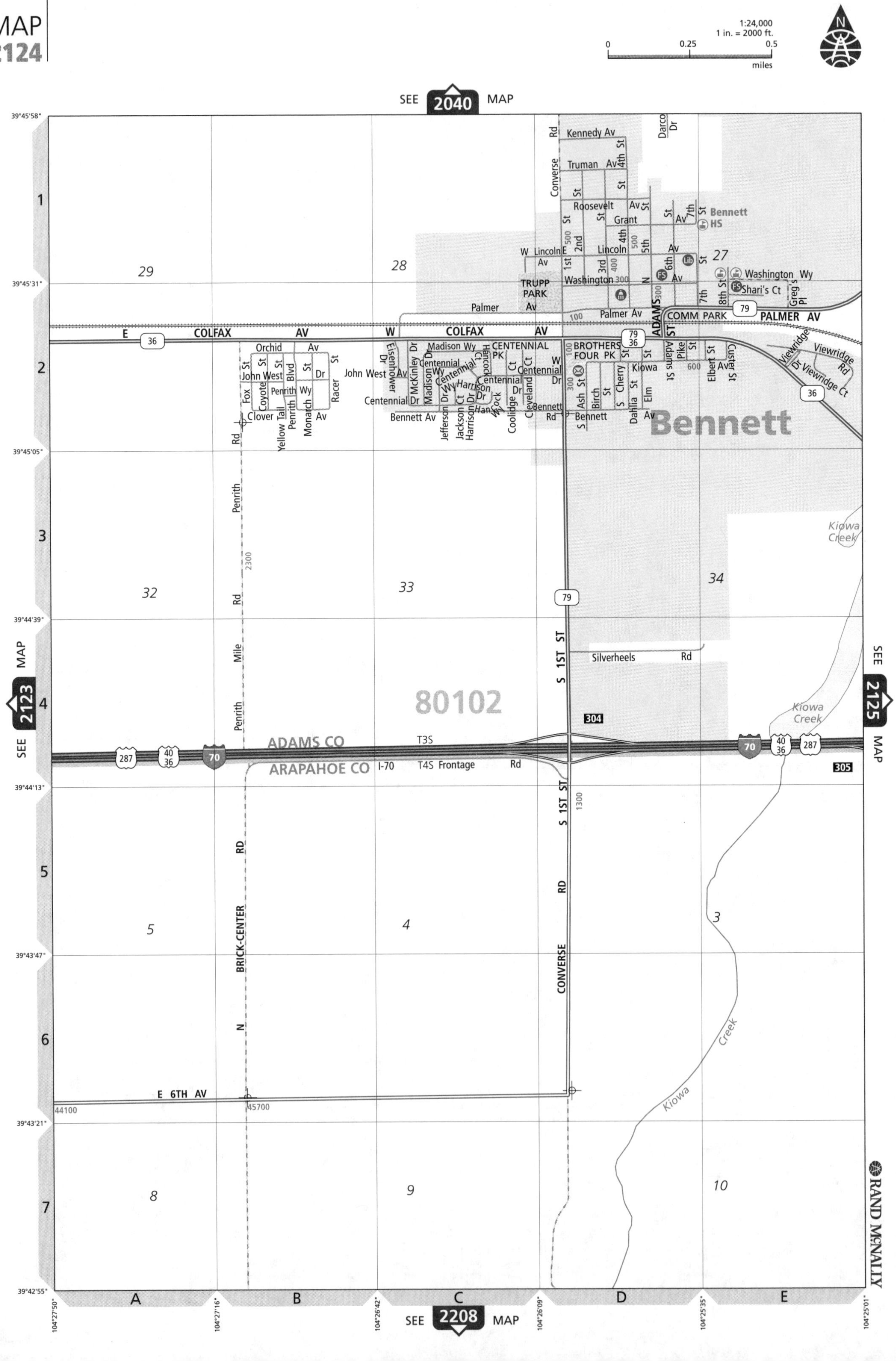

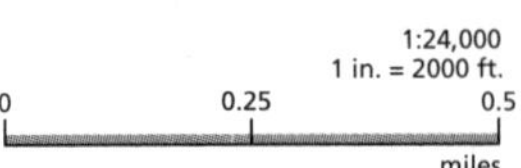

SEE 2040 MAP

Bennett
80102
E COLFAX AV
W COLFAX AV
PALMER AV
ADAMS CO
ARAPAHOE CO
I-70 Frontage Rd
CONVERSE RD
S 1ST ST
BRICK-CENTER RD
Penrith Mile Rd
E 6TH AV
Silverheels Rd
Kiowa Creek
TRUPP PARK
CENTENNIAL PK
BROTHERS FOUR PK
COMM PARK
Bennett HS

SEE 2123 MAP

SEE 2125 MAP

SEE 2208 MAP

1:24,000
1 in. = 2000 ft.
0 0.25 0.5
miles

SEE B MAP

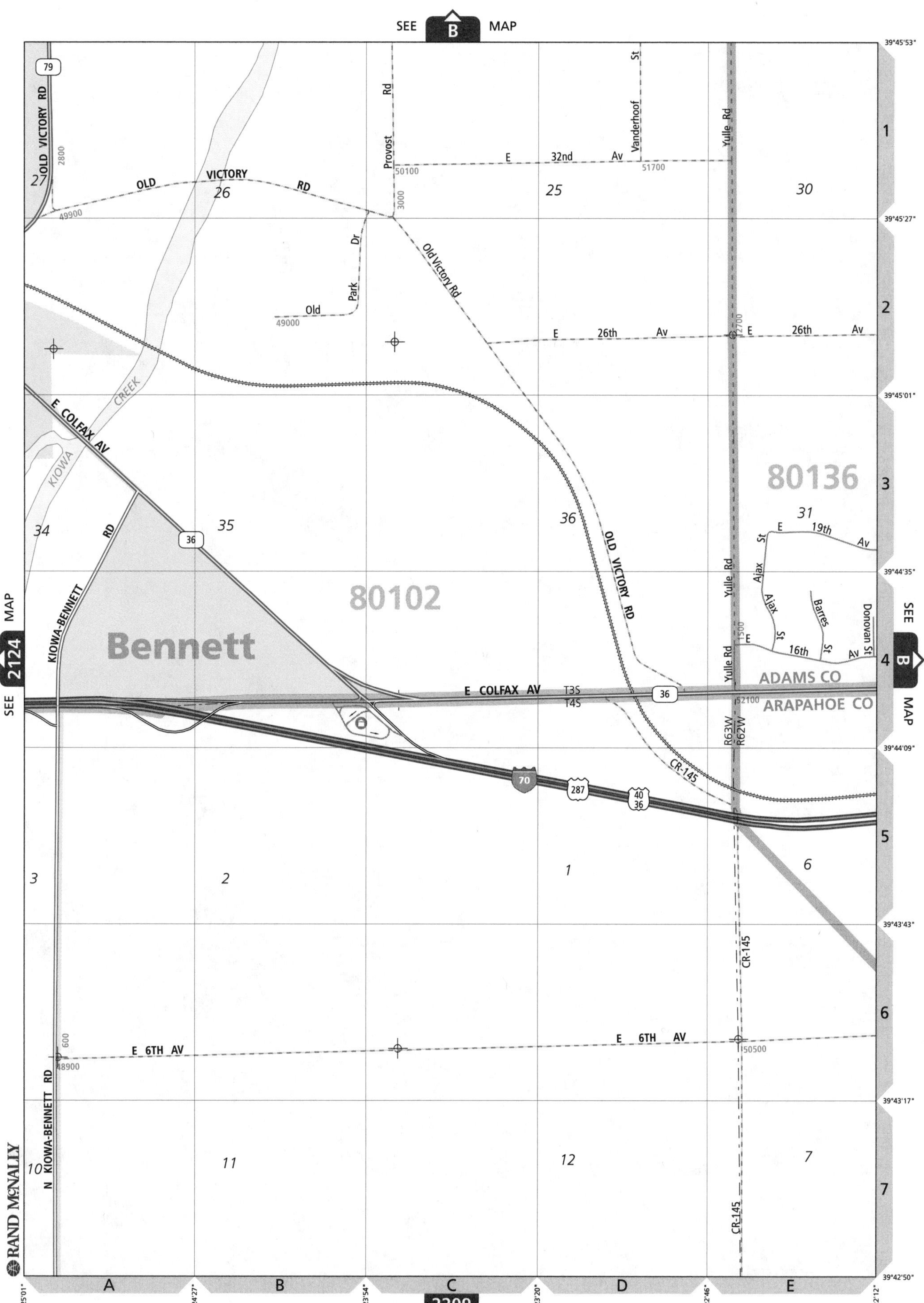

SEE 2124 MAP

SEE B MAP

SEE 2209 MAP

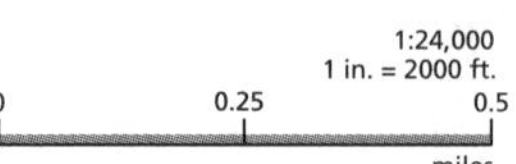

SEE 2101 MAP

Old Glory Rd
Soda Creek Rd
Van Eden Rd
Little Bear Creek Rd
Warren Gulch Rd
Hidden Wilderness Rd
CR-155
Lost Mine Ln
Warren Gulch Rd
Little Bear Creek Rd
Soda Creek Tr
ARAPAHO NATIONAL FOREST
R73W
R72W
80452
103
Tower Rd
Sawmill Ln
SQUAW PASS RD

11 12 7 14 13 18 23 24 19 26 25 30

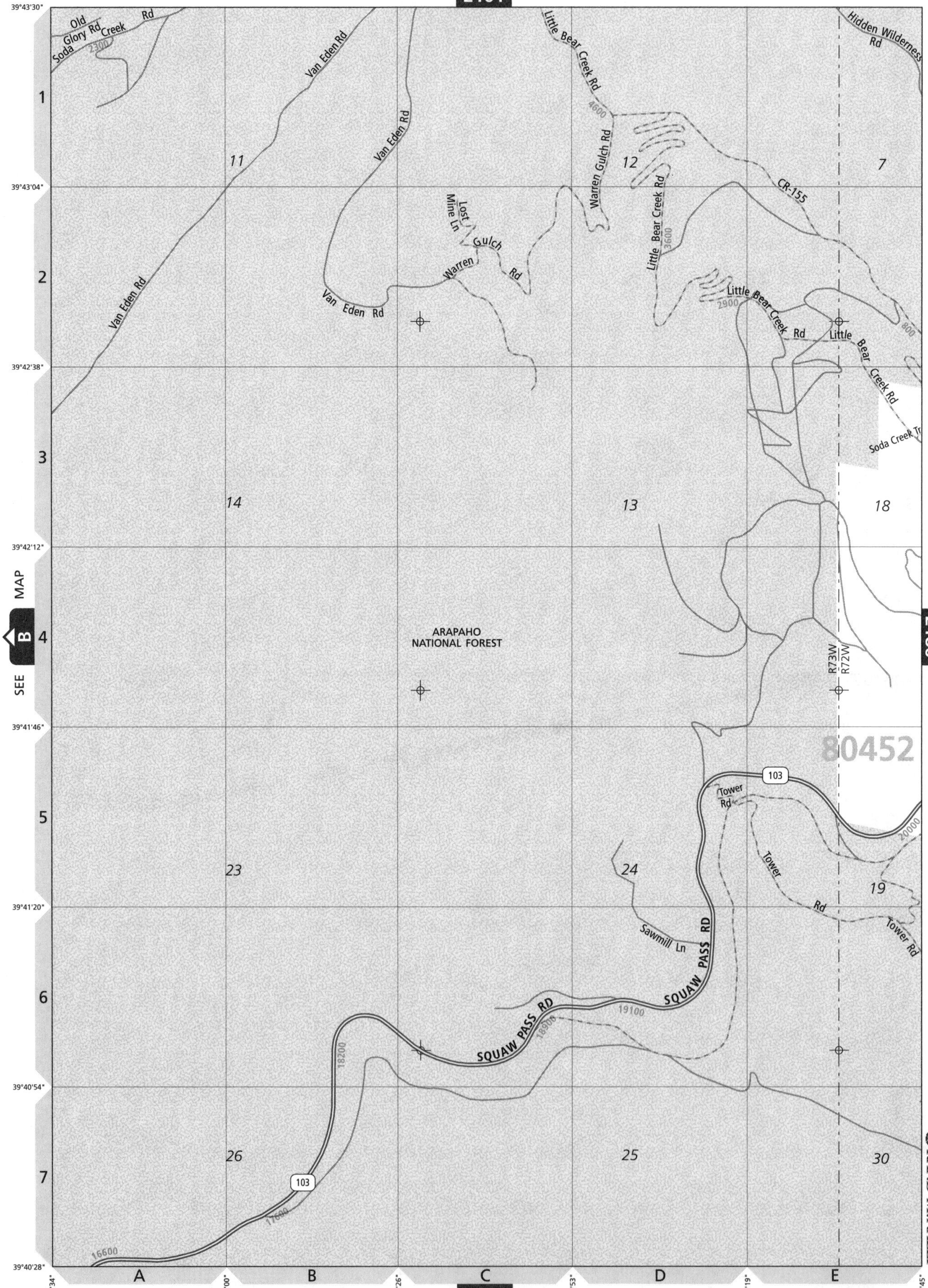

SEE B MAP

SEE 2186 MAP

SEE B MAP

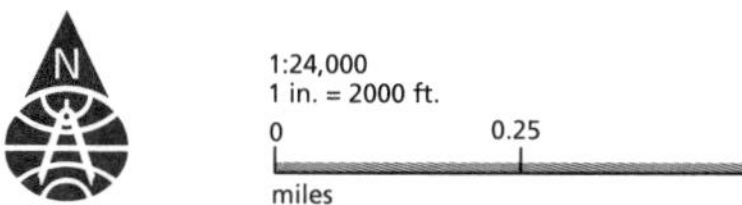

SEE 2102 MAP

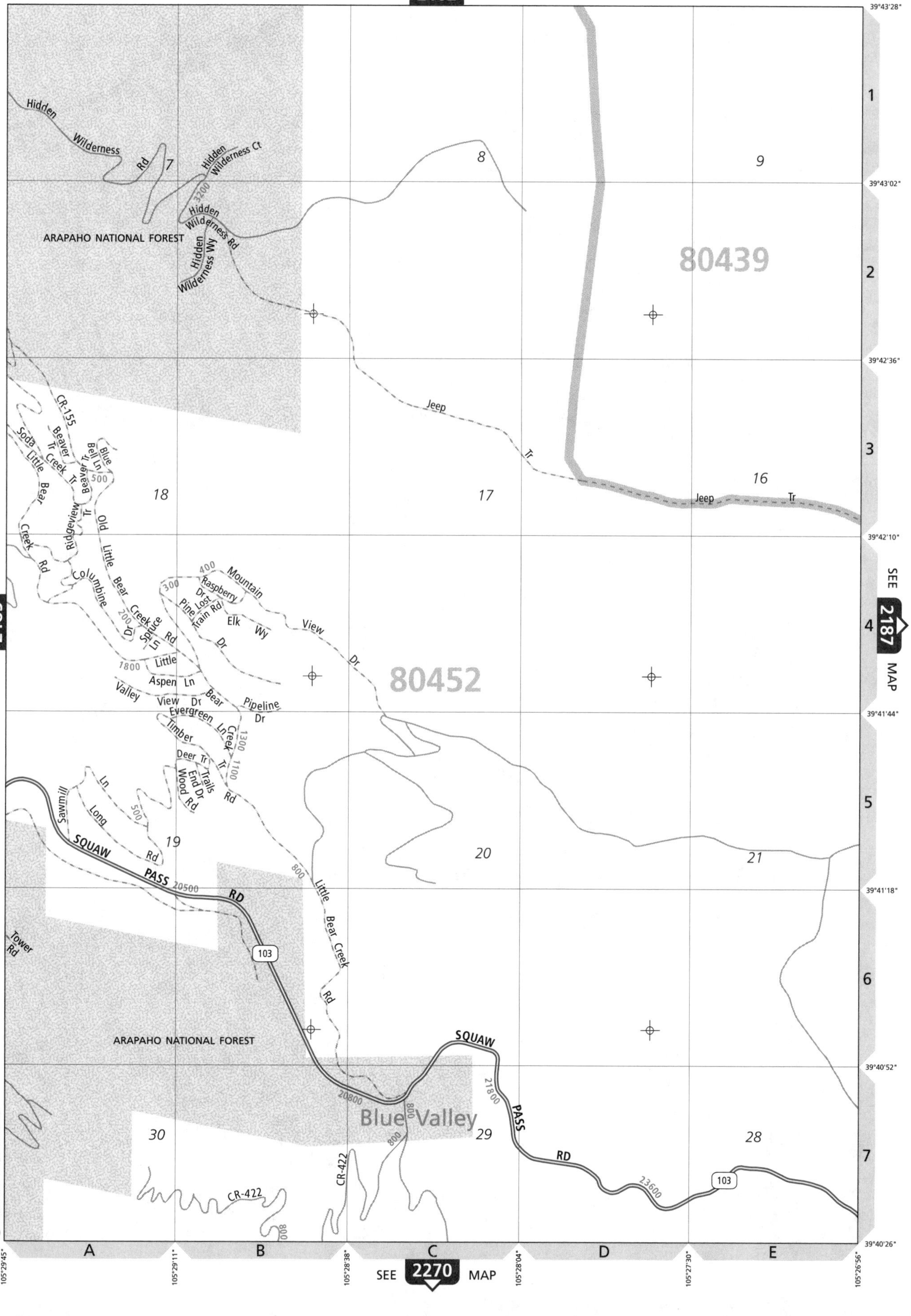

SEE 2185 MAP
SEE 2187 MAP
SEE 2270 MAP

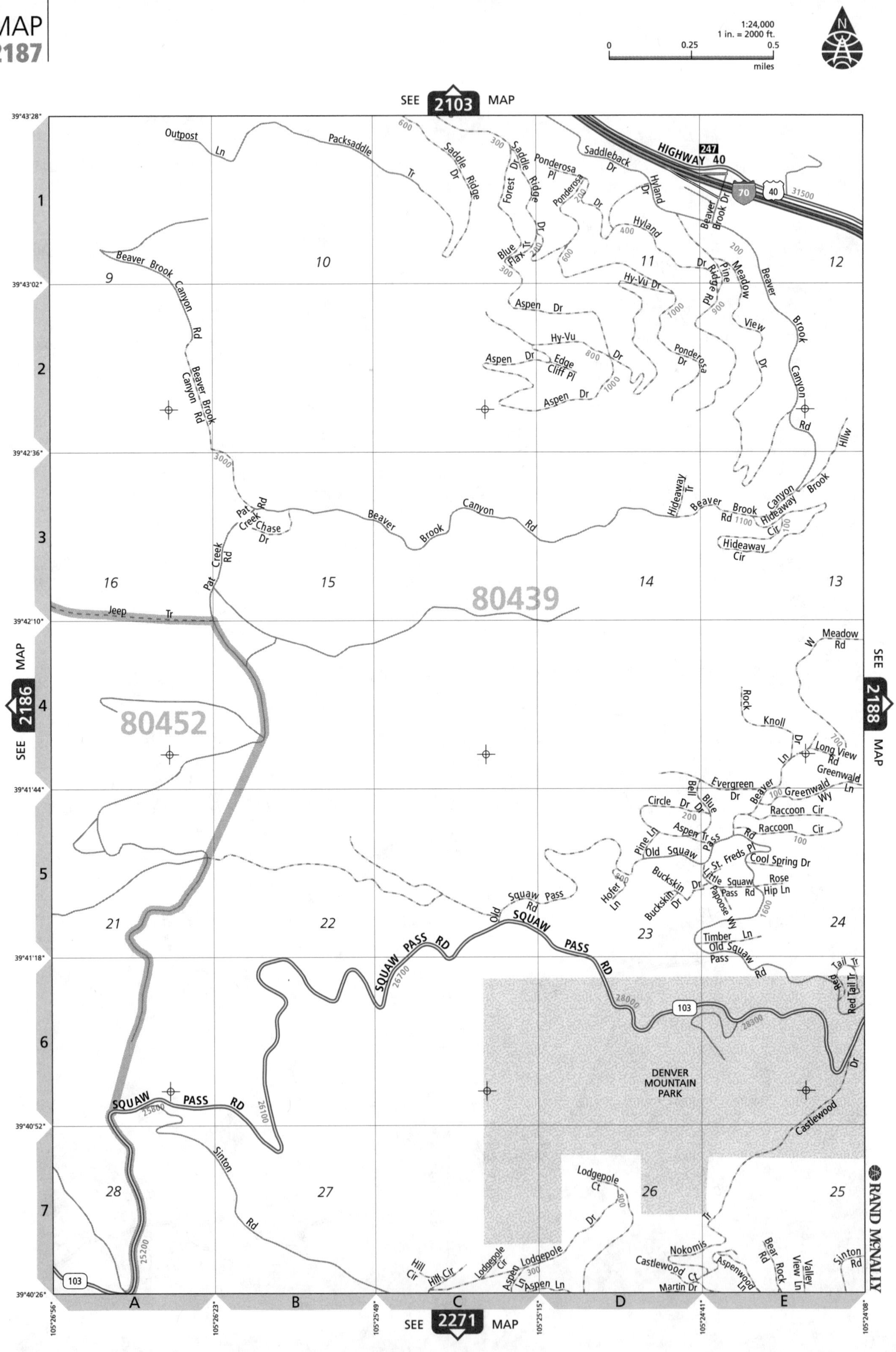

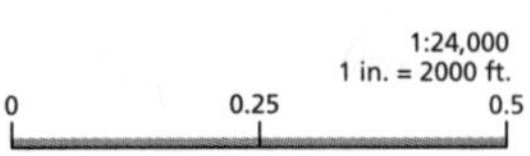

1:24,000
1 in. = 2000 ft.
0
0.25
0.5
miles
N
SEE 2103 MAP
SEE 2186 MAP
SEE 2188 MAP
SEE 2271 MAP
39°43'28"
39°43'02"
39°42'36"
39°42'10"
39°41'44"
39°41'18"
39°40'52"
39°40'26"
105°26'56"
105°26'23"
105°25'49"
105°25'15"
105°24'41"
105°24'05"
1
2
3
4
5
6
7
A
B
C
D
E
Outpost Ln
Packsaddle Tr
Saddle Ridge Dr
Saddle Ridge Dr
Forest Dr
Ponderosa Pl
Ponderosa Dr
Saddleback Dr
HIGHWAY 40
247
70
40
31500
Hyland Dr
Beaver Brook Dr
Hyland
Blue Flax Tr
Beaver Brook Canyon Rd
Beaver Brook Canyon Rd
Hy-Vu Dr
Pine Ridge Rd
Meadow View Dr
Beaver Brook Canyon Rd
Aspen Dr
Hy-Vu Dr
Aspen Dr
Edge Cliff Pl
Aspen Dr
Ponderosa Dr
Hllw
Pat Creek Rd
Chase Dr
Beaver Brook Canyon Rd
Hideaway Tr
Beaver Brook Canyon Rd
Hideaway Cir
Hideaway Cir
Brook
Pat Creek Rd
Jeep Tr
80439
80452
9
10
11
12
16
15
14
13
21
22
23
24
28
27
26
25
W Meadow Rd
Rock Knoll Dr
Ln
Long View Rd
Greenwald Ln
Evergreen Dr
Beaver
Greenwald Wy
Circle Dr
Bell
Blue Dr
Raccoon Cir
Raccoon Cir
Aspen Tr
Pass Rd
Pine Ln
Old Squaw
St. Freds Pl
Cool Spring Dr
Buckskin Dr
Little Squaw Pass Rd
Rose Hip Ln
Hofer Ln
Buckskin Dr
Papoose Wy
Old Squaw Pass Rd
SQUAW PASS RD
Timber Ln
Old Squaw Pass Rd
Red Tail Tr
Red Tail Tr
103
28000
28300
26700
Dr
DENVER
MOUNTAIN
PARK
SQUAW PASS RD
25800
26100
Castlewood
Sinton Rd
Lodgepole Ct
Dr
Tr
Nokomis
Castlewood Ct
Martin Dr
Aspenwood Ln
Bear Rd
Rock
Valley View Ln
Sinton Rd
Hill Cir
Hill Cir
Lodgepole Cir
Aspen Ln
Lodgepole
Aspen Ln
25200
103
RAND McNALLY

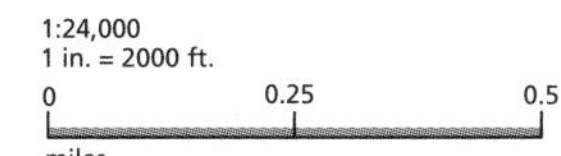

SEE 2104 MAP

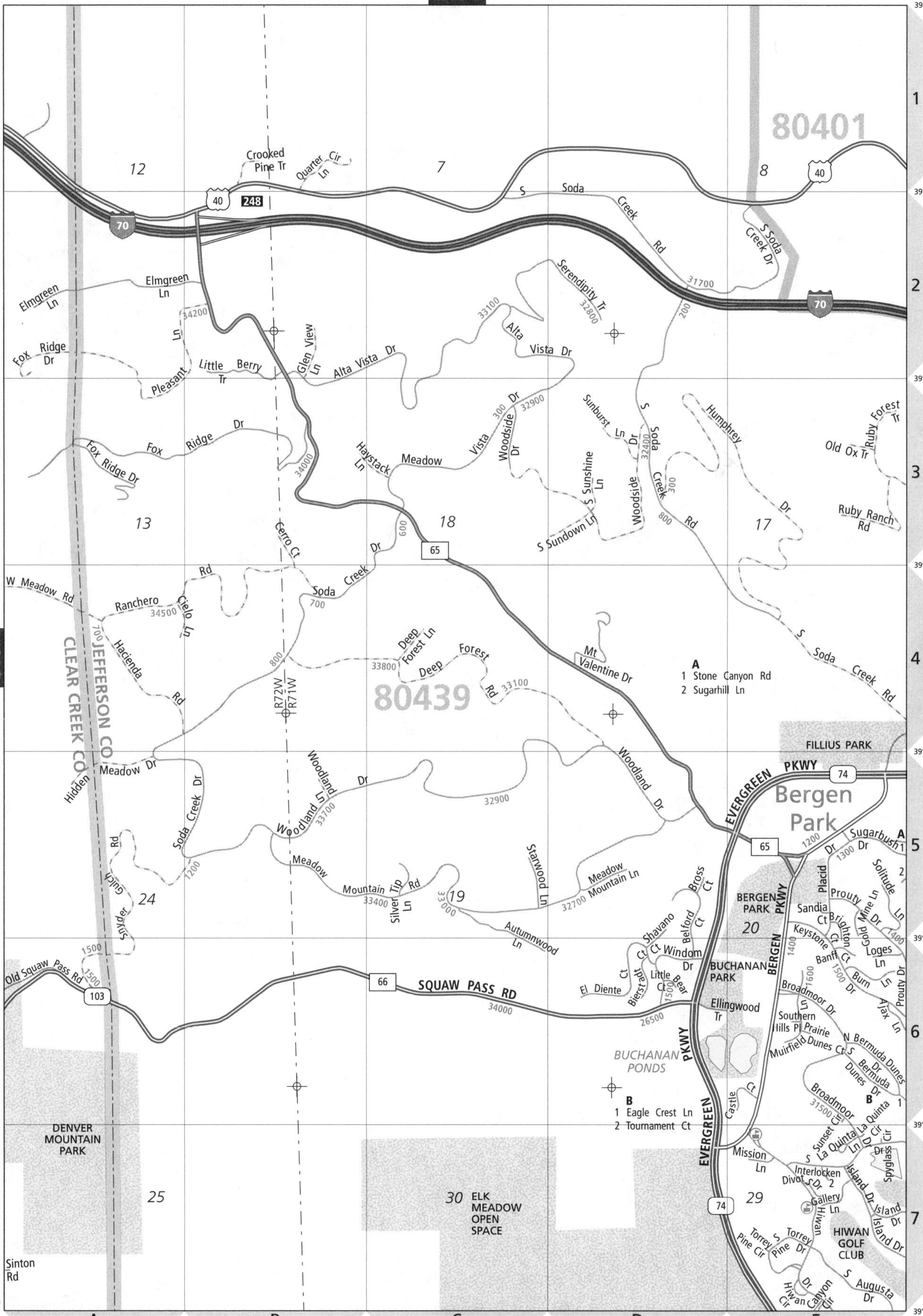

SEE 2187 MAP

SEE 2189 MAP

SEE 2272 MAP

80401
80439
Bergen Park
FILLIUS PARK
BERGEN PARK
BUCHANAN PARK
BUCHANAN PONDS
DENVER MOUNTAIN PARK
ELK MEADOW OPEN SPACE
HIWAN GOLF CLUB
JEFFERSON CO
CLEAR CREEK CO
EVERGREEN PKWY
SQUAW PASS RD

A
1 Stone Canyon Rd
2 Sugarhill Ln

B
1 Eagle Crest Ln
2 Tournament Ct

1:24,000
1 in. = 2000 ft.
0 0.25 0.5
miles

SEE 2105 MAP

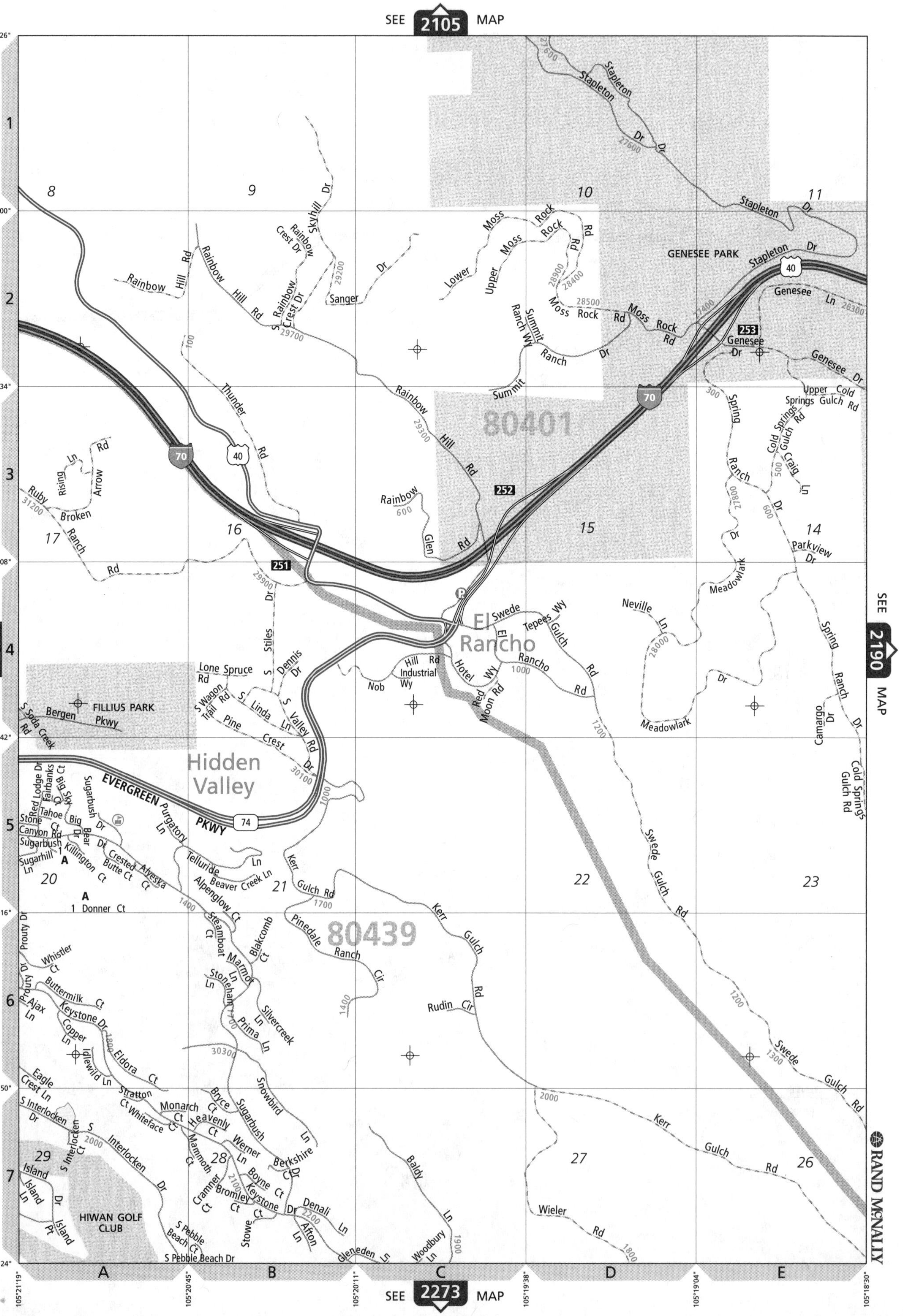

SEE 2188 MAP

SEE 2190 MAP

SEE 2273 MAP

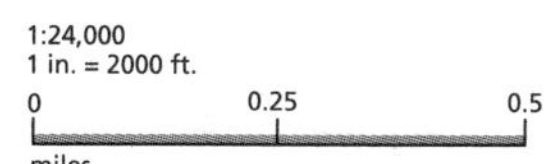

SEE 2106 MAP

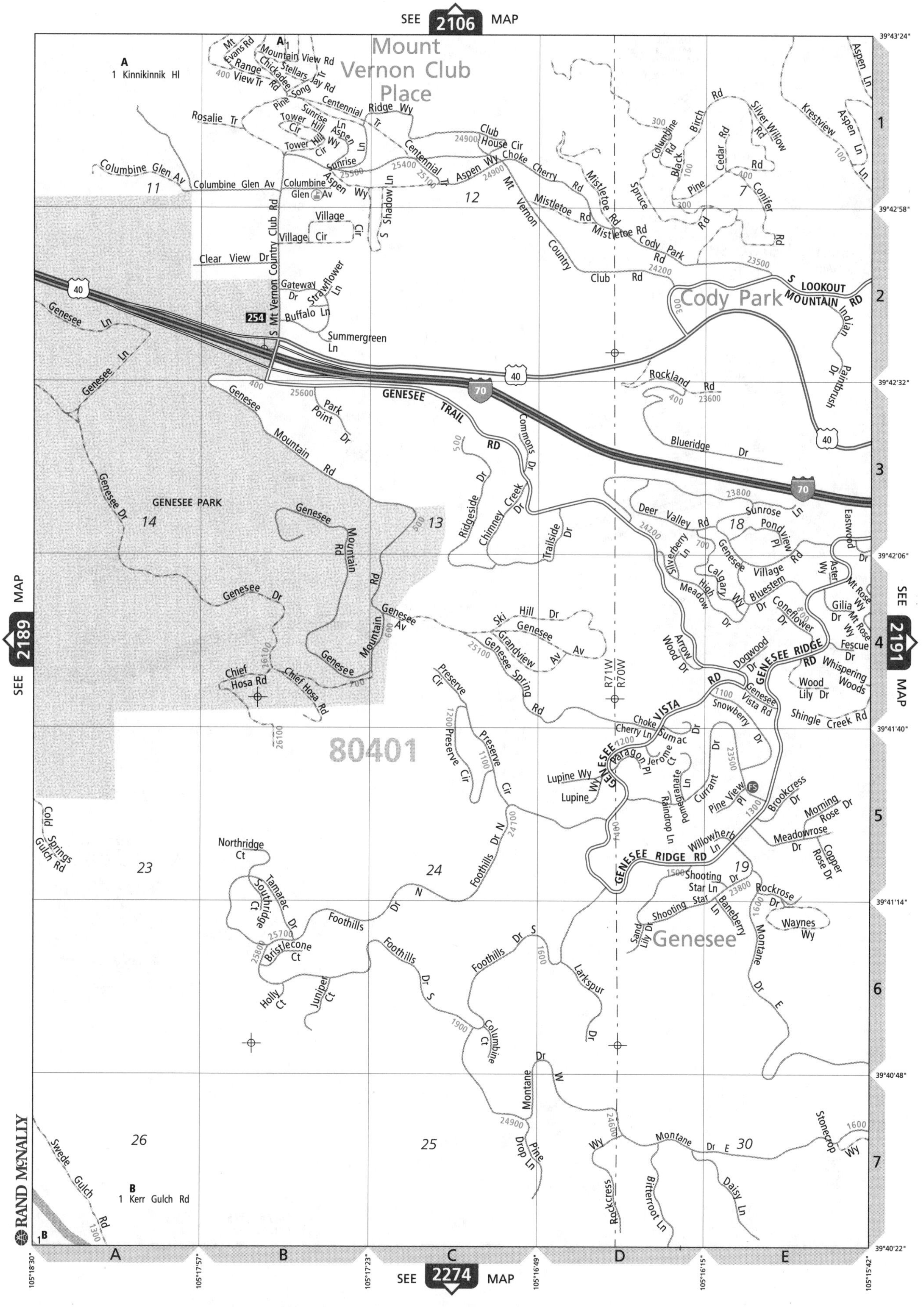

SEE 2189 MAP

SEE 2191 MAP

SEE 2274 MAP

A
1 Kinnikinnik Hl

B
1 Kerr Gulch Rd

Mount Vernon Club Place
Cody Park
Genesee
GENESEE PARK
80401

Mt Evans Rd
Mountain View Rd
Range View Tr
Stellars Jay Rd
Chickadee Rd
Pine Song Tr
Centennial Ridge Wy
Centennial Tr
Rosalie Tr
Sunrise Hill Ln
Tower Hill Cir
Tower Hill Wy
Aspen Cir
Sunrise
Columbine Glen Av
Columbine Glen Av
Aspen Wy
S Shadow Ln
Village Cir
Village Cir
Clear View Dr
S Mt Vernon Country Club Rd
Club House Cir
Aspen Wy
Choke Cherry Rd
Mt Vernon Country Club Rd
Mistletoe Rd
Mistletoe Rd
Mistletoe Rd
Cody Park Rd
Columbine Rd
Black
Birch
Spruce
Cedar Rd
Pine
Rd
Silver Willow Rd
Conifer Rd
Krestview
Aspen Ln
Aspen Ln
S Lookout Mountain Rd
Indian Paintbrush Dr
Gateway Dr
Strawflower Ln
Buffalo Ln
Summergreen Ln
Genesee Ln
Genesee Ln
Rockland Rd
Genesee Trail Rd
Park Point Dr
Genesee Mountain Rd
Commons Dr
Blueridge Dr
Genesee Dr
Genesee Mountain Rd
Ridgeside Dr
Chimney Creek Dr
Trailside Dr
Deer Valley Rd
Sunrose Ln
Pondview Pl
Eastwood Dr
Silverberry Ln
Genesee Village Rd
Calgary Wy
High Meadow Dr
Bluestem Dr
Coneflower Dr
Aster Wy
Mt Rose Wy
Gilia Dr
Mt Rose Wy
Fescue Dr
Genesee Dr
Genesee Mountain Rd
Genesee Av
Ski Hill Dr
Genesee Av
Grandview Av
Genesee Spring Rd
Arrow Wood Dr
Dogwood Dr
Genesee Ridge Rd
Whispering Woods
Wood Lily Dr
Shingle Creek Rd
Chief Hosa Rd
Chief Hosa Rd
Preserve Cir
Preserve Cir
Preserve Cir
Genesee Vista Rd
Genesee Vista Rd
Snowberry Dr
Choke Cherry Ln
Sumac Dr
Genesee Wy
Paragon Pl
Jerome Ct
Pomegranate Ln
Currant Dr
Lupine Wy
Lupine
Raindrop Ln
Pine View Pl
Brookcress Dr
Morning Rose Dr
Meadowrose Dr
Copper Rose Dr
Willowherb Ln
Genesee Ridge Rd
Shooting Star Ln
Shooting Star Ln
Baneberry Dr
Rockrose Dr
Sand Lily Dr
Waynes Wy
Montane Dr E
Cold Springs Gulch Rd
Northridge Ct
Tamarac Dr
Southridge Ct
Foothills Dr N
Foothills Dr N
Bristlecone Ct
Foothills Dr S
Foothills Dr S
Holly Ct
Juniper Ct
Columbine Ct
Larkspur Dr
Montane Dr W
Pine Drop Ln
Montane Dr E
Stonecrop Wy
Wy
Rockcress
Bitterroot Ln
Daisy Ln
Swede Gulch Rd
R71W
R70W

40
254
70

11
12
7
14
13
18
23
24
19
26
25
30

1
2
3
4
5
6
7
A
B
C
D
E

39°43'24"
39°42'58"
39°42'32"
39°42'06"
39°41'40"
39°41'14"
39°40'48"
39°40'22"
105°18'30"
105°17'57"
105°17'23"
105°16'49"
105°16'15"
105°15'42"

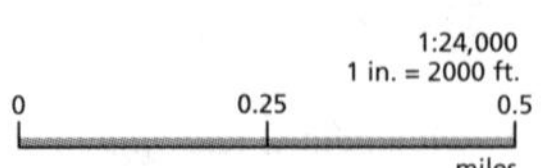

SEE 2107 MAP

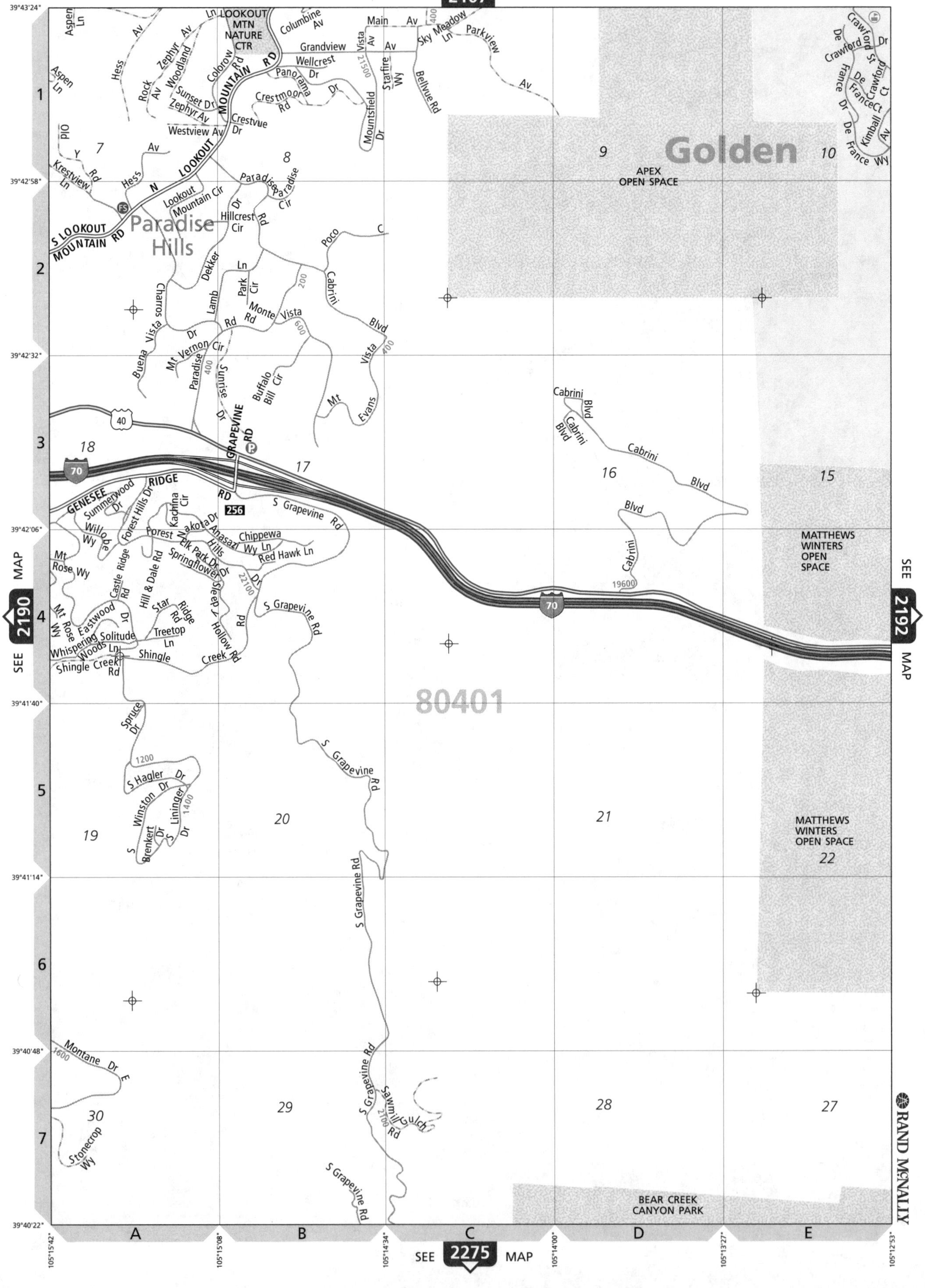

SEE 2190 MAP

SEE 2192 MAP

SEE 2275 MAP

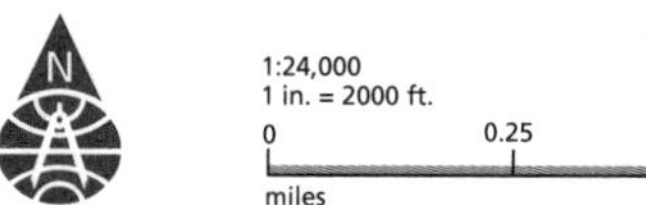

SEE 2108 MAP

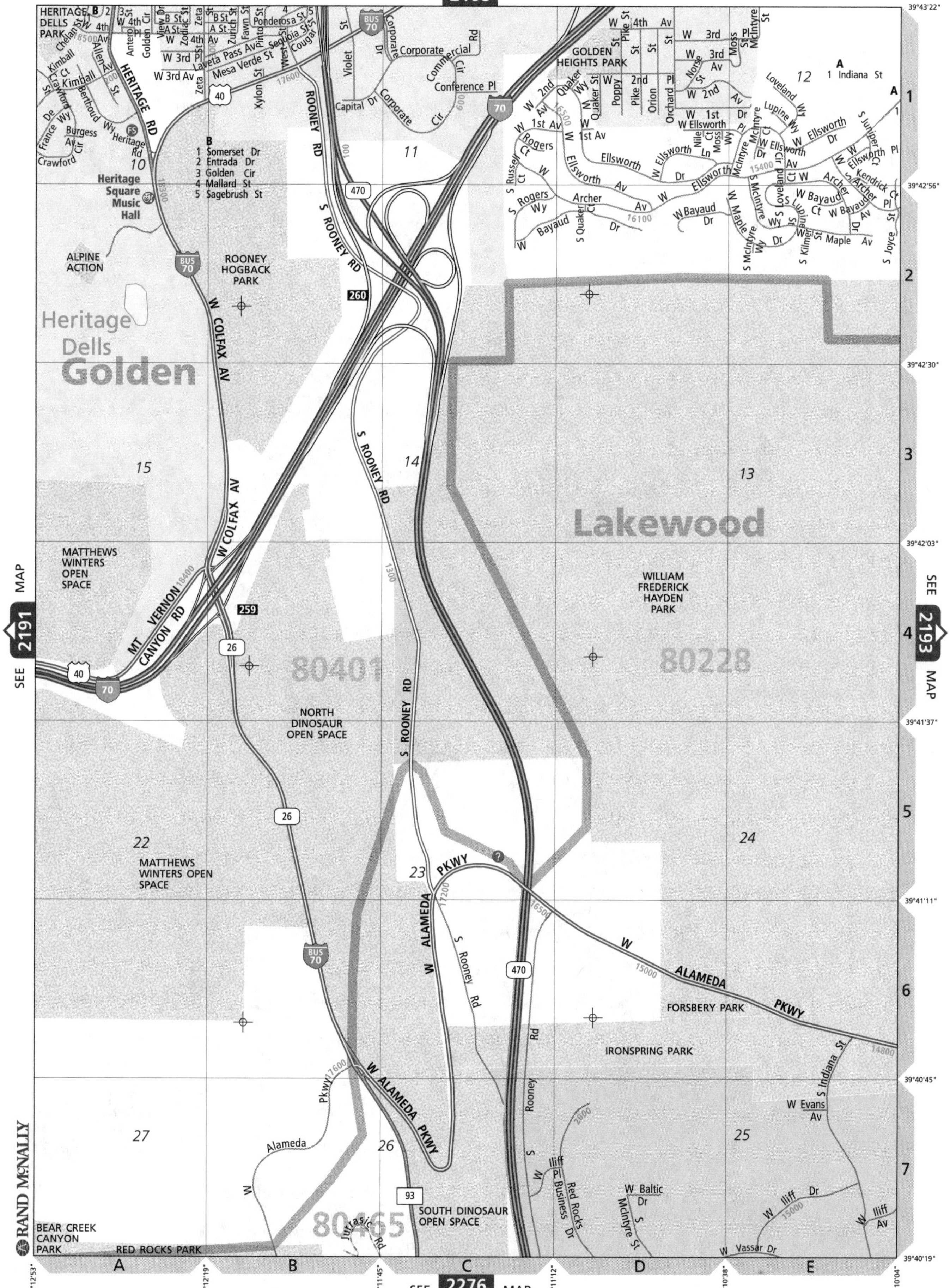

SEE 2191 MAP

SEE 2193 MAP

Golden

Lakewood

Heritage Dells

HERITAGE DELLS PARK

GOLDEN HEIGHTS PARK

ROONEY HOGBACK PARK

ALPINE ACTION

Heritage Square Music Hall

MATTHEWS WINTERS OPEN SPACE

WILLIAM FREDERICK HAYDEN PARK

NORTH DINOSAUR OPEN SPACE

SOUTH DINOSAUR OPEN SPACE

FORSBERY PARK

IRONSPRING PARK

BEAR CREEK CANYON PARK

RED ROCKS PARK

80401

80228

80465

A
1 Indiana St

B
1 Somerset Dr
2 Entrada Dr
3 Golden Cir
4 Mallard St
5 Sagebrush St

W COLFAX AV

MT VERNON CANYON RD

S ROONEY RD

W ALAMEDA PKWY

HERITAGE RD

RAND McNALLY

SEE 2276 MAP

1:24,000
1 in. = 2000 ft.
0 0.25 0.5
miles

SEE 2109 MAP

SEE 2192 MAP

SEE 2194 MAP

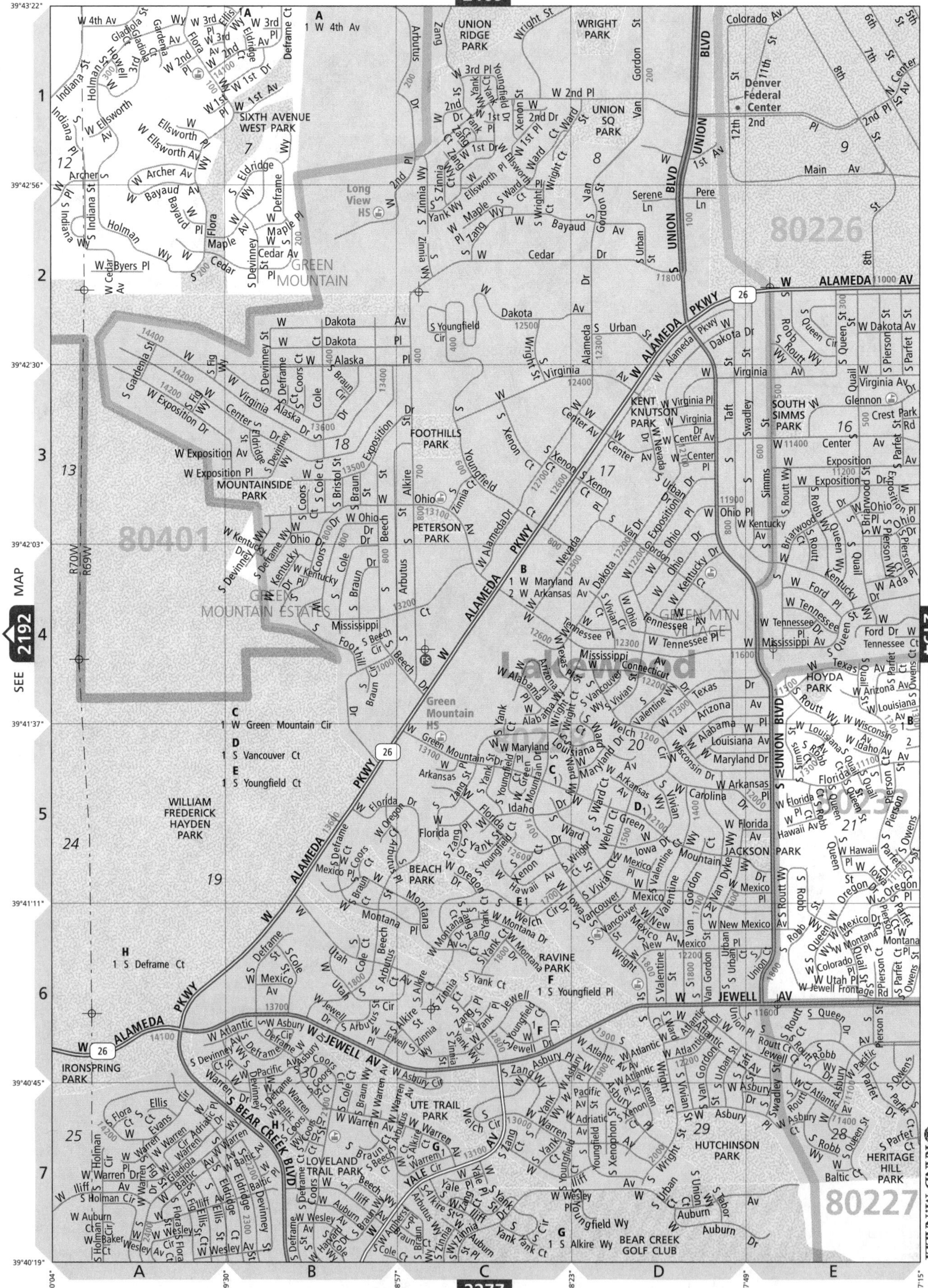

A
1 W 4th Av

B
1 W Maryland Av
2 W Arkansas Av

C
1 W Green Mountain Cir

D
1 S Vancouver Ct

E
1 S Youngfield Ct

F
1 S Youngfield Pl

G
1 S Alkire Wy

H
1 S Deframe Ct

Lakewood

SIXTH AVENUE WEST PARK

UNION RIDGE PARK

WRIGHT PARK

UNION SQ PARK

Denver Federal Center

GREEN MOUNTAIN

FOOTHILLS PARK

PETERSON PARK

MOUNTAINSIDE PARK

GREEN MOUNTAIN ESTATES

KENT KNUTSON PARK

SOUTH SIMMS PARK

GREEN MTN VILLAGE

HOYDA PARK

WILLIAM FREDERICK HAYDEN PARK

BEACH PARK

RAVINE PARK

JACKSON PARK

IRONSPRING PARK

UTE TRAIL PARK

LOVELAND TRAIL PARK

HUTCHINSON PARK

HERITAGE HILL PARK

BEAR CREEK GOLF CLUB

80401

80226

80227

39°43'22" 39°42'56" 39°42'30" 39°42'03" 39°41'37" 39°41'11" 39°40'45" 39°40'19"

105°10'04" 105°09'30" 105°08'57" 105°08'23" 105°07'49" 105°07'15"

A B C D E

1 2 3 4 5 6 7

SEE 2277 MAP

1:24,000
1 in. = 2000 ft.
0 0.25 0.5
miles

SEE 2110 MAP

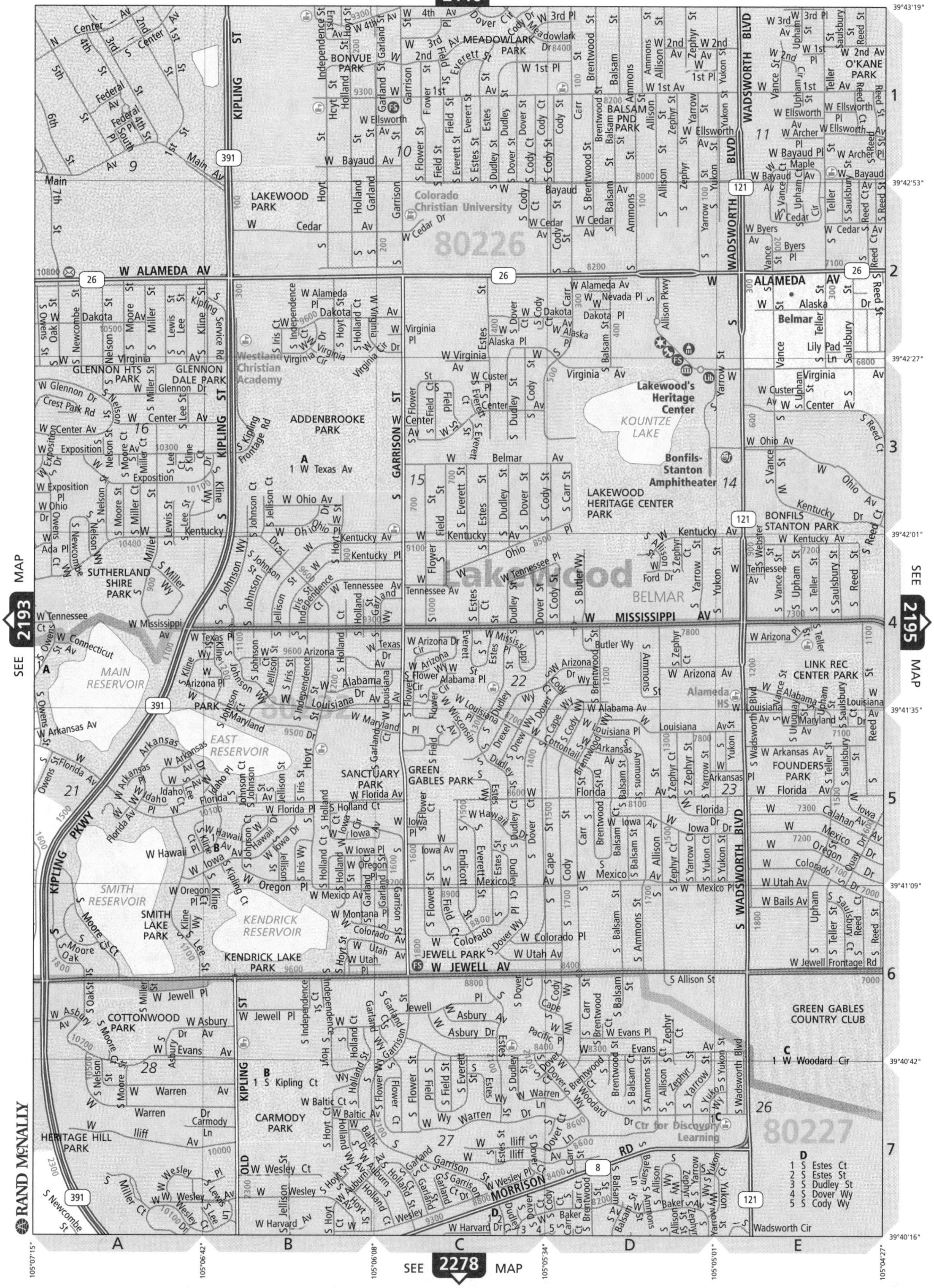

SEE 2193 MAP

SEE 2195 MAP

SEE 2278 MAP

Lakewood
BELMAR
Belmar
80226
80227

W ALAMEDA AV
W MISSISSIPPI AV
W JEWELL AV
MORRISON RD
KIPLING ST
KIPLING PKWY
GARRISON ST
WADSWORTH BLVD
S WADSWORTH BLVD

LAKEWOOD PARK
BONVUE PARK
MEADOWLARK PARK
BALSAM PND PARK
O'KANE PARK
Colorado Christian University
Westland Christian Academy
GLENNON HTS PARK
GLENNON DALE PARK
ADDENBROOKE PARK
Lakewood's Heritage Center
KOUNTZE LAKE
Bonfils-Stanton Amphitheater
LAKEWOOD HERITAGE CENTER PARK
BONFILS STANTON PARK
SUTHERLAND SHIRE PARK
MAIN RESERVOIR
EAST RESERVOIR
SMITH RESERVOIR
KENDRICK RESERVOIR
SMITH LAKE PARK
KENDRICK LAKE PARK
SANCTUARY PARK
GREEN GABLES PARK
JEWELL PARK
LINK REC CENTER PARK
Alameda HS
FOUNDERS PARK
GREEN GABLES COUNTRY CLUB
COTTONWOOD PARK
CARMODY PARK
HERITAGE HILL PARK
Ctr for Discovery Learning

1 W Texas Av
1 S Kipling Ct
1 W Woodard Cir

D
1 S Estes Ct
2 S Estes Ct
3 S Dudley St
4 S Dover Wy
5 S Cody Wy

A B C D E
1 2 3 4 5 6 7

39°43'19"
39°42'53"
39°42'27"
39°42'01"
39°41'35"
39°41'09"
39°40'42"
39°40'16"
105°07'15"
105°06'42"
105°06'08"
105°05'34"
105°05'01"
105°04'27"

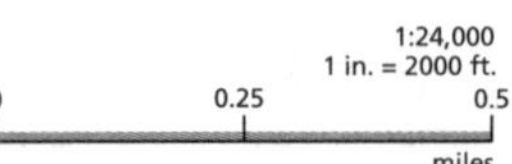

SEE 2111 MAP

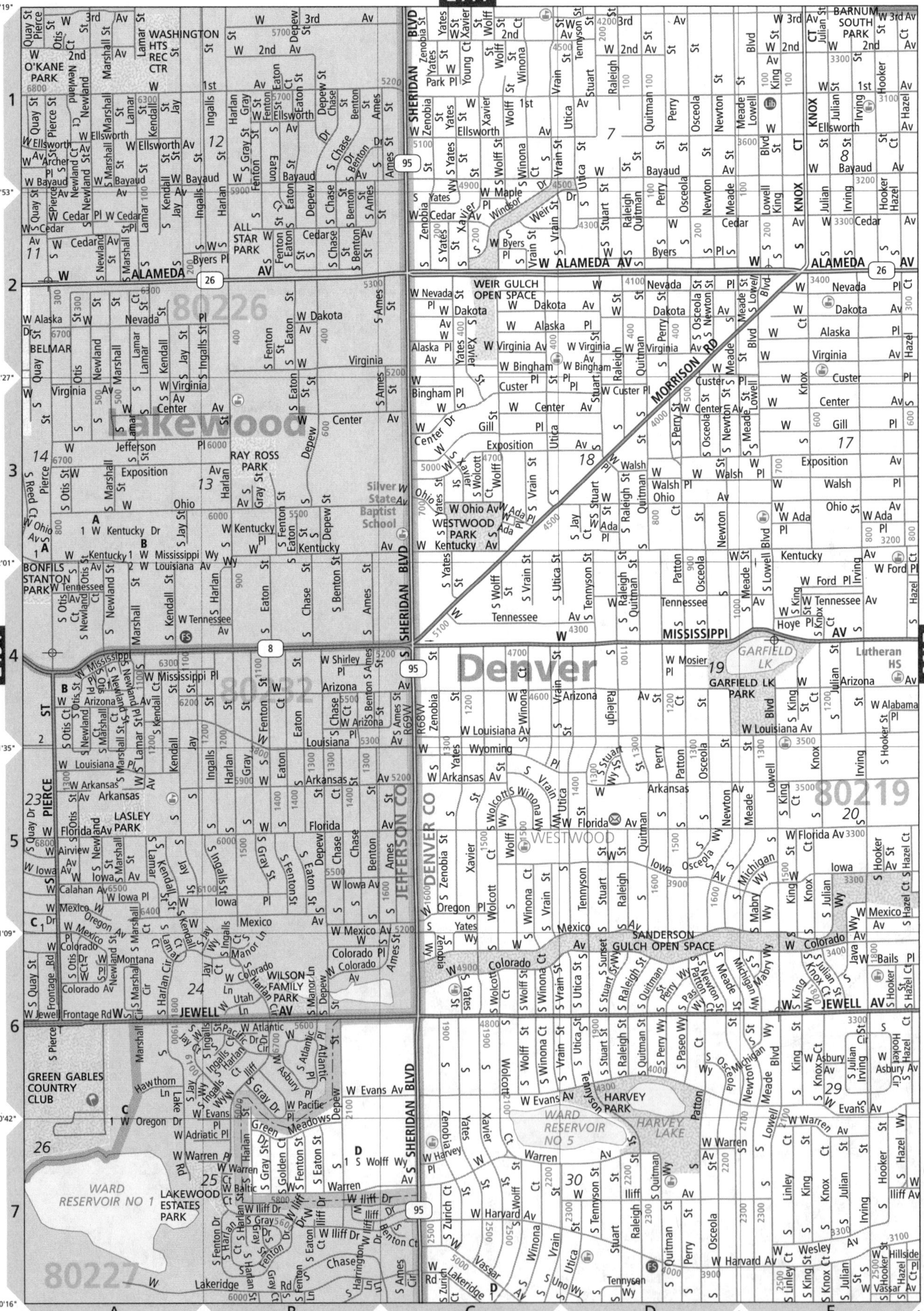

SEE 2194 MAP

SEE 2196 MAP

Lakewood

Denver

80226

80232

80227

80219

WASHINGTON HTS REC CTR

O'KANE PARK

BELMAR

ALL STAR PARK

RAY ROSS PARK

BONFILS STANTON PARK

LASLEY PARK

WILSON FAMILY PARK

GREEN GABLES COUNTRY CLUB

WARD RESERVOIR NO 1

LAKEWOOD ESTATES PARK

WEIR GULCH OPEN SPACE

WESTWOOD PARK

WESTWOOD

Silver State Baptist School

SANDERSON GULCH OPEN SPACE

GARFIELD LK

GARFIELD LK PARK

BARNUM SOUTH PARK

Lutheran HS

HARVEY PARK

HARVEY LAKE

WARD RESERVOIR NO 5

SHERIDAN BLVD

JEFFERSON CO

DENVER CO

W ALAMEDA AV

MORRISON RD

MISSISSIPPI AV

JEWELL AV

KNOX CT

PIERCE ST

A B C D E

1 2 3 4 5 6 7

SEE 2279 MAP

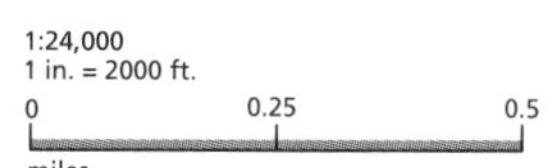

SEE 2112 MAP

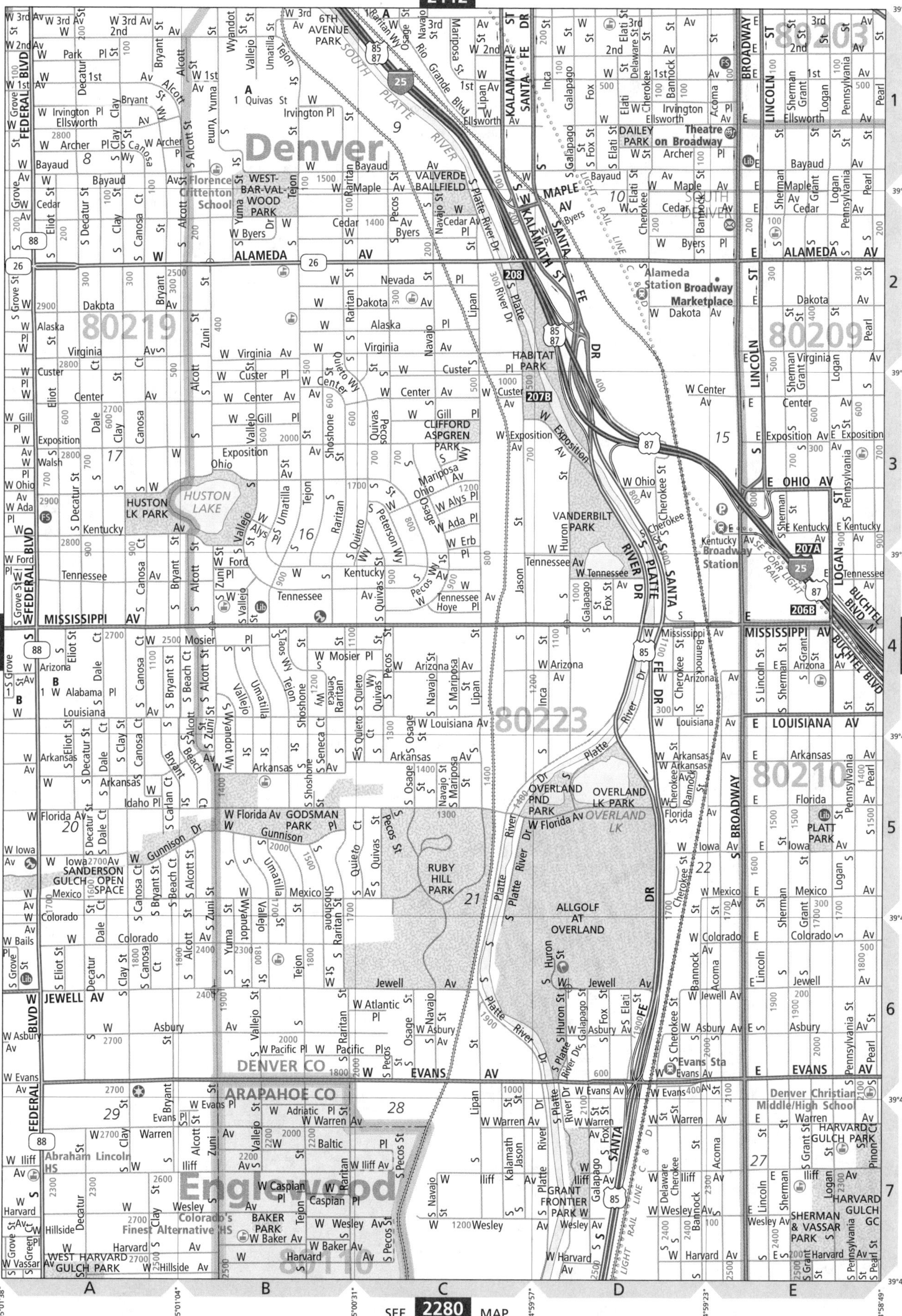

SEE 2195 MAP

SEE 2197 MAP

SEE 2280 MAP

Denver

Englewood

DENVER CO

ARAPAHOE CO

SOUTH DENVER

80219 80223 80203 80209 80210 80110

6TH AVENUE PARK

WEST-BAR-VAL-WOOD PARK

Florence Crittenton School

VALVERDE BALLFIELD

DAILEY PARK

Theatre on Broadway

Alameda Station

Broadway Marketplace

HABITAT PARK

CLIFFORD ASPGREN PARK

HUSTON LK PARK

HUSTON LAKE

VANDERBILT PARK

Broadway Station

GODSMAN PARK

SANDERSON GULCH OPEN SPACE

RUBY HILL PARK

OVERLAND PND PARK

OVERLAND LK PARK

OVERLAND LK

ALLGOLF AT OVERLAND

PLATT PARK

Evans Sta

Denver Christian Middle/High School

HARVARD GULCH PARK

Abraham Lincoln HS

Colorado's Finest Alternative HS

BAKER PARK

GRANT FRONTIER PARK

SHERMAN & VASSAR PARK

HARVARD GULCH GC

WEST HARVARD GULCH PARK

FEDERAL BLVD

ALAMEDA AV

MISSISSIPPI AV

JEWELL AV

EVANS AV

LOUISIANA AV

BROADWAY

LINCOLN ST

LOGAN ST

KALAMATH ST

SANTA FE DR

S PLATTE RIVER DR

BUCHTEL BLVD

E OHIO AV

MAPLE AV

LIGHT RAIL LINE

C & D

SOUTH PLATTE RIVER

Rio Grande Blvd

Gunnison Dr

A B C D E

1 2 3 4 5 6 7

39°43'16" 39°42'50" 39°42'24" 39°41'58" 39°41'32" 39°41'06" 39°40'40" 39°40'13"

105°01'38" 105°01'04" 105°00'31" 104°59'57" 104°59'23" 104°58'49"

1:24,000
1 in. = 2000 ft.
0 0.25 0.5
miles

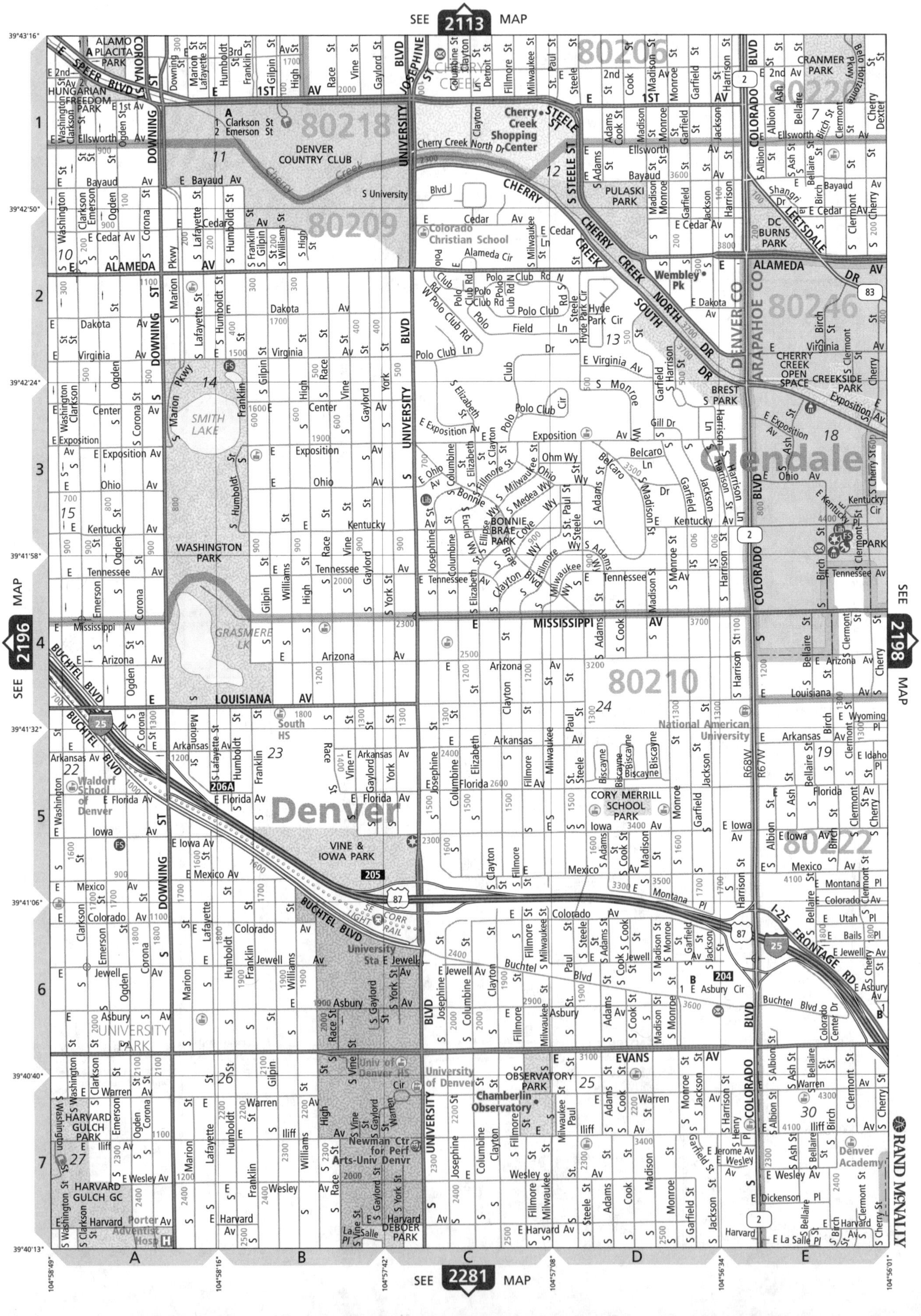

SEE 2113 MAP

SEE 2196 MAP

SEE 2198 MAP

SEE 2281 MAP

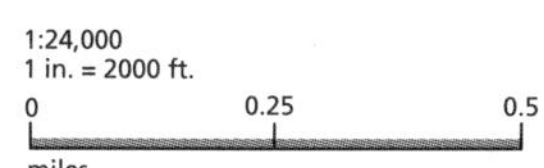

SEE 2114 MAP

SEE 2197 MAP

SEE 2199 MAP

ROBINSON PARK
80220
80246
80230
80224
80247
80222
80231
CRESTMOOR PARK
Wings Over the Rockies Air & Space Mus
JACKIE ROBINSON PARK
Lowry Sports Complex
MIRA VISTA GOLF COURSE
Mizel Center for Arts & Culture
Mizel Mus
Mizel Museum of Judaica
George Washington HS
Glendale
Denver
MIR PARK
CHERRY CREEK OPEN SPACE
FOUR MILE HISTORIC PARK
SUNFISH LAKE
DeVry Inst of Technology
GARLAND PARK
FRANCES WISEBART JACOBS PARK
FAIRMOUNT CEMETERY
ARAPAHOE CO
DENVER CO
CITY OF POTENZA PARK
JUDGE JOSEPH E COOK PARK
Rocky Mtn School
ASH GRV PARK
WELLSHIRE
E ALAMEDA AV
LEETSDALE DR
E MISSISSIPPI AV
CHERRY CREEK NORTH DR
CHERRY CREEK SOUTH DR
S PARKER RD
E EVANS AV
E ILIFF AV
S MONACO PKWY
S QUEBEC ST
FAIRMOUNT DR
S VALENTIA ST
SYRACUSE WY
LOWRY BLVD
RAND McNALLY

A B C D E
1 2 3 4 5 6 7

39°43'13"
39°42'47"
39°42'21"
39°41'54"
39°41'28"
39°41'02"
39°40'36"
39°40'10"
104°56'01"
104°55'27"
104°54'53"
104°54'19"
104°53'46"
104°53'12"

SEE 2282 MAP

1:24,000
1 in. = 2000 ft.
0 0.25 0.5
miles

SEE 2115 MAP

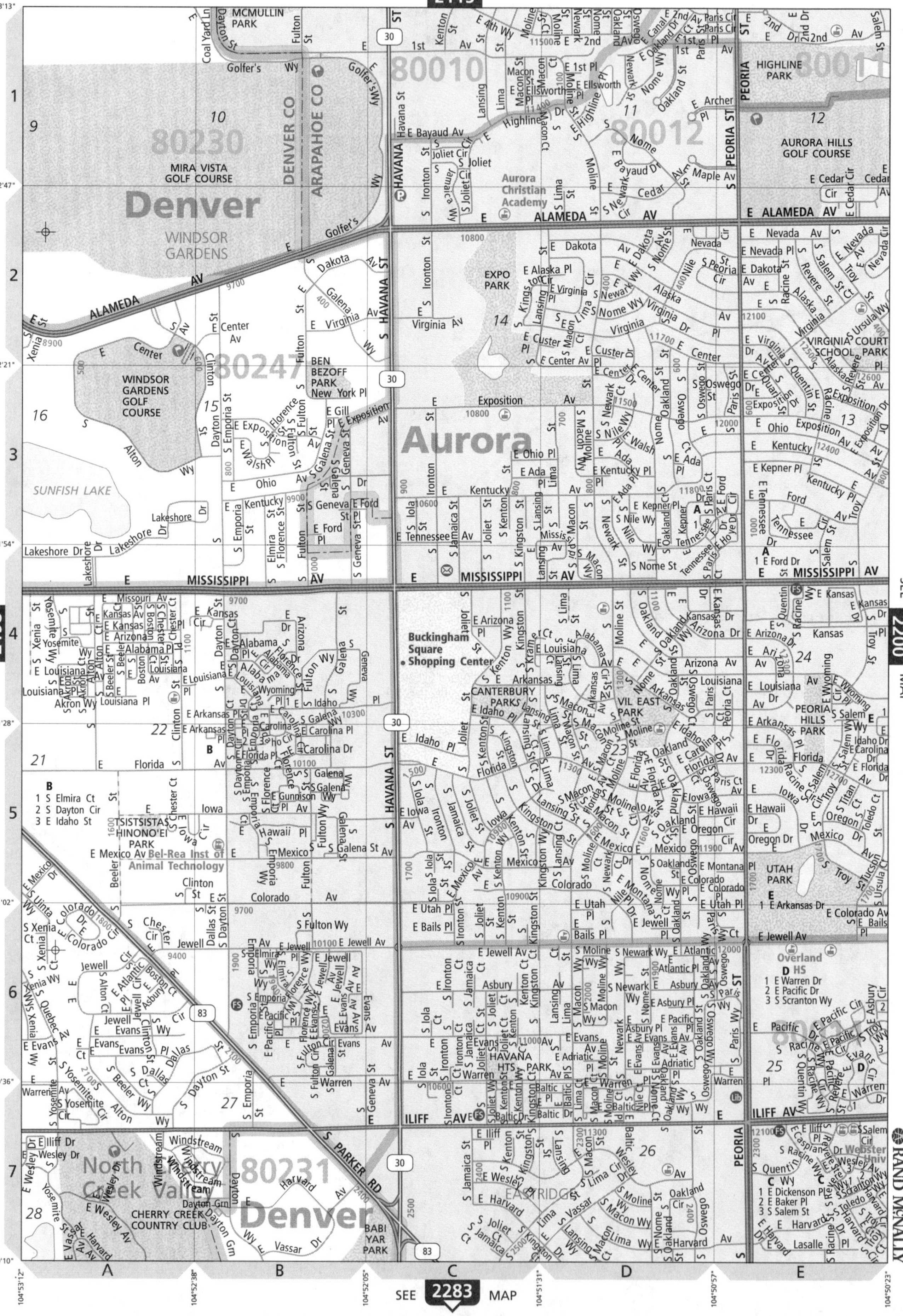

SEE 2198 MAP

SEE 2200 MAP

Denver

Aurora

WINDSOR GARDENS

MIRA VISTA GOLF COURSE

WINDSOR GARDENS GOLF COURSE

SUNFISH LAKE

MCMULLIN PARK

HIGHLINE PARK

AURORA HILLS GOLF COURSE

Aurora Christian Academy

EXPO PARK

BEN BEZOFF PARK

VIRGINIA COURT SCHOOL PARK

Buckingham Square Shopping Center

CANTERBURY PARKS

VIL EAST PARK

PEORIA HILLS PARK

SISTSISTAS HINONO'EI PARK

Bel-Rea Inst of Animal Technology

UTAH PARK

Overland HS

HAVANA HTS PARK

EASTRIDGE

North Cherry Creek Valley

CHERRY CREEK COUNTRY CLUB

BABI YAR PARK

Webster Univ

A
1 E Ford Dr

B
1 S Elmira Ct
2 S Dayton Cir
3 E Idaho St

C
1 E Dickenson Pl
2 E Baker Pl
3 S Salem St

D
1 E Warren Dr
2 E Pacific Dr
3 S Scranton Wy

80010 80011 80012 80230 80247 80231

A B C D E

SEE 2283 MAP

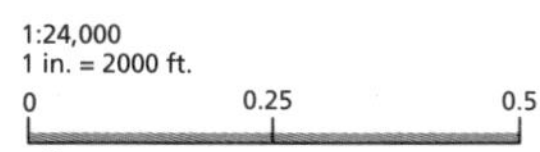

SEE 2116 MAP

SEE 2199 MAP

SEE 2201 MAP

Aurora

AURORA HILLS GOLF COURSE

BICENTENNIAL PARK

Parks Junior College Aurora

Community College of Aurora

CENTRE HILLS GOLF COURSE

CITY CENTER PARK

Aurora History Museum

Delaney Round Barn

Aurora Mall

VIRGINIA COURT SCHOOL PARK

WHEELING PARK

TOLLGATE PARK

ROCKY RIDGE PARK

Abilene Street Market

Gateway HS

VIL GREEN PARK

The Medical Ctr of Aurora-South Campus

TIERRA PARK

HORSESHOE PARK

HEATHER RIDGE COUNTRY CLUB

HEATHER RIDGE CC

WHEEL PARK

80011

80017

80012

80014

E ALAMEDA AV

ALAMEDA PKWY

E EXPOSITION AV

E MISSISSIPPI AV

Jewell Av

E ILIFF AV

S CHAMBERS RD

SABLE BLVD

E HARVARD AV

E YALE AV

225

A B C D E

1 2 3 4 5 6 7

39°43'09" 39°42'43" 39°42'17" 39°41'51" 39°41'25" 39°40'59" 39°40'33" 39°40'07"

104°50'23" 104°49'50" 104°49'16" 104°48'42" 104°48'08" 104°47'35"

SEE 2284 MAP

1:24,000
1 in. = 2000 ft.
0 0.25 0.5
miles

SEE 2117 MAP

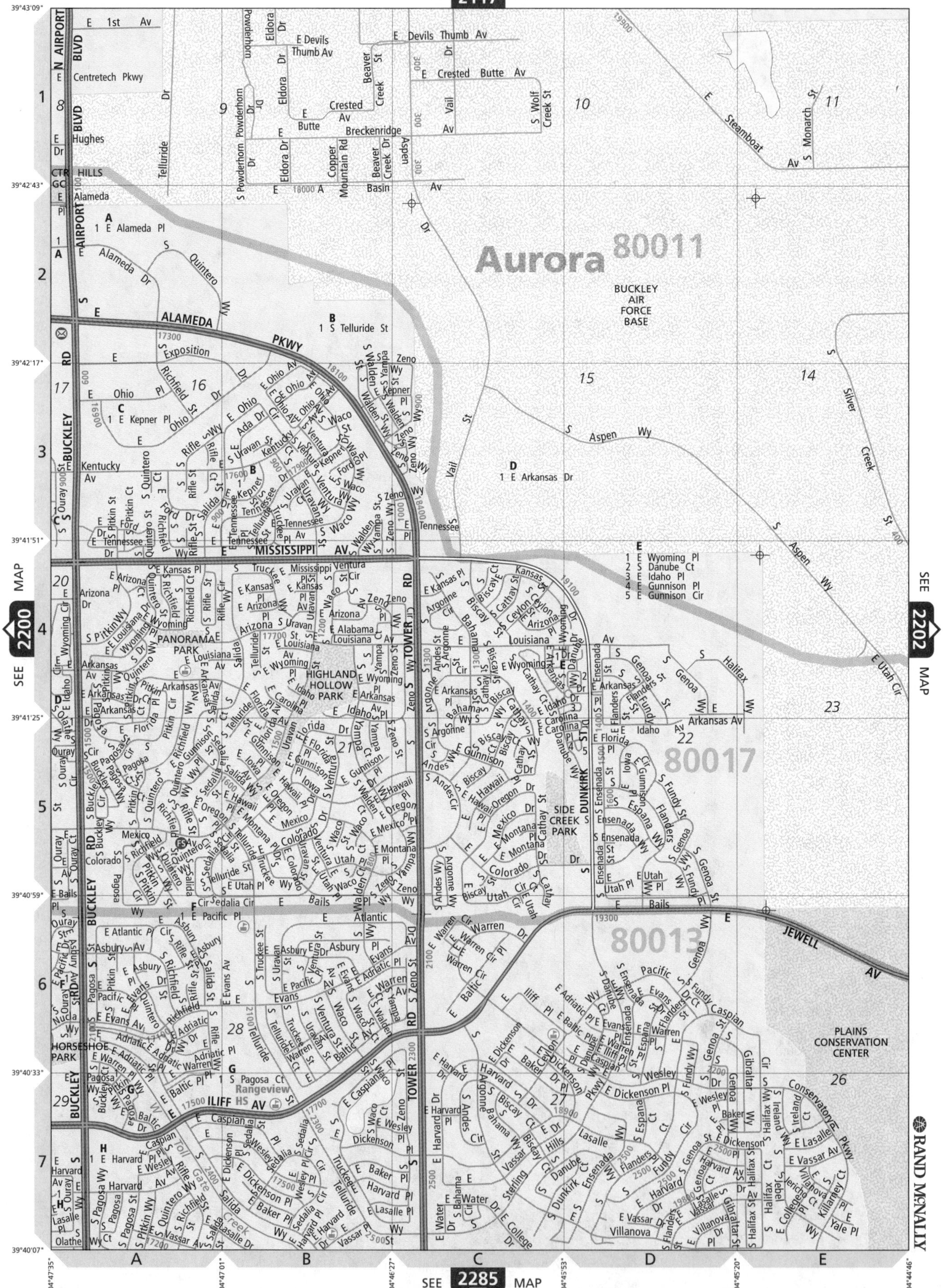

SEE 2200 MAP

SEE 2202 MAP

SEE 2285 MAP

RAND McNALLY

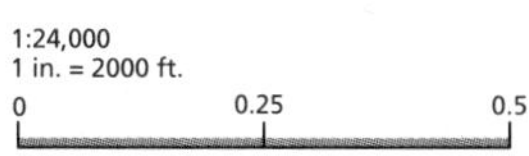

SEE 2118 MAP

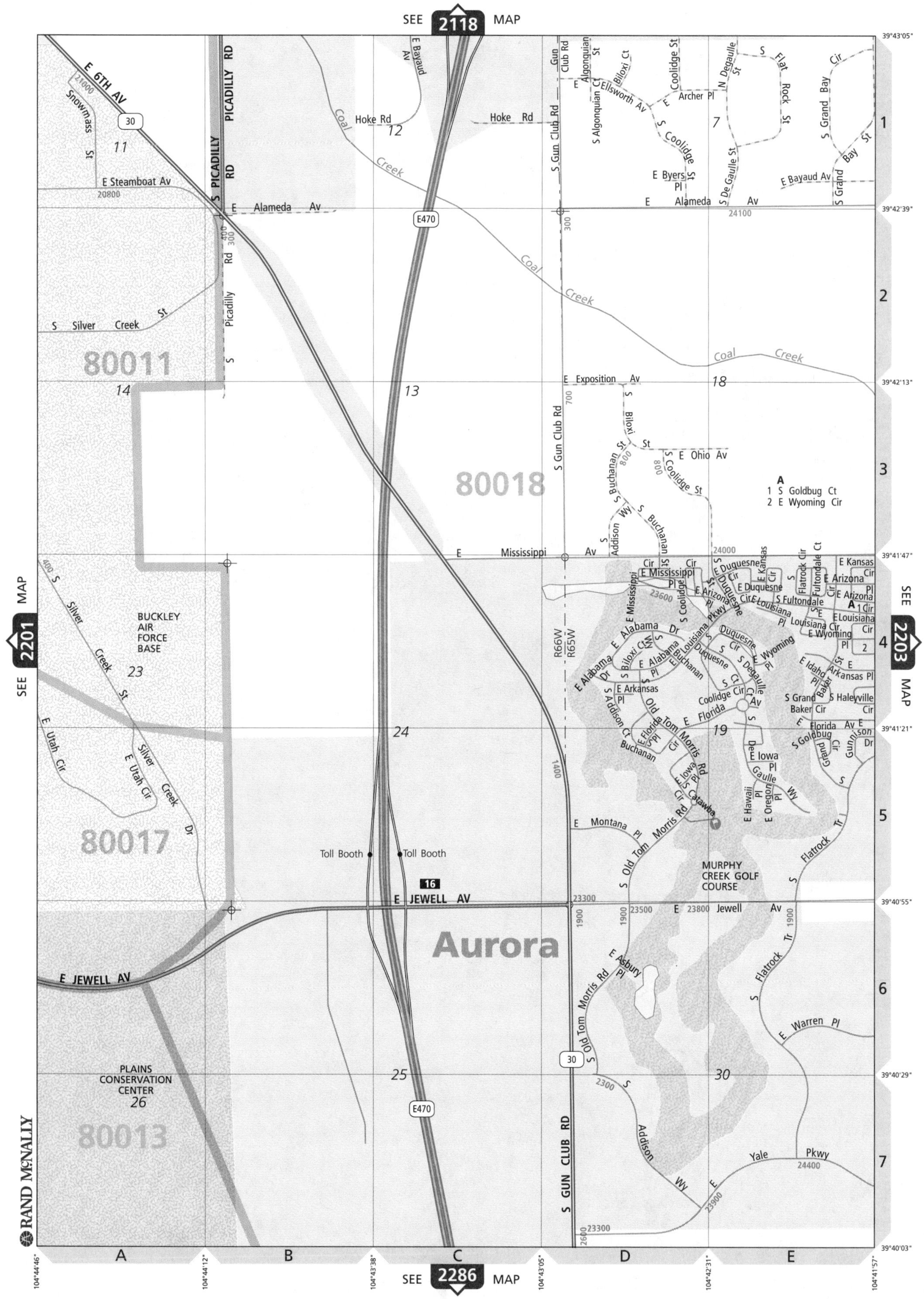

SEE 2201 MAP

SEE 2203 MAP

E 6TH AV
30
Snowmass St
11
E Steamboat Av
S PICADILLY RD
PICADILLY RD
E Alameda Av
S Picadilly Rd
S Silver Creek St
80011
14
E Bayaud Av
Hoke Rd
12
Coal Creek
E470
13
80018
S Gun Club Rd
Gun Club Rd
E Algonquian St
S Algonquian Ct
E Ellsworth Av
Biloxi Ct
Coolidge St
Archer Pl
N Degaulle St
S Flat Rock St
S Grand Bay Cir
7
S Coolidge St
E Byers Pl
S De Gaulle St
E Bayaud Av
S Grand Bay St
E Alameda Av
24100
E Exposition Av
18
S Biloxi St
E Ohio Av
S Buchanan St
S Coolidge St
S Addison Wy
S Buchanan St
A
1 S Goldbug Ct
2 E Wyoming Cir
E Mississippi Av
24000
BUCKLEY AIR FORCE BASE
23
S Silver Creek St
E Utah Cir
E Utah Cir
Silver Creek Dr
80017
24
R66W
R65W
E Mississippi Cir
E Duquesne Cir
E Kansas Cir
E Arizona Pl
S Fultondale Cir
E Louisiana Pl
E Wyoming Cir
E Alabama Dr
S Biloxi Ct
E Alabama Pl
S Duquesne Ct
S Degaulle Ct
E Arkansas Pl
S Addison Ct
Coolidge Cir
E Florida Av
Old Tom Morris Rd
E Florida Pl
Buchanan Cir
19
E Idaho Pl
S Grand Baker Cir
S Haleyville Cir
S Goldbug Cir
Grand Cir
Gunnison Dr
E Iowa Pl
De Gaulle Wy
E Hawaii Pl
E Oregon Pl
S Catawba
E Montana Pl
Toll Booth
Toll Booth
16
E JEWELL AV
MURPHY CREEK GOLF COURSE
S Flatrock Tr
23300
23500
E 23800 Jewell Av
Aurora
E JEWELL AV
E Asbury Pl
S Old Tom Morris Rd
S Flatrock Tr
E Warren Pl
30
PLAINS CONSERVATION CENTER
26
80013
25
E470
30
S Addison Wy
E Yale Pkwy
24400
S GUN CLUB RD
23300

Grid rows: 1, 2, 3, 4, 5, 6, 7
Grid columns: A, B, C, D, E

39°43'05"
39°42'39"
39°42'13"
39°41'47"
39°41'21"
39°40'55"
39°40'29"
39°40'03"
104°44'46"
104°44'12"
104°43'38"
104°43'05"
104°42'31"
104°41'57"

SEE 2286 MAP

1:24,000
1 in. = 2000 ft.
0 0.25 0.5
miles

SEE 2119 MAP

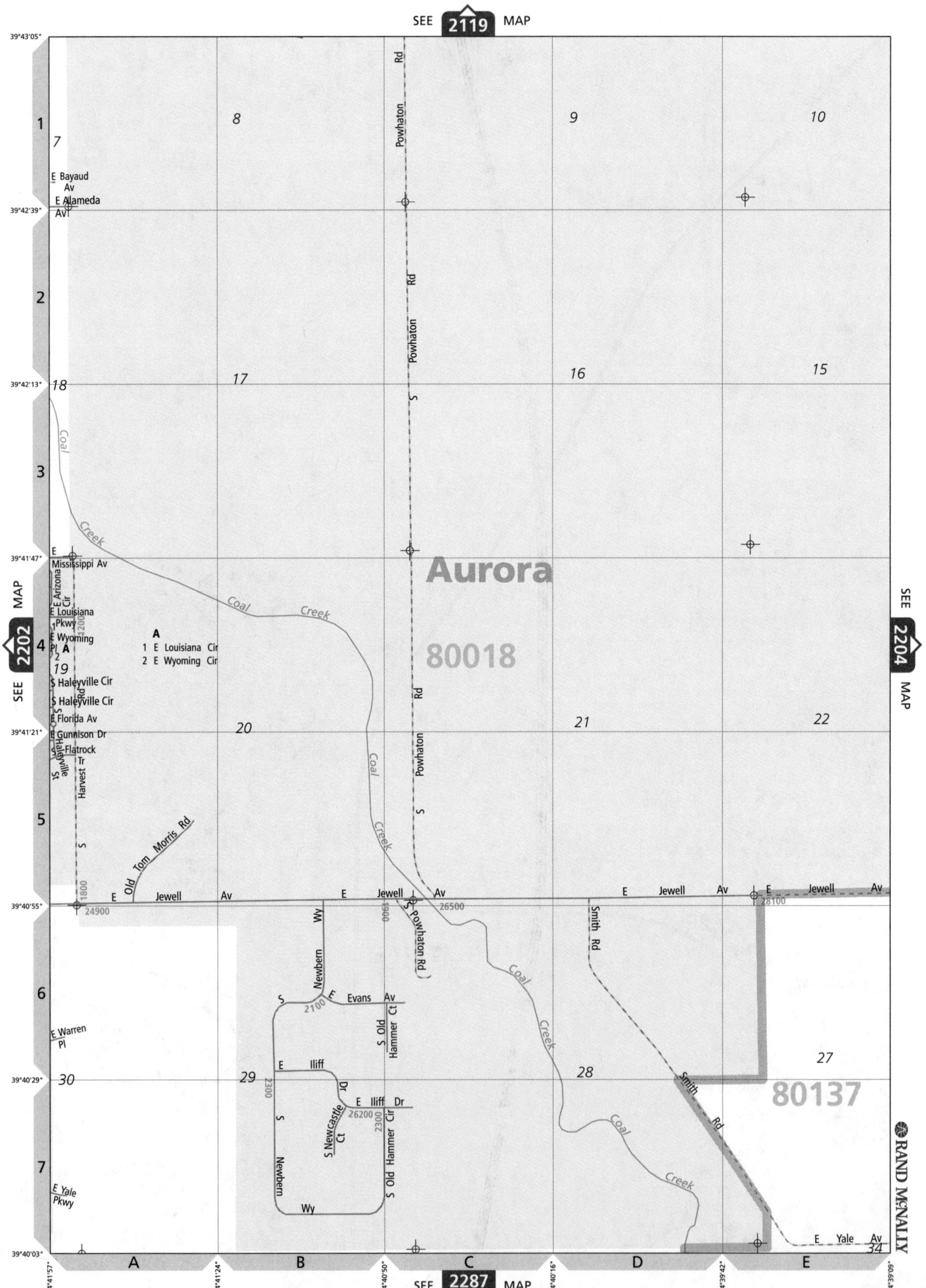

SEE 2202 MAP

SEE 2204 MAP

SEE 2287 MAP

1:24,000
1 in. = 2000 ft.
0 0.25 0.5
miles

SEE 2120 MAP

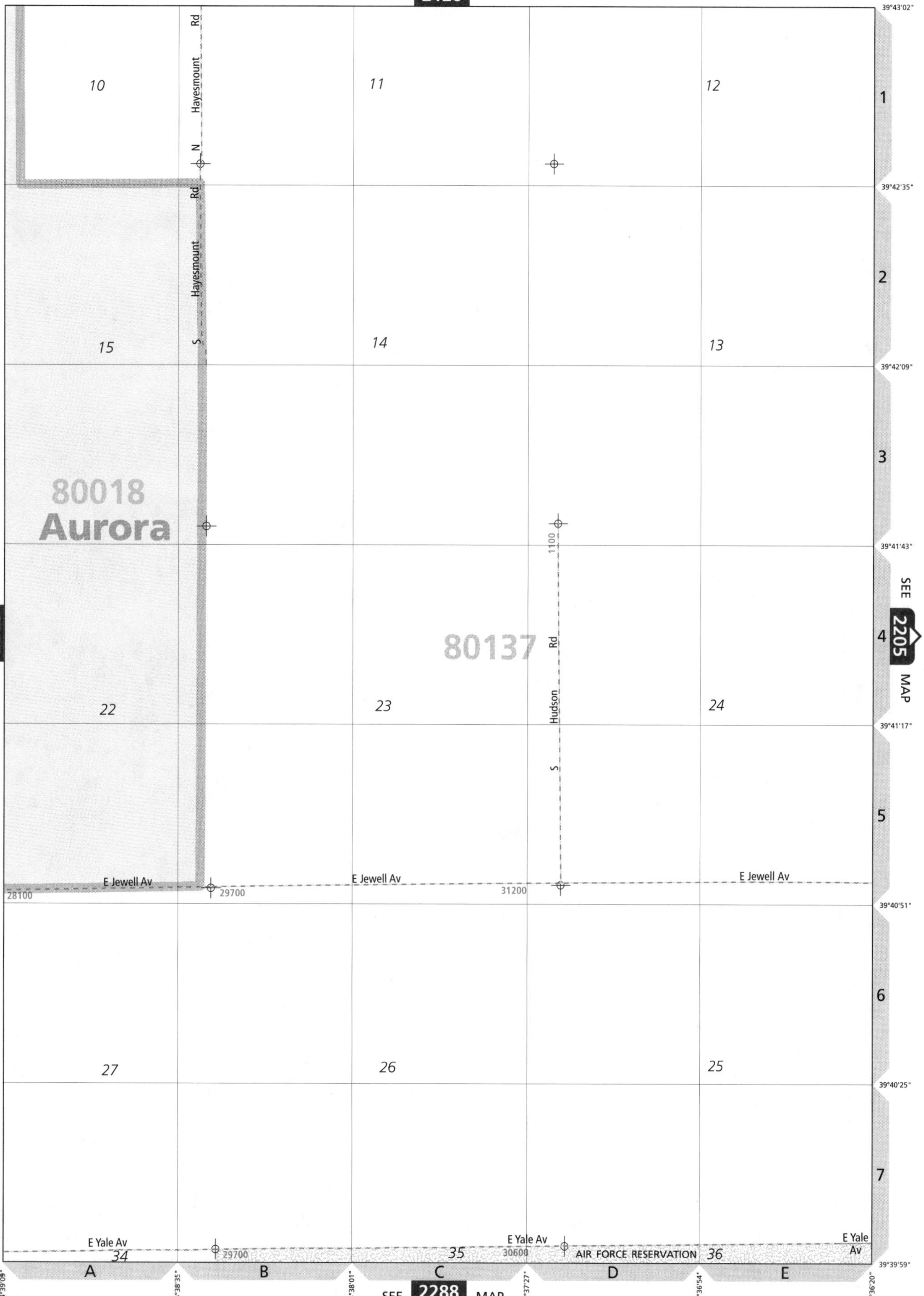

SEE 2203 MAP

SEE 2205 MAP

SEE 2288 MAP

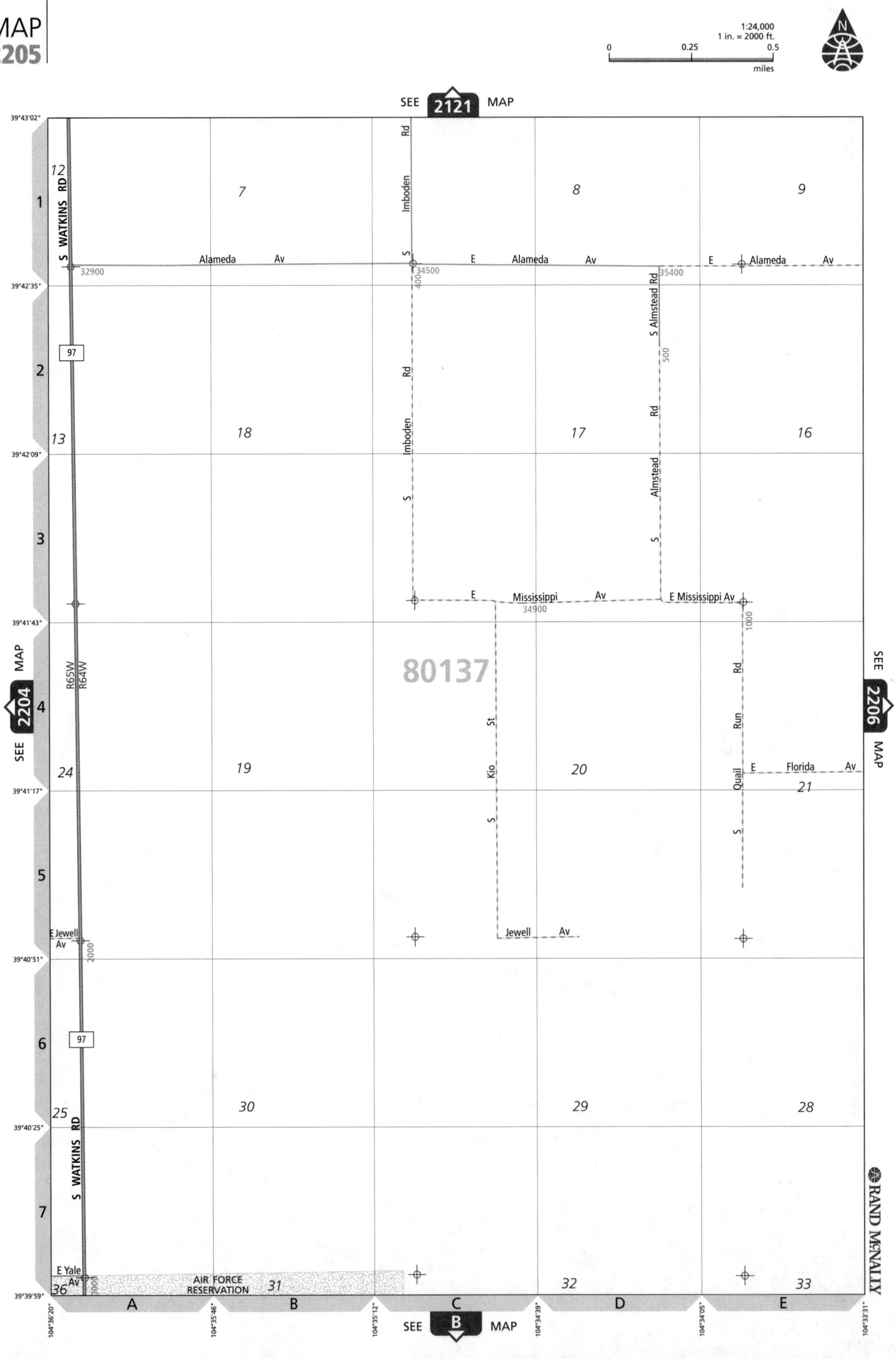

1:24,000
1 in. = 2000 ft.
0 0.25 0.5
miles

SEE 2121 MAP

SEE 2204 MAP

SEE 2206 MAP

SEE B MAP

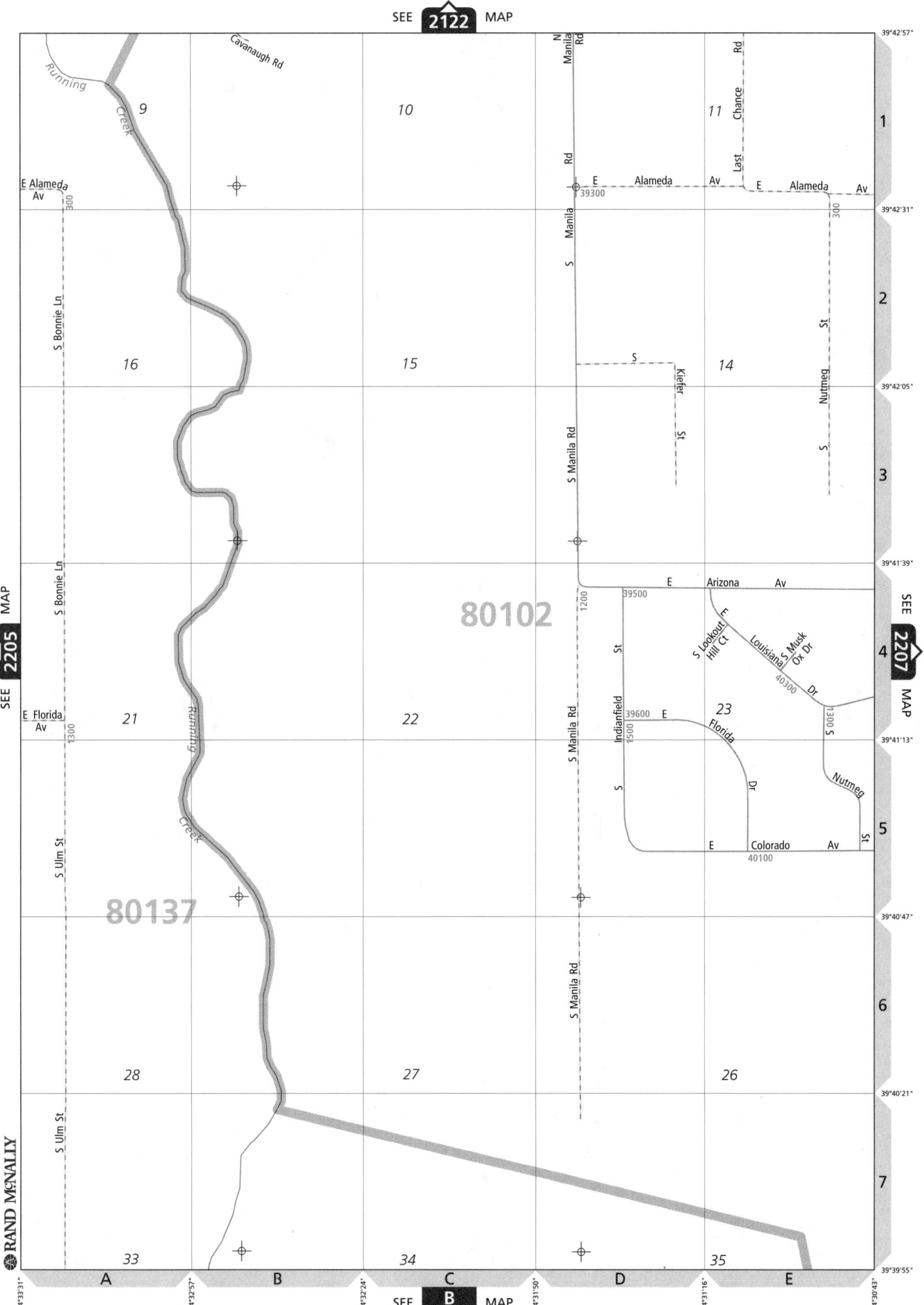
1:24,000
1 in. = 2000 ft.
0 0.25 0.5
miles
SEE 2122 MAP
SEE 2205 MAP
SEE 2207 MAP
SEE B MAP
Cavanaugh Rd
Running Creek
E Alameda Av
N Manila Rd
S Manila Rd
E Alameda Av
Last Chance Rd
39300
300
1300
1200
1500
S Bonnie Ln
S Kiefer St
S Nutmeg St
E Arizona Av
39500
80102
80137
S Lookout Hill Ct
E Louisiana Dr
S Musk Ox Dr
40300
1300 S
S Indianfield St
39600
E Florida Dr
E Florida Av
Nutmeg St
E Colorado Av
40100
S Ulm St
9
10
11
14
15
16
21
22
23
26
27
28
33
34
35
1
2
3
4
5
6
7
A
B
C
D
E
39°42'57"
39°42'31"
39°42'05"
39°41'39"
39°41'13"
39°40'47"
39°40'21"
39°39'55"
104°33'31"
104°32'57"
104°32'24"
104°31'50"
104°31'16"
104°30'43"
RAND McNALLY

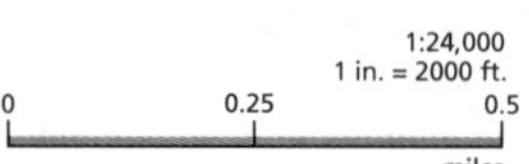

SEE 2123 MAP

SEE 2206 MAP

SEE 2208 MAP

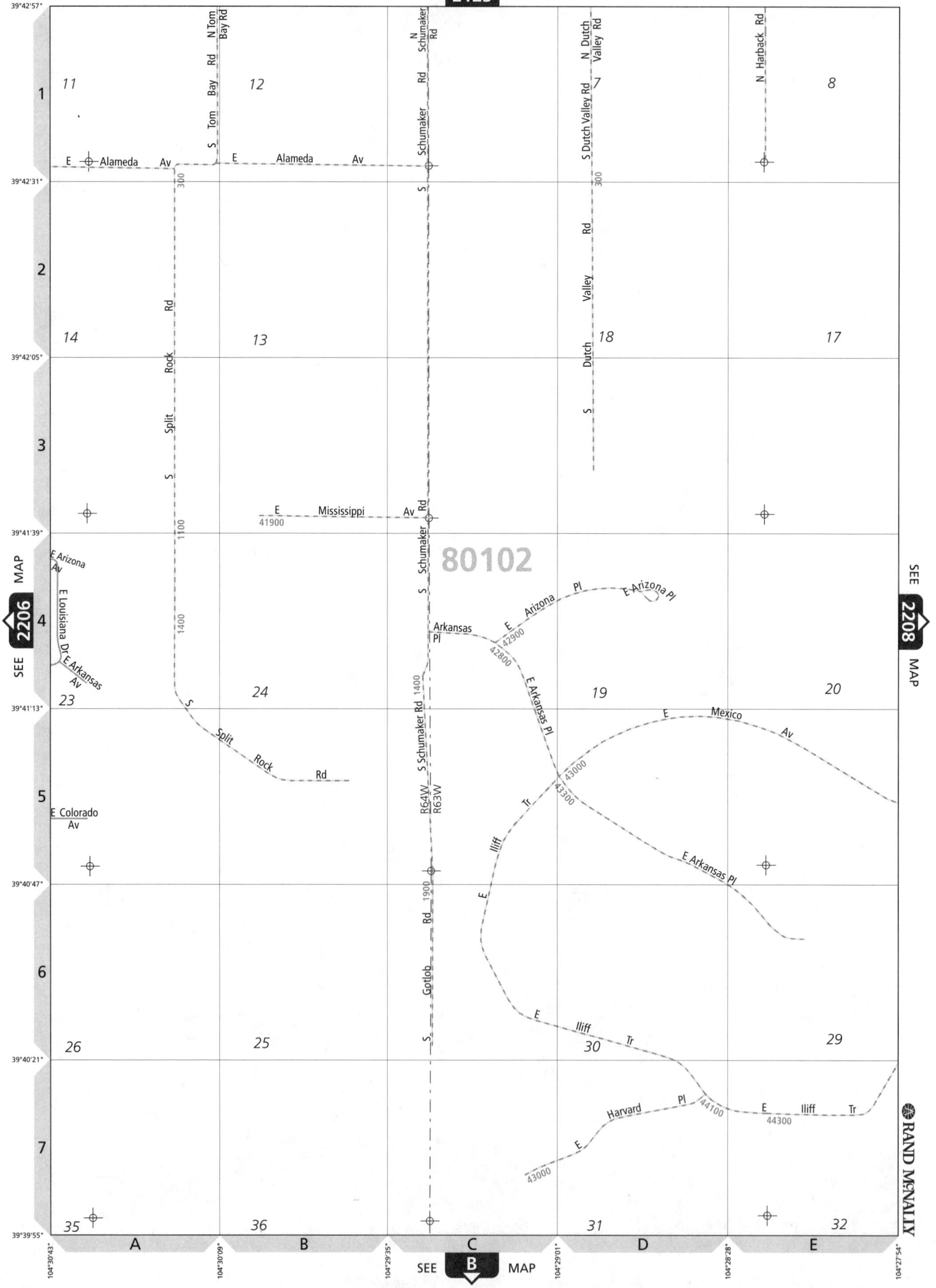

SEE B MAP

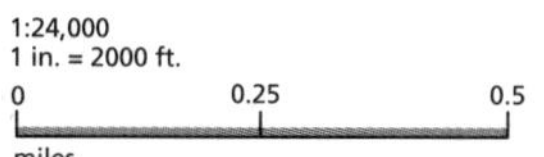

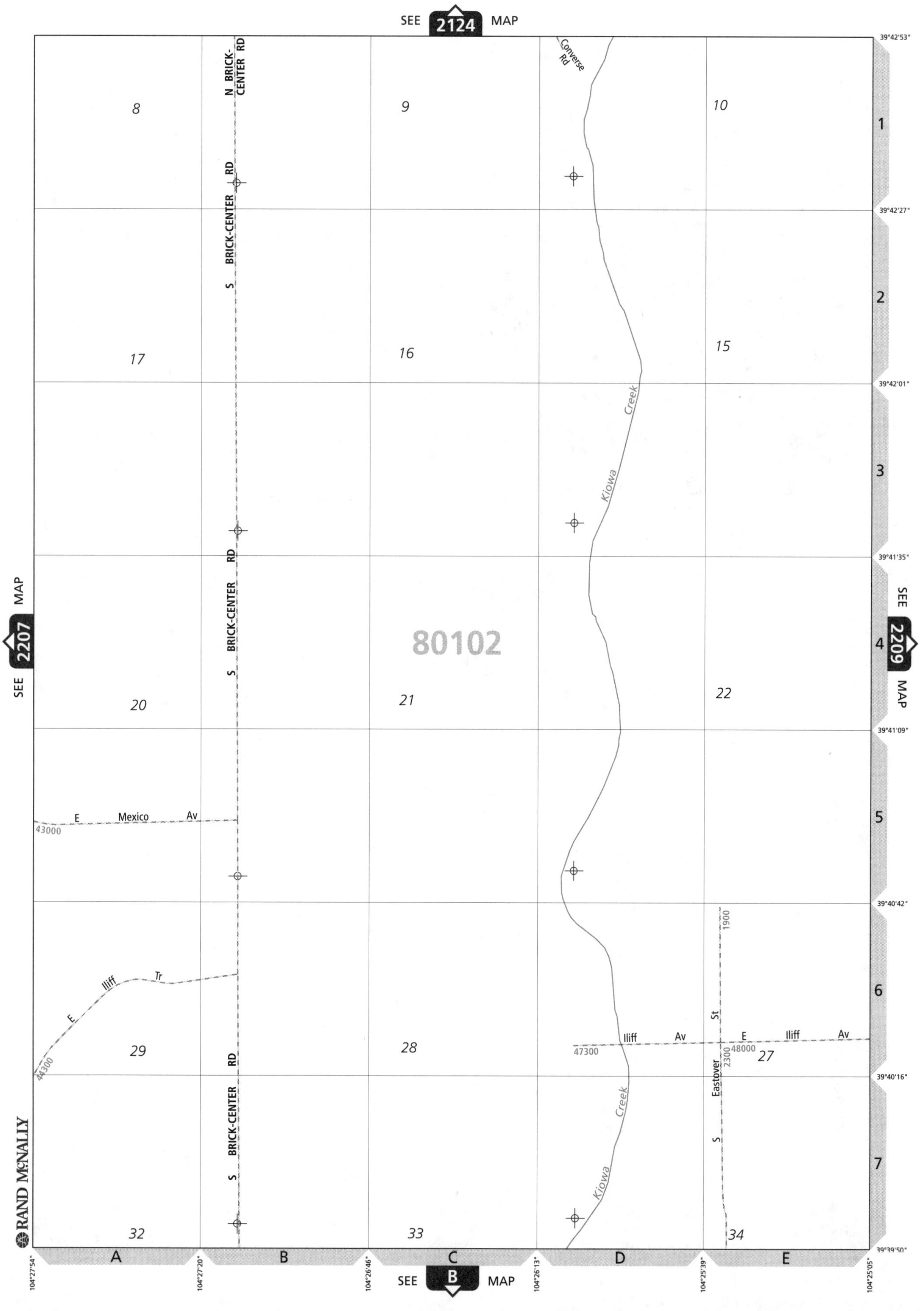

SEE 2124 MAP

SEE 2207 MAP

SEE 2209 MAP

SEE B MAP

1:24,000
1 in. = 2000 ft.
0
0.25
0.5
miles
N
SEE 2125 MAP
SEE 2208 MAP
SEE B MAP
SEE B MAP
39°42'53"
39°42'27"
39°42'01"
39°41'35"
39°41'09"
39°40'42"
39°40'16"
39°39'50"
104°25'05"
104°24'31"
104°23'58"
104°23'24"
104°22'50"
104°22'17"
A
B
C
D
E
1
2
3
4
5
6
7
10
11
12
7
15
14
13
18
22
23
24
19
27
26
25
30
34
35
36
31
ANTELOPE HILLS
GOLF COURSE
Bennett
80102
W Antelope Dr
300
49100
E Antelope Dr
Valley Wy
E Antelope Dr
Columbine Dr
W Antelope Dr
Antelope Hills Blvd
600
700
W Green Gables Wy
Green Gables Ct
Antelope
Green Gables Cir
Dr
E Pinehurst Ct
Antelope Dr
E Mississippi Av
E Mississippi Av
50500
S KIOWA-BENNETT RD
CR-145
CR-145
R63W
R62W
CR-18
1600
S Vanderhoof Ct
S Vanderhoof Ct
E Jewell Av
48900
49600
49900
50500
S Kyle Cir
S Lenaview Cir
E Iliff Av
2300
S KIOWA-BENNETT RD
S Lenaview Cir
RAND McNALLY

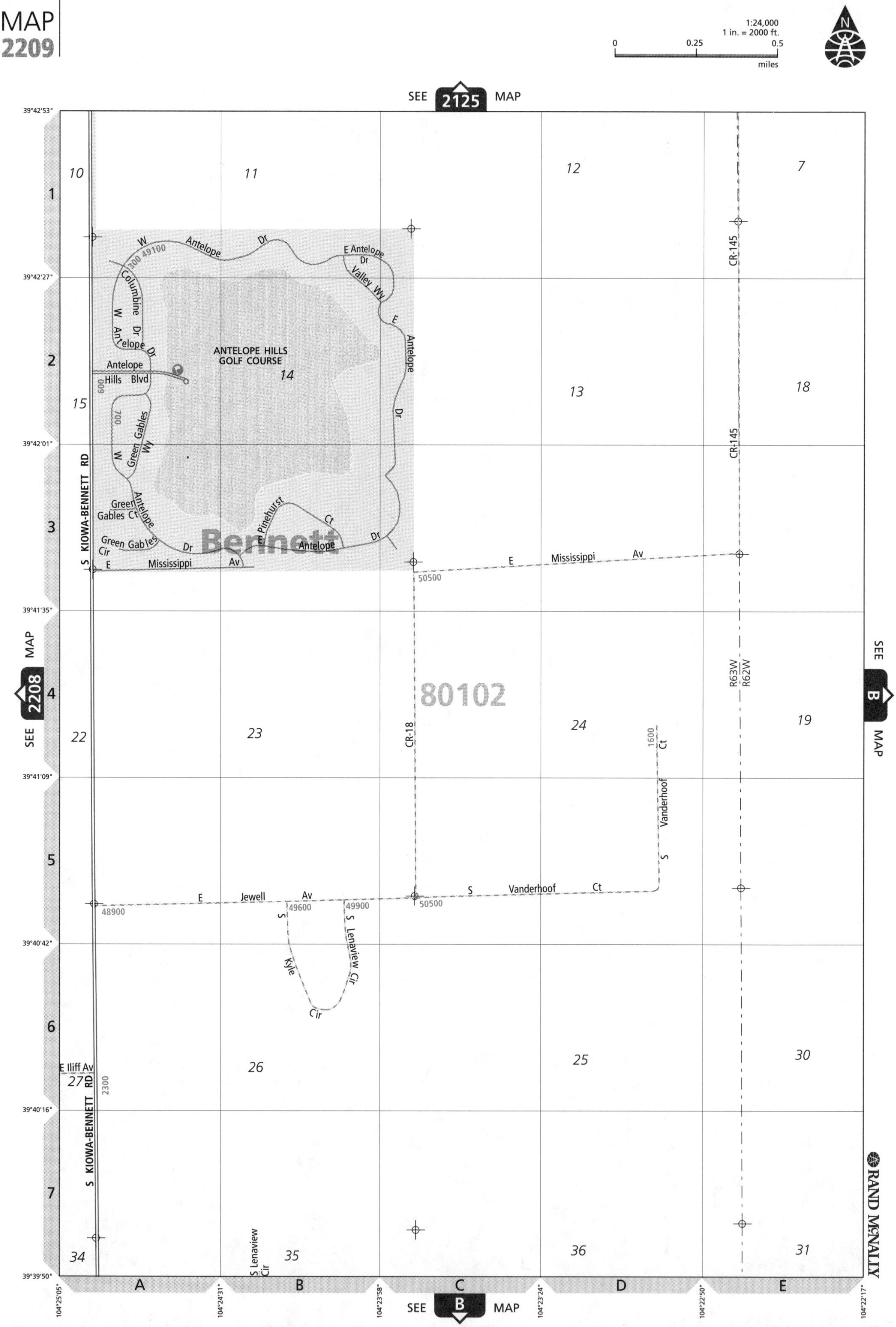

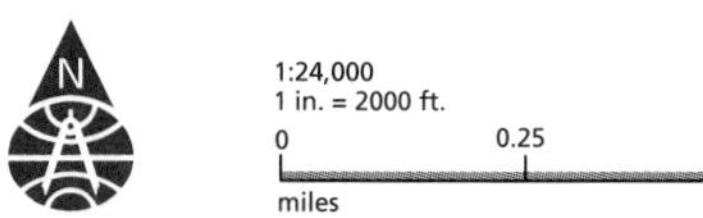

SEE 2186 MAP

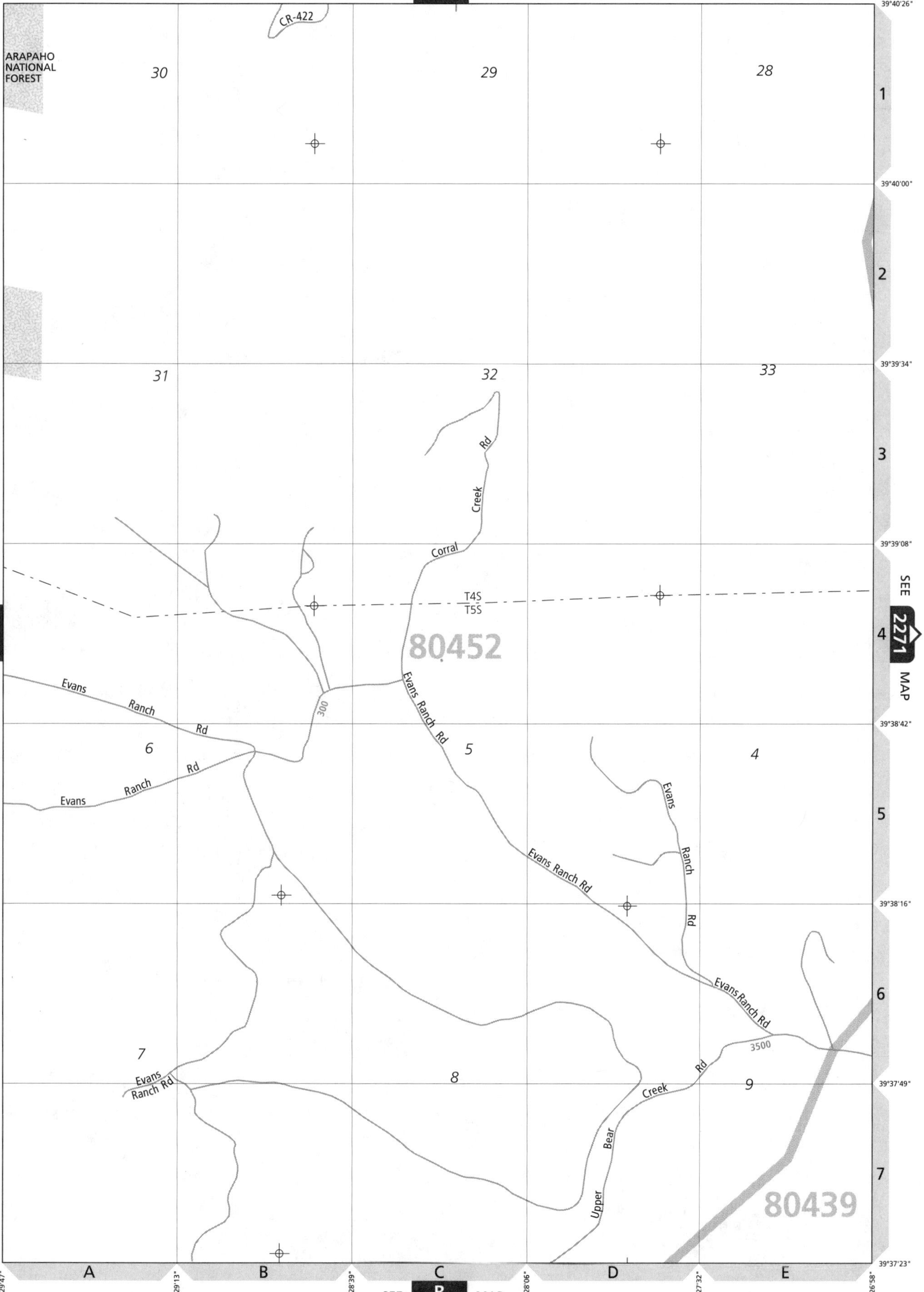

SEE B MAP

SEE 2271 MAP

SEE B MAP

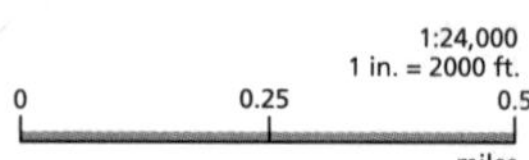

SEE 2187 MAP

Witter Gulch Rd
Sinton Rd
Lodgepole Dr
Meadowlark Dr
Aspen Ln
Aspen Dr
Lodgepole
Castlewood Dr
Martin Dr
Sinton Rd
Aspenwood Ln
Valley View Ln
Juniper Ct
Pinewood Dr
Witter Gulch Rd
Aspenwood Dr
MT EVANS STATE WILDLIFE AREA
Spruce Ct
Jack Pine Ln
Mountain Rd
Witter Gulch Rd
Aspen Pl
Grouse Wy
Evergreen West
Aspen Pl
Aspen Cir
Juniper Ln
Blue Spruce Dr
Snyder Meadow Ln
Juniper Ln
Juniper Ln
Witter Gulch Rd
80452
80439
80452
T4S
T5S
Stagecoach Blvd
Wilderness Cornerstone Rd
N Ponderosa Wy
Deer Ln
James Dr
S Ponderosa Wy
S Ponderosa Wy
Fox Ridge Rd
Circle K Ranch Rd
Mary Beth Rd
Cottonwood Dr
Witter Gulch
Marion Dr
Oak Wy
Bear Dr
Carolyn Dr
Greystone Rd
David Dr
Aspen Ct
Patty Dr
Hillside Rd
Dreher Dr
Nuthatch Rd
Echo Lake Dr
Patty Dr
Murphy Rd
Kings Rd
Sawmill Rd
S Sawmill Rd
Pauls Rd
Teresa Dr
Echo Tr
Siesta Cir
Upper Bear Creek Rd
Bendemeer Valley
Mesa Dr
Bendemeer Dr
Bendemeer Dr
Rock Gulch Rd
Beaver Ct
Bear Creek
Ridge Rd
Fox Hollow Rd
Diamond Dr
Diamond Dr
Diamond Dr
Brookvale
Diamond Dr
Upper Bear Creek Rd
Upper Bear Creek Rd
Grouse Rd
Elk Crossing Ln
Ranch Rd
Grouse Rd
Blue
Blue Potato Patch Rd
Rd
Yankee Creek Rd
Creek
Singing River Ranch Rd
Bear
Bear Meadow Tr
Bear Meadow Tr

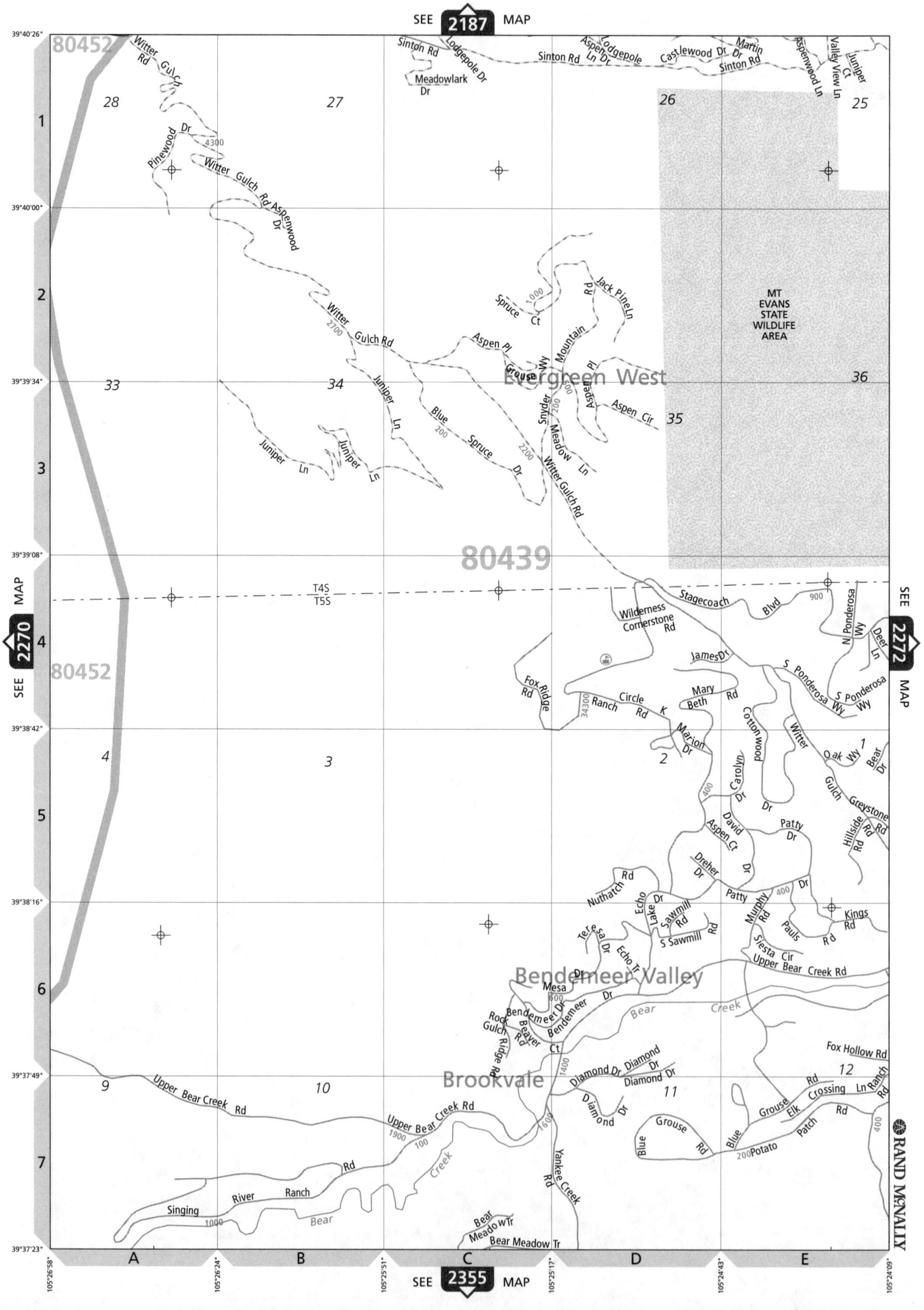

28 27 26 25 33 34 35 36 4 3 2 1 9 10 11 12

1 2 3 4 5 6 7

A B C D E

39°40'26" 39°40'00" 39°39'34" 39°39'08" 39°38'42" 39°38'16" 39°37'49" 39°37'23"

105°26'58" 105°26'24" 105°25'51" 105°25'17" 105°24'43" 105°24'09"

SEE 2270 MAP

SEE 2272 MAP

SEE 2355 MAP

1:24,000
1 in. = 2000 ft.
0 0.25 0.5
miles

SEE 2188 MAP

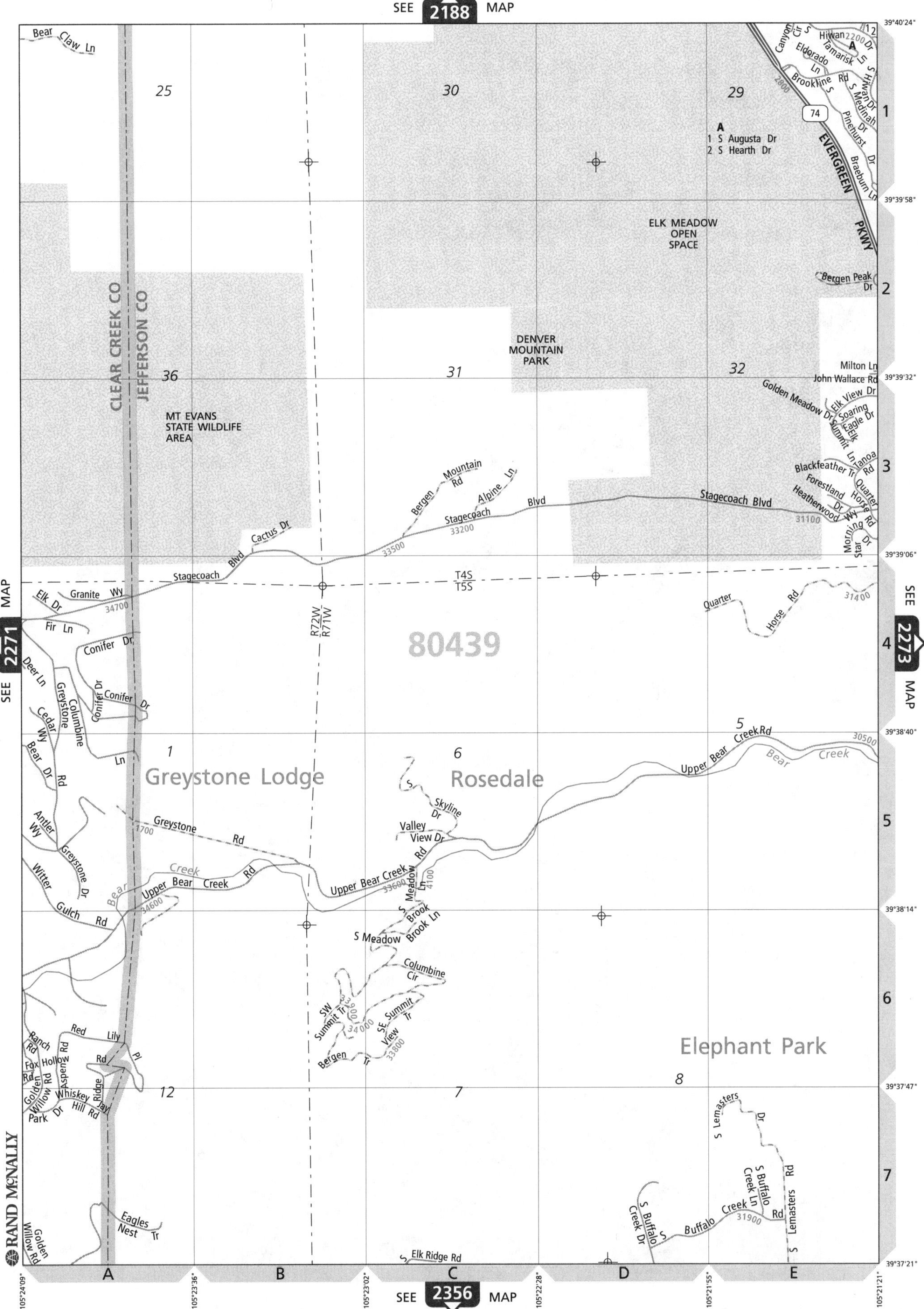
Bear Claw Ln
25
30
29
CLEAR CREEK CO
JEFFERSON CO
ELK MEADOW
OPEN
SPACE
EVERGREEN PKWY
74
A
1 S Augusta Dr
2 S Hearth Dr
Bergen Peak Dr
DENVER
MOUNTAIN
PARK
36
31
32
MT EVANS
STATE WILDLIFE
AREA
Milton Ln
John Wallace Rd
Golden Meadow Dr
Elk View Dr
Soaring Eagle Dr
Blackfeather Tr
Forestland Dr
Heatherwood Wy
Quarter Horse Rd
Morning Star Dr
Bergen Mountain Rd
Alpine Ln
Stagecoach Blvd
Cactus Dr
T4S
T5S
R72W
R71W
Elk Dr
Granite Wy
Fir Ln
Conifer Dr
Deer Ln
Greystone
Columbine
Cedar Wy
Bear Dr
80439
Quarter Horse Rd
5
Upper Bear Creek Rd
Bear Creek
1
6
Greystone Lodge
Rosedale
S Skyline Dr
Valley View Dr
Greystone Rd
Antler Wy
Witter Gulch Rd
Upper Bear Creek Rd
S Meadow Brook Ln
Columbine Cir
SW Summit Tr
SE Summit View Tr
Bergen Tr
Red Lily Pl
Ranch Rd
Fox Hollow Rd
Aspen Rd
Golden Willow Rd
Whiskey Hill Rd
Ridge
Jay
Park Dr
12
7
8
Elephant Park
S Lemasters Dr
S Buffalo Creek Ln
S Buffalo Creek Dr
S Buffalo Creek Rd
S Lemasters Rd
Eagles Nest Tr
Golden Willow Rd
S Elk Ridge Rd
A B C D E
1 2 3 4 5 6 7

SEE 2271 MAP

SEE 2273 MAP

SEE 2356 MAP

1:24,000
1 in. = 2000 ft.
0 0.25 0.5
miles

SEE 2189 MAP

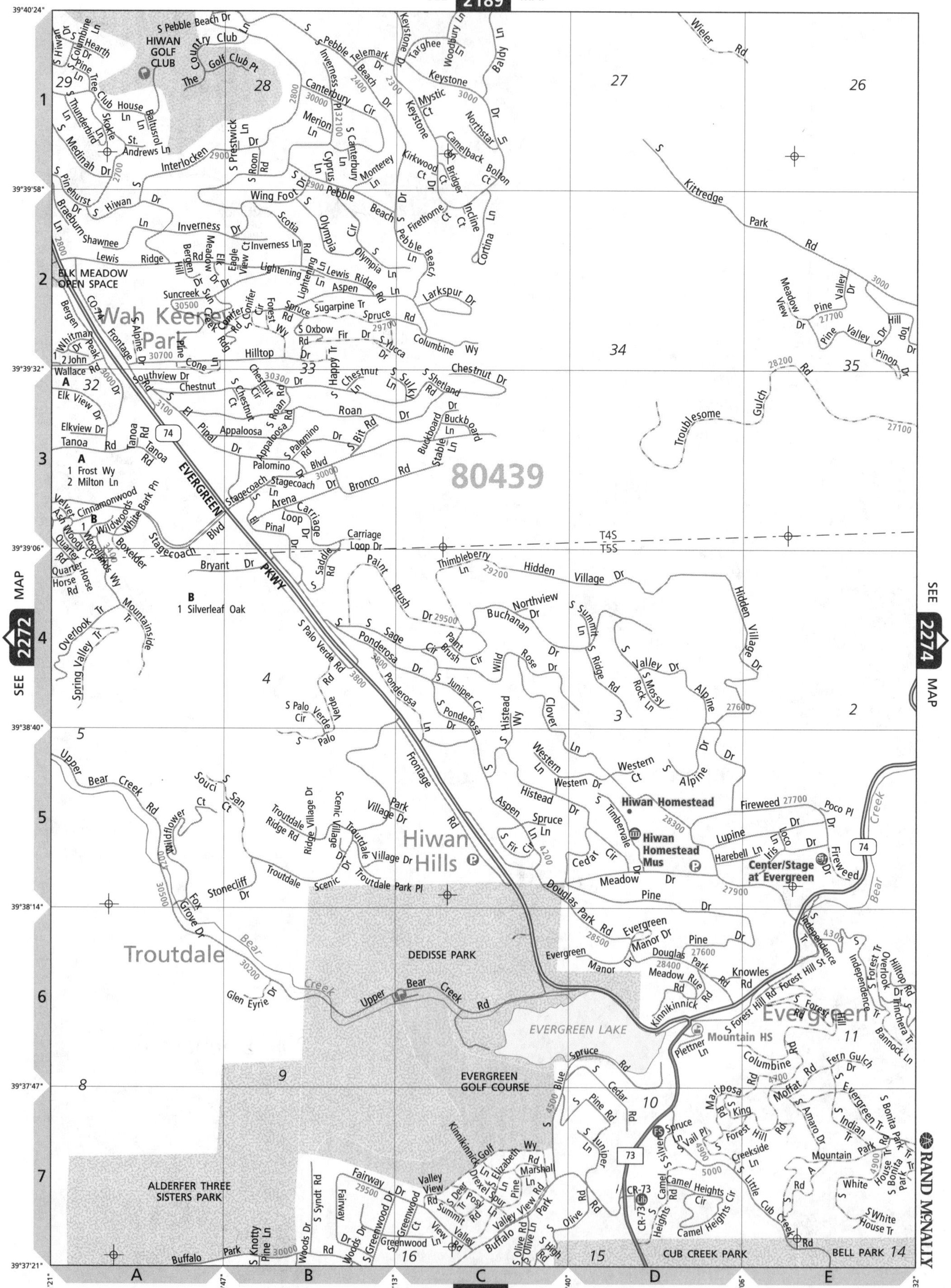

SEE 2272 MAP

SEE 2274 MAP

39°40'24"
39°39'58"
39°39'32"
39°39'06"
39°38'40"
39°38'14"
39°37'47"
39°37'21"

HIWAN GOLF CLUB
S Pebble Beach Dr
Country Club Ln
The Golf Club Pt
S Columbine Dr
S Hearth Dr
Pine Tree Club House Ln
S Thunderbird Ln
Skokie Ln
Baltusrol Ln
St. Andrews Ln
S Medinah Dr
Interlocken
S Prestwick Dr
S Roon Rd
S Pinehurst Dr
S Hiwan Dr
Braeburn Ln
Shawnee Ln
Inverness Dr
Lewis Ridge
Inverness Ln
Wing Foot Dr
Scotia Rd
Olympia Cir
Pebble Beach Dr
Telemark Dr
Inverness Dr
Canterbury Cir
S Canterbury Ln
Merion Ln
Cyprus Ln
Monterey Ln
Keystone Dr
Targhee
Woodbury Ln
Baldy Ln
Keystone
Mystic Ct
Northstar Ln
Camelback Ln
Kirkwood Ct
Bridger Ct
Bolton Ct
Firethorne Ct
Incline Ct
Cortina Ln
S Pebble Beach Dr
Wieler Rd
S Kittredge Park Rd
Meadow View Dr
Pine Valley Dr
Hill Top Dr
Pinon Dr
Troublesome Gulch Rd
ELK MEADOW OPEN SPACE
Bergen Hill Rd
Elk Meadow Dr
Eagle View Ct
Lightening Ln
Lewis Ridge Rd
Suncreek Ln
Sun Creek Rdg
Conifer Rd
Forest Wy
Spruce Rd
Sugarpine Tr
Aspen
Oxbow Rd
Fir Dr
Yucca Dr
Larkspur Dr
Columbine Wy
Wah Keeney Park
CO-74 Frontage Rd
S Alpine Dr
Pine Cone Ln
Hilltop Dr
Happy Tr
Bergen Peak Dr
Whitman Dr
Southview Dr
Chestnut
Chestnut Dr
Chestnut Cir
Chestnut Ct
Roan Rd
Sulky Ln
Shetland Rd
Buckboard Ln
Elk View Dr
Elkview Dr
Tanoa Rd
El Pinal
Appaloosa Dr
Palomino Blvd
Bit Rd
Stable Ln
Stagecoach Dr
Bronco Rd
Arena Loop
Carriage Dr
Carriage Loop Dr
Velvet Ash Dr
Cinnamonwood
Wildwoods
White Bark Pn
Woody Ct
Quarter Horse Rd
Boxelder
Stagecoach Blvd
Bryant Dr
Saddle Rd
Mountainside Tr
Overlook Tr
Spring Valley Tr
EVERGREEN PKWY
T4S
T5S
Thimbleberry Ln
Hidden Village Dr
Paint Brush Dr
Northview Dr
Buchanan Dr
S Summit Ln
S Ridge Rd
Valley Dr
S Mossy Rock Ln
Alpine Dr
S Sage Cir
Ponderosa Dr
S Juniper Cir
Wild Rose Dr
S Palo Verde Rd
S Palo Verde Cir
Histead Wy
Clover Ln
Western Ct
Western Dr
Histead Dr
Aspen Ln
Spruce Ln
Fir Ct
Timbervale Dr
Cedar Cir
Meadow Dr
Pine Dr
Fireweed
Poco Pl
Lupine Dr
Harebell Ln
Iris Ln
Loco Dr
Upper Bear Creek Rd
Souci Ct
S San Ct
Wildflower
Troutdale Ridge Rd
Troutdale Village Dr
Scenic Village Dr
Park Village Dr
Stonecliff Dr
Troutdale Scenic Dr
Troutdale Park Pl
Fox Grove Dr
Glen Eyrie Dr
Douglas Park Rd
Evergreen Manor Dr
Pine Dr
Douglas Park Rd
Knowles Rd
Meadow Rue Rd
Kinnikinnick Rd
Forest Hill Rd
Forest Hill St
Independence Tr
S Forest Tr
Overlook Dr
Hilltop Rd
Trinchera Tr
Bannock Ln
Spruce Rd
Cedar Rd
Pine Rd
Juniper Ln
Blue
Columbine Rd
Fern Gulch Dr
Mariposa Rd
King
Moffat Rd
Evergreen Tr
S Amaro Dr
S Indian Tr
S Bonita Park Tr
Mountain Park Rd
White House Tr
S Spruce Ln
Vail Pl
Silver Camel Rd
Creekside Ln
Little Cub Creek Rd
Camel Heights Cir
Kinnikinnick Golf Wy
S Elizabeth Rd
Marshall
Fairway Dr
Valley View Rd
S Deer Tr
Drexel Post
Summit Rd
Valley View Rd
Buffalo Rd
S Olive Ln
Olive Rd
Greenwood Ln
S Synd Rd
Woods Dr
S Knotty Pine Ln
Buffalo Park Rd
High

80439
Hiwan Hills
Hiwan Homestead
Hiwan Homestead Mus
Center/Stage at Evergreen
Troutdale
Evergreen
Mountain HS
DEDISSE PARK
EVERGREEN LAKE
EVERGREEN GOLF COURSE
ALDERFER THREE SISTERS PARK
CUB CREEK PARK
BELL PARK
Bear Creek
CR-73

A
1 John
2 Wallace Rd

A
1 Frost Wy
2 Milton Ln

B
1 Silverleaf Oak

SEE 2357 MAP

105°21'21" 105°20'47" 105°20'13" 105°19'40" 105°19'06" 105°18'32"

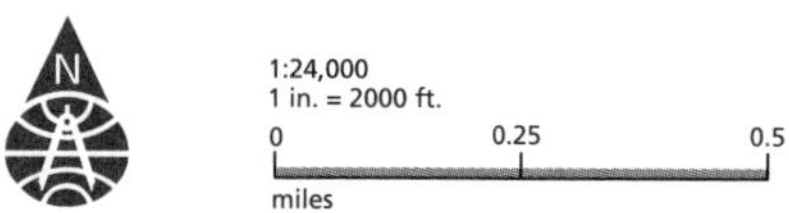

SEE 2190 MAP

Kittredge
80401
80457
80439
BEAR CREEK RD
MEYERS GULCH RD
PARMALEE GULCH RD
LAIR O' THE BEAR PARK
CORWINA PARK
O'FALLON PARK
PENCE PARK
ARROWHEAD COMM PARK
BELL PARK
1 A
A
1 S Bonita Park Tr

SEE 2273 MAP

SEE 2275 MAP

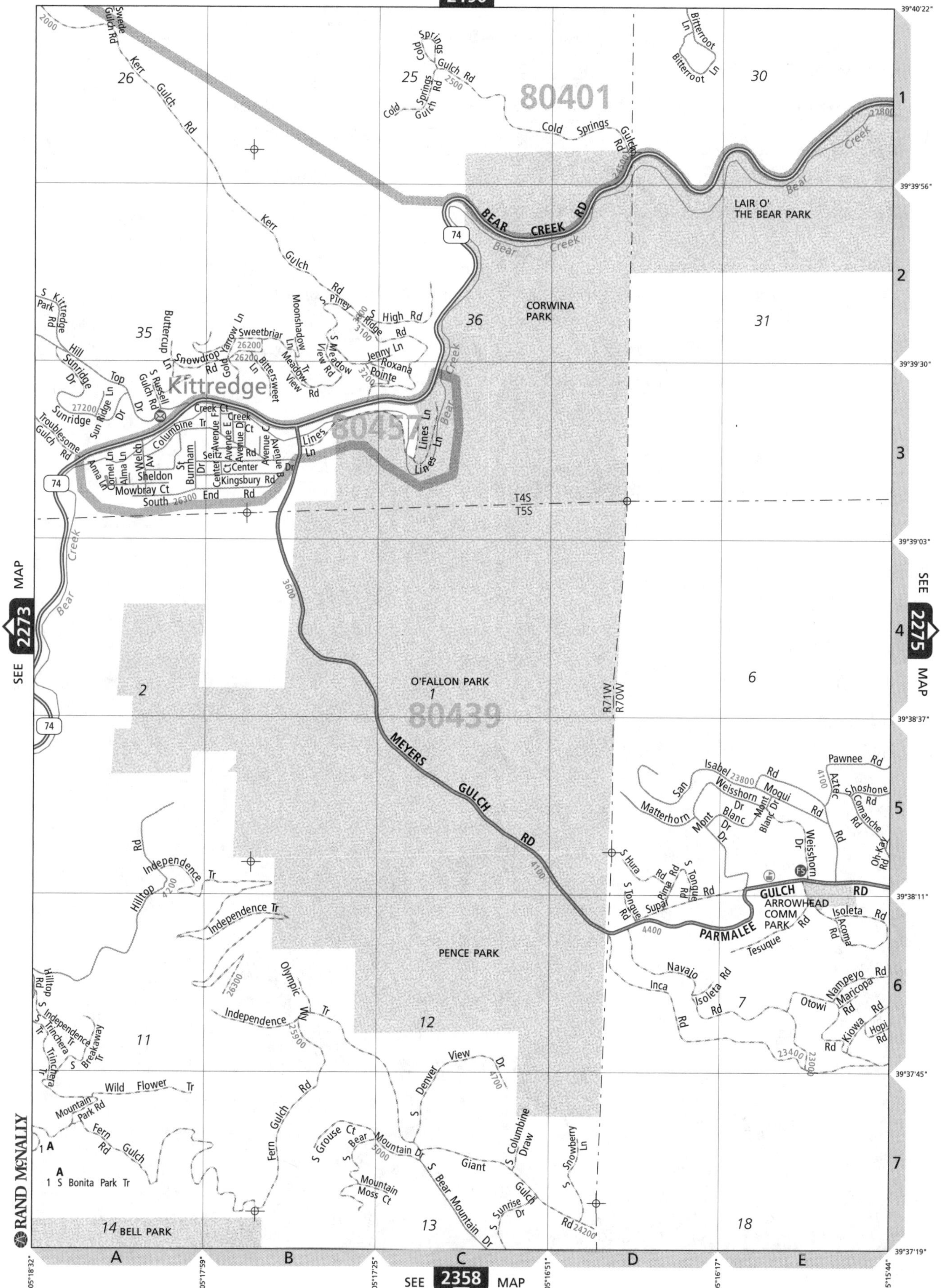

SEE 2358 MAP

RAND McNALLY

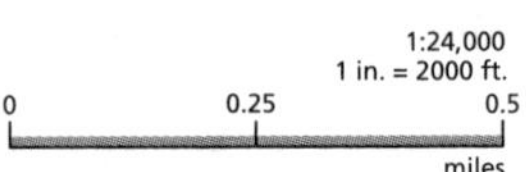

SEE 2191 MAP

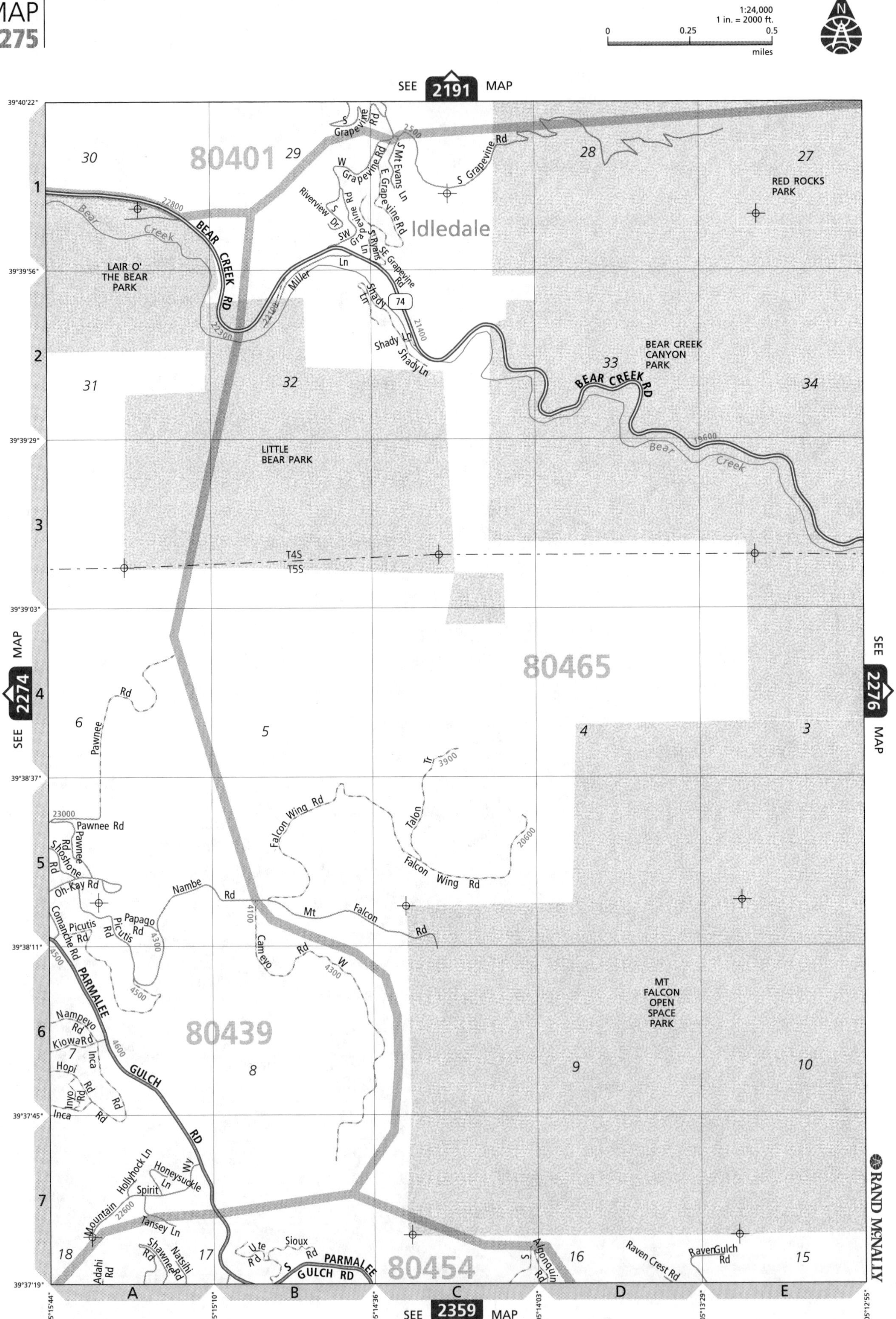

SEE 2274 MAP

SEE 2276 MAP

SEE 2359 MAP

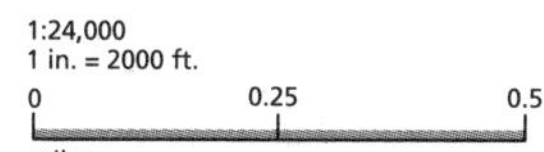

SEE 2192 MAP

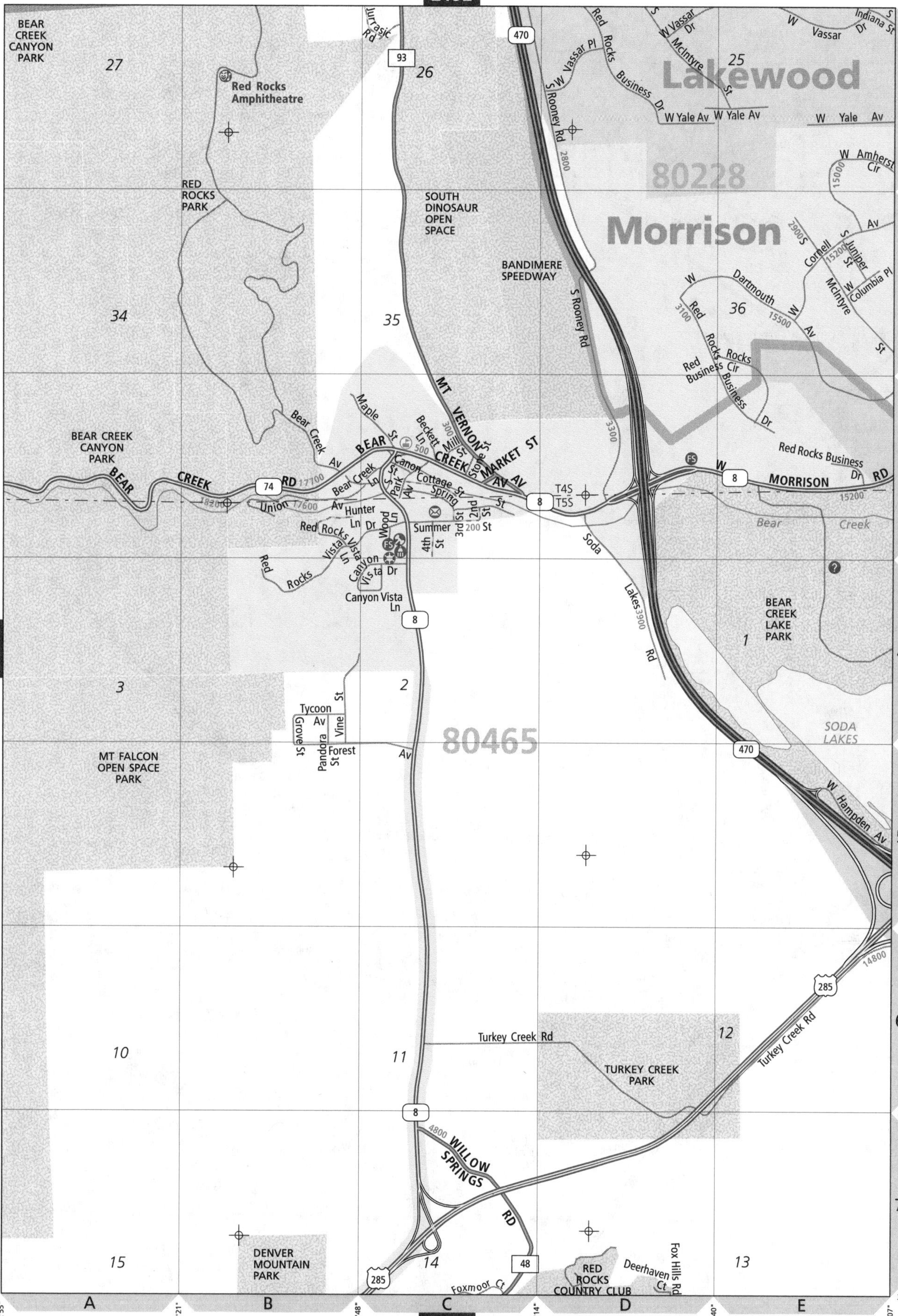

SEE 2275 MAP

SEE 2277 MAP

SEE 2360 MAP

1:24,000
1 in. = 2000 ft.
0 0.25 0.5
miles

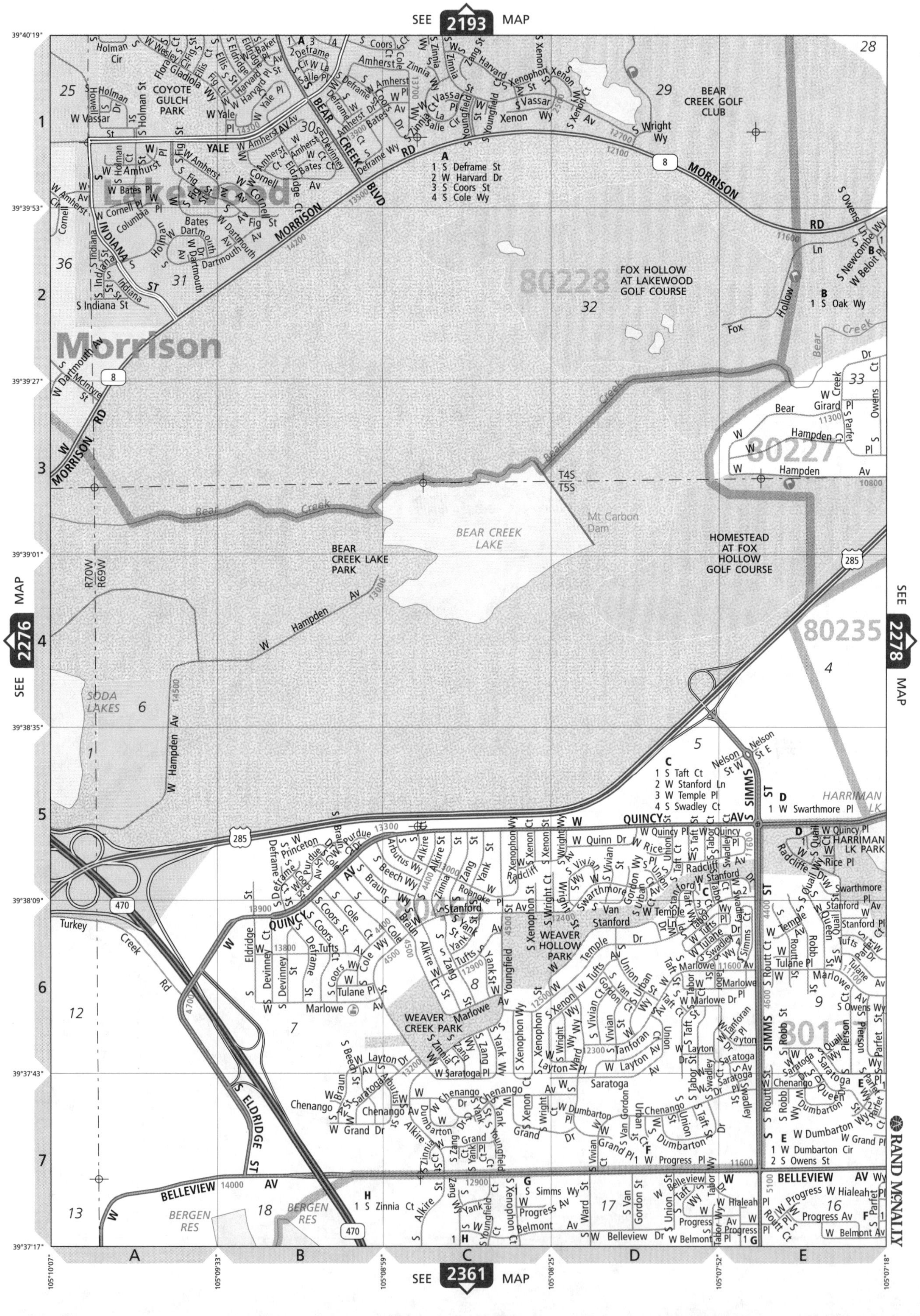

SEE 2193 MAP

SEE 2276 MAP

SEE 2278 MAP

Lakewood
Morrison

COYOTE GULCH PARK
BEAR CREEK GOLF CLUB
FOX HOLLOW AT LAKEWOOD GOLF COURSE
BEAR CREEK LAKE PARK
BEAR CREEK LAKE
Mt Carbon Dam
HOMESTEAD AT FOX HOLLOW GOLF COURSE
SODA LAKES
WEAVER HOLLOW PARK
WEAVER CREEK PARK
HARRIMAN LK
HARRIMAN LK PARK
BERGEN RES

80228
80227
80235

MORRISON RD
BEAR CREEK BLVD
YALE AV
INDIANA ST
W HAMPDEN AV
W QUINCY AV
S SIMMS ST
S ELDRIDGE ST
BELLEVIEW AV
Turkey Creek Rd

A
1 S Deframe St
2 W Harvard Dr
3 S Coors St
4 S Cole Wy

B
1 S Oak Wy

C
1 S Taft Ct
2 W Stanford Ln
3 W Temple Pl
4 S Swadley Ct

D
1 W Swarthmore Pl

E
1 W Dumbarton Cir
2 S Owens St

H
1 S Zinnia Ct

A B C D E

SEE 2361 MAP

RAND McNALLY

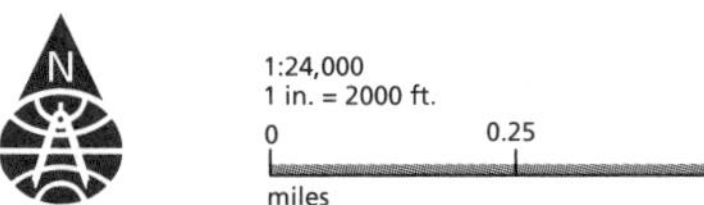

SEE 2194 MAP

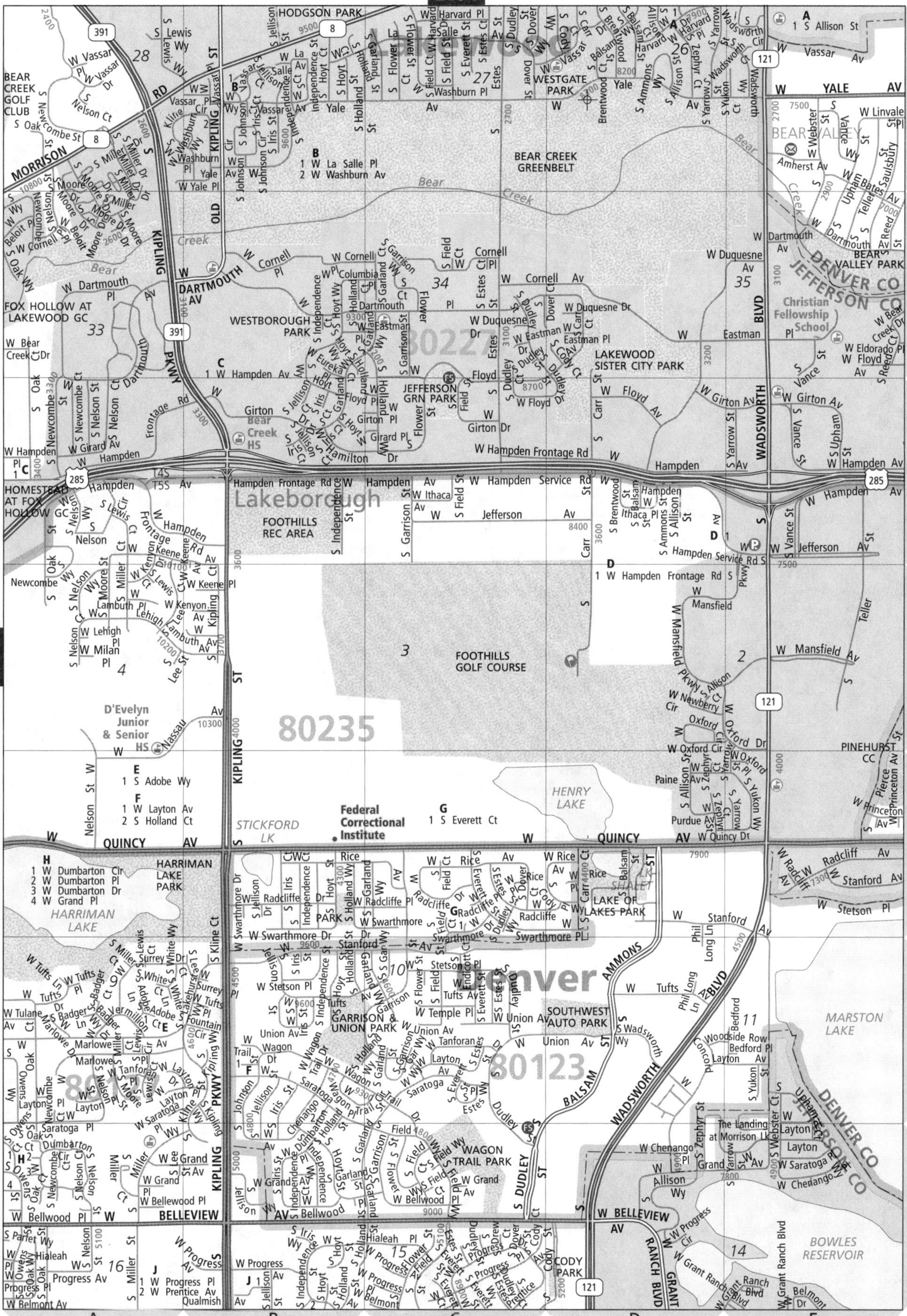

SEE 2277 MAP

SEE 2279 MAP

SEE 2362 MAP

Lakewood

Lakeborough

Denver

BEAR CREEK GOLF CLUB

HODGSON PARK

WESTGATE PARK

BEAR CREEK GREENBELT

BEAR VALLEY

BEAR VALLEY PARK

FOX HOLLOW AT LAKEWOOD GC

WESTBOROUGH PARK

JEFFERSON GRN PARK

LAKEWOOD SISTER CITY PARK

Christian Fellowship School

Bear Creek HS

HOMESTEAD AT FOX HOLLOW GC

FOOTHILLS REC AREA

FOOTHILLS GOLF COURSE

D'Evelyn Junior & Senior HS

PINEHURST CC

HENRY LAKE

STICKFORD LK

Federal Correctional Institute

HARRIMAN LAKE PARK

HARRIMAN LAKE

LAKE OF LAKES PARK

GARRISON & UNION PARK

SOUTHWEST AUTO PARK

MARSTON LAKE

WAGON TRAIL PARK

CODY PARK

BOWLES RESERVOIR

DENVER CO
JEFFERSON CO

80227

80235

80123

A
1 S Allison St

B
1 W La Salle Pl
2 W Washburn Av

C
1 W Hampden Av

D
1 W Hampden Frontage Rd

E
1 S Adobe Wy

F
1 W Layton Av
2 S Holland Ct

G
1 S Everett Ct

H
1 W Dumbarton Cir
2 W Dumbarton Pl
3 W Dumbarton Dr
4 W Grand Pl

J
1 W Progress Pl
2 W Prentice Av

A B C D E

1 2 3 4 5 6 7

39°40'16" 39°39'50" 39°39'24" 39°38'58" 39°38'32" 39°38'06" 39°37'40" 39°37'14"

105°07'18" 105°06'44" 105°06'10" 105°05'37" 105°05'03" 105°04'29"

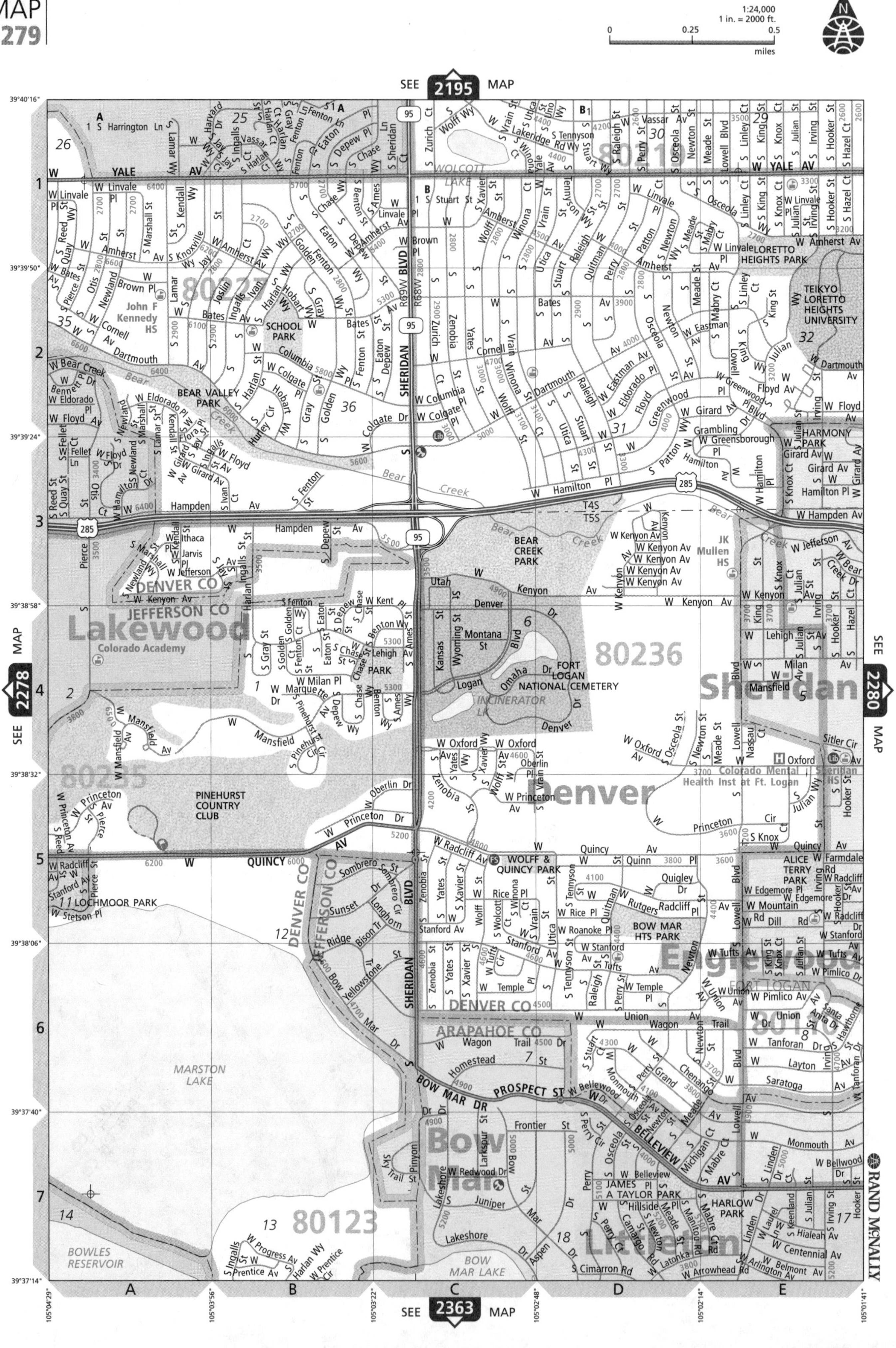

1:24,000
1 in. = 2000 ft.
0 0.25 0.5
miles

SEE 2195 MAP

SEE 2278 MAP

SEE 2280 MAP

Lakewood
Colorado Academy
DENVER CO
JEFFERSON CO
80227
80235
80236
80123
80110
Sheridan
Denver
Englewood
Bow Mar
Littleton
W YALE AV
SHERIDAN BLVD
W QUINCY AV
W Hampden Av
W Kenyon Av
W Oxford Av
W Princeton Av
BOW MAR DR
PROSPECT ST
BELLEVIEW AV
John F Kennedy HS
SCHOOL PARK
BEAR VALLEY PARK
BEAR CREEK PARK
JK Mullen HS
FORT LOGAN NATIONAL CEMETERY
INCINERATOR LK
Colorado Mental Health Inst at Ft. Logan
Sheridan HS
PINEHURST COUNTRY CLUB
LOCHMOOR PARK
WOLFF & QUINCY PARK
BOW MAR HTS PARK
ALICE TERRY PARK
LORETTO HEIGHTS PARK
TEIKYO LORETTO HEIGHTS UNIVERSITY
HARMONY PARK
JAMES A TAYLOR PARK
HARLOW PARK
MARSTON LAKE
BOWLES RESERVOIR
BOW MAR LAKE
WOLCOTT LAKE
ARAPAHOE CO
FORT LOGAN
Bear Creek
T4S
T5S
R69W R68W

39°40'16" 39°39'50" 39°39'24" 39°38'58" 39°38'32" 39°38'06" 39°37'40" 39°37'14"

105°04'29" 105°03'56" 105°03'22" 105°02'48" 105°02'14" 105°01'41"

A B C D E

1 2 3 4 5 6 7

SEE 2363 MAP

1:24,000
1 in. = 2000 ft.
0 0.25 0.5
miles

SEE 2196 MAP

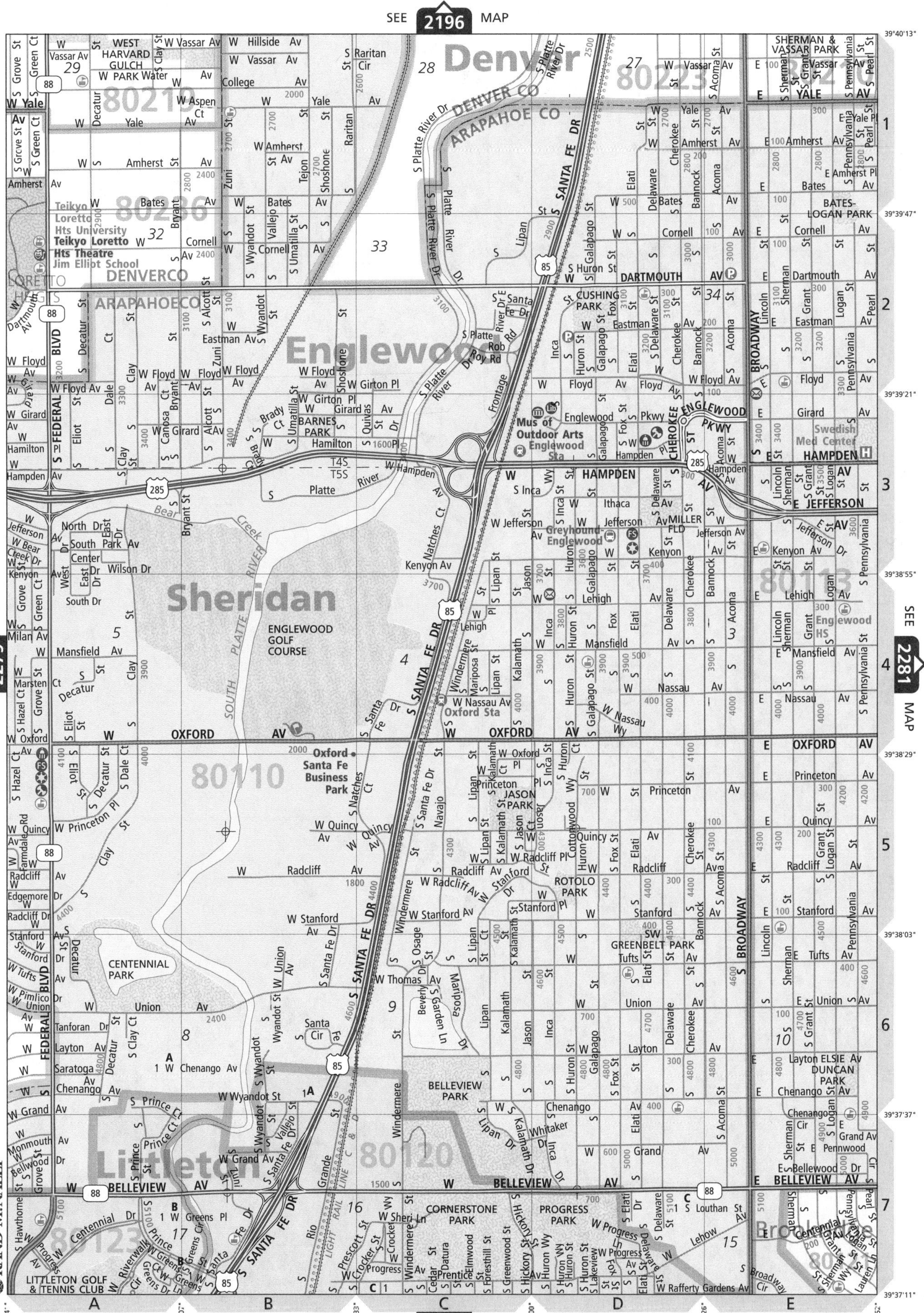

SEE 2279 MAP

SEE 2281 MAP

SEE 2364 MAP

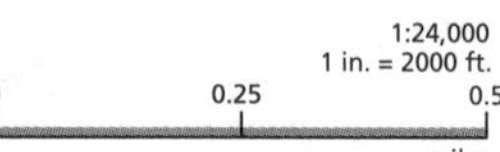

SEE 2197 MAP

SEE 2280 MAP

SEE 2282 MAP

SEE 2365 MAP

Englewood

Denver

Cherry Hills Village

Greenwood Village

DENVER CO

ARAPAHOE CO

80210

80222

80113

80121

UNIV OF DENVER

DEBOER PARK

ROBERT H MCWILLIAMS PARK

BARDE PARK

PACKY ROMANS PARK

MAMIE DOWD EISENHOWER PARK

WELLSHIRE GOLF CLUB

SKEEL RES

MAGNA CARTA PARK

Craig Hosp

BUELL LK

CHERRY HILLS COUNTRY CLUB

CHERRY HILLS LK

THREE POND PARK

DAHLIA HOLLOW PARK

Kent Denver School

JOHN MEADE PARK

BLACKMER LK

GLENMOOR COUNTRY CLUB

WOODIE HOLLOW PARK

GREENWOOD PINE PARK

Theater In the Park

MARJORIE PERRY NATURE PRES

HAMPDEN AV

JEFFERSON AV

QUINCY AV

BELLEVIEW AV

UNIVERSITY BLVD

COLORADO BLVD

DOWNING ST

CLARKSON ST

YALE AV

E OXFORD AV

RAND McNALLY

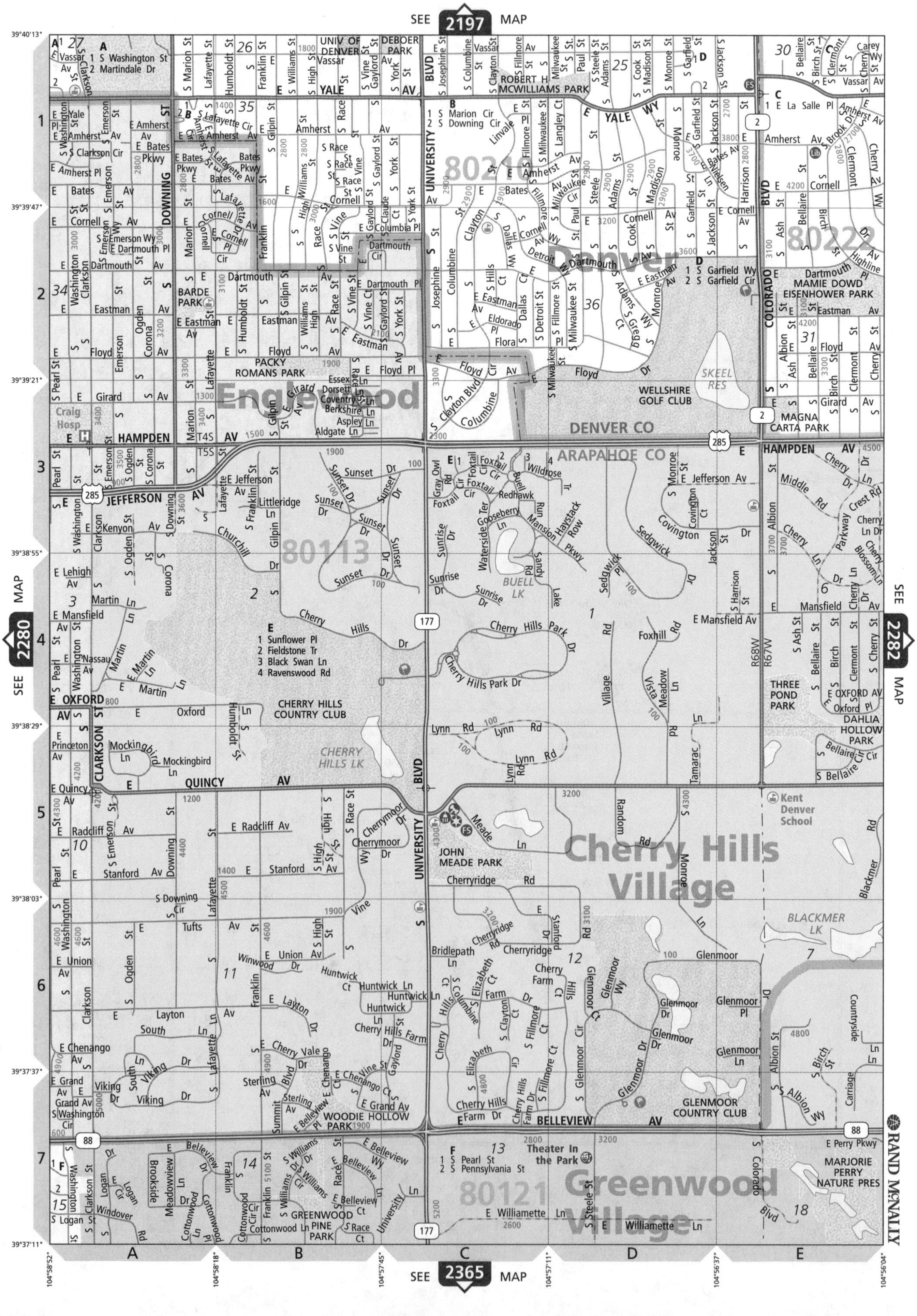

1:24,000
1 in. = 2000 ft.
0 0.25 0.5
miles

SEE 2198 MAP

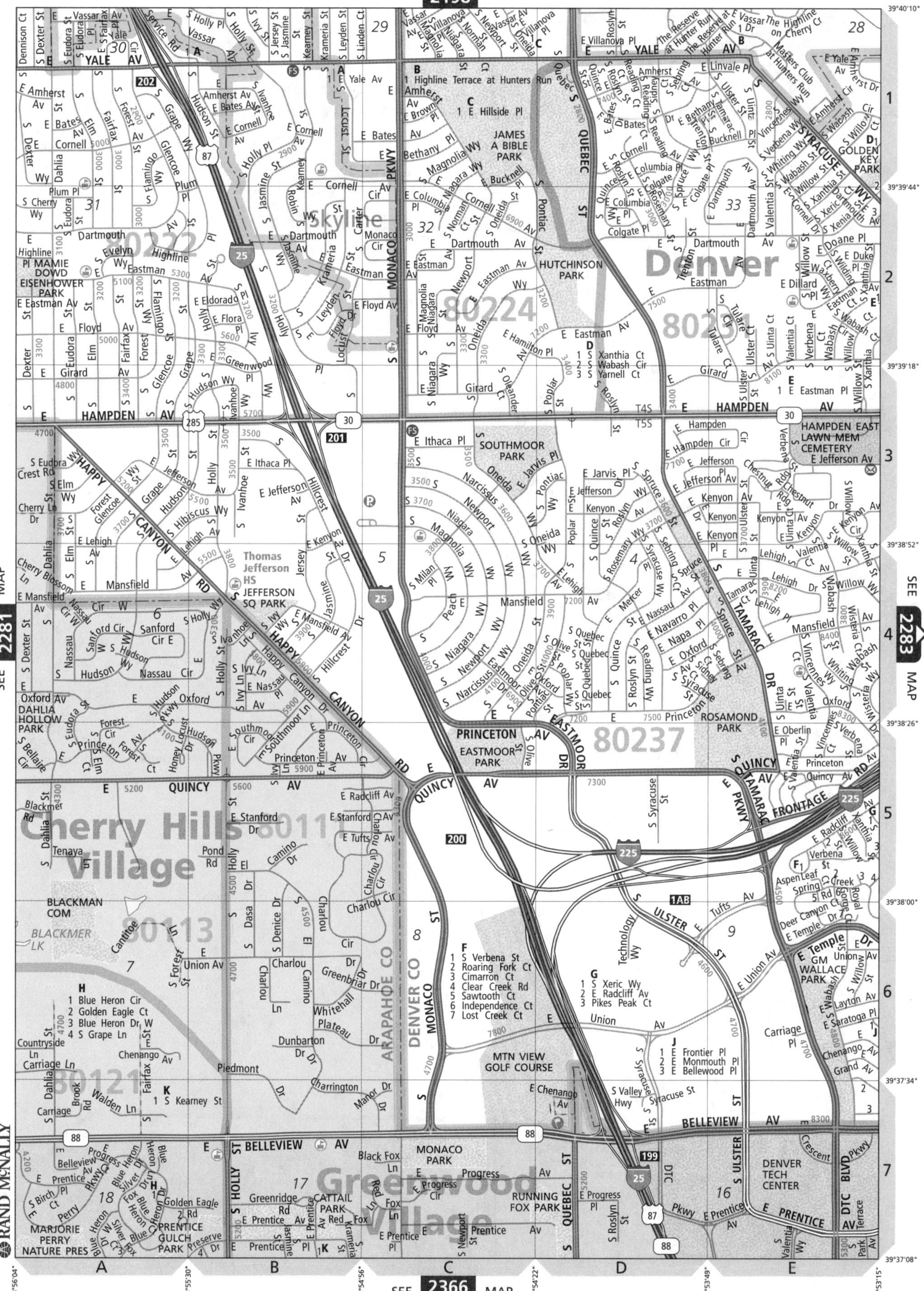

SEE 2281 MAP
SEE 2283 MAP
SEE 2366 MAP

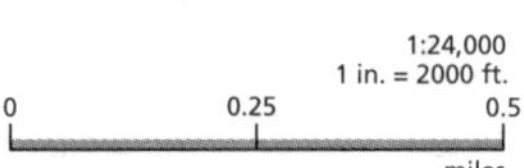

SEE 2199 MAP

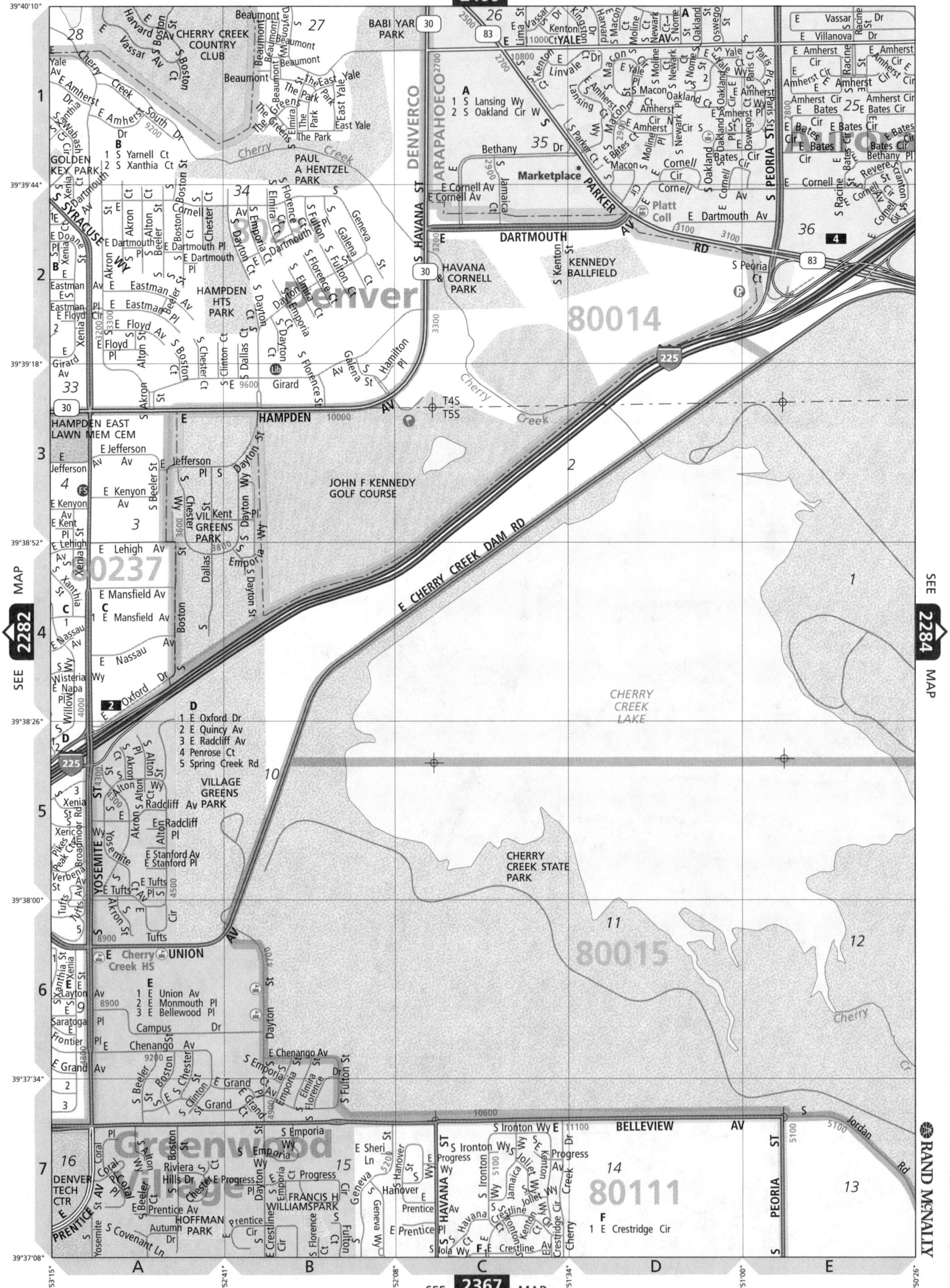

SEE 2282 MAP

SEE 2284 MAP

CHERRY CREEK COUNTRY CLUB
BABI YAR PARK
PAUL A HENTZEL PARK
GOLDEN KEY PARK
HAMPDEN HTS PARK
Denver
HAVANA & CORNELL PARK
KENNEDY BALLFIELD
Marketplace
Platt Coll
Aurora
80014
80237
80015
80111
HAMPDEN EAST LAWN MEM CEM
JOHN F KENNEDY GOLF COURSE
VILLAGE GREENS PARK
E CHERRY CREEK DAM RD
CHERRY CREEK LAKE
CHERRY CREEK STATE PARK
Cherry Creek HS
Greenwood Village
DENVER TECH CTR
HOFFMAN PARK
FRANCIS H WILLIAMS PARK
S SYRACUSE WY
S YOSEMITE ST
S HAVANA ST
DENVERCO
ARAPAHOECO
S PARKER RD
DARTMOUTH AV
HAMPDEN AV
UNION AV
BELLEVIEW AV
S PEORIA ST
YALE AV
PRENTICE AV
T4S
T5S

A
1 S Lansing Wy
2 S Oakland Cir W

B
1 S Yarnell Ct
2 S Xanthia Ct

C
1 E Mansfield Av

D
1 E Oxford Dr
2 E Quincy Av
3 E Radcliff Av
4 Penrose Ct
5 Spring Creek Rd

E
1 E Union Av
2 E Monmouth Pl
3 E Bellewood Pl

F
1 E Crestridge Cir

39°40'10"
39°39'44"
39°39'18"
39°38'52"
39°38'26"
39°38'00"
39°37'34"
39°37'08"
104°53'15"
104°52'41"
104°52'08"
104°51'34"
104°51'00"
104°50'26"

A B C D E

SEE 2367 MAP

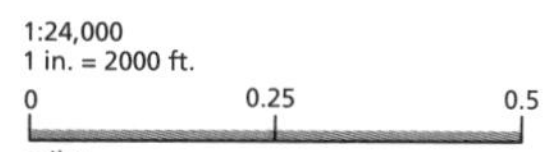

SEE 2200 MAP

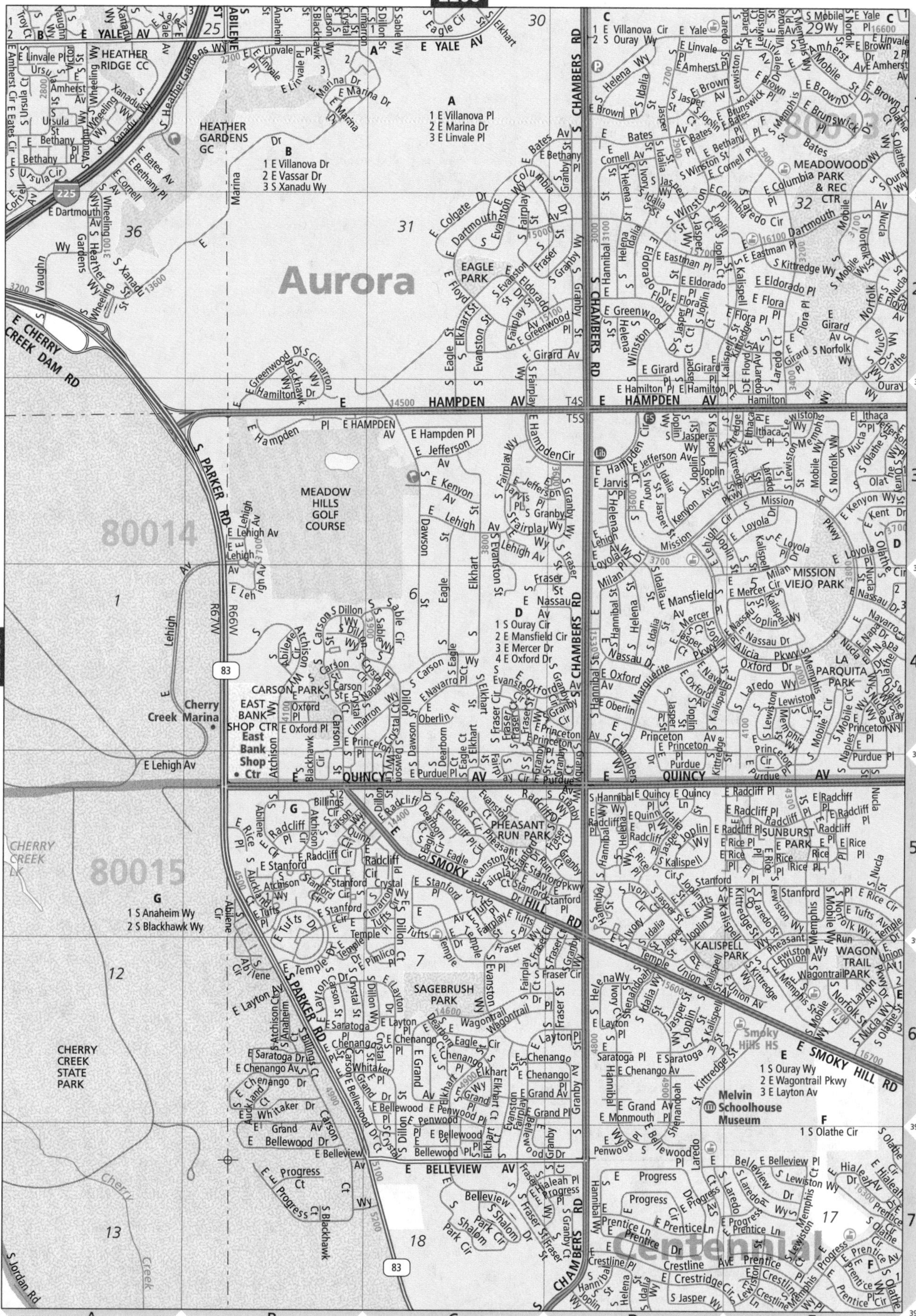

SEE 2283 MAP

SEE 2285 MAP

Aurora

Centennial

HEATHER RIDGE CC

HEATHER GARDENS GC

EAGLE PARK

MEADOWOOD PARK & REC CTR

MEADOW HILLS GOLF COURSE

MISSION VIEJO PARK

LA PARQUITA PARK

CARSON PARK

EAST BANK SHOP CTR

East Bank Shop Ctr

Cherry Creek Marina

CHERRY CREEK STATE PARK

PHEASANT RUN PARK

SUNBURST PARK

KALISPELL PARK

WAGON TRAIL PARK

SAGEBRUSH PARK

Smoky Hills HS

Melvin Schoolhouse Museum

E CHERRY CREEK DAM RD

S PARKER RD

S CHAMBERS RD

E HAMPDEN AV

E QUINCY AV

E YALE AV

E BELLEVIEW AV

E SMOKY HILL RD

80013

80014

80015

A
1 E Villanova Pl
2 E Marina Dr
3 E Linvale Pl

B
1 E Villanova Dr
2 E Vassar Dr
3 S Xanadu Wy

C
1 E Villanova Cir
2 S Ouray Wy

D
1 S Ouray Cir
2 E Mansfield Cir
3 E Mercer Dr
4 E Oxford Dr

E
1 S Ouray Wy
2 E Wagontrail Pkwy
3 E Layton Av

F
1 S Olathe Cir

G
1 S Anaheim Wy
2 S Blackhawk Wy

39°40'07"
39°39'41"
39°39'15"
39°38'49"
39°38'22"
39°37'56"
39°37'30"
39°37'04"

104°50'26"
104°49'53"
104°49'19"
104°48'45"
104°48'12"
104°47'38"

A B C D E

1 2 3 4 5 6 7

SEE 2368 MAP

1:24,000
1 in. = 2000 ft.
0 0.25 0.5
miles

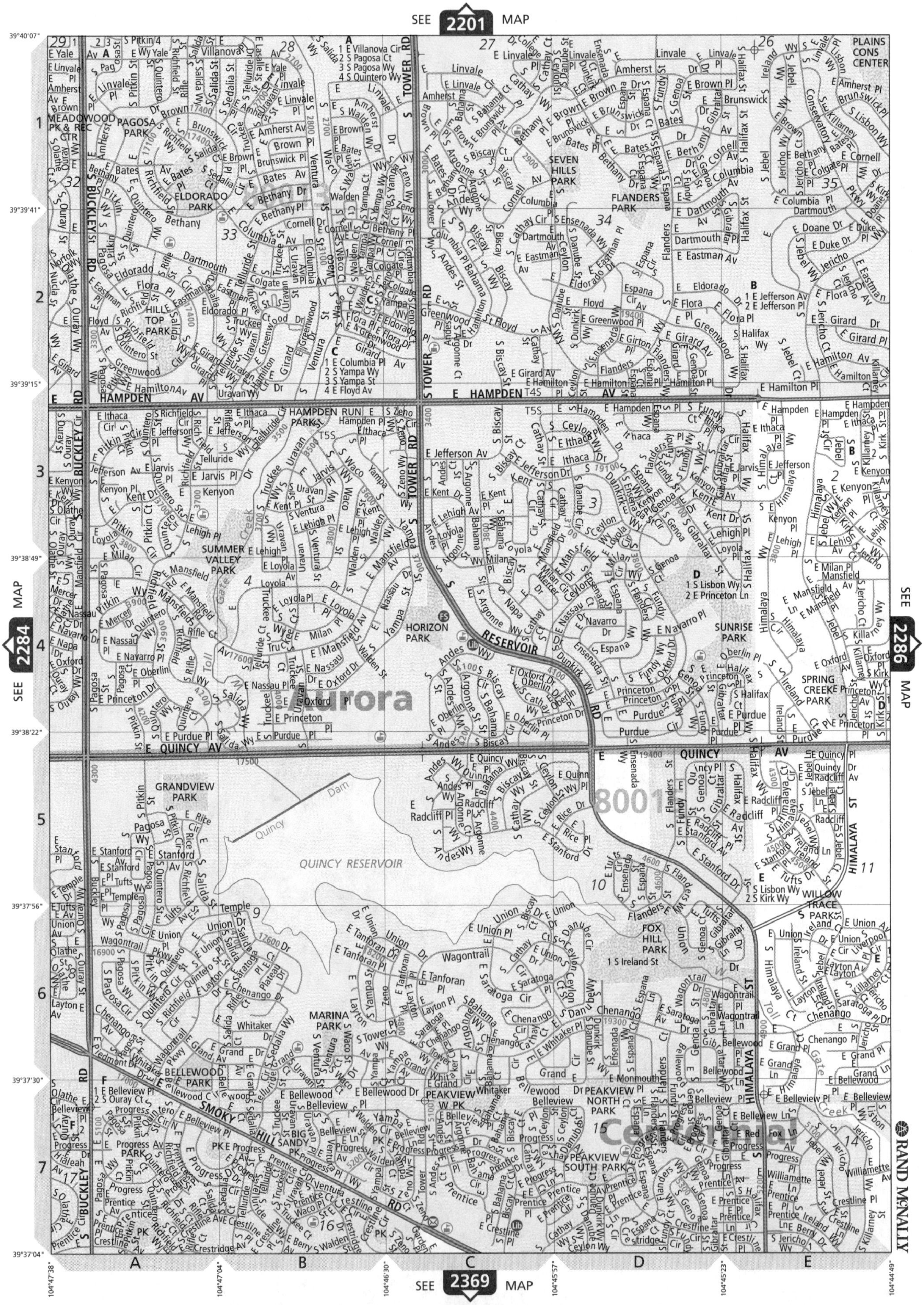

SEE 2201 MAP

SEE 2284 MAP

SEE 2286 MAP

39°40'07"
39°39'41"
39°39'15"
39°38'49"
39°38'22"
39°37'56"
39°37'30"
39°37'04"

MEADOWOOD PK & REC CTR
PAGOSA PARK
ELDORADO PARK
HILLE TOP PARK
SEVEN HILLS PARK
FLANDERS PARK
PLAINS CONS CENTER
HAMPDEN RUN PARK
SUMMER VALLEY PARK
HORIZON PARK
SUNRISE PARK
SPRING CREEK PARK
Aurora
GRANDVIEW PARK
QUINCY RESERVOIR
FOX HILL PARK
WILLOW TRACE PARK
MARINA PARK
BELLEWOOD PARK
PEAKVIEW W PK
PEAKVIEW NORTH PARK
PEAKVIEW SOUTH PARK
BIG SANDY PK
PROGRESS PARK
Centennial

E HAMPDEN AV
E QUINCY AV
S BUCKLEY RD
S TOWER RD
RESERVOIR RD
HIMALAYA ST
SMOKY HILL RD

1 2 3 4 5 6 7
A B C D E

104°47'38"
104°47'04"
104°46'30"
104°45'57"
104°45'23"
104°44'49"

SEE 2369 MAP

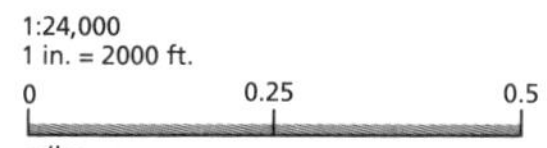

1:24,000
1 in. = 2000 ft.
0 0.25 0.5
miles

SEE 2202 MAP
SEE 2370 MAP
SEE 2285 MAP
SEE 2287 MAP
Toll Booth
E Yale Av
PLAINS CONSERVATION CENTER
Plains Conservation Center
E HAMPDEN AV
Hampden Av
S GUN CLUB RD
E470
30
13
T4S
T5S
R66W
R65W
Aurora
80013
80018
80015
80016
E QUINCY AV
TOLL GATE PARK
Eaglecrest HS
LOOKOUT PARK AND POOL
Centennial
E Chenango Dr
E Belleview Av
E Wagontrail Av
E Bellewood Dr
A
1 E Dartmouth Dr
B
1 E Bellewood Pl
C
1 E Crestone Av
D
1 S Haleyville St
2 S Gold Bug Wy
26
35
36
31
1
6
11
12
7
13
14
18
A
B
C
D
E
1
2
3
4
5
6
7
39°40'03"
39°39'37"
39°39'11"
39°38'45"
39°38'19"
39°37'53"
39°37'27"
39°37'00"
104°44'49"
104°44'16"
104°43'42"
104°43'08"
104°42'34"
104°42'01"
RAND McNALLY

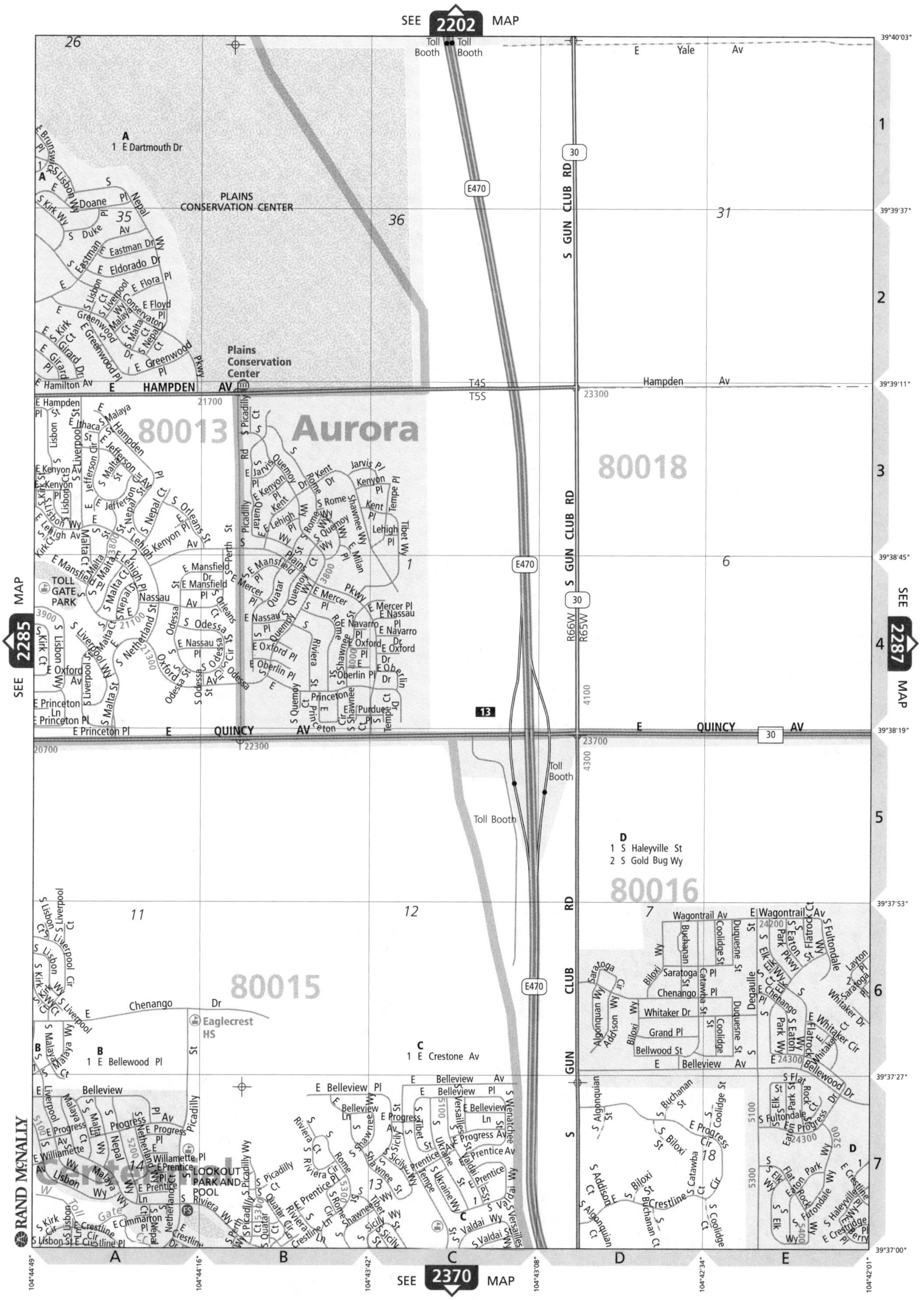

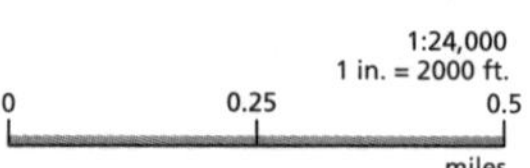

SEE 2203 MAP

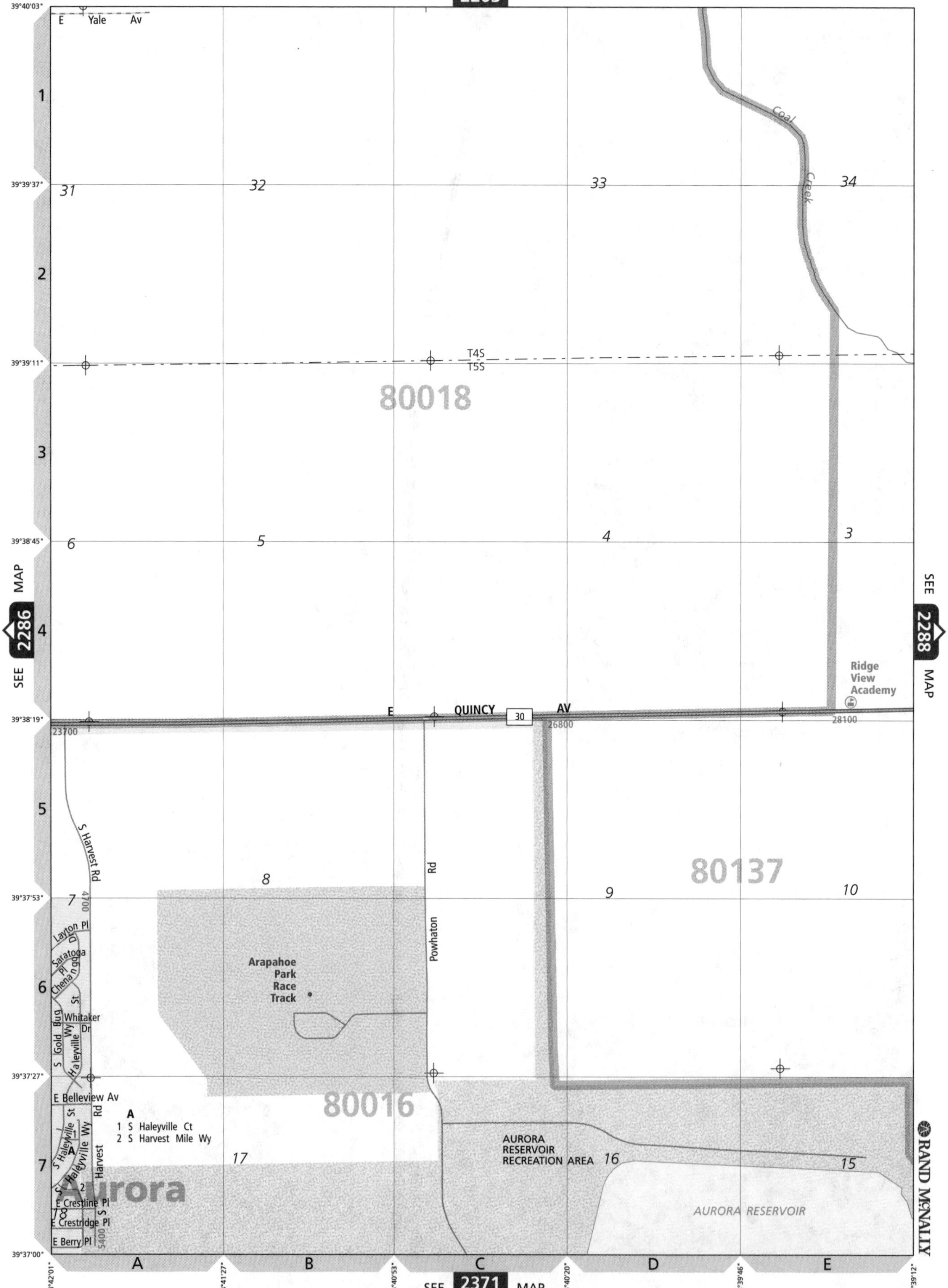

SEE 2286 MAP

SEE 2288 MAP

SEE 2371 MAP

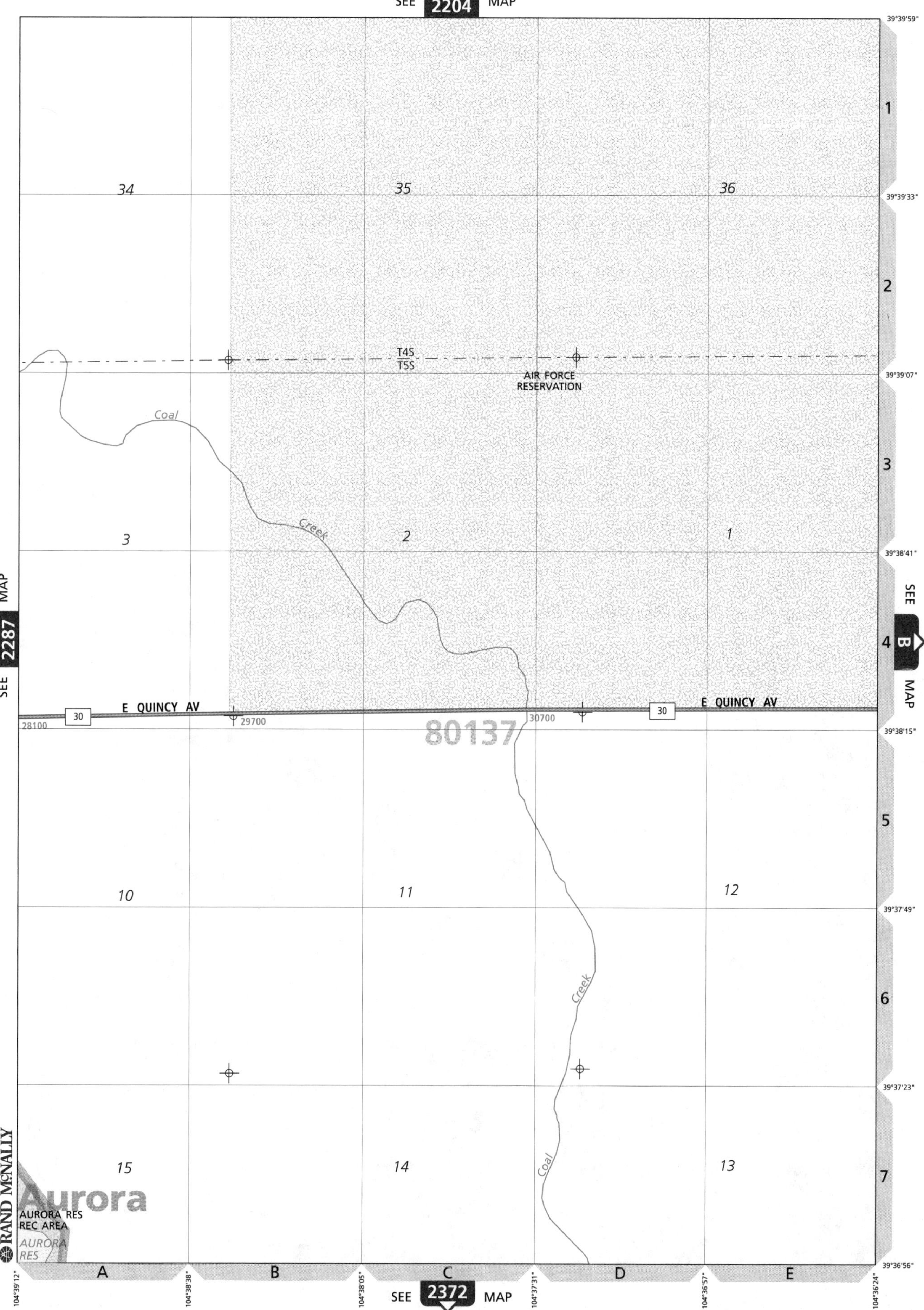
1:24,000
1 in. = 2000 ft.
0
0.25
0.5
miles
SEE 2204 MAP
SEE 2287 MAP
SEE B MAP
SEE 2372 MAP
34
35
36
3
2
1
10
11
12
15
14
13
T4S
T5S
AIR FORCE
RESERVATION
Coal
Creek
E QUINCY AV
30
28100
29700
30700
80137
Aurora
AURORA RES
REC AREA
AURORA
RES
A
B
C
D
E
1
2
3
4
5
6
7
39°39'59"
39°39'33"
39°39'07"
39°38'41"
39°38'15"
39°37'49"
39°37'23"
39°36'56"
104°39'12"
104°38'38"
104°38'05"
104°37'31"
104°36'57"
104°36'24"
RAND McNALLY

1:24,000
1 in. = 2000 ft.
0 0.25 0.5
miles

SEE 2271 MAP

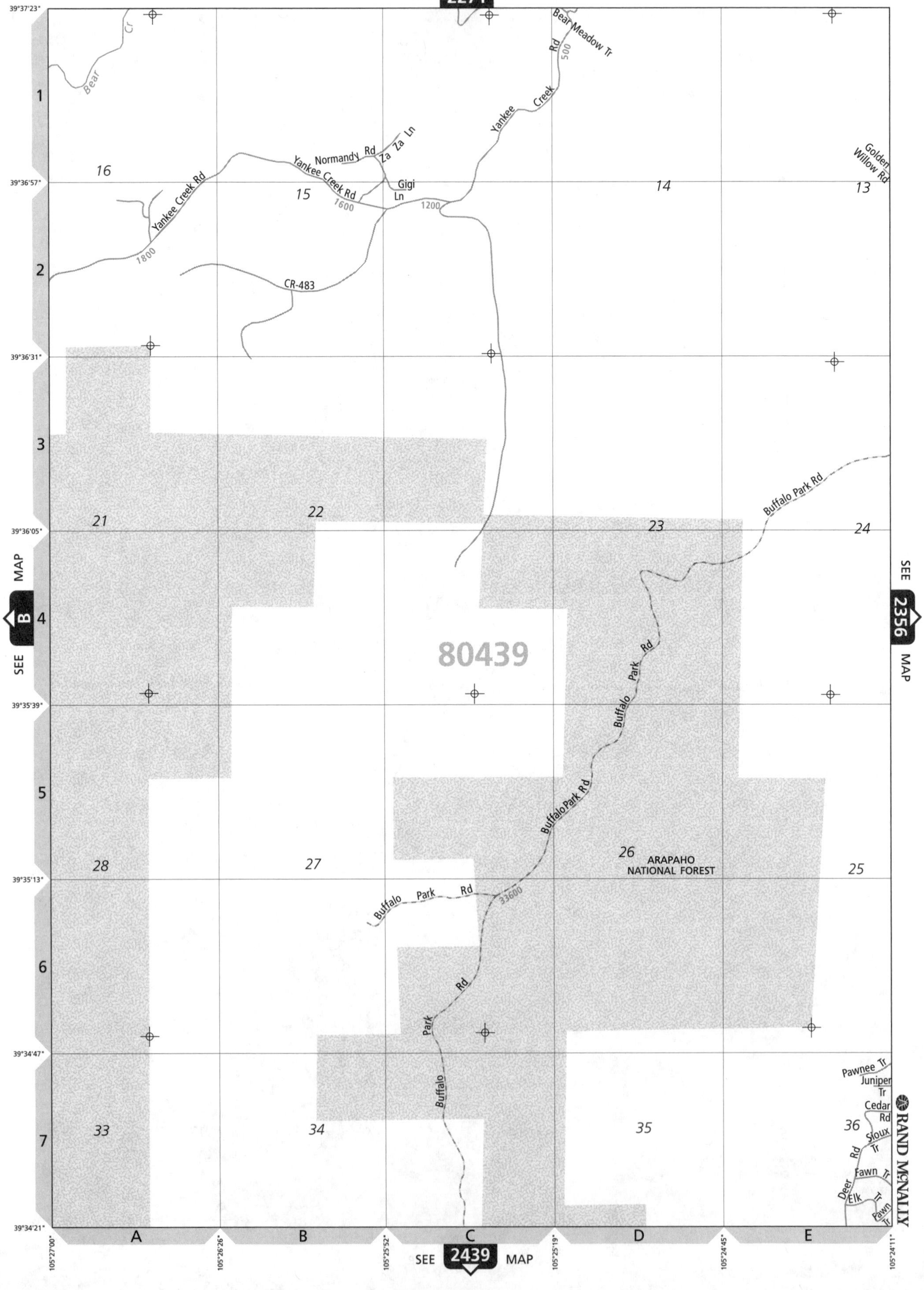

SEE B MAP

SEE 2356 MAP

SEE 2439 MAP

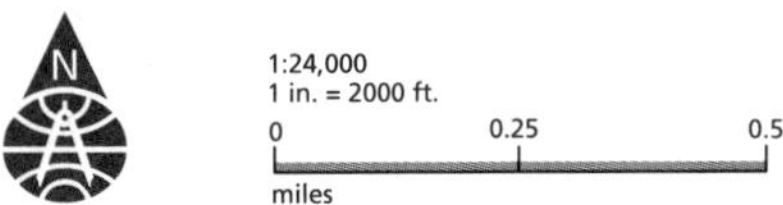

SEE 2272 MAP

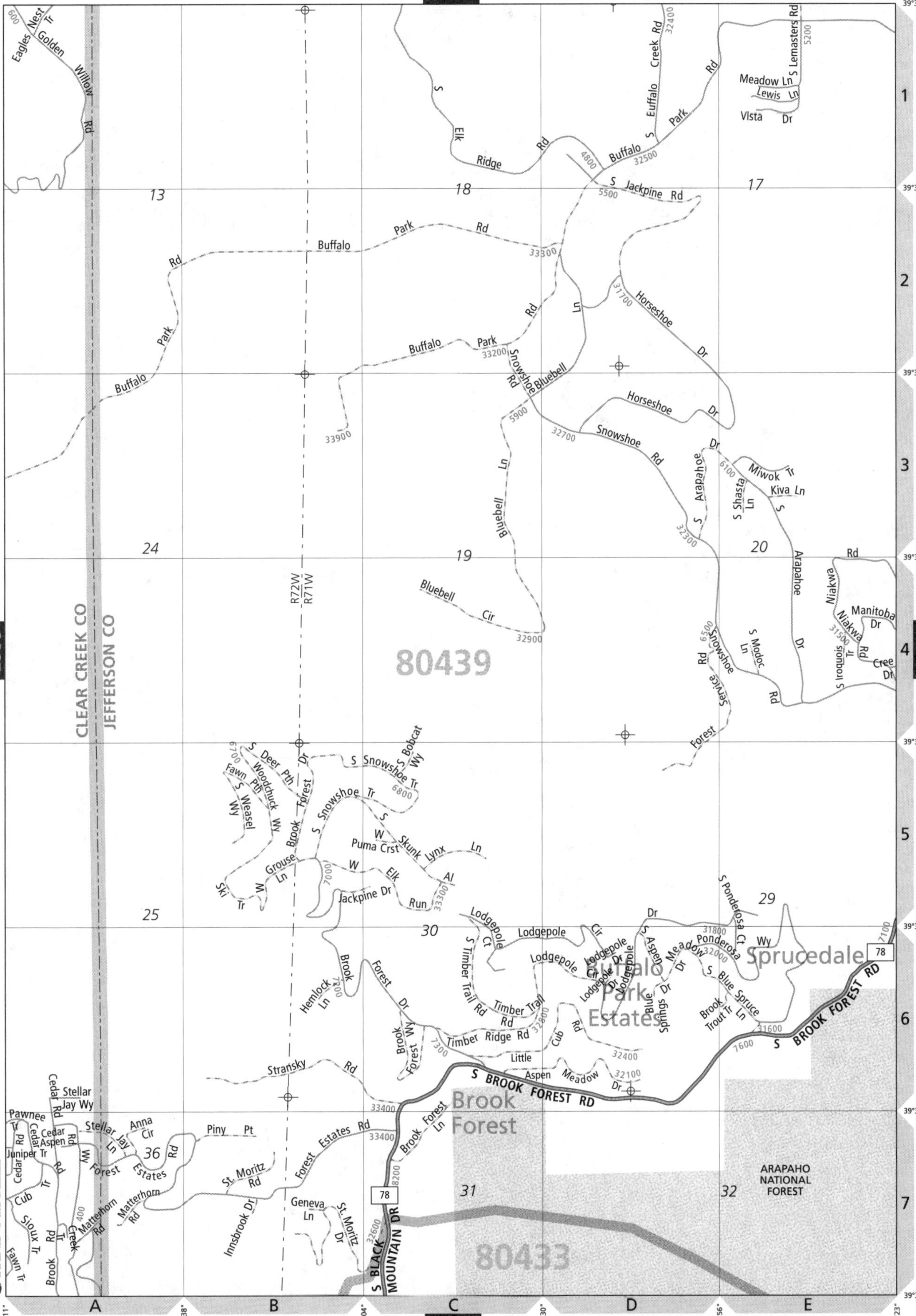

SEE 2355 MAP

SEE 2357 MAP

SEE 2440 MAP

1:24,000
1 in. = 2000 ft.
0 0.25 0.5
miles

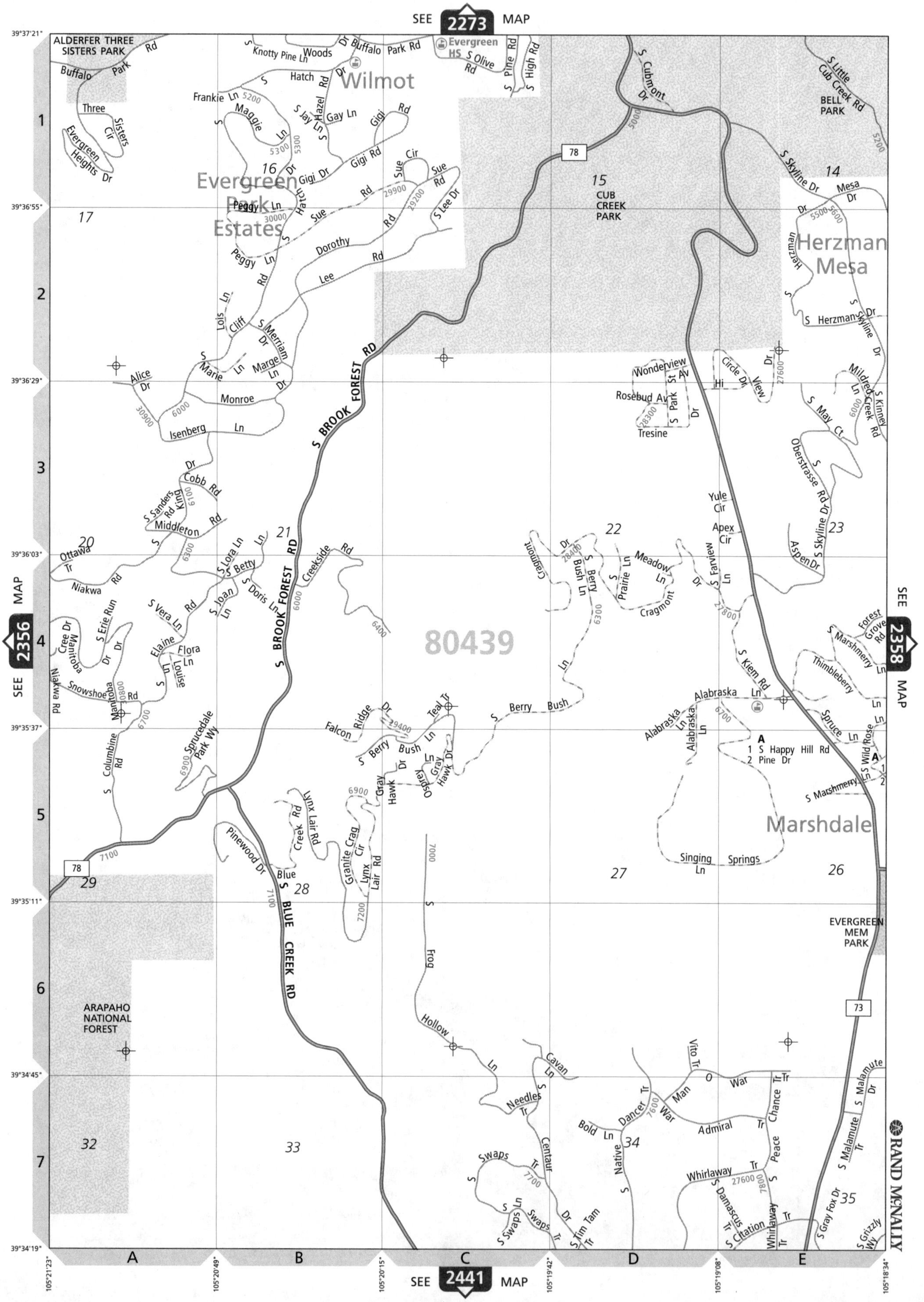

SEE 2273 MAP

ALDERFER THREE SISTERS PARK
Wilmot
Evergreen Park Estates
CUB CREEK PARK
BELL PARK
Herzman Mesa
80439
Marshdale
EVERGREEN MEM PARK
ARAPAHO NATIONAL FOREST

SEE 2356 MAP

SEE 2358 MAP

SEE 2441 MAP

RAND McNALLY

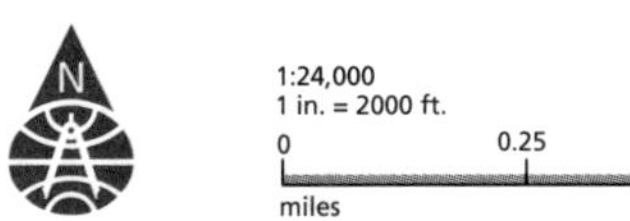

SEE 2274 MAP

Stanley Park
Stanley Park Rd
BELL PARK
Edelweiss Cir
S Twin Spruce Dr
S Sunrise Dr
Sunset Ln
S Bear Mountain Dr
Hawks Cir
Chris Dr
S Burro Ln
N Mountain Park Dr
Mountain Park Dr
S Langdon Dr
Northwood
S Sandrock Dr
S Annapurna Dr
S Little Cub Creek Rd
S Mesa Dr
S Herzman Dr
DENVER MOUNTAIN PARK
S High Dr
Caldwell Ct
S Meadow Dr
S Lone Peak Dr
Lone Peak Tr
80465
S Kilimanjaro Dr
Annapurna Dr
Zugspitz Rd
S Kinney Creek Rd
S Kenya Dr
S Vesuvius Rd
80439
W Loggers Tr
Hilltop Rd
S Olympus Dr
S Jungfrau Wy
S Jungfrau Dr
Timbers Dr
A
1 Thimbleberry Ln
2 S Wild Rose Ln
S Marshmerry Ln
Happy Hill Rd
Vista Ln
Columbine Ln
Coopers Tr
Pine Dr
R70W
R71W
Evergreen Highlands
S Everest Ln
S Silverhorn Dr
S Kilimanjaro Dr
S Willa Ln
Chinook Dr
S Julie Ln
S Ocelot Tr
N TURKEY CREEK RD
Timbers Dr
Silverhorn Ln
Silverhorn Dr
Jura Dr
EVERGREEN MEMORIAL PARK
S Ridge Top Rd
Heiter Hill Rd
Willa Wy
S Monica Ln
Gartner Rd
S Danks Dr
Norman Ln
S Malamute Dr
S Red Fox Dr
Fox
Red
S Armadillo Tr
S Grizzly Wy
Rossman Gulch Rd
14
13
18
23
24
19
26
25
30
35
36
31
1
2
3
4
5
6
7
A
B
C
D
E
39°37'19"
39°36'53"
39°36'27"
39°36'01"
39°35'35"
39°35'09"
39°34'43"
39°34'17"
105°18'34"
105°18'01"
105°17'27"
105°16'53"
105°16'20"
105°15'46"

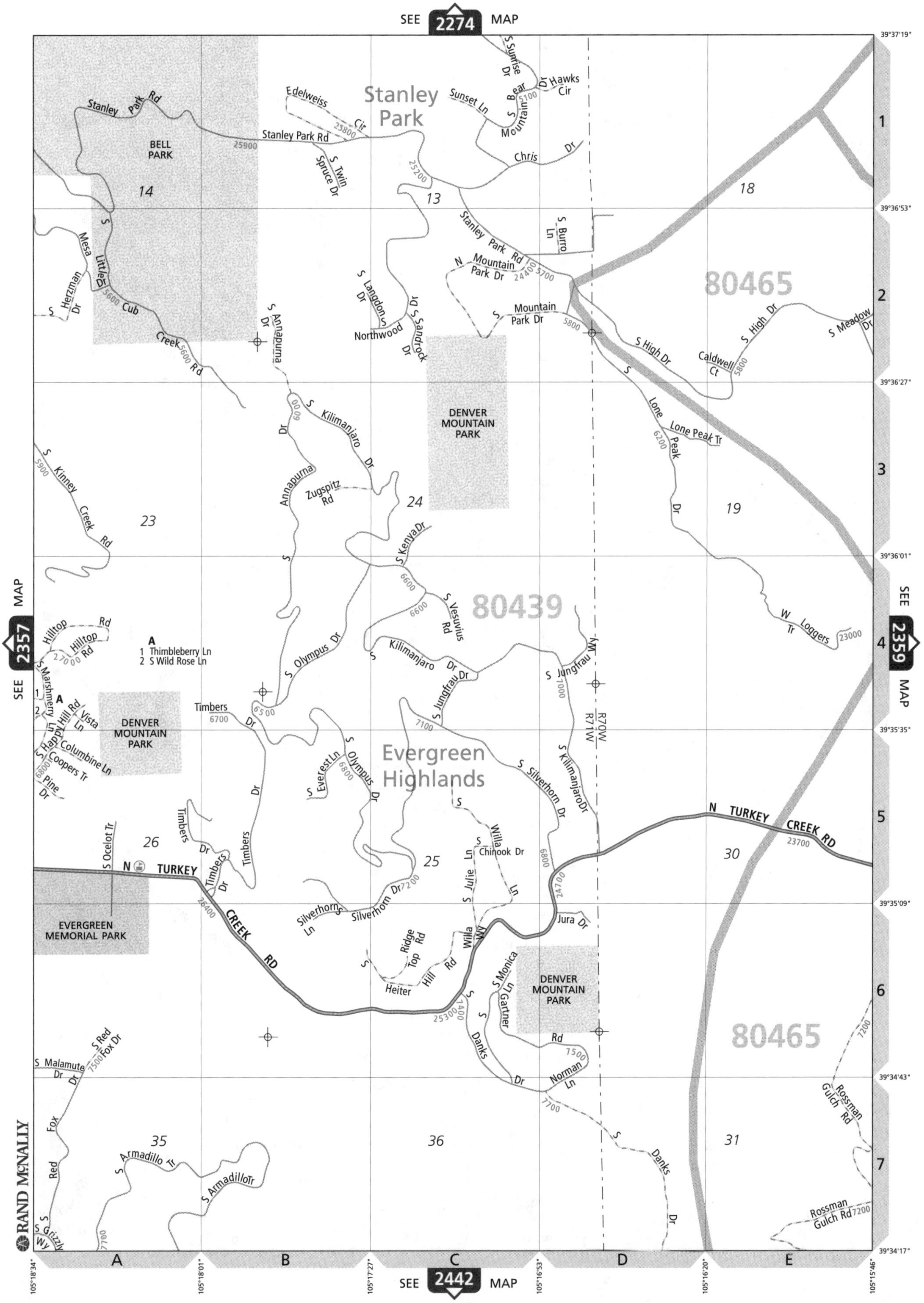

SEE 2357 MAP

SEE 2359 MAP

SEE 2442 MAP

1:24,000
1 in. = 2000 ft.
0 0.25 0.5
miles

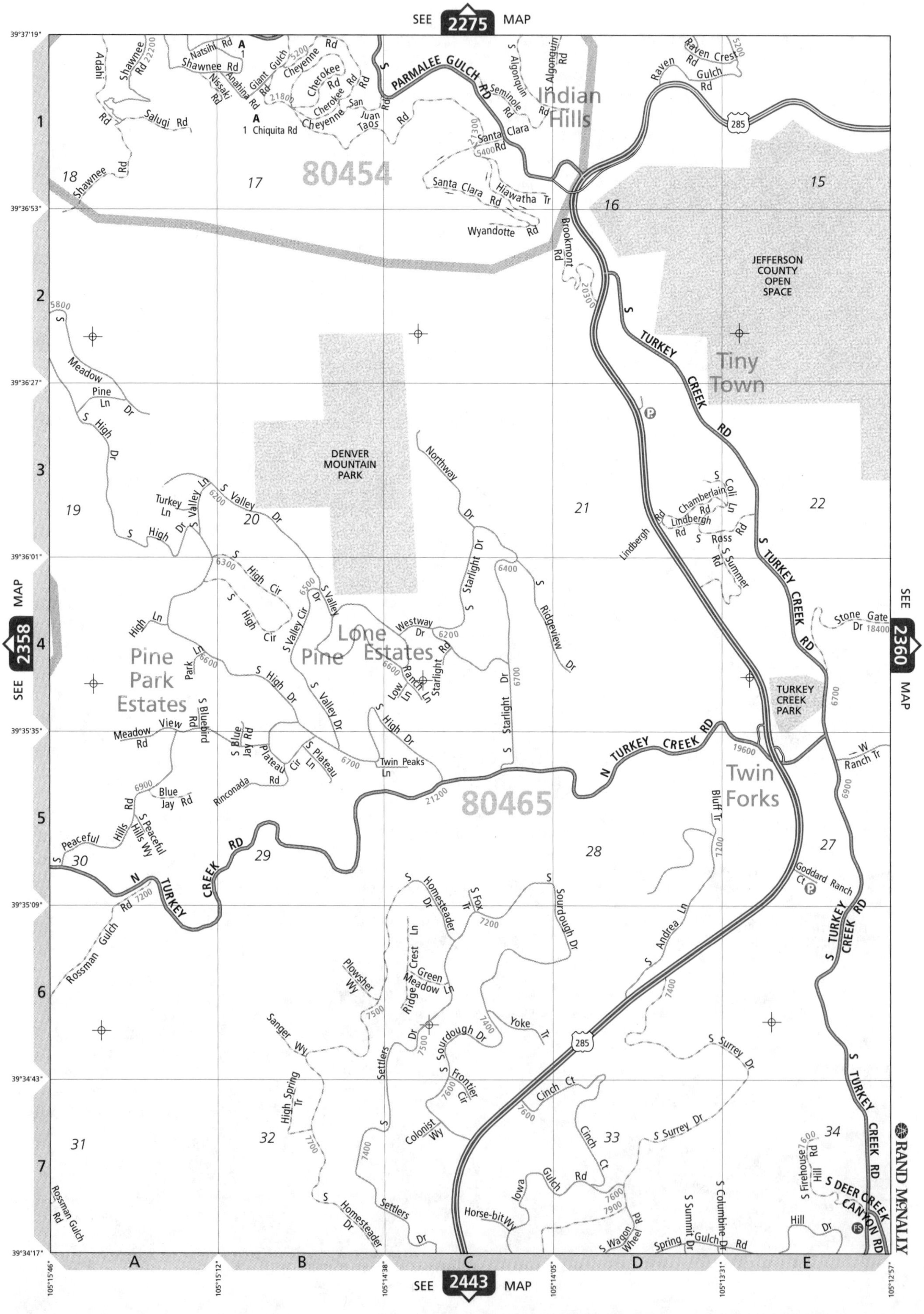

SEE 2275 MAP
SEE 2358 MAP
SEE 2360 MAP
SEE 2443 MAP

1:24,000
1 in. = 2000 ft.
0 0.25 0.5
miles

SEE 2276 MAP

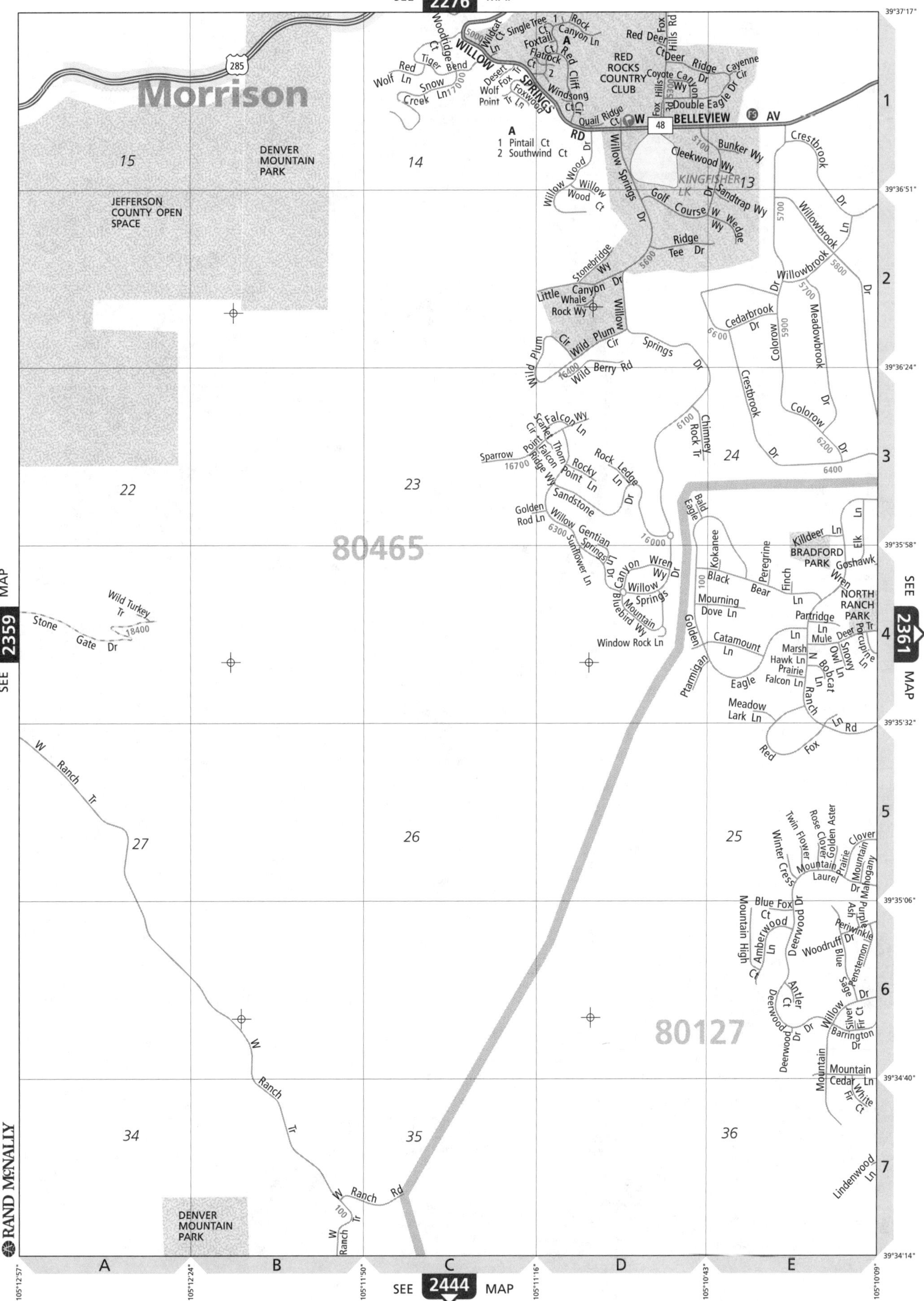

SEE 2359 MAP

SEE 2361 MAP

SEE 2444 MAP

1:24,000
1 in. = 2000 ft.
0 0.25 0.5
miles

SEE 2277 MAP

SEE 2360 MAP

SEE 2362 MAP

A
1 S Tabor Wy
2 W Arlington Dr

B
1 S Owens St
2 S Parfet Ln
3 W Crestline Pl

C
1 S Youngfield Ln
2 S Xenophon Ct

D
1 W Polk Pl
2 S Parfet St

E
1 W Rabbit Ears Pass

F
1 Barrington Dr

G
1 W Cimarrona Peak
2 W Sharkstooth Peak
3 S Storm King Peak
4 Trailrider Pass
5 W Twilight Peak
6 Twilight Peak
7 W Twin Thumbs Pass
8 Red Cloud Peak
9 W Wildhorse Peak
10 W Pyramid Peak
11 S San Juan Range Rd

SEE 2445 MAP

1:24,000
1 in. = 2000 ft.
0 0.25 0.5
miles

SEE 2278 MAP

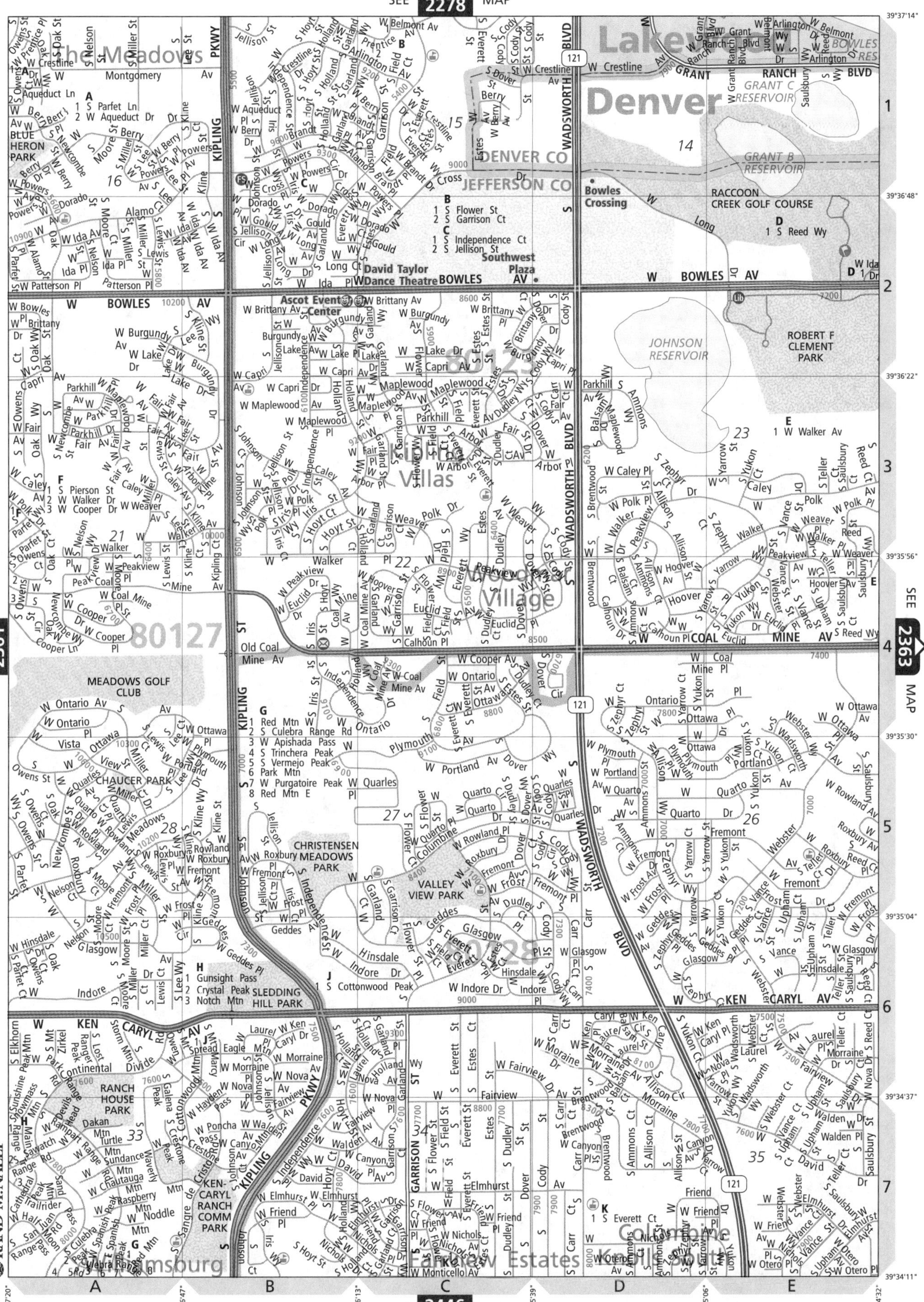

SEE 2361 MAP
SEE 2363 MAP
SEE 2446 MAP

1:24,000
1 in. = 2000 ft.
0 0.25 0.5
miles

SEE 2279 MAP

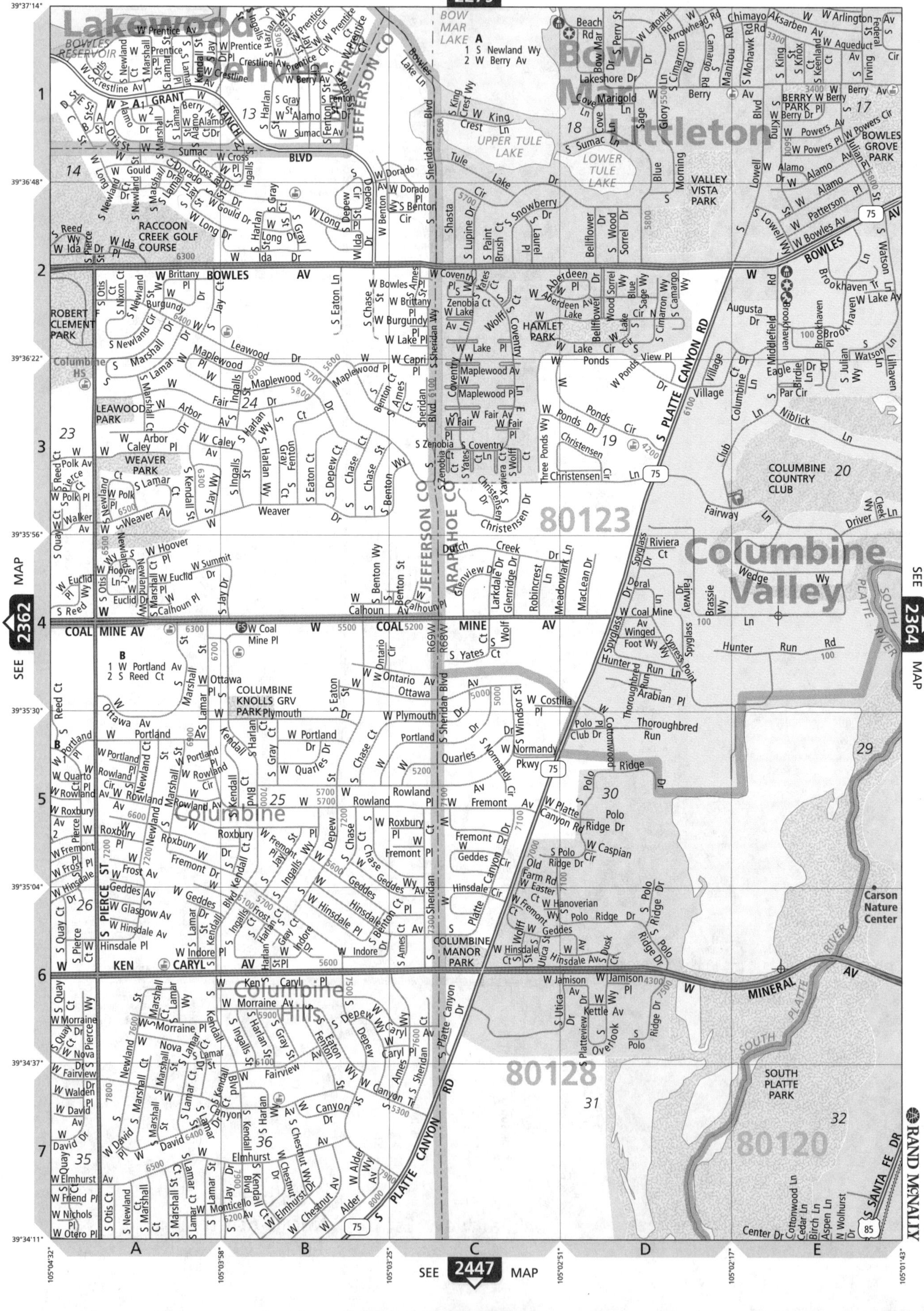

Lakewood
Denver
Bow Mar
Littleton
Columbine Valley
Columbine
Columbine Hills

BOWLES RESERVOIR
BOW MAR LAKE
UPPER TULE LAKE
LOWER TULE LAKE
RACCOON CREEK GOLF COURSE
VALLEY VISTA PARK
BOWLES GROVE PARK
ROBERT F CLEMENT PARK
Columbine HS
LEAWOOD PARK
WEAVER PARK
HAMLET PARK
COLUMBINE COUNTRY CLUB
COLUMBINE KNOLLS GRV PARK
COLUMBINE MANOR PARK
SOUTH PLATTE PARK
Carson Nature Center

80123
80128
80120

A
1 S Newland Wy
2 W Berry Av

B
1 W Portland Av
2 S Reed Ct

W BOWLES AV
W COAL MINE AV
W KEN CARYL AV
W MINERAL AV
S PLATTE CANYON RD
S PIERCE ST
S SHERIDAN BLVD
S SANTA FE DR
W GRANT RANCH BLVD
JEFFERSON CO
ARAPAHOE CO
SOUTH PLATTE RIVER

SEE 2362 MAP
SEE 2364 MAP
SEE 2447 MAP

1:24,000
1 in. = 2000 ft.
0 0.25 0.5
miles

SEE 2280 MAP

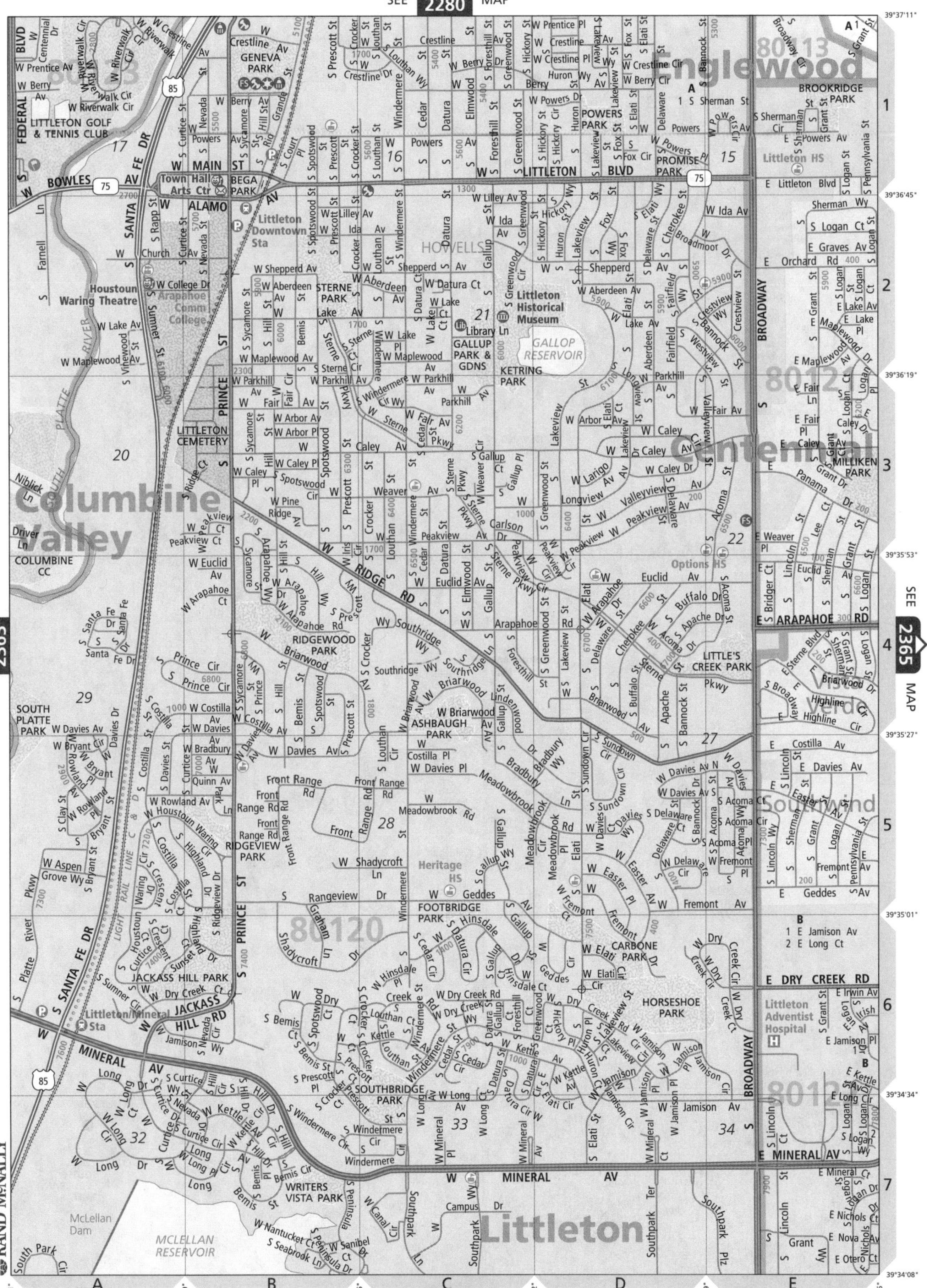

SEE 2448 MAP

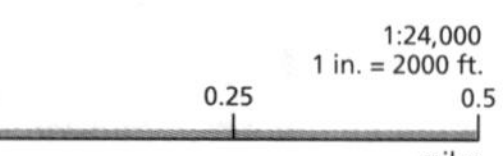

SEE 2281 MAP

Greenwood Village
Littleton
Centennial
Cherry Hill Crest
Dream House Acres
Cherry Hills Manor
Broadway Estates
Southglenn
Cherry Knolls
Nob Hill
Cherrywood Village
80121
80122
MARJORIE PERRY NATURE PRES
ALEXANDER LANE EQUESTRIAN PARK
GREENWOOD PINE PARK
CHERRYVILLE PARK
ROLLIN D BARNARD PARK
CURTIS PARK
Curtis Arts & Humanities Ctr
DEKOEVAND PARK
MILLIKEN PARK
CHAPEL HILL CEMETERY
HERITAGE VIL PARK
ISAAC NEWTON
Southglenn Mall
CHERRY KNOLLS PARK
SOUTHGLENN COUNTRY CLUB
CLARKSON PARK
Arapahoe HS
ARAPAHOE PARK
PUMA PARK
ABBOTT PARK
LINKSVIEW PARK
SOUTH SUBURBAN GOLF COURSE
S UNIVERSITY BLVD
E ARAPAHOE RD
E DRY CREEK RD
MINERAL AV
COLORADO BLVD

A
1 E Maplewood Av
2 E Maplewood Wy

B
1 E Briarwood Dr

C
1 E Irish Av
2 E Jamison Pl
3 S Logan Dr

D
1 E Phillips Dr S
2 S Emerson Wy

SEE 2364 MAP

SEE 2366 MAP

SEE 2449 MAP

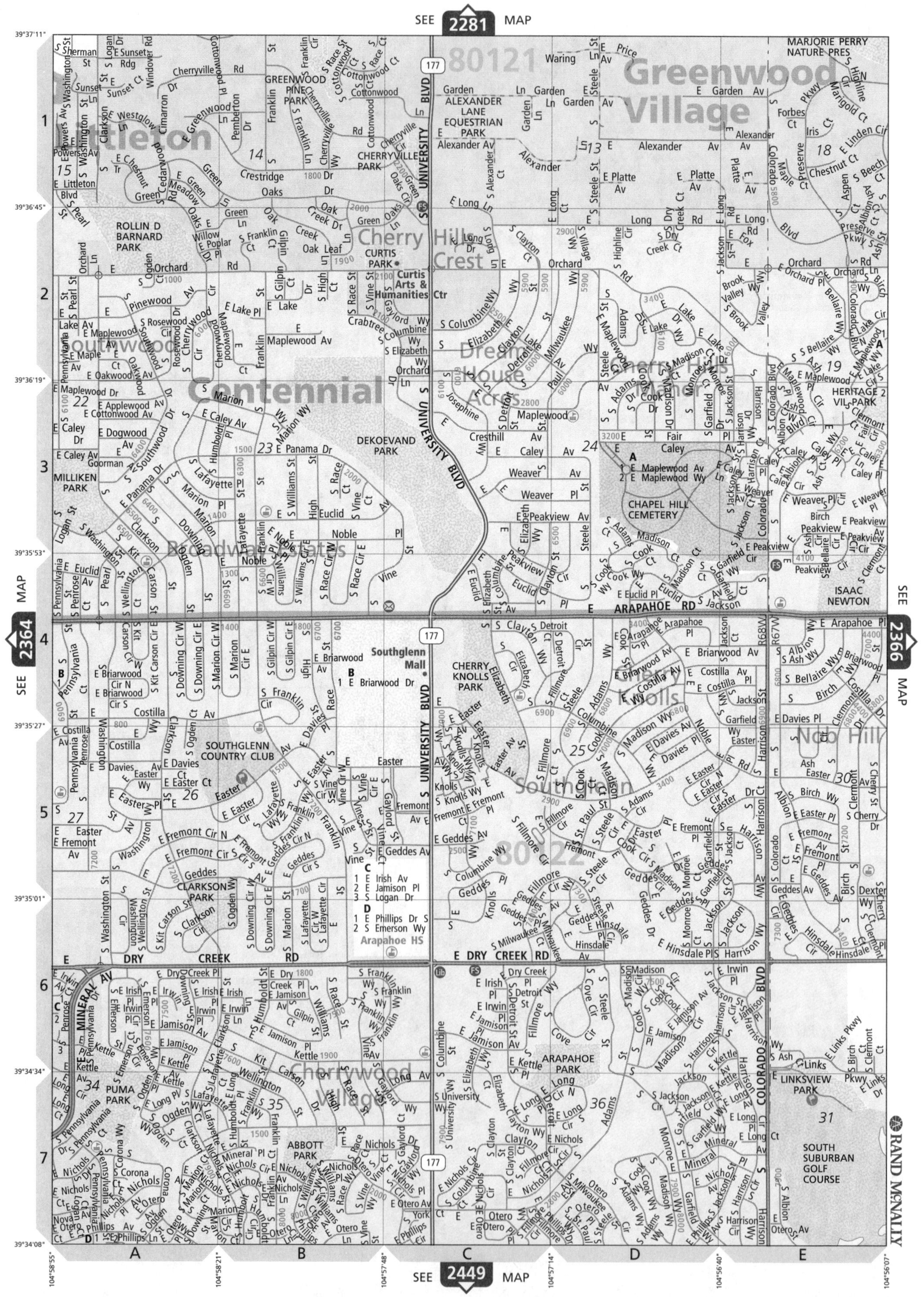

1:24,000
1 in. = 2000 ft.
0 0.25 0.5
miles

SEE 2282 MAP

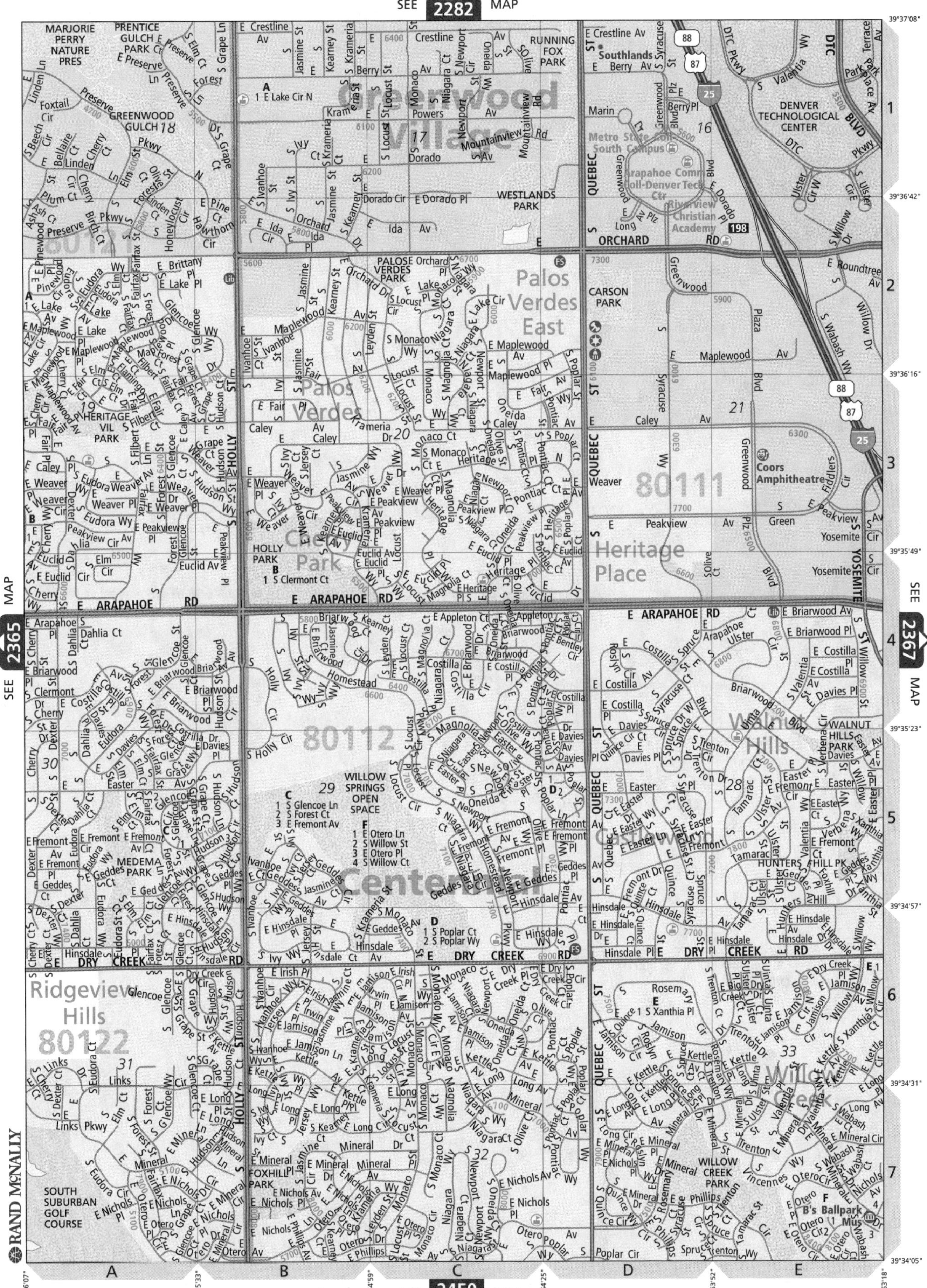

SEE 2365 MAP
SEE 2367 MAP
SEE 2450 MAP

1:24,000
1 in. = 2000 ft.
0 0.25 0.5
miles

SEE 2283 MAP 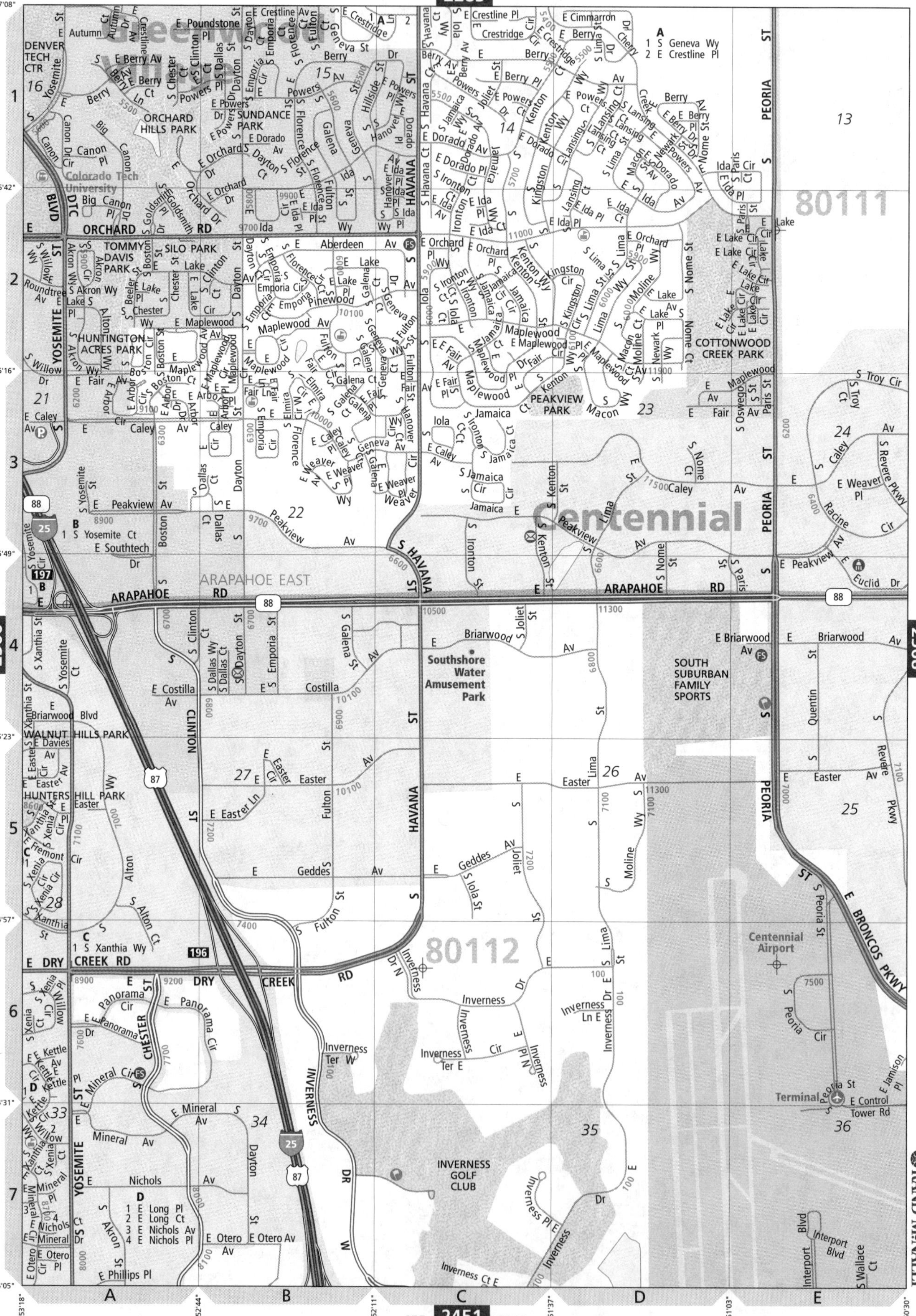
SEE 2366 MAP
SEE 2368 MAP
SEE 2451 MAP

Greenwood Village
Centennial
80111
80112
DENVER TECH CTR
ORCHARD HILLS PARK
SUNDANCE PARK
Colorado Tech University
TOMMY DAVIS PARK
SILO PARK
HUNTINGTON ACRES PARK
COTTONWOOD CREEK PARK
PEAKVIEW PARK
ARAPAHOE EAST
Southshore Water Amusement Park
SOUTH SUBURBAN FAMILY SPORTS
WALNUT HILLS PARK
HUNTERS HILL PARK
Centennial Airport
INVERNESS GOLF CLUB
E ORCHARD RD
ARAPAHOE RD
E DRY CREEK RD
S YOSEMITE ST
S HAVANA ST
S PEORIA ST
S CLINTON ST
INVERNESS DR W
E BRONCOS PKWY

A
1 S Geneva Wy
2 E Crestline Pl

B
1 S Yosemite Ct

C
1 S Xanthia Wy

D
1 E Long Pl
2 E Long Ct
3 E Nichols Av
4 E Nichols Pl

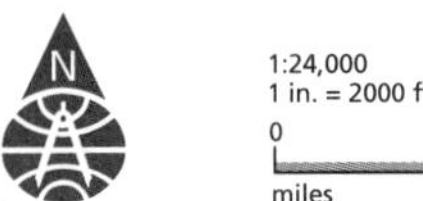

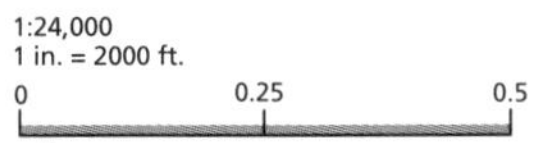

SEE 2284 MAP

Aurora

CHERRY CREEK STATE PARK

A
1 E Crestridge Pl
2 S Kittredge St

Pioneer Hills

S PARKER RD

S CHAMBERS RD

E ORCHARD RD

B
1 E Powers Av

80111

VALLEY COUNTRY CLUB

VIL PARK

Regis Jesuit HS

Arapahoe Crossing

E ARAPAHOE RD

Centennial Medical Plaza

80016

Foxfield

CHERRY CREEK SOCCER COMPLEX

Arapahoe Sports Center

CHERRY CREEK VALLEY ECOLOGICAL PARK

S JORDAN RD

S ATCHISON ST

S BLACKHAWK ST

Centennial

80112

BRONCOS PKWY

C
1 S Norfolk Wy

ARAPAHOE COUNTY COMMUNITY PARK

S POTOMAC ST

S CHAMBERS RD

Centennial Airport

E Control Tower Rd

D
1 E Phillips Dr

E Otero Av

Cherry Creek

13 18 17 19 20 24 25 29 30 31 32 36

1 2 3 4 5 6 7

A B C D E

39°37'04" 39°36'38" 39°36'12" 39°35'46" 39°35'20" 39°34'54" 39°34'28" 39°34'02"

104°50'30" 104°49'56" 104°49'22" 104°48'49" 104°48'15" 104°47'41"

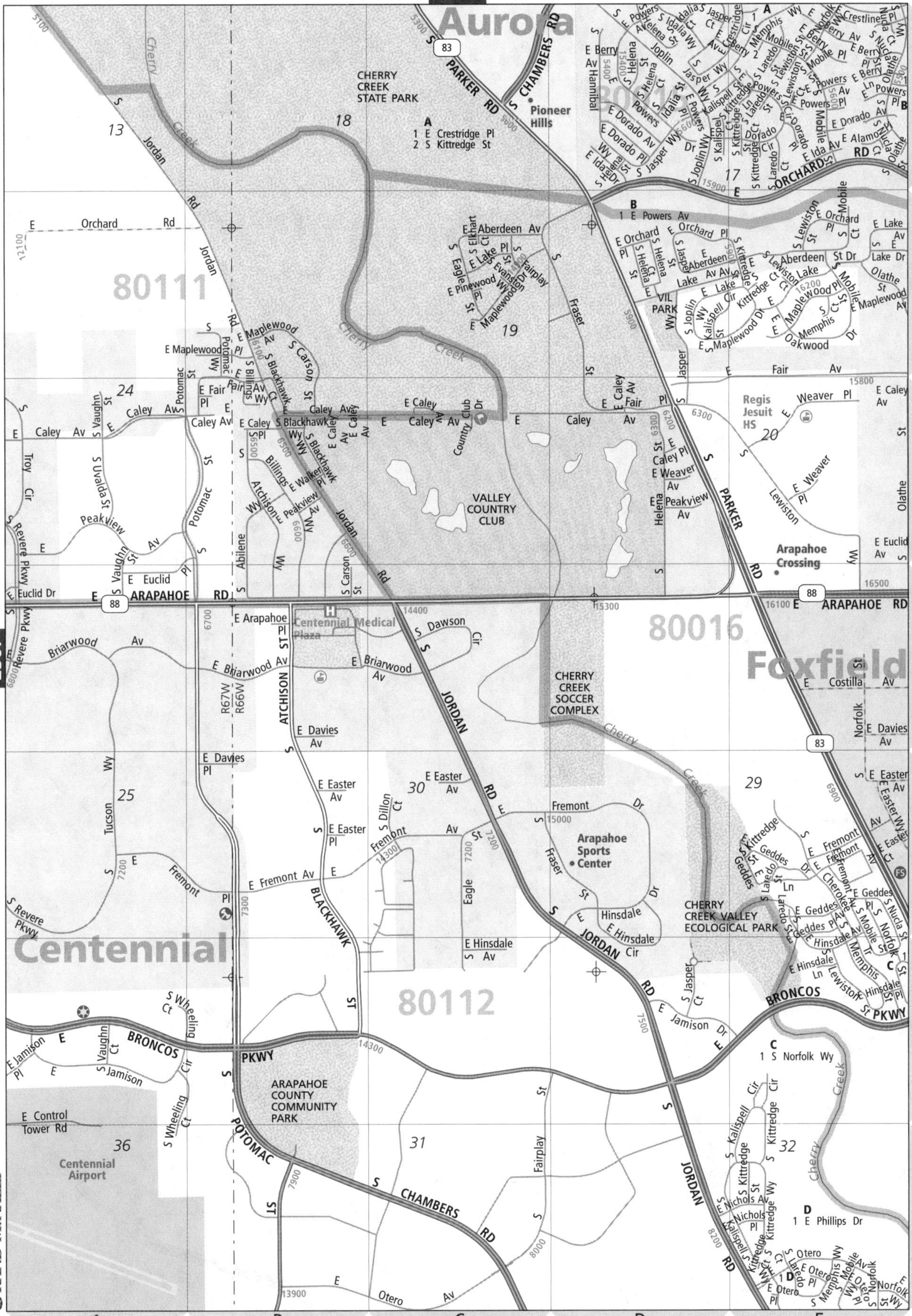

SEE 2367 MAP

SEE 2369 MAP

SEE 2452 MAP

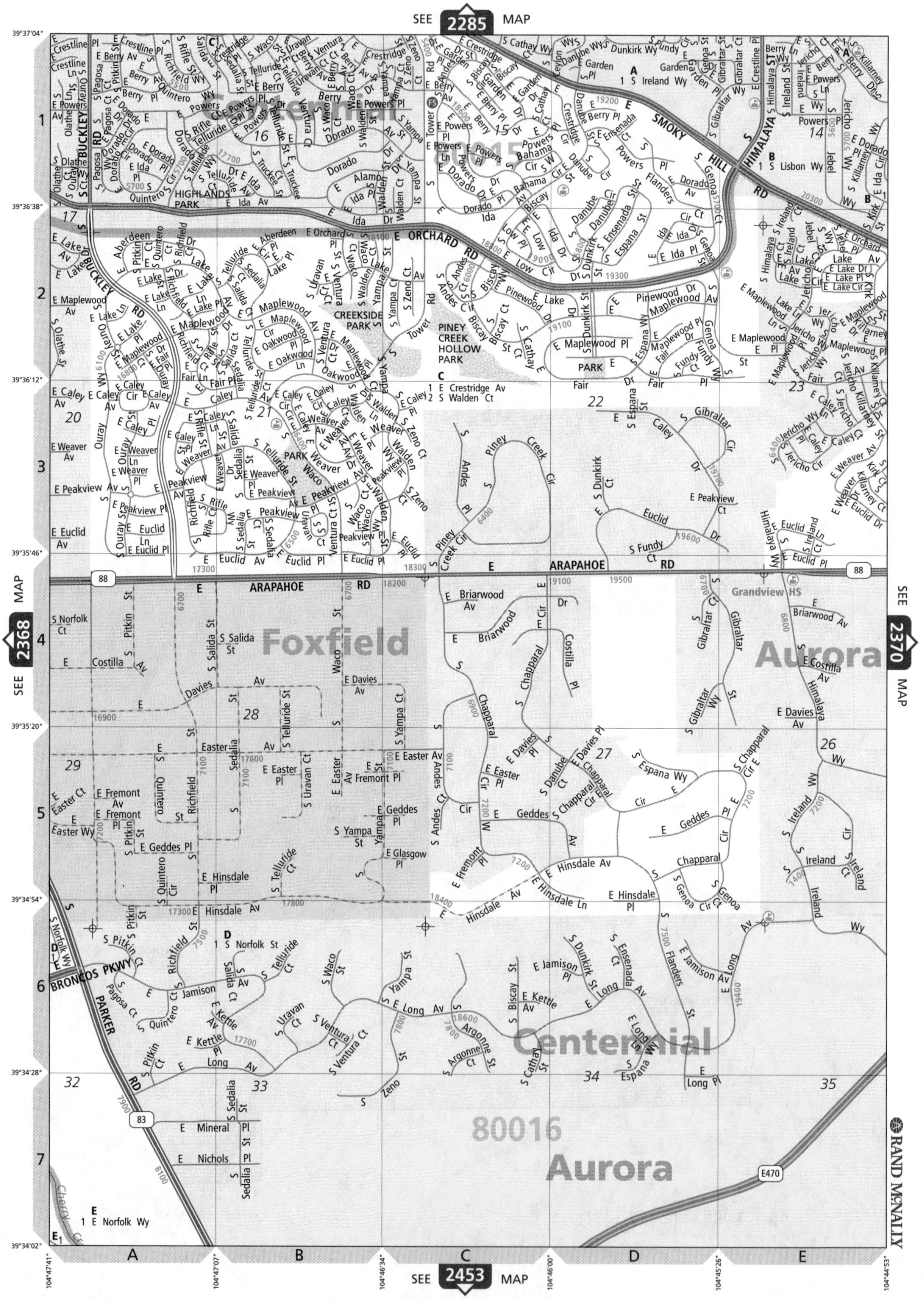

1:24,000
1 in. = 2000 ft.
0 0.25 0.5
miles

SEE 2285 MAP

SEE 2368 MAP

SEE 2370 MAP

Centennial

80015

HIGHLANDS PARK

CREEKSIDE PARK

PINEY CREEK HOLLOW PARK

E ORCHARD RD

E ARAPAHOE RD

S HIMALAYA ST

SMOKY HILL RD

S BUCKLEY RD

BRONCOS PKWY

PARKER RD

Foxfield

Aurora

Grandview HS

Centennial

80016

Aurora

A B C D E

1 2 3 4 5 6 7

SEE 2453 MAP

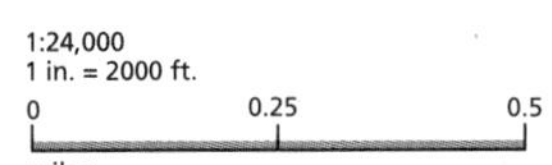

SEE 2286 MAP

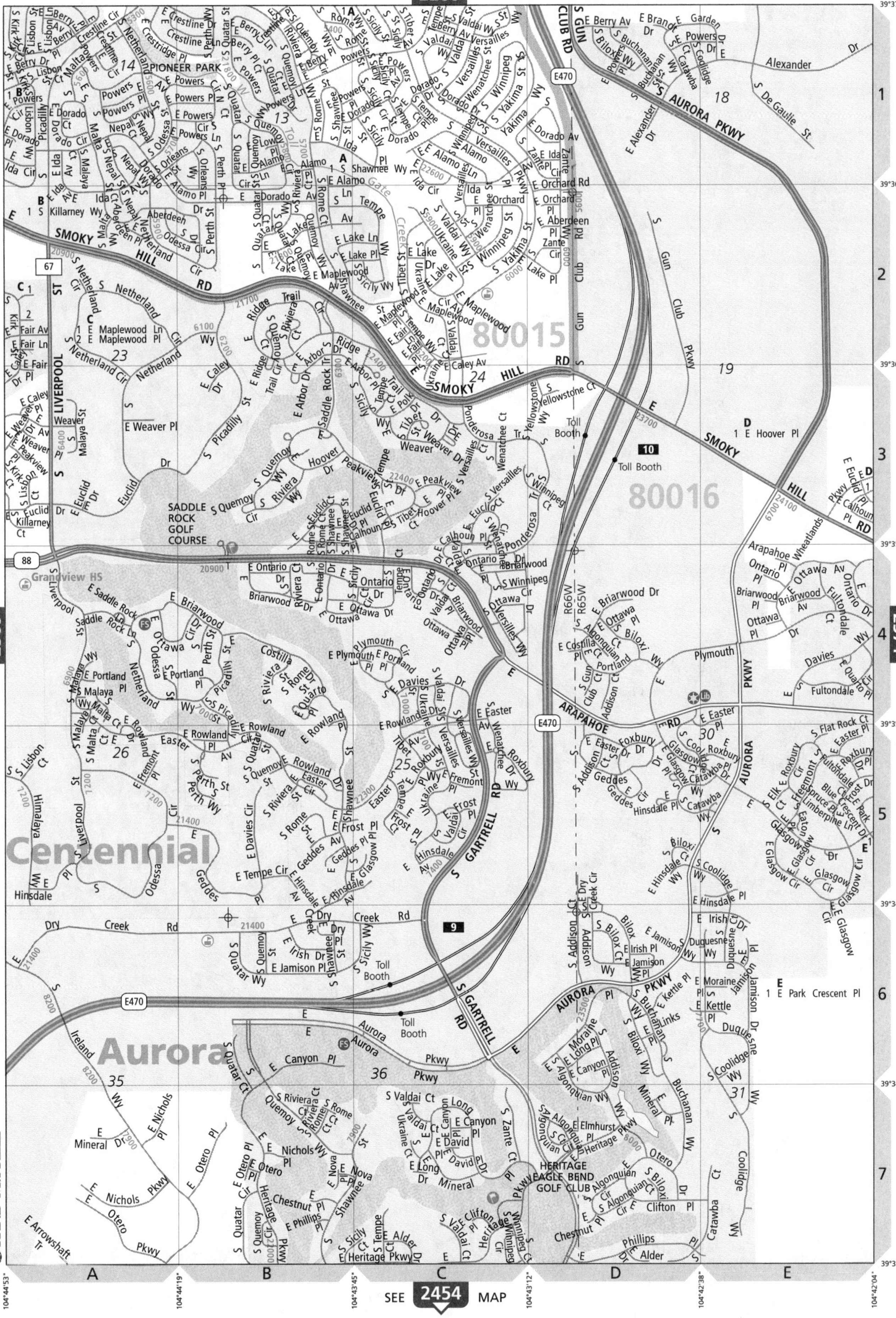

SEE 2369 MAP

SEE 2371 MAP

SEE 2454 MAP

Centennial

Aurora

80015

80016

PIONEER PARK

SADDLE ROCK GOLF COURSE

HERITAGE EAGLE BEND GOLF CLUB

Grandview HS

SMOKY HILL RD

ARAPAHOE RD

AURORA PKWY

S GARTRELL RD

S GUN CLUB RD

LIVERPOOL ST

E470

Dry Creek Rd

Toll Booth

1 2 3 4 5 6 7

A B C D E

39°37'00"
39°36'34"
39°36'08"
39°35'42"
39°35'16"
39°34'50"
39°34'24"
39°33'58"

104°44'53"
104°44'19"
104°43'45"
104°43'12"
104°42'38"
104°42'04"

1:24,000
1 in. = 2000 ft.
0 0.25 0.5
miles

SEE 2287 MAP

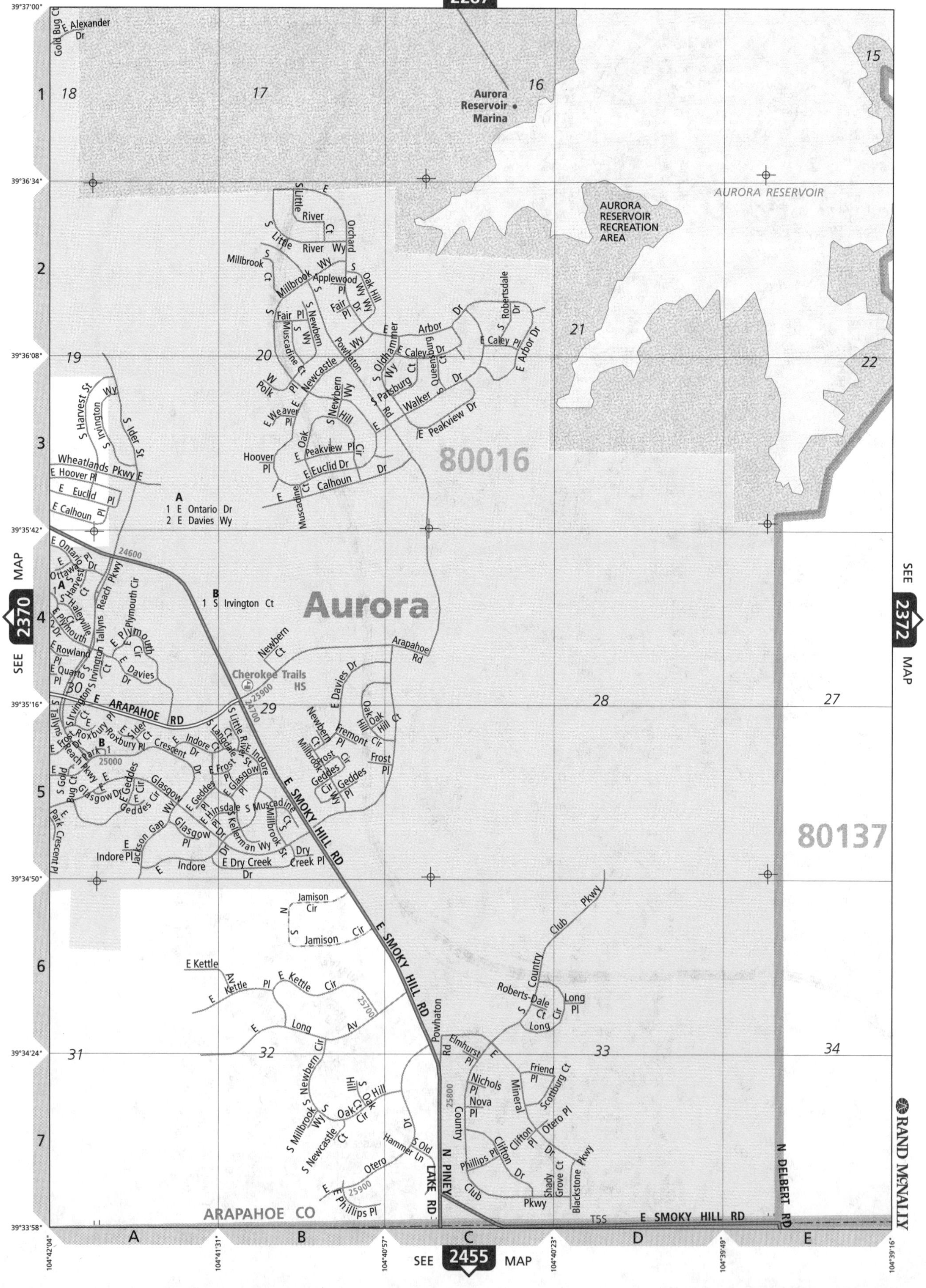

SEE 2370 MAP

SEE 2372 MAP

SEE 2455 MAP

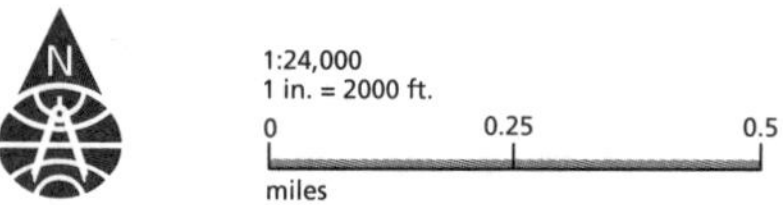

SEE 2288 MAP

SEE 2371 MAP

SEE B MAP

SEE 2456 MAP

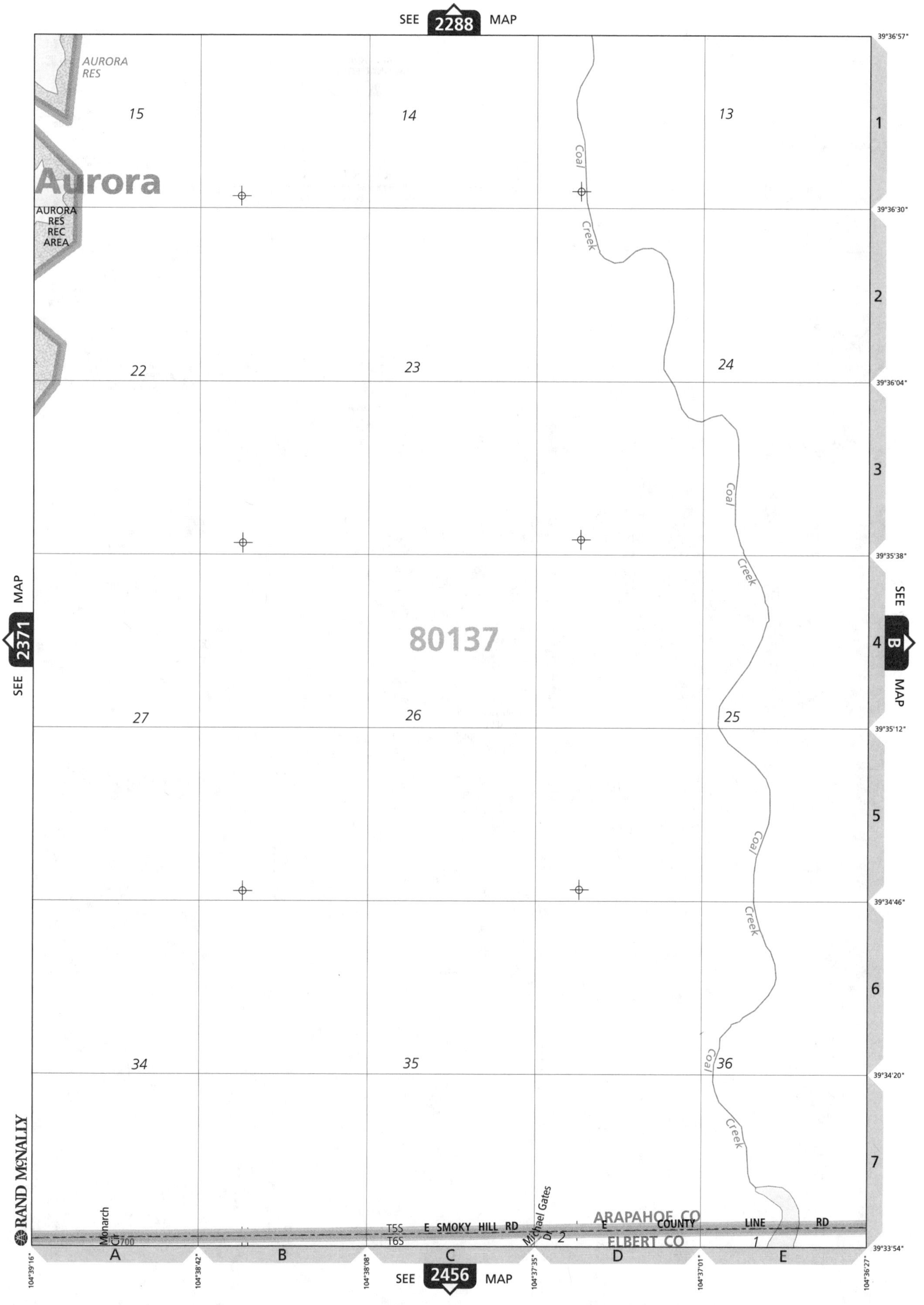

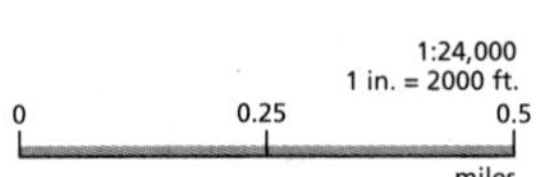

SEE 2355 MAP

ARAPAHO NATIONAL FOREST
Buffalo Park Rd
80439
33
34
35
36
Deer Rd
Ski Tr
Apache Rd
Yuma Tr
Paiute Rd
Paiute Rd
Ouray Rd
Rd
CLEAR CREEK CO
PARK CO
T5S
T6S
80470
4
3
2
1
PIKE NATIONAL FOREST
9
10
11
12
16
15
14
13
Hidden Valley Blvd
Hidden Valley Blvd

39°34'21"
39°33'55"
39°33'29"
39°33'03"
39°32'37"
39°32'10"
39°31'44"
39°31'18"
105°27'01"
105°26'28"
105°25'54"
105°25'20"
105°24'47"
105°24'13"

1 2 3 4 5 6 7
A B C D E

SEE B MAP

SEE 2440 MAP

SEE 2523 MAP

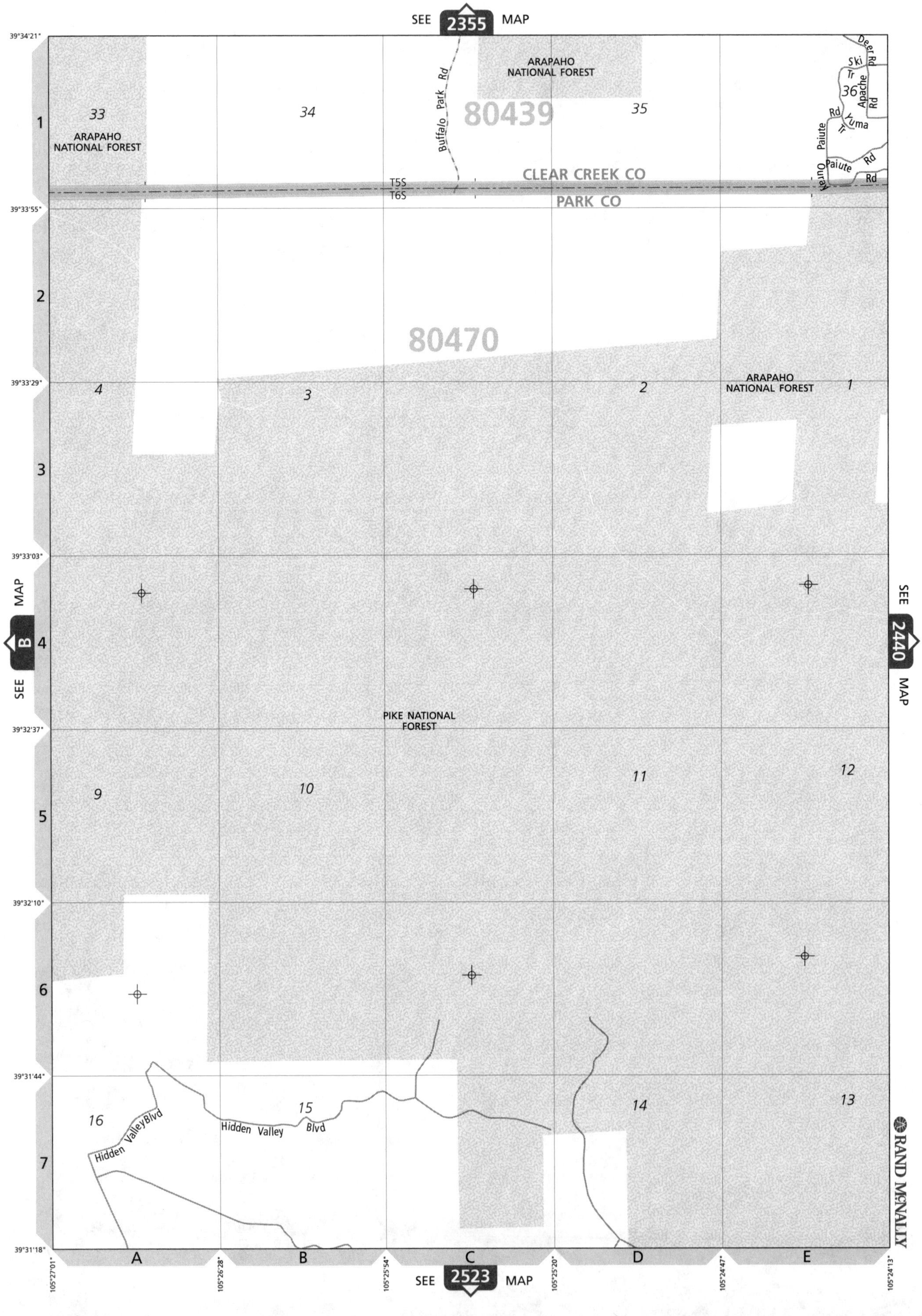

1:24,000
1 in. = 2000 ft.
0 0.25 0.5
miles

SEE 2356 MAP

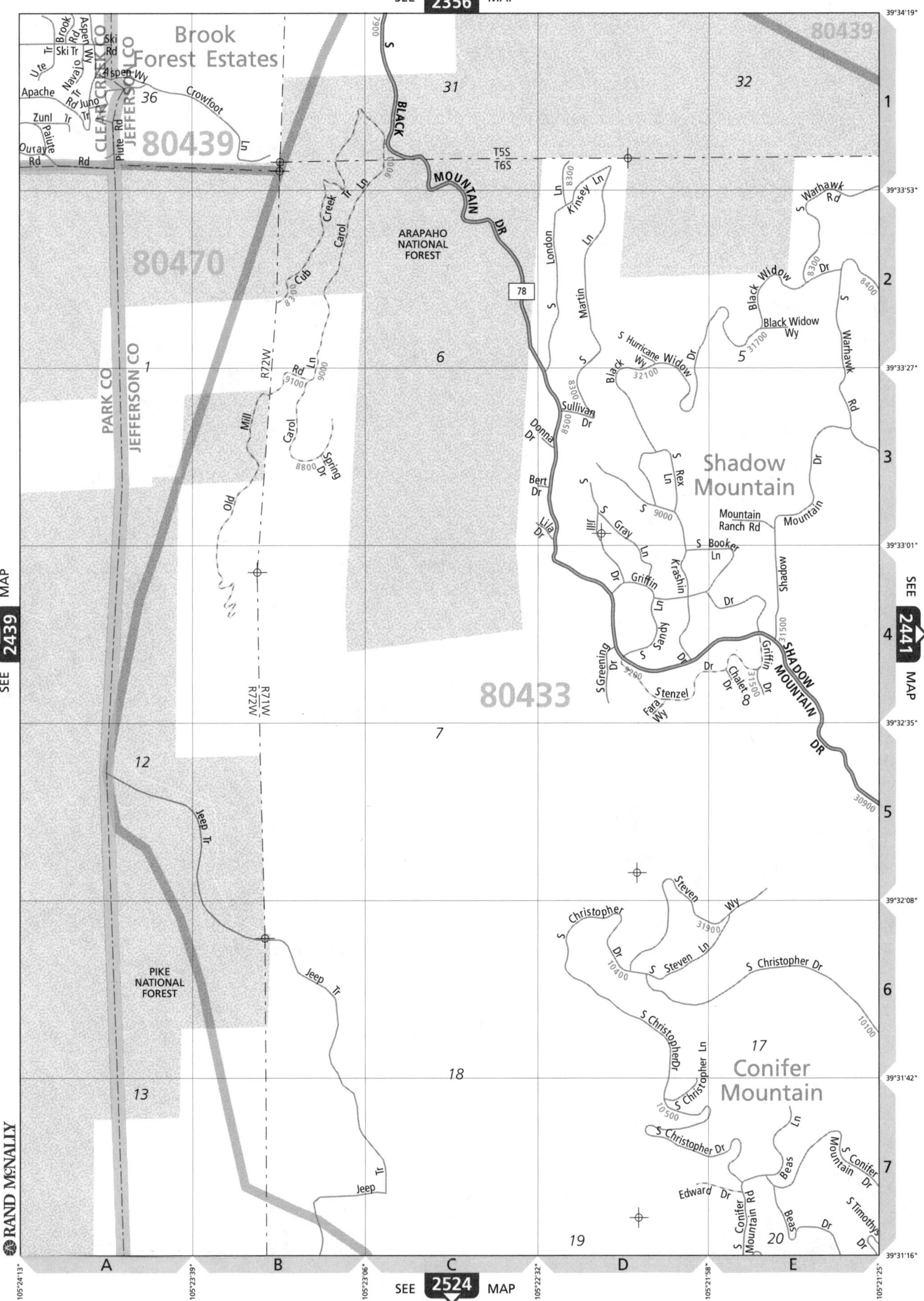

SEE 2439 MAP
SEE 2441 MAP
SEE 2524 MAP

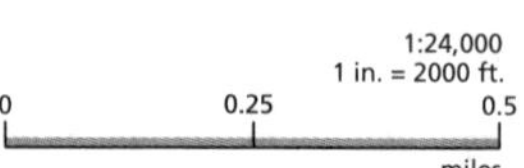

SEE 2357 MAP

SEE 2440 MAP

SEE 2442 MAP

SEE 2525 MAP

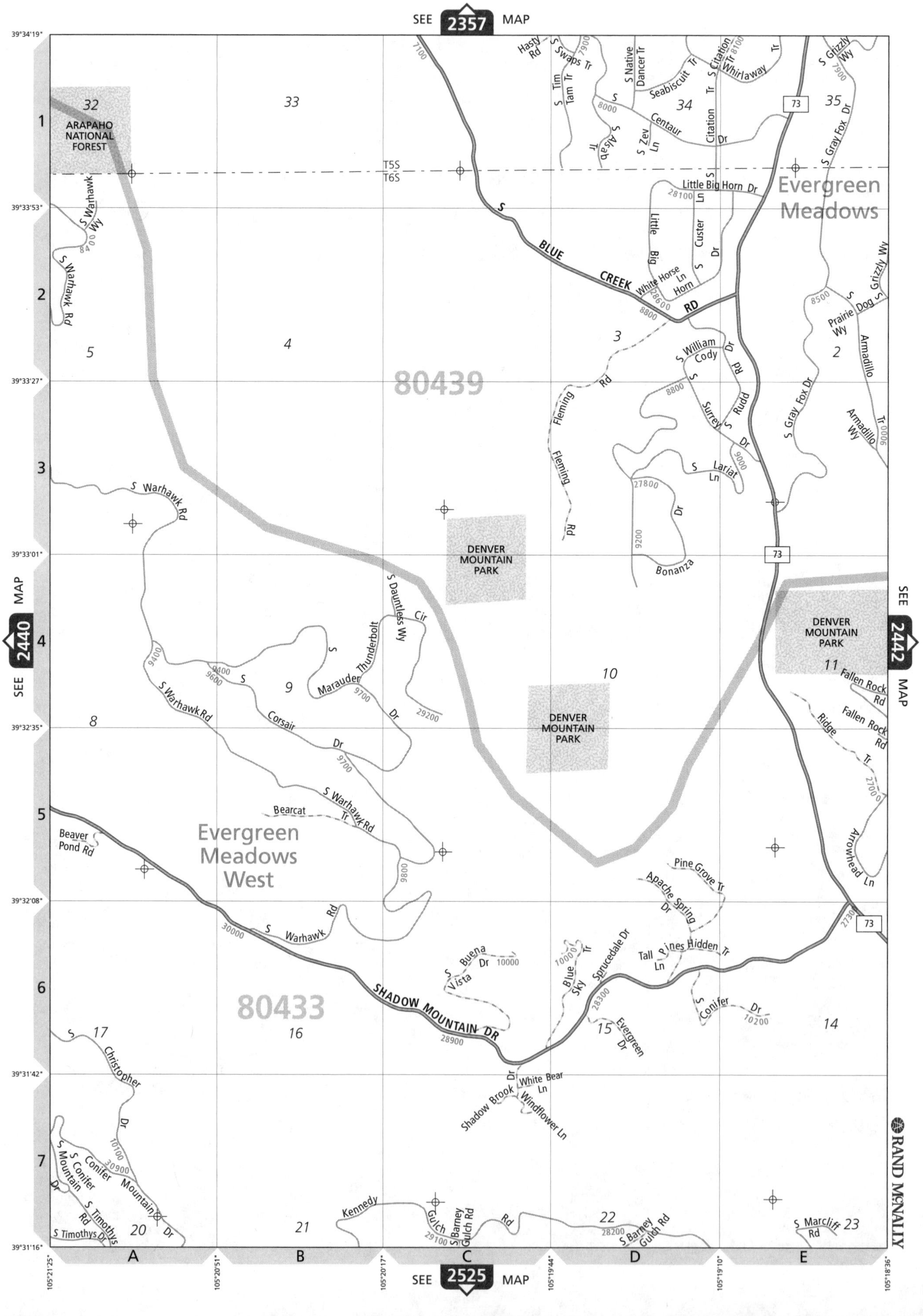

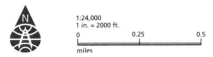

1:24,000
1 in. = 2000 ft.
0 0.25 0.5
miles

SEE 2358 MAP

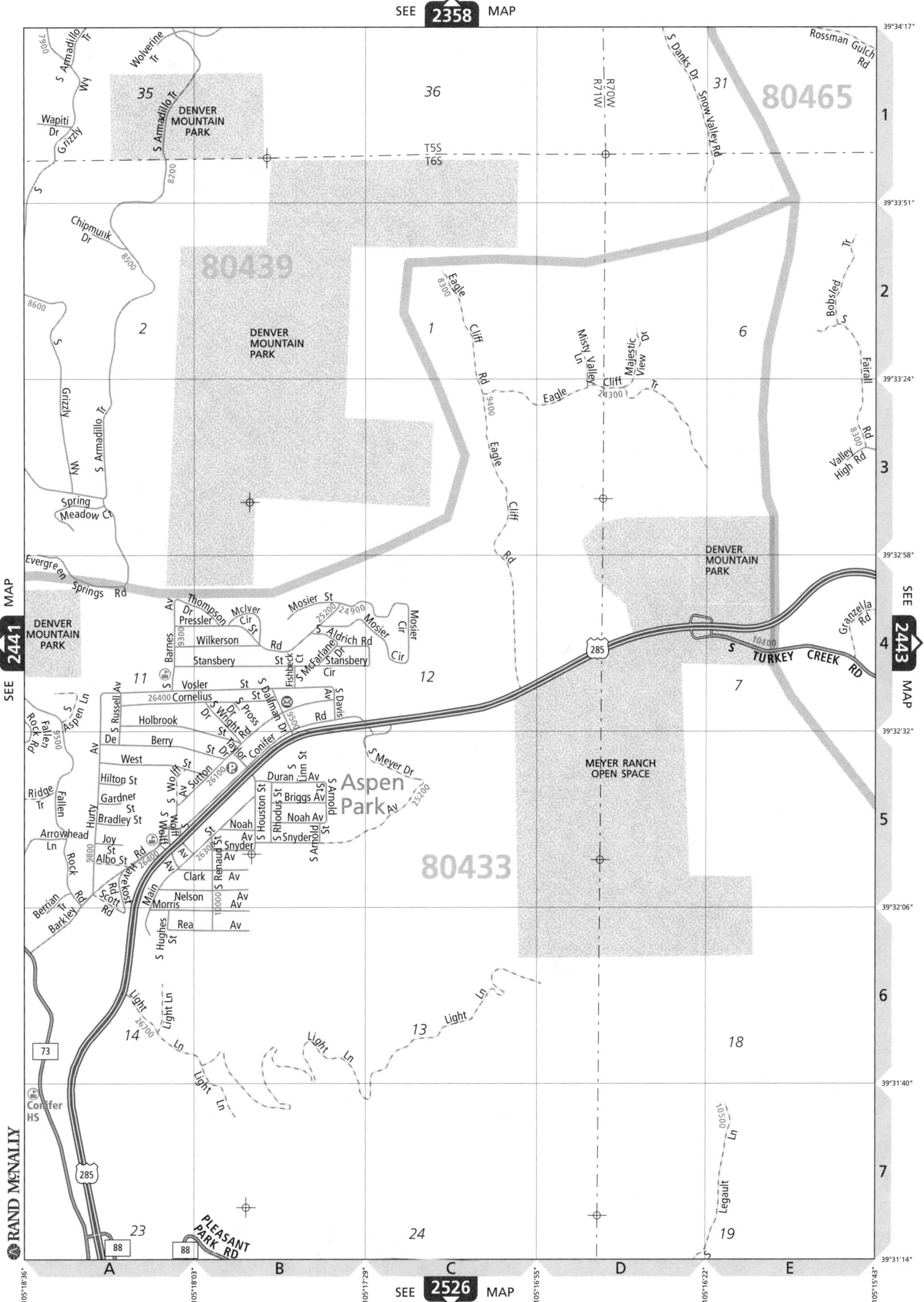

SEE 2441 MAP

SEE 2443 MAP

SEE 2526 MAP

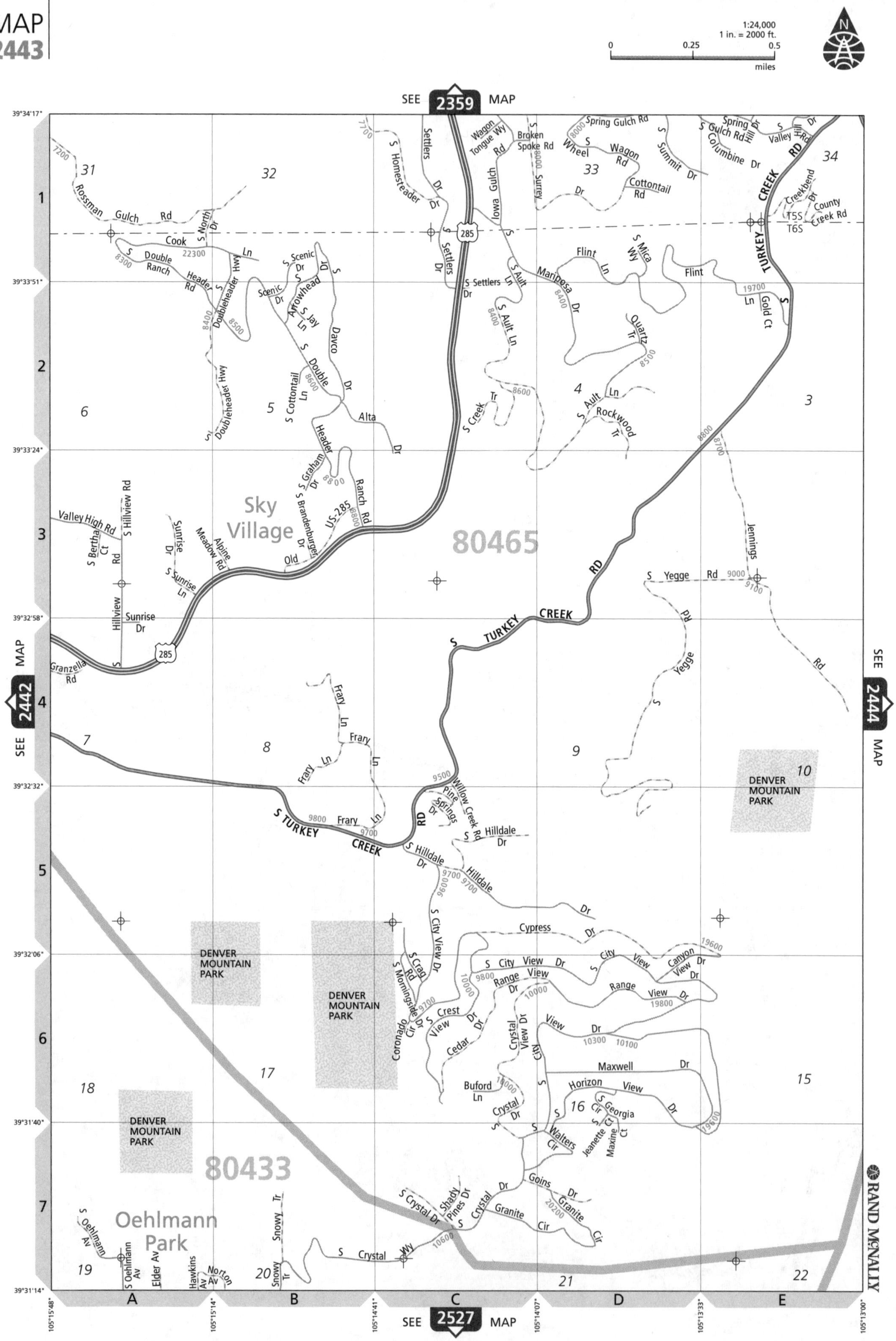

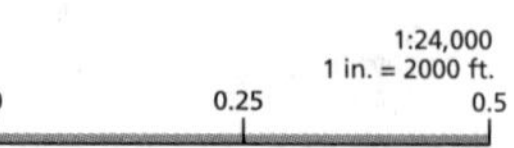

SEE 2359 MAP

SEE 2442 MAP

SEE 2444 MAP

SEE 2527 MAP

Sky Village

80465

80433

Oehlmann Park

DENVER MOUNTAIN PARK

S TURKEY CREEK RD

RAND McNALLY

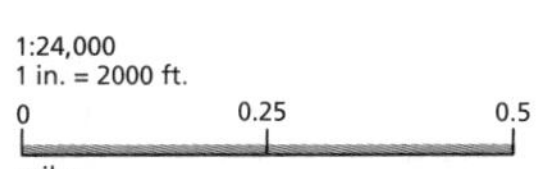

SEE 2360 MAP

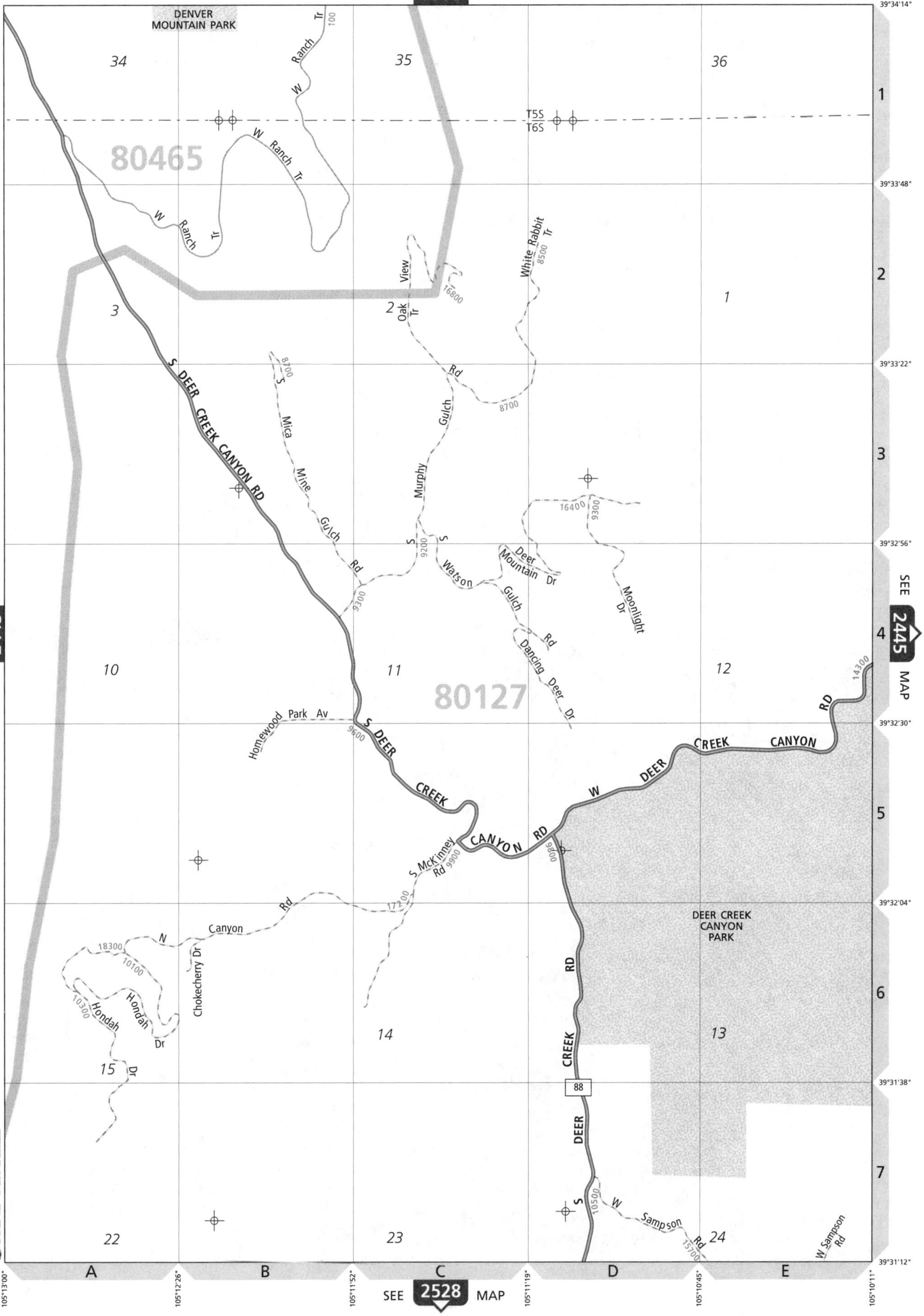

SEE 2443 MAP

SEE 2445 MAP

SEE 2528 MAP

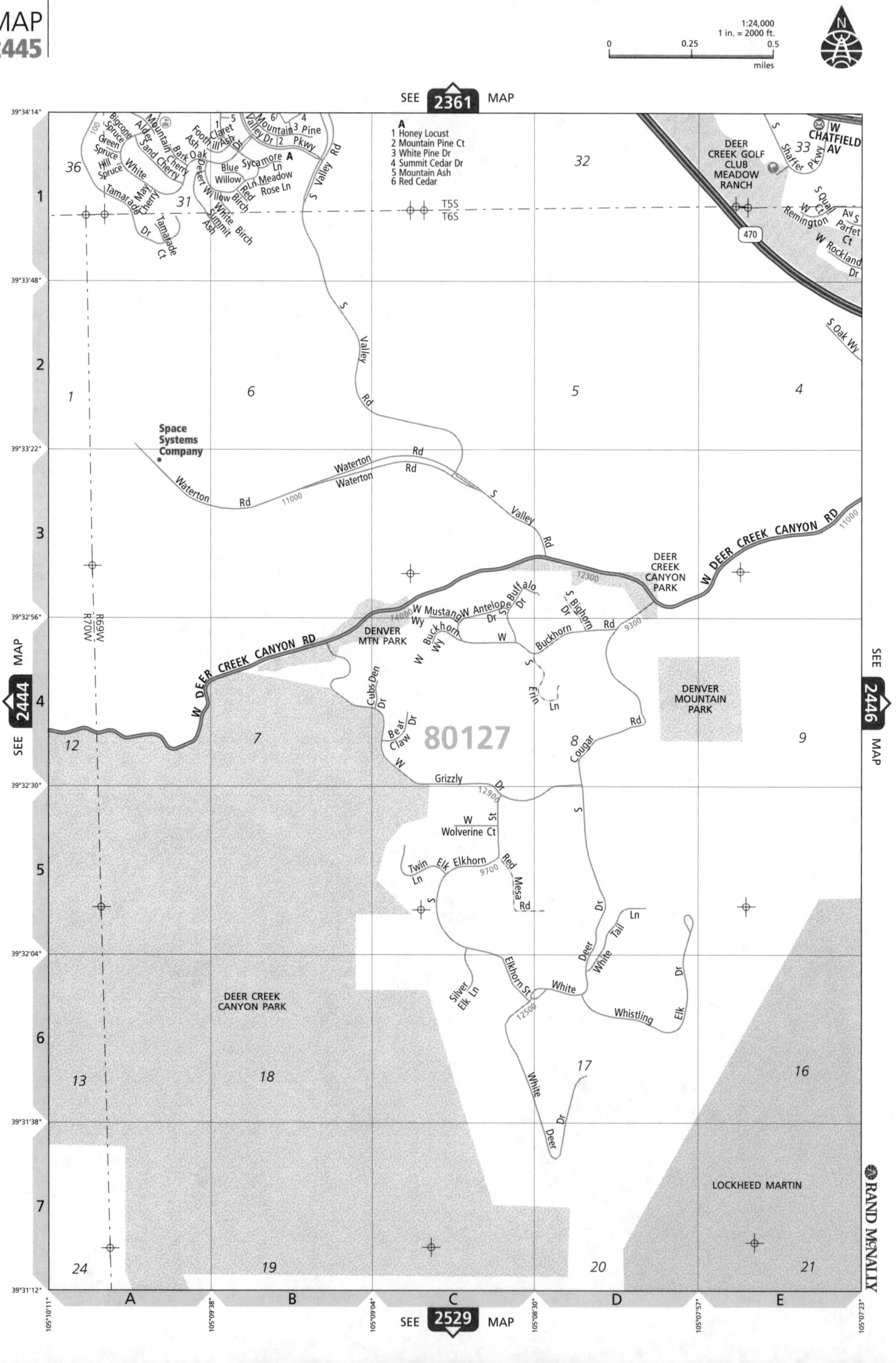

1:24,000
1 in. = 2000 ft.
0 0.25 0.5
miles

SEE 2361 MAP

A
1 Honey Locust
2 Mountain Pine Ct
3 White Pine Dr
4 Summit Cedar Dr
5 Mountain Ash
6 Red Cedar

DEER CREEK GOLF CLUB MEADOW RANCH

W CHATFIELD AV

Space Systems Company

W DEER CREEK CANYON RD

DEER CREEK CANYON PARK

DENVER MTN PARK

80127

DENVER MOUNTAIN PARK

DEER CREEK CANYON PARK

LOCKHEED MARTIN

SEE 2444 MAP

SEE 2446 MAP

SEE 2529 MAP

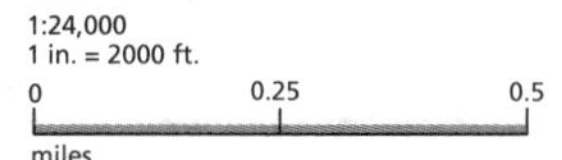

SEE 2362 MAP

W CHATFIELD AV
W DEER CREEK CANYON RD
W UTE AV
KIPLING PKWY
S GARRISON ST
WADSWORTH BLVD
S PLATTE CANYON RD
S OWENS ST

DEER CREEK GOLF CLUB MEADOW RANCH

Chatfield Estates

80128

80127

Chatfield Arboretum

Littleton

FAIRVIEW RESERVOIR

CHATFIELD LAKE

CHATFIELD STATE PARK

LOCKHEED MARTIN

SOUTH PLATTE RIVER

JEFFERSON CO

DOUGLAS CO

A
1 S Lewis Ct

B
1 W Chatfield Pl
2 S Garland Cir

C
1 S Flower Ct

D
1 S Saulsbury St
2 S Saulsbury Wy

E
1 Park Mtn W
2 Park Mtn E
3 W Purgatoire Peak
4 Culebra Range Rd
5 Red Mtn E

F
1 S Garland Ct
2 W Nichols Dr
3 W Monticello Pl

33 34 35 4 3 2 9 10 11 16 15 14 21 22 23

1 2 3 4 5 6 7

A B C D E

39°34'11" 39°33'45" 39°33'19" 39°32'53" 39°32'27" 39°32'01" 39°31'35" 39°31'09"

105°07'23" 105°06'49" 105°06'16" 105°05'42" 105°05'08" 105°04'35"

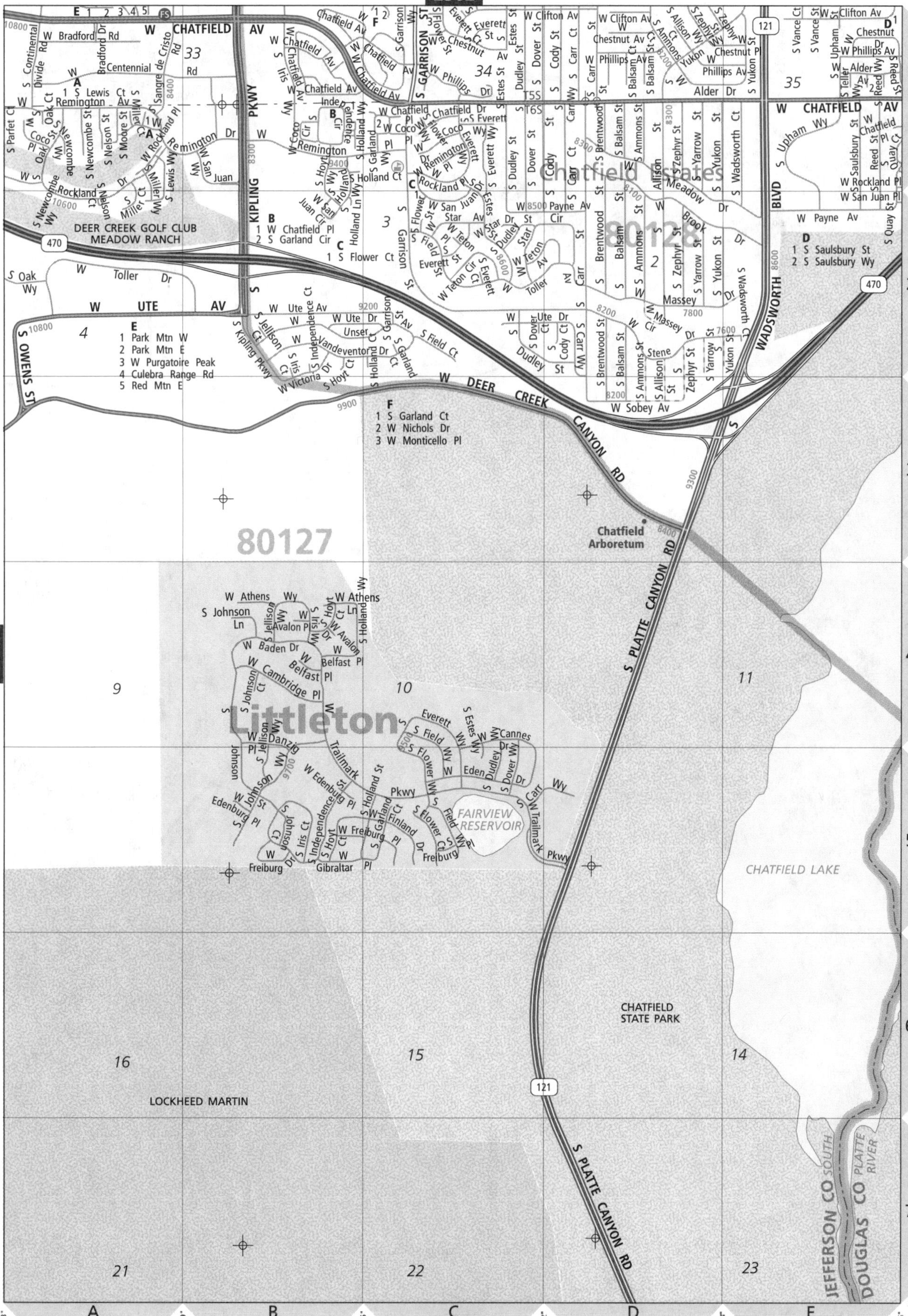

SEE 2445 MAP

SEE 2447 MAP

SEE 2530 MAP

1:24,000
1 in. = 2000 ft.
0 0.25 0.5
miles

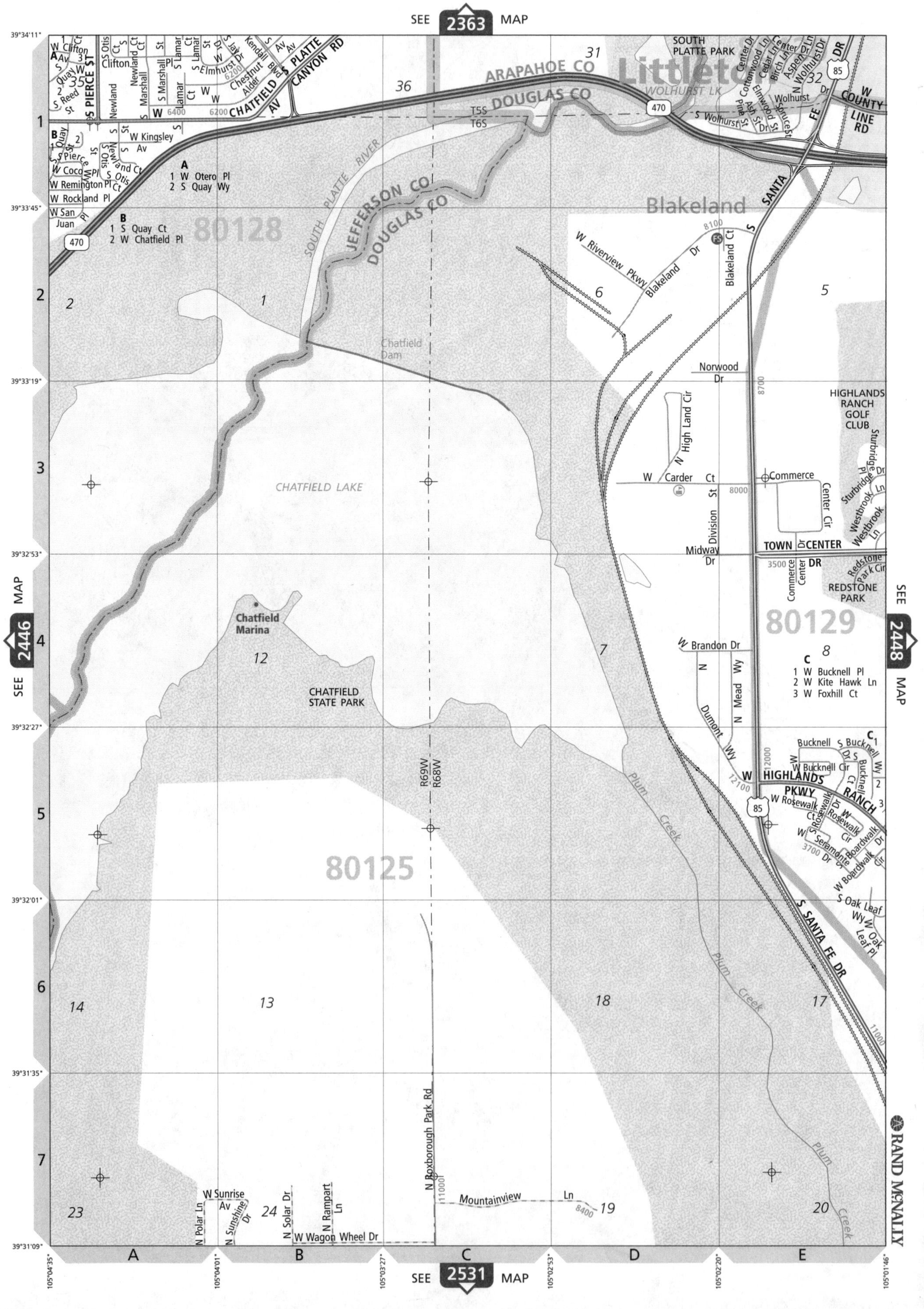

SEE 2363 MAP

SEE 2446 MAP

SEE 2448 MAP

SEE 2531 MAP

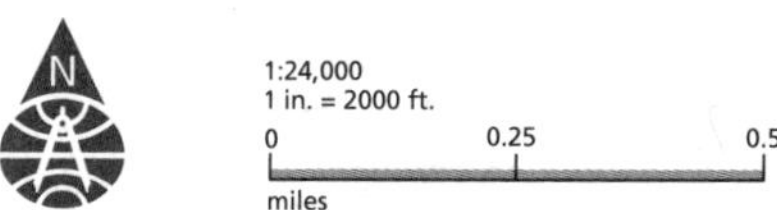

SEE 2364 MAP

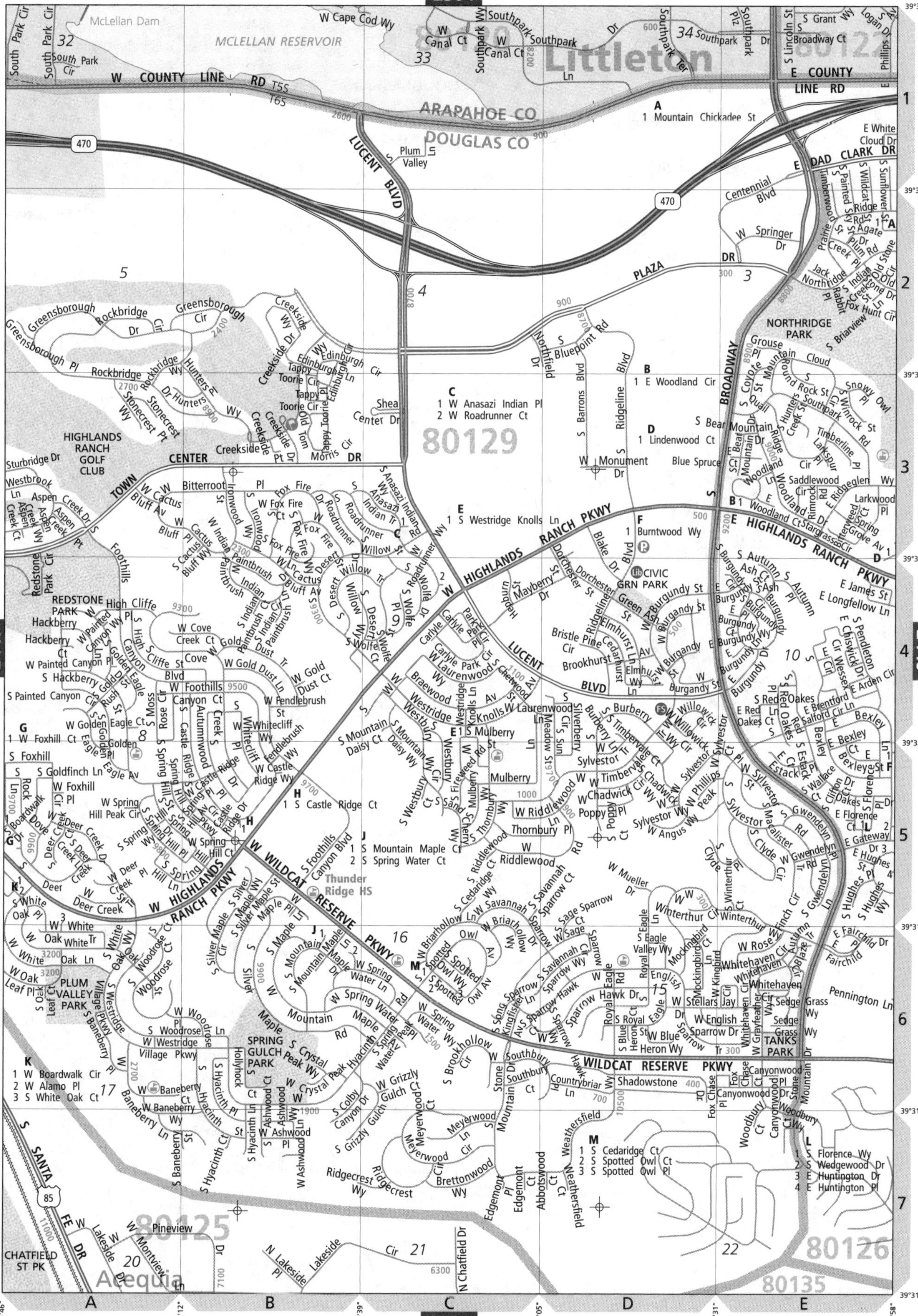

SEE 2447 MAP

SEE 2449 MAP

Littleton

ARAPAHOE CO

DOUGLAS CO

80129

HIGHLANDS RANCH GOLF CLUB

NORTHRIDGE PARK

REDSTONE PARK

PLUM VALLEY PARK

SPRING GULCH PARK

TANKS PARK

CHATFIELD ST PK

Thunder Ridge HS

80125

80126

80135

A
1 Mountain Chickadee St

B
1 E Woodland Cir

C
1 W Anasazi Indian Pl
2 W Roadrunner Ct

D
1 Lindenwood Ct

E
1 S Westridge Knolls Ln

F
1 Burntwood Wy

G
1 W Foxhill Ct

H
1 S Castle Ridge Ct

J
1 S Mountain Maple Ct
2 S Spring Water Ct

K
1 W Boardwalk Cir
2 W Alamo Pl
3 S White Oak Ct

L
1 S Florence Wy
2 S Wedgewood Dr
3 E Huntington Dr
4 E Huntington Pl

M
1 S Cedaridge Ct
2 S Spotted Owl Ct
3 S Spotted Owl Pl

SEE 2532 MAP

1:24,000
1 in. = 2000 ft.
0 0.25 0.5
miles

SEE 2365 MAP

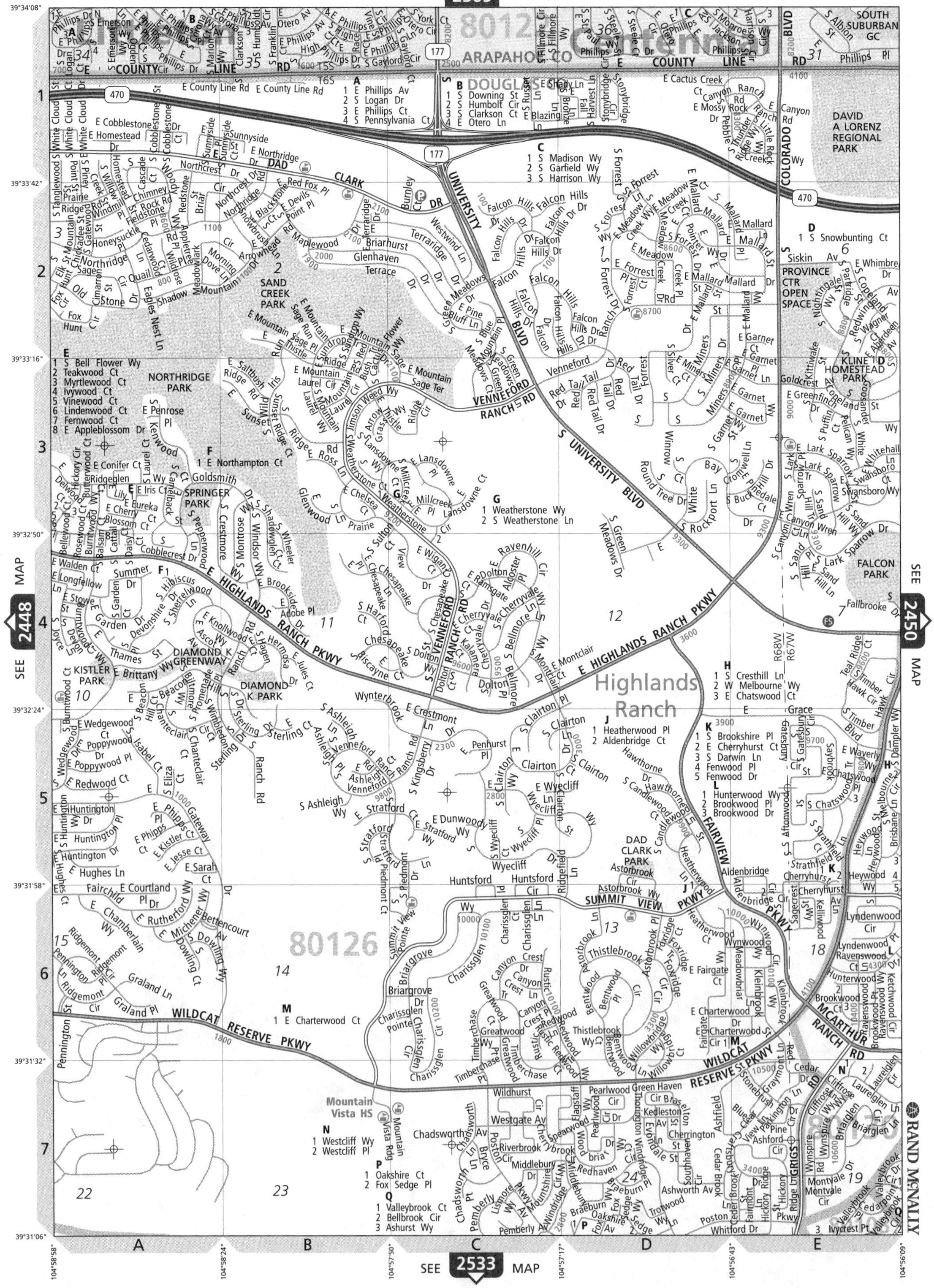

SEE 2448 MAP

SEE 2450 MAP

A
1 E Phillips Av
2 S Logan Dr
3 E Phillips Ct
4 S Pennsylvania Ct

B
1 S Downing St
2 S Humbolt Cir
3 S Clarkson Ct
4 E Otero Ln

C
1 S Madison Wy
2 S Garfield Wy
3 S Harrison Wy

D
1 S Snowbunting Ct

E
1 S Bell Flower Wy
2 Teakwood Ct
3 Myrtlewood Ct
4 Ivywood Ct
5 Vinewood Ct
6 Lindenwood Ct
7 Fernwood Ct
8 E Appleblossom Dr

F
1 E Northampton Ct

G
1 Weatherstone Wy
2 S Weatherstone Ln

H
1 S Cresthill Ln
2 W Melbourne Wy
3 E Chatswood Ct

J
1 Heatherwood Pl
2 Aldenbridge Ct

K
1 S Brookshire Pl
2 E Cherryhurst Ct
3 S Darwin Ln
4 Fenwood Pl
5 Fenwood Dr

L
1 Hunterwood Wy
2 Brookwood Pl
3 Brookwood Dr

M
1 E Charterwood Ct

N
1 Westcliff Wy
2 Westcliff Pl

P
1 Oakshire Ct
2 Fox Sedge Pl

Q
1 Valleybrook Ct
2 Bellbrook Cir
3 Ashurst Wy

SOUTH SUBURBAN GC
DAVID A LORENZ REGIONAL PARK
SAND CREEK PARK
NORTHRIDGE PARK
SPRINGER PARK
DIAMOND K GREENWAY
KISTLER PARK
DIAMOND K PARK
PROVINCE CTR OPEN SPACE
KLINE HOMESTEAD PARK
FALCON PARK
DAD CLARK PARK
Highlands Ranch
Mountain Vista HS
80126
ARAPAHOE CO
DOUGLAS CO

A B C D E

SEE 2533 MAP

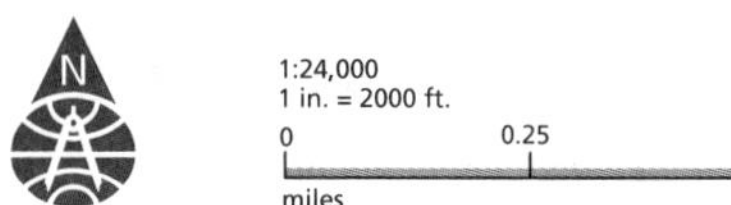

SEE 2366 MAP

A
1 S Niagara Ct
2 S Newport Wy

B
1 E Greenwich Pl
2 S Greenwich Ct

C
1 S Mountain Brush Peak

D
1 S Chestnut Hill Wy
2 E Edgewood Wy

E
1 S Goosander Wy

F
1 S Fallbrooke Dr

G
1 E Wickerdale Pl

H
1 S Brentford Dr

J
1 S Queenscliffe Ct
2 S Dampler Wy

K
1 S Melbourne Cir

L
1 E Buckingham Pl

M
1 Collingswood Ct

N
1 Laurelglen Cir

P
1 Jewelberry Ln

Q
1 Towerbridge Cir
2 Heatherton Tr
3 Fullerton Cir

R
1 Valleybrook Ct

SEE 2449 MAP

SEE 2451 MAP

SEE 2534 MAP

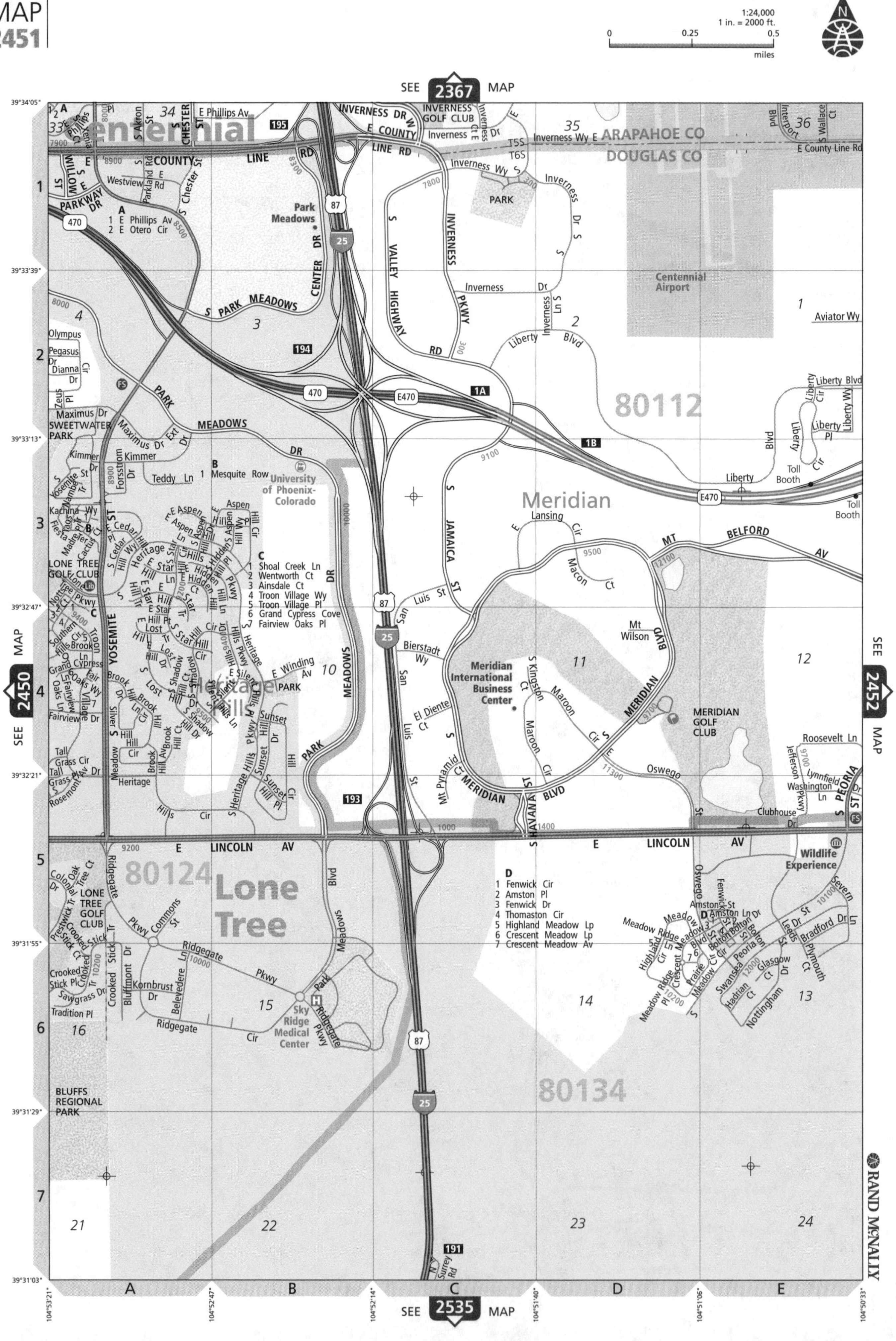

1:24,000
1 in. = 2000 ft.
0
0.25
0.5
miles
N
SEE 2367 MAP
SEE 2450 MAP
SEE 2452 MAP
SEE 2535 MAP
Centennial
ARAPAHOE CO
DOUGLAS CO
E COUNTY LINE RD
E County Line Rd
INVERNESS DR W
INVERNESS GOLF CLUB
Inverness Dr
Inverness Wy E
Inverness Wy
Inverness Dr S
Inverness Pkwy
Inverness Ln S
PARK
Centennial Airport
Aviator Wy
Liberty Blvd
Liberty Cir
Liberty Wy
Liberty Pl
Toll Booth
80112
Meridian
Lansing Cir
Macon Ct
E BELFORD AV
MT
Mt Wilson
MERIDIAN BLVD
Meridian International Business Center
Maroon Cir
S Kingston Ct
MERIDIAN GOLF CLUB
Oswego
Roosevelt Ln
Jefferson Pkwy
Lynnfield Dr
Washington Ln
Clubhouse Dr
S PEORIA ST
S JAMAICA ST
San Luis St
Bierstadt Wy
El Diente Ct
Mt Pyramid Ct
S HAVANA ST
E LINCOLN AV
Wildlife Experience
S VALLEY HIGHWAY
Park Meadows
CENTER DR
S PARK MEADOWS
PARK MEADOWS DR
MEADOWS DR
PARK MEADOWS
University of Phoenix-Colorado
Heritage Hills
Winding Av
E Phillips Av
S Akron St
S CHESTER ST
S Chester St
Westview Rd
Parkland Rd
PARKWAY DR
WILLOW ST
A
1 E Phillips Av
2 E Otero Cir
B
1 Mesquite Row
C
1 Shoal Creek Ln
2 Wentworth Ct
3 Ainsdale Ct
4 Troon Village Wy
5 Troon Village Pl
6 Grand Cypress Cove
7 Fairview Oaks Pl
D
1 Fenwick Cir
2 Amston Pl
3 Fenwick Dr
4 Thomaston Cir
5 Highland Meadow Lp
6 Crescent Meadow Lp
7 Crescent Meadow Av
Olympus
Pegasus Dr
Dianna Cir
Zeus Pl
Maximus Dr
SWEETWATER PARK
Kimmer Dr
Teddy Ln
Forsstrom Dr
S YOSEMITE ST
LONE TREE GOLF CLUB
Lone Tree Pkwy
Troon
Heritage
80124
Lone Tree
RidgeGate Pkwy
Commons St
Crooked Stick Tr
Bluffmont Dr
Kornbrust Dr
Belevedere Ln
Sky Ridge Medical Center
Park Meadows Blvd
LONE TREE GOLF CLUB
Tradition Pl
Sawgrass Dr
BLUFFS REGIONAL PARK
80134
Meadow Ridge
Peoria St
Swansea Ct
Glasgow Dr
Nottingham
Bradford Dr
Plymouth Ct
Severn Ln
Leeds St
Hadrian Ct
Fenwick St
Amston Ln
470
E470
87
25
1A
1B
191
193
194
195
T5S
T6S
1
2
3
4
10
11
12
13
14
15
16
21
22
23
24
33
34
35
36
A
B
C
D
E
1
2
3
4
5
6
7
39°34'05"
39°33'39"
39°33'13"
39°32'47"
39°32'21"
39°31'55"
39°31'29"
39°31'03"
104°53'21"
104°52'47"
104°52'14"
104°51'40"
104°51'06"
104°50'33"
RAND McNALLY

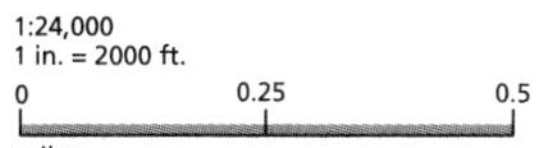

SEE 2368 MAP

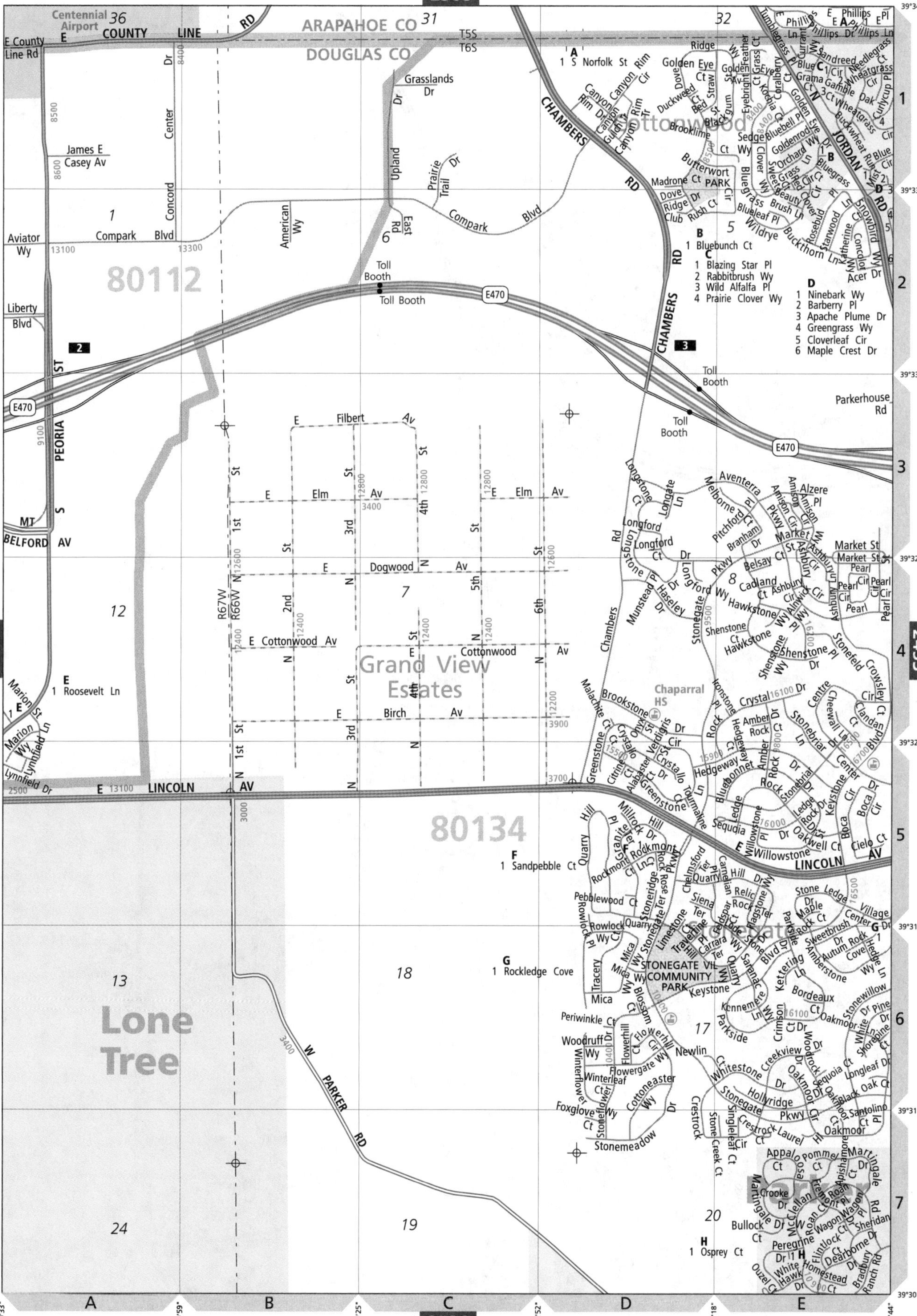

SEE 2451 MAP

SEE 2453 MAP

Centennial Airport
ARAPAHOE CO
DOUGLAS CO
E COUNTY LINE RD
Cottonwood
80112
80134
Grand View Estates
Lone Tree
Parker
Stonegate
Chaparral HS
Butterwort PARK
STONEGATE VIL COMMUNITY PARK
CHAMBERS RD
JORDAN RD
PEORIA ST
E LINCOLN AV
W PARKER RD
E470
Toll Booth

A
1 S Norfolk St

B
1 Bluebunch Ct

C
1 Blazing Star Pl
2 Rabbitbrush Wy
3 Wild Alfalfa Pl
4 Prairie Clover Wy

D
1 Ninebark Wy
2 Barberry Pl
3 Apache Plume Dr
4 Greengrass Wy
5 Cloverleaf Cir
6 Maple Crest Dr

E
1 Roosevelt Ln

F
1 Sandpebble Ct

G
1 Rockledge Cove

H
1 Osprey Ct

RAND McNALLY

SEE 2536 MAP

1:24,000
1 in. = 2000 ft.
0 0.25 0.5
miles

SEE 2369 MAP

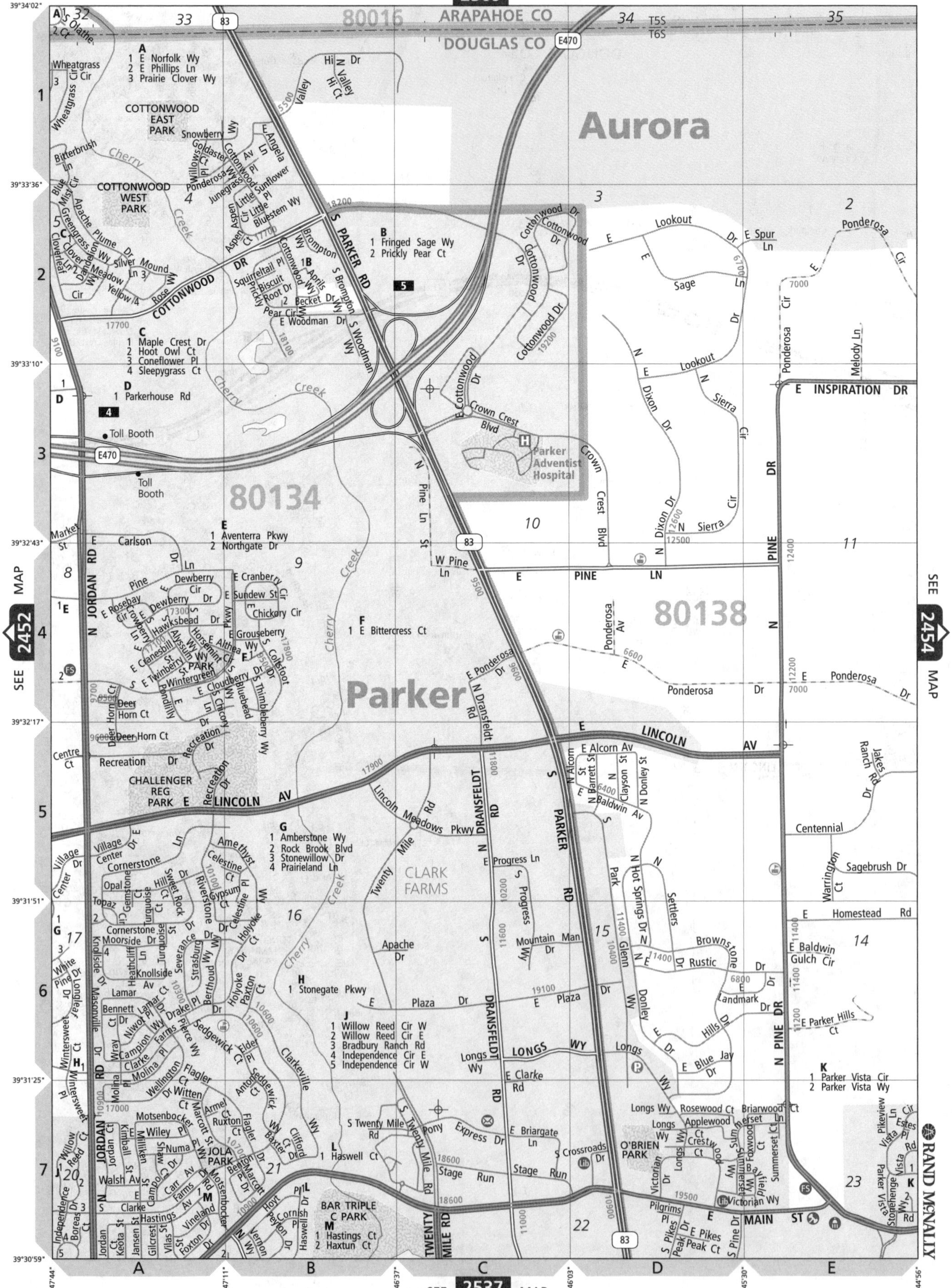

39°34'02"
39°33'36"
39°33'10"
39°32'43"
39°32'17"
39°31'51"
39°31'25"
39°30'59"

80016
ARAPAHOE CO
DOUGLAS CO
T5S
T6S
Aurora
80134
80138
Parker
COTTONWOOD EAST PARK
COTTONWOOD WEST PARK
CHALLENGER REG PARK
CLARK FARMS
JOLA PARK
O'BRIEN PARK
BAR TRIPLE C PARK
Parker Adventist Hospital
Toll Booth
Toll Booth
S PARKER RD
COTTONWOOD DR
E LINCOLN AV
N JORDAN RD
S DRANSFELDT RD
N PINE DR
E INSPIRATION DR
E PINE LN
TWENTY MILE RD
E MAIN ST
LONGS WY
Cherry Creek

A
1 E Norfolk Wy
2 E Phillips Ln
3 Prairie Clover Wy

B
1 Fringed Sage Wy
2 Prickly Pear Ct

C
1 Maple Crest Dr
2 Hoot Owl Ct
3 Coneflower Pl
4 Sleepygrass Ct

D
1 Parkerhouse Rd

E
1 Aventerra Pkwy
2 Northgate Dr

F
1 E Bittercress Ct

G
1 Amberstone Wy
2 Rock Brook Blvd
3 Stonewillow Dr
4 Prairieland Ln

H
1 Stonegate Pkwy

J
1 Willow Reed Cir W
2 Willow Reed Cir E
3 Bradbury Ranch Rd
4 Independence Cir E
5 Independence Cir W

K
1 Parker Vista Cir
2 Parker Vista Wy

L
1 Haswell Ct

M
1 Hastings Ct
2 Haxtun Ct

SEE 2452 MAP

SEE 2454 MAP

A B C D E

104°47'44"
104°47'11"
104°46'37"
104°46'03"
104°45'30"
104°44'56"

SEE 2537 MAP

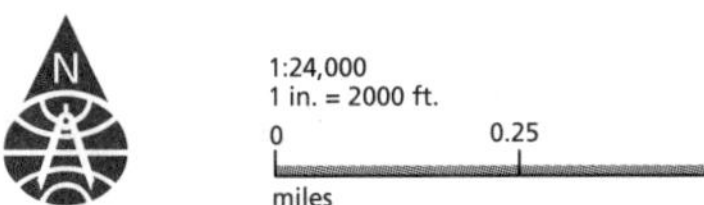

SEE 2370 MAP

ARAPAHOE CO
DOUGLAS CO
Aurora
Livengood Hills
Ponderosa Hills
80138
Parker
HERITAGE EAGLE BEND GOLF CLUB
E INSPIRATION DR
PARKER RD
MAIN ST
CANTERBERRY PKWY

A
1 S Ireland Wy

B
1 S Gartrell Rd

C
1 Parker Vista Ln
2 Parker Vista Pl

D
1 Silver Meadow Ln
2 Wheatfield Ln
3 Silver Meadow Cir

SEE 2453 MAP

SEE 2455 MAP

SEE 2538 MAP

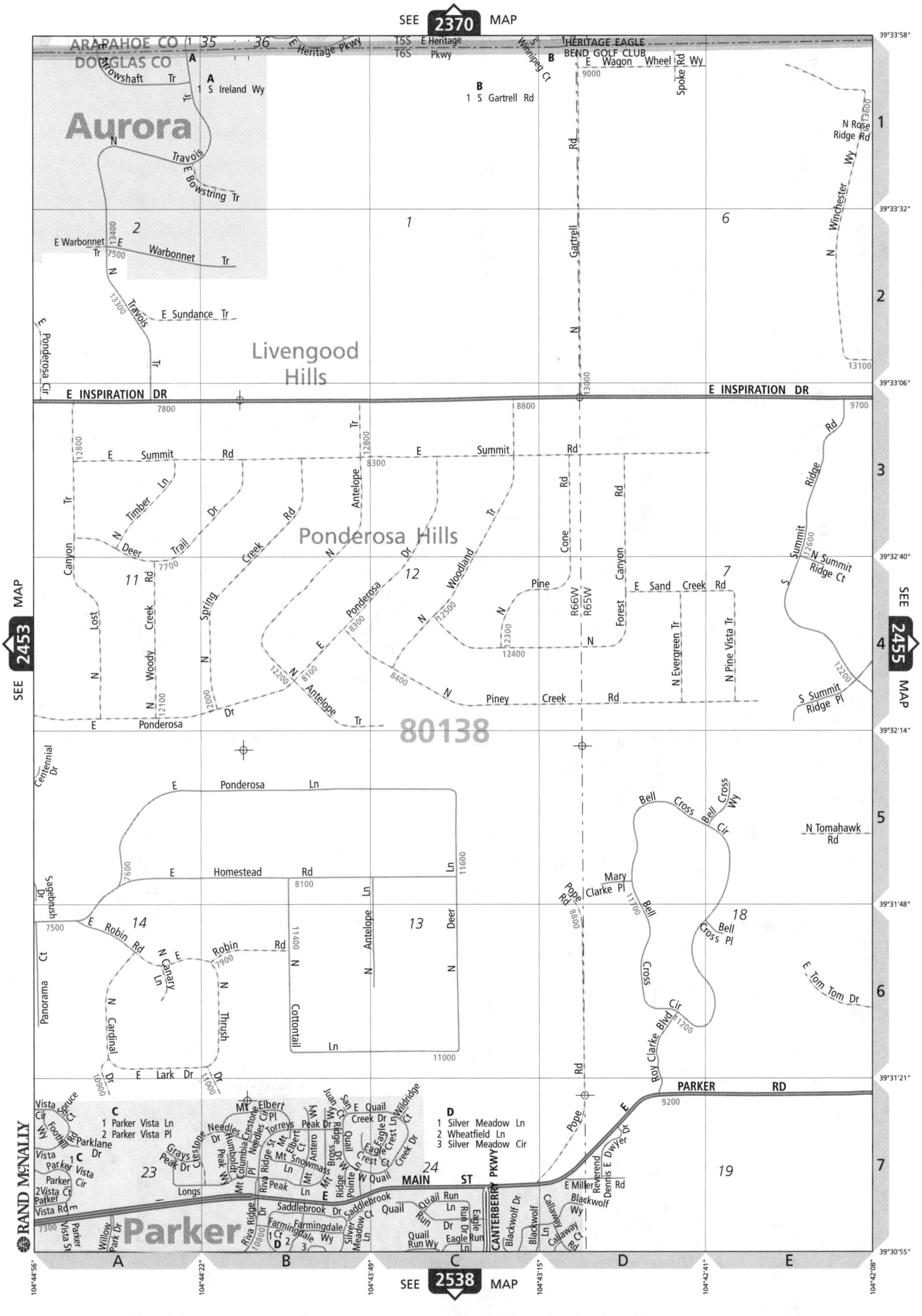

1:24,000
1 in. = 2000 ft.
0 0.25 0.5
miles

SEE 2371 MAP

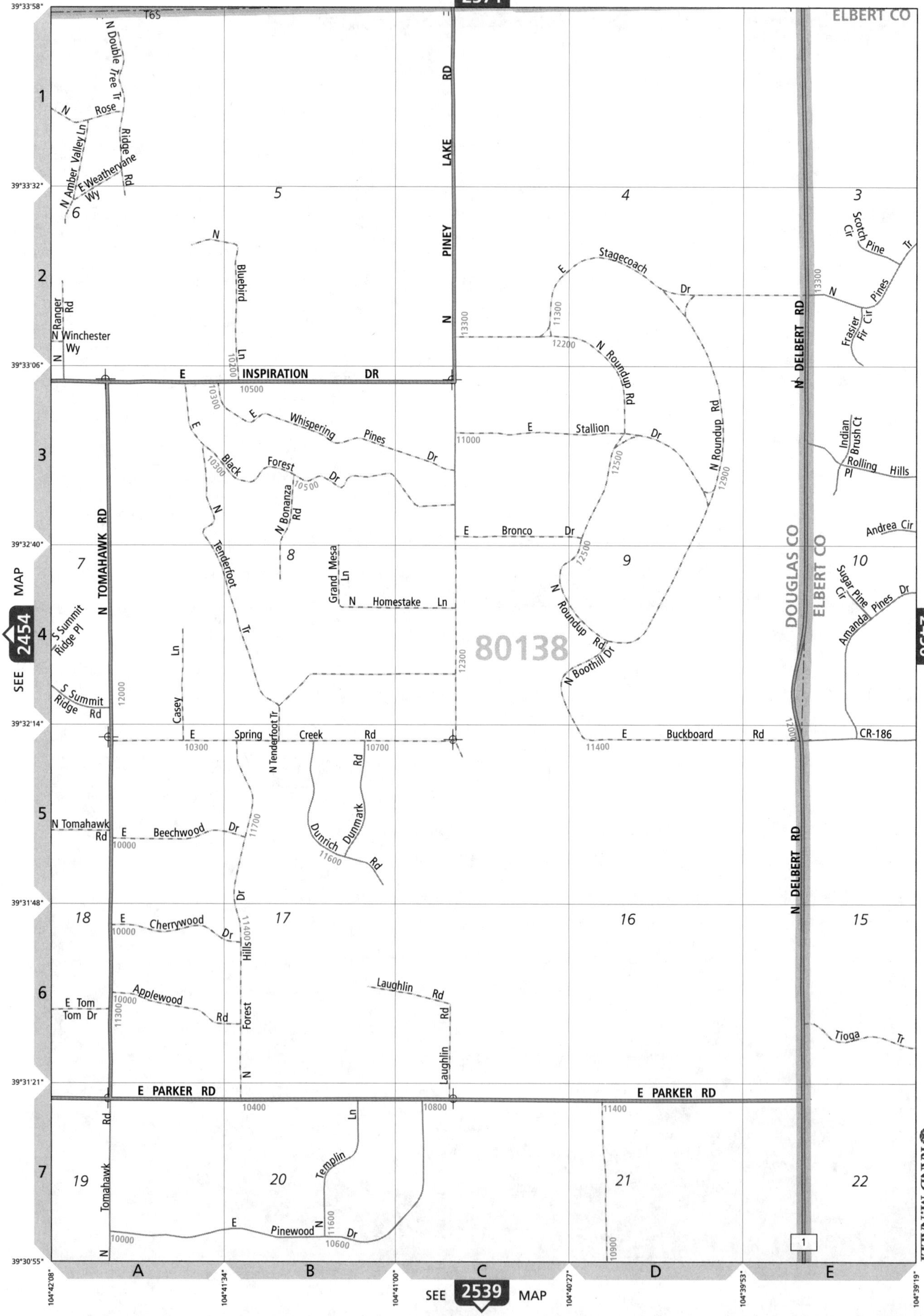

SEE 2454 MAP

SEE 2456 MAP

SEE 2539 MAP

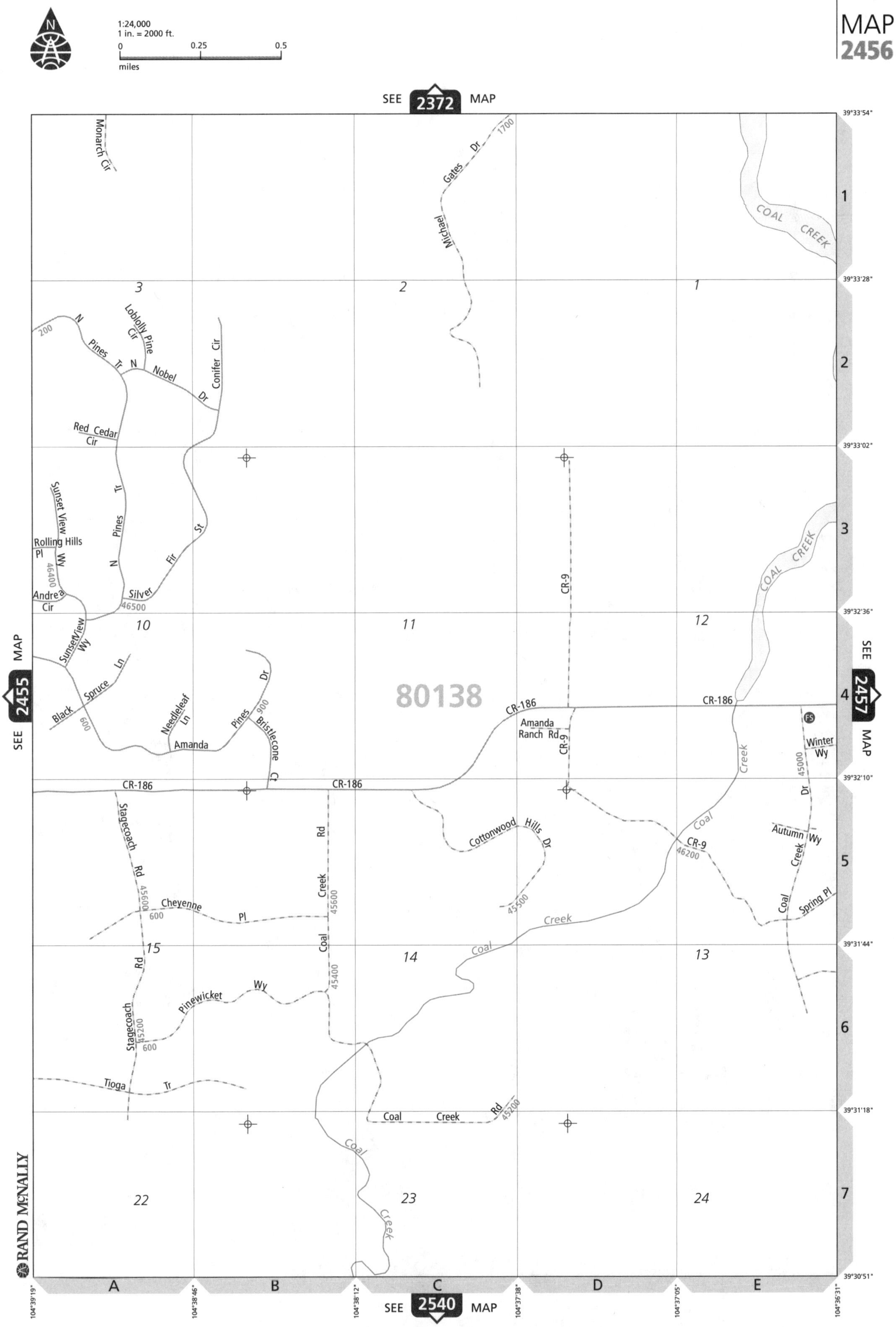

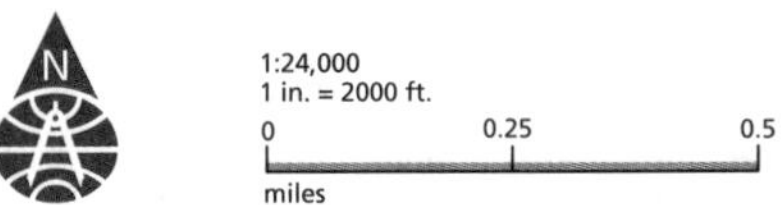

N
1:24,000
1 in. = 2000 ft.
0
0.25
0.5
miles
SEE 2372 MAP
SEE 2455 MAP
SEE 2457 MAP
SEE 2540 MAP
39°33'54"
39°33'28"
39°33'02"
39°32'36"
39°32'10"
39°31'44"
39°31'18"
39°30'51"
104°39'19"
104°38'46"
104°38'12"
104°37'38"
104°37'05"
104°36'31"
A
B
C
D
E
1
2
3
4
5
6
7
80138
Monarch Cir
Gates Dr
1700
Michael
COAL CREEK
3
2
1
200
N Pines Tr
Loblolly Pine Cir
N Nobel Dr
Conifer Cir
Red Cedar Cir
Sunset View Wy
Rolling Hills Pl
46400
Andrea Cir
N Pines Tr
Fir St
Silver
46500
10
11
12
SunsetView Wy
Black Spruce Ln
600
Needleleaf Ln
Amanda
Pines Dr
900
Bristlecone Ct
CR-9
CR-186
Amanda Ranch Rd
Winter Wy
45000
Dr
CR-186
Stagecoach Rd
Rd
Coal Creek
45600
Cottonwood Hills Dr
Coal
CR-9
46200
Autumn Wy
Creek
Coal
Spring Pl
45600
Cheyenne Pl
600
45500
Creek
Coal
15
14
13
Rd
45400
Pinewicket Wy
Stagecoach
45200
600
Tioga Tr
Coal Creek Rd
45200
Coal
Creek
22
23
24
RAND McNALLY

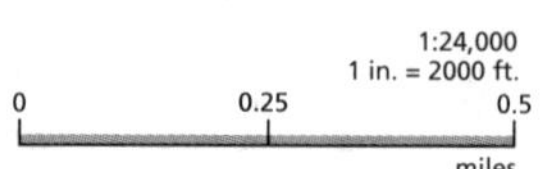

SEE B MAP

SEE 2456 MAP

SEE 2458 MAP

SEE 2541 MAP

RAND McNALLY

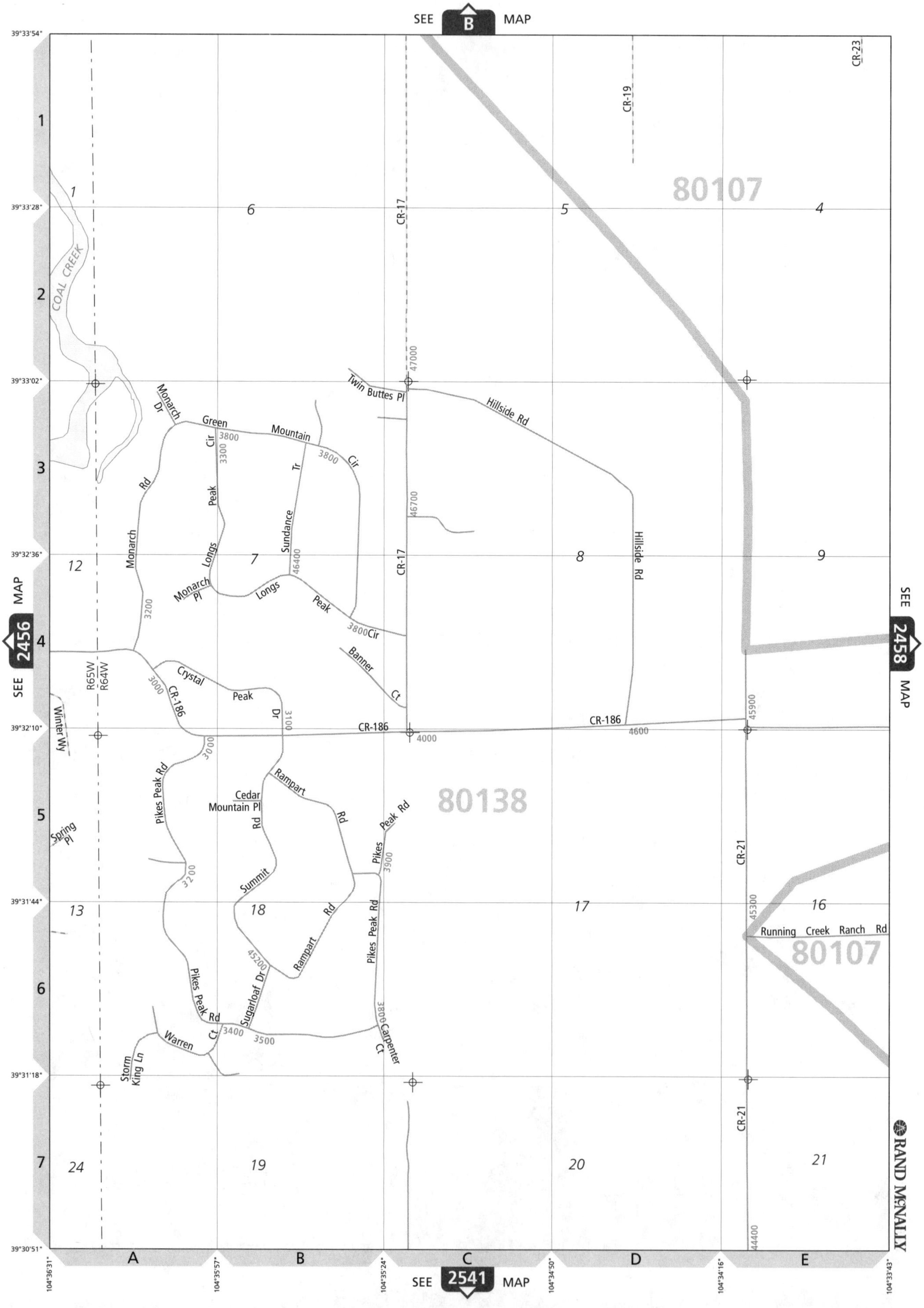

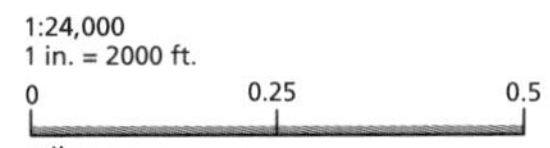

SEE B MAP

CR-29
Patrick Tr
7400
Running
Creek
80107
Eaglecrest Cir
Buckhorn Cir
45300
Deerfield Cir
N Eaglecrest Cir
N Antler Cir
S Antler Cir
Sunset Av
Cactus Cir
S Eaglecrest Cir
80138
Running Creek Ranch Rd
Running

1 2 3 4 5 6 7
A B C D E

4 3 2 9 10 11 16 15 14 21 22 23

39°33'50" 39°33'24" 39°32'58" 39°32'32" 39°32'05" 39°31'39" 39°31'13" 39°30'47"
104°33'43" 104°33'09" 104°32'35" 104°32'02" 104°31'28" 104°30'54"

SEE 2457 MAP
SEE 2459 MAP
SEE 2542 MAP

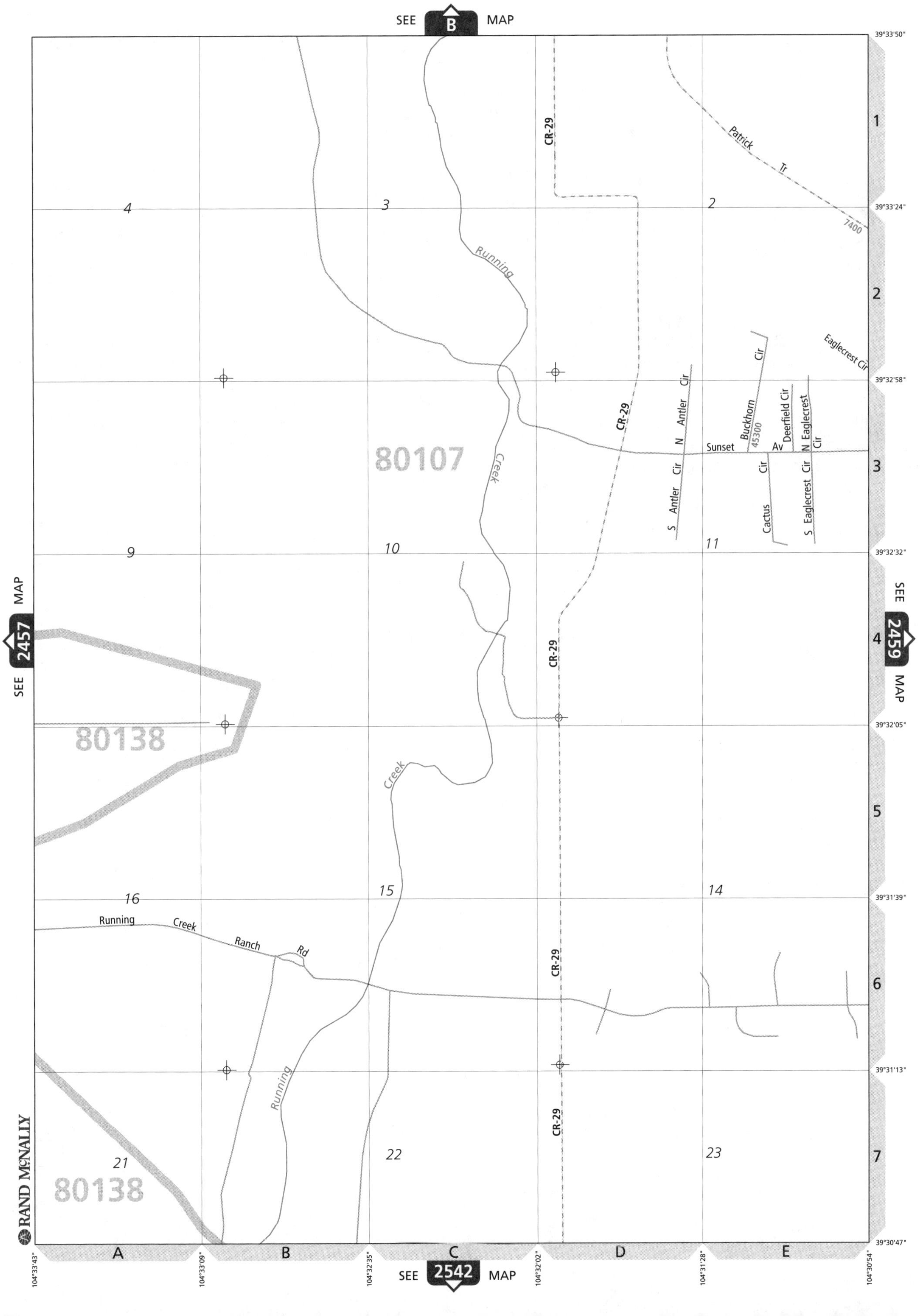

1:24,000
1 in. = 2000 ft.
0 0.25 0.5
miles

SEE B MAP

SEE 2458 MAP

SEE 2460 MAP

SEE 2543 MAP

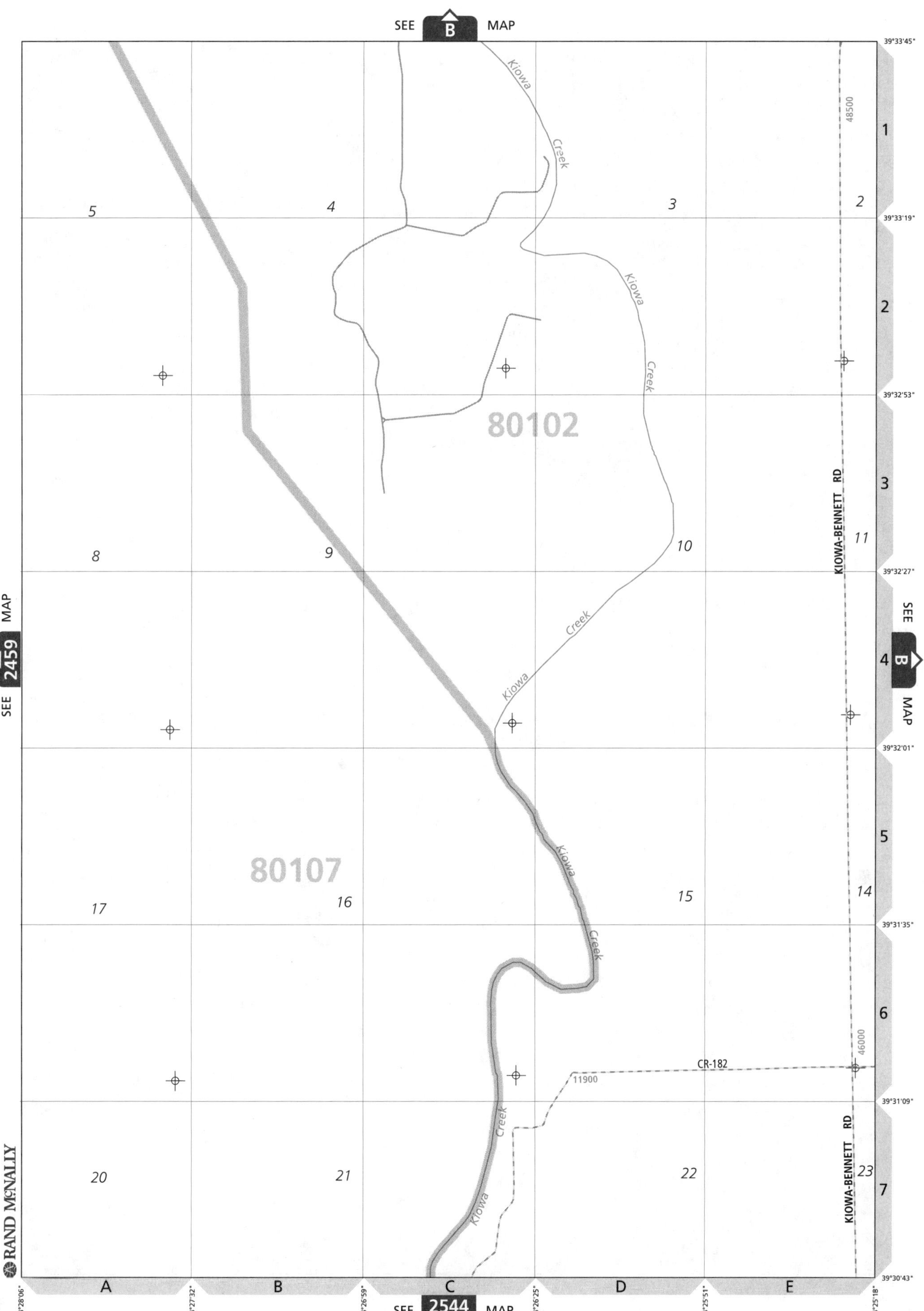
1:24,000
1 in. = 2000 ft.
0
0.25
0.5
miles
SEE B MAP
SEE 2459 MAP
SEE B MAP
SEE 2544 MAP
Kiowa
Creek
80102
80107
KIOWA-BENNETT RD
CR-182
11900
48500
46000
5
4
3
2
8
9
10
11
17
16
15
14
20
21
22
23
A
B
C
D
E
1
2
3
4
5
6
7
39°33'45"
39°33'19"
39°32'53"
39°32'27"
39°32'01"
39°31'35"
39°31'09"
39°30'43"
104°28'06"
104°27'32"
104°26'59"
104°26'25"
104°25'51"
104°25'18"

1:24,000
1 in. = 2000 ft.
0 0.25 0.5
miles

SEE B MAP

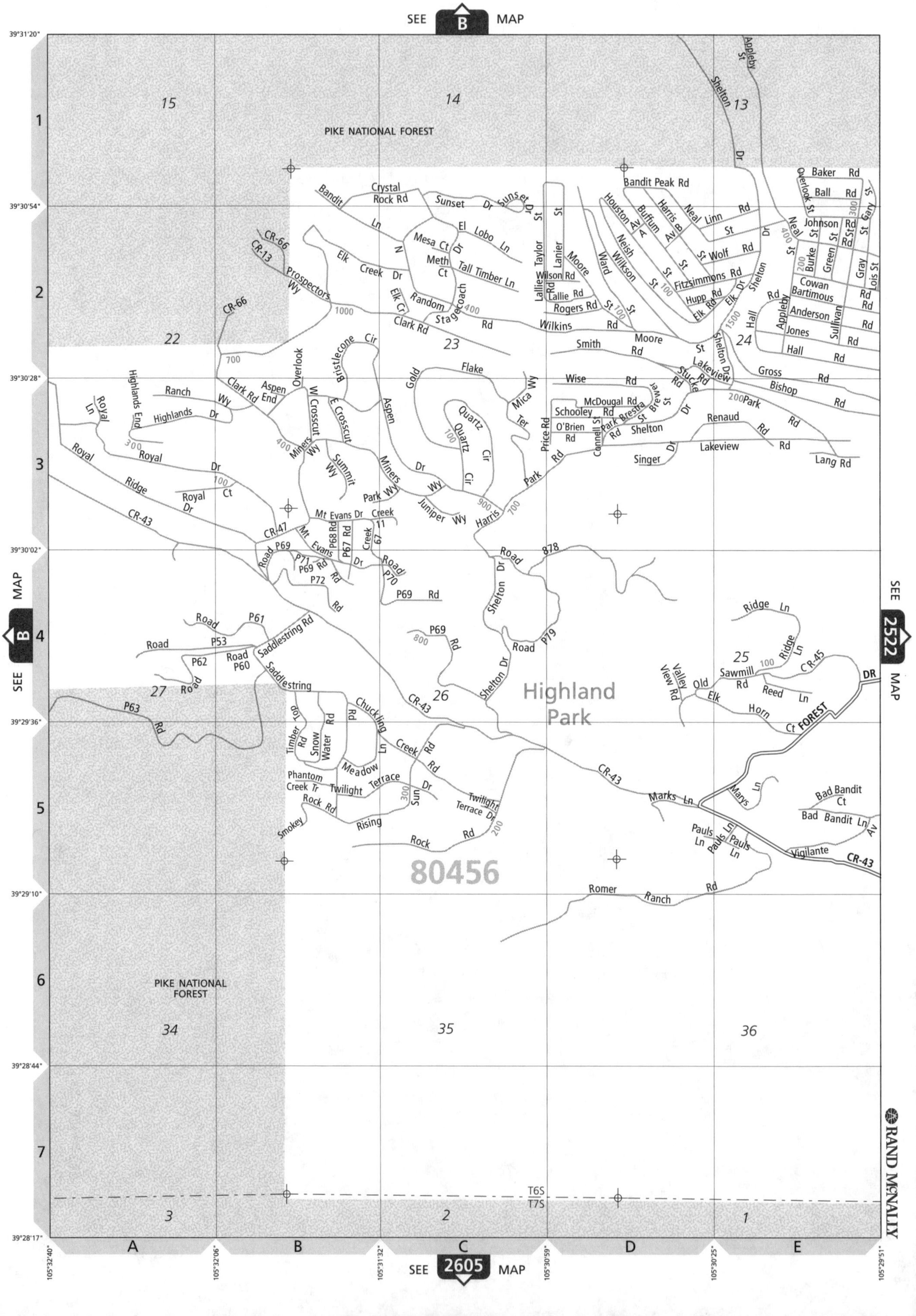

39°31'20"
39°30'54"
39°30'28"
39°30'02"
39°29'36"
39°29'10"
39°28'44"
39°28'17"

1
2
3
4
5
6
7

PIKE NATIONAL FOREST

15
14
13
22
23
24
25
26
27
34
35
36
3
2
1

Highland Park

80456

Appleby St
Shelton Dr
Baker Rd
Overlook St
Ball Rd
Gary St
Johnson Rd
Neal St
Burke St
Green St
Gray St
Lois St
Cowan Rd
Bartimous Rd
Anderson Rd
Jones Rd
Sullivan
Hall Rd
Bandit Peak Rd
Houston Av A
Buffum Av B
Harris St
Neal Linn Rd
Wolf Rd
Fitzsimmons Rd
Hupp Rd
Elk Rd
Elk Dr
Neish St
Wilkson St
Ward St
Moore St
Lanier St
Taylor St
Lallie Rd
Wilson Rd
Rogers Rd
Wilkins Rd
Smith Rd
Moore St
Lakeview Rd
Stucke
Gross Rd
Bishop Rd
Park Rd
Renaud Rd
Lakeview Rd
Lang Rd
Singer Dr
Shelton
Brewer St
Park Brestra St
McDougal Rd
Schooley Rd
O'Brien Rd
Connell St
Price Rd
Wise Rd
Mica Wy
Ter
Park Rd
Harris
Crystal Rock Rd
Sunset Dr
Bandit Ln
El Lobo Ln
Mesa Ct
Meth Ct
Tall Timber Ln
N Dr
Elk Creek Dr
Elk Cr
Random
Stagecoach Rd
Clark Rd
CR-66
CR-13
Prospectors Wy
Bristlecone Cir
Flake
Gold
Quartz Cir
Quartz Cir
Overlook
Aspen End
Aspen
W Crosscut
E Crosscut
Miners Wy
Summit Wy
Miners Wy
Park Wy
Juniper Wy
Clark Rd
Highlands End
Ranch Wy
Highlands Dr
Royal Ln
Royal Dr
Royal Ridge
Royal Ct
Royal Dr
CR-43
CR-47
Mt Evans Dr
Creek 11
Creek 67
P68 Rd
P67 Rd
Mt Evans Dr
Road P69
P71
P69 Rd
P72 Rd
Road P70
P69 Rd
Road 878
Shelton Dr
P69 Rd
Road P79
Shelton Dr
Road P61
Road P53
Road P62
Road P60
Saddlestring Rd
Saddlestring
Road
P63 Rd
Chuckling Ln
Timber Rd
Snow Rd
Water Rd
Rd
Meadow
Phantom Creek Tr
Twilight
Terrace Dr
Rock Rd
Sun
Smokey
Rising
Twilight Terrace Dr
Rock Rd
Creek Rd
CR-43
Marks Ln
Ridge Ln
Ridge Ln
Sawmill Rd
Valley View Rd
Old Elk
Reed Ln
CR-45
Horn Ct
FOREST DR
Marys Ln
Bad Bandit Ct
Bad Bandit Ln
Av
Pauls Ln
Pauls Ln
Pauls Ln
Vigilante
CR-43
Romer Ranch Rd
T6S
T7S

A
B
C
D
E

105°32'40"
105°32'06"
105°31'32"
105°30'59"
105°30'25"
105°29'51"

SEE B MAP

SEE 2522 MAP

SEE 2605 MAP

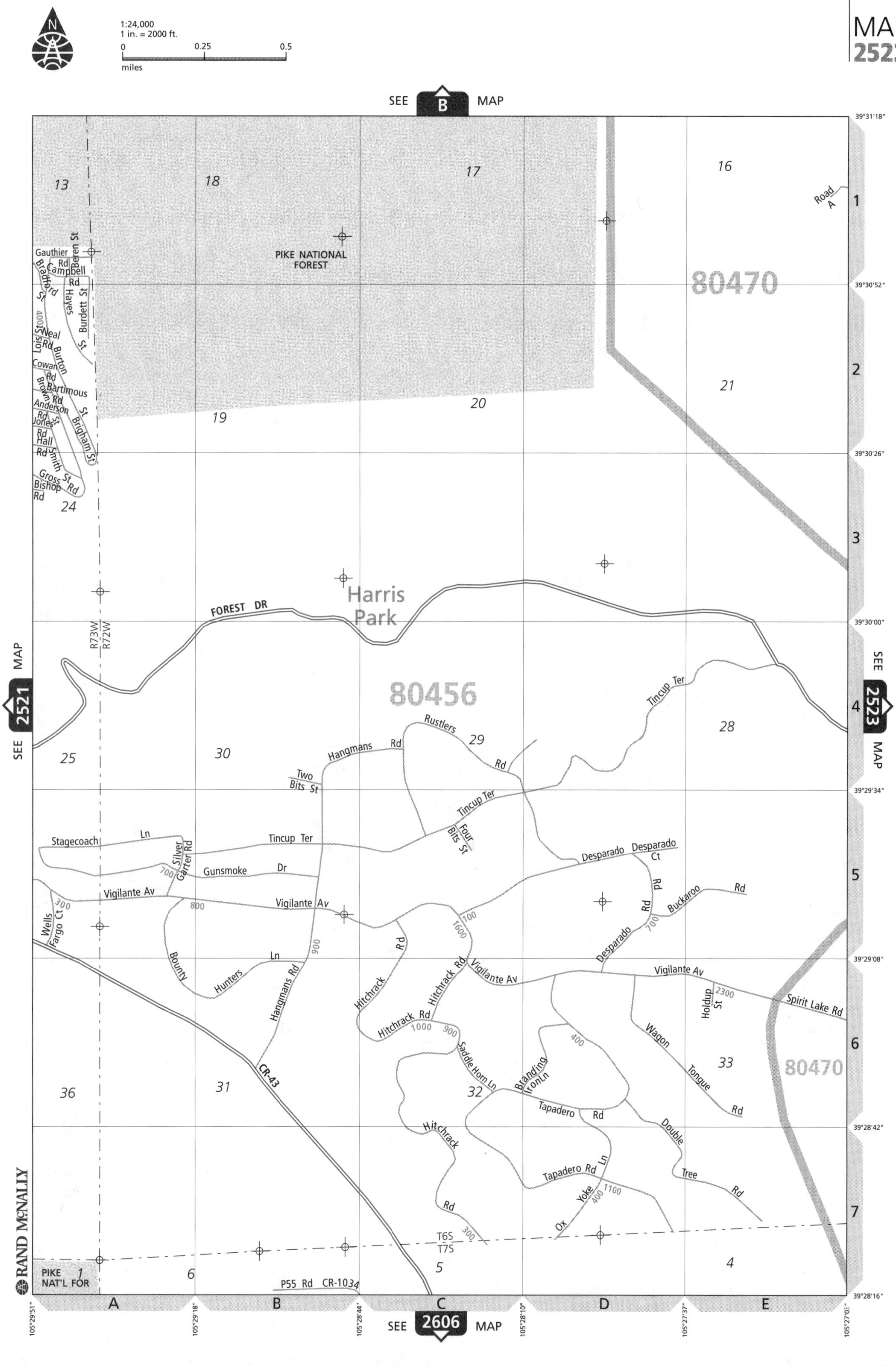

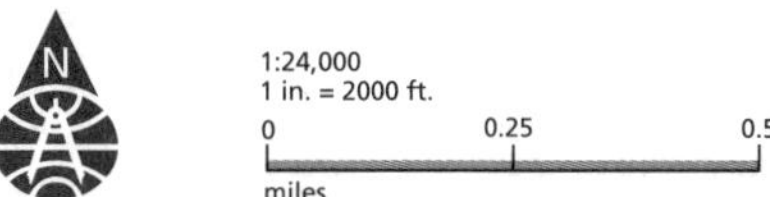

SEE B MAP

SEE 2521 MAP

SEE 2523 MAP

SEE 2606 MAP

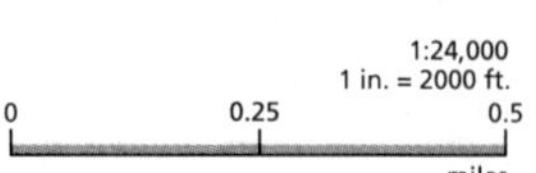

SEE 2439 MAP

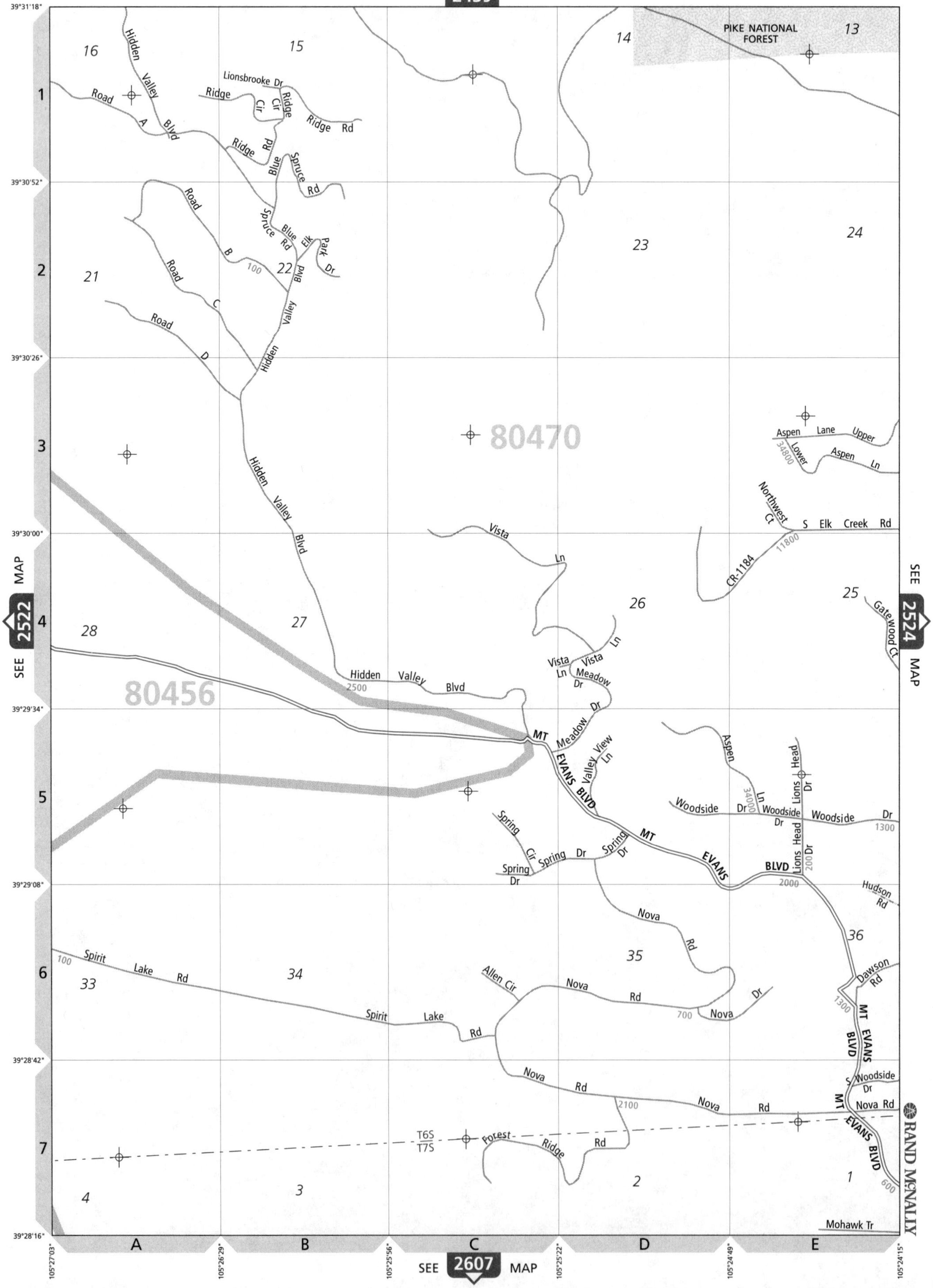

SEE 2522 MAP

SEE 2524 MAP

PIKE NATIONAL FOREST

80470

80456

Hidden Valley Blvd
Road A
Road B
Road C
Road D
Lionsbrooke Dr
Ridge Cir
Ridge Rd
Blue Spruce Rd
Elk Park Dr
Aspen Lane Upper
Lower Aspen Ln
Northwest Ct
S Elk Creek Rd
CR-1184
Vista Ln
Meadow Dr
Valley View Ln
MT EVANS BLVD
Gatewood Ct
Aspen Ln
Lions Head Dr
Woodside Dr
Spring Cir
Spring Dr
Hudson Rd
Nova Rd
Nova Dr
Allen Cir
Spirit Lake Rd
Dawson Rd
S Woodside Dr
Forest Ridge Rd
Mohawk Tr
T6S
T7S

16 15 14 13 21 22 23 24 28 27 26 25 33 34 35 36 4 3 2 1

RAND McNALLY

SEE 2607 MAP

1:24,000
1 in. = 2000 ft.
0 0.25 0.5
miles

SEE 2440 MAP

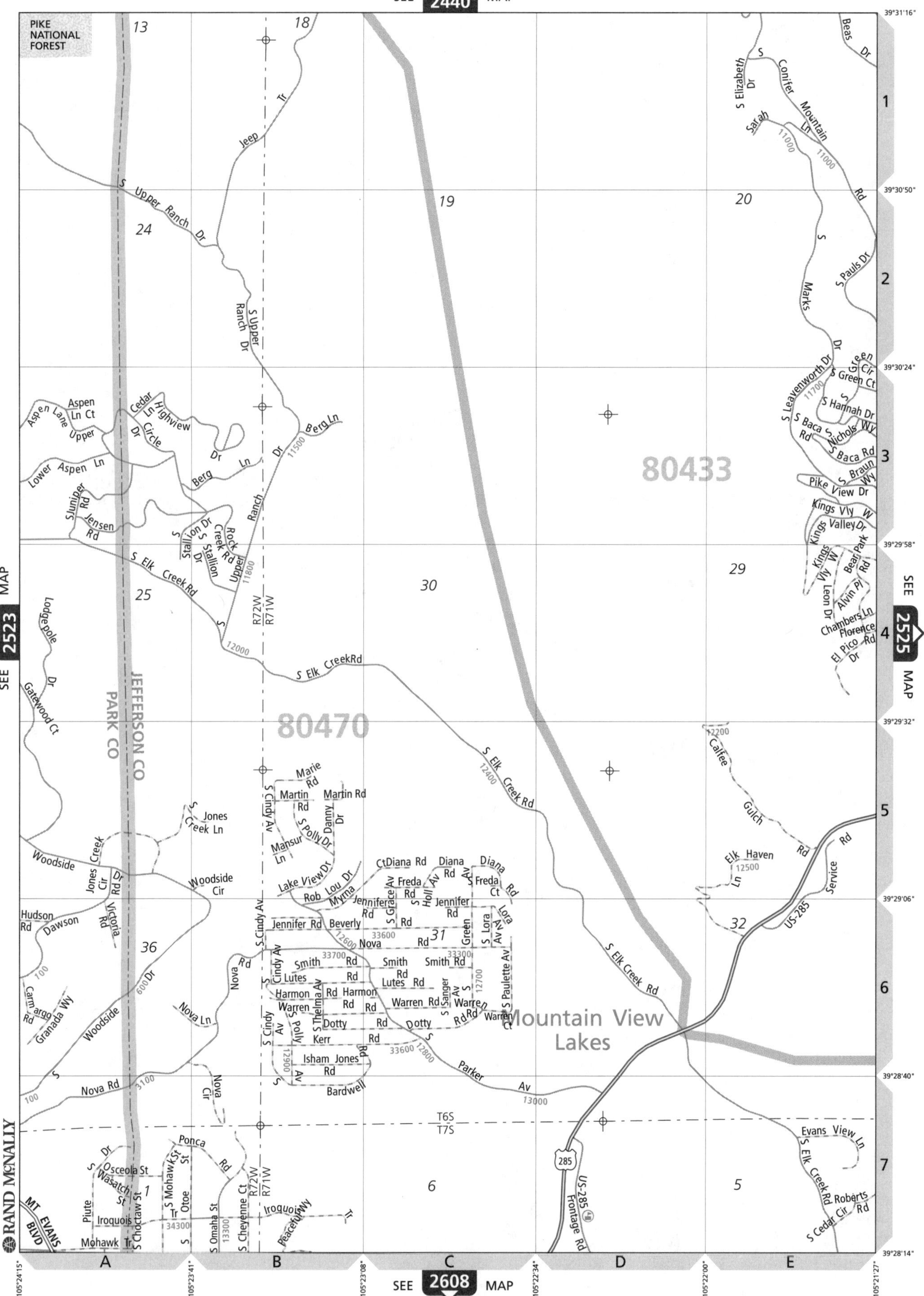

SEE 2523 MAP

SEE 2525 MAP

SEE 2608 MAP

1:24,000
1 in. = 2000 ft.
0 0.25 0.5
miles

SEE 2441 MAP

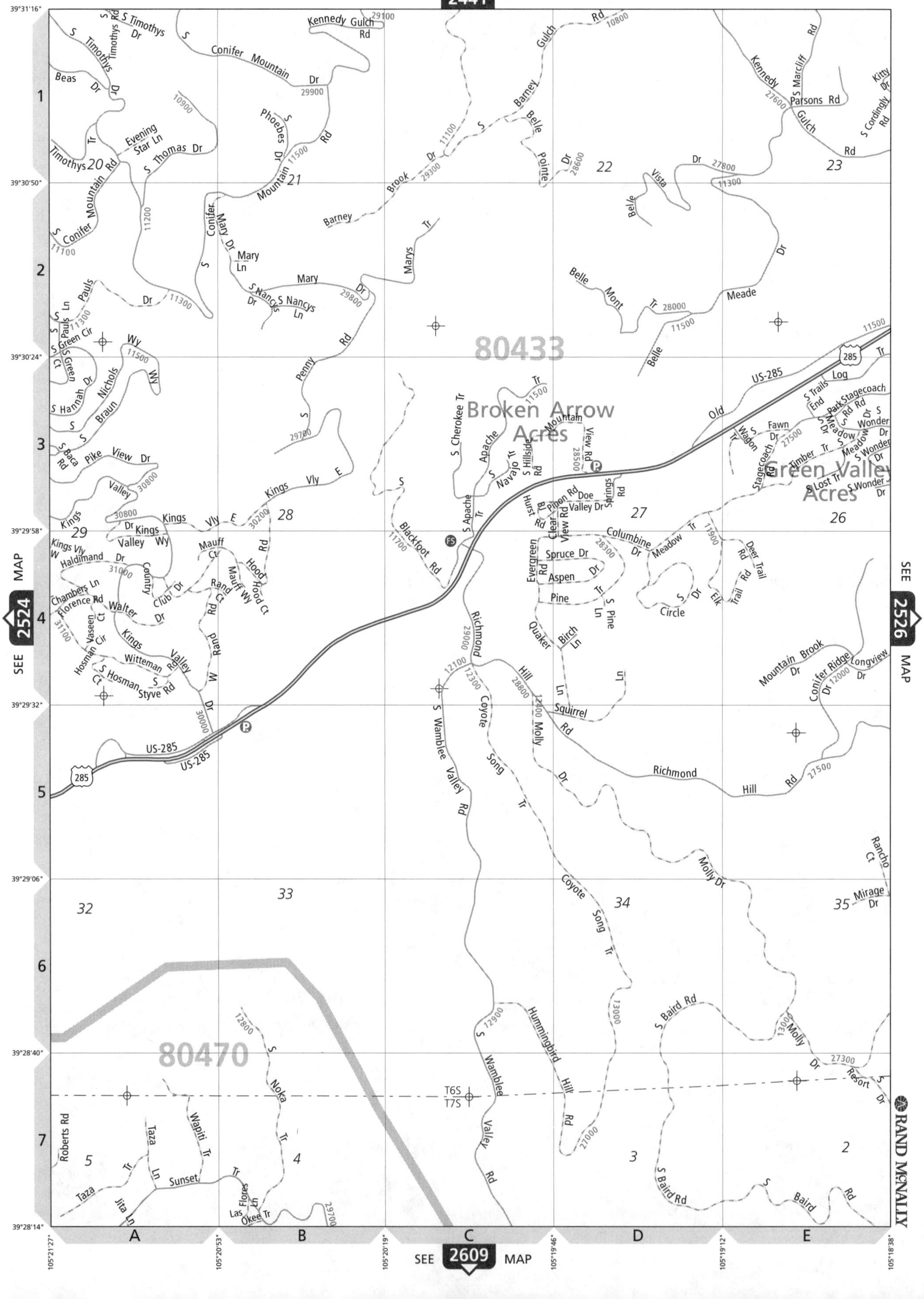

SEE 2524 MAP

SEE 2526 MAP

SEE 2609 MAP

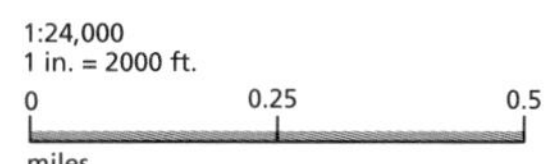

SEE 2442 MAP

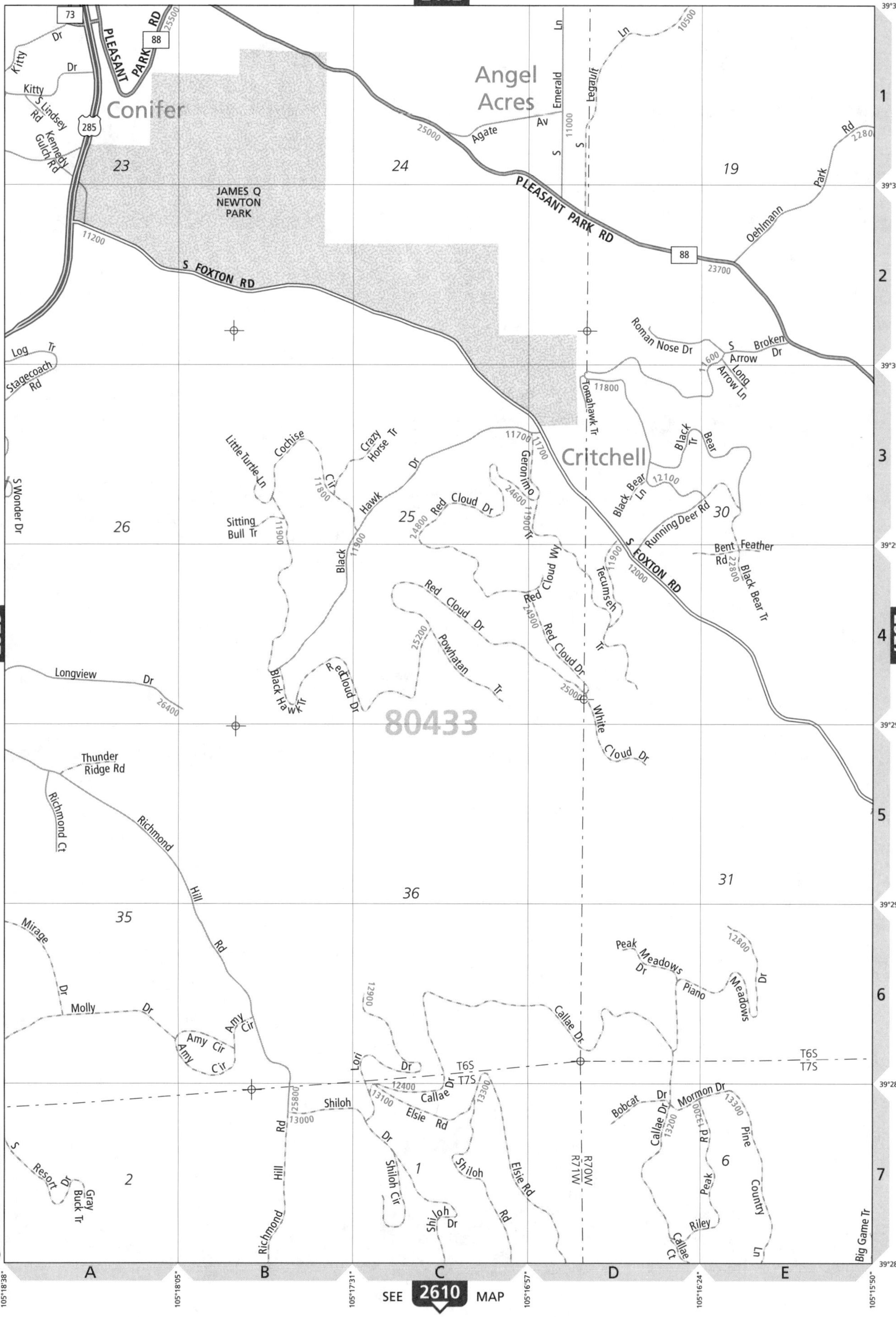

SEE 2525 MAP

SEE 2527 MAP

SEE 2610 MAP

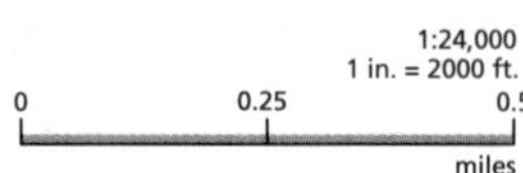

SEE 2443 MAP

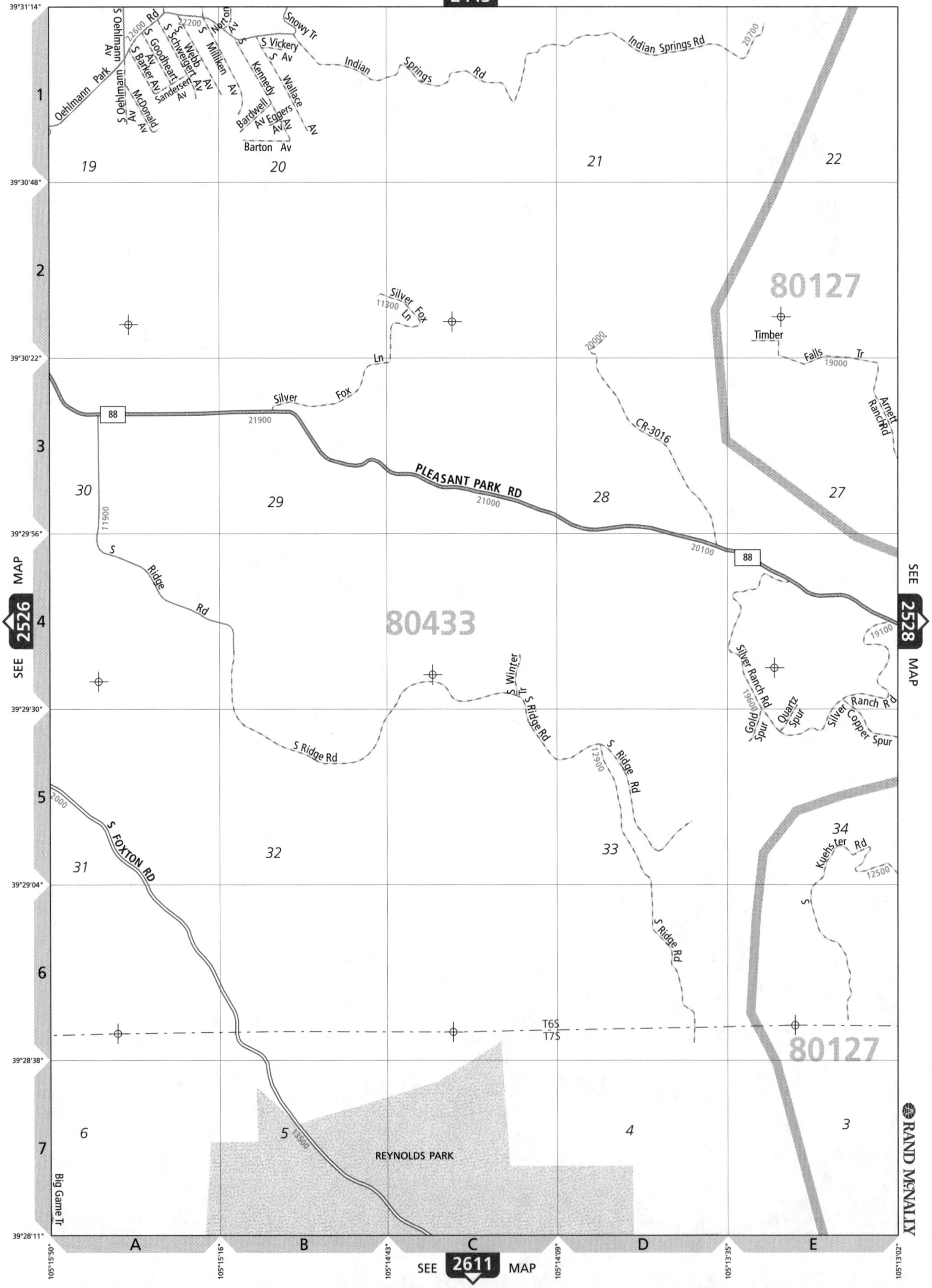

SEE 2526 MAP

SEE 2528 MAP

Oehlmann Park Rd
S Oehlmann Av
S Barker Av
S Goodheart Av
S Schweigert Av
Webb Av
Sandersen Av
McDonald Av
Norton Av
Milliken Av
Kennedy Av
S Vickery Av
Wallace Av
Bardwell Av
Eggers Av
Barton Av
Snowy Tr
Indian Springs Rd
Silver Fox Ln
Timber Falls Tr
Arnett Ranch Rd
CR-3016
PLEASANT PARK RD
S Ridge Rd
S Winter Tr
Silver Ranch Rd
Gold Spur
Quartz Spur
Silver Copper Spur
S Kuehster Rd
S FOXTON RD
Big Game Tr
REYNOLDS PARK
88
80127
80433
T6S
T7S

19 20 21 22 27 28 29 30 31 32 33 34 3 4 5 6

22600 22200 20700 11300 20000 19000 21900 21000 20100 11900 19100 19600 12900 12500 2000 13500

39°31'14" 39°30'48" 39°30'22" 39°29'56" 39°29'30" 39°29'04" 39°28'38" 39°28'11"

105°15'50" 105°15'16" 105°14'43" 105°14'09" 105°13'35" 105°13'02"

1 2 3 4 5 6 7

A B C D E

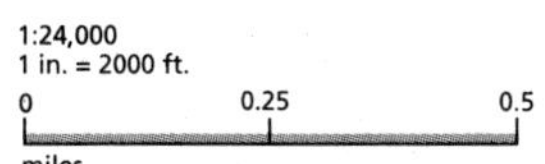

SEE 2444 MAP

39°31'12"
39°30'45"
39°30'19"
39°29'53"
39°29'27"
39°29'01"
39°28'35"
39°28'09"

Deermont
DEER CREEK RD
88
10500
11500
16300
S
Mill Hollow Rd
13800
W Sampson Rd
15700
Hunters Ridge Rd
10000
Sunburst Dr
Rd
W Sampson
24
22
23
26
27
25
HIGH GRADE RD
Maxwell Hill Rd
Antler Tr
11600
Redtail Rd
Arnett Ranch Rd
11500
11900
Elk Tr
11700 Tr
Majestic Eagle Dr
Tr
Mountain Elk
Mountain
Saddle
Mountain
12000
13700
Cottonwood Rd
12300
80433
PLEASANT PARK RD
88
18100
12100
Wild
Trout Tr
Copper Spur
Critchell Ln
S
12300
Samedi Ranch Rd
S Kuehster Rd
80127
Lost Horizon Dr
18400
S Kuehster Rd
12700
S Kuehster 12500 Rd
34
35
36
T6S
T7S
S Kuehster Rd
S Kuehster Rd
3
2
1
13200
Wrangler Tr
Pioneer Tr
Rocky Top Tr
Rocky Ridge Rd
13500

1
2
3
4
5
6
7

A
B
C
D
E

105°13'02"
105°12'28"
105°11'55"
105°11'21"
105°10'47"
105°10'14"

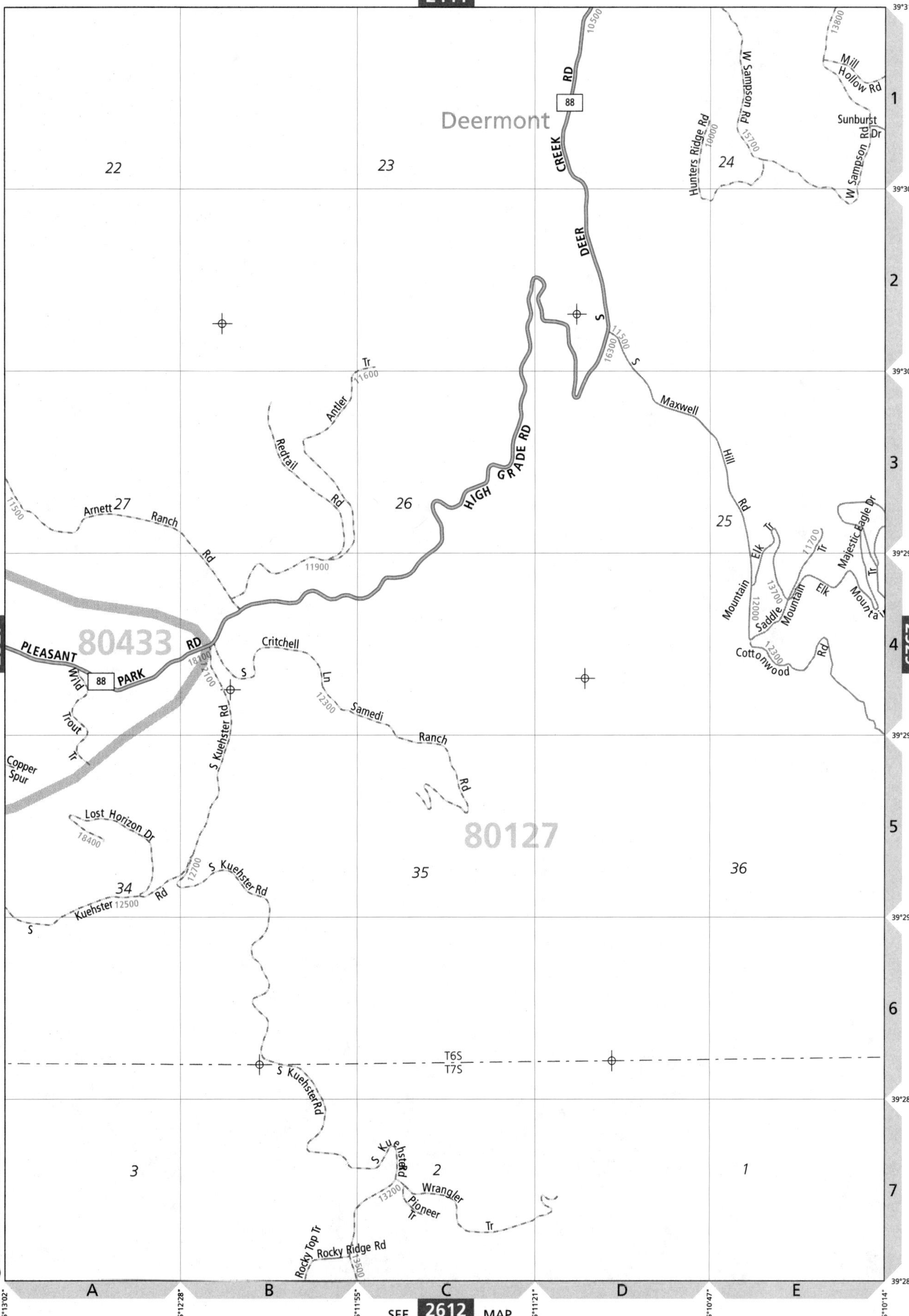

SEE 2527 MAP

SEE 2529 MAP

SEE 2612 MAP

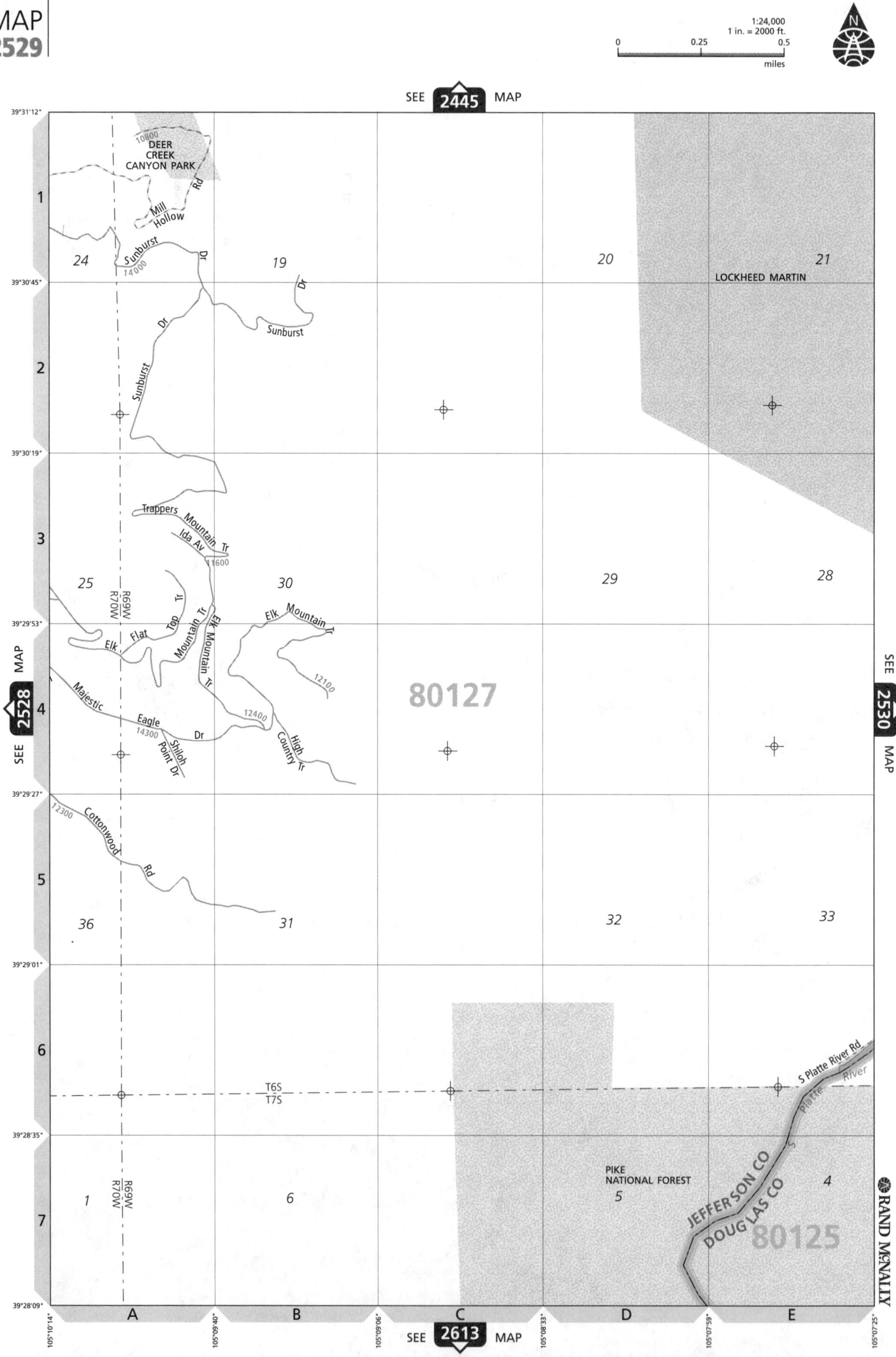

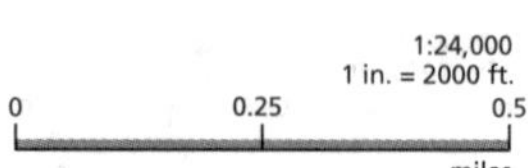

1:24,000
1 in. = 2000 ft.
0
0.25
0.5
miles
N
SEE 2445 MAP
SEE 2528 MAP
SEE 2530 MAP
SEE 2613 MAP
DEER
CREEK
CANYON PARK
Mill
Hollow
Rd
Sunburst
Dr
Sunburst
Trappers
Mountain
Tr
Ida Av
Elk
Flat
Top
Tr
Mountain Tr
Elk Mountain
Elk Mountain Tr
Majestic
Eagle
Dr
Shiloh
Point Dr
High
Country
Tr
Cottonwood
Rd
LOCKHEED MARTIN
80127
PIKE
NATIONAL FOREST
JEFFERSON CO
DOUGLAS CO
80125
S Platte River Rd
S Platte River
T6S
T7S
R69W
R70W
24
19
20
21
25
30
29
28
36
31
32
33
1
6
5
4
10800
14000
11600
12100
12400
14300
12300
1
2
3
4
5
6
7
A
B
C
D
E
39°31'12"
39°30'45"
39°30'19"
39°29'53"
39°29'27"
39°29'01"
39°28'35"
39°28'09"
105°10'14"
105°09'40"
105°09'06"
105°08'33"
105°07'59"
105°07'25"
RAND McNALLY

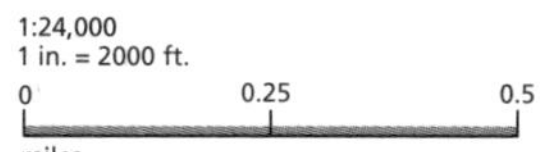

SEE 2446 MAP

SEE 2529 MAP

SEE 2531 MAP

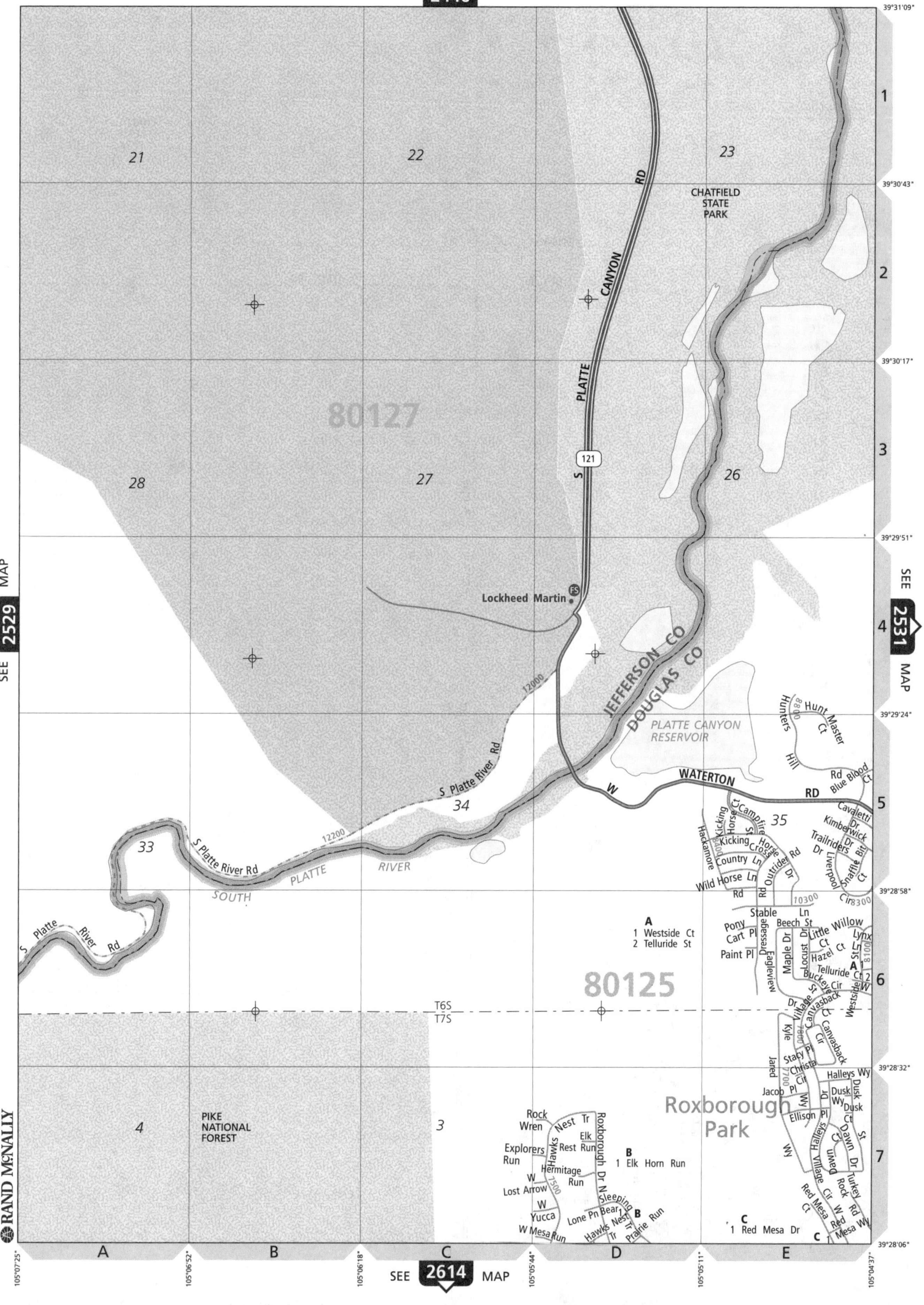

SEE 2614 MAP

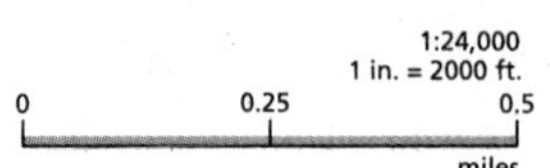

SEE 2447 MAP

CHATFIELD STATE PARK
N Polar Ln
W Sunset Av
N Sunshine Dr
W Ramona Av
N Solar Dr
N Rampart Ln
W Flamingo Wy
W Sunbeam Av
Polo Club Ct
Wildlife Wy
10400
N Roxborough Park Rd
Plum Creek
23
24
19
20
Rangeview Ln
W TITAN RD
9500
9000
7700
N RAMPART RANGE RD
9800
26
25
30
29
R69W
R68W
80125
Blue Blood Ct
W WATERTON RD
35
36
31
32
8500
Cavaletti Dr
Liverpool Cir
A
1 Kimberwick Dr
2 Westside Ct
W Trail North Dr
Arapahoe Dr
W Trail South Dr
Westside Ct
Silvercliff Ln
Lynx Ln
Jasmine Ct
Telluride Pl
Telluride St
Westside Cir
Village Cir
T6S
T7S
Falcon Ln
Fox Ln
Cougar Ln
Big Horn Wy
Village Cir
Fairwood Cir
Den Ct
Falcon Ct
Mule Deer Pl
Garwood St
Firwood Ct
Elmwood St
7600
7700
Mallard Pond Wy
Lone Iris Wy
Rampart Ct
Rampart Wy
Crystal Ct
Bison Ct
Eagle Ct
Perch Ct
Grizzly St
Elk Ct
Chickaree Ct
Lark Ct
Brown Dr
Bear Ct
N Crystal Lake Rd
Lake Pl
Coyote Pl
Red Fox Dr
Pintail Ct
Lark Wy
1
6
5
2
7
B
1 Turkey Rock Rd
S Crystal Lake Cir
Bison Village Cir
Chipmunk Wy
Dovetail Pl
Elk Trail Pl
Hummingbird Pl
Robin Wy
Buffalo Ct
Elk Cir
Mountain Ridge Cir
Marmot
Eagle Wy
Curley Peak Dr
Rock
1 B
C
1 Pintail Pl
2 Marmot Ridge Pl
6200
7400
Lib
CHATFIELD STATE PARK

1
2
3
4
5
6
7

A B C D E

39°31'09"
39°30'43"
39°30'17"
39°29'51"
39°29'24"
39°28'58"
39°28'32"
39°28'06"

105°04'37"
105°04'03"
105°03'30"
105°02'56"
105°02'22"
105°01'49"

SEE 2530 MAP

SEE 2532 MAP

SEE 2615 MAP

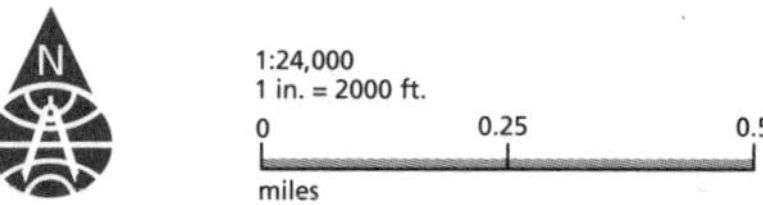

SEE 2448 MAP

CHATFIELD STATE PARK
W Lakeside
W Pineview Dr
Lakeside Cir Dr
W Lakeside Ct
W Chatfield Ln
N Chatfield Dr
N Chatfield Pl
Wildfield Ln
W TITAN RD
Titan Road Industrial Park
Titan Park Cir
Titan Ct
N Chatfield Dr
S SANTA FE DR
Plum Creek
N Moore Rd
80125
80135
Avalanche St
Aspen Leaf Dr
Aspen Leaf Ct
Aspen Leaf Pl
Coachlight Pl
W Trail North Dr
W Trail South Dr
Main St
N Triangle Dr
W Louviers Av
Kelly Av
Kelly Ct
Cora St
N Main St
W Pate Av
N Lavaun Dr
Louviers Industrial Park
Owens Industrial Park
W Airport Rd
Reynolds Dr
N Peterson Rd
Louviers
Louviers Dr
Hill Crest Dr
Valley View Blvd
1st St
2nd St
3rd St
4th St
Elm St
Louviers Blvd
T6S
T7S

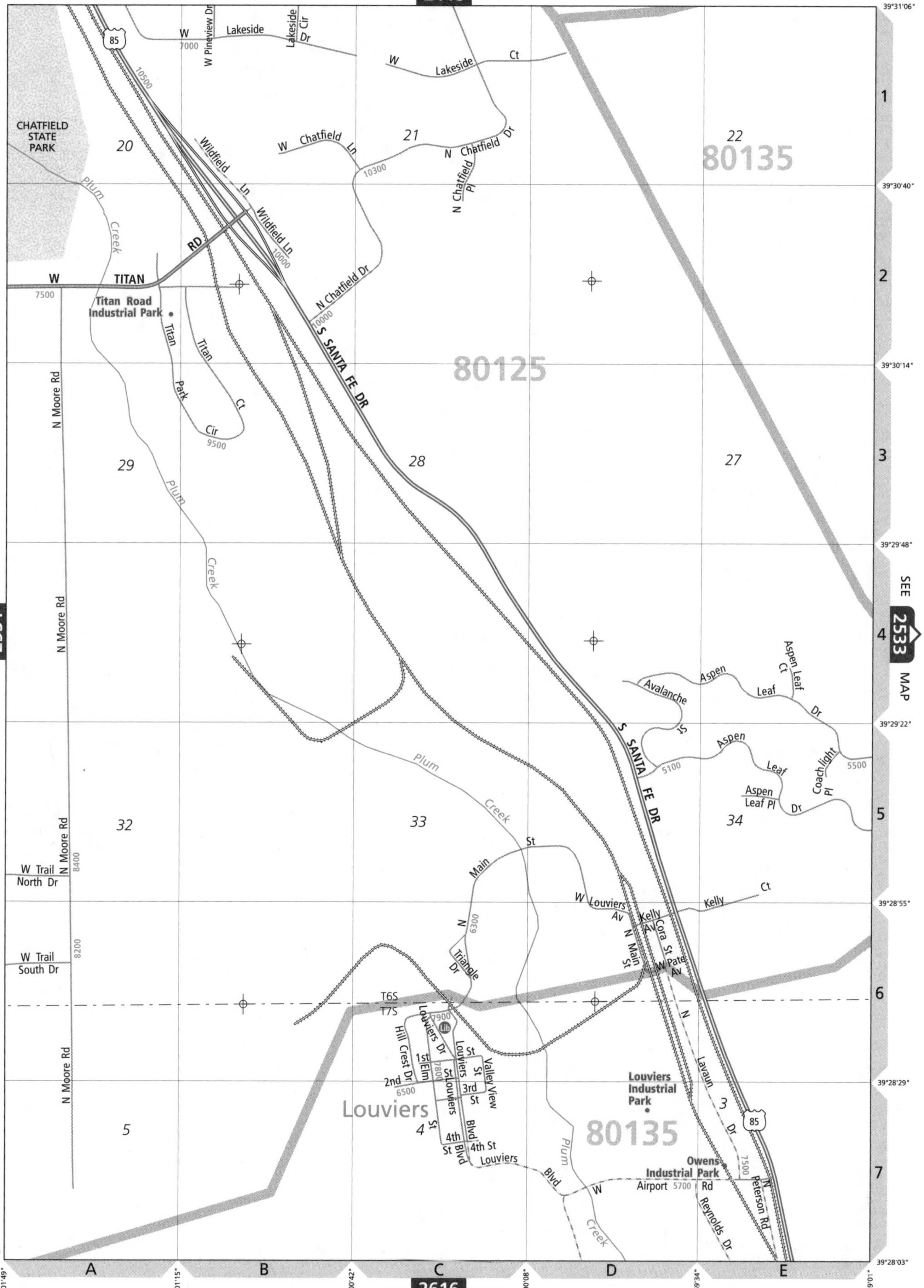

SEE 2531 MAP

SEE 2533 MAP

SEE 2616 MAP

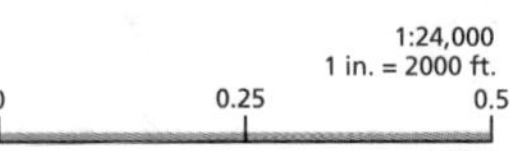

SEE 2449 MAP

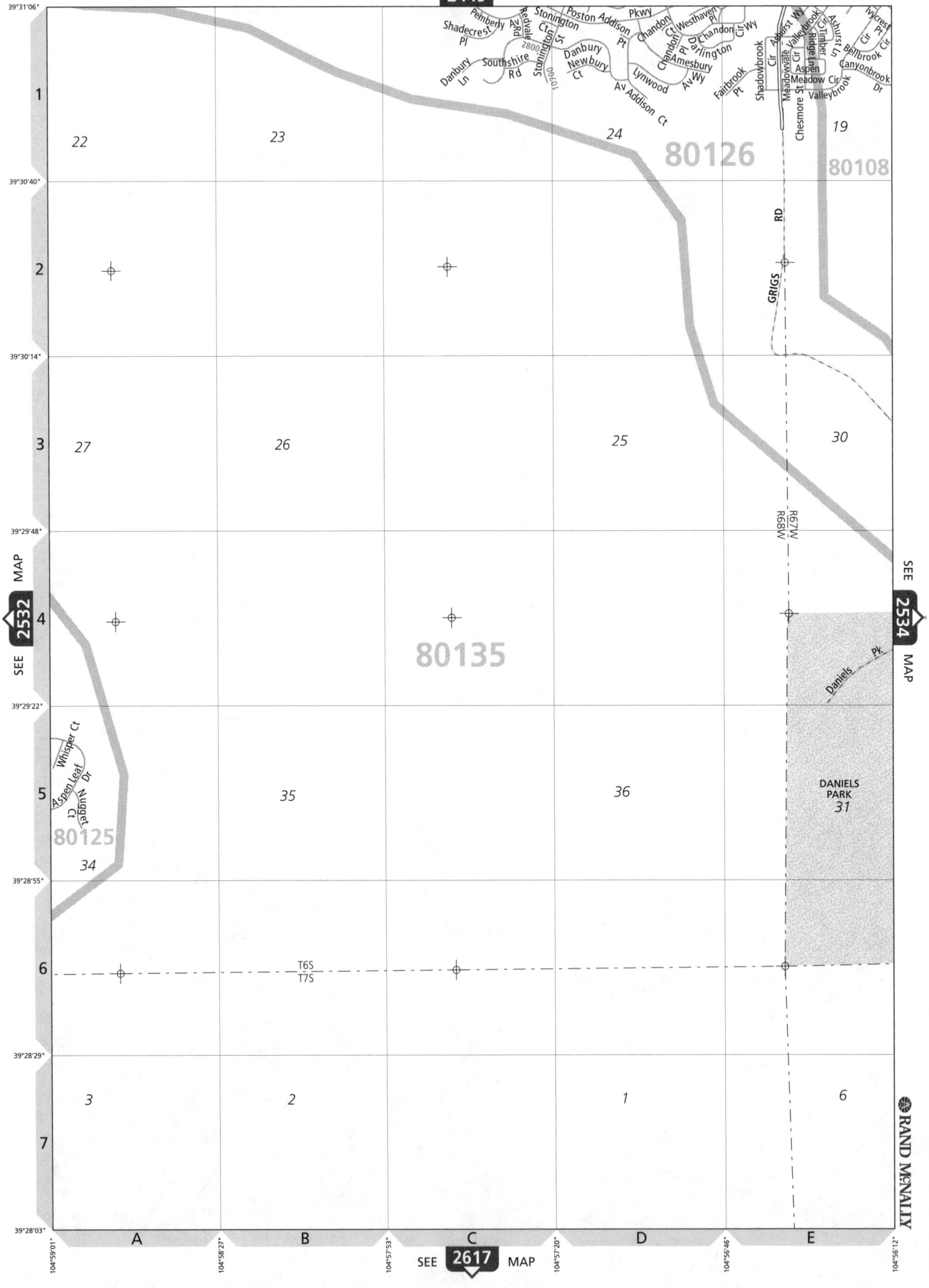

SEE 2532 MAP

SEE 2534 MAP

SEE 2617 MAP

1:24,000
1 in. = 2000 ft.
0 0.25 0.5
miles

SEE 2450 MAP

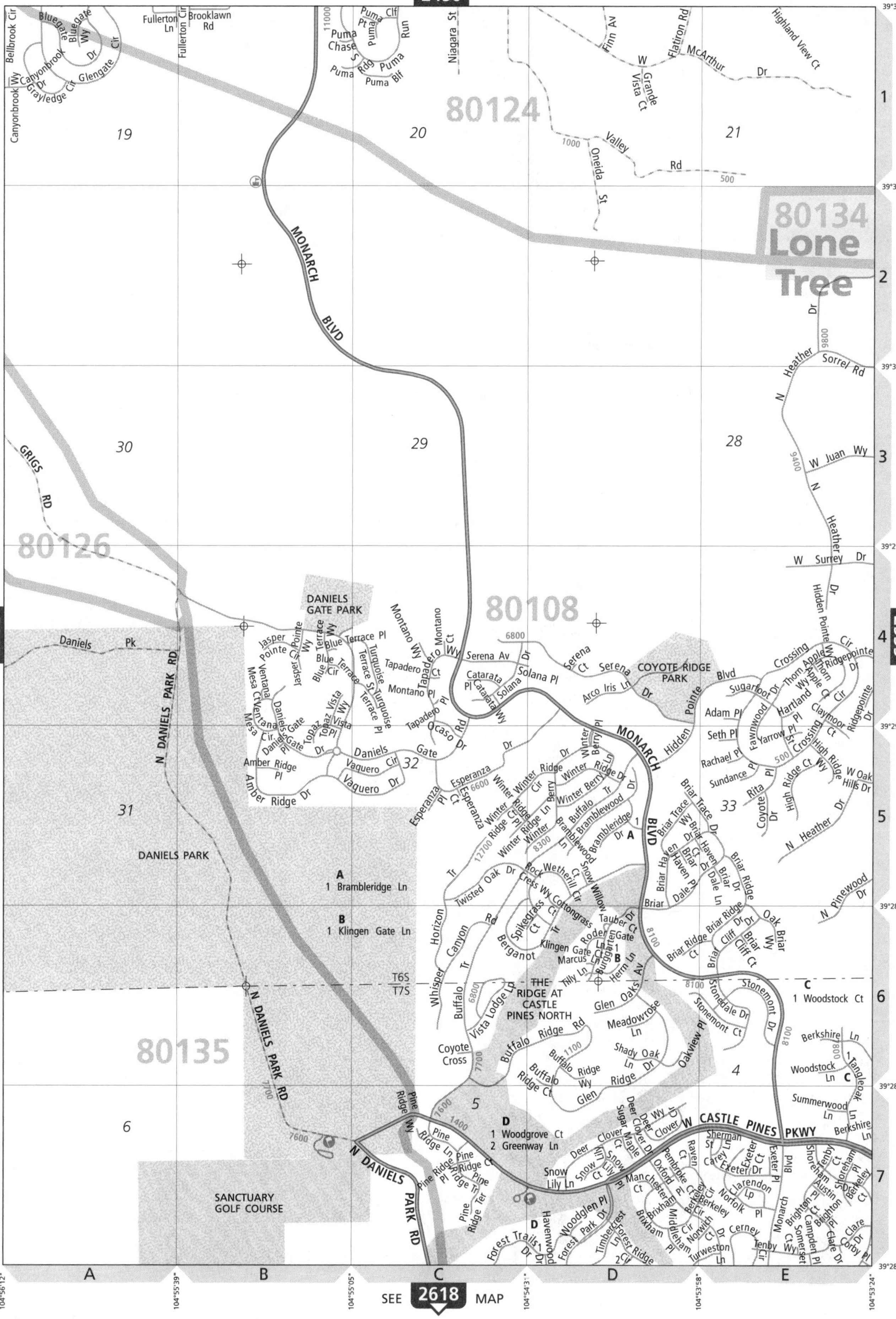

SEE 2533 MAP

SEE 2535 MAP

80124
80134
Lone Tree
80126
80108
80135

MONARCH BLVD
W CASTLE PINES PKWY
N DANIELS PARK RD
GRIGS RD
Daniels Pk
N Heather Dr
W Juan Wy
W Surrey Dr
Sorrel Rd
Valley Rd
Oneida St
Flatiron Rd
McArthur Dr
Highland View Ct
Niagara St
Puma Chase
Fullerton Ln
Brooklawn Rd
Canyonbrook Wy
Glengate Cir
Bluegate Wy

DANIELS GATE PARK
COYOTE RIDGE PARK
DANIELS PARK
THE RIDGE AT CASTLE PINES NORTH
SANCTUARY GOLF COURSE

A
1 Brambleridge Ln

B
1 Klingen Gate Ln

C
1 Woodstock Ct

D
1 Woodgrove Ct
2 Greenway Ln

T6S
T7S

19 20 21 29 28 30 32 33 31 5 4 6

39°31'03"
39°30'37"
39°30'10"
39°29'44"
39°29'18"
39°28'52"
39°28'26"
39°28'00"

104°56'12" 104°55'39" 104°55'05" 104°54'31" 104°53'58" 104°53'24"

A B C D E
1 2 3 4 5 6 7

SEE 2618 MAP

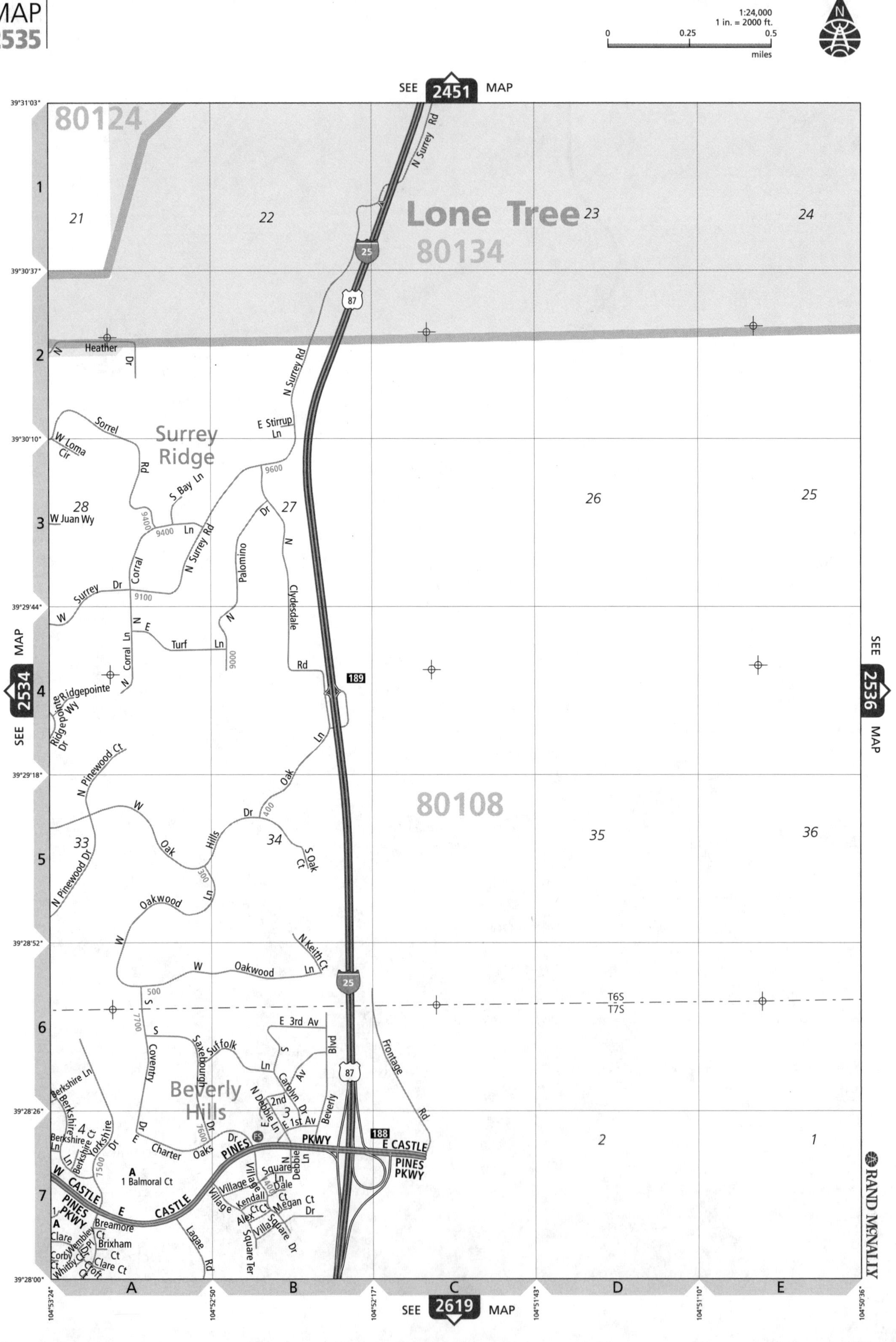

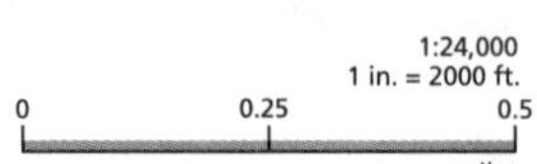

SEE 2451 MAP

80124

Lone Tree

80134

Surrey Ridge

80108

Beverly Hills

21 22 23 24 28 27 26 25 33 34 35 36 4 3 2 1

Heather Dr
N Surrey Rd
Sorrel Rd
W Loma Cir
E Stirrup Ln
S Bay Ln
W Juan Wy
9400 Ln
N Surrey Rd
Palomino Dr
N Clydesdale Rd
W Surrey Dr
Corral
N E Turf Ln
N Corral Ln
Ridgepointe Wy
Ridgepointe Dr
Oak Ln
N Pinewood Ct
W Oak Hills Dr
S Oak Ct
N Pinewood Dr
Oakwood
N Keith Ct
W Oakwood Ln
E 3rd Av
S Coventry Dr
Saxeborough Dr
Suffolk Ln
S Carolyn Av
Beverly Blvd
N Debbie Ln
2nd Dr
E 1st Av
Frontage Rd
Berkshire Ln
Berkshire Ct
Yorkshire Dr
Charter Oaks Dr
PINES PKWY
E CASTLE PINES PKWY
W CASTLE PINES PKWY
E CASTLE
1 Balmoral Ct
Village Square Ln
Dale Ct
Kendall Ct
Megan Ct Dr
Alex Ct
Villa Square Dr
Square Ter
Lagae Rd
Breamore Ct
Wembley Ct
Brixham Ct
Clare Ct
Corby Ct
Whitby Ct
Croft
T6S
T7S
25
87
189
188
9600 9100 9000 400 300 500 7700 7600 1500

SEE 2534 MAP

SEE 2536 MAP

SEE 2619 MAP

A B C D E

1 2 3 4 5 6 7

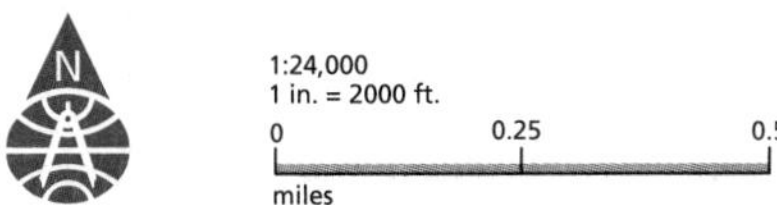

SEE 2452 MAP

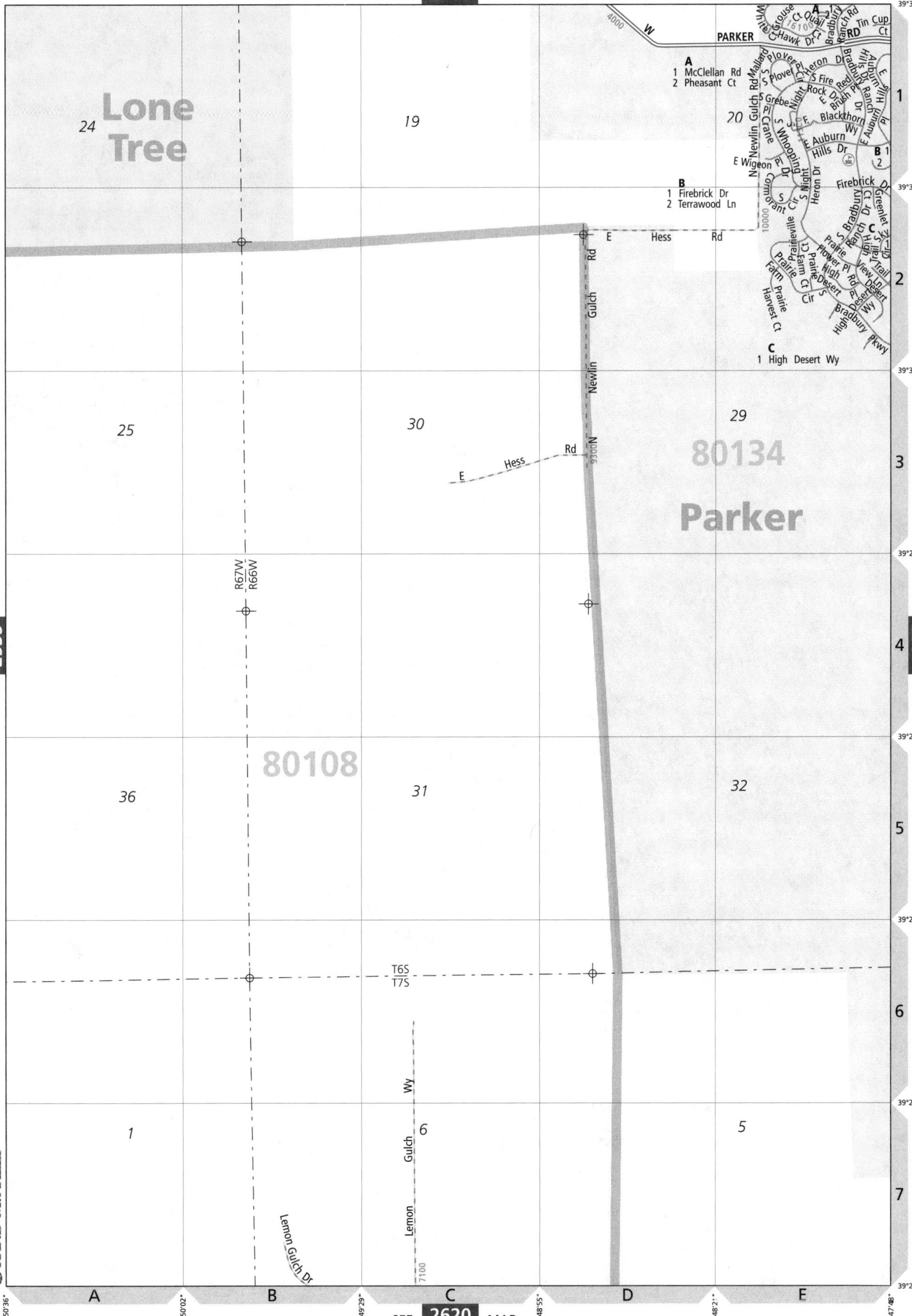

SEE 2535 MAP

SEE 2537 MAP

SEE 2620 MAP

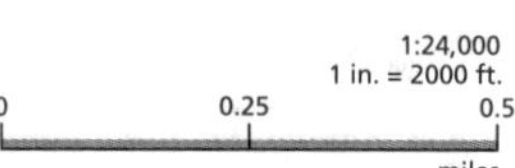

SEE 2453 MAP

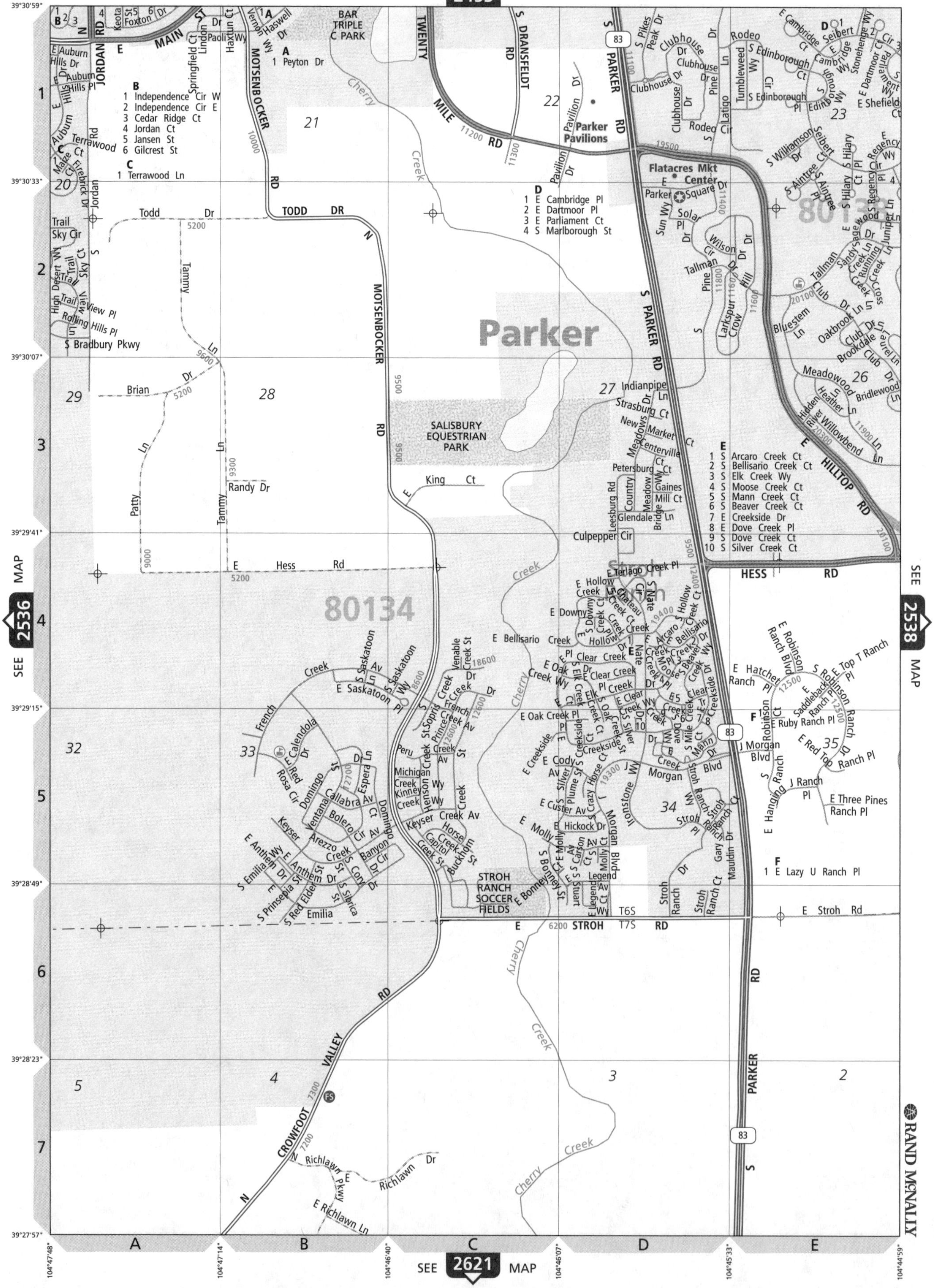

SEE 2536 MAP

SEE 2538 MAP

SEE 2621 MAP

Parker

80134

80138

A
1 Peyton Dr

B
1 Independence Cir W
2 Independence Cir E
3 Cedar Ridge Ct
4 Jordan Ct
5 Jansen St
6 Gilcrest St

C
1 Terrawood Ln

D
1 E Cambridge Pl
2 E Dartmoor Pl
3 E Parliament Ct
4 S Marlborough St

E
1 S Arcaro Creek Ct
2 S Bellisario Creek Ct
3 S Elk Creek Wy
4 S Moose Creek Ct
5 S Mann Creek Ct
6 S Beaver Creek Ct
7 E Creekside Dr
8 E Dove Creek Pl
9 S Dove Creek Ct
10 S Silver Creek Ct

F
1 E Lazy U Ranch Pl

BAR TRIPLE C PARK

Parker Pavilions

Flatacres Mkt Center

SALISBURY EQUESTRIAN PARK

STROH RANCH SOCCER FIELDS

TWENTY MILE RD

S PARKER RD

N MOTSENBOCKER RD

E HILLTOP RD

HESS RD

E STROH RD

N CROWFOOT VALLEY RD

Cherry Creek

39°30'59"
39°30'33"
39°30'07"
39°29'41"
39°29'15"
39°28'49"
39°28'23"
39°27'57"

104°47'48"
104°47'14"
104°46'40"
104°46'07"
104°45'33"
104°44'59"

A B C D E

1 2 3 4 5 6 7

RAND McNALLY

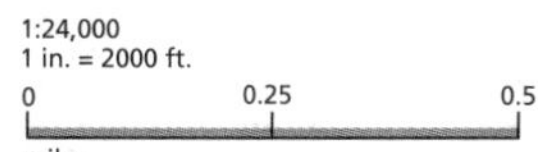

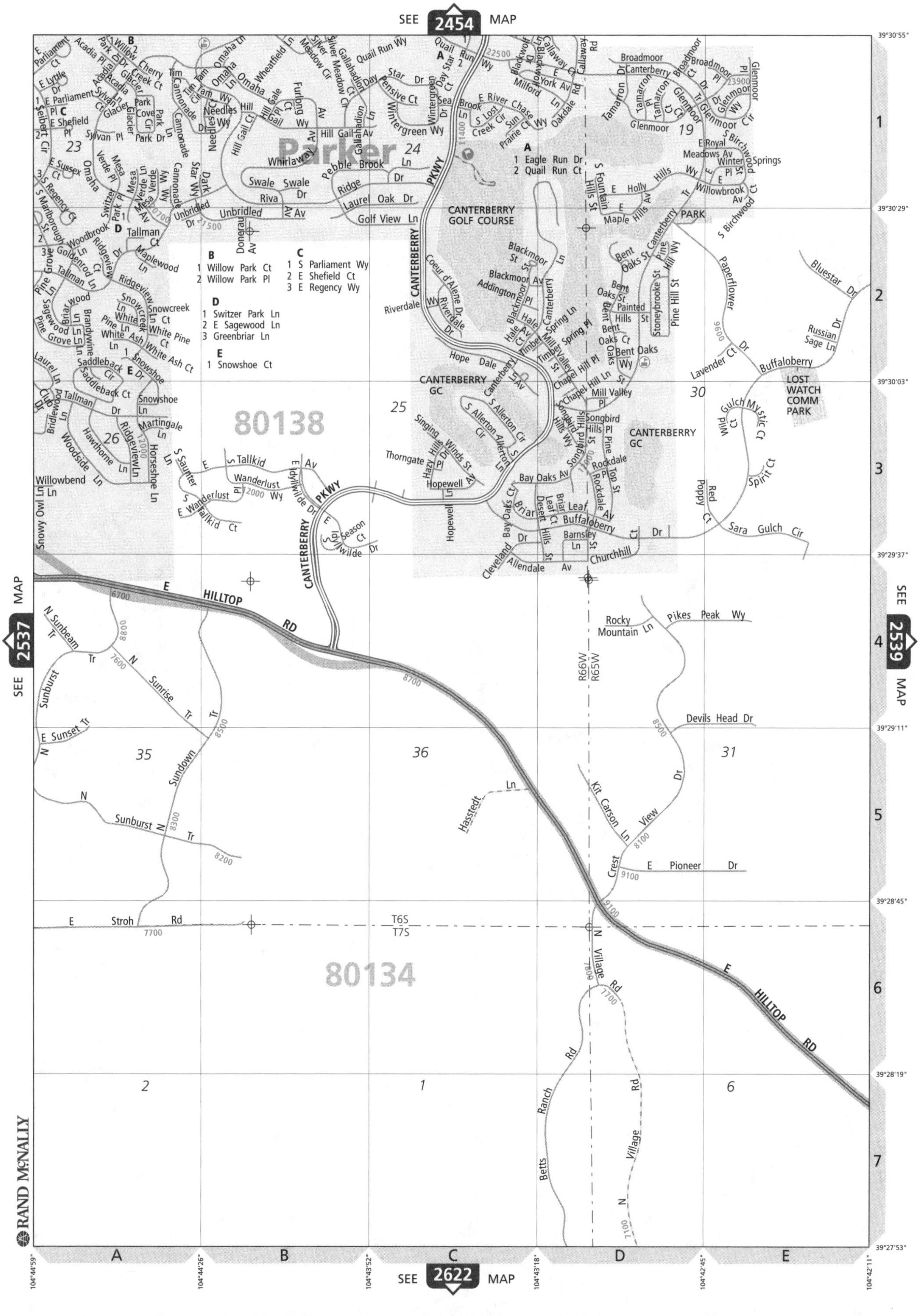

SEE 2454 MAP

SEE 2537 MAP

SEE 2539 MAP

Parker

CANTERBERRY GOLF COURSE

CANTERBERRY GC

LOST WATCH COMM PARK

80138

80134

A
1 Eagle Run Dr
2 Quail Run Ct

B
1 Willow Park Ct
2 Willow Park Pl

C
1 S Parliament Wy
2 E Shefield Ct
3 E Regency Wy

D
1 Switzer Park Ln
2 E Sagewood Ln
3 Greenbriar Ln

E
1 Snowshoe Ct

SEE 2622 MAP

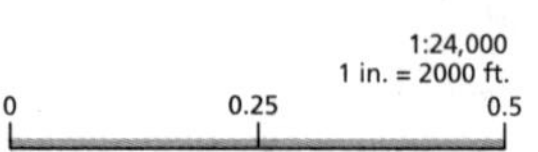

SEE 2455 MAP

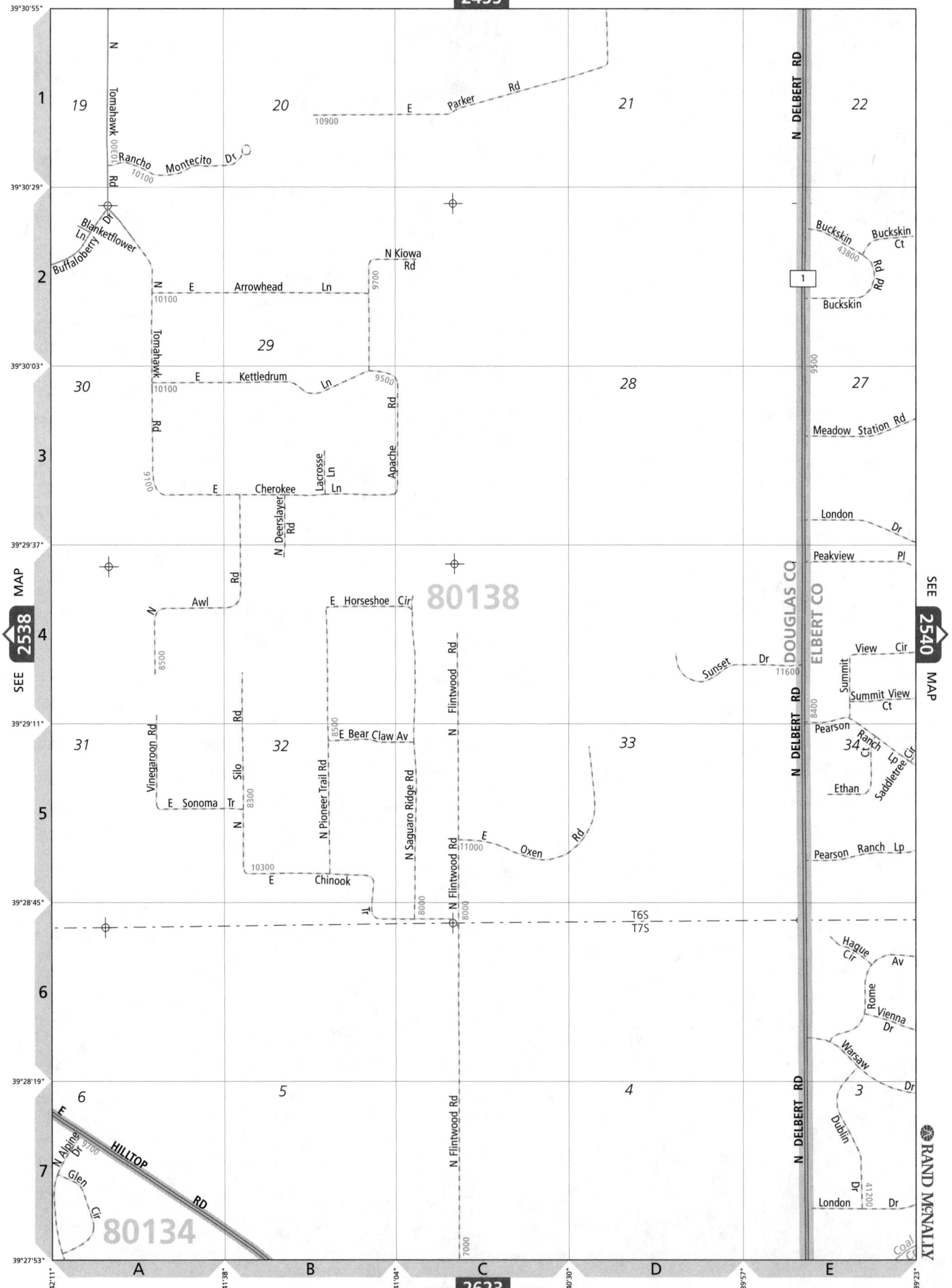

SEE 2538 MAP

SEE 2540 MAP

N Tomahawk Rd
Rancho Montecito Dr
E Parker Rd
N DELBERT RD
Blanketflower Dr
Buffaloberry Ln
N Kiowa Rd
E Arrowhead Ln
Buckskin Rd
Buckskin Ct
E Kettledrum Ln
Apache Rd
Meadow Station Rd
E Cherokee Ln
Lacrosse Ln
N Deerslayer Rd
London Dr
Peakview Pl
N Awl Rd
E Horseshoe Cir
80138
DOUGLAS CO
ELBERT CO
Sunset Dr
Summit View Cir
Summit View Ct
N Flintwood Rd
N Silo Rd
E Bear Claw Av
Vinegaroon Rd
Pearson Ranch Lp
Saddletree Cir
Ethan Ct
N Pioneer Trail Rd
N Saguaro Ridge Rd
E Sonoma Tr
E Oxen Rd
E Chinook Tr
T6S
T7S
Hague Cir
Rome Av
Vienna Dr
Warsaw Dr
Dublin Dr
E HILLTOP RD
N Alpine Dr
Glen Cir
80134
London Dr
Coal Cr

19 20 21 22 29 30 28 27 31 32 33 34 6 5 4 3

1 2 3 4 5 6 7
A B C D E

SEE 2623 MAP

1:24,000
1 in. = 2000 ft.
0 0.25 0.5
miles

SEE 2456 MAP

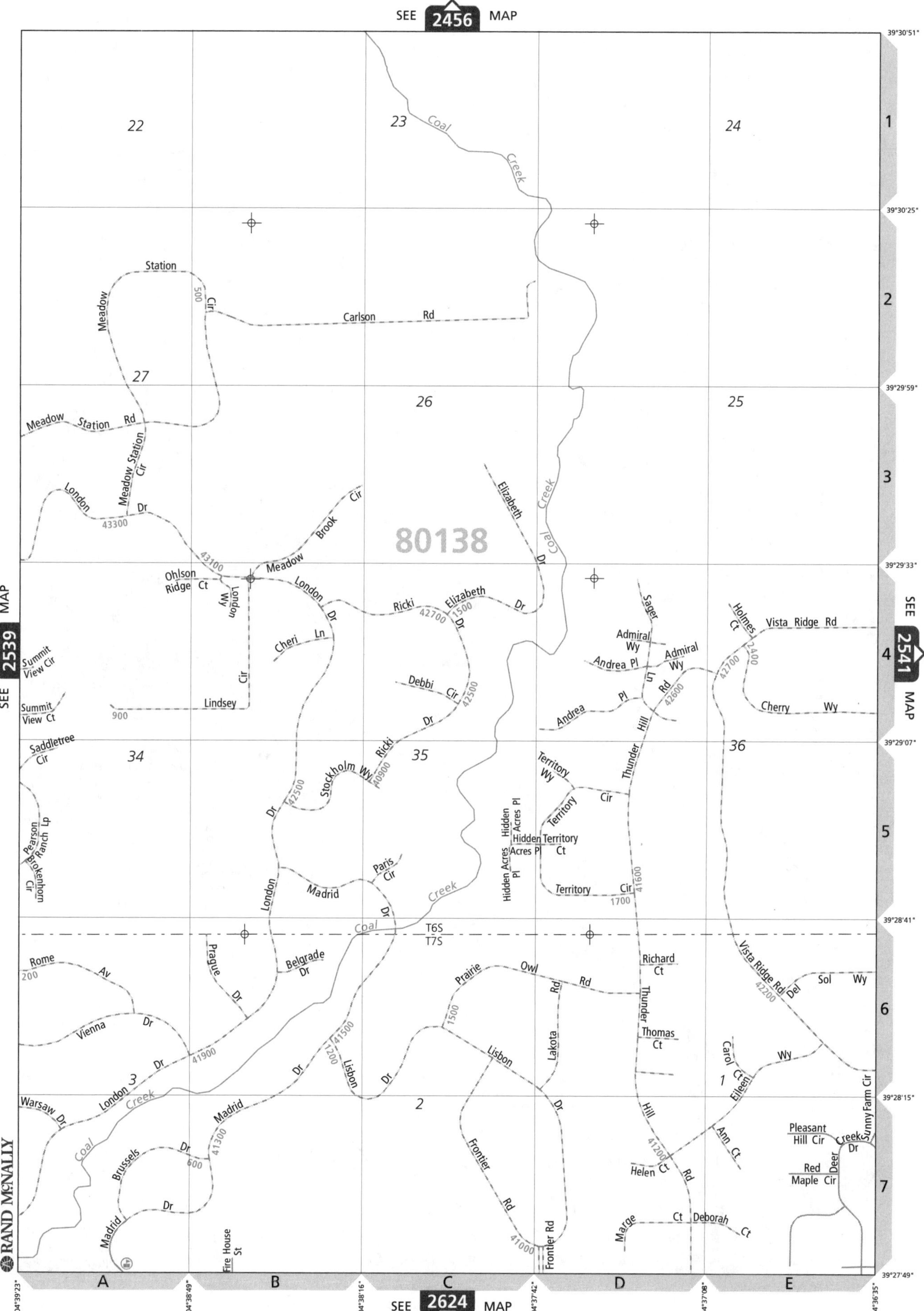

SEE 2539 MAP
SEE 2541 MAP
SEE 2624 MAP

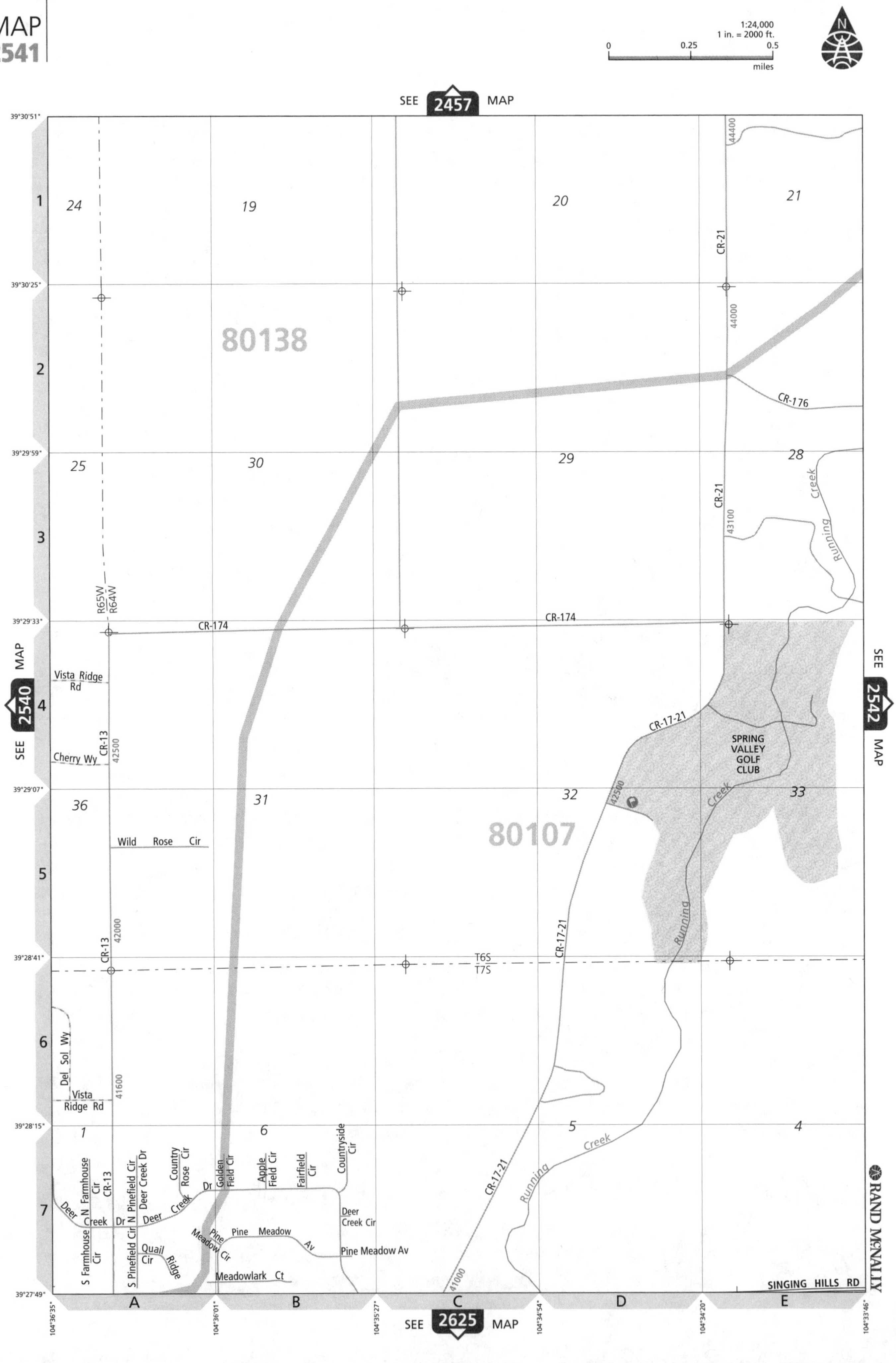

1:24,000
1 in. = 2000 ft.
0 0.25 0.5
miles

SEE 2457 MAP

SEE 2540 MAP

SEE 2542 MAP

SEE 2625 MAP

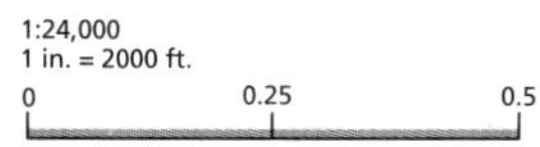

SEE 2458 MAP

Running Creek Ranch Rd
Creek
Running
Creek
Running
80138
21
22
23
CR-29
Shenandoah Ct
Dr
Shenandoah
7500
Morning Star Ct
Pony Express Rd
Dr
Dr
7300
Sun Country Dr
Shenandoah
Shenandoah
Sun Country Dr
Shenandoah Dr
7700
Stampede Ct
Evening Star Ct
S Shenandoah Dr
CR Rd
Evening
Evening Star Ct
28
27
26
CR-176
Taos Tr
CR-29
Taos Tr
CR-174
CR-174
80107
33
34
35
T6S
T7S
Valley View Ct
4
3
2
CR-29
SINGING HILLS RD
SINGING HILLS RD
1
2
3
4
5
6
7
A
B
C
D
E
39°30'47"
39°30'21"
39°29'55"
39°29'29"
39°29'03"
39°28'37"
39°28'11"
39°27'45"
104°33'47"
104°33'13"
104°32'39"
104°32'06"
104°31'32"
104°30'53"

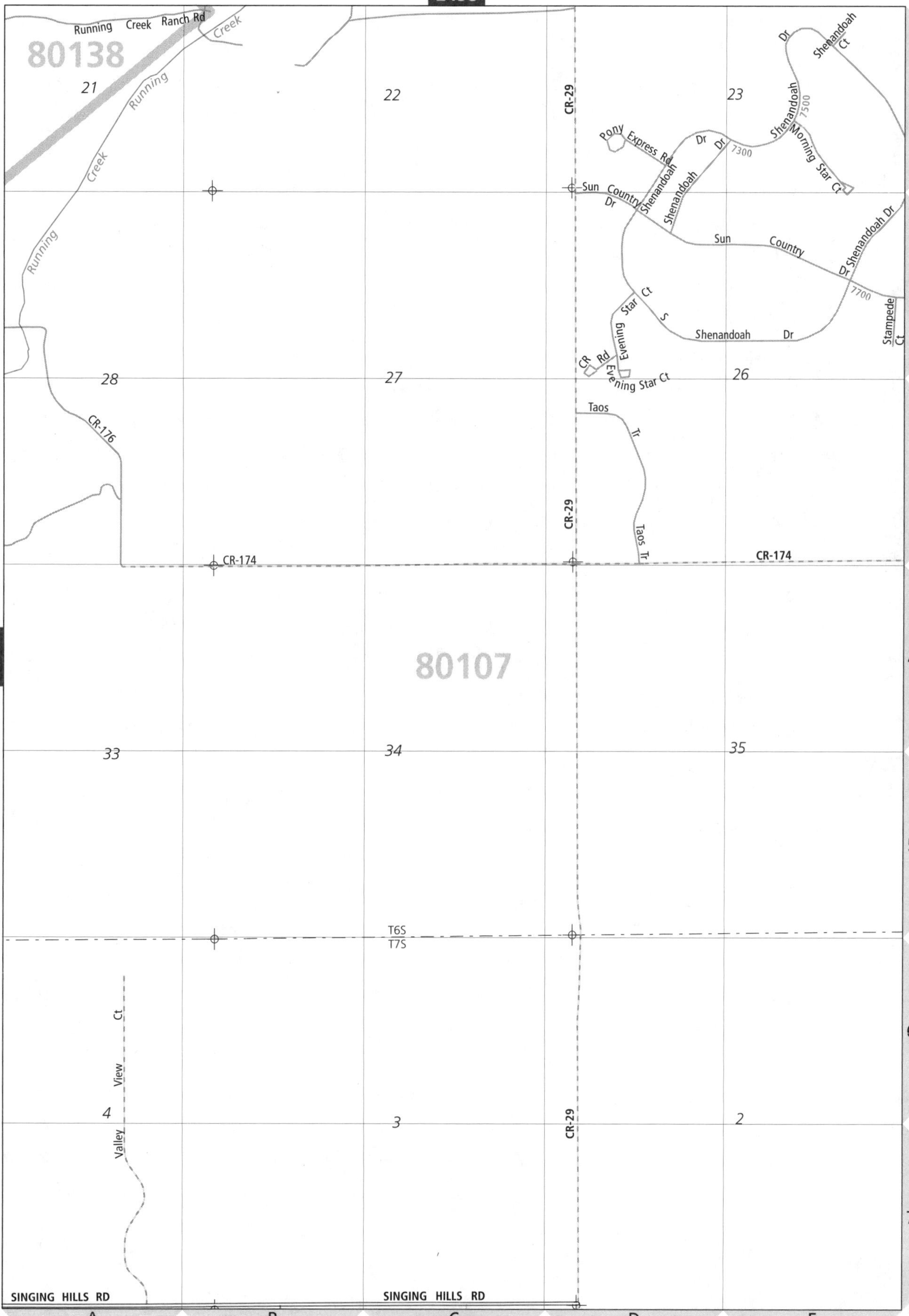

SEE 2541 MAP

SEE 2543 MAP

SEE 2626 MAP

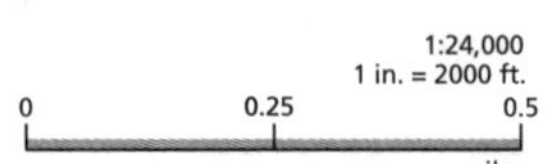

SEE 2459 MAP

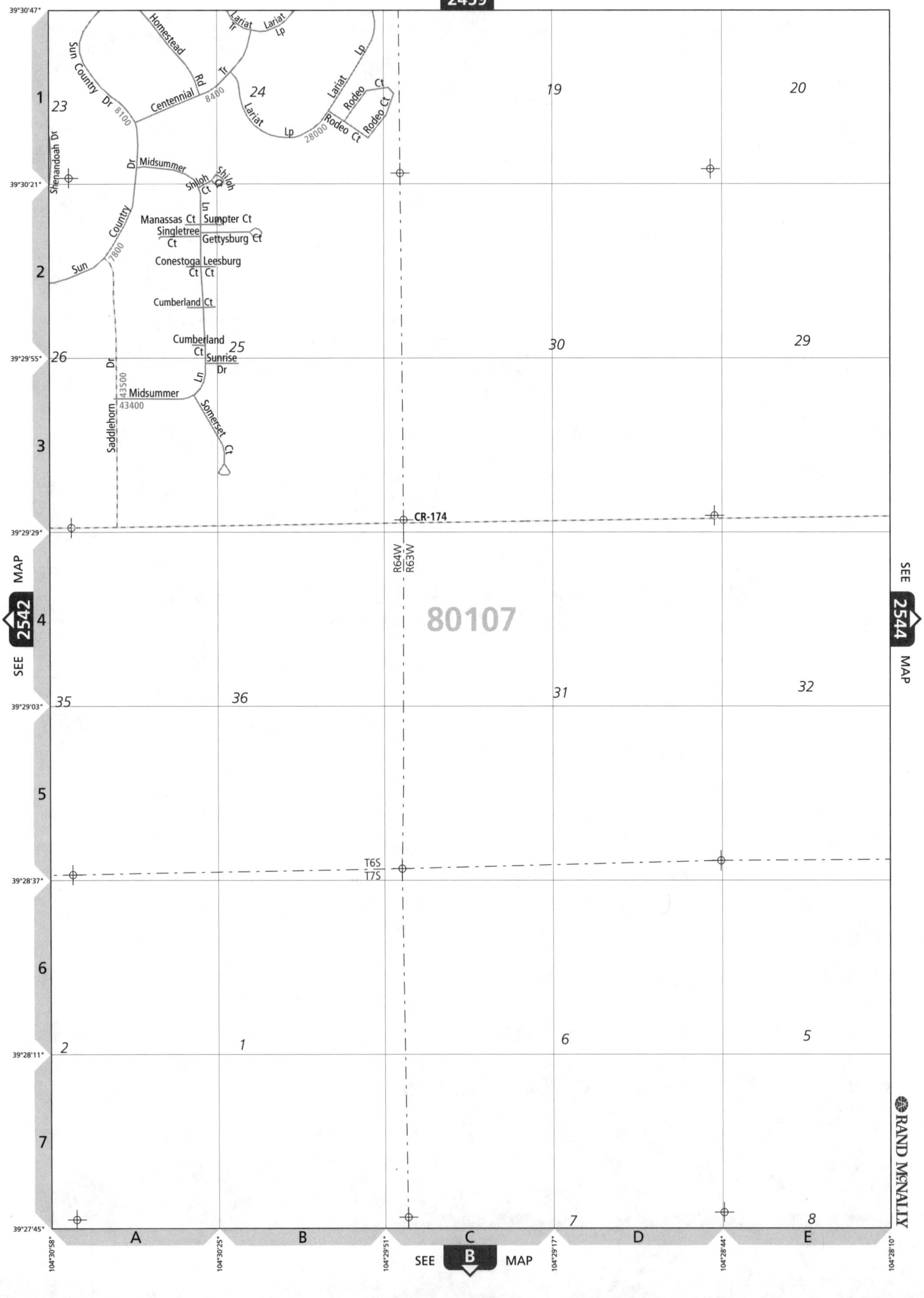

SEE 2542 MAP

SEE 2544 MAP

SEE B MAP

1:24,000
1 in. = 2000 ft.
0
0.25
0.5
miles
SEE 2460 MAP
SEE 2543 MAP
SEE B MAP
SEE B MAP
KIOWA-BENNETT RD
CR-53
CR-174
CR-166
Kiowa Creek
80107
80102
80117
T6S
T7S
43000
42300
41000
20
21
22
23
29
28
27
32
33
34
5
4
3
8
9
10
1
2
3
4
5
6
7
A
B
C
D
E
39°30'43"
39°30'17"
39°29'51"
39°29'25"
39°28'58"
39°28'32"
39°28'06"
39°27'40"
104°28'10"
104°27'36"
104°27'03"
104°26'29"
104°25'55"
104°25'22"
RAND McNALLY

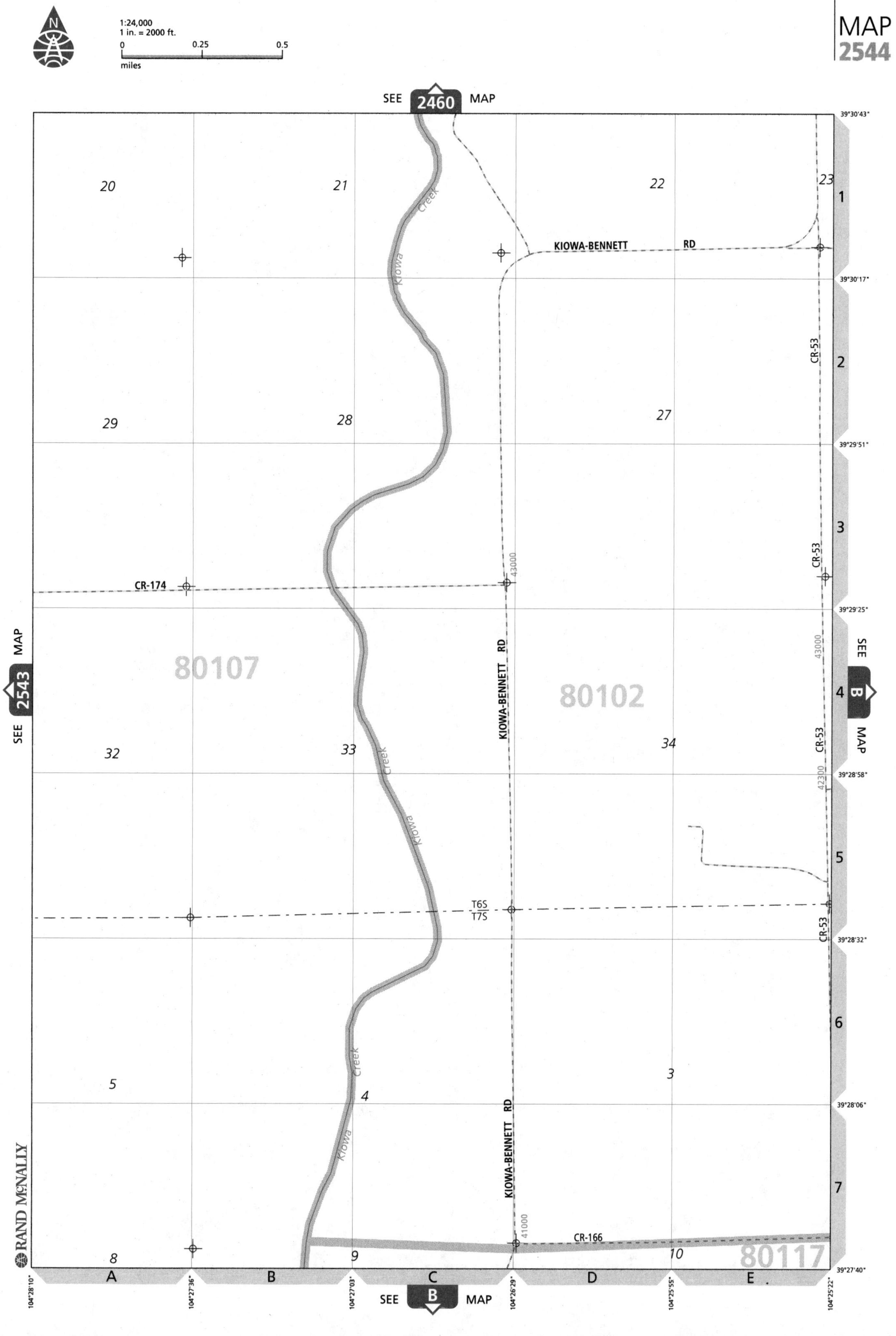

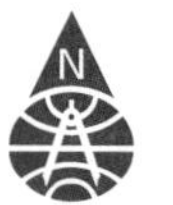

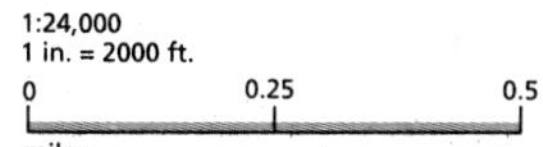

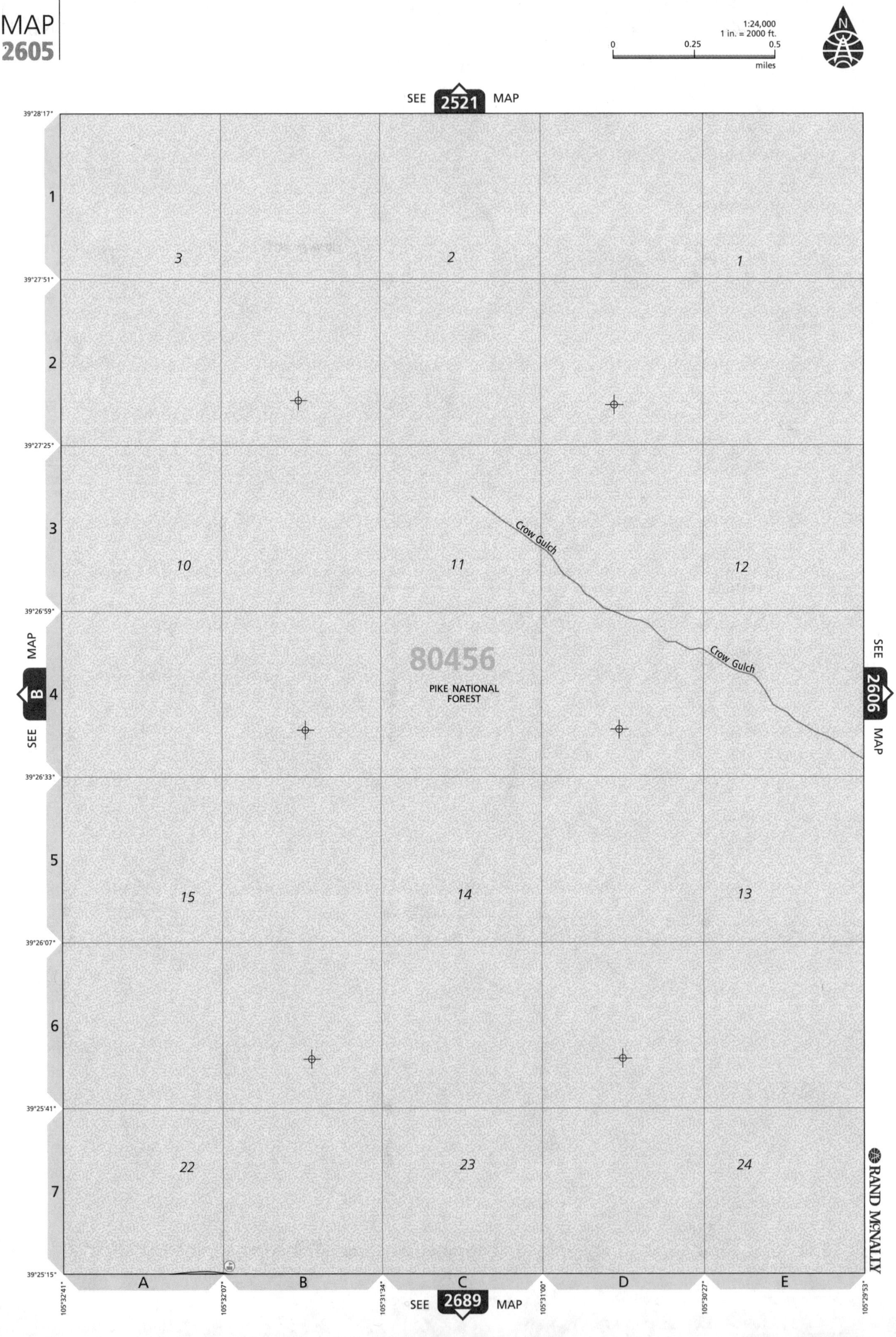

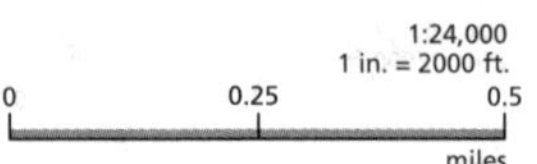

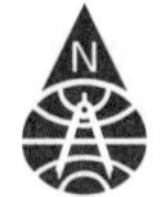

1:24,000
1 in. = 2000 ft.
0
0.25
0.5
miles
N
SEE 2521 MAP
SEE 2689 MAP
SEE B MAP
SEE 2606 MAP
39°28'17"
39°27'51"
39°27'25"
39°26'59"
39°26'33"
39°26'07"
39°25'41"
39°25'15"
105°32'41"
105°32'07"
105°31'34"
105°31'00"
105°30'27"
105°29'53"
1
2
3
4
5
6
7
A
B
C
D
E
3
2
1
10
11
12
15
14
13
22
23
24
Crow Gulch
Crow Gulch
80456
PIKE NATIONAL FOREST
RAND McNALLY

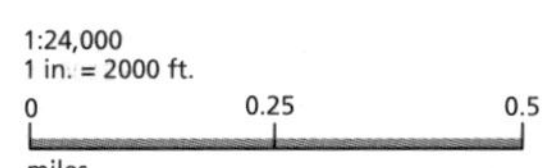

SEE 2522 MAP

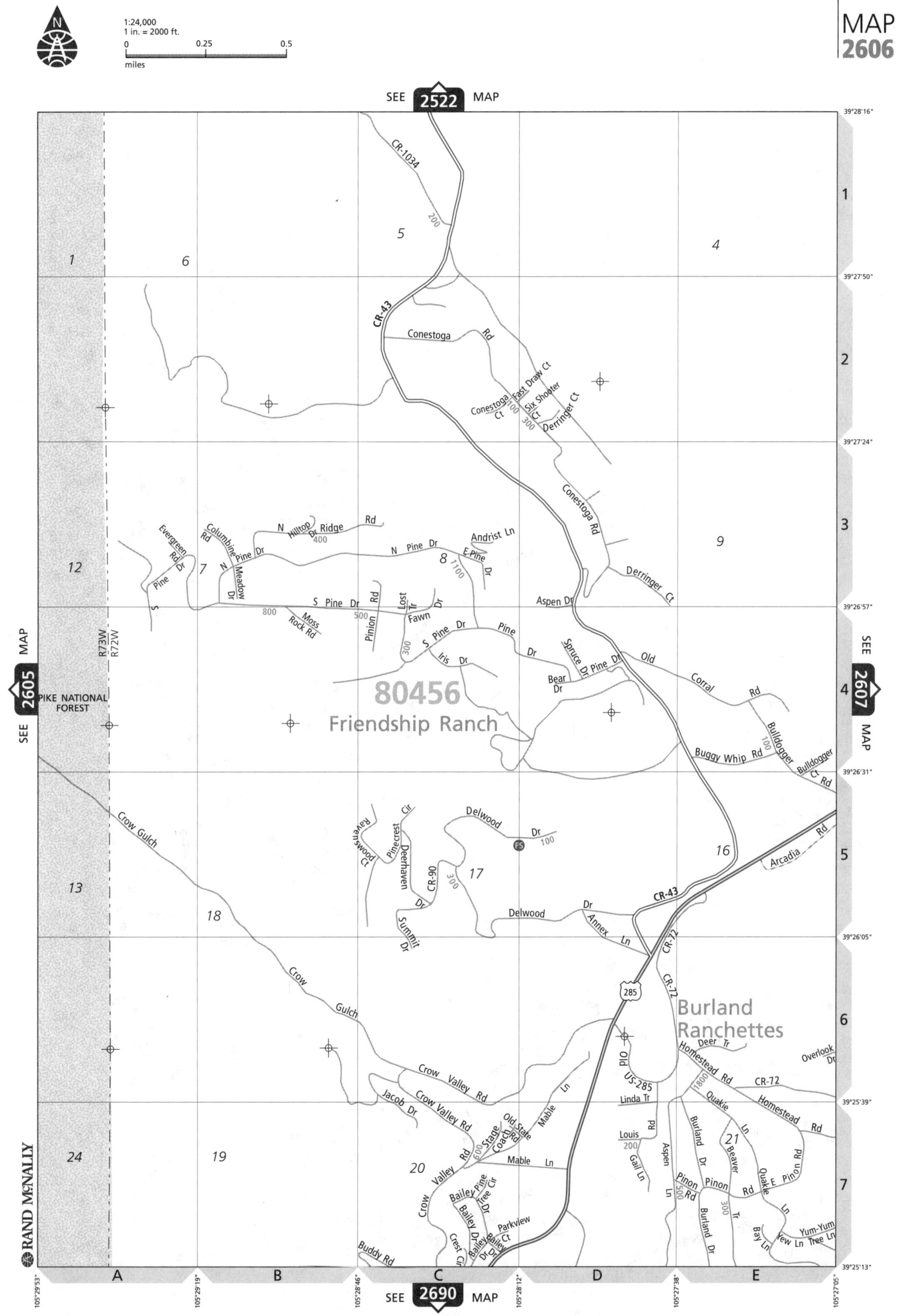

80456
Friendship Ranch

Burland
Ranchettes

PIKE NATIONAL FOREST

CR-43
CR-1034
Conestoga Rd
Conestoga Ct
Fast Draw Ct
Six Shooter Ct
Derringer Ct
N Hilltop Dr
Ridge Rd
Andrist Ln
N Pine Dr
E Pine Dr
Evergreen Rd
Columbine Rd
Pine Dr
N Meadow Dr
S Pine Dr
Moss Rock Rd
Pinion Rd
Lost Fawn Tr
Iris Dr
Aspen Dr
Spruce Dr
Bear Dr
Old Corral Rd
Bulldogger Rd
Bulldogger Ct
Buggy Whip Rd
Crow Gulch
Delwood Dr
Ravenswood Ct
Pinecrest Cir
Deerhaven Dr
CR-90
Summit Dr
Delwood Annex Ln
Arcadia Rd
CR-72
US-285
Old US-285
Deer Tr
Homestead Rd
Overlook Dr
Crow Valley Rd
Jacob Dr
Stage Coach Rd
Old State Rd
Mable Ln
Linda Tr
Louis Rd
Gail Ln
Aspen Ln
Burland Dr
Quakie Ln
Beaver Tr
E Pinon Rd
Pinon Rd
Bay Ln
Yew Ln
Yum-Yum Tree Ln
Bailey Dr
Pine Tree Cir
Bailey Ct
Parkview
Crest Cir
Buddy Rd

1, 4, 5, 6, 7, 8, 9, 12, 13, 16, 17, 18, 19, 20, 21, 24

R73W
R72W

A B C D E
1 2 3 4 5 6 7

39°28'16"
39°27'50"
39°27'24"
39°26'57"
39°26'31"
39°26'05"
39°25'39"
39°25'13"

105°29'53"
105°29'19"
105°28'46"
105°28'12"
105°27'38"
105°27'05"

SEE 2605 MAP

SEE 2607 MAP

SEE 2690 MAP

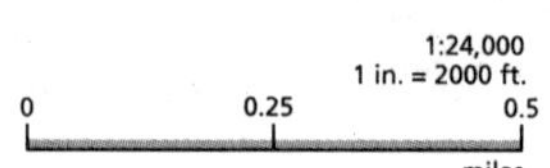

SEE 2523 MAP

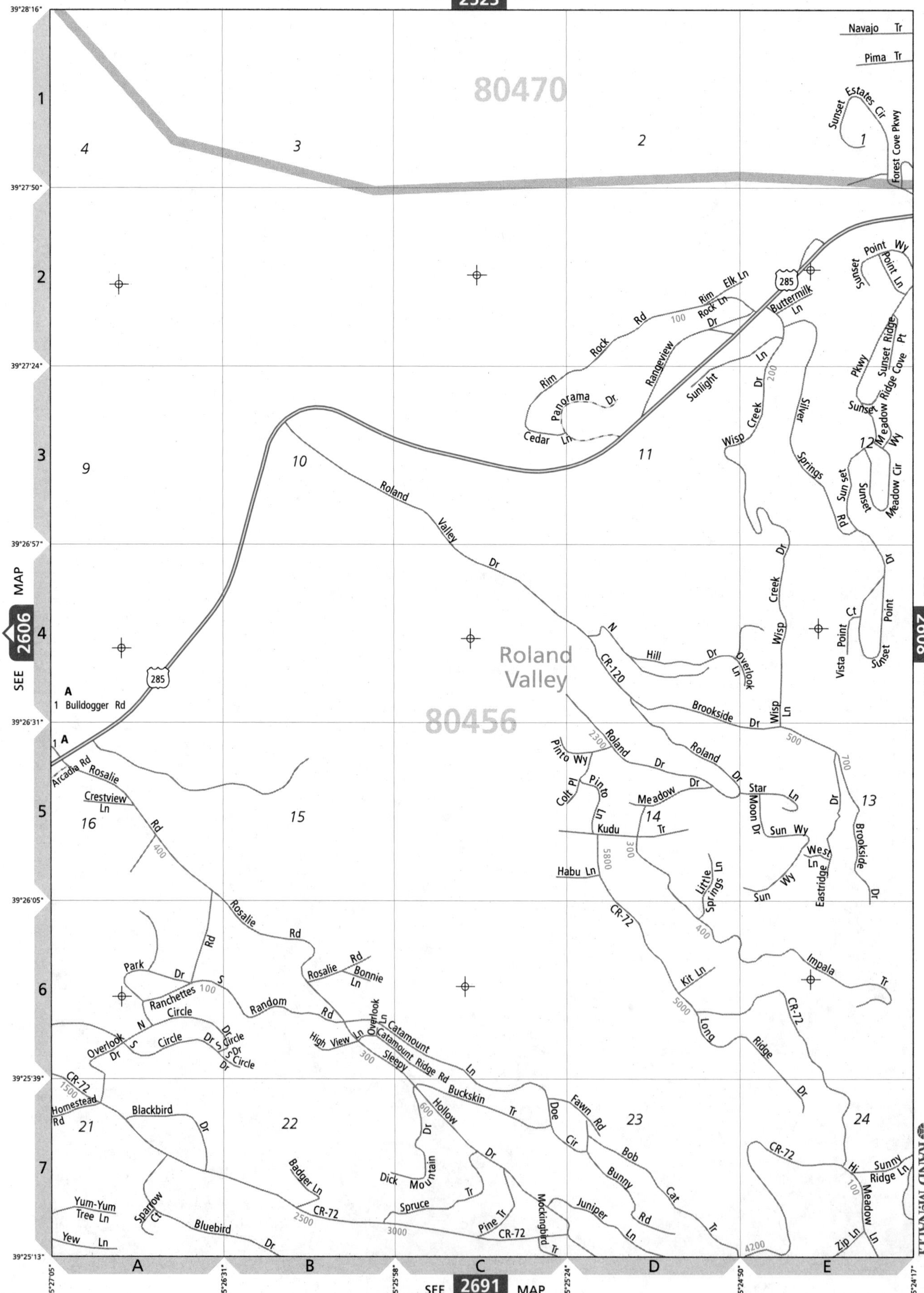

SEE 2606 MAP

SEE 2608 MAP

80470

Roland Valley

80456

Navajo Tr
Pima Tr
Sunset Estates Cir
Forest Cove Pkwy
Point Wy
Point Ln
Sunset
Elk Ln
Rim Rock Ln
Rim Rock Rd
Rangeview Dr
Buttermilk Ln
Panorama Dr
Cedar Ln
Sunlight Ln
Wisp Creek Dr
Silver Springs Rd
Sunset Ridge Pt
Sunset Pkwy
Meadow Ridge Cove Wy
Sunset Meadow Cir
Sun set
Sunset Point Dr
Vista Point Ct
Roland Valley Dr
N Hill Dr
Overlook Ln
CR-120
Brookside Dr
Wisp Ln
Roland Dr
Pinto Wy
Pinto Ln
Colt Pl
Meadow Dr
Star Ln
Moon Dr
Sun Wy
West Ln
Eastridge Dr
Brookside Dr
Kudu Tr
Habu Ln
Little Springs Ln
CR-72
Impala Tr
Kit Ln
Long Ridge Dr
1 Bulldogger Rd
Arcadia Rd
Rosalie Rd
Crestview Ln
Park Dr
Ranchettes Circle
N Circle Dr
S Circle Dr
Overlook Dr
Random Rd
Rosalie Ln
Bonnie Ln
High View Ln
Overlook Ln
Catamount Ln
Catamount Ridge Rd
Sleepy Hollow Dr
Buckskin Tr
Doe Cir
Fawn Rd
Bob Cat Tr
Bunny Rd
Homestead Rd
Blackbird Dr
Badger Ln
Dick Mountain Dr
Spruce Tr
Pine Tr
Mockingbird Tr
Juniper Ln
Yum-Yum Tree Ln
Sparrow Ct
Bluebird Dr
Yew Ln
Hi Sunny Ridge Ln
Meadow Ln
Zip Ln
285

1 2 3 4 9 10 11 12 13 14 15 16 21 22 23 24

A B C D E

1 2 3 4 5 6 7

39°28'16" 39°27'50" 39°27'24" 39°26'57" 39°26'31" 39°26'05" 39°25'39" 39°25'13"

105°27'05" 105°26'31" 105°25'58" 105°25'24" 105°24'50" 105°24'17"

SEE 2691 MAP

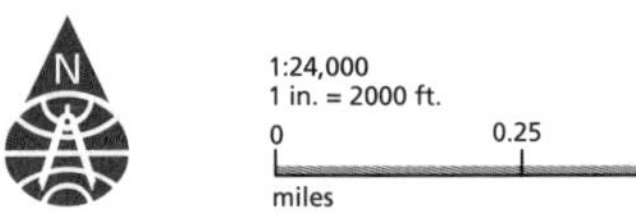

SEE 2524 MAP

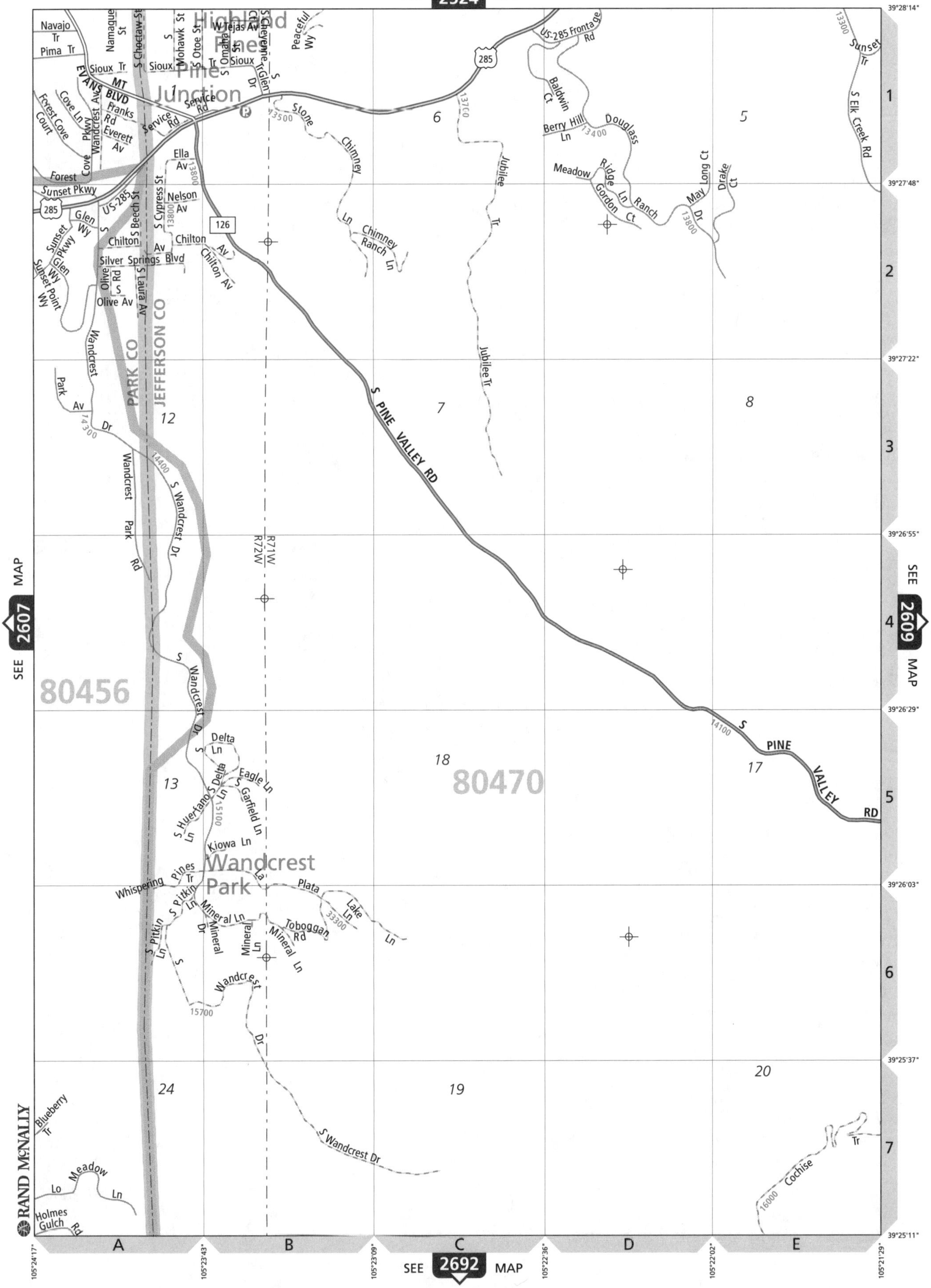

SEE 2607 MAP

SEE 2609 MAP

SEE 2692 MAP

Highland Pines
Pine Junction
Wandcrest Park
80456
80470
PARK CO
JEFFERSON CO
S PINE VALLEY RD
EVANS MT BLVD
US-285
US-285 Frontage Rd
Jubilee Tr
Chimney Ranch Ln
Stone Chimney Ln
S Wandcrest Dr
Wandcrest Park Rd
S Elk Creek Rd
Cochise Tr
Blueberry Tr
Lo Meadow Ln
Holmes Gulch Rd

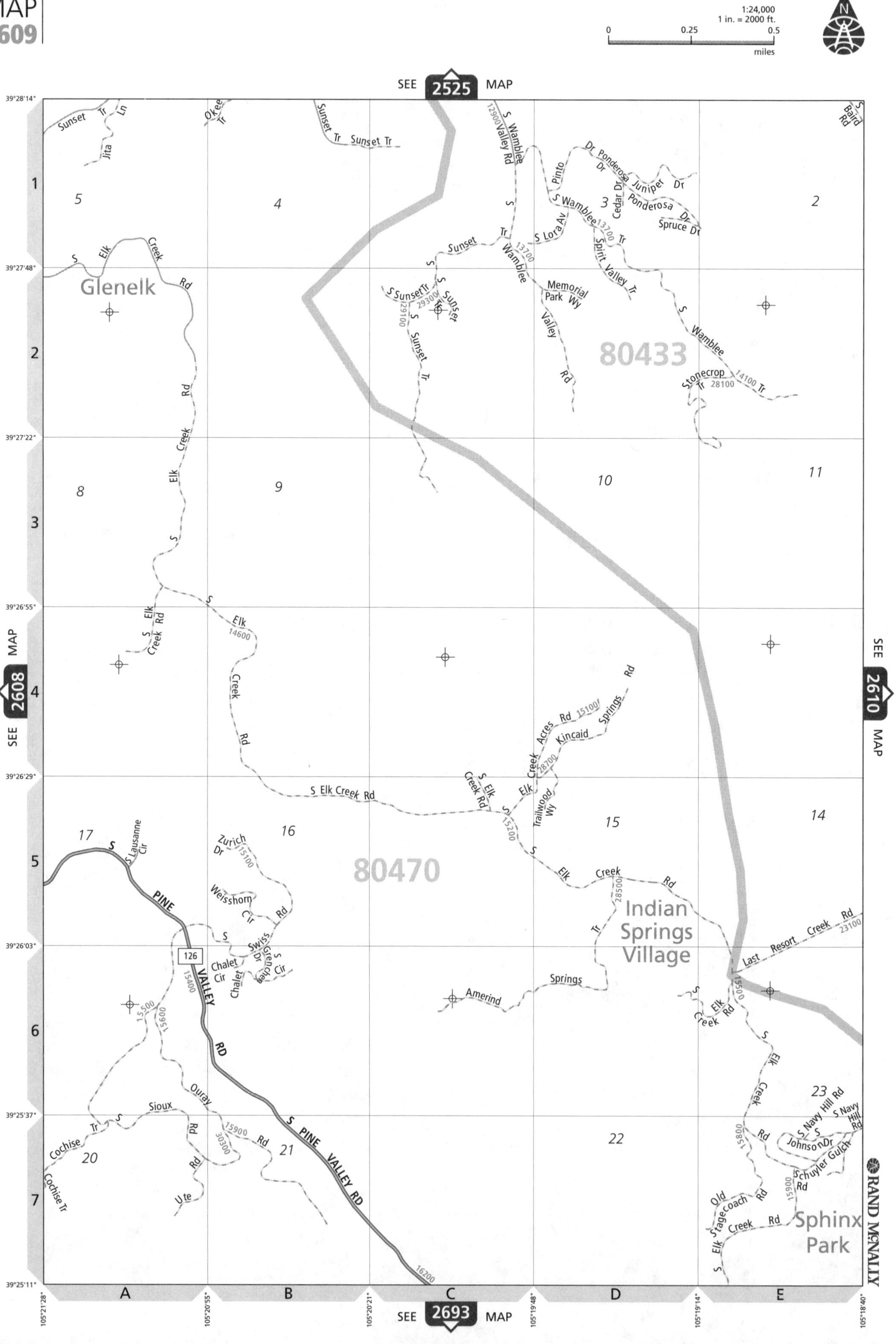

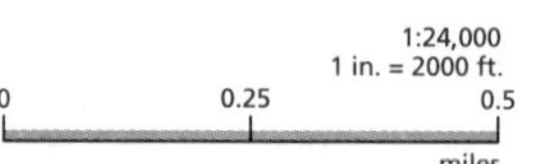

SEE 2525 MAP

SEE 2608 MAP

SEE 2610 MAP

Glenelk

80433

80470

Indian Springs Village

Sphinx Park

S Elk Creek Rd

S Pine Valley Rd

126

S Wamblee Valley Rd

Sunset Tr

S Sunset Tr

Ponderosa Dr

Juniper Dr

Spruce Dr

Cedar Dr

Pinto Dr

S Lora Av

Spirit Valley Tr

Memorial Park Wy

Valley Rd

Stonecrop Tr

Elk Creek Acres Rd

Kincaid

Springs Rd

Trailwood Wy

Last Resort Creek Rd

Amerind

Springs Tr

S Lausanne Cir

Zurich Dr

Weisshorn Cir

Swiss Dr

Chalet Cir

Grenchen Cir

Ouray

Sioux Rd

Cochise Tr

Ute

Old Stagecoach Rd

Johnson Dr

S Navy Hill Rd

Schuyler Gulch Rd

Jita Ln

Okee Tr

S Baird Rd

SEE 2693 MAP

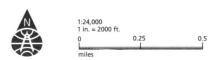

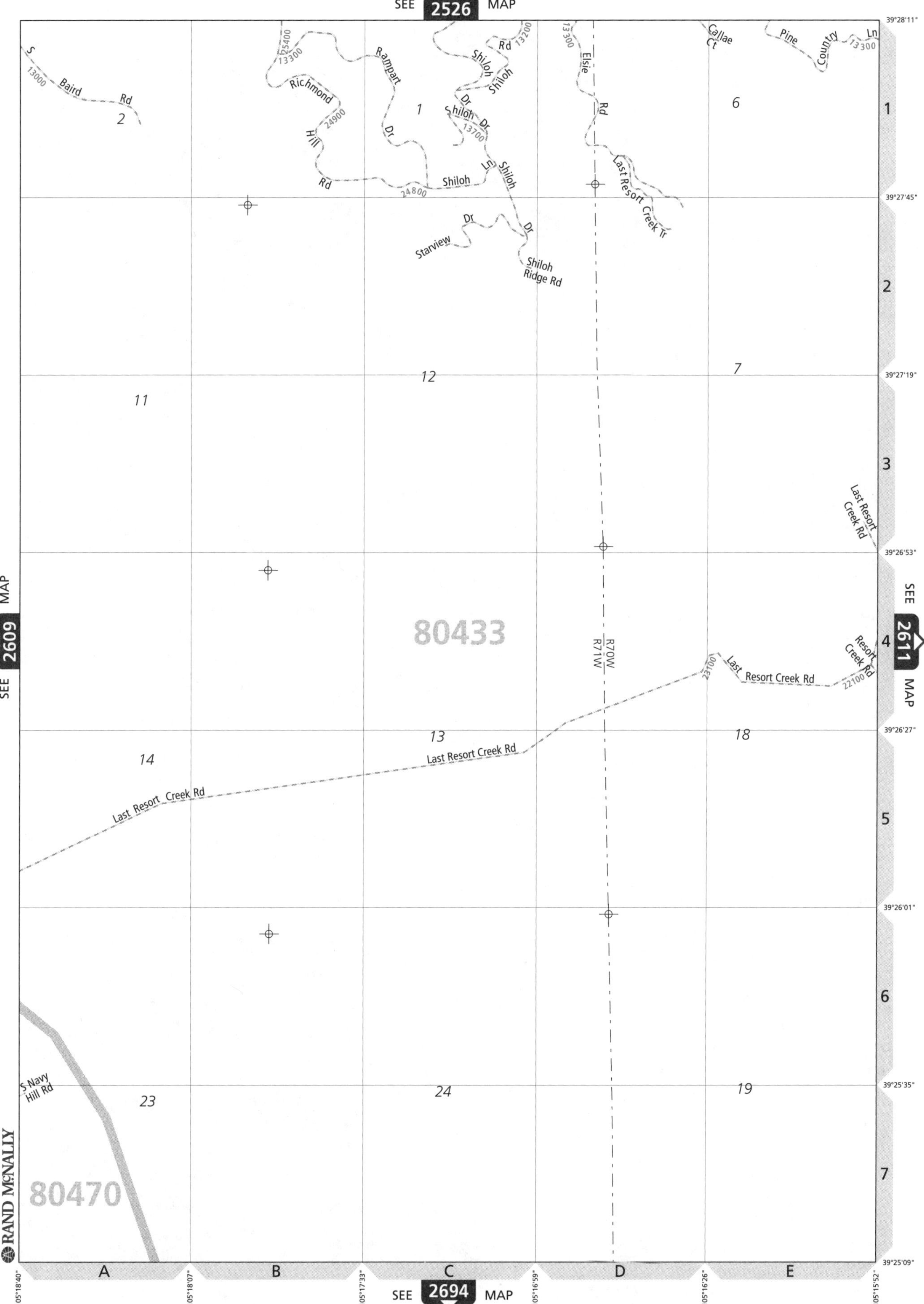
1:24,000
1 in. = 2000 ft.
0 0.25 0.5
miles
SEE 2526 MAP
SEE 2609 MAP
SEE 2611 MAP
SEE 2694 MAP
S Baird Rd
13000
Richmond Hill Rd
Rampart Dr
Shiloh Rd
Shiloh Dr
Shiloh Ln
Shiloh Dr
Starview Dr
Shiloh Ridge Rd
Elsie Rd
Last Resort Creek Tr
Callae Ct
Pine Country Ln
Last Resort Creek Rd
80433
80470
R70W
R71W
S Navy Hill Rd
1
2
6
7
11
12
13
14
18
19
23
24
A
B
C
D
E
39°28'11"
39°27'45"
39°27'19"
39°26'53"
39°26'27"
39°26'01"
39°25'35"
39°25'09"
105°18'40"
105°18'07"
105°17'33"
105°16'59"
105°16'26"
105°15'52"
RAND McNALLY

1:24,000
1 in. = 2000 ft.
0 0.25 0.5
miles

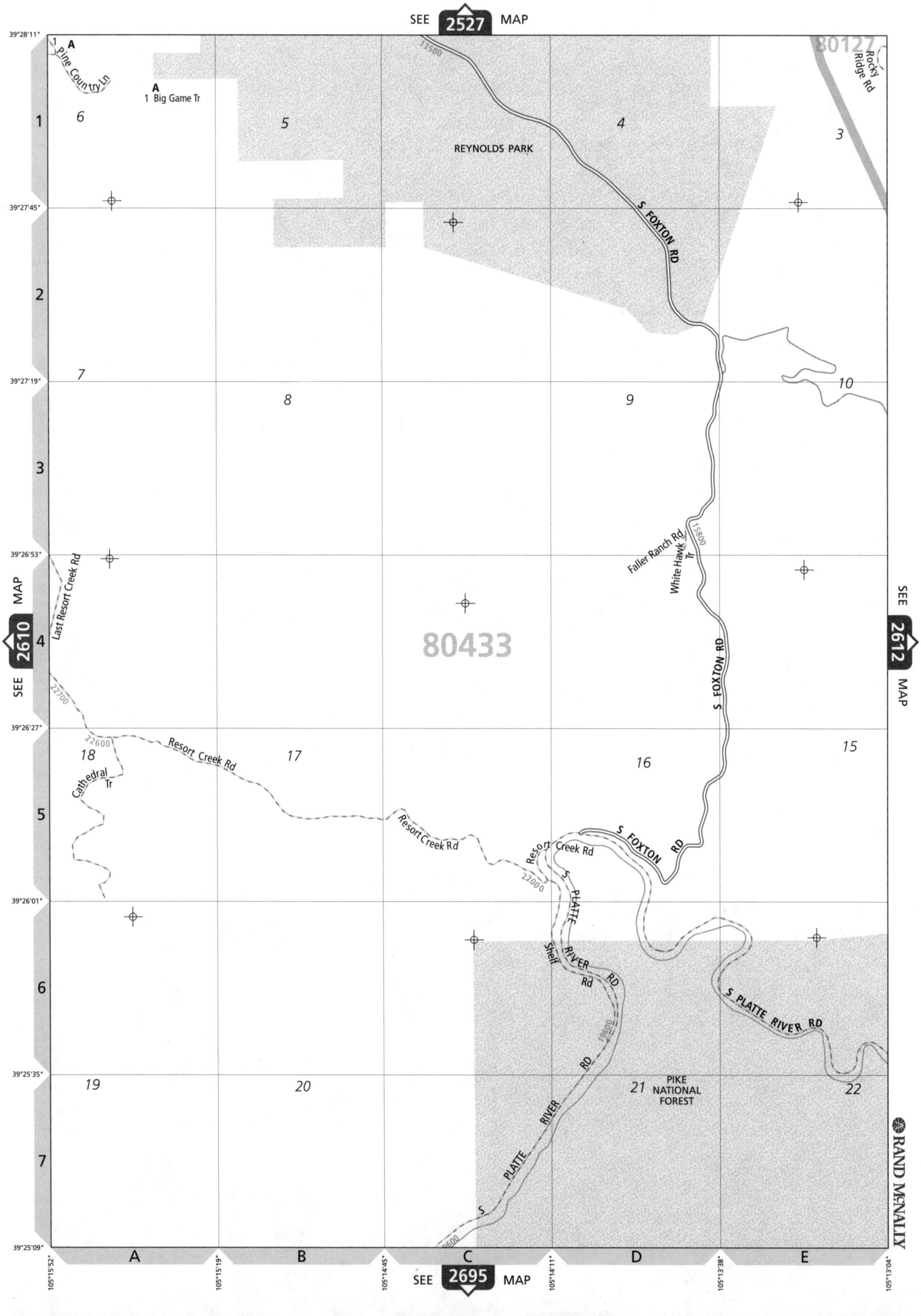

SEE 2527 MAP

REYNOLDS PARK

80127

Rocky Ridge Rd

Pine Country Ln

1 Big Game Tr

S FOXTON RD

Faller Ranch Rd

White Hawk Tr

Last Resort Creek Rd

80433

Resort Creek Rd

Cathedral Tr

S PLATTE RIVER RD

Shelf Rd

PIKE NATIONAL FOREST

SEE 2610 MAP

SEE 2612 MAP

SEE 2695 MAP

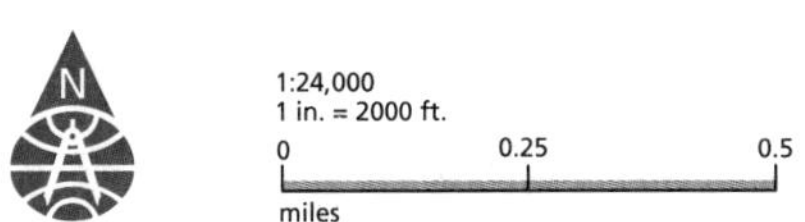

SEE 2528 MAP

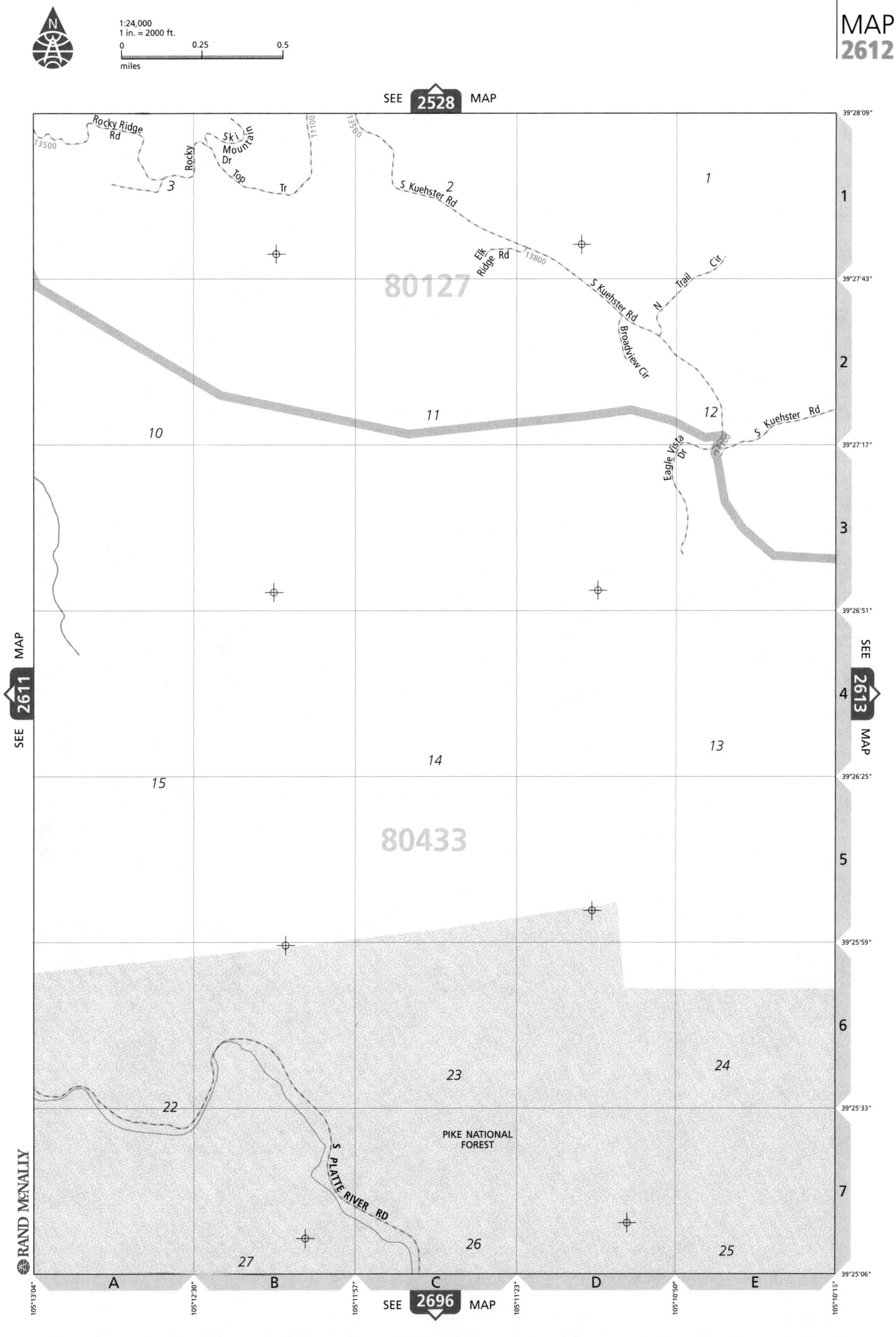

SEE 2611 MAP

SEE 2613 MAP

SEE 2696 MAP

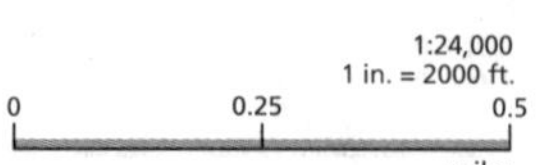

SEE 2529 MAP

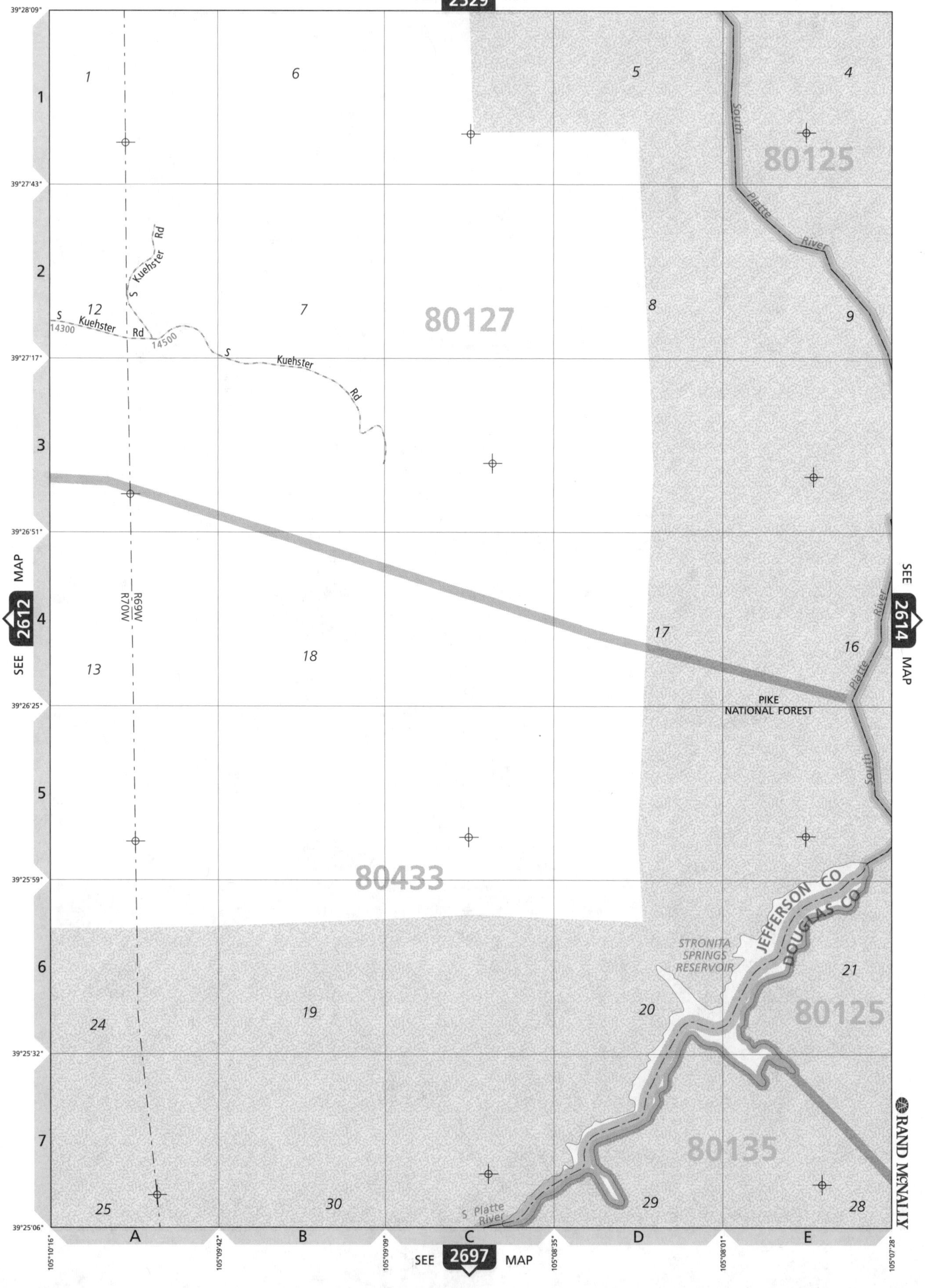

SEE 2612 MAP

SEE 2614 MAP

SEE 2697 MAP

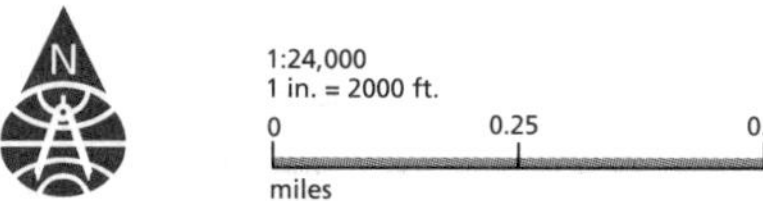

SEE 2530 MAP

W Lookout Run
Hawks Nest
N Wildcat
Bobcat Run
Firethorn
Roxborough
Cougar Run
Pheasant
Bear Run
Council Fire
Ambush Rock
Dr
Dueling Stags
Shadow Rock Run
W Twin Cubs
Sleeping
Expedition
N Arroyo
Roxborough
Dr
W Snow
Cloud
Fairway
Vistas Rd
Buckskin Tr
N Fargo Tr
Surrey Tr
Puma
W Snow Cloud Tr
Beaver Run
N Raspberry Run
Brown
Fox Tr
Roxborough
Dr
Bright Water Tr
Fox Paw Tr
Choke Cherry Wy
Choke Cherry Ct
Briar Rose Tr
N Old Ranch Tr
Roxborough
Big Horn
N Old Ranch Tr
Dr
Old Ranch Tr
A
1 Village Cir W
Red Mesa Dr
Condor Run
Roxborough
Willow Broom Tr
Warriors
Warriors Run
Willow Broom Tr
Dr
B
1 Eagle Feather Pl
Eagle Feather Tr
Woodbine Ct
Sundown
ARROWHEAD GOLF CLUB
Rain Dance Tr
Buffalo Run
Buffalo Run
Silver Thorn Run
Rain Dance Tr
Silver Thorn Run
Roxborough
Mossrock Run
W Harebell Run
Dr
Indian Paint Run
Sandstone Run
Red Fern Ct
Red Fern Run
W Raven Run
Antler Run
Roxborough
Hawthorn Tr
Black Squirrel Run
Black Bear Run
Dr
Totem Run
Dakota Run
Foxcroft Ln
Carpenter Run

DOUGLAS CO
S Platte River
S Platte River
PIKE NATIONAL FOREST
80125
ROXBOROUGH STATE PARK

4
3
2
9
10
11
16
15
14
21
22
23
28
27
26

1
2
3
4
5
6
7
A
B
C
D
E

39°28'06"
39°27'40"
39°27'14"
39°26'48"
39°26'22"
39°25'56"
39°25'30"
39°25'04"
105°07'28"
105°06'54"
105°06'21"
105°05'47"
105°05'13"
105°04'40"

SEE 2613 MAP

SEE 2615 MAP

SEE 2698 MAP

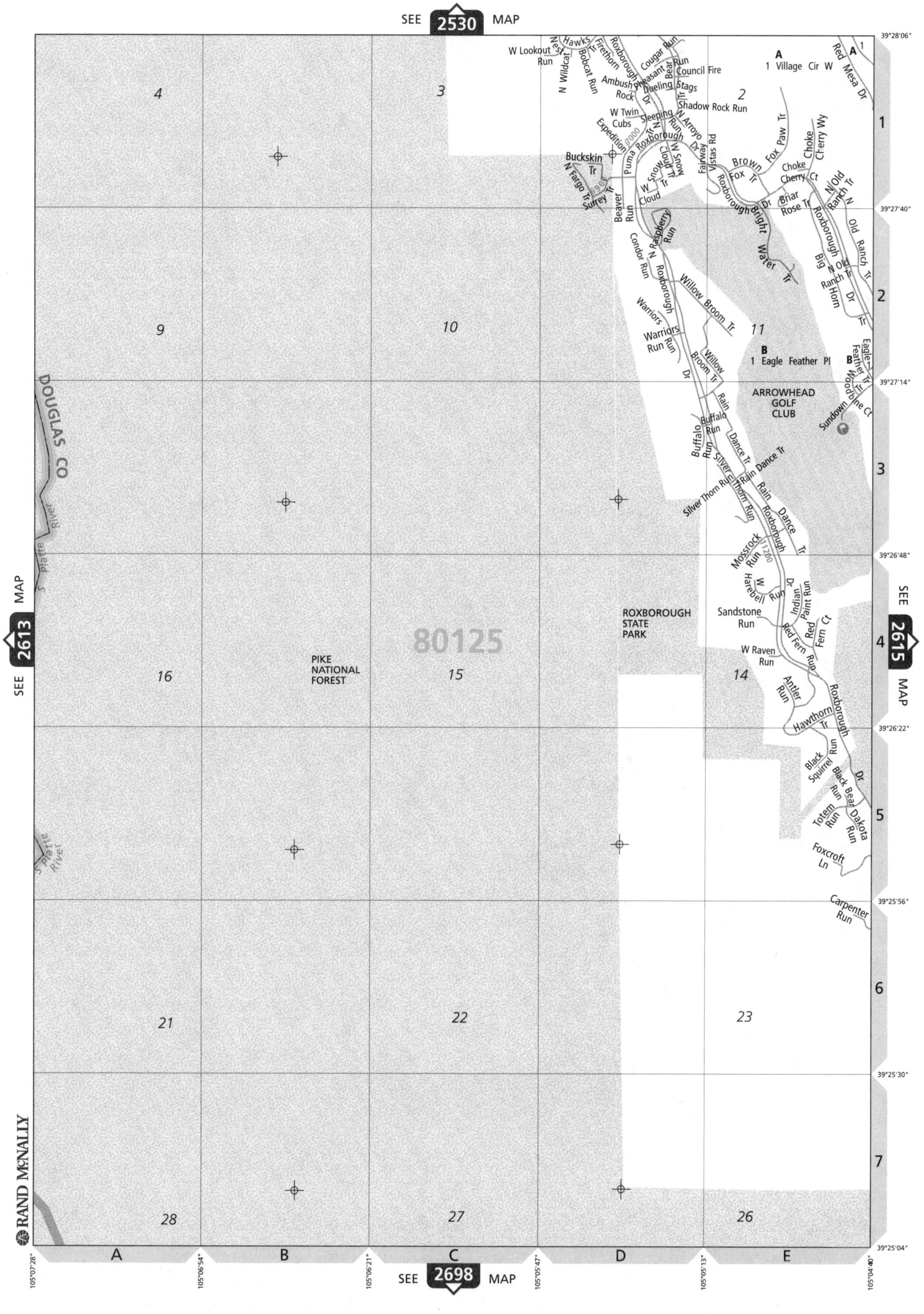

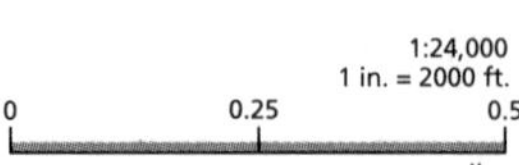

SEE 2531 MAP

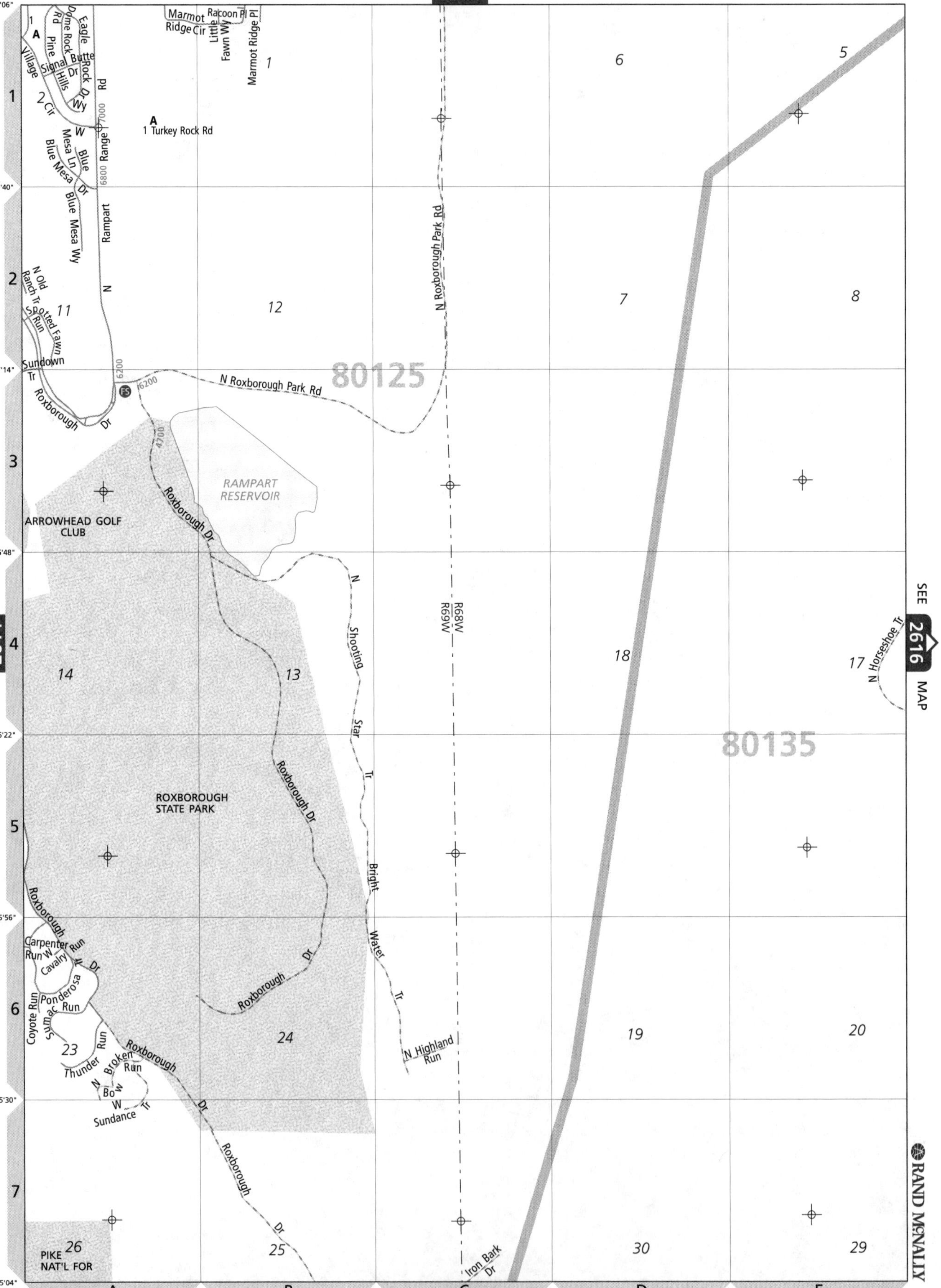

SEE 2614 MAP

SEE 2616 MAP

SEE 2699 MAP

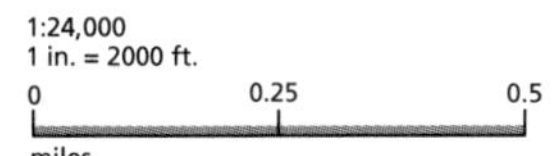

SEE 2532 MAP

SEE 2615 MAP

SEE 2617 MAP

80135

Reynolds Industrial Park

Reynolds Dr

W Airport Rd

N Peterson Rd

Plum Creek

85

5 4 3 8 9 10 17 16 15 20 21 22 29 28 27

Horseshoe Tr

N Horseshoe Tr

N Horseshoe Tr

Hay Meadow Wy

Lambert Ranch Tr

Lambert Ranch Cross

Lehigh Ln

Old Orchard Ln

W Rio Grande Av

Mustang Cir

Hier Valley Rd

W Rainbow Creek Rd

N Rainbow Plz

Creek Rd

N Cherokee Pl

N Chippewa Cir

W Cheyenne Pl

N Seminole Pl

W Cherokee Dr

W Aztec Ct

N Hopi Dr

W Cherokee Dr

N Sioux Ct

W Sioux Dr

W Sioux Ln

Indian Creek Ranch

JARRE CANYON RD

67

5000 5300 5200 4500 4200 4600 4800 4900 7000 6400

39°28'03" 39°27'37" 39°27'11" 39°26'45" 39°26'19" 39°25'53" 39°25'27" 39°25'01"

1 2 3 4 5 6 7

A B C D E

105°01'52" 105°01'18" 105°00'44" 105°00'11" 104°59'37" 104°59'03"

SEE 2700 MAP

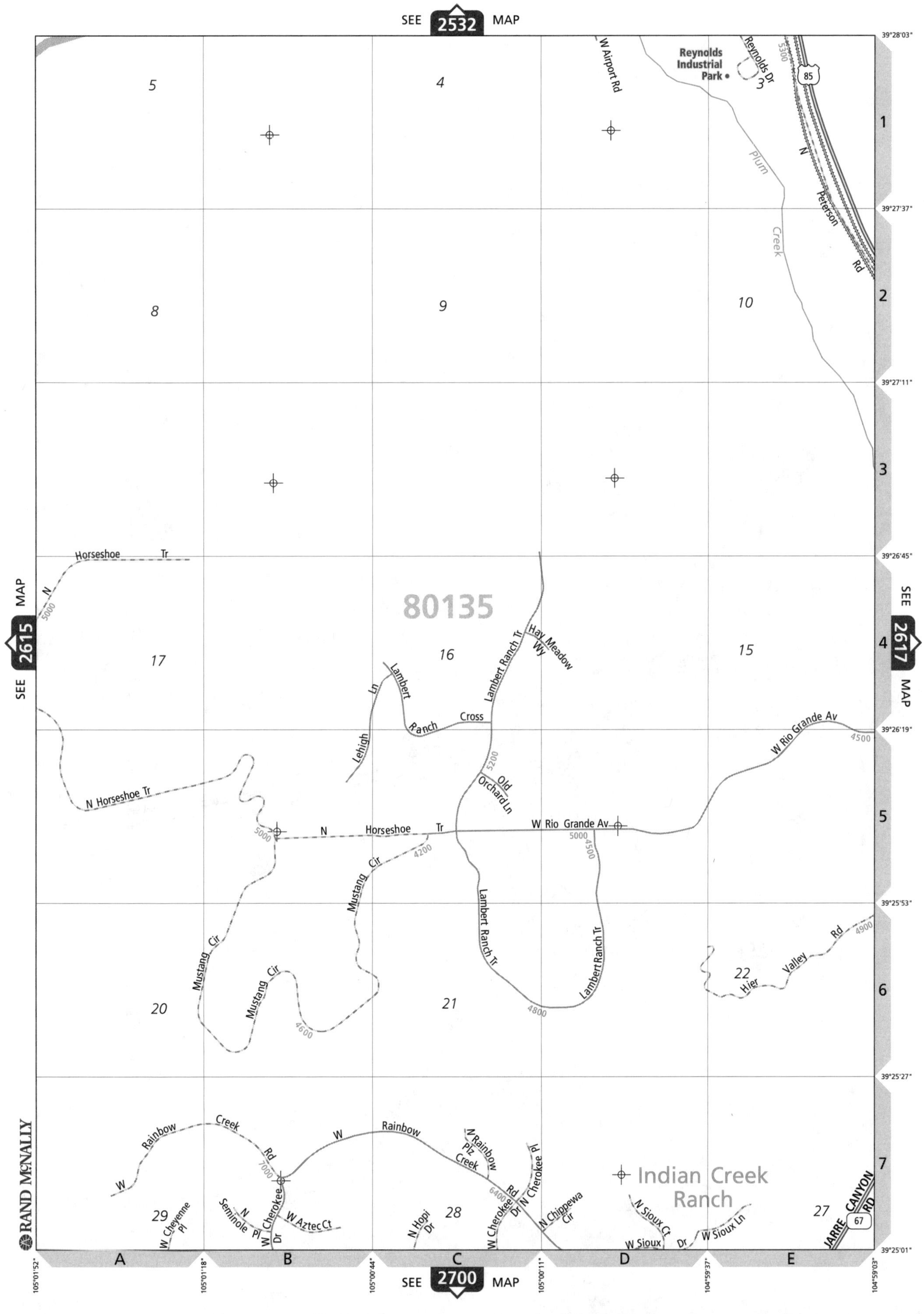

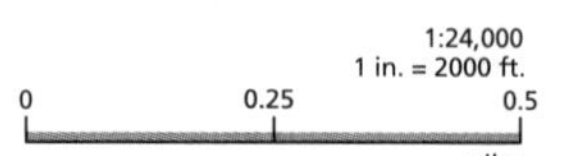

SEE 2533 MAP

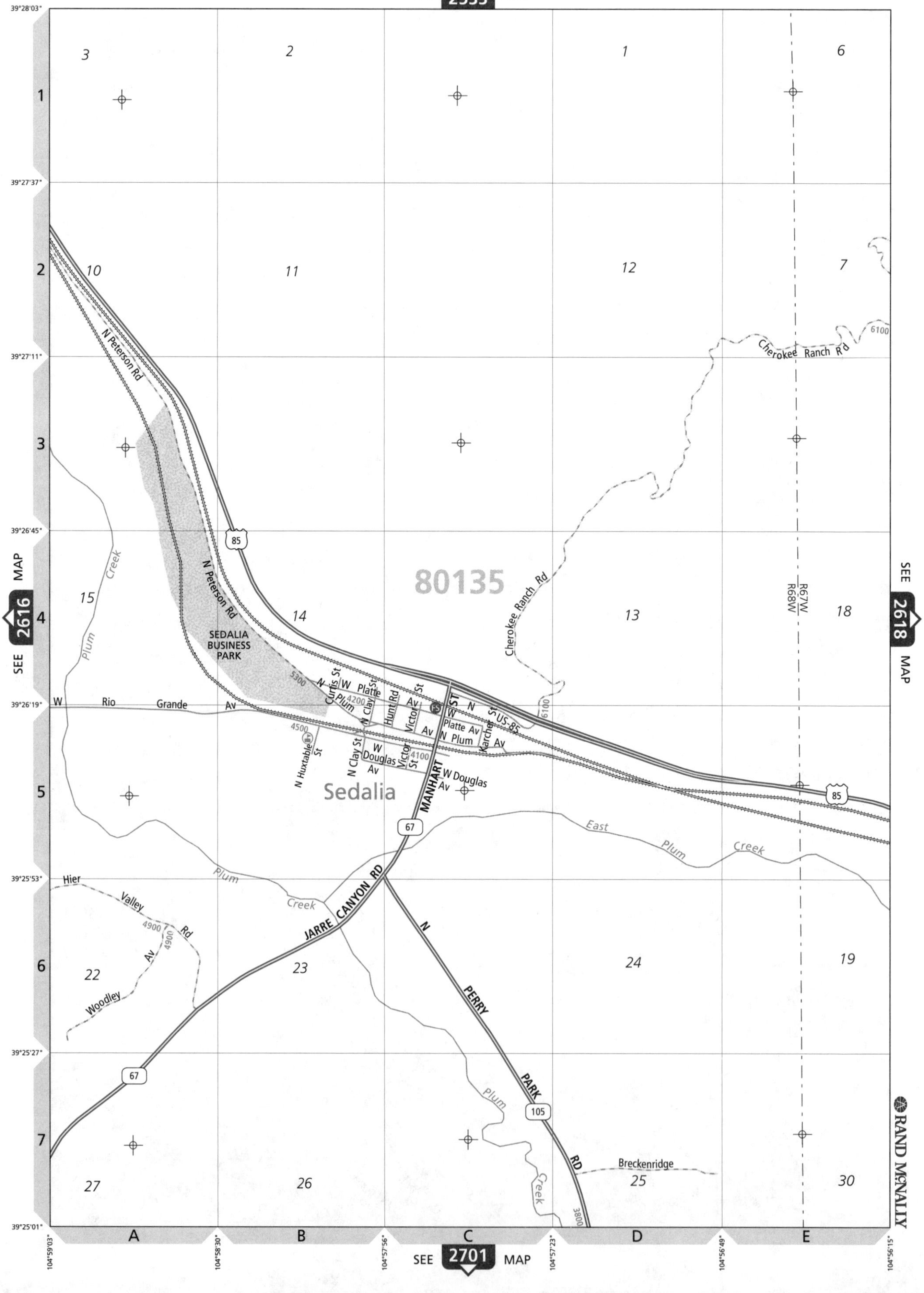

SEE 2616 MAP

SEE 2618 MAP

80135

Sedalia

SEDALIA BUSINESS PARK

N Peterson Rd

W Rio Grande Av

MANHART ST

JARRE CANYON RD

N PERRY PARK RD

Cherokee Ranch Rd

Hier Valley Rd

Woodley Av

Breckenridge

East Plum Creek

Plum Creek

US-85

R67W

R68W

SEE 2701 MAP

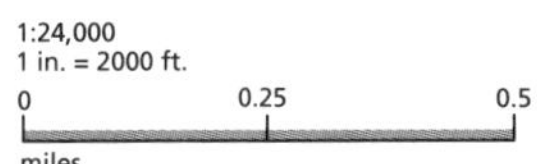

SEE 2534 MAP

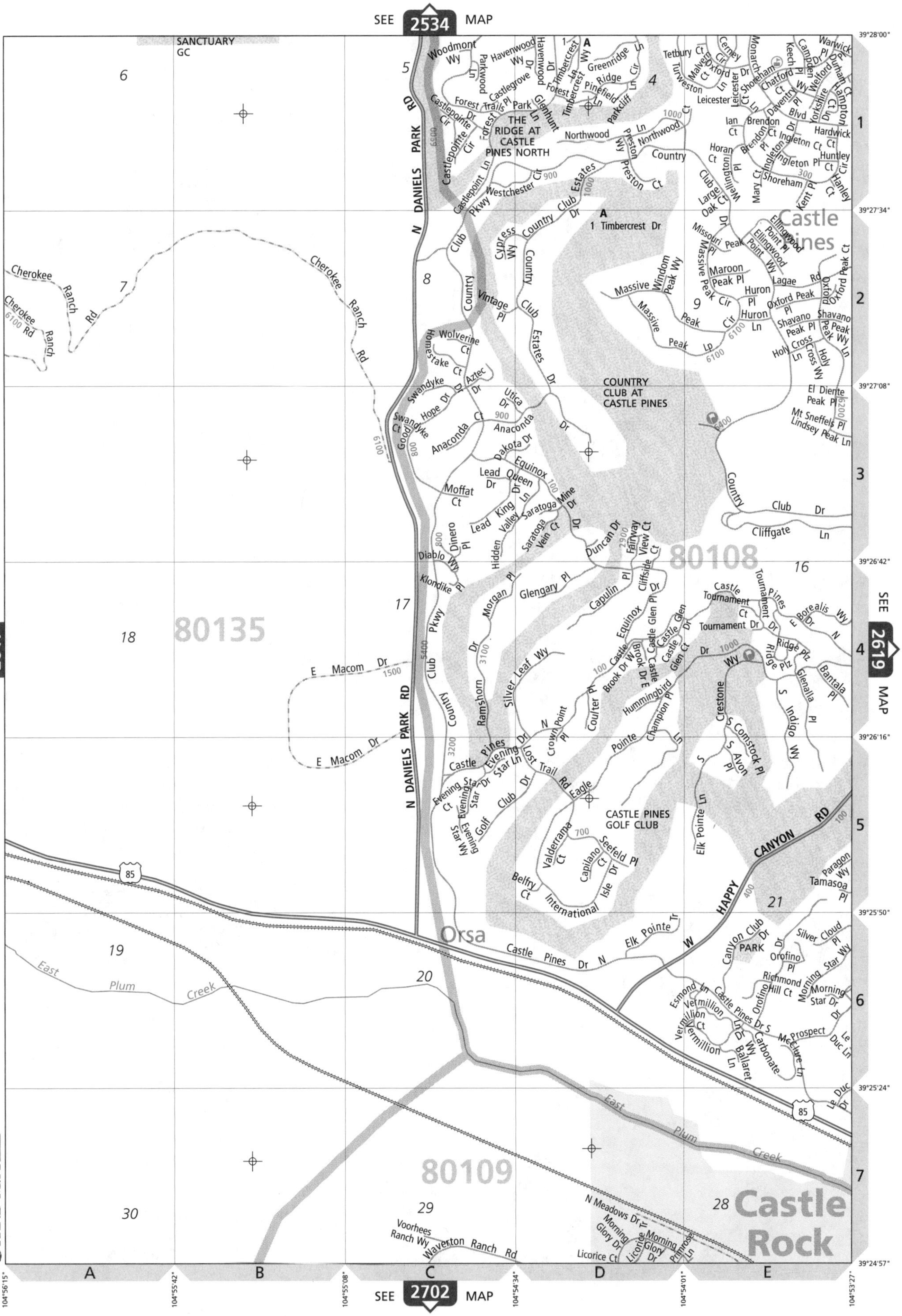

SEE 2617 MAP

SEE 2619 MAP

SEE 2702 MAP

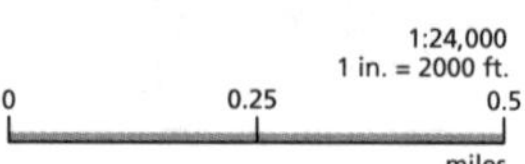

SEE 2535 MAP

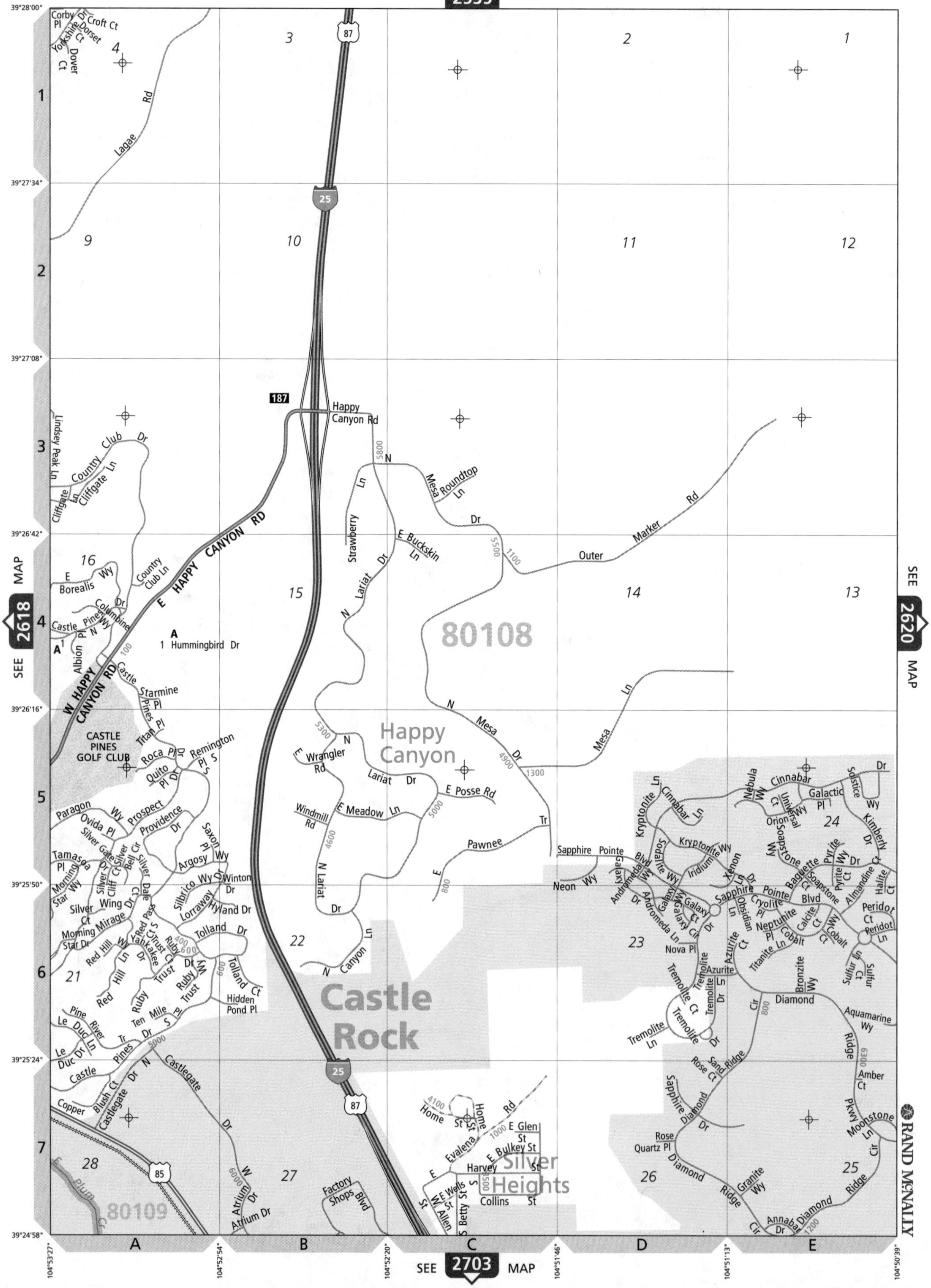

SEE 2618 MAP

SEE 2620 MAP

80108

Happy Canyon

Castle Rock

Silver Heights

CASTLE PINES GOLF CLUB

80109

A 1 Hummingbird Dr

E HAPPY CANYON RD

W HAPPY CANYON RD

Outer Marker Rd

N Mesa Dr

Lagae Rd

A B C D E

1 2 3 4 5 6 7

SEE 2703 MAP

RAND McNALLY

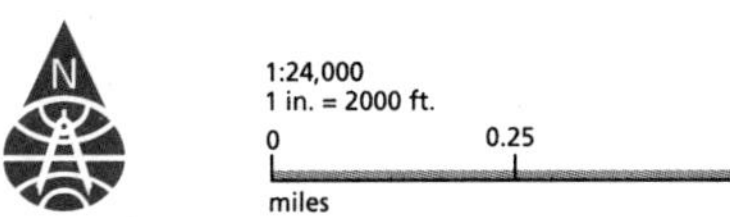

SEE 2536 MAP

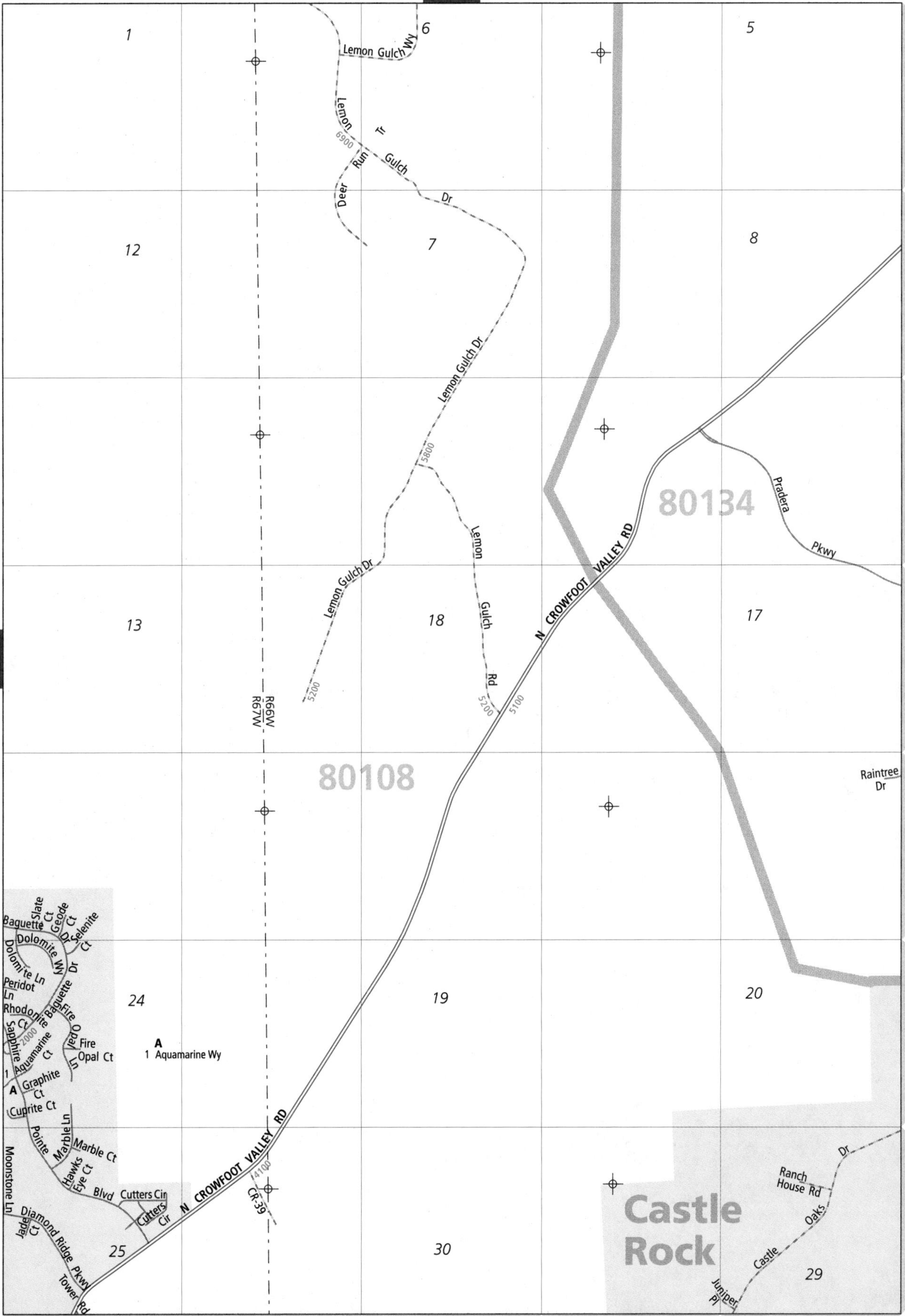

SEE 2619 MAP

SEE 2621 MAP

SEE 2704 MAP

1:24,000
1 in. = 2000 ft.
0 0.25 0.5
miles

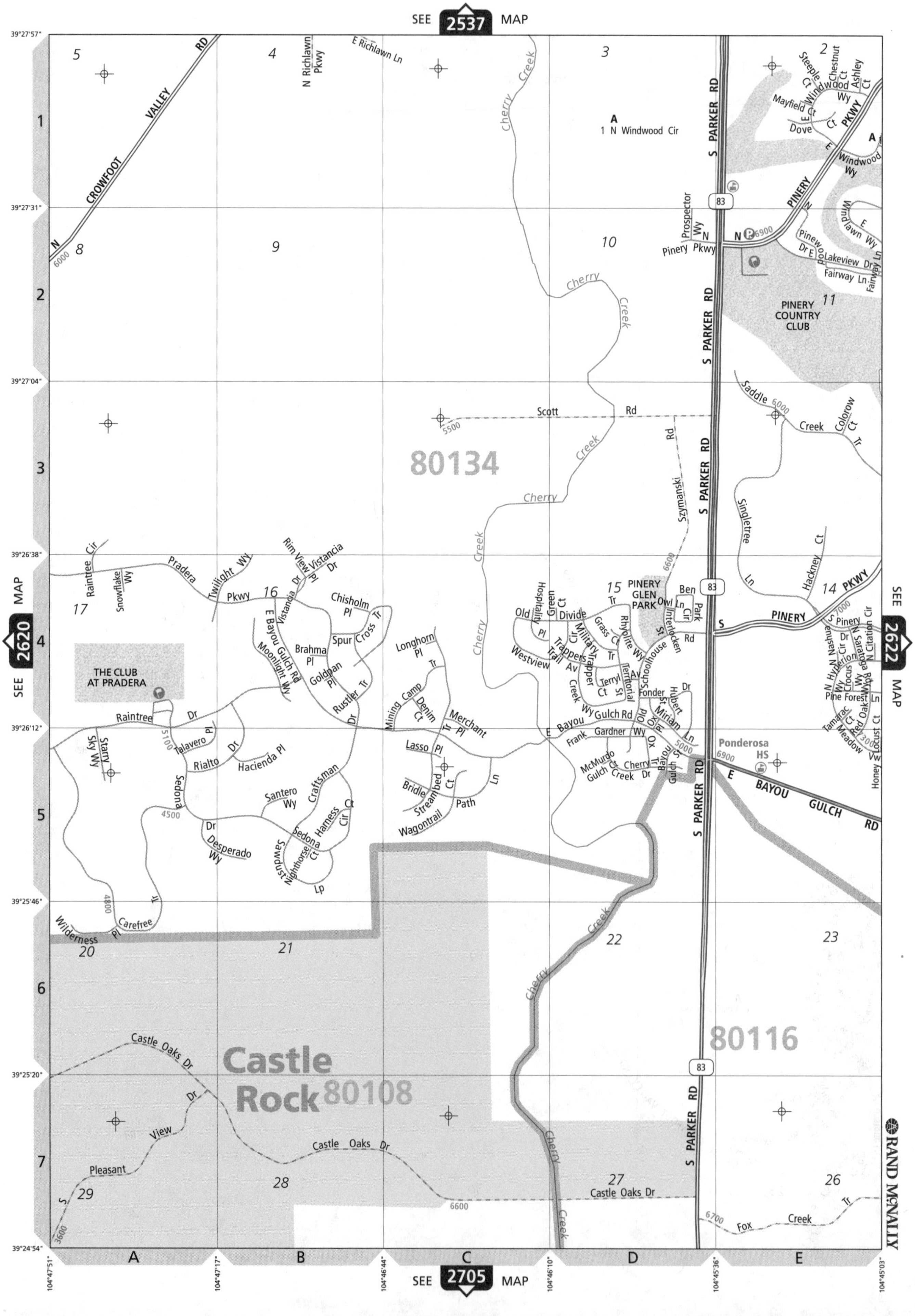

SEE 2537 MAP

SEE 2620 MAP

SEE 2622 MAP

A
1 N Windwood Cir

S PARKER RD
CROWFOOT VALLEY RD
PINERY PKWY
E BAYOU GULCH RD
Cherry Creek
Scott Rd
Szymanski Rd
PINERY COUNTRY CLUB
PINERY GLEN PARK
THE CLUB AT PRADERA
Ponderosa HS
Pradera Pkwy
Raintree Dr
Castle Oaks Dr
Pleasant View Dr
Fox Creek Tr
Saddle Creek Tr
Singletree Ln

80134
80116
Castle Rock 80108

SEE 2705 MAP

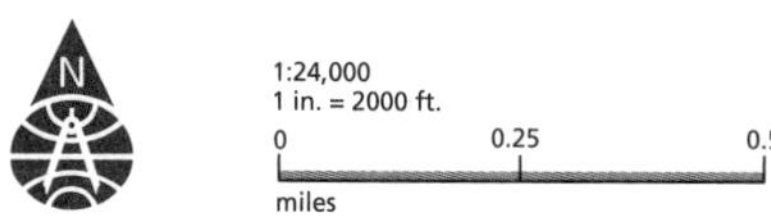

SEE 2538 MAP

N PINERY PKWY
Hillgate Wy
E Windcrest Row
N Windview Cir
N Windpoint Cir
N Windwood Cir
E Windwood Wy
Windlawn Wy
E Windford St
E Windham St
N Windhollow Ct
E Windlawn Wy
Lakeview Dr
N Lakewind Cir
Lakecliff Wy
Fairway Ln
E Windfont Row
N Lakepoint Pl
N Windmont Cir
N Windfield Av
N Windloch Av
N Mountain Manor Ct
N Hillpoint Pl
E Hillview St
N Hillridge Pl
N Hill Ct
N Hillpark Cir
N Ridgeway Cir
Hillcrest Wy
N Hillpark Av
N Hillside Wy
Hillside Cir
Surry Pl
E Carriage Ln
E Carriage Cir
PINERY PARK
The Pinery
N Mountain View Dr
E Green Hollow Ct
N Donner Cir
Pine Hollow Dr
N Hollowview Ct
Lakeview Dr
Piute Row
Pawnee Ct
E Cherokee Rd
E Sunridge Hollow Rd
Arapahoe Ct
N Arapahoe Ct
N Cheyenne Ct
Northwoods Glen Dr
Northstar Ridge Ln
N Mad River Ct
River Mountain Ct
Mad Rd
N Storm Ct
E Thunderbird Cir
Thunderbird Rd
E Thunderbird Ct
Zebulon Cir
N Elbert Pl
Shavano Pl
E Star
N Morning Pl
N Lewis Ct
N Wilder Ct
N Greeley Ct
Powell Rd
N Cantrell Wy
McGill Ct
Beckworth Ct
N Falling Leaf Cir
Ponderosa Rd
E McShane Ct
Riviera Ct
E Derby Wy
Coronado Ct
N Colorado Pl
Belmont Wy
E Villasur Ct
E Elizabeth St
E Huggins Ct
Dorado Ct
E Sadelia Ct
N Villard Ct
A
1 E Ponderosa Ct
Sun Valley Rd
Betts Ranch Rd
Chalet Cir
N Alpine Dr
N Village Rd
PINERY COUNTRY CLUB
BINGHAM LAKE
BINGHAM LAKE PARK
E Lakeshore Ct
Lakeshore Dr
Tempest Ridge Wy
N Lakewood Rd
N Pine View Dr
Hurricane Ct
Lightening Pat Lt
Thunderhill Hts
N Irish
E Captain Meriweather Lewis Dr
E Stetson Rd
N Stetson Ct
Murphy Dr
William Clark Rd
Selly Rd
Angie Ct
Ponderosa Dr
Victoria Ln
N Cantrell Ct
N Quinlin Ct
N Thunderhill Rd
Brush Ct
Autumn Prairie Ct
Crooked Oak Ct
Wild Berry Ct
Lake Fox Run Ct
Silver Bluff Ct
Saddle Creek Tr
S PINERY PKWY
Gooseberry Ct
Nuthatch Rd
Nuthatch Cir
Nuthatch Wy
Kim Ct
S PINERY PKWY
E DEMOCRAT RD
Potentilla Ct
Cistena Wy
Running Fox Wy
Soapweed Cir
Golden Currant Wy
Towhee Rd
Jay Rd
Fox Sparrow Rd
Gopher Ct
Owl Roost Ct
Sage Thrasher Rd
Chickadee Ct
Songbird Wy
Rambling Oak Dr
Forest View Rd
Scenic Pine Dr
Sunshine Meadow Dr
Shade Tree Ln
Serene View Rd
Horned Owl Wy
Warbler Ct
Barn Swallow Wy
Windhaven Dr
Porcupine Pointe
Cistena Wy
Pinyon
N Hillary Cir
N Blandford Cir
S Pinery Dr
N Hyperion Wy
White Ash Pl
Pine Forest Ln
Aster Ct
Bur Oak Pl
Meadow Vw
Side Saddle Ln
Sparrow Rd
Fox
BAYOU GULCH REGIONAL PARK
80134
R66W
R65W
N Bayou Hills Rd
Desert Paint Brush Ct
Moonshine Ridge Tr
N Bayou Hills Rd
E Wild Crocus Cir
E Sand Lily Ln
Bayou Ridge Tr
E Bayou Hills Ln
N Bayou Hills Rd
E BAYOU GULCH RD
80116
Fox Creek Tr
1
2
6
7
11
12
13
14
18
19
23
24
25
26
30
A
B
C
D
E
1
2
3
4
5
6
7
39°27'53"
39°27'27"
39°27'01"
39°26'35"
39°26'09"
39°25'42"
39°25'16"
39°24'50"
104°45'03"
104°44'29"
104°43'56"
104°43'22"
104°42'48"
104°42'15"

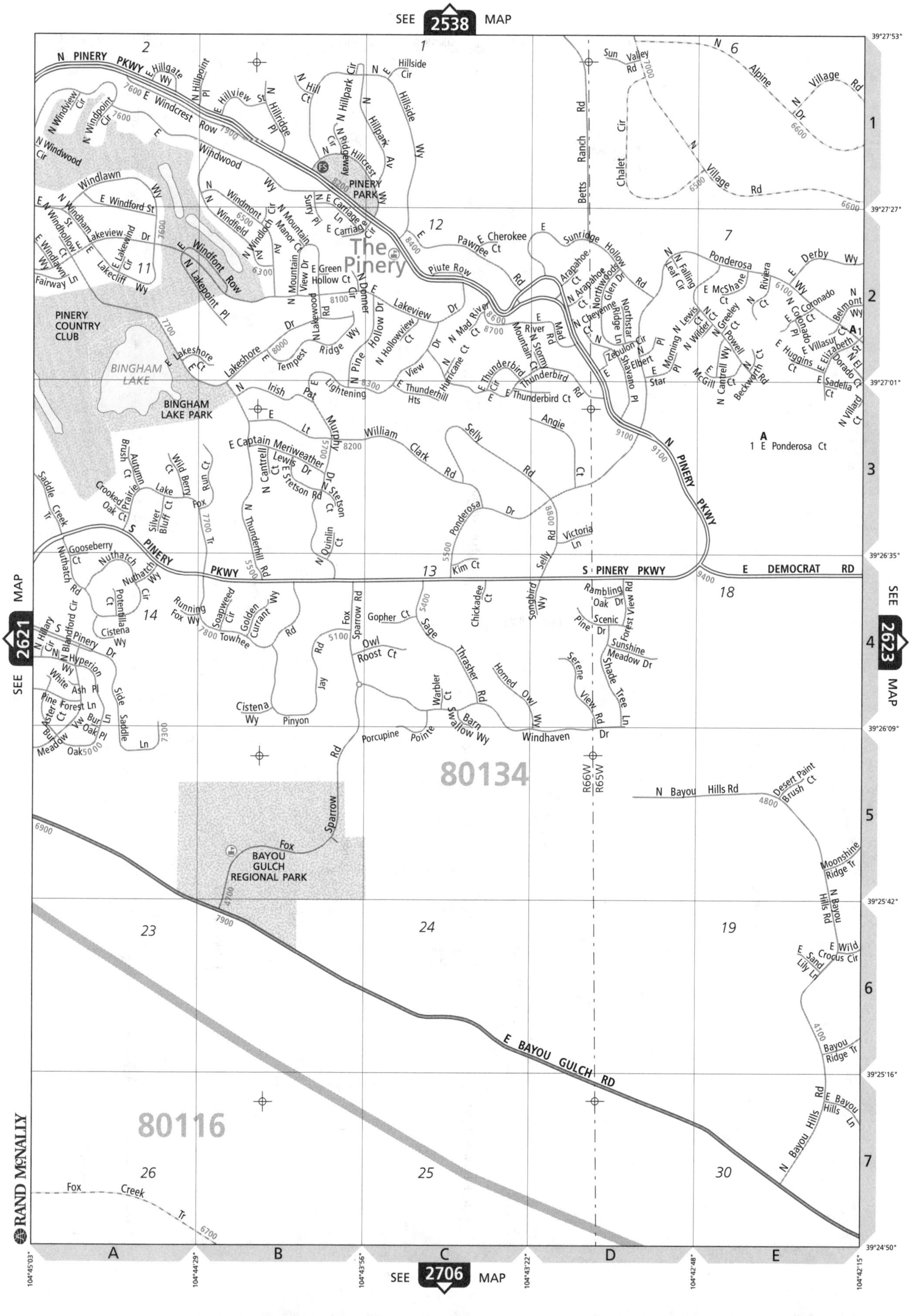

SEE 2621 MAP

SEE 2623 MAP

SEE 2706 MAP

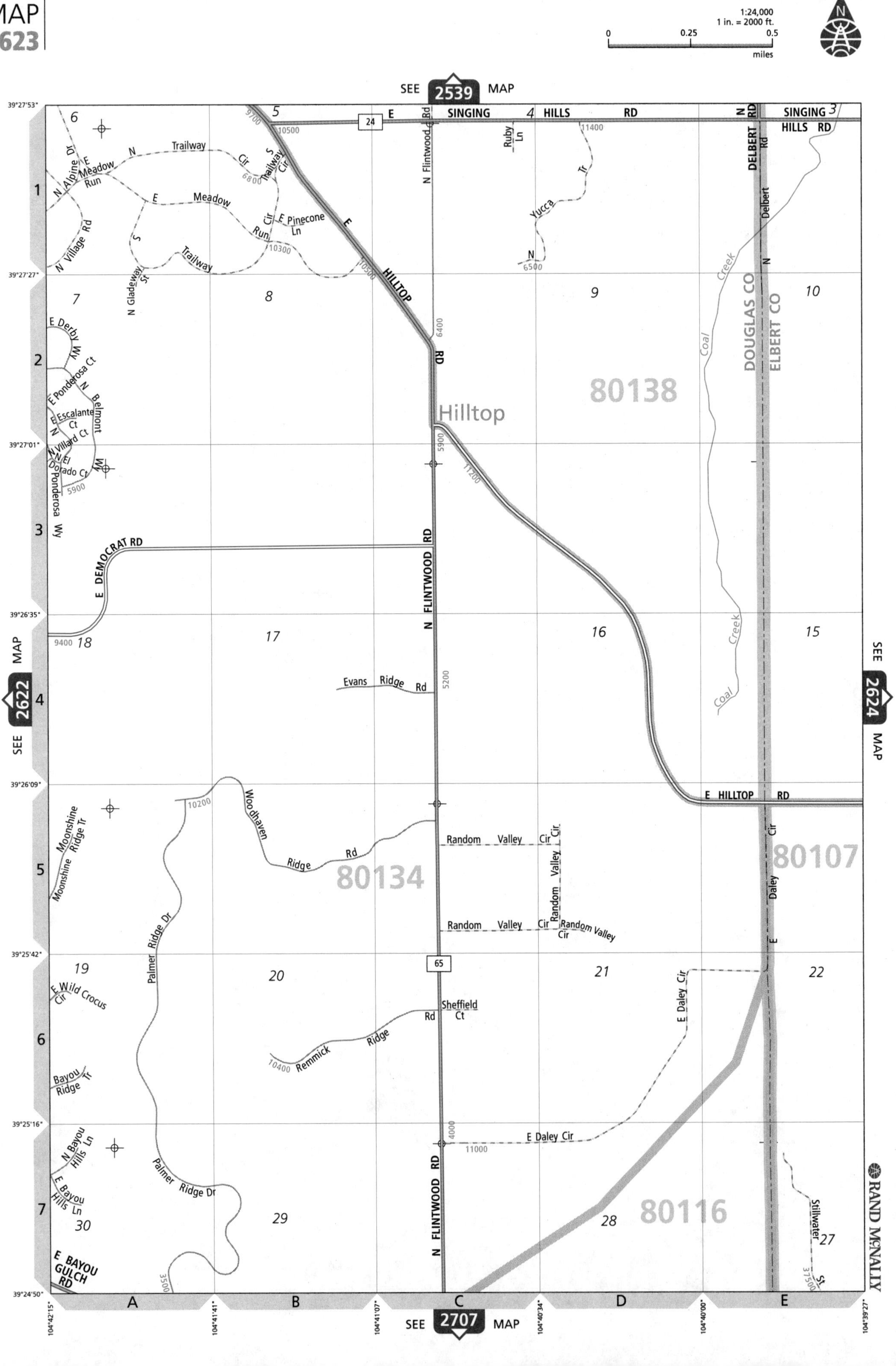

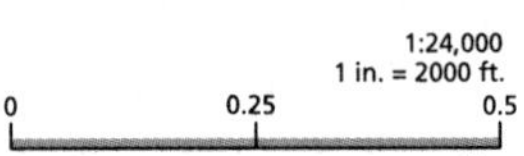

SEE 2539 MAP

E SINGING HILLS RD
SINGING HILLS RD
24
E HILLTOP RD
N FLINTWOOD RD
N DELBERT RD
E DEMOCRAT RD
E HILLTOP RD
Hilltop
80138
80134
80107
80116
DOUGLAS CO
ELBERT CO
65
N Alpine Dr
E Meadow Run
N Trailway Cir
S Trailway Cir
E Meadow Run Cir
E Pinecone Ln
S Trailway
N Village Rd
N Gladeway St
Ruby Ln
Yucca Tr
Coal Creek
E Derby Wy
N Ponderosa Ct
E Ponderosa Wy
N Belmont Wy
E Escalante Ct
N Villard Ct
N El Dorado Ct
N Ponderosa Wy
Evans Ridge Rd
Woodhaven Ridge Rd
Moonshine Ridge Tr
Random Valley Cir
Random Valley Cir
Random Valley Cir
Palmer Ridge Dr
E Wild Crocus Cir
Sheffield Ct
Remmick Ridge Rd
E Daley Cir
E Daley Cir
Bayou Ridge Tr
N Bayou Hills Ln
E Bayou Hills Ln
E BAYOU GULCH RD
Stillwater St

SEE 2622 MAP

SEE 2624 MAP

SEE 2707 MAP

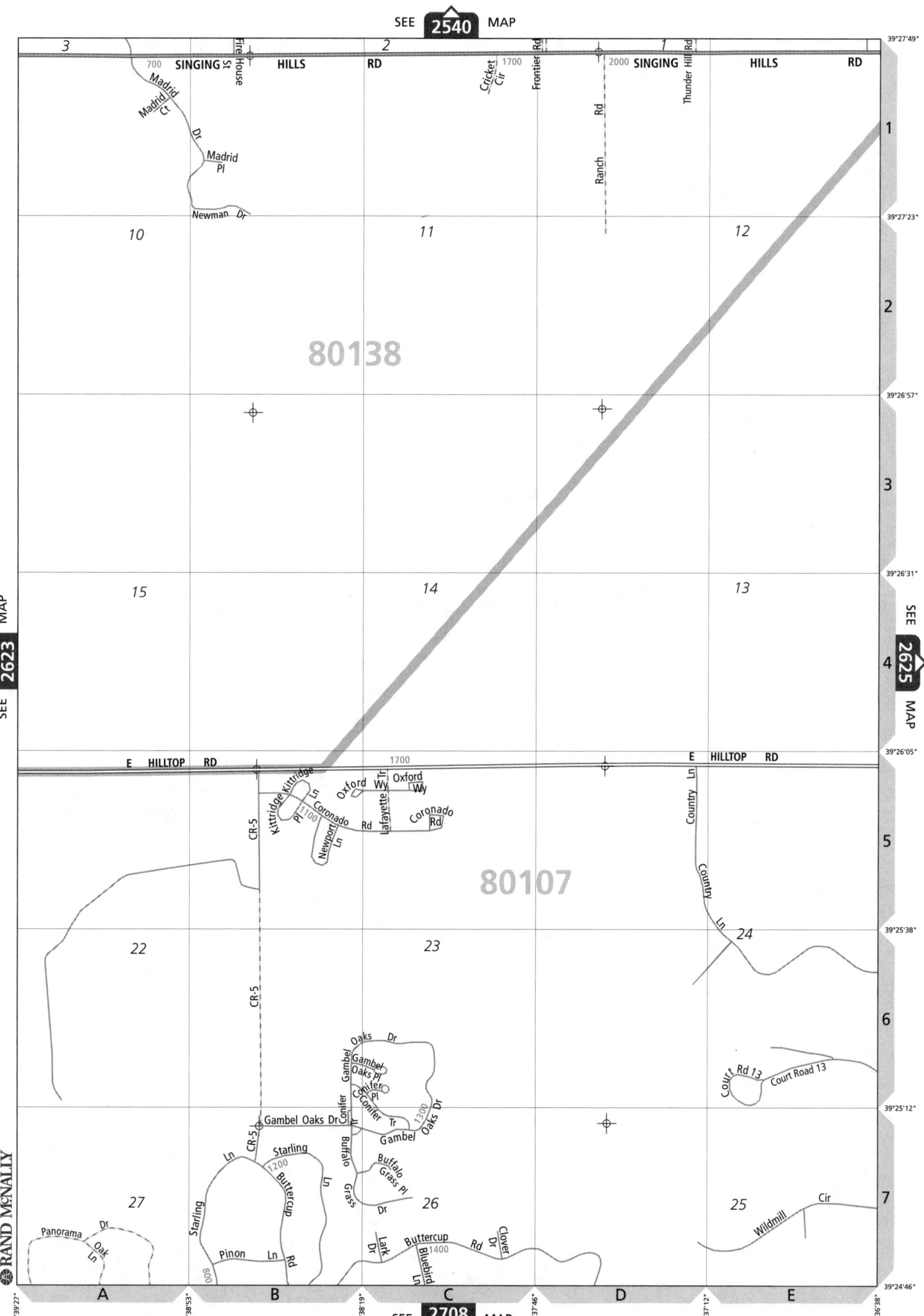

1:24,000
1 in. = 2000 ft.
0
0.25
0.5
miles
SEE 2540 MAP
SEE 2623 MAP
SEE 2625 MAP
SEE 2708 MAP
SINGING HILLS RD
Fire House St
Cricket Cir
Frontier Rd
Ranch Rd
Thunder Hill Rd
Madrid Dr
Madrid Ct
Madrid Pl
Newman Dr
80138
80107
E HILLTOP RD
CR-5
Kittridge Pl
Kittridge Ln
Coronado Rd
Newport Ln
Oxford Wy
Lafayette Tr
Country Ln
Gambel Oaks Dr
Gambel Oaks Pl
Conifer Pl
Conifer Tr
Buffalo Grass Dr
Buffalo Grass Pl
Starling Ln
Buttercup Ln
Buttercup Rd
Pinon Ln
Panorama Dr
Oak Ln
Lark Dr
Bluebird Ln
Clover Dr
Court Rd 13
Court Road 13
Wildmill Cir
RAND McNALLY
A
B
C
D
E
1
2
3
4
5
6
7

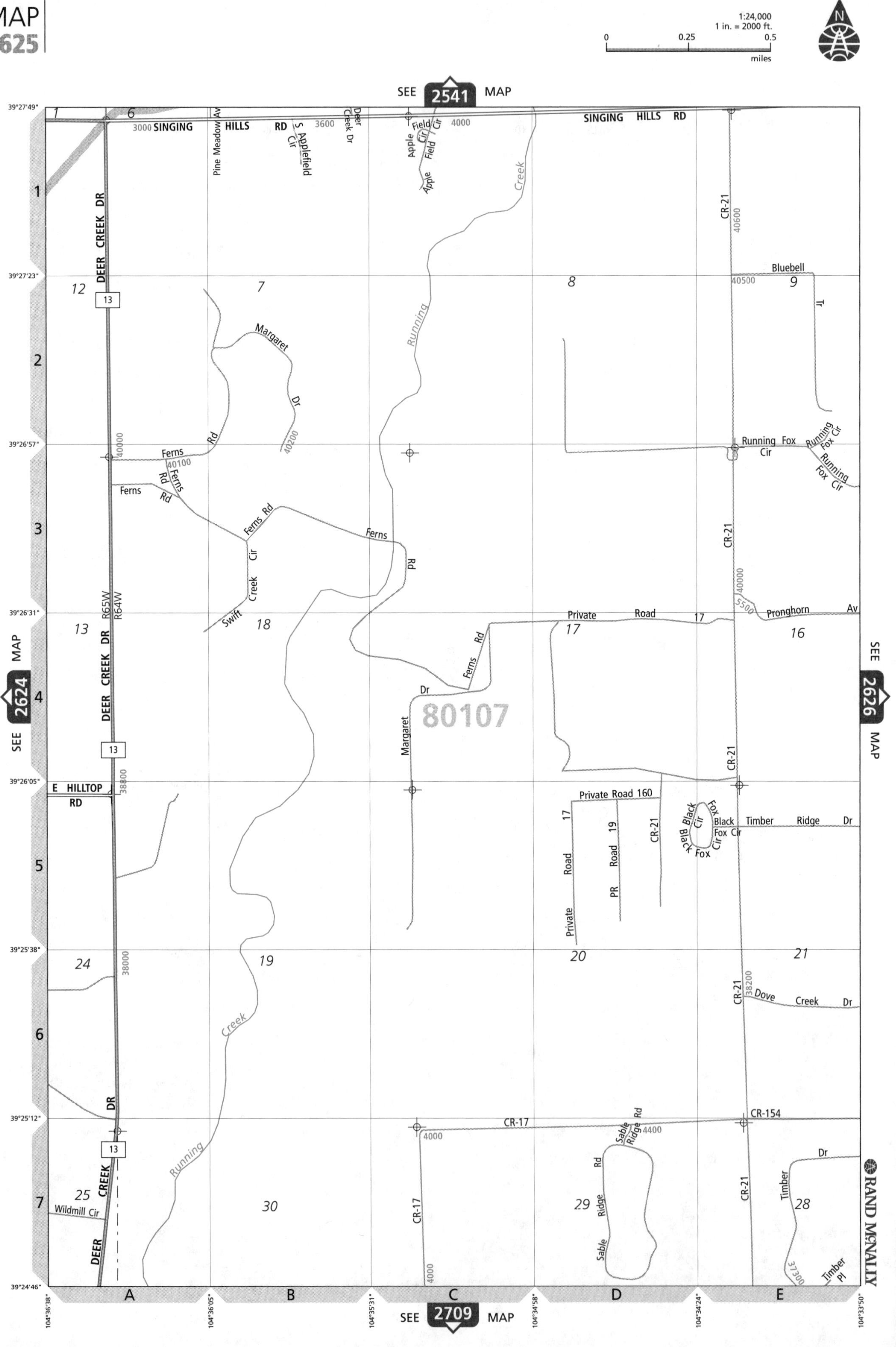

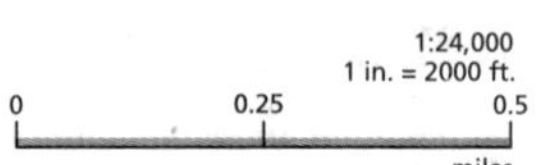

SEE 2541 MAP

SINGING HILLS RD
DEER CREEK DR
Pine Meadow Av
S Applefield Cir
Deer Creek Dr
Apple Field Cir
Creek
Running
CR-21
Bluebell Tr
Margaret Dr
Ferns Rd
Running Fox Cir
Swift Creek Cir
Private Road 17
Pronghorn Av
Margaret Dr
80107
E HILLTOP RD
Private Road 160
Private Road 17
PR Road 19
Black Fox Cir
Timber Ridge Dr
Dove Creek Dr
CR-17
CR-154
Sable Ridge Rd
Timber Dr
Timber Pl
Wildmill Cir
R65W
R64W

SEE 2624 MAP

SEE 2626 MAP

SEE 2709 MAP

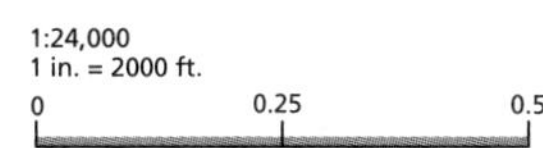

SEE 2542 MAP

Valley View Ct
Rendezvous Cir
Tapadero Cir
CR-29
9
10
11
CR-162
40000
7000
Running Fox Cir
Fox Trot Cir
Long
Pronghorn Av
16
15
14
Elk Cir
Long Elk Cir
80107
39000
CR-158
Timber Ridge Dr
21
22
23
Friendly Rd
Dove Creek Dr
Fawn Meadows Tr
CR-154
5700
5900
Timber Dr
Pheasant Run Rd
28
27
26

1 2 3 4 5 6 7

A B C D E

39°27'45" 39°27'19" 39°26'53" 39°26'26" 39°26'00" 39°25'34" 39°25'08" 39°24'42"

104°33'50" 104°33'17" 104°32'43" 104°32'09" 104°31'36" 104°31'02"

SEE 2625 MAP

SEE B MAP

SEE 2710 MAP

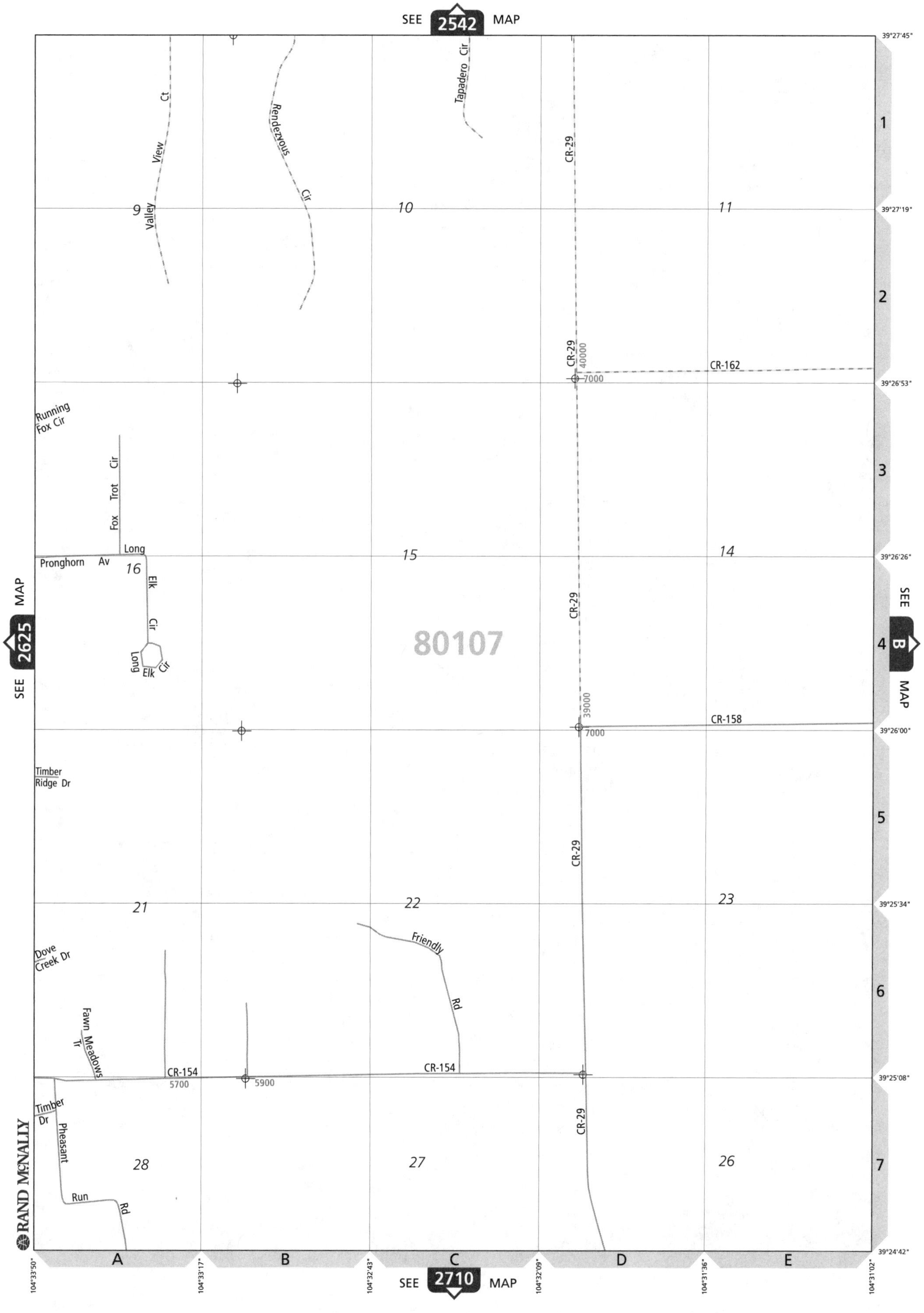

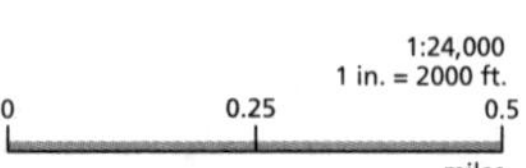

SEE 2605 MAP

SEE B MAP

SEE 2690 MAP

SEE B MAP

80456

PIKE NATIONAL FOREST

Platte Canyon HS

285

Jess-Mar Dr

CR-64

North Rd

Mooredale Rd

Fork South Platte River

Old Stage Coach Rd

CR-64

1500

Old Stage Coach Rd

Glenn Isle Rd

Old Stage Coach Rd

CR-64

CR-64B

CR-64

CR-64

Brookside Tr

Payne Gulch Rd

Payne Gulch Rd

T7S
T8S

22 23 24

27 26 25

34 35 36

3 2 1

10 11 12

1 2 3 4 5 6 7

A B C D E

39°25'15" 39°24'49" 39°24'23" 39°23'57" 39°23'31" 39°23'04" 39°22'38" 39°22'12"

105°32'43" 105°32'09" 105°31'35" 105°31'02" 105°30'28" 105°29'55"

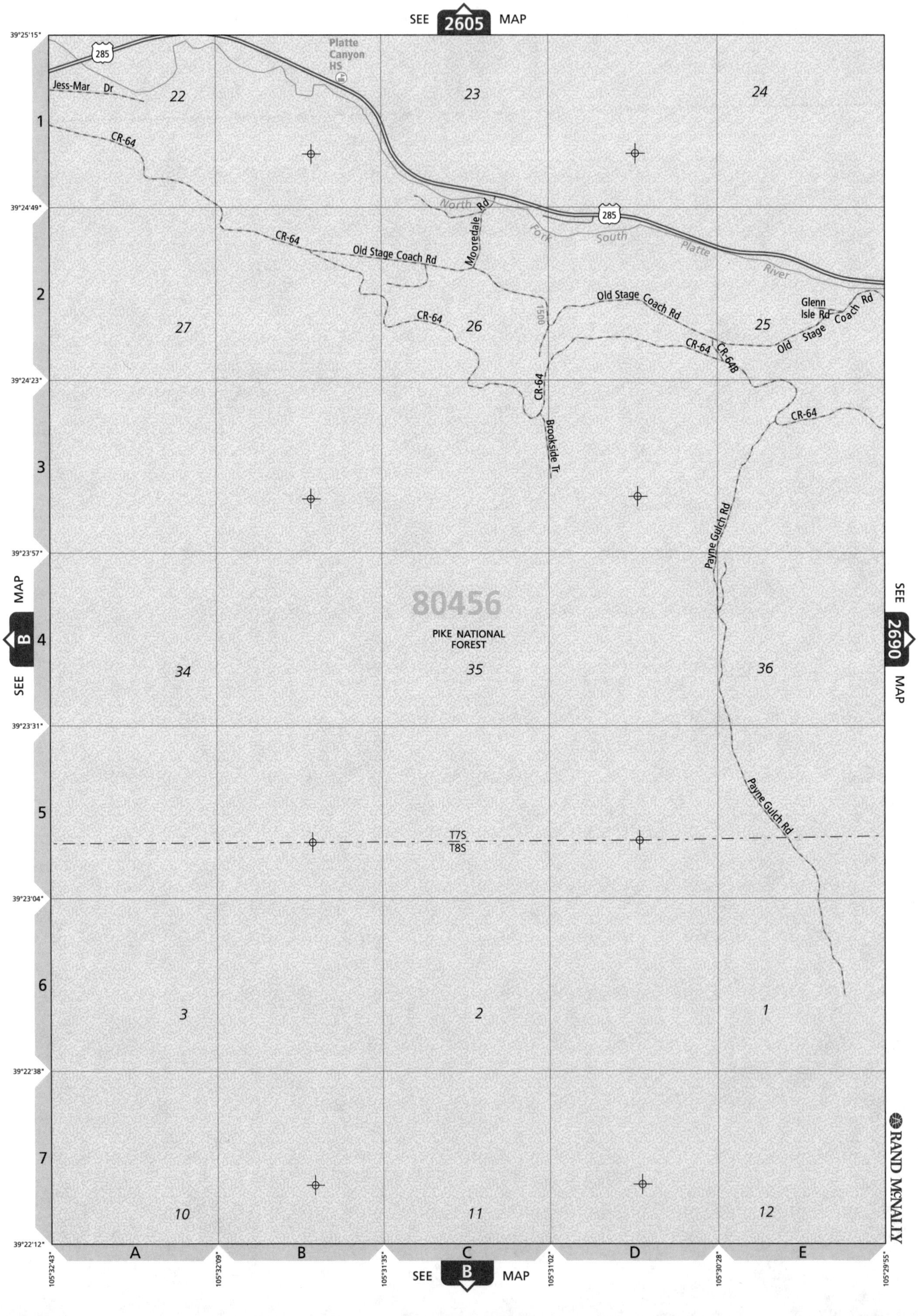

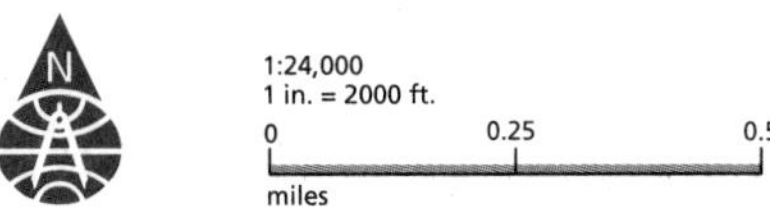

SEE 2606 MAP

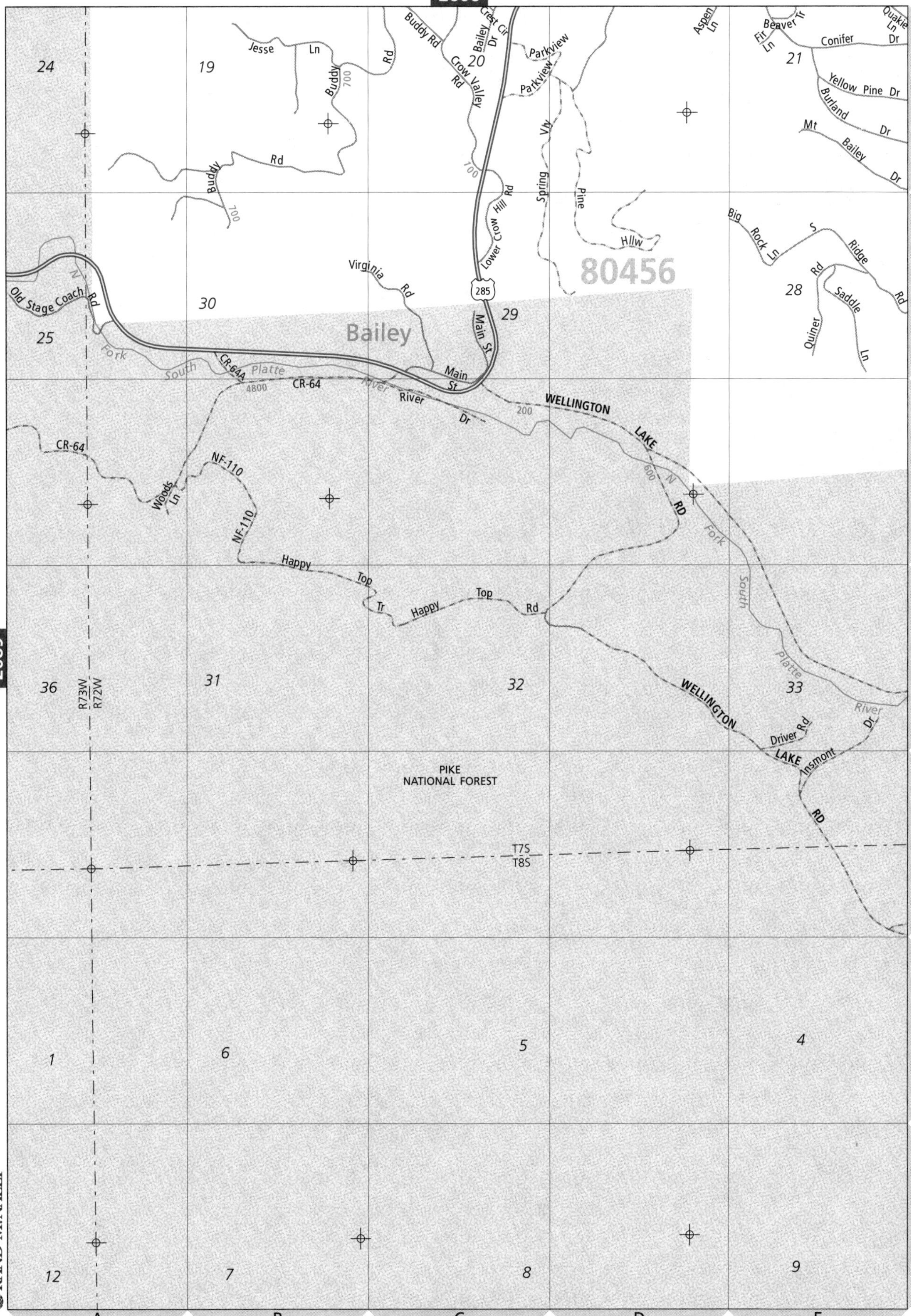

SEE 2689 MAP

SEE 2691 MAP

SEE B MAP

1:24,000
1 in. = 2000 ft.
0
0.25
0.5
miles
N
SEE 2607 MAP
SEE 2690 MAP
SEE 2692 MAP
SEE B MAP
39°25'13"
39°24'47"
39°24'21"
39°23'55"
39°23'29"
39°23'03"
39°22'37"
39°22'11"
105°27'06"
105°26'33"
105°25'59"
105°25'26"
105°24'52"
105°24'18"
A
B
C
D
E
1
2
3
4
5
6
7
Quakie Ln
Conifer Dr
Swift Rd
Hummingbird Ct
Bluebird Dr
Camprobber Ct
Heron Ct
Jaybird Ln
Juniper Ln
Bob Cat Tr
CR-72
Mockingbird Dr
Chickadee Tr
Chickadee Ln
Mockingbird
Raven Dr
Magpie Ln
Teal Ln
Zip Ln
Holmes Gulch Rd
1 Hi Meadow Dr
Yellow Pine Dr
Burland Dr
Bluebird Ln
Grouse Ln
Lark Ln
Mt Bailey Dr
S Columbine Dr
Cedar Dr
Ridge Rd
S Ridge Rd
Raven Tr
Turkey Ln
Lair Ln
Mockingbird
Eagle
Robin Ln
Dr
Burland Dr
Auk Ln
Ptarmigan Tr
80456
21
22
23
24
25
26
27
28
33
34
35
36
4
3
2
1
9
10
11
12
North Fork South Platte River
T7S
T8S
PIKE NATIONAL FOREST
WELLINGTON LAKE RD
CR-837
CR-70
RAND McNALLY

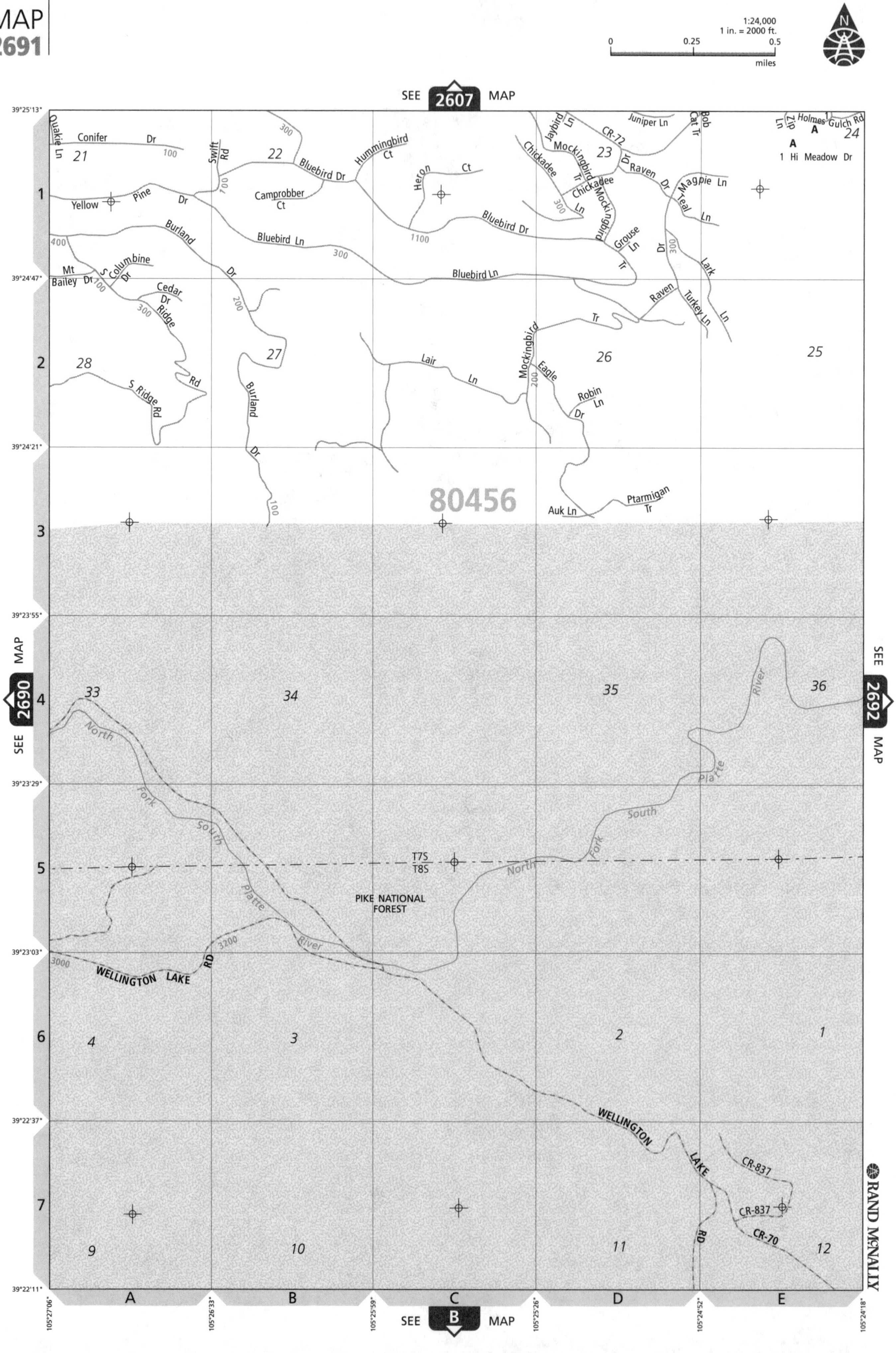

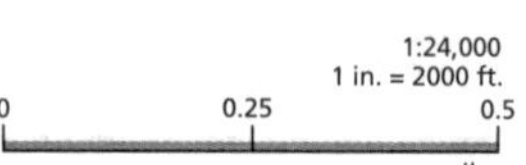

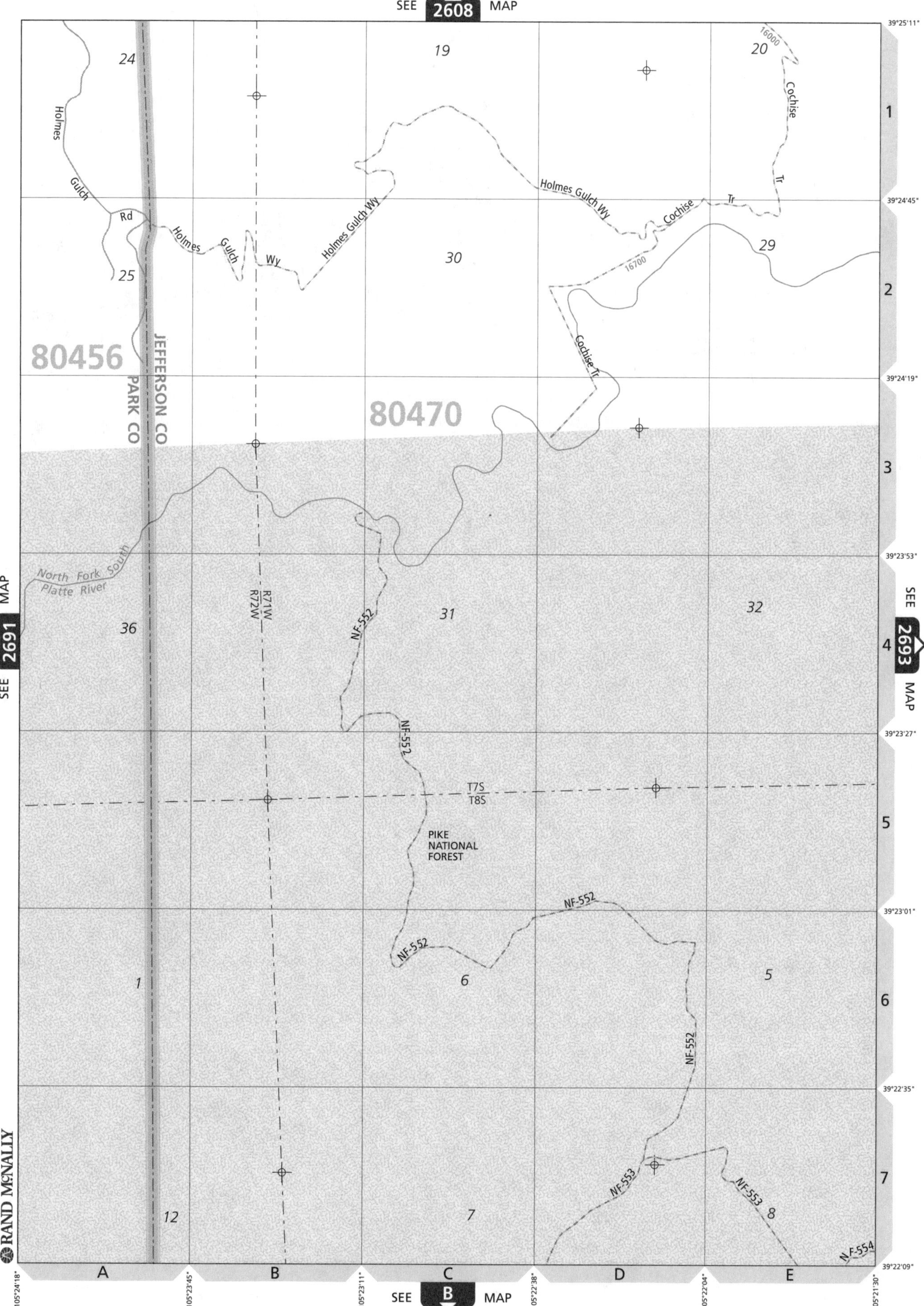
1:24,000
1 in. = 2000 ft.
0
0.25
0.5
miles
SEE 2608 MAP
SEE 2691 MAP
SEE 2693 MAP
SEE B MAP
Holmes Gulch Rd
Holmes Gulch Wy
Holmes Gulch Wy
Cochise Tr
Cochise Tr
16000
16700
80456
80470
JEFFERSON CO
PARK CO
North Fork South Platte River
R71W
R72W
NF-552
NF-553
NF-554
T7S
T8S
PIKE
NATIONAL
FOREST
24
25
36
1
12
19
30
31
6
7
20
29
32
5
8
A
B
C
D
E
1
2
3
4
5
6
7
39°25'11"
39°24'45"
39°24'19"
39°23'53"
39°23'27"
39°23'01"
39°22'35"
39°22'09"
105°24'18"
105°23'45"
105°23'11"
105°22'38"
105°22'04"
105°21'30"
RAND McNALLY

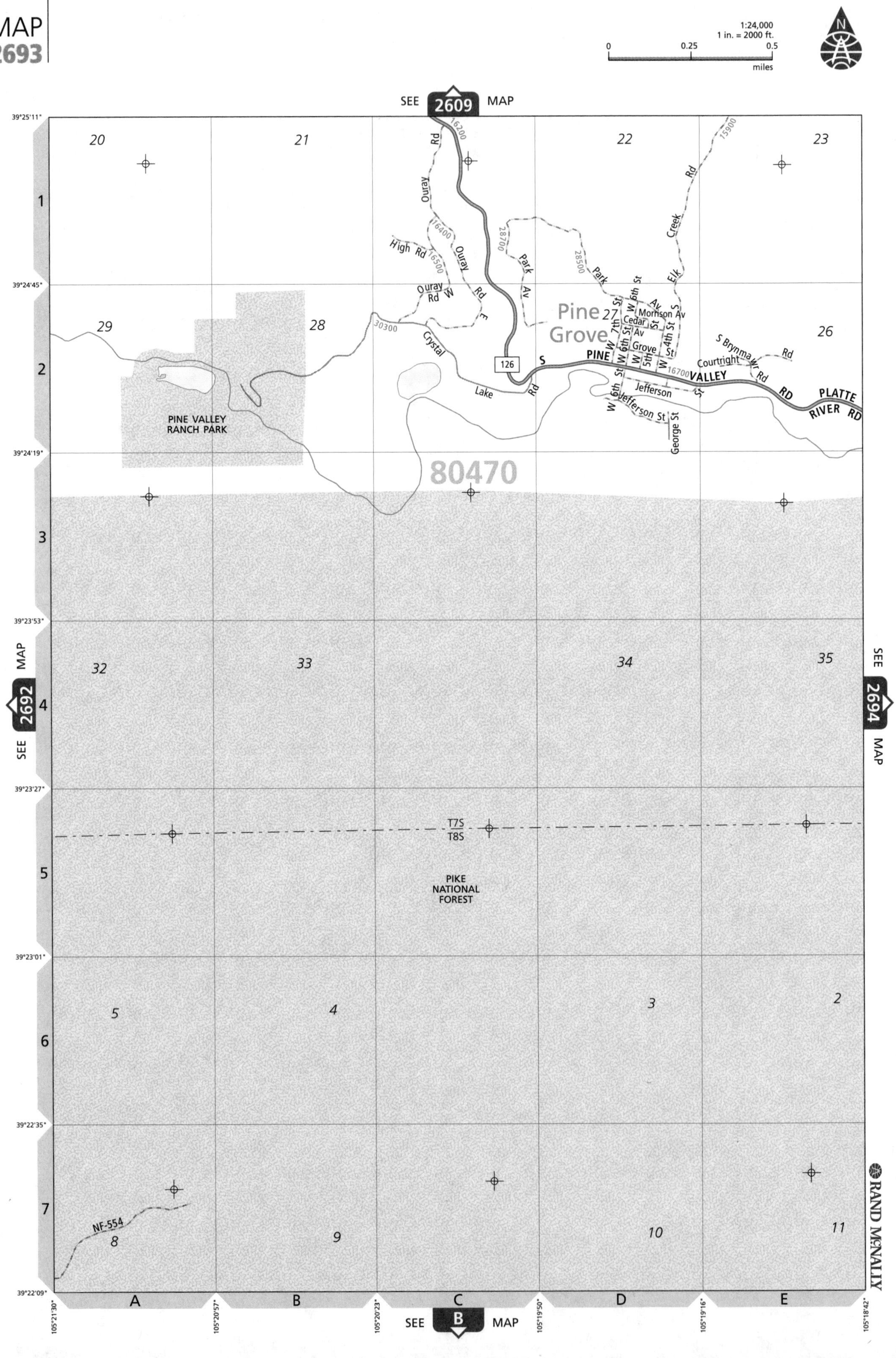

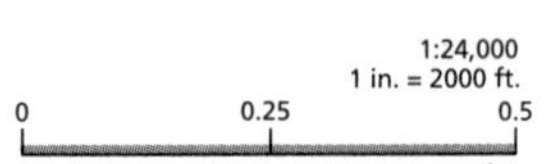

SEE 2609 MAP

20 21 22 23
Ouray Rd
High Rd
Ouray Rd W
Ouray Rd E
Park Av
Park
Creek Rd
Elk
Pine Grove
29 28 27 26
Crystal Lake Rd
126
S PINE VALLEY RD
PLATTE RIVER RD
Morrison Av
Cedar Av
Grove St
Courtright Rd
S Brynmawr Rd
Jefferson St
Jefferson St
George St
PINE VALLEY RANCH PARK
80470
32 33 34 35
T7S
T8S
PIKE NATIONAL FOREST
5 4 3 2
NF-554
8 9 10 11

SEE 2692 MAP

SEE 2694 MAP

SEE B MAP

1:24,000
1 in. = 2000 ft.
0 0.25 0.5
miles

SEE 2610 MAP

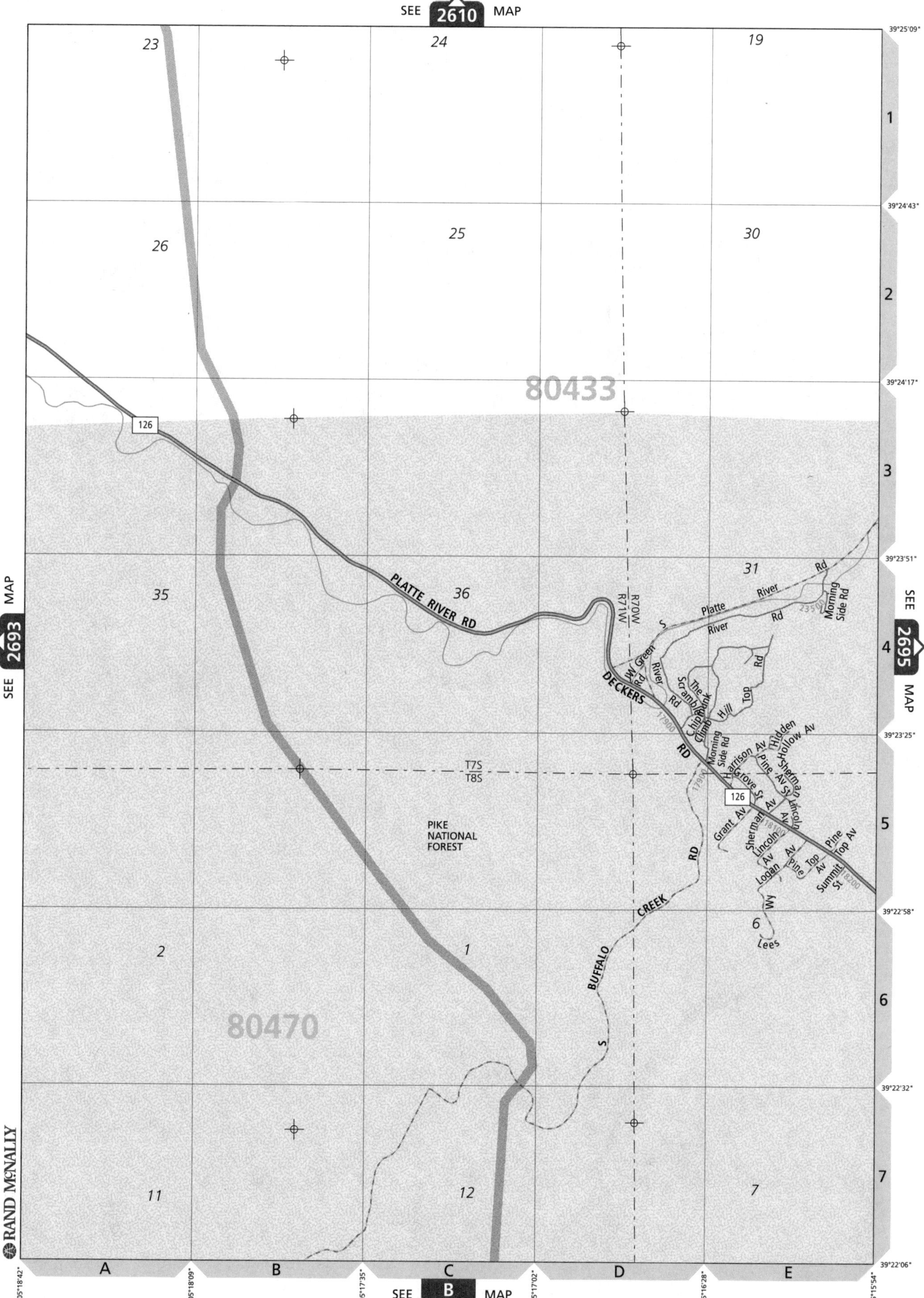

SEE 2693 MAP

SEE 2695 MAP

SEE B MAP

1:24,000
1 in. = 2000 ft.
0
0.25
0.5
miles
N
SEE 2611 MAP
SEE 2694 MAP
SEE 2696 MAP
SEE B MAP
39°25'09"
39°24'43"
39°24'17"
39°23'51"
39°23'25"
39°22'58"
39°22'32"
39°22'06"
105°15'54"
105°15'21"
105°14'47"
105°14'14"
105°13'40"
105°13'06"
1
2
3
4
5
6
7
A
B
C
D
E
19
20
21
22
30
29
28
27
34
33
31
32
6
5
4
3
7
8
9
10
S Platte River Rd
S Platte River Rd
S Platte River Rd
19600
NF-538
NF-538
NF-538
NF-538
NF-538
NF-538
80433
PIKE NATIONAL
FOREST
T7S
T8S
18200
DECKERS
RD
126
RAND McNALLY

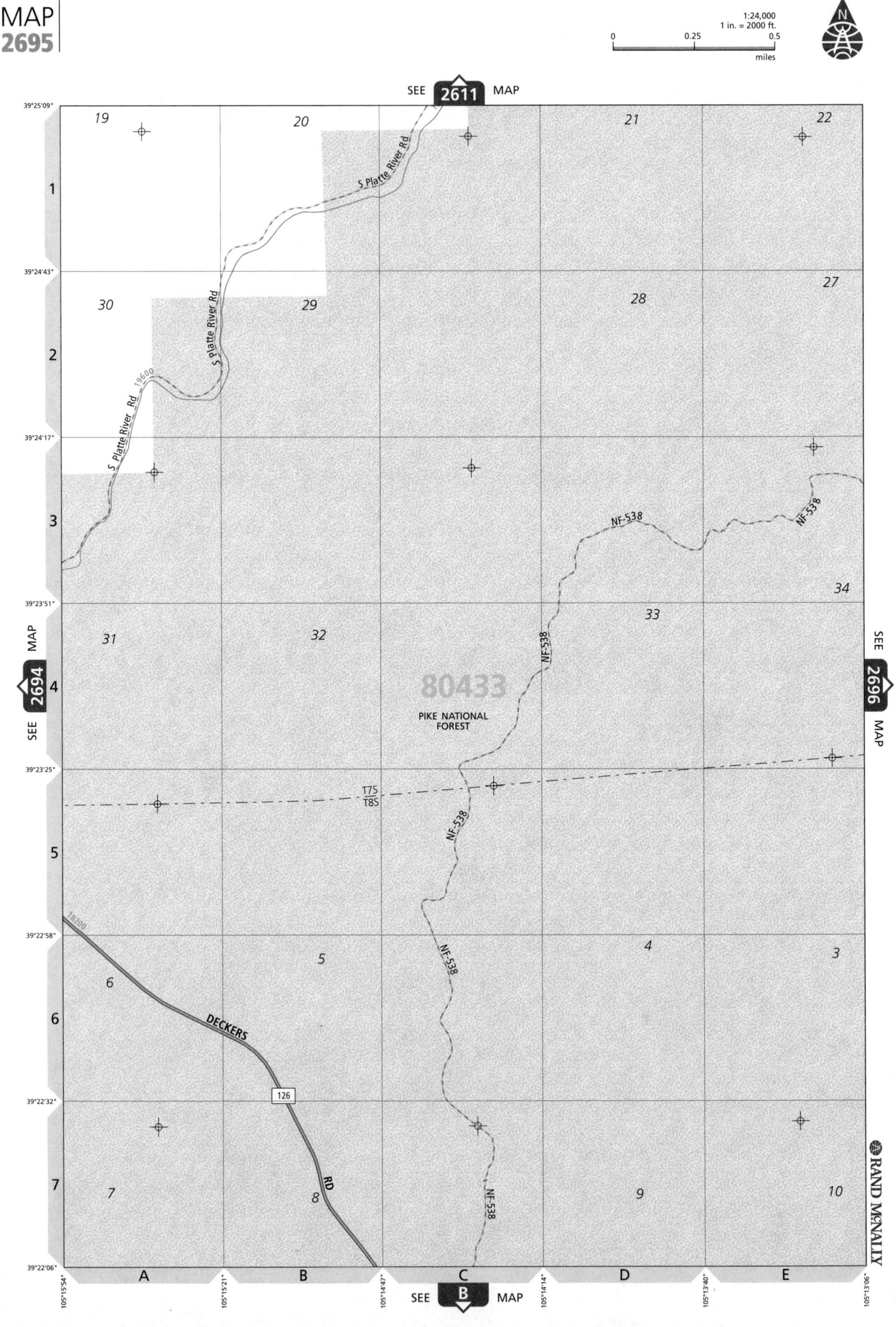

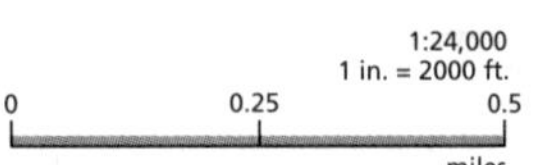

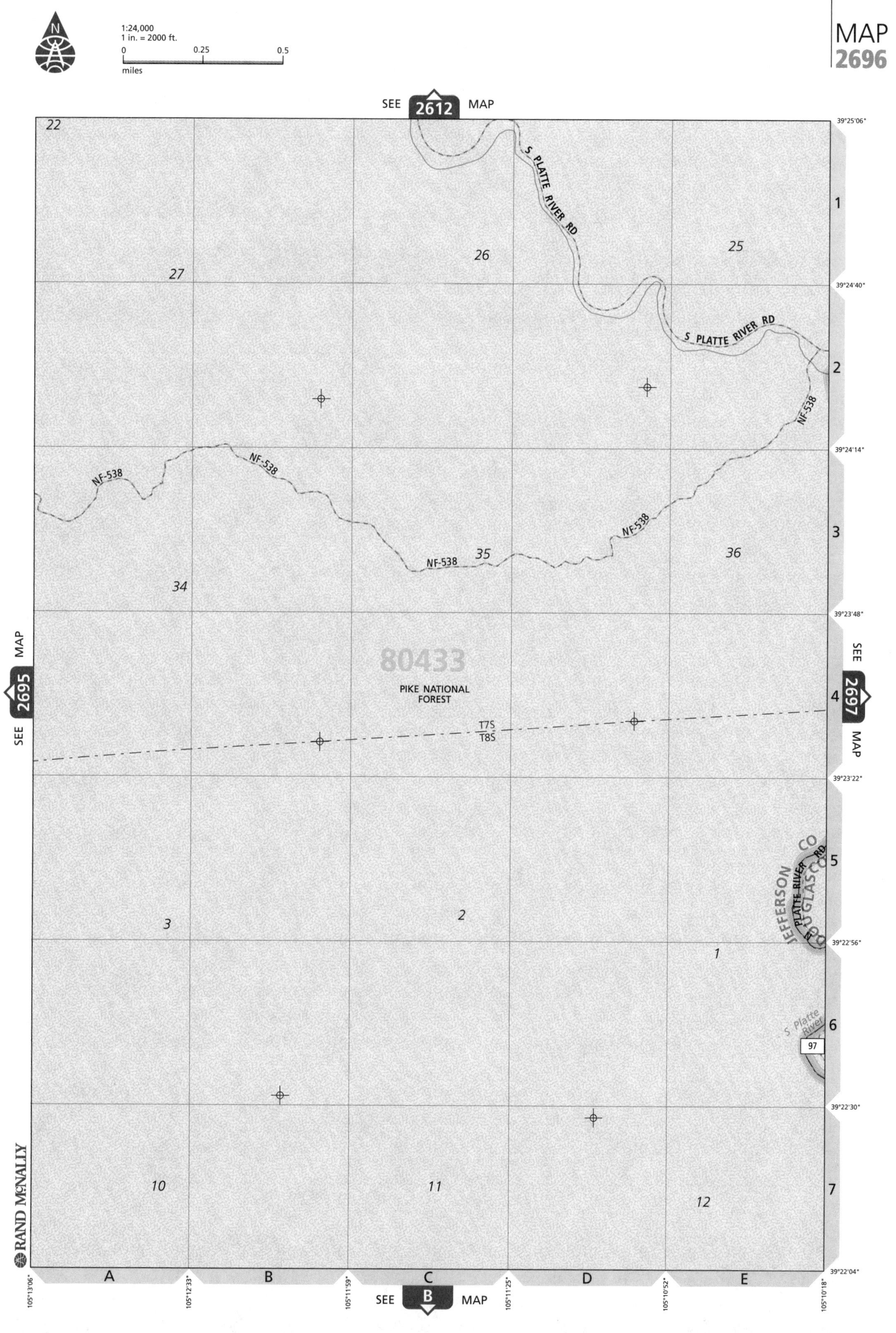

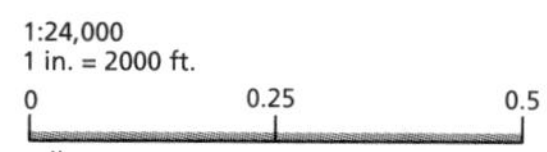

SEE 2612 MAP

S PLATTE RIVER RD
NF-538
80433
PIKE NATIONAL FOREST
T7S
T8S
JEFFERSON CO
DOUGLAS CO
PLATTE RIVER RD
S Platte River
97

22 27 26 25 34 35 36 3 2 1 10 11 12

1 2 3 4 5 6 7

A B C D E

39°25'06"
39°24'40"
39°24'14"
39°23'48"
39°23'22"
39°22'56"
39°22'30"
39°22'04"

105°13'06" 105°12'33" 105°11'59" 105°11'25" 105°10'52" 105°10'18"

SEE 2695 MAP

SEE 2697 MAP

SEE B MAP

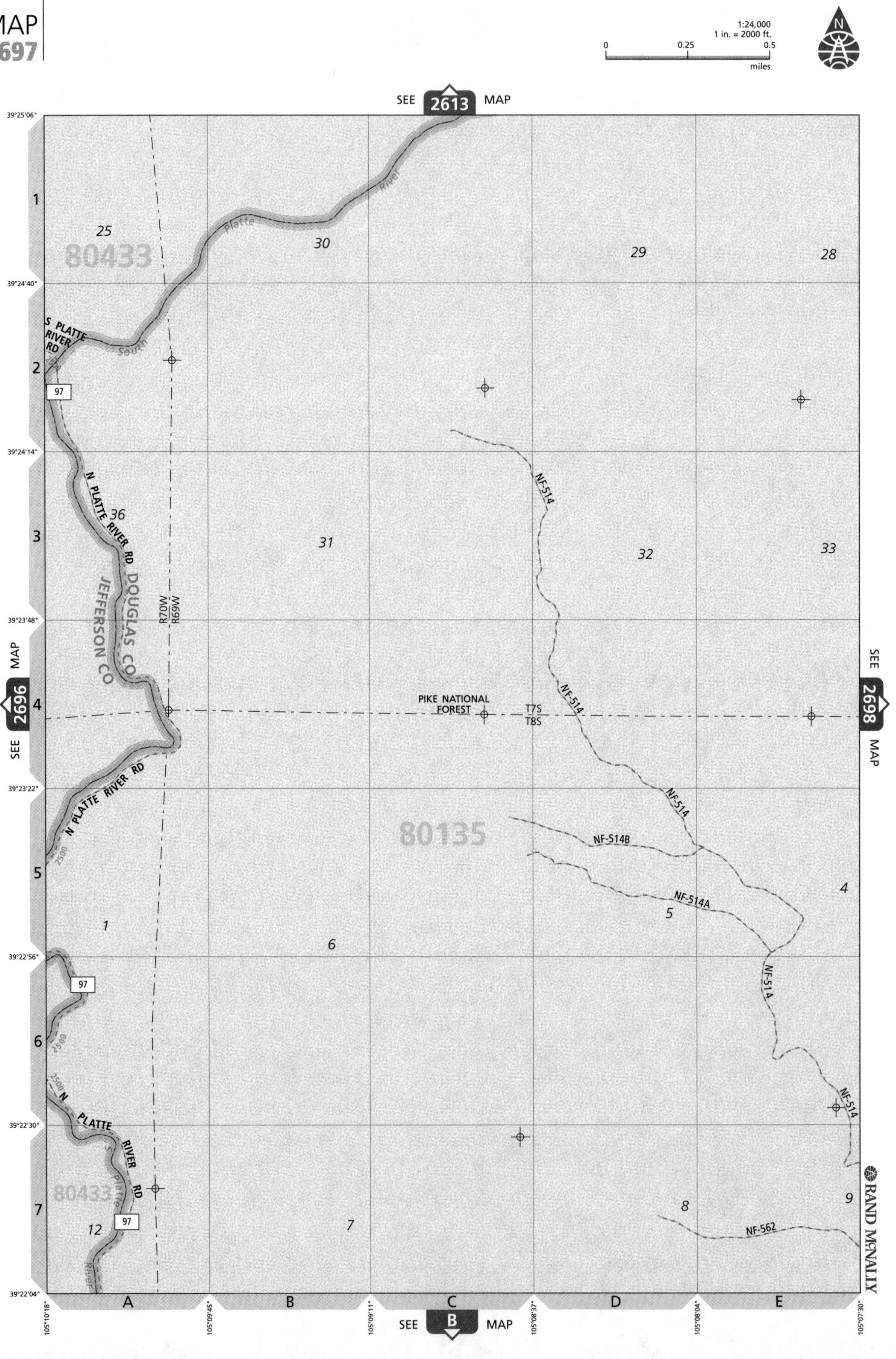

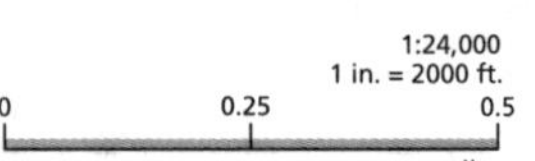

SEE 2613 MAP

25
80433
30
29
28
S PLATTE RIVER RD
97
N PLATTE RIVER RD
36
31
32
33
DOUGLAS CO
JEFFERSON CO
R70W
R69W
PIKE NATIONAL FOREST
T7S
T8S
NF-514
NF-514B
NF-514A
80135
1
6
5
4
NF-514
97
N PLATTE RIVER RD
80433
12
97
7
8
9
NF-562

39°25'06"
39°24'40"
39°24'14"
39°23'48"
39°23'22"
39°22'56"
39°22'30"
39°22'04"

105°10'18"
105°09'45"
105°09'11"
105°08'37"
105°08'04"
105°07'30"

A B C D E
1 2 3 4 5 6 7

SEE 2696 MAP

SEE 2698 MAP

SEE B MAP

1:24,000
1 in. = 2000 ft.
0 0.25 0.5
miles

SEE 2614 MAP

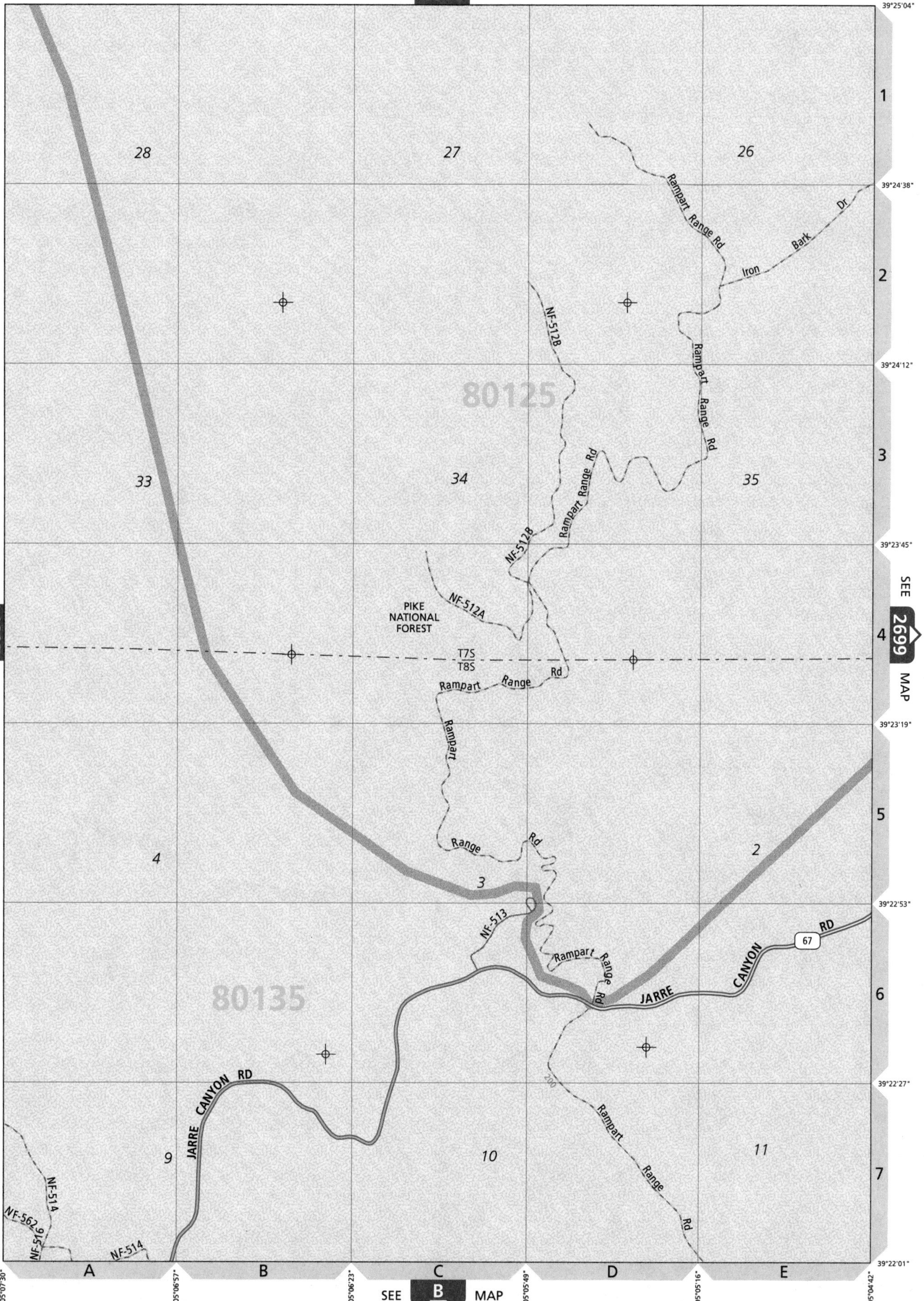

SEE 2697 MAP

SEE 2699 MAP

SEE B MAP

1:24,000
1 in. = 2000 ft.
0 0.25 0.5
miles

SEE 2615 MAP

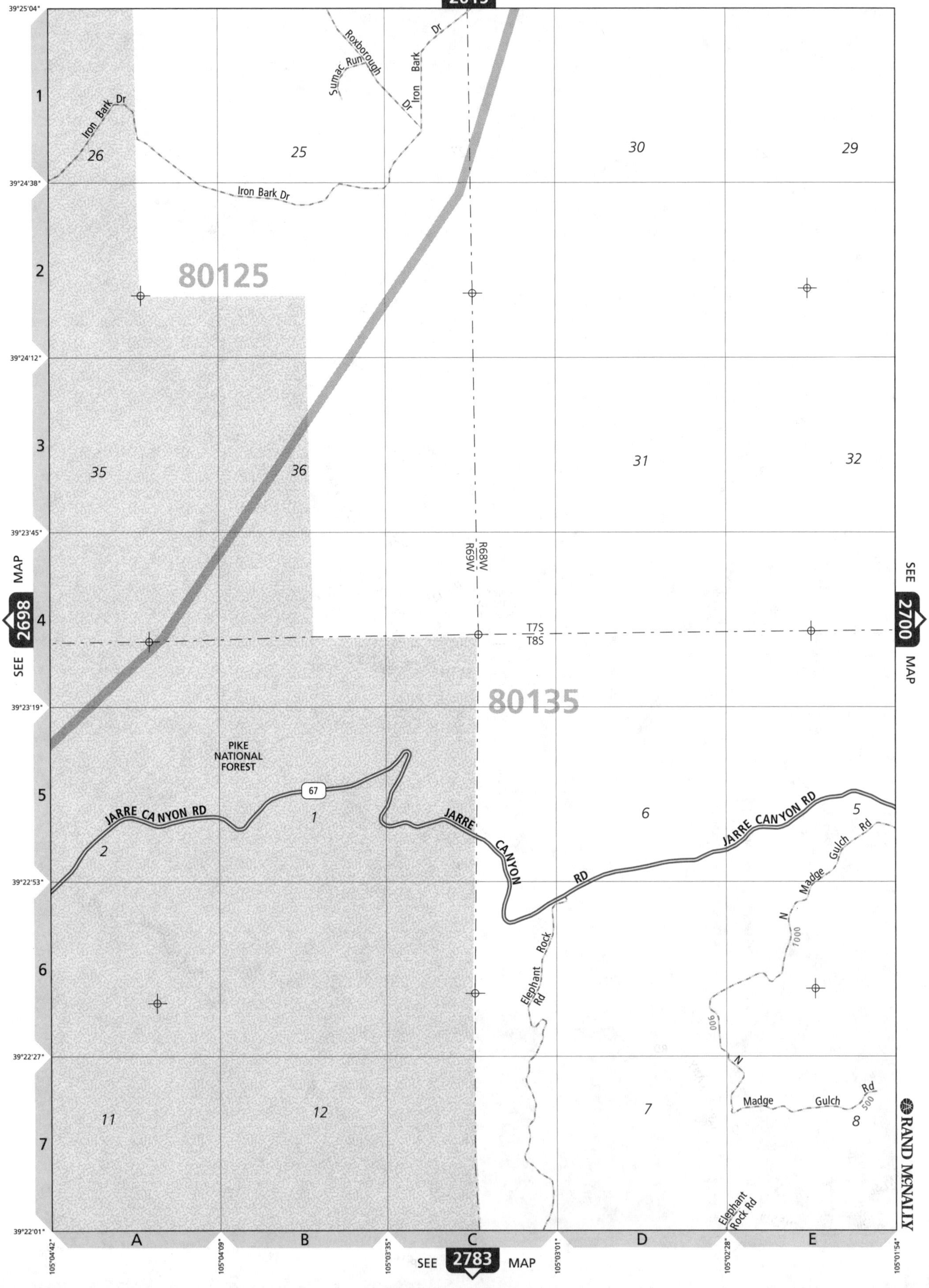

39°25'04"
39°24'38"
39°24'12"
39°23'45"
39°23'19"
39°22'53"
39°22'27"
39°22'01"

1
2
3
4
5
6
7

Iron Bark Dr
Sumac Run
Roxborough Dr
Iron Bark Dr
Dr
Iron Bark Dr

26
25
30
29

80125

35
36
31
32

R68W
R69W

T7S
T8S

80135

PIKE
NATIONAL
FOREST

67
JARRE CANYON RD
1
2
JARRE CANYON RD
6
JARRE CANYON RD
5
Madge Gulch Rd
N
1000
Elephant Rock Rd
900
N
Madge Gulch Rd
500
11
12
7
8
Elephant Rock Rd

SEE 2698 MAP

SEE 2700 MAP

RAND McNALLY

A
B
C
D
E

105°04'42"
105°04'09"
105°03'35"
105°03'01"
105°02'28"
105°01'54"

SEE 2783 MAP

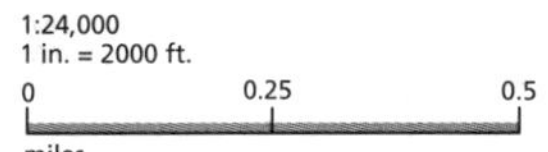

SEE 2616 MAP

W Cheyenne Dr
Piute Dr
7000
W Cherokee Dr
N Hopi Dr
W Cherokee
6500
Dr
N Choctaw Cir
6000
W Sioux Dr
W Blackfoot Cir
N Zuni Pl
Rainbow Creek Rd
N Iriquois Cir
67
W
29
28
N
W Winnebago Wy
Winnebago
W Apache Wy
6600 Dr
2800
Mohawk Dr
JARRE CANYON RD
27
32
33
34
JARRE CANYON RD
80135
T7S
T8S
67
W Meadowbrook Ln
6800
N Hillside Cir
6300
N Oak Valley Rd
1300
5
4
3
W Box Canyon Rd
W Ridgeview Cir
W Rock Oak Cir
N Cathedral Rock Dr
900
N Bee Rock Rd
Oak Valley Rd
1000
500
1300
W Meadowood Ln
6200
8
9
10
N Bee Rock Rd
W Pine Cliff Rd
5800
6200
4000

1
2
3
4
5
6
7

A
B
C
D
E

39°25'01"
39°24'35"
39°24'09"
39°23'42"
39°23'16"
39°22'50"
39°22'24"
39°21'58"

105°01'54"
105°01'21"
105°00'47"
105°00'13"
104°59'40"
104°59'06"

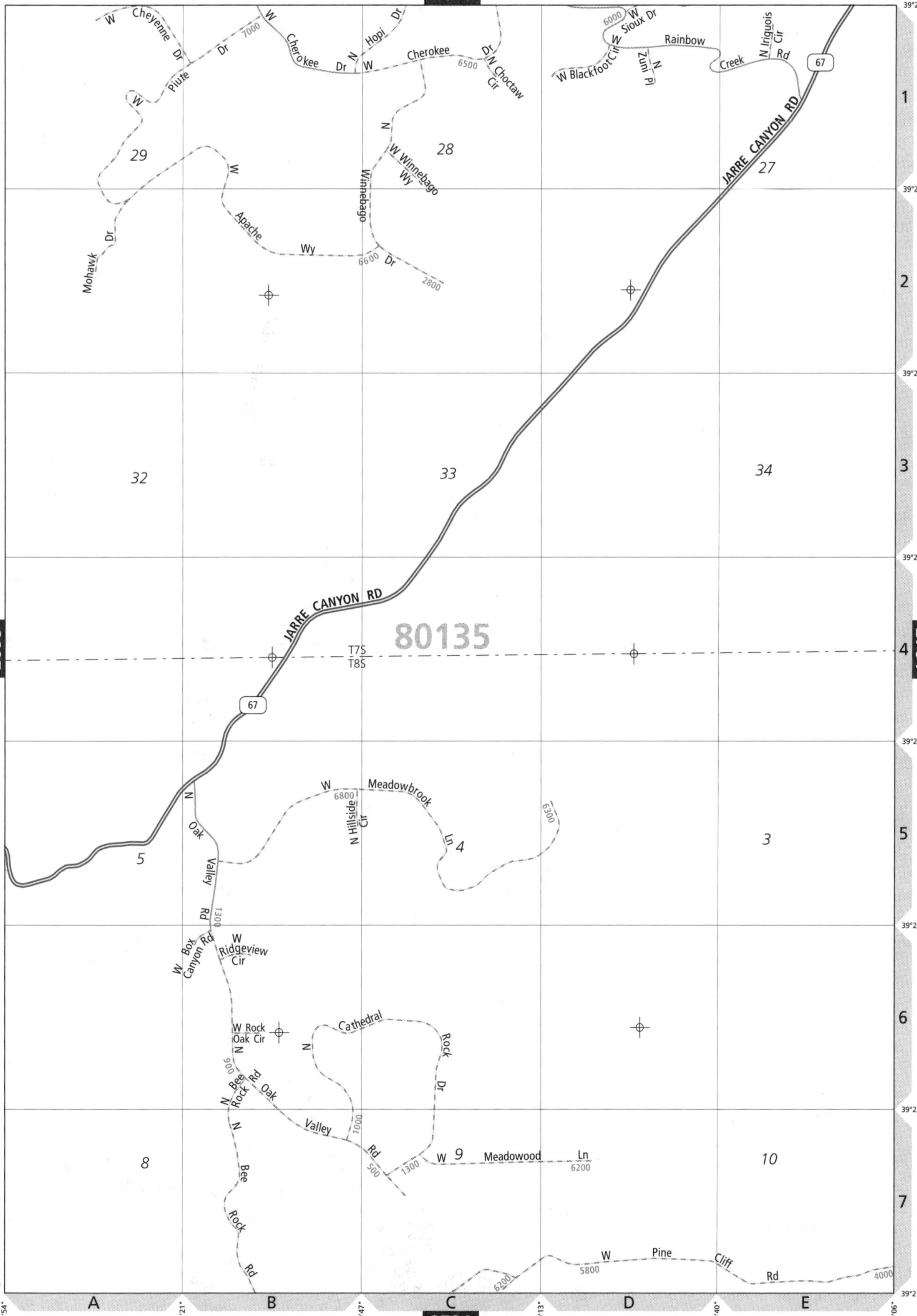

SEE 2699 MAP

SEE 2701 MAP

SEE 2784 MAP

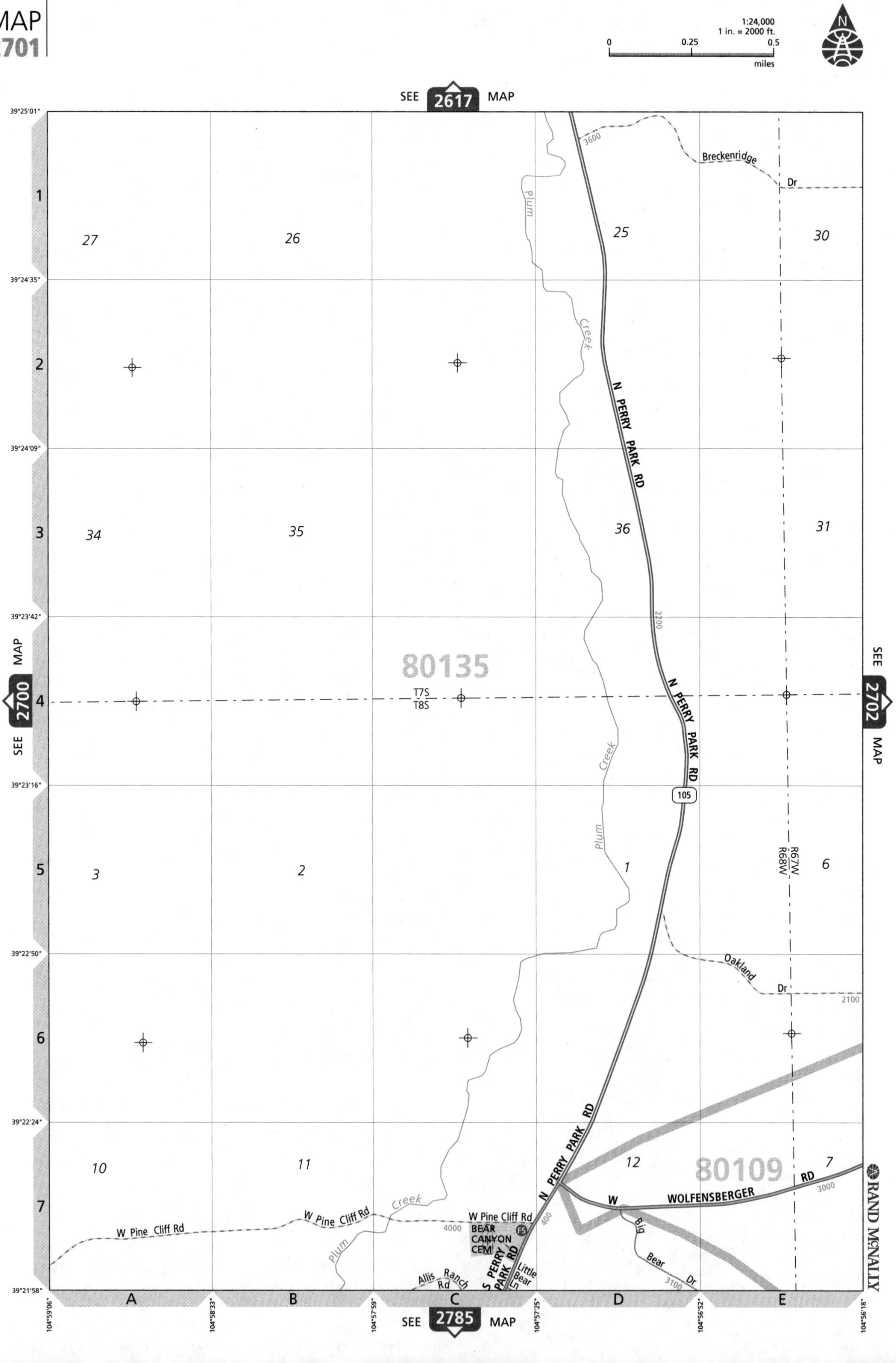

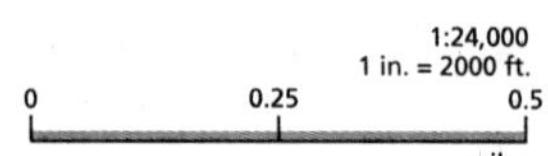

1:24,000
1 in. = 2000 ft.
0 0.25 0.5
miles
N
SEE 2617 MAP
SEE 2700 MAP
SEE 2702 MAP
SEE 2785 MAP
39°25'01"
39°24'35"
39°24'09"
39°23'42"
39°23'16"
39°22'50"
39°22'24"
39°21'58"
104°59'06"
104°58'33"
104°57'59"
104°57'25"
104°56'52"
104°56'18"
A
B
C
D
E
1
2
3
4
5
6
7
27
26
25
30
34
35
36
31
3
2
1
6
10
11
12
7
80135
80109
T7S
T8S
R67W
R68W
N PERRY PARK RD
105
Plum
Creek
Breckenridge
Dr
Oakland
Dr
3600
2200
2100
3000
3100
4000
400
W WOLFENSBERGER RD
W Pine Cliff Rd
BEAR CANYON CEM
Big Bear Dr
Allis Ranch Rd
S PERRY PARK RD
Little Bear Ln
RAND McNALLY

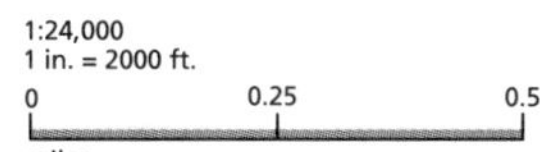

SEE 2618 MAP

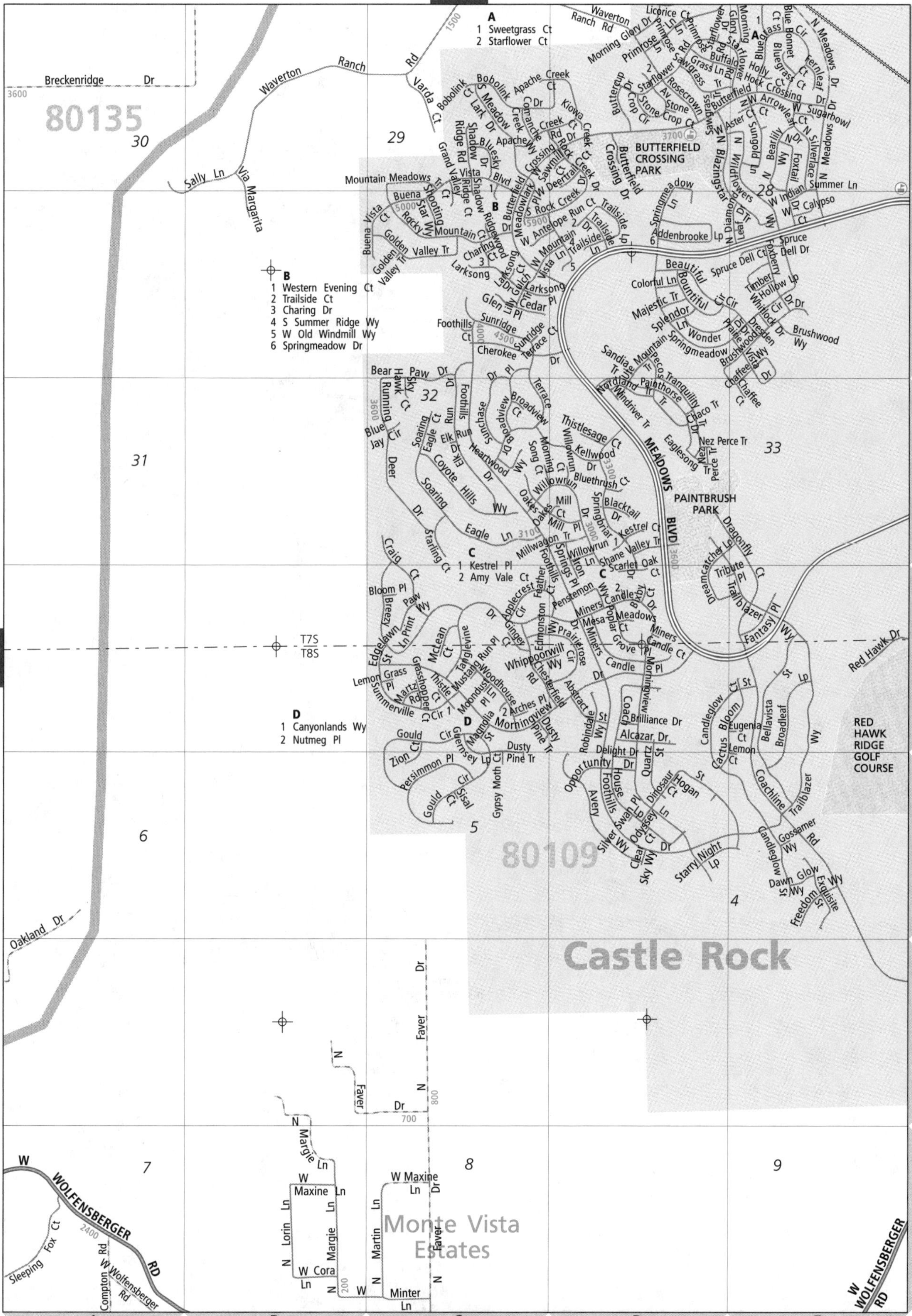

SEE 2701 MAP

SEE 2703 MAP

A
1 Sweetgrass Ct
2 Starflower Ct

B
1 Western Evening Ct
2 Trailside Ct
3 Charing Dr
4 S Summer Ridge Wy
5 W Old Windmill Wy
6 Springmeadow Dr

C
1 Kestrel Pl
2 Amy Vale Ct

D
1 Canyonlands Wy
2 Nutmeg Pl

80135

80109

Castle Rock

Monte Vista Estates

BUTTERFIELD CROSSING PARK

PAINTBRUSH PARK

RED HAWK RIDGE GOLF COURSE

MEADOWS BLVD

W WOLFENSBERGER RD

Waverton Ranch Rd

Breckenridge Dr

Oakland Dr

N Faver Dr

T7S
T8S

29 30 31 32 33 28 6 5 4 7 8 9

1 2 3 4 5 6 7

A B C D E

39°24'57" 39°24'31" 39°24'05" 39°23'39" 39°23'13" 39°22'47" 39°22'21" 39°21'55"

104°56'18" 104°55'45" 104°55'11" 104°54'37" 104°54'04" 104°53'30"

SEE 2786 MAP

1:24,000
1 in. = 2000 ft.
0 0.25 0.5
miles

SEE 2619 MAP

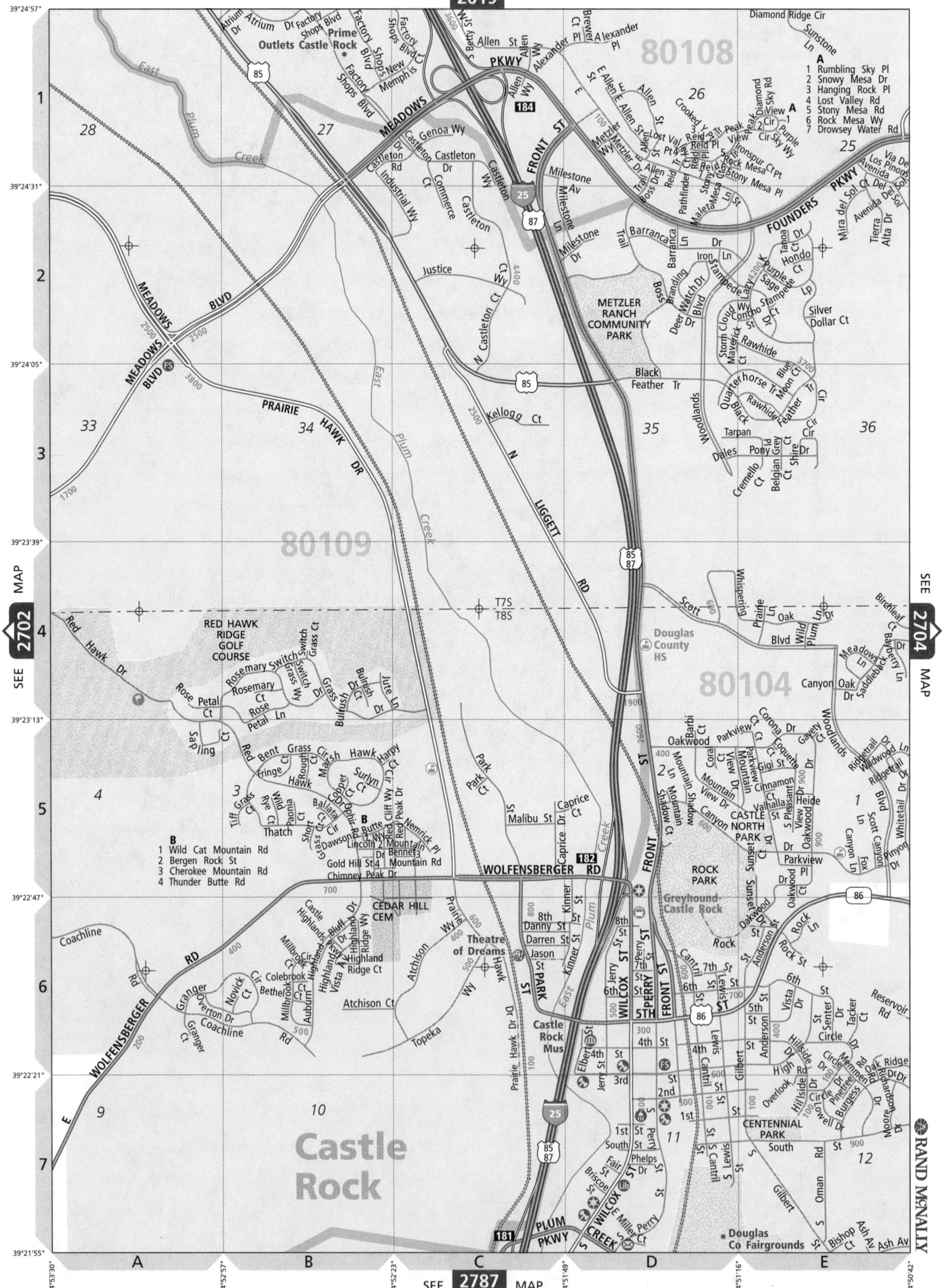

SEE 2702 MAP

SEE 2704 MAP

SEE 2787 MAP

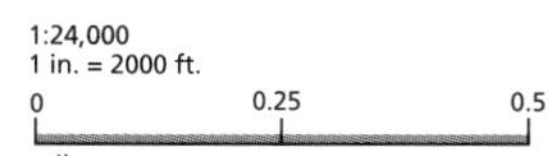

SEE 2620 MAP

SEE 2703 MAP

SEE 2705 MAP

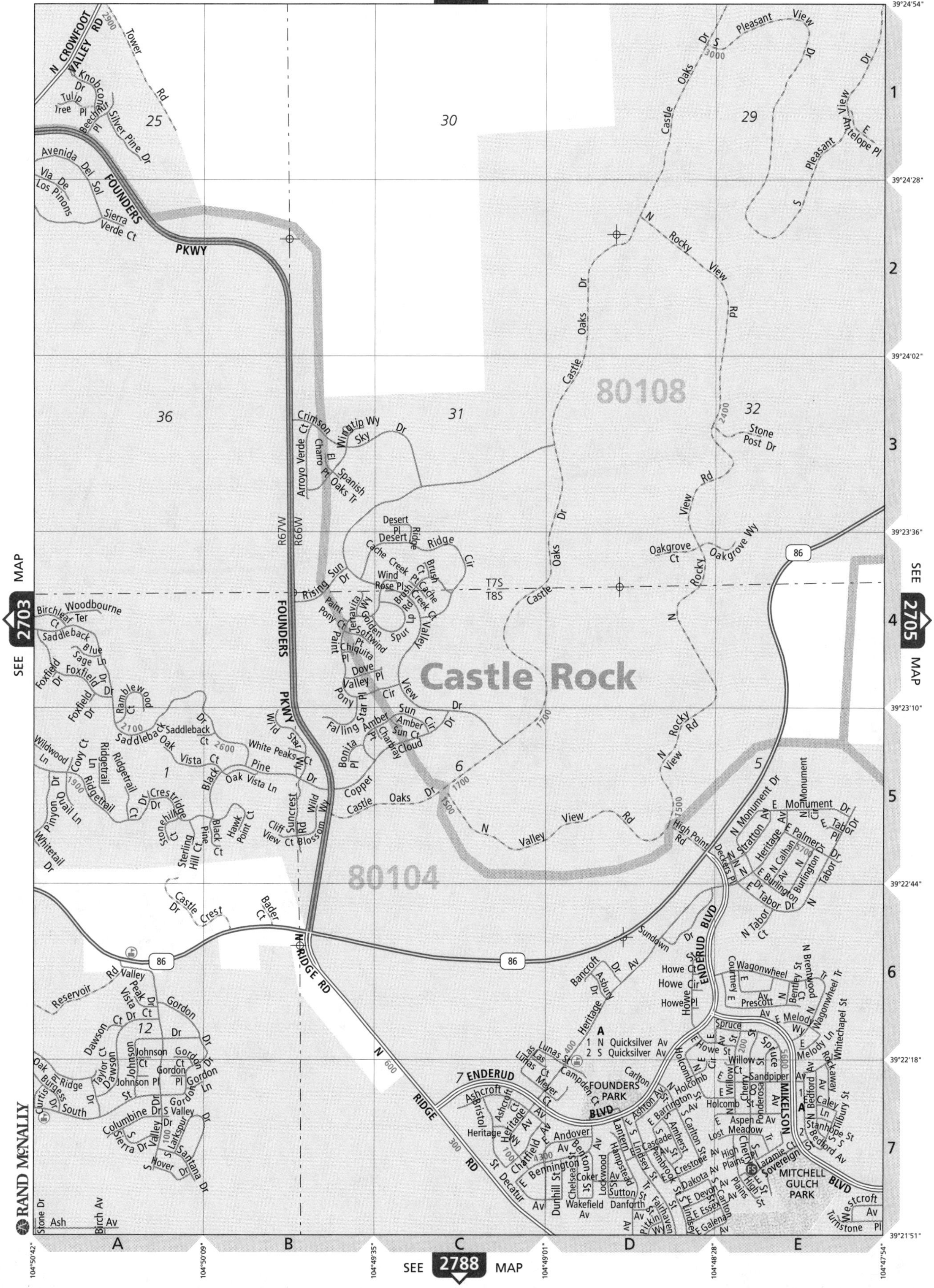

Castle Rock

80108

80104

25 30 29 36 31 32 1 6 5 12 7

R67W R66W

T7S T8S

FOUNDERS PKWY

N RIDGE RD

ENDERUD BLVD

MIKELSON BLVD

FOUNDERS PARK

MITCHELL GULCH PARK

A
1 N Quicksilver Av
2 S Quicksilver Av

1 2 3 4 5 6 7

A B C D E

39°24'54" 39°24'28" 39°24'02" 39°23'36" 39°23'10" 39°22'44" 39°22'18" 39°21'51"

104°50'42" 104°50'09" 104°49'35" 104°49'01" 104°48'28" 104°47'54"

SEE 2788 MAP

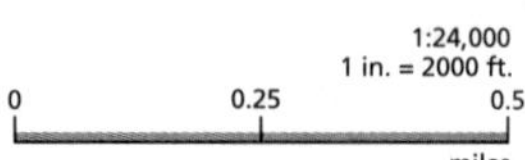

SEE 2621 MAP

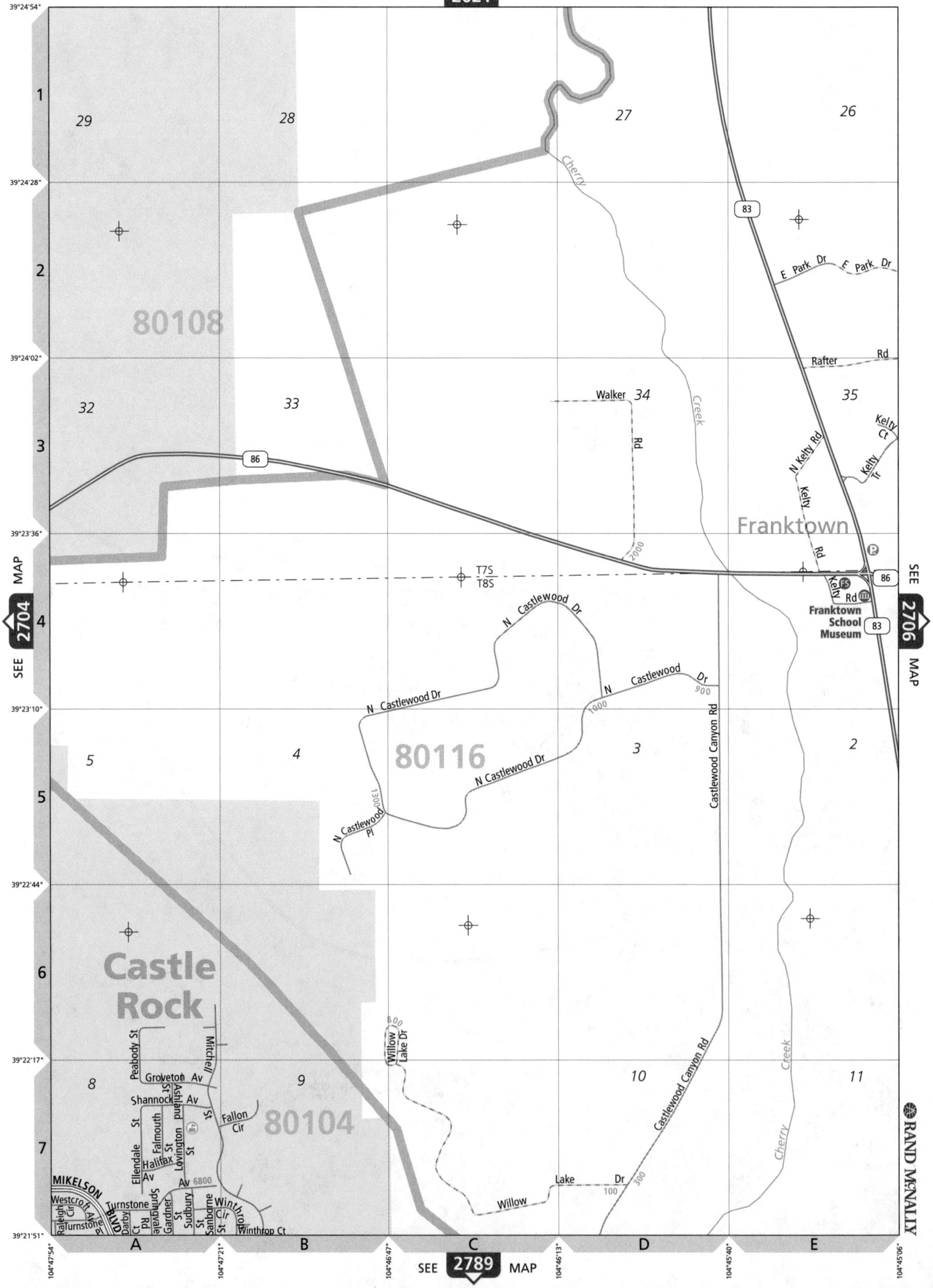

SEE 2704 MAP

SEE 2706 MAP

SEE 2789 MAP

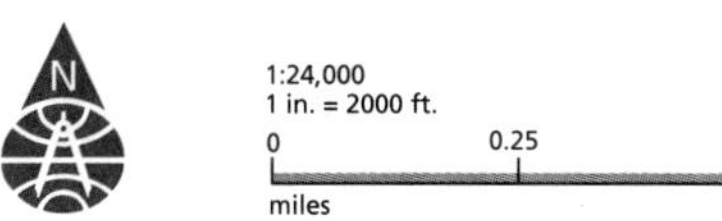

SEE 2622 MAP

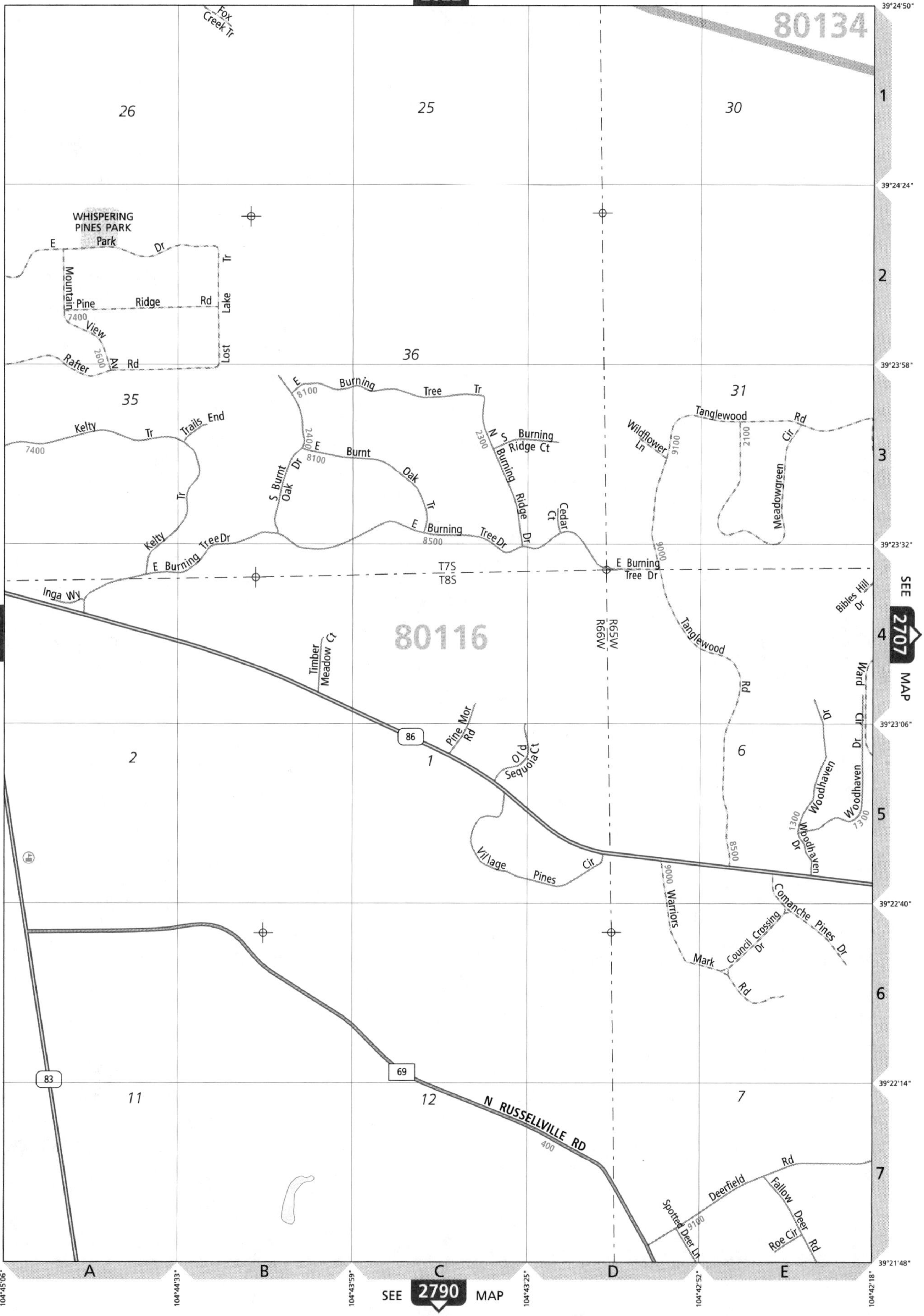

SEE 2705 MAP

SEE 2707 MAP

SEE 2790 MAP

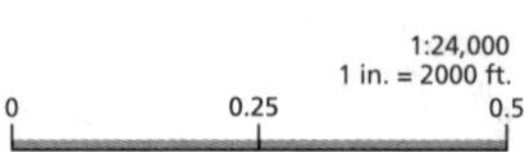

SEE 2623 MAP

E BAYOU GULCH RD
Palmer Ridge Dr
10100
80134
N FLINTWOOD RD
FLINTWOOD RD
Mustang Rd
Bear Creek Dr
Stagecoach
Stillwater St
Tr
Weasel Wy
Racoon Ln
Antelope Run
Ponderosa Ln
Ponderosa Rd
Elkhorn Dr
Bonanza Cir
11300
11200
3100
E Basswood Ln
2800
E Buckhorn Wy
Overlook Rd
Flintwood Hills
Crabapple Dr
11700
Frontier Ln
Tanglewood Rd
9800
Deerpath Tr
N Sycamore Ln
Huckleberry
Dogwood Dr
N Delbert Rd
Bibles Hill Dr
Deerpath Rd
Frontier Ln
2100
Hawthorn Ln
65
E Grant Av
2000
11000
T7S
T8S
E Grant Rd
11600
11800
CR-146
Ward Cir
1900
Holden Cir
10300
Columbine Dr
1800
DOUGLAS CO
ELBERT CO
Holden Cir
10700
Duffy Ln
1500
1400
80116
Rocky Cliff Rd
Ward Cir
Deerpath Tr
Deerpath Rd
80107
E Folsom Point Ln
86
Camelot Dr
N White Tail Dr
700
N Bluff Dr
Deerfield Rd
Deerfield Rd
400
Doe Cir
S White Tail Dr
9900
Fawn Cir
200
N Rocky Cliff Tr
100
N Rocky Cliff Pl
Cliff Rd
Rocky

30 29 28 27
31 32 33 34
6 5 4 3
7 8 9 10

1 2 3 4 5 6 7
A B C D E

39°24'50" 39°24'24" 39°23'58" 39°23'32" 39°23'06" 39°22'40" 39°22'14" 39°21'48"
104°42'18" 104°41'45" 104°41'11" 104°40'37" 104°40'04" 104°39'30"

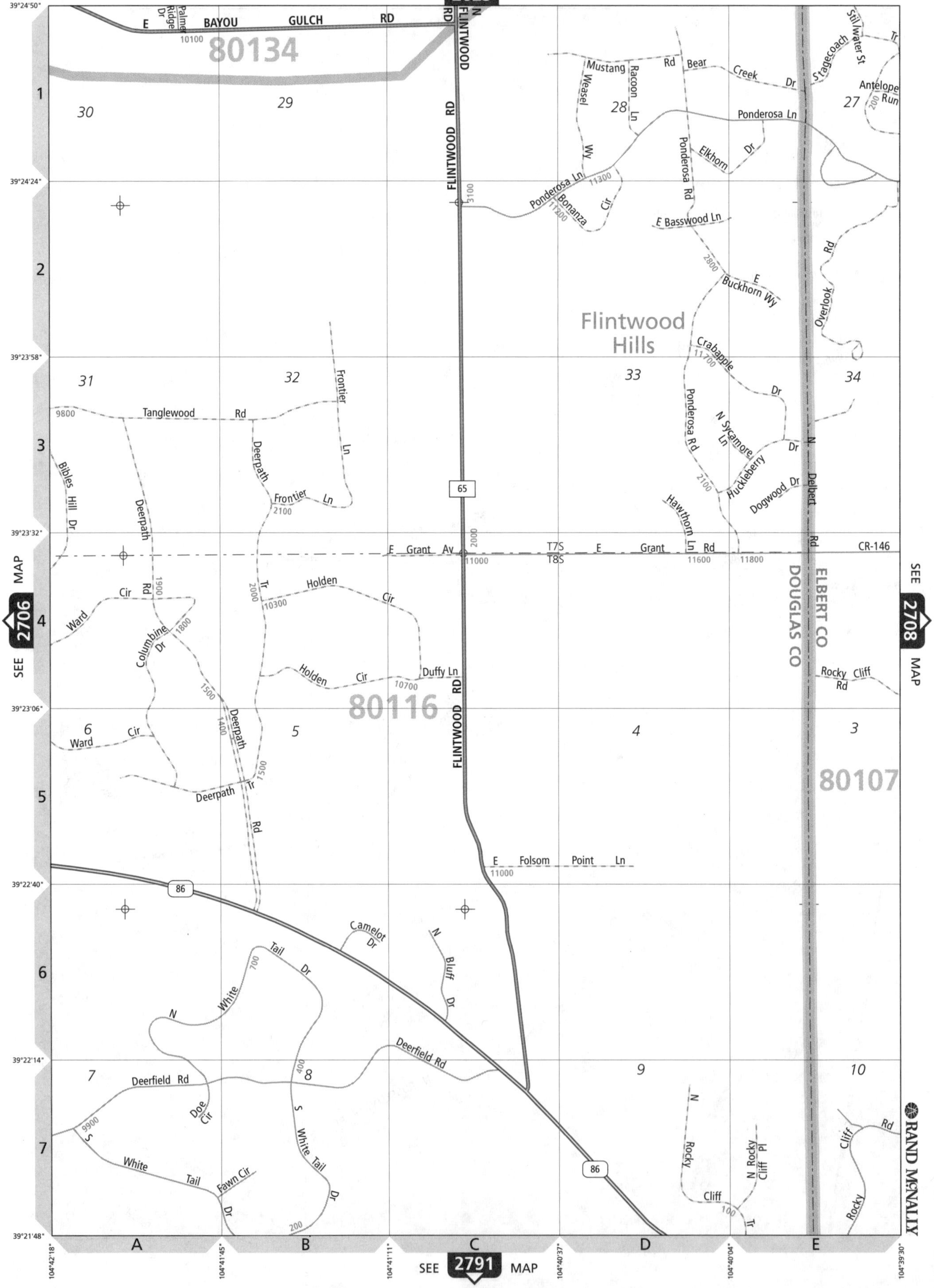

SEE 2706 MAP
SEE 2708 MAP
SEE 2791 MAP

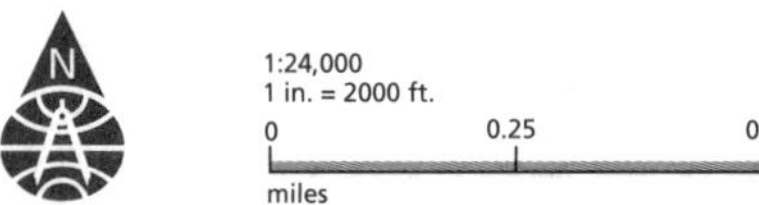

SEE 2624 MAP

Ponderosa Park
80107

Panorama Dr
Oak Ln
500 Verdos Dr
Panorama Dr
Sparrow Ln
Cedar Ln
Verdos Dr
Starling Dr
Antelope Dr
Run
Verdos Dr
Stagecoach Tr
Verdos Ln
Bunny Ln
Cedar Ln
27
Ponderosa Ln
Buttercup Rd
Starling Ln
Mountview Dr
Bluebird Ln
1700
Woodpecker Ln
Grouse Dr
Rd
26
25
Buffalo Tr
1100
800
Buttercup
Woodpecker Ln
Quail Dr
CR-150
1800
Dr
Ponderosa Ln
36400
36900
Ridge View
Coyote Ln
1000
Browning Ct
Ruger Ct
Marlin Ct
Remington Rd
Mossberg Ct
Pawnee Pkwy
Pawnee Ct
Winchester Rd
36400
2800
34
35
36
Osage Ct
CR-5
Shoshone Tr
Savage Rd
1300
1900
1200
Belgian Tr
Colt Ct
CR-146
36000
1300
1000
T7S
T8S
1700
Pawnee Pkwy
Sioux Tr
35500
1900
Tr
CR-3
Rocky Cliff Rd
35500
Cheyenne Tr
3
2
1
CR-142
2800
Cherokee Tr
Kiowa Tr
1600
Belgian
Welch Tr
Morgan Tr
Cimarron Tr
35200
Appaloosa Tr
1700
CR-3
Cherokee Tr
Wagon Wheel Tr
1600
Morgan Tr
34800
1800
Arabian Tr
Shetland Tr
Tr
2000
Stampede Cir
35200
Mustang
Palomino Tr
Wagon Wheel Tr
10
11
12
34500
Tr
Morgan
CR-3
Broken Arrow Cir
Rocky Cliff Rd
Cherokee Tr
Cimarron Tr
34000
Tr
Rawhide Cir
Pinto
Pinto Ct
Wagon Train Tr
Stagecoach Cir
1800

1
2
3
4
5
6
7
A
B
C
D
E

39°24'46"
39°24'20"
39°23'54"
39°23'28"
39°23'02"
39°22'36"
39°22'10"
39°21'44"
104°39'30"
104°38'57"
104°38'23"
104°37'49"
104°37'16"
104°36'42"

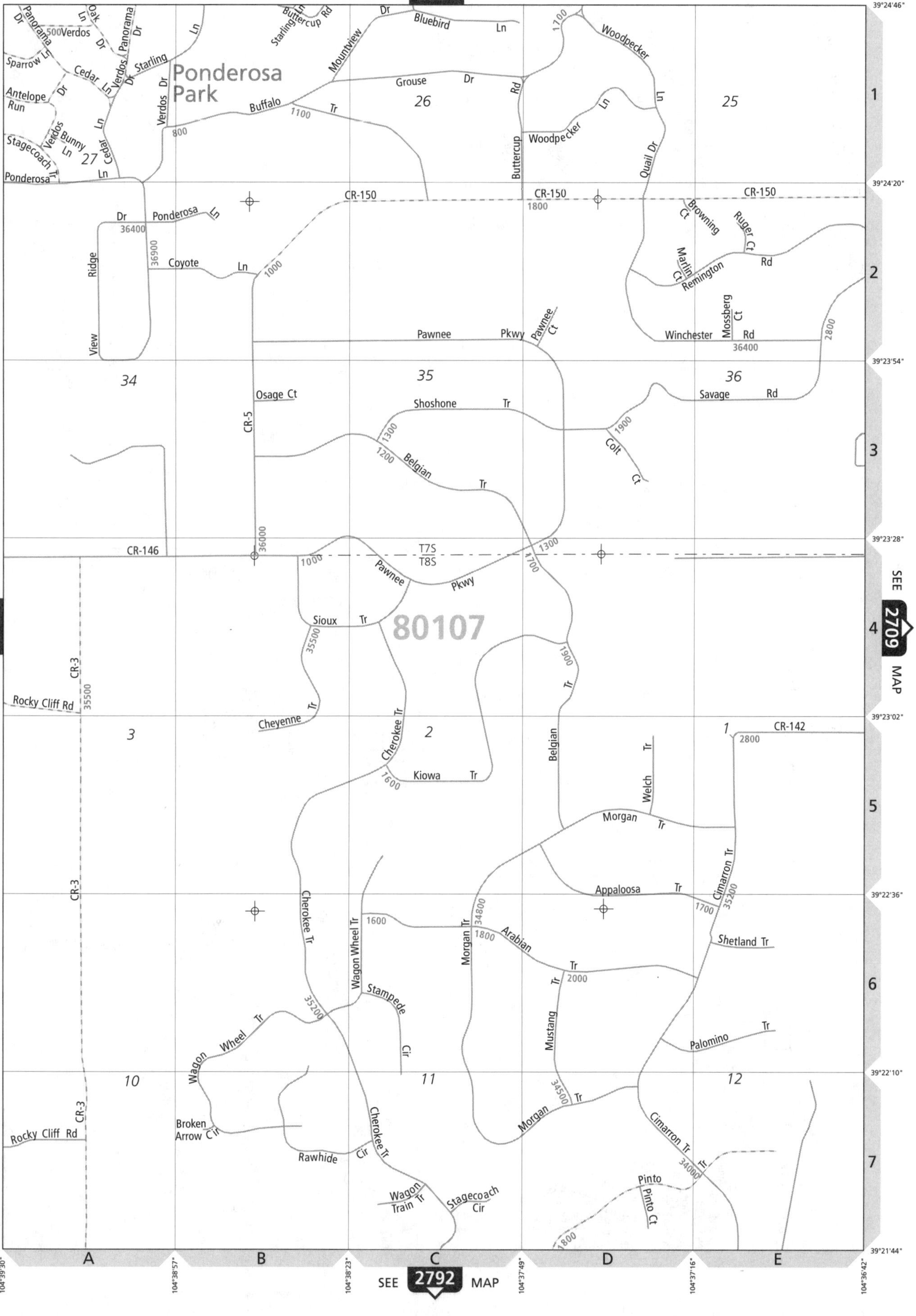

SEE 2707 MAP
SEE 2709 MAP
SEE 2792 MAP

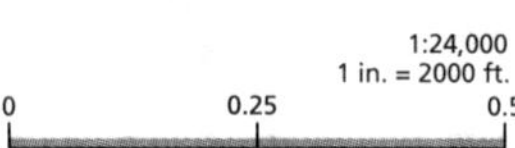

SEE 2625 MAP

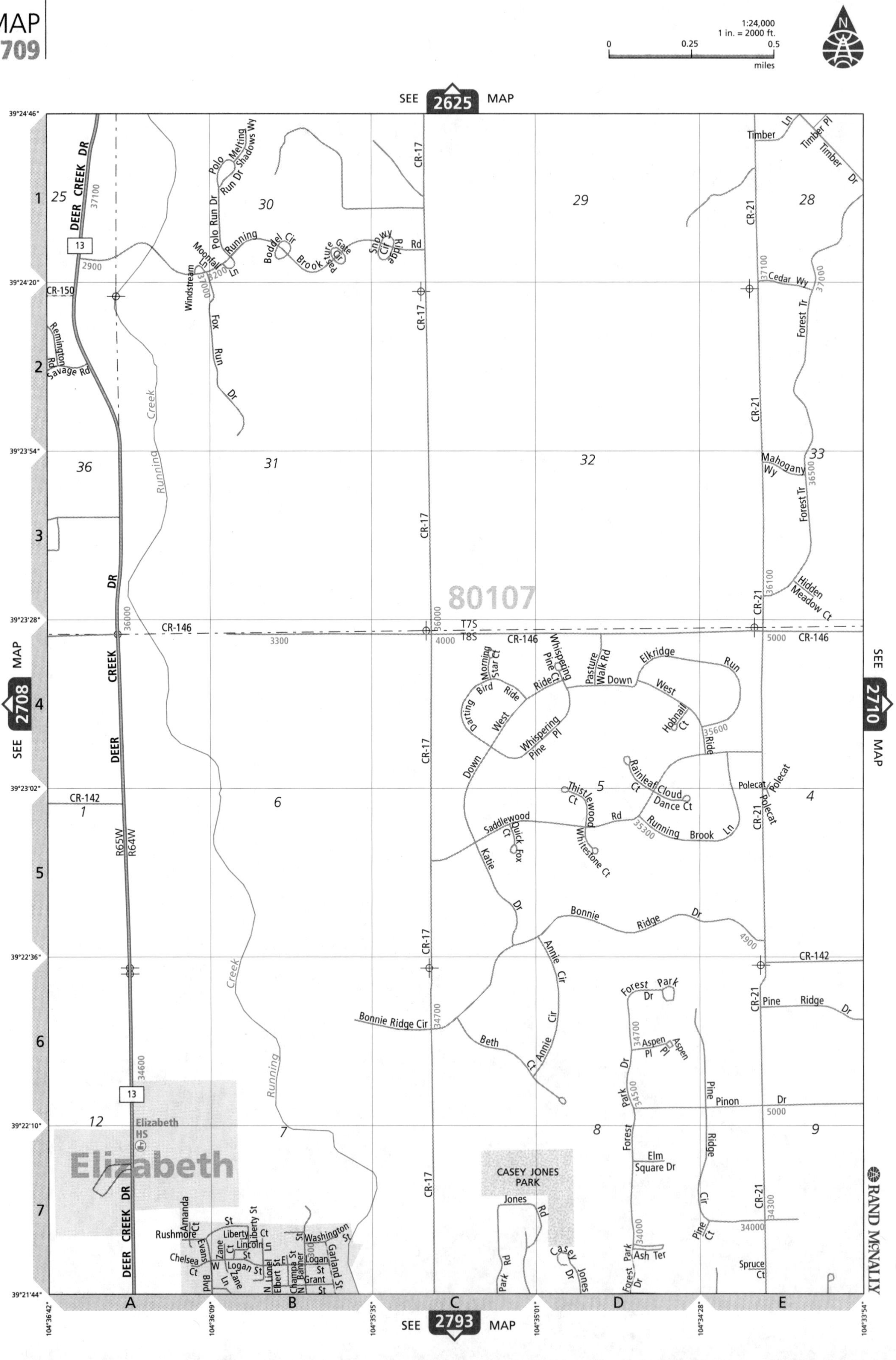

SEE 2708 MAP

SEE 2710 MAP

SEE 2793 MAP

Elizabeth

80107

DEER CREEK DR
CR-17
CR-21
CR-146
CR-142
CR-150
Running Creek
CASEY JONES PARK
Elizabeth HS

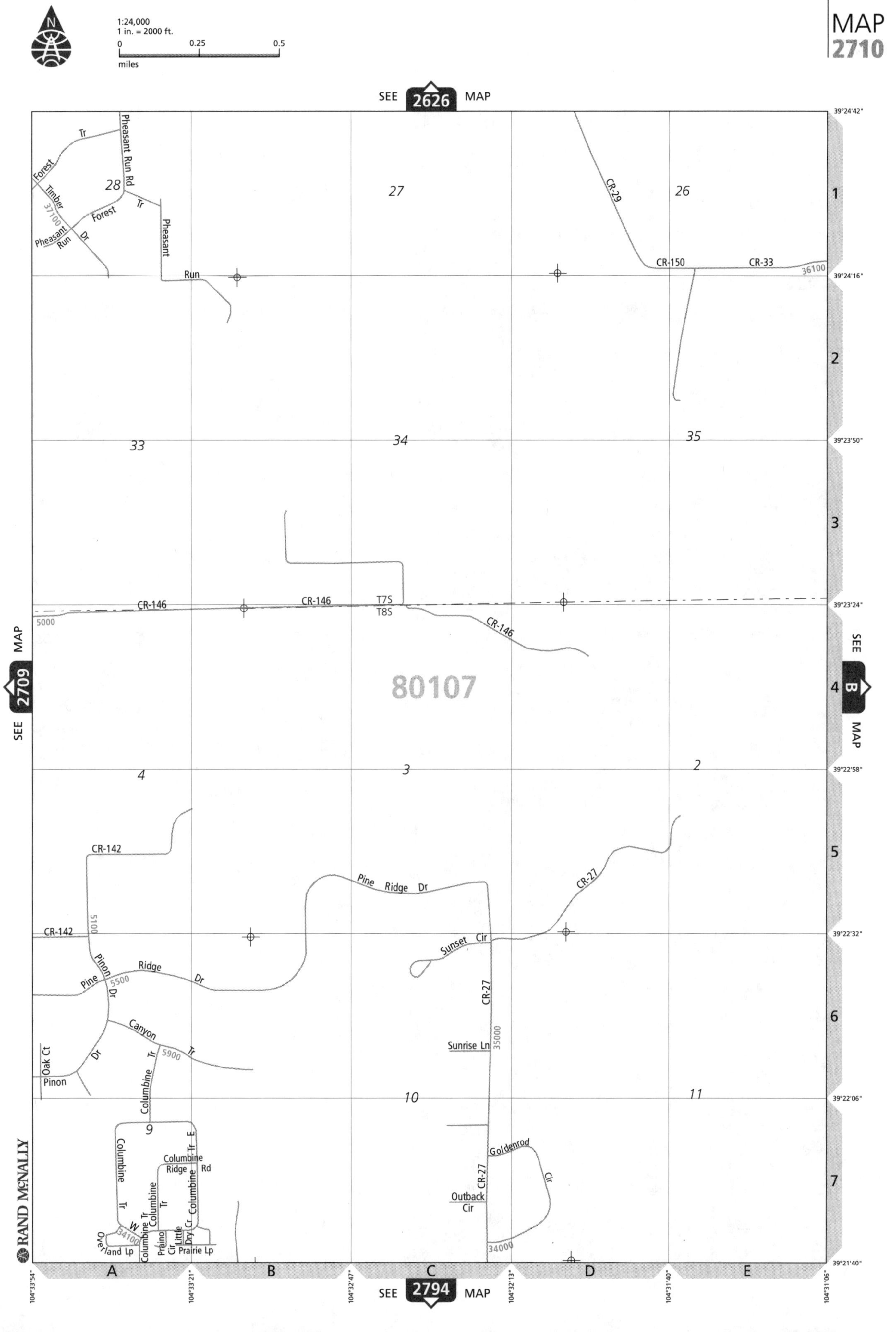

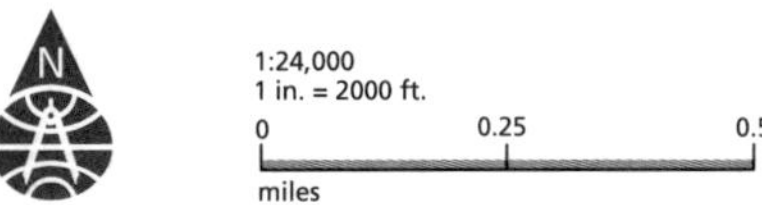

SEE 2626 MAP

SEE 2709 MAP

SEE B MAP

SEE 2794 MAP

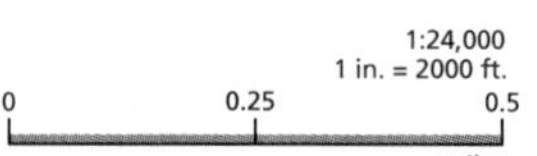

1:24,000
1 in. = 2000 ft.
0 0.25 0.5
miles

SEE 2699 MAP
SEE B MAP
SEE 2784 MAP
SEE B MAP
39°22'01"
39°21'35"
39°21'09"
39°20'43"
39°20'17"
39°19'51"
39°19'25"
39°18'59"
105°04'45"
105°04'11"
105°03'38"
105°03'04"
105°02'30"
105°01'57"
A
B
C
D
E
1
2
3
4
5
6
7
11
12
7
8
14
13
18
17
23
24
19
20
26
25
30
29
35
36
31
32
PIKE NATIONAL FOREST
80135
R68W
R69W
Rampart Range Rd
Elephant Rock Rd
W Jackson Creek Rd
Oak Wy
View
Sunset Ln
Sunset Dr
Valley
W Sprucewood Dr
S Sunset Ln
Columbine Ln
Hidden Valley Rd
8100
1500
RAND McNALLY

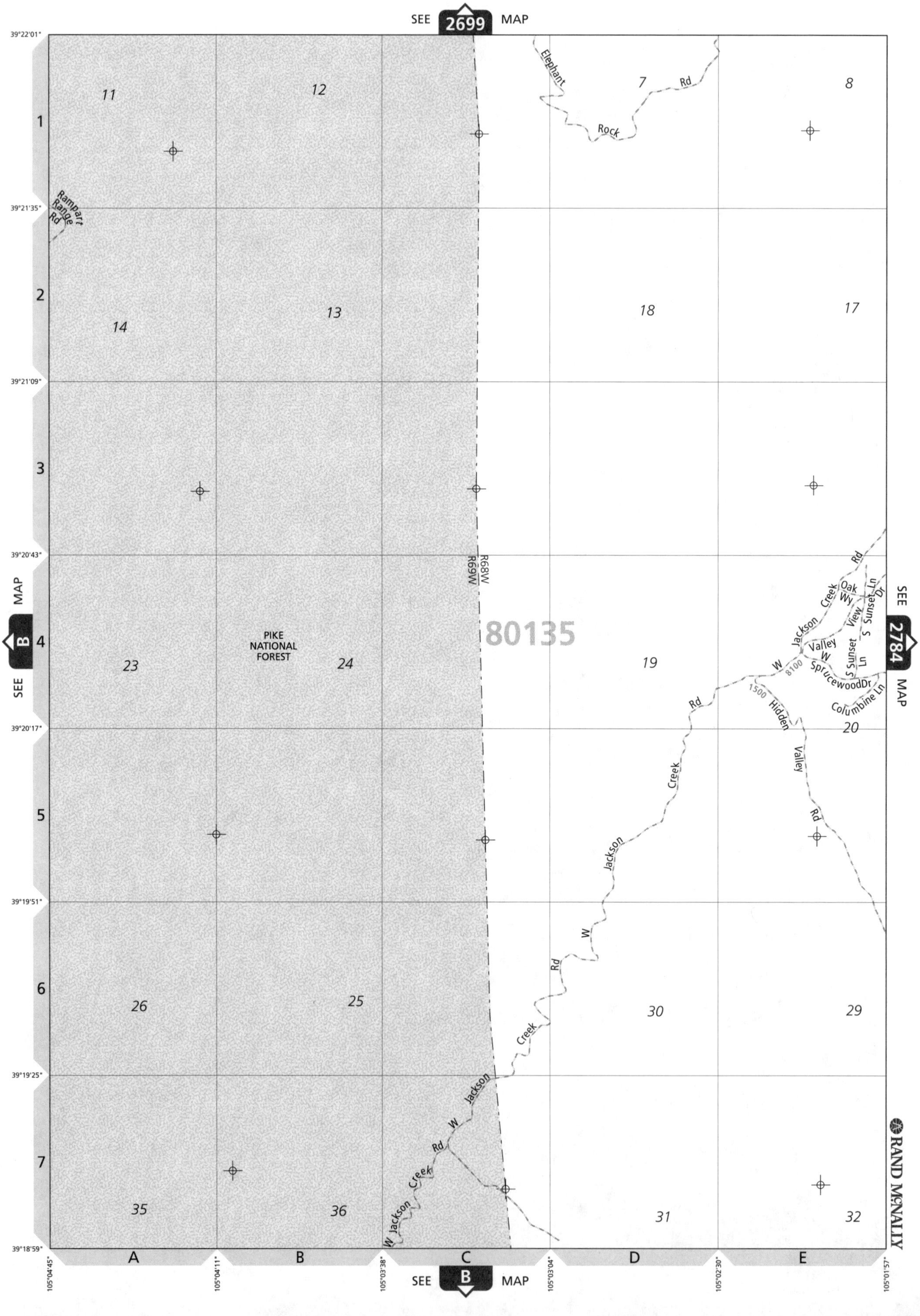

1:24,000
1 in. = 2000 ft.
0 0.25 0.5
miles

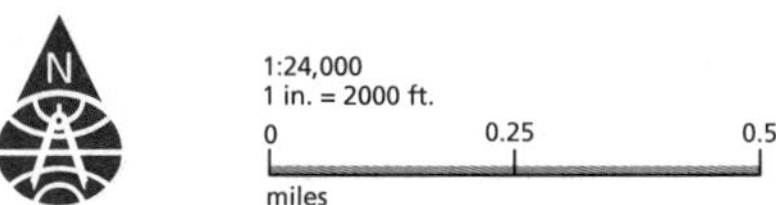

SEE 2700 MAP

8
9
10
N Bee Rock Rd
1
17
16
15
S Coronado Dr
Coronado Dr
2
W Jackson Creek Rd
S Coronado Dr
S
S Coronado Dr
3
W 7600 Jackson Creek Rd
Valley View Dr
6400
W Jackson Creek Rd
5300
21
80135
20
22
W Sprucewood Dr
Hillcrest Cir
4
5
Tall Horse Tr
1500
Hidden Valley Rd
29
28
27
6
Hidden Valley Rd
Majestic Mountain Rd
32
33
34
7
A
B
C
D
E
39°21'58"
39°21'32"
39°21'06"
39°20'40"
39°20'14"
39°19'48"
39°19'22"
39°18'56"
105°01'57"
105°01'23"
105°00'50"
105°00'16"
104°59'43"
104°59'09"

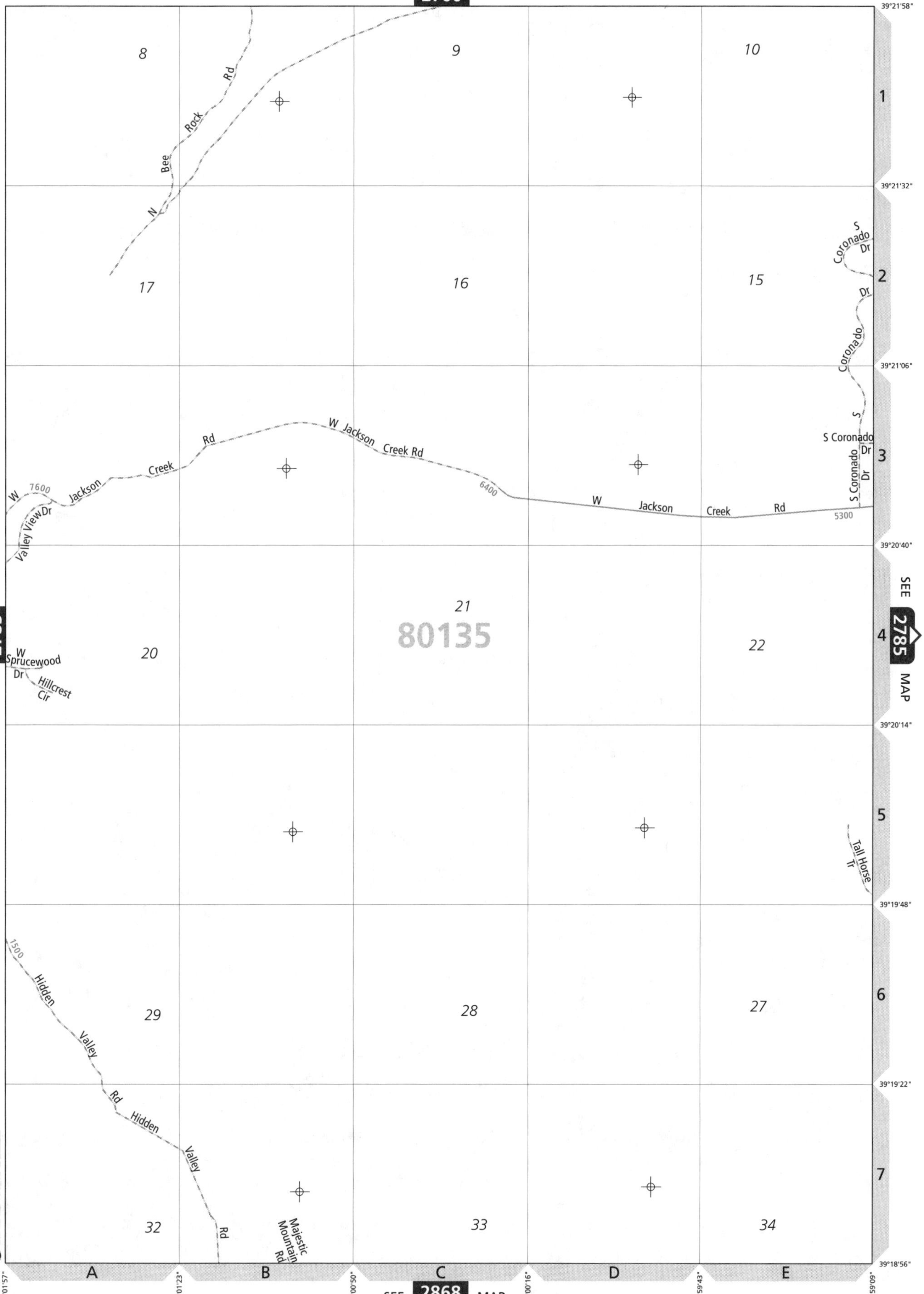

SEE 2783 MAP

SEE 2785 MAP

SEE 2868 MAP

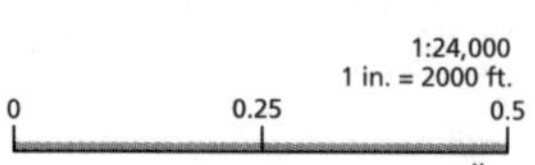

SEE 2701 MAP

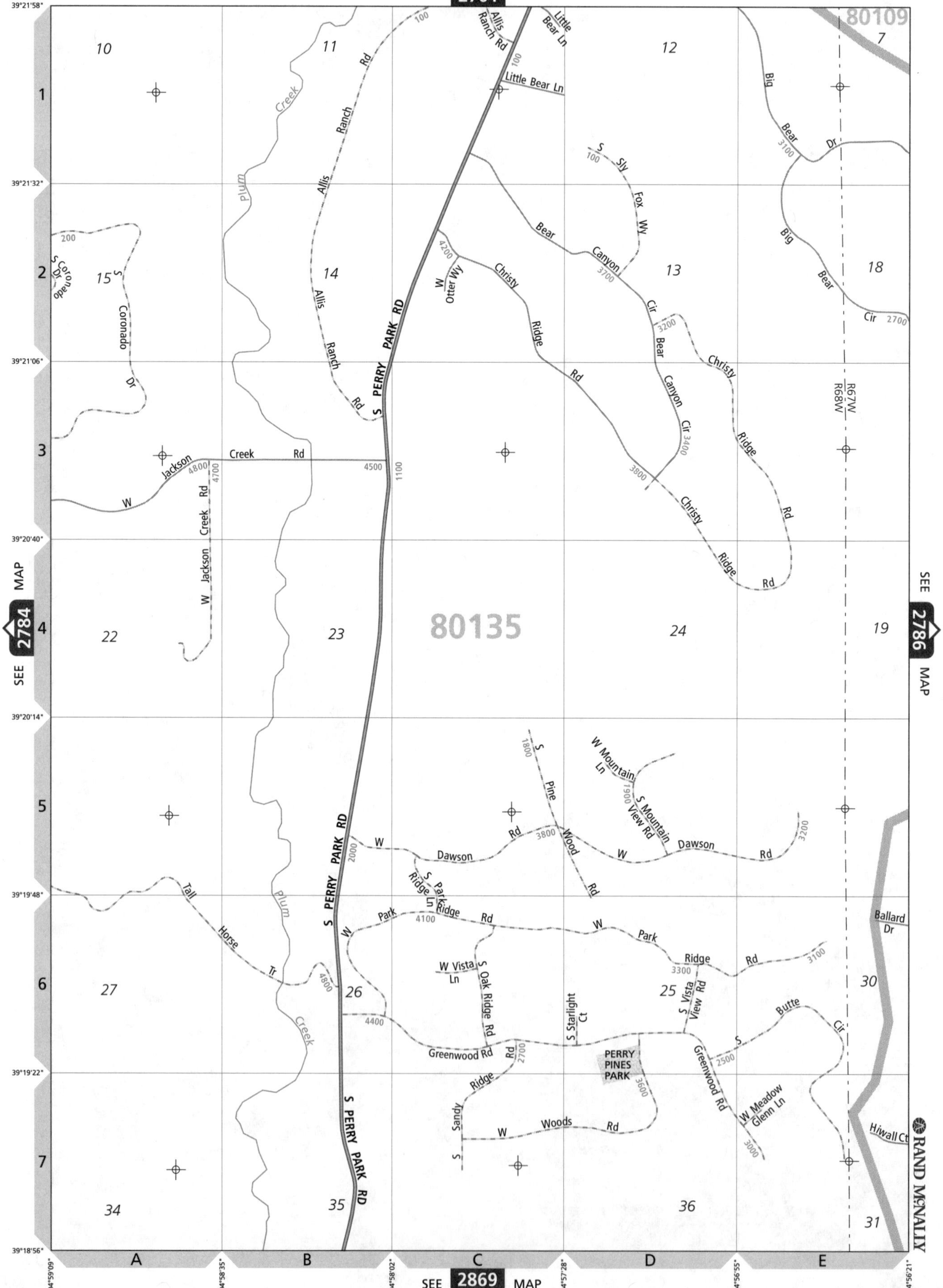

SEE 2784 MAP

SEE 2786 MAP

80135

80109

S PERRY PARK RD

W Jackson Creek Rd

Allis Ranch Rd

Little Bear Ln

Bear Canyon Cir

Christy Ridge Rd

Big Bear Dr

Big Bear Cir

S Sly Fox Wy

W Otter Wy

S Coronado Dr

W Dawson Rd

S Pine Wood Rd

W Mountain Ln

S Mountain View Rd

W Park Ridge Rd

S Park Ridge Ln

Tall Horse Tr

W Vista Ln

S Oak Ridge Rd

S Starlight Ct

S Vista View Rd

Greenwood Rd

S Butte Cir

Sandy Ridge Rd

W Woods Rd

W Meadow Glenn Ln

Ballard Dr

Hiwall Ct

PERRY PINES PARK

Plum Creek

R67W
R68W

SEE 2869 MAP

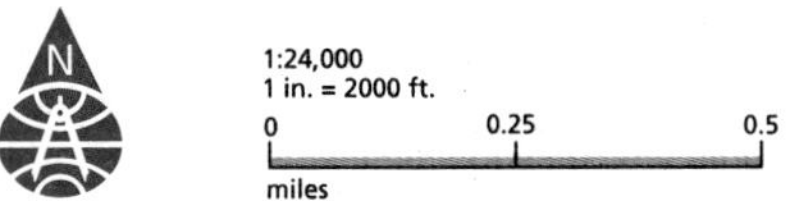

SEE 2702 MAP

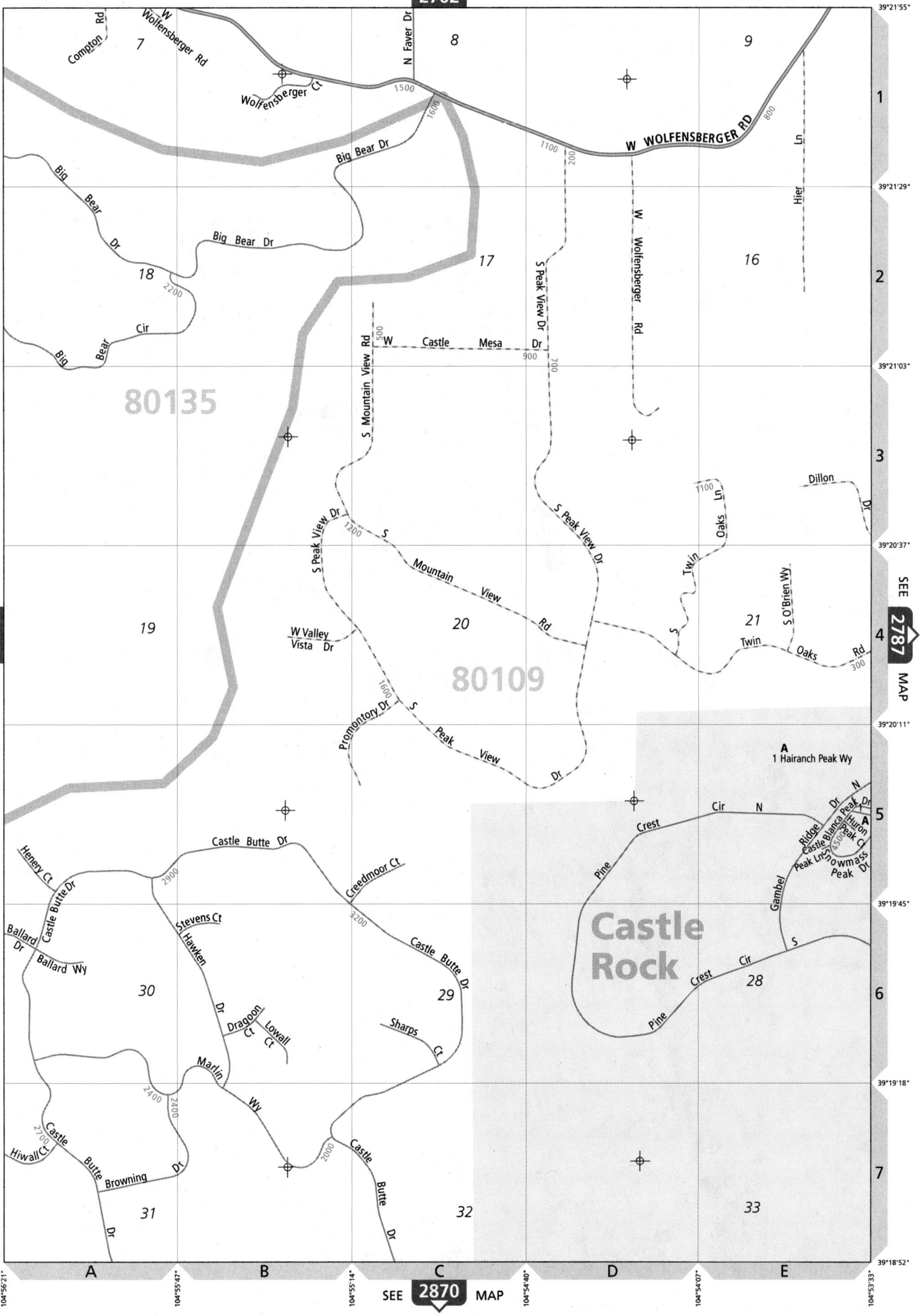

SEE 2785 MAP

SEE 2787 MAP

SEE 2870 MAP

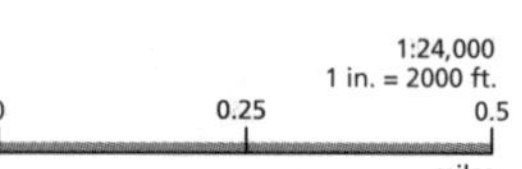

SEE 2703 MAP

Castle Rock

80109

80104

FAIRGROUNDS REGIONAL PARK

DOUGLAS CO FAIRGROUNDS

Daniel C Oakes HS

PLUM CREEK GOLF & CC

PLUM CREEK PARK

A 1 Cherry Hills Ln

B 1 Masters Ct

PLUM CREEK PKWY

W FRONTAGE RD

E FRONTAGE RD

E DOUGLAS LN

CRYSTAL VALLEY PKWY

S WILCOX ST

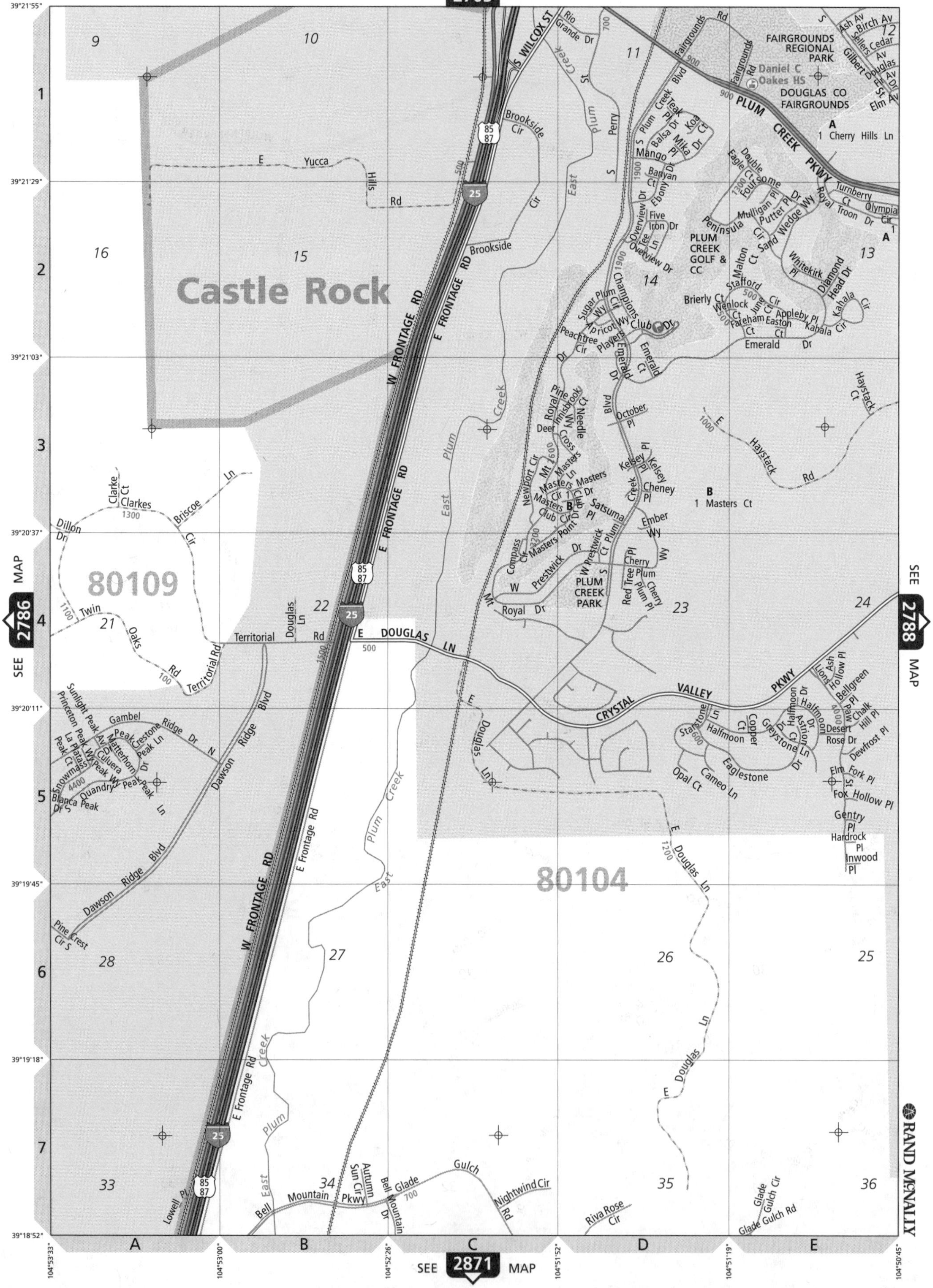

SEE 2786 MAP

SEE 2788 MAP

SEE 2871 MAP

A B C D E

1 2 3 4 5 6 7

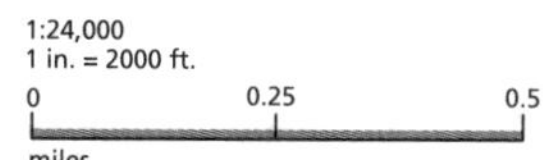

SEE 2704 MAP

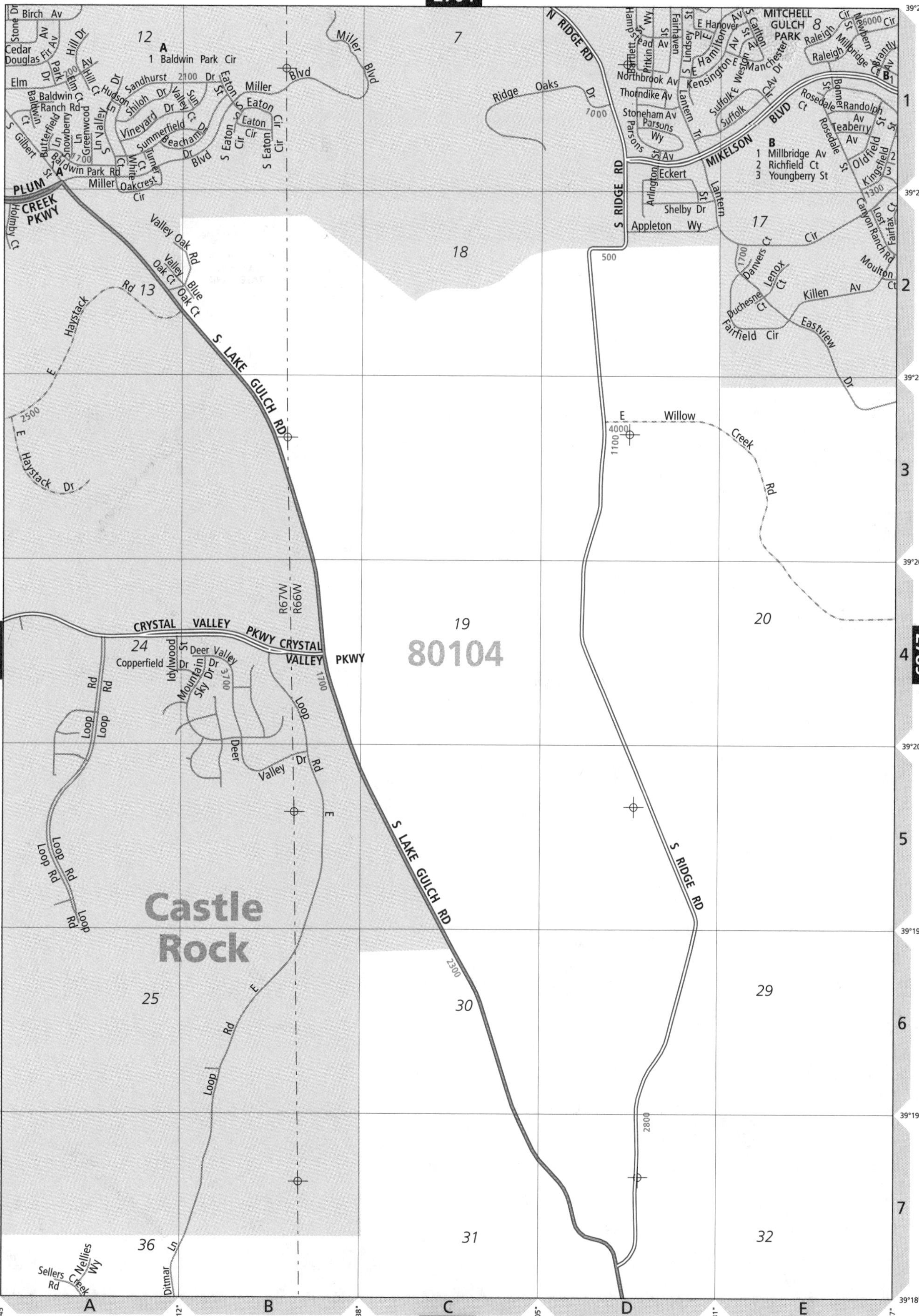

SEE 2787 MAP

SEE 2789 MAP

SEE B MAP

1:24,000
1 in. = 2000 ft.
0
0.25
0.5
miles
N
SEE 2705 MAP
SEE 2788 MAP
SEE 2790 MAP
SEE B MAP
Castle Rock
80116
80104
CASTLEWOOD
CANYON
STATE PARK
Cherry Creek
S Castlewood Canyon Rd
Castlewood Canyon Rd
Castle Pointe Dr
E Willow Creek Rd
Eastview Dr
Lost Canyon Ranch Rd
Moulton Ct
Lost Canyon Ranch Ct
MIKELSON BLVD
Millbridge
Brantly Av
Lancaster Av
Middleton Av
Boyd Ct
Milbury St
Atkinson
Mitchell Ct
Fairdale Ct
Winthrop
Mapleton Ct
Ellsworth
Sanborne
Crenshaw St
Youngberry St
Kittery St
A
1 Gardner St
B
1 Medford Ct
2 Kingsfield St
8
9
10
11
14
15
16
17
20
21
22
23
26
27
28
29
32
33
34
35
800
1000
2500
4000
1
2
3
4
5
6
7
A
B
C
D
E
39°21'51"
39°21'25"
39°20'59"
39°20'33"
39°20'07"
39°19'41"
39°19'15"
39°18'49"
104°47'57"
104°47'24"
104°46'50"
104°46'17"
104°45'43"
104°45'09"
RAND McNALLY

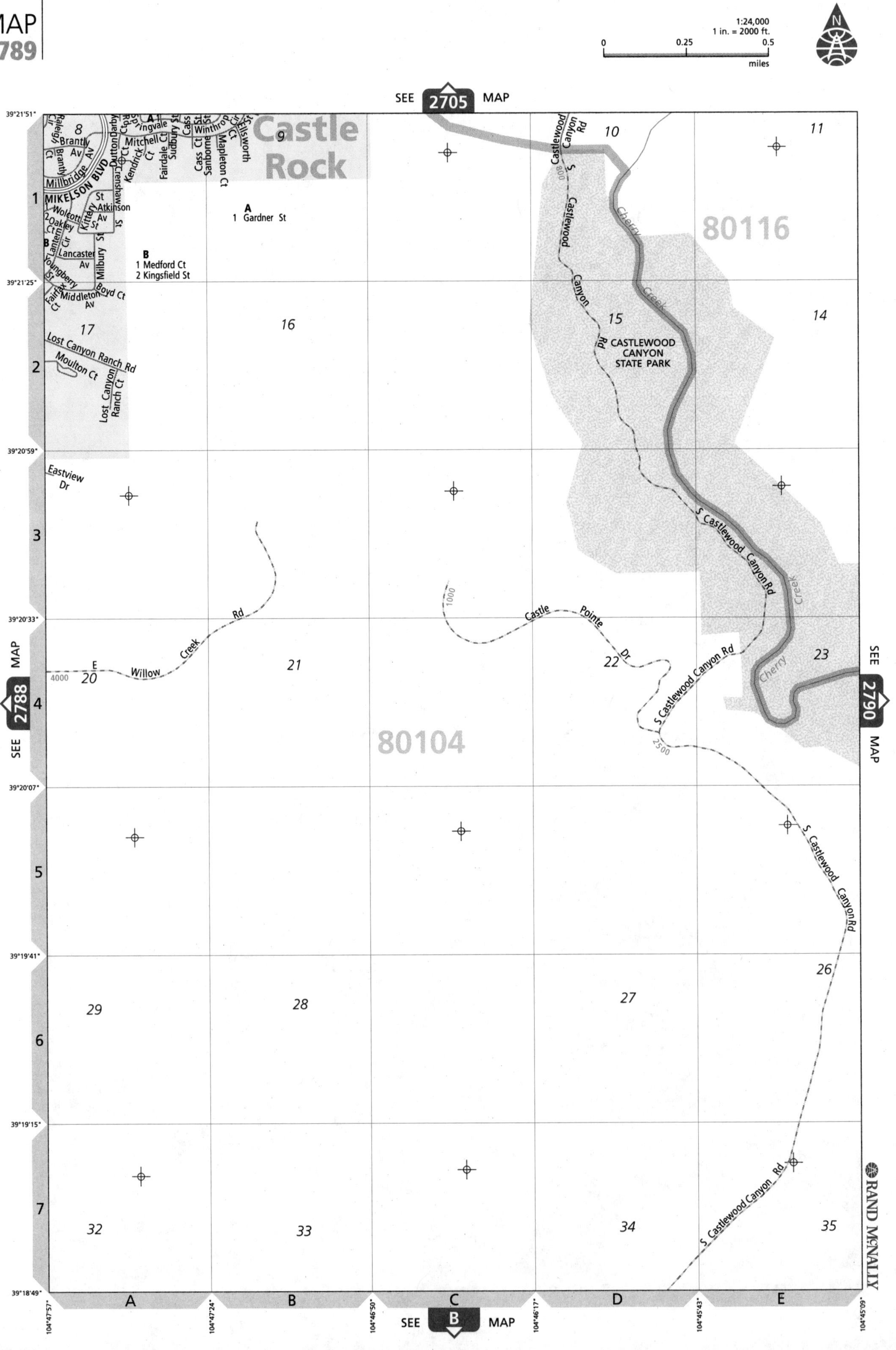

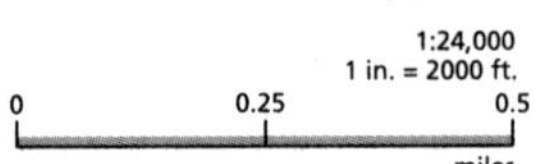

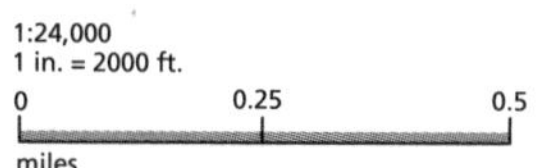

SEE 2706 MAP

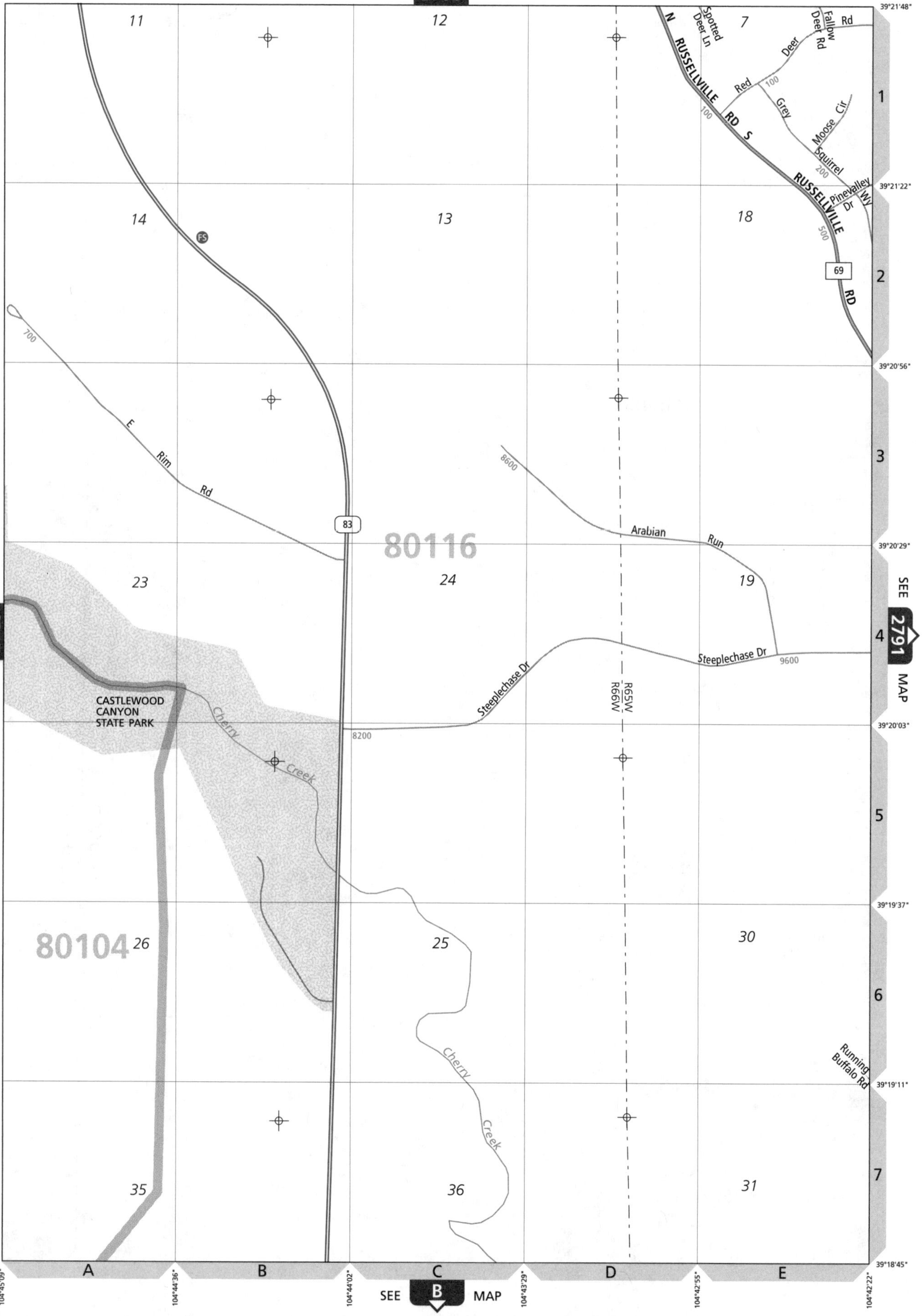

SEE 2789 MAP

SEE 2791 MAP

SEE B MAP

11
12
7
14
13
18
23
24
19
26
25
30
35
36
31

N RUSSELLVILLE RD S
RUSSELLVILLE RD
Spotted Deer Ln
Fallow Deer Rd
Red Deer Rd
Grey Squirrel
Moose Cir
Pinevalley Dr
Wy
69
100
100
200
500
E Rim Rd
700
83
80116
80104
8600
Arabian Run
Steeplechase Dr
9600
8200
R65W
R66W
CASTLEWOOD
CANYON
STATE PARK
Cherry Creek
Running Buffalo Rd
FS

39°21'48"
39°21'22"
39°20'56"
39°20'29"
39°20'03"
39°19'37"
39°19'11"
39°18'45"

104°45'09"
104°44'36"
104°44'02"
104°43'29"
104°42'55"
104°42'22"

1
2
3
4
5
6
7

A
B
C
D
E

RAND McNALLY

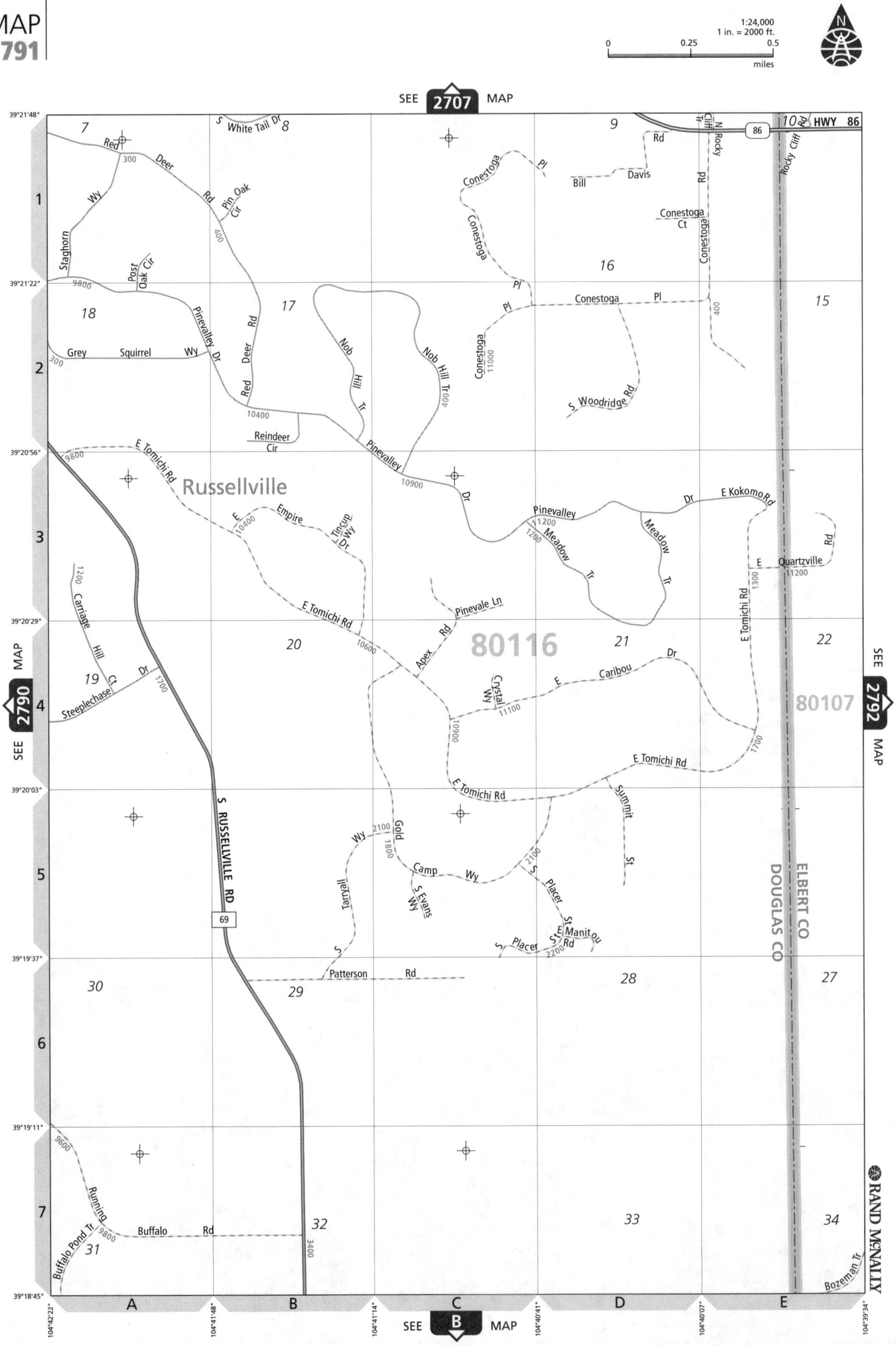

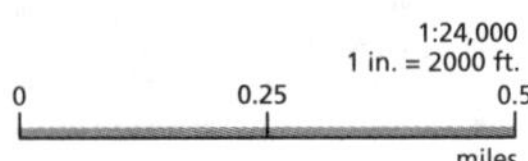

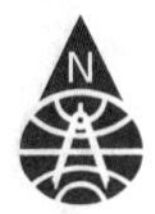

1:24,000
1 in. = 2000 ft.
0 0.25 0.5
miles
SEE 2707 MAP
SEE MAP 2790
SEE 2792 MAP
SEE B MAP
Russellville
80116
80107
S RUSSELLVILLE RD
69
HWY 86
86
ELBERT CO
DOUGLAS CO
Red Deer Rd
Pin Oak Cir
Staghorn Wy
Post Oak Cir
S White Tail Dr
Pinevalley Dr
Grey Squirrel Wy
Reindeer Cir
Nob Hill Tr
Conestoga Pl
Conestoga Ct
Bill Davis Rd
N Rocky Cliff Tr
Rocky Cliff Rd
S Woodridge Rd
E Tomichi Rd
E Empire
Tincup Wy Dr
E Kokomo Rd
Meadow Tr
E Quartzville Rd
Pinevale Ln
Apex Rd
Carriage Hill Ct
Steeplechase Dr
Crystal Wy
E Caribou Dr
Summit St
Gold Camp Wy
S Evans Wy
S Placer St
E Manitou Rd
S Tarryall Wy
S Patterson Rd
Running Buffalo Rd
Buffalo Pond Tr
Bozeman Tr
RAND McNALLY
A B C D E
1 2 3 4 5 6 7
39°21'48" 39°21'22" 39°20'56" 39°20'29" 39°20'03" 39°19'37" 39°19'11" 39°18'45"
104°42'22" 104°41'48" 104°41'14" 104°40'41" 104°40'07" 104°39'34"

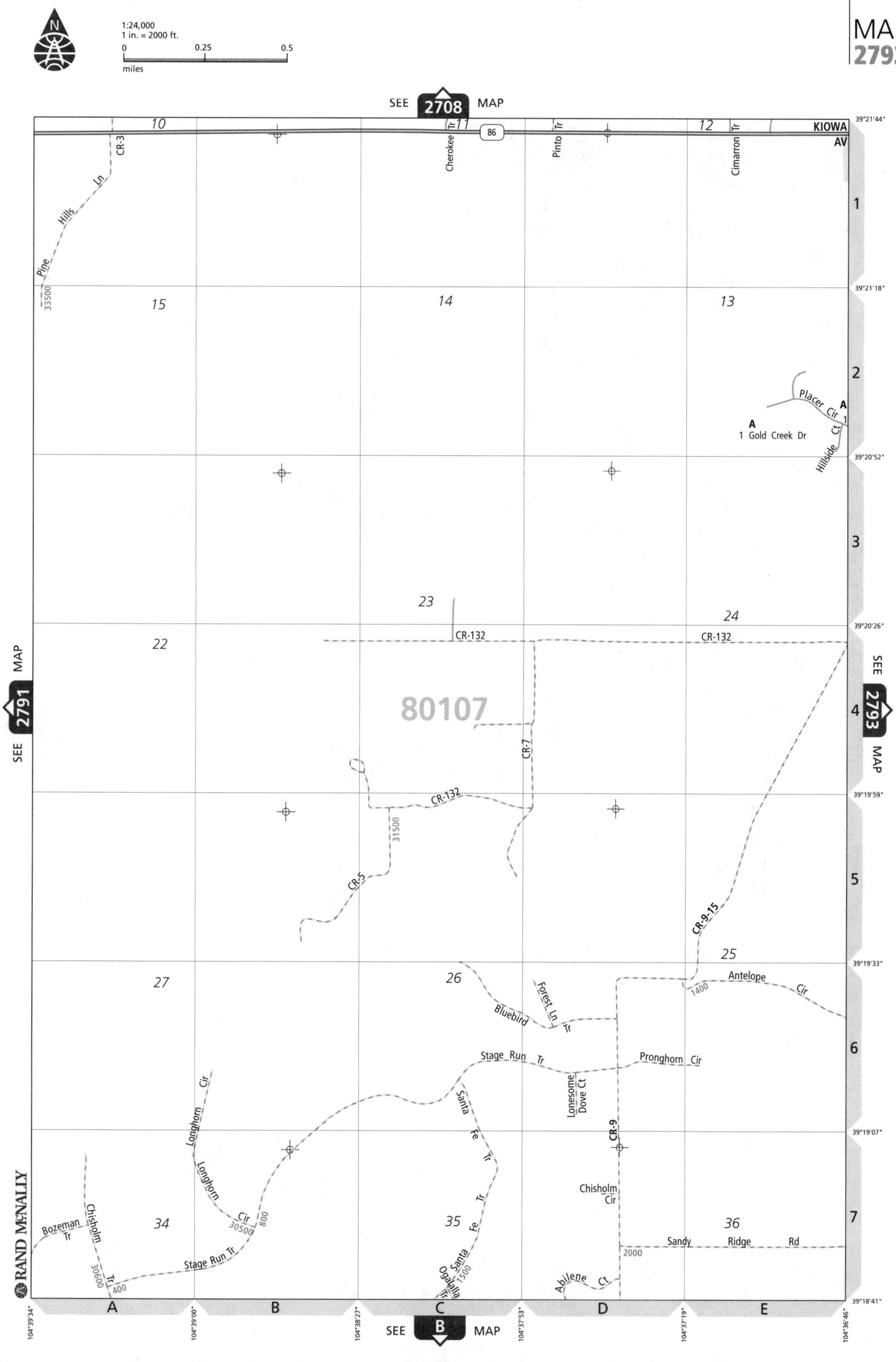

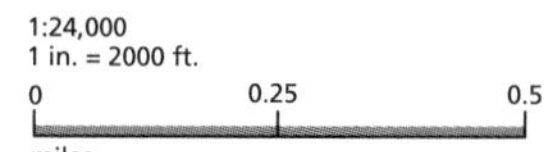

SEE 2708 MAP

SEE 2791 MAP

SEE 2793 MAP

SEE B MAP

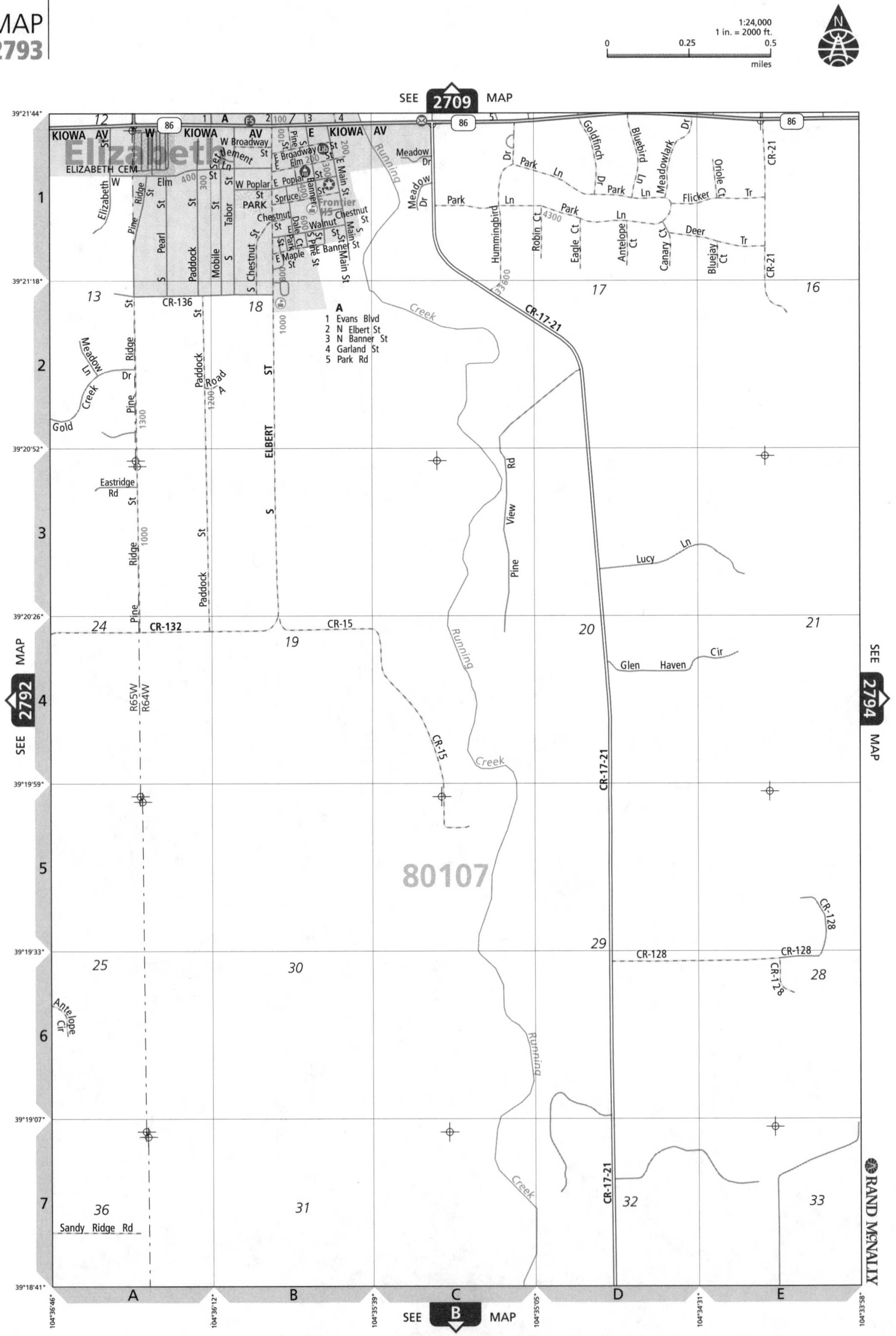

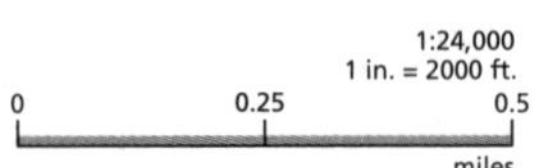

1:24,000
1 in. = 2000 ft.
0 0.25 0.5
miles
N
SEE 2709 MAP
SEE 2792 MAP
SEE 2794 MAP
SEE B MAP
Elizabeth
ELIZABETH CEM
KIOWA AV
W KIOWA AV
E KIOWA AV
W Broadway St
E Broadway St
Settlement Ln
W Poplar St
E Poplar St
PARK
Frontier HS
Spruce
Chestnut St
Walnut
Maple St
Elm
Banner St
S Main St
E Main St
Pine St
Dale Ct
Park St
S Pearl St
Paddock St
Mobile St
S Tabor St
S Chestnut St
Elizabeth St
Pine Ridge St
Meadow Dr
Park Ln
Goldfinch Dr
Bluebird Ln
Meadowlark Dr
Flicker Tr
Oriole Ct
Deer Tr
Hummingbird Dr
Robin Ct
Eagle Ct
Antelope Ct
Canary Ct
Bluejay Ct
CR-21
CR-17-21
CR-136
CR-132
CR-15
CR-128
Meadow Ln
Gold Creek
Dr
Road A
S ELBERT ST
Eastridge Rd
Pine View Rd
Lucy Ln
Glen Haven Cir
Running Creek
R65W
R64W
80107
Antelope Cir
Sandy Ridge Rd
A
1 Evans Blvd
2 N Elbert St
3 N Banner St
4 Garland St
5 Park Rd
86
12 13 16 17 18 19 20 21 24 25 28 29 30 31 32 33 36
1 2 3 4 5 6 7
A B C D E
39°21'44" 39°21'18" 39°20'52" 39°20'26" 39°19'59" 39°19'33" 39°19'07" 39°18'41"
104°36'46" 104°36'12" 104°35'39" 104°35'05" 104°34'31" 104°33'58"
RAND McNALLY

1:24,000
1 in. = 2000 ft.
0 0.25 0.5
miles

SEE 2710 MAP

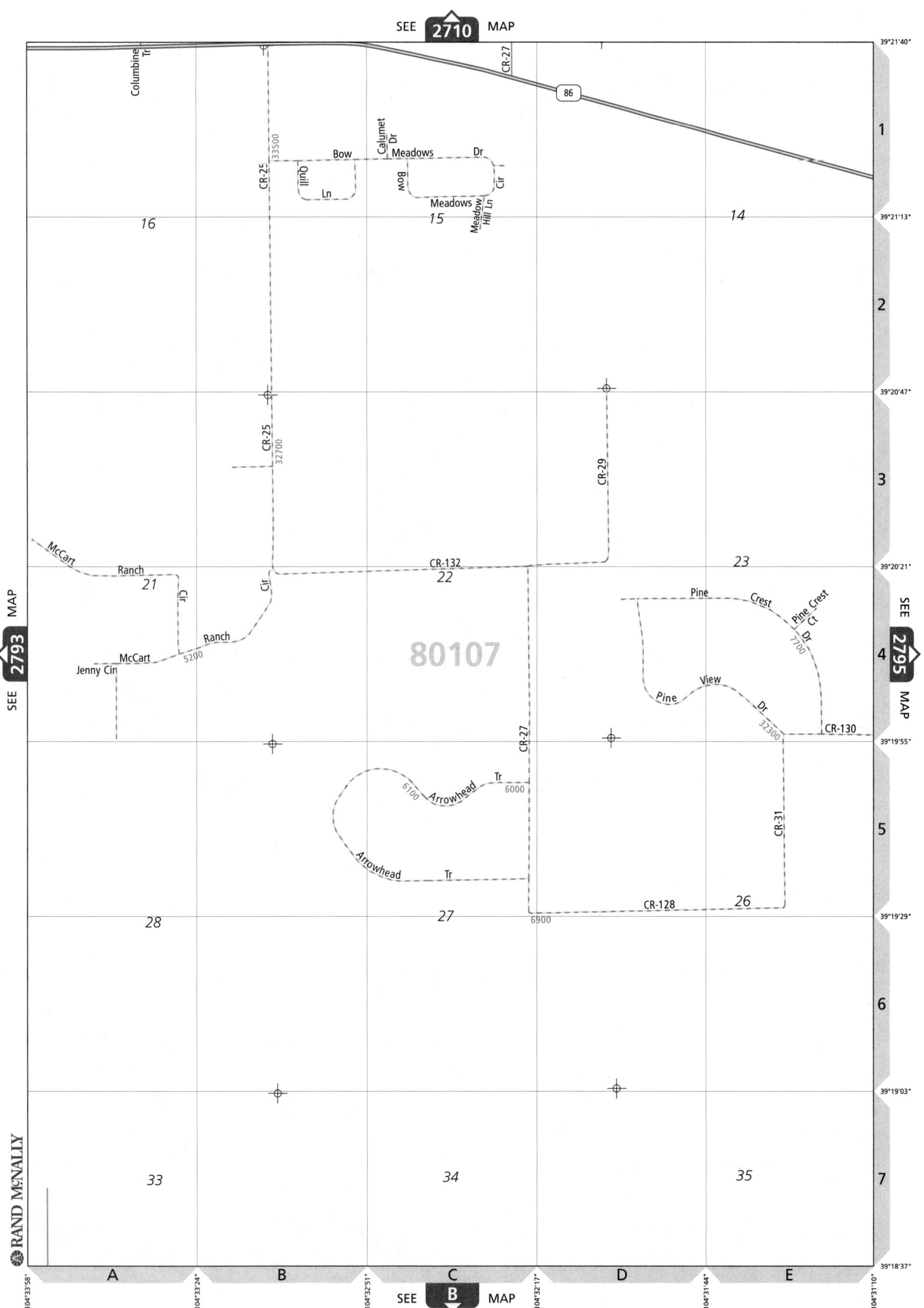

SEE 2793 MAP

SEE 2795 MAP

SEE B MAP

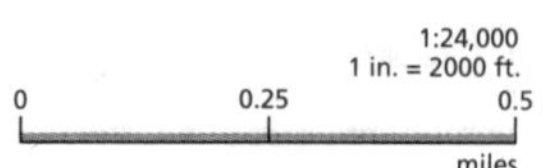

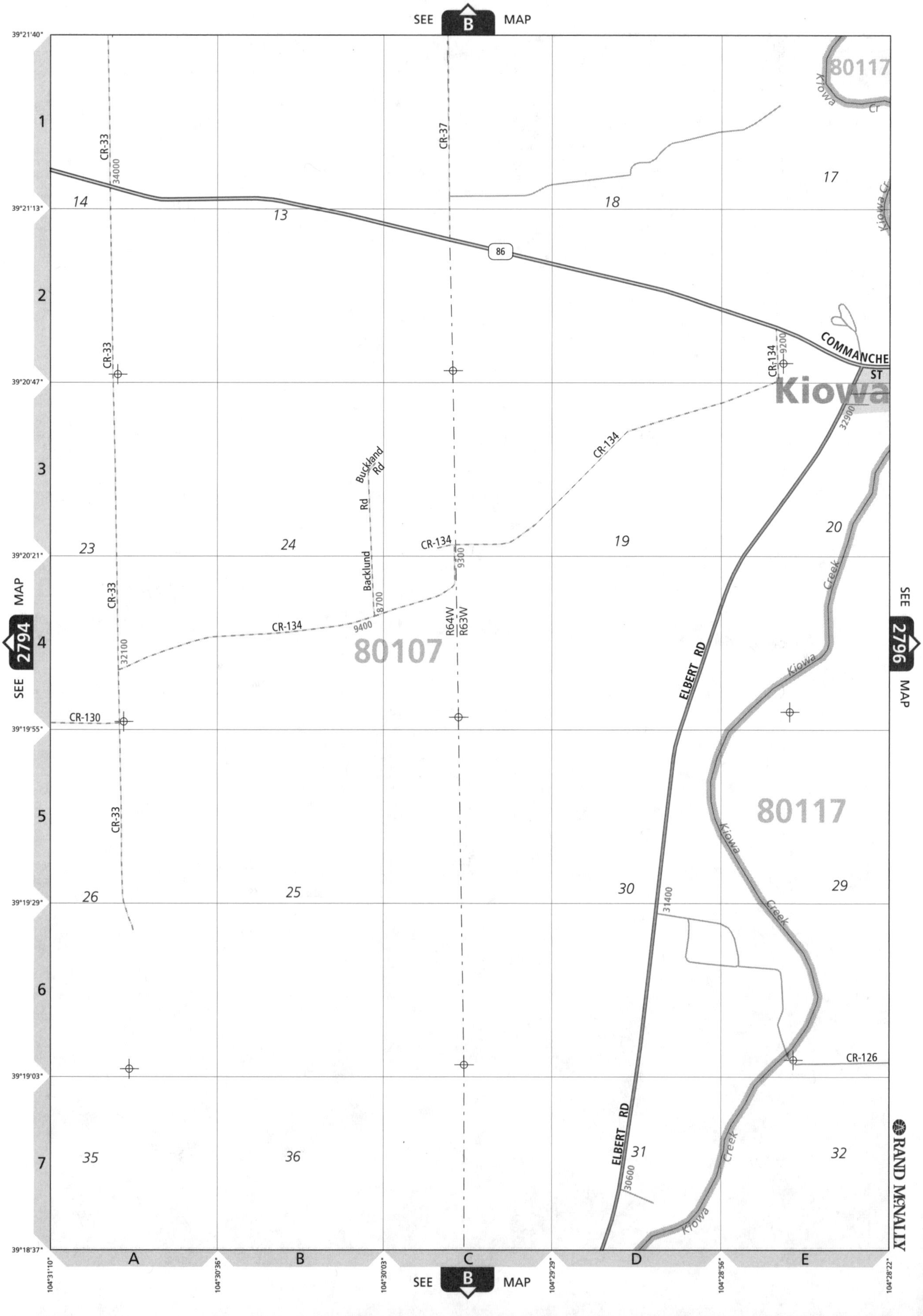

SEE B MAP

SEE MAP 2794

SEE 2796 MAP

SEE B MAP

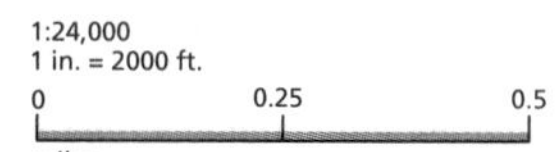

SEE B MAP

SEE MAP 2795

SEE B MAP

SEE B MAP

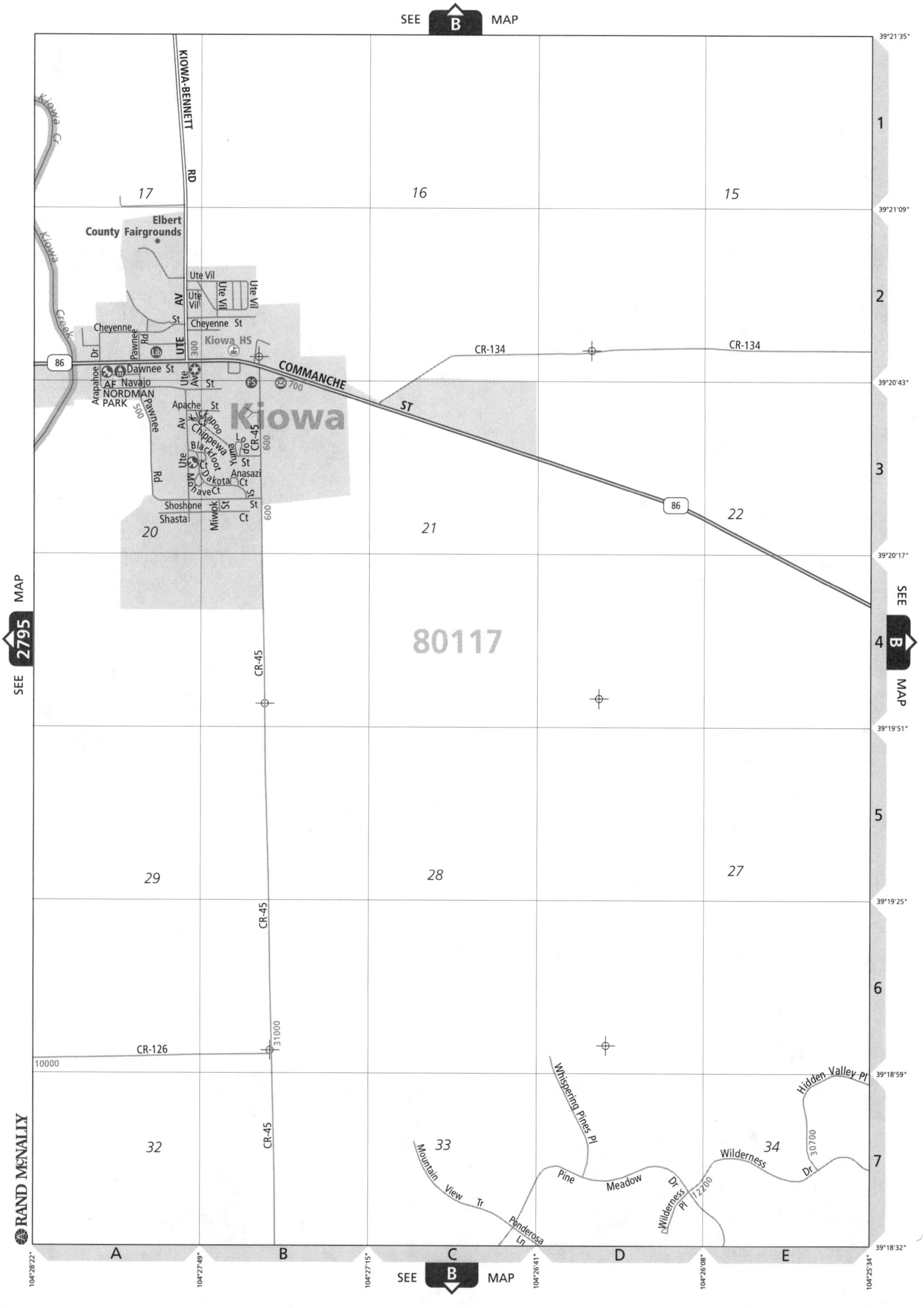

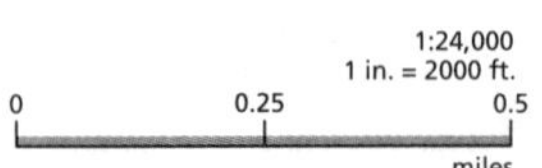

SEE 2784 MAP

SEE B MAP

SEE 2869 MAP

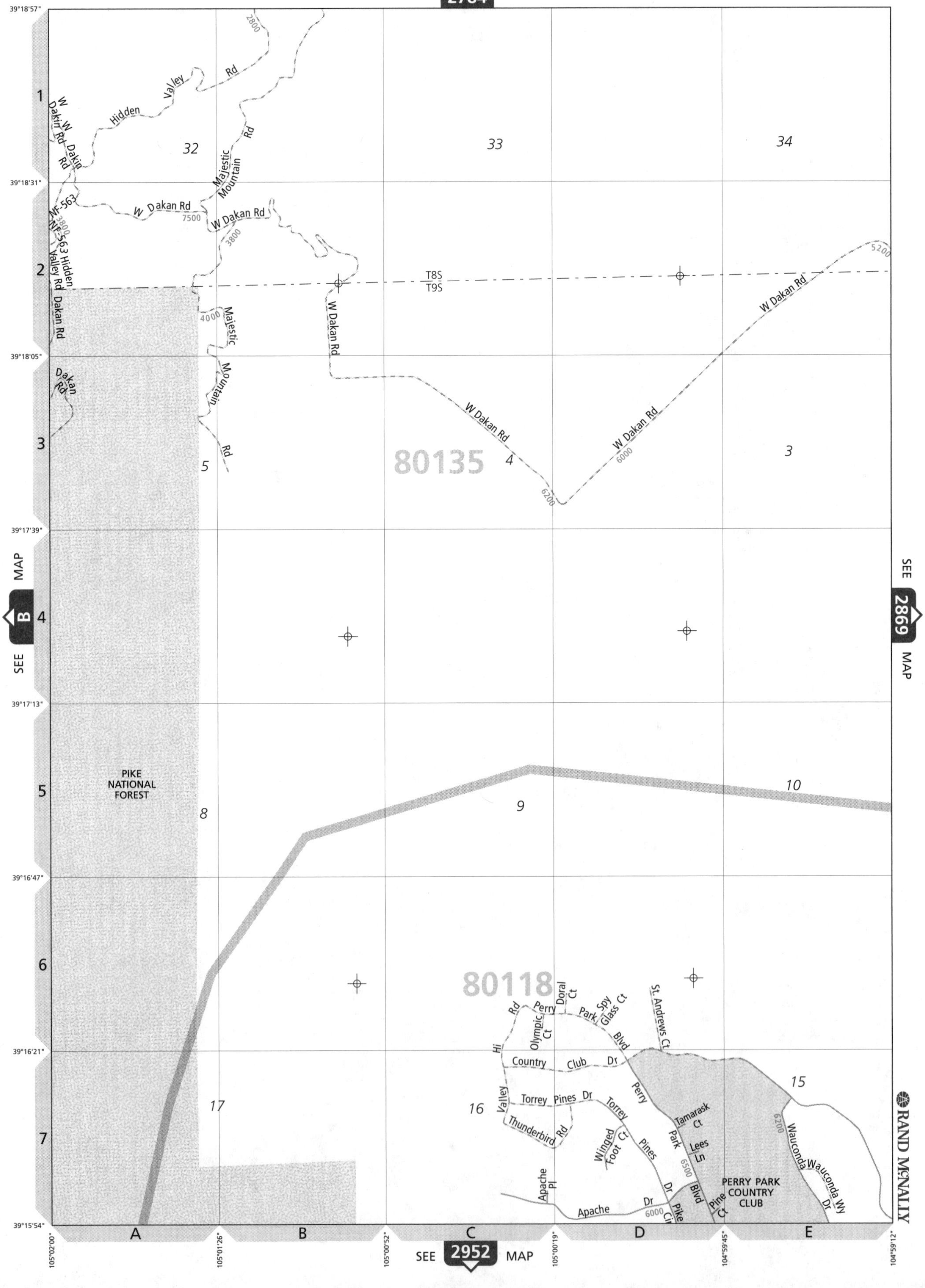

W Dakin Rd
W Dakin Rd
Hidden Valley Rd
Majestic Mountain Rd
W Dakan Rd
NF-563
NF-563 Hidden Valley Rd
Dakan Rd
T8S
T9S
PIKE NATIONAL FOREST
80135
80118
Perry Park Blvd
Country Club Dr
Torrey Pines Dr
Thunderbird Rd
Hi Valley Rd
Olympic Ct
Doral Ct
Spy Glass Ct
St. Andrews Ct
Tamarask Ct
Lees Ln
Winged Foot Ct
Apache Pl
Apache Dr
Pike Cir
Pine Ct
Waucondа Dr
Waucondа Wy
PERRY PARK COUNTRY CLUB

SEE 2952 MAP

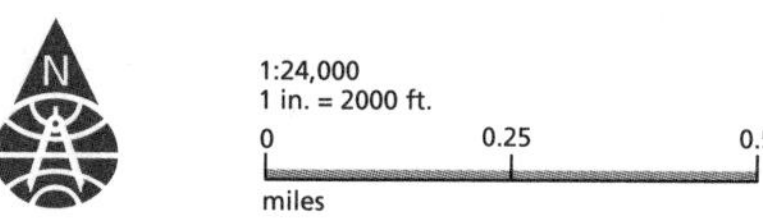

SEE 2785 MAP

S PERRY PARK RD
34
35
36
31
Plum Creek
T8S
T9S
W Dakan Rd
5200
4000
80135
S Perry Park Rd
Plum Creek Meadows Rd
3
2
1
6
Shars Tr
4800
S Perry Park Rd
5000
4900
S PERRY PARK RD
S Perry Park Rd
5100
R67W
R68W
Plum Creek
11
10
12
7
W TOMAH RD
2000
6000
80118
Plum Creek
15
14
13
18
S PERRY PARK RD
Sinclaire Blvd
Wally Av
Perry Park Blvd
Echo Gap Rd
S Perry Park Rd

39°18'54"
39°18'28"
39°18'02"
39°17'36"
39°17'10"
39°16'44"
39°16'17"
39°15'51"

1
2
3
4
5
6
7

A B C D E

104°59'12"
104°58'38"
104°58'05"
104°57'31"
104°56'58"
104°56'24"

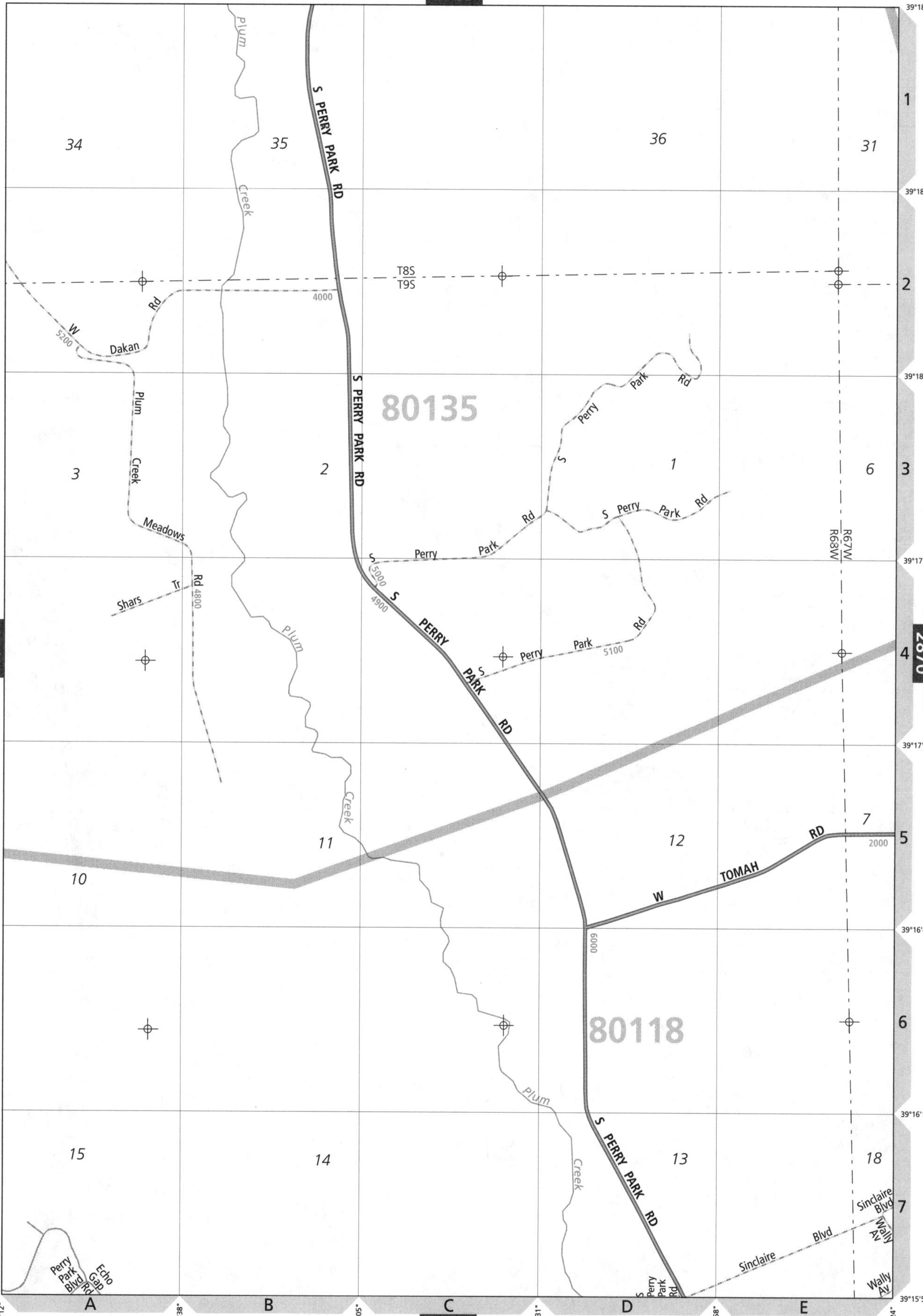

SEE 2868 MAP

SEE 2870 MAP

SEE 2953 MAP

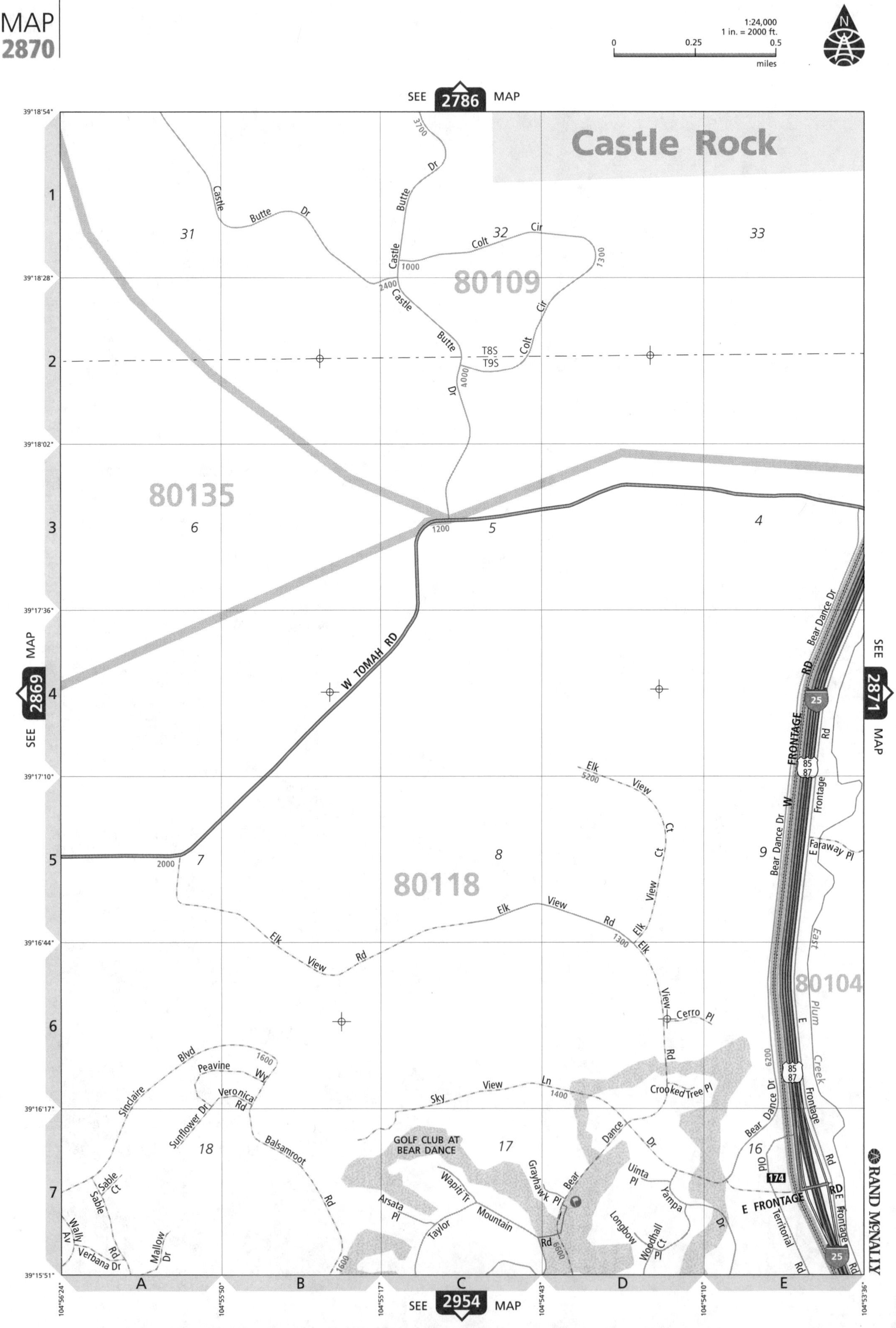

1:24,000
1 in. = 2000 ft.
0 0.25 0.5
miles

SEE 2786 MAP

SEE 2869 MAP

SEE 2871 MAP

SEE 2954 MAP

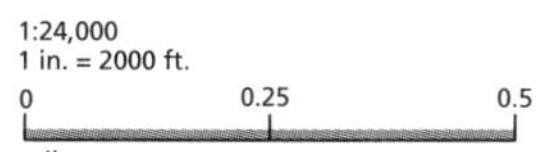

SEE 2787 MAP

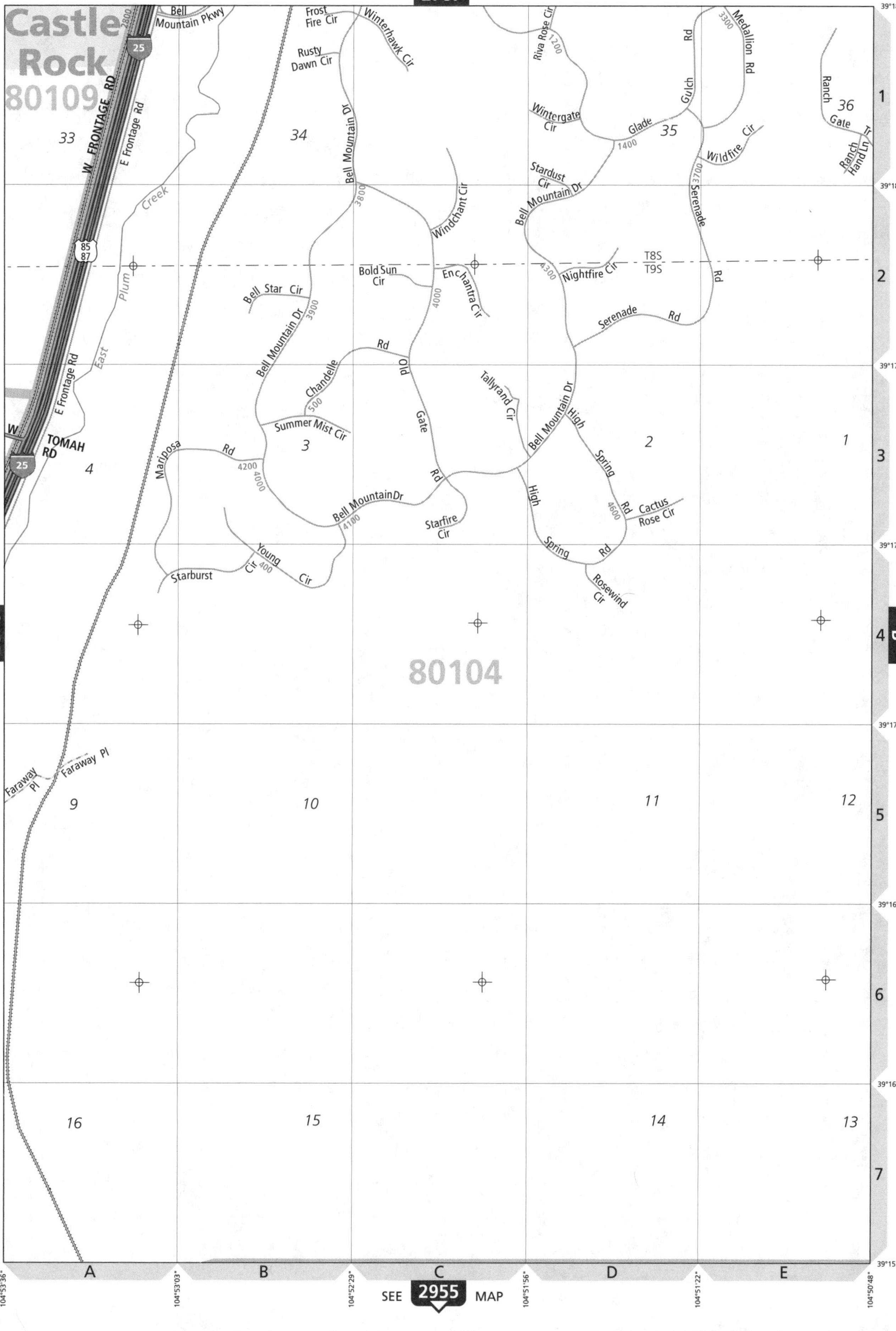

SEE 2870 MAP

SEE B MAP

SEE 2955 MAP

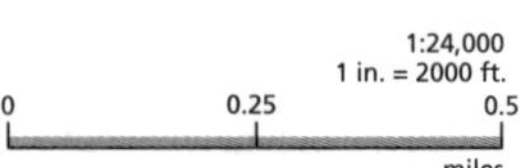

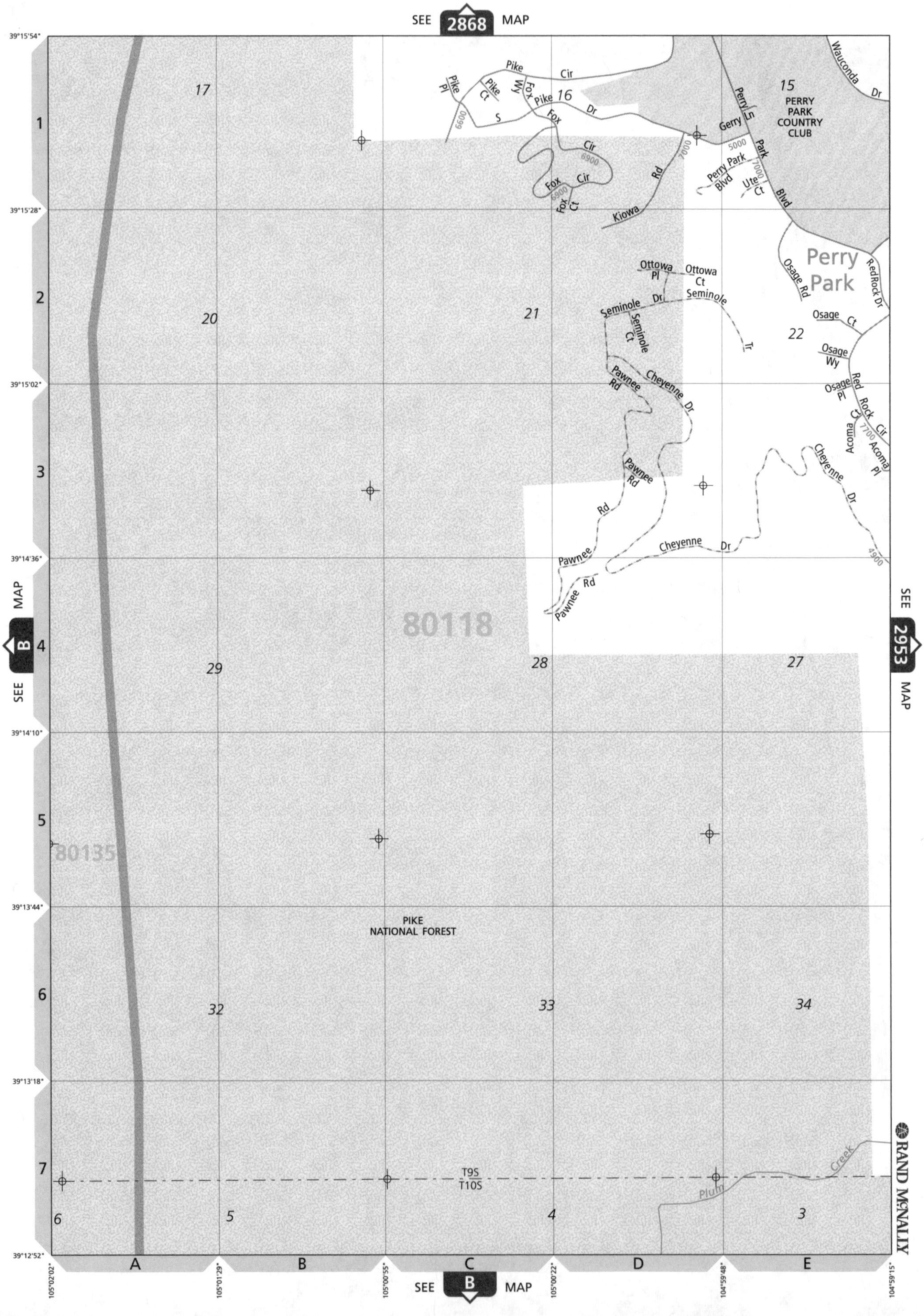

SEE 2868 MAP

SEE B MAP

SEE 2953 MAP

SEE B MAP

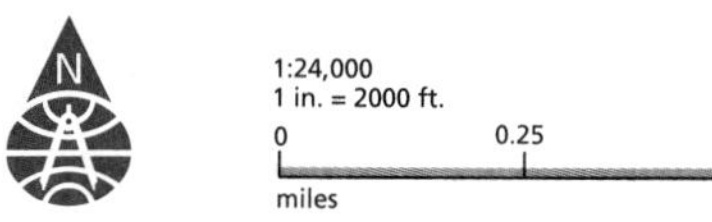

SEE 2869 MAP

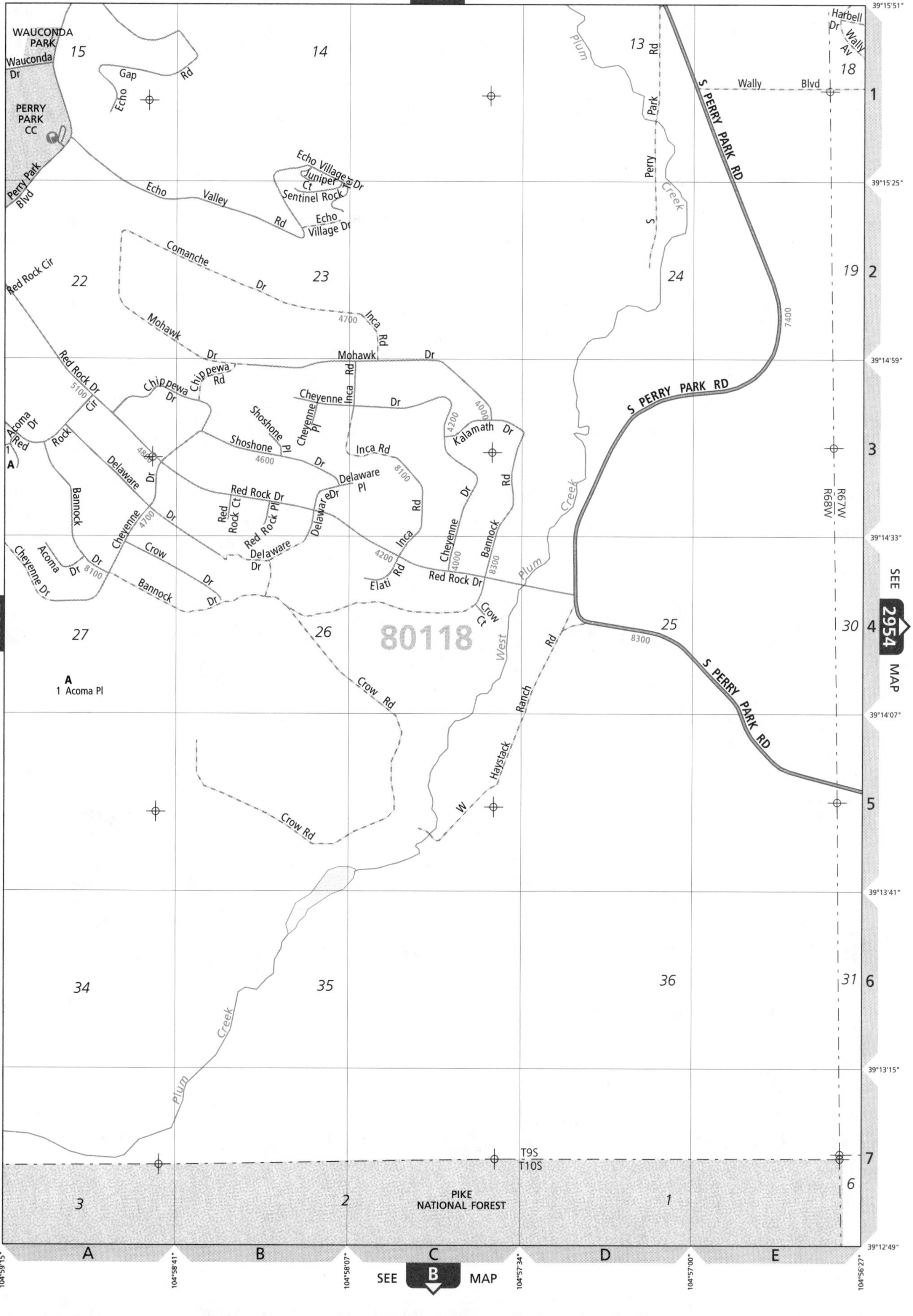

SEE 2952 MAP

SEE 2954 MAP

SEE B MAP

1:24,000
1 in. = 2000 ft.
0 0.25 0.5
miles

SEE 2870 MAP

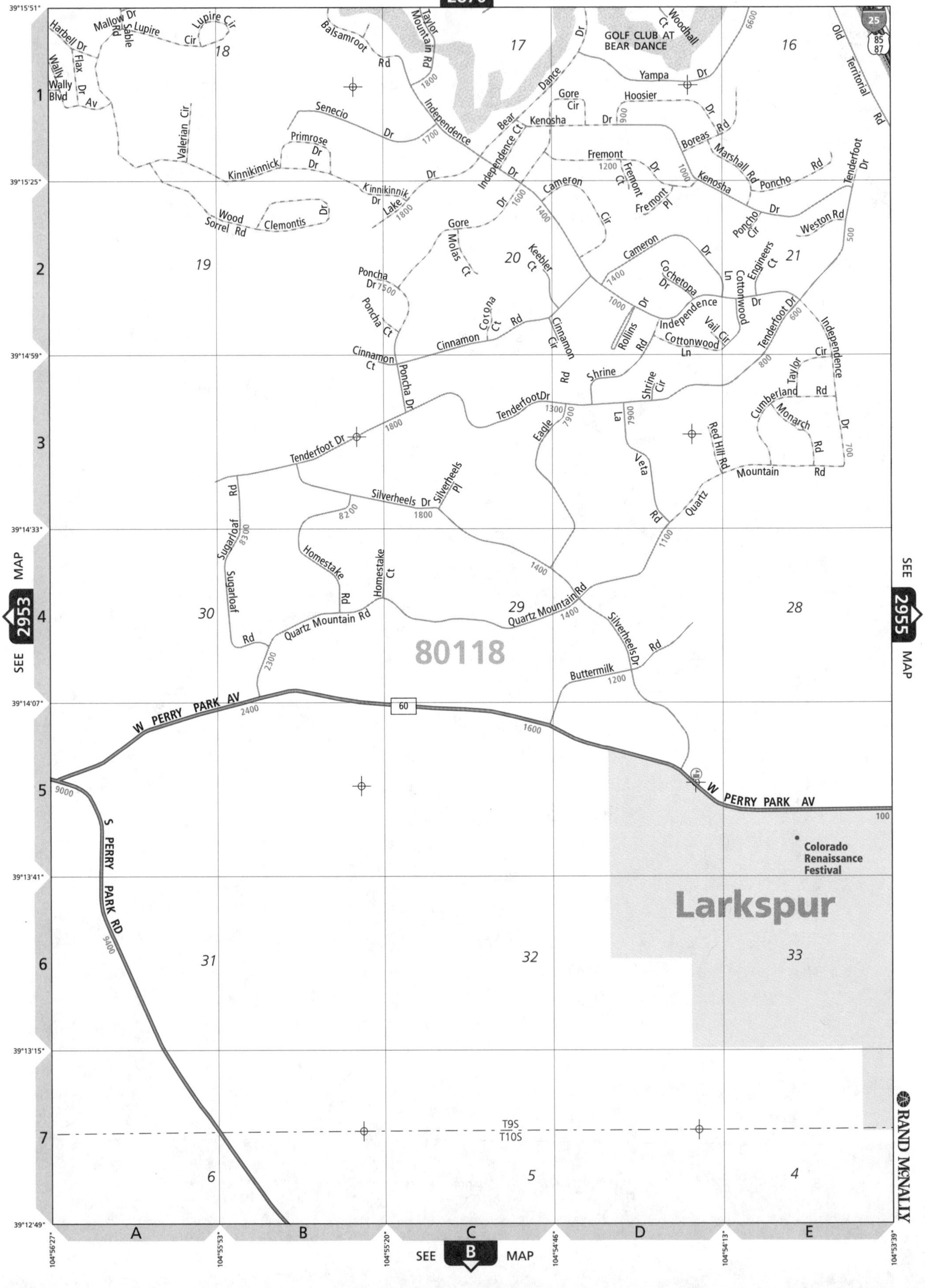

SEE 2953 MAP

SEE 2955 MAP

SEE B MAP

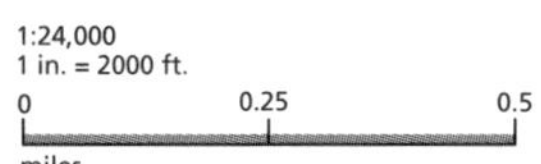

SEE 2871 MAP

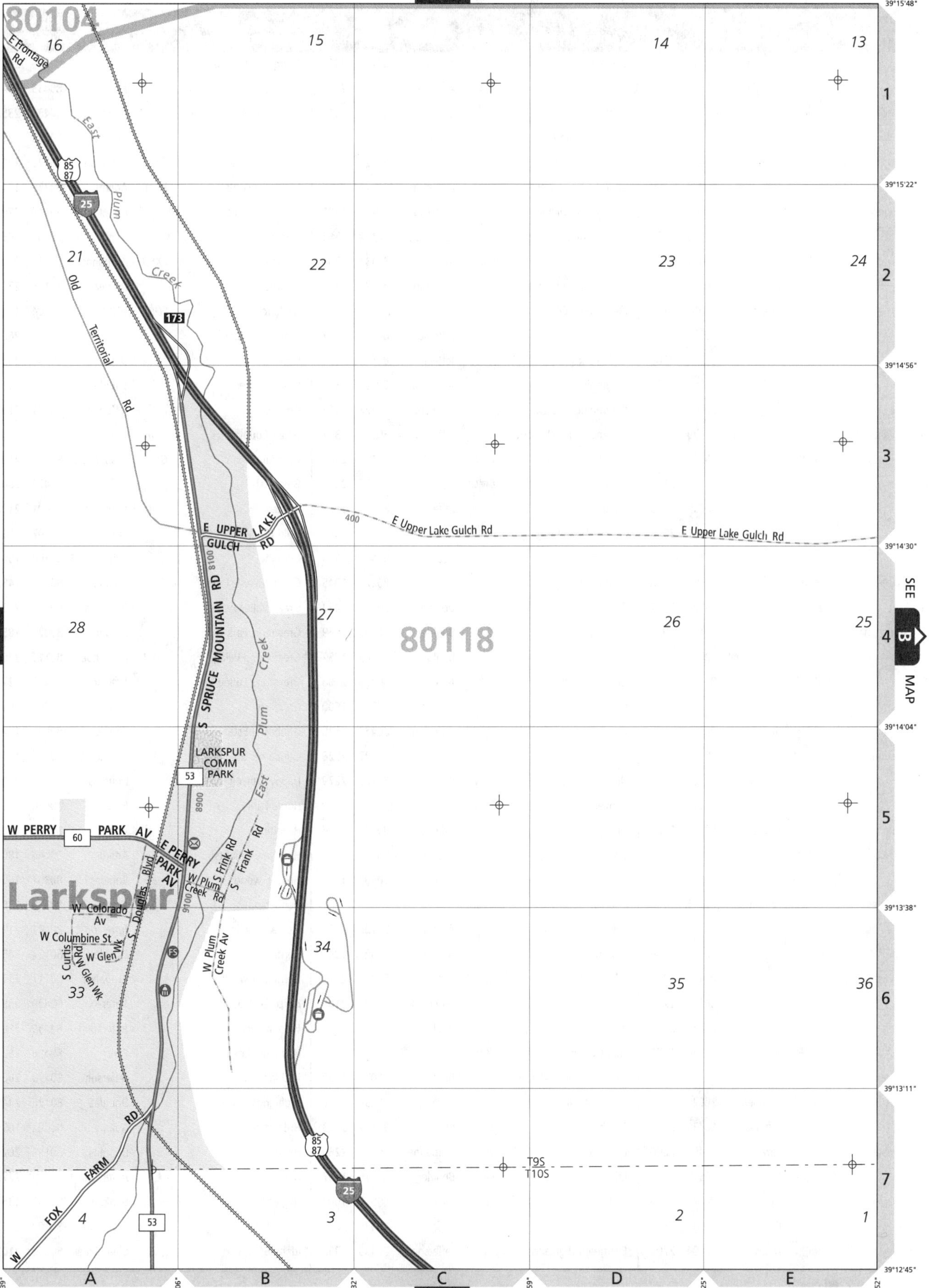

SEE 2954 MAP

SEE B MAP

SEE B MAP

Cities and Communities

Community Name	Abbr.	County	ZIP Code	Map Page
Acequia		Douglas	80125	2448
Acres Green		Douglas	80124	2450
--Adams County	AdmC			
Altona		Boulder	80302	1435
Angel Acres		Jefferson	80433	2526
Applewood		Jefferson	80401	2109
--Arapahoe County	AphC			
* Arvada	ARVD	Adams	80003	2027
* Arvada	ARVD	Jefferson	80004	2026
Aspen Park		Jefferson	80433	2442
* Aurora	AURA	Adams	80011	2117
* Aurora	AURA	Douglas	80138	2453
* Aurora	AURA	Arapahoe	80012	2200
Bailey		Park	80456	2690
Barr Lake		Adams	80603	1781
Bendemeer Valley		Clear Creek	80439	2271
* Bennett	BNNT	Arapahoe	80102	2209
* Bennett	BNNT	Adams	80102	2124
Bergen Park		Jefferson	80439	2188
Berkley		Adams	80221	2028
Beverly Hills		Douglas	80108	2535
* Black Hawk	BKHK	Gilpin	80403	2018
Blakeland		Douglas	80125	2447
Blue Mountain Estates		Jefferson	80403	1938
Blue Valley		Clear Creek	80452	2186
* Boulder	BLDR	Boulder	80302	1686
--Boulder County	BldC			
Boulder Heights		Boulder	80302	1517
Boulder Junction		Boulder	80301	1688
* Bow Mar	BWMR	Jefferson	80123	2279
* Bow Mar	BWMR	Arapahoe	80123	2363
Brigadoon Glen		Boulder	80503	1520
* Brighton	BGTN	Weld	80601	1697
* Brighton	BGTN	Adams	80601	1696
Broadway Estates		Arapahoe	80121	2365
Broken Arrow Acres		Jefferson	80433	2525
Brook Forest		Jefferson	80439	2356
Brook Forest Estates		Clear Creek	80439	2440
Brookridge		Arapahoe	80121	2280
Brookvale		Clear Creek	80439	2271
* Broomfield	BMFD	Broomfield	80020	1859
--Broomfield County	BfdC			
Brownsville		Boulder	80026	1606
Buffalo Park Estates		Jefferson	80439	2356
Burland Ranchettes		Park	80456	2606
Canfield		Boulder	80516	1606
Carriage Club		Douglas	80124	2450
Castle Pines		Douglas	80108	2618
* Castle Rock	CSRK	Douglas	80104	2703
Castlewood		Arapahoe	80112	2366
* Centennial	CTNL	Arapahoe	80111	2367
* Central City	CLCY	Gilpin	80403	2017
Chatfield Estates		Jefferson	80128	2446
Cherry Hills Crest		Arapahoe	80121	2365
Cherry Hills Manor		Arapahoe	80121	2365
* Cherry Hills Village	CHLV	Arapahoe	80113	2281
Cherry Knolls		Arapahoe	80122	2365
Cherry Park		Arapahoe	80111	2366
Cherrywood Village		Arapahoe	80122	2365
--Clear Creek County	CCkC			
Coal Creek		Jefferson	80403	1852
Cody Park		Jefferson	80401	2190
Columbine		Jefferson	80128	2363
Columbine Hills		Jefferson	80128	2363
Columbine Knolls South		Jefferson	80128	2362
* Columbine Valley	CBVL	Arapahoe	80123	2363
* Commerce City	CMCY	Adams	80022	2030
Conifer		Jefferson	80433	2526
Conifer Mountain		Jefferson	80433	2440
Copperdale		Boulder	80403	1853
Coronado		Adams	80229	1945
Cottonwood		Douglas	80134	2452
Crescent		Boulder	80403	1769
Crescent Village		Boulder	80403	1852
Crestview Village		Jefferson	80401	2108
Crisman		Boulder	80302	1600
Critchell		Jefferson	80433	2526
Deermont		Jefferson	80127	2528
* Denver	DNVR	Denver	80123	2279
--Denver County	DvrC			
Derby		Adams	80022	1946
Dominion		Boulder	80503	1438
Dorey Lakes		Gilpin	80403	1934
--Douglas County	DgsC			
Dream House Acres		Arapahoe	80121	2365
Dupont		Adams	80022	1946
* Edgewater	EDGW	Jefferson	80214	2111
El Rancho		Jefferson	80401	2189
El Vado		Boulder	80302	1685
--Elbert County	EbtC			
Eldorado Springs		Boulder	80025	1770
Elephant Park		Jefferson	80439	2272
* Elizabeth	ELIZ	Elbert	80107	2793
* Englewood	EGLD	Arapahoe	80110	2280
* Erie	ERIE	Boulder	80516	1607
* Erie	ERIE	Weld	80516	1607
Evergreen		Jefferson	80439	2273
Evergreen Highlands		Jefferson	80439	2358
Evergreen Meadows		Jefferson	80439	2441
Evergreen Meadows W		Jefferson	80433	2441
Evergreen Park Estates		Jefferson	80439	2357
Evergreen West		Clear Creek	80439	2271
Fairview Estates		Jefferson	80128	2362
* Federal Heights	FLHT	Adams	80260	1944
Flintwood Hills		Douglas	80116	2707
Forest Hills		Gilpin	80403	1933
* Foxfield	FXFD	Arapahoe	80016	2369
Franktown		Douglas	80116	2705
* Frederick	FDRK	Weld	80504	1523
Friendship Ranch		Park	80456	2606
Gateway		Douglas	80130	2450
Gaynor Lakes		Boulder	80504	1521
Genesee		Jefferson	80401	2190
--Gilpin County	GpnC			
* Glendale	GNDL	Arapahoe	80246	2197
Glenelk		Jefferson	80470	2609
* Golden	GOLD	Jefferson	80401	2108
Gold Hill		Boulder	80302	1599
Gooding		Boulder	80504	1522
Grand View Estates		Douglas	80134	2452
Green Valley Acres		Jefferson	80433	2525
Greenway Park		Broomfield	80020	1859
* Greenwood Village	GDVL	Arapahoe	80111	2366
Greystone Lodge		Jefferson	80439	2272
Gunbarrel		Boulder	80301	1605
Gunbarrel Estates		Boulder	80503	1520
Gunbarrel Greens		Boulder	80301	1604
Happy Canyon		Douglas	80108	2619
Harris Park		Park	80456	2522
Hazeltine		Adams	80640	1863
Hazeltine Heights		Adams	80640	1862
Heatherwood		Boulder	80301	1604
Henderson		Adams	80640	1863
Heritage Dells		Jefferson	80401	2192
Heritage Hills		Douglas	80124	2451
Heritage Place		Arapahoe	80111	2366
Herzman Mesa		Jefferson	80439	2357
Hidden Valley		Jefferson	80439	2189
Highland Park		Park	80456	2521
Highland Pines		Jefferson	80470	2608
Highlands Ranch		Douglas	80126	2449
Hi-Land Acres		Adams	80602	1695
Hilltop		Douglas	80138	2623
Hiwan Hills		Jefferson	80439	2273
Hygiene		Boulder	80503	1354
Hyland Hills		Arapahoe	80102	2123
* Idaho Springs	IDSP	Clear Creek	80452	2101

*Indicates incorporated city

Cities and Communities

Community Name	Abbr.	County	ZIP Code	Map Page
Idledale		Jefferson	80465	2275
Indian Creek Ranch		Douglas	80135	2616
Indian Hills		Jefferson	80454	2359
Indian Springs Village		Jefferson	80470	2609
Irondale		Adams	80022	1946
* Jamestown	JMWN	Boulder	80455	1516
--Jefferson County	JfnC			
Ken Caryl		Jefferson	80127	2361
* Kiowa	KIOW	Elbert	80117	2796
Kipling Villas		Jefferson	80123	2362
Kittredge		Jefferson	80457	2274
Kuhlmann Heights		Boulder	80403	1852
* Lafayette	LAFT	Boulder	80026	1690
Lake View		Gilpin	80403	1933
Lakeborough		Jefferson	80235	2278
* Lakeside	LKSD	Jefferson	80212	2027
* Lakewood	LKWD	Jefferson	80226	2194
--Larimer County	LmrC			
* Larkspur	LKSR	Douglas	80118	2955
Leisure Living		Broomfield	80516	1692
Leyden		Jefferson	80007	1940
Leyner		Boulder	80026	1606
Liggett		Boulder	80026	1605
* Littleton	LITN	Douglas	80120	2448
* Littleton	LITN	Arapahoe	80120	2364
Livengood Hills		Douglas	80138	2454
* Lochbuie	LCHB	Weld	80603	1698
Lone Pine Estates		Jefferson	80465	2359
* Lone Tree	LNTR	Douglas	80124	2450
* Longmont	LGMT	Weld	80504	1440
* Longmont	LGMT	Boulder	80501	1439
Lookout Mountain		Jefferson	80401	2107
* Louisville	LSVL	Boulder	80027	1689
Louviers		Douglas	80135	2532
* Lyons	LYNS	Boulder	80540	1352
Lyons Park Estates		Boulder	80540	1352
Mandalay Gardens		Jefferson	80021	1858
Marshall		Boulder	80303	1771
Marshdale		Jefferson	80439	2357
Meridian		Douglas	80112	2451
Monte Vista Estates		Douglas	80109	2702
* Morrison	MRSN	Jefferson	80465	2276
Mount Vernon Club Place		Jefferson	80401	2190
* Mountain View	MNVW	Jefferson	80212	2027
Mountain View Lakes		Jefferson	80470	2524
* Nederland	NDLD	Boulder	80466	1765
Ninemile Corner		Boulder	80026	1690
Niwot		Boulder	80503	1520
Nob Hill		Arapahoe	80122	2365
North Cherry Creek Valley		Arapahoe	80231	2199
North Pecos		Adams	80221	1944
North Washington		Adams	80216	2029
North Washington Hts		Adams	80229	1945
* Northglenn	NHGN	Adams	80233	1860
Oehlmann Park		Jefferson	80433	2443
Orodell		Boulder	80302	1685
Orsa		Douglas	80108	2618
Pactolus		Gilpin	80403	1850
Palos Verdes		Arapahoe	80111	2366
Palos Verdes East		Arapahoe	80111	2366
Panorama Heights		Jefferson	80401	2107
Paradise Hills		Jefferson	80401	2191
Paragon Estates		Boulder	80303	1688
--Park County	PrkC			
* Parker	PARK	Douglas	80138	2453
Perry Park		Douglas	80118	2952
Pine Brook Hill		Boulder	80304	1601
Pine Grove		Jefferson	80470	2693
Pine Junction		Jefferson	80470	2608
Pine Park Estates		Jefferson	80465	2359
Pinecliffe		Gilpin	80403	1767
Pleasant View		Jefferson	80401	2108
Ponderosa Hills		Douglas	80138	2454
Ponderosa Park		Elbert	80107	2708
Rangeview Estates		Boulder	80503	1520
Ridgeview Hills		Arapahoe	80122	2366
Roland Valley		Park	80456	2607
Rolla		Adams	80640	1946
Rollinsville		Gilpin	80474	1849
Rosedale		Jefferson	80439	2272
Roxborough Park		Douglas	80125	2530
Russellville		Douglas	80116	2791
Salina		Boulder	80302	1600
Sedalia		Douglas	80135	2617
Shadow Mountain		Jefferson	80433	2440
Shaw Heights		Adams	80031	1943
Shaw Heights Mesa		Adams	80031	1943
* Sheridan	SRDN	Arapahoe	80110	2280
Sherrelwood		Adams	80221	1944
Silver Heights		Douglas	80108	2619
Silver Spruce		Boulder	80302	1685
Sky Village		Jefferson	80465	2443
Skyline		Arapahoe	80222	2282
Southglenn		Arapahoe	80122	2365
Southwind		Arapahoe	80122	2364
Southwood		Arapahoe	80121	2365
Sphinx Park		Jefferson	80470	2609
Sprucedale		Jefferson	80439	2356
Stanley Park		Jefferson	80439	2358
Stonegate		Douglas	80134	2452
Stroh Ranch		Douglas	80134	2537
Sugarloaf		Boulder	80302	1683
* Superior	SUPE	Jefferson	80027	1856
* Superior	SUPE	Boulder	80027	1772
Surrey Ridge		Douglas	80108	2535
The Meadows		Jefferson	80127	2362
The Pinery		Douglas	80134	2622
* Thornton	TNTN	Adams	80229	1944
Tiny Town		Jefferson	80465	2359
Todd Creek		Adams	80602	1695
Troutdale		Jefferson	80439	2273
Twin Forks		Jefferson	80465	2359
Twin Lakes		Adams	80221	1944
Twin Spruce		Jefferson	80403	1852
Valmont		Boulder	80301	1603
Vista Verde		Arapahoe	80122	2364
Wah Keeney Park		Jefferson	80439	2273
Wallstreet		Boulder	80302	1600
Walnut Hills		Arapahoe	80112	2366
Wandcrest Park		Jefferson	80470	2608
* Ward	WARD	Boulder	80481	1597
Watkins		Arapahoe	80137	2121
Welby		Adams	80229	1945
--Weld County	WldC			
Western Hills		Adams	80221	1944
* Westminster	WSTR	Jefferson	80020	1859
* Westminster	WSTR	Adams	80031	1943
Westminster East		Adams	80221	1944
* Wheat Ridge	WTRG	Jefferson	80033	2110
Williamsburg		Jefferson	80127	2362
Willis Heights		Boulder	80504	1356
Willow Creek		Arapahoe	80112	2366
Willowbrook		Jefferson	80465	2361
Wilmot		Jefferson	80439	2357
Wondervu		Boulder	80403	1852
Woodmar Village		Jefferson	80123	2362

*Indicates incorporated city

List of Abbreviations

Admin	Administration
Agri	Agricultural
Ag	Agriculture
AFB	Air Force Base
Arpt	Airport
Al	Alley
Amer	American
Anx	Annex
Arc	Arcade
Arch	Archaeological
Aud	Auditorium
Avd	Avenida
Av	Avenue
Bfld	Battlefield
Bch	Beach
Bnd	Bend
Bio	Biological
Blf	Bluff
Blvd	Boulevard
Brch	Branch
Br	Bridge
Brk	Brook
Bldg	Building
Bur	Bureau
Byp	Bypass
Bywy	Byway
Cl	Calle
Cljn	Callejon
Cmto	Caminito
Cm	Camino
Cap	Capitol
Cath	Cathedral
Cswy	Causeway
Cem	Cemetery
Ctr	Center
Ctr	Centre
Cir	Circle
Crlo	Circulo
CH	City Hall
Clf	Cliff
Clfs	Cliffs
Clb	Club
Cltr	Cluster
Col	Coliseum
Coll	College
Com	Common
Coms	Commons
Comm	Community
Co.	Company
Cons	Conservation
Conv & Vis Bur	Convention and Visitors Bureau
Cor	Corner
Cors	Corners
Corp	Corporation
Corr	Corridor
Cte	Corte
CC	Country Club
Co	County
Ct	Court
Ct Hse	Court House
Cts	Courts
Cr	Creek
Cres	Crescent
Cross	Crossing
Curv	Curve

Cto	Cut Off
Dept	Department
Dev	Development
Diag	Diagonal
Div	Division
Dr	Drive
Drwy	Driveway
E	East
El	Elevation
Env	Environmental
Est	Estate
Ests	Estates
Exh	Exhibition
Expm	Experimental
Expo	Exposition
Expwy	Expressway
Ext	Extension
Frgds	Fairgrounds
ft	Feet
Fy	Ferry
Fld	Field
Flds	Fields
Flt	Flat
Flts	Flats
For	Forest
Fk	Fork
Ft	Fort
Found	Foundation
Frwy	Freeway
Gdn	Garden
Gdns	Gardens
Gen Hosp	General Hospital
Gln	Glen
GC	Golf Course
Grn	Green
Grds	Grounds
Grv	Grove
Hbr	Harbor/Harbour
Hvn	Haven
HQs	Headquarters
Ht	Height
Hts	Heights
HS	High School
Hwy	Highway
Hl	Hill
Hls	Hills
Hist	Historical
Hllw	Hollow
Hosp	Hospital
Hse	House
Ind Res	Indian Reservation
Info	Information
Inst	Institute
Int'l	International
I	Island
Is	Islands
Isl	Isle
Jct	Junction
Knl	Knoll
Knls	Knolls
Lk	Lake
Lndg	Landing
Ln	Lane
Lib	Library
Ldg	Lodge

Lp	Loop
Mnr	Manor
Mkt	Market
Mdw	Meadow
Mdws	Meadows
Med	Medical
Mem	Memorial
Metro	Metropolitan
Mw	Mews
Mil	Military
Ml	Mill
Mls	Mills
Mon	Monument
Mtwy	Motorway
Mnd	Mound
Mnds	Mounds
Mt	Mount
Mtn	Mountain
Mtns	Mountains
Mun	Municipal
Mus	Museum
Nat'l	National
Nat'l For	National Forest
Nat'l Hist Pk	National Historic Park
Nat'l Hist Site	National Historic Site
Nat'l Mon	National Monument
Nat'l Park	National Park
Nat'l Rec Area	National Recreation Area
Nat'l Wld Ref	National Wildlife Refuge
Nat	Natural
NAS	Naval Air Station
Nk	Nook
N	North
Orch	Orchard
Ohwy	Outer Highway
Ovl	Oval
Ovlk	Overlook
Ovps	Overpass
Pk	Park
Pkwy	Parkway
Pas	Paseo
Psg	Passage
Pass	Passenger
Pth	Path
Pn	Pine
Pns	Pines
Pl	Place
Pln	Plain
Plns	Plains
Plgnd	Playground
Plz	Plaza
Pt	Point
Pnd	Pond
PO	Post Office
Pres	Preserve
Prov	Provincial
Rwy	Railway
Rec	Recreation
Reg	Regional
Res	Reservoir
Rst	Rest
Rdg	Ridge
Rd	Road
Rds	Roads
St.	Saint

Ste.	Sainte
Sci	Science
Sci	Sciences
Sci	Scientific
Shop Ctr	Shopping Center
Shr	Shore
Shrs	Shores
Skwy	Skyway
S	South
Spr	Spring
Sprs	Springs
Sq	Square
Stad	Stadium
St For	State Forest
St Hist Site	State Historic Site
St Nat Area	State Natural Area
St Pk	State Park
St Rec Area	State Recreation Area
Sta	Station
St	Street
Smt	Summit
Sys	Systems
Tech	Technical
Tech	Technological
Tech	Technology
Ter	Terrace
Terr	Territory
Theol	Theological
Thwy	Throughway
Toll Fy	Toll Ferry
TIC	Tourist Information Center
Trc	Trace
Trfwy	Trafficway
Tr	Trail
Tun	Tunnel
Tpk	Turnpike
Unps	Underpass
Univ	University
Vly	Valley
Vet	Veterans
Vw	View
Vil	Village
Wk	Walk
Wall	Wall
Wy	Way
W	West
WMA	Wildlife Management Area

STREET
Block City ZIP Map# Grid

HIGHWAYS

ALT - Alternate Route
BUS - Business Route
CO - County Highway/Road
FM - Farm To Market Road
HIST - Historic Highway
I - Interstate Highway
LP - State Loop
P - Provincial Highway
PK - Park & Recreation Road
RTE - Other Route
SPR - State Spur
SR - State Route/Highway
US - United States Highway

CO-1
9500 DgsC 80138 2539 E2
9900 DgsC 80138 2455 E7
10300 BldC 80501 1440 B2
10300 BldC 80504 1440 B2
10300 LGMT 80501 1440 B2
10300 LGMT 80504 1440 B2
12600 BldC 80504 1357 B2
CO-1 E County Line Rd
10300 BldC 80501 1440 B2
10300 BldC 80504 1440 B2
10300 LGMT 80501 1440 B2
10300 LGMT 80504 1440 B2
12600 BldC 80504 1357 B2
CO-1 N Delbert Rd
9500 DgsC 80138 2539 E2
9900 DgsC 80138 2455 E7
CO-2
19000 AdmC 80603 1698 E4
19000 AdmC 80603 1699 E3
19000 LCHB 80603 1698 E4
19000 WldC 80642 1699 E3
28900 AdmC 80603 1700 A3
28900 WldC 80642 1700 A3
CO-2 E 168th Av
19000 AdmC 80603 1698 E4
19000 AdmC 80603 1699 E3
19000 LCHB 80603 1698 E4
19000 WldC 80642 1699 E3
28900 AdmC 80603 1700 A3
28900 WldC 80642 1700 A3
CO-4
18900 LCHB 80603 1698 E2
18900 WldC 80603 1698 E2
18900 WldC 80603 1699 A2
18900 WldC 80642 1698 E2
18900 WldC 80642 1699 A2
20000 WldC 80642 1700 A1
CO-5
- ERIE 80516 1692 A1
- WldC 80516 1692 A1
CO-6
9500 BldC 80503 1355 D2
9500 BldC 80504 1355 E2
9500 BldC 80504 1356 A2
CO-6 Vermillion Rd
9500 BldC 80503 1355 D2
9500 BldC 80504 1355 E2
9500 BldC 80504 1356 A2
CO-7
- BldC 80516 1692 C4
- BMFD 80020 1692 C4
- BMFD 80516 1692 C4
- ERIE 80516 1692 C4
CO-8
- DgsC 80134 2537 A1
- ERIE 80516 1607 D5
- PARK 80134 2537 A1
- WldC 80516 1607 D5
CO-8 Leon A Wurl Pkwy
- ERIE 80516 1607 C5
- WldC 80516 1607 C5
CO-8 W Parker Rd
- DgsC 80134 2537 A1
- PARK 80134 2537 A1
CO-13
34000 EbtC 80107 2709 A6
34000 ELIZ 80107 2709 A6
37100 EbtC 80107 2625 A7
40000 EbtC 80138 2625 A2
CO-13 Deer Creek Dr
34000 EbtC 80107 2709 A6
34000 ELIZ 80107 2709 A6
37100 EbtC 80107 2625 A7
40000 EbtC 80138 2625 A2
CO-14
- BldC 80516 1523 A6
- WldC 80504 1523 A6
CO-19
- AdmC 80602 1694 E2
- WldC 80603 1694 E2
CO-20.5
- BldC 80501 1440 D6
- WldC 80504 1440 D6
CO-24
10500 DgsC 80134 2623 B1
10500 DgsC 80138 2623 B1
CO-24 E Singing Hills Rd
10500 DgsC 80134 2623 B1
10500 DgsC 80138 2623 B1
CO-25
30000 EbtC 80107 2795 D7
31400 KIOW 80107 2795 E3
CO-25 Elbert Rd
30000 EbtC 80107 2795 D7
31400 KIOW 80107 2795 E3
CO-26
- WldC 80504 1440 C1
CO-27
10 AdmC 80601 1696 C1
10 BGTN 80601 1696 C1
10 BGTN 80603 1696 C1
10 WldC 80603 1696 C1
CO-30
- BldC 80504 1357 E4
23700 AphC 80018 2286 E5
23700 AURA 80016 2286 E5
24700 AphC 80018 2287 C4
26000 AphC 80137 2287 C4
26000 AURA 80016 2287 C4
28100 WldC 80137 2288 A4
CO-30 E Quincy Av
23700 AphC 80018 2286 E5
23700 AURA 80016 2286 E5
26000 AphC 80018 2287 C4
26000 AphC 80137 2287 C4
26000 AURA 80016 2287 C4
28100 AphC 80137 2288 A4
CO-37
600 LCHB 80603 1698 C1
600 WldC 80603 1698 C1
CO-37 Frances Steele Blvd
600 LCHB 80603 1698 C2
600 WldC 80603 1698 C2
CO-41
30000 EbtC 80107 2795 D7
31400 KIOW 80107 2795 E3
CO-41 Elbert Rd
30000 EbtC 80107 2795 D7
31400 KIOW 80107 2795 E3
CO-45
10 AdmC 80603 1700 A1
10 WldC 80642 1700 A1
CO-48
4800 JfnC 80465 2276 C7
4800 MRSN 80465 2276 C7
4900 JfnC 80465 2360 D1
CO-48 Willow Springs Rd
4800 JfnC 80465 2276 C7
4800 MRSN 80465 2276 C7
4900 JfnC 80465 2360 D1
CO-53
7900 DgsC 80118 2955 B5
7900 LKSR 80118 2955 B5
CO-53 S Spruce Mountain Rd
7900 DgsC 80118 2955 B5
7900 LKSR 80118 2955 B5
CO-58
5200 DNVR 80212 2027 B7
5200 MNVW 80212 2027 B7
5900 LKSD 80212 2027 B7
5900 WTRG 80033 2027 B7
5900 WTRG 80212 2027 B7
7400 WTRG 80033 2026 E7
10900 WTRG 80033 2025 E7
CO-58 W 44th Av
5200 DNVR 80212 2027 B7
5200 LKSD 80212 2027 B7
5800 MNVW 80212 2027 B7
5900 WTRG 80033 2027 B7
5900 WTRG 80212 2027 B7
7400 WTRG 80033 2026 E7
10900 WTRG 80033 2025 E7
CO-60
10 DgsC 80118 2954 C5
10 DgsC 80118 2955 A5
10 LKSR 80118 2954 C5
10 LKSR 80118 2955 A5
CO-60 E Perry Park Av
10 DgsC 80118 2955 A5
10 LKSR 80118 2955 A5
CO-60 W Perry Park Av
10 DgsC 80118 2954 C5
10 DgsC 80118 2955 A5
10 LKSR 80118 2954 C5
10 LKSR 80118 2955 A5
CO-65
- JfnC 80439 2188 E5
500 DgsC 80116 2707 C3
3100 DgsC 80134 2707 C3
3500 DgsC 80134 2623 C6
5900 DgsC 80138 2623 C6
CO-65 Flintwood Rd
500 DgsC 80116 2707 C6
3100 DgsC 80134 2707 C1
CO-65 N Flintwood Rd
3500 DgsC 80116 2707 C3
3500 DgsC 80134 2623 C6
3500 DgsC 80134 2707 C3
5900 DgsC 80138 2623 C6
CO-66
34600 CCkC 80439 2188 C6
CO-66 Squaw Pass Rd
34600 CCkC 80439 2188 C6
CO-67
- BldC 80025 1770 D6
- BldC 80303 1770 D7
6000 AphC 80016 2370 A2
6000 CTNL 80015 2370 A2
6000 CTNL 80016 2370 A2
6600 AURA 80016 2370 A2
CO-67 S Liverpool St
6000 AphC 80016 2370 A2
6000 CTNL 80015 2370 A2
6000 CTNL 80016 2370 A2
6600 AURA 80016 2370 A2
CO-69
10 DgsC 80116 2790 E2
100 DgsC 80116 2706 C6
500 DgsC 80116 2791 B5
CO-69 N Russellville Rd
10 DgsC 80116 2790 E2
100 DgsC 80116 2706 C6
CO-69 S Russellville Rd
10 DgsC 80116 2790 E1
500 DgsC 80116 2791 B5
CO-73
- JfnC 80433 2441 E4
- JfnC 80433 2442 A6
- JfnC 80433 2526 A1
- JfnC 80439 2273 D7
- JfnC 80439 2357 E6
- JfnC 80439 2441 E1
CO-78
5000 JfnC 80439 2357 D1
7100 JfnC 80439 2356 E6
7900 JfnC 80433 2356 C7
7900 JfnC 80433 2440 C2
CO-78 S Black Mountain Dr
7900 JfnC 80433 2356 C7
7900 JfnC 80433 2440 C2
7900 JfnC 80439 2356 C7
CO-78 S Brook Forest Rd
5000 JfnC 80439 2357 D1
7100 JfnC 80439 2356 E6
8200 JfnC 80433 2356 C7
CO-80
14800 JfnC 80007 1940 C5
16600 JfnC 80007 1939 D5
16600 JfnC 80403 1939 D5
CO-80 W 82nd Av
16600 JfnC 80007 1939 D5
16600 JfnC 80007 1940 B5
16600 JfnC 80403 1939 D5
CO-80 Leyden Rd
14800 JfnC 80007 1940 C5
CO-88
- JfnC 80433 2442 A7
9800 JfnC 80127 2444 D7
10500 JfnC 80127 2528 D1
18100 JfnC 80433 2528 A4
19000 JfnC 80433 2527 E4
22800 JfnC 80433 2526 D2
CO-88 S Deer Creek Rd
9800 JfnC 80127 2444 D7
10500 JfnC 80127 2528 D1
CO-88 High Grade Rd
16300 JfnC 80127 2528 C2
CO-88 Pleasant Park Rd
- JfnC 80433 2442 A7
18100 JfnC 80127 2528 A4
18100 JfnC 80433 2528 A4
19000 JfnC 80433 2527 E4
22800 JfnC 80433 2526 D2
CO-93
- JfnC 80401 2192 C7
- JfnC 80465 2192 C7
- JfnC 80465 2276 C1
- MRSN 80465 2276 C1
CO-97
10 AphC 80137 2121 A6
10 AphC 80137 2205 A2
2500 DgsC 80135 2696 E6
2500 DgsC 80135 2697 A7
2500 JfnC 80433 2697 A2
CO-97 N Platte River Rd
2500 DgsC 80135 2696 E6
2500 DgsC 80135 2697 A2
2500 JfnC 80433 2697 A6
CO-97 N Watkins Rd
10 AphC 80137 2121 A6
CO-97 S Watkins Rd
10 AphC 80137 2205 A2
CO-126
13700 JfnC 80470 2608 B2
14300 JfnC 80470 2609 A6
16200 JfnC 80470 2693 C2
17200 JfnC 80433 2694 E5
17200 JfnC 80470 2694 A3
18200 JfnC 80433 2695 B6
CO-126 Deckers Rd
17700 JfnC 80433 2694 E5
18200 JfnC 80433 2695 B6
CO-126 S Pine Valley Rd
13700 JfnC 80470 2608 B2
14300 JfnC 80470 2609 A6
16200 JfnC 80470 2693 C2
CO-126 Platte River Rd
- JfnC 80470 2693 E2
17200 JfnC 80433 2694 A3
17200 JfnC 80470 2694 A3
CO-172
3800 JfnC 80403 2108 B1
4100 GOLD 80403 2024 C6
4100 JfnC 80403 2024 C6
6100 ARVD 80007 2024 C3
6100 ARVD 80403 2024 C3
CO-172 Easley Rd
3800 JfnC 80403 2108 B1
4100 GOLD 80403 2024 C6
4100 JfnC 80403 2024 C6
6100 ARVD 80007 2024 C3
6100 ARVD 80403 2024 C3
I-25
- AdmC - 1692 E3
- AdmC - 1776 D1
- AdmC - 1944 E3
- AdmC - 2028 E3
- BMFD - 1692 E1
- BMFD - 1776 D4
- CSRK - 2619 B7
- CSRK - 2703 C2
- CSRK - 2787 A7
- CTNL - 2367 A3
- CTNL - 2451 B1
- DgsC - 2451 C4
- DgsC - 2535 B1
- DgsC - 2619 B2
- DgsC - 2787 B4
- DgsC - 2870 E4
- DgsC - 2871 A3
- DgsC - 2954 E1
- DgsC - 2955 B7
- DNVR - 2028 D5
- DNVR - 2112 C1
- DNVR - 2196 E4
- DNVR - 2197 E6
- DNVR - 2198 A7
- DNVR - 2282 C4
- DvrC - 2282 D7
- GDVL - 2282 D7
- GDVL - 2366 E3
- GDVL - 2367 B7
- LKSR - 2955 A2
- LNTR - 2451 C4
- LNTR - 2535 B1
- NHGN - 1860 D1
- TNTN - 1692 E3
- TNTN - 1776 D4
- TNTN - 1860 D1
- TNTN - 1944 E3
- WSTR - 1776 D4
- WSTR - 1860 D1
I-25 N Valley Hwy
- AdmC - 2028 E3
- DNVR - 2028 E3
- DNVR - 2112 B6
I-70
- AdmC - 2032 B7
- AdmC - 2118 A4
- AdmC - 2119 E5
- AdmC - 2120 C4
- AdmC - 2121 E4
- AdmC - 2122 A4
- AdmC - 2123 D4
- AdmC - 2124 E4
- AdmC - 2125 C5
- AphC - 2118 E5
- AphC - 2119 E5
- AphC - 2125 C5
- ARVD - 2026 E6
- ARVD - 2027 A6
- AURA - 2032 B7
- AURA - 2116 E1
- AURA - 2117 E3
- AURA - 2118 A4
- AURA - 2121 E4
- AURA - 2122 A4
- BNNT - 2124 E4
- BNNT - 2125 C5
- CCkC - 2101 A5
- CCkC - 2102 A5
- CCkC - 2103 B6
- CCkC - 2187 E1
- DNVR - 2027 E6
- DNVR - 2028 A6
- DNVR - 2029 D6
- DNVR - 2030 A6
- DNVR - 2031 B7
- DNVR - 2032 B7
- DvrC - 2032 B7
- GOLD - 2108 D7
- GOLD - 2192 C1
- IDSP - 2101 A5
- IDSP - 2102 E5
- JfnC - 2108 E7
- JfnC - 2109 A6
- JfnC - 2188 E2
- JfnC - 2189 D3
- JfnC - 2190 E3
- JfnC - 2191 A3
- JfnC - 2192 A4
- LKSD - 2027 A6
- LKWD - 2109 C4
- WTRG - 2025 D6
- WTRG - 2026 E6
- WTRG - 2027 A6
- WTRG - 2109 A6
I-70 BUS
- GOLD 80401 2192 A2
10 CCkC 80452 2101 A5
10 DNVR 80202 2112 C5
10 DNVR 80204 2112 C5
10 IDSP 80452 2101 A5
100 DNVR 80203 2112 E5
700 DNVR 80203 2113 A5
1400 DNVR 80218 2113 A5
2700 DNVR 80206 2113 C5
3900 DNVR 80204 2111 E5
3900 DNVR 80220 2113 E5
4700 DNVR 80220 2114 B5
5200 LKWD 80214 2111 B5
6800 LKWD 80214 2110 E5
8300 LKWD 80215 2110 C5
8900 AURA 80010 2115 A5
8900 DNVR 80220 2115 A5
10800 LKWD 80215 2109 E5
11900 JfnC 80401 2109 C5
12100 AURA 80011 2115 E5
12700 AURA 80010 2116 A5
12700 JfnC 80215 2109 C5
13000 AURA 80011 2116 D5
13800 LKWD 80401 2109 B5
14800 JfnC 80401 2108 C7
14800 LKWD 80401 2108 E7
15500 GOLD 80401 2108 E7
16500 AURA 80011 2117 A5
17700 JfnC 80401 2192 B1
20700 AdmC 80011 2118 A5
21400 AURA 80011 2118 A5
I-70 BUS E Colfax Av
10 DNVR 80203 2112 E5
100 DNVR 80202 2112 E5
700 DNVR 80203 2113 A5
1000 DNVR 80218 2113 A5
2700 DNVR 80206 2113 C5
3900 DNVR 80220 2113 E5
4700 DNVR 80220 2114 B5
8900 AURA 80010 2115 A5
8900 DNVR 80220 2115 A5
12100 AURA 80011 2115 E5
12700 AURA 80011 2116 A5
13000 AURA 80010 2116 D5
16500 AURA 80011 2117 A5
20700 AdmC 80011 2118 A5
20700 AURA 80011 2118 A5
I-70 BUS W Colfax Av
- GOLD 80401 2192 A2
10 DNVR 80202 2112 C5
10 DNVR 80203 2112 C5
10 DNVR 80204 2112 C5
3000 DNVR 80204 2111 E5
5100 LKWD 80214 2111 B5
6800 LKWD 80214 2110 E5
8300 LKWD 80215 2110 C5
10800 LKWD 80215 2109 E5
11900 JfnC 80401 2109 C5
12700 JfnC 80215 2109 C5
13800 LKWD 80401 2109 B5
14800 JfnC 80401 2108 C7
14800 LKWD 80401 2108 E7
15500 GOLD 80401 2108 E7
17700 JfnC 80401 2192 B1
I-70 BUS Colorado Blvd
10 CCkC 80452 2101 A5
10 IDSP 80452 2101 A5
I-76
- AdmC - 1698 B5
- AdmC - 1780 E5
- AdmC - 1781 A4
- AdmC - 1862 E7
- AdmC - 1863 A6
- AdmC - 1864 C1
- AdmC - 1945 C7
- AdmC - 1946 C1
- AdmC - 2027 B5
- AdmC - 2028 D2
- AdmC - 2029 A1
- ARVD - 2026 E6
- ARVD - 2027 B5
- BGTN - 1697 D7
- BGTN - 1698 B5
- BGTN - 1780 D7
- BGTN - 1781 D1
- BGTN - 1863 E4
- BGTN - 1864 A3
- CMCY - 1862 E7
- CMCY - 1863 A6
- CMCY - 1864 C1
- CMCY - 1946 C1
- DNVR - 2027 B5
- JfnC - 2027 B5
- LCHB - 1698 E2
- TNTN - 1945 E6
- WldC - 1698 E2
- WTRG - 2027 B5
I-225
- AphC - 2283 D2
- AURA - 2116 B7
- AURA - 2200 B1
- AURA - 2283 A5
- AURA - 2284 A2
- DNVR - 2282 E5
- DNVR - 2283 A5
- DvrC - 2283 A5
- GDVL - 2283 A5
I-270
- AdmC - 1944 E7
- AdmC - 1945 A7
- AdmC - 2029 E3
- CMCY - 2029 D2
- CMCY - 2030 A4
- DNVR - 2030 D6
SR-2
- AdmC 80022 1863 C7
- AdmC 80022 1946 E3
- AdmC 80022 1947 B2
- AdmC 80603 1864 B3
- CMCY 80022 1863 E4
- CMCY 80022 1864 B3
- CMCY 80022 1946 E3
- CMCY 80022 1947 B2
- CMCY 80603 1864 B3
- CMCY 80640 1947 B2
- DNVR 80022 2029 E5
10 BGTN 80601 1696 C6
10 DNVR 80206 2197 E1
10 DNVR 80209 2197 E1
10 DNVR 80220 2197 E1
300 DNVR 80206 2113 E7
300 DNVR 80220 2113 E7
300 DNVR 80246 2197 E1
300 GNDL 80246 2197 E3
500 BGTN 80603 1696 C5
900 AdmC 80601 1780 B2
900 BGTN 80601 1780 B2
1000 DNVR 80210 2197 E3
1200 DNVR 80222 2197 E7
1900 DNVR 80207 2113 E4
2500 DNVR 80205 2113 E4
2600 DNVR 80222 2281 E1
3400 AphC 80222 2281 E3
3400 CHLV 80113 2281 E3
3400 DNVR 80210 2281 E3
3400 DvrC 80210 2281 E3
3800 DNVR 80207 2029 E7
4000 DNVR 80205 2029 E7
4000 DNVR 80216 2029 E7
5100 CMCY 80022 2029 E2
6200 CMCY 80022 2030 A2
12000 AdmC 80601 1864 B1
12000 BGTN 80601 1864 B1
12000 CMCY 80601 1864 B1
SR-2 S 4th Av
10 BGTN 80601 1696 B7
900 AdmC 80601 1780 B1
900 BGTN 80601 1780 B1
SR-2 N 7th Av
10 BGTN 80601 1696 C5
500 BGTN 80603 1696 C5
SR-2 E Bridge St
400 BGTN 80601 1696 C6
SR-2 Colorado Blvd
- DNVR 80022 2029 E5
10 DNVR 80206 2197 E1
10 DNVR 80209 2197 E1
10 DNVR 80220 2197 E1
10 DNVR 80246 2197 E1
300 DNVR 80206 2113 E7
300 DNVR 80220 2113 E7
1800 DNVR 80207 2113 E7
2200 DNVR 80205 2113 E7
3800 DNVR 80207 2029 E7
4000 DNVR 80205 2029 E7
4000 DNVR 80216 2029 E7
5100 CMCY 80022 2029 E5
SR-2 S Colorado Blvd
10 DNVR 80206 2197 E3
10 DNVR 80209 2197 E3
10 DNVR 80220 2197 E3
10 DNVR 80246 2197 E3
300 GNDL 80246 2197 E3
1000 DNVR 80210 2197 E7
1200 DNVR 80222 2197 E7
2600 DNVR 80222 2281 E1
3400 AphC 80210 2281 E3
3400 CHLV 80113 2281 E3
3400 DNVR 80210 2281 E3
3400 DvrC 80222 2281 E3
SR-2 Dahlia St
6000 CMCY 80022 2029 E4
6200 CMCY 80022 2030 A2
SR-2 Sable Blvd
- AdmC 80603 1864 B3
- CMCY 80603 1864 B3
12000 AdmC 80601 1864 B1
12000 BGTN 80601 1864 B1
12000 CMCY 80601 1864 B1
12400 AdmC 80601 1780 B7
12400 BGTN 80601 1780 B7
SR-2 Vasquez Blvd
5500 CMCY 80022 2029 E4
SR-7
- AdmC 80601 1698 A5
- AdmC 80602 1693 B6
- AdmC 80603 1698 A5
- BGTN 80601 1698 A5
- BGTN 80603 1698 A5
- BMFD 80020 1692 B4
- BMFD 80516 1692 B4
- ERIE 80516 1692 B4
- TNTN 80020 1692 B4
- TNTN 80020 1693 B6
- TNTN 80602 1692 B4
10 AdmC 80601 1696 A6
10 BGTN 80601 1696 C6
10 BldC 80503 1352 E2
10 LYNS 80503 1352 E2
100 BldC 80540 1352 D2
200 LYNS 80540 1352 E2
700 BldC 80026 1690 E4
1600 BLDR 80301 1686 E2
1600 BLDR 80302 1686 E2
1600 BLDR 80303 1686 E2
2100 LAFT 80026 1690 B3
2100 TNTN 80602 1693 B6
2200 BLDR 80304 1686 C1
2800 BLDR 80303 1687 A2
2900 BLDR 80304 1602 C7
3000 AdmC 80601 1697 B6
3000 BGTN 80601 1697 B6
3000 BLDR 80301 1687 A2
3000 ERIE 80026 1690 B3
4000 BldC 80503 1353 A3
4000 LYNS 80503 1353 A3
4000 TNTN 80602 1694 A6
4200 BldC 80301 1687 E2
4300 BldC 80303 1687 E2
5000 BldC 80301 1602 C3
5000 BldC 80302 1602 C1
5000 BLDR 80302 1602 C1
5700 BldC 80302 1518 C6
5700 BldC 80503 1518 C6
5700 BLDR 80302 1518 C6
6000 BldC 80301 1688 B2
6000 BldC 80303 1688 B2
6000 BLDR 80301 1688 B2
6000 BLDR 80303 1688 B2
7300 AdmC 80602 1694 E6
8200 BldC 80301 1689 B2
8200 BldC 80303 1689 B2
8600 BldC 80302 1435 C7
8600 BldC 80503 1435 C7
8900 AdmC 80602 1695 B6
9300 LAFT 80026 1689 B2
9700 BldC 80026 1689 E2
9700 BldC 80540 1435 E1
10200 BldC 80503 1436 A1
12000 BldC 80026 1691 A4
12000 ERIE 80026 1691 A4
12300 AdmC 80601 1695 E6
12400 BldC 80516 1691 A4
12400 ERIE 80516 1691 A4
12500 BMFD 80020 1691 A4
12900 AdmC 80602 1696 A6
SR-7 5th Av
100 BldC 80540 1352 D2
100 LYNS 80540 1352 D2
SR-7 28th St
- BldC 80302 1602 C2
- BLDR 80304 1602 C2
1600 BLDR 80301 1686 E2
1600 BLDR 80302 1686 E2
1600 BLDR 80303 1686 E2
5000 BldC 80301 1602 C2
5000 BLDR 80302 1602 C2
SR-7 N 107th St
2100 LAFT 80026 1690 B3
2300 BldC 80026 1690 A2
3000 ERIE 80026 1690 B3
SR-7 E 160th Av
- AdmC 80601 1698 A5
- AdmC 80603 1698 A5
- BGTN 80601 1698 A5
- BGTN 80603 1698 A5
2100 TNTN 80602 1693 B6
4000 TNTN 80602 1694 A6
7300 AdmC 80602 1694 E6
8900 AdmC 80602 1695 B6
12300 AdmC 80601 1695 E6
12900 AdmC 80601 1696 A6
12900 AdmC 80602 1696 A6
12900 BGTN 80601 1696 A6
SR-7 W 168th Av
- BldC 80026 1691 A4
- BMFD 80020 1691 A4
- BMFD 80020 1692 B4
- BMFD 80516 1692 B4
- ERIE 80516 1691 A4
- ERIE 80516 1692 B4
- WldC 80516 1691 A4
SR-7 Arapahoe Av
2800 BLDR 80301 1686 E2
2800 BLDR 80303 1686 E2
2800 BLDR 80303 1687 A2
3000 BLDR 80301 1687 A2
4200 BldC 80301 1687 E2
4300 BldC 80303 1687 E2
SR-7 Arapahoe Rd
- ERIE 80026 1690 B2
6000 BldC 80301 1688 B2
6000 BldC 80303 1687 E2
6000 BldC 80303 1688 B2
6000 BLDR 80301 1687 E2
6000 BLDR 80301 1688 B2
6000 BLDR 80303 1687 E2
6000 BLDR 80303 1688 B2
8200 BldC 80301 1689 B2
8200 BldC 80303 1689 B2
9300 LAFT 80026 1689 B2
9700 BldC 80026 1689 E2
9900 BldC 80026 1690 A2
9900 LAFT 80026 1690 A2
SR-7 Baseline Rd
- BMFD 80020 1692 C4
- BMFD 80516 1692 E4
- TNTN 80020 1692 E4
- TNTN 80602 1692 E4
SR-7 E Baseline Rd
100 LAFT 80026 1690 C4
700 BldC 80026 1690 D4
12000 BldC 80026 1691 A4
12000 ERIE 80026 1691 A4
12400 BldC 80516 1691 B4
12400 ERIE 80516 1691 B4
12500 BMFD 80020 1691 B4
SR-7 W Baseline Rd
100 LAFT 80026 1690 C4
SR-7 Bridge St
- AdmC 80601 1697 E5
- AdmC 80601 1698 A5
- AdmC 80603 1698 A5
- BGTN 80601 1697 E5
- BGTN 80601 1698 A5
- BGTN 80603 1698 A5
SR-7 E Bridge St
10 BGTN 80601 1696 C6
2400 AdmC 80601 1696 D6
3000 AdmC 80601 1697 A6
3000 BGTN 80601 1697 A6
SR-7 W Bridge St
10 AdmC 80601 1696 A6
10 BGTN 80601 1696 A6
SR-7 Broadway St
- BldC 80301 1602 C3
200 LYNS 80540 1352 D1
1800 BLDR 80302 1686 C1
2200 BLDR 80304 1686 C1
2900 BLDR 80304 1602 C7
SR-7 Canyon Blvd
1200 BLDR 80302 1686 D2
2600 BLDR 80301 1686 D2
SR-7 N Foothills Hwy
- BldC 80301 1602 C1
- BldC 80302 1602 C1
- BLDR 80302 1602 C1
- BLDR 80304 1602 C1
5700 BldC 80302 1518 C6
5700 BldC 80503 1518 C6
5700 BLDR 80302 1518 C6
8600 BldC 80302 1435 C7
8600 BldC 80503 1435 C7
9700 BldC 80540 1435 E1
10200 BldC 80503 1353 A7
10200 BldC 80503 1436 A1
SR-7 Main St
300 LYNS 80540 1352 D1
SR-7 E Main St
10 BldC 80503 1352 E2
10 LYNS 80503 1352 E2
10 LYNS 80540 1352 E2
SR-7 S St. Vrain Dr
26000 BldC 80540 1352 B3
32900 LYNS 80540 1352 D2
SR-7 Ute Hwy
4000 BldC 80503 1352 E2
4000 BldC 80503 1353 A3
4000 LYNS 80503 1352 E2
4000 LYNS 80503 1353 A3
4000 LYNS 80540 1352 E2
SR-8
100 MRSN 80465 2276 D3
6200 LKWD 80226 2195 B4
6200 LKWD 80232 2195 B4
7600 LKWD 80227 2194 D7
9200 LKWD 80227 2278 B1
10000 JfnC 80227 2278 A1
11000 JfnC 80227 2277 D1
11000 LKWD 80227 2277 D1
11100 JfnC 80228 2277 D1
11100 LKWD 80228 2277 D1
14500 LKWD 80465 2277 A2
14500 MRSN 80228 2277 A2
14700 JfnC 80465 2276 E3
16400 JfnC 80465 2276 D3
SR-8 Bear Creek Av
100 MRSN 80465 2276 D3
SR-8 W Mississippi Av
5800 LKWD 80232 2195 B4
6200 LKWD 80226 2195 B4
SR-8 Morrison Rd
7600 LKWD 80227 2194 D7
9200 LKWD 80227 2278 B1
10000 JfnC 80227 2278 A1
11000 JfnC 80227 2277 D1
11000 LKWD 80227 2277 D1
11100 JfnC 80228 2277 D1
11100 LKWD 80228 2277 D1
14500 LKWD 80465 2277 A2
14500 MRSN 80228 2277 A2
SR-8 W Morrison Rd
14700 LKWD 80228 2277 A3
14700 LKWD 80465 2276 E3
14700 LKWD 80465 2277 A3
14700 MRSN 80228 2277 A3
16000 MRSN 80465 2276 E3
16400 JfnC 80465 2276 E3
SR-22
10400 AdmC 80601 1863 E1
10400 AdmC 80640 1863 E1
10400 BGTN 80601 1863 E1
10400 BGTN 80640 1863 E1

STREET
Block City ZIP Map# Grid

SR-22
13000 AdmC 80640 1864 A1
13200 AdmC 80601 1864 A1
13200 BGTN 80601 1864 A1
SR-22 E 124th Av
10400 AdmC 80601 1863 E1
10400 AdmC 80640 1863 E1
10400 BGTN 80601 1863 E1
10400 BGTN 80640 1863 E1
13000 AdmC 80640 1864 A1
13200 AdmC 80601 1864 A1
13200 BGTN 80601 1864 A1
SR-26
- GOLD 80401 2192 B5
- JfnC 80401 2192 B5
900 DNVR 80223 2196 B2
2400 DNVR 80219 2196 A2
3100 DNVR 80219 2195 E2
5000 LKWD 80226 2195 B2
6900 LKWD 80226 2194 E2
11000 LKWD 80226 2193 D2
11500 LKWD 80228 2193 D2
14800 JfnC 80228 2192 B5
14800 LKWD 80228 2192 B5
16500 JfnC 80465 2192 B5
SR-26 W Alameda Av
900 DNVR 80223 2196 B2
2400 DNVR 80219 2196 A2
3500 DNVR 80219 2195 E2
5000 LKWD 80226 2195 B2
6900 LKWD 80226 2194 E2
11000 LKWD 80226 2193 D2
11500 LKWD 80228 2193 D2
SR-26 W Alameda Pkwy
11600 LKWD 80226 2193 E2
11600 LKWD 80228 2193 E2
14800 JfnC 80228 2192 D6
14800 LKWD 80228 2192 E6
16500 JfnC 80401 2192 C5
16500 JfnC 80465 2192 C5
SR-30
10 AURA 80010 2199 C1
10 AURA 80012 2199 C1
200 AphC 80012 2199 C3
200 DNVR 80010 2199 C3
200 DNVR 80247 2199 C3
300 AURA 80010 2115 C7
600 AURA 80247 2199 C3
600 DvrC 80247 2199 C3
1400 AURA 80018 2202 D6
1900 AphC 80018 2202 D6
2500 AURA 80014 2199 C7
2500 AURA 80231 2199 C7
2500 DNVR 80014 2199 C7
2500 DNVR 80231 2199 C7
2600 AURA 80014 2283 C1
2600 DNVR 80231 2283 C1
2700 AphC 80018 2286 D1
2700 AURA 80018 2286 D1
3000 DNVR 80014 2283 C2
4100 AURA 80016 2286 D4
5900 DNVR 80222 2282 B3
5900 DNVR 80237 2282 B3
6500 DNVR 80224 2282 B3
7200 DNVR 80231 2282 E3
8700 DNVR 80237 2283 A3
9000 DvrC 80231 2283 A3
9000 GDVL 80014 2283 A3
11500 AURA 80011 2115 E7
12500 AURA 80011 2116 A7
16900 AURA 80011 2117 A7
20500 AURA 80011 2118 A7
21000 AphC 80011 2202 A1
21000 AURA 80011 2202 A1
25900 AphC 80018 2287 C4
25900 AURA 80016 2287 C4
SR-30 E 6th Av
- AphC 80018 2202 B2
10500 AURA 80010 2115 C7
11500 AURA 80011 2115 E7
12500 AURA 80011 2116 A7
16900 AURA 80011 2117 A7
20500 AURA 80011 2118 A7
21000 AphC 80011 2202 A1
21000 AURA 80011 2202 A1
21000 AURA 80018 2202 B1
SR-30 S Gun Club Rd
1400 AURA 80018 2202 D5
1900 AphC 80018 2202 D7
2700 AphC 80018 2286 D1
2700 AURA 80018 2286 D1
4100 AURA 80016 2286 D4
SR-30 E Hampden Av
5900 DNVR 80222 2282 B3
5900 DNVR 80237 2282 B3
6500 DNVR 80224 2282 B3
7200 DNVR 80231 2282 E3
8700 DNVR 80231 2283 A3
8700 DNVR 80237 2283 A3
9000 DvrC 80231 2283 A3
9000 GDVL 80014 2283 A3
9200 DNVR 80014 2283 B3
SR-30 Havana St
10 AURA 80010 2199 C1
10 AURA 80012 2199 C1
300 AURA 80010 2115 C7
SR-30 S Havana St
10 AURA 80010 2199 C1
10 AURA 80012 2199 C1
200 AphC 80012 2199 C3
200 DNVR 80010 2199 C3
200 DNVR 80247 2199 C3
600 AURA 80247 2199 C3
600 DvrC 80247 2199 C3
2500 AURA 80014 2199 C7
2500 AURA 80231 2199 C7
2500 DNVR 80014 2199 C7
2500 DNVR 80231 2199 C7
2600 AURA 80014 2283 C1
2600 DNVR 80231 2283 C1
3000 DNVR 80014 2283 C2
SR-30 E Quincy Av
25900 AphC 80018 2287 C4
25900 AURA 80016 2287 C4

SR-32
1500 AURA 80011 2117 C3
4000 AURA 80011 2033 C7
4000 AURA 80249 2033 C7
4000 DNVR 80239 2033 C7
4000 DNVR 80249 2033 C7
4000 DvrC 80011 2033 C7
4000 DvrC 80239 2033 C7
4000 DvrC 80249 2033 C7
SR-32 Tower Rd
1500 AURA 80011 2117 C3
4000 AURA 80011 2033 C7
4000 AURA 80249 2033 C7
4000 DNVR 80239 2033 C7
4000 DNVR 80249 2033 C7
4000 DvrC 80011 2033 C7
4000 DvrC 80239 2033 C7
4000 DvrC 80249 2033 C7
SR-33
3900 DNVR 80205 2029 E7
3900 DNVR 80207 2029 E7
3900 DNVR 80216 2029 E7
SR-33 E 40th Av
3900 DNVR 80205 2029 E7
3900 DNVR 80207 2029 E7
3900 DNVR 80216 2029 E7
SR-35
- DNVR 80207 2030 D7
3500 DNVR 80207 2114 D1
5000 AdmC 80022 2030 D6
5000 AdmC 80216 2030 D6
5000 CMCY 80022 2030 D6
5000 DNVR 80022 2030 D6
5000 DNVR 80216 2030 D6
SR-35 Quebec St
- DNVR 80207 2030 D7
3500 DNVR 80207 2114 D1
5000 AdmC 80022 2030 D6
5000 AdmC 80216 2030 D6
5000 CMCY 80022 2030 D6
5000 DNVR 80022 2030 D6
5000 DNVR 80216 2030 D6
SR-36
- AdmC 80019 2119 E4
- AdmC 80019 2120 B5
- AdmC 80137 2119 E4
- BNNT 80102 2125 A3
100 AdmC 80102 2124 D2
100 BNNT 80102 2124 D2
30000 AdmC 80137 2120 B5
30300 AURA 80137 2120 B5
32900 AdmC 80137 2121 A4
32900 AURA 80137 2121 A4
36100 AdmC 80137 2122 A2
36100 AURA 80137 2122 A2
37000 AdmC 80102 2122 A2
39300 AdmC 80102 2123 C2
39300 AURA 80102 2123 C2
52100 AdmC 80102 2125 D4
52100 AphC 80136 2125 D4
SR-36 E Colfax Av
- BNNT 80102 2124 A2
- BNNT 80102 2125 C4
100 AdmC 80102 2124 D2
28600 AphC 80019 2120 B5
30000 AdmC 80137 2120 B5
30300 AURA 80137 2120 B5
32900 AdmC 80137 2121 A4
32900 AURA 80137 2121 A4
36100 AdmC 80137 2122 A2
36100 AURA 80137 2122 A2
39300 AdmC 80102 2122 E2
39300 AdmC 80102 2123 C2
39300 AURA 80102 2123 C2
52100 AdmC 80102 2125 E4
52100 AphC 80136 2125 E4
SR-36 W Colfax Av
1100 AdmC 80102 2124 C2
1100 BNNT 80102 2124 C2
SR-36 Tower Rd
- AdmC 80019 2119 E4
- AdmC 80019 2120 A4
- AdmC 80137 2119 E4
- AphC 80137 2120 A4
SR-42
10 LSVL 80027 1689 D7
10 LSVL 80027 1773 E1
200 BldC 80027 1689 D5
300 LAFT 80027 1689 D5
700 BldC 80303 1689 D3
700 LAFT 80026 1689 D5
10200 LSVL 80026 1773 E1
10200 LSVL 80026 1774 A1
10200 LSVL 80027 1774 A1
10300 LAFT 80026 1774 B1
SR-42 N 95th St
- BldC 80027 1689 D5
700 BldC 80303 1689 D3
700 LAFT 80026 1689 D5
700 LAFT 80027 1689 D5
SR-42 N 96th St
100 LSVL 80027 1689 D5
200 BldC 80027 1689 D5
300 LAFT 80027 1689 D5
SR-42 N Courtesy Rd
10 LSVL 80027 1689 D7
10 LSVL 80027 1773 E1
SR-42 Empire Rd
9700 LSVL 80027 1773 E1
10200 LSVL 80026 1773 E1
10200 LSVL 80026 1774 A1
10200 LSVL 80027 1774 A1
10300 LAFT 80026 1774 B1
SR-44
10 NHGN 80229 1860 E6
10 NHGN 80233 1860 B6
10 NHGN 80234 1860 E6
10 NHGN 80260 1860 B6
10 TNTN 80229 1860 E6
200 TNTN 80233 1860 E6
700 NHGN 80233 1861 B6
700 TNTN 80229 1861 B6
1300 NHGN 80229 1861 B6
1400 TNTN 80234 1860 B6

SR-44
1400 TNTN 80260 1860 B6
1900 TNTN 80233 1861 E6
4700 TNTN 80229 1862 A6
4700 TNTN 80233 1862 A6
5000 AdmC 80229 1862 A6
6100 AdmC 80233 1862 A6
7600 AdmC 80640 1862 E6
8100 CMCY 80640 1862 E6
8500 CMCY 80640 1863 A6
11900 CMCY 80022 1863 D6
SR-44 E 104th Av
10 NHGN 80229 1860 D6
10 NHGN 80233 1860 D6
10 NHGN 80260 1860 D6
10 TNTN 80229 1860 E6
200 TNTN 80233 1860 E6
700 NHGN 80233 1861 B6
700 TNTN 80229 1861 B6
1300 NHGN 80229 1861 B6
1900 TNTN 80233 1861 E6
4700 TNTN 80229 1862 A6
4700 TNTN 80233 1862 A6
5000 AdmC 80229 1862 A6
6100 AdmC 80233 1862 A6
7600 AdmC 80640 1862 E6
8100 CMCY 80640 1862 E6
8500 CMCY 80640 1863 A6
11900 CMCY 80022 1863 D6
SR-44 W 104th Av
- NHGN 80233 1860 E6
10 NHGN 80234 1860 B6
10 NHGN 80260 1860 E6
1400 TNTN 80234 1860 B6
1400 TNTN 80260 1860 B6
SR-46
10 GpnC 80403 1934 A5
2800 GpnC 80403 1935 A6
5100 GpnC 80403 2019 E1
5600 GpnC 80403 2020 A2
SR-46 Golden Gate Canyon Rd
10 GpnC 80403 1934 A5
2800 GpnC 80403 1935 A6
5100 GpnC 80403 2019 E1
5600 GpnC 80403 2020 A2
SR-52
7100 BldC 80503 1520 D6
7100 BLDR 80503 1520 D6
7900 BldC 80503 1521 B6
9000 BldC 80504 1521 E6
9500 BldC 80504 1522 A6
11400 BldC 80504 1523 A6
12600 WldC 80516 1523 A6
SR-52 Mineral Rd
7100 BldC 80503 1520 D6
7100 BLDR 80503 1520 D6
7900 BldC 80503 1521 B6
9000 BldC 80504 1521 E6
9500 BldC 80504 1522 A6
11400 BldC 80504 1523 A6
12600 WldC 80516 1523 B6
SR-53
5800 AdmC 80216 2028 E1
6300 AdmC 80221 2028 E1
6700 AdmC 80221 1944 E7
SR-53 E 58th Av
- AdmC 80216 2028 E3
SR-53 Broadway
5800 AdmC 80216 2028 E1
6300 AdmC 80221 2028 E1
6700 AdmC 80221 1944 E7
SR-58
- GOLD - 2107 E2
- GOLD - 2108 A1
- JfnC - 2024 E7
- JfnC - 2025 A7
- JfnC - 2107 E2
- JfnC - 2108 D1
SR-66
10 BldC 80503 1352 E2
10 LYNS 80503 1352 E2
200 LYNS 80540 1352 D1
4000 BldC 80503 1353 A3
4000 LYNS 80503 1353 A3
6300 BldC 80503 1354 A4
7700 BldC 80503 1355 A4
7700 LGMT 80503 1355 A4
9300 BldC 80501 1355 E4
9300 BldC 80504 1355 E4
9300 LGMT 80501 1355 E4
10100 BldC 80504 1356 A4
10100 LGMT 80501 1356 A4
11900 BldC 80504 1357 B4
11900 LGMT 80501 1357 B4
19700 BldC 80540 1352 C1
SR-66 5th Av
500 LYNS 80540 1352 E2
SR-66 Broadway St
200 LYNS 80540 1352 D1
SR-66 Main St
300 LYNS 80540 1352 D1
SR-66 E Main St
10 BldC 80503 1352 E2
10 LYNS 80503 1352 E2
10 LYNS 80540 1352 E2
SR-66 W Main St
500 LYNS 80540 1352 E2
SR-66 N St. Vrain Dr
19700 BldC 80540 1352 C1
19700 LYNS 80540 1352 C1
SR-66 Ute Hwy
4000 BldC 80503 1352 E2
4000 BldC 80503 1353 A3
4000 LYNS 80503 1352 E2
4000 LYNS 80503 1353 A3
4000 LYNS 80540 1352 E2
6300 BldC 80503 1354 A4
7700 BldC 80503 1355 A4
7700 LGMT 80503 1355 A4
9300 BldC 80501 1355 E4
9300 BldC 80504 1355 E4
9300 LGMT 80501 1355 E4
10100 BldC 80504 1356 A4

SR-66 Ute Hwy
10100 LGMT 80501 1356 A4
11900 BldC 80504 1357 A4
11900 LGMT 80501 1357 A4
SR-67
- DgsC 80125 2698 E6
- DgsC 80135 2616 E7
- DgsC 80135 2698 E6
- DgsC 80135 2699 B5
- DgsC 80135 2700 B4
5300 DgsC 80135 2617 C5
SR-67 Jarre Canyon Rd
- DgsC 80125 2698 E6
- DgsC 80135 2616 E7
- DgsC 80135 2617 B6
- DgsC 80135 2698 E6
- DgsC 80135 2699 B5
- DgsC 80135 2700 B4
SR-67 Manhart St
5300 DgsC 80135 2617 C5
SR-72
- ARVD 80007 1939 D2
- ARVD 80007 1940 C3
- ARVD 80403 1938 E1
- ARVD 80403 1939 D2
- ARVD 80403 2025 A1
- BldC 80403 1767 C7
- BldC 80481 1513 E1
- BldC 80481 1514 B3
- BldC 80481 1597 C2
- GpnC 80403 1766 D7
- GpnC 80403 1851 E1
- GpnC 80466 1767 C7
- JfnC 80007 1939 D2
- JfnC 80007 1940 C3
- JfnC 80403 1938 E1
- JfnC 80403 1939 D2
- WARD 80481 1597 D1
10 NDLD 80466 1765 D4
4400 JfnC 80033 2025 D7
4400 WTRG 80033 2025 D7
5000 ARVD 80002 2025 D7
5300 JfnC 80002 2025 D3
6400 ARVD 80007 2025 A1
6700 BldC 80466 1766 D7
7000 ARVD 80007 1941 A7
7000 JfnC 80007 1941 A7
7800 JfnC 80005 1941 A7
8200 ARVD 80005 1941 A7
13700 JfnC 80004 2025 A1
14400 ARVD 80004 2025 A1
23800 ARVD 80403 1854 C7
23800 JfnC 80403 1854 C7
26800 JfnC 80403 1853 E7
31100 BldC 80403 1852 E2
33000 BldC 80466 1765 D2
35700 BldC 80302 1682 A6
35700 BldC 80466 1682 A6
35900 BldC 80466 1681 D2
37700 BldC 80302 1681 D2
39000 BldC 80466 1597 B6
SR-72 W 2nd St
10 NDLD 80466 1765 D3
SR-72 W 64th Av
- ARVD 80403 2025 C2
13700 JfnC 80004 2025 C2
14400 ARVD 80004 2025 C2
14800 ARVD 80007 2025 C2
SR-72 S Bridge St
10 NDLD 80466 1765 D3
700 BldC 80466 1765 C4
SR-72 Coal Creek Canyon Dr
6700 BldC 80466 1765 E6
6700 BldC 80466 1766 B6
SR-72 Coal Creek Canyon Rd
- ARVD 80007 1939 D2
- ARVD 80007 1940 C3
- ARVD 80403 1938 E1
- ARVD 80403 1939 D2
- JfnC 80007 1939 D2
- JfnC 80007 1940 C3
- JfnC 80403 1938 E1
- JfnC 80403 1939 D2
23800 ARVD 80403 1854 C7
23800 JfnC 80403 1854 C7
26800 JfnC 80403 1853 E7
31100 BldC 80403 1852 E2
SR-72 Indiana St
- ARVD 80403 2025 A1
6400 ARVD 80004 2025 A1
6400 ARVD 80007 2025 A1
7000 ARVD 80007 1941 A7
7000 JfnC 80007 1941 A7
7800 JfnC 80005 1941 A7
8200 ARVD 80005 1941 A7
SR-72 Peak to Peak Hwy
- BldC 80481 1513 E1
- BldC 80481 1514 B3
- BldC 80481 1597 C2
- WARD 80481 1597 D1
22800 BldC 80466 1765 D4
33000 NDLD 80466 1765 D2
35700 BldC 80302 1682 A6
35700 BldC 80466 1682 A6
35900 BldC 80466 1681 D2
37700 BldC 80302 1681 D2
39000 BldC 80466 1597 B6
SR-72 Ward Rd
4400 JfnC 80033 2025 D7
4400 WTRG 80033 2025 D7
5000 ARVD 80002 2025 D7
5300 JfnC 80002 2025 D7
5600 ARVD 80004 2025 D7
SR-74
- JfnC 80439 2272 E1
800 JfnC 80401 2189 B5
800 JfnC 80439 2189 B5
1000 JfnC 80439 2188 E5
2900 JfnC 80439 2273 A3
17100 MRSN 80465 2276 B3
17600 JfnC 80465 2276 B3
18300 JfnC 80465 2275 C2

SR-74
22100 JfnC 80439 2275 C2
22600 JfnC 80401 2275 C2
22800 JfnC 80401 2274 C2
22800 JfnC 80439 2274 C2
25200 JfnC 80457 2274 A5
SR-74 Bear Creek Av
17100 MRSN 80465 2276 C3
SR-74 Bear Creek Rd
17400 MRSN 80465 2276 B3
17600 JfnC 80465 2276 B3
18300 JfnC 80465 2275 C2
22100 JfnC 80439 2275 C2
22600 JfnC 80401 2275 C2
22800 JfnC 80401 2274 C2
22800 JfnC 80439 2274 C2
25200 JfnC 80457 2274 C2
SR-74 Evergreen Pkwy
800 JfnC 80401 2189 B5
800 JfnC 80439 2189 B5
1000 JfnC 80439 2188 D7
2800 JfnC 80439 2272 E1
2900 JfnC 80439 2273 A3
SR-75
- LITN 80120 2364 A1
2700 LITN 80123 2364 A1
3100 LITN 80123 2363 D3
3200 CBVL 80123 2363 E2
3600 AphC 80123 2363 E2
6800 AphC 80128 2363 C5
7000 LITN 80128 2363 C5
8000 JfnC 80128 2447 B1
SR-75 W Bowles Av
2700 LITN 80120 2364 A1
2700 LITN 80123 2364 A1
3100 LITN 80123 2363 D3
3600 AphC 80123 2363 E2
3600 CBVL 80123 2363 E2
SR-75 W Littleton Blvd
- LITN 80120 2364 D1
SR-75 S Platte Canyon Rd
5900 AphC 80123 2363 D2
5900 CBVL 80123 2363 D2
5900 LITN 80123 2363 D2
6800 AphC 80128 2363 D5
7000 LITN 80128 2363 C5
8000 JfnC 80128 2447 B1
SR-79
100 AdmC 80102 2124 D2
100 BNNT 80102 2124 D2
2800 AdmC 80102 2125 A1
2800 BNNT 80102 2125 A1
SR-79 S 1st St
100 AdmC 80102 2124 D3
100 BNNT 80102 2124 D3
SR-79 Adams St
- BNNT 80102 2124 D2
SR-79 E Colfax Av
100 AdmC 80102 2124 D2
100 BNNT 80102 2124 D2
SR-79 Kiowa-Bennett Rd
2800 AdmC 80102 2125 A1
2800 BNNT 80102 2125 A1
SR-79 Palmer Av
500 BNNT 80102 2124 E2
700 AdmC 80102 2124 E2
SR-83
- AURA 80014 2199 C7
- AURA 80231 2199 C7
- CSRK 80116 2621 D6
- DgsC 80116 2621 E1
- DgsC 80116 2705 E2
- DgsC 80116 2706 A7
- DgsC 80116 2790 B3
- DgsC 80134 2621 D4
- DNVR 80014 2283 E2
10 DNVR 80209 2197 E2
1000 AphC 80231 2198 C3
1000 AphC 80247 2198 C3
1000 DNVR 80224 2198 C3
1000 DNVR 80231 2198 C3
1000 DNVR 80247 2198 C3
1600 AphC 80231 2199 B6
1600 AphC 80247 2199 B6
2000 AURA 80247 2199 B6
2200 DNVR 80231 2199 B6
2200 DNVR 80247 2199 B6
2300 DNVR 80014 2199 C7
3100 AURA 80014 2283 E2
3200 AphC 80014 2283 E2
3200 AphC 80014 2284 C7
3200 AURA 80014 2284 B4
4000 AURA 80015 2284 B4
4400 DNVR 80246 2197 E2
4400 GNDL 80246 2197 E2
4600 DNVR 80246 2198 A2
4600 GNDL 80246 2198 A2
5100 AphC 80015 2284 C7
5300 AphC 80015 2368 C1
5300 AURA 80015 2368 C1
5600 CTNL 80015 2368 C1
5800 AphC 80016 2368 C1
5800 CTNL 80016 2368 C1
6700 FXFD 80016 2368 E4
7000 AphC 80016 2369 A7
7000 CTNL 80016 2369 A7
7000 FXFD 80016 2369 A7
8000 AURA 80016 2369 A7
8000 AURA 80016 2453 B1
8000 AURA 80138 2453 B1
8000 CTNL 80016 2453 B1
8000 PARK 80138 2453 B1
8100 AphC 80016 2453 B1
8100 AphC 80134 2453 B1
8100 PARK 80134 2453 B1
9300 DgsC 80138 2453 C4
9500 PARK 80134 2537 D1
10900 DgsC 80134 2537 D1
10900 PARK 80138 2537 D1
SR-83 Leetsdale Dr
10 DNVR 80209 2197 E2
10 DNVR 80246 2197 E2
4400 GNDL 80246 2197 E2

SR-83 Leetsdale Dr
4600 DNVR 80246 2198 A2
4600 GNDL 80246 2198 A2
6900 AphC 80247 2198 C3
6900 DNVR 80224 2198 C3
6900 DNVR 80247 2198 C3
SR-83 S Parker Rd
- AURA 80231 2199 C7
- DgsC 80116 2621 E1
- DgsC 80134 2621 D4
1000 AphC 80231 2198 D4
1000 AphC 80247 2198 D4
1000 DNVR 80224 2198 D4
1000 DNVR 80231 2198 D4
1000 DNVR 80247 2198 D4
1600 AphC 80231 2199 B6
1600 AphC 80247 2199 B6
2000 AURA 80247 2199 B6
2200 DNVR 80231 2199 B6
2200 DNVR 80247 2199 B6
2300 AURA 80014 2199 C7
2300 DNVR 80014 2199 C7
2500 AURA 80014 2283 C1
3100 DNVR 80014 2283 E2
3200 AphC 80014 2283 E2
3200 AphC 80014 2284 C7
3200 AURA 80014 2284 B4
4000 AURA 80015 2284 B4
5100 AphC 80015 2284 C7
5300 AphC 80015 2368 C1
5300 AURA 80015 2368 C1
5600 CTNL 80015 2368 C1
6200 AphC 80016 2368 E4
6200 CTNL 80016 2368 E4
6700 FXFD 80016 2368 E4
7000 AphC 80016 2369 A7
7000 CTNL 80016 2369 A7
7000 FXFD 80016 2369 A7
8000 AURA 80016 2369 A7
8000 AURA 80016 2453 B1
8000 AURA 80138 2453 B1
8000 CTNL 80016 2453 B1
8000 PARK 80138 2453 B1
8100 AphC 80016 2453 B1
8100 PARK 80134 2453 B1
9300 DgsC 80134 2453 C4
9300 DgsC 80138 2453 C4
9500 PARK 80134 2537 E5
10900 DgsC 80134 2537 D1
10900 PARK 80138 2537 D1
SR-86
- CSRK 80104 2703 E6
- CSRK 80104 2704 E4
- CSRK 80108 2704 E4
- CSRK 80108 2705 B3
- DgsC 80104 2703 E6
- DgsC 80104 2704 A6
- DgsC 80108 2704 E4
- DgsC 80108 2705 B3
- DgsC 80116 2705 B3
- DgsC 80116 2706 C5
- DgsC 80116 2707 A6
- EbtC 80107 2796 A2
- KIOW 80107 2796 A2
10 DgsC 80116 2791 E1
10 EbtC 80107 2791 E1
10 EbtC 80107 2792 C1
100 ELIZ 80107 2793 A1
200 EbtC 80107 2793 A1
200 KIOW 80117 2796 A2
700 EbtC 80117 2796 A2
2500 ELIZ 80107 2792 C1
5100 EbtC 80107 2794 D1
6900 EbtC 80107 2795 C2
10000 KIOW 80107 2795 C2
SR-86 Commanche St
- EbtC 80107 2795 E2
- EbtC 80107 2796 A2
- KIOW 80107 2795 E2
- KIOW 80107 2796 A2
200 KIOW 80117 2796 A2
700 EbtC 80117 2796 A2
SR-86 Kiowa Av
- ELIZ 80107 2793 C1
2700 EbtC 80107 2793 A1
SR-86 E Kiowa Av
100 ELIZ 80107 2793 B1
300 EbtC 80107 2793 B1
SR-86 W Kiowa Av
100 ELIZ 80107 2793 B1
200 EbtC 80107 2793 A1
SR-88
- GDVL - 2366 D1
10 AphC 80121 2280 E7
10 DNVR 80219 2196 A2
10 EGLD 80110 2280 E7
10 EGLD 80113 2280 E7
10 EGLD 80121 2280 E7
300 DNVR 80204 2112 A7
300 DNVR 80219 2112 A7
500 LITN 80120 2280 E7
700 AphC 80121 2281 A7
700 CHLV 80113 2281 A7
700 EGLD 80113 2281 A7
900 EGLD 80120 2280 E7
1300 GDVL 80113 2281 A7
1700 CHLV 80121 2281 A7
1900 DNVR 80211 2112 A3
2400 GDVL 80121 2281 E7
2400 LITN 80123 2280 A7
2600 DNVR 80219 2280 A1
2600 DNVR 80236 2280 A1
3200 DvrC 80236 2280 A2
3200 SRDN 80110 2280 A2
4100 DNVR 80211 2028 A6
4500 DNVR 80110 2280 A5
4600 CHLV 80121 2282 A7
4600 GDVL 80121 2282 A7
4800 DvrC 80110 2280 A7
5200 CHLV 80111 2282 A7
5200 GDVL 80111 2282 C7
6500 DvrC 80237 2282 C7
6500 GDVL 80237 2282 C7
6600 DvrC 80111 2282 A7

SR-88
6800 DNVR 80237 2282 C7
8900 GDVL 80111 2367 B4
8900 GDVL 80112 2367 B4
9500 CTNL 80111 2367 B4
9600 CTNL 80112 2367 B4
10500 AphC 80112 2367 B4
12100 CTNL 80111 2368 A4
12100 CTNL 80112 2368 A4
12900 AphC 80111 2368 A4
12900 AphC 80112 2368 A4
14300 AphC 80016 2368 E4
16100 CTNL 80016 2368 E4
16100 FXFD 80016 2368 E4
20600 AURA 80016 2369 E4
20700 AphC 80016 2369 E4
20700 AphC 80016 2370 A4
20700 AURA 80016 2370 A4
20700 CTNL 80016 2369 E4
SR-88 E Arapahoe Rd
- CTNL 80111 2367 E4
- GDVL 80111 2367 B4
8900 GDVL 80112 2367 B4
9600 CTNL 80112 2367 B4
10700 AphC 80112 2367 B4
12100 CTNL 80111 2368 A4
12100 CTNL 80112 2368 A4
12900 AphC 80111 2368 A4
12900 AphC 80112 2368 A4
14300 AphC 80016 2368 E4
16100 CTNL 80016 2368 E4
16100 FXFD 80016 2368 E4
20600 AURA 80016 2369 E4
20700 AphC 80016 2369 E4
20700 AphC 80016 2370 A4
20700 AURA 80016 2370 A4
20700 CTNL 80016 2369 E4
SR-88 E Belleview Av
10 AphC 80121 2280 E7
10 EGLD 80110 2280 E7
10 EGLD 80113 2280 E7
10 EGLD 80121 2280 E7
700 AphC 80121 2281 A7
700 CHLV 80113 2281 A7
700 EGLD 80113 2281 A7
700 GDVL 80121 2281 A7
1300 GDVL 80113 2281 A7
2400 CHLV 80121 2281 E7
4600 CHLV 80121 2282 A7
4600 GDVL 80121 2282 A7
5200 CHLV 80111 2282 C7
5200 GDVL 80111 2282 A7
6300 DvrC 80237 2282 A7
6500 DNVR 80237 2282 C7
6500 GDVL 80237 2282 A7
6600 DvrC 80111 2282 C7
SR-88 W Belleview Av
10 EGLD 80110 2280 E7
10 EGLD 80113 2280 E7
500 LITN 80120 2280 D7
900 EGLD 80120 2280 D7
2400 LITN 80123 2280 B7
SR-88 Federal Blvd
10 DNVR 80219 2196 A2
300 DNVR 80204 2112 A7
300 DNVR 80219 2112 A7
1900 DNVR 80211 2112 A3
4100 DNVR 80211 2028 A6
SR-88 S Federal Blvd
10 DNVR 80219 2196 A1
2600 DNVR 80219 2280 A1
2600 DNVR 80236 2280 A1
3200 DvrC 80236 2280 A2
3200 SRDN 80110 2280 A2
4400 EGLD 80110 2280 A5
4500 DNVR 80110 2280 A5
4800 DvrC 80110 2280 A7
5000 LITN 80123 2280 A7
SR-93
- ARVD 80007 1939 D6
- ARVD 80007 2023 E1
- ARVD 80403 1939 B1
- ARVD 80403 2023 E1
- GOLD 80401 2107 C2
- GOLD 80403 2023 D6
- GOLD 80403 2107 C1
- JfnC 80007 1939 C3
- JfnC 80007 2023 E1
- JfnC 80403 1939 C3
- JfnC 80403 2023 E1
- JfnC 80403 2107 C1
10 BLDR 80305 1686 E5
10 BLDR 80305 1687 A6
1000 BldC 80305 1771 C2
1000 BLDR 80305 1771 C2
1100 BLDR 80302 1686 D3
1400 BldC 80303 1771 C2
2800 BldC 80303 1855 C1
2800 BldC 80303 1855 C1
SR-93 Broadway St
100 BLDR 80305 1686 E5
1100 BLDR 80302 1686 D3
SR-93 S Broadway St
10 BLDR 80305 1686 E5
10 BLDR 80305 1687 A6
1200 BLDR 80305 1771 B1
1400 BldC 80305 1771 C1
SR-93 S Foothills Hwy
1000 BldC 80305 1771 C2
1000 BLDR 80305 1771 C2
1400 BldC 80303 1771 C2
2800 BldC 80303 1855 C1
2800 BldC 80303 1855 C1
SR-93 Foothills Rd
- ARVD 80007 1939 D7
- ARVD 80007 2023 E1
- ARVD 80403 1939 C2
- ARVD 80403 2023 E1
- GOLD 80401 2107 C2
- GOLD 80403 2023 D6
- GOLD 80403 2107 C1
- JfnC 80007 1939 C3
- JfnC 80007 2023 E1
- JfnC 80403 1939 C3

STREET Block City ZIP Map# Grid

SR-93 Foothills Rd
- JfnC 80403 2023 E1
- JfnC 80403 2107 C1
SR-95
- ARVD 80002 2027 C4
- DNVR 80235 2279 C3
10 DNVR 80219 2195 C1
10 LKWD 80226 2195 C1
200 DNVR 80204 2111 C7
200 DNVR 80219 2111 C7
400 LKWD 80204 2111 C7
400 LKWD 80219 2195 C1
400 LKWD 80226 2111 C7
700 LKWD 80214 2111 C7
900 LKWD 80232 2195 C4
1800 DNVR 80227 2195 C7
1800 DNVR 80232 2195 C7
2200 DvrC 80227 2195 C7
2200 EDGW 80214 2111 C4
2200 LKWD 80227 2195 C7
2500 DNVR 80212 2111 C4
2500 WTRG 80214 2111 C4
2600 DNVR 80219 2279 C1
2600 DNVR 80227 2279 C1
2600 DNVR 80236 2279 C1
2600 LKWD 80227 2279 C1
3000 WTRG 80212 2111 C1
4100 MNVW 80212 2027 C7
4100 WTRG 80212 2027 C7
4300 LKSD 80212 2027 C7
5100 DNVR 80002 2027 C4
5100 DNVR 80212 2027 C4
5100 JfnC 80002 2027 C4
5400 JfnC 80212 2027 C4
6000 ARVD 80003 2027 C4
6600 ARVD 80030 2027 B1
6700 WSTR 80030 2027 B1
6800 WSTR 80003 2027 B1
7000 WSTR 80030 1943 B7
7300 WSTR 80003 1943 B7
7900 WSTR 80031 1943 B4
8000 ARVD 80003 1943 B4
SR-95 Sheridan Blvd
- ARVD 80002 2027 C4
10 DNVR 80219 2195 C1
10 LKWD 80226 2195 C1
200 DNVR 80204 2111 C7
200 DNVR 80219 2111 C7
400 LKWD 80204 2111 C7
400 LKWD 80226 2111 C7
700 LKWD 80214 2111 C7
2200 EDGW 80214 2111 C4
2500 DNVR 80212 2111 C4
2500 WTRG 80214 2111 C4
3000 WTRG 80212 2111 C1
4100 MNVW 80212 2027 C7
4100 WTRG 80212 2027 C7
4300 LKSD 80212 2027 C7
5100 AdmC 80212 2027 C4
5100 DNVR 80002 2027 C4
5100 DNVR 80212 2027 C4
5400 AdmC 80002 2027 C4
6000 ARVD 80003 2027 C4
6600 ARVD 80030 2027 B1
6700 WSTR 80030 2027 B1
6800 WSTR 80003 2027 B1
7000 WSTR 80030 1943 B7
7300 WSTR 80003 1943 B7
7900 WSTR 80031 1943 B4
8000 ARVD 80003 1943 B4
SR-95 S Sheridan Blvd
- DNVR 80235 2279 C3
10 DNVR 80219 2195 C1
400 LKWD 80226 2195 C1
1200 LKWD 80232 2195 C4
1300 LKWD 80219 2195 C4
1800 DNVR 80227 2195 C7
1800 DNVR 80232 2195 C7
2200 DvrC 80227 2195 C7
2200 LKWD 80227 2195 C7
2600 DNVR 80219 2279 C1
2600 DNVR 80227 2279 C1
2600 LKWD 80227 2279 C1
3200 DNVR 80236 2279 C3
SR-103
10 IDSP 80452 2101 B6
500 CCkC 80452 2101 B6
16600 CCkC 80452 2185 B7
20000 CCkC 80452 2186 B6
25100 CCkC 80439 2187 D6
25100 CCkC 80452 2187 A7
28300 CCkC 80439 2188 A6
SR-103 13th Av
- IDSP 80452 2101 B6
SR-103 Chicago Creek Rd
10 IDSP 80452 2101 C5
500 CCkC 80452 2101 B6
SR-103 Squaw Pass Rd
16600 CCkC 80452 2185 B7
20000 CCkC 80452 2186 B6
25100 CCkC 80439 2187 D6
25100 CCkC 80452 2187 A7
28300 CCkC 80439 2188 A6
SR-105
800 DgsC 80109 2701 D5
800 DgsC 80135 2701 D5
3600 DgsC 80135 2617 C7
SR-105 N Perry Park Rd
800 DgsC 80109 2701 D5
800 DgsC 80135 2701 D5
3600 DgsC 80135 2617 C7
SR-119
- BldC 80501 1439 E3
- BLDR 80301 1602 E7
- CCkC 80403 2104 A4
- CCkC 80439 2103 D6
- GpnC 80403 1849 E2
- GpnC 80403 1850 C7
- GpnC 80403 2018 A4
- GpnC 80403 2102 E1
- GpnC 80403 2103 A1
- GpnC 80474 1849 E2
- JfnC 80439 2104 A4
- LGMT 80501 1440 A3
SR-119
- LGMT 80504 1440 E3
- WldC 80504 1440 E3
10 NDLD 80466 1765 D4
100 BKHK 80403 2017 D2
100 BKHK 80403 2018 A4
100 BldC 80302 1686 A2
200 GpnC 80403 2017 D2
600 LGMT 80501 1439 A4
700 BldC 80466 1765 D4
1200 LGMT 80501 1438 E4
1700 BLDR 80301 1686 E2
2200 BLDR 80302 1686 E1
2200 BLDR 80304 1686 E1
2700 BLDR 80304 1602 E7
2800 BLDR 80301 1603 A6
3700 BldC 80301 1603 E2
4500 BldC 80301 1604 A1
4500 BLDR 80301 1604 A1
6300 BldC 80301 1520 B7
6300 BldC 80503 1520 E3
6300 BLDR 80301 1520 B7
6300 BLDR 80503 1520 B7
7300 BldC 80503 1521 A2
8000 LGMT 80503 1521 B1
8200 BldC 80503 1438 C7
8300 LGMT 80503 1438 C7
10100 GpnC 80403 1933 B7
12500 GpnC 80403 1934 A5
22000 GpnC 80474 1765 E7
26900 BldC 80466 1766 B2
27100 BldC 80466 1682 D7
27100 BldC 80466 1683 E4
27100 BldC 80466 1684 A4
27800 BldC 80302 1684 A4
36700 BldC 80302 1685 A4
SR-119 28th St
1700 BLDR 80301 1686 E2
2200 BLDR 80302 1686 E1
2200 BLDR 80304 1686 E1
2700 BLDR 80301 1602 E7
2700 BLDR 80304 1602 E7
SR-119 Boulder Canyon Dr
26900 BldC 80466 1765 D2
26900 BldC 80466 1766 B2
26900 NDLD 80466 1765 D2
27100 BldC 80466 1682 D7
27100 BldC 80466 1683 E4
27100 BldC 80466 1684 A4
27800 BldC 80302 1684 A4
36700 BldC 80302 1685 A4
39600 BldC 80302 1686 A3
40400 BLDR 80302 1686 A2
SR-119 S Bridge St
10 NDLD 80466 1765 D3
700 BldC 80466 1765 C4
SR-119 Canyon Blvd
100 BldC 80302 1686 A2
100 BLDR 80302 1686 A2
2600 BLDR 80301 1686 D2
SR-119 Clear Creek St
- GpnC 80403 2018 A4
100 BKHK 80403 2017 D2
100 BKHK 80403 2018 A4
200 GpnC 80403 2017 D2
SR-119 Diagonal Hwy
- BLDR 80304 1602 E7
- LGMT 80501 1438 C7
2800 BLDR 80304 1602 E7
2800 BLDR 80301 1603 A6
3700 BldC 80301 1603 E2
4500 BldC 80301 1604 A1
4500 BLDR 80301 1604 A1
6300 BldC 80301 1520 B7
6300 BldC 80503 1520 E3
6300 BLDR 80301 1520 B7
6300 BLDR 80503 1520 B7
7300 BldC 80503 1521 A2
8000 LGMT 80503 1521 B1
8200 BldC 80503 1438 C7
8300 LGMT 80503 1438 C7
SR-119 Highway 119
1000 GpnC 80403 2104 A4
1100 GpnC 80403 2103 C2
9200 GpnC 80403 2017 C1
11900 GpnC 80403 1933 E6
14200 GpnC 80403 1934 C3
SR-119 Ken Pratt Blvd
- BldC 80501 1439 E3
- LGMT 80501 1440 B3
- LGMT 80504 1440 B3
600 LGMT 80501 1439 A4
1200 LGMT 80501 1438 E4
SR-119 Peak to Peak Hwy
22000 BldC 80466 1765 E7
22000 GpnC 80474 1765 E7
23900 NDLD 80466 1765 D4
SR-121
- BMFD 80020 1858 C1
- JfnC 80127 2530 D3
- WTRG 80002 2026 E7
10 LKWD 80226 2194 E2
400 LKWD 80226 2110 E7
600 LKWD 80214 2110 E7
900 LKWD 80232 2194 E3
1900 LKWD 80227 2194 E7
2500 JfnC 80215 2110 E3
2500 WTRG 80033 2110 E3
2600 DNVR 80227 2278 E1
2600 LKWD 80227 2278 E1
2800 JfnC 80227 2278 E1
4000 DNVR 80123 2278 D7
4000 DNVR 80235 2278 E4
4000 LKWD 80235 2278 E4
4800 ARVD 80033 2026 E7
4800 DvrC 80123 2278 D7
4800 LKWD 80123 2278 D7
4800 WTRG 80033 2026 E7
5000 ARVD 80002 2026 E4
5100 DNVR 80123 2362 D4
5100 LKWD 80123 2362 D1
5400 DvrC 80123 2362 D4
5700 ARVD 80003 2026 E4
SR-121
6500 ARVD 80004 2026 D1
6700 JfnC 80128 2362 D4
7000 ARVD 80003 1942 D7
7000 ARVD 80004 1942 D7
7100 ARVD 80005 1942 D7
7700 JfnC 80128 2446 E1
8200 WSTR 80005 1942 D4
9000 WSTR 80021 1942 D2
9400 JfnC 80127 2446 E1
9700 WSTR 80021 1858 C7
10800 JfnC 80021 1858 C2
11200 BMFD 80021 1858 C7
SR-121 S Platte Canyon Rd
- JfnC 80127 2446 D4
- JfnC 80127 2530 D3
- JfnC 80128 2446 D3
SR-121 Wadsworth Blvd
- WTRG 80002 2026 E7
10 LKWD 80226 2194 E1
400 LKWD 80226 2110 E7
600 LKWD 80214 2110 E7
2500 JfnC 80215 2110 E3
2500 WTRG 80033 2110 E3
4800 ARVD 80033 2026 E7
4800 WTRG 80033 2026 E7
5000 ARVD 80002 2026 E4
6500 ARVD 80003 2026 D1
6500 ARVD 80004 2026 D1
7000 ARVD 80003 1942 D7
7000 ARVD 80004 1942 D7
7100 ARVD 80005 1942 D7
8200 WSTR 80005 1942 D4
8700 WSTR 80021 1942 D3
SR-121 S Wadsworth Blvd
10 LKWD 80226 2194 E2
900 LKWD 80232 2194 E3
1900 LKWD 80227 2194 E7
2600 DNVR 80227 2278 E1
2600 LKWD 80227 2278 E1
2800 JfnC 80227 2278 E1
4000 DNVR 80123 2278 D7
4000 DNVR 80235 2278 E4
4000 LKWD 80235 2278 E4
4800 DvrC 80123 2278 D7
4800 LKWD 80123 2278 D7
5100 DNVR 80123 2362 D4
5100 LKWD 80123 2362 D1
5400 DvrC 80123 2362 D4
6700 JfnC 80128 2362 D4
7700 JfnC 80128 2446 E1
9400 JfnC 80127 2446 E1
SR-121 Wadsworth Byp
5200 ARVD 80002 2026 E5
5700 ARVD 80003 2026 E3
SR-121 Wadsworth Pkwy
- BMFD 80020 1858 C1
8800 ARVD 80003 1942 D4
8800 WSTR 80005 1942 D4
9000 WSTR 80021 1942 D2
9700 WSTR 80021 1858 C7
10800 JfnC 80021 1858 C2
11200 BMFD 80021 1858 C7
SR-128
- BfdC 80021 1857 D2
- BldC 80303 1771 C7
- BldC 80303 1855 D1
- BldC 80403 1855 D1
- BMFD 80020 1858 C2
- BMFD 80020 1859 E2
- BMFD 80021 1856 E3
- BMFD 80021 1857 D2
- BMFD 80021 1858 C2
- JfnC 80403 1856 E3
- NHGN 80233 1860 D2
- SUPE 80021 1857 A2
- SUPE 80027 1856 B2
- SUPE 80027 1857 A2
- SUPE 80303 1855 D1
- SUPE 80403 1855 D1
- SUPE 80403 1856 B2
- TNTN 80241 1860 D2
- WSTR 80234 1859 E2
10 NHGN 80234 1860 D2
10 WSTR 80234 1860 D2
1300 NHGN 80233 1861 A2
4500 WSTR 80020 1859 E2
4600 BMFD 80031 1859 A2
4600 WSTR 80031 1859 A2
SR-128 E 120th Av
1300 NHGN 80233 1861 A2
SR-128 W 120th Av
- BldC 80303 1855 E2
- BldC 80403 1855 E2
- NHGN 80233 1860 D2
- SUPE 80027 1856 B2
- SUPE 80303 1855 E2
- SUPE 80403 1855 E2
- SUPE 80403 1856 A2
- TNTN 80241 1860 D2
10 NHGN 80234 1860 D2
10 WSTR 80234 1860 D2
3600 BMFD 80020 1859 E2
3600 WSTR 80031 1859 E2
3600 WSTR 80234 1859 E2
4500 WSTR 80020 1859 E2
4600 BMFD 80031 1859 A2
6400 BMFD 80020 1858 E2
8700 BMFD 80021 1858 C2
SR-128 Interlocken Lp
- BMFD 80021 1857 D2
- BMFD 80021 1858 B2
SR-128 Wadsworth Pkwy
- BMFD 80020 1858 C2
- BMFD 80021 1858 C2
SR-157
- BldC 80301 1603 B7
- BLDR 80301 1603 B7
- BLDR 80301 1687 B2
- BLDR 80303 1687 B1
SR-157 Foothills Pkwy
- BldC 80301 1603 B7
- BLDR 80301 1603 B7
SR-157 Foothills Pkwy
- BLDR 80301 1687 B1
- BLDR 80303 1687 B2
SR-170
300 SUPE 80027 1772 B3
3500 BldC 80025 1770 E6
3500 BldC 80303 1770 E6
3500 BldC 80303 1771 B5
5600 BldC 80027 1772 B3
5600 BldC 80303 1772 B3
6500 SUPE 80303 1772 B3
SR-170 Eldorado Springs Dr
3500 BldC 80025 1770 E6
3500 BldC 80303 1770 E6
3500 BldC 80303 1771 A6
SR-170 Marshall Dr
5200 BldC 80303 1771 B5
5600 BldC 80027 1772 B3
5600 BldC 80303 1772 A3
6500 SUPE 80027 1772 C2
6500 SUPE 80303 1772 C2
SR-170 Marshall Rd
300 BldC 80027 1772 E3
300 SUPE 80027 1772 E3
SR-177
- AphC 80126 2449 C1
- CHLV 80121 2281 C7
3500 CHLV 80113 2281 C4
5100 GDVL 80121 2281 C7
5300 GDVL 80121 2365 C1
5900 CTNL 80121 2365 C1
6600 CTNL 80122 2365 C4
8200 AphC 80122 2449 C1
8200 CTNL 80122 2449 C1
SR-177 S University Blvd
- AphC 80126 2449 C1
- CHLV 80121 2281 C7
3500 CHLV 80113 2281 C4
5100 GDVL 80121 2281 C7
5300 GDVL 80121 2365 C1
5900 CTNL 80121 2365 C1
6600 CTNL 80122 2365 C4
8200 AphC 80122 2449 C1
8200 CTNL 80122 2449 C1
SR-224
- AdmC 80229 1945 B7
10 AdmC 80221 1944 E7
300 AdmC 80229 1944 E7
3800 AdmC 80022 1945 E6
3800 CMCY 80022 1945 E6
3800 TNTN 80022 1945 E6
4800 CMCY 80022 1946 A6
SR-224 E 70th Av
10 AdmC 80221 1944 E7
300 AdmC 80229 1944 E7
700 AdmC 80229 1945 A7
SR-224 E 74th Av
3800 AdmC 80022 1945 D6
3800 CMCY 80022 1945 D6
3800 TNTN 80022 1945 D6
4800 CMCY 80022 1946 A6
SR-265
5100 CMCY 80216 2029 B5
5100 DNVR 80216 2029 B5
5300 CMCY 80022 2029 B5
SR-265 Brighton Blvd
5100 CMCY 80216 2029 B5
5100 DNVR 80216 2029 B5
5300 CMCY 80022 2029 B5
SR-391
- ARVD 80002 2026 B5
- ARVD 80004 2026 B5
10 LKWD 80226 2194 B1
500 LKWD 80226 2110 B7
600 LKWD 80215 2110 B7
900 LKWD 80232 2194 A5
1500 JfnC 80227 2194 A7
1500 JfnC 80232 2194 A7
1500 LKWD 80227 2194 A7
2000 JfnC 80227 2278 A1
2000 LKWD 80227 2278 A1
2500 JfnC 80215 2110 B3
2500 WTRG 80215 2110 B3
3100 WTRG 80033 2110 B1
4700 WTRG 80033 2026 B6
5000 ARVD 80033 2026 B5
5000 WTRG 80002 2026 B5
SR-391 S Kipling Pkwy
900 LKWD 80226 2194 B4
900 LKWD 80232 2194 A4
1500 JfnC 80232 2194 A6
1500 LKWD 80227 2194 A6
1900 JfnC 80227 2194 A6
2000 JfnC 80227 2278 A1
2000 LKWD 80227 2278 A1
SR-391 Kipling St
- ARVD 80002 2026 B5
- ARVD 80004 2026 B5
10 LKWD 80226 2194 B1
500 LKWD 80226 2110 B7
600 LKWD 80215 2110 B7
2500 JfnC 80215 2110 B3
2500 WTRG 80215 2110 B3
3100 WTRG 80033 2110 B1
4700 WTRG 80033 2026 B6
5000 ARVD 80033 2026 B5
5000 WTRG 80002 2026 B5
SR-391 S Kipling St
10 LKWD 80226 2194 B1
SR-470
- DgsC - 2447 A2
- DgsC - 2448 A1
- DgsC - 2449 A1
- DgsC - 2450 E1
- DgsC - 2451 B2
- GOLD - 2192 C6
- JfnC - 2192 C6
- JfnC - 2276 E5
- JfnC - 2277 B7
- JfnC - 2361 B1
- JfnC - 2445 E1
- JfnC - 2446 E2
SR-470
- LITN - 2447 D1
- LITN - 2448 A1
- LKWD - 2192 C6
- LKWD - 2276 E5
- LKWD - 2277 A6
- LNTR - 2450 E1
- LNTR - 2451 B2
- MRSN - 2276 E5
SR-E470
- AdmC - 1692 E7
- AdmC - 1693 A7
- AdmC - 1777 E1
- AdmC - 1778 B2
- AdmC - 1779 B3
- AdmC - 1780 D7
- AdmC - 1864 E1
- AdmC - 1865 D7
- AdmC - 2034 C2
- AdmC - 2118 C1
- AphC - 2118 D4
- AphC - 2202 C7
- AphC - 2286 C1
- AphC - 2370 D1
- AURA - 2034 C2
- AURA - 2118 D4
- AURA - 2202 C7
- AURA - 2286 C4
- AURA - 2369 E7
- AURA - 2370 D1
- AURA - 2453 C1
- BGTN - 1779 B3
- BGTN - 1780 D7
- BMFD - 1692 C6
- CMCY - 1780 D7
- CMCY - 1864 E1
- CMCY - 1865 A2
- CMCY - 1949 D1
- DgsC - 2451 C2
- DgsC - 2452 C2
- DgsC - 2453 A3
- DNVR - 1949 D1
- DNVR - 1950 A7
- DNVR - 2034 C2
- LNTR - 2451 C2
- PARK - 2453 C1
- TNTN - 1692 E7
- TNTN - 1778 D3
US-6
- AdmC - 1698 E2
- AdmC - 1780 D7
- AdmC - 1781 D1
- AdmC - 1862 E6
- AdmC - 1863 A6
- AdmC - 1864 C1
- AdmC - 1946 C1
- BGTN - 1697 E6
- BGTN - 1698 E2
- BGTN - 1780 E5
- BGTN - 1781 A4
- BGTN - 1863 E3
- BGTN - 1864 C1
- CCkC - 2101 E5
- CCkC - 2102 B5
- CCkC 80403 2103 E5
- CCkC 80403 2104 C6
- CCkC 80439 2103 E5
- CMCY - 1862 E6
- CMCY - 1863 A6
- CMCY - 1864 C1
- CMCY - 1946 C1
- DNVR - 2111 A7
- DNVR - 2112 C7
- GOLD 80401 2107 E6
- GOLD 80401 2108 A6
- GOLD 80403 2107 C4
- IDSP - 2101 A5
- IDSP - 2102 B5
- JfnC - 2108 E7
- JfnC - 2109 A7
- JfnC 80401 2104 C6
- JfnC 80401 2105 D5
- JfnC 80401 2106 C5
- JfnC 80401 2107 B4
- JfnC 80403 2105 D5
- JfnC 80403 2106 C5
- JfnC 80403 2107 B4
- JfnC 80439 2104 C6
- LCHB - 1698 E2
- LKWD - 2109 E7
- LKWD - 2110 E7
- LKWD - 2111 E7
- WldC - 1698 E2
4600 DNVR 80216 2029 D6
5300 CMCY 80022 2029 D6
5300 DNVR 80022 2029 D6
US-6 6th Av
- LKWD - 2109 A7
- LKWD - 2110 E7
- LKWD - 2111 B7
US-6 W 6th Av
- DNVR - 2111 A7
- DNVR - 2112 C7
- GOLD 80401 2107 E6
- GOLD 80401 2108 B7
- GOLD 80403 2107 E6
- JfnC - 2109 C7
- JfnC 80401 2107 E6
- JfnC 80401 2108 B7
- LKWD - 2109 C7
- LKWD - 2110 A7
- LKWD - 2111 A7
US-6 Dahlia St
- CMCY 80022 2029 E1
US-6 Vasquez Blvd
4600 DNVR 80216 2029 C6
5300 CMCY 80022 2029 E4
5300 DNVR 80022 2029 E5
US-36
- AdmC - 1944 B6
- AdmC - 1945 B7
- AdmC - 2029 E3
- AdmC - 2032 A7
- AdmC - 2118 E4
US-36
- AdmC - 2119 E4
- AdmC - 2120 D4
- AdmC - 2121 B4
- AdmC - 2122 B4
- AdmC - 2123 E4
- AdmC - 2124 A4
- AdmC - 2125 D5
- AphC - 2119 E4
- AphC - 2125 D5
- AURA - 2032 A7
- AURA - 2116 E1
- AURA - 2117 E3
- AURA - 2118 A4
- AURA - 2121 B4
- AURA - 2122 B4
- BfdC - 1858 E4
- BldC - 1687 D7
- BldC - 1771 E1
- BldC - 1772 B2
- BldC - 1773 B4
- BLDR - 1686 E3
- BLDR - 1687 B5
- BMFD - 1773 B4
- BMFD - 1774 A7
- BMFD - 1858 B1
- BNNT - 2124 E4
- BNNT - 2125 D5
- CMCY - 2029 C2
- CMCY - 2030 E7
- DNVR - 2030 E7
- DNVR - 2031 B7
- DNVR - 2032 A7
- DvrC - 2032 A7
- JfnC - 1858 E4
- JfnC - 1859 A7
- JfnC - 1943 C4
- LSVL - 1772 E3
- LSVL - 1773 B4
- SUPE - 1772 E3
- SUPE - 1773 B4
- WSTR - 1858 E4
- WSTR - 1859 A7
- WSTR - 1943 C4
- WSTR - 1944 B6
10 BldC 80503 1352 E2
10 LYNS 80503 1352 E2
200 LYNS 80540 1352 E2
700 BLDR 80302 1686 E3
700 BLDR 80303 1686 E3
2200 BLDR 80301 1686 E1
2200 BLDR 80304 1686 E1
2700 BLDR 80301 1602 E6
2700 BLDR 80304 1602 E6
4000 BldC 80503 1353 A3
4000 LYNS 80503 1353 A3
4300 BldC 80304 1602 E6
4900 BldC 80301 1602 C1
5000 BldC 80302 1602 C1
5000 BLDR 80302 1602 C1
5700 BldC 80302 1518 C6
5700 BldC 80503 1518 C6
5700 BLDR 80302 1518 C6
8600 BldC 80302 1435 C7
8600 BldC 80503 1435 C7
9700 BldC 80540 1435 E1
10200 BldC 80503 1436 A1
16200 BldC 80540 1269 B5
18000 BldC 80540 1352 C1
19500 LYNS 80540 1269 C7
US-36 5th Av
500 LYNS 80540 1352 E2
US-36 28th St
700 BLDR 80303 1686 E3
1500 BLDR 80301 1686 E3
2200 BLDR 80302 1686 E1
2200 BLDR 80304 1686 E1
2700 BLDR 80301 1602 E6
2700 BLDR 80304 1602 E6
3600 BldC 80301 1602 E6
4300 BldC 80304 1602 E6
5000 BldC 80302 1602 E6
5000 BLDR 80302 1602 E6
US-36 Broadway St
200 LYNS 80540 1352 D1
US-36 Denver-Boulder Tpk
- AdmC - 1944 B6
- BfdC - 1858 E4
- BldC - 1687 D7
- BldC - 1771 E1
- BldC - 1772 B2
- BldC - 1773 B4
- BLDR - 1686 E4
- BLDR - 1687 D7
- BMFD - 1773 B4
- BMFD - 1774 A7
- BMFD - 1858 E4
- JfnC - 1858 E4
- JfnC - 1859 A7
- JfnC - 1943 C4
- LSVL - 1772 E3
- LSVL - 1773 B4
- SUPE - 1772 E3
- SUPE - 1773 B4
- WSTR - 1858 E4
- WSTR - 1859 A7
- WSTR - 1943 E5
- WSTR - 1944 E7
US-36 N Foothills Hwy
- BldC 80301 1602 C1
- BldC 80302 1602 C1
- BLDR 80302 1602 C1
- BLDR 80304 1602 C1
5700 BldC 80302 1518 C6
5700 BldC 80503 1518 C6
5700 BLDR 80302 1518 C6
8600 BldC 80302 1435 C7
8600 BldC 80503 1435 C7
9700 BldC 80540 1435 E1
10200 BldC 80503 1353 A3
10200 BldC 80503 1436 A1
US-36 Main St
300 LYNS 80540 1352 D1
US-36 E Main St
10 BldC 80503 1352 E2
10 LYNS 80503 1352 E2
10 LYNS 80540 1352 E2
US-36 W Main St
500 LYNS 80540 1352 E2
US-36 N St. Vrain Dr
16200 BldC 80540 1269 B5
18000 BldC 80540 1352 C1
19500 LYNS 80540 1269 C7
19500 LYNS 80540 1352 C1
US-36 Ute Hwy
4000 BldC 80503 1352 E2
4000 BldC 80503 1353 A3
4000 LYNS 80503 1352 E2
4000 LYNS 80503 1353 A3
4000 LYNS 80540 1352 E2
US-40
- AdmC - 2118 E5
- AdmC - 2119 E4
- AdmC - 2120 D4
- AdmC - 2121 B4
- AdmC - 2122 B4
- AdmC - 2123 E4
- AdmC - 2124 A4
- AdmC - 2125 D5
- AphC - 2118 E5
- AphC - 2119 B4
- AphC - 2125 D5
- AURA - 2121 B4
- AURA - 2122 B4
- BNNT - 2124 E4
- BNNT - 2125 D5
- CCkC - 2101 A5
- CCkC - 2102 B5
- CCkC - 2103 A5
- IDSP - 2101 A5
- IDSP - 2102 B5
- JfnC - 2189 E2
- JfnC - 2190 A2
- JfnC 80401 2188 E1
- JfnC 80401 2191 A3
- JfnC 80439 2189 B3
10 DNVR 80202 2112 D5
10 DNVR 80204 2112 D5
100 DNVR 80203 2112 E5
700 DNVR 80203 2113 A5
1000 DNVR 80218 2113 A5
2700 DNVR 80206 2113 C5
3900 DNVR 80220 2113 E5
4700 DNVR 80220 2114 A5
5100 LKWD 80214 2111 D5
5200 DNVR 80204 2111 D5
6800 LKWD 80214 2110 E5
8300 LKWD 80215 2110 C5
8900 DNVR 80220 2115 A5
9700 AURA 80010 2115 A5
10900 LKWD 80215 2109 E5
11900 JfnC 80401 2109 D5
12100 AURA 80011 2115 E5
12400 LKWD 80401 2109 A6
12700 AURA 80011 2116 E5
12700 JfnC 80215 2109 D5
13000 AURA 80010 2116 A5
14800 JfnC 80401 2108 C7
14800 LKWD 80401 2108 E6
15500 GOLD 80401 2108 D7
16500 AURA 80011 2117 D5
17700 JfnC 80401 2192 B1
18400 GOLD 80401 2192 A4
20700 AdmC 80011 2118 E5
20700 AURA 80011 2118 E5
31500 CCkC 80439 2187 E1
31500 CCkC 80439 2188 B2
US-40 E Colfax Av
10 DNVR 80203 2112 E5
100 DNVR 80202 2112 E5
700 DNVR 80203 2113 A5
900 DNVR 80218 2113 A5
2700 DNVR 80206 2113 C5
3900 DNVR 80220 2113 E5
4700 DNVR 80220 2114 A5
8900 AURA 80010 2115 A5
8900 DNVR 80220 2115 A5
12100 AURA 80011 2115 E5
12700 AURA 80011 2116 E5
13000 AURA 80010 2116 A5
16500 AURA 80011 2117 D5
20700 AURA 80011 2118 A5
21400 AdmC 80011 2118 A5
US-40 W Colfax Av
- GOLD 80401 2192 A4
10 DNVR 80202 2112 D5
10 DNVR 80203 2112 D5
10 DNVR 80204 2112 D5
3000 DNVR 80204 2111 D5
5200 LKWD 80214 2111 D5
6800 LKWD 80214 2110 E5
8300 LKWD 80215 2110 C5
10800 LKWD 80215 2109 E5
11900 JfnC 80401 2109 D5
12400 LKWD 80401 2109 A6
12700 JfnC 80215 2109 D5
14800 JfnC 80401 2108 C7
14800 LKWD 80401 2108 C7
15500 GOLD 80401 2108 D7
17700 JfnC 80401 2192 B1
US-40 Highway 40
32000 CCkC 80439 2187 E1
US-40 Mt Vernon Canyon Rd
18400 GOLD 80401 2192 A4
18400 JfnC 80401 2192 A4
US-40 S Mt Vernon Cntry Clb Rd
- JfnC 80401 2190 C2
US-85
- AdmC - 1946 C1
- AdmC 80022 1946 A5
- AdmC 80601 1696 B2
- AdmC 80601 1779 D7
- AdmC 80601 1780 A1
- AdmC 80601 1863 D1
- AdmC 80640 1862 E6

STREET
Block City ZIP Map# Grid

US-85
- AdmC 80640 1863 A6
- BGTN 80601 1696 B2
- BGTN 80601 1779 D7
- BGTN 80601 1780 A1
- BGTN 80601 1863 D1
- BGTN 80603 1696 B4
- BGTN 80640 1863 D1
- CMCY - 1946 C1
- CMCY 80640 1863 D1
- CSRK - 2787 C1
- CSRK 80104 2703 C3
- CSRK 80108 2618 E7
- CSRK 80108 2619 A7
- CSRK 80108 2703 B1
- CSRK 80109 2703 C3
- DgsC - 2787 B4
- DgsC - 2870 E6
- DgsC - 2871 A2
- DgsC - 2954 E1
- DgsC - 2955 A1
- DgsC 80108 2618 A5
- DgsC 80108 2619 A7
- DgsC 80120 2447 E1
- DgsC 80135 2532 E7
- DgsC 80135 2616 E1
- DgsC 80135 2617 B4
- DgsC 80135 2618 A5
- DNVR - 2112 B7
- DNVR - 2196 C1
- LKSR - 2955 A1
- WldC 80603 1696 B2
2500 DNVR 80223 2280 D2
2500 DvrC 80223 2280 D2
2500 EGLD 80110 2280 D2
2500 EGLD 80223 2280 D2
3300 SRDN 80110 2280 D2
4600 DNVR 80216 2029 D6
4700 LITN 80120 2280 B6
5300 CMCY 80022 2029 D6
5300 DNVR 80022 2029 D6
5300 LITN 80120 2364 A1
7600 LITN 80120 2363 E7
8200 LITN 80120 2447 E1
8300 DgsC 80125 2447 E1
8300 DgsC 80129 2447 E1
10500 DgsC 80125 2532 A1
10600 DgsC 80125 2448 A7
US-85 Dahlia St
- CMCY 80022 2029 E1
US-85 S Kalamath St
- DNVR 80223 2196 D7
US-85 S Platte River Dr
700 DNVR 80223 2196 D3
US-85 S Santa Fe Dr
- DgsC 80120 2447 E1
700 DNVR 80223 2196 D4
2500 DNVR 80223 2280 D2
2500 DvrC 80223 2280 D2
2500 EGLD 80110 2280 D2
2500 EGLD 80223 2280 D2
3300 SRDN 80110 2280 D2
4700 LITN 80120 2280 B6
5300 LITN 80120 2364 A1
7600 LITN 80120 2363 E7
8200 LITN 80120 2447 E1
8300 DgsC 80125 2447 E1
8300 DgsC 80129 2447 E1
10500 DgsC 80125 2532 A1
10600 DgsC 80125 2448 A7
US-85 Vasquez Blvd
4600 DNVR 80216 2029 C6
5300 CMCY 80022 2029 E4
5300 DNVR 80022 2029 E5
US-86
100 CSRK 80104 2703 D6
US-86 5th St
100 CSRK 80104 2703 D6
US-87
- AdmC - 1692 D7
- AdmC - 1776 D4
- AdmC - 1944 E6
- AdmC - 2028 E2
- BMFD - 1692 E2
- BMFD - 1776 D2
- CSRK - 2619 B1
- CSRK - 2703 C7
- CSRK - 2787 C1
- CTNL - 2367 A5
- CTNL - 2451 B1
- DgsC - 2451 C3
- DgsC - 2535 B2
- DgsC - 2619 B1
- DgsC - 2787 B4
- DgsC - 2870 E6
- DgsC - 2871 A2
- DgsC - 2954 E1
- DgsC - 2955 A1
- DNVR - 2028 E2
- DNVR - 2112 B7
- DNVR - 2196 D2
- DNVR - 2197 E6
- DNVR - 2198 A7
- DNVR - 2282 B1
- DvrC - 2282 D7
- GDVL - 2282 D7
- GDVL - 2366 E3
- GDVL - 2367 A5
- LKSR - 2955 A1
- LNTR - 2451 C3
- LNTR - 2535 B2
- NHGN - 1860 D7
- TNTN - 1692 D7
- TNTN - 1776 D4
- TNTN - 1860 D7
- TNTN - 1944 E6
- WSTR - 1776 D4
- WSTR - 1860 D1
US-87 N Valley Hwy
- AdmC - 2028 E2
- DNVR - 2028 E2
- DNVR - 2112 A4
US-285
- AphC 80236 2279 D3
- DNVR 80227 2279 A3
- DNVR 80235 2279 D3
- DNVR 80236 2279 A3
- JfnC 80227 2278 E3
- JfnC 80235 2277 E4
- JfnC 80235 2278 E3
- JfnC 80433 2442 D4
- JfnC 80433 2524 D7
- JfnC 80433 2525 A5
- JfnC 80433 2526 A1
- JfnC 80454 2359 E1
- JfnC 80465 2276 C7
- JfnC 80465 2277 E4
- JfnC 80465 2359 E1
- JfnC 80465 2360 B1
- JfnC 80465 2442 D4
- JfnC 80465 2443 A4
- JfnC 80470 2524 D7
- LKWD 80227 2277 E4
- LKWD 80227 2278 A3
- LKWD 80227 2279 A3
- LKWD 80235 2278 E3
- LKWD 80465 2276 E6
- LKWD 80465 2277 B5
- MRSN 80465 2276 C7
- MRSN 80465 2360 B1
- PrkC 80456 2690 C2
- SRDN 80110 2279 D3
- SRDN 80110 2280 A3
- SRDN 80236 2279 D3
100 EGLD 80110 2280 D3
200 EGLD 80113 2280 D3
600 EGLD 80113 2281 A3
700 CHLV 80113 2281 E3
2800 CHLV 80210 2281 E3
3200 DvrC 80113 2281 E3
3600 AphC 80210 2281 E3
3600 DNVR 80210 2281 E3
3600 DNVR 80222 2281 E3
3600 DvrC 80222 2281 E3
4700 AphC 80222 2282 B3
4700 CHLV 80113 2282 B3
4700 DNVR 80222 2282 B3
4700 DNVR 80237 2282 B3
13700 JfnC 80470 2608 A2
13700 PrkC 80456 2608 A2
56700 PrkC 80456 2605 A7
56700 PrkC 80456 2689 A1
63000 PrkC 80456 2606 D6
63900 PrkC 80456 2607 A4
US-285 E Hampden Av
1500 CHLV 80113 2281 E3
1500 EGLD 80113 2281 E3
1900 AphC 80113 2281 E3
2300 DvrC 80210 2281 E3
2800 CHLV 80210 2281 E3
3600 AphC 80222 2281 E3
3600 DNVR 80210 2281 E3
3600 DNVR 80222 2281 E3
4700 AphC 80222 2282 B3
4700 CHLV 80113 2282 B3
4700 DNVR 80222 2282 B3
4700 DNVR 80237 2282 B3
US-285 W Hampden Av
- SRDN 80110 2280 A3
100 EGLD 80110 2280 D3
US-285 E Jefferson Av
- EGLD 80110 2280 E3
200 EGLD 80113 2280 E3
600 EGLD 80113 2281 A3
700 CHLV 80113 2281 A3
US-287
- AdmC - 2118 E4
- AdmC - 2119 E4
- AdmC - 2120 E4
- AdmC - 2121 A4
- AdmC - 2122 B4
- AdmC - 2123 E4
- AdmC - 2124 A4
- AdmC - 2125 D5
- AphC - 2119 E4
- AphC - 2125 D5
- AURA - 2121 A4
- AURA - 2122 B4
- BMFD 80020 1858 C1
- BNNT - 2124 E4
- BNNT - 2125 D5
- DNVR 80211 2028 A5
10 DNVR 80202 2112 E5
10 LGMT 80501 1439 B1
100 BldC 80501 1439 B1
100 DNVR 80203 2112 E5
300 DNVR 80204 2112 A5
500 LAFT 80026 1690 C7
500 LAFT 80026 1774 C1
700 DNVR 80203 2113 A5
1000 DNVR 80218 2113 A5
1100 BldC 80026 1774 C1
1300 BldC 80020 1774 C4
1300 LAFT 80020 1774 C4
1400 BldC 80504 1439 B7
1400 LGMT 80504 1439 B7
1600 BMFD 80020 1774 C1
1900 DNVR 80211 2112 A4
2300 BldC 80026 1690 B1
2300 BldC 80504 1356 B4
2300 LGMT 80501 1356 B4
2700 DNVR 80206 2113 C5
3000 ERIE 80026 1690 B1
3300 BldC 80026 1606 B7
3400 ERIE 80026 1606 B5
3500 BMFD 80020 1859 E2
3600 WSTR 80234 1859 E2
3900 DNVR 80220 2113 E5
4300 WSTR 80020 1859 E2
4600 BMFD 80031 1859 A2
4600 WSTR 80031 1859 A2
4700 DNVR 80220 2114 A5
4800 BldC 80504 1606 B1
4800 DNVR 80221 2028 A7
5100 AdmC 80221 2028 A5
5400 BldC 80504 1522 B7
6700 AdmC 80221 2027 E1
6700 WSTR 80030 2027 E1
7000 AdmC 80221 1944 A7
7000 WSTR 80030 1944 A7
7600 AdmC 80221 1943 E6
7600 WSTR 80030 1943 E6
7600 WSTR 80031 1943 E3
8600 FLHT 80031 1943 E3
8600 FLHT 80260 1943 E1
8900 AURA 80010 2115 A5
8900 DNVR 80220 2115 A5
9300 WSTR 80260 1943 E1
9700 FLHT 80031 1859 E6
9700 FLHT 80260 1859 E6
12100 AURA 80011 2115 E5
12700 AURA 80010 2116 E5
13000 AURA 80011 2116 A5
16500 AURA 80011 2117 D5
20700 AURA 80011 2118 E4
21400 AdmC 80011 2118 E4
US-287 N 107th St
1900 BldC 80026 1439 B6
1900 LGMT 80501 1439 B6
1900 LGMT 80504 1439 B6
2100 LAFT 80026 1690 B1
2300 BldC 80026 1690 B1
3000 ERIE 80026 1690 B1
3300 BldC 80026 1606 B7
3400 ERIE 80026 1606 B5
4800 BldC 80504 1606 B1
5400 BldC 80504 1522 B7
12600 BldC 80504 1356 B1
12600 LGMT 80501 1356 B1
US-287 S 112th St
500 LAFT 80026 1690 C7
500 LAFT 80026 1774 C1
1100 BldC 80026 1774 C1
1300 BldC 80020 1774 C1
1300 LAFT 80020 1774 C4
1600 BMFD 80020 1774 C4
US-287 W 120th Av
3600 BMFD 80020 1859 E2
3600 WSTR 80234 1859 E2
4300 WSTR 80020 1859 E2
4600 BMFD 80031 1859 A2
4600 WSTR 80031 1859 A2
6400 BMFD 80020 1858 E2
US-287 E Colfax Av
10 DNVR 80203 2112 E5
100 DNVR 80202 2112 E5
700 DNVR 80203 2113 A5
1000 DNVR 80218 2113 A5
2700 DNVR 80206 2113 C5
3900 DNVR 80220 2113 E5
4700 DNVR 80220 2114 A5
8900 AURA 80010 2115 A5
8900 DNVR 80220 2115 A5
12100 AURA 80011 2115 E5
12700 AURA 80011 2116 E5
13000 AURA 80010 2116 A5
16500 AURA 80011 2117 D5
20700 AdmC 80011 2118 A5
20700 AURA 80011 2118 A5
US-287 W Colfax Av
10 DNVR 80202 2112 D5
10 DNVR 80203 2112 D5
10 DNVR 80204 2112 D5
US-287 Federal Blvd
- DNVR 80211 2028 A5
- WSTR 80031 1859 E2
1500 DNVR 80204 2112 A4
1900 DNVR 80211 2112 A4
4800 DNVR 80221 2028 A7
5100 AdmC 80221 2028 A5
5700 AdmC 80221 2027 E1
6700 WSTR 80030 2027 E1
7000 AdmC 80221 1944 A7
7000 WSTR 80030 1944 A7
7600 AdmC 80221 1943 E6
7600 WSTR 80030 1943 E6
7600 WSTR 80031 1943 E3
8600 FLHT 80031 1943 E3
8600 FLHT 80260 1943 E1
9300 WSTR 80260 1943 E1
9700 FLHT 80031 1859 E7
9700 FLHT 80260 1859 E7
10200 WSTR 80234 1859 E6
US-287 Main St
10 LGMT 80501 1439 B1
1100 LGMT 80501 1356 B6
2300 BldC 80504 1356 B4
US-287 S Main St
10 LGMT 80501 1439 B3
100 BldC 80501 1439 B3
1400 BldC 80504 1439 B6
1400 LGMT 80504 1439 B6

A

A St
- AURA 80011 2116 C4
- CLCY 80403 2017 C4
- DNVR 80123 2363 A1
- LGMT 80501 1356 A6
100 GOLD 80401 2192 B1
Aaron Pl
4400 BLDR 80303 1687 B3
E A Basin Av
17700 AURA 80011 2201 B2
Abbey Dr
500 LGMT 80501 1356 D6
Abbey Pl
200 BLDR 80302 1686 D5
Abbey St
12400 BMFD 80020 1859 C1
Abbotswood Ct
10600 DgsC 80129 2448 D7
Abbott Av
2100 BMFD 80020 1858 C1
E Aberdeen Av
4600 DgsC 80126 2449 E2
4600 DgsC 80126 2450 A2
4700 DgsC 80130 2450 A2
9700 AphC 80111 2367 B2
15700 CTNL 80016 2368 D2
W Aberdeen Av
400 LITN 80120 2364 D2
4200 LITN 80123 2363 C2
S Aberdeen Cir
8600 DgsC 80130 2450 A2
Aberdeen Ct
4400 BldC 80301 1604 D3
Aberdeen Dr
900 BMFD 80020 1859 A1
E Aberdeen Dr
17000 AphC 80016 2369 A2
21200 CTNL 80015 2370 A2
Aberdeen Pl
4400 BldC 80301 1604 D4
E Aberdeen Pl
17700 AphC 80016 2369 B2
21200 CTNL 80015 2370 A2
23200 AphC 80015 2370 D2
W Aberdeen Pl
4400 LITN 80123 2363 C2
E Aberdeen St
16000 CTNL 80016 2368 E2
S Aberdeen St
5900 LITN 80120 2364 D2
Aberdeen Wy
7500 BldC 80301 1604 D4
E Aberdeen Wy
- DgsC 80130 2450 A2
Abernathy Ct
10 DgsC 80130 2450 A3
Abeyta Ct
3800 BldC 80301 1603 A5
Abilene Cir
3200 AURA 80011 2116 B2
S Abilene Cir
4000 AURA 80014 2284 B4
4600 AphC 80015 2284 B6
4600 AURA 80015 2284 B6
Abilene Ct
1700 EbtC 80107 2792 D7
S Abilene Ct
1100 AURA 80012 2200 B4
Abilene Dr
1300 BMFD 80020 1774 E6
Abilene St
10 AURA 80011 2200 B1
10 AURA 80012 2200 B1
3000 AURA 80011 2116 B2
3500 AURA 80011 2032 B7
5500 DNVR 80239 2032 B4
10400 CMCY 80022 1864 A5
10600 AdmC 80022 1864 A5
13200 AdmC 80601 1780 A6
S Abilene St
10 AURA 80011 2200 B1
10 AURA 80012 2200 B1
1500 AURA 80014 2200 B6
2500 AURA 80014 2284 B1
S Abilene Wy
6500 CTNL 80111 2368 B3
Abstract St
- CSRK 80109 2702 D4
Abundance Wy
6700 JfnC 80403 2022 A2
Academy Blvd
- AURA 80011 2116 D4
E Academy Blvd
7700 DNVR 80230 2114 E7
7700 DNVR 80230 2198 D1
Academy St
- CLCY 80403 2017 C4
Acadia Av
200 LAFT 80026 1690 C3
Acadia Dr
21000 PARK 80138 2538 A1
Acadia Ln
10900 PARK 80138 2538 A1
Acadia Pl
10800 PARK 80138 2538 A1
Ace Ct
6400 BldC 80503 1518 E6
Acer Dr
- DgsC 80134 2452 E2
- PARK 80134 2452 E2
Achilles Cir
1100 LAFT 80026 1690 A5
Achilles Dr
13400 DgsC 80124 2450 E2
S Acoma Cir
7100 LITN 80120 2364 E5
Acoma Ct
7500 AdmC 80221 1944 D6
7700 DgsC 80118 2952 E3
S Acoma Ct
7100 LITN 80120 2364 E5
Acoma Dr
8200 DgsC 80118 2953 A4
W Acoma Dr
100 LITN 80120 2364 D4
Acoma Pl
5300 DgsC 80118 2952 E3
5300 DgsC 80118 2953 A3
S Acoma Pl
7200 LITN 80120 2364 E5
Acoma Rd
4400 JfnC 80439 2274 E6
Acoma St
10 DNVR 80223 2196 E1
300 DNVR 80223 2112 D7
700 DNVR 80204 2112 D6
4800 DNVR 80216 2028 D6
8100 AdmC 80221 1944 D4
8100 TNTN 80221 1944 D4
11600 NHGN 80234 1860 D3
S Acoma St
1200 DNVR 80223 2196 E6
2500 DNVR 80223 2280 E1
2600 EGLD 80223 2280 E1
2700 DvrC 80223 2280 E1
2700 EGLD 80110 2280 E1
6300 LITN 80120 2364 E3
Acoma Wy
8200 AdmC 80221 1944 D4
8200 TNTN 80221 1944 D4
8300 TNTN 80260 1944 D4
S Acoma Wy
7100 LITN 80120 2364 E5
Acorn Ln
10 BldC 80304 1602 A6
Acres Green Dr
- CTNL 80112 2450 E1
- LNTR 80124 2450 E1
13300 DgsC 80124 2450 E2
Acropolis Dr
1200 LAFT 80026 1690 A6
E Ada Dr
17700 AURA 80017 2201 B3
E Ada Pl
11800 AURA 80012 2199 D3
16700 AURA 80017 2200 E3
W Ada Pl
- DNVR 80219 2195 C3
1200 DNVR 80223 2196 C3
3000 DNVR 80219 2196 A3
10900 LKWD 80226 2194 A4
11000 LKWD 80226 2193 E4
Adahi Rd
5200 JfnC 80454 2275 A7
5200 JfnC 80454 2359 A1
E Adak Pl
19300 DNVR 80249 2033 D6
Adam Ct
14100 BMFD 80020 1775 E3
Adam Pl
500 DgsC 80108 2534 E4
Adams Av
500 LSVL 80027 1773 C1
1000 LSVL 80027 1689 C7
Adams Cir
1000 BLDR 80303 1687 A3
10500 NHGN 80233 1861 D5
13800 TNTN 80602 1777 C4
S Adams Cir
7100 CTNL 80122 2365 D5
Adams Ct
900 LSVL 80027 1689 C7
8500 AdmC 80229 1945 D3
10700 NHGN 80233 1861 D5
13000 TNTN 80241 1777 D6
S Adams Ct
6500 CTNL 80121 2365 D3
S Adams Dr
200 LSVL 80027 1773 C2
5900 CTNL 80121 2365 D2
Adams Pl
1400 LSVL 80027 1689 C6
10300 TNTN 80229 1861 C6
Adams St
10 DNVR 80206 2197 D1
10 DNVR 80209 2197 D1
100 BNNT 80102 2124 D2
300 DNVR 80206 2113 D7
3200 DNVR 80205 2113 D1
3300 TNTN 80233 1861 C2
3900 DNVR 80205 2029 D7
4000 DNVR 80216 2029 D7
9200 TNTN 80229 1945 D2
10000 TNTN 80229 1861 D7
10700 NHGN 80233 1861 C5
12100 TNTN 80241 1861 D1
13600 TNTN 80602 1777 C4
Adams St SR-79
- BNNT 80102 2124 D2
S Adams St
10 DNVR 80206 2197 D1
10 DNVR 80209 2197 D1
1000 DNVR 80210 2197 D4
2500 DNVR 80210 2281 D1
7500 CTNL 80122 2365 D7
Adams Wy
8200 AdmC 80221 1944 C4
8200 FLHT 80260 1944 C4
8400 AdmC 80229 1945 D4
12100 TNTN 80241 1861 C1
12800 TNTN 80241 1777 C7
S Adams Wy
900 DNVR 80209 2197 D3
3100 DNVR 80210 2281 D2
6700 CTNL 80121 2365 D4
8100 CTNL 80122 2365 D7
Addenbrooke Lp
4400 CSRK 80109 2702 D2
Addington Pl
- PARK 80138 2538 C2
Addish St
13200 AdmC 80022 1782 D5
13400 AdmC 80603 1782 D5
Addison
- TNTN 80260 1944 C3
Addison Ct
- AURA 80016 2370 D4
10600 DgsC 80126 2533 D1
S Addison Ct
1300 AURA 80018 2202 D4
5300 AphC 80016 2286 D7
6900 AURA 80016 2370 D6
Addison Pt
3000 DgsC 80126 2533 D1
Addison Wy
- AURA 80016 2286 D6
N Addison Wy
- AURA 80018 2118 D7
S Addison Wy
1000 AphC 80018 2202 D3
2200 AURA 80018 2202 D7
7600 AURA 80016 2370 D6
S Adelaide Cir
9600 DgsC 80130 2450 A4
S Adelaide Ct
9700 DgsC 80130 2450 A5
E Adelaide Pl
4700 DgsC 80130 2450 A5
Adkinson Av
1600 LGMT 80501 1355 E5
Admiral Wy
2000 EbtC 80138 2540 D4
S Adobe Ct
4600 JfnC 80127 2278 A6
S Adobe Ln
4600 JfnC 80127 2278 A6
E Adobe Pl
1600 DgsC 80126 2449 B4
S Adobe Wy
4600 JfnC 80127 2278 A5
Adonia Cir
1500 LAFT 80026 1690 A6
Adonis Ct
1400 LAFT 80026 1690 A7
W Adriatic Av
12800 LKWD 80228 2193 D7
E Adriatic Dr
17300 AURA 80013 2201 A6
E Adriatic Pl
11400 AURA 80014 2199 D6
14800 AURA 80014 2200 C6
16300 AURA 80013 2200 E6
18200 AURA 80013 2201 B6
W Adriatic Pl
1800 DNVR 80110 2196 B7
1800 DNVR 80223 2196 B7
1800 EGLD 80110 2196 B7
6000 LKWD 80227 2195 A7
14000 LKWD 80228 2193 A7
Aegean Dr
700 LAFT 80026 1690 B5
Aegean Wy
2000 LGMT 80501 1357 A5
Affolter St
- LGMT 80503 1438 C4
Afton Ln
2200 JfnC 80439 2189 B7
S Aftonwood St
9700 DgsC 80126 2449 E5
Agape Wy
1300 LAFT 80026 1690 A6
Agate Av
24500 JfnC 80433 2526 C1
Agate Dr
100 DgsC 80126 2448 E2
Agate Ln
2400 BldC 80304 1602 E5
2400 BLDR 80304 1602 E5
Agate Rd
2400 BldC 80304 1602 E5
2400 BLDR 80304 1602 E5
Agate St
300 BMFD 80020 1858 E1
600 BMFD 80020 1774 E7
Agate Wy
100 BMFD 80020 1858 E1
Aikins Wy
1200 BLDR 80305 1687 C7
1200 BLDR 80305 1771 B1
Ainsdale Ct
8600 LNTR 80124 2450 E3
8600 LNTR 80124 2451 B3
S Aintree Ct
20100 PARK 80138 2537 E2
S Aintree Pl
20100 PARK 80138 2537 E2
Airlawn Rd
6900 DNVR 80216 2030 C7
Airport Blvd
- AURA 80011 2032 E7
- AURA 80011 2033 A7
- AURA 80011 2116 E1
2700 AURA 80011 2117 A3
5100 BLDR 80301 1603 C6
N Airport Blvd
10 AURA 80011 2201 A1
100 AURA 80011 2117 A6
S Airport Blvd
10 AURA 80011 2201 A2
100 AURA 80017 2201 A2
Airport Cir
16300 AURA 80011 2116 E2
Airport Ct
- BMFD 80021 1858 A2
10100 JfnC 80021 1858 A2
10800 JfnC 80021 1857 E2
Airport Dr
3000 BldC 80026 1691 B4
3000 BldC 80516 1691 B4
3000 BMFD 80020 1691 B4
3000 ERIE 80516 1691 B4
Airport Rd
- BldC 80503 1521 B1
600 LGMT 80503 1438 B5
1600 BldC 80503 1355 A7
2400 LGMT 80503 1355 A7
3300 BLDR 80301 1603 C6
10200 BldC 80503 1438 A1
W Airport Rd
5500 DgsC 80135 2532 D7
5800 DgsC 80135 2616 D1
Airport Wy
- AURA 80011 2032 E7
- DvrC 80239 2032 E7
4300 DNVR 80239 2032 E7
12000 BfdC 80021 1858 A2
12000 BMFD 80021 1858 B2
W Airview Av
6800 LKWD 80232 2195 A5
Ajax Ct
2400 SUPE 80027 1773 A7
Ajax Ln
1600 JfnC 80439 2188 E6
1600 JfnC 80439 2189 A6
Ajax St
1500 AdmC 80136 2125 E4
Akers Ct
1400 ERIE 80516 1607 A6
S Akron Cir
5900 GDVL 80111 2367 A2
Akron Ct
2500 DNVR 80238 2115 A3
14800 AdmC 80602 1778 E1
S Akron Ct
1200 AphC 80247 2199 A4
2900 DNVR 80231 2283 A2
4200 GDVL 80111 2283 A5
E Akron Pl
1000 SUPE 80027 1773 B5
Akron St
1100 AURA 80230 2115 A6
1600 AURA 80010 2115 A4
2800 DNVR 80238 2115 A3
10700 AdmC 80640 1863 A4
10700 CMCY 80640 1863 A4
14800 AdmC 80602 1779 A1
14900 AdmC 80602 1778 E1
15400 AdmC 80602 1694 E7
S Akron St
1300 AphC 80247 2199 A4
2900 DNVR 80231 2283 A2
3400 DNVR 80237 2283 A3
4200 GDVL 80111 2283 A5
8000 CTNL 80112 2367 A7
8200 CTNL 80112 2451 A1
8200 LNTR 80112 2451 A1
Akron Wy
600 AURA 80230 2115 A6
600 DNVR 80230 2115 A6
700 DNVR 80230 2114 E6
S Akron Wy
1200 AphC 80247 2199 A4
6000 GDVL 80111 2367 A2
W Aksarben Av
3300 LITN 80123 2363 E1
W Alabama Av
8200 LKWD 80232 2194 D5
E Alabama Cir
9900 AURA 80247 2199 B4
11300 AURA 80012 2199 D4
E Alabama Dr
- AphC 80247 2199 B4
9800 AURA 80247 2199 B4
16000 AURA 80017 2200 E4
23600 AURA 80018 2202 D4
W Alabama Dr
9200 LKWD 80232 2194 B4
E Alabama Pl
- AphC 80247 2198 B4
4800 DNVR 80246 2198 A4
9800 AURA 80247 2199 B4
14700 AURA 80012 2200 C4
16500 AURA 80017 2200 E4
18100 AURA 80017 2201 B4
23600 AURA 80018 2202 D4
W Alabama Pl
3100 DNVR 80219 2195 E4
3100 DNVR 80219 2196 A4
9000 LKWD 80232 2194 C4
12000 JfnC 80232 2193 D5
12500 LKWD 80228 2193 C4
W Alabama Wy
12500 LKWD 80228 2193 C5
Alabaster Ct
9800 DgsC 80134 2452 D5
Alabraska Ln
27900 JfnC 80439 2357 D5
Alameda Av
32900 AphC 80137 2205 A1
E Alameda Av
10 DNVR 80209 2196 E2
10 DNVR 80223 2196 E2
3900 DNVR 80209 2197 E2
3900 DNVR 80246 2197 E2
3900 GNDL 80246 2197 E2
4700 DNVR 80246 2198 C2
4700 GNDL 80246 2198 C2
5500 DNVR 80224 2198 C2
6800 DNVR 80230 2198 C2
7200 DNVR 80247 2198 C2
8900 DNVR 80230 2199 A2
9700 AURA 80010 2199 A2
9700 DNVR 80010 2199 A2
9700 DNVR 80247 2199 A2
10500 AphC 80012 2199 A2
10500 AURA 80012 2199 A2
12900 AURA 80012 2200 A2
15000 AURA 80017 2200 A2
22200 AphC 80011 2202 B2
22200 AURA 80018 2202 B2
23300 AphC 80018 2202 D1
24600 AphC 80018 2203 A1
24600 AURA 80018 2203 A1
34500 AphC 80137 2205 C1
35400 AphC 80137 2206 A1
40000 AphC 80102 2206 E1
41700 AphC 80102 2207 B1
W Alameda Av
10 DNVR 80209 2196 B2
10 DNVR 80223 2196 B2
2400 DNVR 80219 2196 B2
3100 DNVR 80219 2195 E2
5000 LKWD 80226 2195 D2
6900 LKWD 80226 2194 E2
11000 LKWD 80226 2193 E2
11500 LKWD 80228 2193 E2
W Alameda Av SR-26
900 DNVR 80223 2196 B2
2400 DNVR 80219 2196 B2
3100 DNVR 80219 2195 E2
5000 LKWD 80226 2195 D2
6900 LKWD 80226 2194 E2
11000 LKWD 80226 2193 E2
11500 LKWD 80228 2193 E2
E Alameda Cir
2500 DNVR 80209 2197 C2
Alameda Dr
14800 AURA 80012 2200 C2
E Alameda Dr
- AURA 80017 2201 A2
14900 AURA 80012 2200 C2
15000 AURA 80017 2200 D2
W Alameda Dr
12200 LKWD 80228 2193 D2
E Alameda Pkwy
15300 AURA 80017 2200 D2
16300 AURA 80017 2201 A2

STREET Block City ZIP Map# Grid

W Alameda Pkwy
11600 LKWD 80226 2193 D2
11600 LKWD 80228 2193 D2
14800 JfnC 80228 2192 D6
14800 LKWD 80228 2192 D6
16500 JfnC 80401 2192 C6
16500 JfnC 80465 2192 C6
W Alameda Pkwy SR-26
11600 LKWD 80226 2193 D2
11600 LKWD 80228 2193 D2
14800 JfnC 80228 2192 D6
14800 LKWD 80228 2192 D6
16500 JfnC 80401 2192 C6
16500 JfnC 80465 2192 C6
E Alameda Pl
16200 AURA 80017 2200 E2
16600 AURA 80017 2201 A2
W Alameda Pl
9500 LKWD 80226 2194 B2
W Alamo Av
2200 LITN 80120 2364 B2
3400 LITN 80123 2363 E1
S Alamo Ct
5600 DNVR 80123 2363 A1
Alamo Dr
9700 NHGN 80260 1860 D7
E Alamo Dr
18000 CTNL 80015 2369 B1
W Alamo Dr
3500 LITN 80123 2363 E1
5700 DNVR 80123 2363 B1
5700 JfnC 80123 2363 B1
E Alamo Ln
21700 CTNL 80015 2370 B1
22700 AphC 80015 2370 C1
E Alamo Pl
16500 CTNL 80015 2368 E1
22000 CTNL 80015 2370 B1
22400 AphC 80015 2370 C1
W Alamo Pl
- DgsC 80129 2448 A6
3400 LITN 80123 2363 E2
8900 JfnC 80123 2362 B1
9700 JfnC 80127 2362 A2
10900 JfnC 80127 2361 E2
Alamosa Ct
- BGTN 80601 1697 B6
Alan Dr
6800 AdmC 80221 1944 B7
6800 AdmC 80221 2028 B1
Alaska Av
1200 BldC 80501 1438 E3
1200 LGMT 80501 1438 E3
1200 LGMT 80501 1439 A3
E Alaska Av
11500 AURA 80012 2199 D2
12600 AURA 80012 2200 A3
E Alaska Dr
6500 DNVR 80224 2198 C2
15900 AURA 80017 2200 E2
W Alaska Dr
- LKWD 80226 2195 A2
6900 LKWD 80226 2194 E2
13500 LKWD 80228 2193 B3
E Alaska Pl
11200 AURA 80012 2199 C2
12600 AURA 80012 2200 A3
16000 AURA 80017 2200 E2
W Alaska Pl
1200 DNVR 80223 2196 C2
3000 DNVR 80219 2196 A2
4300 DNVR 80219 2195 C2
5000 LKWD 80226 2195 C2
8700 LKWD 80226 2194 C2
13200 LKWD 80228 2193 B2
Alaska Rd
10 BldC 80302 1600 D6
Alaska St
600 GOLD 80403 2107 D1
Albert Ct
8100 AdmC 80221 1944 C5
Albert Dr
10 GpnC 80474 1849 E2
Alberta Ct
4400 BldC 80301 1604 D4
Albion Cir
10900 TNTN 80233 1861 D4
13500 TNTN 80241 1777 E5
Albion Ct
11500 TNTN 80233 1861 D3
S Albion Ct
5800 GDVL 80121 2365 E2
6200 CTNL 80121 2365 E3
Albion Dr
10800 TNTN 80233 1861 D4
Albion Ln
1600 LGMT 80503 1355 B6
Albion Pl
10 DgsC 80108 2619 A4
10800 TNTN 80233 1861 E5
Albion St
- DNVR 80216 2029 E7
10 DNVR 80220 2197 E1
10 DNVR 80246 2197 E1
1500 DNVR 80220 2113 E5
3200 DNVR 80207 2113 E2
4000 DNVR 80207 2029 E7
6500 CMCY 80022 2029 E1
9400 TNTN 80229 1945 E1
11700 TNTN 80233 1861 D2
12400 TNTN 80241 1861 D1
13500 TNTN 80241 1777 D5
S Albion St
10 DNVR 80220 2197 E1
10 DNVR 80246 2197 E1
1500 DNVR 80222 2197 E5
3500 AphC 80222 2281 E3
3500 CHLV 80113 2281 E3
3500 DNVR 80222 2281 E3
4800 CHLV 80121 2281 E6
5000 GDVL 80121 2281 E6
6700 CTNL 80122 2365 E5
8100 CTNL 80122 2449 E1
Albion Wy
1000 BLDR 80305 1687 B7
1100 BLDR 80305 1771 A1
11100 TNTN 80233 1861 E4
S Albion Wy
5000 CHLV 80121 2281 E7
6200 CTNL 80121 2365 E3
6700 CTNL 80122 2365 E4
Albo St
26600 JfnC 80433 2442 A5
Albrook Dr
12500 DNVR 80239 2031 E6
13000 DNVR 80239 2032 A6
Alcazar Dr
- CSRK 80109 2702 D4
E Alcorn Av
6400 DgsC 80138 2453 D5
N Alcorn St
11800 DgsC 80138 2453 D5
Alcoster Pl
9300 DgsC 80126 2449 C4
Alcott Cir
10800 WSTR 80234 1860 A5
13200 BMFD 80020 1776 A6
Alcott Cir N
- FLHT 80260 1944 A1
Alcott Cir S
- FLHT 80260 1944 A2
Alcott Ct
900 BMFD 80020 1776 A6
10800 WSTR 80234 1860 A5
Alcott Dr
500 BMFD 80020 1776 A7
10900 WSTR 80234 1860 A4
Alcott Pl
13000 BMFD 80020 1776 A6
Alcott St
- WSTR 80031 1944 A4
100 DNVR 80219 2196 B1
100 DNVR 80223 2196 B1
600 DNVR 80204 2112 B7
3200 DNVR 80211 2112 A2
4400 DNVR 80211 2028 A7
5100 DNVR 80221 2028 A5
5600 AdmC 80221 2028 A4
7400 WSTR 80030 1944 A6
8300 AdmC 80031 1944 A4
8300 AdmC 80221 1944 A4
10000 FLHT 80260 1860 A7
12500 BMFD 80020 1860 A1
13200 BMFD 80020 1776 A5
N Alcott St
- NHGN 80234 1860 A4
- WSTR 80234 1860 A4
S Alcott St
10 DNVR 80223 2196 B1
100 DNVR 80219 2196 B2
3100 DNVR 80236 2280 B2
3100 DvrC 80236 2280 B2
3100 SRDN 80110 2280 B3
Alcott Wy
900 DNVR 80204 2112 A6
13400 BMFD 80020 1776 A5
N Alcott Wy
10700 WSTR 80234 1860 A5
Aldenbridge Cir
3800 DgsC 80126 2449 D5
Aldenbridge Ct
10200 DgsC 80126 2449 D5
W Alder Av
5400 JfnC 80128 2363 B7
5800 JfnC 80128 2447 B1
7000 JfnC 80128 2446 E1
E Alder Dr
22400 AURA 80016 2370 C7
W Alder Dr
7700 JfnC 80128 2446 D1
Alder Ln
10 BldC 80304 1601 D6
Alder St
2900 FLHT 80260 1860 A7
2900 FLHT 80260 1944 A1
W Alder St
900 LSVL 80027 1688 E7
900 LSVL 80027 1689 A7
1000 BldC 80303 1688 E7
Alder Wy
900 LGMT 80503 1438 B5
W Alder Wy
5600 JfnC 80128 2363 B7
Aldershot Ct
10 DgsC 80130 2450 B2
Aldgate Ln
- EGLD 80113 2281 B3
S Aldrich Rd
9400 JfnC 80433 2442 B4
Alex Ct
400 DgsC 80108 2535 B7
S Alexa Ln
10100 DgsC 80130 2450 C6
E Alexander Av
3200 GDVL 80121 2365 D1
S Alexander Ct
5600 GDVL 80121 2365 C1
E Alexander Dr
- AURA 80016 2371 A1
24100 AURA 80016 2370 E1
Alexander Ln
10 GDVL 80121 2365 C1
Alexander Pl
300 CSRK 80108 2703 D1
Alexandria St
- ERIE 80026 1690 C3
- ERIE 80516 1690 C3
1100 LAFT 80026 1690 C3
Alfalfa Ct
8100 BldC 80503 1520 E3
Algonquan Wy
- AURA 80016 2286 D6
S Algonquian Cir
7900 AURA 80016 2370 D7
S Algonquian Ct
10 AphC 80018 2202 D1
5400 AphC 80016 2286 D7
7900 AURA 80016 2370 D7
Algonquian St
10 AphC 80018 2202 D1
10 AURA 80018 2202 D1
S Algonquian St
5200 AphC 80016 2286 D7
S Algonquian Wy
7600 AURA 80016 2370 D6
Algonquin
- TNTN 80260 1944 C2
S Algonquin Rd
5200 JfnC 80454 2275 C7
5200 JfnC 80454 2359 D1
5200 JfnC 80465 2275 C7
Alice Dr
30600 JfnC 80439 2357 A2
Alice Pl
- DNVR 80216 2029 B6
W Alice Pl
3600 DNVR 80211 2027 D6
3800 DNVR 80212 2027 D6
S Alicia Pkwy
3800 AURA 80013 2284 E4
Aline St
100 LSVL 80027 1773 D1
Aljan Av
9100 BldC 80503 1355 C3
Alkire Ct
6200 ARVD 80004 2025 C3
7300 ARVD 80005 1941 B7
N Alkire Ct
1500 JfnC 80401 2109 C5
S Alkire Ct
1800 LKWD 80228 2193 C6
4300 JfnC 80465 2277 C5
S Alkire Rd
- JfnC 80127 2361 D6
Alkire St
900 LKWD 80401 2109 C6
2000 JfnC 80401 2109 C4
5600 JfnC 80002 2025 B4
5600 JfnC 80004 2025 B4
7400 ARVD 80005 1941 B6
7400 JfnC 80005 1941 B6
N Alkire St
2400 JfnC 80401 2109 C3
8300 ARVD 80005 1941 B3
8300 JfnC 80005 1941 B3
9000 JfnC 80403 1941 B2
9000 WSTR 80005 1941 B2
S Alkire St
200 LKWD 80228 2193 C3
2300 JfnC 80228 2193 C7
4300 JfnC 80465 2277 C5
5000 JfnC 80127 2277 C7
6400 JfnC 80127 2361 C4
Alkire Wy
3200 JfnC 80401 2109 B2
S Alkire Wy
2200 LKWD 80228 2193 D7
Allen Av
- ERIE 80516 1607 A3
Allen Cir
10 PrkC 80470 2523 C6
Allen Ct
1100 ERIE 80516 1607 A3
Allen Dr
500 LGMT 80503 1438 C1
2400 LGMT 80501 1438 C1
Allen St
- LGMT 80504 1439 A6
200 GOLD 80401 2192 A1
E Allen St
- CSRK 80104 2703 D1
10 CSRK 80108 2703 D1
W Allen St
300 CSRK 80108 2703 C1
1000 DgsC 80108 2703 C1
3600 DgsC 80108 2619 C7
Allen Wy
200 CSRK 80108 2703 C1
Allendale Av
- PARK 80138 2538 C4
Allendale Dr
10000 ARVD 80004 2026 A3
10900 ARVD 80004 2025 E3
S Allerton Cir
- PARK 80138 2538 C3
S Allerton Ln
- PARK 80138 2538 C3
Alley A
- BMFD 80020 1776 A4
Alley B
14100 BMFD 80020 1776 A4
Alley C
14000 BMFD 80020 1776 A3
Alley F
- BMFD 80020 1776 A4
Alley I
- BMFD 80020 1776 A3
Alley J
14100 BMFD 80020 1776 A3
Alley L
- BMFD 80020 1776 A3
Alley N
2400 BMFD 80020 1776 A3
Allison Cir
3800 WTRG 80033 2110 D1
S Allison Cir
7600 JfnC 80128 2362 D6
Allison Ct
3500 WTRG 80033 2110 D1
8200 ARVD 80005 1942 D4
9000 WSTR 80021 1942 D3
10000 JfnC 80021 1858 D7
10900 WSTR 80021 1858 D5
S Allison Ct
2000 LKWD 80227 2194 D7
2400 LKWD 80227 2278 D1
3900 LKWD 80235 2278 D4
6500 JfnC 80123 2362 D4
7600 JfnC 80128 2362 D7
8100 JfnC 80128 2446 D1
Allison Dr
8600 WSTR 80005 1942 D3
S Allison Pkwy
300 LKWD 80226 2194 D2
Allison Pl
8000 ARVD 80005 1942 D5
Allison St
10 LKWD 80226 2194 D1
400 LKWD 80226 2110 D7
700 LKWD 80214 2110 D6
3200 JfnC 80215 2110 D2
3900 WTRG 80033 2110 D1
4400 WTRG 80033 2026 D7
4900 ARVD 80033 2026 D5
4900 JfnC 80002 2026 D5
5600 ARVD 80002 2026 D4
5700 ARVD 80004 2026 D3
7700 ARVD 80005 1942 D5
10400 JfnC 80021 1858 D6
11600 BMFD 80020 1858 D2
N Allison St
10000 JfnC 80021 1858 D7
S Allison St
10 LKWD 80226 2194 D2
1100 LKWD 80232 2194 D5
2400 LKWD 80227 2194 D7
3500 JfnC 80235 2278 D3
3500 LKWD 80227 2278 D3
3500 LKWD 80235 2278 D3
6300 JfnC 80123 2362 D3
7600 JfnC 80128 2362 D7
8300 JfnC 80128 2446 D1
Allison Wy
7600 ARVD 80005 1942 D6
9600 JfnC 80021 1942 D1
S Allison Wy
2300 LKWD 80227 2194 D7
5000 DNVR 80123 2278 D7
5000 DvrC 80123 2278 D7
5000 LKWD 80123 2278 D7
6800 JfnC 80128 2362 D5
Allis Ranch Rd
100 DgsC 80135 2701 C7
100 DgsC 80135 2785 C1
Alma Ln
1700 SUPE 80027 1773 B6
3400 JfnC 80457 2274 A3
Almandine Ct
7200 CSRK 80108 2619 E6
Almeria Wy
3100 LGMT 80503 1355 B4
Almi Gateway Pk
- DNVR 80239 2032 D7
Almond Ln
4600 BldC 80301 1603 E3
S Almstead Rd
10 AphC 80137 2205 D2
Alnwick Wy
- DgsC 80134 2452 E4
Alpenglow Ct
1500 JfnC 80439 2189 B5
7100 BldC 80503 1520 C1
Alpha Ct
- EbtC 80107 2709 A7
- ELIZ 80107 2709 A7
Alpine Av
200 BLDR 80304 1686 C1
Alpine Ct
- NDLD 80466 1766 A3
Alpine Dr
- BldC 80466 1765 E4
10 NDLD 80466 1765 E3
10 NDLD 80466 1766 A3
2000 BLDR 80304 1686 D1
3800 JfnC 80439 2273 D4
N Alpine Dr
6300 DgsC 80134 2622 E1
6600 DgsC 80134 2623 A1
7100 DgsC 80134 2539 A7
7300 DgsC 80138 2539 A7
S Alpine Dr
4000 JfnC 80439 2273 D5
Alpine Ln
32900 JfnC 80439 2272 C3
Alpine Pl
10 LGMT 80501 1439 D2
Alpine St
- BldC 80504 1356 D5
100 BldC 80501 1439 D3
100 LGMT 80501 1439 D3
1100 LGMT 80501 1356 D7
Alpine Wy
10 BldC 80304 1601 D5
Alpine Gulch Rd
- BldC 80302 1599 E6
10 BldC 80302 1600 A6
Alpine Meadow Rd
22000 JfnC 80465 2443 B3
Alpine Vista
10 BldC 80466 1682 E6
S Alsab Tr
8000 JfnC 80439 2441 D1
Alsace Wy
1000 LAFT 80026 1690 D3
Alta Dr
800 BMFD 80020 1775 A7
21200 JfnC 80465 2443 B2
Alta St
900 LGMT 80501 1439 A1
Altair Dr
600 DgsC 80124 2450 D2
Alta Vista Dr
8400 ARVD 80004 2026 C2
32700 JfnC 80439 2188 C2
Alter St
300 BMFD 80021 1858 C1
400 BMFD 80020 1858 C1
500 BMFD 80020 1774 C7
Alter Wy
1100 BMFD 80020 1774 C6
E Althea Cir
17400 PARK 80134 2453 A4
Alto Av
- BLDR 80302 1686 A1
Alton Ct
- CMCY 80640 1862 E5
- CMCY 80640 1863 A5
- DNVR 80238 2115 A2
9600 AdmC 80640 1947 A1
S Alton Ct
1100 AphC 80247 2199 A4
2000 AphC 80231 2199 A6
2900 DNVR 80231 2283 A2
4300 GDVL 80111 2283 A5
7400 CTNL 80112 2367 A5
S Alton Pl
4200 GDVL 80111 2283 A5
Alton St
- AdmC 80602 1695 A5
- CMCY 80640 1862 E5
1100 AURA 80230 2115 A6
1700 AURA 80010 2115 A4
2600 DNVR 80238 2115 A3
9700 AdmC 80640 1863 A7
9700 AdmC 80640 1947 A1
9700 CMCY 80640 1863 A7
15900 AdmC 80602 1694 E6
S Alton St
- DNVR 80247 2199 A4
1100 AphC 80247 2199 A4
3300 DNVR 80231 2283 A2
4200 GDVL 80111 2283 A5
Alton Wy
500 DNVR 80230 2115 A7
700 AURA 80230 2115 A6
8700 DNVR 80230 2114 E6
S Alton Wy
500 DNVR 80247 2199 A3
2000 AphC 80231 2199 A7
4300 GDVL 80111 2283 A5
6000 GDVL 80111 2367 A2
6900 CTNL 80112 2367 A5
Altuna St
11800 CMCY 80603 1864 C2
Altura Blvd
1900 AURA 80011 2116 C4
S Altura Ct
100 AURA 80012 2200 C1
Altura St
- CMCY 80022 1864 C6
5500 DNVR 80239 2032 C4
Alvin Dr
10900 NHGN 80233 1861 A5
Alvin Pl
12000 JfnC 80433 2524 E4
Alyeska Ct
1400 JfnC 80439 2189 A5
W Alys Pl
1200 DNVR 80223 2196 C3
Alyssum Dr
100 BGTN 80601 1697 B5
S Alyssum Wy
9400 PARK 80134 2453 A4
Alzere Pl
- DgsC 80134 2452 E3
Amanda Ct
- EbtC 80107 2709 A7
- ELIZ 80107 2709 A7
Amanda Pines Dr
10 EbtC 80138 2455 E4
300 EbtC 80138 2456 A4
Amanda Ranch Rd
1200 EbtC 80138 2456 D4
Amaranth Dr
10 JfnC 80127 2361 A7
S Amaro Dr
4700 JfnC 80439 2273 E7
Amber Ct
1500 CSRK 80108 2619 E7
2000 ERIE 80516 1606 E6
Amber Pl
4100 BLDR 80304 1602 E4
Amber St
4100 BLDR 80304 1602 E4
Amber Ridge Dr
5600 DgsC 80108 2534 B5
Amber Ridge Pl
5700 DgsC 80108 2534 B5
Amber Rock Ct
16000 DgsC 80134 2452 E4
Amber Rock Dr
9800 DgsC 80134 2452 E5
Amberstone Wy
16400 DgsC 80134 2452 E6
16700 DgsC 80134 2453 B5
Amber Sun Cir
- CSRK 80104 2704 B5
- CSRK 80108 2704 B5
Amber Sun Ct
- CSRK 80104 2704 C5
- CSRK 80108 2704 C5
N Amber Valley Ln
13400 DgsC 80138 2455 A2
Amberwood Ln
10 JfnC 80127 2360 E6
Ambush Rock
10900 DgsC 80125 2614 D1
American Wy
8800 DgsC 80112 2452 B2
Americana Rd
500 LGMT 80501 1356 D6
Amerind Springs Tr
28500 JfnC 80470 2609 C6
S Ames Cir
2400 LKWD 80227 2195 C7
N Ames Ct
11300 WSTR 80020 1859 B3
S Ames Ct
6100 JfnC 80123 2363 C3
7400 JfnC 80128 2363 C6
Ames St
10 LKWD 80226 2195 C1
300 LKWD 80226 2111 C7
1000 LKWD 80214 2111 B6
2000 EDGW 80214 2111 B3
2500 WTRG 80214 2111 B3
3900 WTRG 80212 2111 B1
4100 MNVW 80212 2027 B7
4100 WTRG 80212 2027 B7
4800 DNVR 80212 2027 B6
4800 DvrC 80212 2027 B6
4800 LKSD 80212 2027 B6
6000 ARVD 80003 2027 B3
7500 WSTR 80003 1943 B6
8400 ARVD 80003 1943 B4
10000 WSTR 80020 1859 B7
S Ames St
10 LKWD 80226 2195 C1
1400 LKWD 80232 2195 C5
3700 DNVR 80235 2279 C4
5900 JfnC 80123 2363 C2
Ames Wy
5000 DNVR 80212 2027 B5
6800 ARVD 80003 2027 B1
8100 ARVD 80003 1943 B5
S Ames Wy
2600 DNVR 80227 2279 C1
2600 LKWD 80227 2279 C1
3900 DNVR 80235 2279 C4
7500 JfnC 80128 2363 C7
Amesbury St
10 BMFD 80020 1775 B6
Amesbury Wy
10600 DgsC 80126 2533 D1
Amethyst Dr
1900 LGMT 80504 1439 A6
Amethyst Wy
300 SUPE 80027 1857 A1
10100 PARK 80134 2453 A5
E Amherst Av
10 EGLD 80110 2280 E1
10 EGLD 80113 2280 E1
1000 EGLD 80113 2281 A1
1200 DvrC 80210 2281 A1
1600 DNVR 80210 2281 B1
4600 DNVR 80222 2281 E1
5500 AphC 80222 2282 B1
5500 DNVR 80222 2282 B1
6500 DNVR 80224 2282 C1
7300 DNVR 80231 2282 D1
13200 AURA 80014 2284 A1
16200 AURA 80013 2284 E1
16800 AURA 80013 2285 A1
W Amherst Av
10 EGLD 80113 2280 D1
2400 EGLD 80110 2280 B1
3000 DNVR 80236 2280 A1
3600 DNVR 80236 2279 D1
5100 DNVR 80227 2279 B1
7500 DNVR 80227 2278 E1
7500 LKWD 80227 2278 E1
14000 LKWD 80228 2277 B1
E Amherst Cir
- DNVR 80231 2282 E1
1300 DNVR 80210 2281 A1
1300 DvrC 80210 2281 A1
1300 EGLD 80113 2281 A1
8300 AphC 80231 2282 E1
12100 AURA 80014 2283 E1
12400 AURA 80014 2284 A1
E Amherst Cir N
11400 AURA 80014 2283 D1
E Amherst Cir S
11400 AURA 80014 2283 D1
W Amherst Cir
14900 MRSN 80228 2276 E1
14900 MRSN 80228 2277 A1
E Amherst Ct
6700 DgsC 80130 2450 C4
11300 AURA 80014 2283 D1
W Amherst Ct
14000 LKWD 80228 2277 B1
Amherst Dr
1500 LGMT 80503 1355 C6
E Amherst Dr
8600 DNVR 80231 2282 E1
8600 DNVR 80231 2283 A1
16900 AURA 80013 2285 A1
W Amherst Dr
13800 LKWD 80228 2277 B1
E Amherst Pl
500 EGLD 80113 2280 E1
500 EGLD 80113 2281 A1
12000 AURA 80014 2283 D1
15700 AURA 80013 2284 D1
17600 AURA 80013 2285 B1
W Amherst Pl
13500 LKWD 80228 2193 B7
13600 LKWD 80228 2277 B1
Amherst St
1200 SUPE 80027 1773 B5
S Amherst St
10 CSRK 80104 2704 D7
Amherst Wy
1100 SUPE 80027 1773 B5
E Amherst Wy
12000 AURA 80014 2283 E1
W Amherst Wy
13700 LKWD 80228 2277 B1
W Amhurst Pl
14500 LKWD 80228 2277 A1
Amison Cir
9300 DgsC 80134 2452 E3
Amison Wy
- DgsC 80134 2452 E3
Ammons Cir
8200 ARVD 80005 1942 D4
9900 JfnC 80021 1858 D7
Ammons Ct
3200 JfnC 80215 2110 D2
3200 WTRG 80033 2110 D2
9000 WSTR 80021 1942 D3
S Ammons Ct
6500 JfnC 80123 2362 D4
7100 JfnC 80128 2362 D5
8000 JfnC 80128 2446 D1
Ammons Dr
6200 ARVD 80004 2026 D2
Ammons St
100 LKWD 80226 2194 D1
400 LKWD 80226 2110 D7
2200 LKWD 80214 2110 D4
3900 WTRG 80033 2110 D1
4100 WTRG 80033 2026 D7
5600 ARVD 80002 2026 D4
6700 ARVD 80004 2026 D1
7000 ARVD 80004 1942 D7
7100 ARVD 80005 1942 D7
9100 WSTR 80021 1942 D2
10400 JfnC 80021 1858 D6
10900 WSTR 80021 1858 D5
N Ammons St
- WSTR 80021 1942 D2
S Ammons St
- DNVR 80235 2278 D6
- JfnC 80235 2278 D6
10 LKWD 80226 2194 D2
1100 LKWD 80232 2194 D4
1700 LKWD 80227 2194 D6
3100 LKWD 80227 2278 D3
3500 JfnC 80227 2278 D3
3500 LKWD 80235 2278 D3
4300 DNVR 80123 2278 D6
4800 DvrC 80123 2278 D6
4800 LKWD 80123 2278 D6
6900 JfnC 80128 2362 D5
8300 JfnC 80128 2446 D1
Ammons Wy
8000 ARVD 80005 1942 D4
9100 WSTR 80021 1942 D2
S Ammons Wy
2600 LKWD 80227 2278 D1
6100 JfnC 80123 2362 D3
Amston Ln
11700 LNTR 80134 2451 E5
Amston Pl
11800 LNTR 80134 2451 C5
Amston St
10000 LNTR 80134 2451 D5
Amy Cir
26000 JfnC 80433 2526 B6
Amy Vale Ct
2800 CSRK 80109 2702 C4
Anaconda Ct
800 DgsC 80108 2618 C3
Anaconda Dr
900 DgsC 80108 2618 C3
Anaheim Ct
4400 DNVR 80239 2032 A7
S Anaheim Ct
4700 AphC 80015 2284 B6
S Anaheim St
- AURA 80014 2200 B7
- AURA 80014 2284 B1
Anaheim Wy
5500 DNVR 80239 2032 B4
S Anaheim Wy
- AURA 80015 2284 A5
Anahina Rd
5300 JfnC 80454 2359 B1
Anasazi Ct
- KIOW 80117 2796 B3
4600 BLDR 80303 1687 C6
Anasazi Wy
21900 JfnC 80401 2191 A4
W Anasazi Indian Pl
1600 DgsC 80129 2448 C3
S Anasazi Indian Tr
9100 DgsC 80129 2448 C3
S Anasazi Indian Wy
9100 DgsC 80129 2448 C3
Anchor Dr
7800 BldC 80504 1522 A2
Anchor Pl
1600 LAFT 80026 1689 E5
Anchorage Ct
10 LGMT 80501 1356 C7
S Andee Wy
10200 DgsC 80130 2450 C6
Andersen Av
100 JMWN 80455 1516 A2
Anderson Ct
200 ERIE 80516 1607 C5
Anderson Rd
10 PrkC 80456 2521 E2
100 PrkC 80456 2522 A2
Anderson St
300 ERIE 80516 1607 C5
600 CSRK 80104 2703 E6
1900 AdmC 80137 2120 E3
9300 TNTN 80229 1945 C2
S Andes Cir
1500 AURA 80017 2201 C5
2400 AURA 80013 2201 C7
6000 AphC 80016 2369 C2
6900 CTNL 80016 2369 C5
Andes Ct
- DNVR 80249 2033 C5
4000 AURA 80011 2033 C7
4000 DvrC 80249 2033 C7
S Andes Ct
3600 AURA 80013 2285 C3
5200 CTNL 80015 2285 C7
6000 AphC 80016 2369 C2
7200 CTNL 80016 2369 C5
S Andes Pl
6300 CTNL 80016 2369 C3
Andes St
1700 AURA 80011 2117 C4
4300 DNVR 80249 2033 C7
12000 AdmC 80022 1865 C1
S Andes St
1300 AURA 80017 2201 C4
4100 AURA 80013 2285 C4
5100 CTNL 80015 2285 C7
5600 AphC 80015 2369 C1
Andes Wy
2800 AURA 80011 2117 C3
4000 DNVR 80249 2033 C7
S Andes Wy
1400 AURA 80017 2201 C5
4100 AURA 80013 2285 C4
4400 AURA 80015 2285 C5

STREET Block City ZIP Map# Grid

E Andover Av
4300 CSRK 80104 2704 D7
Andrea Cir
200 EbtC 80138 2455 E3
200 EbtC 80138 2456 A3
S Andrea Ln
7000 JfnC 80465 2359 D6
Andrea Pl
2000 EbtC 80138 2540 D4
Andrew Ct
200 LGMT 80501 1439 C2
Andrew Dr
2100 SUPE 80027 1772 E7
2200 SUPE 80027 1773 A7
Andrew Ln
300 SUPE 80027 1773 A6
Andrew Alden St
1900 LGMT 80504 1439 A6
Andrews Dr
12100 DNVR 80239 2031 E5
13000 DNVR 80239 2032 A6
Andrews Pl
20100 DNVR 80249 2033 E7
Andrews Wy
- DNVR 80239 2032 D7
900 BldC 80303 1688 D4
Andrist Ln
10 PrkC 80456 2606 C3
Andromeda Ln
- CSRK 80108 2619 D6
Andromeda Wy
- CSRK 80108 2619 D6
Andrus Rd
6100 BldC 80301 1603 E5
6100 BldC 80301 1604 A5
Andrush Ct
10000 DgsC 80124 2450 D5
Anemone Dr
10 BldC 80302 1601 D7
10 BldC 80302 1685 D1
Angela Ln
8500 PARK 80134 2453 B1
Angelovic Ct
3800 BldC 80301 1603 A5
Angevine Wy
- LAFT 80026 1690 B6
Angie Ct
5700 DgsC 80134 2622 D3
W Angus Wy
400 DgsC 80129 2448 D5
Anhawa Av
9200 BldC 80503 1355 C3
9200 BldC 80504 1355 C3
12600 LGMT 80503 1355 C3
Animas Wy
3800 SUPE 80027 1857 A2
Ann Ct
41200 EbtC 80138 2540 E7
Anna Cir
34800 JfnC 80439 2356 A7
Anna Ln
3400 JfnC 80457 2274 A3
Annabar Dr
1000 CSRK 80108 2619 E7
S Annapurna Dr
5900 JfnC 80439 2358 B2
Anna Thomas Pkwy
300 LAFT 80026 1690 A4
Anne Pl
4600 WldC 80516 1607 D2
Annex Ln
- PrkC 80456 2606 D5
Annie Cir
- EbtC 80107 2709 D6
W Annie Pl
5000 DNVR 80204 2111 C5
5100 LKWD 80214 2111 C5
Anniversary Ln
10 LGMT 80501 1356 B6
Antares Dr
13400 DgsC 80124 2450 D2
Antelope Cir
1400 EbtC 80107 2792 E6
1400 EbtC 80107 2793 A6
Antelope Cross
400 LAFT 80026 1774 B2
Antelope Ct
2800 LAFT 80026 1774 C2
33500 EbtC 80107 2793 D1
Antelope Dr
10 BldC 80540 1352 A1
E Antelope Dr
500 BNNT 80102 2209 C2
W Antelope Dr
300 BNNT 80102 2209 A1
12800 JfnC 80127 2445 C3
N Antelope Ln
11300 DgsC 80138 2454 C6
E Antelope Pl
4000 CSRK 80108 2704 E1
Antelope Pt
200 LAFT 80026 1774 C2
Antelope Run
200 EbtC 80107 2707 E1
200 EbtC 80107 2708 A1
Antelope Tr
- TNTN 80229 1861 E6
N Antelope Tr
12000 DgsC 80138 2454 B4
Antelope Hills Blvd
- AphC 80102 2209 A2
600 BNNT 80102 2209 A2
W Antelope Run Ct
4300 CSRK 80109 2702 C2
Antero Ct
5900 JfnC 80403 2024 A3
Antero Dr
1700 LGMT 80501 1356 C6
Antero Rd
9900 TNTN 80260 1860 B7
Antero St
400 GOLD 80401 2108 A7
400 GOLD 80401 2192 A1
400 JfnC 80401 2192 A1
E Anthem Dr
- PARK 80134 2537 B5
Antioch
- TNTN 80260 1944 C3
N Antler Cir
44800 EbtC 80107 2458 D3
S Antler Cir
- EbtC 80107 2458 D3
Antler Ct
10 JfnC 80127 2360 E6
Antler Dr
10 BldC 80302 1517 C5
Antler Ln
10 GpnC 80403 2020 A1
Antler Run
5400 DgsC 80125 2614 E4
Antler Tr
11600 JfnC 80127 2528 B3
Antler Wy
10 CCkC 80439 2272 A5
Antlers St
13400 BMFD 80020 1775 D5
Anton Ct
17600 PARK 80134 2453 B7
Anvil Ct
5900 JfnC 80403 2024 A3
Anvil Wy
400 GOLD 80401 2108 A7
S Anvil Horn
7500 JfnC 80127 2361 E6
Apache
- AdmC 80022 1946 C3
Apache Ct
6600 BldC 80503 1521 B5
Apache Ct E
3900 BLDR 80303 1687 B5
Apache Ct W
3800 BLDR 80303 1687 B5
Apache Dr
5900 DgsC 80118 2868 D7
18200 PARK 80134 2453 B6
S Apache Dr
6600 LITN 80120 2364 D4
Apache Ln
- LAFT 80026 1690 A3
Apache Pl
200 LCHB 80603 1698 B3
6600 DgsC 80118 2868 C7
Apache Rd
- CCkC 80439 2439 E1
10 CCkC 80439 2440 A1
3200 BLDR 80303 1687 A5
9100 DgsC 80138 2539 C3
Apache St
400 KIOW 80117 2796 A3
S Apache St
6700 LITN 80120 2364 D4
Apache Tr
11500 JfnC 80433 2525 C3
S Apache Tr
11800 JfnC 80433 2525 C3
W Apache Wy
6600 DgsC 80135 2700 B2
Apache Creek Ct
5200 CSRK 80109 2702 C1
Apache Creek Rd
4900 CSRK 80109 2702 C1
Apache Plume Ct
10 BGTN 80601 1697 E5
Apache Plume Dr
8500 DgsC 80134 2452 E2
8500 PARK 80134 2452 E2
8500 PARK 80134 2453 A2
Apache Plume Pl
- BGTN 80601 1697 E5
Apache Plume St
- BGTN 80601 1697 E5
Apache Spring Dr
10000 JfnC 80433 2441 D5
Apelles Cir
1700 LAFT 80026 1690 A6
1700 LSVL 80026 1690 A6
Apex Cir
27800 JfnC 80439 2357 D3
Apex Ln
4300 WSTR 80031 1943 C4
Apex Rd
700 GpnC 80403 1850 D7
1300 DgsC 80116 2791 C4
Apex Valley Rd
700 GpnC 80403 2017 B1
1100 GpnC 80403 1933 A7
W Apishada Pass
10600 JfnC 80127 2362 B5
Apishamore Ct
10600 PARK 80134 2452 E7
Apollo Ct
500 DgsC 80124 2450 E1
500 LNTR 80124 2450 E1
Apollo Dr
10 GpnC 80403 1934 C1
400 BldC 80303 1688 D7
1200 LAFT 80026 1690 A6
E Apollo Bay Dr
4800 DgsC 80130 2450 A5
S Apollo Bay Wy
9900 DgsC 80130 2450 A5
Appaloosa Ct
10700 PARK 80134 2452 E7
Appaloosa Dr
29900 JfnC 80439 2273 B3
Appaloosa Pl
12400 BldC 80020 1775 B2
Appaloosa Rd
3100 JfnC 80439 2273 B3
Appaloosa Tr
1700 EbtC 80107 2708 D5
Apple Ct
700 LSVL 80027 1773 A2
800 LGMT 80501 1438 E1
4300 BldC 80301 1603 A4
Apple Wy
4300 BldC 80301 1603 A4
E Appleblossom Dr
900 DgsC 80126 2449 A3
Appleblossom Ln
3100 WSTR 80030 1943 E5
7800 WSTR 80031 1943 E5
Applebrook Cir
10400 DgsC 80130 2450 A6
Applebrook Ln
5300 DgsC 80130 2450 A7
Appleby Pl
700 CSRK 80104 2787 E2
Appleby St
- PrkC 80456 2521 E1
Applecrest Cir
4300 CSRK 80109 2702 C4
Apple Field Cir
- EbtC 80107 2625 C1
41400 EbtC 80107 2541 B7
S Applefield Cir
40900 EbtC 80107 2625 B1
Apple Ridge Rd
10 BldC 80540 1269 A6
E Appleton Cir
6800 CTNL 80112 2366 C4
Appleton Ct
1500 BGTN 80601 1696 D7
E Appleton Ct
6800 CTNL 80112 2366 C4
Appleton Wy
5000 CSRK 80104 2788 D2
Appletree Ct
- BLDR 80304 1602 D4
Apple Tree Pl
2200 ERIE 80516 1691 D3
Appletree Pl
8700 DgsC 80126 2449 A2
9700 NHGN 80260 1860 C7
9700 TNTN 80260 1860 C7
Apple Valley Rd
10 BldC 80540 1352 B1
10 LYNS 80540 1352 B1
700 BldC 80540 1269 B7
E Applewood Av
800 CTNL 80121 2365 A3
Applewood Cir
- TNTN 80260 1944 B3
Applewood Ct
4400 BLDR 80301 1603 D4
12100 BMFD 80020 1859 D2
19600 PARK 80138 2453 D7
Applewood Dr
700 BldC 80026 1689 C4
800 BldC 80303 1689 C4
1900 LKWD 80215 2109 C4
2100 JfnC 80401 2109 C4
Applewood Ln
- TNTN 80260 1944 B1
7700 AdmC 80221 1944 A5
Applewood Pl
- AURA 80016 2371 B2
Applewood Rd
10000 DgsC 80138 2455 A6
Applewood Center Dr
- WTRG 80033 2109 C2
- WTRG 80401 2109 C2
W Applewood Knolls Dr
11600 LKWD 80215 2109 D3
12000 WTRG 80215 2109 D3
Applewood Ridge Rd
14400 JfnC 80401 2109 A3
Apricot Ct
- BLDR 80304 1602 D4
1800 BGTN 80601 1696 D7
Apricot Pl
1300 ERIE 80516 1691 E3
Apricot Wy
100 CSRK 80104 2787 D2
Aprils Wy
17900 DgsC 80134 2453 B2
17900 PARK 80134 2453 B2
Aqua Ct
10 BMFD 80020 1774 E6
W Aquaduct Dr
11400 JfnC 80127 2361 E1
Aquamarine Ct
1800 CSRK 80108 2620 A6
Aquamarine Pl
- LGMT 80504 1439 A6
Aquamarine Wy
1600 CSRK 80108 2619 E6
1600 CSRK 80108 2620 A6
Aquarius Ct
300 DgsC 80124 2450 E2
W Aqueduct Av
3300 LITN 80123 2363 E1
12800 JfnC 80127 2361 C1
W Aqueduct Dr
10900 JfnC 80127 2361 E1
10900 JfnC 80127 2362 A1
W Aqueduct Ln
10900 JfnC 80127 2361 E1
10900 JfnC 80127 2362 A1
W Aqueduct Pl
9800 JfnC 80123 2362 B1
Arabian Pl
10 CBVL 80123 2363 D4
Arabian Run
8600 DgsC 80116 2790 D3
Arabian Tr
1400 EbtC 80107 2708 C6
Aral Ct
- LGMT 80501 1357 A4
Aral Dr
2300 LGMT 80501 1357 A4
Arapahoe Av
- BldC 80302 1686 A3
100 BLDR 80302 1686 A3
2400 BLDR 80301 1686 E2
2400 BLDR 80303 1686 E2
2800 BLDR 80303 1687 A2
3000 BLDR 80303 1687 A2
4200 BldC 80301 1687 D2
4300 BldC 80303 1687 D2
Arapahoe Av SR-7
2800 BLDR 80301 1686 E2
2800 BLDR 80303 1686 E2
2800 BLDR 80303 1687 A2
3000 BLDR 80301 1687 A2
4200 BldC 80301 1687 D2
4300 BldC 80303 1687 D2
Arapahoe Cir
900 LSVL 80027 1688 E7
900 LSVL 80027 1689 A7
900 LSVL 80027 1772 E1
900 LSVL 80027 1773 A1
Arapahoe Ct
6300 DgsC 80134 2622 D2
E Arapahoe Ct
7800 CTNL 80112 2366 D4
7800 GDVL 80112 2366 D4
N Arapahoe Ct
6200 DgsC 80134 2622 D2
W Arapahoe Ct
2400 LITN 80120 2364 B4
Arapahoe Dr
300 KIOW 80117 2796 A3
1800 LGMT 80501 1438 D2
8000 DgsC 80125 2531 E6
S Arapahoe Dr
6000 JfnC 80439 2356 D3
W Arapahoe Dr
2100 LITN 80120 2364 B4
15200 JfnC 80403 2024 E7
W Arapahoe Ln
300 BldC 80302 1686 B3
300 BLDR 80302 1686 B3
Arapahoe Pl
- AphC 80016 2370 E4
- AURA 80016 2370 E4
E Arapahoe Pl
- AphC 80112 2368 B4
- CTNL 80112 2368 B4
4200 CTNL 80122 2365 E4
4500 CTNL 80122 2366 A4
Arapahoe Rd
- AURA 80016 2371 C4
6000 BldC 80301 1688 B2
6000 BldC 80303 1687 E2
6000 BldC 80303 1688 A2
6000 BLDR 80301 1687 E2
6000 BLDR 80301 1688 A2
6000 BLDR 80303 1687 E2
6000 BLDR 80303 1688 A2
8200 BldC 80301 1689 B2
8200 BldC 80303 1689 B2
9300 LAFT 80026 1689 B2
9700 BldC 80026 1689 B2
9900 LAFT 80026 1690 A2
10100 BldC 80026 1690 A2
10700 ERIE 80026 1690 A2
10700 ERIE 80516 1690 D2
11400 BldC 80516 1690 D2
11900 BldC 80026 1691 A2
11900 BldC 80516 1691 A2
11900 ERIE 80026 1691 A2
11900 ERIE 80516 1691 A2
Arapahoe Rd SR-7
- ERIE 80026 1690 A2
6000 BldC 80301 1688 B2
6000 BldC 80303 1687 E2
6000 BldC 80303 1688 A2
6000 BLDR 80301 1687 E2
6000 BLDR 80301 1688 A2
6000 BLDR 80303 1687 E2
6000 BLDR 80303 1688 A2
8200 BldC 80301 1689 B2
8200 BldC 80303 1689 B2
9300 LAFT 80026 1689 B2
9700 BldC 80026 1689 B2
9900 BldC 80026 1690 A2
9900 LAFT 80026 1690 A2
E Arapahoe Rd
- CTNL 80111 2367 D4
10 CTNL 80121 2364 E4
10 CTNL 80122 2364 E4
10 LITN 80120 2364 E4
600 CTNL 80121 2365 D4
600 CTNL 80122 2365 D4
4500 CTNL 80122 2366 A4
5300 CTNL 80121 2366 A4
5600 CTNL 80111 2366 D4
5600 CTNL 80112 2366 B4
7300 GDVL 80111 2366 D4
7300 GDVL 80112 2366 D4
8700 GDVL 80111 2367 A4
8700 GDVL 80112 2367 A4
9500 CTNL 80112 2367 D4
10500 AphC 80112 2367 D4
12100 CTNL 80111 2368 A4
12100 CTNL 80112 2368 A4
12900 AphC 80111 2368 A4
12900 AphC 80112 2368 A4
14300 AphC 80016 2368 A4
15300 CTNL 80016 2368 E4
16100 FXFD 80016 2368 E4
16600 FXFD 80016 2369 B4
16700 AphC 80016 2369 B4
16700 CTNL 80016 2369 D4
20500 AURA 80016 2369 D4
20600 AURA 80016 2370 D4
20700 AphC 80016 2370 D4
25900 AURA 80016 2371 A5
E Arapahoe Rd SR-88
- CTNL 80111 2367 D4
- GDVL 80111 2367 D4
8900 GDVL 80112 2367 D4
9500 CTNL 80112 2367 D4
10500 AphC 80112 2367 D4
12100 CTNL 80111 2368 A4
12100 CTNL 80112 2368 A4
12900 AphC 80111 2368 A4
12900 AphC 80112 2368 A4
14300 AphC 80016 2368 A4
15300 CTNL 80016 2368 A4
16100 FXFD 80016 2368 A4
20600 AURA 80016 2369 E4
20700 AphC 80016 2369 E4
E Arapahoe Rd SR-88
20700 AphC 80016 2370 A4
20700 AURA 80016 2370 A4
20700 CTNL 80016 2369 E4
W Arapahoe Rd
1900 LITN 80120 2364 B4
Arapahoe St
100 GOLD 80403 2107 D2
700 GOLD 80401 2107 D3
1200 DNVR 80204 2112 C4
1300 DNVR 80202 2112 D4
1900 DNVR 80205 2112 D3
2300 GOLD 80401 2108 A4
3000 DNVR 80205 2113 A2
S Arapahoe Wy
6400 LITN 80120 2364 B3
Aravon Ct
7800 DgsC 80124 2450 D6
Arbol Ct
3800 BldC 80301 1603 A5
W Arbor Av
2000 LITN 80120 2364 B3
6100 JfnC 80123 2363 A3
8600 JfnC 80123 2362 C3
E Arbor Cir
9100 AphC 80111 2367 A3
9100 GDVL 80111 2367 A3
Arbor Dr
400 LAFT 80026 1690 B4
E Arbor Dr
- AURA 80016 2371 C2
9300 AphC 80111 2367 A3
22000 AURA 80016 2370 B2
W Arbor Dr
6400 JfnC 80123 2363 A3
8800 JfnC 80123 2362 C3
11000 JfnC 80127 2361 E3
E Arbor Pl
- AphC 80111 2367 B3
22300 AURA 80016 2370 C3
W Arbor Pl
2000 LITN 80120 2364 B3
8500 JfnC 80123 2362 D3
10000 JfnC 80127 2362 B3
13400 JfnC 80127 2361 B3
Arbor Glen Pl
2700 BLDR 80304 1602 E4
S Arbutus Cir
6500 JfnC 80127 2361 C4
Arbutus Ct
1500 JfnC 80401 2109 B5
6500 ARVD 80004 2025 B1
7300 ARVD 80005 1941 B7
S Arbutus Ct
1800 LKWD 80228 2193 B6
Arbutus Dr
10 LKWD 80228 2193 C1
10 LKWD 80401 2193 C1
200 LKWD 80401 2109 B7
S Arbutus Pl
1400 LKWD 80228 2193 B5
Arbutus St
- ARVD 80005 1941 B4
600 LKWD 80401 2109 B7
1700 JfnC 80401 2109 B5
5200 JfnC 80002 2025 B5
7000 ARVD 80004 1941 B7
7000 ARVD 80004 2025 B1
7000 JfnC 80004 1941 B7
7000 JfnC 80004 2025 B1
N Arbutus St
1500 JfnC 80401 2109 B5
S Arbutus St
600 LKWD 80228 2193 C4
4800 JfnC 80465 2277 C7
S Arbutus Wy
2700 LKWD 80228 2193 C7
4300 JfnC 80465 2277 C5
Arcadia Rd
10 PrkC 80456 2606 E5
10 PrkC 80456 2607 A5
S Arcaro Creek Ct
12400 PARK 80134 2537 E3
E Arcaro Creek Pl
19400 PARK 80134 2537 D4
W Archer Av
14300 JfnC 80401 2193 A1
16100 JfnC 80401 2192 D2
E Archer Cir
14900 AURA 80012 2200 C1
W Archer Dr
15100 JfnC 80401 2192 E1
E Archer Pl
7700 DNVR 80230 2198 D1
11800 AURA 80011 2199 D1
11800 AURA 80012 2199 D1
15100 AURA 80012 2200 C1
23700 AphC 80018 2202 D1
W Archer Pl
10 DNVR 80209 2196 D1
10 DNVR 80223 2196 D1
2500 DNVR 80219 2196 A1
6800 LKWD 80226 2195 A1
7200 LKWD 80226 2194 E1
14800 JfnC 80401 2193 A1
15000 JfnC 80401 2192 E2
Archer St
800 GOLD 80401 2107 E2
Arches Pl
4400 CSRK 80109 2702 C4
Arco Iris Ln
7200 DgsC 80108 2534 D4
E Arden Cir
400 DgsC 80126 2448 E4
Arena Dr
30000 JfnC 80439 2273 B3
Arena Wy
- AdmC 80601 1779 A6
Arezzo Cir
12800 PARK 80134 2537 B5
Argo Ct
10 BMFD 80020 1774 E6
S Argonne Cir
1200 AURA 80017 2201 C4
Argonne Ct
5200 DNVR 80249 2033 C5
S Argonne Ct
2900 AURA 80013 2285 C1
4400 AURA 80015 2285 C5
13000 CTNL 80016 2369 C6
Argonne St
- DNVR 80249 1949 C7
1700 AURA 80011 2117 C4
5100 DNVR 80249 2033 C5
S Argonne St
1300 AURA 80017 2201 C4
2400 AURA 80013 2201 C7
2700 AURA 80013 2285 C1
4800 AURA 80015 2285 C6
5100 CTNL 80015 2285 C7
7500 CTNL 80016 2369 C6
Argonne Wy
4800 DNVR 80249 2033 C5
S Argonne Wy
1600 AURA 80017 2201 C5
3900 AURA 80013 2285 C4
4300 AURA 80015 2285 C5
Argos Cir
800 LAFT 80026 1690 B5
Argosy Wy
400 DgsC 80108 2619 A5
W Argyle Pl
2400 DNVR 80211 2112 A2
Aries Ct
500 DgsC 80124 2450 E1
Arikaree Cir
10 NDLD 80466 1765 C1
E Arizona Av
- GNDL 80246 2197 E4
10 DNVR 80210 2196 E4
10 DNVR 80223 2196 E4
3900 DNVR 80210 2197 E4
3900 DNVR 80246 2197 E4
4800 DNVR 80246 2198 A4
6500 DNVR 80224 2198 C4
11900 AURA 80012 2199 D4
13900 AURA 80012 2200 B4
15300 AURA 80017 2200 D4
17400 AURA 80017 2201 B4
39300 AphC 80102 2206 E4
39900 AphC 80102 2207 A4
W Arizona Av
10 DNVR 80210 2196 D4
800 DNVR 80223 2196 D4
3000 DNVR 80219 2196 A4
3800 DNVR 80219 2195 D4
6400 LKWD 80232 2195 A4
9200 LKWD 80232 2194 B4
10900 JfnC 80232 2193 E4
11500 LKWD 80228 2193 D4
E Arizona Cir
24600 AURA 80018 2202 E4
24700 AURA 80018 2203 A4
E Arizona Dr
7600 AphC 80231 2198 D4
9700 AURA 80247 2199 B4
11900 AURA 80012 2199 D4
16500 AURA 80017 2200 E4
16800 AURA 80017 2201 A4
W Arizona Dr
9000 LKWD 80232 2194 C4
E Arizona Pl
- AphC 80102 2207 D4
9100 AphC 80247 2199 A4
10900 AURA 80012 2199 C4
14800 AURA 80012 2200 C4
16500 AURA 80017 2200 E4
17100 AURA 80017 2201 A4
24600 AURA 80018 2202 E4
W Arizona Pl
5300 LKWD 80232 2195 B4
7300 LKWD 80226 2194 E4
7300 LKWD 80232 2194 E4
12500 LKWD 80228 2193 C4
W Arizona Wy
9000 LKWD 80232 2194 C4
E Arkansas Av
10 DNVR 80210 2196 E5
10 DNVR 80223 2196 E5
2000 DNVR 80210 2197 B5
4000 DNVR 80222 2197 E5
4600 DNVR 80222 2198 A5
7300 AphC 80231 2198 D4
7300 DNVR 80224 2198 D4
7300 DNVR 80231 2198 D4
11700 AURA 80012 2199 D4
13400 AURA 80012 2200 A4
16500 AURA 80017 2200 E4
16800 AURA 80017 2201 A4
40800 AphC 80102 2207 A4
W Arkansas Av
10 DNVR 80210 2196 D5
1200 DNVR 80223 2196 C5
2300 DNVR 80219 2196 B5
4800 DNVR 80219 2195 C5
5100 LKWD 80219 2195 C5
6600 LKWD 80232 2195 A5
7000 LKWD 80232 2194 E5
10900 JfnC 80232 2193 C4
10900 JfnC 80232 2194 A5
12400 LKWD 80228 2193 D5
E Arkansas Dr
12800 AURA 80012 2199 E6
13900 AURA 80012 2200 B4
15800 AURA 80017 2200 E4
19100 AURA 80017 2201 C4
W Arkansas Dr
10000 LKWD 80232 2194 A5
Arkansas Pl
42600 AphC 80102 2207 C4
E Arkansas Pl
- AURA 80247 2199 B5
9600 AphC 80247 2199 B5
12100 AURA 80012 2199 E4
13900 AURA 80012 2200 B4
15800 AURA 80017 2200 D4
18700 AURA 80017 2201 C4
24400 AURA 80018 2202 E4
E Arkansas Pl
42000 AphC 80102 2207 C4
W Arkansas Pl
7600 LKWD 80232 2194 D5
12000 JfnC 80232 2193 D5
13000 LKWD 80228 2193 C5
Arkansas Mountain Rd
10 BldC 80302 1600 C7
10 BldC 80302 1684 B1
Arkins Ct
2500 DNVR 80216 2112 E1
3500 DNVR 80216 2028 E7
3600 DNVR 80216 2029 A7
Arlington
- TNTN 80260 1944 C2
Arlington Av
4200 BMFD 80020 1859 C1
W Arlington Av
3300 LITN 80123 2279 E7
3300 LITN 80123 2363 E1
9000 JfnC 80123 2362 B1
11600 JfnC 80127 2361 E1
Arlington Ct
12400 BMFD 80020 1859 C1
Arlington Dr
7500 BldC 80303 1688 D3
W Arlington Dr
7000 LKWD 80123 2362 E1
11800 JfnC 80127 2361 D2
W Arlington Pl
12500 JfnC 80127 2361 C1
Arlington St
- CSRK 80104 2788 D2
W Arlington Wy
7100 LKWD 80123 2362 E1
Armadillo Dr
10000 DgsC 80124 2450 D5
S Armadillo Tr
7700 JfnC 80439 2358 B7
7700 JfnC 80439 2442 A1
8900 JfnC 80439 2441 E2
Armadillo Wy
27200 JfnC 80439 2441 E3
Armel Ct
17400 PARK 80134 2453 A7
Armer Dr
3700 BLDR 80305 1687 A7
Armour Rd
100 BldC 80455 1516 D7
Arnett St
3000 BLDR 80304 1602 E7
Arnett Ranch Rd
11500 JfnC 80127 2527 E3
11500 JfnC 80127 2528 A3
Arnold Dr
3300 BLDR 80301 1687 A2
S Arnold St
9700 JfnC 80433 2442 B5
Arrow Ct
700 LAFT 80026 1690 E6
Arrow Tr
- AURA 80010 2115 B5
S Arrow Grass Wy
9000 DgsC 80126 2449 B3
Arrowhead Ct
7900 LNTR 80124 2450 E3
W Arrowhead Ct
500 LSVL 80027 1689 B7
Arrowhead Dr
15100 BGTN 80603 1697 B3
S Arrowhead Dr
8300 JfnC 80465 2443 B2
Arrowhead Ln
26800 JfnC 80433 2441 E5
26800 JfnC 80433 2442 A5
E Arrowhead Ln
10100 DgsC 80138 2539 B2
E Arrowhead Rd
1400 DgsC 80126 2449 B2
W Arrowhead Rd
3600 LITN 80123 2279 D7
3600 LITN 80123 2363 D1
W Arrowhead St
500 LSVL 80027 1689 B7
Arrowhead Tr
6000 EbtC 80107 2794 C5
Arrowhead Wy
8100 LNTR 80124 2450 E3
Arrowhead Pass
- TNTN 80229 1861 E6
Arrowleaf Ct
- BLDR 80304 1602 A6
10 BldC 80304 1602 A6
W Arrowleaf Ct
3200 CSRK 80109 2702 E1
E Arrowshaft Tr
7500 AphC 80016 2454 A1
7500 AURA 80138 2454 A1
20700 AphC 80016 2370 A7
Arrow Wood Dr
900 JfnC 80401 2190 D4
Arrowwood Dr
- DgsC 80126 2449 E6
- DgsC 80130 2449 E6
10300 DgsC 80130 2450 A6
Arrowwood Ln
3100 BLDR 80303 1687 A4
Arrowwood St
700 LGMT 80501 1438 B5
N Arroyo Run
7000 DgsC 80125 2614 D1
Arroyo St
300 BGTN 80601 1697 B6
Arroyo Chico
10 BldC 80302 1600 E6
500 BldC 80302 1601 A6
Arroyo Verde Ct
- CSRK 80104 2704 B3
Arsata Pl
1800 DgsC 80118 2870 C7
Artemis Cir
1000 LAFT 80026 1690 B6
Artesian Dr
10 BldC 80025 1770 C7

STREET
Block City ZIP Map# Grid

Arthur Av
1300 LSVL 80027 1773 E2
S Arthur Av
300 LSVL 80027 1773 E2
Arthur Ct
3500 BLDR 80304 1602 E6
S Arthur Ln
9800 DgsC 80130 2450 B5
Arthur St
10 LAFT 80026 1690 E6
Art's Ln
10 GpnC 80474 1849 E2
10 GpnC 80474 1850 A2
Arundel Ln
7800 DgsC 80124 2450 E6
E Asbury Av
10 DNVR 80210 2196 E6
10 DNVR 80223 2196 E6
600 DNVR 80210 2197 A6
4600 DNVR 80222 2197 E6
4800 DNVR 80222 2198 A6
6600 DNVR 80224 2198 C6
6900 AphC 80224 2198 C6
10500 AURA 80014 2199 C6
10500 AURA 80247 2199 C6
14500 AURA 80014 2200 C6
16500 AURA 80013 2200 E6
16800 AURA 80013 2201 A6
W Asbury Av
10 DNVR 80210 2196 D6
1600 DNVR 80223 2196 A6
2200 DNVR 80219 2196 A6
3000 DNVR 80219 2195 E6
10800 JfnC 80227 2194 A6
10800 LKWD 80227 2194 A6
10900 LKWD 80227 2193 E7
E Asbury Cir
4600 DNVR 80222 2197 D6
4600 DNVR 80222 2198 A6
12700 AURA 80014 2199 E6
12700 AURA 80014 2200 A6
17300 AURA 80013 2201 A6
W Asbury Cir
13700 LKWD 80228 2193 B6
W Asbury Ct
11400 LKWD 80227 2193 E7
Asbury Dr
4600 CSRK 80104 2704 D6
E Asbury Dr
13200 AURA 80014 2200 A6
17700 AURA 80013 2201 B6
S Asbury Dr
2000 LKWD 80227 2194 A7
W Asbury Dr
8800 LKWD 80227 2194 C6
13700 LKWD 80228 2193 B6
E Asbury Pl
9300 AphC 80231 2199 A6
11700 AURA 80014 2199 D6
15600 AURA 80013 2200 D6
17900 AURA 80013 2201 B6
23500 AURA 80018 2202 D6
W Asbury Pl
5700 LKWD 80227 2195 B6
12500 LKWD 80228 2193 D7
E Ascot Av
1200 DgsC 80126 2449 A4
Ash Av
100 CSRK 80104 2703 E7
100 CSRK 80104 2787 E1
200 BGTN 80601 1696 A6
200 CSRK 80104 2704 A7
3000 BLDR 80305 1686 E5
3000 BLDR 80305 1687 A5
Ash Cir
11500 TNTN 80233 1861 E3
13300 TNTN 80241 1777 E6
S Ash Cir
6500 CTNL 80121 2365 E3
6900 CTNL 80122 2365 E5
S Ash Cir E
6100 CTNL 80121 2365 E2
S Ash Cir W
6100 CTNL 80121 2365 E3
Ash Ct
10 LGMT 80503 1438 D1
6500 CMCY 80022 2029 E1
7000 AdmC 80022 1945 E7
7000 CMCY 80022 1945 E7
9200 TNTN 80229 1945 E2
10600 TNTN 80233 1861 E5
13100 TNTN 80241 1777 E6
S Ash Ct
5700 GDVL 80121 2365 E1
5700 GDVL 80121 2366 A2
6300 CTNL 80121 2365 E3
7700 CTNL 80122 2365 E6
W Ash Ct
500 LSVL 80027 1689 B6
Ash Dr
11700 TNTN 80233 1861 E3
12400 TNTN 80241 1861 E1
N Ash Pl
10900 TNTN 80233 1861 E4
Ash St
- BMFD 80020 1859 A2
- DgsC 80120 2447 E1
- LITN 80120 2447 E1
- WSTR 80020 1859 A2
10 DNVR 80220 2197 E1
10 DNVR 80246 2197 E1
500 BMFD 80020 1775 A7
2000 DNVR 80220 2113 E4
3200 DNVR 80207 2113 E2
5000 DNVR 80216 2029 E5
5700 GDVL 80121 2366 A2
5800 GDVL 80121 2365 E2
6800 CMCY 80022 2029 E1
6900 AdmC 80022 1945 E7
6900 CMCY 80022 1945 E7
9100 TNTN 80229 1945 E2
9800 FLHT 80260 1860 A7
12400 TNTN 80241 1861 E1
12900 TNTN 80241 1777 D6
N Ash St
11600 TNTN 80233 1861 E2
S Ash St
10 DNVR 80220 2197 E1
10 DNVR 80246 2197 E1
200 BNNT 80102 2124 D2
600 GNDL 80246 2197 E3
1400 DNVR 80222 2197 E5
3400 AphC 80222 2281 E2
3400 DNVR 80222 2281 E2
3900 CHLV 80113 2281 E4
W Ash St
500 LSVL 80027 1689 B6
Ash Ter
- EbtC 80107 2709 D7
Ash Wy
10900 TNTN 80233 1861 E4
S Ash Wy
6700 CTNL 80122 2365 E4
Ashbrook Cir
4800 DgsC 80130 2450 A6
S Ashburn Ct
9200 DgsC 80130 2450 C3
E Ashburn Ln
6300 DgsC 80130 2450 C3
Ashbury Cir
9400 DgsC 80134 2452 E3
Ashbury Ln
- DgsC 80134 2452 E4
Ashcroft Av
3900 CSRK 80104 2704 C7
Ashcroft Ct
1600 LGMT 80501 1439 A6
4100 CSRK 80104 2704 C7
Ashcroft Dr
1300 LGMT 80501 1439 A6
Ashfield Cir
4700 BldC 80301 1604 D3
Ashfield Ct
4600 BldC 80301 1604 D3
Ashfield Dr
4400 BldC 80301 1604 D4
Ashfield St
10500 DgsC 80126 2449 D7
Ashford Cir
1800 LGMT 80501 1356 D5
10700 DgsC 80126 2449 E7
Ashford Dr
500 LGMT 80501 1356 D6
Ash Hollow Pl
1200 CSRK 80104 2787 E4
Ashland St
- CSRK 80104 2705 A7
E Ashleigh Ct
1900 DgsC 80126 2449 B5
S Ashleigh Ln
9700 DgsC 80126 2449 B5
S Ashleigh Pl
9700 DgsC 80126 2449 B5
S Ashleigh Wy
9900 DgsC 80126 2449 B5
Ashley Ct
- BLDR 80301 1603 C7
6900 DgsC 80134 2621 E1
E Ashton Av
4800 CSRK 80104 2704 D7
Ashton Ct
10300 TNTN 80229 1861 B6
Ashurst Ln
10900 DgsC 80108 2533 E1
Ashurst Wy
10900 DgsC 80108 2449 C7
10900 DgsC 80108 2533 E1
10900 DgsC 80126 2533 E1
S Ashwood Ct
10500 DgsC 80129 2448 B7
W Ashwood Ln
2200 DgsC 80129 2448 B7
W Ashwood Pl
2000 DgsC 80129 2448 B7
Ashwood Wy
- DgsC 80129 2448 B7
Ashworth Av
3200 DgsC 80126 2449 D7
E Aspen Av
5200 CSRK 80104 2704 E7
Aspen Cir
- GpnC 80403 1934 B5
10 CCkC 80439 2271 D3
10 GpnC 80403 1850 D5
8600 PARK 80134 2453 B2
Aspen Ct
10 CCkC 80439 2271 D5
300 BMFD 80020 1775 A7
300 BMFD 80020 1859 B1
3600 BLDR 80304 1602 C6
8700 PARK 80134 2453 B2
S Aspen Ct
5700 GDVL 80121 2365 E1
W Aspen Ct
600 LSVL 80027 1773 B2
2400 DNVR 80219 2280 B1
2400 EGLD 80110 2280 B1
Aspen Dr
10 AURA 80011 2201 C1
10 BldC 80403 1852 A2
10 CCkC 80439 2187 C2
10 PrkC 80456 2521 C3
200 BGTN 80601 1696 A6
400 AURA 80011 2117 C7
1500 PrkC 80456 2606 D3
5000 BWMR 80123 2279 D7
9000 TNTN 80229 1945 D2
27500 JfnC 80439 2357 E3
28400 JfnC 80433 2525 D4
Aspen Ln
- LITN 80120 2363 E7
- LITN 80120 2447 E1
10 BldC 80403 1852 A2
10 CCkC 80439 2187 C7
10 CCkC 80439 2271 D1
10 CCkC 80452 2186 A4
10 GpnC 80403 1850 B6
10 PrkC 80456 2606 D7
Aspen Ln
200 GpnC 80403 1933 C7
200 JfnC 80401 2107 A7
200 JfnC 80401 2191 A1
300 GpnC 80403 2017 C1
400 JfnC 80401 2106 E7
400 JfnC 80401 2190 E1
500 PrkC 80456 2690 D1
29600 JfnC 80439 2273 B2
34000 PrkC 80470 2523 D5
S Aspen Ln
4000 JfnC 80439 2273 C5
9500 JfnC 80433 2442 A4
Aspen Pl
- EbtC 80107 2709 D6
10 CCkC 80439 2271 C2
400 GOLD 80403 2107 D1
1300 LGMT 80501 1356 A7
Aspen Rd
- CCkC 80439 2272 A6
500 JfnC 80401 2107 B7
Aspen St
- TNTN 80260 1860 B7
- TNTN 80260 1944 B1
1000 LGMT 80501 1439 A1
1100 BMFD 80020 1775 A6
1100 LGMT 80501 1356 A7
9700 FLHT 80260 1860 A7
Aspen Tr
- LGMT 80501 1439 C6
10 CCkC 80439 2187 D5
10 GpnC 80403 1851 B3
Aspen Wy
- CCkC 80439 2440 A1
10 BldC 80466 1767 A5
100 CCkC 80439 2356 A7
500 LSVL 80027 1773 D1
1000 BMFD 80020 1775 A5
24900 JfnC 80401 2190 C1
S Aspen Wy
10 AURA 80011 2201 D3
W Aspen Wy
600 LSVL 80027 1773 A2
Aspen Creek Ct
9200 DgsC 80129 2448 A3
Aspen Creek Dr
3000 DgsC 80129 2448 A3
4800 BMFD 80020 1775 C5
Aspen Creek Pt
9100 DgsC 80129 2448 A3
Aspen Creek Wy
9200 DgsC 80129 2448 A3
Aspen End
- PrkC 80456 2521 B3
Aspen Grove Ct
10 BldC 80466 1767 C2
W Aspen Grove Wy
- LITN 80120 2364 A5
E Aspen Hill Cir
9400 LNTR 80124 2451 B3
S Aspen Hill Dr
- LNTR 80124 2451 A3
E Aspen Hill Ln
9300 LNTR 80124 2451 A3
E Aspen Hill Pl
9200 LNTR 80124 2451 A3
S Aspen Hill Wy
9400 LNTR 80124 2451 B3
Aspen Lane Upper
- PrkC 80470 2524 A3
35300 PrkC 80470 2523 E3
Aspen Leaf Ct
- DNVR 80237 2282 E5
8800 DgsC 80125 2532 E4
Aspen Leaf Dr
5100 DgsC 80125 2532 E5
5300 DgsC 80125 2533 A5
Aspen Leaf Pl
5500 DgsC 80125 2532 E5
Aspen Ln Ct
34800 PrkC 80470 2524 A3
Aspen Meadow Cir
4100 DgsC 80108 2533 E1
4100 DgsC 80126 2533 E1
Aspen Meadow Dr
32100 JfnC 80439 2356 C6
S Aspen Meadow Dr
7100 JfnC 80439 2356 D6
Aspen Meadow Ln
- GpnC 80403 1935 D1
Aspen Meadows Rd
10 BldC 80466 1767 C2
Aspen Meadows Campground Rd
- GpnC 80403 1935 D2
Aspen Ridge Dr
400 LAFT 80026 1690 B4
Aspenwood Ct
300 LAFT 80026 1774 B1
Aspenwood Dr
10 CCkC 80439 2271 B2
Aspenwood Ln
100 CCkC 80439 2187 E7
100 CCkC 80439 2271 E1
1500 LGMT 80501 1357 A6
Aspley Ln
- EGLD 80113 2281 B3
Aster Ct
1400 SUPE 80027 1857 B1
5100 DgsC 80134 2622 A4
W Aster Ct
3400 CSRK 80109 2702 E1
Aster Wy
800 JfnC 80401 2190 E4
1200 BGTN 80601 1780 D2
Astor Ln
500 BldC 80302 1686 C5
500 BLDR 80302 1686 C5
Astorbrook Cir
3200 DgsC 80126 2449 D5
Astorbrook Ln
10000 DgsC 80126 2449 D6
Astorbrook Pl
- DgsC 80126 2449 D6
Astorbrook Wy
3100 DgsC 80126 2449 D6
Astoria Ct
10000 DgsC 80124 2450 E5
Astoria Ln
2100 LGMT 80501 1356 D5
Astra Wy
37000 AdmC 80137 2038 A5
Astrion Ct
4000 CSRK 80104 2787 E5
Atchison Cir
3200 AURA 80011 2116 B2
S Atchison Cir
4300 AURA 80015 2284 B5
Atchison Ct
1000 CSRK 80109 2703 B6
S Atchison Ct
4700 AphC 80015 2284 B6
Atchison St
- CMCY 80022 1864 B5
3000 AURA 80011 2116 B2
5500 DNVR 80239 2032 B4
S Atchison St
- AphC 80112 2368 B4
- CTNL 80111 2368 B4
- CTNL 80112 2368 B4
Atchison Wy
400 CSRK 80109 2703 C6
5300 DNVR 80239 2032 A5
S Atchison Wy
- AphC 80014 2284 B5
3800 AURA 80014 2284 B4
4200 AURA 80015 2284 B5
6500 CTNL 80111 2368 B3
Athena Rd
10 GpnC 80403 1934 C1
Athene Dr
1400 LAFT 80026 1690 A7
W Athens Ln
9400 LITN 80127 2446 B4
Athens St
1700 BLDR 80302 1686 D3
W Athens Wy
9700 LITN 80127 2446 B4
S Atherton Wy
9800 DgsC 80130 2450 A5
Atkinson Av
1100 CSRK 80104 2789 A1
E Atlantic Av
11700 AURA 80014 2199 D6
W Atlantic Av
11400 LKWD 80227 2193 E7
13800 LKWD 80228 2193 B6
E Atlantic Cir
15600 AURA 80013 2200 D6
E Atlantic Dr
14500 AURA 80014 2200 C6
17900 AURA 80013 2201 B6
W Atlantic Dr
5800 LKWD 80227 2195 B6
12100 LKWD 80228 2193 D6
E Atlantic Pl
4800 DNVR 80222 2198 A6
7000 DNVR 80224 2198 C6
9300 AphC 80231 2199 A6
11700 AURA 80014 2199 D6
16600 AURA 80013 2200 E6
17000 AURA 80013 2201 A6
S Atlantic Pl
- LKWD 80227 2195 B6
- LKWD 80232 2195 B6
W Atlantic Pl
1600 DNVR 80223 2196 C6
5700 LKWD 80227 2195 B6
12200 LKWD 80228 2193 D6
Atlantis Av
1000 LAFT 80026 1690 B5
Atlantis Dr
10 GpnC 80403 1934 C1
Atlas Cir
1000 LAFT 80026 1690 A6
Atrium Dr
- CSRK 80108 2619 B7
- CSRK 80108 2703 B1
Atwood Cir
10500 DgsC 80130 2450 B7
Atwood Ct
1200 LGMT 80501 1356 B7
Atwood St
300 LGMT 80501 1439 B2
1500 LGMT 80501 1356 B7
W Auburn Av
9300 LKWD 80227 2194 B7
11600 JfnC 80228 2193 D7
11600 LKWD 80228 2193 D7
Auburn Ct
1400 LGMT 80503 1355 C7
W Auburn Ct
14600 LKWD 80228 2193 A7
Auburn Dr
- CSRK 80109 2703 B6
W Auburn Dr
11600 JfnC 80228 2193 D7
Auburn Ln
8100 WSTR 80031 1943 D4
W Auburn Pl
13000 JfnC 80228 2193 C7
Auburn St
300 BLDR 80305 1687 A6
E Auburn Hills Dr
- PARK 80134 2537 A1
16600 PARK 80134 2536 E1
E Auburn Hills Pl
- DgsC 80134 2537 A1
- PARK 80134 2537 A1
16500 PARK 80134 2536 E1
Auckland Ct
4400 DNVR 80239 2032 A6
S Auckland Ct
4400 AURA 80015 2284 B5
Auckland Wy
5500 DNVR 80239 2032 B4
Audubon Av
6900 BldC 80503 1521 B4
Audubon Ct
8800 BldC 80503 1521 B5
August Ln
1500 AdmC 80601 1696 D4
1500 BGTN 80601 1696 D4
Augusta Dr
10 CBVL 80123 2363 E2
500 BldC 80027 1773 C3
500 LSVL 80027 1773 C3
4200 BMFD 80020 1775 C3
7200 BLDR 80301 1604 C2
S Augusta Dr
2100 JfnC 80439 2188 E7
2100 JfnC 80439 2272 E1
Augusta Ln
500 BldC 80027 1773 C3
Augusta Pl
8300 LNTR 80124 2450 E5
Auk Ln
10 PrkC 80456 2691 D3
S Ault Ln
8100 JfnC 80465 2443 C1
Auraria Pkwy
- DNVR 80204 2112 B5
Aurora Av
500 BLDR 80302 1686 B4
2800 BLDR 80303 1686 E4
2800 BLDR 80303 1687 A4
E Aurora Pkwy
22200 AURA 80016 2370 C6
S Aurora Pkwy
- AphC 80016 2370 D1
6700 AURA 80016 2370 E5
Aurora Pl
5600 BLDR 80303 1687 D4
Aurora Rd
10 GpnC 80403 1934 C1
Austin Av
- ERIE 80516 1606 E6
- ERIE 80516 1607 A7
Austin Ct
14100 BMFD 80020 1775 E3
Austin Pl
300 DgsC 80108 2534 E7
Autrey Av
400 LAFT 80026 1690 D5
Autumn Ct
10 ERIE 80516 1606 D5
1200 LGMT 80501 1356 D7
4100 BLDR 80304 1602 E4
E Autumn Ct
5400 GDVL 80111 2367 A1
Autumn Dr
5300 GDVL 80111 2283 A7
5400 GDVL 80111 2367 A1
Autumn Wy
2800 EbtC 80138 2456 E5
S Autumn Ash Ct
9300 DgsC 80126 2448 E4
S Autumn Ash Pl
9300 DgsC 80126 2448 E4
Autumn Blaze Tr
10100 DgsC 80129 2448 E6
Autumn Brush Ct
5700 DgsC 80134 2622 A3
Autumn Ridge Blvd
2200 LAFT 80026 1774 C1
Autumn Sun Cir
3200 DgsC 80104 2787 B7
Autumnwood Ln
1400 JfnC 80439 2188 C5
S Autumnwood Pl
9600 DgsC 80129 2448 B4
Autum Rock Cove
16600 DgsC 80134 2452 E6
Avalanche St
- DgsC 80125 2532 D4
- JfnC 80007 1939 E2
- JfnC 80007 1940 A2
Avalon Av
700 LAFT 80026 1690 D6
W Avalon Dr
9500 LITN 80127 2446 B4
W Avalon Pl
9700 LITN 80127 2446 B4
Avante Ct
600 LAFT 80026 1690 C3
Avenida Del Sol
- CSRK 80104 2703 E1
- CSRK 80104 2704 A1
Avenida del Sol
- CSRK 80108 2703 E1
Aventerra Pkwy
- DgsC 80134 2452 E3
- DgsC 80134 2453 B3
Avenue A
- PrkC 80456 2521 D2
Avenue B
10 PrkC 80456 2521 D2
3400 JfnC 80457 2274 B3
Avenue C
3400 JfnC 80457 2274 B3
Avenue D
3300 JfnC 80457 2274 B3
Avenue de Pines Ln
33800 JfnC 80403 1852 B6
Avenue E
3300 JfnC 80457 2274 B3
Avenue F
3300 JfnC 80439 2274 B3
3300 JfnC 80457 2274 B3
Avery St
1200 GOLD 80403 2023 C7
Avery Wy
- CSRK 80109 2702 D5
Avgare Wy
1300 ERIE 80516 1607 A6
Avian Ct
1600 LAFT 80026 1689 D2
Aviator Wy
12400 DgsC 80112 2451 E2
12400 DgsC 80112 2452 A2
Avocado Rd
- BLDR 80304 1602 C4
Avocet Cir
10 TNTN 80241 1777 B6
Avocet Ln
9600 BldC 80026 1605 D5
9600 BldC 80301 1605 D5
Avon Ln
- AdmC 80020 1776 C1
- BMFD 80020 1776 C1
1100 LGMT 80501 1439 A5
S Avon Pl
10 DgsC 80108 2618 E5
W Avondale Dr
3000 DNVR 80204 2111 E5
3000 DNVR 80204 2112 A5
Avrum Dr
6800 AdmC 80221 2028 B1
6900 AdmC 80221 1944 B7
N Awl Rd
8500 DgsC 80138 2539 A4
Azalea Wy
2400 ERIE 80516 1692 A3
Aztec
- AdmC 80022 1946 C3
Aztec Ct
5500 BLDR 80303 1687 D4
W Aztec Ct
6700 DgsC 80135 2616 B7
Aztec Dr
500 BLDR 80303 1687 D4
900 DgsC 80108 2618 C2
Aztec Rd
4100 JfnC 80439 2274 E5
Azure Wy
- BldC 80303 1689 A6
- LSVL 80027 1689 A6
- LSVL 80303 1689 A6
W Azure Wy
700 BldC 80303 1689 A6
700 LSVL 80027 1689 A6
700 LSVL 80303 1689 A6
Azurite Ct
- CSRK 80108 2619 E6
Azurite Ln
- CSRK 80108 2619 D6

B

B St
- AdmC 80022 1946 E4
- AdmC 80022 2030 E1
- AURA 80011 2116 C5
- DNVR 80022 2030 E2
- DNVR 80123 2363 A1
- DNVR 80239 2030 E2
- LGMT 80501 1356 A6
200 GOLD 80401 2192 B1
B & M St
10 WARD 80481 1597 D2
Baca Cir
5400 BldC 80301 1604 C1
S Baca Rd
11600 JfnC 80433 2524 E3
11600 JfnC 80433 2525 A3
Bacchus Dr
1100 LAFT 80026 1690 A6
Bachman Dr
7400 AdmC 80602 1778 C7
7400 TNTN 80602 1778 C7
Backlund Rd
8700 EbtC 80107 2795 B4
Bad Bandit Ct
10 PrkC 80456 2521 E5
Bad Bandit Ln
10 PrkC 80456 2521 E5
Badding Dr
500 TNTN 80229 1860 E7
W Baden Dr
9700 LITN 80127 2446 B4
Bader Ct
1000 DgsC 80104 2704 B6
S Badger Ct
4600 JfnC 80127 2278 A6
Badger Ln
10 PrkC 80456 2607 B7
S Badger Ln
4600 JfnC 80127 2278 A6
Badger Rd
10 GpnC 80403 1933 E6
10 GpnC 80403 1934 A6
Badger Spur
1800 JfnC 80403 2104 A4
S Badger Wy
4600 JfnC 80127 2278 A6
Badger Creek Dr
400 BGTN 80601 1696 E7
Baguette Dr
1100 CSRK 80108 2619 E5
1500 CSRK 80108 2620 A5
S Bahama Cir
2500 AURA 80013 2201 C7
5200 CTNL 80015 2285 C7
S Bahama Cir E
5700 AphC 80015 2369 C1
S Bahama Cir W
5700 AphC 80015 2369 C1
Bahama Ct
- DNVR 80249 2033 D4
S Bahama Ct
2700 AURA 80013 2285 C1
4900 AURA 80015 2285 C7
5100 CTNL 80015 2285 C7
Bahama St
1600 AURA 80011 2117 C4
4300 DNVR 80249 2033 C6
S Bahama St
- CTNL 80015 2285 C7
1100 AURA 80017 2201 C4
2800 AURA 80013 2285 C1
S Bahama Wy
1400 AURA 80017 2201 C4
2400 AURA 80013 2201 C7
3800 AURA 80013 2285 C3
4300 AURA 80015 2285 C5
Bailey Dr
10 PrkC 80456 2606 C7
100 PrkC 80456 2690 C1
1000 BGTN 80603 1697 E1
1000 WldC 80603 1697 E1
W Bails Av
7300 LKWD 80232 2194 E6
E Bails Dr
5300 DNVR 80222 2198 B6
5300 DNVR 80224 2198 B6
15500 AURA 80017 2200 D6
E Bails Pl
4300 DNVR 80222 2197 E6
4500 DNVR 80222 2198 A6
11300 AURA 80012 2199 D6
15000 AURA 80012 2200 C6
16100 AURA 80017 2200 E6
17700 AURA 80017 2201 B6
W Bails Pl
3100 DNVR 80219 2195 E6
3100 DNVR 80219 2196 A6
Bain Ct
1500 ERIE 80516 1607 A6
Bain Dr
1500 ERIE 80516 1607 A6
S Baird Rd
13000 JfnC 80433 2525 D7
13000 JfnC 80433 2609 E1
13000 JfnC 80433 2610 A1
W Baker Av
1800 EGLD 80110 2196 B7
2000 DNVR 80219 2196 B7
8100 LKWD 80227 2194 D7
W Baker Ct
14600 LKWD 80228 2193 A7
Baker Dr
- BLDR 80302 1686 D3
Baker Ln
10 ERIE 80516 1607 C2
E Baker Pl
6400 DNVR 80222 2198 C7
6800 DNVR 80224 2198 C7
12600 AURA 80014 2199 E7
16500 AURA 80013 2200 E7
19000 AURA 80013 2201 C6
W Baker Pl
13900 LKWD 80228 2277 B1
Baker Rd
10 PrkC 80456 2521 E1
7800 JfnC 80403 1936 B6
Baker St
200 LGMT 80501 1439 C2
1200 LGMT 80501 1356 C7
Balarat Rd
- BldC 80455 1515 E1
700 BldC 80455 1516 B1
Balboa Ct
1400 BMFD 80020 1774 E6
Balcolm Ct
300 ERIE 80516 1607 C5
Balcolm St
- ERIE 80516 1607 B4
Bald Eagle
10 JfnC 80127 2360 D3
Balderas St
3700 AdmC 80601 1697 B5
3700 BGTN 80601 1697 B5
E Baldwin Av
6400 DgsC 80138 2453 D5
Baldwin Cir
10 BldC 80025 1770 C7
Baldwin Ct
100 CSRK 80104 2788 A1
4600 DNVR 80216 2029 B6
13400 JfnC 80470 2608 D1
Baldwin Pl
4800 BLDR 80301 1603 B7
E Baldwin Gulch Cir
7000 DgsC 80138 2453 E6
Baldwin Park Cir
1200 CSRK 80104 2788 A1
Baldwin Park Rd
800 CSRK 80104 2788 A1
Baldwin Ranch Rd
100 CSRK 80104 2788 A1
Baldy Ln
1900 JfnC 80439 2189 C7
1900 JfnC 80439 2273 C1
Baler Ct
- BGTN 80601 1697 D4
Ball Rd
10 PrkC 80456 2521 E1
Ballantine Rd
600 JfnC 80401 2107 A7
Ballard Dr
2800 DgsC 80109 2785 E6
2800 DgsC 80109 2786 A6
2800 DgsC 80135 2785 E6
Ballard Wy
2600 DgsC 80109 2786 A6
Ballaret Ln
5000 DgsC 80108 2618 E6
Ballata Ct
1200 CSRK 80109 2703 B5
Balmora St
1100 LAFT 80026 1690 C3
Balmoral Ct
7300 DgsC 80108 2535 A7
Balsa Dr
300 CSRK 80104 2787 D1
Balsam Av
200 BGTN 80601 1696 A6
900 BLDR 80304 1686 C1
Balsam Cir
8100 ARVD 80005 1942 D5
Balsam Ct
9300 WSTR 80021 1942 D2
S Balsam Ct
1400 LKWD 80232 2194 D5
2100 LKWD 80227 2194 D7
6500 JfnC 80123 2362 D4
7600 JfnC 80128 2362 D6
8200 JfnC 80128 2446 D1
9300 DgsC 80126 2449 A4

Denver Regional Street Index

STREET
Block City ZIP Map# Grid

Balsam Dr
- TNTN 80260 1944 C2
1900 BLDR 80304 1686 D1
Balsam Ln
10 BldC 80304 1601 D5
S Balsam Ln
2300 LKWD 80227 2194 D7
Balsam Pl
5800 ARVD 80002 2026 D3
5800 ARVD 80004 2026 D3
Balsam St
100 LKWD 80226 2194 D1
400 LKWD 80226 2110 D7
2100 LKWD 80214 2110 D4
3200 JfnC 80215 2110 D2
3800 WTRG 80033 2110 D1
4400 WTRG 80033 2026 D7
5200 ARVD 80002 2026 D5
6000 ARVD 80004 2026 D3
9300 WSTR 80021 1942 D1
10400 JfnC 80021 1858 D6
10900 WSTR 80021 1858 D5
S Balsam St
- DNVR 80123 2278 D5
- DNVR 80235 2278 D5
10 LKWD 80226 2194 D2
1700 LKWD 80227 2194 D6
1700 LKWD 80232 2194 D6
2400 LKWD 80227 2278 D1
3500 JfnC 80227 2278 D3
3500 JfnC 80235 2278 D3
5000 LKWD 80123 2278 D6
7500 JfnC 80128 2362 D6
8300 JfnC 80128 2446 D1
Balsam Wy
8200 ARVD 80005 1942 C4
9100 WSTR 80021 1942 D2
S Balsam Wy
2400 LKWD 80227 2278 D1
6100 JfnC 80123 2362 D3
Balsamroot Rd
1600 DgsC 80118 2870 B7
1600 DgsC 80118 2954 B1
Balsum Ct
- ARVD 80002 2026 D4
E Baltic Av
17700 AURA 80013 2201 B6
W Baltic Av
9200 LKWD 80227 2194 B7
13800 LKWD 80228 2193 B7
E Baltic Cir
14200 AURA 80014 2200 B6
W Baltic Ct
6000 LKWD 80227 2195 B7
9400 LKWD 80227 2194 B7
11300 LKWD 80227 2193 E7
E Baltic Dr
11100 AURA 80014 2199 D7
17100 AURA 80013 2201 A7
W Baltic Dr
9200 LKWD 80227 2194 B7
13700 LKWD 80228 2193 B7
16200 LKWD 80228 2192 D7
E Baltic Pl
10900 AURA 80014 2199 D7
14100 AURA 80014 2200 C6
15900 AURA 80013 2200 D7
18600 AURA 80013 2201 C6
W Baltic Pl
1600 EGLD 80110 2196 B7
2200 DNVR 80219 2196 B7
13800 LKWD 80228 2193 B7
Baltimore Ct
5500 DNVR 80239 2032 B4
Baltusrol Ln
2500 JfnC 80439 2273 A1
Bamboo Ln
- TNTN 80260 1944 B1
Bancroft Dr
4600 CSRK 80104 2704 D6
Bandit Ln
10 PrkC 80456 2521 B1
Bandit Peak Rd
10 PrkC 80456 2521 D1
W Baneberry Ct
2600 DgsC 80129 2448 A6
Baneberry Ln
1500 JfnC 80401 2190 E6
W Baneberry Ln
2500 DgsC 80129 2448 A6
S Baneberry Pl
10200 DgsC 80129 2448 A6
S Baneberry St
10600 DgsC 80129 2448 A7
W Baneberry Wy
2500 DgsC 80129 2448 A7
Banff Ct
31200 JfnC 80439 2188 E6
Banneks
- LAFT 80026 1690 C5
Banner Cir
1200 ERIE 80516 1607 A2
Banner Ct
3700 EbtC 80138 2457 B4
E Banner St
- EbtC 80107 2793 B1
- ELIZ 80107 2793 B1
N Banner St
100 ELIZ 80107 2709 B7
100 ELIZ 80107 2793 B2
400 EbtC 80107 2709 B7
S Banner St
100 ELIZ 80107 2793 B1
700 EbtC 80107 2793 B1
Bannock Cir
12100 WSTR 80234 1860 D2
Bannock Dr
7900 DgsC 80118 2953 A3
S Bannock Dr
7200 LITN 80120 2364 D5
Bannock Ln
4400 JfnC 80439 2273 E6
Bannock Rd
8200 DgsC 80118 2953 C4
Bannock St
10 DNVR 80223 2196 D1
300 DNVR 80223 2112 D7
800 DNVR 80204 2112 D6
1400 DNVR 80202 2112 D6
4800 AdmC 80216 2028 D6
4800 DNVR 80216 2028 D6
7500 AdmC 80221 1944 D6
10100 NHGN 80260 1860 D6
10800 NHGN 80234 1860 D5
12100 WSTR 80234 1860 D1
15200 BfdC 80020 1776 D1
15200 BMFD 80020 1776 D1
S Bannock St
10 DNVR 80223 2196 D2
2500 DNVR 80223 2280 D1
2600 DvrC 80223 2280 D1
2600 EGLD 80110 2280 D1
2600 EGLD 80223 2280 D1
5300 LITN 80120 2364 E1
6000 LITN 80121 2364 D2
Bantala Pl
10 DgsC 80108 2618 E4
Bantry Ct
7500 DgsC 80124 2450 D6
Banyan Ct
300 CSRK 80104 2787 D1
Banyon Cir
12900 PARK 80134 2537 B5
Banyon Dr
- TNTN 80260 1944 C1
Baranmor Pkwy
12100 AURA 80010 2115 E2
12100 AURA 80011 2115 E2
12700 AURA 80011 2116 A1
Barbados Pl
3300 BLDR 80301 1603 A4
Barbara Cir
1100 WldC 80516 1607 D1
Barbara St
100 LSVL 80027 1773 D1
Barbara Ann Dr
7600 ARVD 80003 2026 D3
7600 ARVD 80004 2026 D3
Barber Dr
7800 JfnC 80021 1858 D6
7800 WSTR 80021 1858 D6
Barber Ln
10 BldC 80025 1770 D7
Barberry
- JfnC 80127 2361 A6
Barberry Av
500 LAFT 80026 1690 B5
Barberry Cir
700 LAFT 80026 1690 B5
W Barberry Cir
800 LSVL 80027 1689 A6
Barberry Ct
1100 BLDR 80305 1686 E7
W Barberry Ct
1800 LSVL 80027 1689 A6
Barberry Dr
600 LGMT 80503 1438 A4
Barberry Pl
8600 PARK 80134 2452 E2
W Barberry Pl
2900 DNVR 80204 2112 A6
Barbi Ct
1000 CSRK 80104 2703 D5
Barcelona Dr
10 BldC 80303 1688 D6
Barclay Ct
10800 AdmC 80640 1862 E5
10800 CMCY 80640 1862 E5
Barcus Ln
- BldC 80027 1772 E4
- SUPE 80027 1772 E4
Bardwell Av
22000 JfnC 80433 2527 B1
S Bardwell Rd
33600 JfnC 80470 2524 B7
Bari Ct
400 BldC 80303 1688 B7
Bark Cherry
10 JfnC 80127 2445 A1
S Barker Av
10900 JfnC 80433 2527 A1
Barker Rd
10 NDLD 80466 1765 E3
Barkley Rd
26400 JfnC 80433 2442 A6
Barkway Ct
7700 DgsC 80124 2450 D5
Barley Ct
- BldC 80503 1520 D4
Barley Ln
- WSTR 80021 1942 D3
Barn Blvd
- AdmC 80601 1779 A7
Barnacle Ct
4500 BldC 80301 1604 A3
Barnacle St
6500 BldC 80301 1604 A3
Barnard Ct
300 LGMT 80501 1438 E4
S Barnes Av
9300 JfnC 80433 2442 A4
Barnes Ln
10600 JfnC 80005 1942 A4
W Barnett Pl
4100 DNVR 80212 2111 D3
Barney Brook Dr
29300 JfnC 80433 2525 B2
S Barney Gulch Rd
10800 JfnC 80433 2525 C1
11100 JfnC 80433 2441 C7
Barnhart St
2500 TNTN 80229 1945 C2
S Barn Owl Dr
- DgsC 80130 2450 C5
Barnsley Ln
- PARK 80138 2538 D3
Barn Swallow Dr
2200 LGMT 80504 1438 D7
Barn Swallow Wy
5000 DgsC 80134 2622 C4
Baron Av
300 LAFT 80026 1690 C3
Baron Ct
300 ERIE 80516 1691 C3
3400 BMFD 80020 1775 E7
Barr Ct
3800 BLDR 80305 1687 A7
Barr Ln
4200 WSTR 80031 1943 C4
Barranca Dr
500 CSRK 80104 2703 D2
Barranca Ln
- CSRK 80104 2703 D2
- CSRK 80108 2703 D2
Barres St
1500 AdmC 80136 2125 E4
Barrett St
- CLCY 80403 2017 C3
N Barrett St
- PARK 80138 2453 D5
11800 DgsC 80138 2453 D5
Barrington
- TNTN 80260 1944 C2
E Barrington Av
4900 CSRK 80104 2704 D7
Barrington Dr
10 JfnC 80127 2360 E6
10 JfnC 80127 2361 B6
S Barrons Blvd
8800 DgsC 80129 2448 D3
Barrow Pl
10 LGMT 80501 1356 C7
Bartimous Rd
10 PrkC 80456 2521 E2
100 PrkC 80456 2522 A2
Bartlett
- TNTN 80260 1944 C2
Bartlett St
700 CSRK 80104 2788 D1
Barton Av
22000 JfnC 80433 2527 B1
Basalt Ct
400 GOLD 80403 2107 D1
3200 SUPE 80027 1857 A1
13600 BMFD 80020 1774 E5
Baseline Pl
700 BGTN 80603 1696 C3
Baseline Rd
- AdmC 80601 1696 B4
- AdmC 80601 1697 C4
- BGTN 80601 1696 B4
- BGTN 80601 1697 C4
- BGTN 80601 1698 A4
- BGTN 80603 1696 B4
- BGTN 80603 1697 C4
- BGTN 80603 1698 A4
- BLDR 80303 1686 E4
- BMFD 80020 1692 D4
- BMFD 80516 1692 D4
- TNTN 80020 1692 D4
- TNTN 80602 1692 D4
- WldC 80603 1696 B4
- WldC 80603 1697 C4
400 BldC 80302 1686 D4
2400 BLDR 80302 1686 E4
2400 BLDR 80305 1686 E4
5200 BldC 80303 1687 E4
5500 BLDR 80303 1687 E4
6000 BldC 80303 1688 A4
Baseline Rd SR-7
- BMFD 80020 1692 D4
- BMFD 80516 1692 D4
- TNTN 80020 1692 D4
- TNTN 80602 1692 D4
E Baseline Rd
100 LAFT 80026 1690 E4
700 BldC 80026 1690 E4
12000 BldC 80026 1691 A4
12000 ERIE 80026 1691 A4
12400 BldC 80516 1691 A4
12400 ERIE 80516 1691 A4
12500 BMFD 80020 1691 A4
E Baseline Rd SR-7
100 LAFT 80026 1690 E4
700 BldC 80026 1690 E4
12000 BldC 80026 1691 A4
12000 ERIE 80026 1691 A4
12400 BldC 80516 1691 A4
12400 ERIE 80516 1691 A4
12500 BMFD 80020 1691 A4
W Baseline Rd
100 LAFT 80026 1690 A4
7800 BldC 80026 1689 E4
7800 BldC 80303 1688 E4
7800 BldC 80303 1689 E4
7800 LSVL 80026 1689 E4
7800 LSVL 80303 1689 E4
9100 BldC 80027 1689 E4
9100 LAFT 80027 1689 E4
9300 LAFT 80026 1689 E4
10000 BldC 80026 1690 A4
W Baseline Rd SR-7
100 LAFT 80026 1690 B4
Basil Pl
2900 SUPE 80027 1773 B7
Bass Cir
100 LAFT 80026 1690 C3
Bassett Cir
- DNVR 80202 2112 C3
Bassett St
1500 DNVR 80202 2112 C3
E Basswood Ln
11500 DgsC 80116 2707 D2
Basswood St
2600 FLHT 80260 1944 A1
E Batavia Dr
15400 AURA 80011 2116 D4
19300 AURA 80011 2117 D4
Batavia Pl
4000 DNVR 80220 2113 E5
6500 DNVR 80220 2114 C4
E Batavia Pl
19300 AURA 80011 2117 D4
Bates Av
300 BLDR 80305 1687 A6
E Bates Av
10 EGLD 80110 2280 E1
10 EGLD 80113 2280 E1
700 EGLD 80113 2281 A1
2300 DNVR 80210 2281 C1
4800 DNVR 80222 2282 A1
5500 AphC 80222 2282 B1
6400 DNVR 80224 2282 C1
13600 AURA 80014 2284 A1
15300 AURA 80013 2284 D1
18800 AURA 80013 2285 D1
W Bates Av
10 EGLD 80113 2280 D1
2300 DNVR 80236 2280 B1
2400 EGLD 80110 2280 B1
3900 DNVR 80236 2279 D2
6900 DNVR 80227 2279 A2
7000 DNVR 80227 2278 E1
13600 LKWD 80228 2277 B1
E Bates Cir
12500 AURA 80014 2283 E1
12500 AURA 80014 2284 A1
E Bates Ct
11400 AURA 80014 2283 D1
W Bates Ct
14000 LKWD 80228 2277 B1
E Bates Dr
7400 DNVR 80231 2282 D1
16100 AURA 80013 2284 E1
19400 AURA 80013 2285 D1
E Bates Pkwy
1200 EGLD 80113 2281 A1
1300 DvrC 80210 2281 A1
1500 DNVR 80210 2281 B1
E Bates Pl
15900 AURA 80013 2284 E1
19300 AURA 80013 2285 D1
W Bates Pl
14500 LKWD 80228 2277 A1
Bates St
300 CLCY 80403 2017 E4
S Bathurst Wy
9800 DgsC 80130 2450 A5
Bauer Ct
9200 LNTR 80124 2450 E3
Bax Ct
6700 CMCY 80022 2030 C1
Baxter Dr
10900 PARK 80134 2453 B7
Baxter Farm Ln
- BldC 80516 1606 C6
- ERIE 80516 1606 C6
Bay Ln
10 PrkC 80456 2606 E7
S Bay Ln
9400 DgsC 80108 2535 A3
E Bayaud Av
- AphC 80018 2202 C1
- AURA 80018 2118 C7
- AURA 80018 2202 C1
10 DNVR 80209 2196 E1
10 DNVR 80223 2196 E1
3100 DNVR 80209 2197 D1
3900 DNVR 80246 2197 E1
4700 DNVR 80246 2198 A1
6500 DNVR 80224 2198 C1
6900 DNVR 80230 2198 C1
10500 AURA 80010 2199 C1
10500 AURA 80012 2199 C1
13600 AURA 80012 2200 A1
24600 AphC 80018 2203 A1
W Bayaud Av
10 DNVR 80209 2196 D1
2400 DNVR 80223 2196 A1
3000 DNVR 80219 2196 A1
3100 DNVR 80219 2195 E1
5100 LKWD 80226 2195 B1
7500 LKWD 80226 2194 E1
12100 LKWD 80228 2193 C2
14300 JfnC 80401 2193 A2
15100 JfnC 80401 2192 E2
W Bayaud Ct
15200 JfnC 80401 2192 E2
E Bayaud Dr
11500 AURA 80012 2199 D1
W Bayaud Dr
16100 JfnC 80401 2192 C2
E Bayaud Pl
15100 AURA 80012 2200 C1
W Bayaud Pl
7200 LKWD 80226 2194 E1
14300 JfnC 80401 2193 A2
Bayberry Ct
5300 BMFD 80020 1775 B5
Bayberry Dr
13700 BMFD 80020 1775 B5
Bayberry Ln
2200 CSRK 80104 2703 E4
Bayberry Wy
2100 ERIE 80516 1692 A2
Bayfield Wy
10800 PARK 80138 2453 E7
Bay Hill Dr
9600 LNTR 80124 2450 E4
Bay Hill Wy
9700 LNTR 80124 2450 E4
Baylor Dr
10 LGMT 80503 1355 B7
2900 BLDR 80305 1686 E7
2900 BLDR 80305 1687 A7
Baylor Ln
8100 WSTR 80031 1943 D4
Baylor Wy
100 LGMT 80503 1355 A7
Bay Oaks Av
22900 PARK 80138 2538 C3
Bay Oaks Ct
12000 PARK 80138 2538 C3
E Bayou Gulch Rd
- DgsC 80116 2621 E5
6900 DgsC 80134 2621 E5
6900 DgsC 80134 2622 C6
9700 DgsC 80134 2623 A7
9700 DgsC 80134 2707 A1
10100 DgsC 80116 2707 A1
Bayou Gulch St
4900 DgsC 80116 2621 D5
4900 DgsC 80134 2621 D5
E Bayou Hills Ln
9700 DgsC 80134 2622 E7
9700 DgsC 80134 2623 A7
N Bayou Hills Ln
3900 DgsC 80134 2623 A7
N Bayou Hills Rd
3600 DgsC 80134 2622 E7
Bayou Ridge Tr
9600 DgsC 80134 2622 E6
9600 DgsC 80134 2623 A6
Bay Point Ln
- BMFD 80020 1776 A3
Beach Cir
1100 BMFD 80020 1776 A6
Beach Ct
400 BMFD 80020 1776 C7
4400 DNVR 80211 2028 A6
5100 DNVR 80221 2028 A6
5400 AdmC 80221 2028 A4
7400 WSTR 80030 1944 A6
S Beach Ct
1100 DNVR 80219 2196 B4
Beach Rd
- BldC 80466 1683 E6
- BldC 80466 1684 A6
5400 BWMR 80123 2363 D1
Beach St
- AdmC 80221 1944 A5
- AdmC 80221 2028 A2
7000 WSTR 80030 1944 A7
10000 FLHT 80260 1860 A7
12400 BMFD 80020 1776 A7
12400 BMFD 80020 1860 A1
Beacham Dr
2100 CSRK 80104 2788 A1
Beachcomber Ct
4500 BldC 80301 1604 A3
Beacon Ct
1900 BldC 80302 1686 B2
1900 BLDR 80302 1686 B2
Beacon Wy
7000 WSTR 80030 1944 A7
7000 WSTR 80030 2028 A1
S Beacon Hill Ct
9600 DgsC 80126 2449 A4
E Beacon Hill Dr
900 DgsC 80126 2449 A4
W Beacon Hill Dr
100 BldC 80026 1690 C3
100 LAFT 80026 1690 C3
Bean Ct
900 ERIE 80516 1607 A7
Bean Mountain Ln
6600 BLDR 80301 1604 A1
Bear Dr
10 CCkC 80439 2271 E5
10 CCkC 80439 2272 A5
10 PrkC 80456 2606 D4
100 GpnC 80403 2019 E1
100 GpnC 80403 2020 A1
S Bear Mtn
7600 JfnC 80127 2361 E6
Bear Rd
3800 JfnC 80403 2022 D7
3800 JfnC 80403 2106 E1
Bear Canyon Cir
3400 DgsC 80135 2785 D2
Bear Canyon Tr
- BldC 80305 1770 C1
- BLDR 80305 1770 C1
Bearcat Tr
29500 JfnC 80433 2441 B5
E Bear Claw Av
10400 DgsC 80138 2539 B5
Bear Claw Dr
9500 JfnC 80127 2445 C4
Bear Claw Ln
- CCkC 80439 2272 A1
Bear Creek Av
100 MRSN 80465 2276 C3
900 JfnC 80465 2276 B3
Bear Creek Av SR-8
100 MRSN 80465 2276 C3
Bear Creek Av SR-74
17100 MRSN 80465 2276 C3
S Bear Creek Blvd
- LKWD 80228 2193 B7
2900 LKWD 80228 2277 B1
Bear Creek Dr
11600 DgsC 80116 2707 D1
11600 EbtC 80107 2707 D1
W Bear Creek Dr
3000 SRDN 80110 2280 A3
3100 SRDN 80110 2279 E3
6800 LKWD 80227 2279 A2
6900 LKWD 80227 2278 E2
10900 JfnC 80227 2277 E3
10900 JfnC 80227 2278 A2
Bear Creek Ln
100 MRSN 80465 2276 B3
Bear Creek Rd
17400 MRSN 80465 2276 A3
17600 JfnC 80465 2276 A3
18300 JfnC 80465 2275 D2
22100 JfnC 80439 2275 A1
22600 JfnC 80401 2275 A1
22800 JfnC 80401 2274 C2
22800 JfnC 80439 2274 C2
25200 JfnC 80457 2274 C2
Bear Creek Rd SR-74
17400 MRSN 80465 2276 A3
17600 JfnC 80465 2276 A3
18300 JfnC 80465 2275 D2
22100 JfnC 80439 2275 A1
22600 JfnC 80401 2275 A1
22800 JfnC 80401 2274 C2
22800 JfnC 80439 2274 C2
25200 JfnC 80457 2274 C2
Bear Dance Dr
6200 DgsC 80118 2870 E7
6700 DgsC 80118 2954 C1
N Bearlily Wy
4600 CSRK 80109 2702 E1
Bear Meadow Tr
- CCkC 80439 2271 C7
- CCkC 80439 2355 D1
Bear Mountain Ct
1200 BLDR 80305 1770 D1
Bear Mountain Dr
1100 BLDR 80305 1686 E7
1200 BLDR 80305 1770 E1
S Bear Mountain Dr
4700 JfnC 80439 2274 B7
5000 JfnC 80439 2358 C1
9000 DgsC 80126 2448 D3
Bear Park Rd
11900 JfnC 80433 2524 E4
Bear Paw Dr
4900 CSRK 80109 2702 C2
Bear Paw Rd
5300 JfnC 80403 2020 B5
Bear Point Tr
- JfnC 80403 2023 A2
Bear Ridge Wy
6500 JfnC 80403 2023 A2
Bear Rock Rd
10 CCkC 80439 2187 E7
Bear Tooth Dr
22100 JfnC 80403 2023 A3
Beas Dr
10400 JfnC 80433 2440 E7
10400 JfnC 80433 2524 E1
10400 JfnC 80433 2525 A1
Beas Ln
10300 JfnC 80433 2440 E7
Beasley Dr
- BldC 80026 1690 B2
- ERIE 80026 1690 B2
3800 ERIE 80516 1690 B2
Beatrice Ct
1400 LGMT 80503 1355 C7
Beaumont
- DNVR 80231 2283 B1
Beauprez Av
500 LAFT 80026 1689 D4
Beautiful Cir
4100 CSRK 80109 2702 D2
Beauty Ln
11600 JfnC 80403 1852 C3
Beauty Brush Ln
16200 DgsC 80134 2452 E2
16200 PARK 80134 2452 E2
Beaver Ct
100 CCkC 80439 2271 C6
Beaver Ln
10 CCkC 80439 2187 E5
Beaver Pt
400 LAFT 80026 1774 B1
Beaver Rd
10 GpnC 80403 1934 A6
N Beaver Rd
10 BldC 80403 1766 C6
Beaver Run
6800 DgsC 80125 2614 D2
Beaver Tr
- CCkC 80452 2186 A3
10 PrkC 80456 2606 E7
300 PrkC 80456 2690 E1
Beaver Wy
10 BldC 80304 1602 A6
Beaver Brook Dr
10 CCkC 80439 2187 E1
Beaver Brook Canyon Rd
10 CCkC 80439 2187 E1
S Beaver Creek Ct
12600 PARK 80134 2537 E3
Beaver Creek Dr
- AURA 80011 2117 B7
- AURA 80011 2201 B1
10 BldC 80466 1765 B3
10 NDLD 80466 1765 B3
Beaver Creek Ln
30200 JfnC 80439 2189 B5
S Beaver Creek Rd
600 GpnC 80403 1850 C5
3700 GpnC 80403 1766 E7
Beaver Creek St
300 AURA 80011 2117 B7
300 AURA 80011 2201 B1
S Beaver Creek Wy
12500 PARK 80134 2537 D4
Beaver Pond Rd
9700 JfnC 80433 2441 A5
Beaver Reservoir Rd
100 BldC 80481 1513 D2
100 BldC 80481 1514 A4
Becket Dr
17900 DgsC 80134 2453 B2
17900 PARK 80134 2453 B2
Beckett Ln
100 MRSN 80465 2276 C3
Beckman Pl
- DNVR 80249 2034 A6
Beckwith Pl
10 LGMT 80501 1356 C4
N Beckworth Ct
6100 DgsC 80134 2622 E3
Becky Cir
46900 EbtC 80107 2459 A1
Bedford
600 DNVR 80123 2278 E6
N Bedford Av
- CSRK 80104 2704 E7
S Bedford Av
- CSRK 80104 2704 E7
Bedford Ct
4600 BldC 80301 1604 D3
5500 DNVR 80239 2032 B4
Bedford Ln
- AdmC 80020 1776 D1
- BMFD 80020 1776 D1
Bedford Pl
700 DNVR 80123 2278 E6
Bedivere Cir
700 LAFT 80026 1690 E6
E Bedivere Cir
1500 LAFT 80026 1690 D6
W Bedivere Cir
1500 LAFT 80026 1690 D6
Bed Straw St
8300 DgsC 80134 2452 D1
Beech Cir
2600 LGMT 80503 1355 C5
S Beech Cir
1000 LKWD 80228 2193 B4
5600 GDVL 80121 2366 A1
6400 JfnC 80127 2361 C3
Beech Ct
100 ERIE 80516 1691 C2
2000 JfnC 80401 2109 C4
6300 ARVD 80004 2025 B2
6800 ARVD 80004 1941 B7
7300 ARVD 80005 1941 B6
S Beech Ct
- JfnC 80127 2361 D6
2200 LKWD 80228 2193 B7
5700 GDVL 80121 2365 E1
Beech Dr
6700 ARVD 80004 2025 B1
S Beech Dr
1000 LKWD 80228 2193 C4
W Beech Pl
500 LSVL 80027 1689 B6
Beech St
800 LKWD 80401 2109 B7
3200 JfnC 80401 2109 B2
5100 JfnC 80002 2025 B5
6800 ARVD 80004 1941 B7
6800 ARVD 80004 2025 B1
7100 ARVD 80005 1941 B7
7300 JfnC 80005 1941 B7
9700 FLHT 80260 1860 A7
10300 DgsC 80125 2530 E6
S Beech St
600 LKWD 80228 2193 B3
4800 JfnC 80465 2277 B6
13800 PrkC 80470 2608 A2
Beech St W
- ARVD 80005 1941 B4
Beech Wy
2700 LGMT 80503 1355 C5
S Beech Wy
2200 LKWD 80228 2193 B7
4300 JfnC 80465 2277 C5
Beechcraft Wy
37300 AdmC 80137 2038 A4
Beechnut Pl
- CSRK 80104 2704 A1
- CSRK 80108 2704 A1
Beechwood Dr
9000 TNTN 80229 1945 D2
E Beechwood Dr
10000 DgsC 80138 2455 A5
Beekman Pl
2600 DNVR 80216 2029 C6
E Beekman Pl
12100 DNVR 80239 2031 E5
W Beekman Pl
1500 DNVR 80221 2028 B5
S Beeler Ct
1100 AphC 80247 2199 A4
5200 GDVL 80111 2283 A7
Beeler St
- AURA 80238 2115 A4
- CMCY 80640 1862 E5
- DNVR 80238 2115 A3
- DvrC 80238 2115 A4
1100 AURA 80230 2115 A5
1400 AURA 80010 2115 A4
9400 CMCY 80640 1863 A4
14600 AdmC 80602 1779 A2
S Beeler St
1200 AphC 80247 2199 A4
1800 AphC 80231 2199 A5
3000 DNVR 80231 2283 A2
3600 DNVR 80237 2283 A3
4900 GDVL 80111 2283 A7
6000 GDVL 80111 2367 A2
6000 GDVL 80111 2367 A2
S Beeler Wy
2100 AphC 80231 2199 A7
N Bee Rock Rd
- DgsC 80135 2700 B6
500 DgsC 80135 2784 A1
Beethoven Dr
10 GpnC 80403 1934 C2
Begole Cir
11800 JfnC 80403 1853 B3
Begonia Wy
1400 SUPE 80027 1773 B7
1400 SUPE 80027 1857 B1
Belcaro Dr
3200 DNVR 80209 2197 D3
Belcaro Ln
3300 DNVR 80209 2197 D3
Belcher Hill Rd
24400 JfnC 80403 2022 C2
26400 JfnC 80403 1937 E7
26400 JfnC 80403 2021 E1
Beldock Ct
200 AdmC 80601 1697 A5
200 BGTN 80601 1697 A5
Beldock St
- BGTN 80601 1697 A5
Belero St
1500 BMFD 80020 1774 E7
Belevedere Ln
- LNTR 80124 2451 A6
W Belfast Pl
9400 LITN 80127 2446 B4
Belford Ct
1400 JfnC 80439 2188 D5

STREET
Block City ZIP Map# Grid

Belford Dr
100 NHGN 80260 1860 D7
Belford Rd
1600 TNTN 80260 1860 B7
Belfry Ct
700 DgsC 80108 2618 D5
Belgian Ct
3300 CSRK 80104 2703 E3
Belgian Tr
1000 EbtC 80107 2708 C3
Belgrade Dr
1100 EbtC 80138 2540 B6
Bell Ct
2000 LKWD 80215 2110 C4
2300 JfnC 80215 2110 C4
Bell Dr
1800 ERIE 80516 1690 C2
3100 BLDR 80301 1603 B7
Bell Ln
300 NHGN 80260 1860 D7
Bellaire Cir
11800 TNTN 80233 1861 E2
12200 TNTN 80241 1861 E1
13200 TNTN 80241 1777 E6
S Bellaire Cir
4200 CHLV 80113 2281 E5
4200 CHLV 80113 2282 A5
6500 CTNL 80121 2365 E4
Bellaire Ct
300 BMFD 80020 1775 A7
300 BMFD 80020 1859 B1
5600 GDVL 80121 2366 A1
10400 TNTN 80233 1861 E6
12300 TNTN 80241 1861 E1
13100 TNTN 80241 1777 E6
Bellaire Dr
9300 TNTN 80229 1945 E2
12400 TNTN 80241 1861 E1
13100 TNTN 80241 1777 E6
N Bellaire Dr
12400 TNTN 80241 1861 E1
Bellaire Pl
10800 TNTN 80233 1861 E5
12100 TNTN 80241 1861 E1
Bellaire St
- AdmC 80229 1945 E2
10 DNVR 80220 2197 E1
10 DNVR 80246 2197 E1
1100 BMFD 80020 1775 B6
1100 DNVR 80220 2113 E6
3200 DNVR 80207 2113 E2
6600 CMCY 80022 2029 E1
9300 TNTN 80229 1945 E2
11900 TNTN 80233 1861 D2
12400 TNTN 80241 1861 E1
13500 TNTN 80241 1777 E5
13500 TNTN 80602 1777 E5
S Bellaire St
10 DNVR 80220 2197 E1
1100 DNVR 80246 2197 E4
1100 GNDL 80246 2197 E4
1700 DNVR 80222 2197 E6
2500 DNVR 80222 2281 E1
3400 AphC 80222 2281 E2
3400 CHLV 80113 2281 E2
Bellaire Wy
12000 TNTN 80233 1861 E2
12000 TNTN 80241 1861 E2
S Bellaire Wy
5900 CTNL 80121 2365 E2
5900 GDVL 80121 2365 E2
6700 CTNL 80122 2365 E4
Bellanca Ct
2400 ERIE 80516 1691 C2
Bella Vista Dr
200 LSVL 80027 1773 C1
4200 LGMT 80503 1438 A6
4400 LGMT 80503 1437 E6
S Bella Vista Dr
10 LSVL 80027 1773 C1
Bella Vista Ln
2600 BLDR 80302 1686 E3
Bellavista St
- CSRK 80109 2702 E4
Bella Vista Wy
- LGMT 80503 1437 E5
Bellbrook Cir
10900 DgsC 80108 2449 C7
10900 DgsC 80108 2533 E1
10900 DgsC 80108 2534 A1
Bell Cross Cir
11200 DgsC 80138 2454 D6
Bell Cross Pl
9300 DgsC 80138 2454 E6
Bell Cross Wy
11800 DgsC 80138 2454 E5
Belle Creek Blvd
- AdmC 80640 1863 A4
- CMCY 80640 1862 E6
10900 CMCY 80640 1863 A4
Belle Meade Dr
11200 JfnC 80433 2525 D3
Belle Mont Tr
28000 JfnC 80433 2525 D2
Belle Pointe Dr
28600 JfnC 80433 2525 C1
E Belleview Av
- AphC 80015 2284 B7
- AphC 80016 2286 C7
- AphC 80016 2287 A7
- AURA 80015 2284 B7
- AURA 80016 2286 D6
- AURA 80016 2287 A7
- CTNL 80015 2284 C7
10 AphC 80121 2280 E7
10 EGLD 80110 2280 E7
10 EGLD 80113 2280 E7
10 EGLD 80121 2280 E7
600 AphC 80121 2281 C7
600 EGLD 80113 2281 C7
700 CHLV 80113 2281 C7
1300 GDVL 80113 2281 C7
2400 CHLV 80121 2281 C7
2400 GDVL 80121 2281 C7
E Belleview Av
4600 CHLV 80121 2282 A7
4600 GDVL 80121 2282 A7
5200 CHLV 80111 2282 D7
5200 GDVL 80111 2282 D7
6500 DNVR 80237 2282 E7
6500 DvrC 80237 2282 B7
6500 GDVL 80237 2282 B7
6600 DvrC 80111 2282 B7
8600 DNVR 80237 2283 D7
8600 DvrC 80237 2283 D7
8600 GDVL 80111 2283 D7
10100 AphC 80111 2283 D7
12100 AphC 80015 2283 D7
22500 AphC 80015 2286 C7
E Belleview Av SR-88
10 AphC 80121 2280 E7
10 EGLD 80110 2280 E7
10 EGLD 80113 2280 E7
10 EGLD 80121 2280 E7
600 AphC 80121 2281 C7
600 EGLD 80113 2281 C7
700 CHLV 80113 2281 C7
700 GDVL 80121 2281 C7
1300 GDVL 80113 2281 C7
2400 CHLV 80121 2281 C7
4600 CHLV 80121 2282 B7
4600 GDVL 80121 2282 B7
5200 CHLV 80111 2282 B7
5200 GDVL 80111 2282 B7
6500 AphC 80237 2282 B7
6500 DNVR 80237 2282 B7
6500 GDVL 80237 2282 B7
6600 DvrC 80111 2282 B7
W Belleview Av
- JfnC 80465 2277 A7
10 EGLD 80110 2280 A7
10 EGLD 80123 2280 C7
500 LITN 80120 2280 C7
900 EGLD 80120 2280 C7
2400 LITN 80123 2280 A7
3100 LITN 80123 2279 D7
3600 EGLD 80110 2279 D7
4300 AphC 80123 2279 D7
4300 BWMR 80123 2279 D7
4300 DNVR 80123 2279 D7
8100 LKWD 80123 2278 D7
8400 DNVR 80123 2278 D7
8400 DvrC 80123 2278 D7
9800 JfnC 80127 2278 A7
10800 JfnC 80127 2277 E7
14000 JfnC 80465 2360 D1
14000 JfnC 80465 2361 A1
W Belleview Av SR-88
10 EGLD 80110 2280 C7
10 EGLD 80123 2280 C7
500 LITN 80120 2280 C7
900 EGLD 80120 2280 C7
2400 LITN 80123 2280 C7
E Belleview Ct
10 GDVL 80121 2281 B7
E Belleview Dr
- CHLV 80113 2281 A7
10 GDVL 80121 2281 A7
14800 AURA 80015 2284 C7
16100 CTNL 80015 2284 E7
W Belleview Dr
11600 JfnC 80127 2277 D7
E Belleview Ln
1900 GDVL 80121 2281 B7
19900 CTNL 80015 2285 E7
22100 AphC 80015 2286 B7
E Belleview Pl
10 CHLV 80113 2281 B7
16200 CTNL 80015 2284 E7
19500 CTNL 80015 2285 D7
20600 AphC 80015 2285 E7
20800 CTNL 80015 2286 A7
22000 AphC 80015 2286 B7
W Belleview Pl
4100 LITN 80123 2279 D7
E Belleview Wy
10 GDVL 80121 2281 B7
Belle Vista Dr
27800 JfnC 80433 2525 D2
Bellevue Dr
10 BLDR 80302 1686 D5
1400 BLDR 80305 1686 D5
E Bellewood Cir
17400 AURA 80015 2285 A7
Bellewood Ct
9300 DgsC 80126 2449 A4
E Bellewood Dr
200 EGLD 80113 2280 E7
14000 AphC 80015 2284 B7
14000 AURA 80015 2284 B7
18000 AURA 80015 2285 B7
19700 CTNL 80015 2285 D6
24200 AURA 80016 2286 E6
W Bellewood Dr
4300 DNVR 80123 2279 D6
4300 DvrC 80123 2279 D6
4300 LITN 80123 2279 D6
E Bellewood Ln
20000 CTNL 80015 2285 D6
E Bellewood Pl
8500 DNVR 80237 2282 D6
8500 DNVR 80237 2283 A6
14300 AURA 80015 2284 C6
20000 CTNL 80015 2285 E6
20300 AphC 80015 2285 E7
20400 AphC 80015 2286 A6
W Bellewood Pl
10200 JfnC 80127 2278 A7
Bellflower
10 JfnC 80127 2361 A6
Bellflower Ct
8000 BldC 80503 1520 E5
Bellflower Dr
- AdmC 80601 1780 D2
- BGTN 80601 1780 D2
5800 LITN 80123 2363 D2
Bellflower Pl
- BGTN 80601 1780 D2
S Bell Flower Wy
9100 DgsC 80126 2449 A3
Bellgreen Pl
1300 CSRK 80104 2787 E4
Bellingham Pl
600 LGMT 80501 1356 D4
S Bellisario Creek Ct
12400 PARK 80134 2537 E3
E Bellisario Creek Dr
19400 PARK 80134 2537 D4
E Bellisario Creek Pl
18900 PARK 80134 2537 C4
Bellmeade Wy
2900 LGMT 80503 1355 B5
S Bellmore Ln
9400 DgsC 80126 2449 C4
Bellmore Pl
9600 DgsC 80126 2449 C4
Bell Mountain Dr
- DgsC 80104 2787 B7
3400 DgsC 80104 2871 B1
Bell Mountain Pkwy
10 DgsC 80104 2787 B7
10 DgsC 80104 2871 A1
Bell Star Cir
400 DgsC 80104 2871 B2
Bellview Ct
300 BldC 80501 1438 D2
300 LGMT 80501 1438 D2
Bellvue Rd
100 JfnC 80401 2191 C1
Bellwood Dr
1400 LGMT 80501 1356 E6
W Bellwood Dr
3000 EGLD 80110 2280 A7
3100 EGLD 80110 2279 E7
W Bellwood Pl
9200 DNVR 80123 2278 B7
10900 JfnC 80127 2278 A7
Bellwood St
- AURA 80016 2286 D6
W Belmar Av
8400 LKWD 80226 2194 C3
W Belmont Av
3300 LITN 80123 2279 E7
9000 JfnC 80123 2362 C1
9100 JfnC 80123 2278 C7
10800 JfnC 80127 2278 A7
10900 JfnC 80127 2277 E7
Belmont Dr
- LGMT 80501 1355 D6
1400 LGMT 80503 1355 D6
W Belmont Dr
7100 LKWD 80123 2278 E7
7100 LKWD 80123 2362 E1
11600 JfnC 80127 2361 D1
W Belmont Pl
11700 JfnC 80127 2277 D7
N Belmont Wy
5900 DgsC 80134 2623 A2
6100 DgsC 80134 2622 E2
Belo Horizonte Pkwy
100 DNVR 80220 2197 E1
W Beloit Pl
10500 JfnC 80227 2278 A2
10800 LKWD 80227 2277 E2
10800 LKWD 80227 2278 A2
Belsay Ct
16100 DgsC 80134 2452 E4
Belvedere St
1700 GOLD 80401 2108 A3
S Bemis Cir
7900 LITN 80120 2364 B7
S Bemis Ct
7500 LITN 80120 2364 B6
S Bemis Pl
7900 LITN 80120 2364 B7
S Bemis St
5700 LITN 80120 2364 B2
Ben Pl
6100 BldC 80301 1688 A2
6100 BLDR 80301 1688 A2
Benchmark Dr
10 BldC 80303 1772 C1
Bendemeer Dr
10 CCkC 80439 2271 D6
Bennet Mountain Rd
1500 CSRK 80109 2703 C5
Bennett Av
- AdmC 80102 2124 C2
- BNNT 80102 2124 C2
Bennett Dr
17000 PARK 80134 2453 A6
W Bennett Pl
6800 LKWD 80227 2279 A2
Bennett Rd
- AdmC 80102 2124 D2
- BNNT 80102 2124 D2
Ben Nevis Av
1300 BMFD 80020 1859 B1
E Bennington Av
4200 CSRK 80104 2704 C7
Ben Park Cir
5300 DgsC 80134 2621 D4
Bent Wy
- LGMT 80501 1438 D4
- LGMT 80503 1438 D4
Bent Feather Rd
23300 JfnC 80433 2526 E4
Bent Grass Cir
1200 CSRK 80109 2703 B5
Benthaven Dr
11200 LKWD 80215 2109 E3
Benthaven Pl
10 BLDR 80305 1770 E1
E Bentley Cir
7100 CTNL 80112 2366 D4
N Bentley St
600 CSRK 80104 2704 E6
Bently St
16100 AdmC 80603 1699 D5
Bent Oaks Ct
23400 PARK 80138 2538 D2
Bent Oaks St
11700 PARK 80138 2538 D2
Bent Oaks Wy
23400 PARK 80138 2538 D2
Benton Cir
6500 ARVD 80003 2027 B2
S Benton Cir
5600 JfnC 80123 2363 C2
Benton Ct
5300 ARVD 80003 2027 B2
6800 WSTR 80003 2027 B1
11500 WSTR 80020 1859 B3
S Benton Ct
2300 LKWD 80227 2195 C7
6100 JfnC 80123 2363 B3
7300 JfnC 80128 2363 B6
S Benton Dr
10 LKWD 80226 2195 B1
Benton Pl
10900 PARK 80134 2453 B7
Benton St
- DNVR 80002 2027 B5
- DNVR 80212 2027 B5
- JfnC 80002 2027 B5
10 LKWD 80226 2195 B1
200 CSRK 80104 2704 D7
500 LKWD 80226 2111 B7
2400 EDGW 80214 2111 B3
3200 WTRG 80214 2111 B2
4000 WTRG 80212 2111 B1
4100 MNVW 80212 2027 B6
4100 WTRG 80212 2027 B7
4800 DvrC 80212 2027 B6
4800 LKSD 80212 2027 B6
5400 LKWD 80214 2111 B4
6400 ARVD 80003 2027 B2
7400 WSTR 80003 1943 B6
8400 ARVD 80003 1943 B4
8800 WSTR 80031 1943 B2
11000 WSTR 80020 1859 B4
14400 BldC 80020 1775 B3
14400 BMFD 80020 1775 B3
N Benton St
10000 WSTR 80020 1859 B7
S Benton St
- JfnC 80123 2363 C4
100 LKWD 80226 2195 B2
1200 LKWD 80232 2195 B4
2600 DNVR 80227 2279 B1
2600 LKWD 80227 2279 B1
Benton Wy
5000 DNVR 80212 2027 B5
8100 ARVD 80003 1943 B5
N Benton Wy
11500 WSTR 80020 1859 B3
S Benton Wy
3700 DNVR 80235 2279 C4
6200 JfnC 80123 2363 C3
W Benton Wy
5700 JfnC 80123 2363 B2
Bentwood Cir
10100 DgsC 80126 2449 D6
Bentwood Ct
10200 DgsC 80126 2449 D6
Bentwood Ln
10200 DgsC 80126 2449 D6
Bentwood Pl
3100 DgsC 80126 2449 D6
Berea Dr
1000 BLDR 80305 1687 A7
1100 BLDR 80305 1771 A1
Beren St
10 PrkC 80456 2522 A1
Berg Ln
33400 JfnC 80470 2524 B3
Berganot Tr
900 DgsC 80108 2534 C6
Bergen Pkwy
- JfnC 80439 2189 A4
1100 JfnC 80439 2188 E6
Bergen Hill Dr
2800 JfnC 80439 2273 A2
Bergen Mountain Rd
33000 JfnC 80439 2272 C3
Bergen Peak Dr
- JfnC 80439 2272 E2
2900 JfnC 80439 2273 A2
Bergen Rock St
1400 CSRK 80109 2703 A5
Bergen View Tr
33800 JfnC 80439 2272 B6
Berkeley Cir
7300 DgsC 80108 2534 D7
Berkeley Ct
1000 LGMT 80503 1438 C1
7400 DgsC 80108 2534 E7
E Berkeley Pl
12200 DNVR 80239 2031 E5
W Berkeley Pl
1500 DNVR 80221 2028 B5
Berkley Av
3400 BLDR 80305 1687 A5
Berkley Ct
3300 BLDR 80305 1687 A5
Berkshire Ct
4700 BldC 80301 1604 D3
7500 DgsC 80108 2535 A7
30000 JfnC 80439 2189 B7
Berkshire Ln
- EGLD 80113 2281 B3
7500 DgsC 80108 2535 A7
7700 DgsC 80108 2534 E6
Berkshire Pl
4600 BldC 80301 1604 D3
Berkshire St
4700 BldC 80301 1604 D3
Berlin Cir
6100 ARVD 80004 2026 A3
N Bermont Av
100 LAFT 80026 1690 C4
S Bermont Av
100 LAFT 80026 1690 C5
S Bermont Dr
500 LAFT 80026 1690 C5
N Bermont St
300 LAFT 80026 1690 C4
N Bermuda Dunes Dr
31300 JfnC 80439 2188 E6
S Bermuda Dunes Dr
31300 JfnC 80439 2188 E6
S Bermuda Run Cir
8900 DgsC 80130 2450 C3
Berrian Tr
26900 JfnC 80433 2442 A6
E Berry Av
- AphC 80015 2369 C1
- AphC 80015 2370 C1
- AphC 80016 2370 D1
- AURA 80016 2370 D1
- CTNL 80015 2369 C1
5600 GDVL 80111 2366 B1
5600 GDVL 80121 2366 B1
8900 GDVL 80111 2367 A1
10700 AphC 80111 2367 C1
16300 CTNL 80015 2368 E1
17800 CTNL 80015 2285 B7
20900 CTNL 80015 2370 A1
W Berry Av
400 LITN 80120 2364 D1
2700 LITN 80123 2364 A1
3300 LITN 80123 2363 E1
5700 DNVR 80123 2363 B1
8700 DNVR 80123 2362 C1
8700 JfnC 80123 2362 C1
10700 JfnC 80127 2362 A1
10800 JfnC 80127 2361 E1
Berry Cir
2700 JfnC 80401 2109 A3
W Berry Cir
500 LITN 80120 2364 D1
E Berry Ct
9100 GDVL 80111 2367 A1
E Berry Dr
9900 GDVL 80111 2367 B1
10400 AphC 80111 2367 B1
17800 CTNL 80015 2369 B1
18500 AphC 80015 2369 C1
20100 CTNL 80015 2285 E7
20800 CTNL 80015 2370 A1
W Berry Dr
900 LITN 80120 2364 C1
3400 LITN 80123 2363 E1
9800 JfnC 80123 2362 B1
10100 JfnC 80127 2362 A1
12800 JfnC 80127 2361 C1
Berry Ln
2700 JfnC 80401 2109 A3
E Berry Ln
- AphC 80015 2370 B1
16500 CTNL 80015 2368 E1
20100 CTNL 80015 2369 E1
21800 CTNL 80015 2370 B1
S Berry Ln
5400 GDVL 80111 2367 A1
E Berry Pl
7800 GDVL 80111 2366 D1
10800 AphC 80111 2367 C1
16300 CTNL 80015 2368 E1
18700 AphC 80015 2369 C1
20200 CTNL 80015 2369 E1
21800 CTNL 80015 2370 B1
22100 AphC 80015 2370 B1
24500 AURA 80016 2286 E7
24600 AURA 80016 2287 A7
W Berry Pl
3400 LITN 80123 2363 E1
9200 JfnC 80123 2362 C1
10600 JfnC 80127 2362 A1
11500 JfnC 80127 2361 E1
Berry Rd
14000 JfnC 80401 2109 A3
S Berry Bush Ln
6300 JfnC 80439 2357 D4
Berry Hill Ln
- JfnC 80470 2608 D1
Berry Turn
2700 JfnC 80401 2109 A3
Bert Dr
32600 JfnC 80433 2440 C3
S Bertha Ct
9000 JfnC 80465 2443 A3
Berthoud St
7100 WSTR 80030 1944 A7
Berthoud Tr
200 BMFD 80020 1774 E4
Berthoud Wy
200 GOLD 80401 2192 A1
200 JfnC 80401 2192 A1
10500 PARK 80134 2453 A6
Berwick Ct
7600 BldC 80301 1604 D3
Beryl St
300 BMFD 80020 1858 E1
600 BMFD 80020 1774 E7
Beryl Wy
100 BMFD 80020 1858 E1
N Beshear Ct
- ERIE 80516 1607 A6
S Beshear Ct
- ERIE 80516 1607 A6
Betasso Rd
10 BldC 80302 1685 A2
Beth Ct
4100 EbtC 80107 2709 C6
Beth Ln
1200 NHGN 80234 1860 C5
E Bethany Cir
17100 AURA 80013 2285 A2
E Bethany Dr
10600 AURA 80014 2283 C1
10600 DNVR 80014 2283 C1
19400 AURA 80013 2285 D1
E Bethany Pl
6400 DNVR 80222 2282 C1
6500 DNVR 80224 2282 C1
7800 DNVR 80231 2282 D1
12400 AURA 80014 2283 E1
13600 AURA 80014 2284 A1
E Bethany Pl
16100 AURA 80013 2284 D1
16900 AURA 80013 2285 A1
Bethel Ct
1300 CSRK 80109 2703 B6
Bethlehem Cir
2700 BMFD 80020 1776 B7
Bettencourt Av
- DgsC 80126 2449 A6
Betts Cir
2500 ERIE 80516 1690 D1
Betts Ranch Rd
- DgsC 80134 2538 D7
- DgsC 80134 2622 D1
S Betty Ln
6300 JfnC 80439 2357 B4
Betty Pl
4600 WldC 80516 1607 E2
S Betty St
3600 DgsC 80108 2619 C7
3600 DgsC 80108 2703 C1
Beverly Blvd
7200 DgsC 80108 2535 B7
Beverly Dr
4600 EGLD 80110 2280 C6
Beverly Ln
4600 WldC 80516 1607 E2
Beverly Rd
33300 JfnC 80470 2524 B6
E Bexley Ct
400 DgsC 80126 2448 E4
S Bexley Dr
9400 DgsC 80126 2448 E4
E Bexley Ln
400 DgsC 80126 2448 E4
E Bexley St
400 DgsC 80126 2448 E5
Bexley Close
10300 TNTN 80229 1861 B6
Bibles Hill Dr
1900 DgsC 80116 2706 E4
1900 DgsC 80116 2707 A3
Bierstadt Ct
1500 JfnC 80439 2188 D6
Bierstadt Rd
9800 TNTN 80260 1860 B7
Bierstadt Wy
10500 DgsC 80112 2451 C4
E Big Bnd
11200 WldC 80504 1440 E2
W Big Bnd
3300 WldC 80504 1440 D2
Big Bear Cir
2200 DgsC 80135 2786 A2
2700 DgsC 80135 2785 E2
Big Bear Dr
1600 DgsC 80109 2786 B1
1600 DgsC 80135 2786 B1
2200 DgsC 80135 2785 E1
3100 DgsC 80109 2701 D7
3100 DgsC 80135 2701 D7
31000 JfnC 80439 2189 A5
Bigbee Rd
10 BldC 80481 1514 D5
Bigbee High Rd
10 BldC 80481 1514 C5
Big Canon Dr
5600 GDVL 80111 2367 A1
Big Canon Pl
8900 GDVL 80111 2367 A2
Bigcone Spruce
10 JfnC 80127 2445 A1
Big Dry Creek Dr
2600 BMFD 80020 1860 A1
12500 BMFD 80020 1776 B7
E Big Dry Creek Dr
8200 CTNL 80112 2366 E6
Big Game Tr
23000 JfnC 80433 2526 E7
23000 JfnC 80433 2527 A7
23000 JfnC 80433 2611 A1
Big Horn Cir
2600 LAFT 80026 1774 C1
Bighorn Ct
1100 LGMT 80501 1356 C7
8200 LNTR 80124 2450 E3
S Bighorn Dr
9100 JfnC 80127 2445 D3
Big Horn Tr
6400 DgsC 80125 2614 E2
Big Horn Wy
9500 DgsC 80125 2531 B6
Big Jack Ct
- BldC 80466 1682 B6
Big Rock Ln
10 PrkC 80456 2690 E2
Big Sky Ct
1100 JfnC 80439 2189 A5
Big Springs Dr
10 NDLD 80466 1765 D3
Bill Davis Rd
10 DgsC 80116 2791 D1
Billings Av
11200 BldC 80026 1606 D5
S Billings Cir
4300 AURA 80015 2284 B5
S Billings Ct
- AURA 80015 2284 B6
4800 AphC 80015 2284 B6
Billings Ln
2200 LGMT 80501 1356 D4
Billings St
3200 AURA 80011 2116 B2
5500 DNVR 80239 2032 B4
10400 CMCY 80022 1864 B5
S Billings St
- AURA 80014 2200 B6
1200 AURA 80012 2200 B4
S Billings Wy
6200 CTNL 80111 2368 B2
Billington Dr
3100 ERIE 80516 1690 B2
S Bilox Ct
- AURA 80016 2370 D6
S Bilox Wy
- AURA 80016 2370 D6
Biloxi Ct
10 AphC 80018 2202 D1
S Biloxi Ct
- AURA 80016 2370 D5
1300 AURA 80018 2202 D4
S Biloxi St
700 AphC 80018 2202 D3
5200 AphC 80016 2286 D7
Biloxi Wy
- AURA 80016 2286 D6
S Biloxi Wy
- AphC 80016 2370 D1
7600 AURA 80016 2370 D6
S Biltmore Wy
9600 DgsC 80126 2449 A4
Bimini Ct
4000 BLDR 80301 1603 A5
W Bingham Pl
4500 DNVR 80219 2195 C2
5000 LKWD 80219 2195 C3
5000 LKWD 80226 2195 C3
Birch Av
100 CSRK 80104 2787 E1
200 BGTN 80601 1696 A6
200 CSRK 80104 2704 A7
200 CSRK 80104 2788 A1
2100 TNTN 80241 1777 B7
3000 BLDR 80305 1687 A5
E Birch Av
3000 DgsC 80134 2452 C4
Birch Cir
300 BGTN 80601 1696 A7
13300 TNTN 80241 1777 E6
S Birch Cir
6400 CTNL 80121 2365 E3
Birch Ct
- TNTN 80233 1861 E5
10 LGMT 80503 1438 C1
5800 GDVL 80121 2366 A2
13300 TNTN 80241 1777 E5
S Birch Ct
5300 GDVL 80121 2282 A7
7700 CTNL 80122 2365 E6
W Birch Ct
600 LSVL 80027 1689 A6
Birch Dr
- TNTN 80260 1944 C2
11600 TNTN 80233 1861 E3
11900 TNTN 80241 1861 E3
12800 TNTN 80241 1777 E7
Birch Ln
- LITN 80120 2363 E7
- LITN 80120 2447 E1
28500 JfnC 80433 2525 D4
Birch St
- TNTN 80229 1861 E6
10 DNVR 80220 2197 E1
10 DNVR 80246 2197 E1
200 BNNT 80102 2124 D2
300 BMFD 80020 1859 B1
1000 GOLD 80401 2107 D3
1700 BMFD 80020 1775 B5
2000 DNVR 80220 2113 E3
2700 FLHT 80260 1860 A7
3200 DNVR 80207 2113 E2
6600 CMCY 80022 2029 E1
6900 AdmC 80022 1945 E7
7000 CMCY 80022 1945 E7
9400 TNTN 80229 1945 E1
11500 TNTN 80233 1861 E3
12200 TNTN 80241 1861 E1
14000 AdmC 80602 1777 E3
S Birch St
10 DNVR 80220 2197 E1
300 GNDL 80246 2197 E2
1100 DNVR 80246 2197 E4
1200 DNVR 80222 2197 E4
2800 DNVR 80222 2281 E2
3400 AphC 80222 2281 E3
3900 CHLV 80113 2281 E4
4900 CHLV 80121 2281 E6
4900 GDVL 80121 2281 E6
7200 CTNL 80122 2365 E5
Birch Wy
- BMFD 80020 1775 B7
13400 TNTN 80241 1777 E5
S Birch Wy
5900 CTNL 80121 2365 E2
6700 CTNL 80122 2365 E4
Birchleaf Ct
1600 CSRK 80104 2703 E4
1600 CSRK 80104 2704 A4
Birchwood Ct
1500 LAFT 80026 1689 E1
S Birchwood Ct
11400 PARK 80138 2538 E2
Birchwood Dr
3800 BLDR 80304 1602 E5
S Birchwood St
11300 PARK 80138 2538 E1
Bird Cliff Wy
6600 BldC 80503 1520 E5
Birdie Ct
4200 BldC 80503 1519 A6
Birdie Ln
10 CBVL 80123 2363 E3
Birdie Rd
1100 BMFD 80020 1775 A7
Birdsill Pl
10 LGMT 80501 1356 C4
Birmingham Ct
10 DgsC 80130 2450 A2
Biscay Cir
1600 AURA 80011 2117 C4
S Biscay Cir
- AphC 80015 2369 C1
- CTNL 80015 2369 C1
3000 AURA 80013 2285 C2
5400 CTNL 80015 2285 C7
Biscay Ct
5100 DNVR 80249 2033 C5

STREET
Block City ZIP Map# Grid

S Biscay Ct
1100 AURA 80017 2201 C4
2400 AURA 80013 2201 C7
2800 AURA 80013 2285 C1
4700 AURA 80015 2285 C6
5100 CTNL 80015 2285 C7
5600 AphC 80015 2369 C1
6000 AphC 80016 2369 C2
Biscay St
1700 AURA 80011 2117 C4
4300 DNVR 80249 2033 C6
S Biscay St
1100 AURA 80011 2201 C4
1100 AURA 80017 2201 C4
2900 AURA 80013 2285 C1
4300 AURA 80015 2285 C5
5700 AphC 80015 2369 C1
6000 AphC 80016 2369 C2
7500 CTNL 80016 2369 C6
S Biscay Wy
1400 AURA 80017 2201 C4
3200 AURA 80013 2285 C2
4300 AURA 80015 2285 C5
6000 AphC 80016 2369 C2
Biscayne
- DNVR 80210 2197 D5
Biscayne Ct
300 LAFT 80026 1690 C3
E Biscayne Ct
2100 DgsC 80126 2449 B4
Biscuit Root Dr
17700 PARK 80134 2453 B2
Bishop Ct
900 CSRK 80104 2703 E7
Bishop Rd
10 PrkC 80456 2521 E3
300 PrkC 80456 2522 A3
Bison Ct
7500 DgsC 80125 2531 A7
Bison Dr
10 BldC 80302 1769 C3
200 BldC 80302 1685 D7
Bison Pl
7400 DgsC 80125 2531 A7
Bison Tr
5300 BWMR 80123 2279 B5
S Bit Rd
3200 JfnC 80439 2273 B3
Bitterbrush Ln
16800 PARK 80134 2453 A1
E Bittercress Ct
17600 PARK 80134 2453 B4
Bitterroot Cir
2400 LAFT 80026 1689 E3
Bitterroot Ln
2100 JfnC 80401 2190 D7
2100 JfnC 80401 2274 D1
W Bitterroot Pl
2200 DgsC 80129 2448 B3
Bittersweet Ln
700 LGMT 80503 1438 A4
3100 JfnC 80439 2274 B3
Bitterweed Ct
9100 DgsC 80126 2448 E3
Bixby Ct
2800 CSRK 80109 2702 D4
Bixby Ln
2900 BLDR 80303 1687 A4
BJ Hurst Rd
11900 JfnC 80433 2525 C3
Black Hls
3300 WldC 80504 1440 D2
Black Bear Ct
2600 LAFT 80026 1774 C2
Black Bear Ln
10 JfnC 80127 2360 E4
24100 JfnC 80433 2526 D3
Black Bear Run
5100 DgsC 80125 2614 E5
Black Bear Tr
22800 JfnC 80433 2526 E4
Black Birch Rd
10 JfnC 80401 2190 D1
S Blackbird Cir
9900 DgsC 80130 2450 C5
Blackbird Ct
1200 BldC 80303 1688 A3
Blackbird Dr
10 PrkC 80456 2607 A7
S Blackbird Pl
9900 DgsC 80130 2450 C5
E Blackbird Wy
- DgsC 80130 2450 C5
Black Cherry Ct
4200 BldC 80301 1603 A4
Black Diamond Dr
400 LAFT 80026 1690 B4
Black Feather Tr
- CSRK 80109 2703 D3
3700 CSRK 80104 2703 D3
Blackfeather Tr
31400 JfnC 80439 2272 E3
W Blackfoot Cir
6000 DgsC 80135 2700 D1
Blackfoot Ct
- KIOW 80117 2796 A3
S Blackfoot Rd
11400 JfnC 80433 2525 C4
Blackfoot St
300 SUPE 80027 1772 D3
E Black Forest Dr
10200 DgsC 80138 2455 B3
Black Fox Cir
- EbtC 80107 2625 D5
Black Fox Ln
10 GDVL 80111 2282 C7
Black Gulch Rd
- GpnC 80403 1851 D2
Blackgum St
8300 DgsC 80134 2452 D1
Blackhawk Cir
3200 AURA 80011 2116 B2
S Blackhawk Cir
4200 AURA 80014 2284 B5
E Blackhawk Ct
6700 DgsC 80130 2450 C5
S Blackhawk Ct
5000 AphC 80015 2284 B7
6200 AphC 80016 2368 B2
6200 CTNL 80111 2368 B2
Black Hawk Dr
11700 JfnC 80433 2526 B4
Blackhawk Ln
300 LAFT 80026 1689 E4
300 LAFT 80026 1690 A4
Blackhawk Rd
500 BLDR 80303 1687 D5
Blackhawk St
- AdmC 80022 1864 B6
- AdmC 80601 1780 B5
- CMCY 80022 1864 B6
200 AURA 80011 2200 B1
3000 AURA 80011 2116 B2
N Blackhawk St
400 AURA 80011 2116 B7
S Blackhawk St
- AURA 80014 2200 B6
- AURA 80014 2284 B1
- CTNL 80112 2368 B5
700 AURA 80012 2200 B3
6600 AphC 80016 2368 B5
6600 AphC 80111 2368 B5
6600 CTNL 80111 2368 B5
7100 AphC 80112 2368 B5
Black Hawk Tr
12200 JfnC 80433 2526 B4
Blackhawk Wy
5500 AdmC 80022 2032 B4
5500 DNVR 80022 2032 B4
5500 DNVR 80239 2032 B4
E Blackhawk Wy
14100 AdmC 80022 1864 B7
14100 CMCY 80022 1864 B7
S Blackhawk Wy
- CTNL 80111 2368 B3
10 AURA 80011 2200 B1
1200 AURA 80012 2200 B4
3400 AURA 80014 2284 B2
4300 AURA 80015 2284 A5
6300 AphC 80016 2368 B3
Blackmer Rd
10 CHLV 80113 2281 E5
10 CHLV 80113 2282 A5
Blackmoor Av
- PARK 80138 2538 C2
Blackmoor St
- PARK 80138 2538 C2
S Black Mountain Dr
7900 JfnC 80433 2356 C7
7900 JfnC 80433 2440 C1
7900 JfnC 80439 2356 C7
S Black Mountain Dr CO-78
7900 JfnC 80433 2356 C7
7900 JfnC 80433 2440 C1
7900 JfnC 80439 2356 C7
Black Oak Ct
16600 DgsC 80134 2452 E6
Black Pine Ct
1300 CSRK 80104 2704 B5
Black Pine Dr
2600 CSRK 80104 2704 B5
Black Spruce Ln
46000 EbtC 80138 2456 A4
Black Squirrel Run
5100 DgsC 80125 2614 E5
E Blackstone Ct
1500 DgsC 80126 2449 B2
Blackstone Pkwy
- AURA 80016 2371 D7
Black Swan Ln
10 CHLV 80113 2281 B4
Blacktail Dr
4000 CSRK 80109 2702 D3
Blacktail Mtn
11600 JfnC 80127 2361 D5
E Blackthorn Wy
16200 PARK 80134 2536 E1
Black Widow Dr
31400 JfnC 80433 2440 E2
Black Widow Wy
31500 JfnC 80433 2440 E2
Blackwolf Dr
11000 PARK 80138 2454 C7
11000 PARK 80138 2538 C1
Blackwolf Ln
11000 PARK 80138 2454 C7
11000 PARK 80138 2538 C1
Blackwolf Wy
22900 PARK 80138 2454 D7
23100 DgsC 80138 2454 D7
Blair Dr
1600 IDSP 80452 2101 C5
Blakcomb Ct
1500 JfnC 80439 2189 B6
Blake Dr
- DgsC 80129 2448 D3
Blake St
1300 DNVR 80204 2112 C4
1400 DNVR 80202 2112 C4
1900 DNVR 80205 2112 D3
3300 DNVR 80205 2113 A1
3700 DNVR 80205 2029 A7
Blakeland Ct
13600 DgsC 80125 2447 E2
Blakeland Dr
8000 DgsC 80125 2447 D2
Blanca Ct
5900 JfnC 80403 2024 A3
6000 ARVD 80403 2024 A3
Blanca Ln
- BMFD 80020 1775 C4
Blanca Rd
9900 TNTN 80260 1860 B7
Blanca St
5600 JfnC 80403 2024 A4
Blanca Peak Ct
3400 SUPE 80027 1857 B1
Blanca Peak Dr
3500 SUPE 80027 1857 A1
4400 CSRK 80109 2786 E5
4400 CSRK 80109 2787 A5
N Blandford Cir
5200 DgsC 80134 2622 A4
Blanketflower Ln
9600 DgsC 80138 2539 A2
E Blazing Ln
2800 DgsC 80126 2449 C1
Blazing Star Pl
8400 PARK 80134 2452 D2
N Blazingstar Tr
4500 CSRK 80109 2702 D1
Block Ct
200 ERIE 80516 1606 D6
Bloom Pl
5100 CSRK 80109 2702 C4
Bloomfield Al
- LYNS 80540 1352 D1
Blossom Ct
10300 DgsC 80134 2452 D6
S Bluebead Wy
9500 PARK 80134 2453 B4
Bluebell Av
1300 BLDR 80302 1686 D5
Bluebell Cir
32900 JfnC 80439 2356 C4
Blue Bell Dr
10 CCkC 80439 2187 E5
Bluebell Dr
1600 BGTN 80601 1780 C2
Blue Bell Ln
10 CCkC 80452 2186 A3
Bluebell Ln
5700 JfnC 80439 2356 D3
Bluebell Pl
16200 DgsC 80134 2452 E1
Bluebell Rd
- BldC 80302 1686 C5
- BLDR 80302 1686 C5
Bluebell Tr
5100 EbtC 80107 2625 E1
Bluebell Wy
1100 BGTN 80601 1780 C2
8200 AdmC 80221 1944 C4
8200 TNTN 80221 1944 C4
Blueberry Cir
- BLDR 80304 1602 D4
Blueberry Tr
10 PrkC 80456 2607 E7
10 PrkC 80456 2608 A7
Bluebird Av
6300 BldC 80503 1520 A3
Bluebird Ct
6300 BldC 80503 1520 A4
Blue Bird Dr
2200 LGMT 80504 1438 E7
Bluebird Dr
10 PrkC 80456 2607 A7
10 PrkC 80456 2691 B1
Blue Bird Ln
700 BldC 80026 1689 B4
700 LSVL 80026 1689 B4
Bluebird Ln
10 PrkC 80456 2691 B1
33000 EbtC 80107 2793 D1
37000 EbtC 80107 2624 C7
37000 EbtC 80107 2708 C1
N Bluebird Ln
10200 DgsC 80138 2455 B2
S Bluebird Rd
6700 JfnC 80465 2359 A4
Bluebird St
1100 BGTN 80601 1779 E1
Bluebird Tr
1500 EbtC 80107 2792 C6
Blue Blood Ct
10000 DgsC 80125 2530 E5
10000 DgsC 80125 2531 A5
Blue Bonnet Ct
5300 CSRK 80109 2702 E1
Blue Bonnet Dr
100 BGTN 80601 1697 B5
Bluebonnet Dr
15900 DgsC 80134 2452 E5
Bluebunch Ct
8600 PARK 80134 2452 D2
Blue Cedar
10 JfnC 80127 2361 B7
Blue Creek Rd
7000 JfnC 80439 2357 B5
S Blue Creek Rd
6900 JfnC 80439 2357 B6
7100 JfnC 80439 2441 C2
Bluefield Av
1500 LGMT 80501 1440 A1
Bluefield Ct
800 LGMT 80501 1440 A1
Blue Flax
1400 BLDR 80305 1770 E1
Blue Flax Tr
10 CCkC 80439 2187 C1
Blue Fox Ct
10 JfnC 80127 2360 E6
Bluefox Ct
7400 LNTR 80124 2450 D3
Bluegate Dr
4700 DgsC 80108 2534 A1
4700 DgsC 80124 2534 A1
4900 DgsC 80124 2450 A7
Bluegate Ln
4800 DgsC 80124 2450 A7
Bluegate Wy
10900 DgsC 80108 2534 A1
10900 DgsC 80124 2534 A1
Blue Grama Ct
8400 PARK 80134 2452 E1
Bluegrass Cir
3200 CSRK 80109 2702 E1
8300 DgsC 80134 2452 E1
8300 PARK 80134 2452 E1
Bluegrass Ct
3200 CSRK 80109 2702 E1
7100 BldC 80301 1604 C4
8600 PARK 80134 2452 E1
Bluegrass Dr
600 LGMT 80503 1438 B4
Bluegrass Wy
700 LGMT 80503 1438 C4
Blue Grouse Rd
10 CCkC 80439 2271 E7
Blue Grouse Ridge Rd
10 JfnC 80127 2361 A5
Blue Heron Cir
100 GDVL 80121 2282 A6
Blue Heron Cir W
2400 LAFT 80026 1689 D1
Blue Heron Ct
10 GDVL 80121 2282 A7
3800 BMFD 80020 1775 B4
S Blue Heron Ct
10300 DgsC 80129 2448 D6
Blue Heron Dr
- CHLV 80121 2282 A7
- GDVL 80121 2282 A7
10 TNTN 80241 1777 B6
Blue Heron Dr W
10 GDVL 80121 2282 A7
10 GDVL 80121 2366 A1
Blue Heron Ln
10 GDVL 80121 2282 A7
Blue Heron Wy
- BldC 80301 1689 D1
2600 LAFT 80026 1689 D1
W Blue Heron Wy
600 DgsC 80129 2448 D6
Bluejay Av
1200 BGTN 80601 1779 E1
Blue Jay Cir
5100 CSRK 80109 2702 C3
Bluejay Ct
33500 EbtC 80107 2793 E1
Blue Jay Dr
500 GOLD 80401 2107 E7
E Blue Jay Dr
6700 DgsC 80138 2453 D6
Blue Jay Ln
10600 NHGN 80233 1860 E5
Blue Jay Rd
22200 JfnC 80465 2359 A5
S Blue Jay Rd
6700 JfnC 80465 2359 B5
Blue Jay St
2800 FLHT 80260 1944 A1
Blue Jay Wy
2800 LAFT 80026 1774 C2
Blue Lake Tr
400 LAFT 80026 1689 C4
Blueleaf Pl
16200 DgsC 80134 2452 E2
Blue Mesa Dr
10000 DgsC 80125 2615 A1
Blue Mesa Ln
6900 DgsC 80125 2615 A1
Blue Mesa Wy
6800 DgsC 80125 2615 A2
Blue Mist Cir
16600 PARK 80134 2452 E1
16600 PARK 80134 2453 A2
Blue Moon Ct
3700 CSRK 80104 2703 E3
Blue Mountain Cir
5600 LGMT 80503 1437 D5
Blue Mountain Dr
8700 JfnC 80403 1938 D3
9600 ARVD 80403 1854 D6
9600 JfnC 80403 1854 D6
9700 ARVD 80403 1938 D1
S Blue Mountain Pl
8800 DgsC 80126 2449 C2
Blue Mountain Rd
10 BldC 80540 1269 B2
1800 WldC 80504 1440 E2
30500 JfnC 80403 1853 A4
Blue Oak Ct
- DgsC 80104 2788 B2
Blue Pine Cir
3800 DgsC 80126 2449 E7
S Bluepoint Rd
- DgsC 80129 2448 D2
Blue Ribbon Rd
10 BldC 80302 1600 D6
Blue Ridge Dr
6000 DgsC 80130 2450 C2
Blueridge Dr
400 JfnC 80401 2190 D3
Blue River Tr
14000 BMFD 80020 1775 B4
Blue Sage
10 JfnC 80127 2360 E6
Blue Sage Ct
1400 BLDR 80305 1770 E1
Blue Sage Dr
5400 LITN 80123 2363 D1
Blue Sage Ln
1800 CSRK 80104 2704 A4
Blue Sage Wy
5900 LITN 80123 2363 D2
Bluesky Dr
4800 CSRK 80109 2702 C1
Blue Sky Tr
10000 JfnC 80433 2441 D6
Blue Springs Dr
32200 JfnC 80439 2356 D6
Bluespruce Ct
900 LGMT 80501 1439 D1
E Blue Spruce Ct
100 DgsC 80126 2448 D3
Blue Spruce Dr
10 CCkC 80439 2271 C3
10 NDLD 80466 1765 E3
10 NDLD 80466 1766 A3
S Blue Spruce Ln
7200 JfnC 80439 2356 E6
Blue Spruce Pl
- AURA 80016 2370 E5
Blue Spruce Rd
10 GpnC 80403 1850 B7
400 GpnC 80403 1934 B1
400 PrkC 80470 2523 B1
N Blue Spruce Rd
10 BldC 80466 1766 B1
S Blue Spruce Rd
4400 JfnC 80439 2273 C6
Blue Spruce Rd S
10 BldC 80466 1766 B1
Bluestar Dr
9700 DgsC 80138 2538 E2
Bluestem Av
3300 LGMT 80503 1438 B7
Bluestem Dr
23400 JfnC 80401 2190 E4
Bluestem Ln
20200 PARK 80138 2537 E2
Blue Stem St
- BGTN 80601 1697 D5
Blue Stem Tr
1100 LAFT 80026 1689 E3
Blue Terrace Cir
6000 DgsC 80108 2534 B4
Blue Terrace Pl
6000 DgsC 80108 2534 B4
Blue Terrace Wy
12300 DgsC 80108 2534 B4
Bluethrush Ct
4000 CSRK 80109 2702 D3
Blue Vista Wy
- BMFD 80020 1775 E3
- BMFD 80020 1776 A3
Blue Willow
10 JfnC 80127 2445 B1
N Bluff Dr
700 DgsC 80116 2707 C6
Bluff Ldg
11100 WldC 80504 1440 E3
Bluff St
2800 BLDR 80301 1686 E1
2800 BLDR 80301 1687 A1
2800 BLDR 80304 1686 E1
3000 BLDR 80301 1603 A7
Bluff Tr
7000 JfnC 80465 2359 D5
Bluffmont Dr
10100 LNTR 80124 2451 A6
W Boardwalk Cir
3500 DgsC 80129 2447 E5
3500 DgsC 80129 2448 A6
S Boardwalk Dr
- DgsC 80129 2448 A5
9900 DgsC 80129 2447 E5
Boatswain Ln
8000 BldC 80504 1522 B1
Boatworks Dr
5400 DgsC 80126 2450 A1
E Bobcat Blf
6100 DgsC 80124 2450 C7
Bobcat Dr
24100 JfnC 80433 2526 D7
Bobcat Ln
10 JfnC 80127 2360 E4
Bobcat Pt
300 LAFT 80026 1774 C1
Bobcat Run
7200 DgsC 80125 2614 D1
S Bobcat Ter
10800 DgsC 80124 2450 B7
Bob Cat Tr
10 PrkC 80456 2607 D7
10 PrkC 80456 2691 E1
Bobcat Wy
10 BldC 80481 1514 E1
S Bobcat Wy
6700 JfnC 80439 2356 C5
Bob-O-Link Ct
- BldC 80301 1603 D7
Bobolink Ct
300 LSVL 80027 1689 C5
4700 CSRK 80109 2702 C1
Bobolink Dr
4300 CSRK 80109 2702 C1
Bobsled Tr
8500 JfnC 80465 2442 E2
Bobtail Rd
- BKHK 80403 2017 E4
- BKHK 80403 2018 A4
Bobtail Hill Cir
- GpnC 80403 2017 D5
Bobwhite Ln
2300 LGMT 80504 1438 D7
Boca Cir
9900 DgsC 80134 2452 E5
Boddel Cir
- EbtC 80107 2709 B1
Bogey Ct
3900 BldC 80503 1518 E5
Bohn Ct
- LYNS 80540 1352 D3
Boise Ct
2100 LGMT 80501 1356 D5
Bold Ln
28400 JfnC 80439 2357 D7
Bold Sun Cir
700 DgsC 80104 2871 C2
Bolero Dr
17900 PARK 80134 2537 B5
E Bolling Dr
14300 DNVR 80239 2032 B6
Bolton Cir
11800 LNTR 80134 2451 E6
Bolton Ct
29200 JfnC 80439 2273 C1
Bolton Dr
11800 LNTR 80134 2451 E5
Bolton St
- LNTR 80134 2451 E5
Bonanza Blvd
- AdmC 80601 1698 B3
200 LCHB 80603 1698 B3
Bonanza Cir
11200 DgsC 80116 2707 D2
Bonanza Dr
- BfdC 80516 1691 D4
- BMFD 80020 1691 D4
- ERIE 80516 1691 D4
10 BldC 80466 1682 B7
10 BldC 80466 1766 A1
10 ERIE 80516 1607 D6
10 WldC 80516 1607 D6
27800 JfnC 80439 2441 D4
N Bonanza Rd
10500 DgsC 80138 2455 B3
Bond Rd
- BldC 80504 1357 A4
Bonita Pl
- CSRK 80104 2704 B5
100 NHGN 80234 1860 D4
S Bonita Park Tr
4900 JfnC 80439 2273 E7
4900 JfnC 80439 2274 A7
Bonner St
- CSRK 80104 2788 E1
E Bonney Ct
19000 PARK 80134 2537 C6
S Bonney St
12900 PARK 80134 2537 C5
Bonnie Cir
1500 WldC 80516 1607 E1
Bonnie Ln
1000 PrkC 80456 2607 B6
S Bonnie Ln
300 AphC 80137 2206 A4
Bonnie Rd
10 BldC 80466 1767 C5
Bonnie Brae Blvd
700 DNVR 80209 2197 C3
1000 DNVR 80210 2197 C3
Bonnie Ridge Cir
3900 EbtC 80107 2709 B6
Bonnie Ridge Dr
3900 EbtC 80107 2709 D5
Bonny Brook Ct
7100 BldC 80503 1521 B4
Bonvue Dr
2100 GOLD 80401 2107 D5
S Booker Ln
9100 JfnC 80433 2440 E4
N Boothill Dr
12000 DgsC 80138 2455 D4
Bordeaux Ct
16300 DgsC 80134 2452 E6
E Borealis Wy
10 DgsC 80108 2618 E4
10 DgsC 80108 2619 A4
Boreas Ct
16800 PARK 80134 2453 A7
Boreas Rd
7000 DgsC 80118 2954 D1
Bosque Ct
3800 BldC 80301 1603 A5
Bosque St
1100 BMFD 80020 1774 E6
Boston Av
- BldC 80501 1439 B3
- BldC 80503 1438 D3
- LGMT 80501 1439 B3
1200 BldC 80501 1438 D3
1200 LGMT 80501 1438 D3
S Boston Cir
6100 AphC 80111 2367 A3
6100 GDVL 80111 2367 A3
Boston Ct
10 LGMT 80501 1439 A3
14900 AdmC 80602 1779 A1
S Boston Ct
- AphC 80231 2199 A6
- AphC 80231 2283 A1
- GDVL 80111 2367 A3
1100 AphC 80247 2199 A4
3000 DNVR 80231 2283 A2
6200 AphC 80111 2367 A3
Boston St
- AdmC 80640 1947 A1
- AURA 80238 2115 A4
- CMCY 80640 1862 E5
- DNVR 80238 2115 A3
- DvrC 80238 2115 A4
1100 AURA 80230 2115 A6
1400 AURA 80010 2115 A4
9100 CMCY 80640 1947 A2
10700 CMCY 80640 1863 A5
15200 AdmC 80602 1695 A7
15200 AdmC 80602 1779 A1
S Boston St
- AphC 80231 2283 A1
1100 AphC 80247 2199 A4
2900 DNVR 80231 2283 A2
3600 DNVR 80014 2283 A4
3600 DNVR 80237 2283 A4
3600 GDVL 80014 2283 A4
4000 AphC 80237 2283 A4
4900 GDVL 80111 2283 A7
6100 GDVL 80111 2367 A2
6300 AphC 80111 2367 A3
6500 GDVL 80112 2367 A3
Botany Ln
- BldC 80026 1606 A7
Bottlebrush Run
- BMFD 80020 1775 B1
Boulder Cir
- BMFD 80020 1775 E5
S Boulder Cir
10 BLDR 80303 1687 D6
Boulder Pt
- BMFD 80020 1775 D5
S Boulder Rd
100 LSVL 80027 1689 D6
5000 BLDR 80303 1687 D6
5400 BldC 80303 1687 D6
7700 BldC 80027 1688 D6
7700 BldC 80303 1688 D6
7700 LSVL 80027 1688 D6
Boulder St
10 BldC 80302 1599 D3
1500 DNVR 80211 2112 B2
W Boulder St
10 NDLD 80466 1765 D3
Boulderado Dr
7700 BldC 80301 1604 D2
Boulder Canyon Dr
26900 BldC 80466 1765 D3
26900 BldC 80466 1766 B1
26900 NDLD 80466 1765 D3
27100 BldC 80466 1682 E7
27100 BldC 80466 1683 B6
27100 BldC 80466 1684 B4
27800 BldC 80302 1684 B4
36700 BldC 80302 1685 A4
39600 BldC 80302 1686 A3
40400 BLDR 80302 1686 A3
Boulder Canyon Dr SR-119
26900 BldC 80466 1765 D3
26900 BldC 80466 1766 B1
26900 NDLD 80466 1765 D3
27100 BldC 80466 1682 E7
27100 BldC 80466 1683 B6
27100 BldC 80466 1684 B4
27800 BldC 80302 1684 B4
36700 BldC 80302 1685 A4
39600 BldC 80302 1686 A3
40400 BldC 80302 1686 A3
Boulder Hills Dr
- BldC 80503 1519 C1
8400 BldC 80503 1436 E7
Boulder View Ln
10 BldC 80304 1602 A6
Boulder View Rd
10 BldC 80302 1684 A2
Bountiful Cir
4000 CSRK 80109 2702 D2
Bountiful Ct
500 AdmC 80221 1944 D7
Bounty St
1800 AURA 80011 2116 B4
Bounty Hunters Ln
10 PrkC 80456 2522 A6
Bourion St
- CLCY 80403 2017 D3
Bowen Cir
100 LGMT 80501 1439 A3
Bowen Ct
5600 CMCY 80022 2030 C4
Bowen St
10 LGMT 80501 1439 A3
2100 LGMT 80501 1356 A5
2300 LGMT 80501 1355 E4
S Bowen St
10 LGMT 80501 1439 A5
Bowie Ct
10 AdmC 80221 1944 D6
W Bowles Av
2700 LITN 80120 2364 A1
2700 LITN 80123 2364 A1
3200 CBVL 80123 2363 E2
3200 LITN 80123 2363 E2
4000 AphC 80123 2363 E2
7200 JfnC 80123 2362 D2
9700 JfnC 80127 2362 A2
10800 JfnC 80127 2361 C2
W Bowles Av SR-75
2700 LITN 80120 2364 A1
2700 LITN 80123 2364 A1
3100 LITN 80123 2363 E2
3600 AphC 80123 2363 E2
3600 CBVL 80123 2363 E2
W Bowles Cir
11600 JfnC 80127 2361 E2
W Bowles Dr
12700 JfnC 80127 2361 C2
W Bowles Pl
5200 JfnC 80123 2363 B2
10800 JfnC 80127 2362 A2
12600 JfnC 80127 2361 C2
W Bowles Pl S
- JfnC 80127 2361 B2
Bowles Lake Ln
5400 BWMR 80123 2363 C1
5400 JfnC 80123 2363 C1
Bowles Ranch Rd
100 GpnC 80403 1850 D4
Bow Line Pl
2800 LGMT 80503 1355 B4
Bowman Pl
1200 NHGN 80233 1861 A3
Bow Mar Dr
4300 DNVR 80123 2279 B6
4500 DvrC 80123 2279 B6
4900 BWMR 80123 2279 C7
5300 BWMR 80123 2363 D1
5400 LITN 80123 2363 D1
Bow Meadows Cir
- EbtC 80107 2794 C1
Bow Meadows Dr
6000 EbtC 80107 2794 B1
Bow Mountain Rd
10 BldC 80302 1601 D3
500 BldC 80304 1601 D3
Bowron Pl
5500 BldC 80503 1604 C1
E Bowstring Tr
7800 AURA 80138 2454 A1
W Box Canyon Rd
7200 DgsC 80135 2700 B6
Boxelder
3300 JfnC 80439 2273 A3
Boxelder Cir
900 BldC 80503 1438 B5
900 LGMT 80503 1438 B5
Boxelder Dr
3400 BldC 80503 1438 B5
3400 LGMT 80503 1438 B5
Boxelder St
1600 LSVL 80027 1773 E2
1600 LSVL 80027 1774 A2
Box Elder Creek Dr
600 BGTN 80601 1696 E7
Boxwood
10 JfnC 80127 2361 A6

Denver Regional Street Index

STREET
Block City ZIP Map# Grid

Boxwood Ct
2400 LAFT 80026 1689 E2
Boxwood Ln
700 LGMT 80503 1438 B4
Boyd Ct
6400 CSRK 80104 2789 A2
Boyd St
200 GOLD 80403 2107 D2
S Boyero Ct
1200 SUPE 80027 1773 B5
Boyne Ct
30100 JfnC 80439 2189 B7
Bozeman Tr
10 EbtC 80107 2791 E7
10 EbtC 80107 2792 A7
Bradburn Blvd
7200 WSTR 80030 1943 D6
11700 WSTR 80031 1859 D2
11900 BMFD 80020 1859 D2
Bradburn Dr
8000 WSTR 80031 1943 D4
8200 AdmC 80031 1943 D4
W Bradbury Av
2400 LITN 80120 2364 B5
Bradbury Ln
10 LITN 80120 2364 C5
S Bradbury Pkwy
- DgsC 80134 2537 A2
- PARK 80134 2536 E2
- PARK 80134 2537 A2
Bradbury Wy
- LITN 80120 2364 D5
Bradbury Ranch Dr
11200 PARK 80134 2536 E1
S Bradbury Ranch Dr
11600 PARK 80134 2536 E2
Bradbury Ranch Rd
- PARK 80134 2453 B6
- PARK 80134 2536 E1
10900 PARK 80134 2452 E7
Bradford Dr
- JfnC 80127 2446 A1
12300 LNTR 80134 2451 E5
W Bradford Rd
10300 JfnC 80127 2446 A1
Bradford St
10 BldC 80540 1352 D3
10 PrkC 80456 2522 A1
Bradley Dr
1400 BLDR 80305 1771 C1
Bradley Pl
2600 TNTN 80229 1945 C2
Bradley St
26600 JfnC 80433 2442 A5
S Brady Ct
3300 SRDN 80110 2280 B3
S Brady Pl
10100 DgsC 80130 2450 B5
Braeburn Ct
2000 LGMT 80503 1438 B6
Braeburn Ln
2600 JfnC 80439 2272 E1
2600 JfnC 80439 2273 A2
Braeburn Pl
3000 DgsC 80126 2449 D7
3700 LGMT 80503 1438 B6
Braeburn Wy
2900 DgsC 80126 2449 D7
W Braewood Av
1200 DgsC 80129 2448 C4
Bragg Pl
900 LGMT 80501 1356 A5
Brahma Pl
- DgsC 80134 2621 B4
Brainard Cir
500 LAFT 80026 1690 A3
S Brainard Dr
12700 BldC 80020 1773 E6
12700 BldC 80020 1774 A7
12700 BMFD 80020 1773 E6
12700 BMFD 80020 1774 A7
12700 BMFD 80021 1774 A7
Bramble Pl
1300 LGMT 80501 1357 A7
Brambleridge Dr
8400 DgsC 80108 2534 D5
Brambleridge Ln
800 DgsC 80108 2534 B5
Bramblewood Dr
800 DgsC 80108 2534 D5
Bramblewood Ln
- DgsC 80108 2534 D5
Bramer Rd
10 BldC 80481 1515 A1
Bramwood Pl
1200 LGMT 80501 1439 A4
S Brandenburger Dr
8900 JfnC 80465 2443 B3
Branding Iron Ct
500 BGTN 80601 1697 B4
Branding Iron Ln
10 PrkC 80456 2522 D6
500 CSRK 80104 2703 D2
Brandon Av
4100 BMFD 80020 1775 C7
S Brandon Ct
500 SUPE 80027 1773 A5
W Brandon Dr
- DgsC 80129 2447 D4
8000 DgsC 80125 2447 D4
Brandon Wy
10300 NHGN 80233 1861 B6
10300 TNTN 80229 1861 B6
Brandon Creek Cir
4800 BLDR 80301 1604 B3
Brandon Creek Dr
4800 BLDR 80301 1604 B2
W Brandt Av
9200 JfnC 80123 2362 B1
11600 JfnC 80127 2361 D1
Brandt Ct
1500 BLDR 80303 1687 D2
E Brandt Dr
- AphC 80016 2370 D1
- AURA 80016 2370 D1
W Brandt Dr
8900 JfnC 80123 2362 C1
13100 JfnC 80127 2361 C1
W Brandt Pl
8900 JfnC 80123 2362 C1
11200 JfnC 80127 2361 E1
Brandywine Ct
5900 BldC 80301 1603 E3
5900 BLDR 80301 1603 E3
Brandywine Ln
11600 PARK 80138 2538 A2
Branham Dr
9300 DgsC 80134 2452 E3
Brantly Av
6000 CSRK 80104 2788 E1
6200 CSRK 80104 2789 A1
Brantly Ct
6100 CSRK 80104 2789 A1
Brantner Pl
2200 BGTN 80601 1696 E7
Braselton St
10600 DgsC 80126 2449 D7
Brassie Wy
10 CBVL 80123 2363 D4
Braun Cir
6200 ARVD 80004 2025 B2
S Braun Cir
500 LKWD 80228 2193 B3
Braun Ct
800 JfnC 80401 2109 B7
800 LKWD 80401 2109 B7
6600 ARVD 80004 2025 B1
6900 ARVD 80004 1941 B7
7500 ARVD 80005 1941 B6
S Braun Ct
1700 LKWD 80228 2193 B5
4300 JfnC 80465 2277 C6
Braun Dr
2000 JfnC 80401 2109 B4
S Braun Dr
900 LKWD 80228 2193 B4
Braun Ln
6300 ARVD 80004 2025 B2
Braun Lp
8400 ARVD 80005 1941 B4
Braun Rd
13200 JfnC 80401 2109 B3
Braun St
600 LKWD 80401 2109 B7
5100 JfnC 80002 2025 B5
7300 ARVD 80005 1941 B7
S Braun St
700 LKWD 80228 2193 B3
4800 JfnC 80465 2277 B7
Braun Wy
6300 ARVD 80004 2025 B3
7200 ARVD 80005 1941 B7
S Braun Wy
2100 LKWD 80228 2193 B7
4300 JfnC 80465 2277 B5
11500 JfnC 80433 2525 A3
11700 JfnC 80433 2524 E3
S Breakaway Tr
4600 JfnC 80439 2274 A6
Breakwater Dr
2900 LGMT 80503 1355 B5
Breakwater Wy
2900 LGMT 80503 1355 B6
Breamore Ct
10 DgsC 80108 2535 A7
Breckenridge
- DgsC 80135 2617 D7
E Breckenridge Av
17700 AURA 80011 2201 B1
Breckenridge Dr
500 BMFD 80020 1775 A5
3600 DgsC 80135 2701 E1
3600 DgsC 80135 2702 A1
Breckenridge Tr
100 BMFD 80020 1774 E4
W Breed St
200 NDLD 80466 1765 C3
Breen Ln
1800 SUPE 80027 1773 B6
Breezy Ln
2500 CSRK 80109 2702 C4
Brendon Ct
400 DgsC 80108 2618 E1
Brendon Pl
6800 DgsC 80108 2618 E1
Brendy Ct
2300 LGMT 80503 1355 D7
2300 LGMT 80503 1438 D1
Brenkert Dr
1500 JfnC 80401 2191 A5
Brennan Ct
1200 ERIE 80516 1607 A3
Brennan St
- ERIE 80516 1606 E6
E Brentford Cir
300 DgsC 80126 2448 E4
S Brentford Dr
9500 DgsC 80130 2450 B4
Brentwood Ct
6400 ARVD 80004 2026 D2
8200 ARVD 80005 1942 C4
N Brentwood Ct
600 CSRK 80104 2704 E6
S Brentwood Ct
2000 LKWD 80227 2194 D6
2500 LKWD 80227 2278 D1
7600 JfnC 80128 2362 D7
Brentwood Dr
10400 JfnC 80021 1858 D6
Brentwood St
100 LKWD 80226 2194 D1
2000 LKWD 80214 2110 D4
2400 JfnC 80215 2110 D4
3800 WTRG 80033 2110 D1
4400 WTRG 80033 2026 D7
5600 ARVD 80002 2026 D4
5800 ARVD 80004 2026 D3
7700 ARVD 80005 1942 C6
9300 WSTR 80021 1942 C1
S Brentwood St
1100 LKWD 80226 2194 D4
1100 LKWD 80232 2194 D4
2100 LKWD 80227 2194 D7
3500 JfnC 80235 2278 D3
3500 LKWD 80227 2278 D3
3500 LKWD 80235 2278 D3
6300 JfnC 80123 2362 D3
7600 JfnC 80128 2362 D7
8300 JfnC 80128 2446 D1
Brentwood Wy
9100 WSTR 80021 1942 C2
10000 JfnC 80021 1858 C7
10000 WSTR 80021 1858 C7
NW Brentwood Wy
9400 WSTR 80021 1942 C1
S Brentwood Wy
1200 LKWD 80232 2194 D5
6400 JfnC 80123 2362 D4
Brestra St
- PrkC 80456 2521 D3
Brettonwood Wy
1200 DgsC 80129 2448 C7
Brewer Ct
- CSRK 80108 2703 D1
Brewer Dr
10400 NHGN 80234 1860 C6
Brewer St
10 PrkC 80456 2521 D3
Brian Dr
5000 DgsC 80134 2537 A3
Briar Cir
1300 DgsC 80126 2449 A2
Briar Cliff Ct
8100 DgsC 80108 2534 E6
Briar Cliff Dr
8100 DgsC 80108 2534 E6
Briar Dale Dr
500 DgsC 80108 2534 D6
Briar Dale Ln
8200 DgsC 80108 2534 E5
E Briargate Ln
18900 PARK 80134 2453 C7
Briarglen Cir
10600 DgsC 80130 2449 E7
Briarglen Ln
4600 DgsC 80130 2449 E7
Briargrove Dr
2200 DgsC 80126 2449 C6
Briargrove Wy
10000 DgsC 80126 2449 C6
Briar Haven Ct
8300 DgsC 80108 2534 D5
Briar Haven Dr
500 DgsC 80108 2534 D5
Briar Haven Pl
8300 DgsC 80108 2534 D5
W Briarhollow Ln
1200 DgsC 80129 2448 C6
W Briarhollow Wy
1100 DgsC 80129 2448 C5
Briarhurst Dr
2100 DgsC 80126 2449 B2
Briar Leaf Av
22800 PARK 80138 2538 C3
Briar Leaf Ct
12100 PARK 80138 2538 D3
Briar Ridge Ct
700 DgsC 80108 2534 D6
4800 BldC 80301 1604 C3
Briar Ridge Dr
8100 DgsC 80108 2534 E6
Briar Ridge Tr
4700 BldC 80301 1604 D3
Briar Rose Tr
6800 DgsC 80125 2614 E1
Briar Trace Dr
8300 DgsC 80108 2534 D5
Briar Trace Wy
8300 DgsC 80108 2534 D5
S Briarview Ln
8800 DgsC 80126 2448 E2
Briarwood Av
- AURA 80016 2370 E4
E Briarwood Av
3600 CTNL 80122 2365 D4
5200 CTNL 80122 2366 A4
8200 CTNL 80112 2366 E4
10500 CTNL 80112 2367 C4
12000 AphC 80112 2367 E4
12200 CTNL 80112 2368 A4
14000 AphC 80112 2368 B4
18600 CTNL 80016 2369 C4
W Briarwood Av
1800 LITN 80120 2364 B4
E Briarwood Blvd
7800 CTNL 80112 2366 E4
8700 CTNL 80112 2367 A4
E Briarwood Cir
5200 CTNL 80122 2366 A4
6800 CTNL 80112 2366 C4
E Briarwood Cir N
800 CTNL 80122 2365 A4
E Briarwood Cir S
800 CTNL 80122 2365 A4
Briarwood Ct
800 LGMT 80501 1438 D1
19900 PARK 80138 2453 E7
Briarwood Dr
- BldC 80305 1770 E2
- GOLD 80401 2107 C3
2500 BLDR 80305 1770 E2
11700 TNTN 80233 1861 E2
13300 BMFD 80020 1775 D6
E Briarwood Dr
- AURA 80016 2370 D4
200 CTNL 80122 2364 E4
500 CTNL 80122 2365 B4
5900 CTNL 80112 2366 B4
18600 CTNL 80016 2369 C4
S Briarwood Dr
700 LKWD 80226 2193 E3
Briarwood Ln
800 LGMT 80501 1438 D1
11500 PARK 80138 2538 A2
Briarwood Pl
- AphC 80016 2370 E4
- AURA 80016 2370 E4
E Briarwood Pl
- AURA 80016 2370 C4
4500 CTNL 80122 2365 E4
4500 CTNL 80122 2366 A4
8200 CTNL 80112 2366 E4
S Briarwood St
700 LKWD 80226 2193 E3
N Brick-Center Rd
- AphC 80102 2124 B6
- AphC 80102 2208 B1
S Brick-Center Rd
- AphC 80102 2208 B4
Brickyard Cir
800 GOLD 80403 2023 C7
Brickyard Rd
1200 GOLD 80403 2023 C7
Bridge St
- AdmC 80601 1697 D5
- AdmC 80601 1698 A5
- AdmC 80603 1698 A5
- BGTN 80601 1697 D5
- BGTN 80601 1698 A5
- BGTN 80603 1698 A5
Bridge St SR-7
- AdmC 80601 1697 D5
- AdmC 80601 1698 A5
- AdmC 80603 1698 A5
- BGTN 80601 1697 D5
- BGTN 80601 1698 A5
- BGTN 80603 1698 A5
E Bridge St
10 BGTN 80601 1696 E6
2400 AdmC 80601 1696 E6
3000 AdmC 80601 1697 A6
3000 BGTN 80601 1697 A6
E Bridge St SR-2
400 BGTN 80601 1696 B6
E Bridge St SR-7
10 BGTN 80601 1696 E6
2400 AdmC 80601 1696 E6
3000 AdmC 80601 1697 A6
3000 BGTN 80601 1697 A6
N Bridge St
10 NDLD 80466 1765 D3
S Bridge St
10 NDLD 80466 1765 C3
700 BldC 80466 1765 C3
S Bridge St SR-72
10 NDLD 80466 1765 C3
700 BldC 80466 1765 C3
S Bridge St SR-119
10 NDLD 80466 1765 C3
700 BldC 80466 1765 C3
W Bridge St
10 AdmC 80601 1696 A6
10 BGTN 80601 1696 A6
W Bridge St SR-7
10 AdmC 80601 1696 A6
10 BGTN 80601 1696 A6
Bridger Ct
2600 JfnC 80439 2273 C1
S Bridger Ct
6600 CTNL 80121 2364 E4
6600 LITN 80120 2364 E4
Bridger Ln
- BLDR 80301 1603 B6
Bridger Pt
700 LAFT 80026 1689 E3
Bridger Tr
10 BldC 80481 1515 A3
3300 BLDR 80301 1603 A6
Bridle Ct
8500 BldC 80503 1436 E7
Bridlegate Ln
10 JfnC 80127 2361 A6
Bridle Path Ln
5800 DgsC 80134 2621 C5
Bridlepath Ln
10 CHLV 80113 2281 C6
Bridlewood Ln
20600 PARK 80138 2537 E3
20600 PARK 80138 2538 A3
Brierly Ct
2100 CSRK 80104 2787 D2
Brigadoon Ct
6100 BldC 80503 1519 E4
6100 BldC 80503 1520 A4
Brigadoon Dr
6000 BldC 80503 1519 E4
Briggs Av
25600 JfnC 80433 2442 B5
Briggs Pl
400 SUPE 80027 1773 A7
Briggs St
100 ERIE 80516 1607 C5
Brigham St
10 PrkC 80456 2522 A2
Bright Angel
3400 WldC 80504 1440 E3
Brighton Blvd
2800 DNVR 80205 2112 E1
2800 DNVR 80216 2112 E1
3500 DNVR 80216 2113 A1
4400 DNVR 80216 2029 A7
5100 CMCY 80216 2029 C4
5300 CMCY 80022 2029 C4
6900 AdmC 80022 1946 A6
6900 CMCY 80022 1946 A6
6900 CMCY 80022 2030 A1
Brighton Blvd SR-265
5100 CMCY 80216 2029 C4
5100 DNVR 80216 2029 C4
5300 CMCY 80022 2029 C4
Brighton Ct
1300 JfnC 80439 2188 E5
7200 DgsC 80108 2534 E7
Brighton Dr
1200 BGTN 80601 1696 C5
Brighton Pl
7200 DgsC 80108 2534 E7
Brighton Rd
8400 AdmC 80640 1946 C2
8400 CMCY 80022 1946 C2
8800 AdmC 80022 1946 C2
9600 AdmC 80640 1862 D7
10000 CMCY 80640 1862 D7
10700 CMCY 80640 1863 A3
11200 AdmC 80640 1863 A3
12300 AdmC 80601 1863 B1
12400 AdmC 80601 1779 C6
13600 BGTN 80601 1779 E3
14700 BGTN 80601 1780 A2
15000 AdmC 80601 1780 A1
Brighton St
500 BGTN 80601 1696 B5
W Brighton St
100 BGTN 80601 1696 A5
Bright Water Tr
- DgsC 80125 2615 B5
6600 DgsC 80125 2614 E2
Brigitte Dr
200 NHGN 80260 1860 D7
Brilliance Dr
- CSRK 80109 2702 D4
Brimble Ct
800 ERIE 80516 1607 A7
Brimble Dr
1400 ERIE 80516 1607 A7
Brisbane Ln
10000 DgsC 80130 2449 E5
Brisbane Wy
10000 DgsC 80130 2450 A5
Briscoe Ln
100 DgsC 80109 2787 A3
Briscoe St
100 CSRK 80104 2703 D7
Bristlecone Cir
10 PrkC 80456 2521 B2
Bristlecone Ct
2700 LAFT 80026 1689 D2
25600 JfnC 80401 2190 B6
46000 EbtC 80138 2456 B4
Bristle Cone Pl
7800 LNTR 80124 2450 E3
Bristlecone St
- BGTN 80601 1697 E5
Bristlecone Wy
10 BldC 80304 1601 D5
10 GpnC 80403 1933 E6
2700 BldC 80301 1689 C2
2700 LAFT 80026 1689 C2
Bristle Pine Cir
600 DgsC 80129 2448 D4
Bristol Ct
2000 LGMT 80501 1356 C5
Bristol Pl
300 LGMT 80501 1356 C5
Bristol St
10 CSRK 80104 2704 C7
2100 SUPE 80027 1772 E6
2100 SUPE 80027 1773 A7
5100 JfnC 80002 2025 B5
S Bristol St
700 LKWD 80228 2193 B3
W Brittany Av
9300 JfnC 80123 2362 C2
12000 JfnC 80127 2361 D2
W Brittany Dr
8500 JfnC 80123 2362 C2
10900 JfnC 80127 2362 A2
11100 JfnC 80127 2361 E2
Brittany Ln
100 BldC 80026 1689 A4
100 LSVL 80026 1689 A4
Brittany Pl
8400 BldC 80503 1521 A4
E Brittany Pl
5300 CTNL 80121 2366 A2
W Brittany Pl
6200 JfnC 80123 2363 A2
8600 JfnC 80123 2362 C2
12700 JfnC 80127 2361 C2
E Brittany Wy
900 DgsC 80126 2449 A4
Britting Av
3700 BLDR 80305 1687 A7
Brixham Cir
7200 DgsC 80108 2534 D7
Brixham Ct
10 DgsC 80108 2535 A7
Brixham Pl
800 DgsC 80108 2534 D7
Broadlands Ct
- BMFD 80020 1775 E3
Broadlands Dr
3100 BMFD 80020 1775 D4
Broadlands Ln
3500 BMFD 80020 1775 D4
Broadlands Marketplace
- BMFD 80020 1775 D3
Broadleaf Lp
- CSRK 80109 2702 E4
Broadmoor Ct
11100 PARK 80138 2538 D1
Broadmoor Dr
23400 PARK 80138 2538 D1
31500 JfnC 80439 2188 E6
W Broadmoor Dr
10 LITN 80120 2364 D2
10 LITN 80121 2364 D2
Broadmoor Lp
3800 BMFD 80020 1775 D4
Broadmoor Pl
23900 PARK 80138 2538 D1
Broadmoor Rd
- DNVR 80237 2283 A5
Broadview Cir
14100 JfnC 80127 2612 D2
Broadview Ct
4500 CSRK 80109 2702 C3
Broadview Dr
7200 LKWD 80214 2110 E7
Broadview Pl
3600 CSRK 80109 2702 C3
Broadway
10 DNVR 80203 2196 E1
10 DNVR 80209 2196 E1
10 DNVR 80223 2196 E1
300 DNVR 80203 2112 E7
300 DNVR 80204 2112 E7
300 DNVR 80223 2112 E7
1400 DNVR 80202 2112 E7
2000 DNVR 80205 2112 E4
2500 DNVR 80216 2112 E2
5100 DNVR 80216 2028 E6
5600 AdmC 80216 2028 E4
6300 AdmC 80221 2028 D3
6700 AdmC 80221 1944 E7
Broadway SR-53
5800 AdmC 80216 2028 D3
6300 AdmC 80221 2028 D3
6700 AdmC 80221 1944 D7
S Broadway
- LITN 80120 2364 E4
10 DNVR 80203 2196 E5
10 DNVR 80209 2196 E5
10 DNVR 80223 2196 E5
900 DNVR 80210 2196 E5
2500 DNVR 80210 2280 E2
2500 DNVR 80223 2280 E2
2600 DvrC 80210 2280 E2
2600 DvrC 80223 2280 E2
2600 EGLD 80110 2280 E2
2600 EGLD 80113 2280 E2
5200 LITN 80120 2280 E6
5300 EGLD 80113 2364 E2
5300 LITN 80113 2364 E2
5400 LITN 80121 2364 E2
6100 CTNL 80121 2364 E2
6700 CTNL 80122 2364 E4
7000 LITN 80122 2364 E4
8000 LITN 80120 2448 E3
8000 LITN 80122 2448 E3
8200 AphC 80126 2448 E3
8200 DgsC 80129 2448 E3
S Broadway Cir
5300 EGLD 80110 2280 E7
5300 EGLD 80113 2280 E7
5300 EGLD 80113 2364 E1
S Broadway Ct
- LITN 80120 2448 E1
- LITN 80122 2448 E1
Broadway St
- BldC 80301 1602 C3
100 BLDR 80305 1686 E4
200 LYNS 80540 1352 C1
1100 BLDR 80302 1686 C2
2200 BLDR 80304 1686 C1
2900 BLDR 80304 1602 C6
Broadway St SR-7
- BldC 80301 1602 C3
200 LYNS 80540 1352 C1
1800 BLDR 80302 1686 C1
2200 BLDR 80304 1686 C1
2900 BLDR 80304 1602 C6
Broadway St SR-66
200 LYNS 80540 1352 C1
Broadway St SR-93
100 BLDR 80305 1686 E4
1100 BLDR 80302 1686 E4
Broadway St US-36
200 LYNS 80540 1352 C1
E Broadway St
200 ELIZ 80107 2793 B1
N Broadway St
5000 BldC 80301 1602 C2
5000 BldC 80302 1602 C2
5000 BLDR 80302 1602 C2
5000 BLDR 80304 1602 C2
S Broadway St
10 BLDR 80305 1686 E5
10 BLDR 80305 1687 B7
1100 BLDR 80305 1771 B1
1400 BldC 80305 1771 B1
S Broadway St SR-93
10 BLDR 80305 1686 E5
10 BLDR 80305 1687 B7
1100 BLDR 80305 1771 B1
1400 BldC 80305 1771 B1
W Broadway St
100 ELIZ 80107 2793 B1
Broadway Frontage St
400 LYNS 80540 1352 C2
Brockway Dr
7000 BldC 80303 1688 D6
Broemel Av
4100 BMFD 80020 1775 C7
Broken Arrow Cir
1000 EbtC 80107 2708 B7
S Broken Arrow Dr
11500 JfnC 80433 2526 E2
Broken Arrow Rd
300 JfnC 80439 2189 A3
N Broken Bow Run
4300 DgsC 80125 2615 A6
Broken Fence Rd
10 BldC 80302 1685 A2
Brokenhorn Cir
42100 EbtC 80138 2540 A5
Broken Spoke Rd
20700 JfnC 80465 2443 C1
W Brome Av
200 LAFT 80026 1690 C3
Brome Ct
5200 WldC 80516 1523 B7
W Brome Pl
700 LAFT 80026 1690 B3
Bromley Ct
30200 JfnC 80439 2189 B7
Bromley Ln
- AdmC 80601 1779 E2
- AdmC 80601 1780 A1
- BGTN 80601 1779 E2
- BGTN 80601 1780 A1
E Bromley Ln
- BGTN 80601 1780 D1
- BGTN 80601 1781 A1
200 AdmC 80601 1780 C1
2900 AdmC 80601 1781 A1
W Bromley Ln
10 BGTN 80601 1780 B1
400 AdmC 80601 1780 A1
Bromley Business Pkwy
100 BGTN 80603 1698 A6
Brompton Wy
8800 PARK 80134 2453 B2
S Brompton Wy
8900 DgsC 80134 2453 B2
E Bronco Dr
11000 DgsC 80138 2455 C3
Bronco Ln
- ARVD 80007 1940 A2
- JfnC 80007 1939 E2
- JfnC 80007 1940 A2
Bronco Rd
400 AdmC 80221 1944 C6
29500 JfnC 80439 2273 B3
E Broncos Pkwy
- AphC 80016 2368 E6
- AphC 80016 2369 A6
- CTNL 80016 2368 E6
- CTNL 80016 2369 A6
7300 AphC 80112 2367 E5
12300 CTNL 80112 2367 E5
12500 AphC 80112 2368 A6
Bronti Cir
9900 DgsC 80124 2450 D5
S Bronze Ln
8300 DgsC 80126 2449 D1
Bronzite Wy
6700 CSRK 80108 2619 E6
Brook Cir
10 BldC 80302 1517 B7
10 BldC 80302 1601 B1
S Brook Dr
2700 DNVR 80222 2281 E1
W Brook Dr
7600 JfnC 80128 2446 D2
Brook Hllw
900 CCkC 80439 2187 E3
Brook Ln
9400 LNTR 80124 2451 A4
Brook Pl
200 BLDR 80302 1686 D5
Brook Rd
10 CCkC 80439 2356 A7
10 CCkC 80439 2440 A1
500 BldC 80302 1601 B1
700 BldC 80302 1517 B7
11500 JfnC 80403 1852 C3
Brookcress Dr
1300 JfnC 80401 2190 E5
Brookdale Ln
20400 PARK 80138 2537 E3
Brookfield Dr
1200 LGMT 80501 1439 A6
1300 LGMT 80501 1438 E6
4300 BLDR 80305 1687 B7
Brook Forest Dr
6700 JfnC 80439 2356 B5
Brook Forest Ln
7400 JfnC 80439 2356 C7
S Brook Forest Rd
5000 JfnC 80439 2357 B3
7100 JfnC 80439 2356 E6
8200 JfnC 80433 2356 C6
S Brook Forest Rd CO-78
5000 JfnC 80439 2357 B3
7100 JfnC 80439 2356 E6
8200 JfnC 80433 2356 C6
Brook Forest Wy
7300 JfnC 80439 2356 C6
Brookhaven Dr
10 CBVL 80123 2363 E2
Brookhaven Ln
10 CBVL 80123 2363 E2
10 LITN 80123 2363 E2
Brookhaven Pl
10 CBVL 80123 2363 E2
Brookhaven Tr
10 CBVL 80123 2363 E2
Brook Hill Av
9600 LNTR 80124 2451 A4
Brook Hill Ct
9600 LNTR 80124 2451 A4
Brook Hill Dr
9500 LNTR 80124 2451 A4
Brook Hill Ln
9500 LNTR 80124 2451 A4
S Brookhollow Cir
10300 DgsC 80129 2448 C6
Brook Hollow Ct
7900 BldC 80301 1688 E2
Brook Hollow Dr
5600 BMFD 80020 1775 B4
Brookhurst Av
500 DgsC 80129 2448 D4
Brooklawn Dr
700 BLDR 80303 1687 C4
Brooklawn Ln
5400 DgsC 80124 2450 B7
Brooklawn Rd
10800 DgsC 80124 2450 B7
10800 DgsC 80124 2534 B1
Brooklime Ct
15900 DgsC 80134 2452 D1
Brookline Rd
31300 JfnC 80439 2272 E1
Brookmont Rd
20300 JfnC 80465 2359 D2
Brooks Av
300 LAFT 80026 1690 D4
N Brooks Av
- LAFT 80026 1690 D4
Brooks Dr
5900 ARVD 80004 2026 B2
Brooks Wy
2100 LGMT 80504 1438 D7

STREET Block City ZIP Map# Grid

S Brookshire Pl
- DgsC 80126 2449 D5
Brookside Cir
1000 CSRK 80104 2787 C1
13900 BMFD 80020 1775 C4
Brookside Ct
- BMFD 80020 1775 B4
200 BldC 80302 1686 B2
Brookside Dr
10 GDVL 80121 2281 A7
10 PrkC 80456 2607 D4
500 LGMT 80501 1439 D1
4800 BMFD 80020 1775 C4
E Brookside Dr
1600 DgsC 80126 2449 B4
Brookside Tr
- PrkC 80456 2689 C3
Brookstone Dr
15600 DgsC 80134 2452 D4
Brook Trout Tr
7300 JfnC 80439 2356 D6
Brook Valley Wy
5900 CTNL 80121 2365 E2
S Brook Valley Wy
5900 CTNL 80121 2365 E2
5900 GDVL 80121 2365 E2
Brookwood Ct
4100 DgsC 80130 2449 E6
Brookwood Dr
- DgsC 80130 2450 A6
4300 DgsC 80130 2449 D5
Brookwood Pl
4200 DgsC 80130 2449 D5
Brookwood Pt
10400 DgsC 80130 2449 E6
S Broome Wy
10000 DgsC 80130 2450 A6
Bross Ct
1300 JfnC 80439 2188 D5
S Bross Ln
1200 LGMT 80501 1439 A5
Bross St
1100 LGMT 80501 1356 A7
1100 LGMT 80501 1439 A1
N Bross St
900 LGMT 80501 1439 A1
S Bross St
800 LGMT 80501 1439 A5
Brown
- BldC 80026 1690 D5
- LAFT 80026 1690 D5
E Brown Av
15700 AURA 80013 2284 D1
Brown Cir
1300 BLDR 80305 1771 C1
E Brown Cir
17100 AURA 80013 2285 A1
Brown Ct
- LAFT 80026 1690 D5
1600 LGMT 80503 1355 A6
E Brown Dr
16500 AURA 80013 2284 E1
19300 AURA 80013 2285 D1
E Brown Pl
2800 AURA 80013 2285 B1
6500 DNVR 80222 2282 C1
6500 DNVR 80224 2282 C1
15300 AURA 80013 2284 D1
15300 AURA 80014 2284 D1
W Brown Pl
5200 DNVR 80227 2279 C1
5200 DNVR 80236 2279 C1
Brown St
10 PrkC 80456 2522 A2
500 NDLD 80466 1765 D2
Brown Bear Ct
7500 DgsC 80125 2531 B7
Brown Bear Wy
7500 DgsC 80125 2531 B7
Brown Fox Tr
10500 DgsC 80125 2614 E1
Browning Ct
36000 EbtC 80107 2708 D2
Browning Dr
2400 DgsC 80109 2786 A7
Brown Squirrel Ln
800 GOLD 80401 2107 E6
N Brownstone Dr
11000 DgsC 80138 2453 D6
11000 PARK 80138 2453 D6
Bruce Ln
200 NHGN 80260 1860 D7
Bruce Pl
10 LGMT 80501 1438 D2
10 LGMT 80503 1438 D2
Bruce St
8800 TNTN 80260 1944 C3
E Bruce Randolph Av
4000 DNVR 80205 2113 E2
4000 DNVR 80207 2113 E2
4700 DNVR 80207 2114 A1
N Bruchez Pkwy
- WSTR 80031 1859 E5
- WSTR 80234 1859 E5
2600 WSTR 80234 1860 A5
Brumm Tr
9000 JfnC 80403 1938 B3
E Brunswick Dr
15800 AURA 80013 2284 E1
19800 AURA 80013 2285 E1
E Brunswick Pl
- AURA 80013 2286 A1
16300 AURA 80013 2284 E1
18900 AURA 80013 2285 C1
Bruntwood Ct
6300 BldC 80303 1688 A3
Brush Ct
- CSRK 80108 2704 C4
Brush Rd
- CSRK 80108 2704 C4
Brushwood Dr
3100 CSRK 80109 2702 D2
Brushwood Wy
3900 CSRK 80109 2702 E2
Brussels Dr
600 EbtC 80138 2540 A7
Bryant Cir
1000 BMFD 80020 1776 A6
11800 WSTR 80234 1860 A2
W Bryant Cir
2800 LITN 80120 2364 A5
Bryant Ct
100 BMFD 80020 1776 A7
10000 FLHT 80260 1860 A7
N Bryant Ct
11100 WSTR 80234 1860 A4
Bryant Dr
- FLHT 80260 1944 A1
2600 BMFD 80020 1776 A6
30300 JfnC 80439 2273 A4
N Bryant Dr
11100 WSTR 80234 1860 A4
Bryant Pl
13100 BMFD 80020 1776 A6
W Bryant Pl
2800 LITN 80120 2364 A5
Bryant St
- FLHT 80260 1944 A3
- WSTR 80031 1944 A3
100 DNVR 80219 2196 A1
400 DNVR 80219 2112 A7
2000 DNVR 80204 2112 A4
2000 DNVR 80211 2112 A4
4400 DNVR 80211 2028 A7
5100 DNVR 80221 2028 A6
5600 AdmC 80221 2028 A4
7400 WSTR 80030 1944 A6
10000 FLHT 80260 1860 A7
12400 BMFD 80020 1860 A1
12500 BMFD 80020 1776 A7
N Bryant St
- FLHT 80234 1860 A6
- FLHT 80260 1860 A6
- WSTR 80234 1860 A6
S Bryant St
- LITN 80120 2364 A5
10 DNVR 80219 2196 A2
2700 DNVR 80219 2280 A2
3000 DvrC 80236 2280 A2
3000 SRDN 80110 2280 A2
3100 DNVR 80236 2280 A3
Bryant Wy
10 DNVR 80219 2196 A1
7000 WSTR 80030 1944 A7
10500 WSTR 80234 1860 A6
13400 BMFD 80020 1776 A5
Bryce
11200 WldC 80504 1440 E2
Bryce Ct
1900 JfnC 80439 2189 B7
Bryce Ln
10600 DgsC 80126 2449 C7
Bryn Mawr Pl
2900 LGMT 80503 1355 C7
S Brynmawr Rd
16700 JfnC 80470 2693 E2
S Buchanan Av
100 LSVL 80027 1773 B1
S Buchanan Cir
200 LSVL 80027 1773 B2
1300 AURA 80018 2202 D5
Buchanan Ct
- AURA 80018 2118 D7
300 LSVL 80027 1773 B1
S Buchanan Ct
100 LSVL 80027 1773 C1
5400 AphC 80016 2286 D7
Buchanan Dr
28500 JfnC 80439 2273 C4
E Buchanan Dr
20300 AURA 80011 2117 E4
Buchanan Ln
600 LGMT 80501 1439 D1
E Buchanan Pl
19300 AURA 80011 2117 D4
Buchanan Pt
2000 LAFT 80026 1690 A4
Buchanan St
- AURA 80016 2286 D6
13200 AdmC 80022 1782 D5
13400 AdmC 80603 1782 D5
S Buchanan St
- AURA 80016 2370 D1
800 AphC 80018 2202 D3
1000 AURA 80018 2202 D3
5100 AphC 80016 2286 D7
S Buchanan Wy
1300 AURA 80018 2202 D4
7600 AURA 80016 2370 D6
Buchtel Blvd
400 DNVR 80209 2196 E4
400 DNVR 80210 2196 E4
600 DNVR 80210 2197 A4
3600 DNVR 80222 2197 E6
Buchtel Blvd N
400 DNVR 80209 2196 E4
500 DNVR 80210 2196 E4
600 DNVR 80210 2197 A4
Buckaroo Rd
10 PrkC 80456 2522 D5
Buckboard Dr
3100 JfnC 80439 2273 C3
Buckboard Ln
29400 JfnC 80439 2273 C3
E Buckboard Rd
11400 DgsC 80138 2455 D5
Buckeye Ct
3600 BLDR 80304 1602 C6
Buckeye St
10400 DgsC 80125 2530 E6
Buckham Wy
- LGMT 80503 1438 A7
S Buck Hill Dr
9100 DgsC 80126 2449 E3
Buckhorn Cir
45300 EbtC 80107 2458 E3
W Buckhorn Rd
12300 JfnC 80127 2445 D4
E Buckhorn Wy
11800 DgsC 80116 2707 D2
W Buckhorn Wy
13100 JfnC 80127 2445 C4
Buckhorn Creek St
12600 PARK 80134 2537 C5
Buckingham Ct
7300 BldC 80301 1604 D2
S Buckingham Ct
9700 DgsC 80130 2450 D5
E Buckingham Pl
7200 DgsC 80130 2450 C5
Buckingham Rd
5000 BldC 80301 1604 C2
7300 BLDR 80301 1604 C2
Buckland Rd
- EbtC 80107 2795 B3
S Buckley Cir
1500 AURA 80017 2201 A5
S Buckley Ct
2200 AURA 80013 2201 A7
Buckley Dr
300 LGMT 80501 1356 B5
Buckley Rd
- AdmC 80022 1864 E3
- DNVR 80249 1948 E7
5600 AdmC 80022 2032 E3
5600 AdmC 80249 2032 E3
5600 DNVR 80022 2032 E3
5600 DNVR 80239 2032 E3
5600 DNVR 80249 2032 E3
8000 AdmC 80022 1948 E1
8000 CMCY 80022 1948 E1
8000 DNVR 80022 1948 E1
12000 AdmC 80603 1864 E1
12000 CMCY 80022 1864 E1
12000 CMCY 80603 1864 E1
12200 AdmC 80603 1780 E6
12200 CMCY 80603 1780 E6
13200 AdmC 80601 1780 E6
13200 BGTN 80601 1780 E6
13200 BGTN 80603 1780 E6
S Buckley Rd
- AphC 80016 2369 A2
- CTNL 80016 2369 A2
500 AURA 80017 2201 A6
1700 AURA 80013 2201 A6
2600 AURA 80013 2285 A1
4200 AURA 80015 2285 A3
5000 CTNL 80015 2285 A7
5400 CTNL 80015 2369 A1
6700 FXFD 80016 2369 A2
Buckley Wy
600 AURA 80011 2116 E7
1900 AURA 80011 2117 A4
S Buckley Wy
1500 AURA 80017 2201 A5
4500 AURA 80015 2285 A5
W Bucknell Cir
3600 DgsC 80129 2447 E5
Bucknell Ct
10 BLDR 80305 1687 A5
S Bucknell Ct
9700 DgsC 80129 2447 E5
W Bucknell Dr
3600 DgsC 80129 2447 E5
E Bucknell Pl
6800 DNVR 80224 2282 C1
7800 DNVR 80231 2282 E1
W Bucknell Pl
3400 DgsC 80129 2447 E4
S Bucknell Wy
9700 DgsC 80129 2447 E5
Buckskin Ct
200 EbtC 80138 2539 E2
Buckskin Dr
- CCkC 80439 2187 D5
E Buckskin Ln
800 DgsC 80108 2619 C4
Buckskin Pl
- BldC 80020 1775 A2
Buckskin Rd
43700 DgsC 80138 2539 E2
Buckskin Tr
10 PrkC 80456 2607 C7
6900 DgsC 80125 2614 D1
Buckthorn Dr
10 JfnC 80127 2361 A7
E Buckthorn Dr
- LGMT 80503 1438 A4
W Buckthorn Dr
- LGMT 80503 1438 A5
Buckthorn Ln
16300 DgsC 80134 2452 E2
Buckthorn Wy
500 LSVL 80027 1773 B1
Buckwheat Run
8500 PARK 80134 2452 E1
Budd Ct
1600 LGMT 80501 1439 A6
Buddy Rd
700 PrkC 80456 2606 C7
700 PrkC 80456 2690 C1
Buell Mansion Pkwy
- AphC 80113 2281 C3
- CHLV 80113 2281 C3
- DNVR 80210 2281 C3
- DvrC 80210 2281 C3
Buena Vista
300 JfnC 80401 2191 A3
Buena Vista Blvd
4700 CSRK 80109 2702 C2
Buena Vista Ct
- BGTN 80601 1697 A7
4400 CSRK 80109 2702 C2
S Buena Vista Dr
10000 JfnC 80433 2441 C6
Buffalo Av
3500 BMFD 80020 1775 D5
Buffalo Ct
900 LGMT 80501 1439 D1
7400 DgsC 80125 2531 B7
S Buffalo Dr
6600 LITN 80120 2364 D4
S Buffalo Dr
9100 JfnC 80127 2445 C3
Buffalo Ln
25800 JfnC 80401 2190 B2
Buffalo Rd
5100 BldC 80516 1607 B1
5300 WldC 80516 1523 B7
Buffalo Run
6200 DgsC 80125 2614 E3
S Buffalo St
6800 LITN 80120 2364 D4
Buffalo Tr
- AURA 80010 2115 B5
500 EbtC 80107 2708 B1
7600 DgsC 80108 2534 C6
Buffaloberry Dr
- DgsC 80138 2539 A2
- PARK 80138 2538 D3
9500 DgsC 80138 2538 E2
Buffalo Bill Cir
300 JfnC 80401 2191 B3
S Buffalo Creek Dr
4800 JfnC 80439 2272 D7
S Buffalo Creek Ln
4900 JfnC 80439 2272 E7
S Buffalo Creek Rd
17900 JfnC 80433 2694 D6
17900 JfnC 80470 2694 D6
31700 JfnC 80439 2272 D7
32400 JfnC 80439 2356 D1
Buffalo Grass Dr
37800 EbtC 80107 2624 B7
Buffalo Grass Ln
3500 CSRK 80109 2702 D1
Buffalo Grass Lp
- BMFD 80020 1775 C1
Buffalo Grass Pl
1200 EbtC 80107 2624 C7
Buffalo Park Rd
- CCkC 80439 2355 C7
- CCkC 80439 2439 C1
- PrkC 80470 2439 C1
28500 JfnC 80439 2273 C7
29100 JfnC 80439 2357 B1
33300 CCkC 80439 2356 A3
Buffalo Pond Tr
3400 DgsC 80116 2791 A7
Buffalo Ridge Ct
1100 DgsC 80108 2534 D6
Buffalo Ridge Rd
900 DgsC 80108 2534 C6
Buffalo Ridge Wy
1000 DgsC 80108 2534 D6
Buffum St
10 PrkC 80456 2521 D2
Buford Ln
20600 JfnC 80465 2443 C6
Buggy Whip Rd
10 PrkC 80456 2606 E4
Bugle Ct
6700 BldC 80301 1604 B3
E Bulkey St
1000 DgsC 80108 2619 C7
Bulldogger Ct
- PrkC 80456 2606 E4
Bulldogger Rd
10 PrkC 80456 2606 E4
10 PrkC 80456 2607 A4
Bullock Ct
10800 DgsC 80134 2452 E7
10800 PARK 80134 2452 E7
Bulrush Ct
2100 CSRK 80109 2703 B4
Bulrush Dr
1000 CSRK 80109 2703 B5
Bungalow Wy
14300 BMFD 80020 1775 C3
Bunker Wy
15700 JfnC 80465 2360 E1
Bunnell Av
400 BldC 80026 1607 B7
400 ERIE 80516 1607 B7
Bunny Ln
300 EbtC 80107 2708 A1
Bunny Rd
10 PrkC 80456 2607 D7
Bunting Dr
700 LAFT 80026 1690 D5
Bunting Cove
800 LAFT 80026 1690 D6
Burbank St
400 BMFD 80020 1858 C1
500 BMFD 80020 1774 C7
S Burberry Ln
9600 DgsC 80129 2448 D4
S Burberry Wy
9600 DgsC 80129 2448 D4
Burdett St
10 PrkC 80456 2522 A2
W Burgandy St
300 DgsC 80129 2448 D4
Burgess Av
100 GOLD 80401 2192 A1
Burgess Dr
10 CSRK 80104 2703 E7
300 CSRK 80104 2704 A7
Burggarten Dr
10 DgsC 80108 2534 D6
W Burgundy Av
9100 JfnC 80123 2362 C2
10100 JfnC 80127 2362 A2
12200 JfnC 80127 2361 D2
S Burgundy Cir
9300 DgsC 80126 2448 E4
E Burgundy Ct
10 DgsC 80126 2448 E4
Burgundy Dr
7000 BldC 80503 1520 E4
E Burgundy Dr
10 DgsC 80126 2448 E4
10 DgsC 80129 2448 E4
S Burgundy Dr
12800 JfnC 80127 2361 C2
W Burgundy Dr
6300 JfnC 80123 2363 A2
8500 JfnC 80123 2362 C2
10000 JfnC 80127 2362 B2
Burgundy Ln
4600 BldC 80301 1604 A3
E Burgundy Ln
10 DgsC 80126 2448 E4
S Burgundy Pl
9400 DgsC 80126 2448 E4
W Burgundy Pl
5200 JfnC 80123 2363 C2
12700 JfnC 80127 2361 C2
E Burgundy St
10 DgsC 80126 2448 E4
10 DgsC 80129 2448 E4
W Burgundy St
300 DgsC 80126 2448 D4
300 DgsC 80129 2448 D4
E Burgundy Wy
10 DgsC 80126 2448 E4
Burke Rd
31200 JfnC 80403 1852 E5
Burke St
10 PrkC 80456 2521 E2
Burland Dr
10 PrkC 80456 2691 B2
400 PrkC 80456 2690 E1
1600 PrkC 80456 2606 E7
11000 JfnC 80403 1853 A5
Burland Rd
30700 JfnC 80403 1853 A5
30800 JfnC 80403 1852 E4
N Burlington Av
100 BldC 80026 1690 D4
100 LAFT 80026 1690 D4
S Burlington Av
100 BldC 80026 1690 D4
100 LAFT 80026 1690 D4
Burlington Blvd
13600 AdmC 80603 1781 A4
13900 BGTN 80601 1781 A3
Burlington Dr
10 LGMT 80501 1439 B6
E Burlington Dr
5400 CSRK 80104 2704 E5
N Burlington Dr
1100 CSRK 80104 2704 E6
S Burlington Ln
9300 DgsC 80130 2450 C4
Burlington Pl
18700 DNVR 80249 2033 C5
E Burlington Pl
12100 DNVR 80239 2031 E5
W Burlington Pl
1500 DNVR 80221 2028 C5
Burlington Wy
10 LGMT 80501 1439 A6
Burn Ln
31300 JfnC 80439 2188 E6
Burnham Dr
3400 JfnC 80457 2274 A3
S Burning Ridge Ct
8700 DgsC 80116 2706 C3
N Burning Ridge Dr
2100 DgsC 80116 2706 C3
E Burning Tree Dr
7600 DgsC 80116 2706 A4
E Burning Tree Tr
8100 DgsC 80116 2706 B3
Burnley Ct
8300 DgsC 80126 2449 C2
S Burnt Oak Dr
2100 DgsC 80116 2706 B3
E Burnt Oak Tr
8100 DgsC 80116 2706 C3
S Burntwood Ct
9700 DgsC 80126 2449 A5
Burntwood Wy
9200 DgsC 80126 2449 A4
9700 DgsC 80126 2448 D3
Bur Oak Ln
4900 DgsC 80134 2622 A5
Bur Oak Pl
7400 DgsC 80134 2622 A4
Burr Pl
4400 BLDR 80303 1687 B3
S Burro Ln
5600 JfnC 80439 2358 D2
Burt St
100 CLCY 80403 2017 C4
Burton St
10 PrkC 80456 2522 A2
S Busch Ln
10 LGMT 80501 1439 A5
Busch St
700 LGMT 80501 1439 A5
Bush St
10 BGTN 80601 1696 B6
E Business Center Dr
6100 DgsC 80130 2450 C1
Butler Cir
4300 BLDR 80305 1687 B7
Butler Ct
200 LGMT 80501 1439 C2
S Butler Wy
900 LKWD 80226 2194 D4
900 LKWD 80232 2194 D4
S Butte Cir
2500 DgsC 80135 2785 E6
Butte Dr
29600 JfnC 80403 1853 B4
Butte Pkwy
400 GOLD 80403 2107 E2
Butte Rd
- LAFT 80026 1691 A7
Butte St
5000 BLDR 80301 1603 C7
Butte Mill Rd
5800 BldC 80301 1603 E7
Buttercup Cir S
- BGTN 80601 1780 D2
Buttercup Dr
4900 CSRK 80109 2702 D1
Buttercup Ln
3100 JfnC 80439 2274 A2
Buttercup Rd
1000 EbtC 80107 2624 B7
1100 EbtC 80107 2708 B1
Butterfield Ln
1200 CSRK 80104 2788 A1
Butterfield Crossing Dr
3700 CSRK 80109 2702 D1
Buttermilk Ct
30900 JfnC 80439 2189 A6
Buttermilk Ln
10 PrkC 80456 2607 E2
Buttermilk Rd
1000 DgsC 80118 2954 D4
Butterwood Ct
9100 DgsC 80126 2449 A3
Butterwort Cir
15800 DgsC 80134 2452 D1
S Buttonhill Ct
9200 DgsC 80130 2450 B3
Button Rock Ct
1100 LGMT 80501 1357 A7
1100 LGMT 80501 1440 A1
Button Rock Dr
900 LGMT 80501 1440 A1
1100 LGMT 80501 1357 A7
Byers Av
- DNVR 80230 2198 C2
E Byers Av
7000 DNVR 80230 2198 D2
W Byers Av
7400 LKWD 80226 2194 E2
W Byers Dr
2100 DNVR 80223 2196 B2
Byers Pl
7200 LKWD 80226 2194 E2
E Byers Pl
23700 AphC 80018 2202 D1
W Byers Pl
10 DNVR 80209 2196 D2
900 DNVR 80223 2196 D2
4700 DNVR 80219 2195 C2
6000 LKWD 80226 2195 A2
14500 JfnC 80401 2193 A2
W Byron Pl
2400 DNVR 80211 2112 A3
3600 DNVR 80211 2111 D3
4300 DNVR 80212 2111 C3
5100 DNVR 80204 2111 C3
5100 EDGW 80214 2111 C3

C

C St
- AdmC 80022 1947 B1
- AdmC 80022 2031 B2
- AURA 80011 2116 C4
- DNVR 80022 2031 B2
- DNVR 80123 2363 A1
- DNVR 80239 2031 B2
- JfnC 80123 2363 A1
- LGMT 80501 1356 A6
1300 GOLD 80401 2108 A7
Caballo Ct
10 BldC 80303 1688 D6
Cabbage Av
- BGTN 80601 1696 B5
S Cabbage Av
10 BGTN 80601 1696 B6
Cabrini Blvd
21500 JfnC 80401 2191 B2
Cache Creek Ct
- CSRK 80108 2704 C4
Cache Creek Pt
- CSRK 80108 2704 B4
Cactus Cir
2600 JfnC 80401 2109 A3
44600 EbtC 80107 2458 E3
Cactus Ct
200 BldC 80304 1602 A5
9100 LNTR 80124 2451 A3
W Cactus Ct
500 LSVL 80027 1689 B7
Cactus Dr
- TNTN 80260 1944 C2
34000 JfnC 80439 2272 B3
Cactus Bloom Ct
- CSRK 80109 2702 D5
W Cactus Bluff Av
2600 DgsC 80129 2448 A3
W Cactus Bluff Pl
2400 DgsC 80129 2448 B3
S Cactus Bluff Wy
9200 DgsC 80129 2448 B4
E Cactus Creek Ct
3700 DgsC 80126 2449 D1
S Cactus Flower Wy
8800 DgsC 80126 2449 B3
Cactus Rose Cir
1400 DgsC 80104 2871 D3
Caddo Pkwy
3600 BLDR 80303 1687 B5
Cade St
- BGTN 80601 1697 B5
Cadland Ct
16100 DgsC 80134 2452 E4
Caesar Rd
- GpnC 80403 1934 B3
Cahita Ct
4200 DNVR 80216 2028 D7
Cairn Ct
- BldC 80301 1603 E5
S Cairns Ct
10000 DgsC 80130 2450 A5
W Caithness Pl
2400 DNVR 80211 2112 A2
Calabria Pl
4500 LGMT 80503 1437 E6
4500 LGMT 80503 1438 A6
W Calahan Av
6800 LKWD 80232 2195 A5
7000 LKWD 80232 2194 E5
Calais Dr
2100 LGMT 80501 1356 E5
Calaveras Ct
2000 LGMT 80501 1356 D5
Calawba St
7700 DNVR 80249 1950 D5
Calcite Ct
7100 CSRK 80108 2619 E6
Caldwell Ct
23700 JfnC 80465 2358 D2
Caledonia Cir
1300 LSVL 80027 1689 C7
Caledonia St
200 LSVL 80027 1689 C7
E Calendola Dr
- PARK 80134 2537 B5
Caleridge Ct
10 DgsC 80130 2450 A2
E Caley Av
- AphC 80015 2370 C3
- AphC 80016 2369 A3
200 CTNL 80121 2364 E3
1200 CTNL 80121 2365 A3
3200 AphC 80121 2365 D3
5300 CTNL 80121 2366 B3
6500 CTNL 80111 2366 C3
7300 AphC 80111 2366 D3
7300 GDVL 80111 2366 D3
8900 GDVL 80111 2367 A3
10800 AphC 80111 2367 D3
10800 CTNL 80111 2367 D3
14000 CTNL 80111 2368 B3
14100 AphC 80111 2368 B3
15400 AphC 80016 2368 D3
15400 CTNL 80016 2368 D3
16700 CTNL 80016 2369 A3
W Caley Av
10 CTNL 80121 2364 D3
10 LITN 80120 2364 D3
10 LITN 80121 2364 D3
6100 JfnC 80123 2363 A3
9500 JfnC 80123 2362 B3
10800 JfnC 80127 2361 E3
10800 JfnC 80127 2362 A3
E Caley Cir
4000 CTNL 80121 2365 E3
9500 AphC 80111 2367 B3
16800 AphC 80016 2369 A3
W Caley Cir
300 LITN 80120 2364 D3
E Caley Dr
- AURA 80016 2371 C2
500 CTNL 80121 2364 E3
500 CTNL 80121 2365 A3
5700 CTNL 80111 2366 B3
18100 AphC 80016 2369 B3
20500 CTNL 80016 2369 E3
20600 CTNL 80016 2370 A3
W Caley Dr
300 LITN 80120 2364 D3
7300 JfnC 80123 2362 E3
E Caley Ln
4300 CTNL 80121 2365 E3
5700 CSRK 80104 2704 E7
17300 AphC 80016 2369 A3
20500 CTNL 80016 2369 E3
Caley Pl
3900 CTNL 80121 2365 E3
E Caley Pl
- AURA 80016 2371 C2
4000 CTNL 80121 2365 E3
4700 CTNL 80121 2366 A3
10000 AphC 80111 2367 B3
14000 CTNL 80111 2368 B3
14100 AphC 80016 2368 B3
15500 CTNL 80016 2368 D3
18200 AphC 80016 2369 C3
20500 CTNL 80016 2369 E3
20700 AphC 80016 2370 A3
W Caley Pl
2000 LITN 80120 2364 B3
6300 JfnC 80123 2363 A3
8000 JfnC 80123 2362 D3
10300 JfnC 80127 2362 A3
Calfee Gulch Rd
12200 JfnC 80433 2524 E5
Calgary Wy
700 JfnC 80401 2190 E4
N Calhan Av
1100 CSRK 80104 2704 E5
W Calhoun Av
- JfnC 80123 2363 B4
E Calhoun Dr
- AURA 80016 2371 B3
W Calhoun Dr
8000 JfnC 80123 2362 D4
E Calhoun PL
- AphC 80016 2370 E3
- AphC 80016 2371 A3
- AURA 80016 2371 A3
E Calhoun Pl
22000 AURA 80016 2370 C3
W Calhoun Pl
6500 JfnC 80123 2363 A4
7900 JfnC 80123 2362 D4
California St
1400 DNVR 80202 2112 D4
1400 DNVR 80204 2112 D4
1900 DNVR 80205 2112 E4
2700 DNVR 80205 2113 A3
California Gulch Rd
- BldC 80455 1597 D5
10 BldC 80481 1597 D3
Calilco Ct
2000 LGMT 80503 1438 A6
Calkins Av
1500 LGMT 80501 1355 E5
Calkins Pl
2600 BMFD 80020 1776 A7
2800 BMFD 80020 1775 E7
Callabra Av
18000 PARK 80134 2537 B5
Callae Ct
13400 JfnC 80433 2526 D7

STREET Block City ZIP Map# Grid

Callae Ct
13400 JfnC 80433 2610 E1
Callae Dr
12400 JfnC 80433 2526 D6
Callan Ct
2800 BMFD 80020 1775 E4
Callaway Ct
11000 PARK 80138 2454 D7
11000 PARK 80138 2538 D1
Callaway Rd
11000 PARK 80138 2454 D7
11000 PARK 80138 2538 D1
Calle Louisa
4500 JfnC 80403 2020 E6
Callisto Dr
13200 DgsC 80124 2450 E2
Calloway Ct
4300 BMFD 80020 1775 C3
Calumet Dr
\- EbtC 80107 2794 C1
Calvin Dr
8600 ARVD 80002 2026 C4
W Calypso Ct
3100 CSRK 80109 2702 E2
Camargo Dr
27400 JfnC 80401 2189 E5
S Camargo Rd
5200 LITN 80123 2279 D7
5300 LITN 80123 2363 D1
S Camargo Wy
5900 AphC 80123 2363 D2
5900 LITN 80123 2363 D2
Cambridge Av
3900 BMFD 80020 1775 D7
E Cambridge Ct
11100 PARK 80138 2537 E1
Cambridge Dr
1500 LGMT 80503 1355 C6
E Cambridge Pl
11100 PARK 80138 2537 C2
W Cambridge Pl
9600 LITN 80127 2446 B4
Cambridge St
4700 BldC 80301 1604 E2
E Cambridge Wy
20200 PARK 80138 2537 E1
Cambro Ln
\- LAFT 80026 1690 D6
Camden Dr
3300 LGMT 80503 1355 B7
Camden Pl
200 BLDR 80302 1686 D5
Camelback Ln
29300 JfnC 80439 2273 C1
S Camelback St
9200 DgsC 80126 2449 A3
Camel Heights Cir
27900 JfnC 80439 2273 D7
S Camel Heights Rd
4900 JfnC 80439 2273 D7
Camelia Ct
6800 BldC 80503 1520 E5
Camelot Dr
10600 DgsC 80116 2707 B6
N Camenish Wy
9000 FLHT 80260 1944 A2
Cameo Ln
4200 CSRK 80104 2787 D5
Cameron Cir
\- DgsC 80118 2954 C2
Cameron Ct
500 LGMT 80501 1439 D2
Cameron Dr
\- BGTN 80603 1864 C2
7400 DgsC 80118 2954 D2
12000 AdmC 80603 1864 C1
12000 CMCY 80603 1864 C2
12400 AdmC 80603 1780 D7
12400 CMCY 80603 1780 D7
Cameron Ln
700 LGMT 80501 1439 D1
Cameyo Rd W
4100 JfnC 80439 2275 B5
4100 JfnC 80465 2275 B5
Camino Bosque
10 BldC 80302 1600 E5
Camino Perdido
4200 JfnC 80403 2021 A7
Campbell Rd
10 PrkC 80456 2522 A1
Campden Ct
4500 CSRK 80104 2704 D7
Campden Pl
7000 DgsC 80108 2618 E1
7100 DgsC 80108 2534 E7
Camp Eden Rd
\- GpnC 80403 1851 E3
10 BldC 80403 1852 B1
Campfire St
\- DgsC 80125 2530 E5
Campground Wy
\- AdmC 80601 1779 A7
Campion Wy
17100 PARK 80134 2453 A6
Campo Ct
3800 BldC 80301 1603 A5
Campo Dr
17000 PARK 80134 2453 A7
Campo St
10 AdmC 80221 1944 D6
Campo Wy
400 SUPE 80027 1773 A6
Camprobber Ct
10 PrkC 80456 2691 B1
Campus Dr
10 BldC 80027 1773 C4
10 LSVL 80027 1773 C4
2600 LAFT 80026 1774 C2
8900 AphC 80015 2283 A6
8900 DNVR 80237 2283 A6
8900 GDVL 80111 2283 A6
8900 GDVL 80237 2283 A6
W Campus Dr
1200 GOLD 80401 2107 D4
1400 LITN 80120 2364 C7
Cana Ct
2400 LAFT 80026 1689 D2
Canadian Crossing Dr
\- LGMT 80501 1356 C5
Canal Av
\- AdmC 80640 1863 D5
\- CMCY 80640 1863 D5
W Canal Cir
1600 LITN 80120 2364 C7
W Canal Ct
\- LITN 80120 2448 C1
E Canal Dr
11700 AURA 80011 2199 D1
11700 AURA 80012 2199 D1
11800 AURA 80011 2115 D7
E Canal Pl
\- AURA 80018 2119 B7
Canary Ct
900 BGTN 80601 1779 D1
900 BGTN 80601 1780 A1
33500 EbtC 80107 2793 D1
Canary Ln
800 BGTN 80601 1696 A7
800 BGTN 80601 1780 B2
N Canary Ln
11200 DgsC 80138 2454 A6
Canary St
9600 FLHT 80260 1944 A1
9700 FLHT 80260 1860 A7
S Canberra Ct
9700 DgsC 80130 2450 A4
S Canberra Dr
9500 DgsC 80130 2450 A4
Candleglow St
\- CSRK 80109 2702 D4
S Candlewood Ct
9900 DgsC 80126 2449 D5
S Candlewood Ln
9900 DgsC 80126 2449 D5
Canna Pl
3000 SUPE 80027 1773 C7
3000 SUPE 80027 1857 B1
W Cannes Dr
8500 LITN 80127 2446 C4
Cannon Cir
1300 LSVL 80027 1689 D6
W Cannon Pl
500 LAFT 80026 1690 B5
Cannon St
1300 LSVL 80027 1689 D7
E Cannon St
100 LAFT 80026 1690 D5
W Cannon St
100 LAFT 80026 1690 C5
Cannonade Dr
10900 PARK 80138 2538 A1
Cannonade Ln
11000 PARK 80138 2538 A1
Cannonade Wy
11400 PARK 80138 2538 A1
Cannon Mountain Dr
1400 LGMT 80503 1437 D6
Cannon Mountain Wy
5400 LGMT 80503 1437 D6
Canon Cir
10 GDVL 80111 2367 A1
Canon Dr
10 GDVL 80111 2367 A1
Canon Pk
10 BldC 80302 1686 A3
Canon Pl
10 GDVL 80111 2367 A1
Canon St
100 MRSN 80465 2276 C3
Canongate Ln
10 DgsC 80130 2450 A2
S Canongate Ln
8600 DgsC 80130 2450 A2
Canon View Rd
10 BldC 80302 1601 B1
Canopus Dr
13100 DgsC 80124 2450 D2
Canosa Ct
\- AdmC 80221 2028 A1
1400 DNVR 80204 2112 A5
7000 WSTR 80030 2028 A1
7200 WSTR 80030 1944 A6
10500 WSTR 80234 1860 A5
S Canosa Ct
100 DNVR 80219 2196 A2
3200 SRDN 80110 2280 A3
Canosa St
10400 WSTR 80234 1860 A6
Canosa Wy
10400 WSTR 80234 1860 A6
S Canosa Wy
10 DNVR 80219 2196 A1
Canossa Dr
2600 BMFD 80020 1860 A1
Canterberry Ln
11300 PARK 80138 2538 D2
Canterberry Pkwy
\- DgsC 80138 2454 C7
\- DgsC 80138 2538 B4
\- PARK 80138 2454 C7
\- PARK 80138 2538 B4
Canterberry Tr
\- DgsC 80138 2538 D2
22500 PARK 80138 2538 D1
Canterbury Cir
3700 BMFD 80020 1775 D7
29400 JfnC 80439 2273 B1
Canterbury Ct
7600 BldC 80301 1604 D3
Canterbury Dr
600 BldC 80026 1690 E5
600 LAFT 80026 1690 E5
4400 BldC 80301 1604 D3
S Canterbury Ln
2600 JfnC 80439 2273 B1
Cantitoe Ln
10 CHLV 80113 2282 A6
N Cantrell Ct
5700 DgsC 80134 2622 B3
N Cantrell Wy
6000 DgsC 80134 2622 E3
Cantril St
10 CSRK 80104 2703 D6
S Cantril St
10 CSRK 80104 2703 D7
Canvasback Cir
7800 DgsC 80125 2530 E6
Canvasback Ct
7900 DgsC 80125 2530 E6
W Canyon Av
5600 JfnC 80128 2363 A7
7900 JfnC 80128 2362 D7
9900 JfnC 80127 2362 B7
Canyon Blvd
100 BldC 80302 1686 B2
100 BLDR 80302 1686 B2
2600 BLDR 80301 1686 E2
Canyon Blvd SR-7
1200 BLDR 80302 1686 B2
2600 BLDR 80301 1686 E2
Canyon Blvd SR-119
100 BldC 80302 1686 B2
100 BLDR 80302 1686 B2
2600 BLDR 80301 1686 E2
Canyon Cir
31600 JfnC 80439 2188 E7
31600 JfnC 80439 2272 E1
Canyon Cr
11200 WldC 80504 1440 E2
Canyon Ct
600 LCHB 80603 1698 B3
Canyon Dr
600 CSRK 80104 2703 D5
W Canyon Dr
5600 JfnC 80128 2363 B7
Canyon Ln
700 LCHB 80603 1698 B3
N Canyon Ln
4300 DgsC 80108 2619 B6
E Canyon Pl
23400 AURA 80016 2370 D6
W Canyon Pl
8300 JfnC 80128 2362 D7
N Canyon Rd
17200 JfnC 80127 2444 B6
Canyon Tr
5600 EbtC 80107 2710 A6
W Canyon Tr
5200 JfnC 80128 2363 B7
Canyon Alder
10 JfnC 80127 2361 A7
Canyonbrook Dr
4300 DgsC 80108 2533 E1
4300 DgsC 80108 2534 A1
Canyonbrook Wy
11000 DgsC 80108 2534 A1
Canyon Cedar
10 JfnC 80127 2361 B7
Canyon Club Dr
4500 DgsC 80108 2618 E6
Canyon Creek Rd
2900 BLDR 80303 1687 A4
Canyon Crest Dr
2700 DgsC 80126 2449 C6
Canyon Crest Ln
2800 DgsC 80126 2449 C6
Canyon Crest Pl
2800 DgsC 80126 2449 C6
Canyon Gulch Tr
\- DgsC 80134 2452 D1
Canyonlands Wy
\- CSRK 80109 2702 B4
Canyon Oak Dr
\- CSRK 80104 2703 E4
Canyon Point Cir
10 GOLD 80403 2107 C2
Canyon Ranch Rd
\- DgsC 80126 2449 D1
E Canyon Ranch Rd
3800 DgsC 80126 2449 E1
Canyon Rim Cir
\- DgsC 80134 2452 D1
Canyon Rim Dr
\- DgsC 80134 2452 D1
Canyon Rim Tr
\- DgsC 80134 2452 D1
Canyonside Dr
10 BldC 80302 1685 D2
Canyon View Dr
500 GOLD 80403 2107 C3
19600 JfnC 80465 2443 D6
Canyon View Rd
10 BldC 80302 1684 E3
10 BldC 80302 1685 A3
Canyon Vista Dr
10 MRSN 80465 2276 B4
Canyon Vista Ln
10 MRSN 80465 2276 B4
Canyonwood Ct
10400 DgsC 80129 2448 E7
Canyonwood Dr
10 DgsC 80129 2448 E6
100 DgsC 80126 2448 E6
Canyonwood Pl
10 DgsC 80129 2448 E6
S Canyon Wren Ct
9200 DgsC 80126 2449 E4
E Canyon Wren Ln
\- DgsC 80126 2449 E3
Canyon Wren Wy
16100 JfnC 80465 2360 D4
S Cape St
1500 LKWD 80232 2194 D5
S Cape Wy
1200 LKWD 80232 2194 D5
1900 LKWD 80227 2194 D6
W Cape Cod Wy
1800 LITN 80120 2448 B1
Capilano Ct
700 DgsC 80108 2618 D5
Capital Dr
100 GOLD 80401 2192 B1
Capitol Ct
\- BMFD 80020 1775 C5
Capitol Creek St
12800 PARK 80134 2537 C5
W Capri Av
8800 JfnC 80123 2362 C2
9800 JfnC 80127 2362 B3
12000 JfnC 80127 2361 D3
W Capri Dr
9400 JfnC 80123 2362 B3
W Capri Pl
5200 JfnC 80123 2363 C3
8400 JfnC 80123 2362 D2
11300 JfnC 80127 2361 E2
Caprice Ct
100 CSRK 80109 2703 D5
Caprice Dr
1000 CSRK 80109 2703 D5
E Captain Meriweather Lewis Dr
7900 DgsC 80134 2622 B3
Capulin Pl
100 DgsC 80108 2618 D4
Carbide Ct
1200 LGMT 80501 1356 D7
Carbon Ct
1000 ERIE 80516 1607 B7
Carbon Pl
\- BLDR 80301 1687 B1
Carbon Rd
9500 BMFD 80020 1773 E5
9900 BldC 80020 1773 E5
Carbon St
\- BLDR 80301 1687 A1
700 ERIE 80516 1607 B4
Carbonate Wy
5000 DgsC 80108 2618 E6
Cardens Ct
\- ERIE 80516 1607 A7
Cardens Pl
\- ERIE 80516 1607 A7
W Carder Ct
8000 DgsC 80125 2447 D3
8000 DgsC 80129 2447 D3
Cardinal Av
1100 BGTN 80601 1779 E1
1100 BGTN 80601 1780 B2
Cardinal Cir
1100 AdmC 80601 1780 A1
1100 BGTN 80601 1780 A1
Cardinal Dr
700 LAFT 80026 1690 D5
N Cardinal Dr
10900 DgsC 80138 2454 A6
Cardinal Ln
7000 BldC 80503 1520 A4
Cardinal St
9600 FLHT 80260 1944 A3
Cardinal Cove
800 LAFT 80026 1690 D6
Carefree Tr
4500 DgsC 80134 2621 A6
Carey Ln
7400 DgsC 80108 2534 E7
S Carey Wy
2500 DNVR 80222 2281 E1
Cargill Dr
1400 AdmC 80221 2028 C3
Caria Dr
100 LAFT 80026 1690 A5
1400 LAFT 80026 1689 E5
Caribou Dr
\- BldC 80466 1681 C6
E Caribou Dr
10900 DgsC 80116 2791 D4
Caribou Pl
100 LGMT 80501 1356 C7
Caribou Rd
10 NDLD 80466 1765 B2
2400 BldC 80466 1765 A1
Caribou St
200 NDLD 80466 1765 C3
S Caribou St
200 NDLD 80466 1765 C3
Caribou Pass Cir
300 LAFT 80026 1689 D4
Caribou Springs Tr
4800 BldC 80503 1436 B1
4900 BldC 80503 1353 B7
Carissa Cir
10 JfnC 80127 2361 A6
Carla Cir
10 BMFD 80020 1774 E5
Carla Wy
10 BMFD 80020 1774 E5
S Carlan Ct
1400 DNVR 80219 2196 A5
Carlile St
11400 NHGN 80233 1861 A3
Carlock Av
3800 BLDR 80305 1687 A7
Carlsbad
\- WldC 80504 1440 E2
Carlson Av
1300 ERIE 80516 1606 E2
1300 ERIE 80516 1607 A2
Carlson Dr
1000 LITN 80120 2364 C3
E Carlson Dr
16900 DgsC 80134 2453 A4
16900 PARK 80134 2453 A4
Carlson Ln
\- BLDR 80301 1603 C7
Carlson Rd
10 EbtC 80138 2540 B2
Carlton Pl
1200 LGMT 80501 1439 A2
N Carlton St
10 CSRK 80104 2704 D7
S Carlton St
10 CSRK 80104 2704 D7
600 CSRK 80104 2788 E1
Carlyle Park Cir
1200 DgsC 80129 2448 C4
Carlyle Park Pl
9400 DgsC 80129 2448 C4
Carmargo Rd
10 PrkC 80470 2524 A6
E Carmel Cir
18700 AURA 80011 2117 C3
Carmel Ct
1300 BMFD 80020 1774 E6
9800 LNTR 80124 2450 E5
Carmel Dr
11700 LKWD 80215 2109 D4
E Carmel Dr
18800 AURA 80011 2117 C3
Carmela Ln
10400 NHGN 80234 1860 B6
Carmen St
300 BldC 80027 1689 E5
400 LAFT 80026 1689 E5
400 LAFT 80027 1689 E5
Carmody Ln
10000 LKWD 80227 2194 A7
Carnation Cir
1300 LGMT 80503 1438 B6
Carnation Pl
7400 AdmC 80022 1945 E6
Carnation Wy
2400 TNTN 80229 1945 C2
Carnegie Dr
2700 BLDR 80305 1686 E6
2700 BLDR 80305 1687 A7
Carnelian Pl
10000 DgsC 80134 2452 E5
Carol Ct
41500 EbtC 80138 2540 E6
Carol Ln
8700 JfnC 80433 2440 B3
Carol Wy
6200 AdmC 80022 1946 B6
S Carole Av
700 LAFT 80026 1690 C5
Carolina Av
1200 LGMT 80501 1438 E1
1200 LGMT 80501 1439 A1
E Carolina Cir
9900 AURA 80247 2199 B4
E Carolina Dr
\- AURA 80247 2199 B5
12800 AURA 80012 2199 E5
14300 AURA 80012 2200 C4
16200 AURA 80017 2200 E5
19200 AURA 80017 2201 C5
W Carolina Dr
12000 JfnC 80232 2193 D5
12000 LKWD 80228 2193 D5
E Carolina Pl
\- AURA 80247 2199 B5
11800 AURA 80012 2199 D5
14800 AURA 80012 2200 C5
17800 AURA 80017 2201 B4
Caroline Av
1500 WldC 80603 1695 E1
1500 WldC 80621 1695 E1
Carolyn Dr
10 CCkC 80439 2271 E5
S Carolyn Dr
7600 DgsC 80108 2535 B6
Carpenter Ct
45100 EbtC 80138 2457 B6
Carpenter Run
4700 DgsC 80125 2614 E6
4700 DgsC 80125 2615 A6
E Carr Av
17000 PARK 80134 2453 A7
N Carr Av
100 LAFT 80026 1690 B4
S Carr Av
100 LAFT 80026 1690 B4
S Carr Av W
300 LAFT 80026 1690 B5
Carr Cir
8100 ARVD 80005 1942 C5
8900 WSTR 80021 1942 C2
Carr Ct
1900 LGMT 80501 1356 A5
2500 JfnC 80215 2110 D3
2500 LKWD 80215 2110 D3
6900 ARVD 80004 2026 C1
8100 ARVD 80005 1942 C5
8500 WSTR 80005 1942 D4
9100 WSTR 80021 1942 C2
S Carr Ct
2300 LKWD 80227 2194 D7
2400 LKWD 80227 2278 D1
4300 DNVR 80123 2278 D5
4300 DNVR 80235 2278 D5
4300 DvrC 80123 2278 D5
4300 JfnC 80235 2278 D5
6100 JfnC 80123 2362 D3
7200 JfnC 80128 2362 D6
8200 JfnC 80128 2446 D1
Carr Dr
1900 LGMT 80501 1356 A5
7400 ARVD 80005 1942 C6
Carr Lp
\- WSTR 80021 1942 C3
8700 WSTR 80005 1942 C3
Carr St
10 LKWD 80226 2194 D1
200 ERIE 80516 1607 C5
400 LKWD 80226 2110 D7
600 LKWD 80214 2110 D7
600 LKWD 80215 2110 D7
2500 JfnC 80215 2110 D5
3800 WTRG 80033 2110 D1
4800 ARVD 80002 2026 D5
4800 JfnC 80002 2026 C6
4800 WTRG 80033 2026 C6
5800 ARVD 80004 2026 D3
7000 ARVD 80004 1942 D7
7100 ARVD 80005 1942 D7
9300 WSTR 80021 1942 C1
11100 BMFD 80020 1858 C2
S Carr St
10 LKWD 80226 2194 D2
1400 LKWD 80232 2194 D5
1700 LKWD 80227 2194 D6
3200 LKWD 80227 2278 D3
3500 JfnC 80235 2278 D3
3500 LKWD 80235 2278 D3
7100 JfnC 80128 2362 D6
8300 JfnC 80128 2446 D2
S Carr Wy
7400 JfnC 80128 2362 D6
8300 JfnC 80128 2446 D1
9700 LITN 80127 2446 C5
Carrara Ter
10200 DgsC 80134 2452 D6
E Carriage Cir
8200 DgsC 80134 2622 B2
Carriage Ct
4000 BldC 80026 1606 C4
Carriage Dr
1200 LGMT 80501 1439 B5
Carriage Ln
10 CHLV 80121 2281 E7
10 CHLV 80121 2282 A6
E Carriage Ln
8100 DgsC 80134 2622 B1
Carriage Pl
\- DNVR 80237 2282 E6
Carriage Brook Rd
10 CHLV 80121 2282 A7
Carriage Club Dr
10200 DgsC 80124 2450 D6
Carriage Hill Ct
1200 DgsC 80116 2791 A3
Carriage Hills Dr
10 BldC 80302 1601 D3
Carriage Loop Dr
29800 JfnC 80439 2273 B3
Carrol Ct
1100 TNTN 80229 1945 A1
Carrol Ln
10600 NHGN 80233 1860 E5
S Carson Cir
10 AURA 80012 2200 B1
Carson Ct
10 BldC 80481 1515 A3
S Carson Ct
900 AURA 80012 2200 B3
5000 AphC 80015 2284 B6
5000 AURA 80015 2284 B6
12900 PARK 80134 2537 D5
Carson St
\- CMCY 80022 1864 B6
3200 AURA 80011 2116 B2
5500 DNVR 80239 2032 B4
S Carson St
1500 AURA 80012 2200 B5
3900 AURA 80014 2284 B4
4000 AURA 80015 2284 B4
6100 AphC 80016 2368 B2
6100 CTNL 80111 2368 B2
Carson Wy
5500 DNVR 80239 2032 B4
10000 CMCY 80022 1864 B6
S Carson Wy
1200 AURA 80012 2200 B4
2500 AURA 80014 2200 B7
4000 AURA 80014 2284 C4
4400 AURA 80015 2284 B5
S Carter Av
200 LSVL 80027 1773 C2
Carter Cir
\- DNVR 80224 2282 B2
3000 AphC 80222 2282 B2
3000 DNVR 80222 2282 B2
Carter Ct
4900 BldC 80301 1604 B2
S Carter Ct
100 LSVL 80027 1773 C1
Carter Dr
\- LYNS 80540 1352 E3
Carter Ln
200 LGMT 80501 1440 B3
Carter Tr
4200 BldC 80301 1604 C4
W Caryl Av
5200 AphC 80128 2363 B6
W Caryl Pl
5300 JfnC 80128 2363 C6
Cascade Av
500 BLDR 80302 1686 B4
5000 BLDR 80303 1687 C4
E Cascade Av
\- CSRK 80104 2704 D7
Cascade Ct
600 GOLD 80403 2107 D1
3500 BMFD 80020 1775 D5
8400 DgsC 80126 2449 A2
Cascade Dr
500 GOLD 80403 2107 D1
2800 FLHT 80260 1944 A1
2900 FLHT 80260 1943 E1
2900 WSTR 80031 1943 E1
Cascade Pl
5600 BLDR 80303 1687 D4
Cascade St
13400 BMFD 80020 1775 E5
Cascade Wy
\- LGMT 80503 1355 B5
Case Cir
3300 BLDR 80305 1687 A7
Casey Ct
1700 LAFT 80026 1689 D1
Casey Ln
12000 DgsC 80138 2455 A4
Casey St
100 CLCY 80403 2017 D4
Casey Jones Dr
\- EbtC 80107 2709 D7
Cash Rd
12200 BldC 80503 1354 C5
Casper Dr
500 LAFT 80026 1690 D7
E Caspian Cir
15600 AURA 80013 2200 D7
19600 AURA 80013 2201 D6
W Caspian Cir
4400 LITN 80128 2363 D5
E Caspian Dr
12300 AURA 80014 2199 E7
E Caspian Pl
14300 AURA 80014 2200 C7
19200 AURA 80013 2201 D6
W Caspian Pl
2000 EGLD 80110 2196 B7
Cass Ct
800 CSRK 80104 2789 A1
Cass St
\- CSRK 80104 2789 A1
Cassin Ct
1400 BLDR 80303 1687 D3
Castle Cir
4500 BMFD 80020 1775 C4
Castle Ct
32000 JfnC 80439 2188 E6
Castle Ln
4400 BMFD 80020 1775 C4
Castle Rd
9800 TNTN 80260 1860 B7
Castle St
\- LAFT 80026 1690 E6
Castle Brook Dr E
2700 DgsC 80108 2618 D4
Castle Brook Dr W
2700 DgsC 80108 2618 D4
Castle Butte Dr
2400 DgsC 80109 2786 A7
2400 DgsC 80109 2870 A1
4000 DgsC 80118 2870 C2
4000 DgsC 80135 2870 C2
Castle Crest Dr
2600 DgsC 80104 2704 A6
Castlegate Dr N
2200 CSRK 80108 2619 A7
Castlegate Dr W
6000 CSRK 80108 2619 A7
Castle Glen Ct
2700 DgsC 80108 2618 D4
Castle Glen Dr
2700 DgsC 80108 2618 D4
Castle Glen Pl
2700 DgsC 80108 2618 D4
Castlegrove Pl
1200 DgsC 80108 2618 C1
Castle Highlands Pkwy
\- CSRK 80109 2703 B6
W Castle Mesa Dr
900 DgsC 80109 2786 C2
Castle Oaks Dr
\- CSRK 80108 2620 E7
1700 CSRK 80104 2704 B5
1700 CSRK 80108 2704 B5
6600 CSRK 80108 2621 D7
6600 CSRK 80116 2621 D7
6600 DgsC 80108 2621 D7
6600 DgsC 80116 2621 D7
Castle Peak Av
2800 SUPE 80027 1773 B7
2900 SUPE 80027 1857 A1
Castle Peak Ln
4600 CSRK 80109 2786 E5
Castle Pines Dr N
10 DgsC 80108 2618 E4
10 DgsC 80108 2619 A4
Castle Pines Dr S
10 DgsC 80108 2619 A4
5000 DgsC 80108 2618 E6
E Castle Pines Pkwy
300 DgsC 80108 2535 C7
W Castle Pines Pkwy
\- DgsC 80108 2535 A7
600 DgsC 80108 2534 E7
1400 DgsC 80135 2534 E7
Castlepoint Ln
6700 DgsC 80108 2618 C1
Castlepointe Cir
1200 DgsC 80108 2618 C1
Castle Pointe Dr
1000 DgsC 80104 2789 D4
S Castle Ridge Cir
9500 DgsC 80129 2448 A4
S Castle Ridge Ct
9800 DgsC 80129 2448 B5
Castle Ridge Dr
\- DgsC 80129 2448 B5
W Castle Ridge Pl
2500 DgsC 80129 2448 B5
Castle Ridge Rd
900 JfnC 80401 2191 A4
W Castle Ridge Wy
2100 DgsC 80129 2448 B5
Castle Rock Dr
10 GOLD 80401 2107 E3
10 JfnC 80401 2107 E3
Castleton Ct
3000 CSRK 80109 2703 C2
N Castleton Ct
4100 CSRK 80109 2703 C2
Castleton Dr
4900 CSRK 80109 2703 C1
Castleton Rd
600 CSRK 80109 2703 B1
Castleton Wy
4500 CSRK 80109 2703 C1
Castlewood Ct
10 CCkC 80439 2187 D7
Castlewood Dr
10 CCkC 80439 2271 D1
300 CCkC 80439 2187 E7
N Castlewood Dr
900 DgsC 80116 2705 D4
N Castlewood Pl
1100 DgsC 80116 2705 B5
Castlewood Canyon Rd
10 DgsC 80104 2789 D1
10 DgsC 80116 2705 D7
10 DgsC 80116 2789 D1

STREET Block City ZIP Map# Grid

S Castlewood Canyon Rd
800 DgsC 80104 2789 E3
800 DgsC 80116 2789 D1
Catalina
- TNTN 80229 1945 D3
Catalpa Cir
1200 BMFD 80020 1774 C6
Catalpa Ct
400 LSVL 80027 1773 B1
Catalpa Pl
- ERIE 80516 1691 E2
Catalpa Wy
3400 BLDR 80304 1602 D6
Catamount Ln
10 JfnC 80127 2360 E4
10 PrkC 80456 2607 B6
Catamount Ridge Rd
10 PrkC 80456 2607 B6
Catarata Pl
6600 DgsC 80108 2534 C4
Catarata Wy
- DgsC 80108 2534 C4
N Catawaba Wy
- AURA 80018 2118 D7
S Catawba Cir
1400 AURA 80018 2202 D5
Catawba Ct
- AURA 80018 2118 D7
S Catawba Ct
5300 AphC 80016 2286 D7
8000 AURA 80016 2370 E7
Catawba St
- AURA 80016 2286 D6
N Catawba Wy
- AURA 80018 2118 D7
S Catawba Wy
7300 AURA 80016 2370 D5
S Cathay Cir
3000 AURA 80013 2285 C2
Cathay Ct
1700 AURA 80011 2117 C4
4900 DNVR 80249 2033 C5
S Cathay Ct
1300 AURA 80017 2201 C4
2700 AURA 80013 2285 C1
4900 AURA 80015 2285 C6
5200 CTNL 80015 2285 C7
5600 AphC 80015 2369 C1
6000 AphC 80016 2369 C2
Cathay St
2200 AURA 80011 2117 C3
4500 DNVR 80249 2033 C6
S Cathay St
1100 AURA 80017 2201 C4
3300 AURA 80013 2285 C2
7800 CTNL 80016 2369 C6
S Cathay Wy
1400 AURA 80017 2201 C5
2700 AURA 80013 2285 C1
4300 AURA 80015 2285 C5
5200 CTNL 80015 2285 C7
5400 CTNL 80015 2369 C1
Cathedral Tr
15300 JfnC 80433 2611 A5
Cathedral Peak
7800 JfnC 80127 2362 A7
N Cathedral Rock Dr
1000 DgsC 80135 2700 B6
Cato Cir
1700 LAFT 80026 1690 A6
1700 LSVL 80026 1690 A6
Cattail Ct
200 LGMT 80501 1440 A3
S Cattail Ct
9300 DgsC 80126 2449 A4
Cattail Dr
8200 BldC 80503 1521 A5
Cattle Trail Dr
10500 JfnC 80403 1853 C6
Cavaletti Dr
10100 DgsC 80125 2530 E5
10100 DgsC 80125 2531 A5
W Cavalry Run
10100 DgsC 80125 2615 A6
Cavan Ct
1400 BldC 80303 1689 C2
Cavan Ln
28500 JfnC 80439 2357 D6
Cavan St
1200 BldC 80026 1689 C3
1200 BldC 80303 1689 C3
1200 LAFT 80026 1689 C3
Cavanaugh Rd
10 AphC 80102 2206 B1
10 AphC 80137 2122 B7
1500 AdmC 80102 2122 B3
1500 AURA 80137 2122 B3
Cavanaugh Mile Rd
- AdmC 80102 2038 B7
- AdmC 80102 2122 B2
- AdmC 80137 2038 B2
- AdmC 80137 2122 B2
- AURA 80102 2038 B7
- AURA 80102 2122 B2
- AURA 80137 2038 B2
- AURA 80137 2122 B2
Cayenne Cir
15700 JfnC 80465 2360 E1
Cayman Pl
3200 BLDR 80301 1603 A4
Cayuga Wy
100 SUPE 80027 1772 D3
Caywood Ct
200 LGMT 80501 1439 D2
Cedar Av
- BldC 80304 1602 B7
100 CSRK 80104 2787 E1
100 CSRK 80104 2788 A1
300 BGTN 80601 1696 A6
900 BLDR 80304 1602 C7
28200 JfnC 80470 2693 D2
E Cedar Av
10 DNVR 80209 2196 E2
10 DNVR 80223 2196 E2
E Cedar Av
2400 DNVR 80209 2197 C2
3900 DNVR 80246 2197 D2
4700 DNVR 80246 2198 A2
5500 DNVR 80224 2198 A2
7300 DNVR 80230 2198 D2
11500 AURA 80012 2199 D2
13900 AURA 80012 2200 B1
W Cedar Av
10 DNVR 80209 2196 D2
1300 DNVR 80223 2196 B2
3000 DNVR 80219 2196 A2
3100 DNVR 80219 2195 E2
5100 LKWD 80226 2195 C2
9200 LKWD 80226 2194 B2
14600 JfnC 80401 2193 A2
Cedar Cir
900 LCHB 80603 1698 B2
28700 JfnC 80439 2273 D5
E Cedar Cir
12300 AURA 80012 2199 E1
S Cedar Cir
7600 LITN 80120 2364 C6
13200 JfnC 80470 2524 E7
W Cedar Cir
7200 LKWD 80226 2194 E2
Cedar Ct
10 BMFD 80020 1774 E6
10 LGMT 80503 1438 C1
2100 DgsC 80116 2706 D3
9300 TNTN 80229 1945 A1
Cedar Dr
10 PrkC 80456 2691 A2
13500 JfnC 80433 2609 D1
20600 JfnC 80465 2443 C6
W Cedar Dr
9100 LKWD 80226 2194 C2
11800 LKWD 80228 2193 C2
Cedar Ln
- LITN 80120 2363 E7
- LITN 80120 2447 E1
10 PrkC 80456 2607 C3
400 EbtC 80107 2708 A1
8500 WSTR 80031 1943 D4
34500 JfnC 80470 2524 A3
E Cedar Ln
3000 DNVR 80209 2197 D2
E Cedar Pl
- DNVR 80224 2198 C2
8100 DNVR 80230 2198 E2
15200 AURA 80012 2200 C1
W Cedar Pl
500 LSVL 80027 1689 B6
6500 LKWD 80226 2195 A2
13900 JfnC 80401 2193 A2
Cedar Rd
10 CCkC 80439 2356 A7
100 JfnC 80401 2190 E1
500 CCkC 80439 2355 E7
S Cedar Rd
4700 JfnC 80439 2273 D7
Cedar St
1400 BMFD 80020 1775 B6
9700 FLHT 80260 1860 A7
S Cedar St
5300 EGLD 80120 2280 C7
5300 LITN 80120 2280 C7
6200 LITN 80120 2364 C3
Cedar Wy
10 CCkC 80439 2272 A4
10 GpnC 80403 1933 D7
5000 EbtC 80107 2709 E1
W Cedar Wy
100 LSVL 80027 1689 C6
Cedarbrook Dr
15600 JfnC 80465 2360 E2
Cedar Brook Ln
10700 DgsC 80126 2449 D7
N Cedar Brook Rd
100 BldC 80304 1602 A4
1100 BldC 80304 1601 E3
S Cedar Brook Rd
10 BldC 80304 1602 A6
Cedarcrest Cir
10600 DgsC 80130 2450 A7
Cedar Glen Pl
4400 CSRK 80109 2702 C2
E Cedar Hill Pl
8900 LNTR 80124 2451 A3
S Cedar Hill Wy
9000 LNTR 80124 2451 A3
Cedarhurst Ln
9400 DgsC 80129 2448 D4
Cedaridge Cir
1800 SUPE 80027 1773 B6
S Cedaridge Ct
10200 DgsC 80129 2448 D7
S Cedaridge Wy
10000 DgsC 80129 2448 C5
Cedar Lake Rd
21100 JfnC 80401 2107 C7
Cedar Mountain Pl
3300 EbtC 80138 2457 B5
Cedarpoint Pl
4300 DgsC 80108 2449 E7
4300 DgsC 80124 2449 E7
Cedar Ridge Ct
16800 PARK 80134 2537 A1
Cedarwood Cir
2200 LAFT 80026 1774 C1
7100 BldC 80301 1604 C2
Cedarwood Dr
1200 LGMT 80501 1356 E7
1600 LGMT 80501 1357 A6
Cedarwood Ln
8700 DgsC 80126 2449 A2
S Cedarwood Rd
5600 GDVL 80121 2365 A1
Ceder Brook St
10700 DgsC 80126 2449 E7
Cedwick Dr
900 LAFT 80026 1690 D5
Celestine Ct
17500 PARK 80134 2453 A5
Celestine Pl
10200 PARK 80134 2453 B6
Cemetery Rd
10 JMWN 80455 1516 B3
Centaur Cir
1100 LAFT 80026 1690 A7
W Centaur Cir
- LSVL 80026 1690 A7
1200 LAFT 80026 1690 A7
Centaur Ct
10 LAFT 80026 1690 A6
S Centaur Dr
7500 JfnC 80439 2357 C7
7900 JfnC 80439 2441 D1
Centaur Plaza Ct
1200 LAFT 80026 1690 A6
Centaur Village Ct
1200 LAFT 80026 1690 A7
Centaur Village Dr
1100 LAFT 80026 1690 A6
E Centennial Av
10 AphC 80121 2280 E7
10 EGLD 80110 2280 E7
10 EGLD 80113 2280 E7
10 EGLD 80121 2280 E7
W Centennial Av
3300 LITN 80123 2279 E7
Centennial Blvd
10 DgsC 80129 2448 E2
Centennial Dr
100 LSVL 80027 1689 D6
500 BNNT 80102 2124 C2
1400 LGMT 80501 1356 C7
7000 DgsC 80138 2453 E5
7300 DgsC 80138 2454 A5
W Centennial Dr
100 BNNT 80102 2124 C2
1700 LSVL 80027 1689 C6
2800 LITN 80123 2280 A7
2900 LITN 80123 2364 A1
Centennial Pkwy
100 LSVL 80027 1772 E2
300 BldC 80027 1772 E2
400 LSVL 80027 1773 A3
W Centennial Rd
10200 JfnC 80127 2446 A1
10200 JfnC 80128 2446 A1
Centennial Tr
5200 BLDR 80303 1687 D3
8100 EbtC 80107 2543 A1
25100 JfnC 80401 2190 C1
Centennial Wy
700 BNNT 80102 2124 C2
Center Al
- IDSP 80452 2101 B5
Center Av
- LKWD 80226 2110 A7
E Center Av
- DNVR 80246 2198 A3
10 DNVR 80209 2196 E3
10 DNVR 80223 2196 E3
600 DNVR 80209 2197 A3
5200 GNDL 80246 2198 A3
5400 DNVR 80224 2198 A3
9100 DNVR 80247 2199 A2
11700 AURA 80012 2199 D2
14500 AURA 80012 2200 C2
14500 AURA 80017 2200 D2
N Center Av
- LKWD 80226 2110 A7
- LKWD 80226 2193 E1
- LKWD 80226 2194 A1
S Center Av
- LKWD 80226 2110 A7
- LKWD 80226 2194 A1
W Center Av
- DNVR 80209 2196 D3
2400 DNVR 80223 2196 A3
3000 DNVR 80219 2196 A3
5200 DNVR 80219 2195 B3
5200 LKWD 80219 2195 B3
5200 LKWD 80226 2195 B3
8400 LKWD 80226 2194 C3
11000 LKWD 80226 2193 E3
12200 LKWD 80228 2193 D3
Center Ct
3400 JfnC 80457 2274 B3
Center Dr
- DgsC 80134 2452 E5
- LITN 80120 2363 E7
- LITN 80120 2447 E1
- SRDN 80110 2280 A3
500 SUPE 80027 1772 E3
26100 JfnC 80457 2274 B3
E Center Dr
11500 AURA 80012 2199 D3
16200 AURA 80017 2200 E2
W Center Dr
5000 DNVR 80219 2195 C3
5000 LKWD 80219 2195 C3
5000 LKWD 80226 2195 C3
13200 LKWD 80228 2193 B3
Center Pl
- BldC 80501 1438 E4
- LGMT 80501 1438 E4
E Center Pl
15700 AURA 80017 2200 D3
W Center Pl
12000 LKWD 80228 2193 D3
Center Green Ct
2900 BLDR 80301 1603 B7
Center Green Dr
3000 BLDR 80301 1603 B7
Centerville Ct
19700 PARK 80134 2537 D3
Central Av
300 BGTN 80601 1696 C7
2000 BLDR 80301 1687 D2
Central Pl
1400 DNVR 80211 2112 B4
Central St
1500 DNVR 80211 2112 B2
Central City Pkwy
- CCkC 80439 2103 A3
Central City Pkwy
- CLCY 80403 2017 C5
- GpnC 80403 2017 C5
- GpnC 80403 2018 B7
- GpnC 80403 2102 D3
- GpnC 80403 2103 A3
- IDSP 80439 2102 C4
200 CCkC 80439 2102 C4
Central Park Blvd
- AURA 80010 2115 A4
- AURA 80238 2115 A4
- DNVR 80220 2115 A4
- DNVR 80238 2115 A4
- DvrC 80238 2115 A4
2600 DNVR 80238 2114 E3
Centre Cir
9700 DgsC 80134 2452 E4
Centre Ct
16700 DgsC 80134 2453 A5
Centrebridge Dr
7900 BldC 80503 1520 E5
Centrepoint Dr
- AURA 80012 2200 C2
E Centretech Cir
- AURA 80011 2116 D7
E Centretech Pkwy
- AURA 80011 2201 A1
15500 AURA 80011 2116 D7
15900 AURA 80011 2200 E1
W Century Cir
200 LSVL 80027 1772 E2
200 LSVL 80027 1773 A3
W Century Dr
- LSVL 80027 1773 A2
1000 LSVL 80027 1772 E2
Century Pl
200 LSVL 80027 1772 E2
Ceran Av
2800 LGMT 80503 1438 C4
Ceres Dr
1200 LAFT 80026 1690 A6
1300 LSVL 80026 1690 A6
Cerillos St
- BGTN 80601 1697 B6
Cerney Cir
7000 DgsC 80108 2534 E7
7000 DgsC 80108 2618 E1
Cerro Ct
500 JfnC 80439 2188 B3
Cerro Pl
800 DgsC 80118 2870 D6
Cessna Dr
10 ERIE 80516 1691 C2
Cessna Wy
37300 AdmC 80137 2038 A4
Ceyl
5100 DNVR 80249 2033 C5
Ceylon Ct
4600 DNVR 80249 2033 C6
S Ceylon Ct
4800 AURA 80015 2285 D6
5100 CTNL 80015 2285 D7
Ceylon St
1500 AURA 80011 2117 C5
4300 DNVR 80249 2033 C6
S Ceylon St
1100 AURA 80017 2201 C4
2700 AURA 80013 2285 D1
4700 AURA 80015 2285 D6
5100 CTNL 80015 2285 C7
S Ceylon Wy
- AURA 80013 2201 C6
2900 AURA 80013 2285 D2
4300 AURA 80015 2285 C5
5400 CTNL 80015 2285 D7
5400 CTNL 80015 2369 D1
Chaco Tr
- CSRK 80109 2702 D3
Chadsworth Av
- DgsC 80126 2449 C7
Chadsworth Ln
10500 DgsC 80126 2449 C7
Chadsworth Pt
10700 DgsC 80126 2449 C7
W Chadwick Cir
500 DgsC 80129 2448 D5
S Chadwick Wy
9800 DgsC 80129 2448 D5
Chadwyck Ct
1900 LGMT 80501 1356 E5
Chaffee Ct
- BGTN 80601 1697 B6
3700 CSRK 80109 2702 E3
E Chaffee Pl
18900 DNVR 80249 2033 C6
W Chaffee Pl
1700 DNVR 80211 2028 B7
Chaffee Wy
3300 CSRK 80109 2702 E3
Chalcis Dr
1800 LAFT 80026 1690 A6
Chalet Cir
6500 DgsC 80134 2622 D1
30200 JfnC 80470 2609 B6
Chalet Dr
- GpnC 80403 1934 B7
31700 JfnC 80433 2440 E4
Chalk Hill Pl
1300 CSRK 80104 2787 E5
Challenger Pl
300 LGMT 80501 1439 B6
Chamberlain Rd
19800 JfnC 80465 2359 D3
E Chamberlain Wy
600 DgsC 80126 2449 A6
S Chambers Cir
- AURA 80017 2200 C4
1300 AURA 80012 2200 C4
Chambers Ct
1000 AURA 80011 2116 D6
9600 CMCY 80022 1864 C7
Chambers Dr
- BLDR 80305 1687 C7
1200 BLDR 80305 1771 C1
Chambers Dr
10100 CMCY 80022 1864 C6
11700 CMCY 80603 1864 C2
Chambers Ln
31200 JfnC 80433 2524 E4
31200 JfnC 80433 2525 A4
Chambers Rd
- AphC 80112 2452 D1
- AURA 80011 2032 C7
- DgsC 80134 2452 D1
- DvrC 80239 2032 C7
10 AURA 80011 2200 D1
10 AURA 80012 2200 D1
10 AURA 80017 2200 D1
100 AURA 80011 2116 D7
4000 DNVR 80239 2032 C7
5500 AdmC 80022 2032 C3
5500 DNVR 80022 2032 C3
9600 AdmC 80022 1948 C1
9600 CMCY 80022 1864 C6
9600 CMCY 80022 1948 C1
10100 AdmC 80022 1864 C6
11400 CMCY 80603 1864 C6
11600 AdmC 80603 1864 C3
11900 BGTN 80603 1864 C3
14400 AdmC 80601 1780 C2
14400 BGTN 80601 1780 C2
N Chambers Rd
1400 AURA 80011 2116 D6
S Chambers Rd
- AphC 80015 2284 D7
- AphC 80112 2368 C7
- AphC 80112 2452 C1
- DgsC 80134 2452 C1
10 AURA 80011 2200 D2
10 AURA 80012 2200 D2
10 AURA 80017 2200 D2
1900 AURA 80013 2200 D6
1900 AURA 80014 2200 D6
2300 AURA 80014 2284 D1
2400 AURA 80013 2284 D2
4200 AURA 80015 2284 D4
4800 CTNL 80015 2284 D7
5400 AURA 80015 2368 C1
5700 AphC 80015 2368 C1
Chambers Wy
300 AURA 80011 2116 D7
N Chambers Wy
- CMCY 80022 1864 C4
S Chambers Wy
- AURA 80015 2284 D4
4200 AURA 80013 2284 D4
4200 AURA 80014 2284 D4
E Chambray Ct
5400 DgsC 80130 2450 B3
S Chambray Ln
9300 DgsC 80130 2450 B4
Champa St
200 ELIZ 80107 2709 B7
1100 DNVR 80204 2112 D4
1300 DNVR 80202 2112 D4
1900 DNVR 80205 2112 D4
2800 DNVR 80205 2113 A2
Champion Cir
900 LGMT 80503 1438 A1
Champion Pl
1000 DgsC 80108 2618 D4
Champions Cir
1900 CSRK 80104 2787 D2
Champlain Dr
2000 BldC 80301 1689 B1
Chandelle Rd
500 DgsC 80104 2871 B3
Chandler Ct
5500 DNVR 80239 2032 B4
Chandler Wy
5100 DNVR 80239 2032 B5
Chandon Ct
3200 DgsC 80126 2533 D1
Chandon Pl
10600 DgsC 80126 2533 D1
Chandon Wy
3200 DgsC 80126 2533 D1
Channel Ct
400 ERIE 80516 1607 C4
S Chanteclair Cir
9600 DgsC 80126 2449 A4
S Chanteclair Ct
9700 DgsC 80126 2449 A5
Chantilly Ct
14100 BMFD 80020 1775 C4
Chaparral Ct
5000 BldC 80301 1604 A2
5000 BLDR 80301 1604 A2
Chaparral Rd
7700 LNTR 80124 2450 D3
Chaparral Village
- AdmC 80229 1945 C3
- TNTN 80229 1945 C3
Chapel Hill Dr
- AdmC 80601 1697 B5
- BGTN 80601 1697 B5
Chapel Hill Ln
23200 PARK 80138 2538 D3
Chapel Hill Pl
23200 PARK 80138 2538 D3
Chapman Dr
- BldC 80302 1685 C3
Chapman Ln
1500 LGMT 80501 1439 A6
Chapman Rd
10 BldC 80302 1684 A2
S Chapparal Cir E
7100 AphC 80016 2369 D5
7100 CTNL 80016 2369 D5
S Chapparal Cir W
6700 CTNL 80016 2369 C4
7200 AphC 80016 2369 C4
Charbray Pt
- CSRK 80104 2704 C5
Charing Ct
4600 CSRK 80109 2702 C2
Charing Dr
4400 CSRK 80109 2702 B2
Charissglen Cir
10200 DgsC 80126 2449 C7
Charissglen Ct
10000 DgsC 80126 2449 C6
Charissglen Ln
10000 DgsC 80126 2449 C6
Charissglen Pointe
2200 DgsC 80126 2449 B6
Charles Dr
1300 LGMT 80503 1355 C7
W Charles St
- BldC 80027 1772 E4
300 SUPE 80027 1772 E4
Charles Wy
8200 AdmC 80221 1944 C4
8200 FLHT 80260 1944 C4
Charlotte Wy
8200 AdmC 80221 1944 C4
8200 FLHT 80260 1944 C4
Charlou Cir
10 CHLV 80111 2282 C5
Charlou Dr
5600 CHLV 80111 2282 B6
5600 CHLV 80113 2282 B6
Charlou Ln
5700 CHLV 80111 2282 B6
Charmatella Dr
- PrkC 80456 2521 B4
Charrington Dr
6200 CHLV 80111 2282 B7
6400 GDVL 80111 2282 B7
Charros Dr
10 JfnC 80401 2191 A2
E Charter Oaks Dr
10 DgsC 80108 2535 A7
E Charterwood Cir
3600 DgsC 80126 2449 D6
E Charterwood Ct
10200 DgsC 80126 2449 B6
E Charterwood Dr
3600 DgsC 80126 2449 D6
Chase Cir
7400 WSTR 80003 1943 B7
7900 ARVD 80003 1943 B5
Chase Ct
3600 BLDR 80305 1687 B5
11700 WSTR 80020 1859 B3
N Chase Ct
11800 WSTR 80020 1859 B2
S Chase Ct
1200 LKWD 80232 2195 B4
6200 JfnC 80123 2363 B3
6900 JfnC 80128 2363 B5
Chase Dr
10 CCkC 80439 2187 B3
7400 WSTR 80003 1943 B6
8700 ARVD 80003 1942 E3
8700 ARVD 80003 1943 A3
S Chase Dr
10 LKWD 80226 2195 B1
S Chase Ln
2400 LKWD 80227 2195 B7
2500 LKWD 80227 2279 B1
2600 DNVR 80227 2279 B1
Chase St
- BMFD 80020 1859 B2
10 LKWD 80226 2195 B1
200 BKHK 80403 2017 E4
300 GpnC 80403 2017 E4
1300 LKWD 80214 2111 B5
2600 EDGW 80214 2111 B3
2800 WTRG 80214 2111 B2
3200 WTRG 80212 2111 B2
4100 MNVW 80212 2027 B7
4100 WTRG 80212 2027 B7
4800 DvrC 80212 2027 B6
4800 LKSD 80212 2027 B6
5100 DNVR 80212 2027 B5
6600 ARVD 80003 2027 B1
7500 WSTR 80003 1943 B6
8400 ARVD 80003 1943 B4
11700 WSTR 80020 1859 B3
S Chase St
100 LKWD 80226 2195 B2
900 LKWD 80232 2195 B4
3700 DNVR 80235 2279 B4
5900 JfnC 80123 2363 B2
Chase Wy
8100 ARVD 80003 1943 B4
11500 WSTR 80020 1859 B3
N Chase Wy
11000 WSTR 80020 1859 B4
S Chase Wy
2700 DNVR 80227 2279 B1
2700 LKWD 80227 2279 B1
3900 DNVR 80235 2279 B4
7100 JfnC 80128 2363 B5
Chase Gulch Rd
- CLCY 80403 2017 C3
100 BKHK 80403 2017 D3
100 GpnC 80403 2017 D3
Chateau Creek Ct
12300 PARK 80134 2537 D4
Chatfield Av
10 CSRK 80104 2704 C7
W Chatfield Av
6200 JfnC 80128 2447 B1
6900 JfnC 80128 2446 E1
9800 JfnC 80127 2446 A1
10800 JfnC 80127 2445 E1
10900 JfnC 80127 2361 E7
N Chatfield Dr
10000 DgsC 80125 2532 B2
10700 DgsC 80125 2448 C7
W Chatfield Dr
9000 JfnC 80128 2446 C1
W Chatfield Ln
6600 DgsC 80125 2532 B1
N Chatfield Pl
10100 DgsC 80125 2532 C2
W Chatfield Pl
6800 JfnC 80128 2447 A2
9300 JfnC 80128 2446 B2
Chatford Ct
6900 DgsC 80108 2618 E1
Chatham Pl
4600 BldC 80301 1604 D3
Chatham St
10 WARD 80481 1597 D1
4600 BldC 80301 1604 D3
Chatham Wy
7500 BldC 80301 1604 D3
E Chatswood Ct
4300 DgsC 80126 2449 E4
E Chatswood Pl
4300 DgsC 80126 2449 E5
S Chatswood Tr
9800 DgsC 80126 2449 E5
W Chautauga Mtn
10500 JfnC 80127 2362 A7
Chautauqua Pk
- BldC 80302 1686 C6
- BLDR 80302 1686 C6
Chautauqua Reservoir Rd
- BldC 80302 1686 C5
- BLDR 80302 1686 C5
Chavez St
- BGTN 80601 1697 A5
Cheesman St
700 BldC 80516 1607 B4
700 ERIE 80516 1607 B4
Cheetah Chase
5600 DgsC 80124 2450 B6
Cheetah Cove
5800 DgsC 80124 2450 B6
Cheetah Tail
10300 DgsC 80124 2450 B6
Cheetah Winds
10400 DgsC 80124 2450 B6
Cheewall Ln
9700 DgsC 80134 2452 E4
Chelan St
400 GOLD 80401 2108 A7
400 GOLD 80401 2192 A1
Chelmsford Ter
10000 DgsC 80134 2452 D5
Chelsea Ct
400 ELIZ 80107 2709 A7
E Chelsea Ct
2000 DgsC 80126 2449 B3
Chelsea St
200 CSRK 80104 2704 D7
Chelsea Manor Ct
6000 BldC 80301 1603 E4
E Chenango Av
- GDVL 80111 2282 D7
10 EGLD 80110 2280 E6
10 EGLD 80113 2280 E6
600 EGLD 80113 2281 A6
700 CHLV 80113 2281 A6
5000 CHLV 80121 2282 A6
8500 DNVR 80237 2282 E6
8500 DNVR 80237 2283 A6
8800 GDVL 80111 2283 A6
8800 GDVL 80237 2283 A6
9700 AphC 80015 2283 B6
13700 AphC 80015 2284 B6
13700 AURA 80015 2284 B6
16900 AURA 80015 2285 A6
W Chenango Av
10 EGLD 80113 2280 D6
2100 LITN 80120 2280 B6
2800 EGLD 80110 2280 A6
3000 EGLD 80110 2279 D6
3300 DNVR 80123 2279 D6
3300 DvrC 80123 2279 D6
3300 LITN 80123 2279 D6
9500 DNVR 80123 2278 B7
12400 JfnC 80465 2277 C7
Chenango Cir
200 EGLD 80113 2280 E7
E Chenango Cir
19000 AURA 80015 2285 C6
E Chenango Ct
1900 CHLV 80113 2281 B7
Chenango Dr
- AURA 80016 2287 A6
E Chenango Dr
- AphC 80015 2286 A6
13800 AphC 80015 2284 B6
13800 AURA 80015 2284 B6
17400 AURA 80015 2285 B6
19200 CTNL 80015 2285 D6
19900 AphC 80015 2285 E6
W Chenango Dr
11300 JfnC 80127 2277 E7
11500 JfnC 80465 2277 D7
Chenango Pl
- AphC 80016 2286 D6
- AURA 80016 2286 D6
E Chenango Pl
- AURA 80016 2286 E6
14400 AURA 80015 2284 C6
18600 AURA 80015 2285 C6
20300 AphC 80015 2285 E6
W Chenango Pl
8000 DNVR 80123 2278 D7
8000 DvrC 80123 2278 D7
8000 LKWD 80123 2278 D7
Cheney Ct
6800 BldC 80503 1521 A5
Cheney Pl
100 CSRK 80104 2787 D3
Cheri Ln
1000 EbtC 80138 2540 B4
Cherokee Av
300 SUPE 80027 1772 D3
Cherokee Ct
200 LCHB 80603 1698 B3
2900 ERIE 80516 1691 C3
6600 BldC 80503 1521 B5
E Cherokee Ct
8500 DgsC 80134 2622 C2
Cherokee Dr
- CSRK 80109 2702 C2
W Cherokee Dr
6300 DgsC 80135 2700 C1

STREET Block City ZIP Map# Grid

W Cherokee Dr
7200 DgsC 80135 2616 B7
E Cherokee Ln
10100 DgsC 80138 2539 B3
Cherokee Pl
200 LCHB 80603 1698 B3
N Cherokee Pl
3900 DgsC 80135 2616 C7
Cherokee Rd
5200 JfnC 80454 2359 B1
Cherokee St
10 DNVR 80223 2196 D1
400 DNVR 80223 2112 D7
900 DNVR 80204 2112 D6
4400 DNVR 80216 2028 D7
8200 AdmC 80221 1944 D4
8300 TNTN 80260 1944 D4
11000 NHGN 80234 1860 D4
S Cherokee St
10 DNVR 80223 2196 D2
2500 DNVR 80223 2280 D1
2600 AphC 80223 2280 D1
2600 EGLD 80110 2280 D1
2600 EGLD 80223 2280 D1
6600 LITN 80120 2364 D4
Cherokee Tr
- AURA 80010 2115 B5
- EbtC 80107 2792 C1
1700 LAFT 80026 1690 C7
34200 EbtC 80107 2708 B6
S Cherokee Tr
7100 AphC 80016 2368 E5
11700 JfnC 80433 2525 C3
Cherokee Wy
100 BLDR 80303 1687 C6
Cherokee Mountain Rd
- CSRK 80109 2703 A5
Cherokee Ranch Rd
6100 DgsC 80135 2617 E2
6100 DgsC 80135 2618 B2
Cherrington St
10600 DgsC 80126 2449 D7
Cherry Av
700 BLDR 80304 1602 B4
Cherry Cir
2400 BGTN 80601 1696 E7
5700 GDVL 80121 2366 A1
11100 TNTN 80233 1861 E4
13300 TNTN 80241 1777 E6
S Cherry Cir
6200 CTNL 80121 2366 A3
Cherry Ct
- TNTN 80233 1862 A3
10 BGTN 80601 1696 B7
10 BGTN 80601 1780 B1
5600 GDVL 80121 2366 A1
6400 BldC 80503 1520 E5
10700 TNTN 80233 1861 E5
13400 TNTN 80241 1777 E5
S Cherry Ct
6100 CTNL 80121 2366 A2
7400 CTNL 80122 2365 E5
7400 CTNL 80122 2366 A6
Cherry Dr
- TNTN 80260 1944 C2
11200 TNTN 80233 1862 A3
11800 TNTN 80233 1861 E2
S Cherry Dr
7000 CTNL 80122 2366 A5
7200 CTNL 80122 2365 E5
Cherry Ln
8500 WSTR 80031 1943 D3
8600 AdmC 80031 1943 D3
9700 TNTN 80229 1861 E7
Cherry Pl
10 BGTN 80601 1696 B7
1400 ERIE 80516 1691 E3
12000 TNTN 80241 1861 E2
Cherry St
10 CSRK 80104 2704 E7
10 DNVR 80220 2197 E1
10 DNVR 80246 2197 E1
300 LCHB 80603 1698 C3
1200 DNVR 80220 2113 E5
1400 LSVL 80027 1773 E2
1500 BGTN 80601 1780 D1
1700 LSVL 80027 1774 A2
2100 BGTN 80601 1696 E7
3200 DNVR 80207 2113 E2
6800 AdmC 80022 1945 E7
6800 CMCY 80022 1945 E7
6800 CMCY 80022 2029 E1
9400 TNTN 80229 1945 E1
9700 FLHT 80260 1860 A7
9700 FLHT 80260 1944 A1
10500 TNTN 80233 1862 A5
10700 TNTN 80233 1861 E5
12400 TNTN 80241 1861 E1
13400 TNTN 80241 1777 E5
13600 TNTN 80602 1777 E5
14400 AdmC 80602 1777 E2
S Cherry St
- BNNT 80102 2124 D2
- GNDL 80246 2197 E2
10 DNVR 80220 2197 E2
100 CSRK 80104 2704 E7
600 DNVR 80246 2197 E3
1200 DNVR 80222 2197 E4
3400 AphC 80222 2281 E2
3400 CHLV 80113 2281 E2
3400 DNVR 80222 2281 E2
6700 CTNL 80122 2366 A4
6800 CTNL 80122 2365 E5
W Cherry St
100 LSVL 80027 1773 C2
Cherry Wy
- TNTN 80602 1777 E4
300 BMFD 80020 1859 C2
1300 BGTN 80601 1696 D7
2400 EbtC 80138 2540 E4
2400 EbtC 80138 2541 A4
13400 TNTN 80241 1777 E5
S Cherry Wy
2800 DNVR 80222 2281 E1
S Cherry Wy
3000 DNVR 80222 2282 A2
6500 CTNL 80121 2366 A3
E Cherry Blossom Ct
900 DgsC 80126 2449 A3
Cherry Blossom Ln
10 CHLV 80113 2281 E4
10 CHLV 80113 2282 A4
Cherrybrook Cir
10500 DgsC 80126 2449 C7
Cherry Creek Ct
10900 PARK 80138 2538 A1
Cherry Creek Dr
5100 AphC 80111 2283 D7
5100 GDVL 80111 2283 D7
5400 AphC 80111 2367 D1
5800 GDVL 80111 2367 D1
6400 DgsC 80134 2621 D5
E Cherry Creek Dam Rd
- AphC 80014 2283 C4
- AphC 80014 2284 A2
- AphC 80015 2283 C4
- AphC 80111 2283 C4
- GDVL 80111 2283 C4
Cherry Creek North Dr
- DNVR 80218 2197 C1
2300 DNVR 80206 2197 C1
3400 DNVR 80209 2197 D2
3700 GNDL 80246 2197 D2
5600 DNVR 80224 2198 B4
5600 DNVR 80246 2198 B4
Cherry Creek South Dr
3700 DNVR 80209 2197 C1
3700 GNDL 80246 2197 C1
4600 DNVR 80246 2197 C1
4700 DNVR 80246 2198 C5
4700 GNDL 80246 2198 C5
6500 DNVR 80224 2198 C5
6900 DNVR 80231 2198 C5
7700 AphC 80231 2198 C5
8800 DNVR 80231 2283 A1
Cherry Hills Dr
10 CHLV 80113 2281 B4
Cherry Hills Ln
1500 CSRK 80104 2787 E1
Cherry Hills Farm Ct
10 CHLV 80113 2281 C6
Cherry Hills Farm Dr
- CHLV 80121 2281 C7
- GDVL 80121 2281 C7
10 CHLV 80113 2281 C6
Cherry Hills Park Dr
10 CHLV 80113 2281 D4
Cherryhurst Av
- DgsC 80126 2449 E6
- DgsC 80130 2449 E6
E Cherryhurst Ct
4100 DgsC 80126 2449 D5
S Cherryhurst Ln
10100 DgsC 80126 2449 E5
Cherry Ln Dr
10 CHLV 80113 2281 E3
10 CHLV 80113 2282 A3
10 DNVR 80237 2282 A3
Cherrymoor Dr
10 CHLV 80113 2281 B5
Cherry Plum Pl
3300 CSRK 80104 2787 D4
Cherry Plum Wy
3000 CSRK 80104 2787 D4
Cherryridge Rd
2400 CHLV 80113 2281 C5
E Cherryvale Ct
2500 DgsC 80126 2449 C4
E Cherry Vale Dr
10 CHLV 80113 2281 B6
S Cherryvale Dr
9400 DgsC 80126 2449 C4
S Cherryvale Ln
9400 DgsC 80126 2449 C4
Cherryvale Rd
10 BldC 80303 1687 E6
10 BLDR 80303 1687 E6
1400 BLDR 80301 1687 E4
S Cherryvale Rd
10 BldC 80303 1687 E7
10 BldC 80303 1771 E2
10 BLDR 80303 1687 E7
Cherryville Cir
2200 GDVL 80121 2365 C1
Cherryville Rd
1200 GDVL 80121 2365 A1
Cherryville Wy
5400 GDVL 80121 2365 B1
Cherrywood Av
100 TNTN 80260 1944 B1
S Cherrywood Cir
5900 CTNL 80121 2365 A2
5900 GDVL 80121 2365 B2
Cherrywood Dr
500 LGMT 80503 1356 D6
1100 BGTN 80601 1696 C4
E Cherrywood Dr
2200 LAFT 80026 1690 C7
2200 LAFT 80026 1774 C1
10000 DgsC 80138 2455 A6
N Cherrywood Dr
200 LAFT 80026 1690 C7
200 LAFT 80026 1774 B1
S Cherrywood Dr
200 LAFT 80026 1774 C1
W Cherrywood Dr
300 LAFT 80026 1774 C1
Cherrywood Ln
100 LSVL 80027 1773 A1
Cherrywood St
12100 BMFD 80020 1859 D1
Cherrywood Wy
1400 LGMT 80501 1356 D7
Cheryl Dr
8700 AdmC 80229 1945 B3
8700 TNTN 80229 1945 B3
S Chesapeake Ct
9400 DgsC 80126 2449 C4
E Chesapeake Ln
1900 DgsC 80126 2449 B4
E Chesapeake Pl
2000 DgsC 80126 2449 B4
S Chesapeake St
9400 DgsC 80126 2449 B4
Chesebro Wy
10 BldC 80025 1770 C7
Cheshire Ct
- BMFD 80020 1776 C1
S Cheshire Ct
9300 DgsC 80130 2450 C4
Chesmore St
10900 DgsC 80126 2533 E1
S Chester Cir
1800 AphC 80247 2199 A6
S Chester Ct
1100 AphC 80247 2199 A4
2900 DNVR 80231 2283 A2
5100 GDVL 80111 2283 A7
5400 GDVL 80111 2367 A1
Chester St
1100 AURA 80230 2115 A6
1400 AURA 80010 2115 A4
E Chester St
100 LAFT 80026 1690 D5
900 BldC 80026 1690 D5
S Chester St
1100 AphC 80247 2199 A4
4900 GDVL 80111 2283 A7
6000 GDVL 80111 2367 A2
7500 CTNL 80112 2367 A6
8100 AphC 80112 2367 A6
8100 CTNL 80112 2451 A1
8100 LNTR 80112 2451 A1
8300 LNTR 80124 2451 A1
W Chester St
100 LAFT 80026 1690 C5
S Chester Wy
3600 GDVL 80014 2283 A3
6000 GDVL 80111 2367 A2
Chesterfield Rd
2400 CSRK 80109 2702 C4
W Chestnut Av
5600 JfnC 80128 2363 B7
5800 JfnC 80128 2447 B1
8800 JfnC 80128 2446 C1
Chestnut Cir
2000 ERIE 80516 1606 D6
3100 JfnC 80439 2273 B3
W Chestnut Cir
800 LSVL 80027 1773 A2
Chestnut Ct
- GDVL 80121 2365 E1
6900 DgsC 80134 2621 E1
S Chestnut Ct
3100 JfnC 80439 2273 B3
W Chestnut Ct
600 LSVL 80027 1773 B2
Chestnut Dr
1000 LGMT 80503 1438 A5
29500 JfnC 80439 2273 A3
W Chestnut Dr
7000 JfnC 80128 2446 E1
7900 JfnC 80128 2363 B7
Chestnut Ln
3600 AdmC 80031 1943 D3
3600 WSTR 80031 1943 D3
4600 BldC 80301 1604 A3
S Chestnut Ln
3100 JfnC 80439 2273 B3
Chestnut Pl
1400 BLDR 80304 1602 C7
1900 DNVR 80202 2112 C3
3500 DNVR 80216 2028 E7
3600 DNVR 80216 2029 A7
3700 LGMT 80503 1438 A5
E Chestnut Pl
22000 AURA 80016 2370 B7
W Chestnut Pl
7700 JfnC 80128 2446 D1
Chestnut Rdg
- DNVR 80237 2282 E3
Chestnut St
100 LSVL 80027 1773 C2
300 ELIZ 80107 2793 B1
2700 FLHT 80260 1860 A7
S Chestnut St
600 EbtC 80107 2793 B1
600 ELIZ 80107 2793 B1
E Chestnut Tr
800 GDVL 80121 2365 A1
Chestnut Wy
400 BMFD 80020 1859 A3
S Chestnut Wy
7900 JfnC 80128 2363 B7
S Chestnut Hill Ct
8800 DgsC 80130 2450 C2
S Chestnut Hill Ln
8800 DgsC 80130 2450 D2
S Chestnut Hill Pl
8800 DgsC 80130 2450 C2
E Chestnut Hill St
6800 DgsC 80130 2450 C2
E Chestnut Hill Tr
7000 DgsC 80130 2450 C2
S Chestnut Hill Wy
8800 DgsC 80130 2450 D3
S Chetwood St
- DgsC 80129 2448 C4
Cheyenne Av
800 LGMT 80501 1356 D5
Cheyenne Ct
1800 LAFT 80026 1690 C7
4700 BLDR 80303 1687 C6
6600 BldC 80503 1521 C5
N Cheyenne Ct
6200 DgsC 80134 2622 D2
S Cheyenne Ct
13200 JfnC 80470 2524 B7
13300 JfnC 80470 2608 B1
Cheyenne Dr
200 LAFT 80026 1690 D7
2400 GOLD 80401 2107 E5
Cheyenne Dr
4500 DgsC 80118 2953 A4
4900 DgsC 80118 2952 D3
W Cheyenne Dr
7200 DgsC 80135 2700 A1
Cheyenne Pl
500 EbtC 80138 2456 A5
1500 DNVR 80202 2112 E5
1500 DNVR 80204 2112 E5
7800 DgsC 80118 2953 B3
W Cheyenne Pl
3800 DgsC 80135 2616 A7
Cheyenne Rd
5200 JfnC 80454 2359 B1
Cheyenne St
10 EbtC 80117 2796 A2
100 GOLD 80403 2107 D2
400 KIOW 80117 2796 A2
700 GOLD 80401 2107 D3
Cheyenne Tr
35500 EbtC 80107 2708 B5
Chicago Creek Rd
10 IDSP 80452 2101 A7
500 CCkC 80452 2101 A7
Chicago Creek Rd SR-103
10 IDSP 80452 2101 A7
500 CCkC 80452 2101 A7
Chickadee Ct
5400 DgsC 80134 2622 C4
Chickadee Dr
10 PrkC 80456 2691 D1
Chickadee Ln
10 PrkC 80456 2691 C1
Chickadee Rd
400 JfnC 80401 2190 B1
500 JfnC 80401 2106 B7
Chickaree Ct
7600 DgsC 80125 2531 B7
Chickaree Pl
7600 DgsC 80125 2531 B7
E Chickory Cir
17600 PARK 80134 2453 B4
Chicory Cir
- BGTN 80601 1697 D5
S Chicory Ln
- PARK 80134 2453 A4
Chief Hosa Rd
26100 JfnC 80401 2190 B4
Childrens Pl
- DNVR 80205 2113 A4
- DNVR 80218 2113 A4
Children's Museum Dr
1900 DNVR 80211 2112 B4
Chilton Av
13600 PrkC 80456 2608 A2
34200 JfnC 80470 2608 A2
Chimayo Rd
3600 LITN 80123 2363 E1
Chimney Creek Dr
600 JfnC 80401 2190 C3
Chimney Hollow Rd
- LmrC 80503 1270 B1
Chimney Peak Dr
1500 CSRK 80109 2703 B5
Chimney Ranch Ln
33400 JfnC 80470 2608 B2
Chimney Rock Rd
900 DgsC 80126 2449 A2
Chimney Rock Tr
6200 JfnC 80465 2360 D3
Chinle Av
800 BLDR 80304 1602 B2
Chinook Av
300 LGMT 80501 1439 D1
S Chinook Dr
7000 JfnC 80439 2358 C5
Chinook Pl
100 LGMT 80501 1439 C1
E Chinook Tr
10300 DgsC 80138 2539 B5
Chinook Wy
1100 BldC 80303 1688 B3
Chipmunk Dr
- GpnC 80403 1934 A6
26700 JfnC 80439 2442 A2
Chipmunk Ln
- GpnC 80403 1934 A6
Chipmunk Pl
7400 DgsC 80125 2531 A7
Chipmunk Climb
17500 JfnC 80433 2694 D4
N Chippewa Cir
3700 DgsC 80135 2616 D7
Chippewa Dr
3800 BLDR 80303 1687 B5
4800 DgsC 80118 2953 A3
Chippewa Ln
22000 JfnC 80401 2191 B4
Chippewa Rd
7700 DgsC 80118 2953 B3
Chippewa St
- KIOW 80117 2796 A3
Chiquita Pl
- CSRK 80104 2704 B4
- CSRK 80108 2704 B4
Chiquita Rd
5200 JfnC 80454 2359 B1
Chiron St
1100 LAFT 80026 1690 B6
Chisholm Cir
1900 EbtC 80107 2792 D7
Chisholm Pl
- DgsC 80134 2621 B4
Chisholm Tr
3300 BLDR 80301 1603 A6
30600 EbtC 80107 2792 A7
E Chiswick Cir
400 DgsC 80126 2448 E4
Chivington Dr
2200 LGMT 80501 1356 A4
2400 LGMT 80501 1355 E4
N Choctaw Cir
3500 DgsC 80135 2700 C1
S Choctaw St
13300 JfnC 80470 2524 A7
13300 JfnC 80470 2608 A1
Choke Cherry Av
4200 BMFD 80020 1775 C7
Choke Cherry Ct
400 GOLD 80403 2023 D7
10400 DgsC 80125 2614 E1
Chokecherry Dr
18000 JfnC 80127 2444 B6
W Choke Cherry Dr
1000 BldC 80303 1688 E6
1000 LSVL 80027 1688 E6
1000 LSVL 80027 1689 A6
Choke Cherry Ln
1000 LGMT 80503 1438 B5
24100 JfnC 80401 2190 D4
Choke Cherry Rd
10 JfnC 80401 2190 C1
Choke Cherry Wy
6900 DgsC 80125 2614 E1
Cholla Ct
3600 BldC 80304 1602 A6
Cholla Ln
1100 BMFD 80020 1774 E7
Chopper Cir
1000 DNVR 80204 2112 C4
Chris Dr
24500 JfnC 80439 2358 C1
Christa Cir
10400 DgsC 80125 2530 E7
Christensen Cir
4400 AphC 80123 2363 D3
Christensen Dr
- LITN 80123 2363 C3
4800 AphC 80123 2363 C3
Christensen Ln
4200 AphC 80123 2363 C3
4200 CBVL 80123 2363 C3
4300 LITN 80123 2363 C3
Christenson Av
- BldC 80027 1772 E6
- SUPE 80027 1772 E6
Christmas Tree Dr
400 BLDR 80302 1686 B4
Christopher Ct
7100 BldC 80503 1521 A3
9200 EbtC 80107 2459 B3
S Christopher Dr
10100 JfnC 80433 2440 E6
10100 JfnC 80433 2441 A6
S Christopher Ln
32000 JfnC 80433 2440 D7
Christopher St
- LAFT 80026 1690 D4
Christy Wy
- SUPE 80027 1773 A6
Christy Ridge Rd
3200 DgsC 80135 2785 D3
Chuckling Creek Rd
100 PrkC 80456 2521 B4
Chuckwagon Cir
- TNTN 80229 1861 E6
Chukar Dr
1400 LGMT 80501 1357 A7
W Church Av
2400 LITN 80120 2364 A2
Church Ln
700 LSVL 80027 1689 B7
Church St
200 BKHK 80403 2017 E4
Churchhill Ct
- PARK 80138 2538 D4
Churchill Dr
10 CHLV 80113 2281 B3
Church Ranch Blvd
- WSTR 80020 1858 D7
7000 JfnC 80021 1858 D7
7000 WSTR 80021 1858 D7
N Church Ranch Wy
10100 WSTR 80021 1858 E6
Chute Rd
200 BldC 80403 1853 D1
Ciancio St
9200 TNTN 80229 1945 C2
Cielo Ct
16600 DgsC 80134 2452 E5
Cielo Ln
700 JfnC 80439 2188 A4
Cimarron Cir
1000 AURA 80011 2116 B6
S Cimarron Cir
4500 AURA 80015 2284 C5
Cimarron Ct
- DNVR 80237 2282 C6
Cimarron Dr
- LSVL 80027 1689 E6
10 GDVL 80121 2365 A1
Cimarron Pl
3100 SUPE 80027 1857 B1
S Cimarron Rd
5300 BWMR 80123 2279 D7
5300 LITN 80123 2279 D7
5300 LITN 80123 2363 D1
Cimarron St
3000 AURA 80011 2116 B2
8700 DgsC 80126 2449 A2
S Cimarron St
2500 AURA 80014 2200 B7
2500 AURA 80014 2284 B1
Cimarron Tr
- EbtC 80107 2792 E1
34000 EbtC 80107 2708 D7
S Cimarron Wy
3400 AURA 80014 2284 B2
5900 LITN 80123 2363 D2
W Cimarrona Peak
11400 JfnC 80127 2361 C7
Cimmaron Wy
200 BLDR 80303 1687 D6
E Cimmarron Dr
11100 AphC 80111 2367 D1
E Cimmarron Pl
21200 CTNL 80015 2286 A7
Cinch Ct
7600 JfnC 80465 2359 D7
S Cindy Av
12300 JfnC 80470 2524 B5
Cindy Ln
1900 GpnC 80403 1849 D7
Cinnabar Dr
- CSRK 80108 2619 E5
Cinnabar Ln
- CSRK 80108 2619 D5
Cinnamon Cir
- BLDR 80304 1602 D3
7800 DgsC 80118 2954 D2
Cinnamon Ct
800 CSRK 80104 2703 E5
1900 DgsC 80118 2954 B2
Cinnamon Ln
900 LSVL 80027 1773 A1
Cinnamon Rd
1300 DgsC 80118 2954 C2
Cinnamon St
1300 LGMT 80501 1356 A7
Cinnamonwood
31100 JfnC 80439 2273 A3
Circle Dr
- TNTN 80229 1861 A6
10 CCkC 80439 2187 D5
10 CSRK 80104 2703 E6
10 LKWD 80215 2110 A3
10 WTRG 80215 2110 A3
400 DNVR 80206 2113 B7
700 BLDR 80302 1686 B4
1600 LSVL 80027 1689 D6
8200 WSTR 80031 1943 D4
8500 AdmC 80031 1943 D4
11000 JfnC 80403 1852 E5
27700 JfnC 80439 2357 E2
34400 JfnC 80470 2524 A3
N Circle Dr
10 PrkC 80456 2607 A6
100 BGTN 80601 1696 E6
S Circle Dr
10 PrkC 80456 2607 B6
12000 JfnC 80433 2525 D4
Circle Rd
10 BldC 80403 1852 A1
Circle Wy
- DNVR 80207 2114 D2
- DNVR 80238 2114 D2
Circle K Ranch Rd
200 CCkC 80439 2271 D4
Circle Point Rd
10800 WSTR 80020 1858 E4
11100 BMFD 80020 1858 E4
Cisne Cir
10 BGTN 80601 1697 E6
Cistena Wy
7500 DgsC 80134 2622 A4
N Citation Dr
5300 DgsC 80134 2621 E4
S Citation Tr
7900 JfnC 80439 2357 E7
8100 JfnC 80439 2441 D1
Citrine Ct
9800 DgsC 80134 2452 D5
City Center Cir
- LAFT 80026 1690 C6
City Center Dr
- WSTR 80020 1943 C1
9400 WSTR 80031 1943 C1
City View Dr
700 AdmC 80229 1945 A3
700 TNTN 80229 1945 A3
S City View Dr
9600 JfnC 80465 2443 C5
Civic Center Dr
9500 TNTN 80229 1944 D1
Claire Cir
11000 NHGN 80234 1860 C4
Claire Ln
800 NHGN 80234 1860 C4
S Clairton Ct
9800 DgsC 80126 2449 D5
E Clairton Dr
2800 DgsC 80126 2449 C5
S Clairton Ln
9700 DgsC 80126 2449 C5
S Clairton Pl
9700 DgsC 80126 2449 C5
S Clairton St
9800 DgsC 80126 2449 C5
S Clairton Wy
9800 DgsC 80126 2449 C5
Clancy Ct
200 BGTN 80601 1696 B7
Clandan Ct
9700 DgsC 80134 2452 E4
Clarabelle Dr
8400 ARVD 80002 2026 C4
Clare Ct
10 DgsC 80108 2535 A7
9200 BldC 80303 1689 C2
Clare Dr
100 DgsC 80108 2535 A7
300 DgsC 80108 2534 E7
Claremont Dr
1100 BLDR 80305 1687 A7
1100 BLDR 80305 1771 A1
Clarendon Dr
600 LGMT 80501 1356 D6
Clarendon Lp
400 DgsC 80108 2534 E7
Claret Ash
10 JfnC 80127 2445 B1
Clark Av
26000 JfnC 80433 2442 A5
Clark Ct
1800 ERIE 80516 1606 E6
6800 AdmC 80221 2028 D1
Clark Dr
1700 ERIE 80516 1606 E6
1700 ERIE 80516 1607 A6
9900 NHGN 80260 1860 D7
Clark Pl
4700 DNVR 80216 2028 E6
Clark Rd
10 PrkC 80456 2521 B3
Clark St
500 GOLD 80403 2107 D2
1800 AURA 80011 2116 B4
Clark Wy
10 LGMT 80501 1356 C5
Clarke Ct
1000 DgsC 80109 2787 A3
E Clarke Rd
18800 PARK 80134 2453 C6
Clarke Farms Dr
- DgsC 80134 2453 A6
17300 PARK 80134 2453 A6
S Clarke Farms Dr
10600 PARK 80134 2453 A7
Clarkes Cir
1100 DgsC 80109 2787 A3
1400 CSRK 80109 2787 A3
Clarkeville Wy
10600 PARK 80134 2453 B6
Clarkson Cir
12800 TNTN 80241 1776 E7
12900 TNTN 80241 1777 A7
S Clarkson Cir
2800 EGLD 80113 2281 A1
7400 CTNL 80122 2365 A6
Clarkson Ct
- DNVR 80205 2113 A3
800 AdmC 80229 1945 A5
10600 NHGN 80233 1861 A5
11800 NHGN 80233 1860 E2
13300 TNTN 80241 1776 E5
13300 TNTN 80241 1777 A5
S Clarkson Ct
8100 CTNL 80122 2449 C1
Clarkson St
10 DNVR 80209 2197 A1
10 DNVR 80218 2197 A1
200 DNVR 80203 2197 B1
300 DNVR 80203 2113 A7
300 DNVR 80218 2113 A7
2000 DNVR 80205 2113 A4
5100 AdmC 80216 2029 A5
5100 DNVR 80216 2029 A5
8400 AdmC 80229 1945 A4
8400 TNTN 80229 1945 A4
11400 NHGN 80233 1860 E3
11400 NHGN 80233 1861 A4
13200 TNTN 80241 1776 E6
S Clarkson St
10 DNVR 80203 2197 A2
10 DNVR 80209 2197 A2
10 DNVR 80218 2197 A2
1000 DNVR 80210 2197 A3
2600 DNVR 80210 2281 A1
2600 EGLD 80210 2281 A1
2700 AphC 80210 2281 A2
2700 EGLD 80113 2281 A2
3500 CHLV 80113 2281 A3
5000 GDVL 80121 2281 A7
5100 AphC 80121 2281 A7
5300 AphC 80121 2365 A1
5300 GDVL 80121 2365 A1
5600 LITN 80121 2365 A1
5900 CTNL 80121 2365 A3
6600 CTNL 80122 2365 A4
8000 CTNL 80122 2449 B1
8200 AphC 80126 2449 B1
Clarkson Wy
12900 TNTN 80241 1776 E6
Claude Ct
4700 DNVR 80216 2029 C6
11800 NHGN 80233 1861 B2
12000 NHGN 80241 1861 B1
12000 TNTN 80241 1861 B1
12300 TNTN 80241 1777 B7
14400 TNTN 80602 1777 B3
S Claude Ct
3000 DNVR 80210 2281 C2
Claude Pl
12800 TNTN 80241 1777 B7
Claude Wy
11800 NHGN 80233 1861 B2
Claudius Rd
- GpnC 80403 1934 B4
Clay Cir
1200 BMFD 80020 1776 A6
Clay Ct
- FLHT 80260 1944 A1
100 BMFD 80020 1776 A7
2600 FLHT 80260 1860 A7
11900 WSTR 80234 1860 A2
S Clay Ct
4700 EGLD 80110 2280 A6
Clay Dr
- FLHT 80260 1944 A1
8000 WSTR 80031 1944 A5
N Clay Dr
11000 WSTR 80234 1860 A4
Clay Pl
13500 BMFD 80020 1776 A5
Clay St
- AdmC 80221 1944 A5
10 DNVR 80219 2196 A1
1500 DNVR 80204 2112 A5
1900 AdmC 80137 2120 E3
2000 DNVR 80211 2112 A4
4100 DNVR 80211 2028 A7
4400 BldC 80301 1603 D3
4800 DNVR 80221 2028 A6
5600 AdmC 80221 2028 A4
6900 WSTR 80030 2028 A1
7300 WSTR 80030 1944 A6
8600 WSTR 80031 1944 A3
9200 FLHT 80260 1944 A2
10300 FLHT 80234 1860 A6
10300 FLHT 80260 1860 A6
10300 WSTR 80234 1860 A6
14400 BMFD 80020 1776 A2
N Clay St
- WSTR 80031 1944 A4

STREET
Block City ZIP Map# Grid

N Clay St
5500 DgsC 80135 2617 B5
S Clay St
10 DNVR 80219 2196 A1
2500 DNVR 80219 2280 A1
3100 DNVR 80236 2280 A2
3100 DvrC 80236 2280 A2
3100 SRDN 80110 2280 A2
4000 EGLD 80110 2280 A5
7000 LITN 80120 2364 A5
Clay Wy
900 DNVR 80204 2112 A6
Clay Commons Ct
4300 BLDR 80303 1687 B4
Claymoor Ct
200 DgsC 80108 2534 E4
N Clayson St
11800 DgsC 80138 2453 D5
S Clayton Blvd
3300 AphC 80113 2281 C3
3300 DNVR 80210 2281 C3
3300 DvrC 80210 2281 C3
Clayton Cir
2200 SUPE 80027 1773 A6
9700 TNTN 80229 1945 C1
S Clayton Cir
7900 CTNL 80122 2365 C7
Clayton Ct
8200 AdmC 80229 1945 C4
11500 TNTN 80233 1861 C3
12400 TNTN 80241 1861 C1
13400 TNTN 80241 1777 C6
S Clayton Ct
4700 CHLV 80113 2281 C6
5800 CTNL 80121 2365 C2
7900 CTNL 80122 2365 C7
Clayton Ln
100 DNVR 80206 2197 C1
Clayton St
- AdmC 80602 1693 C5
- TNTN 80241 1777 C5
200 DNVR 80206 2197 C1
1000 DNVR 80206 2113 C5
2600 DNVR 80205 2113 C3
4000 DNVR 80205 2029 C7
4000 DNVR 80216 2029 C7
6900 AdmC 80229 1945 C7
9500 TNTN 80229 1945 C1
10000 TNTN 80229 1861 C7
11000 NHGN 80233 1861 C4
11400 TNTN 80233 1861 C3
14900 TNTN 80602 1777 C2
E Clayton St
7300 AdmC 80229 1945 C6
S Clayton St
1100 DNVR 80209 2197 C4
1100 DNVR 80210 2197 C4
2600 DNVR 80210 2281 C2
3200 AphC 80113 2281 C2
3200 DvrC 80210 2281 C2
5900 CTNL 80121 2365 C2
6600 CTNL 80122 2365 C4
Clayton Wy
1500 ERIE 80516 1691 C1
12400 TNTN 80241 1861 C1
13100 TNTN 80241 1777 C6
S Clayton Wy
900 DNVR 80209 2197 C4
1000 DNVR 80210 2197 C4
6700 CTNL 80122 2365 C4
Claywood St
12700 BMFD 80020 1776 A7
Clear Creek Dr
5400 DNVR 80002 2027 B5
5400 DNVR 80212 2027 B5
5400 JfnC 80002 2027 B5
E Clear Creek Dr
18900 PARK 80134 2537 D4
Clear Creek Ln
10 GOLD 80401 2107 C3
10 JfnC 80401 2107 C3
E Clear Creek Pl
19100 PARK 80134 2537 D4
Clear Creek Rd
- DNVR 80237 2282 C6
10 CCkC 80439 2103 B7
800 CCkC 80439 2102 E6
Clear Creek St
- GpnC 80403 2018 A4
100 BKHK 80403 2017 E3
100 BKHK 80403 2018 A4
200 GpnC 80403 2017 E3
Clear Creek St SR-119
- GpnC 80403 2018 A4
100 BKHK 80403 2017 E3
100 BKHK 80403 2018 A4
200 GpnC 80403 2017 E3
E Clear Creek Tr
19400 PARK 80134 2537 D4
E Clear Creek Wy
19200 PARK 80134 2537 D4
Clear Creek Service Rd
- JfnC 80403 2108 C1
Clear Sky Wy
- CSRK 80109 2702 D5
Clear View Dr
26000 JfnC 80401 2190 B2
Clear View Ln
10600 DgsC 80126 2449 E7
Clearview Pkwy
400 GOLD 80403 2107 E2
Clear View Rd
11900 JfnC 80433 2525 D4
Clearview Rd
6300 BldC 80303 1688 A4
Clearwater Dr
7900 LNTR 80124 2450 E4
Cleek Wy
10 CBVL 80123 2363 E3
Cleekwood Wy
15700 JfnC 80465 2360 D1
Clematis
- BLDR 80302 1686 C5
Clematis Dr
100 BLDR 80302 1686 C5
Clementis Dr
- DgsC 80118 2954 B2
Clemson Dr
1300 LGMT 80503 1355 B7
Clemson Ln
8200 WSTR 80031 1943 D4
Cleo St
1900 AdmC 80229 1945 B5
Clermont Cir
13200 TNTN 80241 1777 E6
N Clermont Cir
11100 TNTN 80233 1861 E4
Clermont Ct
10500 TNTN 80233 1862 A5
11200 TNTN 80233 1861 E4
12200 TNTN 80241 1861 E1
13100 TNTN 80241 1777 E6
13600 TNTN 80602 1777 E5
S Clermont Ct
6200 CTNL 80121 2365 E3
6400 CTNL 80121 2366 B4
7400 CTNL 80122 2365 E6
Clermont Dr
9100 TNTN 80229 1945 E2
11200 TNTN 80233 1861 E4
S Clermont Dr
2700 DNVR 80222 2281 E1
6800 CTNL 80122 2365 E5
6800 CTNL 80122 2366 A4
Clermont Pl
12300 TNTN 80241 1861 E1
Clermont St
10 DNVR 80220 2197 E1
10 DNVR 80246 2197 E1
1500 DNVR 80220 2113 E5
2000 DNVR 80207 2113 E4
6600 CMCY 80022 2029 E1
7000 AdmC 80022 1945 E7
7000 CMCY 80022 1945 E7
9400 TNTN 80229 1945 E1
10900 TNTN 80233 1861 E5
12400 TNTN 80241 1861 E1
13400 TNTN 80241 1777 E5
S Clermont St
- GNDL 80246 2197 E2
10 DNVR 80220 2197 E2
1200 DNVR 80246 2197 E5
1700 DNVR 80222 2197 E5
2500 DNVR 80222 2281 E1
3400 AphC 80222 2281 E3
3400 CHLV 80113 2281 E3
6700 CTNL 80121 2365 E4
6700 CTNL 80122 2365 E4
Clermont Wy
10500 TNTN 80233 1862 A6
11200 TNTN 80233 1861 E3
Clermont St Pkwy
300 DNVR 80220 2113 E7
Cleveland Av
500 LSVL 80027 1689 B7
500 LSVL 80027 1773 B1
S Cleveland Av
100 LSVL 80027 1773 B2
W Cleveland Cir
700 LAFT 80026 1690 B5
Cleveland Ct
100 BNNT 80102 2124 C2
800 LSVL 80027 1689 B7
Cleveland Dr
22900 PARK 80138 2538 C4
Cleveland Pl
400 BLDR 80302 1686 B4
1400 DNVR 80202 2112 D5
Cleveland St
7800 AdmC 80229 1945 C5
E Cleveland St
100 LAFT 80026 1690 D4
800 BldC 80026 1690 D4
W Cleveland St
100 LAFT 80026 1690 C4
S Cliff Rd
5600 JfnC 80439 2357 B2
Cliffgate Ln
600 DgsC 80108 2618 E3
600 DgsC 80108 2619 A3
Cliffhanger Dr
10 BldC 80302 1517 B7
Cliff Line Rd
300 GOLD 80403 2107 D1
Clifford Ct
10900 PARK 80134 2453 B7
Cliffrose
10 JfnC 80127 2361 A7
Cliffrose Ct
300 LAFT 80026 1689 D5
Cliffrose Ln
- DgsC 80126 2449 E7
2100 LSVL 80027 1689 B5
4200 DgsC 80130 2449 E7
Cliffrose Wy
10500 DgsC 80130 2449 E7
Cliffside Ct
2900 DgsC 80108 2618 D4
Cliff View Ct
2300 CSRK 80104 2704 B5
W Clifton Av
6900 JfnC 80128 2447 A1
8400 JfnC 80128 2446 C1
S Clifton Ct
9800 DgsC 80126 2448 E5
Clifton Dr
- AURA 80016 2371 C7
Clifton Pl
- AURA 80016 2371 C7
E Clifton Pl
23500 AURA 80016 2370 D7
W Clifton Pl
6800 JfnC 80128 2447 A1
Cline Av
- BldC 80301 1603 D7
S Clinton Ct
3300 DNVR 80231 2283 B3
6000 GDVL 80111 2367 B2
6700 GDVL 80112 2367 A4
Clinton St
1100 AURA 80230 2115 A6
1400 AURA 80010 2115 A4
11200 CMCY 80640 1863 A4
14900 AdmC 80602 1779 A1
S Clinton St
- DNVR 80247 2199 A5
1700 AphC 80247 2199 A5
2000 AphC 80231 2199 A6
4900 GDVL 80111 2283 A7
6700 GDVL 80112 2367 A4
6800 CTNL 80112 2367 A4
7400 AphC 80112 2367 A4
Clipper Ct
4400 BldC 80301 1604 A4
Clipper Dr
1900 LAFT 80026 1689 E5
1900 LAFT 80026 1690 A5
Cloud Ct
4600 BldC 80301 1603 E3
E Cloudberry Dr
17300 PARK 80134 2453 A4
Cloud Dance Ct
- EbtC 80107 2709 D5
Clover Av
- AdmC 80102 2124 B2
Clover Cir
900 BldC 80026 1690 B3
900 LAFT 80026 1690 B3
3500 BLDR 80304 1602 D6
Clover Ct
- BldC 80503 1520 E4
Clover Dr
37600 EbtC 80107 2624 C7
Clover Ln
- BldC 80303 1688 D5
4200 BGTN 80601 1697 C5
28300 JfnC 80439 2273 C4
Clover Rd
2700 JfnC 80401 2109 B3
Clover Basin Dr
2300 LGMT 80501 1438 B5
2300 LGMT 80503 1438 B5
4400 LGMT 80503 1437 E6
Clover Basin Rd
5200 LGMT 80503 1437 D6
5400 BldC 80503 1437 D6
Cloverbrook Cir
5300 DgsC 80124 2450 A7
Clover Creek Dr
1400 LGMT 80503 1438 B6
Clover Creek Ln
3600 LGMT 80503 1438 B6
Cloverdale Rd
500 JfnC 80401 2107 A7
Cloverleaf Cir
8600 PARK 80134 2452 E2
8600 PARK 80134 2453 A2
Cloverleaf Dr
3500 BLDR 80304 1602 C5
Clover Meadow Ln
8800 PARK 80134 2453 A2
Clovervale Cir
5200 DgsC 80124 2450 A7
Club Cir
600 LSVL 80027 1773 A3
Club Dr
- PARK 80138 2538 A3
10 JfnC 80127 2361 B7
700 LSVL 80027 1773 B3
11500 PARK 80138 2537 E2
Club Ln
10 CBVL 80123 2363 D3
Club Pl
700 LSVL 80027 1773 A3
Club Crest Dr
7700 ARVD 80005 1942 C5
Club House Cir
24900 JfnC 80401 2190 C1
Clubhouse Cir
4900 BldC 80301 1604 D2
Clubhouse Ct
4900 BldC 80301 1604 C2
Clubhouse Dr
- PARK 80134 2537 D1
- PARK 80138 2537 D1
1200 BMFD 80020 1774 E6
1200 BMFD 80020 1775 A6
5300 BldC 80503 1604 C1
5300 BLDR 80301 1604 C1
9800 DgsC 80112 2451 E5
Club House Ln
30400 JfnC 80439 2273 A1
Clubhouse Rd
5100 BldC 80301 1604 C2
7200 BLDR 80301 1604 C2
Club Rush Ct
15700 DgsC 80134 2452 D2
Club Terrace Dr
- LNTR 80124 2450 E3
S Clyde Cir
9000 DgsC 80129 2448 E5
Clyde Ct
2000 LGMT 80501 1355 D5
S Clyde Pl
9000 DgsC 80129 2448 D5
W Clyde Pl
3000 DNVR 80211 2111 E1
3000 DNVR 80211 2112 A1
N Clydesdale Rd
9000 DgsC 80108 2535 B3
Clynke Ln
- BldC 80303 1688 C6
CO-1 E County Line Rd
10300 BldC 80501 1440 B2
10300 BldC 80504 1440 B2
10300 LGMT 80501 1440 B2
10300 LGMT 80504 1440 B2
12600 BldC 80504 1357 B2
CO-1 N Delbert Rd
9500 DgsC 80138 2539 E2
9900 DgsC 80138 2455 E7
CO-2
6700 CMCY 80022 2030 A1
CO-2 E 168th Av
19000 AdmC 80603 1698 E4
19000 AdmC 80603 1699 E3
19000 LCHB 80603 1698 E4
19000 WldC 80642 1699 E3
28900 AdmC 80603 1700 A3
28900 WldC 80642 1700 A3
CO-4
18900 LCHB 80603 1698 E2
18900 WldC 80603 1698 E2
18900 WldC 80603 1699 A2
18900 WldC 80642 1698 E2
18900 WldC 80642 1699 A2
20000 WldC 80642 1700 A1
CO-5
- ERIE 80516 1692 A1
- WldC 80516 1692 A1
CO-6 Vermillion Rd
9500 BldC 80503 1355 D2
9500 BldC 80504 1355 E2
9500 BldC 80504 1356 A2
CO-7
- BfdC 80516 1692 C4
- BMFD 80020 1692 C4
- BMFD 80516 1692 C4
- ERIE 80516 1692 C4
CO-8
- ERIE 80516 1607 D5
- WldC 80516 1607 D5
CO-8 Leon A Wurl Pkwy
- ERIE 80516 1607 C5
- WldC 80516 1607 C5
CO-8 W Parker Rd
- DgsC 80134 2537 A1
- PARK 80134 2537 A1
CO-13 Deer Creek Dr
34000 EbtC 80107 2709 A6
34000 ELIZ 80107 2709 A6
37100 EbtC 80107 2625 A7
40000 EbtC 80138 2625 A2
CO-14
- BldC 80504 1523 A6
- WldC 80516 1523 E6
CO-19
- AdmC 80602 1694 E2
- WldC 80603 1694 E2
CO-20.5
- BldC 80501 1440 D6
- WldC 80504 1440 D6
CO-24 E Singing Hills Rd
10500 DgsC 80134 2623 B1
10500 DgsC 80138 2623 B1
CO-25 Elbert Rd
30000 EbtC 80107 2795 D7
31400 KIOW 80107 2795 E3
CO-26
- WldC 80504 1440 C1
CO-27
10 AdmC 80601 1696 C1
10 BGTN 80601 1696 C1
10 BGTN 80603 1696 C1
10 WldC 80603 1696 C1
CO-30
- BldC 80504 1357 E4
CO-30 E Quincy Av
23700 AphC 80018 2286 E5
23700 AURA 80016 2286 E5
26000 AphC 80018 2287 C4
26000 AphC 80137 2287 C4
26000 AURA 80016 2287 C4
28100 AphC 80137 2288 A4
CO-37
- WldC 80603 1698 C1
CO-37 Frances Steele Blvd
600 LCHB 80603 1698 C2
600 WldC 80603 1698 C2
CO-41 Elbert Rd
30000 EbtC 80107 2795 D7
31400 KIOW 80107 2795 E3
CO-45
10 AdmC 80603 1700 A1
10 WldC 80642 1700 A1
CO-48 Willow Springs Rd
4800 JfnC 80465 2276 C7
4800 MRSN 80465 2276 C7
4900 JfnC 80465 2360 D1
CO-53 S Spruce Mountain Rd
7900 DgsC 80118 2955 B5
7900 LKSR 80118 2955 B5
CO-58 W 44th Av
5200 DNVR 80212 2027 B7
5200 LKSD 80212 2027 B7
5800 MNVW 80212 2027 B7
5900 WTRG 80033 2027 B7
5900 WTRG 80212 2027 B7
7400 WTRG 80033 2026 E7
10900 WTRG 80033 2025 E7
CO-60 E Perry Park Av
10 DgsC 80118 2955 A5
10 LKSR 80118 2955 A5
CO-60 W Perry Park Av
10 DgsC 80118 2954 C5
10 DgsC 80118 2955 A5
10 LKSR 80118 2954 C5
10 LKSR 80118 2955 A5
CO-65
- JfnC 80439 2188 C3
CO-65 Flintwood Rd
500 DgsC 80116 2707 C6
3100 DgsC 80134 2707 C1
CO-65 N Flintwood Rd
3500 DgsC 80116 2707 C3
3500 DgsC 80134 2623 C6
3500 DgsC 80134 2707 C3
5900 DgsC 80138 2623 C6
CO-66 Squaw Pass Rd
34600 CCkC 80439 2188 C6
CO-67
- BldC 80025 1770 D6
- BldC 80303 1770 D7
CO-67 S Liverpool St
6000 AphC 80016 2370 A2
6000 CTNL 80015 2370 A2
6000 CTNL 80016 2370 A2
6600 AURA 80016 2370 A2
CO-69 N Russellville Rd
10 DgsC 80116 2790 E2
100 DgsC 80116 2706 C6
CO-69 S Russellville Rd
10 DgsC 80116 2790 E1
500 DgsC 80116 2791 B5
CO-72
43300 WARD 80481 1597 C2
CO-73
- JfnC 80433 2441 E4
- JfnC 80433 2442 A6
- JfnC 80433 2526 A1
- JfnC 80439 2357 E6
- JfnC 80439 2441 E1
CO-74 Frontage Rd
- JfnC 80439 2273 A2
CO-78 S Black Mountain Dr
7900 JfnC 80433 2356 C7
7900 JfnC 80433 2440 C2
7900 JfnC 80439 2356 C7
CO-78 S Brook Forest Rd
5000 JfnC 80439 2357 D1
7100 JfnC 80439 2356 E6
8200 JfnC 80433 2356 C7
CO-80 W 82nd Av
16600 JfnC 80007 1939 D5
16600 JfnC 80007 1940 B5
16600 JfnC 80403 1939 D5
CO-80 Leyden Rd
14800 JfnC 80007 1940 C5
CO-88 S Deer Creek Rd
9800 JfnC 80127 2444 D7
10500 JfnC 80127 2528 D1
CO-88 High Grade Rd
16300 JfnC 80127 2528 C2
CO-88 Pleasant Park Rd
- JfnC 80433 2442 A7
18100 JfnC 80127 2528 A4
18100 JfnC 80433 2528 A4
19000 JfnC 80433 2527 E4
22800 JfnC 80433 2526 D2
CO-93
- JfnC 80401 2192 C7
- JfnC 80465 2192 C7
- JfnC 80465 2276 C1
- MRSN 80465 2276 C1
CO-97 N Platte River Rd
2500 DgsC 80135 2696 E6
2500 DgsC 80135 2697 A2
2500 JfnC 80433 2697 A6
CO-97 N Watkins Rd
10 AphC 80137 2121 A6
CO-97 S Watkins Rd
10 AphC 80137 2205 A2
CO-119
500 LGMT 80504 1440 C3
16700 GpnC 80403 1934 C1
17300 GpnC 80403 1850 C6
CO-126 Deckers Rd
17700 JfnC 80433 2694 E5
18200 JfnC 80433 2695 B6
CO-126 S Pine Valley Rd
13700 JfnC 80470 2608 B2
14300 JfnC 80470 2609 A6
16200 JfnC 80470 2693 C2
CO-126 Platte River Rd
- JfnC 80470 2693 E2
17200 JfnC 80433 2694 A3
17200 JfnC 80470 2694 A3
CO-172 Easley Rd
3800 JfnC 80403 2108 B1
4100 GOLD 80403 2024 C6
4100 JfnC 80403 2024 C6
6100 ARVD 80007 2024 C3
6100 ARVD 80403 2024 C3
W Coach Rd
- BldC 80302 1601 B2
Coach House Lp
- CSRK 80109 2702 D4
Coachlight Pl
8600 DgsC 80125 2532 E5
Coachline Rd
- CSRK 80109 2702 E5
- CSRK 80109 2703 A6
Coal Creek Cir
800 BldC 80027 1773 A3
800 LSVL 80027 1773 A3
800 SUPE 80027 1773 A3
Coal Creek Dr
100 SUPE 80027 1772 D4
1300 LAFT 80026 1690 C6
45000 EbtC 80138 2456 E5
E Coal Creek Dr
100 LSVL 80027 1772 D4
100 SUPE 80027 1772 D4
S Coal Creek Dr
100 SUPE 80027 1773 B6
Coal Creek Ln
500 LSVL 80027 1773 B2
Coal Creek Rd
45200 EbtC 80138 2456 C7
Coal Creek Canyon Dr
6700 BldC 80466 1765 E6
6700 BldC 80466 1766 A6
Coal Creek Canyon Dr SR-72
6700 BldC 80466 1765 E6
6700 BldC 80466 1766 A6
Coal Creek Canyon Rd
- ARVD 80007 1939 C2
- ARVD 80007 1940 B3
- ARVD 80403 1938 D1
- ARVD 80403 1939 C2
- JfnC 80007 1939 C2
- JfnC 80007 1940 B3
- JfnC 80403 1938 D1
- JfnC 80403 1939 C2
23800 ARVD 80403 1854 A7
23800 JfnC 80403 1854 A7
26800 JfnC 80403 1853 D7
31100 BldC 80403 1852 C1
Coal Creek Canyon Rd SR-72
- ARVD 80007 1939 C2
- ARVD 80007 1940 B3
- ARVD 80403 1938 D1
- ARVD 80403 1939 C2
- JfnC 80007 1939 C2
- JfnC 80007 1940 B3
- JfnC 80403 1938 D1
- JfnC 80403 1939 C2
23800 ARVD 80403 1854 A7
23800 JfnC 80403 1854 A7
26800 JfnC 80403 1853 D7
31100 BldC 80403 1852 C1
Coal Creek Heights Dr
11300 JfnC 80403 1852 C3
W Coal Mine Av
4500 AphC 80123 2363 D4
4500 CBVL 80123 2363 D4
6600 JfnC 80128 2363 A4
6800 JfnC 80123 2362 D4
8700 JfnC 80128 2362 C4
9900 JfnC 80127 2362 A4
12900 JfnC 80127 2361 B3
W Coal Mine Dr
11600 JfnC 80127 2361 E3
W Coal Mine Pl
6100 JfnC 80128 2363 B4
7600 JfnC 80128 2362 E4
10400 JfnC 80127 2362 A4
Coal Ridge Dr
- SUPE 80027 1773 B6
Coalton Dr
- BldC 80027 1772 D7
- BMFD 80021 1773 E7
- BMFD 80021 1774 A7
- SUPE 80027 1772 D7
1900 SUPE 80027 1773 E7
Coalton Rd
- BldC 80027 1772 E7
- BldC 80027 1773 A7
- SUPE 80021 1773 B7
- SUPE 80027 1772 E7
1500 BMFD 80021 1773 B7
1500 SUPE 80027 1773 B7
Coal Yard Ln
- DNVR 80230 2115 B7
- DNVR 80230 2199 B1
Cobalt Ct
7000 CSRK 80108 2619 E6
Cobalt Wy
900 SUPE 80027 1857 A1
1400 CSRK 80108 2619 E6
Cobb Rd
30400 JfnC 80439 2357 A3
S Cobblecrest Dr
9300 DgsC 80126 2449 A4
Cobblestone Ct
200 LYNS 80540 1352 E2
S Cobblestone Ct
8300 DgsC 80126 2449 A1
E Cobblestone Dr
900 DgsC 80126 2449 A1
S Cobblestone St
8300 DgsC 80126 2449 A1
Cochetopa Dr
1000 DgsC 80118 2954 D2
Cochetopa Pass
- JfnC 80127 2361 E7
Cochise Av
- AdmC 80022 1946 C3
Cochise Cir
11800 JfnC 80433 2526 B3
Cochise Tr
15500 JfnC 80470 2608 E7
15500 JfnC 80470 2609 A7
16000 JfnC 80470 2692 E1
Cockerell Dr
- BLDR 80302 1686 E4
W Coco Cir
9600 JfnC 80128 2446 B1
W Coco Dr
9000 JfnC 80128 2446 C1
W Coco Pl
6800 JfnC 80128 2447 A1
9200 JfnC 80128 2446 C1
10800 JfnC 80127 2446 A1
E Cody Av
19000 PARK 80134 2537 D5
Cody Cir
8100 ARVD 80005 1942 C5
9000 WSTR 80021 1942 C2
S Cody Cir
7100 JfnC 80128 2362 D5
Cody Ct
10 LKWD 80226 2194 C1
1600 LAFT 80026 1690 D6
2500 LKWD 80215 2110 C3
3200 JfnC 80215 2110 C2
3200 WTRG 80033 2110 C2
5800 ARVD 80002 2026 C3
5800 ARVD 80004 2026 C3
8100 ARVD 80005 1942 C5
8500 WSTR 80005 1942 D4
9100 WSTR 80021 1942 C2
S Cody Ct
10 LKWD 80226 2194 C1
1200 LKWD 80232 2194 D4
2400 LKWD 80227 2194 D7
3200 LKWD 80227 2278 D2
5100 JfnC 80123 2278 C7
6100 JfnC 80123 2362 D3
8700 JfnC 80128 2446 D2
Cody Dr
400 LKWD 80226 2110 C7
400 LKWD 80226 2194 C1
7000 ARVD 80004 1942 C7
N Cody Dr
9300 WSTR 80021 1942 C1
Cody Ln
- BLDR 80301 1603 C7
9200 WSTR 80021 1942 C2
Cody St
10 LKWD 80226 2194 D1
1600 LKWD 80215 2110 C4
3800 WTRG 80033 2110 C1
4400 WTRG 80033 2026 D7
5000 JfnC 80002 2026 C5
5400 ARVD 80002 2026 C4
6000 ARVD 80004 2026 C3
9100 WSTR 80021 1942 C2
S Cody St
- DNVR 80123 2362 C1
10 LKWD 80226 2194 D1
900 LKWD 80232 2194 D4
1800 LKWD 80227 2194 D5
5100 DNVR 80123 2278 D7
5100 DvrC 80123 2278 D7
5900 JfnC 80123 2362 D2
7000 JfnC 80128 2362 D5
8300 JfnC 80128 2446 D1
Cody Tr
10 BldC 80481 1515 A2
1300 GOLD 80403 2107 C2
S Cody Wy
1900 LKWD 80227 2194 D6
1900 LKWD 80232 2194 D6
2400 LKWD 80227 2278 D1
4300 JfnC 80123 2278 C5
4400 DNVR 80123 2278 C5
5900 JfnC 80123 2362 D2
7000 JfnC 80128 2362 D5
Cody Park Rd
23500 JfnC 80401 2190 D2
Coeur d'Alene Dr
11500 PARK 80138 2538 C2
Coffman St
100 LGMT 80501 1439 B2
1300 LGMT 80501 1356 B7
S Coffman St
- BldC 80504 1439 A7
10 LGMT 80501 1439 B3
1500 LGMT 80504 1439 A7
Coker Av
4700 CSRK 80104 2704 D7
Colard Ln
10 LmrC 80540 1269 A3
Colby Dr
2800 BLDR 80305 1686 E7
2800 BLDR 80305 1687 A7
S Colby Canyon Dr
10400 DgsC 80129 2448 B6
Cold Spring Dr
700 BldC 80466 1681 E6
700 BldC 80466 1682 A6
Cold Springs Campground Rd
- GpnC 80403 1933 D5
- GpnC 80403 1934 A6
Cold Springs Gulch Rd
300 JfnC 80401 2189 E3
1100 JfnC 80401 2190 A5
2400 JfnC 80401 2274 C1
2800 JfnC 80439 2274 C1
Cole Blvd
1500 JfnC 80401 2109 B5
1500 LKWD 80401 2109 B5
Cole Cir
5300 JfnC 80002 2025 B5
Cole Ct
6500 ARVD 80004 2025 B2
6900 ARVD 80004 1941 B7
7800 JfnC 80005 1941 B6
S Cole Ct
300 LKWD 80228 2193 B3
2700 LKWD 80228 2277 C1
4200 JfnC 80465 2277 B6
Cole Dr
700 JfnC 80401 2109 B7
700 LKWD 80401 2109 B7
5700 ARVD 80004 2025 B4
5700 JfnC 80002 2025 B4
8800 ARVD 80004 2026 C2
S Cole Dr
800 LKWD 80228 2193 B4
Cole Ln
6300 ARVD 80004 2025 B2
Cole St
800 LKWD 80401 2109 B7
3000 JfnC 80401 2109 B2
8300 ARVD 80005 1941 B4
S Cole St
1600 LKWD 80228 2193 B6
4200 JfnC 80465 2277 B5
Cole Wy
5800 JfnC 80002 2025 B3
6200 ARVD 80004 2025 B2
S Cole Wy
2400 LKWD 80228 2193 B7
2400 LKWD 80228 2277 C1
4400 JfnC 80465 2277 B6
Colebrook Ct
1300 CSRK 80109 2703 B6
Coleman
- TNTN 80260 1944 C2
Coleman Dr
600 JfnC 80401 2107 A7
E Colette Wy
- DgsC 80130 2450 C6
E Colfax Av
- AdmC 80102 2124 A2
- BNNT 80102 2124 A2
- BNNT 80102 2125 C4
10 DNVR 80203 2112 E5
100 DNVR 80202 2112 E5
700 DNVR 80203 2113 B5
1400 DNVR 80218 2113 B5
3000 DNVR 80206 2113 D5
3900 DNVR 80220 2113 D5
4700 DNVR 80220 2114 C5
8900 AURA 80010 2115 D5

STREET
Block City ZIP Map# Grid
E Colfax Av
8900 DNVR 80220 2115 D5
12100 AURA 80011 2115 D5
13000 AURA 80010 2116 A5
13000 AURA 80011 2116 A5
16500 AURA 80011 2117 B5
20700 AdmC 80011 2118 A4
20700 AURA 80011 2118 A4
23300 AphC 80018 2118 D5
23300 AURA 80018 2118 D5
23500 AphC 80018 2119 A5
23500 AURA 80018 2119 A5
26300 AphC 80137 2119 D5
28600 AphC 80019 2120 A5
30000 AdmC 80137 2120 C4
30300 AURA 80137 2120 C4
32900 AdmC 80137 2121 A4
32900 AURA 80137 2121 A4
36100 AdmC 80137 2122 C2
36100 AURA 80137 2122 C2
39300 AdmC 80102 2122 D2
39300 AdmC 80102 2123 B2
39300 AURA 80102 2123 B2
52100 AdmC 80102 2125 C4
52100 AphC 80136 2125 C4
E Colfax Av I-70 BUS
10 DNVR 80203 2112 E5
100 DNVR 80202 2112 E5
700 DNVR 80203 2113 B5
1000 DNVR 80218 2113 B5
1800 DNVR 80206 2113 B5
3900 DNVR 80220 2113 D5
4700 DNVR 80220 2114 C5
8900 AURA 80010 2115 D5
8900 DNVR 80220 2115 D5
12100 AURA 80011 2115 D5
13000 AURA 80010 2116 A5
13000 AURA 80011 2116 A5
16500 AURA 80011 2117 B5
20700 AdmC 80011 2118 A4
20700 AURA 80011 2118 A4
E Colfax Av SR-36
- AdmC 80102 2124 A2
- BNNT 80102 2125 A3
100 BNNT 80102 2124 A2
28600 AphC 80019 2120 A5
30000 AdmC 80137 2120 C4
30300 AURA 80137 2120 C4
32900 AdmC 80137 2121 A4
32900 AURA 80137 2121 A4
36100 AdmC 80137 2122 C2
36100 AURA 80137 2122 C2
39300 AdmC 80102 2122 D2
39300 AdmC 80102 2123 B2
39300 AURA 80102 2123 B2
52100 AdmC 80102 2125 C4
52100 AphC 80136 2125 C4
E Colfax Av SR-79
100 AdmC 80102 2124 D2
100 BNNT 80102 2124 D2
E Colfax Av US-40
10 DNVR 80203 2112 E5
100 DNVR 80202 2112 E5
700 DNVR 80203 2113 B5
1000 DNVR 80218 2113 B5
2700 DNVR 80206 2113 D5
3900 DNVR 80220 2113 D5
4700 DNVR 80220 2114 C5
8900 DNVR 80220 2115 D5
9700 AURA 80010 2115 D5
12100 AURA 80011 2115 D5
13000 AURA 80010 2116 A5
13000 AURA 80011 2116 A5
17000 AURA 80011 2117 B5
20700 AdmC 80011 2118 A4
20700 AURA 80011 2118 A4
E Colfax Av US-287
10 DNVR 80203 2112 E5
100 DNVR 80202 2112 E5
700 DNVR 80203 2113 B5
1000 DNVR 80218 2113 B5
1800 DNVR 80206 2113 B5
3900 DNVR 80220 2113 D5
4700 DNVR 80220 2114 C5
8900 AURA 80010 2115 D5
8900 DNVR 80220 2115 D5
12100 AURA 80011 2115 D5
13000 AURA 80010 2116 A5
13000 AURA 80011 2116 A5
16500 AURA 80011 2117 B5
20700 AdmC 80011 2118 A4
20700 AURA 80011 2118 A4
W Colfax Av
- GOLD 80401 2192 B3
10 DNVR 80202 2112 B5
10 DNVR 80203 2112 B5
10 DNVR 80204 2112 B5
1100 AdmC 80102 2124 C2
1100 BNNT 80102 2124 C2
4000 DNVR 80204 2111 D5
5100 LKWD 80214 2111 A5
6800 LKWD 80214 2110 E5
8300 LKWD 80215 2110 E5
10900 LKWD 80215 2109 D5
11900 JfnC 80401 2109 D5
12400 LKWD 80401 2109 D5
12700 JfnC 80215 2109 D5
14800 JfnC 80401 2108 D7
14800 LKWD 80401 2108 D7
15500 GOLD 80401 2108 D7
17700 JfnC 80401 2192 B2
W Colfax Av I-70 BUS
- GOLD 80401 2192 B3
10 DNVR 80202 2112 B5
10 DNVR 80203 2112 B5
10 DNVR 80204 2112 B5
4000 DNVR 80204 2111 D5
5200 LKWD 80214 2111 A5
6800 LKWD 80214 2110 E5
8300 LKWD 80215 2110 E5
10900 LKWD 80215 2109 D5
11900 JfnC 80401 2109 D5
12400 LKWD 80401 2109 D5
12700 JfnC 80215 2109 D5

STREET
Block City ZIP Map# Grid
W Colfax Av I-70 BUS
14800 JfnC 80401 2108 D7
14800 LKWD 80401 2108 D7
15500 GOLD 80401 2108 D7
17700 JfnC 80401 2192 B2
W Colfax Av SR-36
1100 AdmC 80102 2124 C2
1100 BNNT 80102 2124 C2
W Colfax Av US-40
- GOLD 80401 2192 B3
10 DNVR 80202 2112 B5
10 DNVR 80203 2112 B5
10 DNVR 80204 2112 B5
3900 DNVR 80204 2111 D5
5200 LKWD 80214 2111 A5
6800 LKWD 80214 2110 E5
8300 LKWD 80215 2110 E5
10900 LKWD 80215 2109 D5
11900 JfnC 80401 2109 D5
12700 JfnC 80215 2109 D5
13800 LKWD 80401 2109 A6
14800 JfnC 80401 2108 D7
14800 LKWD 80401 2108 D7
15500 GOLD 80401 2108 D7
17700 JfnC 80401 2192 B2
W Colfax Av US-287
10 DNVR 80202 2112 B5
10 DNVR 80203 2112 B5
10 DNVR 80204 2112 B5
Colfax Dr
- LKWD 80401 2109 A6
Colfax A Pl
3400 DNVR 80206 2113 D5
Colfax B Pl
3400 DNVR 80206 2113 D5
E Colgate Cir
18400 AURA 80013 2285 C2
Colgate Ct
10 LGMT 80503 1355 B7
Colgate Dr
2900 LGMT 80503 1355 B7
E Colgate Dr
14700 AURA 80014 2284 C2
W Colgate Dr
5200 DNVR 80227 2279 B2
5200 DNVR 80236 2279 B2
E Colgate Pl
7600 DNVR 80231 2282 D2
18300 AURA 80013 2285 B2
W Colgate Pl
5100 DNVR 80236 2279 C2
5900 DNVR 80227 2279 B2
Colgate St
300 BLDR 80305 1687 A6
S Coli Ln
6200 JfnC 80465 2359 E3
Colinade Dr
9600 LNTR 80124 2450 E4
College Av
400 BLDR 80302 1686 B3
2800 BLDR 80303 1686 E3
2800 BLDR 80303 1687 A3
W College Av
2000 DNVR 80219 2280 B1
2000 EGLD 80110 2280 B1
College Ct
10 LGMT 80503 1355 B6
E College Dr
18700 AURA 80013 2201 C7
18700 AURA 80013 2285 C1
W College Dr
2400 LITN 80120 2364 A2
College Pl
5600 BLDR 80303 1687 D4
E College Pl
20100 AURA 80013 2201 E7
College St
10 BldC 80302 1599 D3
E Collegiate Dr
6200 DgsC 80130 2450 C3
Collingswood Ct
4900 DgsC 80130 2450 B5
Collingswood Dr
4800 DgsC 80130 2450 A6
W Collins Av
10800 LKWD 80215 2109 E6
10800 LKWD 80215 2110 A6
11100 LKWD 80401 2109 E6
S Collins St
3500 DgsC 80108 2619 C7
S Collinsville Pl
4800 DgsC 80130 2450 A5
Collyer St
900 LGMT 80501 1439 B1
1100 LGMT 80501 1356 B7
2400 BldC 80504 1356 B4
S Collyer St
1300 LGMT 80501 1439 B6
Colonial Dr
8400 LNTR 80124 2450 E5
8400 LNTR 80124 2451 A5
Colonist Wy
21200 JfnC 80465 2359 C7
Colony Pl
300 LGMT 80501 1356 B7
Colorado Av
- BldC 80501 1439 B4
- LKWD 80226 2109 E7
- LKWD 80226 2193 D1
10 GpnC 80474 1849 D2
900 LGMT 80501 1439 A4
2400 BLDR 80302 1686 E3
2600 BLDR 80303 1686 E3
2800 BLDR 80303 1687 B3
E Colorado Av
10 DNVR 80210 2196 E6
10 DNVR 80223 2196 E6
2400 DNVR 80210 2197 D6
4300 DNVR 80222 2197 E6
4500 DNVR 80222 2198 A6
5300 DNVR 80224 2198 A5
7100 AphC 80224 2198 C6
7200 DNVR 80231 2198 C6
9200 AphC 80247 2199 B5

STREET
Block City ZIP Map# Grid
E Colorado Av
9600 AURA 80247 2199 B5
10100 AURA 80012 2199 B5
12900 AURA 80012 2200 A6
15500 AURA 80017 2200 D5
16800 AURA 80017 2201 A5
39500 AphC 80102 2206 E5
40700 AphC 80102 2207 A5
W Colorado Av
10 DNVR 80210 2196 E6
100 LKSR 80118 2955 A6
1800 DNVR 80223 2196 A6
3000 DNVR 80219 2195 E6
3000 DNVR 80219 2196 A6
5000 DNVR 80219 2195 B6
5000 LKWD 80219 2195 B6
5000 LKWD 80232 2195 B6
9200 LKWD 80232 2194 B6
Colorado Blvd
- CCkC 80452 2102 A5
- DNVR 80022 2029 D4
- IDSP 80452 2102 A5
10 CCkC 80452 2101 B5
10 DNVR 80206 2197 E1
10 DNVR 80209 2197 E1
10 DNVR 80220 2197 E1
10 DNVR 80246 2197 E1
10 IDSP 80452 2101 B5
300 DNVR 80206 2113 E7
300 DNVR 80220 2113 E7
1800 DNVR 80207 2113 E4
2200 DNVR 80205 2113 E4
3800 DNVR 80205 2029 D7
4000 DNVR 80207 2029 E7
4800 DNVR 80216 2029 E7
5200 CMCY 80022 2029 D4
6800 CMCY 80022 1945 D7
7200 AdmC 80022 1945 D7
8600 AdmC 80229 1945 E3
8600 TNTN 80229 1945 E3
9600 TNTN 80229 1861 D7
10100 TNTN 80233 1861 D7
11900 TNTN 80241 1861 D2
12500 TNTN 80241 1777 D7
13500 TNTN 80602 1777 D4
15100 AdmC 80602 1777 D4
15400 AdmC 80602 1693 D6
15600 TNTN 80602 1693 D6
16000 TNTN 80516 1693 D6
16000 TNTN 80603 1693 D6
Colorado Blvd I-70 BUS
10 CCkC 80452 2101 B5
10 IDSP 80452 2101 B5
Colorado Blvd SR-2
- CMCY 80022 2029 E7
10 DNVR 80206 2197 E1
10 DNVR 80209 2197 E1
10 DNVR 80220 2197 E1
10 DNVR 80246 2197 E1
300 DNVR 80206 2113 E7
300 DNVR 80220 2113 E7
1900 DNVR 80207 2113 E4
2500 DNVR 80205 2113 E4
3800 DNVR 80207 2029 E7
4000 DNVR 80205 2029 E7
4000 DNVR 80216 2029 E7
5100 DNVR 80022 2029 E7
S Colorado Blvd
- CTNL 80121 2365 E2
10 DNVR 80206 2197 E4
10 DNVR 80220 2197 E4
300 DNVR 80209 2197 E4
300 DNVR 80246 2197 E4
300 GNDL 80246 2197 E4
1000 DNVR 80210 2197 E4
1200 DNVR 80222 2197 E4
2600 DNVR 80222 2281 E2
3400 AphC 80210 2281 E2
3400 AphC 80222 2281 E2
3400 CHLV 80113 2281 E2
3400 DNVR 80210 2281 E2
5100 CHLV 80121 2281 E7
5100 GDVL 80121 2281 E7
5900 GDVL 80121 2365 E2
6400 AphC 80121 2365 E3
6600 CTNL 80121 2365 E7
8200 CTNL 80122 2449 E1
8200 CTNL 80126 2449 E1
8200 DgsC 80126 2449 E1
S Colorado Blvd SR-2
10 DNVR 80206 2197 E4
10 DNVR 80220 2197 E4
300 DNVR 80209 2197 E4
300 DNVR 80246 2197 E4
300 GNDL 80246 2197 E4
1000 DNVR 80210 2197 E4
1200 DNVR 80222 2197 E4
2600 DNVR 80222 2281 E2
3400 AphC 80210 2281 E2
3400 CHLV 80113 2281 E2
3400 DNVR 80210 2281 E2
3400 DvrC 80222 2281 E2
E Colorado Cir
9000 AphC 80231 2199 A6
Colorado Ct
8500 AdmC 80229 1945 D3
S Colorado Ct
7200 CTNL 80122 2365 E5
Colorado Dr
- BldC 80504 1522 D3
- BLDR 80303 1687 A3
E Colorado Dr
- AURA 80014 2200 B5
6500 DNVR 80224 2198 C6
8900 AphC 80231 2199 A6
9000 AphC 80247 2199 A6
10800 AURA 80012 2199 D5
11600 AURA 80014 2199 D5
14000 AURA 80012 2200 B6
17700 AURA 80017 2201 B5
W Colorado Dr
6800 LKWD 80232 2195 A6
7000 LKWD 80232 2194 E5
W Colorado Ln
6000 LKWD 80232 2195 B6

STREET
Block City ZIP Map# Grid
E Colorado Pl
11800 AURA 80012 2199 D5
15000 AURA 80012 2200 C5
W Colorado Pl
5300 LKWD 80232 2195 B6
8800 LKWD 80232 2194 C6
11200 JfnC 80232 2193 E6
Colorado St
- CLCY 80403 2017 D4
Colorado Wy
300 LGMT 80501 1439 A4
Colorado Avalanche Blvd
900 DNVR 80204 2112 B5
Colorado Center Dr
- DNVR 80222 2197 E6
Colorado Mills Pkwy
1300 JfnC 80401 2109 A7
1300 LKWD 80401 2109 A7
Colorful Av
2900 LGMT 80504 1440 C3
Colorful Ln
3800 CSRK 80109 2702 D2
Colorow Ct
5900 DgsC 80134 2621 E3
Colorow Dr
5500 JfnC 80465 2360 E2
Colorow Rd
100 JfnC 80401 2191 A1
500 JfnC 80401 2107 B7
Colt Cir
1000 DgsC 80109 2870 C1
Colt Ct
1900 EbtC 80107 2708 D3
Colt Dr
5500 BldC 80503 1604 D1
Colt Pl
10 PrkC 80456 2607 C5
S Coltsfoot Dr
9400 PARK 80134 2453 B4
E Columbia Av
19600 AURA 80013 2285 E1
E Columbia Cir
18400 AURA 80013 2285 C2
Columbia Dr
1100 LGMT 80503 1355 A7
1100 LGMT 80503 1438 A1
E Columbia Dr
6200 DgsC 80130 2450 C3
14800 AURA 80014 2284 C1
Columbia Pl
700 BldC 80303 1688 D4
E Columbia Pl
2100 DNVR 80210 2281 B2
6500 DNVR 80222 2282 C2
6500 DNVR 80224 2282 C2
7600 DNVR 80231 2282 D1
16000 AURA 80013 2284 E1
19000 AURA 80013 2285 C1
W Columbia Pl
5100 DNVR 80227 2279 C2
5100 DNVR 80236 2279 C2
9300 LKWD 80227 2278 B2
14500 LKWD 80228 2277 A2
15000 MRSN 80228 2276 E2
Columbia Rd
9800 TNTN 80260 1860 B7
Columbia St
10 WARD 80481 1597 D2
Columbine Av
200 BMFD 80020 1775 A4
400 JfnC 80401 2107 B7
400 JfnC 80401 2191 B1
1200 BLDR 80302 1686 D4
Columbine Cir
2500 LAFT 80026 1689 D2
13200 TNTN 80241 1777 C6
33600 JfnC 80439 2272 C6
S Columbine Cir
3300 AphC 80113 2281 C3
Columbine Ct
600 LSVL 80027 1689 A7
1800 JfnC 80401 2190 C6
3200 BMFD 80020 1775 E7
6500 BldC 80503 1521 B5
9500 TNTN 80229 1945 C1
9700 TNTN 80229 1861 C7
11100 NHGN 80233 1861 C4
12400 TNTN 80241 1861 C1
13200 TNTN 80241 1777 C6
15000 TNTN 80602 1777 C1
S Columbine Ct
4600 CHLV 80113 2281 C6
8000 CTNL 80122 2365 C7
Columbine Dr
10 PrkC 80456 2691 A1
100 CCkC 80452 2186 A4
300 BNNT 80102 2209 A2
1200 BGTN 80601 1696 C4
1200 CSRK 80104 2704 A7
1200 DgsC 80116 2707 A4
5400 ARVD 80002 2027 A4
12600 BldC 80504 1356 A3
28300 JfnC 80433 2525 D4
S Columbine Dr
8000 JfnC 80465 2359 D7
8000 JfnC 80465 2443 E1
W Columbine Dr
7700 JfnC 80128 2362 C5
Columbine Ln
10 CBVL 80123 2363 E3
10 CCkC 80439 2272 A4
100 GpnC 80403 1850 A6
5200 AdmC 80221 2028 A5
5200 DNVR 80221 2028 A5
7700 DgsC 80135 2783 E4
26800 JfnC 80439 2358 A5
S Columbine Ln
2300 JfnC 80439 2272 E1
2300 JfnC 80439 2273 A1
Columbine Pl
300 LGMT 80501 1356 B7
11600 TNTN 80233 1861 C3
Columbine Rd
10 PrkC 80456 2606 B3

STREET
Block City ZIP Map# Grid
Columbine Rd
100 JfnC 80401 2190 D1
2600 AdmC 80221 2028 A5
2800 DNVR 80221 2028 A5
27800 JfnC 80439 2273 E6
S Columbine Rd
6700 JfnC 80439 2357 A5
Columbine St
200 DNVR 80206 2197 C1
400 DNVR 80206 2113 C7
2600 DNVR 80205 2113 C2
4000 DNVR 80205 2029 C7
5100 CMCY 80216 2029 C5
5100 DNVR 80216 2029 C5
6800 AdmC 80229 2029 C1
9900 TNTN 80229 1861 C7
10900 NHGN 80233 1861 C4
11800 TNTN 80233 1861 C2
12100 TNTN 80241 1861 C1
12700 TNTN 80241 1777 C7
13700 TNTN 80602 1777 C4
16500 AdmC 80602 1693 C5
N Columbine St
700 GOLD 80403 2023 D7
700 GOLD 80403 2107 D1
S Columbine St
700 DNVR 80209 2197 C3
1000 DNVR 80210 2197 C5
2900 DNVR 80210 2281 C2
6600 CTNL 80121 2365 C4
7700 CTNL 80122 2365 C6
W Columbine St
100 LKSR 80118 2955 A6
Columbine Tr
26000 JfnC 80439 2274 A3
26000 JfnC 80457 2274 A3
34000 EbtC 80107 2794 A1
34500 EbtC 80107 2710 A7
Columbine Tr E
34000 EbtC 80107 2710 B7
Columbine Tr W
34000 EbtC 80107 2710 A7
Columbine Wy
10 DgsC 80108 2619 A4
12400 TNTN 80241 1861 B1
13000 TNTN 80241 1777 C7
29500 JfnC 80439 2273 C2
S Columbine Wy
5900 CTNL 80121 2365 C2
5900 GDVL 80121 2365 C2
6900 CTNL 80122 2365 D4
Columbine Campground Rd
- CLCY 80403 2017 A2
- GpnC 80403 2017 A2
S Columbine Draw
4900 JfnC 80439 2274 C7
Columbine Glen Av
25800 JfnC 80401 2190 B1
Columbine Ridge Rd
34000 EbtC 80107 2710 A7
Columbus Wy
5100 DNVR 80239 2032 B5
Comanche Ct
6700 BldC 80503 1521 B5
Comanche Dr
4300 BLDR 80303 1687 B4
4700 DgsC 80118 2953 A2
Comanche Rd
4100 JfnC 80439 2274 E5
4200 JfnC 80439 2275 A5
8700 BldC 80503 1521 B5
Comanche Creek Dr
2400 BGTN 80601 1696 E7
Comanche Creek Wy
4900 CSRK 80109 2702 C1
Comanche Pines Dr
9000 DgsC 80116 2706 E5
Combine Pl
4100 BGTN 80601 1697 C4
Comet Cir
700 TNTN 80260 1944 D3
Commanche St
- EbtC 80107 2795 E2
- EbtC 80107 2796 B2
- KIOW 80107 2795 E2
- KIOW 80107 2796 B2
200 KIOW 80117 2796 B2
700 EbtC 80117 2796 B2
Commanche St SR-86
- EbtC 80107 2795 E2
- EbtC 80107 2796 B2
- KIOW 80107 2795 E2
- KIOW 80107 2796 B2
200 KIOW 80117 2796 B2
700 EbtC 80117 2796 B2
Commander Dr
100 ERIE 80516 1691 C2
Commander Spur
10 BldC 80302 1601 B6
Commerce Ct
1200 LAFT 80026 1690 E7
3000 CSRK 80109 2703 C1
Commerce Dr
- BldC 80503 1437 D4
- LGMT 80503 1437 D4
Commerce St
100 BMFD 80020 1858 C2
1600 BLDR 80301 1687 C2
1600 BLDR 80303 1687 C2
Commerce Center Cir
- DgsC 80125 2447 E3
9100 DgsC 80125 2447 E3
Commerce Center Dr
- DgsC 80129 2447 E4
Commercial Rd
300 GOLD 80401 2192 C1
Commons Dr
500 JfnC 80401 2190 C3
Commons St
- LNTR 80124 2451 A5
Community Center Dr
- NHGN 80234 1860 D4
- WSTR 80234 1860 C4
11400 NHGN 80233 1860 D3

STREET
Block City ZIP Map# Grid
Community Park Dr
- SUPE 80027 1773 B7
Community Park Rd
10 BMFD 80020 1858 E2
10 BMFD 80020 1859 A1
Compark Blvd
- DgsC 80134 2452 C2
13100 DgsC 80112 2452 A2
Compass Av
- LAFT 80026 1690 A4
Compass Cir
3200 CSRK 80104 2787 C4
Compton Rd
- BLDR 80302 1686 E5
- BLDR 80305 1686 E5
700 DgsC 80109 2702 A7
700 DgsC 80109 2786 A1
Compton St
400 BMFD 80020 1774 B7
400 BMFD 80020 1858 B1
Comstock Ct
- BldC 80466 1681 D6
S Comstock Pl
10 DgsC 80108 2618 E4
Concho St
800 CSRK 80104 2703 E2
Concolor Wy
- DgsC 80134 2452 E2
Concord
400 DNVR 80123 2278 D6
Concord Av
400 BLDR 80304 1686 B1
Concord Cir
2400 LAFT 80026 1689 D3
S Concord Ct
9800 DgsC 80130 2450 D5
Concord Dr
7500 BldC 80301 1604 D3
Concord Ln
2000 SUPE 80027 1773 C6
8500 AdmC 80031 1943 D3
8500 WSTR 80031 1943 D3
E Concord Pl
7100 DgsC 80130 2450 D5
Concord Wy
3100 LGMT 80503 1355 B5
Concord Center Dr
8400 AphC 80112 2452 A2
Condor Ct
2000 LGMT 80503 1355 C5
N Condor Run
6600 DgsC 80125 2614 D2
Coneflower Ct
2900 SUPE 80027 1773 B7
2900 SUPE 80027 1857 B1
Coneflower Dr
800 JfnC 80401 2190 E4
Coneflower Pl
8800 PARK 80134 2453 A3
Coneflower Wy
1100 BGTN 80601 1780 C2
W Conejos Pl
3400 DNVR 80204 2111 D5
Conestoga Ct
10 PrkC 80456 2606 C2
5400 BLDR 80301 1687 D2
8200 EbtC 80107 2543 A2
11600 DgsC 80116 2791 D1
Conestoga Pl
11000 DgsC 80116 2791 C2
Conestoga Rd
10 DgsC 80116 2791 E1
10 PrkC 80456 2606 C2
Conestoga St
1600 BLDR 80301 1687 D2
1600 BLDR 80303 1687 D2
Coney Ct
10 BldC 80302 1769 C3
Conference Pl
500 GOLD 80401 2192 C1
Confidence Dr
- BldC 80504 1439 A7
700 LGMT 80504 1439 A7
Conger Ct
- BldC 80466 1681 D6
Conger St
100 NDLD 80466 1765 D3
Conifer Cir
47100 EbtC 80138 2456 B2
S Conifer Cir
2900 JfnC 80439 2273 B2
Conifer Ct
3600 BLDR 80304 1602 C6
6900 BldC 80503 1520 D4
E Conifer Ct
900 DgsC 80126 2449 A3
W Conifer Ct
800 LSVL 80027 1773 A2
Conifer Dr
- BldC 80466 1682 D6
10 PrkC 80456 2691 A1
300 CCkC 80439 2272 A4
300 PrkC 80456 2690 E1
S Conifer Dr
10200 JfnC 80433 2441 D6
Conifer Pl
- EbtC 80107 2624 B6
Conifer Rd
- TNTN 80260 1944 D1
10 JfnC 80401 2190 E1
7400 AdmC 80221 1944 D5
8200 TNTN 80221 1944 D5
25600 JfnC 80433 2442 B5
30200 JfnC 80439 2273 B2
Conifer Tr
- EbtC 80107 2624 B7
S Conifer Mountain Dr
29900 JfnC 80433 2441 A7
29900 JfnC 80433 2525 B1
31300 JfnC 80433 2440 E7
S Conifer Mountain Rd
10600 JfnC 80433 2440 E7
10700 JfnC 80433 2524 E1
11100 JfnC 80433 2525 A2

STREET
Block City ZIP Map# Grid
Conifer Ridge Dr
11400 JfnC 80433 2525 E4
Conley Wy
5400 AphC 80222 2198 A7
5400 DNVR 80222 2198 A7
W Connecticut Av
10800 LKWD 80226 2194 A4
10800 LKWD 80232 2194 A4
W Connecticut Dr
12200 LKWD 80228 2193 D4
Connell St
- PrkC 80456 2521 D3
Connor Wy
- BMFD 80021 1773 C6
- SUPE 80021 1773 C6
- SUPE 80027 1773 C6
Conoco Plz
- LAFT 80026 1690 B4
Conrad Dr
200 ERIE 80516 1607 A6
S Conservatory Pkwy
- AphC 80013 2286 A2
- AURA 80013 2201 E7
- AURA 80013 2285 E1
- AURA 80013 2286 A2
Contestoga Cross
- TNTN 80229 1861 E7
S Continental Divide Rd
7500 JfnC 80127 2362 A6
8300 JfnC 80127 2446 A1
Continental View Dr
10 BldC 80027 1688 E5
10 BldC 80303 1688 E5
10 LSVL 80027 1688 E5
100 BldC 80027 1689 A6
100 BldC 80303 1689 A6
100 LSVL 80027 1689 A6
1800 LSVL 80303 1689 A6
E Control Tower Rd
12100 AphC 80112 2367 E6
12100 AphC 80112 2368 A6
Contumacious Tr
- CMCY 80022 2030 C2
Converse Rd
- AphC 80102 2208 D1
600 AphC 80102 2124 D6
700 BNNT 80102 2124 D1
3300 AdmC 80102 2040 D6
3300 BNNT 80102 2040 D6
Converse Mile Rd
- AdmC 80102 2124 D2
- BNNT 80102 2124 D2
Conway Ct
1300 ERIE 80516 1607 A3
Conway St
1100 ERIE 80516 1607 A3
Cook Cir
12800 TNTN 80241 1777 C7
S Cook Cir
7200 CTNL 80122 2365 D5
Cook Ct
8500 AdmC 80229 1945 D3
10700 NHGN 80233 1861 D5
11300 TNTN 80233 1861 D3
12200 TNTN 80241 1861 D1
13100 TNTN 80241 1777 D6
13900 TNTN 80602 1777 C4
S Cook Ct
6500 CTNL 80121 2365 D4
7000 CTNL 80122 2365 D5
Cook Dr
12800 TNTN 80241 1777 D7
S Cook Dr
6200 CTNL 80121 2365 D3
Cook Ln
21800 JfnC 80465 2443 A1
Cook St
10 DNVR 80206 2197 D1
10 DNVR 80209 2197 D1
1500 DNVR 80206 2113 D5
3200 DNVR 80205 2113 D1
3900 DNVR 80205 2029 D7
4800 DNVR 80216 2029 D5
9200 TNTN 80229 1945 D2
10000 TNTN 80229 1861 D7
10700 NHGN 80233 1861 D5
11800 TNTN 80233 1861 D2
13600 TNTN 80602 1777 C4
S Cook St
1000 DNVR 80209 2197 D4
1000 DNVR 80210 2197 D4
2500 DNVR 80210 2281 D1
5900 CTNL 80121 2365 D2
6200 AphC 80121 2365 D2
6700 CTNL 80122 2365 D4
Cook Wy
8400 AdmC 80229 1945 D4
10300 TNTN 80229 1861 D6
12800 TNTN 80241 1777 D7
S Cook Wy
6500 CTNL 80121 2365 D4
6800 CTNL 80122 2365 D5
Cooke Ct
1000 ERIE 80516 1607 A3
S Coolidge Cir
1100 AURA 80018 2202 D4
Coolidge Ct
100 BNNT 80102 2124 C2
S Coolidge Ct
- AURA 80016 2370 D5
5400 AphC 80016 2286 E7
E Coolidge Dr
20000 AURA 80011 2117 E4
Coolidge Pl
4400 BLDR 80303 1687 B3
E Coolidge Pl
20500 AURA 80011 2117 E4
Coolidge St
- AURA 80016 2286 E6
10 AphC 80018 2202 D1
10 AURA 80018 2202 D1
S Coolidge St
10 AphC 80018 2202 D1
800 AURA 80018 2202 D3

STREET
Block City ZIP Map# Grid

S Coolidge St
5100 AphC 80016 2286 E7
Coolidge Wy
- AURA 80018 2118 D7
S Coolidge Wy
7400 AURA 80016 2370 E5
Cool Spring Dr
10 CCkC 80439 2187 E5
W Cooper Av
8800 JfnC 80128 2362 C4
11700 JfnC 80127 2361 D3
Cooper Ct
1700 CSRK 80109 2703 B5
4100 BLDR 80303 1687 B4
W Cooper Dr
10900 JfnC 80127 2362 A3
12000 JfnC 80127 2361 D3
W Cooper Ln
10700 JfnC 80127 2362 A4
W Cooper Pl
10400 JfnC 80127 2362 A4
11400 JfnC 80127 2361 E4
Coopers Tr
26900 JfnC 80439 2358 A5
S Coors Cir
2000 LKWD 80228 2193 B6
Coors Ct
6700 ARVD 80004 2025 B1
6900 ARVD 80004 1941 B7
8300 ARVD 80005 1941 B4
S Coors Ct
500 LKWD 80228 2193 B3
2700 LKWD 80228 2277 B1
4200 JfnC 80465 2277 B6
Coors Dr
2000 JfnC 80401 2109 B3
7300 ARVD 80005 1941 B6
S Coors Dr
800 LKWD 80228 2193 B4
2800 LKWD 80228 2277 B1
Coors Ln
6300 ARVD 80004 2025 B2
Coors Lp
8400 ARVD 80005 1941 B4
Coors St
600 LKWD 80401 2109 B7
900 JfnC 80401 2109 B6
5200 JfnC 80002 2025 B5
6500 ARVD 80004 2025 B2
8300 ARVD 80005 1941 B4
S Coors St
2100 LKWD 80228 2193 B7
2500 LKWD 80228 2277 C1
4200 JfnC 80465 2277 B5
Coors Wy
6100 ARVD 80004 2025 B3
S Coors Wy
2200 LKWD 80228 2193 B7
4600 JfnC 80465 2277 B6
S Copeland St
8800 DgsC 80126 2449 E2
8800 DgsC 80126 2450 A2
Copeland Wy
500 LGMT 80501 1439 D2
Copper Av
3300 BMFD 80020 1775 E5
Copper Ct
4000 CSRK 80104 2787 E5
Copper Ln
700 LSVL 80027 1773 A3
1700 JfnC 80439 2189 A6
Copper Spur
19000 JfnC 80433 2527 E5
19000 JfnC 80433 2528 A5
Copper St
3500 BLDR 80304 1602 C6
Copper Wy
3400 BMFD 80020 1775 D5
Copper Blush Ct
5100 DgsC 80108 2619 A7
Copper Cloud Dr
- CSRK 80104 2704 B5
- CSRK 80108 2704 B5
Copperdale Ln
10 BldC 80403 1852 C2
Copperfield Dr
- CSRK 80104 2788 A4
Copper Mountain Dr
- AURA 80011 2117 B7
Copper Mountain Rd
- AURA 80011 2201 B1
Copper Rose Dr
1500 JfnC 80401 2190 E5
Coquette Ct
900 CSRK 80104 2703 E5
W Cora Ln
1900 DgsC 80109 2702 B7
Cora St
8100 DgsC 80125 2532 D6
Coral Ct
900 CSRK 80104 2703 D5
Coral Pl
10 GDVL 80111 2283 A7
Coral St
300 BMFD 80020 1858 E1
600 BMFD 80020 1774 E7
Coral Wy
100 BMFD 80020 1858 E1
Coralbells Ct
2000 LGMT 80503 1438 A6
Coralberry Ct
6400 BldC 80503 1521 A6
8400 DgsC 80134 2452 E1
Corby Ct
200 DgsC 80108 2534 E7
200 DgsC 80108 2535 A7
Corby Pl
200 DgsC 80108 2534 E7
200 DgsC 80108 2619 A1
S Cordingly Rd
11000 JfnC 80433 2525 E1
11000 JfnC 80433 2526 A1
Cordova Ct
100 BldC 80303 1688 D7

S Cordova Dr
9500 DgsC 80130 2450 C4
Cordry Ct
2800 BLDR 80303 1686 E3
2800 BLDR 80303 1687 A3
Cordwood Ct
6900 BldC 80301 1604 B2
Corey St
900 LGMT 80501 1439 B1
1700 LGMT 80501 1356 B5
Coring Pl
1200 NHGN 80233 1861 A5
Corinth Cir
1500 LAFT 80026 1690 A6
Corinth Rd
6200 BldC 80503 1436 E3
6200 BldC 80503 1437 A3
S Cormorant Cir
11600 PARK 80134 2536 E1
Cormorant Pl
2900 LGMT 80503 1355 B4
Cornel Ln
3400 JfnC 80457 2274 A3
Cornelius St
100 LAFT 80026 1690 C4
25900 JfnC 80433 2442 A4
E Cornell Av
10 EGLD 80110 2280 E2
10 EGLD 80113 2280 E2
600 EGLD 80113 2281 A2
1500 DNVR 80210 2281 A2
4000 DNVR 80222 2281 E1
5600 DNVR 80222 2282 B1
5700 AphC 80222 2282 B1
6400 DNVR 80224 2282 C2
7300 DNVR 80231 2282 D1
10500 AURA 80014 2283 C2
10500 DNVR 80231 2283 C2
13500 AURA 80014 2284 A1
15300 AURA 80013 2284 D1
19600 AURA 80013 2285 D1
W Cornell Av
10 EGLD 80113 2280 D2
2300 DNVR 80236 2280 B2
2400 EGLD 80110 2280 B2
4200 DNVR 80236 2279 C2
6600 DNVR 80227 2279 A2
8400 LKWD 80227 2278 C2
14800 LKWD 80228 2277 A2
14800 MRSN 80228 2277 A2
15000 MRSN 80228 2276 E2
Cornell Cir
2600 BLDR 80305 1686 E7
E Cornell Cir
11500 AURA 80014 2283 D1
S Cornell Cir
3000 EGLD 80113 2281 A2
9200 DgsC 80130 2450 B3
E Cornell Ct
6200 DgsC 80130 2450 B3
Cornell Dr
10 LGMT 80503 1355 B7
E Cornell Dr
8400 DNVR 80231 2282 E2
17800 AURA 80013 2285 B2
E Cornell Pl
1400 EGLD 80113 2281 B2
16000 AURA 80013 2284 D1
20500 AURA 80013 2285 E1
W Cornell Pl
10600 JfnC 80227 2278 A2
10600 LKWD 80227 2278 A2
14600 LKWD 80228 2277 A2
Cornerstone Dr
16900 PARK 80134 2453 A6
Cornerstone Ln
16900 PARK 80134 2453 A5
Cornish Ct
4700 DNVR 80239 2032 B6
Cornish Pl
17600 PARK 80134 2453 B7
Cornish Wy
4400 DNVR 80239 2032 A7
Cornwall Cir
7700 BldC 80301 1604 D2
E Cornwall Ct
200 LAFT 80026 1690 B3
W Cornwall Ct
200 LAFT 80026 1690 A4
Cornwall Dr
4900 BldC 80301 1604 E2
Corona Ct
600 LAFT 80026 1689 C4
1000 CSRK 80104 2703 E4
7700 DgsC 80118 2954 C2
S Corona Ct
7900 CTNL 80122 2365 A7
8100 CTNL 80122 2449 A1
Corona Dr
11200 NHGN 80233 1861 A4
Corona St
10 DNVR 80209 2197 A1
100 DNVR 80218 2197 A1
300 DNVR 80218 2113 A7
8400 AdmC 80229 1945 A3
8600 TNTN 80229 1945 A3
9700 TNTN 80229 1861 A7
10600 NHGN 80233 1861 A5
13000 TNTN 80241 1777 A6
S Corona St
100 DNVR 80209 2197 A2
1000 DNVR 80210 2197 A5
2800 EGLD 80113 2281 A2
3500 CHLV 80113 2281 A3
Corona Tr
3000 BLDR 80301 1603 A6
S Corona Wy
7900 LITN 80122 2365 A7
8000 CTNL 80122 2365 A7
8100 CTNL 80122 2449 A1
Coronado Cir
9700 JfnC 80465 2443 C6
Coronado Ct
7300 BldC 80303 1688 D6

E Coronado Ct
9500 DgsC 80134 2622 E2
S Coronado Dr
200 DgsC 80135 2784 E3
200 DgsC 80135 2785 A2
Coronado Pkwy N
700 AdmC 80229 1945 A4
Coronado Pkwy S
900 AdmC 80229 1945 B5
Coronado Pl
600 LGMT 80501 1356 D4
N Coronado Pl
6100 DgsC 80134 2622 E2
Coronado Rd
10 EbtC 80107 2624 B5
Corporate Cir
200 GOLD 80401 2192 C1
Corporate Dr
300 GOLD 80401 2192 C1
Corporate Wy
- BMFD 80021 1858 A2
11800 JfnC 80021 1858 A2
Corporate Center Cir
1900 LGMT 80501 1438 D6
1900 LGMT 80504 1438 D6
N Corral Ln
8900 DgsC 80108 2535 A4
Corral Creek Rd
10 CCkC 80452 2270 C4
Corriente Dr
3000 BldC 80301 1603 A5
3200 BLDR 80301 1603 A5
Corriente Pl
4100 BldC 80301 1603 A5
Corrine Ct
14100 BMFD 80020 1775 E3
S Corsair Dr
9400 JfnC 80433 2441 B4
Cortez Ct
13900 BMFD 80020 1775 A4
Cortez Ln
7300 BldC 80303 1688 D6
Cortez St
10 AdmC 80221 1944 D6
Cortina Ln
2600 JfnC 80439 2273 C2
Cortona Ct
- LGMT 80503 1438 A6
S Cory St
- PARK 80134 2537 B5
Cosmos Wy
- BMFD 80020 1775 C1
E Costilla Av
10 CTNL 80122 2364 E5
10 LITN 80120 2364 E5
600 CTNL 80122 2365 A4
4700 CTNL 80122 2366 A4
6300 CTNL 80112 2366 C4
9200 CTNL 80112 2367 A4
9200 GDVL 80112 2367 A4
16200 AphC 80016 2368 E4
16200 FXFD 80016 2368 E4
16500 FXFD 80016 2369 A4
20300 CTNL 80016 2369 E4
W Costilla Av
2400 LITN 80120 2364 B4
E Costilla Blvd
7400 CTNL 80112 2366 D4
E Costilla Cir
6700 CTNL 80112 2366 C4
S Costilla Ct
7300 LITN 80120 2364 A5
E Costilla Dr
4300 CTNL 80122 2365 E4
5200 CTNL 80122 2366 A5
7000 CTNL 80112 2366 C4
21700 AURA 80016 2370 B4
E Costilla Pl
- AURA 80016 2370 D4
3600 CTNL 80122 2365 D4
4800 CTNL 80122 2366 A4
8300 CTNL 80112 2366 E4
18900 CTNL 80016 2369 D4
W Costilla Pl
- AphC 80123 2363 C4
- AphC 80128 2363 C4
- CBVL 80123 2363 C4
1300 LITN 80120 2364 C5
S Costilla St
7000 LITN 80120 2364 A4
E Costilla Wy
800 CTNL 80122 2365 A5
Costillo Ct
- BGTN 80601 1697 B6
Cotoneaster
10 JfnC 80127 2361 A6
Cottage Ln
700 BLDR 80304 1602 B4
Cottage St
- MRSN 80465 2276 C3
Cottage Wy
14300 BMFD 80020 1775 C3
Cotton Creek Dr
4300 WSTR 80031 1859 C5
S Cottoncreek Dr
9900 DgsC 80130 2450 C5
10100 DgsC 80124 2450 C5
Cottoneaster Wy
10500 DgsC 80134 2452 D6
Cottongrass Ct
300 DgsC 80108 2534 D5
W Cottontail Dr
8300 LKWD 80232 2194 D5
N Cottontail Ln
11000 DgsC 80138 2454 B6
S Cottontail Ln
8600 JfnC 80465 2443 B2
Cottontail Rd
10 BldC 80466 1766 A1
20000 JfnC 80465 2443 D1
Cottonwood Av
1400 LAFT 80026 1690 A4
E Cottonwood Av
800 CTNL 80121 2365 A3

E Cottonwood Av
3000 DgsC 80134 2452 B4
Cottonwood Cir
900 GOLD 80401 2107 E5
900 GOLD 80401 2108 A5
1500 GDVL 80121 2281 B7
Cottonwood Ct
300 BldC 80501 1438 D2
300 BMFD 80020 1775 A7
300 BMFD 80020 1859 B1
300 LGMT 80501 1438 D2
S Cottonwood Ct
5400 GDVL 80121 2365 B1
Cottonwood Dr
- AdmC 80221 1943 E5
- TNTN 80260 1944 B1
- WSTR 80030 1943 E5
10 CCkC 80439 2271 E4
700 BMFD 80020 1775 B7
1600 LSVL 80027 1689 C6
2700 AdmC 80221 1944 A5
5000 BldC 80301 1604 B2
16900 DgsC 80134 2453 A2
17700 PARK 80134 2453 C2
18200 DgsC 80138 2453 C2
E Cottonwood Dr
19000 PARK 80134 2453 C3
Cottonwood Ln
- LITN 80120 2363 E7
- LITN 80120 2447 E1
800 DgsC 80118 2954 E2
1500 GDVL 80121 2281 B7
1500 GDVL 80121 2365 B1
S Cottonwood Mtn
7500 JfnC 80127 2362 B7
Cottonwood Pl
1500 GDVL 80121 2281 A7
1500 GDVL 80121 2365 A1
2100 ERIE 80516 1606 D6
W Cottonwood Pl
4400 CBVL 80123 2363 D5
Cottonwood Rd
12300 JfnC 80127 2528 E4
12300 JfnC 80127 2529 A5
Cottonwood St
1400 BMFD 80020 1775 B5
1400 DNVR 80204 2112 B5
Cottonwood Wy
10 EGLD 80110 2280 D5
8500 PARK 80134 2453 B1
8800 DgsC 80134 2453 B2
Cottonwood Hills Dr
45500 EbtC 80138 2456 C5
Cottonwood Lake Blvd
- TNTN 80602 1777 C5
3300 TNTN 80241 1777 C5
S Cottonwood Peak
7500 JfnC 80127 2362 B6
Cougar Ct
400 LAFT 80026 1774 B2
1500 GOLD 80403 2107 C2
Cougar Dr
10 BldC 80302 1769 C3
Cougar Ln
7900 DgsC 80125 2531 A6
S Cougar Rd
9300 JfnC 80127 2445 D4
S Cougar Rdg
10700 DgsC 80124 2450 C7
Cougar Run
10700 DgsC 80125 2614 D1
Cougar St
10 GOLD 80401 2192 B1
S Cougar Canyon
10700 DgsC 80124 2450 C7
Cougar Run Rd
10 BldC 80466 1682 E6
500 BldC 80466 1683 A6
Coughlin Meadows Rd
10 BldC 80302 1682 B3
Coulson St
400 NDLD 80466 1765 C3
Coulter Pl
10 DgsC 80108 2618 D4
Council Crossing Dr
- DgsC 80116 2706 E6
Council Fire
10700 DgsC 80125 2614 D1
Counter Dr
8100 AdmC 80640 1862 E5
8200 CMCY 80640 1862 E5
Countess Ct
1700 LGMT 80501 1356 A6
Country Ct
- LGMT 80501 1439 B6
Country Ln
- BldC 80303 1688 D5
- EbtC 80107 2624 D5
- LGMT 80501 1439 B6
Countrybriar Ln
400 DgsC 80129 2448 D6
Country Club Ct
800 BMFD 80020 1774 D7
2500 WSTR 80234 1860 A2
Country Club Dr
100 DgsC 80108 2619 A3
6200 DgsC 80118 2868 C7
6400 DgsC 80108 2618 E3
11600 WSTR 80234 1860 A3
12000 JfnC 80433 2525 A4
14600 AphC 80016 2368 C3
14600 AphC 80111 2368 C3
Country Club Ln
600 DgsC 80108 2619 A4
11600 WSTR 80234 1860 B3
Country Club Lp N
2200 WSTR 80234 1860 A2
Country Club Lp S
2200 WSTR 80234 1860 A3
Country Club Pkwy
- AURA 80016 2371 C7
200 DgsC 80108 2618 C4
900 DgsC 80135 2618 C2

S Country Club Pkwy
- AURA 80016 2371 C6
Country Club Estates Dr
1000 DgsC 80108 2618 D2
Country Creek Dr
7700 BldC 80503 1520 D5
Country Hills Dr
14000 AdmC 80601 1780 B3
14500 BGTN 80601 1780 C2
Country Meadows Dr
12300 PARK 80134 2537 D3
Country Rose Cir
41300 EbtC 80138 2541 A7
Countryside Cir
41400 EbtC 80107 2541 B7
Countryside Dr
- BldC 80503 1520 E4
N Countryside Dr
10000 WSTR 80021 1858 A6
10800 WSTR 80021 1857 E5
11400 JfnC 80021 1857 E5
Countryside Ln
- BldC 80503 1520 E5
10 CHLV 80121 2281 E6
10 CHLV 80121 2282 A6
Countryside Pk
- BldC 80503 1520 E4
County Rd
10 GpnC 80474 1849 E1
100 LSVL 80027 1773 D1
200 GpnC 80474 1850 A1
W County Rd
200 CLCY 80403 2017 C4
County Creek Rd
8200 JfnC 80465 2443 E1
County Highway 103
- BldC 80466 1765 D1
County Highway 136 N
- BldC 80466 1765 E5
- BldC 80466 1766 A5
E County Line Pl
- AphC 80126 2450 C1
- CTNL 80126 2450 C1
6100 AphC 80112 2450 C1
6100 CTNL 80112 2450 C1
E County Line Rd
- AphC 80112 2451 E1
- AphC 80112 2452 A1
- AphC 80126 2449 B1
- AphC 80138 2372 D7
- BldC 80516 1607 B5
- CTNL 80112 2451 C1
- CTNL 80124 2451 C1
- DgsC 80124 2451 C1
- EbtC 80137 2372 D7
- LNTR 80112 2451 C1
10 DgsC 80126 2448 E1
10 DgsC 80129 2448 E1
10 LITN 80120 2448 E1
10 LITN 80122 2448 E1
600 BldC 80516 1691 B2
600 ERIE 80516 1691 B2
600 WldC 80026 1691 B2
700 AphC 80122 2449 A1
700 CTNL 80122 2449 A1
700 ERIE 80516 1691 B2
700 LITN 80122 2449 A1
2600 BldC 80026 1607 B5
2600 ERIE 80516 1607 B5
3200 CTNL 80126 2449 D1
4100 AphC 80126 2450 A1
4100 CTNL 80122 2450 A1
5300 CTNL 80112 2450 A1
6000 AphC 80112 2450 A1
6000 CTNL 80126 2450 A1
6100 CTNL 80124 2450 D1
6100 LNTR 80124 2450 D1
6200 BldC 80504 1523 B5
6200 WldC 80516 1523 B5
7800 BldC 80501 1440 B5
7800 WldC 80504 1440 B5
8700 LNTR 80124 2451 A1
10000 LGMT 80501 1440 B5
10000 LGMT 80504 1440 B5
11000 BldC 80504 1357 B7
11000 LGMT 80501 1357 B7
E County Line Rd CO-1
10300 BldC 80501 1440 B1
10300 BldC 80504 1440 B1
10300 LGMT 80501 1440 B1
10300 LGMT 80504 1440 B1
12600 BldC 80504 1357 B3
W County Line Rd
10 AphC 80126 2448 A1
10 DgsC 80129 2448 A1
10 LITN 80120 2448 A1
2600 LITN 80129 2448 A1
3500 DgsC 80129 2447 E1
3500 LITN 80120 2447 E1
3500 LITN 80129 2447 E1
County Rd St
200 CLCY 80403 2017 C4
Court Pl
400 BGTN 80601 1696 B6
1300 DNVR 80202 2112 D5
1300 DNVR 80204 2112 D5
2400 DNVR 80205 2113 A3
S Court Pl
5600 LITN 80120 2364 B1
N Courtesy Rd
10 LSVL 80027 1689 D7
10 LSVL 80027 1773 D1
N Courtesy Rd SR-42
10 LSVL 80027 1689 D7
10 LSVL 80027 1773 D1
E Courtland Pl
800 DgsC 80126 2449 A6
E Courtney Av
5300 CSRK 80104 2704 E6
Courtney Wy
300 LAFT 80026 1690 C6
Courtright Rd
27400 JfnC 80470 2693 E2

Court Road 13
- EbtC 80107 2624 E6
S Cove Cir
7500 CTNL 80122 2365 D6
Cove Ct
1700 LGMT 80503 1355 B6
8500 LNTR 80124 2450 E6
Cove Ln
- PrkC 80470 2608 A1
10 BWMR 80123 2363 D1
10 LITN 80123 2363 D1
S Cove Wy
700 DNVR 80209 2197 C3
W Cove Creek Ct
2400 DgsC 80129 2448 B4
S Cove Creek Dr
9300 DgsC 80129 2448 B4
S Covenant Ln
5300 GDVL 80111 2283 A7
Coventry Ct
5000 BldC 80301 1604 C2
S Coventry Dr
7600 DgsC 80108 2535 A6
Coventry Ln
- EGLD 80113 2281 B3
500 LSVL 80027 1773 B2
S Coventry Ln
6300 LITN 80123 2363 C3
S Coventry Ln E
5900 LITN 80123 2363 C2
S Coventry Ln W
5900 LITN 80123 2363 C3
W Coventry Pl
5000 LITN 80123 2363 C2
Covey Ct
9600 NHGN 80260 1944 D1
Covington Ct
10 CHLV 80113 2281 D3
Covington Dr
10 CHLV 80113 2281 D3
Covy Ct
1700 CSRK 80104 2704 A5
Cowan Rd
10 PrkC 80456 2521 E2
200 PrkC 80456 2522 A2
Cowley Dr
2500 LAFT 80026 1689 D2
Coyote Cir
- TNTN 80229 1861 E7
10 GpnC 80403 1933 E7
10 GpnC 80403 1934 A7
1900 GpnC 80403 2018 A1
Coyote Cross
6600 DgsC 80108 2534 C6
Coyote Ct
10 BldC 80302 1682 E2
1500 GOLD 80403 2107 C2
Coyote Dr
8300 DgsC 80108 2534 E5
Coyote Ln
10 JfnC 80127 2361 A4
36900 EbtC 80107 2708 B2
Coyote Pl
7600 DgsC 80125 2531 A7
Coyote Run
4500 DgsC 80125 2615 A6
Coyote Spur
1900 JfnC 80403 2104 B4
Coyote St
- AdmC 80102 2124 B2
S Coyote St
8900 DgsC 80126 2448 E3
Coyote Tr
7200 BldC 80503 1437 C3
7200 LGMT 80503 1437 C3
Coyote Canyon Wy
5400 JfnC 80465 2360 D1
Coyote Hills Wy
3200 CSRK 80109 2702 C3
Coyote Song Tr
12300 JfnC 80433 2525 D6
CR Rd
- EbtC 80107 2542 D2
CR-1.5
- ERIE 80516 1607 C3
- WldC 80516 1607 C3
CR-2
- BldC 80503 1270 B3
13700 AdmC 80601 1696 D3
13700 WldC 80603 1696 D3
CR-2.5
12600 BGTN 80603 1696 B3
12600 WldC 80603 1696 B3
CR-2.25
12400 BGTN 80603 1696 D3
12400 WldC 80603 1696 D3
CR-3
- ERIE 80516 1607 D3
- WldC 80504 1357 D3
- WldC 80516 1523 D7
- WldC 80516 1607 D3
34000 EbtC 80107 2708 A7
34000 EbtC 80107 2792 A1
CR-3.5
- WldC 80504 1440 E1
CR-3.25
- WldC 80504 1523 D4
- WldC 80516 1523 D4
CR-4
- BfdC 80516 1692 D2
- BMFD 80516 1692 D2
- ERIE 80516 1692 A2
- WldC 80516 1693 E2
- WldC 80603 1693 E2
9000 WldC 80603 1694 E2
9000 WldC 80603 1695 A2
12600 WldC 80603 1696 C2
13400 BGTN 80603 1697 B2
13400 WldC 80603 1697 A2
16800 BGTN 80603 1698 A2
16800 WldC 80603 1698 A2
18900 LCHB 80603 1698 E1
18900 WldC 80642 1698 E1
22000 WldC 80642 1700 B1

CR-4.5
10900 WldC 80603 1695 D1
10900 WldC 80621 1695 D1
CR-4.25
13300 WldC 80603 1696 D1
CR-5
31500 EbtC 80107 2792 B5
36000 EbtC 80107 2708 B3
38000 EbtC 80107 2624 B6
38500 EbtC 80138 2624 B5
CR-6
- ERIE 80516 1607 E7
- GpnC 80403 2017 D5
- WldC 80516 1607 E7
CR-7
- EbtC 80107 2792 D4
CR-9
- EbtC 80138 2456 D3
29600 EbtC 80107 2792 D7
CR-9-15
- EbtC 80107 2792 E5
CR-10
- WldC 80516 1607 E3
CR-10.5
- BldC 80516 1607 C2
- ERIE 80516 1607 C2
CR-11
- BMFD 80516 1693 B4
- TNTN 80516 1693 B4
- TNTN 80602 1693 B4
- WldC 80516 1693 B4
CR-12
- GpnC 80403 1849 D6
- WldC 80516 1607 E1
CR-13
- GpnC 80403 1849 E6
- GpnC 80403 1850 A6
- TNTN 80516 1693 D2
- TNTN 80602 1693 D2
- TNTN 80603 1693 D2
- WldC 80516 1693 D2
- WldC 80603 1693 D2
600 PrkC 80456 2521 B2
41000 EbtC 80138 2541 A7
CR-14
- GpnC 80403 1849 C4
- GpnC 80474 1849 C4
CR-15
- EbtC 80107 2793 C4
- TNTN 80602 1694 A1
- TNTN 80603 1694 A1
- WldC 80603 1694 A1
CR-16.5
- BldC 80504 1523 D3
- WldC 80516 1523 D3
CR-17
- AdmC 80602 1694 C3
- WldC 80603 1694 C1
4000 EbtC 80107 2625 C7
4000 EbtC 80107 2709 C1
46000 EbtC 80138 2457 C4
CR-17-21
33300 EbtC 80107 2793 D5
33700 ELIZ 80107 2793 C2
41000 EbtC 80107 2541 C7
41000 EbtC 80107 2625 C1
CR-18
- BldC 80504 1523 B2
50500 AphC 80102 2209 C4
50500 BNNT 80102 2209 C4
CR-19
- EbtC 80107 2457 D1
CR-20
- BldC 80501 1440 B7
- WldC 80504 1440 B7
CR-21
10 AdmC 80602 1695 B1
10 WldC 80603 1695 B1
33500 EbtC 80107 2793 E1
34200 EbtC 80107 2709 E7
37400 EbtC 80107 2625 E7
43000 EbtC 80107 2541 E3
43100 EbtC 80138 2541 E3
44400 EbtC 80107 2457 E5
44400 EbtC 80138 2457 E7
CR-23
1500 WldC 80603 1695 D1
1500 WldC 80621 1695 D1
47700 EbtC 80107 2457 E1
CR-23.5
100 AdmC 80602 1695 E3
100 WldC 80603 1695 E3
700 WldC 80621 1695 D2
CR-23.75
1100 WldC 80603 1695 E2
CR-25
- BldC 80027 1772 B7
- BldC 80027 1856 B1
- JfnC 80403 1856 B1
- SUPE 80027 1772 B7
- SUPE 80403 1856 B1
32500 EbtC 80107 2794 B3
CR-26
- LGMT 80501 1440 E1
- WldC 80504 1440 E1
CR-27
32700 EbtC 80107 2794 C5
35000 EbtC 80107 2710 C7
CR-27.5
13200 WldC 80603 1696 D1
CR-28
- BldC 80504 1357 D6
CR-29
- EbtC 80107 2710 D1
- EbtC 80107 2794 D3
10 AdmC 80602 1696 E3
10 WldC 80603 1696 E3
38000 EbtC 80107 2626 D5
41000 EbtC 80107 2542 D7
47300 EbtC 80107 2458 D3
CR-30
- BldC 80503 1520 D3
CR-31
- AdmC 80601 1697 B3

STREET Block City ZIP Map# Grid

CR-31
- EbtC 80107 2794 E5
500 BGTN 80603 1697 B3
500 WldC 80603 1697 B3
CR-32
- WldC 80504 1357 E2
CR-33
32000 EbtC 80107 2795 A4
36100 EbtC 80107 2710 E1
CR-33.5
1000 BGTN 80603 1697 E2
1000 WldC 80603 1697 E2
CR-33.75
1100 BGTN 80603 1698 A1
1100 WldC 80603 1698 A1
CR-37
34600 EbtC 80107 2795 C1
CR-39
- DgsC 80108 2620 B7
10 LCHB 80603 1698 E3
500 WldC 80642 1698 E3
1000 WldC 80603 1698 E1
CR-41
1000 WldC 80603 1699 B1
1000 WldC 80642 1699 B1
CR-43
2700 PrkC 80456 2606 D5
3100 PrkC 80456 2522 B6
4500 PrkC 80456 2521 E5
CR-43 Rd
5600 PrkC 80456 2521 C5
CR-45
- PrkC 80456 2521 E4
600 EbtC 80117 2796 B4
600 KIOW 80117 2796 B3
CR-47
10 AdmC 80642 1700 C1
10 PrkC 80456 2521 B3
CR-49
1000 WldC 80642 1700 E1
CR-53
41000 EbtC 80102 2544 E5
CR-64
3200 PrkC 80456 2689 D2
4100 PrkC 80456 2690 A3
CR-64A
- PrkC 80456 2690 B2
CR-64B
- PrkC 80456 2689 E2
CR-66
- PrkC 80456 2521 B2
CR-67
- BldC 80303 1770 E7
CR-68
- BldC 80302 1768 C2
- BldC 80303 1770 E7
- BldC 80466 1767 C1
- BldC 80466 1768 A2
CR-69
- BldC 80303 1770 E6
- BldC 80540 1352 D2
CR-70
- PrkC 80456 2691 E7
CR-72
10 PrkC 80456 2607 E7
700 PrkC 80456 2606 D6
3500 PrkC 80456 2691 D1
CR-73
4900 JfnC 80439 2273 D7
CR-83
- BldC 80302 1600 D2
CR-83J
- BldC 80455 1516 C7
- BldC 80455 1600 C1
CR-87S
- BldC 80455 1516 B3
- JMWN 80455 1516 B3
CR-90
- PrkC 80456 2606 C5
CR-92
- BldC 80540 1513 C1
CR-96J
- BldC 80481 1513 B3
CR-97
- BldC 80466 1766 E5
- BldC 80466 1767 A5
- BldC 80481 1513 A2
CR-98
- BldC 80481 1513 A2
CR-99
- BldC 80403 1766 D5
- BldC 80466 1766 D6
CR-100
300 BldC 80481 1513 E7
300 BldC 80481 1514 A6
CR-100J
800 BldC 80481 1514 C4
CR-102N
- BldC 80481 1513 D7
- BldC 80481 1597 D1
CR-103
- BldC 80466 1765 D1
100 BldC 80481 1514 A5
1500 BldC 80466 1681 D4
2000 BldC 80302 1681 D2
CR-104
1900 BldC 80466 1513 A7
1900 BldC 80466 1597 A1
CR-116
- BldC 80466 1597 A7
- BldC 80466 1681 B1
CR-120
- BldC 80302 1681 D2
- BldC 80302 1682 D1
- BldC 80302 1683 B1
- BldC 80466 1681 D2
- PrkC 80456 2607 D4
CR-126
- BldC 80466 1681 D7
- BldC 80466 1765 A1
10000 EbtC 80117 2795 E6
10000 EbtC 80117 2796 A6
CR-126N
- BldC 80466 1681 A7
CR-126S
- BldC 80466 1765 B2
- NDLD 80466 1765 B2
CR-128
- BldC 80466 1765 B2
- EbtC 80107 2793 E5
5200 EbtC 80107 2794 D5
CR-128N
- BldC 80466 1765 A2
CR-130
7500 EbtC 80107 2794 E4
7500 EbtC 80107 2795 A4
CR-132
- EbtC 80107 2792 C5
- EbtC 80107 2793 A4
6000 EbtC 80107 2794 C4
CR-134
- EbtC 80117 2796 C2
- KIOW 80117 2796 C2
9200 EbtC 80107 2795 D3
CR-136
500 EbtC 80107 2793 A2
500 ELIZ 80107 2793 A2
CR-142
2800 EbtC 80107 2708 E5
2800 EbtC 80107 2709 A5
5000 EbtC 80107 2710 A6
CR-145
- AdmC 80102 2125 D5
- AphC 80102 2209 E1
- AphC 80136 2125 D5
CR-146
10 DgsC 80107 2707 E4
10 DgsC 80116 2707 E4
10 EbtC 80107 2708 A4
3000 EbtC 80107 2709 A4
5000 EbtC 80107 2710 A4
CR-150
1000 EbtC 80107 2708 C2
2400 EbtC 80107 2709 A2
36100 EbtC 80107 2710 D1
CR-154
4000 EbtC 80107 2625 E6
5000 EbtC 80107 2626 A6
CR-155
500 CCkC 80452 2186 A3
800 CCkC 80452 2185 E2
CR-158
7000 EbtC 80107 2626 E4
CR-162
7000 EbtC 80107 2626 E2
CR-166
- EbtC 80102 2544 D7
- EbtC 80117 2544 D7
CR-174
- EbtC 80107 2541 A4
- EbtC 80138 2541 A4
7200 EbtC 80107 2542 E3
7200 EbtC 80107 2543 C3
9400 EbtC 80102 2544 A3
9400 EbtC 80107 2544 A3
CR-176
- EbtC 80107 2541 E2
- EbtC 80107 2542 A3
- EbtC 80138 2541 E2
CR-182
11900 EbtC 80102 2460 D6
CR-186
- DgsC 80138 2455 E5
2000 EbtC 80138 2456 E4
2600 EbtC 80138 2457 A4
CR-281
- CCkC 80452 2101 A1
CR-314
- CCkC 80439 2103 A5
900 CCkC 80439 2102 E5
900 CCkC 80452 2102 A5
900 IDSP 80439 2102 A5
900 IDSP 80452 2102 A5
CR-422
800 CCkC 80452 2186 B7
800 CCkC 80452 2270 B1
CR-483
10 CCkC 80439 2355 B2
CR-837
- PrkC 80456 2691 E7
CR-1034
200 PrkC 80456 2522 B7
200 PrkC 80456 2606 C1
CR-1184
11500 PrkC 80470 2523 E4
CR-3016
20000 JfnC 80433 2527 D3
Crabapple Ct
2600 JfnC 80401 2109 B3
Crabapple Dr
11700 DgsC 80116 2707 D2
Crabapple Pl
14000 JfnC 80401 2109 A3
Crabapple Rd
2700 JfnC 80401 2109 B3
N Crabapple Rd
3000 JfnC 80401 2109 B2
Crabapple St
12100 BMFD 80020 1859 D1
Crabtree Dr
2000 CTNL 80121 2365 B2
2000 GDVL 80121 2365 B2
Craft Wy
3000 WSTR 80030 1943 E7
Craftsbury Dr
- DgsC 80130 2449 E7
3400 DgsC 80126 2449 E7
Craftsman Dr
5000 DgsC 80134 2621 B5
Craftsman Wy
14300 BMFD 80020 1775 B3
S Crag Rd
9600 JfnC 80465 2443 C6
Cragmont Dr
27800 JfnC 80439 2357 D4
Cragmoor Rd
2300 BLDR 80305 1770 E2
Cragmore St
10 AdmC 80221 1944 D6
Craig Ct
2800 CSRK 80109 2702 C3
Craig Ln
27000 JfnC 80401 2189 E3
Craig Wy
13900 BMFD 80020 1775 A4
Cramner Ct
2000 JfnC 80439 2189 B7
E Cranberry Cir
17600 PARK 80134 2453 B4
Cranberry Ct
900 LGMT 80503 1438 A5
6400 BldC 80503 1521 A6
Cranbrook Ct
1100 BLDR 80305 1686 E7
Crane Dr
5000 BGTN 80601 1697 D6
Crane St
- BGTN 80601 1697 E6
Crane Hollow Dr
11200 BldC 80503 1354 B7
11200 BldC 80503 1437 C1
E Cranesbill St
17200 PARK 80134 2453 A4
Crannell Dr
7200 BldC 80303 1688 D6
Crawford Cir
100 GOLD 80401 2192 A1
600 LGMT 80501 1439 E2
Crawford Ct
200 GOLD 80401 2191 E1
Crawford Dr
200 GOLD 80401 2191 E1
Crawford St
300 GOLD 80401 2191 E1
300 GOLD 80401 2192 A1
400 GOLD 80401 2107 E7
Crawford Gulch Rd
- GpnC 80403 1935 D7
- GpnC 80403 1936 A6
4500 JfnC 80403 2021 E1
4500 JfnC 80403 2022 B5
8600 JfnC 80403 1937 E7
S Crazy Horse Ct
12800 PARK 80134 2537 D5
Crazy Horse Tr
11700 JfnC 80433 2526 C3
Cree Cir
600 BLDR 80303 1687 D4
Cree Dr
31100 JfnC 80439 2356 E4
31100 JfnC 80439 2357 A4
Creedmoor Ct
1600 DgsC 80109 2786 C5
Creek Ct
1000 LGMT 80503 1438 B5
26200 JfnC 80457 2274 A3
Creek Dr
3900 BMFD 80020 1775 C5
Creek Tr
10 CCkC 80439 2356 A7
S Creek Tr
8600 JfnC 80465 2443 C2
Creek Wy
5100 DgsC 80134 2621 D4
Creek 11
- PrkC 80456 2521 B3
Creek 67
- PrkC 80456 2521 B3
Creek Bed
- GpnC 80403 2017 B7
Creekbend Dr
19200 JfnC 80465 2443 E1
Creek Hollow Rd
8200 BldC 80301 1605 A6
Creekside Ct
500 GOLD 80403 2107 D1
2600 BMFD 80020 1776 A4
S Creekside Ct
12600 PARK 80134 2537 D5
Creekside Dr
- BldC 80504 1438 E7
- BMFD 80020 1775 E4
1900 LGMT 80504 1438 E7
2400 BMFD 80020 1776 A4
8700 DgsC 80129 2448 B3
E Creekside Dr
19600 PARK 80134 2537 D5
Creekside Ln
- BMFD 80020 1776 A4
27900 JfnC 80439 2273 D7
E Creekside Pl
18900 PARK 80134 2537 C5
Creekside Pt
2100 DgsC 80129 2448 B3
Creekside Rd
6400 JfnC 80439 2357 B4
Creekside Wy
8700 DgsC 80129 2448 B2
Creekview Dr
16100 DgsC 80134 2452 E6
Creg Rd
8700 BldC 80503 1438 B5
8800 LGMT 80503 1438 B5
Creighton Dr
2000 JfnC 80401 2109 B3
Cremello Ct
3300 CSRK 80104 2703 E3
Crenshaw St
800 CSRK 80104 2789 A1
S Crescent Ct
7400 LITN 80120 2364 A6
Crescent Dr
700 BLDR 80303 1687 C4
2600 LAFT 80026 1774 D2
8500 AdmC 80031 1943 D3
8500 WSTR 80031 1943 D3
S Crescent Dr
7200 LITN 80120 2364 A5
Crescent Ln
600 LKWD 80214 2110 E7
E Crescent Pkwy
8300 GDVL 80111 2282 E7
Crescent Lake Rd
10 BldC 80403 1852 D2
Crescent Meadow Av
11800 DgsC 80134 2451 C6
Crescent Meadow Blvd
- LNTR 80134 2451 D6
10100 DgsC 80134 2451 D6
Crescent Meadow Lp
- DgsC 80134 2451 C5
Crescent Park Cir
11600 JfnC 80403 1853 A3
Crescent Park Dr
11900 BldC 80403 1853 A3
Cress Ct
1500 BLDR 80304 1602 C5
Cressida Ct
1200 LAFT 80026 1690 A5
Cressman Ct
600 GOLD 80403 2107 D1
Crest Cir
10 PrkC 80456 2606 C7
10 PrkC 80456 2690 C1
Crest Dr
7800 LKWD 80214 2110 D4
Crest Rd
10 CHLV 80113 2281 E3
10 CHLV 80113 2282 A3
Crestbrook Cir
5700 JfnC 80465 2361 A2
Crestbrook Dr
5500 JfnC 80465 2360 E1
5700 JfnC 80465 2361 A2
E Crested Butte Av
18400 AURA 80011 2201 C1
Crested Butte Ct
1300 JfnC 80439 2189 A5
E Cresthill Av
2400 CTNL 80121 2365 C3
Cresthill Dr
7400 BldC 80504 1521 D2
Cresthill Ln
- BldC 80504 1521 E3
S Cresthill Ln
- DgsC 80126 2449 E4
- DgsC 80126 2450 A4
- DgsC 80130 2449 E4
8600 DgsC 80130 2450 A4
E Cresthill Pl
5000 DgsC 80130 2450 A3
E Crestline Av
- AURA 80015 2284 D7
5600 GDVL 80121 2366 B1
6300 GDVL 80111 2366 C1
8900 GDVL 80111 2367 A1
10600 AphC 80111 2283 C7
16300 CTNL 80015 2284 D7
16400 CTNL 80015 2368 E1
17300 CTNL 80015 2285 A7
W Crestline Av
800 LITN 80120 2364 D1
5900 DNVR 80123 2363 B1
7900 DNVR 80123 2362 D1
7900 JfnC 80123 2362 D1
7900 LKWD 80123 2362 D1
12400 JfnC 80127 2361 D1
E Crestline Cir
9700 GDVL 80111 2283 B7
10700 AphC 80111 2283 C7
19400 CTNL 80015 2285 D7
20900 AphC 80015 2286 A7
20900 AphC 80015 2370 A1
20900 CTNL 80015 2286 A7
20900 CTNL 80015 2370 A1
23300 AphC 80016 2286 D7
W Crestline Cir
500 LITN 80120 2364 D1
E Crestline Dr
21400 CTNL 80015 2286 A7
21400 CTNL 80015 2370 A1
W Crestline Dr
1700 LITN 80120 2364 B1
9500 JfnC 80123 2362 B1
10900 JfnC 80127 2362 A1
11200 JfnC 80127 2361 E1
E Crestline Ln
16200 CTNL 80015 2284 E7
16700 CTNL 80015 2368 E1
16700 CTNL 80015 2369 A1
20400 CTNL 80015 2285 E7
21400 CTNL 80015 2370 A1
21600 AphC 80015 2286 B7
E Crestline Pl
10400 AphC 80111 2367 D1
15400 CTNL 80015 2284 D7
16300 CTNL 80015 2368 E1
16900 CTNL 80015 2369 A1
20300 CTNL 80015 2285 E7
20400 AphC 80015 2285 E7
20900 CTNL 80015 2286 A7
20900 CTNL 80015 2370 A1
21900 AphC 80015 2286 A7
21900 AphC 80015 2370 B1
24800 AURA 80016 2286 E7
24800 AURA 80016 2287 A7
W Crestline Pl
800 LITN 80120 2364 D1
11200 JfnC 80127 2361 D2
E Crestmont Ln
2200 DgsC 80126 2449 C5
Crestmoor Dr
10 DNVR 80220 2114 B7
900 BldC 80303 1688 B3
Crestmoor Rd
21800 JfnC 80401 2191 B1
Crestmoore Av
- BldC 80504 1356 A3
S Crestmore Wy
9200 DgsC 80126 2449 A3
E Crestone Av
5000 CSRK 80104 2704 D7
22600 AphC 80015 2286 C6
Crestone Cir
4300 BMFD 80020 1775 C4
5400 BldC 80301 1604 C1
Crestone Ct
1800 LGMT 80501 1356 C6
Crestone Dr
1700 LGMT 80501 1356 C6
W Crestone Mtn
9800 JfnC 80127 2362 B7
Crestone Rd
9900 TNTN 80260 1860 B7
Crestone St
5800 JfnC 80403 2024 A3
6000 ARVD 80403 2024 A3
S Crestone Wy
10 DgsC 80108 2618 E4
Crestone Needles Cir
10400 PARK 80138 2454 B7
Crestone Needles Dr
10400 PARK 80138 2454 A7
S Crestone Peak
7700 JfnC 80127 2362 A7
Crestone Peak Ln
2200 CSRK 80109 2787 A5
Crestone Peak St
4500 BGTN 80601 1697 C6
Crest Park Rd
10600 LKWD 80226 2194 A3
10700 LKWD 80226 2193 E3
E Crestridge Av
17400 CTNL 80015 2369 A1
17600 CTNL 80015 2285 A7
E Crestridge Cir
10700 AphC 80111 2367 C1
11000 AphC 80111 2283 C7
15700 CTNL 80015 2284 D7
15800 CTNL 80015 2368 E1
18700 AphC 80015 2369 D1
19400 CTNL 80015 2285 D7
Crestridge Ct
2500 BldC 80302 1435 A7
Crestridge Dr
1100 GDVL 80121 2365 B1
2300 CSRK 80104 2704 A5
E Crestridge Dr
18000 CTNL 80015 2285 B7
18200 CTNL 80015 2369 B1
18400 AphC 80015 2369 B1
18500 AphC 80015 2285 B7
Crestridge Ln
300 BldC 80501 1438 D2
300 LGMT 80501 1438 D2
E Crestridge Ln
10100 AphC 80111 2367 B1
E Crestridge Pl
15900 CTNL 80015 2368 C1
17700 CTNL 80015 2369 B1
21400 AphC 80015 2370 A1
21400 CTNL 80015 2370 A1
24600 AURA 80016 2286 E7
24600 AURA 80016 2287 A7
Crestridge Rd
10 BldC 80481 1514 E2
Crestrock Cir
15800 DgsC 80134 2452 D6
Crestrock Ct
16100 DgsC 80134 2452 E7
Crestview Ct
100 LSVL 80027 1773 A1
Crest View Dr
10 GpnC 80403 1933 C6
8000 DgsC 80134 2538 D5
8000 DgsC 80138 2538 D5
Crestview Dr
7500 BldC 80504 1521 D3
S Crest View Dr
10000 JfnC 80465 2443 C6
Crestview Ln
10 PrkC 80456 2607 A5
7500 BldC 80504 1521 D2
7800 AdmC 80221 1944 A5
7900 WSTR 80031 1944 A5
S Crestview St
5900 LITN 80120 2364 E2
S Crestview Wy
6000 LITN 80120 2364 E2
Crestvue Cir
2000 GOLD 80401 2107 D5
Crestvue Dr
22100 JfnC 80401 2191 B1
Crestwood Cir
1400 LGMT 80501 1356 E6
Crestwood Ct
100 BldC 80466 1765 B2
19600 PARK 80138 2453 D7
Crete Ct
1400 LAFT 80026 1690 B6
Crey Rd
9900 TNTN 80260 1860 B7
Cricket Cir
1600 EbtC 80138 2624 C1
Crimson Ct
10300 DgsC 80134 2452 E6
Crimson Clover Ln
8600 BldC 80503 1437 D7
Crimson Sky Dr
- CSRK 80104 2704 B3
- CSRK 80108 2704 B3
Crimson Star Dr
- BMFD 80020 1775 C2
Cripple Creek Sq
3400 BLDR 80305 1771 A2
Cripple Creek Tr
3100 BLDR 80305 1771 A2
Crisman
10 BldC 80302 1600 D6
Crisman Dr
800 LGMT 80501 1356 A5
S Critchell Ln
12100 JfnC 80127 2528 B4
Croce Cir
2000 AdmC 80229 1945 B5
S Crocker Ct
7500 LITN 80120 2364 C6
S Crocker St
5200 LITN 80120 2280 C7
5500 LITN 80120 2364 C1
S Crocker Wy
5200 LITN 80120 2280 C7
6600 LITN 80120 2364 C4
Crockett Tr
10 BldC 80481 1515 A3
Crocus Wy
5200 DgsC 80134 2621 E4
Croft Ct
10 DgsC 80108 2535 A7
10 DgsC 80108 2619 A1
Croke Dr
- NHGN 80234 1860 C7
800 TNTN 80260 1944 C1
9600 NHGN 80260 1944 C1
9700 NHGN 80260 1860 C7
9700 TNTN 80260 1860 C7
S Cromwell Ln
9100 DgsC 80126 2449 E3
Crooke Dr
10800 PARK 80134 2452 E7
Crooked Spur
10 BldC 80302 1517 B6
Crooked Oak Ct
7500 DgsC 80134 2622 A3
Crooked Pine Tr
300 JfnC 80439 2188 B1
Crooked Stick Ct
- LNTR 80124 2451 A5
Crooked Stick Pl
8700 LNTR 80124 2451 A6
Crooked Stick Tr
10000 DgsC 80124 2451 A6
10100 LNTR 80124 2451 A6
Crooked Tree Pl
900 DgsC 80118 2870 D6
Crooked Y Pt
- CSRK 80108 2703 D1
Crosby Dr
7600 LNTR 80124 2450 D4
W Cross Av
11600 JfnC 80127 2361 D1
W Cross Dr
6100 JfnC 80123 2363 A1
8400 DNVR 80123 2362 C1
8400 DvrC 80123 2362 C1
12000 JfnC 80127 2361 D1
W Cross Ln
13100 JfnC 80127 2361 C1
W Cross Pl
6100 JfnC 80123 2363 B1
9900 JfnC 80123 2362 B1
13100 JfnC 80127 2361 C1
Crossbill Av
- BGTN 80601 1697 D6
Cross Country Ln
10500 DgsC 80125 2530 E5
Cross Creek Ct
1400 LAFT 80026 1689 C2
Cross Creek Dr
1400 LAFT 80026 1689 C2
Cross Creek Ln
11500 PARK 80138 2537 E2
E Crosscut
10 PrkC 80456 2521 B3
W Crosscut
10 PrkC 80456 2521 B3
Crossing Cir
300 DgsC 80108 2534 E4
Crossing Dr
300 LAFT 80026 1690 B4
Crossland Wy
9400 DgsC 80130 2450 B4
S Crosspointe Dr
9300 DgsC 80130 2450 B4
Crosspointe Ln
- DgsC 80130 2450 B4
S Crossroads Dr
10800 PARK 80134 2453 C7
10800 PARK 80138 2453 C7
Crow Ct
8400 DgsC 80118 2953 C4
Crow Dr
4800 DgsC 80118 2953 A4
Crow Rd
- DgsC 80118 2953 C4
S Crowberry Ln
- PARK 80134 2453 A4
Crowfoot Ln
8100 JfnC 80439 2440 B1
N Crowfoot Valley Rd
3000 CSRK 80104 2703 E1
3000 CSRK 80108 2703 E1
3000 CSRK 80108 2704 A1
3700 CSRK 80108 2620 B7
3700 DgsC 80108 2620 B7
5100 DgsC 80134 2620 D4
6000 DgsC 80134 2537 B7
6000 DgsC 80134 2621 A1
7200 PARK 80134 2537 B7
Crow Gulch
- PrkC 80456 2605 E4
- PrkC 80456 2606 B6
Crow Hill Dr
11500 PARK 80134 2537 E2
Crown Blvd
4200 DNVR 80239 2031 E7
5500 AdmC 80022 2032 B5
5500 DNVR 80022 2032 B5
5500 DNVR 80239 2032 B5
Crown Cir
400 BGTN 80601 1696 A6
2200 LSVL 80027 1689 C5
Crown Crest Blvd
- DgsC 80134 2453 D3
- DgsC 80138 2453 D3
9200 PARK 80134 2453 C3
Crown Point Ct
- BldC 80466 1681 C6
Crown Point Dr
8200 AdmC 80031 1943 E4
8200 WSTR 80031 1943 E4
Crown Point Pl
10 DgsC 80108 2618 D5
Crowsley Ct
9600 DgsC 80134 2452 E4
Crow Valley Rd
10 PrkC 80456 2690 C1
400 PrkC 80456 2606 C7
Cryolite Pl
- CSRK 80108 2619 E6
Crystal Cir
10000 CMCY 80022 1864 B6
S Crystal Cir
4000 AURA 80014 2284 C4
Crystal Ct
700 LAFT 80026 1689 E5
4000 BldC 80301 1604 D3
S Crystal Ct
4100 AURA 80014 2284 B4
5000 AURA 80015 2284 C7
S Crystal Dr
10000 JfnC 80465 2443 C6
10600 JfnC 80433 2443 C7
Crystal Pl
400 LGMT 80501 1356 D7
Crystal St
1800 AURA 80011 2116 B4
5100 DNVR 80239 2032 B5
10000 CMCY 80022 1864 B6
13400 AdmC 80601 1780 B5
S Crystal St
10 AURA 80011 2200 B1
10 AURA 80012 2200 B1
2500 AURA 80014 2200 B7
2500 AURA 80014 2284 B1
4800 AURA 80015 2284 B6
Crystal Wy
1500 DgsC 80116 2791 C4
5500 DNVR 80239 2032 B4
S Crystal Wy
900 AURA 80012 2200 B3
4500 AURA 80015 2284 C5
10600 JfnC 80433 2443 B7
10600 JfnC 80465 2443 B7
Crystal Lake Ct
7500 DgsC 80125 2531 A7
N Crystal Lake Dr
9600 DgsC 80125 2531 A7
S Crystal Lake Dr
9600 DgsC 80125 2531 A7
Crystal Lake Rd
29100 JfnC 80470 2693 C2
Crystallo Ct
9800 DgsC 80134 2452 D4
Crystallo Dr
15500 DgsC 80134 2452 D5
Crystal Peak
7700 JfnC 80127 2362 B6
W Crystal Peak
1900 DgsC 80129 2448 B6
Crystal Peak Dr
3100 EbtC 80138 2457 A4
S Crystal Peak Wy
10300 DgsC 80129 2448 B6
Crystal Rock Rd
100 PrkC 80456 2521 B1
Crystal Valley Pkwy
- CSRK 80104 2788 A4
- DgsC 80104 2788 B4
1100 CSRK 80104 2787 D5
Crystal View Dr
10000 JfnC 80465 2443 C6
Crystal View Ln
11700 BldC 80504 1522 D7
CTC Blvd
- LSVL 80026 1774 A2
100 LSVL 80027 1774 A2
Cub Tr
10 CCkC 80439 2356 A7
Cub Creek Tr
8300 JfnC 80433 2440 B2
S Cubmont Dr
5200 JfnC 80439 2357 D1
Cubs Den Dr
9400 JfnC 80127 2445 C4
Cuchara St
200 AdmC 80221 1944 D6
Culebra Ct
4100 BldC 80301 1603 A5
5900 JfnC 80403 2023 D3
S Culebra Peak
8000 JfnC 80127 2362 A7
Culebra Range Rd
10400 JfnC 80127 2362 A7
10400 JfnC 80127 2446 A3
S Culebra Range Rd
8000 JfnC 80127 2362 B4
Culpepper Cir
19500 PARK 80134 2537 D4
Culuera Peak Wy
2500 CSRK 80109 2787 A5
Culver Ct
1500 BLDR 80301 1686 E3
1500 BLDR 80303 1686 E3
Cumberland Ct
- EbtC 80107 2543 A2
Cumberland Dr
1200 LGMT 80501 1356 E7
1200 LGMT 80501 1439 E1
Cumberland Rd
- DgsC 80118 2954 E3
Cumberland Gap Rd
10 BldC 80466 1767 D3
Cummings Dr
3200 ERIE 80516 1690 B2
Cuprite Ct
1700 CSRK 80108 2620 A6
Curie Ct
4800 BLDR 80301 1603 B7
Curley Peak Wy
- DgsC 80125 2530 E7
- DgsC 80125 2531 A7
Curlycup Pl
8300 PARK 80134 2452 E1

STREET Block City ZIP Map# Grid

Currant Dr
23400 JfnC 80401 2190 D5
Currant Wy
8300 PARK 80134 2452 E1
Curry Ln
- WSTR 80021 1942 D3
S Curtice Cir
7700 LITN 80120 2364 B7
S Curtice Ct
7400 LITN 80120 2364 A6
S Curtice Dr
7700 LITN 80120 2364 A6
S Curtice St
- LITN 80120 2364 A7
S Curtice Wy
7700 LITN 80120 2364 A6
Curtis Ct
10 BMFD 80020 1774 E5
Curtis Pl
10 CSRK 80104 2704 A7
10 LGMT 80501 1438 D2
10 LGMT 80503 1438 D2
S Curtis Rd
9200 LKSR 80118 2955 A6
Curtis St
1300 DNVR 80202 2112 D4
1300 DNVR 80204 2112 D4
1900 DNVR 80205 2112 D3
2900 DNVR 80205 2113 A2
5600 DgsC 80135 2617 B4
Cushman Ct
1500 LGMT 80501 1356 A6
E Custer Av
19100 PARK 80134 2537 C5
W Custer Av
- LKWD 80226 2194 E3
1000 DNVR 80223 2196 C3
E Custer Dr
15700 AURA 80017 2200 D2
S Custer Ln
8300 JfnC 80439 2441 D2
E Custer Pl
- GNDL 80246 2198 A2
5300 DNVR 80224 2198 B2
5300 DNVR 80246 2198 B2
11500 AURA 80012 2199 D2
15600 AURA 80017 2200 D2
W Custer Pl
1000 DNVR 80223 2196 C3
3000 DNVR 80219 2196 A3
3100 DNVR 80219 2195 E3
5000 LKWD 80219 2195 C3
5000 LKWD 80226 2195 C3
8800 LKWD 80226 2194 C3
Custer St
- BNNT 80102 2124 E2
Custy Dr
- WSTR 80234 1860 B2
Cutforth Rd
10 GpnC 80403 1851 A3
Cutter Ln
- BldC 80302 1517 C7
- BldC 80302 1601 C1
Cutters Cir
- CSRK 80108 2620 A7
CW Bixler Blvd
- ERIE 80516 1607 B3
Cyd Dr
7800 AdmC 80221 1944 B5
Cypress Cir
- TNTN 80260 1860 B7
- TNTN 80260 1944 B1
200 BMFD 80020 1859 A3
1400 LAFT 80026 1690 A5
Cypress Dr
700 BLDR 80303 1687 D4
8900 TNTN 80229 1945 D2
19600 JfnC 80465 2443 C5
Cypress Ln
200 BMFD 80020 1859 A3
900 LSVL 80027 1773 A1
Cypress Pt
- BldC 80503 1518 E5
Cypress St
300 BMFD 80020 1859 A3
2100 LGMT 80503 1355 C5
S Cypress St
13700 JfnC 80470 2608 A2
Cypress Wy
1000 DgsC 80108 2618 C2
Cypress Point Cir
9700 LNTR 80124 2450 D5
Cypress Point Wy
10 CBVL 80123 2363 D4
Cyprus Ln
2600 JfnC 80439 2273 B1

D

D St
- AdmC 80022 1947 D1
- AdmC 80022 2031 D1
- AURA 80011 2116 C4
- CLCY 80403 2017 D4
- DNVR 80123 2363 A1
- LGMT 80501 1356 A6
1400 GOLD 80401 2108 A7
Dacre Pl
10500 DgsC 80124 2450 D6
E Dad Clark Dr
300 DgsC 80126 2448 E1
300 DgsC 80129 2448 E1
1700 DgsC 80126 2449 B1
Dagny Wy
2700 LAFT 80026 1689 D2
Dahlia Av
2800 BLDR 80305 1686 E5
2900 BLDR 80305 1687 A5
S Dahlia Cir
500 GNDL 80246 2198 A2
6500 CTNL 80121 2366 A4
Dahlia Ct
11000 TNTN 80233 1861 E4
12100 TNTN 80241 1861 E1
S Dahlia Ct
6700 CTNL 80121 2366 A4
6700 CTNL 80122 2366 A4
W Dahlia Ct
800 LSVL 80027 1773 A2
Dahlia Dr
100 LSVL 80027 1773 C2
11100 TNTN 80233 1862 A4
11800 TNTN 80233 1861 E2
12000 TNTN 80241 1861 E2
12100 TNTN 80241 1862 A1
Dahlia Ln
9700 TNTN 80229 1861 E7
S Dahlia Ln
2400 AphC 80222 2198 A7
2400 DNVR 80222 2198 A7
Dahlia Pl
11000 TNTN 80233 1861 E4
Dahlia St
- AdmC 80602 1777 E2
- DNVR 80022 2029 E4
- DNVR 80216 2029 E4
- TNTN 80602 1778 A4
10 DNVR 80220 2198 A1
10 DNVR 80246 2198 A1
100 BNNT 80102 2124 D2
1500 DNVR 80220 2114 A4
2000 DNVR 80207 2114 A3
3900 DNVR 80207 2030 A7
3900 DNVR 80216 2030 A7
5200 CMCY 80022 2029 E4
6200 CMCY 80022 2030 A2
6800 AdmC 80022 1945 E7
6800 CMCY 80022 1945 E7
7800 TNTN 80022 1945 E5
7900 AdmC 80640 1945 E4
11500 TNTN 80233 1861 E3
13800 TNTN 80602 1777 E4
Dahlia St SR-2
6000 CMCY 80022 2029 E3
6200 CMCY 80022 2030 A2
Dahlia St US-6
- CMCY 80022 2029 E3
Dahlia St US-85
- CMCY 80022 2029 E3
S Dahlia St
10 DNVR 80220 2198 A1
300 GNDL 80246 2198 A2
1000 DNVR 80246 2198 A5
2300 AphC 80222 2198 A7
2300 DNVR 80222 2198 A7
2600 AphC 80222 2282 A4
2600 DNVR 80222 2282 A4
3400 CHLV 80113 2282 A4
3400 DNVR 80237 2282 A4
3900 DvrC 80237 2282 A4
4700 CHLV 80121 2282 A7
4700 GDVL 80121 2282 A7
6900 CTNL 80122 2366 A5
W Dahlia St
- SUPE 80027 1773 A2
100 LSVL 80027 1773 A2
Dahlia Wy
400 LSVL 80027 1773 C2
3600 LGMT 80503 1438 B6
10800 TNTN 80233 1861 E4
11100 TNTN 80233 1862 A4
12500 TNTN 80241 1777 E7
12500 TNTN 80241 1861 D1
Dailey Ln
1900 SUPE 80027 1772 E6
1900 SUPE 80027 1773 A6
Dailey St
2100 SUPE 80027 1773 A6
Daily Ct
1500 ERIE 80516 1607 A7
Daily Dr
1500 ERIE 80516 1607 A6
Daisy Ct
1700 BGTN 80601 1696 D7
1700 BMFD 80020 1774 E5
S Daisy Ct
9200 DgsC 80126 2449 A4
Daisy Ln
2100 JfnC 80401 2190 E7
W Dakan Mtn
10400 JfnC 80127 2362 A7
Dakan Rd
- DgsC 80135 2868 A2
W Dakan Rd
4000 DgsC 80135 2869 A2
5200 DgsC 80135 2868 E2
W Dakin Rd
- DgsC 80135 2868 A1
Dakin St
100 AdmC 80221 1944 D6
Dakota Av
5000 CSRK 80104 2704 D7
E Dakota Av
10 DNVR 80209 2196 E2
10 DNVR 80223 2196 E2
600 DNVR 80209 2197 A2
3900 GNDL 80246 2197 D2
5200 DNVR 80246 2198 A2
6500 DNVR 80224 2198 C2
10200 DNVR 80247 2199 B2
10300 DvrC 80012 2199 B2
11200 AURA 80012 2199 D2
13000 AURA 80012 2200 A2
W Dakota Av
10 DNVR 80209 2196 D2
2400 DNVR 80223 2196 A2
3000 DNVR 80219 2196 A2
4300 DNVR 80219 2195 C2
5600 LKWD 80226 2195 B2
9200 LKWD 80226 2194 B2
10900 LKWD 80226 2193 E2
12300 LKWD 80228 2193 C2
Dakota Blvd
200 BLDR 80302 1602 B2
200 BLDR 80304 1602 B2
Dakota Dr
900 DgsC 80108 2618 C3
W Dakota Dr
11900 LKWD 80228 2193 D2
Dakota Pl
2600 BLDR 80304 1686 B1
E Dakota Pl
13600 AURA 80012 2200 A2
15900 AURA 80017 2200 E2
W Dakota Pl
8200 LKWD 80226 2194 D2
13200 LKWD 80228 2193 B2
Dakota Run
5000 DgsC 80125 2614 E5
Dakota St
400 KIOW 80117 2796 B3
E Dakota Wy
13600 AURA 80012 2200 A2
Dakota Ridge Dr
6400 JfnC 80403 2023 A3
Dakota Ridge Rd
5400 LmrC 80503 1270 B3
Dakota Ridge Tr
- BldC 80304 1602 B7
- BldC 80304 1686 A1
- BLDR 80304 1686 A1
NW Dale Cir
10400 WSTR 80234 1860 A6
Dale Ct
- ELIZ 80107 2793 B1
500 DgsC 80108 2535 B7
600 DNVR 80204 2112 A7
7300 WSTR 80030 1944 A6
10600 WSTR 80234 1860 A6
12500 BMFD 80020 1776 A7
12500 BMFD 80020 1860 A1
S Dale Ct
100 DNVR 80219 2196 A3
3100 DNVR 80236 2280 A3
3100 DvrC 80236 2280 A3
3100 SRDN 80110 2280 A3
Dale Dr
3900 BldC 80026 1606 C5
Dale Pl
10 LGMT 80501 1438 D2
10 LGMT 80503 1438 D2
Dales Pony Dr
800 CSRK 80104 2703 D3
E Daley Cir
- EbtC 80138 2623 E5
4800 DgsC 80134 2623 D7
11000 DgsC 80107 2623 E5
11000 DgsC 80116 2623 E5
Daley Dr
2100 LGMT 80501 1355 E5
S Dallas Ct
2200 AphC 80231 2199 A6
3100 DNVR 80210 2281 C2
3300 DNVR 80231 2283 B2
6400 AphC 80111 2367 B3
6400 GDVL 80111 2367 B3
6800 CTNL 80112 2367 B4
6800 GDVL 80112 2367 B4
Dallas Pl
4400 BLDR 80303 1687 B3
Dallas St
1100 AURA 80230 2115 A6
1500 AURA 80010 2115 A4
9600 AdmC 80640 1863 A7
9600 AdmC 80640 1947 A1
16100 AdmC 80602 1695 A5
S Dallas St
1700 AphC 80247 2199 B6
2100 AphC 80231 2199 A6
3600 GDVL 80014 2283 A4
5400 GDVL 80111 2367 B1
S Dallas Wy
2900 DNVR 80210 2281 C2
6800 CTNL 80112 2367 B4
6800 GDVL 80112 2367 B4
S Dallman Dr
9500 JfnC 80433 2442 B4
Damascus Rd
10 GpnC 80403 1934 D1
1600 GpnC 80403 1850 E5
1600 GpnC 80403 1851 A6
S Damascus Tr
7800 JfnC 80439 2357 E7
Damon Dr
9400 NHGN 80260 1944 D1
9400 TNTN 80260 1944 D1
S Dampler Wy
9700 DgsC 80130 2449 E5
9700 DgsC 80130 2450 B4
S Dan Ct
10200 DgsC 80130 2450 B6
Dana St
- LAFT 80026 1690 C6
Danbury Av
2600 DgsC 80126 2533 D1
Danbury Dr
1700 LGMT 80503 1355 C6
Danbury Ln
2500 DgsC 80126 2533 C1
Dancing Deer Dr
16700 JfnC 80127 2444 C4
Dandelion Wy
16800 PARK 80134 2453 A2
Danforth Av
400 CSRK 80104 2704 D7
Daniels Pk
- DgsC 80135 2533 E4
- DgsC 80135 2534 A4
Daniels Gate Dr
12400 DgsC 80108 2534 B4
Daniels Gate Pl
5700 DgsC 80108 2534 B5
Daniels Gate Rd
6400 DgsC 80108 2534 C5
N Daniels Park Rd
- DgsC 80108 2534 A5
5000 DgsC 80135 2618 C5
7200 DgsC 80135 2534 C7
7700 DgsC 80126 2534 A5
S Danks Dr
7400 JfnC 80439 2358 C6
7700 JfnC 80439 2442 D1
Danny Dr
12300 JfnC 80470 2524 B5
Danny St
10 CSRK 80109 2703 C6
Danny Brook Ct
7800 BldC 80503 1519 D2
Dannys Ct
900 LGMT 80501 1439 A1
S Danube Cir
3600 AURA 80013 2285 D3
4700 AURA 80015 2285 D6
4700 CTNL 80015 2285 D6
5700 AphC 80015 2369 D1
Danube Ct
- DNVR 80249 2033 C4
1700 AURA 80011 2117 C4
S Danube Ct
1300 AURA 80017 2201 D4
2000 AURA 80013 2201 D6
5300 CTNL 80015 2285 D7
7100 CTNL 80016 2369 D5
Danube St
1700 AURA 80011 2117 C4
12000 AdmC 80022 1865 C1
S Danube St
- AphC 80015 2369 D1
3000 AURA 80013 2285 D2
4900 AURA 80015 2285 D6
4900 CTNL 80015 2285 D6
5500 CTNL 80015 2369 D1
Danube Wy
1900 AURA 80011 2117 C4
4300 DNVR 80249 2033 C7
S Danube Wy
1300 AURA 80017 2201 D4
2000 AURA 80013 2201 D6
4800 AURA 80015 2285 D6
4800 CTNL 80015 2285 D6
5400 CTNL 80015 2369 D1
Danvers Ct
5300 CSRK 80104 2788 E2
W Danzig Pl
9600 LITN 80127 2446 B4
Daphne St
600 BMFD 80020 1774 E7
Daphne Wy
10 BMFD 80020 1858 E1
Dapple Ln
4600 BldC 80301 1604 A3
Darby Ct
500 CSRK 80104 2705 A7
500 CSRK 80104 2789 A1
700 LGMT 80501 1439 B2
Darco Dr
900 AdmC 80102 2040 D7
900 AdmC 80102 2124 D1
900 BNNT 80102 2040 D7
Dark Star Wy
11400 PARK 80138 2538 B1
Darlee Ct
1800 LKWD 80215 2110 B4
Darley Av
2600 BLDR 80305 1686 E7
2900 BLDR 80305 1687 A7
Darlington Cir
3300 DgsC 80126 2533 D1
Darren St
10 CSRK 80109 2703 C6
Darting Bird Ride
35200 EbtC 80107 2709 C4
E Dartmoor Ct
11100 PARK 80138 2537 E1
E Dartmoor Pl
11100 PARK 80138 2537 C2
Dartmouth Av
1900 BLDR 80305 1686 E6
2800 BLDR 80305 1687 A6
E Dartmouth Av
10 EGLD 80110 2280 E2
10 EGLD 80113 2280 E2
600 EGLD 80113 2281 A2
2100 AphC 80210 2281 B2
2100 DNVR 80210 2281 B2
4000 DNVR 80222 2281 E2
4500 DNVR 80222 2282 A2
5900 AphC 80222 2282 B2
6600 DNVR 80224 2282 C2
8800 DNVR 80231 2282 E2
8800 DNVR 80231 2283 A2
11000 DNVR 80014 2283 C2
11200 AURA 80014 2284 A2
11600 AURA 80014 2283 D2
15300 AURA 80013 2284 E2
19600 AURA 80013 2285 D2
S Dartmouth Av
14100 LKWD 80228 2277 A2
W Dartmouth Av
- DNVR 80236 2279 E2
10 EGLD 80113 2280 D2
1400 AphC 80223 2280 D2
1400 DNVR 80110 2280 D2
1400 DNVR 80223 2280 D2
1400 DvrC 80110 2280 D2
1400 EGLD 80110 2280 D2
2300 DNVR 80236 2280 A2
2300 DvrC 80236 2280 A2
2300 SRDN 80110 2280 A2
5100 DNVR 80227 2279 A2
7000 DNVR 80227 2278 E2
7300 DvrC 80227 2278 E2
7300 LKWD 80227 2278 E2
14100 LKWD 80228 2277 B2
14900 MRSN 80228 2276 E2
14900 MRSN 80228 2277 A2
15000 LKWD 80465 2276 E2
15200 MRSN 80465 2276 E2
Dartmouth Cir
10 LGMT 80503 1355 B6
E Dartmouth Cir
2100 EGLD 80113 2281 B2
E Dartmouth Dr
20600 AURA 80013 2285 E2
20600 AURA 80013 2286 A1
W Dartmouth Dr
14200 LKWD 80228 2277 A2
E Dartmouth Pl
900 EGLD 80113 2281 A2
2300 DNVR 80210 2281 B2
9900 DNVR 80231 2283 B2
19600 AURA 80013 2285 D2
W Dartmouth Pl
10100 LKWD 80227 2278 A2
Darvey Ln
7700 BldC 80504 1521 E2
Darwin Ct
1000 NHGN 80260 1860 C7
4800 BLDR 80301 1603 B7
S Darwin Ln
9900 DgsC 80130 2450 A5
10000 DgsC 80130 2449 D5
S Dasa Dr
4500 CHLV 80111 2282 B6
S Datura Cir
7600 LITN 80120 2364 C6
S Datura Cir E
7800 LITN 80120 2364 C6
S Datura Cir W
7900 LITN 80120 2364 C6
S Datura Ct
5900 LITN 80120 2364 C2
W Datura Ct
5900 LITN 80120 2364 C2
S Datura St
5300 EGLD 80120 2280 C7
5300 LITN 80120 2280 C7
5300 LITN 80120 2364 C1
S Dauntless Wy
9200 JfnC 80433 2441 C4
S Davco Dr
8300 JfnC 80465 2443 B2
N Davenport Ct
1200 ERIE 80516 1607 A3
S Davenport Ct
1100 ERIE 80516 1607 A3
Davenport St
- DNVR 80239 2032 B6
Davenport Wy
4300 DNVR 80239 2032 B7
Daventry Pl
6900 DgsC 80108 2618 E1
W David Av
6800 JfnC 80128 2363 A7
9200 JfnC 80128 2362 B7
David Dr
10 CCkC 80439 2271 E5
W David Dr
6300 JfnC 80128 2363 A7
7100 JfnC 80128 2362 E7
E David Pl
22800 AURA 80016 2370 C7
W David Pl
6600 JfnC 80128 2363 A7
9500 JfnC 80128 2362 B7
Davidson Pl
3700 BLDR 80305 1687 B5
Davidson Wy
9000 BldC 80026 1689 C4
E Davies Av
100 CTNL 80122 2364 E5
100 LITN 80122 2364 E5
3300 CTNL 80122 2365 D5
7200 CTNL 80112 2366 D5
8600 CTNL 80112 2367 A5
13900 AphC 80112 2368 B4
13900 CTNL 80112 2368 B4
16600 FXFD 80016 2368 E4
18100 FXFD 80016 2369 B4
20100 CTNL 80016 2369 E4
W Davies Av
- CTNL 80122 2364 E5
2800 LITN 80120 2364 A4
W Davies Av N
10 LITN 80120 2364 D5
10 LITN 80122 2364 D5
W Davies Av S
200 LITN 80120 2364 D5
E Davies Cir
21600 CTNL 80016 2370 B5
E Davies Ct
1100 CTNL 80122 2365 A5
7400 CTNL 80112 2366 D4
W Davies Ct
600 LITN 80120 2364 D5
E Davies Dr
- AURA 80016 2371 B4
- CTNL 80122 2366 A5
22500 AURA 80016 2370 C4
W Davies Dr
2800 LITN 80120 2364 A5
E Davies Pl
1900 CTNL 80122 2365 B5
5500 CTNL 80122 2366 B5
8300 CTNL 80112 2366 E4
13600 CTNL 80112 2368 B5
19000 CTNL 80016 2369 C5
W Davies Pl
1300 LITN 80120 2364 C5
S Davies St
7000 LITN 80120 2364 A5
E Davies Wy
- AURA 80016 2371 A3
24500 AURA 80016 2370 E4
W Davies Wy
500 LITN 80120 2364 D4
Da Vinci Dr
3900 LGMT 80503 1438 A5
S Davis Av
9500 JfnC 80433 2442 B4
Davis Ct
- ERIE 80516 1607 A3
Davis Ln
13400 BldC 80504 1356 B2
Davis St
12600 BMFD 80020 1775 C7
S Davis Peak
7600 JfnC 80127 2361 E6
Dawn Ct
- WTRG 80215 2110 A3
4000 BLDR 80304 1602 E5
7500 DgsC 80125 2530 E7
Dawn Dr
7500 DgsC 80125 2530 E7
Dawnee St
200 KIOW 80117 2796 A2
Dawn Glow Wy
- CSRK 80109 2702 E5
Dawn Heath Cir
10 JfnC 80127 2361 A6
Dawn Heath Dr
10 JfnC 80127 2361 A6
Dawson Cir
2200 AURA 80011 2116 C3
S Dawson Cir
4200 AURA 80014 2284 C5
6700 CTNL 80112 2368 C4
Dawson Ct
300 CSRK 80104 2704 A6
S Dawson Ct
2500 AURA 80014 2200 C7
Dawson Dr
100 CSRK 80104 2704 A7
900 AdmC 80229 1945 A4
10400 BldC 80026 1606 A3
Dawson Pl
100 LGMT 80501 1356 C7
Dawson Rd
10 PrkC 80470 2523 E6
10 PrkC 80470 2524 A6
W Dawson Rd
3200 DgsC 80135 2785 D5
Dawson St
600 AURA 80011 2116 C6
8600 AdmC 80229 1945 A3
8600 TNTN 80229 1945 A3
S Dawson St
1500 AURA 80012 2200 C5
3400 AURA 80014 2284 C3
S Dawson Wy
900 AURA 80012 2200 C3
2300 AURA 80014 2200 C7
Dawson Butte Wy
1500 CSRK 80109 2703 B5
Dawson Ridge Blvd
- CSRK 80109 2787 B5
Daydream Rd
4300 JfnC 80403 2021 D6
Daylight Ct
- BGTN 80601 1697 C4
Daylilly Ct
6500 BldC 80503 1521 A5
Day Star Ct
11200 PARK 80138 2538 C1
Day Star Dr
11200 PARK 80138 2538 C1
Dayton Cir
- CMCY 80640 1863 A4
S Dayton Cir
1400 AURA 80247 2199 A5
S Dayton Ct
1200 AURA 80247 2199 B4
2900 DNVR 80231 2283 B2
5400 GDVL 80111 2367 B1
5900 AphC 80111 2367 B2
Dayton Grn
- AphC 80231 2199 A7
- DNVR 80231 2199 A7
Dayton St
- CMCY 80640 1863 A5
- DNVR 80238 2115 B3
- DvrC 80238 2115 B3
100 AURA 80010 2199 B1
100 DNVR 80010 2199 B1
100 DNVR 80230 2199 B1
200 AURA 80230 2199 B1
300 AURA 80230 2115 B7
300 DNVR 80230 2115 B7
1400 AURA 80010 2115 B4
S Dayton St
300 DNVR 80247 2199 B3
1000 AphC 80247 2199 B4
1000 AURA 80247 2199 B4
1900 AphC 80231 2199 B7
3400 DNVR 80014 2283 B3
3400 DNVR 80231 2283 B3
3400 DvrC 80231 2283 B3
3400 GDVL 80014 2283 B3
4700 AphC 80015 2283 B6
4700 GDVL 80015 2283 B6
4700 GDVL 80111 2283 B6
5400 GDVL 80111 2367 B1
5800 AphC 80111 2367 B2
6300 CTNL 80111 2367 B3
6500 CTNL 80112 2367 B4
6500 GDVL 80112 2367 B4
Dayton Wy
10600 CMCY 80640 1863 A5
S Dayton Wy
2300 AphC 80231 2199 B7
2300 DNVR 80231 2199 B7
2600 DNVR 80231 2283 B1
3700 GDVL 80014 2283 B3
Dead Man Gulch
400 JfnC 80401 2107 C7
Dean Dr
700 NHGN 80233 1860 E3
700 NHGN 80233 1861 A3
Dean Pl
1200 BLDR 80302 1686 B3
S Dearborn Cir
700 AURA 80012 2200 C3
S Dearborn Ct
700 AURA 80012 2200 C3
4200 AURA 80014 2284 C5
4300 AURA 80015 2284 C5
Dearborn Pl
700 BldC 80303 1688 D4
Dearborn St
1200 AURA 80011 2116 C5
4300 DNVR 80239 2032 B7
S Dearborn St
1000 AURA 80012 2200 C3
2200 AURA 80014 2200 C7
Dearborn Wy
200 AURA 80011 2116 C7
S Dearborn Wy
900 AURA 80012 2200 C3
Dearborne Dr
10900 PARK 80134 2452 E7
Debbi Cir
1400 EbtC 80138 2540 C4
N Debbie Ln
7600 DgsC 80108 2535 B7
De Berry St
26100 JfnC 80433 2442 A5
Deborah Ct
2300 EbtC 80138 2540 D7
Debra Ann Rd
10 BldC 80403 1852 A2
10 GpnC 80403 1851 E2
Decatur Av
4200 CSRK 80104 2704 C7
Decatur Cir
1300 BMFD 80020 1775 E7
1300 BMFD 80020 1776 A6
N Decatur Cir
11200 WSTR 80234 1860 A4
Decatur Ct
- FLHT 80260 1944 A1
100 BMFD 80020 1776 C7
8000 WSTR 80031 1944 A5
11500 WSTR 80234 1860 A3
Decatur Dr
2700 BMFD 80020 1776 A7
2700 BMFD 80020 1860 A1
N Decatur Dr
11600 WSTR 80234 1860 A3
Decatur Pl
11800 WSTR 80234 1860 A2
13500 BMFD 80020 1776 A5
Decatur St
- AdmC 80221 2028 A2
- WSTR 80234 1860 A6
10 DNVR 80219 2196 A1
400 DNVR 80219 2112 A7
1500 DNVR 80204 2112 A5
3300 DNVR 80211 2112 A1
4400 DNVR 80211 2028 A7
4800 DNVR 80221 2028 A5
7300 WSTR 80030 1944 A6
8600 WSTR 80031 1944 A3
8900 FLHT 80260 1944 A3
9800 FLHT 80260 1860 A7
N Decatur St
1300 WSTR 80234 1859 E4
11500 WSTR 80234 1860 A3
S Decatur St
10 DNVR 80219 2196 A2
2600 DNVR 80219 2280 A1
3000 DvrC 80236 2280 A2
3000 SRDN 80110 2280 A2
3100 DNVR 80236 2280 A2
4500 EGLD 80110 2280 A6
Decatur Wy
- FLHT 80260 1944 A2
N Deckers Pl
1100 CSRK 80104 2704 E5
Deckers Rd
17700 JfnC 80433 2694 D4
18200 JfnC 80433 2695 A6
Deckers Rd CO-126
17700 JfnC 80433 2694 D4
18200 JfnC 80433 2695 A6
Deep Forest Ln
700 JfnC 80439 2188 C4
Deep Forest Rd
32600 JfnC 80439 2188 C4
Deephaven Ct
5000 DNVR 80239 2032 B5
E Deephaven Ct
4800 DNVR 80239 2032 B6
Deer Cir
10 GpnC 80403 1934 B6
Deer Cross
300 CSRK 80104 2787 C3
Deer Ln
10 CCkC 80439 2271 E4
10 CCkC 80439 2272 A4
N Deer Ln
11100 DgsC 80138 2454 C6
S Deer Pth
6700 JfnC 80439 2356 B5
Deer Rd
10 CCkC 80439 2355 E7
400 CCkC 80439 2439 E1
Deer St
10 GOLD 80401 2108 B7
Deer Tr
10 CCkC 80452 2186 B5
300 PrkC 80456 2606 E6
4600 EbtC 80107 2793 D1
S Deer Tr
4900 JfnC 80439 2273 C7
Deer Canyon Ct
- DNVR 80237 2282 E6
Deer Clover Cir
700 DgsC 80108 2534 D7
Deer Clover Dr
- DgsC 80108 2534 D7
Deer Clover Wy
700 DgsC 80108 2534 D7
Deer Creek Cir
41300 EbtC 80107 2541 B7
Deer Creek Ct
5200 BLDR 80301 1604 C1
S Deer Creek Ct
9900 DgsC 80129 2448 A5
Deer Creek Dr
2700 EbtC 80138 2540 E7
2800 EbtC 80138 2541 A7
3400 EbtC 80107 2541 A7
3700 EbtC 80107 2625 B1

Denver Regional Street Index

STREET
Block City ZIP Map# Grid

Deer Creek Dr
34000 EbtC 80107 2709 A7
34000 ELIZ 80107 2709 A7
40000 EbtC 80138 2625 A1
Deer Creek Dr CO-13
34000 EbtC 80107 2709 A7
34000 ELIZ 80107 2709 A7
37100 EbtC 80107 2625 A7
40000 EbtC 80138 2625 A1
W Deer Creek Dr
3000 DgsC 80129 2448 A5
S Deer Creek Ln
9900 DgsC 80129 2448 A5
W Deer Creek Pl
2800 DgsC 80129 2448 A5
S Deer Creek Rd
9800 JfnC 80127 2444 D7
10500 JfnC 80127 2528 D2
S Deer Creek Rd CO-88
9800 JfnC 80127 2444 D7
10500 JfnC 80127 2528 D2
S Deer Creek St
9900 DgsC 80129 2448 A5
W Deer Creek Tr
2800 DgsC 80129 2448 A5
S Deer Creek Canyon Rd
8000 JfnC 80465 2359 E7
8000 JfnC 80465 2443 E1
8000 JfnC 80465 2444 B3
8200 JfnC 80127 2444 B3
W Deer Creek Canyon Rd
8400 JfnC 80127 2446 C3
8400 JfnC 80128 2446 C3
11000 JfnC 80127 2445 E3
14300 JfnC 80127 2444 D5
Deercrest Wy
7300 LNTR 80124 2450 D3
Deerfield Cir
45100 EbtC 80107 2458 E3
Deerfield Ct
1400 LGMT 80501 1356 E7
Deerfield Rd
7400 BldC 80503 1437 C7
9100 DgsC 80116 2706 E7
9500 DgsC 80116 2707 A7
Deerfield Wy
12100 BMFD 80020 1859 D1
Deerhaven Ct
16200 JfnC 80465 2276 D7
Deerhaven Dr
10 PrkC 80456 2606 C5
Deer Horn Ct
9500 PARK 80134 2453 A4
Deer Meadow Ln
300 DgsC 80124 2450 E7
Deer Meadow Tr
5800 JfnC 80403 2023 B4
Deer Mountain Dr
16200 JfnC 80127 2444 C4
Deerpath Rd
1000 DgsC 80116 2707 B5
Deerpath Tr
1200 DgsC 80116 2707 A5
Deer Ridge Dr
15800 JfnC 80465 2360 D1
Deer Run Tr
6500 DgsC 80108 2620 B2
N Deerslayer Rd
8900 DgsC 80138 2539 B3
Deer Springs Ln
1000 GOLD 80403 2023 D7
Deer Trail Cir
10 BldC 80302 1516 E7
W Deertrail Ct
4200 CSRK 80109 2702 D1
Deer Trail Dr
7500 DgsC 80138 2454 A3
Deer Trail Rd
10 BldC 80302 1517 B7
800 BldC 80302 1600 E1
1500 BldC 80302 1516 E7
11900 JfnC 80433 2525 E4
Deer Trail Creek Dr
2200 BGTN 80601 1696 E7
Deer Valley Dr
3500 CSRK 80104 2788 B4
Deer Valley Rd
1700 BLDR 80305 1686 D6
23900 JfnC 80401 2190 D3
Deer Watch Dr
4100 CSRK 80104 2703 D2
Deerwood Dr
- WldC 80504 1440 A2
10 JfnC 80127 2360 E6
900 LGMT 80501 1440 A1
1400 LGMT 80501 1357 A7
1600 LGMT 80501 1356 E6
S Deframe Cir
2600 LKWD 80228 2277 B1
Deframe Ct
300 JfnC 80401 2193 B1
500 JfnC 80401 2109 B7
500 LKWD 80401 2109 B7
6000 ARVD 80004 2025 B3
6900 ARVD 80004 1941 B7
8300 ARVD 80005 1941 B4
S Deframe Ct
500 LKWD 80228 2193 B3
2800 LKWD 80228 2277 B1
4100 JfnC 80465 2277 B5
Deframe Rd
3000 JfnC 80401 2109 B2
Deframe St
800 JfnC 80401 2109 B6
800 LKWD 80401 2109 B6
5100 JfnC 80403 2025 B5
5300 JfnC 80002 2025 B5
6400 ARVD 80004 2025 B1
7300 ARVD 80005 1941 B6
S Deframe St
2000 LKWD 80228 2193 B6
2400 LKWD 80228 2277 C1
4100 JfnC 80465 2277 B5
5500 JfnC 80127 2361 B2
Deframe Wy
6500 ARVD 80004 2025 B2
N Deframe Wy
6300 ARVD 80004 2025 B2
S Deframe Wy
10 JfnC 80401 2193 B2
1900 LKWD 80228 2193 B6
2900 LKWD 80228 2277 B1
De France Ct
300 GOLD 80401 2191 E1
De France Dr
300 GOLD 80401 2191 E1
De France Wy
10 GOLD 80401 2191 E1
100 GOLD 80401 2192 A1
Degaulle Cir
15600 AdmC 80603 1698 D6
S Degaulle Cir
- AURA 80018 2202 E4
N Degaulle St
10 AphC 80018 2202 E1
10 AURA 80018 2202 E1
S De Gaulle St
- AURA 80016 2370 E1
10 AphC 80018 2202 E1
5100 AURA 80016 2286 E7
S Degaulle St
- AURA 80016 2286 E6
S De Gaulle Wy
- AURA 80018 2202 E5
De Gualle Ct
- AURA 80018 2118 D7
De Gualle St
- AURA 80018 2118 E7
Dehesa Ct
3900 BldC 80301 1603 A5
Dehning Wy
- WldC 80504 1440 D3
Dekker Dr
10 JfnC 80401 2191 A2
Delaware Av
700 LGMT 80501 1439 A4
W Delaware Cir
200 LITN 80120 2364 D5
Delaware Ct
11700 NHGN 80234 1860 D3
11800 WSTR 80234 1860 D3
S Delaware Ct
7300 LITN 80120 2364 D5
Delaware Dr
- WSTR 80234 1860 D1
4300 DgsC 80118 2953 B3
Delaware Pl
1800 BldC 80501 1438 E4
1800 LGMT 80501 1438 E4
4300 DgsC 80118 2953 B3
Delaware St
- AdmC 80216 2028 D4
- DNVR 80216 2028 D7
100 DNVR 80223 2196 D1
300 DNVR 80223 2112 D7
1000 DNVR 80204 2112 D6
6400 AdmC 80221 2028 D2
8300 TNTN 80260 1944 D4
8400 AdmC 80221 1944 D4
15200 AdmC 80020 1776 D1
15200 BMFD 80020 1776 D1
N Delaware St
12000 NHGN 80234 1860 D2
12000 WSTR 80234 1860 D2
S Delaware St
- LITN 80120 2280 D7
2000 DNVR 80223 2196 D7
2600 AphC 80223 2280 D1
2600 DNVR 80223 2280 D1
2600 EGLD 80110 2280 D1
2600 EGLD 80223 2280 D1
5300 LITN 80120 2364 D1
N Delbert Rd
2000 DgsC 80107 2707 E3
2000 DgsC 80116 2707 E3
6900 DgsC 80138 2623 E1
7000 DgsC 80138 2539 E7
9900 DgsC 80138 2455 E5
13300 AphC 80137 2371 E7
13300 AURA 80016 2371 E7
13300 EbtC 80138 2371 E7
N Delbert Rd CO-1
9500 DgsC 80138 2539 E1
9900 DgsC 80138 2455 E7
Delgany St
2000 DNVR 80202 2112 D2
2100 DNVR 80216 2112 D2
3600 DNVR 80216 2029 A7
Delight Dr
- CSRK 80109 2702 D5
Della Ct
1600 WldC 80516 1607 E1
Della St
1200 LGMT 80501 1439 B5
Dellwood Av
- BldC 80304 1602 B7
300 BLDR 80304 1602 B7
Del Mar Cir
10 AURA 80010 2115 D6
10 AURA 80011 2115 D6
Del Mar Pkwy
1600 AURA 80010 2115 B4
11900 AURA 80011 2115 C6
E Del Norte St
10 AdmC 80221 1944 D6
Delos Cir
900 LAFT 80026 1690 B5
Delphi Dr
700 LAFT 80026 1690 A5
13400 DgsC 80124 2450 E2
Del Ray Ct
16100 AdmC 80603 1699 E5
Del Rio Ct
4300 DNVR 80239 2032 B6
Del Rosa Ct
1800 BLDR 80304 1602 D6
Del Sol Wy
2500 EbtC 80138 2540 E6
2500 EbtC 80138 2541 A6
Delta Ct
15800 AdmC 80603 1698 D6
Delta Dr
900 LAFT 80026 1690 B6
S Delta Ln
15000 JfnC 80470 2608 B5
Delta St
10 AdmC 80221 1944 D5
E Delta St
10 AdmC 80221 1944 E5
Delwood Ct
600 DgsC 80126 2449 A3
9100 TNTN 80229 1945 D2
Delwood Dr
10 PrkC 80456 2606 C5
E Democrat Rd
9400 DgsC 80134 2622 E4
9400 DgsC 80134 2623 A3
Demott Av
5600 CMCY 80022 2030 B1
Denali Ln
29700 JfnC 80439 2189 B7
Denargo St
3200 DNVR 80216 2112 D2
Denargo Market
10 DNVR 80216 2112 D2
Deneb Dr
13000 DgsC 80124 2450 E3
S Denice Dr
4600 CHLV 80111 2282 B6
Denim Ct
5100 DgsC 80134 2621 C4
Denise Pl
10 LGMT 80501 1355 D7
Denison Cir
1500 LGMT 80503 1355 C7
Denmark Ct
- DNVR 80239 2032 B6
Dennis Dr
900 JfnC 80439 2189 B4
S Dennison Ct
2500 DNVR 80222 2198 A6
2500 DNVR 80222 2282 A1
Dennison Ln
2300 BLDR 80305 1686 E6
Denslow Ln
- SUPE 80027 1773 A6
Denton Av
3000 BLDR 80303 1687 A4
Denver Av
900 AdmC 80137 2120 E4
2400 LGMT 80503 1355 C6
Denver Dr
- DNVR 80235 2279 C4
- DNVR 80236 2279 C4
Denver Pl
800 BGTN 80601 1696 C5
W Denver Pl
2700 DNVR 80211 2112 A1
3000 DNVR 80211 2111 E1
Denver St
100 AdmC 80601 1696 B5
100 BGTN 80601 1696 B5
Denver Wy
10 LGMT 80503 1355 B6
Denver-Boulder Tpk
- AdmC - 1944 C7
- BfdC - 1858 E5
- BldC - 1687 B6
- BldC - 1771 E1
- BldC - 1772 B1
- BldC - 1773 B4
- BLDR - 1686 E4
- BLDR - 1687 B6
- BMFD - 1773 B4
- BMFD - 1774 A7
- BMFD - 1858 C2
- JfnC - 1858 E5
- JfnC - 1859 A6
- JfnC - 1943 B3
- LSVL - 1772 B1
- LSVL - 1773 B4
- SUPE - 1772 B1
- SUPE - 1773 B4
- WSTR - 1858 E5
- WSTR - 1859 A6
- WSTR - 1943 D5
- WSTR - 1944 C7
Denver-Boulder Tpk US-36
- AdmC - 1944 C7
- BfdC - 1858 E5
- BldC - 1687 B6
- BldC - 1771 E1
- BldC - 1772 B1
- BldC - 1773 B4
- BLDR - 1686 E4
- BLDR - 1687 B6
- BMFD - 1773 B4
- BMFD - 1774 A7
- BMFD - 1858 C2
- JfnC - 1858 E5
- JfnC - 1859 A6
- JfnC - 1943 B3
- LSVL - 1772 B1
- LSVL - 1773 B4
- SUPE - 1772 B1
- SUPE - 1773 B4
- WSTR - 1858 E5
- WSTR - 1859 A6
- WSTR - 1943 B3
- WSTR - 1944 C7
S Denver View Dr
4700 JfnC 80439 2274 C7
Denver West Cir
13900 JfnC 80401 2109 B4
14100 LKWD 80401 2109 A5
Denver West Ct
1800 JfnC 80401 2109 A4
1800 LKWD 80401 2109 A4
Denver West Dr
- JfnC 80401 2109 A5
1800 LKWD 80401 2109 A5
Denver West Pkwy
13700 JfnC 80401 2109 A5
13700 LKWD 80401 2109 A5
14900 JfnC 80401 2108 D5
N Denver West Entrance
- LKWD 80401 2109 A6
Denver West-Marriott Blvd
- JfnC 80401 2109 A5
- LKWD 80401 2109 A5
Denver West Pkwy Colorado Mls
- LKWD 80401 2109 B5
Depew Cir
7100 WSTR 80003 1943 B7
S Depew Cir
5600 JfnC 80123 2363 B2
Depew Ct
1100 LKWD 80214 2111 B6
5100 DNVR 80212 2027 B5
6500 ARVD 80003 2027 B1
7100 WSTR 80003 1943 B7
11200 WSTR 80020 1859 B4
S Depew Ct
6100 JfnC 80123 2363 B3
S Depew Dr
10 LKWD 80226 2195 B2
Depew Pl
10800 WSTR 80020 1859 B5
S Depew Pl
2600 DNVR 80227 2279 B1
2600 LKWD 80227 2279 B1
Depew St
- BldC 80020 1775 B2
300 LKWD 80226 2195 B1
500 LKWD 80226 2111 B7
700 LKWD 80214 2111 B6
1600 EDGW 80214 2111 B5
3000 WTRG 80212 2111 B2
3200 WTRG 80214 2111 B2
3800 MNVW 80212 2027 B7
4100 WTRG 80212 2027 B7
4300 LKSD 80212 2027 B7
4800 DNVR 80212 2027 B6
4800 DvrC 80212 2027 B6
6600 ARVD 80003 2027 B1
6700 WSTR 80003 2027 B1
7400 WSTR 80003 1943 B6
8400 ARVD 80003 1943 B4
10000 WSTR 80020 1859 B7
N Depew St
10100 WSTR 80020 1859 B6
S Depew St
- JfnC 80123 2363 B2
10 LKWD 80226 2195 B3
1900 DNVR 80227 2195 B6
1900 DNVR 80232 2195 B6
1900 LKWD 80227 2195 B6
1900 LKWD 80232 2195 B6
2100 DvrC 80227 2195 B6
2700 DNVR 80227 2279 B1
2700 LKWD 80227 2279 B1
3500 DNVR 80235 2279 B3
3600 JfnC 80235 2279 B3
6600 JfnC 80128 2363 B5
Depew Wy
8100 ARVD 80003 1943 B4
11300 WSTR 80020 1859 B4
S Depew Wy
3900 DNVR 80235 2279 B4
7500 JfnC 80128 2363 B6
Depo Dr
3000 LGMT 80503 1438 B5
Depot St
200 GOLD 80401 2107 E2
Depot Hill Rd
1000 BMFD 80020 1774 C7
E Derby Wy
9600 DgsC 80134 2622 E2
9600 DgsC 80134 2623 A2
Derringer Ct
800 PrkC 80456 2606 D3
Derry Ct
- BMFD 80020 1775 E4
Descombes Dr
10 BMFD 80020 1858 E1
10 BMFD 80020 1859 A1
Desert Fox Tr
5400 JfnC 80465 2360 C1
Desert Hills St
12000 PARK 80138 2538 C3
Desert Mountain Ct
5300 BLDR 80301 1604 D1
Desert Paint Brush Ct
9600 DgsC 80134 2622 E5
Desert Pine Ct
5200 BLDR 80301 1604 D2
Desert Ridge Cir
- CSRK 80108 2704 C4
Desert Ridge Pl
- CSRK 80108 2704 C3
Desert Rose Dr
- CSRK 80104 2787 E5
Desert Willow Av
3700 BMFD 80020 1859 D2
Desert Willow Ln
10 JfnC 80127 2445 A1
S Desert Willow Rd
9200 DgsC 80129 2448 B4
S Desert Willow Tr
9300 DgsC 80129 2448 B4
S Desert Willow Wy
9300 DgsC 80129 2448 C4
Desoto St
8600 AdmC 80229 1945 A3
8600 TNTN 80229 1945 A3
Desparado Ct
10 PrkC 80456 2522 D5
Desparado Rd
100 PrkC 80456 2522 D5
Desperado Wy
- DgsC 80134 2621 A5
Despoilation Al
4200 AdmC 80003 2027 D2
S Detroit Cir
6700 CTNL 80122 2365 C4
Detroit Ct
9600 TNTN 80229 1945 C1
10100 TNTN 80229 1861 C7
13300 TNTN 80241 1777 C6
S Detroit Ct
6700 CTNL 80122 2365 D4
Detroit St
100 DNVR 80206 2197 C1
1500 DNVR 80206 2113 C5
9600 TNTN 80229 1861 C7
9600 TNTN 80229 1945 C1
13500 TNTN 80241 1777 C5
13800 TNTN 80602 1777 C4
S Detroit St
3100 DNVR 80210 2281 C2
5900 CTNL 80121 2365 C2
7500 CTNL 80122 2365 C6
Detroit Wy
11000 NHGN 80233 1861 C4
14500 TNTN 80602 1777 C2
S Detroit Wy
2900 DNVR 80210 2281 C2
W Devils Head
10600 JfnC 80127 2362 A7
Devils Head Ct
6100 JfnC 80403 2023 E3
Devils Head Dr
9200 DgsC 80138 2538 D4
E Devils Point Pl
1600 DgsC 80126 2449 B2
E Devils Thumb Av
18100 AURA 80011 2201 C1
Devinney Cir
6200 ARVD 80004 2025 B2
Devinney Ct
400 JfnC 80401 2109 B7
700 LKWD 80401 2109 B7
6600 ARVD 80004 2025 B1
7200 ARVD 80004 1941 B7
7200 ARVD 80005 1941 B7
S Devinney Ct
2000 LKWD 80228 2193 A6
2800 LKWD 80228 2277 B1
4300 JfnC 80465 2277 B6
Devinney St
700 JfnC 80401 2109 B7
700 LKWD 80401 2109 B7
6400 ARVD 80004 2025 B2
8300 ARVD 80005 1941 A4
S Devinney St
10 JfnC 80401 2193 B2
300 LKWD 80228 2193 B3
4300 JfnC 80465 2277 B6
Devinney Wy
6000 ARVD 80004 2025 B3
S Devinney Wy
800 JfnC 80228 2193 B4
800 JfnC 80401 2193 B4
800 LKWD 80228 2193 B4
6000 JfnC 80127 2361 B2
E Devon Av
5100 CSRK 80104 2704 D7
S Devon Ct
9400 DgsC 80126 2449 A4
Devon Pl
200 BLDR 80302 1686 D5
Devonshire Blvd
8400 AdmC 80229 1945 C3
8700 TNTN 80229 1945 C3
Devonshire Ct
2400 AdmC 80229 1945 C3
7700 BldC 80301 1604 D3
S Devonshire Pl
9400 DgsC 80126 2449 A4
Devonshire St
4600 BldC 80301 1604 D3
E Devonshire St
1100 LAFT 80026 1690 B3
W Devonshire St
1200 LAFT 80026 1690 B4
Devonshire Wy
7700 BldC 80301 1604 E3
E Dewberry Cir
17200 PARK 80134 2453 A4
E Dewberry Dr
17000 PARK 80134 2453 A4
Dew Drop St
- WARD 80481 1597 D2
Dewey Av
400 BLDR 80304 1686 B1
Dewfrost Pl
1300 CSRK 80104 2787 E5
Dexter Cir
11200 TNTN 80233 1861 E4
Dexter Ct
3500 DNVR 80207 2113 E1
12700 TNTN 80241 1777 E7
S Dexter Ct
7100 CTNL 80122 2366 A5
Dexter Dr
700 BMFD 80020 1775 B7
2100 LGMT 80501 1356 B5
10700 TNTN 80233 1862 A5
11100 TNTN 80233 1861 E4
Dexter Ln
9700 TNTN 80229 1861 E7
Dexter Pl
- BMFD 80020 1775 B7
11100 TNTN 80233 1861 E4
Dexter St
10 DNVR 80220 2197 E1
10 DNVR 80246 2197 E1
1000 BMFD 80020 1775 B6
2000 DNVR 80220 2113 E3
3200 DNVR 80207 2113 E1
5600 CMCY 80022 2029 E3
6900 CMCY 80022 1945 E7
7400 AdmC 80022 1945 E6
11200 TNTN 80233 1862 A4
12400 TNTN 80241 1861 E1
12800 TNTN 80241 1777 E6
13600 TNTN 80602 1777 E4
S Dexter St
10 DNVR 80220 2197 E1
10 DNVR 80246 2197 E1
10 DNVR 80246 2198 A2
700 GNDL 80246 2198 A3
1900 DNVR 80222 2198 A6
2500 DNVR 80222 2282 A1
3400 AphC 80222 2282 A3
3400 CHLV 80113 2282 A3
6300 CTNL 80121 2366 A3
6600 CTNL 80122 2366 A5
Dexter Wy
12400 TNTN 80241 1861 E1
13400 TNTN 80241 1777 E5
S Dexter Wy
1500 DNVR 80222 2198 A5
2800 DNVR 80222 2282 A1
7300 CTNL 80122 2365 E5
7300 CTNL 80122 2366 A6
7400 AphC 80122 2366 A6
Dharma Av
2700 BMFD 80020 1776 A7
2800 BMFD 80020 1775 E7
Dhu Ct
6000 BldC 80503 1519 E4
Diablo Wy
3300 DgsC 80108 2618 C3
Diagonal Hwy
- BLDR 80301 1602 E6
- BLDR 80304 1602 E6
- LGMT 80501 1438 C7
2800 BLDR 80301 1603 B6
3700 BldC 80301 1603 B6
4500 BldC 80301 1604 A1
4500 BLDR 80301 1604 A1
6300 BldC 80301 1520 C5
6300 BldC 80503 1520 C5
6300 BLDR 80301 1520 C5
6300 BLDR 80503 1520 C5
7800 BldC 80503 1521 A2
8000 LGMT 80503 1521 A2
8200 BldC 80503 1438 C7
8300 LGMT 80503 1438 C7
Diagonal Hwy SR-119
- BLDR 80301 1602 E6
- BLDR 80304 1602 E6
- LGMT 80501 1438 C7
2800 BLDR 80301 1603 B6
3700 BldC 80301 1603 B6
4500 BldC 80301 1604 A1
4500 BLDR 80301 1604 A1
6300 BldC 80301 1520 C5
6300 BldC 80503 1520 C5
6300 BLDR 80301 1520 C5
6300 BLDR 80503 1520 C5
7800 BldC 80503 1521 A2
8000 LGMT 80503 1521 A2
8200 BldC 80503 1438 C7
8300 LGMT 80503 1438 C7
Diamond Cir
300 LSVL 80027 1773 B2
900 LAFT 80026 1690 B3
Diamond Ct
900 BldC 80303 1688 E3
Diamond Dr
300 CCkC 80439 2271 D6
1900 LGMT 80504 1439 A7
Diamond Head Dr
- CSRK 80104 2787 E2
N Diamond Leaf Dr
4400 CSRK 80109 2702 E2
Diamond Ridge Cir
800 CSRK 80108 2619 D7
1000 CSRK 80108 2703 E1
Diamond Ridge Pkwy
5700 CSRK 80108 2620 A7
5700 DgsC 80108 2620 A7
6100 CSRK 80108 2619 E6
Diamond Sky Rd
- CSRK 80108 2703 E1
Diana Rd
33500 JfnC 80470 2524 C5
Diane Av
10 GpnC 80403 1849 D5
S Diane Ct
300 DgsC 80124 2450 E1
Diane Dr
10800 JfnC 80403 1852 B6
Dianna Dr
10 DgsC 80124 2450 E2
10 DgsC 80124 2451 A2
Dichter Ct
1700 TNTN 80229 1945 B2
Dick Connor Av
2500 DNVR 80204 2112 A4
Dickens Ct
800 LGMT 80501 1438 D1
Dickens St
2800 ERIE 80516 1690 C2
E Dickensen Pl
12800 AURA 80014 2200 A7
E Dickenson Dr
18900 AURA 80013 2201 C6
E Dickenson Pl
4000 DNVR 80210 2197 E7
4000 DNVR 80222 2197 E7
5400 AphC 80222 2198 A7
6300 DNVR 80222 2198 B7
6900 DNVR 80224 2198 C7
12500 AURA 80014 2199 E7
16100 AURA 80013 2200 E7
19300 AURA 80013 2201 D7
E Dickinson Dr
14100 AURA 80014 2200 B7
Dick Mountain Dr
10 PrkC 80456 2607 B7
Dickson St
400 LGMT 80501 1439 D2
W Dill Rd
3300 DNVR 80236 2279 E5
3300 EGLD 80110 2279 E5
3300 SRDN 80110 2279 E5
E Dillard Pl
8600 DNVR 80231 2282 E2
Dillion St
14400 DNVR 80239 2032 B6
Dillon Cir
10000 CMCY 80022 1864 B7
S Dillon Ct
4600 AURA 80015 2284 C5
7100 AphC 80112 2368 C5
7100 CTNL 80112 2368 C5
Dillon Dr
300 DgsC 80109 2786 E3
300 DgsC 80109 2787 A3
Dillon Rd
- BldC 80020 1774 E3
- BldC 80027 1773 E3
- LAFT 80020 1774 E3
9600 LSVL 80020 1773 E3
9600 LSVL 80027 1773 E3
10100 LSVL 80020 1774 A3
10100 LSVL 80027 1774 A3
11300 BMFD 80020 1774 E3
12000 BldC 80020 1775 A3
12000 BMFD 80020 1775 A3
W Dillon Rd
- BldC 80027 1772 E3
500 LSVL 80027 1773 A3
700 SUPE 80027 1773 A3
800 BldC 80027 1773 C3
1200 LSVL 80027 1772 E2
8900 LSVL 80020 1773 C3
Dillon St
5100 DNVR 80239 2032 B5
10200 CMCY 80022 1864 B6
13200 AdmC 80601 1780 B6
S Dillon St
- AURA 80014 2284 C5
2300 AURA 80014 2200 C7
4300 AURA 80015 2284 C5
Dillon Wy
600 AURA 80011 2116 B6
1300 SUPE 80027 1773 B6
2300 LGMT 80501 1356 D4
S Dillon Wy
1200 AURA 80012 2200 C4
3900 AURA 80014 2284 B4
4800 AURA 80015 2284 C6
Dime Rd
10 BldC 80302 1600 C6
Dimmit Dr
5800 BldC 80303 1687 E4
Dinero Pl
3300 DgsC 80108 2618 C3
Dinnadan St
- LAFT 80026 1690 E6
Dinosaur St
- CSRK 80109 2702 D5
Dione Pl
400 DgsC 80124 2450 E2
Disc Dr
- BldC 80027 1773 C5
- BMFD 80020 1773 C5
- LSVL 80020 1773 C5
- LSVL 80027 1773 C5
300 BldC 80503 1437 D4
300 LGMT 80503 1437 D4
Disc Pl
- LGMT 80503 1437 E4
Discovery Dr
3100 BLDR 80303 1687 A3
Discovery Pkwy
- SUPE 80027 1772 E4
500 LSVL 80027 1773 A4
500 SUPE 80027 1773 A4
Distel Dr
1100 LAFT 80026 1690 E6
Ditmar Ln
3200 CSRK 80104 2788 A7
3200 DgsC 80104 2788 A7
Divide View Dr
500 BldC 80403 1852 B2
Division St
12900 DgsC 80125 2447 D3
Divot Ct
3900 BldC 80503 1518 E5
Divot Dr
31200 JfnC 80439 2188 E7
W Dixie Pl
1500 DNVR 80221 2028 B6
Dixon Av
1300 LAFT 80026 1690 C6
Dixon Dr
4200 AdmC 80031 1943 C3
4500 WSTR 80031 1943 C3
N Dixon Dr
12500 DgsC 80138 2453 D3
Dixon Rd
10 BldC 80302 1599 D4
E Doane Dr
- AURA 80013 2285 E2
E Doane Pl
- AURA 80013 2285 E2
- AURA 80013 2286 A1
8600 DNVR 80231 2282 E2
8700 DNVR 80231 2283 A2
Dobbins Run
10900 BldC 80026 1606 C4
10900 ERIE 80026 1606 C4
Dodd Ln
2400 LGMT 80501 1356 A4
Dodge Dr
9900 NHGN 80260 1860 D7
Doe Cir
10 PrkC 80456 2607 C7
300 DgsC 80116 2707 A7
Doe Tr
10 NDLD 80466 1766 A3
Doe Valley Dr
28400 JfnC 80433 2525 D3
Dogie Spur
2200 JfnC 80403 2104 B3

STREET
Block City ZIP Map# Grid

Dogleg Ln
13800 BMFD 80020 1775 D4
Dogwood Av
300 BGTN 80601 1696 A7
E Dogwood Av
800 CTNL 80121 2365 A3
3000 DgsC 80134 2452 C4
Dogwood Cir
2100 LSVL 80027 1689 C5
2200 ERIE 80516 1692 B3
Dogwood Ct
1700 BMFD 80020 1774 E5
Dogwood Dr
900 JfnC 80401 2190 E4
2200 ERIE 80516 1692 A3
11900 DgsC 80107 2707 E3
11900 DgsC 80116 2707 E3
Dogwood Ln
1300 LGMT 80501 1356 B7
1600 BLDR 80304 1602 C6
Dogwood St
1700 LSVL 80027 1773 E2
1700 LSVL 80027 1774 A2
Dolomite Ln
7100 CSRK 80108 2620 A6
Dolomite Wy
1800 CSRK 80108 2620 A6
Dolton Ct
9600 DgsC 80126 2449 C4
S Dolton Wy
9400 DgsC 80126 2449 C4
S Dome Peak
7500 JfnC 80127 2361 E6
Dome Rock Rd
7100 DgsC 80125 2615 A1
Domingo Ct
12700 PARK 80134 2537 B5
Domingo Dr
17800 PARK 80134 2537 B5
Dominica Pl
3100 BLDR 80301 1603 B4
E Donald Av
4800 AphC 80222 2198 A7
4800 DNVR 80222 2198 A7
Donald St
- GpnC 80403 1849 D6
Donerau Av
- PARK 80138 2538 B2
N Donley Dr
11000 DgsC 80138 2453 D6
11000 PARK 80138 2453 D6
N Donley St
11800 DgsC 80138 2453 D5
Donn Ct
500 BldC 80303 1688 B7
500 BldC 80303 1772 B1
Donna Dr
32600 JfnC 80433 2440 C3
Donnelly Pl
800 ERIE 80516 1607 D6
N Donner Cir
6200 DgsC 80134 2622 B2
Donner Ct
1300 JfnC 80439 2189 A5
Donovan Ct
100 BldC 80501 1438 E2
100 LGMT 80501 1438 E2
Donovan Dr
1800 BldC 80501 1438 D2
1800 LGMT 80501 1438 D2
Donovan Pl
1500 BldC 80501 1438 E3
1500 LGMT 80501 1438 E3
Donovan St
1600 AdmC 80136 2125 E4
E Dorado Av
- AphC 80015 2369 B1
5700 GDVL 80111 2366 C1
10400 GDVL 80111 2367 C1
10700 AphC 80111 2367 C1
16500 CTNL 80015 2368 E1
17700 CTNL 80015 2369 B1
21700 CTNL 80015 2370 B2
23200 AphC 80015 2370 D1
W Dorado Av
- JfnC 80123 2363 C1
10800 JfnC 80127 2362 A2
11100 JfnC 80127 2361 E2
E Dorado Cir
6300 GDVL 80111 2366 C2
11100 AphC 80111 2367 C1
15900 CTNL 80015 2368 E1
17100 CTNL 80015 2369 A1
20900 CTNL 80015 2370 A1
Dorado Ct
14100 BMFD 80020 1775 C4
E Dorado Ct
6900 DgsC 80130 2450 C5
20900 CTNL 80015 2370 A1
W Dorado Ct
8800 JfnC 80123 2362 C2
E Dorado Dr
16900 CTNL 80015 2369 A1
18600 AphC 80015 2369 C1
20900 CTNL 80015 2370 A1
22300 AphC 80015 2370 C1
S Dorado Dr
22700 AphC 80015 2370 C1
W Dorado Dr
6700 DNVR 80123 2363 A1
6700 DvrC 80123 2363 A1
9500 JfnC 80123 2362 B2
E Dorado Pl
7800 GDVL 80111 2366 E2
10400 GDVL 80111 2367 C1
10600 AphC 80111 2367 C1
16100 CTNL 80015 2368 E1
17100 CTNL 80015 2369 A1
18800 AphC 80015 2369 C2
20700 CTNL 80015 2370 A1
22300 AphC 80015 2370 C1
W Dorado Pl
5300 JfnC 80123 2363 C2
9900 JfnC 80123 2362 B2
12100 JfnC 80127 2361 D2
Doral Ct
- DgsC 80118 2868 D6
14100 BMFD 80020 1775 D4
Doral Dr
3700 LGMT 80503 1438 A1
3800 BldC 80503 1438 A1
7200 BLDR 80301 1604 C1
Doral Ln
10 CBVL 80123 2363 D4
Dorchester Cir
4700 BldC 80301 1604 D3
Dorchester St
- DgsC 80129 2448 D3
Doric Dr
1200 LAFT 80026 1690 A6
Doris Cir
1200 WldC 80516 1607 D1
Doris Ct
6500 CMCY 80022 2030 C1
S Doris Ln
6400 JfnC 80439 2357 B4
Dorothy Blvd
900 TNTN 80229 1945 A1
Dorothy Rd
29200 JfnC 80439 2357 B2
Dorset Ct
10 DgsC 80108 2619 A1
1100 LAFT 80026 1690 B5
Dorsett Ln
- EGLD 80113 2281 B3
Dory Cir
10 GpnC 80403 1934 C5
E Dory Dr
10 GpnC 80403 1934 C4
E Dory Wy
10 GpnC 80403 1934 C4
W Dory Wy
100 GpnC 80403 1934 B4
Dory Hill Rd
700 GpnC 80403 2018 A3
1600 GpnC 80403 1934 B7
Dory Lakes Dr
10 GpnC 80403 1934 B4
E Dory Lakes Dr
200 GpnC 80403 1934 C4
N Dory Lakes Dr
10 GpnC 80403 1934 B5
S Dory Lakes Dr
10 GpnC 80403 1934 B5
Dostal Al
- CLCY 80403 2017 D3
Dotty Rd
33600 JfnC 80470 2524 B6
Double Eagle Ct
1200 CSRK 80104 2787 E1
Double Eagle Dr
15700 JfnC 80465 2360 D1
S Doubleheader Hwy
8300 JfnC 80465 2443 B2
S Double Header Ranch Rd
8300 JfnC 80465 2443 A1
Double Tree Rd
10 PrkC 80456 2522 D7
N Double Tree Tr
13500 DgsC 80138 2455 A1
W Douglas Av
4000 DgsC 80135 2617 C5
S Douglas Blvd
9000 DgsC 80118 2955 A6
9000 LKSR 80118 2955 A6
Douglas Ct
10 BldC 80302 1684 E3
Douglas Dr
300 AdmC 80221 1944 C5
Douglas Dr N
10 BMFD 80020 1774 E5
Douglas Dr S
10 BMFD 80020 1774 E5
Douglas Ln
- CSRK 80109 2787 B4
E Douglas Ln
500 CSRK 80104 2787 C4
500 DgsC 80104 2787 C4
W Douglas Pl
2900 DNVR 80211 2112 A2
W Douglas St
100 SUPE 80027 1772 E4
Douglas Fir Av
100 CSRK 80104 2787 E1
100 CSRK 80104 2788 A1
Douglas Mountain Dr
3900 JfnC 80403 2104 C1
4100 JfnC 80403 2020 D7
Douglas Park Rd
28500 JfnC 80439 2273 C5
Douglass Ranch Dr
13300 JfnC 80470 2608 D1
E Dounce St
600 LAFT 80026 1690 D4
Dove Av
800 BGTN 80601 1696 A7
Dove Ct
7100 DgsC 80134 2621 E1
Dove Dr
700 LAFT 80026 1690 D5
Dove St
2900 FLHT 80260 1944 A1
Dove Cove
800 LAFT 80026 1690 D6
S Dove Creek Ct
12600 PARK 80134 2537 E4
Dove Creek Dr
38100 EbtC 80107 2625 E6
38100 EbtC 80107 2626 A6
E Dove Creek Pl
19600 PARK 80134 2537 E3
S Dove Creek Wy
12500 PARK 80134 2537 D5
S Dover Av
300 LAFT 80026 1690 B5
Dover Cir
6900 ARVD 80004 2026 C1
8100 ARVD 80005 1942 C4
8700 LKWD 80226 2194 C1
8700 WSTR 80005 1942 C3
S Dover Cir
6700 JfnC 80123 2362 D4
Dover Ct
100 DgsC 80108 2619 A1
200 BMFD 80020 1859 B1
1200 BMFD 80020 1775 B6
2500 JfnC 80215 2110 C3
2500 LKWD 80215 2110 C3
5800 ARVD 80002 2026 C3
5800 ARVD 80004 2026 C3
8300 ARVD 80005 1942 C4
8700 WSTR 80005 1942 C3
S Dover Ct
400 LKWD 80226 2194 C2
1900 LKWD 80227 2194 C6
1900 LKWD 80232 2194 C6
3100 LKWD 80227 2278 D2
4300 JfnC 80123 2278 C5
5900 JfnC 80123 2362 D2
7100 JfnC 80128 2362 C5
8700 JfnC 80128 2446 C2
Dover Dr
100 LAFT 80026 1690 B4
2800 BLDR 80305 1686 E6
2800 BLDR 80305 1687 A6
Dover St
10 LKWD 80226 2194 C1
400 LKWD 80226 2110 C7
1300 BMFD 80020 1775 B5
1500 LKWD 80215 2110 C4
3800 WTRG 80033 2110 C1
4800 JfnC 80002 2026 C6
4800 WTRG 80033 2026 C6
5600 ARVD 80002 2026 C4
6800 ARVD 80004 2026 C1
7300 ARVD 80005 1942 C7
8700 WSTR 80005 1942 C3
8700 WSTR 80021 1942 C3
10200 WSTR 80021 1858 C6
N Dover St
10600 JfnC 80021 1858 C5
10600 WSTR 80021 1858 C5
S Dover St
- JfnC 80128 2362 C5
10 LKWD 80226 2194 C1
1000 LKWD 80232 2194 C4
2500 LKWD 80227 2278 C1
5100 JfnC 80123 2278 C7
5400 DNVR 80123 2362 C1
6100 JfnC 80123 2362 D3
8300 JfnC 80128 2446 C1
Dover Wy
- WSTR 80021 1942 C1
1100 BMFD 80020 1775 B6
1400 LKWD 80215 2110 C5
6800 ARVD 80004 2026 C1
6900 ARVD 80004 1942 C7
8400 ARVD 80005 1942 C4
S Dover Wy
1200 LKWD 80232 2194 C5
2100 LKWD 80227 2194 D7
2400 LKWD 80227 2278 C1
6500 JfnC 80123 2362 C4
6800 JfnC 80128 2362 C5
9600 LITN 80127 2446 C5
Dove Ridge Dr
- DgsC 80134 2452 D2
Dove Ridge Wy
8200 DgsC 80134 2452 D1
Dovetail Wy
- DgsC 80125 2531 A7
Dove Valley Pl
- CSRK 80104 2704 B4
- CSRK 80108 2704 B4
Dowdle Dr
10200 GpnC 80403 1852 A7
10300 GpnC 80403 1851 E7
S Dowling Ct
10200 DgsC 80126 2449 A6
S Dowling Wy
10200 DgsC 80126 2449 A6
Downing Cir
9900 TNTN 80229 1861 A7
S Downing Cir
2700 DNVR 80210 2281 C1
2700 EGLD 80113 2281 C1
4500 CHLV 80113 2281 A6
S Downing Cir E
6700 CTNL 80121 2365 A4
6700 CTNL 80122 2365 A4
S Downing Cir W
6700 CTNL 80121 2365 A4
6700 CTNL 80122 2365 A4
Downing Ct
10700 NHGN 80233 1861 A5
Downing Dr
8000 AdmC 80229 1945 A5
9700 TNTN 80229 1861 A7
11300 NHGN 80233 1861 A4
Downing St
- TNTN 80229 1861 A6
- TNTN 80233 1861 A6
10 DNVR 80209 2197 A1
10 DNVR 80218 2197 A1
1500 DNVR 80218 2113 A7
2600 DNVR 80205 2113 A2
5700 AdmC 80216 2029 A3
6200 AdmC 80216 2029 A2
7800 AdmC 80229 1945 A5
8800 TNTN 80229 1945 A3
11400 NHGN 80233 1861 A3
13600 AdmC 80241 1777 A5
13600 AdmC 80602 1777 A5
13600 TNTN 80241 1777 A5
S Downing St
- LITN 80122 2449 C1
10 DNVR 80209 2197 A2
10 DNVR 80218 2197 A2
1000 DNVR 80210 2197 A5
2600 AphC 80210 2281 A2
2600 DNVR 80210 2281 A2
2700 EGLD 80113 2281 A2
3500 CHLV 80113 2281 A3
6400 CTNL 80121 2365 A3
6500 CTNL 80122 2365 A3
8100 CTNL 80122 2449 C1
Downing Wy
700 AdmC 80229 1945 A5
Down West Ride
4100 EbtC 80107 2709 C4
S Downy Creek Ct
12400 PARK 80134 2537 D4
E Downy Creek Pl
19000 PARK 80134 2537 D4
Dragonfly Ct
- CSRK 80109 2702 D3
Dragoon Ct
2000 DgsC 80109 2786 B6
Drake Ct
13600 JfnC 80470 2608 E1
Drake Pl
10400 PARK 80134 2453 A6
Drake St
100 AdmC 80221 1944 D5
400 BLDR 80305 1686 E6
1400 LGMT 80503 1355 B6
N Dransfeldt Rd
9500 PARK 80134 2453 C5
S Dransfeldt Rd
10200 PARK 80134 2453 C6
11000 DgsC 80134 2537 C1
11000 PARK 80134 2537 C1
Dream Canyon Rd
500 BldC 80302 1683 B4
Dreamcatcher Lp
- CSRK 80109 2702 D4
Dreher Dr
10 CCkC 80439 2271 D5
Dresden
- FLHT 80260 1944 C2
- TNTN 80260 1944 C2
Dresden Dr
- CSRK 80109 2702 E2
Dressage Rd
8000 DgsC 80125 2530 E6
Drew Cir
4300 BLDR 80305 1687 B7
4300 BLDR 80305 1771 B1
S Drew Ct
5100 JfnC 80123 2278 C7
S Drew Wy
1200 LKWD 80232 2194 C5
Drew Hill Rd
7200 JfnC 80403 1937 D7
8700 JfnC 80403 1936 D4
Drew Ranch Ln
6600 BLDR 80301 1604 A1
Drexel Spur
29100 JfnC 80439 2273 C7
Drexel St
1100 BLDR 80305 1687 A7
1100 BLDR 80305 1771 A1
S Drexel Wy
1200 LKWD 80232 2194 C5
Drift Pl
700 LGMT 80501 1356 D7
Driftwood Cir
300 LAFT 80026 1689 E5
Driftwood Ln N
- TNTN 80260 1944 B1
Driftwood Ln S
- TNTN 80260 1944 B1
Driftwood Pl
4400 BldC 80301 1604 A4
Drinkwater Ct
1700 ERIE 80516 1606 E5
Driver Ct
4000 BldC 80503 1518 E5
Driver Ln
10 CBVL 80123 2363 E3
10 CBVL 80123 2364 A3
Driver Rd
- PrkC 80456 2690 E4
Drowsey Water Rd
- CSRK 80108 2703 E1
Druid Mine Rd
- GpnC 80403 2017 A7
Dry Creek Cir
800 BldC 80503 1520 E4
E Dry Creek Cir
- AURA 80016 2370 D5
5400 CTNL 80122 2366 A6
7000 CTNL 80112 2366 C6
W Dry Creek Cir
- LITN 80122 2364 E6
10 LITN 80120 2364 E6
Dry Creek Ct
5400 BldC 80301 1604 B1
5400 BLDR 80301 1604 B1
7100 BldC 80503 1520 E4
S Dry Creek Ct
5800 CTNL 80121 2365 D2
5800 GDVL 80121 2365 D2
W Dry Creek Ct
10 LITN 80122 2364 E6
2400 LITN 80120 2364 A6
Dry Creek Dr
900 BldC 80503 1438 C4
900 LGMT 80503 1438 C4
E Dry Creek Dr
- AURA 80016 2371 B5
Drycreek Pkwy
6400 BldC 80503 1520 C6
E Drycreek Pkwy
6200 BldC 80503 1520 D6
W Drycreek Pkwy
6200 BldC 80503 1520 C5
Dry Creek Pl
- AURA 80016 2371 B5
E Dry Creek Pl
1100 CTNL 80122 2365 A6
7000 CTNL 80112 2366 C6
22100 AURA 80016 2370 B6
Dry Creek Rd
7200 BldC 80503 1520 E4
7200 BldC 80503 1521 A3
E Dry Creek Rd
10 LITN 80120 2364 E6
10 LITN 80122 2364 E6
400 LITN 80122 2365 A6
700 CTNL 80122 2365 A6
4200 AphC 80122 2365 C6
4200 AphC 80122 2366 A6
4200 CTNL 80122 2366 A6
5400 CTNL 80112 2366 A6
8600 CTNL 80112 2367 A6
8900 AphC 80112 2367 B6
21400 AURA 80016 2370 A6
W Dry Creek Rd
1200 LITN 80120 2364 C6
W Dry Creek Wy
1400 LITN 80120 2364 C6
DTC Blvd
4500 DNVR 80237 2282 E7
4700 DvrC 80237 2282 E7
4700 GDVL 80111 2282 E7
5300 GDVL 80111 2366 E1
5700 GDVL 80111 2367 A2
DTC Pkwy
5100 GDVL 80111 2282 D7
5300 GDVL 80111 2366 E1
Dublin Dr
41200 EbtC 80138 2539 E7
Du Bois St
200 BKHK 80403 2017 E4
Duchesne Ct
5300 CSRK 80104 2788 E2
Duchess Dr
1700 LGMT 80501 1356 A6
Duckweed Ct
15800 DgsC 80134 2452 D1
Dude's Dr
10 GpnC 80474 1849 E2
10 GpnC 80474 1850 A2
Dudley Cir
6800 ARVD 80004 2026 C1
8100 ARVD 80005 1942 C5
Dudley Ct
5400 ARVD 80002 2026 C4
5900 ARVD 80004 2026 C3
8300 ARVD 80005 1942 C4
8700 WSTR 80005 1942 C3
8800 WSTR 80021 1942 C3
S Dudley Ct
1500 LKWD 80232 2194 C5
2400 LKWD 80227 2194 C7
3200 LKWD 80227 2278 C3
5200 JfnC 80123 2278 C7
6200 JfnC 80123 2362 C3
6700 JfnC 80128 2362 C4
Dudley Dr
6900 ARVD 80004 1942 C7
6900 ARVD 80004 2026 C1
9500 WSTR 80021 1942 B1
Dudley Ln
600 LGMT 80503 1438 C1
Dudley St
10 LKWD 80226 2194 C1
400 LKWD 80226 2110 C7
1700 LKWD 80215 2110 C4
3200 JfnC 80215 2110 C2
3800 WTRG 80033 2110 C1
4600 WTRG 80033 2026 C6
5100 JfnC 80002 2026 C5
5700 ARVD 80002 2026 C4
5700 ARVD 80004 2026 C4
7300 ARVD 80005 1942 C7
9100 WSTR 80021 1942 C2
S Dudley St
- JfnC 80123 2278 C7
1000 LKWD 80226 2194 C4
1000 LKWD 80232 2194 C4
2100 LKWD 80227 2194 C7
3000 LKWD 80227 2278 C2
4500 DNVR 80123 2278 C6
7000 JfnC 80128 2362 C5
7900 JfnC 80128 2446 C1
Dudley Wy
8200 ARVD 80005 1942 C4
9200 WSTR 80021 1942 C2
S Dudley Wy
4400 JfnC 80123 2278 C5
6000 JfnC 80123 2362 C3
9600 LITN 80127 2446 C5
Dueling Stags
10800 DgsC 80125 2614 D1
Duette Wy
10 BMFD 80020 1774 A7
Duffy Ln
10900 DgsC 80116 2707 C4
Duke Cir
2800 BLDR 80305 1686 E7
Duke Ct
12900 BMFD 80020 1775 E7
E Duke Dr
- AURA 80013 2285 E2
E Duke Pl
- AURA 80013 2285 E2
8600 DNVR 80231 2282 E2
S Duke Pl
- AURA 80013 2286 A2
Duluth Ct
5100 DNVR 80239 2032 B5
Duluth Wy
4400 DNVR 80239 2032 B6
Dumas Ct
4400 DNVR 80239 2032 B6
W Dumbarton Cir
10900 JfnC 80127 2277 E7
10900 JfnC 80127 2278 A5
W Dumbarton Dr
10800 JfnC 80127 2278 A5
11200 JfnC 80127 2277 E7
13000 JfnC 80465 2277 C7
W Dumbarton Pl
9500 DNVR 80123 2278 B7
10800 JfnC 80127 2278 A5
12400 JfnC 80465 2277 D7
W Dumbarton Wy
11100 JfnC 80127 2277 E7
N Dumont Wy
12100 DgsC 80125 2447 D4
12100 DgsC 80129 2447 D4
Dump Rd
- CLCY 80403 2017 D4
- GpnC 80403 2017 D4
Dunbar Ct
2200 LGMT 80501 1355 E5
Dunbarton Ct
10 DgsC 80130 2450 B2
Dunbarton Dr
5700 CHLV 80111 2282 B6
Duncan Dr
100 DgsC 80108 2618 D3
Dunes Ct
2900 LGMT 80503 1355 C5
Dunhill St
200 CSRK 80104 2704 D7
W Dunkeld Pl
2400 DNVR 80211 2112 A2
Dunkirk Ct
1600 AURA 80011 2117 D4
4000 DNVR 80249 2033 D7
S Dunkirk Ct
2500 AURA 80013 2201 C7
2700 AURA 80013 2285 D1
6400 CTNL 80016 2369 D3
Dunkirk St
- AURA 80019 2033 C2
- AURA 80249 2033 C3
- DNVR 80019 2033 C3
- DNVR 80249 2033 C2
1500 AURA 80011 2117 D4
S Dunkirk St
- AphC 80015 2369 D2
1300 AURA 80017 2201 D5
1800 AURA 80013 2201 D5
6100 AphC 80016 2369 D2
7500 CTNL 80016 2369 D6
Dunkirk Wy
4300 DNVR 80249 2033 C7
S Dunkirk Wy
3300 AURA 80013 2285 D2
4800 CTNL 80015 2285 D6
5400 CTNL 80015 2369 D1
Dunmark Rd
11700 DgsC 80138 2455 B5
Dunn Rd
200 GOLD 80403 2107 E2
Dunraven Cir
5300 JfnC 80403 2023 E5
Dunraven Ct
5900 JfnC 80403 2023 E3
Dunraven Ln
5500 JfnC 80403 2023 E4
Dunraven Rd
6000 JfnC 80403 2023 E3
Dunraven St
5900 JfnC 80403 2023 E3
6600 ARVD 80007 2023 E1
6600 ARVD 80403 2023 E1
Dunraven Wy
5900 JfnC 80403 2023 E3
Dunrich Rd
11600 DgsC 80138 2455 B5
Dunsford Dr
10200 DgsC 80124 2450 D6
Dunsford Wy
1400 BMFD 80020 1775 A6
E Dunwoody Wy
2500 DgsC 80126 2449 C5
W Duquesne Av
- LKWD 80227 2278 D2
Duquesne Cir
15600 AdmC 80603 1698 D6
E Duquesne Cir
1100 AURA 80018 2202 E4
S Duquesne Cir
- AURA 80018 2202 E4
S Duquesne Ct
1300 AURA 80018 2202 D4
7500 AURA 80016 2370 E6
W Duquesne Dr
8400 LKWD 80227 2278 D2
Duquesne St
- AURA 80016 2286 E6
- AURA 80018 2118 D7
13200 AdmC 80022 1782 D5
13400 AdmC 80603 1782 D5
S Duquesne St
- AphC 80018 2202 E4
- AURA 80018 2202 E4
S Duquesne Wy
7500 AURA 80016 2370 E6
Duran Av
25600 JfnC 80433 2442 B5
Durango Av
13900 BMFD 80020 1775 A4
Durango St
7800 AdmC 80221 1944 D5
Durham Cir
5000 DNVR 80239 2032 B6
7700 BldC 80301 1604 D2
Durham Ct
200 DgsC 80108 2618 E1
5100 DNVR 80239 2032 C5
Durham St
4800 BldC 80301 1604 D2
Durham Wy
7700 BldC 80301 1604 E3
Durian Ct
10 LGMT 80503 1438 C1
Dusk Ct
10200 DgsC 80125 2530 E7
S Dusk Ct
- LITN 80128 2363 D6
Dusk St
7500 DgsC 80125 2530 E7
Dusk Wy
10200 DgsC 80125 2530 E7
Dusty Pine Tr
- CSRK 80109 2702 C4
Dutch Cr
- DgsC 80130 2450 C5
Dutch Ct
2500 LAFT 80026 1689 D2
Dutch Creek Dr
10 AphC 80123 2363 C4
E Dutch Creek St
6300 DgsC 80130 2450 C5
N Dutch Valley Rd
10 AphC 80102 2123 D7
10 AphC 80102 2207 D1
S Dutch Valley Rd
10 AphC 80102 2207 D1
Dutton Ct
700 CSRK 80104 2789 A1
Dyanna Dr
3500 TNTN 80241 1777 D6
Dyer Rd
7100 BldC 80027 1772 D2
7100 BldC 80303 1772 D2
7100 LSVL 80027 1772 D2

E

E St
- AdmC 80022 1948 A1
- AdmC 80022 2032 A1
- AURA 80011 2116 C4
- DNVR 80123 2363 A1
500 GOLD 80401 2108 A7
Eagle Av
2000 SUPE 80027 1773 C6
Eagle Cir
500 AURA 80011 2116 C7
S Eagle Cir
10 AURA 80012 2200 C1
2500 AURA 80014 2200 C7
2500 AURA 80014 2284 C1
4300 AURA 80015 2284 C5
Eagle Ct
100 GOLD 80403 2107 C2
300 LGMT 80501 1439 E3
1000 LSVL 80027 1689 B7
2100 AURA 80011 2116 C3
5100 DNVR 80239 2032 C5
6300 BldC 80503 1519 A6
33500 EbtC 80107 2793 D1
S Eagle Ct
- AURA 80015 2284 C5
2000 AURA 80014 2200 C6
4000 AURA 80014 2284 C4
Eagle Dr
10 CBVL 80123 2363 E3
10 PrkC 80456 2691 D2
100 GOLD 80403 2107 C2
1100 BGTN 80601 1696 C4
Eagle Ln
34000 JfnC 80470 2608 B5
E Eagle Pl
6800 DgsC 80130 2450 C5
Eagle Rd
1100 BMFD 80020 1775 A7
7900 DgsC 80118 2954 C3
Eagle St
2200 AURA 80011 2116 C3
5200 DNVR 80239 2032 C5
S Eagle St
700 AURA 80012 2200 C3
2200 AURA 80014 2200 C7
3800 AURA 80014 2284 C4
5900 CTNL 80016 2368 C2
7200 CTNL 80112 2368 C5
7400 AphC 80112 2368 C5
Eagle Tr
100 PrkC 80456 2691 D3
Eagle Wy
10 BMFD 80020 1774 E7
2900 BLDR 80301 1603 A7
S Eagle Wy
2400 AURA 80014 2200 C7
Eagle Canyon Cir
10 LYNS 80540 1269 C7
Eagle Canyon Dr
- BldC 80540 1269 C7
- LYNS 80540 1269 C7
Eagle Cliff Rd
8300 JfnC 80433 2442 C2
Eagle Cliff Tr
24000 JfnC 80433 2442 D3
Eagle Creek Cir
9800 CMCY 80022 1863 C7
Eagle Creek Pkwy
- AdmC 80022 1947 C1
- CMCY 80022 1947 C1
9600 CMCY 80022 1863 C7
Eaglecrest Cir
- EbtC 80107 2458 E2
- EbtC 80107 2459 A3
N Eaglecrest Cir
- EbtC 80107 2458 E3
S Eaglecrest Cir
- EbtC 80107 2458 E3
Eagle Crest Ct
10700 PARK 80138 2454 B7
Eagle Crest Ln
10700 PARK 80138 2454 C7
30200 JfnC 80439 2188 D6
30200 JfnC 80439 2189 A6
Eagle Feather Ct
7900 LNTR 80124 2450 D3
Eagle Feather Pl
10200 DgsC 80125 2614 E2
Eagle Feather Tr
6300 DgsC 80125 2614 E2
Eagle Feather Wy
7900 LNTR 80124 2450 E3
Eagle Nest Ct
500 GOLD 80401 2107 E7
Eagle Nest Dr
2200 LAFT 80026 1689 E4

STREET
Block City ZIP Map# Grid

Eagle Nest Ln
10 LYNS 80540 1269 C7
Eagle Perch Ct
7600 DgsC 80125 2531 A7
Eagle Pointe Ln
10 DgsC 80108 2618 D5
Eagle Ridge Dr
18600 GOLD 80401 2108 A7
18800 GOLD 80401 2107 E6
Eagle Ridge Rd
500 BldC 80503 1352 E2
500 BldC 80503 1353 A1
500 LYNS 80503 1352 E2
2700 BldC 80503 1269 E6
Eagle River Lp
- BMFD 80020 1775 C2
Eagle River Run
- BMFD 80020 1775 C2
Eagle Rock Dr
7000 DgsC 80125 2615 A1
7300 DgsC 80125 2531 A7
Eagle Run Dr
10900 PARK 80138 2454 C7
10900 PARK 80138 2538 C1
Eagle Run Ln
22300 PARK 80138 2454 C7
22300 PARK 80138 2538 C1
Eagles Dr
10 BldC 80302 1601 D7
Eagle Shadow Av
- TNTN 80602 1694 B4
6400 AdmC 80602 1694 B4
S Eagles Nest Cir
7100 JfnC 80127 2361 D6
Eagles Nest Ln
8800 DgsC 80126 2449 A2
Eagles Nest Tr
- CCkC 80439 2356 A1
600 CCkC 80439 2272 A7
Eaglesong Tr
- CSRK 80109 2702 D3
Eagle Springs Tr
11500 BldC 80503 1353 B7
11500 BldC 80503 1436 B1
Eaglestone Dr
300 CSRK 80104 2787 D5
S Eagle Valley Wy
10000 DgsC 80129 2448 D6
Eagleview Cir
7200 LGMT 80504 1438 D7
Eagle View Ct
2800 JfnC 80439 2273 B2
Eagleview Ct
- LGMT 80504 1438 D7
Eagle View Dr
- WSTR 80021 1857 D7
Eagleview Dr
8000 DgsC 80125 2530 E6
Eagle View Lp
- WSTR 80021 1857 D7
Eagle View Wy
2200 LGMT 80504 1438 E7
Eagle Vista Dr
14400 JfnC 80127 2612 D3
14400 JfnC 80433 2612 D3
Earle Cir
4800 BldC 80301 1604 E3
Easley Rd
- GOLD 80403 2108 B1
3800 JfnC 80403 2108 B1
4100 GOLD 80403 2024 C7
4100 JfnC 80403 2024 C3
5800 ARVD 80403 2024 C3
6100 ARVD 80007 2024 C2
Easley Rd CO-172
3800 JfnC 80403 2108 B1
4100 GOLD 80403 2024 C7
4100 JfnC 80403 2024 C3
6100 ARVD 80007 2024 C3
6100 ARVD 80403 2024 C3
Easley Wy
5200 JfnC 80403 2024 C5
N Easley Wy
3900 GOLD 80403 2108 B1
4000 JfnC 80403 2108 B1
East Dr
- NHGN 80234 1860 C4
- SRDN 80110 2280 A3
- WSTR 80234 1860 C4
East Rd
- DgsC 80112 2452 C2
- DgsC 80134 2452 C2
East St
10 BldC 80302 1599 E3
100 GOLD 80403 2107 D2
100 NDLD 80466 1765 D3
400 BldC 80027 1689 D5
400 LAFT 80027 1689 D5
800 GOLD 80401 2107 E2
1300 JfnC 80401 2107 E3
1700 GOLD 80401 2108 A4
2600 LAFT 80026 1689 D5
N East St
300 LSVL 80027 1689 D7
300 LSVL 80027 1773 D1
E Easter Av
- CTNL 80016 2370 A5
10 CTNL 80122 2364 E5
10 LITN 80120 2364 E5
2400 CTNL 80122 2365 C5
4600 CTNL 80122 2366 A5
6700 CTNL 80112 2366 C5
9500 CTNL 80112 2367 B5
9500 GDVL 80112 2367 B5
10500 AphC 80112 2367 D5
14100 AphC 80112 2368 B5
14500 CTNL 80112 2368 C5
16300 FXFD 80016 2368 E5
16400 FXFD 80016 2369 A5
18400 CTNL 80016 2369 C5
22300 AURA 80016 2370 C5
W Easter Av
400 LITN 80120 2364 D5
E Easter Cir
- AURA 80016 2370 B5
1300 CTNL 80122 2365 B5
8700 CTNL 80112 2367 A5
E Easter Cir N
3600 CTNL 80122 2365 D5
E Easter Cir S
3600 CTNL 80122 2365 D5
Easter Ct
1500 LGMT 80501 1356 B7
E Easter Ct
1100 CTNL 80122 2365 A5
8300 CTNL 80112 2366 E5
16600 FXFD 80016 2368 E5
16600 FXFD 80016 2369 A5
W Easter Ct
4700 LITN 80128 2363 C6
E Easter Dr
- AURA 80016 2370 D5
3700 CTNL 80122 2365 E5
7400 CTNL 80112 2366 D5
E Easter Ln
7700 CTNL 80112 2366 D5
9600 CTNL 80112 2367 B5
E Easter Pl
3800 CTNL 80122 2365 E5
6600 CTNL 80112 2366 C5
8600 CTNL 80112 2367 A5
14100 AphC 80112 2368 B5
17800 FXFD 80016 2369 B5
18800 CTNL 80016 2369 C5
24500 AURA 80016 2370 E5
W Easter Pl
500 LITN 80120 2364 D5
E Easter Wy
900 CTNL 80122 2365 A5
7400 CTNL 80112 2366 D5
16300 FXFD 80016 2368 E5
16700 FXFD 80016 2369 A5
Eastern Av
- BGTN 80601 1696 D6
Eastlake Dr
12500 TNTN 80241 1777 B7
Eastman Av
3200 BLDR 80305 1687 A6
E Eastman Av
- AURA 80013 2286 A2
10 EGLD 80110 2280 E2
10 EGLD 80113 2280 E2
600 EGLD 80113 2281 A2
3300 DNVR 80210 2281 D2
4000 DNVR 80222 2281 E2
6100 AphC 80222 2282 B2
6400 DNVR 80222 2282 B2
6800 DNVR 80224 2282 C2
7000 DNVR 80231 2282 D2
8700 DNVR 80231 2283 A2
19600 AURA 80013 2285 D2
W Eastman Av
10 EGLD 80113 2280 D2
2200 EGLD 80110 2280 B2
2200 SRDN 80110 2280 B2
3600 DNVR 80236 2279 E2
E Eastman Dr
- AURA 80013 2286 A2
17400 AURA 80013 2285 A2
W Eastman Dr
8700 LKWD 80227 2278 C2
E Eastman Pl
8700 DNVR 80231 2282 E3
8700 DNVR 80231 2283 A2
16000 AURA 80013 2284 E2
19300 AURA 80013 2285 D2
W Eastman Pl
9300 LKWD 80227 2278 C2
Eastmoor Dr
7200 DNVR 80237 2282 D5
Easton Ct
600 CSRK 80104 2787 E2
S Eastover St
1900 AphC 80102 2208 E7
East Ridge Av
1200 BLDR 80303 1687 A3
Eastridge Dr
10 PrkC 80456 2607 E5
Eastridge Rd
- EbtC 80107 2793 A3
8800 JfnC 80403 1938 D3
East Ridge Tr
- BldC 80304 1602 A7
Eastview Dr
- BldC 80303 1688 B3
1700 CSRK 80104 2788 E2
2300 DgsC 80104 2788 E2
2300 DgsC 80104 2789 A3
Eastwind Dr
- BldC 80026 1690 E6
- LAFT 80026 1690 E6
Eastwood Ct
3100 BLDR 80304 1602 E7
Eastwood Dr
800 JfnC 80401 2190 E3
800 JfnC 80401 2191 A4
East Yale
- DNVR 80231 2283 B1
Easy St
16800 GpnC 80403 1850 C7
16800 GpnC 80403 1934 C1
Easy Rider Ln
1600 BLDR 80304 1602 C3
Eaton Cir
400 SUPE 80027 1773 A6
NW Eaton Cir
7200 WSTR 80003 1943 B7
S Eaton Cir
1100 CSRK 80104 2788 B1
Eaton Ct
100 LKWD 80226 2195 B1
4200 BLDR 80303 1687 B4
6300 ARVD 80003 2027 B2
7100 WSTR 80003 1943 B7
11700 WSTR 80020 1859 B3
S Eaton Ct
10 LKWD 80226 2195 B1
1100 LKWD 80232 2195 B5
2300 LKWD 80227 2195 B7
6100 JfnC 80123 2363 B3
S Eaton Ln
5900 JfnC 80123 2363 B2
S Eaton Pk
7200 AURA 80016 2370 E5
Eaton Pl
400 LKWD 80226 2111 B7
S Eaton Pl
2600 DNVR 80227 2279 B1
2600 LKWD 80227 2279 B1
Eaton St
- ERIE 80516 1691 C1
10 LKWD 80226 2195 B1
900 CSRK 80104 2788 B1
1300 LKWD 80214 2111 B5
1800 EDGW 80214 2111 B4
2800 WTRG 80214 2111 B2
3000 WTRG 80212 2111 B2
3800 WTRG 80212 2027 B7
4100 MNVW 80212 2027 B7
4800 DvrC 80212 2027 B6
4800 LKSD 80212 2027 B6
5100 DNVR 80002 2027 B5
5100 DNVR 80212 2027 B5
5100 JfnC 80002 2027 B5
6500 ARVD 80003 2027 B1
6700 WSTR 80003 2027 B1
7500 WSTR 80003 1943 B6
7900 ARVD 80003 1943 B5
N Eaton St
3600 WTRG 80212 2111 B1
10800 WSTR 80020 1859 B4
S Eaton St
10 LKWD 80226 2195 B2
1100 LKWD 80232 2195 B4
2100 DNVR 80227 2195 B7
2900 DNVR 80227 2279 C2
3700 DNVR 80235 2279 B4
5500 DNVR 80123 2363 B1
5500 JfnC 80123 2363 B1
6900 JfnC 80128 2363 B4
Eaton Wy
8200 ARVD 80003 1943 B4
11200 WSTR 80020 1859 A4
N Eaton Wy
11800 WSTR 80020 1859 B2
S Eaton Wy
2700 DNVR 80227 2279 B1
2700 LKWD 80227 2279 B1
7600 JfnC 80128 2363 B6
Eaton Park Ct
- AURA 80018 2118 E7
S Eaton Park Pkwy
- AURA 80016 2286 E6
Eaton Park St
- AURA 80018 2118 E7
S Eaton Park St
5100 AURA 80016 2286 E7
S Eaton Park Wy
5200 AURA 80016 2286 E7
Ebony Dr
1300 CSRK 80104 2787 D2
Ebony Ln
- TNTN 80260 1944 B3
Ebony St
1100 AdmC 80221 1944 C6
Echo Dr
12400 BMFD 80020 1775 E5
14800 JfnC 80401 2109 A3
15000 JfnC 80401 2108 E3
Echo Pl
200 BLDR 80302 1686 E5
Echo Tr
10 CCkC 80439 2271 D6
Echo Gap Rd
10 DgsC 80118 2869 A7
10 DgsC 80118 2953 A1
Echo Lake Dr
10 CCkC 80439 2271 D6
Echo Valley Rd
- DgsC 80118 2953 A2
Echo Village Dr
7000 DgsC 80118 2953 B1
Eckert St
4800 CSRK 80104 2788 D1
Eclectic Ct
2900 AdmC 80137 2121 B2
Eclectic St
4100 AdmC 80137 2037 B7
4100 AURA 80137 2037 B7
Eclipse St
2800 AdmC 80137 2121 B2
Eddy Ct
1700 LGMT 80503 1355 C6
Eddy Pl
100 BldC 80303 1688 D6
Edelweiss Cir
25800 JfnC 80439 2358 B1
Edelweiss Ct
7800 BldC 80303 1688 E6
W Eden Dr
8500 LITN 80127 2446 C5
W Edenburg Pl
9500 LITN 80127 2446 B5
Edessa Dr
1700 LAFT 80026 1690 A6
Edge Cliff Pl
10 CCkC 80439 2187 D2
Edgehill Ct
- LGMT 80501 1439 C2
Edgelawn St
- CSRK 80109 2702 C4
Edgemont Ct
10600 DgsC 80129 2448 C7
Edgemont Pl
10600 DgsC 80129 2448 C7
W Edgemore Dr
3000 SRDN 80110 2279 E5
3000 SRDN 80110 2280 A5
W Edgemore Pl
3400 DNVR 80236 2279 E5
3400 SRDN 80110 2279 E5
Edgewater Ct
7700 LITN 80124 2450 E4
Edgewater Pl
9700 LITN 80124 2450 D4
E Edgewood Ct
6900 DgsC 80130 2450 C3
Edgewood Dr
1900 BLDR 80304 1686 D1
2100 BLDR 80304 1602 D7
E Edgewood Dr
6800 DgsC 80130 2450 C3
S Edgewood Ln
8900 DgsC 80130 2450 D3
E Edgewood Pl
6800 DgsC 80130 2450 C3
S Edgewood St
8800 DgsC 80130 2450 C2
E Edgewood Tr
6900 DgsC 80130 2450 D2
E Edgewood Wy
6800 DgsC 80130 2450 D3
Edie Pl
4600 WldC 80516 1607 E2
Edinboro Dr
1000 BLDR 80305 1687 A7
1100 BLDR 80305 1771 A1
S Edinborough Ct
20100 PARK 80138 2537 E1
S Edinborough Pl
20100 PARK 80138 2537 E1
S Edinborough Wy
11200 PARK 80138 2537 E1
Edinburgh Cir
8800 DgsC 80129 2448 B2
Edinburgh Ln
- DgsC 80129 2448 B2
Edison Av
4700 BLDR 80301 1603 B7
Edison Ct
3000 BLDR 80301 1603 B7
Edison Ln
4700 BLDR 80301 1603 B7
Edison Pl
200 SUPE 80027 1773 A6
Edison St
8600 AdmC 80229 1945 A3
8600 TNTN 80229 1945 A3
S Edison Wy
1300 DNVR 80222 2198 A5
1300 DNVR 80246 2198 A5
Edmonston Wy
2700 CSRK 80109 2702 C4
Edmonton Ct
4500 BldC 80301 1604 D3
Edna Dr
- AdmC 80603 1698 D7
Eds Wy
- BldC 80303 1688 B6
Edward Dr
31900 JfnC 80433 2440 D7
Edwards Pl
12300 DNVR 80239 2031 E4
Edwards St
- IDSP 80452 2101 D5
W Egbert Cir
400 BGTN 80601 1696 A6
E Egbert St
10 BGTN 80601 1696 B6
W Egbert St
100 BGTN 80601 1696 A6
Eggers Av
22000 JfnC 80433 2527 B1
Eggleston Dr
7400 BldC 80303 1688 D5
Egret Wy
1600 SUPE 80027 1773 C6
N Egrew Ct
1200 ERIE 80516 1607 A2
S Egrew Ct
1100 ERIE 80516 1607 A3
Ehler Pkwy
- AdmC 80602 1779 A1
8600 AdmC 80602 1778 E2
Eileen Wy
2200 EbtC 80138 2540 E6
Eisenhower Dr
100 AdmC 80102 2124 C2
100 BNNT 80102 2124 C2
300 LSVL 80027 1689 B6
1200 BLDR 80303 1687 C3
Eisenhower Wy
1600 AURA 80011 2117 A4
Elaine Dr
2800 BMFD 80020 1775 E7
2800 BMFD 80020 1776 A7
S Elaine Rd
6300 JfnC 80439 2357 A4
S Elati Cir
7900 LITN 80120 2364 D7
W Elati Cir
700 LITN 80120 2364 D6
Elati Ct
11700 NHGN 80234 1860 D2
S Elati Ct
6100 LITN 80120 2364 D3
S Elati Dr
5100 EGLD 80110 2280 D7
Elati Rd
4200 DgsC 80118 2953 C4
Elati St
10 DNVR 80223 2196 D1
300 DNVR 80223 2112 D7
1100 DNVR 80204 2112 D5
3900 DNVR 80216 2112 D1
4700 DNVR 80216 2028 D6
8200 AdmC 80221 1944 D4
8300 TNTN 80260 1944 D4
11000 NHGN 80234 1860 D4
S Elati St
10 DNVR 80223 2196 D1
2700 DNVR 80223 2280 D1
2700 DvrC 80223 2280 D1
2700 EGLD 80110 2280 D1
2700 EGLD 80223 2280 D1
5300 LITN 80120 2280 D7
7800 LITN 80120 2364 D7
Elati Wy
6800 AdmC 80221 1944 D7
6800 AdmC 80221 2028 D1
S Elati Wy
5700 LITN 80120 2364 D2
S Elbert Ct
1600 SUPE 80027 1773 A6
N Elbert Pl
6100 DgsC 80134 2622 D2
Elbert Rd
1600 TNTN 80260 1860 B7
30000 EbtC 80107 2795 D7
31400 KIOW 80107 2795 D4
Elbert Rd CO-25
30000 EbtC 80107 2795 D7
31400 KIOW 80107 2795 D4
Elbert Rd CO-41
30000 EbtC 80107 2795 D7
31400 KIOW 80107 2795 D4
Elbert St
- BNNT 80102 2124 E2
300 CSRK 80104 2703 D6
500 AdmC 80221 1944 D6
N Elbert St
100 ELIZ 80107 2709 B7
100 ELIZ 80107 2793 B2
S Elbert St
100 ELIZ 80107 2793 B3
800 EbtC 80107 2793 B3
Elbert Wy
200 AdmC 80221 1944 D5
El Camino Dr
5600 CHLV 80111 2282 B5
5600 CHLV 80113 2282 B5
S El Camino Dr
4500 CHLV 80111 2282 B6
El Charro Pt
- CSRK 80104 2704 B3
- CSRK 80108 2704 B3
Elder Av
1200 BLDR 80304 1602 C7
10800 JfnC 80433 2443 A7
Elder Cir
7800 AdmC 80221 1944 C5
Elder Pl
- PARK 80134 2453 B6
Elder St
1100 AdmC 80221 1944 C5
Elderberry Rd
2000 JfnC 80401 2109 A4
Elderberry St
9700 FLHT 80260 1944 A1
El Diente Cir
6000 JfnC 80403 2023 D3
El Diente Ct
5900 JfnC 80403 2023 E4
10500 DgsC 80112 2451 C4
32400 JfnC 80439 2188 D6
El Diente St
5400 JfnC 80403 2023 E4
El Diente Peak Pl
6200 DgsC 80108 2618 E3
Eldora Ct
30600 JfnC 80439 2189 A6
Eldora Dr
- AURA 80011 2117 B7
- AURA 80011 2201 B1
Eldora Pl
700 LGMT 80501 1356 D7
Eldora Rd
10 BldC 80466 1765 A4
10 NDLD 80466 1765 A4
Eldorado Av
- BldC 80466 1765 A5
Eldorado Blvd
400 BMFD 80021 1857 E1
900 BfdC 80021 1857 C1
Eldorado Cir
1600 SUPE 80027 1773 A6
E Eldorado Cir
16900 AURA 80013 2285 A2
N El Dorado Ct
6000 DgsC 80134 2622 E2
6000 DgsC 80134 2623 A3
Eldorado Dr
700 SUPE 80027 1773 A6
E Eldorado Dr
- AURA 80013 2286 A2
14700 AURA 80014 2284 C2
15600 AURA 80013 2284 E2
19100 AURA 80013 2285 D2
Eldorado Ln
900 LSVL 80027 1772 E1
900 LSVL 80027 1773 A1
2300 JfnC 80439 2272 E1
E Eldorado Pl
2500 DNVR 80210 2281 C2
5600 DNVR 80222 2282 B2
15700 AURA 80013 2284 D2
19000 AURA 80013 2285 C2
W Eldorado Pl
3900 DNVR 80236 2279 D2
6300 DNVR 80227 2279 A2
6800 LKWD 80227 2278 E2
6800 LKWD 80227 2279 A2
Eldorado Springs Dr
10 BldC 80025 1770 D6
3300 BldC 80303 1770 D6
4600 BldC 80303 1771 B4
Eldorado Springs Dr SR-170
3500 BldC 80025 1770 D6
3500 BldC 80303 1770 D6
3500 BldC 80303 1771 B4
Eldridge Cir
2500 JfnC 80401 2109 A3
Eldridge Ct
200 JfnC 80401 2193 B1
400 JfnC 80401 2109 A7
5900 JfnC 80004 2025 A3
7000 ARVD 80004 1941 A7
S Eldridge Ct
2200 LKWD 80228 2193 A7
2400 LKWD 80228 2277 B1
Eldridge St
600 JfnC 80401 2109 B7
600 LKWD 80401 2109 B7
4400 JfnC 80403 2025 B7
5800 ARVD 80004 2025 A3
5800 JfnC 80002 2025 A3
5800 JfnC 80004 2025 A3
7000 ARVD 80004 1941 B7
7100 ARVD 80005 1941 A7
7100 JfnC 80007 1941 A7
7800 JfnC 80005 1941 A6
N Eldridge St
2000 JfnC 80401 2109 B3
S Eldridge St
2100 LKWD 80228 2193 B7
2400 LKWD 80228 2277 B1
4200 JfnC 80465 2277 B6
5500 JfnC 80127 2361 B2
S Eldridge Wy
10 JfnC 80401 2193 B1
Electra St
16400 AdmC 80603 1699 E4
16700 WldC 80642 1699 E4
Elephant Rock Rd
- DgsC 80135 2699 C6
- DgsC 80135 2783 C1
Eleuthera Ct
4000 BLDR 80301 1603 A5
Elgin Av
900 LGMT 80501 1439 A4
Elgin Dr
8500 BldC 80026 1689 B4
E Elgin Dr
12900 DNVR 80239 2031 E6
12900 DNVR 80239 2032 A5
E Elgin Pl
600 DNVR 80216 2028 E6
600 DNVR 80216 2029 A6
12900 DNVR 80239 2031 E6
12900 DNVR 80239 2032 A6
Elgin St
- AdmC 80137 2120 E4
Eliot Cir
- WSTR 80234 1859 E5
- WSTR 80234 1860 A5
2700 WSTR 80030 1944 A7
10000 FLHT 80260 1860 A7
Eliot Ct
11400 WSTR 80234 1859 E3
11500 WSTR 80234 1860 A3
13500 BMFD 80020 1775 E5
N Eliot Ct
11100 WSTR 80234 1860 A4
N Eliot Dr
11100 WSTR 80234 1859 E4
Eliot Pl
13500 BMFD 80020 1775 E5
Eliot St
- FLHT 80260 1860 A6
- WSTR 80234 1860 A6
3200 DNVR 80211 2112 A2
4400 DNVR 80211 2028 A7
4800 DNVR 80221 2028 A5
7300 WSTR 80030 1944 A6
8000 AdmC 80221 1944 A5
8000 WSTR 80031 1944 A5
8000 WSTR 80221 1944 A5
12500 BMFD 80020 1776 A7
12500 BMFD 80020 1859 E1
12500 BMFD 80020 1860 A1
S Eliot St
100 DNVR 80219 2196 A2
3300 DNVR 80236 2280 A3
3300 DvrC 80236 2280 A3
3300 SRDN 80110 2280 A3
Elis Cir
1700 LAFT 80026 1690 A6
1700 LSVL 80026 1690 A6
Elitch Cir
- DNVR 80204 2112 B3
S Eliza Ct
9800 DgsC 80126 2449 A5
S Elizabeth Av
400 LAFT 80026 1690 D5
S Elizabeth Cir
4800 CHLV 80113 2281 C6
6800 CTNL 80122 2365 C4
Elizabeth Cir E
11700 TNTN 80233 1861 C2
Elizabeth Cir W
11700 TNTN 80233 1861 B2
Elizabeth Ct
10 BldC 80501 1438 E3
10 LGMT 80501 1438 E3
9500 TNTN 80229 1945 C1
11700 TNTN 80233 1861 C3
12100 TNTN 80241 1861 C1
13300 TNTN 80241 1777 C5
14400 AdmC 80602 1777 C3
S Elizabeth Ct
4600 CHLV 80113 2281 C6
7700 CTNL 80122 2365 C7
Elizabeth Dr
1500 EbtC 80138 2540 C4
S Elizabeth Dr
10900 JfnC 80433 2524 E1
Elizabeth Ln
4500 BMFD 80020 1775 C3
S Elizabeth Ln
4900 JfnC 80439 2273 C7
Elizabeth Pl
11600 TNTN 80233 1861 C3
Elizabeth St
600 DNVR 80206 2113 C7
3500 DNVR 80205 2113 C1
4700 DNVR 80216 2029 C6
5400 CMCY 80022 2029 C4
6800 AdmC 80229 2029 C1
7000 AdmC 80229 1945 C7
9600 TNTN 80229 1945 C1
9900 TNTN 80229 1861 C7
10900 NHGN 80233 1861 C5
12500 TNTN 80241 1861 B1
13100 TNTN 80241 1777 C6
14700 TNTN 80602 1777 C2
16400 AdmC 80602 1693 C5
30000 EbtC 80107 2793 A1
30000 ELIZ 80107 2793 A1
E Elizabeth St
9200 DgsC 80134 2622 E2
S Elizabeth St
500 DNVR 80209 2197 C3
1000 DNVR 80210 2197 C5
6700 CTNL 80121 2365 C4
6700 CTNL 80122 2365 C4
Elizabeth Wy
13300 TNTN 80241 1777 C6
S Elizabeth Wy
5900 CTNL 80121 2365 C2
6100 GDVL 80121 2365 C2
7700 CTNL 80122 2365 C7
Elk Cir
15500 AdmC 80603 1698 D6
Elk Cr
- PrkC 80456 2521 C2
Elk Ct
- AURA 80018 2118 E7
3400 BMFD 80020 1775 E5
7600 DgsC 80125 2531 A7
S Elk Ct
- AURA 80016 2286 E6
7100 AURA 80016 2370 E5
Elk Dr
- WSTR 80030 1943 D7
- WSTR 80030 2027 D1
10 CCkC 80439 2272 A4
10 PrkC 80456 2521 E2
14500 DNVR 80239 2032 B6
Elk Ln
10 JfnC 80127 2360 E3
10 PrkC 80456 2607 D2
Elk Pl
100 LGMT 80501 1439 C1
E Elk Pl
600 DNVR 80216 2028 E6
12900 DNVR 80239 2031 E6
14600 DNVR 80239 2032 B6
W Elk Pl
500 DNVR 80216 2028 D6
1700 DNVR 80211 2028 B6
Elk Rd
10 PrkC 80456 2521 D2
W Elk Run
33300 JfnC 80439 2356 C5
Elk St
- DNVR 80249 1950 E6
S Elk St
5100 AURA 80016 2286 E7
8700 DgsC 80126 2449 A2
Elk Tr
10 CCkC 80439 2355 E7
300 LAFT 80026 1774 B2
Elk Wy
10 CCkC 80452 2186 B4
S Elk Wy
- AURA 80016 2286 E6
S Elk Creek Ct
12500 PARK 80134 2537 D4
Elk Creek Dr
10 PrkC 80456 2521 B2
E Elk Creek Dr
18900 PARK 80134 2537 D4
S Elk Creek Rd
11100 PrkC 80470 2523 E3
11800 JfnC 80470 2524 A4
12400 JfnC 80433 2524 D6
13300 JfnC 80470 2608 E1
13500 JfnC 80470 2609 A1
15400 JfnC 80433 2609 E6
15900 JfnC 80470 2693 D1
S Elk Creek Wy
12500 PARK 80134 2537 E3
S Elk Creek Acres Rd
15100 JfnC 80470 2609 C5
Elk Crossing Ln
10 CCkC 80439 2271 E7
Elken Ct
12200 BMFD 80020 1859 D1
S Elkhart Cir
900 AURA 80012 2200 C4
S Elkhart Ct
2400 AURA 80014 2200 C7
4800 AURA 80015 2284 C6
5900 CTNL 80016 2368 C2
Elkhart St
2200 AURA 80011 2116 C3
5300 DNVR 80239 2032 C4
5500 AdmC 80022 2032 C4
5500 DNVR 80022 2032 C4
11600 CMCY 80603 1864 C2
S Elkhart St
700 AURA 80012 2200 C3
2000 AURA 80014 2200 C6
3300 AURA 80014 2284 C2
4800 AURA 80015 2284 C6
S Elkhart Wy
1000 AURA 80012 2200 C3
4900 AURA 80015 2284 C6
Elk Haven Ln
12500 JfnC 80433 2524 E5
Elk Head Range Rd
11600 JfnC 80127 2361 D7
Elk Horn Ct
200 PrkC 80456 2521 E4
Elkhorn Dr
11700 DgsC 80116 2707 D1
S Elkhorn Mtn
7500 JfnC 80127 2362 A6
Elk Horn Run
10900 DgsC 80125 2530 D7

STREET Block City ZIP Map# Grid
Elkhorn St
9900 JfnC 80127 2445 C6
S Elkhorn St
9600 JfnC 80127 2445 C5
Elkhorn Gulch Rd
- CCkC 80403 2101 D2
Elk Meadow Dr
2800 JfnC 80439 2273 A2
Elk Mountain Cir
9500 DgsC 80125 2531 B7
Elk Mountain Tr
- JfnC 80127 2529 A4
13700 JfnC 80127 2528 E3
Elk Mountain Wy
- BMFD 80020 1775 C6
Elk Park Dr
10 PrkC 80470 2523 B2
800 JfnC 80401 2191 A4
Elk Place Rd
- GpnC 80403 1933 C6
Elk Pointe Ln
10 DgsC 80108 2618 E5
Elk Pointe Tr
10 DgsC 80108 2618 D6
Elk Rest Run
11000 DgsC 80125 2530 D7
Elk Ridge Ln
10 BldC 80302 1517 B6
Elk Ridge Rd
16700 JfnC 80127 2612 C1
Elkridge Rd
- BMFD 80020 1775 C6
S Elk Ridge Rd
4800 JfnC 80439 2272 C7
4800 JfnC 80439 2356 C1
Elkridge Run
35600 EbtC 80107 2709 D4
Elk Run Dr
3500 CSRK 80109 2702 C3
Elk Summit Ln
2900 JfnC 80439 2272 E3
Elk Trail Pl
7400 DgsC 80125 2531 A7
Elk Trail Rd
11900 JfnC 80433 2525 D4
Elk Valley Dr
10 CCkC 80439 2103 B6
Elk View Ct
5200 DgsC 80118 2870 D4
Elk View Dr
2900 JfnC 80439 2272 E3
3000 JfnC 80439 2273 A3
Elkview Dr
3100 JfnC 80439 2273 A3
Elk View Rd
1100 DgsC 80118 2870 D6
Ella Av
34300 JfnC 80470 2608 A1
Ellen Ct
9200 TNTN 80229 1945 A1
Ellen Ln
7600 AdmC 80221 1944 D6
Ellendale St
10 CSRK 80104 2705 A7
Ellingwood Tr
32000 JfnC 80439 2188 D6
Ellingwood Point Pl
6200 DgsC 80108 2618 E2
Ellingwood Point Wy
6200 DgsC 80108 2618 E2
Elliot Cir
1500 BMFD 80020 1775 E7
1500 BMFD 80020 1776 A7
Elliot Ln
- BldC 80403 1852 A2
10 GpnC 80403 1851 E2
Elliot Rd
- BldC 80403 1852 A3
Elliot St
1300 BMFD 80020 1776 A7
Elliott St
400 LGMT 80501 1439 D2
S Ellipse Wy
800 DNVR 80209 2197 C3
Ellis Ct
- ARVD 80005 1941 A4
500 JfnC 80401 2109 A7
5800 JfnC 80004 2025 A3
S Ellis Ct
2100 LKWD 80228 2193 A7
2400 LKWD 80228 2277 A1
Ellis Ln
3000 JfnC 80401 2109 A2
Ellis St
700 LKWD 80401 2109 A7
2000 JfnC 80401 2109 A4
5000 JfnC 80403 2025 A6
8500 ARVD 80005 1941 A4
N Ellis St
4800 JfnC 80403 2025 A6
7000 ARVD 80004 1941 A7
7100 JfnC 80007 1941 A7
S Ellis St
2200 LKWD 80228 2193 A7
2400 LKWD 80228 2277 B1
Ellis Wy
200 JfnC 80401 2193 B1
400 JfnC 80401 2109 B7
Ellison Ln
- BldC 80503 1519 B6
- BLDR 80503 1519 B6
Ellison Pl
2800 BLDR 80304 1602 C7
2800 BLDR 80304 1686 C1
10400 DgsC 80125 2530 E7
El Lobo Ln
10 PrkC 80456 2521 C2
E Ellsworth Av
10 DNVR 80203 2196 E1
10 DNVR 80209 2196 E1
10 DNVR 80223 2196 E1
700 DNVR 80203 2197 A1
700 DNVR 80218 2197 A1
3200 DNVR 80206 2197 D1

E Ellsworth Av
3900 DNVR 80220 2197 E1
4000 DNVR 80209 2197 E1
4000 DNVR 80246 2197 E1
4700 DNVR 80220 2198 A1
4700 DNVR 80246 2198 A1
5500 DNVR 80224 2198 A1
7300 DNVR 80230 2198 D1
13600 AURA 80012 2200 A1
13900 AURA 80011 2200 B1
23300 AphC 80018 2202 D1
23300 AURA 80018 2202 D1
W Ellsworth Av
10 DNVR 80203 2196 D1
10 DNVR 80209 2196 D1
10 DNVR 80223 2196 D1
2500 DNVR 80219 2196 A1
4300 DNVR 80219 2195 C1
6800 LKWD 80226 2195 A1
7200 LKWD 80226 2194 E1
14300 JfnC 80401 2193 A1
15200 JfnC 80401 2192 D2
Ellsworth Ct
700 CSRK 80104 2789 B1
W Ellsworth Dr
15700 JfnC 80401 2192 D1
W Ellsworth Ln
15000 JfnC 80401 2192 D1
Ellsworth Pl
5000 BLDR 80303 1687 C3
E Ellsworth Pl
11500 AURA 80010 2199 D1
W Ellsworth Pl
7000 LKWD 80226 2194 E1
12800 LKWD 80228 2193 C2
14300 JfnC 80401 2193 A1
15600 JfnC 80401 2192 D1
Elm Av
100 CSRK 80104 2787 E1
100 CSRK 80104 2788 A1
300 BGTN 80601 1696 A7
2700 BLDR 80305 1686 E5
2800 BLDR 80305 1687 A5
E Elm Av
3000 DgsC 80134 2452 B3
Elm Cir
- FLHT 80260 1944 A1
700 GOLD 80401 2107 D3
1400 BMFD 80020 1776 A7
11500 TNTN 80233 1861 E3
11500 TNTN 80233 1862 A3
S Elm Cir
6500 CTNL 80121 2366 A4
Elm Ct
- FLHT 80260 1860 A6
200 CSRK 80104 2788 A1
4400 DNVR 80211 2028 A7
4800 DNVR 80221 2028 A5
5400 AdmC 80221 2028 A4
8800 WSTR 80031 1944 A3
9000 FLHT 80260 1944 A2
10100 TNTN 80229 1862 A6
11700 TNTN 80233 1862 A3
S Elm Ct
4200 CHLV 80113 2282 A5
5400 GDVL 80121 2366 A1
5900 CTNL 80121 2366 A2
7300 CTNL 80122 2366 A6
Elm Dr
11800 TNTN 80233 1862 A2
S Elm Dr
2300 AphC 80222 2198 A7
2300 DNVR 80222 2198 A7
Elm Ln
12500 BMFD 80020 1859 E1
12600 BMFD 80020 1775 E7
Elm Pl
900 TNTN 80229 1945 A2
Elm St
- AdmC 80221 1944 A5
- AdmC 80229 1946 A1
- WSTR 80031 1944 A5
- WSTR 80221 1944 A5
10 DNVR 80220 2198 A1
10 DNVR 80246 2198 A1
10 LAFT 80026 1690 B4
200 BNNT 80102 2124 D2
200 LCHB 80603 1698 C3
1300 BMFD 80020 1776 A6
1500 GOLD 80401 2107 D4
1900 DNVR 80220 2114 A4
2000 DNVR 80207 2114 A3
6900 CMCY 80022 1946 A7
6900 CMCY 80022 2030 A1
7000 BldC 80503 1521 B4
7500 DgsC 80135 2532 C6
9700 FLHT 80260 1944 A1
10000 FLHT 80260 1860 A7
12500 TNTN 80241 1778 A7
12500 TNTN 80241 1862 A1
12600 TNTN 80241 1777 E7
13800 TNTN 80602 1778 A4
E Elm St
100 ELIZ 80107 2793 B1
500 LAFT 80026 1690 D4
900 LSVL 80027 1689 D7
S Elm St
10 DNVR 80220 2198 A1
10 DNVR 80246 2198 A1
400 GNDL 80246 2198 A2
1200 DNVR 80222 2198 A5
2700 AphC 80222 2282 A1
2700 DNVR 80222 2282 A1
3400 DNVR 80237 2282 A2
5800 CTNL 80121 2366 A1
5800 GDVL 80121 2366 A1
7000 CTNL 80122 2366 A5
W Elm St
10 LAFT 80026 1690 C4
100 ELIZ 80107 2793 A1
100 LSVL 80027 1773 C1
500 EbtC 80107 2793 A1
Elm Wy
- TNTN 80233 1861 E3

Elm Wy
11400 TNTN 80233 1862 A3
12000 TNTN 80241 1862 A2
12200 TNTN 80241 1861 E1
S Elm Wy
3600 CHLV 80113 2282 A3
3600 DNVR 80237 2282 A3
Elmendorf Dr
- DNVR 80249 2033 C4
Elmendorf Pl
12200 DNVR 80239 2031 E4
13100 DNVR 80239 2032 A4
Elmer Dr
900 NHGN 80233 1861 A4
Elm Fork Pl
1300 CSRK 80104 2787 E5
Elmgreen Ln
10 CCkC 80439 2188 A2
W Elmhurst Av
5600 JfnC 80128 2363 B7
8400 JfnC 80128 2362 C7
Elmhurst Cir
2600 LGMT 80503 1355 C7
Elmhurst Ct
1400 LGMT 80503 1355 C7
Elmhurst Dr
1400 LGMT 80503 1355 C6
W Elmhurst Dr
5700 JfnC 80128 2363 B7
6100 JfnC 80128 2447 A1
9200 JfnC 80128 2362 B7
Elmhurst Ln
1400 LGMT 80503 1355 C7
9400 DgsC 80129 2448 D4
Elmhurst Pl
- AURA 80016 2371 C6
2400 LGMT 80503 1355 C7
3800 BLDR 80305 1687 B6
E Elmhurst Pl
23300 AURA 80016 2370 D7
W Elmhurst Pl
600 BMFD 80020 1858 E1
9400 JfnC 80128 2362 B7
Elmhurst Wy
400 DgsC 80129 2448 D4
S Elmira Cir E
6200 AphC 80111 2367 B3
S Elmira Cir W
6200 AphC 80111 2367 B3
Elmira Ct
15400 AdmC 80602 1695 B7
S Elmira Ct
- AURA 80247 2199 A5
2900 DNVR 80231 2283 B2
Elmira St
- DNVR 80238 2115 B3
- DvrC 80238 2115 B3
1600 AURA 80010 2115 B3
11200 CMCY 80640 1863 B4
15700 AdmC 80602 1695 A7
S Elmira St
900 AURA 80247 2199 B4
900 DNVR 80247 2199 B4
900 DvrC 80247 2199 B4
2700 DNVR 80231 2283 B1
4900 AphC 80015 2283 B7
4900 GDVL 80111 2283 B7
S Elmira Wy
1900 AURA 80247 2199 B6
Elmore Rd
13500 WldC 80504 1357 C5
S Elmoro Ct
1200 SUPE 80027 1773 B5
Elm Square Dr
4600 EbtC 80107 2709 D7
Elmwood Ct
1200 BMFD 80020 1775 B6
Elmwood Dr
7900 AdmC 80221 1944 C5
Elmwood Ln
1000 AdmC 80221 1944 C5
Elmwood Pl
7700 AdmC 80221 1944 A5
Elmwood St
- DgsC 80120 2447 E1
- LITN 80120 2447 E1
1300 BMFD 80020 1775 B6
7500 DgsC 80125 2531 A7
S Elmwood St
5300 EGLD 80120 2280 C7
5300 LITN 80120 2280 C7
5300 LITN 80120 2364 C1
El Norte Ct
- BGTN 80601 1697 B6
El Paso Blvd
400 AdmC 80221 1944 C6
El Paso Cir
7600 AdmC 80221 1944 C6
El Paso Ct
- BGTN 80601 1697 B6
300 AdmC 80221 1944 D5
El Pico Dr
12200 JfnC 80433 2524 E4
S El Pinal Dr
3100 JfnC 80439 2273 A3
El Rancho Rd
900 JfnC 80401 2189 C4
Elsie Rd
13100 JfnC 80433 2526 C7
13300 JfnC 80433 2610 D1
Elysian Tr
1100 LAFT 80026 1690 B7
Elysian Wy
1100 LAFT 80026 1690 B7
Elysian Field Dr
1100 LAFT 80026 1690 B7
Emanuel Wy
10700 JfnC 80403 1852 B6
Ember St
1200 AdmC 80221 1944 C5
Ember Wy
200 CSRK 80104 2787 D3
Emerald Ct
200 CSRK 80104 2787 D2

Emerald Dr
200 CSRK 80104 2787 D2
1900 LGMT 80504 1438 D6
1900 LGMT 80504 1439 A6
Emerald Ln
600 LKWD 80214 2110 E7
7900 BMFD 80020 1858 D2
S Emerald Ln
10700 JfnC 80433 2526 D1
Emerald Rd
2000 BldC 80304 1602 D5
Emerald St
10 BMFD 80020 1858 E2
600 BMFD 80020 1774 E7
Emerald Peak
7700 JfnC 80127 2361 E7
Emerson Av
2600 BLDR 80305 1770 E1
2900 BLDR 80305 1771 A1
Emerson Cir
700 NHGN 80233 1861 A4
S Emerson Cir
- CTNL 80122 2365 A6
Emerson Ct
8500 AdmC 80229 1945 A3
8500 TNTN 80229 1945 A3
S Emerson Ct
7600 CTNL 80122 2365 A6
Emerson Ln
2000 SUPE 80027 1773 A6
Emerson Pl
1000 LGMT 80501 1356 A5
Emerson St
10 DNVR 80209 2197 B1
10 DNVR 80218 2197 B1
100 DNVR 80203 2197 B1
1500 DNVR 80218 2113 A5
2000 DNVR 80205 2113 A4
5100 DNVR 80216 2029 A5
5100 DvrC 80216 2029 A5
8300 AdmC 80229 1945 A4
9000 TNTN 80229 1945 A2
11400 NHGN 80233 1861 A3
13000 TNTN 80241 1776 E5
13100 TNTN 80241 1777 A6
S Emerson St
10 DNVR 80209 2197 A2
10 DNVR 80218 2197 A2
1000 DNVR 80210 2197 A6
2700 AphC 80210 2281 A1
2700 DNVR 80210 2281 A1
3100 EGLD 80113 2281 A2
3500 CHLV 80113 2281 A3
7500 CTNL 80122 2365 A6
S Emerson Wy
3000 EGLD 80113 2281 A2
8100 CTNL 80122 2365 B6
8100 CTNL 80122 2449 A1
8100 LITN 80122 2365 B6
Emerson Gulch Rd
10 BldC 80302 1599 D6
Emery Ct
1400 LGMT 80501 1356 B7
Emery Dr
300 LGMT 80501 1356 B5
Emery Pl
2300 LGMT 80501 1356 B4
Emery Rd
100 NHGN 80233 1860 E4
Emery St
- BldC 80501 1439 B4
900 LGMT 80501 1439 B1
2100 LGMT 80501 1356 B4
S Emery St
1200 LGMT 80501 1439 B6
Emery Wy
10 LGMT 80501 1356 B5
E Emilia Dr
- PARK 80134 2537 B6
S Emilia Wy
- PARK 80134 2537 B5
Emma Ln
1700 BGTN 80601 1696 D7
E Emma St
100 LAFT 80026 1690 D5
800 BldC 80026 1690 D5
W Emma St
100 LAFT 80026 1690 C5
Empire Dr
7200 BldC 80303 1688 C7
7200 BldC 80303 1772 C1
E Empire Dr
10400 DgsC 80116 2791 B3
Empire Pl
10 LGMT 80501 1356 C7
Empire Rd
1300 LSVL 80027 1689 E7
1600 LSVL 80026 1689 E7
9700 LSVL 80027 1773 E1
10000 LSVL 80026 1690 A7
10200 LSVL 80026 1773 E1
10200 LSVL 80026 1774 A1
10200 LSVL 80027 1774 A1
10300 LAFT 80026 1774 A1
Empire Rd SR-42
9700 LSVL 80027 1773 E1
10200 LSVL 80026 1773 E1
10200 LSVL 80026 1774 A1
10200 LSVL 80027 1774 A1
10300 LAFT 80026 1774 A1
Empire St
300 AURA 80010 2115 B7
S Emporia Cir
5500 GDVL 80111 2367 B1
5900 AphC 80111 2367 B2
Emporia Ct
14600 AdmC 80602 1779 A2
S Emporia Ct
1400 AURA 80247 2199 B5
2900 DNVR 80231 2283 B2
4900 GDVL 80111 2283 B6
5400 GDVL 80111 2367 B1
6000 AphC 80111 2367 B2

Emporia Rd
600 BLDR 80305 1686 E7
Emporia St
- DNVR 80238 2115 B3
- DvrC 80238 2115 B3
2000 AURA 80010 2115 B4
9700 AdmC 80640 1863 B7
11200 CMCY 80640 1863 B3
15200 AdmC 80602 1695 A7
15200 AdmC 80602 1779 A1
S Emporia St
- AURA 80247 2199 B5
700 DNVR 80247 2199 B3
2200 AphC 80231 2199 B7
2200 DNVR 80231 2199 B7
4900 AphC 80015 2283 B7
4900 GDVL 80111 2283 B7
6700 CTNL 80112 2367 B4
6700 GDVL 80112 2367 B4
S Emporia Wy
1600 AURA 80247 2199 B5
3600 GDVL 80014 2283 B4
5100 GDVL 80111 2283 B7
Empson Dr
10 LGMT 80501 1356 C6
Enchantra Cir
4000 DgsC 80104 2871 C2
W Enclave Cir
1100 LSVL 80027 1688 E7
1100 LSVL 80027 1772 E1
W Enclave Wy
- LSVL 80027 1772 E1
Enderud Blvd
- CSRK 80104 2704 D6
S Endicott Ct
4500 DNVR 80123 2278 C6
Endicott Dr
3100 BLDR 80305 1771 A1
S Endicott St
1500 LKWD 80232 2194 C5
Engineering Dr
- BLDR 80302 1686 E3
Engineers Ct
7400 DgsC 80118 2954 E2
Englewood Pkwy
10 EGLD 80110 2280 D3
10 EGLD 80113 2280 D3
W English Sparrow Dr
300 DgsC 80129 2448 D6
W English Sparrow Tr
300 DgsC 80129 2448 D6
Enid Ct
5100 DNVR 80239 2032 C5
Enid Wy
4600 DNVR 80239 2032 C6
Ensenada Ct
1900 AURA 80011 2117 D4
S Ensenada Ct
2700 AURA 80013 2285 D1
5600 AphC 80015 2369 D1
7500 CTNL 80016 2369 D6
Ensenada St
1900 AURA 80011 2117 D4
4200 DNVR 80249 2033 D7
S Ensenada St
1300 AURA 80017 2201 D4
2100 AURA 80013 2201 D6
3700 AURA 80013 2285 D3
4600 CTNL 80015 2285 D5
5800 AphC 80015 2369 D2
Ensenada Wy
1600 AURA 80011 2117 D4
S Ensenada Wy
1700 AURA 80017 2201 D5
2000 AURA 80013 2201 D6
3100 AURA 80013 2285 D2
4200 AphC 80015 2285 D5
4900 CTNL 80015 2285 D6
Enterprise St
- BMFD 80020 1858 D2
1800 SUPE 80027 1773 B6
Entrada Dr
400 GOLD 80401 2108 A7
400 GOLD 80401 2192 B1
Environmental Wy
- BMFD 80021 1773 E7
Eolus Rd
2000 TNTN 80260 1860 B7
Ephesus Rd
6200 BldC 80503 1436 E3
6200 BldC 80503 1437 A3
E Eppinger Blvd
300 TNTN 80229 1944 E2
800 TNTN 80229 1945 A2
Equinox Dr
10 DgsC 80108 2618 D4
W Erb Pl
1200 DNVR 80223 2196 C3
Erie Dr
300 BLDR 80303 1687 B5
Erie Ln
2000 SUPE 80027 1773 A6
S Erie Run
6400 JfnC 80439 2357 A4
Erie St
400 AdmC 80221 1944 D6
1700 DNVR 80211 2112 B2
Erie Village Sq
10 ERIE 80516 1607 B3
Erin Ct
7300 BldC 80503 1521 A3
14300 BMFD 80020 1775 C3
S Erin Ln
9300 JfnC 80127 2445 C4
Erin Pl
10300 DgsC 80124 2450 D6
Erin Wy
1600 LAFT 80026 1690 A7
Ermindale Dr
9200 LNTR 80124 2450 D3
Ernst Av
300 LKWD 80226 2194 B1
Ervine Av
1500 LGMT 80501 1355 E6

Erwin Dr
- BldC 80481 1515 A1
E Escalante Ct
9800 DgsC 80134 2623 A2
Escape
10 BldC 80302 1600 C6
Escuela Ct
3900 BldC 80301 1603 A5
Esmond Ln
5000 DgsC 80108 2618 D6
S Espana Cir
3200 AURA 80013 2285 D2
5200 CTNL 80015 2285 D7
S Espana Ct
2400 AURA 80013 2201 D7
2900 AURA 80013 2285 D1
4800 CTNL 80015 2285 D6
S Espana Ln
4800 CTNL 80015 2285 D6
Espana St
1500 AURA 80011 2117 D4
4000 DNVR 80249 2033 D7
S Espana St
2100 AURA 80013 2201 D6
2800 AURA 80013 2285 D1
4600 CTNL 80015 2285 D5
5800 AphC 80015 2369 D2
6200 AphC 80016 2369 D3
6200 CTNL 80016 2369 D3
Espana Wy
1700 AURA 80011 2117 D4
4500 DNVR 80249 2033 D6
S Espana Wy
1600 AURA 80017 2201 D5
3000 AURA 80013 2285 D1
4900 CTNL 80015 2285 D4
6000 AphC 80016 2369 D2
7800 CTNL 80016 2369 D7
Espera Ln
12600 PARK 80134 2537 B5
Esperanza Ct
12600 DgsC 80108 2534 C5
Esperanza Dr
6500 DgsC 80108 2534 C5
Esperanza Pl
12600 DgsC 80108 2534 C5
Esplanade
- DNVR 80206 2113 C4
E Essex Av
5100 CSRK 80104 2704 D7
Essex Cir
4700 BldC 80301 1604 E3
Essex Ct
4700 BldC 80301 1604 E3
Essex Dr
700 AdmC 80229 1945 A4
Essex Ln
- EGLD 80113 2281 B3
Essex Pl
7700 BldC 80301 1604 D3
Essex St
8400 AdmC 80229 1945 A4
8600 TNTN 80229 1945 A4
Estabrook Wy
1800 SUPE 80027 1773 B6
S Estack Ct
9700 DgsC 80126 2448 E5
E Estack Pl
10 DgsC 80126 2448 E5
Estate Cir
7500 BldC 80503 1520 D5
Estes Cir
5200 ARVD 80002 2026 C5
8100 ARVD 80005 1942 C5
Estes Ct
- LYNS 80540 1352 E2
4900 JfnC 80002 2026 C6
5400 ARVD 80002 2026 C4
5900 ARVD 80004 2026 C3
8300 ARVD 80005 1942 C4
8700 WSTR 80005 1942 C3
S Estes Ct
1000 LKWD 80226 2194 C4
1000 LKWD 80232 2194 C4
2400 LKWD 80227 2194 E7
3000 LKWD 80227 2278 C2
7300 JfnC 80128 2362 C6
Estes Dr
6800 ARVD 80004 2026 C1
6900 ARVD 80004 1942 C7
Estes Ln
2000 LGMT 80501 1356 B5
9300 WSTR 80021 1942 C2
Estes Pl
20300 PARK 80138 2453 E7
Estes St
- DNVR 80123 2362 C1
- DvrC 80123 2362 C1
10 LKWD 80226 2194 C1
400 LKWD 80226 2110 C7
2000 LKWD 80215 2110 C4
3200 JfnC 80215 2110 C2
3800 WTRG 80033 2110 C1
4800 JfnC 80002 2026 C6
4800 WTRG 80033 2026 C6
5600 ARVD 80002 2026 C4
5700 ARVD 80004 2026 C4
8000 ARVD 80005 1942 C5
9100 WSTR 80021 1942 C2
S Estes St
- JfnC 80123 2362 C2
- JfnC 80128 2446 C1
- JfnC 80235 2278 C2
- LKWD 80235 2278 C2
10 LKWD 80226 2194 C1
1900 LKWD 80232 2194 C6
2300 LKWD 80227 2194 C7
2400 LKWD 80227 2278 C1
4300 JfnC 80123 2278 C5
4500 DNVR 80123 2278 C6
6700 JfnC 80128 2362 C4
Estes Wy
900 LSVL 80027 1689 A7

S Estes Wy
1400 LKWD 80232 2194 C5
2100 LKWD 80227 2194 C7
4800 DNVR 80123 2278 C6
5200 JfnC 80123 2278 C7
5600 JfnC 80123 2362 C2
9500 LITN 80127 2446 C4
Estrella St
3700 BGTN 80601 1697 A6
Ethan Ct
42700 EbtC 80138 2539 E5
Etna Dr
1200 LAFT 80026 1690 A6
Eucalyptus Ln
- TNTN 80260 1860 D6
- TNTN 80260 1944 B3
Euclid Av
1600 BLDR 80302 1686 D3
4900 BLDR 80303 1687 C3
E Euclid Av
10 CTNL 80121 2364 E4
10 LITN 80120 2364 E4
700 CTNL 80121 2365 B3
3300 CTNL 80122 2365 D4
3800 AphC 80121 2365 D4
4600 CTNL 80121 2366 A4
6000 CTNL 80111 2366 B3
16700 CTNL 80016 2368 E3
16700 CTNL 80016 2369 A3
17400 AphC 80016 2369 B4
W Euclid Av
- CTNL 80121 2364 D4
2400 LITN 80120 2364 B4
8900 JfnC 80123 2362 C4
Euclid Cir
1500 LAFT 80026 1689 E5
1500 LAFT 80026 1690 A5
E Euclid Cir
4600 CTNL 80121 2366 A4
22700 AURA 80016 2370 C3
E Euclid Dr
- AURA 80016 2371 B3
- CTNL 80111 2368 A4
7000 CTNL 80111 2366 C4
12400 CTNL 80111 2367 E4
19100 CTNL 80016 2369 D3
20600 AphC 80016 2369 E3
20700 AphC 80016 2370 A3
21100 CTNL 80016 2370 A3
21900 AURA 80016 2370 B3
W Euclid Dr
6600 JfnC 80123 2363 A4
9600 JfnC 80123 2362 B4
E Euclid Ln
16800 AphC 80016 2369 A3
Euclid Pl
5600 BLDR 80303 1687 D4
E Euclid Pl
- AphC 80016 2370 E3
- AphC 80016 2371 A3
- AphC 80111 2368 A4
- AURA 80016 2371 A3
- CTNL 80111 2368 A4
2700 CTNL 80121 2365 C4
6900 CTNL 80111 2366 C4
18200 AphC 80016 2369 C3
22500 AURA 80016 2370 C3
W Euclid Pl
6500 JfnC 80123 2363 A4
7300 JfnC 80123 2362 E4
S Euclid Wy
900 DNVR 80209 2197 C3
Eudora Cir
11000 TNTN 80233 1861 E4
11000 TNTN 80233 1862 A4
S Eudora Cir
7800 CTNL 80122 2366 A7
Eudora Ct
10100 TNTN 80229 1862 A6
11700 TNTN 80233 1861 E3
12000 TNTN 80241 1861 E3
S Eudora Ct
5900 CTNL 80121 2366 A2
7100 CTNL 80122 2366 A5
Eudora Dr
6800 CMCY 80022 1946 A7
6800 CMCY 80022 2030 A1
7100 AdmC 80022 1946 A7
11800 TNTN 80233 1861 E2
12700 TNTN 80241 1777 E7
12700 TNTN 80241 1778 A7
Eudora Ln
- TNTN 80229 1862 A7
Eudora Pl
11000 TNTN 80233 1861 E4
11100 TNTN 80233 1862 A4
S Eudora Pl
2600 AphC 80222 2282 A1
Eudora St
- AdmC 80229 1862 A7
10 DNVR 80220 2198 A1
10 DNVR 80246 2198 A1
1900 DNVR 80220 2114 A4
2000 DNVR 80207 2114 A3
5600 CMCY 80022 2030 A4
9600 AdmC 80229 1946 A1
11500 TNTN 80233 1862 A3
12400 TNTN 80241 1861 E1
12500 TNTN 80241 1777 E7
13800 TNTN 80602 1777 E4
S Eudora St
10 DNVR 80220 2198 A1
500 GNDL 80246 2198 A2
1200 DNVR 80246 2198 A5
2300 DNVR 80222 2198 A7
2600 DvrC 80222 2282 A1
3000 DNVR 80222 2282 A2
3400 DNVR 80237 2282 A2
4100 CHLV 80113 2282 A5
5900 CTNL 80121 2366 A2
6900 CTNL 80122 2366 A5
Eudora Wy
3800 DNVR 80207 2030 A7
3800 DNVR 80207 2114 A1

STREET Block City ZIP Map# Grid

Eudora Wy
11000 TNTN 80233 1862 A4
S Eudora Wy
3500 CHLV 80113 2282 A3
3500 DNVR 80237 2282 A3
5900 CTNL 80121 2366 A2
7300 CTNL 80122 2366 A5
Eugene Ct
4900 DNVR 80239 2032 C6
Eugene Wy
4300 DNVR 80239 2032 B7
Eugenia Ct
- CSRK 80109 2702 E4
Eureka Ct
4700 DNVR 80239 2032 C6
E Eureka Ct
1200 DgsC 80126 2449 A3
Eureka Ln
1800 SUPE 80027 1773 C6
W Eureka Pl
9400 LKWD 80227 2278 B2
Eureka St
200 CLCY 80403 2017 B4
Eutaw Dr
4100 BLDR 80303 1687 B5
Evalena Rd
900 DgsC 80108 2619 C7
Evans Av
2300 LSVL 80027 1689 C5
E Evans Av
10 DNVR 80210 2196 E6
10 DNVR 80223 2196 E6
700 DNVR 80210 2197 D6
3800 DNVR 80222 2197 D6
4600 DNVR 80222 2198 A6
6900 AphC 80224 2198 E6
6900 DNVR 80224 2198 E6
7100 DNVR 80231 2198 E6
8500 AphC 80231 2198 E6
8700 AphC 80231 2199 A6
10200 AURA 80014 2199 B6
10200 AURA 80247 2199 B6
14800 AURA 80014 2200 C6
15500 AURA 80013 2200 D6
17500 AURA 80013 2201 B6
26100 AURA 80018 2203 B6
W Evans Av
- LKWD 80232 2194 D6
10 DNVR 80210 2196 D6
10 DNVR 80223 2196 C6
1600 AphC 80223 2196 C6
1600 EGLD 80110 2196 C6
1600 EGLD 80223 2196 C6
2200 AphC 80219 2196 C6
2200 DNVR 80219 2196 C6
2200 EGLD 80219 2196 C6
3100 DNVR 80219 2195 E6
5100 DNVR 80227 2195 B6
7600 LKWD 80227 2194 D6
14800 LKWD 80228 2192 E7
Evans Blvd
- ELIZ 80107 2709 A7
- ELIZ 80107 2793 B2
Evans Cir
100 BMFD 80020 1774 E5
100 BMFD 80020 1775 A5
2100 LSVL 80027 1689 C5
E Evans Cir
12500 AURA 80014 2199 E6
W Evans Cir
14000 LKWD 80228 2193 A7
E Evans Ct
9000 AphC 80231 2199 A6
Evans Dr
4000 BLDR 80303 1687 B4
E Evans Dr
14200 AURA 80014 2200 B6
17100 AURA 80013 2201 A6
Evans Pl
2500 DNVR 80219 2196 A7
E Evans Pl
5400 DNVR 80222 2198 A6
9100 AphC 80231 2199 A6
14500 AURA 80014 2200 C6
16000 AURA 80013 2200 E6
19200 AURA 80013 2201 D6
W Evans Pl
2400 DNVR 80219 2196 B7
6000 LKWD 80227 2195 B6
8000 LKWD 80227 2194 D6
Evans St
200 LYNS 80540 1352 D2
700 BldC 80516 1607 B4
700 ERIE 80516 1607 B4
E Evans Wy
9100 AphC 80231 2199 A6
S Evans Wy
2200 DgsC 80116 2791 C5
Evans Ranch Rd
10 CCkC 80452 2270 C4
Evans Ridge Rd
10600 DgsC 80134 2623 B4
Evanston
- TNTN 80260 1944 C2
S Evanston Cir
800 AURA 80012 2200 C3
4100 AURA 80014 2284 C4
Evanston Ct
500 AURA 80011 2116 C7
S Evanston Ct
2000 AURA 80014 2200 C6
4300 AURA 80015 2284 C5
Evanston St
600 AURA 80011 2116 C6
S Evanston St
1400 AURA 80012 2200 C4
1800 AURA 80014 2200 C6
3200 AURA 80014 2284 C4
4400 AURA 80015 2284 C5
S Evanston Wy
- AURA 80017 2200 C1
10 AURA 80011 2200 C1
1000 AURA 80012 2200 C3
3000 AURA 80014 2284 C2
S Evanston Wy
4600 AURA 80015 2284 C6
6000 CTNL 80016 2368 C2
Evans View Dr
10 GpnC 80403 1933 C6
Evans View Ln
31200 JfnC 80470 2524 E7
Evelyn Ct
1600 AdmC 80229 1945 B3
8600 TNTN 80229 1945 B3
S Evelyn Wy
3100 DNVR 80222 2282 A2
Evening Star
10 BldC 80302 1600 C6
Evening Star Ct
- EbtC 80107 2542 D2
700 DgsC 80108 2618 C5
Evening Star Dr
700 DgsC 80108 2618 C5
Evening Star Ln
700 DgsC 80108 2618 C5
2200 LAFT 80026 1689 E4
30700 JfnC 80433 2525 A1
Evening Star Wy
700 DgsC 80108 2618 C5
S Everest Ln
6800 JfnC 80439 2358 B5
Everett Av
10 PrkC 80470 2608 A1
Everett Cir
8700 WSTR 80005 1942 C3
8900 WSTR 80021 1942 C3
Everett Ct
1300 LKWD 80215 2110 C5
4600 WTRG 80033 2026 C6
5400 ARVD 80002 2026 C4
6800 ARVD 80004 2026 C1
8700 WSTR 80005 1942 C3
9500 WSTR 80021 1942 B1
S Everett Ct
500 LKWD 80226 2194 C3
4400 JfnC 80123 2278 C5
6200 JfnC 80123 2362 C3
6800 JfnC 80128 2362 C5
8600 JfnC 80128 2446 C2
Everett Dr
3300 BLDR 80305 1771 A1
4400 WTRG 80033 2026 C7
Everett Pl
1800 LGMT 80501 1355 E5
Everett St
- JfnC 80002 2026 C5
100 LKWD 80226 2194 C1
500 LKWD 80226 2110 C7
700 LKWD 80215 2110 C6
3800 WTRG 80033 2110 C1
4500 WTRG 80033 2026 C7
5600 ARVD 80002 2026 C4
5700 ARVD 80004 2026 C4
8100 ARVD 80005 1942 C4
9100 WSTR 80021 1942 C2
S Everett St
700 LKWD 80226 2194 C3
1100 LKWD 80232 2194 C4
2100 LKWD 80227 2194 C7
2500 LKWD 80227 2278 C1
4300 JfnC 80123 2278 C5
4300 JfnC 80235 2278 C5
4500 DNVR 80123 2278 C6
5200 JfnC 80123 2362 C1
6800 JfnC 80128 2362 C4
8500 JfnC 80128 2446 C2
Everett Wy
8400 ARVD 80005 1942 C4
S Everett Wy
5700 JfnC 80123 2362 B2
8300 JfnC 80128 2446 C1
9500 LITN 80127 2446 C4
Evergreen Av
- BldC 80304 1602 B7
300 BLDR 80304 1602 B7
13800 AURA 80011 2116 B5
Evergreen Dr
- TNTN 80260 1944 B1
10 CCkC 80439 2187 E4
28200 JfnC 80433 2441 D6
Evergreen Ln
10 CCkC 80452 2186 B5
Evergreen Pkwy
- JfnC 80439 2272 E1
800 JfnC 80401 2189 A5
800 JfnC 80439 2189 A5
1000 JfnC 80439 2188 E5
2800 JfnC 80439 2273 A3
Evergreen Pkwy SR-74
- JfnC 80439 2272 E1
800 JfnC 80401 2189 A5
800 JfnC 80439 2189 A5
1000 JfnC 80439 2188 E5
2800 JfnC 80439 2273 A3
Evergreen Pl
10 BMFD 80020 1859 A2
Evergreen Rd
10 GpnC 80403 1933 C7
10 PrkC 80456 2606 A3
200 GpnC 80403 2017 C1
11900 JfnC 80433 2525 C4
Evergreen St
10 BMFD 80020 1859 A2
7400 AdmC 80221 1944 D6
N Evergreen Tr
12100 DgsC 80138 2454 D4
S Evergreen Tr
4700 JfnC 80439 2273 E7
Evergreen Wy
10 BldC 80466 1767 A5
Evergreen Heights Dr
5300 JfnC 80439 2357 A1
Evergreen Manor Dr
28400 JfnC 80439 2273 D6
Evergreen Springs Rd
26800 JfnC 80433 2442 A4
26800 JfnC 80439 2442 A4
Evondale St
10600 DgsC 80126 2449 D7
Ewald
200 LYNS 80540 1352 D2
Ewald Av
100 BldC 80540 1352 D2
100 LYNS 80540 1352 D2
Excalibur St
500 LAFT 80026 1690 D6
Exculpating Rd
5500 BLDR 80301 1687 D2
Exegesis St
800 AURA 80012 2200 C3
Exempla Cir
10 LAFT 80026 1774 C1
Exeter Ct
7400 DgsC 80108 2534 E7
Exeter Dr
7400 DgsC 80108 2534 E7
Exeter Pl
7400 DgsC 80108 2534 E7
Exner Pl
10 LGMT 80501 1438 D2
10 LGMT 80503 1438 D2
Expedition
10900 DgsC 80125 2614 D1
Explorador Calle Av
800 AdmC 80229 1945 A5
Explorers Run
11100 DgsC 80125 2530 C7
E Exposition Av
- DNVR 80209 2197 C3
- DNVR 80224 2198 C3
10 DNVR 80223 2196 E3
400 DNVR 80209 2196 E3
3900 GNDL 80246 2197 E3
4600 GNDL 80246 2198 A3
5200 DNVR 80246 2198 A3
7200 DNVR 80247 2198 C3
9700 DNVR 80247 2199 B3
10300 AURA 80012 2199 B3
10300 AURA 80247 2199 B3
13800 AURA 80012 2200 C3
15000 AURA 80017 2200 C3
23300 AphC 80018 2202 D3
W Exposition Av
1200 DNVR 80223 2196 B3
3000 DNVR 80219 2196 A3
4300 DNVR 80219 2195 C3
5000 LKWD 80219 2195 C3
6000 LKWD 80226 2195 A3
10000 LKWD 80226 2194 A3
10800 LKWD 80226 2193 E3
14000 LKWD 80228 2193 A3
Exposition Dr
1600 BLDR 80301 1687 B2
E Exposition Dr
12100 AURA 80012 2199 E3
12800 AURA 80012 2200 A3
15700 AURA 80017 2200 D3
16900 AURA 80017 2201 A2
W Exposition Dr
10900 LKWD 80226 2193 E3
10900 LKWD 80226 2194 A3
14000 LKWD 80228 2193 A3
W Exposition Pl
10900 LKWD 80226 2193 E3
10900 LKWD 80226 2194 A3
13900 LKWD 80228 2193 A3
Exquisite St
- CSRK 80109 2702 E5
Eyebright Ct
8400 DgsC 80134 2452 E1

F

F St
- AdmC 80022 1948 C1
- AdmC 80022 2032 C1
- AURA 80011 2116 C5
600 GOLD 80401 2108 A7
Factory Shops Blvd
- CSRK 80108 2619 B7
- CSRK 80108 2703 B1
4000 CSRK 80109 2703 B1
E Fair Av
- AphC 80016 2369 E2
- CTNL 80016 2369 E2
- CTNL 80016 2370 A2
5500 CTNL 80111 2366 B3
5500 CTNL 80121 2366 B3
8900 GDVL 80111 2367 A3
10600 AphC 80111 2367 C2
14000 CTNL 80111 2368 B3
15700 AphC 80016 2368 E2
15800 CTNL 80016 2368 E2
W Fair Av
- CTNL 80121 2364 E3
10 LITN 80121 2364 E3
2000 LITN 80120 2364 B3
5000 LITN 80123 2363 C3
8400 JfnC 80123 2362 D3
10000 JfnC 80127 2362 B3
10900 JfnC 80127 2361 E3
E Fair Cir
4400 CTNL 80121 2365 E3
10000 AphC 80111 2367 B2
W Fair Cir
2100 LITN 80120 2364 B3
E Fair Ct
4800 CTNL 80121 2366 A3
E Fair Dr
5100 CTNL 80121 2366 A3
19100 AphC 80016 2369 D3
W Fair Dr
5200 JfnC 80123 2363 A3
8600 JfnC 80123 2362 C3
12400 JfnC 80127 2361 D3
E Fair Ln
200 CTNL 80121 2364 E3
9700 AphC 80111 2367 B3
17300 AphC 80016 2369 A3
20600 CTNL 80016 2370 A2
22400 AphC 80015 2370 C2
Fair Pl
- AURA 80016 2371 B2
200 BLDR 80302 1686 E5
E Fair Pl
- AphC 80016 2368 D3
- CTNL 80016 2368 D3
- CTNL 80111 2368 B3
- CTNL 80121 2364 E3
3200 CTNL 80121 2365 D3
4600 CTNL 80121 2366 A3
5600 CTNL 80111 2366 B3
10600 AphC 80111 2367 C3
16800 AphC 80016 2369 A2
20700 CTNL 80016 2370 A3
22400 AphC 80015 2370 C2
W Fair Pl
5000 LITN 80123 2363 C3
9300 JfnC 80123 2362 C3
Fair St
10 CSRK 80104 2703 D7
S Fairall Rd
8300 JfnC 80465 2442 E2
Fairbairn Wy
10700 DgsC 80124 2450 A7
Fairbanks Ct
1200 JfnC 80439 2189 A5
Fairbanks Pl
100 LGMT 80501 1356 C7
Fairbrook Pt
3700 DgsC 80126 2533 E1
E Fairchild Dr
- DgsC 80129 2448 E6
200 DgsC 80126 2448 E6
200 DgsC 80126 2449 A6
E Fairchild Pl
100 DgsC 80126 2448 E6
Fairdale Ct
700 CSRK 80104 2789 A1
Fairfax Cir
11000 TNTN 80233 1862 A4
Fairfax Ct
1400 CSRK 80104 2788 E2
1400 CSRK 80104 2789 A2
7900 BldC 80503 1520 E4
10100 TNTN 80229 1862 A6
11200 TNTN 80233 1862 A4
S Fairfax Ct
5900 CTNL 80121 2366 A2
7800 CTNL 80122 2366 A7
Fairfax Dr
- TNTN 80233 1862 A3
6900 CMCY 80022 1946 A7
6900 CMCY 80022 2030 A1
7100 AdmC 80022 1946 A7
S Fairfax Dr
2300 AphC 80222 2198 A7
2300 DNVR 80222 2198 A7
S Fairfax Pl
2500 AphC 80222 2198 A6
2500 AphC 80222 2282 A1
2500 DNVR 80222 2282 A1
Fairfax St
- TNTN 80233 1862 A2
10 DNVR 80220 2198 A1
10 DNVR 80246 2198 A1
1900 DNVR 80207 2114 A5
2000 DNVR 80220 2114 A5
5600 CMCY 80022 2030 A4
12000 TNTN 80241 1862 A2
12500 TNTN 80241 1777 E7
12500 TNTN 80241 1861 E1
12700 TNTN 80241 1778 A7
13800 TNTN 80602 1778 A4
S Fairfax St
- CTNL 80121 2366 A2
- GDVL 80121 2366 A2
10 DNVR 80220 2198 A1
10 DNVR 80246 2198 A1
500 GNDL 80246 2198 A3
1100 DNVR 80222 2198 A6
2700 DNVR 80222 2282 A1
3400 DNVR 80237 2282 A2
4800 CHLV 80121 2282 A7
5000 GDVL 80121 2282 A7
7000 CTNL 80122 2366 A5
Fairfax Wy
11000 TNTN 80233 1862 A4
S Fairfax Wy
6300 CTNL 80121 2366 A3
6600 CTNL 80122 2366 A3
Fairfield Cir
5100 CSRK 80104 2788 E2
41400 EbtC 80107 2541 B7
Fairfield Dr
1100 BLDR 80305 1687 A7
1100 BLDR 80305 1771 A1
Fairfield Ln
100 LSVL 80027 1773 B2
S Fairfield St
5900 LITN 80120 2364 D2
S Fairfield Wy
5900 LITN 80120 2364 D2
E Fairgate Ct
3600 DgsC 80126 2449 D6
Fairgate Wy
10000 DgsC 80126 2449 D6
Fairground
- BldC 80501 1438 D4
- LGMT 80501 1438 D4
Fairgrounds Rd
400 CSRK 80104 2787 E1
Fairhaven St
400 CSRK 80104 2704 D7
500 CSRK 80104 2788 D1
Fairlane Av
700 LGMT 80501 1439 A4
Fairlawn Cir
4800 BldC 80301 1604 D3
Fairlawn Ct
4800 BldC 80301 1604 E3
Fairlawn Tr
10300 DgsC 80130 2450 B6
Fairmont Ln
10700 DgsC 80126 2449 E7
Fairmount Dr
8200 DNVR 80247 2198 E2
E Fairmount Dr
8000 DNVR 80230 2198 E1
8100 DNVR 80247 2198 E1
Fair Oaks Wy
8800 LNTR 80124 2451 A4
Fairplay Av
10 BMFD 80020 1774 E5
10 BMFD 80020 1775 A5
S Fairplay Cir
1100 AURA 80012 2200 C4
4200 AURA 80014 2284 C5
S Fairplay Ct
700 AURA 80012 2200 C3
4500 AURA 80015 2284 C5
Fairplay St
2300 AURA 80011 2116 C3
5200 DNVR 80239 2032 C5
5500 AdmC 80022 2032 C4
5500 DNVR 80022 2032 C4
11700 CMCY 80603 1864 C2
13300 AdmC 80601 1780 C5
13300 BGTN 80601 1780 C5
S Fairplay St
1600 AURA 80012 2200 C5
2000 AURA 80014 2200 C6
3000 AURA 80014 2284 C2
4500 AURA 80015 2284 C5
5900 CTNL 80016 2368 C2
7700 AphC 80112 2368 C7
Fairplay Wy
2300 AURA 80011 2116 C3
4400 DNVR 80239 2032 C7
S Fairplay Wy
1000 AURA 80012 2200 C3
2500 AURA 80014 2200 C7
3400 AURA 80014 2284 C3
Fairview Av
7700 AdmC 80221 1944 A5
7900 WSTR 80031 1944 A5
W Fairview Av
5900 JfnC 80128 2363 B7
7800 JfnC 80128 2362 C7
9700 JfnC 80127 2362 B7
Fairview Ct
8400 LNTR 80124 2450 E4
Fairview Dr
- LNTR 80124 2450 E5
- LNTR 80124 2451 A4
6600 BldC 80303 1688 B4
W Fairview Dr
6800 JfnC 80128 2362 E6
6800 JfnC 80128 2363 A7
Fairview Ln
14300 JfnC 80401 2109 A3
Fairview Pkwy
- DgsC 80126 2449 D5
- DgsC 80130 2449 D5
Fairview Pl
9500 LNTR 80124 2450 E4
W Fairview Pl
3200 DNVR 80211 2111 E2
Fairview Rd
7600 BldC 80303 1688 E5
Fairview St
200 LGMT 80504 1440 D3
Fairview Wy
8400 LNTR 80124 2450 E4
Fairview Oaks Ln
8700 LNTR 80124 2451 A4
Fairview Oaks Pl
8800 LNTR 80124 2451 B4
Fairway Ct
1000 BLDR 80303 1687 D3
Fairway Dr
29400 JfnC 80439 2273 B7
E Fairway Dr
- CMCY 80022 1864 D5
Fairway Ln
- AphC 80123 2363 D3
10 CBVL 80123 2363 D3
4300 BMFD 80020 1775 C3
7200 DgsC 80134 2621 E2
7300 DgsC 80134 2622 A2
Fairways Dr
6300 BldC 80503 1518 E5
Fairway View Ct
2900 DgsC 80108 2618 D3
Fairway Vistas Rd
6900 DgsC 80125 2614 D1
Fairwind Cir
14000 BMFD 80020 1776 A4
Fairwind Ln
- BMFD 80020 1776 A3
Fairwood St
9600 DgsC 80125 2531 A6
Faith Ct
800 LGMT 80501 1438 E1
Faith Pl
1800 LGMT 80501 1438 E1
Falcon Ct
- BldC 80301 1603 D7
1000 LSVL 80027 1689 B7
9600 DgsC 80125 2531 B6
Falcon Dr
- BMFD 80020 1775 C2
1100 BGTN 80601 1696 C4
2000 LGMT 80503 1355 C6
Falcon Ln
6100 JfnC 80465 2360 D3
9700 DgsC 80125 2531 A6
Falcon Pt
2800 LAFT 80026 1774 C2
Falcon St
2900 FLHT 80260 1944 A1
S Falcon Creek Dr
9800 DgsC 80130 2450 C5
Falcon Crst
10 BldC 80302 1516 E7
Falcon Hills Dr
10 DgsC 80126 2449 C2
Falcon Ridge Dr
29400 JfnC 80439 2357 B5
Falcon Ridge Wy
6100 JfnC 80465 2360 D3
Falcon Wing Rd
20600 JfnC 80465 2275 C5
Falk Ct
5700 ARVD 80002 2026 C4
E Fall Ln
2900 DgsC 80126 2449 D1
S Fallbrooke Dr
- DgsC 80126 2449 E4
9500 DgsC 80126 2449 E4
9500 DgsC 80130 2450 A3
Fall Creek Dr
13600 BMFD 80020 1775 A5
Fallen Rock Rd
9100 JfnC 80433 2441 E4
9100 JfnC 80433 2442 A4
Faller Ranch Rd
13500 JfnC 80433 2611 D4
N Falling Leaf Cir
6200 DgsC 80134 2622 D2
Falling Star Pl
- CSRK 80104 2704 B5
Fallon Cir
- CSRK 80104 2705 B7
Fallow Deer Rd
10 DgsC 80116 2706 E7
10 DgsC 80116 2790 E1
Fall River Cir
1100 LGMT 80501 1356 E7
Falls Dr
3300 BMFD 80020 1775 E5
Falmouth St
10 CSRK 80104 2705 A7
Fantasy Pl
- CSRK 80109 2702 E4
Far Vw
3200 WldC 80504 1440 D2
Fara Wy
9400 JfnC 80433 2440 D4
Faraday St
1300 AdmC 80229 1945 A4
8600 TNTN 80229 1945 A4
Faraway Pl
10 DgsC 80104 2870 E5
10 DgsC 80104 2871 A5
Fareham Ct
500 CSRK 80104 2787 E2
N Fargo Tr
6800 DgsC 80125 2614 D1
W Farmdale Rd
3100 SRDN 80110 2279 E5
3100 SRDN 80110 2280 A5
Farmer Pl
- BGTN 80601 1697 C4
N Farmhouse Cir
41300 EbtC 80138 2541 A7
S Farmhouse Cir
41200 EbtC 80138 2541 A7
Farmhouse Wy
400 BGTN 80601 1697 B4
Farmingdale Ct
21700 PARK 80138 2454 B7
Farmingdale Wy
21700 PARK 80138 2454 B7
S Farnell Ln
5700 LITN 80123 2364 A2
Farrell Dr
10 GpnC 80403 1850 D2
S Farview Ln
6300 JfnC 80439 2357 D4
Fast Draw Ct
10 PrkC 80456 2606 D2
N Faver Dr
100 DgsC 80109 2786 C1
200 DgsC 80109 2702 C7
Fawn Cir
10200 DgsC 80116 2707 B7
Fawn Ct
13300 BMFD 80020 1775 E6
Fawn Dr
10 PrkC 80456 2606 C4
S Fawn Dr
27500 JfnC 80433 2525 E3
Fawn Ln
10 BldC 80481 1514 A3
Fawn Pth
2800 JfnC 80439 2356 B5
Fawn Rd
10 PrkC 80456 2607 D7
Fawn St
10 GOLD 80401 2108 B7
10 GOLD 80401 2192 B1
Fawn Tr
10 CCkC 80439 2355 E7
10 CCkC 80439 2356 A7
Fawnbrook Ct
10200 DgsC 80130 2450 A6
Fawnbrook Ln
10100 DgsC 80130 2450 A6
Fawn Meadows Tr
38000 EbtC 80107 2626 A6
Fawnwood Dr
8600 DgsC 80108 2534 E5
Fayette St
9000 FLHT 80260 1944 A2
Feather Ct
2800 CSRK 80109 2702 C4
Feather Grass Ct
8300 DgsC 80134 2452 E1
Feather Grass Rd
- BMFD 80020 1775 C1
Feather Reed Av
3300 LGMT 80503 1438 B6
Federal Av
- LKWD 80226 2194 A1
Federal Blvd
- BMFD 80020 1775 E1
- DNVR 80211 2028 A7
- WSTR 80030 1943 E5
- WSTR 80030 1944 A7
- WSTR 80031 1859 E3
10 DNVR 80219 2196 A1
300 DNVR 80204 2112 A7
Federal Blvd
300 DNVR 80219 2112 A7
1900 DNVR 80211 2112 A3
4800 DNVR 80221 2028 A7
5100 AdmC 80221 2028 A7
5700 AdmC 80221 2027 E3
6700 WSTR 80030 2027 E1
7000 AdmC 80221 1944 A7
7600 AdmC 80221 1943 E5
7600 WSTR 80031 1943 E5
8600 FLHT 80031 1943 E3
8600 FLHT 80260 1943 E3
9300 WSTR 80260 1943 E3
9700 FLHT 80031 1859 E7
9700 FLHT 80260 1859 E7
10200 WSTR 80234 1859 E7
Federal Blvd SR-88
10 DNVR 80219 2196 A1
300 DNVR 80204 2112 A7
300 DNVR 80219 2112 A7
1900 DNVR 80211 2112 A3
4100 DNVR 80211 2028 A7
Federal Blvd US-287
- DNVR 80211 2028 A7
- WSTR 80030 1944 A7
- WSTR 80031 1859 E3
1500 DNVR 80204 2112 A3
1900 DNVR 80211 2112 A3
5100 AdmC 80221 2028 A7
5100 DNVR 80221 2028 A7
6700 AdmC 80221 2027 E1
6700 WSTR 80030 2027 E1
7000 AdmC 80221 1944 A7
7000 WSTR 80030 1943 E7
7600 AdmC 80221 1943 E5
7800 WSTR 80031 1943 E5
8600 FLHT 80031 1943 E3
8600 FLHT 80260 1943 E3
9300 WSTR 80260 1943 E3
9700 FLHT 80031 1859 E7
9700 FLHT 80260 1859 E7
10200 WSTR 80234 1859 E7
N Federal Blvd
- WSTR 80031 1859 E2
- WSTR 80234 1859 E2
- WSTR 80234 1860 A1
S Federal Blvd
10 DNVR 80219 2196 A4
2600 DNVR 80219 2280 A3
2600 DNVR 80236 2280 A3
3200 DvrC 80236 2280 A3
3200 SRDN 80110 2280 A3
4400 EGLD 80110 2280 A6
4500 DNVR 80110 2280 A6
4800 DvrC 80110 2280 A6
5100 LITN 80123 2280 A6
5300 LITN 80123 2364 A1
S Federal Blvd SR-88
10 DNVR 80219 2196 A4
2600 DNVR 80219 2280 A3
2600 DNVR 80236 2280 A3
3200 DvrC 80236 2280 A3
3200 SRDN 80110 2280 A3
4400 EGLD 80110 2280 A6
4500 DNVR 80110 2280 A6
4800 DvrC 80110 2280 A6
5000 LITN 80123 2280 A6
Federal Cir
3200 BMFD 80020 1775 E6
S Federal Cir
- LITN 80123 2364 A1
5300 LITN 80123 2363 E1
Federal Ct
13300 BMFD 80020 1775 E5
N Federal Pkwy
- BMFD 80020 1776 A7
- BMFD 80234 1776 A7
- WSTR 80234 1776 A7
- WSTR 80234 1860 B1
Federal Pl
- LKWD 80226 2194 A1
12400 BMFD 80020 1775 D6
Feldspar Ct
10100 DgsC 80134 2452 E6
Feldspar Rd
10 GpnC 80403 1850 B7
S Fellet Ct
3300 LKWD 80227 2279 A3
W Fellet Ln
6800 LKWD 80227 2279 A3
Feltham Pl
1500 LGMT 80501 1355 E6
W Fendlebrush St
2000 DgsC 80129 2448 B4
Fendlebrush Wy
- DgsC 80129 2448 B5
Fenton Cir
7100 WSTR 80003 1943 B7
10900 WSTR 80020 1859 B5
Fenton Ct
4000 WTRG 80212 2027 B7
4000 WTRG 80212 2111 B1
7100 WSTR 80003 1943 A7
8000 ARVD 80003 1943 B5
9300 WSTR 80031 1943 B1
S Fenton Ct
2600 DNVR 80227 2279 B1
2600 LKWD 80227 2279 B1
6100 JfnC 80123 2363 B3
S Fenton Dr
2300 LKWD 80227 2195 B7
S Fenton Ln
2500 LKWD 80227 2195 B7
2500 LKWD 80227 2279 B1
Fenton St
10 LKWD 80226 2195 B1
1700 EDGW 80214 2111 B5
1700 LKWD 80214 2111 B5
3000 WTRG 80212 2111 B3
3200 WTRG 80214 2111 B2
4100 MNVW 80212 2027 B7
4100 WTRG 80212 2027 B7
4800 DvrC 80212 2027 B6
4800 LKSD 80212 2027 B6

STREET
Block City ZIP Map# Grid

Fenton St
4900 DNVR 80212 2027 B6
5400 JfnC 80002 2027 B4
6200 ARVD 80003 2027 B2
7500 WSTR 80003 1943 B6
8400 ARVD 80003 1943 B4
11700 WSTR 80020 1859 B3
14400 BldC 80020 1775 B3
14400 BMFD 80020 1775 B3
S Fenton St
10 LKWD 80226 2195 B1
1100 LKWD 80232 2195 B4
2100 DNVR 80227 2195 B7
2700 DNVR 80227 2279 B1
2700 LKWD 80227 2279 B1
3800 DNVR 80235 2279 B4
5500 DNVR 80123 2363 B1
7500 JfnC 80128 2363 B6
Fenton Wy
8200 ARVD 80003 1943 B4
S Fenton Wy
3700 DNVR 80235 2279 B3
Fenwick Cir
11500 LNTR 80134 2451 C5
Fenwick Dr
- DgsC 80134 2451 C5
- LNTR 80134 2451 C5
Fenwick St
10000 LNTR 80134 2451 E5
Fenwood Dr
4500 DgsC 80130 2449 D5
4600 DgsC 80130 2450 A5
Fenwood Pl
4500 DgsC 80130 2449 E5
4500 DgsC 80130 2450 A5
Ferguson Cir
100 LAFT 80026 1690 C6
Fern Av
4200 BMFD 80020 1859 D1
Fern Cir
1200 BMFD 80020 1774 C6
Fern Dr
2300 AdmC 80030 2028 B1
2300 AdmC 80221 2028 B1
2300 WSTR 80030 2028 B1
Fern Pl
3100 BLDR 80304 1602 D7
Fern St
1100 BMFD 80020 1774 C6
Fern Wy
8900 JfnC 80403 1938 D2
Fernando Rd
7600 AdmC 80221 1944 D6
Fern Gulch Dr
27600 JfnC 80439 2273 E6
Fern Gulch Rd
25900 JfnC 80439 2274 B7
Fern Lake Ct
300 LAFT 80026 1689 C4
Fernleaf Ct
3200 CSRK 80109 2702 E1
Ferns Rd
40100 EbtC 80107 2625 A3
Fernwood Cir
2700 BMFD 80020 1776 C7
Fernwood Ct
9300 DgsC 80126 2449 A3
Fernwood Pl
2600 BMFD 80020 1776 A7
2800 BMFD 80020 1775 E7
Ferrell Wy
- IDSP 80439 2102 B5
Ferris Wy
7600 BldC 80303 1688 D4
Fescue Dr
23300 JfnC 80401 2190 E4
S Fiddlers Green Cir
6300 AphC 80111 2366 E3
6300 GDVL 80111 2366 E3
6400 CTNL 80111 2366 E3
Field Cir
5300 ARVD 80002 2026 C5
8100 ARVD 80005 1942 C5
Field Ct
4600 BldC 80301 1604 C3
4800 JfnC 80002 2026 C6
4800 WTRG 80033 2026 C6
5400 ARVD 80002 2026 C4
8100 ARVD 80005 1942 C4
9500 WSTR 80021 1942 B1
N Field Ct
8700 WSTR 80005 1942 C3
S Field Ct
500 LKWD 80226 2194 C3
1300 LKWD 80232 2194 C5
2500 LKWD 80227 2278 C1
4300 JfnC 80123 2278 C5
4900 DNVR 80123 2278 C7
6200 JfnC 80123 2362 C3
7300 JfnC 80128 2362 C6
8800 JfnC 80128 2446 C2
Field Dr
3800 WTRG 80033 2026 C7
3800 WTRG 80033 2110 C1
Field Ln
9300 WSTR 80021 1942 C2
N Field Pl
8600 WSTR 80005 1942 C3
Field St
100 LKWD 80226 2194 C1
2000 LKWD 80215 2110 C4
3200 JfnC 80215 2110 C2
3200 WTRG 80033 2110 C2
4600 WTRG 80033 2026 C6
5400 ARVD 80002 2026 C4
5700 ARVD 80004 2026 C4
7300 ARVD 80005 1942 C7
8800 WSTR 80005 1942 C3
9100 WSTR 80021 1942 C2
S Field St
10 LKWD 80226 2194 C1
2100 LKWD 80227 2194 C7
3300 LKWD 80227 2278 C3
3500 JfnC 80235 2278 C3

S Field St
5100 DNVR 80123 2278 C7
5100 JfnC 80123 2278 C7
5300 JfnC 80123 2362 C1
6700 JfnC 80128 2362 C4
8500 JfnC 80128 2446 C2
Field Wy
8700 WSTR 80005 1942 C3
S Field Wy
- JfnC 80123 2278 C7
2100 LKWD 80227 2194 C7
4800 DNVR 80123 2278 C7
6300 JfnC 80123 2362 C3
9500 LITN 80127 2446 C4
Fieldcrest Ln
8900 BldC 80503 1355 B3
Fieldstone Pl
900 DgsC 80126 2449 A2
Fieldstone Tr
10 CHLV 80113 2281 B4
Fiesta Ter
8600 LNTR 80124 2451 A3
Fife Ct
3000 DNVR 80211 2112 A2
Fig Ct
5800 JfnC 80002 2025 A4
5800 JfnC 80004 2025 A4
6900 ARVD 80004 2025 A1
N Fig Ct
4700 JfnC 80403 2025 A6
S Fig Ct
2400 LKWD 80228 2277 A1
Fig St
700 JfnC 80401 2109 A7
700 LKWD 80401 2109 A7
5000 JfnC 80403 2025 A6
6400 ARVD 80004 2025 A2
8300 ARVD 80005 1941 A4
N Fig St
4400 JfnC 80403 2025 A7
7000 ARVD 80004 1941 A7
7000 ARVD 80004 2025 A1
S Fig St
2200 LKWD 80228 2193 A7
2400 LKWD 80228 2277 A1
Fig Wy
5600 JfnC 80002 2025 A4
5700 JfnC 80004 2025 A4
S Fig Wy
400 LKWD 80228 2193 A2
Figwood St
- DgsC 80125 2531 A7
E Filbert Av
3000 DgsC 80134 2452 B3
Filbert Ct
1500 DNVR 80220 2114 A5
S Filbert Ct
1700 DNVR 80222 2198 A6
6000 CTNL 80121 2366 A2
S Filbert Ln
6300 CTNL 80121 2366 A3
S Filbert Wy
1400 DNVR 80222 2198 A5
S Fillmore Av
100 LSVL 80027 1773 B1
Fillmore Cir
13000 TNTN 80241 1777 C7
S Fillmore Cir
7100 CTNL 80122 2365 D5
8100 CTNL 80122 2449 C1
Fillmore Ct
400 LSVL 80027 1773 B1
1800 LSVL 80027 1689 B6
9500 TNTN 80229 1945 C1
10700 NHGN 80233 1861 C5
11500 TNTN 80233 1861 C4
12300 TNTN 80241 1861 C1
12800 TNTN 80241 1777 C7
14600 AdmC 80602 1777 C2
S Fillmore Ct
4700 CHLV 80113 2281 C6
7900 CTNL 80122 2365 C7
Fillmore Pl
1400 LSVL 80027 1689 B6
11600 TNTN 80233 1861 C3
Fillmore St
- AdmC 80229 1945 C5
- TNTN 80602 1777 C2
100 DNVR 80206 2197 C1
1500 DNVR 80206 2113 C5
2600 DNVR 80205 2113 C3
4000 DNVR 80205 2029 C7
5100 DNVR 80216 2029 C5
6000 CMCY 80022 2029 C2
9600 TNTN 80229 1945 C1
10100 TNTN 80229 1861 C7
12400 TNTN 80241 1861 C1
13100 TNTN 80241 1777 C6
16400 AdmC 80602 1693 C5
S Fillmore St
1100 DNVR 80209 2197 C5
1100 DNVR 80210 2197 C5
2700 DNVR 80210 2281 C1
Fillmore Wy
11000 NHGN 80233 1861 C4
14800 TNTN 80602 1777 C2
S Fillmore Wy
900 DNVR 80209 2197 C4
1000 DNVR 80210 2197 C4
2900 DNVR 80210 2281 C1
7500 CTNL 80122 2365 C6
8100 CTNL 80122 2449 C1
Filmore Ct
13300 TNTN 80241 1777 C6
Finch
10 JfnC 80127 2360 E4
Finch Av
1200 BGTN 80601 1779 E1
N Finch Av
300 LAFT 80026 1690 D4
S Finch Av
100 LAFT 80026 1690 D5
Findlay Ln
3700 LGMT 80503 1355 A7

Findlay Wy
1400 BLDR 80305 1771 A1
W Finland Dr
9100 LITN 80127 2446 C5
Finn Av
900 DgsC 80124 2450 C7
900 DgsC 80124 2534 D1
Fir Av
5300 WldC 80516 1523 E7
S Fir Cir
4100 JfnC 80439 2273 C5
E Fir Ct
400 LSVL 80027 1773 C1
W Fir Ct
700 LSVL 80027 1773 A1
Fir Dr
- TNTN 80260 1944 B1
8900 TNTN 80229 1945 A2
29700 JfnC 80439 2273 B2
Fir Ln
10 BldC 80304 1602 A6
10 CCkC 80439 2272 A4
10 PrkC 80456 2690 E1
300 BMFD 80020 1859 A3
Fir St
9700 FLHT 80260 1860 A7
9700 FLHT 80260 1944 A1
9700 TNTN 80260 1860 A7
9700 TNTN 80260 1944 A1
N Fir St
- LGMT 80501 1439 B6
S Fir St
- LGMT 80501 1439 B6
W Fir Wy
500 LSVL 80027 1773 B1
Firebrick Dr
16500 PARK 80134 2537 A1
16700 PARK 80134 2536 D2
Firehouse Rd
10 AdmC 80601 1696 E6
10 BGTN 80601 1696 E6
Fire House St
41000 EbtC 80138 2540 B7
41000 EbtC 80138 2624 B1
S Firehouse Hill Rd
7600 JfnC 80465 2359 E7
Fire Opal Ct
2000 CSRK 80108 2620 A6
Fire Opal Ln
6600 CSRK 80108 2620 A6
Firerock Ct
6900 BldC 80301 1604 B3
S Fire Rock Dr
11300 PARK 80134 2536 E1
Fireside St
400 LSVL 80027 1689 C6
Firestone Cir
9800 LNTR 80124 2450 E5
Firestone Wy
2000 SUPE 80027 1773 B6
Firethorn
7200 DgsC 80125 2614 D1
Firethorn Ct
8400 BldC 80503 1521 A5
Firethorne Ct
29400 JfnC 80439 2273 C2
Fireweed Dr
27500 JfnC 80439 2273 E5
S Fireweed Rd
9800 DgsC 80129 2448 C5
Fireweed Tr
- BMFD 80020 1775 C2
Firth Ct
2700 DNVR 80211 2112 A3
Fischer Rd
10600 JfnC 80403 1852 E6
Fishbeck Ct
25800 JfnC 80433 2442 B4
Fisher Dr
3300 BLDR 80301 1687 A2
Fisher Wy
1900 NHGN 80233 1861 B3
Fish Hatchery Rd
- AdmC 80640 1946 A2
- CMCY 80640 1946 A2
Fisk Ct
1500 LGMT 80503 1355 C7
Fitzsimmons Rd
10 PrkC 80456 2521 D2
Fitzsimons Wy
13300 AURA 80011 2116 A3
Five Iron Dr
1800 CSRK 80104 2787 D2
Five Parks Dr
8600 ARVD 80005 1941 B4
Flagg Dr
12000 BldC 80026 1690 E5
12000 BldC 80026 1691 A5
12000 LAFT 80026 1690 E5
12400 ERIE 80026 1691 A5
Flagg St
- CLCY 80403 2017 D4
Flagler Ct
10600 PARK 80134 2453 A6
Flagler Dr
10700 PARK 80134 2453 B7
Flagstaff Dr
2300 LGMT 80501 1356 D4
Flagstaff Rd
- BLDR 80302 1686 C5
4000 BldC 80302 1686 A4
4500 BldC 80302 1685 E5
5100 BldC 80302 1769 B1
8600 BldC 80302 1768 E3
8600 BldC 80403 1768 E3
Flagstaff Wy
- DgsC 80126 2449 D7
Flagstaff Summit Rd
- BldC 80302 1685 D5
Flagstone Pl
600 SUPE 80027 1773 A7
Flagstone Wy
10100 DgsC 80134 2452 E5

S Flamingo Ct
600 DNVR 80246 2198 A3
6100 CTNL 80121 2366 A2
Flamingo Dr
- BldC 80301 1603 D7
700 LAFT 80026 1690 D5
S Flamingo Wy
1500 DNVR 80222 2198 A5
3000 DNVR 80222 2282 A1
W Flamingo Wy
9000 DgsC 80125 2531 B1
Flamingo Cove
800 LAFT 80026 1690 D6
Flanders Ct
- DNVR 80249 2033 D7
S Flanders Ct
2400 AURA 80013 2201 D7
4900 CTNL 80015 2285 D7
5600 AphC 80015 2369 D1
S Flanders Ln
5100 CTNL 80015 2285 D7
Flanders St
- AURA 80019 2033 D3
4200 DNVR 80249 2033 D7
E Flanders Ct
- AURA 80017 2201 D5
S Flanders St
- AURA 80013 2285 D5
- CTNL 80013 2285 D5
1400 AURA 80017 2201 D4
2000 AURA 80013 2201 D6
4500 CTNL 80015 2285 D5
7200 AphC 80016 2369 D6
7500 CTNL 80016 2369 D6
Flanders Wy
4500 DNVR 80249 2033 D5
S Flanders Wy
- AURA 80013 2201 D5
- AURA 80013 2285 D2
1600 AURA 80017 2201 D5
4600 CTNL 80015 2285 D5
Flannagan Ct
1300 ERIE 80516 1607 A2
Flatiron Blvd
400 BMFD 80021 1773 D7
E Flatiron Cir
100 BMFD 80021 1773 E7
W Flatiron Cir
10 BMFD 80021 1773 D7
S Flatiron Ct
1800 BLDR 80301 1687 E2
Flatiron Dr
11000 BldC 80026 1606 C5
11000 ERIE 80026 1606 C5
11600 ERIE 80516 1606 D5
Flatiron Pkwy
5500 BLDR 80301 1687 D1
Flatiron Rd
10600 DgsC 80124 2450 D7
10600 DgsC 80124 2534 D1
Flatiron Marketplace Dr
600 BMFD 80021 1773 E7
Flatirons Ct
800 LSVL 80027 1689 A7
S Flatrock Cir
1100 AURA 80018 2202 E4
Flatrock Ct
5300 JfnC 80465 2360 C1
S Flat Rock Ct
7100 AURA 80016 2370 E5
S Flatrock Ct
4700 AURA 80016 2286 E6
Flat Rock Dr
- AURA 80018 2118 E7
Flat Rock St
- AphC 80018 2118 E7
- AURA 80018 2118 E7
S Flat Rock St
10 AphC 80018 2202 E1
5100 AURA 80016 2286 E7
S Flatrock Tr
- AphC 80018 2202 E5
- AURA 80018 2202 E5
- AURA 80018 2203 A5
S Flat Rock Wy
5300 AURA 80016 2286 E7
S Flatrock Wy
4900 AURA 80016 2286 E6
Flat Top Tr
- JfnC 80127 2529 A4
Flax Dr
- DgsC 80118 2954 A1
Fleetwood Av
9100 BldC 80503 1355 C4
Fleming Dr
1500 LGMT 80501 1355 E4
Fleming Rd
28000 JfnC 80439 2441 D3
Fletcher Dr
- WldC 80516 1607 C3
1100 ERIE 80516 1607 C3
Flicker Av
400 LGMT 80501 1439 B5
Flicker Tr
4400 EbtC 80107 2793 D1
Flint Ct
1600 BMFD 80020 1774 E6
2700 SUPE 80027 1773 A7
Flint Ln
19600 JfnC 80465 2443 D1
Flint Pl
1400 LGMT 80501 1438 E5
Flint Wy
100 BMFD 80020 1858 E2
900 BMFD 80020 1774 E7
Flint Gulch
- BldC 80540 1352 C4
Flint Gulch Dr
10 BldC 80540 1352 B5
Flintlock Ct
16300 PARK 80134 2452 E7
Flintwood Rd
500 DgsC 80116 2707 C5
3100 DgsC 80134 2707 C2

Flintwood Rd CO-65
500 DgsC 80116 2707 C5
3100 DgsC 80134 2707 C2
N Flintwood Rd
3500 DgsC 80116 2707 C1
3500 DgsC 80134 2707 C1
5900 DgsC 80138 2623 C3
6400 DgsC 80134 2623 C1
7000 DgsC 80138 2539 C7
N Flintwood Rd CO-65
3500 DgsC 80116 2707 C1
3500 DgsC 80134 2623 C7
3500 DgsC 80134 2707 C1
5900 DgsC 80138 2623 C3
Flood Ct
- LYNS 80540 1352 D3
Flora Ct
4800 JfnC 80403 2025 A6
6900 ARVD 80004 2025 A1
S Flora Ct
2100 LKWD 80228 2193 A7
2400 LKWD 80228 2277 A1
E Flora Dr
18300 AURA 80013 2285 C2
Flora Ln
3000 JfnC 80401 2109 A2
30500 JfnC 80439 2357 A4
E Flora Pl
- AURA 80013 2286 A2
2300 DNVR 80210 2281 C2
2300 EGLD 80113 2281 C2
5600 DNVR 80222 2282 B2
15700 AURA 80013 2284 D2
17000 AURA 80013 2285 A2
W Flora Pl
6200 DNVR 80227 2279 A3
Flora St
- ARVD 80005 1941 A4
700 JfnC 80401 2109 A7
700 LKWD 80401 2109 A7
5000 JfnC 80403 2025 A6
N Flora St
4400 JfnC 80403 2025 A7
7100 ARVD 80004 1941 A7
S Flora St
2300 LKWD 80228 2193 A7
Flora Wy
- LKWD 80401 2109 A7
10 JfnC 80401 2193 A1
400 JfnC 80401 2109 A7
5800 JfnC 80004 2025 A3
S Flora Wy
10 JfnC 80401 2193 A2
Florado St
7700 AdmC 80221 1944 B5
Floral Dr
1900 BLDR 80304 1602 D7
Florence Ct
1500 LGMT 80503 1437 E6
E Florence Ct
300 DgsC 80126 2448 E5
S Florence Ct
1500 AURA 80247 2199 B5
3000 DNVR 80231 2283 B2
5300 GDVL 80111 2283 B7
5300 GDVL 80111 2367 B1
5900 AphC 80111 2367 B2
S Florence Dr
5000 AphC 80015 2283 B7
5000 AphC 80111 2283 B7
5000 GDVL 80111 2283 B7
S Florence Pl
9800 DgsC 80126 2448 E5
Florence Rd
31200 JfnC 80433 2524 E4
31200 JfnC 80433 2525 A4
Florence St
- DNVR 80238 2115 B3
- DvrC 80238 2115 B3
1500 AURA 80010 2115 B4
4400 DNVR 80238 2031 B6
11200 AdmC 80640 1863 B3
11200 CMCY 80640 1863 B3
15200 AdmC 80602 1695 B7
15200 AdmC 80602 1779 A1
S Florence St
600 DNVR 80247 2199 B3
1300 AURA 80247 2199 B4
3400 DNVR 80014 2283 B3
3400 DNVR 80231 2283 B3
5600 GDVL 80111 2367 B1
5800 AphC 80111 2367 B1
S Florence Wy
- DgsC 80126 2448 E7
1800 AURA 80247 2199 B6
6300 AphC 80111 2367 B3
Florentine Cir
3700 LGMT 80503 1438 A5
Florentine Ct
- LGMT 80503 1438 A6
Florentine Dr
3700 LGMT 80503 1438 A5
E Florida Av
- AURA 80018 2202 D4
10 DNVR 80210 2196 E5
10 DNVR 80223 2196 E5
600 DNVR 80210 2197 A5
3800 DNVR 80222 2197 E5
4700 DNVR 80222 2198 B5
5500 DNVR 80224 2198 B5
7300 AphC 80231 2198 E5
7300 DNVR 80231 2198 E5
8200 AphC 80247 2198 E5
8500 AphC 80247 2199 A5
10300 AURA 80012 2199 A5
10500 AURA 80247 2199 C5
13800 AURA 80012 2200 C5
14900 AURA 80017 2200 D5
17600 AURA 80017 2201 B4
24600 AURA 80018 2203 A4
36100 AphC 80137 2205 E4
36100 AphC 80137 2206 A4
W Florida Av
10 DNVR 80210 2196 D5

W Florida Av
200 DNVR 80223 2196 D5
2000 DNVR 80219 2196 B5
3100 DNVR 80219 2195 E5
5100 LKWD 80219 2195 B5
5100 LKWD 80232 2195 B5
9200 LKWD 80232 2194 B5
10700 JfnC 80232 2194 A5
10900 JfnC 80232 2193 E5
11500 LKWD 80228 2193 D5
E Florida Dr
12100 AURA 80012 2199 E5
12800 AURA 80012 2200 A5
17900 AURA 80017 2201 B5
39600 AphC 80102 2206 E4
W Florida Dr
7700 LKWD 80232 2194 D5
12400 LKWD 80228 2193 C5
E Florida Pl
9700 AURA 80247 2199 B5
14100 AURA 80012 2200 B5
15500 AURA 80017 2200 D5
17000 AURA 80017 2201 A5
23700 AURA 80018 2202 D5
W Florida Pl
9500 LKWD 80232 2194 B5
11400 JfnC 80232 2193 E5
13000 LKWD 80228 2193 C5
Flower Cir
5300 ARVD 80002 2026 C5
8100 ARVD 80005 1942 C5
S Flower Cir
1100 LKWD 80226 2194 C4
1100 LKWD 80232 2194 C4
Flower Ct
4800 JfnC 80002 2026 C6
4800 WTRG 80033 2026 C6
5400 ARVD 80002 2026 C4
8100 ARVD 80005 1942 B4
9300 WSTR 80021 1942 B2
10100 WSTR 80021 1858 B7
N Flower Ct
8700 WSTR 80005 1942 B3
S Flower Ct
1500 LKWD 80232 2194 C5
2100 LKWD 80227 2194 C7
3000 LKWD 80227 2278 C2
7000 JfnC 80128 2362 C5
8500 JfnC 80128 2446 B2
9700 LITN 80127 2446 C5
9800 JfnC 80127 2446 C5
Flower Ln
11600 JfnC 80403 1852 B3
N Flower Pl
8700 WSTR 80005 1942 B3
Flower St
10 LKWD 80226 2194 C1
800 LKWD 80215 2110 C6
3200 JfnC 80215 2110 C2
3200 WTRG 80033 2110 C2
4500 WTRG 80033 2026 C7
5500 ARVD 80002 2026 C4
6700 ARVD 80004 2026 C1
7900 ARVD 80005 1942 C5
9300 WSTR 80021 1942 C2
N Flower St
4600 WTRG 80033 2026 C6
S Flower St
10 LKWD 80226 2194 C1
1000 LKWD 80232 2194 C4
2100 LKWD 80227 2194 C7
3300 LKWD 80227 2278 C3
4500 DNVR 80123 2278 C6
5100 JfnC 80123 2278 C7
5900 JfnC 80123 2362 C2
7000 JfnC 80128 2362 C5
8500 JfnC 80128 2446 C2
S Flower Wy
2100 LKWD 80227 2194 C7
4800 DNVR 80123 2278 C7
6200 JfnC 80123 2362 C3
8300 JfnC 80128 2446 C1
9500 LITN 80127 2446 C5
Flowergate Wy
15300 DgsC 80134 2452 D6
Flowerhill Cir
15500 DgsC 80134 2452 D6
Flowerhill Ct
10400 DgsC 80134 2452 D6
Flowers Ct
- ERIE 80516 1607 A2
E Floyd Av
- DNVR 80224 2282 C2
10 EGLD 80110 2280 E2
10 EGLD 80113 2280 E2
2300 AphC 80113 2281 C2
2300 DNVR 80210 2281 C2
2300 DvrC 80210 2281 C2
2300 EGLD 80113 2281 C2
4100 DNVR 80222 2281 E2
6400 AphC 80222 2282 C2
6500 DNVR 80222 2282 C2
9000 DNVR 80231 2283 A2
14600 AURA 80014 2284 C2
15300 AURA 80013 2284 D2
19100 AURA 80013 2285 D2
W Floyd Av
10 EGLD 80110 2280 E2
10 EGLD 80113 2280 E2
2200 SRDN 80110 2280 B2
2700 DNVR 80236 2280 A2
2700 DvrC 80236 2280 A2
3600 DNVR 80236 2279 D2
6000 DNVR 80227 2279 B3
6800 LKWD 80227 2279 A2
7000 LKWD 80227 2278 E2
E Floyd Cir
- DNVR 80231 2283 A2
E Floyd Dr
2800 AphC 80113 2281 D2
2800 DNVR 80210 2281 D2
6300 AphC 80222 2282 B2
6300 DNVR 80222 2282 B2

W Floyd Dr
6700 LKWD 80227 2279 A3
8700 LKWD 80227 2278 C3
E Floyd Pl
- AURA 80013 2286 A2
2000 AphC 80113 2281 C2
2000 EGLD 80113 2281 C2
9000 DNVR 80231 2283 A2
W Floyd Pl
9300 LKWD 80227 2278 B3
Flycatcher Av
1300 BGTN 80601 1779 E1
Flying Jib Ct
500 LAFT 80026 1689 E5
Folklore Av
500 LGMT 80501 1356 D6
Folsom St
1200 BLDR 80302 1686 E2
2300 BLDR 80304 1686 E1
2400 BLDR 80304 1602 E7
E Folsom Point Ln
11000 DgsC 80116 2707 C5
Fonder Dr
6500 DgsC 80134 2621 D4
Fontaine St
9000 FLHT 80260 1944 A2
Fontana Ct
4700 DNVR 80239 2032 C5
Fontana Wy
4600 DNVR 80239 2032 C7
N Foote Av
100 LAFT 80026 1690 D4
S Foote Av
100 LAFT 80026 1690 D5
Foothill Cir
2500 JfnC 80401 2109 A4
S Foothill Dr
800 LKWD 80228 2193 B4
1000 JfnC 80401 2193 B4
Foothill Ln
14100 JfnC 80401 2109 A3
Foothill Rd
14000 JfnC 80401 2109 A3
17200 JfnC 80401 2108 B2
Foothill Wy
10700 PARK 80138 2454 A7
Foothill Ash
10 JfnC 80127 2445 A1
Foothills Ct
4800 CSRK 80109 2702 C2
Foothills Dr
4000 CSRK 80109 2702 C3
Foothills Dr N
24500 JfnC 80401 2190 C5
Foothills Dr S
1500 JfnC 80401 2190 C6
N Foothills Hwy
- BldC 80301 1602 C2
- BldC 80302 1602 C2
- BLDR 80302 1602 C1
- BLDR 80304 1602 C2
5700 BldC 80302 1518 C7
5700 BldC 80503 1518 C7
5700 BLDR 80302 1518 C7
8600 BldC 80302 1435 C6
8600 BldC 80503 1435 C6
9700 BldC 80540 1435 E2
10200 BldC 80503 1353 A5
10200 BldC 80503 1436 A1
N Foothills Hwy SR-7
- BldC 80301 1602 C2
- BldC 80302 1602 C2
- BLDR 80302 1602 C1
- BLDR 80304 1602 C2
5700 BldC 80302 1518 C7
5700 BldC 80503 1518 C7
5700 BLDR 80302 1518 C7
8600 BldC 80302 1435 C6
8600 BldC 80503 1435 C6
9700 BldC 80540 1435 E2
10200 BldC 80503 1353 A5
10200 BldC 80503 1436 A1
N Foothills Hwy US-36
- BldC 80301 1602 C2
- BldC 80302 1602 C2
- BLDR 80302 1602 C1
- BLDR 80304 1602 C2
5700 BldC 80302 1518 C7
5700 BldC 80503 1518 C7
5700 BLDR 80302 1518 C7
8600 BldC 80302 1435 C6
8600 BldC 80503 1435 C6
9700 BldC 80540 1435 E2
10200 BldC 80503 1353 A5
10200 BldC 80503 1436 A1
S Foothills Hwy
1000 BldC 80305 1771 C3
1000 BLDR 80305 1771 C3
1400 BldC 80303 1771 C3
2800 BldC 80303 1855 C1
2800 BldC 80403 1855 C1
S Foothills Hwy SR-93
1000 BldC 80305 1771 C3
1000 BLDR 80305 1771 C3
1400 BldC 80303 1771 C3
2800 BldC 80303 1855 C1
2800 BldC 80403 1855 C1
Foothills Pkwy
- BldC 80301 1603 B7
- BLDR 80301 1603 B7
- BLDR 80301 1687 B2
- BLDR 80303 1687 B3
Foothills Pkwy SR-157
- BldC 80301 1603 B7
- BLDR 80301 1603 B7
- BLDR 80301 1687 B2
- BLDR 80303 1687 B3
Foothills Rd
- ARVD 80007 1939 D6
- ARVD 80007 2023 E2
- ARVD 80403 1939 C2
- ARVD 80403 2023 E2
- GOLD 80401 2107 C3
- GOLD 80403 2023 C7

STREET
Block City ZIP Map# Grid

Foothills Rd
- GOLD 80403 2107 C3
- JfnC 80007 1939 C2
- JfnC 80007 2023 E2
- JfnC 80403 1939 C2
- JfnC 80403 2023 E2
- JfnC 80403 2107 C3
Foothills Rd SR-93
- ARVD 80007 1939 D6
- ARVD 80007 2023 E2
- ARVD 80403 1939 C2
- ARVD 80403 2023 E2
- GOLD 80401 2107 C3
- GOLD 80403 2023 C7
- GOLD 80403 2107 C3
- JfnC 80007 1939 C2
- JfnC 80007 2023 E2
- JfnC 80403 1939 C2
- JfnC 80403 2023 E2
- JfnC 80403 2107 C3
S Foothills Canyon Blvd
9600 DgsC 80129 2448 B5
W Foothills Canyon Ct
2500 DgsC 80129 2448 B4
Foothills Ranch Dr
- BldC 80503 1435 B5
2900 BldC 80302 1435 B5
Forbes Ct
400 LGMT 80501 1438 E4
400 LGMT 80501 1439 A3
4000 GDVL 80121 2365 E1
Forbes Pl
1200 LGMT 80501 1356 A7
E Ford Av
12100 AURA 80012 2199 E3
E Ford Cir
12000 AURA 80012 2199 E3
15400 AURA 80017 2200 D3
Ford Ct
1500 LSVL 80027 1689 A6
E Ford Dr
11900 AURA 80012 2199 E4
17300 AURA 80017 2201 A3
W Ford Dr
7900 LKWD 80226 2194 D4
11200 LKWD 80226 2193 E4
Ford Pl
1400 LSVL 80027 1689 A6
E Ford Pl
- AURA 80012 2200 D3
10100 DNVR 80247 2199 B3
10300 AURA 80247 2199 B3
15300 AURA 80017 2200 D3
18000 AURA 80017 2201 B3
W Ford Pl
2200 DNVR 80223 2196 B4
3000 DNVR 80219 2195 E4
3000 DNVR 80219 2196 A4
11300 LKWD 80226 2193 E4
Ford St
100 GOLD 80403 2107 D2
800 GOLD 80401 2107 E3
1900 GOLD 80401 2108 A4
N Ford St
800 GOLD 80403 2107 D1
1000 GOLD 80403 2023 D7
Fordham Cir
4600 BldC 80301 1604 E3
Fordham Ct
3400 BLDR 80305 1687 A6
Fordham St
600 BldC 80503 1438 C2
600 LGMT 80503 1438 C2
1100 LGMT 80503 1355 C7
S Fordham St
1200 LGMT 80503 1438 C5
1900 BldC 80503 1438 C5
Forest Av
- BldC 80304 1602 B7
300 BLDR 80304 1602 B7
11000 TNTN 80233 1862 A4
17200 JfnC 80465 2276 B5
17200 MRSN 80465 2276 B5
Forest Cir
5200 TNTN 80241 1777 E7
10900 TNTN 80233 1862 A5
E Forest Cir
- AdmC 80229 1862 A7
- TNTN 80229 1862 A7
S Forest Cir
4200 CHLV 80113 2282 A5
W Forest Cir
- AdmC 80229 1862 A7
- TNTN 80229 1862 A7
Forest Ct
9600 AdmC 80229 1946 A1
10100 TNTN 80229 1862 A6
11700 TNTN 80233 1862 A3
S Forest Ct
4200 CHLV 80113 2282 A5
6000 CTNL 80121 2366 A2
7000 CTNL 80122 2366 A5
8200 CTNL 80122 2450 A1
Forest Dr
- PrkC 80456 2522 B3
10 CCkC 80439 2187 C1
10 PrkC 80456 2521 E5
6000 CMCY 80022 2030 A2
11200 TNTN 80233 1862 A3
12400 TNTN 80241 1862 A1
12500 TNTN 80241 1778 A7
S Forest Dr
2300 AphC 80222 2198 A7
Forest Ln
31500 EbtC 80107 2792 D6
S Forest Ln
5500 GDVL 80121 2366 B1
7100 CTNL 80122 2366 A5
Forest Pkwy
1700 DNVR 80220 2114 A4
1900 DNVR 80207 2114 A4
Forest Rd
10 NDLD 80466 1765 D2
Forest St
10 DNVR 80220 2198 A1
10 DNVR 80246 2198 A1
2000 DNVR 80220 2114 A3
3300 DNVR 80207 2114 A1
3900 DNVR 80207 2030 A7
4600 DNVR 80022 2030 A6
5200 CMCY 80022 2030 A5
5200 DNVR 80216 2030 A5
6900 CMCY 80022 1946 A7
12500 TNTN 80241 1778 A7
12500 TNTN 80241 1862 A1
13100 TNTN 80241 1777 E6
13800 TNTN 80602 1778 A4
S Forest St
10 DNVR 80220 2198 A1
500 GNDL 80246 2198 A3
1100 DNVR 80246 2198 A4
1500 DNVR 80222 2198 A5
2700 DNVR 80222 2282 A1
3400 DNVR 80237 2282 A2
4600 CHLV 80113 2282 A6
5700 GDVL 80121 2366 A2
6400 CTNL 80121 2366 A3
6800 CTNL 80122 2366 A4
Forest Tr
36000 EbtC 80107 2709 E3
37300 EbtC 80107 2710 A1
S Forest Tr
4400 JfnC 80439 2273 E6
Forest Wy
2900 JfnC 80439 2273 B2
10900 TNTN 80233 1862 A4
12000 TNTN 80241 1862 A2
12800 TNTN 80241 1777 E7
S Forest Wy
- CTNL 80111 2366 A4
1300 DNVR 80222 2198 A4
1300 DNVR 80246 2198 A4
3700 CHLV 80113 2282 A3
3700 DNVR 80237 2282 A3
6400 CTNL 80121 2366 A4
6900 CTNL 80122 2366 A4
Forest Canyon
3400 WldC 80504 1440 D2
N Forest Canyon Rd
12300 DgsC 80138 2454 D4
Forest Cove Court
- PrkC 80470 2608 A1
Forest Cove Pkwy
- PrkC 80456 2607 E1
- PrkC 80456 2608 A1
- PrkC 80470 2607 E1
- PrkC 80470 2608 A1
Forest Estates Rd
35000 CCkC 80439 2356 A7
Forest Grove Rd
27200 JfnC 80439 2357 E4
S Foresthill Ct
7700 LITN 80120 2364 C6
Forest Hill Rd
10 GpnC 80403 1934 B6
S Forest Hill Rd
4400 JfnC 80439 2273 D6
Forest Hill St
27800 JfnC 80439 2273 E6
S Foresthill St
5300 EGLD 80120 2280 C7
5300 LITN 80120 2280 C7
5500 LITN 80120 2364 C1
Forest Hills Dr
22800 JfnC 80401 2191 A4
N Forest Hills Dr
11000 DgsC 80138 2455 B6
Forestland Dr
31400 JfnC 80439 2272 E3
Forest Park Cir
1300 LAFT 80026 1689 D2
Forest Park Dr
- DgsC 80108 2534 D7
- DgsC 80108 2618 C1
34000 EbtC 80107 2709 D7
Forest Ridge Cir
6900 DgsC 80108 2618 D1
7200 DgsC 80108 2534 D7
Forest Ridge Rd
10 PrkC 80470 2523 C7
Forest Service Rd
6500 JfnC 80439 2356 D5
Forest Star Dr
1700 GpnC 80403 1934 D1
Forest Trails Dr
1100 DgsC 80108 2534 C7
1200 DgsC 80108 2618 C1
Forest View Rd
5300 DgsC 80134 2622 D4
Forest View St
12400 BMFD 80020 1859 C1
12500 BMFD 80020 1775 C7
N Fork Ct
5400 BLDR 80301 1604 B1
N Fork Dr
1900 LAFT 80026 1690 A4
2000 LAFT 80026 1689 E4
S Fork Dr
1900 LAFT 80026 1690 A5
2000 LAFT 80026 1689 E4
W Fork Wy
- AphC 80102 2122 A6
700 AphC 80137 2122 A5
S Forrest Ct
8700 DgsC 80126 2449 D2
S Forrest Dr
8600 DgsC 80126 2449 D2
Forrest Ln
10 BldC 80302 1517 A7
S Forrest Ln
8500 DgsC 80126 2449 D2
E Forrest Pl
3200 DgsC 80126 2449 D2
S Forrest St
8500 DgsC 80126 2449 D1
S Forrest Wy
8600 DgsC 80126 2449 D2
Forsstrom Dr
- LNTR 80124 2451 A3
Forsyth Dr
10 LGMT 80501 1356 C6
Forsythe Pl
5000 BLDR 80303 1687 C3
Forsythe Rd
10 BldC 80466 1767 D1
200 BldC 80466 1683 D7
Forsythe Tr
10 BldC 80466 1767 D1
Forsythia Ct
2600 ERIE 80516 1692 A3
Forsythia Pl
2600 ERIE 80516 1692 A3
Forsythia St
- ERIE 80516 1692 A3
Fortune Ct
15700 AdmC 80603 1698 E6
Fortune Tr
- AURA 80010 2115 B5
Forum Dr
1200 LAFT 80026 1690 A6
Foster Ct
1500 LGMT 80501 1438 E6
Foster Dr
1600 LGMT 80501 1438 E6
Founders Pkwy
- CSRK 80104 2704 A2
- CSRK 80108 2704 A2
- DgsC 80104 2704 B4
10 CSRK 80108 2703 E2
5000 CSRK 80104 2703 E2
Foundry Pl
- BLDR 80301 1687 A1
S Fountain Cir
4600 JfnC 80127 2278 B6
Fountain Ct
1800 LGMT 80503 1438 B6
Fountain St
4800 BLDR 80304 1602 B3
Fountain Hill Ct
2900 AdmC 80137 2121 B2
S Fountain Hills St
11300 PARK 80138 2538 D1
Fountaintree Ln
10 BldC 80304 1601 E3
Four Bits St
10 PrkC 80456 2522 C5
Fourmile Canyon Dr
10 BldC 80302 1601 B7
10 BldC 80302 1685 C1
1900 BldC 80302 1600 E6
6400 BldC 80302 1599 D6
10600 BldC 80302 1598 B6
Four Rivers Rd
7100 BldC 80301 1604 C2
Foursome Dr
800 CSRK 80104 2787 E2
Fowler Dr
11200 NHGN 80233 1861 A3
Fowler Ln
10 BldC 80025 1770 C7
1700 BldC 80503 1355 A6
3700 LGMT 80503 1355 A6
Fox
- AdmC 80022 1946 C3
Fox Cir
6800 DgsC 80118 2952 D1
S Fox Cir
5600 LITN 80120 2364 D1
Fox Ct
300 BLDR 80303 1687 B5
7100 DgsC 80118 2952 D1
10300 NHGN 80260 1860 D6
Fox Dr
200 BLDR 80303 1687 B5
8800 TNTN 80260 1944 D3
Fox Ln
300 SUPE 80027 1772 D3
Fox Rd
10 GpnC 80403 1934 A6
Fox St
- AdmC 80102 2124 B2
10 DNVR 80223 2196 D1
300 DNVR 80223 2112 D7
400 LGMT 80501 1439 D2
1200 DNVR 80204 2112 D5
3100 DNVR 80202 2112 D2
3700 DNVR 80216 2112 D1
5000 AdmC 80216 2028 D5
5000 DNVR 80216 2028 D5
8200 AdmC 80221 1944 D4
8200 TNTN 80221 1944 D4
9600 NHGN 80260 1944 D1
9600 TNTN 80260 1944 D1
S Fox St
10 DNVR 80223 2196 D1
2900 EGLD 80110 2280 D2
5000 LITN 80120 2280 D7
5600 LITN 80120 2364 D1
E Fox Tr
3800 CTNL 80121 2365 E2
3800 GDVL 80121 2365 E2
S Fox Tr
7100 JfnC 80465 2359 C5
Fox Wy
6800 AdmC 80221 2028 D1
6800 DgsC 80118 2952 C1
6900 AdmC 80221 1944 D7
S Fox Wy
5800 LITN 80120 2364 D2
Foxberry Dr
4200 CSRK 80109 2702 E2
Foxborough Ct
5200 DgsC 80130 2450 A6
S Foxbury Dr
- AURA 80016 2370 D5
Fox Canyon Ln
1300 CSRK 80104 2703 E5
Fox Chase Ct
10300 DgsC 80129 2448 E6
Fox Chase Pl
10300 DgsC 80129 2448 D7
Fox Creek Tr
6700 DgsC 80116 2621 E7
6700 DgsC 80116 2622 A7
6700 DgsC 80116 2706 B1
Foxcroft Ln
10300 DgsC 80125 2614 E5
Fox Den Dr
9500 DgsC 80125 2531 A6
W Fox Farm Rd
10 DgsC 80118 2955 A7
10 LKSR 80118 2955 A7
Foxfield Dr
1700 CSRK 80104 2704 A4
W Fox Fire Ct
2200 DgsC 80129 2448 B3
S Fox Fire Dr
9100 DgsC 80129 2448 B3
S Fox Fire Ln
9200 DgsC 80129 2448 B3
W Fox Fire St
1900 DgsC 80129 2448 B3
S Fox Fire Wy
9100 DgsC 80129 2448 B3
Foxglove Ct
15300 DgsC 80134 2452 D7
Foxglove Dr
100 BGTN 80601 1697 B5
Foxglove Tr
- BMFD 80020 1775 B2
Fox Grove Dr
- JfnC 80439 2273 A5
Fox Haven Ct
18500 LCHB 80603 1698 D3
18500 WldC 80603 1698 D3
Foxhaven Ct
- BldC 80503 1521 A4
S Foxhill Cir
9700 DgsC 80129 2448 A5
Fox Hill Ct
700 BldC 80303 1688 B4
W Foxhill Ct
3400 DgsC 80129 2447 E4
3400 DgsC 80129 2448 A5
Fox Hill Dr
1000 LGMT 80501 1439 E2
8000 BldC 80501 1439 E2
E Foxhill Pl
8300 CTNL 80112 2366 E5
W Foxhill Pl
3100 DgsC 80129 2448 A5
Foxhill Rd
10 CHLV 80113 2281 D4
Fox Hills Rd
- JfnC 80465 2276 D7
5300 JfnC 80465 2360 D1
Fox Hollow Ct
13900 BMFD 80020 1775 B4
Fox Hollow Dr
5800 BMFD 80020 1775 A4
Fox Hollow Ln
800 GOLD 80401 2107 E6
Fox Hollow Ln S
- LKWD 80227 2277 E2
- LKWD 80228 2277 E2
Fox Hollow Pl
1300 CSRK 80104 2787 E5
Fox Hollow Rd
10 CCkC 80439 2271 E6
10 CCkC 80439 2272 A6
Fox Hunt Cir
400 DgsC 80126 2448 E2
400 DgsC 80126 2449 A2
Fox Hunt Ct
7200 BldC 80503 1521 B4
Fox Meadow Dr
5100 DgsC 80130 2450 A6
Foxmoor Ct
- JfnC 80465 2276 C7
- JfnC 80465 2360 C1
Fox Paw Tr
6900 DgsC 80125 2614 E1
Foxridge Cir
10100 DgsC 80126 2449 D6
Fox Ridge Ct
5800 BMFD 80020 1775 B4
Foxridge Ct
10000 DgsC 80126 2449 D6
Fox Ridge Dr
10 CCkC 80439 2188 A2
13800 BMFD 80020 1775 B4
Fox Ridge Rd
34300 CCkC 80439 2271 C4
Foxridge Tr
3400 DgsC 80126 2449 D6
Fox Run Cir
- NHGN 80233 1861 C5
Fox Run Ct
5700 DgsC 80134 2622 B3
Fox Run Dr
37000 EbtC 80107 2709 B2
Fox Run Pkwy
- TNTN 80229 1861 C4
- TNTN 80233 1861 C4
10900 NHGN 80233 1861 C4
Fox Sedge Ln
3000 DgsC 80126 2449 D7
Fox Sedge Pl
3000 DgsC 80126 2449 B7
3000 DgsC 80126 2533 D1
Fox Sedge Wy
10800 DgsC 80126 2449 D7
Fox Sparrow Rd
5100 DgsC 80134 2622 B4
Fox Tail Cir
100 GpnC 80403 1933 D7
Foxtail Cir
10 CHLV 80113 2281 C3
4500 GDVL 80121 2366 A1
Foxtail Ct
300 BLDR 80305 1686 D6
16700 JfnC 80465 2360 C1
Foxtail Dr
10 GpnC 80403 1933 E6
1300 BMFD 80020 1774 D7
N Foxtail Dr
4500 CSRK 80109 2702 E1
Foxtail Ln
11500 PARK 80138 2537 E2
Foxtail Pl
3500 LGMT 80503 1438 B6
Foxton Dr
17000 PARK 80134 2453 A7
17000 PARK 80134 2537 A1
S Foxton Rd
11200 JfnC 80433 2526 B2
12000 JfnC 80433 2527 A5
13500 JfnC 80433 2611 D2
Fox Trot Cir
39600 EbtC 80107 2626 A3
Foxwood Ct
10700 PARK 80138 2453 E7
Foxwood Dr
- EbtC 80107 2459 B1
Foxwood Ln
16600 JfnC 80465 2360 C1
Foxwood Pl
10200 EbtC 80107 2459 C4
Frailey Dr
3900 BldC 80026 1606 D5
Frala Ct
- AdmC 80601 1697 A5
- BGTN 80601 1697 A5
Frances Pl
8800 JfnC 80215 2110 C3
8800 LKWD 80215 2110 C3
Frances Steele Blvd
600 LCHB 80603 1698 C3
600 WldC 80603 1698 C3
Frances Steele Blvd CO-37
600 LCHB 80603 1698 C3
600 WldC 80603 1698 C3
Francis St
100 BldC 80501 1438 E1
300 LGMT 80501 1438 E1
1100 LGMT 80501 1355 E7
2400 BldC 80504 1355 E7
S Francis St
300 BldC 80501 1438 E4
1300 LGMT 80501 1438 E5
Francis Wy
1600 LGMT 80501 1355 E6
S Frank Rd
9000 LKSR 80118 2955 B5
Frank St
- AURA 80011 2117 C3
Frankfort Wy
4600 DNVR 80239 2032 C7
Frank Gardner Wy
6400 DgsC 80134 2621 D5
Frankie Ln
30200 JfnC 80439 2357 A1
N Franklin Av
2400 LSVL 80027 1689 C5
S Franklin Cir
10 GDVL 80121 2281 B7
5200 GDVL 80121 2365 B1
6800 CTNL 80122 2365 B4
Franklin Ct
16500 TNTN 80602 1693 A4
N Franklin Ct
1400 LSVL 80027 1689 B7
S Franklin Ct
5800 CTNL 80121 2365 B2
5800 GDVL 80121 2365 B2
7900 CTNL 80122 2365 B7
8100 CTNL 80122 2449 B1
Franklin Dr
- BLDR 80302 1686 E3
4700 BLDR 80301 1603 B7
8400 AdmC 80229 1945 A4
S Franklin Ln
5400 GDVL 80121 2365 B1
Franklin St
- CMCY 80216 2029 B4
10 BldC 80503 1520 D4
100 DNVR 80218 2197 B1
1200 DNVR 80218 2113 B5
2700 DNVR 80205 2113 B2
3900 DNVR 80205 2029 B7
5200 AdmC 80216 2029 B4
5200 DNVR 80216 2029 B4
6100 AdmC 80229 2029 B2
8000 AdmC 80229 1945 A4
8600 TNTN 80229 1945 A4
9800 TNTN 80229 1861 A7
11200 NHGN 80233 1861 A3
13500 TNTN 80241 1777 A5
13600 AdmC 80602 1777 A5
13600 TNTN 80602 1777 A5
E Franklin St
1200 TNTN 80229 1861 A7
S Franklin St
100 DNVR 80209 2197 B2
1000 DNVR 80210 2197 B5
2500 DNVR 80210 2281 B1
2700 DvrC 80210 2281 B2
2700 EGLD 80113 2281 B2
3500 CHLV 80113 2281 B3
5000 GDVL 80121 2281 B7
5200 GDVL 80121 2365 B1
5900 CTNL 80121 2365 B2
6600 CTNL 80122 2365 B5
Franklin Wy
10400 NHGN 80233 1861 B6
S Franklin Wy
7100 CTNL 80122 2365 B5
Franks Rd
10 JfnC 80470 2608 A1
Frary Ln
9700 JfnC 80465 2443 B4
S Fraser Cir
- AURA 80015 2284 C6
1000 AURA 80012 2200 C3
4100 AURA 80014 2284 C4
Fraser Ct
1700 AURA 80011 2116 C4
S Fraser Ct
100 AURA 80012 2200 D1
4100 AURA 80014 2284 C4
4600 AURA 80015 2284 D6
Fraser St
3200 AURA 80011 2116 C1
3800 AURA 80011 2032 C7
11600 CMCY 80603 1864 C2
N Fraser St
5100 DNVR 80239 2032 C5
S Fraser St
700 AURA 80012 2200 C3
2100 AURA 80014 2200 C6
4100 AURA 80014 2284 C4
5100 AURA 80015 2284 C7
5900 CTNL 80016 2368 D2
7200 CTNL 80112 2368 C5
Fraser Wy
2300 AURA 80011 2116 C3
5000 DNVR 80239 2032 C6
S Fraser Wy
- AURA 80017 2200 C3
800 AURA 80012 2200 C3
4100 AURA 80014 2284 C4
4500 AURA 80015 2284 C6
Frasier Fir Cir
47000 EbtC 80138 2455 E2
Fred Dr
9500 NHGN 80260 1944 D1
9500 TNTN 80260 1944 D1
Fred St
10 BldC 80302 1600 C6
S Freda Ct
33500 JfnC 80470 2524 C5
Freda Rd
33300 JfnC 80470 2524 C5
Frederick Cir
4000 LGMT 80503 1438 A6
Fredericks Ct
3800 BldC 80301 1603 A5
Freedom Wy
- CSRK 80109 2702 E5
Freeland Dr
10 IDSP 80452 2101 D6
Freeman Ct
2500 ERIE 80516 1690 D1
E Freemont Dr
24200 AURA 80016 2370 E5
E Freeport Dr
6300 DgsC 80130 2450 C3
Freeport Wy
4900 DNVR 80239 2032 C6
W Freiburg Dr
9700 LITN 80127 2446 B5
S Freiburg Pl
9000 LITN 80127 2446 C5
W Freiburg Pl
9300 LITN 80127 2446 B5
Fremont
- TNTN 80260 1944 C2
E Fremont Av
- FXFD 80016 2368 E5
600 CTNL 80122 2364 E5
4200 CTNL 80122 2365 E5
4600 CTNL 80122 2366 A5
7100 CTNL 80112 2366 D5
13500 AphC 80112 2368 B5
13500 CTNL 80112 2368 B5
16300 AphC 80016 2368 E5
16900 FXFD 80016 2369 A5
W Fremont Av
10 LITN 80120 2364 D5
10 LITN 80122 2364 D5
5000 AphC 80128 2363 C5
8700 JfnC 80128 2362 E5
10200 JfnC 80127 2362 B5
11100 JfnC 80127 2361 E5
E Fremont Cir
4800 CTNL 80122 2366 A5
8200 CTNL 80112 2366 E5
8700 CTNL 80112 2367 A5
E Fremont Cir N
1000 CTNL 80122 2365 A5
E Fremont Cir S
1000 CTNL 80122 2365 A5
Fremont Ct
1200 LGMT 80501 1356 E7
7200 DgsC 80118 2954 D1
E Fremont Ct
2400 CTNL 80122 2365 C5
8300 CTNL 80112 2366 E5
W Fremont Ct
800 LITN 80120 2364 D5
4700 LITN 80128 2363 C6
Fremont Dr
1000 DgsC 80118 2954 D1
10700 PARK 80134 2452 E7
E Fremont Dr
2900 CTNL 80122 2365 D5
7300 CTNL 80112 2366 D5
14400 CTNL 80112 2368 D5
W Fremont Dr
400 LITN 80120 2364 D6
5000 AphC 80128 2363 C5
7200 JfnC 80128 2362 E5
11400 JfnC 80127 2361 E5
Fremont Pl
- AURA 80016 2371 B5
7200 DgsC 80118 2954 D2
E Fremont Pl
2600 CTNL 80122 2365 C5
4600 CTNL 80122 2366 A5
7200 CTNL 80112 2366 D5
13200 CTNL 80112 2368 A5
18100 FXFD 80016 2369 B5
18700 CTNL 80016 2369 C5
21300 CTNL 80016 2370 A5
22600 AURA 80016 2370 C5
W Fremont Pl
10 CTNL 80122 2364 E5
10 LITN 80120 2364 E5
10 LITN 80122 2364 E5
5300 JfnC 80128 2363 C5
6800 JfnC 80128 2362 E5
10300 JfnC 80127 2362 A5
11100 JfnC 80127 2361 E5
Fremont St
2400 BLDR 80304 1602 E7
French Ct
1500 ERIE 80516 1607 A6
French Creek Av
18200 PARK 80134 2537 C4
Fresno Ct
1300 BMFD 80020 1774 E6
Friar Tuck Ct
1500 LAFT 80026 1690 D6
W Friend Av
8800 JfnC 80128 2362 C7
W Friend Dr
7700 JfnC 80128 2362 D7
Friend Pl
- AURA 80016 2371 C7
W Friend Pl
6800 JfnC 80128 2363 A7
7700 JfnC 80128 2362 D7
Friendly Rd
- EbtC 80107 2626 C6
Friends Pl
5500 BLDR 80303 1687 D4
Fringe Ct
1800 CSRK 80109 2703 B5
Fringed Sage Wy
17800 PARK 80134 2453 B2
S Frink Rd
9000 LKSR 80118 2955 B5
S Frog Hollow Ln
7000 JfnC 80439 2357 C6
Front St
100 LSVL 80027 1773 D1
500 LSVL 80027 1689 D7
2300 CSRK 80104 2703 D5
2600 CSRK 80109 2703 D5
4700 CSRK 80108 2703 C1
E Front St N
32500 AdmC 80137 2120 E3
32500 AdmC 80137 2121 A3
E Front St S
32500 AdmC 80137 2120 E4
32500 AdmC 80137 2121 A4
N Front St
- AdmC 80137 2120 E4
S Front St
- AdmC 80137 2120 E4
Frontage Rd
- AdmC 80601 1698 A5
- AdmC 80603 1697 E7
- BGTN 80601 1698 A5
- BGTN 80601 1781 D1
- BGTN 80603 1697 E7
- BGTN 80603 1698 A5
- BldC 80303 1688 D4
- DgsC 80108 2535 C6
- DNVR 80237 2282 E5
- DNVR 80237 2283 A5
- JfnC 80439 2273 C5
- WldC 80642 1698 D2
600 LGMT 80501 1438 E4
700 LCHB 80603 1698 A5
700 WldC 80603 1698 D2
3100 EGLD 80110 2280 C3
3200 SRDN 80110 2280 C3
5200 ARVD 80002 2027 B4
5200 JfnC 80002 2027 B4
E Frontage Rd
- DgsC 80118 2870 E7
10 CSRK 80104 2787 C3
10 DgsC 80104 2787 B5
3200 DgsC 80104 2871 A1
4100 DgsC 80104 2870 E5
6800 DgsC 80104 2954 E1
6800 DgsC 80104 2955 A1
W Frontage Rd
- AdmC 80601 1697 E7
- AdmC 80601 1698 A6
- AdmC 80603 1698 A6
- BGTN 80601 1697 E7
- BGTN 80601 1698 A6
- BGTN 80603 1697 E7
- BGTN 80603 1698 A6
10 CSRK 80104 2787 C3
500 CSRK 80109 2787 C3
500 DgsC 80104 2787 C3
2800 DgsC 80104 2871 A1
4100 DgsC 80104 2870 E4
Fronterra Dr
- CMCY 80022 1864 D7
Frontier Av
2500 BLDR 80301 1687 B1
3100 BMFD 80020 1775 E6
Frontier Cir
7600 JfnC 80465 2359 C6
Frontier Dr
1100 LGMT 80501 1355 D7
1100 LGMT 80501 1438 D1
Frontier Ln
10 BldC 80466 1767 B1
2100 DgsC 80116 2707 B3
Frontier Pl
10 LGMT 80501 1355 D7
500 LCHB 80603 1698 B3
E Frontier Pl
8700 DNVR 80237 2282 E6
8700 DNVR 80237 2283 A6
Frontier Rd
- EbtC 80138 2624 D1
41000 EbtC 80138 2540 C7
Frontier St
2100 LGMT 80501 1355 D5
4400 BWMR 80123 2279 C7
4400 LITN 80123 2279 C7
Front Neck Mine Rd
- GpnC 80403 2017 C7
- GpnC 80403 2101 C1
Front Range Av
- BLDR 80304 1602 B3
Front Range Dr
900 BLDR 80304 1602 C3

STREET Block City ZIP Map# Grid

Front Range Dr
1400 BMFD 80020 1776 A6
Front Range Pkwy
- AURA 80137 2038 A5
5000 AdmC 80137 2038 A5
Front Range Rd
- BldC 80302 1435 B7
- BldC 80302 1518 B1
800 LITN 80120 2364 B5
Front View Cres
2600 DNVR 80211 2112 A4
W Frost Av
6600 JfnC 80128 2363 A5
8600 JfnC 80128 2362 C5
11000 JfnC 80127 2361 E5
Frost Cir
- AURA 80016 2371 B5
E Frost Dr
24300 AURA 80016 2370 E5
24500 AURA 80016 2371 A5
W Frost Dr
5700 JfnC 80128 2363 B6
7100 JfnC 80128 2362 E5
Frost Pl
- AURA 80016 2371 B5
E Frost Pl
- AURA 80016 2371 B5
22700 AURA 80016 2370 C5
W Frost Pl
6800 JfnC 80128 2363 A5
9700 JfnC 80128 2362 B5
10300 JfnC 80127 2362 A5
11400 JfnC 80127 2361 E6
Frost Wy
31300 JfnC 80439 2273 A3
Frost Fire Cir
500 DgsC 80104 2871 B1
Frying Pan Rd
6800 BldC 80301 1604 B2
Fuller Ct
3900 BLDR 80305 1687 B6
Fullerton Cir
5500 DgsC 80124 2450 C7
5500 DgsC 80124 2534 B1
Fullerton Ct
4500 DNVR 80239 2032 C7
Fullerton Ln
5200 DgsC 80124 2534 A1
Fulton Av
- AdmC 80601 1780 B1
- BGTN 80601 1780 B1
600 BGTN 80601 1696 B7
Fulton Cir
3000 BLDR 80301 1603 B7
S Fulton Cir
2100 AURA 80247 2199 B6
S Fulton Ct
3000 DNVR 80231 2283 B2
5300 GDVL 80111 2283 B7
5300 GDVL 80111 2367 B1
Fulton Dr
500 BGTN 80601 1696 B7
Fulton St
- DNVR 80238 2115 B3
- DvrC 80238 2115 B3
100 AURA 80010 2199 B1
100 AURA 80230 2199 B1
100 DNVR 80010 2199 B1
100 DNVR 80230 2199 B1
1700 AURA 80010 2115 B4
10600 AdmC 80640 1863 B5
15200 AdmC 80602 1695 B7
15200 AdmC 80602 1779 B1
S Fulton St
900 AURA 80247 2199 B4
900 DNVR 80247 2199 B4
900 DvrC 80247 2199 B4
4900 AphC 80015 2283 B7
4900 AphC 80111 2283 B7
4900 GDVL 80111 2283 B7
5900 AphC 80111 2367 B2
5900 GDVL 80111 2367 B2
6900 CTNL 80112 2367 B5
6900 GDVL 80112 2367 B5
7300 AphC 80112 2367 B6
S Fulton Wy
1300 AURA 80247 2199 B4
5600 GDVL 80111 2367 B1
S Fultondale Cir
1100 AURA 80018 2202 E4
6900 AURA 80016 2370 E4
Fultondale Ct
- AphC 80016 2370 E4
- AURA 80016 2370 E4
S Fultondale Ct
1100 AURA 80018 2202 E4
5100 AURA 80016 2286 E7
7200 AURA 80016 2370 E5
S Fultondale Wy
4700 AURA 80016 2286 E6
S Fundy Cir
2400 AURA 80013 2201 D7
3900 AURA 80013 2285 D4
5400 CTNL 80015 2285 D7
5400 CTNL 80015 2369 D1
S Fundy Ct
2000 AURA 80013 2201 D6
2900 AURA 80013 2285 D1
5400 CTNL 80015 2285 D7
6100 AphC 80016 2369 D2
6600 CTNL 80016 2369 D3
Fundy St
4900 DNVR 80249 2033 D5
S Fundy St
1600 AURA 80017 2201 D5
2800 AURA 80013 2285 D1
4300 CTNL 80015 2285 D5
Fundy Wy
1600 AURA 80011 2117 D4
S Fundy Wy
1800 AURA 80017 2201 D5
2200 AURA 80013 2201 D7
3600 AURA 80013 2285 D3
6100 AphC 80016 2369 D2

Furlong Ct
10900 PARK 80138 2538 B1
Furman Wy
600 BLDR 80305 1686 E7
Furrow Wy
700 BldC 80026 1690 A3
700 LAFT 80026 1690 A3
S Futondale Wy
5300 AURA 80016 2286 E7

G

G St
- AURA 80011 2116 C4
400 CLCY 80403 2017 C4
700 GOLD 80401 2108 A7
Gadsden Ct
15200 AdmC 80603 1699 E7
Gadsden Dr
15200 AdmC 80603 1699 E6
29300 AdmC 80603 1700 A7
Gail Ct
9300 TNTN 80229 1945 B1
Gail Ln
10 PrkC 80456 2606 D7
Gaillardia Ln
200 BLDR 80302 1686 C5
Gaines Mill Ct
19700 PARK 80134 2537 D3
Galactic Pl
- CSRK 80108 2619 E5
Galapago Ct
11700 NHGN 80234 1860 C2
Galapago St
10 DNVR 80223 2196 D1
300 DNVR 80223 2112 D7
1300 DNVR 80204 2112 D5
2900 DNVR 80202 2112 D2
3700 DNVR 80216 2112 D1
6800 AdmC 80221 2028 D1
7000 AdmC 80221 1944 D7
S Galapago St
10 DNVR 80223 2196 D1
2900 EGLD 80110 2280 D2
5000 LITN 80120 2280 D6
Galapagos Pl
1400 BldC 80504 1357 A4
1400 LGMT 80501 1356 E4
1400 LGMT 80501 1357 A4
Galatia Ct
- BldC 80503 1437 A3
10300 BldC 80503 1436 D3
Galatia Rd
5600 BldC 80503 1436 D3
6200 BldC 80503 1437 A3
Galaxy Cir
- CSRK 80108 2619 D6
500 TNTN 80260 1944 D3
Galaxy Ct
- CSRK 80108 2619 D6
Galaxy Dr
- CSRK 80108 2619 D5
Galaxy Wy
- CSRK 80108 2619 D6
Gale Av
1000 BldC 80303 1688 A4
Gale Blvd
800 TNTN 80260 1944 C2
Gale Dr
6100 BldC 80303 1688 A3
Galen Ct
8600 AdmC 80229 1945 B3
8600 TNTN 80229 1945 B3
E Galena Av
5100 CSRK 80104 2704 D7
5100 CSRK 80104 2788 D1
Galena Ct
14500 AdmC 80602 1779 B2
S Galena Ct
3200 DNVR 80231 2283 B2
6200 AphC 80111 2367 B3
Galena St
- DNVR 80238 2115 B4
- DvrC 80238 2115 B4
1400 AURA 80010 2115 B5
15400 AdmC 80602 1695 B7
S Galena St
- DNVR 80247 2199 B4
- DvrC 80247 2199 B4
900 AURA 80247 2199 B3
3400 DNVR 80014 2283 B2
3400 DNVR 80231 2283 B2
5500 GDVL 80111 2367 B1
6700 CTNL 80112 2367 B4
Galena Wy
3000 BLDR 80305 1771 A2
S Galena Wy
- DNVR 80230 2199 B2
300 AURA 80010 2199 B2
300 DNVR 80010 2199 B2
300 DNVR 80247 2199 B2
500 AURA 80012 2199 B2
1400 AURA 80247 2199 B4
6100 AphC 80111 2367 B3
S Galena Peak
7600 JfnC 80127 2362 A6
Galileo Ln
3100 BLDR 80301 1603 B7
Gallagher Ct
200 ERIE 80516 1607 C2
Gallahadion Ct
11200 PARK 80138 2538 B1
Gallahadion Ln
11200 PARK 80138 2538 B1
Gallatin
3400 WldC 80504 1440 E2
Gallatin Pl
5000 BLDR 80303 1687 C3
Gallee Ln
1400 BldC 80504 1357 A5
1400 LGMT 80501 1357 A5
Gallery Ln
31600 JfnC 80439 2188 E7

Galley Ct
4400 BldC 80301 1604 B4
S Gallup Ct
6300 LITN 80120 2364 C3
S Gallup Pl
6300 LITN 80120 2364 C3
S Gallup St
5700 LITN 80120 2364 C2
S Gallup Wy
7400 LITN 80120 2364 C5
Galt Wy
- LAFT 80026 1689 D2
Galway Ct
- BMFD 80020 1775 E4
Galway Rd
9100 BldC 80303 1689 C3
Gambel Oaks Dr
1200 EbtC 80107 2624 C7
Gambel Oaks Pl
- EbtC 80107 2624 B6
Gambel Ridge Dr N
- CSRK 80109 2786 E6
- CSRK 80109 2787 A5
Gamble Gulch Rd
1700 GpnC 80403 1849 B7
1700 GpnC 80403 1933 B1
3500 GpnC 80474 1849 D4
Gamble Oak Ct
8400 PARK 80134 2452 E1
Gamow Ln
3100 BLDR 80301 1603 B7
Gandhi Dr
5300 BLDR 80303 1687 C2
Gap Rd
- GpnC 80403 1850 C7
300 GpnC 80403 1934 E1
2000 GpnC 80403 1935 A1
4400 GpnC 80403 1936 A2
W Gap Rd
- GpnC 80403 1936 A1
33300 JfnC 80403 1852 C6
S Gar Wy
4500 DNVR 80123 2278 C6
Garcia Av
- BGTN 80601 1697 B5
E Garden Av
3000 GDVL 80121 2365 D1
Garden Cir
1300 LGMT 80501 1356 A6
14300 JfnC 80401 2109 A3
Garden Ct
6900 CMCY 80022 1946 C6
S Garden Ct
9400 DgsC 80126 2449 A4
Garden Ctr
10 BMFD 80020 1858 D1
E Garden Dr
- AphC 80016 2370 D1
- AURA 80016 2370 D1
800 DgsC 80126 2449 A4
18900 AphC 80015 2369 C1
19600 CTNL 80015 2369 D1
Garden Ln
2800 GDVL 80121 2365 C1
6900 CMCY 80022 1946 C6
S Garden Ln
4600 EGLD 80110 2280 C6
Garden Pl
1300 LGMT 80501 1356 A6
E Garden Pl
18500 AphC 80015 2285 C7
18500 AphC 80015 2369 C1
19800 CTNL 80015 2369 D1
Garden Rd
2700 JfnC 80401 2109 A3
Garden St
300 GOLD 80403 2107 D2
Garden Glen Ct
400 GOLD 80403 2107 D2
Gardenia Ct
200 JfnC 80401 2193 A1
600 LKWD 80401 2109 A7
6900 ARVD 80004 2025 A1
Gardenia St
600 LKWD 80401 2109 A7
3000 JfnC 80401 2109 A2
4400 JfnC 80403 2025 A7
6300 ARVD 80004 2025 A2
6300 JfnC 80004 2025 A2
N Gardenia St
7100 ARVD 80004 1941 A7
S Gardenia St
500 LKWD 80228 2193 A3
Gardenia Wy
3000 SUPE 80027 1857 B1
Gardenwall Wy
1900 LGMT 80501 1356 D6
Gardner Ct
10 LGMT 80501 1356 C6
Gardner Dr
10 LGMT 80501 1356 C6
Gardner St
400 CSRK 80104 2705 A7
400 CSRK 80104 2789 A1
26600 JfnC 80433 2442 A5
Garfield Av
600 LSVL 80027 1689 C7
Garfield Cir
8300 AdmC 80229 1945 D4
10100 TNTN 80229 1861 D6
11800 TNTN 80233 1861 D2
12800 TNTN 80241 1777 D7
S Garfield Cir
2600 DNVR 80210 2281 D2
Garfield Ct
1400 LSVL 80027 1689 C6
8500 AdmC 80229 1945 D3
9900 TNTN 80229 1861 D7
13400 TNTN 80241 1777 D6
S Garfield Ct
6500 CTNL 80121 2365 D4
7300 CTNL 80122 2365 D5
Garfield Dr
13000 TNTN 80241 1777 D6

Garfield Dr
13900 TNTN 80602 1777 D4
S Garfield Dr
6100 CTNL 80121 2365 D3
S Garfield Ln
34000 JfnC 80470 2608 B5
Garfield Pkwy
13200 TNTN 80241 1777 D6
Garfield Pl
12200 TNTN 80241 1861 D1
13200 TNTN 80241 1777 D6
13800 TNTN 80602 1777 D4
Garfield St
10 DNVR 80206 2197 D1
10 DNVR 80209 2197 D1
300 DNVR 80206 2113 D7
3500 DNVR 80205 2113 D1
5300 DNVR 80216 2029 D4
9200 TNTN 80229 1945 D2
10100 TNTN 80229 1861 D7
11800 TNTN 80233 1861 D2
13400 TNTN 80241 1777 D5
13900 TNTN 80602 1777 D4
14400 AdmC 80602 1777 D3
S Garfield St
10 DNVR 80206 2197 D2
10 DNVR 80209 2197 D2
1000 DNVR 80210 2197 D5
2700 DNVR 80210 2281 D1
7200 CTNL 80122 2365 D5
Garfield Wy
8400 AdmC 80229 1945 D4
9300 TNTN 80229 1945 D1
11500 TNTN 80233 1861 D3
13500 TNTN 80241 1777 D5
S Garfield Wy
2600 DNVR 80210 2281 D2
6500 CTNL 80121 2365 E4
7900 CTNL 80122 2365 D7
8100 CTNL 80122 2449 C1
S Garland Cir
8300 JfnC 80128 2446 B2
Garland Ct
6700 ARVD 80004 2026 B1
8400 ARVD 80005 1942 B4
9500 WSTR 80021 1942 B1
9800 WSTR 80021 1858 B7
S Garland Ct
1300 LKWD 80232 2194 C5
1900 LKWD 80227 2194 C6
2900 LKWD 80227 2278 C2
6100 JfnC 80123 2362 C3
7200 JfnC 80128 2362 C5
8700 JfnC 80128 2446 C2
9700 LITN 80127 2446 C5
Garland Dr
10 NHGN 80233 1860 E5
700 NHGN 80233 1861 A5
8100 ARVD 80005 1942 B5
9800 WSTR 80021 1858 B7
Garland Ln
1700 BLDR 80304 1602 D7
9900 WSTR 80021 1858 C6
Garland Pl
9900 WSTR 80021 1858 B7
Garland St
100 ELIZ 80107 2709 B7
100 ELIZ 80107 2793 B2
300 LKWD 80226 2194 C1
400 LKWD 80226 2110 B7
800 LKWD 80215 2110 B7
2000 JfnC 80215 2110 B4
3200 WTRG 80215 2110 C2
3800 WTRG 80033 2110 C1
4500 WTRG 80033 2026 B7
5500 ARVD 80002 2026 B4
5900 ARVD 80004 2026 B3
7400 ARVD 80005 1942 B6
9200 WSTR 80021 1942 B2
N Garland St
10000 WSTR 80021 1858 B7
S Garland St
10 LKWD 80226 2194 B2
1600 LKWD 80232 2194 C6
2300 LKWD 80227 2194 C7
2500 LKWD 80227 2278 C1
4700 DNVR 80123 2278 C6
5000 JfnC 80123 2278 C7
6100 JfnC 80123 2362 C3
7500 JfnC 80128 2362 C6
8000 JfnC 80128 2446 C1
Garland Wy
10400 WSTR 80021 1858 B6
S Garland Wy
900 LKWD 80226 2194 C4
900 LKWD 80232 2194 C4
1900 LKWD 80227 2194 B6
3100 LKWD 80227 2278 C2
4300 JfnC 80123 2278 C5
4500 DNVR 80123 2278 B6
5600 JfnC 80123 2362 B2
8100 JfnC 80128 2446 C1
E Garnet Ct
3900 DgsC 80126 2449 E2
Garnet Ln
4000 BldC 80304 1602 D5
4400 BLDR 80304 1602 D5
E Garnet Ln
3800 DgsC 80126 2449 E3
E Garnet Pl
3900 DgsC 80126 2449 E3
Garnet St
100 BMFD 80020 1858 E1
1600 BMFD 80020 1774 D6
S Garnet St
9000 DgsC 80126 2449 D3
E Garnet Wy
3800 DgsC 80126 2449 E3
Garrison Cir
7800 ARVD 80005 1942 B5
Garrison Ct
7400 ARVD 80005 1942 B7
9400 WSTR 80021 1942 B2
10200 WSTR 80021 1858 B7

S Garrison Ct
2300 LKWD 80227 2194 C7
6400 JfnC 80123 2362 C3
7200 JfnC 80128 2362 C5
Garrison Dr
9200 WSTR 80021 1942 C2
Garrison Ln
9700 WSTR 80021 1942 B1
Garrison St
10 LKWD 80226 2194 C1
400 LKWD 80226 2110 C7
2000 LKWD 80215 2110 C4
3200 JfnC 80215 2110 C2
3800 WTRG 80033 2110 C1
4400 WTRG 80033 2026 C7
4800 JfnC 80002 2026 C7
4900 ARVD 80033 2026 C7
4900 WTRG 80002 2026 C4
5700 ARVD 80002 2026 C4
5700 ARVD 80004 2026 C4
6800 ARVD 80004 1942 C7
9000 WSTR 80021 1942 B2
10400 WSTR 80021 1858 B5
N Garrison St
8400 ARVD 80005 1942 B3
8400 WSTR 80005 1942 B3
8600 ARVD 80021 1942 B3
8600 WSTR 80021 1942 B3
10000 WSTR 80021 1858 B7
S Garrison St
- JfnC 80123 2278 C6
10 LKWD 80226 2194 C2
1000 LKWD 80232 2194 C3
1800 LKWD 80227 2194 C6
3100 LKWD 80227 2278 C2
3500 JfnC 80235 2278 C3
3500 LKWD 80235 2278 C3
4900 DNVR 80123 2278 C7
6100 JfnC 80123 2362 C3
6900 JfnC 80128 2362 C4
8100 JfnC 80128 2446 C1
Garrison Wy
9800 WSTR 80021 1858 B7
S Garrison Wy
2900 LKWD 80227 2278 C2
7900 DNVR 80123 2278 C6
7900 JfnC 80128 2362 C7
8100 JfnC 80128 2446 C1
S Gartner Rd
7500 JfnC 80439 2358 C6
N Gartrell Rd
13000 DgsC 80138 2454 D2
S Gartrell Rd
- AphC 80138 2454 C1
- AURA 80016 2454 C1
7200 AURA 80016 2370 C5
Garwood St
9700 DgsC 80125 2531 A6
Gary
- TNTN 80260 1944 C2
Gary St
- PrkC 80456 2521 E2
Gary Mauldin Dr
- PARK 80134 2537 D5
E Gate Dr
- BGTN 80601 1697 A6
S Gatesbury Cir
9700 DgsC 80126 2449 E5
Gateway Av
- DNVR 80239 2032 C5
Gateway Cir
700 LAFT 80026 1690 B4
Gateway Dr
25800 JfnC 80401 2190 B2
E Gateway Dr
100 DgsC 80126 2448 E5
100 DgsC 80129 2448 E5
500 DgsC 80126 2449 A5
Gateway Ln
- BldC 80027 1688 E5
- BldC 80027 1689 A6
- BldC 80303 1688 E5
Gatewood Ct
10 PrkC 80470 2523 E4
10 PrkC 80470 2524 A4
S Gatewood St
8500 DgsC 80126 2449 A2
Gatling Ln
3100 BLDR 80301 1603 C7
Gauthier Rd
10 PrkC 80456 2522 A1
Gaviota Av
10 BGTN 80601 1697 D6
Gawain St
10 LAFT 80026 1690 E6
Gay Cir
1300 LGMT 80501 1356 A6
S Gay Dr
10 LGMT 80501 1439 A5
Gay Ln
29700 JfnC 80439 2357 B1
Gay St
- BldC 80504 1356 A4
900 LGMT 80501 1439 A1
1100 LGMT 80501 1356 A7
S Gay St
700 LGMT 80501 1439 A4
Gayety Ct
800 CSRK 80104 2703 E5
S Gaylord Cir
8200 CTNL 80122 2449 B1
Gaylord Ct
14100 AdmC 80602 1777 B3
S Gaylord Ct
7900 CTNL 80122 2365 C7
8200 CTNL 80122 2449 C1
Gaylord Pl
1900 TNTN 80241 1777 B5
Gaylord St
100 DNVR 80206 2197 C1
1000 DNVR 80206 2113 B5
1800 DNVR 80205 2113 B4
4600 DNVR 80216 2029 B6
8200 AdmC 80229 1945 B4

Gaylord St
9100 TNTN 80229 1945 B2
10300 TNTN 80229 1861 B6
10900 NHGN 80233 1861 B4
13300 TNTN 80241 1777 B6
13800 AdmC 80602 1777 B4
14800 TNTN 80602 1777 B2
S Gaylord St
300 DNVR 80209 2197 B3
2200 DNVR 80210 2197 B7
3000 DNVR 80210 2281 B2
3100 EGLD 80113 2281 C2
4800 CHLV 80113 2281 C6
7200 CTNL 80122 2365 C5
Gaylord Wy
11700 NHGN 80233 1861 B2
S Gaylord Wy
5900 GDVL 80121 2365 C2
7900 CTNL 80122 2365 C7
Gaynor Dr
7900 BldC 80504 1522 A2
Gaynor Lake Wy
- BldC 80504 1522 B2
E Geddes Av
10 CTNL 80122 2364 E5
10 LITN 80120 2364 E5
10 LITN 80122 2364 E5
2100 CTNL 80122 2365 C5
5000 CTNL 80122 2366 A5
6300 CTNL 80112 2366 C6
10100 AphC 80112 2367 C5
10500 CTNL 80112 2367 C5
16200 AphC 80016 2368 E5
18800 AphC 80016 2369 C5
18800 CTNL 80016 2369 C5
22100 AURA 80016 2370 B5
W Geddes Av
800 LITN 80120 2364 C5
4400 LITN 80128 2363 C6
6600 JfnC 80128 2363 A6
9900 JfnC 80127 2362 B6
9900 JfnC 80128 2362 B6
11100 JfnC 80127 2361 E6
Geddes Cir
- AURA 80016 2371 B5
E Geddes Cir
- AURA 80016 2370 D5
- AURA 80016 2371 A5
4000 CTNL 80122 2365 E6
5700 CTNL 80112 2366 B5
E Geddes Cir N
1600 CTNL 80122 2365 B5
E Geddes Cir S
1700 CTNL 80122 2365 B5
W Geddes Cir
800 LITN 80120 2364 D6
5000 AphC 80128 2363 C5
10000 JfnC 80127 2362 B6
E Geddes Ct
4900 CTNL 80122 2366 A5
E Geddes Dr
- CTNL 80122 2365 D5
15900 AphC 80016 2368 E5
15900 CTNL 80016 2368 E5
S Geddes Dr
- AURA 80016 2370 D5
W Geddes Dr
6300 JfnC 80128 2363 A6
E Geddes Ln
6700 CTNL 80112 2366 C5
15900 AphC 80016 2368 E5
15900 CTNL 80016 2368 E5
Geddes Pl
- AURA 80016 2371 B5
E Geddes Pl
2400 CTNL 80122 2365 C5
5400 CTNL 80122 2366 B5
8400 CTNL 80112 2366 E5
16400 AphC 80016 2368 E5
18100 FXFD 80016 2369 C5
19500 AphC 80016 2369 D5
21400 CTNL 80016 2370 B5
22100 AURA 80016 2370 B5
25300 AURA 80016 2371 A5
W Geddes Pl
5200 JfnC 80128 2363 B5
8500 JfnC 80128 2362 C6
10000 JfnC 80127 2362 B6
Geer Canyon Dr
10 BldC 80302 1435 A6
Gemini Ct
400 DgsC 80124 2450 E2
Gemstone Ct
10200 PARK 80134 2453 A6
Gene Amole Wy
- DNVR 80204 2112 D5
Genesee Av
24200 JfnC 80401 2190 C4
Genesee Ct
10 BLDR 80303 1687 D6
10000 DgsC 80124 2450 D5
Genesee Dr
26100 JfnC 80401 2190 B4
27600 JfnC 80401 2189 E2
Genesee Ln
26300 JfnC 80401 2189 E2
26300 JfnC 80401 2190 A3
Genesee Mountain Rd
400 JfnC 80401 2190 B3
Genesee Ridge Rd
700 JfnC 80401 2190 E4
700 JfnC 80401 2191 A3
Genesee Spring Rd
24900 JfnC 80401 2190 C4
Genesee Trail Rd
23700 JfnC 80401 2190 C3
Genesee Village Rd
23400 JfnC 80401 2190 E3
Genesee Vista Rd
1000 JfnC 80401 2190 E4
E Geneseo St
700 LAFT 80026 1690 D4
W Geneseo St
100 LAFT 80026 1690 B4

Geneva Av
500 BLDR 80302 1686 B3
Geneva Cir
1600 LGMT 80503 1355 C6
S Geneva Cir
6300 AphC 80111 2367 B3
Geneva Ct
7000 LKWD 80214 2110 E4
16000 AdmC 80602 1695 B6
S Geneva Ct
6000 AphC 80111 2367 C2
Geneva Ln
32800 JfnC 80439 2356 B7
Geneva Pl
2700 LGMT 80503 1355 C6
Geneva Rd
7800 JfnC 80403 1936 B6
Geneva St
- DNVR 80238 2115 B4
- DNVR 80239 2031 B6
- DvrC 80238 2115 B4
1400 AURA 80010 2115 B5
4700 DNVR 80238 2031 B6
S Geneva St
700 AURA 80247 2199 B3
900 DNVR 80247 2199 B4
1000 DvrC 80247 2199 B4
3000 DNVR 80231 2283 B2
5100 AphC 80111 2283 B7
5100 GDVL 80111 2283 B7
5200 AphC 80111 2367 B1
5500 GDVL 80111 2367 B1
S Geneva Wy
1300 AURA 80247 2199 B4
5200 AphC 80111 2283 B7
6100 AphC 80111 2367 B2
Geneva's Wy
- GpnC 80403 1849 E4
S Genoa Cir
3700 AURA 80013 2285 D3
7400 AphC 80016 2369 D5
S Genoa Ct
2500 AURA 80013 2201 D7
3800 AURA 80013 2285 D4
4700 CTNL 80015 2285 D6
5700 AphC 80015 2369 D1
7400 AphC 80016 2369 E5
Genoa St
- AURA 80019 2033 D3
- AURA 80249 2033 D3
- DNVR 80019 2033 D3
1600 AURA 80011 2117 D4
4900 DNVR 80249 2033 D5
S Genoa St
1800 AURA 80013 2201 D5
2900 AURA 80013 2285 D1
4800 CTNL 80015 2285 D6
5400 CTNL 80015 2369 D1
6100 AphC 80015 2369 D2
6100 AphC 80016 2369 D2
19300 AURA 80017 2201 D4
Genoa Wy
500 CSRK 80109 2703 C1
S Genoa Wy
1700 AURA 80017 2201 D5
2200 AURA 80013 2201 D7
3500 AURA 80013 2285 D3
5200 CTNL 80015 2285 D7
Gentian Ln
16300 JfnC 80465 2360 D3
Gentry Ct
2700 AdmC 80137 2121 B2
Gentry Pl
1300 CSRK 80104 2787 E5
2500 AdmC 80137 2121 B3
Geode Ct
7300 CSRK 80108 2620 A5
George St
16600 JfnC 80470 2693 D2
Georgetown Rd
1100 BLDR 80305 1687 C7
1100 BLDR 80305 1771 B2
S Georgia Cir
10300 JfnC 80465 2443 D6
Georgian Cir
11400 JfnC 80403 1853 A4
Germain St
2000 FLHT 80260 1944 B2
German Ct
1300 ERIE 80516 1607 A2
Geronimo Tr
11700 JfnC 80433 2526 C3
Gerry Ln
5700 DgsC 80118 2952 E1
Gettysburg Ct
- EbtC 80107 2543 A2
Giant Gulch Rd
5200 JfnC 80454 2359 B1
24200 JfnC 80439 2274 C7
Gibbs Av
4700 BLDR 80301 1603 B7
S Gibraltar Cir
3500 AURA 80013 2285 E3
6300 CTNL 80016 2369 D3
S Gibraltar Ct
5100 CTNL 80015 2285 E7
5400 CTNL 80015 2369 E1
6700 CTNL 80016 2369 D4
S Gibraltar Ln
4700 CTNL 80015 2285 E6
W Gibraltar Pl
9300 LITN 80127 2446 B5
Gibraltar St
4800 DNVR 80249 2033 D6
S Gibraltar St
2600 AURA 80013 2201 D7
4200 AURA 80013 2285 D4
4300 CTNL 80015 2285 D5
5400 CTNL 80015 2369 E1
6700 CTNL 80016 2369 E4
S Gibraltar Wy
- AphC 80015 2369 D1
2100 AURA 80013 2201 E6
4900 CTNL 80015 2285 D6

STREET Block City ZIP Map# Grid

S Gibraltar Wy
5600 CTNL 80015 2369 D1
6900 CTNL 80016 2369 D4
Gibralter St
1600 AURA 80011 2117 D4
Gibralter Wy
4500 DNVR 80249 2033 D6
S Gibson Ct
1300 SUPE 80027 1773 A5
Gifford Dr
1500 LGMT 80501 1355 E5
E Gifford Dr
6500 CMCY 80022 2030 C2
Gigi Dr
29700 JfnC 80439 2357 B1
Gigi Ln
10 CCkC 80439 2355 C2
Gigi Rd
29400 JfnC 80439 2357 B1
Gigi St
800 CSRK 80104 2703 E5
Gilbert St
- JfnC 80403 2023 E4
10 CSRK 80104 2703 E6
900 BLDR 80302 1686 B4
S Gilbert St
10 CSRK 80104 2703 E7
500 CSRK 80104 2787 E1
1000 CSRK 80104 2788 A1
Gilcrest St
11200 PARK 80134 2453 A7
11200 PARK 80134 2537 A1
Gilia Dr
900 JfnC 80401 2190 E4
Gill Dr
3700 DNVR 80209 2197 D3
E Gill Pl
5400 DNVR 80224 2198 B3
5400 DNVR 80246 2198 B3
10100 DNVR 80247 2199 B3
W Gill Pl
1200 DNVR 80223 2196 C3
3000 DNVR 80219 2196 A3
4300 DNVR 80219 2195 C3
5000 LKWD 80219 2195 C3
5000 LKWD 80226 2195 C3
E Gill Wy
500 SUPE 80027 1773 A5
Gillaspie Dr
500 BLDR 80305 1687 A7
1200 BLDR 80305 1771 A1
Gillespie Spur
- BldC 80455 1516 A3
Gillespie Spur Rd
100 BldC 80455 1516 A3
Gillette Ct
1600 LGMT 80501 1438 E6
Gilmore St
1900 AdmC 80137 2120 E3
S Gilpin Cir E
6700 CTNL 80121 2365 B4
6700 CTNL 80122 2365 B4
S Gilpin Cir W
6700 CTNL 80121 2365 B4
6700 CTNL 80122 2365 B4
Gilpin Ct
5800 CTNL 80121 2365 B2
5800 GDVL 80121 2365 B2
S Gilpin Ct
5800 CTNL 80121 2365 B2
7600 CTNL 80122 2365 B6
Gilpin Dr
700 BLDR 80303 1687 B4
Gilpin Rd
10 GpnC 80403 1849 E4
10 GpnC 80403 1850 A5
Gilpin St
- BMFD 80516 1693 B4
10 DNVR 80218 2197 B1
1200 DNVR 80218 2113 B5
3200 DNVR 80205 2113 B2
9600 TNTN 80229 1945 B1
9800 TNTN 80229 1861 B7
11700 NHGN 80233 1861 A2
16400 TNTN 80602 1693 B4
S Gilpin St
200 DNVR 80209 2197 B2
1000 DNVR 80210 2197 B4
3000 DvrC 80210 2281 B2
3000 EGLD 80113 2281 B2
3100 DNVR 80210 2281 B2
3500 CHLV 80113 2281 B3
Gilson Av
100 IDSP 80452 2101 E5
Ginger Ct
4400 CSRK 80109 2702 C4
S Ginger Cir
1600 DNVR 80222 2198 A5
Ginny Wy
2300 LAFT 80026 1689 E1
E Girard Av
10 EGLD 80110 2280 E3
10 EGLD 80113 2280 E3
600 EGLD 80113 2281 A3
1600 CHLV 80113 2281 B3
4000 DNVR 80210 2281 E3
4000 DNVR 80222 2281 E3
6500 DNVR 80222 2282 C3
6500 DNVR 80224 2282 C3
7600 DNVR 80231 2282 D3
8600 DNVR 80231 2283 A3
10100 DNVR 80014 2283 B3
15000 AURA 80014 2284 C2
16400 AURA 80013 2284 E2
18300 AURA 80013 2285 B2
W Girard Av
1600 EGLD 80110 2280 B3
3000 SRDN 80110 2280 A3
3300 DNVR 80110 2279 E3
3300 SRDN 80110 2279 E3
3600 DNVR 80236 2279 E2
6100 DNVR 80227 2279 A3
10600 LKWD 80227 2278 A3
E Girard Dr
20300 AURA 80013 2285 E2
20500 AURA 80013 2286 A2
E Girard Pl
16200 AURA 80013 2284 E2
17600 AURA 80013 2285 A2
20400 AURA 80013 2286 A2
W Girard Pl
9300 LKWD 80227 2278 C3
10900 JfnC 80227 2277 E3
W Girton Av
7300 LKWD 80227 2278 E3
W Girton Dr
8800 LKWD 80227 2278 C3
E Girton Pl
19500 AURA 80013 2285 D2
W Girton Pl
1700 SRDN 80110 2280 B3
9300 LKWD 80227 2278 B3
Glacier Pl
- BldC 80303 1688 B3
Glacier Pt
11400 WldC 80504 1440 E2
Glacier Park Cir
10900 PARK 80138 2538 A1
Glacier Park Dr
10900 PARK 80138 2538 A1
Glacier Park Cove
21000 PARK 80138 2538 A1
Glacier Rim Tr
3600 BMFD 80020 1775 D5
Glacier View Rd
7100 BldC 80301 1604 C1
7100 BLDR 80301 1604 C1
7300 BldC 80503 1520 C7
7300 BldC 80503 1604 C1
Glade Gulch Cir
3100 DgsC 80104 2787 E7
Glade Gulch Rd
- DgsC 80104 2787 C7
900 DgsC 80104 2871 D1
N Gladeway St
6500 DgsC 80134 2623 A2
Gladiola Ct
300 JfnC 80401 2193 A1
6300 ARVD 80004 2025 A2
6300 JfnC 80004 2025 A2
Gladiola St
- JfnC 80401 2109 A7
300 JfnC 80401 2193 A1
700 LKWD 80401 2109 A7
5200 JfnC 80002 2025 A5
5200 JfnC 80403 2025 A5
6800 ARVD 80004 2025 A1
N Gladiola St
7000 ARVD 80004 1941 A7
7000 ARVD 80004 2025 A1
S Gladiola Wy
2200 LKWD 80228 2193 A7
2500 LKWD 80228 2277 A1
Gladstone Cir
300 BMFD 80020 1775 A5
W Glasgow Av
6600 JfnC 80128 2363 A6
10200 JfnC 80127 2362 A6
11100 JfnC 80127 2361 E6
E Glasgow Cir
24300 AURA 80016 2370 E5
Glasgow Ct
12100 LNTR 80134 2451 E6
E Glasgow Dr
24300 AURA 80016 2370 E5
24900 AURA 80016 2371 A5
Glasgow Pl
- AURA 80016 2371 A5
E Glasgow Pl
- AURA 80016 2371 B5
18300 FXFD 80016 2369 C5
23700 AURA 80016 2370 D5
W Glasgow Pl
8500 JfnC 80128 2362 C6
Glen Cir
7100 DgsC 80134 2539 A7
13400 BMFD 80020 1775 E5
Glen Ct
1300 BLDR 80305 1770 E1
S Glen Dr
13500 JfnC 80470 2608 B1
E Glen St
1100 DgsC 80108 2619 C7
W Glen Wk
- LKSR 80118 2955 A6
Glen Wy
- PrkC 80456 2608 A2
Glenalla Pl
10 DgsC 80108 2618 E4
Glenarbor Cir
600 LGMT 80501 1356 D5
Glenarbor Ct
2000 LGMT 80501 1356 D5
Glenarbor Wy
1900 LGMT 80501 1356 D5
Glenarm Pl
1200 DNVR 80204 2112 D5
2000 DNVR 80202 2112 E4
2000 DNVR 80203 2112 E4
2000 DNVR 80205 2112 E4
2800 DNVR 80205 2113 A3
Glen Ayr Dr
1500 LKWD 80215 2110 C4
Glen Bar Dr
- LKWD 80215 2110 C5
Glenco Dr
6900 CMCY 80022 1946 A7
Glencoe
- TNTN 80260 1944 C2
Glencoe Cir
11700 TNTN 80233 1862 A2
S Glencoe Cir
7100 CTNL 80122 2366 A5
Glencoe Ct
5800 CMCY 80022 2030 A3
9600 AdmC 80229 1946 A1
10100 AdmC 80229 1862 A6
Glencoe Ct
10100 TNTN 80229 1862 A6
11700 TNTN 80233 1862 A3
S Glencoe Ct
6300 CTNL 80121 2366 A3
6800 CTNL 80122 2366 A4
Glencoe Dr
11900 TNTN 80233 1862 A2
S Glencoe Ln
7100 CTNL 80122 2366 B5
Glencoe Pl
10900 TNTN 80233 1862 A5
Glencoe St
- CMCY 80022 2030 A1
- CTNL 80121 2366 A3
- TNTN 80233 1862 A2
100 DNVR 80220 2198 A1
800 DNVR 80220 2114 A6
1900 DNVR 80207 2114 A4
4500 DNVR 80216 2030 A6
7000 CMCY 80022 1946 A7
12000 TNTN 80241 1862 A2
13800 TNTN 80602 1778 A4
S Glencoe St
10 DNVR 80220 2198 A1
600 GNDL 80246 2198 A2
1100 DNVR 80222 2198 A4
1100 DNVR 80246 2198 A4
2700 DNVR 80222 2282 A1
3500 DNVR 80237 2282 A3
6700 CTNL 80121 2366 A4
6700 CTNL 80122 2366 A4
S Glencoe Wy
5900 CTNL 80121 2366 A2
7300 CTNL 80122 2366 A5
Glencoe Valley Rd
6600 JfnC 80403 2023 A1
6900 JfnC 80403 2022 E1
7000 JfnC 80403 1938 E7
7700 ARVD 80403 1938 C5
Glencove Pl
4400 BldC 80301 1604 D4
Glendale
- TNTN 80260 1944 C2
Glen Dale Dr
1700 LKWD 80215 2110 C5
Glendale Ln
19500 PARK 80134 2537 D3
Glendale Gulch Cir
5400 BLDR 80301 1604 B2
Glendale Gulch Rd
- BldC 80302 1516 D7
10 BldC 80455 1516 D7
Glen Dee Dr
1500 LKWD 80215 2110 C5
Gleneagles Village Pkwy
5100 DgsC 80130 2450 B3
Gleneden Ln
29500 JfnC 80439 2189 B7
29500 JfnC 80439 2273 C1
Glenellen Dr
8500 ARVD 80002 2026 C4
Glen Eyrie Dr
30100 JfnC 80439 2273 B6
Glen Garry Dr
1700 LKWD 80215 2110 C5
Glengary Pl
100 DgsC 80108 2618 D4
Glengate Cir
10800 DgsC 80108 2534 A1
10800 DgsC 80124 2534 A1
11000 DgsC 80124 2450 A7
Glengate Lp
10700 DgsC 80124 2450 A7
Glen Gyle Dr
1800 LKWD 80215 2110 C4
Glen Haven Cir
4500 EbtC 80107 2793 D4
Glenhaven Ct
700 BldC 80303 1688 E4
Glenhaven Dr
2000 DgsC 80126 2449 B3
Glenhunt Ln
6900 DgsC 80108 2618 D1
Glen Mawr Dr
10 GpnC 80403 1850 A5
Glenmoor Cir
11100 DgsC 80138 2538 D1
11100 PARK 80138 2538 D1
S Glenmoor Cir
10 CHLV 80113 2281 D7
Glenmoor Ct
10 CHLV 80113 2281 D6
11100 PARK 80138 2538 D1
Glen Moor Dr
1600 LKWD 80215 2110 C5
Glenmoor Dr
- CHLV 80121 2281 D7
10 CHLV 80113 2281 D6
100 GDVL 80121 2281 D6
23400 PARK 80138 2538 D1
23900 DgsC 80138 2538 D1
Glenmoor Ln
10 CHLV 80113 2281 E6
Glen Moor Pkwy
1600 LKWD 80215 2110 C5
Glenmoor Pl
10 CHLV 80113 2281 E6
11100 DgsC 80138 2538 E1
11100 PARK 80138 2538 E1
Glenmoor Rd
6300 BldC 80303 1688 A3
Glenmoor Wy
10 CHLV 80113 2281 D6
23900 DgsC 80138 2538 E1
23900 PARK 80138 2538 E1
Glenneyre Dr
3700 LGMT 80503 1438 A7
Glenn Isle Rd
100 PrkC 80456 2689 E2
W Glennon Dr
10600 LKWD 80226 2193 E3
10600 LKWD 80226 2194 A3
Glen Oaks Av
800 DgsC 80108 2534 D6
Glen Ridge Dr
7400 DgsC 80108 2534 D7
Glenridge Dr
10 AphC 80123 2363 C4
Glen Shiel Dr
1900 LKWD 80215 2110 C4
S Glenstone Cir
9900 DgsC 80130 2450 B5
E Glenstone Dr
5600 DgsC 80130 2450 B5
E Glenstone Ln
5700 DgsC 80130 2450 B5
S Glenstone Tr
9800 DgsC 80130 2450 B5
Glenview Ct
300 LGMT 80501 1439 E3
Glenview Dr
10 AphC 80123 2363 C4
Glen View Ln
100 JfnC 80439 2188 B2
Glenwood Ct
2700 BLDR 80304 1602 E7
Glenwood Dr
600 LAFT 80026 1690 C3
1900 BLDR 80304 1602 D7
2700 BLDR 80301 1602 E7
2800 BLDR 80301 1603 A7
E Glenwood Ln
1700 DgsC 80126 2449 B3
Globeville Rd
3700 DNVR 80216 2028 D7
3700 DNVR 80216 2112 D1
Goatbarn Ln
10 BldC 80302 1601 C6
Goddard Pl
2100 BLDR 80305 1686 E7
Goddard Ranch Ct
19300 JfnC 80465 2359 E5
Goins Dr
20100 JfnC 80465 2443 C7
Gold Ct
3300 BMFD 80020 1775 E6
8300 JfnC 80465 2443 E2
Gold Spur
12400 JfnC 80433 2527 E5
Gold Tr
10 BldC 80302 1599 D4
Gold Wy
700 SUPE 80027 1773 A7
Goldaster Ct
8500 PARK 80134 2453 A1
S Goldbug Cir
1500 AURA 80018 2202 E5
Gold Bug Ct
- AURA 80016 2371 A1
S Gold Bug Ct
7200 AURA 80016 2371 A5
S Goldbug Ct
- AURA 80018 2202 E3
S Gold Bug Wy
- AURA 80016 2286 D5
- AURA 80016 2287 A6
Gold Camp Wy
1500 DgsC 80116 2791 C5
Goldco Cir
200 GOLD 80403 2107 D2
Gold Creek Dr
10 EbtC 80107 2792 E2
10 EbtC 80107 2793 A2
Goldcrest Av
- DgsC 80126 2449 E3
W Gold Dust Ct
2000 DgsC 80129 2448 B4
W Gold Dust Ln
2100 DgsC 80129 2448 B4
W Gold Dust Tr
2100 DgsC 80129 2448 B4
Gold Dust Peak
7700 JfnC 80127 2361 E7
Golden Cir
400 GOLD 80401 2108 A7
400 GOLD 80401 2192 A1
1400 JfnC 80401 2192 A1
Golden Ct
4800 DNVR 80212 2027 B6
4800 DvrC 80212 2027 B6
4800 LKSD 80212 2027 B6
S Golden Ct
2100 DNVR 80227 2195 B7
3700 DNVR 80235 2279 B4
Golden Ln
400 LGMT 80501 1439 E2
S Golden Rd
- JfnC 80401 2109 A6
- LKWD 80401 2109 A6
17200 GOLD 80401 2108 B5
17500 JfnC 80401 2108 B5
Golden St
- BldC 80503 1438 C3
S Golden Wy
2700 DNVR 80227 2279 B1
Golden Aster
10 JfnC 80127 2360 E5
Golden Bear Dr
1600 LGMT 80501 1356 E6
Golden Currant Wy
5400 DgsC 80134 2622 B4
S Golden Eagle Av
9600 DgsC 80129 2448 A4
Golden Eagle Cir
600 GOLD 80401 2107 E7
2800 LAFT 80026 1774 C2
Golden Eagle Ct
10 GDVL 80121 2282 A6
1800 BMFD 80020 1775 A5
W Golden Eagle Ct
2700 DgsC 80129 2448 A4
Golden Eagle Dr
300 BMFD 80020 1775 A5
S Golden Eagle Dr
9600 DgsC 80129 2448 A4
Golden Eagle Ln
10 JfnC 80127 2360 D4
Golden Eagle Pkwy
10 AdmC 80601 1697 E6
5000 BGTN 80601 1697 D7
S Golden Eagle Pl
9500 DgsC 80129 2448 A5
Golden Eagle Rd
10 GDVL 80121 2282 A7
Golden Eagle Run
- BMFD 80020 1775 C2
Golden Eye Av
- DgsC 80134 2452 E1
Golden Eye Ct
15800 DgsC 80134 2452 D1
Golden Eye Dr
8400 DgsC 80134 2452 E1
8400 PARK 80134 2452 E1
Goldeneye Ln
1400 BGTN 80601 1779 E1
Goldeneye Pl
3100 SUPE 80027 1857 B1
Golden Field Cir
41400 EbtC 80107 2541 B7
41400 EbtC 80138 2541 B7
Golden Gate Dr
- GOLD 80403 2107 C1
10 GpnC 80403 2019 E1
600 GpnC 80403 2020 A1
Golden Gate Canyon Rd
10 GpnC 80403 1934 A5
2800 GpnC 80403 1935 B6
5100 GpnC 80403 2019 D1
5600 GpnC 80403 2020 C3
20100 GOLD 80403 2023 B7
20100 GOLD 80403 2107 B1
20100 JfnC 80403 2023 B7
20100 JfnC 80403 2106 C1
20100 JfnC 80403 2107 B1
23100 JfnC 80403 2022 A6
25200 JfnC 80403 2021 D6
Golden Gate Canyon Rd SR-46
10 GpnC 80403 1934 A5
2800 GpnC 80403 1935 B6
5100 GpnC 80403 2019 D1
5600 GpnC 80403 2020 A2
Golden Hills Pl
17100 GOLD 80401 2108 C5
Golden Hills Rd
1400 GOLD 80401 2108 C5
1400 JfnC 80401 2108 C5
Golden Meadow Dr
31500 JfnC 80439 2272 E3
Golden Park Dr
900 GOLD 80403 2107 D2
Golden Park Pl
900 GOLD 80403 2107 C2
Golden Point Dr
800 JfnC 80401 2107 A7
Golden Ridge Rd
500 GOLD 80401 2108 A7
Goldenrod Cir
1100 BMFD 80020 1774 C6
34000 EbtC 80107 2710 C7
Golden Rod Ct
100 BldC 80501 1439 D3
100 LGMT 80501 1439 D3
Goldenrod Dr
600 BLDR 80302 1686 C5
Golden Rod Ln
16600 JfnC 80465 2360 C3
Goldenrod Ln
20400 PARK 80138 2538 A2
Goldenrod Wy
16200 DgsC 80134 2452 E1
16200 PARK 80134 2452 E1
Golden Spur Lp
- CSRK 80108 2704 B4
Golden Valley Tr
5100 CSRK 80109 2702 C2
Goldenvue Dr
1900 GOLD 80401 2107 D4
Golden Willow Rd
- CCkC 80439 2355 E1
10 CCkC 80439 2272 A7
400 CCkC 80439 2271 E7
600 CCkC 80439 2356 A1
Goldfinch Ct
2000 LGMT 80503 1355 C5
Goldfinch Dr
33800 EbtC 80107 2793 D1
S Goldfinch Ln
9700 DgsC 80129 2448 A5
Goldfinch St
5500 BGTN 80601 1697 E6
Gold Flake Ter
10 PrkC 80456 2521 C3
Gold Hill Dr
100 LAFT 80026 1689 E4
200 LAFT 80026 1690 A4
Gold Hill Rd
9900 BldC 80302 1599 C3
10700 BldC 80302 1598 E4
14200 BldC 80302 1597 E6
14200 BldC 80455 1597 E6
14200 BldC 80455 1598 A5
14200 BldC 80466 1597 C6
14200 BldC 80481 1597 C6
Gold Hill St
1500 CSRK 80109 2703 B5
Gold Lake Rd
- BldC 80455 1515 C3
- BldC 80481 1515 B4
10 BldC 80481 1513 E7
10 BldC 80481 1597 E1
400 BldC 80481 1514 C7
400 BldC 80481 1598 A1
Gold Maple St
1600 BGTN 80601 1697 E5
Gold Mine Ln
1300 JfnC 80439 2188 E6
Gold Mine Gulch
- TNTN 80229 1861 E6
Gold Mountain Rd
- CLCY 80403 2017 D5
- GpnC 80403 2017 D5
Gold Nugget Dr
7100 BldC 80503 1521 B4
Goldpan Pl
- DgsC 80134 2621 B4
Gold Run Rd
600 BldC 80302 1600 B4
1600 BldC 80302 1599 E4
Gold Run St
300 BldC 80302 1599 D3
S Gold Rush St
9300 DgsC 80129 2448 A4
E Goldsmith Dr
1100 DgsC 80126 2449 A3
S Goldsmith Dr
5800 GDVL 80111 2367 A2
S Goldsmith Pl
5700 GDVL 80111 2367 A2
Gold Yarrow Ln
3100 JfnC 80439 2274 B3
Golf Wy
28900 JfnC 80439 2273 C7
Golf Club Dr
700 DgsC 80108 2618 C5
6600 BldC 80503 1519 A5
Golf Club Pt
30400 JfnC 80439 2273 A1
Golf Course Dr
5100 JfnC 80465 2360 D2
Golf Course Wy
- AdmC 80601 1779 A7
E Golfer's Wy
- AURA 80230 2199 B1
- DNVR 80230 2199 B1
- DNVR 80247 2199 B2
300 DNVR 80230 2115 A7
10100 AURA 80010 2199 B1
Golf View Ln
22000 PARK 80138 2538 B2
Good Friday Rd
10 BldC 80302 1683 E3
S Goodheart Av
10800 JfnC 80433 2527 A1
Good Hope Dr
800 DgsC 80108 2618 C3
Goodhue Blvd
7300 BldC 80303 1688 D5
E Goorman Av
800 CTNL 80121 2365 A3
S Goosander Wy
8700 DgsC 80126 2449 E3
9000 DgsC 80126 2450 A3
Gooseberry Ct
7400 DgsC 80134 2622 A4
N Gooseberry Ct
600 LAFT 80026 1690 B5
S Gooseberry Ct
700 LAFT 80026 1690 C6
Gooseberry Dr
600 LGMT 80503 1438 A4
Gooseberry Ln
- CHLV 80113 2281 C3
Goose Haven Dr
10300 BldC 80026 1606 A4
Goose Point Ct
6900 BldC 80503 1520 C1
Gopher Ct
8300 DgsC 80134 2622 C4
Gorce Ct
2400 ERIE 80516 1606 D6
Gordon Ct
200 CSRK 80104 2704 A6
1900 ERIE 80516 1606 E6
2400 LGMT 80501 1356 A4
13400 JfnC 80470 2608 D2
Gordon Dr
10 CSRK 80104 2704 A7
1700 ERIE 80516 1606 E6
4600 BLDR 80305 1687 B7
Gordon Ln
10 CSRK 80104 2704 A7
Gordon Pl
100 CSRK 80104 2704 A7
Gordon Creek Rd
10 BldC 80302 1682 B4
Gore Cir
- DgsC 80118 2954 D1
Gore Dr
1600 DgsC 80118 2954 C2
S Gore Range Rd
7200 JfnC 80127 2361 E6
Gorham Ct
300 LSVL 80027 1689 C5
Goshawk
10 JfnC 80127 2360 E4
10 JfnC 80127 2361 A4
Goshawk Ct
5000 BGTN 80601 1697 D7
Goshawk Dr
1500 LGMT 80501 1357 A7
Goshawk St
5200 BGTN 80601 1697 E6
Goss Cir E
2200 BLDR 80302 1686 E2
Goss Cir W
2100 BLDR 80302 1686 D2
Goss Dr
600 LGMT 80501 1439 D2
Goss St
2300 BLDR 80302 1686 E2
Gossamer Wy
- CSRK 80109 2702 E5
S Gotlob Rd
1900 AphC 80102 2207 C6
N Gough Av
400 LAFT 80026 1690 D4
S Gough Av
100 LAFT 80026 1690 D5
W Gould Av
9700 JfnC 80123 2362 B2
Gould Cir
- CSRK 80109 2702 C4
W Gould Dr
6400 JfnC 80123 2363 A1
12500 JfnC 80127 2361 D2
W Gould Wy
8800 JfnC 80123 2362 C2
S Grace Av
12500 JfnC 80470 2524 C6
E Grace Blvd
- DgsC 80130 2449 E5
3900 DgsC 80126 2449 E5
Grace Ct
8000 AdmC 80221 1944 E5
Grace Pl
7600 AdmC 80221 1944 E6
E Grace Pl
100 AdmC 80221 1944 E6
Graham Cir
- ERIE 80516 1607 A7
Graham Ct
4200 BLDR 80305 1687 B6
S Graham Dr
8800 JfnC 80465 2443 B3
Graham Ln
1700 LITN 80120 2364 B5
Graham Wy
- ERIE 80516 1607 A7
Grain Ct
- BGTN 80601 1697 C4
Graland Ln
800 DgsC 80126 2449 A6
Graland Pl
800 DgsC 80126 2449 A6
W Grambling Dr
3600 DNVR 80236 2279 E2
Granada Ct
100 LGMT 80501 1439 C1
Granada Rd
7300 AdmC 80221 1944 C6
Granada Wy
10 PrkC 80470 2524 A6
S Granby Cir
700 AURA 80012 2200 C3
4100 AURA 80014 2284 D4
Granby Ct
1700 AURA 80011 2116 C4
S Granby Ct
100 AURA 80012 2200 C1
4100 AURA 80014 2284 D5
4400 AURA 80015 2284 D5
5200 CTNL 80015 2284 D7
Granby St
2200 AURA 80011 2116 C3
5300 DNVR 80239 2032 C5
11700 CMCY 80603 1864 C2
13400 AdmC 80601 1780 C5
13400 BGTN 80601 1780 C5
S Granby St
1500 AURA 80012 2200 D5
2800 AURA 80014 2284 D1
4800 AURA 80015 2284 D6
Granby Wy
100 AURA 80011 2200 D1
2300 AURA 80011 2116 C3
4500 DNVR 80239 2032 C7
S Granby Wy
900 AURA 80012 2200 C3
2400 AURA 80014 2200 D7
3100 AURA 80014 2284 D2
4300 AURA 80015 2284 D5
Grand Av
800 LGMT 80501 1439 A4
1300 LGMT 80501 1438 E4
E Grand Av
500 EGLD 80113 2280 E7
700 CHLV 80113 2281 A7
700 EGLD 80113 2281 A7
8500 DNVR 80237 2282 E6
8500 DNVR 80237 2283 A6
9200 GDVL 80111 2283 A7
10000 AphC 80015 2283 A7
10000 AphC 80111 2283 A7
14900 AURA 80015 2284 C6
17400 AURA 80015 2285 A6
W Grand Av
2100 LITN 80120 2280 B7
3000 EGLD 80110 2279 D6
3000 EGLD 80110 2280 A7
3300 LITN 80123 2279 D6
3600 DNVR 80123 2279 D6
3600 DvrC 80123 2279 D6
7800 DNVR 80123 2278 D7
7800 DvrC 80123 2278 D7
7900 LKWD 80123 2278 D7
10000 JfnC 80127 2278 B7
E Grand Cir
19000 AURA 80015 2285 C6
Grand Ct
400 GOLD 80401 2108 A4
E Grand Ct
9500 GDVL 80111 2283 B7
E Grand Dr
14200 AURA 80015 2284 B6
17400 AURA 80015 2285 B6
W Grand Dr
13300 JfnC 80465 2277 B7
E Grand Ln
20400 AphC 80015 2285 E6
Grand Pl
- AURA 80016 2286 D6
E Grand Pl
9500 GDVL 80111 2283 B7
14800 AURA 80015 2284 C6
20400 AphC 80015 2285 E6
W Grand Pl
10200 JfnC 80127 2278 A7
10900 JfnC 80127 2277 E7
12300 JfnC 80465 2277 D7
S Grand Baker Cir
1400 AURA 80018 2202 E4
S Grand Baker St
- AphC 80018 2202 E5
1400 AURA 80018 2202 E5
S Grand Bay Cir
10 AphC 80018 2202 E1

STREET
Block City ZIP Map# Grid

S Grand Bay St
10 AphC 80018 2118 E7
10 AphC 80018 2202 E1
Grand Cypress Ln
8600 LNTR 80124 2451 A4
Grand Cypress Cove
9500 LNTR 80124 2451 B4
Grande Vista Ct
10300 DgsC 80124 2534 D1
Grand Mesa Ln
12300 DgsC 80138 2455 B4
Grand Valley Ct
4600 CSRK 80109 2702 C1
Grandview Av
1900 BLDR 80302 1686 D3
6300 ARVD 80002 2026 E4
6300 ARVD 80002 2027 A4
21400 JfnC 80401 2191 B1
24800 JfnC 80401 2190 C4
Grandview Dr
12600 BldC 80504 1356 A4
Grandview Meadows Dr
600 LGMT 80503 1437 E5
Grange Creek Dr
11000 TNTN 80233 1862 A4
Grange Hall Cir
- TNTN 80229 1861 E7
Granger Cir
1600 CSRK 80109 2703 A6
Granger Ct
500 CSRK 80109 2703 A6
Granite Av
- BLDR 80304 1602 B2
Granite Cir
20200 JfnC 80465 2443 D7
Granite Ct
900 LGMT 80501 1439 D1
Granite Dr
10 BldC 80302 1601 D7
10 BldC 80302 1685 D1
Granite Wy
10 CCkC 80439 2272 A4
5800 CSRK 80108 2619 E7
Granite Crag Cir
6900 JfnC 80439 2357 B5
Granite Hill Dr
10000 DgsC 80134 2452 D5
Granite Peak Ln
28700 JfnC 80403 1853 C3
Grant Av
300 BNNT 80102 2124 D1
400 LSVL 80027 1773 C1
800 LSVL 80027 1689 D7
24100 JfnC 80433 2694 E5
E Grant Av
10600 DgsC 80116 2707 C4
Grant Cir
- TNTN 80241 1860 E1
Grant Cir E
12900 TNTN 80241 1776 E6
Grant Cir N
- TNTN 80241 1776 D6
Grant Cir W
- TNTN 80241 1776 D6
Grant Ct
1600 LGMT 80501 1356 A6
S Grant Ct
200 LSVL 80027 1773 C2
6300 CTNL 80121 2364 E3
Grant Dr
10400 NHGN 80233 1860 E5
12400 TNTN 80241 1776 E7
12400 TNTN 80241 1860 E1
S Grant Dr
6300 CTNL 80121 2364 E3
Grant Pl
700 BldC 80302 1686 C4
700 BLDR 80302 1686 C4
7300 ARVD 80002 2026 E4
E Grant Rd
11000 DgsC 80116 2707 D4
11800 DgsC 80107 2707 D4
Grant St
10 DNVR 80203 2196 E1
10 DNVR 80209 2196 E1
100 BldC 80501 1438 E3
100 ELIZ 80107 2709 B7
200 LGMT 80501 1438 E2
300 DNVR 80203 2112 E7
600 LGMT 80501 1439 A1
1900 DNVR 80205 2112 E4
2100 LGMT 80501 1355 E5
5100 AdmC 80216 2028 E5
5100 DNVR 80216 2028 E5
7800 AdmC 80229 1944 E5
8100 TNTN 80229 1944 E5
9600 TNTN 80229 1860 E6
10300 TNTN 80233 1860 E6
11600 NHGN 80233 1860 E2
12000 TNTN 80241 1860 E2
S Grant St
- LGMT 80501 1438 E3
10 DNVR 80203 2196 E2
10 DNVR 80209 2196 E2
1100 DNVR 80210 2196 E4
1300 LGMT 80501 1439 A6
2500 DNVR 80210 2280 E1
2600 AphC 80210 2280 E1
2600 EGLD 80113 2280 E2
5100 AphC 80121 2280 E7
5200 AphC 80121 2364 E1
5500 LITN 80121 2364 E1
5900 CTNL 80121 2364 E2
6600 CTNL 80122 2364 E4
7500 LITN 80122 2364 E6
Grant Wy
100 AdmC 80229 1944 E4
100 TNTN 80229 1944 E4
S Grant Wy
- LITN 80120 2364 E7
8000 LITN 80122 2364 E7
8000 LITN 80122 2448 E1
W Grant Ranch Blvd
- DNVR 80123 2362 E1

STREET
Block City ZIP Map# Grid

W Grant Ranch Blvd
- DvrC 80123 2363 A1
- LKWD 80123 2278 D7
6900 DNVR 80123 2363 A1
6900 LKWD 80123 2363 A1
7000 LKWD 80123 2362 D1
Granzella Rd
9300 JfnC 80465 2442 E4
9300 JfnC 80465 2443 A4
Grape Av
- BldC 80304 1602 A6
600 BLDR 80304 1602 B7
Grape Cir
11300 TNTN 80233 1862 A3
Grape Ct
9600 AdmC 80229 1946 A1
10100 AdmC 80229 1862 A6
10100 TNTN 80229 1862 A6
11700 TNTN 80233 1862 A2
13000 TNTN 80241 1778 A6
S Grape Ct
5500 GDVL 80121 2366 B1
6100 CTNL 80121 2366 A2
7100 CTNL 80122 2366 B5
Grape Dr
6000 CMCY 80022 2030 A2
Grape Ln
300 BLDR 80304 1602 B7
S Grape Ln
5300 GDVL 80121 2282 A6
5300 GDVL 80121 2366 B1
7100 CTNL 80122 2366 A5
Grape St
10 DNVR 80220 2198 A1
10 DNVR 80246 2198 A1
1700 DNVR 80220 2114 A4
3300 DNVR 80207 2114 A1
3900 DNVR 80207 2030 A7
4500 DNVR 80216 2030 A6
6400 CMCY 80022 2030 A2
7000 CMCY 80022 1946 A7
11700 TNTN 80233 1862 A3
12000 TNTN 80241 1862 A2
12800 TNTN 80241 1778 A7
13900 TNTN 80602 1778 A4
S Grape St
10 DNVR 80220 2198 A1
1100 DNVR 80246 2198 A5
2100 AphC 80222 2198 A7
2100 DNVR 80222 2198 A7
3200 DNVR 80222 2282 A3
3500 DNVR 80237 2282 A3
7100 CTNL 80122 2366 A5
Grape Wy
- TNTN 80233 1862 A2
12000 TNTN 80241 1862 A1
S Grape Wy
2800 DNVR 80222 2282 A1
7000 CTNL 80122 2366 A5
Grapevine Rd
- JfnC 80401 2191 B3
E Grapevine Rd
- JfnC 80401 2275 C1
2300 JfnC 80465 2275 C1
S Grapevine Rd
800 JfnC 80401 2191 B3
2100 JfnC 80401 2275 B1
2500 JfnC 80465 2275 C1
SE Grapevine Rd
2700 JfnC 80465 2275 C1
SW Grapevine Rd
2700 JfnC 80465 2275 B1
W Grapevine Rd
2400 JfnC 80401 2275 B1
2400 JfnC 80465 2275 B1
Grapewood Ln
2600 BLDR 80304 1602 E7
Graphite Ct
1800 CSRK 80108 2620 A6
Graphite Wy
700 SUPE 80027 1857 A1
Grasmere Dr
7800 BldC 80301 1604 E3
Grass Ct
6400 DgsC 80134 2621 D4
Grasshopper Ct
- CSRK 80109 2702 C4
Grasslands Dr
14400 DgsC 80134 2452 C1
E Graves Av
200 CTNL 80121 2364 E2
Graves Ct
1700 NHGN 80233 1861 B4
Gray Cir
6800 ARVD 80003 2027 B1
6800 WSTR 80003 2027 B1
8000 ARVD 80003 1943 B5
10800 WSTR 80020 1859 A5
Gray Ct
500 LKWD 80214 2111 B7
500 LKWD 80226 2111 B7
3500 ARVD 80002 2027 B5
6700 ARVD 80003 2027 B1
8400 ARVD 80003 1943 B4
9300 WSTR 80031 1943 A1
N Gray Ct
11800 WSTR 80020 1859 A2
S Gray Ct
- JfnC 80123 2363 B2
2500 LKWD 80227 2195 B7
2500 LKWD 80227 2279 B1
7000 JfnC 80128 2363 B5
Gray Dr
6800 ARVD 80003 2027 B1
S Gray Dr
2000 LKWD 80227 2195 B6
S Gray Ln
9000 JfnC 80433 2440 D3
Gray St
10 LKWD 80226 2195 B1
10 PrkC 80456 2521 E2
300 LKWD 80226 2111 B7
800 LKWD 80214 2111 B6
1700 EDGW 80214 2111 B3

STREET
Block City ZIP Map# Grid

Gray St
3000 WTRG 80214 2111 B2
3500 WTRG 80212 2111 B1
4800 DvrC 80212 2027 B6
4800 LKSD 80212 2027 B6
5100 DNVR 80002 2027 B5
5100 DNVR 80212 2027 B5
5500 ARVD 80002 2027 B4
5500 JfnC 80002 2027 B4
6400 ARVD 80003 2027 B2
8400 ARVD 80003 1943 B4
9300 WSTR 80031 1943 B2
11700 WSTR 80020 1859 B3
N Gray St
4100 WTRG 80212 2027 B7
4300 LKSD 80212 2027 B7
S Gray St
10 LKWD 80226 2195 B1
1100 LKWD 80232 2195 B5
2100 DNVR 80227 2195 B7
2300 LKWD 80227 2195 B7
3000 DNVR 80227 2279 B2
3800 DNVR 80235 2279 B4
5300 DNVR 80123 2363 B1
5700 JfnC 80123 2363 B2
7600 JfnC 80128 2363 B6
Gray Wy
7600 WSTR 80003 1943 B6
11700 WSTR 80020 1859 A3
S Gray Wy
2800 DNVR 80227 2279 B2
Gray Buck Tr
26500 JfnC 80433 2526 A7
Grayden Ct
1900 SUPE 80027 1773 B6
W Grayfeather Wy
- DgsC 80129 2448 E6
E Gray Fox Ct
7100 DgsC 80130 2450 D5
S Gray Fox Dr
7800 JfnC 80439 2357 E7
7800 JfnC 80439 2441 E1
E Gray Fox Ln
7100 DgsC 80130 2450 D6
Gray Hawk Dr
29000 JfnC 80439 2357 C5
Grayhawk Pl
1300 DgsC 80118 2870 C7
Grayledge Cir
11000 DgsC 80108 2534 A1
Graymont Ln
10500 DgsC 80126 2449 E7
Gray Owl Rd
10 CHLV 80113 2281 C3
Grays Peak Dr
800 SUPE 80027 1857 A1
1300 LGMT 80501 1356 C7
21400 PARK 80138 2454 A7
Greatrock Ct
15300 AdmC 80603 1700 A7
Greatrock Rd
15200 AdmC 80603 1700 A6
29300 AdmC 80603 1699 E5
Great Rock St
16300 AdmC 80603 1700 A4
Greatrock Wy
16200 AdmC 80603 1700 A5
Great Western Dr
- LGMT 80504 1440 A4
1600 LGMT 80501 1440 A4
1800 BldC 80501 1440 A4
Great Western Rd
10 BGTN 80601 1696 B5
300 AdmC 80601 1696 B5
800 BGTN 80603 1696 B3
800 WldC 80603 1696 B3
Greatwood Ct
10200 DgsC 80126 2449 C6
Greatwood Pt
10200 DgsC 80126 2449 C6
Greatwood Wy
2600 DgsC 80126 2449 C6
S Grebe Pl
16100 PARK 80134 2536 E1
N Greeley Ct
6200 DgsC 80134 2622 E2
S Green Av
12400 JfnC 80470 2524 C6
Green Cir
1100 BLDR 80305 1686 E7
13400 BMFD 80020 1775 E5
S Green Cir
11500 JfnC 80433 2524 E2
11500 JfnC 80433 2525 A2
Green Ct
3100 DNVR 80211 2111 E2
4100 DNVR 80211 2027 E7
4900 DNVR 80221 2027 E6
5400 DgsC 80134 2621 D4
6600 AdmC 80221 2027 E1
7800 WSTR 80030 1943 E5
8300 WSTR 80031 1943 E4
13500 BMFD 80020 1775 E5
N Green Ct
9300 WSTR 80031 1943 E1
9500 FLHT 80260 1943 E1
9500 WSTR 80260 1943 E1
10100 WSTR 80031 1859 E6
S Green Ct
2600 DNVR 80219 2196 A7
2600 DNVR 80219 2280 A1
2600 DNVR 80236 2280 A1
3700 SRDN 80110 2280 A4
11500 JfnC 80433 2524 E3
11500 JfnC 80433 2525 A3
Green Dr
- AdmC 80603 1698 E7
Green Pl
1500 BldC 80501 1438 E2
1500 LGMT 80501 1438 E2
13500 BMFD 80020 1775 E5
Green St
10 PrkC 80456 2521 E2

STREET
Block City ZIP Map# Grid

Green Ash St
300 DgsC 80129 2448 D4
Greenbriar Blvd
1300 BLDR 80305 1771 B1
3400 BldC 80305 1771 A2
Greenbriar Cir
7800 BldC 80301 1604 E2
Greenbriar Ct
4600 BLDR 80305 1771 B1
Greenbriar Dr
6300 CHLV 80111 2282 B6
Greenbriar Ln
11500 PARK 80138 2538 B2
Greenfield Ln
- BMFD 80020 1776 A1
E Greenfinch Dr
4200 DgsC 80126 2449 E3
Green Gables Cir
900 BNNT 80102 2209 A3
Green Gables Ct
800 BNNT 80102 2209 A3
Green Gables Wy
600 BNNT 80102 2209 A3
Greengrass Wy
8600 PARK 80134 2452 E2
8600 PARK 80134 2453 A2
Green Haven Cir
3100 DgsC 80126 2449 D7
E Green Hollow Ct
8100 DgsC 80134 2622 B2
Greening Av
1200 ERIE 80516 1607 A3
S Greening Dr
9300 JfnC 80433 2440 D4
Green Island Cir
8300 LNTR 80124 2450 E4
Green Island Pl
9400 LNTR 80124 2450 E4
Greenleaf Ln
7700 AdmC 80221 1944 A5
Greenlee Wy
1500 LAFT 80026 1690 A3
Greenlet Ct
11700 PARK 80134 2536 E2
Green Meadow Ln
10 BldC 80302 1517 B7
21200 JfnC 80465 2359 C6
E Green Meadow Ln
1100 GDVL 80121 2365 A1
S Green Meadows Ct
8900 DgsC 80126 2449 C3
Green Meadows Dr
5600 DNVR 80227 2195 B7
S Green Meadows Dr
8800 DgsC 80126 2449 C2
S Green Meadows Ln
8900 DgsC 80126 2449 C3
Green Mountain Cir
3000 EbtC 80138 2457 A3
W Green Mountain Cir
12400 LKWD 80228 2193 B5
W Green Mountain Dr
11600 JfnC 80232 2193 D5
12500 LKWD 80228 2193 C5
Green Mountain St
- BLDR 80302 1686 D4
Green Oaks Cir
2200 GDVL 80121 2365 C1
Green Oaks Dr
900 GDVL 80121 2365 A1
5800 CTNL 80121 2365 A1
Green Oaks Ln
2000 GDVL 80121 2365 B2
Greenridge Ln
800 DgsC 80108 2618 D1
Greenridge Rd
10 GDVL 80111 2282 B7
10 GDVL 80121 2282 B7
Green River Dr
- DgsC 80130 2450 B1
Green Rock Dr
100 BldC 80302 1686 A2
100 BLDR 80302 1686 A2
S Greens Cir
5200 LITN 80123 2280 B7
W Greens Ct
2700 LITN 80123 2280 A7
W Greens Dr
2700 LITN 80123 2280 A7
W Greens Ln
- LITN 80123 2280 A7
Greens Pl
4000 BldC 80503 1518 E6
W Greens Pl
2700 LITN 80123 2280 B7
Greensborough Cir
2400 DgsC 80129 2448 B2
Greensborough Dr
2300 DgsC 80129 2448 A2
Greensborough Pl
8700 DgsC 80129 2448 A2
W Greensborough Pl
3600 DNVR 80236 2279 E3
Greenspointe Ct
9000 DgsC 80130 2450 B3
Greenspointe Ln
8900 DgsC 80130 2450 B3
Greenspointe Pl
5700 DgsC 80130 2450 B3
Greenspointe Wy
5700 DgsC 80130 2450 B3
Green Spruce
10 JfnC 80127 2445 A1
Greenstone Cir
15300 DgsC 80134 2452 D5
Greenstone Ln
15500 DgsC 80134 2452 D5
Greensview Cir
9800 LNTR 80124 2450 E5
Greenwald Ln
- CCkC 80439 2187 E4
Greenwald Wy
10 CCkC 80439 2187 E5

STREET
Block City ZIP Map# Grid

Greenway Cir E
200 BMFD 80020 1859 A3
Greenway Cir W
200 BMFD 80020 1859 A2
Greenway Dr
10 BMFD 80020 1859 A2
Greenway Dr E
6000 BMFD 80020 1859 A2
6000 WSTR 80020 1859 A2
Greenway Dr N
- BMFD 80020 1859 A2
Greenway Dr S
11600 BMFD 80020 1859 A3
11600 WSTR 80020 1859 A3
Greenway Dr W
- BMFD 80020 1859 C2
6700 BMFD 80020 1858 D3
Greenway Ln
400 BMFD 80020 1859 A3
900 DgsC 80108 2534 C7
S Greenwich Ct
8900 DgsC 80130 2450 A3
E Greenwich Dr
4800 DgsC 80130 2450 A3
E Greenwich Ln
4900 DgsC 80130 2450 A3
E Greenwich Pl
4800 DgsC 80130 2450 A3
S Greenwich St
8800 DgsC 80130 2450 A3
E Greenwich Wy
4900 DgsC 80130 2450 A2
Green Willow Ct
6900 BldC 80301 1604 B3
E Green Willow Ln
1300 GDVL 80121 2365 B2
Greenwood Blvd
10 AdmC 80221 1944 C6
8300 FLHT 80260 1944 C5
8300 TNTN 80221 1944 C5
8300 TNTN 80260 1944 C5
E Greenwood Cir
16900 AURA 80013 2285 A2
S Greenwood Cir
5900 LITN 80120 2364 C2
Greenwood Ct
8000 AdmC 80221 1944 C5
S Greenwood Ct
5000 JfnC 80439 2273 C7
7700 LITN 80120 2364 D6
Greenwood Dr
- BldC 80503 1521 A5
E Greenwood Dr
13800 AURA 80014 2284 B3
15400 AURA 80013 2284 D2
17800 AURA 80013 2285 B2
20700 AURA 80013 2286 A2
S Greenwood Dr
5000 JfnC 80439 2273 B7
Greenwood Ln
400 LGMT 80501 1439 E2
1200 CSRK 80104 2788 A1
29300 JfnC 80439 2273 B7
E Greenwood Ln
1300 GDVL 80121 2365 A1
Greenwood Pl
8200 BldC 80503 1521 A5
E Greenwood Pl
5600 DNVR 80222 2282 B2
14800 AURA 80014 2284 C2
18500 AURA 80013 2285 C2
20900 AURA 80013 2286 A2
W Greenwood Pl
3600 DNVR 80236 2279 D2
Greenwood Rd
3000 DgsC 80135 2785 D6
S Greenwood St
5300 EGLD 80120 2280 C7
5300 LITN 80120 2280 C7
5500 LITN 80120 2364 C1
Greenwood Plaza Blvd
5900 GDVL 80111 2366 D2
6200 AphC 80111 2366 E3
6200 CTNL 80111 2366 E3
6500 GDVL 80112 2366 E3
S Gregg Ct
3200 DNVR 80210 2281 D2
Gregory Dr
300 GOLD 80403 2107 D2
Gregory Ln
400 BldC 80302 1686 B4
400 BLDR 80302 1686 B4
Gregory St
100 BKHK 80403 2018 A4
200 BKHK 80403 2017 D4
200 CLCY 80403 2017 D4
Gregory Canyon Rd
- BldC 80302 1686 B5
- BLDR 80302 1686 B5
Greg's Pl
300 AdmC 80102 2124 E2
300 BNNT 80102 2124 E2
S Grenchen Dr
15300 JfnC 80470 2609 B6
Grenfell Ct
1800 ERIE 80516 1690 C2
Grey Ct
3400 CSRK 80104 2703 E3
Greylock St
4600 BldC 80301 1604 E3
Grey Squirrel Wy
100 DgsC 80116 2790 E1
300 DgsC 80116 2791 A2
Greystone Dr
200 CCkC 80439 2272 A5
Greystone Ln
4100 CSRK 80104 2787 E5
Greystone Rd
10 CCkC 80439 2271 E5
1700 CCkC 80439 2272 A5
Grey Swallow St
400 BGTN 80601 1697 D7
Grey Wolf Pl
4900 BMFD 80020 1775 B3

STREET
Block City ZIP Map# Grid

Griffin Dr
31500 JfnC 80433 2440 E4
Griffith Pl
1900 LGMT 80501 1355 E6
E Griffith Pl
- DgsC 80130 2450 A4
Griffith St
300 NDLD 80466 1765 C3
900 LSVL 80027 1689 D6
W Griffith St
300 LSVL 80027 1689 B6
Grigs Rd
- DgsC 80108 2449 E7
- DgsC 80108 2534 A3
- DgsC 80126 2449 E7
- DgsC 80126 2533 E2
- DgsC 80126 2534 A3
- DgsC 80130 2449 E7
Grinnell Av
4200 BLDR 80305 1687 B7
Grinnell Dr
2700 LGMT 80503 1355 C7
Grizzly Ct
7600 DgsC 80125 2531 A7
Grizzly Dr
10 BldC 80481 1514 E1
W Grizzly Dr
12500 JfnC 80127 2445 C4
Grizzly Wy
- BldC 80481 1514 E1
S Grizzly Wy
7800 JfnC 80439 2357 E7
7800 JfnC 80439 2358 A7
7800 JfnC 80439 2441 E1
8600 JfnC 80439 2442 A3
S Grizzly Gulch
10400 DgsC 80129 2448 B7
W Grizzly Gulch Ct
1700 DgsC 80129 2448 C6
Groover Dr
10 BldC 80540 1269 B7
Grosbeak St
5000 AdmC 80601 1697 D6
5000 BGTN 80601 1697 D6
Gross Rd
10 PrkC 80456 2521 E2
10 PrkC 80456 2522 A3
Gross Dam Rd
- BldC 80302 1768 E4
10 BldC 80403 1852 E2
500 BldC 80403 1853 A2
1900 BldC 80403 1769 B7
3900 BldC 80403 1768 E4
Ground Squirrel Ct
- BldC 80503 1354 A2
Grouse Av
1200 BGTN 80601 1779 E1
Grouse Ct
300 LSVL 80027 1773 B1
1200 LGMT 80501 1357 A7
11000 PARK 80134 2536 E1
S Grouse Ct
4900 JfnC 80439 2274 B7
Grouse Dr
1400 EbtC 80107 2708 C1
Grouse Ln
10 PrkC 80456 2691 D1
W Grouse Ln
34000 JfnC 80439 2356 B5
Grouse Pl
100 DgsC 80126 2448 E2
Grouse Wy
10 CCkC 80439 2271 C2
E Grouseberry Wy
17600 PARK 80134 2453 B4
Grove Cir
13000 BMFD 80020 1775 E6
N Grove Cir
9800 WSTR 80031 1859 E7
Grove Cir E
2200 BLDR 80302 1686 E2
Grove Cir W
2100 BLDR 80302 1686 E2
Grove Ct
10 BldC 80302 1600 E1
1100 LSVL 80027 1689 A7
1700 LGMT 80501 1355 E6
10800 WSTR 80031 1859 E5
13300 BMFD 80020 1775 E6
Grove Dr
900 LSVL 80027 1689 A7
Grove Ln
10700 WSTR 80031 1859 E5
N Grove Lp
- WSTR 80031 1859 E7
Grove Pl
2400 BGTN 80601 1696 E7
9900 WSTR 80031 1859 E7
13100 BMFD 80020 1775 E6
Grove St
- BGTN 80601 1697 A7
10 DNVR 80219 2196 A1
200 DNVR 80204 2196 A1
300 DNVR 80219 2112 A7
800 DNVR 80204 2112 A6
1500 BLDR 80302 1686 D2
1500 DNVR 80204 2111 E5
3100 DNVR 80211 2111 E1
3900 JfnC 80465 2276 B4
4700 DNVR 80211 2027 E6
4800 DNVR 80221 2027 E6
6600 AdmC 80221 2027 E1
7800 WSTR 80030 1943 E5
8000 WSTR 80031 1943 E5
8800 AdmC 80031 1943 E2
10700 WSTR 80031 1859 E5
12500 BMFD 80020 1859 E1
12600 BMFD 80020 1775 E7
18000 JfnC 80433 2694 E5
28200 JfnC 80470 2693 D2
N Grove St
9200 AdmC 80031 1943 E2
9200 WSTR 80031 1943 E2
10500 WSTR 80031 1859 E5

STREET
Block City ZIP Map# Grid

S Grove St
10 DNVR 80219 2196 A2
2600 DNVR 80219 2280 A1
2600 DNVR 80236 2280 A1
3600 SRDN 80110 2280 A4
5000 EGLD 80110 2280 A7
5000 LITN 80123 2280 A7
11500 WSTR 80031 1859 E3
Grove Wy
9900 WSTR 80031 1859 E7
12900 BMFD 80020 1775 E6
12900 BMFD 80020 1776 A6
Groveton Av
- CSRK 80104 2705 A7
Guadeloupe St
4000 BLDR 80301 1603 A5
Guava Pl
- BLDR 80304 1602 D4
Guernsey Lp
- CSRK 80109 2702 C4
Guinivere St
10 LAFT 80026 1690 E6
N Gulch Rd
10 BldC 80302 1683 E3
Gull St
5000 BGTN 80601 1697 D6
9600 FLHT 80260 1860 A7
9600 FLHT 80260 1944 A1
Gunbarrel Av
5800 BldC 80301 1603 E3
5800 BLDR 80301 1603 E3
6100 BldC 80301 1604 A3
6100 BLDR 80301 1604 A3
Gunbarrel Cir
5300 BldC 80503 1604 C1
Gunbarrel Rd
5600 BldC 80503 1520 C7
5600 BldC 80503 1604 C1
Gunbarrel Ridge Rd
9100 BldC 80026 1605 C2
9100 BldC 80301 1605 C2
S Gun Club Ct
- AURA 80016 2370 D4
S Gun Club Pkwy
- AURA 80016 2370 D2
Gun Club Rd
- AdmC 80019 2118 E4
- AphC 80018 2118 D5
- AURA 80019 2118 E4
- DNVR 80249 1950 C6
10 AphC 80018 2202 D1
10 AURA 80018 2202 D1
100 AURA 80018 2118 D7
12800 AdmC 80022 1782 C6
13400 AdmC 80603 1782 C6
15200 AdmC 80603 1698 C7
S Gun Club Rd
1400 AURA 80018 2202 D7
1900 AphC 80018 2202 D7
2700 AphC 80018 2286 D2
2700 AURA 80018 2286 D2
4100 AURA 80016 2286 D6
4300 AphC 80016 2286 D6
5400 AURA 80016 2370 D1
5500 AphC 80015 2370 D2
5500 AphC 80016 2370 D2
S Gun Club Rd SR-30
1400 AURA 80018 2202 D7
1900 AphC 80018 2202 D7
2700 AphC 80018 2286 D2
2700 AURA 80018 2286 D2
4100 AURA 80016 2286 D4
Gun Club Mile Rd
- AdmC 80022 1782 C7
- AdmC 80022 1866 C1
2000 AdmC 80019 2118 D3
2000 AURA 80019 2118 D3
2600 AURA 80019 2034 D7
E Gunnison Cir
19200 AURA 80017 2201 D4
E Gunnison Dr
24700 AURA 80018 2202 E5
24700 AURA 80018 2203 A5
W Gunnison Dr
2400 DNVR 80219 2196 A5
2400 DNVR 80223 2196 A5
E Gunnison Pl
5600 DNVR 80222 2198 B5
5600 DNVR 80224 2198 B5
7500 DNVR 80231 2198 D5
10000 AURA 80247 2199 B5
14500 AURA 80012 2200 C5
15700 AURA 80017 2200 E5
19200 AURA 80017 2201 D4
W Gunnison Pl
1800 DNVR 80223 2196 B5
2300 DNVR 80219 2196 B5
Gunnison Wy
13800 BMFD 80020 1775 A4
Gunpark Dr E
6500 BldC 80301 1604 A2
6500 BLDR 80301 1604 A2
Gunpark Dr W
6300 BldC 80301 1604 A2
6300 BLDR 80301 1604 A2
Gunsight Pass
7700 JfnC 80127 2361 E7
7700 JfnC 80127 2362 B6
Gunsmoke Dr
10 PrkC 80456 2522 B5
Guy Ct
15500 AdmC 80603 1864 D1
Guy Hill Rd
29100 JfnC 80403 2021 C7
S Gwendelyn Ln
- DgsC 80129 2448 E5
S Gwendelyn Pl
9900 DgsC 80129 2448 E5
W Gwendelyn Rd
- DgsC 80129 2448 E5
- DgsC 80129 2448 E5
Gyda Dr
8900 ARVD 80002 2026 C4

STREET
Block City ZIP Map# Grid

Gypsum Ct
3600 SUPE 80027 1857 A1
17500 PARK 80134 2453 A5
Gypsy Moth Ct
- CSRK 80109 2702 C5
Gyros Cir
2000 LAFT 80026 1689 E6
2000 LSVL 80027 1689 E6

H

H St
100 CLCY 80403 2017 C4
800 GOLD 80401 2108 B7
Habitat Dr
6100 BldC 80301 1603 E3
6100 BldC 80301 1604 A3
6100 BLDR 80301 1604 A3
Habu Ln
10 PrkC 80456 2607 C5
Hacienda Pl
5300 DgsC 80134 2621 B5
Hacienda Rd
700 JfnC 80439 2188 A4
Hackamore Rd
8300 DgsC 80125 2530 D5
Hackberry Cir
2100 LGMT 80501 1355 E5
Hackberry Ct
2900 DgsC 80129 2448 A4
Hackberry Ln
9400 DgsC 80129 2448 A4
S Hackberry St
9500 DgsC 80129 2448 A4
W Hackberry St
500 LSVL 80027 1773 B1
Hackberry Hill Rd
7000 ARVD 80003 1942 E7
7000 ARVD 80004 1942 E7
Hackney Ct
5400 DgsC 80134 2621 E4
Hadar Dr
13100 DgsC 80124 2450 D3
Haddon Rd
3900 DNVR 80205 2113 D3
3900 DNVR 80207 2113 D3
Hadrian Ct
10200 LNTR 80134 2451 E6
S Hagen Ct
9500 DgsC 80126 2449 B4
S Hagler Dr
22600 JfnC 80401 2191 A5
Hague Cir
100 EbtC 80138 2539 E6
S Hahns Peak
7600 JfnC 80127 2361 E6
Hairanch Peak Wy
2800 CSRK 80109 2786 E5
Haldimand Dr
31000 JfnC 80433 2525 A4
Hale Av
- PARK 80138 2538 C2
Hale Ct
- PARK 80138 2538 C2
Hale Pkwy
4100 DNVR 80220 2113 E6
4700 DNVR 80220 2114 A6
S Haleyville Cir
1400 AURA 80018 2202 E4
1400 AURA 80018 2203 A4
S Haleyville Ct
- AURA 80016 2371 A4
5200 AURA 80016 2287 A7
Haleyville St
- AURA 80016 2287 A6
S Haleyville St
1400 AURA 80018 2203 A5
5100 AURA 80016 2287 A7
5200 AURA 80016 2286 D5
S Haleyville Wy
5200 AURA 80016 2287 A7
5300 AURA 80016 2286 E7
Half Dr
- LGMT 80504 1439 A7
Half Measures Dr
800 LGMT 80504 1439 B6
Halfmoon Dr
600 CSRK 80104 2787 D5
W Half Moon Pass
10800 JfnC 80127 2362 A7
11000 JfnC 80127 2361 E7
Halifax Av
6600 CSRK 80104 2705 A7
S Halifax Cir
5300 CTNL 80015 2285 E7
Halifax Ct
4900 DNVR 80249 2033 D5
S Halifax Ct
2500 AURA 80013 2201 E7
4200 AURA 80013 2285 E4
Halifax St
1900 AURA 80011 2117 D4
4800 DNVR 80249 2033 D6
S Halifax St
2500 AURA 80013 2201 E7
3700 AURA 80013 2285 E4
4300 CTNL 80015 2285 E5
Halifax Wy
1600 AURA 80011 2117 E4
4800 DNVR 80249 2033 D5
S Halifax Wy
- AphC 80013 2285 E5
1200 AURA 80017 2201 D4
2400 AURA 80013 2201 E7
3300 AURA 80013 2285 E2
4300 AphC 80015 2285 E5
4300 AURA 80015 2285 E5
Halite Ct
7200 CSRK 80108 2619 E6
Hall Rd
10 PrkC 80456 2521 E2
200 PrkC 80456 2522 A2
Hallet Peak Dr
1600 LGMT 80503 1437 D6
Halleys Dr
7500 DgsC 80125 2530 E7
Halleys Wy
10200 DgsC 80125 2530 E7
Hallmark Ln
700 LGMT 80501 1356 D6
Halter Wy
- CCkC 80439 2103 B7
Halyard Ct
1600 LAFT 80026 1689 E5
Hamal Dr
700 DgsC 80124 2450 D3
E Hamilton Av
5100 CSRK 80104 2788 D1
5200 CSRK 80104 2704 E7
20400 AURA 80013 2285 E2
20500 AURA 80013 2286 A3
W Hamilton Av
- SRDN 80110 2279 D3
3600 DNVR 80236 2279 D3
E Hamilton Cir
20400 AURA 80013 2285 E2
Hamilton Ct
4400 BLDR 80305 1687 B6
8600 LNTR 80124 2450 E4
8600 LNTR 80124 2451 A4
Hamilton Dr
- LGMT 80501 1356 B6
E Hamilton Dr
13700 AURA 80014 2284 B3
18500 AURA 80013 2285 C2
W Hamilton Dr
6600 DNVR 80227 2279 A3
6600 LKWD 80227 2279 A3
9100 LKWD 80227 2278 B3
Hamilton Pl
- DNVR 80231 2283 B3
E Hamilton Pl
7100 DNVR 80224 2282 C2
15800 AURA 80013 2284 D3
20300 AURA 80013 2285 E3
W Hamilton Pl
1600 SRDN 80110 2280 B3
3000 SRDN 80110 2279 E3
4200 DNVR 80236 2279 D3
Hamilton St
- AdmC 80137 2120 E4
Hampden Av
23300 AphC 80018 2286 D3
E Hampden Av
- AphC 80014 2284 B3
10 EGLD 80110 2280 E3
10 EGLD 80113 2280 E3
1500 CHLV 80113 2281 E3
1500 EGLD 80113 2281 A3
2300 DvrC 80113 2281 E3
2800 CHLV 80210 2281 E3
3600 AphC 80210 2281 E3
3600 DNVR 80210 2281 E3
3600 DNVR 80222 2281 E3
3600 DvrC 80222 2281 E3
4700 AphC 80222 2282 A3
4700 CHLV 80113 2282 A3
4700 DNVR 80222 2282 A3
4700 DNVR 80237 2282 A3
6500 DNVR 80224 2282 E3
7200 DNVR 80231 2282 E3
8700 DNVR 80231 2283 B3
8700 DNVR 80237 2283 B3
9000 DvrC 80231 2283 B3
9000 GDVL 80014 2283 B3
9200 DNVR 80014 2283 B3
14200 AURA 80014 2284 B3
15000 AURA 80013 2284 D3
16800 AURA 80013 2285 A3
20000 AphC 80013 2285 C3
21700 AphC 80013 2286 A3
21700 AphC 80018 2286 A3
21700 AURA 80013 2286 A3
21700 AURA 80018 2286 A3
E Hampden Av SR-30
5900 DNVR 80222 2282 A3
5900 DNVR 80237 2282 A3
6500 DNVR 80224 2282 E3
7200 DNVR 80231 2282 E3
8700 DNVR 80231 2283 B3
8700 DNVR 80237 2283 B3
9000 DvrC 80231 2283 B3
9000 GDVL 80014 2283 B3
9200 DNVR 80014 2283 B3
E Hampden Av US-285
1500 CHLV 80113 2281 E3
1500 EGLD 80113 2281 E3
1900 AphC 80113 2281 E3
2800 CHLV 80210 2281 E3
3600 AphC 80210 2281 E3
3600 AphC 80222 2281 E3
3600 DNVR 80210 2281 E3
3600 DNVR 80222 2281 E3
4700 AphC 80222 2282 B3
4700 CHLV 80113 2282 B3
4700 DNVR 80222 2282 B3
4700 DNVR 80237 2282 B3
W Hampden Av
- SRDN 80110 2280 D3
10 EGLD 80110 2280 E3
100 EGLD 80110 2280 E3
3000 SRDN 80110 2279 E3
3300 AphC 80236 2279 E3
3300 DNVR 80236 2279 E3
5500 DNVR 80227 2279 B3
5500 DNVR 80235 2279 B3
5500 DvrC 80235 2279 B3
6300 LKWD 80227 2279 B3
6300 LKWD 80235 2279 B3
6800 LKWD 80235 2278 E3
9000 LKWD 80227 2278 C3
9200 JfnC 80235 2278 C3
10000 JfnC 80235 2278 A3
10800 JfnC 80227 2277 E3
13000 LKWD 80465 2277 B4
14900 LKWD 80465 2276 E5
W Hampden Av US-285
- SRDN 80110 2280 D3
100 EGLD 80110 2280 D3
E Hampden Cir
7800 DNVR 80237 2282 D3
14900 AURA 80014 2284 C3
15200 AURA 80013 2284 D3
E Hampden Dr
19000 AURA 80013 2285 D3
E Hampden Pl
14600 AURA 80014 2284 C3
18200 AURA 80013 2285 B3
20600 AphC 80013 2285 E3
20900 AphC 80013 2286 A3
W Hampden Pl
300 EGLD 80110 2280 D3
10800 JfnC 80227 2278 A3
10900 JfnC 80227 2277 E3
Hampden Frontage Rd
- JfnC 80227 2278 B3
- JfnC 80235 2278 B3
- LKWD 80227 2278 B3
- LKWD 80235 2278 B3
W Hampden Frontage Rd
- JfnC 80227 2278 A3
8400 LKWD 80227 2278 C3
10100 JfnC 80235 2278 A3
W Hampden Frontage Rd S
- JfnC 80235 2278 D4
- LKWD 80235 2278 D4
W Hampden Service Rd
8400 JfnC 80235 2278 C3
8400 LKWD 80227 2278 C3
8400 LKWD 80235 2278 C3
W Hampden Service Rd S
- LKWD 80235 2278 D3
Hampshire St
4600 BldC 80301 1604 E3
Hampstead Av
10 CSRK 80104 2704 D7
400 CSRK 80104 2788 D1
S Hampton Cir
4100 BLDR 80301 1603 B5
Hampton Ct
6900 DgsC 80108 2618 E1
Hamron Ct
1900 ERIE 80516 1606 E5
Hancock Ct
100 BNNT 80102 2124 C2
Hancock Dr
1100 BLDR 80303 1687 C3
Hancock Wy
200 BNNT 80102 2124 C2
Handles Rd
9800 TNTN 80260 1860 B6
Hangar Ct
11900 JfnC 80021 1858 A2
E Hanging J Ranch Pl
20000 DgsC 80134 2537 E5
Hanging Rock Pl
- CSRK 80108 2703 E1
Hangmans Rd
100 PrkC 80456 2522 B6
Hanley Ct
6700 DgsC 80108 2618 E1
S Hannah Dr
11500 JfnC 80433 2525 A3
11600 JfnC 80433 2524 E3
Hannibal Ct
5500 DNVR 80239 2032 D4
9700 CMCY 80022 1864 D7
S Hannibal Ct
1900 AURA 80013 2200 D6
Hannibal Dr
800 AURA 80011 2116 D6
Hannibal St
5100 DNVR 80239 2032 D5
9900 CMCY 80022 1864 D7
11800 CMCY 80603 1864 C2
S Hannibal St
1900 AURA 80013 2200 D6
2900 AURA 80013 2284 D2
4500 AURA 80015 2284 D5
5400 CTNL 80015 2284 D7
S Hannibal Wy
900 AURA 80017 2200 D3
2000 AURA 80013 2200 D6
4300 AURA 80015 2284 D5
5100 CTNL 80015 2284 D7
5400 CTNL 80015 2368 D1
Hanover Av
4000 BLDR 80305 1687 B7
Hanover Ct
2900 AdmC 80137 2121 B2
15200 AdmC 80602 1695 B7
15200 AdmC 80602 1779 B1
S Hanover Ct
6300 AphC 80111 2367 C3
Hanover Ct E
9700 CMCY 80640 1863 B7
Hanover Ct W
9600 CMCY 80640 1863 B7
9600 CMCY 80640 1947 B1
E Hanover Pl
5100 CSRK 80104 2788 D1
Hanover St
- DNVR 80238 2115 C3
- DvrC 80238 2115 C3
1500 AURA 80010 2115 B4
14800 AdmC 80602 1779 B1
S Hanover St
5100 AphC 80111 2283 C7
Hanover Wy
500 AURA 80010 2115 C7
S Hanover Wy
5100 AphC 80111 2283 B7
5700 GDVL 80111 2367 C2
W Hanoverian Wy
4600 LITN 80128 2363 C6
Hapgood St
400 BLDR 80302 1686 B3
Happy Tr
3000 JfnC 80439 2273 B3
S Happy Canyon Dr
5700 CHLV 80111 2282 B4
Happy Canyon Rd
- DgsC 80108 2619 B3
4800 AphC 80222 2282 A3
4800 CHLV 80113 2282 A3
4800 DNVR 80222 2282 A3
4800 DNVR 80237 2282 A3
5500 AphC 80113 2282 A3
5500 AphC 80237 2282 A3
5500 CHLV 80111 2282 A3
E Happy Canyon Rd
100 DgsC 80108 2619 A4
S Happy Canyon Rd
5600 AphC 80113 2282 B4
5600 CHLV 80111 2282 B4
5600 CHLV 80113 2282 B4
5600 DNVR 80237 2282 B4
6300 DvrC 80237 2282 B4
W Happy Canyon Rd
100 DgsC 80108 2618 E5
100 DgsC 80108 2619 A4
S Happy Hill Rd
6700 JfnC 80439 2358 A5
6800 JfnC 80439 2357 E5
Happy Top Rd
- PrkC 80456 2690 C4
Happy Top Tr
- PrkC 80456 2690 B3
N Harback Rd
10 AphC 80102 2207 E1
1500 AdmC 80102 2123 E3
4000 AdmC 80102 2039 E7
Harbell Dr
- DgsC 80118 2953 E1
- DgsC 80118 2954 A1
Harbor Ln
1700 LGMT 80503 1355 B6
Harbortown Pl
8200 LNTR 80124 2450 E6
Harbour Dr
- DNVR 80247 2198 E4
Harding Ct
- BLDR 80305 1771 A2
S Harding Ct
200 LSVL 80027 1773 B2
Hardrock Pl
1300 DgsC 80104 2787 E5
Hardscrabble Dr
1900 BLDR 80305 1771 A2
Hardscrabble Pl
1900 BLDR 80305 1770 E2
Hardscrabble Rd
10 BldC 80403 1852 A1
Hardt Rd
- BldC 80503 1435 E5
Hardwick Ct
200 DgsC 80108 2618 E1
Hard Wy Rd
10 BldC 80481 1514 E5
Harebell Ln
28000 JfnC 80439 2273 D5
W Harebell Run
10500 DgsC 80125 2614 E4
S Harford Ct
9500 DgsC 80126 2449 B4
Harkwood Run Tr
30500 JfnC 80403 2104 D2
S Harlan Cir
- LKWD 80227 2195 B6
1800 LKWD 80232 2195 A6
Harlan Ct
4400 WTRG 80033 2027 B7
8200 ARVD 80003 1943 A5
9400 WSTR 80031 1943 A1
S Harlan Ct
1900 LKWD 80227 2195 B6
2500 LKWD 80227 2279 B1
6900 JfnC 80128 2363 B5
Harlan St
- DNVR 80212 2027 B6
10 LKWD 80226 2195 B1
300 LKWD 80226 2111 B7
600 LKWD 80214 2111 B6
1700 EDGW 80214 2111 B4
3000 WTRG 80033 2111 B2
3000 WTRG 80212 2111 B2
3000 WTRG 80214 2111 B2
4100 WTRG 80212 2027 B6
4400 WTRG 80033 2027 B6
4800 DvrC 80212 2027 B6
4800 LKSD 80212 2027 B6
4900 DNVR 80033 2027 B6
5300 ARVD 80002 2027 B3
5300 JfnC 80002 2027 B3
6000 ARVD 80003 2027 B3
7500 WSTR 80003 1943 B5
7600 ARVD 80003 1943 B5
8800 WSTR 80031 1943 A3
9400 JfnC 80031 1943 A1
9500 JfnC 80021 1943 A1
9500 WSTR 80021 1943 A1
11400 WSTR 80020 1859 A3
S Harlan St
10 LKWD 80226 2195 B2
1000 LKWD 80232 2195 B5
2100 DNVR 80227 2195 B7
2200 DvrC 80227 2195 B7
2200 LKWD 80227 2195 B7
2400 LKWD 80227 2279 B1
3500 DNVR 80227 2279 B3
3500 DNVR 80235 2279 B3
3500 DvrC 80235 2279 B3
5500 DNVR 80123 2363 B1
5700 JfnC 80123 2363 B2
7400 JfnC 80128 2363 B6
Harlan Wy
7400 WSTR 80003 1943 B6
S Harlan Wy
900 LKWD 80226 2195 B4
2800 DNVR 80227 2279 B2
5200 DNVR 80123 2279 B7
5200 DNVR 80123 2363 B1
6200 JfnC 80123 2363 B3
7700 JfnC 80128 2363 B7
Harlequin Dr
1500 LGMT 80501 1357 A7
1500 LGMT 80501 1440 A1
Harmon Pl
1000 LGMT 80501 1356 A5
Harmon Rd
33600 JfnC 80470 2524 B6
Harmon St
300 LAFT 80026 1690 C5
Harmony Ln
- CMCY 80022 1865 A5
10600 CMCY 80022 1864 E5
Harmony Pkwy
- BMFD 80020 1776 A6
12900 WSTR 80234 1776 A6
N Harmony Park Dr
1900 WSTR 80234 1776 A6
Harness Ct
- BGTN 80601 1697 C5
- DgsC 80134 2621 B5
Harper St
10 LSVL 80027 1689 C6
W Harper St
300 LSVL 80027 1689 B6
Harper Lake Ct
1200 LSVL 80027 1689 A7
Harper Lake Dr
1100 LSVL 80027 1689 A7
Harpy Ct
900 CSRK 80109 2703 B5
S Harrington Ln
2500 LKWD 80227 2195 B7
2500 LKWD 80227 2279 A1
Harris Cir
9600 TNTN 80229 1945 B1
Harris Ct
- ERIE 80516 1606 E7
9600 TNTN 80229 1945 B1
9700 TNTN 80229 1861 B7
Harris Rd
- GpnC 80403 2017 A7
Harris St
10 PrkC 80456 2521 D2
1600 SUPE 80027 1773 C5
8300 AdmC 80229 1945 B4
9100 TNTN 80229 1945 B2
10100 TNTN 80229 1861 B7
Harris Wy
11100 TNTN 80233 1862 B4
Harrison Av
1200 BLDR 80303 1687 C3
18000 JfnC 80433 2694 E5
N Harrison Av
100 LAFT 80026 1690 C4
S Harrison Av
100 LAFT 80026 1690 C5
Harrison Cir
8300 AdmC 80229 1945 D4
S Harrison Cir
7700 CTNL 80122 2365 E6
8000 CTNL 80122 2449 E1
Harrison Ct
1200 BLDR 80303 1687 B3
1500 LSVL 80027 1689 A6
8500 AdmC 80229 1945 D3
13400 TNTN 80241 1777 D5
S Harrison Ct
6300 CTNL 80121 2365 E3
7100 CTNL 80122 2365 E5
Harrison Dr
200 BNNT 80102 2124 C2
700 LAFT 80026 1690 C3
13000 TNTN 80241 1777 D6
13900 TNTN 80602 1777 D4
S Harrison Dr
6100 CTNL 80121 2365 E3
S Harrison Ln
600 DNVR 80209 2197 D3
Harrison Pl
12200 TNTN 80241 1861 D1
Harrison St
10 DNVR 80206 2197 E1
10 DNVR 80209 2197 E1
1500 DNVR 80206 2113 D5
3300 DNVR 80205 2113 D1
3900 DNVR 80205 2029 D7
5200 DNVR 80216 2029 D5
9200 TNTN 80229 1945 D2
9600 TNTN 80229 1861 D7
11800 TNTN 80233 1861 D2
13500 TNTN 80241 1777 D5
13900 TNTN 80602 1777 D4
14500 AdmC 80602 1777 D2
S Harrison St
10 DNVR 80206 2197 E2
10 DNVR 80209 2197 E2
1000 DNVR 80210 2197 E4
2700 DNVR 80210 2281 E1
3700 CHLV 80113 2281 E4
6800 CTNL 80122 2365 E5
Harrison Wy
8400 AdmC 80229 1945 D4
S Harrison Wy
6300 CTNL 80121 2365 E3
7500 CTNL 80122 2365 E6
8000 CTNL 80122 2449 C1
Harris Park Rd
500 PrkC 80456 2521 C3
Harrow Ct
- BGTN 80601 1697 C5
Harry St
- GpnC 80403 1849 D5
Harry B Combs Pkwy
7800 DNVR 80249 1951 C5
Hartford Dr
500 BLDR 80305 1686 E7
500 BLDR 80305 1687 A6
1100 BLDR 80305 1771 B2
Hartland Pl
400 DgsC 80108 2534 E4
Hartley Ct
1600 LGMT 80501 1438 E6
Hartwick Cir
2800 LGMT 80503 1355 C7
Harvard
- DNVR 80210 2197 E7
- DNVR 80222 2197 E7
E Harvard Av
- AphC 80231 2199 A7
- AphC 80231 2283 A1
10 DNVR 80210 2196 E7
10 DNVR 80223 2196 E7
1400 DNVR 80210 2197 B7
4200 DNVR 80222 2197 E7
6400 DNVR 80222 2198 C7
6500 DNVR 80224 2198 C7
7300 AphC 80231 2198 D7
7300 DNVR 80231 2198 D7
9800 DNVR 80231 2199 B7
10200 AURA 80014 2199 B7
10200 AURA 80247 2199 B7
10200 DNVR 80014 2199 B7
10200 DNVR 80247 2199 B7
14500 AURA 80014 2200 C7
16500 AURA 80013 2200 E7
19800 AURA 80013 2201 D7
W Harvard Av
10 DNVR 80210 2196 D7
10 DNVR 80223 2196 D7
2400 EGLD 80110 2196 A7
3000 DNVR 80219 2196 A7
3100 DNVR 80219 2195 D7
5100 LKWD 80227 2195 C7
9700 LKWD 80227 2194 B7
12600 JfnC 80228 2277 C1
13900 LKWD 80228 2277 B1
E Harvard Cir
7900 AphC 80231 2198 E7
12500 AURA 80014 2199 E7
12600 AURA 80014 2200 A7
Harvard Ct
2100 LGMT 80503 1355 C5
E Harvard Dr
10800 AURA 80014 2199 C7
11100 AURA 80014 2283 D1
18600 AURA 80013 2201 C6
S Harvard Dr
9300 DgsC 80130 2450 C4
W Harvard Dr
6000 LKWD 80227 2279 B1
7800 LKWD 80227 2278 D1
8800 LKWD 80227 2194 C7
13700 LKWD 80228 2193 B7
13700 LKWD 80228 2277 C1
Harvard Ln
300 BLDR 80305 1687 A6
E Harvard Ln
4800 AphC 80222 2198 A7
6200 DgsC 80130 2450 C4
E Harvard Pl
16800 AURA 80013 2200 E7
17800 AURA 80013 2201 B7
43000 AphC 80102 2207 D7
W Harvard Pl
8800 LKWD 80227 2278 C1
14100 LKWD 80228 2277 B1
Harvard St
2000 LGMT 80503 1355 C4
Harvest Ct
15600 AdmC 80603 1698 E6
S Harvest Ct
- AURA 80016 2371 A4
Harvest Dr
1400 LAFT 80026 1690 A3
Harvest Ln
4000 BGTN 80601 1697 B4
S Harvest Ln
- AphC 80126 2449 D1
- CTNL 80122 2449 D1
- CTNL 80126 2449 D1
Harvest Rd
6700 BldC 80301 1604 B1
12800 AdmC 80022 1782 E6
13600 AdmC 80603 1698 E7
13600 AdmC 80603 1782 E3
16000 LCHB 80603 1698 E5
S Harvest Rd
- AphC 80016 2287 A7
- AphC 80018 2287 A5
- AURA 80016 2287 A7
1100 AphC 80018 2203 A5
1100 AURA 80018 2203 A5
Harvest St
200 LGMT 80501 1440 A3
S Harvest St
- AphC 80016 2371 A3
- AURA 80016 2371 A3
Harvest Mile Rd
- AdmC 80019 2034 E5
- AdmC 80019 2119 A2
- AdmC 80022 1782 E7
- AdmC 80022 1866 E1
- AdmC 80249 2034 E2
- AdmC 80249 2035 A2
- AURA 80019 2034 E5
- AURA 80019 2035 A7
- AURA 80019 2119 A2
S Harvest Mile Wy
5300 AURA 80016 2287 A7
Harvest Point Dr
100 ERIE 80516 1606 E6
W Harvey Pl
5100 DNVR 80219 2195 C7
5100 DNVR 80227 2195 C7
E Harvey St
800 DgsC 80108 2619 C7
Harwich St
4600 BldC 80301 1604 E3
Haseley Dr
15700 DgsC 80134 2452 D4
Haskell Ct
2700 AdmC 80137 2121 B2
Haskell Pl
2500 AdmC 80137 2121 C2
Haskell Wy
2200 AdmC 80137 2121 B3
Hasstedt Ln
- DgsC 80134 2538 C5
- DgsC 80138 2538 C5
Hastings Av
17000 PARK 80134 2453 A7
Hastings Ct
17000 PARK 80134 2453 B7
Hastings Dr
4400 BLDR 80305 1771 B1
Hastings Wy
8800 AdmC 80031 1943 E3
8800 WSTR 80031 1943 E3
Hasty Rd
28700 JfnC 80439 2357 D7
28700 JfnC 80439 2441 C1
Haswell Ct
11300 PARK 80134 2453 B7
Haswell Dr
11300 PARK 80134 2453 B7
11300 PARK 80134 2537 B1
S Hatch Dr
5100 JfnC 80439 2357 B1
E Hatchet Ranch Pl
20000 DgsC 80134 2537 E4
Hathaway Ln
10 DgsC 80130 2450 A2
Hauck St
1700 ERIE 80516 1690 C2
Haul Rd
10 BldC 80466 1765 D5
Hauptman Ct
3800 BldC 80301 1603 A5
Havana Ct
- AdmC 80640 1863 B6
- CMCY 80640 1863 B6
15900 AdmC 80602 1695 B6
S Havana Ct
5300 AphC 80111 2283 C7
5700 AphC 80111 2367 C2
Havana St
- AdmC 80602 1779 B1
- DvrC 80238 2115 C3
10 AURA 80010 2199 C1
10 AURA 80012 2199 C1
2300 AURA 80010 2115 C3
3600 DNVR 80238 2115 C1
3700 DNVR 80239 2031 C7
3700 DNVR 80239 2115 C1
3800 DNVR 80238 2031 B7
5400 AdmC 80022 2031 B4
5400 DNVR 80022 2031 B4
9600 CMCY 80640 1947 B1
10400 AdmC 80640 1863 B6
10400 CMCY 80640 1863 B6
15500 AdmC 80602 1695 B7
Havana St SR-30
10 AURA 80010 2199 C1
10 AURA 80012 2199 C1
300 AURA 80010 2115 C7
S Havana St
- DgsC 80112 2451 D5
- DgsC 80134 2451 D5
- GDVL 80111 2283 C7
10 AURA 80010 2199 C2
200 AphC 80012 2199 C2
200 AURA 80012 2199 C2
200 DNVR 80010 2199 C2
200 DNVR 80247 2199 C2
600 DvrC 80247 2199 C2
1000 AURA 80247 2199 C5
1800 AURA 80014 2199 C5
2500 AURA 80231 2199 C5
2500 DNVR 80014 2199 C5
2500 DNVR 80231 2199 C5
2600 AURA 80014 2283 C2
2600 DNVR 80231 2283 C2
3000 DNVR 80014 2283 C2
5300 AphC 80111 2283 C7
5600 AphC 80111 2367 C2
5600 GDVL 80111 2367 C2
6300 CTNL 80111 2367 C4
6600 CTNL 80112 2367 C4
7100 AphC 80112 2367 C5
S Havana St SR-30
10 AURA 80010 2199 C2
10 AURA 80012 2199 C2
200 AphC 80012 2199 C2
200 DNVR 80010 2199 C2
200 DNVR 80247 2199 C2
600 AURA 80247 2199 C2
600 DvrC 80247 2199 C2
2500 AURA 80014 2199 C5
2500 AURA 80231 2199 C5
2500 DNVR 80014 2199 C5
2500 DNVR 80231 2199 C5
2600 AURA 80014 2283 C2
2600 DNVR 80231 2283 C2
3000 DNVR 80014 2283 C2
Havana Wy
- AURA 80010 2115 C2
- DNVR 80010 2115 C2
- DNVR 80238 2115 C2
- DvrC 80010 2115 C2
15600 AdmC 80602 1695 B6
Havekost Rd
9900 JfnC 80433 2442 A5
Havenwood Dr
7100 DgsC 80108 2618 D1
7200 DgsC 80108 2534 D7
Havenwood Wy
1200 DgsC 80108 2618 C1
Havilah St
- CLCY 80403 2017 E4
W Hawaii Av
10000 LKWD 80232 2194 B5
11400 JfnC 80232 2193 E5
12500 LKWD 80228 2193 C5
E Hawaii Cir
11900 AURA 80012 2199 D5
14200 AURA 80012 2200 B5
E Hawaii Dr
12100 AURA 80012 2199 E5
18700 AURA 80017 2201 C5
W Hawaii Dr
8600 LKWD 80232 2194 C5

STREET
Block City ZIP Map# Grid

E Hawaii Ln
8400 AphC 80231 2198 E5
8400 AphC 80247 2198 E5
E Hawaii Pl
- AURA 80018 2202 E5
9800 AURA 80247 2199 B5
14500 AURA 80012 2200 C5
17600 AURA 80017 2201 B5
W Hawaii Pl
10100 LKWD 80232 2194 A5
11100 JfnC 80232 2193 E5
Hawk Ct
1000 LSVL 80027 1689 B7
2900 LAFT 80026 1774 C2
Hawk Ln
10 BldC 80304 1601 D5
Hawk St
2600 FLHT 80260 1944 A1
2600 TNTN 80260 1944 A1
2900 FLHT 80260 1860 A7
Hawk Wy
10 GpnC 80403 1933 E6
Hawken Dr
2200 DgsC 80109 2786 B6
Hawkins Av
10800 JfnC 80433 2443 A7
Hawk Point Ct
2600 CSRK 80104 2704 B5
Hawk Ridge Dr
1200 ERIE 80516 1690 D2
1200 LAFT 80026 1690 D2
Hawk Ridge Rd
1100 LAFT 80026 1690 D3
Hawks Cir
24400 JfnC 80439 2358 D1
E Hawksbead Dr
17100 PARK 80134 2453 A4
Hawks Eye Ct
6100 CSRK 80108 2620 A7
Hawks Nest Tr
7300 DgsC 80125 2530 D7
7300 DgsC 80125 2614 D1
Hawkstone Pl
16200 DgsC 80134 2452 E4
Hawkstone Wy
9500 DgsC 80134 2452 E4
Hawthorn
4200 BMFD 80020 1859 C1
Hawthorn Av
200 BldC 80304 1602 B6
200 BLDR 80304 1602 B6
Hawthorn Cir
5500 GDVL 80121 2366 A2
W Hawthorn Ct
300 LSVL 80027 1689 B6
Hawthorn Hllw
3200 BLDR 80304 1602 C7
Hawthorn Ln
2000 DgsC 80116 2707 D3
6300 LKWD 80227 2195 A6
Hawthorn Pl
1700 BLDR 80304 1602 D6
W Hawthorn St
500 LSVL 80027 1689 A6
Hawthorn Tr
5300 DgsC 80125 2614 E5
Hawthorne Cir
3900 LGMT 80503 1438 A5
Hawthorne Dr
- LGMT 80503 1438 A5
3300 DgsC 80126 2449 D5
Hawthorne Ln
21000 PARK 80138 2538 A3
Hawthorne Pl
2600 BLDR 80304 1602 E7
4100 LGMT 80503 1438 A5
E Hawthorne Pl
2100 DNVR 80206 2113 B7
W Hawthorne Pl
3000 AdmC 80221 2027 E2
Hawthorne Rd
1200 JfnC 80401 2109 B5
1200 LKWD 80401 2109 B5
Hawthorne St
9800 DgsC 80126 2449 D5
S Hawthorne St
4700 DNVR 80110 2279 E6
4700 EGLD 80110 2279 E6
5000 EGLD 80110 2280 A7
5000 LITN 80123 2280 A7
Haxtun Ct
11200 PARK 80134 2453 B7
11200 PARK 80134 2537 B1
Hayden Ct
700 BldC 80503 1438 C1
700 LGMT 80503 1438 C1
Hayden Pl
3400 BLDR 80301 1603 A7
W Hayden Pass
10200 JfnC 80127 2362 B7
Hayes St
10 PrkC 80456 2522 A2
Hayesmount Rd
10400 AdmC 80022 1868 A3
10400 DNVR 80022 1868 A3
10400 DNVR 80249 1868 A5
10400 DNVR 80642 1868 A5
12000 AdmC 80022 1784 A7
13100 AdmC 80603 1784 A4
14800 AdmC 80603 1700 A5
16600 WldC 80642 1700 A5
N Hayesmount Rd
10 AphC 80137 2120 B7
10 AphC 80137 2204 B1
10 AURA 80137 2120 B7
S Hayesmount Rd
10 AphC 80018 2204 B2
10 AphC 80137 2204 B2
10 AURA 80018 2204 B2
Hayloft Wy
400 BGTN 80601 1697 B4
Hay Meadow Wy
6200 DgsC 80135 2616 C4

Hays Cir
700 LGMT 80501 1439 E1
Hays Ct
1500 ERIE 80516 1690 C1
1500 LSVL 80027 1689 A6
Hays Dr
1700 LSVL 80027 1689 A6
Haysmount Mile Rd
- AURA 80137 1952 A7
- AURA 80137 2036 B1
- AURA 80249 1952 A7
- DNVR 80249 1952 A7
- DNVR 80249 2036 B1
- DvrC 80249 1952 A7
Haystack Ct
800 CSRK 80104 2787 E3
8400 BldC 80503 1521 A5
E Haystack Dr
1000 CSRK 80104 2788 A3
Haystack Ln
- BGTN 80601 1697 C4
- WSTR 80031 1942 D3
33600 JfnC 80439 2188 B3
E Haystack Rd
1000 CSRK 80104 2787 E3
2500 CSRK 80104 2788 A2
2500 DgsC 80104 2788 A2
Haystack Row
10 CHLV 80113 2281 D3
Haystack Wy
1400 LAFT 80026 1690 A3
W Haystack Ranch Rd
- DgsC 80118 2953 C5
Hayward Pl
1800 LGMT 80501 1355 E6
W Hayward Pl
3200 DNVR 80211 2111 E2
4000 DNVR 80212 2111 D2
Hazel Ct
10 DNVR 80219 2195 E1
200 DNVR 80204 2195 E1
800 DNVR 80204 2111 E6
2600 DNVR 80211 2111 E3
9200 AdmC 80031 1943 E2
9200 WSTR 80031 1943 E2
10300 DgsC 80125 2530 E6
13000 BMFD 80020 1775 E6
S Hazel Ct
10 DNVR 80219 2195 E2
2600 DNVR 80219 2279 E1
2600 DNVR 80236 2279 E1
3400 SRDN 80110 2279 E4
3900 SRDN 80110 2280 A4
Hazel Dr
12900 BMFD 80020 1775 E7
Hazel Pl
3200 WSTR 80031 1943 E2
13400 BMFD 80020 1775 E5
S Hazel Rd
5100 JfnC 80439 2357 B1
Hazel St
12500 BMFD 80020 1859 E1
12600 BMFD 80020 1775 E7
Hazel Wy
12800 BMFD 80020 1775 E7
S Hazel Wy
2100 DNVR 80219 2195 E7
Hazelwood Ct
3600 BLDR 80304 1602 E6
Hazelwood Dr
10 BldC 80466 1767 B1
Hazy Hills Dr
11900 PARK 80138 2538 C3
Health Park Dr
10 BldC 80027 1773 B4
10 LSVL 80027 1773 B4
S Hearth Dr
2300 JfnC 80439 2272 E1
2300 JfnC 80439 2273 A1
Heart Lake Wy
- BMFD 80020 1775 D6
E Heartland Dr
- CMCY 80022 1864 D5
E Heartstrong St
600 SUPE 80027 1773 A5
Heartwood Ct
2300 LAFT 80026 1774 C1
Heartwood Wy
4500 CSRK 80109 2702 C3
Heathcliff Ln
10300 PARK 80134 2453 A6
Heather Ct
5300 BMFD 80020 1775 B4
N Heather Dr
8300 DgsC 80108 2534 E5
9800 LNTR 80108 2534 E3
9900 LNTR 80108 2535 A2
9900 LNTR 80134 2535 A2
10000 DgsC 80108 2535 A2
Heather Ln
20300 PARK 80138 2537 E3
Heather Pl
7500 AdmC 80221 1944 A6
Heather Rd
2700 JfnC 80401 2109 A3
Heather Wy
10 JfnC 80401 2109 A3
5900 BldC 80503 1519 E4
S Heather Gardens Wy
2700 AURA 80014 2284 A1
Heatherglen Ct
10300 DgsC 80130 2450 A6
Heatherglen Dr
5000 DgsC 80130 2450 A6
Heatherglen Pt
10200 DgsC 80130 2450 A6
Heatherhill Cir
- LGMT 80503 1438 A7
Heatherton Cir
10800 DgsC 80124 2450 A7
Heatherton Ln
5200 DgsC 80124 2450 A7
Heatherton St
- DgsC 80130 2450 A7

Heatherton St
10800 DgsC 80124 2450 A7
Heatherton Tr
10800 DgsC 80124 2450 C7
Heatherwood Ct
4700 BldC 80301 1604 D2
10000 DgsC 80126 2449 D6
Heatherwood Dr
4400 BldC 80301 1604 D3
Heatherwood Ln
9900 DgsC 80126 2449 D5
Heatherwood Pl
10000 DgsC 80126 2449 D5
Heatherwood Wy
3600 JfnC 80439 2272 E3
Heavenly Ct
30400 JfnC 80439 2189 B7
E Hecla Dr
1300 LSVL 80027 1689 E6
Hecla Wy
1400 LSVL 80027 1689 E6
Hedge Ln
10200 DgsC 80134 2452 E6
Hedgerow Cir
2600 LAFT 80027 1689 D4
Hedgerow Ln
500 BGTN 80601 1697 D4
Hedgeway Ct
9800 DgsC 80134 2452 E4
Hedgeway Dr
15900 DgsC 80134 2452 D5
Heide
- CSRK 80104 2703 E5
Heidelberg Dr
2600 BLDR 80305 1770 E1
2700 BLDR 80305 1771 A1
Heinze Wy
9200 CMCY 80640 1947 A1
10300 CMCY 80640 1863 B7
Heirloom Wy
1600 LGMT 80501 1356 D6
S Heiter Hill Rd
7200 JfnC 80439 2358 C6
Helen Ct
2000 EbtC 80138 2540 D7
Helena Cir
10 DgsC 80124 2450 E2
S Helena Cir
1400 AURA 80017 2200 D4
Helena Ct
5500 DNVR 80239 2032 D4
9800 CMCY 80022 1864 D7
N Helena Ct
400 AURA 80011 2116 D7
S Helena Ct
5600 CTNL 80015 2368 D1
5900 CTNL 80016 2368 D2
Helena Pl
3100 AURA 80011 2116 D2
Helena St
- CMCY 80603 1864 D1
1700 AURA 80011 2116 D4
5200 DNVR 80239 2032 D5
9900 CMCY 80022 1864 D7
S Helena St
- AphC 80016 2368 D3
1700 AURA 80017 2200 D6
1800 AURA 80013 2200 D6
2900 AURA 80013 2284 D1
5400 CTNL 80015 2284 D7
5400 CTNL 80015 2368 D1
5900 CTNL 80016 2368 D2
S Helena Wy
900 AURA 80017 2200 D3
2700 AURA 80013 2284 D1
4300 AURA 80015 2284 D5
W Hemlock Cir
700 LSVL 80027 1773 A1
S Hemlock Ct
9600 DgsC 80130 2450 C4
W Hemlock Dr
- LSVL 80027 1773 B1
Hemlock Ln
33800 JfnC 80439 2356 B6
Hemlock Pl
3300 BLDR 80304 1602 D6
Hemlock St
100 BMFD 80020 1858 D1
Hemlock Wy
10 BMFD 80020 1858 D2
1600 BMFD 80020 1774 D5
Hendee Ct
500 ERIE 80516 1607 A6
Henderson Ct
4800 BldC 80026 1606 B2
Henderson Rd
8900 AdmC 80601 1778 E7
8900 AdmC 80601 1779 A7
8900 AdmC 80602 1778 E7
8900 AdmC 80602 1779 A7
10300 AdmC 80601 1863 B1
10300 AdmC 80602 1863 B1
10300 AdmC 80640 1863 B1
S Hendricks St
- BldC 80466 1765 C4
- NDLD 80466 1765 C4
Henery Ct
2100 DgsC 80109 2786 A5
Hennington Ct
1800 LGMT 80501 1356 A5
S Henry Pl
2300 DNVR 80210 2197 E7
Henson Dr
- BldC 80504 1357 B3
Henson Creek St
12700 PARK 80134 2537 C5
Hepburn St
- DgsC 80129 2448 C4
Hera Ct
1100 LAFT 80026 1690 B7
Hercules Cir
900 LAFT 80026 1690 B5
Heritage Av
10 CSRK 80104 2704 C7

N Heritage Av
1200 CSRK 80104 2704 E5
E Heritage Pkwy
21600 AphC 80016 2370 B7
21600 AURA 80016 2370 B7
22000 AphC 80138 2454 B1
22000 AURA 80016 2454 B1
E Heritage Pl N
6500 CTNL 80111 2366 C3
E Heritage Pl S
6600 CTNL 80111 2366 C4
6800 CTNL 80112 2366 C4
S Heritage Pl E
6400 CTNL 80111 2366 D3
S Heritage Pl W
6400 CTNL 80111 2366 C3
Heritage Rd
- GOLD 80401 2192 A1
- JfnC 80401 2192 A1
600 GOLD 80401 2108 A7
Heritage Wy
4100 CSRK 80104 2704 C7
Heritage Hills Cir
9300 LNTR 80124 2451 A5
S Heritage Hills Pkwy
- DgsC 80124 2451 B4
9200 LNTR 80124 2451 A3
Herman Pl
900 LGMT 80501 1356 A5
Hermes Cir
700 LAFT 80026 1690 B5
Hermitage Run
11000 DgsC 80125 2530 D7
Hermosa Ct
10800 NHGN 80234 1860 D5
Hermosa Dr
2000 BLDR 80304 1602 D7
E Hermosa Dr
1400 DgsC 80126 2449 B4
Heron Ct
10 PrkC 80456 2691 C1
2000 LGMT 80503 1355 C5
Heron St
100 AdmC 80601 1697 D6
100 BGTN 80601 1697 D6
Herrn Ln
10 DgsC 80108 2534 D6
Hershey Ct
400 ERIE 80516 1606 E6
S Herzman Dr
5500 JfnC 80439 2357 E2
5800 JfnC 80439 2358 A2
Hess Av
200 JfnC 80401 2191 A1
300 JfnC 80401 2107 A7
Hess Rd
- DgsC 80134 2537 E4
- PARK 80134 2537 E4
1200 BldC 80403 1852 B2
E Hess Rd
- DgsC 80108 2536 D2
- DgsC 80134 2536 D2
- PARK 80134 2536 C3
5100 DgsC 80134 2537 B4
5100 PARK 80134 2537 B4
Hessie Ct
500 LAFT 80026 1689 C4
Heterodox View Av
6100 BldC 80303 1688 A3
Hexton Ct
10200 DgsC 80124 2450 D6
Heywood Ln
10000 DgsC 80130 2449 E5
S Heywood St
9900 DgsC 80130 2449 E5
Heywood Wy
4300 DgsC 80130 2449 E5
E Hialeah Av
16600 CTNL 80015 2284 E7
16800 CTNL 80015 2285 A7
W Hialeah Av
3300 LITN 80123 2279 E7
E Hialeah Dr
16300 CTNL 80015 2284 E7
E Hialeah Pl
15200 AURA 80015 2284 C7
W Hialeah Pl
9100 JfnC 80123 2278 C7
10800 JfnC 80127 2278 A7
10900 JfnC 80127 2277 E7
Hiawatha Tr
5500 JfnC 80454 2359 C1
S Hibiscus Dr
9400 DgsC 80126 2449 A4
S Hibiscus Wy
3600 DNVR 80237 2282 A3
Hickman Pl
12300 DNVR 80239 2031 E4
E Hickock Dr
19000 PARK 80134 2537 D5
Hickok Pl
3300 BLDR 80301 1603 A6
Hickok Tr
10 BldC 80481 1515 A2
Hickory Av
5300 BLDR 80303 1687 D4
Hickory Cir
9100 DgsC 80126 2449 A3
S Hickory Cir
5600 LITN 80120 2364 D1
Hickory Ct
1400 ERIE 80516 1691 E2
W Hickory Ct
600 LSVL 80027 1689 B7
Hickory Dr
1200 ERIE 80516 1691 E2
Hickory Ln N
- TNTN 80260 1944 B1
Hickory Ln S
- TNTN 80260 1944 A1
Hickory Pl
400 BMFD 80020 1859 A3
8900 TNTN 80229 1945 B2

S Hickory Pl
7700 LITN 80120 2364 D6
Hickory St
- LGMT 80501 1439 B6
300 BMFD 80020 1859 A3
S Hickory St
5100 EGLD 80110 2280 C7
5100 EGLD 80120 2280 C7
5300 LITN 80120 2280 C7
5600 LITN 80120 2364 D1
W Hickory St
600 LSVL 80027 1689 A7
Hickory Wy
1200 ERIE 80516 1691 D3
S Hickory Wy
5700 LITN 80120 2364 D2
Hickory Ridge Ln
10700 DgsC 80126 2449 E7
Hickory Ridge St
10700 DgsC 80126 2449 E7
Hidden Tr
10100 JfnC 80433 2441 D6
Hidden Acres Pl
1700 EbtC 80138 2540 C5
E Hidden Hill Ct
9200 LNTR 80124 2451 A3
E Hidden Hill Ln
9300 LNTR 80124 2451 A3
S Hidden Hill Pl
- LNTR 80124 2451 B3
Hidden Hollow Av
23800 JfnC 80433 2694 E5
Hidden Meadow Ct
5000 EbtC 80107 2709 E3
Hidden Meadow Dr
34700 CCkC 80439 2188 A5
Hidden Pointe Blvd
500 DgsC 80108 2534 D5
Hidden Pointe Wy
- DgsC 80108 2534 E4
Hidden Pond Pl
5000 DgsC 80108 2619 B6
Hidden River Ln
- PARK 80134 2537 E3
- PARK 80138 2537 E3
Hidden Valley Blvd
- PrkC 80470 2439 B7
- PrkC 80470 2523 A1
Hidden Valley Ln
200 DgsC 80108 2618 C4
Hidden Valley Pl
30700 EbtC 80117 2796 E7
Hidden Valley Rd
1500 DgsC 80135 2783 E4
1500 DgsC 80135 2784 A6
2800 DgsC 80135 2868 A1
Hidden Village Dr
27600 JfnC 80439 2273 D4
Hidden Wilderness Ct
10 CCkC 80452 2186 B1
Hidden Wilderness Rd
- CCkC 80452 2101 E7
10 CCkC 80452 2185 E1
10 CCkC 80452 2186 B2
Hidden Wilderness Wy
10 CCkC 80452 2186 B2
Hideaway Cir
100 CCkC 80439 2187 E3
Hideaway Tr
10 CCkC 80439 2187 D3
Hidee Mine Rd
- GpnC 80403 2017 E6
- GpnC 80403 2018 A6
Hier Ln
10 DgsC 80109 2786 E2
Hier Valley Rd
4900 DgsC 80135 2616 E6
4900 DgsC 80135 2617 A6
High Cir
13500 TNTN 80241 1777 B5
S High Cir
6300 JfnC 80465 2359 B4
High Ct
3500 WTRG 80033 2110 E1
S High Ct
5900 CTNL 80121 2365 B2
5900 GDVL 80121 2365 B2
8200 CTNL 80122 2449 B1
S High Dr
5700 JfnC 80439 2358 D2
5700 JfnC 80465 2358 D2
5800 JfnC 80465 2359 A3
High Ln
22400 JfnC 80465 2359 A4
High Pkwy
100 GOLD 80403 2107 E2
High Rd
29400 JfnC 80470 2693 C1
S High Rd
2900 JfnC 80439 2274 C2
5200 JfnC 80439 2273 C7
5200 JfnC 80439 2357 C1
High St
- AdmC 80602 1777 B3
- TNTN 80602 1693 B5
10 GpnC 80474 1849 D2
10 IDSP 80452 2101 B5
10 JMWN 80455 1516 B2
100 DNVR 80206 2197 B1
100 DNVR 80218 2197 B1
200 BKHK 80403 2017 E4
200 CLCY 80403 2017 E4
200 LYNS 80540 1352 D1
300 CSRK 80104 2703 E6
300 DNVR 80218 2113 B7
300 ERIE 80516 1607 B4
900 CCkC 80452 2101 B5
1200 BLDR 80304 1686 C1
1200 DNVR 80206 2113 B5
3000 DNVR 80205 2113 B2
3900 DNVR 80205 2029 B7
4600 DNVR 80216 2029 B6
5500 AdmC 80216 2029 B4
8200 AdmC 80229 1945 B4

High St
9300 TNTN 80229 1945 B1
9700 TNTN 80229 1861 B7
11700 NHGN 80233 1861 B2
13000 TNTN 80241 1777 B6
14500 TNTN 80602 1777 B2
E High St
10 CLCY 80403 2017 D4
S High St
200 DNVR 80209 2197 B2
1000 DNVR 80210 2197 B4
3000 DvrC 80210 2281 B2
3000 EGLD 80113 2281 B2
3100 DNVR 80210 2281 B2
4300 CHLV 80113 2281 B5
6300 CTNL 80121 2365 B3
6500 CTNL 80122 2365 B4
W High St
- CLCY 80403 2017 C4
W High Cliffe Pl
2700 DgsC 80129 2448 A4
S High Cliffe St
9400 DgsC 80129 2448 A4
High Country Ct
100 LAFT 80026 1689 E4
5500 BLDR 80301 1604 B2
High Country Dr
100 LAFT 80026 1689 E4
High Country Tr
100 LAFT 80026 1689 E4
12200 JfnC 80127 2529 B4
High Desert Pl
- PARK 80134 2536 E2
High Desert Rd
- PARK 80134 2536 E2
High Desert Wy
- PARK 80134 2536 E2
- PARK 80134 2537 A2
High Grade Rd
- JfnC 80433 2528 C3
16300 JfnC 80127 2528 C3
High Grade Rd CO-88
16300 JfnC 80127 2528 C3
High Lake Dr
100 BldC 80481 1515 B1
Highland Av
400 BldC 80302 1686 B2
400 BLDR 80302 1686 B2
N High Land Cir
- DgsC 80125 2447 D3
S Highland Ct
7400 LITN 80120 2364 B6
Highland Dr
400 LGMT 80501 1439 D1
4500 BldC 80503 1353 B3
7000 LKWD 80214 2110 E7
S Highland Dr
7200 LITN 80120 2364 B5
Highland Pl
3100 AdmC 80031 1943 E2
9200 ARVD 80002 2026 B5
N Highland Run
- DgsC 80125 2615 C6
Highland Bluff Dr
1000 CSRK 80109 2703 B6
Highlander Rd
- JfnC 80403 1852 A3
Highland Meadow Cir
10100 DgsC 80134 2451 D6
Highland Meadow Lp
10100 DgsC 80134 2451 C5
Highland Park Dr
900 BMFD 80020 1859 B1
W Highland Park Pl
3000 DNVR 80211 2111 E2
3000 DNVR 80211 2112 A2
Highland Ridge Ct
- CSRK 80109 2703 B6
Highland Ridge Wy
1000 CSRK 80109 2703 B6
Highlands Dr
10 PrkC 80456 2521 A3
5300 BldC 80503 1519 C2
Highlands End
- PrkC 80456 2521 A2
E Highlands Ranch Pkwy
10 DgsC 80126 2448 E3
10 DgsC 80129 2448 E3
3600 DgsC 80126 2449 D4
W Highlands Ranch Pkwy
- DgsC 80125 2447 E5
- DgsC 80129 2447 E5
500 DgsC 80126 2448 C4
500 DgsC 80129 2448 C4
Highland View Ct
10700 DgsC 80124 2450 E7
10700 DgsC 80124 2534 E1
Highland Vista Av
1000 CSRK 80109 2703 B6
E Highline Cir
10 CTNL 80122 2364 E4
10 LITN 80120 2364 E4
S Highline Cir
- GDVL 80121 2365 E1
5800 CTNL 80121 2365 D2
Highline Dr
11200 NHGN 80233 1860 E4
E Highline Dr
11100 AURA 80010 2199 C1
11100 AURA 80012 2199 C1
Highline Pl
4400 DNVR 80222 2281 E2
5200 DNVR 80222 2282 A2
E Highline Pl
11500 AURA 80012 2199 D1
Highline Vw
- DNVR 80224 2198 C7
- DNVR 80231 2198 C7
Hghline Terrace at Hunters Run
- AphC 80231 2282 C1
High Lonesome Pt
200 LAFT 80026 1689 D5

High Lonesome Tr
2300 LAFT 80026 1689 E4
2300 LAFT 80027 1689 E4
High Meadow Dr
23800 JfnC 80401 2190 D4
High Plains Ct
1400 LAFT 80026 1689 D2
1600 SUPE 80027 1772 E6
High Plains Dr
1600 SUPE 80027 1772 E6
1600 SUPE 80027 1773 A6
High Plains Pl
5300 CSRK 80104 2704 E7
High Plains St
100 CSRK 80104 2704 E7
Highpoint Cir
10 GpnC 80403 1934 C5
High Point Dr
500 GOLD 80403 2107 C3
High Point Rd
- CSRK 80104 2704 D5
- CSRK 80108 2704 D5
High Prairie Wy
- BMFD 80020 1775 E1
- BMFD 80020 1776 A1
High Ridge Ct
8400 DgsC 80108 2534 E5
High Ridge Wy
300 DgsC 80108 2534 E5
High Spring Rd
4500 DgsC 80104 2871 D3
High Spring Tr
7600 JfnC 80465 2359 B7
High View Dr
10 BldC 80304 1601 E5
Highview Dr
34200 JfnC 80470 2524 A3
High View Ln
10 BldC 80302 1517 B7
10 PrkC 80456 2607 B6
Highway 40
32000 CCkC 80439 2187 D1
Highway 40 US-40
32000 CCkC 80439 2187 D1
Highway 119
1000 GpnC 80403 2104 A4
1100 GpnC 80403 2103 E3
9200 GpnC 80403 2017 C1
11900 GpnC 80403 1933 E6
14200 GpnC 80403 1934 C3
Highway 119 SR-119
1000 GpnC 80403 2104 A4
1100 GpnC 80403 2103 E3
9200 GpnC 80403 2017 C1
11900 GpnC 80403 1933 E6
14200 GpnC 80403 1934 C3
Hi Land Cir
16000 AdmC 80602 1695 A6
Hilary Ct
3900 BMFD 80020 1775 D7
S Hilary Ct
11400 PARK 80138 2537 E2
S Hilary Pl
11300 PARK 80138 2537 E1
Hill Cir
10 CCkC 80439 2187 C7
S Hill Cir
7700 LITN 80120 2364 B6
Hill Ct
200 CSRK 80104 2788 A1
N Hill Ct
6900 DgsC 80134 2622 B1
Hill Dr
100 CSRK 80104 2788 A1
19300 JfnC 80465 2359 E7
19300 JfnC 80465 2443 E1
N Hill Dr
10 PrkC 80456 2607 D4
S Hill Dr
7700 LITN 80120 2364 B6
Hill St
10 BldC 80302 1599 D3
S Hill St
5900 LITN 80120 2364 B2
S Hill Wy
6600 LITN 80120 2364 B4
Hill & Dale Rd
800 JfnC 80401 2191 A4
N Hillary Cir
5300 DgsC 80134 2622 A4
Hillcrest Cir
7700 DgsC 80135 2784 A4
22300 JfnC 80401 2191 B2
Hill Crest Dr
7800 DgsC 80135 2532 C6
Hillcrest Dr
- FLHT 80260 1944 B2
10 GpnC 80403 1850 B5
12600 BldC 80504 1356 A4
12600 LGMT 80501 1356 A4
S Hillcrest Dr
3900 AphC 80237 2282 B4
3900 CHLV 80111 2282 B4
3900 DNVR 80237 2282 B4
Hillcrest Rd
11500 JfnC 80403 1852 C3
N Hillcrest Wy
8100 DgsC 80134 2622 B1
Hilldale Dr
9700 JfnC 80465 2443 C5
S Hilldale Dr
9700 JfnC 80465 2443 C5
Hill Gail Av
22000 PARK 80138 2538 B1
Hill Gail Ct
11000 PARK 80138 2538 B1
Hill Gail Wy
21500 PARK 80138 2538 B1
Hill Gale Pl
21600 PARK 80138 2538 B1
E Hillgate Wy
7600 DgsC 80134 2622 A1
N Hillpark Av
6600 DgsC 80134 2622 C1

Denver Regional Street Index

STREET
Block City ZIP Map# Grid

N Hillpark Cir
6900 DgsC 80134 2622 B1
N Hillpoint Pl
6800 DgsC 80134 2622 A1
N Hillridge Pl
6700 DgsC 80134 2622 B1
S Hillrose Ln
1500 SUPE 80027 1773 B5
S Hills Ct
3100 DNVR 80210 2281 C2
E Hills Dr
6600 DgsC 80138 2453 D6
Hillsdale Cir
2000 BLDR 80305 1686 E7
Hillsdale Wy
2300 BLDR 80305 1686 E7
Hillside
- TNTN 80260 1944 C2
W Hillside Av
2000 DNVR 80219 2280 B1
2000 EGLD 80110 2280 B1
2400 DNVR 80219 2196 A7
2400 EGLD 80110 2196 A7
E Hillside Cir
8400 DgsC 80134 2622 C1
N Hillside Cir
1500 DgsC 80135 2700 B5
Hillside Ct
- BMFD 80020 1775 E1
10 BldC 80302 1517 A7
800 LGMT 80501 1438 D1
33000 EbtC 80107 2792 E3
Hillside Dr
10 LKWD 80215 2110 A3
10 WTRG 80033 2110 A3
10 WTRG 80215 2110 A3
200 CSRK 80104 2703 E6
Hillside Ln
1100 LSVL 80027 1772 E1
E Hillside Pl
6900 DNVR 80224 2282 C1
W Hillside Pl
3000 DNVR 80219 2195 E7
3000 DNVR 80219 2196 A7
3800 LITN 80123 2279 D7
Hillside Rd
- EbtC 80138 2457 D3
10 CCkC 80439 2271 E5
1500 BLDR 80302 1686 D3
S Hillside Rd
11800 JfnC 80433 2525 C3
Hillside St
100 BKHK 80403 2017 E3
100 BKHK 80403 2018 A4
1100 AURA 80010 2115 B6
S Hillside St
5500 GDVL 80111 2367 B1
Hillside Ter
2300 LAFT 80026 1689 E2
N Hillside Wy
6500 DgsC 80134 2622 C1
Hill Spruce
10 JfnC 80127 2445 A1
Hills View Dr
9200 BldC 80503 1521 C6
9200 BldC 80504 1521 C6
Hilltop Cir
7500 AdmC 80221 1944 C6
Hill Top Dr
26200 JfnC 80439 2274 A2
26200 JfnC 80457 2274 A2
27200 JfnC 80439 2273 E2
Hilltop Dr
10 PrkC 80456 2606 B3
1300 LGMT 80501 1356 D7
15300 AdmC 80601 1697 B7
29900 JfnC 80439 2273 B2
Hill Top Rd
- JfnC 80433 2694 E4
31400 JfnC 80403 1852 E4
Hilltop Rd
4100 JfnC 80439 2274 A6
4200 JfnC 80439 2273 E6
27000 JfnC 80439 2358 A4
E Hilltop Rd
- DgsC 80134 2537 E3
- PARK 80134 2538 B4
10 DgsC 80107 2623 E5
10 DgsC 80134 2623 E5
10 EbtC 80107 2624 A5
10 EbtC 80138 2623 E5
10 EbtC 80138 2624 A5
2300 EbtC 80107 2625 A5
6700 DgsC 80138 2538 B4
6700 PARK 80138 2538 B4
8700 DgsC 80134 2538 E6
9100 DgsC 80134 2539 A7
9100 DgsC 80138 2539 A7
19500 PARK 80134 2537 E3
19500 PARK 80138 2537 E3
Hilltop St
500 LGMT 80501 1439 D1
Hill View Dr
- BldC 80503 1521 C6
S Hillview Rd
8800 JfnC 80465 2443 A3
E Hillview St
7800 DgsC 80134 2622 B1
Hilton St
26600 JfnC 80433 2442 A5
Himalaya Av
200 BMFD 80020 1774 E4
200 BMFD 80020 1775 A4
S Himalaya Cir
4000 AphC 80013 2285 E4
4300 AphC 80015 2285 E5
Himalaya Ct
300 BMFD 80020 1775 A4
E Himalaya Ct
5000 AphC 80015 2285 E7
S Himalaya Ct
3600 AphC 80013 2285 E3
4300 AphC 80015 2285 E5
5900 CTNL 80016 2369 E2
Himalaya Rd
1500 AURA 80011 2117 E4
4200 DNVR 80249 2033 D6
10800 AdmC 80022 1865 D5
10800 CMCY 80022 1865 D5
Himalaya St
- AdmC 80022 1865 D7
- AdmC 80022 1949 D1
- CMCY 80022 1865 D7
- CMCY 80022 1949 D1
S Himalaya St
- AphC 80013 2285 E3
- AURA 80013 2285 E5
- AURA 80015 2285 E5
4900 AphC 80015 2285 E7
4900 CTNL 80015 2285 E7
5400 CTNL 80015 2369 E1
S Himalaya Wy
- AphC 80013 2285 E3
- AURA 80013 2285 E3
5500 CTNL 80015 2369 E1
6600 AphC 80016 2369 E3
6700 CTNL 80016 2369 E4
7100 CTNL 80016 2370 A5
Hi Meadow Dr
10 PrkC 80456 2691 E1
Hi Meadow Ln
10 PrkC 80456 2607 E7
600 PrkC 80456 2691 E1
E Hinsdale Av
- AURA 80016 2370 C5
3000 CTNL 80122 2365 D6
7300 CTNL 80112 2366 D6
14700 CTNL 80112 2368 C6
16100 AphC 80016 2368 E6
16900 FXFD 80016 2369 A6
18400 AphC 80016 2369 D5
18400 CTNL 80016 2369 D5
22000 CTNL 80016 2370 B5
W Hinsdale Av
4300 LITN 80128 2363 C6
6600 JfnC 80128 2363 A6
E Hinsdale Cir
4000 CTNL 80122 2365 E6
5500 CTNL 80122 2366 A6
15300 CTNL 80112 2368 D6
W Hinsdale Cir
- LITN 80128 2363 C6
5000 AphC 80128 2363 C6
E Hinsdale Ct
5300 CTNL 80122 2366 A6
7300 CTNL 80112 2366 D6
W Hinsdale Ct
1000 LITN 80120 2364 C6
4700 LITN 80128 2363 C6
E Hinsdale Dr
7300 CTNL 80112 2366 D6
14900 AphC 80112 2368 D5
14900 CTNL 80112 2368 D5
W Hinsdale Dr
1100 LITN 80120 2364 C6
6900 JfnC 80128 2362 E6
6900 JfnC 80128 2363 A6
10700 JfnC 80127 2362 A6
11000 JfnC 80127 2361 E6
E Hinsdale Ln
16100 AphC 80016 2368 E6
19000 AphC 80016 2369 C5
19000 CTNL 80016 2369 C5
E Hinsdale Pl
- AphC 80016 2368 E6
3600 CTNL 80122 2365 D6
4400 CTNL 80122 2366 A6
6900 CTNL 80112 2366 C6
17400 FXFD 80016 2369 B5
19300 AphC 80016 2369 D5
20700 CTNL 80016 2370 A5
23700 AURA 80016 2370 D5
25400 AURA 80016 2371 A5
W Hinsdale Pl
1600 LITN 80120 2364 C6
6600 JfnC 80128 2363 A6
8500 JfnC 80128 2362 C6
E Hinsdale Wy
- AURA 80016 2370 D5
Histead Dr
28800 JfnC 80439 2273 C5
S Histead Wy
3900 JfnC 80439 2273 C4
Hitching Post Rd
- TNTN 80229 1861 E7
Hitchrack Rd
10 PrkC 80456 2522 C7
Hi View Dr
27600 JfnC 80439 2357 E3
Hiwall Ct
2800 DgsC 80109 2785 E7
2800 DgsC 80109 2786 A7
Hiwan Cir
2200 JfnC 80439 2188 E7
S Hiwan Dr
1000 JfnC 80439 2188 E7
2200 JfnC 80439 2272 E1
2300 JfnC 80439 2273 A1
S Hobart Wy
2800 DNVR 80227 2279 B2
Hobbit Ln
10400 WSTR 80031 1859 E6
Hobnail Ct
- EbtC 80107 2709 D4
Hofer Ln
10 CCkC 80439 2187 D5
Hoffman Blvd
12400 AURA 80011 2115 E6
13000 AURA 80011 2116 A6
Hoffman Dr
1200 ERIE 80516 1607 A6
Hoffman Wy
9400 TNTN 80229 1945 A1
Hoffman Wy N
1600 TNTN 80229 1945 B3
1800 AdmC 80229 1945 B3
Hoffman Wy S
1600 TNTN 80229 1945 A2
1800 AdmC 80229 1945 A2
Hogan Ct
- CSRK 80109 2702 D5
4400 BldC 80503 1519 A5
Hog Back Dr
700 GOLD 80403 2023 C6
700 JfnC 80403 2023 C6
Hoke Rd
22300 AphC 80018 2202 B1
22900 AURA 80018 2202 C1
Holbrook St
100 ERIE 80516 1607 B5
26100 JfnC 80433 2442 A4
E Holcomb Cir
200 CSRK 80104 2704 D7
E Holcomb St
5200 CSRK 80104 2704 D7
N Holcomb St
10 CSRK 80104 2704 D6
Holden Cir
10300 DgsC 80116 2707 B4
Holden Ct
1300 ERIE 80516 1607 A2
W Holden Pl
2800 DNVR 80204 2112 A6
Holdup St
10 PrkC 80456 2522 E6
Holeman Dr
1500 ERIE 80516 1690 D1
Holiday Blvd
- FLHT 80260 1944 B2
Holiday Bnd
- FLHT 80260 1944 B1
Holiday Cir
- FLHT 80260 1944 B1
Holiday Cor
- FLHT 80260 1944 B2
Holiday Cres
- FLHT 80260 1944 B2
Holiday Ct
- FLHT 80260 1944 B3
Holiday Dr
- BLDR 80304 1602 C3
- FLHT 80260 1944 B2
1500 LGMT 80501 1356 B6
Holiday Gdn
- FLHT 80260 1944 B2
Holiday Gln
- FLHT 80260 1944 A1
Holiday Hts
- FLHT 80260 1944 A2
Holiday Ln
- FLHT 80260 1944 B1
Holiday Lp
- FLHT 80260 1944 B1
- TNTN 80260 1944 B1
Holiday Pkwy
- FLHT 80260 1944 B2
Holiday Pl
- FLHT 80260 1944 B1
Holiday Rd
- FLHT 80260 1944 B1
Holiday Run
- FLHT 80260 1944 B1
Holiday Sq
- FLHT 80260 1944 B3
Holiday Ter
- FLHT 80260 1944 B1
Holiday Tr
- FLHT 80260 1944 B2
Holiday Vw
- FLHT 80260 1944 B2
Holiday Wy
- FLHT 80260 1944 B1
Holiday Mall
- FLHT 80260 1944 A3
Holiday Pass
- FLHT 80260 1944 B2
Holiday Vale
- FLHT 80260 1944 B1
Holiday Vista
- FLHT 80260 1944 B2
S Holl Av
12400 JfnC 80470 2524 C6
Holland Cir
6400 ARVD 80004 2026 B2
9700 WSTR 80021 1858 B7
9700 WSTR 80021 1942 A1
Holland Ct
- ARVD 80002 2026 B4
3500 WTRG 80033 2110 B2
6600 ARVD 80004 2026 B1
8200 ARVD 80005 1942 B4
9200 WSTR 80021 1942 B2
9900 WSTR 80021 1858 B7
S Holland Ct
900 LKWD 80226 2194 B4
900 LKWD 80232 2194 B4
1900 LKWD 80227 2194 B6
3000 LKWD 80227 2278 B2
4800 DNVR 80123 2278 A5
6400 JfnC 80123 2362 C3
7500 JfnC 80128 2362 B6
8400 JfnC 80128 2446 C1
Holland Dr
5400 ARVD 80002 2026 B4
S Holland Ln
8500 JfnC 80128 2446 B2
Holland Pl
10400 WSTR 80021 1858 B7
Holland St
10 LKWD 80226 2194 B1
1200 LKWD 80215 2110 B6
3200 JfnC 80215 2110 B2
3200 WTRG 80033 2110 B2
3200 WTRG 80215 2110 B2
4400 WTRG 80033 2026 B7
5300 ARVD 80002 2026 B5
5900 ARVD 80004 2026 B3
7000 ARVD 80004 1942 B7
7300 ARVD 80005 1942 B7
9200 WSTR 80021 1942 B2
10600 WSTR 80021 1858 B6
S Holland St
10 LKWD 80226 2194 B2
900 LKWD 80232 2194 B4
1900 LKWD 80227 2194 B7
2500 LKWD 80227 2278 B1
5100 DNVR 80123 2278 B7
5100 JfnC 80123 2278 B7
6100 JfnC 80123 2362 B3
7500 JfnC 80128 2362 B6
9700 LITN 80127 2446 C5
Holland Wy
10400 WSTR 80021 1858 B6
S Holland Wy
2200 LKWD 80227 2194 B7
3200 LKWD 80227 2278 C3
4300 JfnC 80123 2278 B5
4800 DNVR 80123 2278 B6
5900 JfnC 80123 2362 B3
6700 JfnC 80128 2362 B4
8300 JfnC 80128 2446 C1
9300 JfnC 80127 2446 C4
9300 LITN 80127 2446 C4
Hollings Wy
30400 BldC 80403 1853 A2
S Hollow Creek Ct
12400 PARK 80134 2537 D4
E Hollow Creek Dr
18900 PARK 80134 2537 D4
E Hollow Creek Ln
18900 PARK 80134 2537 D4
N Hollowview Ct
6100 DgsC 80134 2622 C2
Holly Av
1200 LGMT 80501 1439 A5
1300 LGMT 80501 1438 E5
S Holly Cir
6900 CTNL 80112 2366 B5
6900 CTNL 80122 2366 B5
Holly Cir N
- TNTN 80241 1778 A7
- TNTN 80602 1778 A7
- TNTN 80602 1862 B1
Holly Cir S
- TNTN 80241 1778 A7
- TNTN 80602 1778 A7
- TNTN 80602 1862 B1
Holly Ct
2200 JfnC 80401 2190 B6
Holly Dr
2200 ERIE 80516 1692 A3
Holly Dr E
1300 BMFD 80020 1774 D6
Holly Dr W
1300 BMFD 80020 1774 D6
Holly Pl
1200 BLDR 80303 1687 A3
S Holly Pl
2300 AphC 80222 2198 A7
2300 DNVR 80222 2198 A7
2700 AphC 80222 2282 B1
2900 DNVR 80222 2282 B1
Holly St
10 DNVR 80220 2198 B1
10 DNVR 80224 2198 B1
10 DNVR 80246 2198 B1
800 DNVR 80220 2114 B6
1900 DNVR 80207 2114 B4
3900 DNVR 80207 2030 B7
4700 DNVR 80022 2030 A6
4700 DNVR 80216 2030 A6
5400 CMCY 80022 2030 B3
6800 CMCY 80022 1946 A7
7100 AdmC 80022 1946 A7
8800 AdmC 80640 1946 A2
8800 CMCY 80640 1946 A2
10800 AdmC 80233 1862 A4
10800 TNTN 80233 1862 A4
11700 AdmC 80602 1862 A1
11900 TNTN 80241 1862 A1
12300 TNTN 80602 1862 A1
12500 TNTN 80241 1778 A7
13200 TNTN 80602 1778 A7
14000 AdmC 80602 1778 A3
15200 AdmC 80602 1694 A5
15200 TNTN 80602 1694 A5
16000 TNTN 80603 1694 A5
16000 WldC 80603 1694 A5
S Holly St
10 DNVR 80220 2198 B1
10 DNVR 80224 2198 B1
10 DNVR 80246 2198 B1
1200 DNVR 80222 2198 B7
2100 AphC 80222 2198 B7
2700 AphC 80222 2282 B1
2700 DNVR 80222 2282 B1
3400 DNVR 80237 2282 B3
3800 AphC 80113 2282 B4
3800 AphC 80237 2282 B4
3800 CHLV 80113 2282 B4
4300 CHLV 80111 2282 B5
4700 CHLV 80121 2282 B7
5000 GDVL 80111 2282 B7
5200 GDVL 80121 2282 B7
5400 GDVL 80111 2366 B3
5400 GDVL 80121 2366 B3
5800 CTNL 80121 2366 B3
6000 CTNL 80111 2366 B3
6500 CTNL 80112 2366 B3
6800 CTNL 80122 2366 B7
8100 AphC 80126 2450 B1
8100 CTNL 80112 2450 B1
8100 CTNL 80122 2450 B1
N Holly Wy
12000 AdmC 80602 1862 A1
S Holly Wy
3900 AphC 80113 2282 B4
3900 AphC 80237 2282 B4
3900 CHLV 80111 2282 B4
3900 CHLV 80113 2282 B4
3900 DNVR 80237 2282 B4
Hollyberry Ln
300 BLDR 80305 1686 D6
E Holly Hills Wy
23400 PARK 80138 2538 D1
Hollyhock Cir
2000 LGMT 80503 1438 A6
Holly Hock Ct
3300 CSRK 80109 2702 E1
S Hollyhock Ct
10400 DgsC 80129 2448 B6
Hollyhock Ln
4900 JfnC 80439 2275 A7
8500 BldC 80026 1689 B4
Holly Oak
10 JfnC 80127 2361 A7
Hollyridge Dr
16000 DgsC 80134 2452 E6
Hollywood St
7700 AdmC 80022 1946 A5
7700 CMCY 80022 1946 A5
S Holman Cir
2200 LKWD 80228 2193 A7
2400 LKWD 80228 2277 A1
Holman Ct
6300 ARVD 80004 2025 A2
S Holman Ct
2700 LKWD 80228 2277 A1
Holman St
4800 JfnC 80403 2025 A6
6100 ARVD 80004 2025 A2
6100 JfnC 80004 2025 A2
N Holman St
4400 JfnC 80403 2025 A7
S Holman St
3000 LKWD 80228 2277 A2
Holman Wy
100 JfnC 80401 2193 A1
S Holman Wy
10 JfnC 80401 2193 A2
Holmby Ct
- CSRK 80104 2788 A2
Holmes Ct
2300 EbtC 80138 2540 E4
Holmes Pl
5200 BLDR 80303 1687 D3
Holmes Gulch Rd
- JfnC 80470 2692 A1
10 PrkC 80456 2607 E7
10 PrkC 80456 2608 A7
10 PrkC 80456 2691 E1
10 PrkC 80456 2692 A1
Holmes Gulch Wy
34600 PrkC 80456 2692 A2
34600 PrkC 80470 2692 A2
Holy Cross Ln
6300 DgsC 80108 2618 E2
Holy Cross Rd
9700 TNTN 80260 1860 B6
Holy Cross Wy
6200 DgsC 80108 2618 E2
Holyoke Ct
17500 PARK 80134 2453 B6
Holyoke Dr
2200 BLDR 80305 1686 E7
10500 PARK 80134 2453 B6
Holyoke Ln
2100 SUPE 80027 1773 B6
Home St
3900 DgsC 80108 2619 C7
N Home Farm Av
800 WSTR 80234 1776 C7
N Home Farm Cir
900 WSTR 80234 1776 C7
N Home Farm Ct
12400 WSTR 80234 1776 C7
12400 WSTR 80234 1860 C1
N Home Farm Dr
12700 WSTR 80234 1776 C7
N Home Farm Ln
12600 WSTR 80234 1776 C7
Homer Cir
900 LAFT 80026 1690 B5
Homestake Ct
800 DgsC 80108 2618 C2
8200 DgsC 80118 2954 B4
Homestake Dr
800 GOLD 80401 2107 E5
800 GOLD 80401 2108 A5
N Homestake Ln
12300 DgsC 80138 2455 B4
Homestake Rd
8200 DgsC 80118 2954 B4
Homestake Peak
11500 JfnC 80127 2361 E7
Homestead Ct
16400 PARK 80134 2452 E7
E Homestead Dr
700 DgsC 80126 2449 A1
Homestead Pkwy
- LGMT 80501 1356 C5
S Homestead Pkwy
5900 CTNL 80111 2366 B4
5900 CTNL 80112 2366 B4
Homestead Pl
4900 TNTN 80229 1861 E6
4900 TNTN 80229 1862 A6
Homestead Rd
10 PrkC 80456 2607 A7
500 PrkC 80456 2606 E6
7800 JfnC 80403 1937 D6
44200 EbtC 80107 2459 A7
44200 EbtC 80107 2543 A1
E Homestead Rd
7000 DgsC 80138 2453 E6
7500 DgsC 80138 2454 B5
Homestead St
400 LAFT 80026 1690 A4
4500 BWMR 80123 2279 C6
8300 DgsC 80126 2449 A1
Homestead Wy
200 BGTN 80601 1697 C5
5400 BldC 80301 1604 B1
5400 BLDR 80301 1604 B1
S Homesteader Dr
7200 JfnC 80465 2359 C5
7700 JfnC 80465 2443 C1
Homewood Park Av
17400 JfnC 80127 2444 B5
Hondah Dr
10100 JfnC 80127 2444 A6
Hondo Ct
1100 CSRK 80104 2703 E2
S Honey Wy
1100 DNVR 80224 2198 B4
1300 DNVR 80222 2198 B4
Honey Creek Ln
2100 SUPE 80027 1773 C6
Honey Locust
10 JfnC 80127 2361 A7
10 JfnC 80127 2445 C1
Honeylocust Cir
5700 GDVL 80171 2366 A2
Honey Locust Ct
5000 DgsC 80134 2621 E5
Honey Locust Dr
4200 CHLV 80113 2282 A5
Honeysuckle Cir
1100 BMFD 80020 1774 C7
Honeysuckle Ct
- BGTN 80601 1780 D2
Honeysuckle Ln
1000 LSVL 80027 1688 D7
1000 LSVL 80027 1689 B7
4900 JfnC 80439 2275 A7
Honeysuckle Pl
700 DgsC 80126 2449 A2
Honeysuckle Wy
4000 LGMT 80503 1438 A4
Hood Ct
12000 JfnC 80433 2525 B4
Hood Rd
30200 JfnC 80433 2525 B4
S Hooker Cir
1900 DNVR 80219 2195 E6
Hooker Ct
10000 WSTR 80031 1859 E7
N Hooker Ct
11500 WSTR 80031 1859 E3
Hooker Pl
10000 WSTR 80031 1859 E7
Hooker St
10 DNVR 80219 2195 E1
200 DNVR 80204 2195 E1
300 DNVR 80219 2111 E7
800 DNVR 80204 2111 E6
1900 DNVR 80211 2111 E4
4400 DNVR 80211 2027 E7
4800 DNVR 80221 2027 E6
6600 AdmC 80221 2027 E1
N Hooker St
7600 WSTR 80030 1943 E6
7900 WSTR 80031 1943 E5
9200 AdmC 80031 1943 E2
11500 WSTR 80031 1859 E3
S Hooker St
10 DNVR 80219 2195 E2
2600 DNVR 80219 2279 E1
2600 DNVR 80236 2279 E1
4100 SRDN 80110 2279 E5
5000 EGLD 80110 2279 E7
5200 LITN 80123 2279 E7
Hooker Wy
8800 AdmC 80031 1943 E3
8800 WSTR 80031 1943 E3
10000 WSTR 80031 1859 E7
Hooper St
100 CLCY 80403 2017 C5
Hoosier Ct
10 BldC 80466 1682 B6
Hoosier Dr
900 DgsC 80118 2954 D1
Hoosier Hill Rd
10 BldC 80302 1600 A4
Hoot Owl Ct
16800 PARK 80134 2453 A2
N Hoover Av
100 LSVL 80027 1773 C1
700 LSVL 80027 1689 C7
S Hoover Av
100 LSVL 80027 1773 C2
W Hoover Av
8100 JfnC 80123 2362 D4
12400 JfnC 80127 2361 D4
Hoover Ct
200 LSVL 80027 1773 C1
E Hoover Dr
22000 AURA 80016 2370 B3
W Hoover Ln
- JfnC 80123 2363 A4
Hoover Pl
- AURA 80016 2371 B3
E Hoover Pl
- AphC 80016 2370 E3
- AphC 80016 2371 A3
22500 AURA 80016 2370 C3
W Hoover Pl
6500 JfnC 80123 2363 A4
7800 JfnC 80123 2362 D4
Hope Ct
8400 AdmC 80229 1945 C3
Hope Dale Av
22500 PARK 80138 2538 C2
Hopewell Av
22600 PARK 80138 2538 C3
Hopewell Ln
- PARK 80138 2538 C3
E Hopi
- AdmC 80022 1946 C3
W Hopi
- AdmC 80022 1946 C3
N Hopi Dr
3500 DgsC 80135 2616 C7
3500 DgsC 80135 2700 C1
Hopi Pl
200 BLDR 80303 1687 B5
Hopi Rd
4600 JfnC 80439 2274 E6
4600 JfnC 80439 2275 A6
Hopkins Av
200 LAFT 80026 1690 C4
Hopkins Dr
1600 AdmC 80229 1945 B3
8700 TNTN 80229 1945 B3
Hopkins Pl
4800 BLDR 80301 1603 B6
Hopper Pl
- BGTN 80601 1697 C4
Hoptree Ct
500 LSVL 80027 1689 B7
Horan Ct
600 DgsC 80108 2618 E1
Horiuchi Ct
- BGTN 80601 1697 A5
Horiuchi St
- BGTN 80601 1697 B5
Horizon Av
- LAFT 80026 1690 E7
1300 LAFT 80026 1691 A7
Horizon Dr
1000 LYNS 80540 1269 D7
16600 AdmC 80601 1697 B4
Horizon Ln
1300 LGMT 80501 1356 A4
6300 BldC 80503 1520 D6
Horizon Pkwy
- BldC 80503 1355 B5
- LGMT 80503 1355 B5
Horizon Tr
12700 DgsC 80108 2534 C6
S Horizon View Dr
10100 JfnC 80465 2443 D6
Horned Owl Wy
5000 DgsC 80134 2622 C4
W Hornsilver Mtn
11600 JfnC 80127 2361 D6
Horse-bit Wy
20900 JfnC 80465 2359 C7
Horse Creek St
18600 PARK 80134 2537 C5
S Horsemint Wy
9400 PARK 80134 2453 A4
Horseradish Gulch Rd
4800 JfnC 80403 2021 D6
E Horseshoe Cir
10400 DgsC 80138 2539 B4
Horseshoe Dr
31400 JfnC 80439 2356 D2
Horseshoe Ln
- WSTR 80021 1942 D3
11800 PARK 80138 2538 A3
Horseshoe Pl
- BGTN 80601 1697 C4
10 BldC 80466 1765 E2
N Horseshoe Tr
5000 DgsC 80135 2615 E4
5000 DgsC 80135 2616 A5
Horsfal St
10 BldC 80302 1599 E3
Horton Ct
- AdmC 80216 2029 A4
Hosman Cir
12100 JfnC 80433 2525 A4
S Hosman Ct
12200 JfnC 80433 2525 A4
Hospitality Pl
5300 DgsC 80134 2621 C4
Hot Sprs
11400 WldC 80504 1440 E2
Hotel Wy
29100 JfnC 80401 2189 C4
N Hot Springs Dr
11400 DgsC 80138 2453 D5
Hottman St
3400 BGTN 80601 1697 A7
Houston St
10 PrkC 80456 2521 D1
S Houston St
9700 JfnC 80433 2442 B5
S Houstoun Waring Cir
7200 LITN 80120 2364 A6
W Houstoun Waring Cir
2400 LITN 80120 2364 A5
Hover Dr
2300 CSRK 80104 2704 A7
S Hover Rd
1500 LGMT 80501 1438 D6
1500 LGMT 80503 1438 D6
1900 BldC 80503 1438 D6
1900 LGMT 80504 1438 D6
Hover St
- BldC 80501 1355 D5
- BldC 80503 1355 D5
- BldC 80504 1355 D5
- LGMT 80501 1355 D5
10 BldC 80501 1438 D2
10 BldC 80503 1438 D2
200 LGMT 80501 1438 D2
200 LGMT 80503 1438 D2
1200 LGMT 80503 1355 D5
S Hover St
- BldC 80504 1438 D5
- LGMT 80503 1438 D5
- LGMT 80504 1438 D5
100 BldC 80501 1438 D5
100 BldC 80503 1438 D5
400 LGMT 80501 1438 D5
Hover Ridge Cir
900 LGMT 80501 1438 D1
Howard Pl
2200 BLDR 80305 1686 E7
W Howard Pl
2800 DNVR 80204 2112 A5
3100 DNVR 80204 2111 E5
Howe Cir
600 CSRK 80104 2704 D6
Howe Ct
600 CSRK 80104 2704 D6
3800 BldC 80301 1603 A5
Howe Pl
500 CSRK 80104 2704 D6
Howe St
500 CSRK 80104 2704 D6
E Howe St
5200 CSRK 80104 2704 D6

STREET
Block City ZIP Map# Grid

Howell Ct
5600 JfnC 80002 2025 A4
Howell Rd
3100 JfnC 80401 2109 A2
Howell St
300 JfnC 80401 2193 A1
4800 JfnC 80403 2025 A6
6800 ARVD 80004 2025 A1
N Howell St
5200 JfnC 80002 2025 A5
5200 JfnC 80403 2025 A5
S Howell St
2600 LKWD 80228 2277 A1
Hoya Ct
3900 BldC 80301 1603 A5
E Hoye Dr
12000 AURA 80012 2199 E3
W Hoye Pl
1200 DNVR 80223 2196 C4
3400 DNVR 80219 2195 E4
Hoyt Cir
7700 ARVD 80005 1942 B6
Hoyt Ct
3500 WTRG 80033 2110 B1
4200 WTRG 80033 2026 B7
5100 ARVD 80002 2026 B5
6000 ARVD 80004 2026 B3
7400 ARVD 80005 1942 B6
9000 WSTR 80021 1942 B3
10400 WSTR 80021 1858 B6
S Hoyt Ct
2100 LKWD 80227 2194 B7
3300 LKWD 80227 2278 B3
6400 JfnC 80123 2362 B3
7700 JfnC 80128 2362 B7
8800 JfnC 80128 2446 B3
9300 LITN 80127 2446 B4
Hoyt Dr
2000 TNTN 80229 1945 B3
5400 ARVD 80002 2026 B4
Hoyt Ln
9900 WSTR 80021 1858 B7
Hoyt Pl
10400 WSTR 80021 1858 B6
17600 PARK 80134 2453 B7
Hoyt St
400 BMFD 80020 1774 B7
400 BMFD 80020 1858 B1
400 LKWD 80226 2110 B7
400 LKWD 80226 2194 B1
2000 JfnC 80215 2110 B4
2000 LKWD 80215 2110 B4
3500 WTRG 80033 2110 B1
4500 WTRG 80033 2026 B7
5100 ARVD 80002 2026 B5
6000 ARVD 80004 2026 B3
7300 ARVD 80005 1942 B7
9200 WSTR 80021 1942 B2
10400 WSTR 80021 1858 B6
N Hoyt St
10600 WSTR 80021 1858 B5
S Hoyt St
- JfnC 80235 2278 B5
10 LKWD 80226 2194 B2
1800 LKWD 80232 2194 B6
2300 LKWD 80227 2194 B7
2500 LKWD 80227 2278 B1
4300 JfnC 80123 2278 B5
4500 DNVR 80123 2278 B6
6400 JfnC 80123 2362 B3
7500 JfnC 80128 2362 B7
Hoyt Wy
8000 ARVD 80005 1942 B4
10400 WSTR 80021 1858 B6
S Hoyt Wy
1900 LKWD 80227 2194 B6
3000 LKWD 80227 2278 B2
6400 JfnC 80123 2362 B4
8400 JfnC 80128 2446 B1
Hubbard Dr
600 LGMT 80501 1439 D2
Hubert St
5100 DgsC 80134 2621 D4
Huckleberry Dr
11700 DgsC 80116 2707 E3
11900 DgsC 80107 2707 E3
Hudson Cir
5500 TNTN 80241 1778 A6
S Hudson Cir
7100 CTNL 80122 2366 B5
Hudson Ct
9600 AdmC 80229 1946 A1
10100 AdmC 80229 1862 A6
10100 TNTN 80229 1862 A6
11000 TNTN 80233 1862 A5
12000 TNTN 80241 1862 A2
12900 TNTN 80241 1778 A7
S Hudson Ct
6200 CTNL 80121 2366 B3
7500 CTNL 80122 2366 B6
Hudson Ln
- CSRK 80104 2788 A1
S Hudson Ln
7100 CTNL 80122 2366 B5
S Hudson Pkwy
- CHLV 80113 2282 A4
Hudson Pl
11100 TNTN 80233 1862 A4
Hudson Rd
- AdmC 80642 1700 C4
10 PrkC 80470 2523 E6
10 PrkC 80470 2524 A6
N Hudson Rd
1500 AdmC 80019 2120 D4
1500 AdmC 80137 2120 D4
1500 AURA 80137 2120 D4
1800 AURA 80019 2120 D4
2600 AdmC 80019 2036 D6
2600 AdmC 80137 2036 D6
2600 AURA 80019 2036 C3
2600 AURA 80137 2036 D6
5400 AdmC 80249 1952 C7
5400 AURA 80137 1952 C7
S Hudson Rd
1100 AphC 80137 2204 D4
Hudson St
10 DNVR 80220 2198 A1
800 DNVR 80220 2114 A6
3200 DNVR 80207 2114 A2
6400 CMCY 80022 2030 A2
10000 TNTN 80229 1862 A7
10100 AdmC 80229 1862 A7
11500 TNTN 80233 1862 A3
12900 TNTN 80241 1778 A6
13800 TNTN 80602 1778 A4
S Hudson St
10 DNVR 80220 2198 A1
1200 DNVR 80246 2198 B5
2100 AphC 80222 2198 B7
2100 DNVR 80222 2198 B7
2700 DNVR 80222 2282 B1
2900 AphC 80222 2282 B1
3500 DNVR 80237 2282 A3
6300 CTNL 80121 2366 B3
7800 CTNL 80122 2366 B7
Hudson Wy
13800 TNTN 80602 1778 A4
S Hudson Wy
3400 DNVR 80222 2282 B3
3900 AphC 80237 2282 A4
3900 CHLV 80113 2282 A4
3900 DNVR 80237 2282 A4
7600 CTNL 80122 2366 B6
Hudson Mile Rd
8800 DNVR 80249 1952 C2
11000 AdmC 80642 1868 C5
11000 DNVR 80249 1868 C5
11000 DNVR 80642 1868 C5
16400 AdmC 80603 1700 B4
16400 WldC 80642 1700 B4
S Huerfano Ln
15100 JfnC 80470 2608 A5
Huerfano St
- BGTN 80601 1697 A6
Huey Cir
4600 BLDR 80305 1687 B7
E Huggins Ct
9500 DgsC 80134 2622 E2
S Hughes Ct
10000 DgsC 80126 2449 A5
E Hughes Dr
- AURA 80011 2200 E1
- AURA 80011 2201 A1
E Hughes Ln
700 DgsC 80126 2449 A5
S Hughes Pl
10000 DgsC 80126 2448 E5
E Hughes St
400 DgsC 80126 2448 E5
S Hughes St
10000 JfnC 80433 2442 A6
S Hughes Wy
10000 DgsC 80126 2448 E5
Hughesville Rd
600 GpnC 80403 2017 D1
1200 GpnC 80403 1933 D7
Hughs Dr
2600 ERIE 80516 1690 C2
Humboldt Cir
2800 LGMT 80503 1355 C7
7800 AdmC 80229 1945 A5
S Humboldt Cir
8100 CTNL 80122 2365 B7
8100 CTNL 80122 2449 B1
Humboldt Dr
11800 NHGN 80233 1861 A2
13200 TNTN 80241 1777 A6
Humboldt Pl
2800 LGMT 80503 1355 C7
S Humboldt Pl
6200 CTNL 80121 2365 A3
Humboldt St
10 WARD 80481 1597 D1
100 DNVR 80218 2197 B1
300 DNVR 80218 2113 B7
3200 DNVR 80205 2113 A2
5000 DNVR 80216 2029 A5
5800 AdmC 80216 2029 A3
9600 TNTN 80229 1945 A1
11400 NHGN 80233 1861 A3
16400 TNTN 80602 1693 A5
S Humboldt St
100 DNVR 80209 2197 B2
1300 DNVR 80210 2197 B5
2500 DNVR 80210 2281 B1
2700 DvrC 80210 2281 B1
2700 EGLD 80113 2281 B1
4100 CHLV 80113 2281 B4
7500 CTNL 80122 2365 B6
Humboldt Wy
900 SUPE 80027 1857 A2
13400 TNTN 80241 1777 A5
Humboldt Peak Wy
10500 PARK 80138 2454 B7
S Humbolt Cir
8100 CTNL 80122 2365 B7
8100 CTNL 80122 2449 C1
Hummer Dr
10 BldC 80466 1682 B6
Hummingbird Cir
1300 BGTN 80601 1779 E1
Hummingbird Ct
10 PrkC 80456 2691 B1
Hummingbird Dr
10 DgsC 80108 2618 D4
10 DgsC 80108 2619 A4
33500 EbtC 80107 2793 C1
Hummingbird Ln
10 BldC 80403 1852 D2
Hummingbird Pl
9700 DgsC 80125 2531 A7
Hummingbird Hill Rd
27000 JfnC 80433 2525 C6
Humphrey Dr
300 JfnC 80439 2188 D3
Hunt Ct
2900 ERIE 80516 1690 C1
4100 BLDR 80303 1687 B4
Hunt Rd
5600 DgsC 80135 2617 C5
Hunter Ct
400 ERIE 80516 1606 E6
1200 LGMT 80501 1355 D7
Hunter Ln
100 JfnC 80465 2276 B3
100 MRSN 80465 2276 B3
Hunter Pl
6900 BldC 80301 1604 B1
Hunter St
9000 AdmC 80031 1943 E2
Hunter Wy
8800 AdmC 80031 1943 E3
8800 WSTR 80031 1943 E3
Hunter Run Ln
10 AphC 80123 2363 D4
10 CBVL 80123 2363 D4
Hunter Run Rd
10 CBVL 80123 2363 D4
Hunters Pl
2500 DgsC 80129 2448 A3
Hunters Wy
8800 DgsC 80129 2448 B2
S Hunters Creek St
9000 DgsC 80126 2448 E3
E Hunters Hill Dr
8200 CTNL 80112 2366 E6
Hunters Hill Rd
8600 DgsC 80125 2530 E4
Hunters Ridge Rd
10000 JfnC 80127 2528 D1
Hunterwood Dr
- DgsC 80126 2449 E6
4300 DgsC 80130 2449 E6
4500 DgsC 80130 2450 A6
Hunterwood Wy
10200 DgsC 80130 2449 D5
10200 DgsC 80130 2450 A6
Huntington Ct
10 LGMT 80503 1355 C7
E Huntington Dr
600 DgsC 80126 2448 E7
600 DgsC 80126 2449 A5
E Huntington Pl
600 DgsC 80126 2448 E7
600 DgsC 80126 2449 A5
S Huntington Wy
- DgsC 80126 2449 A5
Huntley Ct
200 DgsC 80108 2618 E1
Huntley Creek Ct
100 ERIE 80516 1607 C5
Hunt Master Ct
10300 DgsC 80125 2530 E4
Huntsford Cir
2700 DgsC 80126 2449 C5
Huntsford Pl
2500 DgsC 80126 2449 C5
Huntwick Ct
10 CHLV 80113 2281 B6
Huntwick Ln
10 CHLV 80113 2281 B6
S Huntwick Pl
4900 DgsC 80124 2450 A7
S Huntwick St
10700 DgsC 80124 2450 A7
Hupp Rd
10 PrkC 80456 2521 D2
S Hura Rd
4300 JfnC 80439 2274 D5
S Hurley Cir
3000 DNVR 80227 2279 B3
Huron Ct
10 BLDR 80303 1687 D6
S Huron Ct
4100 EGLD 80110 2280 D5
7700 LITN 80120 2364 D6
Huron Ln
6100 DgsC 80108 2618 E2
Huron Pl
6100 DgsC 80108 2618 E2
S Huron Pl
7700 LITN 80120 2364 D6
Huron St
- AdmC 80221 2028 D2
2900 DNVR 80202 2112 D2
8400 AdmC 80221 1944 C2
8400 FLHT 80260 1944 C2
8400 TNTN 80221 1944 C2
8400 TNTN 80260 1944 C2
9600 NHGN 80260 1944 C2
9700 NHGN 80260 1860 C6
10200 NHGN 80234 1860 C6
N Huron St
10400 NHGN 80234 1860 C4
10400 NHGN 80260 1860 C4
11100 WSTR 80234 1860 C4
13400 BMFD 80020 1776 C6
13400 WSTR 80020 1776 C6
13400 WSTR 80234 1776 C6
14700 AdmC 80020 1776 C3
15200 AdmC 80020 1692 C7
15400 BMFD 80020 1692 C7
16000 BMFD 80516 1692 C7
S Huron St
700 DNVR 80223 2196 D3
3000 EGLD 80110 2280 D2
5000 LITN 80120 2280 D7
5300 LITN 80120 2364 D1
S Huron Wy
5200 LITN 80120 2280 D7
5300 LITN 80120 2364 D1
Huron Peak Av
900 SUPE 80027 1857 A1
Huron Peak Ct
2900 CSRK 80109 2786 E5
Huron Peak Pl
3000 SUPE 80027 1857 B1
N Hurricane Ct
6100 DgsC 80134 2622 C3
S Hurricane Wy
8600 JfnC 80433 2440 D2
Hurricane Hill Dr
10 BldC 80466 1766 A1
W Hurst Pl
4900 DNVR 80204 2111 C7
Hurty Av
9500 JfnC 80433 2442 A5
Hutchinson St
400 LSVL 80027 1773 C1
Hutton St
- AURA 80010 2115 E5
N Huxtable St
5400 DgsC 80135 2617 B5
S Hyacinth Ct
10600 DgsC 80129 2448 B7
S Hyacinth Ln
10500 DgsC 80129 2448 B7
S Hyacinth Pl
10400 DgsC 80129 2448 B6
W Hyacinth Rd
1900 DgsC 80129 2448 B6
S Hyacinth St
10300 DgsC 80129 2448 B6
Hyacinth Wy
1300 SUPE 80027 1857 B1
Hyde Park Cir
10 DNVR 80209 2197 D2
Hygiene Rd
4300 BldC 80503 1353 B6
6200 BldC 80503 1354 A6
7500 BldC 80503 1355 A6
7500 LGMT 80503 1355 A6
Hyland Dr
10 CCkC 80439 2187 D1
400 DgsC 80108 2619 A6
Hyland Greens Pl
4600 WSTR 80031 1859 C7
N Hyperion Wy
7100 DgsC 80134 2622 A4
7200 DgsC 80134 2621 E4
Hy-Vu Dr
10 CCkC 80439 2187 D1

I

I-25
- AdmC - 1692 E3
- AdmC - 1776 D1
- AdmC - 1944 E3
- AdmC - 2028 D5
- BMFD - 1692 E1
- BMFD - 1776 D4
- CSRK - 2619 B2
- CSRK - 2703 C2
- CSRK - 2787 A7
- CTNL - 2367 B7
- CTNL - 2451 B1
- DgsC - 2451 C4
- DgsC - 2535 B1
- DgsC - 2619 B7
- DgsC - 2787 A7
- DgsC - 2870 E4
- DgsC - 2871 A3
- DgsC - 2954 E1
- DgsC - 2955 A2
- DNVR - 2112 B7
- DNVR - 2196 E4
- DNVR - 2197 A4
- DNVR - 2198 A7
- DNVR - 2282 C4
- DvrC - 2282 D7
- GDVL - 2282 D7
- GDVL - 2366 E3
- GDVL - 2367 A3
- LKSR - 2955 A2
- LNTR - 2451 C4
- LNTR - 2535 B6
- NHGN - 1860 D7
- TNTN - 1692 E3
- TNTN - 1776 D1
- TNTN - 1860 D7
- TNTN - 1944 D1
- WSTR - 1776 D1
- WSTR - 1860 D1
I-25 Frontage Rd
- DNVR 80210 2197 E6
- DNVR 80222 2197 E6
E I-25 Frontage Rd
10 BMFD 80516 1692 E2
10 TNTN 80020 1692 E2
W I-25 Frontage Rd
10 BMFD 80020 1692 E4
10 BMFD 80516 1692 E4
I-25 N Valley Hwy
- AdmC - 2028 E3
- DNVR - 2028 E3
- DNVR - 2112 C1
I-70
- AdmC - 2032 B7
- AdmC - 2118 A4
- AdmC - 2119 E5
- AdmC - 2120 C4
- AdmC - 2121 E4
- AdmC - 2122 E4
- AdmC - 2123 D4
- AdmC - 2124 E4
- AdmC - 2125 C5
- AphC - 2118 E5
- AphC - 2119 A4
- AphC - 2122 A4
- AphC - 2125 C5
- ARVD - 2026 E6
- ARVD - 2027 E6
- AURA - 2032 B7
- AURA - 2116 E1
- AURA - 2117 E3
- AURA - 2118 A4
- AURA - 2121 E4
- AURA - 2122 A4
- BNNT - 2124 E4
- BNNT - 2125 C5
- CCkC - 2101 A5
- CCkC - 2102 E5
- CCkC - 2103 B6
- CCkC - 2187 E1
- DNVR - 2027 E6
- DNVR - 2028 A6
- DNVR - 2029 D6
- DNVR - 2030 A6
- DNVR - 2031 B7
- DNVR - 2032 B7
- DvrC - 2032 B7
- GOLD - 2108 D7
- GOLD - 2192 A4
- IDSP - 2101 A5
- IDSP - 2102 A5
- JfnC - 2108 E7
- JfnC - 2109 C4
- JfnC - 2188 A2
- JfnC - 2189 A3
- JfnC - 2190 E3
- JfnC - 2191 A3
- JfnC - 2192 C1
- LKSD - 2027 A6
- LKWD - 2109 C4
- WTRG - 2025 C7
- WTRG - 2026 E6
- WTRG - 2027 A6
- WTRG - 2109 C1
I-70 BUS
- AURA 80011 2116 D5
- GOLD 80401 2192 B4
- JfnC 80401 2192 B4
I-70 BUS E Colfax Av
10 DNVR 80203 2112 E5
100 DNVR 80202 2112 E5
700 DNVR 80203 2113 A5
1000 DNVR 80218 2113 A5
2700 DNVR 80206 2113 C5
3900 DNVR 80220 2113 E5
4700 DNVR 80220 2114 B5
8900 AURA 80010 2115 A5
8900 DNVR 80220 2115 A5
12100 AURA 80011 2115 E5
12700 AURA 80011 2116 A5
13000 AURA 80010 2116 D5
16500 AURA 80011 2117 A5
20700 AdmC 80011 2118 A5
20700 AURA 80011 2118 A5
I-70 BUS W Colfax Av
- GOLD 80401 2192 A2
10 DNVR 80202 2112 C5
10 DNVR 80203 2112 C5
10 DNVR 80204 2112 C5
3000 DNVR 80204 2111 E5
5100 LKWD 80214 2111 B5
6800 LKWD 80214 2110 E5
8300 LKWD 80215 2110 C5
10800 LKWD 80215 2109 E5
11900 JfnC 80401 2109 C5
12700 JfnC 80215 2109 C5
13800 LKWD 80401 2109 B5
14800 JfnC 80401 2108 C7
14800 LKWD 80401 2108 E7
15500 GOLD 80401 2108 E7
17700 JfnC 80401 2192 B1
I-70 BUS Colorado Blvd
10 CCkC 80452 2101 A5
10 IDSP 80452 2101 A5
I-70 Frontage Rd
10 AphC 80102 2124 C4
I-70 Frontage Rd N
10000 WTRG 80033 2026 A6
10800 WTRG 80033 2025 D6
12200 JfnC 80033 2025 D6
N I-70 Service Rd
7800 ARVD 80002 2026 C6
7800 ARVD 80033 2026 C6
7800 JfnC 80002 2026 C6
7800 WTRG 80033 2026 C6
8000 JfnC 80033 2026 C6
8000 WTRG 80002 2026 C6
W I-70 Service Rd
5200 DNVR 80212 2027 B6
5200 LKSD 80212 2027 B6
5700 WTRG 80033 2027 B6
I-70 S Service Rd
10000 WTRG 80033 2026 A6
10500 WTRG 80033 2025 E6
I-76
- AdmC - 1698 B5
- AdmC - 1780 E5
- AdmC - 1781 A4
- AdmC - 1862 E7
- AdmC - 1863 A6
- AdmC - 1864 C1
- AdmC - 1945 C7
- AdmC - 1946 C1
- AdmC - 2027 B5
- AdmC - 2028 D2
- AdmC - 2029 A1
- ARVD - 2026 E6
- ARVD - 2027 B5
- BGTN - 1697 D7
- BGTN - 1698 B5
- BGTN - 1780 D7
- BGTN - 1781 D1
- BGTN - 1863 E4
- BGTN - 1864 A3
- CMCY - 1862 E7
- CMCY - 1863 A6
- CMCY - 1864 C1
- CMCY - 1946 C1
- DNVR - 2027 B5
- JfnC - 2027 B5
- LCHB - 1698 E2
- TNTN - 1945 E6
- WldC - 1698 E2
- WTRG - 2027 B5
I-76 Frontage Rd
8800 AdmC 80022 1946 B3
8800 AdmC 80640 1946 B3
8800 CMCY 80022 1946 B3
19000 WldC 80603 1698 E1
19000 WldC 80642 1698 E1
I-76 Service Rd
7800 AdmC 80022 1945 E6
7800 TNTN 80022 1945 E6
8000 AdmC 80022 1946 A4
8000 CMCY 80022 1946 A4
I-225
- AphC - 2283 A5
- AURA - 2116 B7
- AURA - 2200 B1
- AURA - 2283 A5
- AURA - 2284 A2
- DNVR - 2282 D5
- DNVR - 2283 A5
- GDVL - 2283 A5
I-270
- AdmC - 1944 E7
- AdmC - 1945 A7
- AdmC - 2029 E3
- CMCY - 2029 D2
- CMCY - 2030 D6
- DNVR - 2030 D6
Ian Ct
500 DgsC 80108 2618 E1
IBM Dr
- BldC 80503 1520 B6
- BLDR 80503 1520 B6
Icarus Dr
1800 LAFT 80026 1690 A6
Ida Av
- JfnC 80127 2529 A3
E Ida Av
6400 GDVL 80111 2366 C2
9700 GDVL 80111 2367 B1
10400 AphC 80111 2367 C2
16300 CTNL 80015 2368 E1
17700 CTNL 80015 2369 B1
18600 AphC 80015 2369 C2
20900 CTNL 80015 2370 A1
22500 AphC 80015 2370 C2
W Ida Av
10 LITN 80120 2364 E2
10 LITN 80121 2364 E2
10100 JfnC 80127 2362 B2
11300 JfnC 80127 2361 E2
E Ida Cir
5600 GDVL 80111 2366 B2
9700 GDVL 80111 2367 B2
11800 AphC 80111 2367 D1
19600 AphC 80015 2369 D2
20600 CTNL 80015 2369 E1
20600 CTNL 80015 2370 A1
22600 AphC 80015 2370 C2
E Ida Ct
11300 AphC 80111 2367 D2
E Ida Dr
15300 CTNL 80015 2368 D1
18000 CTNL 80015 2369 B2
19600 AphC 80015 2369 D2
W Ida Dr
5500 JfnC 80123 2363 B2
6800 JfnC 80123 2362 E2
E Ida Pl
- GDVL 80111 2367 B2
5800 GDVL 80111 2366 B2
10700 AphC 80111 2367 C2
17100 CTNL 80015 2369 A1
19500 AphC 80015 2369 D2
22100 CTNL 80015 2370 B1
23200 AphC 80015 2370 D1
S Ida Pl
- GDVL 80111 2367 C2
W Ida Pl
6600 JfnC 80123 2363 A2
8800 JfnC 80123 2362 B2
10400 JfnC 80127 2362 A2
Ida St
400 AdmC 80601 1696 B4
400 BGTN 80603 1696 B4
400 WldC 80603 1696 B4
E Idaho Av
19700 AURA 80017 2201 D5
W Idaho Av
10200 LKWD 80232 2194 A5
11100 JfnC 80232 2193 E5
E Idaho Cir
9900 AURA 80247 2199 B5
16800 AURA 80017 2200 E4
16800 AURA 80017 2201 A4
E Idaho Dr
12800 AURA 80012 2199 E5
12800 AURA 80012 2200 A5
19200 AURA 80017 2201 C4
W Idaho Dr
12300 LKWD 80228 2193 C5
E Idaho Pl
- AURA 80247 2199 C5
4600 DNVR 80222 2197 E5
4600 DNVR 80222 2198 A5
9700 AphC 80247 2199 B4
10300 AURA 80012 2199 B4
13100 AURA 80012 2200 A5
15300 AURA 80017 2200 D4
17900 AURA 80017 2201 B4
24500 AURA 80018 2202 E4
W Idaho Pl
2600 DNVR 80219 2196 A5
10100 LKWD 80232 2194 B5
Idaho St
600 GOLD 80403 2107 D1
1400 IDSP 80452 2101 C5
E Idaho St
9800 AURA 80247 2199 A5
Idahoe Mall
- IDSP 80452 2101 C5
Idalia Cir
800 AURA 80011 2116 D6
S Idalia Cir
1600 AURA 80017 2200 D5
Idalia Ct
1300 AURA 80011 2116 D5
N Idalia Ct
10 AURA 80011 2200 D1
100 AURA 80011 2116 D7
S Idalia Ct
1200 SUPE 80027 1773 B5
1500 AURA 80017 2200 D5
5400 CTNL 80015 2368 D1
Idalia Pl
- CMCY 80603 1864 D1
Idalia St
- DNVR 80239 2032 D4
2500 AURA 80011 2116 D3
9900 CMCY 80022 1864 D7
10100 AdmC 80022 1864 D7
11800 CMCY 80603 1864 D2
N Idalia St
10800 CMCY 80022 1864 D4
S Idalia St
1100 AURA 80017 2200 D4
2000 AURA 80013 2200 D6
3900 AURA 80013 2284 D4
4600 AURA 80015 2284 D5
5600 CTNL 80015 2368 D1
S Idalia Wy
4300 AURA 80015 2284 D5
5400 CTNL 80015 2284 D7
5400 CTNL 80015 2368 D1
Idaua Wy
10700 CMCY 80022 1864 D5
S Ider Ct
7100 AURA 80016 2371 A5
S Ider St
- AURA 80016 2371 A3
Idlewild Ln
30800 JfnC 80439 2189 A6
Idlewild St
7700 CMCY 80022 1946 A5
7800 AdmC 80022 1946 B5
E Idyllwilde Dr
21900 DgsC 80138 2538 B3
Idylwild Ct
6700 BldC 80301 1604 B3
Idylwild Tr
4800 BldC 80301 1604 B2
5300 BLDR 80301 1604 B1
Idylwood St
- CSRK 80104 2788 A4
Iliad Wy
1000 LAFT 80026 1690 B6
Iliff Av
47300 AphC 80102 2208 D6
E Iliff Av
10 DNVR 80210 2196 E7
10 DNVR 80223 2196 E7
500 DNVR 80210 2197 A7
3900 DNVR 80222 2197 E7
5100 AphC 80222 2198 A7
5500 DNVR 80222 2198 A7
6900 DNVR 80224 2198 E7
7300 AphC 80231 2198 E7
8500 AphC 80231 2199 C7
9500 DNVR 80231 2199 C7
9800 AURA 80247 2199 C7
9800 DNVR 80247 2199 C7
12100 AURA 80014 2199 E7
12700 AURA 80014 2200 B7
15100 AURA 80013 2200 E7
16600 AURA 80013 2201 A7
19100 AURA 80017 2201 A7
48000 AphC 80102 2208 E6
48000 AphC 80102 2209 A6
W Iliff Av
10 DNVR 80210 2196 D7
10 DNVR 80223 2196 D7
1600 EGLD 80110 2196 C7
3000 DNVR 80219 2195 E7
3000 DNVR 80219 2196 A7
10000 LKWD 80227 2194 A7
12500 LKWD 80228 2193 D7
14700 LKWD 80228 2192 E7
E Iliff Dr
- AphC 80231 2198 E7
- AphC 80231 2199 A7
26000 AURA 80018 2203 B6
W Iliff Dr
5200 DNVR 80219 2195 B7
6700 LKWD 80227 2195 B6
6700 LKWD 80232 2195 B6
12800 JfnC 80228 2193 C7
14800 LKWD 80228 2192 E7
W Iliff Ln
8000 LKWD 80227 2194 C7
E Iliff Pl
- AURA 80013 2201 D6
6800 DNVR 80224 2198 C7
10800 AURA 80014 2199 C7
14900 AURA 80014 2200 C7
15900 AURA 80013 2200 D7
W Iliff Pl
16600 LKWD 80228 2192 D7
Iliff St
2600 BLDR 80305 1770 E1
2700 BLDR 80305 1771 A1
E Iliff Tr
43000 AphC 80102 2207 D6
44300 AphC 80102 2208 A6
E Iliff Wy
1000 SUPE 80027 1773 B5
Ilium Cir
1200 LAFT 80026 1690 A6
Ilium Dr
1200 LAFT 80026 1690 A6
Illini Ct
10 BLDR 80303 1687 D6
Illini Wy
5100 BLDR 80303 1687 D6
Illinois St
- IDSP 80452 2101 D5
400 GOLD 80403 2107 D2
700 GOLD 80401 2107 D3
3000 GOLD 80401 2108 A6
N Imboden Rd
2000 AdmC 80137 2121 C3
2000 AURA 80137 2121 C3
2800 AdmC 80137 2037 C7
2800 AURA 80137 2037 C7
5600 AdmC 80137 1953 C7

STREET Block City ZIP Map# Grid

N Imboden Rd
5600 AdmC 80249 1953 C7
5600 AURA 80137 1953 C7
5600 AURA 80249 1953 C7
7200 AdmC 80102 1953 B2
S Imboden Rd
10 AphC 80137 2121 C7
10 AphC 80137 2205 C1
Imboden Mile Rd
700 AphC 80137 2121 C6
Impala Tr
10 PrkC 80456 2607 E6
Imperial Ln
2000 SUPE 80027 1773 B6
Imperial Wy
1100 SUPE 80027 1773 B6
E Inca
- AdmC 80022 1946 C3
W Inca
- AdmC 80022 1946 C3
Inca Ct
8400 FLHT 80260 1944 C4
9400 TNTN 80260 1944 C1
N Inca Ct
14400 WSTR 80020 1776 C2
S Inca Dr
4900 EGLD 80110 2280 D7
5000 LITN 80120 2280 D7
Inca Pkwy
100 BLDR 80303 1687 B4
Inca Rd
7800 DgsC 80118 2953 C3
22200 JfnC 80439 2275 A6
22900 JfnC 80439 2274 D6
Inca St
- DNVR 80204 2112 D5
10 DNVR 80223 2196 D1
300 DNVR 80223 2112 D7
2900 DNVR 80202 2112 C2
3800 DNVR 80211 2112 C1
4000 DNVR 80211 2028 C7
7200 AdmC 80221 1944 C7
10400 NHGN 80234 1860 C6
10400 NHGN 80260 1860 C6
S Inca St
1100 DNVR 80223 2196 D4
3300 EGLD 80110 2280 D2
Inca Wy
7000 AdmC 80221 1944 C7
S Inca Wy
3500 EGLD 80110 2280 C3
Incline Ct
2700 JfnC 80439 2273 C2
Incorrigible Cir
800 LGMT 80504 1439 B6
W Independence Av
11600 JfnC 80401 2109 D5
11600 LKWD 80215 2109 D5
11600 LKWD 80401 2109 D5
Independence Cir
9000 WSTR 80021 1942 B2
10400 WSTR 80021 1858 B6
S Independence Cir
8300 JfnC 80128 2446 B1
Independence Cir E
10900 PARK 80134 2453 B6
11000 PARK 80134 2537 A1
Independence Cir W
10900 PARK 80134 2453 B6
10900 PARK 80134 2537 A1
Independence Ct
- DgsC 80118 2954 C2
- DNVR 80237 2282 C6
3200 JfnC 80215 2110 B2
3200 WTRG 80215 2110 B2
3400 WTRG 80033 2110 B2
6400 ARVD 80004 2026 B2
S Independence Ct
400 LKWD 80226 2194 B2
1000 LKWD 80232 2194 B4
1900 LKWD 80227 2194 B6
3100 LKWD 80227 2278 B2
4300 JfnC 80123 2278 B5
5000 DNVR 80123 2278 B7
5600 JfnC 80123 2362 C2
8800 JfnC 80128 2446 B2
Independence Dr
- BLDR 80301 1603 B6
400 LGMT 80501 1356 D7
700 DgsC 80118 2954 E2
10900 PARK 80134 2453 A7
N Independence Dr
8800 ARVD 80005 1942 B2
8800 ARVD 80021 1942 B2
8800 WSTR 80021 1942 B2
Independence Pl
3800 WTRG 80033 2110 B1
4100 WTRG 80033 2026 B7
Independence Rd
4800 BldC 80301 1603 C6
4800 BLDR 80301 1603 C6
Independence St
400 LKWD 80226 2110 B7
400 LKWD 80226 2194 B1
1600 LKWD 80215 2110 B5
3500 WTRG 80033 2110 B1
4800 WTRG 80033 2026 B7
5000 ARVD 80002 2026 B7
6900 ARVD 80004 2026 B1
7000 ARVD 80004 1942 B7
8200 ARVD 80005 1942 B4
10400 WSTR 80021 1858 B5
N Independence St
9700 WSTR 80021 1858 B7
9700 WSTR 80021 1942 B1
S Independence St
- LITN 80127 2446 B5
1200 LKWD 80232 2194 B4
1900 LKWD 80227 2194 B6
2500 LKWD 80227 2278 B1
3500 JfnC 80227 2278 B3
3500 JfnC 80235 2278 B3
3500 LKWD 80235 2278 B3
4500 DNVR 80123 2278 B6

S Independence St
5100 JfnC 80123 2278 B7
5900 JfnC 80123 2362 B3
6700 JfnC 80128 2362 B4
Independence Tr
26300 JfnC 80439 2274 B6
S Independence Tr
- JfnC 80439 2273 E6
4600 JfnC 80439 2274 A6
Independence Wy
- ARVD 80005 1942 B3
- ARVD 80021 1942 B3
6400 ARVD 80004 2026 B2
9700 WSTR 80021 1858 C6
9700 WSTR 80021 1942 A1
S Independence Wy
4900 DNVR 80123 2278 B7
7600 JfnC 80128 2362 B7
Independent Dr
10 GpnC 80403 1849 D7
Indian Rd
3100 BldC 80301 1603 E7
S Indian Tr
4800 JfnC 80439 2273 E7
Indiana Ct
6900 ARVD 80007 2024 E1
S Indiana Pl
10 JfnC 80401 2193 A1
Indiana St
- ARVD 80403 2025 A2
- SUPE 80027 1773 A7
10 JfnC 80401 2192 E1
10 JfnC 80401 2193 A1
300 LKWD 80401 2109 A7
600 JfnC 80401 2109 A7
4400 JfnC 80403 2025 A7
5100 JfnC 80002 2025 A5
5700 JfnC 80004 2025 A4
6400 ARVD 80004 2025 A2
6400 ARVD 80007 2025 A2
7000 ARVD 80007 1941 A6
7000 JfnC 80007 1941 A6
7800 JfnC 80005 1941 A5
8200 ARVD 80005 1941 A5
8900 ARVD 80005 1940 E1
8900 ARVD 80007 1940 E1
8900 JfnC 80005 1940 E1
8900 JfnC 80403 1940 E1
8900 WSTR 80403 1940 E1
9700 WSTR 80403 1856 E4
10400 BldC 80403 1856 E4
10400 BMFD 80021 1856 E4
11600 SUPE 80027 1856 E4
Indiana St SR-72
- ARVD 80403 2025 A2
6400 ARVD 80004 2025 A2
6400 ARVD 80007 2025 A2
7000 ARVD 80007 1941 A6
7000 JfnC 80007 1941 A6
7800 JfnC 80005 1941 A5
8200 ARVD 80005 1941 A5
N Indiana St
2700 JfnC 80401 2109 A3
S Indiana St
10 JfnC 80401 2193 A2
1600 SUPE 80027 1773 A6
2000 LKWD 80228 2192 E7
2500 LKWD 80228 2276 E1
2500 LKWD 80228 2277 A2
2700 SUPE 80027 1857 A1
S Indiana Wy
100 JfnC 80401 2193 A2
Indiana Gulch Rd
15000 BldC 80455 1597 E3
15700 BldC 80481 1597 E3
15700 WARD 80481 1597 E3
Indian Brush Ct
46400 EbtC 80138 2455 E3
S Indian Creek St
8800 DgsC 80126 2448 E2
S Indianfield St
1200 AphC 80102 2206 D4
Indian Head Rd
21000 JfnC 80007 1939 B5
22400 JfnC 80403 1939 A5
Indian Hills St
16300 AdmC 80603 1700 A4
Indian Lookout Rd
600 LYNS 80540 1352 C1
Indian Paint Run
5600 DgsC 80125 2614 E4
W Indian Paintbrush Cir
2200 DgsC 80129 2448 B4
S Indian Paintbrush Ct
9400 DgsC 80129 2448 B4
Indian Paintbrush Dr
- AdmC 80601 1780 C2
- BGTN 80601 1780 C2
10 JfnC 80401 2190 E2
W Indian Paintbrush Dr
2100 DgsC 80129 2448 B3
Indian Paintbrush Ln
1300 LGMT 80503 1438 B5
S Indian Paintbrush Ln
9400 DgsC 80129 2448 B4
Indian Peak Rd
1400 BldC 80403 1852 A1
1400 GpnC 80403 1851 E1
Indian Peaks Cir
2100 LGMT 80504 1438 E7
Indian Peaks Dr
- LAFT 80026 1689 E4
10 BldC 80466 1765 A1
700 NDLD 80466 1765 A1
Indian Peaks Tr
- BldC 80026 1689 D3
- BldC 80303 1689 D3
- LAFT 80026 1690 A4
2300 LAFT 80026 1689 D3
6900 BldC 80301 1604 C2
Indian Peaks Tr W
- BldC 80027 1689 C4
- LAFT 80027 1689 C4
500 BldC 80026 1689 C3

Indian Peaks Tr W
500 BldC 80303 1689 C3
500 LAFT 80026 1689 C3
Indianpipe Ln
- PARK 80134 2537 D3
Indian Springs Rd
20700 JfnC 80433 2527 D1
Indian Summer Ct
5400 BLDR 80301 1604 B1
W Indian Summer Ln
3100 CSRK 80109 2702 E2
Indian Wells Ct
7400 LNTR 80124 2450 D4
Indian Wells Dr
9600 LNTR 80124 2450 D5
Indian Wells Ln
7400 LNTR 80124 2450 D5
Indian Wells Pl
7500 LNTR 80124 2450 D5
Indian Wells Wy
7400 LNTR 80124 2450 D5
Indian Wells Cove
7400 LNTR 80124 2450 D4
Indigo Ct
6100 BldC 80301 1603 E3
6100 BldC 80301 1604 A3
Indigo Dr
- AdmC 80601 1780 C2
1300 BGTN 80601 1780 C2
S Indigo Wy
10 DgsC 80108 2618 E4
E Indore Dr
25400 AURA 80016 2371 A5
W Indore Dr
5400 JfnC 80128 2363 B6
9200 JfnC 80128 2362 B6
10300 JfnC 80127 2362 A6
E Indore Pl
- AURA 80016 2371 A5
W Indore Pl
5900 JfnC 80128 2363 B6
8500 JfnC 80128 2362 C6
12600 JfnC 80127 2361 D6
E Indore St
- AURA 80016 2371 B5
Industrial Cir
1800 LGMT 80501 1438 D5
Industrial Ln
2000 BMFD 80020 1858 C1
2100 BMFD 80021 1858 C1
2200 BMFD 80021 1774 A7
Industrial Wy
3000 CSRK 80109 2703 B1
29300 JfnC 80439 2189 C4
Infinite Dr
1400 LSVL 80027 1772 D2
Inga Wy
7500 DgsC 80116 2706 A4
Ingalls Cir
6000 ARVD 80003 2027 A3
8500 ARVD 80003 1943 A3
10800 WSTR 80020 1859 A5
Ingalls Ct
3000 WTRG 80214 2111 A2
4100 WTRG 80033 2027 A7
6500 ARVD 80003 2027 A1
7000 WSTR 80003 1943 A7
7900 ARVD 80003 1943 A5
S Ingalls Ct
1800 LKWD 80232 2195 B6
1900 LKWD 80227 2195 B6
2600 LKWD 80227 2279 B1
7200 JfnC 80128 2363 B6
Ingalls Pl
3800 WTRG 80033 2111 A1
Ingalls St
10 LKWD 80226 2195 B1
100 LKWD 80226 2111 A7
1400 LKWD 80214 2111 A5
2900 EDGW 80214 2111 B3
2900 WTRG 80214 2111 B3
3000 WTRG 80033 2111 B3
4800 WTRG 80033 2027 A6
5200 DNVR 80002 2027 A5
5200 DvrC 80002 2027 A5
6900 ARVD 80003 2027 A1
7000 ARVD 80003 1943 A7
7200 WSTR 80003 1943 A7
9400 WSTR 80031 1943 A1
11500 WSTR 80020 1859 A3
S Ingalls St
10 LKWD 80226 2195 B2
1100 LKWD 80232 2195 B5
1900 LKWD 80227 2195 B6
3200 DNVR 80227 2279 A3
3600 DNVR 80235 2279 B3
5200 DNVR 80123 2279 B7
5300 DNVR 80123 2363 B1
5600 DvrC 80123 2363 B1
7600 JfnC 80128 2363 B6
S Ingalls Wy
2000 LKWD 80227 2195 B6
2700 DNVR 80227 2279 B2
7100 JfnC 80128 2363 B5
Ingersoll Pl
5000 BLDR 80303 1687 C3
Ingleton Ct
300 DgsC 80108 2618 E1
Ingleton Dr
6700 DgsC 80108 2618 E1
Ingleton Pl
300 DgsC 80108 2618 E1
Ingram Ct
4600 BLDR 80305 1687 B6
Innisbrook Ct
2500 CSRK 80104 2787 D3
Innovation Dr
1200 BLDR 80303 1687 A3
Innsbrook Dr
7700 JfnC 80439 2356 B7
Insmont Dr
200 PrkC 80456 2690 E5
E Inspiration Dr
7000 DgsC 80138 2453 E3

E Inspiration Dr
7300 DgsC 80138 2454 A3
9700 DgsC 80138 2455 B3
Inspiration Rd
11400 JfnC 80403 1852 D3
W Inspiration Rd
32400 JfnC 80403 1852 C3
Inspiration Point Dr
- DNVR 80212 2027 B5
Interlocken Blvd
200 BMFD 80021 1858 A1
400 BMFD 80021 1857 E1
500 BMFD 80021 1773 E7
Interlocken Cres
300 BMFD 80021 1857 E1
300 BMFD 80021 1858 A1
S Interlocken Ct
2000 JfnC 80439 2189 A7
S Interlocken Dr
1800 JfnC 80439 2188 E7
1900 JfnC 80439 2189 A7
2000 JfnC 80439 2273 A1
Interlocken Lp
- BMFD 80021 1773 D7
- BMFD 80021 1857 D1
- BMFD 80021 1858 A2
Interlocken Lp SR-128
- BMFD 80021 1857 D2
- BMFD 80021 1858 A2
Interlocken Pkwy
100 BMFD 80021 1858 A1
Interlocken St
5400 DgsC 80134 2621 D4
International Ct
300 BMFD 80021 1858 A1
International Isle Dr
700 DgsC 80108 2618 D5
Interport Blvd
8000 AphC 80112 2367 E7
8100 AphC 80112 2451 E1
Inverness Cir E
10 AphC 80112 2367 C6
Inverness Ct E
- AphC 80112 2367 C7
10 AphC 80112 2451 C1
Inverness Dr
1300 LAFT 80026 1690 D2
32100 JfnC 80439 2273 A2
Inverness Dr E
10 AphC 80112 2367 D7
10 AphC 80112 2451 C1
Inverness Dr N
- AphC 80112 2367 C6
Inverness Dr S
300 DgsC 80112 2451 D1
Inverness Dr W
- CTNL 80112 2451 B1
100 AphC 80112 2367 B6
200 AphC 80112 2451 B1
Inverness Ln
30200 JfnC 80439 2273 B2
Inverness Ln E
10 AphC 80112 2367 D6
Inverness Ln S
- DgsC 80112 2451 D2
Inverness Pkwy
400 AphC 80112 2451 C1
S Inverness Pl
2400 JfnC 80439 2273 B1
Inverness Pl E
- AphC 80112 2367 C7
Inverness Pl N
- AphC 80112 2367 C6
Inverness St
200 BMFD 80020 1859 B1
1100 BMFD 80020 1775 B6
Inverness Ter E
10 AphC 80112 2367 C6
Inverness Ter W
- AphC 80112 2367 B6
Inverness Wy E
10 AphC 80112 2451 D1
Inverness Wy S
10 AphC 80112 2451 C1
Inwood Pl
1300 DgsC 80104 2787 E5
Inyo Rd
4700 JfnC 80439 2275 A6
Inyokern Ct
- AphC 80137 2121 C6
Io Ct
1600 LAFT 80026 1690 A7
S Iola Ct
2000 AURA 80014 2199 C6
6200 AphC 80111 2367 C3
Iola St
1600 AURA 80010 2115 C4
10900 CMCY 80640 1863 C3
15000 AdmC 80602 1779 B1
15400 AdmC 80602 1695 B7
S Iola St
900 AURA 80012 2199 C3
2200 AURA 80014 2199 C6
7300 AphC 80112 2367 C5
S Iola Wy
5400 AphC 80111 2283 C7
5400 AphC 80111 2367 C1
Ionic Dr
1800 LAFT 80026 1690 A7
Ionosphere Dr
1900 LGMT 80504 1439 B7
Iowa Av
900 LGMT 80501 1439 A5
1300 LGMT 80501 1438 E5
E Iowa Av
- AURA 80012 2200 A5
10 DNVR 80210 2196 E5
10 DNVR 80223 2196 E5
600 DNVR 80210 2197 A5
3800 DNVR 80222 2197 E5
4900 DNVR 80222 2198 A5
7300 DNVR 80224 2198 D5
7300 DNVR 80231 2198 D5
9200 AphC 80247 2199 B5

E Iowa Av
9500 AURA 80247 2199 B5
11900 AURA 80012 2199 D5
16100 AURA 80017 2200 E5
17800 AURA 80017 2201 B5
N Iowa Av
100 LAFT 80026 1690 D4
S Iowa Av
100 LAFT 80026 1690 D5
W Iowa Av
10 DNVR 80210 2196 D5
10 DNVR 80223 2196 D5
2700 DNVR 80219 2196 A5
3600 DNVR 80219 2195 D5
5200 LKWD 80219 2195 B5
6800 LKWD 80232 2195 A5
8000 LKWD 80232 2194 D5
E Iowa Cir
9500 AphC 80247 2199 A5
19400 AURA 80017 2201 D5
W Iowa Cir
9300 LKWD 80232 2194 B5
Iowa Ct
300 GOLD 80403 2107 D1
Iowa Dr
200 GOLD 80403 2107 D1
E Iowa Dr
8300 AphC 80231 2198 E5
10800 AURA 80012 2199 C5
14000 AURA 80012 2200 B5
17700 AURA 80017 2201 B5
W Iowa Dr
7600 LKWD 80232 2194 D5
11100 JfnC 80232 2193 E5
12300 LKWD 80228 2193 D5
E Iowa Pl
8500 AphC 80231 2198 E5
15300 AURA 80017 2200 D5
23800 AURA 80018 2202 D5
W Iowa Pl
5800 LKWD 80232 2195 B5
9100 LKWD 80232 2194 C5
Iowa St
- AURA 80011 2117 E4
600 GOLD 80403 2107 D2
Iowa Gulch Rd
7600 JfnC 80465 2359 C7
7700 JfnC 80465 2443 C1
Ipswich St
4600 BldC 80301 1604 E3
Iran St
4600 DNVR 80249 2033 D6
Iredell St
16500 AdmC 80603 1700 A4
S Ireland Cir
7200 CTNL 80016 2369 E5
Ireland Ct
4800 DNVR 80249 2033 E6
S Ireland Ct
2400 AURA 80013 2201 E7
4100 AphC 80013 2285 E4
4700 AphC 80015 2285 E6
5800 CTNL 80015 2369 E2
5900 CTNL 80016 2369 E2
6600 AphC 80016 2369 E3
S Ireland Ln
4400 AphC 80015 2285 E5
Ireland St
- DNVR 80249 2033 E6
S Ireland St
4200 AphC 80013 2285 E4
4500 AphC 80015 2285 E5
5400 CTNL 80015 2285 D6
5400 CTNL 80015 2369 E1
S Ireland Wy
- AURA 80013 2285 E1
2400 AURA 80013 2201 E7
5200 CTNL 80015 2285 E7
5500 CTNL 80015 2369 E1
7100 CTNL 80016 2369 E5
7400 AURA 80016 2369 E5
7900 AphC 80016 2370 A6
7900 AURA 80016 2370 A6
8200 AphC 80016 2454 B1
8200 AphC 80138 2454 B1
8200 AURA 80138 2454 B1
Irene Av
10 GpnC 80403 1849 D6
Irene Ct
10 BMFD 80020 1774 E6
Iridium Wy
- CSRK 80108 2619 D5
N Iriquois Cir
3600 DgsC 80135 2700 E1
Iris Av
- BLDR 80301 1602 E6
1200 BLDR 80304 1602 E6
2800 BLDR 80301 1603 A6
Iris Cir
1300 BMFD 80020 1774 D6
W Iris Cir
1800 LITN 80120 2364 B3
Iris Ct
- GDVL 80121 2365 E1
3400 BLDR 80304 1602 C6
3700 WTRG 80033 2110 B1
4200 WTRG 80033 2026 B7
6300 ARVD 80004 2026 B2
8200 ARVD 80005 1942 B4
8800 WSTR 80021 1942 B3
E Iris Ct
1200 DgsC 80126 2449 A3
N Iris Ct
3200 JfnC 80215 2110 B2
3200 WTRG 80033 2110 B2
3200 WTRG 80215 2110 B2
S Iris Ct
- JfnC 80235 2278 B5
400 LKWD 80226 2194 B2
3300 LKWD 80227 2278 B3
4300 JfnC 80123 2278 B5
6400 JfnC 80123 2362 B3
7100 JfnC 80128 2362 B5
8800 JfnC 80128 2446 B2

S Iris Ct
9700 LITN 80127 2446 B5
Iris Dr
10 PrkC 80456 2606 C4
1100 LKWD 80215 2110 B6
27700 JfnC 80439 2273 E5
S Iris Dr
3300 LKWD 80227 2278 B3
Iris Rd
- GpnC 80403 1934 C1
Iris St
100 BMFD 80020 1858 D1
1500 LKWD 80215 2110 B5
1600 BMFD 80020 1774 D5
2500 JfnC 80215 2110 B4
5100 WTRG 80033 2026 B5
5700 ARVD 80002 2026 B4
6600 ARVD 80004 2026 B1
8700 ARVD 80005 1942 B3
9700 WSTR 80021 1858 B7
9700 WSTR 80021 1942 B1
S Iris St
900 LKWD 80226 2194 B4
900 LKWD 80232 2194 B4
2400 LKWD 80227 2278 B1
4500 DNVR 80123 2278 B6
6400 JfnC 80123 2362 B3
6700 JfnC 80128 2362 B4
Iris Wy
6000 ARVD 80004 2026 B3
10400 WSTR 80021 1858 B5
S Iris Wy
1600 LKWD 80232 2194 B5
5100 JfnC 80123 2278 B7
5600 JfnC 80123 2362 B1
7900 JfnC 80128 2362 B7
8100 JfnC 80128 2446 B1
9300 LITN 80127 2446 B4
E Irish Av
400 LITN 80122 2364 E6
400 LITN 80122 2365 B5
E Irish Dr
- AURA 80016 2370 E6
E Irish Ln
1400 CTNL 80122 2365 B6
E Irish Pl
- AURA 80016 2370 D6
2700 CTNL 80122 2365 C6
5700 CTNL 80112 2366 B6
Iris Hollow Pl
2600 BLDR 80304 1602 E6
N Irish Pat Murphy Dr
5500 DgsC 80134 2622 B3
Iris Walk Ct
3300 BLDR 80304 1602 E6
Irma Dr
- TNTN 80229 1861 B5
11800 NHGN 80233 1861 A2
12000 NHGN 80241 1861 A2
12000 TNTN 80241 1861 A2
Irma Wy
- NHGN 80233 1861 A2
Iron Ct
- BldC 80503 1438 B1
- LGMT 80503 1438 B1
3900 BldC 80503 1518 E5
Iron Bark Dr
- DgsC 80125 2615 C7
- DgsC 80125 2698 E2
- DgsC 80125 2699 B2
Iron Forge Pl
- BLDR 80301 1687 A1
Iron Horse Dr
1600 LGMT 80501 1440 A3
Iron Springs Pl
2900 CSRK 80109 2702 D4
Ironspur Ct
- CSRK 80108 2703 E1
Ironstone Pl
9700 DgsC 80134 2452 D4
Ironstone Wy
12700 PARK 80134 2537 D5
Ironton Ct
500 AURA 80010 2115 C7
S Ironton Ct
2000 AURA 80014 2199 C6
5300 AphC 80111 2283 C7
5700 AphC 80111 2367 C1
Ironton St
1400 AURA 80010 2115 C4
4500 DNVR 80239 2031 C6
9600 CMCY 80022 1863 C7
9600 CMCY 80022 1947 C1
11200 CMCY 80640 1863 C3
15200 AdmC 80602 1779 B1
15300 AdmC 80602 1695 C7
S Ironton St
100 AURA 80010 2199 C2
100 AURA 80012 2199 C2
1800 AURA 80014 2199 C6
6500 CTNL 80111 2367 C3
6500 CTNL 80112 2367 C3
S Ironton Wy
5100 AphC 80111 2283 C7
Ironwood Cir
2700 ERIE 80516 1691 E3
Ironwood Pl
1200 BMFD 80020 1775 A6
2600 ERIE 80516 1691 E3
Ironwood St
9100 DgsC 80129 2448 B3
Ironwood Wy
- ERIE 80516 1691 E4
S Ironwood Wy
9100 DgsC 80129 2448 B3
Iroquois Dr
100 BLDR 80303 1687 C5
Iroquois Tr
33400 JfnC 80470 2524 B7
S Iroquois Tr
6500 JfnC 80439 2356 E4
Irving Cir
12600 BMFD 80020 1775 E7
12600 BMFD 80020 1859 E1

Irving Ct
9700 WSTR 80031 1859 E7
13000 BMFD 80020 1775 E6
N Irving Ct
10800 WSTR 80031 1859 E5
Irving Dr
- WSTR 80031 1859 E4
12400 BMFD 80020 1859 E1
12400 WSTR 80020 1859 E1
12400 WSTR 80234 1859 E1
N Irving Dr
- WSTR 80031 1859 E4
Irving St
- WSTR 80031 1943 E1
10 DNVR 80219 2195 E1
300 DNVR 80219 2111 E7
800 DNVR 80204 2111 E6
1900 DNVR 80211 2111 E5
4000 DNVR 80211 2027 E7
4800 DNVR 80221 2027 E6
5200 DvrC 80221 2027 E5
8000 WSTR 80030 1943 E5
8100 AdmC 80031 1943 E4
10000 WSTR 80031 1859 E7
12500 BMFD 80020 1859 E1
14400 BMFD 80020 1775 E2
N Irving St
7100 WSTR 80030 1943 E6
9200 AdmC 80031 1943 E2
9200 WSTR 80031 1943 E2
11500 WSTR 80031 1859 E3
S Irving St
10 DNVR 80219 2195 E2
2500 DNVR 80219 2279 E1
3500 SRDN 80110 2279 E4
3700 SRDN 80236 2279 E4
4100 DNVR 80236 2279 E5
4200 DvrC 80236 2279 E5
4400 EGLD 80110 2279 E5
4600 DNVR 80110 2279 E6
4800 AphC 80110 2279 E6
5100 LITN 80123 2279 E7
5200 LITN 80123 2363 E1
S Irvington Ct
7000 AURA 80016 2371 A4
E Irvington Pl
6700 DNVR 80224 2198 C1
6700 DNVR 80230 2198 C1
W Irvington Pl
10 DNVR 80203 2196 D1
10 DNVR 80223 2196 D1
2700 DNVR 80219 2196 A1
S Irvington Wy
- AphC 80016 2371 A3
- AURA 80016 2371 A3
E Irwin Av
400 LITN 80122 2364 E6
400 LITN 80122 2365 A6
E Irwin Ln
1400 CTNL 80122 2365 B6
Irwin Pl
200 ERIE 80516 1606 D6
E Irwin Pl
1100 CTNL 80122 2365 A6
6300 CTNL 80112 2366 C6
S Isabel Ct
9700 DgsC 80126 2449 A5
Isabell Ct
2900 JfnC 80401 2108 E2
5700 JfnC 80403 2024 E4
Isabell Dr
4600 JfnC 80403 2024 E6
4600 JfnC 80403 2025 A6
Isabell St
600 LKWD 80401 2109 A7
1100 JfnC 80401 2108 E6
1100 JfnC 80401 2109 A6
4700 JfnC 80403 2024 E6
Isabelle Rd
9500 BldC 80026 1605 D6
9500 BldC 80026 1606 A6
9500 BldC 80301 1605 D6
10900 BldC 80516 1606 B6
10900 ERIE 80516 1606 B6
Isabelle Wy
- BMFD 80020 1775 C6
Isenberg Ln
30100 JfnC 80439 2357 A3
Isham Jones Rd
33700 JfnC 80470 2524 B6
Island Cir
7300 BldC 80301 1604 D3
Island Dr
2800 BLDR 80301 1603 A6
2900 BldC 80301 1603 A6
31100 JfnC 80439 2189 A7
31400 JfnC 80439 2188 E7
Island Ln
2000 JfnC 80439 2189 A7
Island Pt
2100 JfnC 80439 2189 A7
Island Green Dr
7200 BLDR 80301 1604 C1
Isle Of Pines Rd
- BldC 80403 1766 E6
- GpnC 80403 1767 A6
Isoleta Rd
23000 JfnC 80439 2274 E6
Itasca
- TNTN 80260 1944 C2
W Ithaca Av
300 EGLD 80110 2280 D3
9000 JfnC 80235 2278 C3
E Ithaca Cir
17000 AURA 80013 2285 A3
Ithaca Ct
1500 LGMT 80503 1355 B7
Ithaca Dr
500 BLDR 80305 1686 E7
800 BLDR 80305 1687 A7
1100 BLDR 80305 1771 A1
E Ithaca Dr
18900 AURA 80013 2285 D3

E Ithaca Pl
6500 DNVR 80237 2282 C3
16000 AURA 80013 2284 E3
18300 AURA 80013 2285 B3
20600 AphC 80013 2285 E3
W Ithaca Pl
6300 DNVR 80235 2279 A3
8200 JfnC 80235 2278 D3
E Ithaca St
20900 AphC 80013 2286 A3
Ithaca Wy
8800 AdmC 80031 1943 E3
8800 WSTR 80031 1943 E3
S Ivan Ct
3400 DNVR 80227 2279 B3
S Ivan Wy
2700 DNVR 80227 2279 B2
Ivanhoe Cir
12000 AdmC 80602 1862 B2
N Ivanhoe Cir
12200 AdmC 80602 1862 B1
S Ivanhoe Cir
7500 CTNL 80112 2366 B6
Ivanhoe Ct
12000 AdmC 80602 1862 B2
N Ivanhoe Ct
12200 AdmC 80602 1862 C2
S Ivanhoe Ct
6100 CTNL 80111 2366 B2
7200 CTNL 80112 2366 B5
S Ivanhoe Ln
4000 AphC 80237 2282 B4
4000 CHLV 80111 2282 B4
4000 CHLV 80113 2282 B4
4000 DNVR 80237 2282 B4
S Ivanhoe Pl
2400 AphC 80222 2198 A7
Ivanhoe St
- AdmC 80602 1694 A4
10 DNVR 80220 2198 B1
10 DNVR 80224 2198 B1
10 DNVR 80246 2198 B1
1500 DNVR 80220 2114 B4
3200 DNVR 80207 2114 B2
6300 CMCY 80022 2030 B2
7100 CMCY 80022 1946 B7
8000 AdmC 80022 1946 B5
12300 AdmC 80602 1862 A1
13000 TNTN 80602 1778 A6
S Ivanhoe St
1800 DNVR 80224 2198 B6
2100 DNVR 80222 2198 B6
2800 AphC 80222 2282 B1
3500 DNVR 80222 2282 B3
3500 DNVR 80237 2282 B3
5700 GDVL 80111 2366 B1
6100 CTNL 80111 2366 B2
S Ivanhoe Wy
1100 DNVR 80222 2198 B4
1100 DNVR 80224 2198 B4
3400 DNVR 80222 2282 B3
3400 DNVR 80237 2282 B3
7500 CTNL 80112 2366 B6
S Ivory Cir
300 AURA 80011 2116 D7
900 AURA 80017 2200 D3
1600 AURA 80012 2200 D5
4600 AURA 80015 2284 D5
S Ivory Ct
1800 AURA 80017 2200 D6
1900 AURA 80013 2200 D6
2900 AURA 80013 2284 D1
4600 AURA 80015 2284 D5
S Ivory St
2000 AURA 80013 2200 D6
S Ivory Wy
1900 AURA 80013 2200 D6
Ivy Cir
3500 BLDR 80304 1602 D6
N Ivy Cir
12000 AdmC 80602 1862 B2
Ivy Ct
13200 TNTN 80602 1778 A6
N Ivy Ct
12200 AdmC 80602 1862 B1
S Ivy Ct
5600 GDVL 80111 2366 B1
6300 CTNL 80111 2366 B3
7200 CTNL 80112 2366 B5
Ivy Ln
10 DNVR 80220 2114 B7
S Ivy Ln
4000 CHLV 80111 2282 B4
Ivy Pl
1500 SUPE 80027 1857 B1
12300 AdmC 80602 1862 B1
13100 TNTN 80602 1778 A6
N Ivy Pl
- AdmC 80602 1862 B1
Ivy St
- AdmC 80602 1694 A4
10 DNVR 80220 2198 B1
10 DNVR 80224 2198 B1
1700 DNVR 80220 2114 B4
2600 DNVR 80207 2114 B2
4500 DNVR 80022 2030 B6
4500 DNVR 80216 2030 B6
6300 CMCY 80022 2030 B2
7100 CMCY 80022 1946 B7
8000 AdmC 80022 1946 B5
12500 TNTN 80602 1862 A1
12900 TNTN 80602 1778 A6
N Ivy St
11600 TNTN 80233 1862 B3
S Ivy St
- CTNL 80112 2366 B4
10 DNVR 80220 2198 B1
10 DNVR 80224 2198 B1
2500 AphC 80222 2198 B7
2500 AphC 80222 2282 B1
5700 GDVL 80111 2366 B1
6000 CTNL 80111 2366 B3
Ivy Wy
2400 ERIE 80516 1692 A3
6200 CMCY 80022 2030 B2
N Ivy Wy
12200 AdmC 80602 1862 C2
S Ivy Wy
600 DNVR 80224 2198 B3
3200 DNVR 80222 2282 B2
3300 DNVR 80237 2282 B2
3900 AphC 80237 2282 B4
3900 CHLV 80111 2282 B4
6700 CTNL 80112 2366 B4
Ivycrest Pt
4300 DgsC 80108 2449 E7
4300 DgsC 80108 2533 E1
Ivywood Ct
700 DgsC 80126 2449 A3
Ivywood St
7800 AdmC 80022 1946 B5

J

E Jack Pl
5700 DgsC 80130 2450 B5
W Jackass Hill Rd
2400 LITN 80120 2364 A6
S Jackdaw St
8800 DgsC 80126 2450 A2
Jack Pine Ct
500 BLDR 80304 1602 B6
Jackpine Dr
33600 JfnC 80439 2356 B5
Jack Pine Ln
10 CCkC 80439 2271 D2
S Jackpine Rd
5500 JfnC 80439 2356 D2
Jack Rabbit Pl
10 DgsC 80126 2448 E2
Jackson
11400 WldC 80504 1440 D2
Jackson Cir
100 LSVL 80027 1689 B7
4700 BLDR 80303 1687 C3
8300 AdmC 80229 1945 D4
11800 TNTN 80233 1861 D2
S Jackson Cir
7700 CTNL 80122 2365 D7
Jackson Ct
200 BNNT 80102 2124 C2
1300 LSVL 80027 1689 C7
8500 AdmC 80229 1945 D3
10300 TNTN 80233 1861 D5
E Jackson Ct
6500 DgsC 80130 2450 C3
S Jackson Ct
6500 AphC 80121 2365 E3
6500 CTNL 80121 2365 E3
7200 CTNL 80122 2365 E5
Jackson Dr
- TNTN 80602 1777 D5
100 LSVL 80027 1689 C5
300 GOLD 80403 2107 D2
13500 TNTN 80241 1777 D5
E Jackson Ln
6500 DgsC 80130 2450 C3
Jackson Pl
- TNTN 80602 1777 D4
300 GOLD 80403 2107 C1
12200 TNTN 80241 1861 D1
13400 TNTN 80241 1777 D5
Jackson St
- CHLV 80113 2281 D4
- TNTN 80229 1861 D7
10 DNVR 80206 2197 E1
10 DNVR 80209 2197 E1
300 LAFT 80026 1690 D7
400 GOLD 80403 2107 D2
900 GOLD 80401 2107 D3
1500 DNVR 80206 2113 D5
2000 GOLD 80401 2108 A4
3300 DNVR 80205 2113 D1
3900 DNVR 80205 2029 D7
5200 DNVR 80216 2029 D5
6200 CMCY 80022 2029 D2
9200 TNTN 80229 1945 D2
11400 TNTN 80233 1861 D3
13500 TNTN 80241 1777 D5
13900 TNTN 80602 1777 D4
14500 AdmC 80602 1777 D2
15800 AdmC 80602 1693 D6
15800 TNTN 80602 1693 D6
N Jackson St
100 NDLD 80466 1765 C3
900 GOLD 80403 2023 C7
900 GOLD 80403 2107 C1
S Jackson St
10 DNVR 80206 2197 D2
10 DNVR 80209 2197 D2
100 NDLD 80466 1765 C3
1000 DNVR 80210 2197 D5
2400 DNVR 80210 2281 D1
5800 GDVL 80121 2365 E2
6200 AphC 80121 2365 E3
6400 CTNL 80121 2365 E3
7900 CTNL 80122 2365 E7
8200 CTNL 80122 2449 D1
Jackson Wy
3200 TNTN 80233 1861 D4
8400 AdmC 80229 1945 D4
S Jackson Wy
6900 CTNL 80122 2365 E4
W Jackson Creek Rd
4500 DgsC 80135 2785 A3
5300 DgsC 80135 2784 D3
7600 DgsC 80135 2783 E4
Jackson Gap St
- DNVR 80249 1951 A6
Jackson Gap Wy
- AURA 80016 2371 A5
Jacob Dr
10 PrkC 80456 2606 C6
Jacob Pl
10400 DgsC 80125 2530 E7
Jacques Wy
600 ERIE 80516 1691 C1
Jade Ct
1600 BMFD 80020 1774 D6
2900 SUPE 80027 1773 A7
5900 CSRK 80108 2620 A7
7600 BldC 80303 1688 D4
Jade Ln
1300 LGMT 80504 1438 E7
1300 LGMT 80504 1439 A7
Jade St
100 BMFD 80020 1858 D1
1000 BMFD 80020 1774 D7
11800 BldC 80516 1606 E4
11800 ERIE 80026 1606 E4
Jade Wy
10 BldC 80540 1352 C4
2100 LGMT 80504 1438 E7
Jaguar Dr
10500 DgsC 80124 2450 B7
Jaguar Gln
10500 DgsC 80124 2450 B7
Jaguar Pt
10500 DgsC 80124 2450 B7
Jaguar Wy
5400 DgsC 80130 2450 B6
5500 DgsC 80124 2450 B6
Jakes Ranch Rd
11900 DgsC 80138 2453 E5
Jalna Ct
16300 AdmC 80603 1700 B4
Jalna St
- WldC 80642 1700 B3
16700 AdmC 80603 1700 B3
S Jamaica Cir
6400 AphC 80111 2367 C3
Jamaica Ct
900 AURA 80010 2115 C6
S Jamaica Ct
2000 AURA 80014 2199 C6
2900 AURA 80014 2283 C1
2900 DNVR 80014 2283 C1
6000 AphC 80111 2367 C2
Jamaica Dr
15700 AdmC 80602 1695 C6
Jamaica St
- AdmC 80602 1779 B1
1600 AURA 80010 2115 C4
11200 CMCY 80640 1863 C3
S Jamaica St
1500 AURA 80012 2199 C5
2300 AURA 80014 2199 C7
9100 DgsC 80112 2451 C3
S Jamaica Wy
- GDVL 80111 2283 C7
100 AURA 80012 2199 C1
5100 AphC 80111 2283 C7
5500 AphC 80111 2367 C1
James Cir
10 LGMT 80501 1439 A6
1100 LAFT 80026 1690 B6
12600 BMFD 80020 1775 C6
12600 BMFD 80020 1859 E1
James Ct
1100 LAFT 80026 1690 B6
7900 BldC 80503 1520 E4
12400 BMFD 80020 1859 E1
12600 BMFD 80020 1775 E7
James Dr
10 CCkC 80439 2271 D4
James Pt
12500 BMFD 80020 1775 E7
James St
700 LGMT 80501 1439 A4
12400 BMFD 80020 1859 E1
E James St
500 DgsC 80126 2448 E4
James Wy
1300 ERIE 80516 1607 A2
3300 WSTR 80030 1943 E6
James Basin Rd
10 BldC 80481 1513 D7
James Canyon Dr
10 BldC 80302 1516 E3
10 BldC 80302 1517 A4
10 BldC 80455 1516 C3
3500 BldC 80455 1515 E1
3500 JMWN 80455 1515 E1
3500 JMWN 80455 1516 A2
James E Casey Av
13100 DgsC 80112 2452 A1
Jameston St
4600 BldC 80301 1604 E3
E Jamison Av
400 LITN 80122 2364 E6
1500 CTNL 80122 2365 B6
8500 CTNL 80112 2366 E6
16900 CTNL 80016 2369 A6
19700 AURA 80016 2369 D6
W Jamison Av
100 LITN 80120 2364 D7
100 LITN 80122 2364 D7
4500 LITN 80128 2363 D6
E Jamison Cir
7300 CTNL 80112 2366 D6
12800 AphC 80112 2368 A6
E Jamison Cir N
8300 CTNL 80112 2366 E6
E Jamison Cir S
6200 CTNL 80112 2366 B6
N Jamison Cir
25700 AphC 80016 2371 B6
25700 AURA 80016 2371 B6
S Jamison Cir
25700 AphC 80016 2371 B6
25700 AURA 80016 2371 B6
W Jamison Cir
200 LITN 80120 2364 D6
E Jamison Dr
- CTNL 80112 2366 D6
15600 AphC 80112 2368 D6
24000 AURA 80016 2370 E6
E Jamison Ln
5900 CTNL 80112 2366 B6
Jamison Pl
1600 LGMT 80501 1355 E4
E Jamison Pl
400 LITN 80122 2364 E6
400 LITN 80122 2365 B5
3900 CTNL 80122 2365 E6
5900 CTNL 80112 2366 B6
12500 AphC 80112 2367 E6
12500 AphC 80112 2368 A6
19200 CTNL 80016 2369 C6
21900 AURA 80016 2370 B6
W Jamison Pl
300 LITN 80120 2364 D6
4400 LITN 80128 2363 D6
E Jamison Wy
- AURA 80016 2370 D6
W Jamison Wy
2100 LITN 80120 2364 A6
Janelle Cir
33000 JfnC 80403 1852 C4
Janelle Ln
32600 JfnC 80403 1852 C4
Janice Ct
300 NHGN 80233 1860 E4
Janice Wy
6100 ARVD 80004 2026 A2
Jankowski Dr
10 GpnC 80403 1934 D2
Jansen St
11200 PARK 80134 2453 A7
11200 PARK 80134 2537 A1
Japonica Wy
400 BLDR 80304 1602 B6
Jared Ct
14100 BMFD 80020 1775 E3
Jared Wy
7500 DgsC 80125 2530 E6
Jarosa Ln
2000 SUPE 80027 1773 B6
Jarre Canyon Rd
- DgsC 80125 2698 D6
- DgsC 80135 2616 E7
- DgsC 80135 2617 B6
- DgsC 80135 2698 D6
- DgsC 80135 2699 C5
- DgsC 80135 2700 B4
Jarre Canyon Rd SR-67
- DgsC 80125 2698 D6
- DgsC 80135 2616 E7
- DgsC 80135 2617 B6
- DgsC 80135 2698 D6
- DgsC 80135 2699 C5
- DgsC 80135 2700 B4
Jarvis Pl
- AURA 80018 2286 B3
E Jarvis Pl
7300 DNVR 80237 2282 D3
15000 AURA 80014 2284 C3
15300 AURA 80013 2284 D3
17200 AURA 80013 2285 A3
21700 AURA 80018 2286 B3
W Jarvis Pl
6300 DNVR 80235 2279 A3
Jasmine Cir
900 BLDR 80304 1602 C6
S Jasmine Cir
7900 CTNL 80112 2366 B7
Jasmine Ct
5900 CMCY 80022 2030 B2
10000 DgsC 80125 2531 A6
12900 TNTN 80602 1778 B7
N Jasmine Ct
11600 TNTN 80233 1862 B2
S Jasmine Ct
6800 CTNL 80112 2366 B4
8200 CTNL 80112 2450 B1
Jasmine Dr
7800 CMCY 80022 1946 B5
Jasmine Pl
900 LAFT 80026 1690 B6
12300 AdmC 80602 1862 B1
13000 TNTN 80602 1778 B6
S Jasmine Pl
2400 AphC 80222 2198 B7
Jasmine St
- AdmC 80233 1862 B3
- AdmC 80602 1694 B5
- TNTN 80602 1862 B3
10 DNVR 80220 2198 B1
10 DNVR 80224 2198 B1
1500 DNVR 80220 2114 B5
3200 DNVR 80207 2114 B1
6800 CMCY 80022 2030 B1
7000 CMCY 80022 1946 B7
8000 AdmC 80022 1946 B5
11300 TNTN 80233 1862 B3
12000 AdmC 80602 1862 B2
12800 TNTN 80602 1778 B6
S Jasmine St
10 DNVR 80220 2198 B1
10 DNVR 80224 2198 B1
2100 DNVR 80222 2198 B7
2400 AphC 80222 2198 B7
3000 AphC 80222 2282 B2
3000 DNVR 80222 2282 B2
3900 AphC 80237 2282 B4
3900 CHLV 80111 2282 B4
3900 DNVR 80237 2282 B4
5300 GDVL 80111 2282 B7
5900 CTNL 80111 2366 B2
5900 GDVL 80111 2366 B2
Jasmine Wy
12900 TNTN 80602 1778 B6
S Jasmine Wy
600 DNVR 80224 2198 B3
3100 AphC 80222 2282 B2
3100 DNVR 80222 2282 B2
6300 CTNL 80111 2366 B3
7500 CTNL 80112 2366 B6
Jason Ct
2600 ERIE 80516 1690 D2
8400 FLHT 80260 1944 C4
9000 BldC 80303 1689 C3
9000 TNTN 80260 1944 C1
N Jason Ct
12400 WSTR 80234 1860 C1
12500 WSTR 80234 1776 C7
S Jason Ct
4300 EGLD 80110 2280 C5
N Jason Dr
14400 WSTR 80020 1776 C3
Jason St
10 CSRK 80109 2703 C6
3600 DNVR 80211 2112 C1
4000 DNVR 80211 2028 C7
8400 FLHT 80260 1944 C4
S Jason St
500 DNVR 80223 2196 C4
3500 EGLD 80110 2280 C4
Jason Wy
9400 TNTN 80260 1944 C1
S Jasper Cir
200 AURA 80017 2200 D2
Jasper Ct
2300 BLDR 80304 1602 D6
4800 DNVR 80239 2032 D5
S Jasper Ct
- AphC 80112 2368 D6
- CTNL 80112 2368 D6
3300 AURA 80013 2284 D2
5400 CTNL 80015 2368 D1
Jasper Dr
10 BldC 80540 1352 C4
9800 CMCY 80022 1864 D7
Jasper Ln
- BMFD 80020 1775 C5
Jasper Rd
10700 BldC 80026 1606 E3
11000 ERIE 80026 1606 E3
11800 BldC 80516 1606 E3
12000 BldC 80516 1607 A4
12000 ERIE 80516 1607 A4
Jasper St
- AdmC 80022 1948 D1
- CMCY 80022 1948 D1
1500 AURA 80011 2116 D4
5500 DNVR 80239 2032 D4
9800 CMCY 80022 1864 D7
10100 AdmC 80022 1864 D7
11800 CMCY 80603 1864 D2
N Jasper St
10800 CMCY 80022 1864 D4
S Jasper St
600 AURA 80017 2200 D3
2700 AURA 80013 2284 D1
4300 AURA 80015 2284 D5
5900 CTNL 80016 2368 D2
Jasper Wy
400 SUPE 80027 1857 A1
S Jasper Wy
- CTNL 80016 2368 D2
2200 AURA 80013 2200 D7
3000 AURA 80013 2284 D1
5400 CTNL 80015 2284 D7
5400 CTNL 80015 2368 D1
6100 AphC 80016 2368 D2
Jasper Peak Ct
300 LAFT 80026 1689 D4
Jasper Pointe Cir
5600 DgsC 80108 2534 B4
Jasper Pointe Wy
12300 DgsC 80108 2534 B4
Java Ct
2600 DNVR 80211 2111 E3
S Java Wy
1600 DNVR 80219 2195 E6
Jay Cir
8200 ARVD 80003 1943 A4
11100 WSTR 80020 1859 A4
S Jay Cir
- DvrC 80123 2363 B1
5300 DNVR 80123 2363 B1
Jay Ct
1800 LKWD 80232 2195 B6
6900 ARVD 80003 2027 A1
8600 ARVD 80003 1943 A3
S Jay Ct
800 DNVR 80219 2195 D3
1900 LKWD 80227 2195 A6
2600 LKWD 80227 2279 B1
5900 JfnC 80123 2363 B2
S Jay Dr
5300 DNVR 80123 2363 A1
6500 JfnC 80123 2363 B4
6500 JfnC 80128 2363 B4
8000 JfnC 80128 2447 B1
S Jay Ln
5300 JfnC 80439 2357 B1
8400 JfnC 80465 2443 B2
Jay Rd
2600 BLDR 80304 1602 E4
2800 BldC 80301 1602 E4
2800 BldC 80301 1603 A4
2900 BLDR 80301 1603 A4
5900 BldC 80301 1604 B4
12000 BldC 80516 1607 A4
12100 BldC 80026 1607 A4
12100 ERIE 80516 1607 A4
Jay St
10 LKWD 80226 2195 A1
100 LKWD 80226 2111 A7
1100 BLDR 80302 1686 B3
1300 LKWD 80214 2111 A5
1800 EDGW 80214 2111 A4
2900 WTRG 80214 2111 A2
4000 WTRG 80033 2111 A1
4500 WTRG 80033 2027 A6
6600 ARVD 80003 2027 A1
7100 WSTR 80003 1943 A7
7900 ARVD 80003 1943 A5
10800 WSTR 80020 1859 A5
N Jay St
- WSTR 80021 1859 A7
S Jay St
- JfnC 80123 2363 A1
10 LKWD 80226 2195 A2
1100 LKWD 80232 2195 A4
2700 DNVR 80227 2279 A1
2700 LKWD 80227 2279 A1
3600 DNVR 80235 2279 B3
7200 JfnC 80128 2363 B5
S Jay Wy
1800 LKWD 80232 2195 B6
2000 LKWD 80227 2195 A6
2500 LKWD 80227 2279 B1
6300 JfnC 80123 2363 A3
Jaybird Ln
100 PrkC 80456 2691 D1
S Jeanette Ct
10300 JfnC 80465 2443 D7
S Jebel Cir
3500 AphC 80013 2285 E3
S Jebel Ct
3300 AURA 80013 2285 E2
4300 AphC 80015 2285 E5
5900 AphC 80016 2369 E2
5900 CTNL 80016 2369 E2
S Jebel Ln
4400 AphC 80015 2285 E5
Jebel St
1600 AURA 80011 2117 E4
4400 DNVR 80249 2033 E6
S Jebel St
- AphC 80015 2285 E6
5100 CTNL 80015 2285 E7
S Jebel Wy
- AURA 80013 2285 E1
2400 AURA 80013 2201 E7
3900 AphC 80013 2285 E4
4400 AphC 80015 2285 E5
5200 CTNL 80015 2285 E7
5500 CTNL 80015 2369 E1
5900 AphC 80016 2369 E2
Jed Smith Rd
10 BldC 80481 1515 A3
Jeep Tr
- CCkC 80439 2186 E3
- CCkC 80439 2187 A3
- CCkC 80452 2186 C3
- CCkC 80452 2187 A3
- JfnC 80433 2440 B6
- JfnC 80470 2440 B5
- JfnC 80470 2524 B1
Jeffco Airport Av
- BfdC 80021 1858 B2
8600 BMFD 80021 1858 B2
Jefferson Av
- BldC 80501 1438 E2
- LGMT 80501 1438 E2
400 LSVL 80027 1773 D1
500 LSVL 80027 1689 D7
E Jefferson Av
- EGLD 80110 2280 E3
200 EGLD 80113 2280 E3
600 EGLD 80113 2281 A3
700 CHLV 80113 2281 A3
5200 DNVR 80237 2282 A3
8500 DNVR 80237 2283 A3
14600 AURA 80014 2284 C3
15500 AURA 80013 2284 D3
16900 AURA 80013 2285 A3
20600 AphC 80013 2285 E2
21000 AphC 80013 2286 A3
E Jefferson Av US-285
- EGLD 80110 2280 E3
200 EGLD 80113 2280 E3
600 EGLD 80113 2281 A3
700 CHLV 80113 2281 A3
S Jefferson Av
200 LSVL 80027 1773 C2
W Jefferson Av
10 EGLD 80110 2280 D3
10 EGLD 80113 2280 D3
3000 SRDN 80110 2279 E3
3000 SRDN 80110 2280 A3
6000 DNVR 80235 2279 A3
6000 JfnC 80235 2279 A3
6900 LKWD 80235 2278 E3
8400 JfnC 80235 2278 C3
E Jefferson Cir
21000 AphC 80013 2286 A3
Jefferson Dr
100 BNNT 80102 2124 C2
300 AdmC 80102 2124 C2
E Jefferson Dr
200 EGLD 80113 2280 E3
7300 DNVR 80237 2282 D3
17300 AURA 80013 2285 B3
Jefferson Pkwy
- DgsC 80134 2451 E4
9700 DgsC 80112 2451 E4
Jefferson Pl
- BMFD 80020 1859 B2
- WSTR 80020 1859 B2
E Jefferson Pl
- DNVR 80237 2283 A3
- GDVL 80014 2283 A3
7700 DNVR 80237 2282 D3
15100 AURA 80014 2284 C3
16700 AURA 80013 2284 E3
17200 AURA 80013 2285 A3
20600 AphC 80013 2285 E2
W Jefferson Pl
6000 LKWD 80226 2195 A3
Jefferson St
3000 BLDR 80304 1602 C7
16600 JfnC 80470 2693 D2
N Jefferson St
10 NDLD 80466 1765 D3
S Jefferson St
100 NDLD 80466 1765 D3
Jefferson County Pkwy
- GOLD 80401 2108 B7
Jellison Cir
7600 ARVD 80005 1942 B6
N Jellison Cir
10700 WSTR 80021 1858 B5
S Jellison Cir
5700 JfnC 80123 2362 B2
5700 JfnC 80127 2362 B2
Jellison Ct
3400 WTRG 80033 2110 B2
5100 ARVD 80002 2026 B5
5100 WTRG 80033 2026 B5
6900 ARVD 80004 2026 B1
8200 ARVD 80005 1942 B4
8800 WSTR 80021 1942 B3
S Jellison Ct
700 LKWD 80226 2194 B3
3300 LKWD 80227 2278 B3
7200 JfnC 80128 2362 B5
8700 JfnC 80128 2446 B2
S Jellison Dr
- JfnC 80123 2278 B5
Jellison St
- WSTR 80005 1942 B3
2500 LKWD 80215 2110 B3
3200 JfnC 80215 2110 B2
3200 WTRG 80033 2110 B2
3200 WTRG 80215 2110 B2
5100 WTRG 80033 2026 B5
5600 ARVD 80002 2026 B4
6000 ARVD 80004 2026 B3
8600 ARVD 80005 1942 B3
9700 WSTR 80021 1858 B7
9700 WSTR 80021 1942 B1
S Jellison St
- JfnC 80123 2362 C2
900 LKWD 80226 2194 B4
900 LKWD 80232 2194 B4
2300 LKWD 80227 2194 B7
2500 LKWD 80227 2278 B1
4500 DNVR 80123 2278 B6
5200 JfnC 80123 2278 B7
5200 JfnC 80127 2362 B1
7000 JfnC 80128 2362 B5
Jellison Wy
6100 ARVD 80004 2026 A2
9600 WSTR 80021 1942 B1
10400 WSTR 80021 1858 B5
S Jellison Wy
5000 DNVR 80123 2278 B7
5000 DvrC 80123 2278 B7
5000 JfnC 80127 2278 B7
9300 LITN 80127 2446 B4
Jennie Dr
400 AdmC 80221 1944 D7
6900 AdmC 80221 2028 D1
Jennie Ln
10 BldC 80403 1852 A1
Jennifer Ct
1900 AdmC 80601 1696 D4
1900 BGTN 80601 1696 D4
Jennifer Rd
33200 JfnC 80470 2524 C6
Jennine Pl
1500 BLDR 80304 1602 C6
Jennings Rd
8700 JfnC 80465 2443 E3
Jenny Cir
31900 EbtC 80107 2794 A4
Jenny Ln
25600 JfnC 80439 2274 B2
Jensen Rd
34400 JfnC 80470 2524 A3
S Jericho Cir
6400 CTNL 80016 2369 E3
Jericho Ct
4800 DNVR 80249 2033 E6
S Jericho Ct
- AURA 80013 2285 E1
2500 AURA 80013 2201 E7
3800 AphC 80013 2285 E3
4800 AphC 80015 2285 E6
5400 CTNL 80015 2369 E1
6100 CTNL 80016 2369 E2
Jericho St
4800 DNVR 80249 2033 E6
S Jericho St
- AphC 80016 2369 E2
- CTNL 80016 2369 E2
4200 AphC 80013 2285 E4
4900 AphC 80015 2285 E6
5100 CTNL 80015 2285 E7
S Jericho Wy
- AphC 80013 2285 E2
2800 AURA 80013 2285 E2
5200 AphC 80015 2285 E7
5200 CTNL 80015 2285 E7
5500 CTNL 80015 2369 E1
6100 CTNL 80016 2369 E2
E Jerome Av
3900 DNVR 80210 2197 D7
3900 DNVR 80222 2197 D7
Jerome Ct
24000 JfnC 80401 2190 D5
Jerry St
300 CSRK 80104 2703 D7
Jersey Av
600 LGMT 80501 1439 A5
Jersey Cir
11300 TNTN 80233 1862 A3
Jersey Cir E
- TNTN 80602 1778 B7
Jersey Cir W
12600 TNTN 80602 1778 A7
Jersey Ct
12800 TNTN 80602 1778 A6
S Jersey Ct
6300 CTNL 80111 2366 B3
7200 CTNL 80112 2366 B5
Jersey Dr
11300 TNTN 80233 1862 A3
Jersey Ln
11300 TNTN 80233 1862 B3
Jersey St
10 DNVR 80220 2198 B1
10 DNVR 80224 2198 B1
600 DNVR 80220 2114 B6
11300 TNTN 80233 1862 A3
13000 TNTN 80602 1778 A6
S Jersey St
- CTNL 80112 2366 B6
10 DNVR 80220 2198 B2
10 DNVR 80224 2198 B2

STREET Block City ZIP Map# Grid
S Jersey St
2400 AphC 80222 2198 B7
2400 DNVR 80222 2198 B7
2500 AphC 80222 2282 B1
3900 AphC 80237 2282 B4
3900 CHLV 80111 2282 B4
3900 DNVR 80237 2282 B4
Jersey Wy
11300 TNTN 80233 1862 B3
S Jersey Wy
1300 DNVR 80224 2198 B5
7700 CTNL 80112 2366 B7
E Jesse Ct
1100 DgsC 80126 2449 A5
Jesse Ln
10 PrkC 80456 2690 B1
Jess-Mar Dr
- PrkC 80456 2689 A1
Jessup St
10 BGTN 80601 1696 B7
W Jessup St
10 BGTN 80601 1696 A7
W Jewel Av
- DNVR 80223 2196 D6
Jewel Dr
1700 LGMT 80501 1356 B6
Jewel St
2200 LGMT 80501 1356 B4
Jewelberry Cir
10600 DgsC 80130 2450 B7
Jewelberry Ln
- DgsC 80130 2450 B7
Jewelberry Tr
10500 DgsC 80130 2450 B7
Jewel Creek Ct
5400 BLDR 80301 1604 B1
Jewell Av
34900 AphC 80137 2205 C5
E Jewell Av
- AURA 80013 2202 A6
- AURA 80017 2202 A6
10 DNVR 80210 2196 E6
10 DNVR 80223 2196 E6
600 DNVR 80210 2197 A6
4100 DNVR 80222 2197 E6
4700 DNVR 80222 2198 A6
5400 DNVR 80224 2198 C6
7300 AphC 80224 2198 C6
7800 DNVR 80231 2198 E6
9400 AphC 80231 2199 A6
9400 AphC 80247 2199 A6
9400 AURA 80247 2199 A6
10100 AURA 80012 2199 B6
10100 AURA 80014 2199 B6
13200 AURA 80014 2200 A6
14100 AURA 80012 2200 B6
19200 AURA 80013 2201 E6
19200 AURA 80017 2201 E6
23300 AURA 80018 2202 E6
24300 AphC 80018 2202 E6
24400 AphC 80018 2203 A5
24400 AURA 80018 2203 A5
27200 AphC 80137 2203 E5
28100 AphC 80018 2204 A5
28100 AphC 80137 2204 A5
28100 AURA 80018 2204 A5
31200 AphC 80137 2205 A5
48900 AphC 80102 2209 B5
W Jewell Av
10 DNVR 80210 2196 E6
1200 DNVR 80223 2196 C6
2300 DNVR 80219 2196 A6
3100 DNVR 80219 2195 E6
5100 DNVR 80232 2195 A6
5100 LKWD 80232 2195 A6
5200 DNVR 80227 2195 A6
5200 LKWD 80227 2195 A6
7400 LKWD 80232 2194 C6
7700 LKWD 80227 2194 C6
10800 JfnC 80227 2194 C6
10800 JfnC 80232 2194 C6
10900 JfnC 80232 2193 D6
10900 LKWD 80227 2193 D6
11200 LKWD 80228 2193 D6
E Jewell Cir
9300 AphC 80231 2199 A6
9300 AphC 80247 2199 A6
W Jewell Cir
12700 LKWD 80228 2193 C6
W Jewell Dr
11200 LKWD 80227 2193 E6
13300 LKWD 80228 2193 B6
E Jewell Pl
9900 AURA 80247 2199 B6
11700 AURA 80012 2199 D6
15500 AURA 80013 2200 D6
W Jewell Pl
10100 LKWD 80227 2194 A6
10100 LKWD 80232 2194 A6
13200 LKWD 80228 2193 B6
W Jewell Frontage Rd
6900 LKWD 80232 2195 A6
7000 LKWD 80232 2194 E6
10900 JfnC 80232 2193 E6
Jib Ct
6400 BldC 80301 1604 A4
S Jill Av
10100 DgsC 80130 2450 C6
S Jill Dr
9000 JfnC 80433 2440 D3
Jimson Ct
1600 BLDR 80304 1602 C6
S Jimson Weed Wy
8900 DgsC 80126 2449 B3
Jita Ln
13500 JfnC 80470 2525 A7
13500 JfnC 80470 2609 A1
JJ Kelly Rd
10 BldC 80540 1269 A7
10 BldC 80540 1352 A1
J Morgan Blvd
- DgsC 80134 2537 E5
- PARK 80134 2537 D5
Joan Dr
10 AdmC 80221 1944 D5
S Joan Ln
6400 JfnC 80439 2357 B4
Joan St
7000 AdmC 80221 1944 C7
Joanie Dr
30800 JfnC 80403 1852 E5
30800 JfnC 80403 1853 A5
Joanie Rd
30800 JfnC 80403 1852 E5
30800 JfnC 80403 1853 A5
Joann Ct
1900 AdmC 80601 1696 D4
1900 BGTN 80601 1696 D4
Jodel Ln
1200 LGMT 80503 1438 C5
Jodelle Ln
- WldC 80504 1357 B4
John F Kirby Dr
700 LKWD 80214 2111 A7
Johnson Av
600 LSVL 80027 1689 C7
Johnson Cir
7000 BldC 80503 1520 E4
7000 BldC 80503 1521 A3
S Johnson Cir
2600 LKWD 80227 2278 B1
Johnson Ct
200 CSRK 80104 2704 A6
1400 BLDR 80303 1687 C3
5600 ARVD 80002 2026 A4
8200 ARVD 80005 1942 B4
9800 WSTR 80021 1942 B1
10400 WSTR 80021 1858 B6
S Johnson Ct
800 LKWD 80226 2194 B3
1300 LKWD 80232 2194 B4
2500 LKWD 80227 2278 B1
6200 JfnC 80123 2362 B3
7800 JfnC 80127 2362 B7
7900 JfnC 80128 2362 B7
9300 LITN 80127 2446 B4
Johnson Dr
10 CSRK 80104 2704 A7
S Johnson Dr
15700 JfnC 80470 2609 E7
Johnson Ln
3000 BfdC 80516 1692 C2
3000 BMFD 80516 1692 C2
S Johnson Ln
9300 LITN 80127 2446 B4
Johnson Pl
100 CSRK 80104 2704 A7
Johnson Rd
10 PrkC 80456 2521 E2
600 GOLD 80401 2108 B6
Johnson St
- NDLD 80466 1765 C2
600 LSVL 80027 1773 D1
1100 LKWD 80215 2110 B6
3500 WTRG 80033 2110 B1
5100 WTRG 80033 2026 B5
5600 ARVD 80002 2026 B4
6800 ARVD 80004 2026 A1
8700 ARVD 80005 1942 B3
10400 WSTR 80021 1858 B5
S Johnson St
100 NDLD 80466 1765 D3
1000 LKWD 80226 2194 B4
1000 LKWD 80232 2194 B4
4700 DNVR 80123 2278 B6
5600 JfnC 80123 2362 B1
7000 JfnC 80128 2362 B5
7500 JfnC 80127 2362 B6
9400 LITN 80127 2446 B5
Johnson Wy
6000 ARVD 80004 2026 A2
S Johnson Wy
900 LKWD 80226 2194 B4
900 LKWD 80232 2194 B4
6300 JfnC 80123 2362 B3
9600 LITN 80127 2446 B5
Johnston Ct
- LGMT 80501 1439 B6
John Wallace Rd
31200 JfnC 80439 2272 E3
31200 JfnC 80439 2273 A2
John West Av
1200 BNNT 80102 2124 B2
John West Dr
- AdmC 80102 2124 B2
Jolene Cir
8200 AdmC 80229 1945 B4
Jolene Dr
1600 AdmC 80229 1945 B4
Jolene Wy
8200 AdmC 80229 1945 B4
Joliet Cir
9700 CMCY 80022 1863 C7
S Joliet Cir
100 AURA 80012 2199 C1
Joliet Ct
15300 AdmC 80602 1695 C7
S Joliet Ct
2000 AURA 80014 2199 C6
Joliet St
1400 AURA 80010 2115 C6
3700 DNVR 80239 2115 C1
4500 DNVR 80239 2031 C6
5500 AdmC 80022 2031 C4
5500 DNVR 80022 2031 C4
11200 CMCY 80640 1863 C4
S Joliet St
900 AURA 80012 2199 C3
1800 AURA 80014 2199 C6
5500 AphC 80111 2367 C1
6700 CTNL 80112 2367 C4
7100 AphC 80112 2367 C5
Joliet Wy
1800 BLDR 80305 1771 A2
S Joliet Wy
2200 AURA 80014 2199 C7
5200 AphC 80111 2283 C7
Jonathan Pl
2100 BLDR 80304 1602 D6
Jones Ct
400 ERIE 80516 1607 B7
Jones Rd
- EbtC 80107 2709 C7
10 PrkC 80456 2521 E2
200 PrkC 80456 2522 A2
1900 GOLD 80401 2107 E4
Jones Creek Cir
10 JfnC 80470 2524 A5
S Jones Creek Ln
10 JfnC 80470 2524 B5
Jonquil Ct
2400 LAFT 80026 1689 E2
Jonquil Pl
700 BLDR 80304 1602 B6
S Joplin Cir
800 AURA 80017 2200 E3
Joplin Ct
4800 DNVR 80239 2032 D5
11800 CMCY 80603 1864 D2
N Joplin Ct
1000 AURA 80011 2116 D5
S Joplin Ct
1100 AURA 80017 2200 D4
2800 AURA 80013 2284 D1
Joplin St
600 AURA 80011 2116 D7
4800 DNVR 80239 2032 D6
10700 CMCY 80022 1864 D5
12100 CMCY 80603 1864 D1
N Joplin St
1000 AURA 80011 2116 D6
S Joplin St
- AURA 80013 2200 D7
200 AURA 80017 2200 D2
3500 AURA 80013 2284 D3
4500 AURA 80015 2284 D5
S Joplin Wy
- CTNL 80015 2284 D7
900 AURA 80017 2200 D3
2100 AURA 80013 2200 D6
3500 AURA 80013 2284 D3
4300 AURA 80015 2284 D5
5700 CTNL 80015 2368 D1
6000 AphC 80016 2368 D2
Joppa Ct
16600 AdmC 80603 1700 B4
Joppa St
16300 AdmC 80603 1700 B4
Jordan Ct
10700 PARK 80134 2453 A7
11100 PARK 80134 2537 A1
Jordan Dr
1700 AdmC 80221 1944 B7
6800 AdmC 80221 2028 B1
Jordan Pl
2100 BLDR 80304 1602 D6
Jordan Rd
5900 AphC 80111 2368 B3
6100 CTNL 80111 2368 B2
6200 AphC 80016 2368 B3
6600 CTNL 80112 2368 B3
N Jordan Rd
- AphC 80112 2452 E1
- DgsC 80134 2452 E1
- PARK 80134 2452 E1
9100 DgsC 80134 2453 A4
9100 PARK 80134 2453 A4
10500 DgsC 80134 2537 A1
10500 PARK 80134 2537 A1
S Jordan Rd
5100 AphC 80015 2283 E7
5100 AphC 80015 2284 A7
5100 AphC 80015 2368 A1
5100 AphC 80111 2283 E7
5100 AphC 80111 2284 A7
5100 AphC 80111 2368 A1
6700 AphC 80016 2368 C4
6700 CTNL 80111 2368 C4
6700 CTNL 80112 2368 C4
7200 AphC 80112 2368 D6
8200 AphC 80112 2452 E1
8200 DgsC 80134 2452 E1
8200 PARK 80134 2452 E1
9100 DgsC 80134 2537 A2
9100 PARK 80134 2537 A2
12100 GDVL 80111 2283 E7
Jordan Wy
500 LCHB 80603 1698 E2
500 WldC 80603 1698 E2
S Joseph Dr
10100 DgsC 80130 2450 B6
Josephine Cir
11600 TNTN 80233 1861 C3
Josephine Ct
12300 TNTN 80241 1861 B1
12800 TNTN 80241 1777 B7
13600 TNTN 80602 1777 B5
Josephine Pl
9600 TNTN 80229 1945 C1
Josephine St
200 DNVR 80206 2197 C1
500 DNVR 80206 2113 C7
2600 DNVR 80205 2113 C2
4000 DNVR 80205 2029 C7
4000 DNVR 80216 2029 C7
9700 TNTN 80229 1861 C7
9700 TNTN 80229 1945 D1
10900 NHGN 80233 1861 C5
11800 TNTN 80233 1861 C2
12400 TNTN 80241 1861 C1
12500 TNTN 80241 1777 B7
14900 TNTN 80602 1777 B1
16500 AdmC 80602 1693 B5
S Josephine St
800 DNVR 80209 2197 C4
1800 DNVR 80210 2197 C6
2900 DNVR 80210 2281 C2
Josephine Wy
11000 NHGN 80233 1861 C4
S Josephine Wy
6100 CTNL 80121 2365 C3
S Joslin Ct
2700 DNVR 80227 2279 B2
2700 LKWD 80227 2279 B2
Joslyn Ct
1900 BLDR 80304 1602 D6
Joslyn Pl
1900 BLDR 80304 1602 D6
Jotipa Dr
9100 BldC 80503 1355 C4
9100 LGMT 80503 1355 C4
Journey Ln
- BldC 80503 1355 A2
Joy St
26600 JfnC 80433 2442 A5
Joyce Dr
- ARVD 80007 2024 E2
6200 ARVD 80403 2024 E2
S Joyce Ln
9400 DgsC 80126 2449 A4
Joyce St
700 LKWD 80401 2108 E7
1300 JfnC 80401 2108 E5
5200 JfnC 80403 2024 E5
6800 ARVD 80007 2024 E1
S Joyce St
10 JfnC 80401 2192 E2
Joyce Wy
2900 JfnC 80401 2108 E2
W Juan Wy
10 DgsC 80108 2534 E3
10 DgsC 80108 2535 A3
Jubilee Tr
13700 JfnC 80470 2608 C1
Judicial Center Dr
1000 BGTN 80601 1781 C1
Judson Dr
1100 BLDR 80305 1687 A7
1200 BLDR 80305 1771 A1
1400 BLDR 80305 1770 E1
1600 LGMT 80501 1355 E6
Judson St
100 BldC 80501 1438 E2
300 LGMT 80501 1438 E2
2100 LGMT 80501 1355 E5
8800 AdmC 80031 1943 E3
8800 WSTR 80031 1943 E3
S Judson St
1300 LGMT 80501 1438 E5
Juhls Dr
5600 BldC 80301 1603 D4
Juilliard St
2600 BLDR 80305 1770 E1
2900 BLDR 80305 1771 A1
E Jules Ct
1700 DgsC 80126 2449 B4
Julian Cir
700 LAFT 80026 1690 A5
S Julian Cir
1900 DNVR 80219 2195 E6
Julian Ct
9900 WSTR 80031 1859 E7
12400 BMFD 80020 1859 E1
12700 BMFD 80020 1775 E7
Julian Pt
12600 BMFD 80020 1775 E7
Julian St
- BMFD 80020 1775 E6
10 DNVR 80219 2195 E1
300 DNVR 80219 2111 E7
1300 DNVR 80204 2111 E5
1900 DNVR 80211 2111 E5
4400 DNVR 80211 2027 E7
4800 DNVR 80221 2027 E6
6800 AdmC 80221 2027 E1
7800 WSTR 80030 1943 E5
8000 WSTR 80031 1943 E5
8100 AdmC 80031 1943 E5
11400 WSTR 80031 1859 E3
S Julian St
10 DNVR 80219 2195 E2
2500 DNVR 80219 2279 E1
3300 AphC 80236 2279 E2
3300 DNVR 80236 2279 E2
3800 SRDN 80236 2279 E4
4500 EGLD 80110 2279 E6
4500 SRDN 80110 2279 E6
5000 LITN 80123 2279 E7
5400 LITN 80123 2363 E1
Julian Wy
1900 DNVR 80204 2111 E4
1900 DNVR 80211 2111 E4
7100 WSTR 80030 1943 E7
10100 WSTR 80031 1859 E6
N Julian Wy
9200 AdmC 80031 1943 E2
9200 WSTR 80031 1943 E2
11400 WSTR 80031 1859 E3
S Julian Wy
1600 DNVR 80219 2195 E5
3000 DNVR 80236 2279 E2
6000 CBVL 80123 2363 E3
6000 LITN 80123 2363 E3
S Julie Ln
7000 JfnC 80439 2358 C5
June Ct
2000 CSRK 80104 2787 E2
Juneau Pl
10 LGMT 80501 1356 C7
Juneau Rd
- BldC 80301 1602 E5
- BldC 80301 1603 A5
- BLDR 80304 1602 E5
Junegrass Pl
17600 PARK 80134 2453 A2
S Jungfrau Dr
6000 JfnC 80439 2358 C4
S Jungfrau Wy
6200 JfnC 80439 2358 D4
Juniper Av
2200 BLDR 80304 1602 E6
S Juniper Cir
3800 JfnC 80439 2273 C4
Juniper Ct
10 CCkC 80439 2271 E1
500 LSVL 80027 1773 C2
2100 BLDR 80304 1602 D6
2200 JfnC 80401 2190 B6
4000 DgsC 80118 2953 B1
5200 JfnC 80403 2024 E5
15000 JfnC 80401 2108 E3
S Juniper Ct
10 JfnC 80401 2192 E1
W Juniper Ct
600 LSVL 80027 1773 B2
Juniper Dr
- GpnC 80403 1934 C5
- TNTN 80260 1944 C2
2700 JfnC 80401 2108 E3
27900 JfnC 80433 2609 D1
Juniper Ln
10 CCkC 80439 2271 B3
10 PrkC 80456 2607 D7
10 PrkC 80456 2691 D1
11500 PARK 80138 2537 E2
S Juniper Ln
4800 JfnC 80439 2273 D7
Juniper Pl
3600 CSRK 80108 2620 D7
Juniper Rd
10 GpnC 80403 1933 E6
S Juniper Rd
11600 JfnC 80470 2524 A3
Juniper St
100 LSVL 80027 1773 C2
700 LKWD 80401 2108 E7
1300 JfnC 80401 2108 E5
1700 LGMT 80501 1355 E6
11800 BldC 80516 1606 E4
11800 ERIE 80026 1606 E4
S Juniper St
2900 MRSN 80228 2276 E2
5000 BWMR 80123 2279 C7
Juniper Tr
10 CCkC 80439 2355 E7
10 CCkC 80439 2356 A7
Juniper Wy
10 PrkC 80456 2521 C3
1900 ERIE 80516 1692 A3
7200 JfnC 80007 1940 E7
Juniper Heights Rd
10 BldC 80403 1769 A7
Juno Tr
10 CCkC 80439 2440 A1
Jupiter Dr
200 DgsC 80124 2450 E2
Jura Dr
24700 JfnC 80439 2358 D6
Jurrasic Rd
17300 JfnC 80465 2192 B7
17300 JfnC 80465 2276 C1
Justice Wy
600 CSRK 80109 2703 C2
Jute Ln
2100 CSRK 80109 2703 B4
JW Green Rd
- JfnC 80433 2694 D4
K
Kachina Cir
700 JfnC 80401 2191 A3
Kachina Wy
8800 LNTR 80124 2451 A3
Kahala Cir
2000 CSRK 80104 2787 E2
Kahler Pl
- BMFD 80020 1775 E4
S Kalahari Ct
10500 DgsC 80124 2450 C7
Kalamath Cir
9500 TNTN 80260 1944 C1
Kalamath Ct
8400 FLHT 80260 1944 C4
9400 TNTN 80260 1944 C1
12600 WSTR 80234 1776 C7
14800 AdmC 80020 1776 C2
N Kalamath Ct
12400 WSTR 80234 1860 C1
12700 WSTR 80234 1776 C7
14600 WSTR 80020 1776 C2
S Kalamath Ct
4100 EGLD 80110 2280 C5
Kalamath Dr
3900 DgsC 80118 2953 C3
S Kalamath Dr
4900 EGLD 80110 2280 C7
Kalamath St
10 DNVR 80223 2196 C1
300 DNVR 80204 2112 C6
300 DNVR 80223 2112 C6
3500 DNVR 80211 2112 C1
4000 DNVR 80211 2028 C7
4800 AdmC 80221 2028 C5
4800 DNVR 80221 2028 C5
8000 AdmC 80221 1944 C4
8400 FLHT 80260 1944 C4
10700 NHGN 80234 1860 C5
13400 WSTR 80234 1776 C5
N Kalamath St
- BMFD 80020 1776 C5
- WSTR 80234 1776 C5
S Kalamath St
10 DNVR 80223 2196 C2
3700 EGLD 80110 2280 C4
S Kalamath St US-85
- DNVR 80223 2196 D3
W Kalamath St
- WSTR 80234 1776 D5
Kalamere Ct
9500 DgsC 80126 2449 C4
S Kalispell Cir
2400 AURA 80013 2200 D7
4300 AURA 80015 2284 D5
7900 AphC 80112 2368 E7
Kalispell Ct
1700 AURA 80011 2116 D4
S Kalispell Ct
3100 AURA 80013 2284 E2
5700 CTNL 80015 2368 D1
Kalispell St
- AdmC 80022 1948 D1
- CMCY 80022 1948 D1
1800 AURA 80011 2116 D4
4800 DNVR 80239 2032 D5
10700 CMCY 80022 1864 D5
12100 CMCY 80603 1864 D1
S Kalispell St
500 AURA 80017 2200 D2
4000 AURA 80013 2284 D4
4600 AURA 80015 2284 D6
5600 CTNL 80015 2368 D1
6000 AphC 80016 2368 D2
S Kalispell Wy
300 AURA 80017 2200 D2
4500 AURA 80015 2284 D5
7900 AphC 80112 2368 D7
Kalmia Av
- BldC 80301 1603 B6
400 BldC 80304 1602 B6
1000 BLDR 80304 1602 C6
2700 BLDR 80301 1602 E6
2800 BLDR 80301 1603 A6
Kalmia Cir
2100 BLDR 80304 1602 D6
Kalmia Ct
- BLDR 80301 1602 E6
- BLDR 80304 1602 E6
Kalmia Wy
600 BMFD 80020 1774 D7
600 BMFD 80020 1858 D1
Kalua Rd
6400 BldC 80301 1604 A3
Kane Dr
900 LGMT 80501 1439 A5
Kanemoto Ln
1200 ERIE 80516 1607 A2
Kanemoto Wy
1200 ERIE 80516 1607 A2
Kansas Av
800 LGMT 80501 1439 A5
1300 LGMT 80501 1438 E5
E Kansas Av
9100 AphC 80247 2199 A4
E Kansas Cir
- AURA 80247 2199 B4
9500 AphC 80247 2199 B4
24300 AURA 80018 2202 E4
E Kansas Dr
4800 DNVR 80246 2198 A4
12400 AURA 80012 2199 E4
12800 AURA 80012 2200 A4
16500 AURA 80017 2200 E4
18900 AURA 80017 2201 C4
E Kansas Pl
9300 AphC 80247 2199 A4
12100 AURA 80012 2199 E4
14800 AURA 80012 2200 C4
16500 AURA 80017 2200 E4
17800 AURA 80017 2201 B4
Kansas St
- DNVR 80236 2279 C4
Karcher St
5500 DgsC 80135 2617 C5
Karlann Dr
10 GpnC 80403 1934 C1
Karly Wy
- BMFD 80020 1775 C3
Karsh Dr
400 LGMT 80501 1439 E2
E Karval Pl
900 SUPE 80027 1773 A5
Kassler Pl
3100 WSTR 80031 1943 E1
Katherine Av
11600 LKWD 80215 2109 D6
11600 LKWD 80401 2109 D6
Katherine Ct
8700 DgsC 80134 2452 E2
8900 BldC 80303 1689 B3
Katherine Wy
8300 AdmC 80221 1944 B4
8300 FLHT 80260 1944 B4
Katie Dr
4000 EbtC 80107 2709 C5
Katie Ln
10 BldC 80403 1852 A2
Kattell St
100 ERIE 80516 1607 C5
Katy Ln
1000 LGMT 80504 1439 A6
Kay Ct
1000 LGMT 80501 1438 D1
Kay St
2100 LGMT 80501 1355 D5
Kearney Cir
11700 TNTN 80233 1862 B2
12400 TNTN 80602 1862 A1
S Kearney Cir
6400 CTNL 80111 2366 B3
Kearney Ct
- AdmC 80602 1694 B5
7000 CMCY 80022 1946 B7
S Kearney Ct
6700 CTNL 80112 2366 B4
Kearney Dr
7600 AdmC 80022 1946 B6
S Kearney Ln
- DNVR 80220 2198 B1
- DNVR 80224 2198 B1
Kearney St
10 DNVR 80220 2198 B1
1500 DNVR 80220 2114 B5
1900 DNVR 80207 2114 B5
3900 DNVR 80207 2030 B7
4200 DNVR 80216 2030 B7
6000 CMCY 80022 2030 B2
7200 AdmC 80022 1946 B6
7200 CMCY 80022 1946 B6
12200 AdmC 80602 1862 B1
12500 TNTN 80602 1862 B1
Kearney St
12800 TNTN 80602 1778 B6
S Kearney St
10 DNVR 80220 2198 B1
1300 DNVR 80224 2198 B5
2300 AphC 80222 2198 B7
2500 DNVR 80222 2198 B7
2600 DNVR 80222 2282 B1
2700 AphC 80222 2282 B1
5300 GDVL 80111 2282 A7
5700 GDVL 80111 2366 B2
5900 CTNL 80111 2366 B2
8200 CTNL 80112 2450 B1
Kearney Wy
11300 TNTN 80233 1862 B3
12900 TNTN 80602 1778 B6
S Kearney Wy
1900 DNVR 80224 2198 B6
Kedleston Av
3100 DgsC 80126 2449 D7
Keebler Ct
7600 DgsC 80118 2954 C2
Keech Wy
6900 DgsC 80108 2618 E1
Keel Ct
1800 LAFT 80026 1689 E5
4500 BldC 80301 1604 A3
S Keenan St
9700 DgsC 80130 2450 B5
W Keene Av
10100 JfnC 80235 2278 B3
W Keene Pl
10000 JfnC 80235 2278 B4
Keenen Ct
5700 DgsC 80130 2450 B5
S Keenland Ct
5000 EGLD 80110 2279 E7
5000 LITN 80123 2279 E7
5400 LITN 80123 2363 E1
Keith Ct
14300 BMFD 80020 1775 C3
N Keith Ct
8000 DgsC 80108 2535 B6
Keller Farm Dr
2300 BLDR 80304 1602 E5
S Kellerman Wy
7200 AURA 80016 2371 B5
Kelling Dr
- LYNS 80540 1352 D2
Kelliwood Wy
10100 DgsC 80126 2449 E6
Kellogg Cir
4700 BLDR 80303 1687 C3
Kellogg Ct
10 CSRK 80109 2703 C3
Kellogg Pl
3300 WSTR 80031 1943 D1
Kellwood Dr
4300 CSRK 80109 2702 D3
Kelly Av
5700 DgsC 80125 2532 D6
Kelly Ct
5400 DgsC 80125 2532 E6
Kelly Ln
- AdmC 80601 1696 E4
- WldC 80603 1696 E4
Kelly Pl
900 LGMT 80501 1356 A4
15000 DNVR 80239 2032 C7
20900 DNVR 80249 2033 E6
20900 DNVR 80249 2034 B7
Kelly Rd E
10 BldC 80302 1684 E2
10 BldC 80302 1685 A3
Kelly Rd W
500 BldC 80302 1684 E3
Kelsey Pl
100 CSRK 80104 2787 D3
Kelso Rd
- BldC 80301 1602 E2
- BldC 80301 1603 A2
Kelty Ct
2300 DgsC 80116 2705 E3
Kelty Rd
1800 DgsC 80116 2705 E4
N Kelty Rd
- DgsC 80116 2705 E3
Kelty Tr
7100 DgsC 80116 2705 E3
7300 DgsC 80116 2706 A3
Kemper Dr
9400 LNTR 80124 2450 D4
Kempton Ct
1400 ERIE 80516 1607 A2
1500 LGMT 80501 1438 E6
W Ken Caryl Av
5000 AphC 80128 2363 A6
5000 LITN 80128 2363 A6
6800 JfnC 80128 2362 E6
9200 JfnC 80127 2362 A6
11500 JfnC 80127 2361 E6
W Ken Caryl Cir
8000 JfnC 80128 2362 D6
W Ken Caryl Dr
9700 JfnC 80127 2362 B6
W Ken Caryl Pl
5600 JfnC 80128 2363 B6
8200 JfnC 80128 2362 D6
S Kendall Blvd
6700 JfnC 80128 2363 B5
8100 JfnC 80128 2447 B1
Kendall Cir
11600 WSTR 80020 1859 A3
Kendall Ct
300 DgsC 80108 2535 B7
500 LKWD 80226 2111 A7
5600 ARVD 80002 2027 A4
5600 JfnC 80002 2027 A4
8600 ARVD 80003 1943 A3
N Kendall Ct
9600 WSTR 80021 1943 A1
9900 WSTR 80021 1859 A7
S Kendall Ct
1100 LKWD 80232 2195 A4

Denver Regional Street Index

STREET Block City ZIP Map# Grid

S Kendall Ct
6900 JfnC 80128 2363 B5
Kendall Dr
1400 BLDR 80305 1770 E1
1400 BLDR 80305 1771 A1
10900 WSTR 80020 1859 A4
Kendall St
10 LKWD 80226 2195 A1
300 LKWD 80226 2111 A7
1400 LKWD 80214 2111 A5
1800 EDGW 80214 2111 A5
2900 WTRG 80214 2111 A2
3800 WTRG 80033 2111 A1
4200 WTRG 80033 2027 A7
6600 ARVD 80003 2027 A1
7300 WSTR 80003 1943 A7
7900 ARVD 80003 1943 A5
9300 WSTR 80031 1943 A1
11200 WSTR 80020 1859 A4
11500 BMFD 80020 1859 A4
S Kendall St
10 LKWD 80226 2195 A2
1100 LKWD 80232 2195 A5
3200 DNVR 80227 2279 A2
3500 DNVR 80235 2279 A3
5300 DNVR 80123 2363 A1
6200 JfnC 80123 2363 A3
Kendall Wy
10900 WSTR 80020 1859 A4
S Kendall Wy
2700 DNVR 80227 2279 A1
2700 LKWD 80227 2279 A1
Kendrick Ct
700 CSRK 80104 2789 A1
5200 JfnC 80403 2024 E5
S Kendrick Ct
10 JfnC 80401 2192 E1
Kendrick Dr
6600 ARVD 80007 2024 E2
6600 ARVD 80403 2024 E2
Kendrick St
1300 JfnC 80401 2108 E5
4600 JfnC 80403 2024 E6
7200 JfnC 80007 1940 E7
Kendrick Wy
7300 JfnC 80007 1940 E7
Ken Mar Ct
500 LGMT 80501 1438 D2
Kennedy Av
- AdmC 80102 2124 D1
- BNNT 80102 2124 D1
13400 AdmC 80601 1780 C5
13500 BGTN 80601 1780 C5
N Kennedy Av
1200 LSVL 80027 1689 A6
1400 BldC 80027 1689 A6
S Kennedy Av
11000 JfnC 80433 2527 B1
Kennedy Ct
1400 BLDR 80303 1687 C3
Kennedy Dr
- BldC 80503 1437 D3
- LGMT 80503 1437 D3
100 NHGN 80234 1860 D5
Kennedy Gulch Rd
- JfnC 80433 2526 A1
27600 JfnC 80433 2441 B7
29100 JfnC 80433 2525 B1
Kennemere Ln
10300 DgsC 80134 2452 E6
Kenneys Cr
1400 GOLD 80401 2107 E3
Kenogha St
- GpnC 80403 2017 A5
Kenosha Ct
16700 AdmC 80603 1700 B4
Kenosha Dr
- BLDR 80301 1603 C7
700 DgsC 80118 2954 D1
Kenosha Rd
11600 BldC 80504 1606 D1
11600 BldC 80516 1606 D1
11900 BldC 80516 1607 A1
11900 ERIE 80516 1606 D1
11900 ERIE 80516 1607 A1
Ken Pratt Blvd
- BldC 80501 1439 C4
- LGMT 80501 1440 A3
- LGMT 80504 1440 A3
600 LGMT 80501 1439 C4
1200 LGMT 80501 1438 D5
Ken Pratt Blvd SR-119
- BldC 80501 1439 C4
- LGMT 80501 1440 A3
- LGMT 80504 1440 A3
600 LGMT 80501 1439 C4
1200 LGMT 80501 1438 D5
Kensing Ct
2500 DNVR 80211 2112 B2
E Kensington Av
5100 CSRK 80104 2788 D1
Kensington St
600 LGMT 80501 1439 C2
W Kent Av
900 TNTN 80260 1944 C3
E Kent Cir
18900 AURA 80013 2285 C3
Kent Dr
- AURA 80018 2286 B3
E Kent Dr
16700 AURA 80013 2284 E3
17100 AURA 80013 2285 A3
21700 AURA 80018 2286 B3
Kent Pl
- AURA 80018 2286 C3
6700 DgsC 80108 2618 E1
9600 GDVL 80014 2283 A3
E Kent Pl
8700 DNVR 80237 2283 A3
18800 AURA 80013 2285 C3
W Kent Pl
5300 DNVR 80235 2279 C3
Kent St
1000 BLDR 80303 1687 A4

Kent St
8800 AdmC 80031 1943 E3
8800 WSTR 80031 1943 E3
Kentmere Dr
1900 LGMT 80501 1356 E5
Kenton Cir
9800 CMCY 80022 1863 C7
S Kenton Ct
2100 AURA 80014 2199 C6
2600 AURA 80014 2283 C1
5300 AphC 80111 2283 C7
5500 AphC 80111 2367 C1
Kenton St
100 AURA 80010 2199 C1
1600 AURA 80010 2115 C4
11200 CMCY 80640 1863 C3
S Kenton St
- DNVR 80014 2283 C2
700 AURA 80012 2199 C3
1800 AURA 80014 2199 C6
5700 AphC 80111 2367 C2
6300 CTNL 80111 2367 D3
6500 AphC 80112 2367 C3
6500 CTNL 80112 2367 C3
S Kenton Wy
1100 AURA 80012 2199 C4
2200 AURA 80014 2199 C7
5100 AphC 80111 2283 C7
5500 AphC 80111 2367 C1
E Kentucky Av
- DNVR 80223 2196 D3
10 DNVR 80209 2196 E3
600 DNVR 80209 2197 A3
3900 GNDL 80246 2197 D3
4700 GNDL 80246 2198 A3
4900 DvrC 80246 2198 A3
5400 DNVR 80246 2198 B3
5500 DNVR 80224 2198 B3
10500 AURA 80012 2199 C3
10500 AURA 80247 2199 C3
12800 AURA 80012 2200 A3
16000 AURA 80017 2200 E3
16800 AURA 80017 2201 A3
W Kentucky Av
2200 DNVR 80223 2196 A3
2400 DNVR 80219 2196 A3
3200 DNVR 80219 2195 E3
5000 LKWD 80226 2195 C3
7400 LKWD 80226 2194 D4
11700 LKWD 80226 2193 E3
11700 LKWD 80228 2193 E3
E Kentucky Cir
4500 GNDL 80246 2197 E3
4800 AphC 80246 2198 A3
4800 DNVR 80246 2198 A3
4800 GNDL 80246 2198 A3
E Kentucky Dr
9700 DNVR 80247 2199 B3
9900 AURA 80247 2199 B3
9900 DvrC 80247 2199 B3
10300 AURA 80012 2199 B3
14500 AURA 80012 2200 C3
W Kentucky Dr
6800 LKWD 80226 2195 A3
6900 LKWD 80226 2194 E3
9500 LKWD 80232 2194 A4
11000 LKWD 80226 2193 E4
11500 LKWD 80228 2193 E4
13800 JfnC 80401 2193 B3
E Kentucky Pl
4500 GNDL 80246 2197 E3
11500 AURA 80012 2199 D3
13400 AURA 80012 2200 B3
W Kentucky Pl
5800 LKWD 80226 2195 B3
9200 LKWD 80226 2194 B4
13700 LKWD 80228 2193 B4
Kenuil Ct
16700 AdmC 80603 1700 B4
Kenuil St
16600 AdmC 80603 1700 B4
S Kenwood Ct
8900 DgsC 80126 2449 A3
Kenwood Dr
2300 BLDR 80305 1686 E6
Kenwood St
7600 AdmC 80022 1946 B5
7600 CMCY 80022 1946 B5
S Kenya Dr
6300 JfnC 80439 2358 C3
Kenyon Av
- EGLD 80110 2280 C3
- SRDN 80110 2280 C3
E Kenyon Av
10 EGLD 80110 2280 E3
10 EGLD 80113 2280 E3
800 CHLV 80113 2281 A3
800 EGLD 80113 2281 A3
3600 AphC 80013 2286 A3
7800 DNVR 80237 2282 E3
8900 DNVR 80237 2283 A3
14600 AURA 80014 2284 C3
15500 AURA 80013 2284 D3
19900 AURA 80013 2285 D3
20600 AphC 80013 2285 E3
W Kenyon Av
10 EGLD 80110 2280 D3
10 EGLD 80113 2280 D3
3000 SRDN 80110 2280 A4
3100 SRDN 80110 2279 E3
3400 SRDN 80236 2279 E3
3500 DNVR 80236 2279 E3
4900 DNVR 80235 2279 C3
6200 DvrC 80235 2279 A3
10000 JfnC 80235 2278 A4
Kenyon Cir
2800 BLDR 80305 1770 E1
2800 BLDR 80305 1771 A1
E Kenyon Dr
7800 DNVR 80237 2282 E3
17200 AURA 80013 2285 A3
W Kenyon Dr
10300 JfnC 80235 2278 A4

Kenyon Ln
- WldC 80504 1523 C2
3600 LGMT 80503 1355 B6
E Kenyon Ln
700 CHLV 80113 2281 A3
700 EGLD 80113 2281 A3
Kenyon Pl
- AURA 80018 2286 B3
E Kenyon Pl
7900 DNVR 80237 2282 E3
19400 AURA 80013 2285 D3
20100 AphC 80013 2285 E3
21400 AphC 80013 2286 A3
21700 AURA 80018 2286 B3
E Kenyon Wy
16600 AURA 80013 2284 E3
16800 AURA 80013 2285 A3
Keota Ln
1700 SUPE 80027 1773 B6
Keota St
11200 PARK 80134 2453 A7
11200 PARK 80134 2537 A1
Keough Dr
11700 NHGN 80233 1860 E3
11700 NHGN 80233 1861 A3
E Kepner Dr
11800 AURA 80012 2199 D3
15800 AURA 80017 2200 D3
17600 AURA 80017 2201 B3
E Kepner Pl
12100 AURA 80012 2199 E3
16500 AURA 80017 2200 E3
18300 AURA 80017 2201 B3
Kerr Rd
33600 JfnC 80470 2524 B6
Kerr Gulch Rd
1100 JfnC 80439 2189 B5
2000 JfnC 80439 2190 A7
2000 JfnC 80439 2274 B2
3200 JfnC 80457 2274 B2
Kerry Rd
9100 BldC 80303 1689 C2
Kestrel Ct
3900 CSRK 80109 2702 D3
Kestrel Ln
- BldC 80026 1605 C3
- BldC 80301 1605 C3
- LGMT 80501 1439 B6
Kestrel Pl
4000 CSRK 80109 2702 C4
Ketchwood Cir
4400 DgsC 80130 2449 E6
4400 DgsC 80130 2450 A6
Ketchwood Ct
10400 DgsC 80130 2450 A7
Kettering Ln
10300 DgsC 80134 2452 E6
E Kettle Av
400 LITN 80122 2364 E6
500 LITN 80122 2365 A6
1100 CTNL 80122 2365 A6
5500 CTNL 80122 2366 B6
5600 CTNL 80112 2366 B6
8600 CTNL 80112 2367 A6
18900 CTNL 80016 2369 C6
25100 AphC 80016 2371 A6
W Kettle Av
1500 LITN 80120 2364 C6
4400 LITN 80128 2363 D6
E Kettle Cir
8600 CTNL 80112 2366 E6
8700 CTNL 80112 2367 A7
25700 AphC 80016 2371 B6
W Kettle Cir
2400 LITN 80120 2364 B7
E Kettle Ct
7700 CTNL 80112 2366 D6
E Kettle Pl
700 LITN 80122 2365 A6
2800 CTNL 80122 2365 C6
8000 CTNL 80112 2366 E6
8700 CTNL 80112 2367 A6
17500 CTNL 80016 2369 A6
23900 AURA 80016 2370 E6
25300 AphC 80016 2371 B6
E Kettledrum Ln
10100 DgsC 80138 2539 B3
Kevin Ct
14300 BMFD 80020 1775 C3
Kewanee Dr
5300 BLDR 80303 1687 D5
Key Ct
2400 LGMT 80501 1356 A4
Keyser Creek Av
18200 PARK 80134 2537 B5
E Keystone Av
18500 AURA 80011 2117 B7
Keystone Blvd
16500 DgsC 80134 2452 E5
Keystone Ct
1000 LAFT 80026 1690 B5
1300 LGMT 80501 1356 B7
2300 BLDR 80304 1602 E6
Keystone Dr
1400 JfnC 80439 2188 E5
1600 JfnC 80439 2189 A6
2200 JfnC 80439 2273 C1
Keystone Tr
100 BMFD 80020 1774 E4
Kickapoo Ct
- KIOW 80117 2796 A3
Kicking Horse Ct
8500 DgsC 80125 2530 E5
Kicking Horse Dr
10400 DgsC 80125 2530 E5
Kidder Dr
6800 AdmC 80221 2028 D1
6900 AdmC 80221 1944 D7
S Kiefer St
800 AphC 80102 2206 D2
S Kiem Rd
6500 JfnC 80439 2357 E4
S Kilimanjaro Dr
6000 JfnC 80439 2358 B3

Kilkenny St
- BldC 80301 1689 C3
1300 BldC 80303 1689 C3
S Killarney Ct
- AphC 80013 2285 E2
- AURA 80013 2285 E2
2500 AURA 80013 2201 E7
4700 AphC 80015 2285 E6
6200 CTNL 80016 2369 E2
6200 CTNL 80016 2370 A3
6400 AphC 80016 2369 E3
6400 AphC 80016 2370 A3
S Killarney Dr
6100 CTNL 80016 2369 E2
Killarney St
1600 AURA 80011 2117 E4
S Killarney St
3500 AphC 80013 2285 E3
5400 AphC 80015 2285 E7
5400 CTNL 80015 2285 E7
5400 CTNL 80015 2369 E1
6200 CTNL 80016 2369 E3
6300 AphC 80016 2369 E3
S Killarney Wy
2800 AURA 80013 2285 E1
3900 AphC 80013 2285 E4
5600 CTNL 80015 2369 E1
5600 CTNL 80015 2370 A2
Killdeer Ln
10 JfnC 80127 2360 E3
Killdeer St
5200 BGTN 80601 1697 E6
Killen Av
5400 CSRK 80104 2788 E2
Killington Ct
1300 JfnC 80439 2189 A5
Kilmer Ct
6700 ARVD 80007 2024 E1
Kilmer Dr
6400 ARVD 80007 2024 E2
6400 ARVD 80403 2024 E2
Kilmer St
900 JfnC 80401 2108 E6
5200 JfnC 80403 2024 E5
6800 ARVD 80007 2024 E1
S Kilmer St
100 JfnC 80401 2192 E2
Kim Ct
8600 DgsC 80134 2622 C4
Kimball Av
100 GOLD 80401 2191 E1
100 GOLD 80401 2192 A1
200 JfnC 80401 2192 A1
Kimball Ct
300 GOLD 80401 2192 A1
Kimball St
10700 PARK 80134 2453 A7
Kimbark Dr
15200 AdmC 80601 1697 B7
Kimbark St
- BldC 80501 1439 B4
100 LAFT 80026 1690 C5
900 LGMT 80501 1439 B1
1900 LGMT 80501 1356 B6
S Kimbark St
- LGMT 80501 1439 B4
Kimberly Dr
- CSRK 80108 2619 E5
- FLHT 80260 1944 A1
Kimberly St
7700 AdmC 80022 1946 B5
7700 CMCY 80022 1946 B5
Kimberwick Dr
10100 DgsC 80125 2530 E5
10100 DgsC 80125 2531 A5
Kimblewyck Cir
- NHGN 80233 1861 C5
Kimmer Dr
9000 LNTR 80124 2451 A3
Kimwood Rd
10 GpnC 80403 1851 B4
Kincaid Pl
2100 BLDR 80304 1602 D6
Kincaid Springs Rd
28700 JfnC 80470 2609 D4
Kincross Ct
4700 BldC 80301 1605 A3
Kincross Dr
7900 BldC 80301 1604 E3
8100 BldC 80301 1605 A3
Kincross Wy
8000 BldC 80301 1604 E3
8100 BldC 80301 1605 A3
King Av
- BLDR 80305 1686 D5
1700 BLDR 80302 1686 D5
King Cir
13000 BMFD 80020 1775 E6
N King Cir
10400 WSTR 80031 1859 D6
King Ct
5300 AdmC 80221 2027 E5
9100 BldC 80026 1689 C5
11400 WSTR 80031 1859 E3
15100 BMFD 80020 1775 D1
E King Ct
5900 DgsC 80134 2537 C3
S King Ct
1400 DNVR 80219 2195 E5
S King Dr
6000 JfnC 80439 2357 A3
King Pt
12600 BMFD 80020 1775 D7
S King Rd
4700 JfnC 80439 2273 D7
King St
- BMFD 80020 1775 D7
- BMFD 80020 1859 D1
10 DNVR 80219 2195 E1
300 DNVR 80219 2111 E7
400 BldC 80026 1689 C5
500 LAFT 80026 1689 C5
1500 DNVR 80204 2111 E5
1900 DNVR 80211 2111 E4

King St
4400 DNVR 80211 2027 E7
4800 DNVR 80221 2027 E6
7000 AdmC 80221 2027 E1
8000 WSTR 80030 1943 E5
8000 WSTR 80031 1943 E5
10400 WSTR 80031 1859 E5
12400 WSTR 80234 1859 D1
N King St
8200 AdmC 80031 1943 E4
8200 WSTR 80031 1943 E4
11400 WSTR 80031 1859 E4
S King St
10 DNVR 80219 2195 E2
2500 DNVR 80219 2279 E1
2600 DNVR 80236 2279 E1
3500 SRDN 80236 2279 E4
4500 EGLD 80110 2279 E6
4500 SRDN 80110 2279 E6
5500 LITN 80123 2363 E1
King Wy
1900 DNVR 80211 2111 E4
2000 DNVR 80204 2111 E4
9700 WSTR 80031 1943 D1
11400 WSTR 80031 1859 D3
N King Wy
9200 AdmC 80031 1943 E2
9200 WSTR 80031 1943 E2
S King Wy
1800 DNVR 80219 2195 E6
3100 DNVR 80236 2279 E2
W Kingbird Cir
300 DgsC 80129 2448 E6
W King Crest Ln
5000 BWMR 80123 2363 C1
5000 LITN 80123 2363 C1
5100 LITN 80123 2363 C1
S King Crest Wy
5500 BWMR 80123 2363 C1
5500 LITN 80123 2363 C1
Kingfisher Av
- DgsC 80129 2448 C6
1300 BGTN 80601 1779 E1
King Flats Rd
- CLCY 80403 2017 A4
200 GpnC 80403 2017 A5
King Lake Tr
- BMFD 80020 1775 C5
Kinglet Ct
800 BGTN 80601 1779 E1
Kings Ct
10 LAFT 80026 1690 E6
Kings Pl
10 NDLD 80466 1765 D2
Kings Rd
- GpnC 80403 2017 A5
10 CCkC 80439 2271 E6
Kings Vly E
29700 JfnC 80433 2525 B3
Kings Vly W
31200 JfnC 80433 2524 E3
31400 JfnC 80433 2525 A4
S Kingsberry Dr
9700 DgsC 80126 2449 C5
Kingsbury Ct
1400 JfnC 80401 2109 C5
1400 LKWD 80215 2109 C5
Kingsbury Rd
26000 JfnC 80457 2274 B3
Kingsfield St
1000 CSRK 80104 2788 E1
1000 CSRK 80104 2789 A1
W Kingsley Av
6400 JfnC 80128 2447 A1
Kings Mill Ln
9600 LNTR 80124 2450 E4
Kings Mill Pl
9600 LNTR 80124 2450 E4
Kings Ridge Blvd
4700 BLDR 80301 1603 B7
S Kingston Av
4800 DgsC 80130 2450 A5
S Kingston Cir
400 AURA 80012 2199 C2
6000 AphC 80111 2367 D2
Kingston Ct
1900 LGMT 80503 1355 C6
15200 AdmC 80602 1695 C7
15200 AdmC 80602 1779 C1
S Kingston Ct
1900 AURA 80012 2199 C6
2000 AURA 80014 2199 C6
2600 AURA 80014 2283 D1
9500 DgsC 80130 2451 C4
10000 DgsC 80130 2450 A5
Kingston St
1400 AURA 80010 2115 C5
4500 DNVR 80239 2031 C6
11200 CMCY 80640 1863 C4
15300 AdmC 80602 1695 C7
S Kingston St
1000 AURA 80012 2199 C4
2300 AURA 80014 2199 C7
S Kingston Wy
1600 AURA 80012 2199 D5
5600 AphC 80111 2367 C2
Kingstown Pl
3900 BldC 80301 1603 A5
3900 BLDR 80301 1603 A5
Kings Valley Dr
30000 JfnC 80433 2525 A4
30800 JfnC 80433 2524 E3
Kings Valley Wy
30800 JfnC 80433 2525 A4
Kingwood Pl
1300 BLDR 80304 1602 C6
Kinner St
700 CSRK 80109 2703 D6
S Kinney Creek Rd
5900 JfnC 80439 2357 E3
5900 JfnC 80439 2358 A3
Kinney Creek Wy
18200 PARK 80134 2537 C5

Kinnikinic Rd
10 BldC 80302 1686 C5
10 BLDR 80302 1686 C5
Kinnikinnick Ct
1200 LGMT 80501 1356 D7
Kinnikinnick Dr
- DgsC 80118 2954 B1
Kinnikinnick Ln
28900 JfnC 80439 2273 C7
Kinnikinnick Rd
28000 JfnC 80439 2273 D6
Kinnikinnik Dr
1900 DgsC 80118 2954 B2
1900 ERIE 80516 1692 A3
Kinnikinnik Hl
600 JfnC 80401 2106 B7
600 JfnC 80401 2190 A1
Kinsey Ln
32500 JfnC 80433 2440 D2
Kio Ct
700 AphC 80137 2121 C6
S Kio St
1100 AphC 80137 2205 C4
E Kiowa
- AdmC 80022 1946 C3
W Kiowa
- AdmC 80022 1946 C3
Kiowa Av
- ELIZ 80107 2793 A1
200 BNNT 80102 2124 D2
2700 EbtC 80107 2792 E1
2700 EbtC 80107 2793 A1
2700 ELIZ 80107 2792 E1
Kiowa Av SR-86
- ELIZ 80107 2793 A1
2700 EbtC 80107 2792 E1
2700 EbtC 80107 2793 A1
2700 ELIZ 80107 2792 E1
E Kiowa Av
100 ELIZ 80107 2793 B1
300 EbtC 80107 2793 B1
E Kiowa Av SR-86
100 ELIZ 80107 2793 B1
300 EbtC 80107 2793 B1
W Kiowa Av
100 ELIZ 80107 2793 A1
200 EbtC 80107 2793 A1
W Kiowa Av SR-86
100 ELIZ 80107 2793 A1
200 EbtC 80107 2793 A1
Kiowa Ln
34000 JfnC 80470 2608 B5
Kiowa Pl
200 BLDR 80303 1687 B5
Kiowa Rd
7000 DgsC 80118 2952 D2
22800 JfnC 80439 2274 E6
22800 JfnC 80439 2275 A6
N Kiowa Rd
9500 DgsC 80138 2539 C2
Kiowa Tr
700 EbtC 80107 2708 C5
Kiowa-Bennett Rd
- BNNT 80102 2125 A4
2800 AdmC 80102 2125 A4
33000 EbtC 80117 2796 A1
33000 KIOW 80117 2796 A1
40000 EbtC 80117 2544 C7
44000 EbtC 80102 2460 E7
44000 EbtC 80102 2544 D1
Kiowa-Bennett Rd SR-79
2800 AdmC 80102 2125 A1
2800 BNNT 80102 2125 A1
N Kiowa-Bennett Rd
1400 AdmC 80102 2125 A7
1400 BNNT 80102 2125 A7
S Kiowa-Bennett Rd
10 AphC 80102 2209 A3
10 BNNT 80102 2209 A3
Kiowa Creek Ct
4900 CSRK 80109 2702 D1
Kiowa Creek Dr
2400 BGTN 80601 1696 E7
Kipling Ct
10400 WSTR 80021 1858 A6
S Kipling Ct
1500 LKWD 80232 2194 B7
3600 JfnC 80235 2278 B4
6400 JfnC 80127 2362 B4
S Kipling Pkwy
- LKWD 80227 2278 A2
900 LKWD 80226 2194 A6
900 LKWD 80232 2194 A6
1500 JfnC 80232 2194 A6
1500 LKWD 80227 2194 A6
1900 JfnC 80227 2194 A6
2000 JfnC 80227 2278 A2
4300 DNVR 80123 2278 B7
4300 JfnC 80127 2278 B7
4300 JfnC 80235 2278 B7
4800 JfnC 80123 2278 B7
5200 JfnC 80123 2362 B1
5200 JfnC 80127 2362 B1
7500 JfnC 80128 2362 B7
8100 JfnC 80127 2446 B2
8100 JfnC 80128 2446 B2
S Kipling Pkwy SR-391
900 LKWD 80226 2194 A6
900 LKWD 80232 2194 A6
1500 JfnC 80232 2194 A6
1500 LKWD 80227 2194 A6
1900 JfnC 80227 2194 A6
2000 JfnC 80227 2278 A2
2000 LKWD 80227 2278 A2
Kipling Pl
10500 WSTR 80021 1858 A6
Kipling St
- ARVD 80004 2026 B4
10 LKWD 80226 2194 B1
500 LKWD 80226 2110 B6
600 LKWD 80215 2110 B6
2500 JfnC 80215 2110 B3
2500 WTRG 80215 2110 B3
3100 WTRG 80033 2110 B3

Kipling St
4700 WTRG 80033 2026 B7
4900 ARVD 80033 2026 B7
5000 ARVD 80002 2026 A4
5000 WTRG 80002 2026 A4
7100 ARVD 80005 1942 A7
7200 ARVD 80004 1942 A7
8500 WSTR 80005 1942 A5
9700 WSTR 80021 1942 A1
Kipling St SR-391
- ARVD 80002 2026 B7
- ARVD 80004 2026 B7
10 LKWD 80226 2194 B1
500 LKWD 80226 2110 B6
600 LKWD 80215 2110 B6
2500 JfnC 80215 2110 B3
2500 WTRG 80215 2110 B3
3100 WTRG 80033 2110 B3
4700 WTRG 80033 2026 B7
5000 ARVD 80033 2026 B7
5000 WTRG 80002 2026 B7
S Kipling St
10 LKWD 80226 2194 B3
3500 LKWD 80227 2278 B5
3900 JfnC 80235 2278 B5
4000 JfnC 80123 2278 B5
4000 JfnC 80127 2278 B5
5900 JfnC 80123 2362 B4
5900 JfnC 80127 2362 B4
6600 JfnC 80128 2362 B4
S Kipling St SR-391
10 LKWD 80226 2194 B3
Kipling Wy
10500 WSTR 80021 1942 B1
10500 WSTR 80021 1858 A5
S Kipling Wy
4700 JfnC 80127 2278 B6
S Kipling Frontage Rd
- LKWD 80226 2194 B3
S Kipling Service Rd
400 LKWD 80226 2194 A2
Kirby Ct
- AphC 80137 2121 C6
S Kirk Cir
5400 AphC 80015 2286 A7
5400 AphC 80015 2370 A1
5400 CTNL 80015 2286 A7
5400 CTNL 80015 2370 A1
Kirk Ct
4300 DNVR 80249 2033 E6
S Kirk Ct
3300 AURA 80013 2286 A2
3800 AphC 80013 2286 A3
4000 AphC 80013 2285 E4
4800 AphC 80015 2286 A6
5500 CTNL 80015 2370 A1
6400 AphC 80016 2369 E3
6600 AphC 80016 2370 A3
Kirk St
4800 DNVR 80249 2033 E6
S Kirk St
3500 AphC 80013 2285 E3
3500 AphC 80013 2286 A3
4200 AURA 80013 2285 E4
4200 AURA 80015 2285 E4
5600 CTNL 80015 2370 A1
5800 CTNL 80015 2369 E2
5900 AphC 80016 2369 E2
6100 CTNL 80016 2369 E2
6100 CTNL 80016 2370 A2
E Kirk Wy
900 SUPE 80027 1773 A5
S Kirk Wy
- AURA 80013 2285 E1
3100 AURA 80013 2286 A2
3600 AphC 80013 2285 E3
4800 AphC 80015 2285 E6
4800 AphC 80015 2286 A6
Kirkwall St
2800 BMFD 80020 1859 B1
Kirkwood Ct
4600 BldC 80301 1605 A3
29500 JfnC 80439 2273 C1
S Kirkwood Ct
2300 DNVR 80222 2198 C7
Kirkwood Pl
3500 BLDR 80304 1602 D6
Kirkwood St
4600 BldC 80301 1604 E3
4600 BldC 80301 1605 A3
E Kistler Ct
1100 DgsC 80126 2449 A5
Kit Ln
10 PrkC 80456 2607 D6
S Kit Carson Cir E
6700 CTNL 80121 2365 A4
6700 CTNL 80122 2365 A4
S Kit Carson Cir W
6700 CTNL 80121 2365 A4
6700 CTNL 80122 2365 A4
S Kit Carson Dr
7600 CTNL 80122 2365 B6
Kit Carson Ln
8800 DgsC 80138 2538 D5
S Kit Carson St
6500 CTNL 80121 2365 A4
6600 CTNL 80122 2365 A4
W Kite Hawk Ln
- DgsC 80129 2447 E4
Kiteley Ln
1200 LGMT 80503 1355 C7
Kittery St
900 CSRK 80104 2789 A1
S Kittiwake St
8900 DgsC 80126 2449 E3
S Kittredge Cir
7700 AphC 80112 2368 E7
Kittredge Ct
1700 AURA 80011 2116 D4
S Kittredge Ct
2500 AURA 80013 2200 E7
5700 CTNL 80015 2368 E1
6000 AphC 80016 2368 E1
8000 AphC 80112 2368 E7

STREET
Block City ZIP Map# Grid

S Kittredge Ln
5600 CTNL 80015 2368 E1
Kittredge St
- CMCY 80022 1948 D1
1800 AURA 80011 2116 D4
4200 AURA 80011 2032 D7
4200 DNVR 80239 2032 D7
4200 DvrC 80239 2032 D7
9600 CMCY 80022 1864 D7
12100 CMCY 80603 1864 D1
S Kittredge St
- AphC 80016 2368 E2
1100 AURA 80017 2200 E4
4200 AURA 80013 2284 D5
4500 AURA 80015 2284 E5
5500 CTNL 80015 2368 C1
5900 CTNL 80016 2368 E2
7900 AphC 80112 2368 E7
S Kittredge Wy
1000 AURA 80017 2200 D3
2100 AURA 80013 2200 E6
3100 AURA 80013 2284 E2
4600 AURA 80015 2284 E6
7900 AphC 80112 2368 E7
Kittredge Loop Rd
- BLDR 80302 1686 E4
S Kittredge Park Rd
2500 JfnC 80439 2273 D1
3000 JfnC 80439 2274 A2
Kittrell Ct
3100 BLDR 80305 1771 A1
Kittridge Ln
38800 EbtC 80107 2624 B5
Kittridge Pl
38800 EbtC 80107 2624 B5
Kitty Dr
10700 JfnC 80433 2525 E1
10700 JfnC 80433 2526 A1
Kiva Ln
31600 JfnC 80439 2356 E3
Kleinbrook St
10100 DgsC 80126 2449 E6
Kleinbrook Wy
10100 DgsC 80126 2449 E6
S Kline Cir
2600 LKWD 80227 2278 A1
Kline Ct
7100 ARVD 80004 1942 A7
8000 ARVD 80005 1942 A5
S Kline Ct
700 LKWD 80226 2194 A3
1500 LKWD 80232 2194 A5
4500 JfnC 80127 2278 B6
6400 JfnC 80127 2362 B4
Kline Dr
- LGMT 80501 1438 D5
800 LKWD 80215 2110 B6
7400 ARVD 80005 1942 A6
W Kline Dr
10000 LKWD 80215 2110 A6
Kline St
2400 LKWD 80215 2110 A3
3900 WTRG 80033 2110 A1
6400 ARVD 80004 2026 A2
8100 ARVD 80005 1942 A4
9800 WSTR 80021 1858 A7
9800 WSTR 80021 1942 A1
S Kline St
300 LKWD 80226 2194 B2
1100 LKWD 80232 2194 B4
4700 JfnC 80127 2278 B6
5500 JfnC 80127 2362 B1
Kline Wy
10500 WSTR 80021 1858 A6
S Kline Wy
700 LKWD 80226 2194 B3
1100 LKWD 80232 2194 A4
7000 JfnC 80127 2362 B5
Klingen Gate Ct
10 DgsC 80108 2534 D6
Klingen Gate Ln
10 DgsC 80108 2534 B6
Klondike Pl
3300 DgsC 80108 2618 C4
Kneale Rd
10 BldC 80025 1770 B7
1200 BldC 80025 1769 E6
Knight Ct
12900 BMFD 80020 1775 E6
Knight St
10 LAFT 80026 1690 E6
Knob Ct
700 BldC 80026 1690 B3
700 LAFT 80026 1690 B3
Knobcone Dr
5200 CSRK 80108 2704 A1
S Knoll Cir
10100 DgsC 80130 2450 B6
S Knoll Ct
10200 DgsC 80130 2450 B6
Knoll Dr
- DgsC 80124 2450 B6
- DgsC 80130 2450 B6
E Knoll Pl
5400 DgsC 80130 2450 B5
Knoll Crest Ct
5700 BldC 80301 1603 E6
S Knolls Wy
6900 CTNL 80122 2365 C6
Knollside Av
17000 PARK 80134 2453 A6
Knollside Dr
17000 PARK 80134 2453 A6
Knollwood Dr
2100 BldC 80302 1686 A2
E Knollwood Wy
1300 DgsC 80126 2449 A4
Knotty Pine Av
- TNTN 80260 1860 B7
- TNTN 80260 1944 B1
S Knotty Pine Ln
5100 JfnC 80439 2273 B7
5100 JfnC 80439 2357 B1
Knowles Rd
27900 JfnC 80439 2273 D6
Knox Cir
3500 WSTR 80030 1943 E6
Knox Ct
10 DNVR 80219 2195 E1
300 DNVR 80219 2111 E7
800 DNVR 80204 2111 E6
4100 DNVR 80211 2027 E7
4800 DNVR 80221 2027 E6
6600 AdmC 80221 2027 E1
7800 WSTR 80030 1943 E5
8000 WSTR 80031 1943 E5
9100 AdmC 80031 1943 E2
11400 WSTR 80031 1859 E3
12400 BMFD 80020 1859 E1
N Knox Ct
9200 AdmC 80031 1943 D2
9200 WSTR 80031 1943 D2
S Knox Ct
10 DNVR 80219 2195 E2
2500 DNVR 80219 2279 E1
3300 DNVR 80110 2279 E3
3300 DNVR 80236 2279 E3
3400 AphC 80236 2279 E3
3600 SRDN 80236 2279 E3
4500 EGLD 80110 2279 E6
4500 SRDN 80110 2279 E6
5400 LITN 80123 2363 E1
Knox Dr
1300 BLDR 80305 1771 B1
Knox Pl
7400 WSTR 80030 1943 E6
Knox Pt
12600 BMFD 80020 1775 E7
Knox St
- AdmC 80221 2027 E1
S Knoxville Wy
2700 DNVR 80227 2279 A1
2700 LKWD 80227 2279 A1
Koa Ct
1100 CSRK 80104 2787 D1
Kochia Ct
8400 DgsC 80134 2452 E1
Kodiak Ct
10 LGMT 80501 1356 C7
Kohinoor Pl
10 GOLD 80401 2107 D4
Kohl St
- BMFD 80020 1774 E5
100 BMFD 80020 1858 D1
Kohler Dr
1800 BLDR 80305 1686 D6
Kokai Cir
1400 AdmC 80221 1944 C5
Kokanee
10 JfnC 80127 2360 E4
E Kokomo Rd
11800 DgsC 80116 2791 E3
Kola Dr
- TNTN 80260 1944 C1
Kolar Ct
10 ERIE 80516 1607 A5
Kornbrust Dr
- LNTR 80124 2451 A6
Korte Pkwy
600 BldC 80501 1438 E4
600 LGMT 80501 1438 E4
Korte Pl
1800 BldC 80501 1438 D4
1800 LGMT 80501 1438 D4
Kramer Ct
900 AURA 80010 2115 C6
S Kramer Ct
1200 AURA 80012 2199 C4
Kramer Dr
- ERIE 80026 1606 C5
- ERIE 80516 1606 C5
Krameria Ct
- AdmC 80602 1694 B4
12000 AdmC 80602 1862 B1
S Krameria Ct
5600 GDVL 80111 2366 B1
7700 CTNL 80112 2366 B6
Krameria Dr
7200 AdmC 80022 1946 B6
7200 CMCY 80022 1946 B6
Krameria St
- TNTN 80602 1778 B5
100 DNVR 80220 2198 B1
1500 DNVR 80220 2114 B5
3200 DNVR 80207 2114 B2
6500 CMCY 80022 2030 B1
7000 CMCY 80022 1946 B7
8000 AdmC 80022 1946 B5
12200 AdmC 80602 1862 B1
S Krameria St
200 DNVR 80224 2198 B2
2300 AphC 80222 2198 B7
2500 DNVR 80222 2198 B7
2600 DNVR 80222 2282 B1
3000 AphC 80222 2282 B2
5300 GDVL 80111 2282 B7
5300 GDVL 80111 2366 B1
5900 CTNL 80111 2366 B3
7300 CTNL 80112 2366 B6
Krameria Wy
- AdmC 80602 1694 B4
- TNTN 80602 1778 B4
S Krameria Wy
1700 DNVR 80224 2198 B6
6400 CTNL 80111 2366 B3
6600 CTNL 80112 2366 B3
8200 CTNL 80112 2450 B1
S Krashin Dr
8900 JfnC 80433 2440 D4
Krestview Ln
10 JfnC 80401 2190 E1
10 JfnC 80401 2191 A1
100 JfnC 80401 2106 E7
Kristal Wy
2000 AdmC 80221 1944 B6
Kristy Ct
1800 LGMT 80501 1439 B6
Kristy Ct
1800 LGMT 80504 1439 B6
Kryptonite Dr
- CSRK 80108 2619 D5
Kryptonite Ln
- CSRK 80108 2619 D5
Kudu Tr
10 PrkC 80456 2607 D5
S Kuehster Rd
12100 JfnC 80127 2528 B5
12100 JfnC 80433 2528 B5
12500 JfnC 80127 2527 E5
13500 JfnC 80127 2612 C1
14000 JfnC 80433 2612 E2
14300 JfnC 80127 2613 A2
N Kuner Rd
10 BGTN 80601 1696 B5
200 AdmC 80601 1696 B5
S Kuner Rd
10 BGTN 80601 1696 A7
600 BGTN 80601 1780 B2
Kunst Rd
7900 JfnC 80403 1936 B6
S Kyle Cir
1900 AphC 80102 2209 B6
Kyle Wy
7600 DgsC 80125 2530 E6
Kylie Dr
1600 LGMT 80501 1440 A3

L

L Rd
10 BldC 80403 1852 A1
Labelle Rd
10 BldC 80302 1599 E7
10 BldC 80302 1683 D1
Lacey Ct
7200 BldC 80503 1521 A4
La Chula Rd
700 GpnC 80403 1850 E2
700 GpnC 80403 1851 A2
Lackland Dr
12900 DNVR 80239 2031 E4
13100 DNVR 80239 2032 A4
Lackland Pl
14900 DNVR 80239 2032 C4
Lacosta Ln
9400 LNTR 80124 2450 D4
Lacrosse Ln
9100 DgsC 80138 2539 B3
Ladean St
8100 AdmC 80229 1945 B4
Ladies Tresses Pl
- BMFD 80020 1775 B3
Ladore St
7700 AdmC 80022 1946 B5
7700 CMCY 80022 1946 B5
La Farge Av
500 LSVL 80027 1689 D7
500 LSVL 80027 1773 D1
S Lafayette Cir
2700 DNVR 80210 2281 A1
S Lafayette Cir E
7300 CTNL 80122 2365 B6
S Lafayette Cir W
7300 CTNL 80122 2365 B6
Lafayette Ct
13400 TNTN 80241 1777 B5
S Lafayette Ct
7700 CTNL 80122 2365 A7
Lafayette Dr
2600 BLDR 80305 1770 E2
2600 BLDR 80305 1771 A2
S Lafayette Dr
2900 EGLD 80113 2281 B1
S Lafayette Ln
4800 CHLV 80113 2281 B6
S Lafayette Pl
6200 CTNL 80121 2365 A3
Lafayette St
- NHGN 80233 1861 A2
- TNTN 80241 1861 A1
100 DNVR 80218 2197 A1
100 LSVL 80027 1689 C7
1500 DNVR 80218 2113 A5
3300 DNVR 80205 2113 A2
8000 AdmC 80229 1945 A5
9600 TNTN 80229 1945 A1
9800 TNTN 80229 1861 A7
13400 TNTN 80241 1777 A5
16400 TNTN 80602 1693 A5
S Lafayette St
100 DNVR 80209 2197 A2
1300 DNVR 80210 2197 B5
2500 DNVR 80210 2281 A1
2700 DvrC 80210 2281 B1
3400 CHLV 80113 2281 B3
3500 EGLD 80113 2281 B3
6300 CTNL 80121 2365 B3
6600 CTNL 80122 2365 B3
W Lafayette St
100 LSVL 80027 1689 B7
Lafayette Tr
38800 EbtC 80107 2624 C5
Lafayette Wy
7800 AdmC 80229 1945 A5
13300 TNTN 80241 1777 A6
S Lafayette Wy
7000 CTNL 80122 2365 B5
Lagae Rd
- DgsC 80108 2618 E2
- DgsC 80108 2619 A1
7200 DgsC 80108 2535 A7
W La Garita Pass
11400 JfnC 80127 2361 E7
La Grange Cir
2800 BLDR 80305 1686 E7
2800 BLDR 80305 1687 A7
E Laguna Cir
6100 DgsC 80130 2450 B3
Laguna Pl
4300 BLDR 80303 1687 C4
Lair Ln
500 PrkC 80456 2691 C2
S Laird Ct
1200 SUPE 80027 1773 B5
Lake Av
2100 TNTN 80241 1777 B7
2100 TNTN 80241 1861 B1
13600 AdmC 80603 1781 B4
E Lake Av
- AphC 80016 2369 A2
400 CTNL 80121 2364 E2
600 CTNL 80121 2365 A2
2500 GDVL 80121 2365 C7
4600 CTNL 80121 2366 A2
9300 GDVL 80111 2367 A2
9600 AphC 80111 2367 A2
16700 CTNL 80016 2368 E2
20200 CTNL 80016 2369 E2
21800 AphC 80015 2370 B2
22100 CTNL 80015 2370 B2
W Lake Av
- LITN 80120 2364 A2
3200 CBVL 80123 2363 E2
3200 LITN 80123 2363 E2
9400 JfnC 80123 2362 B2
12000 JfnC 80127 2361 D2
E Lake Cir
6700 CTNL 80111 2366 C2
11900 GDVL 80111 2367 E2
15700 AphC 80016 2368 D2
20100 AphC 80016 2369 E2
20100 CTNL 80016 2369 E2
E Lake Cir N
4400 CTNL 80121 2365 E2
4500 CTNL 80121 2366 B1
E Lake Cir S
4400 CTNL 80121 2365 E2
4400 CTNL 80121 2366 A2
W Lake Cir N
4100 LITN 80123 2363 D2
W Lake Cir S
4300 LITN 80123 2363 D2
E Lake Ct
3600 CTNL 80121 2365 D2
W Lake Ct
1400 LITN 80120 2364 C2
Lake Dr
- BldC 80503 1354 A4
100 LmrC 80540 1269 A2
1600 DgsC 80118 2954 C2
E Lake Dr
- AphC 80015 2370 C2
1600 CTNL 80121 2365 B2
10000 AphC 80111 2367 B2
16000 AphC 80016 2368 E2
16200 CTNL 80016 2368 E2
16700 CTNL 80016 2369 A2
18900 AphC 80016 2369 C2
N Lake Dr
12800 TNTN 80241 1777 B7
W Lake Dr
9300 JfnC 80123 2362 C2
10100 JfnC 80127 2362 A2
11300 JfnC 80127 2361 E2
Lake Ln
33100 JfnC 80470 2608 B6
E Lake Ln
16800 AphC 80016 2369 A2
20200 CTNL 80016 2369 E2
22200 CTNL 80015 2370 B2
E Lake Pl
400 CTNL 80121 2364 E2
1400 CTNL 80121 2365 B2
5300 CTNL 80121 2366 A2
6500 CTNL 80111 2366 C2
9200 GDVL 80111 2367 A2
10100 AphC 80111 2367 B2
14700 CTNL 80016 2368 C2
17700 AphC 80016 2369 B2
22200 CTNL 80015 2370 C2
23200 AphC 80015 2370 D2
W Lake Pl
1600 LITN 80120 2364 C2
5000 LITN 80123 2363 C2
5200 JfnC 80123 2363 C2
9400 JfnC 80123 2362 B2
S Lake Rd
1900 LKWD 80227 2195 A6
1900 LKWD 80232 2195 A6
Lake St
- GpnC 80403 1849 D6
E Lake Wy
3400 CTNL 80121 2365 D2
Lake Avery Dr
- TNTN 80241 1777 B6
Lakebriar Dr
3700 BLDR 80304 1602 B5
Lake Cir Dr
2000 TNTN 80241 1777 B6
E Lakecliff Wy
7500 DgsC 80134 2622 A2
Lakecrest At Gateway
- DNVR 80239 2032 D6
Lake Front Dr
10 GpnC 80403 1933 C6
Lake Gulch Rd
- GpnC 80403 2017 D5
- GpnC 80403 2018 A6
S Lake Gulch Rd
10 CSRK 80104 2788 B2
400 DgsC 80104 2788 B2
S Lakehurst Wy
4500 DNVR 80123 2278 B6
4500 JfnC 80127 2278 B6
Lake Isle Ln
2400 BMFD 80020 1776 A4
Lake Meadow Dr
2500 BldC 80301 1689 D1
2500 LAFT 80026 1689 D1
Lake Park Ct
2100 LGMT 80503 1355 C5
Lake Park Dr
2100 LGMT 80503 1355 C5
2300 BldC 80503 1355 C5
Lake Park Wy
3200 LGMT 80503 1355 B4
N Lakepoint Pl
6200 DgsC 80134 2622 A2
W Lakeridge Rd
4400 DNVR 80219 2279 C1
4800 DNVR 80219 2195 C7
5100 LKWD 80227 2195 C7
N Lakeridge Tr
2700 BldC 80302 1435 B6
S Lakeridge Tr
- BldC 80503 1435 B7
2700 BldC 80302 1435 B7
E Lakeshore Ct
7800 DgsC 80134 2622 A2
Lakeshore Dr
- AphC 80247 2199 A4
- DNVR 80247 2198 E3
- DNVR 80247 2199 A3
10 BldC 80302 1768 D3
10 BldC 80403 1768 D3
2900 LGMT 80503 1355 C6
4900 BWMR 80123 2279 C7
5300 BWMR 80123 2363 D1
5400 LITN 80123 2363 D1
E Lakeshore Dr
7400 DgsC 80134 2622 B2
W Lakeshore Dr
- DNVR 80204 2111 D4
- DNVR 80212 2111 D4
Lake Shore Pl
1700 EDGW 80214 2111 B4
1700 LKWD 80214 2111 B4
Lakeshore Park Rd
100 BldC 80302 1768 D3
Lakeside Cir
6300 DgsC 80125 2448 B7
6800 DgsC 80125 2532 B1
Lakeside Ct
8800 BldC 80301 1689 B1
W Lakeside Ct
6300 DgsC 80125 2532 C1
Lakeside Dr
8800 BldC 80301 1689 B1
W Lakeside Dr
6600 DgsC 80125 2532 B1
7000 DgsC 80125 2448 A7
Lakeside Ln
10 LKSD 80212 2027 B6
10 WTRG 80033 2027 B6
N Lakeside Pl
10700 DgsC 80125 2448 B7
Lake Song Ln
13900 BMFD 80020 1776 A4
Lake Valley Dr
4400 BldC 80503 1518 E5
4500 BldC 80503 1519 A5
Lakeview Cir
3400 LGMT 80503 1355 B6
Lakeview Ct
200 NDLD 80466 1765 D3
1100 BGTN 80601 1696 C4
S Lakeview Ct
7700 LITN 80120 2364 D6
Lake View Dr
10 GpnC 80403 1933 C6
33800 JfnC 80470 2524 B5
Lakeview Dr
10 NDLD 80466 1765 D3
6200 LITN 80120 2364 D3
6500 BldC 80303 1688 B4
E Lakeview Dr
7000 DgsC 80134 2621 E2
7300 DgsC 80134 2622 A2
Lakeview Ln
- BMFD 80020 1776 A3
Lakeview Pl
100 NDLD 80466 1765 D3
Lake View Pt
- BldC 80503 1518 E4
Lakeview Rd
100 PrkC 80456 2521 D2
S Lakeview St
5300 LITN 80120 2280 D7
5600 LITN 80120 2364 D1
S Lakeview Wy
5400 LITN 80120 2364 D1
Lake Vista Dr
- BMFD 80020 1776 A3
E Lakewind Cir
6400 DgsC 80134 2622 A2
Lakewood Dr
- FLHT 80260 1944 B2
Lakewood Pl
6800 LKWD 80214 2110 E5
6800 LKWD 80214 2111 A5
N Lakewood Rd
6200 DgsC 80134 2622 B2
Lakewood St
13000 AdmC 80022 1784 B5
13000 AdmC 80603 1784 B4
14900 AdmC 80603 1700 B7
Lakewood Heights Dr
10 LKWD 80215 2110 B5
Lakewood Village Dr
700 LKWD 80215 2110 C6
Lakota Rd
41500 EbtC 80138 2540 D6
Lakota Ridge Ln
7000 LmrC 80513 1270 E1
Lallie Rd
100 PrkC 80456 2521 C2
Lamaica Dr
- AdmC 80640 1863 C4
- CMCY 80640 1863 C4
Lamar Cir
8700 ARVD 80003 1943 A3
11000 WSTR 80020 1859 A4
Lamar Ct
500 LKWD 80226 2111 A7
7200 WSTR 80003 1943 A7
7500 ARVD 80003 1943 A6
17500 PARK 80134 2453 A6
S Lamar Ct
- JfnC 80123 2363 A3
300 LKWD 80226 2195 A2
1800 LKWD 80232 2195 A6
7700 JfnC 80128 2363 A7
8000 JfnC 80128 2447 A1
Lamar Dr
8500 ARVD 80003 1943 A4
8700 ARVD 80031 1943 A3
8700 WSTR 80031 1943 A3
17000 PARK 80134 2453 A6
S Lamar Dr
6000 JfnC 80123 2363 A3
S Lamar Ln
5700 JfnC 80123 2363 A2
Lamar Pl
6300 ARVD 80003 2027 A2
8200 ARVD 80003 1943 A4
N Lamar Pl
9600 WSTR 80021 1943 A1
S Lamar Pl
- DNVR 80123 2363 A1
Lamar St
10 BMFD 80020 1859 A2
100 LKWD 80226 2195 A1
300 LKWD 80226 2111 A7
900 LKWD 80214 2111 A6
2000 EDGW 80214 2111 A3
3000 WTRG 80214 2111 A2
3800 WTRG 80033 2111 A1
4100 WTRG 80033 2027 A7
5600 ARVD 80002 2027 A4
5700 ARVD 80003 2027 A4
7100 WSTR 80003 1943 A7
8000 ARVD 80003 1943 A5
8100 ARVD 80003 1942 E5
9400 WSTR 80031 1943 A1
11500 WSTR 80020 1859 A3
N Lamar St
4500 WTRG 80033 2027 A7
S Lamar St
10 LKWD 80226 2195 A2
1100 LKWD 80232 2195 A5
2700 DNVR 80227 2279 A2
2700 LKWD 80227 2279 A2
5300 DNVR 80123 2363 A1
6700 JfnC 80123 2363 A5
7800 JfnC 80128 2363 A7
8000 JfnC 80128 2447 A1
S Lamar Wy
2500 DNVR 80227 2279 A1
2500 LKWD 80227 2279 A1
7500 JfnC 80128 2363 A6
Lamb Ln
100 JfnC 80401 2191 A2
Lambert Cir
1200 LAFT 80026 1690 A4
Lambert Ln
900 NHGN 80234 1860 C4
Lambert Ranch Cross
6400 DgsC 80135 2616 C4
Lambert Ranch Tr
4500 DgsC 80135 2616 D6
W Lambuth Av
10000 JfnC 80235 2278 A4
W Lambuth Pl
10500 JfnC 80235 2278 A4
S Lameria Dr
9600 DgsC 80130 2450 C4
Lamertine Pl
- IDSP 80452 2101 D5
La Mesa Dr
2200 BldC 80303 1771 A5
Lamplighted Dr
- FLHT 80260 1944 B2
Lamplighter Dr
1300 LGMT 80501 1356 C6
Lancaster Av
6200 CSRK 80104 2789 A1
E Lance Pl
5900 DgsC 80130 2450 B5
Lancelot St
10 LAFT 80026 1690 E5
Lander Ln
1600 LAFT 80026 1690 D6
Lander St
8800 AdmC 80031 1943 E3
8800 WSTR 80031 1943 E3
Landis Ct
1400 BLDR 80303 1687 C3
Landmark Dr
- AdmC 80022 1864 E6
- CMCY 80022 1864 E6
- CMCY 80022 1865 A7
E Landmark Dr
6800 DgsC 80138 2453 D6
Lane Ct
3100 BLDR 80305 1771 A1
Lane St
9600 TNTN 80260 1944 C1
9700 NHGN 80260 1860 C7
9700 TNTN 80260 1860 C7
Lane A
- IDSP 80452 2101 E5
Lane B
- IDSP 80452 2101 E5
Lane C
- IDSP 80452 2101 E5
Lane D
- IDSP 80452 2101 E5
Lanewood St
12800 AdmC 80022 1784 B6
Lang Rd
10 PrkC 80456 2521 E3
S Langdale Ct
- AURA 80016 2371 A5
S Langdon Dr
5700 JfnC 80439 2358 B2
S Langley Ct
2700 DNVR 80210 2281 D1
Lanier St
10 PrkC 80456 2521 D2
E Lansdowne Ct
2400 DgsC 80126 2449 C3
E Lansdowne Pl
2300 DgsC 80126 2449 C3
S Lansdowne Wy
9100 DgsC 80126 2449 B3
Lansing Cir
9600 CMCY 80022 1863 C7
9600 CMCY 80022 1947 C1
E Lansing Cir
11000 DgsC 80112 2451 D3
S Lansing Ct
1300 AURA 80012 2199 D4
1900 AURA 80014 2199 D6
5500 AphC 80111 2367 D1
Lansing St
- AURA 80012 2199 D4
10 AURA 80010 2199 C1
1400 AURA 80010 2115 C4
11200 CMCY 80640 1863 C4
15000 AdmC 80602 1779 C1
S Lansing St
900 AURA 80012 2199 D3
2300 AURA 80014 2199 D7
S Lansing Wy
2400 AURA 80014 2199 D7
2400 AURA 80014 2283 C1
5500 AphC 80111 2367 D1
Lantana
10 JfnC 80127 2361 A6
Lantana Dr
- BMFD 80020 1775 B1
Lantern Cir
- CSRK 80104 2788 D1
- CSRK 80104 2789 A1
Lantern Tr
- CSRK 80104 2704 D7
- CSRK 80104 2788 D1
Lanyon Dr
2300 LGMT 80503 1355 D7
2400 LGMT 80503 1438 C1
Lanyon Ln
1200 LGMT 80503 1355 D7
Laodicea Rd
6200 BldC 80503 1436 E3
6200 BldC 80503 1437 A3
La Paz Pl
200 LGMT 80501 1356 B5
La Place Ct
8000 WSTR 80031 1943 D5
La Plata Cir
5400 BldC 80301 1604 B1
La Plata Ct
3900 BGTN 80601 1697 B6
La Plata Ln
33300 JfnC 80470 2608 B5
La Plata Rd
9900 TNTN 80260 1860 B7
La Plata Peak Ct
2700 CSRK 80109 2787 A5
La Quinta Cir
1800 JfnC 80439 2188 E7
La Quinta Ct
7400 LNTR 80124 2450 D4
La Quinta Dr
9400 LNTR 80124 2450 D4
La Quinta Ln
1900 JfnC 80439 2188 E7
7400 LNTR 80124 2450 D4
La Quinta Pl
7400 LNTR 80124 2450 D4
La Quinta Bay
7400 LNTR 80124 2450 D4
Larado St
9700 AdmC 80022 1864 E7
Laramie Blvd
200 BLDR 80304 1602 B2
Laramie Ct
10 CSRK 80104 2704 E7
2100 LGMT 80501 1356 D5
Larch Ct
1100 BMFD 80020 1774 D5
Larchmont Ct
1800 LAFT 80026 1689 D1
S Laredo Cir
500 AURA 80017 2200 E3
2900 AURA 80013 2284 E2
Laredo Ct
5500 DNVR 80239 2032 E4
E Laredo Ct
7200 DgsC 80130 2450 D4
S Laredo Ct
1300 AURA 80017 2200 E4
2500 AURA 80013 2200 E7
3300 AURA 80013 2284 E2
5100 CTNL 80015 2284 E7
5700 CTNL 80015 2368 E1
8000 AphC 80112 2368 E7
Laredo Dr
- AdmC 80022 1948 D1
- CMCY 80022 1948 D1
9800 AdmC 80022 1864 D7
9800 CMCY 80022 1864 D7
Laredo Pl
100 LCHB 80603 1698 B3
Laredo St
- AdmC 80022 2032 E4
- AURA 80011 2116 E3
- CMCY 80603 1864 D2
- DNVR 80022 2032 E4
5500 DNVR 80239 2032 E4
10400 CMCY 80022 1864 D5
N Laredo St
200 AURA 80011 2200 E1
1300 AURA 80011 2116 E4
S Laredo St
1400 AURA 80017 2200 E5
2200 AURA 80013 2200 E7
3600 AURA 80013 2284 E3
4800 AURA 80015 2284 D7
4800 CTNL 80015 2284 D7
5400 CTNL 80015 2368 E1
7300 AphC 80016 2368 E5
9600 DgsC 80130 2450 C5
Laredo Wy
- CMCY 80022 1864 D5

STREET Block City ZIP Map# Grid

Laredo Wy
300 LCHB 80603 1698 B2
5500 DNVR 80239 2032 E4
S Laredo Wy
1000 AURA 80017 2200 E3
4100 AURA 80013 2284 E4
5100 CTNL 80015 2284 E7
Large Oak Ct
6100 DgsC 80108 2618 E1
N Lariat Dr
4500 DgsC 80108 2619 B5
S Lariat Ln
9000 JfnC 80439 2441 D3
Lariat Lp
16500 EbtC 80107 2543 B1
20200 EbtC 80107 2459 B7
Lariat Tr
9000 EbtC 80107 2459 A7
9000 EbtC 80107 2543 B1
Lariat Wy
4300 BldC 80301 1604 C4
Lariat Loop Rd
1300 GOLD 80401 2107 C4
1300 JfnC 80401 2107 C4
W Larigo Av
700 LITN 80120 2364 D3
Larimer St
900 DNVR 80204 2112 D4
1300 DNVR 80202 2112 D4
1900 DNVR 80205 2112 D4
3100 DNVR 80205 2113 A1
Lark Av
1200 BGTN 80601 1779 E1
S Lark Av
200 LSVL 80027 1773 A2
Lark Ct
1300 BldC 80303 1688 A3
9500 DgsC 80125 2531 B7
Lark Dr
37600 EbtC 80107 2624 C7
E Lark Dr
7600 DgsC 80138 2454 A6
Lark Ln
- BldC 80301 1603 D7
10 PrkC 80456 2691 E1
1100 BGTN 80601 1779 E1
Lark St
1200 LGMT 80501 1439 B5
9600 FLHT 80260 1944 A1
Lark Wy
- DgsC 80125 2531 B7
Lark Bunting Dr
9300 WSTR 80021 1942 C1
Lark Bunting Ln
10 JfnC 80127 2361 A3
14500 AdmC 80603 1781 D1
Lark Bunting Pl
1500 LGMT 80501 1357 A7
Larkdale Dr
10 AphC 80123 2363 C4
Larksong Ct
4300 CSRK 80109 2702 C2
Larksong Dr
4500 CSRK 80109 2702 C2
Larksong Pl
4400 CSRK 80109 2702 C2
S Lark Sparrow Dr
9200 DgsC 80126 2449 E4
9300 DgsC 80126 2450 A3
S Lark Sparrow Pl
9100 DgsC 80126 2449 E3
E Lark Sparrow St
4000 DgsC 80126 2449 E3
S Lark Sparrow Tr
9100 DgsC 80126 2449 E3
Larkspur Cir
3500 LGMT 80503 1438 B6
Larkspur Ct
800 LSVL 80027 1773 A1
3500 LGMT 80503 1438 B6
N Larkspur Ct
1400 LAFT 80026 1689 D2
S Larkspur Ct
1400 LAFT 80026 1689 C2
Larkspur Dr
200 BGTN 80601 1697 B5
400 JfnC 80401 2107 B7
1700 JfnC 80401 2190 D6
3300 LGMT 80503 1438 B5
11500 PARK 80134 2537 D2
29500 JfnC 80439 2273 C2
S Larkspur Dr
200 CSRK 80104 2704 A7
Larkspur Ln
900 LSVL 80027 1772 E1
900 LSVL 80027 1773 A1
Larkspur Pl
400 DgsC 80126 2448 E3
Larkspur Rd
8300 BldC 80302 1518 B1
Larkspur St
4900 BWMR 80123 2279 C7
Larkwood Ct
3600 BLDR 80304 1602 E6
Larkwood Pl
600 DgsC 80126 2448 E3
Larkwood St
7700 AdmC 80022 1946 B5
7700 CMCY 80022 1946 B5
Larry Ct
1900 AdmC 80229 1945 B3
Larry Dr
10600 NHGN 80233 1861 A5
Larsh Dr
6800 AdmC 80221 2028 B1
7400 AdmC 80221 1944 B6
Larson Ct
1800 ERIE 80516 1690 D2
Larson Dr
10500 NHGN 80233 1861 A5
Larson Ln
11200 NHGN 80233 1861 A3
W La Salle Av
8800 LKWD 80227 2278 C1
La Salle Cir
13000 JfnC 80228 2277 C1
E Lasalle Dr
17500 AURA 80013 2285 B1
19600 AURA 80013 2201 D7
La Salle Pl
2100 DNVR 80210 2197 B7
9000 AdmC 80031 1943 E2
9000 WSTR 80031 1943 E2
E La Salle Pl
4300 DNVR 80222 2197 E7
4300 DNVR 80222 2281 E1
4700 AphC 80222 2198 A7
4700 DNVR 80222 2198 A7
6500 DNVR 80224 2198 C7
E Lasalle Pl
12100 AURA 80014 2199 E7
16300 AURA 80013 2200 E7
18600 AURA 80013 2201 D7
W La Salle Pl
9800 LKWD 80227 2278 B1
13800 LKWD 80228 2277 B1
Lasalle St
900 SUPE 80027 1773 A6
Las Colinas Dr
9500 LNTR 80124 2450 D4
Laser Dr
100 LAFT 80026 1690 C6
Las Flores Ln
30400 JfnC 80470 2525 B7
Lashley Ln
100 BLDR 80305 1686 E5
S Lashley Ln
10 BLDR 80305 1686 E5
10 BLDR 80305 1687 A5
Lashley St
200 LGMT 80501 1439 C2
1000 LGMT 80501 1356 C7
Las Lomas St
100 BGTN 80601 1697 B6
Las Lunas Ct
4300 CSRK 80104 2704 C6
Las Lunas St
100 CSRK 80104 2704 C6
Lasso Pl
5800 DgsC 80134 2621 C5
Last Chance Ct
10 BldC 80466 1682 A6
Last Chance Rd
10 AphC 80102 2122 E7
10 AphC 80102 2206 E1
W Last Dollar Pass
11300 JfnC 80127 2361 E7
Last Resort Creek Rd
- JfnC 80433 2610 E3
- JfnC 80433 2611 A4
- JfnC 80470 2609 E6
23100 JfnC 80433 2609 E6
Last Resort Creek Tr
24000 JfnC 80433 2610 D1
Latigo Ln
11100 PARK 80138 2537 D1
W Latonka Rd
3600 LITN 80123 2279 D7
4100 LITN 80123 2363 D1
Laughlin Rd
- DgsC 80138 2455 B6
Laura Av
10 GpnC 80403 1849 D6
S Laura Av
13900 PrkC 80470 2608 A2
Laurel Av
800 BLDR 80303 1687 C4
W Laurel Av
7400 JfnC 80128 2362 E6
Laurel Ct
1300 LGMT 80501 1356 E7
1700 BMFD 80020 1774 D5
S Laurel Ct
9000 DgsC 80126 2449 A3
W Laurel Ct
500 LSVL 80027 1689 B6
Laurel Dr
8600 AdmC 80022 1946 C3
8600 AdmC 80640 1946 C3
8600 CMCY 80022 1946 C3
8600 CMCY 80640 1946 C3
W Laurel Dr
8100 JfnC 80128 2362 D6
Laurel Hl
16200 DgsC 80134 2452 E7
Laurel Ln
11600 PARK 80138 2537 E2
11600 PARK 80138 2538 A2
W Laurel Ln
3300 LITN 80123 2279 E7
S Laurel Pl
5800 LITN 80123 2363 C2
W Laurel Pl
9300 JfnC 80128 2362 C6
9800 JfnC 80127 2362 B6
Laurel St
10 BMFD 80020 1858 D1
200 BGTN 80601 1696 B7
1300 BMFD 80020 1774 D6
Laurel Wy
300 LAFT 80026 1689 E4
Laurelglen Cir
10500 DgsC 80130 2449 E7
10500 DgsC 80130 2450 B7
Laurelglen Ln
4500 DgsC 80130 2449 E7
4500 DgsC 80130 2450 A7
Laurel Oak Dr
22000 PARK 80138 2538 B1
S Lauren Ct
10100 DgsC 80130 2450 C6
Lauren Ln
5300 AphC 80121 2280 E7
W Laurenwood Ln
1000 DgsC 80129 2448 C4
W Laurenwood Wy
1100 DgsC 80129 2448 C4
Laurus
10 JfnC 80127 2361 B6
S Lausanne Cir
15100 JfnC 80470 2609 A5
N Lavaun Dr
7500 DgsC 80125 2532 E6
7500 DgsC 80135 2532 E6
Lavender Ct
9300 DgsC 80138 2538 D2
Lavender Hill Ln
2300 LAFT 80026 1689 D4
La Veta Rd
7900 DgsC 80118 2954 D3
Laveta Pass Av
300 GOLD 80401 2192 A1
Lavinia Ln
11700 NHGN 80233 1861 B2
Lavinia Wy
11800 NHGN 80233 1861 B2
La Vista Pl
7100 BldC 80503 1520 C5
7100 BLDR 80503 1520 C5
Lawley Dr
100 ERIE 80516 1607 B4
Lawn St
900 BldC 80303 1688 A4
Lawrence Rd
- BldC 80305 1686 E5
Lawrence St
100 CLCY 80403 2017 D4
1300 DNVR 80202 2112 D4
1300 DNVR 80204 2112 D4
1900 DNVR 80205 2112 D4
3100 DNVR 80205 2113 A2
Lawry Ln
- BLDR 80302 1686 C2
Lawson Av
- ERIE 80516 1691 D1
Lawson Ct
- ERIE 80516 1691 D1
E Layton Av
- AURA 80015 2284 B6
10 EGLD 80110 2280 E6
10 EGLD 80113 2280 E6
600 EGLD 80113 2281 A6
700 CHLV 80113 2281 A6
8500 DNVR 80237 2282 E6
8700 DNVR 80237 2283 A6
13800 AphC 80015 2284 B6
16700 AURA 80015 2285 A6
20400 AphC 80015 2285 E6
W Layton Av
- LKWD 80123 2278 D6
10 EGLD 80113 2280 D6
2900 DNVR 80110 2280 A6
2900 EGLD 80110 2280 A6
3000 DNVR 80110 2279 E6
3300 DNVR 80123 2279 E6
9900 DNVR 80123 2278 A5
12000 JfnC 80465 2277 D6
E Layton Dr
1600 CHLV 80113 2281 B6
14100 AURA 80015 2284 B6
17300 AURA 80015 2285 A6
W Layton Dr
10100 JfnC 80127 2278 A6
11600 JfnC 80127 2277 E6
11600 JfnC 80465 2277 E6
E Layton Ln
20200 AphC 80015 2285 E6
Layton Pl
- AphC 80016 2287 A6
- AURA 80016 2286 E6
- AURA 80016 2287 A6
E Layton Pl
14300 AURA 80015 2284 C6
18200 AURA 80015 2285 B6
20400 AphC 80015 2285 E6
W Layton Pl
7400 LKWD 80123 2278 E7
10100 JfnC 80127 2278 A6
12400 JfnC 80465 2277 C6
W Layton Wy
7400 LKWD 80123 2278 E7
7600 DNVR 80123 2278 E7
7600 JfnC 80123 2278 E7
Lazy K Dr
3900 CSRK 80104 2703 E2
E Lazy U Ranch Pl
20000 DgsC 80134 2537 E5
Lazy Z Rd
10 BldC 80466 1766 E4
10 BldC 80466 1767 A4
2100 BldC 80466 1768 A4
Leader Cir
500 LSVL 80027 1689 C5
Lead King Dr
200 DgsC 80108 2618 C3
Lead Queen Dr
200 DgsC 80108 2618 C3
Leaf Ct
4800 DNVR 80216 2028 E6
S Leavenworth Dr
11600 JfnC 80433 2524 E3
W Leawood Dr
5200 AphC 80123 2363 B2
5200 LITN 80123 2363 B2
Lebrun Ct
7500 DgsC 80124 2450 D6
Ledge Rock Dr
16400 DgsC 80134 2452 E5
Le Duc Dr
5100 DgsC 80108 2618 E7
5100 DgsC 80108 2619 A6
Le Duc Ln
5100 DgsC 80108 2618 E6
5100 DgsC 80108 2619 A6
Lee Cir
3800 WTRG 80033 2110 A1
4700 BLDR 80303 1687 C3
Lee Ct
7200 ARVD 80004 1942 A7
8000 ARVD 80005 1942 A5
S Lee Ct
700 LKWD 80226 2194 A3
1400 LKWD 80232 2194 A5
2400 LKWD 80227 2194 B7
3600 JfnC 80235 2278 A4
4500 JfnC 80127 2278 B6
5700 JfnC 80127 2362 A2
6500 CTNL 80121 2364 E3
6600 CTNL 80122 2364 E3
Lee Dr
8000 ARVD 80005 1942 A5
S Lee Dr
5400 JfnC 80439 2357 C2
Lee Ln
10000 LKWD 80215 2110 A4
Lee Rd
29000 JfnC 80439 2357 B2
Lee St
- ARVD 80033 2026 A5
800 LSVL 80027 1689 D7
1000 LKWD 80215 2110 A6
3500 WTRG 80033 2110 A1
6400 ARVD 80004 2026 A2
6900 ARVD 80004 1942 A7
7900 ARVD 80005 1942 A5
10000 WSTR 80021 1858 A7
N Lee St
4400 WTRG 80033 2026 A7
S Lee St
500 LKWD 80226 2194 A3
1500 LKWD 80232 2194 A6
3800 JfnC 80235 2278 A4
5000 JfnC 80127 2278 A7
5500 JfnC 80127 2362 A1
Lee Wy
1000 LGMT 80501 1356 A7
S Lee Wy
5900 JfnC 80127 2362 B2
Leeds St
- LNTR 80134 2451 E5
Lee Hill Dr
10 BldC 80302 1602 B2
10 BLDR 80302 1602 B2
200 BLDR 80304 1602 B2
1300 BldC 80302 1601 E1
4800 BldC 80302 1516 E6
4800 BldC 80302 1517 A6
4800 BldC 80455 1516 E6
Lee Hill Rd
1200 BLDR 80304 1602 C3
1500 BldC 80301 1602 C3
1500 BLDR 80301 1602 C3
Lees Ln
5900 DgsC 80118 2868 D7
Lees Wy
23000 JfnC 80433 2694 E6
Leesburg Ct
8200 EbtC 80107 2543 A2
Leesburg Rd
12500 PARK 80134 2537 D3
Leetsdale Dr
10 DNVR 80209 2197 E2
4400 DNVR 80246 2197 E2
4400 GNDL 80246 2197 E2
4600 DNVR 80246 2198 C3
4600 GNDL 80246 2198 C3
6900 AphC 80247 2198 C3
6900 DNVR 80224 2198 C3
6900 DNVR 80247 2198 C3
Leetsdale Dr SR-83
10 DNVR 80209 2197 E2
4400 DNVR 80246 2197 E2
4400 GNDL 80246 2197 E2
4600 DNVR 80246 2198 C3
4600 GNDL 80246 2198 C3
5500 DNVR 80224 2198 C3
6900 AphC 80247 2198 C3
6900 DNVR 80247 2198 C3
Left Fork Rd
10 BldC 80302 1600 A7
10 BldC 80302 1684 A1
Left Hand Cir
6700 BldC 80301 1604 B1
6700 BLDR 80301 1604 B1
Lefthand Cir
1800 LGMT 80501 1438 D6
Lefthand Dr
1100 LGMT 80501 1439 A6
1300 LGMT 80501 1438 E6
Lefthand Canyon Dr
10 BldC 80302 1435 A7
10 BldC 80503 1435 A7
800 BldC 80302 1517 C4
800 BldC 80302 1518 A1
3500 BldC 80302 1516 D6
3500 BldC 80455 1516 D6
7700 BldC 80455 1600 A1
8900 BldC 80455 1599 B2
10000 BldC 80455 1597 E4
10000 BldC 80455 1598 C3
Legacy Dr
- BldC 80503 1438 C4
- LGMT 80503 1438 C4
Legacy Ridge Ct
10800 WSTR 80031 1859 E5
Legacy Ridge Pkwy
3500 WSTR 80031 1859 D4
Legacy Ridge Wy
10800 WSTR 80031 1859 E5
S Legault Ln
10500 JfnC 80433 2442 E7
10500 JfnC 80433 2526 D1
E Legend Av
19100 PARK 80134 2537 D5
19200 DgsC 80134 2537 D5
E Legend Ct
19200 PARK 80134 2537 D6
Legend Tr
13700 BMFD 80020 1775 D4
Legend Wy
13700 BMFD 80020 1775 D4
Legend Ridge Tr
- BldC 80503 1521 B6
E Lehigh Av
- AphC 80013 2285 E3
- AphC 80013 2286 A3
- AphC 80014 2284 A4
- AURA 80014 2284 B3
- AURA 80018 2286 A3
- CHLV 80113 2281 A4
- EGLD 80113 2281 A4
10 EGLD 80110 2280 E4
10 EGLD 80113 2280 E4
5000 DNVR 80237 2282 A4
8900 DNVR 80014 2283 A4
8900 DNVR 80237 2283 A4
8900 GDVL 80014 2283 A4
15300 AURA 80013 2284 D3
18600 AURA 80013 2285 C3
W Lehigh Av
- DNVR 80236 2279 C4
10 EGLD 80110 2280 D4
10 EGLD 80113 2280 D4
3300 SRDN 80110 2279 E4
3300 SRDN 80236 2279 E4
5200 DNVR 80235 2279 C4
10000 JfnC 80235 2278 A4
Lehigh Cir
- ERIE 80516 1607 D6
E Lehigh Cir
15900 AURA 80013 2284 D3
E Lehigh Dr
8000 DNVR 80237 2282 E4
Lehigh Ln
5100 DgsC 80135 2616 B5
Lehigh Pl
- AURA 80018 2286 C3
E Lehigh Pl
- AphC 80013 2286 A4
8200 DNVR 80237 2282 E4
17800 AURA 80013 2285 B3
20100 AphC 80013 2285 E3
21700 AURA 80018 2286 B3
W Lehigh Pl
1200 EGLD 80110 2280 C4
10500 JfnC 80235 2278 A4
Lehigh St
1000 BLDR 80305 1686 E7
1300 BLDR 80305 1770 E1
1800 BLDR 80305 1771 A2
W Lehow Av
10 EGLD 80110 2280 D7
10 EGLD 80113 2280 D7
10 LITN 80110 2280 D7
10 LITN 80120 2280 D7
Leicester Ct
6900 DgsC 80108 2618 E1
Leicester Ln
500 DgsC 80108 2618 E1
S Lemasters Dr
4700 JfnC 80439 2272 E7
S Lemasters Rd
4800 JfnC 80439 2272 E7
5200 JfnC 80439 2356 E1
Lemon Ct
- CSRK 80109 2702 E4
Lemon Pl
- BLDR 80304 1602 C3
Lemon Grass Pl
- CSRK 80109 2702 B4
Lemon Gulch Dr
5200 DgsC 80108 2620 B4
7000 DgsC 80108 2536 B7
Lemon Gulch Rd
5200 DgsC 80108 2620 C3
Lemon Gulch Wy
7100 DgsC 80108 2536 C7
7100 DgsC 80108 2620 B1
S Lenaview Cir
2000 AphC 80102 2209 B5
Lenox Ct
5300 CSRK 80104 2788 E2
Leo Ct
13600 DgsC 80124 2450 D2
Leo Ln
400 TNTN 80260 1944 D4
700 FLHT 80260 1944 D4
Leon Dr
11900 JfnC 80433 2524 E4
Leon Ln
10 BldC 80403 1852 A2
10 GpnC 80403 1851 E2
Leona Dr
400 AdmC 80221 1944 D5
Leonard Ln
10 NHGN 80233 1860 E4
Leonards Rd
10 BldC 80302 1601 B6
Leon A Wurl Pkwy
- WldC 80516 1607 D5
11900 ERIE 80516 1606 E6
11900 ERIE 80516 1607 A6
Leon A Wurl Pkwy CO-8
- ERIE 80516 1607 D5
- WldC 80516 1607 D5
Leopard Dr
7000 DgsC 80124 2450 D7
Leopard Gate
7000 DgsC 80124 2450 D7
Leroy Dr
800 NHGN 80233 1861 B5
N Lessig St
38500 AdmC 80137 2121 A4
Letcher St
- GpnC 80403 2017 A5
Levi Cir
12200 AdmC 80640 1863 E1
Lewark Av
10 BldC 80403 1852 A1
Lewis Cir
10700 WSTR 80021 1858 A6
S Lewis Cir
4700 JfnC 80127 2278 A6
Lewis Ct
1800 LKWD 80215 2110 A4
6100 ARVD 80004 2026 A3
8400 ARVD 80005 1942 A3
10700 WSTR 80021 1858 A5
N Lewis Ct
6200 DgsC 80134 2622 D2
S Lewis Ct
3700 JfnC 80235 2278 A4
4700 JfnC 80127 2278 A6
6800 JfnC 80127 2362 A5
8400 JfnC 80127 2446 A1
Lewis Dr
800 LKWD 80215 2110 A6
Lewis Ln
1100 BldC 80503 1269 E4
31700 JfnC 80439 2356 E1
S Lewis Ln
2400 LKWD 80227 2194 B7
Lewis St
- ARVD 80002 2026 A4
10 CSRK 80104 2703 D6
2300 LKWD 80215 2110 A4
3500 WTRG 80033 2110 A1
6500 ARVD 80004 2026 A2
7500 ARVD 80005 1942 A6
10700 WSTR 80021 1858 A5
S Lewis St
10 CSRK 80104 2703 D7
300 LKWD 80226 2194 A2
5700 JfnC 80127 2362 A2
S Lewis Wy
2500 LKWD 80227 2278 A1
7100 JfnC 80127 2362 A5
8500 JfnC 80127 2446 A1
Lewis Ridge Rd
29800 JfnC 80439 2273 B2
S Lewiston Cir
4100 AURA 80013 2284 E4
Lewiston Ct
5500 DNVR 80239 2032 E4
S Lewiston Ct
1400 AURA 80017 2200 E4
5300 CTNL 80015 2284 E7
5600 CTNL 80015 2368 E1
6000 AphC 80016 2368 E2
Lewiston St
- DNVR 80239 2032 E7
- DvrC 80239 2032 E7
1800 AURA 80011 2116 E4
3800 AURA 80011 2032 E7
10700 CMCY 80022 1864 D5
11700 CMCY 80603 1864 D2
S Lewiston St
1100 AURA 80017 2200 E4
2100 AURA 80013 2200 E6
3600 AURA 80013 2284 E3
5300 CTNL 80015 2284 E7
5500 CTNL 80015 2368 E1
5900 CTNL 80016 2368 E2
7400 AphC 80016 2368 E6
S Lewiston Wy
- FXFD 80016 2368 E3
1000 AURA 80017 2200 E4
3500 AURA 80013 2284 E3
4500 AURA 80015 2284 E5
5100 CTNL 80015 2284 E7
6300 AphC 80016 2368 E3
6500 CTNL 80016 2368 E3
Lewistown Ct
14400 AdmC 80601 1780 D2
14400 BGTN 80601 1780 D2
Lewistown St
11200 AdmC 80022 1864 E3
Lexi Cir
4200 BMFD 80020 1775 C3
N Lexington Av
800 WSTR 80020 1776 C4
Lexington Cir
14000 BMFD 80020 1776 B4
14000 WSTR 80020 1776 B4
N Lexington Dr
13900 WSTR 80020 1776 C4
N Lexington Pl
13800 WSTR 80020 1776 C4
Lexington St
2400 LAFT 80026 1689 D3
Leyden Cir
11300 TNTN 80233 1862 B3
Leyden Ct
- TNTN 80602 1778 B5
12000 AdmC 80602 1862 B2
S Leyden Ct
6700 CTNL 80112 2366 C4
8200 CTNL 80112 2450 C1
Leyden Ln
7600 AdmC 80022 1946 B6
Leyden Rd
14800 JfnC 80007 1940 D5
Leyden Rd CO-80
14800 JfnC 80007 1940 D5
Leyden St
- AdmC 80602 1694 B5
100 DNVR 80220 2198 B1
1700 DNVR 80220 2114 B4
1900 DNVR 80207 2114 B4
4600 CMCY 80216 2030 B6
4600 DNVR 80022 2030 B6
4600 DNVR 80216 2030 B6
6800 CMCY 80022 2030 B1
7300 CMCY 80022 1946 B6
7700 AdmC 80022 1946 B5
11300 TNTN 80233 1862 B3
12000 AdmC 80602 1862 B2
12900 TNTN 80602 1778 B6
S Leyden St
700 DNVR 80224 2198 B4
2300 AphC 80222 2198 B7
2400 DNVR 80222 2198 B7
3000 AphC 80222 2282 B2
3200 DNVR 80222 2282 B2
5900 CTNL 80111 2366 C2
8000 CTNL 80112 2366 C7
Leyden Wy
- TNTN 80233 1862 B3
Leyner Dr
1300 ERIE 80516 1607 A6
Libby Dr
- BLDR 80302 1686 E3
Liberty Blvd
12300 DgsC 80112 2451 E2
13000 DgsC 80112 2452 A2
Liberty Cir
8900 DgsC 80112 2451 E2
Liberty Ct
200 ELIZ 80107 2709 B7
1500 LGMT 80501 1356 C7
Liberty Pl
- DgsC 80112 2451 E2
Liberty St
300 EbtC 80107 2709 B7
300 ELIZ 80107 2709 B7
Liberty Wy
- DgsC 80112 2451 E2
Libra Ct
13600 DgsC 80124 2450 D2
Library Ln
- LITN 80120 2364 C2
Lichen Ln
10 BldC 80403 1852 E2
Lichen Pl
5200 BldC 80301 1604 C1
Lickskillet Rd
10 BldC 80302 1599 D2
100 BldC 80455 1599 D2
Licorice Ct
3800 CSRK 80109 2618 D7
3800 CSRK 80109 2702 D1
Licorice Tr
3700 CSRK 80109 2618 D7
3700 CSRK 80109 2702 D1
Lieter Pl
10500 DgsC 80124 2450 D7
N Liggett Rd
1900 CSRK 80104 2703 C3
1900 CSRK 80109 2703 C3
Light Ln
10400 JfnC 80433 2442 A6
Lightening Ln
30100 JfnC 80439 2273 B2
E Lightning View Dr
8100 DgsC 80134 2622 B3
Lila Dr
31800 JfnC 80433 2440 D3
Lilac Cir
200 LSVL 80027 1773 C2
300 LCHB 80603 1698 B2
1000 BMFD 80020 1774 B7
2500 ERIE 80516 1692 B3
Lilac Ct
400 LSVL 80027 1773 C2
1000 BMFD 80020 1774 B7
W Lilac Ct
600 LSVL 80027 1773 B2
Lilac Dr
1000 LCHB 80603 1698 C2
W Lilac Dr
300 LCHB 80603 1698 C2
300 WldC 80603 1698 C2
Lilac Ln
5200 AdmC 80221 2028 A5
5200 DNVR 80221 2028 A5
Lilac Pl
800 LAFT 80026 1690 B6
Lilac St
800 BMFD 80020 1774 B7
900 LGMT 80501 1438 E1
13800 TNTN 80602 1778 B4
Lilhaven Ln
- CBVL 80123 2363 E3
- LITN 80123 2363 E3
W Lilley Av
1000 LITN 80120 2364 C2
Lillian Ln
9400 TNTN 80229 1945 B1
Lillis Dr
11700 JfnC 80403 1852 D3
Lillis Ln
11500 JfnC 80403 1852 D3
Lillis Pl
31700 JfnC 80403 1852 D3
Lillis Wy
- JfnC 80403 1852 E3
Lilly Ct
9300 TNTN 80229 1945 A1
Lilly Dr
1800 TNTN 80229 1945 B3
Lilly Gulch Tr
4200 CSRK 80109 2702 C2
E Lily Ct
900 DgsC 80126 2449 A3
Lily Ln
200 GOLD 80403 2107 E2
Lily Pad Ln
- LKWD 80226 2194 E2
Lima Cir
- CMCY 80022 1863 C7
S Lima Cir
400 AURA 80012 2199 D2
2300 AURA 80014 2199 D7
Lima Ct
11400 CMCY 80640 1863 C3
S Lima Ct
1400 AURA 80012 2199 D5
2200 AURA 80014 2199 D7
Lima St
- DNVR 80010 2115 D3
- DvrC 80010 2115 D3
10 AURA 80010 2199 C1
10 AURA 80012 2199 C1
1400 AURA 80010 2115 D5
3700 AdmC 80239 2115 D1
3700 AURA 80239 2115 D1
3700 DNVR 80239 2115 D1
4700 DNVR 80239 2031 C5
11200 CMCY 80640 1863 C3
12300 AdmC 80602 1695 C6
S Lima St
- AURA 80012 2199 D2
1800 AURA 80014 2199 D7
2600 AURA 80014 2283 C1

STREET
Block City ZIP Map# Grid

S Lima St
5600 AphC 80111 2367 D1
6400 CTNL 80111 2367 D3
6600 CTNL 80112 2367 D5
6700 AphC 80112 2367 D5
S Lima Wy
2400 AURA 80014 2199 D7
5900 AphC 80111 2367 D2
Limber Wy
- LNTR 80124 2450 E4
Limberpine Ln
- AURA 80016 2370 E5
Limestone Ct
10200 DgsC 80134 2452 D6
Limestone Pl
2700 SUPE 80027 1773 A7
Lincoln Av
100 LSVL 80027 1689 C7
100 LSVL 80027 1773 C1
23800 JfnC 80433 2694 E5
E Lincoln Av
- DgsC 80124 2450 E5
- DgsC 80130 2450 E5
- DgsC 80138 2453 D5
- PARK 80138 2453 D5
100 BNNT 80102 2124 D1
1000 DgsC 80134 2451 D5
1000 LNTR 80134 2451 D5
1200 DgsC 80112 2451 D5
2500 LNTR 80134 2452 A5
3700 DgsC 80134 2452 E5
8600 LNTR 80124 2450 E5
8600 LNTR 80124 2451 B5
16500 DgsC 80134 2453 A5
16900 PARK 80134 2453 A5
S Lincoln Av
200 LSVL 80027 1773 C2
W Lincoln Av
100 BNNT 80102 2124 D1
Lincoln Cir
100 LSVL 80027 1773 C1
1400 LGMT 80501 1356 A6
Lincoln Ct
300 LSVL 80027 1773 C1
1600 LGMT 80501 1356 A6
10400 NHGN 80233 1860 E6
S Lincoln Ct
7800 LITN 80122 2364 E7
Lincoln Dr
1800 LGMT 80501 1355 E6
1800 LGMT 80501 1356 A6
5700 AdmC 80216 2028 E4
11300 NHGN 80233 1860 E3
Lincoln Pl
10 LGMT 80501 1439 A3
1600 BLDR 80302 1686 C2
Lincoln St
- DNVR 80205 2112 E6
- TNTN 80241 1776 E7
10 DNVR 80203 2196 E1
10 DNVR 80209 2196 E1
100 ELIZ 80107 2709 B7
300 DNVR 80203 2112 E6
800 LGMT 80501 1439 A1
1400 DNVR 80202 2112 E6
2100 LGMT 80501 1355 E4
2100 LGMT 80501 1356 A5
5200 DNVR 80216 2028 E4
5400 AdmC 80216 2028 E4
11700 NHGN 80233 1860 E3
S Lincoln St
- DNVR 80223 2196 E3
10 DNVR 80203 2196 E3
10 DNVR 80209 2196 E3
700 LGMT 80501 1439 A4
1100 DNVR 80210 2196 E4
2500 DNVR 80210 2280 E2
2600 DvrC 80210 2280 E2
2600 EGLD 80113 2280 E2
6500 CTNL 80121 2364 E4
6600 CTNL 80122 2364 E4
7000 LITN 80122 2364 E5
8000 LITN 80122 2448 E1
Lincoln Wy
7600 AdmC 80221 1944 D6
S Lincoln Wy
7100 CTNL 80122 2364 E5
7100 LITN 80120 2364 E5
Lincoln Meadows Pkwy
- PARK 80134 2453 B5
Lincoln Mountain Dr
- CSRK 80109 2703 B5
Lincoln Park Homes
- DNVR 80204 2112 C5
Linda Cir
7800 AdmC 80221 1944 D5
Linda Ln
100 AdmC 80221 1944 D6
S Linda Ln
900 JfnC 80439 2189 B4
Linda Tr
10 PrkC 80456 2606 D7
Lindark St
15000 AdmC 80603 1784 B1
Linda Sue Ln
10 NHGN 80233 1860 E4
Linda Vista
12600 BldC 80504 1357 A4
Linda Vista Dr
2100 LKWD 80215 2110 A3
10700 LKWD 80215 2109 E3
Lindbergh Rd
19800 JfnC 80465 2359 D3
Linden Av
10 BldC 80304 1602 B6
10 BLDR 80304 1602 B6
Linden Cir
1100 BLDR 80304 1602 C6
E Linden Cir
4100 GDVL 80121 2365 E1
Linden Ct
5200 GDVL 80121 2366 A2
13800 TNTN 80602 1778 B4
S Linden Ct
1900 DNVR 80224 2198 C6
2300 DNVR 80222 2198 B7
2600 DNVR 80222 2282 C1
Linden Dr
10 BldC 80304 1602 A5
1500 BldC 80304 1601 E4
S Linden Dr
5000 EGLD 80110 2279 E7
5000 LITN 80123 2279 E7
E Linden Ln
4000 GDVL 80121 2365 E1
4000 GDVL 80121 2366 A1
Linden Pl
2200 ERIE 80516 1691 E2
Linden St
1700 LGMT 80501 1355 E6
W Linden St
500 LSVL 80027 1689 B6
800 BldC 80027 1689 A6
Linden Wy
1400 ERIE 80516 1691 E2
S Linden Wy
1800 DNVR 80224 2198 C6
Linden Park Ct
500 BLDR 80304 1602 B6
Linden Park Dr
500 BLDR 80304 1602 B6
Lindenwood Ct
500 DgsC 80126 2448 D3
500 DgsC 80126 2449 A3
Lindenwood Dr
10 LITN 80120 2364 C4
Lindenwood Ln
10 JfnC 80127 2360 E7
10 JfnC 80127 2361 A7
Lindon Dr
17300 PARK 80134 2537 A1
Lindsey Cir
900 EbtC 80138 2540 B4
Lindsey Rd
400 JfnC 80401 2107 A7
1600 TNTN 80260 1860 B7
S Lindsey Rd
11000 JfnC 80433 2526 A1
S Lindsey St
10 CSRK 80104 2704 D7
600 CSRK 80104 2788 D1
Lindsey Peak Ln
- DgsC 80108 2618 E3
- DgsC 80108 2619 A3
Lines Ln
- JfnC 80457 2274 B3
S Lininger Dr
1100 JfnC 80401 2191 A5
E Links Cir
- CTNL 80112 2366 A6
4800 CTNL 80122 2366 A6
Links Dr
2800 BLDR 80301 1603 A6
E Links Dr
4600 CTNL 80122 2365 E7
4600 CTNL 80122 2366 A7
E Links Pkwy
4000 CTNL 80122 2365 E6
4600 CTNL 80122 2366 A7
Links Pl
2200 ERIE 80516 1691 D3
E Links Pl
23600 AURA 80016 2370 D6
Linley Ct
800 DNVR 80204 2111 E6
S Linley Ct
2200 DNVR 80219 2195 E7
2500 DNVR 80219 2279 E1
2800 DNVR 80236 2279 E2
Linn Ln
10 BldC 80403 1852 A2
Linn Rd
10 PrkC 80456 2521 D2
S Linn St
9700 JfnC 80433 2442 B5
E Linvale Av
15800 AURA 80013 2284 E1
E Linvale Cir
18700 AURA 80013 2285 C1
E Linvale Dr
11000 AURA 80014 2283 C1
18100 AURA 80013 2285 B1
E Linvale Pl
2700 DNVR 80210 2281 C1
8000 DNVR 80231 2282 E1
13900 AURA 80014 2284 B1
15700 AURA 80013 2284 D1
19200 AURA 80013 2285 D1
W Linvale Pl
5200 DNVR 80236 2279 C1
6500 DNVR 80227 2279 A1
7000 DNVR 80227 2278 E1
Lion Pt
10 BldC 80302 1601 E2
Lionel Ln
100 ELIZ 80107 2709 B7
11700 JfnC 80403 1852 C3
E Lions Pt
6200 DgsC 80124 2450 C6
S Lions Pth
10300 DgsC 80124 2450 C6
Lionsbrooke Dr
- PrkC 80470 2523 B1
Lions Head Dr
10 PrkC 80470 2523 E5
E Lionshead Pkwy
6500 DgsC 80124 2450 C7
Lionshead Tr
- DgsC 80124 2450 C6
- DgsC 80130 2450 C6
S Lions Heart
10300 DgsC 80124 2450 C6
Lions Paw St
- CSRK 80104 2787 E4
4600 DgsC 80104 2787 E4
Lipan Ct
8400 FLHT 80260 1944 C4
8900 TNTN 80260 1944 C2
13900 WSTR 80020 1776 C4
N Lipan Ct
12400 WSTR 80234 1860 C1
S Lipan Ct
4500 EGLD 80110 2280 C6
Lipan Dr
1100 AdmC 80221 1944 C6
S Lipan Dr
4900 EGLD 80110 2280 C7
Lipan St
- AdmC 80020 1776 C2
10 DNVR 80223 2196 C1
400 DNVR 80223 2112 C7
500 DNVR 80204 2112 C6
3400 DNVR 80211 2112 C1
4000 DNVR 80211 2028 C7
7200 AdmC 80221 1944 C7
8400 FLHT 80260 1944 C4
8800 TNTN 80260 1944 C3
10400 NHGN 80234 1860 C6
14400 WSTR 80020 1776 C3
15200 AdmC 80020 1692 C7
S Lipan St
200 DNVR 80223 2196 C2
2900 EGLD 80110 2280 C2
Lipan Wy
100 BLDR 80303 1687 B5
Lisbon Ct
4800 DNVR 80249 2033 E6
S Lisbon Ct
3200 AURA 80013 2286 A2
3700 AphC 80013 2286 A3
4700 AphC 80015 2286 A6
5600 CTNL 80015 2370 A1
6500 AphC 80016 2370 A3
7100 CTNL 80016 2370 A5
Lisbon Dr
1200 EbtC 80138 2540 B6
S Lisbon Ln
- AphC 80015 2286 A7
5400 CTNL 80015 2286 A7
5400 CTNL 80015 2370 A1
Lisbon St
- DNVR 80249 2034 B7
1600 AURA 80011 2117 E4
4200 DNVR 80249 2033 E6
S Lisbon St
3500 AphC 80013 2286 A3
5400 CTNL 80015 2286 A7
5400 CTNL 80015 2370 A1
S Lisbon Wy
- AURA 80013 2285 E1
- AURA 80013 2286 A1
3700 AphC 80013 2286 A3
4100 AphC 80013 2285 D4
4700 AphC 80015 2285 E5
4700 AphC 80015 2286 A6
5100 CTNL 80015 2285 E7
5100 CTNL 80015 2286 A7
5600 CTNL 80015 2370 A1
5800 CTNL 80015 2369 E1
Lismore Wy
10700 DgsC 80126 2449 C7
Lithgow
- DgsC 80130 2450 A5
Little Bear Ct
1800 LGMT 80501 1356 C6
32300 JfnC 80439 2188 D6
Little Bear Dr
1700 LGMT 80501 1356 C6
Little Bear Ln
3800 DgsC 80135 2701 C7
3800 DgsC 80135 2785 C1
Little Bear Rd
2000 TNTN 80260 1860 B6
Little Bear Creek Rd
10 CCkC 80452 2186 B6
2400 CCkC 80452 2185 E2
4600 CCkC 80452 2101 C7
Little Berry Tr
34100 JfnC 80439 2188 B2
Little Big Horn Dr
27700 JfnC 80439 2441 D1
Little Bluestem Wy
8600 PARK 80134 2453 B2
Little Canyon Dr
16300 JfnC 80465 2360 D2
Little Cub Rd
32400 JfnC 80439 2356 C6
S Little Cub Creek Rd
4800 JfnC 80439 2273 E7
5200 JfnC 80439 2357 E1
5200 JfnC 80439 2358 A2
Little Dry Cr
- EbtC 80107 2710 A7
Little Fawn Wy
7200 DgsC 80125 2615 B1
Little Fox Ct
500 LGMT 80501 1440 A2
S Little Gull Ct
8700 DgsC 80126 2450 A2
W Little Haystack Mtn
12100 JfnC 80127 2361 D5
Little John Ct
1300 LAFT 80026 1690 D6
Little Leaf Ct
900 LGMT 80503 1438 A5
Little League Ln
- BldC 80503 1520 D6
Little Raven St
1400 DNVR 80202 2112 C3
1400 DNVR 80204 2112 B3
Little Raven Tr
8900 BldC 80503 1521 B6
Little Raven Wy
- BMFD 80020 1775 C6
Littleridge Ln
10 CHLV 80113 2281 B3
S Little River Ct
- AURA 80016 2371 B2
Little River St
- AURA 80018 2119 B7
S Little River Wy
- AURA 80016 2371 B2
S Little Rock Wy
8400 DgsC 80126 2449 E1
Little Springs Ln
10 PrkC 80456 2607 D5
Little Squaw Pass Rd
10 CCkC 80439 2187 E5
Little Sunflower Pl
8600 PARK 80134 2453 B2
E Littleton Blvd
10 CTNL 80121 2364 E1
10 LITN 80121 2364 E1
600 CTNL 80121 2365 A1
600 GDVL 80121 2365 A1
600 LITN 80121 2365 A1
W Littleton Blvd
- LITN 80120 2364 C1
10 LITN 80121 2364 C1
W Littleton Blvd SR-75
- LITN 80120 2364 C1
Little Turtle Ln
11700 JfnC 80433 2526 B3
Little Willow Ct
10200 DgsC 80125 2530 E6
Lively Ct
- LYNS 80540 1352 E3
Liverpool Cir
8200 DgsC 80125 2531 A5
8300 DgsC 80125 2530 E5
S Liverpool Cir
4700 AphC 80015 2285 E6
4700 AphC 80015 2286 A6
Liverpool Ct
4300 DNVR 80249 2034 A6
S Liverpool Ct
4700 AphC 80015 2286 A6
Liverpool St
800 AphC 80018 2118 A6
800 AURA 80011 2118 A6
4000 DNVR 80249 2034 A7
4300 DNVR 80249 2033 E6
S Liverpool St
- AphC 80013 2286 A4
- AURA 80013 2286 A3
6000 AphC 80016 2370 A3
6000 CTNL 80015 2370 A3
6000 CTNL 80016 2370 A3
6600 AURA 80016 2370 A4
S Liverpool St CO-67
6000 AphC 80016 2370 A3
6000 CTNL 80015 2370 A3
6000 CTNL 80016 2370 A3
6600 AURA 80016 2370 A3
E Liverpool Wy
- AURA 80011 2118 A4
S Liverpool Wy
- AphC 80013 2286 A4
- AphC 80015 2285 E6
- AphC 80015 2286 A7
3200 AURA 80013 2286 A3
5100 CTNL 80015 2286 A7
Livingston Dr
10400 NHGN 80260 1860 C6
11100 NHGN 80234 1860 C4
11100 WSTR 80234 1860 C4
Lloyd Cir
2600 BLDR 80304 1602 E6
Loblolly Pine Cir
47200 EbtC 80138 2456 A2
Loch Lomond Av
1300 BMFD 80020 1859 B1
Lochmore Dr
1800 LGMT 80501 1357 A5
1900 LGMT 80501 1356 E5
Loch Ness Av
1100 BMFD 80020 1859 B1
Lock St
1200 LSVL 80027 1773 D1
E Lockheed Dr
15900 AURA 80011 2116 D7
Locksley St
- LAFT 80026 1690 E6
Lockwood St
100 CSRK 80104 2704 D7
Loco Ln
4200 JfnC 80439 2273 E5
Locust Av
600 BLDR 80304 1602 B4
E Locust Av
500 LCHB 80603 1698 C3
W Locust Av
100 LCHB 80603 1698 B3
S Locust Cir
6000 CTNL 80111 2366 C2
7000 CTNL 80112 2366 C5
Locust Ct
7800 CMCY 80022 1946 B5
12000 AdmC 80602 1862 B2
13700 TNTN 80602 1778 B4
S Locust Ct
6100 CTNL 80111 2366 C3
6700 CTNL 80112 2366 C4
W Locust Ct
600 LSVL 80027 1689 B6
Locust Dr
8100 DgsC 80125 2530 E6
Locust Ln
200 DNVR 80220 2114 C7
200 DNVR 80220 2198 B1
Locust Pl
400 BLDR 80304 1602 B4
900 TNTN 80229 1945 A2
12500 TNTN 80602 1862 B1
S Locust Pl
7000 CTNL 80112 2366 C5
Locust St
10 DNVR 80220 2198 C1
600 DNVR 80220 2114 B6
3200 DNVR 80207 2114 B1
6000 CMCY 80022 2030 B3
7200 CMCY 80022 1946 B7
7700 AdmC 80022 1946 B5
11200 TNTN 80233 1862 B3
12000 AdmC 80602 1862 B2
13800 TNTN 80602 1778 B4
S Locust St
100 DNVR 80224 2198 B2
2300 DNVR 80222 2198 C7
3200 AphC 80222 2282 B2
3200 DNVR 80222 2282 B2
3400 DNVR 80237 2282 B2
5400 GDVL 80111 2366 C1
6000 CTNL 80111 2366 C3
7600 CTNL 80112 2366 C6
8200 CTNL 80112 2450 C1
Locust Wy
- TNTN 80602 1778 B7
12500 TNTN 80602 1862 B1
S Locust Wy
6300 CTNL 80111 2366 C4
8200 CTNL 80112 2450 C1
Lode Ct
- BLDR 80303 1687 D3
Lode Stone Wy
10100 DgsC 80134 2452 E6
Lodge Ct
1400 BLDR 80303 1687 D3
Lodge Ln
1400 BLDR 80303 1687 D3
Lodge Pl
5400 BLDR 80303 1687 D3
Lodgepole Cir
10 CCkC 80439 2187 C7
32500 JfnC 80439 2356 C6
Lodgepole Ct
- CCkC 80439 2187 D7
6900 BldC 80301 1604 B3
7100 JfnC 80439 2356 C5
Lodge Pole Dr
10 GpnC 80403 1934 D4
Lodgepole Dr
10 CCkC 80439 2187 C7
10 PrkC 80470 2524 A4
800 CCkC 80439 2271 D1
1800 ERIE 80516 1692 A3
31700 JfnC 80439 2356 D6
Lodgepole Ln
100 GpnC 80403 1933 E6
Lodgepole Tr
7900 LNTR 80124 2450 E3
Lodge Pole Wy
10 GpnC 80403 1934 C5
Lodgewood Ln
300 LAFT 80026 1689 D4
Lodgewood Pt
300 LAFT 80026 1689 D4
Lofton Ct
1400 AdmC 80221 1944 C5
Log Tr
26800 JfnC 80433 2525 E3
26800 JfnC 80433 2526 A2
Logan Av
23700 JfnC 80433 2694 E5
Logan Blvd
- DNVR 80235 2279 C4
- DNVR 80236 2279 C4
E Logan Cir
900 GDVL 80121 2281 A7
Logan Ct
5600 AdmC 80216 2028 E4
10600 NHGN 80233 1860 E5
S Logan Ct
5900 CTNL 80121 2364 E2
8000 LITN 80122 2365 A7
8200 LITN 80122 2449 A1
S Logan Dr
- LITN 80122 2449 B1
5100 GDVL 80121 2281 A7
5300 GDVL 80121 2365 A1
7500 LITN 80122 2364 E6
7600 LITN 80122 2365 B6
7900 LITN 80122 2448 E1
Logan Ln
2100 LGMT 80501 1355 E5
S Logan Pl
6100 CTNL 80121 2364 E3
Logan St
10 DNVR 80203 2196 E1
10 DNVR 80209 2196 E1
300 DNVR 80203 2112 E7
1800 LGMT 80501 1355 E6
1900 DNVR 80205 2112 E5
5100 DNVR 80216 2028 E5
5600 AdmC 80216 2028 E4
8100 AdmC 80229 1944 E4
8100 TNTN 80229 1944 E4
9800 TNTN 80229 1860 E7
11700 NHGN 80233 1860 E3
13000 TNTN 80241 1776 E6
E Logan St
100 ELIZ 80107 2709 B7
S Logan St
- GDVL 80121 2281 A7
10 DNVR 80203 2196 E2
10 DNVR 80209 2196 E2
1000 DNVR 80210 2196 E5
2500 DNVR 80210 2280 E2
2600 AphC 80210 2280 E2
2600 EGLD 80113 2280 E2
5000 AphC 80121 2280 E7
5200 AphC 80121 2281 A7
5700 LITN 80121 2364 E1
5900 CTNL 80121 2364 E2
6500 CTNL 80121 2365 A3
6600 CTNL 80122 2364 E4
7700 LITN 80122 2364 E7
W Logan St
100 ELIZ 80107 2709 B7
S Logan Wy
7800 LITN 80122 2364 E7
Logan Mill Rd
10 BldC 80302 1600 C7
Loges Ln
31300 JfnC 80439 2188 E6
W Loggers Tr
23000 JfnC 80439 2358 E4
Logic Dr
3000 LGMT 80503 1438 B7
Lois Cir
100 LSVL 80027 1773 C1
Lois Ct
1700 LAFT 80026 1689 E2
W Lois Ct
700 LSVL 80027 1773 B1
Lois Dr
400 LSVL 80027 1773 D1
Lois Ln
5700 JfnC 80439 2357 B2
Lois Pl
10 LGMT 80501 1356 B6
Lois St
10 PrkC 80456 2521 E2
10 PrkC 80456 2522 A2
W Lois Wy
500 LSVL 80027 1773 B1
Loki Av
4700 BldC 80301 1603 B2
W Loma Cir
10 DgsC 80108 2535 A3
Loma Pl
2800 BldC 80301 1603 A5
2800 BLDR 80301 1603 A5
Loma Linda Dr
700 BGTN 80601 1696 D7
Lomand Cir
16000 AdmC 80602 1695 A5
Lombard St
2500 LAFT 80026 1689 D3
Lombardi St
1100 ERIE 80516 1607 A2
1400 BldC 80516 1607 A2
Lombardy Dr
1600 BLDR 80304 1602 C6
Lombardy Ln
900 LKWD 80215 2110 B6
Lombardy St
1700 LGMT 80503 1437 E6
Lo Meadow Ln
10 PrkC 80456 2607 E7
10 PrkC 80456 2608 A7
London Av
200 LAFT 80026 1690 B5
London Dr
41300 EbtC 80138 2540 A7
43300 DgsC 80138 2539 E3
S London Ln
8300 JfnC 80433 2440 D2
London Wy
42500 EbtC 80138 2540 B4
Lone Pn
11000 DgsC 80125 2530 D7
Lone Eagle Ct
5400 BLDR 80301 1604 B1
Lone Eagle Pt
300 LAFT 80026 1689 E3
Lone Eagle Rd
6400 JfnC 80403 2020 A2
Lone Iris Pl
9500 DgsC 80125 2531 B7
S Lone Lynx
10300 DgsC 80124 2450 C6
Lone Maple Ln
8100 LNTR 80124 2450 E3
Lone Oak Ct
8100 LNTR 80124 2450 E3
S Lone Peak Dr
5700 JfnC 80439 2358 D3
5700 JfnC 80465 2358 D3
Lone Peak Tr
23500 JfnC 80439 2358 D3
Lone Pine Dr
7600 JfnC 80403 1939 A4
Lonesome Dove Ct
31000 EbtC 80107 2792 D6
Lone Spruce Rd
30300 JfnC 80439 2189 B4
Lone Tree Pkwy
8500 LNTR 80124 2451 A3
9800 DgsC 80124 2450 D5
9900 LNTR 80124 2450 D5
E Long Av
- AphC 80016 2369 A6
2200 CTNL 80122 2365 C7
6800 CTNL 80112 2366 C7
7300 GDVL 80111 2366 D2
17100 CTNL 80016 2369 A6
19400 AURA 80016 2369 E6
25500 AphC 80016 2371 B6
26300 AURA 80016 2371 B6
W Long Av
- JfnC 80123 2362 B2
- LITN 80120 2364 B7
Long Cir
- AURA 80016 2371 C6
E Long Cir
500 LITN 80122 2364 E7
500 LITN 80122 2365 A7
7300 CTNL 80112 2366 D7
E Long Cir N
2800 CTNL 80122 2365 D7
6100 CTNL 80112 2366 C6
E Long Cir S
3000 CTNL 80122 2365 D7
6100 CTNL 80112 2366 B7
W Long Cir
2800 LITN 80120 2364 A7
E Long Ct
500 LITN 80122 2364 E7
500 LITN 80122 2365 A7
2800 CTNL 80121 2365 D1
2800 GDVL 80121 2365 D1
3800 CTNL 80122 2365 E7
8800 CTNL 80112 2367 A7
W Long Ct
1200 LITN 80120 2364 C7
8800 JfnC 80123 2362 B2
E Long Dr
2400 CTNL 80121 2365 C2
2400 GDVL 80121 2365 C2
22500 AURA 80016 2370 C7
W Long Dr
2700 LITN 80120 2364 A6
6400 JfnC 80123 2363 A1
8300 DNVR 80123 2362 D2
9600 JfnC 80123 2362 B2
E Long Ln
2400 CTNL 80121 2365 C1
2400 GDVL 80121 2365 C1
5200 CTNL 80122 2366 B7
19500 CTNL 80016 2369 D6
S Long Ln
5800 CTNL 80121 2365 C2
5800 GDVL 80121 2365 C2
Long Pl
- AURA 80016 2371 D6
E Long Pl
2700 CTNL 80122 2365 C7
5400 CTNL 80122 2366 B7
8100 CTNL 80112 2366 E6
8600 CTNL 80112 2367 A6
19700 CTNL 80016 2369 D7
23400 AURA 80016 2370 D6
W Long Pl
2600 LITN 80120 2364 B7
5600 JfnC 80123 2363 B2
Long Rd
10 CCkC 80452 2186 A5
E Long Rd
2400 GDVL 80121 2365 D2
3800 CTNL 80121 2365 E2
Long Spur
- JfnC 80127 2361 A5
Long Arrow Ln
23500 JfnC 80433 2526 E3
Longate Ln
9200 DgsC 80134 2452 D3
Long Bow Ct
1600 LAFT 80026 1690 D6
Longbow Ct
- BldC 80301 1603 E3
- BLDR 80301 1603 E3
Longbow Dr
5900 BLDR 80301 1603 E2
6200 BLDR 80301 1604 A2
Longbow Pl
900 DgsC 80118 2870 D7
Longdon St
1100 LGMT 80501 1356 C7
Long Elk Cir
- EbtC 80107 2626 A3
E Longfellow Ln
400 DgsC 80126 2448 E4
600 DgsC 80126 2449 A4
W Longfellow Pl
3000 AdmC 80221 2027 E2
Longford Ct
15600 DgsC 80134 2452 D3
Longford Dr
15600 DgsC 80134 2452 D3
Longford Wy
9500 DgsC 80134 2452 D4
Longhorn
4400 BWMR 80123 2279 C5
5200 DNVR 80236 2279 C5
Longhorn Cir
30500 EbtC 80107 2792 B7
Longhorn Dr
- BldC 80026 1606 C4
Longhorn Pl
5900 DgsC 80134 2621 C4
Longhorn Rd
3100 BldC 80302 1518 C7
3100 BLDR 80302 1518 C7
3200 BldC 80503 1518 D7
Longhurst Pl
500 BGTN 80601 1696 E7
Longleaf Dr
10300 DgsC 80134 2452 E6
10300 DgsC 80134 2453 A6
N Longmont Av
100 LAFT 80026 1690 C4
S Longmont Av
100 LAFT 80026 1690 C5
Long Ridge Dr
10 PrkC 80456 2607 D6
Longs Ct
- BMFD 80020 1775 C4
Longs Rd
9800 TNTN 80260 1860 B7
Longs Wy
10600 DgsC 80138 2453 D7
10700 PARK 80138 2453 D7
18000 PARK 80134 2453 C6
Longs Peak Av
- LGMT 80501 1438 D2
10 LGMT 80501 1439 A2
2100 LGMT 80503 1438 D2
E Longs Peak Av
1000 LGMT 80501 1439 E1
Longs Peak Cir
3300 EbtC 80138 2457 A4
Longs Peak Dr
10 BMFD 80021 1858 B2
100 LYNS 80540 1352 D1
600 BldC 80303 1688 D7
1600 LSVL 80027 1689 C6
9200 CMCY 80640 1863 A5
Longs Peak Ln
- LGMT 80501 1438 D2
10400 PARK 80138 2454 A7
Longs Peak St
- BGTN 80601 1696 D5
- BGTN 80601 1697 B5
1700 WldC 80516 1523 E7
Longspeak St
200 BGTN 80601 1696 C5
E Longs Peak St
100 BGTN 80601 1696 B5
S Long Springs Butte
7200 JfnC 80127 2361 D5
Longspur Dr
200 BGTN 80601 1697 E6
400 BGTN 80603 1697 E6

STREET
Block City ZIP Map# Grid

Longstone Ct
9200 DgsC 80134 2452 D3
Longstone Dr
9200 DgsC 80134 2452 D3
Long Trail Rd
2200 GpnC 80403 1934 C1
W Longview Av
500 LITN 80120 2364 D3
Longview Blvd
- WldC 80504 1440 D3
E Longview Blvd
11100 WldC 80504 1440 E2
N Longview Blvd
3200 WldC 80504 1440 D2
S Longview Blvd
3200 WldC 80504 1440 E2
W Longview Blvd
11100 WldC 80504 1440 E2
Longview Ct
400 LGMT 80501 1438 D2
Longview Dr
6600 BldC 80503 1520 E6
6600 BldC 80503 1521 A4
9900 DgsC 80124 2450 E6
26400 JfnC 80433 2525 E4
26400 JfnC 80433 2526 A4
Long View Rd
10 CCkC 80439 2187 E4
S Longview St
6000 LITN 80120 2364 D3
Longwood Av
3200 BLDR 80305 1771 A2
Longwood Cir
5400 DgsC 80130 2450 B6
Longwood Wy
10300 DgsC 80130 2450 B6
Lookout Dr
- BldC 80504 1606 C1
E Lookout Dr
6400 DgsC 80138 2453 D3
Lookout Pl
- BLDR 80301 1604 C1
7100 BldC 80503 1604 C1
Lookout Rd
6100 BLDR 80301 1603 E2
6100 BLDR 80301 1604 A1
6500 BldC 80301 1604 B1
6800 BldC 80503 1604 B1
7900 BldC 80301 1605 A1
7900 BldC 80503 1605 A1
9300 BldC 80026 1605 D1
9500 BldC 80026 1606 C1
9500 BldC 80504 1606 C1
W Lookout Run
11100 DgsC 80125 2614 C1
S Lookout Hill Ct
1300 AphC 80102 2206 E4
Lookout Mountain Cir
10 JfnC 80401 2191 A2
Lookout Mountain Rd
2000 GOLD 80401 2107 C5
2000 JfnC 80401 2107 C5
N Lookout Mountain Rd
10 JfnC 80401 2191 A1
300 JfnC 80401 2107 B7
S Lookout Mountain Rd
10 JfnC 80401 2191 A2
100 JfnC 80401 2190 E2
Lookout Ridge Dr
- BldC 80503 1605 C2
5300 BldC 80301 1605 C2
Lookout View Ct
200 GOLD 80401 2108 A4
Lookout View Dr
200 GOLD 80401 2108 A4
Loomis Ct
600 LGMT 80501 1438 D2
Loomis Wy
29300 JfnC 80403 1853 B4
Loop Rd
- AdmC 80601 1779 A6
- CSRK 80104 2788 A4
E Loop Rd
- BldC 80503 1520 B6
- BLDR 80503 1520 B6
W Loop Rd
- BldC 80503 1520 A6
- BLDR 80503 1520 A6
Loop Rd E
- CSRK 80104 2788 B4
Lora Av
33100 JfnC 80470 2524 C6
S Lora Av
12500 JfnC 80470 2524 C6
28500 JfnC 80433 2609 D1
S Lora Ln
6300 JfnC 80439 2357 B4
Loren Ln
10600 NHGN 80233 1861 A5
Loretta Dr
8100 AdmC 80221 1944 D4
8100 TNTN 80221 1944 D4
Lori Dr
12900 JfnC 80433 2526 C6
N Lorin Ln
200 DgsC 80109 2702 B7
Lorraine Ct
2900 BLDR 80304 1602 D7
Lorraway Dr
400 DgsC 80108 2619 A6
Lost Tr
10 PrkC 80456 2606 C3
S Lost Tr
11800 JfnC 80433 2525 E3
Lost Angel Rd
10 BldC 80302 1684 A2
200 BldC 80302 1683 E3
W Lost Arrow
11100 DgsC 80125 2530 C7
N Lost Canyon Tr
12100 DgsC 80138 2454 A4
Lost Canyon Ranch Ct
1900 CSRK 80104 2789 A2
Lost Canyon Ranch Rd
6000 CSRK 80104 2788 E2
6100 CSRK 80104 2789 A2
6500 DgsC 80104 2789 A2
S Lost Creek Cir
11200 PARK 80138 2538 C1
Lost Creek Ct
- DNVR 80237 2282 C6
Lost Creek Ln
- LAFT 80026 1689 E3
E Lost Hill Dr
9100 LNTR 80124 2451 A4
S Lost Hill Dr
9100 LNTR 80124 2451 A4
E Lost Hill Tr
9000 LNTR 80124 2451 A4
Lost Horizon
10 BldC 80403 1852 A1
Lost Horizon Dr
18400 JfnC 80127 2528 A5
Lost Lake Tr
2500 DgsC 80116 2706 B2
Lost Lake Wy
- BMFD 80020 1775 D6
Lost Meadow Tr
5200 CSRK 80104 2704 E7
Lost Mine Ln
- CCkC 80452 2185 C2
S Lost Ranger Peak
7500 JfnC 80127 2362 A6
Lost Trail Rd
700 DgsC 80108 2618 D5
Lost Train Rd
10 CCkC 80452 2186 B4
Lost Valley Pt
- CSRK 80108 2703 D1
Lost Valley Rd
4800 CSRK 80108 2703 E1
Lotus Ct
1900 LGMT 80501 1356 D5
Lotus Wy
600 BMFD 80020 1774 D7
600 BMFD 80020 1858 D1
Lou Dr
9400 NHGN 80260 1944 D1
9400 TNTN 80260 1944 D1
9700 NHGN 80260 1860 D7
Louis Rd
10 PrkC 80456 2606 D7
Louise Dr
8000 AdmC 80221 1944 C4
8200 FLHT 80260 1944 C4
Louise Ln
6600 JfnC 80439 2357 A4
E Louisiana Av
10 DNVR 80210 2196 E4
10 DNVR 80223 2196 E4
3600 DNVR 80210 2197 E4
3900 DNVR 80222 2197 E4
3900 DNVR 80246 2197 E4
4600 DNVR 80222 2198 A4
4600 DNVR 80246 2198 A4
5500 DNVR 80224 2198 A4
7200 AphC 80231 2198 C4
9300 AphC 80247 2199 A4
11100 AURA 80012 2199 D4
13000 AURA 80012 2200 A4
15300 AURA 80017 2200 D4
17900 AURA 80017 2201 B4
W Louisiana Av
10 DNVR 80210 2196 D4
800 DNVR 80223 2196 C4
2400 DNVR 80219 2196 A4
5100 LKWD 80232 2195 C4
5200 DNVR 80219 2195 C4
7600 LKWD 80232 2194 D5
10900 JfnC 80232 2193 E4
12300 LKWD 80228 2193 C5
E Louisiana Cir
24400 AURA 80018 2202 E4
24700 AURA 80018 2203 A4
E Louisiana Dr
9800 AphC 80247 2199 B4
9800 AURA 80247 2199 B4
12100 AURA 80012 2199 E4
15000 AURA 80012 2200 C4
16500 AURA 80017 2200 E4
17000 AURA 80017 2201 A4
39900 AphC 80102 2206 E4
40700 AphC 80102 2207 A4
E Louisiana Pkwy
- AURA 80018 2202 D4
- AURA 80018 2203 A4
Louisiana Pl
1000 LGMT 80501 1439 A5
E Louisiana Pl
8900 AphC 80247 2199 A4
13900 AURA 80012 2200 B4
16200 AURA 80017 2200 E4
24100 AURA 80018 2202 E4
W Louisiana Pl
6400 LKWD 80232 2195 A5
8800 LKWD 80232 2194 C5
S Louthan Cir
7000 LITN 80120 2364 C5
S Louthan Ct
7700 LITN 80120 2364 C6
S Louthan St
5300 LITN 80120 2280 D7
5600 LITN 80120 2364 C1
S Louthan Wy
5400 LITN 80120 2364 C1
W Louviers Av
5700 DgsC 80125 2532 D6
Louviers Blvd
7500 DgsC 80135 2532 C7
8000 DgsC 80125 2532 C6
Louviers Dr
7900 DgsC 80135 2532 C6
Love Ct
1000 BLDR 80303 1687 D3
Loveland Ct
7600 JfnC 80007 1940 E6
S Loveland Ct
10 JfnC 80401 2192 E2
Loveland St
600 JfnC 80401 2108 E7
4300 JfnC 80403 2024 E7
Loveland Wy
10 JfnC 80401 2192 E1
Lovington St
10 CSRK 80104 2705 A7
E Low Cir
18900 AphC 80015 2369 C2
E Low Dr
18900 AphC 80015 2369 C2
Low Ln
6700 JfnC 80465 2359 C4
E Low Pl
18900 AphC 80015 2369 C2
21900 CTNL 80015 2370 B1
Lowall Ct
2500 DgsC 80109 2786 B6
Lowell Av
10000 WSTR 80031 1859 D7
Lowell Blvd
- BfdC 80516 1691 D5
- BMFD 80020 1691 D5
- BMFD 80020 1859 D2
- ERIE 80516 1691 D5
10 DNVR 80219 2195 E1
300 DNVR 80219 2111 E7
1800 DNVR 80204 2111 E5
1800 DNVR 80211 2111 E3
4000 DNVR 80211 2027 E7
5100 AdmC 80221 2027 E5
5100 DNVR 80221 2027 E5
5500 AdmC 80003 2027 D3
6500 AdmC 80030 2027 D2
6700 WSTR 80030 2027 D2
7000 AdmC 80221 1943 D7
7000 WSTR 80030 1943 D7
7900 WSTR 80031 1943 D4
8100 AdmC 80031 1943 D4
11900 WSTR 80031 1859 D2
11900 WSTR 80234 1859 D2
13600 BMFD 80020 1775 D4
S Lowell Blvd
10 DNVR 80219 2195 E2
2500 DNVR 80219 2279 E1
3400 AphC 80236 2279 E2
3400 DNVR 80236 2279 E2
3500 SRDN 80236 2279 E4
4300 SRDN 80110 2279 E7
4400 EGLD 80110 2279 E5
4600 DNVR 80110 2279 E5
4700 DNVR 80123 2279 E7
4800 DvrC 80110 2279 E7
4800 DvrC 80123 2279 E7
4800 LITN 80123 2279 E7
5300 LITN 80123 2363 E1
Lowell Ct
8800 AdmC 80031 1943 D3
9600 WSTR 80031 1943 D1
12400 BMFD 80020 1859 D1
13000 BMFD 80020 1775 D7
N Lowell Ct
10400 WSTR 80031 1859 D6
Lowell Dr
10 CSRK 80104 2703 E7
N Lowell Dr
10500 WSTR 80031 1859 D5
Lowell Ln
3000 BfdC 80516 1692 C3
3000 BMFD 80516 1692 C3
Lowell Pl
3200 CSRK 80109 2787 A7
3200 DgsC 80104 2787 A7
Lowell Wy
8800 AdmC 80031 1943 D3
S Lowell Wy
- CBVL 80123 2363 E2
5700 LITN 80123 2363 E2
Lower Aspen Ln
34800 PrkC 80470 2523 E3
34800 PrkC 80470 2524 A3
Lower Crow Hill Rd
10 PrkC 80456 2690 C2
Lower Gulch Rd
600 GpnC 80474 1849 C3
Lower Moss Rock Rd
28400 JfnC 80401 2189 C2
Lower Russell Gulch Rd
- GpnC 80403 2017 B7
E Lowry Blvd
- AURA 80010 2115 A7
7300 DNVR 80230 2198 D1
8400 DNVR 80230 2114 E7
9000 AURA 80230 2115 A7
9000 DNVR 80230 2115 A7
E Lowry Pl
9700 AURA 80230 2115 B7
10500 AURA 80010 2115 C6
E Loyola Av
17800 AURA 80013 2285 B4
E Loyola Cir
18900 AURA 80013 2285 C3
Loyola Ct
3300 BLDR 80305 1771 A1
E Loyola Dr
15900 AURA 80013 2284 E3
17600 AURA 80013 2285 B4
E Loyola Pl
16000 AURA 80013 2284 E3
16900 AURA 80013 2285 A3
E Lt William Clark Rd
7900 DgsC 80134 2622 B3
Lucca Dr
4300 LGMT 80503 1438 A6
4400 LGMT 80503 1437 E6
Lucent Blvd
- DgsC 80126 2448 C4
- LITN 80120 2448 B1
8700 DgsC 80129 2448 B1
Lucerne Dr
100 LAFT 80026 1690 C3
W Lucerne Dr
300 BldC 80026 1690 B3
300 LAFT 80026 1690 B3
Lucerne Wy
100 LAFT 80026 1690 C3
Lucille Ct
1300 NHGN 80233 1861 A4
Lucy Ln
- EbtC 80107 2793 D3
Ludlow St
4300 BLDR 80305 1771 B1
4600 BLDR 80305 1687 B7
Lunceford Ct
9900 NHGN 80260 1860 C7
Lunceford Ln
9800 NHGN 80260 1860 C7
Lunceford St
9600 TNTN 80260 1944 C1
Lunnonhaus Dr
1400 GOLD 80401 2108 B5
Lupine Cir
6700 ARVD 80007 2024 E1
Lupine Ct
1300 LGMT 80503 1438 C6
3200 JfnC 80401 2108 E2
Lupine Dr
27600 JfnC 80439 2273 D5
S Lupine Dr
5700 LITN 80123 2363 C2
Lupine Ln
700 BldC 80302 1686 C5
700 BLDR 80302 1686 C5
Lupine St
800 JfnC 80401 2108 E6
7200 JfnC 80007 1940 E7
S Lupine St
10 JfnC 80401 2192 E2
Lupine Wy
10 JfnC 80401 2192 E1
1200 JfnC 80401 2190 D5
6700 ARVD 80007 2024 E1
Lupire Cir
- DgsC 80118 2954 A1
Lutes Rd
33600 JfnC 80470 2524 B6
Lutheran Pkwy
3200 JfnC 80215 2110 D2
3200 WTRG 80033 2110 D2
Lutheran Pkwy W
- WTRG 80033 2110 C1
Lydia Dr
1400 LAFT 80026 1689 E6
1400 LAFT 80026 1690 A6
1400 LSVL 80026 1690 A6
Lykins Av
500 BLDR 80304 1602 B2
Lykins Pl
- BldC 80503 1435 D5
Lykins Gulch Rd
- BldC 80501 1438 C4
- LGMT 80501 1438 C4
- LGMT 80503 1438 C4
Lyle Ct
3100 DNVR 80211 2112 B2
Lyndenwood Cir
4300 DgsC 80130 2449 E6
4600 DgsC 80130 2450 A6
Lyndenwood Pt
4300 DgsC 80130 2449 E6
Lynn Dr
5300 ARVD 80002 2026 B4
Lynn Rd
10 CHLV 80113 2281 C5
Lynne Av
10900 BldC 80026 1606 B4
10900 ERIE 80026 1606 B4
Lynnfield Dr
- DgsC 80112 2451 E5
- DgsC 80112 2452 A5
Lynnfield Ln
- DgsC 80112 2452 A5
Lynnwood Ln
10 GpnC 80403 1851 B4
Lynwood Av
3100 DgsC 80126 2533 D1
Lynx Ct
10500 DgsC 80124 2450 C6
Lynx Dr
10 BldC 80481 1514 E1
Lynx Ln
10100 DgsC 80125 2530 E6
10100 DgsC 80125 2531 A6
33000 JfnC 80439 2356 C5
Lynx Run
10400 DgsC 80124 2450 C6
S Lynx Bay
10400 DgsC 80124 2450 C6
S Lynx Cove
6500 DgsC 80124 2450 C6
Lynx Lair Rd
6900 JfnC 80439 2357 B5
Lyonesse St
1700 LAFT 80026 1690 D7
Lyons St
18600 GOLD 80401 2108 A7
E Lyttle Dr
20800 PARK 80138 2538 A1
Lyttle Dowdle Dr
33200 JfnC 80403 1852 B7

M

Mable Av
1600 AdmC 80229 1945 B4
Mable Ln
10 PrkC 80456 2606 D7
S Mabre Ct
5000 LITN 80123 2279 E7
S Mabry Ct
2700 DNVR 80236 2279 E1
S Mabry Wy
1800 DNVR 80219 2195 E6
S Macalister Tr
9900 DgsC 80129 2448 E5
MacArthur Dr
- BldC 80301 1687 C2
- BldC 80303 1687 C2
1500 BLDR 80303 1687 C2
MacArthur Ln
4600 BLDR 80303 1687 C2
Macaw St
800 BGTN 80601 1696 A7
800 BGTN 80601 1780 B2
MacCullen Dr
1500 ERIE 80516 1690 C2
Macedonia St
10200 BldC 80503 1436 E2
Macintosh Pl
4800 BLDR 80301 1603 B7
S Mackay Dr
9900 DgsC 80130 2450 A5
MacKenzie Ct
10 DgsC 80130 2450 A3
Macky Dr
- BLDR 80302 1686 D3
Macky Wy
4600 BLDR 80305 1771 B1
MacLean Dr
10 AphC 80123 2363 D4
E Macom Dr
1500 DgsC 80135 2618 B5
S Macon Cir
2700 AURA 80014 2283 D1
Macon Ct
10 AURA 80010 2199 D1
11100 DgsC 80112 2451 D3
S Macon Ct
10 AURA 80010 2199 D1
500 AURA 80012 2199 D2
2200 AURA 80014 2199 D7
2600 AURA 80014 2283 D1
6100 AphC 80111 2367 D2
Macon St
10 AURA 80010 2199 C1
10 AURA 80012 2199 C1
2200 AURA 80010 2115 D3
11900 CMCY 80640 1863 C2
S Macon St
1400 AURA 80012 2199 D5
2300 AURA 80014 2199 D7
2700 AURA 80014 2283 D1
5700 AphC 80111 2367 D1
S Macon Wy
700 AURA 80012 2199 D3
1900 AURA 80014 2199 D6
6100 AphC 80111 2367 D3
Macoun Wy
- BldC 80301 1603 A4
Madeleine St
9000 FLHT 80260 1944 A2
Madera Ct
2800 BldC 80301 1603 A5
Madero St
1200 BMFD 80020 1774 E7
N Madge Gulch Rd
500 DgsC 80135 2699 E7
Madison Av
300 AdmC 80601 1696 B5
300 BGTN 80601 1696 B5
3000 BLDR 80303 1687 A3
S Madison Av
100 LSVL 80027 1773 B1
S Madison Cir
7500 CTNL 80122 2365 D6
Madison Ct
- BMFD 80020 1775 E3
800 ERIE 80516 1606 E7
1500 LSVL 80027 1689 B6
8500 AdmC 80229 1945 D3
11200 TNTN 80233 1861 D4
12300 TNTN 80241 1861 D1
S Madison Ct
6100 CTNL 80121 2365 D2
6500 AphC 80121 2365 D3
7000 CTNL 80122 2365 D5
Madison Dr
100 BNNT 80102 2124 C2
2000 ERIE 80516 1606 D7
2700 LGMT 80503 1355 C4
S Madison Dr
6100 CTNL 80121 2365 D3
Madison Ln
- BMFD 80020 1776 A3
3000 BMFD 80020 1775 E3
Madison Pl
11900 TNTN 80233 1861 D2
Madison St
- TNTN 80241 1861 C1
10 DNVR 80206 2197 D1
10 DNVR 80209 2197 D1
300 DNVR 80206 2113 D7
3200 DNVR 80205 2113 D2
3900 DNVR 80205 2029 D7
4300 DNVR 80216 2029 D7
9900 TNTN 80229 1861 D7
10500 NHGN 80233 1861 D5
11300 TNTN 80233 1861 D3
12600 TNTN 80241 1777 D7
13900 TNTN 80602 1777 D4
14400 AdmC 80602 1777 C2
S Madison St
10 DNVR 80206 2197 D2
10 DNVR 80209 2197 D4
1000 DNVR 80209 2197 D4
1000 DNVR 80210 2197 D4
2700 DNVR 80210 2281 D1
Madison Wy
600 BNNT 80102 2124 C2
2000 ERIE 80516 1606 E7
8400 AdmC 80229 1945 D4
10700 NHGN 80233 1861 D5
S Madison Wy
6800 CTNL 80122 2365 D5
8100 CTNL 80122 2449 C1
Madison Park Appartment
- TNTN 80233 1861 C2
- TNTN 80241 1861 D2
S Madras Ct
9100 DgsC 80130 2450 B3
Madras Dr
- DgsC 80130 2450 B3
Madras Ln
- DgsC 80130 2450 B3
Madre Pl
9100 LNTR 80124 2451 A3
Madrid Ct
600 EbtC 80138 2624 A1
Madrid Dr
40500 EbtC 80138 2624 A1
41000 EbtC 80138 2540 A7
Madrid Pl
800 EbtC 80138 2624 B1
N Mad River Ct
6100 DgsC 80134 2622 C2
E Mad River Rd
8600 DgsC 80134 2622 D2
Madrone Ct
15700 DgsC 80134 2452 D1
S Maggie Ln
5300 JfnC 80439 2357 B1
Maggie St
200 LGMT 80501 1440 A3
S Magnolia Cir
7000 CTNL 80112 2366 C5
Magnolia Ct
- TNTN 80602 1778 B7
S Magnolia Ct
6100 CTNL 80111 2366 C3
6700 CTNL 80112 2366 C4
Magnolia Dr
10 BldC 80302 1685 A4
10 BldC 80466 1685 A4
100 BldC 80466 1684 E4
3500 BldC 80466 1683 D7
5800 BldC 80466 1767 C1
7000 BldC 80466 1766 E4
9100 BldC 80466 1765 E4
S Magnolia Ln
500 DNVR 80224 2198 C2
Magnolia Pl
- TNTN 80602 1778 B7
Magnolia St
- CSRK 80109 2702 C4
- TNTN 80602 1778 B6
100 DNVR 80220 2198 C1
600 DNVR 80220 2114 C6
3200 DNVR 80207 2114 C2
3900 DNVR 80207 2030 C7
6400 CMCY 80022 2030 C2
7400 CMCY 80022 1946 B6
7700 AdmC 80022 1946 C5
16600 AdmC 80602 1694 B4
S Magnolia St
300 DNVR 80224 2198 C2
3100 DNVR 80224 2282 C2
Magnolia Wy
12100 AdmC 80602 1862 C1
12800 TNTN 80602 1778 B6
S Magnolia Wy
1300 DNVR 80224 2198 C5
2900 DNVR 80224 2282 C1
3700 DNVR 80237 2282 C3
7800 CTNL 80112 2366 C7
Magpie Av
1200 BGTN 80601 1779 E1
Magpie Ct
1400 GOLD 80403 2107 C3
Magpie Ln
10 PrkC 80456 2691 D1
Mahlon Ct
1000 LAFT 80026 1690 C2
W Mahogany Cir
800 LSVL 80027 1773 A2
Mahogany Wy
5000 EbtC 80107 2709 E3
Mahonia
- JfnC 80127 2361 A6
Maiden Wy
11800 NHGN 80233 1861 B2
Maid Marion Ct
1400 LAFT 80026 1690 D6
Main Av
- LKWD 80226 2193 E1
- LKWD 80226 2194 A2
21400 JfnC 80401 2191 B1
Main St
- EbtC 80107 2793 B1
- ELIZ 80107 2793 B1
- GpnC 80403 2017 C7
10 BldC 80302 1599 D3
10 BMFD 80020 1858 E2
10 GpnC 80474 1849 E2
10 JMWN 80455 1516 B3
10 LGMT 80501 1439 B1
10 PrkC 80456 2690 C2
100 BldC 80455 1516 A2
100 CLCY 80403 2017 D3
100 LSVL 80027 1773 D1
200 BKHK 80403 2018 A4
300 ERIE 80516 1607 B4
300 LYNS 80540 1352 D1
500 BMFD 80020 1774 E7
600 LSVL 80027 1689 D7
1100 LGMT 80501 1356 B7
2300 BldC 80504 1356 B5
3800 WSTR 80031 1859 D2
11200 WSTR 80020 1858 E3
26000 JfnC 80433 2442 A5
Main St SR-7
300 LYNS 80540 1352 D1
Main St SR-66
300 LYNS 80540 1352 D1
Main St US-36
300 LYNS 80540 1352 D1
Main St US-287
10 LGMT 80501 1439 B1
1100 LGMT 80501 1356 B7
2300 BldC 80504 1356 B5
E Main St
- DgsC 80134 2537 A1
- PARK 80134 2537 A1
10 BldC 80503 1352 E2
10 LYNS 80503 1352 E2
10 LYNS 80540 1352 E2
100 ELIZ 80107 2793 B1
6900 DgsC 80138 2453 E7
7300 PARK 80138 2454 C7
8200 DgsC 80138 2454 C7
19200 PARK 80138 2453 E7
19300 PARK 80134 2453 E7
E Main St SR-7
10 BldC 80503 1352 E2
10 LYNS 80503 1352 E2
10 LYNS 80540 1352 E2
E Main St SR-66
10 BldC 80503 1352 E2
10 LYNS 80503 1352 E2
10 LYNS 80540 1352 E2
E Main St US-36
10 BldC 80503 1352 E2
10 LYNS 80503 1352 E2
10 LYNS 80540 1352 E2
N Main St
10 BGTN 80601 1696 B5
300 AdmC 80601 1696 B5
400 BGTN 80603 1696 B5
7900 DgsC 80135 2532 C5
8100 DgsC 80125 2532 D6
S Main St
- BldC 80516 1691 B2
- ERIE 80516 1691 B2
10 BGTN 80601 1696 B7
10 LGMT 80501 1439 B4
100 BldC 80501 1439 B4
600 BGTN 80601 1780 A1
700 EbtC 80107 2793 B1
700 ELIZ 80107 2793 B1
1400 BldC 80504 1439 B4
1400 LGMT 80504 1439 B4
2500 BldC 80026 1691 B3
S Main St US-287
10 LGMT 80501 1439 B4
100 BldC 80501 1439 B4
1400 BldC 80504 1439 B4
1400 LGMT 80504 1439 B4
W Main St
500 LYNS 80540 1352 D1
2200 LITN 80120 2364 B1
W Main St SR-66
500 LYNS 80540 1352 D1
W Main St US-36
500 LYNS 80540 1352 D1
Main Range Tr
10900 JfnC 80127 2362 A7
11000 JfnC 80127 2361 E7
Maize Ct
11600 PARK 80134 2537 A1
Maize Ln
- BGTN 80601 1697 C4
Majestic Dr
- BldC 80504 1521 E3
1700 LAFT 80026 1690 E7
1700 LAFT 80026 1691 A7
9500 BldC 80503 1521 D3
Majestic Tr
3800 CSRK 80109 2702 D2
Majestic Eagle Dr
- JfnC 80127 2528 E4
14200 JfnC 80127 2529 A4
Majestic Mountain Rd
3100 DgsC 80135 2784 B7
3100 DgsC 80135 2868 B1
Majestic View Dr
200 BldC 80303 1688 E7
300 LSVL 80027 1688 E7
8600 JfnC 80433 2442 D2
Malachite Ct
9700 DgsC 80134 2452 D4
S Malamute Dr
7500 JfnC 80439 2357 E7
7500 JfnC 80439 2358 A6
S Malamute Tr
7700 JfnC 80439 2357 E7
Malaya Ct
3900 DNVR 80249 2034 A7
S Malaya Ct
3200 AURA 80013 2286 A2
4900 AphC 80015 2286 A6
5100 CTNL 80015 2286 A7
5800 CTNL 80015 2370 A1
7000 AURA 80016 2370 A5
Malaya St
800 AphC 80018 2118 A6
900 AURA 80011 2118 A6
900 AURA 80018 2118 A6
3900 DNVR 80249 2034 A7
S Malaya St
3500 AphC 80013 2286 A3
6300 CTNL 80016 2370 A3
S Malaya Wy
- AphC 80015 2286 A7
5100 CTNL 80015 2286 A7
6900 AURA 80016 2370 A4
Maleta Ln
700 CSRK 80104 2703 D2
700 CSRK 80108 2703 D2
Malibu St
200 CSRK 80109 2703 C5
Mallard Cir
2400 LGMT 80504 1438 D7
Mallard Ct
1200 BldC 80303 1687 E3
11000 PARK 80134 2536 E1
E Mallard Ct
8500 DgsC 80126 2449 D2
Mallard Dr
1800 SUPE 80027 1773 C6
E Mallard Dr
3500 DgsC 80126 2449 D2
Mallard Ln
1300 BGTN 80601 1779 E1
E Mallard Ln
3800 DgsC 80126 2449 E2
Mallard Pl
2100 LGMT 80504 1438 D7

STREET
Block City ZIP Map# Grid

S Mallard Pl
8500 DgsC 80126 2449 D2
Mallard St
100 GOLD 80401 2192 B2
E Mallard St
3600 DgsC 80126 2449 E2
E Mallard Wy
- DgsC 80126 2449 E2
Mallard Pond Ct
- BldC 80303 1688 C4
Mallard Pond Dr
700 BldC 80303 1688 C4
Mallard Pond Wy
9500 DgsC 80125 2531 B7
Malley Dr
100 NHGN 80233 1860 E3
700 NHGN 80233 1861 A3
Mallow Dr
- DgsC 80118 2870 A7
- DgsC 80118 2954 A1
Malory St
900 LAFT 80026 1690 D6
S Malta Ct
- AphC 80013 2286 A3
3300 AURA 80013 2286 A2
6900 AURA 80016 2370 A4
Malta St
4500 DNVR 80249 2034 A6
S Malta St
- AphC 80013 2286 A4
- AURA 80013 2286 A4
- AURA 80015 2286 A4
5500 CTNL 80015 2370 A1
S Malta Wy
5100 CTNL 80015 2286 A7
5900 CTNL 80015 2370 A2
Malthusian Wy
6600 CMCY 80022 2029 D1
Malton Ct
1700 CSRK 80104 2787 E2
Malvern Ct
600 DgsC 80108 2618 E1
Mammoth
3200 WldC 80504 1440 D2
Mammoth Ct
2000 JfnC 80439 2189 B7
Mammoth View Ln
400 CLCY 80403 2017 D5
Manassas Ct
8300 EbtC 80107 2543 A2
Manchester Ct
7400 DgsC 80108 2534 D7
E Manchester Dr
5300 CSRK 80104 2788 E1
Mandel St
9000 FLHT 80260 1944 B2
Manet Wy
900 NHGN 80234 1860 C4
Mango Dr
400 CSRK 80104 2787 D1
Manhart St
5300 DgsC 80135 2617 C5
Manhart St SR-67
5300 DgsC 80135 2617 C5
Manhattan Cir
5200 BLDR 80303 1687 D6
Manhattan Dr
10 BLDR 80303 1687 D6
Manhattan Pl
600 BLDR 80303 1687 C4
N Manila Rd
- AdmC 80102 2038 D3
- AdmC 80137 2038 D3
10 AphC 80102 2206 D1
1500 AdmC 80102 2122 D3
2600 AURA 80102 2038 D7
2600 AURA 80102 2122 D1
S Manila Rd
10 AphC 80102 2206 D2
Manilla Pl
7700 BldC 80503 1520 D5
Manitoba Dr
30800 JfnC 80439 2357 A4
30900 JfnC 80439 2356 E4
E Manitou Rd
11200 DgsC 80116 2791 D5
S Manitou Rd
5200 LITN 80123 2279 D7
5300 LITN 80123 2363 D1
S Mann Creek Ct
12500 PARK 80134 2537 E3
E Mann Creek Dr
19600 PARK 80134 2537 D5
Manor Dr
6400 CHLV 80111 2282 C7
S Manor Ln
- LKWD 80227 2195 B6
1800 LKWD 80232 2195 B6
Manor Wy
1400 BGTN 80601 1696 D5
Manor House Rd
10 JfnC 80127 2361 A5
Manorwood Ct
600 LSVL 80027 1773 B2
Manorwood Ln
600 LSVL 80027 1773 B2
Man O War Tr
27600 JfnC 80439 2357 D7
N Manposa Ct
14600 WSTR 80020 1776 C2
E Mansfield Av
10 EGLD 80110 2280 E4
10 EGLD 80113 2280 E4
500 EGLD 80113 2281 A4
3700 CHLV 80113 2281 D4
4600 CHLV 80113 2282 A4
4700 AphC 80237 2282 A4
4800 DNVR 80237 2282 A4
8600 DNVR 80237 2283 A4
8900 GDVL 80014 2283 A4
15800 AURA 80013 2284 D4
18200 AURA 80013 2285 B4
20400 AphC 80013 2285 E4
W Mansfield Av
10 EGLD 80110 2280 D4
10 EGLD 80113 2280 D4
2700 SRDN 80110 2280 A4
3300 SRDN 80236 2279 E4
3500 DNVR 80236 2279 E4
6400 DNVR 80235 2279 A4
6500 LKWD 80235 2279 A4
7200 LKWD 80235 2278 E4
E Mansfield Cir
16600 AURA 80013 2284 C4
16600 AURA 80013 2285 A4
E Mansfield Dr
3900 AphC 80013 2286 A4
19000 AURA 80013 2285 C3
E Mansfield Ln
- AphC 80013 2285 E4
W Mansfield Pkwy
7600 LKWD 80235 2278 D4
E Mansfield Pl
20400 AphC 80013 2285 E4
21400 AphC 80013 2286 A4
21700 AURA 80018 2286 B4
E Mansfield Rd
17300 AURA 80013 2285 A4
Mansur Ln
33800 JfnC 80470 2524 B5
Manzanita
10 JfnC 80127 2361 A5
E Maple Av
10 DNVR 80209 2196 E1
10 DNVR 80223 2196 E1
500 CTNL 80121 2365 A2
7600 DNVR 80230 2198 D1
11800 AURA 80012 2199 D1
W Maple Av
10 DNVR 80209 2196 D1
1300 DNVR 80223 2196 C2
7200 LKWD 80226 2194 E1
14000 JfnC 80401 2193 A2
15000 JfnC 80401 2192 E2
Maple Cir
1100 BMFD 80020 1774 B6
3400 BGTN 80601 1697 A7
Maple Ct
- LGMT 80501 1439 C6
1100 BMFD 80020 1774 B6
4500 BLDR 80301 1603 E4
5700 GDVL 80111 2365 E1
7300 DNVR 80230 2198 C1
W Maple Ct
900 LSVL 80027 1689 A6
Maple Dr
- TNTN 80260 1944 B1
1100 BMFD 80020 1774 B6
8100 DgsC 80125 2530 E6
W Maple Dr
15500 JfnC 80401 2192 E2
S Maple Ln
10000 DgsC 80129 2448 B6
E Maple Pl
14800 AURA 80012 2200 C1
W Maple Pl
2000 DgsC 80129 2448 B5
4800 DNVR 80219 2195 C2
12900 LKWD 80228 2193 C2
13800 JfnC 80401 2193 B2
Maple Rd
10800 BldC 80026 1774 C2
10800 LAFT 80026 1774 C2
Maple St
- LGMT 80501 1439 C6
100 MRSN 80465 2276 B3
300 LAFT 80026 1690 B4
500 GOLD 80403 2107 D2
900 GOLD 80401 2107 D3
E Maple St
- EbtC 80107 2793 B1
- ELIZ 80107 2793 B1
W Maple St
100 SUPE 80027 1772 E3
Maple Crest Dr
- DgsC 80134 2452 E2
- PARK 80134 2452 E2
16800 PARK 80134 2453 A2
E Maple Hills Av
23400 PARK 80138 2538 D2
Maple Rock Ct
16300 DgsC 80134 2452 E5
Mapleton Av
100 BldC 80302 1686 B1
100 BLDR 80302 1686 B1
400 BLDR 80304 1686 B1
2700 BLDR 80301 1686 E1
2800 BLDR 80301 1687 A1
Mapleton Cir
2400 LGMT 80503 1355 C5
Mapleton Ct
800 CSRK 80104 2789 B1
2500 LGMT 80503 1355 C4
E Maplewood Av
- AphC 80015 2370 C2
- CTNL 80015 2370 B2
- CTNL 80111 2366 A3
300 CTNL 80121 2364 E2
1500 CTNL 80121 2365 B2
5600 CTNL 80111 2366 B2
7900 GDVL 80111 2366 D2
9400 AphC 80111 2367 A3
9400 GDVL 80111 2367 A2
14100 AphC 80111 2368 B2
14100 CTNL 80111 2368 B2
16700 CTNL 80016 2368 E2
16700 CTNL 80016 2369 A2
19000 AphC 80016 2369 D2
W Maplewood Av
2800 LITN 80120 2364 A2
5000 LITN 80123 2363 C3
9100 JfnC 80123 2362 C3
11300 JfnC 80127 2361 E3
E Maplewood Cir
- GDVL 80111 2367 B3
9600 AphC 80111 2367 B3
17700 AphC 80016 2369 B2
Maplewood Cir E
2400 LGMT 80503 1355 D4
Maplewood Cir W
2400 LGMT 80503 1355 C4
E Maplewood Ct
1400 CTNL 80121 2365 B2
Maplewood Dr
100 ERIE 80516 1606 E6
E Maplewood Dr
300 CTNL 80121 2364 E2
500 CTNL 80121 2365 A3
4900 CTNL 80121 2366 A2
10500 AphC 80111 2367 C3
14700 CTNL 80016 2368 C2
15900 AphC 80016 2368 D2
16800 AphC 80016 2369 A2
S Maplewood Dr
8600 DgsC 80126 2449 B2
W Maplewood Dr
- JfnC 80127 2362 A3
5500 JfnC 80123 2363 B3
8600 JfnC 80123 2362 C3
11300 JfnC 80127 2361 E3
Maplewood Ln
11500 PARK 80138 2538 A2
E Maplewood Ln
20500 CTNL 80016 2369 E2
20700 CTNL 80016 2370 A2
22500 AphC 80015 2370 C2
E Maplewood Pl
4100 CTNL 80121 2365 E2
5200 CTNL 80121 2366 A2
6900 CTNL 80111 2366 C3
7200 GDVL 80111 2366 C3
11100 AphC 80111 2367 C2
13900 CTNL 80111 2368 A2
16100 AphC 80016 2368 E2
19100 AphC 80016 2369 D2
20100 CTNL 80016 2369 E2
20700 CTNL 80016 2370 A2
22400 AphC 80015 2370 C2
W Maplewood Pl
5000 LITN 80123 2363 C3
5500 JfnC 80123 2363 B3
9300 JfnC 80123 2362 C3
E Maplewood Wy
4400 CTNL 80121 2365 D3
4400 CTNL 80121 2366 A3
Maplson Ct
1700 LSVL 80027 1689 B6
Marathon Rd
8800 BldC 80503 1521 B5
S Marauder Dr
9400 JfnC 80433 2441 B4
Marble Cir
10 GOLD 80401 2108 B7
Marble Ct
1000 BldC 80303 1688 E3
1300 BMFD 80020 1774 D6
2000 CSRK 80108 2620 A7
Marble Dr
1100 BldC 80303 1688 E3
Marble Ln
2700 SUPE 80027 1773 A7
2800 SUPE 80027 1857 A1
6200 CSRK 80108 2620 A7
Marble St
400 BMFD 80020 1858 D1
600 BMFD 80020 1774 D7
March Ct
1900 ERIE 80516 1690 C2
March Dr
14500 DNVR 80239 2032 B4
March Pl
15300 DNVR 80239 2032 D4
Marchant St
100 BKHK 80403 2017 E4
100 BKHK 80403 2018 A4
S Marcliff Rd
10700 JfnC 80433 2441 E7
10700 JfnC 80433 2525 E1
Marcott Dr
10900 PARK 80134 2453 B7
Marcott St
10700 PARK 80134 2453 A7
Marcus Ln
10 DgsC 80108 2534 D6
Marfell Ct
2000 ERIE 80516 1606 E7
Marfell St
- BldC 80026 1606 E7
800 ERIE 80516 1606 E7
Margaret Dr
- EbtC 80107 2625 C4
Marge Ct
2000 EbtC 80138 2540 D7
Marge Ln
30100 JfnC 80439 2357 B2
N Margie Ln
200 DgsC 80109 2702 B7
S Marguerite Pkwy
4000 AURA 80013 2284 D4
Maria Cir
12500 BMFD 80020 1775 D7
12500 BMFD 80020 1859 D1
Maria St
7800 WSTR 80030 1943 D5
Maribou Ct
8900 DgsC 80130 2450 C3
Maricopa Rd
23000 JfnC 80439 2274 E6
Marie Ln
30200 JfnC 80439 2357 A2
Marie Rd
33700 JfnC 80470 2524 B5
Marigold Ct
- GDVL 80121 2365 E1
1300 LAFT 80026 1690 B6
Marigold Dr
10 AdmC 80221 1944 C4
1400 LAFT 80026 1690 B6
E Marigold Dr
10 AdmC 80221 1944 E4
Marigold Ln
4400 BWMR 80123 2363 D1
4400 LITN 80123 2363 D1
Marin Ct
7600 DgsC 80124 2450 D5
Marin Dr
- GDVL 80111 2366 D1
E Marina Dr
13600 AURA 80014 2284 B2
Marine St
1700 BLDR 80302 1686 D2
2800 BLDR 80303 1686 E3
7800 BLDR 80303 1687 A2
Mariner Dr
2200 BldC 80503 1355 B5
2200 LGMT 80503 1355 B5
Mariner Ln
3200 LGMT 80503 1355 B5
Marion Cir
7900 AdmC 80229 1945 A5
S Marion Cir
2700 DNVR 80210 2281 C1
7900 CTNL 80122 2365 A7
S Marion Cir E
6700 CTNL 80121 2365 B4
6700 CTNL 80122 2365 B4
S Marion Cir W
6700 CTNL 80121 2365 B4
6700 CTNL 80122 2365 B4
Marion Ct
7900 AdmC 80229 1945 A5
S Marion Ct
7900 CTNL 80122 2365 A7
Marion Dr
10 CCkC 80439 2271 D5
13400 TNTN 80241 1777 A5
S Marion Pkwy
100 DNVR 80209 2197 A2
S Marion Pl
6400 CTNL 80121 2365 A3
Marion St
- TNTN 80229 1861 A6
100 DNVR 80218 2197 A1
300 DNVR 80218 2113 A7
2500 DNVR 80205 2113 A3
5400 DNVR 80216 2029 A4
5800 AdmC 80216 2029 A3
9700 DgsC 80112 2452 A4
11400 NHGN 80233 1861 A3
13300 TNTN 80241 1777 A5
16400 TNTN 80602 1693 A5
S Marion St
1300 DNVR 80210 2197 A4
2400 DNVR 80210 2281 A1
2900 EGLD 80113 2281 A2
3500 CHLV 80113 2281 A3
6400 CTNL 80121 2365 A3
6600 CTNL 80122 2365 A3
Marion Wy
9600 TNTN 80229 1945 A1
10400 NHGN 80233 1861 A6
12800 DgsC 80112 2452 A5
S Marion Wy
6100 CTNL 80121 2365 B3
8200 CTNL 80122 2449 A1
Mariposa Av
1200 BLDR 80302 1686 D5
Mariposa Ct
13300 WSTR 80234 1776 C5
14600 AdmC 80020 1776 C2
N Mariposa Ct
12400 WSTR 80234 1776 D7
12400 WSTR 80234 1860 C1
Mariposa Dr
1200 AdmC 80221 1944 C6
S Mariposa Dr
4600 EGLD 80110 2280 C6
8200 JfnC 80465 2443 D1
Mariposa Rd
4200 DgsC 80104 2871 A3
27700 JfnC 80439 2273 D7
Mariposa St
- AdmC 80221 1944 C5
100 DNVR 80223 2196 C1
1300 DNVR 80204 2112 C5
3300 DNVR 80211 2112 C1
4200 DNVR 80211 2028 C7
6900 AdmC 80221 2028 C1
8400 FLHT 80260 1944 C4
8500 TNTN 80260 1944 C3
13200 WSTR 80234 1776 C6
N Mariposa St
12000 WSTR 80234 1860 C2
S Mariposa St
1100 DNVR 80223 2196 C4
3900 EGLD 80110 2280 C4
Mariposa Wy
4400 DNVR 80211 2028 C7
S Mariposa Wy
700 DNVR 80223 2196 C3
Market St
- DgsC 80134 2452 E3
- DgsC 80134 2453 A3
100 MRSN 80465 2276 C3
1300 DNVR 80202 2112 C4
1300 DNVR 80204 2112 C4
1900 DNVR 80205 2112 D3
S Marks Dr
11000 JfnC 80433 2524 E2
Marks Ln
10 PrkC 80456 2521 D5
S Marlborough St
11400 PARK 80138 2537 C2
11400 PARK 80138 2538 A1
Marlin Ct
36600 EbtC 80107 2708 D2
Marlin Dr
3100 LGMT 80503 1355 B5
Marlin Wy
2000 DgsC 80109 2786 B6
W Marlowe Av
10100 JfnC 80127 2278 A6
11000 JfnC 80127 2277 E6
11500 JfnC 80465 2277 D6
W Marlowe Dr
10600 JfnC 80127 2278 A6
11700 JfnC 80465 2277 D6
W Marlowe Pl
10100 JfnC 80127 2278 A6
11600 JfnC 80465 2277 E6
Marmot Ct
900 LGMT 80501 1439 D1
Marmot Ln
1600 JfnC 80439 2189 B6
Marmot Pt
300 LAFT 80026 1774 C1
Marmot Ridge Cir
9500 DgsC 80125 2531 A7
9600 DgsC 80125 2615 A1
Marmot Ridge Pl
7200 DgsC 80125 2531 B7
7200 DgsC 80125 2615 B1
Maroon
- TNTN 80260 1860 B7
Maroon Cir
4400 BMFD 80020 1775 C5
9500 DgsC 80112 2451 D4
Maroon Peak
7700 JfnC 80127 2361 E7
Maroon Peak Cir
700 SUPE 80027 1857 A2
Maroon Peak Pl
6100 DgsC 80108 2618 E2
W Marquette Dr
5700 DNVR 80235 2279 B4
Mars Ct
500 DgsC 80124 2450 E2
Marshall Cir
8000 ARVD 80003 1943 A5
S Marshall Cir
- LKWD 80227 2195 A6
- LKWD 80232 2195 A6
Marshall Ct
500 LKWD 80226 2111 A7
2300 ERIE 80516 1606 D6
6000 ARVD 80003 2027 A3
7200 WSTR 80003 1943 A7
8000 ARVD 80003 1943 A5
8800 WSTR 80031 1943 A2
11500 WSTR 80020 1859 A3
N Marshall Ct
2900 WTRG 80214 2111 A2
S Marshall Ct
1200 LKWD 80232 2195 A4
5700 JfnC 80123 2363 A2
6600 JfnC 80128 2363 A4
7900 JfnC 80128 2447 A1
Marshall Dr
5200 BldC 80303 1771 D3
5600 BldC 80027 1772 A3
5600 BldC 80303 1772 A3
6500 SUPE 80027 1772 D2
6500 SUPE 80303 1772 D2
Marshall Dr SR-170
5200 BldC 80303 1771 D3
5600 BldC 80027 1772 A3
5600 BldC 80303 1772 A3
6500 SUPE 80027 1772 D2
6500 SUPE 80303 1772 D2
S Marshall Dr
6000 JfnC 80123 2363 A3
Marshall Ln
28900 JfnC 80439 2273 C7
Marshall Pl
100 LGMT 80501 1439 C2
9100 WSTR 80031 1943 A2
Marshall Rd
- BldC 80303 1771 D3
300 BldC 80027 1772 E3
300 SUPE 80027 1772 E3
700 BldC 80305 1771 C2
7100 DgsC 80118 2954 D1
Marshall Rd SR-170
300 BldC 80027 1772 E3
300 SUPE 80027 1772 E3
Marshall St
- ARVD 80033 2027 A6
100 LKWD 80226 2195 A1
1200 BLDR 80302 1686 B3
2000 EDGW 80214 2111 A4
2000 LKWD 80214 2111 A4
3200 WTRG 80214 2111 A2
3500 WTRG 80033 2111 A1
4700 WTRG 80033 2027 A6
5000 ARVD 80002 2027 A5
5000 JfnC 80002 2027 A5
5000 JfnC 80033 2027 A5
6300 ARVD 80003 2027 A2
7000 WSTR 80003 1943 A7
7800 ARVD 80003 1943 A5
11500 WSTR 80020 1859 A3
S Marshall St
200 LKWD 80226 2195 A2
900 LKWD 80232 2195 A4
2700 DNVR 80227 2279 A1
5300 DNVR 80123 2363 A1
6700 JfnC 80123 2363 A4
6900 JfnC 80128 2363 A5
8000 JfnC 80128 2447 A1
N Marshall Wy
9700 WSTR 80021 1859 A7
9700 WSTR 80021 1943 A1
S Marshall Wy
3600 DNVR 80235 2279 A3
Marshallville Ditch Rd
- BldC 80301 1689 B2
- BldC 80303 1689 B2
Marsh Hawk Cir
1600 CSRK 80109 2703 B5
Marsh Hawk Ln
10 JfnC 80127 2360 E4
S Marshmerry Ln
6500 JfnC 80439 2357 E4
6600 JfnC 80439 2358 A4
W Marsten Ct
3000 SRDN 80110 2280 A4
Marston Tr
800 GOLD 80401 2107 E6
Marti Cir
1900 BldC 80501 1440 B4
1900 LGMT 80501 1440 B4
Martin Cir E
15800 JfnC 80401 2108 D2
Martin Cir W
15800 JfnC 80401 2108 D2
Martin Dr
10 CCkC 80439 2187 D7
10 CCkC 80439 2271 E1
200 BLDR 80305 1687 A6
Martin Ln
10 CHLV 80113 2281 A4
10 EGLD 80113 2281 A4
E Martin Ln
- EGLD 80113 2281 A4
10 CHLV 80113 2281 A4
N Martin Ln
200 DgsC 80109 2702 C7
S Martin Ln
8300 JfnC 80433 2440 D2
Martin Rd
900 LGMT 80501 1439 C1
1000 LGMT 80501 1356 C7
33700 JfnC 80470 2524 B5
Martin St
100 BldC 80501 1439 C3
100 LGMT 80501 1439 C3
1300 LGMT 80501 1356 C7
S Martin St
10 BldC 80501 1439 C3
10 LGMT 80501 1439 C3
Martindale Dr
600 AphC 80210 2281 A1
600 DNVR 80210 2281 A1
600 EGLD 80113 2281 A1
600 EGLD 80210 2281 A1
Martinez Pl
10 LGMT 80501 1356 B5
Martingale Dr
16400 PARK 80134 2452 E7
Martingale Dr W
16100 PARK 80134 2452 E7
Martingale Ln
21200 PARK 80138 2538 A3
Martinique Av
3100 BLDR 80301 1603 A4
Martin Luther King Blvd
1100 DNVR 80205 2113 B2
3800 DNVR 80207 2113 E2
4700 DNVR 80207 2114 A2
Martin Luther King Jr Blvd
7300 DNVR 80207 2114 D2
7300 DNVR 80238 2114 D2
Martz Rd
- CSRK 80109 2702 C4
Mar Vista Pl
6500 DNVR 80224 2198 B2
Mary Ct
6700 DgsC 80108 2618 E1
Mary Dr
29100 JfnC 80433 2525 B2
Mary Ln
30300 JfnC 80433 2525 B2
Mary Beth Rd
10 CCkC 80439 2271 D4
Mary Clarke Pl
9000 DgsC 80138 2454 D5
W Maryland Av
7300 LKWD 80232 2194 E5
10900 JfnC 80232 2193 C4
W Maryland Dr
9500 LKWD 80232 2194 B5
12000 JfnC 80232 2193 D5
12000 LKWD 80228 2193 D5
W Maryland Pl
9100 LKWD 80232 2194 B5
12500 LKWD 80228 2193 C5
Marylin Jean Dr
7600 ARVD 80003 2026 D3
7600 ARVD 80004 2026 D3
Marys Ln
10 PrkC 80456 2521 E5
Marys Tr
11300 JfnC 80433 2525 C2
Masey St
7000 AdmC 80221 1944 C7
Mason Cir
8300 AdmC 80031 1943 D4
Mason St
- ERIE 80516 1607 B7
Masonville Dr
11600 PARK 80134 2453 A6
W Massey Cir
8000 JfnC 80128 2446 D2
W Massey Dr
7600 JfnC 80128 2446 D2
Massive Rd
9800 TNTN 80260 1860 B7
Massive Peak Cir
6100 DgsC 80108 2618 E2
Massive Peak Lp
6100 DgsC 80108 2618 D2
Mast Rd
4400 BldC 80301 1604 A4
Masters Ct
1500 SUPE 80027 1773 A6
2900 CSRK 80104 2787 D3
Masters Dr
200 CSRK 80104 2787 D3
Masters Ln
2800 CSRK 80104 2787 D3
Masters Club Cir
2800 CSRK 80104 2787 C3
Masters Club at Hunters Run
- AphC 80231 2282 E1
- DNVR 80231 2282 E1
Masters Point Dr
2900 CSRK 80104 2787 C4
Matai Ct
7600 BldC 80503 1520 D4
Matchless St
200 LSVL 80027 1689 C6
Mather Cir
100 BGTN 80601 1696 B7
Mather St
2700 BGTN 80601 1696 E6
2900 BGTN 80601 1697 A6
Mathews Cir
500 ERIE 80516 1607 A7
Mathews Wy
- ERIE 80516 1607 A7
Matsuno St
- BGTN 80601 1697 B5
Matterhorn Dr
23800 JfnC 80439 2274 D5
Matterhorn Pl
7700 JfnC 80439 2356 A7
Matterhorn Peak Ln
2400 CSRK 80109 2787 A5
S Matthew Ln
10000 DgsC 80130 2450 B5
Mattive Pl
2200 BGTN 80601 1696 E7
Mauff Ct
30400 JfnC 80433 2525 A4
Mauff Wy
12000 JfnC 80433 2525 B4
Maverick Ct
3800 CSRK 80104 2703 D2
Maximus Dr
10 DgsC 80124 2451 A2
10 LNTR 80124 2451 A2
100 DgsC 80124 2450 E2
Maximus Dr Ext
9000 LNTR 80124 2451 A2
Maxine Ct
10400 JfnC 80465 2443 D7
W Maxine Ln
1900 DgsC 80109 2702 B7
Maxwell Av
200 BLDR 80302 1686 B1
200 BLDR 80304 1686 B1
Maxwell Dr
19600 JfnC 80465 2443 D6
Maxwell Pl
- AURA 80019 2034 A4
- DNVR 80249 2033 E4
- DNVR 80249 2034 A4
13100 DNVR 80239 2032 B4
E Maxwell Pl
16000 DNVR 80239 2032 D4
S Maxwell Hill Rd
11500 JfnC 80127 2528 D3
S May Ct
5900 JfnC 80439 2357 E3
Maya Pl
2800 BldC 80301 1603 A5
2800 BLDR 80301 1603 A5
Mayberry Dr
1200 DgsC 80129 2448 C4
May Cherry
10 JfnC 80127 2445 A1
Mayeda Ct
- BGTN 80601 1697 B5
Mayeda St
- AdmC 80601 1697 B5
- BGTN 80601 1697 B5
Mayfield Cir
1400 LGMT 80501 1438 E6
Mayfield Ct
7100 DgsC 80134 2621 E1
Mayfield Ln
1500 LGMT 80501 1438 E6
May Long Ct
13600 JfnC 80470 2608 D2
N Maywood Ct
14400 AdmC 80603 1784 B2
McAfee Cir
100 ERIE 80516 1607 D5
McAfee Ct
600 ERIE 80516 1607 D5
W McArthur Dr
10 DgsC 80124 2534 D1
1000 DgsC 80124 2450 C7
McArthur Ranch Rd
- DgsC 80126 2449 E6
- DgsC 80130 2449 E6
1700 DgsC 80124 2450 C7
5700 DgsC 80130 2450 A7
McCall Al
- LYNS 80540 1352 D1
McCall Dr
- BldC 80503 1354 A4
McCall Pl
1900 LGMT 80501 1356 B5
McCartney Dr
- BldC 80303 1688 E7
- LSVL 80027 1688 E7
McCart Ranch Cir
5200 EbtC 80107 2794 A4
McCaslin Blvd
- BldC 80027 1688 E6
- BldC 80027 1772 E4
- BldC 80303 1688 E6
- JfnC 80403 1856 E3
- LSVL 80027 1688 E6
100 LSVL 80027 1773 A1
2000 LSVL 80027 1772 E4
2000 SUPE 80027 1772 E4
2000 SUPE 80027 1773 A5
3400 BldC 80027 1856 E3
3400 SUPE 80027 1856 E3
3400 SUPE 80027 1857 A1
S McCaslin Blvd
- BldC 80027 1772 E3
- SUPE 80027 1772 E3
10 LSVL 80027 1773 A2
400 LSVL 80027 1772 E3
McCella Ct
7800 WSTR 80030 1943 D5
12400 BMFD 80020 1775 D7
McClellan Rd
- PARK 80134 2536 D1
10800 PARK 80134 2452 E7

STREET Block City ZIP Map# Grid

McCloskey Av
13300 AURA 80010 2116 A4
McClure Ct
600 ERIE 80516 1607 A7
McClure Dr
1300 LGMT 80501 1439 E1
3200 ERIE 80516 1690 B2
McClure Ln
5000 DgsC 80108 2618 E6
McClure Wy
- ERIE 80516 1606 E7
- ERIE 80516 1607 A7
McConnell Dr
- LYNS 80540 1352 E3
McCoy Pl
8900 AdmC 80031 1943 D3
McCrumb Dr
11800 NHGN 80233 1861 A2
McData Pkwy
- BMFD 80021 1857 D5
- WSTR 80021 1857 D5
McDonald Av
11000 JfnC 80433 2527 A1
McDonald Ct
100 ERIE 80516 1606 E5
McDougal Rd
10 PrkC 80456 2521 D3
McDougal St
1900 AdmC 80229 1945 B3
McElwain Blvd
2000 AdmC 80229 1945 B4
8600 TNTN 80229 1945 B4
McFarland Dr
- DNVR 80216 2029 A7
S McFarlane Dr
9400 JfnC 80433 2442 B4
E McGill Ct
9300 DgsC 80134 2622 D2
McIntire St
800 BLDR 80303 1687 C4
McIntosh Av
900 BMFD 80020 1859 B1
McIntosh Dr
2900 LGMT 80503 1355 B6
McIntyre Cir
10 JfnC 80401 2192 E1
McIntyre Ct
10 JfnC 80401 2192 E1
6200 ARVD 80403 2024 D3
6400 ARVD 80007 2024 E2
7100 ARVD 80007 1940 E7
7700 JfnC 80007 1940 D5
McIntyre Pkwy
- ARVD 80007 2024 E3
- ARVD 80403 2024 E3
McIntyre St
400 GOLD 80401 2108 E7
400 GOLD 80401 2192 E1
400 JfnC 80401 2192 E1
700 JfnC 80401 2108 E6
3200 JfnC 80403 2108 E2
4200 JfnC 80403 2024 E5
4300 GOLD 80403 2024 E5
6400 ARVD 80007 2024 E2
6400 ARVD 80403 2024 E2
7200 ARVD 80007 1940 E7
7200 JfnC 80007 1940 E7
S McIntyre St
2200 LKWD 80228 2192 D7
2400 LKWD 80228 2276 D1
2900 MRSN 80228 2276 E2
3200 LKWD 80228 2277 A3
3200 MRSN 80228 2277 A3
McIntyre Wy
6200 ARVD 80403 2024 E2
S McIntyre Wy
10 JfnC 80401 2192 E2
McIver Cir
25000 JfnC 80433 2442 B4
McKay Ln
- BLDR 80303 1687 D3
McKay Rd
10000 AdmC 80229 1862 B6
10000 TNTN 80229 1862 B6
10000 TNTN 80233 1862 B6
McKay Landing Pkwy
2500 BMFD 80020 1776 A4
McKay Park Cir
- BMFD 80020 1776 A4
McKay Park Dr
- BMFD 80020 1776 A4
McKenzie Ct
12500 BMFD 80020 1775 D7
McKinley Av
2300 LSVL 80027 1689 C5
S McKinley Ct
300 LSVL 80027 1773 C2
McKinley Dr
100 AdmC 80102 2124 C2
100 BNNT 80102 2124 C2
4700 BLDR 80303 1687 C3
McKinley Pl
1400 LSVL 80027 1689 C6
McKinley Park Ln
200 LSVL 80027 1689 C7
S McKinney Rd
9900 JfnC 80127 2444 C5
McLean Ct
2500 CSRK 80109 2702 C4
McMurdo Gulch Ct
6400 DgsC 80134 2621 D5
E McShane Ct
9300 DgsC 80134 2622 E2
McSorley Ln
5900 BldC 80303 1687 E3
Meachum Wy
1500 ERIE 80516 1607 A7
Mead Ct
600 LSVL 80027 1773 C1
Mead Dr
2000 BldC 80301 1689 C1
Mead St
700 LSVL 80027 1773 D1

N Mead Wy
12200 DgsC 80125 2447 E4
Meade Cir
9700 WSTR 80031 1859 D7
9700 WSTR 80031 1943 D1
Meade Ct
6500 AdmC 80003 2027 D2
8800 AdmC 80031 1943 D3
9600 WSTR 80031 1943 D1
10900 WSTR 80031 1859 D5
12400 BMFD 80020 1859 D1
N Meade Ct
11000 WSTR 80031 1859 D4
Meade Ln
10 CHLV 80113 2281 C5
Meade Lp
10300 WSTR 80031 1859 D6
Meade St
- WSTR 80031 1943 D1
10 DNVR 80219 2195 E1
300 DNVR 80204 2111 D7
300 DNVR 80219 2111 D7
1900 DNVR 80211 2111 E4
4700 DNVR 80211 2027 D6
4800 DNVR 80221 2027 D6
5100 AdmC 80221 2027 D5
8000 WSTR 80030 1943 D5
8800 AdmC 80031 1943 D3
12600 BMFD 80020 1775 D7
N Meade St
9200 WSTR 80031 1943 D2
S Meade St
- DNVR 80236 2279 E4
500 DNVR 80219 2195 E3
2500 DNVR 80219 2279 E1
4700 DNVR 80123 2279 D7
4800 DvrC 80123 2279 D7
4800 LITN 80123 2279 D7
Meade Wy
7500 WSTR 80030 1943 D6
Meadow Av
2100 BLDR 80304 1602 D6
3100 BMFD 80020 1775 E7
Meadow Ct
1000 LSVL 80027 1689 A7
2100 LGMT 80501 1356 B5
7300 BldC 80301 1604 C4
S Meadow Ct
7300 BldC 80301 1604 C4
Meadow Dr
- EbtC 80107 2793 C1
- ELIZ 80107 2793 C1
- PrkC 80456 2606 B3
10 PrkC 80456 2607 D5
10 PrkC 80470 2523 D5
1900 LGMT 80501 1356 B5
27800 JfnC 80439 2273 D5
S Meadow Dr
4300 BldC 80301 1604 C4
5800 JfnC 80465 2358 E2
5800 JfnC 80465 2359 A2
11700 JfnC 80433 2525 E3
W Meadow Dr
7600 JfnC 80128 2446 D1
Meadow Ln
- BGTN 80601 1697 D4
10 CCkC 80439 2271 C3
10 CHLV 80113 2281 D4
10 PrkC 80456 2521 B5
1800 LGMT 80501 1356 B6
6300 JfnC 80439 2357 D4
7200 BldC 80503 1521 B4
31700 JfnC 80439 2356 E1
33200 EbtC 80107 2793 A2
E Meadow Ln
800 DgsC 80108 2619 B5
W Meadow Rd
500 CCkC 80439 2187 E4
500 CCkC 80439 2188 A4
Meadow Run
900 GOLD 80403 2107 D1
E Meadow Run
10000 DgsC 80134 2623 A1
10300 DgsC 80138 2623 A1
Meadow St
1100 LGMT 80501 1439 C1
2100 LGMT 80501 1356 B4
2400 BldC 80504 1356 B4
Meadow Tr
1200 DgsC 80116 2791 D3
28000 JfnC 80433 2525 D4
Meadow Vw
7200 DgsC 80134 2621 E5
7300 DgsC 80134 2622 A5
Meadow Wy
- PrkC 80456 2607 E3
10 GpnC 80403 1850 C5
Meadowbriar Ln
10000 DgsC 80126 2449 E6
Meadow Bridge Wy
12400 PARK 80134 2537 D3
Meadow Brook Cir
- EbtC 80138 2540 B4
Meadowbrook Cir
10 LITN 80120 2364 D5
Meadowbrook Ct
13700 BMFD 80020 1775 B5
Meadowbrook Dr
600 BLDR 80303 1687 B5
2100 AdmC 80221 1944 B6
5700 JfnC 80465 2360 E2
13800 BMFD 80020 1775 B4
S Meadow Brook Ln
4100 JfnC 80439 2272 C5
W Meadowbrook Ln
6300 DgsC 80135 2700 C5
Meadowbrook Pl
10 LITN 80120 2364 D5
Meadowbrook Rd
10 LITN 80120 2364 C5
W Meadowbrook Rd
1500 LITN 80120 2364 C5
E Meadow Creek Ct
3500 DgsC 80126 2449 D2

S Meadow Creek Dr
8500 DgsC 80126 2449 D2
E Meadow Creek Pl
3300 DgsC 80126 2449 D2
Meadow Creek Rd
600 LKWD 80214 2111 A7
E Meadow Creek Wy
3400 DgsC 80126 2449 D2
Meadowcross Ln
- BldC 80301 1603 C3
Meadowdale Ct
8100 BldC 80503 1520 E3
Meadowdale Dr
7200 BldC 80503 1520 E4
Meadowdale Sq
8000 BldC 80503 1520 E4
Meadow Glen Dr
700 BLDR 80303 1687 D4
Meadow Glen Isl
- BLDR 80303 1687 D3
W Meadow Glenn Ln
3400 DgsC 80135 2785 E7
Meadowgreen Cir
2100 DgsC 80116 2706 E3
Meadow Hill Cir
8900 LNTR 80124 2451 A4
Meadow Hill Ln
33300 EbtC 80107 2794 C2
Meadowlake Dr
200 GpnC 80403 1850 D7
Meadow Lake Rd
7900 BldC 80503 1520 E5
Meadowland Ct
10 BldC 80466 1767 D2
Meadowlark Cir
10 LCHB 80603 1698 B3
8600 DgsC 80126 2449 A2
Meadowlark Ct
3300 EbtC 80107 2541 B7
Meadowlark Dr
10 CCkC 80439 2271 C1
300 LKWD 80226 2110 C7
700 LAFT 80026 1690 D5
1200 BldC 80303 1688 B3
8400 LKWD 80226 2194 C1
27800 JfnC 80401 2189 E4
33700 EbtC 80107 2793 D1
S Meadow Lark Dr
4700 CSRK 80109 2702 C1
Meadow Lark Ln
10 JfnC 80127 2360 E4
Meadowlark Ln
10 AphC 80123 2363 D4
600 LCHB 80603 1698 B3
1500 GOLD 80403 2107 C2
14100 AdmC 80601 1780 E3
14100 BGTN 80601 1780 E3
Meadowlark Pl
5800 CSRK 80109 2702 C2
Meadowlark Wy
- BldC 80304 1602 A4
Meadowlark Cove
800 LAFT 80026 1690 D6
Meadowlook Wy
10 BldC 80304 1602 A4
Meadow Mountain Dr
4900 BMFD 80020 1775 C4
Meadow Mountain Ln
32400 JfnC 80439 2188 D5
Meadow Mountain Rd
32300 JfnC 80439 2188 B5
Meadow Mountain Tr
2700 LAFT 80026 1689 D4
Meadowood Ln
11700 PARK 80138 2537 E3
W Meadowood Ln
6200 DgsC 80135 2700 C7
Meadow Park Ln
13300 BMFD 80020 1775 D6
Meadow Ridge Ln
11700 DgsC 80134 2451 D5
32300 JfnC 80470 2608 D1
Meadow Ridge Pl
10200 DgsC 80134 2451 D6
Meadowrose Dr
1400 JfnC 80401 2190 E5
Meadow Rose Ln
10 JfnC 80127 2445 B1
Meadowrose Ln
800 DgsC 80108 2534 D6
Meadow Rue Rd
28200 JfnC 80439 2273 D6
Meadows Blvd
1700 CSRK 80109 2702 D3
2500 CSRK 80109 2703 A2
N Meadows Dr
3300 CSRK 80109 2618 D7
3300 CSRK 80109 2702 E1
W Meadows Dr
- JfnC 80128 2362 A5
10000 JfnC 80127 2362 A5
10900 JfnC 80127 2361 E6
Meadows Ln
2300 CSRK 80104 2703 D4
Meadows Pkwy
10 CSRK 80108 2703 B1
10 CSRK 80109 2703 B1
Meadow Station Cir
300 EbtC 80138 2540 A2
Meadow Station Rd
10 DgsC 80138 2539 E3
10 EbtC 80138 2540 A3
Meadow Sweet Ln
2000 ERIE 80516 1606 D6
Meadowsweet Rd
1200 JfnC 80401 2109 B5
1200 LKWD 80401 2109 B5
Meadow Sweet Farm Pkwy
- ERIE 80516 1606 E6
Meadowvale Cir
10900 DgsC 80126 2533 E1
Meadow View Dr
10 CCkC 80439 2187 E1
27700 JfnC 80439 2273 E2

Meadowview Ln
10 GDVL 80121 2281 A7
Meadow View Pkwy
- BldC 80026 1606 D5
- ERIE 80516 1606 D5
Meadow View Rd
3200 JfnC 80439 2274 B2
22000 JfnC 80465 2359 A5
S Meadow View Rd
3100 JfnC 80439 2274 B2
Meadow Vista Dr
300 JfnC 80439 2188 C3
N Meadow Woods St
14400 AdmC 80603 1784 C2
Medallion Rd
3300 DgsC 80104 2871 E1
S Medea Wy
800 DNVR 80209 2197 C3
Medford Ct
6100 CSRK 80104 2788 E1
6100 CSRK 80104 2789 A1
Medford St
2100 LGMT 80501 1356 D5
S Medinah Dr
2400 JfnC 80439 2272 E1
2400 JfnC 80439 2273 A1
Medvina Hill Rd
10 BldC 80302 1600 B5
S Meeker Ct
300 LSVL 80027 1773 A2
Meeker Dr
1400 LGMT 80501 1356 C7
Meeker Pl
300 LGMT 80501 1439 D1
Meeker St
600 LGMT 80501 1439 C1
Megan Ct
500 DgsC 80108 2535 B7
700 LGMT 80501 1439 D1
Meilly St
- LYNS 80540 1352 D2
500 BldC 80540 1352 C2
Melborne Ct
9200 DgsC 80134 2452 D3
S Melbourne Cir
- DgsC 80130 2450 B5
9900 DgsC 80130 2449 E5
Melbourne Pl
9900 DgsC 80130 2450 A5
W Melbourne Wy
4500 DgsC 80130 2449 E4
Melissa Ln
3000 BldC 80301 1605 A7
Meller St
- BldC 80026 1607 A6
500 ERIE 80516 1607 A6
Melody Cir
600 NHGN 80260 1860 D7
Melody Dr
200 NHGN 80260 1860 D7
11600 NHGN 80234 1860 D3
12000 WSTR 80234 1860 D2
Melody Ln
13000 DgsC 80138 2453 E3
E Melody Ln
5600 CSRK 80104 2704 E6
E Melody Wy
5600 CSRK 80104 2704 E6
Melrose Dr
7900 WTRG 80033 2110 D1
Melting Shadows Wy
37400 EbtC 80107 2709 B1
Memmen Dr
10 CSRK 80104 2703 E6
Memorial Park Wy
28500 JfnC 80433 2609 D2
Memory Ln
700 LGMT 80501 1356 D6
Memphis Ct
- AURA 80011 2032 E7
- DNVR 80239 2032 E7
- DvrC 80239 2032 E7
10700 CMCY 80022 1864 D5
S Memphis Ct
5100 CTNL 80015 2284 E7
6100 AphC 80016 2368 E2
Memphis St
- AdmC 80022 1864 E7
- CMCY 80022 1864 E5
1800 AURA 80011 2116 E4
11800 CMCY 80603 1864 E2
N Memphis St
- AdmC 80022 2032 E5
- DNVR 80022 2032 E5
5200 DNVR 80239 2032 E5
S Memphis St
1100 AURA 80017 2200 E4
2100 AURA 80013 2200 E6
2800 AURA 80013 2284 E1
4200 AURA 80015 2284 E5
7300 AphC 80016 2368 E6
S Memphis Wy
- CTNL 80015 2284 E7
- CTNL 80015 2368 E1
300 AURA 80017 2200 E2
2400 AURA 80013 2200 E7
3500 AURA 80013 2284 E3
8100 AphC 80112 2368 E7
Mercator Av
100 LAFT 80026 1690 A5
E Mercer Cir
15900 AURA 80013 2284 E4
E Mercer Dr
16700 AURA 80013 2284 C4
16700 AURA 80013 2285 A4
E Mercer Pl
7300 DNVR 80237 2282 D4
15700 AURA 80013 2284 D4
21700 AURA 80018 2286 B4
Merchant Pl
6000 DgsC 80134 2621 C4
Mercury Cir
700 DgsC 80124 2450 D3

Mercury Dr
900 LAFT 80026 1690 B6
13000 DgsC 80124 2450 E3
Meredith Ct
9200 LNTR 80124 2450 E3
Meredith Wy
4800 BLDR 80303 1687 C2
Merideth Ln
10 LGMT 80501 1356 B6
S Meridian Blvd
9200 DgsC 80112 2451 C5
S Merimbula St
9600 DgsC 80130 2450 B5
Merion Ln
30100 JfnC 80439 2273 B1
Merion Pl
1100 BMFD 80020 1775 A6
Merl Pl
1300 LGMT 80501 1356 A5
Merlin Dr
500 LAFT 80026 1690 D6
S Merriam Dr
5800 JfnC 80439 2357 B2
Merriman Pl
1100 LGMT 80501 1439 E2
Merritt Dr
1100 BLDR 80303 1687 C3
Merry Ln
700 BldC 80303 1771 E1
Mesa Cir
100 LAFT 80026 1690 A4
Mesa Ct
10 PrkC 80456 2521 C2
100 LSVL 80027 1773 A1
800 BMFD 80020 1774 D6
1200 GOLD 80403 2023 D7
S Mesa Ct
1200 SUPE 80027 1773 B5
Mesa Dr
- GOLD 80403 2107 D1
10 CCkC 80439 2271 C6
1900 BLDR 80304 1686 D1
6000 BldC 80303 1771 E1
26800 JfnC 80439 2358 A2
27000 JfnC 80439 2357 E1
N Mesa Dr
4800 DgsC 80108 2619 C5
Mesa Ln
1300 DgsC 80108 2619 D5
W Mesa Run
11100 DgsC 80125 2530 D7
Mesa St
10 BldC 80455 1516 A3
10 JMWN 80455 1516 A3
100 BGTN 80601 1697 A6
N Mesa Tr
- BldC 80302 1686 B6
- BldC 80302 1770 B1
- BldC 80305 1770 C1
- BLDR 80305 1770 C1
S Mesa Tr
- BldC 80025 1770 C6
- BldC 80302 1770 C4
- BldC 80305 1770 C6
- BLDR 80305 1770 B1
Mesa Canyon Dr
- BLDR 80302 1686 C5
- BLDR 80305 1686 C5
Mesa Meadows Ct
4000 CSRK 80109 2702 D4
Mesa Oak
10 JfnC 80127 2361 B7
Mesa Park Pl
400 AdmC 80229 1861 E7
400 TNTN 80229 1861 E7
Mesa Point Pl
- LSVL 80027 1689 B6
Mesa Top Ct
5400 BLDR 80301 1604 B1
Mesa Verde
3300 WldC 80504 1440 D2
Mesa Verde Ln
11200 PARK 80138 2538 A1
Mesa Verde Pl
11300 PARK 80138 2538 A1
Mesa Verde St
100 GOLD 80401 2192 B1
Mesa Verde Wy
11200 PARK 80138 2538 A2
Mesa View Dr
300 GOLD 80403 2107 C2
Mesa View Wy
300 GOLD 80403 2107 C1
Mesquite Row
8800 LNTR 80124 2451 B3
Messmer Rd
- GpnC 80403 1851 D1
Meth Ct
- PrkC 80456 2521 C2
Metropolitan Dr
1600 LGMT 80501 1356 E6
Metzler Dr
100 CSRK 80108 2703 D1
Metzler Wy
4900 CSRK 80108 2703 D1
E Mexico Av
10 DNVR 80210 2196 E5
10 DNVR 80223 2196 E5
700 DNVR 80210 2197 A5
3900 DNVR 80222 2197 E5
5600 DNVR 80222 2198 B5
6900 DNVR 80224 2198 C5
7900 DNVR 80231 2198 E5
9200 AphC 80247 2199 A5
9300 AURA 80247 2199 B5
11600 AURA 80012 2199 E5
15300 AURA 80012 2200 E5
15300 AURA 80017 2200 E5
16800 AURA 80017 2201 A5
43000 AphC 80102 2207 D5
43000 AphC 80102 2208 A5
W Mexico Av
10 DNVR 80210 2196 E5
1600 DNVR 80223 2196 B5

W Mexico Av
2300 DNVR 80219 2196 B5
5100 DNVR 80219 2195 B6
5200 DNVR 80219 2195 B6
5200 DNVR 80232 2195 B6
8000 LKWD 80232 2194 D5
12000 JfnC 80232 2193 D5
12000 LKWD 80228 2193 D5
E Mexico Dr
8700 AphC 80231 2199 A5
8700 AphC 80247 2199 A5
11400 AURA 80012 2199 D5
14900 AURA 80012 2200 C5
14900 AURA 80014 2200 C5
15200 AURA 80017 2200 C5
17700 AURA 80017 2201 B5
W Mexico Dr
6800 LKWD 80232 2194 E5
6800 LKWD 80232 2195 A5
10900 JfnC 80232 2193 E6
E Mexico Pl
18300 AURA 80017 2201 B5
W Mexico Pl
6600 LKWD 80232 2195 A5
7600 LKWD 80232 2194 D6
12000 JfnC 80232 2193 E5
13800 LKWD 80228 2193 B5
Meyer Ct
4400 CSRK 80104 2704 C7
S Meyer Dr
9600 JfnC 80433 2442 C5
Meyers Gulch Rd
3300 JfnC 80439 2274 C5
3300 JfnC 80457 2274 C5
Meyerwood Cir
1200 DgsC 80129 2448 C7
Meyerwood Ct
10400 DgsC 80129 2448 C7
Meyerwood Ln
1200 DgsC 80129 2448 C7
S Miami Ct
300 DNVR 80224 2198 C2
Miami Wy
900 BLDR 80305 1687 A7
Mica Ct
3000 SUPE 80027 1773 A7
3000 SUPE 80027 1857 A1
Mica Rd
10 GpnC 80403 1850 B6
Mica Wy
10 PrkC 80456 2521 C3
10200 DgsC 80134 2452 D6
S Mica Wy
8300 JfnC 80465 2443 D1
S Mica Mine Gulch Rd
8700 JfnC 80127 2444 B3
Mica Mountain Rd
4900 JfnC 80403 2021 D6
Michael Gates Dr
1700 AphC 80137 2372 C7
1700 EbtC 80138 2372 C7
1700 EbtC 80138 2456 C1
Michelle Ct
- LAFT 80026 1690 C6
E Michener Wy
2500 DgsC 80126 2449 A6
N Michigan Av
100 LAFT 80026 1690 D4
S Michigan Av
100 LAFT 80026 1690 D5
S Michigan Ct
5000 LITN 80123 2279 D7
S Michigan Wy
1800 DNVR 80219 2195 D6
Michigan Creek Wy
18200 PARK 80134 2537 C5
Middle Rd
10 CHLV 80113 2281 E3
Middlebury Dr
2700 DgsC 80126 2449 C7
Middlebury Wy
10700 DgsC 80126 2449 D7
Middle Crest Rd
8300 BldC 80302 1518 B1
S Middlefield Rd
10 CBVL 80123 2363 E2
5900 LITN 80123 2363 E2
Middle Fork Rd
10 BldC 80302 1435 B7
2700 BldC 80302 1518 B1
Middleham Pl
7200 DgsC 80108 2534 D7
Middlepark Rd
- BldC 80302 1518 A2
Middleton Av
6100 CSRK 80104 2789 A2
Middleton Rd
30400 JfnC 80439 2357 A3
Midland Ct
- BGTN 80601 1697 C4
Midland Pl
1900 BGTN 80601 1696 D4
Midland St
- BGTN 80601 1697 C4
500 BGTN 80601 1696 B4
Midsummer Ln
43300 EbtC 80107 2543 A3
E Midway Blvd
- BMFD 80020 1774 E7
- BMFD 80020 1859 A1
900 BMFD 80020 1775 B7
W Midway Blvd
- BMFD 80020 1773 E6
- BMFD 80021 1773 E6
- BMFD 80021 1774 A7
100 BMFD 80020 1774 E7
100 BMFD 80020 1858 D1
Midway Dr
10 GpnC 80403 1850 C5
8000 DgsC 80125 2447 D4
8000 DgsC 80129 2447 D4
Mika Pl
1200 CSRK 80104 2787 D1

Mikelson Blvd
- CSRK 80104 2704 E7
- CSRK 80104 2705 A7
- CSRK 80104 2788 D1
- CSRK 80104 2789 A1
W Milan Av
3000 SRDN 80110 2280 A4
3100 SRDN 80110 2279 E4
3100 SRDN 80236 2279 E4
3500 DNVR 80236 2279 E4
E Milan Cir
19400 AURA 80013 2285 D4
E Milan Dr
15300 AURA 80013 2284 D4
E Milan Pl
18800 AURA 80013 2285 C4
20400 AphC 80013 2285 E4
22100 AURA 80018 2286 B4
S Milan Pl
6500 DNVR 80237 2282 C4
W Milan Pl
5500 DNVR 80235 2279 B4
10600 JfnC 80235 2278 A4
Milano Ln
4000 LGMT 80503 1438 A5
Milbury St
1300 CSRK 80104 2789 A1
Mildred Dr
10800 NHGN 80233 1861 A5
Mildred Ln
27300 JfnC 80439 2357 E2
S Mile Creek Ct
12600 PARK 80134 2537 D5
Mile High Wk
- DNVR 80204 2112 A5
Mile High Stadium Cir
1500 DNVR 80204 2112 A4
1900 DNVR 80211 2112 A4
Mile High Stadium Cir W
- DNVR 80204 2112 A4
- DNVR 80211 2112 A4
Miles Dr
9200 LNTR 80124 2450 E3
Milestone Av
- CSRK 80108 2703 C1
Milestone Dr
- CSRK 80104 2703 D2
- CSRK 80109 2703 D2
Milestone Ln
- CSRK 80104 2703 C2
- CSRK 80108 2703 C2
Milford Ln
- PARK 80138 2538 C1
Military Tr
5300 DgsC 80134 2621 D4
Milky Wy
600 FLHT 80260 1944 D3
600 TNTN 80260 1944 D3
Mill Rd
- ERIE 80516 1607 D6
Mill St
10 BldC 80302 1516 B3
10 BldC 80455 1516 B3
10 JMWN 80455 1516 B3
100 MRSN 80465 2276 C3
Millard Rd
10 BldC 80403 1852 A1
Millbridge Av
6000 CSRK 80104 2788 E1
6000 CSRK 80104 2789 A1
Millbridge Ct
5900 CSRK 80104 2788 E1
Millbrook Cir
500 CSRK 80109 2703 B6
Millbrook Ct
- AURA 80018 2119 B7
1400 CSRK 80109 2703 B6
S Millbrook Ct
- AURA 80016 2371 B2
Millbrook St
- AURA 80018 2119 B7
S Millbrook St
7300 AURA 80016 2371 B5
Millbrook Wy
- AURA 80016 2371 B5
S Millbrook Wy
- AURA 80016 2371 B2
8000 AphC 80016 2371 B7
S Millcreek Ct
9200 DgsC 80126 2449 C3
E Millcreek Pl
2200 DgsC 80126 2449 C3
Miller Av
10 AdmC 80601 1696 A6
10 BGTN 80601 1696 A6
N Miller Av
100 LAFT 80026 1690 C4
S Miller Av
100 LAFT 80026 1690 C5
Miller Blvd
3000 CSRK 80104 2788 B1
Miller Cir
8000 ARVD 80005 1942 A4
Miller Ct
2000 LKWD 80215 2110 A4
3500 WTRG 80033 2110 A1
8100 ARVD 80005 1942 A4
10700 WSTR 80021 1858 A5
E Miller Ct
300 CSRK 80104 2703 D7
S Miller Ct
700 LKWD 80226 2194 A3
2200 LKWD 80227 2194 A7
3600 JfnC 80235 2278 A4
4500 JfnC 80127 2278 A6
5700 JfnC 80127 2362 A2
8400 JfnC 80127 2446 A1
Miller Dr
1900 LGMT 80501 1438 D6
1900 LGMT 80504 1438 D6
S Miller Dr
- JfnC 80227 2278 A1
- LKWD 80227 2278 A2

STREET
Block City ZIP Map# Grid

Miller Ln
21600 JfnC 80465 2275 B2
Miller Pl
1100 GOLD 80401 2107 D3
E Miller Rd
8800 DgsC 80138 2454 D7
8800 PARK 80138 2454 D7
Miller St
- ERIE 80516 1607 A7
2200 LKWD 80215 2110 A3
3200 WTRG 80215 2110 A2
3500 WTRG 80033 2110 A1
4100 WTRG 80033 2026 A7
4900 ARVD 80033 2026 A5
5200 ARVD 80002 2026 A5
5800 ARVD 80004 2026 A3
8400 ARVD 80005 1942 A4
10000 WSTR 80021 1858 A7
N Miller St
7200 ARVD 80004 1942 A7
7200 ARVD 80005 1942 A7
S Miller St
300 LKWD 80226 2194 A2
1900 LKWD 80227 2194 A6
1900 LKWD 80232 2194 A6
5100 JfnC 80127 2278 A7
5500 JfnC 80127 2362 A1
Miller Wy
4000 WTRG 80033 2110 A1
S Miller Wy
900 LKWD 80226 2194 A4
4900 JfnC 80127 2278 A7
8500 JfnC 80127 2446 A1
Millet Cir
600 BGTN 80601 1697 C4
Mill Hollow Rd
10800 JfnC 80127 2528 E1
10800 JfnC 80127 2529 A1
Millikan Rd
- BLDR 80302 1686 E5
- BLDR 80305 1686 E5
S Milliken Av
10800 JfnC 80433 2527 A1
Milliken Ct
4200 BLDR 80303 1687 B4
Milliken St
10700 PARK 80134 2453 A7
Millionaire Dr E
10 BldC 80302 1684 D2
Millionaire Dr W
10 BldC 80302 1684 C2
Millrock Ter
9900 DgsC 80134 2452 D5
Mills St
400 LAFT 80026 1690 A4
S Millstone Ct
9600 DgsC 80130 2450 C4
E Millstone Pl
6500 DgsC 80130 2450 C4
E Millstone St
6500 DgsC 80130 2450 C4
Mill Valley Pl
23300 PARK 80138 2538 D3
Mill Valley St
11700 PARK 80138 2538 D2
Mill Village Blvd
200 LGMT 80501 1440 A3
Millwagon Tr
4200 CSRK 80109 2702 C3
Milne Wy
- BLDR 80301 1687 D1
Milner Ct
1200 LGMT 80503 1355 C7
Milner Ln
1200 LGMT 80503 1355 C7
1200 LGMT 80503 1438 C1
Milo Cir
900 LAFT 80026 1690 B6
Milton Ln
31200 JfnC 80439 2272 E2
31200 JfnC 80439 2273 A3
Milwaukee Cir
11600 TNTN 80233 1861 C3
S Milwaukee Cir
2900 DNVR 80210 2281 D1
Milwaukee Ct
9700 TNTN 80229 1861 C7
9700 TNTN 80229 1945 C1
10600 NHGN 80233 1861 C5
11500 TNTN 80233 1861 C3
12300 TNTN 80241 1861 C1
13300 TNTN 80241 1777 C6
13700 TNTN 80602 1777 C4
S Milwaukee Ct
7400 CTNL 80122 2365 C6
Milwaukee Pl
11600 TNTN 80233 1861 C3
13000 TNTN 80241 1777 C7
Milwaukee St
- AdmC 80602 1693 C5
- TNTN 80241 1777 C5
- TNTN 80602 1777 C5
100 DNVR 80206 2197 C1
1500 DNVR 80206 2113 C5
3200 DNVR 80205 2113 C1
4000 DNVR 80205 2029 C7
5000 DNVR 80216 2029 C5
9800 TNTN 80229 1861 C7
10500 NHGN 80233 1861 C5
11500 TNTN 80233 1861 C3
S Milwaukee St
200 DNVR 80209 2197 C2
1100 DNVR 80210 2197 D5
2700 DNVR 80210 2281 C1
7900 CTNL 80122 2365 D7
S Milwaukee Wy
900 DNVR 80209 2197 D4
1000 DNVR 80210 2197 D4
5900 CTNL 80121 2365 D2
7300 CTNL 80122 2365 C6
Mimas Pl
400 DgsC 80124 2450 E3
Mine Ln
10 BldC 80302 1600 E1
Mineola Ct
10 BLDR 80303 1687 D6
Miner St
1400 IDSP 80452 2101 B5
E Mineral Av
100 LITN 80120 2364 E7
100 LITN 80122 2364 E7
500 LITN 80122 2365 A6
1400 CTNL 80122 2365 A6
6500 CTNL 80112 2366 C7
8900 CTNL 80112 2367 A7
W Mineral Av
- LITN 80120 2363 E6
100 LITN 80122 2364 C7
1100 LITN 80120 2364 C7
4300 LITN 80128 2363 E6
5000 AphC 80128 2363 E6
E Mineral Cir
4800 CTNL 80122 2366 A7
8400 CTNL 80112 2366 E7
8400 CTNL 80112 2367 A7
E Mineral Ct
400 LITN 80122 2364 E7
W Mineral Ct
- LITN 80120 2364 D7
Mineral Dr
34300 JfnC 80470 2608 B6
E Mineral Dr
- AURA 80016 2371 C7
6000 CTNL 80112 2366 B7
8800 CTNL 80112 2367 A7
21000 AphC 80016 2370 A7
Mineral Ln
34000 JfnC 80470 2608 B6
E Mineral Ln
5200 CTNL 80122 2366 A7
E Mineral Pl
1400 CTNL 80122 2365 B7
7500 CTNL 80112 2366 D7
8000 CTNL 80122 2366 B7
8800 CTNL 80112 2367 A7
17200 CTNL 80016 2369 A7
17500 AURA 80016 2369 A7
23600 AURA 80016 2370 D7
W Mineral Pl
- LITN 80120 2364 C7
Mineral Rd
300 WldC 80504 1523 C6
7100 BldC 80503 1520 D6
7100 BLDR 80503 1520 D6
7900 BldC 80503 1521 C6
9000 BldC 80504 1521 C6
9500 BldC 80504 1522 A6
12600 WldC 80516 1523 A6
Mineral Rd SR-52
7100 BldC 80503 1520 D6
7100 BLDR 80503 1520 D6
7900 BldC 80503 1521 C6
9000 BldC 80504 1521 C6
9500 BldC 80504 1522 A6
11400 BldC 80504 1523 A6
12600 WldC 80516 1523 A6
Miners Al
1100 GOLD 80401 2107 D4
E Miners Ct
3500 DgsC 80126 2449 D3
Miners Dr
100 LAFT 80026 1690 C6
S Miners Dr
8800 DgsC 80126 2449 D3
S Miners Pl
8800 DgsC 80126 2449 D3
S Miners St
8800 DgsC 80126 2449 D3
Miners Wy
- PrkC 80456 2521 B3
Miners Candle Ct
3900 CSRK 80109 2702 D4
Miners Candle Dr
3900 CSRK 80109 2702 D4
Miners Candle Pl
3800 CSRK 80109 2702 D4
Miners Mesa Rd
- BKHK 80403 2018 A4
Mines Pk
10 GOLD 80401 2107 D5
Mining Camp Tr
5100 DgsC 80134 2621 C4
E Minnesota Dr
5600 DNVR 80224 2198 B4
5600 DNVR 80246 2198 B4
Minnow Ln
5000 BMFD 80020 1775 B4
Minos Ct
1600 LAFT 80026 1690 A7
Minot Pl
500 LGMT 80501 1356 D5
Minotaur Cir
800 LAFT 80026 1690 B6
Minshal Dr
- BldC 80301 1603 D7
- BLDR 80301 1603 D7
W Minter Ln
1700 DgsC 80109 2702 C7
Minturn Av
10 BMFD 80020 1774 E5
Mira del Sol Ct
4400 CSRK 80104 2703 E2
Mirage Dr
4500 DgsC 80108 2619 A6
26600 JfnC 80433 2526 A6
26700 JfnC 80433 2525 E6
Miramonte Blvd
1800 BMFD 80020 1774 D6
Miramonte Ct
1300 BMFD 80020 1774 E6
Miramonte Rd
- BldC 80403 1768 D7
32000 BldC 80403 1852 C1
Miramonte St
1100 BMFD 80020 1774 E7
Miriam Ln
5000 DgsC 80134 2621 D4
Miro Ct
6900 BldC 80503 1520 E4
Mirror Lake Wy
- BMFD 80020 1775 C6
Mission Ln
31800 JfnC 80439 2188 E7
S Mission Pkwy
3600 AURA 80013 2284 E3
Mission Wy
14300 BMFD 80020 1775 C3
E Mississippi Av
- AphC 80231 2198 C4
- DNVR 80231 2198 C4
10 DNVR 80209 2196 E4
10 DNVR 80223 2196 E4
500 DNVR 80210 2196 E4
1600 DNVR 80209 2197 C4
3900 DNVR 80210 2197 C4
3900 GNDL 80246 2197 C4
4300 DNVR 80246 2197 C4
4600 DNVR 80246 2198 A4
4600 GNDL 80246 2198 A4
6100 DNVR 80224 2198 C4
7800 AphC 80247 2198 E4
7800 DNVR 80247 2198 E4
8800 AphC 80247 2199 A4
8800 DNVR 80247 2199 A4
9400 AURA 80247 2199 A4
10300 AURA 80012 2199 C4
12800 AURA 80012 2200 C4
14900 AURA 80017 2200 C4
16600 AURA 80017 2201 B4
18500 AURA 80011 2201 B4
22700 AphC 80018 2202 C4
22700 AURA 80018 2202 C4
24600 AphC 80018 2203 A4
24600 AURA 80018 2203 A4
34500 AphC 80137 2205 C3
41900 AphC 80102 2207 B3
48900 AphC 80102 2209 A3
48900 BNNT 80102 2209 A3
W Mississippi Av
10 DNVR 80209 2196 D4
10 DNVR 80210 2196 D4
10 DNVR 80223 2196 D4
2400 DNVR 80219 2196 A4
3200 DNVR 80219 2195 D4
5100 LKWD 80232 2195 D4
5200 LKWD 80226 2195 D4
6800 LKWD 80226 2194 D4
6800 LKWD 80232 2194 D4
11400 LKWD 80226 2193 E4
11500 LKWD 80228 2193 D4
W Mississippi Av SR-8
5800 LKWD 80232 2195 B4
6200 LKWD 80226 2195 A4
E Mississippi Cir
23600 AURA 80018 2202 D4
W Mississippi Ct
13000 LKWD 80228 2193 B4
E Mississippi Dr
7500 AphC 80231 2198 D4
7500 DNVR 80231 2198 D4
E Mississippi Pl
- AURA 80018 2202 D4
14100 AURA 80012 2200 B4
17800 AURA 80017 2201 B4
W Mississippi Pl
6500 LKWD 80232 2195 A4
8600 LKWD 80232 2194 C4
W Mississippi Wy
6500 LKWD 80232 2195 A3
Missouri Av
600 LGMT 80501 1439 A5
1400 LGMT 80501 1438 E6
E Missouri Av
4800 DNVR 80246 2198 A4
9300 AphC 80247 2199 A4
Missouri Gulch Rd
10 GpnC 80403 1933 B6
Missouri Peak Pl
6100 DgsC 80108 2618 E2
Mistletoe Rd
10 JfnC 80401 2190 D2
Misty Ct
- BMFD 80020 1775 D6
Misty Rd
27600 JfnC 80403 1937 E6
27600 JfnC 80403 1938 A6
Misty St
13300 BMFD 80020 1775 E6
Misty Wy
6000 BldC 80503 1519 E4
6000 BldC 80503 1520 A4
Misty Vale Ct
10 BldC 80302 1600 D3
Misty Valley Ln
8600 JfnC 80433 2442 D2
Mitchell Cir
19800 DNVR 80249 2033 D6
Mitchell Ct
9400 BldC 80503 1355 C3
9400 BldC 80504 1355 C3
Mitchell Dr
19400 DNVR 80249 2033 D7
Mitchell Ln
3300 BLDR 80301 1603 B6
Mitchell Pl
- DNVR 80249 2034 A6
15000 DNVR 80239 2032 C7
19800 DNVR 80249 2033 D7
Mitchell St
- CSRK 80104 2705 A6
- CSRK 80104 2789 A1
Mitze Dr
8100 AdmC 80221 1944 C4
8300 FLHT 80260 1944 C4
Mitze Wy
8200 AdmC 80221 1944 C4
8200 FLHT 80260 1944 C4
Miwok St
800 KIOW 80117 2796 B3
Miwok Tr
31700 JfnC 80439 2356 E3
S Mobile Cir
4100 AURA 80013 2284 E4
Mobile Ct
- AdmC 80022 1864 E7
- AdmC 80022 1948 E1
- CMCY 80022 1948 E1
- CMCY 80603 1864 E2
S Mobile Ct
5900 CTNL 80016 2368 E2
Mobile St
- AdmC 80022 1864 E7
10 LGMT 80501 1439 A3
200 EbtC 80107 2793 B1
200 ELIZ 80107 2793 B1
700 AURA 80011 2116 E6
14400 AdmC 80601 1780 E2
14400 BGTN 80601 1780 E2
S Mobile St
1900 AURA 80013 2200 E6
1900 AURA 80017 2200 E6
2700 AURA 80013 2284 E1
5500 CTNL 80015 2368 E1
6000 AphC 80016 2368 E2
6000 CTNL 80016 2368 E2
Mobile Wy
10400 CMCY 80022 1864 E5
S Mobile Wy
2100 AURA 80013 2200 E7
2900 AURA 80013 2284 E2
4500 AURA 80015 2284 E5
8100 AphC 80112 2368 E7
Mockingbird Ct
400 DgsC 80129 2448 D6
Mockingbird Ln
10 CHLV 80113 2281 A5
600 BGTN 80601 1695 E7
700 BGTN 80601 1779 D1
4100 LGMT 80503 1438 A6
10000 DgsC 80129 2448 D6
Mockingbird St
600 BGTN 80601 1695 E7
600 BGTN 80601 1779 D1
1000 BGTN 80601 1780 A1
Mockingbird Tr
1600 PrkC 80456 2607 C7
1600 PrkC 80456 2691 D1
Model T Rd
10 BldC 80302 1601 B6
Modena Ln
6300 BldC 80503 1520 A3
S Modoc Ln
6500 JfnC 80439 2356 E4
Modoc St
10 WARD 80481 1597 D1
Modred St
900 LAFT 80026 1690 D6
Moffat Ct
800 DgsC 80108 2618 C3
W Moffat Pl
2200 AdmC 80221 2028 B4
Moffat Rd
27600 JfnC 80439 2273 E7
Moffat St
600 ERIE 80516 1607 B4
Moffit Ct
3700 BLDR 80304 1602 C5
Mohave Ct
- KIOW 80117 2796 A3
Mohawk Cir
100 SUPE 80027 1772 D4
Mohawk Dr
100 BLDR 80303 1687 C5
3000 DgsC 80135 2700 A2
4000 DgsC 80118 2953 B3
S Mohawk Rd
5300 LITN 80123 2363 E1
S Mohawk St
13100 JfnC 80470 2524 A7
13300 JfnC 80470 2608 A1
Mohawk Tr
10 PrkC 80470 2523 E7
34700 JfnC 80470 2524 A7
Molas Ct
7500 DgsC 80118 2954 C2
Molina Pl
16900 PARK 80134 2453 A6
Moline Ct
- CMCY 80640 1863 D2
200 AURA 80010 2199 D1
Moline Pl
- CMCY 80640 1863 D2
S Moline Pl
2900 AURA 80014 2283 D1
Moline St
- CMCY 80640 1863 D2
10 AURA 80012 2199 D1
200 AURA 80010 2199 C1
1300 AURA 80010 2115 D5
2400 DNVR 80010 2115 D3
2400 DvrC 80010 2115 D3
4700 DNVR 80239 2031 D6
12100 AdmC 80640 1863 D1
S Moline St
10 AURA 80012 2199 D1
2100 AURA 80014 2199 D6
S Moline Wy
1900 AURA 80012 2199 D6
1900 AURA 80014 2199 D6
5900 AphC 80111 2367 D2
S Moline Wy S
7100 AphC 80112 2367 D5
E Molly Av
19000 PARK 80134 2537 C5
19200 DgsC 80134 2537 D5
Molly Cir
- BMFD 80020 1775 D3
S Molly Ct
12900 PARK 80134 2537 D5
Molly Dr
12400 JfnC 80433 2525 D5
26400 JfnC 80433 2526 A6
Molly Ln
- BMFD 80020 1775 D3
Mona Ct
7800 AdmC 80221 1944 D5
S Monaco Cir
3100 AphC 80222 2282 C2
3100 DNVR 80222 2282 C2
3100 DNVR 80224 2282 C2
8000 CTNL 80112 2366 C7
S Monaco Cir E
7600 CTNL 80112 2366 C6
S Monaco Cir W
7600 CTNL 80112 2366 C6
Monaco Ct
12000 AdmC 80602 1862 B2
S Monaco Ct
6300 CTNL 80111 2366 C3
7800 CTNL 80112 2366 C7
8200 CTNL 80112 2450 C1
Monaco Dr
6500 AdmC 80602 1862 B1
Monaco Pkwy
10 DNVR 80220 2198 C1
10 DNVR 80224 2198 C1
600 DNVR 80220 2114 C6
1900 DNVR 80207 2114 C6
3900 DNVR 80207 2030 C7
3900 DNVR 80216 2030 C7
S Monaco Pkwy
10 DNVR 80220 2198 C2
1800 DNVR 80224 2198 C7
2000 DNVR 80222 2198 C7
2600 DNVR 80224 2282 C2
2900 AphC 80222 2282 C2
3200 DNVR 80222 2282 C2
3400 DNVR 80237 2282 C2
Monaco St
- DNVR 80207 2030 C7
- DNVR 80237 2282 C5
4800 DNVR 80022 2030 B6
4800 DNVR 80216 2030 B6
5300 CMCY 80022 2030 B4
6900 CMCY 80022 1946 B7
7400 AdmC 80022 1946 B6
8800 AdmC 80640 1946 B2
8800 CMCY 80640 1946 B2
9700 AdmC 80229 1862 B7
9700 AdmC 80640 1862 B7
12000 AdmC 80602 1862 B2
15200 AdmC 80602 1694 B7
15200 AdmC 80602 1778 B1
15200 TNTN 80602 1694 B7
15200 TNTN 80602 1778 B1
S Monaco St
- DNVR 80237 2282 C6
- DvrC 80111 2282 C6
- DvrC 80237 2282 C6
- GDVL 80237 2282 C6
5100 CHLV 80111 2282 C6
5100 GDVL 80111 2282 C6
5400 GDVL 80111 2366 C1
5800 CTNL 80111 2366 C1
7300 CTNL 80112 2366 C6
10700 DgsC 80124 2450 C7
Monaco Wy
6600 AdmC 80602 1862 B1
12900 TNTN 80602 1778 B6
S Monaco Wy
5900 CTNL 80111 2366 C2
7500 CTNL 80112 2366 C6
Monaco St Pkwy
2200 DNVR 80207 2114 C2
Monaghan Rd
- DNVR 80249 2035 D1
Monaghan Mile Rd
- AdmC 80019 2119 E4
- AURA 80019 2035 D5
- AURA 80019 2119 E4
- DNVR 80249 2035 D3
- DvrC 80249 2035 D3
Monarch Av
1200 LGMT 80501 1356 E7
Monarch Blvd
- DgsC 80108 2618 E1
8100 DgsC 80108 2534 E7
11000 DgsC 80124 2450 B7
11000 DgsC 80124 2534 B2
Monarch Cir
47900 AphC 80137 2372 A7
47900 EbtC 80138 2372 A7
47900 EbtC 80138 2456 A1
Monarch Ct
100 LSVL 80027 1689 B5
1300 LGMT 80501 1356 E7
12900 BMFD 80020 1775 E7
30400 JfnC 80439 2189 A7
Monarch Dr
- BLDR 80301 1603 C7
1200 LGMT 80501 1356 E7
46900 EbtC 80138 2457 A3
Monarch Pl
3200 EbtC 80138 2457 A4
Monarch Rd
- BldC 80503 1521 D5
- DgsC 80118 2954 E3
3000 EbtC 80138 2457 A4
5600 BldC 80503 1519 D5
5600 BldC 80503 1520 A5
5600 BLDR 80503 1520 A5
9800 BldC 80504 1521 E5
10300 BldC 80504 1522 A5
Monarch St
- AdmC 80102 2124 B2
100 LSVL 80027 1689 C5
S Monarch St
4900 AURA 80011 2201 E1
Monarch Tr
200 BMFD 80020 1774 E5
Monarch Wy
900 SUPE 80027 1773 A6
Monarch Park Ct
6400 BldC 80503 1520 E6
Monarch Park Pl
6200 BldC 80503 1520 D6
Monares Ln
100 ERIE 80516 1607 D5
Moncrief Rd
- AURA 80010 2115 E4
E Moncrieff Pl
13800 AURA 80011 2116 C1
W Moncrieff Pl
3300 DNVR 80211 2111 E2
4400 DNVR 80212 2111 C2
5100 WTRG 80212 2111 C2
S Monica Ln
7300 JfnC 80439 2358 C6
W Monmouth Av
3000 EGLD 80110 2279 E7
3000 EGLD 80110 2280 A7
3400 LITN 80123 2279 E7
3800 DNVR 80123 2279 D6
3800 DvrC 80123 2279 D6
E Monmouth Pl
8500 DNVR 80237 2282 D6
8500 DNVR 80237 2283 A6
15300 AURA 80015 2284 D6
19400 CTNL 80015 2285 D7
Monroe Cir
8300 AdmC 80229 1945 D4
13400 TNTN 80241 1777 D6
Monroe Ct
8500 AdmC 80229 1945 D3
13100 TNTN 80241 1777 D6
S Monroe Ct
200 LSVL 80027 1773 C2
6100 CTNL 80121 2365 D2
7300 CTNL 80122 2365 D5
Monroe Dr
1000 BLDR 80303 1687 B3
9900 TNTN 80229 1861 D7
12200 TNTN 80241 1861 D1
13000 TNTN 80241 1777 D6
29800 JfnC 80439 2357 B3
S Monroe Dr
6100 CTNL 80121 2365 D3
S Monroe Ln
4300 CHLV 80113 2281 D5
Monroe Pl
1400 LSVL 80027 1689 C6
12200 TNTN 80241 1861 D1
Monroe St
10 DNVR 80206 2197 D1
10 DNVR 80209 2197 D1
300 DNVR 80206 2113 D7
3500 DNVR 80205 2113 D1
5100 DNVR 80216 2029 D5
6700 CMCY 80022 2029 D1
8800 TNTN 80229 1945 D3
10100 TNTN 80229 1861 D7
11600 TNTN 80233 1861 D3
13400 TNTN 80241 1777 D5
13800 TNTN 80602 1777 D4
S Monroe St
- DNVR 80210 2281 D3
10 DNVR 80206 2197 D1
10 DNVR 80209 2197 D1
1000 DNVR 80210 2197 D5
3500 CHLV 80113 2281 D3
3500 DvrC 80113 2281 D3
3500 DvrC 80210 2281 D3
Monroe Wy
900 SUPE 80027 1773 A6
8400 AdmC 80229 1945 D4
11900 TNTN 80233 1861 D2
13200 TNTN 80241 1777 D6
S Monroe Wy
600 DNVR 80209 2197 D3
7700 CTNL 80122 2365 D7
8100 CTNL 80122 2449 D1
W Montana Av
12800 LKWD 80228 2193 C5
E Montana Cir
14300 AURA 80012 2200 C5
E Montana Dr
18800 AURA 80017 2201 C5
W Montana Dr
12900 LKWD 80228 2193 C6
E Montana Pl
3300 DNVR 80210 2197 D5
4300 DNVR 80222 2197 E5
4500 DNVR 80222 2198 A5
6900 DNVR 80224 2198 C5
12000 AURA 80012 2199 D5
16100 AURA 80017 2200 E5
17700 AURA 80017 2201 B5
23300 AURA 80018 2202 D5
W Montana Pl
6600 LKWD 80232 2195 A6
9300 LKWD 80232 2194 B6
10900 JfnC 80232 2193 E6
13200 LKWD 80228 2193 B6
Montana St
- DNVR 80236 2279 C4
Montane Dr
10 IDSP 80452 2101 D5
Montane Dr E
1500 JfnC 80401 2190 E6
1600 JfnC 80401 2191 A6
Montane Dr W
23900 JfnC 80401 2190 C7
Montano Ct
12300 DgsC 80108 2534 C4
Montano Pl
6400 DgsC 80108 2534 C4
Montano Wy
12300 DgsC 80108 2534 C4
Mont Blanc Dr
23600 JfnC 80439 2274 E5
E Montclair Ct
2900 DgsC 80126 2449 D4
S Montclair Dr
9600 DgsC 80126 2449 C4
Montclair Ln
3900 BLDR 80301 1603 B5
Montclair Pl
7000 DNVR 80220 2114 C6
Monte Wy
- NHGN 80233 1861 A3
Monterey Cir
10200 NHGN 80260 1860 C6
Monterey Ct
1400 BMFD 80020 1774 E6
Monterey Dr
1300 BMFD 80020 1774 E6
Monterey Ln
29800 JfnC 80439 2273 B1
Monterey Pl
3700 BldC 80301 1603 A5
3700 BLDR 80301 1603 A5
E Monterey Pl
6200 DgsC 80130 2450 B3
Monte Vista Av
8500 BldC 80503 1521 A5
Monte Vista Rd
300 JfnC 80401 2191 B2
Monte Vista St
300 BGTN 80601 1697 B6
Montezuma St
100 BGTN 80601 1697 B6
W Montgomery Av
10000 JfnC 80127 2362 A1
Montgomery Cir
1700 LGMT 80501 1357 A5
S Montgomery Ct
1200 SUPE 80027 1773 A5
Montgomery Dr
10 ERIE 80516 1607 C5
10 WldC 80516 1607 C5
W Monticello Av
6200 JfnC 80128 2363 A7
9100 JfnC 80128 2362 C7
W Monticello Pl
9100 JfnC 80128 2446 C3
S Montrose Wy
9200 DgsC 80126 2449 B4
Montvale Cir
10700 DgsC 80130 2449 E7
Montvale Dr
- DgsC 80126 2449 E7
4900 DgsC 80130 2449 E7
Montview Blvd
- AURA 80011 2116 D4
4000 DNVR 80206 2113 E4
4000 DNVR 80207 2113 E4
4000 DNVR 80220 2113 E4
4700 DNVR 80207 2114 A4
4700 DNVR 80220 2114 A4
7600 DNVR 80238 2114 E4
8800 AURA 80010 2115 A4
8800 AURA 80238 2115 A4
8800 DNVR 80220 2115 A4
8800 DNVR 80238 2115 A4
8800 DvrC 80238 2115 A4
E Montview Blvd
12100 AURA 80010 2115 E4
12800 AURA 80010 2116 A4
18500 AURA 80011 2117 C4
E Montview Dr
19500 AURA 80011 2117 D4
W Montview Ln
7000 DgsC 80125 2448 A7
N Monument Cir
1400 CSRK 80104 2704 E5
E Monument Dr
5500 CSRK 80104 2704 E5
N Monument Dr
1200 CSRK 80104 2704 E5
W Monument Dr
600 DgsC 80129 2448 D3
Moon Cir
2300 TNTN 80229 1945 C2
Moon Ct
9000 TNTN 80229 1945 C2
Moon Dr
10 PrkC 80456 2607 E5
Moondust Pl
4600 CSRK 80109 2702 C4
Mooney Pl
100 ERIE 80516 1691 C3
Moonfall Ln
- EbtC 80107 2709 A1
Moon Gulch Rd
- GpnC 80403 1849 D2
- GpnC 80474 1849 B3
Moonlight Dr
9200 JfnC 80127 2444 D4
Moonlight Wy
5300 DgsC 80134 2621 B4
Moonshadow Ln
3100 JfnC 80439 2274 B2
Moonshine Ridge Tr
4600 DgsC 80134 2622 E5
4600 DgsC 80134 2623 A5
Moonstone Ct
- BldC 80504 1438 E7
- LGMT 80504 1438 E7
Moonstone Ln
1600 CSRK 80108 2619 E7
1600 CSRK 80108 2620 A7
Moore Cir
6300 ARVD 80004 2026 A2
10700 WSTR 80021 1858 A5
S Moore Cir
1600 LKWD 80232 2194 A6
Moore Ct
3400 WTRG 80033 2110 A1
4400 WTRG 80033 2026 A7
8300 ARVD 80005 1942 A4
10600 WSTR 80021 1858 A6
S Moore Ct
700 LKWD 80226 2194 A3
1600 LKWD 80232 2194 A6
1800 LKWD 80227 2194 A6
7100 JfnC 80127 2362 A5
Moore Dr
10 CSRK 80104 2703 E7
S Moore Dr
- JfnC 80227 2278 A1

Denver Regional Street Index

STREET Block City ZIP Map# Grid

S Moore Dr
2600 LKWD 80227 2278 A1
N Moore Rd
7500 DgsC 80125 2532 A7
Moore St
10 PrkC 80456 2521 D2
2500 LKWD 80215 2110 A3
2500 WTRG 80215 2110 A3
3200 WTRG 80033 2110 A2
4200 WTRG 80033 2026 A7
6500 ARVD 80004 2026 A1
8000 JfnC 80005 1942 A5
8200 ARVD 80005 1942 A4
10600 WSTR 80021 1858 A5
S Moore St
300 LKWD 80226 2194 A2
2100 LKWD 80227 2194 A7
3600 JfnC 80235 2278 A4
4700 JfnC 80127 2278 A6
5700 JfnC 80127 2362 A2
8400 JfnC 80127 2446 A1
Moore Wy
10700 WSTR 80021 1858 A5
Mooredale Rd
10 PrkC 80456 2689 C2
Moorhead Av
2700 BLDR 80305 1686 E4
2700 BLDR 80305 1687 A4
Moorhead Cir
4800 BldC 80305 1687 C7
4800 BLDR 80305 1687 C7
E Moorhead Cir
700 BldC 80305 1687 C7
800 BLDR 80305 1687 C7
W Moorhead Cir
700 BLDR 80305 1687 B7
Mooring Rd
10300 BldC 80504 1522 A1
Moorside Dr
17000 PARK 80134 2453 A6
Moose Cir
100 DgsC 80116 2790 E1
S Moose Creek Ct
12500 PARK 80134 2537 E3
S Moose Creek Pl
12500 PARK 80134 2537 D4
Moqui Rd
23300 JfnC 80439 2274 E5
W Moraine Dr
8400 JfnC 80128 2362 D6
E Moraine Pl
24000 AURA 80016 2370 E6
Morgan Dr
700 BLDR 80303 1687 C4
Morgan Pl
- LGMT 80501 1356 A7
100 DgsC 80108 2618 C4
Morgan Rd
400 LGMT 80501 1439 D2
Morgan Tr
34400 EbtC 80107 2708 D7
Mormon Dr
23800 JfnC 80433 2526 D7
Morning Dove Dr
900 LGMT 80501 1440 A1
Morning Dove Ln
8700 DgsC 80126 2449 A2
S Morning Glory Ct
9500 DgsC 80130 2450 A4
Morning Glory Dr
100 BLDR 80302 1686 C5
3600 CSRK 80109 2618 D7
3800 CSRK 80109 2702 D1
S Morning Glory Ln
5300 LITN 80123 2363 D1
9300 DgsC 80130 2450 A4
E Morning Glory Pl
5000 DgsC 80130 2450 A4
S Morning Glory Wy
9300 DgsC 80130 2450 A4
Morning Rose Dr
23300 JfnC 80401 2190 E5
Morningside Dr
10 LKWD 80215 2110 A3
10 WTRG 80033 2110 A3
10 WTRG 80215 2110 A3
1400 LGMT 80501 1356 E7
1400 LGMT 80501 1357 A7
S Morningside Dr
9900 JfnC 80465 2443 C6
Morning Side Rd
17500 JfnC 80433 2694 E4
Morningside Rd
2700 BLDR 80304 1686 B1
Morning Song Ct
3300 CSRK 80109 2702 C3
Morning Star Ct
- EbtC 80107 2709 C4
43900 EbtC 80107 2542 E1
Morning Star Dr
4200 DgsC 80108 2618 E6
4200 DgsC 80108 2619 A6
31300 JfnC 80439 2272 E3
Morning Star Ln
300 LAFT 80026 1689 E4
E Morning Star Pl
9100 DgsC 80134 2622 D2
Morning Star Wy
10 DgsC 80108 2619 A6
300 DgsC 80108 2618 E6
Morningview Dr
- CSRK 80109 2702 C4
Morningview Ln
- CSRK 80109 2702 D4
W Morraine Av
5800 JfnC 80128 2363 B6
8100 JfnC 80128 2362 D6
9700 JfnC 80127 2362 B6
W Morraine Dr
6800 JfnC 80128 2363 A6
7000 JfnC 80128 2362 E6
W Morraine Pl
6300 JfnC 80128 2363 A6
9900 JfnC 80127 2362 B6

Morris Av
25000 JfnC 80433 2442 A6
Morris Ct
- AURA 80011 2115 E2
- ERIE 80516 1690 C2
Morrison Al
400 BLDR 80302 1686 B2
Morrison Av
28300 JfnC 80470 2693 D2
Morrison Ct
- SUPE 80027 1773 B6
Morrison Dr
6800 AdmC 80221 2028 B1
6900 AdmC 80221 1944 A7
Morrison Rd
1400 DNVR 80204 2112 A5
5100 DNVR 80219 2195 D3
5100 LKWD 80226 2195 D3
5100 LKWD 80232 2195 D3
7600 LKWD 80227 2194 C7
9200 LKWD 80227 2278 A1
10000 JfnC 80227 2278 A1
11000 JfnC 80227 2277 D1
11000 LKWD 80227 2277 D1
11100 JfnC 80228 2277 D1
11100 LKWD 80228 2277 D1
14500 LKWD 80465 2277 B2
14500 MRSN 80228 2277 B2
Morrison Rd SR-8
7600 LKWD 80227 2194 C7
9200 LKWD 80227 2278 A1
10000 JfnC 80227 2278 A1
11000 JfnC 80227 2277 D1
11000 LKWD 80227 2277 D1
11100 JfnC 80228 2277 D1
11100 LKWD 80228 2277 D1
14500 LKWD 80465 2277 B2
14500 MRSN 80228 2277 B2
W Morrison Rd
14700 LKWD 80228 2277 A3
14700 LKWD 80465 2276 E3
14700 LKWD 80465 2277 A3
14700 MRSN 80228 2277 A3
14700 MRSN 80465 2276 E3
16000 MRSN 80465 2276 E3
16400 JfnC 80465 2276 E3
W Morrison Rd SR-8
14700 LKWD 80228 2277 A3
14700 LKWD 80465 2276 E3
14700 LKWD 80465 2277 A3
14700 MRSN 80228 2277 A3
16000 MRSN 80465 2276 E3
16400 JfnC 80465 2276 E3
Morton Rd
- BldC 80503 1521 B4
Moselle Ct
2000 FLHT 80260 1944 B2
Moselle St
2000 FLHT 80260 1944 B2
Mosier Cir
24900 JfnC 80433 2442 C4
W Mosier Pl
2100 DNVR 80223 2196 B4
2400 DNVR 80219 2196 B4
3900 DNVR 80219 2195 D4
Mosier St
25600 JfnC 80433 2442 B4
Mosko Ct
3400 AdmC 80221 2027 E1
Moss Cir
6400 ARVD 80007 2024 D2
Moss Ct
6600 ARVD 80007 2024 D2
7000 ARVD 80007 1940 D7
Moss St
300 GOLD 80401 2192 E1
700 GOLD 80401 2108 D7
1300 JfnC 80401 2108 E6
7000 ARVD 80007 1940 E7
Moss Wy
10 JfnC 80401 2192 D1
Mossberg Ct
36600 EbtC 80107 2708 E2
Mossrock Ct
- BldC 80503 1270 B4
Mossrock Dr
- BldC 80503 1270 B4
Moss Rock Pl
1400 BLDR 80304 1602 C6
Moss Rock Rd
10 PrkC 80456 2606 B4
28400 JfnC 80401 2189 D2
Mossrock Run
10400 DgsC 80125 2614 E4
S Moss Rose Cir
9600 DgsC 80129 2448 A4
E Mossy Rock Dr
3800 DgsC 80126 2449 D1
S Mossy Rock Ln
3800 JfnC 80439 2273 D4
Motsenbocker Rd
- PARK 80134 2453 A7
N Motsenbocker Rd
7400 DgsC 80134 2537 B2
9800 PARK 80134 2537 B1
11700 PARK 80134 2453 B7
Motsenbocker Wy
17000 PARK 80134 2453 A7
Moulton Ct
6000 CSRK 80104 2788 E2
6100 CSRK 80104 2789 A2
Mountain Dr
- LGMT 80503 1437 D5
W Mountain Ln
3300 DgsC 80135 2785 D5
W Mountain Rd
3300 DNVR 80236 2279 E5
3300 SRDN 80110 2279 E5
Mountain Alder
10 JfnC 80127 2445 A1
Mountain Ash
10 JfnC 80127 2445 C1
Mountain Base Rd
- GpnC 80403 1934 E3
- GpnC 80403 1935 A2

Mountain Birch
10 JfnC 80127 2361 A5
Mountain Bluebird Wy
16100 JfnC 80465 2360 D4
Mountain Brook Dr
27400 JfnC 80433 2525 E4
E Mountain Brush Cir
6900 DgsC 80130 2450 C3
S Mountain Brush Ct
9100 DgsC 80130 2450 C3
E Mountain Brush Ln
7200 DgsC 80130 2450 D3
S Mountain Brush Pl
9100 DgsC 80130 2450 C3
S Mountain Brush St
9200 DgsC 80130 2450 C3
S Mountain Brush Tr
9200 DgsC 80130 2450 D3
S Mountain Brush Peak
9200 DgsC 80130 2450 B3
Mountain Cedar Ln
10 JfnC 80127 2360 E6
Mountain Chickadee St
300 DgsC 80126 2448 D1
300 DgsC 80126 2449 A2
Mountain Cloud Cir
100 DgsC 80126 2448 E2
S Mountain Daisy Ct
1800 DgsC 80129 2448 B4
S Mountain Daisy Wy
9600 DgsC 80129 2448 C4
Mountain Gold Run
- BMFD 80020 1775 B2
Mountain High Ct
10 JfnC 80127 2360 E6
Mountain House Rd
- GpnC 80403 1935 A5
3000 GpnC 80403 1934 E5
Mountain King Rd
10 BldC 80302 1600 A7
E Mountain Laurel Cir
1800 DgsC 80126 2449 B3
Mountain Laurel Dr
10 JfnC 80127 2360 E5
10 JfnC 80127 2361 A5
Mountain Laurel Pl
3700 BLDR 80304 1602 C6
S Mountain Laurel Wy
8900 DgsC 80126 2449 B3
Mountain Mahogany
10 JfnC 80127 2360 E5
Mountain Man Dr
- PARK 80134 2453 C6
N Mountain Manor Ct
6400 DgsC 80134 2622 B2
W Mountain Maple Av
1500 DgsC 80129 2448 B6
S Mountain Maple Ct
10100 DgsC 80129 2448 C5
S Mountain Maple Dr
10100 DgsC 80129 2448 B6
S Mountain Maple Ln
10100 DgsC 80129 2448 B6
S Mountain Meadows Dr
100 GpnC 80403 1850 C5
Mountain Meadows Rd
10 BldC 80302 1684 B2
Mountain Meadows Tr
4700 CSRK 80109 2702 B1
Mountain Moss Ct
25500 JfnC 80439 2274 B7
Mountain Oak
10 JfnC 80127 2361 B7
N Mountain Park Dr
24400 JfnC 80439 2358 C2
S Mountain Park Dr
24400 JfnC 80439 2358 C2
Mountain Park Rd
26700 JfnC 80439 2274 A7
27100 JfnC 80439 2273 E7
Mountain Pine Ct
- JfnC 80127 2445 C1
Mountain Pine Dr
10 JfnC 80127 2361 B7
10 JfnC 80127 2445 B1
Mountain Pines Rd
1200 BldC 80302 1684 B1
Mountain Ranch Rd
9100 JfnC 80433 2440 E3
Mountain Ridge Dr
- BldC 80503 1435 B6
9100 BldC 80302 1435 B6
Mountain Ridge Pl
- BldC 80503 1435 B5
9500 BldC 80302 1435 B5
E Mountain Sage Dr
1800 DgsC 80126 2449 B2
E Mountain Sage Pl
1800 DgsC 80126 2449 B2
E Mountain Sage Run
1800 DgsC 80126 2449 B2
E Mountain Sage Ter
2200 DgsC 80126 2449 C3
Mountain Shadow Ct
10 CSRK 80104 2703 D5
Mountain Shadow Ln
10 CSRK 80104 2703 D5
Mountain Shadows Dr
3000 LKWD 80215 2109 D2
3000 WTRG 80215 2109 D2
Mountainside Tr
10 JfnC 80439 2273 A4
Mountain Sky Dr
2400 CSRK 80104 2788 B4
Mountain Spirit Wy
22200 JfnC 80439 2275 A7
Mountain View Av
10 LGMT 80501 1356 B7
1400 LGMT 80501 1355 E7
2600 DgsC 80116 2706 A2
2800 LGMT 80503 1355 C7
3800 BldC 80503 1355 B7
E Mountain View Av
- BldC 80501 1356 D7

E Mountain View Av
- LGMT 80501 1357 A7
10 LGMT 80501 1356 C7
Mountain View Blvd
- BMFD 80020 1692 A3
- ERIE 80516 1691 E3
- ERIE 80516 1692 A3
Mountain View Cir
- BMFD 80020 1691 E7
- BMFD 80020 1692 A7
Mountain View Ct
100 LSVL 80027 1773 A1
3600 LGMT 80503 1355 B7
Mountain View Dr
- FLHT 80260 1944 B2
10 CCkC 80452 2186 B4
10 GpnC 80403 1849 D7
900 CSRK 80104 2703 D5
N Mountain View Dr
6300 DgsC 80134 2622 B2
Mountain View Ln
8900 BldC 80303 1689 B3
Mountainview Ln
8400 DgsC 80125 2447 C7
Mountain View Rd
400 BldC 80302 1686 B2
400 BLDR 80302 1686 B2
500 BldC 80302 1768 D3
25900 JfnC 80401 2190 B1
28500 JfnC 80433 2525 D3
Mountainview Rd
10 GDVL 80111 2366 C1
S Mountain View Rd
500 DgsC 80109 2786 C3
1800 DgsC 80135 2785 D5
Mountain View St
1700 WldC 80516 1523 E7
Mountain View Tr
30500 EbtC 80117 2796 C7
Mountain View Mobile Ct
- LGMT 80501 1356 A7
W Mountain Vista Ln
4300 CSRK 80109 2702 C2
Mountain Vista Rdg
10500 DgsC 80126 2449 C7
Mountain Willow Dr
- JfnC 80127 2361 A6
10 JfnC 80127 2360 E7
Mt Antero Wy
10700 PARK 80138 2454 B7
Mt Audubon Pl
5500 BldC 80503 1604 C1
Mt Bailey Dr
10 PrkC 80456 2690 E1
10 PrkC 80456 2691 A1
Mt Belford Av
12100 DgsC 80112 2451 D3
12400 DgsC 80112 2452 A3
Mt Belford Dr
4800 BGTN 80601 1697 D6
Mt Belford St
400 BGTN 80601 1697 D6
Mt Berstadt St
- BGTN 80601 1697 D6
Mt Bross St
- AdmC 80601 1697 D6
- BGTN 80601 1697 D6
Mt Bross Wy
10700 PARK 80138 2454 B7
Mt Cameron Dr
4700 BGTN 80601 1697 C6
Mt Cameron St
400 BGTN 80601 1697 D7
Mt Columbia Pl
10500 PARK 80138 2454 B7
Mt Elbert Ct
10700 PARK 80138 2454 B7
Mt Elbert Pl
21600 PARK 80138 2454 B7
Mt Elbert St
- BGTN 80601 1697 C6
Mt Eolus St
400 BGTN 80601 1697 D6
Mt Evans Blvd
- PrkC 80456 2523 C5
10 JfnC 80470 2608 A1
600 PrkC 80470 2523 E7
600 PrkC 80470 2524 A7
Mt Evans Ct
800 LSVL 80027 1689 A7
Mt Evans Dr
- PrkC 80456 2521 B3
1300 LGMT 80501 1356 C7
S Mt Evans Ln
2500 JfnC 80401 2275 C1
2500 JfnC 80465 2275 C1
Mt Evans Pl
- BLDR 80301 1604 C1
5200 BldC 80503 1604 C1
Mt Evans Rd
400 JfnC 80401 2106 B7
400 JfnC 80401 2190 B1
Mt Evans St
500 LGMT 80501 1439 D2
4600 BGTN 80601 1697 D6
Mt Evans Vista
400 JfnC 80401 2191 B3
Mt Falcon Rd
21000 JfnC 80465 2275 B5
Mt Harvard St
- BGTN 80601 1697 C6
S Mt Holy Cross
7100 JfnC 80127 2361 D5
Mt Lincoln St
- BGTN 80601 1697 C6
Mt Lindsey St
300 BGTN 80601 1697 D6
S Mt Marcy
7500 JfnC 80127 2362 B6
Mt Massive Dr
4800 BGTN 80601 1697 D6
Mt Massive Wy
100 LGMT 80501 1356 C5

Mt Meeker Rd
5400 BLDR 80301 1604 B1
7100 BldC 80301 1604 C1
7100 BldC 80503 1604 C1
7300 BldC 80503 1520 D7
S Mt Owen
7500 JfnC 80127 2362 A6
Mt Oxford St
- BGTN 80601 1697 C6
W Mt Powell
12100 JfnC 80127 2361 D5
Mt Princeton St
4500 BGTN 80601 1697 C6
Mt Pyramid Ct
9700 DgsC 80112 2451 C5
Mt Rose Wy
900 JfnC 80401 2190 E4
900 JfnC 80401 2191 A4
Mt Royal Dr
400 CSRK 80104 2787 C4
Mt Sanitas Av
5600 LGMT 80503 1437 D5
5700 BldC 80503 1437 D5
Mt Sanitas Dr
- BldC 80302 1686 A1
- BLDR 80302 1686 A1
- BLDR 80304 1686 A1
Mt Sanitas Tr
- BldC 80302 1686 A1
- BldC 80304 1602 A7
- BldC 80304 1686 A1
- BLDR 80302 1686 A1
Mountsfield Dr
21500 JfnC 80401 2191 B1
Mt Shavano St
- BGTN 80601 1697 C6
Mt Sherman Rd
7100 BldC 80301 1604 C1
7100 BldC 80503 1604 C1
7400 BldC 80503 1520 D7
Mt Sherman St
- BGTN 80601 1697 D6
Mountshire Cir
10700 DgsC 80126 2449 C7
Mt Sneffels Pl
6200 DgsC 80108 2618 E3
Mt Sneffels St
1800 LGMT 80501 1356 C5
4500 BGTN 80601 1697 C6
Mt Snowmass Ln
21700 PARK 80138 2454 B7
Mount Sopris Pkwy
- SUPE 80027 1857 A1
Mt Sopris Pkwy
- SUPE 80027 1857 A1
Mt Valentine Dr
32600 JfnC 80439 2188 D4
Mt Vernon Av
200 MRSN 80465 2276 C3
300 JfnC 80465 2276 C3
Mt Vernon Cir
300 JfnC 80401 2191 A3
Mt Vernon Rd
16000 JfnC 80401 2108 C7
16100 GOLD 80401 2108 C7
Mt Vernon Canyon Rd
18400 GOLD 80401 2192 A4
18400 JfnC 80401 2192 A4
Mt Vernon Canyon Rd US-40
18400 GOLD 80401 2192 A4
18400 JfnC 80401 2192 A4
Mt Vernon Country Club Rd
10 JfnC 80401 2190 C1
S Mt Vernon Country Club Rd
10 JfnC 80401 2190 B2
S Mt Vernon Cntry Clb Rd US-40
- JfnC 80401 2190 B2
Mountview Dr
1100 EbtC 80107 2708 B1
Mt Wilson
9400 DgsC 80112 2451 D4
Mt Wilson St
400 BGTN 80601 1697 C6
Mt Zion Dr
1800 GOLD 80401 2107 D4
S Mt Zirkel
7500 JfnC 80127 2362 A6
Mourning Dove Ln
10 JfnC 80127 2360 D4
700 GOLD 80401 2107 E7
Mouse Ear Ln
34700 JfnC 80403 2020 B5
Mowbray Ct
26300 JfnC 80457 2274 A3
Mowry Pl
3300 WSTR 80031 1943 E1
W Mueller Dr
700 DgsC 80129 2448 D5
Muirfield Cir
400 LSVL 80027 1773 B3
13800 BMFD 80020 1775 D4
Muirfield Ct
400 LSVL 80027 1773 B3
5300 BLDR 80301 1604 C1
13800 BMFD 80020 1775 D4
Muirfield Ln
1600 JfnC 80439 2188 E6
Muirfield Pt
13800 BMFD 80020 1775 D4
Mulberry Cir
300 BMFD 80020 1858 E3
300 BMFD 80020 1859 A3
Mulberry Ct
4500 BLDR 80301 1603 E4
W Mulberry Ln
1000 DgsC 80129 2448 C5
W Mulberry Pl
2000 DNVR 80204 2112 B6
S Mulberry St
9700 DgsC 80129 2448 C4

W Mulberry St
500 LSVL 80027 1773 A1
S Mulberry Wy
9800 DgsC 80129 2448 C5
Mule Deer Pl
7600 DgsC 80125 2531 B6
Mule Deer Tr
10 JfnC 80127 2360 E4
10 JfnC 80127 2361 A3
Mulligan Pl
1400 CSRK 80104 2787 E2
Mumford Av
100 LGMT 80501 1356 B4
Mumford Pl
10 LGMT 80501 1356 C4
Munoz Ct
500 ERIE 80516 1607 A6
Munstead Pl
- DgsC 80134 2452 D4
Muriel Dr
100 NHGN 80233 1860 E4
700 NHGN 80233 1861 A4
4000 TNTN 80233 1861 E4
Muriel Pl
11000 TNTN 80233 1861 E4
Murphy Rd
10 CCkC 80439 2271 E6
S Murphy Gulch Rd
8700 JfnC 80127 2444 C3
Murray Dr
10600 NHGN 80233 1861 A4
Murray St
100 BldC 80503 1520 E4
Muscadine Ct
- AURA 80016 2371 B3
S Muscadine Ct
- AURA 80016 2371 B5
Muscadne Ct
- AURA 80018 2119 B7
Muscadne St
- AURA 80018 2119 B7
S Musk Ox Dr
1200 AphC 80102 2206 E4
Muskrat Rd
10 GpnC 80403 1934 B7
200 GpnC 80403 2018 B1
Mustang Cir
4200 DgsC 80135 2616 B6
Mustang Rd
11200 DgsC 80116 2707 D1
Mustang Tr
34500 EbtC 80107 2708 D6
W Mustang Wy
13000 JfnC 80127 2445 C3
Mustang Run Pl
4700 CSRK 80109 2702 C4
Mustique Ct
4000 BLDR 80301 1603 B4
Myrna Ct
33500 JfnC 80470 2524 B6
Myrna Pl
9100 TNTN 80229 1945 B2
W Myrtle Pl
1900 DNVR 80204 2112 B5
Myrtle St
1100 BGTN 80601 1696 D5
Myrtlewood Ct
600 DgsC 80126 2449 A3
Myrtlewood Ln
2100 JfnC 80401 2109 C4
2100 LKWD 80215 2109 C4
Mystic Ct
9400 DgsC 80138 2538 E3
29500 JfnC 80439 2273 C1

N

Nadm Dr
33500 JfnC 80403 1852 B6
Nagel Dr
9100 TNTN 80229 1945 A1
Naiad Dr
800 NHGN 80234 1860 C5
Nakota Dr
22400 JfnC 80401 2191 A4
Namaque St
34700 PrkC 80470 2608 A1
Nambe Rd
4200 JfnC 80439 2275 A5
4200 JfnC 80465 2275 A5
Nambe Tr
9100 LNTR 80124 2451 A3
Nampeyo Rd
22800 JfnC 80439 2274 E6
22800 JfnC 80439 2275 A6
Nancy Mine Rd
10 BldC 80302 1600 A6
S Nancys Dr
11400 JfnC 80433 2525 B2
S Nancys Ln
29900 JfnC 80433 2525 B2
W Nantucket Ct
2000 LITN 80120 2364 B7
E Napa Dr
16700 AURA 80013 2284 E4
18700 AURA 80013 2285 C4
E Napa Pl
7600 DNVR 80237 2282 D4
8500 DNVR 80237 2283 A4
14200 AURA 80014 2284 C4
16600 AURA 80013 2284 E4
S Naples Ct
1900 AURA 80013 2200 E6
Naples Ln
1500 LGMT 80503 1438 A6
Naples St
800 AURA 80011 2116 E6
S Naples St
1700 AURA 80017 2200 E5
Naples Wy
600 AURA 80011 2116 E7
S Naples Wy
800 AURA 80017 2200 E3
2100 AURA 80013 2200 E6

S Naples Wy
4100 AURA 80013 2284 E5
S Narcissus Wy
3500 DNVR 80237 2282 C3
N Nashua Cir
5200 DgsC 80134 2621 E4
Nassau Av
- JfnC 80235 2278 B4
E Nassau Av
10 EGLD 80110 2280 E4
10 EGLD 80113 2280 E4
600 EGLD 80113 2281 A4
700 CHLV 80113 2281 A4
7600 DNVR 80237 2282 D4
8500 DNVR 80237 2283 A4
8900 GDVL 80014 2283 A4
15100 AURA 80014 2284 C4
15300 AURA 80013 2284 C4
21300 AphC 80013 2286 A4
W Nassau Av
10 EGLD 80110 2280 D4
10 EGLD 80113 2280 D4
10300 JfnC 80235 2278 A4
Nassau Cir E
5200 CHLV 80113 2282 A4
Nassau Cir W
4900 CHLV 80113 2282 A4
Nassau Ct
- DNVR 80236 2279 E4
- SRDN 80236 2279 E4
E Nassau Ct
6200 DgsC 80130 2450 C3
E Nassau Dr
16600 AURA 80013 2284 E4
18200 AURA 80013 2285 C4
Nassau Pl
4000 BLDR 80301 1603 B5
E Nassau Pl
- AURA 80013 2284 E4
5700 CHLV 80111 2282 B4
17100 AURA 80013 2285 A4
21400 AphC 80013 2286 A4
22300 AURA 80018 2286 C4
W Nassau Wy
700 EGLD 80110 2280 D4
Natches Ct
3500 SRDN 80110 2280 C3
S Natches Ct
4100 SRDN 80110 2280 C5
S Nate Cir
12300 PARK 80134 2537 D4
Nate Dr
- PARK 80134 2537 D4
National Pl
300 LGMT 80501 1356 B7
National Western Dr
4600 DNVR 80216 2029 A6
S Native Dancer Tr
7500 JfnC 80439 2357 D7
7700 JfnC 80439 2441 D1
Natsihi Rd
22100 JfnC 80454 2359 A1
22300 JfnC 80454 2275 A7
Nautilus Ct
1100 LAFT 80026 1690 A5
Nautilus Ct N
4900 BLDR 80301 1604 A2
Nautilus Ct S
4600 BLDR 80301 1604 A3
Nautilus Dr
6300 BldC 80301 1604 A3
6300 BLDR 80301 1604 A3
E Navajo
- AdmC 80022 1946 C3
W Navajo
- AdmC 80022 1946 C3
N Navajo Cir
11300 WSTR 80234 1860 C3
N Navajo Ct
12400 WSTR 80234 1860 C1
Navajo Pl
4400 BLDR 80303 1687 C6
Navajo Rd
23000 JfnC 80439 2274 D6
Navajo St
- BMFD 80020 1776 B5
- DNVR 80211 2028 C6
- NHGN 80234 1860 C4
- WSTR 80234 1776 B5
- WSTR 80234 1860 C4
200 KIOW 80117 2796 A3
300 DNVR 80223 2112 C7
300 DNVR 80223 2196 C1
700 DNVR 80204 2112 C6
3200 DNVR 80211 2112 C1
6800 AdmC 80221 2028 C1
8200 AdmC 80221 1944 C4
8200 FLHT 80260 1944 C4
15200 AdmC 80020 1776 B1
15400 AdmC 80020 1692 C7
N Navajo St
11500 WSTR 80234 1860 C3
S Navajo St
100 DNVR 80223 2196 C2
4200 EGLD 80110 2280 C5
Navajo Tr
10 CCkC 80439 2440 A1
10 NDLD 80466 1765 C2
10 PrkC 80470 2607 E1
10 PrkC 80470 2608 A1
2000 LAFT 80026 1689 E3
2000 LAFT 80026 1690 A3
S Navajo Tr
11600 JfnC 80433 2525 C3
E Navarro Dr
16600 AURA 80013 2284 E4
19400 AURA 80013 2285 D4
22300 AURA 80018 2286 C4
E Navarro Pl
7600 DNVR 80237 2282 D4
14600 AURA 80014 2284 C4
15800 AURA 80013 2284 D4
19600 AURA 80013 2285 D4
22200 AURA 80018 2286 B4

STREET
Block City ZIP Map# Grid

S Navy Hill Rd
- JfnC 80470 2610 A6
15800 JfnC 80470 2609 E6
Neal Rd
10 PrkC 80456 2521 E2
600 PrkC 80456 2522 A2
Neal St
10 PrkC 80456 2521 D2
Nebo Rd
3100 BldC 80302 1518 C2
Nebraska Wy
5300 DNVR 80246 2198 B4
5500 DNVR 80224 2198 B4
7200 BldC 80504 1522 D3
Nebrina Pl
2800 BldC 80301 1603 A5
2800 BLDR 80301 1603 A5
Nebula Wy
- CSRK 80108 2619 E5
Needlegrass Ct
8300 PARK 80134 2452 E1
Needleleaf Ln
46000 EbtC 80138 2456 A4
Needles Ct
11000 PARK 80138 2538 B1
Needles Tr
28800 JfnC 80439 2357 C7
Needles Wy
21500 PARK 80138 2538 B1
Neher Ln
10 BLDR 80304 1602 D5
Neil Pl
3600 DNVR 80205 2113 D2
Neil St
8800 TNTN 80260 1944 C3
Neish St
10 PrkC 80456 2521 D2
Nellies Wy
3100 DgsC 80104 2788 A7
Nelson Av
26000 JfnC 80433 2442 A5
34300 JfnC 80470 2608 A2
S Nelson Cir
3500 JfnC 80235 2278 A3
3500 LKWD 80227 2278 A3
Nelson Ct
3000 LKWD 80215 2110 A2
5800 ARVD 80002 2026 A3
5800 ARVD 80004 2026 A3
8400 ARVD 80005 1942 A4
10300 WSTR 80021 1857 E6
10400 WSTR 80021 1858 A6
S Nelson Ct
2600 JfnC 80227 2278 A1
3300 LKWD 80227 2278 A3
3800 JfnC 80235 2278 A4
4900 JfnC 80127 2278 A7
7100 JfnC 80127 2362 A5
8500 JfnC 80127 2446 A2
Nelson Dr
3000 LKWD 80215 2110 A2
4200 BMFD 80020 1775 C3
8400 ARVD 80005 1941 E4
Nelson Pl
2200 LKWD 80215 2110 A3
Nelson Rd
1400 LGMT 80501 1438 E4
1800 BldC 80501 1438 E4
2800 BldC 80302 1435 E5
2800 BldC 80503 1435 E5
4100 BldC 80503 1436 A5
5500 BldC 80503 1437 A4
6400 LGMT 80503 1437 E4
8100 LGMT 80503 1438 C4
8600 BldC 80503 1438 C4
Nelson St
10 WARD 80481 1597 D1
2500 WTRG 80215 2110 A3
3200 LKWD 80215 2110 A2
3800 WTRG 80033 2110 A1
4700 WTRG 80033 2026 A6
5400 ARVD 80002 2026 A4
6500 ARVD 80004 2026 A1
7000 ARVD 80004 1942 A7
7600 ARVD 80005 1942 A6
8000 JfnC 80005 1942 A5
10000 WSTR 80021 1857 E7
10600 WSTR 80021 1858 A6
S Nelson St
300 LKWD 80226 2194 A3
2100 LKWD 80227 2194 A7
2800 JfnC 80227 2278 A2
2800 LKWD 80227 2278 A2
4700 JfnC 80127 2278 A6
5800 JfnC 80127 2362 A2
8400 JfnC 80127 2446 A1
Nelson St E
- JfnC 80465 2277 E5
Nelson St W
- JfnC 80127 2278 A5
- JfnC 80235 2278 A5
- JfnC 80465 2277 E5
S Nelson Wy
800 LKWD 80226 2194 A3
3500 LKWD 80227 2278 A3
3600 JfnC 80235 2278 A4
6400 JfnC 80127 2362 A3
Nelson Park Cir
700 LGMT 80503 1438 B5
Nelson Park Dr
600 LGMT 80503 1438 B4
Nelson Park Ln
600 BldC 80503 1438 C4
600 LGMT 80503 1438 C4
Nemrick Pl
1400 CSRK 80109 2703 C5
Neon Wy
- CSRK 80108 2619 D6
- DgsC 80108 2619 D6
Neon Forest Cir
700 LGMT 80504 1439 A6
S Nepal Ct
3300 AURA 80013 2286 A2
3600 AphC 80013 2286 A3
5400 CTNL 80015 2286 A7
5900 CTNL 80015 2370 A2
Nepal St
- AdmC 80019 2034 A4
- DNVR 80019 2034 A4
4500 DNVR 80249 2034 A6
N Nepal St
800 AphC 80018 2118 A6
900 AURA 80018 2118 A6
S Nepal St
3600 AphC 80013 2286 A3
5800 CTNL 80015 2370 A1
S Nepal Wy
3100 AURA 80013 2286 A1
5100 CTNL 80015 2286 A7
5600 CTNL 80015 2370 A1
Neptune Ct
300 DgsC 80124 2450 E2
Neptune Dr
1100 LAFT 80026 1690 A6
Neptunite Pl
- CSRK 80108 2619 E6
Nero Rd
10 GpnC 80403 1934 B3
S Netherland Cir
5800 CTNL 80015 2370 A2
6100 CTNL 80016 2370 A2
Netherland Ct
5500 DNVR 80249 2034 A4
S Netherland Ct
5400 CTNL 80015 2286 A7
Netherland St
4300 DNVR 80249 2034 A6
S Netherland St
- AphC 80013 2286 A4
- AphC 80015 2370 A1
5500 CTNL 80015 2370 A1
S Netherland Wy
5100 CTNL 80015 2286 A7
6100 CTNL 80016 2370 A3
6800 AURA 80016 2370 A4
Network Pkwy
- BMFD 80021 1857 E2
Neva Rd
- BldC 80302 1518 D4
- BldC 80503 1518 D4
4100 BldC 80503 1519 A4
7900 BldC 80503 1520 E4
8200 BldC 80503 1521 A4
E Nevada Av
12800 AURA 80012 2199 E2
12800 AURA 80012 2200 A2
E Nevada Cir
11900 AURA 80012 2199 D2
12800 AURA 80012 2200 A2
S Nevada Cir
7500 LITN 80120 2364 B6
S Nevada Dr
7700 LITN 80120 2364 A7
W Nevada Dr
12100 LKWD 80228 2193 D3
E Nevada Pl
6500 DNVR 80224 2198 C2
12100 AURA 80012 2199 E2
13600 AURA 80012 2200 B2
W Nevada Pl
1200 DNVR 80223 2196 C2
5000 DNVR 80219 2195 C2
5000 LKWD 80226 2195 C2
8200 LKWD 80226 2194 D2
12100 LKWD 80228 2193 C4
Nevada St
- GpnC 80403 2017 B4
100 CLCY 80403 2017 C4
S Nevada St
5400 LITN 80120 2364 B1
Nevadaville Rd
1000 GpnC 80403 2017 B5
Neville Ln
800 JfnC 80401 2189 D4
Nevis St
4000 BLDR 80301 1603 A5
4100 BldC 80301 1603 A5
S Newark Cir
200 AURA 80012 2199 D2
Newark Ct
500 AURA 80010 2115 D7
11200 CMCY 80640 1863 D4
S Newark Ct
600 AURA 80012 2199 D3
2600 AURA 80014 2283 D1
S Newark Pl
2800 AURA 80014 2283 D1
Newark St
10 AURA 80012 2199 D1
200 AURA 80010 2199 D1
1600 AURA 80010 2115 D4
11300 CMCY 80640 1863 D3
S Newark St
900 AURA 80012 2199 D3
5700 AphC 80111 2367 D1
S Newark Wy
400 AURA 80012 2199 D2
1900 AURA 80014 2199 D6
6100 AphC 80111 2367 D2
S Newbern Cir
7800 AphC 80016 2371 B7
Newbern Ct
- AURA 80016 2371 B5
Newbern St
- CSRK 80104 2788 E1
S Newbern Wy
- AURA 80016 2371 B2
1900 AURA 80018 2203 B6
W Newberry Cir
7800 LKWD 80235 2278 D4
S Newberry Ct
2400 DNVR 80224 2198 C7
Newborn Wy
- AURA 80018 2119 B7
Newbury Ct
2800 DgsC 80126 2533 D1
Newby Pl
10 LGMT 80501 1356 C4
S Newcastle Ct
2300 AURA 80018 2203 B7
8000 AphC 80016 2371 B7
S Newcastle Dr
9600 DgsC 80130 2450 A4
New Castle St
8100 DNVR 80249 1951 B4
Newcastle Wy
- AURA 80018 2119 B7
E Newcastle Wy
- AURA 80016 2371 B3
N Newcomb St
4200 WTRG 80033 2026 A7
Newcombe Ct
5800 ARVD 80002 2026 A3
6400 ARVD 80004 2026 A2
10200 WSTR 80021 1857 E6
S Newcombe Ct
3300 LKWD 80227 2278 A3
4800 JfnC 80127 2278 A6
8500 JfnC 80127 2446 A2
Newcombe Dr
1900 LKWD 80215 2110 A4
Newcombe St
2500 LKWD 80215 2110 A3
2500 WTRG 80215 2110 A3
6600 ARVD 80004 2026 A1
8400 ARVD 80005 1941 E4
10300 WSTR 80021 1857 E6
10600 WSTR 80021 1858 A6
S Newcombe St
- JfnC 80127 2362 A3
300 LKWD 80226 2194 A2
2400 JfnC 80227 2194 A7
2400 JfnC 80227 2278 A1
2700 LKWD 80227 2278 A1
8400 JfnC 80127 2446 A1
Newcombe Wy
4800 WTRG 80033 2026 A6
10600 WSTR 80021 1858 A5
S Newcombe Wy
800 LKWD 80226 2194 A4
2800 JfnC 80227 2278 A2
2800 LKWD 80227 2277 E2
2800 LKWD 80227 2278 A2
3600 JfnC 80235 2278 A4
6700 JfnC 80127 2362 A4
8400 JfnC 80127 2446 A1
New Forest Ln
8400 BldC 80503 1521 A1
E Newhall Dr
7000 DgsC 80130 2450 D4
7100 LITN 80124 2450 D4
New Haven Ct
4000 BLDR 80301 1603 B5
Newland Cir
7900 ARVD 80003 1943 A5
S Newland Cir
6500 JfnC 80123 2363 A2
Newland Ct
10 LKWD 80226 2195 A1
700 BldC 80303 1688 B4
1700 LKWD 80214 2111 A4
1900 EDGW 80214 2111 A4
2800 WTRG 80214 2111 A3
8200 ARVD 80003 1943 A4
N Newland Ct
9600 WSTR 80021 1859 A7
9600 WSTR 80021 1943 A1
S Newland Ct
10 LKWD 80226 2195 A1
1200 LKWD 80232 2195 A4
3400 LKWD 80227 2279 A3
5300 DNVR 80123 2363 A1
5700 JfnC 80123 2363 A2
7900 JfnC 80128 2363 A7
7900 JfnC 80128 2447 A1
Newland Dr
8400 ARVD 80003 1943 A3
S Newland Pl
1100 LKWD 80232 2195 A4
Newland St
10 LKWD 80226 2195 A1
300 LKWD 80226 2111 A7
2000 LKWD 80214 2111 A4
2600 EDGW 80214 2111 A3
3100 WTRG 80033 2111 A3
3200 WTRG 80214 2111 A2
4200 WTRG 80033 2027 A7
5300 ARVD 80002 2027 A5
6400 ARVD 80003 2027 A2
7000 WSTR 80003 1943 A7
7600 ARVD 80003 1943 A6
11500 WSTR 80020 1859 A3
S Newland St
- DNVR 80123 2363 A2
- DvrC 80123 2363 A2
10 LKWD 80226 2195 A2
1000 LKWD 80232 2195 A4
2700 DNVR 80227 2279 A2
3500 DNVR 80235 2279 A3
6900 JfnC 80128 2363 A5
7900 JfnC 80128 2447 A1
Newland Wy
5500 ARVD 80002 2027 A4
S Newland Wy
- DNVR 80123 2363 C1
- JfnC 80123 2363 A4
Newlin Ct
10500 DgsC 80134 2452 D6
N Newlin Gulch Rd
9300 DgsC 80108 2536 D3
10000 DgsC 80134 2536 E1
10000 PARK 80134 2536 E1
Newman Av
100 GpnC 80403 1849 D5
Newman Cir
400 LGMT 80501 1439 E2
Newman Dr
800 EbtC 80138 2624 B2
Newman St
3800 WTRG 80033 2110 A1
6600 ARVD 80004 2026 A1
7800 ARVD 80005 1942 A5
8000 JfnC 80005 1942 A5
New Market Ct
19700 PARK 80134 2537 D3
Newmarket St
10 WARD 80481 1597 D1
New Memphis Ct
800 CSRK 80108 2703 C1
W New Mexico Av
11400 JfnC 80232 2193 D6
12200 LKWD 80228 2193 D6
W New Mexico Pl
11600 JfnC 80232 2193 D6
11600 LKWD 80228 2193 D6
Newport Cir
2700 CSRK 80104 2787 C3
S Newport Cir
5400 GDVL 80111 2366 C1
Newport Ct
12300 AdmC 80602 1862 C1
16600 AdmC 80602 1694 B4
S Newport Ct
6300 CTNL 80111 2366 C3
7100 CTNL 80112 2366 C5
8100 CTNL 80112 2450 C1
Newport Dr
12100 AdmC 80602 1862 C1
Newport Ln
3800 BLDR 80304 1602 B5
38700 EbtC 80107 2624 B5
S Newport Ln
9100 DgsC 80130 2450 C4
Newport St
- TNTN 80602 1778 C6
100 DNVR 80220 2198 C1
600 DNVR 80220 2114 C5
3200 DNVR 80207 2114 C1
3900 DNVR 80207 2030 C7
4800 CMCY 80216 2030 C6
4800 DNVR 80022 2030 C6
4800 DNVR 80216 2030 C6
6400 CMCY 80022 2030 C2
7400 CMCY 80022 1946 C6
7700 AdmC 80022 1946 C5
11300 TNTN 80233 1862 B4
S Newport St
1800 AphC 80224 2198 C6
1900 DNVR 80224 2198 C6
2800 DNVR 80224 2282 C2
5300 GDVL 80111 2282 C7
5500 GDVL 80111 2366 C1
6000 CTNL 80111 2366 C2
7000 CTNL 80112 2366 C5
Newport Vil
- TNTN 80229 1945 D3
Newport Wy
12800 TNTN 80602 1778 B7
S Newport Wy
300 DNVR 80224 2198 C2
3500 DNVR 80237 2282 C3
7100 CTNL 80112 2366 C5
8100 CTNL 80112 2450 C1
Newton Ct
6600 AdmC 80003 2027 D1
13400 BMFD 80020 1775 D5
N Newton Ct
10200 WSTR 80031 1859 D6
Newton Dr
11700 WSTR 80031 1859 D3
N Newton Lp
- WSTR 80031 1859 D6
Newton Pl
- WSTR 80031 1859 D3
Newton St
10 DNVR 80219 2195 D1
300 DNVR 80219 2111 D7
1900 DNVR 80204 2111 D4
2900 DNVR 80211 2111 D2
4600 DNVR 80211 2027 D6
4800 DNVR 80221 2027 D6
5100 AdmC 80221 2027 D6
6400 AdmC 80003 2027 D2
7900 WSTR 80030 1943 D5
8800 AdmC 80031 1943 D3
9700 WSTR 80031 1943 D1
11700 WSTR 80031 1859 D3
12400 BMFD 80020 1859 D1
N Newton St
9200 WSTR 80031 1943 D2
S Newton St
10 DNVR 80219 2195 D2
2500 DNVR 80219 2279 D1
4300 DNVR 80236 2279 D6
4700 DNVR 80123 2279 E6
5000 DvrC 80123 2279 D7
5200 LITN 80123 2279 D7
Newton Wy
7400 WSTR 80030 1943 D6
12500 BMFD 80020 1775 C7
S Newton Wy
2700 DNVR 80236 2279 D1
New York Pl
10100 DNVR 80247 2199 B3
Nez Perce Tr
- CSRK 80109 2702 D3
NF-105
- GpnC 80474 1849 B2
NF-108
- PrkC 80456 2521 E1
NF-110
- PrkC 80456 2690 B3
NF-112
- BldC 80466 1513 A7
- BldC 80466 1597 B1
- BldC 80481 1597 C1
- WARD 80481 1597 D1
NF-226
- BldC 80466 1681 E3
NF-233A
- BldC 80302 1682 A1
NF-233C
- BldC 80302 1682 B1
NF-298
- BldC 80466 1681 A3
NF-512A
- DgsC 80125 2698 C4
NF-512B
- DgsC 80125 2698 C4
NF-513
- DgsC 80125 2698 C6
- DgsC 80135 2698 C6
NF-514
- DgsC 80135 2697 D4
- DgsC 80135 2698 A7
NF-514A
- DgsC 80135 2697 D5
NF-514B
- DgsC 80135 2697 D5
NF-516
- DgsC 80135 2698 A7
NF-538
- JfnC 80433 2695 D4
- JfnC 80433 2696 E2
NF-552
- JfnC 80470 2692 C6
NF-553
- JfnC 80470 2692 E7
NF-554
- JfnC 80470 2692 E7
- JfnC 80470 2693 A7
NF-562
- DgsC 80135 2697 E7
- DgsC 80135 2698 A7
NF-563
- DgsC 80135 2868 A2
S Niagara Cir
7100 CTNL 80112 2366 C5
Niagara Ct
12100 AdmC 80602 1862 C1
S Niagara Ct
5400 GDVL 80111 2366 C1
6000 CTNL 80111 2366 C2
6700 CTNL 80112 2366 C4
8100 CTNL 80112 2450 C1
Niagara St
- TNTN 80602 1778 C6
100 DNVR 80220 2198 C1
1100 DNVR 80220 2114 C5
1900 DNVR 80207 2114 C4
3900 DNVR 80207 2030 C7
4300 DNVR 80216 2030 C7
6400 CMCY 80022 2030 C2
7400 CMCY 80022 1946 C6
7700 AdmC 80022 1946 C5
10000 DgsC 80124 2450 C7
10000 DgsC 80124 2534 C1
11300 TNTN 80233 1862 B3
12100 AdmC 80602 1862 C1
16500 AdmC 80602 1694 B5
S Niagara St
1900 AphC 80224 2198 C6
1900 DNVR 80224 2198 C6
3200 DNVR 80224 2282 C2
5900 CTNL 80111 2366 C2
5900 GDVL 80111 2366 C2
8100 CTNL 80112 2366 C7
8100 CTNL 80112 2450 C1
8200 AphC 80112 2450 C1
8200 AphC 80126 2450 C1
Niagara Wy
- TNTN 80602 1778 B6
S Niagara Wy
1700 AphC 80224 2198 C6
1700 DNVR 80224 2198 C6
2900 DNVR 80224 2282 C2
3700 DNVR 80237 2282 C3
6100 CTNL 80111 2366 C2
7600 CTNL 80112 2366 C7
Niakwa Rd
30700 JfnC 80439 2356 E4
30700 JfnC 80439 2357 A4
Niblick Ct
3900 BldC 80503 1518 E6
Niblick Dr
3900 BldC 80503 1518 E5
4100 BldC 80503 1519 A6
Niblick Ln
10 CBVL 80123 2363 E3
10 CBVL 80123 2364 A3
Nicholl St E
2200 BLDR 80304 1602 D7
Nicholl St W
2200 BLDR 80304 1602 D7
E Nichols Av
800 LITN 80122 2365 A7
1300 CTNL 80122 2365 A7
6000 CTNL 80112 2366 B7
8900 CTNL 80112 2367 A7
15900 AphC 80112 2368 E7
W Nichols Av
7700 JfnC 80128 2362 D7
E Nichols Cir
2800 CTNL 80122 2365 C7
E Nichols Ct
500 LITN 80122 2364 E7
500 LITN 80122 2365 A7
8800 CTNL 80112 2367 A7
E Nichols Dr
500 LITN 80122 2364 E7
600 LITN 80122 2365 A7
1400 CTNL 80122 2365 B7
5100 CTNL 80122 2366 A7
W Nichols Dr
8800 JfnC 80128 2362 C7
9300 JfnC 80128 2446 C3
E Nichols Ln
1600 CTNL 80122 2365 B7
5600 CTNL 80122 2366 B7
6100 CTNL 80122 2366 B7
E Nichols Pkwy
21000 AphC 80016 2370 A7
Nichols Pl
- AURA 80016 2371 C7
E Nichols Pl
2300 CTNL 80122 2365 C7
5000 CTNL 80122 2366 A7
7400 CTNL 80112 2366 D7
8800 CTNL 80112 2367 A7
15900 AphC 80112 2368 E7
17300 CTNL 80016 2369 A7
17600 AURA 80016 2369 A7
21300 AphC 80016 2370 A7
21900 AURA 80016 2370 B7
W Nichols Pl
6900 JfnC 80128 2363 A7
9200 JfnC 80128 2362 B7
S Nichols Wy
11500 JfnC 80433 2524 E3
11500 JfnC 80433 2525 A3
Nickel Ct
1300 BMFD 80020 1774 D6
Nickel St
10 BMFD 80020 1858 D1
600 BMFD 80020 1774 D7
Nicklaus Ct
4400 BldC 80503 1519 A5
S Nickolas Av
10100 DgsC 80130 2450 B5
10200 DgsC 80124 2450 B5
E Nielsen Ln
3400 DNVR 80210 2281 D1
Nightfire Cir
1200 DgsC 80104 2871 D2
Nighthawk Cir
- BMFD 80020 1775 C2
700 LSVL 80027 1773 A1
Nighthawk Ln
2700 JfnC 80403 2021 E4
Nighthawk Pkwy
5000 BGTN 80601 1697 D6
S Night Heron Dr
11000 PARK 80134 2536 E1
Nighthorse Ct
- DgsC 80134 2621 B5
Nightingale Ct
1900 LGMT 80501 1356 D5
S Nightingale Wy
8800 DgsC 80126 2449 E2
Nightshade Dr
10 BldC 80302 1682 E2
Night Sky Ln
2100 LAFT 80026 1689 E4
Nightwind Cir
1000 DgsC 80104 2787 C7
Nikau Ct
7400 BldC 80503 1520 E5
Nikau Dr
7400 BldC 80503 1520 D4
Nile Cir
6400 ARVD 80007 2024 D2
7800 JfnC 80007 1940 D6
Nile Ct
10 JfnC 80401 2192 D1
800 GOLD 80401 2108 D7
800 JfnC 80401 2108 D7
6900 ARVD 80007 2024 D1
7000 JfnC 80007 2024 D1
7900 JfnC 80007 1940 D5
S Nile Ct
1500 AURA 80012 2199 D5
2200 AURA 80014 2199 D7
Nile St
700 GOLD 80401 2108 D7
800 AURA 80010 2115 D6
1200 JfnC 80401 2108 D6
5300 JfnC 80403 2024 D5
7300 ARVD 80007 1940 D7
7700 JfnC 80007 1940 D6
S Nile St
300 AURA 80012 2199 D2
Nile Wy
7000 ARVD 80007 1940 D7
7500 JfnC 80007 1940 D6
S Nile Wy
600 AURA 80012 2199 D3
N Niles St
600 JfnC 80401 2108 D7
Nimbus Rd
- BldC 80503 1518 D3
3500 BldC 80302 1518 D3
6300 BldC 80503 1520 B3
Ninebark Ln
900 LGMT 80503 1438 A5
Ninebark Wy
16600 PARK 80134 2452 E2
Nissaki Rd
5200 JfnC 80454 2359 A1
Nissen Ct
1300 BMFD 80020 1775 A6
Nissen Pl
1300 BMFD 80020 1775 A6
Niver Av
500 NHGN 80260 1860 D7
1000 TNTN 80260 1860 C7
Niver Ct
1300 AdmC 80229 1945 A4
Niwot Pl
17200 PARK 80134 2453 A6
Niwot Rd
4400 BldC 80503 1519 B4
7300 BldC 80503 1520 D4
8100 BldC 80503 1521 A4
9200 BldC 80504 1521 C4
11500 BldC 80504 1522 E4
11500 BldC 80504 1523 A4
Niwot Sq
6700 BldC 80503 1520 D5
Niwot St
10 WARD 80481 1597 D1
Niwot Tr
- BMFD 80020 1775 D6
Niwot Meadow Farm Rd
8300 BldC 80503 1521 A3
Niwot Ridge Ln
700 LAFT 80026 1689 E3
Niwot Ridge Rd
800 BldC 80466 1597 A7
S Nixon Ct
5900 JfnC 80123 2363 A2
Noah Av
25600 JfnC 80433 2442 B5
Nob Wy
11700 JfnC 80403 1853 B3
N Nobel Dr
600 EbtC 80138 2456 A2
Nob Hill Rd
800 JfnC 80401 2189 C4
800 JfnC 80439 2189 C4
Nob Hill Tr
300 DgsC 80116 2791 C2
Noble Ct
800 JfnC 80401 2108 D7
3000 BLDR 80301 1603 C7
6900 ARVD 80007 2024 D1
6900 JfnC 80007 2024 D1
7900 JfnC 80007 1940 D5
E Noble Pl
1700 CTNL 80121 2365 B3
E Noble Rd
3400 CTNL 80121 2365 D5
3400 CTNL 80122 2365 D5
Noble St
700 GOLD 80401 2108 D7
1000 JfnC 80401 2108 D6
6200 ARVD 80403 2024 D2
6200 JfnC 80403 2024 D2
7600 JfnC 80007 1940 D6
Noble Park Pl
4900 BLDR 80301 1603 B7
W Noddle Mtn
10400 JfnC 80127 2362 A7
Noel Av
400 LGMT 80501 1439 B5
Nogales Ct
2900 BldC 80301 1603 A5
S Noka Tr
12800 JfnC 80470 2525 B7
Nokomis Tr
10 CCkC 80439 2187 D7
Nola Dr
8000 AdmC 80221 1944 B4
Nolan Ct
- ARVD 80002 2027 A4
Nolan St
5300 ARVD 80002 2027 A5
5800 ARVD 80003 2027 A3
Noland Ct
- LYNS 80540 1352 E3
Nome Ct
10 LGMT 80501 1356 C7
S Nome Ct
1800 AURA 80012 2199 D5
2200 AURA 80014 2199 D7
6100 AphC 80111 2367 D2
6300 CTNL 80111 2367 D3
Nome St
- DNVR 80010 2115 D2
- DvrC 80010 2115 D2
200 AURA 80010 2199 D1
1500 AURA 80010 2115 D4
3700 AdmC 80239 2115 D1
3700 AURA 80239 2115 D1
3700 DNVR 80239 2115 D1
4700 DNVR 80239 2031 D5
11200 CMCY 80640 1863 D3
S Nome St
10 AURA 80012 2199 D1
1900 AURA 80014 2199 D6
2600 AURA 80014 2283 D1
5900 AphC 80111 2367 D2
6600 CTNL 80111 2367 D4
6600 CTNL 80112 2367 D4
Nome Wy
10 AURA 80011 2199 D1
10 AURA 80012 2199 D1
S Nome Wy
400 AURA 80012 2199 D2
Nonaham Ln
1200 ERIE 80516 1607 A2
Nordland Tr
3900 CSRK 80109 2702 D3
Norfolk Ct
10400 CMCY 80022 1864 E5
S Norfolk Ct
1400 AURA 80017 2200 E5
6700 FXFD 80016 2369 A4
Norfolk Pl
7300 DgsC 80108 2534 E7
Norfolk St
- AdmC 80022 1864 E6
1500 AURA 80011 2116 E4
2200 ERIE 80516 1692 A3
10700 CMCY 80022 1864 E5
S Norfolk St
700 AURA 80017 2200 E3
2100 AURA 80013 2200 E7
3000 AURA 80013 2284 E2
4700 AURA 80015 2284 E6
6700 FXFD 80016 2368 E4
7300 AphC 80016 2368 E5
7400 AphC 80016 2369 B6
8100 AphC 80112 2368 E7
8100 AphC 80112 2452 D1
Norfolk Wy
600 AURA 80011 2116 E6
E Norfolk Wy
8100 AphC 80112 2368 E7
8100 AphC 80112 2369 A7
8200 AphC 80112 2453 A1
S Norfolk Wy
3100 AURA 80013 2285 A2
3200 AURA 80013 2284 E2
4500 AURA 80015 2284 E5
5400 CTNL 80015 2368 E1
7400 AphC 80016 2368 E6
7400 AphC 80016 2369 A6
S Norman Ct
3000 DNVR 80224 2282 C2
Norman Ln
24500 JfnC 80439 2358 D7
S Normandy Cir
7100 AphC 80128 2363 C5

STREET
Block City ZIP Map# Grid

W Normandy Pkwy
5000 AphC 80128 2363 C5
5000 CBVL 80123 2363 C5
Normandy Rd
10 CCkC 80439 2355 B1
1200 JfnC 80401 2109 B5
1200 LKWD 80401 2109 B5
Normans St
100 GOLD 80403 2107 D1
Norse St
200 GOLD 80401 2192 D1
5300 JfnC 80403 2024 D5
6400 ARVD 80007 2024 D2
North Av
- LKWD 80226 2109 E7
- LKWD 80226 2110 A7
- LKWD 80228 2109 D7
North Dr
- SRDN 80110 2280 A3
S North Dr
8200 JfnC 80465 2443 A1
North St
- CLCY 80403 2017 C3
- GpnC 80403 2017 C3
600 LAFT 80026 1690 D5
900 BLDR 80304 1686 C1
E Northampton Ct
1000 DgsC 80126 2449 B3
Northaven Cir
- TNTN 80233 1861 D1
12000 TNTN 80241 1861 D1
Northbrook Av
4800 CSRK 80104 2788 D1
Northbrook Dr
3800 BLDR 80304 1602 E5
Northbrook Pl
2700 BLDR 80304 1602 E5
Northcrest Dr
1200 DgsC 80126 2449 A1
Northern Av
1100 BGTN 80601 1696 C6
Northern Wy
800 SUPE 80027 1773 A6
Northfield Ct
4500 BldC 80301 1604 D3
Northfield Dr
- DgsC 80129 2448 C2
Northfield Ln
1500 LAFT 80026 1689 E1
Northgate Dr
16800 DgsC 80134 2453 B4
Northglenn Dr
10800 NHGN 80233 1860 D5
Northmoor Dr
1200 BMFD 80020 1775 B6
Northpark Av
- FLHT 80031 1859 E6
- FLHT 80260 1859 E6
3200 WSTR 80031 1859 E6
Northpark Dr
3300 WSTR 80031 1859 D6
Northridge Ct
800 JfnC 80401 2190 B5
1000 ERIE 80516 1607 C3
1300 BLDR 80304 1602 C5
Northridge Dr
- WldC 80516 1607 C2
1000 ERIE 80516 1607 C2
E Northridge Dr
1500 DgsC 80126 2449 B1
Northridge Rd
- DgsC 80129 2448 E2
200 DgsC 80126 2448 E2
200 DgsC 80126 2449 A2
Northstar Ct
500 BLDR 80304 1602 B5
Northstar Dr
8600 TNTN 80260 1944 D3
Northstar Ln
29200 JfnC 80439 2273 C1
Northstar Ridge Ln
6200 DgsC 80134 2622 D2
North View Dr
1000 ERIE 80516 1607 C2
Northview Dr
29100 JfnC 80439 2273 C4
Northway Dr
6300 JfnC 80465 2359 C3
Northwest Ct
11800 PrkC 80470 2523 E3
Northwest Pkwy
- BldC - 1774 D2
- BMFD - 1691 D7
- BMFD - 1692 A6
- BMFD - 1774 A3
- BMFD - 1775 A1
- BMFD 80020 1773 D5
- LSVL - 1774 A3
- LSVL 80027 1773 D5
Northwestern Rd
1300 LGMT 80503 1355 B6
Northwood Ct
900 DgsC 80108 2618 D1
S Northwood Dr
5500 JfnC 80439 2358 B2
Northwood Ln
1000 DgsC 80108 2618 D1
Northwoods Glen Ct
9000 DgsC 80134 2622 D2
Northwoods Glen Dr
6200 DgsC 80134 2622 D2
Norton Av
10800 JfnC 80433 2443 A7
10800 JfnC 80433 2527 B1
Norton Dr
200 GpnC 80403 1934 B6
Norton St
300 BLDR 80305 1686 E6
Norwich Ct
700 DgsC 80108 2534 D7
Norwich St
8500 AdmC 80031 1943 D3
Norwich Wy
4000 AdmC 80031 1943 D3
4000 WSTR 80031 1943 D3
Norwood Av
1200 BLDR 80304 1602 D5
Norwood Ct
3800 BLDR 80304 1602 E5
Norwood Dr
- TNTN 80260 1944 C2
3600 DgsC 80125 2447 D2
3600 DgsC 80129 2447 D2
Notabon Ct
3100 LAFT 80026 1689 C4
Notch Mtn
7000 JfnC 80127 2362 B6
Nottingham Ct
3500 BLDR 80304 1602 E6
Nottingham Dr
10100 LNTR 80134 2451 E6
Nottingham St
1100 LAFT 80026 1690 B5
Nottinghill Gate
6200 BldC 80301 1604 A3
Notts Ct
9300 LNTR 80124 2451 A3
E Nova Av
500 LITN 80122 2364 E7
500 LITN 80122 2365 A7
W Nova Av
9400 JfnC 80128 2362 C6
9700 JfnC 80127 2362 B6
Nova Cir
10 JfnC 80470 2524 B7
Nova Dr
10 PrkC 80470 2523 D6
W Nova Dr
6200 JfnC 80128 2363 A6
7000 JfnC 80128 2362 E6
Nova Ln
10 JfnC 80470 2524 A6
Nova Pl
- AURA 80016 2371 C7
- CSRK 80108 2619 D6
E Nova Pl
22200 AURA 80016 2370 C7
W Nova Pl
7700 JfnC 80128 2362 E6
9900 JfnC 80127 2362 B6
Nova Rd
10 PrkC 80470 2523 D6
33100 JfnC 80470 2524 C6
Novick Ct
600 CSRK 80109 2703 B6
Nucla Ct
10600 CMCY 80022 1864 E5
S Nucla Ct
5400 CTNL 80015 2368 E1
Nucla Dr
- AdmC 80022 1864 E7
Nucla St
- AdmC 80022 1948 D1
- CMCY 80022 1948 D1
1100 AURA 80011 2116 E5
10600 CMCY 80022 1864 E5
11200 AdmC 80022 1864 E3
N Nucla St
1200 AURA 80011 2116 E5
S Nucla St
1000 AURA 80017 2200 E3
3000 AURA 80013 2284 E2
3200 AURA 80013 2285 A2
4200 AURA 80015 2284 E5
5500 CTNL 80015 2368 E1
7300 AphC 80016 2368 E5
Nucla Wy
600 AURA 80011 2116 E6
S Nucla Wy
2000 AURA 80013 2200 E6
2100 AURA 80013 2201 A6
3300 AURA 80013 2284 E2
4800 AURA 80015 2284 E6
Nueva Vista Dr
1300 AdmC 80229 1945 A4
Nugget Ct
1600 BLDR 80304 1602 C6
8300 DgsC 80125 2533 A5
Nugget Dr
10 BldC 80302 1517 B5
Nugget Hill Rd
100 BldC 80455 1516 C7
Numa Pl
17000 PARK 80134 2453 A7
Nuthatch Cir
5400 DgsC 80134 2622 A4
Nuthatch Rd
10 CCkC 80439 2271 D6
5500 DgsC 80134 2622 A4
Nuthatch Wy
7600 DgsC 80134 2622 A4
Nutmeg Pl
4600 CSRK 80109 2702 B4
S Nutmeg St
300 AphC 80102 2206 E3
Nyland Wy
3500 BldC 80026 1689 B5
3500 LSVL 80026 1689 B5

O

Oak Av
1500 BLDR 80304 1602 D5
Oak Cir
1400 BLDR 80304 1602 C5
10000 WSTR 80021 1857 E7
S Oak Cir
6500 JfnC 80127 2362 A4
Oak Cir N
3000 BMFD 80020 1774 B6
Oak Cir S
10 BMFD 80020 1774 B7
Oak Ct
1300 BLDR 80304 1602 C5
5300 ARVD 80002 2025 E5
5500 ARVD 80002 2026 A4
6300 ARVD 80004 2025 E2
10000 WSTR 80021 1857 E7
34500 EbtC 80107 2710 A6
S Oak Ct
- BldC 80501 1439 B5
- LGMT 80501 1439 B5
3100 JfnC 80227 2278 A3
3400 LKWD 80227 2278 A3
4600 JfnC 80127 2278 A6
6400 JfnC 80127 2362 A4
8400 DgsC 80108 2535 B5
8400 JfnC 80127 2446 A1
W Oak Ct
800 LSVL 80027 1689 A6
Oak Dr
- TNTN 80260 1944 A1
2600 LKWD 80215 2109 E3
2600 LKWD 80215 2110 A3
Oak Ln
300 BMFD 80020 1859 A2
400 DgsC 80108 2535 B5
37500 EbtC 80107 2624 A7
37500 EbtC 80107 2708 A1
Oak Pl
900 TNTN 80229 1945 A3
1400 BLDR 80304 1602 C5
Oak St
2400 DNVR 80212 2111 C3
2600 WTRG 80215 2110 A3
2800 LKWD 80215 2109 E3
2800 LKWD 80215 2110 A3
3100 WTRG 80033 2110 A2
4600 WTRG 80033 2026 A6
5400 ARVD 80002 2026 A4
5800 ARVD 80004 2026 A3
6500 ARVD 80004 2025 E1
7000 ARVD 80004 1941 E7
8000 ARVD 80005 1941 E5
8000 JfnC 80005 1941 E5
E Oak St
300 LAFT 80026 1690 D4
N Oak St
- LGMT 80501 1439 B6
10000 WSTR 80021 1857 E7
10600 WSTR 80021 1858 A5
S Oak St
- LGMT 80501 1439 B6
300 LKWD 80226 2194 A2
1700 LKWD 80232 2194 A6
1800 LKWD 80227 2194 A6
3600 JfnC 80227 2278 A4
3600 JfnC 80235 2278 A4
3600 LKWD 80227 2278 A4
5100 JfnC 80127 2278 A7
5600 JfnC 80127 2362 A2
8400 JfnC 80127 2446 A1
W Oak St
300 LAFT 80026 1690 B4
Oak Wy
10 CCkC 80439 2271 E5
6800 ARVD 80004 2025 E1
7800 DgsC 80135 2783 E4
8400 ARVD 80005 1941 E4
S Oak Wy
2900 LKWD 80227 2277 E2
2900 LKWD 80227 2278 A2
5100 JfnC 80127 2278 A7
5900 JfnC 80127 2362 A2
8600 JfnC 80127 2445 E2
8600 JfnC 80127 2446 A2
Oak Briar Wy
8100 DgsC 80108 2534 E6
Oakbrook Ln
20400 PARK 80138 2537 E2
Oakbrush Wy
9300 LNTR 80124 2450 E4
S Oak Creek Ct
12600 PARK 80134 2537 D5
Oak Creek Dr
1800 GDVL 80121 2365 B2
Oak Creek Ln
5700 GDVL 80121 2365 B2
5800 CTNL 80121 2365 B2
E Oak Creek Pl
19000 PARK 80134 2537 C5
E Oak Creek Wy
18900 PARK 80134 2537 C4
Oakcrest Cir
1800 CSRK 80104 2788 A2
Oakdale Pl
1000 BLDR 80304 1602 C5
Oakdale Rd
- PARK 80138 2538 D1
Oakes Mill Ct
4300 CSRK 80109 2702 C3
Oakes Mill Pl
3200 CSRK 80109 2702 C3
Oakgrove Ct
2000 CSRK 80108 2704 D4
Oakgrove Wy
4200 CSRK 80108 2704 D4
Oak Hill Cir
- AURA 80016 2371 B3
S Oak Hill Cir
8000 AphC 80016 2371 B7
Oak Hill Ct
- AURA 80016 2371 B5
S Oak Hill Ct
7900 AphC 80016 2371 B7
Oak Hill St
- DNVR 80249 1951 B6
W Oak Hills Dr
10 DgsC 80108 2535 A5
8400 DgsC 80108 2534 E5
S Oak Hill Wy Wy
- AURA 80016 2371 B2
Oakhurst Dr
1100 BMFD 80020 1775 A6
S Oakland Cir
2400 AURA 80014 2199 D7
S Oakland Cir E
2700 AURA 80014 2283 D1
S Oakland Cir W
2700 AURA 80014 2283 C1
Oakland Ct
100 AURA 80011 2199 D1
500 AURA 80010 2115 D7
S Oakland Ct
900 AURA 80012 2199 D3
2800 AURA 80014 2283 D1
Oakland Dr
2100 DgsC 80135 2701 E6
2100 DgsC 80135 2702 A6
11200 CMCY 80640 1863 D3
S Oakland Pl
2800 AURA 80014 2283 D1
Oakland St
- AdmC 80640 1863 D4
10 AURA 80011 2199 D1
10 AURA 80012 2199 D1
200 AURA 80010 2199 D1
400 AURA 80011 2115 D7
1600 AURA 80010 2115 D4
4700 DNVR 80239 2031 D6
12000 CMCY 80640 1863 D2
12300 BGTN 80640 1863 D1
S Oakland St
600 AURA 80012 2199 D3
1800 AURA 80014 2199 D6
2500 AURA 80014 2283 D1
S Oakland Wy
- AURA 80012 2199 D4
1900 AURA 80014 2199 D6
Oakleaf Cir
1200 BLDR 80304 1602 C5
S Oak Leaf Ct
10200 DgsC 80129 2448 A6
Oak Leaf Ln
1900 GDVL 80121 2365 B2
W Oak Leaf Pl
3200 DgsC 80129 2447 E6
3200 DgsC 80129 2448 A6
S Oak Leaf Wy
10000 DgsC 80129 2447 E6
Oakley Ct
6100 CSRK 80104 2789 A1
Oakley Ln
1300 ERIE 80516 1607 A2
Oakmont Ln
10 JfnC 80127 2361 B7
Oakmoor Cir
10500 DgsC 80134 2452 E6
Oakmoor Ct
10600 DgsC 80134 2452 E6
Oakmoor Ln
10500 DgsC 80134 2452 E6
Oakmoor Pl
16300 DgsC 80134 2452 E7
Oak Ridge Dr
10 CSRK 80104 2703 E6
10 CSRK 80104 2704 A7
Oak Ridge Ln
1600 LGMT 80501 1355 E6
S Oak Ridge Rd
2300 DgsC 80135 2785 C6
Oakshire Av
10800 DgsC 80126 2449 D7
Oakshire Ct
2900 DgsC 80126 2449 B7
Oak Terrace Rd
- GpnC 80403 1850 A6
Oak Tree Ct
5300 BLDR 80301 1604 C1
10000 LNTR 80124 2451 A5
N Oak Valley Rd
400 DgsC 80135 2700 B6
Oakview Pl
7700 DgsC 80108 2534 D6
Oak View Tr
16800 JfnC 80127 2444 C2
16800 JfnC 80465 2444 C2
Oak Vista Ct
2300 CSRK 80104 2704 A5
Oak Vista Ln
2600 CSRK 80104 2704 B5
Oakwell Ct
16400 DgsC 80134 2452 E5
E Oakwood Av
800 CTNL 80121 2365 A2
Oakwood Ct
900 CSRK 80104 2703 E6
E Oakwood Ct
800 CTNL 80121 2365 A2
Oakwood Dr
- WSTR 80030 1943 D4
400 CSRK 80104 2703 D5
3600 LGMT 80503 1438 A4
4300 WSTR 80031 1943 D4
E Oakwood Dr
16100 AphC 80016 2368 E2
E Oakwood Ln
17700 AphC 80016 2369 B2
W Oakwood Ln
300 DgsC 80108 2535 A5
Oakwood Pl
300 BLDR 80304 1602 B5
E Oakwood Pl
17700 AphC 80016 2369 B2
Oakwood St
8200 AdmC 80031 1943 D3
8200 WSTR 80031 1943 D3
Oard Ct
700 LGMT 80501 1439 D2
Oban Ct
7800 DgsC 80124 2450 E6
E Oberlin Dr
19000 AURA 80013 2285 C4
22300 AURA 80018 2286 C4
W Oberlin Dr
- DNVR 80236 2279 C5
5200 DNVR 80235 2279 C5
E Oberlin Pl
8000 DNVR 80237 2282 E5
14500 AURA 80014 2284 C4
15400 AURA 80013 2284 D4
18600 AURA 80013 2285 C4
21800 AURA 80018 2286 B4
W Oberlin Pl
4600 DNVR 80236 2279 C4
Oberon Rd
6300 ARVD 80004 2026 B1
S Oberstrasse Rd
6000 JfnC 80439 2357 E3
O'Brian Wy
12400 AdmC 80603 1864 D1
O'Brien Rd
10 PrkC 80456 2521 D3
S O'Brien Wy
1300 DgsC 80109 2786 E4
Obsidian Ln
- CSRK 80108 2619 E6
Ocaso Dr
6500 DgsC 80108 2534 C5
S Ocelot Tr
6900 JfnC 80439 2358 A5
O'Connor Rd
- BldC 80303 1688 E6
Octillo St
100 BGTN 80601 1697 A6
October Pl
100 CSRK 80104 2787 D3
O'Dell Dr
2600 ERIE 80516 1690 C1
O'Dell Pl
6400 BLDR 80301 1604 A1
S Odessa Cir
4000 AphC 80013 2286 B4
5900 CTNL 80015 2370 A2
7100 CTNL 80016 2370 A5
Odessa Ct
- DNVR 80249 2034 A4
800 AphC 80018 2118 A6
800 AURA 80018 2118 A6
S Odessa St
4000 AphC 80013 2286 A4
5600 CTNL 80015 2370 A1
6900 AURA 80016 2370 A4
Odessa Wy
3300 AURA 80011 2118 A1
Odin Av
5200 BldC 80301 1603 B1
Odyssey Ct
- CSRK 80109 2702 D5
1100 LAFT 80026 1690 B6
S Oehlmann Av
10600 JfnC 80433 2443 A7
10600 JfnC 80433 2527 A1
Oehlmann Park Rd
21900 JfnC 80433 2527 A1
22800 JfnC 80433 2526 E2
Ogalalla Tr
30200 EbtC 80107 2792 C7
Ogallala Rd
3900 BldC 80503 1518 E1
8700 BldC 80503 1521 B1
8700 BldC 80504 1521 B1
Ogden Cir
700 NHGN 80233 1861 A4
S Ogden Cir
8200 CTNL 80122 2449 A1
8200 LITN 80122 2449 A1
Ogden Ct
7900 AdmC 80229 1945 A5
9600 TNTN 80229 1945 A1
9700 TNTN 80229 1861 A7
S Ogden Ct
5900 CTNL 80121 2365 A2
5900 GDVL 80121 2365 A2
6900 CTNL 80122 2365 A5
Ogden Dr
11200 NHGN 80233 1861 A4
Ogden St
- TNTN 80241 1777 A7
- TNTN 80241 1861 A1
10 DNVR 80209 2197 A1
10 DNVR 80218 2197 A1
300 DNVR 80218 2113 A7
1900 DNVR 80205 2113 A4
5800 AdmC 80216 2029 A3
8200 AdmC 80229 1945 A4
8600 TNTN 80229 1945 A3
9700 TNTN 80229 1861 A7
11400 NHGN 80233 1861 A3
S Ogden St
10 DNVR 80209 2197 A2
10 DNVR 80218 2197 A2
1400 DNVR 80210 2197 A6
2700 AphC 80210 2281 A2
2700 DNVR 80210 2281 A2
2700 EGLD 80113 2281 A2
3600 CHLV 80113 2281 A4
6500 CTNL 80121 2365 A4
6600 CTNL 80122 2365 A4
8100 LITN 80122 2365 A7
S Ogden Wy
7300 CTNL 80122 2365 B6
O'Hayre Ct
3000 LKWD 80215 2110 A2
3000 WTRG 80033 2110 A2
E Ohio Av
10 DNVR 80209 2196 E3
10 DNVR 80223 2196 E3
700 DNVR 80209 2197 A3
4000 GNDL 80246 2197 E3
6100 DNVR 80224 2198 B3
9700 DNVR 80247 2199 B3
11900 AURA 80012 2199 E3
13600 AURA 80012 2200 B3
15100 AURA 80017 2200 C3
18000 AURA 80017 2201 B3
23500 AphC 80018 2202 D3
W Ohio Av
- DNVR 80223 2196 D3
2400 DNVR 80219 2196 B3
4600 DNVR 80219 2195 C3
5000 LKWD 80219 2195 C3
5000 LKWD 80226 2195 C3
7300 LKWD 80226 2194 E3
12900 LKWD 80228 2193 C3
E Ohio Cir
17500 AURA 80017 2201 B3
W Ohio Cir
12300 LKWD 80228 2193 D4
E Ohio Dr
6900 DNVR 80224 2198 C3
16900 AURA 80017 2201 A3
W Ohio Dr
10900 LKWD 80226 2193 E3
10900 LKWD 80226 2194 A3
13600 LKWD 80228 2193 B3
E Ohio Pl
11000 AURA 80012 2199 C3
16300 AURA 80017 2200 E3
16900 AURA 80017 2201 A3
W Ohio Pl
9500 LKWD 80226 2194 B3
11000 LKWD 80226 2193 E3
11900 LKWD 80228 2193 D3
Ohio Wy
2900 DNVR 80209 2197 C3
Oh-Kay Rd
4200 JfnC 80439 2275 A5
23000 JfnC 80439 2274 E5
Ohlson Ridge Ct
600 EbtC 80138 2540 A4
Ohm Wy
3000 DNVR 80209 2197 C3
Oh My God Rd
- CCkC 80452 2101 A1
10 GpnC 80403 2017 A7
10 GpnC 80403 2101 A1
Okee Tr
30100 JfnC 80470 2525 B7
30100 JfnC 80470 2609 B1
S Olathe Cir
3700 AURA 80013 2284 E3
3700 AURA 80013 2285 A3
5000 CTNL 80015 2284 E7
5000 CTNL 80015 2285 A7
S Olathe Ct
2800 AURA 80013 2284 E1
2800 AURA 80013 2285 A1
5700 CTNL 80015 2369 A1
8200 AphC 80112 2453 A1
S Olathe Ln
5500 CTNL 80015 2369 A1
Olathe St
- AdmC 80022 1864 E6
- CMCY 80022 1864 E6
800 AURA 80011 2116 E6
S Olathe St
- AURA 80013 2285 A3
- FXFD 80016 2368 E3
1000 AURA 80017 2200 E3
1900 AURA 80013 2200 E6
3500 AURA 80013 2284 E3
4700 AURA 80015 2284 E6
4700 AURA 80015 2285 A6
5700 CTNL 80015 2368 E1
6000 CTNL 80016 2368 E2
6000 CTNL 80016 2369 A2
Olathe Wy
- AdmC 80022 1864 E6
600 AURA 80011 2116 E6
10400 CMCY 80022 1864 E5
S Olathe Wy
1200 AURA 80017 2200 E4
1400 AURA 80017 2201 A5
2500 AURA 80013 2200 E4
2600 AURA 80013 2201 A7
2800 AURA 80013 2284 E1
3000 AURA 80013 2285 A2
4700 AURA 80015 2284 E6
4700 AURA 80015 2285 A6
5300 CTNL 80015 2284 E7
5300 CTNL 80015 2368 E1
5700 CTNL 80015 2369 A1
Old Brompton Rd
6000 BldC 80301 1603 E3
6100 BldC 80301 1604 A4
Old Carter Lake Rd
10 BldC 80403 1852 A1
Old Coal Mine Av
9700 JfnC 80123 2362 B4
9700 JfnC 80128 2362 B4
Old Corral Rd
10 PrkC 80456 2606 D4
Old CR-52
1500 WldC 80516 1523 E6
Old Divide Tr
6200 DgsC 80134 2621 C4
Old Dory Hill Rd
10 GpnC 80403 1934 C5
Olde Stage Rd
5000 BldC 80302 1518 A7
5000 BldC 80302 1602 A2
6900 BldC 80302 1517 E3
Olde Wadsworth Blvd
5200 ARVD 80002 2026 E4
5700 ARVD 80003 2026 E4
5700 ARVD 80004 2026 E4
Olde Wadsworth Ct
6200 ARVD 80003 2026 E2
6200 ARVD 80004 2026 E2
Old Farm Rd
7100 LITN 80128 2363 C5
Oldfield St
1000 CSRK 80104 2788 E1
Old Gate Rd
3800 DgsC 80104 2871 C3
Old Glory Rd
10 CCkC 80452 2185 A1
Old Gold Rd
10 GpnC 80403 1850 B6
S Old Hammer Cir
2300 AURA 80018 2203 C7
S Old Hammer Ct
2100 AURA 80018 2203 C6
S Old Hammer Ln
8100 AphC 80016 2371 C7
S Oldhammer Wy
- AURA 80016 2371 B3
Old Hughesville Rd
- GpnC 80403 1933 E7
- GpnC 80403 2017 E1
- GpnC 80403 2018 A1
Old Kipling St
1900 LKWD 80227 2194 B7
1900 LKWD 80232 2194 B7
2400 LKWD 80227 2278 B2
Old Laramie Tr
100 LAFT 80026 1690 C7
Old Little Bear Creek Rd
10 CCkC 80452 2186 A3
Old Main St
200 LYNS 80540 1352 D1
Old Mill Rd
9100 JfnC 80433 2440 B3
Old Mill Tr N
7300 BldC 80301 1604 D3
Old Mill Tr S
7300 BldC 80301 1604 D3
Old Orchard Ln
5900 DgsC 80135 2616 C5
Old Ox Tr
31500 JfnC 80439 2188 E3
Old Park Dr
49000 AdmC 80102 2125 B2
Old Post Cir
4800 BldC 80301 1604 D2
Old Post Ct
4700 BldC 80301 1604 C3
Old Post Rd
7200 BldC 80301 1604 C3
Old Post Office Rd
10 BldC 80302 1683 E1
Old Quarry Rd
2200 JfnC 80401 2109 A4
N Old Ranch Tr
6500 DgsC 80125 2615 A2
6600 DgsC 80125 2614 E2
Old St. Vrain Rd
200 BldC 80540 1352 C3
Old Sawmill Rd
10 PrkC 80456 2521 D4
Old Schoolhouse Rd
5000 DgsC 80134 2621 D4
Old Sequoia Ct
1400 DgsC 80116 2706 C5
Old Squaw Pass Rd
10 CCkC 80439 2187 C5
2500 CCkC 80439 2188 A6
Old Stage Rd
- GpnC 80403 1934 B4
Old Stagecoach Rd
- GpnC 80474 1765 E7
- GpnC 80474 1849 E1
Old Stage Coach Rd
300 PrkC 80456 2690 A2
500 PrkC 80456 2689 E2
Old Stagecoach Rd
15800 JfnC 80470 2609 E7
Old Stagecoach Trail Rd
100 GpnC 80474 1849 E1
Old State Rd
- PrkC 80456 2606 C7
Old Stone Cir
200 DgsC 80126 2448 E2
Old Stone Dr
200 DgsC 80126 2448 E2
300 DgsC 80126 2449 A2
Old Sunshine Tr
10 BldC 80302 1601 C6
Old Tale Rd
1100 BldC 80303 1687 E3
1200 BLDR 80301 1687 E3
1200 BLDR 80303 1687 E3
Old Territorial Rd
- DgsC 80104 2870 E7
- DgsC 80118 2870 E7
- DgsC 80118 2954 E1
- DgsC 80118 2955 A2
- LKSR 80118 2955 A2
Old Tom Morris Cir
8900 DgsC 80129 2448 B3
Old Tom Morris Rd
1700 AURA 80018 2203 A5
S Old Tom Morris Rd
- AURA 80018 2202 D4
Old Townsite Rd
10 BldC 80302 1683 D2
Old Tram Rd
- CLCY 80403 2017 C4
Old US-285
- JfnC 80465 2443 B3
- PrkC 80456 2606 D6
11500 JfnC 80433 2525 D3
Old Victory Rd
- BNNT 80102 2125 A1
2700 AdmC 80102 2125 D3
Old Wadsworth Blvd
11200 BMFD 80021 1858 C2
Old Westbury Ct
4000 BLDR 80301 1603 B5
Old Whiskey Rd
100 BldC 80466 1684 D5
W Old Windmill Wy
4300 CSRK 80109 2702 B2
Old Y Rd
10 JfnC 80401 2191 A1
S Oleander Ct
3400 DNVR 80224 2282 C3
3400 DNVR 80237 2282 C3
Olin Ct
900 ERIE 80516 1607 A7
S Olive Av
13900 PrkC 80470 2608 A2
S Olive Cir
7600 CTNL 80112 2366 C6
Olive Ct
1300 ERIE 80516 1691 E3
5100 GDVL 80121 2366 A1
S Olive Ct
6600 CTNL 80111 2366 C4
6700 CTNL 80112 2366 D4
Olive Dr
- TNTN 80260 1944 C2

Denver Regional Street Index

STREET Block City ZIP Map# Grid

S Olive Ln
5100 JfnC 80439 2273 C7
Olive Rd
34700 PrkC 80470 2608 A2
S Olive Rd
4900 JfnC 80439 2273 D7
5200 JfnC 80439 2357 C1
Olive St
100 LAFT 80026 1690 B4
200 DNVR 80220 2198 C1
1900 DNVR 80220 2114 C4
3200 DNVR 80207 2114 C1
3900 DNVR 80207 2030 C7
4800 CMCY 80216 2030 C6
4800 DNVR 80022 2030 C6
4800 DNVR 80216 2030 C6
6000 CMCY 80022 2030 C2
7200 CMCY 80022 1946 C7
7700 AdmC 80022 1946 C5
16600 AdmC 80602 1694 C4
S Olive St
100 DNVR 80230 2198 C2
1800 DNVR 80224 2198 C6
1900 AphC 80224 2198 C6
4200 DNVR 80237 2282 C5
5400 GDVL 80111 2366 C1
6300 CTNL 80111 2366 C3
7000 CTNL 80112 2366 C5
Olive Wy
- TNTN 80602 1778 C6
S Olive Wy
- DNVR 80230 2198 C2
300 DNVR 80224 2198 C2
6800 CTNL 80112 2366 C4
Ollie Ln
- BldC 80303 1688 C6
Olmstead Pl
15700 DNVR 80239 2032 D4
Olmsted Dr
12200 DNVR 80239 2031 E4
14300 DNVR 80239 2032 B4
Olmsted Pl
12900 DNVR 80239 2031 E4
15500 DNVR 80239 2032 D4
Olson Dr
- BLDR 80302 1686 E3
- BLDR 80303 1686 E3
2800 BLDR 80303 1687 A3
Olympia Av
300 LGMT 80501 1356 D4
Olympia Cir
1500 CSRK 80104 2787 E2
S Olympia Cir
2700 JfnC 80439 2273 B2
Olympia Ct
- BMFD 80020 1775 E4
S Olympia Ln
2800 JfnC 80439 2273 B2
Olympian Cir
1300 LAFT 80026 1690 B6
Olympic Ct
- DgsC 80118 2868 C6
Olympic Wy
4600 JfnC 80439 2274 B6
Olympus Cir
10 DgsC 80124 2450 E2
10 DgsC 80124 2451 A2
S Olympus Dr
6400 JfnC 80439 2358 B4
Omaha Av
20700 PARK 80138 2538 A1
Omaha Dr
- DNVR 80236 2279 C4
Omaha Ln
10800 PARK 80138 2538 B1
Omaha Pl
5400 BldC 80303 1687 D5
5400 BLDR 80303 1687 D5
S Omaha St
13100 JfnC 80470 2524 B7
13300 JfnC 80470 2608 B1
S Oman Rd
10 CSRK 80104 2703 E7
Omega Cir
13300 DgsC 80124 2450 D2
Omega Dr
13300 DgsC 80124 2450 D2
Omega Ln
600 DgsC 80124 2450 D2
On A Hill Rd
1800 GpnC 80403 1934 C1
O'Neal Cir
3200 BLDR 80301 1603 A7
O'Neal Pkwy
3300 BLDR 80301 1603 A7
S Oneida Cir
7000 CTNL 80112 2366 C5
Oneida Ct
- DNVR 80220 2198 C1
200 DNVR 80220 2114 C7
S Oneida Ct
6300 CTNL 80111 2366 C3
6700 CTNL 80112 2366 C4
Oneida Dr
7100 CMCY 80022 1946 C6
Oneida Pl
1100 DNVR 80220 2114 C6
Oneida St
- AdmC 80602 1778 C6
- CMCY 80022 1946 C5
- TNTN 80602 1778 C6
100 DNVR 80220 2198 C1
200 BLDR 80303 1687 D5
600 DNVR 80220 2114 C6
1900 DNVR 80207 2114 C4
3900 DNVR 80207 2030 C7
4100 DNVR 80216 2030 C7
5800 CMCY 80022 2030 C3
7600 AdmC 80022 1946 C5
10100 DgsC 80124 2534 D1
16400 AdmC 80602 1694 C5
S Oneida St
- CTNL 80112 2366 C4
100 DNVR 80230 2198 C2
1800 AphC 80224 2198 C6
1900 DNVR 80224 2198 C6
2900 DNVR 80224 2282 C2
3900 DNVR 80237 2282 C4
S Oneida Wy
300 DNVR 80224 2198 C3
3200 DNVR 80224 2282 C2
3400 DNVR 80237 2282 C3
5400 GDVL 80111 2366 C1
6100 CTNL 80111 2366 C3
7600 CTNL 80112 2366 C6
W Ontario Av
5200 AphC 80123 2363 C4
5200 AphC 80128 2363 C4
8800 JfnC 80128 2362 C4
10500 JfnC 80127 2362 A4
11100 JfnC 80127 2361 E4
W Ontario Cir
6700 JfnC 80128 2363 B4
Ontario Ct
10 BLDR 80303 1687 D6
E Ontario Dr
- AphC 80016 2371 A4
- AURA 80016 2371 A3
21900 AURA 80016 2370 B4
W Ontario Dr
9100 JfnC 80128 2362 C4
Ontario Pl
- AphC 80016 2370 E4
- AURA 80016 2370 E4
5400 BLDR 80303 1687 D6
W Ontario Pl
7600 JfnC 80128 2362 D4
10500 JfnC 80127 2362 A4
Onyx Cir
1200 LGMT 80504 1439 A7
1300 LGMT 80504 1438 E7
Onyx St
- DgsC 80134 2452 D4
Onyx Wy
300 SUPE 80027 1857 A1
2100 LGMT 80504 1439 A7
Ooranson Ct
- LYNS 80540 1352 E3
Opal Ct
4200 CSRK 80104 2787 D5
Opal Ln
3200 SUPE 80027 1857 A1
Opal St
- BMFD 80020 1858 C1
1000 BMFD 80020 1774 D7
Opal Wy
400 SUPE 80027 1857 A1
700 BMFD 80020 1774 D7
Opal Hill Dr
17000 PARK 80134 2453 A5
Ophir Av
10 BMFD 80020 1774 E4
Ophir Rd
1400 CSRK 80109 2703 B5
Opportunity Dr
- CSRK 80109 2702 D5
Orange Ct
400 DNVR 80220 2114 C7
3800 BLDR 80304 1602 C5
Orange Dr
- BLDR 80304 1602 D4
Orange Ln
3700 BLDR 80304 1602 C6
Orange Pl
1000 BLDR 80304 1602 C5
Orangewood Dr
9600 TNTN 80260 1860 C7
9600 TNTN 80260 1944 C1
9700 NHGN 80260 1860 C7
Orchard Av
1100 BLDR 80304 1602 C5
Orchard Ct
700 LSVL 80027 1773 A2
3900 BLDR 80304 1602 B5
5000 GOLD 80403 2024 D6
5400 JfnC 80403 2024 D4
6900 ARVD 80007 2024 D1
7300 WSTR 80030 1943 D7
Orchard Dr
400 LSVL 80027 1773 A2
1400 JfnC 80401 2109 B5
1500 LKWD 80401 2109 B5
1600 AdmC 80221 1944 B4
E Orchard Dr
- AURA 80016 2371 B2
5600 GDVL 80121 2366 B2
6100 CTNL 80111 2366 B2
6200 GDVL 80111 2366 B2
9400 GDVL 80111 2367 B1
Orchard Ln
10 CTNL 80121 2365 A2
10 GDVL 80121 2365 A2
E Orchard Ln
4300 CTNL 80121 2365 E2
E Orchard Pl
4200 CTNL 80121 2365 E2
6600 CTNL 80111 2366 C2
11400 AphC 80111 2367 D2
16200 CTNL 80016 2368 E2
20400 AphC 80016 2369 E2
22800 AphC 80015 2370 C2
Orchard Rd
1200 JfnC 80401 2109 B5
1200 LKWD 80401 2109 B5
E Orchard Rd
- AphC 80015 2370 D2
- AURA 80016 2370 D2
10 CTNL 80121 2364 E2
10 LITN 80121 2364 E2
600 GDVL 80121 2365 A2
3700 CTNL 80121 2365 E2
5400 GDVL 80111 2366 D2
5600 CTNL 80121 2366 D2
5600 GDVL 80121 2366 D2
5900 CTNL 80111 2366 D2
8500 GDVL 80111 2367 A2
9600 AphC 80111 2367 A2
E Orchard Rd
12100 AphC 80111 2368 A2
15100 AphC 80016 2368 E1
15100 CTNL 80016 2368 E1
15300 AphC 80015 2368 E1
15300 CTNL 80015 2368 E1
16400 CTNL 80015 2369 C2
18100 AphC 80015 2369 C2
18100 AphC 80016 2369 C2
19700 CTNL 80016 2369 C2
Orchard St
100 GOLD 80401 2192 D1
500 GOLD 80401 2108 D7
1200 JfnC 80401 2108 D6
5300 JfnC 80403 2024 D5
7000 ARVD 80007 1940 D7
Orchard Wy
400 LSVL 80027 1773 B2
N Orchard Creek Cir
5700 BLDR 80301 1603 D3
S Orchard Creek Cir
5700 BLDR 80301 1603 D4
5800 BldC 80301 1603 D4
Orchard Creek Ln
5700 BLDR 80301 1603 D4
5800 BldC 80301 1603 D4
Orchard Grass Ln
16200 DgsC 80134 2452 E1
16200 PARK 80134 2452 E1
Orchid Av
- AdmC 80102 2124 B2
Orchid Ct
1400 LAFT 80026 1690 B6
Ord Dr
300 BldC 80303 1688 E5
W Oregon Av
6500 LKWD 80232 2195 A5
E Oregon Cir
11900 AURA 80012 2199 D5
W Oregon Ct
13400 LKWD 80228 2193 B5
E Oregon Dr
12800 AURA 80012 2199 E5
14500 AURA 80012 2200 C5
18700 AURA 80017 2201 C5
W Oregon Dr
6800 LKWD 80232 2194 E5
6800 LKWD 80232 2195 A7
10900 JfnC 80232 2193 E5
12900 LKWD 80228 2193 C5
E Oregon Pl
- AURA 80018 2202 E5
6100 DNVR 80224 2198 B5
8500 AphC 80231 2198 E5
17800 AURA 80017 2201 B5
W Oregon Pl
4800 DNVR 80219 2195 C5
5100 LKWD 80219 2195 C5
5100 LKWD 80232 2195 C5
9300 LKWD 80232 2194 B5
10900 JfnC 80232 2193 E5
Oriole Cir
1000 BGTN 80601 1779 E1
1000 BGTN 80601 1780 B2
Oriole Ct
33700 EbtC 80107 2793 E1
Oriole Dr
700 LAFT 80026 1690 D5
Oriole Ln
7000 BldC 80503 1520 B4
Oriole St
2800 FLHT 80260 1944 A1
Oriole Cove
800 LAFT 80026 1690 D6
Orion Cir
5500 JfnC 80403 2024 D4
Orion Ct
500 LGMT 80501 1440 A2
3800 BLDR 80304 1602 B5
5600 JfnC 80403 2024 D4
6900 ARVD 80007 2024 D1
7900 JfnC 80007 1940 D5
Orion Dr
700 LAFT 80026 1690 B5
Orion Ln
7000 ARVD 80007 1940 E7
7000 ARVD 80007 2024 D1
Orion Pl
1500 LGMT 80501 1440 A2
6400 ARVD 80007 2024 D2
Orion St
- ARVD 80007 1940 D7
- ARVD 80007 2024 D1
100 GOLD 80401 2192 D1
1100 JfnC 80401 2108 D6
7600 JfnC 80007 1940 D6
N Orion St
7200 JfnC 80007 1940 D7
Orion Wy
- CSRK 80108 2619 E5
6400 ARVD 80007 2024 D2
7900 JfnC 80007 1940 D5
Orlando Wy
8000 JfnC 80005 1941 E4
Orleans Cir
11500 AdmC 80022 1866 A2
Orleans Ct
4000 DNVR 80249 2034 A7
S Orleans Ct
4000 AphC 80013 2286 B4
Orleans Ln
- FLHT 80260 1944 A2
Orleans St
4500 DNVR 80249 2034 A5
9000 FLHT 80260 1944 A2
S Orleans St
3700 AphC 80013 2286 A3
5700 CTNL 80015 2370 A1
S Orleans Wy
- AURA 80011 2118 A4
- AURA 80019 2118 A4
5800 CTNL 80015 2370 B1
Orman Dr
800 BLDR 80303 1687 B4
Orofino Dr
300 DgsC 80108 2618 E6
Orofino Pl
4400 DgsC 80108 2618 E6
Osage
- AdmC 80022 1946 B3
10 JfnC 80127 2361 A7
N Osage Cir
11200 WSTR 80234 1860 B4
Osage Ct
- DgsC 80118 2952 E2
1000 EbtC 80107 2708 B3
N Osage Ct
13800 WSTR 80020 1776 B4
Osage Dr
4400 BLDR 80303 1687 C6
Osage Pl
5500 DgsC 80118 2952 E3
Osage Rd
7200 DgsC 80118 2952 E2
Osage St
300 DNVR 80223 2112 C7
300 DNVR 80223 2196 C1
1000 DNVR 80204 2112 C5
3200 DNVR 80211 2112 C2
4000 DNVR 80211 2028 C7
5100 AdmC 80221 2028 C6
5100 DNVR 80221 2028 C6
7600 AdmC 80221 1944 C6
8700 TNTN 80260 1944 C3
11100 NHGN 80234 1860 C4
13400 WSTR 80234 1776 B5
N Osage St
12000 WSTR 80234 1860 C2
S Osage St
700 DNVR 80223 2196 C3
4500 EGLD 80110 2280 C6
Osage Wy
5500 DgsC 80118 2952 E2
8300 AdmC 80221 1944 C4
8300 FLHT 80260 1944 C4
Osceola Ct
6600 AdmC 80003 2027 D1
10200 WSTR 80031 1859 D6
N Osceola Ct
11100 WSTR 80031 1859 D4
N Osceola Dr
10500 WSTR 80031 1859 D5
Osceola Lp
10600 WSTR 80031 1859 D5
Osceola St
- WSTR 80031 1859 D3
10 DNVR 80219 2195 D1
300 DNVR 80219 2111 D7
2000 DNVR 80204 2111 D3
2000 DNVR 80211 2111 D3
2000 DNVR 80212 2111 D3
3900 DNVR 80211 2027 D7
4800 DNVR 80212 2027 D5
5100 AdmC 80212 2027 D5
5100 AdmC 80221 2027 D5
5100 DNVR 80221 2027 D5
6200 AdmC 80003 2027 D2
8000 WSTR 80030 1943 D5
9600 WSTR 80031 1943 D1
12600 BMFD 80020 1775 D7
34500 JfnC 80470 2524 A7
N Osceola St
9000 WSTR 80031 1943 D2
S Osceola St
10 DNVR 80219 2195 D2
2500 DNVR 80219 2279 D1
2800 DNVR 80236 2279 D2
5000 DNVR 80123 2279 D7
5000 DvrC 80123 2279 D7
5000 LITN 80123 2279 D7
S Osceola Wy
1500 DNVR 80219 2195 D5
2700 DNVR 80219 2279 E1
2700 DNVR 80236 2279 E1
Osprey Cir
10 TNTN 80241 1777 B6
Osprey Ct
800 LSVL 80027 1689 B7
10900 PARK 80134 2452 D7
E Osprey Ct
6800 DgsC 80130 2450 C5
Osprey Dr
- BMFD 80020 1775 C1
Osprey Ln
6800 JfnC 80439 2357 C5
Osprey St
1200 BGTN 80601 1779 E1
Ostia Cir
1700 LAFT 80026 1690 A6
1700 LSVL 80026 1690 A6
Oswego Ct
300 AURA 80010 2115 D7
400 AURA 80011 2115 D7
S Oswego Ct
1500 AURA 80012 2199 D5
2800 AURA 80014 2283 E1
Oswego St
200 AURA 80010 2199 D1
400 AURA 80011 2115 D7
1400 AURA 80010 2115 D5
5400 AdmC 80022 2031 D4
5400 DNVR 80022 2031 D4
5400 DNVR 80239 2031 D4
9900 DgsC 80134 2451 D5
9900 LNTR 80134 2451 D5
11200 CMCY 80640 1863 D3
E Oswego St
11300 DgsC 80112 2451 D4
11600 DgsC 80134 2451 D4
11600 LNTR 80134 2451 D4
S Oswego St
600 AURA 80012 2199 D3
2200 AURA 80014 2199 D7
2500 AURA 80014 2283 D1
6200 GDVL 80111 2367 E3
S Oswego Wy
1900 AURA 80012 2199 E6
1900 AURA 80014 2199 E6
E Otero Av
- CTNL 80112 2367 B7
1600 CTNL 80122 2449 B1
2300 CTNL 80122 2365 C7
5500 CTNL 80112 2366 B7
5500 CTNL 80122 2366 B7
9500 AphC 80112 2367 B7
16100 AphC 80112 2368 E7
W Otero Av
8100 JfnC 80128 2362 D7
E Otero Cir
1700 CTNL 80122 2365 B7
3100 CTNL 80122 2449 D1
5000 CTNL 80122 2366 A7
5200 CTNL 80122 2450 A1
8200 CTNL 80112 2366 E7
8500 CTNL 80112 2450 E1
8700 CTNL 80112 2367 A7
8700 CTNL 80112 2451 A1
E Otero Ct
500 LITN 80122 2364 E7
500 LITN 80122 2365 A7
E Otero Dr
5200 CTNL 80122 2366 A7
5900 CTNL 80112 2366 B7
23400 AURA 80016 2370 D7
25900 AphC 80016 2371 B7
26300 AURA 80016 2371 B7
E Otero Ln
1600 CTNL 80122 2365 B7
1900 CTNL 80122 2449 C1
8400 CTNL 80112 2366 C5
E Otero Pkwy
21000 AphC 80016 2370 A7
Otero Pl
- AURA 80016 2371 C7
E Otero Pl
2600 CTNL 80122 2365 C7
5100 CTNL 80122 2366 A7
8300 CTNL 80112 2366 E7
8700 CTNL 80112 2367 A7
16100 AphC 80112 2368 E7
21500 AphC 80016 2370 B7
21800 AURA 80016 2370 B7
W Otero Pl
6900 JfnC 80128 2363 A7
6900 JfnC 80128 2447 A1
7200 JfnC 80128 2362 E7
Otis Cir
7900 ARVD 80003 1943 A5
10800 WSTR 80020 1858 E5
10800 WSTR 80020 1859 A5
Otis Ct
200 LKWD 80226 2195 A1
2400 EDGW 80214 2111 A3
2900 WTRG 80214 2111 A2
5500 ARVD 80002 2027 A4
6600 ARVD 80003 2027 A1
7000 ARVD 80003 1943 A7
7200 WSTR 80003 1943 A7
N Otis Ct
9800 WSTR 80021 1858 E7
S Otis Ct
1000 LKWD 80226 2195 A4
1200 LKWD 80232 2195 A4
3400 LKWD 80227 2279 A3
5300 DNVR 80123 2363 A1
5900 JfnC 80123 2363 A2
7900 JfnC 80128 2363 A7
7900 JfnC 80128 2447 A1
Otis Dr
8300 ARVD 80003 1943 A3
N Otis Dr
9600 WSTR 80021 1942 E1
9700 WSTR 80021 1859 A7
S Otis Pl
1100 LKWD 80232 2195 A4
Otis St
300 LKWD 80226 2111 A7
2000 LKWD 80214 2111 A4
2400 EDGW 80214 2111 A3
3200 WTRG 80214 2111 A2
3500 WTRG 80033 2111 A1
4600 WTRG 80033 2027 A6
5300 ARVD 80002 2027 A5
6900 ARVD 80003 2027 A1
7000 WSTR 80003 1943 A7
7400 ARVD 80003 1943 A6
11100 WSTR 80020 1859 A4
11200 WSTR 80020 1858 E4
N Otis St
- WSTR 80021 1858 E7
7200 WSTR 80003 1943 A7
9400 WSTR 80021 1943 A1
S Otis St
300 LKWD 80226 2195 A2
1100 LKWD 80232 2195 A4
2700 DNVR 80227 2279 A2
5500 DNVR 80123 2363 A1
8300 JfnC 80128 2447 A1
S Otis Wy
6500 JfnC 80123 2363 A4
S Otoe St
13100 JfnC 80470 2524 A7
13300 JfnC 80470 2608 A1
Otowi Rd
23100 JfnC 80439 2274 E6
E Ottawa Av
- AphC 80016 2370 E4
- AURA 80016 2370 E4
W Ottawa Av
4900 AphC 80128 2363 C4
8700 JfnC 80128 2362 C4
10200 JfnC 80127 2362 A5
E Ottawa Cir
22200 AURA 80016 2370 B4
E Ottawa Dr
22100 AURA 80016 2370 C4
S Ottawa Dr
- AURA 80016 2370 C4
W Ottawa Dr
7700 JfnC 80128 2362 D5
Ottawa Pl
- AphC 80016 2370 E4
- AURA 80016 2370 C4
4400 BLDR 80303 1687 C6
E Ottawa Pl
- AURA 80016 2370 D4
- AURA 80016 2371 A4
W Ottawa Pl
6500 JfnC 80128 2363 A4
7600 JfnC 80128 2362 D4
10200 JfnC 80127 2362 B4
Ottawa Tr
31100 JfnC 80439 2357 A4
Otter Ct
2500 LAFT 80026 1774 C1
W Otter Wy
400 DgsC 80135 2785 C2
Ottowa Ct
- DgsC 80118 2952 D2
Ottowa Pl
- DgsC 80118 2952 D2
Ouray Av
- LYNS 80540 1352 E1
200 BMFD 80020 1775 A5
S Ouray Cir
1500 AURA 80017 2201 A5
3500 AURA 80013 2284 C4
3500 AURA 80013 2285 A3
S Ouray Ct
1700 AURA 80017 2201 A5
4100 AURA 80013 2284 E4
4100 AURA 80013 2285 A4
5100 CTNL 80015 2285 A7
5700 CTNL 80015 2369 A1
6200 AphC 80016 2369 A2
Ouray Dr
7800 BldC 80503 1519 C1
8100 BldC 80503 1436 D7
Ouray Rd
10 CCkC 80439 2439 E1
10 PrkC 80470 2439 E1
200 CCkC 80439 2440 A1
15300 JfnC 80470 2609 A6
16300 JfnC 80470 2693 C1
Ouray Rd E
16400 JfnC 80470 2693 C1
Ouray Rd W
16200 JfnC 80470 2693 C2
Ouray St
- CMCY 80022 1864 E6
800 AURA 80011 2116 E5
10100 AdmC 80022 1864 E6
S Ouray St
700 AURA 80017 2200 E3
900 AURA 80017 2201 A3
1900 AURA 80013 2201 A6
2500 AURA 80013 2200 E7
3000 AURA 80013 2285 A1
3600 AURA 80013 2284 E3
4700 AURA 80013 2285 A6
5500 CTNL 80015 2369 A1
6000 AphC 80016 2369 A2
Ouray Wy
600 AURA 80011 2116 E6
S Ouray Wy
2500 AURA 80013 2200 E7
2500 AURA 80013 2201 A7
2800 AURA 80013 2285 A1
2900 AURA 80013 2284 E1
4500 AURA 80015 2285 A6
4700 AURA 80015 2284 E6
6100 AphC 80016 2369 A3
Outback Cir
6600 EbtC 80107 2710 C7
Outback Ct
5600 BLDR 80301 1604 B1
Outer Marker Rd
1100 DgsC 80108 2619 D4
Outlook Tr
2200 BMFD 80020 1774 E5
Outpost Ln
- CCkC 80439 2187 A1
Outrider Rd
8200 DgsC 80125 2530 E5
Outrigger Ct
6400 BldC 80301 1604 A3
Ouzel Ct
11000 PARK 80134 2452 E7
Overbrook Dr
7000 BldC 80503 1521 B4
Overhill Rd
1300 JfnC 80401 2109 C6
1400 LKWD 80215 2109 C6
Overland Ct
100 LAFT 80026 1689 E5
Overland Dr
2000 BGTN 80601 1696 D5
Overland Lp
34000 EbtC 80107 2710 A7
Overland Rd
- BldC 80455 1516 A2
- JMWN 80455 1516 A2
6800 BldC 80481 1515 A1
7800 BldC 80481 1514 E1
Overland Tr
15000 BGTN 80603 1697 B3
44500 EbtC 80107 2459 B7
Overlook
10 PrkC 80456 2521 B3
Overlook Dr
10 PrkC 80456 2607 A6
300 BLDR 80305 1686 E6
400 PrkC 80456 2606 E6
1300 LAFT 80026 1690 E7
1300 LAFT 80026 1691 A7
2300 BMFD 80020 1774 C6
11500 JfnC 80403 1852 D3
27300 JfnC 80439 2273 E6
Overlook Ln
10 BldC 80302 1600 E1
10 PrkC 80456 2607 D4
Overlook Rd
10 EbtC 80107 2707 E2
100 CSRK 80104 2703 E7
Overlook St
10 PrkC 80456 2521 E1
Overlook Tr
3300 JfnC 80439 2273 A4
S Overlook Wy
7500 LITN 80128 2363 D6
Overton Dr
1700 CSRK 80109 2703 A6
Overton St
15100 AdmC 80603 1700 C7
15100 AdmC 80603 1784 C1
Overview Dr
1900 CSRK 80104 2787 D2
Ovida Pl
10 DgsC 80108 2619 A5
Owens Cir
10400 WSTR 80021 1857 E6
Owens Ct
3000 LKWD 80215 2109 E2
3100 WTRG 80033 2109 E2
6500 ARVD 80004 2025 E1
7800 ARVD 80005 1941 E5
S Owens Ct
700 LKWD 80226 2194 A3
1100 JfnC 80232 2193 E4
2000 LKWD 80227 2193 E6
3200 JfnC 80227 2277 E3
4900 JfnC 80127 2278 A7
5900 JfnC 80127 2362 A3
Owens Dr
10000 WSTR 80021 1857 E7
S Owens Ln
- JfnC 80227 2277 E1
- LKWD 80227 2277 E1
Owens St
1500 LKWD 80215 2109 E5
3600 WTRG 80033 2109 E1
4200 WTRG 80033 2025 E5
5300 ARVD 80002 2025 E5
6400 ARVD 80004 2025 E2
7000 ARVD 80004 1941 E7
7800 ARVD 80005 1941 E5
N Owens St
10500 WSTR 80021 1857 E6
10700 WSTR 80021 1858 A5
S Owens St
1000 LKWD 80226 2194 A4
1000 LKWD 80232 2194 A4
1100 JfnC 80232 2194 A4
1800 JfnC 80232 2193 E6
4900 JfnC 80127 2277 E7
4900 JfnC 80127 2278 A7
6500 JfnC 80127 2362 A4
7000 JfnC 80127 2361 E5
8700 JfnC 80127 2446 A2
Owens Wy
8000 ARVD 80005 1941 E5
8000 JfnC 80005 1941 E5
S Owens Wy
4700 JfnC 80127 2277 E6
4700 JfnC 80127 2278 A6
7000 JfnC 80127 2362 A5
Owl Ct
700 LSVL 80027 1689 B7
Owl Dr
10 GpnC 80474 1849 D2
300 LSVL 80027 1773 B1
800 LSVL 80027 1689 B7
Owl Ln
- DgsC 80134 2621 D4
9400 BldC 80026 1605 C3
9400 BldC 80301 1605 C3
Owl Wy
- BGTN 80601 1697 D7
Owl Creek Rd
10 BldC 80302 1683 E3
Owl Roost Ct
8200 DgsC 80134 2622 C4
Ox Pl
- DgsC 80134 2621 D4
Ox Tr
5000 DgsC 80134 2621 D5
Oxbow Dr
- BGTN 80601 1697 C4
S Oxbow Rd
2900 JfnC 80439 2273 B2
E Oxen Rd
11000 DgsC 80138 2539 C5
E Oxford Av
- AphC 80013 2285 E4
- AphC 80013 2286 A4
- AURA 80018 2286 A4
10 EGLD 80110 2280 E4
10 EGLD 80113 2280 E4
600 EGLD 80113 2281 A4
700 CHLV 80113 2281 A4
4800 CHLV 80113 2282 A4
5300 CHLV 80111 2282 A4
7000 DNVR 80237 2282 D4
14900 AURA 80014 2284 C4
15400 AURA 80013 2284 D4
W Oxford Av
10 EGLD 80110 2280 C4
10 EGLD 80113 2280 C4
1500 SRDN 80110 2280 C4
3100 SRDN 80110 2279 E4
3200 DNVR 80110 2279 E4
4600 DNVR 80236 2279 C4
5100 DNVR 80235 2279 C4
W Oxford Cir
7800 LKWD 80235 2278 D4
Oxford Dr
- DgsC 80108 2618 E1
7200 DgsC 80108 2534 D7
E Oxford Dr
8000 DNVR 80237 2282 E4
8900 AphC 80237 2283 A4
8900 DNVR 80237 2283 A4
8900 GDVL 80111 2283 A4
9200 GDVL 80014 2283 A4
16700 AURA 80013 2284 C4
19700 AURA 80013 2285 D4
22300 AURA 80018 2286 C4

STREET
Block City ZIP Map# Grid

W Oxford Dr
7600 LKWD 80235 2278 E4
Oxford Ln
1900 SUPE 80027 1773 C6
E Oxford Ln
800 CHLV 80113 2281 A4
800 EGLD 80113 2281 A4
E Oxford Pl
4400 CHLV 80113 2281 E4
13900 AURA 80014 2284 B4
17900 AURA 80013 2285 B4
20600 AphC 80013 2285 E4
21800 AURA 80018 2286 B4
W Oxford Pl
1000 EGLD 80110 2280 C5
7700 LKWD 80235 2278 E5
Oxford Rd
4100 BldC 80503 1518 E2
4100 BldC 80503 1519 A2
5600 BldC 80503 1520 A2
9500 BldC 80503 1521 D2
9500 BldC 80504 1521 D2
9900 BldC 80504 1522 A2
11800 BldC 80504 1523 A2
Oxford Wy
10 EbtC 80107 2624 B5
Oxford Peak Ct
6200 DgsC 80108 2618 E2
Oxford Peak Ln
6100 DgsC 80108 2618 E2
Oxford Peak Pl
6200 DgsC 80108 2618 E2
Ox Yoke Ln
10 PrkC 80456 2522 D7

P

P55 Rd
- PrkC 80456 2522 B7
P63 Rd
- PrkC 80456 2521 A4
P67 Rd
10 PrkC 80456 2521 B4
P68 Rd
10 PrkC 80456 2521 B3
P69 Rd
200 PrkC 80456 2521 C4
P71 Rd
- PrkC 80456 2521 B4
P72 Rd
10 PrkC 80456 2521 B4
Pace St
- BldC 80504 1356 E7
400 LGMT 80501 1439 E2
1000 BldC 80501 1356 E7
1000 BldC 80501 1439 E2
1000 LGMT 80501 1356 E7
W Pacific Av
13800 LKWD 80228 2193 B6
E Pacific Cir
12600 AURA 80014 2199 E6
12600 AURA 80014 2200 A6
W Pacific Cir
5800 LKWD 80227 2195 B6
W Pacific Ct
11100 LKWD 80227 2193 E6
E Pacific Dr
12700 AURA 80014 2199 E6
12700 AURA 80014 2200 A6
16600 AURA 80013 2200 E6
16800 AURA 80013 2201 A6
E Pacific Pl
4800 DNVR 80222 2198 A6
8200 AphC 80231 2198 E6
9800 AURA 80247 2199 B6
11700 AURA 80014 2199 D6
14500 AURA 80014 2200 C6
15500 AURA 80013 2200 D6
16800 AURA 80013 2201 A6
W Pacific Pl
2000 DNVR 80223 2196 B6
5700 LKWD 80227 2195 B6
8500 LKWD 80227 2194 C6
Packer Ln
- BLDR 80301 1603 C7
Packer Gulch Rd
10 BldC 80302 1600 C6
Packsaddle Tr
- CCkC 80439 2187 B1
Pactolus Lake Rd
10 GpnC 80403 1850 D2
700 GpnC 80474 1850 D2
Paddock St
300 EbtC 80107 2793 A1
800 ELIZ 80107 2793 A2
Padfield Pl
1300 ERIE 80516 1607 A2
S Pagosa Cir
1500 AURA 80017 2201 A5
4400 AURA 80015 2285 A5
Pagosa Ct
- CMCY 80022 1864 E6
- CMCY 80022 1865 A6
S Pagosa Ct
1600 AURA 80017 2201 A5
2200 AURA 80013 2201 B7
4000 AURA 80013 2285 A4
5600 CTNL 80015 2369 A1
7600 CTNL 80016 2369 A6
Pagosa St
- CMCY 80022 1865 A6
1900 AURA 80011 2117 A4
10400 CMCY 80022 1864 E5
S Pagosa St
1400 AURA 80017 2201 A4
1900 AURA 80013 2201 A6
2600 AURA 80013 2285 A1
5000 AphC 80015 2285 A6
5000 AURA 80015 2285 A6
5000 CTNL 80015 2285 A6
Pagosa Wy
1600 AURA 80011 2117 A4
E Pagosa Wy
- AURA 80013 2201 A7
S Pagosa Wy
1700 AURA 80017 2201 A5
2100 AURA 80013 2201 A7
3300 AURA 80013 2285 A2
4400 AURA 80015 2285 A5
5200 CTNL 80015 2285 A7
5700 CTNL 80015 2369 A1
W Paine Av
7800 LKWD 80235 2278 D5
Paint Pl
10500 DgsC 80125 2530 E6
Paint Brush Cir
29300 JfnC 80439 2273 C4
S Paint Brush Ct
5800 LITN 80123 2363 C2
Paint Brush Dr
10 GpnC 80403 1850 A6
29500 JfnC 80439 2273 B4
Paint Brush Ln
2500 LAFT 80026 1689 D4
Paint Brush Rd
10 GpnC 80403 1850 A6
Paint Brush Tr
7100 BldC 80301 1604 C4
S Painted Canyon Cir
9300 DgsC 80129 2448 A4
W Painted Canyon Pl
2800 DgsC 80129 2448 A4
W Painted Canyon Wy
2800 DgsC 80129 2448 A4
Painted Hills St
23400 PARK 80138 2538 D2
S Painted Sky St
8400 DgsC 80126 2448 E1
Painthorse Dr
- CSRK 80109 2702 D3
Paint Pony Cir
- CSRK 80104 2704 B4
- CSRK 80108 2704 B4
Paint Pony Ct
- CSRK 80108 2704 B4
Paiute Av
6600 BldC 80503 1521 C5
Paiute Ct
6600 BldC 80503 1521 C5
Paiute Rd
- CCkC 80470 2440 A1
10 CCkC 80439 2439 E1
300 CCkC 80439 2440 A1
Palamino Ln
10 BldC 80302 1601 B1
Palermo Pl
- LGMT 80503 1437 E6
4400 LGMT 80503 1438 A6
Paley St
10500 NHGN 80234 1860 B6
Pali Wy
4300 BldC 80301 1604 C4
S Palisade Ct
800 LSVL 80027 1773 A2
9300 DgsC 80130 2450 C4
E Palisade Dr
7000 DgsC 80130 2450 C4
7200 LNTR 80124 2450 C4
Palmer Av
100 AdmC 80102 2124 D2
100 BNNT 80102 2124 D2
Palmer Av SR-79
500 BNNT 80102 2124 E2
700 AdmC 80102 2124 E2
Palmer Ct
4500 BldC 80503 1519 A5
E Palmer Dr
5600 CSRK 80104 2704 E5
Palmer Ln
1500 ERIE 80516 1607 A6
9700 NHGN 80260 1860 C7
Palmer Ridge Dr
3500 DgsC 80134 2623 A7
3500 DgsC 80134 2707 A1
Palm Tree Cir
- TNTN 80260 1944 B1
Palo Pkwy
2800 BldC 80301 1602 E5
2800 BLDR 80301 1602 E5
2800 BLDR 80304 1602 E5
2900 BldC 80301 1603 A5
2900 BLDR 80301 1603 A5
Paloma Av
10 BGTN 80601 1697 E6
Paloma St
5000 BGTN 80601 1697 D6
Palomino Dr
30100 JfnC 80439 2273 B3
N Palomino Dr
9000 DgsC 80108 2535 B3
E Palomino Pkwy
6200 DgsC 80130 2450 C2
S Palomino Rd
3200 JfnC 80439 2273 B3
Palomino Tr
2200 EbtC 80107 2708 E6
S Palo Verde Cir
3900 JfnC 80439 2273 B4
S Palo Verde Rd
3800 JfnC 80439 2273 B5
Palo Verde St
9200 TNTN 80229 1945 C2
Pampas Ct
2500 BLDR 80304 1602 E5
Pan Ct
600 LAFT 80026 1690 B5
E Panama Dr
10 CTNL 80121 2364 E3
10 LITN 80120 2364 E3
10 LITN 80121 2364 E3
400 CTNL 80121 2365 A3
Pandora Ct
1100 LAFT 80026 1690 A7
Pandora St
3900 JfnC 80465 2276 B5
Panorama Av
2300 BLDR 80304 1686 E1
Panorama Cir
800 LGMT 80501 1438 D1
E Panorama Cir
9000 AphC 80112 2367 A6
9000 CTNL 80112 2367 A6
Panorama Ct
7300 BldC 80303 1772 D1
11200 DgsC 80138 2454 A6
Panorama Dr
10 PrkC 80456 2607 C3
200 EbtC 80107 2624 A7
200 EbtC 80107 2708 A1
800 JfnC 80401 2107 C7
7200 BldC 80303 1772 D1
21600 JfnC 80401 2191 B1
E Panorama Dr
8900 AphC 80112 2367 A6
8900 CTNL 80112 2367 A6
E Panorama Ln
6700 AphC 80224 2198 C6
6700 DNVR 80224 2198 C6
Panorama Pt
- LAFT 80026 1691 A7
Panther Trc
10400 DgsC 80124 2450 B6
Panther Butte
5900 DgsC 80124 2450 B6
Panther Hollows
5900 DgsC 80124 2450 B6
Paoli Wy
17300 PARK 80134 2537 A1
Paonia
10 JfnC 80127 2361 A7
Paonia Ct
1600 CSRK 80109 2703 B5
Papago Rd
4300 JfnC 80439 2275 A5
Paperflower Dr
- PARK 80138 2538 E2
9500 DgsC 80138 2538 E2
Papoose Wy
10 CCkC 80439 2187 E5
Par Cir
10 CBVL 80123 2363 E3
Paradise Cir
21900 JfnC 80401 2191 B2
Paradise Ln
9200 BldC 80020 1773 D4
9200 BldC 80027 1773 D4
9200 LSVL 80020 1773 D4
9500 BMFD 80020 1773 D4
Paradise Rd
10 JfnC 80401 2191 B2
Paragon Dr
100 BldC 80303 1688 E6
Paragon Pl
24300 JfnC 80401 2190 D5
Paragon Rd
- BldC 80303 1688 C7
Paragon Wy
10 DgsC 80108 2618 E5
10 DgsC 80108 2619 A5
Paramount Ct
2300 LSVL 80027 1689 C5
Paramount Pkwy
10 LKWD 80215 2110 A3
10 WTRG 80215 2110 A3
Paramount Pl
1400 LGMT 80501 1356 A4
Parfet Ct
2600 LKWD 80215 2109 E3
5800 ARVD 80002 2025 E3
6100 ARVD 80004 2025 E3
7000 ARVD 80004 1941 E7
7600 ARVD 80005 1941 E6
10500 WSTR 80021 1857 E6
S Parfet Ct
1100 JfnC 80232 2193 E4
2100 LKWD 80227 2193 E7
3400 JfnC 80227 2277 E3
4500 JfnC 80127 2277 E6
7100 JfnC 80127 2361 E5
7300 JfnC 80127 2362 A6
8400 JfnC 80127 2445 E1
8400 JfnC 80127 2446 A1
Parfet Dr
2800 LKWD 80215 2109 E2
S Parfet Dr
1900 LKWD 80227 2193 E6
S Parfet Ln
5300 JfnC 80127 2361 D2
5300 JfnC 80127 2362 A1
Parfet St
- ARVD 80002 2026 A4
600 LKWD 80215 2110 A7
2500 LKWD 80215 2109 E3
3200 WTRG 80033 2109 E2
4200 WTRG 80033 2025 E7
5800 ARVD 80002 2025 E3
6800 ARVD 80004 2025 E1
6900 ARVD 80004 1941 E7
7900 ARVD 80005 1941 E5
10600 WSTR 80021 1857 E5
S Parfet St
300 LKWD 80226 2193 E2
4700 JfnC 80127 2277 E6
5600 JfnC 80127 2361 E1
5700 JfnC 80127 2362 A2
N Parfet Wy
8000 ARVD 80005 1941 E5
8000 JfnC 80005 1941 E5
S Parfet Wy
4900 JfnC 80127 2277 E7
5100 JfnC 80127 2278 A7
6400 JfnC 80127 2361 E3
6400 JfnC 80127 2362 A3
Parfet Estates Dr
1700 GOLD 80401 2107 D4
Paris Cir
100 AURA 80011 2199 D1
1300 EbtC 80138 2540 C5
Paris Ct
11400 CMCY 80640 1863 D3
S Paris Ct
900 AURA 80012 2199 D3
2800 AURA 80014 2283 E1
5800 AphC 80111 2367 E1
S Paris Pl
2700 AURA 80014 2283 E1
Paris St
100 AURA 80011 2199 D1
100 AURA 80012 2199 D1
900 AURA 80011 2115 D6
2300 AURA 80010 2115 D3
3700 AdmC 80239 2115 D1
3700 AURA 80239 2115 D1
3700 DNVR 80239 2115 D1
4600 DNVR 80239 2031 D6
11200 CMCY 80640 1863 D3
S Paris St
- AphC 80111 2367 E2
- GDVL 80111 2367 E2
600 AURA 80012 2199 E3
2800 AURA 80014 2283 E1
6600 CTNL 80111 2367 E4
6600 CTNL 80112 2367 E4
S Paris Wy
2000 AURA 80014 2199 E6
Park
- LSVL 80027 1689 D7
Park Av
- PrkC 80456 2608 A3
1500 DNVR 80218 2113 A4
1900 DNVR 80203 2113 A4
1900 DNVR 80205 2113 A4
28300 JfnC 80470 2693 D1
S Park Av
10 MRSN 80465 2276 C3
Park Av W
- DNVR 80203 2113 A4
- DNVR 80218 2113 A4
100 DNVR 80205 2113 A4
200 DNVR 80205 2112 D1
3400 DNVR 80202 2112 D1
3400 DNVR 80216 2112 D1
Park Blvd
- AdmC 80601 1779 A7
- AdmC 80602 1779 A7
Park Cir
200 JfnC 80401 2191 B2
7300 BldC 80301 1604 C3
Park Ct
300 CSRK 80109 2703 C5
4300 BldC 80301 1604 D4
Park Dr
- CCkC 80439 2272 A7
10 PrkC 80456 2607 A6
100 CSRK 80104 2788 A1
500 LYNS 80540 1352 C1
E Park Dr
6900 DgsC 80116 2705 E2
7300 DgsC 80116 2706 A2
N Park Dr
1300 LAFT 80026 1689 D2
Park Ln
100 LGMT 80501 1439 A4
600 LKWD 80214 2110 E7
800 BLDR 80302 1686 B4
2400 LITN 80120 2364 B5
2500 LAFT 80026 1689 D2
4000 EbtC 80107 2793 C1
22300 JfnC 80465 2359 A4
Park Mtn
8000 JfnC 80127 2362 B5
8000 JfnC 80127 2446 A1
Park Mtn E
10500 JfnC 80127 2446 A2
Park Mtn W
10600 JfnC 80127 2446 A2
Park Pl
1300 BMFD 80020 1775 A6
2000 DNVR 80205 2113 B4
7300 BldC 80301 1604 D4
W Park Pl
2700 DNVR 80219 2196 A1
4900 DNVR 80219 2195 C1
Park Rd
- BLDR 80503 1520 A6
- EbtC 80107 2709 C7
- EbtC 80107 2793 B2
10 PrkC 80456 2521 E3
S Park Rd
11700 JfnC 80433 2525 E3
Park St
10 BMFD 80020 1858 C2
200 CSRK 80109 2703 C6
300 LYNS 80540 1352 D2
700 ELIZ 80107 2793 B1
700 GOLD 80403 2107 D2
1600 LAFT 80026 1690 D6
S Park St
5900 JfnC 80439 2357 D3
Park Wy
10 PrkC 80456 2521 B3
Park Centre Dr
- WSTR 80234 1860 B1
Parkcliff Ln
800 DgsC 80108 2618 D1
Park Cove Dr
- BMFD 80020 1775 E4
- BMFD 80020 1776 A4
Park Cove Wy
- BMFD 80020 1775 E3
- BMFD 80020 1776 A3
E Park Crescent Dr
24600 AURA 80016 2370 E5
24600 AURA 80016 2371 A5
E Park Crescent Pl
24500 AURA 80016 2370 E5
24500 AURA 80016 2371 A5
Parkdale Cir
- ERIE 80516 1691 D2
N Parkdale Cir
1600 ERIE 80516 1691 D1
S Parkdale Cir
1600 ERIE 80516 1691 C2
Parkdale Ct
1800 ERIE 80516 1691 D2
Parkdale Pl
700 ERIE 80516 1691 C1
Park East Rd
11600 AURA 80010 2115 D7
S Parker Av
12500 JfnC 80470 2524 C6
S Parker Ct
2900 AURA 80014 2283 D1
Parker Dr
900 LGMT 80501 1356 A4
E Parker Rd
8900 DgsC 80138 2454 D7
8900 PARK 80138 2454 D7
9200 DgsC 80138 2455 A7
10900 DgsC 80138 2539 C1
S Parker Rd
- AURA 80231 2199 B7
- DgsC 80116 2621 D5
- DgsC 80134 2621 D5
1000 AphC 80231 2198 E5
1000 AphC 80247 2198 E5
1000 DNVR 80224 2198 E5
1000 DNVR 80231 2198 E5
1000 DNVR 80247 2198 E5
1600 AphC 80231 2199 B7
1600 AphC 80247 2199 B7
2000 AURA 80247 2199 B7
2200 DNVR 80231 2199 B7
2200 DNVR 80247 2199 B7
2300 AURA 80014 2199 B7
2300 DNVR 80014 2199 B7
2500 AURA 80014 2283 D2
3100 DNVR 80014 2283 D2
3200 AphC 80014 2283 D2
3200 AphC 80014 2284 B6
3200 AURA 80014 2284 B3
4000 AURA 80015 2284 B6
5100 AphC 80015 2284 B6
5300 AphC 80015 2368 C1
5300 AURA 80015 2368 C1
5600 CTNL 80015 2368 C1
5800 AphC 80016 2368 C1
5800 CTNL 80016 2368 C1
6700 FXFD 80016 2368 D3
7000 AphC 80016 2369 A6
7000 CTNL 80016 2369 A6
7000 FXFD 80016 2369 A6
8000 AURA 80016 2369 A6
8000 AURA 80016 2453 B2
8000 AURA 80138 2453 B2
8000 CTNL 80016 2453 B2
8000 PARK 80138 2453 B2
8100 AphC 80016 2453 B2
8100 PARK 80134 2453 B2
9300 DgsC 80134 2453 B2
9300 DgsC 80138 2453 B2
9500 PARK 80134 2537 D2
10900 DgsC 80134 2537 D2
10900 PARK 80138 2537 D1
S Parker Rd SR-83
- AURA 80231 2199 B7
- DgsC 80116 2621 D5
- DgsC 80134 2621 D5
1000 AphC 80231 2198 E5
1000 AphC 80247 2198 E5
1000 DNVR 80224 2198 E5
1000 DNVR 80231 2198 E5
1000 DNVR 80247 2198 E5
1600 AphC 80231 2199 B7
1600 AphC 80247 2199 B7
2000 AURA 80247 2199 B7
2200 DNVR 80231 2199 B7
2200 DNVR 80247 2199 B7
2300 AURA 80014 2199 B7
2300 DNVR 80014 2199 B7
2500 AURA 80014 2283 D2
3100 DNVR 80014 2283 D2
3200 AphC 80014 2283 D2
3200 AphC 80014 2284 B6
3200 AURA 80014 2284 B3
4000 AphC 80015 2284 B6
5100 AURA 80015 2284 B6
5300 AphC 80015 2368 C1
5300 AURA 80015 2368 C1
5600 CTNL 80015 2368 C1
5800 AphC 80016 2368 C1
6200 CTNL 80016 2368 D3
6700 FXFD 80016 2368 D3
7000 AphC 80016 2369 A6
7000 CTNL 80016 2369 A6
7000 FXFD 80016 2369 A6
8000 AURA 80016 2369 A6
8000 AURA 80016 2453 B2
8000 AURA 80138 2453 B2
8000 PARK 80134 2453 B2
8100 AphC 80016 2453 B2
8100 PARK 80134 2453 B2
9300 DgsC 80134 2453 B2
9300 DgsC 80138 2453 B2
9500 PARK 80134 2537 D1
10300 PARK 80134 2453 C5
10900 PARK 80138 2537 D1
12400 DgsC 80134 2537 D2
W Parker Rd
3000 DgsC 80134 2452 B6
3000 LNTR 80134 2452 B6
3700 PARK 80134 2452 B6
4000 DgsC 80134 2536 E1
4600 PARK 80134 2536 E1
4800 DgsC 80134 2537 A1
4800 PARK 80134 2537 A1
W Parker Rd CO-8
- DgsC 80134 2537 A1
- PARK 80134 2537 A1
E Parker Hills Ct
7000 DgsC 80138 2453 E6
Parkerhouse Rd
16500 DgsC 80134 2452 E3
16500 DgsC 80134 2453 A3
16500 PARK 80134 2453 A3
E Parker Square Dr
19500 PARK 80134 2537 D2
Parker Vista Cir
10800 PARK 80138 2454 A7
20500 PARK 80138 2453 E7
Parker Vista Ct
20700 PARK 80138 2454 A7
Parker Vista Ln
10800 PARK 80138 2454 A7
Parker Vista Pl
10900 PARK 80138 2454 A7
Parker Vista Rd
10800 PARK 80138 2453 E7
20600 PARK 80138 2454 A7
E Parker Vista St
- PARK 80138 2454 A7
Parker Vista Wy
10900 PARK 80138 2453 E7
S Park Glenn Wy
10100 DgsC 80138 2453 D5
10100 PARK 80134 2453 D5
10100 PARK 80138 2453 D5
W Parkhill Av
2200 LITN 80120 2364 B3
8300 JfnC 80123 2362 D3
10600 JfnC 80127 2362 A3
W Parkhill Dr
10600 JfnC 80127 2362 A3
11300 JfnC 80127 2361 E3
W Parkhill Pl
10600 JfnC 80127 2362 A3
12100 JfnC 80127 2361 D3
Parkington Ln
10500 DgsC 80126 2449 E7
Park Lake Dr
1600 BldC 80301 1689 B1
1600 BldC 80303 1689 B1
2400 BldC 80301 1605 B7
S Parkland Rd
- LNTR 80112 2451 A1
8300 LNTR 80124 2451 A1
Parklane Dr
20700 PARK 80138 2454 A7
E Park Ln Dr
12200 AURA 80011 2115 E2
12700 AURA 80011 2116 A2
Park Ln Rd
5600 BldC 80503 1520 C7
7100 BldC 80503 1604 C1
Park Meadows Blvd
- LNTR 80124 2451 B6
Park Meadows Dr
7300 DgsC 80130 2450 D1
7300 LNTR 80130 2450 D1
7700 LNTR 80124 2450 D1
10000 LNTR 80124 2451 B4
S Park Meadows Center Dr
8300 CTNL 80112 2451 B2
8300 LNTR 80112 2451 B2
8300 LNTR 80124 2451 B2
Park Place Av
5600 GDVL 80111 2366 E1
Park Point Dr
400 JfnC 80401 2190 B3
W Park Range Rd
10700 JfnC 80127 2362 A6
11000 JfnC 80127 2361 E6
Parkridge Av
10500 BldC 80504 1356 A4
S Park Ridge Ln
2100 DgsC 80135 2785 C5
W Park Ridge Rd
3100 DgsC 80135 2785 D6
Park Saddle Ct
5700 BLDR 80301 1604 B2
Parkside Cir
1600 LAFT 80026 1690 D6
Parkside Dr
15900 DgsC 80134 2452 E6
E Parkside Dr
16600 CMCY 80022 1864 E6
16900 CMCY 80022 1865 A5
N Parkside Dr
400 LGMT 80501 1439 B5
S Parkside Dr
- LGMT 80501 1439 B5
Parkside Pkwy
- FLHT 80260 1944 A3
Park Terrace Av
8300 GDVL 80111 2366 E1
S Park Terrace Av
5400 GDVL 80111 2282 E7
5400 GDVL 80111 2366 E1
Parkview
10 PrkC 80456 2690 C1
Parkview Av
100 GOLD 80401 2191 C1
100 JfnC 80401 2191 C1
400 JfnC 80401 2107 C7
800 LSVL 80027 1773 D1
Parkview Ct
10 PrkC 80456 2606 C7
500 GOLD 80403 2107 D3
1000 CSRK 80104 2703 D5
Park View Dr
15200 AdmC 80601 1697 B7
Parkview Dr
900 CSRK 80104 2703 E5
2100 LGMT 80504 1438 E7
2300 BldC 80504 1438 E7
27300 JfnC 80401 2189 E3
E Parkview Dr
12200 AURA 80011 2115 E7
12600 AURA 80011 2116 A7
Parkview Mtn
7500 JfnC 80127 2361 E6
Parkview Pl
- BMFD 80020 1775 E5
800 CSRK 80104 2703 E5
E Parkview Pl
- AURA 80018 2119 B7
Park Village Dr
29800 JfnC 80439 2273 C5
Park Vista Dr
11100 NHGN 80234 1860 B4
Parkway Dr
10 AphC 80222 2281 E3
10 CHLV 80113 2281 E3
10 DNVR 80222 2281 E3
900 BLDR 80303 1687 D3
E Parkway Dr
- CTNL 80112 2450 E1
- CTNL 80124 2450 E1
- LNTR 80124 2451 A1
6000 CMCY 80022 2030 A3
7400 LNTR 80124 2450 E1
Parkwood Ln
7100 DgsC 80108 2618 C1
E Parliament Ct
20800 PARK 80138 2537 E1
20800 PARK 80138 2538 A1
E Parliament Pl
20800 PARK 80138 2538 A1
S Parliament Wy
11200 PARK 80138 2537 E1
11200 PARK 80138 2538 B2
Parmalee Gulch Rd
4400 JfnC 80439 2274 D6
4500 JfnC 80439 2275 A6
4600 JfnC 80454 2275 A6
S Parmalee Gulch Rd
5000 JfnC 80439 2275 B7
5000 JfnC 80454 2275 B7
5100 JfnC 80454 2359 C1
5500 JfnC 80465 2359 C1
Parr Rd
1100 BMFD 80020 1775 A6
S Parramatta Pl
9500 DgsC 80130 2450 A4
Parsons Av
900 CSRK 80104 2788 D1
Parsons Rd
27200 JfnC 80433 2525 E1
Parsons Wy
4800 CSRK 80104 2788 D1
Parthenon Ct
600 LAFT 80026 1690 B5
Parthenon Pl
1000 LAFT 80026 1690 B6
Partridge Cir
600 GOLD 80403 2107 D1
Partridge Ln
10 JfnC 80127 2360 E4
S Partridge St
8700 DgsC 80126 2449 E2
Pasadena Wy
4700 BMFD 80020 1775 C3
Paschal Dr
700 BldC 80026 1689 D5
700 BldC 80027 1689 D5
700 LAFT 80026 1689 D5
S Paseo Wy
1800 DNVR 80219 2195 D6
Paseo del Prado St
3600 BLDR 80301 1602 D5
3700 BldC 80301 1603 A5
3700 BLDR 80301 1603 A5
Pasque Dr
900 LGMT 80501 1439 E1
Pasture Gate Cir
- EbtC 80107 2709 B1
Pasture Walk Rd
- EbtC 80107 2709 D4
Pat Creek Rd
- CCkC 80439 2187 B3
10 CCkC 80452 2187 A3
W Pate Av
5800 DgsC 80125 2532 D6
5800 DgsC 80135 2532 D6
Pathfinder Ct
- CSRK 80108 2703 D2
Patricia Dr
7800 AdmC 80229 1944 E5
Patricia Rd
10 GpnC 80474 1849 E2
300 GpnC 80474 1850 A2
Patrick Tr
7100 EbtC 80107 2458 E1
7100 EbtC 80107 2459 A2
S Patsburg Ct
- AURA 80016 2371 C3
Patsburg St
- DNVR 80249 1951 B6
Patterson Ct
10800 NHGN 80234 1860 D4
W Patterson Pl
3400 LITN 80123 2363 E2
10600 JfnC 80127 2362 A2
11400 JfnC 80127 2361 E2
Patterson Rd
10800 DgsC 80116 2791 B6
Patti Pl
10 BMFD 80020 1774 E6
Patton Cir
1500 BLDR 80303 1687 C2
S Patton Ct
500 DNVR 80219 2195 D4
2600 DNVR 80219 2279 D1
2600 DNVR 80236 2279 D1
Patton Dr
1400 BLDR 80303 1687 D3
Patton St
12600 BMFD 80020 1775 D7
S Patton Wy
3300 DNVR 80236 2279 D3
Patty Dr
10 CCkC 80439 2271 E5
Patty Ln
9000 DgsC 80134 2537 A3
9000 PARK 80134 2537 A3
Paula Av
10 GpnC 80403 1849 D5
S Paulette Av
12500 JfnC 80470 2524 C6
S Pauls Dr
11100 JfnC 80433 2524 E2
11300 JfnC 80433 2525 A2
Pauls Ln
10 PrkC 80456 2521 E5

STREET / Block City ZIP Map# Grid

S Pauls Ln
11400 JfnC 80433 2525 A2
Pauls Rd
10 CCkC 80439 2271 E6
Pavilion Dr
11100 DgsC 80134 2537 D1
Pawnee Ct
36600 EbtC 80107 2708 D2
Pawnee Dr
10 BLDR 80303 1687 C6
Pawnee Ln
- BMFD 80020 1775 C5
8300 BldC 80503 1521 A5
Pawnee Pkwy
1000 EbtC 80107 2708 C4
Pawnee Pl
4600 BLDR 80303 1687 C6
Pawnee Pt
2000 LAFT 80026 1690 A4
Pawnee Rd
- DgsC 80118 2952 D2
300 KIOW 80117 2796 A2
500 EbtC 80117 2796 A3
22800 JfnC 80439 2275 A5
23000 JfnC 80465 2275 A4
23100 JfnC 80439 2274 E5
E Pawnee Rd
8400 DgsC 80134 2622 C2
Pawnee Tr
10 CCkC 80439 2355 E7
10 CCkC 80439 2356 A7
E Pawnee Tr
800 DgsC 80108 2619 C5
Pawnee Wy
6900 BldC 80503 1521 A4
Paw Paw Av
- TNTN 80260 1944 B1
Paw Print Wy
2600 CSRK 80109 2702 C4
Paxton Ct
10500 PARK 80134 2453 B6
W Payne Av
7100 JfnC 80128 2446 E2
Payne Ct
1900 AURA 80011 2117 A4
2500 ERIE 80516 1690 D1
Payne Wy
1700 AURA 80011 2117 A4
Payne Gulch Rd
- PrkC 80456 2689 D4
Peabody St
- CSRK 80104 2705 A7
S Peace Chance Tr
7500 JfnC 80439 2357 E7
Peaceful Wy
13300 JfnC 80470 2524 B7
13300 JfnC 80470 2608 B1
S Peaceful Hills Rd
6800 JfnC 80465 2359 A5
S Peaceful Hills Wy
6900 JfnC 80465 2359 A5
Peach Ct
- BLDR 80304 1602 C4
700 LSVL 80027 1773 A2
1500 BGTN 80601 1696 D7
4300 BldC 80301 1603 A4
Peach Dr
- TNTN 80260 1944 C2
Peach Pl
1400 ERIE 80516 1691 E3
Peach Wy
4200 BldC 80301 1603 A4
S Peach Wy
3600 DNVR 80237 2282 C4
Peachtree Cir
10 CSRK 80104 2787 D2
Peacock Dr
13000 DgsC 80124 2450 D2
Peacock St
9700 FLHT 80260 1944 A3
Peak Av
2900 LGMT 80504 1440 C2
5200 BLDR 80301 1687 C2
S Peak Ln
10 BldC 80302 1683 C1
S Peak Rd
10 BldC 80302 1683 C1
S Peak Tr
10 BldC 80302 1683 C2
Peak Meadows Dr
23900 JfnC 80433 2526 D6
Peak to Peak Hwy
- BldC 80481 1513 E1
- BldC 80481 1514 B2
- BldC 80481 1597 C3
- WARD 80481 1597 D1
22000 GpnC 80474 1765 E7
23900 NDLD 80466 1765 D4
33000 BldC 80466 1765 D1
35700 BldC 80302 1682 A6
35700 BldC 80466 1682 A6
35900 BldC 80466 1681 D3
37700 BldC 80302 1681 D2
39000 BldC 80466 1597 C7
Peak to Peak Hwy SR-72
- BldC 80481 1513 E1
- BldC 80481 1514 B2
- BldC 80481 1597 C3
- WARD 80481 1597 D1
23900 NDLD 80466 1765 D4
33000 BldC 80466 1765 D1
35700 BldC 80302 1682 A6
35700 BldC 80466 1682 A6
35900 BldC 80466 1681 D3
37700 BldC 80302 1681 D2
39000 BldC 80466 1597 C7
Peak to Peak Hwy SR-119
22000 BldC 80466 1765 D6
22000 GpnC 80474 1765 E7
23900 NDLD 80466 1765 D4
E Peakview Av
- AphC 80016 2368 B3
2700 CTNL 80121 2365 C3
4400 CTNL 80121 2366 A3
6200 CTNL 80111 2366 C3
7700 GDVL 80111 2366 D3
8900 GDVL 80111 2367 A3
9300 AphC 80111 2367 B3
9500 CTNL 80111 2367 B3
12800 AphC 80111 2368 A3
12800 CTNL 80111 2368 A3
15500 CTNL 80016 2368 D3
16700 CTNL 80016 2369 A3
18100 AphC 80016 2369 B3
W Peakview Av
100 LITN 80120 2364 D3
7200 JfnC 80123 2362 E4
Peak View Cir
- CSRK 80108 2703 E1
Peakview Cir
1000 BldC 80302 1517 C5
E Peakview Cir
4000 AphC 80121 2365 E3
4000 CTNL 80121 2365 E3
W Peakview Cir
1000 LITN 80120 2364 C3
E Peakview Ct
19900 CTNL 80016 2369 D3
W Peakview Ct
2400 LITN 80120 2364 B3
Peak View Dr
10 GpnC 80403 1934 C5
Peakview Dr
10 BldC 80466 1765 D4
10 NDLD 80466 1765 D4
E Peakview Dr
- AURA 80016 2371 C3
21900 AURA 80016 2370 B3
S Peak View Dr
200 DgsC 80109 2786 D2
W Peakview Dr
7700 JfnC 80123 2362 D3
10600 JfnC 80127 2362 A4
Peakview Pl
10 DgsC 80138 2539 E4
E Peakview Pl
- AURA 80016 2371 B3
5200 CTNL 80121 2366 A3
6600 CTNL 80111 2366 C3
18200 AphC 80016 2369 B3
20700 AphC 80016 2370 A3
22500 AURA 80016 2370 C3
W Peakview Pl
10400 JfnC 80127 2362 A4
Peakview Rd
10 BldC 80302 1517 B6
Peak Vista Ct
2200 CSRK 80104 2704 A6
Pear Ct
700 LSVL 80027 1773 A2
1700 BGTN 80601 1696 D7
Pearl Cir
9500 DgsC 80134 2452 E4
10900 NHGN 80233 1860 E4
13200 TNTN 80241 1776 E5
Pearl Ct
10800 NHGN 80233 1860 E5
Pearl Pkwy
- BldC 80301 1603 D7
3300 BLDR 80301 1687 B1
4900 BldC 80301 1687 B1
Pearl St
- BldC 80301 1603 D7
- BldC 80301 1687 C1
- DgsC 80134 2452 E4
10 BldC 80302 1686 B2
10 DNVR 80203 2196 E1
10 DNVR 80209 2196 E1
900 DNVR 80203 2112 E6
1400 BLDR 80302 1686 E1
1900 DNVR 80205 2112 E5
2800 BLDR 80301 1686 E1
4700 BLDR 80301 1687 B1
4800 DNVR 80216 2028 E6
5500 AdmC 80216 2028 E4
8000 AdmC 80229 1944 E5
9600 TNTN 80229 1944 E1
9800 TNTN 80229 1860 E7
11600 NHGN 80233 1860 E3
13200 TNTN 80241 1776 E5
S Pearl St
10 DNVR 80203 2196 E1
10 DNVR 80209 2196 E1
200 EbtC 80107 2793 A1
200 ELIZ 80107 2793 A1
1000 DNVR 80210 2196 E5
2500 DNVR 80210 2280 E1
2600 AphC 80210 2280 E1
2600 EGLD 80113 2280 E1
2600 EGLD 80210 2280 E1
3200 EGLD 80113 2281 A3
5100 AphC 80121 2280 E7
5100 AphC 80121 2281 C7
5700 LITN 80121 2365 A2
5900 CTNL 80121 2365 A2
5900 GDVL 80121 2365 A2
6600 CTNL 80122 2365 A4
Pearl Wy
10900 NHGN 80233 1860 E4
Pearl East Cir
4700 BLDR 80301 1687 B1
Pearl Street Mall
1100 BLDR 80302 1686 C2
Pearlwood Cir
10500 DgsC 80126 2449 D7
Pearson Ranch Lp
42400 EbtC 80138 2540 A5
43300 DgsC 80138 2539 E5
Peavine Wy
- DgsC 80118 2870 A6
Pebble Ct
7300 BldC 80503 1520 E3
Pebble Rd
7800 BldC 80503 1520 E3
Pebble Beach Ct
- BldC 80503 1518 E5
S Pebble Beach Ct
2200 JfnC 80439 2189 A7
Pebble Beach Dr
3900 BldC 80503 1518 E6
4000 BldC 80503 1519 A6
S Pebble Beach Dr
2300 JfnC 80439 2189 A7
2300 JfnC 80439 2273 B1
Pebble Beach Ln
9800 LNTR 80124 2450 D5
S Pebble Beach Ln
2700 JfnC 80439 2273 C2
Pebble Brook Ln
22200 PARK 80138 2538 B1
S Pebble Creek Wy
8300 DgsC 80126 2449 D1
Pebbles Pl
4900 BMFD 80020 1775 C3
Pebblewood Ct
15500 DgsC 80134 2452 D5
Pecan Ct
- LGMT 80501 1439 B6
Pecan St
- LGMT 80501 1439 B6
Peck Dr
600 LGMT 80503 1438 A5
N Pecos Ct
13400 WSTR 80234 1776 B5
Pecos St
- AdmC 80020 1692 B7
- AdmC 80020 1776 B1
1200 DNVR 80204 2112 C6
3200 DNVR 80211 2112 C1
4000 DNVR 80211 2028 C7
5100 AdmC 80221 2028 C7
5100 DNVR 80221 2028 C7
6900 AdmC 80221 1944 B6
8300 FLHT 80260 1944 C5
8400 TNTN 80260 1944 C5
9700 NHGN 80260 1860 B7
9700 TNTN 80260 1860 B7
10300 TNTN 80234 1860 B7
11200 NHGN 80234 1860 B4
11200 WSTR 80234 1860 B4
14500 WSTR 80020 1776 B2
N Pecos St
11500 WSTR 80234 1860 B2
13400 WSTR 80234 1776 B5
S Pecos St
- EGLD 80110 2196 C7
10 DNVR 80223 2196 C2
Pecos Tr
3700 CSRK 80109 2702 D2
Pecos Wy
1600 AdmC 80221 1944 B4
5300 AdmC 80221 2028 B5
S Pecos Wy
900 DNVR 80223 2196 C4
Peerless St
300 LSVL 80027 1689 C6
Peery Dr
500 GOLD 80403 2107 D1
Peery Pkwy
300 GOLD 80403 2107 E2
Pegasus Dr
10 DgsC 80124 2450 E2
10 DgsC 80124 2451 A2
Pegasus Pl
1000 LAFT 80026 1690 B6
Peggy Ln
30000 JfnC 80439 2357 B2
Pelican Av
10 BGTN 80601 1697 E6
Pelican St
5000 AdmC 80601 1697 D7
5000 BGTN 80601 1697 D7
Pelon Dr
9400 NHGN 80260 1944 D1
9400 TNTN 80260 1944 D1
Pemberly Av
2600 DgsC 80126 2533 C1
2700 DgsC 80126 2449 C7
Pemberton Dr
5400 GDVL 80121 2365 B1
Pembroke Ct
7400 DgsC 80108 2534 D7
Pembroke Gdns
4400 BldC 80301 1603 E4
S Pembrook St
10 CSRK 80104 2704 D7
Pena Blvd
- DNVR - 1949 A6
- DNVR - 1950 D6
- DNVR - 1951 A6
- DNVR - 2032 E6
- DNVR - 2033 A1
Pendleton Av
700 LGMT 80501 1439 D2
S Pendleton Dr
9400 DgsC 80126 2448 E4
Penhurst Cir
600 LGMT 80501 1356 D6
E Penhurst Pl
2500 DgsC 80126 2449 C5
Peninsula Cir
1300 CSRK 80104 2787 D2
S Peninsula Dr
8100 LITN 80120 2364 B7
Pennington Ln
10200 DgsC 80126 2448 E6
10200 DgsC 80126 2449 A6
Pennington St
- DgsC 80126 2449 A7
Pennock Wy
2400 LGMT 80501 1355 E4
Pennsylvania Av
- BLDR 80303 1686 D5
900 BLDR 80302 1686 C3
2800 BLDR 80303 1687 A3
Pennsylvania Cir
13100 TNTN 80241 1776 E6
Pennsylvania Ct
7600 AdmC 80229 1944 E6
S Pennsylvania Ct
8000 LITN 80122 2365 A7
8200 LITN 80122 2449 B1
Pennsylvania Dr
9800 TNTN 80229 1860 E7
S Pennsylvania Dr
7500 LITN 80122 2365 A6
Pennsylvania Pl
5600 BLDR 80303 1687 D3
Pennsylvania St
- TNTN 80233 1860 E2
- TNTN 80241 1860 E2
10 DNVR 80203 2196 E1
10 DNVR 80209 2196 E1
700 DNVR 80203 2112 E6
1900 DNVR 80205 2112 E5
4600 DNVR 80216 2028 E6
5500 AdmC 80216 2028 E4
8100 AdmC 80229 1944 E4
8100 TNTN 80229 1944 E4
11700 NHGN 80233 1860 E3
13000 TNTN 80241 1776 E6
S Pennsylvania St
10 DNVR 80203 2196 E2
10 DNVR 80209 2196 E2
1100 DNVR 80210 2196 E5
2500 DNVR 80210 2280 E1
2600 AphC 80210 2280 E1
2600 EGLD 80113 2280 E1
2600 EGLD 80210 2280 E1
5100 AphC 80121 2280 E7
5100 AphC 80121 2281 C7
5700 CTNL 80121 2364 E1
5700 LITN 80121 2364 E1
5900 CTNL 80121 2365 A2
6600 CTNL 80122 2365 A4
7100 CTNL 80122 2364 E5
7900 LITN 80122 2365 A7
Pennsylvania Wy
8100 AdmC 80229 1944 E4
Pennsylvania Gulch Rd
- BldC 80302 1598 B7
- BldC 80466 1681 D2
10 BldC 80302 1681 E1
10 BldC 80302 1682 A1
E Pennwood Cir
400 EGLD 80113 2280 E7
500 AphC 80121 2280 E7
S Penny Rd
11400 JfnC 80433 2525 B3
Penrith Blvd
- AdmC 80102 2124 B2
Penrith Rd
2300 AdmC 80102 2124 B3
4100 AdmC 80102 2040 B6
Penrith Wy
- AdmC 80102 2124 B2
Penrith Mile Rd
- AdmC 80102 2124 B4
Penrose Ct
- DNVR 80237 2283 A5
S Penrose Ct
6600 CTNL 80121 2365 A4
6600 CTNL 80122 2365 A4
7500 LITN 80122 2365 A6
Penrose Pl
3300 BLDR 80301 1603 A6
E Penrose Pl
1200 DgsC 80126 2449 A3
Pensacola Dr
14300 DNVR 80239 2032 B4
Pensacola Pl
12900 DNVR 80239 2031 E4
15400 DNVR 80239 2032 D4
Pensive Ct
22000 PARK 80138 2538 C1
Penstemon
10 JfnC 80127 2360 E6
Penstemon Wy
2800 CSRK 80109 2702 D4
E Penwood Pl
14800 AURA 80015 2284 C6
S Peoria Cir
300 AURA 80012 2199 D2
7500 AphC 80112 2367 E6
S Peoria Ct
1300 AURA 80012 2199 E4
3100 AURA 80014 2283 E2
Peoria St
10 AURA 80011 2199 E1
10 AURA 80012 2199 E1
800 AURA 80010 2115 E7
1400 AURA 80011 2115 E4
3700 AdmC 80239 2115 E1
3700 AURA 80239 2115 E1
3700 DNVR 80239 2115 E1
5500 AdmC 80022 2031 E6
5500 DNVR 80022 2031 E6
5500 DNVR 80239 2031 E6
9600 AdmC 80022 1863 D7
9600 AdmC 80022 1947 D1
9600 CMCY 80022 1863 D7
9600 CMCY 80022 1947 D1
10400 AdmC 80640 1863 D1
10400 BGTN 80640 1863 D1
10400 CMCY 80640 1863 D1
N Peoria St
- AdmC 80239 2115 E2
- DNVR 80239 2115 E2
2200 AURA 80010 2115 E2
2600 AURA 80011 2115 E2
3600 AURA 80239 2115 E2
S Peoria St
- AphC 80112 2452 A3
- DgsC 80112 2451 E5
- DgsC 80134 2451 E6
10 AURA 80011 2199 E1
10 AURA 80012 2199 E1
1900 AURA 80014 2199 E7
2500 AURA 80014 2283 E1
5100 AphC 80111 2367 E1
5100 GDVL 80111 2283 E7
5100 GDVL 80111 2367 E1
6600 CTNL 80111 2367 E3
6600 CTNL 80112 2367 E3
7100 AphC 80112 2367 E5
10000 LNTR 80134 2451 E6
Peoria Wy
3900 DNVR 80239 2031 D7
Peppertree Ct
6800 BldC 80503 1520 D5
Peppertree Dr
6800 BldC 80503 1520 D5
Peppertree Ln
6800 BldC 80503 1520 D4
S Pepperwood Ln
9200 DgsC 80126 2449 A3
Peppler Dr
- LGMT 80501 1356 C4
Percival St
- LAFT 80026 1690 E6
Pere Ln
- LKWD 80228 2193 D2
Peregrine
10 JfnC 80127 2360 E4
Peregrine Cir
100 BMFD 80020 1774 E5
300 BMFD 80020 1775 A5
500 LGMT 80501 1440 A2
Peregrine Ct
1600 BMFD 80020 1774 E6
1700 LAFT 80026 1689 E2
1800 BMFD 80020 1775 A6
Peregrine Dr
16100 PARK 80134 2452 E7
Peregrine Ln
1700 BMFD 80020 1775 A5
E Peregrine Wy
6900 DgsC 80130 2450 C5
Peridot Ct
1500 CSRK 80108 2619 E6
Peridot Ln
1600 CSRK 80108 2619 E6
1700 CSRK 80108 2620 A6
Periwinkle
10 JfnC 80127 2360 E6
Periwinkle Ct
15300 DgsC 80134 2452 D6
Periwinkle Dr
1200 BLDR 80304 1602 C5
Periwinkle Pl
4000 LGMT 80503 1438 A5
S Perry Cir
5100 LITN 80123 2279 D7
Perry Ct
6600 AdmC 80003 2027 D1
9900 WSTR 80031 1859 D7
N Perry Ct
11000 WSTR 80031 1859 D5
S Perry Ct
5200 LITN 80123 2279 D7
N Perry Dr
- WSTR 80031 1859 D5
E Perry Pkwy
4200 GDVL 80121 2281 E7
4200 GDVL 80121 2282 A7
Perry Pl
7700 WSTR 80030 1943 D6
Perry St
10 DNVR 80219 2195 D1
100 ERIE 80516 1607 C5
100 WldC 80516 1607 C5
300 DNVR 80219 2111 D7
700 CSRK 80104 2703 D6
2000 DNVR 80204 2111 D5
2000 DNVR 80212 2111 D3
4000 DNVR 80212 2027 D7
5100 AdmC 80212 2027 D5
6400 AdmC 80003 2027 D2
9600 WSTR 80031 1943 D1
11700 WSTR 80031 1859 D2
N Perry St
- WSTR 80031 1859 D2
9000 WSTR 80031 1943 D2
12000 BMFD 80020 1859 D2
12200 BMFD 80020 1775 D7
S Perry St
10 DNVR 80219 2195 D2
100 CSRK 80104 2703 D7
700 CSRK 80104 2787 D1
2500 DNVR 80219 2279 D1
2700 DNVR 80236 2279 D2
4700 DNVR 80123 2279 D6
5000 DvrC 80123 2279 D6
5000 LITN 80123 2279 D7
5300 LITN 80123 2363 D1
Perry Wy
9700 WSTR 80031 1859 D7
S Perry Wy
1800 DNVR 80219 2195 D6
E Perry Park Av
10 DgsC 80118 2955 A5
10 LKSR 80118 2955 A5
E Perry Park Av CO-60
10 DgsC 80118 2955 A5
10 LKSR 80118 2955 A5
W Perry Park Av
10 DgsC 80118 2954 E5
10 DgsC 80118 2955 A5
10 LKSR 80118 2954 E5
10 LKSR 80118 2955 A5
W Perry Park Av CO-60
10 DgsC 80118 2954 E5
10 DgsC 80118 2955 A5
10 LKSR 80118 2954 E5
10 LKSR 80118 2955 A5
Perry Park Blvd
6000 DgsC 80118 2868 C6
6200 DgsC 80118 2869 A7
6200 DgsC 80118 2953 A2
6700 DgsC 80118 2952 E1
N Perry Park Rd
10 DgsC 80135 2701 D7
400 DgsC 80109 2701 D7
3600 DgsC 80135 2617 C6
N Perry Park Rd SR-105
800 DgsC 80109 2701 D7
800 DgsC 80135 2701 D7
3600 DgsC 80135 2617 C6
S Perry Park Rd
10 DgsC 80135 2701 C7
10 DgsC 80135 2785 B3
2600 DgsC 80135 2869 B1
5100 DgsC 80118 2869 D7
6700 DgsC 80118 2953 E1
8300 DgsC 80118 2954 A5
Perseverance Tr
26800 JfnC 80403 2022 A1
Persimmon Dr
- BLDR 80304 1602 C3
Persimmon Pl
- CSRK 80109 2702 C5
Perth Cir
4200 DNVR 80249 2034 A6
Perth Ct
5200 DNVR 80249 2034 A4
E Perth Pl
- DgsC 80130 2450 A4
S Perth Pl
5700 CTNL 80015 2370 B1
Perth St
- AURA 80011 2118 A2
4500 DNVR 80249 2034 A6
N Perth St
800 AphC 80018 2118 A6
800 AURA 80018 2118 A6
S Perth St
3800 AphC 80013 2286 B4
5900 CTNL 80015 2370 B2
6800 AURA 80016 2370 B4
S Perth Wy
5400 AphC 80015 2286 B7
5400 CTNL 80015 2286 B7
5400 CTNL 80015 2370 B1
7200 AURA 80016 2370 B5
Peru Creek Av
18200 PARK 80134 2537 C5
Petersburg Ct
19700 PARK 80134 2537 D3
Peterson Ct
4800 DNVR 80221 2028 B6
Peterson Pl
1500 LGMT 80501 1355 E4
N Peterson Rd
- AdmC 80102 2039 A3
- AURA 80102 2039 A5
- AURA 80102 2123 A2
200 AphC 80102 2123 A7
5300 DgsC 80135 2532 E7
5300 DgsC 80135 2616 E1
5300 DgsC 80135 2617 A2
S Peterson Wy
700 DNVR 80223 2196 C3
Petursdale Ct
7100 BldC 80301 1604 C4
Peyton Dr
17600 PARK 80134 2453 B7
17600 PARK 80134 2537 B1
Phantom Creek Tr
10 PrkC 80456 2521 B5
Pheasant Av
10 BGTN 80601 1697 E6
Pheasant Cir
400 LAFT 80026 1774 C1
Pheasant Ct
11000 PARK 80134 2536 D1
Pheasant Dr
2500 LGMT 80503 1355 C5
Pheasant Ln
- BldC 80301 1603 D6
10 JfnC 80127 2361 A4
Pheasant Run
100 LSVL 80027 1689 B6
10800 DgsC 80125 2614 D1
37000 EbtC 80107 2710 A1
Pheasant St
2600 FLHT 80260 1944 A1
2600 TNTN 80260 1944 A1
S Pheasant Run Pkwy
- AphC 80015 2284 E6
14800 AURA 80014 2284 C5
14800 AURA 80015 2284 C5
Pheasant Run Rd
- EbtC 80107 2626 A7
- EbtC 80107 2710 A1
Phelps Dr
10 CSRK 80104 2703 D7
Philippi Wy
10200 BldC 80503 1437 A3
E Phillips Av
- AphC 80112 2451 B1
400 AphC 80126 2448 E1
400 LITN 80122 2448 E1
500 LITN 80122 2365 A7
500 LITN 80122 2449 B1
800 CTNL 80122 2365 A7
900 CTNL 80122 2449 A1
5900 CTNL 80112 2450 B1
6200 CTNL 80112 2366 B7
8600 CTNL 80112 2367 A7
8600 CTNL 80112 2451 A1
W Phillips Av
8100 JfnC 80128 2446 D1
E Phillips Cir
1700 CTNL 80122 2365 B7
1700 CTNL 80122 2449 B1
7600 CTNL 80112 2450 D1
8000 CTNL 80112 2366 D7
Phillips Ct
1700 ERIE 80516 1606 E6
E Phillips Ct
1000 CTNL 80122 2449 A1
1000 LITN 80122 2449 A1
Phillips Dr
700 NHGN 80233 1860 E3
700 NHGN 80233 1861 A3
E Phillips Dr
1100 LITN 80122 2449 A1
1900 CTNL 80122 2449 B1
2900 CTNL 80122 2365 C7
16100 AphC 80112 2368 E7
16100 AphC 80112 2452 E1
E Phillips Dr N
500 LITN 80122 2449 A1
E Phillips Dr S
500 LITN 80122 2449 A1
700 LITN 80122 2365 B6
W Phillips Dr
9100 JfnC 80128 2446 C1
E Phillips Ln
800 CTNL 80122 2365 A7
800 LITN 80122 2365 A7
900 CTNL 80122 2449 A1
16200 AphC 80112 2452 E1
16500 AphC 80112 2453 A1
Phillips Pl
- AURA 80016 2371 C7
E Phillips Pl
1000 CTNL 80122 2449 A1
1000 LITN 80122 2449 A1
4400 CTNL 80122 2450 A1
6200 CTNL 80112 2450 B1
8700 CTNL 80112 2451 A1
8900 CTNL 80112 2367 A7
16400 AphC 80112 2452 E1
22100 AURA 80016 2370 B7
26000 AphC 80016 2371 B7
Phillips Rd
9500 BldC 80026 1605 D3
9500 BldC 80301 1605 D3
9900 BldC 80026 1606 A3
W Phillips Rd
- BldC 80026 1605 C3
8700 BldC 80301 1605 C3
W Phillips Peak
200 DgsC 80129 2448 D5
Phil Long Ln
- DNVR 80123 2278 D5
E Phipps Ct
1100 DgsC 80126 2449 A5
E Phipps Pl
1000 DgsC 80126 2449 A5
S Phoebes Dr
11000 JfnC 80433 2525 B1
Phoenix Ct
1400 TNTN 80229 1945 A2
Photinia
10 JfnC 80127 2361 A6
Piano Meadows Dr
12800 JfnC 80433 2526 D6
S Picadilly Ct
3500 AURA 80018 2286 B3
5200 AphC 80015 2286 B7
5400 CTNL 80015 2286 B7
Picadilly Rd
10 AURA 80018 2202 B1
200 AphC 80018 2118 B7
200 AURA 80018 2118 B7
1500 AdmC 80011 2118 B4
1500 AdmC 80019 2118 B4
1500 AURA 80011 2118 B4
1500 AURA 80019 2118 B4
3200 AURA 80249 2118 B2
3200 DNVR 80249 2118 B2
3200 DvrC 80249 2118 B2
3800 AdmC 80019 2034 B5
3800 AURA 80019 2034 B7
3800 DNVR 80249 2034 B7
3800 DvrC 80249 2034 B5
4800 AURA 80249 2034 B5
5500 DNVR 80019 2034 A3
11200 AdmC 80022 1866 A3
11200 DNVR 80022 1866 A3
11200 DNVR 80249 1866 A3
12000 AdmC 80022 1782 A7
13300 AdmC 80603 1782 A4
14400 AdmC 80603 1698 A7
S Picadilly Rd
- AURA 80015 2286 B3
10 AphC 80011 2202 B1
10 AURA 80018 2202 B1
300 AphC 80018 2202 B2
3500 AphC 80013 2286 B3
3500 AURA 80013 2286 B3
3500 AURA 80018 2286 B3
S Picadilly St
- AphC 80015 2370 B3
- AURA 80015 2370 B3
- AURA 80016 2370 B3
- CTNL 80015 2370 B3
5100 AphC 80015 2286 A7
5100 CTNL 80015 2286 A7
5800 AphC 80016 2370 A1
6100 CTNL 80016 2370 B3
S Picadilly Wy
5200 AphC 80015 2286 B7
Picardy Pl
1200 LAFT 80026 1690 C2
Picket Ln
700 LGMT 80501 1356 D6
Pickett Ct
1600 ERIE 80516 1690 C1
Picutis Rd
4200 JfnC 80439 2275 A5
Piedmont Av
1000 BldC 80303 1688 A3
S Piedmont Ct
10100 DgsC 80126 2449 B5
Piedmont Dr
5600 CHLV 80111 2282 B6
5600 CHLV 80113 2282 B6
5600 CHLV 80121 2282 B6
E Piedmont Dr
16900 AURA 80015 2285 A6
S Piedmont Dr
10000 DgsC 80126 2449 C5
Piedra Ct
4100 BldC 80301 1602 E5
4100 BldC 80301 1603 A5
Piedra Pl
4100 BldC 80301 1603 A5
S Pierce Av
600 LSVL 80020 1773 E3

STREET
Block City ZIP Map# Grid

S Pierce Av
700 LSVL 80027 1773 E3
Pierce Ct
5500 ARVD 80002 2027 A4
8200 ARVD 80003 1942 E4
S Pierce Ct
6300 JfnC 80123 2363 A3
6900 JfnC 80128 2363 A5
Pierce St
10 LKWD 80226 2195 A1
100 ERIE 80516 1607 C4
200 LKWD 80226 2111 A7
900 LKWD 80214 2111 A6
1900 EDGW 80214 2111 A5
2500 WTRG 80033 2111 A4
2500 WTRG 80214 2111 A4
4100 WTRG 80033 2027 A7
5800 ARVD 80002 2026 E3
5800 ARVD 80003 2026 E3
5800 ARVD 80003 2027 A2
7100 WSTR 80003 1942 E7
7600 ARVD 80003 1943 A5
7800 ARVD 80003 1942 E5
12600 WSTR 80234 1776 B7
N Pierce St
- ARVD 80003 1942 E3
- WSTR 80003 1942 E3
- WSTR 80021 1942 E3
9300 WSTR 80021 1943 A2
9800 WSTR 80021 1858 E7
S Pierce St
- JfnC 80123 2363 A2
10 LKWD 80226 2195 A2
1000 LKWD 80232 2195 A5
3000 DNVR 80227 2279 A3
3000 DvrC 80227 2279 A3
3000 LKWD 80227 2279 A3
3500 DNVR 80235 2279 A3
3800 DNVR 80235 2278 E5
3800 LKWD 80235 2278 E5
3800 LKWD 80235 2279 A5
4100 JfnC 80235 2278 E5
4100 LKWD 80123 2278 E5
4200 DNVR 80123 2279 A5
4200 DvrC 80235 2279 A5
4200 LKWD 80123 2279 A5
6700 JfnC 80128 2363 A6
7900 JfnC 80128 2447 A1
Pierce Wy
- PARK 80134 2453 A6
6700 ARVD 80003 2026 E1
8700 ARVD 80003 1942 E3
8700 ARVD 80003 1943 A3
S Pierce Wy
7500 JfnC 80128 2363 A6
8300 JfnC 80128 2447 A1
S Pierce Frontage Rd
1700 LKWD 80232 2195 A6
Pierre St
4900 BLDR 80304 1602 B2
Pierson Cir
10500 WSTR 80021 1857 E5
Pierson Ct
- ARVD 80004 1941 E7
3800 WTRG 80033 2109 E1
6800 ARVD 80004 2025 E1
8000 ARVD 80005 1941 E5
8000 JfnC 80005 1941 E5
S Pierson Ct
900 LKWD 80226 2193 E3
1100 JfnC 80232 2193 E5
4700 JfnC 80127 2277 E6
5900 JfnC 80127 2361 E2
Pierson St
2500 LKWD 80215 2109 E3
3200 WTRG 80033 2109 E2
4400 WTRG 80033 2025 E7
5800 ARVD 80002 2025 E3
6900 ARVD 80004 1941 E7
6900 ARVD 80004 2025 E2
7600 ARVD 80005 1941 E6
10600 WSTR 80021 1857 E5
N Pierson St
4200 WTRG 80033 2025 E7
S Pierson St
300 LKWD 80226 2193 E2
1400 JfnC 80232 2193 E5
1900 LKWD 80227 2193 E6
5600 JfnC 80127 2361 E2
6300 JfnC 80127 2362 A3
Pierson Wy
2800 LKWD 80215 2109 E2
7800 ARVD 80005 1941 E5
S Pierson Wy
900 LKWD 80226 2193 E3
4700 JfnC 80127 2277 E6
6400 JfnC 80127 2361 E4
Pierson Mountain Av
5500 LGMT 80503 1437 D6
Pika Pt
300 LAFT 80026 1774 B1
Pika Rd
10 BldC 80302 1769 B3
Pike Cir
6000 DgsC 80118 2868 D7
6000 DgsC 80118 2952 C1
Pike Ct
- LGMT 80503 1438 B6
6800 DgsC 80118 2952 C1
6900 ARVD 80007 2024 D1
7000 ARVD 80007 1940 D7
S Pike Dr
5000 DgsC 80118 2952 C1
Pike Pl
6800 DgsC 80118 2952 C1
Pike Rd
- WldC 80501 1440 A6
- WldC 80504 1440 A6
1800 LGMT 80501 1438 D6
1800 LGMT 80504 1438 D6
3800 LGMT 80503 1438 A6
6500 BldC 80503 1437 C6
6500 LGMT 80503 1437 C6
10300 LGMT 80501 1439 A6

Pike Rd
10300 LGMT 80504 1439 A6
Pike St
- ARVD 80007 2024 D2
100 BNNT 80102 2124 D2
100 NHGN 80233 1860 E5
400 GOLD 80401 2192 D1
700 GOLD 80401 2108 D7
1100 JfnC 80401 2108 D6
5400 JfnC 80403 2024 D4
Pikeminnow Pl
14200 BMFD 80020 1775 C4
Pikes Rd
9700 TNTN 80260 1860 A7
Pikes Peak Ct
- DNVR 80237 2282 E5
- DNVR 80237 2283 A5
800 LSVL 80027 1689 A7
E Pikes Peak Ct
19700 PARK 80138 2453 D7
Pikes Peak Dr
- FLHT 80260 1944 B2
- TNTN 80260 1944 B2
S Pikes Peak Dr
10400 PARK 80138 2453 D7
11100 PARK 80138 2537 D1
Pikes Peak Ln
900 LSVL 80027 1689 A7
Pikes Peak Pl
200 LGMT 80501 1356 C6
Pikes Peak Rd
3000 EbtC 80138 2457 A5
Pikes Peak St
1700 WldC 80516 1523 E7
1700 WldC 80516 1607 E1
Pikes Peak Wy
9200 DgsC 80138 2538 D4
Pikeview Ct
7400 LKWD 80214 2110 E3
Pike View Dr
30800 JfnC 80433 2524 E3
30800 JfnC 80433 2525 A3
Pikeview Ln
10700 PARK 80138 2453 E7
Pikeview St
1000 LKWD 80215 2110 B6
Pilgrims Pl
19500 PARK 80138 2453 D7
Pima Ct
10 BLDR 80303 1687 C6
Pima Rd
4300 JfnC 80439 2274 D5
Pima Tr
10 PrkC 80470 2607 E1
10 PrkC 80470 2608 A1
W Pimlico Av
3300 DNVR 80110 2279 E6
3300 DNVR 80236 2279 E6
3300 EGLD 80110 2279 E6
Pimlico Ct
800 BldC 80303 1688 E4
W Pimlico Dr
3000 DNVR 80110 2279 E6
3000 EGLD 80110 2279 E6
3000 EGLD 80110 2280 A6
E Pimlico Pl
14300 AURA 80015 2284 C6
Pinal Rd
1800 GOLD 80401 2107 D4
Pindar Cir
1700 LAFT 80026 1690 A6
1700 LSVL 80026 1690 A6
Pine Cir
- GpnC 80403 1934 C5
Pine Ct
- LGMT 80501 1439 B6
5700 DgsC 80118 2868 D7
34200 EbtC 80107 2709 E7
E Pine Ct
5500 GDVL 80121 2366 B2
W Pine Ct
1200 LSVL 80027 1772 E1
Pine Dr
10 CCkC 80452 2186 B4
10 GpnC 80403 1850 B5
10 PrkC 80456 2606 D4
26900 JfnC 80439 2357 E5
26900 JfnC 80439 2358 A5
27600 JfnC 80439 2273 D6
E Pine Dr
10 PrkC 80456 2606 C3
N Pine Dr
10 PrkC 80456 2606 B3
10700 DgsC 80138 2453 E6
10800 PARK 80138 2453 E6
S Pine Dr
- PARK 80138 2453 D7
- PARK 80138 2537 D1
10 PrkC 80456 2606 C4
11400 PARK 80134 2537 D2
Pine Hllw
10 PrkC 80456 2690 D2
Pine Ln
- DgsC 80134 2453 A4
- PARK 80134 2453 A4
10 CCkC 80439 2187 D5
22600 JfnC 80465 2359 A3
E Pine Ln
6000 DgsC 80138 2453 D4
6000 PARK 80134 2453 D4
S Pine Ln
12100 JfnC 80433 2525 D4
W Pine Ln
- PARK 80134 2453 C4
Pine Pl
10 BMFD 80020 1859 A2
Pine Rd
10 BldC 80403 1852 D2
10 JfnC 80401 2190 D1
28800 JfnC 80439 2273 C7
S Pine Rd
4600 JfnC 80439 2273 D7
5200 JfnC 80439 2357 C1

Pine St
- DgsC 80120 2447 E1
- LGMT 80501 1439 B6
10 JMWN 80455 1516 B3
100 BldC 80455 1516 A3
100 BMFD 80020 1859 A2
100 ELIZ 80107 2793 B1
100 LSVL 80027 1689 D7
200 CLCY 80403 2017 D4
400 BldC 80302 1599 D3
400 BldC 80302 1686 B2
1700 BLDR 80302 1686 D1
1800 ERIE 80516 1692 A3
2300 FLHT 80260 1944 A1
2300 TNTN 80260 1944 A1
2700 BLDR 80301 1686 D1
2700 FLHT 80260 1860 A7
2900 FLHT 80031 1859 E7
2900 FLHT 80260 1859 E7
2900 WSTR 80031 1859 E7
18000 JfnC 80433 2694 E5
E Pine St
10 NDLD 80466 1765 D3
S Pine St
700 EbtC 80107 2793 B1
700 ELIZ 80107 2793 B1
W Pine St
10 NDLD 80466 1765 D3
100 LSVL 80027 1773 B1
500 LSVL 80027 1689 B7
700 BldC 80466 1765 C3
Pine Tr
10 PrkC 80456 2607 C7
28300 JfnC 80433 2525 D4
Pine Wy
100 BMFD 80020 1859 A2
E Pine Bluff Ln
2500 DgsC 80126 2449 C2
Pine Brook Rd
10 BldC 80304 1601 E4
S Pinebrook St
9500 DgsC 80130 2450 C4
Pinebrook Loop Rd
10 BldC 80304 1601 D4
300 BldC 80302 1601 E4
W Pine Cliff Rd
3700 DgsC 80135 2701 C7
4000 DgsC 80135 2700 D7
Pinecliffe Rd
200 BldC 80466 1767 B7
200 GpnC 80403 1767 B7
Pinecliffe Tr
10 NDLD 80466 1765 E3
Pine Cone Cir
300 BldC 80481 1514 B4
Pine Cone Ct
7100 BldC 80503 1521 B4
Pine Cone Dr
100 BldC 80481 1514 B3
Pine Cone Ln
30500 JfnC 80439 2273 A2
Pinecone Ln
8800 BldC 80503 1521 B4
E Pinecone Ln
10500 DgsC 80134 2623 B1
N Pine Cone Rd
12300 DgsC 80138 2454 C4
Pinecone St
10 GOLD 80401 2108 B7
Pine Country Ln
13300 JfnC 80433 2526 E7
13300 JfnC 80433 2610 E1
13300 JfnC 80433 2611 A1
Pinecrest Cir
10 PrkC 80456 2606 C5
Pine Crest Cir N
- CSRK 80109 2786 D5
Pine Crest Cir S
- CSRK 80109 2786 D6
- CSRK 80109 2787 A6
Pine Crest Ct
32300 EbtC 80107 2794 E4
Pine Crest Dr
7200 EbtC 80107 2794 D4
29000 JfnC 80439 2189 B4
Pinecrest Rd
- JfnC 80401 2107 A7
22700 JfnC 80401 2191 A1
E Pinedale Ct
3900 DgsC 80126 2449 E3
Pinedale Ranch Cir
1400 JfnC 80439 2189 B6
Pine Drop Ln
2100 JfnC 80401 2190 C7
N Pinefield Cir
41300 EbtC 80138 2541 A7
S Pinefield Cir
41200 EbtC 80138 2541 A7
Pinefield Ln
900 DgsC 80108 2618 D1
Pine Forest Ln
7100 DgsC 80134 2621 E4
7200 DgsC 80134 2622 A4
Pine Glade Dr
400 GpnC 80403 1850 E6
Pine Glade Rd
10 BldC 80466 1767 B2
Pine Grove Ln
11500 PARK 80138 2537 E2
11500 PARK 80138 2538 A2
Pine Grove Tr
9800 JfnC 80433 2441 D5
Pine Hill St
11500 PARK 80138 2538 D2
Pine Hill Wy
11500 PARK 80138 2538 D2
Pine Hills Ln
33500 EbtC 80107 2792 A1
Pine Hills Wy
7000 DgsC 80125 2615 A1
N Pine Hollow Dr
6000 DgsC 80134 2622 B2
Pinehurst Cir
- BMFD 80020 1775 E4

S Pinehurst Cir
3900 DNVR 80235 2279 B4
Pinehurst Ct
700 LSVL 80027 1773 B3
900 BNNT 80102 2209 B3
5300 BLDR 80301 1604 C1
Pinehurst Dr
5200 BLDR 80301 1604 C1
S Pinehurst Dr
2400 JfnC 80439 2272 E1
2600 JfnC 80439 2273 A1
N Pine Ln St
12400 PARK 80134 2453 C3
Pine Meadow Av
- EbtC 80107 2625 B1
3400 EbtC 80107 2541 B7
Pine Meadow Cir
41300 EbtC 80107 2541 A7
Pine Meadow Dr
- EbtC 80117 2796 D7
Pine Mor Rd
1500 DgsC 80116 2706 C5
Pine Needle Ln
700 LSVL 80027 1773 B1
Pine Needle Rd
10 BldC 80304 1602 A4
Pine Needle Wy
300 CSRK 80104 2787 C3
W Pine Ridge Av
2000 LITN 80120 2364 B3
Pine Ridge Cir
34000 EbtC 80107 2709 E6
Pine Ridge Ct
1300 DgsC 80108 2534 C7
Pine Ridge Dr
5000 EbtC 80107 2709 E6
5000 EbtC 80107 2710 A6
5000 JfnC 80403 2023 B6
Pine Ridge Ln
1400 DgsC 80108 2534 C7
9100 BldC 80302 1435 B6
34800 JfnC 80403 1852 A3
Pine Ridge Pl
1400 DgsC 80108 2534 C7
Pine Ridge Rd
10 CCkC 80439 2187 E1
4300 GOLD 80403 2023 C7
4400 JfnC 80403 2023 C7
7400 DgsC 80116 2706 A2
Pine Ridge St
300 EbtC 80107 2793 A1
300 ELIZ 80107 2793 A1
Pine Ridge Ter
7500 DgsC 80108 2534 C7
Pine Ridge Tr
7500 DgsC 80108 2534 C7
Pine Ridge Wy
7400 DgsC 80108 2534 C7
Pine River Tr
5100 DgsC 80108 2619 A6
S Pinery Dr
- DgsC 80134 2621 E4
- DgsC 80134 2622 A4
N Pinery Pkwy
6900 DgsC 80134 2621 D2
7300 DgsC 80134 2622 A1
S Pinery Pkwy
6900 DgsC 80134 2621 E4
7000 DgsC 80134 2622 A3
N Pines Tr
10 DgsC 80138 2455 E2
200 EbtC 80138 2456 A2
Pine Slope Rd
- IDSP 80452 2101 C6
600 CCkC 80452 2101 C6
Pine Song Tr
300 JfnC 80401 2190 B1
400 JfnC 80401 2106 B7
Pine Springs Dr
9500 JfnC 80465 2443 C5
Pine Top Av
23600 JfnC 80433 2694 E5
Pine Top St
11900 PARK 80138 2538 D3
Pine Tree Cir
10 PrkC 80456 2606 C7
Pine Tree Ln
10 BldC 80304 1601 D5
2300 JfnC 80439 2273 A1
Pinetree Rd
10 CSRK 80104 2703 E7
Pinevale Ln
11100 DgsC 80116 2791 C3
Pine Valley Ct
5300 BLDR 80301 1604 C1
Pine Valley Dr
27200 JfnC 80439 2273 E2
Pinevalley Dr
9700 DgsC 80116 2790 E2
9800 DgsC 80116 2791 A2
S Pine Valley Rd
13700 JfnC 80470 2608 C3
14300 JfnC 80470 2609 A5
16200 JfnC 80470 2693 D2
S Pine Valley Rd CO-126
13700 JfnC 80470 2608 C3
14300 JfnC 80470 2609 A5
16200 JfnC 80470 2693 D2
Pine View Dr
32200 EbtC 80107 2794 D4
W Pineview Dr
7000 DgsC 80125 2532 B1
7100 DgsC 80125 2448 A7
Pineview Ln
10 BldC 80302 1517 B6
Pine View Pl
1400 JfnC 80401 2190 E5
Pine View Rd
- EbtC 80107 2793 C3
1200 GOLD 80403 2023 D7
N Pine Vista Tr
12100 DgsC 80138 2454 E4
Pinewalk Wy
10700 DgsC 80124 2450 A7

Pinewicket Wy
10 EbtC 80138 2456 A6
E Pinewood Av
800 CTNL 80121 2365 A2
9700 AphC 80111 2367 B2
Pinewood Cir
400 LAFT 80026 1774 B1
E Pinewood Cir
- GDVL 80121 2366 A2
4600 CTNL 80121 2366 A2
Pinewood Ct
1400 LGMT 80501 1356 E7
N Pinewood Ct
8600 DgsC 80108 2535 A5
Pinewood Dr
10 CCkC 80439 2271 A1
7100 JfnC 80439 2357 B5
E Pinewood Dr
10000 DgsC 80138 2455 B7
19300 AphC 80016 2369 D2
N Pinewood Dr
6400 DgsC 80134 2621 E2
8100 DgsC 80108 2534 E5
8100 DgsC 80108 2535 A5
E Pinewood Pl
4700 CTNL 80121 2366 A2
14800 CTNL 80016 2368 C2
S Pine Wood Rd
1800 DgsC 80135 2785 C5
S Piney Creek Cir
6600 CTNL 80016 2369 C3
N Piney Creek Rd
8300 DgsC 80138 2454 C4
N Piney Lake Rd
- AphC 80016 2371 C7
- AphC 80138 2371 C7
- AURA 80016 2371 C7
12100 DgsC 80138 2455 C2
S Piney Peak
7300 JfnC 80127 2361 D6
S Piney Point St
8400 DgsC 80126 2449 A1
S Piney Ridge Rd
3000 JfnC 80439 2274 B2
Piney River Rd
14100 BMFD 80020 1775 C4
Pinion Dr
8400 BldC 80302 1518 A1
Pinion Pl
10 BMFD 80020 1859 A2
Pinion Rd
10 PrkC 80456 2606 C4
Pinion St
100 BMFD 80020 1859 A2
N Pinion St
- LGMT 80501 1439 C6
S Pinion St
- LGMT 80501 1439 C6
Pin Oak Cir
100 DgsC 80116 2791 B1
Pin Oak Dr
10 JfnC 80127 2361 B7
Pinon Cir
- TNTN 80260 1860 B7
- TNTN 80260 1944 B1
10 GpnC 80403 1933 C7
2100 ERIE 80516 1692 A3
Pinon Cr
- GpnC 80403 1933 C7
Pinon Ct
900 LGMT 80501 1439 D1
S Pinon Ct
2200 DNVR 80210 2196 E7
Pinon Dr
2100 ERIE 80516 1692 A2
3800 BLDR 80303 1687 B5
4600 EbtC 80107 2709 E6
5500 EbtC 80107 2710 A6
S Pinon Dr
3100 JfnC 80439 2273 E2
Pinon Ln
900 EbtC 80107 2624 B7
Pinon Pl
2000 ERIE 80516 1692 A2
Pinon Rd
10 PrkC 80456 2606 E7
11900 JfnC 80433 2525 D3
E Pinon Rd
200 PrkC 80456 2606 E7
Pinon Tr
9300 LNTR 80124 2450 E4
Pinon Wy
10 BldC 80466 1767 A6
Pintail Av
800 BGTN 80601 1696 A7
Pintail Cir
1100 BldC 80303 1688 A3
Pintail Ct
1100 BldC 80303 1688 A3
5200 JfnC 80465 2360 C1
7500 DgsC 80125 2531 B7
Pintail Dr
- BldC 80503 1438 D7
2000 LGMT 80504 1438 D7
Pintail Pl
7400 DgsC 80125 2531 B7
Pinto Ct
34000 EbtC 80107 2708 D7
Pinto Dr
10 BldC 80302 1601 D3
28400 JfnC 80433 2609 D1
Pinto Ln
10 PrkC 80456 2607 D5
Pinto St
100 GOLD 80401 2108 B7
100 GOLD 80401 2192 B1
Pinto Tr
1800 EbtC 80107 2708 D7
1800 EbtC 80107 2792 D1
Pinto Wy
10 PrkC 80456 2607 C5
Piny Pt
34200 JfnC 80439 2356 B7

Pinyon Cir
600 LCHB 80603 1698 B2
Pinyon Dr
1300 CSRK 80104 2703 E5
1300 CSRK 80104 2704 A5
4900 BWMR 80123 2279 C7
11000 NHGN 80234 1860 D4
W Pinyon Wy
700 LSVL 80027 1773 A1
Pinyon Jay Rd
5100 DgsC 80134 2622 B4
Pinyon Pine Ln
10 JfnC 80127 2361 B7
Pinyon Pine Rd
10 JfnC 80127 2361 B7
Pioneer Cir
- TNTN 80229 1861 E6
E Pioneer Dr
9100 DgsC 80138 2538 D5
Pioneer Pl
10 BGTN 80601 1697 C5
10300 TNTN 80229 1861 E6
10300 TNTN 80229 1862 A6
Pioneer Rd
100 GpnC 80403 1935 D1
5500 BldC 80301 1603 D3
Pioneer Tr
13400 JfnC 80127 2528 C7
Pioneer Wy
10 BGTN 80601 1697 C3
10 BGTN 80603 1697 C3
N Pioneer Trail Rd
8200 DgsC 80138 2539 B5
Pipeline Dr
10 CCkC 80452 2186 B4
Piper Dr
100 ERIE 80516 1691 C3
Piper Dr S
2900 ERIE 80516 1691 C3
2900 WldC 80516 1691 C3
Piper St
1900 SUPE 80027 1773 C6
Pipit Rd
- BldC 80501 1439 E6
- BldC 80501 1440 A6
Pirlot Pl
7400 DgsC 80124 2450 D6
Pisa Ct
- LGMT 80503 1438 A5
Pisces Ct
13600 DgsC 80124 2450 E2
Pitchford Pl
16000 DgsC 80134 2452 E3
S Pitkin Av
800 SUPE 80027 1773 A5
S Pitkin Cir
1400 AURA 80017 2201 A5
3500 AURA 80013 2285 A3
E Pitkin Ct
- CMCY 80022 1865 A7
S Pitkin Ct
900 AURA 80017 2201 A3
3500 AURA 80013 2285 A3
4700 AURA 80015 2285 A6
5200 CTNL 80015 2285 A7
5900 AphC 80016 2369 A2
7500 CTNL 80016 2369 A6
Pitkin Dr
4600 BLDR 80303 1687 B4
S Pitkin Ln
15400 JfnC 80470 2608 A6
Pitkin St
- AdmC 80022 1865 A3
- AdmC 80229 1945 C5
- CMCY 80022 1865 A7
1800 AURA 80011 2117 A4
S Pitkin St
900 AURA 80017 2201 A3
1900 AURA 80013 2201 A6
3100 AURA 80013 2285 A2
4200 AURA 80015 2285 A5
5100 CTNL 80015 2285 A7
5400 CTNL 80015 2369 A1
6700 AphC 80016 2369 A4
6700 FXFD 80016 2369 A4
7400 CTNL 80016 2369 A6
Pitkin Wy
- CMCY 80022 1865 A6
500 CSRK 80104 2704 D7
500 CSRK 80104 2788 D1
S Pitkin Wy
- AURA 80017 2201 A4
2200 AURA 80013 2201 A7
3000 AURA 80013 2285 A1
4700 AURA 80015 2285 A6
Piute Dr
13100 JfnC 80470 2524 A7
W Piute Dr
7000 DgsC 80135 2700 A1
Piute Rd
34700 CCkC 80439 2440 A1
Piute Row
8500 DgsC 80134 2622 C2
Placer Av
10 LGMT 80501 1439 C1
Placer Cir
- EbtC 80107 2792 E2
Placer St
1700 IDSP 80452 2101 C5
S Placer St
2000 DgsC 80116 2791 D5
Placid Dr
1300 JfnC 80439 2188 E5
2100 BldC 80301 1689 C1
S Plains Pkwy
- AphC 80013 2286 B4
- AURA 80015 2286 B4
- AURA 80018 2286 B4
Plains View Rd
10 BldC 80302 1684 B1
Plainview Rd
10000 ARVD 80403 1938 E1
10000 JfnC 80403 1854 E6
10000 JfnC 80403 1938 E1

Planet Pl
6100 TNTN 80260 1944 D3
Plaster Cir
13600 BMFD 80020 1775 E5
Plaster Pt
- BMFD 80020 1775 E5
Plateau Cir
21700 JfnC 80465 2359 B5
Plateau Dr
- TNTN 80229 1861 E7
6100 CHLV 80111 2282 B6
E Plateau Dr
17400 AURA 80015 2285 B6
S Plateau Ln
6800 JfnC 80465 2359 B5
Plateau Pkwy
100 GOLD 80403 2107 E2
Plateau Rd
- LGMT 80503 1437 E7
- LGMT 80503 1438 A7
3100 BldC 80302 1435 C7
3100 BldC 80503 1435 C7
6200 BldC 80503 1436 E7
7400 BldC 80503 1437 D7
9500 BldC 80503 1438 E7
9500 BldC 80504 1438 E7
9500 LGMT 80504 1438 E7
10100 LGMT 80504 1439 A7
10400 BldC 80504 1439 A7
Platinum Ct
2700 SUPE 80027 1773 B7
Plato's Ct
- LYNS 80540 1352 D1
E Platte Av
3300 GDVL 80121 2365 D1
W Platte Av
3700 DgsC 80135 2617 C5
Platte St
1000 DNVR 80211 2112 B3
S Platte Canyon Dr
7100 AphC 80128 2363 C6
S Platte Canyon Rd
- JfnC 80127 2446 D7
- JfnC 80127 2530 D3
- JfnC 80128 2446 D4
5900 AphC 80123 2363 D3
5900 CBVL 80123 2363 D3
5900 LITN 80123 2363 D3
6800 AphC 80128 2363 D3
7000 LITN 80128 2363 C7
8000 JfnC 80128 2447 B1
S Platte Canyon Rd SR-75
5900 AphC 80123 2363 D3
5900 CBVL 80123 2363 D3
5900 LITN 80123 2363 D3
6800 AphC 80128 2363 D3
7000 LITN 80128 2363 C7
8000 JfnC 80128 2447 B1
S Platte Canyon Rd SR-121
- JfnC 80127 2446 D4
- JfnC 80127 2530 D3
- JfnC 80128 2446 D7
W Platte Canyon Rd
3400 AphC 80128 2363 D5
3400 LITN 80128 2363 D5
Platte River Blvd
- AdmC 80601 1780 A1
- BGTN 80601 1696 A7
- BGTN 80601 1780 A1
S Platte River Dr
100 DNVR 80223 2196 C2
2400 DvrC 80223 2280 C1
2400 EGLD 80223 2280 C1
2500 EGLD 80110 2280 D1
3000 DNVR 80110 2280 C1
3000 DNVR 80223 2280 C1
3000 DvrC 80110 2280 C1
3100 SRDN 80110 2280 B3
S Platte River Dr US-85
700 DNVR 80223 2196 D4
S Platte River Dr E
3100 EGLD 80110 2280 C2
S Platte River Pkwy
7300 LITN 80120 2364 A6
Platte River Rd
- JfnC 80470 2693 E2
17200 JfnC 80433 2694 C4
17200 JfnC 80470 2694 C4
Platte River Rd CO-126
- JfnC 80470 2693 E2
17200 JfnC 80433 2694 C4
17200 JfnC 80470 2694 C4
N Platte River Rd
2500 DgsC 80135 2696 E5
2500 DgsC 80135 2697 A5
2500 JfnC 80433 2697 A6
N Platte River Rd CO-97
2500 DgsC 80135 2696 E5
2500 DgsC 80135 2697 A5
2500 JfnC 80433 2697 A6
S Platte River Rd
- JfnC 80433 2612 B7
- JfnC 80433 2696 D1
- JfnC 80433 2697 A2
12000 JfnC 80127 2530 C5
12200 JfnC 80125 2530 A6
12200 JfnC 80127 2529 E6
17000 JfnC 80433 2694 E4
17000 JfnC 80433 2695 A3
19600 JfnC 80433 2611 C7
S Platteview Dr
7500 LITN 80128 2363 D6
Platte View Landing Apartments
- AdmC 80601 1696 A6
- BGTN 80601 1696 A6
Players Club Dr
100 CSRK 80104 2787 D2
Plaza Ct N
1300 LAFT 80026 1690 A6
Plaza Dr
10 DgsC 80126 2448 D2

STREET Block City ZIP Map# Grid

Plaza Dr
10 DgsC 80129 2448 D2
1700 LSVL 80027 1689 E6
E Plaza Dr
17800 PARK 80134 2453 C6
19100 PARK 80138 2453 C6
W Pleasant Av
11600 LKWD 80215 2109 D6
11600 LKWD 80401 2109 D6
Pleasant Ln
34700 CCkC 80439 2188 A3
Pleasant St
600 BLDR 80302 1686 C3
Pleasant Hill Cir
2100 EbtC 80138 2540 E7
Pleasant Park Rd
- JfnC 80433 2442 B7
18100 JfnC 80127 2528 A4
18100 JfnC 80433 2528 A4
19000 JfnC 80433 2527 C3
22800 JfnC 80433 2526 C2
Pleasant Park Rd CO-88
18100 JfnC 80127 2528 A4
18100 JfnC 80433 2528 A4
19000 JfnC 80433 2527 C3
22800 JfnC 80433 2526 C2
25500 JfnC 80433 2442 B7
Pleasant Ridge Rd
4400 BldC 80301 1603 A3
Pleasant Street Ct
- BLDR 80302 1686 C3
S Pleasant View Dr
900 CSRK 80104 2703 E5
3000 CSRK 80108 2704 E1
3600 CSRK 80108 2621 A7
Pless Dr
- AdmC 80601 1781 B1
15200 AdmC 80601 1697 B7
Plettner Ln
4500 JfnC 80439 2273 D6
S Plover Cir
11100 PARK 80134 2536 E1
S Plover Pl
16200 PARK 80134 2536 E1
Plowsher Wy
7200 JfnC 80465 2359 B6
Plum Av
800 LCHB 80603 1698 C2
N Plum Av
4800 DgsC 80135 2617 C5
W Plum Cir
900 LSVL 80027 1689 A6
1000 BldC 80027 1689 A6
Plum Ct
- BLDR 80304 1602 D4
1200 ERIE 80516 1691 E3
1500 BGTN 80601 1696 D7
4200 BldC 80301 1603 A4
4200 GDVL 80121 2366 A2
Plum Pl
5300 DNVR 80222 2282 A2
Plumb Pl
- ERIE 80516 1606 D5
Plum Bumpy Ln
- BldC 80503 1520 A3
W Plum Creek Av
- DgsC 80118 2955 B6
- LKSR 80118 2955 B6
S Plum Creek Blvd
900 CSRK 80104 2787 D1
Plum Creek Pkwy
- CSRK 80104 2788 A2
10 CSRK 80104 2703 C7
900 CSRK 80104 2787 E1
Plum Creek Pl
100 DgsC 80126 2448 E2
W Plum Creek Rd
100 LKSR 80118 2955 B5
Plum Creek Meadows Rd
4100 DgsC 80135 2869 A3
S Plum Valley Ln
1700 DgsC 80129 2448 C1
Pluto Ct
400 DgsC 80124 2450 E2
Plutus Dr
10 GpnC 80403 1934 C1
W Plymouth Av
8600 JfnC 80128 2362 C5
E Plymouth Cir
22300 AURA 80016 2370 C4
25000 AURA 80016 2371 A4
Plymouth Ct
10100 LNTR 80134 2451 E6
E Plymouth Dr
- AphC 80016 2370 E4
- AURA 80016 2370 E4
- AURA 80016 2371 A4
W Plymouth Dr
5600 JfnC 80128 2363 B5
10200 JfnC 80127 2362 B5
E Plymouth Pl
22300 AURA 80016 2370 B4
W Plymouth Pl
7600 JfnC 80128 2362 D5
S Pochard St
8700 DgsC 80130 2450 A2
Poco Pl
4200 JfnC 80439 2273 E5
Poco C
100 JfnC 80401 2191 B2
Point Ln
- PrkC 80456 2607 E2
E Pointer Wy
3600 DgsC 80126 2449 D2
Point of Pines Dr
2300 BldC 80302 1602 A2
Point View Ln
11600 BldC 80503 1353 A6
N Polar Ln
10600 DgsC 80125 2447 A7
10600 DgsC 80125 2531 A1
Polaris Pl
200 TNTN 80260 1944 D3

Polecat
5000 EbtC 80107 2709 E5
Polk Av
100 LSVL 80027 1773 B1
1800 LSVL 80027 1689 B6
S Polk Av
100 LSVL 80027 1773 B1
W Polk Av
6800 JfnC 80123 2362 E3
6800 JfnC 80123 2363 A3
Polk Ct
1700 LSVL 80027 1689 B6
1900 AURA 80011 2117 A4
E Polk Dr
22400 AURA 80016 2370 C3
W Polk Dr
9600 JfnC 80123 2362 B3
10800 JfnC 80127 2362 A3
10900 JfnC 80127 2361 E3
W Polk Pl
- AURA 80016 2371 B3
6800 JfnC 80123 2363 A3
9700 JfnC 80123 2362 B3
11000 JfnC 80127 2361 D4
S Polly Av
12800 JfnC 80470 2524 B6
S Polly Dr
12300 JfnC 80470 2524 B5
Polo Dr
1700 LGMT 80501 1356 D6
Polo Pl
12400 BldC 80020 1775 B3
Polo Wy
1700 LGMT 80501 1356 D6
Polo Club Cir
10 DNVR 80209 2197 C3
Polo Club Ct
9500 DgsC 80125 2531 A1
Polo Club Dr
10 AphC 80128 2363 D5
10 CBVL 80123 2363 D5
10 DNVR 80209 2197 C3
Polo Club Ln
10 DNVR 80209 2197 C2
Polo Club Rd
10 DNVR 80209 2197 C2
W Polo Club Rd
10 DNVR 80209 2197 C2
Polo Club Rd N
- DNVR 80209 2197 C2
Polo Club Rd S
- DNVR 80209 2197 C2
Polo Field Ln
10 DNVR 80209 2197 C2
Polo Ridge Dr
- AphC 80128 2363 D5
- LITN 80128 2363 D5
S Polo Ridge Dr
6900 AphC 80128 2363 D5
6900 CBVL 80123 2363 D5
6900 LITN 80128 2363 D5
Polo Run Dr
37300 EbtC 80107 2709 B1
Pomegranate Ln
1200 JfnC 80401 2190 D5
Pommel Ct
10600 PARK 80134 2452 E7
Pomona Dr
6000 ARVD 80003 1943 A4
6800 ARVD 80003 1942 E4
7500 ARVD 80005 1942 E4
N Pomona Dr
6900 ARVD 80003 1942 E4
8000 ARVD 80005 1942 C4
W Pomona Dr
- ARVD 80003 1942 D4
7700 ARVD 80005 1942 D4
Pompey Wy
10400 NHGN 80234 1860 B5
Ponca Pl
300 BLDR 80303 1687 C5
Ponca Rd
34100 JfnC 80470 2524 A7
Poncha Ct
1900 DgsC 80118 2954 B2
Poncha Dr
7500 DgsC 80118 2954 B2
W Poncha Pass
10300 JfnC 80127 2362 B7
Poncho Cir
7300 DgsC 80118 2954 E2
Poncho Rd
- DgsC 80118 2954 E2
N Pond Dr
1000 BGTN 80601 1696 C5
Pond Rd
10 CHLV 80111 2282 B5
10 CHLV 80113 2282 B5
Ponderosa Av
- DgsC 80138 2453 D4
17500 PARK 80134 2453 A2
Ponderosa Cir
- DgsC 80138 2453 E3
1000 LGMT 80501 1356 D7
1000 LGMT 80501 1439 D1
E Ponderosa Cir
7000 AURA 80138 2453 E2
7000 DgsC 80138 2453 E2
7500 DgsC 80138 2454 A2
Ponderosa Ct
600 LSVL 80027 1773 B1
4200 BldC 80301 1603 A5
E Ponderosa Ct
9800 DgsC 80134 2622 E3
9800 DgsC 80134 2623 A2
S Ponderosa Ct
7100 JfnC 80439 2356 E5
Ponderosa Dr
- FLHT 80260 1944 B2
10 CCkC 80439 2187 D1
10 NDLD 80466 1765 D3
100 BldC 80303 1688 E7
5500 DgsC 80134 2622 C3
13500 JfnC 80433 2609 D1

E Ponderosa Dr
6400 DgsC 80138 2453 D4
6400 PARK 80134 2453 C4
7000 DgsC 80138 2454 A4
S Ponderosa Dr
2900 JfnC 80439 2273 B4
Ponderosa Ln
10 DgsC 80107 2707 E1
10 DgsC 80116 2707 E1
200 EbtC 80107 2708 A1
3700 JfnC 80439 2273 B4
11900 EbtC 80117 2796 C7
E Ponderosa Ln
7600 DgsC 80138 2454 B5
Ponderosa Pl
10 BMFD 80020 1859 A2
10 CCkC 80439 2187 D1
2200 ERIE 80516 1692 A3
Ponderosa Rd
2000 DgsC 80116 2707 D3
Ponderosa St
10 CSRK 80104 2704 E7
100 BMFD 80020 1859 A2
100 GOLD 80401 2192 B1
Ponderosa Tr
4600 DgsC 80125 2615 A6
Ponderosa Tr S
- AphC 80015 2370 C3
- AphC 80016 2370 C3
6400 AURA 80016 2370 C3
Ponderosa Wy
10 BldC 80466 1767 B5
1000 CCkC 80439 2271 E4
31600 JfnC 80439 2356 D6
N Ponderosa Wy
10 CCkC 80439 2271 E4
5900 DgsC 80134 2623 A3
6000 DgsC 80134 2622 E2
S Ponderosa Wy
100 CCkC 80439 2271 E4
E Pondlilly Dr
17200 PARK 80134 2453 A4
W Ponds Cir
4200 AphC 80123 2363 D3
4200 CBVL 80123 2363 D3
4400 LITN 80123 2363 D3
W Ponds Dr
- CBVL 80123 2363 D3
- LITN 80123 2363 D3
4400 AphC 80123 2363 D3
W Ponds View Pl
4200 AphC 80123 2363 D3
Pondview Pl
23500 JfnC 80401 2190 E3
S Pontiac Ct
6300 CTNL 80111 2366 C3
6700 CTNL 80112 2366 D4
Pontiac St
100 DNVR 80220 2198 C1
600 DNVR 80220 2114 C6
2100 DNVR 80207 2114 C3
4800 DNVR 80022 2030 C6
4800 DNVR 80216 2030 C6
6000 CMCY 80022 2030 C2
7000 CMCY 80022 1946 C7
8000 AdmC 80022 1946 C4
S Pontiac St
- CTNL 80112 2366 C4
100 DNVR 80230 2198 C2
600 DNVR 80224 2198 C3
1900 AphC 80224 2198 C6
2900 DNVR 80224 2282 D2
4100 DNVR 80237 2282 C4
6200 CTNL 80111 2366 D3
S Pontiac Wy
2000 AphC 80224 2198 C6
2000 DNVR 80224 2198 C6
3600 DNVR 80237 2282 D3
7200 CTNL 80112 2366 D6
Pony Cart Pl
10500 DgsC 80125 2530 E6
Pony Express Dr
18400 PARK 80134 2453 C7
Pony Express Rd
- EbtC 80107 2542 D1
Poorman Rd
10 BldC 80302 1601 C6
Pope Ct
700 ERIE 80516 1606 D7
Pope Dr
700 ERIE 80516 1606 D7
Pope Rd
8800 DgsC 80138 2454 D7
8800 PARK 80138 2454 D7
Poplar Av
1500 BLDR 80304 1602 C5
Poplar Cir
400 BGTN 80601 1696 A7
S Poplar Cir
8100 CTNL 80112 2366 D7
8100 CTNL 80112 2450 D1
Poplar Ct
7000 CMCY 80022 1946 C7
16600 AdmC 80602 1694 C4
S Poplar Ct
6300 CTNL 80111 2366 D3
6700 CTNL 80112 2366 D4
Poplar Ln
1900 BldC 80304 1602 D5
1900 BLDR 80304 1602 D5
S Poplar Ln
7100 CTNL 80112 2366 C5
Poplar Pl
900 BLDR 80304 1602 B5
6100 CMCY 80022 2030 C2
E Poplar Pl
1300 GDVL 80121 2365 A2
Poplar St
100 DNVR 80220 2198 D1
100 LCHB 80603 1698 C3
600 DNVR 80220 2114 C7
3300 DNVR 80207 2114 C1
3900 DNVR 80207 2030 C7
6400 CMCY 80022 2030 C1

Poplar St
7000 CMCY 80022 1946 C7
7700 AdmC 80022 1946 C5
E Poplar St
100 ELIZ 80107 2793 B1
S Poplar St
- DNVR 80224 2198 D5
100 DNVR 80230 2198 D2
1800 AphC 80224 2198 D6
3400 DNVR 80224 2282 D3
3400 DNVR 80237 2282 D3
6100 CTNL 80111 2366 D2
7100 CTNL 80112 2366 D5
W Poplar St
100 ELIZ 80107 2793 B1
Poplar Wy
1200 BMFD 80020 1774 B6
S Poplar Wy
300 DNVR 80224 2198 D2
1700 AphC 80224 2198 D5
4000 DNVR 80237 2282 D4
7700 CTNL 80112 2366 D7
8100 CTNL 80112 2450 C1
8500 DgsC 80130 2450 D2
S Poplar Wy E
7700 CTNL 80112 2366 D6
Poplar Grove Pl
2600 CSRK 80109 2702 D4
Poppy Ct
1700 LAFT 80026 1689 E1
5600 JfnC 80403 2024 D4
6900 ARVD 80007 2024 D1
S Poppy Ct
9800 DgsC 80129 2448 D5
Poppy Dr
400 BGTN 80601 1696 D7
800 AdmC 80601 1780 D1
800 BGTN 80601 1780 D1
W Poppy Pl
600 DgsC 80129 2448 D5
Poppy St
100 GOLD 80401 2192 D1
700 GOLD 80401 2108 D7
700 JfnC 80401 2108 D7
6400 ARVD 80007 2024 D2
7400 JfnC 80007 1940 D7
Poppy Wy
600 BMFD 80020 1774 C7
5700 JfnC 80403 2024 D4
N Poppy Wy
7200 JfnC 80007 1940 D7
E Poppywood Dr
700 DgsC 80126 2449 A5
E Poppywood Pl
700 DgsC 80126 2449 A5
Porcupine Ln
10 JfnC 80127 2360 E4
10 JfnC 80127 2361 A4
Porcupine Pointe
8400 DgsC 80134 2622 C5
Porphyry Vw
10 BldC 80455 1516 B3
Porter Wy
6400 CMCY 80022 2030 C2
Porter Ranch Rd
- BldC 80466 1684 A6
10 BldC 80466 1683 E6
Portico Dr
- LGMT 80503 1437 D6
7600 BldC 80503 1437 D6
Portico Ln
8600 BldC 80503 1437 D7
W Portland Av
6300 JfnC 80128 2363 A5
7100 JfnC 80128 2362 E5
W Portland Dr
5800 JfnC 80128 2363 B5
Portland Pl
900 BLDR 80304 1686 C1
E Portland Pl
22400 AURA 80016 2370 C4
W Portland Pl
6800 JfnC 80128 2363 A5
10200 JfnC 80127 2362 A5
E Portland Wy
- AURA 80016 2370 D4
Portofino Dr
4000 LGMT 80503 1438 A5
4500 LGMT 80503 1437 E5
Portside Ct
500 LAFT 80026 1689 E5
Portside Wy
4600 BldC 80301 1604 A3
E Posse Rd
900 DgsC 80108 2619 C5
Post Boy Rd
10 BldC 80302 1684 B1
Post Oak Cir
300 DgsC 80116 2791 A1
Poston Pkwy
- DgsC 80108 2449 D7
- DgsC 80126 2449 C7
- DgsC 80130 2449 D7
3500 DgsC 80126 2533 D1
Poston Wy
7300 BLDR 80301 1604 C2
Posy Ln
29000 JfnC 80439 2273 C7
Potato Gulch Rd
- BldC 80302 1598 E6
- BldC 80302 1599 A6
- GpnC 80403 1850 A7
Potato Patch Rd
200 CCkC 80439 2271 E7
Potentilla Ct
5400 DgsC 80134 2622 A4
Potentilla St
5300 BGTN 80601 1697 E5
Potomac Cir
800 AURA 80011 2116 B6
S Potomac Cir
400 AURA 80012 2200 A2
S Potomac Ct
900 AURA 80012 2200 A3

Potomac St
- BGTN 80601 1780 A6
- CMCY 80022 1864 A6
9600 AdmC 80022 1864 A7
9600 AdmC 80022 1948 A1
9600 CMCY 80022 1948 A1
10700 AdmC 80603 1864 A4
10700 CMCY 80603 1864 A4
11600 BGTN 80601 1864 A1
11600 CMCY 80601 1864 A1
12000 AdmC 80601 1864 A1
13600 AdmC 80601 1780 A4
N Potomac St
10 AURA 80011 2200 B1
10 AURA 80012 2200 B1
1400 AURA 80010 2116 B6
1400 AURA 80011 2116 B4
S Potomac St
- AphC 80112 2368 B3
- CTNL 80112 2368 B3
10 AURA 80011 2200 B1
10 AURA 80012 2200 B1
1700 AURA 80014 2200 A5
6200 AphC 80111 2368 A3
6200 CTNL 80111 2368 A3
Potomac Wy
300 AURA 80011 2116 B7
5500 AdmC 80022 2032 B4
5500 DNVR 80022 2032 B4
5500 DNVR 80239 2032 B4
S Potomac Wy
- AphC 80111 2368 B2
300 AURA 80012 2200 B3
6100 CTNL 80111 2368 B2
Potter Ct
2300 DNVR 80205 2112 D2
Pouder Ct
10000 DgsC 80124 2450 D5
E Poundstone Pl
9300 GDVL 80111 2367 A1
Powder Tr
- CLCY 80403 2017 D5
Powderhorn Dr
10 AURA 80011 2201 B1
200 AURA 80011 2117 B7
7300 DgsC 80124 2450 D5
S Powderhorn Dr
10 AURA 80011 2201 B2
Powderhorn Ln
2300 BLDR 80305 1770 E1
Powderhorn Pl
10 LGMT 80501 1356 C7
Powderhorn Tr
200 BMFD 80020 1774 E5
Powder River Dr
1700 LAFT 80026 1690 D7
Powder Run Dr
- CLCY 80403 2017 D5
400 GpnC 80403 2017 D5
N Powell Rd
5800 DgsC 80134 2622 E2
Powell St
1600 ERIE 80516 1690 C1
Powerhouse Pl
- DNVR 80230 2114 E7
E Powers Av
- AphC 80015 2370 B1
- CTNL 80015 2368 D1
- CTNL 80015 2370 B1
10 LITN 80120 2364 E1
10 LITN 80121 2364 E1
300 LITN 80121 2365 A1
5600 GDVL 80111 2366 C1
5600 GDVL 80121 2366 C1
9700 GDVL 80111 2367 B1
11500 AphC 80111 2367 D1
16700 CTNL 80015 2369 A1
W Powers Av
10 LITN 80120 2364 D1
10 LITN 80121 2364 D1
3400 LITN 80123 2363 E1
10200 JfnC 80127 2362 A1
11000 JfnC 80127 2361 E1
E Powers Cir
15900 CTNL 80015 2368 E1
20700 CTNL 80015 2370 A1
E Powers Cir N
21500 CTNL 80015 2370 B1
E Powers Cir S
21500 CTNL 80015 2370 B1
W Powers Cir
100 LITN 80120 2364 E1
3300 LITN 80123 2363 E1
9500 JfnC 80123 2362 B1
E Powers Ct
10900 AphC 80111 2367 C1
E Powers Dr
- AURA 80016 2370 D1
9600 GDVL 80111 2367 B1
10600 AphC 80111 2367 C1
15400 CTNL 80015 2368 D1
17400 CTNL 80015 2369 A1
18600 AphC 80015 2369 C1
21800 AphC 80015 2370 B1
21800 CTNL 80015 2370 B1
W Powers Dr
800 LITN 80120 2364 D1
9500 JfnC 80123 2362 B1
E Powers Ln
- AphC 80015 2370 B1
- CTNL 80015 2370 B1
18600 AphC 80015 2369 C1
20300 CTNL 80015 2369 E1
E Powers Pl
- AURA 80016 2370 D1
9500 GDVL 80111 2367 A1
16500 CTNL 80015 2368 E1
18100 CTNL 80015 2369 B1
18600 AphC 80015 2369 C1
21100 CTNL 80015 2370 A1
22200 AphC 80015 2370 B1
W Powers Pl
200 LITN 80120 2364 D1
3400 LITN 80123 2363 E1

W Powers Pl
8800 JfnC 80123 2362 C1
10800 JfnC 80127 2362 A2
11000 JfnC 80127 2361 E2
Powhatan Tr
12100 JfnC 80433 2526 C4
Powhaton Rd
- AphC 80016 2287 C6
- AphC 80016 2371 C6
- AphC 80018 2287 C6
- AURA 80016 2287 C6
- AURA 80016 2371 C6
10 AURA 80018 2119 C7
10 AURA 80018 2203 C1
600 AphC 80018 2119 C5
1900 AdmC 80019 2119 C3
1900 AURA 80019 2119 C3
12000 AdmC 80022 1783 B7
12000 AdmC 80022 1867 B1
12000 DNVR 80022 1867 B1
12000 DNVR 80249 1867 B1
13400 AdmC 80603 1783 B4
13700 AdmC 80603 1699 B7
S Powhaton Rd
- AURA 80016 2371 B2
10 AURA 80018 2203 C2
1500 AdmC 80019 2119 C4
1500 AphC 80018 2119 C4
1500 AURA 80019 2119 C4
Powhaton St
- DNVR 80249 1951 B6
Powhaton Mile Rd
- AdmC 80249 1951 B7
- AdmC 80249 2035 B1
- DNVR 80249 1951 B7
Powo Wy
10 NDLD 80466 1765 D2
Poze Blvd
2000 TNTN 80229 1945 B3
8800 AdmC 80229 1945 B3
Pradera Pkwy
- DgsC 80134 2620 E3
5100 DgsC 80134 2621 A4
Prado Dr
4200 BldC 80303 1771 B5
Prague Dr
41800 EbtC 80138 2540 B6
Praino Cir
- EbtC 80107 2710 A7
Prairie Av
500 LCHB 80603 1698 B3
3200 BLDR 80301 1687 A1
Prairie Cir
7800 LNTR 80124 2450 E3
Prairie Dr
100 BGTN 80601 1697 C5
Prairie Ln
2400 CSRK 80104 2703 E4
S Prairie Ln
6300 JfnC 80439 2357 D4
Prairie Lp
34000 EbtC 80107 2710 A7
Prairie Pl
- BMFD 80020 1776 A1
Prairie Run
10900 DgsC 80125 2530 D7
10900 DgsC 80125 2614 D1
Prairie Wy
1700 LSVL 80027 1774 A1
Prairie Clover
10 JfnC 80127 2360 E5
10 JfnC 80127 2361 A5
Prairie Clover Wy
8300 PARK 80134 2453 A1
8400 PARK 80134 2452 D2
Prairie Dog Wy
27100 JfnC 80439 2441 E2
Prairie Dunes Ct
31600 JfnC 80439 2188 E6
S Prairie Falcon Ct
9900 DgsC 80130 2450 D5
Prairie Falcon Ln
10 JfnC 80127 2360 E4
1500 BMFD 80020 1775 A5
S Prairie Falcon Ln
9800 DgsC 80130 2450 C5
Prairie Falcon Pkwy
10 BGTN 80601 1697 E6
N Prairie Falcon Pkwy
10 BGTN 80601 1697 E5
Prairie Farm Cir
16300 PARK 80134 2536 E2
Prairie Farm Ct
- PARK 80134 2536 E2
Prairie Fire Cir
4100 LGMT 80503 1438 A5
Prairie Flower Pl
- PARK 80134 2536 E2
Prairie Harvest Ct
- PARK 80134 2536 E2
Prairie Hawk Dr
- CSRK 80109 2703 B3
1500 LGMT 80501 1440 A1
Prairie Knoll Dr
8800 BldC 80503 1355 B4
Prairie Lake Tr
7600 DgsC 80134 2622 A3
Prairieland Ln
- DgsC 80134 2453 B5
- PARK 80134 2453 B5
Prairie Meadow Cir
10100 DgsC 80134 2451 D6
Prairie Owl Rd
1500 EbtC 80138 2540 C6
Prairie Ridge Ct
2700 LAFT 80026 1689 C2
Prairie Ridge Dr
2700 LAFT 80026 1689 D2
Prairie Ridge Rd
10 DgsC 80126 2448 E2
500 DgsC 80126 2449 A2
Prairierose Cir
4200 CSRK 80109 2702 D4

Prairie Song Pl
1500 LGMT 80501 1440 A1
Prairie Trail Dr
8500 DgsC 80134 2452 C1
S Prairie View Dr
9100 DgsC 80126 2449 B3
Prairieville Ct
- PARK 80134 2536 E2
Prairie Vista Dr
3200 CSRK 80109 2702 D2
Prarie Sky Ln
- BMFD 80020 1775 B2
S Pratt Pkwy
- LGMT 80504 1439 A6
10 LGMT 80501 1439 A3
Pratt Pl
10 LGMT 80501 1439 A4
8600 AdmC 80031 1943 D3
Pratt St
800 LGMT 80501 1439 A1
2100 LGMT 80501 1356 A5
2300 BldC 80504 1356 A5
8400 AdmC 80031 1943 C4
Pratt Wy
1400 LGMT 80501 1439 A6
Preble Creek Pkwy
- BMFD 80020 1691 E5
- BMFD 80020 1692 A5
Premier Pl
2400 BLDR 80304 1602 E5
E Prentice Av
- AphC 80015 2286 C7
5500 GDVL 80121 2282 B7
7900 GDVL 80111 2282 E7
9100 GDVL 80111 2283 A7
10400 AphC 80111 2283 C7
16400 CTNL 80015 2284 E7
18900 CTNL 80015 2285 D7
W Prentice Av
400 LITN 80120 2280 C7
900 EGLD 80120 2280 C7
3000 LITN 80123 2364 A1
6000 DNVR 80123 2279 B7
6200 DNVR 80123 2363 A1
8500 JfnC 80123 2278 C7
8900 JfnC 80123 2362 C1
E Prentice Cir
9600 GDVL 80111 2283 B7
16700 CTNL 80015 2284 E7
17300 CTNL 80015 2285 A7
W Prentice Cir
5500 DNVR 80123 2279 B7
5500 DNVR 80123 2363 B1
W Prentice Ct
5400 DNVR 80123 2363 B1
E Prentice Dr
15400 CTNL 80015 2284 D7
17700 CTNL 80015 2285 B7
W Prentice Dr
12400 JfnC 80127 2361 C1
E Prentice Ln
15400 CTNL 80015 2284 D7
19300 CTNL 80015 2285 D7
21200 CTNL 80015 2286 A7
E Prentice Pl
5600 GDVL 80121 2282 B7
6400 GDVL 80111 2282 C7
10300 AphC 80111 2283 C7
16100 CTNL 80015 2284 E7
18600 CTNL 80015 2285 C7
21300 CTNL 80015 2286 A7
22700 AphC 80015 2286 C7
W Prentice Pl
- DNVR 80123 2363 B1
800 LITN 80120 2364 D1
10800 JfnC 80127 2362 A1
12200 JfnC 80127 2361 D1
E Prescott Av
5200 CSRK 80104 2704 E6
S Prescott Ct
7600 LITN 80120 2364 B6
S Prescott Pl
7600 LITN 80120 2364 B6
S Prescott St
5200 LITN 80120 2280 B7
5600 LITN 80120 2364 B1
S Prescott Wy
6600 LITN 80120 2364 B4
Preserve Cir
1100 JfnC 80401 2190 C5
E Preserve Ct
4900 GDVL 80121 2366 A1
Preserve Dr
5300 GDVL 80111 2282 B7
5300 GDVL 80121 2282 B7
5300 GDVL 80121 2366 A1
5500 GDVL 80111 2366 A1
E Preserve Ln
4900 GDVL 80121 2366 A1
Preserve Pkwy N
4000 GDVL 80121 2365 E1
4400 GDVL 80121 2366 A1
Preserve Pkwy S
4000 GDVL 80121 2365 E2
4200 GDVL 80121 2366 A2
Pressler St
26000 JfnC 80433 2442 A4
Preston Ct
900 DgsC 80108 2618 D1
Preston Dr
1700 LGMT 80501 1356 D6
Preston Wy
- DgsC 80108 2618 D1
Prestwick Ct
2000 LGMT 80501 1356 E5
W Prestwick Ct
100 CSRK 80104 2787 D4
W Prestwick Dr
100 CSRK 80104 2787 C4
S Prestwick Ln
2500 JfnC 80439 2273 B1
Prestwick Tr
- LNTR 80124 2451 A5
10100 LNTR 80124 2450 E6

STREET Block City ZIP Map# Grid

E Price Av
5500 GDVL 80121 2365 D1
Price Rd
- LGMT 80501 1438 E4
- PrkC 80456 2521 D3
200 LGMT 80501 1439 A3
Prickly Pear Cir
8800 PARK 80134 2453 B2
8900 DgsC 80134 2453 B2
Prickly Pear Ct
8900 PARK 80134 2453 B2
Prima Ln
1700 JfnC 80439 2189 B6
Primos Rd
400 BldC 80302 1682 E3
400 BldC 80302 1683 A3
Primrose Cir
- BGTN 80601 1780 C3
Primrose Ct
- BGTN 80601 1780 D3
100 LGMT 80501 1439 D3
3900 BMFD 80020 1775 D7
Primrose Dr
- DgsC 80118 2954 B1
Primrose Ln
3500 CSRK 80109 2618 D7
3500 CSRK 80109 2702 D1
5300 AdmC 80221 2028 A5
5300 DNVR 80221 2028 A5
6500 BldC 80503 1521 B5
Primrose Ln N
1000 LAFT 80026 1690 B6
Primrose Rd
400 BldC 80302 1686 C5
400 BLDR 80302 1686 C5
Prince Cir
2800 ERIE 80516 1690 C1
3000 BMFD 80020 1775 E7
S Prince Cir
6800 LITN 80120 2364 A4
Prince Ct
12900 BMFD 80020 1775 E6
S Prince Ct
2500 LITN 80123 2280 A6
Prince St
10 LGMT 80501 1439 A3
S Prince St
5000 LITN 80123 2280 A7
5200 LITN 80120 2280 A7
5300 LITN 80120 2364 B3
S Prince Wy
6800 LITN 80120 2364 B4
Prince Creek Dr
12500 PARK 80134 2537 C5
N Princess Cir
2900 BMFD 80020 1775 E7
S Princess Cir
3000 BMFD 80020 1775 E7
Princess Ct
3400 BMFD 80020 1775 E7
Princess Dr
1700 LGMT 80501 1356 A6
E Princeton Av
10 EGLD 80110 2280 E5
10 EGLD 80113 2280 E5
500 EGLD 80113 2281 A5
700 CHLV 80113 2281 A5
4700 CHLV 80113 2282 A5
5700 CHLV 80111 2282 B5
6200 AphC 80237 2282 B5
8000 DNVR 80237 2282 E5
15100 AURA 80014 2284 D4
15400 AURA 80013 2284 D4
20400 AphC 80013 2285 E4
W Princeton Av
10 EGLD 80110 2280 D5
10 EGLD 80113 2280 D5
4600 DNVR 80236 2279 C5
6700 DNVR 80235 2279 A5
7100 DNVR 80235 2278 E5
7100 LKWD 80235 2278 E5
Princeton Cir
10 LGMT 80503 1355 B7
E Princeton Cir
5900 CHLV 80111 2282 B5
16200 AURA 80013 2284 E4
22000 AURA 80018 2286 B4
S Princeton Cir
9300 DgsC 80130 2450 C4
W Princeton Cir
3400 DNVR 80236 2279 D5
Princeton Ct
1200 LGMT 80503 1355 B7
W Princeton Ct
900 LSVL 80027 1773 A2
Princeton Dr
1000 LGMT 80503 1438 C1
1100 LGMT 80503 1355 C7
E Princeton Dr
19000 AURA 80013 2285 C4
19000 AURA 80015 2285 C4
21900 AURA 80018 2286 B4
W Princeton Dr
5200 DNVR 80235 2279 B5
13500 JfnC 80465 2277 B5
E Princeton Ln
20700 AphC 80013 2285 D4
20700 AphC 80013 2286 A4
S Princeton Ln
9300 DgsC 80130 2450 C4
Princeton Pl
600 LAFT 80026 1689 D4
E Princeton Pl
- AphC 80013 2286 A5
15100 AURA 80014 2284 C4
16500 AURA 80013 2284 E4
19800 AURA 80013 2285 D4
20500 AphC 80013 2285 E4
W Princeton Pl
1000 EGLD 80110 2280 C5
2800 SRDN 80110 2280 A5
Princeton St
8600 AdmC 80031 1943 D3

S Princeton St
9100 DgsC 80130 2450 C3
Princeton Peak Wy
2600 CSRK 80109 2787 A4
S Prinsepia St
- PARK 80134 2537 B6
Private Road 17
- EbtC 80107 2625 D4
Private Road 160
- EbtC 80107 2625 D5
Prize Mine Rd
- GpnC 80403 2017 A5
S Proctor Ct
1500 SUPE 80027 1773 B5
Professional Ln
1500 LGMT 80501 1439 B6
E Progress Av
- AphC 80015 2286 A7
- CTNL 80015 2284 D7
- CTNL 80015 2286 A7
6500 GDVL 80111 2282 C7
10900 AphC 80111 2283 C7
16900 CTNL 80015 2285 A7
W Progress Av
- LITN 80123 2280 A7
400 LITN 80120 2280 D7
1600 EGLD 80120 2280 C7
6000 DNVR 80123 2279 B7
9600 JfnC 80123 2278 B7
9800 JfnC 80127 2278 B7
12600 JfnC 80127 2277 C7
E Progress Cir
6500 GDVL 80111 2282 C7
9700 GDVL 80111 2283 B7
15400 CTNL 80015 2284 D7
19400 CTNL 80015 2285 D7
23300 AphC 80016 2286 D7
E Progress Cir N
16900 CTNL 80015 2285 A7
E Progress Cir S
- CTNL 80015 2285 D7
W Progress Cir
- LKWD 80123 2278 D7
E Progress Ct
4900 GDVL 80121 2282 A7
13700 AphC 80015 2284 B7
E Progress Dr
16300 CTNL 80015 2284 E7
16800 CTNL 80015 2285 A7
24100 AURA 80016 2286 E7
W Progress Dr
8500 JfnC 80123 2278 C7
E Progress Ln
6200 PARK 80134 2453 C5
19800 CTNL 80015 2285 D7
W Progress Ln
400 LITN 80120 2280 D7
E Progress Pl
7300 GDVL 80111 2282 D7
9500 GDVL 80111 2283 B7
15200 AURA 80015 2284 D7
16100 CTNL 80015 2284 E7
17900 CTNL 80015 2285 B7
21300 CTNL 80015 2286 A7
W Progress Pl
9800 JfnC 80123 2278 A7
10800 JfnC 80127 2278 A7
11400 JfnC 80127 2277 E7
E Progress Wy
- AphC 80111 2283 C7
13700 AphC 80015 2284 B7
S Progress Wy
10200 PARK 80134 2453 C5
Promenade Dr S
- WSTR 80020 1858 E5
- WSTR 80020 1859 A5
S Promenade Pl
9600 DgsC 80126 2449 A4
Promontory Ct
3800 BLDR 80304 1602 B5
Promontory Dr
1700 DgsC 80109 2786 B5
Pronghorn Av
5000 EbtC 80107 2625 E4
5000 EbtC 80107 2626 A4
Pronghorn Cir
2000 EbtC 80107 2792 D6
Pronghorn St
12600 BMFD 80020 1775 C6
Prospect Dr
10 DgsC 80108 2619 A5
4300 DgsC 80108 2618 E6
Prospect Rd
5500 BldC 80503 1436 D7
5500 BldC 80503 1437 A7
8700 BldC 80503 1438 A7
8700 LGMT 80503 1438 A7
10700 BldC 80504 1439 C7
10700 LGMT 80504 1439 C7
Prospect St
- BldC 80302 1599 D3
400 LYNS 80540 1352 D2
4400 AphC 80123 2279 C6
4400 BWMR 80123 2279 C6
4400 DNVR 80123 2279 C6
4400 LITN 80123 2279 C6
Prospector Wy
6300 DgsC 80134 2621 D2
Prospectors Wy
10 PrkC 80456 2521 B2
S Pross Dr
9500 JfnC 80433 2442 B4
Prosser St
- CLCY 80403 2017 C4
Prouty Dr
1300 JfnC 80439 2188 E5
1500 JfnC 80439 2189 A6
Providence Dr
500 DgsC 80108 2619 A5
Provost Rd
3000 AdmC 80102 2125 C1
PR Road 19
39100 EbtC 80107 2625 D5

Ptarmigan
10 JfnC 80127 2360 D4
Ptarmigan Cir
5400 BldC 80301 1604 C1
Ptarmigan Ct
1200 LAFT 80026 1690 D2
Ptarmigan Dr
1100 LGMT 80501 1357 A7
13800 BMFD 80020 1775 B4
Ptarmigan Ln
5300 BMFD 80020 1775 B5
Ptarmigan St
300 GOLD 80403 2107 D2
Ptarmigan Tr
10 PrkC 80456 2691 D3
9200 LNTR 80124 2450 D4
N Public Rd
100 LAFT 80026 1690 C4
S Public Rd
- LAFT 80026 1774 C1
100 LAFT 80026 1690 C5
Pueblo Ct
1500 TNTN 80229 1945 A2
Pueblo Pl
5400 BldC 80303 1687 D5
5400 BLDR 80303 1687 D5
S Puffin Ct
4200 DgsC 80126 2449 E3
Puma Blf
6100 DgsC 80124 2534 C1
Puma Clf
10900 DgsC 80124 2534 C1
Puma Dr
10 BldC 80302 1769 C3
Puma Pt
6100 DgsC 80124 2534 C1
Puma Rdg
6000 DgsC 80124 2534 B1
S Puma Run
10900 DgsC 80124 2450 C7
10900 DgsC 80124 2534 C1
Puma Tr
6900 DgsC 80125 2614 D1
Puma Wk
10 BldC 80302 1600 C6
Puma Chase
6000 DgsC 80124 2534 B1
W Puma Crst
33500 JfnC 80439 2356 B5
Puma Point Wy
6300 JfnC 80403 2023 A3
Puma Sands
6100 DgsC 80124 2450 C7
Purcel St
- BGTN 80601 1696 E7
2900 BGTN 80601 1697 A7
Purcell Pl
2400 BGTN 80601 1696 E7
E Purdue Av
15100 AURA 80014 2284 D5
W Purdue Av
7900 LKWD 80235 2278 D5
13400 JfnC 80465 2277 B5
E Purdue Cir
19300 AURA 80013 2285 D5
Purdue Ct
10 LGMT 80503 1355 B7
Purdue Dr
- LGMT 80501 1438 C1
1000 LGMT 80503 1438 C1
1100 LGMT 80503 1355 B7
E Purdue Dr
15600 AURA 80013 2284 D5
W Purdue Dr
13400 JfnC 80465 2277 B5
E Purdue Pl
4200 AURA 80018 2286 B4
14700 AURA 80014 2284 C5
16200 AURA 80013 2284 E5
19400 AURA 80013 2285 D4
20200 AphC 80013 2285 E5
W Purgatoire Peak
10400 JfnC 80127 2362 B5
10400 JfnC 80127 2446 A2
Purgatory Ln
1300 JfnC 80439 2189 A5
Purple Ash
10 JfnC 80127 2360 E6
Purple Plum
10 JfnC 80127 2361 A7
Purple Sage Lp
900 CSRK 80104 2703 E2
Purple Sky Wy
- CSRK 80108 2703 E1
Pussy Willow Ct
4500 BLDR 80301 1603 E3
Putney Curl
10300 TNTN 80229 1861 B6
Putter Ct
6600 BldC 80503 1518 E5
Putter Pl
1400 CSRK 80104 2787 E2
Pyramid Cir
4600 BMFD 80020 1775 C5
Pyramid Ct
3900 SUPE 80027 1857 A2
Pyramid Rd
2000 TNTN 80260 1860 B7
W Pyramid Peak
11000 JfnC 80127 2361 C7
Pyrite Ct
7300 CSRK 80108 2619 E5
Pyrite Rd
10 GpnC 80403 1850 B7
10 GpnC 80403 1934 B1
Pyrite Wy
10 BldC 80540 1352 C5
7400 CSRK 80108 2619 E5

Q

Quail Cir
300 BLDR 80304 1602 B5
900 BGTN 80601 1780 A1

Quail Cir
1900 LSVL 80027 1689 B6
S Quail Cir
7400 JfnC 80127 2361 E6
Quail Ct
1400 GOLD 80403 2107 C2
1800 LSVL 80027 1689 B6
1900 LKWD 80215 2109 E4
3800 WTRG 80033 2109 E1
5500 ARVD 80002 2025 E4
6000 ARVD 80004 2025 E3
10500 WSTR 80021 1857 E5
11000 PARK 80134 2536 E1
S Quail Ct
- JfnC 80127 2361 E4
1400 JfnC 80232 2193 E5
4300 JfnC 80127 2277 E5
8400 JfnC 80127 2445 E1
Quail Dr
700 LAFT 80026 1690 D5
2000 LKWD 80215 2109 E4
37100 EbtC 80107 2708 D1
Quail Ln
1500 CSRK 80104 2704 A5
S Quail Ln
6700 JfnC 80127 2361 E4
Quail Pl
800 DgsC 80126 2449 A2
Quail Rd
3600 LGMT 80503 1438 B5
8700 BldC 80503 1438 B5
10700 LGMT 80501 1439 B5
10800 BldC 80501 1439 B5
Quail St
1100 BGTN 80601 1780 A1
2500 LKWD 80215 2109 E3
3100 WTRG 80033 2109 E3
5200 ARVD 80033 2025 E5
5200 WTRG 80033 2025 E5
5800 ARVD 80002 2025 E4
6900 ARVD 80004 2025 E1
7200 ARVD 80004 1941 E7
7200 ARVD 80005 1941 E7
7900 JfnC 80005 1941 E5
10500 WSTR 80021 1857 E5
N Quail St
- WSTR 80021 1857 E5
4300 WTRG 80033 2025 E7
S Quail St
1100 LKWD 80226 2193 E4
1500 JfnC 80232 2193 E5
1800 LKWD 80227 2193 E6
4300 JfnC 80127 2277 E6
5400 JfnC 80127 2361 E1
Quail Wy
10200 WSTR 80021 1857 E6
S Quail Wy
700 LKWD 80226 2193 E4
4300 JfnC 80127 2277 E5
5900 JfnC 80127 2361 E2
Quail Cove
800 LAFT 80026 1690 D6
Quail Creek Dr
- BMFD 80020 1775 E4
2400 BMFD 80020 1776 A4
E Quail Creek Dr
10700 PARK 80138 2454 C7
W Quail Creek Dr
10700 PARK 80138 2454 C7
Quail Creek Ln
4600 BldC 80301 1604 B3
Quail Hollow Ct
5200 BLDR 80301 1604 C2
Quail Ridge Cir
200 DgsC 80126 2448 E3
3300 EbtC 80138 2541 A7
Quail Ridge Ct
16400 JfnC 80465 2360 D1
Quail Ridge Dr
13800 BMFD 80020 1775 A4
Quail Ridge Dr W
10700 PARK 80138 2454 B7
Quail Run Ct
10900 PARK 80138 2538 C1
Quail Run Dr
22300 PARK 80138 2454 C7
Quail Run Ln
22300 PARK 80138 2454 C7
Quail Run Rd
900 AphC 80137 2121 E6
N Quail Run Rd
1400 AdmC 80137 2121 E4
1400 AURA 80137 2121 E4
4800 AURA 80137 2037 E5
5200 AdmC 80137 2037 E3
S Quail Run Rd
1000 AphC 80137 2205 E4
Quail Run Wy
22300 PARK 80138 2454 C7
22300 PARK 80138 2538 B1
Quail Run Mile Rd
- AdmC 80137 1953 D2
- AdmC 80137 2037 E2
8200 AdmC 80102 1953 D4
Quaker Cir
700 GOLD 80401 2108 D7
Quaker Ct
6400 ARVD 80007 2024 D2
S Quaker Ct
- JfnC 80401 2192 D2
Quaker Ln
4800 GOLD 80403 2024 D6
4800 JfnC 80403 2024 D6
12100 JfnC 80433 2525 C4
Quaker St
100 GOLD 80401 2192 D1
800 GOLD 80401 2108 D6
800 JfnC 80401 2108 D6
5000 GOLD 80403 2024 D6
6200 ARVD 80007 2024 D3
6200 ARVD 80403 2024 D3
6200 JfnC 80403 2024 D3
7000 ARVD 80007 1940 D7
7200 JfnC 80007 1940 D7

Quaker Wy
100 JfnC 80401 2192 D1
Quakie Ln
10 PrkC 80456 2606 E7
10 PrkC 80456 2690 E1
10 PrkC 80456 2691 A1
Quality 1st Av
- BldC 80027 1773 D5
- LSVL 80027 1773 D5
Qualla Ct
10 BLDR 80303 1687 C6
Qualla Dr
4600 BLDR 80303 1687 C6
Qualmish Av
5200 JfnC 80123 2278 B7
Quam Dr
11700 NHGN 80233 1861 A2
Quandary Rd
9800 TNTN 80260 1860 B6
S Quandry Peak Dr
4100 CSRK 80109 2787 A5
Quandry Peak St
1500 BGTN 80601 1697 C6
S Quantum St
10 DNVR 80230 2198 D1
Quari Ct
- AURA 80010 2115 E4
800 AURA 80011 2115 E6
Quari St
200 AURA 80011 2199 E1
1300 AURA 80011 2115 E5
4900 DNVR 80239 2031 E5
S Quari St
600 AURA 80012 2199 E3
Quari Wy
1700 AURA 80010 2115 E4
W Quarles Av
10500 JfnC 80127 2362 A5
W Quarles Dr
5800 JfnC 80128 2363 B5
8400 JfnC 80128 2362 D5
W Quarles Pl
9200 JfnC 80128 2362 C5
Quarry Ct
5600 BLDR 80301 1604 B2
S Quarry Mtn
7300 JfnC 80127 2361 D6
Quarry Rd
600 DgsC 80124 2450 D7
Quarry Wy
- DgsC 80134 2452 E6
Quarry Hill Dr
15500 DgsC 80134 2452 D6
Quarry Hill Pl
10000 DgsC 80134 2452 D5
Quarter Cir Ln
300 JfnC 80439 2188 B1
Quarter Horse Rd
31200 JfnC 80439 2272 E3
31200 JfnC 80439 2273 A3
Quarterhorse Tr
700 CSRK 80104 2703 D3
W Quarto Av
7500 JfnC 80128 2362 E5
W Quarto Cir
8700 JfnC 80128 2362 C5
W Quarto Dr
7700 JfnC 80128 2362 D5
10600 JfnC 80127 2362 A5
E Quarto Pl
24600 AURA 80016 2370 E4
24600 AURA 80016 2371 A4
W Quarto Pl
6800 JfnC 80128 2363 A5
8900 JfnC 80128 2362 C5
10500 JfnC 80127 2362 A5
Quartz Cir
10 PrkC 80456 2521 C3
6400 ARVD 80007 2024 C2
Quartz Ct
900 LGMT 80501 1439 E1
Quartz Dr
1300 BMFD 80020 1774 C6
Quartz Lp
6100 ARVD 80403 2024 C3
Quartz Rd
10 GpnC 80403 1850 B7
Quartz Spur
12300 JfnC 80433 2527 E5
Quartz St
- CSRK 80109 2702 D5
1400 JfnC 80401 2108 D5
7200 JfnC 80007 1940 C6
N Quartz St
7600 ARVD 80007 1940 C6
7600 JfnC 80007 1940 C6
Quartz Tr
8400 JfnC 80465 2443 D2
Quartz Wy
10 BldC 80540 1352 C5
600 BMFD 80020 1774 C7
2800 SUPE 80027 1773 A7
6700 ARVD 80007 2024 C1
Quartz Mountain Rd
600 DgsC 80118 2954 D3
Quartz Valley Rd
100 GpnC 80403 2017 C3
E Quartzville Rd
11200 DgsC 80116 2791 E3
11200 EbtC 80107 2791 E3
Quary Ct
10600 CMCY 80022 1864 E5
S Quatar Cir
5300 AphC 80015 2286 B7
5700 CTNL 80015 2370 B1
7000 AphC 80016 2370 B7
8100 AphC 80016 2454 B1
8100 AURA 80016 2370 B7
8100 AURA 80016 2454 B1
S Quatar Ct
- AURA 80016 2370 B6
5400 AphC 80015 2286 B7
5700 CTNL 80015 2370 B1
5900 AphC 80015 2370 B2

S Quatar St
3800 AURA 80018 2286 B4
5800 AphC 80015 2370 B2
5800 CTNL 80015 2370 B2
7100 AURA 80016 2370 B5
S Quatar Wy
- AURA 80016 2370 B6
3500 AURA 80018 2286 B3
5900 AphC 80015 2370 B2
5900 CTNL 80015 2370 B2
Quay Cir
7100 ARVD 80003 1942 E7
Quay Ct
5500 ARVD 80002 2026 E4
6800 ARVD 80003 2026 E1
8200 ARVD 80003 1942 E4
S Quay Ct
6300 JfnC 80123 2363 A4
7600 JfnC 80128 2363 A6
8000 JfnC 80128 2447 A1
8300 JfnC 80128 2446 E1
Quay Dr
8200 ARVD 80003 1942 E4
8300 ARVD 80003 1943 A4
S Quay Dr
1500 LKWD 80232 2194 E5
1500 LKWD 80232 2195 A5
Quay Lp
9700 WSTR 80021 1858 E7
9700 WSTR 80021 1942 E1
Quay St
10 LKWD 80226 2195 A1
200 LKWD 80226 2111 A7
2500 LKWD 80214 2110 E3
3800 WTRG 80033 2110 E1
4100 WTRG 80033 2026 E7
5400 ARVD 80002 2026 E5
6600 ARVD 80003 2026 E1
7600 ARVD 80003 1942 E6
11900 BMFD 80020 1858 E2
N Quay St
9300 JfnC 80021 1942 E2
9300 WSTR 80021 1942 E2
S Quay St
- JfnC 80128 2446 E2
- JfnC 80128 2447 A1
100 LKWD 80226 2195 A2
1700 LKWD 80232 2195 A6
3400 LKWD 80227 2279 A3
Quay Wy
9800 WSTR 80021 1858 E7
S Quay Wy
2700 DNVR 80227 2279 A1
8200 JfnC 80128 2447 A1
Quebec Av
300 LGMT 80501 1439 B6
Quebec Ct
300 DNVR 80230 2114 D7
S Quebec Ct
7100 CTNL 80112 2366 D5
Quebec St
- DNVR 80207 2030 C7
- DNVR 80220 2114 D7
- DNVR 80224 2198 D1
- DNVR 80247 2198 D1
10 DNVR 80220 2198 D1
10 DNVR 80230 2198 D1
500 DNVR 80230 2114 D7
2200 DNVR 80238 2114 D3
2800 DNVR 80207 2114 D3
4000 DNVR 80216 2030 C7
5000 AdmC 80022 2030 D6
5000 AdmC 80216 2030 D6
5000 CMCY 80022 2030 D6
5000 DNVR 80022 2030 D6
7800 CMCY 80022 1946 D6
8000 AdmC 80022 1946 D6
11900 AdmC 80602 1862 C2
12500 AdmC 80602 1778 C7
12500 TNTN 80602 1778 C7
15200 AdmC 80602 1694 C7
15200 TNTN 80602 1694 C7
16600 WldC 80603 1694 C5
Quebec St SR-35
3500 DNVR 80207 2114 D1
5000 AdmC 80022 2030 D6
5000 AdmC 80216 2030 D6
5000 CMCY 80022 2030 D6
5000 DNVR 80022 2030 D6
5000 DNVR 80216 2030 D6
S Quebec St
900 AphC 80247 2198 D4
900 DNVR 80224 2198 D4
900 DNVR 80247 2198 D4
1000 DNVR 80231 2198 D4
1700 AphC 80224 2198 D6
2100 AphC 80231 2198 D7
2600 AphC 80231 2282 D1
2600 DNVR 80224 2282 D1
2600 DNVR 80231 2282 D1
4800 DNVR 80237 2282 D7
5000 AphC 80237 2282 D7
5100 GDVL 80111 2282 D7
5100 GDVL 80237 2282 D7
5400 GDVL 80111 2366 D1
5700 CTNL 80111 2366 D1
6500 CTNL 80112 2366 D3
8100 CTNL 80112 2450 D2
8100 CTNL 80124 2450 D2
8100 DgsC 80126 2450 D2
8100 LNTR 80124 2450 D2
8500 DgsC 80130 2450 D2
8500 LNTR 80130 2450 D2
8600 DgsC 80124 2450 D2
S Quebec Wy
10 DNVR 80230 2198 D1
1100 AphC 80231 2198 D5
1100 DNVR 80224 2198 D5
1100 DNVR 80231 2198 D5
1900 AphC 80231 2199 A6
Queen Cir
6900 ARVD 80004 1941 E7
6900 ARVD 80004 2025 E1
7400 ARVD 80005 1941 E6

S Queen Cir
300 LKWD 80226 2193 E2
Queen Ct
3100 BMFD 80020 1775 E7
4600 WTRG 80033 2025 E6
6000 ARVD 80004 2025 E3
S Queen Ct
1500 JfnC 80232 2193 E5
6400 JfnC 80127 2361 E4
S Queen Dr
1900 LKWD 80227 2193 E6
S Queen Ln
6800 JfnC 80127 2361 E4
S Queen Rd
6700 JfnC 80127 2361 E4
Queen St
2500 LKWD 80215 2109 E3
5800 ARVD 80002 2025 E3
6600 ARVD 80004 2025 E1
7000 ARVD 80004 1941 E7
7600 ARVD 80005 1941 E6
8000 JfnC 80005 1941 E4
10500 WSTR 80021 1857 E5
S Queen St
300 LKWD 80226 2193 E2
1500 JfnC 80232 2193 E5
2200 JfnC 80227 2193 E7
2200 LKWD 80227 2193 E7
4400 JfnC 80127 2277 E6
5600 JfnC 80127 2361 E2
S Queen Wy
700 LKWD 80226 2193 E3
1700 JfnC 80232 2193 E6
6000 JfnC 80127 2361 E2
Queens Dr
1700 LGMT 80501 1356 A6
S Queensburg Ct
- AURA 80016 2371 C3
Queensburg St
11100 DNVR 80249 1867 C4
S Queenscliffe Ct
9500 DgsC 80130 2450 B4
S Queenscliffe Dr
9500 DgsC 80130 2450 A4
S Quemoy Cir
- CTNL 80015 2370 B1
5500 AphC 80015 2370 B1
6600 AURA 80016 2370 B3
S Quemoy Ct
3800 AURA 80018 2286 B4
5600 CTNL 80015 2370 B1
6100 AphC 80015 2370 B2
6200 AURA 80016 2370 B2
S Quemoy St
7100 AURA 80016 2370 B5
S Quemoy Wy
3500 AphC 80013 2286 B3
3800 AURA 80018 2286 B4
5700 CTNL 80015 2370 B1
5900 AphC 80015 2370 B2
6400 AURA 80016 2370 B3
Quency St
- AdmC 80022 1866 B5
- DNVR 80249 1866 B5
Quency Wy
- AdmC 80022 1866 C3
- DNVR 80022 1866 C3
- DNVR 80249 1866 C3
Quentin St
- AdmC 80022 2031 E4
- DNVR 80022 2031 E4
- DNVR 80239 2031 E4
1300 AURA 80011 2115 E5
1600 AURA 80010 2115 E4
3700 AdmC 80239 2115 E1
3700 AURA 80239 2115 E1
3700 DNVR 80239 2115 E1
S Quentin St
600 AURA 80012 2199 E3
6800 CTNL 80112 2367 E4
Quentin Wy
- AURA 80014 2199 E7
S Quentin Wy
2100 AURA 80014 2199 E6
Quick Fox Ct
- EbtC 80107 2709 C5
N Quicksilver Av
10 CSRK 80104 2704 D6
S Quicksilver Av
10 CSRK 80104 2704 D6
Quicksilver Rd
11900 BldC 80501 1439 E5
11900 BldC 80501 1440 A5
11900 BldC 80504 1440 A5
Quieto Ct
4400 DNVR 80211 2028 B7
S Quieto Ct
1300 DNVR 80223 2196 C5
S Quieto Wy
500 DNVR 80223 2196 B2
Quiet Retreat Ct
7000 BldC 80503 1521 C4
W Quigley Dr
3800 DNVR 80236 2279 D5
Quigley St
8600 AdmC 80031 1943 D3
Quill Ln
33500 EbtC 80107 2794 B1
Quince Av
800 BLDR 80304 1602 C5
1700 BldC 80304 1602 C5
Quince Cir
600 BLDR 80304 1602 B5
S Quince Cir
7000 CTNL 80112 2366 D5
Quince Ct
- TNTN 80602 1778 C6
4200 BldC 80301 1603 A5
S Quince Ct
7300 CTNL 80112 2366 D5
Quince Dr
- TNTN 80260 1944 C2
Quince St
1100 DNVR 80230 2114 D6

STREET
Block City ZIP Map# Grid

Quince St
1200 DNVR 80220 2114 D5
2200 DNVR 80207 2114 D3
2200 DNVR 80238 2114 D3
7800 AdmC 80022 1946 C5
8800 CMCY 80022 1946 C3
8800 CMCY 80640 1946 C3
12400 AdmC 80602 1862 C1
12500 AdmC 80602 1778 C7
12700 TNTN 80602 1778 C7
N Quince St
- DNVR 80230 2198 D1
S Quince St
100 DNVR 80230 2198 D2
900 AphC 80231 2198 D4
900 AphC 80247 2198 D4
900 DNVR 80247 2198 D4
1900 DNVR 80231 2198 D6
2700 DNVR 80231 2282 D1
3700 DNVR 80237 2282 D3
6800 CTNL 80112 2366 D5
S Quince Wy
1100 AphC 80231 2198 D4
1100 DNVR 80231 2198 D4
3000 DNVR 80231 2282 D2
7900 CTNL 80112 2366 D7
E Quincy Av
- AphC 80013 2285 D5
- AphC 80015 2286 B5
10 EGLD 80110 2280 E5
10 EGLD 80113 2280 E5
500 EGLD 80113 2281 A5
800 CHLV 80113 2281 A5
4300 CHLV 80113 2282 A5
5500 CHLV 80111 2282 A5
6400 AphC 80237 2282 C5
6400 DNVR 80237 2282 C5
8700 DNVR 80237 2283 A5
13400 AphC 80014 2284 D5
13400 AphC 80015 2284 D5
13400 AURA 80014 2284 D5
13400 AURA 80015 2284 D5
15300 AURA 80013 2284 D5
16600 AURA 80015 2285 A5
18900 AphC 80015 2285 D5
18900 AURA 80013 2285 D5
20700 AphC 80013 2286 B5
20700 AURA 80013 2286 B5
20700 AURA 80015 2286 B5
20700 AURA 80018 2286 B5
23300 AphC 80018 2286 D5
23300 AURA 80016 2286 D5
23700 AphC 80018 2287 C4
23700 AURA 80016 2287 C4
26000 AphC 80137 2287 C4
28100 AphC 80137 2288 A4
E Quincy Av CO-30
23700 AphC 80018 2286 D5
23700 AURA 80016 2286 D5
23700 AURA 80016 2287 C4
26000 AphC 80018 2287 C4
26000 AphC 80137 2287 C4
28100 AphC 80137 2288 A4
E Quincy Av SR-30
25900 AphC 80018 2287 C4
25900 AURA 80016 2287 C4
W Quincy Av
10 EGLD 80110 2280 D5
10 EGLD 80113 2280 D5
1600 SRDN 80110 2280 C5
3000 DvrC 80236 2279 E5
3000 SRDN 80110 2279 E5
3200 SRDN 80236 2279 E5
4500 DNVR 80236 2279 D5
5200 DNVR 80123 2279 B5
5200 DNVR 80235 2279 B5
6200 DvrC 80235 2279 B5
6200 LKWD 80123 2279 B5
7000 DNVR 80235 2278 D5
7000 JfnC 80235 2278 D5
7000 LKWD 80235 2278 D5
7200 DNVR 80123 2278 D5
7200 LKWD 80235 2278 D5
8200 DvrC 80123 2278 D5
9700 JfnC 80127 2278 A5
10500 JfnC 80127 2277 D5
10500 JfnC 80235 2277 D5
10500 JfnC 80465 2277 D5
E Quincy Dr
20300 AphC 80015 2285 E5
W Quincy Dr
7700 LKWD 80235 2278 D5
E Quincy Ln
15600 AURA 80015 2284 D5
E Quincy Pl
15500 AURA 80015 2284 D5
18700 AURA 80015 2285 C5
19600 CTNL 80015 2285 D5
20300 AphC 80015 2285 E5
W Quincy Pl
11200 JfnC 80127 2277 E5
12000 JfnC 80465 2277 D5
Quiner Rd
- PrkC 80456 2690 E2
N Quinlin Ct
5500 DgsC 80134 2622 B3
W Quinn Av
2400 LITN 80120 2364 B5
E Quinn Cir
14000 AURA 80015 2284 B5
W Quinn Dr
12200 JfnC 80465 2277 D5
E Quinn Pl
15500 AURA 80015 2284 D5
19000 AURA 80015 2285 D5
W Quinn Pl
3800 DNVR 80236 2279 D5
Quinn St
900 BLDR 80303 1687 A4
Quintana Ln
800 ERIE 80516 1691 D2
S Quintero Cir
3700 AURA 80013 2285 A3
4700 AURA 80015 2285 A6
5600 CTNL 80015 2369 A1
7300 FXFD 80016 2369 A5
S Quintero Ct
1100 AURA 80017 2201 A4
4200 AURA 80013 2285 A4
5200 CTNL 80015 2285 A7
5900 AphC 80016 2369 A2
7600 CTNL 80016 2369 A6
Quintero St
- AdmC 80022 1865 A3
1600 AURA 80011 2117 A4
10200 CMCY 80022 1865 A6
S Quintero St
1000 AURA 80017 2201 A4
1900 AURA 80013 2201 A6
3000 AURA 80013 2285 A2
4500 AURA 80015 2285 A5
5100 CTNL 80015 2285 A7
7100 FXFD 80016 2369 A5
S Quintero Wy
1300 AURA 80017 2201 A4
2500 AURA 80013 2201 A7
3000 AURA 80013 2285 A1
5400 CTNL 80015 2369 A1
Quitman Ct
- BMFD 80020 1859 D1
6600 AdmC 80003 2027 D1
Quitman Ln
11900 WSTR 80031 1859 D2
Quitman Pl
- WSTR 80031 1859 D2
Quitman St
10 DNVR 80219 2195 D1
300 DNVR 80219 2111 D7
2000 DNVR 80204 2111 D5
2000 DNVR 80212 2111 D3
5100 AdmC 80212 2027 D5
5100 DNVR 80212 2027 D5
6400 AdmC 80003 2027 D2
7800 WSTR 80030 1943 D5
11800 WSTR 80031 1859 D3
N Quitman St
9200 WSTR 80031 1943 D2
S Quitman St
10 DNVR 80219 2195 D2
2600 DNVR 80219 2279 D2
2600 DNVR 80236 2279 D2
Quitman Wy
7400 WSTR 80030 1943 D6
9700 WSTR 80031 1859 D7
S Quitman Wy
2200 DNVR 80219 2195 D7
Quito Pl
300 DgsC 80108 2619 A5
Quivas Cir
11600 WSTR 80234 1860 B3
Quivas Lp
11200 WSTR 80234 1860 B3
Quivas St
- AdmC 80020 1776 B2
300 DNVR 80223 2112 C7
300 DNVR 80223 2196 B1
1100 DNVR 80204 2112 B6
3200 DNVR 80211 2112 B1
4600 DNVR 80211 2028 B6
4800 DNVR 80221 2028 B6
5500 AdmC 80221 2028 B4
7400 AdmC 80221 1944 B6
10000 TNTN 80260 1860 B7
10200 TNTN 80234 1860 B7
10400 NHGN 80234 1860 B6
15200 AdmC 80020 1692 B7
N Quivas St
13400 WSTR 80234 1776 B5
13500 BMFD 80020 1776 B5
13500 WSTR 80020 1776 B5
S Quivas St
500 DNVR 80223 2196 C3
3200 SRDN 80110 2280 C3
Quivas Wy
8300 AdmC 80221 1944 B4
8300 FLHT 80260 1944 B4
11400 WSTR 80234 1860 B3
N Quivas Wy
12900 WSTR 80234 1776 B6
Quiver Ct
1700 LAFT 80026 1690 E6
Quivira Dr
1200 AdmC 80229 1945 A4
S Quray St
- CTNL 80015 2285 A7

R

Rabbit Dr
12200 LKWD 80401 2109 D6
12300 JfnC 80401 2109 D6
Rabbitbrush Wy
8400 PARK 80134 2452 D2
W Rabbit Ears Pass
12100 JfnC 80127 2361 D6
Rabbit Mountain Rd
- BMFD 80020 1775 D6
6400 BldC 80503 1354 C2
Rabbit Run Dr
800 GOLD 80401 2107 E6
Raccoon Cir
10 CCkC 80439 2187 E5
Raccoon Ct
2600 LAFT 80026 1774 B2
S Race Cir E
6500 CTNL 80121 2365 B4
S Race Cir W
6500 CTNL 80121 2365 B4
Race Ct
300 DNVR 80206 2113 B7
4900 DNVR 80216 2029 B5
13000 TNTN 80241 1777 B6
13600 AdmC 80602 1777 B5
S Race Ct
5300 GDVL 80121 2281 B7
5300 GDVL 80121 2365 B1
6300 CTNL 80121 2365 B3
7900 CTNL 80122 2365 B7
8200 CTNL 80122 2449 B1
Race St
- AdmC 80602 1693 B5
- TNTN 80602 1693 B5
100 DNVR 80206 2197 B1
1000 DNVR 80206 2113 B5
1800 DNVR 80205 2113 B5
3900 DNVR 80205 2029 B7
4600 DNVR 80216 2029 B6
6800 AdmC 80229 2029 B1
8200 AdmC 80229 1945 B4
8800 TNTN 80229 1945 B3
9700 TNTN 80229 1861 B7
12000 NHGN 80233 1861 B2
12000 NHGN 80241 1861 B2
13300 TNTN 80241 1777 B6
14900 TNTN 80602 1777 B2
S Race St
300 DNVR 80209 2197 B2
1000 DNVR 80210 2197 B5
2600 DNVR 80210 2281 B1
3000 DvrC 80210 2281 B2
3100 EGLD 80113 2281 B2
5100 CHLV 80113 2281 B7
5100 CHLV 80121 2281 B7
5100 GDVL 80121 2281 B7
5900 CTNL 80121 2365 B2
5900 GDVL 80121 2365 B2
6700 CTNL 80122 2365 B4
Race Wy
9600 TNTN 80229 1945 B1
S Race Wy
8000 CTNL 80122 2365 B7
Racer St
- AdmC 80102 2124 B2
Rachael Pl
500 DgsC 80108 2534 E5
Racine Cir
- CMCY 80022 1863 E5
S Racine Cir
1500 AURA 80012 2199 E5
6200 CTNL 80111 2367 E3
Racine Ct
- CMCY 80022 1863 E5
11800 AdmC 80640 1863 E2
11800 BGTN 80640 1863 E2
11800 CMCY 80640 1863 E2
Racine St
- CMCY 80022 1863 E5
1300 AURA 80011 2115 E5
1700 AURA 80010 2115 E4
5500 DNVR 80239 2031 E4
12400 AdmC 80640 1779 E7
12400 AdmC 80640 1863 E1
S Racine St
- AURA 80014 2199 E7
300 AURA 80012 2199 E2
2900 AURA 80014 2283 E2
Racine Wy
1600 AURA 80010 2115 E4
S Racine Wy
1100 AURA 80012 2199 E4
2100 AURA 80014 2199 E6
Racoon Ln
3200 DgsC 80116 2707 D1
Racoon Pl
9500 DgsC 80125 2615 B1
Racquet Ln
5500 BLDR 80303 1687 D4
E Radcliff Av
- DNVR 80111 2283 A5
- DNVR 80237 2283 A5
- GDVL 80111 2283 A5
10 EGLD 80110 2280 E5
10 EGLD 80113 2280 E5
600 EGLD 80113 2281 A5
1400 CHLV 80113 2281 B5
6300 CHLV 80111 2282 B5
8400 DNVR 80237 2282 E5
19900 CTNL 80015 2285 E5
20400 AphC 80015 2285 E5
W Radcliff Av
10 EGLD 80113 2280 D5
1000 EGLD 80110 2280 C5
1800 SRDN 80110 2280 B5
3000 SRDN 80110 2279 E5
4800 DNVR 80236 2279 C5
7000 LKWD 80123 2279 A5
7500 DNVR 80123 2278 E5
7500 LKWD 80123 2278 E5
11600 JfnC 80465 2277 D5
E Radcliff Cir
14200 AURA 80015 2284 C5
E Radcliff Dr
- AphC 80015 2285 E5
14400 AURA 80014 2284 C5
14400 AURA 80015 2284 C5
W Radcliff Dr
3000 EGLD 80110 2280 A5
3000 SRDN 80110 2280 A5
3100 EGLD 80110 2279 E5
3100 SRDN 80110 2279 E5
E Radcliff Pl
9100 GDVL 80111 2283 A5
15400 AURA 80015 2284 D5
18700 AURA 80015 2285 C5
18700 CTNL 80015 2285 D5
20100 AphC 80015 2285 E5
W Radcliff Pl
1000 EGLD 80110 2280 C5
W Radcliffe Dr
- JfnC 80127 2278 B5
- JfnC 80465 2277 E5
8900 JfnC 80123 2278 A5
11200 JfnC 80127 2277 E5
Radcliffe Pl
1600 LGMT 80503 1355 A6
W Radcliffe Pl
9200 JfnC 80123 2278 C5
W Rafferty Gardens Av
10 EGLD 80110 2280 D7
10 EGLD 80113 2280 D7
10 LITN 80110 2280 D7
10 LITN 80120 2280 D7
Rafter Rd
7000 DgsC 80116 2705 E3
7400 DgsC 80116 2706 A2
Railroad Av
300 LYNS 80540 1352 D2
Railroad Access Rd
- ARVD 80403 1938 D1
- JfnC 80403 1938 D1
Rainbow Av
8400 AdmC 80229 1945 B3
8700 TNTN 80229 1945 B3
Rainbow Dr
2200 AdmC 80229 1945 B3
Rainbow Ln
- BMFD 80020 1775 C5
N Rainbow Plz
4000 DgsC 80135 2616 C7
Rainbow Wy
900 BldC 80303 1688 A4
W Rainbow Creek Rd
5500 DgsC 80135 2700 D1
6000 DgsC 80135 2616 C7
Rainbow Crest Dr
10 JfnC 80401 2189 B2
S Rainbow Crest Dr
10 JfnC 80401 2189 B2
Rainbow Glen Rd
600 JfnC 80401 2189 C3
Rainbow Hill Rd
30100 JfnC 80401 2189 A2
Rain Dance Tr
6000 DgsC 80125 2614 E3
Raindrop Ln
1300 JfnC 80401 2190 D5
Rainleaf Ct
- EbtC 80107 2709 D4
Rain Lilly Ln
800 BLDR 80304 1602 C5
Raintree Cir
5300 DgsC 80134 2621 A4
E Raintree Ct
100 LSVL 80027 1773 C1
W Raintree Ct
700 LSVL 80027 1773 A1
Raintree Dr
- DgsC 80134 2620 E5
4800 DgsC 80134 2621 A4
S Raintree Ln
100 LSVL 80027 1773 C1
Raleigh Cir
5600 CSRK 80104 2705 A7
5600 CSRK 80104 2788 E1
5600 CSRK 80104 2789 A1
Raleigh Ct
6600 AdmC 80003 2027 D1
N Raleigh Ct
11000 WSTR 80031 1859 D4
W Raleigh Ct
9300 WSTR 80031 1943 D1
Raleigh Pl
7800 WSTR 80030 1943 C5
7800 WSTR 80031 1943 C5
11800 WSTR 80031 1859 D2
Raleigh St
10 DNVR 80219 2195 D1
400 DNVR 80219 2111 D7
1200 DNVR 80204 2111 D5
2400 DNVR 80212 2111 D3
5100 AdmC 80212 2027 D6
5100 DNVR 80212 2027 D6
6400 AdmC 80003 2027 D2
13600 BMFD 80020 1775 D5
N Raleigh St
6900 WSTR 80030 2027 D1
7800 WSTR 80030 1943 D5
9000 WSTR 80031 1943 D2
9900 WSTR 80031 1859 D7
S Raleigh St
10 DNVR 80219 2195 D2
2500 DNVR 80219 2279 D1
2600 DNVR 80236 2279 D1
Ralph Ct
800 AdmC 80221 1944 C4
Ralph Ln
8100 AdmC 80221 1944 C4
8200 FLHT 80260 1944 C4
Ralston Pl
- ARVD 80004 2025 C1
Ralston Rd
- ARVD 80002 2027 A3
- JfnC 80002 2027 A3
6300 ARVD 80003 2027 A3
6800 ARVD 80003 2026 D3
7500 ARVD 80003 2026 D3
9600 ARVD 80002 2026 A2
10800 ARVD 80004 2025 D2
Ralston St
5000 BLDR 80304 1602 B2
Ralston Creek Rd
1000 GpnC 80403 1936 A5
Ralston Frontage Rd
6400 ARVD 80002 2027 A3
6400 ARVD 80003 2027 A3
6800 ARVD 80002 2026 E4
Ramblewood Ct
5700 CSRK 80104 2704 A5
Rambling Oak Dr
9000 DgsC 80134 2622 D4
W Ramona Av
9000 DgsC 80125 2531 B1
Ramona Rd
10 BldC 80403 1852 A1
Rampart Ct
10000 DgsC 80125 2531 A7
Rampart Dr
13300 JfnC 80433 2610 C1
N Rampart Ln
10500 DgsC 80125 2531 B1
10800 DgsC 80125 2447 B7
Rampart Rd
45200 EbtC 80138 2457 B6
Rampart St
9000 FLHT 80260 1944 A2
Rampart Wy
100 DNVR 80230 2198 D1
300 DNVR 80230 2114 D7
7600 DgsC 80125 2531 A7
Rampart Range Rd
200 DgsC 80135 2698 D7
200 DgsC 80135 2783 A1
3200 DgsC 80125 2698 D1
N Rampart Range Rd
6200 DgsC 80125 2615 A2
7700 DgsC 80125 2531 A3
S Rampart Range Rd
7700 JfnC 80127 2362 A7
E Ramsgate Ct
2500 DgsC 80126 2449 C4
S Ramshead Ct
9900 DgsC 80130 2450 D5
Ramshorn Dr
100 DgsC 80108 2618 C4
Ranch Cir
- TNTN 80229 1861 E6
Ranch Dr
2100 NHGN 80234 1860 A4
2100 WSTR 80234 1860 A4
Ranch Ln
6700 JfnC 80465 2359 C4
Ranch Pl
11200 WSTR 80234 1860 B4
Ranch Rd
- TNTN 80229 1861 E6
10 BldC 80481 1515 A2
10 CCkC 80439 2271 E7
10 CCkC 80439 2272 A6
40500 EbtC 80138 2624 D1
N Ranch Rd
10 JfnC 80127 2360 E4
10 JfnC 80127 2361 A3
S Ranch Rd
9900 DgsC 80126 2449 B5
W Ranch Rd
10 JfnC 80127 2360 B7
10 JfnC 80465 2360 B7
W Ranch Tr
10 JfnC 80465 2359 E5
10 JfnC 80465 2360 B7
10 JfnC 80465 2444 B1
Ranch Wy
10 PrkC 80456 2521 A3
Ranch Elsie Dr
30800 JfnC 80403 1852 E4
30800 JfnC 80403 1853 A4
Ranch Elsie Rd
11100 JfnC 80403 1853 A4
11400 JfnC 80403 1852 E3
W Ranch Elsie Rd
11600 JfnC 80403 1852 D3
Ranchero Rd
33800 JfnC 80439 2188 A4
Ranchettes Rd
10 PrkC 80456 2607 A6
Ranch Gate Tr
2000 DgsC 80104 2871 E1
Ranch Hand Ln
3700 DgsC 80104 2871 E1
Ranch House Rd
- CSRK 80104 2620 E7
Rancho Ct
12600 JfnC 80433 2525 E5
Rancho Montecito Dr
10100 DgsC 80138 2539 A1
Ranch Reserve Ln
2600 WSTR 80234 1860 A3
2800 WSTR 80234 1859 E3
Ranch Reserve Pkwy
- WSTR 80031 1859 E3
- WSTR 80234 1859 E3
11200 WSTR 80234 1860 A3
Ranch Reserve Rdg
2300 WSTR 80234 1860 A3
Rand Ct
30400 JfnC 80433 2525 A4
W Rand Rd
30400 JfnC 80433 2525 B4
Rand Wy
1000 SUPE 80027 1773 B6
Randall Ridge Rd
10 GpnC 80403 1851 B4
Randolph Av
5800 CSRK 80104 2788 E1
Randolph Pl
12200 DNVR 80239 2031 E4
12900 DNVR 80239 2032 A4
21200 DNVR 80249 2034 A4
Random Ct
11100 BldC 80026 1606 C5
Random Rd
10 CHLV 80113 2281 D5
N Random Rd
10 PrkC 80456 2521 C2
S Random Rd
10 PrkC 80456 2607 B6
Random Wy
11100 BldC 80026 1606 C4
Random Valley Cir
11200 DgsC 80134 2623 C5
Randy Dr
5400 DgsC 80134 2537 B3
Range Rd
10 BldC 80466 1767 B3
Range St
1600 BLDR 80301 1687 C2
1600 BLDR 80303 1687 C2
N Ranger Rd
13000 DgsC 80138 2455 A2
Rangeview Cir
10 WTRG 80215 2110 B2
Rangeview Ct
10 GpnC 80403 1934 C7
10 GpnC 80403 2018 B1
Range View Dr
19800 JfnC 80465 2443 D6
Rangeview Dr
- GpnC 80403 1934 B7
- GpnC 80403 2018 B1
10 LKWD 80215 2110 A2
10 PrkC 80456 2607 D3
10 WTRG 80215 2110 A2
S Rangeview Dr
100 LITN 80120 2364 B5
Rangeview Ln
900 LGMT 80501 1438 D1
9200 DgsC 80125 2531 B2
Rangeview Pl
- AdmC 80229 1861 E7
TNTN 80229 1861 E7
10 WTRG 80215 2110 A2
Range View Tr
300 JfnC 80401 2190 B1
400 JfnC 80401 2106 A7
Rannoch Dr
1800 LGMT 80501 1357 A5
Rap Av
- DNVR 80249 1951 B3
Rapp Ln
9700 NHGN 80260 1860 C7
S Rapp St
5700 LITN 80120 2364 A2
S Raritan Cir
2600 EGLD 80110 2280 C1
Raritan Ct
4500 DNVR 80211 2028 B7
13100 WSTR 80234 1776 B6
Raritan Pl
5400 BLDR 80303 1687 D5
Raritan St
4400 DNVR 80211 2028 B7
4800 DNVR 80221 2028 B6
5300 AdmC 80221 2028 B5
7400 AdmC 80221 1944 B6
11200 NHGN 80234 1860 B4
11200 WSTR 80234 1860 B4
14900 AdmC 80020 1776 B2
N Raritan St
13100 WSTR 80234 1776 B5
S Raritan St
1900 DNVR 80223 2196 B6
2000 AphC 80223 2196 B7
2000 EGLD 80110 2196 B7
2000 EGLD 80223 2196 B7
2100 AphC 80110 2196 B7
2100 DNVR 80110 2196 B7
2500 EGLD 80110 2280 B1
Raritan Wy
300 DNVR 80223 2196 C1
400 DNVR 80204 2112 B7
400 DNVR 80223 2112 B7
5300 AdmC 80221 2028 B4
10000 TNTN 80260 1860 B7
N Raritan Wy
13400 WSTR 80234 1776 B5
Raspberry Dr
10 CCkC 80452 2186 B4
W Raspberry Mtn
10500 JfnC 80127 2362 A7
Raspberry Run
6800 DgsC 80125 2614 D2
Rattlesnake Dr
7300 DgsC 80124 2450 D5
Raven Ct
7400 DgsC 80108 2534 D7
7700 BldC 80303 1688 E4
Raven Dr
10 PrkC 80456 2691 D1
Raven Run
- BMFD 80020 1775 C1
W Raven Run
10500 DgsC 80125 2614 E4
Raven Crest Rd
19700 JfnC 80465 2275 D7
19700 JfnC 80465 2359 D1
Raven Gulch Rd
5200 JfnC 80465 2275 D7
5200 JfnC 80465 2359 D1
E Ravenhill Cir
2600 DgsC 80126 2449 C4
Ravenswood Ct
10 PrkC 80456 2606 C5
4200 DgsC 80130 2449 E6
Ravenswood Ln
10200 DgsC 80130 2449 E6
Ravenswood Rd
10 CHLV 80113 2281 B4
Ravenswood Wy
10300 DgsC 80130 2449 E6
Ravenwood Ln
2500 LAFT 80026 1689 D4
Ravenwood Rd
900 BldC 80303 1688 B3
Ravine Ct
10 LCHB 80603 1698 B3
Ravine Pl
100 LCHB 80603 1698 B3
Ravine Wy
300 LCHB 80603 1698 B2
Rawhide Cir
- EbtC 80107 2708 B7
3600 CSRK 80104 2703 E3
Rawhide Ct
5800 BldC 80302 1518 C7
Rawlins Wy
400 LAFT 80026 1690 D6
Raymer Ln
1000 SUPE 80027 1773 B5
Raymond Ct
- LYNS 80540 1352 E3
Ray Smith Rd
- GpnC 80403 2017 A6
Rea Av
25700 JfnC 80433 2442 A6
Rea Rd
- GpnC 80403 1934 E5
S Reading Ct
2900 DNVR 80231 2282 D1
S Reading Wy
4000 DNVR 80237 2282 D4
Reasoner Wy
15700 AdmC 80603 1780 C7
15800 AdmC 80603 1864 D1
Recreation Dr
- DgsC 80134 2453 A5
- PARK 80134 2453 A5
Red Mtn
8000 JfnC 80127 2362 A7
Red Mtn E
10300 JfnC 80127 2362 B5
10300 JfnC 80127 2446 A3
Red Mtn W
10400 JfnC 80127 2362 B4
Red Ash Ln
- BldC 80303 1772 B2
1100 BldC 80027 1772 C2
1100 SUPE 80027 1772 C2
1100 SUPE 80303 1772 C2
Red Birch
10 JfnC 80127 2445 B1
Redbird St
1200 LGMT 80501 1439 B5
E Red Brush Pl
16500 PARK 80134 2536 E1
Red Bud St
- BGTN 80601 1697 E5
S Red Bush Tr
8800 DgsC 80126 2449 B2
Red Canyon Dr
6200 DgsC 80130 2450 C2
Red Cedar
10 JfnC 80127 2445 C1
Red Cedar Cir
- EbtC 80138 2456 A2
Red Cedar Dr
3900 DgsC 80126 2449 E6
3900 DgsC 80130 2449 E6
Red Cliff Cir
16500 JfnC 80465 2360 D1
Red Cliff Wy
1400 CSRK 80109 2703 B5
Red Cloud Dr
24600 JfnC 80433 2526 C3
Red Cloud Rd
1700 LGMT 80501 1356 C5
Red Cloud St
2000 TNTN 80260 1860 B7
Red Cloud Wy
12000 JfnC 80433 2526 D4
Red Cloud Peak
11400 JfnC 80127 2361 C7
Red Clover Ct
8600 PARK 80134 2452 E1
Red Clover Wy
- AdmC 80601 1780 D2
- BGTN 80601 1780 D2
Redcone Pl
5000 DgsC 80130 2450 A7
Redcone Wy
10500 DgsC 80130 2450 A7
Red Cross Wy
300 DNVR 80230 2114 D7
Red Deer Ct
16200 JfnC 80465 2360 D1
Red Deer Dr
7300 BldC 80301 1688 C1
Red Deer Rd
10 DgsC 80116 2790 E1
100 DgsC 80116 2791 A1
Red Deer Tr
- BMFD 80020 1775 C6
3000 LAFT 80026 1689 C3
S Red Elder St
- PARK 80134 2537 B6
Red Falcon Wy
- LGMT 80501 1440 A2
Red Feather Pt
2000 LAFT 80026 1690 A4
Red Fern Ct
5600 DgsC 80125 2614 E4
Redfern Pl
1600 LGMT 80501 1438 E6
Red Fern Run
5500 DgsC 80125 2614 E4
Redfield Cir
2100 LGMT 80501 1356 D5
S Red Fox Dr
7500 JfnC 80439 2358 A6
Red Fox Ln
10 GDVL 80111 2282 C7
10 JfnC 80127 2360 E5
E Red Fox Ln
19900 CTNL 80015 2285 E7
E Red Fox Pl
1600 DgsC 80126 2449 B2
Red Fox Tr
4500 BldC 80301 1604 B3
Red Fox Wy
7300 DgsC 80125 2531 A7
Red Gulch Rd
10 BldC 80540 1352 D3
Redhaven Wy
2900 DgsC 80126 2449 D7
Red Hawk Dr
- CSRK 80109 2702 E4
1900 CSRK 80109 2703 B5
Red Hawk Ln
22100 JfnC 80401 2191 B4
Red Hawk Pkwy
5200 BGTN 80601 1697 E6
Redhawk Run
10 CHLV 80113 2281 C3
Red Hill Cir
6700 BldC 80302 1518 A5
Red Hill Ln
600 DgsC 80108 2619 A6
Red Hill Rd
- DgsC 80118 2954 D3
6400 BldC 80302 1518 A6
6500 BldC 80302 1517 E5
Red Hill Wy
5200 DgsC 80108 2619 A6
Red Lily Pl
10 CCkC 80439 2272 A6

STREET
Block City ZIP Map# Grid

Red Lion Rd
- BldC 80302 1685 B4
Red Ln St
- AdmC 80642 1700 D4
Red Locust
10 JfnC 80127 2361 A7
Red Lodge Dr
1200 JfnC 80439 2189 A5
Red Maple
10 JfnC 80127 2361 B7
Red Maple Cir
2100 EbtC 80138 2540 E7
Red Mesa Ct
7100 DgsC 80125 2530 E7
Red Mesa Dr
7000 DgsC 80125 2530 E7
7000 DgsC 80125 2614 E1
Red Mesa Rd
9800 JfnC 80127 2445 C5
Red Mesa Wy
- DgsC 80125 2530 E7
Redmond Dr
- LGMT 80503 1437 E5
4400 LGMT 80503 1438 A4
Red Moon Rd
1000 JfnC 80401 2189 C4
Red Mountain Ct
1300 LGMT 80501 1439 E1
Red Mountain Dr
1200 LGMT 80501 1439 E1
1400 LGMT 80501 1440 A1
Red Oak Ct
10 ERIE 80516 1606 E5
Red Oak Dr
900 LGMT 80501 1356 E7
Red Oak Wy
5000 DgsC 80134 2621 E5
E Red Oakes Ct
10 DgsC 80126 2448 E4
S Red Oakes Dr
9500 DgsC 80126 2448 E4
S Red Oakes Ln
9600 DgsC 80126 2448 E4
S Red Oakes Pl
9600 DgsC 80126 2448 E4
Red Pass Ct S
5200 DgsC 80108 2619 A6
Red Peak Dr
1400 CSRK 80109 2703 C5
Red Poppy Ct
9100 DgsC 80138 2538 E3
Red Poppy Dr
1600 BGTN 80601 1780 D2
Red Poppy Wy
- BGTN 80601 1780 D2
Red Rock Cir
7600 DgsC 80118 2952 E2
7600 DgsC 80118 2953 A2
Red Rock Ct
8100 DgsC 80118 2953 B3
Red Rock Dr
3800 DgsC 80118 2953 C4
5300 DgsC 80118 2952 E2
Red Rock Pl
8100 DgsC 80118 2953 B4
Red Rocks Business Cir
15600 MRSN 80465 2276 D2
15700 LKWD 80465 2276 D2
15700 MRSN 80228 2276 D2
Red Rocks Business Dr
2000 LKWD 80228 2192 D7
2200 LKWD 80228 2276 D1
3100 MRSN 80228 2276 D2
3200 MRSN 80465 2276 D2
Red Rocks Vista Dr
100 MRSN 80465 2276 B4
Red Rocks Vista Ln
100 MRSN 80465 2276 B3
Red Rosa Cir
12700 PARK 80134 2537 B5
Redstone Dr
500 BMFD 80020 1775 A5
15400 BldC 80503 1270 C4
Redstone Ln
3000 BLDR 80305 1771 A2
Redstone Rd
3100 BLDR 80305 1771 A2
Redstone St
8500 DgsC 80126 2449 A2
Redstone Park Cir
- DgsC 80129 2448 A4
3200 DgsC 80129 2447 E4
Redtail Ct
1500 LGMT 80501 1356 E6
Red Tail Dr
10 DgsC 80126 2449 C3
Redtail Dr
10 BMFD 80020 1774 E5
100 BMFD 80020 1775 A5
Redtail Rd
11800 JfnC 80127 2528 B3
Red Tail Tr
10 CCkC 80439 2187 E6
Redtop Ct
1800 LGMT 80503 1438 B7
E Red Top Ranch Pl
20300 DgsC 80134 2537 E5
Red Tree Pl
3200 CSRK 80104 2787 D4
Redvale Rd
10600 DgsC 80126 2533 C1
S Redwing Av
8700 DgsC 80126 2449 E2
8700 DgsC 80126 2450 A2
8700 DgsC 80130 2450 A2
Redwing Ln
1400 BMFD 80020 1775 A5
Redwing Pl
6400 BldC 80503 1520 A4
Red Wolf Ln
17100 JfnC 80465 2360 C1
Redwood Av
1200 BLDR 80304 1602 C5
1500 BldC 80304 1602 C5
2200 LAFT 80026 1774 C1
Redwood Cir
200 BMFD 80020 1858 E3
200 BMFD 80020 1859 A3
Redwood Ct
2400 LGMT 80503 1355 C4
4200 BldC 80301 1603 A4
E Redwood Ct
700 DgsC 80126 2449 A5
W Redwood Dr
4800 BWMR 80123 2279 C7
Redwood Pl
4200 BldC 80301 1603 A5
Reed Cir
7100 ARVD 80003 1942 E7
Reed Ct
10 LKWD 80226 2194 E1
2600 LKWD 80214 2110 E3
2600 WTRG 80033 2110 E3
5500 ARVD 80002 2026 E4
6600 ARVD 80003 2026 E1
7000 BMFD 80020 1858 E3
8200 ARVD 80003 1942 E5
N Reed Ct
9400 WSTR 80021 1942 E1
S Reed Ct
100 LKWD 80226 2194 E2
600 LKWD 80226 2195 A3
1800 LKWD 80232 2194 E6
3000 LKWD 80227 2278 E2
6300 JfnC 80123 2362 E3
6300 JfnC 80123 2363 A3
6800 JfnC 80128 2363 A5
6900 JfnC 80128 2362 E5
Reed Dr
2100 LKWD 80214 2110 E4
Reed Ln
10 PrkC 80456 2521 E4
Reed Pl
100 LGMT 80501 1439 C2
Reed St
200 LKWD 80226 2194 E1
400 LKWD 80226 2110 E7
1700 EDGW 80214 2110 E5
2400 LKWD 80214 2110 E3
3800 WTRG 80033 2110 E1
4100 WTRG 80033 2026 E7
5700 ARVD 80002 2026 E4
6600 ARVD 80003 2026 E1
7600 ARVD 80003 1942 E6
10500 JfnC 80021 1858 E6
N Reed St
- JfnC 80021 1858 E6
9800 WSTR 80021 1858 E7
11900 BMFD 80020 1858 E2
S Reed St
100 LKWD 80226 2194 E2
1100 LKWD 80232 2194 E5
2700 DNVR 80227 2279 A1
2800 DNVR 80227 2278 E2
3400 LKWD 80227 2278 E3
3400 LKWD 80227 2279 A3
4300 DNVR 80235 2279 A5
4300 DvrC 80235 2279 A5
4300 LKWD 80123 2279 A5
8200 JfnC 80128 2447 A1
8300 JfnC 80128 2446 E1
N Reed Wy
9300 JfnC 80021 1942 E2
9300 WSTR 80021 1942 E2
S Reed Wy
- DNVR 80123 2362 E1
- JfnC 80128 2362 E4
- LKWD 80123 2362 E1
5800 JfnC 80123 2362 E2
5800 JfnC 80123 2363 A2
8200 JfnC 80128 2446 E1
Reed Ranch Rd
- BldC 80302 1517 D6
Rees Ct
700 LGMT 80501 1439 C1
Reese Ct
- ERIE 80516 1606 E7
Reese St
400 LYNS 80540 1352 D1
Regal Ct
1700 LSVL 80027 1689 C6
Regal Pl
200 LSVL 80027 1689 C6
W Regal St
100 LSVL 80027 1689 C6
S Regency Ct
11400 PARK 80138 2538 A1
S Regency Pl
11400 PARK 80138 2537 E2
E Regency Wy
20500 PARK 80138 2537 E1
20500 PARK 80138 2538 B2
Regent Dr
- BLDR 80302 1686 E4
Regina Ln
1100 NHGN 80233 1861 A5
Regis Av
2600 BLDR 80305 1686 E6
2600 BLDR 80305 1687 A6
3000 DNVR 80221 2027 E5
Regis Blvd
3300 DNVR 80221 2027 E5
Regis Rd
5200 AdmC 80221 2027 E5
Regulus Dr
13100 DgsC 80124 2450 E2
Reid Pl
600 CSRK 80108 2703 D1
Reid Tr
- CSRK 80108 2703 D1
Reindeer Cir
10300 DgsC 80116 2791 B2
Reindeer Dr
10 BldC 80481 1514 A3
Reindeer Ln
- BldC 80481 1514 A3
Reliance Cir
1600 SUPE 80027 1773 B6
Reliance Ct
1600 SUPE 80027 1773 B6
Reliance Dr
- ERIE 80516 1691 D1
Relic Rock Ter
16000 DgsC 80134 2452 E5
Rembrandt Rd
10 BldC 80302 1517 E4
W Remington Av
10000 JfnC 80127 2446 A1
11200 JfnC 80127 2445 E1
W Remington Dr
10300 JfnC 80127 2446 A1
W Remington Pl
6800 JfnC 80128 2447 A1
9400 JfnC 80128 2446 B1
9800 JfnC 80127 2446 B1
Remington Pl S
500 DgsC 80108 2619 A5
Remington Rd
2000 EbtC 80107 2708 D2
2500 EbtC 80107 2709 A2
Remmick Ridge Rd
10400 DgsC 80134 2623 B6
Remuda Ct
- BldC 80302 1518 C7
Remuda Ln
200 LAFT 80026 1774 C1
Renaissance Dr
- LGMT 80503 1438 A6
Renaud Rd
10 PrkC 80456 2521 E3
S Renaud St
9800 JfnC 80433 2442 B5
Rendezvous Cir
40000 EbtC 80107 2626 B1
Rendezvous Dr
100 LAFT 80027 1689 D4
300 LAFT 80026 1689 D4
Reno Dr
6700 ARVD 80002 2027 A4
7600 ARVD 80002 2026 D4
S Renoir Dr
9000 DgsC 80126 2450 A3
Rensselaer Dr
9600 ARVD 80004 2026 B2
Rental Wy
- NDLD 80466 1765 D3
Repplier St
3100 BLDR 80304 1602 D7
Reserve Dr
1200 LGMT 80501 1356 E6
6000 BldC 80303 1687 E3
6100 BldC 80303 1688 A3
Reservoir Rd
- BKHK 80403 2018 A3
- BldC 80301 1603 D1
- BLDR 80301 1603 D1
2500 CSRK 80104 2703 E6
2500 CSRK 80104 2704 A6
2500 DgsC 80104 2704 A6
S Reservoir Rd
3700 AURA 80013 2285 C4
4200 AphC 80015 2285 C4
4300 CTNL 80015 2285 C4
4400 AURA 80015 2285 C4
S Resort Dr
13200 JfnC 80433 2525 E7
13200 JfnC 80433 2526 A7
Resort Creek Rd
14600 JfnC 80433 2611 C5
22700 JfnC 80433 2610 E4
Retrievers Tr
33300 JfnC 80403 1936 B5
Reunion Dr
- CMCY 80022 1864 E5
10600 CMCY 80022 1865 A5
Reunion Pkwy
- AdmC 80022 1865 A7
- CMCY 80022 1865 A7
N Reunion Pkwy
- CMCY 80022 1865 A5
Revere Ct
- AURA 80010 2115 E4
- CMCY 80022 1863 E5
12500 AURA 80011 2115 E2
S Revere Pkwy
6300 CTNL 80111 2367 E3
6500 CTNL 80111 2368 A3
6700 CTNL 80112 2368 A4
6800 CTNL 80112 2367 E5
Revere St
- AdmC 80022 2031 E4
- CMCY 80022 1863 E6
- DNVR 80022 2031 E4
1300 AURA 80011 2115 E5
3700 AdmC 80239 2115 E1
3700 AURA 80239 2115 E1
3700 DNVR 80239 2115 E1
5500 DNVR 80239 2031 E4
S Revere St
- AURA 80014 2199 E7
200 AURA 80012 2200 A1
300 AURA 80012 2199 E2
2900 AURA 80014 2283 E1
S Revere Wy
2400 AURA 80014 2199 E7
Reverend Dennis E Dwyer Dr
- DgsC 80138 2454 D7
S Rex Ln
8900 JfnC 80433 2440 D3
Rex St
800 LSVL 80027 1773 D1
Reynolds Dr
7100 DgsC 80135 2616 E1
7200 DgsC 80135 2532 E7
Reynolds Farm Ln
900 LGMT 80503 1438 C1
Rhodonite Ct
1700 CSRK 80108 2620 A6
S Rhodus St
9700 JfnC 80433 2442 B5
Rhyolite Wy
5300 DgsC 80134 2621 D4
Rialto Dr
5000 DgsC 80134 2621 A5
Riata Ct
- BldC 80302 1518 C7
Ricara Dr
4600 BLDR 80303 1687 C5
W Rice Av
8400 DNVR 80123 2278 D5
9200 JfnC 80123 2278 B5
E Rice Cir
16600 AURA 80015 2284 E5
17300 AURA 80015 2285 A5
E Rice Dr
19100 AURA 80015 2285 D5
19200 AphC 80015 2285 D5
19200 CTNL 80015 2285 D5
E Rice Pl
- AphC 80015 2284 B5
15900 AURA 80015 2284 E5
19200 AURA 80015 2285 D5
W Rice Pl
4600 DNVR 80236 2279 C5
8400 DNVR 80123 2278 D5
8600 JfnC 80123 2278 C5
11200 JfnC 80127 2277 E5
12000 JfnC 80465 2277 D5
Rice St
1800 LGMT 80501 1355 E5
Richard Ct
2200 EbtC 80138 2540 D6
Richard Rd
8400 AdmC 80229 1945 B3
Richard Allen Ct
2900 DNVR 80205 2113 D2
Richards Ct
1100 ERIE 80516 1607 A2
Richardson Rd
10 CSRK 80104 2703 E7
S Richfield Cir
3500 AURA 80013 2285 A3
4800 AURA 80015 2285 A6
Richfield Ct
6100 CSRK 80104 2788 E1
S Richfield Ct
1100 AURA 80017 2201 A4
5300 CTNL 80015 2285 A7
5900 AphC 80016 2369 A2
Richfield St
- AdmC 80022 1865 A3
- CMCY 80022 1865 A6
1000 AURA 80011 2117 A5
S Richfield St
- AphC 80016 2369 A2
1100 AURA 80017 2201 A4
2000 AURA 80013 2201 A6
2800 AURA 80013 2285 A1
4200 AURA 80015 2285 A5
5100 AphC 80015 2285 A7
5100 CTNL 80015 2285 A7
6700 FXFD 80016 2369 A5
7500 CTNL 80016 2369 A6
Richfield Wy
- CMCY 80022 1865 B7
S Richfield Wy
900 AURA 80017 2201 A3
2100 AURA 80013 2201 A6
2800 AURA 80013 2285 A1
5400 CTNL 80015 2285 A7
5400 CTNL 80015 2369 A1
E Richlawn Dr
5600 DgsC 80134 2537 B7
E Richlawn Ln
5700 DgsC 80134 2537 B7
5700 DgsC 80134 2621 B1
N Richlawn Pkwy
7000 DgsC 80134 2537 B7
7000 DgsC 80134 2621 B1
Richman St
100 BKHK 80403 2018 A4
100 GpnC 80403 2018 A3
Richmond Ct
12400 JfnC 80433 2526 A5
Richmond Dr
- TNTN 80260 1944 C2
Richmond Hill Ct
5200 DgsC 80108 2618 E6
Richmond Hill Rd
24800 JfnC 80433 2610 B1
25400 JfnC 80433 2526 B7
26900 JfnC 80433 2525 D5
E Richthofen Cir
13700 AURA 80011 2116 B5
Richthofen Pkwy
6500 DNVR 80220 2114 C6
Richthofen Pl
7300 DNVR 80220 2114 D6
8900 AURA 80010 2115 A6
8900 DNVR 80220 2115 A6
Ricki Dr
40900 EbtC 80138 2540 C5
S Riddlewood Ct
800 DgsC 80129 2448 C5
W Riddlewood Ln
800 DgsC 80129 2448 C5
W Riddlewood Rd
900 DgsC 80129 2448 C5
Rider Ridge Dr
500 LGMT 80501 1439 E2
Rider Ridge Pl
700 LGMT 80501 1439 D2
Rider Ridge Rd
600 LGMT 80501 1439 D1
Ridge Av
400 LGMT 80501 1439 B6
Ridge Cir
10 PrkC 80470 2523 B1
2300 BMFD 80020 1774 C6
S Ridge Ct
2400 LITN 80120 2364 B3
Ridge Dr
10 BldC 80304 1602 A3
2100 BMFD 80020 1774 C6
S Ridge Dr
2000 BMFD 80020 1774 C7
Ridge Ln
10 PrkC 80456 2521 E4
Ridge Pkwy
11600 BMFD 80021 1857 B2
11800 SUPE 80027 1857 B2
Ridge Pl
- LSVL 80027 1773 A3
Ridge Plz
2100 DgsC 80108 2618 E4
Ridge Rd
- PrkC 80470 2523 B1
10 BldC 80303 1688 E6
10 BldC 80466 1765 E1
10 CCkC 80439 2272 A7
10 NDLD 80466 1765 E1
100 BldC 80466 1766 A1
100 BldC 80481 1514 E3
100 BldC 80481 1515 A3
400 GOLD 80403 2107 D1
500 CCkC 80439 2271 C6
1000 GOLD 80403 2023 D7
1900 BldC 80466 1682 C7
3800 BldC 80466 1683 A6
4000 JfnC 80403 2108 B1
8400 ARVD 80002 2026 C4
10000 ARVD 80033 2026 A5
10200 WTRG 80033 2026 A5
10400 WTRG 80033 2025 E5
10900 ARVD 80033 2025 E5
12000 BldC 80403 1852 C2
N Ridge Rd
10 CSRK 80104 2704 C7
10 CSRK 80104 2788 D1
10 PrkC 80456 2606 B3
900 DgsC 80104 2704 B6
S Ridge Rd
10 CSRK 80104 2788 D2
10 PrkC 80456 2691 A2
300 PrkC 80456 2690 E2
400 DgsC 80104 2788 D2
3700 JfnC 80439 2273 D4
11800 JfnC 80433 2527 A4
W Ridge Rd
10 CTNL 80122 2364 C4
10 LITN 80120 2364 C4
Ridge Tr
5200 BWMR 80123 2279 B6
5200 DNVR 80236 2279 B6
5200 DvrC 80236 2279 B6
5400 DNVR 80123 2279 B6
5400 DvrC 80123 2279 B6
26900 JfnC 80433 2442 A5
27000 JfnC 80433 2441 E4
Ridge Wy
10 GpnC 80403 1850 D5
24900 JfnC 80401 2190 C1
Ridge Creek Ct
1700 LGMT 80501 1439 E1
Ridgecrest Cir
10500 DgsC 80129 2448 C7
Ridge Crest Ln
7400 JfnC 80465 2359 C6
Ridgecrest Wy
1700 DgsC 80129 2448 B7
Ridgefield Ln
10000 DgsC 80126 2449 D6
Ridgegate Cir
10100 LNTR 80124 2451 A6
Ridgegate Pkwy
- LNTR 80124 2451 A5
E Ridgeglen Wy
400 DgsC 80126 2448 E3
600 DgsC 80126 2449 A3
Ridgeline Blvd
9200 DgsC 80129 2448 D4
S Ridgeline Blvd
8700 DgsC 80129 2448 D3
Ridgemont Cir
500 DgsC 80126 2449 A6
Ridgemont Pl
600 DgsC 80126 2449 A6
Ridge Oaks Dr
1000 CSRK 80104 2788 C1
Ridgepointe Dr
8700 DgsC 80108 2535 A4
8800 DgsC 80108 2534 E4
Ridge Pointe Ln
10800 PARK 80138 2454 B7
Ridgepointe Wy
8800 DgsC 80108 2535 A4
Ridgeside Dr
500 JfnC 80401 2190 C3
Ridge Tee Dr
15800 JfnC 80465 2360 D2
Ridge Top Rd
25300 JfnC 80439 2358 C6
E Ridge Trail Cir
21900 AURA 80016 2370 B2
Ridgetrail Ct
1500 CSRK 80104 2704 A5
Ridgetrail Dr
- CSRK 80104 2703 E5
1900 CSRK 80104 2704 A5
E Ridge Trail Dr
22000 AURA 80016 2370 B2
22600 AphC 80016 2370 B2
Ridgetrail Ln
1600 CSRK 80104 2704 A5
Ridgeview Av
400 BMFD 80020 1774 D6
W Ridgeview Cir
1000 BMFD 80020 1774 D5
7000 DgsC 80135 2700 B6
Ridgeview Ct
11500 PARK 80138 2538 A2
Ridge View Dr
3100 BMFD 80516 1692 A4
3100 ERIE 80516 1692 A4
Ridgeview Dr
500 LSVL 80027 1773 A2
1500 LSVL 80027 1689 B6
1900 LGMT 80501 1438 E6
1900 LGMT 80504 1438 E6
S Ridgeview Dr
6300 JfnC 80465 2359 C4
7200 LITN 80120 2364 B6
Ridgeview Ln
10 BldC 80302 1517 B7
10 BldC 80302 1601 B1
11600 PARK 80138 2538 A2
Ridgeview Tr
10 CCkC 80452 2186 A4
Ridgeview Wy
2000 LGMT 80504 1438 E7
Ridge Village Dr
4100 JfnC 80439 2273 B5
N Ridgeway Cir
6700 DgsC 80134 2622 B1
Ridgewood Ct
4500 CSRK 80109 2702 C2
Riglea Wy
900 BldC 80303 1688 B3
S Rifle Cir
1100 AURA 80017 2201 B4
Rifle Ct
- BldC 80302 1518 C7
S Rifle Ct
800 AURA 80017 2201 A3
3900 AURA 80013 2285 A4
4900 AURA 80015 2285 B6
5400 CTNL 80015 2285 A7
5600 CTNL 80015 2369 A1
6500 AphC 80016 2369 A3
Rifle St
- AdmC 80022 1865 A3
- CMCY 80022 1865 A3
2200 AURA 80011 2117 A3
S Rifle St
900 AURA 80017 2201 A3
2000 AURA 80013 2201 A6
3100 AURA 80013 2285 A2
5400 CTNL 80015 2369 A1
6100 AphC 80016 2369 A2
Rifle Wy
400 BMFD 80020 1775 A4
S Rifle Wy
800 AURA 80017 2201 A3
2100 AURA 80013 2201 A6
4000 AURA 80013 2285 A4
6500 AphC 80016 2369 A3
Rifleman Phillips Campgrnd Rd
- GpnC 80403 1935 E2
- GpnC 80403 1936 A2
Rigdon Ct
- LYNS 80540 1352 D3
Rigel Dr
13000 DgsC 80124 2450 D2
Riggi Pl
4400 CMCY 80022 2029 E1
Riley Ct
- LGMT 80503 1438 A6
Riley Dr
4000 LGMT 80503 1438 A6
Riley Peak Rd
13200 JfnC 80433 2526 D7
N Rim
3200 WldC 80504 1440 D2
S Rim
11200 WldC 80504 1440 D2
Rim Dr
2300 BMFD 80020 1774 C6
Rim Rd
- BldC 80302 1600 A5
10 BldC 80302 1599 E4
E Rim Rd
700 DgsC 80116 2790 A3
Rimrock Cir
2300 LAFT 80026 1689 E4
Rim Rock Ct
5600 BLDR 80301 1604 B1
Rimrock Dr
17200 GOLD 80401 2108 B5
Rim Rock Ln
10 PrkC 80456 2607 D2
Rim Rock Rd
10 PrkC 80456 2607 C3
Rimrock Rd
9100 DgsC 80126 2448 E3
Rimrock St
1700 GOLD 80401 2108 C5
Rim View Pl
5500 DgsC 80134 2621 B3
Rinconada Rd
21800 JfnC 80465 2359 B5
Ringsby Ct
3100 DNVR 80216 2028 E7
3100 DNVR 80216 2112 E1
Rio Ct
1300 DNVR 80204 2112 B5
W Rio Grande Av
4100 DgsC 80135 2617 A5
4500 DgsC 80135 2616 E5
Rio Grande Blvd
10 DNVR 80223 2196 C1
Rio Grande Dr
100 CSRK 80104 2787 D1
Rio Grande St
- BGTN 80601 1697 B6
S Rio Grande St
4900 LITN 80120 2280 B7
5100 LITN 80120 2364 B1
Rio Rancho Wy
500 BGTN 80601 1697 A7
Rising Ln
31000 JfnC 80439 2189 A3
Rising Sun Dr
- CSRK 80104 2704 B4
- CSRK 80108 2704 B4
Rising Sun Rd
10 PrkC 80456 2521 B5
Risky Dr
22900 JfnC 80403 2021 D1
Risky Rd
7300 JfnC 80403 2021 C1
Risse Ct
10 ERIE 80516 1606 E5
Rita Pl
400 DgsC 80108 2534 E5
Ritenour Ct
9200 LNTR 80124 2450 E3
Riva Ridge Dr
10800 PARK 80138 2454 B7
10800 PARK 80138 2538 B1
Riva Ridge St
- PARK 80138 2454 B7
Riva Rose Cir
1200 DgsC 80104 2787 D7
1200 DgsC 80104 2871 D1
River Dr
10 PrkC 80456 2690 C3
W River Dr
2500 DNVR 80211 2112 A4
River Rd
- BldC 80501 1438 E3
- LGMT 80501 1438 E3
23500 JfnC 80433 2694 E4
Rivera St
12500 BMFD 80020 1775 D7
12500 BMFD 80020 1859 D1
S Riverbend Ct
1200 SUPE 80027 1773 A5
S Riverbend Ln
1600 SUPE 80027 1773 B6
Riverbend Rd
4800 BldC 80301 1687 C2
4800 BLDR 80301 1687 C2
E Riverbend St
900 SUPE 80027 1773 B5
E Riverbend Wy
- SUPE 80027 1773 A5
Riverbend Trailer Pth
- LYNS 80540 1352 C1
Riverbrook Cir
10600 DgsC 80126 2449 C7
E River Chase Wy
22500 PARK 80138 2538 C1
Riverdale Av
4800 AdmC 80229 1945 E1
4900 AdmC 80229 1946 A1
Riverdale Dr
11600 PARK 80138 2538 C2
Riverdale Ln
- AdmC 80229 1862 A7
5200 AdmC 80229 1946 A1
Riverdale Rd
8800 AdmC 80229 1945 E2
8900 TNTN 80229 1945 E2
9700 AdmC 80229 1861 E7
9700 TNTN 80229 1861 E7
10100 TNTN 80229 1862 A4
10300 TNTN 80233 1862 A4
10800 AdmC 80233 1862 A4
11200 AdmC 80602 1862 D2
12300 AdmC 80601 1778 E6
12300 AdmC 80602 1778 E6
12600 TNTN 80602 1778 E6
13200 AdmC 80601 1779 B4
13200 AdmC 80602 1779 B4
13500 AdmC 80602 1695 D7
Riverdale Wy
- PARK 80138 2538 C2
5200 AdmC 80229 1862 A7
River Glen Ct
- BMFD 80020 1776 A4
River Rock Ln
5000 BMFD 80020 1775 B4
River Run Cir
11400 CMCY 80640 1863 C2
River Run Ct
11500 CMCY 80640 1863 D3
River Run Pkwy
11200 CMCY 80640 1863 C3
River Run Pl
11300 CMCY 80640 1863 C2
Riverside Av
1900 BldC 80304 1602 D4
1900 BLDR 80304 1602 D4
Riverside Dr
600 BLDR 80302 1686 B2
2200 IDSP 80452 2101 D5
2900 IDSP 80452 2102 A5
Riverside Ln
10 BldC 80481 1515 A1
2000 BldC 80304 1602 D4
2000 BLDR 80304 1602 D4
Riverstone Dr
10100 PARK 80134 2453 A5
Riverton Rd
300 LAFT 80026 1690 C6
Riverview Ct
200 BldC 80501 1440 A3
200 LGMT 80501 1440 A3
River View Dr
- BMFD 80020 1775 E4
S Riverview Dr
2600 JfnC 80465 2275 B1
W Riverview Pkwy
8300 DgsC 80125 2447 D2
W Riverwalk Cir
- LITN 80123 2280 A7
2900 LITN 80123 2364 A1
River Walk Ln
2000 LGMT 80504 1438 D7
S Riviera Cir
5200 AphC 80015 2286 B7
Riviera Ct
10 CBVL 80123 2363 D4
N Riviera Ct
6200 DgsC 80134 2622 E2
S Riviera Ct
5100 AphC 80015 2286 B7
5800 CTNL 80015 2370 B2
6200 AURA 80016 2370 B2

STREET
Block City ZIP Map# Grid

S Riviera Ln
5300 AphC 80015 2286 B7
Riviera Pl
2200 LGMT 80501 1438 D1
2200 LGMT 80503 1438 D1
S Riviera St
4000 AURA 80018 2286 B4
6900 AURA 80016 2370 B4
S Riviera Wy
- AURA 80015 2370 B3
5400 AphC 80015 2286 A7
5400 CTNL 80015 2286 A7
5700 AphC 80015 2370 B1
5700 CTNL 80015 2370 B1
6500 AURA 80016 2370 B3
Riviera Hills Dr
9300 GDVL 80111 2283 A7
Road 11A
- GpnC 80403 1850 D5
Road 11B
- GpnC 80403 1850 D4
Road 11C
- GpnC 80403 1850 E4
Road 878
- PrkC 80456 2521 C4
Road A
- EbtC 80107 2793 B2
- PrkC 80470 2522 E1
- PrkC 80470 2523 A1
S Road A
4900 JfnC 80439 2273 E7
Road B
10 PrkC 80470 2523 A2
Road C
10 PrkC 80470 2523 A2
Road D
10 PrkC 80470 2523 A2
Road P53
400 PrkC 80456 2521 A4
Road P60
10 PrkC 80456 2521 B4
Road P61
10 PrkC 80456 2521 A4
Road P62
- PrkC 80456 2521 A4
Road P69
10 PrkC 80456 2521 B4
Road P70
10 PrkC 80456 2521 C4
Road P79
10 PrkC 80456 2521 C4
W Roadrunner Ct
1400 DgsC 80129 2448 C3
S Roadrunner Dr
9100 DgsC 80129 2448 B3
S Roadrunner St
9100 DgsC 80129 2448 B3
W Roadrunner Wy
1500 DgsC 80129 2448 C4
Roan Ct
16300 PARK 80134 2452 E7
Roan Dr
29100 JfnC 80439 2273 B3
Roan Pl
16400 PARK 80134 2452 E7
S Roan Rd
3100 JfnC 80439 2273 B3
W Roanoke Pl
4100 DNVR 80236 2279 D5
12800 JfnC 80465 2277 C5
Roaring Fork Cir
14000 BMFD 80020 1775 C4
Roaring Fork Ct
- DNVR 80237 2282 C6
Roaring Fork Tr
6800 BldC 80301 1604 B2
Robb Cir
2800 LKWD 80215 2109 E2
3100 WTRG 80033 2109 E2
8400 ARVD 80005 1941 E4
10500 WSTR 80021 1857 D5
Robb Ct
2500 LKWD 80215 2109 E3
5900 ARVD 80004 2025 E3
7600 ARVD 80005 1941 E6
10400 WSTR 80021 1857 E6
S Robb Ct
1300 JfnC 80232 2193 E5
6000 JfnC 80127 2361 E2
Robb Dr
7200 ARVD 80005 1941 E7
10400 WSTR 80021 1857 D6
S Robb Ln
6600 JfnC 80127 2361 E4
Robb Pkwy
8000 ARVD 80005 1941 E5
8000 JfnC 80005 1941 E5
Robb St
2500 LKWD 80215 2109 E3
3800 WTRG 80033 2109 E1
4800 ARVD 80033 2025 E5
4800 WTRG 80033 2025 E6
6000 ARVD 80004 2025 E3
6900 ARVD 80004 1941 E7
7600 ARVD 80005 1941 E6
10200 WSTR 80021 1857 E7
S Robb St
1600 JfnC 80232 2193 E6
4400 JfnC 80127 2277 E6
5600 JfnC 80127 2361 E2
Robb Wy
7400 ARVD 80005 1941 E7
S Robb Wy
300 LKWD 80226 2193 E2
1500 JfnC 80232 2193 E5
1900 LKWD 80227 2193 E6
4900 JfnC 80127 2277 E7
6000 JfnC 80127 2361 E3
Roberts Av
9600 BldC 80027 1689 D5
9600 LAFT 80027 1689 D5
Roberts Rd
31100 JfnC 80470 2524 E7
31100 JfnC 80470 2525 A7

Roberts-Dale Ct
- AURA 80016 2371 C6
S Robertsdale Dr
- AURA 80016 2371 C2
Robertsdale St
- DNVR 80249 1951 C6
Robin Ct
- BldC 80301 1603 D7
9600 DgsC 80125 2531 B7
33500 EbtC 80107 2793 D1
Robin Dr
800 LAFT 80026 1690 D5
6300 BldC 80503 1520 A3
Robin Ln
10 PrkC 80456 2691 D2
600 BGTN 80601 1696 C4
7800 AdmC 80221 1944 A5
E Robin Rd
7500 DgsC 80138 2454 A6
Robin St
- LAFT 80026 1690 C6
Robin Wy
3000 AphC 80222 2282 B2
Robin Cove
800 LAFT 80026 1690 D5
Robincrest Ln
10 AphC 80123 2363 C4
Robindale Wy
- CSRK 80109 2702 D4
Robin Hood St
1300 LAFT 80026 1690 D6
Robins Dr
12900 DNVR 80239 2032 A4
Robinson Pl
4500 BldC 80301 1603 E3
4500 BldC 80301 1604 A3
Robinson Wy
7400 ARVD 80003 2026 D3
7400 ARVD 80004 2026 D3
Robinson Hill Rd
10 GpnC 80403 2019 B4
1400 GpnC 80403 2020 A6
30000 JfnC 80403 2021 A6
E Robinson Ranch Blvd
12500 DgsC 80134 2537 E4
S Robinson Ranch Ct
12500 DgsC 80134 2537 E5
S Robinson Ranch Dr
12500 DgsC 80134 2537 E4
Rob Lou Dr
33700 JfnC 80470 2524 B6
Rob Roy Rd
- EGLD 80110 2280 C2
Roca Pl
300 DgsC 80108 2619 A5
Rock Av
100 JfnC 80401 2191 A1
Rock Ln
10 CSRK 80104 2703 E6
12300 BldC 80504 1357 A4
12300 LGMT 80501 1357 A4
Rock Pt
- BMFD 80020 1775 E5
Rock Rd
10 PrkC 80456 2521 C5
Rock St
- BGTN 80601 1697 A7
10 CSRK 80104 2703 E6
Rockaway Av
10 CSRK 80104 2704 E6
Rockbridge Cir
2700 DgsC 80129 2448 A2
Rockbridge Dr
2400 DgsC 80129 2448 A3
Rockbridge Wy
2500 DgsC 80129 2448 A3
Rock Brook Blvd
- DgsC 80134 2453 B5
- PARK 80134 2453 B5
Rock Canyon Ln
5300 JfnC 80465 2360 D1
Rock Creek Cir
- BMFD 80021 1773 B7
- SUPE 80027 1773 B7
1200 BldC 80020 1774 E1
1200 LAFT 80026 1774 E1
Rock Creek Ct
1100 LAFT 80026 1690 E7
Rock Creek Dr
3000 BMFD 80020 1774 B6
4900 CSRK 80109 2702 D1
S Rock Creek Dr
5600 CSRK 80109 2702 C2
Rock Creek Pkwy
1000 SUPE 80027 1772 E5
1000 SUPE 80027 1773 A4
S Rock Creek Pkwy
- SUPE 80027 1773 A5
2400 BMFD 80021 1773 B7
Rock Creek Rd
34000 JfnC 80470 2524 B3
Rock Cress Wy
- DgsC 80108 2534 D5
Rockcress Wy
2100 JfnC 80401 2190 D7
Rock Crystal Dr
15900 DgsC 80134 2452 D4
Rockdale Pl
23300 PARK 80138 2538 D3
Rockdale St
12000 PARK 80138 2538 D3
S Rock Dove Ln
9700 DgsC 80129 2448 A5
Rock Gulch Rd
10 CCkC 80439 2271 C6
E Rockhampton Cir
5300 DgsC 80130 2450 B4
S Rockhampton Wy
9600 DgsC 80130 2450 A4
Rockies Ct
1700 LAFT 80026 1689 E1
Rock Knoll Dr
10 CCkC 80439 2187 E4

Rock Lake Rd
200 BldC 80481 1515 A2
900 BldC 80481 1514 E3
W Rockland Dr
10300 JfnC 80127 2446 A2
10800 JfnC 80127 2445 E1
W Rockland Pl
6800 JfnC 80128 2447 A1
9000 JfnC 80128 2446 C1
10300 JfnC 80127 2446 A1
Rockland Rd
23600 JfnC 80401 2190 D2
Rock Ledge Ln
6200 JfnC 80465 2360 D3
Rockledge Cove
16700 DgsC 80134 2452 C6
Rock Mesa Pt
- CSRK 80108 2703 D1
Rock Mesa Wy
- CSRK 80108 2703 E1
Rockmont Cir
1400 BLDR 80305 1770 D1
Rockmont Ct
15500 DgsC 80134 2452 D5
Rockmont Dr
3300 DNVR 80211 2112 C2
Rockmont Ln
15600 DgsC 80134 2452 D5
Rockmount Dr
3300 DNVR 80211 2112 C2
W Rock Oak Cir
7000 DgsC 80135 2700 B6
E Rock Pipit Ct
4700 DgsC 80126 2450 A3
S Rockport Ln
9200 DgsC 80126 2449 D3
Rock Rose Ct
800 LSVL 80027 1689 A7
10000 DgsC 80134 2452 D5
Rockrose Dr
23700 JfnC 80401 2190 E5
Rockspray Ct
2100 LGMT 80503 1355 C5
Rockview Cir
1500 SUPE 80027 1772 E6
Rockview Dr
200 SUPE 80027 1772 E5
200 SUPE 80027 1773 A4
Rockway Pl
700 BldC 80303 1688 E4
Rockwood Tr
20300 JfnC 80465 2443 D2
Rock Wren
11100 DgsC 80125 2530 D7
Rocky Wy
10 BldC 80403 1852 A1
N Rocky Cliff Pl
10 DgsC 80116 2707 E7
Rocky Cliff Rd
- DgsC 80116 2707 E4
- EbtC 80107 2791 E1
10 EbtC 80107 2707 E7
10 EbtC 80107 2708 A7
N Rocky Cliff Tr
10 DgsC 80116 2707 D7
10 DgsC 80116 2791 E1
Rocky Knob Ln
10 BldC 80466 1682 E6
Rocky Mountain Dr
5000 CSRK 80109 2702 C2
8000 LKWD 80214 2110 D4
Rocky Mountain Ln
9000 DgsC 80138 2538 D4
Rocky Mountain Pl
700 LGMT 80501 1439 D2
Rocky Point Ln
16400 JfnC 80465 2360 D3
Rocky Ridge Rd
13500 JfnC 80127 2528 B7
13500 JfnC 80127 2611 E1
13500 JfnC 80127 2612 A1
Rocky Top Tr
11100 JfnC 80127 2528 B7
11100 JfnC 80127 2612 A1
N Rocky View Rd
1500 CSRK 80104 2704 D5
1500 CSRK 80108 2704 D5
Rodeo Cir
11000 PARK 80138 2537 E1
Rodeo Ct
400 NDLD 80466 1765 D3
1200 LGMT 80503 1438 C5
44000 EbtC 80107 2543 B1
Rodeo Dr
7400 BldC 80504 1522 D3
Rodeo Pl
- TNTN 80229 1861 E7
Roder Gate Ln
10 DgsC 80108 2534 D6
Rodriquez Ct
1100 LGMT 80501 1356 A7
1100 LGMT 80501 1439 A1
Roe Cir
9400 DgsC 80116 2706 E7
Rogers Cir
6000 ARVD 80403 2024 C3
Rogers Ct
10 JfnC 80401 2192 C1
1500 JfnC 80401 2108 C5
5500 JfnC 80403 2024 C4
6100 ARVD 80403 2024 C3
6400 ARVD 80007 2024 C2
Rogers Rd
10 PrkC 80456 2521 D2
4000 LGMT 80503 1437 E3
4000 LGMT 80503 1438 A3
5000 BldC 80503 1436 B3
8300 BldC 80501 1438 C3
8300 BldC 80503 1438 C3
E Rogers Rd
10 LGMT 80501 1439 C3
200 BldC 80501 1439 C3
Rogers St
1400 JfnC 80401 2108 C5

Rogers St
6300 ARVD 80007 2024 C2
6300 JfnC 80007 2024 C2
6300 JfnC 80403 2024 C2
7600 ARVD 80007 1940 C6
7600 JfnC 80007 1940 C6
S Rogers Wy
10 JfnC 80401 2192 C2
E Roggen Wy
900 SUPE 80027 1773 A5
Roland Dr
10 PrkC 80456 2607 D5
Roland Valley Dr
- PrkC 80456 2607 B3
Rolfe Ct
3900 WTRG 80033 2109 E1
Rolling Hills Dr
- FLHT 80260 1944 B3
Rolling Hills Pl
- DgsC 80138 2455 E3
200 EbtC 80138 2456 A3
16700 PARK 80134 2537 A2
Rollins Dr
7500 DgsC 80118 2954 D2
Rollins Pass Rd
10 GpnC 80474 1849 D2
S Rollinsville Rd
600 NDLD 80466 1765 C4
S Rollinsville St
400 NDLD 80466 1765 C3
Roma Ct
1700 LGMT 80503 1438 A6
Roman Nose Dr
23800 JfnC 80433 2526 D2
Romblon Wy
10400 NHGN 80234 1860 B6
Rome Av
10 EbtC 80138 2539 E6
200 EbtC 80138 2540 A6
S Rome Cir
5300 AphC 80015 2286 B7
S Rome Ct
- AURA 80016 2370 B3
5800 CTNL 80015 2370 B2
S Rome St
4000 AURA 80018 2286 B4
5200 AphC 80015 2286 B7
5600 AphC 80015 2370 B1
5600 CTNL 80015 2370 B1
6600 AURA 80016 2370 B4
S Rome Wy
3500 AURA 80018 2286 B3
5500 AphC 80015 2370 C1
Romer Ranch Rd
- PrkC 80456 2521 D5
Rona Ct
- BldC 80302 1518 C7
Ronald Ln
10400 NHGN 80234 1860 C6
Ronnie Rd
10 BldC 80403 1852 A2
100 GpnC 80403 1851 E2
S Roon Rd
2600 JfnC 80439 2273 B1
Rooney Rd
10 GOLD 80401 2192 B1
10 JfnC 80401 2192 B1
S Rooney Rd
- JfnC 80228 2192 C7
- LKWD 80228 2192 C7
100 GOLD 80401 2192 B2
100 JfnC 80401 2192 B2
100 LKWD 80401 2192 B3
1300 JfnC 80465 2192 C6
1900 LKWD 80465 2192 C7
2800 JfnC 80228 2276 D2
2800 JfnC 80465 2276 D2
2800 LKWD 80228 2276 D1
2800 MRSN 80228 2276 D2
2800 MRSN 80465 2276 D2
Roosevelt Av
- AdmC 80102 2124 D1
100 LSVL 80027 1773 D1
400 BNNT 80102 2124 D1
2400 TNTN 80229 1945 C2
N Roosevelt Av
100 LAFT 80026 1690 C4
S Roosevelt Av
100 LAFT 80026 1690 C5
100 LSVL 80027 1773 D1
Roosevelt Ln
12500 DgsC 80112 2451 E4
12500 DgsC 80112 2452 A4
Roosevelt Wy
1500 AURA 80011 2117 A4
Rosalie Dr
10600 NHGN 80233 1861 A5
Rosalie Rd
10 PrkC 80456 2607 A5
Rosalie Tr
26200 JfnC 80401 2190 A1
Rose Ct
800 BGTN 80601 1696 D7
800 BGTN 80601 1780 D1
9200 TNTN 80229 1945 A1
Rose Dr
600 BGTN 80601 1696 D7
Rose Ln
1700 BGTN 80601 1696 D7
5800 CMCY 80022 2030 B3
Rose St
100 LSVL 80027 1773 D1
900 LGMT 80501 1438 E1
Roseanna Dr
1100 NHGN 80234 1860 C5
E Rosebay Cir
17000 PARK 80134 2453 A4
Rosebud Av
28300 JfnC 80439 2357 D3
Rosebud Pl
8600 DgsC 80134 2452 E2
Rose Clover
10 JfnC 80127 2360 E5

Rosecrown Av
- CSRK 80109 2702 D1
Rosedale Ct
900 CSRK 80104 2788 E1
Rosedale St
1000 CSRK 80104 2788 E1
W Rose Finch Cir
300 DgsC 80129 2448 E6
Rosehill Dr
1000 BLDR 80302 1686 B4
Rose Hip Ln
10 CCkC 80439 2187 E5
Roseland Av
- BldC 80504 1356 A3
S Rosemary Cir
7500 CTNL 80112 2366 D6
Rosemary Ct
1500 CSRK 80109 2703 B4
S Rosemary Ct
8000 CTNL 80112 2366 D7
Rosemary Dr
1200 CSRK 80109 2703 B4
Rosemary Ln
2600 AdmC 80221 2028 A4
Rosemary St
- TNTN 80602 1778 D6
1100 DNVR 80220 2114 D6
1100 DNVR 80230 2114 D6
2200 DNVR 80207 2114 D3
2200 DNVR 80238 2114 D3
8000 AdmC 80022 1946 D4
8000 CMCY 80022 1946 D4
8700 AdmC 80640 1946 D4
8700 CMCY 80640 1946 D4
S Rosemary St
10 DNVR 80230 2198 D1
900 DNVR 80220 2114 D6
900 DNVR 80230 2114 D6
1600 AphC 80231 2198 D5
1600 DNVR 80231 2198 D5
2900 DNVR 80231 2282 D2
S Rosemary Wy
- DNVR 80247 2198 D4
1100 AphC 80231 2198 D4
1100 DNVR 80231 2198 D4
3700 DNVR 80237 2282 D4
7700 CTNL 80112 2366 E6
S Rosemont Av
- LNTR 80124 2450 E5
9700 LNTR 80124 2451 A5
Rose Petal Ct
1800 CSRK 80109 2703 A4
Rose Petal Ln
1400 CSRK 80109 2703 B4
Rose Quartz Pl
400 CSRK 80108 2619 D7
N Rose Ridge Rd
13500 DgsC 80138 2455 A1
13800 DgsC 80138 2454 E1
W Rosewalk Cir
3600 DgsC 80129 2447 E5
W Rosewalk Ct
3700 DgsC 80129 2447 E5
S Rosewalk Dr
9800 DgsC 80129 2447 E5
Rosewind Cir
1200 DgsC 80104 2871 D4
Rosewood Av
1000 BLDR 80304 1602 B3
S Rosewood Cir
6100 CTNL 80121 2365 A2
Rosewood Ct
9300 DgsC 80126 2449 A4
19600 DgsC 80138 2453 D7
19600 PARK 80138 2453 D7
Rosewood Dr
2000 LKWD 80215 2109 C4
S Rosewood Dr
6100 CTNL 80121 2365 A2
Rosewood St
1000 BLDR 80304 1602 C4
Roslyn Cir
2000 DNVR 80207 2114 D4
2000 DNVR 80220 2114 D4
S Roslyn Cir
6800 CTNL 80112 2366 D4
S Roslyn Ct
900 DNVR 80220 2114 D6
900 DNVR 80230 2114 D6
7600 CTNL 80112 2366 D6
Roslyn St
- TNTN 80602 1778 D6
100 DNVR 80230 2198 D1
900 DNVR 80220 2114 D6
1100 DNVR 80230 2114 D6
2200 DNVR 80207 2114 D3
2400 DNVR 80238 2114 D3
5400 AdmC 80022 2030 D4
5400 DNVR 80022 2030 D4
5400 DNVR 80216 2030 D4
7800 AdmC 80022 1946 C5
8400 CMCY 80022 1946 D4
S Roslyn St
- DNVR 80224 2282 D3
- DNVR 80231 2282 D1
- DNVR 80237 2282 D3
100 DNVR 80230 2198 D1
1500 DNVR 80231 2198 D5
2500 AphC 80231 2198 D7
2500 AphC 80231 2282 D1
5300 GDVL 80111 2282 D7
S Roslyn Wy
3600 DNVR 80237 2282 D3
7900 CTNL 80112 2366 D7
Ross Ct
10600 WSTR 80021 1857 E5
E Ross Ln
1700 DgsC 80126 2449 B3
Ross Pl
10500 WSTR 80021 1857 E5
S Ross Rd
6200 JfnC 80465 2359 D3
Ross St
10500 WSTR 80021 1857 E5

Rossman Gulch Rd
7200 BldC 80465 2358 E7
7200 JfnC 80465 2359 A7
7200 JfnC 80465 2442 E1
7200 JfnC 80465 2443 A1
Rotherwood Cir
10200 DgsC 80130 2450 A6
Rothrock Pl
100 LGMT 80501 1439 C2
Rough Ct
1800 CSRK 80109 2703 B5
S Round Rock St
8900 DgsC 80126 2448 E2
Round Table Dr
10 LAFT 80026 1690 E6
Roundtop Ln
800 DgsC 80108 2619 C3
E Roundtree Av
8700 GDVL 80111 2366 E2
8700 GDVL 80111 2367 A2
Roundtree Ct
3600 BLDR 80304 1602 E6
S Round Tree Dr
9100 DgsC 80126 2449 D3
Roundup Pl
900 LGMT 80501 1356 E4
N Roundup Rd
12200 DgsC 80138 2455 D2
Routt Cir
2900 LKWD 80215 2109 E2
Routt Ct
5800 ARVD 80002 2025 E3
5800 ARVD 80004 2025 E3
7600 ARVD 80005 1941 E6
10700 WSTR 80021 1857 E5
S Routt Ct
800 LKWD 80226 2193 E4
1900 LKWD 80227 2193 E6
1900 LKWD 80228 2193 E6
4700 JfnC 80127 2277 E6
Routt Dr
7200 ARVD 80005 1941 E7
Routt Ln
7400 ARVD 80005 1941 E6
N Routt Ln
10400 WSTR 80021 1857 D6
Routt St
3100 LKWD 80215 2109 E2
3200 WTRG 80033 2109 E2
4500 WTRG 80033 2025 E6
6700 ARVD 80004 2025 E1
7000 ARVD 80004 1941 E7
7300 ARVD 80005 1941 E7
8000 JfnC 80005 1941 D5
N Routt St
10500 WSTR 80021 1857 E5
S Routt St
4400 JfnC 80127 2277 E6
5600 JfnC 80127 2361 E2
NW Routt Wy
10500 WSTR 80021 1857 D5
S Routt Wy
400 LKWD 80226 2193 E2
700 LKWD 80228 2193 E3
1100 JfnC 80232 2193 E4
5300 JfnC 80127 2361 E1
Rowena Pl
100 LAFT 80026 1689 E4
Rowena St
1100 TNTN 80229 1945 A1
W Rowland Av
2400 LITN 80120 2364 A5
6600 JfnC 80128 2363 A5
6800 JfnC 80128 2362 E5
10600 JfnC 80127 2362 A5
11000 JfnC 80127 2361 E5
E Rowland Cir
21700 AURA 80016 2370 B5
W Rowland Cir
6300 JfnC 80128 2363 A5
E Rowland Dr
- AURA 80016 2370 B5
W Rowland Dr
11000 JfnC 80127 2361 E5
E Rowland Pl
24700 AURA 80016 2370 B5
24700 AURA 80016 2371 A4
W Rowland Pl
2800 LITN 80120 2364 A5
5200 AphC 80128 2363 B5
8600 JfnC 80128 2362 C5
10500 JfnC 80127 2362 A5
Rowlock Pl
10000 DgsC 80134 2452 D5
Rowlock Wy
10200 DgsC 80134 2452 D6
Roworth St
200 CLCY 80403 2017 C5
Roxana Pointe
25600 JfnC 80439 2274 C3
Roxborough Dr
- DgsC 80125 2699 B1
6100 DgsC 80125 2615 A3
6500 DgsC 80125 2614 D1
Roxborough Dr N
- DgsC 80125 2530 D7
- DgsC 80125 2614 D1
N Roxborough Park Rd
6200 DgsC 80125 2531 C5
6200 DgsC 80125 2615 B3
10800 DgsC 80125 2447 C7
W Roxbury Av
- JfnC 80128 2362 B5
6800 JfnC 80128 2363 A5
10000 JfnC 80127 2362 B5
11000 JfnC 80127 2361 E5
E Roxbury Cir
24200 AURA 80016 2370 E5
E Roxbury Dr
- AURA 80016 2370 C5
W Roxbury Dr
6300 JfnC 80128 2363 A5
8700 JfnC 80128 2362 C5
11400 JfnC 80127 2361 E5

Roxbury Ln
10 BldC 80302 1516 E7
E Roxbury Pl
24500 AURA 80016 2370 E5
24900 AURA 80016 2371 A5
W Roxbury Pl
5800 JfnC 80128 2363 B5
7000 JfnC 80128 2362 E5
10200 JfnC 80127 2362 A5
11400 JfnC 80127 2361 E5
Roxwood Ln
800 BLDR 80303 1687 D4
Royal Ct
10 PrkC 80456 2521 A3
12800 BMFD 80020 1775 E7
Royal Dr
10 PrkC 80456 2521 A3
Royal Ln
100 PrkC 80456 2521 A3
Royal St
10 LGMT 80501 1439 A3
9000 FLHT 80260 1944 B2
Royal Arch Wy
- BMFD 80020 1775 D6
S Royal Eagle Ln
10000 DgsC 80129 2448 D6
Royal Eagle Rd
- DgsC 80129 2448 D6
S Royal Eagle St
10200 DgsC 80129 2448 D6
Royal Gorge Ct
- DNVR 80237 2282 E5
E Royal Meadows Av
23900 PARK 80138 2538 E1
Royal Pine St
5500 BGTN 80601 1697 E5
Royal Ridge Dr
- PrkC 80456 2521 A3
Royal Troon Dr
1200 CSRK 80104 2787 E2
Roy Clarke Blvd
11100 DgsC 80138 2454 D6
Roy Smith Rd
- GpnC 80403 2017 A6
Rozena Dr
7000 BldC 80503 1354 C5
Rubey Dr
10 GOLD 80403 2107 C2
N Rubey Dr
100 GOLD 80403 2107 C2
Ruby Ln
6800 DgsC 80138 2623 C1
Ruby St
4400 BldC 80304 1602 D4
Ruby Wy
1300 LGMT 80504 1439 A6
3100 SUPE 80027 1857 A1
Ruby Forest Tr
300 JfnC 80439 2188 E3
E Ruby Ranch Pl
20000 DgsC 80134 2537 E5
Ruby Ranch Rd
29600 JfnC 80401 2189 A3
29600 JfnC 80439 2189 A3
31200 JfnC 80439 2188 E3
Ruby Trust Ct
600 DgsC 80108 2619 A6
Ruby Trust Dr
600 DgsC 80108 2619 A6
Ruby Trust Wy
600 DgsC 80108 2619 A6
S Rudd Rd
8700 JfnC 80439 2441 E3
Rudi Ln
10 BldC 80403 1852 A2
100 GpnC 80403 1851 E2
Rudi Ln W
10 GpnC 80403 1852 A2
Rudin Cir
29200 JfnC 80439 2189 C6
Rue de Trust
1000 WldC 80516 1607 D2
Rufous Wy
- LAFT 80026 1689 D2
Ruger Ct
36800 EbtC 80107 2708 E2
Rumbling Sky Pl
- CSRK 80108 2703 E1
Running Brook Ln
35300 EbtC 80107 2709 D5
Running Brook Rd
2800 EbtC 80107 2709 B1
Running Buffalo Rd
9600 DgsC 80116 2790 E6
9600 DgsC 80116 2791 A7
Running Creek Ln
11500 PARK 80138 2537 E2
Running Creek Ranch Rd
- EbtC 80107 2457 E6
- EbtC 80107 2458 A6
- EbtC 80107 2542 A1
- EbtC 80138 2457 E6
- EbtC 80138 2542 A1
Running Deer Dr
3100 CSRK 80109 2702 C3
Running Deer Rd
23700 JfnC 80433 2526 D3
Running Fox Cir
- EbtC 80107 2625 E3
- EbtC 80107 2626 A3
Running Fox Wy
7700 DgsC 80134 2622 A4
Rushmore
3300 WldC 80504 1440 D2
Rushmore St
100 EbtC 80107 2709 A7
100 ELIZ 80107 2709 A7
Russel Gulch Rd
- GpnC 80403 2017 A7
S Russell Av
9500 JfnC 80433 2442 A4
Russell Blvd
300 TNTN 80229 1944 E2
700 TNTN 80229 1945 A2

STREET Block City ZIP Map# Grid

Russell Ct
6100 ARVD 80403 2024 C3
7000 ARVD 80007 1940 C7
7200 JfnC 80007 1940 C7
S Russell Ct
10 JfnC 80401 2192 C1
Russell Ln
6000 ARVD 80403 2024 C3
Russell St
800 GOLD 80401 2108 C6
1400 JfnC 80401 2108 C5
6000 ARVD 80403 2024 C3
6000 JfnC 80403 2024 C3
Russell Wy
1400 TNTN 80229 1945 B2
6400 ARVD 80007 2024 C2
Russell Gulch Rd
10 GpnC 80403 2017 B7
S Russell Gulch Rd
3300 JfnC 80439 2274 A3
N Russellville Rd
10 DgsC 80116 2790 D1
100 DgsC 80116 2706 C7
N Russellville Rd CO-69
10 DgsC 80116 2790 D1
100 DgsC 80116 2706 C7
S Russellville Rd
10 DgsC 80116 2790 E1
500 DgsC 80116 2791 B5
S Russellville Rd CO-69
10 DgsC 80116 2790 E1
500 DgsC 80116 2791 A4
S Russet Ln
8300 DgsC 80126 2449 C1
Russian Sage Ln
9600 DgsC 80138 2538 E2
E Rustic Dr
6500 DgsC 80138 2453 D6
6500 PARK 80138 2453 D6
Rustic Tr
4400 BldC 80301 1604 C3
Rustic Knolls Dr
5700 BldC 80301 1603 D5
Rustic Redwood Ct
10200 DgsC 80126 2449 C6
Rustic Redwood Ln
10200 DgsC 80126 2449 C6
Rustic Redwood Wy
10100 DgsC 80126 2449 C6
Rustler Tr
5200 DgsC 80134 2621 B4
Rustlers Rd
10 PrkC 80456 2522 C4
Rustlers Ravine
- TNTN 80229 1861 E6
Rusty Dawn Cir
500 DgsC 80104 2871 B1
N Rutgers Ct
11000 WSTR 80031 1859 D4
W Rutgers Pl
3800 DNVR 80236 2279 D5
Rutgers Rd
3700 LGMT 80503 1355 A7
Rutgers St
8300 AdmC 80031 1943 C4
Ruth Dr
1100 TNTN 80229 1945 A1
Ruth Rd
10 BMFD 80020 1774 E6
Ruth Rd E
10 BMFD 80020 1774 E6
Ruth Wy
6800 AdmC 80221 2028 B1
6900 AdmC 80221 1944 B7
E Rutherford Wy
900 DgsC 80126 2449 A6
Ruxton Ct
17500 PARK 80134 2453 A7
S Ryans Ln
2800 JfnC 80465 2275 C1
Rye Ct
8100 BldC 80503 1520 E4
Rye Gulch Rd
4900 JfnC 80403 2021 C5

S

Sable Blvd
- AdmC 80603 1864 B2
- CMCY 80022 1864 B6
- CMCY 80603 1864 B2
12000 AdmC 80601 1864 B2
12000 BGTN 80601 1864 B2
12000 CMCY 80601 1864 B2
12400 AdmC 80601 1780 B7
12400 BGTN 80601 1780 B7
Sable Blvd SR-2
- AdmC 80603 1864 B2
- CMCY 80603 1864 B2
12000 AdmC 80601 1864 B2
12000 BGTN 80601 1864 B2
12000 CMCY 80601 1864 B2
12400 AdmC 80601 1780 B7
12400 BGTN 80601 1780 B7
N Sable Blvd
10 AURA 80011 2200 C1
10 AURA 80012 2200 C1
1300 AURA 80011 2116 C6
3800 AURA 80011 2032 B7
S Sable Blvd
10 AURA 80011 2200 C2
10 AURA 80012 2200 C2
2200 AURA 80014 2200 B7
S Sable Cir
3900 AURA 80014 2284 C4
Sable Ct
- DgsC 80118 2870 A7
Sable Rd
- DgsC 80118 2870 A7
- DgsC 80118 2954 A1
Sable St
5500 DNVR 80239 2032 B4
S Sable Wy
2500 AURA 80014 2200 C7

S Sable Wy
2500 AURA 80014 2284 C1
Sable Ridge Rd
37500 EbtC 80107 2625 D7
Saddle Ln
10 PrkC 80456 2690 E2
S Saddle Rd
3400 JfnC 80439 2273 B4
Saddleback Cir
21000 PARK 80138 2538 A2
Saddleback Ct
2400 CSRK 80104 2704 A5
11800 PARK 80138 2538 A2
Saddleback Dr
10 CCkC 80439 2103 C7
10 CCkC 80439 2187 D1
1300 CSRK 80104 2703 E4
1400 CSRK 80104 2704 A4
Saddleback Ln
- BldC 80303 1771 C4
- WSTR 80021 1942 D3
E Saddleback Ranch Pl
20300 DgsC 80134 2537 E5
Saddlebrook Ct
21800 PARK 80138 2454 B7
Saddlebrook Dr
21700 PARK 80138 2454 B7
Saddle Creek Tr
5600 DgsC 80134 2621 E3
5600 DgsC 80134 2622 A3
Saddlehorn Dr
43000 EbtC 80107 2543 A3
Saddle Horn Ln
10 PrkC 80456 2522 C6
S Saddlehorn Ln
10000 DgsC 80130 2450 D5
Saddle Mountain Tr
11700 JfnC 80127 2528 E4
Saddle Ridge Dr
10 CCkC 80439 2187 C1
300 CCkC 80439 2103 C7
Saddle Rock Ln
21200 AURA 80016 2370 A4
E Saddle Rock Ln
21200 AURA 80016 2370 A4
Saddle Rock Tr S
- AphC 80015 2370 B3
- AphC 80016 2370 B3
- AURA 80015 2370 B3
6300 AURA 80016 2370 B3
Saddlestring
10 PrkC 80456 2521 B5
Saddlestring Rd
300 PrkC 80456 2521 B4
Saddletree Cir
42500 EbtC 80138 2539 E5
42500 EbtC 80138 2540 A5
Saddlewood Cir
200 DgsC 80126 2448 E3
Saddlewood Rd
4000 EbtC 80107 2709 C5
E Sadelia Ct
9700 DgsC 80134 2622 E3
Sage Cir
500 DgsC 80126 2449 A2
1900 GOLD 80401 2107 D4
S Sage Cir
3700 JfnC 80439 2273 B4
Sage Ct
4300 BldC 80301 1604 C4
Sage Dr
- BGTN 80601 1697 B5
1900 GOLD 80401 2107 D5
E Sage Ln
6600 DgsC 80138 2453 D2
Sage Pl
700 LGMT 80501 1439 D1
Sage St
900 BMFD 80020 1774 D6
Sage Brush Ct
5000 BMFD 80020 1775 B4
Sagebrush Ct
7900 BldC 80301 1688 E2
W Sagebrush Ct
500 LSVL 80027 1689 B7
Sage Brush Dr
4900 BMFD 80020 1775 C4
Sagebrush Dr
7100 DgsC 80138 2453 E5
7200 DgsC 80138 2454 A5
W Sagebrush Dr
600 LSVL 80027 1689 B7
Sage Brush St
- BGTN 80601 1697 E5
Sagebrush St
10 GOLD 80401 2108 B7
10 GOLD 80401 2192 B2
Sagebrush Tr
9100 LNTR 80124 2450 D3
Sagebrush Wy
1000 LSVL 80027 1689 B7
Sagecrest St
10100 DgsC 80126 2449 E6
Sager Ln
42600 EbtC 80138 2540 D4
W Sage Sparrow Cir
800 DgsC 80129 2448 D6
S Sage Sparrow Ct
10000 DgsC 80129 2448 D5
Sage Thrasher Rd
5100 DgsC 80134 2622 C4
Sage Valley Rd
8800 BldC 80503 1435 C7
Sagewood Ln
11500 PARK 80138 2538 A2
E Sagewood Ln
20400 PARK 80138 2537 E2
20400 PARK 80138 2538 B2
Sagrimore Cir
800 LAFT 80026 1690 E6
E Sagrimore Cir
1500 LAFT 80026 1690 D7
W Sagrimore Cir
1500 LAFT 80026 1690 D6

N Saguaro Ridge Rd
8000 DgsC 80138 2539 C5
Sailor Ct
10300 BldC 80504 1522 A2
St. Andrews Ct
- DgsC 80118 2868 D6
St. Andrews Dr
500 LGMT 80501 1356 D6
1400 BMFD 80020 1775 A5
St. Andrews Ln
500 BldC 80027 1773 B3
600 LSVL 80027 1773 B4
30800 JfnC 80439 2273 A1
E St. Clair Av
100 LGMT 80501 1439 C2
W St. Clair Pl
4400 AdmC 80212 2027 C5
St. Croix St
4100 BldC 80301 1603 A4
4100 BLDR 80301 1603 A4
St. Francis Wy
1000 DNVR 80204 2112 C4
St. Freds Pl
10 CCkC 80439 2187 E5
St. James St
300 CLCY 80403 2017 D3
St. John St
1100 ERIE 80516 1607 A3
St. Johns St
- BldC 80301 1603 B5
- BLDR 80301 1603 B5
St. Lucia St
4000 BLDR 80301 1603 A5
St. Moritz Dr
32600 JfnC 80433 2356 B7
32600 JfnC 80439 2356 B7
St. Moritz Rd
7600 JfnC 80439 2356 B7
St. Paul Cir
11800 TNTN 80233 1861 C2
13100 TNTN 80241 1777 C6
St. Paul Ct
4700 DNVR 80216 2029 D6
9400 TNTN 80229 1945 C1
10600 NHGN 80233 1861 C5
11500 TNTN 80233 1861 C4
12300 TNTN 80241 1861 C1
13100 TNTN 80241 1777 D6
St. Paul Dr
10100 TNTN 80229 1861 C7
13100 TNTN 80241 1777 C6
St. Paul St
- AdmC 80602 1693 C5
100 DNVR 80206 2197 D1
1500 DNVR 80206 2113 D5
2600 DNVR 80205 2113 C3
4000 DNVR 80205 2029 D7
5000 DNVR 80216 2029 C5
9500 TNTN 80229 1945 C1
10000 TNTN 80229 1861 C7
11700 TNTN 80233 1861 C3
13300 TNTN 80241 1777 D5
13800 TNTN 80602 1777 C4
S St. Paul St
1100 DNVR 80209 2197 D5
1100 DNVR 80210 2197 D5
2600 DNVR 80210 2281 D2
7100 CTNL 80122 2365 D5
St. Paul Wy
10800 NHGN 80233 1861 C5
S St. Paul Wy
5900 CTNL 80121 2365 C3
8100 CTNL 80122 2365 D7
8100 CTNL 80122 2449 D1
St. Petersburg St
3900 BLDR 80301 1603 B5
St. Vincent Pl
3200 BLDR 80301 1603 A5
N St. Vrain Dr
16200 BldC 80540 1269 A5
18000 BldC 80540 1352 C1
19500 LYNS 80540 1269 C7
19500 LYNS 80540 1352 C1
N St. Vrain Dr SR-66
19700 BldC 80540 1352 C1
19700 LYNS 80540 1352 C1
N St. Vrain Dr US-36
16200 BldC 80540 1269 A5
18000 BldC 80540 1352 C1
19500 LYNS 80540 1269 C7
19500 LYNS 80540 1352 C1
S St. Vrain Dr
26000 BldC 80540 1352 B3
32900 LYNS 80540 1352 B3
S St. Vrain Dr SR-7
26000 BldC 80540 1352 B3
32900 LYNS 80540 1352 B3
St. Vrain Rd
4300 BldC 80503 1435 E1
4300 BldC 80503 1436 C1
4300 BldC 80504 1435 E1
5700 BldC 80503 1437 B1
7500 BldC 80503 1438 A2
7500 LGMT 80503 1437 D3
7500 LGMT 80503 1438 A2
St. Vrain Tr
10 BldC 80481 1515 A2
St. Vrain Canal Dr
- LYNS 80540 1352 E2
Sakata St
- BGTN 80601 1697 B5
Sal St
700 BldC 80026 1690 D5
700 LAFT 80026 1690 D5
S Salem Cir
1500 AURA 80012 2199 E5
2300 AURA 80014 2199 E7
Salem Ct
- CMCY 80022 1863 E5
500 AURA 80011 2115 E7
S Salem Ct
200 AURA 80012 2200 A1
9600 DgsC 80130 2450 D4

Salem St
200 AURA 80011 2199 E1
400 AURA 80011 2116 A7
1300 AURA 80011 2115 E5
3700 AdmC 80239 2115 E1
3700 AURA 80239 2115 E1
3700 DNVR 80239 2115 E1
3900 DNVR 80239 2031 E7
11300 BGTN 80640 1863 E3
11900 CMCY 80640 1863 E2
12400 AdmC 80640 1779 E7
12400 AdmC 80640 1863 E1
S Salem St
- AURA 80014 2199 E7
300 AURA 80012 2199 E2
S Salem Wy
1400 AURA 80012 2199 E4
S Salford Ln
- DgsC 80129 2448 E4
9500 DgsC 80126 2448 E4
S Salida Cir
1700 AURA 80017 2201 A5
S Salida Ct
1500 AURA 80017 2201 A4
2800 AURA 80013 2285 A1
4700 AURA 80015 2285 B6
5300 CTNL 80015 2285 A7
6000 AphC 80016 2369 B2
7500 CTNL 80016 2369 B6
Salida St
- AdmC 80022 1865 A3
- AURA 80011 2033 A7
1500 AURA 80011 2117 A4
10400 CMCY 80022 1865 A5
S Salida St
900 AURA 80017 2201 A3
2000 AURA 80013 2201 A6
2700 AURA 80013 2285 B1
4500 AURA 80015 2285 A5
5400 CTNL 80015 2369 A1
6300 AphC 80016 2369 B3
6700 FXFD 80016 2369 B4
Salida Wy
600 AURA 80011 2117 A6
S Salida Wy
- AURA 80015 2285 B5
1100 AURA 80017 2201 B4
2300 AURA 80013 2201 B7
3200 AURA 80013 2285 A2
Salina St
100 LAFT 80026 1689 E5
100 LAFT 80026 1690 A4
Salisbury Ct
2000 BldC 80026 1690 A2
Sally Ln
2300 DgsC 80109 2702 B1
E Saltbush Ridge Rd
1400 DgsC 80126 2449 B3
Salugi Rd
22300 JfnC 80454 2359 A1
Salvia Ct
1500 JfnC 80401 2108 C5
5500 JfnC 80403 2024 C4
6100 ARVD 80403 2024 C3
6600 ARVD 80007 2024 C1
7200 ARVD 80007 1940 C7
7200 JfnC 80007 1940 C7
Salvia Ln
6100 ARVD 80403 2024 C2
Salvia St
- ARVD 80403 2024 C2
- JfnC 80007 1940 C7
800 GOLD 80401 2108 C6
1600 JfnC 80401 2108 C5
4100 GOLD 80403 2024 C7
4100 GOLD 80403 2108 C1
4100 JfnC 80403 2024 C7
4100 JfnC 80403 2108 C1
6900 ARVD 80007 2024 C1
7000 ARVD 80007 1940 C7
Salvia Wy
6100 ARVD 80403 2024 C3
Samedi Ranch Rd
12300 JfnC 80127 2528 B4
Samos Cir
1500 LAFT 80026 1690 A7
1500 LSVL 80026 1690 A7
W Sampson Rd
13800 JfnC 80127 2528 E1
15700 JfnC 80127 2444 D7
Samuel Dr
1700 AdmC 80221 1944 B6
2100 WSTR 80030 1944 B6
E Samuel Peak
5500 DgsC 80130 2450 B5
Sanborn Pl
1400 LGMT 80501 1355 E7
Sanborne St
500 CSRK 80104 2705 A7
500 CSRK 80104 2789 B1
Sanctuary Cir
800 LGMT 80501 1356 E6
Sanctuary Ln
700 LGMT 80501 1356 D7
Sand Mtn
7800 JfnC 80127 2362 A7
W Sandbar Cir
500 LSVL 80027 1773 B1
Sand Cherry
10 JfnC 80127 2445 A1
Sandcherry Pl
4000 LGMT 80503 1438 A4
Sand Cherry St
- BGTN 80601 1697 E5
S Sand Cherry Wy
9800 DgsC 80129 2448 C5
Sand Creek Dr
- CMCY 80022 2030 B5
- CMCY 80216 2030 B5
- DNVR 80216 2030 B5
N Sand Creek Dr
- CMCY 80022 2030 B4
Sand Creek Dr S
- CMCY 80022 2030 D6

Sand Creek Dr S
- CMCY 80216 2030 D6
- DNVR 80022 2030 D6
- DNVR 80216 2030 D6
E Sand Creek Rd
9100 DgsC 80138 2454 D4
Sand Dollar Cir
2100 LGMT 80503 1355 B5
Sand Dollar Ct
2900 LGMT 80503 1355 B5
Sand Dollar Dr
2100 LGMT 80503 1355 B5
Sander Rd
10 BldC 80403 1852 A2
S Sanderling Wy
8900 DgsC 80126 2450 A3
8900 DgsC 80130 2450 A3
Sanders Cir
200 ERIE 80516 1607 A6
Sanders Pl
10 BGTN 80601 1696 B7
S Sanders Rd
6200 JfnC 80439 2357 A3
Sandersen Av
- JfnC 80433 2527 A1
Sandhill Ct
9500 DgsC 80126 2450 A4
E Sand Hill Ln
4100 DgsC 80126 2449 E4
S Sand Hill Pl
9400 DgsC 80126 2449 E4
S Sand Hill St
9200 DgsC 80126 2450 A3
9200 DgsC 80130 2450 A3
S Sand Hill Tr
9200 DgsC 80126 2449 E3
S Sand Hill Wy
9300 DgsC 80126 2449 E3
Sandhurst Dr
1900 CSRK 80104 2788 A1
Sandia Ct
31300 JfnC 80439 2188 E5
Sandia Tr
4000 CSRK 80109 2702 D2
Sandler Dr
100 LAFT 80026 1690 C4
W Sandlewood Ct
600 LSVL 80027 1689 A7
Sand Lily Dr
1600 JfnC 80401 2190 D6
E Sand Lily Ln
9600 DgsC 80134 2622 E6
Sandoval St
- BGTN 80601 1697 A5
Sandown Rd
- DNVR 80207 2030 D7
6300 DNVR 80216 2030 C7
Sandpebble Ct
10000 DgsC 80134 2452 C5
E Sandpiper Av
5200 CSRK 80104 2704 E7
Sandpiper Cir
10 TNTN 80241 1777 B6
4400 BldC 80301 1604 B4
Sandpiper Ct
4400 BldC 80301 1604 A3
Sandpiper Dr
2300 LAFT 80026 1689 E5
Sandpiper Ln
1100 BGTN 80601 1779 E1
1100 BGTN 80601 1780 B2
Sandpiper Pl
2900 LGMT 80503 1355 B5
Sandpoint Dr
500 LGMT 80501 1356 D5
Sandra Ln
10 BMFD 80020 1774 E5
Sandra Pl
- BMFD 80020 1774 E5
Sandra Wy
5300 ARVD 80002 2026 B5
Sandra Jean's Wy
14500 WldC 80504 1357 B3
Sandreed Cir
8300 DgsC 80134 2452 E1
8300 PARK 80134 2452 E1
S Sandrock Dr
5800 JfnC 80439 2358 C2
Sand Rose Ct
6300 CSRK 80108 2619 D7
Sandstone Ct
1300 BLDR 80305 1770 E1
Sandstone Dr
- BldC 80540 1352 B4
- LGMT 80504 1440 D3
16000 JfnC 80465 2360 D3
Sandstone Run
10500 DgsC 80125 2614 E4
Sandstone Wy
900 SUPE 80027 1857 A1
Sandtrap Cir
13800 BMFD 80020 1775 D4
Sandtrap Ct
13800 BMFD 80020 1775 D4
Sandtrap Ln
- BMFD 80020 1775 D4
Sandtrap Wy
15700 JfnC 80465 2360 E2
Sand Wedge Wy
1500 CSRK 80104 2787 E2
Sandy Cir
1600 WldC 80516 1607 E1
Sandy Dr
10 BldC 80302 1684 E2
S Sandy Ln
9200 JfnC 80433 2440 D4
Sandy Creek Ln
11500 PARK 80138 2537 E2
Sandy Lake Rd
10 CHLV 80113 2281 C4
Sandy Ridge Rd
2000 EbtC 80107 2792 D7
2000 EbtC 80107 2793 A7

S Sandy Ridge Rd
2700 DgsC 80135 2785 C7
Sanford Cir E
5200 CHLV 80113 2282 A4
Sanford Cir W
4900 CHLV 80113 2282 A4
S Sanger Av
12600 JfnC 80470 2524 C6
Sanger Dr
29200 JfnC 80401 2189 B2
Sanger Wy
7500 JfnC 80465 2359 B6
S Sangre de Cristo Rd
7500 JfnC 80127 2362 B7
8200 JfnC 80127 2446 A1
W Sanibel Ct
1900 LITN 80120 2364 B7
San Isabel Rd
23400 JfnC 80439 2274 D5
Sanitas Valley Tr
- BldC 80304 1602 A7
- BldC 80304 1686 A1
- BLDR 80304 1686 A1
San Joaquin Rdg
11200 JfnC 80127 2361 E7
W San Juan Cir
9500 JfnC 80128 2446 B2
San Juan Ct
10700 PARK 80138 2454 B7
W San Juan Dr
8900 JfnC 80128 2446 C2
W San Juan Pl
6800 JfnC 80128 2446 E2
6800 JfnC 80128 2447 A2
San Juan Rd
21300 JfnC 80454 2359 B1
W San Juan Wy
- JfnC 80128 2446 B1
10000 JfnC 80127 2446 B1
S San Juan Range Rd
7900 JfnC 80127 2362 A7
8100 JfnC 80127 2361 C7
W San Juan Range Rd
11100 JfnC 80127 2361 E7
San Luis St
- DgsC 80112 2451 C4
- LNTR 80134 2451 C4
San Marco Dr
4000 LGMT 80503 1438 A6
S San Souci Ct
4100 JfnC 80439 2273 B5
Santa Anita Dr
3200 DNVR 80110 2279 E6
Santa Anna St
- BLDR 80301 1603 C7
Santa Clara Pl
5100 BLDR 80303 1687 C5
Santa Clara Rd
5400 JfnC 80454 2359 C1
S Santa Fe Cir
4700 EGLD 80110 2280 B6
Santa Fe Ct
- BGTN 80601 1697 B6
Santa Fe Dr
- NHGN 80234 1860 C4
- WSTR 80234 1860 C4
10 DNVR 80223 2196 C1
300 DNVR 80204 2112 D7
300 DNVR 80223 2112 D7
2100 LGMT 80501 1356 D4
6800 AdmC 80221 2028 C1
7000 AdmC 80221 1944 C7
8600 FLHT 80260 1944 C3
8600 TNTN 80260 1944 C3
S Santa Fe Dr
- DgsC 80120 2447 E1
10 DNVR 80223 2196 D2
2500 DNVR 80223 2280 D1
2500 DvrC 80223 2280 D1
2500 EGLD 80110 2280 D1
2500 EGLD 80223 2280 D1
3300 SRDN 80110 2280 C2
4700 LITN 80120 2280 B6
5300 LITN 80120 2364 A2
7600 LITN 80120 2363 E7
8200 LITN 80120 2447 E1
8300 DgsC 80125 2447 E1
8300 DgsC 80129 2447 E1
10500 DgsC 80125 2532 B2
10600 DgsC 80125 2448 A7
S Santa Fe Dr US-85
- DgsC 80120 2447 E1
700 DNVR 80223 2196 D4
2500 DNVR 80223 2280 D1
2500 DvrC 80223 2280 D1
2500 EGLD 80110 2280 D1
2500 EGLD 80223 2280 D1
3300 SRDN 80110 2280 D1
4700 LITN 80120 2280 C6
5300 LITN 80120 2364 A2
7600 LITN 80120 2363 E7
8200 LITN 80120 2447 E1
8300 DgsC 80125 2447 E1
8300 DgsC 80129 2447 E1
10500 DgsC 80125 2532 B2
10600 DgsC 80125 2448 A7
Santa Fe St
- AdmC 80020 1692 C7
- AdmC 80020 1776 C1
- BMFD 80020 1692 C7
10700 NHGN 80234 1860 C5
Santa Fe Tr
600 EbtC 80107 2792 C7
Santa Fe Mountain Dr
10 CCkC 80439 2103 A7
1500 CCkC 80439 2102 E7
Santana Dr
1500 CSRK 80104 2704 A7
Santero Wy
- DgsC 80134 2621 B5
Santolino Ct
16600 DgsC 80134 2452 E7
Sapling Ct
1800 CSRK 80109 2703 A5

Sapphire Dr
400 CSRK 80108 2619 D7
Sapphire Ln
1300 LGMT 80504 1439 A7
Sapphire Wy
900 SUPE 80027 1857 A1
Sapphire Pointe Blvd
- DgsC 80108 2619 D5
- DgsC 80108 2620 A6
6700 CSRK 80108 2620 A6
6800 CSRK 80108 2619 D6
Sara Gulch Cir
9300 DgsC 80138 2538 E3
E Sarah Ct
1200 DgsC 80126 2449 A5
Sarah Ln
31700 JfnC 80433 2524 E1
Saranac Wy
10300 DgsC 80134 2452 E6
E Saratoga Av
19500 CTNL 80015 2285 D6
W Saratoga Av
2900 DNVR 80110 2280 A6
2900 EGLD 80110 2280 A6
3000 DNVR 80110 2279 E6
3300 DNVR 80123 2279 E6
11600 JfnC 80465 2277 E6
Saratoga Cir
- AURA 80016 2286 D6
E Saratoga Cir
18800 AURA 80015 2285 C6
Saratoga Ct
900 BldC 80303 1688 E3
Saratoga Dr
1500 LAFT 80026 1690 D7
E Saratoga Dr
13800 AphC 80015 2284 B6
W Saratoga Dr
11400 JfnC 80127 2277 E7
13200 JfnC 80465 2277 B7
Saratoga Pl
- AURA 80016 2286 D6
- AURA 80016 2287 A6
E Saratoga Pl
8500 DNVR 80237 2282 E6
8600 DNVR 80237 2283 A6
14100 AphC 80015 2284 B6
15300 AURA 80015 2284 D6
17400 AURA 80015 2285 B6
20400 AphC 80015 2285 E6
W Saratoga Pl
7400 LKWD 80123 2278 E7
9700 DNVR 80123 2278 B6
9900 JfnC 80127 2278 A6
11000 JfnC 80127 2277 E6
12900 JfnC 80465 2277 C7
N Saratoga Rd
5300 DgsC 80134 2621 E4
Saratoga Mine Dr
200 DgsC 80108 2618 D3
Saratoga Vein Ct
200 DgsC 80108 2618 D3
S Saskatoon Ln
- PARK 80134 2537 B4
E Saskatoon Pl
18100 PARK 80134 2537 B4
S Saskatoon Wy
- PARK 80134 2537 C4
Sassafras Ln
900 BMFD 80020 1774 D7
Satsuma Pl
100 CSRK 80104 2787 D3
Saturn Dr
13000 DgsC 80124 2450 E3
Saturn Pl
300 DgsC 80124 2450 E2
Saulsbury Cir
8200 ARVD 80003 1942 E4
N Saulsbury Cir
9300 JfnC 80021 1942 E1
Saulsbury Ct
3400 WTRG 80033 2110 E2
5500 ARVD 80002 2026 E4
6400 ARVD 80003 2026 E2
8200 ARVD 80003 1942 E4
N Saulsbury Ct
9400 JfnC 80021 1942 E1
9400 WSTR 80021 1942 E1
S Saulsbury Ct
1800 LKWD 80232 2194 E6
6300 JfnC 80123 2362 E3
7100 JfnC 80128 2362 E6
Saulsbury St
200 LKWD 80226 2194 E1
400 LKWD 80226 2110 E7
900 LKWD 80214 2110 E6
3000 WTRG 80033 2110 E2
4400 WTRG 80033 2026 E7
5700 ARVD 80002 2026 E4
6600 ARVD 80003 2026 E1
7600 ARVD 80003 1942 E6
11900 BMFD 80020 1858 E2
N Saulsbury St
3400 WTRG 80033 2110 E1
S Saulsbury St
100 LKWD 80226 2194 E2
900 LKWD 80232 2194 E4
2700 DNVR 80227 2278 E1
6300 JfnC 80123 2362 E4
6800 JfnC 80128 2362 E5
8300 JfnC 80128 2446 E1
S Saulsbury Wy
5300 DNVR 80123 2362 E1
5300 LKWD 80123 2362 E1
8200 JfnC 80128 2446 E2
S Saunter Ln
- DgsC 80138 2538 A3
Saurini Blvd
4100 CMCY 80022 2029 E1
Savage Rd
1900 EbtC 80107 2708 E3
2300 EbtC 80107 2709 A2
Savannah Ct
3900 BLDR 80301 1603 A5

STREET Block City ZIP Map# Grid

Savannah Ct
4000 BldC 80301 1603 A5
Savannah Pl
3900 BLDR 80301 1603 A5
S Savannah Sparrow Ct
10000 DgsC 80129 2448 D5
W Savannah Sparrow Dr
1100 DgsC 80129 2448 C5
S Savannah Sparrow Wy
10100 DgsC 80129 2448 D6
S Sawatch Range Rd
7800 JfnC 80127 2361 E7
7800 JfnC 80127 2362 A7
Sawdust Ct
10 CCkC 80439 2103 C7
Sawdust Lp
5500 DgsC 80134 2621 B5
Sawgrass Dr
8100 LNTR 80124 2450 E6
8500 LNTR 80124 2451 A6
Sawgrass Tr
3500 CSRK 80109 2702 D1
W Sawmill Ct
4300 CSRK 80109 2702 C1
Saw Mill Ln
- WSTR 80021 1942 D3
Sawmill Ln
- CCkC 80452 2185 D6
10 CCkC 80452 2186 A5
Sawmill Rd
10 BldC 80302 1598 A4
10 BldC 80455 1597 E4
10 BldC 80455 1598 A4
10 CCkC 80439 2271 D6
S Sawmill Rd
10 CCkC 80439 2271 D6
Sawmill Creek Rd
- CCkC 80439 2102 E6
- CCkC 80439 2103 A6
Sawmill Gulch Rd
2100 JfnC 80401 2191 B7
Sawtooth Ct
- DNVR 80237 2282 C6
Sawtooth Ln
- BldC 80503 1520 E4
8200 BldC 80503 1521 A4
Sawtooth Pt
500 LAFT 80026 1690 A4
S Saxebourgh Dr
7600 DgsC 80108 2535 A6
Saxon Pl
400 DgsC 80108 2619 A5
S Saybrook St
9700 DgsC 80126 2449 E5
Scarlet Oak Ct
3900 CSRK 80109 2702 D4
Scarlet Thorn Cir
6100 JfnC 80465 2360 D3
Scarsdale Ct
1800 LAFT 80026 1689 D1
Scarsdale Pl
4300 BLDR 80301 1603 B5
Scenic Ct
400 GOLD 80401 2108 A4
Scenic Dr
7700 BldC 80303 1688 E4
21800 JfnC 80465 2443 B2
S Scenic Dr
8400 JfnC 80465 2443 B1
Scenic Pl
2500 LGMT 80503 1355 C7
Scenic Rd
10 GpnC 80403 1850 B7
Scenic Pine Dr
8900 DgsC 80134 2622 D4
Scenic View Ct
5500 BLDR 80303 1687 D3
Scenic Village Dr
4200 JfnC 80439 2273 B5
N Schaffer Pkwy
- JfnC 80127 2361 D6
Schlagel St
9400 BldC 80503 1438 B5
Schneider Ln
- WldC 80504 1523 C2
Schneider Wy
6500 ARVD 80003 2026 D1
6500 ARVD 80004 2026 D1
School Rd
- NDLD 80466 1765 C2
Schooley Rd
10 PrkC 80456 2521 D3
Schoolhouse Rd
27600 JfnC 80403 1937 D7
27600 JfnC 80403 2021 E1
Schooner St
2200 LAFT 80026 1689 E5
N Schumaker Rd
10 AphC 80102 2207 C1
600 AdmC 80102 2123 C3
2600 AdmC 80102 2039 C7
2600 AURA 80102 2039 C7
S Schumaker Rd
10 AphC 80102 2207 C4
Schuyler Gulch Rd
27100 JfnC 80470 2609 E7
S Schweigert Av
10800 JfnC 80433 2527 A1
Scorpio Dr
600 DgsC 80124 2450 E2
Scorpios Cir
1200 LAFT 80026 1690 B6
Scotch Pn
10 JfnC 80127 2361 B7
Scotch Heather
10 JfnC 80127 2361 A6
Scotch Pine Cir
10 EbtC 80138 2455 E2
Scotia Rd
2700 JfnC 80439 2273 B2
Scotswood Ct
5900 BldC 80301 1603 E4
Scott Blvd
400 CSRK 80104 2703 D4

Scott Blvd
400 CSRK 80109 2703 D4
E Scott Cir
20600 DNVR 80249 2033 E6
Scott Ct
2400 LGMT 80501 1356 A4
Scott Dr
14400 AdmC 80601 1779 E3
Scott Dr N
10 BMFD 80020 1774 E6
Scott Dr S
10 BMFD 80020 1774 E6
E Scott Pl
14700 DNVR 80239 2032 B7
19100 DNVR 80249 2033 C6
21000 DNVR 80249 2034 A6
W Scott Pl
1700 DNVR 80211 2028 B6
3000 DNVR 80211 2027 E7
Scott Rd
5500 DgsC 80134 2621 C3
10000 JfnC 80433 2442 A5
Scottburg Ct
- AURA 80016 2371 C7
Scott Canyon Ln
1400 CSRK 80104 2703 E5
Scranton Ct
700 AURA 80011 2116 A6
4900 DNVR 80239 2031 E5
Scranton St
200 AURA 80011 2200 A1
700 AURA 80011 2116 A6
1400 AURA 80011 2115 E5
2200 AURA 80010 2115 E3
4900 DNVR 80239 2031 E5
S Scranton St
2900 AURA 80014 2283 E1
Scranton Wy
- CMCY 80022 1863 E6
S Scranton Wy
2100 AURA 80014 2199 E6
2100 AURA 80014 2200 A6
Scrub Oak Cir
1200 BLDR 80305 1686 E7
1200 BLDR 80305 1770 E1
Scrub Oak Dr
9200 LNTR 80124 2450 E4
Seabiscuit Tr
28100 JfnC 80439 2441 D1
Sea Brook Ln
- PARK 80138 2538 C1
S Seabrook Ln
8200 LITN 80120 2364 B7
S Season Ct
12200 DgsC 80138 2538 B3
Seattle Ln
10 LGMT 80501 1439 B6
Seaver Dr
29600 JfnC 80403 1853 B2
Seaway Ct
2100 LGMT 80503 1355 B5
S Sebring Ct
2800 DNVR 80231 2282 D1
3700 DNVR 80237 2282 D4
Secrest Cir
6600 ARVD 80007 2024 C2
Secrest Ct
1500 JfnC 80401 2108 C5
5700 JfnC 80403 2024 C4
6100 ARVD 80403 2024 D3
6900 ARVD 80007 1940 C7
6900 ARVD 80007 2024 C1
7400 JfnC 80007 1940 C7
Secrest Dr
5800 ARVD 80003 2026 E3
Secrest Ln
6200 ARVD 80403 2024 D3
Secrest St
1600 GOLD 80401 2108 C5
1600 JfnC 80401 2108 C5
6300 ARVD 80403 2024 C2
Secrest Wy
6300 ARVD 80403 2024 D3
Security Av
11600 JfnC 80401 2109 D5
11600 LKWD 80215 2109 D5
11600 LKWD 80401 2109 D5
W Security Av
11500 LKWD 80215 2109 E5
11500 LKWD 80401 2109 E5
E Security Dr
14100 AURA 80012 2200 B3
E Security Pl
14700 AURA 80011 2116 C5
E Security Wy
14700 AURA 80011 2116 C5
S Sedalia Cir
1700 AURA 80017 2201 A5
2300 AURA 80013 2201 B7
S Sedalia Ct
2800 AURA 80013 2285 A1
5100 CTNL 80015 2285 B7
6000 AphC 80016 2369 B2
E Sedalia St
10000 CMCY 80022 1865 A6
S Sedalia St
- AURA 80013 2201 B7
1500 AURA 80017 2201 A5
2700 AURA 80013 2285 B1
5400 CTNL 80015 2369 B1
6200 AphC 80016 2369 B2
6900 FXFD 80016 2369 B5
7900 CTNL 80016 2369 B7
8000 AURA 80016 2369 B7
Sedalia Wy
1500 AURA 80011 2117 A4
S Sedalia Wy
3100 AURA 80013 2285 A2
4900 AURA 80015 2285 B6
Sedge Wy
- DgsC 80134 2452 E1
900 BldC 80026 1690 B3
900 LAFT 80026 1690 B3

Sedge Grass Wy
10200 DgsC 80129 2448 E6
Sedgewick Ct
10600 PARK 80134 2453 A6
Sedgewick Wy
10600 PARK 80134 2453 B6
Sedgwick Dr
- CHLV 80210 2281 D3
- DNVR 80210 2281 D3
- DvrC 80210 2281 D3
10 CHLV 80113 2281 D3
Sedgwick Pl
10 CHLV 80113 2281 D4
Sedona Cir
- DgsC 80134 2621 B5
Sedona Dr
5100 DgsC 80134 2621 A5
Seefeld Pl
700 DgsC 80108 2618 D5
Seibert Cir
- PARK 80138 2537 E1
- PARK 80138 2538 A1
S Seibert Ct
1400 SUPE 80027 1773 B5
Seidler Ct
1900 ERIE 80516 1606 E6
Seitz Rd
26100 JfnC 80457 2274 B3
Selack St
- BKHK 80403 2018 A3
Seldom Seen Rd
- GpnC 80403 2019 E2
- GpnC 80403 2020 A2
Selenite Ct
2000 CSRK 80108 2620 A5
Sellers Dr
100 CSRK 80104 2787 E1
Sellers Creek Rd
- DgsC 80104 2788 A7
Selly Rd
8600 DgsC 80134 2622 C3
Selworthy Ct
1100 LAFT 80026 1690 B5
Seminole Ct
- DgsC 80118 2952 D2
Seminole Dr
- DgsC 80118 2952 D2
100 BLDR 80303 1687 C5
N Seminole Pl
3700 DgsC 80135 2616 B7
Seminole Rd
600 DNVR 80204 2112 B7
20500 JfnC 80454 2359 C1
Seminole Tr
- DgsC 80118 2952 D2
Senator Ct
2300 LSVL 80027 1689 C5
Senator Dr
2400 LSVL 80027 1689 C5
Senda Roscosa St
1700 BldC 80303 1771 B4
Seneca Cir
1500 LAFT 80026 1690 A7
1500 LSVL 80026 1690 A7
S Seneca Ct
1300 DNVR 80223 2196 B5
Seneca Pl
5400 BldC 80303 1687 D5
5400 BLDR 80303 1687 D5
S Seneca Wy
1200 DNVR 80223 2196 B4
Senecio Ct
800 LAFT 80026 1690 C3
Senecio Dr
1700 DgsC 80118 2954 B1
Senter Dr
400 CSRK 80104 2703 E6
Sentinel Dr
3300 BLDR 80301 1603 B6
Sentinel Rock Ln
10 BldC 80302 1517 B7
Sentinel Rock Ter
4000 DgsC 80118 2953 B2
Sequerra St
1100 BMFD 80020 1774 E7
Sequoia Ct
700 BLDR 80304 1602 B6
16400 DgsC 80134 2452 E6
Sequoia Dr
15900 DgsC 80134 2452 E5
Sequoia St
10 GOLD 80401 2192 B1
N Sequoia St
- LGMT 80501 1439 C6
S Sequoia St
- LGMT 80501 1439 C6
W Seramonte Dr
3700 DgsC 80129 2447 E5
Serena Av
6600 DgsC 80108 2534 C4
Serena Ct
12300 DgsC 80108 2534 D4
Serena Dr
6800 DgsC 80108 2534 D4
Serenade Rd
3600 DgsC 80104 2871 D2
Serendipity Tr
32800 JfnC 80439 2188 D2
Serene Ln
- LKWD 80228 2193 D2
Serene View Rd
5000 DgsC 80134 2622 D4
E Serengeti Cir
6400 DgsC 80124 2450 C7
S Serengeti Dr
10500 DgsC 80124 2450 C7
E Serengeti Pl
6400 DgsC 80124 2450 C7
Serenity Cir
1400 LGMT 80501 1356 D7
Serenity Ln
800 LGMT 80501 1356 D7
Service Dr
- GOLD 80403 2024 D7

Service Dr
- JfnC 80403 2024 D7
S Service Dr
- JfnC 80403 2108 A2
Service Rd
- AphC 80222 2282 A1
- BldC 80503 1520 B6
- BLDR 80503 1520 B6
- DNVR 80222 2198 A7
- DNVR 80222 2282 A1
- DvrC 80222 2198 A7
- JfnC 80403 2023 B4
- JfnC 80470 2608 A1
N Service Rd
- GOLD 80401 2107 E2
- GOLD 80401 2108 A2
- JfnC 80401 2107 E2
- JfnC 80401 2108 A2
- JfnC 80403 2108 A2
S Service Rd
- JfnC 80401 2108 D1
- JfnC 80403 2108 D1
Seth Pl
500 DgsC 80108 2534 E5
Seton Ct
11000 WSTR 80031 1859 D5
W Seton Pl
11100 WSTR 80031 1859 D4
Seton St
8600 AdmC 80031 1943 C3
8900 WSTR 80031 1943 C3
Settlement Ln
200 ELIZ 80107 2793 B1
Settlers Dr
7400 JfnC 80465 2359 C7
7400 JfnC 80465 2443 C1
N Settlers Dr
11400 DgsC 80138 2453 D5
S Settlers Dr
7300 JfnC 80465 2359 B6
7900 JfnC 80465 2443 C1
Seven Arrows Dr
9100 LNTR 80124 2450 E3
Seven Hills Dr
10 BldC 80302 1601 D7
200 BldC 80302 1685 D1
Severance Dr
10300 PARK 80134 2453 A6
Severance Lodge Rd
10 GpnC 80403 1850 A4
E Severn Dr
7500 DNVR 80230 2114 D6
Severn Ln
10000 LNTR 80134 2451 E5
E Severn Pl
- DNVR 80230 2115 A6
4800 DNVR 80220 2114 A7
7200 DNVR 80230 2114 C6
9000 AURA 80230 2115 A6
16100 AURA 80011 2116 E6
W Severn Pl
2800 DNVR 80204 2112 A7
3200 DNVR 80204 2111 E6
Seward St
300 LYNS 80540 1352 D1
Shadecrest Pl
2500 DgsC 80126 2533 C1
Shadecrest Pt
10900 DgsC 80126 2533 C1
Shade Tree Ln
5000 DgsC 80134 2622 D4
S Shadow Ln
10 JfnC 80401 2190 C2
Shadowbrook Cir
10900 DgsC 80126 2533 E1
Shadow Brook Dr
10400 JfnC 80433 2441 C7
Shadow Canyon Tr
3600 BMFD 80020 1775 D5
Shadow Creek Dr
2800 BLDR 80303 1687 A3
S Shadowglen Ct
9200 DgsC 80126 2449 B3
S Shadow Hill Cir
- DgsC 80124 2451 A4
9300 LNTR 80124 2451 A4
S Shadow Hill Ct
9900 LNTR 80124 2451 A4
S Shadow Hill Dr
10000 LNTR 80124 2451 A4
Shadow Mountain Dr
800 DgsC 80126 2449 A2
27300 JfnC 80433 2441 B6
30900 JfnC 80433 2440 E4
Shadow Ridge Ct
4700 CSRK 80109 2702 C1
Shadow Ridge Rd
4800 CSRK 80109 2702 C1
Shadow Rock Run
10700 DgsC 80125 2614 D1
Shadowstone Dr
300 DgsC 80129 2448 D6
Shadow Wood Ct
14200 AdmC 80603 1784 D2
16600 AdmC 80642 1700 D4
Shadow Wood St
14500 AdmC 80603 1700 D7
14500 AdmC 80603 1784 D2
Shady Hllw E
2900 BLDR 80304 1602 E7
Shady Hllw W
2900 BLDR 80304 1602 E7
Shady Ln
21400 JfnC 80465 2275 B2
E Shady Ln
2800 DgsC 80126 2449 C1
Shadycroft Dr
300 LITN 80120 2364 B6
W Shadycroft Ln
300 LITN 80120 2364 C5
Shady Grove Ct
- AURA 80016 2371 C7
Shady Grove St
7800 DNVR 80249 1951 C5

Shady Hollow Rd
10 BldC 80466 1682 E6
Shady Oak Ln
800 DgsC 80108 2534 D6
Shady Pines Dr
10600 JfnC 80465 2443 C7
Shaffer Dr
- JfnC 80127 2361 E7
S Shaffer Ln
7400 JfnC 80127 2361 D6
N Shaffer Pkwy
7700 JfnC 80127 2361 D7
S Shaffer Pkwy
8300 JfnC 80127 2445 E1
11700 JfnC 80127 2361 E7
Shaffer Pl
8300 JfnC 80127 2361 D7
Shalako Pl
- BldC 80303 1772 B1
Shale Ct
2900 SUPE 80027 1773 B7
Shallot Cir
700 LAFT 80026 1690 D7
S Shalom Park Cir
5100 AURA 80015 2284 C7
Shamrock Dr
1800 SUPE 80027 1773 C6
Shane Valley Tr
3900 CSRK 80109 2702 D3
Shangri la Dr
4100 DNVR 80246 2197 E1
Shannock Av
6600 CSRK 80104 2705 A7
Shannon Dr
3100 BMFD 80020 1775 E3
9600 ARVD 80004 2026 B2
S Shannon Tr
6200 DgsC 80130 2450 C6
Shari's Ct
800 BNNT 80102 2124 E2
W Sharkstooth Peak
11400 JfnC 80127 2361 C7
Sharon Ln
8900 ARVD 80002 2026 C4
Sharon Pkwy
400 GOLD 80403 2107 E2
Sharpe Ct
10 LGMT 80501 1438 D1
Sharpe Pl
1300 LGMT 80501 1439 A1
1400 LGMT 80501 1438 E1
Sharps Ct
1600 DgsC 80109 2786 C6
Shars Tr
3000 DgsC 80135 2869 A4
Shasta Cir
5700 LITN 80123 2363 C2
Shasta Ct
300 KIOW 80117 2796 A3
S Shasta Ln
6100 JfnC 80439 2356 E3
Shavano Ct
1400 JfnC 80439 2188 D6
N Shavano Pl
5900 DgsC 80134 2622 D2
Shavano Rd
9800 TNTN 80260 1860 B7
Shavano St
1700 LGMT 80501 1356 C6
Shavano Peak Dr
900 SUPE 80027 1857 A1
Shavano Peak Pl
6200 DgsC 80108 2618 E2
Shavano Peak Wy
6200 DgsC 80108 2618 E2
Shaw Blvd
3600 WSTR 80031 1943 D4
4000 AdmC 80031 1943 C3
Shaw Ct
10800 PARK 80134 2453 A7
S Shawnee Ct
4200 AURA 80018 2286 B4
6600 AURA 80016 2370 B3
Shawnee Ln
300 SUPE 80027 1772 D3
30800 JfnC 80439 2273 A2
Shawnee Pl
4600 BLDR 80303 1687 C5
Shawnee Rd
22100 JfnC 80454 2359 A1
22200 JfnC 80454 2275 A7
22600 JfnC 80465 2359 A1
S Shawnee St
3900 AURA 80018 2286 B4
5100 AphC 80015 2286 B7
5600 AphC 80015 2370 B1
6000 CTNL 80015 2370 B2
6600 AURA 80016 2370 B3
Shawnee Wy
- AURA 80018 2286 B3
S Shawnee Wy
5100 AphC 80015 2286 B7
5400 AphC 80015 2370 C1
Shea Pl
- BMFD 80020 1775 E3
E Shea Pl
6200 DgsC 80130 2450 C5
Shea Center Dr
1700 DgsC 80129 2448 C3
Sheader Av
300 LAFT 80026 1690 C4
S Sheephorn Mtn
7200 JfnC 80127 2361 D6
Sheep Patch Rd
4500 JfnC 80403 2021 C6
Sheffield Ct
11000 DgsC 80134 2623 C6
E Shefield Ct
20500 PARK 80138 2537 E1
20500 PARK 80138 2538 B2
Shefield Dr
3700 BMFD 80020 1775 D7
E Shefield Pl
20800 PARK 80138 2538 A1

Shelby Dr
4800 CSRK 80104 2788 D2
Sheldon Av
2300 AdmC 80221 1944 A7
2500 WSTR 80030 1944 A7
Sheldon Dr
700 AdmC 80229 1945 A3
700 TNTN 80229 1944 E3
700 TNTN 80229 1945 A3
Sheldon St
26200 JfnC 80457 2274 A3
Sheley Ct
300 LGMT 80501 1438 E4
Shelf Rd
- BldC 80466 1765 A5
- JfnC 80433 2611 C6
Shelton Dr
1200 PrkC 80456 2521 E2
Shelton Ranch Rd
800 GOLD 80401 2107 E6
Shenandoah Ct
44300 EbtC 80107 2542 E1
Shenandoah Dr
7100 EbtC 80107 2542 D2
7600 EbtC 80107 2543 A2
S Shenandoah Dr
- EbtC 80107 2542 D2
S Shenandoah Wy
4700 AURA 80015 2284 D7
Shenstone Ct
16000 DgsC 80134 2452 D4
Shenstone Dr
9400 DgsC 80134 2452 E4
Shenstone Wy
9500 DgsC 80134 2452 E4
W Shepperd Av
200 LITN 80120 2364 D2
Sheramdi St
12700 BldC 80503 1355 C4
S Sheraton Pl
10 BGTN 80601 1696 D6
E Sheri Ln
10200 AphC 80111 2283 B7
W Sheri Ln
1600 EGLD 80120 2280 C7
1600 LITN 80120 2280 C7
Sheridan Blvd
- AdmC 80002 2027 C3
- WSTR 80020 1859 B2
10 DNVR 80219 2195 C1
10 LKWD 80226 2195 C1
200 DNVR 80204 2111 C7
200 DNVR 80219 2111 C7
200 LKWD 80226 2111 C7
700 LKWD 80214 2111 C7
1200 LKWD 80204 2111 C6
2200 EDGW 80214 2111 C3
2400 DNVR 80212 2111 C3
2500 WTRG 80214 2111 C3
3000 WTRG 80212 2111 C3
4100 MNVW 80212 2027 C7
4100 WTRG 80212 2027 C7
4300 LKSD 80212 2027 C7
4700 DNVR 80212 2027 C6
5100 DNVR 80002 2027 C6
5100 JfnC 80212 2027 C6
5600 ARVD 80002 2027 C3
5800 AdmC 80003 2027 C3
6000 ARVD 80003 2027 C3
6600 ARVD 80030 2027 C3
6700 WSTR 80030 2027 C3
6800 WSTR 80003 2027 C3
6900 WSTR 80030 1943 B7
7300 WSTR 80003 1943 B7
7900 ARVD 80003 1943 B7
7900 WSTR 80031 1943 B7
9400 WSTR 80020 1943 C1
12000 BMFD 80020 1859 B2
12000 WSTR 80031 1859 B2
12600 BMFD 80020 1775 B6
14200 BldC 80020 1775 B6
Sheridan Blvd SR-95
- ARVD 80002 2027 C3
10 DNVR 80219 2195 C1
10 LKWD 80226 2195 C1
200 DNVR 80204 2111 C7
200 DNVR 80219 2111 C7
400 LKWD 80204 2111 C7
400 LKWD 80226 2111 C7
700 LKWD 80214 2111 C7
2200 EDGW 80214 2111 C3
2500 DNVR 80212 2111 C3
2500 WTRG 80214 2111 C3
3000 WTRG 80212 2111 C3
4100 MNVW 80212 2027 C7
4100 WTRG 80212 2027 C7
4300 LKSD 80212 2027 C7
5100 DNVR 80002 2027 C6
5100 DNVR 80212 2027 C6
5400 AdmC 80002 2027 C3
5400 JfnC 80212 2027 C6
6000 ARVD 80003 2027 C3
6600 ARVD 80030 2027 C3
6700 WSTR 80030 2027 C3
6800 WSTR 80003 2027 C3
6900 WSTR 80030 1943 B7
7300 WSTR 80003 1943 B7
7900 WSTR 80031 1943 B7
8000 ARVD 80003 1943 B7
N Sheridan Blvd
9700 WSTR 80031 1859 B6
11200 WSTR 80020 1859 B3
11800 BMFD 80020 1859 B3
S Sheridan Blvd
10 DNVR 80219 2195 C4
10 LKWD 80226 2195 C4
400 LKWD 80219 2195 C4
900 LKWD 80232 2195 C4
1800 DNVR 80227 2195 C7
1800 DNVR 80232 2195 C7
2200 DvrC 80227 2195 C7
2200 LKWD 80227 2195 C7
2600 DNVR 80219 2279 C2
2600 DNVR 80227 2279 C2

S Sheridan Blvd
2600 DNVR 80236 2279 C2
2600 LKWD 80227 2279 C2
3500 DNVR 80235 2279 C2
4300 BWMR 80123 2279 C6
4300 DvrC 80235 2279 C6
4300 DvrC 80236 2279 C6
5600 BWMR 80123 2363 C1
5600 LITN 80123 2363 C1
5700 AphC 80123 2363 C1
6800 AphC 80128 2363 C5
S Sheridan Blvd SR-95
- DNVR 80235 2279 C2
10 DNVR 80219 2195 C4
10 LKWD 80226 2195 C4
400 LKWD 80219 2195 C4
900 LKWD 80232 2195 C4
1800 DNVR 80227 2195 C7
1800 DNVR 80232 2195 C7
2200 DvrC 80227 2195 C7
2200 LKWD 80227 2195 C7
2600 DNVR 80219 2279 C2
2600 DNVR 80227 2279 C2
2600 DNVR 80236 2279 C2
2600 LKWD 80227 2279 C2
Sheridan Ct
8100 ARVD 80003 1943 B4
S Sheridan Ct
2600 DNVR 80227 2279 C1
2600 LKWD 80227 2279 C1
7500 JfnC 80128 2363 C7
Sheridan Dr
16300 PARK 80134 2452 E7
Sheridan Pkwy
- BfdC 80020 1775 C1
- BfdC 80516 1692 B4
- BMFD 80020 1691 E7
- BMFD 80020 1692 A7
- BMFD 80020 1775 B3
- BMFD 80516 1692 B4
- ERIE 80516 1692 B4
Sheridan Wy
- LAFT 80026 1690 D7
S Sheridan Wy
5900 JfnC 80123 2363 C2
Sherman Av
23900 JfnC 80433 2694 E5
S Sherman Cir
5500 LITN 80121 2364 E1
Sherman Ct
10 BldC 80501 1438 E3
10 LGMT 80501 1438 E3
Sherman Dr
1200 LGMT 80501 1438 E4
1200 LGMT 80501 1439 A4
11300 NHGN 80233 1860 E3
Sherman Pl
7600 AdmC 80221 1944 E5
Sherman St
10 DNVR 80203 2196 E1
10 DNVR 80209 2196 E1
200 BldC 80501 1438 E2
300 LGMT 80501 1438 E2
600 DgsC 80108 2534 E7
1500 DNVR 80203 2112 E5
1900 DNVR 80205 2112 E5
2100 LGMT 80501 1355 E5
5100 AdmC 80216 2028 E5
5100 DNVR 80216 2028 E5
7300 AdmC 80221 1944 E5
11600 NHGN 80233 1860 E3
S Sherman St
10 DNVR 80203 2196 E2
10 DNVR 80209 2196 E2
600 LGMT 80501 1438 E5
1100 DNVR 80210 2196 E4
2500 DNVR 80210 2280 E1
2600 DvrC 80210 2280 E1
2600 EGLD 80113 2280 E2
5100 AphC 80121 2280 E7
5300 AphC 80121 2364 E1
5400 AphC 80121 2365 A1
5400 GDVL 80121 2365 A1
5500 LITN 80121 2364 E1
6500 CTNL 80121 2364 E4
6600 CTNL 80122 2364 E4
Sherman Wy
1600 LGMT 80501 1355 E6
8000 AdmC 80221 1944 E5
S Sherman Wy
5400 AphC 80121 2280 E7
5800 CTNL 80121 2364 E2
Sherrelwood Cir
1800 AdmC 80221 1944 B5
Sherrelwood Dr
1600 AdmC 80221 1944 B5
S Sherrelwood Ln
9400 DgsC 80126 2449 A4
Sherri Mar Ct
1100 LGMT 80501 1355 D7
1100 LGMT 80501 1438 D1
Sherri Mar Pl
2000 LGMT 80501 1355 D7
Sherri Mar St
2100 LGMT 80501 1355 D5
Sherwood Cir
2600 BLDR 80304 1602 E6
Sherwood Ct
200 LGMT 80501 1356 C6
Sherwood Rd
10 BldC 80466 1682 B7
10 BldC 80466 1766 A1
Shetland Ct
10 DgsC 80130 2450 B3
S Shetland Rd
3100 JfnC 80439 2273 C3
Shetland Tr
2300 EbtC 80107 2708 E6
Shetland Wy
9000 DgsC 80130 2450 A3
Shiloh Cir
25300 JfnC 80433 2526 C7
Shiloh Ct
- EbtC 80107 2543 B1

STREET Block City ZIP Map# Grid

Shiloh Dr
1900 CSRK 80104 2788 A1
13000 JfnC 80433 2526 B7
13300 JfnC 80433 2610 C1
Shiloh Ln
24700 JfnC 80433 2610 C1
Shiloh Rd
13200 JfnC 80433 2526 C7
13200 JfnC 80433 2610 C1
Shiloh Point Dr
- JfnC 80127 2529 A4
Shiloh Ridge Rd
14000 JfnC 80433 2610 C2
Shimley Ln
11200 JfnC 80403 1852 B4
Shimley Rd
11200 JfnC 80403 1852 B4
Shingle Creek Rd
22100 JfnC 80401 2191 A4
23200 JfnC 80401 2190 E4
Shining Oak Ct
10 JfnC 80127 2361 A7
Shining Oak Dr
10 JfnC 80127 2361 A7
Shining Star Tr
- BldC 80302 1599 E5
- BldC 80302 1600 A5
Shiny Rock Ranch Rd
- BldC 80455 1597 E3
Shire Cir
3300 CSRK 80104 2703 E3
W Shirley Pl
5300 LKWD 80232 2195 B4
Shoal Cir
2800 LGMT 80503 1355 C6
Shoal Creek Ln
8800 LNTR 80124 2451 B3
Shooting Star Dr
1400 JfnC 80401 2190 D6
Shooting Star Ln
23800 JfnC 80401 2190 D5
N Shooting Star Tr
- DgsC 80125 2615 B4
Shooting Star Wy
4500 CSRK 80109 2702 C2
N Shore Dr
- BldC 80503 1355 B4
1900 LGMT 80503 1355 B5
Shore Pn
10 JfnC 80127 2361 B7
Shoreham Cir
200 DgsC 80108 2618 E1
Shoreham Dr
7000 DgsC 80108 2618 E1
7100 DgsC 80108 2534 E7
Shoreham Pl
7300 DgsC 80108 2534 E7
Shorepine Ct
10400 DgsC 80134 2452 E6
Short Ct
1300 LSVL 80027 1689 C7
Short Pl
200 LSVL 80027 1689 C7
1700 LGMT 80501 1438 E2
W Short Pl
2700 DNVR 80204 2112 A7
2800 DNVR 80219 2112 A7
4500 DNVR 80204 2111 C7
Short Rd
- BldC 80303 1688 E5
Short St
1000 LSVL 80027 1689 D7
Short Dirt Rd
10 GpnC 80403 1935 A6
Short Grass Ct
1400 CSRK 80109 2703 B5
Shortridge Ct
2300 ERIE 80516 1606 D6
Shoshone
11200 WldC 80504 1440 E2
Shoshone Ct
100 BLDR 80303 1687 C6
Shoshone Dr
4300 DgsC 80118 2953 B3
Shoshone Pl
7000 DgsC 80118 2953 B3
Shoshone Rd
22900 JfnC 80439 2274 E5
22900 JfnC 80439 2275 A5
Shoshone St
- AdmC 80020 1776 B2
300 EbtC 80117 2796 A3
300 KIOW 80117 2796 A3
1200 DNVR 80204 2112 B5
3200 DNVR 80211 2112 B1
4500 DNVR 80211 2028 B6
5100 DNVR 80221 2028 B5
5300 AdmC 80221 2028 B4
8200 AdmC 80221 1944 B4
8300 FLHT 80260 1944 B4
13100 WSTR 80234 1776 B5
S Shoshone St
500 DNVR 80223 2196 B3
3100 DNVR 80223 2280 B2
3100 DvrC 80110 2280 B2
3100 DvrC 80223 2280 B2
3100 EGLD 80110 2280 B2
3100 SRDN 80110 2280 B2
Shoshone Tr
1300 EbtC 80107 2708 C3
2700 LAFT 80026 1689 C4
Shoshone Wy
10000 TNTN 80260 1860 B6
11600 WSTR 80234 1860 B3
Shoshoni Rd
- GpnC 80474 1849 E1
- GpnC 80474 1850 A1
Shoshoni Wy
10 BldC 80466 1765 C1
10 NDLD 80466 1765 C1
Shoup Pl
4700 BLDR 80303 1687 C3
Shrine Cir
7500 DgsC 80118 2954 D3
Shrine Rd
7400 DgsC 80118 2954 D3
Shull Ct
400 BGTN 80601 1696 B7
Shupe Pl
- LGMT 80501 1439 E2
Shuttleworth Dr
800 ERIE 80516 1607 A7
S Sibrica St
- PARK 80134 2537 B6
S Sicily Cir
5600 AphC 80015 2370 C1
S Sicily Ct
5600 AphC 80015 2370 C1
6800 AURA 80016 2370 C4
Sicily Dr
1500 LGMT 80503 1437 E6
S Sicily St
5100 AphC 80015 2286 C7
5700 AphC 80015 2370 C1
5700 CTNL 80015 2370 C1
S Sicily Wy
5200 AphC 80015 2286 C7
5400 AphC 80015 2370 C1
6000 CTNL 80015 2370 C2
6200 AURA 80016 2370 C3
Side Saddle Ln
7300 DgsC 80134 2622 A4
S Sidney Ct
2700 AphC 80231 2282 D1
2700 DNVR 80231 2282 D1
4100 DNVR 80237 2282 D4
Sidney Rd E
11700 JfnC 80403 1852 B3
Sidney Rd W
33300 JfnC 80403 1852 B3
Sidon Cir
1500 LAFT 80026 1689 E7
1500 LSVL 80026 1689 E7
1500 LSVL 80027 1689 E7
Siegal Ct
6400 CMCY 80022 2030 A2
Siegel Cir
- DNVR 80204 2112 C4
Siena Ter
15800 DgsC 80134 2452 D5
Siena Wy
7200 BldC 80301 1604 C2
Sierra Av
400 LGMT 80501 1439 B5
N Sierra Cir
12500 DgsC 80138 2453 D3
Sierra Dr
1400 BLDR 80302 1686 D5
1400 BLDR 80305 1686 D5
9300 ARVD 80005 1942 A6
S Sierra Dr
1300 CSRK 80104 2704 A7
Sierra Rd
- AdmC 80601 1697 B6
- BGTN 80601 1697 B6
Sierra Verde Ct
- CSRK 80104 2704 A2
Siesta Cir
10 CCkC 80439 2271 E6
Signal Butte Dr
10000 DgsC 80125 2615 A1
Signal Creek Blvd
2700 TNTN 80241 1777 C6
Signal Creek Dr
2600 TNTN 80241 1777 C5
Signal Creek Pl
2700 TNTN 80241 1777 C5
Signal Rock Rd
10 BldC 80403 1852 A1
Signature Cir
1000 LGMT 80501 1356 E6
Signature Ct
1800 LGMT 80501 1356 E6
Silbrico Wy
400 DgsC 80108 2619 A6
S Silent Hills Dr
9300 LNTR 80124 2451 B4
9400 DgsC 80124 2451 B4
Silent Hills Ln
9500 DgsC 80124 2451 A4
9500 LNTR 80124 2451 A4
E Silent Hills Pl
9500 DgsC 80124 2451 B4
9500 LNTR 80124 2451 B4
Silo Ct
- BGTN 80601 1697 D4
Silo Ln
- WSTR 80021 1942 D3
N Silo Rd
8000 DgsC 80138 2539 B5
Silver Av
3500 BMFD 80020 1775 D6
S Silver Ct
8900 DgsC 80126 2449 D3
Silver Pl
2700 SUPE 80027 1773 A7
Silver Rd
10 GpnC 80403 1850 B7
Silver Aspen
10 JfnC 80127 2361 A7
Silver Bell Cir
4500 DgsC 80108 2619 A5
Silverberry
10 JfnC 80127 2361 A7
S Silverberry Cir
9600 DgsC 80129 2448 D4
Silverberry Ct
700 LAFT 80026 1690 B5
Silverberry Ln
700 JfnC 80401 2190 D4
Silver Bluff Ct
5600 DgsC 80134 2622 A3
Silver Cliff Ct
4500 DgsC 80108 2619 A6
Silvercliff Ln
10000 DgsC 80125 2531 A6
Silver Cloud Ln
10 BldC 80302 1517 A7
Silver Cloud Pl
10 DgsC 80108 2618 E6
S Silver Creek Ct
12600 PARK 80134 2537 E4
Silver Creek Dr
- AURA 80011 2202 A5
- AURA 80017 2202 A5
Silvercreek Ln
1600 JfnC 80439 2189 B6
S Silver Creek St
400 AphC 80011 2202 A2
400 AphC 80018 2202 A2
400 AURA 80011 2201 E3
400 AURA 80011 2202 A2
400 AURA 80017 2202 A4
12500 PARK 80134 2537 D5
Silver Dale Ct
4500 DgsC 80108 2619 A5
Silver Dollar Ct
1100 CSRK 80104 2703 E2
Silver Elk Ln
12900 JfnC 80127 2445 C6
Silver Feather Cir
- BMFD 80020 1775 B1
Silver Feather Wy
- BMFD 80020 1775 B2
Silver Fir Ct
10 JfnC 80127 2360 E6
Silver Fir St
46500 EbtC 80138 2456 A3
Silver Fox Cir
10 GDVL 80121 2282 A7
Silver Fox Ct
100 GDVL 80121 2282 A7
Silver Fox Dr
10 GDVL 80121 2282 A7
Silver Fox Ln
11300 JfnC 80433 2527 C2
Silver Garter Rd
10 PrkC 80456 2522 A5
Silver Gate Dr
4500 DgsC 80108 2619 A5
Silver Gulch Rd
- BKHK 80403 2018 B4
- GpnC 80403 2018 B4
Silverheels Dr
1100 DgsC 80118 2954 D4
1100 LKSR 80118 2954 D4
Silverheels Pl
8100 DgsC 80118 2954 C3
Silverheels Rd
10 AdmC 80102 2124 D4
10 BNNT 80102 2124 D4
Silver Hill Cir
9500 LNTR 80124 2451 A4
S Silverhorn Dr
6800 JfnC 80439 2358 C5
Silverhorn Ln
27700 JfnC 80439 2358 B6
N Silverlace Dr
4700 CSRK 80109 2702 E1
Silver Lake Av
700 BLDR 80304 1602 B4
Silver Leaf Wy
100 DgsC 80108 2618 C4
Silverleaf Oak
31100 JfnC 80439 2273 A4
S Silver Maple Cir
10000 DgsC 80129 2448 B6
S Silver Maple Rd
9800 DgsC 80129 2448 B6
S Silver Maple St
- DgsC 80129 2448 B6
S Silver Maple Wy
9900 DgsC 80129 2448 B5
Silver Meadow Cir
21800 PARK 80138 2454 B7
21800 PARK 80138 2538 B1
Silver Meadow Ln
21700 PARK 80138 2538 B1
21800 PARK 80138 2454 B7
Silver Mesa Dr
6400 DgsC 80130 2450 B2
Silvermound
10 JfnC 80127 2361 A6
Silver Mound Ln
17100 PARK 80134 2453 A2
Silver Pine Dr
4600 CSRK 80108 2704 A1
Silver Plume Cir
3800 BLDR 80305 1771 B2
Silver Plume Ln
3600 BLDR 80305 1771 A2
Silver Plume Pl
3500 BLDR 80305 1771 A2
S Silver Plume St
12800 PARK 80134 2537 D5
Silver Point Dr
900 BldC 80466 1681 C6
Silver Ranch Rd
19100 JfnC 80433 2527 E5
Silver Sage Ct
4800 BldC 80301 1604 C3
Silver Springs Blvd
34400 JfnC 80470 2608 A2
34700 PrkC 80456 2608 A2
Silver Springs Rd
10 PrkC 80456 2607 E3
Silver Spruce
10 BldC 80302 1685 A4
10 BldC 80466 1685 A4
S Silver Spruce Ln
4800 JfnC 80439 2273 D7
Silver Spur Ln
9500 DgsC 80130 2450 C4
Silver Star Ct
600 LGMT 80501 1439 E2
Silver Swan Pl
- CSRK 80109 2702 D5
Silver Thorn Run
6000 DgsC 80125 2614 D3
Silver Tip Ln
1200 JfnC 80439 2188 C5
Silverton Dr
13600 BMFD 80020 1775 A5
Silverweed Wy
7700 LNTR 80124 2450 D3
Silver Willow Rd
100 JfnC 80401 2190 E1
Silver Wing Ct
4500 DgsC 80108 2619 A6
Simmons Ct
400 ERIE 80516 1607 A5
Simmons Dr
6000 BldC 80303 1687 E3
6000 BldC 80303 1688 A3
Simmons St
300 ERIE 80516 1607 A6
Simmons Wy
24800 JfnC 80403 1938 C2
Simms Ct
3800 WTRG 80033 2109 D1
6800 ARVD 80004 2025 D1
8100 ARVD 80005 1941 D4
S Simms Ct
4500 JfnC 80465 2277 E6
6000 JfnC 80127 2361 E3
Simms Dr
2800 LKWD 80215 2109 D3
2900 WTRG 80215 2109 D3
Simms Pl
2100 LKWD 80215 2109 E4
5000 ARVD 80033 2025 D5
5000 WTRG 80033 2025 D5
Simms St
- LKWD 80228 2109 E7
- LKWD 80401 2109 E7
600 LKWD 80215 2109 E7
3100 WTRG 80033 2109 E3
3100 WTRG 80215 2109 E3
4400 WTRG 80033 2025 E6
5800 ARVD 80002 2025 D3
6400 ARVD 80004 2025 E2
7000 ARVD 80004 1941 E7
7500 JfnC 80005 1941 D6
8300 ARVD 80005 1941 E4
N Simms St
10400 JfnC 80021 1857 D6
10800 BMFD 80021 1857 D4
10800 WSTR 80021 1857 D4
S Simms St
300 LKWD 80226 2193 E3
300 LKWD 80228 2193 E3
1200 JfnC 80232 2193 E5
4300 JfnC 80465 2277 E6
5100 JfnC 80127 2277 E6
5200 JfnC 80127 2361 E2
S Simms Wy
5200 JfnC 80127 2277 C7
5500 JfnC 80127 2361 E1
W Simpson Pl
700 LAFT 80026 1690 B4
E Simpson St
100 LAFT 80026 1690 D4
700 BldC 80026 1690 D4
W Simpson St
100 LAFT 80026 1690 C4
Sinclaire Blvd
1600 DgsC 80118 2869 E7
1600 DgsC 80118 2870 A7
Singer Dr
10 PrkC 80456 2521 D3
Singing Hills Ct
7400 BldC 80301 1604 D2
Singing Hills Dr
7400 BldC 80301 1604 D2
7400 BLDR 80301 1604 D2
Singing Hills Rd
10 DgsC 80138 2623 E1
10 EbtC 80138 2624 A1
2700 EbtC 80107 2625 A1
2700 EbtC 80138 2625 A1
5000 EbtC 80107 2541 E7
5000 EbtC 80107 2542 A7
E Singing Hills Rd
10500 DgsC 80134 2623 C1
10500 DgsC 80138 2623 C1
E Singing Hills Rd CO-24
10500 DgsC 80134 2623 C1
10500 DgsC 80138 2623 C1
Singing River Ranch Rd
20500 JfnC 80439 2271 A7
Singing Springs Ln
6700 JfnC 80439 2357 D5
Singing Winds St
11900 PARK 80138 2538 C3
Singleleaf Ct
10600 DgsC 80134 2452 E7
Single Tree Ct
16600 JfnC 80465 2360 C1
Singletree Ct
8300 EbtC 80107 2543 A2
Singletree Ln
- BGTN 80601 1697 C5
5400 DgsC 80134 2621 E3
Sinton Rd
10 CCkC 80439 2187 B7
10 CCkC 80439 2271 C1
2800 CCkC 80439 2188 A7
N Sioux Ct
3800 DgsC 80135 2616 D7
Sioux Dr
5100 BLDR 80303 1687 C5
5400 BldC 80303 1687 D5
W Sioux Dr
5500 DgsC 80135 2616 D7
5500 DgsC 80135 2700 D1
W Sioux Ln
5600 DgsC 80135 2616 E7
Sioux Rd
21600 JfnC 80454 2275 B7
S Sioux Rd
15500 JfnC 80470 2609 A6
Sioux St
- AdmC 80022 1946 C3
Sioux Tr
- TNTN 80229 1861 E7
10 CCkC 80439 2355 E7
10 CCkC 80439 2356 A7
1000 EbtC 80107 2708 B4
33900 JfnC 80470 2608 B1
Sir Galahad Dr
500 LAFT 80026 1690 D5
Sirus Dr
13500 DgsC 80124 2450 D2
Sisal Ct
- CSRK 80109 2702 C5
Siskin Av
- DgsC 80126 2449 E2
100 BGTN 80601 1697 E6
Sitler Cir
- DNVR 80110 2279 E4
- DNVR 80236 2279 E4
- SRDN 80110 2279 E4
- SRDN 80236 2279 E4
Sitting Bull Tr
25800 JfnC 80433 2526 B3
Six St
- JfnC 80007 1939 E2
Six Shooter Ct
10 PrkC 80456 2606 D2
Skeel St
10 BGTN 80601 1696 B6
Ski Rd
10 CCkC 80439 2440 A1
Ski Tr
100 CCkC 80439 2440 A1
300 CCkC 80439 2439 E1
7000 JfnC 80439 2356 B5
Ski Hill Dr
24400 JfnC 80401 2190 C4
Ski Mountain Dr
13500 JfnC 80127 2612 B1
Skokie Ln
31000 JfnC 80439 2273 A1
S Skunk Al
6900 JfnC 80439 2356 C5
Skunk Canyon Tr
- BldC 80302 1686 C6
- BldC 80305 1686 C6
- BLDR 80305 1686 C6
Sky Cove Dr
13900 BMFD 80020 1776 A4
E Skye Ln
10 DgsC 80130 2450 B2
E Skye Pl
10 DgsC 80130 2450 B2
Skyhaven Dr
- FLHT 80260 1944 B2
Sky Hawk Ct
3700 CSRK 80109 2702 C3
Skyhill Dr
10 JfnC 80401 2189 B2
Skyland Dr
8500 BldC 80503 1521 B5
Skylane Dr
200 ERIE 80516 1691 D3
Skylark Cir
200 LAFT 80026 1690 D5
Skylark Ct
2000 LGMT 80503 1355 C5
Skylark Dr
200 LAFT 80026 1690 D5
S Skylark St
8700 DgsC 80126 2450 A2
Sky Lark Wy
200 BldC 80303 1688 D5
Skyline
10 BldC 80403 1852 A1
Skyline Dr
- ERIE 80516 1692 A3
10 JfnC 80215 2110 A2
10 LKWD 80215 2110 A2
10 WTRG 80215 2110 A2
700 CCkC 80452 2101 A7
2500 WSTR 80030 1944 A6
30400 JfnC 80403 1853 A4
33700 JfnC 80403 1852 B6
S Skyline Dr
3800 JfnC 80439 2272 C5
5400 JfnC 80439 2357 E1
Skyline Ln
1500 LGMT 80501 1356 D6
Sky Meadow Ln
20500 JfnC 80401 2107 C7
20700 JfnC 80401 2191 C1
Sky Ranch Rd
2200 AURA 80011 2117 D3
Skysail Ct
2400 LGMT 80503 1355 B4
Sky Trail Rd
10 BldC 80302 1601 A1
Sky Trail St
5200 BWMR 80123 2279 C7
Skyview Ct
100 LSVL 80027 1773 A1
N Skyview Dr
10 BldC 80466 1766 B1
S Skyview Dr
10 BldC 80466 1766 B1
Sky View Ln
1300 DgsC 80118 2870 C6
Sky Vu Dr
33700 JfnC 80403 1852 B6
Skywalker Pt
700 LAFT 80026 1689 D4
Skyway Ct
7400 BldC 80303 1772 D1
Skyway Dr
- LGMT 80504 1440 D3
700 BldC 80303 1772 D1
1500 WldC 80504 1440 D3
Slate Ct
2700 SUPE 80027 1773 A7
7300 CSRK 80108 2620 A5
Slaughterhouse Gulch Rd
200 BldC 80455 1516 B3
200 JMWN 80455 1516 B3
Sleeping Bear Tr
7100 DgsC 80125 2614 D1
7300 DgsC 80125 2530 D7
Sleeping Fox Ct
2400 DgsC 80109 2702 A7
Sleeping Owl Pt
500 LAFT 80026 1689 E4
Sleepygrass Ct
8900 PARK 80134 2453 A3
Sleepy Hollow Dr
10 PrkC 80456 2607 B6
Sleepy Hollow Rd
900 JfnC 80401 2191 A4
Sleepytime Dr
- BldC 80301 1603 E3
4600 BLDR 80301 1603 D3
Slick Rock Ct
5600 BLDR 80301 1604 B1
S Sly Fox Wy
100 DgsC 80135 2785 D1
Small Dr
6100 CMCY 80022 2030 B1
Smiley Dr
- BLDR 80303 1687 A3
Smith Cir
200 ERIE 80516 1607 D6
Smith Ct
2300 LGMT 80501 1356 A5
Smith Dr
2200 LGMT 80501 1356 A5
E Smith Dr
13700 AURA 80011 2116 B2
Smith Rd
- AdmC 80137 2120 A4
- AphC 80019 2120 A4
- AphC 80137 2203 D7
- AURA 80018 2203 D6
- AURA 80137 2203 D7
10 PrkC 80456 2521 D2
1800 GOLD 80401 2107 D5
10500 AURA 80010 2115 C1
10500 DNVR 80238 2115 C1
11400 AURA 80011 2115 D1
12700 AURA 80011 2116 C2
16200 AURA 80011 2117 A3
19200 AdmC 80011 2118 A3
19200 AdmC 80019 2118 A3
19200 AURA 80011 2118 A3
19200 AURA 80019 2118 A3
23300 AdmC 80019 2119 A4
23300 AURA 80019 2119 A4
33400 JfnC 80470 2524 C6
E Smith Rd
4000 DNVR 80216 2029 E7
4400 DNVR 80216 2030 A7
5600 DNVR 80207 2030 D7
7300 DNVR 80207 2114 E1
8800 DNVR 80207 2115 A1
Smith St
10 PrkC 80456 2522 A3
Smith Wy
- AphC 80231 2198 C7
- DNVR 80224 2198 C7
- DNVR 80231 2198 C7
1500 AdmC 80019 2118 D4
1500 AURA 80019 2118 D4
Smith Hill Rd
10 GpnC 80403 2019 A4
2200 GpnC 80403 2018 E6
Smokey Rock Rd
10 PrkC 80456 2521 B5
E Smoky Hill Rd
- AphC 80137 2371 D7
- DgsC 80138 2371 D7
700 AphC 80137 2372 C7
700 EbtC 80138 2372 C7
14200 AURA 80015 2284 C5
16500 AphC 80015 2284 E6
16700 CTNL 80015 2284 E6
16700 CTNL 80015 2285 A7
16900 AURA 80015 2285 A7
18500 AphC 80015 2285 A7
18500 CTNL 80015 2369 D1
19200 AphC 80015 2369 D1
20100 CTNL 80016 2369 D1
20300 AphC 80016 2369 D1
20700 CTNL 80015 2370 A2
20700 CTNL 80016 2370 A2
21000 AphC 80015 2370 A2
21000 AURA 80015 2370 A2
23100 AphC 80016 2370 E3
23100 AURA 80016 2370 E3
24300 AphC 80016 2371 B5
24300 AURA 80016 2371 B5
Smuggler Cir
3500 BLDR 80305 1771 A2
Smuggler Pl
3600 BLDR 80305 1771 A2
Smuggler Wy
3500 BLDR 80305 1771 A2
Snaffle Bit Ct
8300 DgsC 80125 2530 E5
Snakes Rd
- DNVR 80249 1951 B3
Snapdragon Ct
1500 SUPE 80027 1857 B1
Snead Ct
6600 BldC 80503 1519 B5
Sneffels
- TNTN 80260 1860 B7
Snowbank Ct
1200 LGMT 80501 1356 D7
Snowberry Ct
- BldC 80503 1521 A5
400 GOLD 80403 2107 C1
700 LAFT 80026 1690 B5
4300 BLDR 80304 1602 C4
Snowberry Dr
1100 JfnC 80401 2190 E4
S Snowberry Dr
5700 LITN 80123 2363 C2
Snowberry Ln
1200 BMFD 80020 1774 D7
1200 CSRK 80104 2788 A1
Snowberry Ln
6300 BldC 80503 1521 B6
S Snowberry Ln
4900 JfnC 80439 2274 D7
Snowberry St
600 LGMT 80503 1438 A5
Snowberry Wy
17600 PARK 80134 2453 A1
Snowbird Av
4100 BMFD 80020 1775 C7
Snowbird Ln
700 LAFT 80026 1689 E3
30000 JfnC 80439 2189 B6
Snowbird Wy
8700 DgsC 80134 2452 E2
S Snowbrush Ln
8600 DgsC 80126 2449 B2
S Snowbunting Ct
8800 DgsC 80126 2449 E2
Snowcap Ln
- BMFD 80020 1775 C2
W Snow Cloud Tr
10800 DgsC 80125 2614 D1
Snowcreek Ct
21300 PARK 80138 2538 A2
Snow Creek Ln
17000 JfnC 80465 2360 C1
Snowcreek Ln
11600 PARK 80138 2538 A2
Snowcrest Dr
- BMFD 80020 1775 C2
Snowdrop Rd
26200 JfnC 80439 2274 A3
Snowflake Wy
- DgsC 80134 2621 A4
Snow Goose St
5200 BGTN 80601 1697 E6
Snow Lake Ct
900 AphC 80137 2121 E5
Snow Lily Ct
1000 DgsC 80108 2534 D7
Snow Lily Ln
1100 DgsC 80108 2534 D7
Snow Lily Pl
7400 DgsC 80108 2534 D7
Snowmass Cir
2100 BMFD 80020 1774 D5
N Snowmass Cir
500 SUPE 80027 1857 A2
S Snowmass Cir
600 SUPE 80027 1857 A2
Snowmass Ct
1400 BLDR 80305 1770 E1
Snowmass Mtn
26200 JfnC 80127 2362 A7
Snowmass Pl
10 LGMT 80501 1439 C1
Snowmass Rd
1800 TNTN 80260 1860 A7
Snowmass St
- AphC 80011 2202 A1
- AURA 80011 2202 A1
Snowmass Peak Dr
4100 CSRK 80109 2787 A5
4500 CSRK 80109 2786 E5
Snow Peak Ct
7100 BldC 80503 1521 B4
Snowpeak Ln
600 BldC 80026 1689 B4
Snowshoe Ct
21100 PARK 80138 2538 B2
Snowshoe Dr
11800 PARK 80138 2538 A2
Snowshoe Ln
21200 PARK 80138 2538 A3
Snowshoe Rd
31100 JfnC 80439 2357 A4
31200 JfnC 80439 2356 D4
S Snowshoe Tr
6700 JfnC 80439 2356 C5
Snow Valley Rd
24400 JfnC 80439 2442 D1
Snow Water Rd
10 PrkC 80456 2521 B5
Snow Willow Ct
8200 DgsC 80108 2534 D5
Snowy Tr
10500 JfnC 80433 2443 B7
10700 JfnC 80433 2527 B1
Snowy Mesa Dr
- CSRK 80108 2703 E1
Snowy Owl Dr
1400 BMFD 80020 1775 A5
Snowy Owl Ln
- PARK 80138 2538 A3
10 JfnC 80127 2360 E4
Snowy Owl Pl
400 DgsC 80126 2448 E3
Snowy Ridge Cir
3800 EbtC 80107 2709 C1
Snyder Av
25200 JfnC 80433 2442 B5
Snyder St
100 NDLD 80466 1765 D3
Snyder Wy
1100 SUPE 80027 1773 B5
Snyder Gulch Rd
1200 JfnC 80439 2188 A5
Snyder Mountain Rd
10 CCkC 80439 2271 C3
Soapstone Ct
7300 CSRK 80108 2619 E5
Soapstone Wy
7400 CSRK 80108 2619 E5
Soapweed Cir
5400 DgsC 80134 2622 B4
Soaring Eagle Ct
3500 CSRK 80109 2702 C3
Soaring Eagle Dr
31400 JfnC 80439 2272 E3
Soaring Eagle Ln
3100 CSRK 80109 2702 C3
W Sobey Av
7900 JfnC 80128 2446 D3

STREET
Block City ZIP Map# Grid

Soda Creek Dr
600 JfnC 80439 2188 B4
S Soda Creek Dr
31700 JfnC 80401 2188 E2
31700 JfnC 80439 2188 E2
Soda Creek Rd
10 IDSP 80452 2101 D6
200 CCkC 80452 2101 C7
1500 CCkC 80452 2185 A1
S Soda Creek Rd
10 JfnC 80439 2188 D2
1000 JfnC 80439 2189 A4
Soda Creek Tr
- CCkC 80452 2185 E3
10 CCkC 80452 2186 A3
Soda Lakes Rd
3500 JfnC 80465 2276 D3
3500 MRSN 80465 2276 D3
Sodalite Wy
- CSRK 80108 2619 D5
Softwind Pt
- CSRK 80104 2704 B4
- CSRK 80108 2704 B4
Solana Dr
1200 AdmC 80229 1945 A4
6600 DgsC 80108 2534 C4
Solana Pl
6900 DgsC 80108 2534 C4
N Solar Dr
10500 DgsC 80125 2531 B1
10800 DgsC 80125 2447 B7
Solar Pl
- PARK 80134 2537 D2
Solitude Ln
1300 JfnC 80439 2188 E5
22800 JfnC 80401 2191 A4
Solstice Wy
- CSRK 80108 2619 E5
Sombrero Cir
4400 BWMR 80123 2279 C5
Sombrero St
5300 BWMR 80123 2279 B5
5300 DNVR 80123 2279 B5
Somerset Ct
7200 DgsC 80108 2534 E7
43300 EbtC 80107 2543 A3
Somerset Dr
400 GOLD 80401 2108 A7
400 GOLD 80401 2192 B1
6200 BldC 80503 1521 A5
Somerset St
1100 LAFT 80026 1690 B4
Sommerset Cir
1300 LGMT 80501 1356 E7
1300 LGMT 80501 1357 B6
Sonata Bay Ct
2900 LGMT 80503 1355 C5
Songbird Cir
6000 BldC 80303 1687 E3
6000 BldC 80303 1688 A3
Songbird Ct
1300 BldC 80303 1688 A3
Songbird Wy
5000 DgsC 80134 2622 D4
Songbird Hills Pl
23300 PARK 80138 2538 D3
Songbird Hills St
11900 PARK 80138 2538 D3
Songbird Hills Wy
23100 PARK 80138 2538 D3
S Song Sparrow Ln
10200 DgsC 80129 2448 C6
Sonoma Cir
1000 LGMT 80501 1356 E5
E Sonoma Tr
10100 DgsC 80138 2539 A5
S Sopris Creek Dr
12500 PARK 80134 2537 C5
Sorento Pl
200 LGMT 80501 1439 C2
Sorrel Ct
1400 LGMT 80501 1357 B7
Sorrel Dr
- BMFD 80020 1775 C2
Sorrel Rd
9400 DgsC 80108 2535 A2
9900 DgsC 80108 2534 E2
Sorrel Run
- BMFD 80020 1775 C2
S Sourdough Dr
7200 JfnC 80465 2359 D5
South Dr
- SRDN 80110 2280 A4
South Ln
10 CHLV 80113 2281 A6
South Pl
- LKWD 80226 2194 A1
300 LSVL 80027 1689 B7
South St
400 LSVL 80027 1689 C7
500 CSRK 80104 2703 E7
1100 CSRK 80104 2704 A7
2300 BLDR 80302 1686 E2
Southard St
1700 ERIE 80516 1690 D1
E South Boulder Rd
- BldC 80026 1690 E6
- BldC 80026 1691 A6
- LAFT 80026 1691 A6
100 LAFT 80026 1690 D6
W South Boulder Rd
100 LAFT 80026 1690 A6
100 LSVL 80027 1690 A6
800 BldC 80027 1689 A6
1300 LSVL 80026 1690 A6
Southbury Ct
1000 DgsC 80129 2448 C6
W Southbury Pl
1000 DgsC 80129 2448 C6
South End Rd
26100 JfnC 80457 2274 A3
Southern St
- AdmC 80601 1697 D6
- BGTN 80601 1697 A7
E Southern St
- AdmC 80601 1697 A7
400 BGTN 80601 1696 C7
2000 AdmC 80601 1696 E7
3000 BGTN 80601 1697 A7
W Southern St
300 BGTN 80601 1696 A7
400 AdmC 80601 1696 A7
Southern Hills Cir
9400 LNTR 80124 2450 E4
9400 LNTR 80124 2451 A4
Southern Hills Pl
31600 JfnC 80439 2188 E6
Southhaven Cir
10700 DgsC 80126 2449 D7
Southlawn Cir
- CMCY 80022 1865 A6
E Southlawn Pkwy
- CMCY 80022 1865 A6
South Loop Dr
- BldC 80305 1687 C6
- BLDR 80305 1687 C6
E Southmoor Cir
5600 CHLV 80111 2282 B5
Southmoor Dr
10 DNVR 80220 2198 B1
10 DNVR 80224 2198 B1
Southmoor Ln
5600 CHLV 80111 2282 B5
South Park Av
- SRDN 80110 2280 A3
South Park Cir
8000 LITN 80120 2364 A7
8000 LITN 80120 2448 A1
8000 LITN 80129 2448 A1
Southpark Dr
600 LITN 80120 2448 C1
Southpark Ln
- LITN 80120 2364 C7
8100 LITN 80120 2448 C1
8200 AphC 80129 2448 C1
Southpark Plz
7900 LITN 80120 2364 E7
7900 LITN 80120 2448 E1
Southpark Rd
10 DgsC 80126 2448 E3
10 DgsC 80129 2448 E3
Southpark Ter
7900 LITN 80120 2364 D7
8200 AphC 80129 2448 D1
8200 LITN 80120 2448 D1
Southpark Wy
- LITN 80120 2364 C7
8000 LITN 80120 2448 C1
Southpointe Dr
2600 LAFT 80026 1774 C1
Southridge Ct
1300 JfnC 80401 2190 B5
Southridge Ln
- BldC 80504 1521 D3
S Southridge Ln
6700 LITN 80120 2364 C4
Southridge Pl
300 LGMT 80501 1439 B6
Southridge Wy
10 LITN 80120 2364 C4
Southshire Rd
2700 DgsC 80126 2533 C1
E Southtech Dr
9100 GDVL 80111 2367 A3
Southview Dr
30700 JfnC 80439 2273 A3
Southwind Ct
5400 JfnC 80465 2360 C1
S Southwood Dr
800 CTNL 80121 2365 A2
E Sovereign St
5400 CSRK 80104 2704 E7
Spangler Dr
1100 NHGN 80260 1860 C6
Spangler Pl
- LGMT 80501 1356 C7
Spangler St
- NHGN 80260 1860 C6
- TNTN 80260 1860 C6
Spanish Oaks Tr
- CSRK 80108 2704 B3
E Spanish Peak
10500 JfnC 80127 2362 A7
W Spanish Peak
8000 JfnC 80127 2362 A7
Sparrow Ct
10 PrkC 80456 2607 A7
Sparrow Ln
- BldC 80301 1603 D7
300 EbtC 80107 2708 A1
Sparrow St
5000 BGTN 80601 1697 D7
Sparrow Wy
5000 BGTN 80601 1697 D7
S Sparrow Hawk Ct
10300 DgsC 80129 2448 C6
Sparrow Hawk Dr
900 LGMT 80501 1440 A1
W Sparrow Hawk Dr
700 DgsC 80129 2448 D6
S Sparrow Hawk Wy
10300 DgsC 80129 2448 D6
Sparrow Point Wy
16400 JfnC 80465 2360 C3
Sparta Dr
800 LAFT 80026 1690 A5
Spaulding Cir
1800 SUPE 80027 1773 C5
E Spaulding St
100 LAFT 80026 1690 D5
W Spaulding St
100 LAFT 80026 1690 C5
Spearwood Dr
3000 DgsC 80126 2449 C7
Speer Blvd
- DNVR 80211 2112 B3
600 DNVR 80203 2112 D6
600 DNVR 80204 2112 D6
E Speer Blvd
- DNVR 80204 2112 E7
10 DNVR 80203 2112 E7
600 DNVR 80203 2197 A1
700 DNVR 80218 2197 A1
N Speer Blvd
2700 DNVR 80211 2112 A2
3000 DNVR 80211 2111 E2
Spencer St
900 LGMT 80501 1438 D1
1700 LGMT 80501 1355 D5
2400 BldC 80501 1355 D5
2400 BldC 80504 1355 D5
Sperry St
10400 NHGN 80234 1860 B5
Spica Dr
13000 DgsC 80124 2450 E2
Spikegrass Ct
8100 DgsC 80108 2534 C6
Spindrift Dr
2200 LGMT 80503 1355 C4
Spine Rd
4200 BLDR 80301 1603 E4
4600 BldC 80301 1603 E3
5100 BldC 80301 1604 A2
5100 BLDR 80301 1604 A2
Spinnaker Cir
2200 LGMT 80503 1355 B4
Spinnaker Dr
3000 LGMT 80503 1355 B4
Spinnaker Pl
2900 LGMT 80503 1355 B4
Spinnaker Wy
7900 BldC 80504 1522 A2
Spinning Wheel Dr
- BGTN 80601 1697 D4
Spirit Ct
9200 DgsC 80138 2538 E3
Spirit Horse Tr
8200 JfnC 80403 1936 B5
Spirit Lake Rd
10 PrkC 80456 2522 E6
10 PrkC 80470 2522 E6
10 PrkC 80470 2523 B6
Spirit Valley Tr
13000 JfnC 80433 2609 D1
Splendor Ln
3700 CSRK 80109 2702 D2
S Split Rock Rd
300 AphC 80102 2207 A3
Spoke Rd
- DgsC 80138 2454 D1
Sports Blvd
- DNVR 80230 2198 E1
E Sports Park Dr
- AURA 80011 2117 D5
S Spotswood Cir
6300 LITN 80120 2364 B3
S Spotswood Ct
7500 LITN 80120 2364 B6
Spotswood Pl
2200 BLDR 80304 1602 D4
S Spotswood St
5600 LITN 80120 2364 B1
Spotted Deer Ln
10 DgsC 80116 2706 D7
10 DgsC 80116 2790 E1
Spotted Fawn Run
6300 DgsC 80125 2615 A2
Spotted Horse Tr
5200 BldC 80301 1604 B1
S Spotted Owl Av
- DgsC 80129 2448 C6
S Spotted Owl Ct
10200 DgsC 80129 2448 D7
S Spotted Owl Pl
10200 DgsC 80129 2448 D7
S Spotted Owl Wy
1300 DgsC 80129 2448 C6
W Spread Eagle Mtn
9800 JfnC 80127 2362 B6
Spring Cir
10 PrkC 80470 2523 C5
Spring Ct
7100 BldC 80303 1772 C1
Spring Dr
- BldC 80303 1688 D7
10 PrkC 80470 2523 D5
7100 BldC 80303 1772 C1
8800 JfnC 80433 2440 B3
11700 NHGN 80233 1860 E3
11700 NHGN 80233 1861 A2
Spring Ln
10 BldC 80302 1517 B7
Spring Pl
- EbtC 80138 2456 E5
- EbtC 80138 2457 A5
Spring St
100 CLCY 80403 2017 D4
100 MRSN 80465 2276 C3
300 JfnC 80465 2276 C3
W Spring St
200 NDLD 80466 1765 C3
Spring Vly
100 PrkC 80456 2690 C2
Springbriar Dr
3000 CSRK 80109 2702 D3
Spring Creek Cir
7200 BldC 80503 1521 B3
Spring Creek Cross
1500 LAFT 80026 1689 E2
Spring Creek Ct
1200 LGMT 80501 1356 E7
Spring Creek Dr
1500 LAFT 80026 1689 E1
Spring Creek Pl
3400 BLDR 80301 1603 A6
Spring Creek Rd
- DNVR 80237 2282 E5
- DNVR 80237 2283 A5
E Spring Creek Rd
10000 DgsC 80138 2455 B5
N Spring Creek Rd
12000 DgsC 80138 2454 B4
Spring Creek Tr
8800 BldC 80503 1521 B4
S Spring Creek Pass
8100 JfnC 80127 2361 E7
Springdale Ln
2800 BLDR 80303 1686 D5
2800 BLDR 80303 1687 A3
Springdale Pl
10 LGMT 80501 1439 C1
W Springer Dr
10 DgsC 80129 2448 E2
Springfield Ct
17200 DgsC 80134 2537 A1
17200 PARK 80134 2537 A1
Springflower Dr
22000 JfnC 80401 2191 A4
Spring Grove Av
400 DgsC 80126 2448 E3
Spring Gulch Dr
- LmrC 80540 1269 A2
Spring Gulch Rd
- BldC 80455 1599 C1
10 BldC 80481 1597 E1
10 BldC 80481 1598 A1
10 CCkC 80452 2101 A6
200 LmrC 80540 1269 A1
19600 JfnC 80465 2359 E7
20100 JfnC 80465 2443 D1
Spring Harbor Ln
- BMFD 80020 1775 E3
- BMFD 80020 1776 A3
Spring Harbor Wy
- BMFD 80020 1775 E3
S Spring Hill Av
- DgsC 80129 2448 B5
W Spring Hill Ct
2500 DgsC 80129 2448 B5
Springhill Dr
6800 BldC 80503 1520 E4
6800 BldC 80503 1521 A4
S Spring Hill Dr
9700 DgsC 80129 2448 A5
S Spring Hill Ln
9700 DgsC 80129 2448 A5
S Spring Hill Pkwy
- DgsC 80129 2448 A5
S Spring Hill Pl
9700 DgsC 80129 2448 A5
S Spring Hill St
9700 DgsC 80129 2448 A5
S Spring Hill Wy
- DgsC 80129 2448 A5
W Spring Hill Peak Cir
2800 DgsC 80129 2448 A5
Springmeadow Cir
3100 CSRK 80109 2702 D2
Spring Meadow Ct
9100 JfnC 80439 2442 A3
Springmeadow Dr
4400 CSRK 80109 2702 B2
Springmeadow Ln
4500 CSRK 80109 2702 D2
Spring Ranch Dr
300 JfnC 80401 2189 E3
Springs Dr
200 LSVL 80027 1773 B2
Springs Pl
2100 LGMT 80504 1438 D7
Springs Rd
11800 JfnC 80433 2525 D3
Springs Cove
100 LSVL 80027 1773 C2
Springvale Rd
500 CSRK 80104 2705 A7
500 CSRK 80104 2789 A1
Spring Valley Rd
3700 BldC 80304 1602 B5
3700 BLDR 80304 1602 B5
Spring Valley Tr
3700 JfnC 80439 2273 A4
S Spring Water Ct
10100 DgsC 80129 2448 C5
W Spring Water Ln
1600 DgsC 80129 2448 C6
W Spring Water Pl
1500 DgsC 80129 2448 B6
W Spring Water Wy
1500 DgsC 80129 2448 C6
S Spring Water Peak
10300 DgsC 80129 2448 C6
N Springwood Ct
2300 LAFT 80026 1774 B1
S Springwood Ct
2400 LAFT 80026 1774 B1
Spruce Av
100 LCHB 80603 1698 C3
1200 LGMT 80501 1439 A2
1300 LGMT 80501 1438 E2
1800 BldC 80501 1438 D2
5400 CSRK 80104 2704 E6
E Spruce Av
5200 CSRK 80104 2704 E6
Spruce Cir
- LSVL 80027 1689 C7
500 LSVL 80027 1773 B1
S Spruce Cir
6900 CTNL 80112 2366 D4
Spruce Ct
- BLDR 80302 1686 B2
10 CCkC 80439 2271 C2
200 BldC 80302 1686 B2
1900 ERIE 80516 1692 A3
4800 EbtC 80107 2709 E7
20300 PARK 80138 2454 A7
S Spruce Ct
900 DNVR 80220 2114 D6
900 DNVR 80230 2114 D6
7700 CTNL 80112 2366 D6
Spruce Dr
10 PrkC 80456 2606 D4
1200 JfnC 80401 2191 A5
1700 WldC 80516 1523 E7
1700 WldC 80516 1607 E1
13800 JfnC 80433 2609 D1
Spruce Dr
28400 JfnC 80433 2525 C4
S Spruce Dr E
6900 CTNL 80112 2366 D5
S Spruce Dr W
6900 CTNL 80112 2366 D5
Spruce Ln
- IDSP 80452 2101 E5
10 CCkC 80452 2186 A4
27200 JfnC 80439 2357 E4
28900 JfnC 80439 2273 C5
W Spruce Ln
400 LSVL 80027 1689 B7
Spruce Pl
- TNTN 80602 1778 D6
800 LCHB 80603 1698 B2
Spruce Rd
10 JfnC 80401 2190 D1
29500 JfnC 80439 2273 B2
Spruce St
- AphC 80120 2447 E1
- BMFD 80020 1692 A7
- BMFD 80020 1775 E1
- BMFD 80020 1776 A1
- DNVR 80230 2198 D1
- LITN 80120 2447 E1
- TNTN 80602 1778 D6
10 BldC 80455 1516 B3
100 CLCY 80403 2017 C4
100 ELIZ 80107 2793 B1
100 JMWN 80455 1516 B3
200 BldC 80302 1686 B2
500 BLDR 80302 1686 B2
900 DNVR 80230 2114 D6
1100 LSVL 80027 1689 D7
1200 DNVR 80220 2114 D4
1900 DNVR 80238 2114 D4
2700 BLDR 80301 1686 E1
S Spruce St
1800 DNVR 80231 2198 D6
3500 DNVR 80237 2282 D3
6700 CTNL 80112 2366 D4
6700 GDVL 80112 2366 D4
W Spruce St
100 LSVL 80027 1689 C7
600 NDLD 80466 1765 C3
Spruce Tr
10 PrkC 80456 2607 C7
Spruce Wy
10 BldC 80466 1767 A5
10 GpnC 80403 1933 C7
S Spruce Wy
2900 DNVR 80231 2282 D2
W Spruce Wy
500 LSVL 80027 1689 B7
Spruce Canyon Cir
11700 JfnC 80403 1853 B2
Spruce Canyon Dr
29200 JfnC 80403 1853 B3
Sprucedale Dr
10000 JfnC 80433 2441 D6
Sprucedale Park Wy
6900 JfnC 80439 2357 A5
Spruce Dell Ct
3300 CSRK 80109 2702 D2
Spruce Dell Dr
3200 CSRK 80109 2702 E2
Spruce Meadows Dr
- AdmC 80020 1776 A1
- BMFD 80020 1775 E1
- BMFD 80020 1776 A1
S Spruce Mountain Rd
7900 DgsC 80118 2955 B4
7900 LKSR 80118 2955 B4
S Spruce Mountain Rd CO-53
7900 DgsC 80118 2955 B4
7900 LKSR 80118 2955 B4
Sprucewood Ct
300 LAFT 80026 1690 B7
300 LAFT 80026 1774 B1
W Sprucewood Dr
7600 DgsC 80135 2784 A4
7800 DgsC 80135 2783 E4
Spur Ct
10 BldC 80481 1515 A2
500 GOLD 80403 2023 D7
E Spur Ln
6900 AURA 80138 2453 E2
6900 DgsC 80138 2453 E2
Spur Cross Tr
5300 DgsC 80134 2621 B4
Spyderco Wy
800 GOLD 80403 2023 C7
Spyglass Cir
800 LSVL 80027 1773 B3
1800 JfnC 80439 2188 E7
Spy Glass Ct
- DgsC 80118 2868 D6
7400 BldC 80301 1604 D2
Spyglass Dr
10 CBVL 80123 2363 D4
4700 BMFD 80020 1775 B3
Spy Glass Ln
4000 BldC 80503 1518 E6
4000 BldC 80503 1519 A6
Squaw Pass Rd
16600 CCkC 80452 2185 C6
20000 CCkC 80452 2186 A5
25100 CCkC 80439 2187 A6
25100 CCkC 80452 2187 A6
28300 CCkC 80439 2188 C6
Squaw Pass Rd CO-66
34600 CCkC 80439 2188 C6
Squaw Pass Rd SR-103
16600 CCkC 80452 2185 C6
20000 CCkC 80452 2186 A5
25100 CCkC 80439 2187 A6
25100 CCkC 80452 2187 A6
28300 CCkC 80439 2188 C6
Squires Cir
4400 BLDR 80305 1687 B7
Squires Ct
2300 LGMT 80501 1356 A5
Squires St
2100 LGMT 80501 1356 A5
Squirrel Ln
28300 JfnC 80433 2525 D5
Squirreltail Pl
17700 PARK 80134 2453 B2
SR-2
- AdmC 80022 1863 C7
- AdmC 80022 1946 E3
- AdmC 80022 1947 B2
- AdmC 80603 1864 A4
- CMCY 80022 1863 E4
- CMCY 80022 1864 A4
- CMCY 80022 1946 E3
- CMCY 80022 1947 B2
- CMCY 80022 2029 E2
- CMCY 80022 2030 A2
- CMCY 80603 1864 A4
- CMCY 80640 1947 B2
- DNVR 80022 2029 E2
- DNVR 80216 2029 E2
SR-2 S 4th Av
10 BGTN 80601 1696 B7
900 AdmC 80601 1780 B1
900 BGTN 80601 1780 B1
SR-2 N 7th Av
10 BGTN 80601 1696 C5
500 BGTN 80603 1696 C5
SR-2 E Bridge St
400 BGTN 80601 1696 C6
SR-2 Colorado Blvd
- DNVR 80022 2029 E5
10 DNVR 80206 2197 E1
10 DNVR 80209 2197 E1
10 DNVR 80220 2197 E1
10 DNVR 80246 2197 E1
300 DNVR 80206 2113 E7
300 DNVR 80220 2113 E7
1800 DNVR 80207 2113 E7
2200 DNVR 80205 2113 E7
3800 DNVR 80207 2029 E7
4000 DNVR 80205 2029 E7
4000 DNVR 80216 2029 E7
5100 DNVR 80022 2029 E5
SR-2 S Colorado Blvd
10 DNVR 80206 2197 E3
10 DNVR 80209 2197 E3
10 DNVR 80220 2197 E3
300 DNVR 80246 2197 E3
300 GNDL 80246 2197 E3
1000 DNVR 80210 2197 E7
1200 DNVR 80222 2197 E7
2600 DNVR 80222 2281 E1
3400 AphC 80210 2281 E3
3400 CHLV 80113 2281 E3
3400 DNVR 80210 2281 E3
3400 DvrC 80222 2281 E3
SR-2 Dahlia St
6000 CMCY 80022 2029 E4
6200 CMCY 80022 2030 A2
SR-2 Sable Blvd
- AdmC 80603 1864 B3
- CMCY 80603 1864 B3
12000 AdmC 80601 1864 B1
12000 BGTN 80601 1864 B1
12000 CMCY 80601 1864 B1
12400 AdmC 80601 1780 B7
12400 BGTN 80601 1780 B7
SR-2 Vasquez Blvd
5500 CMCY 80022 2029 E4
SR-7
- AdmC 80602 1693 A5
- BldC 80301 1602 C2
- BLDR 80304 1602 C2
- TNTN 80020 1692 E4
- TNTN 80020 1693 A5
- TNTN 80602 1692 E4
- TNTN 80602 1693 B6
SR-7 5th Av
100 BldC 80540 1352 D2
100 LYNS 80540 1352 D2
SR-7 28th St
- BldC 80302 1602 C2
- BLDR 80304 1602 C2
1600 BLDR 80301 1686 E2
1600 BLDR 80302 1686 E2
1600 BLDR 80303 1686 E2
5000 BldC 80301 1602 C2
5000 BLDR 80302 1602 C2
SR-7 N 107th St
2100 LAFT 80026 1690 B3
2300 BldC 80026 1690 A2
3000 ERIE 80026 1690 B3
SR-7 E 160th Av
- AdmC 80601 1698 A5
- AdmC 80603 1698 A5
- BGTN 80601 1698 A5
- BGTN 80603 1698 A5
2100 TNTN 80602 1693 B6
4000 TNTN 80602 1694 A6
7300 AdmC 80602 1694 E6
8900 AdmC 80602 1695 B6
12300 AdmC 80601 1695 E6
12900 AdmC 80601 1696 A6
12900 AdmC 80602 1696 A6
12900 BGTN 80601 1696 A6
SR-7 W 168th Av
- BldC 80026 1691 A4
- BMFD 80020 1691 A4
- BMFD 80020 1692 B4
- BMFD 80516 1692 B4
- ERIE 80516 1691 A4
- ERIE 80516 1692 B4
- WldC 80516 1691 A4
SR-7 Arapahoe Av
2800 BLDR 80301 1686 E2
2800 BLDR 80303 1686 E2
2800 BLDR 80303 1687 A2
3000 BLDR 80301 1687 A2
4200 BldC 80301 1687 E2
4300 BldC 80303 1687 E2
SR-7 Arapahoe Rd
- ERIE 80026 1690 B2
6000 BldC 80301 1688 B2
SR-7 Arapahoe Rd
6000 BldC 80303 1687 E2
6000 BldC 80303 1688 B2
6000 BLDR 80301 1687 E2
6000 BLDR 80301 1688 B2
6000 BLDR 80303 1687 E2
6000 BLDR 80303 1688 B2
8200 BldC 80301 1689 B2
8200 BldC 80303 1689 B2
9300 LAFT 80026 1689 B2
9700 BldC 80026 1689 E2
9900 BldC 80026 1690 A2
9900 LAFT 80026 1690 A2
SR-7 Baseline Rd
- BMFD 80020 1692 C4
- BMFD 80516 1692 E4
- TNTN 80020 1692 E4
- TNTN 80602 1692 E4
SR-7 E Baseline Rd
100 LAFT 80026 1690 C4
700 BldC 80026 1690 D4
12000 BldC 80026 1691 A4
12000 ERIE 80026 1691 A4
12400 BldC 80516 1691 B4
12400 ERIE 80516 1691 B4
12500 BMFD 80020 1691 B4
SR-7 W Baseline Rd
100 LAFT 80026 1690 C4
SR-7 Bridge St
- AdmC 80601 1697 E5
- AdmC 80601 1698 A5
- AdmC 80603 1698 A5
- BGTN 80601 1697 E5
- BGTN 80601 1698 A5
- BGTN 80603 1698 A5
SR-7 E Bridge St
10 BGTN 80601 1696 C6
2400 AdmC 80601 1696 D6
3000 AdmC 80601 1697 A6
3000 BGTN 80601 1697 A6
SR-7 W Bridge St
10 AdmC 80601 1696 A6
10 BGTN 80601 1696 A6
SR-7 Broadway St
- BldC 80301 1602 C3
200 LYNS 80540 1352 D1
1800 BLDR 80302 1686 C1
2200 BLDR 80304 1686 C1
2900 BLDR 80304 1602 C7
SR-7 Canyon Blvd
1200 BLDR 80302 1686 D2
2600 BLDR 80301 1686 D2
SR-7 N Foothills Hwy
- BldC 80301 1602 C1
- BldC 80302 1602 C1
- BLDR 80302 1602 C1
- BLDR 80304 1602 C1
5700 BldC 80302 1518 C6
5700 BldC 80503 1518 C6
5700 BLDR 80302 1518 C6
8600 BldC 80302 1435 C7
8600 BldC 80503 1435 C7
9700 BldC 80540 1435 E1
10200 BldC 80503 1353 A7
10200 BldC 80503 1436 A1
SR-7 Main St
300 LYNS 80540 1352 D1
SR-7 E Main St
10 BldC 80503 1352 E2
10 LYNS 80503 1352 E2
10 LYNS 80540 1352 E2
SR-7 S St. Vrain Dr
26000 BldC 80540 1352 B3
32900 LYNS 80540 1352 D2
SR-7 Ute Hwy
4000 BldC 80503 1352 E2
4000 BldC 80503 1353 A3
4000 LYNS 80503 1352 E2
4000 LYNS 80503 1353 A3
4000 LYNS 80540 1352 E2
SR-8
- JfnC 80465 2276 C7
- MRSN 80465 2276 C7
SR-8 Bear Creek Av
100 MRSN 80465 2276 D3
SR-8 W Mississippi Av
5800 LKWD 80232 2195 B4
6200 LKWD 80226 2195 B4
SR-8 Morrison Rd
7600 LKWD 80227 2194 D7
9200 LKWD 80227 2278 B1
10000 JfnC 80227 2278 A1
11000 JfnC 80227 2277 D1
11000 LKWD 80227 2277 D1
11100 JfnC 80228 2277 D1
11100 LKWD 80228 2277 D1
14500 LKWD 80465 2277 A2
14500 MRSN 80228 2277 A2
SR-8 W Morrison Rd
14700 LKWD 80228 2277 A3
14700 LKWD 80465 2276 E3
14700 LKWD 80465 2277 A3
14700 MRSN 80228 2277 A3
16000 MRSN 80465 2276 E3
16400 JfnC 80465 2276 E3
SR-22 E 124th Av
10400 AdmC 80601 1863 E1
10400 AdmC 80640 1863 E1
10400 BGTN 80601 1863 E1
10400 BGTN 80640 1863 E1
13000 AdmC 80640 1864 A1
13200 AdmC 80601 1864 A1
13200 BGTN 80601 1864 A1
SR-26
- GOLD 80401 2192 B5
- JfnC 80401 2192 B5
- JfnC 80465 2192 B5
SR-26 W Alameda Av
900 DNVR 80223 2196 B2
2400 DNVR 80219 2196 A2
3500 DNVR 80219 2195 E2
5000 LKWD 80226 2195 B2
6900 LKWD 80226 2194 E2
11000 LKWD 80226 2193 D2

STREET
Block City ZIP Map# Grid

SR-26 W Alameda Av
11500 LKWD 80228 2193 D2
SR-26 W Alameda Pkwy
11600 LKWD 80226 2193 E2
11600 LKWD 80228 2193 E2
14800 JfnC 80228 2192 D6
14800 LKWD 80228 2192 E6
16500 JfnC 80401 2192 C5
16500 JfnC 80465 2192 C5
SR-30
- AphC 80011 2202 A1
- AphC 80018 2202 A1
- AURA 80018 2202 A1
SR-30 E 6th Av
- AphC 80018 2202 B2
10500 AURA 80010 2115 C7
11500 AURA 80011 2115 E7
12500 AURA 80011 2116 A7
16900 AURA 80011 2117 A7
20500 AURA 80011 2118 A7
21000 AphC 80011 2202 A1
21000 AURA 80011 2202 A1
21000 AURA 80018 2202 B1
SR-30 S Gun Club Rd
1400 AURA 80018 2202 D5
1900 AphC 80018 2202 D7
2700 AphC 80018 2286 D1
2700 AURA 80018 2286 D1
4100 AURA 80016 2286 D4
SR-30 E Hampden Av
5900 DNVR 80222 2282 B3
5900 DNVR 80237 2282 B3
6500 DNVR 80224 2282 B3
7200 DNVR 80231 2282 E3
8700 DNVR 80231 2283 A3
8700 DNVR 80237 2283 A3
9000 DvrC 80231 2283 A3
9000 GDVL 80014 2283 A3
9200 DNVR 80014 2283 B3
SR-30 Havana St
10 AURA 80010 2199 C1
10 AURA 80012 2199 C1
300 AURA 80010 2115 C7
SR-30 S Havana St
10 AURA 80010 2199 C1
10 AURA 80012 2199 C1
200 AphC 80012 2199 C3
200 DNVR 80010 2199 C3
200 DNVR 80247 2199 C3
600 AURA 80247 2199 C3
600 DvrC 80247 2199 C3
2500 AURA 80014 2199 C7
2500 AURA 80231 2199 C7
2500 DNVR 80014 2199 C7
2500 DNVR 80231 2199 C7
2600 AURA 80014 2283 C1
2600 DNVR 80231 2283 C1
3000 DNVR 80014 2283 C2
SR-30 E Quincy Av
25900 AphC 80018 2287 C4
25900 AURA 80016 2287 C4
SR-32 Tower Rd
1500 AURA 80011 2117 C3
4000 AURA 80011 2033 C7
4000 AURA 80249 2033 C7
4000 DNVR 80239 2033 C7
4000 DNVR 80249 2033 C7
4000 DvrC 80011 2033 C7
4000 DvrC 80239 2033 C7
4000 DvrC 80249 2033 C7
SR-33 E 40th Av
3900 DNVR 80205 2029 E7
3900 DNVR 80207 2029 E7
3900 DNVR 80216 2029 E7
SR-35 Quebec St
- DNVR 80207 2030 D7
3500 DNVR 80207 2114 D1
5000 AdmC 80022 2030 D6
5000 AdmC 80216 2030 D6
5000 CMCY 80022 2030 D6
5000 DNVR 80022 2030 D6
5000 DNVR 80216 2030 D6
SR-36
- AdmC 80102 2125 A3
- BNNT 80102 2125 A3
SR-36 E Colfax Av
- BNNT 80102 2124 A2
- BNNT 80102 2125 C4
100 AdmC 80102 2124 D2
28600 AphC 80019 2120 B5
30000 AdmC 80137 2120 B5
30300 AURA 80137 2120 B5
32900 AdmC 80137 2121 A4
32900 AURA 80137 2121 A4
36100 AdmC 80137 2122 A2
36100 AURA 80137 2122 A2
39300 AdmC 80102 2122 E2
39300 AdmC 80102 2123 C2
39300 AURA 80102 2123 C2
52100 AdmC 80102 2125 E4
52100 AphC 80136 2125 E4
SR-36 W Colfax Av
1100 AdmC 80102 2124 C2
1100 BNNT 80102 2124 C2
SR-36 Tower Rd
- AdmC 80019 2119 E4
- AdmC 80019 2120 A4
- AdmC 80137 2119 E4
- AphC 80137 2120 A4
SR-42 N 95th St
- BldC 80027 1689 D5
700 BldC 80303 1689 D3
700 LAFT 80026 1689 D5
700 LAFT 80027 1689 D5
SR-42 N 96th St
100 LSVL 80027 1689 D5
200 BldC 80027 1689 D5
300 LAFT 80027 1689 D5
SR-42 N Courtesy Rd
10 LSVL 80027 1689 D7
10 LSVL 80027 1773 E1
SR-42 Empire Rd
9700 LSVL 80027 1773 E1
10200 LSVL 80026 1773 E1
10200 LSVL 80026 1774 A1
10200 LSVL 80027 1774 A1
10300 LAFT 80026 1774 B1
SR-44 E 104th Av
10 NHGN 80229 1860 D6
10 NHGN 80233 1860 D6
10 NHGN 80260 1860 D6
10 TNTN 80229 1860 E6
200 TNTN 80233 1860 E6
700 NHGN 80233 1861 B6
700 TNTN 80229 1861 B6
1300 NHGN 80229 1861 B6
1900 TNTN 80233 1861 E6
4700 TNTN 80229 1862 A6
4700 TNTN 80233 1862 A6
5000 AdmC 80229 1862 A6
6100 AdmC 80233 1862 A6
7600 AdmC 80640 1862 E6
8100 CMCY 80640 1862 E6
8500 CMCY 80640 1863 A6
11900 CMCY 80022 1863 D6
SR-44 W 104th Av
- NHGN 80233 1860 E6
10 NHGN 80234 1860 B6
10 NHGN 80260 1860 E6
1400 TNTN 80234 1860 B6
1400 TNTN 80260 1860 B6
SR-46 Golden Gate Canyon Rd
10 GpnC 80403 1934 A5
2800 GpnC 80403 1935 A6
5100 GpnC 80403 2019 E1
5600 GpnC 80403 2020 A2
SR-52
- BldC 80504 1523 A6
- WldC 80516 1523 E6
SR-52 Mineral Rd
7100 BldC 80503 1520 D6
7100 BLDR 80503 1520 D6
7900 BldC 80503 1521 B6
9000 BldC 80504 1521 E6
9500 BldC 80504 1522 A6
11400 BldC 80504 1523 A6
12600 WldC 80516 1523 B6
SR-53 E 58th Av
- AdmC 80216 2028 E3
SR-53 Broadway
5800 AdmC 80216 2028 E1
6300 AdmC 80221 2028 E1
6700 AdmC 80221 1944 E7
SR-58
- GOLD - 2107 E2
- GOLD - 2108 A1
- JfnC - 2024 E7
- JfnC - 2025 A7
- JfnC - 2107 E2
- JfnC - 2108 A1
SR-66
- BldC 80504 1357 B4
SR-66 5th Av
500 LYNS 80540 1352 E2
SR-66 Broadway St
200 LYNS 80540 1352 D1
SR-66 Main St
300 LYNS 80540 1352 D1
SR-66 E Main St
10 BldC 80503 1352 E2
10 LYNS 80503 1352 E2
10 LYNS 80540 1352 E2
SR-66 W Main St
500 LYNS 80540 1352 E2
SR-66 N St. Vrain Dr
19700 BldC 80540 1352 C1
19700 LYNS 80540 1352 C1
SR-66 Ute Hwy
4000 BldC 80503 1352 E2
4000 BldC 80503 1353 A3
4000 LYNS 80503 1352 E2
4000 LYNS 80503 1353 A3
4000 LYNS 80540 1352 E2
6300 BldC 80503 1354 A4
7700 BldC 80503 1355 A4
7700 LGMT 80503 1355 A4
9300 BldC 80501 1355 E4
9300 BldC 80504 1355 E4
9300 LGMT 80501 1355 E4
10100 BldC 80504 1356 A4
10100 LGMT 80501 1356 A4
11900 BldC 80504 1357 A4
11900 LGMT 80501 1357 A4
SR-67 Jarre Canyon Rd
- DgsC 80125 2698 E6
- DgsC 80135 2616 E7
- DgsC 80135 2617 B6
- DgsC 80135 2698 E6
- DgsC 80135 2699 B5
- DgsC 80135 2700 B4
SR-67 Manhart St
5300 DgsC 80135 2617 C5
SR-72
- ARVD 80004 2025 A2
- ARVD 80007 2025 A2
- ARVD 80403 2025 A2
- BldC 80403 1766 D7
- BldC 80403 1767 C7
- BldC 80403 1852 A1
- BldC 80466 1767 C7
- GpnC 80403 1851 E1
- GpnC 80466 1766 D7
SR-72 W 2nd St
10 NDLD 80466 1765 D3
SR-72 W 64th Av
- ARVD 80403 2025 C2
13700 JfnC 80004 2025 C2
14400 ARVD 80004 2025 C2
14800 ARVD 80007 2025 C2
SR-72 S Bridge St
10 NDLD 80466 1765 D3
700 BldC 80466 1765 C4
SR-72 Coal Creek Canyon Dr
6700 BldC 80466 1765 E6
6700 BldC 80466 1766 B6
SR-72 Coal Creek Canyon Rd
- ARVD 80007 1939 D2
- ARVD 80007 1940 C3
- ARVD 80403 1938 E1
- ARVD 80403 1939 D2
- JfnC 80007 1939 D2
- JfnC 80007 1940 C3
- JfnC 80403 1938 E1
- JfnC 80403 1939 D2
23800 ARVD 80403 1854 C7
23800 JfnC 80403 1854 C7
26800 JfnC 80403 1853 E7
31100 BldC 80403 1852 E2
SR-72 Indiana St
- ARVD 80403 2025 A1
6400 ARVD 80004 2025 A1
6400 ARVD 80007 2025 A1
7000 ARVD 80007 1941 A7
7000 JfnC 80007 1941 A7
7800 JfnC 80005 1941 A7
8200 ARVD 80005 1941 A7
SR-72 Peak to Peak Hwy
- BldC 80481 1513 E1
- BldC 80481 1514 B3
- BldC 80481 1597 C2
- WARD 80481 1597 D1
22800 BldC 80466 1765 D4
33000 NDLD 80466 1765 D2
35700 BldC 80302 1682 A6
35700 BldC 80466 1682 A6
35900 BldC 80466 1681 D2
37700 BldC 80302 1681 D2
39000 BldC 80466 1597 B6
SR-72 Ward Rd
4400 JfnC 80033 2025 D7
4400 WTRG 80033 2025 D7
5000 ARVD 80002 2025 D7
5300 JfnC 80002 2025 D7
5600 ARVD 80004 2025 D7
SR-74
- JfnC 80439 2273 E5
- JfnC 80439 2274 A5
- JfnC 80457 2274 A5
SR-74 Bear Creek Av
17100 MRSN 80465 2276 C3
SR-74 Bear Creek Rd
17400 MRSN 80465 2276 B3
17600 JfnC 80465 2276 B3
18300 JfnC 80465 2275 C2
22100 JfnC 80439 2275 C2
22600 JfnC 80401 2275 C2
22800 JfnC 80401 2274 C2
22800 JfnC 80439 2274 C2
25200 JfnC 80457 2274 C2
SR-74 Evergreen Pkwy
800 JfnC 80401 2189 B5
800 JfnC 80439 2189 B5
1000 JfnC 80439 2188 D7
2800 JfnC 80439 2272 E1
2900 JfnC 80439 2273 A3
SR-75 W Bowles Av
2700 LITN 80120 2364 A1
2700 LITN 80123 2364 A1
3100 LITN 80123 2363 D3
3600 AphC 80123 2363 E2
3600 CBVL 80123 2363 E2
SR-75 W Littleton Blvd
- LITN 80120 2364 D1
SR-75 S Platte Canyon Rd
5900 AphC 80123 2363 D2
5900 CBVL 80123 2363 D2
5900 LITN 80123 2363 D2
6800 AphC 80128 2363 D5
7000 LITN 80128 2363 C5
8000 JfnC 80128 2447 B1
SR-79
- AdmC 80102 2124 E2
- BNNT 80102 2124 E2
SR-79 S 1st St
100 AdmC 80102 2124 D3
100 BNNT 80102 2124 D3
SR-79 Adams St
- BNNT 80102 2124 D2
SR-79 E Colfax Av
100 AdmC 80102 2124 D2
100 BNNT 80102 2124 D2
SR-79 Kiowa-Bennett Rd
2800 AdmC 80102 2125 A1
2800 BNNT 80102 2125 A1
SR-79 Palmer Av
500 BNNT 80102 2124 E2
700 AdmC 80102 2124 E2
SR-83
- CSRK 80116 2621 D7
- DgsC 80116 2621 D6
- DgsC 80116 2705 E2
- DgsC 80116 2706 A7
- DgsC 80116 2790 B3
SR-83 Leetsdale Dr
10 DNVR 80209 2197 E2
10 DNVR 80246 2197 E2
4400 GNDL 80246 2197 E2
4600 DNVR 80246 2198 A2
4600 GNDL 80246 2198 A2
6900 AphC 80247 2198 C3
6900 DNVR 80224 2198 C3
6900 DNVR 80247 2198 C3
SR-83 S Parker Rd
- AURA 80231 2199 C7
- DgsC 80116 2621 E1
- DgsC 80134 2621 D4
1000 AphC 80231 2198 D4
1000 AphC 80247 2198 D4
1000 DNVR 80224 2198 D4
1000 DNVR 80231 2198 D4
1000 DNVR 80247 2198 D4
1600 AphC 80231 2199 B6
1600 AphC 80247 2199 B6
2000 AURA 80247 2199 B6
2200 DNVR 80231 2199 B6
2200 DNVR 80247 2199 B6
2300 AURA 80014 2199 C7
2300 DNVR 80014 2199 C7
2500 AURA 80014 2283 C1
3100 DNVR 80014 2283 E2
3200 AphC 80014 2283 E2
3200 AphC 80014 2284 C7
3200 AURA 80014 2284 B4
4000 AURA 80015 2284 B4
5100 AphC 80015 2284 C7
5300 AphC 80015 2368 C1
5300 AURA 80015 2368 C1
5600 CTNL 80015 2368 C1
6200 AphC 80016 2368 E4
6200 CTNL 80016 2368 E4
6700 FXFD 80016 2368 E4
7000 AphC 80016 2369 A7
7000 CTNL 80016 2369 A7
7000 FXFD 80016 2369 A7
8000 AURA 80016 2369 A7
8000 AURA 80016 2453 B1
8000 AURA 80138 2453 B1
8000 CTNL 80016 2453 B1
8000 PARK 80138 2453 B1
8100 AphC 80016 2453 B1
8100 PARK 80134 2453 B1
9300 DgsC 80134 2453 C4
9300 DgsC 80138 2453 C4
9500 PARK 80134 2537 E5
10900 DgsC 80134 2537 D1
10900 PARK 80138 2537 D1
SR-86
- CSRK 80104 2703 E6
- CSRK 80104 2704 E4
- CSRK 80108 2704 E4
- CSRK 80108 2705 B3
- DgsC 80104 2703 E6
- DgsC 80104 2704 A6
- DgsC 80108 2704 E4
- DgsC 80108 2705 B3
- DgsC 80116 2705 B3
- DgsC 80116 2706 C5
- DgsC 80116 2707 A6
4000 EbtC 80107 2793 C1
4000 ELIZ 80107 2793 C1
5100 EbtC 80107 2794 D1
6900 EbtC 80107 2795 C2
10000 KIOW 80107 2795 C2
11300 EbtC 80117 2796 B3
11300 KIOW 80117 2796 B3
SR-86 Commanche St
- EbtC 80107 2795 E2
- EbtC 80107 2796 A2
- KIOW 80107 2795 E2
- KIOW 80107 2796 A2
200 KIOW 80117 2796 A2
700 EbtC 80117 2796 A2
SR-86 Kiowa Av
- ELIZ 80107 2793 C1
2700 EbtC 80107 2793 A1
SR-86 E Kiowa Av
100 ELIZ 80107 2793 B1
300 EbtC 80107 2793 B1
SR-86 W Kiowa Av
100 ELIZ 80107 2793 B1
200 EbtC 80107 2793 A1
SR-88
- GDVL - 2282 D7
- GDVL - 2366 D1
- GDVL - 2367 A3
SR-88 E Arapahoe Rd
- CTNL 80111 2367 E4
- GDVL 80111 2367 B4
8900 GDVL 80112 2367 B4
9600 CTNL 80112 2367 B4
10700 AphC 80112 2367 B4
12100 CTNL 80111 2368 A4
12100 CTNL 80112 2368 A4
12900 AphC 80111 2368 A4
12900 AphC 80112 2368 A4
14300 AphC 80016 2368 E4
16100 CTNL 80016 2368 E4
16100 FXFD 80016 2368 E4
20600 AURA 80016 2369 E4
20700 AphC 80016 2369 E4
20700 AphC 80016 2370 A4
20700 AURA 80016 2370 A4
20700 CTNL 80016 2369 E4
SR-88 E Belleview Av
10 AphC 80121 2280 E7
10 EGLD 80110 2280 E7
10 EGLD 80113 2280 E7
10 EGLD 80121 2280 E7
700 AphC 80121 2281 A7
700 CHLV 80113 2281 A7
700 EGLD 80113 2281 A7
700 GDVL 80121 2281 A7
1300 GDVL 80113 2281 A7
2400 CHLV 80121 2281 E7
4600 CHLV 80121 2282 A7
4600 GDVL 80121 2282 A7
5200 CHLV 80111 2282 C7
5200 GDVL 80111 2282 C7
6300 DvrC 80237 2282 A7
6500 DNVR 80237 2282 C7
6500 GDVL 80237 2282 A7
6600 DvrC 80111 2282 C7
SR-88 W Belleview Av
10 EGLD 80110 2280 E7
10 EGLD 80113 2280 E7
500 LITN 80120 2280 D7
900 EGLD 80120 2280 D7
2400 LITN 80123 2280 B7
SR-88 Federal Blvd
10 DNVR 80219 2196 A1
300 DNVR 80204 2112 A7
300 DNVR 80219 2112 A7
1900 DNVR 80211 2112 A3
4100 DNVR 80211 2028 A6
SR-88 S Federal Blvd
10 DNVR 80219 2196 A1
2600 DNVR 80219 2280 A1
2600 DNVR 80236 2280 A1
3200 DvrC 80236 2280 A2
3200 SRDN 80110 2280 A2
4400 EGLD 80110 2280 A5
4500 DNVR 80110 2280 A5
4800 DvrC 80110 2280 A7
5000 LITN 80123 2280 A7
SR-93
- ARVD 80007 1939 B1
- ARVD 80403 1939 B1
- BldC 80303 1855 C2
- BldC 80403 1855 C2
- JfnC 80403 1939 B1
SR-93 Broadway St
100 BLDR 80305 1686 E5
1100 BLDR 80302 1686 D3
SR-93 S Broadway St
10 BLDR 80305 1686 E5
10 BLDR 80305 1687 A6
1200 BLDR 80305 1771 B1
1400 BldC 80305 1771 C1
SR-93 S Foothills Hwy
1000 BldC 80305 1771 C2
1000 BLDR 80305 1771 C2
1400 BldC 80303 1771 C2
2800 BldC 80303 1855 C1
2800 BldC 80403 1855 C1
SR-93 Foothills Rd
- ARVD 80007 1939 D7
- ARVD 80007 2023 E1
- ARVD 80403 1939 C2
- ARVD 80403 2023 E1
- GOLD 80401 2107 C2
- GOLD 80403 2023 D6
- GOLD 80403 2107 C1
- JfnC 80007 1939 C3
- JfnC 80007 2023 E1
- JfnC 80403 1939 C3
- JfnC 80403 2023 E1
- JfnC 80403 2107 C1
SR-95 Sheridan Blvd
- ARVD 80002 2027 C4
10 DNVR 80219 2195 C1
10 LKWD 80226 2195 C1
200 DNVR 80204 2111 C7
200 DNVR 80219 2111 C7
400 LKWD 80204 2111 C7
400 LKWD 80226 2111 C7
700 LKWD 80214 2111 C7
2200 EDGW 80214 2111 C4
2500 DNVR 80212 2111 C4
2500 WTRG 80214 2111 C4
3000 WTRG 80212 2111 C1
4100 MNVW 80212 2027 C7
4100 WTRG 80212 2027 C7
4300 LKSD 80212 2027 C7
5100 AdmC 80212 2027 C4
5100 DNVR 80002 2027 C4
5100 DNVR 80212 2027 C4
5400 AdmC 80002 2027 C4
6000 ARVD 80003 2027 C4
6600 ARVD 80030 2027 B1
6700 WSTR 80030 2027 B1
6800 WSTR 80003 2027 B1
7000 WSTR 80030 1943 B7
7300 WSTR 80003 1943 B7
7900 WSTR 80031 1943 B4
8000 ARVD 80003 1943 B4
SR-95 S Sheridan Blvd
- DNVR 80235 2279 C3
10 DNVR 80219 2195 C1
400 LKWD 80226 2195 C1
1200 LKWD 80232 2195 C4
1300 LKWD 80219 2195 C4
1800 DNVR 80227 2195 C7
1800 DNVR 80232 2195 C7
2200 DvrC 80227 2195 C7
2200 LKWD 80227 2195 C7
2600 DNVR 80219 2279 C1
2600 DNVR 80227 2279 C1
2600 LKWD 80227 2279 C1
3200 DNVR 80236 2279 C3
SR-103 13th Av
- IDSP 80452 2101 B6
SR-103 Chicago Creek Rd
10 IDSP 80452 2101 C5
500 CCkC 80452 2101 B6
SR-103 Squaw Pass Rd
16600 CCkC 80452 2185 B7
20000 CCkC 80452 2186 B6
25100 CCkC 80439 2187 D6
25100 CCkC 80452 2187 A7
28300 CCkC 80439 2188 A6
SR-105 N Perry Park Rd
800 DgsC 80109 2701 D5
800 DgsC 80135 2701 D5
3600 DgsC 80135 2617 C7
SR-119
- BldC 80466 1765 E7
- CCkC 80403 2104 C6
- CCkC 80439 2103 D6
- GpnC 80403 1849 E2
- GpnC 80403 1850 C7
- GpnC 80403 1933 D6
- GpnC 80403 1934 D1
- GpnC 80403 2017 D1
- GpnC 80403 2018 C5
- GpnC 80403 2102 E1
- GpnC 80403 2103 A1
- GpnC 80474 1765 E7
- GpnC 80474 1849 E2
- JfnC 80439 2104 C6
- LGMT 80501 1440 A3
- LGMT 80504 1440 B3
- WldC 80504 1440 E3
SR-119 28th St
1700 BLDR 80301 1686 E2
2200 BLDR 80302 1686 E1
2200 BLDR 80304 1686 E1
2700 BLDR 80301 1602 E7
2700 BLDR 80304 1602 E7
SR-119 Boulder Canyon Dr
26900 BldC 80466 1765 D2
26900 BldC 80466 1766 B2
26900 NDLD 80466 1765 D2
27100 BldC 80466 1682 D7
27100 BldC 80466 1683 E4
27100 BldC 80466 1684 A4
27800 BldC 80466 1684 A4
36700 BldC 80302 1685 A4
39600 BldC 80302 1686 A3
40400 BLDR 80302 1686 A2
SR-119 S Bridge St
10 NDLD 80466 1765 D3
700 BldC 80466 1765 C4
SR-119 Canyon Blvd
100 BldC 80302 1686 A2
100 BLDR 80302 1686 A2
2600 BLDR 80301 1686 D2
SR-119 Clear Creek St
- GpnC 80403 2018 A4
100 BKHK 80403 2017 D2
100 BKHK 80403 2018 A4
200 GpnC 80403 2017 D2
SR-119 Diagonal Hwy
- BLDR 80304 1602 E7
- LGMT 80501 1438 C7
2800 BLDR 80301 1602 E7
2800 BLDR 80301 1603 A6
3700 BldC 80301 1603 E2
4500 BldC 80301 1604 A1
4500 BLDR 80301 1604 A1
6300 BldC 80301 1520 B7
6300 BldC 80503 1520 E3
6300 BLDR 80301 1520 B7
6300 BLDR 80503 1520 B7
7300 BldC 80503 1521 A2
8000 LGMT 80503 1521 B1
8200 BldC 80503 1438 C7
8300 LGMT 80503 1438 C7
SR-119 Highway 119
1000 GpnC 80403 2104 A4
1100 GpnC 80403 2103 C2
9200 GpnC 80403 2017 C1
11900 GpnC 80403 1933 E6
14200 GpnC 80403 1934 C3
SR-119 Ken Pratt Blvd
- BldC 80501 1439 E3
- LGMT 80501 1440 B3
- LGMT 80504 1440 B3
600 LGMT 80501 1439 A4
1200 LGMT 80501 1438 E4
SR-119 Peak to Peak Hwy
22000 BldC 80466 1765 E7
22000 GpnC 80474 1765 E7
23900 NDLD 80466 1765 D4
SR-121
- BMFD 80020 1858 C2
8200 BMFD 80021 1858 C1
SR-121 S Platte Canyon Rd
- JfnC 80127 2446 D4
- JfnC 80127 2530 D3
- JfnC 80128 2446 D3
SR-121 Wadsworth Blvd
- WTRG 80002 2026 E7
10 LKWD 80226 2194 E1
400 LKWD 80226 2110 E7
600 LKWD 80214 2110 E7
2500 JfnC 80215 2110 E3
2500 WTRG 80033 2110 E3
4800 ARVD 80033 2026 E7
4800 WTRG 80033 2026 E7
5000 ARVD 80002 2026 E4
6500 ARVD 80003 2026 D1
6500 ARVD 80004 2026 D1
7000 ARVD 80003 1942 D7
7000 ARVD 80004 1942 D7
7100 ARVD 80005 1942 D7
8200 WSTR 80005 1942 D4
8700 WSTR 80021 1942 D3
SR-121 S Wadsworth Blvd
10 LKWD 80226 2194 E2
900 LKWD 80232 2194 E3
1900 LKWD 80227 2194 E7
2600 DNVR 80227 2278 E1
2600 LKWD 80227 2278 E1
2800 JfnC 80227 2278 E1
4000 DNVR 80123 2278 D7
4000 DNVR 80235 2278 E4
4000 LKWD 80235 2278 E4
4800 DvrC 80123 2278 D7
4800 LKWD 80123 2278 D7
5100 DNVR 80123 2362 D4
5100 LKWD 80123 2362 D1
5400 DvrC 80123 2362 D4
6700 JfnC 80128 2362 D4
7700 JfnC 80128 2446 E1
9400 JfnC 80127 2446 E1
SR-121 Wadsworth Byp
5200 ARVD 80002 2026 E5
5700 ARVD 80003 2026 E3
SR-121 Wadsworth Pkwy
- BMFD 80020 1858 C1
8800 ARVD 80003 1942 D4
8800 WSTR 80005 1942 D4
9000 WSTR 80021 1942 D2
9700 WSTR 80021 1858 C7
10800 JfnC 80021 1858 C2
11200 BMFD 80021 1858 C7
SR-128
- BfdC 80021 1857 B2
- BldC 80303 1771 C7
- BldC 80303 1855 D1
- BldC 80403 1855 D1
- BMFD 80020 1858 D2
- BMFD 80021 1856 E3
- BMFD 80021 1857 D2
- BMFD 80021 1858 D2
- JfnC 80403 1856 E3
- SUPE 80021 1857 A2
- SUPE 80027 1856 B2
- SUPE 80027 1857 B2
- SUPE 80303 1855 D1
- SUPE 80403 1855 D1
- SUPE 80403 1856 B2
SR-128 E 120th Av
1300 NHGN 80233 1861 A2
SR-128 W 120th Av
- BldC 80303 1855 E2
- BldC 80403 1855 E2
- NHGN 80233 1860 D2
- SUPE 80027 1856 B2
- SUPE 80303 1855 E2
- SUPE 80403 1855 E2
- SUPE 80403 1856 A2
- TNTN 80241 1860 D2
10 NHGN 80234 1860 D2
10 WSTR 80234 1860 D2
3600 BMFD 80020 1859 E2
3600 WSTR 80031 1859 E2
3600 WSTR 80234 1859 E2
4500 WSTR 80020 1859 E2
4600 BMFD 80031 1859 A2
6400 BMFD 80020 1858 E2
8700 BMFD 80021 1858 C2
SR-128 Interlocken Lp
- BMFD 80021 1857 D2
- BMFD 80021 1858 B2
SR-128 Wadsworth Pkwy
- BMFD 80020 1858 C2
- BMFD 80021 1858 C2
SR-157 Foothills Pkwy
- BldC 80301 1603 B7
- BLDR 80301 1603 B7
- BLDR 80301 1687 B1
- BLDR 80303 1687 B2
SR-170 Eldorado Springs Dr
3500 BldC 80025 1770 E6
3500 BldC 80303 1770 E6
3500 BldC 80303 1771 A6
SR-170 Marshall Dr
5200 BldC 80303 1771 B5
5600 BldC 80027 1772 B3
5600 BldC 80303 1772 A3
6500 SUPE 80027 1772 C2
6500 SUPE 80303 1772 C2
SR-170 Marshall Rd
300 BldC 80027 1772 E3
300 SUPE 80027 1772 E3
SR-177 S University Blvd
- AphC 80126 2449 C1
- CHLV 80121 2281 C7
3500 CHLV 80113 2281 C4
5100 GDVL 80121 2281 C7
5300 GDVL 80121 2365 C1
5900 CTNL 80121 2365 C1
6600 CTNL 80122 2365 C4
8200 AphC 80122 2449 C1
8200 CTNL 80122 2449 C1
SR-224
- AdmC 80022 1945 D6
- AdmC 80229 1945 B7
- TNTN 80022 1945 D6
SR-224 E 70th Av
10 AdmC 80221 1944 E7
300 AdmC 80229 1944 E7
700 AdmC 80229 1945 A7
SR-224 E 74th Av
3800 AdmC 80022 1945 D6
3800 CMCY 80022 1945 D6
3800 TNTN 80022 1945 D6
4800 CMCY 80022 1946 A6
SR-265 Brighton Blvd
5100 CMCY 80216 2029 B5
5100 DNVR 80216 2029 B5
5300 CMCY 80022 2029 B5
SR-391 S Kipling Pkwy
900 LKWD 80226 2194 B4
900 LKWD 80232 2194 A4
1500 JfnC 80232 2194 A6
1500 LKWD 80227 2194 A6
1900 JfnC 80227 2194 A6
2000 JfnC 80227 2278 A1
2000 LKWD 80227 2278 A1
SR-391 Kipling St
- ARVD 80002 2026 B5
- ARVD 80004 2026 B5
10 LKWD 80226 2194 B1
500 LKWD 80226 2110 B7
600 LKWD 80215 2110 B7
2500 JfnC 80215 2110 B3
2500 WTRG 80215 2110 B3
3100 WTRG 80033 2110 B1
4700 WTRG 80033 2026 B6
5000 ARVD 80033 2026 B5
5000 WTRG 80002 2026 B5
SR-391 S Kipling St
10 LKWD 80226 2194 B1
SR-470
- DgsC - 2447 D1
- DgsC - 2448 A1
- DgsC - 2449 A1
- DgsC - 2450 E1
- DgsC - 2451 B2
- GOLD - 2192 B2
- JfnC - 2192 C6
- JfnC - 2276 C1
- JfnC - 2277 B7
- JfnC - 2361 B1
- JfnC - 2445 E1
- JfnC - 2446 E2
- JfnC - 2447 A2
- LITN - 2447 D1
- LITN - 2448 A1
- LKWD - 2192 C6
- LKWD - 2276 E5
- LKWD - 2277 A6
- LNTR - 2450 E1
- LNTR - 2451 A1
- MRSN - 2276 C1
SR-E470
- AdmC - 1692 E7
- AdmC - 1693 A7
- AdmC - 1777 E1
- AdmC - 1778 B2
- AdmC - 1779 E6
- AdmC - 1780 D7

STREET
Block City ZIP Map# Grid

SR-E470
- AdmC - 1864 E1
- AdmC - 1865 D7
- AdmC - 2034 C2
- AdmC - 2118 C1
- AphC - 2118 D4
- AphC - 2202 C7
- AphC - 2286 C6
- AphC - 2370 D1
- AURA - 2034 C2
- AURA - 2118 D4
- AURA - 2202 C2
- AURA - 2286 C1
- AURA - 2369 E7
- AURA - 2453 C1
- BGTN - 1779 E6
- BGTN - 1780 D7
- BMFD - 1692 C6
- CMCY - 1780 D7
- CMCY - 1864 E1
- CMCY - 1865 A2
- CMCY - 1949 D1
- DgsC - 2451 C2
- DgsC - 2452 C2
- DgsC - 2453 A3
- DNVR - 1949 D1
- DNVR - 1950 A7
- DNVR - 2034 C2
- LNTR - 2451 C2
- PARK - 2453 A3
- TNTN - 1692 E7
- TNTN - 1778 D3
Stable Dr
7100 BldC 80503 1521 A4
Stable Ln
3200 JfnC 80439 2273 C3
10300 DgsC 80125 2530 E6
Stacy Ct
500 LAFT 80026 1690 C6
Stacy Dr
1900 AdmC 80221 1944 B4
2300 AdmC 80031 1944 B4
2300 WSTR 80031 1944 B4
8300 FLHT 80260 1944 B4
Stacy Pl
- DgsC 80125 2530 E6
Stadium Dr
- BLDR 80302 1686 D3
Stafford Cir
500 CSRK 80104 2787 E2
Stage Run
18600 PARK 80134 2453 C7
Stage Coach
10 PrkC 80456 2606 C7
Stagecoach Blvd
10 CCkC 80439 2272 A4
300 CCkC 80439 2271 D4
28900 JfnC 80439 2273 B3
Stagecoach Cir
1500 EbtC 80107 2708 C7
Stagecoach Dr
300 PrkC 80456 2521 C2
E Stagecoach Dr
11000 DgsC 80138 2455 D2
Stagecoach Ln
10 PrkC 80456 2522 A5
30200 JfnC 80439 2273 B3
Stagecoach Rd
10 BldC 80302 1598 B5
26800 JfnC 80433 2525 E3
26800 JfnC 80433 2526 A3
45000 EbtC 80138 2456 A6
Stagecoach Tr
10 DgsC 80107 2707 E1
10 DgsC 80116 2707 E1
200 EbtC 80107 2708 A1
Stage Run Tr
400 EbtC 80107 2792 A7
Staghorn Dr
3700 LGMT 80503 1438 A4
Staghorn Wy
10 DgsC 80116 2791 A1
E Stallion Dr
11000 DgsC 80138 2455 D3
S Stallion Dr
11600 JfnC 80470 2524 A4
Stampede Cir
34300 EbtC 80107 2708 C6
Stampede Ct
1000 CSRK 80104 2703 E2
43500 EbtC 80107 2542 E2
Stampede Dr
600 LCHB 80603 1698 B3
3900 CSRK 80104 2703 D2
Stampede Wy
10 LCHB 80603 1698 B3
Standing Pines Rd
9700 JfnC 80403 1936 C1
9900 JfnC 80403 1852 C7
Stanford Av
2500 BLDR 80305 1686 E6
2600 BLDR 80305 1687 A6
E Stanford Av
10 EGLD 80110 2280 E5
10 EGLD 80113 2280 E5
600 EGLD 80113 2281 A5
700 CHLV 80113 2281 A5
6000 CHLV 80111 2282 B5
9100 GDVL 80111 2283 A5
15000 AURA 80015 2284 C5
16900 AURA 80015 2285 A5
19700 CTNL 80015 2285 D5
W Stanford Av
10 EGLD 80113 2280 D5
1300 EGLD 80110 2280 C5
1700 SRDN 80110 2280 B5
3000 EGLD 80110 2279 E5
4900 DNVR 80236 2279 C5
7000 LKWD 80123 2278 E5
7000 LKWD 80123 2279 A5
7800 DNVR 80123 2278 D5
9800 JfnC 80127 2278 B6
11200 JfnC 80127 2277 E6
12400 JfnC 80465 2277 C6
E Stanford Cir
- AURA 80015 2284 B5
Stanford Ct
3400 BLDR 80305 1687 A6
E Stanford Dr
2600 CHLV 80113 2281 D6
5600 CHLV 80111 2282 B5
5600 CHLV 80113 2282 B5
14900 AURA 80015 2284 C5
18800 AURA 80015 2285 C5
19700 CTNL 80015 2285 D5
W Stanford Dr
800 EGLD 80110 2280 C5
11600 JfnC 80465 2277 D5
Stanford Ln
10 LGMT 80503 1355 B7
W Stanford Ln
11600 JfnC 80465 2277 D5
E Stanford Pl
9100 GDVL 80111 2283 A5
13800 AURA 80015 2284 C5
16600 AURA 80015 2285 A5
20100 AphC 80015 2285 E5
W Stanford Pl
1000 EGLD 80110 2280 C5
11100 JfnC 80127 2277 E6
11800 JfnC 80465 2277 D6
Stanhope St
5700 CSRK 80104 2704 E7
Stanley Dr
1500 ERIE 80516 1607 A6
Stanley Rd
- CCkC 80452 2101 A5
- IDSP 80452 2101 A5
Stanley Park Rd
24300 JfnC 80439 2358 C2
Stansbery Cir
24500 JfnC 80433 2442 B4
Stansbery St
25600 JfnC 80433 2442 B4
Stanton Dr
10200 GpnC 80403 1852 A7
Stapleton Dr
27600 JfnC 80401 2105 C7
27600 JfnC 80401 2189 D1
E Stapleton Dr N
4500 DNVR 80216 2030 A6
E Stapleton Dr S
4600 DNVR 80216 2029 E6
4600 DNVR 80216 2030 A6
W Star Av
8800 JfnC 80128 2446 C2
W Star Cir
8400 JfnC 80128 2446 C2
W Star Dr
8700 JfnC 80128 2446 C2
Star Ln
10 PrkC 80456 2607 E5
Starboard Ct
4500 BldC 80301 1604 A3
Starboard Dr
4500 BldC 80301 1604 A3
Starburst Cir
100 DgsC 80104 2871 B4
Star Creek Dr
- BMFD 80020 1775 E4
- BMFD 80020 1776 A4
Stardance Cir
1500 LGMT 80501 1440 A2
Stardance Wy
500 LGMT 80501 1440 A2
Stardust Cir
1200 DgsC 80104 2871 D1
Starfire Cir
4600 DgsC 80104 2871 C3
Starfire Wy
200 JfnC 80401 2191 C1
Starflower Ct
5100 CSRK 80109 2702 C1
Starflower Rd
3500 CSRK 80109 2702 D1
Stargazer Dr
- BMFD 80020 1775 B2
Stargrass Cir
9100 DgsC 80126 2448 E3
S Star Hill Cir
9200 LNTR 80124 2451 A3
E Star Hill Ln
9100 LNTR 80124 2451 A3
E Star Hill Pt
9100 LNTR 80124 2451 A4
E Star Hill Tr
9100 LNTR 80124 2451 A3
Starkey Ct
600 ERIE 80516 1607 A7
S Starlight Ct
3800 DgsC 80135 2785 D6
S Starlight Dr
6200 JfnC 80465 2359 C4
Starlight Rd
200 TNTN 80260 1944 D3
6500 JfnC 80465 2359 C4
Starline Av
100 LAFT 80026 1690 C3
Starling Ct
3000 CSRK 80109 2702 C3
6300 BldC 80503 1520 A4
Starling Ln
800 EbtC 80107 2624 B7
1200 EbtC 80107 2708 B1
Starmine Pl
300 DgsC 80108 2619 A4
Star Park Ct
- BMFD 80020 1775 E4
Starr Ln
100 AdmC 80601 1697 A4
100 WldC 80603 1697 A4
Star Ridge Rd
1000 JfnC 80401 2191 A4
Starry Night Lp
- CSRK 80109 2702 D5
Starry Sky Wy
4900 DgsC 80134 2621 A5
Starstone Ln
- CSRK 80104 2787 D5
Star View Dr
5800 BMFD 80020 1775 A4
Starview Dr
24700 JfnC 80433 2610 C2
Starwood Ln
- PARK 80134 2452 E2
1200 JfnC 80439 2188 C5
8700 DgsC 80134 2452 E2
State Park Rd
- GpnC 80403 1850 E7
- GpnC 80403 1934 E1
- GpnC 80403 1935 A1
Stazio Dr
2400 BldC 80301 1603 E7
2400 BldC 80301 1687 E1
E Steamboat Av
17600 AURA 80011 2117 B7
19900 AURA 80011 2201 D1
20600 AURA 80011 2202 A1
20800 AphC 80011 2202 A1
20800 AphC 80018 2202 A1
Steamboat Ct
1500 JfnC 80439 2189 B6
Steamboat Valley Rd
- BldC 80503 1269 C4
- BldC 80540 1269 C5
10 LYNS 80540 1352 C1
100 LYNS 80540 1269 D7
Stearman Ct
100 ERIE 80516 1691 C2
Stearns Av
900 BldC 80303 1688 A4
Steavenson Pl
2300 DNVR 80216 2029 C6
S Steele Cir
7200 CTNL 80122 2365 D5
Steele Ct
12800 TNTN 80241 1777 C7
13600 TNTN 80602 1777 C5
S Steele Ct
8200 CTNL 80122 2449 D1
Steele Dr
9400 TNTN 80229 1945 C1
13000 TNTN 80241 1777 D6
Steele St
- AdmC 80602 1693 C5
- TNTN 80233 1861 C6
- TNTN 80516 1693 C5
- TNTN 80602 1693 C5
10 DNVR 80209 2197 D1
100 DNVR 80206 2197 D1
2100 DNVR 80206 2113 D4
2100 LGMT 80501 1355 D5
2600 DNVR 80205 2113 D3
3900 DNVR 80205 2029 D7
5200 DNVR 80216 2029 D5
7800 AdmC 80229 1945 C4
7800 TNTN 80229 1945 C4
9700 TNTN 80229 1861 C7
10700 NHGN 80233 1861 C5
12200 TNTN 80241 1861 C1
N Steele St
10900 NHGN 80233 1861 C4
S Steele St
10 DNVR 80206 2197 D1
10 DNVR 80209 2197 D1
1000 DNVR 80210 2197 D5
2700 DNVR 80210 2281 D1
5100 CHLV 80113 2281 D7
5100 CHLV 80121 2281 D7
5100 GDVL 80121 2281 D7
5600 GDVL 80121 2365 D1
6200 AphC 80121 2365 D2
6700 CTNL 80121 2365 D4
6700 CTNL 80122 2365 D4
8200 CTNL 80122 2449 D1
Steel Works Dr
- BLDR 80301 1687 A1
Steeple Ct
6900 DgsC 80134 2621 E1
Steeplechase Dr
- BldC 80503 1519 D1
5500 BldC 80503 1436 D7
8200 DgsC 80116 2790 C4
9600 DgsC 80116 2791 A4
Stein St
900 LAFT 80026 1690 C3
Stellar Jay Ln
10 CCkC 80439 2356 A7
Stellar Jay Wy
10 CCkC 80439 2356 A6
W Stellars Jay Dr
300 DgsC 80129 2448 D6
Stellars Jay Rd
25500 JfnC 80401 2190 B1
W Stene Dr
7600 JfnC 80128 2446 D2
Stenzel Dr
31500 JfnC 80433 2440 D4
S Stephen Pl
10100 DgsC 80130 2450 B6
Stephens Rd
2500 BLDR 80305 1686 E7
Sterling Av
1600 CHLV 80113 2281 B7
Sterling Cir
- BLDR 80301 1603 D7
Sterling Cir E
3000 BLDR 80301 1603 D7
Sterling Cir W
3000 BLDR 80301 1603 D7
Sterling Ct
2900 BLDR 80301 1603 B7
E Sterling Ct
1700 DgsC 80126 2449 B5
Sterling Dr
4700 BLDR 80301 1687 B1
5300 BLDR 80301 1603 C7
S Sterling Dr
9600 DgsC 80126 2449 A5
Sterling Hill Ct
1300 CSRK 80104 2704 A5
S Sterling Hills Pkwy
- AURA 80013 2201 C7
Sterling Park Appartments
- BGTN 80601 1781 B1
E Sterne Blvd
200 CTNL 80121 2364 E4
200 CTNL 80122 2364 E4
S Sterne Cir
6100 LITN 80120 2364 B2
S Sterne Ct
6000 LITN 80120 2364 B2
S Sterne Pkwy
6000 LITN 80120 2364 B2
W Sterne Pkwy
10 CTNL 80122 2364 D4
1400 LITN 80120 2364 C3
Stetson Ct
400 BGTN 80601 1697 C4
N Stetson Ct
5700 DgsC 80134 2622 B3
W Stetson Pl
6900 DNVR 80123 2278 E5
6900 DNVR 80123 2279 A5
6900 LKWD 80123 2278 E5
6900 LKWD 80123 2279 A5
E Stetson Rd
8000 DgsC 80134 2622 B3
S Steven Ln
10000 JfnC 80433 2440 D6
Steven Wy
31700 JfnC 80433 2440 D5
Stevens Cir
- ERIE 80516 1690 C2
Stevens Cir N
3000 ERIE 80516 1690 C2
Stevens Cir S
3000 ERIE 80516 1690 C2
Stevens Ct
- DNVR 80221 2028 B5
2200 DgsC 80109 2786 B6
Stevens St
300 CLCY 80403 2017 E4
Stickney Al
- LYNS 80540 1352 D1
Stickney Av
200 LYNS 80540 1352 D1
S Stiles Dr
700 JfnC 80439 2189 B4
Stillwater St
37400 EbtC 80107 2623 E7
37400 EbtC 80107 2707 E1
Stillwater Wy
1800 BldC 80026 1690 B2
Stinky Gulch Rd
- BldC 80466 1765 D1
10 NDLD 80466 1765 D1
Stirrup Ct
8400 BldC 80503 1436 D7
Stirrup Ln
8400 BldC 80503 1519 D1
8500 BldC 80503 1436 D7
E Stirrup Ln
500 DgsC 80108 2535 B2
Stockholm Wy
1200 EbtC 80138 2540 B5
Stockley Av
6100 CMCY 80022 2030 B1
Stockton Dr
1200 ERIE 80516 1607 A6
Stoll Pl
14400 DNVR 80239 2032 B5
21300 DNVR 80249 2034 A5
E Stoll Pl
12100 DNVR 80239 2031 E5
W Stoll Pl
1500 DNVR 80221 2028 B5
Stone Cir
- BMFD 80020 1775 E5
Stone Dr
10 CSRK 80104 2704 A7
100 CSRK 80104 2788 A1
Stone Pl
4000 BldC 80301 1603 A5
Stone St
100 MRSN 80465 2276 C3
Stonebriar Dr
15900 DgsC 80134 2452 E5
Stonebriar Ln
9700 DgsC 80134 2452 E4
Stonebridge Wy
5600 JfnC 80465 2360 D2
Stonebrush Dr
- DgsC 80130 2449 E7
3800 DgsC 80126 2449 E7
Stone Canyon Rd
10 BldC 80503 1352 E2
10 BldC 80503 1353 A1
10 LYNS 80503 1352 E2
100 JfnC 80439 2188 D4
100 JfnC 80439 2189 A5
1100 BldC 80503 1269 E3
1100 BldC 80503 1270 A5
Stone Chimney Ln
13500 JfnC 80470 2608 B1
Stonecliff Dr
4200 JfnC 80439 2273 A5
Stone Creek Ct
10600 DgsC 80134 2452 D7
Stonecrest Pt
2700 DgsC 80129 2448 A3
Stonecrest Wy
8900 DgsC 80129 2448 A3
Stone Crop Cir
5000 CSRK 80109 2702 D1
Stone Crop Ct
5000 CSRK 80109 2702 D1
Stonecrop Tr
28100 JfnC 80433 2609 D2
Stonecrop Wy
2100 JfnC 80401 2190 E7
2100 JfnC 80401 2191 A7
Stonedale Dr
7800 DgsC 80108 2534 E6
Stonefeld Pl
16300 DgsC 80134 2452 E4
Stoneflower Dr
10300 DgsC 80134 2452 D7
Stone Gate Dr
18300 JfnC 80465 2360 A4
18400 JfnC 80465 2359 E4
Stonegate Pkwy
- DgsC 80134 2453 B6
- PARK 80134 2453 B6
9500 DgsC 80134 2452 D4
Stoneglen Tr
10100 LNTR 80124 2450 E5
Stonegrass Pt
3900 BMFD 80020 1775 D4
Stoneham Av
4800 CSRK 80104 2788 D1
Stoneham Ln
1600 JfnC 80439 2189 B6
Stoneham St
1000 SUPE 80027 1773 B5
Stonehaven Av
900 BMFD 80020 1859 B1
Stonehaven Ct
10 DgsC 80130 2450 B3
Stonehenge Cir
2000 BldC 80026 1690 B1
Stonehenge Dr
1700 BldC 80026 1690 B2
Stonehenge Wy
- PARK 80138 2453 E7
- PARK 80138 2537 E1
Stonehill Ct
1400 CSRK 80104 2704 A5
Stone Ledge Dr
16300 DgsC 80134 2452 E5
Stonemeadow Dr
10500 DgsC 80134 2452 D7
Stonemont Ct
600 DgsC 80108 2534 D6
Stonemont Dr
500 DgsC 80108 2534 E6
Stone Mountain Dr
- DgsC 80126 2448 E6
- DgsC 80129 2448 E6
S Stone Mountain Dr
- DgsC 80129 2448 C6
Stone Post Dr
4300 CSRK 80108 2704 E3
Stoneridge Ter
8300 BldC 80302 1518 A1
10100 DgsC 80134 2452 D5
Stones Peak Dr
1400 LGMT 80503 1437 D6
1700 BldC 80503 1437 D6
Stonewall Ln
2500 LAFT 80027 1689 D4
Stonewall Pl
5500 BLDR 80303 1687 D4
Stonewillow Dr
10300 DgsC 80134 2453 B5
10400 DgsC 80134 2452 E6
Stoney Dr
3800 BldC 80026 1606 D5
Stoney Brook Dr
5300 BMFD 80020 1775 B4
Stoneybrooke St
11600 PARK 80138 2538 D2
Stoney Creek Wy
- BMFD 80020 1775 C2
Stonington Ct
2800 DgsC 80126 2533 C1
Stonington St
10500 DgsC 80126 2533 C1
Stonybridge Cir
- AphC 80126 2449 D1
- CTNL 80122 2449 D1
- CTNL 80126 2449 D1
Stony Hill Rd
1900 BLDR 80305 1770 D1
Stony Mesa Ct
- CSRK 80108 2703 D2
Stony Mesa Pl
- CSRK 80108 2703 D1
Stony Mesa Rd
- CSRK 80108 2703 E1
Storage Tek Dr
- BMFD 80020 1773 D6
- BMFD 80021 1773 D6
- LSVL 80027 1773 D6
S Storm Mtn
7500 JfnC 80127 2362 A6
Storm Cloud Wy
3700 CSRK 80104 2703 D2
Storm King Ln
45000 EbtC 80138 2457 A6
S Storm King Peak
8100 JfnC 80127 2361 C7
N Stormy Mountain Ct
6100 DgsC 80134 2622 D2
Stout St
1100 DNVR 80204 2112 C5
1300 DNVR 80202 2112 C5
1900 DNVR 80205 2112 C5
2800 DNVR 80205 2113 A3
Stowe Ct
30100 JfnC 80439 2189 B7
E Stowe St
700 DgsC 80126 2449 A4
Stransky Rd
33400 JfnC 80439 2356 B6
Strasburg Ct
19700 PARK 80134 2537 D3
Strasburg Wy
10400 PARK 80134 2453 A6
E Stratford Ct
2000 DgsC 80126 2449 B5
Stratford Ln
1800 LGMT 80503 1355 C6
S Stratford Ln
9900 DgsC 80126 2449 B5
S Stratford Pl
9900 DgsC 80126 2449 B5
E Stratford Wy
2300 DgsC 80126 2449 C5
N Stratford Lakes Dr
3300 WSTR 80031 1859 E3
3300 WSTR 80234 1859 E3
Strath St
7000 BldC 80503 1519 E4
S Strathfield Ct
4200 DgsC 80126 2449 E5
S Strathfield Ln
9900 DgsC 80126 2449 E5
Strathmore Ln
400 LAFT 80026 1690 C6
Strathmore St
1900 LSVL 80027 1689 C6
N Stratton Av
1200 CSRK 80104 2704 E5
Stratton Ct
30700 JfnC 80439 2189 A7
Straw Ct
- BGTN 80601 1697 C5
Strawberry Ct
6400 BldC 80503 1521 A5
Strawberry Ln
5500 DgsC 80108 2619 B4
8400 BldC 80503 1521 A5
Strawberry Wy
- BLDR 80304 1602 D3
Strawflower
10 JfnC 80127 2361 A6
Strawflower Ln
10 JfnC 80401 2190 B2
Streambed Tr
4800 DgsC 80134 2621 C5
Streamcrest Dr
8600 BldC 80302 1435 B7
Stroh Pl
1800 LGMT 80501 1355 D7
E Stroh Rd
6000 DgsC 80134 2537 D6
6000 PARK 80134 2537 D6
7300 DgsC 80134 2538 A6
Stroh Ranch Ct
- DgsC 80134 2537 D6
- PARK 80134 2537 D5
Stroh Ranch Dr
12900 DgsC 80134 2537 D6
12900 PARK 80134 2537 D6
Stroh Ranch Pl
- PARK 80134 2537 D5
Stroh Ranch Wy
12700 PARK 80134 2537 D5
Stroilway St
16600 AdmC 80642 1700 D4
Strong St
10 BGTN 80601 1696 B5
Stuart Cir
10800 WSTR 80031 1859 D5
Stuart Ct
2400 DNVR 80212 2111 D3
6600 AdmC 80003 2027 C1
6600 AdmC 80030 2027 C1
11000 WSTR 80031 1859 D5
13300 BMFD 80020 1775 C5
N Stuart Ct
- BMFD 80020 1859 D1
S Stuart Ct
5000 DNVR 80123 2279 D6
Stuart Pl
7800 WSTR 80030 1943 C5
8000 WSTR 80031 1943 C5
Stuart St
- AdmC 80003 2027 D2
- AdmC 80031 1943 D2
10 DNVR 80219 2195 D1
300 DNVR 80219 2111 D7
1000 LGMT 80501 1438 D1
1200 DNVR 80204 2111 D5
2000 DNVR 80212 2111 D4
2100 LGMT 80501 1355 D5
4700 DNVR 80212 2027 D6
5100 AdmC 80212 2027 D5
7800 WSTR 80031 1943 C5
8000 WSTR 80030 1943 C5
13600 BMFD 80020 1775 C5
N Stuart St
- WSTR 80031 1859 C5
9200 WSTR 80031 1943 D2
S Stuart St
1800 DNVR 80219 2195 D6
2700 DNVR 80219 2279 D2
2700 DNVR 80236 2279 D2
S Stuart Wy
1300 DNVR 80219 2195 D5
2600 DNVR 80219 2279 D1
13000 PARK 80134 2537 D6
Stucke Rd
10 PrkC 80456 2521 D2
Sturbridge Dr
3200 DgsC 80129 2447 E3
3200 DgsC 80129 2448 A3
Sturbridge Pl
9000 DgsC 80129 2447 E3
S Styve Rd
12200 JfnC 80433 2525 A4
Sudbury St
400 CSRK 80104 2705 A7
500 CSRK 80104 2789 A1
Sue Cir
29300 JfnC 80439 2357 C1
Sue Rd
29200 JfnC 80439 2357 C1
Sue St
700 BldC 80026 1690 D5
700 LAFT 80026 1690 D5
Suffolk Av
5100 CSRK 80104 2788 E1
Suffolk Cir
5200 CSRK 80104 2788 D1
Suffolk Ln
200 DgsC 80108 2535 B6
Sugar Ct
10 BldC 80302 1684 B2
Sugar Dr
- BMFD 80020 1775 C4
Sugarbin Ct
200 LGMT 80501 1440 A4
W Sugarbowl Ct
3100 CSRK 80109 2702 E1
Sugarbush Dr
1200 JfnC 80439 2188 E5
1400 JfnC 80439 2189 A5
Sugarfoot St
400 DgsC 80108 2534 E4
Sugarhill Ln
31200 JfnC 80439 2188 E5
31200 JfnC 80439 2189 A5
Sugarloaf Dr
45200 EbtC 80138 2457 B6
Sugarloaf Rd
10 BldC 80302 1685 A3
900 BldC 80302 1684 E2
3600 BldC 80302 1683 D2
6300 BldC 80302 1682 E4
8000 DgsC 80118 2954 B4
8700 BldC 80466 1682 A6
Sugarloaf Mountain Rd
- BldC 80302 1598 D7
- BldC 80302 1599 A7
10 BldC 80302 1683 C1
Sugar Maple Ct
7400 DgsC 80108 2534 D7
Sugar Mill Av
600 LGMT 80501 1439 D1
Sugar Mill Pl
500 LGMT 80501 1439 D1
Sugar Mill Rd
600 BldC 80501 1439 D3
600 LGMT 80501 1439 D3
Sugar Pine Cir
46300 EbtC 80138 2455 E4
Sugarpine Tr
2900 JfnC 80439 2273 B2
Sugar Plum Wy
100 CSRK 80104 2787 D2
S Sugarstone Cir
9100 DgsC 80130 2450 B3
Sulfur Ct
6800 CSRK 80108 2619 E6
Sulfur Ln
6900 CSRK 80108 2619 E6
S Sulky Ln
3100 JfnC 80439 2273 C3
Sullivan Dr
32500 JfnC 80433 2440 D3
Sullivan St
10 PrkC 80456 2521 E2
Sully Wy
10600 NHGN 80234 1860 B5
S Sulton Ct
9300 DgsC 80126 2449 B4
Sumac
- BldC 80302 1686 C4
- BLDR 80302 1686 C4
Sumac Av
1700 BldC 80304 1602 C4
2400 BLDR 80304 1602 E4
W Sumac Av
5700 JfnC 80123 2363 B1
6100 DNVR 80123 2363 A1
Sumac Ct
4200 BldC 80301 1603 A4
W Sumac Ct
400 LSVL 80027 1773 B1
Sumac Dr
24000 JfnC 80401 2190 D5
S Sumac Ln
4400 BWMR 80123 2363 D1
4400 LITN 80123 2363 D1
Sumac Pl
1900 LGMT 80501 1355 D7
Sumac Run
- DgsC 80125 2699 B1
10000 DgsC 80125 2615 A6
Sumac St
900 LGMT 80501 1438 D1
2000 LGMT 80501 1355 D5
Summer Dr
900 DgsC 80126 2449 A4
S Summer Rd
6300 JfnC 80465 2359 E4
Summer St
100 JfnC 80465 2276 C3
100 MRSN 80465 2276 C3
Summer Bay Ln
14000 BMFD 80020 1776 A4
Summerfield Ct
100 ERIE 80516 1607 A5
Summerfield Dr
1900 CSRK 80104 2788 A1
Summergreen Ln
25700 JfnC 80401 2190 B2
Summer Hawk Dr
700 LGMT 80501 1440 B1
Summer Heaven Dr
1800 GpnC 80403 1934 C1
Summerlin Dr
- BldC 80503 1438 A7
- LGMT 80503 1438 A7
Summer Mist Cir
500 DgsC 80104 2871 B3
S Summer Ridge Wy
5900 CSRK 80109 2702 B2
Summerset Ct
20000 PARK 80138 2453 E7
Summerset Ln
19700 PARK 80138 2453 D7
19900 DgsC 80138 2453 D7
Summerset Wy
10800 PARK 80138 2453 D7
Summer Star Ln
6300 JfnC 80403 2022 B1
Summerville Cir
5200 CSRK 80109 2702 C4
Summerwood Dr
700 JfnC 80401 2191 A3

STREET
Block City ZIP Map# Grid

Summerwood Ln
200 DgsC 80108 2534 E7
Summit Blvd
100 CHLV 80113 2281 B7
100 GDVL 80121 2281 B7
200 BMFD 80021 1773 C7
Summit Cir
200 LAFT 80026 1690 C3
Summit Dr
10 PrkC 80456 2606 C5
S Summit Dr
8000 JfnC 80465 2359 D7
8000 JfnC 80465 2443 D1
W Summit Dr
6100 JfnC 80123 2363 A4
S Summit Ln
3700 JfnC 80439 2273 D4
Summit Pl
- ERIE 80026 1690 B1
1600 BldC 80026 1690 B1
Summit Rd
29100 JfnC 80439 2273 C7
45200 EbtC 80138 2457 B5
E Summit Rd
7500 DgsC 80138 2454 A3
Summit St
1900 DgsC 80116 2791 D5
23600 JfnC 80433 2694 E5
Summit Tr
100 BMFD 80020 1774 E4
SE Summit Tr
4500 JfnC 80439 2272 C6
SW Summit Tr
4500 JfnC 80439 2272 B6
Summit Wy
10 PrkC 80456 2521 B3
Summit Ash
10 JfnC 80127 2445 A1
Summit Cedar Dr
10 JfnC 80127 2361 B7
10 JfnC 80127 2445 C1
Summit Grove Pkwy
3100 TNTN 80241 1777 D5
13100 TNTN 80241 1778 A6
Summit Ranch Dr
28600 JfnC 80401 2189 C3
Summit Ranch Wy
10 JfnC 80401 2189 D2
N Summit Ridge Ct
9600 DgsC 80138 2454 E4
S Summit Ridge Pl
9500 DgsC 80138 2454 E4
9700 DgsC 80138 2455 A4
S Summit Ridge Rd
12000 DgsC 80138 2454 E3
12000 DgsC 80138 2455 A4
Summit View Cir
10 EbtC 80138 2539 E4
10 EbtC 80138 2540 A4
Summit View Ct
42600 EbtC 80138 2539 E4
42600 EbtC 80138 2540 A4
Summit View Dr
- BldC 80027 1689 D5
1200 LSVL 80027 1689 D5
Summitview Dr
2000 LGMT 80504 1438 E7
Summit View Pkwy
3300 DgsC 80126 2449 D6
Summit View Pointe
10100 DgsC 80126 2449 C6
S Sumner Cir
7400 LITN 80120 2364 A6
Sumner St
200 LGMT 80501 1438 E2
1700 LGMT 80501 1355 E6
S Sumner St
5900 LITN 80120 2364 A2
Sumpter Ct
- EbtC 80107 2543 A2
Sun Wy
10 PrkC 80456 2607 E5
11500 PARK 80134 2537 D2
W Sunbeam Av
9600 DgsC 80125 2531 A1
N Sunbeam Tr
8800 DgsC 80134 2538 A4
Sunbird Av
1100 BGTN 80601 1779 E1
Sunblaze Lp
- BMFD 80020 1775 D3
Sunburst Ct
1000 LAFT 80026 1690 B5
Sunburst Dr
13800 JfnC 80127 2528 E1
13800 JfnC 80127 2529 A1
Sunburst Ln
32400 JfnC 80439 2188 D3
N Sunburst Tr
- PARK 80138 2538 A4
8200 DgsC 80134 2537 E5
8200 DgsC 80134 2538 A4
8800 DgsC 80138 2538 A4
Sunchase Dr
3700 CSRK 80109 2702 C3
Sun Country Dr
7100 EbtC 80107 2542 D1
7800 EbtC 80107 2543 A2
8100 EbtC 80107 2459 A7
Suncreek Dr
30300 JfnC 80439 2273 A2
Sun Creek Rdg
2900 JfnC 80439 2273 A2
Suncrest Rd
1200 CSRK 80104 2704 B5
Sundance Cir
10 NDLD 80466 1765 C2
Sundance Ct
1800 LGMT 80501 1357 A5
2000 BldC 80504 1357 A5
W Sundance Mtn
10400 JfnC 80127 2362 A7
Sundance Pl
500 DgsC 80108 2534 E5
1600 LGMT 80501 1357 A6
Sundance Sq
4900 BldC 80301 1604 D2
Sundance Tr
46400 EbtC 80138 2457 B3
E Sundance Tr
7700 DgsC 80138 2454 A2
W Sundance Tr
9900 DgsC 80125 2615 A7
E Sundew St
17600 PARK 80134 2453 B4
Sun Dial Pl
5200 BldC 80301 1604 C2
S Sundown Cir
7200 LITN 80120 2364 D5
Sundown Dr
800 CSRK 80104 2704 D6
Sundown Ln
400 AdmC 80221 1944 D5
2800 BLDR 80303 1686 E3
2800 BLDR 80303 1687 A3
10300 TNTN 80229 1862 A6
S Sundown Ln
500 JfnC 80439 2188 D3
Sundown Tr
- DgsC 80125 2615 A2
10800 DgsC 80125 2614 E3
44500 EbtC 80107 2459 B7
N Sundown Tr
10 NDLD 80466 1765 C2
7600 DgsC 80134 2538 A5
8500 DgsC 80138 2538 A5
S Sundown Tr
10 NDLD 80466 1765 C2
Sundrop Ln
- BGTN 80601 1780 D2
Sundrop Pl
- BGTN 80601 1780 D2
E Sundrop Tr
1800 DgsC 80126 2449 B2
S Sundrop Wy
8800 DgsC 80126 2449 B2
Sunflower Cir
3600 LGMT 80503 1438 B6
Sunflower Dr
- DgsC 80118 2870 A7
Sunflower Ln
16400 JfnC 80465 2360 D3
Sunflower Pl
10 CHLV 80113 2281 B4
Sunflower St
900 LSVL 80027 1688 E7
900 LSVL 80027 1689 B7
900 LSVL 80027 1772 E1
12100 BMFD 80020 1859 D1
S Sunflower St
8400 DgsC 80126 2448 E1
N Sungold Ln
4900 CSRK 80109 2702 E1
Sunland St
200 LSVL 80027 1689 C5
Sunlight Dr
1700 LGMT 80501 1356 C5
10400 BldC 80026 1606 A3
Sunlight Ln
10 PrkC 80456 2607 D3
4600 BMFD 80020 1775 C5
Sunlight Rd
9800 TNTN 80260 1860 B7
Sunlight Wy
800 SUPE 80027 1857 A1
S Sunlight Peak
8000 JfnC 80127 2361 E7
Sunlight Peak Av
- CSRK 80109 2787 A4
S Sun Meadow St
9600 DgsC 80129 2448 D5
Sunningdale Blvd
9800 LNTR 80124 2450 D4
Sunny Dr
10 BldC 80403 1852 A2
Sunny Wy
800 BldC 80026 1689 C4
800 BldC 80303 1689 C4
Sunny Farm Cir
41400 EbtC 80138 2540 E7
Sunny Ridge Ln
10 PrkC 80456 2607 E7
Sunnyside Cir
1900 LSVL 80027 1689 C5
S Sunnyside Ct
8300 DgsC 80126 2449 B1
Sunnyside Ln
300 LGMT 80501 1439 C2
400 BLDR 80302 1686 E4
600 BLDR 80305 1686 E4
S Sunnyside Pl
8300 DgsC 80126 2449 A1
Sunnyside St
300 LSVL 80027 1689 C6
E Sunnyside St
1200 DgsC 80126 2449 B1
Sun Prairie Ct
11300 PARK 80138 2538 C1
Sunridge Cir
2000 BMFD 80020 1774 C6
Sunridge Dr
27100 JfnC 80439 2274 A3
Sun Ridge Ln
3200 JfnC 80439 2274 A3
E Sunridge Hollow Rd
8700 DgsC 80134 2622 D2
Sunridge Terrace Ct
4000 CSRK 80109 2702 C2
Sunridge Terrace Dr
3400 CSRK 80109 2702 C2
W Sunrise Av
9500 DgsC 80125 2447 B7
Sunrise Ct
2500 LSVL 80027 1689 C5
4100 BLDR 80304 1602 E5
Sunrise Dr
- BldC 80503 1353 A5
- BldC 80540 1353 A5
10 CHLV 80113 2281 C3
300 JfnC 80401 2191 B3
8200 EbtC 80107 2543 A3
8900 JfnC 80465 2443 A3
S Sunrise Dr
5000 JfnC 80439 2274 C7
5000 JfnC 80439 2358 C1
Sunrise Ln
10 BldC 80302 1601 B1
6600 EbtC 80107 2710 C6
25500 JfnC 80401 2190 B1
S Sunrise Ln
8200 JfnC 80465 2443 A3
N Sunrise Tr
7600 DgsC 80134 2538 A4
Sunrise Ranch Dr
5900 BldC 80503 1519 E3
5900 BldC 80503 1520 A2
Sunrose Ln
23500 JfnC 80401 2190 E3
Sunset Av
- EbtC 80107 2458 E3
- EbtC 80107 2459 A3
W Sunset Av
9600 DgsC 80125 2531 A1
Sunset Blvd
1400 BLDR 80304 1686 C1
Sunset Cir
10 LGMT 80501 1438 E1
1800 JfnC 80439 2188 E7
6600 EbtC 80107 2710 C6
Sunset Ct
900 CSRK 80104 2703 E5
E Sunset Ct
900 GDVL 80121 2365 A1
Sunset Dr
- BGTN 80601 1696 C6
- ERIE 80516 1691 D3
10 CHLV 80113 2281 B3
10 PrkC 80456 2521 C1
300 GOLD 80401 2108 A4
500 LSVL 80027 1689 C6
700 CSRK 80104 2703 E5
700 LKWD 80214 2110 D7
2400 LGMT 80501 1355 D4
5200 BWMR 80123 2279 B5
5200 DNVR 80236 2279 B5
5200 DvrC 80236 2279 B5
5400 DNVR 80123 2279 B5
11600 DgsC 80138 2539 D4
22300 JfnC 80401 2191 A1
44500 EbtC 80107 2459 A7
W Sunset Dr
2400 LITN 80120 2364 A6
Sunset Ln
- BldC 80504 1521 D3
10 GDVL 80121 2365 A1
25000 JfnC 80439 2358 C1
S Sunset Ln
1400 DgsC 80135 2783 E4
Sunset Pkwy
- PrkC 80456 2607 E3
- PrkC 80456 2608 A2
- PrkC 80470 2607 E3
Sunset Pl
1800 LGMT 80501 1438 E5
8000 EbtC 80107 2459 A7
E Sunset Rdg
900 AphC 80121 2365 A1
900 GDVL 80121 2365 A1
Sunset St
10 BldC 80501 1438 E3
100 LGMT 80501 1438 E3
1700 LGMT 80501 1355 E6
S Sunset St
- BldC 80504 1438 E7
10 BldC 80501 1438 E4
100 LGMT 80501 1438 E5
1600 LGMT 80504 1438 E7
Sunset Tr
29700 JfnC 80470 2525 A7
30800 JfnC 80470 2608 E1
30800 JfnC 80470 2609 A1
E Sunset Tr
7400 DgsC 80134 2538 A5
S Sunset Tr
29100 JfnC 80433 2609 C2
29100 JfnC 80470 2609 C2
Sunset Wy
2000 LGMT 80501 1438 D5
S Sunset Wy
1800 DNVR 80219 2195 D6
Sunset Estates Cir
- PrkC 80470 2607 E1
Sunset Hill Cir
9600 LNTR 80124 2451 B4
Sunset Hill Dr
9500 LNTR 80124 2451 B4
Sunset Hill Pl
9600 LNTR 80124 2451 B5
Sunset Meadow Cir
- PrkC 80456 2607 E3
Sunset Point Dr
- PrkC 80456 2607 E4
Sunset Point Wy
- PrkC 80456 2607 E2
- PrkC 80456 2608 A2
Sunset Ridge Cove
- PrkC 80456 2607 E3
S Sunset Ridge Ct
8900 DgsC 80126 2449 B3
Sunset Ridge Pt
- PrkC 80456 2607 E3
E Sunset Ridge Rd
1400 DgsC 80126 2449 B3
Sunset View Wy
46300 EbtC 80138 2456 A4
Sunshine Av
- BldC 80302 1686 B2
- BLDR 80302 1686 B2
- BLDR 80304 1686 B2
N Sunshine Dr
10500 DgsC 80125 2531 B1
10600 DgsC 80125 2447 B7
S Sunshine Ln
400 JfnC 80439 2188 D3
Sunshine Pkwy
300 GOLD 80403 2107 E2
Sunshine Wy
400 BGTN 80601 1697 C4
Sunshine Canyon Dr
10 BldC 80302 1686 A1
10 BLDR 80302 1686 A1
10 BLDR 80304 1686 A1
600 BldC 80302 1685 E1
1400 BldC 80302 1601 D7
4700 BldC 80302 1600 E4
7000 BldC 80302 1599 E2
Sunshine Meadow Dr
9000 DgsC 80134 2622 D4
Sunshine Peak
7600 JfnC 80127 2361 E7
7600 JfnC 80127 2362 A7
Sunstone Ln
5400 CSRK 80108 2703 E1
Sun Valley Ct
2200 CSRK 80104 2788 B1
Sun Valley Rd
6500 DgsC 80134 2622 D1
Supai Rd
23700 JfnC 80439 2274 D6
Superior Plaza Wy
100 SUPE 80027 1772 E3
100 SUPE 80027 1773 A3
Surlyn Ct
1000 CSRK 80109 2703 B5
S Surrey Dr
7400 JfnC 80465 2359 E6
7900 JfnC 80465 2443 C1
8700 JfnC 80439 2441 D3
W Surrey Dr
10 DgsC 80108 2534 E4
10 DgsC 80108 2535 A3
10100 JfnC 80127 2278 A6
W Surrey Pl
10000 JfnC 80127 2278 B6
N Surrey Rd
- LNTR 80134 2451 C7
9100 DgsC 80108 2535 A3
9600 LNTR 80134 2535 B2
Surrey Tr
6700 DgsC 80125 2614 D1
Surrey Ridge Rd
- BldC 80302 1601 C2
N Surry Pl
6500 DgsC 80134 2622 B1
E Sussex Ct
7900 BldC 80503 1520 D4
20800 PARK 80138 2538 A1
W Sussex Ct
7900 BldC 80503 1520 E4
Sussex St
1700 LAFT 80026 1690 D7
Sutherland Ct
10 DgsC 80130 2450 B2
E Sutton Cir
100 LAFT 80026 1690 B5
W Sutton Cir
100 LAFT 80026 1690 B5
Sutton Rd
25600 JfnC 80433 2442 B5
Sutton St
4700 CSRK 80104 2704 D7
Swadley Cir
7100 ARVD 80004 1941 D7
Swadley Ct
7000 ARVD 80004 2025 D1
7100 ARVD 80004 1941 D7
8300 ARVD 80005 1941 D4
S Swadley Ct
4300 JfnC 80465 2277 E5
5600 JfnC 80127 2361 E1
W Swadley Ct
4500 JfnC 80465 2277 E5
Swadley Dr
11700 LKWD 80215 2109 D2
11700 WTRG 80215 2109 D2
Swadley St
2500 LKWD 80215 2109 D3
3200 WTRG 80033 2109 D2
3200 WTRG 80215 2109 D2
5000 ARVD 80033 2025 D5
5000 WTRG 80033 2025 D5
6500 ARVD 80004 2025 D2
8200 ARVD 80005 1941 D4
8200 JfnC 80005 1941 D4
S Swadley St
300 LKWD 80228 2193 E3
4700 JfnC 80465 2277 E7
S Swadley Wy
4600 JfnC 80465 2277 D6
5900 JfnC 80127 2361 E2
Swale Av
21600 PARK 80138 2538 B1
Swale Dr
21800 PARK 80138 2538 B1
Swallow Ct
1300 BldC 80303 1688 A3
Swallow Ln
- BldC 80301 1603 D7
6300 BldC 80303 1688 A3
Swan Av
1400 BGTN 80601 1779 E2
Swandyke Ct
800 DgsC 80108 2618 C3
Swandyke Dr
800 DgsC 80108 2618 C3
E Swansboro Ct
4500 DgsC 80126 2449 E3
E Swansboro Wy
4300 DgsC 80126 2449 E3
Swansea Dr
11800 LNTR 80134 2451 E6
S Swaps Ln
7900 JfnC 80439 2357 C7
S Swaps Tr
7700 JfnC 80439 2357 C7
8000 JfnC 80439 2441 D1
W Swarthmore Av
12000 JfnC 80465 2277 D6
W Swarthmore Dr
9000 DNVR 80123 2278 C6
9200 JfnC 80123 2278 C5
W Swarthmore Pl
4300 JfnC 80127 2277 E5
8400 DNVR 80123 2278 C6
8400 DvrC 80123 2278 C6
Swede Gulch Rd
700 JfnC 80401 2189 C4
1300 JfnC 80401 2190 A7
1300 JfnC 80401 2274 A1
Sweeney Pl
1800 LGMT 80501 1355 D6
Sweetbriar Tr
26000 JfnC 80439 2274 B2
Sweetbrush Dr
16400 DgsC 80134 2452 E6
Sweet Clover Wy
8400 DgsC 80134 2452 E1
Sweetgrass Ct
5300 CSRK 80109 2702 C1
Sweet Rock Ct
10200 PARK 80134 2453 A5
Sweet Valley Ct
200 LGMT 80501 1440 A3
Sweetwater Cir
2500 LAFT 80026 1689 D5
Sweetwater Ct
6900 BldC 80301 1604 B3
Sweet Water Rd
7800 LNTR 80124 2450 E3
Swift Rd
10 PrkC 80456 2691 B1
Swift Creek Cir
39600 EbtC 80107 2625 B4
S Swiss Rd
15100 JfnC 80470 2609 B6
Switch Grass Ct
1400 CSRK 80109 2703 B4
Switch Grass Dr
900 CSRK 80109 2703 B4
Switch Grass Wy
2300 CSRK 80109 2703 B4
Switzer Ln
400 NHGN 80260 1944 C1
400 TNTN 80260 1944 C1
Switzerland Tr
- BldC 80455 1597 E4
- BldC 80455 1598 A4
- BldC 80481 1597 C2
- WARD 80481 1597 D2
10 BldC 80466 1765 E2
300 BldC 80302 1681 D2
900 BldC 80302 1682 A1
2000 BldC 80302 1598 E5
2000 BldC 80302 1599 A5
Switzerland Park Rd
10 BldC 80302 1683 B4
900 BldC 80302 1682 E5
Switzer Park Ln
11400 PARK 80138 2538 B2
Switzer Park Pl
11400 PARK 80138 2538 A2
Sycamore Av
800 BLDR 80303 1687 D4
W Sycamore Cir
500 LSVL 80027 1773 B1
W Sycamore Ct
400 LSVL 80027 1773 B1
Sycamore Ln
10 JfnC 80127 2445 B1
N Sycamore Ln
2200 DgsC 80116 2707 D3
W Sycamore Ln
100 LSVL 80027 1773 C1
Sycamore St
- BldC 80027 1772 E3
- SUPE 80027 1772 E3
S Sycamore St
5500 LITN 80120 2364 B1
W Sycamore St
500 LSVL 80027 1773 C1
500 SUPE 80027 1772 E3
E Sydney Av
5100 DgsC 80130 2450 B5
S Sydney Ln
9600 DgsC 80130 2450 A5
E Sydney Pl
5500 DgsC 80130 2450 B4
Sylvan Ct
11000 PARK 80138 2538 A1
Sylvan Ln
3200 WldC 80504 1440 D2
Sylvan Pl
11000 PARK 80138 2538 A1
Sylvan Rd
31700 JfnC 80403 1852 D4
Sylvan St
7000 BldC 80503 1519 E4
W Sylvestor Ct
9600 DgsC 80129 2448 E5
W Sylvestor Pl
10 DgsC 80129 2448 D5
S Sylvestor Rd
- DgsC 80126 2448 E5
9700 DgsC 80129 2448 E5
W Sylvestor St
10 DgsC 80129 2448 E5
W Sylvestor Tr
400 DgsC 80129 2448 D5
W Sylvestor Wy
400 DgsC 80129 2448 D5
Sylvia Dr
11800 NHGN 80233 1860 E2
11800 NHGN 80233 1861 A2
Sylvia Ln
4600 WldC 80516 1607 D2
S Syndt Rd
5000 JfnC 80439 2273 B7
Syracuse Ct
2600 DNVR 80238 2114 D3
S Syracuse Ct
900 DNVR 80220 2114 D6
900 DNVR 80230 2114 D6
6900 CTNL 80112 2366 D4
8200 CTNL 80112 2450 D1
Syracuse St
- TNTN 80602 1778 D6
900 DNVR 80220 2114 D6
900 DNVR 80230 2114 D6
1900 DNVR 80207 2114 D4
1900 DNVR 80238 2114 D4
8100 CMCY 80022 1946 D4
S Syracuse St
10 DNVR 80230 2198 D1
1500 DNVR 80231 2198 D5
4100 DNVR 80237 2282 D4
4600 DvrC 80237 2282 D7
4600 GDVL 80111 2282 D7
4600 GDVL 80237 2282 D7
5400 GDVL 80111 2366 D1
7100 CTNL 80112 2366 D5
S Syracuse Wy
2200 AphC 80231 2198 D7
2200 DNVR 80224 2198 D7
2200 DNVR 80231 2198 D7
2600 DNVR 80231 2282 E1
2700 AphC 80231 2282 E1
3000 DNVR 80231 2283 A2
3800 DNVR 80237 2282 D4
6000 GDVL 80111 2366 D3
6300 AphC 80111 2366 D3
6300 CTNL 80111 2366 D3
6600 CTNL 80112 2366 D3
6600 GDVL 80112 2366 D3
Szymanski Rd
6600 DgsC 80134 2621 D3

T

Table Dr
1900 GOLD 80401 2108 A4
Table Heights Dr
2300 GOLD 80401 2108 A4
Table Mesa Ct
2600 BLDR 80305 1686 E7
Table Mesa Dr
- BLDR 80303 1687 C7
1800 BLDR 80305 1686 C7
3000 BLDR 80305 1687 A7
4700 BldC 80305 1687 C7
Table Mountain Ct
- BldC 80503 1354 E3
- BldC 80503 1355 A3
Table Mountain Dr
4300 GOLD 80403 2024 D7
Table Mountain Pkwy
15700 GOLD 80403 2024 D6
15700 JfnC 80403 2024 D6
Table Mountain Rd
- BldC 80503 1354 E3
Table Top Ct
5600 BLDR 80301 1604 B1
Table View Dr
14300 JfnC 80401 2109 A5
14300 LKWD 80401 2109 A5
Tabor Ct
3600 WTRG 80033 2109 D1
5600 ARVD 80002 2025 D4
7000 ARVD 80004 2025 D1
8300 ARVD 80005 1941 D4
10500 JfnC 80021 1857 D6
N Tabor Ct
800 CSRK 80104 2704 E6
S Tabor Ct
4300 JfnC 80465 2277 D5
6400 JfnC 80127 2361 D3
Tabor Dr
11800 LKWD 80215 2109 D2
11800 WTRG 80033 2109 D2
11800 WTRG 80215 2109 D2
E Tabor Dr
5400 CSRK 80104 2704 E6
N Tabor Dr
1000 CSRK 80104 2704 E5
Tabor Pl
2100 LKWD 80215 2109 E4
8400 ARVD 80005 1941 D4
E Tabor Pl
5800 CSRK 80104 2704 E5
Tabor St
700 LKWD 80401 2109 D7
2600 LKWD 80215 2109 D3
5100 ARVD 80033 2025 D5
5100 WTRG 80033 2025 D5
5600 ARVD 80002 2025 D4
6700 ARVD 80004 2025 D1
7500 ARVD 80005 1941 D6
S Tabor St
100 ELIZ 80107 2793 B1
600 EbtC 80107 2793 B1
4600 JfnC 80465 2277 D6
5900 JfnC 80127 2361 E2
S Tabor Wy
- JfnC 80465 2277 D7
2300 JfnC 80228 2193 D7
5100 JfnC 80127 2277 E7
5300 JfnC 80127 2361 D2
Tabriz Pl
2600 BLDR 80304 1602 E6
Tacker Ct
400 CSRK 80104 2703 E6
Taft Cir
6800 ARVD 80004 2025 D1
Taft Ct
1500 LSVL 80027 1689 A6
2500 LKWD 80215 2109 D3
3600 WTRG 80033 2109 D1
5200 WTRG 80033 2025 D5
5600 ARVD 80002 2025 D4
7000 ARVD 80004 2025 D1
7600 ARVD 80005 1941 D5
7600 JfnC 80005 1941 D5
S Taft Ct
200 LSVL 80027 1773 A2
4400 JfnC 80465 2277 D5
5300 JfnC 80127 2361 D1
Taft Dr
1900 LKWD 80215 2109 D4
2500 BLDR 80302 1686 E3
2500 BLDR 80303 1686 E3
Taft Pl
1400 LSVL 80027 1689 A6
Taft St
2600 LKWD 80215 2109 D3
5600 ARVD 80002 2025 D4
7000 ARVD 80004 1941 D7
7000 ARVD 80004 2025 D1
8300 ARVD 80005 1941 D4
S Taft St
300 LKWD 80228 2193 D3
900 LKWD 80226 2193 D3
4300 JfnC 80465 2277 D5
5500 JfnC 80127 2361 D1
S Taft Wy
4500 JfnC 80465 2277 D5
5100 JfnC 80127 2277 D7
5900 JfnC 80127 2361 D3
Tahoe Ct
8800 BldC 80301 1689 B2
31100 JfnC 80439 2189 A5
Tahoe Ln
8800 BldC 80301 1689 C2
Talavero Pl
5200 DgsC 80134 2621 A5
Talbot Dr
4600 BLDR 80303 1687 C4
Talisman Dr
3300 BLDR 80301 1603 B7
Talisman Pl
3700 BLDR 80301 1603 B6
Tall Grass Cir
9700 LNTR 80124 2451 A4
Tall Grass Pl
8700 LNTR 80124 2450 E5
8700 LNTR 80124 2451 A5
Tall Grass Tr
- JfnC 80403 2023 A4
Tall Horse Tr
4800 DgsC 80135 2784 E5
4800 DgsC 80135 2785 A5
E Tallkid Av
21400 DgsC 80138 2538 B3
S Tallkid Ct
12000 DgsC 80138 2538 A3
Tallman Ct
21200 PARK 80138 2538 A2
Tallman Dr
- PARK 80134 2537 D2
20100 PARK 80138 2537 E2
21500 PARK 80138 2538 A2
Tallman Ln
2100 LGMT 80501 1438 D1
2200 LGMT 80503 1438 D1
Tall Pine Ln
10 BldC 80302 1517 A7
Tall Pines Ln
10200 JfnC 80433 2441 D6
Tall Spruce Cir
- BGTN 80601 1697 E4
Tall Spruce St
200 BGTN 80601 1697 E5
Tall Timber Ln
10 PrkC 80456 2521 C2
Tally Ho Ct
4600 BldC 80301 1604 B3
Tally Ho Tr
4500 BldC 80301 1604 B3
S Tallyns Reach Pkwy
- AURA 80016 2371 A4
Tallyrand Cir
4300 DgsC 80104 2871 C3
Talon Tr
3900 JfnC 80465 2275 C5
Tamarac Ct
7100 DgsC 80134 2621 E4
S Tamarac Ct
3900 DNVR 80237 2282 E4
7000 CTNL 80112 2366 E5
Tamarac Dr
1400 JfnC 80401 2190 B5
S Tamarac Dr
3100 DNVR 80224 2282 E4
3100 DNVR 80231 2282 E4
3500 DNVR 80237 2282 E4
Tamarac Ln
10 CHLV 80113 2281 D5
S Tamarac Pkwy
4300 DNVR 80237 2282 E5
Tamarac Pl
- TNTN 80602 1778 D6
Tamarac St
- AdmC 80640 1946 D3
- CMCY 80022 1946 D3
- TNTN 80602 1778 D6
1200 DNVR 80220 2114 E5
2600 DNVR 80238 2114 D3
S Tamarac St
10 DNVR 80230 2198 D1
1100 AphC 80247 2198 E4
1100 DNVR 80247 2198 E4
1800 DNVR 80231 2198 E6
2900 DNVR 80231 2282 E1
7000 CTNL 80112 2366 E5
8200 CTNL 80112 2450 D1
Tamarack Av
2100 BldC 80304 1602 D4
2100 BLDR 80304 1602 D4
Tamarack Ct
4200 BLDR 80304 1602 E4
Tamarack Dr
2200 BLDR 80304 1602 E4
Tamarade Ct
10 JfnC 80127 2445 A1
Tamarade Dr
- JfnC 80127 2361 A7
10 JfnC 80127 2445 A1

STREET
Block City ZIP Map# Grid
Tamarak Wy
1800 ERIE 80516 1692 A3
Tamarask Ct
5900 DgsC 80118 2868 D7
Tamarisk Ct
600 LSVL 80027 1689 B7
Tamarisk Ln
31300 JfnC 80439 2272 E1
W Tamarisk St
700 LSVL 80027 1689 A7
Tamarron Ct
11100 PARK 80138 2538 D1
Tamarron Dr
11100 PARK 80138 2538 D1
Tamarron Ln
2200 LAFT 80026 1689 E4
Tamarron Pl
11100 PARK 80138 2538 D1
Tamasoa Pl
10 DgsC 80108 2618 E5
10 DgsC 80108 2619 A5
Tamerlain Ct
10 DgsC 80130 2450 A2
Tammy Ln
9000 DgsC 80134 2537 B3
9000 PARK 80134 2537 B3
Tammywood St
12500 BMFD 80020 1775 C7
12500 BMFD 80020 1859 C1
Tanager Cir
700 LGMT 80501 1440 A1
Tanager Pl
1500 LGMT 80501 1440 A1
Tanager St
5100 BGTN 80601 1697 D7
Tanager Tr
- BMFD 80020 1775 C2
Tanaka Dr
1500 ERIE 80516 1607 A6
S Tananger Ct
100 LSVL 80027 1773 A1
Tanbark Dr
- JfnC 80127 2361 A5
Tancred St
10400 NHGN 80234 1860 B5
W Tanforan Av
12000 JfnC 80465 2277 D6
E Tanforan Dr
18200 AURA 80015 2285 B6
W Tanforan Dr
2900 DNVR 80110 2280 A6
2900 EGLD 80110 2280 A6
3300 DNVR 80110 2279 E6
3300 DNVR 80123 2279 E6
8700 DNVR 80123 2278 C6
E Tanforan Pl
18200 AURA 80015 2285 B6
W Tanforan Pl
10300 JfnC 80127 2278 A6
11700 JfnC 80465 2277 E6
Tangleoak Ln
7500 DgsC 80108 2534 E6
Tanglevine Dr
4400 CSRK 80109 2702 C4
Tanglewood Ct
4800 BldC 80301 1604 D3
Tanglewood Rd
8500 DgsC 80116 2706 D4
9800 DgsC 80116 2707 A3
S Tanglewood St
8400 DgsC 80126 2449 A2
Tanglewood Tr
4500 BldC 80301 1604 D3
Tanner Peak Tr
- BGTN 80601 1697 C6
Tanoa Ct
4500 CSRK 80104 2703 E2
Tanoa Rd
30800 JfnC 80439 2273 A3
31100 JfnC 80439 2272 E3
Tansey Ln
5000 JfnC 80439 2275 A7
5000 JfnC 80454 2275 A7
Tantra Dr
- BldC 80305 1687 C7
- BLDR 80305 1687 C7
Tantra Park Cir
1000 BLDR 80305 1687 B7
Taos Rd
21300 JfnC 80454 2359 B1
Taos Tr
8700 LNTR 80124 2451 A3
43000 EbtC 80107 2542 D3
S Taos Wy
1100 DNVR 80223 2196 B4
Tapadero Cir
40600 EbtC 80107 2626 C1
Tapadero Ct
6500 DgsC 80108 2534 C4
Tapadero Pl
6500 DgsC 80108 2534 C5
Tapadero Rd
10 PrkC 80456 2522 D6
Tapadero Wy
12300 DgsC 80108 2534 C4
Tape Dr
- BldC 80027 1773 C5
- BMFD 80020 1773 D5
- LSVL 80027 1773 D5
Tappy Toorie Cir
8800 DgsC 80129 2448 B2
Tappy Toorie Pl
8900 DgsC 80129 2448 B3
E Tarcoola Ln
4800 DgsC 80130 2450 A5
S Tarcoola Pl
10000 DgsC 80130 2450 A5
Targhee Ln
29300 JfnC 80439 2273 C1
Targhee Pt
2400 LAFT 80026 1689 E3
Tarpan Pl
700 CSRK 80104 2703 D3
S Tarryall Wy
2100 DgsC 80116 2791 B5
Tatum Ln
1000 BLDR 80303 1687 D4
Tauber Ct
10 DgsC 80108 2534 D6
Taurus Cir
1200 LAFT 80026 1690 A5
S Taylor Av
100 LSVL 80027 1773 E2
1700 LSVL 80027 1774 A1
Taylor Cir
- DgsC 80118 2954 E3
Taylor Ct
- BMFD 80020 1775 E4
10 CSRK 80104 2704 A7
Taylor Dr
10 GpnC 80403 1851 A2
9600 JfnC 80433 2442 B5
Taylor Ln
800 ERIE 80516 1691 D2
Taylor St
10 PrkC 80456 2521 C2
Taylor Mountain Dr
1500 LGMT 80503 1437 E6
Taylor Mountain Rd
1400 DgsC 80118 2870 C7
1600 DgsC 80118 2954 C1
Taza Ln
13200 JfnC 80470 2525 A7
Taza Tr
30600 JfnC 80470 2525 A7
Teaberry Av
5800 CSRK 80104 2788 E1
Teak Pl
1000 CSRK 80104 2787 D1
Teakwood Ct
600 DgsC 80126 2449 A3
Teakwood Ln
- TNTN 80260 1944 B1
Teal Cir
500 LGMT 80503 1438 C2
N Teal Ct
1300 BldC 80303 1688 A3
S Teal Ct
1200 BldC 80303 1688 A3
Teal Ln
10 PrkC 80456 2691 D1
Teal St
100 NHGN 80233 1860 E5
Teal Tr
6700 JfnC 80439 2357 C4
Teal Creek Ct
13700 BMFD 80020 1775 B5
Teal Creek Dr
13800 BMFD 80020 1775 B4
Teal Ridge Ct
9600 DgsC 80126 2449 E4
S Technology Ct
100 BMFD 80021 1858 A1
Technology Dr
100 BMFD 80021 1858 A1
4600 GOLD 80403 2024 D6
Technology Wy
7600 DNVR 80237 2282 D6
Tecoma Cir
10 JfnC 80127 2361 A6
Tecumseh Tr
11900 JfnC 80433 2526 D4
Teddy Ln
9200 LNTR 80124 2451 A3
Tee Ln
1900 CSRK 80104 2787 D2
Teepee Dr
- BldC 80301 1688 D1
W Tejas Av
34100 JfnC 80470 2608 B1
Tejas Ln
10 NDLD 80466 1765 C2
Tejon Ct
8100 AdmC 80221 1944 B5
N Tejon Ct
13000 WSTR 80234 1776 B6
Tejon St
10 DNVR 80223 2196 B1
800 DNVR 80204 2112 B6
3000 DNVR 80211 2112 B2
4000 DNVR 80211 2028 B7
5100 AdmC 80221 2028 B5
5100 DNVR 80221 2028 B5
8300 AdmC 80221 1944 B4
8300 FLHT 80260 1944 B4
14400 AdmC 80020 1776 B2
14400 WSTR 80020 1776 B2
15300 AdmC 80020 1692 B7
N Tejon St
- BMFD 80020 1776 B5
- WSTR 80020 1776 B5
- WSTR 80234 1776 B5
8400 FLHT 80260 1944 B4
11800 WSTR 80234 1860 B2
S Tejon St
10 DNVR 80223 2196 B2
2000 AphC 80223 2196 B7
2000 EGLD 80110 2196 B7
2000 EGLD 80223 2196 B7
2500 EGLD 80110 2280 B1
3000 DNVR 80110 2280 B1
3000 DNVR 80223 2280 B1
3000 DvrC 80110 2280 B1
3000 DvrC 80223 2280 B1
Tejon Wy
- FLHT 80260 1944 B3
10000 TNTN 80260 1860 B7
Telemark Dr
29600 JfnC 80439 2273 B1
Telleen Av
1000 ERIE 80516 1607 A5
Teller Cir
900 BLDR 80303 1687 C4
Teller Ct
2500 LKWD 80214 2110 E3
2500 WTRG 80033 2110 E3
6800 ARVD 80003 2026 E1
Teller Ct
8200 ARVD 80003 1942 E4
9600 WSTR 80021 1942 E1
9700 WSTR 80021 1858 E7
S Teller Ct
6300 JfnC 80123 2362 E3
7100 JfnC 80128 2362 E5
Teller Ln
9700 WSTR 80021 1942 E1
Teller St
10 LKWD 80226 2194 E1
400 LKWD 80226 2110 E7
1000 LKWD 80214 2110 E5
2500 WTRG 80033 2110 E3
4100 WTRG 80033 2026 E7
5600 ARVD 80002 2026 E4
5600 ARVD 80003 2026 E4
8700 ARVD 80003 1942 E3
8700 WSTR 80003 1942 E3
8700 WSTR 80021 1942 E3
11500 BMFD 80020 1858 E3
N Teller St
9200 JfnC 80021 1942 E2
9200 WSTR 80021 1942 E1
S Teller St
10 LKWD 80226 2194 E2
1200 LKWD 80232 2194 E4
2700 DNVR 80227 2278 E2
3500 LKWD 80227 2278 E4
3500 LKWD 80235 2278 E4
7400 JfnC 80128 2362 E6
S Teller Wy
8200 JfnC 80128 2446 E1
Teller Lake Wy
- BMFD 80020 1775 D6
Telluride Cir
3700 BLDR 80305 1771 A2
S Telluride Cir
3500 AURA 80013 2285 B3
6000 AphC 80016 2369 B2
Telluride Ct
10200 DgsC 80125 2530 E6
10400 CMCY 80022 1865 A5
S Telluride Ct
2100 AURA 80013 2201 B6
3900 AURA 80013 2285 B4
5300 CTNL 80015 2285 B7
5700 CTNL 80015 2369 A1
6200 AphC 80016 2369 B3
7400 FXFD 80016 2369 B5
7500 CTNL 80016 2369 B6
Telluride Dr
- AURA 80011 2117 A7
- AURA 80011 2201 A1
13600 BMFD 80020 1775 A5
13800 BMFD 80020 1774 E4
Telluride Ln
3700 BLDR 80305 1771 B2
30200 JfnC 80439 2189 B5
Telluride Pl
- DgsC 80125 2531 A6
10 LGMT 80501 1356 C7
10 LGMT 80501 1439 C1
3800 BLDR 80305 1771 B2
Telluride St
- AdmC 80601 1781 B4
- CMCY 80022 1865 A7
600 AURA 80011 2117 B6
10000 DgsC 80125 2531 A6
10100 DgsC 80125 2530 D6
13800 AdmC 80601 1781 B4
15200 AdmC 80601 1697 A7
15600 BGTN 80601 1697 A7
16600 WldC 80603 1697 A4
S Telluride St
900 AURA 80017 2201 B3
1900 AURA 80013 2201 B7
3000 AURA 80013 2285 B2
5000 AURA 80015 2285 B7
5000 CTNL 80015 2285 B7
5500 CTNL 80015 2369 B1
6100 AphC 80016 2369 B2
6900 FXFD 80016 2369 B5
Telluride Wy
10000 CMCY 80022 1865 A6
S Telluride Wy
3500 AURA 80013 2285 A3
5300 CTNL 80015 2285 B7
5700 CTNL 80015 2369 A1
E Tempe Cir
7300 AURA 80016 2370 B5
7300 CTNL 80016 2370 B5
S Tempe Ct
4200 AURA 80018 2286 C4
5700 AphC 80015 2370 C1
6300 AURA 80016 2370 C3
Tempe Pl
- AURA 80018 2286 C3
S Tempe St
- AphC 80015 2370 C1
5000 AphC 80015 2286 C7
6500 AURA 80016 2370 C3
S Tempe Wy
5900 CTNL 80015 2370 C2
6100 AphC 80015 2370 C2
E Tempest Ridge Wy
7000 DgsC 80134 2622 B2
W Temple Av
11400 JfnC 80127 2277 E6
E Temple Dr
- DNVR 80237 2282 E6
8800 DNVR 80237 2283 A6
14000 AphC 80015 2284 B6
16600 AURA 80015 2284 E5
17400 AURA 80015 2285 B6
W Temple Dr
11600 JfnC 80127 2277 D6
11600 JfnC 80465 2277 D6
W Temple Ln
11800 JfnC 80465 2277 D6
E Temple Pl
15300 AURA 80015 2284 D6
16900 AURA 80015 2285 A5
W Temple Pl
4600 DNVR 80236 2279 C6
8900 DNVR 80123 2278 C6
11800 JfnC 80465 2277 D5
N Templin Ln
11600 DgsC 80138 2455 B7
Tempted Ways Dr
800 LGMT 80504 1439 A6
Tenacity Dr
- BldC 80504 1439 A6
700 LGMT 80504 1439 A6
Tenaya Ln
10 CHLV 80113 2282 A5
Tenby Ct
7400 DgsC 80108 2534 E7
Tenby Ln
10300 TNTN 80229 1861 B6
Tenby Wy
7100 DgsC 80108 2534 E7
Tenderfoot Dr
400 DgsC 80118 2954 E1
N Tenderfoot Tr
12000 DgsC 80138 2455 A4
Tenino Av
5200 BLDR 80303 1687 D5
5400 BldC 80303 1687 D5
Ten Mile Pl
5000 DgsC 80108 2619 A6
E Tennessee Av
- GNDL 80246 2198 A4
400 DNVR 80209 2196 E4
1600 DNVR 80209 2197 B4
4400 DNVR 80246 2197 E4
4400 GNDL 80246 2197 E4
5600 DNVR 80246 2198 B4
6100 DNVR 80224 2198 B4
10500 DNVR 80247 2199 C3
11700 AURA 80012 2199 D4
13300 AURA 80012 2200 A4
16400 AURA 80017 2200 E3
17800 AURA 80017 2201 B3
W Tennessee Av
2400 DNVR 80223 2196 B4
3000 DNVR 80219 2196 A4
3600 DNVR 80219 2195 D4
6000 LKWD 80226 2195 A4
7500 LKWD 80226 2194 E4
12200 LKWD 80228 2193 D4
E Tennessee Cir
12400 AURA 80012 2199 E3
W Tennessee Cir
11100 LKWD 80226 2193 E4
11100 LKWD 80226 2194 A4
E Tennessee Dr
12200 AURA 80012 2199 E3
14500 AURA 80012 2200 C3
17500 AURA 80017 2201 B3
W Tennessee Dr
11300 LKWD 80226 2193 E4
E Tennessee Pl
15800 AURA 80017 2200 D3
18400 AURA 80017 2201 C3
W Tennessee Pl
8500 LKWD 80226 2194 C4
11400 LKWD 80226 2193 E4
12400 LKWD 80228 2193 C4
Tennyson Cir
- LAFT 80026 1690 D6
Tennyson Ct
10300 WSTR 80031 1859 C6
N Tennyson Ct
10000 WSTR 80031 1859 D7
Tennyson Pl
11000 WSTR 80031 1859 C4
Tennyson St
- BfdC 80516 1691 C5
- BMFD 80020 1691 C5
- WSTR 80031 1859 C3
300 DNVR 80219 2111 D7
300 DNVR 80219 2195 D1
1200 DNVR 80204 2111 D6
2600 DNVR 80212 2111 D3
5100 AdmC 80212 2027 D7
5200 DNVR 80212 2027 D5
5400 AdmC 80002 2027 D5
5400 AdmC 80221 2027 D5
5800 AdmC 80003 2027 C3
5800 ARVD 80002 2027 C3
5800 ARVD 80003 2027 C3
5800 ARVD 80221 2027 C3
6400 AdmC 80030 2027 D2
6400 ARVD 80030 2027 D2
8000 WSTR 80030 1943 C4
8000 WSTR 80031 1943 C4
N Tennyson St
- BMFD 80020 1859 C2
- WSTR 80020 1859 C2
9200 WSTR 80031 1943 D2
10800 WSTR 80031 1859 D5
S Tennyson St
900 DNVR 80219 2195 D4
4400 DNVR 80236 2279 D5
N Tennyson Wy
10700 WSTR 80031 1859 C5
S Tennyson Wy
2500 DNVR 80219 2195 D7
2500 DNVR 80219 2279 D1
2600 DNVR 80236 2279 D1
Tepees Wy
28600 JfnC 80401 2189 D4
Teresa Dr
10 CCkC 80439 2271 D6
E Terlago Creek Pl
19100 PARK 80134 2537 D4
Tern St
9700 FLHT 80260 1944 A1
Terrace Cir N
700 BLDR 80304 1602 B2
Terrace Cir S
700 BLDR 80304 1602 B2
Terrace Dr
1300 LGMT 80501 1356 E7
1300 LGMT 80501 1357 A7
1900 DgsC 80126 2449 B2
Terrace Pl
7200 BldC 80303 1688 C6
E Terraridge Dr
2100 DgsC 80126 2449 B2
Terra Vista St
100 BGTN 80601 1697 A6
Terravita Wy
- CSRK 80108 2704 B4
Terrawood Ct
11500 PARK 80134 2537 A1
Terrawood Ln
11500 PARK 80134 2536 D2
11500 PARK 80134 2537 A1
Territorial Rd
- CSRK 80109 2787 A4
- DgsC 80104 2787 B4
- DgsC 80109 2787 A4
Territorial St
5100 DgsC 80134 2621 D4
Territory Cir
1700 EbtC 80138 2540 D5
Territory Ct
42800 EbtC 80138 2540 D5
Territory Wy
42400 EbtC 80138 2540 D5
Terry Cir
7100 ARVD 80007 1940 C7
Terry Ct
6100 ARVD 80403 2024 C3
6600 ARVD 80007 2024 C1
7100 ARVD 80007 1940 C7
7400 JfnC 80007 1940 C6
Terry Dr
- BldC 80504 1357 A4
Terry Ln
6000 ARVD 80403 2024 C3
Terry St
800 JfnC 80401 2108 C6
900 LGMT 80501 1439 A1
1700 LGMT 80501 1356 A6
6400 ARVD 80007 2024 C2
6400 ARVD 80403 2024 C2
7200 JfnC 80007 1940 C7
16900 JfnC 80403 2024 C3
S Terry St
700 LGMT 80501 1439 A5
Terry Wy
6100 ARVD 80403 2024 C3
Terryl Av
- DgsC 80134 2621 D4
Tesla Cir
4900 BLDR 80301 1603 C7
Tesla Ct
4900 BLDR 80301 1603 B7
Tesuque Rd
23300 JfnC 80439 2274 E6
Tetbury Ct
600 DgsC 80108 2618 D1
Teton
3200 WldC 80504 1440 D2
W Teton Av
8500 JfnC 80128 2446 C2
W Teton Cir
8800 JfnC 80128 2446 C2
Teton Ct
10000 DgsC 80124 2450 D5
W Teton Pl
8900 JfnC 80128 2446 C2
Teton Pt
- LAFT 80026 1689 D3
W Texas Av
10900 JfnC 80232 2194 B3
10900 LKWD 80232 2194 B3
11000 JfnC 80232 2193 E4
11200 LKWD 80226 2193 E4
W Texas Dr
9200 LKWD 80232 2194 C4
12000 JfnC 80226 2193 D4
12000 JfnC 80228 2193 D4
12000 LKWD 80226 2193 D4
12000 LKWD 80228 2193 D4
Texas Ln
10 LGMT 80501 1439 B6
W Texas Pl
10100 LKWD 80232 2194 B4
12500 LKWD 80228 2193 C4
Texas St
600 GOLD 80403 2107 C1
E Thames St
800 DgsC 80126 2449 A4
Thatch Cir
1100 CSRK 80109 2703 B5
Thea Gulch Rd
25800 JfnC 80403 2022 A5
The Country Club Ln
2600 JfnC 80439 2273 A1
The Covington
- AphC 80231 2198 D6
The Greens
- DNVR 80231 2283 B1
The Highline on Cherry Cr
- AphC 80231 2198 E7
- AphC 80231 2282 E1
The Landing at Morrison Lk
- DNVR 80123 2278 D7
- DvrC 80123 2278 D7
- LKWD 80123 2278 D7
The Lane Rd
10 BldC 80403 1852 D2
S Thelma Av
12800 JfnC 80470 2524 B6
The Park
- DNVR 80231 2283 B1
Theresa Dr
- BldC 80303 1688 E4
The Reserve at Hunter Run
- AphC 80231 2282 D1
- DNVR 80231 2282 D1
The Scramble
17600 JfnC 80433 2694 D4
Thimbleberry Ln
27100 JfnC 80439 2357 E4
27100 JfnC 80439 2358 A4
29200 JfnC 80439 2273 C4
S Thimbleberry Wy
9500 PARK 80134 2453 B4
Thistle Ct
- CSRK 80109 2702 C4
Thistle Pl
400 LGMT 80501 1439 D1
Thistlebrook Cir
3000 DgsC 80126 2449 D6
Thistlebrook Wy
- DgsC 80126 2449 D6
E Thistle Ridge Cir
2100 DgsC 80126 2449 B3
E Thistle Ridge Rd
1500 DgsC 80126 2449 B2
Thistlesage Ct
4100 CSRK 80109 2702 D3
Thistlewood Ct
- EbtC 80107 2709 D5
W Thomas Av
1400 EGLD 80110 2280 C6
Thomas Ct
2100 EbtC 80138 2540 D6
Thomas Dr
700 BLDR 80303 1687 C4
S Thomas Dr
10900 JfnC 80433 2525 A1
Thomas Ln
- BldC 80305 1771 A3
W Thomas St
- SUPE 80027 1772 E4
Thomaston Cir
11700 LNTR 80134 2451 C5
Thompson Ct
5100 DNVR 80216 2029 C5
Thompson Dr
26100 JfnC 80433 2442 A4
Thor Av
- BldC 80301 1603 C2
Thor Ct
400 DgsC 80124 2450 E2
Thorington Ln
10600 DgsC 80126 2449 D7
Thorn Apple Ct
8700 DgsC 80108 2534 E4
Thorn Apple Wy
300 DgsC 80108 2534 E4
Thornbird Pl
2600 BLDR 80304 1602 E6
Thornbury Pl
1000 DgsC 80129 2448 C5
S Thornbury Wy
9800 DgsC 80129 2448 C5
Thorncreek Cir
13400 TNTN 80241 1777 A5
Thorncreek Ct
900 TNTN 80241 1777 A5
Thorndike Av
4800 CSRK 80104 2788 D1
Thorndyke Pl
4100 BMFD 80020 1775 C7
Thorne Cir
10 GpnC 80403 1850 E7
Thorngate Pl
22600 PARK 80138 2538 C3
Thornton Ests
- TNTN 80229 1945 D3
Thornton Pkwy
- TNTN 80229 1944 E1
- TNTN 80260 1944 E1
10 TNTN 80229 1945 A1
W Thornton Pkwy
- FLHT 80260 1944 D2
- TNTN 80229 1944 D2
800 TNTN 80260 1944 D2
Thornwood Cir
700 LGMT 80503 1438 A4
Thornwood Wy
3800 LGMT 80503 1438 A4
Thorodin Dr
10200 GpnC 80403 1851 E7
10200 GpnC 80403 1852 A7
Thoroughbred Run
- LITN 80128 2363 D5
10 CBVL 80123 2363 D5
W Three Acre Ln
7600 WTRG 80033 2026 D7
E Three Pines Ranch Pl
20300 DgsC 80134 2537 E5
Three Ponds Wy
6000 AphC 80123 2363 C3
6000 LITN 80123 2363 C3
Three Sisters Cir
5300 JfnC 80439 2357 A1
Threshing Dr
4200 BGTN 80601 1697 C5
E Thrill Pl
4800 DNVR 80207 2114 A2
N Thrush Dr
11000 DgsC 80138 2454 B6
Thunder Rd
100 BldC 80503 1270 C3
100 JfnC 80401 2189 B3
Thunder Run
10000 DgsC 80125 2615 A6
Thunderbird
11000 WldC 80504 1440 D3
Thunderbird Cir
4800 BLDR 80303 1687 C6
E Thunderbird Cir
8600 DgsC 80134 2622 C2
E Thunderbird Ct
8700 DgsC 80134 2622 C3
Thunderbird Ct E
500 BLDR 80303 1687 C5
Thunderbird Dr
100 BLDR 80303 1687 C6
S Thunderbird Ln
2400 JfnC 80439 2273 A1
Thunderbird Rd
- DgsC 80118 2868 C7
E Thunderbird Pl
8500 DgsC 80134 2622 C3
Thunderbolt Cir
29200 JfnC 80433 2441 B4
Thunder Butte Rd
1400 CSRK 80109 2703 A5
Thunderhead Dr
8300 BldC 80302 1518 B1
E Thunderhill Hts
8400 DgsC 80134 2622 C3
Thunder Hill Rd
41000 EbtC 80138 2540 D6
41000 EbtC 80138 2624 D1
N Thunderhill Rd
5500 DgsC 80134 2622 B3
Thunderlake Cir
- BldC 80303 1689 C3
2900 LAFT 80026 1689 C3
Thunder Ridge Rd
26400 JfnC 80433 2526 A5
Thunder Ridge Rd S
- BldC 80466 1682 D7
S Thunder Ridge Wy
8400 DgsC 80126 2449 E1
S Tibet Ct
6600 AURA 80016 2370 C3
Tibet St
- DNVR 80249 1950 B5
S Tibet St
5100 AphC 80015 2286 C7
5400 AphC 80015 2370 C1
6400 AURA 80016 2370 C3
Tibet Wy
- AURA 80018 2286 C3
S Tibet Wy
7000 AURA 80016 2370 C5
Tiburon Ct
9900 DgsC 80124 2450 D5
Tichy Blvd
5600 CMCY 80022 2030 B1
Tierra Alta Dr
4400 CSRK 80104 2703 E2
Tiffany Pl
900 LGMT 80501 1356 A4
Tiff Grass Ct
1500 CSRK 80109 2703 B5
Tiger Pt
10500 DgsC 80124 2450 C7
Tiger Run
10400 DgsC 80124 2450 C6
Tiger Wk
- DgsC 80124 2450 C7
S Tiger Wk
6700 DgsC 80124 2450 C7
Tiger Bend Ln
5300 JfnC 80465 2360 C1
Tiger Chase
10500 DgsC 80124 2450 C7
Tiger Grotto
10500 DgsC 80124 2450 C7
Tiger Paw
6600 DgsC 80124 2450 C6
S Tigers Eye
10500 DgsC 80124 2450 C6
E Tiger Tooth
6600 DgsC 80124 2450 C6
S Tilbury St
100 CSRK 80104 2704 E7
S Tilden St
200 NDLD 80466 1765 C3
Tilghman Rd
10 BldC 80481 1515 A2
Tiller Dr
- LGMT 80501 1356 C5
Tilly Ln
10 DgsC 80108 2534 D6
Timber Ct
900 LGMT 80501 1439 D1
Timber Dr
10 GpnC 80403 1934 C6
36000 EbtC 80107 2710 A1
37100 EbtC 80107 2709 E1
37300 EbtC 80107 2625 E7
37300 EbtC 80107 2626 A7
Timber Ln
10 BldC 80304 1601 E5
10 CCkC 80439 2187 E5
5000 EbtC 80107 2709 E1
N Timber Ln
12700 DgsC 80138 2454 A3
Timber Pl
5100 EbtC 80107 2625 E7
5100 EbtC 80107 2709 E1
Timber Rd
- GpnC 80403 1934 B2
Timber Tr
10 BldC 80302 1601 D7
10 BldC 80302 1685 D1
10 CCkC 80452 2186 A5
27200 JfnC 80433 2525 E3
Timberchase Pt
2500 DgsC 80126 2449 C7
Timberchase Tr
2600 DgsC 80126 2449 C6
Timber Cove St
16200 AdmC 80642 1700 C4
Timbercrest Dr
1000 DgsC 80108 2618 D2
Timbercrest Ln
7100 DgsC 80108 2618 D1
7200 DgsC 80108 2534 D7
Timbercrest Wy
7000 DgsC 80108 2618 D1
Timber Falls Tr
19000 JfnC 80127 2527 E2
S Timber Hawk Cir
9600 DgsC 80126 2449 E4
9600 DgsC 80130 2449 E4
Timber Hollow Lp
4100 CSRK 80109 2702 E2
Timberline Dr
10 BldC 80466 1766 A2
Timberline Pl
400 DgsC 80126 2448 E3

STREET
Block City ZIP Map# Grid

Timberline Rd
7300 DgsC 80130 2450 D4
7300 LNTR 80124 2450 D4
E Timberline Rd
- DgsC 80124 2450 C4
- LNTR 80124 2450 C4
6600 DgsC 80130 2450 C4
Timber Meadow Ct
1600 DgsC 80116 2706 B4
Timber Ridge Dr
5000 EbtC 80107 2625 E5
5000 EbtC 80107 2626 A5
Timber Ridge Ln
10900 DgsC 80108 2533 E1
Timber Ridge Rd
3200 JfnC 80439 2356 C6
Timbers Dr
7100 JfnC 80439 2358 B5
Timber Spring Ln
23100 PARK 80138 2538 C2
Timber Spring Pl
23100 PARK 80138 2538 D2
Timber Top Rd
10 PrkC 80456 2521 B5
Timber Trail Rd
7100 JfnC 80439 2356 C6
S Timber Trail Rd
7100 JfnC 80439 2356 C6
S Timbervale Ct
9600 DgsC 80129 2448 D4
S Timbervale Dr
4000 JfnC 80439 2273 D5
W Timbervale Tr
400 DgsC 80129 2448 D5
S Timberwood St
8400 DgsC 80126 2448 E1
Timon Cir
2000 LAFT 80026 1689 E6
2000 LSVL 80026 1689 E6
2000 LSVL 80027 1689 E6
Timothy Dr
600 LGMT 80503 1438 B4
Timothy Pl
7200 BldC 80503 1521 A3
S Timothys Dr
10700 JfnC 80433 2440 E7
10700 JfnC 80433 2441 A7
10700 JfnC 80433 2525 A1
S Timothys Rd
10600 JfnC 80433 2441 A7
10600 JfnC 80433 2525 A1
Timothys Tr
31200 JfnC 80433 2525 A1
Tim Tam Cir
21400 PARK 80138 2538 A1
S Tim Tam Tr
7900 JfnC 80439 2357 D7
7900 JfnC 80439 2441 D1
Tim Tam Wy
10900 PARK 80138 2538 A1
Tincup Cir
2800 BLDR 80305 1771 A2
13900 BMFD 80020 1774 E4
Tin Cup Ct
16600 PARK 80134 2536 E1
Tincup Ct
1900 BLDR 80305 1771 A2
Tincup Ter
10 PrkC 80456 2522 B5
Tincup Wy
1000 DgsC 80116 2791 B3
Tioga Tr
10 DgsC 80138 2455 E6
10 EbtC 80138 2456 A6
Tipperary St
1200 BldC 80026 1689 C3
1200 BldC 80303 1689 C3
1200 LAFT 80026 1689 C3
Titan Ct
400 AURA 80011 2116 A7
4700 DNVR 80239 2032 A6
4800 DNVR 80239 2031 E5
9500 DgsC 80125 2532 B2
S Titan Ct
1500 AURA 80012 2199 E5
Titan Pl
300 DgsC 80108 2619 A5
3900 BldC 80026 1606 C5
W Titan Rd
7200 DgsC 80125 2532 A2
7500 DgsC 80125 2531 D2
Titan St
200 AURA 80011 2116 A7
200 AURA 80011 2200 A1
Titan Wy
4900 DNVR 80239 2031 E5
Titanite Ln
1000 CSRK 80108 2619 E6
Titan Park Cir
9500 DgsC 80125 2532 A2
Titus St
- DNVR 80249 1951 C6
Toboggan Rd
15400 JfnC 80470 2608 B6
Todd Dr
5000 DgsC 80134 2537 A2
Toedtli Dr
700 BLDR 80305 1687 B7
1200 BLDR 80305 1771 B1
S Toledo Ct
1600 AURA 80012 2199 E5
2200 AURA 80014 2200 A7
Toledo St
200 AURA 80011 2116 A7
S Toledo Wy
2400 AURA 80014 2199 E7
2400 AURA 80014 2200 A7
Tolland Ct
500 DgsC 80108 2619 B6
Tolland Dr
400 DgsC 80108 2619 A6
W Toller Av
8400 JfnC 80128 2446 C2
W Toller Dr
10800 JfnC 80127 2446 A2
Tollgate Dr
9100 BldC 80503 1435 E6
Tom Ct
5900 DgsC 80130 2450 B6
W Tomah Rd
- DgsC 80104 2871 A3
- DgsC 80118 2871 A3
10 DgsC 80109 2870 B4
10 DgsC 80118 2870 B4
10 DgsC 80135 2870 B4
2000 DgsC 80118 2869 E5
N Tomahawk Rd
9100 DgsC 80138 2539 A2
11700 DgsC 80138 2454 E5
11700 DgsC 80138 2455 A5
Tomahawk Tr
- TNTN 80229 1861 E7
11600 JfnC 80433 2526 D3
N Tom Bay Rd
10 AphC 80102 2123 A7
10 AphC 80102 2207 A1
S Tom Bay Rd
10 AphC 80102 2207 A1
E Tomichi Rd
1100 DgsC 80116 2791 E4
E Tom Tom Dr
9600 DgsC 80138 2454 E6
9600 DgsC 80138 2455 A6
S Tongue Rd
4300 JfnC 80439 2274 D5
Tonkin Pl
1400 BldC 80504 1357 A4
1400 LGMT 80501 1356 E4
1400 LGMT 80501 1357 A4
Tony Pl
900 LGMT 80501 1356 A5
Topaz Cir
10200 PARK 80134 2453 A6
Topaz Ct
1100 LGMT 80504 1439 A6
Topaz Dr
2000 BldC 80304 1602 D4
2400 BLDR 80304 1602 D4
Topaz St
10 GOLD 80401 2108 B7
700 SUPE 80027 1773 A7
Topaz Vista Pl
5900 DgsC 80108 2534 B5
Topaz Vista Wy
12400 DgsC 80108 2534 B5
Topeka Ct
4600 DNVR 80239 2032 A6
4700 DNVR 80239 2031 E6
Topeka Wy
500 CSRK 80109 2703 C6
E Top T Ranch Pl
20300 DgsC 80134 2537 E4
Torrey Ct
6400 ARVD 80007 2024 C2
Torrey Ln
6000 ARVD 80403 2024 D3
Torrey Rd
9800 TNTN 80260 1860 B7
Torrey St
900 JfnC 80401 2108 C6
6000 ARVD 80403 2024 C2
6900 ARVD 80007 2024 C1
7000 ARVD 80007 1940 B7
7200 JfnC 80007 1940 C7
Torrey Wy
6300 ARVD 80403 2024 C2
Torrey Pine Cir
31800 JfnC 80439 2188 E7
S Torrey Pine Dr
2100 JfnC 80439 2188 E7
Torrey Pines Dr
6000 DgsC 80118 2868 D7
Torreys Peak Dr
1300 LGMT 80501 1356 C7
10300 PARK 80138 2454 B7
N Torreys Peak Dr
2700 SUPE 80027 1773 A7
2900 SUPE 80027 1857 B1
S Torreys Peak Dr
3800 SUPE 80027 1857 A2
W Torreys Peak Dr
3000 SUPE 80027 1857 A1
E Tory Pointe
5600 DgsC 80130 2450 B6
Totara Pl
6800 BldC 80503 1520 E4
Totem Run
10200 DgsC 80125 2614 E5
Tourmaline Ct
9800 DgsC 80134 2452 D5
Tourmaline Ln
27800 JfnC 80403 2021 D4
Tournament Ct
2000 JfnC 80439 2188 D7
2500 DgsC 80108 2618 E4
Tournament Dr
2500 DgsC 80108 2618 E4
Tower Rd
- AdmC 80019 2119 E4
- AdmC 80019 2120 A4
- AdmC 80137 2119 E4
- AdmC 80601 1781 B2
- AphC 80137 2120 A4
- BGTN 80601 1781 B2
- BGTN 80603 1781 B2
- CCkC 80452 2185 E6
- CCkC 80452 2186 A6
1300 AURA 80011 2117 C5
2900 CSRK 80108 2620 A7
2900 CSRK 80108 2704 A1
2900 DgsC 80108 2620 A7
2900 DgsC 80108 2704 A1
3700 AURA 80011 2033 B7
3700 DNVR 80249 2033 B7
4000 AURA 80249 2033 B7
4000 DNVR 80239 2033 B6
4000 DvrC 80011 2033 B7
Tower Rd
4000 DvrC 80239 2033 B7
4000 DvrC 80249 2033 B7
7200 DNVR 80249 1949 B1
8100 CMCY 80022 1949 B1
8100 DNVR 80022 1949 B1
8800 AdmC 80022 1949 B1
9600 AdmC 80022 1865 B5
9600 CMCY 80022 1865 B5
12100 AdmC 80022 1781 B7
12100 CMCY 80022 1781 B7
15200 AdmC 80601 1697 B7
16000 BGTN 80601 1697 B4
16600 BGTN 80603 1697 B4
Tower Rd SR-32
1500 AURA 80011 2117 C4
4000 AURA 80011 2033 C7
4000 AURA 80249 2033 C7
4000 DNVR 80239 2033 C6
4000 DNVR 80249 2033 C7
4000 DvrC 80011 2033 C7
4000 DvrC 80239 2033 C7
4000 DvrC 80249 2033 C7
Tower Rd SR-36
- AdmC 80019 2119 E4
- AdmC 80019 2120 A4
- AdmC 80137 2119 E4
- AdmC 80137 2120 A4
N Tower Rd
700 AURA 80011 2117 C6
S Tower Rd
- AphC 80016 2369 C2
1100 AURA 80017 2201 C4
1900 AURA 80013 2201 C7
2600 AURA 80013 2285 C1
5000 AURA 80015 2285 C7
5000 CTNL 80015 2285 C7
5200 AphC 80015 2285 C7
5400 AphC 80015 2369 C1
5400 CTNL 80015 2369 C1
S Tower Wy
2800 AURA 80013 2285 C1
4800 AURA 80015 2285 B6
Towerbridge Cir
10700 DgsC 80124 2450 C7
Towerbridge Ln
10700 DgsC 80124 2450 B7
Towerbridge Rd
- DgsC 80124 2450 B7
- DgsC 80130 2450 B7
Tower Hill Cir
10 JfnC 80401 2190 B1
Towhee Rd
7800 DgsC 80134 2622 B4
Town Center Dr
- DgsC 80129 2448 A3
3500 DgsC 80125 2447 E3
3500 DgsC 80129 2447 E3
Townley Cir
1000 LGMT 80501 1356 A7
E Townsend Dr
7000 DgsC 80130 2450 C4
7000 LNTR 80124 2450 C4
S Townsville Cir
9500 DgsC 80130 2450 A4
Tracery Ct
10200 DgsC 80134 2452 D6
Tracewood Cir
10400 DgsC 80130 2450 A7
Tracewood Ct
10300 DgsC 80130 2450 A7
Tracewood Dr
10300 DgsC 80130 2450 A6
Trade Centre Av
- LGMT 80501 1438 C5
2400 LGMT 80503 1438 C5
Tradition Pl
10200 LNTR 80124 2451 A6
N Trail Cir
13000 JfnC 80127 2612 E2
Trail Rdg
3200 WldC 80504 1440 D3
Trailblazer Wy
- CSRK 80109 2702 E4
Trail Boss Dr
- CSRK 80104 2703 D2
- CSRK 80108 2703 D2
Trailhead Rd
6000 DgsC 80130 2450 C4
W Trailmark Pkwy
- JfnC 80127 2446 C5
- LITN 80127 2446 C5
W Trail North Dr
7500 DgsC 80125 2531 E5
7500 DgsC 80125 2532 A5
Trailrider Pass
10700 JfnC 80127 2362 A7
11000 JfnC 80127 2361 C7
Trailriders Dr
10200 DgsC 80125 2530 E5
Trail Ridge Cir
700 LSVL 80027 1689 A7
Trail Ridge Ct
- LGMT 80501 1439 C2
Trail Ridge Dr
700 LSVL 80027 1689 A7
800 LSVL 80027 1773 A1
E Trailridge Dr
2500 LAFT 80026 1689 D3
W Trailridge Dr
2600 LAFT 80026 1689 D3
Trail Ridge Rd
- BldC 80501 1356 E7
1200 LGMT 80501 1356 E7
1200 LGMT 80501 1439 E1
Trails Av
3100 BMFD 80020 1775 E6
Trails End
2300 DgsC 80116 2706 B3
S Trails End
11600 JfnC 80433 2525 E3
Trails End Dr
10 CCkC 80452 2186 B5
Trailside Ct
4200 CSRK 80109 2702 B2
Trailside Dr
600 JfnC 80401 2190 D3
4500 CSRK 80109 2702 D2
Trailside Ln
4400 CSRK 80109 2702 D2
Trailside Lp
4400 CSRK 80109 2702 D2
Trail Sky Cir
- PARK 80134 2536 E2
16700 PARK 80134 2537 A2
Trail Sky Ct
11800 PARK 80134 2537 A2
W Trail South Dr
7500 DgsC 80125 2531 E6
7500 DgsC 80125 2532 A6
Trail View Ln
- PARK 80134 2536 E2
- PARK 80134 2537 A2
Trail View Pl
- PARK 80134 2537 A2
N Trailway Cir
6800 DgsC 80134 2623 A1
S Trailway Cir
6800 DgsC 80134 2623 B1
6800 DgsC 80138 2623 B1
Trailwood Wy
14900 JfnC 80470 2609 D5
Tranquility Tr
- CSRK 80109 2702 D3
Trapper Ct
6400 DgsC 80134 2621 D4
Trappers Mountain Tr
11600 JfnC 80127 2529 A3
Trappers Trail Av
6300 DgsC 80134 2621 D4
Travertine Pl
10200 DgsC 80134 2452 D6
Travis St
9300 TNTN 80229 1945 C1
9900 TNTN 80229 1861 C7
Travis Gulch Rd
10 GpnC 80403 1849 D4
10 GpnC 80474 1849 D4
N Travois Tr
13900 AphC 80016 2454 A1
13900 AphC 80138 2454 A1
13900 AURA 80138 2454 A1
Tree Haven St
16400 AdmC 80642 1700 D4
Treetop Ln
22500 JfnC 80401 2191 A4
Trefoil Cir
- BGTN 80601 1780 D2
Trefoil Ct
- BGTN 80601 1780 D2
Tremolite Ct
- DgsC 80108 2619 D6
Tremolite Dr
- CSRK 80108 2619 D6
- DgsC 80108 2619 D6
Tremolite Ln
- DgsC 80108 2619 D6
Tremont Pl
- DNVR 80203 2112 E4
1200 DNVR 80204 2112 D5
1300 DNVR 80202 2112 D5
2100 DNVR 80205 2112 E4
2700 DNVR 80205 2113 A3
S Trenton Cir
7000 CTNL 80112 2366 D5
S Trenton Ct
- AphC 80231 2198 D7
1500 DNVR 80231 2198 D5
7500 CTNL 80112 2366 D6
S Trenton Dr
6900 CTNL 80112 2366 D5
Trenton Pl
- TNTN 80602 1778 D6
Trenton St
- DNVR 80238 2114 D2
500 DNVR 80230 2114 D7
1200 DNVR 80220 2114 D5
2800 TNTN 80602 1778 D7
S Trenton St
10 DNVR 80230 2198 D1
1600 DNVR 80231 2198 D5
2900 DNVR 80231 2282 D1
7800 CTNL 80112 2366 E7
S Trenton Wy
2100 AphC 80231 2198 D7
8100 CTNL 80112 2366 E7
8100 CTNL 80112 2450 D1
Tresine Dr
28100 JfnC 80439 2357 D3
Trevarton Ln
6100 BldC 80503 1436 E2
6100 BldC 80503 1437 A2
Triangle Ct
- AdmC 80640 1863 D4
Triangle Dr
8000 DgsC 80125 2532 C6
Tribute Pl
- CSRK 80109 2702 D4
Trinchera Tr
26700 JfnC 80439 2274 A6
S Trinchera Tr
4600 JfnC 80439 2273 E6
4600 JfnC 80439 2274 A6
S Trinchera Peak
8000 JfnC 80127 2362 B5
Trinity Mountain Ranch Rd
- GpnC 80403 1850 E6
Tripp Dr
400 GOLD 80401 2107 E7
400 GOLD 80401 2108 A7
Trojan Ct
11000 WSTR 80031 1859 C4
Troon Cir
3700 BMFD 80020 1775 D4
Troon Ct
300 LSVL 80027 1773 B4
13700 BMFD 80020 1775 D5
Troon Village Dr
9400 LNTR 80124 2451 A4
Troon Village Pl
8700 LNTR 80124 2451 B4
Troon Village Wy
9400 LNTR 80124 2451 B3
Trotter Ln
7900 DgsC 80124 2450 E5
Trotwood Wy
10800 DgsC 80126 2449 D7
Troublesome Gulch Rd
27100 JfnC 80439 2273 D3
27100 JfnC 80439 2274 A3
27100 JfnC 80457 2274 A3
Trout Ct
- BLDR 80303 1687 D3
Trout Creek Cir
1100 LGMT 80501 1356 E7
Trout Creek Pl
1300 LGMT 80501 1356 E7
Troutdale Park Pl
29800 JfnC 80439 2273 B5
Troutdale Ridge Rd
29900 JfnC 80439 2273 B5
Troutdale Scenic Dr
29700 JfnC 80439 2273 B5
Troutdale Village Dr
4200 JfnC 80439 2273 B5
Troxell Av
2800 LGMT 80503 1438 B1
2900 BldC 80503 1438 B1
Troy Cir
1400 LAFT 80026 1690 A5
S Troy Cir
200 AURA 80012 2200 A2
6200 CTNL 80111 2367 E3
6200 CTNL 80111 2368 A3
Troy Ct
700 AURA 80011 2116 A6
S Troy Ct
2500 AURA 80014 2199 E7
2500 AURA 80014 2200 A7
2600 AURA 80014 2284 A1
6200 CTNL 80111 2367 E3
Troy St
- AURA 80010 2115 E4
- CMCY 80022 1863 E5
200 AURA 80011 2200 A1
700 AURA 80011 2116 A6
900 BldC 80026 1690 C3
900 LAFT 80026 1690 C3
1300 AURA 80011 2115 E5
3700 AdmC 80239 2116 A1
3700 AURA 80239 2116 A1
3700 DNVR 80239 2116 A1
3800 DNVR 80239 2032 A7
4800 DNVR 80239 2031 E5
12400 AdmC 80640 1779 E7
12400 AdmC 80640 1863 E1
S Troy St
300 AURA 80012 2199 E2
400 AURA 80012 2200 A3
2300 AURA 80014 2200 A7
Troy Wy
- CMCY 80022 1863 E5
S Troy Wy
2100 AURA 80014 2199 E6
2100 AURA 80014 2200 A6
Truckee Ct
- CMCY 80022 1865 A6
S Truckee Ct
3100 AURA 80013 2285 B2
5300 CTNL 80015 2285 B7
5600 CTNL 80015 2369 B1
Truckee St
- AdmC 80601 1697 A7
10400 CMCY 80022 1865 A5
S Truckee St
900 AURA 80017 2201 B3
1900 AURA 80013 2201 B6
2700 AURA 80013 2285 B1
5100 CTNL 80015 2285 B7
5700 CTNL 80015 2369 B1
S Truckee Wy
1100 AURA 80017 2201 B4
2300 AURA 80013 2201 B7
3200 AURA 80013 2285 B2
Truda Dr
1000 NHGN 80233 1861 A2
Truman Av
200 AdmC 80102 2124 D1
200 BNNT 80102 2124 D1
Truman Ct
1400 LSVL 80027 1689 A7
Trussville St
- AdmC 80022 1867 C2
- DNVR 80022 1867 C2
- DNVR 80249 1867 C4
Tschaikovsky Dr
10 GpnC 80403 1934 C2
Tschaikovsky Rd
- GpnC 80403 1934 C2
Tucker Gulch Dr
1000 GOLD 80403 2023 C7
1000 GOLD 80403 2107 C1
Tucker Gulch Wy
900 GOLD 80403 2107 C1
S Tucson Cir
200 AURA 80012 2200 A2
2500 AURA 80014 2200 A7
Tucson Ct
2300 LGMT 80501 1356 D4
Tucson St
200 AURA 80011 2200 A1
700 AURA 80011 2116 A6
1000 AURA 80011 2115 E5
5500 AdmC 80022 2031 E4
5500 DNVR 80022 2031 E4
5500 DNVR 80239 2031 E4
10400 CMCY 80022 1863 E6
12400 AdmC 80640 1779 E7
12400 AdmC 80640 1863 E1
12800 AdmC 80601 1779 E6
16000 AdmC 80602 1695 E5
16000 WldC 80601 1695 E5
16000 WldC 80603 1695 E5
S Tucson St
- AURA 80014 2199 E5
1500 AURA 80012 2199 E5
Tucson Wy
2000 AURA 80010 2116 A4
2200 LGMT 80501 1356 D5
5000 DNVR 80239 2031 E5
S Tucson Wy
300 AURA 80012 2199 E2
300 AURA 80012 2200 A2
2500 AURA 80014 2200 A7
6800 CTNL 80112 2368 A5
Tufts Av
- DNVR 80237 2283 A6
E Tufts Av
10 EGLD 80110 2280 E6
10 EGLD 80113 2280 E6
600 EGLD 80113 2281 A6
700 CHLV 80113 2281 A6
6100 CHLV 80111 2282 B5
7800 DNVR 80237 2282 E6
8900 DNVR 80237 2283 A5
8900 GDVL 80111 2283 A5
8900 GDVL 80237 2283 A5
14500 AURA 80015 2284 C5
16700 AURA 80015 2285 A6
W Tufts Av
10 EGLD 80110 2280 D6
10 EGLD 80113 2280 D6
3300 EGLD 80110 2279 E6
3800 DNVR 80236 2279 D6
5100 BWMR 80123 2279 D6
8900 DNVR 80123 2278 C6
13600 JfnC 80465 2277 B6
E Tufts Cir
9100 GDVL 80111 2283 A6
19300 CTNL 80015 2285 D5
W Tufts Cir
4600 DNVR 80236 2279 C6
E Tufts Dr
14000 AURA 80015 2284 B5
19700 CTNL 80015 2285 D6
20200 AphC 80015 2285 E5
W Tufts Dr
10600 JfnC 80127 2278 A6
10700 JfnC 80127 2277 E6
W Tufts Ln
10600 JfnC 80127 2278 A6
E Tufts Pl
9100 GDVL 80111 2283 A5
14200 AURA 80015 2284 C5
16900 AURA 80015 2285 A5
W Tufts Pl
10600 JfnC 80127 2278 A6
11700 JfnC 80465 2277 D6
W Tulane Av
10800 JfnC 80127 2277 E6
10800 JfnC 80127 2278 A6
Tulane Ct
10 LGMT 80503 1355 B7
W Tulane Dr
11700 JfnC 80465 2277 D6
W Tulane Pl
11500 JfnC 80127 2277 E6
13600 JfnC 80465 2277 B6
Tulane St
2000 FLHT 80260 1944 B2
S Tulare Cir
3200 DNVR 80231 2282 E2
S Tulare Ct
3200 DNVR 80231 2282 E2
Tularosa Ln
- LGMT 80501 1356 C5
Tule Lake Dr
4400 LITN 80123 2363 C1
4800 JfnC 80123 2363 C1
Tulip Ct
1500 LGMT 80501 1355 E7
Tulip St
900 LGMT 80501 1438 D1
2000 LGMT 80501 1355 D5
Tulip Wy
2300 LGMT 80501 1355 D5
Tulip Tree Pl
1700 CSRK 80108 2704 A1
Tulsa Ct
4500 DNVR 80239 2031 E6
Tulsa Wy
5100 DNVR 80239 2031 E4
5500 DNVR 80239 2032 A4
Tumblegrass Pl
8300 PARK 80134 2452 E1
Tumbleweed Dr
300 BGTN 80601 1697 C4
10300 TNTN 80229 1861 E6
Tumbleweed Wy
11100 PARK 80138 2537 E1
Tumwater Ln
2600 BLDR 80304 1602 E6
Tundra Pl
700 LGMT 80501 1439 D1
Tungsten Pl
400 LGMT 80501 1356 D7
Tungsten Rd
- BldC 80466 1765 E2
Tungsten Tr
- BldC 80466 1765 E2
Tunnel 19 Rd
200 BldC 80403 1852 E2
200 BldC 80403 1853 A1
E Turf Ln
100 DgsC 80108 2535 A4
Turin Dr
- BldC 80503 1437 D6
1400 LGMT 80503 1437 D6
Turkey Ln
10 PrkC 80456 2691 D2
22400 JfnC 80465 2359 A3
Turkey Creek Rd
14600 JfnC 80465 2277 A6
14600 LKWD 80465 2277 A6
14800 JfnC 80465 2276 E6
14800 MRSN 80465 2276 C6
N Turkey Creek Rd
19200 JfnC 80465 2359 D5
23000 JfnC 80465 2358 E5
23700 JfnC 80439 2358 E5
S Turkey Creek Rd
5800 JfnC 80465 2359 D2
7900 JfnC 80465 2443 E1
9800 JfnC 80465 2442 E4
10200 JfnC 80433 2442 E4
Turkey Rock Rd
7200 DgsC 80125 2531 A7
7200 DgsC 80125 2615 A1
7300 DgsC 80125 2530 E7
Turnagain Ct
10 BldC 80302 1685 D2
Turnberry Cir
1000 LSVL 80027 1773 A3
Turnberry Ct
1400 CSRK 80104 2787 E2
13900 BMFD 80020 1775 D4
Turnberry Pkwy
- CMCY 80022 1863 E5
- CMCY 80022 1864 A5
Turnberry Pt
13900 BMFD 80020 1775 D4
Turner Ct
2000 CSRK 80104 2788 A1
Turner Dr
7400 AdmC 80221 1944 B6
Turnpike Dr
- WSTR 80031 1943 D5
3600 WSTR 80030 1943 D5
N Turnpike Dr
7500 WSTR 80030 1943 E6
Turnstone Av
6400 CSRK 80104 2705 A7
Turnstone Pl
5800 CSRK 80104 2704 E7
6100 CSRK 80104 2705 A7
Turquoise Ct
10200 PARK 80134 2453 A6
Turquoise Dr
1100 BldC 80504 1439 A7
1100 LGMT 80504 1439 A7
Turquoise St
- PARK 80134 2453 A6
Turquoise Terrace Pl
12400 DgsC 80108 2534 C4
Turquoise Terrace St
12300 DgsC 80108 2534 C4
W Turtle Mtn
10400 JfnC 80127 2362 A7
Turweston Ln
7000 DgsC 80108 2534 D7
7000 DgsC 80108 2618 D1
Tuscany Ct
1700 LGMT 80503 1437 E6
E Tuscany Ct
5100 DgsC 80130 2450 A2
S Tuscany Ln
8800 DgsC 80130 2450 A2
E Tuscany Pl
5100 DgsC 80130 2450 A3
E Tuscany Wy
- DgsC 80130 2450 A2
Tuscon Wy
- CMCY 80022 1863 E5
Twenty Mile Rd
- PARK 80134 2453 B5
- PARK 80134 2537 C1
11200 DgsC 80134 2537 C1
S Twenty Mile Rd
10700 PARK 80134 2453 B7
Twilight Ct
1700 LGMT 80501 1357 A5
Twilight Dr
10 LKWD 80215 2110 A3
10 WTRG 80215 2110 A3
1600 LGMT 80501 1357 A5
Twilight Ln
- BldC 80503 1353 A5
Twilight St
11900 BldC 80503 1353 A6
11900 BldC 80540 1353 A6
Twilight Wy
5500 DgsC 80134 2621 B4
Twilight Peak
11000 JfnC 80127 2361 C7
W Twilight Peak
11000 JfnC 80127 2361 C7
Twilight Terrace Dr
10 PrkC 80456 2521 B5
E Twinberry St
17200 PARK 80134 2453 A4
Twin Buttes Pl
3800 EbtC 80138 2457 B3
W Twin Cubs
10900 DgsC 80125 2614 D1
Twin Elk Ln
13000 JfnC 80127 2445 C5
Twin Flower
10 JfnC 80127 2360 E5
Twin Lakes Rd
4800 BldC 80301 1604 B3
4800 BLDR 80301 1604 B3
Twin Lakes Wy
4800 BldC 80301 1604 B2
S Twin Oaks Ln
1100 DgsC 80109 2786 D4
Twin Oaks Rd
10 CSRK 80109 2787 A4
10 DgsC 80109 2787 A4
300 DgsC 80109 2786 E4
Twin Peaks Cir
- BldC 80503 1355 A7
1100 LGMT 80503 1355 A7
1100 LGMT 80503 1438 B1
Twin Peaks Ln
21200 JfnC 80465 2359 C5

STREET Block City ZIP Map# Grid

Twin Peaks Golf Course
- LGMT 80503 1355 B7
Twin Sisters Dr
1400 LGMT 80501 1356 C7
Twin Sisters Rd
10 BldC 80466 1683 E7
10 BldC 80466 1767 E1
10 BldC 80466 1768 A1
S Twin Spruce Dr
5400 JfnC 80439 2358 B1
Twin Spruce Rd
9500 JfnC 80403 1852 C6
10800 JfnC 80403 1853 A5
W Twin Thumbs Pass
11100 JfnC 80127 2361 C7
Twisted Oak Dr
6600 DgsC 80108 2534 C5
Twisted Pine Cir N
- TNTN 80260 1944 A1
Twisted Pine Cir S
- TNTN 80260 1944 B1
Two Bits St
10 PrkC 80456 2522 B4
Two Brothers Rd
- CCkC 80452 2101 B3
- IDSP 80452 2101 B3
Tycoon Av
17500 JfnC 80465 2276 B4
Tyler Av
300 LSVL 80027 1773 B1
1700 LSVL 80027 1689 B6
1800 LGMT 80501 1355 D5
S Tyler Av
100 LSVL 80027 1773 B1
Tyler Dr
9600 ARVD 80004 2026 B2
S Tyler Dr
- SUPE 80027 1773 C7
2200 BMFD 80021 1773 C7
Tyler Pl
1200 ERIE 80516 1607 B2
Tyler Rd
1900 BLDR 80304 1686 D1
Tynan Ct
400 ERIE 80516 1606 E6
Tynan Dr
300 ERIE 80516 1606 E5
300 ERIE 80516 1607 A5
Tyrrhenian Ct
2200 LGMT 80501 1357 A5
Tyrrhenian Dr
2200 BldC 80504 1357 A5
2200 LGMT 80501 1356 E4
2400 LGMT 80501 1357 A4

U

S Uinta Ct
1300 AphC 80231 2198 E5
3300 DNVR 80231 2282 E2
3700 DNVR 80237 2282 E3
7600 CTNL 80112 2366 E6
Uinta Pl
1000 DgsC 80118 2870 D7
S Uinta Pl
7500 CTNL 80112 2366 E6
Uinta St
- TNTN 80602 1778 D6
1200 DNVR 80220 2114 E5
1900 DNVR 80238 2114 E5
8400 AdmC 80022 1946 E4
8400 CMCY 80022 1946 E4
14500 AdmC 80602 1778 D2
S Uinta St
2700 AphC 80231 2282 E1
2700 DNVR 80231 2282 E1
3700 DNVR 80237 2282 E4
6700 CTNL 80112 2366 E4
6700 GDVL 80112 2366 E4
S Uinta Wy
1500 AphC 80231 2198 E5
1700 AphC 80231 2199 A6
S Ukraine Cir
6000 AphC 80015 2370 C2
S Ukraine Ct
6300 AphC 80015 2370 C3
7800 AURA 80016 2370 C7
S Ukraine St
5100 AphC 80015 2286 C7
5900 AphC 80015 2370 C2
7000 AURA 80016 2370 C4
S Ukraine Wy
5300 AphC 80015 2286 C7
S Ulm St
1300 AphC 80137 2206 A7
S Ulster Cir
6800 CTNL 80112 2366 E4
S Ulster Cir E
5700 GDVL 80111 2366 E1
Ulster Cir W
5700 GDVL 80111 2366 E1
Ulster Ct
- DNVR 80230 2114 E7
S Ulster Ct
3300 DNVR 80231 2282 E2
7300 CTNL 80112 2366 E5
S Ulster Pl
7500 CTNL 80112 2366 E6
Ulster St
- DNVR 80207 2114 D1
1200 DNVR 80220 2114 E5
2800 DNVR 80238 2114 E2
3900 DNVR 80207 2030 E7
8300 AdmC 80022 1946 D4
8300 CMCY 80022 1946 D4
8700 AdmC 80640 1946 D4
15500 TNTN 80602 1694 D7
S Ulster St
- AphC 80247 2198 E4
10 DNVR 80230 2198 E1
1300 AphC 80231 2198 E4
1300 DNVR 80231 2198 E4
2700 AphC 80231 2282 E1
2700 DNVR 80231 2282 E1
3400 DNVR 80237 2282 E3
4700 DvrC 80111 2282 E7
4700 DvrC 80237 2282 E7
4700 GDVL 80111 2282 E7
7000 CTNL 80112 2366 E5
Ulster Wy
500 DNVR 80230 2114 E6
Ulysses Ct
1600 GOLD 80401 2108 C5
1600 JfnC 80401 2108 C5
Ulysses St
1300 JfnC 80401 2108 C5
1600 GOLD 80401 2108 C5
5200 JfnC 80403 2024 C5
7000 ARVD 80007 1940 B7
7000 ARVD 80007 2024 C1
Ulysses Wy
4100 JfnC 80403 2024 B7
4100 JfnC 80403 2108 B1
N Umatilla Ct
12900 WSTR 80234 1776 B6
Umatilla St
- AdmC 80020 1776 B2
200 DNVR 80223 2196 B1
1100 DNVR 80204 2112 B6
3800 DNVR 80211 2112 B1
4100 DNVR 80211 2028 B7
5000 DNVR 80221 2028 B6
5400 AdmC 80221 2028 B4
8300 AdmC 80260 1944 B4
8400 AdmC 80221 1944 B4
8400 FLHT 80260 1944 B4
13100 WSTR 80234 1776 A5
S Umatilla St
1100 DNVR 80223 2196 B4
2900 EGLD 80110 2280 B2
3300 SRDN 80110 2280 B3
Umatilla Wy
10000 TNTN 80260 1860 B7
Umber Cir
- ARVD 80007 2024 B2
6200 ARVD 80403 2024 B2
Umber Ct
7000 ARVD 80007 1940 B7
7000 ARVD 80007 2024 B1
8900 JfnC 80007 1940 B3
Umber St
6000 ARVD 80403 2024 B3
7000 ARVD 80007 1940 B7
7000 ARVD 80007 2024 B1
Umbria Ln
- LGMT 80503 1438 A5
Umpire Ct
- AdmC 80642 1700 D4
Umpire St
- AdmC 80102 1868 E6
- AdmC 80642 1868 E6
14300 AdmC 80603 1784 D2
14700 AdmC 80603 1700 D7
16300 AdmC 80642 1700 D4
Unbridled Av
21500 PARK 80138 2538 B2
Unbridled Dr
21300 PARK 80138 2538 A2
Undergrove Cir
7600 DNVR 80249 1951 C5
Undergrove St
27500 DNVR 80249 1951 D6
Union Av
200 JfnC 80465 2276 B3
200 MRSN 80465 2276 B3
500 BLDR 80304 1602 B4
E Union Av
10 EGLD 80110 2280 E6
10 EGLD 80113 2280 E6
600 EGLD 80113 2281 A6
700 CHLV 80113 2281 A6
5300 CHLV 80111 2282 B6
5300 CHLV 80113 2282 B6
7600 DNVR 80237 2282 D6
8900 AphC 80111 2283 A6
8900 DNVR 80111 2283 A6
8900 DNVR 80237 2283 A6
8900 GDVL 80111 2283 A6
8900 GDVL 80237 2283 A6
9500 AphC 80015 2283 A6
16600 AURA 80015 2284 E6
16600 AURA 80015 2285 A6
20400 AphC 80015 2285 E6
W Union Av
10 EGLD 80110 2280 D6
10 EGLD 80113 2280 D6
1800 SRDN 80110 2280 A6
2900 DNVR 80110 2280 A6
3100 DNVR 80110 2279 E6
3100 EGLD 80110 2279 E6
3600 DNVR 80236 2279 E6
8400 DNVR 80123 2278 D6
Union Blvd
- LKWD 80401 2109 D7
10 LKWD 80228 2193 D1
400 LKWD 80228 2109 D7
S Union Blvd
10 LKWD 80228 2193 D2
900 LKWD 80226 2193 E5
1100 JfnC 80226 2193 E5
1100 JfnC 80228 2193 E5
1100 JfnC 80232 2193 E5
1800 LKWD 80227 2193 E5
Union Cir
- ARVD 80002 2025 D4
8500 ARVD 80005 1941 D4
E Union Cir
20400 AphC 80015 2285 E6
Union Ct
3600 WTRG 80033 2109 D1
5200 ARVD 80002 2025 D5
5200 WTRG 80033 2025 D5
6200 ARVD 80004 2025 D2
7100 ARVD 80004 1941 D7
8300 ARVD 80005 1941 D4
N Union Ct
3800 WTRG 80033 2109 D1
S Union Ct
1400 SUPE 80027 1773 B5
1700 LKWD 80228 2193 E6
2300 JfnC 80228 2193 D7
4400 JfnC 80465 2277 D5
5900 JfnC 80127 2361 D2
Union Dr
2000 LKWD 80215 2109 D4
E Union Dr
18200 AURA 80015 2285 B6
19600 CTNL 80015 2285 D6
20100 AphC 80015 2285 E6
E Union Pl
17100 AURA 80015 2285 A6
S Union Pl
1900 LKWD 80228 2193 D6
Union Rd
4900 BldC 80503 1353 B4
Union St
1100 LKWD 80401 2109 D6
1200 JfnC 80401 2109 D6
3000 LKWD 80215 2109 D2
3000 WTRG 80215 2109 D2
3300 WTRG 80033 2109 D2
5600 ARVD 80002 2025 D4
6700 ARVD 80004 2025 D1
7000 ARVD 80004 1941 D7
8200 ARVD 80005 1941 D4
S Union St
4300 JfnC 80465 2277 D5
5100 JfnC 80127 2277 D7
5900 JfnC 80127 2361 D2
Union Wy
2100 LKWD 80215 2109 D4
5300 ARVD 80002 2025 D5
10500 JfnC 80021 1857 D5
S Union Wy
6500 JfnC 80127 2361 D3
Unita St
2600 DNVR 80238 2114 E3
N Unita Wy
- DNVR 80220 2114 E6
400 DNVR 80230 2114 E7
400 DNVR 80230 2198 E1
Unity Pkwy
- CMCY 80022 1865 A5
10500 CMCY 80022 1864 E5
Universal Ct
- CSRK 80108 2619 E5
University Av
400 BLDR 80302 1686 B3
2900 LGMT 80503 1355 B6
University Blvd
10 DNVR 80206 2197 C1
10 DNVR 80218 2197 C1
300 DNVR 80206 2113 C7
S University Blvd
- CHLV 80121 2281 C5
10 DNVR 80206 2197 B1
10 DNVR 80209 2197 B1
10 DNVR 80218 2197 B1
1000 DNVR 80210 2197 C3
2600 DNVR 80210 2281 C1
3000 DvrC 80210 2281 C1
3000 EGLD 80113 2281 C1
3200 AphC 80113 2281 C1
3300 CHLV 80113 2281 C5
5100 GDVL 80121 2281 C5
5300 GDVL 80121 2365 C1
5900 CTNL 80121 2365 C3
6600 CTNL 80122 2365 C5
8200 AphC 80122 2449 C1
8200 AphC 80126 2449 C1
8200 CTNL 80122 2449 C1
9600 DgsC 80126 2450 B4
9600 DgsC 80130 2450 B4
S University Blvd SR-177
- CHLV 80121 2281 C5
- CTNL 80122 2449 C1
3500 CHLV 80113 2281 C5
5100 GDVL 80121 2281 C5
5300 GDVL 80121 2365 C1
5900 CTNL 80121 2365 C3
6600 CTNL 80122 2365 C5
8200 AphC 80122 2449 C1
8200 AphC 80126 2449 C1
University Cir
10 LGMT 80503 1355 B6
University Dr
10 LGMT 80503 1355 B6
University Ln
10 GDVL 80121 2281 C7
S University Wy
7800 CTNL 80122 2365 C7
University Heights Av
2400 BLDR 80302 1686 E3
Uno St
6000 ARVD 80003 2027 C3
S Uno Wy
2500 DNVR 80219 2195 C7
2500 DNVR 80219 2279 D1
W Unser Av
9100 JfnC 80128 2446 B2
9800 JfnC 80127 2446 B2
Upham Cir
7300 ARVD 80003 1942 E7
Upham Ct
900 LKWD 80214 2110 E6
3000 WTRG 80033 2110 E2
8200 ARVD 80003 1942 E4
9800 WSTR 80021 1858 E7
S Upham Ct
- DNVR 80123 2278 E6
10 LKWD 80226 2194 E2
4700 LKWD 80123 2278 E6
7200 JfnC 80128 2362 E6
Upham Dr
6600 ARVD 80003 2026 E1
9800 WSTR 80021 1858 E7
Upham St
200 LKWD 80226 2194 E1
400 LKWD 80226 2110 E7
2600 LKWD 80214 2110 E3
3800 WTRG 80033 2110 E1
4400 WTRG 80033 2026 E7
5600 ARVD 80002 2026 E4
6400 ARVD 80003 2026 E1
7600 ARVD 80003 1942 E6
11800 BMFD 80020 1858 E2
S Upham St
- LKWD 80226 2194 E3
900 LKWD 80232 2194 E4
2700 DNVR 80227 2278 E2
3300 LKWD 80227 2278 E3
6600 JfnC 80123 2362 E4
7200 JfnC 80128 2362 E6
8200 JfnC 80128 2446 E1
N Upham Wy
9200 JfnC 80021 1942 E2
S Upham Wy
8300 JfnC 80128 2446 E1
Upland Av
1200 BLDR 80304 1602 C4
1700 BldC 80304 1602 C4
Upland Dr
8400 DgsC 80112 2452 C1
8400 DgsC 80134 2452 C1
Upland Spur
2300 LKWD 80215 2109 E3
Upper Apex Rd
2500 CLCY 80403 2017 B3
2500 GpnC 80403 2017 A2
Upper Bear Creek Rd
300 CCkC 80439 2271 E6
1900 CCkC 80439 2270 D7
1900 CCkC 80452 2270 D7
29000 JfnC 80439 2273 B6
30500 JfnC 80439 2272 D5
Upper Cold Springs Gulch Rd
26900 JfnC 80401 2189 E3
Upper Elk Valley Dr
10 CCkC 80439 2103 A6
Upper Hughesville Rd
- GpnC 80403 1933 E6
- GpnC 80403 1934 A6
E Upper Lake Gulch Rd
10 DgsC 80118 2955 B3
10 LKSR 80118 2955 B3
Upper Main St
- BKHK 80403 2018 A4
Upper Moon Gulch Rd
1200 GpnC 80474 1849 C3
Upper Moss Rock Rd
28900 JfnC 80401 2189 C2
S Upper Ranch Dr
11500 JfnC 80470 2524 B2
Upton Ct
4900 DNVR 80239 2032 A5
Upton St
10600 NHGN 80234 1860 B5
Ura Ln
1700 NHGN 80234 1860 B5
10000 TNTN 80260 1860 B6
10300 TNTN 80234 1860 B6
S Uravan Ct
1000 AURA 80017 2201 B3
5000 AURA 80015 2285 B6
5300 CTNL 80015 2285 B7
5400 CTNL 80015 2369 B1
6000 AphC 80016 2369 B2
7100 FXFD 80016 2369 B5
7700 CTNL 80016 2369 B6
S Uravan Pl
5100 CTNL 80015 2285 B7
Uravan St
2200 AURA 80011 2117 B3
10100 CMCY 80022 1865 B6
15200 AdmC 80601 1697 A7
S Uravan St
- AURA 80015 2285 B4
800 AURA 80017 2201 B3
2000 AURA 80013 2201 B6
3000 AURA 80013 2285 B2
5100 CTNL 80015 2285 B7
S Uravan Wy
3100 AURA 80013 2285 B2
Urban Cir
6700 ARVD 80004 2025 D1
Urban Ct
700 LKWD 80401 2109 D7
3500 WTRG 80033 2109 D2
6100 ARVD 80004 2025 D3
7300 JfnC 80005 1941 D6
7600 ARVD 80005 1941 D5
S Urban Ct
1700 LKWD 80228 2193 D6
2300 JfnC 80228 2193 D7
4400 JfnC 80465 2277 D6
6400 JfnC 80127 2361 D3
Urban Dr
2000 LKWD 80215 2109 D4
7200 ARVD 80004 1941 D7
7200 ARVD 80005 1941 D7
S Urban Dr
700 LKWD 80228 2193 D3
Urban St
400 LKWD 80228 2109 D7
1100 LKWD 80401 2109 D5
1500 JfnC 80401 2109 D5
1500 LKWD 80215 2109 D5
3500 WTRG 80033 2109 D2
5800 ARVD 80002 2025 D3
5800 ARVD 80004 2025 D3
7100 ARVD 80004 1941 D7
7100 JfnC 80005 1941 D7
7500 ARVD 80005 1941 D6
10500 JfnC 80021 1857 D5
N Urban St
3800 WTRG 80033 2109 D1
S Urban St
100 LKWD 80228 2193 D2
5600 JfnC 80127 2361 D1
Urban Wy
7000 ARVD 80004 1941 D7
7500 ARVD 80005 1941 C6
S Urban Wy
1300 LKWD 80228 2193 D6
4600 JfnC 80465 2277 D6
S Ursula Cir
3000 AURA 80014 2284 A1
Ursula Ct
2000 AURA 80010 2116 A4
S Ursula Ct
1500 AURA 80012 2200 A5
1700 AURA 80012 2199 E5
2800 AURA 80014 2284 A1
Ursula St
- AURA 80011 2200 A1
1400 AURA 80011 2116 A5
2300 AURA 80010 2116 A3
4900 DNVR 80239 2031 E5
4900 DNVR 80239 2032 A5
10400 CMCY 80022 1864 A5
12200 AdmC 80640 1863 E1
12200 AdmC 80640 1864 A1
N Ursula St
- AURA 80010 2116 A4
1500 AURA 80011 2116 A4
S Ursula St
100 AURA 80012 2200 A2
2800 AURA 80014 2284 A1
Ursula Wy
- CMCY 80022 1864 A5
4900 DNVR 80239 2031 E5
5100 DNVR 80239 2032 A5
S Ursula Wy
300 AURA 80012 2199 E2
300 AURA 80012 2200 A2
S Uruguay St
1200 LKWD 80232 2194 E5
US-6
- AdmC - 1698 E2
- AdmC - 1780 E5
- AdmC - 1781 D1
- AdmC - 1862 E6
- AdmC - 1863 A6
- AdmC - 1864 C1
- AdmC - 1946 C1
- AdmC 80022 1946 A5
- BGTN - 1697 E6
- BGTN - 1698 E2
- BGTN - 1780 E5
- BGTN - 1781 D1
- BGTN - 1863 E3
- BGTN - 1864 C1
- CCkC - 2101 A5
- CCkC - 2102 E5
- CCkC 80403 2103 E5
- CCkC 80403 2104 C6
- CCkC 80439 2103 E5
- CCkC 80439 2104 C6
- CMCY - 1862 E6
- CMCY - 1863 A6
- CMCY - 1864 C1
- CMCY - 1946 C1
- CMCY 80022 2029 E2
- GOLD 80401 2107 C4
- GOLD 80403 2107 C4
- IDSP - 2101 A5
- IDSP - 2102 E5
- JfnC 80401 2104 C6
- JfnC 80401 2105 D5
- JfnC 80401 2106 C5
- JfnC 80401 2107 B4
- JfnC 80403 2105 D5
- JfnC 80403 2106 C5
- JfnC 80403 2107 B4
- LCHB - 1698 E2
- WldC - 1698 E2
US-6 6th Av
- LKWD - 2109 A7
- LKWD - 2110 A7
- LKWD - 2111 B7
US-6 W 6th Av
- DNVR - 2111 A7
- DNVR - 2112 C7
- GOLD 80401 2107 E6
- GOLD 80401 2108 B7
- GOLD 80403 2107 E6
- JfnC - 2109 C7
- JfnC 80401 2107 E6
- JfnC 80401 2108 B7
- LKWD - 2109 C7
- LKWD - 2110 E7
- LKWD - 2111 A7
US-6 Dahlia St
- CMCY 80022 2029 E1
US-6 Vasquez Blvd
4600 DNVR 80216 2029 C6
5300 CMCY 80022 2029 E4
5300 DNVR 80022 2029 E5
US-36
- AdmC - 1944 E7
- AdmC - 1945 B7
- AdmC - 2029 C2
- AdmC - 2032 A7
- AdmC - 2118 A4
- AdmC - 2119 E4
- AdmC - 2120 D4
- AdmC - 2121 B4
- AdmC - 2122 D4
- AdmC - 2123 E4
- AdmC - 2124 A4
- AdmC - 2125 D5
- AphC - 2119 E4
- AphC - 2122 B4
- AphC - 2125 D5
- AURA - 2032 A7
- AURA - 2116 E1
- AURA - 2117 E3
- AURA - 2118 A4
- AURA - 2121 B4
- AURA - 2122 B4
- BNNT - 2124 E4
- BNNT - 2125 D5
- CMCY - 2029 E3
- CMCY - 2030 E7
- DNVR - 2030 E7
- DNVR - 2031 B7
- DNVR - 2032 A7
- DvrC - 2032 A7
US-36 5th Av
500 LYNS 80540 1352 E2
US-36 28th St
700 BLDR 80303 1686 E3
1500 BLDR 80301 1686 E3
2200 BLDR 80302 1686 E1
2200 BLDR 80304 1686 E1
2700 BLDR 80301 1602 E6
2700 BLDR 80304 1602 E6
3600 BldC 80301 1602 E6
4300 BldC 80304 1602 E6
5000 BldC 80302 1602 E6
5000 BLDR 80302 1602 E6
US-36 Broadway St
200 LYNS 80540 1352 D1
US-36 Denver-Boulder Tpk
- AdmC - 1944 B6
- BfdC - 1858 E4
- BldC - 1687 D7
- BldC - 1771 E1
- BldC - 1772 B2
- BldC - 1773 B4
- BLDR - 1686 E4
- BLDR - 1687 B5
- BMFD - 1773 B4
- BMFD - 1774 A7
- BMFD - 1858 B1
- JfnC - 1858 E4
- JfnC - 1859 A7
- JfnC - 1943 B1
- LSVL - 1772 E3
- LSVL - 1773 B4
- SUPE - 1772 E3
- SUPE - 1773 B4
- WSTR - 1858 E4
- WSTR - 1859 A7
- WSTR - 1943 B1
- WSTR - 1944 E7
US-36 N Foothills Hwy
- BldC 80301 1602 C1
- BldC 80302 1602 C1
- BLDR 80302 1602 C1
- BLDR 80304 1602 C1
5700 BldC 80302 1518 C6
5700 BldC 80503 1518 C6
5700 BLDR 80302 1518 C6
8600 BldC 80302 1435 C7
8600 BldC 80503 1435 C7
9700 BldC 80540 1435 E1
10200 BldC 80503 1353 A3
10200 BldC 80503 1436 A1
US-36 Main St
300 LYNS 80540 1352 D1
US-36 E Main St
10 BldC 80503 1352 E2
10 LYNS 80503 1352 E2
10 LYNS 80540 1352 E2
US-36 W Main St
500 LYNS 80540 1352 E2
US-36 N St. Vrain Dr
16200 BldC 80540 1269 B5
18000 BldC 80540 1352 C1
19500 LYNS 80540 1269 C7
19500 LYNS 80540 1352 C1
US-36 Ute Hwy
4000 BldC 80503 1352 E2
4000 BldC 80503 1353 A3
4000 LYNS 80503 1352 E2
4000 LYNS 80503 1353 A3
4000 LYNS 80540 1352 E2
US-40
- CCkC 80439 2103 B5
- AdmC - 2118 E5
- AdmC - 2119 E4
- AdmC - 2120 D4
- AdmC - 2121 B4
- AdmC - 2122 B4
- AdmC - 2123 E4
- AdmC - 2124 A4
- AdmC - 2125 D5
- AphC - 2118 E5
- AphC - 2119 B4
- AphC - 2125 D5
- AURA - 2121 B4
- AURA - 2122 B4
- AURA 80011 2116 D5
- BNNT - 2124 E4
- BNNT - 2125 D5
- CCkC - 2101 E5
- CCkC - 2102 E5
- CCkC - 2103 A5
- GOLD 80401 2192 A4
- IDSP - 2101 A5
- IDSP - 2102 B5
- JfnC - 2189 E2
- JfnC - 2190 A2
- JfnC 80401 2188 E1
- JfnC 80401 2191 A3
- JfnC 80401 2192 A4
- JfnC 80439 2189 B3
31500 CCkC 80439 2187 E1
31500 CCkC 80439 2188 B2
US-40 E Colfax Av
10 DNVR 80203 2112 E5
100 DNVR 80202 2112 E5
700 DNVR 80203 2113 A5
900 DNVR 80218 2113 A5
2700 DNVR 80206 2113 C5
3900 DNVR 80220 2113 E5
4700 DNVR 80220 2114 A5
8900 AURA 80010 2115 A5
8900 DNVR 80220 2115 A5
12100 AURA 80011 2115 E5
12700 AURA 80011 2116 E5
13000 AURA 80010 2116 A5
16500 AURA 80011 2117 D5
20700 AURA 80011 2118 A5
21400 AdmC 80011 2118 A5
US-40 W Colfax Av
- GOLD 80401 2192 A4
10 DNVR 80202 2112 D5
10 DNVR 80203 2112 D5
10 DNVR 80204 2112 D5
3000 DNVR 80204 2111 D5
5200 LKWD 80214 2111 D5
6800 LKWD 80214 2110 E5
8300 LKWD 80215 2110 C5
10800 LKWD 80215 2109 E5
11900 JfnC 80401 2109 D5
12400 LKWD 80401 2109 A6
12700 JfnC 80215 2109 D5
14800 JfnC 80401 2108 C7
14800 LKWD 80401 2108 C7
15500 GOLD 80401 2108 D7
17700 JfnC 80401 2192 B1
US-40 Highway 40
32000 CCkC 80439 2187 E1
US-40 Mt Vernon Canyon Rd
18400 GOLD 80401 2192 A4
18400 JfnC 80401 2192 A4
US-40 S Mt Vernon Cntry Clb Rd
- JfnC 80401 2190 C2
US-85
- AdmC - 1946 A5
- AdmC 80022 1946 A5
- AdmC 80601 1696 B2
- AdmC 80601 1779 D7
- AdmC 80601 1780 A1
- AdmC 80601 1863 D1
- AdmC 80603 1696 B4
- AdmC 80640 1862 E6
- AdmC 80640 1863 A6
- BGTN 80601 1696 B4
- BGTN 80601 1779 D7
- BGTN 80601 1780 A1
- BGTN 80601 1863 D1
- BGTN 80603 1696 B4
- BGTN 80640 1863 D1
- CMCY - 1946 C1
- CMCY 80022 2029 E2
- CMCY 80640 1863 D1
- CSRK - 2703 C7
- CSRK - 2787 C1
- CSRK 80108 2618 E7
- CSRK 80108 2619 A7
- CSRK 80108 2703 B1
- CSRK 80109 2703 B1
- DgsC - 2787 B4
- DgsC - 2870 E6
- DgsC - 2871 A2
- DgsC - 2954 E1
- DgsC - 2955 A1
- DgsC 80108 2618 A5
- DgsC 80108 2619 A7
- DgsC 80125 2532 E7
- DgsC 80135 2532 E7
- DgsC 80135 2616 E1
- DgsC 80135 2617 B4
- DgsC 80135 2618 A5
- DNVR - 2112 B7
- DNVR - 2196 C1
- LKSR - 2955 A1
N US-85
5500 DgsC 80135 2617 C5
US-85 Dahlia St
- CMCY 80022 2029 E1
US-85 S Kalamath St
- DNVR 80223 2196 D7
US-85 S Platte River Dr
700 DNVR 80223 2196 D3
US-85 S Santa Fe Dr
- DgsC 80120 2447 E1
700 DNVR 80223 2196 D4
2500 DNVR 80223 2280 D2
2500 DvrC 80223 2280 D2
2500 EGLD 80110 2280 D2
2500 EGLD 80223 2280 D2
3300 SRDN 80110 2280 D2
4700 LITN 80120 2280 B6
5300 LITN 80120 2364 A1
7600 LITN 80120 2363 E7
8200 LITN 80120 2447 E1
8300 DgsC 80125 2447 E1
8300 DgsC 80129 2447 E1
10500 DgsC 80125 2532 A1
10600 DgsC 80125 2448 A7
US-85 Vasquez Blvd
4600 DNVR 80216 2029 C6
5300 CMCY 80022 2029 E4
5300 DNVR 80022 2029 E5
US-86
- CSRK 80104 2703 D6
US-86 5th St
100 CSRK 80104 2703 D6
US-87
- AdmC - 1692 D7
- AdmC - 1776 D4
- AdmC - 1944 E6
- AdmC - 2028 D5
- BMFD - 1692 E2
- BMFD - 1776 D2
- CSRK - 2619 B7
- CSRK - 2703 C7
- CSRK - 2787 B4
- CTNL - 2367 A5
- CTNL - 2451 B1
- DgsC - 2451 C3
- DgsC - 2535 B2
- DgsC - 2619 B1
- DgsC - 2787 C1
- DgsC - 2870 E6
- DgsC - 2871 A2
- DgsC - 2954 E1
- DgsC - 2955 B7
- DNVR - 2112 B7
- DNVR - 2196 D3
- DNVR - 2197 C6
- DNVR - 2198 A7
- DNVR - 2282 B1
- DvrC - 2282 D7
- GDVL - 2282 D7

STREET
Block City ZIP Map# Grid

US-87
- GDVL - 2366 E3
- GDVL - 2367 A5
- LKSR - 2955 A1
- LNTR - 2451 C3
- LNTR - 2535 B2
- NHGN - 1860 D7
- TNTN - 1692 D7
- TNTN - 1776 D4
- TNTN - 1860 D7
- TNTN - 1944 D2
- WSTR - 1776 D4
- WSTR - 1860 D1
US-87 N Valley Hwy
- AdmC - 2028 E2
- DNVR - 2028 E2
- DNVR - 2112 A4
US-285
12200 JfnC 80433 2525 A5
12900 JfnC 80470 2608 A2
12900 PrkC 80456 2608 A2
- AphC 80236 2279 D3
- DNVR 80227 2279 A3
- DNVR 80235 2279 D3
- DNVR 80236 2279 A3
- JfnC 80227 2278 E3
- JfnC 80235 2277 E4
- JfnC 80235 2278 E3
- JfnC 80433 2442 D4
- JfnC 80433 2524 D7
- JfnC 80433 2525 A5
- JfnC 80433 2526 A1
- JfnC 80454 2359 E1
- JfnC 80465 2276 E6
- JfnC 80465 2277 E4
- JfnC 80465 2359 E1
- JfnC 80465 2360 B1
- JfnC 80465 2442 D4
- JfnC 80465 2443 A4
- JfnC 80470 2524 D7
- LKWD 80227 2277 E4
- LKWD 80227 2278 A3
- LKWD 80227 2279 A3
- LKWD 80235 2278 E3
- LKWD 80465 2276 C7
- LKWD 80465 2277 B5
- MRSN 80465 2276 C7
- MRSN 80465 2360 B1
- PrkC 80456 2690 C2
- SRDN 80110 2279 D3
- SRDN 80110 2280 B3
- SRDN 80236 2279 D3
13700 JfnC 80470 2608 A2
13700 PrkC 80456 2608 A2
56700 PrkC 80456 2605 A7
56700 PrkC 80456 2689 A1
63000 PrkC 80456 2606 D6
63900 PrkC 80456 2607 A4
US-285 Frontage Rd
13200 JfnC 80470 2524 D7
13200 JfnC 80470 2608 D1
US-285 E Hampden Av
1500 CHLV 80113 2281 E3
1500 EGLD 80113 2281 E3
1900 AphC 80113 2281 E3
2300 DvrC 80210 2281 E3
2800 CHLV 80210 2281 E3
3600 AphC 80222 2281 E3
3600 DNVR 80210 2281 E3
3600 DNVR 80222 2281 E3
4700 AphC 80222 2282 B3
4700 CHLV 80113 2282 B3
4700 DNVR 80222 2282 B3
4700 DNVR 80237 2282 B3
US-285 W Hampden Av
- SRDN 80110 2280 A3
100 EGLD 80110 2280 D3
US-285 E Jefferson Av
- EGLD 80110 2280 E3
200 EGLD 80113 2280 E3
600 EGLD 80113 2281 A3
700 CHLV 80113 2281 A3
US-285 Service Rd
12700 JfnC 80433 2524 E6
US-287
- AdmC - 2118 E4
- AdmC - 2119 E4
- AdmC - 2120 E4
- AdmC - 2121 A4
- AdmC - 2122 B4
- AdmC - 2123 E4
- AdmC - 2124 A4
- AdmC - 2125 D5
- AphC - 2119 E4
- AphC - 2125 D5
- AURA - 2121 A4
- AURA - 2122 B4
- AURA 80011 2116 D5
- BldC 80020 1774 C5
- BMFD 80020 1774 C5
- BMFD 80020 1858 E2
- BNNT - 2124 E4
- BNNT - 2125 D5
- LAFT 80026 1690 B4
US-287 N 107th St
1900 BldC 80504 1439 B6
1900 LGMT 80501 1439 B6
1900 LGMT 80504 1439 B6
2100 LAFT 80026 1690 B1
2300 BldC 80026 1690 B1
3000 ERIE 80026 1690 B1
3300 BldC 80026 1606 B7
3400 ERIE 80026 1606 B5
4800 BldC 80504 1606 B1
5400 BldC 80504 1522 B7
12600 BldC 80504 1356 B1
12600 LGMT 80501 1356 B1
US-287 S 112th St
500 LAFT 80026 1690 C7
500 LAFT 80026 1774 C1
1100 BldC 80026 1774 C1
1300 BldC 80020 1774 C1
1300 LAFT 80020 1774 C4
1600 BMFD 80020 1774 C4
US-287 W 120th Av
3600 BMFD 80020 1859 E2
3600 WSTR 80234 1859 E2
4300 WSTR 80020 1859 E2
4600 BMFD 80031 1859 A2
4600 WSTR 80031 1859 A2
6400 BMFD 80020 1858 E2
US-287 E Colfax Av
10 DNVR 80203 2112 E5
100 DNVR 80202 2112 E5
700 DNVR 80203 2113 A5
1000 DNVR 80218 2113 A5
2700 DNVR 80206 2113 C5
3900 DNVR 80220 2113 E5
4700 DNVR 80220 2114 A5
8900 AURA 80010 2115 A5
8900 DNVR 80220 2115 A5
12100 AURA 80011 2115 E5
12700 AURA 80011 2116 E5
13000 AURA 80010 2116 A5
16500 AURA 80011 2117 D5
20700 AdmC 80011 2118 A5
20700 AURA 80011 2118 A5
US-287 W Colfax Av
10 DNVR 80202 2112 D5
10 DNVR 80203 2112 D5
10 DNVR 80204 2112 D5
US-287 Federal Blvd
- DNVR 80211 2028 A5
- WSTR 80031 1859 E2
1500 DNVR 80204 2112 A4
1900 DNVR 80211 2112 A4
4800 DNVR 80221 2028 A7
5100 AdmC 80221 2028 A5
5700 AdmC 80221 2027 E1
6700 WSTR 80030 2027 E1
7000 AdmC 80221 1944 A7
7000 WSTR 80030 1944 A7
7600 AdmC 80221 1943 E6
7600 WSTR 80030 1943 E6
7600 WSTR 80031 1943 E3
8600 FLHT 80031 1943 E3
8600 FLHT 80260 1943 E1
9300 WSTR 80260 1943 E1
9700 FLHT 80031 1859 E7
9700 FLHT 80260 1859 E7
10200 WSTR 80234 1859 E6
US-287 Main St
10 LGMT 80501 1439 B1
1100 LGMT 80501 1356 B6
2300 BldC 80504 1356 B4
US-287 S Main St
10 LGMT 80501 1439 B3
100 BldC 80501 1439 B3
1400 BldC 80504 1439 B6
1400 LGMT 80504 1439 B6
Uscombe Pl
- BldC 80503 1520 D1
Usufruct Av
- BLDR 80503 1520 A6
W Utah Av
7300 LKWD 80232 2194 E6
12800 LKWD 80228 2193 E6
E Utah Cir
- AURA 80011 2201 E4
- AURA 80011 2202 A5
- AURA 80017 2202 A5
13900 AURA 80012 2200 B5
18700 AURA 80017 2201 C6
W Utah Cir
13200 LKWD 80228 2193 B6
Utah Ct
1600 GOLD 80401 2108 C5
8800 TNTN 80229 1945 B3
Utah Dr
1700 GOLD 80401 2108 B5
W Utah Ln
6000 LKWD 80232 2195 B6
E Utah Pl
4300 DNVR 80222 2197 E6
5300 DNVR 80222 2198 A6
5300 DNVR 80224 2198 A6
11300 AURA 80012 2199 D6
15000 AURA 80012 2200 C5
15800 AURA 80017 2200 D6
17900 AURA 80017 2201 B5
W Utah Pl
9200 LKWD 80232 2194 B6
11200 JfnC 80232 2193 E6
Utah St
- DNVR 80236 2279 C3
1400 GOLD 80401 2108 B5
1400 JfnC 80401 2108 B5
Utah Wy
- LGMT 80501 1439 A6
Ute Av
- KIOW 80117 2796 A3
10 EbtC 80117 2796 A2
W Ute Av
8400 JfnC 80128 2446 B2
9200 JfnC 80127 2446 B2
Ute Ct
5800 DgsC 80118 2952 E1
Ute Dr
8800 JfnC 80403 1938 C3
W Ute Dr
8400 JfnC 80128 2446 C2
Ute Hwy
4000 BldC 80503 1352 E2
4000 BldC 80503 1353 B3
4000 LYNS 80503 1352 E2
4000 LYNS 80503 1353 B3
4000 LYNS 80540 1352 E2
6300 BldC 80503 1354 A4
7700 BldC 80503 1355 B4
7700 LGMT 80503 1355 B4
9300 BldC 80501 1355 B4
9300 BldC 80504 1355 B4
9300 LGMT 80501 1355 B4
10100 BldC 80504 1356 B4
10100 LGMT 80501 1356 B4
11900 BldC 80504 1357 A4
11900 LGMT 80501 1357 A4
Ute Hwy SR-7
4000 BldC 80503 1352 E2
4000 BldC 80503 1353 B3
4000 LYNS 80503 1352 E2
4000 LYNS 80503 1353 B3
4000 LYNS 80540 1352 E2
Ute Hwy SR-66
4000 BldC 80503 1352 E2
4000 BldC 80503 1353 B3
4000 LYNS 80503 1352 E2
4000 LYNS 80503 1353 B3
4000 LYNS 80540 1352 E2
6300 BldC 80503 1354 A4
7700 BldC 80503 1355 B4
7700 LGMT 80503 1355 B4
9300 BldC 80501 1355 B4
9300 BldC 80504 1355 B4
9300 LGMT 80501 1355 B4
10100 BldC 80504 1356 B4
10100 LGMT 80501 1356 B4
11900 BldC 80504 1357 A4
11900 LGMT 80501 1357 A4
Ute Hwy US-36
4000 BldC 80503 1352 E2
4000 BldC 80503 1353 B3
4000 LYNS 80503 1352 E2
4000 LYNS 80503 1353 B3
4000 LYNS 80540 1352 E2
Ute Rd
5000 JfnC 80454 2275 B7
30300 JfnC 80470 2609 A7
Ute St
- BLDR 80301 1603 C7
Ute Tr
10 CCkC 80439 2440 A1
Ute Vil
- KIOW 80117 2796 B2
Ute Wy
10 NDLD 80466 1765 D2
Ute Creek Dr
1800 LGMT 80501 1356 E5
1800 LGMT 80501 1357 A6
Ute Mountain Tr
3700 CSRK 80109 2702 D2
Utica Av
400 BLDR 80304 1602 B4
Utica Cir
900 BLDR 80304 1602 C4
12600 BMFD 80020 1775 C7
Utica Ct
500 BLDR 80304 1602 B4
5400 AdmC 80212 2027 C4
6300 ARVD 80003 2027 C2
9200 WSTR 80031 1943 C2
11000 WSTR 80031 1859 C4
12300 BMFD 80020 1859 C1
N Utica Ct
9000 WSTR 80031 1943 C2
Utica Dr
900 DgsC 80108 2618 C3
S Utica Dr
7500 LITN 80128 2363 D6
Utica Pl
12200 BMFD 80020 1859 C1
Utica St
10 DNVR 80219 2195 D1
10 WARD 80481 1597 D2
400 DNVR 80219 2111 D7
1300 DNVR 80204 2111 D5
3200 DNVR 80212 2111 D2
5000 DNVR 80212 2027 C5
5400 AdmC 80212 2027 C4
6500 ARVD 80003 2027 C2
6800 AdmC 80030 2027 C1
6800 WSTR 80030 2027 C1
7200 WSTR 80030 1943 C7
8800 AdmC 80031 1943 C3
9200 WSTR 80031 1943 C1
10800 WSTR 80031 1859 C5
12200 BMFD 80020 1859 C1
12500 BMFD 80020 1775 C7
13200 BldC 80455 1597 D2
13200 BldC 80481 1597 D2
N Utica St
9000 WSTR 80031 1943 D2
S Utica St
10 DNVR 80219 2195 D1
2500 DNVR 80219 2279 C1
2700 DNVR 80236 2279 D1
7400 LITN 80128 2363 C6
N Utica Wy
11700 WSTR 80031 1859 C3
Utopia Ct
4900 DNVR 80239 2032 A5
Utrillo Ln
10400 NHGN 80234 1860 B6
S Uvalda Cir
400 AURA 80012 2200 A2
Uvalda Ct
1900 AURA 80010 2116 A4
Uvalda St
- CMCY 80022 1863 E5
- CMCY 80022 1864 A5
3000 AURA 80011 2116 A2
5500 AdmC 80022 2032 A5
5500 DNVR 80022 2032 A5
5500 DNVR 80239 2032 A5
S Uvalda St
300 AURA 80012 2200 A2
13000 AphC 80111 2368 A3

V

Vail Cir
7600 DgsC 80118 2954 D2
Vail Dr
10 AURA 80011 2201 C1
100 AURA 80011 2117 C7
Vail Ln
1200 LGMT 80503 1355 C7
1200 LGMT 80503 1438 C1
S Vail Pl
4800 JfnC 80439 2273 D7
S Vail St
10 AURA 80011 2201 C3
10 AURA 80017 2201 C3
W Vail Pass
12000 JfnC 80127 2361 D6
Vail Pass St
- BLDR 80301 1603 C7
Valdai Av
700 LCHB 80603 1698 C2
700 WldC 80603 1698 C2
S Valdai Cir
7200 AURA 80016 2370 C5
S Valdai Ct
- AURA 80016 2370 C4
6200 AphC 80015 2370 C2
Valdai St
100 LCHB 80603 1698 B3
S Valdai St
5100 AphC 80015 2286 C7
5400 AphC 80015 2370 C1
7000 AURA 80016 2370 C4
S Valdai Wy
5300 AphC 80015 2286 C7
5900 AphC 80015 2370 C2
Valderrama Ct
700 DgsC 80108 2618 D5
Vale Dr
5200 DNVR 80246 2198 A3
5500 DNVR 80224 2198 A3
S Vale Rd
5800 BldC 80303 1771 E2
Vale Wy
2400 ERIE 80516 1691 E3
S Valentia Ct
3300 DNVR 80231 2282 E2
3800 DNVR 80237 2282 E4
Valentia St
- AdmC 80602 1778 D7
- DNVR 80230 2114 E6
- TNTN 80602 1778 D7
1200 DNVR 80220 2114 E5
2600 DNVR 80238 2114 E3
8400 AdmC 80022 1946 E3
8400 CMCY 80022 1946 E3
S Valentia St
1000 AphC 80247 2198 E4
1000 DNVR 80247 2198 E3
1900 AphC 80231 2198 E6
1900 DNVR 80231 2198 E6
2800 AphC 80231 2282 E2
2800 DNVR 80231 2282 E2
4000 DNVR 80237 2282 E4
6900 CTNL 80112 2366 E4
S Valentia Wy
5300 GDVL 80111 2282 E7
5300 GDVL 80111 2366 E1
7100 CTNL 80112 2366 E5
S Valentine Ct
1600 LKWD 80228 2193 D5
Valentine Ln
10 LGMT 80501 1356 B6
S Valentine St
1700 LKWD 80228 2193 D6
S Valentine Wy
1100 LKWD 80228 2193 D4
Valerian Cir
- DgsC 80118 2954 A1
Valhalla Dr
4900 BldC 80301 1603 B2
5000 BLDR 80301 1603 B2
Valhalla St
800 CSRK 80104 2703 E5
Valkyrie Dr
4800 BldC 80301 1603 B2
Vallejo Cir
- WSTR 80234 1776 A6
N Vallejo Cir
12800 WSTR 80234 1776 B6
Vallejo Ct
- WSTR 80234 1776 B7
N Vallejo Ct
13200 WSTR 80234 1776 A6
Vallejo St
100 DNVR 80223 2196 B1
400 DNVR 80223 2112 B7
800 DNVR 80204 2112 B6
3800 DNVR 80211 2112 B1
4500 DNVR 80211 2028 B7
5000 DNVR 80221 2028 B6
5600 AdmC 80221 2028 B4
8300 AdmC 80221 1944 B4
8300 AdmC 80260 1944 B4
11800 WSTR 80234 1860 B2
13000 WSTR 80234 1776 A5
S Vallejo St
500 DNVR 80223 2196 B3
2000 AphC 80223 2196 B7
2000 EGLD 80110 2196 B7
2000 EGLD 80223 2196 B7
2700 EGLD 80110 2280 B2
4900 LITN 80120 2280 B7
S Valley Cir
6300 JfnC 80465 2359 B4
Valley Dr
400 CSRK 80104 2704 A6
500 CSRK 80104 2704 A6
S Valley Dr
- CSRK 80104 2788 A1
10 CSRK 80104 2704 A7
3600 JfnC 80439 2273 D4
6100 JfnC 80465 2359 B3
N Valley Hwy
- AdmC - 2028 E3
- DNVR - 2028 E3
- DNVR - 2112 B2
N Valley Hwy I-25
- AdmC - 2028 E3
- DNVR - 2028 E3
- DNVR - 2112 B6
N Valley Hwy US-87
- AdmC - 2028 E3
- DNVR - 2028 E3
- DNVR - 2112 B6
S Valley Hwy
5000 DNVR 80237 2282 D7
Valley Ln
- BldC 80301 1603 D6
10 BldC 80302 1517 E5
10 BldC 80302 1518 A5
S Valley Ln
6200 JfnC 80465 2359 A3
Valley Pkwy
- JfnC 80127 2361 A6
- JfnC 80127 2445 B1
Valley Rd
10 BldC 80466 1766 B1
500 DgsC 80124 2534 D1
1000 DgsC 80124 2450 C7
S Valley Rd
- JfnC 80127 2361 B7
- JfnC 80127 2445 B1
900 JfnC 80439 2189 B4
19300 JfnC 80465 2443 E1
Valley Wy
400 BNNT 80102 2209 B1
Valleybrook Cir
10800 DgsC 80108 2449 E7
10800 DgsC 80126 2533 E1
10900 DgsC 80108 2450 A7
10900 DgsC 80108 2533 E1
10900 DgsC 80124 2449 E7
10900 DgsC 80124 2450 A7
Valleybrook Ct
10700 DgsC 80124 2449 C7
10700 DgsC 80124 2450 B7
Valleybrook Dr
- DgsC 80130 2450 A7
4400 DgsC 80124 2449 E7
4400 DgsC 80124 2450 A7
Valleyhead St
- AdmC 80249 1951 D7
- AdmC 80249 2035 D1
- AURA 80019 2035 D3
6900 DNVR 80249 1951 D7
N Valley Hi Ct
13800 AURA 80138 2453 B1
E Valley Hi Dr
5500 AURA 80138 2453 B1
5500 DgsC 80138 2453 B1
5500 PARK 80134 2453 B1
Valley Hi Rd
6000 DgsC 80118 2868 C7
Valley High Rd
22800 JfnC 80465 2443 A3
23100 JfnC 80465 2442 E3
S Valley Highway Rd
7800 DgsC 80112 2451 C1
Valley Oak Ct
- CSRK 80104 2788 A2
- DgsC 80104 2788 A2
Valley Oak Rd
- CSRK 80104 2788 A2
- DgsC 80104 2788 A2
W Valleyview Av
200 LITN 80120 2364 D3
Valley View Ct
1500 GOLD 80403 2107 C2
40500 EbtC 80107 2626 A2
41000 EbtC 80107 2542 A7
Valley View Dr
- CSRK 80108 2704 C4
10 CCkC 80452 2186 A4
300 BLDR 80304 1686 B1
1200 DgsC 80135 2783 E4
1200 DgsC 80135 2784 A4
33400 JfnC 80439 2272 C5
Valleyview Dr
10 NDLD 80466 1765 D3
2000 AdmC 80221 1944 B5
Valley View Ln
10 CCkC 80439 2187 E7
10 CCkC 80439 2271 E1
10 PrkC 80470 2523 D5
Valley View Rd
10 PrkC 80456 2521 D4
29100 JfnC 80439 2273 C7
N Valley View Rd
1500 CSRK 80104 2704 C5
1500 CSRK 80108 2704 C5
Valley View St
7700 DgsC 80135 2532 C6
S Valleyview St
6000 LITN 80120 2364 D3
Valley View Wy
10 BldC 80304 1601 E4
10 BldC 80304 1602 A4
Valley Vista Dr
- FLHT 80260 1944 B3
W Valley Vista Dr
1800 DgsC 80109 2786 B4
Valley Vista Ln
10 BldC 80302 1517 B7
Valmont Dr
5800 BldC 80301 1603 E7
Valmont Rd
2300 BLDR 80304 1602 E7
2700 BLDR 80301 1602 E7
2800 BLDR 80301 1603 C7
5300 BldC 80301 1603 C7
6200 BldC 80301 1604 A7
8300 BldC 80026 1605 A6
8300 BldC 80301 1605 A6
Valtec Ct
7100 BldC 80303 1688 C2
Valtec Ln
1600 BldC 80303 1688 C2
Van Bibber Dr
5600 JfnC 80403 2023 D4
Van Buren Ct
300 LSVL 80027 1773 C1
Van Buren Wy
1600 AURA 80011 2117 A4
N Vance Ct
9200 JfnC 80021 1942 E2
9500 WSTR 80021 1942 E1
S Vance Ct
10 LKWD 80226 2194 E2
7200 JfnC 80128 2362 E5
8000 JfnC 80128 2446 E1
Vance Dr
7700 ARVD 80003 1942 E5
7700 ARVD 80005 1942 E5
Vance St
100 LKWD 80226 2194 E1
500 LKWD 80226 2110 E7
2000 LKWD 80214 2110 E4
3600 WTRG 80033 2110 E1
4400 WTRG 80033 2026 E7
5800 ARVD 80002 2026 E3
6800 ARVD 80003 2026 E1
7400 ARVD 80003 1942 E6
9000 WSTR 80021 1942 E2
11800 BMFD 80020 1858 D2
S Vance St
200 LKWD 80226 2194 E2
900 LKWD 80232 2194 E4
3200 LKWD 80227 2278 E3
3500 LKWD 80235 2278 E3
6400 JfnC 80123 2362 E3
7200 JfnC 80128 2362 E6
7900 JfnC 80128 2446 E1
S Vance Wy
2700 DNVR 80227 2278 E1
S Vancouver Ct
1400 LKWD 80228 2193 B5
S Vancouver St
1700 LKWD 80228 2193 D6
S Vancouver Wy
1100 LKWD 80228 2193 D4
S Vanderhoof Ct
1600 AphC 80102 2209 D5
Vanderhoof St
3300 AdmC 80102 2125 D1
W Vandeventor Dr
9100 JfnC 80128 2446 B2
9500 JfnC 80127 2446 B2
Vandriver St
7600 DNVR 80249 1951 D5
S Van Dyke Wy
1400 LKWD 80228 2193 D5
Van Eden Rd
- CCkC 80452 2101 C7
- CCkC 80452 2185 B1
Van Gordon Ct
700 LKWD 80401 2109 D7
6500 ARVD 80004 2025 D2
7000 ARVD 80004 1941 D7
8500 ARVD 80005 1941 D4
S Van Gordon Ct
600 LKWD 80228 2193 D3
4500 JfnC 80465 2277 D6
Van Gordon Dr
2600 LKWD 80215 2109 D3
Van Gordon St
10 LKWD 80228 2193 D1
400 LKWD 80228 2109 D7
800 LKWD 80401 2109 D6
1100 JfnC 80401 2109 D6
2500 LKWD 80215 2109 D3
4800 WTRG 80033 2025 D6
5800 ARVD 80002 2025 D3
6700 ARVD 80004 2025 D1
7100 ARVD 80004 1941 D7
S Van Gordon St
10 LKWD 80228 2193 D2
4900 JfnC 80465 2277 D7
5100 JfnC 80127 2277 D7
5900 JfnC 80127 2361 D2
Van Gordon Wy
10500 JfnC 80021 1857 D5
S Van Gordon Wy
4300 JfnC 80465 2277 D6
5300 JfnC 80127 2361 D1
Vanguard Dr
8100 AdmC 80221 1944 B4
Vaquero Cir
6000 DgsC 80108 2534 B5
Vaquero Dr
10 BldC 80303 1688 D7
6000 DgsC 80108 2534 B5
Varda Ct
3300 DgsC 80109 2702 C1
Varese Ln
10700 NHGN 80234 1860 A5
Vaseen Ct
12000 JfnC 80433 2525 A4
Vasquez Blvd
4600 DNVR 80216 2029 C6
5200 CMCY 80022 2029 D5
5300 DNVR 80022 2029 D5
Vasquez Blvd SR-2
5500 CMCY 80022 2029 E4
Vasquez Blvd US-6
4600 DNVR 80216 2029 D6
5300 CMCY 80022 2029 E4
5300 DNVR 80022 2029 E4
Vasquez Blvd US-85
4600 DNVR 80216 2029 D6
5300 CMCY 80022 2029 E4
5300 DNVR 80022 2029 E4
Vasquez Ct
300 BldC 80540 1269 D7
300 LYNS 80540 1269 D7
Vasquez Dr
300 LYNS 80540 1269 D7
Vasquez St
- GOLD 80401 2107 E2
E Vassar Av
- AphC 80231 2199 A7
- AphC 80231 2283 A1
10 DNVR 80210 2280 E1
10 DNVR 80223 2280 E1
1200 DNVR 80210 2281 B1
4300 DNVR 80222 2281 E1
4800 AphC 80222 2282 A1
5500 DNVR 80222 2282 B1
6200 DNVR 80222 2198 B7
6600 DNVR 80224 2198 C7
6600 DNVR 80224 2282 C1
16000 AURA 80013 2200 E7
20100 AURA 80013 2201 E7
W Vassar Av
10 DNVR 80210 2280 D1
10 DNVR 80223 2280 D1
2000 EGLD 80110 2280 B1
2400 DNVR 80219 2280 B1
3000 DNVR 80219 2196 A7
3300 DNVR 80219 2279 D1
4700 DNVR 80219 2195 D7
5100 LKWD 80227 2195 C7
7100 DNVR 80227 2278 E1
7100 LKWD 80227 2278 E1
12700 JfnC 80228 2277 C1
Vassar Cir
1900 BLDR 80305 1686 D6
Vassar Ct
10 LGMT 80503 1355 B7
Vassar Dr
1900 BLDR 80305 1686 E6
2600 BLDR 80305 1687 A6
E Vassar Dr
7900 AphC 80231 2198 D7
7900 AphC 80231 2282 E1
9700 DNVR 80231 2199 B7
10900 AURA 80014 2199 C7
12100 AURA 80014 2283 E1
12400 AURA 80014 2284 B1
18500 AURA 80013 2201 C7
W Vassar Dr
8300 LKWD 80227 2278 D1
10500 JfnC 80227 2278 A1
14600 LKWD 80228 2277 A1
14900 LKWD 80228 2192 E7
15300 LKWD 80228 2276 D1
E Vassar Ln
4800 AphC 80222 2198 A7
4800 DNVR 80222 2198 A7
E Vassar Pl
18100 AURA 80013 2201 B7
W Vassar Pl
2600 LKWD 80227 2278 B1
10600 JfnC 80227 2278 A1
13000 JfnC 80228 2277 C1
16400 LKWD 80228 2276 D1
W Vassar Wy
5800 DNVR 80227 2279 B1
5800 LKWD 80227 2279 B1
9800 LKWD 80227 2278 B1
S Vaughn Cir
1400 AURA 80012 2200 A4
Vaughn Ct
10500 CMCY 80022 1864 A5
S Vaughn Ct
1600 AURA 80012 2200 A5
7600 AphC 80112 2368 A6
Vaughn St
3000 AURA 80011 2116 A2
5100 DNVR 80239 2032 A5
10400 CMCY 80022 1864 A5
N Vaughn St
200 AURA 80011 2200 A1
1400 AURA 80010 2116 A5
1400 AURA 80011 2116 A5
S Vaughn St
- AphC 80111 2368 A3
- AphC 80112 2368 A4
- CTNL 80111 2368 A3
- CTNL 80112 2368 A4
1600 AURA 80012 2200 A5
Vaughn Wy
- CMCY 80022 1864 A5
1600 AURA 80010 2116 A4
5000 DNVR 80239 2032 A5
S Vaughn Wy
- AphC 80014 2284 A2
300 AURA 80012 2200 A2
2300 AURA 80014 2200 A7
2800 AURA 80014 2284 A1
VCF Rd
- BLDR 80503 1520 A5
Velvet Ash
3300 JfnC 80439 2273 A3
Venable Creek St
12500 PARK 80134 2537 C4
Venice Ln
1400 LGMT 80503 1438 A6
Venice St
1100 LGMT 80501 1356 A7
1100 LGMT 80501 1439 A1
Venneford Ranch Rd
8700 DgsC 80126 2449 C3
S Venneford Ranch Rd
2200 DgsC 80126 2449 C4
Ventana St
12700 PARK 80134 2537 B5
Ventana Mesa Cir
12400 DgsC 80108 2534 B4
Ventana Mesa Ct
12400 DgsC 80108 2534 B4
S Ventura Cir
1100 AURA 80017 2201 B4
Ventura Ct
16400 AdmC 80601 1697 A4
16400 BGTN 80601 1697 A4
S Ventura Ct
900 AURA 80017 2201 B3
5000 AURA 80015 2285 B6
5300 CTNL 80015 2285 B7
5600 CTNL 80015 2369 B1
6000 AphC 80016 2369 B2
7800 CTNL 80016 2369 B6
Ventura St
600 AURA 80011 2117 B6
10100 CMCY 80022 1865 B6
S Ventura St
900 AURA 80017 2201 B3
2000 AURA 80013 2201 B6
2700 AURA 80013 2285 B1
5000 AURA 80015 2285 B6
S Ventura Wy
900 AURA 80017 2201 B3
3500 AURA 80013 2285 B3
5100 CTNL 80015 2285 B7

Venus Ct
400 DgsC 80124 2450 E1
Venus Rd
10 GpnC 80403 1934 C1
S Vera Ln
6400 JfnC 80439 2357 A4
Vera Marie Ln
10 GpnC 80474 1849 E2
Verbana Dr
- DgsC 80118 2870 A7
S Verbena Cir
7000 CTNL 80112 2366 E5
Verbena Ct
14700 AdmC 80602 1778 E2
S Verbena Ct
3300 DNVR 80231 2282 E2
Verbena St
- DNVR 80216 2030 E6
- DNVR 80237 2282 E5
- DNVR 80237 2283 A5
- GDVL 80111 2283 A5
- GDVL 80237 2283 A5
1100 DNVR 80220 2114 E6
1100 DNVR 80230 2114 E6
1900 DNVR 80238 2114 E4
8600 AdmC 80022 1946 E3
8600 CMCY 80022 1946 E3
16000 AdmC 80602 1694 D5
S Verbena St
3500 DNVR 80231 2282 E3
3500 DNVR 80237 2282 E3
S Verbena Wy
2900 AphC 80231 2282 E1
2900 DNVR 80231 2282 E1
7100 CTNL 80112 2366 E5
Verdant Cir
400 LGMT 80501 1439 D1
Verdi Dr
10 GpnC 80403 1934 C2
Verdigris St
- DgsC 80134 2452 D5
Verdos Dr
300 EbtC 80107 2708 A1
S Vermejo Peak
8000 JfnC 80127 2362 B5
8000 JfnC 80127 2446 A1
Vermillion Ct
5000 DgsC 80108 2618 D6
Vermillion Dr
5000 DgsC 80108 2618 E6
W Vermillion Dr
10300 JfnC 80127 2278 A6
Vermillion Ln
5000 DgsC 80108 2618 E6
Vermillion Rd
8700 BldC 80503 1355 C2
8700 BldC 80504 1355 C2
9500 BldC 80504 1356 D2
11600 BldC 80504 1357 A2
Vermillion Rd CO-6
9500 BldC 80503 1355 D2
9500 BldC 80504 1355 D2
9500 BldC 80504 1356 A2
Vermillion Tr
13400 BldC 80504 1356 E1
13400 BldC 80504 1357 A1
Verna Ln
10800 NHGN 80234 1860 D4
Vernier Av
300 LAFT 80026 1690 B5
Vernier Ct
400 LAFT 80026 1690 B5
Vernon Dr
2000 GOLD 80401 2108 A4
Vernon Ln
1700 SUPE 80027 1773 A6
Vernon Wy
11300 PARK 80134 2453 B7
11300 PARK 80134 2537 B1
Veronica Rd
- DgsC 80118 2870 B6
S Versailles Ct
6400 AURA 80016 2370 C3
S Versailles Pkwy
6000 AphC 80015 2370 C1
Versailles St
100 LCHB 80603 1698 C3
S Versailles St
5100 AphC 80015 2286 C7
5800 AphC 80015 2370 C2
7000 AURA 80016 2370 C5
S Versailles Wy
5400 AphC 80015 2286 C7
5400 AphC 80015 2370 C1
6700 AURA 80016 2370 C4
S Versilles Wy
- AURA 80016 2370 C4
Vesta Cir
1300 LAFT 80026 1690 A6
Vestal Rd
5300 BldC 80503 1353 C2
S Vesuvius Rd
6400 JfnC 80439 2358 C4
Vetch Cir
900 BldC 80026 1690 B3
900 LAFT 80026 1690 B3
Via Appia Wy
500 LSVL 80027 1689 B7
800 LSVL 80027 1773 A1
Via Capri
- LSVL 80027 1689 B6
N Via Capri
- LSVL 80027 1689 B6
Via De Los Pinons
- CSRK 80104 2703 E1
- CSRK 80104 2704 A1
Vialpando St
- BGTN 80601 1697 B5
Via Margarita
3100 DgsC 80109 2702 B1
Via Roma
- LSVL 80027 1689 B6
S Via Vara
- BMFD 80020 1773 E4
Via Varra
- BMFD 80020 1773 E4
S Vickery Av
10900 JfnC 80433 2527 B1
Victor St
200 AURA 80011 2200 A1
700 AURA 80011 2116 A5
1900 AURA 80010 2116 A4
5500 DgsC 80135 2617 C5
5500 DNVR 80239 2032 A4
10400 CMCY 80022 1864 A5
S Victor St
300 AURA 80012 2200 A2
2100 AURA 80014 2200 A6
2700 AURA 80014 2284 A1
Victor Wy
5000 DNVR 80239 2032 A5
S Victor Wy
400 AURA 80012 2200 A3
Victoria Ct
700 LAFT 80026 1689 E5
W Victoria Dr
9500 JfnC 80128 2446 B3
9800 JfnC 80127 2446 B3
Victoria Ln
8900 DgsC 80134 2622 D3
Victoria Rd
10 PrkC 80470 2524 A6
Victorian Dr
10700 PARK 80138 2453 D7
Victorian Wy
19800 PARK 80138 2453 D7
Vienna Dr
100 EbtC 80138 2539 E6
100 EbtC 80138 2540 A6
View Dr
10 GOLD 80401 2108 A7
10 GOLD 80401 2192 A1
Viewpoint Dr
12100 LKWD 80401 2109 D6
12300 JfnC 80401 2109 D6
View Point Rd
1500 JfnC 80401 2109 D5
1500 LKWD 80215 2109 D5
1700 BLDR 80305 1770 E1
Viewpoint Wy
3800 BldC 80026 1606 C5
3900 ERIE 80026 1606 C5
Viewridge Ct
10 BNNT 80102 2124 E2
View Ridge Dr
36400 EbtC 80107 2708 A2
Viewridge Dr
- BNNT 80102 2124 E2
Viewridge Rd
1100 BNNT 80102 2124 E2
Vigilante Av
- PrkC 80456 2521 E5
10 PrkC 80456 2522 A5
2300 PrkC 80470 2522 D6
Viking Ct
200 ERIE 80516 1691 D2
Viking Dr
10 CHLV 80113 2281 A7
10 EGLD 80113 2281 A7
S Vilas Ct
1500 SUPE 80027 1773 B6
Vilas St
11200 PARK 80134 2453 A7
Villa Dr
400 DgsC 80108 2535 B7
Village Cir
12100 CMCY 80603 1864 D1
25100 JfnC 80401 2190 B2
Village Cir E
- DgsC 80125 2531 A6
Village Cir W
- DgsC 80125 2614 E1
- DgsC 80125 2615 A1
8000 DgsC 80125 2530 E6
8000 DgsC 80125 2531 A6
Village Ct
10 AphC 80123 2363 D3
10 CBVL 80123 2363 D3
Village Dr
10 CBVL 80123 2363 D3
E Village Dr
200 BGTN 80601 1697 A6
W Village Dr
10 BGTN 80601 1696 E6
10 BGTN 80601 1697 A6
Village Hl
- AdmC 80601 1697 A6
200 BGTN 80601 1697 A6
Village Ln
2300 LGMT 80503 1438 C2
Village Pkwy
9200 LKWD 80215 2110 B5
Village Rd
10 CHLV 80113 2281 D4
N Village Rd
6500 DgsC 80134 2623 A1
6600 DgsC 80134 2622 E1
7100 DgsC 80134 2538 D7
7800 DgsC 80138 2538 D6
S Village Wy
5800 CTNL 80121 2365 D2
5800 GDVL 80121 2365 D2
Village Center Dr
16800 DgsC 80134 2452 E5
16800 DgsC 80134 2453 A5
Village Center Dr E
16900 DgsC 80134 2453 A5
16900 PARK 80134 2453 A5
Village Garden Dr
- AdmC 80601 1696 E6
10 BGTN 80601 1696 E6
10 BGTN 80601 1697 A6
Village Pines Cir
8900 DgsC 80116 2706 C5
Village Square Dr
7000 DgsC 80108 2535 B7
Village Square Ln
300 DgsC 80108 2535 B7
Village Square Ter
7200 DgsC 80108 2535 A7
E Villanova Cir
16700 AURA 80013 2200 D7
16700 AURA 80013 2284 D1
16700 AURA 80013 2285 B1
Villanova Ct
2700 LGMT 80503 1355 C7
E Villanova Dr
12100 AURA 80014 2283 E1
12400 AURA 80014 2284 B1
19800 AURA 80013 2201 D7
E Villanova Pl
6600 DNVR 80224 2282 C1
7300 AphC 80231 2282 D1
14300 AURA 80014 2284 C1
16200 AURA 80013 2284 E1
16500 AURA 80013 2200 E7
17400 AURA 80013 2285 A1
20300 AURA 80013 2201 E7
N Villard Ct
5900 DgsC 80134 2622 E3
5900 DgsC 80134 2623 A3
E Villasur Ct
9700 DgsC 80134 2622 E2
Villiage Cir
- CMCY 80603 1864 C1
Vinca
10 JfnC 80127 2361 A7
Vinca Ct
4200 BLDR 80304 1602 D4
Vinca Pl
1400 SUPE 80027 1857 B1
S Vincennes Ct
3900 DNVR 80237 2282 E4
S Vincennes Wy
2800 AphC 80231 2282 E1
2800 DNVR 80231 2282 E1
7900 CTNL 80112 2366 E7
Vine Av
- BldC 80304 1602 D4
- BLDR 80304 1602 D4
S Vine Cir E
7100 CTNL 80122 2365 B5
S Vine Cir W
7100 CTNL 80122 2365 B5
Vine Ct
6500 AdmC 80229 2029 B1
10200 TNTN 80229 1861 B6
S Vine Ct
3100 EGLD 80113 2281 B2
6300 CTNL 80121 2365 B3
7200 CTNL 80122 2365 B5
Vine Pl
2400 BLDR 80304 1602 E4
8300 AdmC 80229 1945 B4
Vine St
100 DNVR 80206 2197 B1
1000 DNVR 80206 2113 B5
1800 DNVR 80205 2113 B5
3900 JfnC 80465 2276 B4
3900 MRSN 80465 2276 B4
4600 DNVR 80216 2029 B6
8200 AdmC 80229 1945 B4
9100 TNTN 80229 1945 B2
9800 TNTN 80229 1861 B7
13400 TNTN 80241 1777 B5
14900 TNTN 80602 1777 B2
S Vine St
300 DNVR 80209 2197 B3
1000 DNVR 80210 2197 B5
3000 DvrC 80210 2281 B2
3000 EGLD 80113 2281 B2
3100 DNVR 80210 2281 B2
4800 CHLV 80113 2281 B7
5900 CTNL 80121 2365 B2
5900 GDVL 80121 2365 B2
6500 CTNL 80122 2365 C4
7200 AphC 80122 2365 B5
8100 CTNL 80122 2449 B1
S Vine Wy
4400 CHLV 80113 2281 B6
8000 CTNL 80122 2365 B7
Vinegaroon Rd
8200 DgsC 80138 2539 A5
Vineland Dr
17000 PARK 80134 2453 A7
Vinewood Ct
500 DgsC 80126 2449 A3
S Vinewood St
6000 LITN 80120 2364 A2
Vineyard Dr
1900 CSRK 80104 2788 A1
Vineyard Ln
4300 BLDR 80304 1602 D4
Vineyard Pl
2200 BLDR 80304 1602 E4
Vintage Pl
1000 DgsC 80108 2618 C2
Violet Av
900 BLDR 80304 1602 B4
1300 BldC 80304 1602 C4
2400 BldC 80301 1602 C4
Violet Ct
6300 ARVD 80403 2024 B2
Violet Pl
6000 ARVD 80403 2024 B3
Violet St
200 GOLD 80401 2192 B1
1600 GOLD 80401 2108 B5
Violet Wy
- ARVD 80007 2024 B2
- ARVD 80403 2024 B3
- JfnC 80403 2024 B3
Vireo Ct
800 LGMT 80501 1440 A1
Virgil Ct
5800 JfnC 80403 2024 B3
5900 ARVD 80403 2024 B3
Virgil St
3200 JfnC 80401 2108 B2
6000 ARVD 80403 2024 B2
Virgil Wy
6300 ARVD 80007 2024 B2
Virgil Wy
6300 ARVD 80403 2024 B2
E Virginia Av
10 DNVR 80209 2196 E2
10 DNVR 80223 2196 E2
4000 DNVR 80209 2197 E2
4000 GNDL 80246 2197 E2
4600 GNDL 80246 2198 A2
4900 DNVR 80246 2198 A2
5800 DNVR 80224 2198 B2
7200 DNVR 80247 2198 C2
10100 DNVR 80247 2199 B2
10300 AURA 80012 2199 C2
10300 DvrC 80012 2199 C2
W Virginia Av
2400 DNVR 80223 2196 A2
3000 DNVR 80219 2196 A2
4500 DNVR 80219 2195 C2
5000 LKWD 80219 2195 B2
5000 LKWD 80226 2195 B2
8100 LKWD 80226 2194 D3
11300 LKWD 80226 2193 E3
11400 LKWD 80228 2193 D3
W Virginia Cir
9600 LKWD 80226 2194 B2
E Virginia Ct
- AURA 80012 2199 E2
E Virginia Dr
11200 AURA 80012 2199 D2
W Virginia Dr
9200 LKWD 80226 2194 B2
13000 LKWD 80228 2193 B3
E Virginia Pl
11500 AURA 80012 2199 D2
12800 AURA 80012 2200 A3
W Virginia Pl
9200 LKWD 80226 2194 C2
12000 LKWD 80228 2193 D3
Virginia Rd
- PrkC 80456 2690 B2
Virginia St
10 IDSP 80452 2101 B5
600 GOLD 80403 2023 C7
Virginia Canyon Rd
- GpnC 80403 2101 A1
300 CCkC 80452 2101 C4
300 CLCY 80403 2017 B7
300 GpnC 80403 2017 B7
300 IDSP 80452 2101 C4
Virgo Ct
13400 DgsC 80124 2450 D2
Virgo Dr
13300 DgsC 80124 2450 E2
Visionaries Dr
- DNVR 80205 2113 B4
- DNVR 80218 2113 B4
Vista Av
300 JfnC 80401 2191 B1
Vista Cir
20300 PARK 80138 2453 E7
20300 PARK 80138 2454 A7
Vista Dr
400 CSRK 80104 2703 E6
1900 BLDR 80304 1602 D7
31700 JfnC 80439 2356 E1
Vista Ln
100 LSVL 80027 1773 A1
100 PrkC 80470 2523 C3
600 LKWD 80214 2110 E7
26800 JfnC 80439 2358 A4
W Vista Ln
4100 DgsC 80135 2785 C6
Vista Pkwy
- BldC 80026 1691 D2
- BMFD 80020 1691 D2
- ERIE 80516 1691 D2
Vista Rd
10 CHLV 80113 2281 D4
10700 PARK 80138 2453 E7
10700 PARK 80138 2454 A7
Vista Lodge Lp
6700 DgsC 80108 2534 C6
Vistancia Dr
5500 DgsC 80134 2621 B4
Vista Point Ct
- PrkC 80456 2607 E4
Vista Ridge Rd
41500 EbtC 80138 2540 E6
42800 EbtC 80138 2541 A4
Vista View Dr
- LGMT 80504 1440 D3
1400 WldC 80504 1440 D3
W Vista View Dr
10300 JfnC 80127 2362 A5
S Vista View Rd
2400 DgsC 80135 2785 D6
Vito Tr
7500 JfnC 80439 2357 D6
Vivian Cir
1000 BLDR 80303 1687 C3
5400 ARVD 80002 2025 D4
Vivian Ct
700 LKWD 80401 2109 D7
3600 WTRG 80033 2109 D1
6000 ARVD 80004 2025 D3
7000 ARVD 80004 1941 D7
8500 ARVD 80005 1941 C4
S Vivian Ct
1700 LKWD 80228 2193 D5
4600 JfnC 80465 2277 D6
4900 JfnC 80127 2277 D7
5900 JfnC 80127 2361 D2
Vivian Dr
3200 WTRG 80033 2109 D2
3200 WTRG 80215 2109 D2
Vivian St
100 BldC 80501 1438 E3
300 LGMT 80501 1438 E2
800 LKWD 80401 2109 D7
1000 JfnC 80401 2109 D6
2100 LGMT 80501 1355 E5
2400 LKWD 80215 2109 D3
2900 WTRG 80215 2109 D2
3100 WTRG 80033 2109 D2
Vivian St
5200 ARVD 80002 2025 D5
5200 WTRG 80033 2025 D5
6700 ARVD 80004 2025 D1
8300 ARVD 80005 1941 C4
N Vivian St
4200 WTRG 80033 2025 D7
S Vivian St
800 LKWD 80228 2193 D4
1400 LGMT 80501 1438 E6
4400 JfnC 80465 2277 D5
5900 JfnC 80127 2361 D2
S Vivian Wy
1400 LKWD 80228 2193 D5
4300 JfnC 80465 2277 D5
Voiles Dr
400 BGTN 80601 1696 D7
Voiles Pl
600 BGTN 80601 1696 C7
Voiles St
400 BGTN 80601 1696 C7
Voilet Av
2800 BldC 80301 1602 E4
S Vona Ct
1500 SUPE 80027 1773 B6
Vonnie Claire Rd
11700 JfnC 80403 1852 D3
Voorhees Ranch Wy
1400 DgsC 80109 2618 C7
Voorhis Wy
- ARVD 80004 2026 D3
Vosler St
25600 JfnC 80433 2442 A4
Vrain Cir
12300 BMFD 80020 1859 C1
Vrain Ct
5400 AdmC 80212 2027 C4
9200 WSTR 80031 1943 C2
11000 WSTR 80031 1859 C4
Vrain Dr
11200 WSTR 80031 1859 C4
Vrain St
10 DNVR 80219 2195 D1
300 DNVR 80219 2111 C7
1300 DNVR 80204 2111 C5
3800 DNVR 80212 2111 C1
4900 DNVR 80212 2027 C5
5300 AdmC 80212 2027 C5
6400 ARVD 80003 2027 C2
6800 AdmC 80030 2027 C1
6800 ARVD 80030 2027 C1
7200 WSTR 80030 1943 C7
8800 AdmC 80031 1943 C3
11000 WSTR 80031 1859 C4
12500 BMFD 80020 1775 C7
N Vrain St
9000 WSTR 80031 1943 C2
S Vrain St
10 DNVR 80219 2195 D1
2700 DNVR 80219 2279 D1
2700 DNVR 80236 2279 D1
S Vrain Wy
1400 DNVR 80219 2195 C5
Vulcan St
200 LSVL 80027 1689 C5

W

S Wabash Cir
2800 DNVR 80231 2282 E1
2800 DNVR 80231 2283 A1
S Wabash Ct
3200 DNVR 80231 2282 E2
7800 CTNL 80112 2366 E7
8100 CTNL 80112 2450 E1
Wabash Pl
- AdmC 80602 1778 E7
- TNTN 80602 1778 E7
Wabash St
- CMCY 80022 1946 E3
1100 DNVR 80220 2114 E5
1100 DNVR 80230 2114 E5
2600 DNVR 80238 2114 E3
4500 DNVR 80216 2030 E6
S Wabash St
2100 AphC 80231 2198 E7
2900 DNVR 80231 2282 E1
4600 DNVR 80237 2282 E6
5000 DvrC 80237 2282 E6
5000 GDVL 80111 2282 E6
7900 CTNL 80112 2366 E7
Wabash Wy
14500 AdmC 80602 1778 E2
S Wabash Wy
6100 GDVL 80111 2366 E2
S Waco Ct
1700 AURA 80017 2201 B5
2100 AURA 80013 2201 B6
3000 AURA 80013 2285 B2
5100 CTNL 80015 2285 B7
5500 CTNL 80015 2369 B1
5900 AphC 80016 2369 B2
Waco St
- AdmC 80022 1781 B7
- AdmC 80601 1697 B5
- BGTN 80601 1697 B5
- CMCY 80022 1865 B6
- WldC 80603 1697 B4
N Waco St
500 AURA 80011 2117 B6
S Waco St
1100 AURA 80017 2201 B4
2100 AURA 80013 2201 B6
2800 AURA 80013 2285 B2
4900 AURA 80015 2285 B6
5200 CTNL 80015 2285 B7
5900 AphC 80016 2369 B2
5900 CTNL 80015 2369 B2
5900 CTNL 80016 2369 B2
6700 FXFD 80016 2369 B4
S Waco Wy
900 AURA 80017 2201 B3
2700 AURA 80013 2285 B1
6500 AphC 80016 2369 B3
Wade Rd
600 BldC 80503 1438 B1
600 LGMT 80503 1438 B1
Wadsworth Blvd
- BfdC 80020 1858 D2
- WSTR 80020 1858 D2
- WSTR 80021 1858 D2
- WTRG 80002 2026 E7
10 LKWD 80226 2194 E1
400 LKWD 80226 2110 E6
600 LKWD 80214 2110 E6
2500 JfnC 80215 2110 E3
2500 WTRG 80033 2110 E3
4800 ARVD 80033 2026 E7
4800 WTRG 80033 2026 E7
5800 ARVD 80002 2026 E3
5800 ARVD 80003 2026 E3
6500 ARVD 80004 2026 D1
7000 ARVD 80003 1942 D7
7000 ARVD 80004 1942 D7
7100 ARVD 80005 1942 D7
8200 WSTR 80005 1942 D7
9200 JfnC 80021 1942 D1
9200 WSTR 80021 1942 D1
11000 JfnC 80021 1858 D2
11100 BMFD 80021 1858 D2
11500 BMFD 80020 1858 D2
Wadsworth Blvd SR-121
- WTRG 80002 2026 E7
10 LKWD 80226 2194 E1
400 LKWD 80226 2110 E6
600 LKWD 80214 2110 E6
2500 JfnC 80215 2110 E3
2500 WTRG 80033 2110 E3
4800 ARVD 80033 2026 E7
4800 WTRG 80033 2026 E7
5000 ARVD 80002 2026 E7
6500 ARVD 80003 2026 D1
6500 ARVD 80004 2026 D1
7000 ARVD 80003 1942 D7
7000 ARVD 80004 1942 D7
7100 ARVD 80005 1942 D7
8200 WSTR 80005 1942 D7
8700 WSTR 80021 1942 D7
S Wadsworth Blvd
10 LKWD 80226 2194 E2
1200 LKWD 80232 2194 E6
2000 LKWD 80227 2194 E7
2600 DNVR 80227 2278 E3
2600 LKWD 80227 2278 E3
2800 JfnC 80227 2278 E3
4000 DNVR 80235 2278 D6
4000 LKWD 80235 2278 D6
4400 DNVR 80123 2278 D6
4800 DvrC 80123 2278 D6
4900 LKWD 80123 2278 D6
5100 DNVR 80123 2362 D1
5100 LKWD 80123 2362 D1
5400 DvrC 80123 2362 D1
6700 JfnC 80128 2362 D5
7700 JfnC 80128 2446 E2
9400 JfnC 80127 2446 E2
S Wadsworth Blvd SR-121
10 LKWD 80226 2194 E2
900 LKWD 80232 2194 E6
1900 LKWD 80227 2194 E6
2600 DNVR 80227 2278 E3
2600 LKWD 80227 2278 E3
2800 DvrC 80227 2278 E3
4000 DNVR 80123 2278 D6
4000 DNVR 80235 2278 D6
4000 LKWD 80235 2278 D6
4800 JfnC 80123 2278 D6
4800 LKWD 80123 2278 D6
5100 DNVR 80123 2362 D3
5100 LKWD 80123 2362 D1
5400 DvrC 80123 2362 D1
6700 JfnC 80128 2362 D5
7700 JfnC 80128 2446 E2
9400 JfnC 80127 2446 E2
Wadsworth Byp
5200 ARVD 80002 2026 E2
5700 ARVD 80003 2026 E2
Wadsworth Byp SR-121
5200 ARVD 80002 2026 E2
5700 ARVD 80003 2026 E2
Wadsworth Cir
200 LGMT 80501 1439 C2
S Wadsworth Cir
2600 LKWD 80227 2194 E7
2600 LKWD 80227 2278 D1
Wadsworth Ct
300 LGMT 80501 1439 C2
S Wadsworth Ct
2500 LKWD 80227 2278 D1
6800 JfnC 80128 2362 E5
8300 JfnC 80128 2446 E1
Wadsworth Pkwy
- BMFD 80020 1858 C3
8800 ARVD 80003 1942 C1
8800 WSTR 80005 1942 C1
9000 WSTR 80021 1942 C1
9700 WSTR 80021 1858 C6
10800 JfnC 80021 1858 C3
11200 BMFD 80021 1858 C3
Wadsworth Pkwy SR-121
- BMFD 80020 1858 C3
8800 ARVD 80003 1942 C1
8800 WSTR 80005 1942 C1
9000 WSTR 80021 1942 C1
9700 WSTR 80021 1858 C6
10800 JfnC 80021 1858 C3
11200 BMFD 80021 1858 C3
Wadsworth Pkwy SR-128
- BMFD 80020 1858 C3
- BMFD 80021 1858 C6
S Wadsworth Wy
2500 LKWD 80227 2278 E1
4300 DNVR 80235 2278 D6
7800 JfnC 80128 2362 E7
Wagner Cir
10 BldC 80304 1601 D4
S Wagner Ct
8800 DgsC 80126 2449 E2
Wagner Dr
4100 AdmC 80031 1943 C3
8400 WSTR 80031 1943 C3
Wagner Ln
8800 AdmC 80031 1943 C3
N Wagner Ln
- WSTR 80031 1859 C7
Wagner St
8800 AdmC 80031 1943 C3
8800 WSTR 80031 1943 C3
Wagon Ct
16300 PARK 80134 2452 E7
Wagon Pl
16400 PARK 80134 2452 E7
Wagon Rd
- WSTR 80234 1860 D2
Wagon Tr
11700 JfnC 80433 2525 E3
Wagon Box Cir
- DgsC 80124 2450 A7
- DgsC 80130 2450 A7
Wagon Box Pl
5000 DgsC 80130 2450 A7
Wagon Box Wy
10600 DgsC 80130 2450 A7
Wagon Tongue Rd
10 PrkC 80456 2522 D6
Wagon Tongue Wy
20700 JfnC 80465 2443 C1
Wagontrail Av
- AURA 80016 2286 D6
E Wagontrail Av
24300 AURA 80016 2286 E6
E Wagontrail Cir
18500 AURA 80015 2285 C6
W Wagon Trail Cir
9300 DNVR 80123 2278 B6
Wagontrail Ct
4800 DgsC 80134 2621 C5
E Wagontrail Dr
16200 AURA 80015 2284 E6
19700 CTNL 80015 2285 D6
W Wagon Trail Dr
3300 DNVR 80110 2279 D6
3300 DNVR 80236 2279 D6
4500 BWMR 80123 2279 C6
4500 DNVR 80123 2279 C6
9800 DNVR 80123 2278 B6
E Wagontrail Ln
20000 CTNL 80015 2285 E6
E Wagontrail Pkwy
16600 AURA 80015 2284 E6
16700 AURA 80015 2285 A6
17300 AphC 80015 2285 A6
17300 CTNL 80015 2285 A6
E Wagontrail Pl
14900 AURA 80015 2284 C6
20000 CTNL 80015 2285 D6
S Wagon Trail Rd
900 JfnC 80439 2189 B4
Wagon Train Tr
- EbtC 80107 2708 C7
Wagon Wheel Dr
- WldC 80603 1697 B3
15100 BGTN 80603 1697 B3
W Wagon Wheel Dr
9000 DgsC 80125 2447 B7
S Wagon Wheel Rd
7700 JfnC 80465 2359 D7
8000 JfnC 80465 2443 D1
Wagon Wheel Tr
- EbtC 80107 2708 C6
Wagonwheel Tr
5400 CSRK 80104 2704 E6
N Wagonwheel Tr
300 CSRK 80104 2704 E6
E Wagon Wheel Wy
9000 DgsC 80138 2454 D1
Wagonwheel Gap Rd
10 BldC 80302 1601 D3
10 BldC 80302 1602 A2
Waite Dr
800 BLDR 80303 1687 C4
Wakefield Av
4500 CSRK 80104 2704 D7
W Walden Av
9200 JfnC 80128 2362 B7
9800 JfnC 80127 2362 B7
Walden Cir
600 BLDR 80305 1687 C6
S Walden Cir
5100 CTNL 80015 2285 B7
Walden Ct
1300 LGMT 80501 1356 E7
E Walden Ct
600 DgsC 80126 2449 A4
S Walden Ct
1600 AURA 80017 2201 B5
2900 AURA 80013 2285 B1
5400 CTNL 80015 2369 C3
5900 AphC 80016 2369 B2
W Walden Dr
7100 JfnC 80128 2362 E7
Walden Ln
10 CHLV 80121 2282 A7
S Walden Ln
6300 AphC 80016 2369 B3
W Walden Pl
6800 JfnC 80128 2363 A7
7100 JfnC 80128 2362 E7
Walden St
- CMCY 80022 1865 B5
2800 AURA 80011 2117 B2
12500 AdmC 80022 1781 B7
N Walden St
600 AURA 80011 2117 B6
S Walden St
900 AURA 80017 2201 B2
2200 AURA 80013 2201 B6
2800 AURA 80013 2285 B1
5100 CTNL 80015 2285 B7
5600 CTNL 80015 2369 B1
6500 AphC 80016 2369 B3

STREET
Block City ZIP Map# Grid

S Walden Wy
1000 AURA 80017 2201 B4
1900 AURA 80013 2201 B6
2700 AURA 80013 2285 B1
6200 AphC 80016 2369 C3
Walden Ponds
- BldC 80301 1604 C5
Waldenwood Dr
4600 DgsC 80130 2450 A6
Waldenwood Pl
4700 DgsC 80130 2450 A6
Waldorf Pl
10 IDSP 80452 2101 D5
Walker Av
6700 BldC 80503 1521 B4
W Walker Av
- JfnC 80123 2362 A3
6800 JfnC 80123 2363 A3
10000 JfnC 80127 2362 A3
Walker Ct
6600 BldC 80503 1521 B5
E Walker Dr
- AURA 80016 2371 C3
W Walker Dr
7200 JfnC 80123 2362 E3
10900 JfnC 80127 2361 E3
10900 JfnC 80127 2362 A3
E Walker Pl
- AphC 80016 2368 B3
- AphC 80111 2368 B3
- CTNL 80111 2368 B3
W Walker Pl
7200 JfnC 80123 2362 E3
10400 JfnC 80127 2362 A3
12400 JfnC 80127 2361 D4
Walker Rd
2000 DgsC 80116 2705 D3
8800 BldC 80503 1521 B5
Walker St
1500 ERIE 80516 1690 C2
Walkway
- BLDR 80302 1686 D3
Wall St
- BldC 80302 1599 E6
- BldC 80302 1600 A6
1800 IDSP 80452 2101 D5
S Wallace Av
10900 JfnC 80433 2527 B1
S Wallace Ct
8200 AphC 80112 2367 E7
8200 DgsC 80112 2451 E1
9800 DgsC 80126 2448 E5
Wallace St
100 NHGN 80234 1860 D5
Wally Av
- DgsC 80118 2869 E7
- DgsC 80118 2870 A7
- DgsC 80118 2953 E1
- DgsC 80118 2954 A1
Wally Blvd
- DgsC 80118 2953 E1
- DgsC 80118 2954 A1
Walnut Ct
- LGMT 80501 1439 C6
Walnut Dr
1500 BGTN 80601 1696 D5
Walnut Ln
200 LSVL 80027 1689 B7
Walnut St
- BLDR 80301 1686 E1
- BLDR 80302 1686 E1
- LGMT 80501 1439 C6
100 DNVR 80204 2112 B4
300 BGTN 80601 1696 B5
1000 LSVL 80027 1689 D7
2300 DNVR 80205 2112 D3
3000 BLDR 80301 1687 A2
3200 DNVR 80205 2113 A1
3800 DNVR 80205 2029 B7
E Walnut St
100 ELIZ 80107 2793 B1
S Walnut St
- BLDR 80302 1686 E2
W Walnut St
10 BGTN 80601 1696 A5
200 LSVL 80027 1689 C7
Walnut Hollow Ln
1800 BLDR 80302 1686 D2
Walnut Ln Ln
- BLDR 80302 1686 D2
Walsh Av
17000 PARK 80134 2453 A7
E Walsh Dr
14600 AURA 80012 2200 C3
E Walsh Pl
6900 DNVR 80224 2198 C3
9800 DNVR 80247 2199 B3
11600 AURA 80012 2199 D3
14500 AURA 80012 2200 C3
16100 AURA 80017 2200 E3
W Walsh Pl
3000 DNVR 80219 2196 A3
4000 DNVR 80219 2195 D3
Walter Dr
30800 JfnC 80433 2525 A4
Walter Wy
10 BMFD 80020 1774 E6
S Walters Cir
10400 JfnC 80465 2443 D7
Walters Dr
2400 ERIE 80516 1606 D5
S Wamblee Tr
13500 JfnC 80433 2609 D1
S Wamblee Valley Rd
12100 JfnC 80433 2525 C5
12900 JfnC 80433 2609 C1
Wanda Ln
10700 NHGN 80234 1860 C5
Wandcrest Av
10 PrkC 80470 2608 A1
S Wandcrest Dr
- PrkC 80470 2608 A2
14400 JfnC 80456 2608 A3

Wandcrest Park Rd
- JfnC 80456 2608 A3
E Wanderlust Pl
21300 DgsC 80138 2538 A3
S Wanderlust Wy
12000 DgsC 80138 2538 B3
Waneka Pkwy
10 LAFT 80026 1690 C6
Waneka Lake Tr
2300 LAFT 80026 1689 E4
S Wangaratta Ct
9500 DgsC 80130 2450 B4
E Wangaratta Wy
5200 DgsC 80130 2450 A4
Wapiti Ct
6900 BldC 80301 1604 B3
Wapiti Dr
26900 JfnC 80439 2442 A1
Wapiti Pl
100 BldC 80481 1515 A3
Wapiti Tr
6400 DgsC 80118 2870 C7
13000 JfnC 80470 2525 A7
War Admiral Tr
27700 JfnC 80439 2357 D7
Warbler Ct
5100 DgsC 80134 2622 C4
S Warbler Ct
100 LSVL 80027 1773 A1
Warbler Ct
2600 FLHT 80260 1944 A1
2600 TNTN 80260 1944 A1
E Warbonnet Tr
7500 AURA 80138 2454 A2
7500 DgsC 80138 2454 A2
Ward Cir
1200 DgsC 80116 2706 E4
1200 DgsC 80116 2707 A4
Ward Ct
10 LKWD 80228 2193 C1
2900 LKWD 80215 2109 D2
2900 WTRG 80215 2109 D2
3100 WTRG 80033 2109 D2
8500 ARVD 80005 1941 C4
S Ward Ct
1400 LKWD 80228 2193 D5
Ward Dr
2300 LKWD 80215 2109 D3
Ward Rd
- JfnC 80005 1941 C6
3200 WTRG 80033 2109 D2
3200 WTRG 80215 2109 D2
4400 JfnC 80033 2025 C4
4400 WTRG 80033 2025 C4
5000 ARVD 80002 2025 C4
5300 JfnC 80002 2025 C4
6400 ARVD 80004 2025 C2
7000 ARVD 80004 1941 C7
8500 ARVD 80005 1941 C4
Ward Rd SR-72
4400 JfnC 80033 2025 C4
4400 WTRG 80033 2025 C4
5000 ARVD 80002 2025 C4
5300 JfnC 80002 2025 C4
5600 ARVD 80004 2025 C4
Ward St
- BldC 80455 1515 E3
- GpnC 80403 1849 D6
- JMWN 80455 1515 E3
10 JMWN 80455 1516 A3
10 PrkC 80456 2521 D2
100 LKWD 80228 2193 C1
S Ward St
1400 LKWD 80228 2193 C5
5100 JfnC 80127 2277 D7
5100 JfnC 80465 2277 D7
5900 JfnC 80127 2361 D1
S Ward Wy
1300 LKWD 80228 2193 C5
4500 JfnC 80465 2277 D6
5300 JfnC 80127 2361 D1
Wardenburg Dr
- BLDR 80302 1686 D4
Warehouse Pl
- DNVR 80230 2115 A7
S Warhawk Rd
8400 JfnC 80433 2440 E2
9000 JfnC 80433 2441 A3
S Warhawk Wy
8300 JfnC 80433 2441 A2
Waring Ln
10 GDVL 80121 2365 C1
Warner Dr
700 GOLD 80401 2108 A7
W Warner Pl
200 DNVR 80216 2028 D6
Warren Av
1400 LGMT 80501 1438 E1
E Warren Av
10 DNVR 80210 2196 E7
10 DNVR 80223 2196 E7
600 DNVR 80210 2197 A7
3900 DNVR 80222 2197 E7
4800 AphC 80222 2198 A7
4800 DNVR 80222 2198 A7
8500 AphC 80231 2198 E7
9800 AphC 80231 2199 B7
9800 AURA 80247 2199 B7
10500 AURA 80014 2199 C6
14500 AURA 80014 2200 C6
16300 AURA 80013 2200 E6
18200 AURA 80013 2201 B6
W Warren Av
10 DNVR 80210 2196 D7
1700 AphC 80110 2196 B7
1700 DNVR 80110 2196 B7
1700 DNVR 80223 2196 B7
1700 DvrC 80223 2196 B7
1700 EGLD 80110 2196 B7
2200 DNVR 80219 2196 A7
2200 EGLD 80219 2196 A7
3300 DNVR 80219 2195 E7
5100 DNVR 80227 2195 B7
10000 LKWD 80227 2194 A7

W Warren Av
13400 LKWD 80228 2193 B7
Warren Cir
- DNVR 80210 2197 C7
E Warren Cir
7500 AphC 80231 2198 D6
18900 AURA 80013 2201 C6
18900 AURA 80017 2201 C6
W Warren Cir
13100 LKWD 80228 2193 C7
Warren Ct
900 LGMT 80501 1438 E1
3200 EbtC 80138 2457 A6
33100 JfnC 80470 2524 C6
W Warren Ct
6000 LKWD 80227 2195 B7
Warren Dr
6800 AdmC 80221 2028 B1
6900 AdmC 80221 1944 B7
E Warren Dr
- AURA 80014 2199 E7
- AURA 80014 2200 A6
7000 DNVR 80224 2198 C7
7300 AphC 80224 2198 D6
7300 AphC 80231 2198 D6
18700 AURA 80013 2201 C6
W Warren Dr
- LKWD 80228 2193 A7
10000 LKWD 80227 2194 A7
W Warren Ln
8600 LKWD 80227 2194 C7
E Warren Pl
- AURA 80013 2201 D6
11900 AURA 80014 2199 E7
14400 AURA 80014 2200 C6
16000 AURA 80013 2200 E6
24300 AphC 80018 2203 A6
24300 AURA 80018 2202 E6
24300 AURA 80018 2203 A6
W Warren Pl
6000 LKWD 80227 2195 A7
14200 LKWD 80228 2193 A7
Warren Rd
33300 JfnC 80470 2524 C6
Warren Gulch Rd
10 CCkC 80452 2185 D2
Warrens Rd
31800 JfnC 80403 1852 D4
Warrington Ct
11500 DgsC 80138 2453 E5
Warrior Wy
- LSVL 80026 1690 A6
1200 LAFT 80026 1690 A6
Warriors Run
6400 DgsC 80125 2614 D2
Warriors Mark Rd
9000 DgsC 80116 2706 D5
Warsaw Dr
- DgsC 80138 2539 E6
100 EbtC 80138 2540 A7
Warwick Pl
200 DgsC 80108 2618 E1
Wasach Dr
1800 LGMT 80501 1357 A5
Wasatch Pt
1300 LAFT 80026 1689 D3
S Wasatch St
13200 JfnC 80470 2524 A7
Washburn Av
1200 ERIE 80516 1607 B2
W Washburn Av
- LKWD 80227 2278 B1
Washburn Ct
1100 ERIE 80516 1607 A2
W Washburn Pl
9000 LKWD 80227 2278 C1
Washburn St
1300 ERIE 80516 1607 A2
W Washburn Wy
10100 LKWD 80227 2278 B1
Washington Av
- LSVL 80027 1688 E7
10 GOLD 80403 2107 D2
100 BNNT 80102 2124 D2
700 GOLD 80401 2107 E4
1400 LSVL 80027 1689 B6
N Washington Av
- GOLD 80403 2107 C1
S Washington Av
100 LSVL 80027 1773 B1
Washington Cir
2000 GOLD 80401 2107 E4
S Washington Cir
600 EGLD 80113 2281 A7
7300 CTNL 80122 2365 A6
Washington Ct
700 AdmC 80229 1945 A5
Washington Ln
12500 DgsC 80112 2451 E5
Washington St
10 DNVR 80203 2197 A1
10 DNVR 80209 2197 A1
100 GOLD 80403 2107 C2
300 ELIZ 80107 2709 B7
1900 DNVR 80205 2113 A4
2000 DNVR 80203 2113 A4
2000 DNVR 80218 2113 A4
3000 BLDR 80304 1602 C7
4600 DNVR 80216 2028 E7
5100 AdmC 80216 2029 A4
5100 DNVR 80216 2029 A4
6200 AdmC 80229 2029 A2
6800 AdmC 80229 1945 A7
7300 AdmC 80229 1944 E6
8000 TNTN 80229 1944 E4
9600 TNTN 80229 1860 E7
10200 TNTN 80233 1860 E7
10400 NHGN 80233 1860 E5
12000 TNTN 80241 1860 E2
12800 TNTN 80241 1776 E6
13500 AdmC 80602 1776 E6
13500 TNTN 80020 1776 E6
14400 AdmC 80020 1776 E3
15100 AdmC 80020 1692 E5

Washington St
16700 BMFD 80516 1692 E5
16700 TNTN 80020 1692 E5
S Washington St
10 DNVR 80203 2197 A2
10 DNVR 80209 2197 A2
1000 DNVR 80210 2197 A5
2700 AphC 80210 2281 A1
2700 DNVR 80210 2281 A1
2700 EGLD 80210 2281 A1
3900 EGLD 80113 2281 A4
5000 AphC 80121 2281 A7
5000 GDVL 80121 2281 A7
5300 AphC 80121 2365 A1
5300 GDVL 80121 2365 A1
5500 LITN 80121 2365 A1
6500 CTNL 80121 2365 A3
6500 CTNL 80122 2365 A3
Washington Wy
800 BNNT 80102 2124 E1
10400 NHGN 80233 1860 E6
S Washington Wy
7100 CTNL 80122 2365 A5
Washington Center Pkwy
- NHGN 80233 1861 A1
- TNTN 80241 1860 E1
12100 TNTN 80241 1861 A1
Watada Dr
3400 BGTN 80601 1697 A7
Watada St
3400 BGTN 80601 1697 A7
W Water Av
2400 DNVR 80219 2280 A1
2400 EGLD 80110 2280 A1
E Water Dr
18600 AURA 80013 2201 C7
Water St
- IDSP 80452 2101 D5
500 GOLD 80401 2107 E3
600 DNVR 80211 2112 B3
Waterbury Rd
10500 BldC 80504 1356 A4
Water Cress Ct
2300 LGMT 80504 1438 D7
Waterford Ct
7000 BldC 80503 1521 A4
S Waterford Ct
9300 DgsC 80130 2450 D4
Waterford Wy
8500 BldC 80503 1521 A4
Waterford Place Apartments
- TNTN 80233 1861 C1
- TNTN 80241 1861 C2
Watermill Dr
- BGTN 80601 1697 D4
Waterside Ln
- BMFD 80020 1776 A3
Waterside Ter
- CHLV 80113 2281 C4
Watersong Cir
2200 LGMT 80504 1438 D6
Waterstone Dr
5200 BldC 80301 1603 C3
Waterton Rd
- JfnC 80127 2445 B3
W Waterton Rd
10600 DgsC 80125 2531 A5
10700 DgsC 80125 2530 D5
11300 JfnC 80127 2530 D5
Watkins Rd
- AdmC 80642 1868 E1
13600 AdmC 80603 1784 E5
13600 AdmC 80642 1784 E5
16000 AdmC 80603 1700 E5
16000 AdmC 80642 1700 E4
N Watkins Rd
1600 AdmC 80137 2121 A7
N Watkins Rd CO-97
10 AphC 80137 2121 A5
S Watkins Rd
10 AphC 80137 2205 A1
S Watkins Rd CO-97
10 AphC 80137 2205 A1
Watkins Mile Rd
- AdmC 80102 1952 E4
- AdmC 80137 1952 E7
- AdmC 80137 2036 E1
- AdmC 80137 2121 A4
- AdmC 80249 1952 E4
- AdmC 80642 1868 E2
- AURA 80137 1952 E7
- AURA 80137 2036 E1
- AURA 80249 1952 E6
N Watkins Mile Rd
- AdmC 80137 2121 A3
- AURA 80137 2121 A3
Watonga Wy
7600 BldC 80303 1688 D4
S Watson Ln
200 CBVL 80123 2363 E2
400 LITN 80123 2363 E2
S Watson Gulch Rd
9200 JfnC 80127 2444 C4
Wauconda Dr
- DgsC 80118 2953 A1
6200 DgsC 80118 2868 E7
6300 DgsC 80118 2952 E1
Wauconda Wy
- DgsC 80118 2868 E7
S Waverly Mtn
7600 JfnC 80127 2362 A7
E Waverly Wy
4300 DgsC 80126 2449 E5
Waverton Ranch Rd
1100 CSRK 80109 2702 D1
1100 DgsC 80109 2618 C7
1100 DgsC 80109 2702 D1
S Waxberry Wy
3100 DNVR 80231 2282 E2
Waxwing Av
1300 BGTN 80601 1779 E1
Waxwing Ct
6000 BldC 80503 1520 A4

Waynes Wy
23400 JfnC 80401 2190 E6
Wazee St
- DNVR 80205 2112 D3
1300 DNVR 80204 2112 C4
1400 DNVR 80202 2112 C4
3400 DNVR 80205 2113 A1
3400 DNVR 80216 2113 A1
Weasel Wy
10 GpnC 80403 1934 A7
3000 DgsC 80116 2707 D1
S Weasel Wy
6800 JfnC 80439 2356 B5
Weathersfield Ct
10600 DgsC 80129 2448 D7
Weathersfield Wy
10500 DgsC 80129 2448 D7
E Weatherstone Cir
2100 DgsC 80126 2449 B3
S Weatherstone Ct
9100 DgsC 80126 2449 B3
S Weatherstone Ln
9300 DgsC 80126 2449 C3
Weatherstone Wy
- DgsC 80126 2449 C3
E Weathervane Wy
9900 DgsC 80138 2455 A1
E Weaver Av
- CTNL 80016 2370 A3
2600 CTNL 80121 2365 C3
5400 CTNL 80111 2366 B3
5400 CTNL 80121 2366 A3
10000 AphC 80111 2367 B3
15500 CTNL 80016 2368 D3
16700 CTNL 80016 2369 A3
17300 AphC 80016 2369 A3
20600 AphC 80016 2370 A3
W Weaver Av
1200 LITN 80120 2364 C3
6400 JfnC 80123 2363 A3
8700 JfnC 80123 2362 C3
10500 JfnC 80127 2362 A3
E Weaver Cir
4600 CTNL 80121 2366 A3
5600 CTNL 80111 2366 B3
10300 AphC 80111 2367 C3
W Weaver Cir
1200 LITN 80120 2364 C3
Weaver Dr
10 BldC 80302 1600 D7
10 BldC 80302 1684 D1
E Weaver Dr
5100 CTNL 80121 2366 A3
6200 CTNL 80111 2366 C3
18100 AphC 80016 2369 B3
20700 AphC 80016 2370 A3
22400 AURA 80016 2370 C3
W Weaver Dr
5400 JfnC 80123 2363 B3
9100 JfnC 80123 2362 C3
E Weaver Ln
16800 AphC 80016 2369 A3
E Weaver Pl
- AURA 80016 2371 B3
10 CTNL 80121 2364 E3
10 LITN 80120 2364 E3
4100 CTNL 80121 2365 E3
5100 CTNL 80121 2366 A3
5600 CTNL 80111 2366 B3
10100 AphC 80111 2367 B3
12400 CTNL 80111 2367 E3
15600 CTNL 80016 2368 E3
16300 AphC 80016 2368 E3
18200 AphC 80016 2369 B3
20800 AphC 80016 2370 A3
21200 CTNL 80016 2370 A3
W Weaver Pl
7200 JfnC 80123 2362 E3
Weaver St
- BldC 80503 1436 D7
Weaver Park Rd
200 BldC 80501 1439 D3
200 LGMT 80501 1439 D3
S Webb Av
10800 JfnC 80433 2527 A1
Webber Ct
400 ERIE 80516 1607 A6
N Webster Ct
9200 JfnC 80021 1942 E1
S Webster Ct
4700 LKWD 80123 2278 E7
7500 JfnC 80128 2362 E6
Webster Dr
8400 ARVD 80003 1942 E3
Webster St
500 LKWD 80214 2110 E7
500 LKWD 80226 2110 E7
3300 WTRG 80033 2110 E2
4600 WTRG 80033 2026 E6
5600 ARVD 80002 2026 E4
5700 ARVD 80003 2026 E4
8100 ARVD 80003 1942 E4
S Webster St
900 LKWD 80226 2194 E4
2700 DNVR 80227 2278 E1
2900 DvrC 80227 2278 E1
2900 LKWD 80227 2278 E1
6500 JfnC 80123 2362 E4
6700 JfnC 80128 2362 E5
Webster Wy
7600 ARVD 80003 1942 E6
9400 JfnC 80021 1942 D1
S Webster Wy
6800 JfnC 80128 2362 E4
Wedge Ct
3900 BldC 80503 1518 E5
Wedge Wy
10 CBVL 80123 2363 E4
W Wedge Wy
15600 JfnC 80465 2360 E2
Wedge Rock Dr
10 LmrC 80540 1269 A1
E Wedgewood Ct
700 DgsC 80126 2449 A5

S Wedgewood Dr
9700 DgsC 80126 2449 A5
9800 DgsC 80126 2448 E7
Wedgwood Av
2300 LGMT 80501 1355 C6
2300 LGMT 80503 1355 C6
Wedgwood Rd
10 GpnC 80403 1850 E3
10 GpnC 80403 1851 A3
Weeden Pl
10300 DgsC 80124 2450 D6
E Weeping Willow Cir
5000 DgsC 80130 2450 A4
S Weeping Willow Ct
9100 DgsC 80130 2450 A3
S Weeping Willow Pl
9200 DgsC 80130 2450 A3
S Weeping Willow Wy
- DgsC 80130 2450 B3
Weiman Ct
6900 CMCY 80022 1946 A7
S Weir Dr
100 DNVR 80219 2195 C2
Weisshorn Cir
30100 JfnC 80470 2609 B5
Weisshorn Dr
23400 JfnC 80439 2274 E5
Welby Cir
9200 TNTN 80229 1945 D2
Welby Rd
8500 AdmC 80229 1945 C2
8700 TNTN 80229 1945 C2
Welby Rd Ter
9300 TNTN 80229 1945 D1
Welch Av
3400 JfnC 80439 2274 A3
3400 JfnC 80457 2274 A3
S Welch Cir
1100 LKWD 80228 2193 D5
Welch Ct
200 LYNS 80540 1352 D2
700 LKWD 80401 2109 D7
900 JfnC 80401 2109 D6
6700 ARVD 80004 2025 C1
7000 ARVD 80004 1941 C7
S Welch Ct
1400 LKWD 80228 2193 D5
Welch Dr
- AdmC 80601 1697 B7
200 LYNS 80540 1352 D2
Welch St
800 JfnC 80401 2109 D6
800 LKWD 80401 2109 D6
1500 LKWD 80215 2109 D5
6000 ARVD 80004 2025 C3
Welch Tr
35300 EbtC 80107 2708 D5
S Weldona Ln
1200 SUPE 80027 1773 B5
E Weldona Wy
1300 SUPE 80027 1773 B5
Welford Pl
6900 DgsC 80108 2618 E1
Wellcrest Dr
- JfnC 80401 2191 B1
Wellington Av
100 LAFT 80026 1690 B5
S Wellington Ct
6600 CTNL 80121 2365 A4
6600 CTNL 80122 2365 A4
Wellington Dr
17000 PARK 80134 2453 A7
Wellington Pkwy
5200 ARVD 80003 2027 B3
Wellington Pl
6700 DgsC 80108 2618 E1
Wellington Rd
4400 BldC 80301 1603 E4
4400 BLDR 80301 1603 E4
Wellington St
100 NHGN 80234 1860 D5
S Wellington St
7300 CTNL 80122 2365 A6
Wellington Lake Rd
200 PrkC 80456 2690 D3
3000 PrkC 80456 2691 A6
Wells Dr
600 BldC 80303 1688 D7
W Wells Pl
4700 DNVR 80204 2111 C6
Wells St
100 ERIE 80516 1607 C4
E Wells St
900 DgsC 80108 2619 C7
Wells Wy
1500 LGMT 80501 1356 B7
Wells Fargo Ct
10 PrkC 80456 2522 A5
Wellshire Cir
1100 BMFD 80020 1775 A6
Wellshire Ct
7900 BldC 80503 1520 E4
Welsh Ct
800 LSVL 80027 1689 B7
Welsh Pl
4000 BldC 80301 1602 E5
Welton St
1100 DNVR 80204 2112 D5
1300 DNVR 80202 2112 D5
1900 DNVR 80205 2112 E4
2600 DNVR 80205 2113 A3
Wembley Pl
7200 DgsC 80108 2535 A7
S Wenatchee Ct
6400 AURA 80016 2370 C3
Wenatchee Ct
10 LCHB 80603 1698 C3
S Wenatchee St
- AURA 80016 2370 C3
5100 AphC 80015 2286 C7
5500 AphC 80015 2370 C1
S Wenatchee Wy
7100 AURA 80016 2370 C5

Wendeleen Wy
10 BldC 80302 1600 D6
Wenlock Ct
400 CSRK 80104 2787 D2
Wentworth Ct
8700 LNTR 80124 2451 B3
Werchester St
- CMCY 80022 1864 A5
Werner Ln
2000 JfnC 80439 2189 B7
E Wesley Av
- AphC 80231 2198 C7
- AphC 80231 2199 A7
- DNVR 80231 2198 C7
10 DNVR 80210 2196 E7
10 DNVR 80223 2196 E7
3800 DNVR 80210 2197 E7
4000 DNVR 80222 2197 E7
6300 DNVR 80222 2198 B7
6800 DNVR 80224 2198 C7
12400 AURA 80014 2199 E7
14300 AURA 80014 2200 C7
15900 AURA 80013 2200 E7
17000 AURA 80013 2201 A7
W Wesley Av
10 DNVR 80210 2196 D7
900 DNVR 80223 2196 C7
2000 DNVR 80219 2196 B7
2000 EGLD 80110 2196 B7
3300 DNVR 80219 2195 E7
9400 LKWD 80227 2194 B7
13300 LKWD 80228 2193 B7
W Wesley Cir
14300 LKWD 80228 2193 A7
14300 LKWD 80228 2277 A1
W Wesley Ct
9700 LKWD 80227 2194 B7
E Wesley Dr
- AphC 80231 2198 E7
- AphC 80231 2199 A7
- AURA 80013 2201 D7
W Wesley Dr
9200 LKWD 80227 2194 C7
E Wesley Pl
4800 DNVR 80222 2198 A7
12600 AURA 80014 2199 C7
14300 AURA 80014 2200 B7
19700 AURA 80013 2201 D7
W Wesley Pl
8600 LKWD 80227 2194 C7
12600 JfnC 80228 2193 C7
E Wessex Cir
300 DgsC 80126 2448 E4
West Dr
- NHGN 80234 1860 C4
- SRDN 80110 2280 A4
- WSTR 80234 1860 C4
200 GOLD 80403 2107 C2
West Ln
10 PrkC 80456 2607 E5
West St
10 GOLD 80401 2192 B1
300 LSVL 80027 1773 C1
26100 JfnC 80433 2442 A5
Westbrook Ln
3100 DgsC 80129 2448 A3
3300 DgsC 80129 2447 E3
S Westbury Cir
9700 DgsC 80129 2448 C5
S Westbury Ct
9800 DgsC 80129 2448 C5
S Westbury Wy
9600 DgsC 80129 2448 C4
Westchester Cir
900 DgsC 80108 2618 C1
Westchester Dr
2400 AdmC 80221 1944 A6
N Westcliff Pkwy
- WSTR 80021 1858 E7
9700 JfnC 80021 1943 A1
9700 WSTR 80021 1859 A7
9700 WSTR 80021 1943 A1
Westcliff Pl
10500 DgsC 80130 2449 B7
Westcliff Wy
10500 DgsC 80130 2449 B7
Westcroft Av
5900 CSRK 80104 2704 E7
5900 CSRK 80104 2705 A7
Western Av
- BldC 80301 1687 C2
- BLDR 80301 1687 C2
Western Ct
28500 JfnC 80439 2273 D5
Western Dr
28700 JfnC 80439 2273 C5
Western Ln
28900 JfnC 80439 2273 C5
Western Evening Ct
4700 CSRK 80109 2702 B2
West Fork Rd
8300 BldC 80302 1518 B1
Westgate Av
2600 DgsC 80126 2449 C7
E Westglow Ln
800 GDVL 80121 2365 A1
800 LITN 80121 2365 A1
Westhampton Ct
13900 BMFD 80020 1775 D4
Westhampton Pt
14000 BMFD 80020 1775 D3
Westhaven Pl
3300 DgsC 80126 2533 D1
Westin Dr
1400 ERIE 80516 1607 A7
Westlake Ct
2600 LGMT 80503 1355 C5
Westlake Dr
- BMFD 80020 1775 E5
2100 LGMT 80503 1355 C5
Westlake Pl
13000 BMFD 80020 1775 E6
Westminster Blvd
- BMFD 80020 1858 E4

STREET
Block City ZIP Map# Grid

Westminster Blvd
- JfnC 80021 1943 A1
- WSTR 80020 1858 E4
- WSTR 80020 1943 A1
- WSTR 80021 1943 A1
10300 WSTR 80020 1859 A5
Westminster Pl
3300 WSTR 80030 1943 E7
N Westmoor Cir
- BMFD 80021 1857 E4
- WSTR 80021 1857 E4
Westmoor Dr
- BMFD 80021 1857 E4
- JfnC 80021 1857 E4
- WSTR 80021 1857 E4
10000 WSTR 80021 1858 A5
E Weston Av
5300 CSRK 80104 2788 E1
Weston Cir
- ERIE 80516 1606 E7
Weston Dr
- ERIE 80516 1607 A7
Weston Rd
600 DgsC 80118 2954 E2
Weston St
3000 DNVR 80216 2112 D1
Westridge Dr
- BldC 80301 1603 C3
Westridge Rd
24700 JfnC 80403 1938 C3
25200 ARVD 80403 1938 C3
W Westridge Knolls Av
- DgsC 80129 2448 C4
Westridge Knolls Ln
- DgsC 80129 2448 C4
S Westridge Knolls Ln
- DgsC 80129 2448 C3
S Westridge Village Pkwy
- DgsC 80129 2448 A6
W Westridge Village Pkwy
- DgsC 80129 2448 A6
Westside Cir
10000 DgsC 80125 2531 A6
Westside Ct
10000 DgsC 80125 2530 D6
10000 DgsC 80125 2531 A5
Westside St
8000 DgsC 80125 2530 E6
8100 DgsC 80125 2531 A6
Westview Av
22300 JfnC 80401 2191 A1
Westview Cir
6100 DgsC 80134 2621 C4
Westview Ct
300 LGMT 80501 1439 E2
1000 LAFT 80026 1690 B4
Westview Dr
800 BldC 80303 1688 B3
1500 BldC 80301 1688 B3
7700 LKWD 80214 2110 D6
West View Rd
10 BldC 80516 1523 B7
E Westview Rd
9000 LNTR 80124 2451 A1
S Westview St
6000 LITN 80120 2364 D2
Westward Dr
1600 LAFT 80026 1689 D2
Westway Dr
21100 JfnC 80465 2359 C4
Westwind Ln
8700 DgsC 80126 2449 C2
Westwood Ct
3100 BLDR 80304 1602 E7
Westwood Dr
400 DNVR 80206 2113 B7
West Woods Cir
6400 ARVD 80007 2024 D2
Wetherill Cir
8100 DgsC 80108 2534 D5
Wetterborn Rd
1600 TNTN 80260 1860 B7
Wetterhorn Wy
100 LGMT 80501 1356 C6
Wewatta St
- DNVR 80202 2112 D3
- DNVR 80216 2112 D3
1400 DNVR 80204 2112 C3
Wewoka Dr
400 BldC 80303 1688 E5
Wexford Rd
9100 BldC 80303 1689 C3
Whale Rock Wy
5800 JfnC 80465 2360 D2
Whaley Dr
6000 BldC 80303 1688 B7
Wharton Ct
2500 ERIE 80516 1690 D2
Wheat Av
- LAFT 80026 1690 A4
Wheat Berry Ct
2000 ERIE 80516 1606 E6
Wheat Berry Dr
300 ERIE 80516 1606 D6
Wheatfield Ln
- BGTN 80601 1697 C4
10700 PARK 80138 2454 C7
10700 PARK 80138 2538 B1
Wheatgrass Cir
- PARK 80134 2452 E1
8300 PARK 80134 2453 A1
Wheatlands Pkwy E
- AphC 80016 2370 E4
- AphC 80016 2371 A3
- AURA 80016 2370 E4
- AURA 80016 2371 A3
S Wheeler Ct
9200 DgsC 80126 2449 B4
S Wheeling Cir
1400 AURA 80012 2200 A5
Wheeling Ct
12200 AdmC 80640 1864 A1
S Wheeling Ct
7700 AphC 80112 2368 A7
Wheeling St
1500 AURA 80010 2116 A4
3700 AdmC 80239 2116 A1
3700 AURA 80011 2116 A1
3700 DNVR 80011 2116 A1
3700 DNVR 80239 2116 A1
5100 DNVR 80239 2032 A5
10700 CMCY 80022 1864 A5
12000 AdmC 80601 1864 A1
12000 CMCY 80601 1864 A1
S Wheeling St
400 AURA 80012 2200 A3
3300 AURA 80014 2284 A2
Wheeling Wy
5000 DNVR 80239 2032 A5
S Wheeling Wy
300 AURA 80012 2200 A2
2700 AURA 80014 2284 A1
Wheel Park Cir
- AURA 80013 2200 D7
Whiles Ct
500 ERIE 80516 1607 A6
E Whimbrel Dr
4600 DgsC 80126 2449 E2
4600 DgsC 80126 2450 A2
4700 DgsC 80130 2450 A2
Whippoorwill Dr
1500 LKWD 80215 2109 C5
Whippoorwill St
12500 BMFD 80020 1775 D7
12500 BMFD 80020 1859 C2
Whippoorwill Wy
4300 CSRK 80109 2702 C4
Whirlaway Av
21600 PARK 80138 2538 B1
Whirlaway Tr
27600 JfnC 80439 2357 D7
27600 JfnC 80439 2441 E1
Whiskey Jay Hill Rd
10 CCkC 80439 2272 A7
Whisper Ct
8500 DgsC 80125 2533 A5
Whisper Canyon Rd
12900 DgsC 80108 2534 C6
Whispering Ct
- EbtC 80107 2709 D4
Whispering Oak Dr
600 CSRK 80104 2703 D4
Whispering Pine Ct
- EbtC 80107 2709 D4
Whispering Pine Pl
35600 EbtC 80107 2709 C4
Whispering Pines
10 BldC 80302 1600 E3
E Whispering Pines Dr
10300 DgsC 80138 2455 B3
Whispering Pines Pl
30500 EbtC 80117 2796 D6
Whispering Pines Tr
34400 JfnC 80470 2608 A6
Whispering Woods
23000 JfnC 80401 2190 E4
23000 JfnC 80401 2191 A4
Whistlepig Dr
- BMFD 80020 1775 A3
Whistlepig Ln
1700 BMFD 80020 1775 A4
Whistler Ct
31000 JfnC 80439 2189 A6
Whistler Dr
2300 LGMT 80501 1356 C5
Whistling Elk Dr
9900 JfnC 80127 2445 D6
E Whitaker Cir
- AURA 80016 2286 E6
18500 AURA 80015 2285 C7
E Whitaker Ct
- AURA 80016 2286 E6
Whitaker Dr
- AphC 80016 2287 A6
- AURA 80016 2286 D6
- AURA 80016 2287 A6
1000 EGLD 80110 2280 D7
E Whitaker Dr
13800 AURA 80015 2284 B6
17400 AURA 80015 2285 B6
E Whitaker Pl
14200 AURA 80015 2284 B6
19000 AURA 80015 2285 C6
19100 CTNL 80015 2285 C6
Whitby Ct
7100 DgsC 80108 2535 A7
White Ct
1900 CSRK 80104 2788 A1
S White Ct
4600 JfnC 80127 2278 A6
White Ln
1000 ERIE 80516 1607 B2
S White Ln
4600 JfnC 80127 2278 A6
White Pl
5400 BLDR 80303 1687 D3
S White Wy
4500 JfnC 80127 2278 A6
White Alder
10 JfnC 80127 2361 A7
White Ash Ct
21300 PARK 80138 2538 A2
White Ash Dr
1100 GOLD 80403 2107 C1
White Ash Ln
21100 PARK 80138 2538 A2
White Ash Pl
7400 DgsC 80134 2622 A4
White Bark Pn
3300 JfnC 80439 2273 A5
E White Bay Dr
3300 DgsC 80126 2449 D3
White Bear Ln
28800 JfnC 80433 2441 C7
White Birch
10 JfnC 80127 2445 B1
Whitechapel St
5700 CSRK 80104 2704 E6
S Whitecliff Pl
9600 DgsC 80129 2448 B4
W Whitecliff Wy
- DgsC 80129 2448 B4
S White Cloud Ct
8300 DgsC 80126 2449 A1
White Cloud Dr
12300 JfnC 80433 2526 D4
E White Cloud Dr
500 DgsC 80126 2448 E1
500 DgsC 80126 2449 A1
S White Cloud St
8300 DgsC 80126 2449 A1
White Deer Dr
12500 JfnC 80127 2445 D6
Whiteface Ct
30600 JfnC 80439 2189 A7
White Feather Dr
1700 LGMT 80501 1440 A2
White Fir Ct
10 JfnC 80127 2360 E7
Whitehall Dr
1200 LGMT 80501 1356 E6
1400 LGMT 80501 1357 A6
4700 CHLV 80111 2282 B6
E Whitehall Ln
4500 DgsC 80126 2449 E3
4500 DgsC 80126 2450 A3
Whitehaven Cir
100 DgsC 80129 2448 E6
White Hawk Dr
16100 PARK 80134 2536 E1
16200 PARK 80134 2452 E7
White Hawk Tr
14000 JfnC 80433 2611 D4
White Hawk Ranch Dr
1100 BldC 80303 1689 C3
White Horse Ln
8600 JfnC 80439 2441 D2
S White House Tr
4900 JfnC 80439 2273 E7
Whitekirk Pl
1000 CSRK 80104 2787 E2
E White Oak Ct
2700 LAFT 80026 1689 D2
S White Oak Ct
10000 DgsC 80129 2448 A6
W White Oak Ct
2700 LAFT 80026 1689 C2
White Oak Dr
- JfnC 80127 2361 A7
10 JfnC 80127 2445 A1
W White Oak Ln
3000 DgsC 80129 2448 A6
S White Oak Pl
10000 DgsC 80129 2448 A5
W White Oak St
2700 DgsC 80129 2448 A6
W White Oak Tr
2900 DgsC 80129 2448 A6
S White Oak Wy
10100 DgsC 80129 2448 A6
White Peaks Ct
2900 CSRK 80104 2704 B5
White Pelican Cir
10 TNTN 80241 1777 B6
S White Pelican Wy
9000 DgsC 80126 2449 E3
White Pine Ct
21300 PARK 80138 2538 A2
White Pine Dr
10 JfnC 80127 2361 B7
10 JfnC 80127 2445 C1
10400 DgsC 80134 2452 E6
10400 DgsC 80134 2453 A6
White Pine Ln
21100 PARK 80138 2538 A2
White Pine Pl
10 JfnC 80127 2361 B7
White Rabbit Tr
8500 JfnC 80127 2444 D2
White Raven Ln
- BMFD 80021 1773 B7
- SUPE 80027 1773 B7
White Rock Cir
4600 BldC 80301 1603 E3
4600 BLDR 80301 1603 E3
Whitestone Ct
- EbtC 80107 2709 D5
Whitestone Dr
16000 DgsC 80134 2452 E6
Whitetail Cir
2800 LAFT 80026 1774 C1
Whitetail Dr
1300 CSRK 80104 2703 E5
1300 CSRK 80104 2704 A5
N White Tail Dr
400 DgsC 80116 2707 B6
S White Tail Dr
10 DgsC 80116 2707 A7
200 DgsC 80116 2791 B1
White Tail Ln
9900 JfnC 80127 2445 D6
Whitewater Rd
- CCkC 80439 2102 B5
- IDSP 80439 2102 B5
Whitford Dr
3400 DgsC 80126 2533 D1
3500 DgsC 80126 2449 D7
S Whiting Wy
2900 AphC 80231 2282 E1
2900 DNVR 80231 2282 E1
3900 DNVR 80237 2282 E4
Whitlock Dr
- CSRK 80109 2702 E2
Whitman Dr
3000 JfnC 80439 2273 A2
Whitney Cir
- BMFD 80020 1775 E3
Whitney Pl
4200 BLDR 80305 1687 B7
S Whooping Crane Dr
11300 PARK 80134 2536 E1
S Wickerdale Ct
9400 DgsC 80130 2450 B4
E Wickerdale Ln
5400 DgsC 80130 2450 A4
E Wickerdale Pl
5500 DgsC 80130 2450 B4
Wicklow St
- BldC 80301 1689 C3
1200 BldC 80303 1689 C3
Wide Acres Rd
12000 JfnC 80401 2109 C6
12000 LKWD 80215 2109 C6
12400 LKWD 80401 2109 C6
Widgeon Dr
300 LGMT 80503 1438 D2
Widgeon Ln
300 LGMT 80503 1438 C2
Wieler Rd
1800 JfnC 80439 2189 D7
1800 JfnC 80439 2273 D1
Wier Wy
6300 ARVD 80403 2024 B2
E Wigan Ct
2300 DgsC 80126 2449 C4
E Wigeon Pl
16100 PARK 80134 2536 E1
Wiggett Ct
100 ERIE 80516 1606 E5
E Wiggins St
600 SUPE 80027 1773 A5
Wigham St
9100 TNTN 80229 1945 C2
9900 TNTN 80229 1861 C7
Wikiup Dr
- AdmC 80022 1946 C3
- AdmC 80640 1946 C3
- CMCY 80022 1946 C3
E Wikiup Dr
- AdmC 80022 1946 C3
W Wikiup Dr
- AdmC 80022 1946 B3
Wilcox St
10 CSRK 80104 2703 D6
S Wilcox St
10 CSRK 80104 2703 D7
400 CSRK 80104 2787 C1
Wild Alfalfa Pl
8300 PARK 80134 2452 D2
Wild Basin
11000 WldC 80504 1440 D3
Wild Basin Wy
- BMFD 80020 1775 C5
Wild Berry Ct
5700 DgsC 80134 2622 A3
Wild Berry Rd
16200 JfnC 80465 2360 D3
Wild Blossom Wy
1400 CSRK 80104 2704 B5
N Wildcat
7200 DgsC 80125 2614 D1
Wildcat Ct
5300 JfnC 80465 2360 C1
Wildcat Ln
10 BldC 80304 1601 D5
Wildcat Rdg
- DgsC 80124 2450 B6
S Wildcat St
8400 DgsC 80126 2448 E1
Wild Cat Mountain Rd
1500 CSRK 80109 2703 A5
Wildcat Reserve Pkwy
- DgsC 80126 2448 D6
- DgsC 80126 2450 A4
- DgsC 80129 2448 D6
- DgsC 80130 2450 A4
1800 DgsC 80126 2449 A6
4100 DgsC 80130 2449 D7
W Wildcat Reserve Pkwy
1700 DgsC 80129 2448 B5
E Wild Crocus Cir
9700 DgsC 80134 2622 E6
9700 DgsC 80134 2623 A6
Wild Dunes Ct
5300 BLDR 80301 1604 D1
N Wilder Ct
6100 DgsC 80134 2622 E2
Wilderman Pl
1700 AURA 80011 2116 B4
Wilderness Dr
12200 EbtC 80117 2796 E7
Wilderness Pl
- EbtC 80117 2796 D7
2800 BLDR 80301 1687 A1
2900 BLDR 80301 1603 B7
4700 DgsC 80134 2621 A6
Wilderness Cornerstone Rd
100 CCkC 80439 2271 D4
Wildewood Dr
10 NDLD 80466 1765 E3
10 NDLD 80466 1766 A3
Wildewood Ln
10 NDLD 80466 1765 E4
Wildfield Ln
10000 DgsC 80125 2532 B2
Wildfire Cir
1700 DgsC 80104 2871 E1
Wildfire Ct
1200 LGMT 80503 1438 B5
Wild Flower Ct
10 BldC 80466 1767 D3
Wildflower Ct
- BldC 80303 1771 D3
1500 BGTN 80601 1780 C2
4100 JfnC 80439 2273 A5
Wild Flower Dr
- AdmC 80601 1780 D2
1100 BGTN 80601 1780 D2
Wildflower Dr
- BGTN 80601 1780 D2
Wildflower Ln
9000 DgsC 80116 2706 D3
Wildflower Pl
1500 BGTN 80601 1780 C1
8400 LNTR 80124 2450 E3
Wildflower St
13300 BMFD 80020 1775 E6
Wild Flower Tr
26000 JfnC 80439 2274 A7
N Wildflowers Wy
4500 CSRK 80109 2702 E1
Wildgoose Ln
7400 BldC 80503 1520 A3
Wild Gulch Ct
9400 DgsC 80138 2538 E3
Wild Horse Cir
200 BldC 80304 1601 D4
Wild Horse Ln
10500 DgsC 80125 2530 E5
Wildhorse Rdg
- DNVR 80249 2033 C3
W Wildhorse Peak
11100 JfnC 80127 2361 C7
Wildhurst Cir
10500 DgsC 80126 2449 C7
S Wilding Ct
3100 DNVR 80231 2282 E2
S Wild Iris Run
8800 DgsC 80126 2449 B3
Wildlife Pl
1700 LGMT 80501 1357 A6
Wildlife Wy
10000 DgsC 80125 2531 A2
Wildmill Cir
2200 EbtC 80107 2624 E7
2200 EbtC 80107 2625 A7
Wild Plum Cir
16200 JfnC 80465 2360 D2
Wild Plum Ct
3700 BldC 80304 1602 B6
3700 BLDR 80304 1602 B6
Wild Plum Ln
- CSRK 80104 2703 E4
Wild Ridge Cir
600 LAFT 80026 1690 D3
Wildridge Ct
10700 PARK 80138 2454 C7
Wild Ridge Ln
500 LAFT 80026 1690 C3
Wild Rose Cir
3100 EbtC 80138 2541 A5
Wild Rose Ct
1500 GOLD 80403 2107 C2
Wildrose Ct
500 LSVL 80027 1689 B7
1300 LGMT 80503 1438 B6
8700 DgsC 80126 2449 A2
Wild Rose Dr
28200 JfnC 80439 2273 C4
Wildrose Dr
1400 LGMT 80503 1438 B6
S Wild Rose Ln
6700 JfnC 80439 2357 E5
6700 JfnC 80439 2358 A4
Wildrose Pl
3600 LGMT 80503 1438 B6
Wild Rose Rd
500 BLDR 80302 1686 C5
Wildrose Tr
10 CHLV 80113 2281 C3
Wildrose Wy
500 LSVL 80027 1689 B7
Wildrye Cir
8600 DgsC 80134 2452 E2
8600 PARK 80134 2452 E2
Wild Rye Ct
1600 CSRK 80109 2703 B5
Wild Star Wy
1700 CSRK 80104 2704 B5
Wild Tiger Ln
10 BldC 80302 1684 B2
Wild Tiger Rd
10 BldC 80302 1684 B1
Wild Trout Tr
12400 JfnC 80127 2528 A4
12400 JfnC 80433 2528 A4
Wild Turkey Ln
10 JfnC 80127 2361 A4
Wild Turkey Tr
10 BldC 80302 1600 C6
6300 JfnC 80465 2360 A4
Wildwood Cir
1200 BLDR 80305 1686 D7
Wildwood Ct
1300 BLDR 80305 1770 D1
Wildwood Ln
10 BldC 80304 1601 E4
1300 CSRK 80104 2703 E5
1300 CSRK 80104 2704 A5
1400 BLDR 80305 1770 E1
Wildwood Rd
1100 BLDR 80305 1686 E7
1200 BLDR 80305 1770 D1
Wildwoods
31000 JfnC 80439 2273 A3
Wiley Cir
8500 AdmC 80031 1943 C4
8500 WSTR 80031 1943 C4
S Wiley Ct
900 SUPE 80027 1773 A5
E Wiley Pl
17000 PARK 80134 2453 A7
Wilkerson Rd
25200 JfnC 80433 2442 B4
Wilkerson Wy
1300 LGMT 80501 1356 E7
Wilkins Rd
10 PrkC 80456 2521 C2
Wilkson
10 PrkC 80456 2521 D2
S Willa Ln
6800 JfnC 80439 2358 C5
Willa Wy
7200 JfnC 80439 2358 C6
E Willamette Pl
21300 CTNL 80015 2286 A7
Willard Loop Dr
- BLDR 80302 1686 E4
E William St
100 SUPE 80027 1772 D4
W William St
- SUPE 80027 1772 E4
400 BldC 80027 1772 E4
S William Cody Dr
8600 JfnC 80439 2441 D2
E Williamette Av
20500 AphC 80015 2285 E7
20500 AphC 80015 2286 A7
20500 CTNL 80015 2285 E7
20500 CTNL 80015 2286 A7
E Williamette Ln
2600 GDVL 80121 2281 C7
19900 CTNL 80015 2285 E7
S Williams Cir
5100 GDVL 80121 2281 B7
8000 CTNL 80122 2365 B7
S Williams Cir E
6500 CTNL 80121 2365 B4
S Williams Cir W
6600 CTNL 80121 2365 B4
Williams Ct
1800 ERIE 80516 1690 C2
9600 TNTN 80229 1945 B1
9800 TNTN 80229 1861 B7
S Williams Ct
8000 CTNL 80122 2365 B7
S Williams Dr
5100 GDVL 80121 2281 B7
Williams St
400 DNVR 80218 2113 B7
2100 DNVR 80205 2113 B3
3900 DNVR 80205 2029 B7
4600 DNVR 80216 2029 B6
7400 AdmC 80229 1945 B6
10000 TNTN 80229 1861 B7
10400 NHGN 80233 1861 B6
13400 TNTN 80241 1777 B5
14900 TNTN 80602 1777 B2
S Williams St
200 DNVR 80209 2197 B2
1000 DNVR 80210 2197 B4
2400 DNVR 80210 2281 B1
3100 DvrC 80210 2281 B2
3100 EGLD 80113 2281 B2
6300 CTNL 80121 2365 B3
7500 CTNL 80122 2365 B6
Williams Wy
10000 TNTN 80229 1861 B7
11800 NHGN 80233 1861 B2
S Williams Wy
8000 CTNL 80122 2365 B7
Williams Fork Tr
5100 BldC 80301 1604 A2
S Williamson Dr
20100 PARK 80138 2537 E1
Willie's Ln
10 GpnC 80474 1849 E1
Willobe Wy
800 JfnC 80401 2191 A4
Willodene Dr
1500 LGMT 80501 1356 C6
Willow Av
16000 AdmC 80602 1694 E5
Willow Cir
- DNVR 80230 2114 E7
- TNTN 80260 1944 C1
S Willow Cir
3700 DNVR 80237 2282 E3
7500 CTNL 80112 2366 E6
7500 CTNL 80112 2367 A6
Willow Ct
500 LCHB 80603 1698 D3
1000 LGMT 80503 1438 C5
2000 LKWD 80215 2109 C4
2400 LGMT 80503 1355 C4
5200 CSRK 80104 2704 E7
S Willow Ct
1600 AphC 80231 2198 E5
2800 DNVR 80231 2282 E1
7900 CTNL 80112 2366 C5
W Willow Ct
500 LSVL 80027 1689 B6
Willow Ct N
100 BMFD 80020 1858 E2
100 BMFD 80020 1859 A2
Willow Ct S
100 BMFD 80020 1858 E2
100 BMFD 80020 1859 A2
Willow Dr
- TNTN 80260 1944 C1
100 LCHB 80603 1698 C3
S Willow Dr
5900 GDVL 80111 2366 E2
6000 GDVL 80111 2367 A2
Willow Ln
10 GpnC 80403 1850 D7
1700 LKWD 80215 2109 C4
6100 BldC 80301 1603 E3
6100 BldC 80301 1604 A3
8200 BldC 80503 1521 A5
12500 JfnC 80401 2109 C4
Willow Pl
100 BMFD 80020 1859 C2
500 LCHB 80603 1698 C3
1000 LAFT 80026 1690 B5
1000 LSVL 80027 1688 E7
Willow Pl N
100 BMFD 80020 1858 E2
100 BMFD 80020 1859 C2
Willow Pl S
100 BMFD 80020 1858 E3
100 BMFD 80020 1859 C2
Willow St
- LGMT 80501 1439 C6
1100 DNVR 80220 2114 E4
1100 DNVR 80230 2114 E4
2600 DNVR 80238 2114 E2
8600 AdmC 80022 1946 E3
8600 CMCY 80022 1946 E3
8700 AdmC 80640 1946 E3
Willow St
16200 AdmC 80602 1694 E5
N Willow St
10 CSRK 80104 2704 E7
S Willow St
- CTNL 80112 2451 A1
1100 AphC 80247 2198 E4
1100 DNVR 80247 2198 E4
2900 DNVR 80231 2282 E2
3400 DNVR 80237 2282 E3
6700 CTNL 80112 2366 E4
8300 LNTR 80124 2451 A1
W Willow St
500 LSVL 80027 1689 A7
900 BldC 80027 1689 A7
1000 BldC 80027 1688 E7
1000 LSVL 80027 1688 E7
Willow Wy
1600 JfnC 80401 2109 C5
S Willow Wy
3800 DNVR 80237 2282 E4
3800 DNVR 80237 2283 A4
5900 GDVL 80111 2367 A2
7500 CTNL 80112 2366 E6
7800 CTNL 80112 2367 A7
Willow Bend Ct
8000 BldC 80301 1688 E1
Willowbend Ln
20200 PARK 80138 2537 E3
20600 PARK 80138 2538 A3
Willowbridge Ct
10200 DgsC 80126 2449 D7
Willowbridge Wy
10200 DgsC 80126 2449 D6
E Willowbrook Av
23800 PARK 80138 2538 D1
Willowbrook Cir
2000 ERIE 80516 1606 D6
Willowbrook Dr
1400 LGMT 80501 1357 A6
5600 JfnC 80465 2360 E2
5800 JfnC 80465 2361 A3
Willowbrook Ln
15100 JfnC 80465 2360 E2
Willowbrook Rd
700 BLDR 80302 1686 B4
Willow Broom Tr
6400 DgsC 80125 2614 D2
Willow Creek Cir
1000 LGMT 80503 1438 B5
Willow Creek Ct
8000 BldC 80301 1688 E1
Willow Creek Dr
- BldC 80503 1438 B5
1600 BldC 80301 1688 E2
1600 BldC 80303 1688 E2
2100 BldC 80301 1689 A1
2100 GOLD 80401 2108 A4
3100 LGMT 80503 1438 B5
Willow Creek Rd
9500 JfnC 80465 2443 C4
E Willow Creek Rd
4000 DgsC 80104 2788 D3
4000 DgsC 80104 2789 A4
S Willow Creek St
8400 DgsC 80126 2449 A1
Willow Glen Ct
200 BldC 80302 1686 B2
Willowherb Ln
23700 JfnC 80401 2190 D5
W Willowick Cir
100 DgsC 80129 2448 D4
Willow Lake Dr
100 DgsC 80116 2705 C7
Willowleaf Dr
10 JfnC 80127 2361 A6
E Willowmore Ct
6100 DgsC 80130 2450 B2
Willow Oak
10 JfnC 80127 2361 B7
S Willow Park Ct
10800 PARK 80138 2538 B2
Willow Park Dr
- PARK 80138 2454 A7
- PARK 80138 2538 A1
Willow Park Pl
21100 PARK 80138 2538 B2
Willow Reed Cir E
10800 PARK 80134 2453 B6
Willow Reed Cir W
10800 PARK 80134 2453 B6
Willow Reed Ct
10700 PARK 80134 2453 A7
Willowrun Ct
3400 CSRK 80109 2702 D3
Willowrun Dr
2900 CSRK 80109 2702 C3
Willowrun Ln
4200 CSRK 80109 2702 D3
Willow Run Pkwy
- BMFD 80020 1776 A7
- BMFD 80234 1776 A7
- WSTR 80234 1776 A7
Willows Pl
8400 PARK 80134 2453 A1
Willow Springs Dr
6300 JfnC 80465 2360 D3
Willow Springs Rd
4800 JfnC 80465 2276 C7
4800 MRSN 80465 2276 C7
4900 JfnC 80465 2360 C1
Willow Springs Rd CO-48
4800 JfnC 80465 2276 C7
4800 MRSN 80465 2276 C7
4900 JfnC 80465 2360 C1
Willowstone Pl
9900 DgsC 80134 2452 E5
Willowstone St
16100 DgsC 80134 2452 E5
Willow Wood Ct
13900 BMFD 80020 1775 B4
16400 JfnC 80465 2360 D1
Willow Wood Dr
5400 JfnC 80465 2360 D2

STREET Block City ZIP Map# Grid

Willow Wood Dr
13900 BMFD 80020 1775 B4
S Wilmington Ct
9300 DgsC 80130 2450 D4
Wilson Cir
1700 ERIE 80516 1606 E6
11400 PARK 80134 2537 D2
Wilson Ct
1600 BLDR 80304 1602 C5
3000 DNVR 80205 2113 D2
7300 WSTR 80030 1943 D6
Wilson Dr
- SRDN 80110 2280 A3
Wilson Pl
1400 LSVL 80027 1689 C6
Wilson Rd
- PrkC 80456 2521 C2
9800 TNTN 80260 1860 B7
Wilson St
300 LAFT 80026 1690 B4
E Wiltshire Ct
7200 DgsC 80130 2450 D4
7200 LNTR 80124 2450 D4
S Wiltshire Dr
9200 DgsC 80130 2450 D3
9200 LNTR 80124 2450 D3
9300 DgsC 80124 2450 D3
E Wiltshire Pl
7200 DgsC 80130 2450 D3
S Wimbledon Ct
9700 DgsC 80126 2449 A5
Winchester Cir
6700 BLDR 80301 1604 B1
7000 BldC 80503 1520 B7
7000 BLDR 80301 1520 B7
Winchester Rd
36000 EbtC 80107 2708 D2
N Winchester Wy
13100 DgsC 80138 2454 E2
13100 DgsC 80138 2455 A2
Windchant Cir
3700 DgsC 80104 2871 C2
E Windcrest Row
7600 DgsC 80134 2622 A1
Windemere Ln
10 BldC 80303 1688 E6
Winder Pl
24300 JfnC 80403 1938 D3
S Windermere Cir
6100 LITN 80120 2364 C3
S Windermere St
3700 EGLD 80110 2280 C4
4800 EGLD 80120 2280 C7
4800 LITN 80120 2280 C7
5300 LITN 80120 2364 C1
S Windermere Wy
6000 LITN 80120 2364 C2
N Windfield Av
6300 DgsC 80134 2622 B2
Windflower Dr
800 LGMT 80501 1440 A1
Windflower Ln
- DgsC 80124 2450 A7
5200 DgsC 80130 2450 A7
28800 JfnC 80433 2441 C7
E Windfont Row
7700 DgsC 80134 2622 A2
E Windford St
7400 DgsC 80134 2622 A1
N Windham St
- DgsC 80134 2622 A2
Windhaven Dr
8300 DgsC 80134 2622 C5
N Windhollow Ct
6400 DgsC 80134 2622 A2
E Winding Av
- DgsC 80124 2451 B4
- LNTR 80124 2451 B4
Winding Dr
2400 BldC 80504 1356 C4
2400 LGMT 80501 1356 C4
Winding River Ct
14000 BMFD 80020 1776 B4
Winding River Dr
2500 BMFD 80020 1776 A4
Winding River Rd
- BMFD 80020 1776 B4
Winding Trail Dr
- LGMT 80501 1356 C5
2700 BLDR 80304 1602 E5
3700 BldC 80301 1602 E6
3700 BLDR 80301 1602 E6
Winding Trail Village
- BLDR 80304 1602 D5
E Windlawn Wy
7300 DgsC 80134 2621 E1
7300 DgsC 80134 2622 A2
Windler St
- BGTN 80601 1696 D4
N Windloch Cir
6500 DgsC 80134 2622 B2
Windmill Dr
- LGMT 80501 1356 C4
4200 BGTN 80601 1697 C5
Windmill Pl
700 DgsC 80126 2449 A2
Windmill Rd
200 DgsC 80108 2619 B5
N Windmont Av
6300 DgsC 80134 2622 B1
Windom Dr
1500 JfnC 80439 2188 D6
Windom Ln
- BMFD 80020 1775 C4
Windom Rd
2000 TNTN 80260 1860 B7
Windom Peak Dr
900 SUPE 80027 1857 A1
Windom Peak Wy
6100 DgsC 80108 2618 D2
Windover Rd
10 GDVL 80121 2281 A7
10 GDVL 80121 2365 A1

Window Rock Ln
6600 JfnC 80465 2360 D4
N Windpoint Cir
6700 DgsC 80134 2622 A1
Windridge Cir
2800 DgsC 80126 2449 C7
Windridge Ct
10700 DgsC 80126 2449 D7
Windriver Tr
3700 CSRK 80109 2702 D3
Wind Rose Pl
- CSRK 80108 2704 C4
Windrow Ln
2400 LAFT 80027 1689 D4
Windrower Ct
- BGTN 80601 1697 D4
Windsong Ct
5400 JfnC 80465 2360 D1
Windsor Dr
3400 AURA 80011 2117 D1
7300 BldC 80301 1604 C2
7300 BLDR 80301 1604 C2
S Windsor Dr
100 DNVR 80219 2195 C2
S Windsor St
7000 AphC 80128 2363 C5
S Windsor Wy
9200 DgsC 80126 2449 B3
Windstream
- AphC 80231 2199 A7
- DNVR 80231 2199 A7
Windstream Ln
3100 EbtC 80107 2709 A2
N Windview Cir
6800 DgsC 80134 2622 A1
N Windwood Cir
7300 DgsC 80134 2621 D1
7300 DgsC 80134 2622 A1
E Windwood Wy
7100 DgsC 80134 2621 E1
7300 DgsC 80134 2622 A1
Windy Ct
5900 JfnC 80403 2024 B3
Windy St
5800 JfnC 80403 2024 B3
5900 ARVD 80403 2024 B3
Winegate Av
500 BLDR 80304 1602 B2
Winfield Cir
1600 LKWD 80215 2109 C5
Winfield Dr
1800 LKWD 80215 2109 D4
Winfield Pl
13200 JfnC 80401 2109 B5
Winged Foot Ct
6400 DgsC 80118 2868 D7
Winged Foot Wy
10 CBVL 80123 2363 D4
Winger Dr
10 BldC 80466 1767 B1
Wing Foot Dr
30100 JfnC 80439 2273 B2
Wingler Pl
2200 BGTN 80601 1696 E7
Wingtip Wy
- CSRK 80108 2704 B3
N Winnebago Dr
2800 DgsC 80135 2700 B1
W Winnebago Wy
6500 DgsC 80135 2700 C1
S Winnipeg Cir
6700 AURA 80016 2370 C4
S Winnipeg Ct
6500 AURA 80016 2370 D3
8200 AURA 80016 2454 C1
Winnipeg St
200 LCHB 80603 1698 C3
S Winnipeg St
- AphC 80015 2370 C1
Winona Cir
12600 BMFD 80020 1775 C7
Winona Ct
10 DNVR 80219 2195 C1
400 DNVR 80219 2111 C7
1200 DNVR 80204 2111 C5
3800 DNVR 80212 2111 C1
4100 DNVR 80212 2027 C7
5300 AdmC 80212 2027 C5
6400 ARVD 80003 2027 C2
7200 WSTR 80030 1943 C7
8800 AdmC 80031 1943 C3
9200 WSTR 80031 1943 C2
10800 WSTR 80031 1859 C5
12500 BMFD 80020 1859 C1
N Winona Ct
9000 WSTR 80031 1943 C2
11600 WSTR 80031 1859 C3
S Winona Ct
10 DNVR 80219 2195 C1
2600 DNVR 80219 2279 C1
2700 DNVR 80236 2279 C1
Winona Dr
12200 BMFD 80020 1859 C1
Winona Pl
4400 BMFD 80020 1859 C1
Winona St
5300 AdmC 80212 2027 C5
6300 ARVD 80003 2027 C2
6800 ARVD 80030 2027 C1
N Winona St
9900 WSTR 80031 1859 C7
S Winona Wy
1400 DNVR 80219 2195 C5
S Winrock St
8900 DgsC 80126 2448 C3
S Winrow Ct
9100 DgsC 80126 2449 D3
Winslow Cir
1100 LGMT 80501 1439 E2
Winslow Ct
1500 ERIE 80516 1607 A5
S Winston Dr
1300 JfnC 80401 2191 A5

S Winston St
2900 AURA 80013 2284 D1
S Winter Tr
12300 JfnC 80433 2527 C4
Winter Wy
- LNTR 80124 2450 E3
2600 EbtC 80138 2456 E4
2600 EbtC 80138 2457 A4
Winter Berry Dr
8300 DgsC 80108 2534 D5
Winter Berry Ln
7100 DgsC 80108 2534 D5
Winter Berry Pl
- DgsC 80108 2534 D5
Winter Cress
10 JfnC 80127 2360 E5
Winterflower Wy
10400 DgsC 80134 2452 D6
Wintergate Cir
1100 DgsC 80104 2871 D1
Wintergreen Dr
11200 PARK 80138 2538 C1
S Wintergreen Pkwy
- DgsC 80134 2453 A4
- PARK 80134 2453 A4
Wintergreen Wy
22000 PARK 80138 2538 C1
Winterhawk Cir
3500 DgsC 80104 2871 C1
Winterleaf Ct
15400 DgsC 80134 2452 D6
E Winterpark Av
17400 AURA 80011 2117 B7
Winter Ridge Cir
6900 DgsC 80108 2534 C5
Winter Ridge Ct
6800 DgsC 80108 2534 C5
Winter Ridge Dr
7000 DgsC 80108 2534 D5
Winter Ridge Ln
6900 DgsC 80108 2534 C5
Winter Ridge Pl
6900 DgsC 80108 2534 C5
E Winter Springs Pl
23800 PARK 80138 2538 E1
Wintersweet Ct
10500 DgsC 80134 2453 A6
Wintersweet Pl
10500 DgsC 80134 2453 A6
W Winterthur Cir
400 DgsC 80129 2448 D5
S Winterthur Ct
10000 DgsC 80129 2448 E5
W Winterthur Wy
- DgsC 80126 2448 E5
300 DgsC 80129 2448 E5
Winthrop Cir
6800 CSRK 80104 2705 B7
7000 CSRK 80104 2789 A1
Winthrop Ct
7100 CSRK 80104 2705 B7
Winton Dr
400 DgsC 80108 2619 B5
Winton Wy
- LAFT 80026 1690 D6
Winwood Dr
10 CHLV 80113 2281 B6
W Wisconsin Av
9000 LKWD 80232 2194 C5
11100 JfnC 80232 2193 E5
W Wisconsin Dr
12000 JfnC 80232 2193 D5
12000 LKWD 80228 2193 D5
Wise Rd
10 PrkC 80456 2521 D3
Wisp Ln
10 PrkC 80456 2607 E4
Wisp Creek Dr
10 PrkC 80456 2607 D3
Wistera Wy
- BMFD 80020 1775 B2
S Wisteria Ct
3800 DNVR 80237 2282 E4
Wisteria Dr
2400 ERIE 80516 1692 A3
Wisteria Wy
300 LAFT 80026 1689 D4
S Wisteria Wy
4000 DNVR 80237 2282 E4
4000 DNVR 80237 2283 A4
Witney Pl
7800 DgsC 80124 2450 E6
Witteman Rd
30800 JfnC 80433 2525 A4
Witten Ct
17300 PARK 80134 2453 A7
Witter Gulch Rd
10 CCkC 80439 2272 A5
200 CCkC 80439 2271 E5
4300 CCkC 80439 2187 A7
4300 CCkC 80452 2187 A7
4300 CCkC 80452 2271 A1
Woburn Keep
10300 TNTN 80229 1861 B6
S Wodley Ct
8200 ARVD 80005 1941 D5
S Wolcott Ct
700 DNVR 80219 2195 C3
4400 DNVR 80236 2279 C5
Wolcott Ln
8800 AdmC 80031 1943 C3
Wolcott St
- CSRK 80104 2789 A1
S Wolcott Wy
1400 DNVR 80219 2195 C5
Wolf Ct
12300 BMFD 80020 1859 C1
S Wolf Ct
6700 AphC 80123 2363 C4
Wolf Rd
10 GpnC 80403 1934 A7
10 PrkC 80456 2521 E2
Wolf Creek Dr
900 BldC 80501 1439 E1

Wolf Creek Dr
900 LGMT 80501 1356 E7
900 LGMT 80501 1439 E1
2400 BGTN 80601 1696 E7
S Wolf Creek St
10 AURA 80011 2201 C1
Wolf Creek Tr
100 BMFD 80020 1774 E5
Wolfdale Dr
9200 LNTR 80124 2450 D3
Wolfe Ct
11500 WSTR 80031 1859 C3
S Wolfe Ct
9400 DgsC 80129 2448 C4
S Wolfe Dr
9300 DgsC 80129 2448 C4
S Wolfe Pl
9300 DgsC 80129 2448 C4
Wolfe St
- WSTR 80031 1859 C4
S Wolfe St
9300 DgsC 80129 2448 B4
Wolfensberger Ct
1900 DgsC 80109 2786 B1
Wolfensberger Rd
- CSRK 80104 2703 C5
10 CSRK 80109 2703 C5
E Wolfensberger Rd
100 CSRK 80109 2703 A6
100 DgsC 80109 2703 A6
W Wolfensberger Rd
10 CSRK 80109 2703 A7
10 DgsC 80109 2702 E7
10 DgsC 80109 2703 A7
10 DgsC 80109 2786 D1
1100 DgsC 80135 2786 D1
2600 DgsC 80109 2701 D7
2800 DgsC 80135 2701 D7
S Wolff Av
9800 JfnC 80433 2442 A5
Wolff Ct
7800 WSTR 80030 1943 C5
8600 WSTR 80031 1943 C3
8700 AdmC 80031 1943 C3
9800 WSTR 80031 1859 C7
12200 BMFD 80020 1859 C1
12700 BMFD 80020 1775 C7
S Wolff Ct
5900 LITN 80123 2363 C2
Wolff Dr
12200 BMFD 80020 1859 B1
Wolff Pl
12200 BMFD 80020 1859 C1
Wolff St
200 DNVR 80219 2195 C1
400 DNVR 80219 2111 C7
600 DNVR 80204 2111 C7
2900 DNVR 80212 2111 C2
4100 DNVR 80212 2027 C7
5000 WSTR 80031 1859 C7
5300 AdmC 80212 2027 C5
6400 ARVD 80003 2027 C2
6900 WSTR 80030 2027 C1
8000 WSTR 80030 1943 C5
8000 WSTR 80031 1943 C5
12500 BMFD 80020 1859 C1
12700 BMFD 80020 1775 C7
N Wolff St
- WSTR 80031 1859 C2
S Wolff St
10 DNVR 80219 2195 C1
2700 DNVR 80219 2279 C1
2700 DNVR 80236 2279 C1
7400 LITN 80128 2363 C6
Wolff Wy
11000 WSTR 80031 1859 C4
N Wolff Wy
10600 WSTR 80031 1859 C5
S Wolff Wy
2600 DNVR 80219 2195 B7
2600 DNVR 80219 2279 C1
Wolf Point Tr
5400 JfnC 80465 2360 C1
Wolf Tongue Ct
10 NDLD 80466 1765 C3
Wolftongue Rd
10 BldC 80466 1682 C6
W Wolf Tooth Pass
11300 JfnC 80127 2361 E7
Wolhurst Dr
- AphC 80120 2447 E1
- LITN 80120 2447 E1
N Wolhurst Dr
- LITN 80120 2363 E7
- LITN 80120 2447 E1
S Wolhurst Dr
- AphC 80120 2447 D1
- LITN 80120 2447 D1
Wolverine Ct
600 DgsC 80108 2618 C2
W Wolverine Ct
12900 JfnC 80127 2445 C5
Wolverine Tr
26200 JfnC 80439 2442 A1
Wonder Dr
3400 CSRK 80109 2702 D2
S Wonder Dr
11700 JfnC 80433 2525 E3
11700 JfnC 80433 2526 A3
Wonderland Av
10 BldC 80403 1852 A1
Wonderland Tr
10 BldC 80403 1852 A1
Wonderland Hill Av
3900 BLDR 80304 1602 B5
Wonderland Hill Cir
3700 BLDR 80304 1602 B5
Wonderview Av
28000 JfnC 80439 2357 D2
Wonderview Ct
1400 BldC 80303 1687 E3
6000 BLDR 80303 1687 E3
Wood Ct
- BldC 80503 1438 B1

Wood Ct
- LGMT 80503 1438 B1
Wood Ln
100 MRSN 80465 2276 C3
Wood Rd
100 CCkC 80452 2186 B5
W Woodard Cir
7700 LKWD 80227 2194 E7
W Woodard Dr
7600 LKWD 80227 2194 D7
Woodbine Ct
6200 DgsC 80125 2614 E2
Woodbine Pl
10 GpnC 80403 1767 B7
Woodbourne Ter
1800 CSRK 80104 2704 A7
Woodbourne Hollow Rd
5700 BldC 80301 1603 D5
Woodbriar Dr
2900 DgsC 80126 2449 D7
Woodbrook Ln
20400 PARK 80138 2538 A2
Woodbury Ct
10500 DgsC 80129 2448 E7
Woodbury Ln
2300 JfnC 80439 2189 C7
2300 JfnC 80439 2273 C1
Woodbury Wy
10400 DgsC 80129 2448 E7
10500 DgsC 80126 2448 E7
Woodchuck Wy
6700 JfnC 80439 2356 B5
Woodfern
10 JfnC 80127 2361 A7
Woodglen Blvd
4000 TNTN 80233 1861 E3
Woodglen Pl
7300 DgsC 80108 2534 D7
Woodgrove Ct
7300 DgsC 80108 2534 C7
Woodhall Ct
6700 DgsC 80118 2870 D7
6700 DgsC 80118 2954 D1
Woodhaven Dr
1200 DgsC 80116 2706 E5
Woodhaven Ridge Rd
10200 DgsC 80134 2623 B5
Woodhouse Ln
2300 CSRK 80109 2702 C4
E Woodland Cir
10 DgsC 80126 2448 D3
Woodland Ct
1100 BLDR 80305 1686 E7
E Woodland Ct
100 DgsC 80126 2448 E3
Woodland Dr
9000 DgsC 80126 2448 E3
12600 BldC 80504 1356 A4
32200 JfnC 80439 2188 D5
Woodland Ln
- DgsC 80126 2448 E3
100 JfnC 80401 2191 A1
1100 JfnC 80439 2188 B5
N Woodland Tr
12300 DgsC 80138 2454 C4
Woodlands Blvd
- CSRK 80104 2703 D3
- CSRK 80108 2703 D3
- DgsC 80104 2703 E4
Woodlands Wy
3400 JfnC 80439 2273 A3
Woodley Av
4900 DgsC 80135 2617 A6
Wood Lily Dr
900 JfnC 80401 2190 E4
E Woodman Dr
18100 DgsC 80134 2453 B2
18100 PARK 80134 2453 B2
S Woodman Wy
9000 PARK 80134 2453 B2
Woodmont Wy
1300 DgsC 80108 2618 C1
Woodpecker Ln
1900 EbtC 80107 2708 D1
Woodridge Ct
17000 JfnC 80465 2360 C1
S Woodridge Rd
10 DgsC 80116 2791 D2
Woodrock Dr
10500 DgsC 80134 2452 E6
S Woodrose Ct
10100 DgsC 80129 2448 A6
S Woodrose Ln
10100 DgsC 80129 2448 A6
W Woodrose Pl
2500 DgsC 80129 2448 B6
Woodruff Dr
- JfnC 80127 2360 E6
10 JfnC 80127 2361 A6
Woodruff Wy
15300 DgsC 80134 2452 D6
Woods Dr
29700 JfnC 80439 2273 B7
29700 JfnC 80439 2357 B1
Woods Ln
- PrkC 80456 2690 A3
W Woods Rd
3600 DgsC 80135 2785 C7
Woodside Cir
10 JfnC 80470 2524 B5
Woodside Dr
10 JfnC 80470 2524 A5
1300 PrkC 80470 2523 E5
32400 JfnC 80439 2188 D3
S Woodside Dr
100 JfnC 80470 2524 A6
100 PrkC 80470 2523 E7
Woodside Ln
20900 PARK 80138 2538 A3
Woodside Rd
1000 LGMT 80501 1356 E7
Woodside Row
500 DNVR 80123 2278 D6

Woodson Dr
300 ERIE 80516 1607 A6
Wood Sorrel
10 JfnC 80127 2361 A7
S Wood Sorrel Dr
5800 LITN 80123 2363 D2
Wood Sorrel Rd
- DgsC 80118 2954 B2
Wood Sorrel Wy
5900 LITN 80123 2363 D2
Woodstock Ct
7700 DgsC 80108 2534 E6
Woodstock Ln
200 DgsC 80108 2534 E6
Woodstock Pl
2500 BLDR 80305 1770 E1
Woodward St
1500 ERIE 80516 1690 C2
Woody Cr
3400 JfnC 80439 2273 A3
S Woody Wy
8400 DgsC 80126 2449 A1
N Woody Creek Rd
12100 DgsC 80138 2454 A4
Worchelle Wy
- CMCY 80022 1864 A5
Worchester Ct
2200 AURA 80010 2116 A3
S Worchester Ct
2400 AURA 80014 2200 A7
Worchester St
- AdmC 80022 2032 A4
- DNVR 80022 2032 A4
3000 AURA 80011 2116 A2
5100 DNVR 80239 2032 A4
10400 CMCY 80022 1864 A6
S Worchester St
600 AURA 80012 2200 A3
S Worchester Wy
400 AURA 80012 2200 A2
2000 AURA 80014 2200 B6
Worley Dr
1000 AdmC 80221 1944 C7
Wrangler Rd
- TNTN 80229 1861 E7
E Wrangler Rd
400 DgsC 80108 2619 B5
Wrangler Tr
16800 JfnC 80127 2528 C7
Wray Ct
11500 PARK 80134 2453 A6
Wren
10 JfnC 80127 2360 E4
Wren Ct
- LGMT 80501 1439 B5
Wren St
9700 FLHT 80260 1944 A1
Wren Cove
800 LAFT 80026 1690 D6
Wright Av
3100 BLDR 80301 1603 C7
Wright Cir
3300 BLDR 80301 1603 B7
Wright Ct
10 LKWD 80228 2193 C1
900 JfnC 80401 2109 C6
2100 LGMT 80501 1356 A5
2800 LKWD 80215 2109 C3
2900 WTRG 80215 2109 C2
3800 WTRG 80033 2109 C1
6700 ARVD 80004 2025 C1
7000 ARVD 80004 1941 C7
S Wright Ct
1200 LKWD 80228 2193 C5
4300 JfnC 80465 2277 D6
5900 JfnC 80127 2361 C2
S Wright Dr
9500 JfnC 80433 2442 B4
Wright St
- ARVD 80004 2025 C2
200 LKWD 80228 2109 D7
200 LKWD 80228 2193 C1
700 LKWD 80401 2109 C7
1100 JfnC 80401 2109 C6
2900 WTRG 80215 2109 D2
3100 WTRG 80033 2109 D2
8400 ARVD 80005 1941 C4
N Wright St
4300 WTRG 80033 2025 C7
S Wright St
400 LKWD 80228 2193 C2
2300 JfnC 80228 2193 D7
4400 JfnC 80465 2277 D5
5900 JfnC 80127 2361 D2
Wright Wy
14200 BMFD 80020 1775 C3
S Wright Wy
- JfnC 80228 2277 D1
- LKWD 80228 2277 D1
4300 JfnC 80465 2277 D5
Wyandot Cir
11800 WSTR 80234 1860 A2
N Wyandot Ct
13000 WSTR 80234 1776 A6
Wyandot Dr
2000 AdmC 80221 1944 B5
Wyandot St
- AdmC 80020 1776 A2
200 DNVR 80223 2112 B7
200 DNVR 80223 2196 B1
700 DNVR 80204 2112 B6
3200 DNVR 80211 2112 B1
4500 DNVR 80211 2028 B6
5200 DNVR 80211 2028 B5
5600 AdmC 80221 2028 B4
8300 AdmC 80221 1944 B4
8300 AdmC 80260 1944 B4
11200 NHGN 80234 1860 B4
11200 WSTR 80234 1860 B4
13500 WSTR 80234 1776 A5
S Wyandot St
1500 DNVR 80223 2196 B5
2900 EGLD 80110 2280 B2
4700 LITN 80120 2280 B6

S Wyandot St
4700 SRDN 80110 2280 B6
W Wyandot St
2200 LITN 80120 2280 B6
Wyandot Wy
- WSTR 80234 1776 A6
S Wyandot Wy
1200 DNVR 80223 2196 B4
Wyandott Cir N
10100 TNTN 80260 1860 A7
Wyandott Cir S
10000 TNTN 80260 1860 A7
Wyandotte Rd
20700 JfnC 80454 2359 C2
Wyco Dr
11500 NHGN 80233 1861 B3
S Wyecliff Ct
10000 DgsC 80126 2449 C5
S Wyecliff Dr
9800 DgsC 80126 2449 C5
E Wyecliff Ln
2900 DgsC 80126 2449 C5
S Wyecliff Pl
9900 DgsC 80126 2449 C5
E Wyecliff Wy
2800 DgsC 80126 2449 C5
Wyman Wy
6800 WSTR 80030 2027 C1
Wyndemere Cir
1000 LGMT 80501 1356 E5
Wyndemere Dr
700 LGMT 80501 1356 D5
Wyndham Park Dr
6100 ARVD 80004 2025 B3
6100 JfnC 80004 2025 B3
Wynkoop St
1400 DNVR 80202 2112 C3
3400 DNVR 80216 2113 A1
4400 DNVR 80216 2029 B7
Wynspire Rd
10600 DgsC 80130 2449 E7
Wynspire Wy
10500 DgsC 80130 2449 E7
Wynterbrook Dr
2100 DgsC 80126 2449 B4
Wynwood Cir
3800 DgsC 80126 2449 D6
Wynwood Wy
10000 DgsC 80126 2449 E6
Wyoming Cir
400 GOLD 80403 2023 D7
E Wyoming Cir
12700 AURA 80012 2199 E4
16800 AURA 80017 2200 E6
16800 AURA 80017 2201 A4
24600 AURA 80018 2202 E3
24700 AURA 80018 2203 A4
E Wyoming Dr
- AURA 80012 2200 D4
16300 AURA 80017 2200 E4
16900 AURA 80017 2201 A4
E Wyoming Pl
4500 DNVR 80222 2197 E4
4500 DNVR 80222 2198 A4
6900 DNVR 80224 2198 C4
9900 AURA 80247 2199 B4
12700 AURA 80012 2199 E4
14400 AURA 80012 2200 B4
17800 AURA 80017 2201 B4
24600 AURA 80018 2202 E4
24600 AURA 80018 2203 A4
W Wyoming Pl
4400 DNVR 80219 2195 C5
5100 LKWD 80219 2195 C5
5100 LKWD 80232 2195 C5
Wyoming St
- DNVR 80236 2279 C4
500 GOLD 80403 2023 C7

X

Xanadle St
- CMCY 80022 1864 A5
Xanadu St
1400 AURA 80011 2116 A5
1700 AURA 80010 2116 B4
5500 DNVR 80239 2032 A4
10600 CMCY 80022 1864 A5
S Xanadu St
300 AURA 80012 2200 A2
3200 AURA 80014 2284 A2
S Xanadu Wy
2400 AURA 80014 2200 A7
2600 AURA 80014 2284 A1
Xanthia Ct
2600 DNVR 80238 2114 E3
S Xanthia Ct
2900 DNVR 80231 2282 D2
3300 DNVR 80231 2283 A1
7500 CTNL 80112 2366 E6
7900 CTNL 80112 2367 A7
S Xanthia Pl
7500 CTNL 80112 2366 D6
Xanthia St
700 DNVR 80230 2114 E6
1100 DNVR 80220 2114 E5
2600 DNVR 80238 2114 E3
8600 AdmC 80022 1946 E3
8600 CMCY 80022 1946 E3
S Xanthia St
3000 DNVR 80231 2282 E2
3800 DNVR 80237 2282 E3
3800 DNVR 80237 2283 A4
6700 GDVL 80112 2367 A4
7000 CTNL 80112 2367 A4
7200 CTNL 80112 2366 E5
Xanthia Wy
- DNVR 80238 2114 E3
S Xanthia Wy
7200 CTNL 80112 2366 E5
7200 CTNL 80112 2367 A5
Xanthippe Ln
- BLDR 80302 1686 D3

Xapary St
1200 AURA 80011 2116 A5
S Xapary St
300 AURA 80012 2200 A2
Xapary Wy
5500 DNVR 80239 2032 A4
S Xapary Wy
- AURA 80014 2200 A7
Xavier Cir
6800 ARVD 80030 2027 C1
Xavier Ct
6100 ARVD 80003 2027 C3
7700 WSTR 80030 1943 C6
11500 WSTR 80031 1859 C3
N Xavier Ct
11700 WSTR 80031 1859 C2
Xavier Dr
11200 WSTR 80031 1859 C4
Xavier Ln
13600 BMFD 80020 1775 C5
Xavier St
200 DNVR 80219 2195 C1
400 DNVR 80219 2111 C7
1000 DNVR 80204 2111 C6
3800 DNVR 80212 2111 C1
4100 DNVR 80212 2027 C7
5300 AdmC 80212 2027 C5
6400 ARVD 80003 2027 C2
7800 WSTR 80030 1943 C5
7900 WSTR 80031 1943 C5
8800 AdmC 80031 1943 C3
10300 WSTR 80031 1859 C6
12600 BMFD 80020 1859 C1
12700 BMFD 80020 1775 C7
S Xavier St
10 DNVR 80219 2195 C2
2700 DNVR 80219 2279 C1
4400 DNVR 80236 2279 C5
Xavier Wy
7100 WSTR 80030 1943 C7
N Xavier Wy
11600 WSTR 80031 1859 C3
S Xavier Wy
4100 DNVR 80236 2279 C4
S Xaviera Ct
6300 LITN 80123 2363 C3
S Xenia Cir
7100 CTNL 80112 2367 A5
Xenia Ct
16200 AdmC 80602 1694 E5
S Xenia Ct
1800 AphC 80231 2199 A6
3000 DNVR 80231 2283 A2
7900 CTNL 80112 2367 A7
8200 CTNL 80112 2451 A1
Xenia Pl
- AdmC 80022 1946 E3
S Xenia Pl
7500 CTNL 80112 2367 A6
Xenia St
1100 DNVR 80230 2114 E6
1300 DNVR 80220 2114 E5
1900 DNVR 80238 2114 E5
8600 AdmC 80022 1946 E3
8600 AdmC 80640 1946 E3
8600 CMCY 80022 1946 E3
16100 AdmC 80602 1694 E5
S Xenia St
- DNVR 80230 2199 A2
- DNVR 80247 2199 A2
1100 AphC 80247 2199 A4
3000 DNVR 80231 2282 E2
3100 DNVR 80231 2283 A2
3700 DNVR 80237 2283 A4
S Xenia Wy
1900 AphC 80231 2198 E6
1900 AphC 80231 2199 A6
Xenon Ct
900 JfnC 80401 2109 C6
5600 JfnC 80002 2025 C4
7000 ARVD 80004 1941 C7
7000 ARVD 80004 2025 C1
8200 ARVD 80005 1941 C4
N Xenon Ct
1900 LKWD 80215 2109 C4
S Xenon Ct
600 LKWD 80228 2193 C3
2500 JfnC 80228 2277 D1
4300 JfnC 80465 2277 C5
6400 JfnC 80127 2361 C4
Xenon Dr
6700 ARVD 80004 2025 C1
Xenon Ln
- CSRK 80108 2619 E5
Xenon St
- JfnC 80005 1941 C4
100 LKWD 80228 2193 C1
700 LKWD 80401 2109 C7
1000 JfnC 80401 2109 C6
2800 LKWD 80215 2109 C3
2800 WTRG 80215 2109 C3
3100 WTRG 80033 2109 C3
4100 WTRG 80033 2025 C7
6000 ARVD 80004 2025 C3
8300 ARVD 80005 1941 C4
S Xenon St
1900 LKWD 80228 2193 D7
2500 JfnC 80228 2277 C1
4300 JfnC 80465 2277 C5
5300 JfnC 80127 2361 C1
Xenon Wy
5600 JfnC 80002 2025 C4
5700 ARVD 80004 2025 C4
5700 JfnC 80004 2025 C4
S Xenon Wy
2400 JfnC 80228 2277 D1
4600 JfnC 80465 2277 D6
5700 JfnC 80127 2361 C2
Xenophon Ct
900 JfnC 80401 2109 C6
S Xenophon Ct
5100 JfnC 80127 2277 C7
5900 JfnC 80127 2361 C3
Xenophon St
700 LKWD 80401 2109 C7
1000 JfnC 80401 2109 C6
6000 ARVD 80004 2025 C3
S Xenophon St
2000 LKWD 80228 2193 D7
2500 JfnC 80228 2277 C1
4300 JfnC 80465 2277 C6
6400 JfnC 80127 2361 C4
S Xenophon Wy
- JfnC 80127 2361 C3
4300 JfnC 80465 2277 C5
Xenophone Ct
8200 ARVD 80005 1941 C4
S Xeric Ct
3000 DNVR 80231 2282 E2
S Xeric Wy
- GDVL 80111 2283 A5
4400 DNVR 80237 2282 D6
4400 DNVR 80237 2283 A5
Xylon St
- GOLD 80401 2192 B1

Y

Yakima Ct
500 LCHB 80603 1698 C2
Yakima St
100 LCHB 80603 1698 C3
S Yakima St
5900 AphC 80015 2370 C2
S Yakima Wy
5500 AphC 80015 2370 C1
E Yale Av
- AphC 80018 2286 D1
- AphC 80018 2287 A1
- AURA 80013 2200 C7
- AURA 80018 2286 D1
10 DNVR 80210 2280 E1
10 DNVR 80223 2280 E1
10 DvrC 80223 2280 E1
10 EGLD 80110 2280 E1
10 EGLD 80113 2280 E1
200 AphC 80210 2280 E1
400 EGLD 80210 2280 E1
600 AphC 80210 2281 B1
600 EGLD 80113 2281 B1
600 EGLD 80210 2281 B1
700 DNVR 80210 2281 B1
4000 DNVR 80222 2281 B1
5500 AphC 80222 2282 A1
5500 DNVR 80222 2282 A1
6400 DNVR 80224 2282 B1
7000 DNVR 80231 2282 D1
7300 DvrC 80231 2282 D1
8100 AphC 80231 2198 E7
9000 DNVR 80231 2283 C1
10200 AURA 80014 2283 C1
13600 AURA 80014 2284 A1
14800 AURA 80014 2200 C7
15300 AURA 80013 2284 D1
16800 AURA 80013 2285 A1
28100 AphC 80137 2203 E7
28100 AphC 80137 2204 A7
32800 AphC 80137 2205 A7
W Yale Av
10 DNVR 80210 2280 D1
10 DvrC 80210 2280 D1
10 EGLD 80113 2280 D1
10 EGLD 80223 2280 D1
200 AphC 80223 2280 D1
300 DNVR 80223 2280 D1
1900 LKWD 80228 2193 C7
2400 EGLD 80110 2280 A1
3000 DNVR 80219 2280 A1
3000 DNVR 80236 2280 A1
3100 DNVR 80219 2279 E1
3100 DNVR 80236 2279 E1
5100 DNVR 80227 2279 A1
5100 LKWD 80227 2279 A1
7000 DNVR 80227 2278 E1
7500 LKWD 80227 2278 D1
14800 LKWD 80228 2277 A1
14800 MRSN 80228 2276 E1
15900 LKWD 80228 2276 E1
Yale Cir
1000 BLDR 80305 1687 A7
E Yale Cir
5100 DNVR 80222 2282 A1
E Yale Ct
11800 AURA 80014 2283 D1
W Yale Ct
900 LSVL 80027 1773 A2
Yale Dr
3600 LGMT 80503 1355 B7
E Yale Dr
6500 DgsC 80130 2450 C4
S Yale Ln
9300 DgsC 80130 2450 C4
E Yale Pkwy
23300 AphC 80018 2202 E7
23300 AURA 80018 2202 E7
24400 AphC 80018 2203 A7
24400 AURA 80018 2203 A7
E Yale Pl
600 EGLD 80113 2280 E1
600 EGLD 80113 2281 A1
11400 AURA 80014 2283 D1
16500 AURA 80013 2284 E1
17800 AURA 80013 2285 B1
20400 AURA 80013 2201 E7
W Yale Pl
10100 LKWD 80227 2278 B1
13100 JfnC 80228 2193 C7
13100 LKWD 80228 2193 C7
14500 LKWD 80228 2277 B1
Yale Rd
500 BLDR 80305 1687 A7
Yale Wy
3600 LGMT 80503 1355 A7
E Yale Wy
3200 DNVR 80210 2281 D1
11400 AURA 80014 2283 D1
S Yampa Cir
5100 CTNL 80015 2285 B7
Yampa Ct
7000 BldC 80301 1604 C2
S Yampa Ct
1300 AURA 80017 2201 B4
2200 AURA 80013 2201 B6
2900 AURA 80013 2285 B1
5000 AURA 80015 2285 C6
5100 CTNL 80015 2285 B6
5500 CTNL 80015 2369 C1
6000 AphC 80016 2369 C2
6900 FXFD 80016 2369 C5
Yampa Dr
6500 DgsC 80118 2870 D7
6600 DgsC 80118 2954 D1
Yampa St
- AdmC 80022 1865 B3
- CMCY 80022 1865 B3
- DNVR 80249 2033 B1
7000 DNVR 80249 1949 B7
12500 AdmC 80022 1781 B7
S Yampa St
1000 AURA 80017 2201 B3
4700 AURA 80015 2285 B6
5200 CTNL 80015 2285 B7
5600 CTNL 80015 2369 C1
5900 AphC 80016 2369 B2
7100 FXFD 80016 2369 B5
7500 CTNL 80016 2369 C6
18300 AURA 80013 2285 B3
Yampa Wy
16400 AdmC 80601 1697 B4
16400 BGTN 80601 1697 B4
S Yampa Wy
1300 AURA 80017 2201 B5
2800 AURA 80013 2285 C1
S Yank Cir
2300 JfnC 80228 2193 C7
Yank Ct
200 LKWD 80228 2193 C1
1900 JfnC 80401 2109 C4
5100 JfnC 80002 2025 C5
6400 ARVD 80004 2025 C2
7900 ARVD 80005 1941 C5
S Yank Ct
1200 LKWD 80228 2193 C4
2400 JfnC 80228 2193 C7
4900 JfnC 80465 2277 C7
5100 JfnC 80127 2277 C7
5500 JfnC 80127 2361 C1
S Yank Pl
1800 LKWD 80228 2193 C6
Yank St
700 LKWD 80401 2109 C7
1300 JfnC 80401 2109 C5
S Yank St
1300 LKWD 80228 2193 C5
2300 JfnC 80228 2193 C7
4300 JfnC 80465 2277 C5
Yank Wy
10 LKWD 80228 2193 C1
5200 JfnC 80002 2025 C5
6300 ARVD 80004 2025 B1
S Yank Wy
1800 LKWD 80228 2193 C6
4700 JfnC 80465 2277 C6
5900 JfnC 80127 2361 C2
Yankakee Dr
600 DgsC 80108 2619 A6
Yankee Creek Rd
10 CCkC 80439 2271 D7
10 CCkC 80439 2355 C1
Yarmouth Av
1200 BLDR 80304 1602 C3
1900 BLDR 80301 1602 C3
2000 BldC 80301 1602 D3
S Yarnell Ct
3000 DNVR 80231 2282 D3
3000 DNVR 80231 2283 A1
Yarro Pl
- BldC 80503 1520 E4
E Yarrow Cir
1500 SUPE 80027 1857 B1
2900 SUPE 80027 1773 B7
W Yarrow Cir
1400 SUPE 80027 1857 B1
2900 SUPE 80027 1773 B7
Yarrow Ct
2500 BLDR 80305 1686 E7
3200 JfnC 80215 2110 D2
3200 WTRG 80033 2110 D2
4100 WTRG 80033 2026 D7
8200 ARVD 80005 1942 D4
9800 JfnC 80021 1858 D7
S Yarrow Ct
1600 LKWD 80232 2194 D5
4200 LKWD 80235 2278 E5
6800 JfnC 80128 2362 D4
Yarrow Pl
400 DgsC 80108 2534 E5
Yarrow St
- BGTN 80601 1697 E5
- BldC 80026 1689 E2
- LAFT 80026 1689 E2
10 LKWD 80226 2194 D1
2500 LKWD 80214 2110 D3
3200 JfnC 80215 2110 D2
3900 WTRG 80033 2110 D1
4400 WTRG 80033 2026 D7
4900 ARVD 80002 2026 D6
5700 ARVD 80004 2026 D4
8000 ARVD 80005 1942 D5
9000 WSTR 80021 1942 D2
9900 JfnC 80021 1858 D7
11000 WSTR 80021 1858 D4
S Yarrow St
- LKWD 80123 2278 E7
900 LKWD 80226 2194 D4
900 LKWD 80232 2194 D4
2100 LKWD 80227 2194 D7
2400 LKWD 80227 2278 D1
4000 LKWD 80235 2278 E5
6300 JfnC 80123 2362 E3
S Yarrow St
7000 JfnC 80128 2362 E5
8300 JfnC 80128 2446 D1
S Yarrow Wy
2300 LKWD 80227 2194 D7
6500 JfnC 80123 2362 E4
7200 JfnC 80128 2362 D6
Yates Cir
4800 BMFD 80020 1775 B7
Yates Ct
4700 BMFD 80020 1859 C1
6100 ARVD 80003 2027 C2
7000 WSTR 80030 1943 C7
10300 WSTR 80031 1859 C6
S Yates Ct
5900 LITN 80123 2363 C2
6700 AphC 80123 2363 C4
Yates Dr
8700 AdmC 80031 1943 C3
8700 WSTR 80031 1943 C3
N Yates Dr
10600 WSTR 80031 1859 C5
Yates Pl
5100 BMFD 80020 1859 B1
Yates St
200 DNVR 80219 2195 C1
400 DNVR 80219 2111 C7
1200 DNVR 80204 2111 C6
3700 DNVR 80212 2111 C1
4100 DNVR 80212 2027 C7
5300 AdmC 80212 2027 C5
6900 WSTR 80030 2027 C1
7700 WSTR 80030 1943 C5
7800 WSTR 80031 1943 C5
9700 WSTR 80031 1859 C7
12600 BMFD 80020 1859 C1
12700 BMFD 80020 1775 C7
N Yates St
9000 AdmC 80031 1943 C2
9000 WSTR 80031 1943 C2
S Yates St
10 DNVR 80219 2195 C1
2700 DNVR 80219 2279 C2
2700 DNVR 80236 2279 C2
N Yates Wy
11600 WSTR 80031 1859 C3
S Yates Wy
100 DNVR 80219 2195 C2
4100 DNVR 80236 2279 C4
Yaupon Av
1400 BLDR 80304 1602 C3
Yeager Dr
1000 LGMT 80501 1356 A6
Yeager Pl
900 LGMT 80501 1356 A5
S Yegge Rd
9000 JfnC 80465 2443 D4
Yellow Field Wy
100 ERIE 80516 1606 E6
Yellow Flax
10 JfnC 80127 2361 A7
Yellow Locust
10 JfnC 80127 2361 A7
Yellow Pine Av
1700 BLDR 80304 1602 C3
Yellow Pine Dr
10 PrkC 80456 2691 A1
800 PrkC 80456 2690 E1
Yellow Rose Wy
17100 PARK 80134 2453 A2
S Yellowstone Ct
6300 AphC 80016 2370 D3
Yellowstone Rd
11000 WldC 80504 1440 D3
Yellowstone St
2100 JfnC 80401 2109 C4
5200 BWMR 80123 2279 B6
5200 DNVR 80236 2279 B6
S Yellowstone Wy
6300 AphC 80015 2370 D3
6300 AphC 80016 2370 D3
Yellow Tail St
- AdmC 80102 2124 B2
Yew Ct
900 LGMT 80501 1439 D1
Yew Ln
10 PrkC 80456 2606 E7
100 PrkC 80456 2607 A7
Yoke Tr
20600 JfnC 80465 2359 C6
E York Av
23000 PARK 80138 2538 D1
S York Ct
8100 CTNL 80122 2365 C7
8100 CTNL 80122 2449 C1
York Pl
10200 TNTN 80229 1861 B6
York St
600 DNVR 80206 2113 C5
1800 DNVR 80205 2113 C2
3800 DNVR 80205 2029 C7
3800 DNVR 80216 2029 C7
5400 CMCY 80022 2029 C3
5600 AdmC 80216 2029 C3
5600 CMCY 80216 2029 C3
5800 AdmC 80229 2029 B2
8800 AdmC 80229 1945 C3
9600 TNTN 80229 1945 C1
9700 TNTN 80229 1861 C7
10300 TNTN 80233 1861 B6
11200 NHGN 80233 1861 B4
12100 TNTN 80241 1861 B1
12500 TNTN 80241 1777 B7
13500 AdmC 80602 1777 B5
13500 TNTN 80602 1777 B5
15200 AdmC 80602 1693 B7
15600 TNTN 80602 1693 B5
16600 TNTN 80516 1693 B5
S York St
300 DNVR 80209 2197 C3
1900 DNVR 80210 2197 C6
2500 DNVR 80210 2281 C1
3100 EGLD 80113 2281 C2
York Wy
11000 NHGN 80233 1861 B4
13300 TNTN 80241 1777 B6
Yorkshire Dr
- DgsC 80108 2618 E1
- DgsC 80108 2619 A1
7400 DgsC 80108 2535 A7
Yosemite
11100 WldC 80504 1440 D3
Yosemite Cir
1400 DNVR 80230 2114 E7
S Yosemite Cir
2200 AphC 80231 2199 A7
6500 GDVL 80111 2366 E4
6500 GDVL 80111 2367 A4
S Yosemite Ct
4300 GDVL 80111 2283 A5
6500 GDVL 80111 2367 A3
6800 CTNL 80112 2367 A4
Yosemite St
- AdmC 80022 1946 E3
- AURA 80230 2115 A6
700 DNVR 80230 2114 E6
1000 DNVR 80230 2115 A6
1100 DvrC 80010 2115 A6
1400 AURA 80010 2115 A6
1500 DNVR 80220 2115 A6
1900 AURA 80238 2115 A2
1900 DNVR 80238 2115 A2
1900 DvrC 80238 2115 A2
8800 AdmC 80640 1946 E3
8800 CMCY 80022 1946 E3
9000 CMCY 80640 1946 E2
13100 TNTN 80602 1778 E6
14500 AdmC 80602 1778 E1
15200 AdmC 80602 1694 E7
16300 WldC 80603 1694 E5
S Yosemite St
- AphC 80237 2283 A5
2100 AphC 80231 2199 A7
3200 DNVR 80237 2283 A5
3500 DNVR 80231 2283 A5
4300 DNVR 80111 2283 A5
4400 GDVL 80237 2283 A5
4900 GDVL 80111 2283 A7
5400 GDVL 80111 2367 A1
6300 GDVL 80111 2366 E4
6600 GDVL 80112 2366 E4
6700 CTNL 80112 2366 E4
6800 CTNL 80112 2367 A7
8000 CTNL 80112 2451 A3
8100 LNTR 80112 2451 A3
8100 LNTR 80124 2451 A3
Yosemite Wy
- AdmC 80640 1862 E6
S Yosemite Wy
1100 AphC 80247 2199 A4
1100 DNVR 80247 2199 A4
Yost Ct
5500 DNVR 80239 2032 A4
Yost St
1300 AURA 80011 2116 A5
S Yost St
10 AURA 80011 2200 A1
300 AURA 80012 2200 A2
Young Cir
300 DgsC 80104 2871 B4
Young Ct
100 DNVR 80219 2195 C1
400 ERIE 80516 1607 B7
Young Dr
14500 AdmC 80601 1780 C2
14500 BGTN 80601 1780 C2
Youngberry St
- CSRK 80104 2788 E1
- CSRK 80104 2789 A1
Youngfield Cir
6600 ARVD 80004 2025 C1
S Youngfield Cir
400 LKWD 80228 2193 C2
Youngfield Ct
1700 JfnC 80401 2109 C5
5100 JfnC 80002 2025 C5
6700 ARVD 80004 2025 C1
S Youngfield Ct
400 LKWD 80228 2193 C3
2600 JfnC 80228 2277 C1
5000 JfnC 80465 2277 C7
5100 JfnC 80127 2277 C7
6400 JfnC 80127 2361 C3
Youngfield Dr
200 LKWD 80228 2193 C1
1500 JfnC 80401 2109 C5
1500 LKWD 80215 2109 C5
S Youngfield Ln
5900 JfnC 80127 2361 C3
S Youngfield Pl
1800 LKWD 80228 2193 C6
Youngfield St
1000 JfnC 80401 2109 C5
1400 JfnC 80215 2109 C5
1500 LKWD 80215 2109 C5
1500 LKWD 80401 2109 C5
2700 WTRG 80215 2109 C3
3100 WTRG 80033 2109 C3
3100 WTRG 80401 2109 C3
4000 WTRG 80033 2025 C7
4000 WTRG 80401 2025 C7
4900 JfnC 80033 2025 C6
4900 JfnC 80403 2025 C6
5600 JfnC 80002 2025 C4
6000 ARVD 80004 2025 C3
7200 JfnC 80004 1941 C7
7200 JfnC 80005 1941 C7
8000 ARVD 80005 1941 C5
S Youngfield St
1900 LKWD 80228 2193 D7
2600 JfnC 80228 2277 C1
2600 LKWD 80228 2277 C1
4300 JfnC 80465 2277 C6
5400 JfnC 80127 2361 C1
S Youngfield Wy
2300 JfnC 80228 2193 D7
2300 LKWD 80228 2193 D7
S Youngfield Wy
5500 JfnC 80127 2361 C1
W Youngfield Wy
5200 JfnC 80002 2025 C5
Youngfield Frontage Rd
3200 JfnC 80401 2109 C1
3200 WTRG 80401 2109 C1
Yuba St
- AURA 80010 2116 A5
- AURA 80011 2116 A5
S Yuba St
10 AURA 80011 2200 A1
10 AURA 80012 2200 A1
Yuba Wy
5500 DNVR 80239 2032 B4
W Yucca
11100 DgsC 80125 2530 D7
Yucca Ct
900 LGMT 80501 1439 D1
1800 GOLD 80401 2107 D4
7300 BldC 80301 1604 C3
S Yucca Dr
3000 JfnC 80439 2273 B2
N Yucca Tr
6500 DgsC 80138 2623 D1
Yucca Wy
8900 TNTN 80229 1945 C2
E Yucca Hills Rd
10 CSRK 80104 2787 B1
10 DgsC 80109 2787 B1
Yukon Ct
3700 WTRG 80033 2110 D1
4400 WTRG 80033 2026 D7
6200 ARVD 80004 2026 D2
8200 ARVD 80005 1942 D5
9600 JfnC 80021 1942 D1
S Yukon Ct
1600 LKWD 80232 2194 D5
2300 LKWD 80227 2194 D7
2600 LKWD 80227 2278 E1
6300 JfnC 80123 2362 E3
7200 JfnC 80128 2362 E6
Yukon St
100 LKWD 80226 2194 E1
400 LKWD 80226 2110 D7
1900 LKWD 80214 2110 D4
5600 ARVD 80002 2026 D4
5700 ARVD 80004 2026 D4
8600 ARVD 80005 1942 D4
8600 WSTR 80005 1942 D4
8700 WSTR 80021 1942 D3
10600 JfnC 80021 1858 D5
10900 WSTR 80021 1858 D5
N Yukon St
9400 WSTR 80021 1942 D1
S Yukon St
10 LKWD 80226 2194 E2
900 LKWD 80232 2194 E4
2100 LKWD 80227 2194 E7
4800 DNVR 80123 2278 E6
6300 JfnC 80123 2362 E4
6700 JfnC 80128 2362 D4
8300 JfnC 80128 2446 D1
Yukon Wy
10400 JfnC 80021 1858 D6
S Yukon Wy
2300 LKWD 80227 2194 E7
4100 LKWD 80235 2278 E5
6500 JfnC 80123 2362 E4
6800 JfnC 80128 2362 E5
8000 JfnC 80128 2446 D1
Yule Cir
27800 JfnC 80439 2357 D3
Yulle Rd
- AphC 80102 2125 E4
1500 AdmC 80136 2125 E4
Yuma
- AdmC 80022 1946 C3
Yuma Cir
500 BLDR 80303 1687 D5
Yuma Loop
- KIOW 80117 2796 B3
Yuma St
10 DNVR 80223 2196 B1
400 DNVR 80219 2112 B7
400 DNVR 80223 2112 B7
900 DNVR 80204 2112 B6
S Yuma St
10 DNVR 80223 2196 B1
Yuma Tr
10 CCkC 80439 2439 E1
Yum-Yum Tree Ln
100 PrkC 80456 2606 E7
100 PrkC 80456 2607 A7

Z

Zachery Ct
700 LGMT 80501 1439 D1
Zamia Av
1400 BLDR 80304 1602 C3
Zamia Ct
700 BLDR 80304 1602 B3
Zane Ct
200 ELIZ 80107 2709 B7
Zane Ln
- ELIZ 80107 2709 B7
Zane St
2300 AdmC 80221 1944 B6
Zang Cir
6500 ARVD 80004 2025 C1
Zang Ct
100 LKWD 80228 2193 C1
6500 ARVD 80004 2025 C1
7700 ARVD 80005 1941 C4
S Zang Ct
1700 LKWD 80228 2193 C6
2300 JfnC 80228 2193 C7
4700 JfnC 80465 2277 C6
5400 JfnC 80127 2361 C1
S Zang Pl
1800 LKWD 80228 2193 C6
Zang St
100 LKWD 80228 2193 C1
Zang St
300 LKWD 80228 2109 C7
500 BMFD 80021 1773 D7
700 LKWD 80401 2109 C7
1700 JfnC 80401 2109 C4
5100 JfnC 80002 2025 C5
6500 ARVD 80004 2025 C1
7700 ARVD 80005 1941 C6
S Zang St
1400 LKWD 80228 2193 C5
2500 JfnC 80228 2277 C1
4300 JfnC 80465 2277 C5
5500 JfnC 80127 2361 C1
Zang St W
- ARVD 80005 1941 C5
- JfnC 80005 1941 C5
Zang Wy
100 LKWD 80228 2193 C1
2800 JfnC 80401 2109 C3
5900 JfnC 80002 2025 C3
5900 JfnC 80004 2025 C3
6000 ARVD 80004 2025 C3
S Zang Wy
1900 LKWD 80228 2193 C6
4700 JfnC 80465 2277 C6
5100 JfnC 80127 2277 C7
S Zante Cir
5600 AphC 80015 2370 D1
Zante Ct
300 LCHB 80603 1698 C2
S Zante Ct
7700 AURA 80016 2370 C7
Zante St
100 LCHB 80603 1698 C3
Zante Wy
400 LCHB 80603 1698 B2
S Zante Wy
5600 AphC 80015 2370 D1
Za Za Ln
10 CCkC 80439 2355 C1
E Zebulon Cir
9000 DgsC 80134 2622 D2
Zenith Av
100 LAFT 80026 1690 A4
S Zeno Cir
1200 AURA 80017 2201 C4
3500 AURA 80013 2285 C3
Zeno Ct
17900 AdmC 80601 1697 B4
18200 BGTN 80601 1697 B4
S Zeno Ct
2900 AURA 80013 2285 C2
5200 CTNL 80015 2285 C7
5500 CTNL 80015 2369 C1
5900 AphC 80016 2369 C2
Zeno St
- AdmC 80022 1781 B7
1400 AURA 80011 2117 B5
S Zeno St
1300 AURA 80017 2201 C4
2100 AURA 80013 2201 C6
4700 AURA 80015 2285 C6
5400 CTNL 80015 2285 C7
5400 CTNL 80015 2369 C1
7800 CTNL 80016 2369 C7
S Zeno Wy
1000 AURA 80017 2201 B3
3600 AURA 80013 2285 C3
5200 CTNL 80015 2285 C7
Zenobia Cir
6800 ARVD 80030 2027 C1
10100 WSTR 80031 1859 C7
Zenobia Ct
6100 ARVD 80003 2027 C3
7700 WSTR 80030 1943 C5
10300 WSTR 80031 1859 C6
N Zenobia Ct
11600 WSTR 80031 1859 B3
S Zenobia Ct
5900 LITN 80123 2363 C2
Zenobia Lp
6700 ARVD 80003 2027 C1
6700 ARVD 80030 2027 C1
N Zenobia Lp
11700 WSTR 80031 1859 B3
Zenobia Pl
7000 WSTR 80030 1943 C7
Zenobia St
200 DNVR 80219 2195 C1
400 DNVR 80219 2111 C7
1200 DNVR 80204 2111 C5
3700 DNVR 80212 2111 C1
4100 DNVR 80212 2027 C7
5300 AdmC 80212 2027 C5
6500 ARVD 80003 2027 C2
6800 ARVD 80030 2027 C1
7800 WSTR 80030 1943 C5
7900 WSTR 80031 1943 C5
S Zenobia St
10 DNVR 80219 2195 C2
2700 DNVR 80219 2279 C2
2700 DNVR 80236 2279 C2
S Zenobia Wy
1600 DNVR 80219 2195 C6
1600 LKWD 80219 2195 C6
1600 LKWD 80232 2195 C6
Zephyr Av
300 JfnC 80401 2191 A1
Zephyr Cir
7000 ARVD 80004 1942 D7
Zephyr Ct
3200 JfnC 80215 2110 D2
3200 WTRG 80033 2110 D2
8400 ARVD 80005 1942 D4
9000 WSTR 80021 1942 D2
10800 JfnC 80021 1858 D5
10800 WSTR 80021 1858 D5
S Zephyr Ct
900 LKWD 80226 2194 D4
1100 LKWD 80232 2194 D4
2000 LKWD 80227 2194 D6
2500 LKWD 80227 2278 D1
4000 LKWD 80235 2278 D5
6300 JfnC 80123 2362 D3

STREET Block City ZIP Map# Grid

S Zephyr Ct
6800 JfnC 80128 2362 D4
Zephyr Dr
9700 JfnC 80021 1858 D7
9700 JfnC 80021 1942 D1
Zephyr St
100 LKWD 80226 2194 D1
200 LKWD 80226 2110 D7
2500 JfnC 80215 2110 D3
2500 LKWD 80214 2110 D3
3800 WTRG 80033 2110 D1
4400 WTRG 80033 2026 D7
5600 ARVD 80002 2026 D4
5700 ARVD 80004 2026 D4
8200 ARVD 80005 1942 D4
10800 WSTR 80021 1858 D4
S Zephyr St
- DNVR 80123 2278 D5
- DNVR 80235 2278 D5
10 LKWD 80226 2194 D2
1300 LKWD 80232 2194 D5
2100 LKWD 80227 2194 D7
4100 LKWD 80235 2278 D5
4800 JfnC 80123 2278 D7
4800 LKWD 80123 2278 D7
6800 JfnC 80128 2362 D4
8000 JfnC 80128 2446 D1
W Zephyr St
10100 JfnC 80021 1858 D6
10100 WSTR 80021 1858 D6
S Zephyr Wy
2300 LKWD 80227 2194 D7
7100 JfnC 80128 2362 D5
8000 JfnC 80128 2446 D1
Zeta St
10 GOLD 80401 2108 A7
10 GOLD 80401 2192 A1
200 JfnC 80401 2192 A1
Zeus Dr
1700 LAFT 80026 1690 A7
Zeus Pl
- DgsC 80124 2451 A2
S Zev Ln
8200 JfnC 80439 2441 D1
Zinger St
4700 BLDR 80301 1603 E3
Zinnia Cir
1400 LAFT 80026 1689 E2
Zinnia Ct
3200 JfnC 80401 2109 C2
5800 JfnC 80002 2025 C3
6000 ARVD 80004 2025 C3
8400 ARVD 80005 1941 B4
N Zinnia Ct
3100 JfnC 80401 2109 C2
S Zinnia Ct
600 LKWD 80228 2193 C3
2600 JfnC 80228 2277 C1
5000 JfnC 80465 2277 C7
5200 JfnC 80127 2277 B7
5200 JfnC 80127 2361 C1
Zinnia St
700 LKWD 80401 2109 C7
3100 JfnC 80401 2109 C2
3100 WTRG 80401 2109 C2
5100 JfnC 80002 2025 C5
6500 ARVD 80004 2025 C2
8000 ARVD 80005 1941 C5
8800 JfnC 80005 1941 C3
S Zinnia St
1800 LKWD 80228 2193 C6
2400 JfnC 80228 2193 C7
2400 JfnC 80228 2277 C1
4300 JfnC 80465 2277 C5
5500 JfnC 80127 2361 C1
Zinnia Wy
2100 JfnC 80401 2109 C4
S Zinnia Wy
200 LKWD 80228 2193 C2
2400 JfnC 80228 2193 C7
2400 JfnC 80228 2277 C1
4800 JfnC 80465 2277 C6
Zion
11000 WldC 80504 1440 E3
Zion Ct
- CSRK 80109 2702 C5
5500 DNVR 80239 2032 B4
Zion St
200 AURA 80011 2200 B1
3000 AURA 80011 2116 B2
Zip Ln
10 PrkC 80456 2607 E7
10 PrkC 80456 2691 E1
Zircon Wy
500 SUPE 80027 1857 A2
Zodiac St
10 GOLD 80401 2108 A7
10 GOLD 80401 2192 A1
Zugspitz Rd
25600 JfnC 80439 2358 B3
Zuni Dr
- WSTR 80234 1860 A5
N Zuni Dr
10700 NHGN 80234 1860 A5
10700 WSTR 80234 1860 A5
N Zuni Pl
3500 DgsC 80135 2700 D1
Zuni St
800 DNVR 80204 2112 B6
2500 DNVR 80211 2112 B3
4100 DNVR 80211 2028 B7
5000 AdmC 80221 2028 B4
5000 DNVR 80221 2028 B4
7200 WSTR 80030 1944 B7
7500 AdmC 80221 1944 B5
8100 AdmC 80031 1944 B5
8100 WSTR 80031 1944 B5
8100 WSTR 80221 1944 B5
8300 AdmC 80260 1944 B5
9600 FLHT 80260 1860 A7
9600 FLHT 80260 1944 A1
9600 TNTN 80260 1860 A7
9600 TNTN 80260 1944 A1
10300 FLHT 80234 1860 A7
Zuni St
10300 TNTN 80234 1860 A7
10300 WSTR 80234 1860 A7
10400 NHGN 80234 1860 A6
12400 BMFD 80234 1776 A7
12800 WSTR 80234 1776 A7
13200 WSTR 80020 1776 A3
14100 AdmC 80020 1776 A3
15000 BMFD 80020 1776 A3
15300 BfdC 80020 1692 A7
15600 BMFD 80020 1692 A7
N Zuni St
11700 WSTR 80234 1860 A2
S Zuni St
1300 DNVR 80219 2196 B7
2000 AphC 80219 2196 B7
2000 AphC 80223 2196 B7
2000 DNVR 80223 2196 B7
2000 EGLD 80110 2196 B7
2000 EGLD 80219 2196 B7
2000 EGLD 80223 2196 B7
2500 DNVR 80219 2280 B1
2500 EGLD 80110 2280 B1
2700 DNVR 80236 2280 B2
3000 AphC 80236 2280 B2
3000 SRDN 80110 2280 B2
4900 LITN 80120 2280 B7
Zuni Tr
10 CCkC 80439 2440 A1
S Zurich Ct
2200 DNVR 80219 2195 C7
2600 DNVR 80219 2279 C1
2600 DNVR 80236 2279 C2
Zurich Dr
30200 JfnC 80470 2609 B5
Zurich St
10 GOLD 80401 2108 B7
10 GOLD 80401 2192 B1
Zweck Ct
800 BldC 80503 1438 B1
800 LGMT 80503 1438 B1
Zwieback St
1400 DNVR 80205 2113 A4
1400 DNVR 80218 2113 A4

#

1st Av
- AphC 80018 2118 D7
- AURA 80018 2118 D7
- IDSP 80452 2101 B5
- LGMT 80501 1439 C3
10 BldC 80501 1439 C3
100 BldC 80503 1520 D4
1200 BldC 80501 1438 E3
1200 LGMT 80501 1438 E3
8000 JfnC 80007 1940 D5
E 1st Av
- AdmC 80603 1781 A4
- AURA 80011 2201 A1
- AURA 80018 2119 B7
10 DNVR 80203 2196 E1
10 DNVR 80223 2196 E1
100 BMFD 80020 1858 E2
300 DgsC 80108 2535 B7
600 DNVR 80203 2197 A1
1000 BMFD 80020 1859 B2
1200 DNVR 80218 2197 B1
1800 DNVR 80206 2197 B1
3900 DNVR 80220 2197 D1
6400 DNVR 80220 2198 C1
7200 DNVR 80230 2198 D1
8100 DNVR 80230 2114 E7
9700 AURA 80010 2199 C1
9700 AURA 80230 2199 C1
9700 DNVR 80010 2199 C1
9700 DNVR 80230 2199 C1
11700 AURA 80012 2199 D1
11800 AURA 80011 2199 D1
15300 AURA 80011 2200 D1
15500 AURA 80011 2116 D7
N 1st Av
10 BGTN 80601 1696 B5
S 1st Av
10 BGTN 80601 1696 B6
10 SUPE 80027 1772 E4
W 1st Av
- LKWD 80228 2193 D1
10 DNVR 80203 2196 D1
10 DNVR 80223 2196 D1
600 BMFD 80020 1858 D2
2300 DNVR 80219 2196 B1
3100 DNVR 80219 2195 E1
5100 LKWD 80226 2195 C1
6900 LKWD 80226 2194 E1
13900 JfnC 80401 2193 B1
16400 JfnC 80401 2192 D1
E 1st Dr
14200 AURA 80011 2200 B1
14200 AURA 80012 2200 B1
W 1st Dr
12900 LKWD 80228 2193 C1
13900 JfnC 80401 2193 B1
15600 GOLD 80401 2192 D1
15600 JfnC 80401 2192 D1
1st Pl
- AURA 80018 2118 D7
E 1st Pl
- AURA 80018 2119 B7
6900 DNVR 80220 2198 C1
7500 DNVR 80230 2114 D7
7500 DNVR 80230 2198 D1
11500 AURA 80010 2199 D1
11800 AURA 80011 2199 D1
W 1st Pl
7200 LKWD 80226 2194 E1
12900 LKWD 80228 2193 C1
14300 JfnC 80401 2193 A1
1st St
- LKWD 80226 2110 A7
- LKWD 80226 2194 A1
300 AdmC 80102 2124 D1
300 BNNT 80102 2124 D1
400 GOLD 80403 2107 D2
1st St
500 CSRK 80104 2703 D7
1300 DNVR 80204 2112 C4
6400 DgsC 80135 2532 C6
12300 NHGN 80241 1861 B1
12300 TNTN 80241 1861 B1
12500 TNTN 80241 1777 B7
E 1st St
10 NDLD 80466 1765 D3
N 1st St
12000 DgsC 80134 2452 B5
12000 LNTR 80134 2452 B5
S 1st St
100 AdmC 80102 2124 D4
100 BNNT 80102 2124 D4
S 1st St SR-79
100 AdmC 80102 2124 D4
100 BNNT 80102 2124 D4
W 1st St
10 NDLD 80466 1765 C3
S 1st Wy
500 BGTN 80601 1696 B7
2nd Av
- IDSP 80452 2101 B5
- LYNS 80540 1352 E1
10 BldC 80503 1520 D4
10 SUPE 80027 1772 E4
300 LGMT 80501 1439 A3
8100 JfnC 80007 1940 C5
E 2nd Av
10 BldC 80501 1439 C3
10 DNVR 80203 2196 E1
10 DNVR 80223 2196 E1
10 LGMT 80501 1439 C3
300 DgsC 80108 2535 B6
600 DNVR 80203 2197 A1
700 DNVR 80218 2197 A1
2300 DNVR 80206 2197 D1
4000 DNVR 80220 2197 E1
4700 DNVR 80220 2198 A1
11500 AURA 80010 2199 D1
11900 AURA 80011 2115 D7
11900 AURA 80011 2199 D1
12100 AURA 80012 2199 D1
14500 AURA 80011 2116 C7
14800 AURA 80012 2200 C1
16100 AURA 80011 2200 C1
16500 AURA 80011 2117 A7
S 2nd Av
- AdmC 80601 1780 B1
- BGTN 80601 1780 B1
10 LYNS 80540 1352 E3
200 BGTN 80601 1696 B6
W 2nd Av
10 DNVR 80203 2196 D1
100 BMFD 80020 1858 E1
2000 DNVR 80223 2196 A1
3000 DNVR 80219 2196 A1
4300 DNVR 80219 2195 C1
5100 LKWD 80226 2195 C1
8600 LKWD 80226 2194 C1
13800 JfnC 80401 2193 B1
15700 GOLD 80401 2192 D1
15700 JfnC 80401 2192 D1
W 2nd Cir
7300 LKWD 80226 2194 E1
2nd Ct
- LYNS 80540 1352 D3
E 2nd Ct
31700 AdmC 80137 2120 E4
2nd Dr
- AphC 80018 2118 E7
- AURA 80018 2118 D7
E 2nd Dr
12100 AURA 80011 2199 E1
W 2nd Dr
12400 LKWD 80228 2193 C1
2nd Pl
- LKWD 80226 2193 E1
- LKWD 80228 2193 E1
E 2nd Pl
- AURA 80018 2119 B7
S 2nd Pl
100 BGTN 80601 1696 B6
W 2nd Pl
11800 LKWD 80228 2193 D1
13000 LKWD 80401 2193 C1
14300 JfnC 80401 2193 A1
16000 GOLD 80401 2192 D1
2nd St
- LKWD 80226 2110 A7
- LKWD 80226 2194 A1
300 CSRK 80104 2703 D7
400 BNNT 80102 2124 D1
600 GOLD 80403 2107 D2
3200 BldC 80304 1602 B6
3500 JfnC 80465 2276 C3
3500 MRSN 80465 2276 C3
5000 BLDR 80302 1602 B2
5000 BLDR 80304 1602 B2
6400 DgsC 80135 2532 C7
12400 NHGN 80241 1861 B1
12400 TNTN 80241 1861 B1
12500 TNTN 80241 1777 B7
E 2nd St
10 NDLD 80466 1765 D3
N 2nd St
- AdmC 80137 2120 E3
12000 DgsC 80134 2452 B4
W 2nd St
10 NDLD 80466 1765 C3
W 2nd St SR-72
10 NDLD 80466 1765 C3
2nd Av Pkwy
- DNVR 80220 2198 C1
- DNVR 80230 2114 D7
- DNVR 80230 2198 C1
7000 DNVR 80220 2114 C7
3rd Av
- BldC 80503 1438 D2
- IDSP 80452 2101 B5
- LGMT 80503 1438 D2
10 LGMT 80501 1439 A2
10 SUPE 80027 1772 E4
3rd Av
100 BldC 80503 1520 E4
800 LYNS 80540 1352 D1
1200 LGMT 80501 1438 D2
1800 BldC 80501 1438 D2
8100 JfnC 80007 1940 C5
E 3rd Av
- AURA 80018 2119 B7
- BldC 80501 1439 D3
- BMFD 80020 1858 E1
- DNVR 80206 2197 B1
- DNVR 80230 2114 D7
- LGMT 80501 1439 D3
- LGMT 80501 1440 A3
- AURA 80018 2119 B7
10 DNVR 80203 2196 E1
10 DNVR 80223 2196 E1
300 DgsC 80108 2535 B6
800 DNVR 80203 2197 B1
800 DNVR 80218 2197 B1
900 BMFD 80020 1859 B1
1900 DNVR 80206 2113 B7
3900 DNVR 80220 2113 E7
6900 DNVR 80220 2114 C7
9700 AURA 80230 2115 B7
9700 DNVR 80230 2115 B7
9900 AURA 80010 2115 B7
12000 AURA 80011 2115 D7
S 3rd Av
10 BGTN 80601 1696 B6
W 3rd Av
10 DNVR 80203 2196 D1
10 DNVR 80223 2196 D1
800 BMFD 80020 1858 D1
3000 DNVR 80204 2196 A1
3000 DNVR 80219 2196 A1
3100 DNVR 80204 2195 E1
3300 DNVR 80219 2195 E1
5200 LKWD 80226 2195 B1
7200 LKWD 80226 2194 E1
14100 JfnC 80401 2193 A1
15700 GOLD 80401 2192 D1
18200 JfnC 80401 2192 A1
3rd Pl
- AURA 80018 2118 D7
E 3rd Pl
- AURA 80018 2119 B7
- DNVR 80206 2113 C7
W 3rd Pl
6700 LKWD 80226 2111 A7
7000 LKWD 80226 2110 E7
7200 LKWD 80226 2194 E1
12800 LKWD 80228 2193 C1
14100 JfnC 80401 2193 A1
15600 JfnC 80401 2192 D1
18200 GOLD 80401 2192 A1
3rd St
- AdmC 80137 2120 E4
- BLDR 80304 1686 B1
- JfnC 80465 2276 C3
- LKWD 80226 2110 A7
- LKWD 80226 2194 A1
- MRSN 80465 2276 C3
100 CSRK 80104 2703 D7
200 BNNT 80102 2124 D1
900 GOLD 80403 2107 D2
1900 BLDR 80302 1686 B2
2900 BLDR 80304 1602 B7
6400 DgsC 80135 2532 C7
12500 TNTN 80241 1777 B7
E 3rd St
- CLCY 80403 2017 D4
10 NDLD 80466 1765 D3
N 3rd St
12400 DgsC 80134 2452 B3
W 3rd St
10 NDLD 80466 1765 C3
W 3rd Av Dr
100 BMFD 80020 1858 E1
3rd Av Pl
2400 BldC 80501 1438 C2
2400 BldC 80503 1438 C2
2400 LGMT 80501 1438 C2
2400 LGMT 80503 1438 C2
4-H Rd
- AdmC 80601 1779 A7
4th Av
- IDSP 80452 2101 B5
10 LGMT 80501 1439 B2
10 SUPE 80027 1772 E4
100 BldC 80503 1520 E4
800 LYNS 80540 1352 D1
E 4th Av
10 DNVR 80203 2112 E7
10 DNVR 80204 2112 E7
10 DNVR 80223 2112 E7
100 LGMT 80501 1439 C2
700 DNVR 80203 2113 A7
1100 DNVR 80218 2113 B7
3900 DNVR 80220 2113 E7
4000 DNVR 80206 2113 E7
6400 DNVR 80220 2114 B7
7200 DNVR 80230 2114 D7
13700 AURA 80011 2116 B7
N 4th Av
- BGTN 80601 1696 B5
S 4th Av
10 BGTN 80601 1696 B7
600 AdmC 80601 1780 B1
600 BGTN 80601 1780 B1
S 4th Av SR-2
10 BGTN 80601 1696 B7
600 AdmC 80601 1780 B1
600 BGTN 80601 1780 B1
W 4th Av
10 DNVR 80203 2112 D7
10 DNVR 80204 2112 D7
10 GOLD 80401 2192 A1
800 BMFD 80020 1858 D1
1100 DNVR 80223 2112 C7
2300 DNVR 80219 2112 B7
3200 DNVR 80204 2111 E7
4400 DNVR 80219 2111 C7
5200 LKWD 80226 2111 B7
7600 LKWD 80226 2110 D7
W 4th Av
8700 LKWD 80226 2194 C1
12000 LKWD 80228 2109 D7
14100 JfnC 80401 2109 D7
14100 JfnC 80401 2193 B1
18200 JfnC 80401 2192 A1
E 4th Cir
13700 AURA 80011 2116 B7
E 4th Dr
- AphC 80018 2118 E7
- AURA 80018 2118 E7
E 4th Pl
- AURA 80011 2116 D7
- AURA 80018 2119 B7
1900 DNVR 80206 2113 B7
W 4th Pl
6600 LKWD 80226 2111 A7
8800 LKWD 80226 2110 C7
14300 JfnC 80401 2109 A7
18500 GOLD 80401 2192 A1
4th St
- AdmC 80137 2120 E4
- BNNT 80102 2124 D1
- LKWD 80226 2194 A1
300 MRSN 80465 2276 C3
500 CSRK 80104 2703 D6
900 GOLD 80403 2107 D2
2100 BldC 80302 1686 B2
2100 BLDR 80302 1686 B2
2300 BLDR 80304 1686 B2
2900 BLDR 80304 1602 B7
3300 BldC 80304 1602 B7
6400 DgsC 80135 2532 C7
E 4th St
- CLCY 80403 2017 D4
10 NDLD 80466 1765 D2
N 4th St
12600 DgsC 80134 2452 C3
W 4th St
- CLCY 80403 2017 C4
600 NDLD 80466 1765 C2
16700 JfnC 80470 2693 D2
E 4th Wy
10500 AURA 80010 2115 C7
11000 AURA 80010 2199 C1
W 4th Av Dr
100 BMFD 80020 1858 E1
W 4th Av Pl
400 BMFD 80020 1858 E1
4WD Rd
- BldC 80302 1768 C3
- BldC 80481 1513 B2
- BldC 80540 1513 B2
5th Av
- BldC 80027 1772 E3
- IDSP 80452 2101 B5
- SUPE 80027 1772 E3
10 LGMT 80501 1439 B2
100 BldC 80503 1520 E4
100 BldC 80540 1352 D2
100 LYNS 80540 1352 D2
1000 BldC 80540 1269 D7
1000 LYNS 80540 1269 D7
5th Av SR-7
100 BldC 80540 1352 D2
100 LYNS 80540 1352 D2
5th Av SR-66
500 LYNS 80540 1352 D2
5th Av US-36
500 LYNS 80540 1352 D2
E 5th Av
- AURA 80018 2118 D7
E 5th Av
10 DNVR 80203 2112 E7
10 DNVR 80204 2112 E7
10 LGMT 80501 1439 D2
600 DNVR 80203 2113 A7
1100 DNVR 80218 2113 A7
2300 DNVR 80206 2113 C7
3900 DNVR 80220 2113 E7
6100 DNVR 80220 2114 B7
8100 DNVR 80230 2114 E7
9700 AURA 80010 2115 B7
9700 AURA 80230 2115 B7
9700 DNVR 80230 2115 B7
13100 AURA 80011 2116 A7
N 5th Av
10 BGTN 80601 1696 B5
800 BGTN 80603 1696 B3
800 WldC 80603 1696 B3
S 5th Av
10 BGTN 80601 1696 B6
800 AdmC 80601 1780 B1
800 BGTN 80601 1780 B1
W 5th Av
- DNVR 80204 2112 A7
10 DNVR 80203 2112 D7
1900 BMFD 80020 1858 C1
3300 DNVR 80204 2111 E7
5100 LKWD 80204 2111 C7
5100 LKWD 80226 2111 C7
9200 LKWD 80226 2110 B7
13800 JfnC 80401 2109 A7
15800 GOLD 80401 2108 D7
E 5th Cir
14800 AURA 80011 2116 C7
S 5th Ct
700 BGTN 80601 1696 B7
E 5th Dr
- AURA 80018 2118 D7
E 5th Pl
- AURA 80018 2118 E7
- AURA 80018 2119 B7
10600 AURA 80010 2115 C7
13300 AURA 80011 2116 A7
S 5th Pl
- AURA 80018 2118 D7
W 5th Pl
6200 LKWD 80226 2111 A7
8400 LKWD 80226 2110 D7
5th St
- CSRK 80109 2703 D6
- LKWD 80226 2109 E7
- LKWD 80226 2193 E1
5th St
- LKWD 80226 2194 A1
10 NDLD 80466 1765 C2
500 GOLD 80403 2107 D2
800 CSRK 80104 2703 E6
1100 DNVR 80204 2112 B4
2000 BLDR 80302 1686 B2
2300 BLDR 80304 1686 B2
2900 BLDR 80304 1602 B7
5th St US-86
100 CSRK 80104 2703 D6
E 5th St
- CLCY 80403 2017 D4
10 NDLD 80466 1765 D2
N 5th St
300 BNNT 80102 2124 D1
700 AdmC 80102 2124 D1
12000 DgsC 80134 2452 C4
W 5th St
800 NDLD 80466 1765 C2
16800 JfnC 80470 2693 D2
E 5th Av Pkwy
- DNVR 80220 2114 D7
7300 DNVR 80230 2114 D7
6th Av
- AdmC 80022 2030 D2
- AdmC 80022 2031 B2
- AdmC 80022 2032 D2
- CMCY 80022 2030 D2
- DNVR 80022 2030 D2
- DNVR 80022 2031 A2
- DNVR 80239 2030 D2
- DNVR 80239 2031 A2
- IDSP 80452 2101 B5
- LKWD - 2109 E7
- LKWD - 2110 A7
- LKWD - 2111 B7
600 LGMT 80501 1439 A2
1200 LGMT 80501 1438 E2
6th Av US-6
- LKWD - 2109 E7
- LKWD - 2110 E7
- LKWD - 2111 B7
E 6th Av
- AphC 80018 2202 A1
- AphC 80137 2119 E6
- AphC 80137 2120 A6
- AURA 80137 2120 A6
10 DNVR 80203 2112 E7
10 DNVR 80204 2112 E7
10 LGMT 80501 1439 C2
600 DNVR 80203 2113 A7
700 DNVR 80218 2113 A7
900 BMFD 80020 1775 B7
1800 DNVR 80206 2113 A7
3900 DNVR 80220 2113 D7
9700 AURA 80010 2115 C7
9700 AURA 80230 2115 C7
9700 DNVR 80230 2115 C7
11500 AURA 80011 2115 C7
14700 AURA 80011 2116 A7
16900 AURA 80011 2117 A7
20500 AphC 80011 2202 A1
20500 AURA 80011 2202 A1
21000 AURA 80018 2202 A1
21600 AphC 80018 2118 A7
21600 AURA 80011 2118 A7
21600 AURA 80018 2118 A7
23300 AphC 80018 2119 A6
23300 AURA 80018 2119 A6
32900 AphC 80137 2121 B6
37600 AphC 80102 2122 C6
37600 AphC 80137 2122 C6
40100 AphC 80102 2123 A6
44100 AphC 80102 2124 A6
48900 AphC 80102 2125 A6
48900 BNNT 80102 2125 A6
E 6th Av SR-30
- AphC 80018 2202 A1
10500 AURA 80010 2115 C7
11500 AURA 80011 2115 C7
12500 AURA 80011 2116 A7
18300 AURA 80011 2117 A7
20500 AphC 80011 2202 A1
20500 AURA 80011 2202 A1
21000 AURA 80018 2202 A1
N 6th Av
10 BGTN 80601 1696 B5
S 6th Av
10 BGTN 80601 1696 C6
700 AdmC 80601 1780 C1
700 BGTN 80601 1780 C1
W 6th Av
- DNVR - 2112 A7
- GOLD 80401 2107 E5
- GOLD 80403 2107 E5
- JfnC - 2108 E7
- JfnC - 2109 A7
- JfnC 80401 2107 E5
- LKWD - 2109 E7
- LKWD - 2110 C7
- LKWD - 2111 B7
10 DNVR 80203 2112 A7
1000 BMFD 80020 1858 D1
1300 BMFD 80020 1774 C7
3300 DNVR 80204 2111 E7
5200 LKWD 80214 2111 B7
5200 LKWD 80226 2111 B7
6600 LKWD 80226 2110 C7
6800 LKWD 80214 2110 C7
10800 LKWD 80215 2109 E7
12200 LKWD 80401 2109 C7
15700 GOLD 80401 2108 E7
W 6th Av US-6
- DNVR - 2111 C7
- DNVR - 2112 A7
- GOLD 80401 2107 E5
- GOLD 80401 2108 A7
- GOLD 80403 2107 E5
- JfnC - 2108 E7
- JfnC - 2109 A7
- JfnC 80401 2107 E5
- LKWD - 2109 E7
- LKWD - 2110 A7
W 6th Av US-6
- LKWD - 2111 C7
E 6th Cir
1000 BMFD 80020 1775 B7
W 6th Dr
12600 LKWD 80401 2109 C7
6th Pkwy
- AphC 80018 2118 D7
- AURA 80018 2118 D7
E 6th Pkwy
22400 AURA 80018 2118 C7
E 6th Pl
7500 DNVR 80230 2114 D7
10500 AURA 80010 2115 C7
12200 AURA 80011 2115 E7
16200 AURA 80011 2116 E7
W 6th Pl
4700 DNVR 80204 2111 C7
8100 LKWD 80214 2110 D7
10300 LKWD 80215 2110 A7
12700 LKWD 80401 2109 C7
13700 JfnC 80401 2109 B7
6th St
- LKWD 80226 2109 E7
- LKWD 80226 2193 E1
- LKWD 80226 2194 A1
300 BNNT 80102 2124 D1
600 GOLD 80403 2107 D2
700 BldC 80302 1686 B4
800 CSRK 80104 2703 E6
2100 BLDR 80302 1686 B2
2600 BLDR 80304 1686 B1
4300 BLDR 80304 1602 B4
E 6th St
- CLCY 80403 2017 D4
N 6th St
12000 DgsC 80134 2452 D4
W 6th St
- CLCY 80403 2017 D4
- NDLD 80466 1765 C2
16700 JfnC 80470 2693 D2
E 6th Av Pkwy
- AURA 80018 2118 C7
4000 DNVR 80206 2113 E7
4000 DNVR 80220 2113 E7
4800 DNVR 80220 2114 A7
7300 DNVR 80230 2114 D7
W 6th Avenue North Dr
3500 DNVR 80204 2111 C7
W 6th Avenue South Dr
- LKWD 80204 2111 C7
- LKWD 80214 2111 C7
3500 DNVR 80204 2111 C7
7th Av
- AdmC 80022 1946 D7
- AdmC 80022 1947 A7
- AdmC 80022 1948 B7
- CMCY 80022 1946 D7
- IDSP 80452 2101 B5
E 7th Av
- DNVR 80204 2112 E7
10 DNVR 80203 2112 E7
700 DNVR 80203 2113 A7
700 DNVR 80218 2113 A7
900 BMFD 80020 1775 B7
4000 DNVR 80206 2113 E7
4000 DNVR 80220 2113 E7
4700 DNVR 80220 2114 A7
7300 DNVR 80230 2114 D7
9700 AURA 80010 2115 B7
9700 AURA 80230 2115 B7
11800 AURA 80011 2115 D7
16400 AURA 80011 2116 E6
16800 AURA 80011 2117 A6
34500 AphC 80137 2121 C6
N 7th Av
10 BGTN 80601 1696 C4
500 BGTN 80603 1696 C4
N 7th Av SR-2
10 BGTN 80601 1696 C4
500 BGTN 80603 1696 C4
S 7th Av
10 BGTN 80601 1696 C6
700 AdmC 80601 1780 C1
700 BGTN 80601 1780 C1
W 7th Av
2400 DNVR 80204 2112 A7
4700 DNVR 80204 2111 C7
5600 LKWD 80214 2111 B7
8400 LKWD 80214 2110 D7
8400 LKWD 80215 2110 C7
12300 LKWD 80401 2109 C7
13600 JfnC 80401 2109 A7
15700 JfnC 80401 2108 D7
15800 GOLD 80401 2108 D7
E 7th Cir
1100 BMFD 80020 1775 B7
15300 AURA 80011 2116 D6
E 7th Dr
16100 AURA 80011 2116 E6
W 7th Dr
13200 JfnC 80401 2109 B7
13200 LKWD 80401 2109 B7
7th Pl
500 GOLD 80403 2107 D2
E 7th Pl
9000 AURA 80230 2115 A7
9100 AURA 80010 2115 A7
16500 AURA 80011 2116 E6
W 7th Pl
8200 LKWD 80214 2110 D7
10400 LKWD 80215 2110 A7
12000 LKWD 80401 2109 D7
7th St
- LKWD 80226 2109 E7
- LKWD 80226 2193 E1
- LKWD 80226 2194 A2
300 CSRK 80104 2703 D6
600 BNNT 80102 2124 D1
700 BldC 80302 1686 C4
700 GOLD 80401 2107 D2
1000 DNVR 80204 2112 B4
2200 DNVR 80211 2112 B3
2300 BLDR 80302 1686 B2

STREET Block	City	ZIP	Map#	Grid
7th St				
2700	BLDR	80304	1686	B1
2900	BLDR	80304	1602	B7
W 7th St				
16700	JfnC	80470	2693	D2
W 7th Av Dr				
700	BMFD	80020	1774	E7
700	BMFD	80020	1858	D1
E 7th Av Pkwy				
1800	DNVR	80206	2113	B7
1800	DNVR	80218	2113	B7
3900	DNVR	80220	2113	D7
8th Av				
-	AdmC	80022	1946	E5
-	AdmC	80022	1947	D5
-	AdmC	80022	1948	A5
300	CCkC	80452	2101	B5
300	IDSP	80452	2101	B5
1000	LGMT	80501	1439	A1
1200	LGMT	80501	1438	E1
E 8th Av				
-	DNVR	80230	2114	D6
10	DNVR	80203	2112	E6
10	DNVR	80204	2112	E6
100	LGMT	80501	1439	C1
700	DNVR	80203	2113	B6
700	DNVR	80218	2113	B6
900	BMFD	80020	1775	B7
1800	DNVR	80206	2113	B6
3900	DNVR	80220	2113	E6
4800	DNVR	80220	2114	A6
9700	AURA	80010	2115	B6
9700	AURA	80230	2115	B6
15500	AURA	80011	2116	D6
17500	AURA	80011	2117	B6
N 8th Av				
10	BGTN	80601	1696	C5
S 8th Av				
10	BGTN	80601	1696	C7
700	AdmC	80601	1780	C1
700	BGTN	80601	1780	C1
W 8th Av				
10	DNVR	80203	2112	D6
2000	DNVR	80204	2112	B6
4700	DNVR	80204	2111	C6
5200	LKWD	80214	2111	C6
8000	LKWD	80214	2110	D7
8400	LKWD	80215	2110	C7
10900	LKWD	80215	2109	E7
11200	LKWD	80401	2109	D7
12300	JfnC	80401	2109	D7
15000	LKWD	80401	2108	E7
16100	JfnC	80401	2108	D7
16200	GOLD	80401	2108	D7
W 8th Byp				
-	DNVR	80204	2111	E7
-	DNVR	80204	2112	A7
E 8th Cir				
15800	AURA	80011	2116	D6
N 8th Ct				
500	BGTN	80601	1696	C4
E 8th Dr				
15700	AURA	80011	2116	D6
E 8th Pl				
7300	DNVR	80220	2114	D6
7300	DNVR	80230	2114	D6
16300	AURA	80011	2116	E6
W 8th Pl				
-	LKWD	80215	2109	E6
-	LKWD	80401	2109	E6
6300	LKWD	80214	2111	A6
7000	LKWD	80214	2110	E6
10000	LKWD	80215	2110	A6
12400	JfnC	80401	2109	C6
16800	JfnC	80401	2108	C6
17100	GOLD	80401	2108	C6
8th St				
-	AdmC	80102	2124	E2
-	LKWD	80226	2109	E7
-	LKWD	80226	2193	E2
10	CSRK	80109	2703	C6
200	CSRK	80104	2703	D6
300	BNNT	80102	2124	E2
700	BldC	80302	1686	C4
800	GOLD	80401	2107	D3
900	DNVR	80204	2112	C5
2000	BLDR	80302	1686	B2
2700	BLDR	80304	1686	B1
4500	BLDR	80304	1602	B3
W 8th Av Dr				
800	BMFD	80020	1774	D7
W 8th Avenue Viaduct				
-	DNVR	80204	2112	B6
9th Av				
-	AdmC	80022	1947	A3
-	AdmC	80022	1948	D3
-	BldC	80503	1438	C1
-	IDSP	80452	2101	C5
10	LGMT	80501	1439	A1
1400	LGMT	80501	1438	C1
2200	LGMT	80503	1438	C1
E 9th Av				
-	BldC	80504	1440	A1
10	DNVR	80203	2112	E6
10	DNVR	80204	2112	E6
10	LGMT	80501	1439	E1
700	DNVR	80203	2113	A6
900	BMFD	80020	1775	B7
1400	BldC	80501	1439	E1
1400	LGMT	80501	1440	A1
1900	DNVR	80218	2113	B6
2800	DNVR	80206	2113	D6
3900	DNVR	80220	2113	E6
7300	DNVR	80220	2114	D6
7300	DNVR	80230	2114	D6
N 9th Av				
10	BGTN	80601	1696	C5
700	BGTN	80603	1696	C4
S 9th Av				
10	BGTN	80601	1696	C6
700	AdmC	80601	1780	C1
700	BGTN	80601	1780	C1
W 9th Av				
10	BMFD	80020	1774	E7
10	DNVR	80203	2112	D6
2400	DNVR	80204	2112	A6
4400	DNVR	80204	2111	B6
5100	LKWD	80214	2111	B6
8300	LKWD	80214	2110	D6
8300	LKWD	80215	2110	D6
13100	JfnC	80401	2109	C6
16400	JfnC	80401	2108	C6
17100	GOLD	80401	2108	C6
W 9th Dr				
10000	LKWD	80215	2110	A6
E 9th Pl				
21000	AphC	80018	2118	A6
N 9th Pl				
400	BGTN	80601	1696	C4
W 9th Pl				
6300	LKWD	80214	2111	A6
6900	LKWD	80214	2110	E6
10400	LKWD	80215	2110	A6
13400	JfnC	80401	2109	B6
9th St				
-	DNVR	80204	2112	B4
400	GOLD	80401	2107	E2
700	BLDR	80302	1686	C4
2200	BLDR	80304	1686	B1
4200	BLDR	80304	1602	B4
W 9th Av Pl				
3100	BMFD	80020	1774	B7
10th Av				
-	IDSP	80452	2101	C5
100	LGMT	80501	1439	A1
2100	LGMT	80501	1438	D1
2200	LGMT	80503	1438	D1
8500	LKWD	80215	2110	C6
E 10th Av				
10	DNVR	80203	2112	E6
10	DNVR	80204	2112	E6
100	BMFD	80020	1774	E7
100	BMFD	80020	1775	A7
700	DNVR	80203	2113	A6
700	DNVR	80218	2113	A6
2700	DNVR	80206	2113	D6
3900	DNVR	80220	2113	D6
5700	DNVR	80220	2114	B6
7200	DNVR	80230	2114	C6
9700	AURA	80230	2115	B6
12100	AURA	80010	2115	E6
12100	AURA	80011	2115	E6
14500	AURA	80011	2116	C6
16900	AURA	80011	2117	A6
N 10th Av				
10	BGTN	80601	1696	C5
S 10th Av				
10	BGTN	80601	1696	C6
700	AdmC	80601	1780	C1
700	BGTN	80601	1780	C1
W 10th Av				
10	DNVR	80203	2112	D6
900	BMFD	80020	1774	C7
2600	DNVR	80204	2112	A6
3100	DNVR	80204	2111	E6
5100	LKWD	80214	2111	B6
6800	LKWD	80214	2110	E6
8300	LKWD	80215	2110	D6
12400	JfnC	80401	2109	C6
12400	LKWD	80401	2109	C6
15100	JfnC	80401	2108	D6
17100	GOLD	80401	2108	B6
E 10th Ct				
1100	BMFD	80020	1775	B6
E 10th Dr				
-	DNVR	80230	2114	E7
-	DNVR	80230	2115	A6
9100	AURA	80230	2115	A6
15900	AURA	80011	2116	D6
35100	AphC	80137	2121	C6
E 10th Pl				
15600	AURA	80011	2116	D6
W 10th Pl				
6400	LKWD	80214	2111	A6
10th St				
-	BLDR	80304	1602	C4
10	GOLD	80401	2107	E2
2000	BLDR	80302	1686	C2
2800	BLDR	80304	1686	C1
W 10th Av Cir				
2900	BMFD	80020	1774	B7
W 10th Av Pl				
3100	BMFD	80020	1774	B7
11th Av				
-	IDSP	80452	2101	C5
10	LGMT	80501	1439	B1
1400	LGMT	80501	1438	E1
2200	LGMT	80503	1438	D1
E 11th Av				
10	DNVR	80203	2112	E6
10	DNVR	80204	2112	E6
100	BMFD	80020	1775	A7
600	DNVR	80203	2113	A6
1900	DNVR	80218	2113	B6
2400	DNVR	80206	2113	D6
3900	DNVR	80220	2113	E6
5600	DNVR	80220	2114	B6
7200	DNVR	80230	2114	C6
8900	AURA	80010	2115	A6
8900	AURA	80230	2115	A6
8900	DNVR	80220	2115	A6
8900	DNVR	80230	2115	A6
11700	AURA	80011	2115	E6
13000	AURA	80011	2116	A6
16800	AURA	80011	2117	A6
20900	AphC	80018	2118	A6
20900	AURA	80011	2118	A6
20900	AURA	80018	2118	A6
N 11th Av				
10	BGTN	80601	1696	C4
10	BGTN	80603	1696	C4
S 11th Av				
10	BGTN	80601	1696	C6
700	AdmC	80601	1780	C1
700	BGTN	80601	1780	C1
W 11th Av				
10	DNVR	80203	2112	D6
800	BMFD	80020	1774	D7
2400	DNVR	80204	2112	A6
5200	DNVR	80204	2111	C6
5200	LKWD	80214	2111	B6
6800	LKWD	80214	2110	E6
9000	LKWD	80215	2110	B6
13000	JfnC	80401	2109	C6
15700	JfnC	80401	2108	D6
N 11th Ct				
200	BGTN	80601	1696	C5
W 11th Ct				
900	BMFD	80020	1774	D7
E 11th Dr				
800	AURA	80230	2115	A6
W 11th Dr				
17000	JfnC	80401	2108	C6
E 11th Pl				
100	BMFD	80020	1775	A6
16500	AURA	80011	2116	E6
33800	AphC	80137	2121	B5
W 11th Pl				
6200	LKWD	80214	2111	A6
12600	JfnC	80401	2109	C6
17000	JfnC	80401	2108	C6
11th St				
-	LKWD	80226	2193	E1
600	GOLD	80401	2107	D3
1500	DNVR	80204	2112	C4
1800	BLDR	80302	1686	C2
2800	BLDR	80304	1686	C1
2900	BLDR	80304	1602	C7
W 11th Av Cir				
2900	BMFD	80020	1774	B7
W 11th Av Ct				
3100	BMFD	80020	1774	B7
W 11th Av Dr				
3100	BMFD	80020	1774	A7
W 11th Av Pl				
3200	BMFD	80020	1774	A7
12th Av				
-	IDSP	80452	2101	C5
1100	LGMT	80501	1356	A7
1400	LGMT	80501	1355	E7
2300	LGMT	80503	1355	D7
E 12th Av				
-	BMFD	80020	1774	E6
10	DNVR	80203	2112	E6
10	DNVR	80204	2112	E6
700	DNVR	80203	2113	A6
1100	BMFD	80020	1775	B6
1900	DNVR	80206	2113	B6
1900	DNVR	80218	2113	B6
3900	DNVR	80220	2113	E6
6500	DNVR	80220	2114	C5
8900	AURA	80010	2115	A5
8900	DNVR	80220	2115	A5
8900	DvrC	80010	2115	A5
15300	AURA	80011	2116	D5
N 12th Av				
10	BGTN	80601	1696	C5
S 12th Av				
10	BGTN	80601	1696	C6
700	BGTN	80601	1780	C1
W 12th Av				
10	DNVR	80203	2112	D6
1200	BMFD	80020	1774	D6
1400	DNVR	80204	2112	B6
3100	DNVR	80204	2111	E6
5200	LKWD	80204	2111	B6
5200	LKWD	80214	2111	B6
7000	LKWD	80214	2110	D6
8300	LKWD	80215	2110	D6
11600	LKWD	80215	2109	D6
11600	LKWD	80401	2109	D6
16900	JfnC	80401	2108	C6
17000	GOLD	80401	2108	C6
E 12th Ct				
1100	BMFD	80020	1775	B6
N 12th Ct				
-	BGTN	80601	1696	C4
W 12th Dr				
16400	JfnC	80401	2108	C5
W 12th Ln				
10600	LKWD	80215	2110	A6
E 12th Pl				
37000	AphC	80137	2121	E5
37000	AphC	80137	2122	A5
W 12th Pl				
1800	DNVR	80204	2112	B5
6600	LKWD	80214	2111	A6
8200	LKWD	80214	2110	D6
9400	LKWD	80215	2110	B6
12400	JfnC	80401	2109	D6
12400	LKWD	80401	2109	D6
16400	JfnC	80401	2108	C6
12th St				
-	DNVR	80204	2112	B4
-	LKWD	80226	2193	D1
10	BldC	80455	1516	B3
10	JMWN	80455	1516	B3
500	BLDR	80302	1686	C4
500	GOLD	80401	2107	E3
500	JfnC	80401	2107	E3
W 12th St				
-	BMFD	80020	1774	D6
W 12th Av Ct				
3000	BMFD	80020	1774	B6
W 12th Av Pl				
2600	BMFD	80020	1774	C6
13th Av				
-	CCkC	80452	2101	C5
-	IDSP	80452	2101	C5
13th Av SR-103				
-	IDSP	80452	2101	C5
E 13th Av				
10	DNVR	80203	2112	E5
10	DNVR	80204	2112	E5
600	DNVR	80203	2113	A5
700	DNVR	80218	2113	B5
1000	BMFD	80020	1775	B6
1800	DNVR	80206	2113	C5
3900	DNVR	80220	2113	E5
4800	DNVR	80220	2114	A5
8900	AURA	80010	2115	A5
8900	DNVR	80220	2115	A5
8900	DvrC	80010	2115	A5
11900	AURA	80011	2115	E5
15300	AURA	80011	2116	D5
17700	AURA	80011	2117	B5
N 13th Av				
10	BGTN	80601	1696	D5
S 13th Av				
10	BGTN	80601	1696	D6
700	AdmC	80601	1780	C1
700	BGTN	80601	1780	C1
W 13th Av				
10	DNVR	80203	2112	D5
10	DNVR	80204	2112	D5
1200	BMFD	80020	1774	D6
3400	DNVR	80204	2111	D5
5100	LKWD	80204	2111	C5
6600	LKWD	80214	2111	A5
6800	LKWD	80214	2110	E5
10000	LKWD	80215	2110	A6
11200	LKWD	80215	2109	E6
12000	LKWD	80401	2109	D6
14900	JfnC	80401	2109	A5
15000	JfnC	80401	2108	E6
E 13th Cir				
14600	AURA	80011	2116	C5
E 13th Pl				
-	AURA	80011	2116	D5
10	BMFD	80020	1774	E6
12200	AURA	80011	2115	E5
33800	AphC	80137	2121	B5
W 13th Pl				
10300	LKWD	80215	2110	A5
16000	JfnC	80401	2108	D5
13th St				
100	GOLD	80401	2107	E3
100	JfnC	80401	2107	E3
800	DNVR	80204	2112	C4
1700	BLDR	80302	1686	C2
2700	BLDR	80304	1686	C1
4300	BLDR	80304	1602	C4
14th Av				
-	IDSP	80452	2101	C5
300	LGMT	80501	1356	B7
1400	LGMT	80501	1355	E7
2200	LGMT	80503	1355	E7
E 14th Av				
-	BMFD	80020	1774	E6
10	DNVR	80203	2112	E5
10	DNVR	80204	2112	E5
700	DNVR	80203	2113	A5
700	DNVR	80218	2113	A5
1000	BMFD	80020	1775	B6
1800	DNVR	80206	2113	C5
3900	DNVR	80220	2113	E5
4800	DNVR	80220	2114	B5
8900	DNVR	80220	2115	A5
11700	AURA	80010	2115	E5
11900	AURA	80011	2115	E5
13000	AURA	80011	2116	A5
18000	AURA	80011	2117	B5
N 14th Av				
200	BGTN	80601	1696	D5
S 14th Av				
200	BGTN	80601	1696	D6
W 14th Av				
-	LKWD	80215	2109	D5
10	DNVR	80203	2112	D5
2700	DNVR	80204	2112	A5
3000	DNVR	80204	2111	E5
5100	LKWD	80204	2111	C5
6800	LKWD	80214	2110	E5
10200	LKWD	80215	2110	A5
11600	LKWD	80401	2109	D5
14900	JfnC	80401	2109	A5
16200	JfnC	80401	2108	D5
17600	GOLD	80401	2108	B5
E 14th Ct				
100	BMFD	80020	1775	A6
N 14th Ct				
-	BGTN	80601	1696	D5
S 14th Ct				
500	BGTN	80601	1696	D7
E 14th Dr				
-	AURA	80011	2117	A5
E 14th Pl				
10	BMFD	80020	1774	E6
10	BMFD	80020	1775	A6
15300	AURA	80011	2116	D5
W 14th Pl				
10000	LKWD	80215	2110	A5
12800	JfnC	80401	2109	C5
15800	JfnC	80401	2108	D5
14th St				
200	DNVR	80202	2112	C4
500	GOLD	80401	2107	E3
1500	DNVR	80202	2112	C4
1700	BLDR	80302	1686	C2
2700	BLDR	80304	1686	C1
3800	BLDR	80304	1602	C5
S 14th Av Dr				
10	BGTN	80601	1696	D6
15th Av				
-	IDSP	80452	2101	C5
10	LGMT	80501	1356	B7
1900	LGMT	80501	1355	D7
2200	LGMT	80503	1355	C7
E 15th Av				
10	LGMT	80501	1356	C7
1000	BMFD	80020	1775	B5
N 15th Av				
-	BGTN	80603	1696	D4
600	BGTN	80601	1696	D4
S 15th Av				
600	BGTN	80601	1696	D7
800	AdmC	80601	1780	D1
800	BGTN	80601	1780	D1
W 15th Av				
1100	BMFD	80020	1774	D6
16900	GOLD	80401	2108	C5
16900	JfnC	80401	2108	C5
N 15th Ct				
100	BGTN	80601	1696	D5
S 15th Dr				
500	BGTN	80601	1696	D7
W 15th Dr				
12800	JfnC	80401	2109	C5
12800	LKWD	80215	2109	C5
12800	LKWD	80401	2109	C5
E 15th Pl				
17400	AURA	80011	2117	A5
W 15th Pl				
8400	LKWD	80214	2110	D5
9500	LKWD	80215	2110	B5
12600	LKWD	80215	2109	C5
17200	GOLD	80401	2108	B5
15th St				
10	BldC	80455	1516	B2
10	JMWN	80455	1516	B2
100	DNVR	80202	2112	D4
100	DNVR	80204	2112	D4
500	GOLD	80401	2107	E3
2200	BLDR	80302	1686	C1
2200	DNVR	80211	2112	C3
2700	BLDR	80304	1686	C1
3800	BLDR	80304	1602	C5
S 15th Av Dr				
100	BGTN	80601	1696	D6
16th Av				
-	IDSP	80452	2101	C5
-	LGMT	80503	1355	D6
1000	LGMT	80501	1356	A6
1400	LGMT	80501	1355	E6
E 16th Av				
10	DNVR	80202	2112	E5
10	DNVR	80203	2112	E5
400	LGMT	80501	1356	D6
700	DNVR	80203	2113	A5
700	DNVR	80218	2113	A5
1000	BMFD	80020	1775	B5
2800	DNVR	80206	2113	D5
4000	DNVR	80220	2113	E5
7300	DNVR	80220	2114	D5
8900	AURA	80010	2115	A5
8900	DNVR	80220	2115	A5
16000	AURA	80011	2116	D4
18900	AURA	80011	2117	C4
52000	AdmC	80102	2125	E4
52000	AdmC	80136	2125	E4
N 16th Av				
300	BGTN	80601	1696	D5
S 16th Av				
400	BGTN	80601	1696	D7
W 16th Av				
2100	DNVR	80202	2112	C3
3000	DNVR	80204	2112	A5
3100	DNVR	80204	2111	E5
5100	LKWD	80214	2111	C5
7400	LKWD	80214	2110	E5
8200	LKWD	80215	2110	D5
11400	LKWD	80215	2109	E5
16900	GOLD	80401	2108	B5
16900	JfnC	80401	2108	B5
16th Cir				
3400	BLDR	80304	1602	C6
S 16th Ct				
800	BGTN	80601	1696	D7
E 16th Dr				
17300	AURA	80011	2117	A5
N 16th Dr				
100	BGTN	80601	1696	D5
W 16th Dr				
12800	JfnC	80401	2109	C5
12800	LKWD	80215	2109	C5
12800	LKWD	80401	2109	C5
16th Pl				
1500	LGMT	80501	1355	D6
E 16th Pl				
-	AURA	80010	2116	A4
14400	AURA	80011	2116	B4
18700	AURA	80011	2117	C4
W 16th Pl				
7000	LKWD	80214	2110	E5
8200	LKWD	80215	2110	D5
12400	LKWD	80215	2109	C5
12700	JfnC	80401	2109	C5
12700	LKWD	80401	2109	C5
16800	GOLD	80401	2108	C5
16800	JfnC	80401	2108	C5
16th St				
-	BldC	80455	1516	A3
-	JMWN	80455	1516	A3
300	GOLD	80401	2107	E3
1500	BLDR	80302	1686	D2
1600	DNVR	80202	2112	C3
2500	DNVR	80211	2112	B2
2800	BLDR	80304	1686	D1
3400	BLDR	80304	1602	C6
S 16th Av Dr				
100	BGTN	80601	1696	D6
16th St Mall				
100	DNVR	80202	2112	D4
17th Av				
-	JMWN	80455	1516	A3
10	LGMT	80501	1356	A6
200	IDSP	80452	2101	C5
1400	LGMT	80501	1355	C6
2200	LGMT	80503	1355	C6
8500	BldC	80503	1355	C6
E 17th Av				
-	BldC	80504	1357	A6
10	DNVR	80202	2112	E5
10	DNVR	80203	2112	E5
10	LGMT	80501	1356	D6
700	DNVR	80203	2113	A4
700	DNVR	80218	2113	A4
1000	BMFD	80020	1775	B5
1800	DNVR	80206	2113	C4
3900	DNVR	80220	2113	D4
6500	DNVR	80220	2114	C4
8900	AURA	80010	2115	A4
8900	DNVR	80220	2115	A4
12500	BldC	80501	1357	A6
12500	LGMT	80501	1357	A6
14900	AURA	80011	2116	C4
18600	AURA	80011	2117	C4
N 17th Av				
-	AdmC	80601	1696	D4
-	BGTN	80601	1696	D4
S 17th Av				
-	AdmC	80601	1780	D1
-	BGTN	80601	1780	D1
400	BGTN	80601	1696	D7
W 17th Av				
3000	DNVR	80204	2112	A4
3100	DNVR	80204	2111	E4
5100	EDGW	80214	2111	B4
5100	LKWD	80214	2111	B4
6800	LKWD	80214	2110	E4
8200	LKWD	80215	2110	D5
10800	LKWD	80215	2109	E5
N 17th Ct				
100	BGTN	80601	1696	D5
W 17th Ct				
1000	BMFD	80020	1774	D5
W 17th Dr				
1700	GOLD	80401	2108	B4
E 17th Pl				
12300	AURA	80010	2115	E4
12600	AURA	80010	2116	A4
15800	AURA	80011	2116	E4
19500	AURA	80011	2117	D4
W 17th Pl				
10000	LKWD	80215	2110	A4
11400	LKWD	80215	2109	E4
17200	GOLD	80401	2108	B5
17th St				
300	DNVR	80202	2112	D4
400	GOLD	80401	2107	E3
2200	BLDR	80302	1686	D1
2500	DNVR	80211	2112	B2
2700	BLDR	80304	1686	D1
4100	BLDR	80304	1602	D4
S 17th Av Dr				
10	BGTN	80601	1696	D6
E 17th Av Pkwy				
4000	DNVR	80220	2113	E4
4800	DNVR	80220	2114	A4
18th Av				
1800	LGMT	80501	1355	D6
E 18th Av				
10	DNVR	80202	2112	E4
10	DNVR	80203	2112	E4
700	DNVR	80203	2113	A4
700	DNVR	80218	2113	A4
1100	BMFD	80020	1775	B5
4000	DNVR	80206	2113	E4
4000	DNVR	80220	2113	E4
6500	DNVR	80220	2114	C4
15300	AURA	80011	2116	D4
16900	AURA	80011	2117	A4
N 18th Av				
-	BGTN	80601	1696	D5
S 18th Av				
10	BGTN	80601	1696	D6
W 18th Av				
900	BMFD	80020	1774	D5
2900	DNVR	80204	2112	A4
3100	DNVR	80204	2111	E4
5600	LKWD	80214	2111	B4
6000	EDGW	80214	2111	A4
8300	LKWD	80215	2110	D4
8400	LKWD	80214	2110	D4
11200	LKWD	80215	2109	E4
N 18th Ct				
-	BGTN	80601	1696	D5
W 18th Dr				
9600	LKWD	80215	2110	B4
11900	LKWD	80215	2109	D5
E 18th Pl				
15800	AURA	80011	2116	E4
19500	AURA	80011	2117	D4
W 18th Pl				
10200	LKWD	80215	2110	A4
12200	LKWD	80215	2109	D4
18th St				
-	DNVR	80202	2112	C2
300	GOLD	80401	2108	A3
500	GOLD	80401	2107	E4
1600	BLDR	80302	1686	D2
2300	BLDR	80304	1686	D1
2500	DNVR	80211	2112	B2
2900	BLDR	80304	1602	D7
19th Av				
-	IDSP	80452	2101	D5
1000	LGMT	80501	1356	A5
1400	LGMT	80501	1355	E5
E 19th Av				
-	AdmC	80019	2118	D4
-	AURA	80010	2115	E4
-	AURA	80019	2118	D4
10	DNVR	80202	2112	E4
10	DNVR	80203	2112	E4
600	DNVR	80203	2113	A4
700	DNVR	80218	2113	A4
1000	BMFD	80020	1775	B5
1800	DNVR	80206	2113	B4
4000	DNVR	80220	2113	E4
6500	DNVR	80220	2114	C4
8900	DNVR	80220	2115	A4
12700	AURA	80010	2116	A4
15500	AURA	80011	2116	D4
18500	AURA	80011	2117	C4
52300	AdmC	80136	2125	E3
N 19th Av				
-	WldC	80603	1696	D5
10	BGTN	80601	1696	D5
600	AdmC	80601	1696	D5
W 19th Av				
2900	DNVR	80204	2112	A4
3100	DNVR	80204	2111	E4
5800	EDGW	80214	2111	B4
5800	LKWD	80214	2111	B4
8000	LKWD	80214	2110	D4
10000	LKWD	80215	2110	B4
12800	JfnC	80401	2109	C4
12800	LKWD	80215	2109	C4
E 19th Dr				
-	AURA	80010	2116	A4
E 19th Pl				
-	AURA	80010	2116	A4
12300	AURA	80010	2115	E4
14200	AURA	80011	2116	B4
17000	AURA	80011	2117	A4
W 19th Pl				
6700	LKWD	80214	2111	A4
12300	LKWD	80215	2109	D4
12600	JfnC	80401	2109	D4
19th St				
300	GOLD	80401	2108	A4
600	GOLD	80401	2107	E4
1700	BLDR	80302	1686	D2
2200	DNVR	80202	2112	D3
2300	DNVR	80211	2112	D3
2400	BLDR	80304	1686	D1
2900	BLDR	80304	1602	D7
4400	BldC	80304	1602	D4
20th Av				
-	IDSP	80452	2101	D5
600	LGMT	80501	1356	B5
1600	LGMT	80501	1355	E5
E 20th Av				
10	DNVR	80202	2112	E4
10	DNVR	80203	2112	E4
100	DNVR	80205	2112	E4
500	DNVR	80203	2113	A4
500	DNVR	80205	2113	A4
1100	DNVR	80218	2113	A4
1900	DNVR	80206	2113	B4
N 20th Av				
400	BGTN	80601	1696	D4
S 20th Av				
10	BGTN	80601	1696	D6
200	AdmC	80601	1696	D6
W 20th Av				
2900	DNVR	80204	2112	A4
2900	DNVR	80211	2112	A4
3100	DNVR	80204	2111	E4
3400	DNVR	80211	2111	E4
3800	DNVR	80212	2111	D4
5200	EDGW	80214	2111	A4
5400	LKWD	80214	2111	A4
6800	EDGW	80214	2110	E4
6800	LKWD	80214	2110	E4
8300	LKWD	80215	2110	A4
10800	LKWD	80215	2109	E4
12700	JfnC	80401	2109	B4
13300	LKWD	80401	2109	B4
W 20th Pl				
3400	DNVR	80211	2111	E4
13600	JfnC	80401	2109	B4
20th St				
-	DNVR	80211	2112	D3
200	BLDR	80305	1686	D5
400	GOLD	80401	2108	A4
500	DNVR	80203	2112	D3
500	DNVR	80205	2112	D3
700	GOLD	80401	2107	E4
1600	BLDR	80302	1686	D2
1600	DNVR	80202	2112	D3
2000	LGMT	80501	1355	D5
2000	LGMT	80503	1355	D5
2200	BLDR	80304	1686	D1
3900	BLDR	80304	1602	D5
21st Av				
-	LGMT	80503	1355	D5
10	LGMT	80501	1356	A5
1300	LGMT	80501	1355	D5
E 21st Av				
100	LGMT	80501	1356	C5
1200	DNVR	80205	2113	B4
2200	DNVR	80206	2113	B4
7400	DNVR	80207	2114	D4
12700	AURA	80010	2115	E4
12900	AURA	80010	2116	A4
14500	AURA	80011	2116	C4
N 21st Av				
600	BGTN	80601	1696	D4
S 21st Av				
200	AdmC	80601	1696	E6
200	BGTN	80601	1696	E6
W 21st Av				
2700	DNVR	80211	2112	A4
3100	DNVR	80211	2111	E4
3800	DNVR	80212	2111	E4
7800	LKWD	80214	2110	D4
10500	LKWD	80215	2110	A4
12800	LKWD	80215	2109	C4
13400	JfnC	80401	2109	B4
E 21st Cir				
19000	AURA	80011	2117	C4
S 21st Ct				
700	BGTN	80601	1696	E7
S 21st Pl				
200	BGTN	80601	1696	E6
W 21st Pl				
10000	LKWD	80215	2110	B4
11700	LKWD	80215	2109	D4
13400	JfnC	80401	2109	B4
21st St				
-	DNVR	80202	2112	D2
200	GOLD	80401	2108	A4
300	DNVR	80203	2112	E4
300	DNVR	80205	2112	E4
1000	GOLD	80401	2107	E4
2000	BldC	80301	1602	D3
2000	LGMT	80501	1355	D5
2000	LGMT	80503	1355	D5
2100	BLDR	80302	1686	D1
2200	BLDR	80304	1686	D1
3800	BLDR	80304	1602	D5
W 21st Wy				
11700	LKWD	80215	2109	D4
22nd Av				
-	IDSP	80452	2101	D5
2200	LGMT	80501	1355	D5
2300	LGMT	80503	1355	C5
E 22nd Av				
-	DNVR	80238	2115	A3
700	DNVR	80205	2113	A4
2200	DNVR	80206	2113	B4

Denver Regional Street Index

STREET
Block City ZIP Map# Grid

E 22nd Av
4000 DNVR 80207 2113 E4
6500 DNVR 80207 2114 C3
7600 DNVR 80238 2114 D3
9500 AURA 80010 2115 B3
12700 AURA 80010 2116 A3
14700 AURA 80011 2116 C3
17400 AURA 80011 2117 A3
S 22nd Av
- AdmC 80601 1780 E1
- BGTN 80601 1780 E1
10 BGTN 80601 1696 E6
300 AdmC 80601 1696 E7
W 22nd Av
2700 DNVR 80211 2112 A4
3000 DNVR 80211 2111 E4
3800 DNVR 80212 2111 E4
5200 DNVR 80204 2111 B4
5200 EDGW 80214 2111 B4
7400 LKWD 80214 2110 E4
13700 JfnC 80401 2109 B4
22nd Ct
2500 LGMT 80503 1355 C4
22nd Dr
2500 LGMT 80503 1355 C4
E 22nd Dr
18800 AURA 80011 2117 C3
E 22nd Pl
14000 AURA 80011 2116 B3
18500 AURA 80011 2117 C3
W 22nd Pl
9600 LKWD 80215 2110 B4
11600 LKWD 80215 2109 D4
13300 JfnC 80401 2109 B4
22nd St
- BLDR 80304 1686 D1
300 DNVR 80205 2112 D3
300 GOLD 80401 2108 A4
800 GOLD 80401 2107 E4
1600 DNVR 80216 2112 D3
2000 BLDR 80302 1686 D1
4300 BLDR 80304 1602 D4
W 22nd Wy
8100 LKWD 80214 2110 D4
S 22nd Av Ct
300 BGTN 80601 1696 E6
23rd Av
- IDSP 80452 2101 D5
100 LGMT 80501 1356 A5
2100 LGMT 80501 1355 D4
E 23rd Av
- DNVR 80238 2115 A3
700 DNVR 80205 2113 C3
2200 DNVR 80206 2113 C3
3500 DNVR 80207 2113 E3
4800 DNVR 80207 2114 A3
7200 DNVR 80238 2114 D3
9500 AURA 80010 2115 B3
12700 AURA 80010 2116 A3
13700 AURA 80011 2116 B3
17400 AURA 80011 2117 A3
S 23rd Av
300 BGTN 80601 1696 E6
W 23rd Av
2500 DNVR 80211 2112 A3
3100 DNVR 80211 2111 E3
3800 DNVR 80212 2111 E3
7800 LKWD 80214 2110 D3
10000 LKWD 80215 2110 A4
12700 LKWD 80401 2109 C4
12800 LKWD 80215 2109 C4
13800 JfnC 80401 2109 B4
W 23rd Cir
2300 JfnC 80401 2109 C4
W 23rd Pl
7600 LKWD 80214 2110 E3
10400 LKWD 80215 2110 A4
12000 LKWD 80215 2109 D4
13300 JfnC 80401 2109 B3
23rd St
300 GOLD 80401 2108 A4
700 GOLD 80401 2107 E4
1700 BLDR 80302 1686 E2
2200 BLDR 80304 1686 D1
4400 BLDR 80304 1602 D4
W 23rd Av Dr
10700 LKWD 80215 2109 E3
10700 LKWD 80215 2110 A3
24th Av
2300 LGMT 80501 1355 C4
2300 LGMT 80503 1355 C4
E 24th Av
700 DNVR 80205 2113 A3
6500 DNVR 80207 2114 C3
7700 DNVR 80238 2114 D3
14500 AURA 80011 2116 C3
S 24th Av
300 BGTN 80601 1696 E6
W 24th Av
2600 DNVR 80211 2112 A3
3100 DNVR 80211 2111 E3
3800 DNVR 80212 2111 D3
5200 DNVR 80204 2111 A4
5200 EDGW 80214 2111 A4
7000 EDGW 80214 2110 E3
7600 LKWD 80214 2110 D3
8400 LKWD 80215 2110 C3
E 24th Dr
17400 AURA 80011 2117 A3
24th Pl
- BLDR 80302 1686 E1
E 24th Pl
- DNVR 80238 2114 E3
- DNVR 80238 2115 A3
W 24th Pl
8000 LKWD 80214 2110 D3
12800 JfnC 80401 2109 C3
12800 LKWD 80215 2109 C3
12800 LKWD 80401 2109 C3
24th St
400 DNVR 80205 2112 E3
400 GOLD 80401 2108 A4
600 GOLD 80401 2107 E5
2100 BLDR 80302 1686 E1
24th St
2200 BLDR 80304 1686 E1
2900 BLDR 80304 1602 E7
W 24th Pl Cir
11600 LKWD 80215 2109 D3
25th Av
- IDSP 80452 2101 E5
E 25th Av
700 DNVR 80205 2113 A3
4000 DNVR 80207 2113 E3
4800 DNVR 80207 2114 B3
7200 DNVR 80238 2114 D3
9600 AURA 80010 2115 B3
13300 AURA 80011 2116 A3
33800 AdmC 80137 2121 B3
34300 AURA 80137 2121 B3
S 25th Av
200 BGTN 80601 1696 E6
W 25th Av
2600 DNVR 80211 2112 A3
3100 DNVR 80211 2111 E3
3800 DNVR 80212 2111 D3
5200 DNVR 80204 2111 C3
5200 EDGW 80214 2111 C3
6800 LKWD 80214 2111 A3
7800 LKWD 80214 2110 D3
8400 LKWD 80215 2110 C3
11600 LKWD 80215 2109 D3
13400 JfnC 80401 2109 B3
E 25th Dr
8500 DNVR 80238 2114 E3
8900 DNVR 80238 2115 A3
15300 AURA 80011 2116 D3
17400 AURA 80011 2117 B3
W 25th Ln
6500 EDGW 80214 2111 A3
E 25th Pl
7800 DNVR 80238 2114 D3
14000 AURA 80011 2116 B3
W 25th Pl
7000 LKWD 80214 2110 E3
8300 LKWD 80215 2110 D3
11100 LKWD 80215 2109 E3
13300 JfnC 80401 2109 B3
25th St
- BLDR 80302 1686 E1
- BLDR 80304 1686 E1
300 DNVR 80205 2113 A3
500 DNVR 80205 2112 E3
3300 BLDR 80304 1602 E7
E 26th Av
- AdmC 80102 2123 A2
- AdmC 80102 2125 D2
- AdmC 80136 2125 E2
- AURA 80010 2115 D3
- AURA 80102 2123 A2
- DNVR 80010 2115 C3
- DvrC 80010 2115 C3
- DvrC 80238 2115 C3
4000 DNVR 80205 2113 E3
4000 DNVR 80207 2113 E3
4800 DNVR 80207 2114 B3
7200 DNVR 80238 2114 D3
9000 DNVR 80238 2115 A3
14000 AURA 80011 2116 B3
20100 AURA 80011 2117 E3
21700 AdmC 80019 2118 B3
21700 AURA 80011 2118 B3
21700 AURA 80019 2118 B3
23300 AdmC 80019 2119 A2
23300 AURA 80019 2119 A2
27900 AURA 80019 2120 A2
28100 AURA 80137 2120 E2
31300 AdmC 80137 2120 E2
31300 AdmC 80137 2121 A2
31300 AURA 80137 2121 A2
S 26th Av
300 BGTN 80601 1696 E6
W 26th Av
2400 DNVR 80211 2112 A3
3000 DNVR 80211 2111 E3
3800 DNVR 80212 2111 E3
5100 EDGW 80214 2111 C3
5100 WTRG 80214 2111 A3
6600 LKWD 80214 2111 A3
6700 WTRG 80033 2111 A3
6900 LKWD 80214 2110 E3
6900 WTRG 80033 2110 E3
7300 JfnC 80215 2110 D3
8300 LKWD 80215 2110 D3
9800 WTRG 80215 2110 A3
12700 LKWD 80215 2109 C3
12800 LKWD 80401 2109 C3
13100 JfnC 80401 2109 B3
15200 JfnC 80401 2108 E3
E 26th Pl
- AURA 80010 2115 C3
W 26th Pl
7200 WTRG 80033 2110 E3
11000 LKWD 80215 2109 E3
26th St
- BldC 80301 1602 D2
400 DNVR 80205 2113 C3
600 DNVR 80205 2112 E3
1800 BLDR 80302 1686 E2
2200 BLDR 80304 1686 E1
3400 BLDR 80304 1602 E6
3900 BldC 80304 1602 E4
N 26th St
4300 BldC 80301 1602 E3
4300 BLDR 80304 1602 E3
E 26th Wy
14500 AURA 80011 2116 C3
E 26th Av Pkwy
3500 DNVR 80205 2113 D3
3800 DNVR 80207 2113 D3
27th Av
- IDSP 80452 2101 E5
E 27th Av
1200 DNVR 80205 2113 A3
14000 AURA 80011 2116 B3
S 27th Av
- AdmC 80601 1780 E1
- BGTN 80601 1780 E1
S 27th Av
10 AdmC 80601 1696 E6
10 BGTN 80601 1696 E6
W 27th Av
2200 DNVR 80211 2112 B3
3300 DNVR 80211 2111 E3
4400 DNVR 80212 2111 C3
5300 WTRG 80214 2111 B3
7200 WTRG 80033 2110 E3
10000 JfnC 80215 2110 A3
10000 WTRG 80215 2110 A3
11000 LKWD 80215 2109 E3
12700 JfnC 80401 2109 C3
12700 LKWD 80401 2109 C3
W 27th Dr
11700 LKWD 80215 2109 D3
27th Pl
- IDSP 80452 2101 E5
W 27th Pl
11000 LKWD 80215 2109 E3
27th St
300 BLDR 80305 1686 E5
600 DNVR 80205 2113 A3
700 DNVR 80205 2112 E3
2100 BLDR 80302 1686 E1
2200 BLDR 80304 1686 E1
27th Wy
400 BLDR 80302 1686 E5
400 BLDR 80305 1686 E5
E 28th Av
1200 DNVR 80205 2113 A3
3900 DNVR 80207 2113 E3
6500 DNVR 80207 2114 C2
7300 DNVR 80238 2114 E3
8800 DNVR 80238 2115 A3
13200 AURA 80011 2116 B2
16900 AURA 80011 2117 A2
S 28th Av
300 BGTN 80601 1696 E6
W 28th Av
2500 DNVR 80211 2112 A3
3000 DNVR 80211 2111 E3
4400 DNVR 80212 2111 C3
5200 WTRG 80214 2111 B3
5900 EDGW 80214 2111 B3
6700 WTRG 80033 2111 A3
7200 WTRG 80033 2110 E3
11200 LKWD 80215 2109 E3
13000 JfnC 80401 2109 C3
E 28th Dr
8100 DNVR 80238 2114 E2
E 28th Pl
7800 DNVR 80238 2114 E2
9100 DNVR 80238 2115 A2
W 28th Pl
7000 WTRG 80033 2110 E3
10700 LKWD 80215 2109 E3
10700 LKWD 80215 2110 A3
13100 JfnC 80401 2109 C3
28th St
- BldC 80302 1602 C2
200 BLDR 80305 1686 E5
400 DNVR 80205 2113 A3
700 BLDR 80303 1686 E5
900 DNVR 80205 2112 E2
1500 BLDR 80301 1686 E2
1600 BLDR 80302 1686 E2
2200 BLDR 80304 1686 E2
2700 BLDR 80301 1602 E7
3600 BldC 80301 1602 E4
4300 BldC 80304 1602 E4
4900 BLDR 80304 1602 C2
5000 BLDR 80302 1602 C2
28th St SR-7
- BldC 80302 1602 C2
- BLDR 80304 1602 C2
1600 BLDR 80301 1686 E2
1600 BLDR 80302 1686 E2
1600 BLDR 80303 1686 E2
5000 BldC 80301 1602 C2
5000 BLDR 80302 1602 C2
28th St SR-119
1700 BLDR 80301 1686 E2
1700 BLDR 80302 1686 E2
2200 BLDR 80304 1686 E2
2700 BLDR 80301 1602 E7
2700 BLDR 80304 1602 E7
28th St US-36
- BldC 80302 1602 C2
700 BLDR 80303 1686 E2
1500 BLDR 80301 1686 E2
1600 BLDR 80302 1686 E2
2200 BLDR 80304 1686 E2
2700 BLDR 80301 1602 E7
3600 BldC 80301 1602 E4
4300 BldC 80304 1602 E4
4900 BLDR 80304 1602 C2
5000 BLDR 80302 1602 C2
28th St Frontage Rd
- BLDR 80303 1687 A4
1200 BLDR 80303 1686 E3
E 29th Av
1200 DNVR 80205 2113 B2
3900 DNVR 80207 2113 E2
4800 DNVR 80207 2114 A2
7300 DNVR 80238 2114 D2
8800 DNVR 80238 2115 A2
33700 AdmC 80137 2121 B2
34400 AURA 80137 2121 B2
S 29th Av
300 BGTN 80601 1696 E6
W 29th Av
600 DNVR 80202 2112 A2
2100 DNVR 80211 2112 A2
3100 DNVR 80211 2111 E2
3800 DNVR 80212 2111 E2
5100 WTRG 80214 2111 C2
5800 EDGW 80214 2111 B2
6700 WTRG 80033 2111 B2
6900 WTRG 80033 2110 E3
7400 JfnC 80215 2110 E3
10000 WTRG 80215 2110 A2
12400 LKWD 80215 2109 C3
12400 WTRG 80215 2109 C3
W 29th Av
12900 JfnC 80401 2109 C3
14800 JfnC 80401 2108 E3
E 29th Pl
- DNVR 80238 2114 E2
- DNVR 80238 2115 A2
W 29th Pl
6100 WTRG 80214 2111 B2
7000 WTRG 80033 2110 E2
12000 LKWD 80215 2109 D3
12000 WTRG 80215 2109 D3
15000 JfnC 80401 2108 E2
29th St
200 BLDR 80305 1686 E5
300 BLDR 80305 1687 A5
800 DNVR 80205 2113 A2
1000 DNVR 80205 2112 E2
1500 BLDR 80301 1687 A3
1500 BLDR 80303 1687 A3
2600 BLDR 80301 1603 A7
W 29th St
1800 DNVR 80216 2112 E1
E 30th Av
- AdmC 80102 2038 E4
- AdmC 80102 2122 D2
- AdmC 80137 2038 E4
- AURA 80102 2122 D2
- DNVR 80205 2113 E2
4000 DNVR 80207 2113 E2
6500 DNVR 80207 2114 C2
11400 AURA 80010 2115 D2
11700 AURA 80011 2115 D2
12700 AURA 80011 2116 A2
17300 AURA 80011 2117 A2
S 30th Av
300 BGTN 80601 1697 A6
W 30th Av
- DNVR 80202 2112 D2
2000 DNVR 80211 2112 B2
3200 DNVR 80211 2111 D2
3800 DNVR 80212 2111 D2
6100 WTRG 80214 2111 B2
6600 WTRG 80033 2111 A2
7200 WTRG 80033 2110 E2
7400 JfnC 80215 2110 E2
10000 WTRG 80215 2110 A2
10800 LKWD 80215 2109 E2
10800 LKWD 80215 2110 A2
14600 JfnC 80401 2109 A2
W 30th Dr
13000 JfnC 80401 2109 C2
N 30th Ln
14000 JfnC 80401 2109 A2
W 30th Pl
11700 LKWD 80215 2109 D2
12100 WTRG 80215 2109 D2
13600 JfnC 80401 2109 B2
30th St
100 BLDR 80305 1686 E5
200 BLDR 80305 1687 A5
500 DNVR 80205 2113 A2
1200 DNVR 80205 2112 E2
1500 BLDR 80301 1687 A2
1600 BLDR 80303 1687 A2
2800 BLDR 80301 1603 A7
3800 BldC 80301 1603 A4
E 31st Av
3300 DNVR 80205 2113 B2
12200 AURA 80011 2115 E2
13000 AURA 80011 2116 A2
S 31st Av
300 BGTN 80601 1697 A6
W 31st Av
600 DNVR 80202 2112 D2
600 DNVR 80216 2112 D2
2000 DNVR 80211 2112 B2
3300 DNVR 80211 2111 E2
4400 DNVR 80212 2111 C2
6400 WTRG 80214 2111 A2
6600 WTRG 80033 2111 A2
6900 WTRG 80033 2110 E2
10000 JfnC 80215 2110 B2
10400 LKWD 80215 2110 A2
10400 WTRG 80215 2110 A2
10800 LKWD 80215 2109 E2
12400 WTRG 80215 2109 C2
13600 JfnC 80401 2109 B2
E 31st Cir
21100 AURA 80011 2118 A2
E 31st Pl
- AURA 80010 2115 D2
- AURA 80011 2115 D2
W 31st Pl
7200 WTRG 80033 2110 E2
10500 LKWD 80215 2110 A2
10800 LKWD 80215 2109 E2
12000 WTRG 80215 2109 D2
31st St
- BLDR 80301 1687 A1
100 BLDR 80305 1687 A5
700 BLDR 80303 1687 A4
1000 DNVR 80205 2113 A2
1700 DNVR 80216 2112 E1
2500 DNVR 80216 2028 D7
3100 DNVR 80205 2112 E1
S 31st St
10 BLDR 80305 1687 A5
E 32nd Av
13700 AURA 80011 2116 D2
16900 AURA 80011 2117 A2
50100 AdmC 80102 2125 D1
51700 AdmC 80136 2125 D1
S 32nd Av
300 BGTN 80601 1697 A6
W 32nd Av
1600 DNVR 80211 2112 A2
3200 DNVR 80211 2111 E2
3800 DNVR 80212 2111 E2
5100 WTRG 80212 2111 A2
5100 WTRG 80214 2111 A2
5900 WTRG 80033 2111 A2
6800 WTRG 80033 2110 E2
7500 JfnC 80215 2110 E2
9000 WTRG 80215 2110 B2
W 32nd Av
10300 LKWD 80215 2110 B2
10800 LKWD 80215 2109 B2
10800 WTRG 80033 2109 B2
11500 WTRG 80215 2109 B2
12600 JfnC 80401 2109 B2
12600 WTRG 80401 2109 B2
14900 JfnC 80401 2108 C2
W 32nd Dr
12000 WTRG 80033 2109 D2
12000 WTRG 80215 2109 D2
14900 JfnC 80401 2108 E2
E 32nd Pkwy
18500 AURA 80011 2117 C2
20800 AURA 80011 2118 A2
21400 AdmC 80019 2118 A2
E 32nd Pl
- AURA 80011 2116 D1
17000 AURA 80011 2117 B2
W 32nd Pl
6800 WTRG 80033 2111 A2
8800 WTRG 80033 2110 C2
11700 WTRG 80033 2109 D2
14900 JfnC 80401 2108 E2
32nd St
- BLDR 80301 1603 A7
- BLDR 80301 1687 A1
200 BLDR 80305 1687 A5
700 BLDR 80303 1687 A4
700 DNVR 80205 2113 A2
1300 DNVR 80205 2112 E1
7600 BldC 80302 1518 C3
7600 BldC 80503 1518 C3
S 32nd St
10 BLDR 80305 1687 A5
E 33rd Av
1200 DNVR 80205 2113 A2
4600 DNVR 80207 2113 E2
6500 DNVR 80207 2114 C2
11400 AURA 80010 2115 D1
12300 AURA 80011 2115 E1
12500 AURA 80011 2116 A1
S 33rd Av
300 BGTN 80601 1697 A6
W 33rd Av
1400 DNVR 80211 2112 C2
3300 DNVR 80211 2111 E2
3800 DNVR 80212 2111 E2
5100 WTRG 80212 2111 B2
5900 WTRG 80033 2111 B2
6900 WTRG 80033 2110 E2
11700 WTRG 80033 2109 D2
13100 JfnC 80401 2109 C2
E 33rd Dr
- AdmC 80019 2118 A1
16300 AURA 80011 2116 E1
21100 AURA 80011 2118 A2
E 33rd Pl
13800 AURA 80011 2116 C1
W 33rd Pl
10400 WTRG 80033 2110 A2
11700 WTRG 80033 2109 D2
13200 JfnC 80401 2109 C2
33rd St
- BLDR 80301 1603 A7
- BLDR 80301 1687 A1
900 DNVR 80205 2113 A1
1500 DNVR 80205 2112 E1
1600 BLDR 80303 1687 A2
S 33rd St
10 BLDR 80305 1687 A6
E 34th Av
5000 DNVR 80207 2114 A1
S 34th Av
- AdmC 80601 1781 A1
- BGTN 80601 1781 A1
600 BGTN 80601 1697 A7
W 34th Av
3000 DNVR 80211 2112 A2
3600 DNVR 80211 2111 D2
4400 DNVR 80212 2111 C2
5100 WTRG 80212 2111 C2
5800 WTRG 80033 2111 B2
9700 WTRG 80033 2110 B2
11700 WTRG 80033 2109 D2
13500 JfnC 80401 2109 B2
34th Ct
7600 BldC 80302 1518 C3
7600 BldC 80503 1518 C3
S 34th Ct
- BGTN 80601 1697 A7
E 34th Dr
19400 AURA 80011 2117 D2
W 34th Dr
7800 WTRG 80033 2110 D2
W 34th Pl
7200 WTRG 80033 2110 E2
12000 WTRG 80033 2109 D2
34th St
700 BLDR 80303 1687 A4
1000 DNVR 80205 2113 A1
3300 BLDR 80301 1603 A6
3400 BldC 80301 1603 A6
S 34th St
10 BLDR 80305 1687 A6
E 35th Av
1200 DNVR 80205 2113 B1
3900 DNVR 80207 2113 E1
4800 DNVR 80207 2114 B1
7300 DNVR 80238 2114 D1
15300 AURA 80011 2116 D1
W 35th Av
1300 DNVR 80211 2112 C1
3600 DNVR 80211 2111 C1
3800 DNVR 80212 2111 E1
5100 WTRG 80212 2111 C1
5900 WTRG 80033 2111 B2
6800 WTRG 80033 2110 E1
11600 WTRG 80033 2109 D2
S 35th Ct
- BGTN 80601 1697 A7
E 35th Dr
- AURA 80011 2117 E2
- AURA 80011 2118 A1
E 35th Pl
13800 AURA 80011 2116 C1
W 35th Pl
6100 WTRG 80033 2111 A1
7200 WTRG 80033 2110 E1
10600 WTRG 80033 2109 E1
35th St
700 BLDR 80303 1687 A4
1100 DNVR 80205 2113 A1
1600 DNVR 80216 2113 A1
1800 DNVR 80216 2112 E1
7600 BldC 80302 1518 D3
7600 BldC 80503 1518 D3
N 35th St
- BldC 80302 1518 D2
S 35th St
10 BLDR 80305 1687 A5
E 36th Av
1200 DNVR 80205 2113 B1
3900 DNVR 80207 2113 E1
6500 DNVR 80207 2114 C1
15500 AURA 80011 2116 D1
S 36th Av
600 BGTN 80601 1697 A7
W 36th Av
1100 DNVR 80211 2112 C1
3000 DNVR 80211 2111 E1
4400 DNVR 80212 2111 C1
5100 WTRG 80212 2111 C1
6700 WTRG 80033 2111 A1
10400 WTRG 80033 2110 A1
10600 WTRG 80033 2109 E1
E 36th Dr
20100 AURA 80011 2117 E1
20100 AURA 80011 2118 A1
E 36th Pl
15500 AURA 80011 2116 D1
W 36th Pl
4500 DNVR 80212 2111 C1
5600 WTRG 80212 2111 B1
6700 WTRG 80033 2111 A1
10500 WTRG 80033 2110 A1
11800 WTRG 80033 2109 D1
36th St
700 BLDR 80303 1687 B4
1300 DNVR 80205 2113 A1
1600 DNVR 80216 2113 A1
1800 DNVR 80216 2029 A7
1900 DNVR 80216 2028 E7
S 36th St
10 BLDR 80305 1687 A5
E 37th Av
1200 DNVR 80205 2113 A1
3900 DNVR 80207 2113 D1
10500 DNVR 80238 2115 C1
11200 AdmC 80239 2115 C1
11200 AURA 80239 2115 C1
11200 DNVR 80239 2115 C1
12800 AdmC 80239 2116 A1
12800 DNVR 80239 2116 A1
12900 AURA 80011 2116 A1
12900 AURA 80239 2116 A1
12900 DNVR 80011 2116 A1
12900 DvrC 80011 2116 A1
W 37th Av
1000 DNVR 80211 2112 C1
3600 DNVR 80211 2111 D1
4500 DNVR 80212 2111 C1
5100 WTRG 80212 2111 C1
5900 WTRG 80033 2111 B1
9200 WTRG 80033 2110 B1
11600 WTRG 80033 2109 E1
E 37th Dr
- AURA 80011 2117 D1
E 37th Pl
- AURA 80011 2116 A1
- DNVR 80011 2116 A1
- DNVR 80239 2116 A1
W 37th Pl
4500 DNVR 80212 2111 C1
5800 WTRG 80033 2111 B1
5800 WTRG 80212 2111 B1
10200 WTRG 80033 2110 A1
11600 WTRG 80033 2109 E1
37th St
700 BLDR 80303 1687 B4
E 38th Av
- DNVR 80207 2113 D1
3200 DNVR 80205 2113 D1
4800 DNVR 80207 2114 A1
12000 DNVR 80239 2115 D1
13000 AdmC 80239 2116 A1
13000 AURA 80011 2116 A1
13000 DNVR 80011 2116 A1
13000 DNVR 80239 2116 A1
42500 AdmC 80102 2039 C7
42500 AURA 80102 2039 C7
44000 AdmC 80102 2040 A7
45700 BNNT 80102 2040 C7
W 38th Av
- DNVR 80216 2112 C1
1000 DNVR 80211 2112 C1
3000 DNVR 80211 2111 E1
3800 DNVR 80212 2111 E1
5100 WTRG 80212 2111 B1
5800 WTRG 80033 2111 B1
6900 WTRG 80033 2110 D1
10800 WTRG 80033 2109 E1
12700 WTRG 80401 2109 C1
W 38th Dr
12400 WTRG 80033 2109 C1
E 38th Pl
20600 DNVR 80249 2033 E7
21400 DNVR 80249 2034 A7
W 38th Pl
8200 WTRG 80033 2110 D1
10800 WTRG 80033 2109 E1
38th St
1400 DNVR 80205 2113 A1
1400 DNVR 80216 2113 A1
1600 BLDR 80301 1687 B2
1600 BLDR 80303 1687 B2
1600 DNVR 80216 2029 A7
S 38th St
10 BLDR 80305 1687 A6
39th Av
20700 DNVR 80249 2033 E7
20800 DNVR 80249 2034 A7
E 39th Av
1500 DNVR 80205 2113 B1
3900 DNVR 80239 2031 E7
4800 DNVR 80207 2030 A7
5600 DNVR 80207 2114 B1
12800 DNVR 80239 2032 A7
13800 AURA 80011 2032 C7
21300 DNVR 80249 2034 A7
W 39th Av
500 DNVR 80216 2112 D1
2700 DNVR 80211 2112 A1
3600 DNVR 80211 2111 D1
4400 DNVR 80212 2111 C1
5800 WTRG 80033 2111 B1
6000 WTRG 80212 2111 A1
7900 WTRG 80033 2110 D1
10800 WTRG 80033 2109 E1
W 39th Cir
11600 WTRG 80033 2109 D1
E 39th Pl
19100 DNVR 80249 2033 C7
W 39th Pl
5900 WTRG 80033 2111 A1
5900 WTRG 80212 2111 A1
10800 WTRG 80033 2109 E1
10800 WTRG 80033 2110 A1
39th St
- BldC 80503 1518 E4
700 BLDR 80303 1687 B4
1700 DNVR 80216 2029 A7
N 39th St
- BldC 80503 1518 E3
8200 BldC 80503 1435 E6
S 39th St
200 BLDR 80305 1687 B6
E 40th Av
1400 DNVR 80205 2029 B7
2000 DNVR 80216 2029 B7
3900 DNVR 80207 2029 E7
7700 DNVR 80207 2030 D7
7700 DNVR 80216 2030 D7
10500 DNVR 80238 2031 D7
10500 DNVR 80239 2031 D7
14700 AURA 80011 2032 D7
15300 DNVR 80239 2032 D7
17800 AURA 80011 2033 B7
17800 AURA 80011 2117 B1
20700 DNVR 80249 2033 E7
21500 DNVR 80249 2034 A7
33900 AdmC 80137 2037 B7
33900 AURA 80137 2037 B7
E 40th Av SR-33
3900 DNVR 80205 2029 E7
3900 DNVR 80207 2029 E7
3900 DNVR 80216 2029 E7
N 40th Av
- AdmC 80601 1697 B5
- BGTN 80601 1697 B5
- BGTN 80603 1697 B4
W 40th Av
500 DNVR 80216 2112 D1
2700 DNVR 80211 2112 A1
3000 DNVR 80211 2111 E1
6000 WTRG 80212 2111 A1
6100 WTRG 80033 2111 A1
8200 WTRG 80033 2110 D1
11100 WTRG 80033 2109 E1
E 40th Cir
16400 AURA 80011 2032 E7
16400 AURA 80011 2116 E1
W 40th Cir
11600 WTRG 80033 2109 D1
E 40th Dr
19500 DNVR 80249 2033 D7
E 40th Pl
18600 AURA 80011 2033 C7
18600 DNVR 80249 2033 C7
18600 DvrC 80249 2033 C7
21100 DNVR 80249 2034 A7
40th St
1300 DNVR 80205 2029 A7
1300 DNVR 80205 2113 A1
1700 DNVR 80216 2029 A7
S 40th St
200 BLDR 80305 1687 B6
E 41st Av
2700 DNVR 80216 2029 C7
4800 DNVR 80207 2030 A7
7400 DNVR 80216 2030 D7
19300 DNVR 80249 2033 D7
21000 DNVR 80249 2034 A7
W 41st Av
500 DNVR 80216 2028 D7
1400 DNVR 80211 2028 C7
3000 DNVR 80211 2027 E7
3800 DNVR 80212 2027 D7
5100 MNVW 80212 2027 C7
5100 WTRG 80212 2027 C7
5900 WTRG 80033 2027 A7
9600 WTRG 80033 2026 B7
10400 WTRG 80033 2110 A1
10800 WTRG 80033 2109 E1
E 41st Pl
20900 DNVR 80249 2033 E7
20900 DNVR 80249 2034 A7
W 41st Pl
10800 WTRG 80033 2025 E7
10800 WTRG 80033 2026 A7
N 41st St
7600 BldC 80503 1518 E2
S 41st St
200 BLDR 80305 1687 B6
E 42nd Av
2700 DNVR 80216 2029 C7
5600 DNVR 80216 2030 B7
12400 DNVR 80239 2031 E7
14100 DNVR 80239 2032 A7
20100 DNVR 80249 2033 E7
20800 DNVR 80249 2034 A7

STREET Block City ZIP Map# Grid

E 42nd Av
23300 AdmC 80019 2034 D6
23300 AURA 80019 2034 D6
N 42nd Av
- BGTN 80601 1697 C5
W 42nd Av
400 DNVR 80216 2028 D7
900 DNVR 80211 2028 C7
3000 DNVR 80211 2027 E7
4000 DNVR 80212 2027 D7
6100 WTRG 80033 2027 A7
10400 WTRG 80033 2026 A7
12200 WTRG 80033 2025 D7
E 42nd Pl
20100 DNVR 80249 2033 E7
21400 DNVR 80249 2034 A7
S 42nd St
100 BLDR 80305 1687 B6
E 43rd Av
10 DNVR 80216 2028 E7
2000 DNVR 80216 2029 B7
14400 DNVR 80239 2032 B7
20100 DNVR 80249 2033 E7
20900 DNVR 80249 2034 A7
W 43rd Av
200 DNVR 80216 2028 D7
1000 DNVR 80211 2028 C7
3800 DNVR 80211 2027 D7
3800 DNVR 80212 2027 D7
5100 MNVW 80212 2027 B7
5700 WTRG 80212 2027 B7
5900 WTRG 80033 2027 B7
9700 WTRG 80033 2026 B7
15200 JfnC 80403 2024 E7
W 43rd Dr
17200 JfnC 80403 2024 B7
E 43rd Pl
20100 DNVR 80249 2033 E6
W 43rd Pl
7000 WTRG 80033 2026 E7
43rd St
1700 DNVR 80216 2029 B7
S 43rd St
300 BLDR 80305 1687 B6
E 44th Av
10 DNVR 80216 2028 E7
1900 DNVR 80216 2029 B7
12300 DNVR 80239 2031 E7
14400 DNVR 80239 2032 B7
20300 DNVR 80249 2033 E6
21100 DNVR 80249 2034 A6
W 44th Av
10 DNVR 80216 2028 D7
2000 DNVR 80211 2028 A7
3000 DNVR 80211 2027 E7
3800 DNVR 80212 2027 E7
5100 MNVW 80212 2027 B7
5800 LKSD 80212 2027 B7
5900 WTRG 80033 2027 B7
5900 WTRG 80212 2027 B7
8000 WTRG 80033 2026 C7
10900 WTRG 80033 2025 D7
12800 JfnC 80403 2025 D7
14800 JfnC 80403 2024 D7
15300 GOLD 80403 2024 D7
16400 GOLD 80403 2108 A1
16400 JfnC 80403 2108 A1
18000 GOLD 80401 2108 A1
18000 JfnC 80401 2108 A1
W 44th Av CO-58
5200 DNVR 80212 2027 B7
5700 WTRG 80212 2027 B7
5800 MNVW 80212 2027 B7
5900 LKSD 80212 2027 B7
5900 WTRG 80033 2027 B7
10500 WTRG 80033 2026 A7
10900 WTRG 80033 2025 D7
W 44th Dr
14200 JfnC 80403 2025 A7
E 44th Pl
18800 DNVR 80249 2033 C6
W 44th Pl
6300 WTRG 80033 2027 A7
8000 WTRG 80033 2026 D7
10800 WTRG 80033 2025 E7
14100 JfnC 80403 2025 A7
44th St
- DNVR 80216 2029 B6
S 44th St
300 BLDR 80305 1687 B6
E 45th Av
- DNVR 80238 2031 C6
10 DNVR 80216 2028 E7
2300 DNVR 80216 2029 C6
10500 DNVR 80239 2031 C6
14400 DNVR 80239 2032 B6
18500 DNVR 80239 2033 C6
20400 DNVR 80249 2033 E6
21500 DNVR 80249 2034 A6
33700 AdmC 80137 2037 B6
33700 AURA 80137 2037 B6
N 45th Av
- BGTN 80603 1697 C4
10 BGTN 80601 1697 C5
S 45th Av
100 BGTN 80601 1697 C6
W 45th Av
300 DNVR 80216 2028 D7
2700 DNVR 80211 2028 A7
3600 DNVR 80211 2027 E7
3800 DNVR 80212 2027 C7
5100 LKSD 80212 2027 C7
6000 WTRG 80033 2027 A7
10300 WTRG 80033 2026 A7
10600 WTRG 80033 2025 E7
W 45th Dr
14200 JfnC 80403 2025 A7
16100 GOLD 80403 2024 D7
E 45th Pl
- DNVR 80239 2032 E7
W 45th Pl
6200 WTRG 80033 2027 A7
7400 WTRG 80033 2026 E7
11400 WTRG 80033 2025 E7
14200 JfnC 80403 2025 A7
N 45th St
7100 BldC 80503 1519 A4
S 45th St
300 BLDR 80305 1687 B6
46th Av
- DNVR 80216 2029 B6
E 46th Av
10 DNVR 80216 2028 E6
700 DNVR 80216 2029 A6
5000 DNVR 80216 2030 A6
12900 DNVR 80239 2031 E6
12900 DNVR 80239 2032 A6
18700 DNVR 80249 2033 D6
21000 DNVR 80249 2034 A6
N 46th Av
- BGTN 80601 1697 C4
W 46th Av
1000 DNVR 80211 2028 C6
3000 DNVR 80211 2027 E6
3800 DNVR 80212 2027 E6
5100 LKSD 80212 2027 C6
6000 WTRG 80033 2027 A7
8100 WTRG 80033 2026 D6
11100 WTRG 80033 2025 E7
14100 JfnC 80403 2025 A7
W 46th Cir
8000 WTRG 80033 2026 D7
W 46th Dr
14400 JfnC 80403 2025 A7
E 46th Pl
20100 DNVR 80249 2033 D6
W 46th Pl
6800 WTRG 80033 2027 A6
8800 WTRG 80033 2026 C6
11100 WTRG 80033 2025 E6
46th St
1000 BLDR 80305 1687 B7
S 46th St
500 BLDR 80305 1687 B7
E 46th Av Dr
6700 DNVR 80216 2030 C6
46th Avenue South Dr
- DNVR 80216 2028 E7
E 47th Av
10 DNVR 80216 2028 E6
1400 DNVR 80216 2029 B6
5200 DNVR 80216 2030 A6
9900 DNVR 80238 2031 B6
10500 DNVR 80239 2031 C6
12900 DNVR 80239 2032 A6
18900 DNVR 80249 2033 C6
21400 DNVR 80249 2034 A6
W 47th Av
- LKSD 80212 2027 A6
2900 DNVR 80211 2028 A6
3100 DNVR 80211 2027 E6
3800 DNVR 80212 2027 D6
6000 WTRG 80033 2027 A6
10800 WTRG 80033 2025 E6
10800 WTRG 80033 2026 A6
E 47th Dr
14300 DNVR 80239 2032 B6
E 47th Pl
20200 DNVR 80249 2033 D6
W 47th Pl
6100 WTRG 80033 2027 A6
10300 WTRG 80033 2026 A6
47th St
2200 BLDR 80301 1687 B1
2600 BLDR 80301 1603 B7
3700 BldC 80301 1603 B6
E 47th Av Cir
12900 DNVR 80239 2032 A6
E 47th Av Dr
- CMCY 80022 2030 C6
- DNVR 80022 2030 C6
- DNVR 80216 2030 C6
E 48th Av
- AdmC 80019 2034 A6
- AURA 80019 2035 A5
- DNVR 80216 2028 E6
- DNVR 80216 2029 A6
- DNVR 80249 2033 E6
- DNVR 80249 2034 A6
- DvrC 80249 2034 A6
4800 CMCY 80022 2030 A6
4800 DNVR 80022 2030 A6
4800 DNVR 80216 2030 A6
5800 CMCY 80216 2030 B6
12100 DNVR 80239 2031 E6
12900 DNVR 80239 2032 A6
18500 DNVR 80239 2033 A6
34100 AdmC 80137 2037 B5
34100 AURA 80137 2037 B5
36100 AURA 80137 2038 A5
37300 AdmC 80137 2038 A5
37800 AURA 80102 2038 A5
39300 AdmC 80102 2038 E5
40300 AURA 80102 2039 A5
41000 AdmC 80102 2039 A5
44000 AdmC 80102 2040 A5
N 48th Av
- BGTN 80603 1697 D4
400 BGTN 80601 1697 D4
S 48th Av
500 BGTN 80601 1697 D4
600 BGTN 80603 1697 D4
W 48th Av
- DNVR 80221 2028 C6
- WTRG 80212 2027 B6
10 DNVR 80216 2028 E6
3600 DNVR 80211 2027 D6
3600 DNVR 80221 2027 D6
5200 DNVR 80212 2027 B6
5200 DvrC 80212 2027 B6
5200 LKSD 80212 2027 B6
6000 WTRG 80033 2027 A6
6800 WTRG 80033 2026 E6
14000 JfnC 80403 2025 A6
14900 JfnC 80403 2024 E6
15200 GOLD 80403 2024 E6
W 48th Cir
7300 WTRG 80033 2026 E6
48th Dr
20300 DNVR 80249 2033 E6
E 48th Dr
20300 DNVR 80249 2033 D5
21200 DNVR 80249 2034 A6
E 48th Pl
15600 DNVR 80239 2032 D6
19600 DNVR 80249 2033 D5
21200 DNVR 80249 2034 A6
W 48th Pl
6200 WTRG 80033 2027 A6
8500 JfnC 80002 2026 C6
14300 JfnC 80403 2025 A6
16900 JfnC 80403 2024 C6
48th St
1500 BldC 80301 1687 C2
1500 BldC 80303 1687 C2
1500 BLDR 80301 1687 C2
1500 BLDR 80303 1687 C2
W 48th Avenue South Dr
2000 DNVR 80211 2028 A6
3600 DNVR 80211 2027 D6
3800 DNVR 80212 2027 D6
49th Av
20300 DNVR 80249 2033 E6
21500 DNVR 80249 2034 A5
E 49th Av
- DNVR 80249 2034 A6
10 DNVR 80216 2028 E6
700 DNVR 80216 2029 A6
10300 DNVR 80238 2031 B5
10400 DNVR 80239 2031 B5
19600 DNVR 80249 2033 D5
W 49th Av
10 DNVR 80216 2028 E6
1800 DNVR 80221 2028 A6
3000 DNVR 80221 2027 E6
5200 DNVR 80212 2027 B6
5900 WTRG 80033 2027 B6
8800 JfnC 80002 2026 C6
9200 WTRG 80033 2026 B6
11700 WTRG 80033 2025 D6
12400 JfnC 80033 2025 C6
14800 JfnC 80403 2024 E6
14800 JfnC 80403 2025 A6
E 49th Dr
6000 CMCY 80022 2030 C6
7100 CMCY 80216 2030 C6
7100 DNVR 80216 2030 C6
W 49th Dr
5900 DNVR 80002 2027 A5
5900 JfnC 80002 2027 A5
5900 WTRG 80033 2027 A5
49th Pl
4900 DNVR 80239 2032 C6
21000 DNVR 80249 2034 A6
E 49th Pl
19600 DNVR 80249 2033 D5
21200 DNVR 80249 2034 A5
W 49th Pl
6000 DNVR 80033 2027 A6
6000 DNVR 80212 2027 A6
6000 WTRG 80033 2027 A6
8800 ARVD 80002 2026 C6
8800 ARVD 80033 2026 C6
8800 JfnC 80002 2026 C6
8800 WTRG 80033 2026 C6
12300 JfnC 80033 2025 D6
12300 WTRG 80033 2025 D6
14800 JfnC 80403 2025 A6
15000 JfnC 80403 2024 E6
49th St
2400 BLDR 80301 1687 C1
N 49th St
7000 BldC 80503 1519 B3
10200 BldC 80503 1436 B2
50th Av
15600 DNVR 80239 2032 D5
E 50th Av
- AURA 80019 2034 A5
- AURA 80249 2034 A5
- DNVR 80216 2029 A5
- DNVR 80249 2034 A5
10 DNVR 80216 2028 E5
4800 DNVR 80216 2030 A5
5800 CMCY 80022 2030 C5
12200 DNVR 80239 2031 E5
14000 DNVR 80239 2032 A5
19600 DNVR 80249 2033 D5
37300 AdmC 80137 2038 A5
S 50th Av
15200 AdmC 80601 1697 D7
15200 BGTN 80601 1697 D7
W 50th Av
10 DNVR 80216 2028 D5
1500 DNVR 80221 2028 B5
3600 DNVR 80221 2027 D5
3800 DNVR 80212 2027 D5
5400 DNVR 80033 2027 B5
5400 WTRG 80033 2027 B5
6500 ARVD 80002 2027 A5
8000 ARVD 80002 2026 D5
8800 ARVD 80033 2026 C5
8800 JfnC 80002 2026 C5
10400 WTRG 80033 2026 A5
11000 WTRG 80033 2025 E5
14000 JfnC 80403 2025 A6
15600 GOLD 80403 2024 D6
15600 JfnC 80403 2024 D6
E 50th Dr
- DNVR 80249 2033 D5
14900 DNVR 80239 2032 C6
E 50th Pl
- DNVR 80249 2033 D5
14900 DNVR 80239 2032 C6
21200 DNVR 80249 2034 A5
W 50th Pl
12000 JfnC 80033 2025 D5
12000 WTRG 80033 2025 D5
14100 JfnC 80403 2025 A5
N 50th St
16000 BGTN 80601 1697 D4
16600 BGTN 80603 1697 D4
E 50th Wy
15000 DNVR 80239 2032 C6
E 51st Av
- AdmC 80137 2038 A5
10 DNVR 80216 2028 E5
2300 DNVR 80216 2029 C5
10500 DNVR 80238 2031 B5
10500 DNVR 80239 2031 C5
13100 DNVR 80239 2032 A5
18700 DNVR 80249 2033 C5
21300 DNVR 80249 2034 A5
W 51st Av
10 DNVR 80216 2028 E5
1500 DNVR 80221 2028 B5
3600 DNVR 80221 2027 D5
3800 DNVR 80212 2027 D5
6500 ARVD 80002 2027 A5
6500 JfnC 80002 2027 A5
6500 JfnC 80033 2027 A5
6500 WTRG 80033 2027 A5
7600 ARVD 80002 2026 D5
8400 JfnC 80002 2026 C5
8600 WTRG 80002 2026 B5
9500 WTRG 80033 2026 B5
13500 JfnC 80002 2025 B5
13500 JfnC 80403 2025 B5
16400 JfnC 80403 2024 C5
E 51st Dr
15600 DNVR 80239 2032 D5
21300 DNVR 80249 2034 A5
W 51st Ln
16100 JfnC 80403 2024 D5
E 51st Pl
15600 DNVR 80239 2032 D5
18700 DNVR 80249 2033 C5
21300 DNVR 80249 2034 A5
W 51st Pl
5500 DNVR 80212 2027 B5
9600 ARVD 80002 2026 B5
9600 WTRG 80033 2026 B5
9900 ARVD 80033 2026 B5
9900 WTRG 80002 2026 B5
13600 JfnC 80002 2025 B5
15200 JfnC 80403 2024 E5
E 51st St
700 DNVR 80216 2029 A5
N 51st St
- BldC 80503 1353 C3
4200 BldC 80301 1603 C1
5000 BLDR 80301 1603 C1
5500 BldC 80503 1519 C7
5500 BLDR 80301 1519 C7
10000 BldC 80503 1436 C4
W 51st St
13900 JfnC 80403 2025 B5
E 52nd Av
- AURA 80019 2034 A5
- AURA 80249 2034 A5
10 AdmC 80216 2028 E5
10 DNVR 80216 2028 E5
800 AdmC 80216 2029 A5
800 DNVR 80216 2029 A5
4200 CMCY 80022 2029 E5
4200 DNVR 80022 2029 E5
4800 CMCY 80022 2030 A5
4800 CMCY 80216 2030 A5
4800 DNVR 80022 2030 A5
4800 DNVR 80216 2030 A5
8700 DNVR 80249 2033 C5
14100 DNVR 80239 2032 B5
21300 DNVR 80249 2034 A5
37300 AdmC 80137 2038 A4
W 52nd Av
900 AdmC 80221 2028 C5
900 DNVR 80221 2028 C5
3600 AdmC 80221 2027 C5
3600 DNVR 80221 2027 C5
4400 DNVR 80212 2027 C5
4400 JfnC 80212 2027 C5
6000 DNVR 80002 2027 A5
6100 ARVD 80002 2027 A5
6100 DvrC 80002 2027 A5
9200 ARVD 80002 2026 B5
11500 ARVD 80033 2025 D5
11500 WTRG 80033 2025 D5
11700 ARVD 80002 2025 D5
12300 JfnC 80033 2025 D5
12500 JfnC 80002 2025 C5
13800 JfnC 80403 2025 A5
14800 JfnC 80403 2024 E5
W 52nd Cir
- ARVD 80033 2026 A5
- WTRG 80033 2026 A5
W 52nd Dr
15600 JfnC 80403 2024 D5
19400 JfnC 80403 2023 E5
E 52nd Pl
6800 CMCY 80022 2030 C5
12200 DNVR 80239 2031 E5
18800 DNVR 80249 2033 C4
W 52nd Pl
- ARVD 80002 2027 A5
- ARVD 80033 2026 A5
1600 AdmC 80221 2028 B5
3200 AdmC 80221 2027 E5
4400 AdmC 80212 2027 C5
8400 ARVD 80002 2026 C5
11900 ARVD 80002 2025 D5
12800 JfnC 80002 2025 C5
16400 JfnC 80403 2024 C5
E 52nd Av Dr
12200 DNVR 80239 2031 E5
E 53rd Av
10 AdmC 80216 2028 E5
3200 DNVR 80216 2029 D5
8700 DNVR 80249 2033 C4
10900 DNVR 80239 2031 D4
14500 DNVR 80239 2032 C5
21300 DNVR 80249 2034 A4
W 53rd Av
- ARVD 80002 2025 E5
2000 AdmC 80221 2028 B5
3000 AdmC 80221 2027 E5
5200 JfnC 80002 2027 B5
5200 JfnC 80212 2027 B5
5300 ARVD 80002 2026 E5
6100 ARVD 80002 2027 A5
14800 JfnC 80002 2025 A5
14800 JfnC 80403 2024 E5
14800 JfnC 80403 2025 A5
W 53rd Cir
10100 ARVD 80033 2026 A5
W 53rd Ct
- AdmC 80221 2028 C5
W 53rd Dr
1700 AdmC 80221 2028 B4
17200 JfnC 80403 2024 B5
W 53rd Ln
19500 JfnC 80403 2023 E5
E 53rd Pl
6800 CMCY 80022 2030 D6
6800 DNVR 80216 2030 D6
21300 DNVR 80249 2034 A4
W 53rd Pl
- ARVD 80002 2026 E5
- JfnC 80002 2027 C5
300 AdmC 80216 2028 D4
2300 AdmC 80221 2028 B5
4600 AdmC 80212 2027 C5
11700 ARVD 80002 2025 D5
11700 ARVD 80033 2025 D5
12800 JfnC 80002 2025 C5
15000 JfnC 80403 2024 E5
N 53rd St
13000 BldC 80503 1353 C3
E 53rd Wy
6400 CMCY 80022 2030 B4
W 53rd Wy
16500 JfnC 80403 2024 C5
54th Av
- DNVR 80216 2030 D4
E 54th Av
10 AdmC 80216 2028 E4
700 AdmC 80216 2029 A4
700 DNVR 80216 2029 A4
6300 CMCY 80022 2030 B4
10500 DNVR 80239 2031 C4
14800 DNVR 80239 2032 C4
21500 DNVR 80249 2034 A4
W 54th Av
- ARVD 80033 2026 A5
2800 AdmC 80221 2028 A4
3000 AdmC 80221 2027 E4
5100 JfnC 80212 2027 C4
6000 ARVD 80002 2027 A4
6000 JfnC 80002 2027 A4
7600 ARVD 80002 2026 D4
11000 ARVD 80033 2025 E4
12000 ARVD 80002 2025 D5
13200 JfnC 80002 2025 B5
14800 JfnC 80403 2025 A5
15600 JfnC 80403 2024 D5
W 54th Av N
- AdmC 80212 2027 C4
W 54th Av S
- AdmC 80212 2027 C5
W 54th Dr
12000 ARVD 80002 2025 D4
12300 JfnC 80002 2025 D4
W 54th Ln
10700 ARVD 80002 2025 E4
10700 ARVD 80002 2026 A4
E 54th Pl
6800 CMCY 80022 2030 C4
6800 DNVR 80216 2030 C4
21500 DNVR 80249 2034 A4
W 54th Pl
2000 AdmC 80221 2028 B4
6500 ARVD 80002 2027 A4
8000 ARVD 80002 2026 D4
10800 ARVD 80002 2025 E4
12800 JfnC 80002 2025 C5
17200 JfnC 80403 2024 B4
19500 JfnC 80403 2023 E4
E 54th Av Dr
12200 DNVR 80239 2031 E4
E 55th Av
10 AdmC 80216 2028 E4
6100 CMCY 80022 2030 B4
12100 DNVR 80239 2031 E4
16200 DNVR 80239 2032 E4
21500 DNVR 80249 2034 A4
W 55th Av
2200 AdmC 80221 2028 A4
3000 AdmC 80221 2027 E4
6000 ARVD 80002 2027 A4
6000 JfnC 80002 2027 A4
8800 ARVD 80002 2026 C4
W 55th Dr
8500 ARVD 80002 2026 C4
16400 JfnC 80403 2024 D4
19400 JfnC 80403 2023 E4
W 55th Ln
10700 ARVD 80002 2025 E4
10700 ARVD 80002 2026 A4
19500 JfnC 80403 2023 E4
E 55th Pl
21300 DNVR 80249 2034 A4
W 55th Pl
- ARVD 80002 2026 A4
1600 AdmC 80221 2028 B4
3000 AdmC 80221 2027 E4
4800 AdmC 80212 2027 C4
6000 JfnC 80002 2027 A4
11000 ARVD 80002 2025 E4
12800 JfnC 80002 2025 C5
16200 JfnC 80403 2024 D4
19500 JfnC 80403 2023 E4
55th St
10 BldC 80303 1687 D5
1500 BLDR 80301 1687 D2
1600 BLDR 80303 1687 D2
2500 BldC 80301 1687 D1
2800 BldC 80301 1603 D7
2800 BLDR 80301 1603 D7
N 55th St
4200 BldC 80301 1603 D4
5700 BldC 80503 1519 D5
5700 BLDR 80301 1519 D5
5700 BLDR 80503 1519 D5
8500 BldC 80503 1436 D7
13600 BldC 80503 1270 D6
13600 BldC 80503 1353 D1
E 56th Av
- AdmC 80019 2035 A3
- AdmC 80022 2031 E3
- AdmC 80022 2032 D4
- AdmC 80102 2038 C3
- AdmC 80102 2039 B3
- AdmC 80137 2038 E3
- AdmC 80249 2032 D4
- AdmC 80249 2034 C4
- AdmC 80249 2035 D3
- AURA 80019 2034 D3
- AURA 80019 2035 D3
- AURA 80137 2038 C3
- AURA 80249 2035 A3
- DNVR 80216 2031 A4
- DNVR 80239 2030 E4
- DNVR 80249 2035 D3
10 AdmC 80216 2028 E4
1200 AdmC 80216 2029 A4
1200 DNVR 80216 2029 A4
3100 CMCY 80022 2029 D4
4900 CMCY 80022 2030 A4
5600 AdmC 80137 2036 D3
5600 AdmC 80137 2037 A3
5600 AURA 80019 2036 D3
5600 AURA 80137 2036 D3
5600 AURA 80137 2037 A3
7000 AdmC 80022 2030 E4
7000 DNVR 80022 2030 E4
7000 DNVR 80216 2030 E4
10500 DNVR 80022 2031 A4
10500 DNVR 80239 2031 A4
12900 DNVR 80022 2032 A4
12900 DNVR 80239 2032 A4
16500 DNVR 80249 2032 D4
16900 DNVR 80239 2033 A4
18500 AURA 80019 2033 E3
18500 AURA 80249 2033 E3
18500 DNVR 80019 2033 E3
18500 DNVR 80249 2033 E3
19000 AdmC 80019 2033 E3
19900 AdmC 80019 2034 A3
19900 DNVR 80019 2034 A3
19900 DNVR 80249 2034 A3
45700 AdmC 80102 2040 B3
W 56th Av
- JfnC 80403 2023 E4
10 AdmC 80216 2028 D4
1600 AdmC 80221 2028 A4
5200 JfnC 80002 2027 B4
6500 ARVD 80002 2027 A4
6600 ARVD 80002 2026 E4
W 56th Cir
11700 ARVD 80002 2025 D4
W 56th Dr
11700 ARVD 80002 2025 D4
14500 JfnC 80002 2025 A4
14600 JfnC 80403 2025 A4
16400 JfnC 80403 2024 C4
19500 JfnC 80403 2023 E4
W 56th Ln
19300 JfnC 80403 2023 E4
W 56th Pl
2200 AdmC 80221 2028 B4
6400 ARVD 80002 2027 A4
9900 ARVD 80002 2026 B4
11800 ARVD 80002 2025 D4
12400 JfnC 80002 2025 C4
15600 JfnC 80403 2024 D4
19400 JfnC 80403 2023 E4
56th St
1600 BLDR 80301 1687 D2
1600 BLDR 80303 1687 D2
W 56th Wy
- AdmC 80002 2027 C4
- AdmC 80221 2027 D4
14300 JfnC 80002 2025 A4
E 57th Av
- AURA 80019 2033 C3
- DNVR 80249 2033 C3
200 AdmC 80216 2028 E4
800 AdmC 80216 2029 A4
W 57th Av
2300 AdmC 80221 2028 A4
7300 ARVD 80002 2026 D4
11800 ARVD 80002 2025 D4
16800 JfnC 80403 2024 C4
19200 JfnC 80403 2023 E4
E 57th Cir
19300 AURA 80019 2033 D3
W 57th Cir
19400 JfnC 80403 2023 E4
57th Ct N
1900 BLDR 80301 1687 D1
57th Ct S
1800 BLDR 80301 1687 D2
W 57th Dr
12700 JfnC 80002 2025 C4
14800 JfnC 80403 2024 E4
14800 JfnC 80403 2025 A4
W 57th Ln
- JfnC 80403 2024 C4
E 57th Pl
7000 AdmC 80022 2030 C3
7000 CMCY 80022 2030 C3
18700 DNVR 80249 2033 C3
W 57th Pl
2200 AdmC 80221 2028 B4
9600 ARVD 80002 2026 B4
14400 JfnC 80002 2025 A4
17100 JfnC 80403 2024 C4
19300 JfnC 80403 2023 E4
N 57th St
2300 BldC 80301 1687 D1
3600 BldC 80301 1603 D5
3600 BLDR 80301 1603 D5
E 58th Av
10 AdmC 80216 2028 E3
700 AdmC 80216 2029 A3
4800 CMCY 80022 2030 A3
7200 AdmC 80022 2030 B3
18800 DNVR 80249 2033 C3
19300 AURA 80019 2033 D3
E 58th Av SR-53
- AdmC 80216 2028 E3
W 58th Av
2500 AdmC 80221 2028 A3
3000 AdmC 80221 2027 E3
4400 AdmC 80002 2027 C3
4400 ARVD 80002 2027 C3
9600 ARVD 80002 2026 A4
10400 ARVD 80004 2026 A4
10900 ARVD 80002 2025 E4
10900 ARVD 80004 2025 E4
12200 JfnC 80002 2025 E4
12400 JfnC 80004 2025 A4
14300 JfnC 80403 2025 A4
15600 JfnC 80403 2024 D3
19000 JfnC 80403 2023 E4
W 58th Ct
18400 JfnC 80403 2024 A4
E 58th Dr
19300 AURA 80019 2033 D3
W 58th Dr
13700 ARVD 80004 2025 B3
18200 JfnC 80403 2024 A3
E 58th Pl
4800 CMCY 80022 2030 A3
19300 AURA 80019 2033 D3
W 58th Pl
- ARVD 80002 2026 B3
2200 AdmC 80221 2028 B3
6600 ARVD 80003 2026 E3
6600 ARVD 80003 2027 A3
10100 ARVD 80004 2026 A3
13700 ARVD 80004 2025 B3
13700 JfnC 80004 2025 B3
14500 JfnC 80403 2025 A3
18200 JfnC 80403 2024 A4
W 58th Wy
- AdmC 80002 2027 D3
- AdmC 80221 2027 D3
- ARVD 80002 2027 D3
- ARVD 80221 2027 D3
W 58th Frontage Rd
7000 ARVD 80002 2026 E3
E 59th Av
6500 CMCY 80022 2030 C3
7200 AdmC 80022 2030 C3
19300 AURA 80019 2033 D3
19300 DNVR 80249 2033 D3
W 59th Av
5800 ARVD 80003 2027 B3
7300 ARVD 80003 2026 E3
7400 ARVD 80004 2026 E3
10900 ARVD 80004 2025 E3
14000 JfnC 80004 2025 A3
17800 JfnC 80403 2024 B3
E 59th Dr
19300 AURA 80019 2033 D3
W 59th Dr
13500 ARVD 80004 2025 B3
13900 JfnC 80004 2025 B3
17700 JfnC 80403 2024 B3
18800 JfnC 80403 2023 E4
E 59th Pl
19300 AURA 80019 2033 D3
W 59th Pl
2200 AdmC 80221 2028 B3
10800 ARVD 80004 2026 A3
10900 ARVD 80004 2025 E3
14000 JfnC 80004 2025 A3
17500 JfnC 80403 2024 B3
18900 JfnC 80403 2023 E3
N 59th St
11000 BldC 80503 1353 E7
11000 BldC 80503 1436 D1
E 60th Av
- AURA 80019 2033 D3
- AURA 80249 2033 D3
- DNVR 80249 2033 D3
1300 AdmC 80216 2029 A3
4100 CMCY 80022 2029 E3
4900 CMCY 80022 2030 A3
7200 AdmC 80022 2030 C3
W 60th Av
1800 AdmC 80221 2028 A3
4400 AdmC 80003 2027 C3
6400 ARVD 80003 2027 A3
7400 ARVD 80004 2026 E3
7600 ARVD 80003 2026 D3
10900 ARVD 80004 2025 E3
17100 ARVD 80403 2024 C3
17100 JfnC 80403 2024 C3
W 60th Ct
17200 ARVD 80403 2024 C3
W 60th Dr
16600 ARVD 80403 2024 C3
18900 JfnC 80403 2023 E3
W 60th Ln
17500 ARVD 80403 2024 B3
19100 JfnC 80403 2023 E3
E 60th Pl
6700 CMCY 80022 2030 C3
W 60th Pl
10 AdmC 80216 2028 D3
5500 ARVD 80003 2027 B3
13200 ARVD 80004 2025 C3
18800 ARVD 80403 2024 A3
18800 JfnC 80403 2023 E3
18800 JfnC 80403 2024 A3
E 60th Wy
7100 AdmC 80022 2030 C3
7100 CMCY 80022 2030 C3
E 61st Av
1200 AdmC 80216 2029 A3
4400 CMCY 80022 2029 E3
5600 CMCY 80022 2030 B3
W 61st Av
- AdmC 80221 2027 E2

STREET
Block City ZIP Map# Grid

W 61st Av
1600 AdmC 80221 2028 B3
4400 AdmC 80003 2027 D3
6000 ARVD 80003 2027 A3
7400 ARVD 80003 2026 E3
7600 ARVD 80004 2026 D3
10800 ARVD 80004 2025 E3
18800 ARVD 80403 2024 A3
18800 JfnC 80403 2023 E3
18800 JfnC 80403 2024 A3
W 61st Cir
12900 ARVD 80004 2025 C3
W 61st Ct
17200 ARVD 80403 2024 B3
W 61st Dr
- ARVD 80403 2024 D3
- JfnC 80403 2024 D3
5700 ARVD 80003 2027 B3
W 61st Ln
13500 ARVD 80004 2025 B3
16700 ARVD 80403 2024 C3
E 61st Pl
6700 CMCY 80022 2030 C2
W 61st Pl
4000 AdmC 80003 2027 D3
4400 ARVD 80003 2027 C3
11400 ARVD 80004 2025 D3
16400 ARVD 80403 2024 C3
18800 JfnC 80403 2023 E3
18800 JfnC 80403 2024 A3
61st St
3200 BldC 80301 1603 E6
N 61st St
3100 BldC 80301 1603 E7
11800 BldC 80503 1353 E6
11800 BldC 80503 1354 A5
E 61st Wy
5300 CMCY 80022 2030 A2
W 61st Wy
17200 ARVD 80403 2024 B3
E 62nd Av
10 AdmC 80216 2028 E2
700 AdmC 80216 2029 A2
4900 CMCY 80022 2030 A2
7200 AdmC 80022 2030 B2
W 62nd Av
10 AdmC 80216 2028 C2
2800 AdmC 80221 2028 A2
3000 AdmC 80221 2027 E2
4300 AdmC 80003 2027 D2
4300 ARVD 80003 2027 D2
6800 ARVD 80003 2026 E3
7400 ARVD 80004 2026 D2
10900 ARVD 80004 2025 E2
14000 JfnC 80004 2025 A3
18800 JfnC 80403 2023 E3
18800 JfnC 80403 2024 A3
W 62nd Cir
14600 ARVD 80004 2025 A2
17000 ARVD 80403 2024 C2
W 62nd Ct
- AdmC 80221 2028 A2
17200 ARVD 80403 2024 B3
W 62nd Dr
13500 ARVD 80004 2025 B3
W 62nd Ln
13700 ARVD 80004 2025 B3
16800 ARVD 80403 2024 C2
E 62nd Pl
6100 CMCY 80022 2030 B2
W 62nd Pl
4000 AdmC 80003 2027 D2
6400 ARVD 80003 2027 A2
7600 ARVD 80003 2026 D2
7600 ARVD 80004 2026 D2
11900 ARVD 80004 2025 D2
16700 ARVD 80403 2024 C2
62nd St
1600 BldC 80301 1688 A2
1600 BldC 80303 1688 A2
E 62nd Wy
6500 CMCY 80022 2030 C2
W 62nd Wy
7700 ARVD 80004 2026 D2
E 63rd Av
4500 CMCY 80022 2029 E2
7000 CMCY 80022 2030 C2
7200 AdmC 80022 2030 C2
18600 DNVR 80249 2033 C2
W 63rd Av
- JfnC 80004 2025 B2
2700 AdmC 80221 2028 A2
3000 AdmC 80221 2027 E2
3800 AdmC 80003 2027 D2
4800 ARVD 80003 2027 C2
7100 ARVD 80003 2026 E2
9600 ARVD 80004 2026 B2
14000 ARVD 80004 2025 A2
15600 ARVD 80403 2024 D2
W 63rd Cir
13600 ARVD 80004 2025 B2
16900 ARVD 80403 2024 C2
W 63rd Ct
- AdmC 80221 2028 A2
W 63rd Dr
- AdmC 80003 2027 C2
4400 ARVD 80003 2027 C2
10600 ARVD 80004 2026 A2
16900 ARVD 80403 2024 D3
W 63rd Ln
13500 ARVD 80004 2025 B3
16800 ARVD 80403 2024 C2
E 63rd Pl
5600 CMCY 80022 2030 B2
W 63rd Pl
3800 AdmC 80003 2027 D2
4400 ARVD 80003 2027 C2
8400 ARVD 80004 2026 C2
14000 ARVD 80004 2025 A2
14000 JfnC 80004 2025 A2
16400 JfnC 80403 2024 C2
16600 ARVD 80007 2024 C2
16800 ARVD 80403 2024 D3
63rd St
- BldC 80503 1437 A2
1400 BldC 80301 1688 A2
1400 BldC 80303 1688 A2
1600 BldC 80301 1687 E1
2200 BldC 80301 1603 E7
N 63rd St
3700 BldC 80301 1604 A1
4400 BLDR 80301 1604 A2
5400 BLDR 80503 1604 A1
5600 BLDR 80503 1520 A7
6200 BldC 80503 1520 A7
7800 BldC 80503 1437 A6
12200 BldC 80503 1354 A5
12700 BldC 80503 1353 E4
W 63rd Wy
10600 ARVD 80004 2026 A2
13500 ARVD 80004 2025 B2
E 64th Av
- AdmC 80102 2038 C1
- AdmC 80137 2038 C1
- AdmC 80249 2034 B1
- AdmC 80249 2035 A1
- AURA 80137 2036 A1
- CMCY 80022 2030 A1
- DNVR 80249 2035 E1
- DNVR 80249 2036 A1
10 AdmC 80216 2028 E2
10 AdmC 80221 2028 E2
400 AdmC 80229 2028 E2
700 AdmC 80216 2029 A2
700 AdmC 80229 2029 A2
3200 CMCY 80022 2029 D2
7200 AdmC 80022 2030 B2
16900 AdmC 80022 2032 E2
16900 DNVR 80249 2032 E2
16900 DNVR 80249 2033 A2
18600 AdmC 80019 2033 E1
18600 AdmC 80019 2034 A1
18600 AURA 80019 2033 E1
18600 AURA 80019 2034 A1
18600 AURA 80249 2033 E1
18600 AURA 80249 2034 A1
42500 AdmC 80102 2039 C1
42500 AdmC 80102 2040 A1
W 64th Av
10 AdmC 80216 2028 D2
1600 AdmC 80221 2028 B2
3000 AdmC 80221 2027 D2
3500 AdmC 80003 2027 D2
4200 ARVD 80003 2027 D2
6800 ARVD 80003 2026 E2
9000 ARVD 80004 2026 C2
13700 JfnC 80004 2025 A2
14400 ARVD 80004 2025 A2
14800 ARVD 80007 2024 E2
14800 ARVD 80007 2025 A2
14800 ARVD 80403 2025 A2
15500 JfnC 80403 2024 E2
16400 JfnC 80007 2024 E2
17200 ARVD 80403 2024 B2
18600 ARVD 80007 2023 E1
18600 ARVD 80403 2023 E1
18900 JfnC 80007 2023 E1
18900 JfnC 80403 2023 E1
W 64th Av SR-72
- ARVD 80403 2025 A2
13700 JfnC 80004 2025 A2
14400 ARVD 80004 2025 A2
14800 ARVD 80007 2025 A2
W 64th Cir
4400 ARVD 80003 2027 C2
15900 ARVD 80007 2024 D2
W 64th Dr
12900 ARVD 80004 2025 C2
16900 ARVD 80007 2024 C2
W 64th Ln
15900 ARVD 80007 2024 D2
E 64th Pl
7100 CMCY 80022 2030 C2
W 64th Pl
4400 ARVD 80003 2027 C2
7200 ARVD 80003 2026 E2
9800 ARVD 80004 2026 B2
11100 ARVD 80004 2025 E2
15600 ARVD 80007 2024 D2
W 64th Wy
9400 ARVD 80004 2026 B2
16000 ARVD 80007 2024 D2
E 65th Av
6100 CMCY 80022 2030 B2
W 65th Av
2400 AdmC 80221 2028 A2
3000 AdmC 80221 2027 E2
3300 AdmC 80003 2027 E2
4400 ARVD 80003 2027 C2
7600 ARVD 80003 2026 E2
8800 ARVD 80004 2026 C2
13200 ARVD 80004 2025 B2
15600 ARVD 80403 2024 E2
W 65th Cir
10900 ARVD 80004 2025 E1
16700 ARVD 80007 2024 C2
W 65th Dr
13200 ARVD 80004 2025 B2
E 65th Pl
7100 CMCY 80022 2030 C1
7200 AdmC 80022 2030 C1
W 65th Pl
2400 AdmC 80221 2028 A1
3900 AdmC 80003 2027 D1
4900 ARVD 80003 2027 C2
9800 ARVD 80004 2026 B2
10800 ARVD 80004 2025 E2
15600 ARVD 80007 2024 D2
N 65th St
9800 BldC 80503 1437 A2
E 65th Wy
5300 CMCY 80022 2030 A1
W 65th Wy
8500 ARVD 80004 2026 C2
10900 ARVD 80004 2025 E1
14600 ARVD 80007 2025 A2
E 66th Av
300 AdmC 80229 2028 E1
700 AdmC 80229 2029 A1
7000 CMCY 80022 2030 C1
7200 AdmC 80022 2030 C1
W 66th Av
10 AdmC 80221 2028 D1
3000 AdmC 80221 2027 E1
3500 AdmC 80003 2027 E1
3500 AdmC 80030 2027 E1
4300 ARVD 80003 2027 C1
4300 ARVD 80030 2027 C1
6800 ARVD 80003 2026 E1
8800 ARVD 80004 2026 C1
10800 ARVD 80004 2025 E1
W 66th Cir
9900 ARVD 80004 2026 B1
12600 ARVD 80004 2025 C1
15700 ARVD 80007 2024 D1
W 66th Dr
13800 ARVD 80004 2025 B1
W 66th Ln
16800 ARVD 80007 2024 C2
E 66th Pl
6500 CMCY 80022 2030 C1
7000 AdmC 80022 2030 C1
W 66th Pl
2400 AdmC 80221 2028 A1
9700 ARVD 80004 2026 B1
11200 ARVD 80004 2025 E1
14700 ARVD 80007 2025 A2
16800 ARVD 80007 2024 C1
66th St
- BldC 80503 1354 A3
1500 BldC 80027 1772 B5
1500 SUPE 80027 1772 B5
2000 BldC 80303 1772 B5
N 66th St
11000 BldC 80503 1354 A7
11000 BldC 80503 1437 A1
E 66th Wy
5200 CMCY 80022 2030 A1
W 66th Wy
- AdmC 80221 2028 D2
13600 ARVD 80004 2025 B1
67th Av
- ARVD 80007 2024 B1
E 67th Av
2000 AdmC 80229 2029 B1
7000 AdmC 80022 2030 C1
7000 CMCY 80022 2030 C1
W 67th Av
3000 AdmC 80221 2027 E1
3500 AdmC 80030 2027 E1
5200 ARVD 80030 2027 B1
6300 ARVD 80003 2027 A1
7100 ARVD 80003 2026 E1
7600 ARVD 80004 2026 D1
11200 ARVD 80004 2025 E1
15300 ARVD 80007 2024 E2
W 67th Av N
11600 ARVD 80004 2025 D1
W 67th Cir
6700 ARVD 80003 2027 A1
13600 ARVD 80004 2025 B1
16400 ARVD 80007 2024 D1
W 67th Ct
13800 ARVD 80004 2025 B1
W 67th Dr
13300 ARVD 80004 2025 B1
W 67th Ln
17000 ARVD 80007 2024 C1
67th Pl
- ARVD 80007 2024 B1
E 67th Pl
6300 CMCY 80022 2030 B1
7100 AdmC 80022 2030 C1
W 67th Pl
2700 AdmC 80221 2028 A1
6100 ARVD 80003 2027 A1
7100 ARVD 80003 2026 E1
9700 ARVD 80004 2026 B1
13200 ARVD 80004 2025 B1
16800 ARVD 80007 2024 C1
N 67th St
7500 BldC 80503 1520 B3
8800 BldC 80503 1437 B6
W 67th Wy
8700 ARVD 80004 2026 C1
13700 ARVD 80004 2025 B1
68th Av
- DNVR 80249 2033 C1
E 68th Av
700 AdmC 80229 2029 B1
3700 CMCY 80022 1945 D7
4000 CMCY 80022 2029 E1
6100 CMCY 80022 2030 B1
26700 DNVR 80249 1951 C7
W 68th Av
800 AdmC 80221 2028 C1
3000 AdmC 80221 2027 D1
4300 AdmC 80030 2027 C1
5200 ARVD 80030 2027 B1
5200 WSTR 80030 2027 B1
5500 WSTR 80003 2027 B1
6400 ARVD 80003 2027 A1
6800 ARVD 80003 2026 E1
9900 ARVD 80004 2026 A1
11400 ARVD 80004 2025 E1
14800 ARVD 80007 2024 E1
14800 ARVD 80007 2025 A1
19200 ARVD 80007 2023 E1
19500 JfnC 80007 2023 E1
19800 JfnC 80403 2023 E1
W 68th Cir
6200 ARVD 80003 2027 A1
15200 ARVD 80007 2024 E1
W 68th Dr
13700 ARVD 80004 2025 B1
E 68th Pl
2000 AdmC 80229 2029 B1
6900 CMCY 80022 2030 C1
7100 AdmC 80022 2030 C1
W 68th Pl
3400 AdmC 80221 2027 E1
6200 ARVD 80003 2027 A1
6900 ARVD 80003 2026 E1
9200 ARVD 80004 2026 B1
12100 ARVD 80004 2025 D1
13300 ARVD 80004 1941 B7
15000 ARVD 80007 2024 E1
S 68th St
10 BldC 80303 1688 B7
400 BldC 80303 1772 B1
E 68th Wy
5700 CMCY 80022 2030 B1
W 68th Wy
800 AdmC 80221 2028 C1
10700 ARVD 80004 2026 A1
13800 ARVD 80004 2025 B1
69th Av
- ARVD 80007 2024 B1
- DNVR 80249 1949 B7
E 69th Av
1400 AdmC 80229 2029 B1
4200 CMCY 80022 1945 E7
4600 CMCY 80022 2029 E1
5700 CMCY 80022 2030 B1
7100 AdmC 80022 1946 C7
7100 CMCY 80022 1946 C7
W 69th Av
- ARVD 80007 2025 A1
1600 AdmC 80221 2028 B1
3300 AdmC 80221 2027 E1
4500 WSTR 80030 2027 C1
5100 WSTR 80003 2027 C1
5200 ARVD 80003 2027 B1
7200 ARVD 80003 2026 E1
7500 ARVD 80004 2026 E1
12400 ARVD 80004 2025 D1
13700 ARVD 80004 1941 B7
14900 ARVD 80007 2024 E1
W 69th Cir
16500 ARVD 80007 2024 C1
W 69th Ct
4900 WSTR 80030 2027 C1
W 69th Dr
4500 WSTR 80030 1943 C7
4700 WSTR 80030 2027 C1
8300 ARVD 80004 2026 D1
14300 ARVD 80004 2025 A1
W 69th Lp
5000 WSTR 80030 1943 C7
5000 WSTR 80030 2027 C1
E 69th Pl
2300 AdmC 80229 1945 C7
4200 CMCY 80022 1945 E7
6400 CMCY 80022 1946 B7
6900 AdmC 80022 1946 C7
W 69th Pl
3600 AdmC 80221 2027 D1
3600 WSTR 80030 2027 D1
6200 ARVD 80003 2027 A1
6800 ARVD 80003 2026 E1
7300 ARVD 80003 1942 D7
7500 ARVD 80004 1942 D7
9500 ARVD 80004 2026 B1
11000 ARVD 80004 2025 E1
13300 ARVD 80004 1941 B7
16000 ARVD 80007 2024 D1
69th St
900 BldC 80303 1688 C4
E 69th Wy
- AdmC 80229 2029 C1
2700 AdmC 80229 1945 C7
6700 CMCY 80022 1946 C7
W 69th Wy
6400 ARVD 80003 2027 A1
8300 ARVD 80004 2026 D1
11400 ARVD 80004 2025 E1
70th Av
- DNVR 80249 1949 C7
E 70th Av
10 AdmC 80221 1944 E7
300 AdmC 80229 1944 E7
700 AdmC 80229 1945 A7
4000 AdmC 80022 1945 E7
4000 CMCY 80022 1945 E7
4800 CMCY 80022 1946 A7
7200 AdmC 80022 1946 C7
E 70th Av SR-224
10 AdmC 80221 1944 E7
300 AdmC 80229 1944 E7
700 AdmC 80229 1945 A7
W 70th Av
2400 AdmC 80030 2028 A1
2400 AdmC 80221 2028 A1
2400 WSTR 80030 2028 A1
2700 AdmC 80221 1944 A7
2700 WSTR 80030 1944 A7
4400 WSTR 80030 1943 C7
5100 WSTR 80003 1943 C7
6000 ARVD 80003 1943 A7
7100 ARVD 80003 1942 E7
9400 ARVD 80004 1942 B7
9600 ARVD 80004 2026 B1
10800 ARVD 80004 1941 E7
12100 ARVD 80004 2025 D1
15800 ARVD 80007 2024 D1
15800 JfnC 80007 2024 D1
W 70th Ct
5000 WSTR 80030 1943 C7
W 70th Dr
6200 ARVD 80003 1943 A7
7600 ARVD 80003 1942 D7
10100 ARVD 80004 1942 A7
10200 ARVD 80005 1942 A7
14000 ARVD 80004 1941 A7
14500 ARVD 80007 1941 A7
14500 JfnC 80004 1941 A7
14500 JfnC 80007 1941 A7
15700 ARVD 80007 1940 D7
E 70th Pl
6400 CMCY 80022 1946 C7
W 70th Pl
- AdmC 80221 1944 C7
4200 WSTR 80030 1943 D7
6200 ARVD 80003 1943 A7
8100 ARVD 80004 1942 D7
13400 ARVD 80004 1941 B7
14200 ARVD 80004 2025 A1
16100 ARVD 80007 1940 D7
W 70th Wy
8500 ARVD 80004 1942 C7
11900 ARVD 80004 1941 D7
N 71 Rd
10 BldC 80540 1269 B5
71st Av
- DNVR 80249 1949 C7
E 71st Av
700 AdmC 80229 1945 A7
4000 CMCY 80022 1945 E7
4800 AdmC 80022 1945 E7
4800 AdmC 80022 1946 A7
5300 CMCY 80022 1946 A7
27100 DNVR 80249 1951 C7
W 71st Av
400 AdmC 80221 1944 D7
2600 WSTR 80030 1944 A7
3000 WSTR 80030 1943 E7
5600 WSTR 80003 1943 B7
6200 ARVD 80003 1943 A7
7100 ARVD 80003 1942 E7
7600 ARVD 80005 1942 D7
9200 ARVD 80004 1942 B7
13900 ARVD 80004 1941 A7
16700 ARVD 80007 1940 C7
W 71st Cir
5600 WSTR 80003 1943 B7
8500 ARVD 80004 1942 C7
16100 ARVD 80007 1940 D7
W 71st Ct
5000 WSTR 80030 1943 C7
W 71st Dr
14200 ARVD 80004 1941 A7
E 71st Pl
6100 CMCY 80022 1946 B7
W 71st Pl
1100 AdmC 80221 1944 C7
4900 WSTR 80030 1943 C7
5600 WSTR 80003 1943 B7
6200 ARVD 80003 1943 A7
6900 ARVD 80003 1942 E7
8100 ARVD 80004 1942 D7
10800 ARVD 80004 1941 E7
16200 ARVD 80007 1940 D7
N 71st Rd
10 BldC 80540 1269 B3
71st St
- BldC 80503 1520 C6
- BLDR 80503 1520 C6
N 71st St
5400 BldC 80301 1604 C1
5400 BldC 80503 1520 C5
5400 BldC 80503 1604 C1
5400 BLDR 80301 1520 C5
5400 BLDR 80301 1604 C1
6500 BLDR 80503 1520 C5
W 71st Wy
3000 WSTR 80030 1943 E7
E 72nd Av
- AdmC 80137 1953 D6
- AdmC 80249 1953 A6
- AURA 80137 1953 A6
- AURA 80249 1953 A6
4000 AdmC 80022 1945 E7
4000 CMCY 80022 1945 E7
4800 AdmC 80022 1946 A7
4800 CMCY 80022 1946 A7
16900 DNVR 80249 1949 A7
30800 AdmC 80137 1952 C6
30800 AdmC 80249 1952 C6
30800 AURA 80137 1952 C6
30800 AURA 80249 1952 C6
W 72nd Av
- ARVD 80003 1942 B7
800 AdmC 80221 1944 D7
2300 WSTR 80030 1944 A7
5000 WSTR 80030 1943 A7
5700 ARVD 80003 1943 A7
6000 WSTR 80003 1943 A7
6700 WSTR 80003 1942 E7
8100 ARVD 80004 1942 B7
10000 ARVD 80005 1942 B7
10600 ARVD 80004 1941 E7
10600 ARVD 80005 1941 E7
12000 JfnC 80005 1941 E7
12300 JfnC 80004 1941 E7
13900 JfnC 80007 1941 A7
14100 ARVD 80007 1941 A7
14800 JfnC 80007 1940 E7
16400 ARVD 80007 1940 C7
17400 ARVD 80007 2024 B1
W 72nd Cir
13200 ARVD 80005 1941 B7
13200 JfnC 80005 1941 B7
15600 ARVD 80007 1940 D7
15600 JfnC 80007 1940 D7
W 72nd Dr
6300 WSTR 80003 1943 A7
13400 ARVD 80005 1941 B7
13900 JfnC 80007 1941 A7
15900 ARVD 80007 1940 D7
E 72nd Pl
- AdmC 80022 1946 B7
7000 CMCY 80022 1946 C7
W 72nd Pl
4900 WSTR 80030 1943 C7
7200 ARVD 80003 1942 E7
10200 ARVD 80005 1942 A7
13900 ARVD 80005 1941 A7
13900 JfnC 80007 1941 A7
15200 JfnC 80007 1940 E7
E 72nd Wy
4600 AdmC 80022 1945 E7
4600 CMCY 80022 1945 E7
W 72nd Wy
3800 WSTR 80030 1943 D7
E 73rd Av
10 AdmC 80221 1944 E7
700 AdmC 80229 1945 A7
6400 CMCY 80022 1946 C6
7000 AdmC 80022 1946 C6
W 73rd Av
1700 AdmC 80221 1944 B7
2600 WSTR 80030 1944 A7
4800 WSTR 80030 1943 C7
5600 WSTR 80003 1943 A7
7200 ARVD 80003 1942 E7
8700 ARVD 80005 1942 C7
13900 ARVD 80005 1941 A7
15100 JfnC 80007 1940 E7
W 73rd Cir
7400 ARVD 80003 1942 E7
W 73rd Dr
11800 ARVD 80005 1941 D7
16500 JfnC 80007 1940 C7
E 73rd Pl
- AdmC 80022 1945 E6
- CMCY 80022 1945 E6
6600 CMCY 80022 1946 C6
W 73rd Pl
1900 AdmC 80221 1944 B6
2000 WSTR 80030 1944 B6
6300 WSTR 80003 1943 A7
7400 ARVD 80003 1942 E7
8700 ARVD 80005 1942 B7
10000 ARVD 80005 1941 E6
16900 JfnC 80007 1940 C7
N 73rd St
7000 BldC 80503 1520 C3
8400 BldC 80503 1437 C7
E 73rd Wy
4400 AdmC 80022 1945 E6
4400 CMCY 80022 1945 E6
74th Av
- DNVR 80249 1950 E6
- DNVR 80249 1951 A6
E 74th Av
300 AdmC 80229 1944 E6
2000 AdmC 80229 1945 E6
3800 AdmC 80022 1945 E6
3800 CMCY 80022 1945 E6
3800 TNTN 80022 1945 E6
5800 CMCY 80022 1946 A6
7200 AdmC 80022 1946 A6
E 74th Av SR-224
3800 AdmC 80022 1945 E6
3800 CMCY 80022 1945 E6
3800 TNTN 80022 1945 E6
4800 CMCY 80022 1946 A6
W 74th Av
2000 AdmC 80221 1944 B6
2100 WSTR 80030 1944 B6
3000 WSTR 80030 1943 E6
5300 WSTR 80003 1943 B6
6800 ARVD 80003 1942 E7
6800 WSTR 80003 1942 E7
8400 ARVD 80005 1942 B6
11200 ARVD 80005 1941 E7
15600 ARVD 80007 1940 D7
15600 JfnC 80007 1940 D7
W 74th Cir
6200 ARVD 80003 1943 A6
W 74th Dr
8400 ARVD 80005 1942 C6
13400 ARVD 80005 1941 B7
13400 JfnC 80005 1941 B7
14100 ARVD 80007 1941 A6
14100 JfnC 80007 1941 A6
16100 JfnC 80007 1940 D6
E 74th Pl
2100 AdmC 80229 1945 B6
6500 CMCY 80022 1946 B6
7200 AdmC 80022 1946 B6
W 74th Pl
5600 WSTR 80003 1943 B6
6200 ARVD 80003 1943 A6
6900 ARVD 80003 1942 E6
10000 ARVD 80005 1942 A6
11600 ARVD 80005 1941 D6
14000 JfnC 80007 1941 A6
16500 JfnC 80007 1940 C6
E 74th Wy
4700 AdmC 80022 1945 E6
4700 CMCY 80022 1945 E6
W 74th Wy
1600 AdmC 80221 1944 B6
9300 ARVD 80005 1942 B6
13900 ARVD 80005 1941 B6
E 75th Av
700 AdmC 80229 1945 A6
6900 AdmC 80022 1946 C6
6900 CMCY 80022 1946 C6
24500 DNVR 80249 1950 E6
24500 DNVR 80249 1951 A6
W 75th Av
4300 WSTR 80030 1943 C6
5600 WSTR 80003 1943 B6
6000 ARVD 80003 1943 B6
7400 ARVD 80003 1942 E6
9500 ARVD 80005 1942 B6
11700 JfnC 80005 1941 D6
12400 ARVD 80005 1941 C6
75th Cir
27000 DNVR 80249 1951 C6
W 75th Cir
8900 ARVD 80005 1942 C6
11600 ARVD 80005 1941 D6
W 75th Dr
5500 WSTR 80003 1943 B6
6100 ARVD 80003 1943 A6
11700 ARVD 80005 1941 D6
W 75th Ln
11900 ARVD 80005 1941 D6
E 75th Pl
700 AdmC 80229 1945 A6
6800 CMCY 80022 1946 C6
6900 AdmC 80022 1946 C6
W 75th Pl
3500 WSTR 80030 1943 E6
5500 WSTR 80003 1943 B6
6100 ARVD 80003 1943 A6
6800 ARVD 80003 1942 E6
9100 ARVD 80005 1942 B6
11900 ARVD 80005 1941 D6
12300 JfnC 80005 1941 C6
16500 ARVD 80007 1940 C6
16500 JfnC 80007 1940 C6
75th St
- BldC 80301 1604 D1
- BldC 80503 1520 D7
- BldC 80503 1604 D1
- BLDR 80301 1604 D1
N 75th St
- BldC 80503 1604 D4
- BLDR 80301 1604 D4
700 BldC 80303 1688 D3
1200 BldC 80301 1688 D3
2500 BldC 80301 1604 D4
8600 BldC 80503 1437 D7
8600 LGMT 80503 1437 D7
11000 BldC 80503 1354 D7
W 75th Wy
8500 ARVD 80005 1942 C6
76th Av
- DNVR 80249 1951 D6
E 76th Av
300 AdmC 80229 1944 E6
2300 AdmC 80229 1945 C6
5400 AdmC 80022 1946 B6
5400 CMCY 80022 1946 B6
W 76th Av
1600 AdmC 80221 1944 B6
5100 WSTR 80030 1943 B6
5600 WSTR 80003 1943 B6
6100 ARVD 80003 1943 A6
6800 ARVD 80003 1942 E6
7500 ARVD 80005 1942 E6
11600 ARVD 80005 1941 D6
11600 JfnC 80005 1941 D6
15800 JfnC 80007 1940 D6
W 76th Dr
5600 WSTR 80003 1943 B6
10600 ARVD 80005 1942 A6
10800 ARVD 80005 1941 E6
11600 JfnC 80005 1941 D5
14800 JfnC 80007 1940 E6
14800 JfnC 80007 1941 A6
16400 ARVD 80007 1940 C6
W 76th Ln
11600 ARVD 80005 1941 D6
11600 JfnC 80005 1941 D6
E 76th Pl
6500 AdmC 80022 1946 C6
W 76th Pl
6700 ARVD 80003 1943 A5
6800 ARVD 80003 1942 E6
9700 ARVD 80005 1942 B6
11000 ARVD 80005 1941 E6
11500 JfnC 80005 1941 E6
N 76th St
10 BldC 80303 1688 D5
S 76th St
1400 BldC 80027 1772 D3
1400 SUPE 80027 1772 D3
W 76th Wy
11200 ARVD 80005 1941 E6
E 77th Av
400 AdmC 80229 1944 E6
1600 AdmC 80229 1945 B6
4800 AdmC 80022 1945 E6
4800 CMCY 80022 1945 E6
4800 CMCY 80022 1946 A6
6300 AdmC 80022 1946 B6
W 77th Av
- WSTR 80030 1943 C6
5600 WSTR 80003 1943 B6
6400 ARVD 80003 1943 A6
9700 ARVD 80005 1942 B6
10800 ARVD 80005 1941 E6
W 77th Cir
8800 ARVD 80005 1942 C5
E 77th Dr
400 AdmC 80229 1944 E5
W 77th Dr
5000 WSTR 80030 1943 C6
5700 WSTR 80003 1943 B6
6100 ARVD 80003 1943 A6
7600 ARVD 80003 1942 D6
7600 ARVD 80005 1942 D6
11600 ARVD 80005 1941 D5
11600 JfnC 80005 1941 D5
14800 JfnC 80007 1941 A6
16300 ARVD 80007 1940 C6
16300 JfnC 80007 1940 C6
E 77th Pl
400 AdmC 80229 1944 E5
6500 AdmC 80022 1946 C5
W 77th Pl
4000 WSTR 80030 1943 D6
6400 ARVD 80003 1943 A6
8900 ARVD 80005 1942 C6
10700 ARVD 80005 1941 E6
15900 JfnC 80007 1940 D6
N 77th St
- BldC 80503 1520 D3
E 77th Wy
5600 AdmC 80022 1946 A5
W 77th Wy
8300 ARVD 80005 1942 C6
E 78th Av
400 AdmC 80229 1944 E5
700 AdmC 80229 1945 A5
4800 AdmC 80022 1945 E5
6200 AdmC 80022 1946 B5
6500 CMCY 80022 1946 C5
23400 DNVR 80249 1950 E5
24000 DNVR 80249 1951 A5
W 78th Av
- ARVD 80003 1942 E5
- WSTR 80003 1943 C5
3600 WSTR 80030 1943 D5
6100 ARVD 80003 1943 A5
10000 ARVD 80005 1942 A5
10700 ARVD 80005 1941 E5

Denver Regional Street Index

STREET Block City ZIP Map# Grid

W 78th Av
14500 JfnC 80005 1941 A5
14500 JfnC 80007 1941 A5
16600 JfnC 80007 1940 C6
W 78th Av N
13200 ARVD 80005 1941 B6
13200 JfnC 80005 1941 B6
W 78th Cir
1200 AdmC 80221 1944 C5
6500 ARVD 80003 1943 A5
8900 ARVD 80005 1942 C5
12800 ARVD 80005 1941 C6
W 78th Dr
11000 ARVD 80005 1941 E5
E 78th Pl
300 AdmC 80229 1944 E5
2200 AdmC 80229 1945 B5
5600 AdmC 80022 1946 B5
7200 CMCY 80022 1946 C5
W 78th Pl
100 AdmC 80221 1944 D5
5200 WSTR 80003 1943 B5
5200 WSTR 80030 1943 B5
6000 ARVD 80003 1943 A5
7000 ARVD 80003 1942 E5
10000 ARVD 80005 1942 A5
13300 JfnC 80005 1941 B5
16500 JfnC 80007 1940 C5
E 78th Wy
6300 CMCY 80022 1946 B5
6400 AdmC 80022 1946 B5
W 78th Wy
3900 WSTR 80030 1943 D5
8000 ARVD 80005 1942 D5
E 79th Av
2400 AdmC 80229 1945 C5
6500 CMCY 80022 1946 C5
7400 AdmC 80022 1946 D5
W 79th Av
3600 WSTR 80030 1943 D5
5200 WSTR 80003 1943 B5
6000 ARVD 80003 1943 A5
6700 ARVD 80003 1942 E5
8700 ARVD 80005 1942 C5
10800 ARVD 80005 1941 E5
W 79th Cir
6700 ARVD 80003 1942 E5
E 79th Ct
6300 AdmC 80022 1946 B5
6300 CMCY 80022 1946 B5
W 79th Ct
200 AdmC 80221 1944 D5
6800 ARVD 80003 1942 E5
8400 ARVD 80005 1942 C5
W 79th Dr
6800 ARVD 80003 1942 E5
11200 ARVD 80005 1941 E5
11200 JfnC 80005 1941 E5
16400 JfnC 80007 1940 C5
E 79th Pl
6500 AdmC 80022 1946 C5
6500 CMCY 80022 1946 C5
W 79th Pl
900 AdmC 80221 1944 C5
5600 ARVD 80003 1943 B5
8400 ARVD 80005 1942 C5
10800 ARVD 80005 1941 E5
13000 JfnC 80005 1941 B5
15600 JfnC 80007 1940 D5
E 79th St
- AdmC 80229 1945 C5
N 79th St
5400 BldC 80301 1604 E1
5400 BldC 80503 1604 E1
8400 BldC 80503 1437 E7
8400 BldC 80503 1520 E1
W 79th Wy
1600 AdmC 80221 1944 B5
9000 ARVD 80005 1942 B5
E 80th Av
10 AdmC 80221 1944 E5
300 AdmC 80229 1944 E5
5600 AdmC 80022 1946 B5
6400 CMCY 80022 1946 B5
27500 DNVR 80249 1951 D5
W 80th Av
10 AdmC 80221 1944 D5
2400 WSTR 80031 1944 A5
2800 WSTR 80221 1944 A5
3000 AdmC 80221 1943 E5
3000 WSTR 80030 1943 E5
5100 ARVD 80003 1943 B5
5200 WSTR 80031 1943 B5
6300 ARVD 80003 1942 B5
7500 ARVD 80005 1942 B5
10200 JfnC 80005 1942 B5
10800 ARVD 80005 1941 D5
10800 JfnC 80005 1941 D5
13600 JfnC 80007 1941 A5
W 80th Cir
5700 ARVD 80003 1943 B5
6600 ARVD 80003 1942 E5
7800 ARVD 80005 1942 D5
W 80th Dr
3700 WSTR 80031 1943 D5
6400 ARVD 80003 1942 E5
6400 ARVD 80003 1943 A5
8900 ARVD 80005 1942 C5
E 80th Pl
1400 AdmC 80229 1945 A5
W 80th Pl
2000 AdmC 80221 1944 B5
2600 WSTR 80031 1944 A5
4100 WSTR 80031 1943 D5
5500 ARVD 80003 1943 B5
7000 ARVD 80003 1942 E5
7800 ARVD 80005 1942 D5
12800 ARVD 80005 1941 C5
S 80th St
- BldC 80027 1688 E6
- BldC 80303 1688 E6
100 LSVL 80027 1688 E6
W 80th Wy
2600 WSTR 80031 1944 A4
E 81st Av
- CMCY 80022 1946 C4
10 AdmC 80221 1944 E5
5600 AdmC 80022 1946 B4
18000 DNVR 80022 1949 B4
18000 DNVR 80249 1949 B4
W 81st Av
10 AdmC 80221 1944 D5
2900 WSTR 80031 1944 A4
3600 WSTR 80031 1943 D5
6400 ARVD 80003 1943 A5
7400 ARVD 80003 1942 E5
9400 ARVD 80005 1942 B5
10600 JfnC 80005 1941 E5
10600 JfnC 80005 1942 A5
12800 ARVD 80005 1941 C5
W 81st Cir
5700 ARVD 80003 1943 B5
10000 ARVD 80005 1942 A4
W 81st Dr
9800 ARVD 80005 1942 B4
10800 JfnC 80005 1941 E5
W 81st Ln
10000 ARVD 80005 1942 A4
E 81st Pl
10 AdmC 80221 1944 D4
1700 AdmC 80229 1945 B4
W 81st Pl
1400 AdmC 80221 1944 C4
4800 WSTR 80031 1943 C5
5700 ARVD 80003 1943 B5
7400 ARVD 80003 1942 E5
10300 ARVD 80005 1942 A4
12900 ARVD 80005 1941 C5
N 81st St
7800 BldC 80503 1520 E1
E 82nd Av
7300 AdmC 80022 1946 D4
7300 CMCY 80022 1946 D4
W 82nd Av
3200 AdmC 80031 1943 E4
5200 ARVD 80003 1943 B4
5200 WSTR 80003 1943 B4
5200 WSTR 80031 1943 B4
10400 ARVD 80005 1942 A4
11100 JfnC 80005 1941 D5
13200 ARVD 80005 1941 A5
13200 JfnC 80007 1941 A5
16600 JfnC 80007 1939 E4
16600 JfnC 80007 1940 A4
16600 JfnC 80403 1939 E4
W 82nd Av CO-80
16600 JfnC 80007 1939 E4
16600 JfnC 80007 1940 A4
16600 JfnC 80403 1939 E4
W 82nd Cir
5700 ARVD 80003 1943 B4
E 82nd Dr
300 AdmC 80229 1944 E5
300 TNTN 80229 1944 E5
W 82nd Dr
- WSTR 80031 1944 A4
6400 ARVD 80003 1943 A4
10000 ARVD 80005 1942 A4
W 82nd Ln
10000 ARVD 80005 1942 A4
12600 ARVD 80005 1941 C4
82nd Pl
11600 ARVD 80005 1941 D4
11600 JfnC 80005 1941 D4
E 82nd Pl
2200 AdmC 80229 1945 B4
7300 AdmC 80022 1946 D4
7300 CMCY 80022 1946 D4
W 82nd Pl
1600 AdmC 80221 1944 B4
2400 AdmC 80031 1944 A4
2400 WSTR 80031 1944 A4
6000 ARVD 80003 1943 A4
6900 ARVD 80003 1942 E4
10400 ARVD 80005 1942 A4
10800 JfnC 80005 1941 E4
11700 ARVD 80005 1941 D4
W 82nd Wy
2500 WSTR 80031 1944 A4
7300 ARVD 80003 1942 E4
W 83 Av
12400 ARVD 80005 1941 C4
12400 JfnC 80005 1941 C4
E 83rd Av
- AdmC 80229 1945 C4
6000 AdmC 80022 1946 B4
7300 CMCY 80022 1946 D4
W 83rd Av
- WSTR 80031 1944 A4
200 AdmC 80221 1944 D4
600 TNTN 80221 1944 D4
3000 WSTR 80031 1943 E4
3400 AdmC 80031 1943 E4
5300 ARVD 80003 1943 B4
7400 ARVD 80003 1942 E4
9500 ARVD 80005 1942 B4
11900 ARVD 80005 1941 D4
12100 JfnC 80005 1941 D4
E 83rd Dr
300 AdmC 80229 1944 E4
300 TNTN 80229 1944 E4
1600 AdmC 80229 1945 B4
W 83rd Dr
10400 ARVD 80005 1942 A4
12400 ARVD 80005 1941 C4
12600 JfnC 80005 1941 C4
W 83rd Ln
11600 JfnC 80005 1941 D4
11900 ARVD 80005 1941 D4
E 83rd Pl
700 AdmC 80229 1945 A4
5900 AdmC 80022 1946 B4
W 83rd Pl
10 AdmC 80221 1944 D4
10 TNTN 80221 1944 D4
6000 ARVD 80003 1943 A4
10400 ARVD 80005 1942 A4
11600 ARVD 80005 1941 D4
83rd St
- BldC 80503 1521 A4
N 83rd St
7000 BldC 80503 1521 A3
W 83rd Wy
6100 ARVD 80003 1943 A4
6900 ARVD 80003 1942 E4
12400 ARVD 80005 1941 C4
E 84th Av
10 TNTN 80221 1944 E4
10 TNTN 80260 1944 E4
200 TNTN 80229 1944 E4
600 AdmC 80229 1944 E4
1600 AdmC 80229 1945 B4
5800 AdmC 80022 1946 B4
7300 CMCY 80022 1946 D4
W 84th Av
- ARVD 80005 1941 B4
- WSTR 80003 1943 C4
10 AdmC 80221 1944 D4
10 TNTN 80221 1944 D4
10 TNTN 80260 1944 D4
600 FLHT 80260 1944 D4
2100 AdmC 80260 1944 A4
2300 WSTR 80031 1944 A4
3100 AdmC 80031 1943 E4
5200 WSTR 80031 1943 C4
6100 ARVD 80003 1943 A4
8400 ARVD 80005 1942 C4
12400 JfnC 80005 1941 C4
W 84th Cir
6500 ARVD 80003 1942 E4
6500 ARVD 80003 1943 A4
8600 ARVD 80005 1942 C4
12500 ARVD 80005 1941 C4
E 84th Ct
- TNTN 80229 1944 E4
W 84th Ct
7800 ARVD 80005 1942 D4
E 84th Dr
3200 AdmC 80229 1945 C4
W 84th Dr
12400 ARVD 80005 1941 C4
W 84th Ln
11600 ARVD 80005 1941 D4
E 84th Pl
1400 AdmC 80229 1945 A4
W 84th Pl
1100 FLHT 80260 1944 C4
6500 ARVD 80003 1943 A3
10200 ARVD 80005 1942 A4
12800 ARVD 80005 1941 C4
W 84th Wy
6000 ARVD 80003 1943 A4
6500 ARVD 80003 1942 E4
7500 WSTR 80005 1942 E3
E 85th Av
- AdmC 80022 1946 E3
- CMCY 80022 1946 E3
10 TNTN 80229 1944 E4
600 AdmC 80229 1944 E4
700 AdmC 80229 1945 A4
700 TNTN 80229 1945 A4
W 85th Av
- AdmC 80260 1944 A4
- TNTN 80260 1944 D4
- WSTR 80031 1944 A4
1000 FLHT 80260 1944 C3
3600 WSTR 80031 1943 D4
6100 ARVD 80003 1943 A3
9900 ARVD 80005 1942 B4
11700 ARVD 80005 1941 D4
W 85th Cir
12500 ARVD 80005 1941 C4
E 85th Dr
3200 AdmC 80229 1945 D4
W 85th Dr
13400 ARVD 80005 1941 B4
E 85th Pl
1000 AdmC 80229 1945 A3
W 85th Pl
6000 ARVD 80003 1943 A3
9900 ARVD 80005 1942 B4
10800 ARVD 80005 1941 E4
W 85th Wy
9900 ARVD 80005 1942 B4
E 86th Av
200 TNTN 80229 1944 E3
2700 AdmC 80229 1945 C3
3200 TNTN 80229 1945 C3
7300 CMCY 80022 1946 D3
8100 AdmC 80022 1946 E3
W 86th Av
- FLHT 80260 1944 B3
2700 WSTR 80031 1944 A3
2900 WSTR 80031 1943 E3
6000 ARVD 80003 1943 A3
8600 WSTR 80005 1942 D4
9100 ARVD 80005 1942 C3
12400 ARVD 80005 1941 C3
12400 JfnC 80005 1941 C3
W 86th Cir
8500 WSTR 80005 1942 C3
13500 ARVD 80005 1941 B4
W 86th Ct
8600 WSTR 80005 1942 C3
W 86th Dr
8700 WSTR 80005 1942 C3
13200 ARVD 80005 1941 B4
W 86th Pkwy
- ARVD 80007 1941 A4
10000 ARVD 80005 1942 A4
10000 WSTR 80005 1942 A4
12600 ARVD 80005 1941 B4
E 86th Pl
1500 AdmC 80229 1945 A3
W 86th Pl
9200 WSTR 80005 1942 B3
9800 ARVD 80005 1942 B3
14100 ARVD 80005 1941 A4
E 87th Av
500 TNTN 80229 1944 E3
8000 AdmC 80022 1946 E3
8600 CMCY 80022 1946 E3
W 87th Av
4500 AdmC 80031 1943 C3
4500 WSTR 80031 1943 C3
9900 ARVD 80005 1942 B3
12800 JfnC 80005 1941 C3
W 87th Cir
9600 ARVD 80005 1942 B3
W 87th Dr
7600 ARVD 80003 1942 D3
7600 WSTR 80005 1942 D3
8300 WSTR 80021 1942 D3
W 87th Pl
- WSTR 80031 1944 A3
500 TNTN 80260 1944 D3
4500 AdmC 80031 1943 C3
4500 WSTR 80031 1943 C3
8900 WSTR 80005 1942 C3
9200 ARVD 80005 1942 B3
N 87th St
12600 BldC 80503 1355 B3
12600 LGMT 80503 1355 B3
W 87th Wy
6900 ARVD 80003 1942 E3
E 88th Av
- AdmC 80022 1947 A3
- AdmC 80640 1947 A3
- CMCY 80022 1947 A3
- CMCY 80640 1947 A3
10 TNTN 80229 1944 E3
10 TNTN 80260 1944 E3
700 AdmC 80229 1945 A3
700 TNTN 80229 1945 A3
4000 AdmC 80640 1945 E3
4000 TNTN 80022 1945 E3
4100 CMCY 80022 1945 E3
4100 TNTN 80640 1945 E3
4800 AdmC 80022 1946 B3
4800 CMCY 80022 1946 B3
4800 CMCY 80640 1946 B3
6100 AdmC 80640 1946 B3
15500 AdmC 80022 1948 E3
15500 CMCY 80022 1948 E3
15500 CMCY 80022 1949 A3
15500 DNVR 80022 1948 E3
15500 DNVR 80022 1949 A3
17400 CMCY 80022 1950 B2
17400 DNVR 80022 1950 B2
17400 DNVR 80249 1949 E3
17400 DNVR 80249 1950 B2
31300 AdmC 80102 1952 D2
31300 AdmC 80102 1953 A2
31300 AdmC 80137 1953 A2
31300 AdmC 80249 1953 A2
31300 DNVR 80249 1952 D2
31300 DvrC 80249 1952 D2
W 88th Av
10 TNTN 80260 1944 D3
1500 FLHT 80260 1944 C3
2900 WSTR 80031 1944 A3
3000 AdmC 80031 1943 E3
3000 FLHT 80031 1943 E3
3000 FLHT 80260 1943 E3
5200 WSTR 80031 1943 A3
6000 ARVD 80003 1943 A3
6000 ARVD 80031 1943 A3
6000 WSTR 80003 1943 A3
6500 WSTR 80021 1942 E3
6500 WSTR 80031 1942 E3
6800 WSTR 80003 1942 E3
7200 ARVD 80003 1942 E3
7200 WSTR 80005 1942 E3
9000 ARVD 80005 1942 E3
9000 ARVD 80021 1942 E3
12500 JfnC 80005 1941 C3
12500 WSTR 80005 1941 C3
E 88th Cir N
3600 TNTN 80229 1945 D3
E 88th Cir S
3600 TNTN 80229 1945 D3
W 88th Cir
9100 WSTR 80021 1942 C3
W 88th Ct
- AdmC 80031 1943 D3
W 88th Pl
5000 AdmC 80031 1943 B3
5000 WSTR 80031 1943 B3
8500 WSTR 80021 1942 C3
S 88th St
1800 BldC 80027 1773 B4
1800 LSVL 80027 1773 B4
2300 SUPE 80027 1773 B5
W 88th Wy
3600 AdmC 80031 1943 D3
3600 WSTR 80031 1943 D3
E 89th Av
3500 TNTN 80229 1945 D3
5500 AdmC 80022 1946 B3
5500 CMCY 80640 1946 B3
8900 AdmC 80640 1946 E3
8900 AdmC 80640 1947 A2
W 89th Av
- FLHT 80260 1944 A3
3400 AdmC 80031 1943 D3
8800 ARVD 80005 1941 A3
8800 ARVD 80007 1941 A3
8800 JfnC 80005 1941 A3
8800 JfnC 80007 1941 A3
9400 WSTR 80021 1942 B3
W 89th Cir
9400 WSTR 80021 1942 B3
W 89th Ct
9100 WSTR 80021 1942 B2
W 89th Dr
8500 WSTR 80021 1942 C2
E 89th Pl
3600 TNTN 80229 1945 D3
W 89th Pl
3400 AdmC 80031 1943 E2
9400 WSTR 80021 1942 B3
N 89th St
9400 BldC 80503 1438 B5
9400 LGMT 80503 1438 B5
W 89th Wy
3600 AdmC 80031 1943 D2
9600 WSTR 80021 1942 B3
E 90th Av
2100 TNTN 80229 1945 B2
5100 CMCY 80640 1946 A2
8900 AdmC 80640 1946 E2
8900 AdmC 80640 1947 A2
W 90th Av
1600 FLHT 80260 1944 B2
1600 TNTN 80260 1944 B2
2900 FLHT 80031 1943 E2
2900 FLHT 80260 1943 E2
3600 AdmC 80031 1943 D2
4200 WSTR 80031 1943 C2
6800 WSTR 80021 1942 E2
W 90th Cir
9200 WSTR 80021 1942 B2
W 90th Ct
9100 WSTR 80021 1942 C2
W 90th Dr
6800 JfnC 80021 1942 E2
9300 WSTR 80021 1942 B2
E 90th Pl
2400 TNTN 80229 1945 C2
W 90th Pl
2600 FLHT 80260 1944 A2
3100 AdmC 80031 1943 E2
3600 WSTR 80031 1943 D2
9100 WSTR 80021 1942 B2
W 90th Wy
3700 WSTR 80031 1943 D2
E 91st Av
1400 TNTN 80229 1945 A2
7000 AdmC 80640 1946 C2
W 91st Av
- AdmC 80031 1943 D2
500 TNTN 80260 1944 D2
2600 FLHT 80260 1944 A2
2900 FLHT 80260 1943 E2
3600 WSTR 80031 1943 D2
6500 WSTR 80021 1943 A2
8400 WSTR 80021 1942 C2
W 91st Cir
400 TNTN 80260 1944 D2
W 91st Ct
6800 JfnC 80021 1942 E2
6800 WSTR 80021 1942 E2
6800 WSTR 80021 1943 A2
E 91st Dr
4100 TNTN 80229 1945 E2
W 91st Dr
500 TNTN 80260 1944 D2
2400 FLHT 80260 1944 A2
E 91st Pl
700 TNTN 80229 1945 A2
W 91st Pl
2500 FLHT 80260 1944 A2
2900 FLHT 80260 1943 E2
3700 WSTR 80031 1943 D2
8400 WSTR 80021 1942 C2
91st St
- BldC 80503 1438 C3
E 91st Wy
800 TNTN 80229 1945 A2
E 92nd Av
- AdmC 80640 1946 E2
- AdmC 80640 1947 A2
- CMCY 80640 1946 E2
- CMCY 80640 1947 A2
900 TNTN 80229 1945 A2
W 92nd Av
1600 FLHT 80260 1944 A2
1600 TNTN 80260 1944 A2
3000 AdmC 80031 1943 E2
3000 FLHT 80260 1943 E2
5800 WSTR 80031 1943 B2
6600 WSTR 80021 1943 A2
6800 JfnC 80021 1942 E2
8900 WSTR 80021 1942 E2
E 92nd Ct
4300 TNTN 80229 1945 E2
W 92nd Dr
5800 WSTR 80031 1943 B2
W 92nd Ln
6900 JfnC 80021 1942 E2
6900 WSTR 80021 1942 E2
E 92nd Pl
3600 TNTN 80229 1945 D2
W 92nd Pl
3200 WSTR 80031 1943 E2
7100 JfnC 80021 1942 E2
8500 WSTR 80021 1942 C2
E 93rd Av
- TNTN 80229 1945 D2
W 93rd Av
- FLHT 80260 1944 A2
- JfnC 80021 1942 E2
- WSTR 80021 1942 E2
3100 WSTR 80031 1943 E1
W 93rd Cir
8000 WSTR 80021 1942 D2
E 93rd Dr
4300 TNTN 80229 1945 E2
W 93rd Dr
- FLHT 80260 1944 A2
E 93rd Pl
4300 TNTN 80229 1945 E1
W 93rd Pl
- FLHT 80260 1944 A2
5900 WSTR 80031 1943 B2
7400 JfnC 80021 1942 E1
7500 WSTR 80021 1942 E1
W 93rd Wy
7300 JfnC 80021 1942 E2
8000 WSTR 80021 1942 D2
E 94th Av
3500 TNTN 80229 1945 D1
W 94th Av
- FLHT 80260 1944 A1
3000 FLHT 80260 1943 E1
3600 WSTR 80031 1943 D1
6800 JfnC 80021 1942 E1
6800 WSTR 80021 1942 E1
E 94th Dr
4300 TNTN 80229 1945 E1
4500 AdmC 80229 1945 E1
W 94th Dr
- FLHT 80260 1944 A1
E 94th Ln
3000 TNTN 80229 1945 C1
W 94th Ln
- FLHT 80260 1944 A1
E 94th Pl
4100 TNTN 80229 1945 E1
W 94th Pl
- FLHT 80260 1944 A1
6700 WSTR 80021 1943 A1
7200 JfnC 80021 1942 D1
9200 WSTR 80021 1942 B2
E 95th Av
700 TNTN 80229 1944 E1
700 TNTN 80229 1945 A1
W 95th Av
- FLHT 80260 1944 A1
- JfnC 80031 1943 A1
3000 FLHT 80260 1943 E1
3000 WSTR 80260 1943 E1
6300 WSTR 80031 1943 A1
7000 JfnC 80021 1942 E1
9000 WSTR 80021 1942 B2
W 95th Cir
1100 TNTN 80260 1944 C1
E 95th Dr
3100 TNTN 80229 1945 C1
W 95th Dr
- FLHT 80260 1944 A1
- JfnC 80021 1942 D1
8400 WSTR 80021 1942 C1
W 95th Pl
- FLHT 80260 1944 A1
1000 TNTN 80260 1944 C1
3700 WSTR 80031 1943 D1
6400 WSTR 80021 1943 A1
6700 WSTR 80021 1942 E1
N 95th St
- BldC 80027 1689 D4
- BldC 80503 1438 D7
- BldC 80504 1438 D7
- LGMT 80504 1438 D7
700 BldC 80303 1689 D4
700 LAFT 80026 1689 D4
700 LAFT 80027 1689 D4
1500 BldC 80301 1689 D1
2300 BldC 80026 1689 D1
2400 BldC 80026 1605 D7
2400 BldC 80301 1605 D7
5000 BldC 80503 1605 D3
5400 BldC 80026 1521 D6
5400 BldC 80503 1521 D6
5400 BldC 80504 1521 D6
12600 BldC 80501 1355 D1
12600 BldC 80503 1355 D1
12600 BldC 80504 1355 D1
12600 LGMT 80501 1355 D1
12600 LGMT 80503 1355 D1
N 95th St SR-42
- BldC 80027 1689 D4
700 BldC 80303 1689 D4
700 LAFT 80026 1689 D4
700 LAFT 80027 1689 D4
W 95th Wy
7700 WSTR 80021 1942 D1
E 96th Av
- AdmC 80022 1949 C1
- AdmC 80022 1950 A1
- AdmC 80229 1945 E1
- AdmC 80229 1946 A1
- CMCY 80022 1949 E1
- CMCY 80022 1950 A1
- DNVR 80249 1950 A1
- DNVR 80249 1952 B1
- TNTN 80229 1945 E1
6500 AdmC 80640 1946 E1
7700 CMCY 80640 1946 E1
8400 AdmC 80640 1947 A1
9400 CMCY 80640 1947 A1
10400 AdmC 80022 1947 A1
10400 CMCY 80022 1947 A1
11300 AdmC 80022 1948 C1
11300 CMCY 80022 1948 C1
31300 AdmC 80102 1868 E7
31300 DNVR 80102 1868 E7
31300 DNVR 80249 1868 E7
W 96th Av
- JfnC 80403 1857 B7
- WSTR 80005 1857 B7
- WSTR 80005 1941 B1
- WSTR 80021 1857 B7
- WSTR 80403 1857 B7
500 NHGN 80260 1944 D1
1400 TNTN 80260 1944 C1
2300 FLHT 80260 1944 B1
2900 FLHT 80260 1943 E1
2900 WSTR 80260 1943 E1
5200 WSTR 80020 1943 B1
5200 WSTR 80031 1943 B1
6500 WSTR 80021 1943 A1
7200 JfnC 80021 1942 D1
7200 WSTR 80021 1942 D1
13200 JfnC 80005 1941 B1
13200 JfnC 80403 1941 B1
13200 WSTR 80403 1941 B1
E 96th Cir
1700 TNTN 80229 1945 B1
15600 CMCY 80022 1864 D7
W 96th Cir
3200 WSTR 80031 1943 E1
W 96th Ct
6700 WSTR 80021 1942 E1
E 96th Dr
1300 TNTN 80229 1945 A1
4800 AdmC 80229 1945 E1
4800 AdmC 80229 1946 A1
W 96th Dr
- FLHT 80260 1944 A1
- WSTR 80021 1942 D2
6400 WSTR 80021 1943 A1
E 96th Ln
1400 TNTN 80229 1945 A1
W 96th Ln
- FLHT 80260 1944 A1
E 96th Pl
1000 TNTN 80229 1861 A7
1100 TNTN 80229 1945 A1
4800 AdmC 80229 1945 E1
4800 AdmC 80229 1946 A1
11200 CMCY 80022 1947 C1
16400 AdmC 80022 1948 E1
16400 CMCY 80022 1948 E1
W 96th Pl
800 TNTN 80260 1944 C1
6300 WSTR 80021 1943 A1
N 96th St
100 LSVL 80027 1689 D5
200 BldC 80027 1689 D5
300 LAFT 80027 1689 D5
N 96th St SR-42
100 LSVL 80027 1689 D5
200 BldC 80027 1689 D5
300 LAFT 80027 1689 D5
S 96th St
- BMFD 80020 1773 D4
400 BldC 80027 1773 D2
400 LSVL 80027 1773 D2
1400 LSVL 80020 1773 D4
E 96th Wy
- AdmC 80022 1864 E7
1600 TNTN 80229 1861 B7
1600 TNTN 80229 1945 B1
15500 CMCY 80022 1864 D7
E 97th Av
- AdmC 80229 1945 E1
1200 TNTN 80229 1861 A7
2200 TNTN 80229 1945 C1
15600 CMCY 80022 1864 D7
16400 AdmC 80022 1864 E7
W 97th Av
800 NHGN 80260 1944 C1
800 TNTN 80260 1944 C1
1200 TNTN 80260 1860 C7
3000 FLHT 80260 1943 E1
3000 WSTR 80031 1943 E1
7500 JfnC 80021 1942 E1
7500 WSTR 80021 1942 E1
E 97th Cir
2100 TNTN 80229 1945 B1
W 97th Cir
6700 WSTR 80021 1942 E1
E 97th Ct
1500 TNTN 80229 1861 A7
W 97th Ct
6600 WSTR 80021 1858 E7
6600 WSTR 80021 1859 A7
9700 WSTR 80021 1942 B1
E 97th Dr
1800 TNTN 80229 1861 B7
4800 AdmC 80229 1861 E7
4900 AdmC 80229 1862 A7
W 97th Dr
9700 WSTR 80021 1942 B1
E 97th Pl
- AdmC 80022 1864 E7
1200 TNTN 80229 1861 A7
3400 TNTN 80229 1945 D1
4800 AdmC 80229 1861 E7
4900 AdmC 80229 1862 A7
9600 AdmC 80640 1863 A7
15700 CMCY 80022 1864 D7
W 97th Pl
3900 WSTR 80031 1859 D7
6400 WSTR 80021 1943 A1
6700 WSTR 80021 1858 E7
6700 WSTR 80021 1859 A7
7200 WSTR 80021 1942 E1
E 97th Wy
16000 AdmC 80022 1864 D7
16000 CMCY 80022 1864 D7
W 97th Wy
4100 WSTR 80031 1859 D7
E 98th Av
1800 TNTN 80229 1861 B7
16000 AdmC 80022 1864 D7
16000 CMCY 80022 1864 D7
W 98th Av
- FLHT 80031 1859 E7
- FLHT 80260 1859 E7
- WSTR 80021 1858 E7
800 NHGN 80260 1860 C7
1100 TNTN 80260 1860 C7
5100 WSTR 80020 1859 C7
5200 WSTR 80031 1859 C7
7600 JfnC 80021 1942 D1
9300 WSTR 80021 1942 B1
W 98th Cir
2800 FLHT 80260 1860 A7
6700 WSTR 80021 1858 E7
W 98th Ct
5000 WSTR 80031 1859 C7
6400 WSTR 80021 1859 A7
9300 WSTR 80021 1858 B7
E 98th Dr
3300 TNTN 80229 1861 D7
W 98th Dr
2600 FLHT 80260 1860 A7
6200 WSTR 80021 1858 E7
6200 WSTR 80021 1859 A7
E 98th Pl
300 TNTN 80229 1860 E7
1800 TNTN 80229 1861 B7
15300 CMCY 80022 1864 D7
W 98th Pl
5000 WSTR 80031 1859 C7
6600 WSTR 80021 1859 A7
9200 WSTR 80021 1858 C7
E 98th Wy
- CMCY 80022 1865 A7
2400 TNTN 80229 1861 C7
15900 AdmC 80022 1864 D7
15900 CMCY 80022 1864 D7
W 98th Wy
9200 WSTR 80021 1858 C7

Denver Regional Street Index

STREET
Block City ZIP Map# Grid

E 99th Av
- AdmC 80022 1864 E7
- AdmC 80022 1865 A7
- CMCY 80022 1865 A7
1700 TNTN 80229 1861 B7
15300 CMCY 80022 1864 D7
W 99th Av
300 NHGN 80260 1860 D7
1100 TNTN 80260 1860 C7
3100 WSTR 80031 1859 E7
6400 WSTR 80021 1859 A7
6600 WSTR 80021 1858 E7
7600 JfnC 80021 1858 D7
9800 WSTR 80021 1942 A1
E 99th Cir
3800 TNTN 80229 1861 D7
W 99th Cir
2800 FLHT 80260 1860 A7
3400 WSTR 80031 1859 E7
E 99th Ct
3600 TNTN 80229 1861 D7
W 99th Ct
5100 WSTR 80031 1859 C7
E 99th Dr
3300 TNTN 80229 1861 D7
E 99th Ln
3500 TNTN 80229 1861 D7
E 99th Pl
- AdmC 80022 1864 E7
10 TNTN 80229 1860 E7
2000 TNTN 80229 1861 B7
9600 AdmC 80640 1863 A7
15300 CMCY 80022 1864 D7
W 99th Pl
2400 FLHT 80260 1860 A7
3700 WSTR 80031 1859 D7
7600 JfnC 80021 1858 D7
7600 WSTR 80021 1858 D7
E 99th Wy
2300 TNTN 80229 1861 C7
15300 CMCY 80022 1864 D7
W 99th Wy
9400 WSTR 80021 1858 B7
100 Year Party Ct
- BldC 80504 1439 B7
1900 LGMT 80504 1439 B6
E 100th Av
- AdmC 80022 1864 B7
- CMCY 80022 1864 D7
- CMCY 80022 1865 A7
700 TNTN 80229 1861 B7
4900 AdmC 80229 1861 E7
4900 AdmC 80229 1862 A7
4900 TNTN 80229 1862 A7
7500 AdmC 80640 1862 D7
W 100th Av
600 NHGN 80260 1860 D7
1000 TNTN 80260 1860 C7
2500 FLHT 80260 1860 A7
2800 FLHT 80031 1859 E7
2800 FLHT 80260 1859 E7
3600 WSTR 80031 1859 D7
5200 WSTR 80020 1859 B7
8300 JfnC 80021 1858 C7
8900 WSTR 80021 1858 A7
11600 WSTR 80021 1857 C7
W 100th Cir
9200 WSTR 80021 1858 B7
E 100th Ct
3400 TNTN 80229 1861 D7
4900 TNTN 80229 1862 A7
15300 CMCY 80022 1864 C6
W 100th Ct
4700 WSTR 80031 1859 C7
5200 WSTR 80020 1859 B7
10100 WSTR 80021 1858 A7
E 100th Dr
4800 AdmC 80229 1862 A7
4800 TNTN 80229 1862 A7
W 100th Dr
2700 FLHT 80260 1860 A7
10800 WSTR 80021 1857 E7
E 100th Ln
1100 TNTN 80229 1861 A7
4800 AdmC 80229 1862 A7
4800 TNTN 80229 1862 A7
14100 AdmC 80022 1864 B6
14100 CMCY 80022 1864 B6
E 100th Pl
1100 TNTN 80229 1861 A7
5200 TNTN 80229 1862 A7
14100 AdmC 80022 1864 B7
14100 CMCY 80022 1864 B7
W 100th Pl
- WSTR 80021 1858 A7
400 NHGN 80260 1860 D7
1200 TNTN 80260 1860 C7
2500 FLHT 80260 1860 A7
3500 WSTR 80031 1859 D7
5400 WSTR 80020 1859 B7
11500 WSTR 80021 1857 E7
E 100th Wy
2400 TNTN 80229 1861 C7
5200 TNTN 80229 1862 A7
W 100th Wy
9200 WSTR 80021 1858 B7
10900 WSTR 80021 1857 E7
E 101st Av
1200 TNTN 80229 1861 A7
14100 AdmC 80022 1864 B6
14100 CMCY 80022 1864 B6
W 101st Av
- FLHT 80260 1860 A7
- TNTN 80260 1860 A7
800 NHGN 80260 1860 C7
5100 WSTR 80031 1859 C7
5400 WSTR 80020 1859 B7
7600 JfnC 80021 1858 D7
10100 WSTR 80021 1858 A7
11500 WSTR 80021 1857 D7
W 101st Cir
2100 TNTN 80260 1860 B7
3500 WSTR 80031 1859 D6
E 101st Ct
1900 TNTN 80229 1861 B6
4800 AdmC 80229 1862 A6
4800 TNTN 80229 1862 A6
W 101st Ct
1900 TNTN 80260 1860 B7
W 101st Dr
10000 WSTR 80021 1858 A7
101st Ln
- TNTN 80229 1862 A6
E 101st Pl
- TNTN 80229 1861 C6
5400 TNTN 80229 1862 A6
14100 AdmC 80022 1864 B6
14100 CMCY 80022 1864 B6
W 101st Pl
800 NHGN 80260 1860 C6
1100 TNTN 80260 1860 C6
2500 FLHT 80260 1860 A7
3400 WSTR 80031 1859 E7
10200 WSTR 80021 1858 A7
10500 WSTR 80021 1857 E7
E 101st Wy
2300 TNTN 80229 1861 C6
15500 CMCY 80022 1864 D6
E 102nd Av
- AdmC 80022 1864 E6
- CMCY 80022 1865 A6
300 TNTN 80229 1860 E6
2000 TNTN 80229 1861 B6
9600 AdmC 80640 1863 B6
9600 CMCY 80640 1863 B6
14100 CMCY 80022 1864 B6
W 102nd Av
- FLHT 80031 1859 E6
- FLHT 80260 1859 E6
- FLHT 80260 1860 A6
- WSTR 80031 1859 E6
800 NHGN 80260 1860 C6
1100 TNTN 80260 1860 C6
5200 WSTR 80020 1859 B6
7700 JfnC 80021 1858 D6
8800 WSTR 80021 1858 C6
10500 WSTR 80021 1857 E7
E 102nd Cir
1900 TNTN 80229 1861 B6
W 102nd Cir
3200 WSTR 80031 1859 E6
10900 WSTR 80021 1857 E7
102nd Ct
- TNTN 80229 1862 A6
E 102nd Ct
3200 TNTN 80229 1861 D6
W 102nd Ct
10900 WSTR 80021 1857 E6
E 102nd Dr
- CMCY 80022 1865 A6
3200 TNTN 80229 1861 D6
W 102nd Dr
11100 WSTR 80021 1857 E7
102nd Ln
- TNTN 80229 1862 A6
E 102nd Pl
- CMCY 80022 1864 E6
- CMCY 80022 1865 A6
3200 TNTN 80229 1861 C6
14100 AdmC 80022 1864 B6
W 102nd Pl
800 NHGN 80260 1860 C6
1100 TNTN 80260 1860 C6
4600 WSTR 80031 1859 C6
5400 WSTR 80020 1859 B6
7600 JfnC 80021 1858 D6
10500 WSTR 80021 1858 A6
10600 WSTR 80021 1857 E7
E 102nd Wy
- AdmC 80022 1864 E6
- CMCY 80022 1864 E6
E 103rd Av
1900 TNTN 80229 1861 B6
W 103rd Av
800 NHGN 80260 1860 C6
1600 FLHT 80260 1860 B6
2100 TNTN 80260 1860 A6
3800 WSTR 80031 1859 D6
5400 WSTR 80020 1859 B6
6800 WSTR 80021 1858 E6
7200 JfnC 80021 1858 E6
11200 WSTR 80021 1857 E6
E 103rd Cir
3500 TNTN 80229 1861 D6
W 103rd Cir
4600 WSTR 80031 1859 C6
10900 WSTR 80021 1857 E6
E 103rd Ct
2200 TNTN 80229 1861 B6
W 103rd Ct
3900 WSTR 80031 1859 C6
10900 WSTR 80021 1857 E6
E 103rd Dr
3200 TNTN 80229 1861 D6
W 103rd Dr
3600 WSTR 80031 1859 D6
11200 WSTR 80021 1857 E6
E 103rd Pl
2100 TNTN 80229 1861 B6
W 103rd Pl
1100 NHGN 80260 1860 C6
1100 TNTN 80260 1860 C6
4800 WSTR 80031 1859 C6
10900 WSTR 80021 1857 E6
E 104th Av
- AdmC 80022 1865 B6
- DNVR 80102 1868 E5
10 NHGN 80229 1860 E6
10 NHGN 80233 1860 E6
10 NHGN 80260 1860 E6
10 TNTN 80229 1860 E6
10 TNTN 80233 1860 E6
200 TNTN 80233 1860 E6
700 NHGN 80233 1861 A6
700 TNTN 80229 1861 A6
1300 NHGN 80229 1861 A6
1900 TNTN 80233 1861 A6
4700 TNTN 80229 1862 C6
4700 TNTN 80233 1862 C6
5000 AdmC 80229 1862 C6
6100 AdmC 80233 1862 C6
7600 AdmC 80640 1862 C6
8100 CMCY 80640 1862 C6
8500 CMCY 80640 1863 A6
11900 CMCY 80022 1863 E6
13700 AdmC 80022 1864 A6
16400 CMCY 80022 1864 D6
16500 CMCY 80022 1865 B6
29600 AdmC 80642 1868 B5
29600 DNVR 80249 1868 B5
29600 DNVR 80642 1868 B5
38200 AdmC 80102 1868 E5
E 104th Av SR-44
10 NHGN 80229 1860 E6
10 NHGN 80233 1860 E6
10 NHGN 80260 1860 E6
10 TNTN 80229 1860 E6
200 TNTN 80233 1860 E6
700 NHGN 80233 1861 A6
700 TNTN 80229 1861 A6
1300 NHGN 80229 1861 A6
1900 TNTN 80233 1861 A6
4700 TNTN 80229 1862 C6
4700 TNTN 80233 1862 C6
5000 AdmC 80229 1862 C6
6100 AdmC 80233 1862 C6
7600 AdmC 80640 1862 C6
8100 CMCY 80640 1862 C6
8500 CMCY 80640 1863 A6
11900 CMCY 80022 1863 A6
W 104th Av
- FLHT 80260 1859 E6
- NHGN 80233 1860 D6
- WSTR 80234 1859 E6
10 NHGN 80234 1860 D6
10 NHGN 80260 1860 D6
1400 TNTN 80234 1860 B6
1400 TNTN 80260 1860 B6
2000 FLHT 80234 1860 B6
2000 FLHT 80260 1860 B6
2000 WSTR 80234 1860 B6
4600 WSTR 80020 1859 C6
4600 WSTR 80031 1859 C6
9600 WSTR 80021 1858 B6
10700 WSTR 80021 1857 E6
W 104th Av SR-44
- NHGN 80233 1860 D6
10 NHGN 80234 1860 D6
10 NHGN 80260 1860 D6
1400 TNTN 80234 1860 D6
1400 TNTN 80260 1860 D6
W 104th Cir
2500 WSTR 80234 1860 A6
10900 WSTR 80021 1857 E6
W 104th Ct
2600 WSTR 80234 1860 A6
9400 WSTR 80021 1858 B6
10900 WSTR 80021 1857 E6
E 104th Dr
12900 CMCY 80022 1863 E6
13900 CMCY 80022 1864 B6
W 104th Dr
3700 WSTR 80031 1859 D6
9300 WSTR 80021 1858 A6
10900 WSTR 80021 1857 E6
W 104th Ln
2700 WSTR 80234 1860 A6
E 104th Pl
- CMCY 80022 1865 B5
- CMCY 80640 1863 A5
100 NHGN 80233 1860 E6
3500 NHGN 80233 1861 D6
8500 AdmC 80640 1862 E6
8500 CMCY 80640 1862 E6
13800 CMCY 80022 1864 B5
W 104th Pl
1200 NHGN 80234 1860 C6
2700 WSTR 80234 1860 A6
3400 WSTR 80031 1859 E6
7800 JfnC 80021 1858 D6
9200 WSTR 80021 1858 B6
10700 WSTR 80021 1857 E6
S 104th St
100 LSVL 80027 1774 A1
600 LSVL 80026 1774 A1
700 LSVL 80020 1774 A4
1300 BMFD 80020 1774 A4
1700 BldC 80020 1774 A4
E 104th Wy
8100 AdmC 80640 1862 E6
8100 CMCY 80640 1862 E6
16300 CMCY 80022 1864 E5
17000 CMCY 80022 1865 A5
W 104th Wy
9400 WSTR 80021 1858 B6
E 105th Av
- CMCY 80022 1863 E5
- CMCY 80022 1865 B5
- CMCY 80640 1863 A5
10 NHGN 80233 1860 E6
4100 TNTN 80233 1861 E5
8200 AdmC 80640 1862 E5
8200 CMCY 80640 1862 E5
16100 CMCY 80022 1864 D5
W 105th Av
- WSTR 80020 1859 B6
- WSTR 80031 1859 E6
- WSTR 80234 1859 E6
8000 JfnC 80021 1858 D6
9900 WSTR 80021 1858 A6
E 105th Cir
16200 CMCY 80022 1864 E5
E 105th Ct
3300 NHGN 80233 1861 D5
8500 AdmC 80640 1862 E5
16000 CMCY 80022 1864 D5
W 105th Ct
2500 WSTR 80234 1860 A6
E 105th Dr
- CMCY 80022 1864 A5
- CMCY 80640 1863 A5
4600 TNTN 80233 1862 A5
W 105th Dr
- WSTR 80031 1859 E6
- WSTR 80234 1859 E6
2600 WSTR 80234 1860 A6
11400 WSTR 80021 1857 D6
E 105th Pl
- CMCY 80022 1863 E5
- CMCY 80640 1862 E5
- CMCY 80640 1863 A5
700 NHGN 80233 1860 E6
700 NHGN 80233 1861 A5
13800 CMCY 80022 1864 B5
W 105th Pl
2300 NHGN 80234 1860 A5
2400 WSTR 80234 1860 A5
4000 WSTR 80031 1859 D6
7700 JfnC 80021 1858 D6
9500 WSTR 80021 1858 B5
11400 WSTR 80021 1857 E5
N 105th St
- BldC 80504 1439 A7
- LGMT 80504 1439 A7
E 105th Wy
- CMCY 80022 1864 A5
- CMCY 80022 1865 A5
W 105th Wy
4000 WSTR 80031 1859 D6
9600 WSTR 80021 1858 B5
11400 WSTR 80021 1857 E6
E 106th Av
- CMCY 80022 1863 E5
10 NHGN 80233 1860 E5
3000 NHGN 80233 1861 C5
3500 TNTN 80233 1861 D5
9400 CMCY 80640 1863 A5
10100 AdmC 80640 1863 B5
16700 CMCY 80022 1864 E5
17000 CMCY 80022 1865 A4
W 106th Av
1400 NHGN 80234 1860 B5
7600 JfnC 80021 1858 D5
9200 WSTR 80021 1858 B5
10800 WSTR 80021 1857 E5
E 106th Cir
5000 TNTN 80233 1862 A5
13900 CMCY 80022 1864 B5
W 106th Cir
2700 WSTR 80234 1860 A6
E 106th Ct
3300 NHGN 80233 1861 D5
4100 TNTN 80233 1861 E5
16000 CMCY 80022 1864 D5
W 106th Ct
10500 WSTR 80021 1858 A6
E 106th Dr
4400 TNTN 80233 1861 E5
4700 TNTN 80233 1862 A5
9400 CMCY 80640 1863 A5
16600 CMCY 80022 1864 E5
W 106th Dr
4800 WSTR 80031 1859 C5
W 106th Lp
- WSTR 80234 1860 A5
E 106th Pl
10 NHGN 80233 1860 E5
3000 NHGN 80233 1861 C5
4200 TNTN 80233 1861 E5
9400 CMCY 80640 1863 A5
16600 CMCY 80022 1864 E5
W 106th Pl
- WSTR 80031 1859 D5
2700 WSTR 80234 1860 A5
9900 WSTR 80021 1858 B5
10900 WSTR 80021 1857 E5
11800 JfnC 80021 1857 D5
E 106th Wy
- CMCY 80022 1863 E5
16900 CMCY 80022 1864 E5
17000 CMCY 80022 1865 A5
W 106th Wy
10500 WSTR 80021 1858 A5
11400 WSTR 80021 1857 E6
E 107th Av
- CMCY 80022 1864 A5
10 NHGN 80233 1860 E5
3400 NHGN 80233 1861 D5
3500 TNTN 80233 1861 D5
9100 CMCY 80640 1863 A5
13800 AdmC 80022 1864 B5
17000 CMCY 80022 1865 A5
W 107th Av
3300 WSTR 80031 1859 E5
10500 WSTR 80021 1858 A5
11600 JfnC 80021 1857 D5
11600 WSTR 80021 1857 D5
E 107th Cir
4400 TNTN 80233 1861 E5
W 107th Cir
4400 WSTR 80031 1859 C5
10700 WSTR 80021 1858 A5
E 107th Ct
3100 NHGN 80233 1861 C5
4100 TNTN 80233 1861 E5
16600 CMCY 80022 1864 E5
W 107th Ct
2700 WSTR 80234 1860 A5
5000 WSTR 80031 1859 C5
10300 WSTR 80021 1858 A5
E 107th Dr
4700 TNTN 80233 1862 A5
9100 AdmC 80640 1863 A4
9100 CMCY 80640 1863 A4
W 107th Dr
2400 WSTR 80234 1860 A5
4300 WSTR 80031 1859 C5
9400 WSTR 80021 1858 B5
W 107th Lp
4900 WSTR 80031 1859 C5
E 107th Pl
10 NHGN 80233 1860 E5
4400 TNTN 80233 1861 E5
4700 TNTN 80233 1862 A5
9200 CMCY 80640 1863 A5
10100 AdmC 80640 1863 B5
13800 CMCY 80022 1864 B5
W 107th Pl
- WSTR 80234 1859 E5
2500 WSTR 80234 1860 A5
4100 WSTR 80031 1859 C5
9900 WSTR 80021 1858 B5
11400 WSTR 80021 1857 E5
N 107th St
1900 BldC 80504 1439 B7
1900 LGMT 80501 1439 B7
1900 LGMT 80504 1439 B7
2100 LAFT 80026 1690 B1
2300 BldC 80026 1690 B1
3000 ERIE 80026 1690 B1
3300 BldC 80026 1606 B7
3400 ERIE 80026 1606 B7
4800 BldC 80504 1606 B3
5400 BldC 80504 1522 B5
12600 BldC 80504 1356 B1
12600 LGMT 80501 1356 B1
N 107th St SR-7
2100 LAFT 80026 1690 B1
2300 BldC 80026 1690 B1
3000 ERIE 80026 1690 B1
N 107th St US-287
1900 BldC 80504 1439 B7
1900 LGMT 80501 1439 B7
1900 LGMT 80504 1439 B7
2100 LAFT 80026 1690 B1
2300 BldC 80026 1690 B1
3000 ERIE 80026 1690 B1
3300 BldC 80026 1606 B7
3400 ERIE 80026 1606 B7
4800 BldC 80504 1606 B3
5400 BldC 80504 1522 B5
12600 BldC 80504 1356 B1
12600 LGMT 80501 1356 B1
E 107th Wy
15600 CMCY 80022 1864 D5
E 108th Av
- AdmC 80022 1864 B5
- CMCY 80022 1864 B5
500 NHGN 80233 1860 E5
1100 NHGN 80233 1861 A5
3700 TNTN 80233 1861 D5
5100 TNTN 80233 1862 A5
9200 CMCY 80640 1863 A5
10500 AdmC 80640 1863 C5
19300 AdmC 80022 1865 D4
W 108th Av
2500 WSTR 80234 1860 A5
3000 WSTR 80031 1859 E5
3000 WSTR 80234 1859 E5
5700 WSTR 80020 1859 A5
6700 WSTR 80020 1858 E5
7600 JfnC 80021 1858 D5
8500 WSTR 80021 1858 D5
10800 WSTR 80021 1857 E5
11000 JfnC 80021 1857 E5
W 108th Cir
5800 WSTR 80020 1859 A5
9200 WSTR 80021 1858 B4
E 108th Ct
15800 CMCY 80022 1864 D4
E 108th Dr
- CMCY 80022 1864 E5
3100 NHGN 80233 1861 C5
9200 CMCY 80640 1863 A4
W 108th Dr
6900 WSTR 80020 1858 E5
11800 JfnC 80021 1857 D5
E 108th Pl
1200 NHGN 80233 1861 A5
5300 TNTN 80233 1862 A5
9200 CMCY 80640 1863 A4
19300 AdmC 80022 1865 D4
W 108th Pl
2500 WSTR 80234 1860 A5
4600 WSTR 80031 1859 C5
6000 WSTR 80020 1859 A5
7900 WSTR 80021 1858 C5
E 108th Wy
15400 CMCY 80022 1864 D4
E 109th Av
10 NHGN 80233 1860 E5
2400 NHGN 80233 1861 C4
3200 TNTN 80233 1861 E5
9200 CMCY 80640 1863 A4
15300 CMCY 80022 1864 D4
W 109th Av
2500 WSTR 80234 1860 A5
4600 WSTR 80031 1859 C5
5700 WSTR 80020 1859 A5
7800 WSTR 80021 1858 D5
W 109th Cir
3300 WSTR 80031 1859 E5
5600 WSTR 80020 1859 B5
E 109th Ct
2600 NHGN 80233 1861 C4
4600 TNTN 80233 1861 E5
4900 TNTN 80233 1862 A4
W 109th Ct
3300 WSTR 80031 1859 E5
E 109th Dr
2200 NHGN 80233 1861 B4
E 109th Pl
10 NHGN 80233 1860 E4
2200 NHGN 80233 1861 B4
4600 TNTN 80233 1861 E5
4700 TNTN 80233 1862 A5
W 109th Pl
4600 WSTR 80031 1859 C5
6300 WSTR 80020 1859 A4
7700 WSTR 80021 1858 D5
N 109th St
3400 BldC 80026 1606 B5
3400 ERIE 80026 1606 B5
4400 BldC 80504 1606 B2
E 110th Av
- AdmC 80022 1865 C4
- AdmC 80233 1862 A4
- CMCY 80022 1865 C4
2500 NHGN 80233 1861 C4
3200 TNTN 80233 1861 E4
4900 TNTN 80233 1862 A4
W 110th Av
2500 WSTR 80234 1860 A4
3700 WSTR 80031 1859 D5
6200 WSTR 80020 1859 A4
7600 WSTR 80021 1858 D4
W 110th Cir
4500 WSTR 80031 1859 C5
5600 WSTR 80020 1859 B4
E 110th Ct
2600 NHGN 80233 1861 C4
W 110th Ct
2700 WSTR 80234 1860 A4
3900 WSTR 80031 1859 D4
E 110th Dr
2300 NHGN 80233 1861 B4
W 110th Dr
6900 WSTR 80020 1858 E4
7800 WSTR 80021 1858 D4
110th Pl
- TNTN 80233 1861 D4
- WSTR 80020 1859 A4
E 110th Pl
1200 NHGN 80233 1861 A4
4800 TNTN 80233 1861 E4
4800 TNTN 80233 1862 A4
W 110th Pl
2800 WSTR 80234 1859 E4
2800 WSTR 80234 1860 A4
3500 WSTR 80031 1859 E4
6000 WSTR 80020 1859 A4
7800 WSTR 80021 1858 D4
W 111th Av
1100 NHGN 80234 1860 C4
2500 WSTR 80234 1860 A4
2900 WSTR 80234 1859 E4
4400 WSTR 80031 1859 C4
6000 WSTR 80020 1859 A4
6700 WSTR 80020 1858 E4
7600 JfnC 80021 1858 D4
W 111th Cir
4100 WSTR 80031 1859 D4
E 111th Ct
5200 TNTN 80233 1862 B4
W 111th Ct
2400 NHGN 80234 1860 A4
2400 WSTR 80234 1860 A4
E 111th Dr
2200 NHGN 80233 1861 B4
5300 TNTN 80233 1862 A4
5500 AdmC 80233 1862 A4
W 111th Dr
3000 WSTR 80031 1859 E4
W 111th Lp
2700 WSTR 80234 1860 A4
3200 WSTR 80031 1859 E4
E 111th Pl
100 NHGN 80233 1860 E4
900 NHGN 80233 1861 A4
5500 TNTN 80233 1862 A4
W 111th Pl
1100 NHGN 80234 1860 C4
2400 WSTR 80234 1860 A4
3000 WSTR 80031 1859 E4
5700 WSTR 80020 1859 B4
6700 WSTR 80020 1858 E4
N 111th St
300 LAFT 80026 1690 C3
1200 ERIE 80026 1690 C1
1600 BldC 80026 1690 C1
1600 ERIE 80516 1690 C1
1800 BldC 80516 1690 C1
2000 BldC 80026 1606 C7
2000 BldC 80516 1606 C7
2000 ERIE 80516 1606 C7
W 111th Wy
- NHGN 80234 1860 B4
2800 WSTR 80234 1860 A4
2900 WSTR 80234 1859 E4
E 112th Av
- NHGN 80233 1860 E4
600 NHGN 80233 1861 A4
1800 TNTN 80233 1861 A4
4800 TNTN 80233 1862 B4
5200 AdmC 80233 1862 B4
9200 AdmC 80640 1863 B4
9200 CMCY 80640 1863 B4
11700 BGTN 80640 1863 D4
13000 AdmC 80603 1864 D4
13000 CMCY 80022 1864 D4
13000 CMCY 80603 1864 D4
13600 AdmC 80022 1864 D4
16500 AdmC 80022 1865 C3
16500 CMCY 80022 1865 C3
20100 AdmC 80022 1866 A3
20100 DNVR 80249 1866 A3
21700 DNVR 80022 1866 D3
W 112th Av
- WSTR 80021 1857 C4
400 NHGN 80234 1860 D4
700 WSTR 80234 1860 A4
2900 WSTR 80031 1859 D4
2900 WSTR 80234 1859 E4
4600 WSTR 80020 1859 C4
6600 BMFD 80020 1858 E4
6600 WSTR 80020 1858 E4
11600 BMFD 80021 1857 C4
11600 JfnC 80021 1857 C4
E 112th Cir
300 NHGN 80233 1860 E4
N 112th Cir
3500 WSTR 80031 1859 D4
W 112th Cir
4800 WSTR 80031 1859 C4
E 112th Ct
- AdmC 80640 1863 A4
- CMCY 80640 1863 A4
5000 TNTN 80233 1862 A4
W 112th Ct
4600 WSTR 80031 1859 C4
E 112th Dr
200 NHGN 80233 1860 E4
9500 CMCY 80640 1863 A4
E 112th Pl
- AdmC 80022 1865 B3
- CMCY 80022 1864 B4
- CMCY 80022 1865 B3
100 NHGN 80233 1860 E4
700 NHGN 80233 1861 B4
4300 TNTN 80233 1861 E4
5300 TNTN 80233 1862 A4
9500 CMCY 80640 1863 A4
W 112th Pl
4800 WSTR 80031 1859 C4
5400 WSTR 80020 1859 B4
S 112th St
500 LAFT 80026 1690 C7
500 LAFT 80026 1774 C3
1100 BldC 80026 1774 C3
1300 BldC 80020 1774 C3
1300 LAFT 80020 1774 C3
1600 BMFD 80020 1774 C3
S 112th St US-287
500 LAFT 80026 1690 C7
500 LAFT 80026 1774 C3
1100 BldC 80026 1774 C3
1300 LAFT 80020 1774 C3
1600 BfdC 80020 1774 C3
1600 BMFD 80020 1774 C3
E 112th Wy
- AdmC 80640 1863 C3
4800 TNTN 80233 1861 E4
10600 CMCY 80640 1863 C3
E 113th Av
1800 NHGN 80233 1861 B4
4200 TNTN 80233 1861 E4
5800 TNTN 80233 1862 B3
10600 CMCY 80640 1863 C3
W 113th Av
1600 WSTR 80234 1860 B3
3200 WSTR 80031 1859 E4
4900 WSTR 80020 1859 C4
6500 WSTR 80020 1858 E4
E 113th Cir
5800 TNTN 80233 1862 A3
W 113th Cir
- WSTR 80234 1860 C4
113th Ct
2800 WSTR 80234 1860 A4
E 113th Ct
16700 AdmC 80022 1864 E3
W 113th Ct
- WSTR 80031 1859 E4
- WSTR 80234 1859 E4
E 113th Pl
- AdmC 80022 1865 B3
- CMCY 80022 1865 B3
100 NHGN 80233 1860 E3
1700 NHGN 80233 1861 B3
4100 TNTN 80233 1861 E3
5300 TNTN 80233 1862 A3
W 113th Pl
6300 WSTR 80020 1859 A4
6700 BMFD 80020 1858 E4
6700 WSTR 80020 1858 E4
N 113th St
5300 BldC 80504 1606 C1
E 114th Av
- AdmC 80022 1865 B3
- AdmC 80022 1866 D3
- CMCY 80022 1865 B3
- CMCY 80640 1863 C3
- DNVR 80249 1866 D3
- DNVR 80249 1867 A3
- DvrC 80249 1866 D3
1700 NHGN 80233 1861 B3
6100 TNTN 80233 1862 B3
12100 BGTN 80640 1863 E3
W 114th Av
300 NHGN 80234 1860 D3
600 WSTR 80234 1860 D3
6400 WSTR 80020 1859 A3
N 114th Cir
3300 WSTR 80031 1859 E3
E 114th Ct
600 NHGN 80233 1860 E3
16100 AdmC 80022 1864 D3
W 114th Ct
2700 WSTR 80234 1860 A3
2800 WSTR 80234 1859 E3
E 114th Dr
3200 TNTN 80233 1861 D3
11400 CMCY 80640 1863 D3
W 114th Dr
4800 WSTR 80031 1859 C3
E 114th Pl
700 NHGN 80233 1861 A3
5900 TNTN 80233 1862 B3
11700 CMCY 80640 1863 D3
W 114th Pl
300 NHGN 80234 1860 D3
3300 WSTR 80031 1859 E3
5700 WSTR 80020 1859 B3
E 114th Wy
4200 TNTN 80233 1861 E3
W 114th Wy
300 NHGN 80234 1860 D3
E 115th Av
600 NHGN 80233 1860 E3
700 NHGN 80233 1861 A3
2700 TNTN 80233 1861 D3
4900 TNTN 80233 1862 A3
11300 CMCY 80640 1863 C3
12100 BGTN 80640 1863 E3
21000 AdmC 80022 1866 A3
W 115th Av
400 NHGN 80234 1860 D3
600 WSTR 80234 1860 D3
3100 WSTR 80031 1859 E3
5200 WSTR 80020 1859 C3
6600 WSTR 80020 1858 E3
E 115th Cir
4600 TNTN 80233 1861 E3

STREET
Block City ZIP Map# Grid

W 115th Cir
1600 WSTR 80234 1860 B3
E 115th Ct
4600 TNTN 80233 1861 E3
4700 TNTN 80233 1862 A3
W 115th Ct
5600 WSTR 80020 1859 B3
E 115th Dr
3200 TNTN 80233 1861 C3
11800 CMCY 80640 1863 D3
W 115th Dr
2400 WSTR 80234 1860 A3
5400 WSTR 80020 1859 B3
W 115th Lp
5300 WSTR 80020 1859 B3
E 115th Pl
800 NHGN 80233 1861 A3
4000 TNTN 80233 1861 E3
10900 CMCY 80640 1863 C3
W 115th Pl
3100 WSTR 80031 1859 E3
5200 WSTR 80020 1859 B3
N 115th St
4900 BldC 80504 1606 D1
7000 BldC 80504 1522 D3
12600 BldC 80504 1356 D1
12600 LGMT 80501 1356 D1
E 115th Wy
2800 TNTN 80233 1861 C3
E 116th Av
500 NHGN 80233 1860 E3
1800 NHGN 80233 1861 B3
3500 TNTN 80233 1861 D3
4900 TNTN 80233 1862 A3
11800 CMCY 80640 1863 D3
W 116th Av
200 NHGN 80234 1860 C3
700 WSTR 80234 1860 C3
3200 WSTR 80031 1859 E3
5200 WSTR 80020 1859 C3
6700 BMFD 80020 1858 E3
6700 WSTR 80020 1858 E3
8000 BMFD 80021 1858 C3
E 116th Cir
12100 BGTN 80640 1863 D2
12100 CMCY 80640 1863 D2
W 116th Cir
1700 WSTR 80234 1860 B3
5200 WSTR 80020 1859 B3
8800 BMFD 80021 1858 C3
E 116th Ct
2300 TNTN 80233 1861 C3
12600 BGTN 80640 1863 E3
16500 AdmC 80022 1864 E3
W 116th Ct
1600 WSTR 80234 1860 B3
4800 WSTR 80031 1859 C3
8800 BMFD 80021 1858 C3
E 116th Dr
- BGTN 80640 1863 D3
1900 NHGN 80233 1861 B3
4800 TNTN 80233 1861 E3
4900 TNTN 80233 1862 A3
11800 CMCY 80640 1863 D3
14800 CMCY 80603 1864 C3
W 116th Dr
2800 WSTR 80234 1860 A3
W 116th Ln
4700 WSTR 80031 1859 C3
E 116th Pl
1800 NHGN 80233 1861 B3
2300 TNTN 80233 1861 C3
4800 TNTN 80233 1862 A3
11800 CMCY 80640 1863 D2
14800 CMCY 80603 1864 C2
W 116th Pl
200 NHGN 80234 1860 D3
700 WSTR 80234 1860 D3
2800 WSTR 80031 1859 E3
2800 WSTR 80234 1859 E3
5600 WSTR 80020 1859 B3
7200 BMFD 80020 1858 E3
E 116th Wy
- NHGN 80233 1861 C3
2300 TNTN 80233 1861 C3
W 116th Wy
- WSTR 80031 1859 D3
200 NHGN 80234 1860 D3
E 117th Av
- AdmC 80602 1862 A3
- CMCY 80603 1864 D2
300 NHGN 80233 1860 E3
4300 TNTN 80233 1861 E3
4800 TNTN 80233 1862 A3
11800 CMCY 80640 1863 D2
W 117th Av
400 NHGN 80234 1860 D3
4400 WSTR 80031 1859 C3
5200 WSTR 80020 1859 C3
6800 BMFD 80020 1858 E3
E 117th Cir
5500 TNTN 80233 1862 A2
E 117th Ct
1800 NHGN 80233 1861 B3
2800 TNTN 80233 1861 C2
5100 TNTN 80233 1862 A2
12600 BGTN 80640 1863 E2
W 117th Ct
4200 WSTR 80031 1859 C2
E 117th Dr
3400 TNTN 80233 1861 D2
5000 TNTN 80233 1862 A3
15100 CMCY 80603 1864 C2
E 117th Pl
300 NHGN 80233 1860 E3
3100 TNTN 80233 1861 D2
11800 CMCY 80640 1863 D2
14800 CMCY 80603 1864 C2
W 117th Pl
5500 WSTR 80020 1859 B2
E 117th Wy
1800 NHGN 80233 1861 B3
2600 TNTN 80233 1861 C2

W 117th Wy
2700 WSTR 80234 1860 A3
4800 WSTR 80031 1859 C2
E 118th Av
300 NHGN 80233 1860 E2
3500 TNTN 80233 1861 D2
4900 TNTN 80233 1862 A2
11400 CMCY 80640 1863 D2
15300 CMCY 80603 1864 D2
18500 AdmC 80022 1865 C2
18500 CMCY 80022 1865 C2
21100 AdmC 80022 1866 A2
W 118th Av
- WSTR 80031 1859 C2
400 NHGN 80234 1860 D2
700 WSTR 80234 1860 D2
5500 WSTR 80020 1859 B2
5900 BMFD 80020 1859 B2
E 118th Cir
2600 TNTN 80233 1861 C2
W 118th Cir
5600 WSTR 80020 1859 B2
E 118th Ct
4300 TNTN 80233 1861 E2
12600 BGTN 80640 1863 E2
W 118th Ct
4600 WSTR 80031 1859 C2
W 118th Mw
3800 WSTR 80031 1859 D2
E 118th Pl
300 NHGN 80233 1860 E2
4300 TNTN 80233 1861 E2
5000 TNTN 80233 1862 A2
11400 CMCY 80640 1863 D2
14800 CMCY 80603 1864 C2
W 118th Pl
- WSTR 80031 1859 B2
5200 WSTR 80020 1859 B2
7200 BMFD 80020 1858 E2
N 118th St
4300 ERIE 80026 1606 E3
E 118th Wy
3600 TNTN 80233 1861 D2
W 118th Wy
4200 WSTR 80031 1859 C2
E 119th Av
- AdmC 80233 1862 A2
- AdmC 80602 1862 A2
- BGTN 80640 1863 D2
- CMCY 80603 1864 D2
- TNTN 80233 1862 A2
- TNTN 80602 1862 A2
3500 TNTN 80233 1861 D2
11400 CMCY 80640 1863 D2
W 119th Av
2800 WSTR 80031 1859 E2
2800 WSTR 80234 1859 E2
2800 WSTR 80234 1860 A2
6800 BMFD 80020 1858 E2
18800 BldC 80303 1855 D2
18800 BldC 80403 1855 D2
18800 SUPE 80303 1855 D2
18800 SUPE 80403 1855 D2
E 119th Ct
4800 TNTN 80233 1861 E2
4900 TNTN 80233 1862 A2
12600 BGTN 80640 1863 E2
W 119th Dr
9400 BMFD 80021 1858 B2
9400 JfnC 80021 1858 B2
W 119th Mw
3800 WSTR 80031 1859 D2
E 119th Pl
1000 NHGN 80233 1861 A2
3200 TNTN 80233 1861 D2
5100 TNTN 80233 1862 A2
11400 CMCY 80640 1863 D2
W 119th Pl
7000 BMFD 80020 1858 E2
E 119th St
3400 TNTN 80233 1861 D2
N 119th St
700 BldC 80026 1690 E1
700 LAFT 80026 1690 E1
1600 BldC 80026 1606 E7
1600 ERIE 80516 1606 E7
3700 ERIE 80026 1606 E4
4200 BldC 80516 1606 E4
7800 BldC 80504 1439 E7
7800 BldC 80504 1522 E1
8700 BldC 80501 1439 E5
9900 LGMT 80501 1439 E3
E 119th Wy
4300 TNTN 80233 1861 E2
5100 TNTN 80233 1862 A2
E 120th Av
- AdmC 80022 1867 A2
- AdmC 80601 1864 A2
- AdmC 80640 1864 A2
- CMCY 80640 1862 D2
- DNVR 80022 1867 A2
- DNVR 80249 1867 A2
10 TNTN 80241 1860 E2
300 NHGN 80233 1860 E2
500 TNTN 80233 1860 E2
700 NHGN 80233 1861 B2
700 TNTN 80241 1861 E2
2300 TNTN 80233 1861 B2
4700 TNTN 80233 1862 A2
4700 TNTN 80241 1862 A2
5400 AdmC 80602 1862 A2
10100 AdmC 80640 1863 A2
10100 CMCY 80640 1863 C2
12600 CMCY 80601 1864 A2
12600 CMCY 80640 1864 A2
13300 BGTN 80601 1864 A2
14300 AdmC 80603 1864 A2
14300 CMCY 80603 1864 E2
14800 BGTN 80603 1864 A2
16000 CMCY 80022 1864 E2
16900 CMCY 80022 1865 B2
17700 AdmC 80022 1865 B2
21100 AdmC 80022 1866 A1
29600 AdmC 80022 1868 B1

E 120th Av
32000 AdmC 80642 1868 E1
E 120th Av SR-128
1300 NHGN 80233 1861 A2
W 120th Av
- BldC 80303 1855 E2
- BldC 80403 1855 E2
- NHGN 80233 1860 B2
- SUPE 80027 1856 A2
- SUPE 80303 1855 E2
- SUPE 80403 1855 E2
- SUPE 80403 1856 A2
- TNTN 80241 1860 B2
10 NHGN 80234 1860 B2
10 WSTR 80234 1860 B2
3600 BMFD 80020 1859 D2
3600 WSTR 80234 1859 D2
4300 WSTR 80020 1859 C2
4600 BMFD 80031 1859 C2
4600 WSTR 80031 1859 C2
6400 BMFD 80020 1858 E2
8800 BMFD 80021 1858 B2
9800 BfdC 80021 1858 A2
10600 BfdC 80021 1857 E2
10600 BMFD 80021 1857 E2
W 120th Av SR-128
- BldC 80303 1855 E2
- BldC 80403 1855 E2
- NHGN 80233 1860 B2
- SUPE 80027 1856 A2
- SUPE 80303 1855 E2
- SUPE 80403 1856 A2
- TNTN 80241 1860 B2
- WSTR 80234 1859 D2
10 NHGN 80234 1860 B2
10 WSTR 80234 1860 B2
3600 BMFD 80020 1859 D2
4300 WSTR 80020 1859 D2
4500 WSTR 80031 1859 D2
4600 BMFD 80031 1859 A2
6400 BMFD 80020 1858 E2
8700 BMFD 80021 1858 B2
W 120th Av US-287
- BMFD 80020 1859 D2
3600 WSTR 80234 1859 D2
4300 WSTR 80020 1859 D2
4600 BMFD 80031 1859 A2
4600 WSTR 80031 1859 A2
6400 BMFD 80020 1858 E2
E 120th Dr
6600 AdmC 80602 1862 C2
E 120th Pl
3500 TNTN 80233 1861 D2
4800 TNTN 80241 1861 E2
5000 TNTN 80241 1862 A2
5600 AdmC 80602 1862 A2
18600 AdmC 80022 1865 C1
N 120th St
10 BldC 80026 1690 E5
10 LAFT 80026 1690 E5
S 120th St
- BMFD 80020 1774 E1
10 BldC 80026 1690 E7
10 LAFT 80026 1690 E7
600 BldC 80020 1690 E7
600 LAFT 80020 1690 E7
700 BldC 80020 1774 E1
700 LAFT 80026 1774 E1
800 LAFT 80020 1774 E1
E 121st Av
- CMCY 80603 1864 D1
4900 TNTN 80241 1861 E1
4900 TNTN 80241 1862 A2
11800 AdmC 80640 1863 D1
W 121st Av
1300 WSTR 80234 1860 B2
E 121st Ct
4500 TNTN 80241 1861 E2
E 121st Dr
6100 AdmC 80602 1862 B1
W 121st Dr
- BMFD 80020 1859 D1
E 121st Pl
2600 TNTN 80241 1861 C1
5300 TNTN 80241 1862 A1
6100 AdmC 80602 1862 B1
13400 AdmC 80601 1864 A1
13400 BGTN 80601 1864 A1
18600 AdmC 80022 1865 C1
18600 CMCY 80022 1865 C1
W 121st Pl
3600 WSTR 80234 1859 D2
4300 BMFD 80020 1859 C1
E 121st Wy
4400 TNTN 80241 1861 E1
E 121st Cir Dr
16500 AdmC 80603 1864 E1
16800 CMCY 80022 1864 E1
16800 CMCY 80603 1864 E1
E 122nd Av
- AdmC 80640 1863 D1
- CMCY 80603 1864 D1
4300 TNTN 80241 1861 E1
6200 AdmC 80602 1862 B1
W 122nd Av
800 WSTR 80234 1860 C1
3600 BMFD 80020 1859 D1
3600 WSTR 80234 1859 D1
E 122nd Cir
5100 TNTN 80241 1862 A1
E 122nd Ct
4400 TNTN 80241 1861 E1
E 122nd Dr
5600 AdmC 80602 1862 B1
W 122nd Dr
4300 BMFD 80020 1859 D1
E 122nd Pl
5800 AdmC 80602 1862 B1
W 122nd Pl
4300 BMFD 80020 1859 D1
W 122nd St
4400 BMFD 80020 1859 D1

E 123rd Av
- AdmC 80640 1863 B1
2500 TNTN 80241 1861 C1
5700 TNTN 80241 1862 B1
6200 AdmC 80602 1862 B1
15900 CMCY 80603 1864 D1
W 123rd Av
200 WSTR 80234 1860 D1
E 123rd Cir
6600 AdmC 80602 1862 B1
E 123rd Ct
5100 TNTN 80241 1862 A1
E 123rd Dr
2500 TNTN 80241 1861 B1
6200 AdmC 80602 1862 B1
W 123rd Dr
4200 BMFD 80020 1859 C1
E 123rd Pl
6200 AdmC 80602 1862 B1
W 123rd Pl
4400 BMFD 80020 1859 C1
W 123rd St
4200 BMFD 80020 1859 D1
E 123rd Wy
2400 TNTN 80241 1861 C1
6100 AdmC 80602 1862 B1
E 124th Av
- CMCY 80603 1864 A1
400 TNTN 80241 1860 E1
2300 NHGN 80241 1861 D1
2300 TNTN 80241 1861 D1
10400 AdmC 80601 1863 D1
10400 AdmC 80640 1863 D1
10400 BGTN 80601 1863 D1
10400 BGTN 80640 1863 D1
13000 AdmC 80640 1864 A1
13200 AdmC 80601 1864 A1
13200 BGTN 80601 1864 A1
E 124th Av SR-22
10400 AdmC 80601 1863 D1
10400 AdmC 80640 1863 D1
10400 BGTN 80601 1863 D1
10400 BGTN 80640 1863 D1
13000 AdmC 80640 1864 A1
13200 AdmC 80601 1864 A1
13200 BGTN 80601 1864 A1
W 124th Av
800 WSTR 80234 1860 C1
2900 BMFD 80020 1859 E1
2900 WSTR 80020 1859 E1
2900 WSTR 80234 1859 E1
E 124th Cir
2700 TNTN 80241 1861 C1
E 124th Ct
2300 TNTN 80241 1861 B1
W 124th Ct
1100 WSTR 80234 1776 B7
E 124th Dr
2400 TNTN 80241 1861 C1
W 124th Dr
900 WSTR 80234 1860 C1
1000 WSTR 80234 1776 C7
E 124th Pl
2500 TNTN 80241 1861 C1
124th St
- BldC 80516 1607 A4
- ERIE 80516 1607 A4
N 124th St
4200 BldC 80516 1607 A4
4200 ERIE 80516 1607 A4
S 124th St
2000 BMFD 80020 1775 A4
2300 BldC 80020 1775 A4
E 124th Wy
2800 TNTN 80241 1861 C1
4900 TNTN 80241 1862 A1
5600 AdmC 80602 1862 A1
E 125th Av
- AdmC 80022 1781 B7
4000 TNTN 80241 1861 D1
4200 TNTN 80241 1777 E7
4900 TNTN 80241 1862 A1
W 125th Av
- BMFD 80020 1776 B7
- BMFD 80020 1859 E1
2700 BMFD 80020 1860 A1
E 125th Cir
2700 TNTN 80241 1777 C7
E 125th Ct
2300 TNTN 80241 1861 B1
W 125th Dr
1000 WSTR 80234 1776 B7
3400 BMFD 80020 1859 E1
E 125th Pl
1900 TNTN 80241 1777 B7
2500 TNTN 80241 1861 C1
W 125th Pl
- BMFD 80020 1859 E1
W 125th Pt
3400 BMFD 80020 1859 E1
E 125th Wy
2000 TNTN 80241 1777 B7
E 126th Av
- TNTN 80241 1776 E7
- TNTN 80241 1861 A1
2200 TNTN 80241 1777 B7
10800 AdmC 80601 1779 C7
17600 AdmC 80022 1781 A7
17600 AdmC 80603 1781 A7
W 126th Av
2700 BMFD 80020 1776 A7
3700 BMFD 80020 1775 D7
W 126th Cir
5000 BMFD 80020 1859 B1
E 126th Ct
1900 TNTN 80241 1777 B7
5100 TNTN 80241 1778 A7
W 126th Ct
1100 WSTR 80234 1776 B7
W 126th Dr
- BMFD 80020 1775 E7
3300 BMFD 80020 1859 E1
E 126th Lp
2300 TNTN 80241 1777 B7

E 126th Pl
- TNTN 80602 1778 B7
4300 TNTN 80241 1777 E7
W 126th Pl
- BMFD 80020 1859 E1
800 WSTR 80234 1776 C7
3500 BMFD 80020 1775 C6
E 126th Wy
2500 TNTN 80241 1777 C7
E 127th Av
4700 TNTN 80241 1777 E7
5800 TNTN 80602 1778 A7
W 127th Av
3700 BMFD 80020 1775 D7
4800 BMFD 80020 1859 C1
E 127th Cir
1900 TNTN 80241 1777 B7
E 127th Ct
2400 TNTN 80241 1777 C7
5100 TNTN 80241 1778 A7
8500 AdmC 80602 1778 E7
W 127th Ct
800 WSTR 80234 1776 C7
E 127th Dr
- TNTN 80602 1778 A7
2300 TNTN 80241 1777 B7
5200 TNTN 80241 1778 A7
E 127th Ln
- TNTN 80602 1778 A7
3700 TNTN 80241 1777 D7
E 127th Pl
- AdmC 80602 1778 E7
- TNTN 80602 1778 B7
2300 TNTN 80241 1777 B7
W 127th Pl
1000 WSTR 80234 1776 C7
4700 BMFD 80020 1775 C7
E 127th Wy
4300 TNTN 80241 1777 E7
5000 TNTN 80241 1778 A7
E 128th Av
- AdmC 80603 1784 E6
- AdmC 80642 1784 E6
10 TNTN 80241 1776 E7
10 WSTR 80234 1776 E7
2200 TNTN 80241 1777 B7
5000 TNTN 80241 1778 C7
5400 TNTN 80602 1778 C7
6200 AdmC 80602 1778 C7
16900 AdmC 80603 1780 E7
16900 AdmC 80603 1781 A7
16900 CMCY 80603 1780 E7
18400 AdmC 80022 1781 C6
18400 AdmC 80022 1782 A6
24800 AdmC 80022 1783 A6
26400 AdmC 80022 1784 A6
W 128th Av
10 TNTN 80241 1776 B7
2100 BMFD 80020 1776 B7
2100 BMFD 80234 1776 B7
2100 WSTR 80234 1776 B7
2900 BMFD 80020 1775 E7
E 128th Cir
5200 TNTN 80241 1778 A7
E 128th Ct
5200 TNTN 80241 1777 E7
5400 TNTN 80241 1778 A7
E 128th Dr
1900 TNTN 80241 1777 B7
5200 TNTN 80241 1778 A7
E 128th Pl
3200 TNTN 80241 1777 D7
8100 TNTN 80602 1778 E7
W 128th Pl
- BMFD 80020 1776 C7
4600 BMFD 80020 1775 C7
E 128th Wy
5200 TNTN 80241 1778 A7
E 129th Av
800 TNTN 80241 1776 E7
4400 TNTN 80241 1777 E6
5200 TNTN 80241 1778 A6
5800 TNTN 80602 1778 B6
E 129th Cir
4100 TNTN 80241 1777 E6
E 129th Ct
4700 TNTN 80241 1777 E7
E 129th Dr
1900 TNTN 80241 1777 B7
W 129th Dr
1700 WSTR 80234 1776 B7
E 129th Pl
5100 TNTN 80241 1777 E6
5200 TNTN 80241 1778 A7
5700 TNTN 80602 1778 A6
W 129th Pl
600 BMFD 80020 1776 A7
E 129th Wy
4000 TNTN 80241 1777 E6
5200 TNTN 80241 1778 A6
E 130th Av
- TNTN 80602 1778 B6
500 TNTN 80241 1776 E6
800 TNTN 80241 1777 A6
4700 TNTN 80241 1778 A6
W 130th Av
- BMFD 80020 1776 A6
- BMFD 80234 1776 A6
- WSTR 80234 1776 A6
E 130th Cir
- TNTN 80602 1778 D6
900 TNTN 80241 1777 A6
5200 TNTN 80241 1778 A6
E 130th Ct
500 TNTN 80241 1776 E6
5200 TNTN 80241 1777 E6
W 130th Ct
1600 WSTR 80234 1776 B6
E 130th Dr
900 TNTN 80241 1777 A6
5500 TNTN 80241 1778 A6
W 130th Dr
1600 WSTR 80234 1776 B6

E 130th Pl
- TNTN 80602 1778 D6
1000 TNTN 80241 1777 A6
5300 TNTN 80241 1778 A6
W 130th Pl
1700 WSTR 80234 1776 B6
3400 BMFD 80020 1775 D6
E 130th Wy
500 TNTN 80241 1776 E6
5200 TNTN 80241 1777 E6
5200 TNTN 80241 1778 A6
5600 TNTN 80602 1778 A6
E 131st Av
- TNTN 80602 1778 C6
400 TNTN 80241 1776 E6
2500 TNTN 80241 1777 C6
29600 AdmC 80022 1784 B6
W 131st Av
3400 BMFD 80020 1775 D6
E 131st Cir
1600 TNTN 80241 1777 B6
W 131st Cir
3100 BMFD 80020 1775 E6
E 131st Ct
500 TNTN 80241 1776 E6
4000 TNTN 80241 1777 D6
W 131st Ct
1700 WSTR 80234 1776 B6
E 131st Dr
5200 TNTN 80241 1777 E6
5200 TNTN 80241 1778 A6
6700 TNTN 80602 1778 C6
W 131st Dr
1800 WSTR 80234 1776 B6
W 131st Ln
1800 WSTR 80234 1776 B6
E 131st Pl
800 TNTN 80241 1776 E6
4200 TNTN 80241 1777 E6
5600 TNTN 80602 1778 A6
W 131st Pl
1900 WSTR 80234 1776 B6
3400 BMFD 80020 1775 D6
E 131st Wy
500 TNTN 80241 1776 E6
2800 TNTN 80241 1777 C6
5300 TNTN 80241 1778 A6
6700 TNTN 80602 1778 C6
W 131st Wy
2100 WSTR 80234 1776 B6
2900 BMFD 80020 1775 E6
E 132nd Av
- ININ 80241 1776 E6
- TNTN 80602 1778 C6
800 TNTN 80241 1777 A6
11700 AdmC 80601 1779 E6
11700 BGTN 80601 1779 E6
12900 AdmC 80601 1780 A6
21000 AdmC 80022 1781 E5
23300 AdmC 80022 1782 D5
W 132nd Av
1900 WSTR 80234 1776 B6
2200 BMFD 80020 1776 A6
E 132nd Cir
800 TNTN 80241 1776 E5
900 TNTN 80241 1777 A6
W 132nd Cir
3100 BMFD 80020 1775 E6
E 132nd Ct
3100 TNTN 80241 1777 D6
W 132nd Ct
3100 BMFD 80020 1775 D6
3100 BMFD 80020 1776 A6
E 132nd Dr
800 TNTN 80241 1776 E6
800 TNTN 80241 1777 A6
E 132nd Pl
1000 TNTN 80241 1777 A6
W 132nd Pl
1100 WSTR 80234 1776 C6
3400 BMFD 80020 1775 D6
E 132nd Wy
400 TNTN 80241 1776 E6
1000 TNTN 80241 1777 A6
6000 TNTN 80602 1778 B6
W 132nd Wy
2500 BMFD 80020 1776 A6
E 133rd Av
800 TNTN 80241 1776 E6
1200 TNTN 80241 1777 A6
W 133rd Av
2800 BMFD 80020 1776 A6
3100 BMFD 80020 1775 E6
E 133rd Cir
4000 TNTN 80241 1777 D6
25900 AdmC 80022 1783 B5
W 133rd Cir
900 WSTR 80234 1776 C5
2500 BMFD 80020 1776 A6
3100 BMFD 80020 1775 E6
E 133rd Ct
500 TNTN 80241 1776 E5
3700 TNTN 80241 1777 D6
W 133rd Ct
1100 WSTR 80234 1776 C5
E 133rd Dr
900 TNTN 80241 1777 A5
13800 AdmC 80601 1780 B5
E 133rd Ln
2900 TNTN 80241 1777 C6
E 133rd Pl
800 TNTN 80241 1776 E5
800 TNTN 80241 1777 A5
14200 AdmC 80601 1780 B5
E 133rd Wy
400 TNTN 80241 1776 E6
1000 TNTN 80241 1777 A5
W 133rd Wy
1000 WSTR 80234 1776 C5
E 134th Av
400 TNTN 80241 1776 E5
4600 TNTN 80241 1777 E5
14100 AdmC 80601 1780 B5
23300 AdmC 80022 1782 D5

W 134th Av
800 WSTR 80234 1776 C5
2800 BMFD 80020 1775 E5
2800 BMFD 80020 1776 A5
E 134th Cir
1800 TNTN 80241 1777 B5
W 134th Cir
2500 BMFD 80020 1776 A5
2900 BMFD 80020 1775 E5
E 134th Ct
3700 TNTN 80241 1777 D6
W 134th Ct
2800 BMFD 80020 1775 D6
2800 BMFD 80020 1776 A6
E 134th Dr
3500 TNTN 80241 1777 D5
W 134th Dr
1300 WSTR 80234 1776 B5
E 134th Pl
3500 TNTN 80241 1777 D5
14500 AdmC 80601 1780 B5
W 134th Pl
1100 WSTR 80234 1776 B5
2800 BMFD 80020 1776 A5
3800 BMFD 80020 1775 D5
E 134th Wy
1800 TNTN 80241 1777 B5
W 134th Wy
2000 WSTR 80234 1776 B5
3000 BMFD 80020 1775 E5
E 135th Av
1300 TNTN 80241 1777 A5
14500 AdmC 80601 1780 B5
W 135th Av
1800 WSTR 80234 1776 B5
2500 BMFD 80020 1776 A5
2900 BMFD 80020 1775 E5
E 135th Ct
3500 TNTN 80241 1777 D5
W 135th Ct
2000 WSTR 80234 1776 B5
E 135th Dr
3700 TNTN 80241 1777 D5
W 135th Dr
1100 WSTR 80234 1776 C5
E 135th Ln
4600 TNTN 80241 1777 E5
W 135th Ln
- WSTR 80234 1776 C5
E 135th Pl
1200 TNTN 80241 1777 A5
W 135th Pl
1700 WSTR 80234 1776 B5
13400 BMFD 80020 1775 E5
E 135th Wy
3700 TNTN 80241 1777 D5
W 135th Wy
1600 WSTR 80234 1776 B5
E 136th Av
- AdmC 80022 1783 A4
- AdmC 80603 1782 E4
- BGTN 80603 1781 A5
- TNTN 80020 1776 E5
- TNTN 80241 1776 E5
10 AdmC 80602 1776 E5
1200 AdmC 80241 1777 A5
1200 AdmC 80602 1777 A5
1200 TNTN 80241 1777 A5
1900 TNTN 80602 1777 C5
4600 TNTN 80602 1778 A5
7300 AdmC 80602 1778 D5
8900 AdmC 80602 1779 A5
11800 AdmC 80601 1779 D5
11800 BGTN 80601 1779 D5
12700 AdmC 80601 1780 A5
14300 BGTN 80601 1780 E5
16900 AdmC 80601 1781 A5
16900 BGTN 80601 1781 A5
17300 AdmC 80603 1781 A5
23400 AdmC 80022 1782 E4
W 136th Av
- TNTN 80020 1776 B5
- TNTN 80241 1776 B5
10 BMFD 80020 1776 B5
10 WSTR 80020 1776 B5
10 WSTR 80234 1776 B5
2400 BMFD 80020 1775 C5
6500 BMFD 80020 1774 E5
E 136th Pl
4500 TNTN 80602 1777 E5
6300 TNTN 80602 1778 B5
136th Pl E
3200 TNTN 80602 1777 C5
E 137th Av
- AdmC 80602 1777 B5
2400 TNTN 80602 1777 B5
6300 TNTN 80602 1778 B4
18200 AdmC 80603 1781 B4
137th Av E
- TNTN 80602 1777 C5
E 137th Pl
- TNTN 80602 1777 E4
- TNTN 80602 1778 B4
18000 AdmC 80603 1781 B4
E 137th Wy
32100 AdmC 80603 1784 E4
32100 AdmC 80642 1784 E4
E 138th Av
- AdmC 80602 1777 B5
- AdmC 80602 1779 A4
- TNTN 80602 1778 B4
2200 TNTN 80602 1777 B5
E 138th Ct
2600 TNTN 80602 1777 C4
9000 AdmC 80602 1778 E4
9000 AdmC 80602 1779 A4
E 138th Dr
- TNTN 80602 1777 E4
E 138th Pl
3500 TNTN 80602 1777 D4
E 139th Av
3500 TNTN 80602 1777 D4
6300 TNTN 80602 1778 B4

Block	City	ZIP	Map#	Grid
E 139th Ct				
-	AdmC	80602	1778	E4
9000	AdmC	80602	1779	A4
W 139th Ct				
900	WSTR	80020	1776	C4
E 139th Dr				
2700	TNTN	80602	1777	C4
E 139th Pl				
3700	TNTN	80602	1777	D4
W 139th Pl				
1200	WSTR	80020	1776	C4
E 140th Av				
-	AdmC	80601	1780	B4
-	BGTN	80601	1780	B4
-	TNTN	80602	1778	A4
2700	TNTN	80602	1777	C4
W 140th Dr				
800	WSTR	80020	1776	C4
E 140th Wy				
32200	AdmC	80603	1784	E3
32200	AdmC	80642	1784	E3
E 141st Av				
1200	AdmC	80602	1777	A4
E 142nd Av				
1600	AdmC	80602	1777	B3
2200	TNTN	80602	1777	B3
9900	AdmC	80602	1779	B3
E 143rd Av				
1200	AdmC	80602	1777	B3
2200	TNTN	80602	1777	B3
32400	AdmC	80603	1784	E3
32400	AdmC	80642	1784	E3
E 143rd Wy				
10000	AdmC	80602	1779	B3
E 144th Av				
-	AdmC	80603	1781	E2
-	AdmC	80603	1783	E2
-	BGTN	80603	1781	B3
10	AdmC	80602	1776	E3
10	TNTN	80020	1776	E3
10	WSTR	80020	1776	E3
700	AdmC	80602	1777	A3
700	TNTN	80020	1777	A3
700	TNTN	80602	1777	A3
1200	AdmC	80020	1777	A3
4500	TNTN	80602	1778	A3
7300	AdmC	80602	1778	D3
12500	AdmC	80601	1779	E3
12500	BGTN	80601	1779	E3
12800	AdmC	80601	1780	A3
12800	BGTN	80601	1780	A3
16700	BGTN	80601	1781	A3
21000	AdmC	80603	1782	B2
29500	AdmC	80603	1784	A2
W 144th Av				
10	TNTN	80020	1776	A3
10	WSTR	80020	1776	A3
1300	AdmC	80020	1776	A3
1900	BMFD	80020	1776	A3
2600	BMFD	80020	1775	C3
9500	BldC	80020	1775	C3
W 144th Ct				
1000	WSTR	80020	1776	C3
2700	BMFD	80020	1776	A3
E 144th Dr				
1700	TNTN	80602	1777	B3
E 144th Pl				
2000	TNTN	80602	1777	B3
W 144th Pl				
1000	WSTR	80020	1776	C3
E 144th Wy				
1900	TNTN	80602	1777	B3
E 145th Av				
-	AdmC	80603	1784	D2
2400	TNTN	80602	1777	B3
9100	AdmC	80602	1778	E3
9100	AdmC	80602	1779	A3
E 145th Ct				
2300	TNTN	80602	1777	B3
E 145th Pl				
2100	TNTN	80602	1777	B2
8200	AdmC	80602	1778	E2
W 145th Pl				
1300	AdmC	80020	1776	C2
1300	WSTR	80020	1776	C2
W 145th Wy				
900	WSTR	80020	1776	C3
E 146th Av				
3800	AdmC	80602	1777	D2
8500	AdmC	80602	1778	E2
9200	AdmC	80602	1779	A2
30800	AdmC	80603	1784	B2
E 146th Pl				
2500	TNTN	80602	1777	C2
9800	AdmC	80602	1779	B2
E 147th Av				
-	TNTN	80602	1777	B2
9400	AdmC	80602	1779	A2
32400	AdmC	80603	1784	E2
32400	AdmC	80642	1784	E2
W 147th Ct				
2800	BMFD	80020	1776	A2
3300	BMFD	80020	1775	E2
E 147th Pl				
9200	AdmC	80602	1779	A2
E 148th Av				
-	AdmC	80601	1779	E2
-	AdmC	80602	1777	E2
2000	TNTN	80602	1777	B2
12700	AdmC	80601	1780	A2
12700	BGTN	80601	1779	E2
12700	BGTN	80601	1780	A2
29000	AdmC	80603	1783	E1
29000	AdmC	80603	1784	A1
W 148th Av				
1000	WSTR	80020	1776	C2
2800	BMFD	80020	1775	E2
E 148th Cir				
8900	AdmC	80602	1778	E2
9100	AdmC	80602	1779	A2
E 148th Ct				
30500	AdmC	80603	1784	B1
W 148th Ct				
2500	BMFD	80020	1776	A2
E 148th Dr				
1900	TNTN	80602	1777	B2
E 148th Pl				
2400	TNTN	80602	1777	C2
9700	AdmC	80602	1779	B2
W 148th Pl				
-	AdmC	80020	1776	B2
E 149th Av				
2400	TNTN	80602	1777	B2
32600	AdmC	80603	1784	E1
32600	AdmC	80642	1784	E1
W 149th Av				
800	AdmC	80020	1776	C2
2000	BMFD	80020	1776	B2
2700	BMFD	80020	1775	E2
E 149th Ct				
9800	AdmC	80602	1779	B1
W 149th Ct				
3200	BMFD	80020	1775	E2
W 149th Pl				
1400	AdmC	80020	1776	B1
E 150th Av				
2400	TNTN	80602	1777	B1
9500	AdmC	80602	1779	A1
30500	AdmC	80603	1784	B1
W 150th Av				
-	AdmC	80020	1776	B1
-	BMFD	80020	1776	A1
W 150th Ct				
3000	WSTR	80031	1859	E6
3500	BMFD	80020	1775	D1
E 150th Pl				
2400	TNTN	80602	1777	C1
10800	AdmC	80602	1779	C1
W 150th Pl				
1400	AdmC	80020	1776	B1
E 151st Av				
3400	AdmC	80602	1777	D1
30600	AdmC	80603	1784	C1
32600	AdmC	80642	1784	E1
E 151st Ct				
9900	AdmC	80602	1779	B1
W 151st Ct				
3100	BMFD	80020	1775	E1
E 151st Pl				
10600	AdmC	80602	1779	C1
E 152nd Av				
-	AdmC	80601	1781	C1
-	BGTN	80601	1781	A1
4000	AdmC	80602	1777	E1
5600	TNTN	80602	1778	C1
9000	AdmC	80602	1778	E1
10500	AdmC	80602	1779	B1
18900	AdmC	80601	1697	C7
19300	BGTN	80601	1697	C7
20100	AdmC	80603	1697	E7
20100	BGTN	80603	1697	E7
20700	AdmC	80603	1698	B7
25200	AdmC	80603	1699	C7
29200	AdmC	80603	1700	A7
32400	AdmC	80642	1700	E7
W 152nd Av				
300	AdmC	80020	1776	D1
300	BMFD	80020	1776	D1
2200	BMFD	80020	1775	E1
152nd Av E				
-	AdmC	80020	1776	E1
-	AdmC	80020	1777	A1
-	AdmC	80602	1777	A1
-	TNTN	80020	1776	E1
W 152nd Pl				
2200	AdmC	80020	1776	A1
2200	BMFD	80020	1776	A1
E 153rd Av				
8900	AdmC	80602	1694	E7
8900	AdmC	80602	1695	A7
W 153rd Av				
10	AdmC	80020	1776	D1
E 153rd Cir				
24700	AdmC	80603	1698	E7
E 153rd Dr				
10500	AdmC	80602	1695	B7
10800	AdmC	80602	1779	C1
W 153rd Pl				
1900	AdmC	80020	1692	A7
1900	BMFD	80020	1692	A7
E 154th Av				
10100	AdmC	80602	1695	B7
W 154th Av				
800	AdmC	80020	1692	C7
800	BMFD	80020	1692	C7
E 154th Cir				
24700	AdmC	80603	1698	E7
E 154th Pl				
17700	AdmC	80601	1697	A7
W 154th Pl				
1800	AdmC	80020	1692	A7
1800	BMFD	80020	1692	A7
E 155th Av				
-	AdmC	80601	1697	B7
8900	AdmC	80602	1694	E7
9800	AdmC	80602	1695	B7
E 155th Ct				
10500	AdmC	80602	1695	B7
E 155th Dr				
9000	AdmC	80602	1694	E7
9000	AdmC	80602	1695	A7
E 155th Pl				
-	BGTN	80601	1697	A7
10700	AdmC	80602	1695	C7
17800	AdmC	80601	1697	A7
W 155th Pl				
2200	AdmC	80020	1692	A7
2200	BMFD	80020	1692	A7
E 155th Wy				
23000	AdmC	80603	1698	D7
E 156th Av				
2300	AdmC	80602	1693	C7
23300	AdmC	80603	1698	D6
29600	AdmC	80603	1700	A6
W 156th Av				
800	AdmC	80020	1692	B7
800	BMFD	80020	1692	B7
E 156th Ct				
8100	TNTN	80602	1694	D7
33000	AdmC	80603	1700	E6
33000	AdmC	80642	1700	E6
E 157th Av				
-	AdmC	80602	1695	A7
9000	AdmC	80602	1694	E6
23400	AdmC	80603	1698	C6
E 157th Ct				
8100	TNTN	80602	1694	D6
10600	AdmC	80602	1695	B6
E 157th Pl				
-	AdmC	80602	1695	A6
E 158th Av				
-	TNTN	80602	1694	D6
9300	AdmC	80602	1695	A6
E 158th Ct				
10500	AdmC	80602	1695	B6
E 158th Pl				
9600	AdmC	80602	1695	A6
E 159th Av				
8900	AdmC	80602	1694	E6
9700	AdmC	80602	1695	A6
E 159th Ct				
8100	TNTN	80602	1694	D6
E 159th Pl				
9700	AdmC	80602	1695	A6
E 160th Av				
-	AdmC	80601	1698	B5
-	AdmC	80602	1693	A6
-	BGTN	80601	1698	B5
10	AdmC	80020	1692	E6
10	BMFD	80020	1692	E6
10	TNTN	80020	1692	E6
700	AdmC	80020	1693	A6
700	TNTN	80020	1693	A6
1300	TNTN	80602	1693	A6
4000	TNTN	80602	1694	A6
7300	AdmC	80602	1694	E6
8900	AdmC	80602	1695	B6
12300	AdmC	80601	1695	B6
12900	AdmC	80601	1696	A6
12900	AdmC	80602	1696	A6
12900	BGTN	80601	1696	A6
21700	AdmC	80603	1698	B5
21700	BGTN	80603	1698	B5
28200	AdmC	80603	1699	D5
33000	AdmC	80603	1700	E5
33000	AdmC	80642	1700	E5
E 160th Av SR-7				
-	AdmC	80601	1698	A5
-	AdmC	80603	1698	A5
-	BGTN	80601	1698	A5
-	BGTN	80603	1698	A5
2100	TNTN	80602	1693	E6
4000	TNTN	80602	1694	A6
7300	AdmC	80602	1694	E6
8900	AdmC	80602	1695	B6
12300	AdmC	80601	1695	B6
12900	AdmC	80601	1696	A6
12900	AdmC	80602	1696	A6
12900	BGTN	80601	1696	A6
W 160th Av				
10	BMFD	80020	1692	D6
10	TNTN	80020	1692	D6
2500	BMFD	80020	1691	D6
E 160th Ct				
29000	AdmC	80603	1699	E5
29000	AdmC	80603	1700	A5
E 160th Pl				
8400	AdmC	80602	1694	E6
9500	AdmC	80602	1695	A6
28500	AdmC	80603	1699	E5
E 161st Av				
-	AdmC	80602	1694	E5
-	AdmC	80602	1695	A6
E 161st Pl				
-	AdmC	80602	1694	E5
-	AdmC	80602	1695	A5
E 162nd Av				
-	AdmC	80602	1693	A5
-	AdmC	80602	1694	E5
-	AdmC	80602	1695	A5
29200	AdmC	80603	1699	E5
29200	AdmC	80603	1700	A5
E 162nd Ct				
28300	AdmC	80603	1699	E5
E 163rd Av				
8400	AdmC	80602	1694	E5
E 163rd Ct				
8400	AdmC	80602	1694	E5
E 163rd Pl				
8600	AdmC	80602	1694	E5
28200	AdmC	80603	1699	E5
29700	AdmC	80603	1700	A5
E 164th Av				
-	AdmC	80602	1693	C5
-	TNTN	80020	1692	E5
-	TNTN	80602	1693	B5
17700	AdmC	80601	1697	B5
17700	BGTN	80601	1697	B5
E 164th Pl				
-	AdmC	80602	1693	B5
1600	TNTN	80602	1693	A5
E 165th Av				
-	TNTN	80602	1693	B5
2300	AdmC	80602	1693	C5
29700	AdmC	80603	1700	A4
E 165th Ct				
6400	AdmC	80602	1694	B5
E 165th Pl				
-	AdmC	80602	1694	B5
E 166th Av				
-	TNTN	80020	1693	A4
-	TNTN	80602	1693	A4
2500	AdmC	80602	1693	C4
29000	AdmC	80603	1699	E4
29000	AdmC	80603	1700	A4
31300	AdmC	80642	1700	C4
E 166th Ct				
32200	AdmC	80642	1700	D4
E 166th Dr				
1900	TNTN	80602	1693	B5
E 166th Pl				
6600	AdmC	80602	1694	C4
29700	AdmC	80603	1700	A4
E 167th Av				
6600	AdmC	80602	1694	B4
29000	AdmC	80603	1699	E4
29000	AdmC	80603	1700	A4
31300	AdmC	80642	1700	C4
E 167th Dr				
32100	AdmC	80642	1700	D3
E 167th Pl				
7000	AdmC	80602	1694	C4
29700	AdmC	80603	1700	A4
E 168th Av				
-	TNTN	80020	1692	E4
-	TNTN	80602	1692	E4
1000	BMFD	80516	1693	A4
2200	TNTN	80516	1693	A4
2700	TNTN	80602	1693	A4
4000	TNTN	80603	1693	E4
6700	TNTN	80602	1694	A4
6700	TNTN	80603	1694	A4
7000	AdmC	80602	1694	A4
7000	WldC	80603	1694	A4
9100	AdmC	80602	1695	A4
9100	WldC	80603	1695	A4
12700	AdmC	80601	1695	D4
12900	WldC	80603	1696	A4
15500	BGTN	80601	1696	D4
15500	BGTN	80603	1696	D4
16000	AdmC	80601	1696	D4
16600	BGTN	80601	1698	B4
16600	BGTN	80603	1698	B4
16700	AdmC	80601	1697	A4
16700	WldC	80603	1697	A4
18000	LCHB	80603	1698	B4
18000	WldC	80603	1698	B4
19000	AdmC	80603	1699	D3
19000	WldC	80642	1699	D3
22600	AdmC	80601	1698	B4
28900	AdmC	80603	1700	A3
28900	WldC	80642	1700	A3
E 168th Av CO-2				
19000	AdmC	80603	1698	E4
19000	AdmC	80603	1699	D3
19000	LCHB	80603	1698	E4
19000	WldC	80642	1699	D3
28900	AdmC	80603	1700	A3
28900	WldC	80642	1700	A3
W 168th Av				
-	BldC	80026	1691	D4
-	BldC	80516	1691	D4
-	BMFD	80020	1691	D4
-	BMFD	80020	1692	B4
-	BMFD	80516	1692	B4
-	ERIE	80516	1691	D4
-	ERIE	80516	1692	B4
W 168th Av SR-7				
-	BldC	80026	1691	D4
-	BldC	80516	1691	D4
-	BMFD	80020	1691	D4
-	BMFD	80020	1692	B4
-	BMFD	80516	1692	B4
-	ERIE	80516	1691	D4
-	ERIE	80516	1692	B4
175th Av				
2300	WldC	80516	1692	B2

Denver Regional Points of Interest Index

Airports

FEATURE NAME / Address City ZIP Code	MAP#	GRID
Aurora Airpark, AphC	2119	E6
Boulder Municipal, BLDR	1603	C6
Centennial, CTNL	2367	E6
Denver International, DNVR	1950	B3
Erie Municipal, BldC	1691	C3
Front Range, AURA	2037	D4
Jefferson County, JfnC	1858	A3
Vance Brand Municipal, LGMT	1438	A3

Beaches, Harbors & Water Rec

FEATURE NAME / Address City ZIP Code	MAP#	GRID
Aurora Reservoir Marina, AURA	2371	C1
Boulder Reservoir Marina, BldC	1603	C2
Chatfield Marina, DgsC	2447	B4
Cherry Creek Marina, AphC	2284	B4

Buildings

FEATURE NAME / Address City ZIP Code	MAP#	GRID
Boulder Technical Center BldC, 80503	1520	C6
Brighton Business Center W Bromley Ln, BGTN, 80601	1780	A1
Centennial Valley Business Park BldC, 80027	1772	D2
Colorado Technological Center LSVL, 80020	1773	E2
Coors Brewing 1201 Ford St, GOLD, 80401	2107	E3
Coors Technology Center W 45th Dr, GOLD, 80403	2024	D6
Denver Business Center DNVR, 80239	2031	C4
Denver Technological Center GDVL, 80111	2366	E1
Flatiron Business Park 55th St, BLDR, 80301	1687	D1
Gunbarrel Business Park 6175 Longbow Dr, BLDR, 80301	1603	E2
Hunter Douglas Business Park W Midway Blvd, BMFD, 80020	1774	B7
IBM 6300 Diagonal Hwy, BLDR, 80503	1520	B6
Ideal Industrial Park W 6th Av, BMFD, 80020	1774	C7
Lockheed Martin 12257 S Platte Canyon Rd, JfnC, 80127	2530	C4
Louviers Industrial Park W Airport Rd, DgsC, 80135	2532	D6
Meridian International Business Center Maroon Cir, DgsC, 80112	2451	C4
Montbello Industrial Park DNVR, 80239	2031	C6
Owens Industrial Park W Airport Rd, DgsC, 80135	2532	D7
Oxford Santa Fe Business Park W Oxford Av, SRDN, 80110	2280	B5
Reynolds Industrial Park Reynolds Dr, DgsC, 80135	2616	D1
Sedalia Business Park DgsC, 80135	2617	A4
Space Systems Company 12999 W Deer Creek Canyon Rd, JfnC, 80127	2445	A2
Titan Road Industrial Park Titan Park Cir, DgsC, 80125	2532	A2
Turnpike Industrial Park W Midway Blvd, BMFD, 80020	1858	B1
Washington Square Business Center NHGN, 80233	1860	E1

Buildings - Governmental

FEATURE NAME / Address City ZIP Code	MAP#	GRID
Adams County Court 1100 Judicial Center Dr, BGTN, 80601	1781	C1
Adams County Detention Facility 150 N 19th Av, BGTN, 80601	1696	D5
Adams County Municipal Court 22 S 4th Av, BGTN, 80601	1696	B6
Adams County Municipal Court 5291 E 60th Av, CMCY, 80022	2030	A3
Adams County Municipal Court 11701 Community Center Dr, NHGN, 80233	1860	D3
Adams County Municipal Court 9500 Civic Center Dr, TNTN, 80229	1944	E1
Adams/Jefferson County Municipal Court 3030 Turnpike Dr, WSTR, 80030	1943	E6
Administration & Support Office 4300 Cherry Creek South Dr, GNDL, 80246	2197	E3
Administration Building 450 S 4th Av, BGTN, 80601	1696	B7
Arapahoe County Administration Building 5334 S Prince St, LITN, 80120	2364	B1
Arapahoe County Court 15400 E 14th Pl, AURA, 80011	2116	D5
Arapahoe County Court 1790 W Littleton Blvd, LITN, 80120	2364	C1
Arapahoe County District Court 7325 S Potomac St, CTNL, 80112	2368	B5
Arapahoe County Municipal Court 2450 E Quincy Av, CHLV, 80113	2281	C5
Arapahoe County Municipal Court 3400 S Elati St, EGLD, 80110	2280	D3
Arapahoe County Municipal Court 6060 S Quebec St, GDVL, 80111	2366	D2
Arapahoe County Municipal Court 950 S Birch St, GNDL, 80246	2197	E3
Arapahoe County Municipal Court 2255 W Berry Av, LITN, 80120	2364	B1
Arapahoe County Municipal Court 4101 S Federal Blvd, SRDN, 80110	2280	A5
Arapahoe/Jefferson County Municipal Court 5931 S Middlefield Rd, CBVL, 80123	2363	E2
Arvada City Hall 8101 Ralston Rd, ARVD, 80004	2026	D3
Bennett Town Hall 355 4th St, BNNT, 80102	2124	D2
Black Hawk City Hall 201 Selack St, BKHK, 80403	2018	A4
Boulder City Hall 1777 Broadway St, BLDR, 80302	1686	C2
Boulder County Court 505 4th Av, LGMT, 80501	1439	B2
Boulder County District Court 2025 14th St, BLDR, 80302	1686	C2
Boulder County Municipal Court 1777 6th St, BLDR, 80302	1686	B2
Boulder County Municipal Court 1 Descombes Dr, BMFD, 80020	1859	A1
Boulder County Municipal Court 1290 S Public Rd, LAFT, 80026	1690	C6
Boulder County Municipal Court 408 3rd Av, LGMT, 80501	1439	B2
Boulder County Municipal Court 749 Main St, LSVL, 80027	1689	D7
Boulder County Municipal Court 432 5th Av, LYNS, 80540	1352	D2
Boulder County Municipal Court 30 E 1st St, NDLD, 80466	1765	D3
Bow Mar Town Hall 5395 Lakeshore Dr, BWMR, 80123	2363	C1
Brighton City Hall 22 S 4th Av, BGTN, 80601	1696	B6
Broomfield City Hall 1 Descombes Dr, BMFD, 80020	1859	A1
Castle Rock Town Hall 680 Wilcox St, CSRK, 80104	2703	D7
Centennial City Hall 12503 E Euclid Dr, CTNL, 80111	2367	E4
Central City City Hall 141 Nevada St, CLCY, 80403	2017	D4
Cherry Hills Village City Hall 2450 E Quincy Av, CHLV, 80113	2281	C5
Colorado Correctional Center 15000 S Golden Rd, JfnC, 80401	2108	E6
Colorado Governor's Mansion 400 E 8th Av, DNVR, 80203	2112	E6
Colorado State Capitol 200 E Colfax Av, DNVR, 80203	2112	E5
Columbine Valley Town Hall 5931 S Middlefield Rd, CBVL, 80123	2363	E2
Commerce City City Hall 5291 E 60th Av, CMCY, 80022	2030	A3
County Court 3280 Downing St, DNVR, 80205	2113	A2
County Court 1865 W Mississippi Av, DNVR, 80223	2196	B4
County Court 3100 S Sheridan Blvd, DNVR, 80236	2279	C3
Denver Administrative Office 1313 Sherman St, DNVR, 80203	2112	E5
Denver City Hall 1437 Bannock St, DNVR, 80204	2112	D5
Denver County Court 1351 Cherokee St, DNVR, 80204	2112	D5
Denver County Jail 10500 Smith Rd, DNVR, 80238	2115	C1
Denver County Supreme Court 2 E 14th Av, DNVR, 80203	2112	E5
Denver Federal Center 2nd Pl, LKWD, 80226	2193	E1
Denver Women's Correctional Facility 10900 Smith Rd, DNVR, 80238	2115	C1
District Court 1391 Speer Blvd, DNVR, 80204	2112	D5
District Court 1611 S Federal Blvd, DNVR, 80219	2196	A5
Douglas County Court 355 S Wilcox St, CSRK, 80104	2703	D7
Douglas County District Court 100 3rd St, CSRK, 80104	2703	D7
Douglas County Municipal Court 318 S Perry St, CSRK, 80104	2703	D7
Douglas County Municipal Court 20120 E Main St, PARK, 80138	2453	E7
Edgewater City Hall 2401 Sheridan Blvd, EDGW, 80214	2111	C3
Elbert County District Court 751 Ute Av, KIOW, 80117	2796	A3
Elizabeth Town Hall 321 S Banner St, ELIZ, 80107	2793	B1
Englewood City Hall 3400 S Elati St, EGLD, 80110	2280	D3
Erie Town Hall 645 Holbrook St, ERIE, 80516	1607	C4
Federal Correctional Institute 9595 W Quincy Av, JfnC, 80235	2278	B5
Federal Heights Police Department 2380 W 90th Av, FLHT, 80260	1944	A2
Gilpin County Jail 2960 Dory Hill Rd, GpnC, 80403	1934	B6
Glendale City Hall 950 S Birch St, GNDL, 80246	2197	E3
Golden City Hall 911 10th St, GOLD, 80401	2107	D3
Greenwood Village City Hall 6060 S Quebec St, GDVL, 80111	2366	D2
Idaho Springs City Hall 1711 Miner St, IDSP, 80452	2101	D5
Jamestown Town Hall 118 Main St, JMWN, 80455	1516	B2
Jefferson County Building 100 Jefferson County Pkwy, GOLD, 80401	2108	B7
Jefferson County Court 100 Jefferson County Pkwy, GOLD, 80401	2108	B7
Jefferson County Government Center 700 Jefferson County Pkwy, GOLD, 80401	2108	A6
Jefferson County Jail 200 Jefferson County Pkwy, GOLD, 80401	2108	B6
Jefferson County Municipal Court 8101 Ralston Rd, ARVD, 80004	2026	D3
Jefferson County Municipal Court 4800 W Redwood Dr, BWMR, 80123	2279	C7
Jefferson County Municipal Court 2401 Sheridan Blvd, EDGW, 80214	2111	C3
Jefferson County Municipal Court 911 10th St, GOLD, 80401	2107	D3
Jefferson County Municipal Court 445 S Allison Pkwy, LKWD, 80226	2194	D2
Jefferson County Municipal Court MRSN, 80465	2276	C3
Jefferson County Municipal Court 7500 W 29th Av, WTRG, 80033	2110	E3
Judiciary Courts State of Colorado 1301 Pennsylvania St, DNVR, 80203	2112	E5
Lafayette City Hall 1290 S Public Rd, LAFT, 80026	1690	C6
Lakewood Municipal Center 480 S Allison Pkwy, LKWD, 80226	2194	D2
Larkspur Town Hall 9524 S Spruce Mountain Rd, LKSR, 80118	2955	A6
Littleton City Hall 2255 W Berry Av, LITN, 80120	2364	B1
Lochbuie Town Hall 703 Frances Steele Blvd, LCHB, 80603	1698	C2
Lone Tree City Hall 8527 Lone Tree Pkwy, LNTR, 80124	2450	E3
Longmont City Hall 350 Kimbark St, LGMT, 80501	1439	B2
Longmont Municipal Court 225 Kimbark St, LGMT, 80501	1439	B3
Louisville City Hall 749 Main St, LSVL, 80027	1689	D7
Lyons City Hall 432 5th Av, LYNS, 80540	1352	D2
Morrison Town Hall MRSN, 80465	2276	C3
Mountain View City Hall 4176 Benton St, MNVW, 80212	2027	B7
National Institute of Standards and Tech Broadway St, BLDR, 80302	1686	E5
National Renewable Energy Laboratory 15003 Denver West Pkwy, JfnC, 80401	2108	E5
Nederland Town Hall 45 W 1st St, NDLD, 80466	1765	D3
Northglenn City Hall 11701 Community Center Dr, NHGN, 80233	1860	D2
Parker Town Hall 20120 E Main St, PARK, 80138	2453	E7
Sheridan City Hall 4101 S Federal Blvd, SRDN, 80110	2280	A4
Superior City Hall 124 E Coal Creek Dr, SUPE, 80027	1772	E4
Thornton City Hall 9500 Civic Center Dr, TNTN, 80229	1944	E1
United States Court of Appeals 1823 Stout St, DNVR, 80202	2112	D4
United States District Court 1929 Stout St, DNVR, 80202	2112	D4
United States Mint 320 W Colfax Av, DNVR, 80204	2112	D5
Webb City Building Court Pl, DNVR, 80202	2112	D5
Westminster City Hall 4800 W 92nd Av, WSTR, 80031	1943	C2
Wheat Ridge City Hall 7500 W 29th Av, WTRG, 80033	2110	E3

Cemeteries

FEATURE NAME / Address City ZIP Code	MAP#	GRID
Arvada Cem, ARVD	2026	B4
Bear Canyon Cem, DgsC	2701	C7
Cedar Hill Cem, CSRK	2703	B6
Chapel Hill Cem, AphC	2365	D3
Coal Creek Cem, LSVL	1774	A1
Columbia Cem, BLDR	1686	C3
Crown Hill Cem, JfnC	2110	D3
Eastlawn Memorial Gardens, AURA	2117	E3
Elizabeth Cem, ELIZ	2793	A1
Elmwood Cem, AdmC	1780	A2
Evergreen Memorial Park, JfnC	2358	A6
Fairmount Cem, DNVR	2198	D4
Fort Logan National Cem, DNVR	2279	D4
Golden Cem, JfnC	2108	B7
Golden Hill Cem, JfnC	2109	D5
Green Mountain Cem, BLDR	1686	D5
Hampden East Lawn Memorial Cem, DNVR	2282	E3
Highland Memorial Gardens Cem, NHGN	1860	E6
Idaho Springs Cem, CCkC	2101	B6
Lafayette Cem, LAFT	1690	C4
Lakeview Cem, BMFD	1774	E7
Littleton Cem, LITN	2364	B3
Lyons Cem, LYNS	1352	D1
Mountain View Cem, BldC	1603	A6
Mountain View Cem, LGMT	1356	A7
Mount Nebo Cem, AURA	2115	D5
Mount Olivet Cem, JfnC	2025	B6
Niwot Cem, BldC	1520	C3
Riverside Cem, CMCY	2029	B4
Rosehill Cem, CMCY	2030	C2
Sacred Heart Cem, BldC	1688	B5
Superior Cem, BldC	1773	A5
Valmont Cem, BldC	1604	A7
Wesley Chapel Cem, WSTR	1860	C2

Colleges & Universities

FEATURE NAME / Address City ZIP Code	MAP#	GRID
Arapahoe Community College 5900 S Santa Fe Dr, LITN, 80120	2364	A2
Arapahoe Community College-Denver Tech Ctr 5660 Greenwood Plaza Blvd, GDVL, 80111	2366	D1
Bel-Rea Institute of Animal Technology 1681 S Dayton St, AphC, 80247	2199	A5
Cambridge College 12500 E Iliff Av, AURA, 80014	2199	E7
Colorado Christian University 180 S Garrison St, LKWD, 80226	2194	C2
Colorado Institute of Art 1200 Lincoln St, DNVR, 80203	2112	E5
Colorado School of Mines 1500 Illinois St, GOLD, 80401	2107	D4
Colorado State University-Denver 110 16th St Mall, DNVR, 80202	2112	D5
Colorado Technical University 5775 DTC Blvd, GDVL, 80111	2367	A1
Columbia College 14707 E 2nd Av, AURA, 80011	2116	C7
Community College of Aurora 16000 E Centretech Pkwy, AURA, 80011	2200	D1

Denver Regional Points of Interest Index

Colleges & Universities

FEATURE NAME Address City ZIP Code	MAP#	GRID
Community College of Denver-Auraria 1111 W Colfax Av, DNVR, 80204	2112	C5
DeVry Institute of Technology 925 S Niagara St, DNVR, 80224	2198	C3
DeVry University 12202 Airport Wy, BMFD, 80021	1858	B2
DeVry University 1870 W 122nd Av, WSTR, 80234	1860	B1
Front Range Community College 3645 W 112th Av, WSTR, 80031	1859	D4
Johnson & Wales University 7150 Montview Blvd, DNVR, 80220	2114	C4
Metro State College-Main Campus 1601 11th St, DNVR, 80204	2112	C4
Metro State College-North Campus 11990 Grant St, NHGN, 80233	1860	E2
Metro State College-South Campus 5660 Greenwood Plaza Blvd, GDVL, 80111	2366	D1
Naropa University 2130 Arapahoe Av, BLDR, 80302	1686	E2
National American University 1325 S Colorado Blvd, DNVR, 80210	2197	D4
Parks Junior College-Aurora 6 Abilene St, AURA, 80011	2200	B1
Parks Junior College-Thornton 9065 Grant St, TNTN, 80229	1944	D2
Platt College 3100 S Parker Rd, AURA, 80014	2283	D2
Red Rocks Community College-Main 13300 W 6th Av, LKWD, 80401	2109	B7
Regis University-Denver 3333 Regis Blvd, DNVR, 80221	2027	E5
Regis Universtiy-Boulder 6235 Lookout Rd, BLDR, 80301	1604	A2
Rocky Mountain College of Art & Design 1600 Pierce St, LKWD, 80214	2111	A4
Teikyo Loretto Heights University 3001 S Federal Blvd, DNVR, 80236	2280	A1
UC-Denver School of the Arts 1250 14th St, DNVR, 80204	2112	C4
University of Colorado-Boulder 1305 University Av, BLDR, 80302	1686	D3
University of Colorado-Denver 1200 Larimer St, DNVR, 80204	2112	C4
University of Colorado-East Campus Marine St, BLDR, 80303	1687	A2
University of Colorado Health Sciences Ctr 4200 E 9th Av, DNVR, 80220	2113	E6
University of Colorado-Research Park Foothills Pkwy, BLDR, 80303	1687	B3
University of Colorado-Williams Village Baseline Rd, BLDR, 80303	1687	A4
University of Denver 2199 S University Blvd, DNVR, 80210	2197	C6
University of Denver-College of Law 7039 E 18th Av, DNVR, 80220	2114	C4
University of Phoenix-Colorado 10004 Park Meadows Dr, LNTR, 80124	2451	B3
University of Phoenix-Westminster 8700 Turnpike Dr, WSTR, 80031	1943	C3
Webster University 12510 E Iliff Av, AURA, 80014	2199	E7
Westwood College of Technology 7350 Broadway, AdmC, 80221	1944	E6

Entertainment & Sports

FEATURE NAME Address City ZIP Code	MAP#	GRID
Adams County Fairgrounds 9755 Henderson Rd, AdmC, 80601	1779	A7
Arapahoe Park Race Track 26000 Powhaton Rd, AphC, 80016	2287	B6
Arvada Center for Arts & Humanities 6901 Wadsworth Blvd, ARVD, 80004	2026	D1
Ascot Event Center 9136 W Bowles Av, JfnC, 80123	2362	B2
Aurora Fox Arts Center 9900 E Colfax Av, AURA, 80010	2115	B5
Avenue Theater 417 E 17th Av, DNVR, 80203	2112	E4
Bandimere Speedway JfnC, 80228	2276	C2
Bandshell Broadway St, BLDR, 80302	1686	C2
Big Bear Ice Arena 8500 E Lowry Blvd, DNVR, 80230	2114	E7
Bluebird Theatre 3317 E Colfax Av, DNVR, 80206	2113	D5
Bonfils-Stanton Amphitheater 797 S Wadsworth Blvd, LKWD, 80226	2194	E3
Boulder County Fairgrounds Park Boston Av, BldC, 80501	1438	D3
Bovine Metropolis Theatre 1527 Champa St, DNVR, 80202	2112	D4
Bullwhackers Casino 101 Gregory St, CLCY, 80403	2017	E4
Center/Stage at Evergreen 27608 Fireweed Dr, JfnC, 80439	2273	E5
Chatfield Arboretum 8500 W Deer Creek Canyon Rd, JfnC, 80127	2446	D3
Chautauqua Auditorium 900 Baseline Rd, BLDR, 80302	1686	C4
Coal Creek Arena 21000 E 6th Av, AURA, 80011	2117	E7
Colorado Convention Center 700 14th St, DNVR, 80204	2112	D5
Coors Amphitheatre 6350 Greenwood Plaza Blvd, GDVL, 80111	2366	E3
Coors Events & Conference Center Regent Dr, BLDR, 80302	1686	E4
Coors Field 2001 Blake St, DNVR, 80205	2112	D3
David Taylor Dance Theatre 9132 W Bowles Av, JfnC, 80123	2362	C2
Denver Botanic Gardens 1005 York St, DNVR, 80206	2113	B6
Denver Center for Performing Arts 1245 Champa St, DNVR, 80204	2112	C4
Denver Civic Theatre 721 Santa Fe Dr, DNVR, 80204	2112	D7
Denver Coliseum 4600 44th St, DNVR, 80216	2029	A7
Denver Merchandise Mart 451 E 58th Av, AdmC, 80216	2028	E3
Denver Zoo Steele St, DNVR, 80206	2113	D4
Douglas County Fairgrounds 500 Fairgrounds Rd, CSRK, 80104	2703	D7
Elbert County Fairgrounds 75 Ute Av, KIOW, 80117	2796	A2
Festival Playhouse 5665 Olde Wadsworth Blvd, ARVD, 80002	2026	D4
Fillmore Auditorium 1510 Clarkson St, DNVR, 80218	2113	A5
Folsom Field Colorado Av, BLDR, 80302	1686	D3
Gateway Park Fun Center 4800 28th St, BldC, 80301	1602	C3
Germinal Stage Denver 2450 W 44th Av, DNVR, 80211	2028	A7
Harrah's Casino Main St, CLCY, 80403	2017	D4
Helen Bonfils Theatre Complex 1050 13th St, DNVR, 80204	2112	C4
Heritage Square Music Hall 18301 W Colfax Av, GOLD, 80401	2192	A1
Historic Oriental Theater 4335 W 44th Av, DNVR, 80212	2027	C7
Houstoun Waring Theatre 5900 S Santa Fe Dr, LITN, 80120	2364	A2
Hyland Hills Water World 1800 W 89th Av, FLHT, 80260	1944	B3
Imagination Makers Theater Company 2590 Walnut St, BLDR, 80302	1686	E2
Invesco Field at Mile High 1701 Mile High Stadium Cir, DNVR, 80204	2112	A4
Jeffco North Area Stadium Complex Foothills Rd, ARVD, 80403	2023	E2
Jefferson County Fairgrounds 15200 W 6th Av, JfnC, 80401	2108	E7
Jefferson County Stadium 9700 Kipling St, LKWD, 80226	2110	B7
Joseph B Gould Paramount Theatre 1621 Glenarm Pl, DNVR, 80202	2112	D4
Lakeside Amusement Park 4601 Sheridan Blvd, LKSD, 80212	2027	B6
Longmont Theatre Company 513 Main St, LGMT, 80501	1439	B2
Mary Rippon Theatre 1305 University Av, BLDR, 80302	1686	D3
Mile High Greyhound Park 6200 Dahlia St, CMCY, 80022	2030	A2
Miners Alley Playhouse 1224 Washington Av, GOLD, 80401	2107	E3
National Western Complex Arena 4655 Humboldt St, DNVR, 80216	2029	A6
National Western Complex Expo Hall 4655 Humboldt St, DNVR, 80216	2029	A6
Newman Center for Perf Arts-Univ Denvr 2344 E Iliff Av, DNVR, 80210	2197	B7
Northglenn Recreation Center Theatre 11801 Community Center Dr, NHGN, 80233	1860	D2
Ocean Journey 700 Water St, DNVR, 80211	2112	B3
Pepsi Center 1000 Chopper Cir, DNVR, 80204	2112	B4
Rattlebrain Theater Co 1601 Arapahoe St, DNVR, 80202	2112	D4
Red Rocks Amphitheatre JfnC, 80465	2276	B1
Rocky Mountain Speedway Buckley Rd, AdmC, 80022	1948	E1
Second Creek Raceway 17010 E 88th Av, CMCY, 80022	1949	A2
Six Flags Elitch Gardens 2000 Elitch Cir, DNVR, 80204	2112	B4
Southshore Water Amusement Park 10750 E Briarwood Av, CTNL, 80112	2367	C4
Teikyo Loretto Heights Theatre 3001 S Federal Blvd, DNVR, 80236	2280	A2
Theater In the Park 5151 S Steele St, GDVL, 80121	2281	C7
Theatre of Dreams 735 Park St, CSRK, 80109	2703	C6
Theatre on Broadway 13 S Broadway, DNVR, 80223	2196	D1
Town Hall Arts Center 2450 W Main St, LITN, 80120	2364	A1
Walden Family Playhouse 14500 W Colfax Av, LKWD, 80401	2109	B6
Wembley Park 351 S Jackson St, DNVR, 80209	2197	D2

Golf Courses

FEATURE NAME Address City ZIP Code	MAP#	GRID
AllGolf at Overland, DNVR	2196	D5
Antelope Hills GC, BNNT	2209	A2
Applewood GC, JfnC	2109	B2
Arrowhead GC, DgsC	2614	E3
Aurora Hills GC, AURA	2199	E1
Bear Creek GC, JfnC	2277	D1
Boulder CC, BldC	1604	C2
Box Elder GC, AdmC	1784	C2
Broadlands GC, BMFD	1775	D3
Buffalo Run GC, CMCY	1864	D4
Canterberry GC, PARK	2538	C1
Castle Pines GC, DgsC	2618	E4
Centre Hills GC, AURA	2200	E1
Cherry Creek CC, AphC	2199	A7
Cherry Hills CC, CHLV	2281	C4
City Park GC, DNVR	2113	C3
Coal Creek GC, LSVL	1773	B3
Columbine CC, CBVL	2363	E3
Country Club at Castle Pines, DgsC	2618	E3
Deer Creek GC Meadow Ranch, JfnC	2445	E1
Denver CC, DNVR	2197	B1
Eagle Trace GC, BMFD	1775	A6
Englewood GC, SRDN	2280	B4
Evergreen GC, JfnC	2273	C6
Fitzsimons GC, AURA	2115	E3
Flatirons GC, BLDR	1687	D2
Foothills GC, JfnC	2278	D4
Fossil Trace GC, GOLD	2108	A6
Fox Hill CC, BldC	1440	A3
Fox Hollow at Lakewood GC, LKWD	2277	E2
Glenmoor CC, CHLV	2281	D7
Golf Club at Bear Dance, DgsC	2870	D7
Green Gables CC, LKWD	2195	A6
Green Valley Ranch GC, DNVR	2033	D5
Greenway Park GC, BMFD	1859	A2
Harvard Gulch GC, DNVR	2197	A7
Haystack Mountain GC, BldC	1519	E4
Heather Gardens GC, AURA	2284	A1
Heather Ridge CC, AURA	2200	A7
Heritage Eagle Bend GC, AURA	2370	C7
Heritage GC at Westmoor, WSTR	1857	E5
Heritage GC at Westmoor, WSTR	1858	A4
Highlands Ranch GC, DgsC	2448	B3
Hiwan GC, JfnC	2273	A1
Homestead at Fox Hollow GC, JfnC	2277	E3
Hyland Hills GC, WSTR	1943	C1
Indian Peaks GC, LAFT	1689	E4
Indian Tree GC, ARVD	1942	D6
Inverness GC, AphC	2367	C7
John F Kennedy GC, DNVR	2283	C3
Lake Arbor GC, ARVD	1942	E3
Lake Valley GC, BldC	1519	A5
Lakewood CC, LKWD	2111	A6
Legacy Ridge GC, WSTR	1859	D5
Links at Highlands Ranch, DgsC	2450	B2
Littleton Golf & Tennis Club, LITN	2364	A1
Lone Tree GC, DgsC	2450	E6
Meadow Hills GC, AURA	2284	C3
Meadows GC, JfnC	2361	C5
Meridian GC, DgsC	2451	D4
Mira Vista GC, AURA	2199	B1
Mountain View GC, DNVR	2282	D7
Murphy Creek GC, AURA	2202	E5
Omni Interlocken Resort GC, BMFD	1857	D1
Park Hill GC, DNVR	2113	E1
Perry Park CC, DgsC	2953	A1
Pinehurst CC, DNVR	2279	A5
Pinery CC, DgsC	2621	E2
Plum Creek Golf & CC, CSRK	2787	D2
Raccoon Creek GC, JfnC	2362	E2
Red Hawk Ridge GC, CSRK	2703	A4
Red Rocks CC, JfnC	2360	D1
Riverdale GC, AdmC	1779	A5
Rolling Hills CC, JfnC	2108	E3
Saddle Rock GC, AURA	2370	B4
Sanctuary GC, DgsC	2534	B7
Southglenn CC, CTNL	2365	B5
South Suburban Family Sports, AphC	2367	E4
South Suburban GC, CTNL	2365	E7
Springhill GC, AURA	2117	B6
Spring Valley GC, EbtC	2541	D5
Stoney Creek GC, WSTR	1941	A1
Sunset GC, LGMT	1438	D1
The Club at Pradera, DgsC	2621	A4
The Ranch CC, WSTR	1860	B2
The Ridge at Castle Pines North, DgsC	2534	D7
Thorncreek GC, TNTN	1776	E5
Twin Peaks GC, LGMT	1355	B7
Ute Creek GC, LGMT	1356	E5
Valley CC, AphC	2368	C3
Vista Ridge GC, ERIE	1691	E3
Wellshire GC, DNVR	2281	E2
West Woods GC, ARVD	2024	D2
Willis Case GC, DNVR	2027	C6
Windsor Gardens GC, DNVR	2199	A2

Historic Sites

FEATURE NAME Address City ZIP Code	MAP#	GRID
Boettcher Mansion 900 Colorow Rd, JfnC, 80401	2107	B6
Byers-Evans House 1310 Bannock St, DNVR, 80204	2112	D5
Centennial House 1671 Galena St, AURA, 80010	2115	B4
Central City Opera House 200 Eureka St, CLCY, 80403	2017	C4
Colorado State Historical Society 1300 Broadway, DNVR, 80203	2112	E5
Delaney Round Barn 170 S Chambers Rd, AURA, 80017	2200	D1
Golden's 12th St Historic District 12th St, GOLD, 80401	2107	D3
Grant-Humphreys Mansion 770 Pennsylvania St, DNVR, 80203	2112	E6
Historic Boulder 646 Pearl St, BLDR, 80302	1686	B2
Hiwan Homestead 4208 S Timbervale Dr, JfnC, 80439	2273	D5
Lower Downtown District 17th St, DNVR, 80202	2112	D3
Pearce-McAllister Cottage 1880 Gaylord St, DNVR, 80206	2113	B4
Teller House 120 Eureka St, CLCY, 80403	2017	C4

Hospitals

FEATURE NAME Address City ZIP Code	MAP#	GRID
Boulder Community Hosp 1100 Balsam Av, BLDR, 80304	1686	C1
Centennial Medical Plaza 14200 E Arapahoe Rd, CTNL, 80112	2368	B4
Centennial Peaks Health 2255 S 88th St, LSVL, 80027	1773	B4
Centura-Avista Adventist Hosp 100 Health Park Dr, LSVL, 80027	1773	B4
Children's Hosp 1056 E 19th Av, DNVR, 80218	2113	A4
Colorado Mental Health Inst at Ft. Logan 3520 W Oxford Av, DNVR, 80236	2279	E4
Craig Hosp 3425 S Clarkson St, EGLD, 80113	2281	A3
Denver Health Med Ctr 777 Bannock St, DNVR, 80204	2112	D7
Exempla Good Samaritan Med Ctr 200 Exempla Cir, LAFT, 80026	1774	D1

Denver Regional Points of Interest Index

Hospitals

FEATURE NAME	Address City ZIP Code	MAP#	GRID
Exempla Lutheran Med Ctr	8300 W 38th Av, WTRG, 80033	2110	D1
Exempla St Joseph Hosp	1835 Franklin St, DNVR, 80218	2113	A4
Kindred Hosp	1920 High St, DNVR, 80206	2113	B4
Littleton Adventist Hosp	7700 S Broadway, LITN, 80122	2364	E6
Longmont United Hosp	1950 Mountain View Av, LGMT, 80501	1355	D7
Mediplex Specialty Hosp	8451 Pearl St, TNTN, 80229	1944	E4
National Jewish Medical and Research Center	1400 Jackson St, DNVR, 80206	2113	D5
North Suburban Med Ctr	9191 Grant St, TNTN, 80229	1944	E2
Parker Adventist Hosp	9395 Crown Crest Blvd, PARK, 80134	2453	C3
Platte Valley Med Ctr	1850 E Egbert St, BGTN, 80601	1696	D6
Porter Adventist Hosp	AphC, 80210	2281	A1
Porter Adventist Hosp	2525 S Downing St, DNVR, 80210	2197	A7
Presbyterian-St. Lukes Med Ctr	1719 E 19th Av, DNVR, 80218	2113	B4
Rose Med Ctr	4567 E 9th Av, DNVR, 80220	2113	E6
St. Anthony's Hosp-Central	4231 W 16th Av, DNVR, 80204	2111	D4
St. Anthony's Hosp-North	2551 W 84th Av, WSTR, 80031	1944	A4
Sky Ridge Med Ctr	10101 Ridgegate Pkwy, LNTR, 80124	2451	B6
Swedish Med Ctr	501 E Hampden Av, EGLD, 80113	2280	E3
The Med Ctr of Aurora-North Campus	700 N Potomac St, AURA, 80011	2116	B6
The Med Ctr of Aurora-South Campus	1501 S Potomac St, AURA, 80012	2200	A5
University of Colorado Hosp	4200 E 9th Av, DNVR, 80220	2113	D6
VA Eastern CO Health Care Sys	1055 Clermont St, DNVR, 80220	2113	E6

Law Enforcement

FEATURE NAME	Address City ZIP Code	MAP#	GRID
Adams County Sheriff's Dept	1901 E Bridge St, BGTN, 80601	1696	D6
Arapahoe County Sheriff's Dept	13101 E Broncos Pkwy, AphC, 80112	2368	A6
Arvada Police Dept	8101 Ralston Rd, ARVD, 80004	2026	D3
Aurora Police Dept-District 1	1400 Dallas St, AURA, 80010	2115	B5
Aurora Police Dept-Mini Station	14200 E Alameda Av, AURA, 80012	2200	B2
Boulder County Sheriff's Dept	1777 6th St, BLDR, 80302	1686	B2
Boulder Police Dept	1805 33rd St, BLDR, 80301	1687	A2
Bow Mar Police Dept	5395 Lakeshore Dr, BWMR, 80123	2363	D1
Brighton Police Dept	36 S Main St, BGTN, 80601	1696	B6
Broomfield Police Dept	1 Descombes Dr, BMFD, 80020	1859	A1
Castle Rock Police Dept	318 S Perry St, CSRK, 80104	2703	D7
Central City Police Dept	141 Nevada St, CLCY, 80403	2017	D4
Cherry Hills Village Police Dept	2450 E Quincy Av, CHLV, 80113	2281	C5
Colorado Highway Patrol-Aurora	18500 E Colfax Av, AURA, 80011	2117	C5
Colorado Highway Patrol-Broomfield	7701 W 120th Av, BMFD, 80020	1858	D2
Colorado Highway Patrol-Castle Rock	900 Wilcox St, CSRK, 80104	2703	D5
Colorado Highway Patrol-Denver	700 Kipling St, LKWD, 80215	2110	B7
Colorado Highway Patrol-Golden	1096 McIntyre St, JfnC, 80401	2108	E6
Columbine Valley Police Dept	5931 S Middlefield Rd, CBVL, 80123	2363	E2
Commerce City Police Dept	5291 E 60th Av, CMCY, 80022	2030	A3
Denver County Sheriff's Dept	10500 Smith Rd, DNVR, 80238	2115	C1
Denver Police Dept	3921 Holly St, DNVR, 80207	2030	A7
Denver Police Dept	4685 Peoria St, DNVR, 80239	2031	D6
Denver Police Dept-District 1	2195 Decatur St, DNVR, 80211	2112	A4
Denver Police Dept-District 2	3555 Colorado Blvd, DNVR, 80205	2113	E1
Denver Police Dept-District 3	1625 S University Blvd, DNVR, 80210	2197	C5
Denver Police Dept-District 4	2100 S Clay St, DNVR, 80219	2196	A6
Denver Police Dept-District 5	4685 Pearl St, DNVR, 80216	2028	E6
Denver Police Dept-Headquarters	1331 Cherokee St, DNVR, 80204	2112	D5
Denver Police Dept-Safety	700 Kipling St, LKWD, 80215	2110	B7
Douglas County Sheriff's Dept	355 S Wilcox St, CSRK, 80104	2703	D7
Edgewater Police Dept	5901 W 25th Av, EDGW, 80214	2111	B3
Elizabeth Police Dept	425 E Main St, ELIZ, 80107	2793	B1
Englewood Police Dept	3615 S Elati St, EGLD, 80110	2280	D3
Erie Police Dept	645 Holbrook St, ERIE, 80516	1607	C4
Federal Heights City Hall	2380 W 90th Av, FLHT, 80260	1944	A3
Glendale Police Dept	950 S Birch St, GNDL, 80246	2197	E3
Golden Police Dept	911 10th St, GOLD, 80401	2107	D3
Greenwood Village Police Dept	6060 S Quebec St, GDVL, 80111	2366	D2
Idaho Springs Police Dept	1711 Miner St, IDSP, 80452	2101	C5
Jefferson County Sheriff's Dept	200 Jefferson County Pkwy, GOLD, 80401	2108	B7
Kiowa Police Dept	404 Commanche St, KIOW, 80117	2796	A2
Lafayette Police Dept	1290 S Public Rd, LAFT, 80026	1690	C6
Lakewood Police Dept	445 S Allison Pkwy, LKWD, 80226	2194	D2
Littleton Police Dept	2255 W Berry Av, LITN, 80120	2364	B1
Lochbuie Police Dept	152 Poplar St, LCHB, 80603	1698	C3
Longmont Police Dept	225 Kimbark St, LGMT, 80501	1439	B3
Louisville Police Dept	749 Main St, LSVL, 80027	1689	D7
Lyons Police Dept	432 5th Av, LYNS, 80540	1352	D1
Morrison Police Dept	MRSN, 80465	2276	C4
Mountain View Police Dept	4176 Benton St, MNVW, 80212	2027	B7
Nederland Police Dept	750 Peak to Peak Hwy, NDLD, 80466	1765	C2
Northglenn Police Dept	11701 Community Center Dr, NHGN, 80233	1860	D3
Parker Police Dept	19600 E Parker Square Dr, PARK, 80134	2537	D2
Sheridan Police Dept	4101 S Federal Blvd, SRDN, 80110	2280	A5
Tallyn's Reach Police	23911 E Arapahoe Rd, AURA, 80016	2370	D4
Thornton Police Dept	9500 Civic Center Dr, TNTN, 80229	1944	E1
Westminster Police Dept	8800 Sheridan Blvd, WSTR, 80031	1943	B3
Wheat Ridge Police Dept	7500 W 29th Av, WTRG, 80033	2110	E3

Libraries

FEATURE NAME	Address City ZIP Code	MAP#	GRID
Adams County-Bennett Branch	495 7th St, BNNT, 80102	2124	D1
Adams County-Thornton	8992 Washington St, TNTN, 80229	1945	A2
Arapahoe County-Castlewood Xpress	6739 S Uinta St, CTNL, 80112	2366	E4
Arapahoe County-Glendale	999 S Clermont St, GNDL, 80246	2197	E3
Arapahoe County-Koelbel Main	5955 S Holly St, CTNL, 80121	2366	B2
Arapahoe County-Sheridan	3201 W Oxford Av, SRDN, 80110	2279	E4
Arapahoe County-Smoky Hill	5430 S Biscay Cir, CTNL, 80015	2285	C7
Arapahoe County-Southglenn	7500 S University Blvd, CTNL, 80122	2365	C6
Aurora	3981 S Reservoir Rd, AURA, 80013	2285	C4
Aurora-Iliff Square	2245 S Peoria St, AURA, 80014	2199	E7
Aurora-Martin L King Jr	9901 E 16th Av, AURA, 80010	2115	B4
Aurora-North Branch	1298 Peoria St, AURA, 80011	2115	E5
Aurora Public-Central	14949 E Alameda Av, AURA, 80012	2200	C2
Aurora Public-Chambers Plaza	15057 E Colfax Av, AURA, 80011	2116	C5
Aurora-South Branch	15324 E Hampden Cir, AURA, 80013	2284	D3
Aurora-Tallyn's Reach	23911 E Arapahoe Rd, AURA, 80016	2370	E4
Boulder-Carnegie Branch for Local History	1125 Pine St, BLDR, 80302	1686	C2
Boulder-George Reynolds	3595 Table Mesa Dr, BLDR, 80305	1687	A6
Boulder-Main Branch	1000 Canyon Blvd, BLDR, 80302	1686	C2
Boulder-Meadows	4800 Baseline Rd, BLDR, 80303	1687	C4
Denver-Athmar Park	1055 S Tejon St, DNVR, 80223	2196	B4
Denver-Bear Valley	5171 W Dartmouth Av, DNVR, 80236	2279	C2
Denver-Byers	675 Santa Fe Dr, DNVR, 80204	2112	C7
Denver-Central	10 W 14th Av, DNVR, 80204	2112	E5
Denver-Dahlia	3380 Dahlia St, DNVR, 80207	2114	A1
Denver-Decker	1501 S Logan St, DNVR, 80210	2196	E5
Denver-Eugene Field	810 S University Blvd, DNVR, 80209	2197	C3
Denver-Ford Warren	2825 High St, DNVR, 80205	2113	B2
Denver-Hadley	1890 S Grove St, DNVR, 80219	2196	A6
Denver-Hampden	9755 E Girard Av, DNVR, 80231	2283	B3
Denver-Montbello	12955 Albrook Dr, DNVR, 80239	2031	E6
Denver-Montclair	932 Jersey St, DNVR, 80220	2114	B6
Denver-Park Hill	4705 Montview Blvd, DNVR, 80207	2113	E4
Denver-Ross-Barnum	3570 W 1st Av, DNVR, 80219	2195	E1
Denver-Ross-Broadway	33 E Bayaud Av, DNVR, 80209	2196	E1
Denver-Ross-Cherry Creek	305 Milwaukee St, DNVR, 80206	2113	C7
Denver-Smiley	4501 W 46th Av, DNVR, 80212	2027	C6
Denver-Valdez Perry Branch	4690 Vine St, DNVR, 80216	2029	B6
Denver-Virginia Village	1500 S Dahlia St, DNVR, 80222	2198	A5
Denver-Woodbury	3265 Federal Blvd, DNVR, 80211	2112	A2
Douglas County-Lone Tree	8827 Lone Tree Pkwy, LNTR, 80124	2451	A3
Douglas County-Louviers	7885 Louviers Blvd, DgsC, 80135	2532	C6
Douglas County-Parker	19801 E Main St, PARK, 80138	2453	D7
Douglas County-PS Miller	100 S Wilcox St, CSRK, 80104	2703	D7
Elbert County	331 Commanche St, KIOW, 80117	2796	A2
Elizabeth Branch	207 E Main St, ELIZ, 80107	2793	B1
Englewood Public	1000 Englewood Pkwy, EGLD, 80110	2280	D3
Gilpin County	15131 Highway 119, GpnC, 80403	1934	C2
Highlands Ranch	9292 Ridgeline Blvd, DgsC, 80129	2448	D4
Idaho Springs Public	219 14th Av, IDSP, 80452	2101	C5
Jefferson County-Arvada	8555 W 57th Av, ARVD, 80002	2026	C4
Jefferson County-Belmar	555 S Allison Pkwy, LKWD, 80226	2194	D3
Jefferson County-Columbine	7706 W Bowles Av, JfnC, 80123	2362	E2
Jefferson County-Edgewater	5843 W 25th Av, EDGW, 80214	2111	B3
Jefferson County-Evergreen	5000 CR-73, JfnC, 80439	2273	D7
Jefferson County-Golden	1019 10th St, GOLD, 80401	2107	D3
Jefferson County-Standley Lake	8485 Kipling St, ARVD, 80005	1942	A4
Jefferson County-Wheat Ridge	5475 W 32nd Av, WTRG, 80212	2111	B2
Koelbel Public	5955 Holly St, CMCY, 80022	2030	A3
Lafayette Public	775 W Baseline Rd, LAFT, 80026	1690	B4
Lakewood Public	10200 W 20th Av, LKWD, 80215	2110	A4
Littleton-Bemis	6014 S Datura St, LITN, 80120	2364	C2
Longmont Public	409 4th Av, LGMT, 80501	1439	B2
Louisville Public	950 Spruce St, LSVL, 80027	1689	D7
Lyons Depot	430 5th Av, LYNS, 80540	1352	D2
Mamie Doud Eisenhower	1 Descombes Dr, BMFD, 80020	1859	A1
Mamie Doud Eisenhower Public	3 Community Park Rd, BMFD, 80020	1858	E1
Nederland Community	750 Peak to Peak Hwy, NDLD, 80466	1765	C2
Parker Branch	10851 S Crossroads Dr, PARK, 80134	2453	D7
Pauline Robinson Branch	5575 E 33rd Av, DNVR, 80207	2114	A1
Rangeview District-Brighton	575 S 8th Av, BGTN, 80601	1696	C7
Rangeview District-Commerce City	7185 Monaco St, CMCY, 80022	1946	B7
Rangeview District-Northglenn	10530 N Huron St, NHGN, 80234	1860	C5
Rangeview District-Perl Mack	7611 Hilltop Cir, AdmC, 80221	1944	C6
Ross-University Hills	4310 E Amherst Av, DNVR, 80222	2281	E1
Roxborough	7999 N Rampart Range Rd, DgsC, 80125	2531	A5
Westminster-Irving Street	7392 N Irving St, WSTR, 80030	1943	E6
Westminster-Kings Mill	9018 Field St, WSTR, 80021	1942	C3
Westminster Public-College Hill	3705 W 112th Av, WSTR, 80031	1859	D4

Military Installations

FEATURE NAME	Address City ZIP Code	MAP#	GRID
Air Force Reservation	AphC, 80137	2288	C3
Buckley Air Force Base	AURA, 80011	2201	D2
Camp George West	JfnC, 80401	2108	E4
Table Mountain Antenna Fields Sites	BldC, 80503	1436	B6

Museums

FEATURE NAME	Address City ZIP Code	MAP#	GRID
Adams County Mus Complex	9601 Henderson Rd, AdmC, 80601	1779	A7
Argo Gold Mill & Mine Mus	2350 Riverside Dr, IDSP, 80452	2101	E5
Arvada Flour Mill Mus	5590 Olde Wadsworth Blvd, ARVD, 80002	2026	D4
Astor House Mus	822 12th St, GOLD, 80401	2107	D3
Aurora History Mus	15051 E Alameda Av, AURA, 80012	2200	C2
Black American West Mus	3091 California St, DNVR, 80205	2113	A2
Boulder Mus of Contemporary Art	1750 13th St, BLDR, 80302	1686	D2
Boulder Mus of History	1206 Euclid Av, BLDR, 80302	1686	C4
Bowles House Mus	3924 W 72nd Av, WSTR, 80030	1943	D7

Denver Regional Points of Interest Index

Museums

FEATURE NAME Address City ZIP Code	MAP#	GRID
B's Ballpark Mus 8611 E Otero Pl, CTNL, 80112	2366	E7
Castle Rock Mus 420 Elbert St, CSRK, 80104	2703	C6
Children's Mus of Denver 2121 Children's Museum Dr, DNVR, 80211	2112	B3
Colorado History Mus 1300 Broadway, DNVR, 80203	2112	D5
Colorado Military History Mus 1141 Oneida St, DNVR, 80220	2114	C6
Colorado Railroad Mus 17155 W 44th Av, JfnC, 80403	2108	C1
CO School of Mines Geology Mus 1516 Illinois St, GOLD, 80401	2107	D4
CU Heritage Center 1305 University Av, BLDR, 80302	1686	D3
Denver Art Mus 100 W 14th Av, DNVR, 80204	2112	D5
Denver Firefighters Mus 1326 Tremont Pl, DNVR, 80204	2112	D5
Denver Mus of Miniatures & Toys 1880 Gaylord St, DNVR, 80206	2113	C4
Denver Mus of Nature & Science 2001 Colorado Blvd, DNVR, 80206	2113	D4
Foothills Art Center 809 15th St, GOLD, 80401	2107	E3
Forney Transportation Mus 4303 Brighton Blvd, DNVR, 80216	2029	A7
Franktown School Mus DgsC, 80116	2705	E4
Gilpin History Mus 228 E High St, CLCY, 80403	2017	D4
Golden Pioneer Mus 923 10th St, GOLD, 80401	2107	D3
Historical Society & Mus 209 Eureka St, CLCY, 80403	2017	C4
Hiwan Homestead Mus 4208 S Timbervale Dr, JfnC, 80439	2273	D5
Idaho Springs Heritage Mus 2060 Miner St, IDSP, 80452	2101	D5
Lakewood's Heritage Center LKWD, 80226	2194	D3
Leanin' Tree Mus of Western Art 6055 Longbow Dr, BLDR, 80301	1603	E2
Littleton Historical Mus 6028 S Gallup St, LITN, 80120	2364	C2
Longmont Mus & Cultural Center 400 Quail Rd, LGMT, 80501	1439	B5
Louisville Historical Mus 1001 Main St, LSVL, 80027	1689	D7
Lyons Redstone Mus 340 High St, LYNS, 80540	1352	D1
Melvin Schoolhouse Mus 4950 S Laredo St, AURA, 80015	2284	E6
Miners Mus 108 E Simpson St, LAFT, 80026	1690	C5
Mizel Center for Arts & Culture 350 S Dahlia St, DNVR, 80246	2198	A2
Mizel Mus 400 S Kearney St, DNVR, 80224	2198	B2
Mizel Mus of Judaica 560 S Monaco Pkwy, DNVR, 80224	2198	B2
Molly Brown House Mus 1340 Pennsylvania St, DNVR, 80203	2112	E5
Museo de Las Americas 861 Santa Fe Dr, DNVR, 80204	2112	C6
Museum of Contemporary Art-Denver 1275 19th St, DNVR, 80202	2112	D3
Museum of Outdoor Arts 1000 Englewood Pkwy, EGLD, 80110	2280	D3
Plains Conservation Center 21901 E Hampden Av, AURA, 80013	2286	B2
Rocky Mountain Quilt Mus 1111 Washington Av, GOLD, 80401	2107	E3
Stiles African American Heritage Center 2607 Glenarm Pl, DNVR, 80205	2113	A3
Trianon Mus & Art Gallery 335 14th St, DNVR, 80202	2112	D5
Underhill Mus 1416 Miner St, IDSP, 80452	2101	C5
Wildlife Experience 10035 S Peoria St, LNTR, 80134	2451	E5
Wings Over the Rockies Air & Space Mus 7711 E Academy Blvd, DNVR, 80230	2198	E1
WOW Children's Mus 110 N Harrison Av, LAFT, 80026	1690	D4

Open Space

FEATURE NAME	MAP#	GRID
Betasso Preserve, BldC	1685	B2
Carolyn Holmberg Preserve, BldC	1774	B5
Jim Hamm Nature Area, BldC	1357	A6
Leon A Wurl Wildlife Sanctuary, LSVL	1689	A7
Marjorie Perry Nature Preserve, GDVL	2281	E7
Mount Evans State Wildlife Area, CCkC	2271	E2
Rocky Mountain Arsenal NWR, AdmC	1948	C4
Standley Lake Pk Wildlife Refuge, JfnC	1941	C2
Two Ponds National Wildlife Refuge, ARVD	1942	B5
Walden Ponds Wildlife Habitat, BldC	1604	B6

Other

FEATURE NAME Address City ZIP Code	MAP#	GRID
16th Street Mall 511 16th St Mall, DNVR, 80202	2112	D4
Adam's Mark Hotel-Denver 1550 Court Pl, DNVR, 80202	2112	D5
Alpine Action GOLD, 80401	2192	A2
Brown Palace Hotel 321 17th St, DNVR, 80202	2112	E4
Carson Nature Center 7301 S Platte River Pkwy, LITN, 80120	2363	E6
Chamberlin Observatory 2930 E Warren Av, DNVR, 80210	2197	C7
Clear Creek History Park 11th St, GOLD, 80401	2107	D3
Colorado Renaissance Festival W Perry Park Av, LKSR, 80118	2954	E5
Curtis Arts & Humanities Center 2349 E Orchard Rd, GDVL, 80121	2365	C2
Fiske Planetarium Regent Dr, BLDR, 80302	1686	E4
Gates Planetarium 2001 Colorado Blvd, DNVR, 80206	2113	D4
Hotel Monaco 1717 Champa St, DNVR, 80202	2112	D4
Hyatt Regency-Denver 1750 Welton St, DNVR, 80202	2112	D4
Larimer Square 1400 Larimer St, DNVR, 80202	2112	C4
Lookout Mountain Nature Center 910 Colorow Rd, JfnC, 80401	2107	B7
Marriott-Denver City Center 1701 California St, DNVR, 80202	2112	D4
National Center for Atmospheric Research 1850 Table Mesa Dr, BLDR, 80305	1686	C7
Oxford Hotel 1600 17th St, DNVR, 80202	2112	C3
Pearl Street Mall Pearl St, BLDR, 80302	1686	C2
The Splash at Fossil Trace Illinois St, GOLD, 80401	2108	A6

Park & Ride

FEATURE NAME	MAP#	GRID
Park & Ride, BldC	1522	B4
Park & Ride, EGLD	2280	D2
Park & Ride-Airport Blvd/40th Av, AURA	2033	A7
Park & Ride-Arapahoe, GDVL	2367	A3
Park & Ride-Aspen Park, JfnC	2442	B5
Park & Ride-Avoca, LKWD	2278	E3
Park & Ride-Bloomfield, BMFD	1858	C2
Park & Ride-Boyd's Crossing, ARVD	2026	E4
Park & Ride-Brighton, BGTN	1696	B5
Park & Ride-Broadway, AdmC	1944	D7
Park & Ride-Church of the Nazarene, EGLD	2280	E2
Park & Ride-Church Ranch Boulevard, JfnC	1858	E6
Park & Ride-Coal Creek, ARVD	1939	C2
Park & Ride-Coal Creek Improvement, BldC	1852	E2
Park & Ride-Cold Springs, LKWD	2109	E7
Park & Ride-Commerce City, AdmC	1946	A7
Park & Ride-Downing & 30th, DNVR	2113	A2
Park & Ride-El Ranco, JfnC	2189	C4
Park & Ride-Evergreen, JfnC	2273	C5
Park & Ride-Fitzsimons, AURA	2116	B5
Park & Ride-Flatiron, BLDR	1686	E5
Park & Ride-Foothills, BLDR	1687	B1
Park & Ride-Franktown, DgsC	2705	E4
Park & Ride-Goose Haven, BldC	1606	B4
Park & Ride-Green Valley, JfnC	2525	D3
Park & Ride-Highlands Ranch, DgsC	2449	C2
Park & Ride-Highlands Ranch Town, DgsC	2448	D3
Park & Ride-I-25 & Broadway, DNVR	2196	E3
Park & Ride-Ken Caryl & C-470, JfnC	2361	D6
Park & Ride-Kings Valley, JfnC	2525	B5
Park & Ride-Lafayette Park, LAFT	1690	C6
Park & Ride-Littleton, LITN	2364	A6
Park & Ride-Littleton Downtown, LITN	2364	B2
Park & Ride-Littleton Overflow, LITN	2364	B1
Park & Ride-Lutheran Church of The Cross, -JfnC	2273	D5
Park & Ride-Lyons, LYNS	1352	D1
Park & Ride-Montbello, DNVR	2031	E6
Park & Ride-Nederland, NDLD	1765	D3
Park & Ride-Nine Mile, DNVR	2283	D2
Park & Ride-Niwot, BldC	1520	D4
Park & Ride-Olympic, AURA	2284	D1
Park & Ride-Paradise Hills, JfnC	2191	B3
Park & Ride-Parker, PARK	2453	D6
Park & Ride-Pine Junction, JfnC	2608	B1
Park & Ride-Pinery, DgsC	2621	E2
Park & Ride-Roosevelt Park, LGMT	1439	B1
Park & Ride-Smoky Hill Cut Off, AURA	2199	C2
Park & Ride-Southmoor, DNVR	2282	C3
Park & Ride-Superior/Louisville, SUPE	1772	E3
Park & Ride-Table Mesa, BLDR	1687	C6
Park & Ride-Thornton, TNTN	1944	E3
Park & Ride-Twin Forks, JfnC	2359	D3
Park & Ride-US-36 & E Flatiron Circle, BMFD	1773	E6
Park & Ride-Wagon Road, WSTR	1860	C2
Park & Ride-Ward Road, JfnC	2025	C6
Park & Ride-Westminster Center, WSTR	1943	B2
Park & Ride-Wonervu, BldC	1852	A1

Parks & Recreation

FEATURE NAME Address City ZIP Code	MAP#	GRID
6th Avenue Pk, DNVR	2112	B6
36th & Holly Pk, TNTN	1778	A5
Abbott Pk, CTNL	2365	B7
Adams County Regional Pk, AdmC	1863	A1
Addenbrooke Pk, LKWD	2194	B3
Admiral Arleigh A Burke Pk, BLDR	1687	C5
Affolter Pk, LGMT	1438	E5
AF Nordman Pk, KIOW	2796	A3
Alamo Placita Pk, DNVR	2197	A1
Albert E Anderson Pk, WTRG	2026	C7
Albion & 35th Pk, DNVR	2113	E1
Alderfer Three Sisters Pk, JfnC	2273	A7
Alexander Lane Equestrian Pk, GDVL	2365	C1
Alice Sweet Thomas Pk, JfnC	1941	D5
Alice Terry Pk, SRDN	2279	E5
Allendale Pk, ARVD	2025	E3
All Star Pk, LKWD	2195	B2
Altair Pk, DgsC	2450	D2
Alta Pk, LGMT	1439	A1
Altura Pk, AURA	2116	C4
Alvin B Thomas Memorial Pk, NHGN	1861	B5
Amhurst Pk, WSTR	1776	B6
Annette Brand Pk, BldC	1689	A6
Apache Mesa Pk, AURA	2116	E6
Apex Open Space, GOLD	2191	D1
Applemeadows Pk, JfnC	2023	E3
Applewood Pk, JfnC	2109	B4
Arapahoe County Community Pk, AphC	2368	B6
Arapahoe Pk, CTNL	2365	C6
Arapahoe Pk, JfnC	2025	A7
Arapahoe Ridge Pk, BLDR	1687	C3
Arapahoe Sports Center, CTNL	2368	D5
Arapaho National Forest, CCkC	2185	C4
Argo Pk, DNVR	2028	E6
Arrowhead Community Pk, JfnC	2274	E6
Arrow Wood Pk, BLDR	1687	A4
Asel Open Space, JfnC	1853	C5
Ashbaugh Pk, LITN	2364	C4
Ash Grove Pk, DNVR	2198	A5
Ashland Pk, DNVR	2112	A2
Aspen Pk, TNTN	1945	D2
Aurora 7 Pk, BLDR	1687	B4
Aurora Pk, AURA	2115	A6
Aurora Reservoir Rec Area, AphC	2371	D2
Aurora Sports Pk, AURA	2117	D5
Autumn Ash Pk, BldC	1690	C3
Aviation Pk, LKWD	2110	E4
Aviator Pk, DNVR	2114	D3
Babi Yar Pk, AURA	2283	B1
Baker Pk, EGLD	2196	B7
Bald Mountain Pk, BldC	1601	A5
Balsam Pond Pk, LKWD	2194	D1
Barberry Pk, LAFT	1690	B5
Barde Pk, EGLD	2281	A2
Barnes Pk, SRDN	2280	B3
Barnum East Pk, DNVR	2112	A7
Barnum North Pk, DNVR	2111	E7
Barnum South Pk, DNVR	2111	E7
Barr Lake State Pk, AdmC	1781	E6
Bar Triple C Pk, PARK	2453	B7
Bates-Logan Pk, EGLD	2280	E1
Bayou Gulch Regional Pk, DgsC	2622	B5
Beach Pk, BLDR	1686	C4
Beach Pk, LKWD	2193	C5
Bear Creek Canyon Pk, JfnC	2275	D2
Bear Creek Greenbelt, JfnC	2278	C1
Bear Creek Lake Pk, JfnC	2277	B3
Bear Creek Pk, DNVR	2279	C3
Bear Valley Pk, DNVR	2279	A2
Beech Open Space, BldC	1518	A5
Bega Pk, LITN	2364	B1
Belleview Acres Pk, JfnC	2361	C1
Belleview Pk, LITN	2280	C6
Bellewood Pk, AURA	2285	A6
Bellows Pk, LKWD	2109	E6
Bell Pk, JfnC	2358	A1
Bell Roth Pk, TNTN	1944	C3
Ben Bezoff Pk, DNVR	2199	B2
Benedict Fountain Pk, DNVR	2112	E4
Benedict Pk, AdmC	1696	D6
Bergen Pk, JfnC	2188	E5
Berkeley Lake Pk, DNVR	2027	C6
Berry Pk, LITN	2363	E1
Beverly Heights Pk, GOLD	2107	D5
Bicentennial Pk, AURA	2200	A1
Big Sandy Pk, CTNL	2285	B7
Bingham Lake Pk, DgsC	2622	A3
Birch Pk, BMFD	1775	A7
Bishop Square Pk, WSTR	1943	E5
Bjaa Pk, BGTN	1696	C5
Blackman Common, CHLV	2282	A6
Blue Heron Pk, JfnC	2361	E1
Blue Heron Pk, LAFT	1689	D1
Blue Star Memorial Pk, BMFD	1774	C7
Bluffs Regional Pk, DgsC	2450	E6
Bohn Pk, BldC	1352	D2
Bonfils Stanton Pk, LKWD	2194	E3
Bonnie Brae Pk, DNVR	2197	C3
Bonvue Pk, LKWD	2194	B1
Boulder Mountain Pk, BldC	1686	B5
Boulder Reservoir Pk, BldC	1603	B1
Bowles Grove Pk, LITN	2363	E1
Bow Mar Heights Pk, DNVR	2279	D5
Bradford Pk, JfnC	2360	E4
Brandon Place Pk, TNTN	1945	E1
Brandywine North Pk, BMFD	1775	D7
Brandywine Pk, BMFD	1859	D1
Brest Pk, DNVR	2197	D3
Briar Ridge Pk, TNTN	1861	E3
Bridgeside Pk, ARVD	2025	D3
Brighton Memorial Pkway Pk, AdmC	1696	C7
Brighton Pk, BGTN	1696	C4
Bromley Pk, BGTN	1697	E6
Brookridge Pk, EGLD	2364	E1
Brookshire Pk, TNTN	1861	C2
Broomfield Community Pk, BMFD	1859	A1
Brothers Four Pk, BNNT	2124	D2
Buchanan Pk, JfnC	2188	D6
Buckingham Pk, BldC	1517	E3
Bullhead Gulch Open Space, LAFT	1689	E2
Burgess Pk, GOLD	2107	E3
Butterfield Crossing Pk, CSRK	2702	D1
Camenisch Pk, FLHT	1944	B3
Campbel Pk, BGTN	1696	B7
Canterbury Pk, AURA	2199	C4
Canyon Pk, BLDR	1686	D2
Carbone Pk, LITN	2364	D6
Carmody Pk, LKWD	2194	B7
Carroll Butts Pk, WSTR	1943	D1
Carr Pk, LGMT	1355	E5
Carson Pk, AURA	2284	B4
Carson Pk, GDVL	2366	D2
Casey Jones Pk, EbtC	2709	C7
Casey Pk, BLDR	1686	C1
Castle North Pk, CSRK	2703	D5
Castlewood Canyon State Pk, DgsC	2789	D2
Cattail Pk, GDVL	2282	B7
Centennial Gardens, DNVR	2112	B3
Centennial Pk, BldC	1686	A2
Centennial Pk, BNNT	2124	C2
Centennial Pk, CSRK	2703	E7
Centennial Pk, EGLD	2280	A6
Centennial Pk, LSVL	1689	C6
Central Pk, BLDR	1686	C2
Central Pk, BMFD	1858	A1
Central Pk, NHGN	1861	C5
Chaffee Pk, DNVR	2028	B7
Challenger Regional Pk, PARK	2453	A5
Charles Whitlock Recreation Pk, LKWD	2110	C5
Chatfield State Pk, AphC	2447	B4
Chaucer Pk, JfnC	2362	A5
Chautauqua Pk, BldC	1686	C5
Cheese Ranch Pk, DgsC	2450	B3
Cheesman Pk, DNVR	2113	B6

FEATURE NAME Address City ZIP Code	MAP#	GRID
Cherry Creek Open Space, DNVR	2197	E2
Cherry Creek Soccer Complex, AphC	2368	D4
Cherry Creek State Pk, AphC	2283	C5
Cherry Creek Valley Ecological Pk, AphC	2368	D5
Cherry Knolls Pk, CTNL	2365	C4
Cherry Pk, TNTN	1861	E3
Cherryville Pk, GDVL	2365	B1
Cherrywood Pk, LAFT	1774	C1
Cherrywood Pk, TNTN	1777	D4
Chester Portsmouth Pk, LKWD	2109	C3
Chipeta Pk, NDLD	1765	D3
Christensen Meadows Pk, JfnC	2362	B5
Christensen Pk, BLDR	1603	B7
Ciancio Pk, DNVR	2028	C7
Circle Pk, SUPE	1773	B6
Citizens Pk, EDGW	2111	B4
City Center Pk, AURA	2200	C1
City of Axum Pk, DNVR	2113	E2
City of Cuernavaca Pk, DNVR	2112	C2
City of Nairobi Pk, DNVR	2113	D1
City of Potenza Pk, DNVR	2198	A4
City Pk, AURA	2115	B4
City Pk, DNVR	2113	C4
City Pk, LAFT	1690	C4
City Pk Esplanade, DNVR	2113	C4
Civic Center Pk, DNVR	2112	E5
Civic Green Pk, DgsC	2448	D4
Clark Centennial Pk, LGMT	1439	C1
Clarkson Pk, CTNL	2365	A5
Clear Creek Pk, AdmC	1945	C7
Clear Creek White Water Golf Course, JfnC	2107	C3
Clear Creek Whitewater Pk, GOLD	2107	D3
Cleo Mudrock Pk, LSVL	1773	C1
Clifford Aspgren Pk, DNVR	2196	C3
Club Crest North Pk, ARVD	1942	B6
Club Crest South Pk, ARVD	1942	B6
Coal Creek at Avalon Open Space, LAFT	1690	E7
Coal Creek Corridor, LAFT	1690	C7
Coal Creek Pk, ERIE	1607	C4
Cobblestone Pk, WSTR	1944	A4
Cody Pk, JfnC	2278	D7
Collyer Pk, LGMT	1439	B2
Colorado Pk, BGTN	1696	A6
Colorado Rockies Baseball Complex, TNTN	1777	B4
Columbia Pk, TNTN	1945	D2
Columbine Knolls Grove Pk, JfnC	2363	B4
Columbine Manor Pk, AphC	2363	C6
Columbine Pk, ARVD	2027	A5
Columbine Pk, BLDR	1602	D7
Columbine Pk, BMFD	1775	D7
Columbus Pk, DNVR	2112	C1
Commons Pk, DNVR	2112	C3
Community Pk, BNNT	2124	D2
Community Pk, SUPE	1773	A7
Community Pk, TNTN	1945	B1
Confluence Pk, DNVR	2112	B3
Congress Pk, DNVR	2113	C6
Conoco Pk, BMFD	1775	D7
Coral Creek Corridor, LAFT	1690	A7
Cornerstone Pk, EGLD	2280	C7
Corwina Pk, JfnC	2274	C2
Cory Merrill School Pk, DNVR	2197	D5
Cotton Creek Pk, WSTR	1859	C4
Cottonwood Creek Pk, AphC	2367	D2
Cottonwood East Pk, PARK	2453	A1
Cottonwood Pk, AURA	2116	B3
Cottonwood Pk, BMFD	1775	E6
Cottonwood Pk, LAFT	1690	B7
Cottonwood Pk, LKWD	2194	A6
Cottonwood Pk, LSVL	1689	C6
Cottonwood Pk, TNTN	1777	D6
Cottonwood West Pk, PARK	2453	A2
Country Estates Pk, BMFD	1775	A5
Country West Pk, JfnC	2361	D1
Coyote Gulch Pk, LKWD	2277	A1
Coyote Ridge Pk, DgsC	2534	D4
Cranmer Pk, DNVR	2197	E1
Creekside Pk, AphC	2369	B2
Creekside Pk, ARVD	2026	E3
Creekside Pk, DNVR	2027	A5
Creekside Pk, GNDL	2197	E3
Crescent Pk, DNVR	2114	D6
Cressman Gulch Pk, GOLD	2023	D7
Crestmoor Pk, DNVR	2198	B1
Crestview Pk, BLDR	1602	C4
Crestview Pk, JfnC	2024	E5
Cross Ridge Pk, LAFT	1689	D2
Crown Hill Pk, JfnC	2110	C2
Cub Creek Pk, JfnC	2357	D1
Curtis Pk, DNVR	2113	A2
Curtis Pk, GDVL	2365	B2
Cushing Pk, EGLD	2280	D2
Dad Clark Pk, DgsC	2449	D5
Dahlia Hollow Pk, CHLV	2282	A4
Dailey Pk, DNVR	2196	D1
Daniels Gate Pk, DgsC	2534	B4
Daniels Pk, DgsC	2534	A5
Daniels Pk, JfnC	2109	C5
Danny Kendrick West Pk, JfnC	2025	C1
David A Lorenz Regional Pk, AphC	2449	E1
Davis Lane Pk, ARVD	2025	E1
Dawson Pk, BldC	1355	B6
DC Burns Pk, DNVR	2197	E2
Deboer Pk, DNVR	2197	C7
Dedisse Pk, JfnC	2273	C6
Deer Creek Canyon Pk, JfnC	2444	D6
Dekoevand Pk, CTNL	2365	B3
Del Mar Pk, AURA	2115	E7
Denison Pk, DNVR	2114	C6
Denver Center Performing Arts Pk, DNVR	2112	C4
Denver Mountain Pk, CCkC	2187	D6
Denver Mountain Pk, JfnC	2108	D3
Diamond K Greenway, DgsC	2449	A4
Diamond K Pk, DgsC	2449	B4
Dover Square Pk, WSTR	1942	C3
Dunham Pk, DNVR	2029	C7
Dutch Creek Pk, BldC	1773	C2
Eagle Pk, AURA	2284	C2
Eagleview Pk, TNTN	1777	C5
East Boulder Community Pk, BldC	1687	D5

FEATURE NAME Address City ZIP Code	MAP#	GRID
Eastglen Pk, TNTN	1777	E7
Eastlake Shores Pk, TNTN	1777	C7
East Mapleton Ballfield, BLDR	1687	A1
Eastmoor Pk, DNVR	2282	C5
Eastridge Activity Area, DgsC	2450	D4
Eaton Pk, BldC	1604	A2
Eben G Fine Pk, BldC	1686	A3
EB Rains Jr Memorial Pk, NHGN	1860	E3
Edward Sell Smith Pk, BLDR	1686	B4
Eldorado Canyon State Pk, BldC	1769	C7
Eldorado Pk, AURA	2285	A1
Elk Meadow Open Space, JfnC	2272	D2
Elmendorf Pk, DNVR	2031	E4
Elsie Duncan Pk, EGLD	2280	E6
Elvira Pk, DNVR	2029	B6
Elysian Pk, JMWN	1516	B3
Emerald Pk, BMFD	1858	E1
Emil Schneider Pk, ARVD	1942	D7
England Pk, WSTR	1943	D7
Enrietto Pk, LSVL	1689	C6
Expo Pk, AURA	2199	C2
Fairfax Pk, CMCY	2030	A1
Fairgrounds Regional Pk, CSRK	2787	E1
Fairmount Pk, JfnC	2024	D5
Fairplay Pk, AURA	2116	C3
Fairview Cemetery, AdmC	1697	A5
Falcon Pk, DgsC	2449	E4
Falcon Pk, DNVR	2032	A4
Far Horizon Pk, ARVD	1943	B4
Farmstead Pk, ARVD	1941	B7
Faversham Pk, WSTR	1943	B7
Fillius Pk, JfnC	2189	A4
Fitzmorris Pk, ARVD	2026	B2
Flagg Pk, BldC	1691	B5
Flanders Pk, AURA	2285	D1
Flanders Pk, BldC	1355	B5
FM Day Pk, AdmC	1944	B7
Footbridge Pk, LITN	2364	C5
Foothills Pk, LKWD	2193	C3
Foothills Rec Area, JfnC	2278	B3
Ford Pk, DNVR	2032	C5
Forest Pk, LAFT	1689	D2
Forsbery Pk, LKWD	2192	D6
Founders Pk, CSRK	2704	D7
Founders Pk, LKWD	2194	E5
Founder's Pk, WTRG	2111	A1
Fourmile Creek Canyon Open Space, BldC	1601	C3
Four Mile Historic Pk, DNVR	2198	A3
Fox Hill Pk, CTNL	2285	D6
Foxhill Pk, CTNL	2366	B7
Foxshire Pk, WSTR	1860	A5
Frances Wisebart Jacobs Pk, DNVR	2198	C4
Francis H Williams Pk, GDVL	2283	B7
Frank Varra Pk, BMFD	1773	D6
Frederick Law Olmstead Jr Pk, BLDR	1602	C7
Fred N Thomas Memorial Pk, DNVR	2114	D3
Freedom Pk, AURA	2116	A5
Freedom Pk, CMCY	2030	C2
Fruitdaly Pk, WTRG	2026	A6
Fuller Pk, DNVR	2113	B2
Fulton Pk, AURA	2115	B6
Gallup Pk & Gardens, LITN	2364	C2
Garden Acres Pk, LGMT	1355	D6
Garfield Lake Pk, DNVR	2195	D4
Garland Pk, DNVR	2198	B4
Garrison & Union Pk, DNVR	2278	B6
Gary R McDonald Pk, LKWD	2109	D6
Gates Crescent Pk, DNVR	2112	B4
Generals Pk, AURA	2115	E5
Genesee Pk, JfnC	2190	A3
Geneva Pk, LITN	2364	B1
George Morrison Sr Pk, DNVR	2113	A2
Glencoe Pk, TNTN	1862	A4
Glennon Dale Pk, LKWD	2194	A3
Glennon Heights Pk, LKWD	2194	A3
Globeville Landing, DNVR	2029	A7
GM Wallace Pk, DvrC	2282	E6
Godsman Pk, DNVR	2196	B5
Golden Gate Canyon State Pk, GpnC	1935	B2
Golden Gate Canyon State Pk, JfnC	1853	B7
Golden Heights Pk, JfnC	2192	D1
Golden Key Pk, DNVR	2282	E1
Golden Ponds Pk & Nature Area, BldC	1438	C2
Governor's Pk, DNVR	2112	E7
Graham Pk, LKWD	2109	E3
Grandview Pk, AURA	2285	A5
Grange Creek Pk, TNTN	1861	E4
Grant Frontier Pk, DNVR	2196	D7
Grant Pk, NHGN	1860	E6
Great Pk, BldC	1690	D4
Green Gables Pk, LKWD	2194	C5
Green Valley East Ranch Pk, DNVR	2033	E6
Greenway Pk, DNVR	2114	E3
Greenwood Gulch, GDVL	2366	A1
Greenwood Pine Pk, GDVL	2281	B7
Gregory Hills Pk, WSTR	1943	E5
Guson Pk, DNVR	2114	A3
Habitat Pk, DNVR	2196	C2
Hackberry Pk, ARVD	1942	E6
Hallack Pk, DNVR	2111	E4
Hamlet Pk, LITN	2363	C2
Hampden Heights Pk, DNVR	2283	A2
Hampden Run Pk, AURA	2285	B3
Hampshire Pk, WSTR	1859	C7
Harlow Pk, LITN	2279	E7
Harlow Platts Pk, BLDR	1771	A1
Harmony Pk, SRDN	2279	E2
Harold D Lutz Sports Complex, ARVD	2026	A4
Harriman Lake Pk, JfnC	2278	A5
Harvard Gulch Pk, DNVR	2197	A7
Harvey Pk, DNVR	2195	D6
Haskin Pk, ARVD	1941	A4
Havana & Cornell Pk, DNVR	2283	C2
Havana Heights Pk, AURA	2199	C6
Havana Pk, AURA	2115	C6
Hayward Pk, WTRG	2110	E3
Heritage Dells Pk, GOLD	2192	A1
Heritage Hill Pk, LKWD	2193	E2
Heritage Pk, LSVL	1773	B2
Heritage Village Pk, CTNL	2366	A3

FEATURE NAME Address City ZIP Code	MAP#	GRID
Highland Heritage Regional Pk, DgsC	2450	B4
Highland Hollow Pk, AURA	2201	B4
Highland Pk, BMFD	1859	A1
Highland Pk, DNVR	2111	E2
Highlands Pk, CTNL	2369	A1
Highline Pk, AURA	2199	E1
Highridge Court Pk, TNTN	1860	A7
Hillside Pk, ARVD	1943	A6
Hill Top Pk, AURA	2285	A2
Hirshorn Pk, DNVR	2112	B2
Hodgson Pk, LKWD	2278	B1
Hoffman Pk, AURA	2115	E6
Hoffman Pk, GDVL	2283	A7
Holbrook Pk, LKWD	2110	C7
Holly Pk, AdmC	1862	A4
Holly Pk, CTNL	2366	B3
Homestead Pk, ARVD	2027	B2
Hoover Pk, LGMT	1355	C7
Horace E Randall Pk, WTRG	2027	A7
Horizon Pk, AURA	2285	C4
Horseshoe Pk, AURA	2200	E6
Horseshoe Pk, LITN	2364	D6
Hoskinson Pk, ARVD	2026	C3
Howard H Heuston Pk, BLDR	1603	A7
Hoyda Pk, JfnC	2193	E4
Hugh Danahy Pk, NHGN	1860	C5
Hungarian Freedom Pk, DNVR	2197	A1
Hunters Glen Lake Pk, TNTN	1777	A6
Hunters Hill Pk, CTNL	2366	E5
Huntington Acres Pk, GDVL	2367	A2
Huston Lake Pk, DNVR	2196	A3
Hutchinson Pk, DNVR	2282	D2
Hutchinson Pk, JfnC	2193	D7
Hyland Hills Sports Complex, FLHT	1944	B3
Idalia Pk, DNVR	2032	D5
Independence Pk, ARVD	2026	B1
Indiana Street Open Space, JfnC	1941	A6
Indian Peaks Pk, LAFT	1689	C4
Inspiration Point Pk, DNVR	2027	B5
Ironspring Pk, JfnC	2192	D6
Isaac Newton, CTNL	2365	E4
Isaak Walton Pk, BldC	1438	E3
Jackass Hill Pk, LITN	2364	A6
Jackie Robinson Pk, DNVR	2198	E1
Jackson Pk, LKWD	2193	D5
James A Bible Pk, DNVR	2282	C1
James A Taylor Pk, LITN	2279	D7
James N Manley Pk, DNVR	2113	C7
James Q Newton Pk, JfnC	2526	B2
James Richey Pk, LKWD	2110	C5
Jason Pk, EGLD	2280	C5
Jaycee Pk, NHGN	1861	B5
Jefferson County Open Space, JfnC	2360	A2
Jefferson Green Pk, LKWD	2278	C3
Jefferson Pk, DNVR	2112	A3
Jefferson Square Pk, DNVR	2282	B4
Jewell Pk, AURA	2115	E5
Jewell Pk, LKWD	2194	C6
Joel H Greenstein Memorial Baseball Pk, BLDR	1602	C6
John Meade Pk, CHLV	2281	C5
Johnson Pk, DNVR	2029	B6
Johnson Pk, WTRG	2026	D6
Jola Pk, PARK	2453	A7
Judge Joseph E Cook Pk, DNVR	2198	C5
Kalispell Pk, AURA	2284	D6
Kamemoto Pk, LGMT	1439	A5
Keith Helart Pk, LSVL	1689	B5
Ken-Caryl Ranch Community Center Pk, JfnC	2361	B7
Ken-Caryl Ranch Community Pk, JfnC	2362	B7
Kendrick Lake Pk, LKWD	2194	B6
Kennedy Ballfield, DNVR	2283	D2
Kensington Pk, LGMT	1439	C1
Kensington Pk, WSTR	1858	A6
Kent Knutson Pk, LKWD	2193	D3
Ketring Pk, LITN	2364	C2
Kimbark Pk, LGMT	1439	B1
King Mill Pk, WSTR	1942	C2
Kistler Pk, DgsC	2449	A4
Kittredge Pk, DNVR	2114	C6
Kiwanis Pk, NHGN	1860	E5
Kline Homestead Pk, DgsC	2449	E3
Kohl Pk, BMFD	1774	D7
Lac Amora Pk, BMFD	1774	C6
Ladybug Pk, ARVD	2026	C2
Lagerman Reservoir Open Space, LGMT	1437	C6
Lair O' the Bear Pk, JfnC	2274	E2
Lake Arbor Pk, ARVD	1943	A4
Lakecrest Pk, JfnC	1942	A4
Lake of Lakes Pk, JfnC	2278	D5
Lake Pk, LSVL	1689	C6
Lake Village IV Pk, TNTN	1777	C7
Lakewood & Dry Gulch Pk, DNVR	2111	D6
Lakewood Estates Pk, LKWD	2195	A7
Lakewood Heritage Center Pk, LKWD	2194	D3
Lakewood Pk, LKWD	2194	B2
Lakewood Sister City Pk, LKWD	2278	D2
Lamont Does Memorial Pk, LAFT	1690	D6
Lamplighter Pk, ARVD	1941	E6
Lanyon Pk, LGMT	1356	B5
La Parquita Pk, AURA	2284	E4
Larkspur Community Pk, LKSR	2955	B5
Larson Pk, NHGN	1861	A5
Lasley Pk, LKWD	2195	A5
Leawood Pk, JfnC	2363	A3
Lefthand Creek Pk, LGMT	1438	E6
Left Hand Valley Grange Pk, BldC	1521	A4
Legion Pk, BldC	1688	B2
Lewis Meadows Pk, WTRG	2109	D2
Lew Walsh Pk, ARVD	2027	A1
Leyden Creek Pk, ARVD	1941	D7
Liberty Hills Pk, TNTN	1945	D1
Library Pk, LAFT	1690	B4
Lily Pk, TNTN	1945	B2
Lincoln Pk, DNVR	2112	C6
Lindenwood Pk, LAFT	1690	D3
Lindsley Pk, DNVR	2113	E6
Link Recreation Center Pk, LKWD	2194	E4
Linksview Pk, CTNL	2365	E7
Little Bear Pk, JfnC	2275	B3
Little Dry Creek Pk, ARVD	1943	A5

Parks & Recreation

Denver Regional Points of Interest Index

Parks & Recreation

FEATURE NAME Address City ZIP Code	MAP#	GRID
Little's Creek Pk, LITN	2364	E4
Lochmoor Pk, DNVR	2279	A5
Loma Linda Pk, TNTN	1860	E7
Lonesome Pine Pk, DgsC	2450	E2
Long Lake Regional Pk, ARVD	2024	A2
Longmont-Hygiene Buffer, BldC	1354	E5
Longmont-Niwot Buffer, BldC	1521	C2
Lookout Pk and Pool, CTNL	2286	A7
Loomiller Pk, LGMT	1355	E7
Loomis Pk, TNTN	1945	A2
Loretto Heights Pk, DNVR	2279	E1
Lost Watch Community Pk, DgsC	2538	E3
Louisville Sports Complex, LSVL	1689	D7
Loveland Mine Pk, GOLD	2107	C3
Loveland Trail Pk, LKWD	2193	B7
Lowry Sports Complex, DNVR	2198	E1
Lu Murray Pk, TNTN	1945	A1
Magna Carta Pk, AphC	2281	E3
Majestic View Pk, ARVD	1942	C7
Malcom Pk, BGTN	1696	B6
Mamie Dowd Eisenhower Pk, DNVR	2281	E2
Maplegrove Pk, JfnC	2109	A2
Maple Valley Pk, ARVD	2025	A1
Marge Roberts Pk, ARVD	2026	A3
Marina Pk, AURA	2285	B6
Martinez Pk, DNVR	2111	D6
Martin Luther King Pk, DNVR	2114	C1
Martin Pk, BLDR	1687	A6
Matthews Winters Open Space, JfnC	2191	E4
Maximus Trail Pk, DgsC	2450	E2
Mayeda Pk, BGTN	1696	B7
Mayfair Pk, DNVR	2114	B6
McIlvoy Pk, ARVD	2026	E4
McKinley Pk, LSVL	1689	C7
McMullin Pk, AURA	2199	B1
McNichols Pk, DNVR	2114	D4
Meadowbrook Village Trail Pk, JfnC	2024	D4
Meadowlark Pk, LKWD	2194	C1
Meadow Mountain Pk, LAFT	1689	D4
Meadowood Pk & Recreation Center, AURA	2284	E1
Meadow Pk, LYNS	1352	C1
Meadows Pk, ARVD	2024	D2
Meadows Pk, LSVL	1773	A3
Medema Pk, CTNL	2366	A5
Melody Pk, BLDR	1602	C6
Melvin F Silverman Pk, DNVR	2031	E5
Memorial Pk, ARVD	2026	D3
Memory Square Pk, LSVL	1689	C7
Mesa Reservoir Pk, BldC	1603	A2
Messina Pk, FLHT	1944	B2
Metzler Ranch Community Pk, CSRK	2703	D2
Meyer Ranch Open Space, JfnC	2442	D5
Michael Northey Pk, JfnC	1941	D4
Miller Field, EGLD	2280	D3
Miller Gardens, LAFT	1690	C5
Milliken Pk, CTNL	2365	A3
Miramonte Pk, BMFD	1774	E6
Mir Pk, DNVR	2198	A3
Mission Viejo Pk, AURA	2284	E4
Mitchell Gulch Pk, CSRK	2704	E7
Molholm Pk, LKWD	2111	A6
Monaco Pk, CHLV	2282	C7
Monaco Pk, CMCY	2030	B3
Monarch Pk, BldC	1520	D5
Montbello Central Pk, DNVR	2032	A6
Montbello Civic Center Pk, DNVR	2031	E6
Montclair Pk, DNVR	2114	C5
Montoya Pk, BGTN	1696	C5
Montview Pk, AURA	2115	A4
Moon Gulch Pk, ARVD	1941	B7
Moorehead Pk, AURA	2115	C3
Morse Pk, LKWD	2110	D4
Mountainside Pk, JfnC	2193	A3
Mountair Pk, LKWD	2111	B5
Mount Falcon Open Space Pk, JfnC	2275	D6
Nome Pk, AURA	2115	D5
Norfolk Glen Pk, AURA	2116	D4
Norman D Memorial Pk, GOLD	2107	C1
Norse Glenn Pk, NHGN	1860	C7
Northaven Pk, TNTN	1861	E1
North Boulder Community Pk, BLDR	1602	B3
North Boulder Pk, BLDR	1686	B1
North Dinosaur Open Space, JfnC	2192	B4
Northeast Denver Community Pk, DNVR	2113	D2
North Jeffco Pk, ARVD	2026	C3
North Midway Pk, BMFD	1858	D1
Northmoor Pk, BMFD	1775	B6
North Pk, NHGN	1861	C4
North Ranch Pk, JfnC	2360	E4
Northridge Pk, DgsC	2449	A3
Northstar Pk, TNTN	1944	D3
Northwest Open Space, NHGN	1860	B4
Nyland Open Space, LSVL	1689	B5
Oakhurst Pk, WSTR	1942	C1
Oak Pk, ARVD	2026	A1
Oakwood Pk, WSTR	1943	C4
O'Brien Pk, PARK	2453	D7
Observatory Pk, DNVR	2197	C7
O'Fallon Pk, JfnC	2274	C4
O'Kane Pk, LKWD	2195	A1
Old Mill Pk, LGMT	1439	A3
Orchard Hills Pk, GDVL	2367	A1
Orchard Pk, BldC	1603	B4
Outlook Pk, BMFD	1774	E5
Overland Lake Pk, DNVR	2196	D5
Overland Pond Pk, DNVR	2196	D5
Packy Romans Pk, EGLD	2281	B2
Pagosa Pk, AURA	2285	A1
Paintbrush Pk, CSRK	2702	D3
Palisade Pk, WldC	1692	D3
Palos Verdes Pk, CTNL	2366	C2
Panorama Pk, AURA	2201	A4
Panorama Pk, WTRG	2111	B2
Paramount Pk, WTRG	2110	A3
Parfet Pk, GOLD	2107	E3
Park East Pk, BLDR	1687	B3
Parklane Pk, AURA	2116	A2
Park Ridge Village Pk, TNTN	1777	E6
Parkside Pk, BLDR	1602	E6
Park Village Pk, TNTN	1777	D5

FEATURE NAME Address City ZIP Code	MAP#	GRID
Paul A Hentzel Pk, DNVR	2283	B1
Peakview North Pk, CTNL	2285	D7
Peakview Pk, AphC	2367	C3
Peakview South Pk, CTNL	2285	D7
Peakview West Pk, AURA	2285	C7
Pearce Pk, JfnC	1941	B5
Pecos Pk, TNTN	1944	C1
Pence Pk, JfnC	2274	C6
Peoria Hills Pk, AURA	2199	E4
Perry Pines Pk, DgsC	2785	D6
Peterson Pk, LKWD	2193	C3
Pferdesteller Pk, DNVR	2111	C2
Pheasant Ridge Pk, BGTN	1697	B6
Pheasant Run Pk, AURA	2284	C5
Pike National Forest, PrkC	2605	C4
Pinery Glen Pk, DgsC	2621	D4
Pinery Pk, DgsC	2622	B1
Pine Valley Ranch Pk, JfnC	2693	A2
Pine View Pk, BLDR	1602	D6
Piney Creek Hollow Pk, AphC	2369	C2
Pinion Pk, BMFD	1775	D7
Pioneer Pk, CTNL	2370	A1
Pioneer Pk, JfnC	1941	D5
Pirates Pk, LSVL	1689	D6
Plains Conservation Center, AphC	2286	B1
Platte River Ranch Pk, BGTN	1695	E7
Platt Pk, DNVR	2196	E5
Playway Pk, TNTN	1861	D3
Plum Creek Pk, CSRK	2787	D4
Plum Valley Pk, DgsC	2448	A6
Powderhorn Pk, JfnC	2361	E3
Powers Pk, LITN	2364	D1
Pratt Pk, LGMT	1355	B7
Prentice Gulch Pk, GDVL	2366	A1
Progress Pk, EGLD	2280	D7
Promise Pk, LITN	2364	D1
Prospect Pk, WTRG	2025	E7
Province Center Open Space, DgsC	2449	E2
Pulaski Pk, DNVR	2197	D1
Puma Pk, CTNL	2365	A7
Purple Pk, SUPE	1773	A5
Quaker Acres Pk, JfnC	1940	B6
Rabbit Mountain Open Space, BldC	1270	D5
Raber Pk, LGMT	1355	E5
Rainbow Ridge Pk, JfnC	2025	D4
Ralston Cove Pk, ARVD	2026	B3
Ralston Recreation Pk, ARVD	2025	E2
Ralston Valley Pk, ARVD	2025	B1
Ranch House Pk, JfnC	2362	A6
Ravine Pk, LKWD	2193	C6
Ray Ross Pk, LKWD	2195	B3
Red Oak Pk, LAFT	1690	A7
Red Rocks Pk, JfnC	2276	B1
Redstone Pk, DgsC	2448	A4
Redtail Ridge Open Space, BldC	1270	E2
Reynolds Pk, JfnC	2611	C1
Richard Hart Estate Pk, EDGW	2111	B3
Richard S Steele Pk, BMFD	1774	B7
Ridge Regional Pk Athletic Fields, JfnC	2361	D4
Ridgeview Pk, LITN	2364	B5
Ridgewood Pk, LITN	2364	B4
Riverdale Pk, TNTN	1861	E6
Robbi Farrifino Pk, ARVD	1942	C6
Robert F Clement Pk, JfnC	2362	E2
Robert H McWilliams Pk, DNVR	2281	C1
Robinson Pk, DNVR	2198	A1
Rock Pk, CSRK	2703	D5
Rocky Flats Open Space, BMFD	1857	A6
Rocky Mountain Lake Pk, DNVR	2027	E6
Rocky Ridge Pk, AURA	2200	E4
Rollin D Barnard Pk, CTNL	2365	A2
Rooney Hogback Pk, GOLD	2192	B2
Roosevelt National Forest, BldC	1681	C4
Roosevelt Pk, LGMT	1439	A1
Rosamond Pk, DNVR	2282	D4
Rotary Pk, NHGN	1860	B5
Rotello Pk, AdmC	1945	B5
Rothrock Dell Pk, LGMT	1439	D2
Rotolo Pk, EGLD	2280	D5
Roxborough State Pk, DgsC	2615	A5
Ruby Hill Pk, DNVR	2196	C5
Rude Pk, DNVR	2112	A5
Running Fox Pk, GDVL	2282	C7
Russell Pk, DNVR	2113	B1
Ruston Pk, FLHT	1860	A7
Ruth Roberts Pk, BldC	1774	D4
Saddlewood Pk, JfnC	2361	D5
Sagebrush Pk, AURA	2284	C6
St. Charles Pk, DNVR	2113	A1
Salberg Memorial Pk, BLDR	1602	D7
Salisbury Equestrian Pk, DgsC	2537	C3
Sanchez Pk, DNVR	2111	E6
Sanctuary Pk, LKWD	2194	B5
Sand Creek Pk, AURA	2116	A2
Sand Creek Pk, DgsC	2449	B2
Sanderson Gulch Open Space, DNVR	2195	D6
Sandstone Pk, LYNS	1352	D1
Sandstone Ranch Community Pk, LGMT	1440	C3
Sandstone Ranch District Pk, WldC	1440	C4
Schafer Pk, DNVR	2113	C1
School Pk, DNVR	2279	B2
Scott Carpenter Pk, BLDR	1687	A3
Secrest Pk, ARVD	2026	E2
Seven Hills Pk, AURA	2285	D1
Shadow Ridge Pk, TNTN	1777	D5
Sherman & Vassar Pk, DNVR	2196	E7
Sherrelwood Pk, AdmC	1944	C5
Sherwood Hills Pk, TNTN	1861	C7
Sherwood Pk, WSTR	1859	A4
Side Creek Pk, AURA	2201	C5
Sierra Pk, ARVD	1941	E5
Silo Pk, GDVL	2367	A2
Sixth Avenue West Pk, JfnC	2193	B1
Skylake Pk, TNTN	1861	E2
Skyland Pk, DNVR	2114	B1
Skyline Pk, DNVR	2112	D4
Sledding Hill Pk, JfnC	2362	B6
Sloan's Lake Pk, DNVR	2111	C4
Smith Lake Pk, LKWD	2194	A6
Smith Pk, AdmC	1696	A5

FEATURE NAME Address City ZIP Code	MAP#	GRID
Sonny Lawson Pk, DNVR	2112	E3
Southbridge Pk, LITN	2364	C6
South Dinosaur Open Space, JfnC	2276	C2
South Midway Pk, BMFD	1858	D1
Southmoor Pk, DNVR	2282	C3
South Pk, NHGN	1861	D5
South Platte Pk, LITN	2363	E7
Southridge Pk, GOLD	2108	B5
South Simms Pk, LKWD	2193	E3
South Table Mountain Pk, JfnC	2109	A4
Southwest Auto Pk, DNVR	2278	D6
Spangler Pk, LGMT	1356	B7
Spencer Garrett Pk, AURA	2115	C4
Sperry Pk, NHGN	1860	B5
Spring Creek Pk, AphC	2285	E4
Springer Pk, DgsC	2449	A3
Spring Gulch Pk, DgsC	2448	B6
Springvale Pk, TNTN	1778	A5
Spruce Pk, BMFD	1775	E5
Squires Pk, WSTR	1859	D7
Stazio Recreational Fields, BldC	1687	E1
Steele Pk, TNTN	1861	C4
Sterne Pk, LITN	2364	B2
Stites Pk, WTRG	2111	A2
Stonegate Village Community Pk, DgsC	2452	D6
Stratford Pk, WSTR	1859	A4
Stroh Ranch Soccer Fields, PARK	2537	C5
Summer Valley Pk, AURA	2285	A3
Summit Grove Pk, TNTN	1777	D5
Sunburst Pk, AURA	2284	E5
Sundance Pk, GDVL	2367	B1
Sundance Pk, LSVL	1773	C1
Sunken Gardens, DNVR	2112	D6
Sunrise Pk, AURA	2285	D4
Sunset Maple Pk, LAFT	1690	B4
Sunset Pk, LGMT	1438	E2
Sunset Pk, LKWD	2110	A6
Sunset Pk, WSTR	1943	C5
Sutherland Shire Pk, JfnC	2194	A4
Swansea Pk, DNVR	2029	C6
Sweetwater Pk, DgsC	2450	E3
SW Greenbelt Pk, EGLD	2280	D6
Table Mountain Pk, JfnC	2024	A3
Taft Pk, LKWD	2109	D3
Tanglewood Pk, JfnC	2109	B4
Tanks Pk, DgsC	2448	E6
Tantra Pk, BLDR	1687	B7
Tennyson Knolls Pk, AdmC	2027	C2
Tennyson Pk, DNVR	2027	C7
Terrace Pk, ARVD	2026	C5
Terrace Pk, AURA	2117	C3
Territory Pk, JfnC	2361	E6
The Farm Open Space, LSVL	1689	A4
Thomas Ernest McClain Pk, DNVR	2114	D2
Thompson Pk, LGMT	1439	A2
Three Pond Pk, CHLV	2281	E4
Thunderbolt Pk, DNVR	2113	B2
Thundercloud Pk, ARVD	1942	E7
Tierra Pk, AURA	2200	C6
Toll Gate Pk, AphC	2286	A4
Tollgate Pk, AURA	2200	D3
Tomlinson Pk, ARVD	2026	B5
Tommy Davis Pk, GDVL	2367	A2
Tom Watson Pk, BLDR	1520	A6
Tony Grampsas Sports Complex, GOLD	2024	C7
Trailhead Pk, AdmC	1945	C6
Triangle Pk, AURA	2117	D4
Truman Pk, ARVD	2025	D1
Trupp Pk, AdmC	2124	C2
Tsistsistas Hinono'ei Pk, AphC	2199	A5
Turkey Creek Pk, JfnC	2359	E4
Twin Lakes Pk, AdmC	2028	D1
Ulysses Pk, GOLD	2108	B6
Union Reservoir Rec Area, WldC	1357	E7
Union Ridge Pk, LKWD	2109	C7
Union Square Pk, LKWD	2193	D1
Utah Pk, AURA	2199	E5
Ute Trail Pk, JfnC	2193	C7
Valley Pk, LGMT	1438	C1
Valley View Pk, JfnC	2362	C5
Valley Vista Pk, LITN	2363	D1
Valverde Ballfield, DNVR	2196	C1
Van Bibber Pk, JfnC	2025	B4
Vanderbilt Pk, DNVR	2196	D3
Vanover Pk, GOLD	2107	E3
Verbena Pk, DNVR	2114	E6
Veterans Memorial Pk, CMCY	2030	A3
Veterans Pk, AdmC	1696	A5
Viking Pk, DNVR	2112	A2
Village East Pk, AURA	2199	D4
Village Green Pk, AURA	2200	C4
Village Greens Pk, AphC	2283	A3
Village Pk, AphC	2368	D2
Village Place Pk, DNVR	2032	A6
Vine & Iowa Pk, DNVR	2197	B5
Virginia Court School Pk, AURA	2199	E2
Volunteer Fire Fighters Pk, ARVD	1942	B4
Wadsworth Pk, ARVD	2026	D2
Wagon Trail Pk, AURA	2284	E6
Wagon Trail Pk, DNVR	2278	C7
Walker Branch Pk, EDGW	2111	B4
Walker Ranch Pk, BldC	1769	B5
Walnut Hills Pk, CTNL	2366	E4
Walton Heath Pk, TNTN	1861	C2
Waneka Lake Pk, LAFT	1690	A5
Waneka Landing Open Space, LAFT	1689	E5
Warembourg Open Space, LAFT	1690	D7
Washington Heights Recreation Center, LKWD	2195	A1
Washington Pk, DNVR	2197	A3
Wauconda Pk, DgsC	2953	A1
Weaver Creek Pk, JfnC	2277	C6
Weaver Hollow Pk, JfnC	2277	C6
Weaver Pk, JfnC	2363	A3
Weir Gulch Marina Pk, DNVR	2112	A6
Weir Gulch Open Space, DNVR	2195	C2
Welchester Tree Grant Pk, JfnC	2109	C6
West-Bar-Val-Wood Pk, DNVR	2196	B2
Westborough Pk, LKWD	2278	B2
Westgate Pk, LKWD	2278	C1
West Harvard Gulch Pk, DNVR	2280	A1

Denver Regional Points of Interest Index

FEATURE NAME Address City ZIP Code	MAP#	GRID
West Highland Pk, BLDR	1686	D6
Westlake Pk, BMFD	1776	A5
Westlands Pk, CTNL	2366	C2
Westminster City Pk, WSTR	1859	B5
West Ranch Pk, DNVR	2033	C6
Westree Pk, ARVD	1942	D4
Westwood Pk, ARVD	1940	C7
Westwood Pk, DNVR	2195	C3
Wheat Ridge Historical Pk, WTRG	2025	E6
Wheeling Pk, AURA	2200	A3
Wheel Pk, AURA	2200	D7
Whispering Meadows Pk, LAFT	1690	B6
Whispering Pines Pk, DgsC	2706	A2
White Ash Mine Pk, GOLD	2107	C2
White Ranch Open Space, JfnC	2022	D2
White Tail Pk, LAFT	1774	C1
Wildcat Ridge Pk, DgsC	2450	B6
William Frederick Hayden Pk, JfnC	2192	D4
Willowbrook Pk, WSTR	1860	D1
Willow Creek Pk, BldC	1438	B5
Willow Creek Pk, CTNL	2366	D7
Willow Pk North, BMFD	1775	E6
Willow Pk South, BMFD	1775	E6
Willow Springs Open Space, CTNL	2366	B5
Willow Trace Pk, AphC	2285	E5
Wilson Family Pk, LKWD	2195	B6
Winburn Pk, NHGN	1860	C4
Windsor Pk, WSTR	1859	D5
Windy Saddle Pk, JfnC	2107	B5
Wolff & Quincy Pk, DNVR	2279	C5
Wolff Run Pk, WSTR	1943	C6
Wonderland Lake Pk, BLDR	1602	B5
Woodbridge Station Pk, TNTN	1778	A6
Woodglen Meadows Pk, TNTN	1777	E7
Woodglen Pk, TNTN	1861	C3
Woodhaven Pk, TNTN	1861	C3
Woodie Hollow Pk, CHLV	2281	B7
Woodrun Pk, ARVD	1942	B5
Wright Pk, LKWD	2193	D1
Writers Vista Pk, LITN	2364	B7
Wyco Pk, NHGN	1861	B3
Wyndham Pk, JfnC	2025	B3
Yankee Doodle Pk, ARVD	2025	C2
Yarrow Pk, LAFT	1689	E2
Yorkborough Pk, TNTN	1861	C7
Youth Memorial Sports Complex, ARVD	1941	B6
Zangs Spur Pk, BMFD	1774	C7
Zuni Pk, DNVR	2028	B5

Post Offices

FEATURE NAME Address City ZIP Code	MAP#	GRID
Adams City Station 6655 Brighton Blvd, CMCY, 80022	2029	E1
Alcott Station 3700 Tennyson St, DNVR, 80212	2111	D1
Altura Station 15355 E Colfax Av, AURA, 80011	2116	D5
Arvada Main 5885 Allison St, ARVD, 80004	2026	D3
Aurora Main 16890 E Alameda Pkwy, AURA, 80017	2201	A2
Bear Valley 7555 W Amherst Av, DNVR, 80227	2278	E1
Bennett Main 205 S Ash St, BNNT, 80102	2124	D2
Black Hawk Main 345 Clear Creek St, BKHK, 80403	2017	E3
Boulder Main 1905 15th St, BLDR, 80302	1686	D2
Brighton 90 N 4th Av, BGTN, 80601	1696	B5
Broomfield Main 280 E 1st Av, BMFD, 80020	1859	A2
Buckingham Plaza Station 1074 S Ironton St, AURA, 80012	2199	C4
Capitol Hill Retail 1541 Marion St, DNVR, 80218	2113	A5
Castle Rock Main 300 E Miller Ct, CSRK, 80104	2703	D7
Centennial Branch 2221 E Arapahoe Rd, CTNL, 80121	2365	C4
Central City Main 149 Gregory St, CLCY, 80403	2017	D4
Cherry Creek 245 Columbine St, DNVR, 80206	2197	C1
Columbine Hills Station 6698 S Iris St, JfnC, 80123	2362	B4
Commerce City Main 7351 Magnolia St, CMCY, 80022	1946	C6
Conifer Main 9546 S Dallman Dr, JfnC, 80433	2442	B4
Downtown Station 951 20th St, DNVR, 80205	2112	D3
Dupont Main 8096 Brighton Rd, AdmC, 80022	1946	B5
Eagle View 8800 W 116th Cir, BMFD, 80021	1858	C4
Edgewater Branch 1990 Depew St, EDGW, 80214	2111	B4
Elizabeth Main 795 Kiowa Av, EbtC, 80107	2793	C1
Englewood Downtown Station 3330 S Broadway, EGLD, 80113	2280	E2
Englewood Mail Processing Center 6555 S Kenton St, CTNL, 80111	2367	C3
Englewood Main 915 W Lehigh Av, EGLD, 80110	2280	D4
Erie Main 150 Wells St, ERIE, 80516	1607	C4
Fitzsimons Station 13001 E 17th Pl, AURA, 80010	2116	A4
Flat Irons Annex 1860 38th St, BLDR, 80301	1687	B2
Fletcher Station 1550 Dayton St, AURA, 80010	2115	B5
Gateway Station 2500 S Abilene St, AURA, 80014	2200	B7
Glendale Station 945 S Birch St, GNDL, 80246	2197	E3
Golden Downtown Station 619 12th St, GOLD, 80401	2107	E3
Golden Main 1100 Johnson Rd, GOLD, 80401	2108	B6
Greenwood Village Branch 6855 S Dayton St, GDVL, 80112	2367	B4
Harris Park Station 7262 Meade St, WSTR, 80030	1943	D7
Henderson Main 12210 Brighton Rd, AdmC, 80640	1863	B1
Highlands Ranch 9609 S University Blvd, DgsC, 80126	2450	A4
High Mar 4985 Moorhead Av, BLDR, 80305	1687	C6
Hoffman Heights Station 738 Peoria St, AURA, 80011	2115	E6
Idaho Springs Main 2420 Colorado Blvd, IDSP, 80452	2101	D5
Indian Tree Station 7765 Wadsworth Blvd, ARVD, 80005	1942	D5
Jamestown Main 133 Main St, JMWN, 80455	1516	A2
Ken Caryl Ranch 8200 W Chatfield Av, JfnC, 80127	2445	E1
Kiowa Main 708 Commanche St, KIOW, 80117	2796	B3
Kittredge JfnC, 80439	2274	A3
Lafayette Main 603 S Public Rd, LAFT, 80026	1690	C5
Lakewood Branch 10799 W Alameda Av, LKWD, 80226	2194	A2
Larkspur Main 9080 S Spruce Mountain Rd, LKSR, 80118	2955	B5
Littleton Main 5753 S Prince St, LITN, 80120	2364	B1
Longmont Main 201 Coffman St, LGMT, 80501	1439	B3
Louisville Downtown 637 Front St, LSVL, 80027	1689	D7
Louisville Main 566 S McCaslin Blvd, LSVL, 80027	1773	A2
Lyons Main 305 Railroad Av, LYNS, 80540	1352	D1
Mile High Station 501 W 14th Av, DNVR, 80204	2112	D5
Montbello Station 4710 Nome St, DNVR, 80239	2031	D6
Montclair Station 8275 E 11th Av, DNVR, 80220	2114	E6
Morrison Main 151 Summer St, MRSN, 80465	2276	C3
Nederland Main 350 East St, NDLD, 80466	1765	D3
Northglenn Branch 11887 Washington St, NHGN, 80233	1860	E2
North Pecos Station 1411 Cortez St, AdmC, 80221	1944	C6
Northview Carrier Annex 850 W 112th Av, NHGN, 80234	1860	C4
Parker Main 18695 Pony Express Dr, PARK, 80134	2453	C7
Park Hill 3355 Hudson St, DNVR, 80207	2114	A1
South Denver Station 225 S Broadway, DNVR, 80223	2196	E2
Stockyards Station 4910 Brighton Blvd, DNVR, 80216	2029	B5
Sullivan Station 8700 E Jefferson Av, DNVR, 80237	2282	E3
Sunnyside Station 1766 W 46th Av, DNVR, 80211	2028	B6
Thornton Branch 8804 Washington St, TNTN, 80229	1945	A3
Tower 18555 E Smoky Hill Rd, CTNL, 80015	2285	C7
Twin Peaks 1845 Skyway Dr, WldC, 80504	1440	E3
University Park Station 3800 Buchtel Blvd, DNVR, 80210	2197	D6
Ward Main 1 Columbia St, WARD, 80481	1597	D2
Wellshire Station 2080 S Holly St, DNVR, 80222	2198	B6
Westwood Station 4259 W Florida Av, DNVR, 80219	2195	D5
Wheat Ridge Main 4210 Wadsworth Blvd, WTRG, 80033	2026	E7

Schools

FEATURE NAME Address City ZIP Code	MAP#	GRID
Ability Plus Academy of Colorado 3286 S Wadsworth Blvd, LKWD, 80227	2278	E3
ABN Christian School 5231 S Santa Fe Dr, LITN, 80120	2280	B7
Abraham Lincoln High School 2285 S Federal Blvd, DNVR, 80219	2196	A7
Academy Charter School 1551 Prairie Hawk Dr, CSRK, 80109	2703	C5
Accelerated School 2160 S Cook St, DNVR, 80210	2197	D6
Acres Green Elementary School 13524 Acres Green Dr, DgsC, 80124	2450	E2
Adams City High School 4625 E 68th Av, CMCY, 80022	2029	E1
Adams City Middle School 4451 E 72nd Av, CMCY, 80022	1945	E7
Adams Elementary School 6450 W 95th Pl, WSTR, 80021	1943	A1
Alameda High School 1255 S Wadsworth Blvd, LKWD, 80232	2194	D4
Alice Terry Elementary School 4485 S Irving St, SRDN, 80110	2279	E5
Allendale Elementary School 5900 Oak St, ARVD, 80004	2026	A3
All Souls Catholic School 4951 S Pennsylvania St, EGLD, 80113	2280	E6
Alsup Elementary School 7101 Birch St, CMCY, 80022	1945	E7
Altura Elementary School 1650 Altura Blvd, AURA, 80011	2116	C4
Ames Elementary School 7300 S Clermont Dr, CTNL, 80122	2365	E5
Amesse Elementary School 5440 Scranton St, DNVR, 80239	2031	E4
Angevine Middle School 1150 W South Boulder Rd, LAFT, 80026	1690	B6
Antelope Ridge Elementary School 5455 S Tempe St, AphC, 80015	2286	C7
Arapahoe High School 2201 E Dry Creek Rd, AphC, 80122	2365	B6
Arapahoe Ridge Elementary School 13095 N Pecos St, WSTR, 80234	1776	B6
Arapahoe Ridge High School 6600 Arapahoe Rd, BldC, 80303	1688	B2
Arkansas Elementary School 17301 E Arkansas Av, AURA, 80017	2201	A4
Arrowhead Elementary School 19100 E Bates Av, AURA, 80013	2285	C1
Arrowwood Elementary School 10345 Arrowwood Dr, DgsC, 80130	2450	A6
Arrupe Jesuit High School 4343 Utica St, DNVR, 80212	2027	C7
Arts Cultural Academy at Manual 1700 E 28th Av, DNVR, 80205	2113	B3
Arvada High School 7951 W 65th Av, ARVD, 80004	2026	D2
Arvada Middle School 5751 Balsam St, ARVD, 80002	2026	D4
Arvada West High School 11325 Allendale Dr, ARVD, 80004	2025	E2
Asbury Elementary School 1320 E Asbury Av, DNVR, 80210	2197	A6
Ashley Elementary School 1914 Syracuse St, DNVR, 80220	2114	D4
Aspen Creek K-8 School 5500 Aspen Creek Dr, BMFD, 80020	1775	B4
Assumption School 2341 E 78th Av, AdmC, 80229	1945	C5
Aurora Central High School 11700 E 11th Av, AURA, 80010	2115	D6
Aurora Christian Academy 11001 E Alameda Av, AURA, 80012	2199	C1
Aurora Hills Middle School 1009 S Uvalda St, AURA, 80012	2200	A3
Aurora Quest Academy 472 S Wheeling St, AURA, 80012	2200	A3
Aurora Seventh Day Adventist School 1159 S Moline St, AURA, 80012	2199	D4
Baker Elementary School 3555 W 64th Av, AdmC, 80221	2027	E2
Baker Middle School 574 W 6th Av, DNVR, 80204	2112	D7
Barnum Elementary School 85 Hooker St, DNVR, 80219	2195	E1
Barrett Elementary School 2900 Richard Allen Ct, DNVR, 80205	2113	D2
Base Line Middle School 700 20th St, BLDR, 80302	1686	E4
Beach Court Elementary School 4950 Beach Ct, DNVR, 80221	2028	A6
Beacon Country Day School 6100 E Belleview Av, GDVL, 80111	2282	B7
Bear Canyon Elementary School 9660 S Salford Ln, DgsC, 80126	2449	A4
Bear Creek Elementary School 2500 Table Mesa Dr, BLDR, 80305	1686	E7
Bear Creek Elementary School 3125 Old Kipling St, LKWD, 80227	2278	B2
Bear Creek High School 3490 S Kipling Pkwy, LKWD, 80227	2278	B3
Belleview Christian School 3455 W 83rd Av, AdmC, 80031	1943	D4
Belleview Elementary School 4851 S Dayton St, GDVL, 80111	2283	B6
Bell Middle School 1001 Ulysses St, GOLD, 80401	2108	C6
Belmar Elementary School 885 S Garrison St, LKWD, 80226	2194	C3
Bennett Elementary School 462 8th St, BNNT, 80102	2124	E1
Bennett High School 610 7th St, BNNT, 80102	2124	E1
Bennett Middle School 455 8th St, BNNT, 80102	2124	E1
Bergen Meadows Elementary School 1892 Bergen Pkwy, JfnC, 80439	2188	E7
Bergen Valley Elementary School 1422 Sugarbush Dr, JfnC, 80439	2189	A5
Berkeley Gardens Elementary School 5301 Lowell Blvd, AdmC, 80221	2027	D5
Bertha Heid Elementary School 9100 Poze Blvd, TNTN, 80229	1945	B2
Beth Eden Baptist School 2600 Wadsworth Blvd, WTRG, 80033	2110	E3
Bethel Christian School 1450 N Airport Blvd, AURA, 80011	2117	A5
Beth Jacob High School 5100 W 14th Av, DNVR, 80204	2111	C5
Bethlehem Lutheran School 2100 Wadsworth Blvd, LKWD, 80214	2110	E4
Birch Elementary School 1035 Birch St, BMFD, 80020	1775	B7
Bishop Machebeuf Catholic High School 458 N Unita Wy, DNVR, 80230	2114	E7
Bixby School 4760 Table Mesa Dr, BLDR, 80305	1687	C6
Blessed Sacrament School 1973 Elm St, DNVR, 80220	2114	A4
Blue Heron Elementary School 5987 W Dorado Dr, JfnC, 80123	2363	B2
Boston Elementary School 1365 Boston St, AURA, 80010	2115	A5
Boulder Comm School of Integrated Studies 3995 Aurora Av, BLDR, 80303	1687	B4
Boulder Country Day School 4820 Nautilus Ct N, BLDR, 80301	1604	A3
Boulder High School 1604 Arapahoe Av, BLDR, 80302	1686	D2

Denver Regional Points of Interest Index

FEATURE NAME / Address City ZIP Code	MAP#	GRID
Boulder Jewish Day School 7415 Lookout Rd, BldC, 80503	1604	C1
Boulder Prep Charter High School 5075 Chaparral Ct, BLDR, 80301	1604	A2
Boulder Technical Education Center 6600 Arapahoe Rd, BldC, 80303	1688	A2
Bradford Intermediate School 2 Woodruff Dr, JfnC, 80127	2361	A6
Bradford Primary School 1 White Oak Dr, JfnC, 80127	2445	A1
Bradley Elementary School 3051 S Elm St, DNVR, 80222	2282	A1
Bridge School 6717 S Boulder Rd, BldC, 80303	1688	B6
Brighton Adventist Academy 820 S 5th Av, BGTN, 80601	1696	B7
Brighton Charter School 1931 E Bridge St, BGTN, 80601	1696	D6
Brighton Heritage Academy 830 E Bridge St, BGTN, 80601	1696	C6
Brighton High School 270 S 8th Av, BGTN, 80601	1696	C6
Brighton High School 10724 Tancred St, NHGN, 80234	1860	B5
Bromley East Charter School 356 Longspur Dr, BGTN, 80601	1697	E6
Bromwell Elementary School 2500 E 4th Av, DNVR, 80206	2113	C7
Broomfield Heights Middle School 1555 Daphne St, BMFD, 80020	1774	E6
Broomfield High School 1 Eagle Wy, BMFD, 80020	1774	E7
Brown Elementary School 2550 Lowell Blvd, DNVR, 80211	2111	E3
Bruce Randolph Middle School 3955 Steele St, DNVR, 80205	2029	D7
Bryant Webster Elementary School 3635 Quivas St, DNVR, 80211	2112	B1
Buffalo Ridge Elementary School 7075 Shoreham Dr, DgsC, 80108	2618	E1
Burlington Elementary School 1051 S Pratt Pkwy, LGMT, 80501	1439	A5
Campbell Elementary School 6500 Oak St, ARVD, 80004	2026	A2
Campus Middle School 4785 S Dayton St, GDVL, 80111	2283	B6
Canyon Creek Elementary School 6070 S Versailles Pkwy, AphC, 80015	2370	C2
CARE Middle School 14076 E Briarwood Av, CTNL, 80112	2368	B4
Carmody Middle School 2050 Old Kipling St, LKWD, 80227	2194	B6
Carson Elementary School 5420 E 1st Av, DNVR, 80220	2198	A1
Casey Middle School 2410 13th St, BLDR, 80304	1686	C1
Castle Rock Elementary School 1103 Canyon Dr, CSRK, 80104	2703	E5
Castle Rock Middle School 2575 Meadows Blvd, CSRK, 80109	2702	E1
Castro Elementary School 845 S Lowell Blvd, DNVR, 80219	2195	E3
Centaurus High School 10300 W South Boulder Rd, LSVL, 80026	1690	A6
Centennial Elementary School 13200 Westlake Dr, BMFD, 80020	1775	E6
Centennial Elementary School 4665 Raleigh St, DNVR, 80212	2027	D6
Centennial Elementary School 3306 W Berry Av, LITN, 80123	2363	E1
Centennial Middle School 2205 Norwood Av, BLDR, 80304	1602	D5
Center for Discovery Learning 7700 W Woodard Dr, LKWD, 80227	2194	E7
Central Elementary School 6450 Holly St, CMCY, 80022	2030	B2
Central Elementary School 1020 4th Av, LGMT, 80501	1439	A2
Century Elementary School 2500 S Granby Wy, AURA, 80014	2200	D7
Century Middle School 13000 Lafayette St, TNTN, 80241	1777	A6
Challenges Choices Images Charter School 1537 Alton St, AURA, 80010	2115	A4
Chaparral High School 15655 Brookstone Dr, DgsC, 80134	2452	D4
Charles Hay Elementary School 3195 S Lafayette St, EGLD, 80113	2281	A2
Charles S Semper Elementary School 7575 W 96th Av, WSTR, 80021	1942	D1
Chaslou Academy 3188 W 37th Av, DNVR, 80211	2111	E1
Chatfield High School 7227 S Simms St, JfnC, 80127	2361	D5
Cheltenham Elementary School 1580 Julian St, DNVR, 80204	2111	E5
Cherokee Trail Elementary School 17302 Clarke Farms Dr, PARK, 80134	2453	A6
Cherokee Trails High School 25901 E Arapahoe Rd, AURA, 80016	2371	B4
Cherrelyn Elementary School 4500 S Lincoln St, EGLD, 80113	2280	E5
Cherry Creek Academy 6260 S Dayton St, AphC, 80111	2367	B3
Cherry Creek High School 9300 E Union Av, GDVL, 80111	2283	A6
Cherry Creek School 4700 S Yosemite St, GDVL, 80111	2283	A6
Cherry Drive Elementary School 11500 Cherry Dr, TNTN, 80233	1862	A3
Cherry Hills Christian School 3651 S Colorado Blvd, CHLV, 80113	2281	E3
Cherry Hills Village Elementary School 2400 E Quincy Av, CHLV, 80113	2281	C5
Children's Garden Montessori School 444 Detroit St, DNVR, 80206	2113	C7
Chinook Alternatives School 6600 Arapahoe Rd, BldC, 80303	1688	B2
Christian Fellowship School 7350 W Eastman Pl, LKWD, 80227	2278	E2
Christian School of Lakewood 3241 W 44th Av, DNVR, 80211	2027	E7
Christ the King Catholic School 860 Elm St, DNVR, 80220	2114	A6
Cimarron Elementary School 17373 E Lehigh Pl, AURA, 80013	2285	A3
Clara E Metz Elementary School 2341 Sherrelwood Dr, AdmC, 80221	1944	B5
Clayton Charter School 3605 Martin Luther King Blvd, DNVR, 80205	2113	D2
Clayton Elementary School 4600 S Fox St, EGLD, 80110	2280	D6
Clayton Elementary School 2410 Poze Blvd, TNTN, 80229	1945	C2
Clear Creek Middle School 320 Chicago Creek Rd, IDSP, 80452	2101	C6
Clear Lake Middle School 1941 Elmwood Ln, AdmC, 80221	1944	B5
Clyde Miller Elementary School 1701 Espana St, AURA, 80011	2117	D4
Coal Creek Elementary School 11719 Ranch Elsie Rd, JfnC, 80403	1852	E4
Coal Creek Elementary School 801 W Tamarisk St, LSVL, 80027	1689	A7
Cole Middle School 3240 Humboldt St, DNVR, 80205	2113	B2
Colfax Elementary School 1526 Tennyson St, DNVR, 80204	2111	D5
College View Elementary School 2675 S Decatur St, DNVR, 80219	2280	A1
Colorado Academy 3800 S Pierce St, LKWD, 80235	2279	A4
Colorado Catholic Academy 11180 W 44th Av, WTRG, 80033	2025	E7
Colorado Christian School 200 S University Blvd, DNVR, 80209	2197	C2
Colorado's Finest Alternative High School 2323 W Baker Av, EGLD, 80110	2196	B7
Colorow Elementary School 6317 S Estes St, JfnC, 80123	2362	C3
Columbia Middle School 17600 E Columbia Av, AURA, 80013	2285	B2
Columbian Elementary School 2925 W 40th Av, DNVR, 80211	2028	A7
Columbine Elementary School 3130 Repplier St, BLDR, 80304	1602	D7
Columbine Elementary School 2540 E 29th Av, DNVR, 80205	2113	C2
Columbine Elementary School 111 Longs Peak Av, LGMT, 80501	1439	C2
Columbine High School 6201 S Pierce St, JfnC, 80123	2363	A3
Columbine Hills Elementary School 6005 W Canyon Av, JfnC, 80128	2363	B7
Columbine Primary Center 2727 Columbine St, DNVR, 80205	2113	C3
Community Challenge Charter School 948 Santa Fe Dr, DNVR, 80204	2112	D6
Community Christian School 11980 Irma Dr, NHGN, 80233	1861	A2
Community Montessori Elementary School 805 Gillaspie Dr, BLDR, 80305	1687	A7
Compass Montessori School 10399 W 44th Av, WTRG, 80033	2026	A7
Compass Montessori Secondary School 4441 Salvia St, JfnC, 80403	2024	C7
Conifer High School JfnC, 80433	2442	A7
Contemporary Learning Acad Alt High School 2211 W 27th Av, DNVR, 80211	2112	A2
Core Knowledge Charter School 11661 N Pine Dr, DgsC, 80138	2453	E5
Cornerstone Montessori School 15970 W 50th Av, JfnC, 80403	2024	D6
Coronado Elementary School 7922 S Carr St, JfnC, 80128	2362	D7
Coronado Hills Elementary School 8300 Downing Dr, AdmC, 80229	1945	A4
Cory Elementary School 1550 S Steele St, DNVR, 80210	2197	D5
Cotton Creek Elementary School 11100 Vrain St, WSTR, 80031	1859	C4
Cottonwood Creek Elementary School 11200 E Orchard Rd, AphC, 80111	2367	D2
Cougar Run Elementary School 8780 Venneford Ranch Rd, DgsC, 80126	2449	D2
Country Acres Day School DgsC, 80104	2704	A6
Cowell Elementary School 4540 W 10th Av, DNVR, 80204	2111	C6
Coyote Creek Elementary School 2861 W Baneberry Ct, DgsC, 80129	2448	A6
Coyote Ridge Elementary School 13770 Broadlands Dr, BMFD, 80020	1775	C4
Crawford Elementary School 1600 Florence St, AURA, 80010	2115	B4
Creekside Elementary School 3740 Martin Dr, BLDR, 80305	1687	A6
Creekside Elementary School 19993 E Long Av, CTNL, 80016	2369	E6
Creighton Middle School W 1st Av, LKWD, 80226	2194	B1
Cresthill Middle School 9195 S Cresthill Ln, DgsC, 80130	2450	A3
Crest View Elementary School 1897 Sumac Av, BLDR, 80304	1602	D4
Crossroad Alternative School 9451 Hoffman Wy, TNTN, 80229	1945	A1
Crown Pointe Academy 7281 N Irving St, WSTR, 80030	1943	E7
Dakota Ridge High School 13399 W Coal Mine Av, JfnC, 80127	2361	C2
Dakota Valley Elementary School 3950 S Kirk Wy, AphC, 80013	2286	A4
Dalton Elementary School 17401 E Dartmouth Av, AURA, 80013	2285	A2
Daniel C Oakes High School 961 Plum Creek Pkwy, CSRK, 80104	2787	E1
Dartmouth Elementary School 3050 S Laredo St, AURA, 80013	2284	E1
DCS Montessori Charter School 8218 W Carder Ct, DgsC, 80125	2447	D3
Deane Elementary School 580 S Harlan St, LKWD, 80226	2195	B3
Deer Creek Middle School 9201 W Columbine Dr, JfnC, 80128	2362	C5
Del Pueblo Elementary School 750 Galapago St, DNVR, 80204	2112	D7
Dennison Elementary School 401 Independence St, LKWD, 80226	2194	B1
Dennison Montessori School 1821 S Yates St, DNVR, 80219	2195	C6
Denver Academy 4400 E Iliff Av, DNVR, 80222	2197	E7
Denver Academy of Torah 400 S Kearney St, DNVR, 80224	2198	B2
Denver Christian Middle/High School 2135 S Pearl St, DNVR, 80210	2196	E6
Denver International School 1101 S Race St, DNVR, 80210	2197	B4
Denver School for the Arts 7111 Montview Blvd, DNVR, 80207	2114	C3
Denver Waldorf School 940 Fillmore St, DNVR, 80206	2113	C6
Desiderata School 2243 Mountain View Av, LGMT, 80501	1355	D7
D'Evelyn Junior & Senior High School 10359 W Nassau Av, JfnC, 80235	2278	A4
Devinney Elementary School 1725 S Wright St, LKWD, 80228	2193	D6
Dora Moore K-8 School 846 Corona St, DNVR, 80218	2113	A6
Douglas County High School 2842 Front St, CSRK, 80104	2703	D4
Douglas Elementary School 840 N 75th St, BldC, 80303	1688	D4
Doull Elementary School 2520 S Utica St, DNVR, 80219	2195	D7
Drake Middle School 12550 W 52nd Av, JfnC, 80033	2025	C5
Dry Creek Elementary School 7686 E Hinsdale Av, CTNL, 80112	2366	D6
Dunstan Middle School 1855 S Wright St, LKWD, 80228	2193	D6
Dupont Elementary School 7970 Kimberly St, AdmC, 80022	1946	B5
Dutch Creek Elementary School 7304 W Roxbury Pl, JfnC, 80128	2362	E5
Eagle Crest Elementary School 4444 Clover Basin Dr, LGMT, 80503	1437	E5
Eaglecrest High School 5100 S Picadilly St, AphC, 80015	2286	B6
Eagle Ridge Elementary School 7716 Timberline Rd, LNTR, 80124	2450	D3
Eagleton Elementary School 880 Hooker St, DNVR, 80204	2111	E6
Eagleview Elementary School 4601 Summit Grove Pkwy, TNTN, 80241	1777	E6
East Elementary School 5933 S Fairfield St, LITN, 80120	2364	E2
East High School 1545 Detroit St, DNVR, 80206	2113	C5
East Middle School 1275 Fraser St, AURA, 80011	2116	C5
Eastridge Community Elementary School 11777 E Wesley Av, AURA, 80014	2199	D7
Ebert Elementary School 410 Park Av W, DNVR, 80205	2112	E4
Edgewater Elementary School 5570 W 24th Av, EDGW, 80214	2111	B3
Edison Elementary School 3350 Quitman St, DNVR, 80212	2111	D2
Eiber Elementary School 1385 Independence St, LKWD, 80215	2110	B5
Eisenhower Elementary School 1220 Eisenhower Dr, BLDR, 80303	1687	C3
Eldorado Elementary School 1305 W Timbervale Tr, DgsC, 80129	2448	C5
Eldorado K-8 School 3351 S Indiana St, SUPE, 80027	1857	A1
Elizabeth High School 34500 Deer Creek Dr, ELIZ, 80107	2709	A7
Elk Creek Elementary School 13304 US-285 Frontage Rd, JfnC, 80470	2524	D7
Elkhart Elementary School 1020 Eagle St, AURA, 80011	2116	C6
Ellis Elementary School 1651 S Dahlia St, DNVR, 80222	2198	A5
Elmwood Baptist Academy 13100 E 144th Av, AdmC, 80601	1779	E3
Emerald Elementary School 755 W Elmhurst Pl, BMFD, 80020	1858	E1
Emily Griffith Opportunity School 1250 Welton St, DNVR, 80204	2112	D5
Englewood High School 3800 S Logan St, EGLD, 80113	2280	E4
Erie Elementary School 4137 E County Line Rd, ERIE, 80516	1607	B4
Erie Middle & High School 650 Main St, ERIE, 80516	1607	B4
Escuela Tlatelolco 2949 Federal Blvd, DNVR, 80211	2112	A2
Euclid Middle School 777 W Euclid Av, LITN, 80120	2364	D4
Eugene Field Elementary School 5402 S Sherman Wy, AphC, 80121	2280	E7
Evergreen Academy 27826 Alabraska Ln, JfnC, 80439	2357	E4
Evergreen High School 29300 Buffalo Park Rd, JfnC, 80439	2357	C1
Evergreen Middle School 2059 S Hiwan Dr, JfnC, 80439	2188	E7
Everitt Middle School 3900 Kipling St, WTRG, 80033	2110	B1
Excel Academy 11500 W 84th Pl, ARVD, 80005	1941	D4
Fairmont Elementary School 520 W 3rd Av, DNVR, 80223	2196	D1
Fairmount Elementary School 15975 W 50th Av, JfnC, 80403	2024	D6

Denver Regional Points of Interest Index

FEATURE NAME	Address City ZIP Code	MAP#	GRID
Fairview Elementary School	7826 Fairview Av, AdmC, 80221	1944	A5
Fairview Elementary School	2715 W 11th Av, DNVR, 80204	2112	A6
Fairview High School	1515 Greenbriar Blvd, BLDR, 80305	1771	B1
Faith Baptist School	833 15th Av, LGMT, 80501	1356	A6
Faith Christian Academy	6210 Ward Rd, ARVD, 80004	2025	D2
Falcon Bluffs Middle School	8449 S Garrison St, JfnC, 80128	2446	C1
Falcon Creek Middle School	6100 S Genoa St, AphC, 80016	2369	E2
Fallis Elementary School	6700 E Virginia Av, DNVR, 80224	2198	C2
Fall River Elementary School	1400 Deerwood Dr, LGMT, 80501	1357	A7
Family Star Montessori School	1331 E 33rd Av, DNVR, 80205	2113	A2
Federal Heights Elementary School	2500 W 96th Av, TNTN, 80260	1944	B1
Fireside Elementary School	845 W Dahlia St, LSVL, 80027	1773	A2
Fitzmorris Elementary School	6250 Independence St, ARVD, 80004	2026	B2
Fitzsimmons Middle School	PrkC, 80456	2605	B7
Flagstone Elementary School	104 Lovington St, CSRK, 80104	2705	A7
Flatirons Elementary School	1150 7th St, BLDR, 80302	1686	C3
Fletcher Elementary School	10455 E 25th Av, AURA, 80010	2115	C3
Flood Middle School	3695 S Lincoln St, EGLD, 80113	2280	E3
Florence Crittenton School	96 S Zuni St, DNVR, 80223	2196	B1
Flynn Elementary School	8731 Lowell Blvd, AdmC, 80031	1943	D3
Foothill Elementary School	1001 Hawthorn Av, BLDR, 80304	1602	C6
Foothills Academy	4725 Miller St, WTRG, 80033	2026	A6
Foothills Elementary School	13165 W Ohio Av, LKWD, 80228	2193	C3
Force Elementary School	1550 S Wolff St, DNVR, 80219	2195	C5
Ford Elementary School	14500 Maxwell Pl, DNVR, 80239	2032	C4
Fort Logan Elementary School	3700 S Knox Ct, SRDN, 80110	2279	E4
Foster Elementary School	5300 Saulsbury Ct, ARVD, 80002	2026	E5
Fox Creek Elementary School	6585 E Collegiate Dr, DgsC, 80130	2450	C3
Fox Hollow Elementary School	6363 S Waco St, AphC, 80016	2369	B3
Francis M Day Elementary School	1740 Jordan Dr, AdmC, 80221	1944	B7
Franklin Elementary School	1603 E Euclid Av, CTNL, 80121	2365	B3
Franktown Elementary School	DgsC, 80116	2706	A5
Fremont Elementary School	6420 Urban St, ARVD, 80004	2025	D2
Friends' School	5465 Pennsylvania Av, BLDR, 80303	1687	D3
Frontier High School	589 S Banner St, ELIZ, 80107	2793	B1
Frontier Valley Elementary School	23919 Canterberry Tr, PARK, 80138	2538	D2
Front Range Christian School	6500 W Coal Mine Av, JfnC, 80128	2363	A4
Front Range Christian School	4100 S Wadsworth Blvd, LKWD, 80235	2278	E5
Fulton Elementary School	755 Fulton St, AURA, 80010	2115	B6
Garden Place Elementary School	4425 Lincoln St, DNVR, 80216	2028	E7
Gateway Academy Smoky Hill	5637 S Himalaya St, CTNL, 80015	2369	E1
Gateway High School	1300 S Sable Blvd, AURA, 80012	2200	C4
George Washington High School	655 S Monaco Pkwy, DNVR, 80224	2198	B3
Gethsemane Lutheran School	10675 Washington St, NHGN, 80233	1860	E5
Gilliam School	2844 Downing St, DNVR, 80205	2113	A2
Gilpin Elementary School	2409 Arapahoe St, DNVR, 80205	2112	E3
Glacier Peak Elementary School	12060 Jasmine St, AdmC, 80602	1862	B2
Glennon Heights Elementary School	11025 W Glennon Dr, LKWD, 80226	2193	E3
Goddard Middle School	3800 W Berry Av, LITN, 80123	2363	E1
Godsman Elementary School	2120 W Arkansas Av, DNVR, 80223	2196	B5
Golden High School	701 24th St, GOLD, 80401	2108	A4
Goldrick Elementary School	1050 S Zuni St, DNVR, 80223	2196	B4
Gove Middle School	4050 E 14th Av, DNVR, 80220	2113	E5
Governor's Ranch Elementary School	5354 S Field St, JfnC, 80123	2362	C1
Graland Country Day School	30 S Birch St, DNVR, 80246	2197	E1
Grandview High School	20500 E Arapahoe Rd, AURA, 80016	2370	A4
Grandview High School	20500 E Arapahoe Rd, CTNL, 80016	2369	E4
Grant Middle School	1751 S Washington St, DNVR, 80210	2197	A6
Green Gables Elementary School	8701 W Woodard Dr, LKWD, 80227	2194	C6
Greenlee Elementary School	1150 Lipan St, DNVR, 80204	2112	C6
Green Mountain Elementary School	12250 W Kentucky Dr, LKWD, 80228	2193	D4
Green Mountain High School	13175 W Green Mountain Dr, LKWD, 80228	2193	C4
Green Valley Elementary School	4100 Jericho St, DNVR, 80249	2033	E7
Greenwood Elementary School	5550 S Holly St, GDVL, 80111	2366	B1
Guardian Angels School	1843 W 52nd Av, AdmC, 80221	2028	B5
Gust Elementary School	3440 W Yale Av, DNVR, 80236	2279	E1
Hackberry Hill Elementary School	7300 W 76th Av, ARVD, 80003	1942	E6
Hallett Elementary School	2950 Jasmine St, DNVR, 80207	2114	B2
Hamilton Middle School	8600 E Dartmouth Av, DNVR, 80231	2282	E2
Hanson Elementary School	7133 E 73rd Av, CMCY, 80022	1946	C6
Harrington Elementary School	2401 E 37th Av, DNVR, 80205	2113	C1
Harris Park Elementary School	4300 W 75th Av, WSTR, 80030	1943	C6
Heatherwood Elementary School	7750 Concord Dr, BldC, 80301	1604	D3
Henderson Elementary School	12301 E 124th Av, BGTN, 80640	1863	E1
Henry Middle School	3005 S Golden Wy, DNVR, 80227	2279	B2
Heritage Christian School	1301 S Clinton St, AphC, 80247	2199	A4
Heritage Elementary School	6867 E Heritage Pl S, CTNL, 80111	2366	C4
Heritage Elementary School	3350 Summit View Pkwy, DgsC, 80126	2449	D6
Heritage High School	1401 W Geddes Av, LITN, 80120	2364	C5
Heritage Middle School	233 E Mountain View Av, LGMT, 80501	1356	D7
Highland Elementary School	711 E Euclid Av, CTNL, 80121	2365	A4
Highlands Ranch Christian School	1733 E Dad Clark Dr, DgsC, 80126	2449	B1
Highlands Ranch High School	9375 S Cresthill Ln, DgsC, 80130	2450	A4
Highline Community Elementary School	11000 E Exposition Av, AURA, 80012	2199	C3
High Peaks Elementary School	3995 Aurora Av, BLDR, 80303	1687	B4
High Plains Elementary School	6100 S Fulton St, AphC, 80111	2367	B2
High Plains High School	455 E Eppinger Blvd, TNTN, 80229	1944	E2
Hillcrest Elementary School	10335 Croke Dr, NHGN, 80260	1860	C6
Hillel Academy	450 S Hudson St, DNVR, 80246	2198	B2
Hill Middle School	451 Clermont St Pkwy, DNVR, 80220	2113	E7
Hinkley High School	1250 N Chambers Rd, AURA, 80011	2116	D5
Holly Hills Elementary School	6161 E Cornell Av, AphC, 80222	2282	B1
Holly Ridge Primary School	3301 S Monaco Pkwy, DNVR, 80222	2282	C2
Holm Elementary School	3185 S Willow St, DNVR, 80231	2282	E2
Holy Family Grade School	4343 Utica St, DNVR, 80212	2027	C7
Holy Family High School	5195 W 144th Av, BMFD, 80020	1775	C3
Holy Trinity School	3050 W 76th Av, WSTR, 80030	1943	E6
Homestead Elementary School	7451 S Homestead Pkwy, CTNL, 80112	2366	C6
Hopkins Elementary School	7171 S Pennsylvania St, CTNL, 80122	2365	A5
Horace Mann Middle School	4130 Navajo St, DNVR, 80211	2028	C7
Horizon Middle School	3981 S Reservoir Rd, AURA, 80013	2285	C4
Horizon Senior High School	5321 E 136th Av, TNTN, 80602	1778	A5
Horizons K-8 Alternative School	4545 Sioux Dr, BLDR, 80303	1687	C5
Hulstrom Elementary School	10604 Grant Dr, NHGN, 80233	1860	E5
Humanex Academy	2700 S Zuni St, EGLD, 80110	2280	B1
Hunters Glen Elementary School	13222 Corona St, TNTN, 80241	1777	A6
Huron Middle School	10900 N Huron St, NHGN, 80234	1860	C5
Hutchinson Elementary School	12900 W Utah Av, LKWD, 80228	2193	C6
Hygiene Elementary School	11968 N 75th St, BldC, 80503	1354	D6
Hyland Christian School	5255 W 98th Av, WSTR, 80020	1859	B7
Independence Elementary School	4700 S Memphis St, AURA, 80015	2284	E6
Indian Peaks Elementary School	1335 S Judson St, LGMT, 80501	1438	E5
Indian Ridge Elementary School	16501 E Progress Dr, AphC, 80015	2284	E7
Iowa Elementary School	16701 E Iowa Av, AURA, 80017	2200	E5
Iron Horse Elementary School	20151 Tallman Dr, PARK, 80138	2537	E2
Iver C Ranum High School	2401 W 80th Av, AdmC, 80221	1944	A5
Jamaica Elementary School	800 Jamaica St, AURA, 80010	2115	C6
Jarrow Montessori School	3900 Orange Ct, BLDR, 80304	1602	C5
Jefferson Academy Charter School	9955 Yarrow St, JfnC, 80021	1858	D7
Jefferson Academy High School	9955 Yarrow St, JfnC, 80021	1858	D7
Jefferson County Academy	331 14th St, DNVR, 80202	2112	D5
Jefferson County Open Elementary School	7655 W 10th Av, LKWD, 80214	2110	E6
Jefferson County Open Junior/High School	7655 W 10th Av, LKWD, 80214	2110	D6
Jefferson High School	2305 Pierce St, EDGW, 80214	2111	A4
Jessie Whaley Maxwell Elementary School	14390 E Bolling Dr, DNVR, 80239	2032	B6
Jewell Elementary School	14601 E Jewell Av, AURA, 80012	2200	C6
J Hodgkins Middle School	3475 W 67th Av, AdmC, 80221	2027	E1
Jim Elliot School	3001 S Federal Blvd, DNVR, 80236	2280	A2
JK Mullen High School	3601 S Lowell Blvd, DNVR, 80236	2279	E3
John Dewey Middle School	7480 Conifer Rd, AdmC, 80221	1944	E6
John F Kennedy High School	2855 S Lamar St, DNVR, 80227	2279	A2
Johnson Elementary School	1850 S Irving St, DNVR, 80219	2195	E6
John W Thimmig Elementary School	11453 Oswego St, CMCY, 80640	1863	D3
Kaiser Elementary School	4500 S Quitman St, DNVR, 80236	2279	D6
Kearney Middle School	6160 Kearney St, CMCY, 80022	2030	B2
Kemp Elementary School	6775 Oneida St, CMCY, 80022	2030	C1
Ken Caryl Middle School	6509 W Ken Caryl Av, JfnC, 80128	2363	A6
Kendallvue Elementary School	13658 W Marlowe Av, JfnC, 80465	2277	B6
Kendrick Lakes Elementary School	1350 S Hoyt St, LKWD, 80232	2194	B5
Kent Denver School	4000 E Quincy Av, CHLV, 80113	2281	E5
Kenton Elementary School	1255 Kenton St, AURA, 80010	2115	C5
Kepner Middle School	911 S Hazel Ct, DNVR, 80219	2195	E3
King-Murphy Elementary School	425 Circle K Ranch Rd, CCkC, 80439	2271	D4
Kiowa High School	525 Commanche St, KIOW, 80117	2796	B2
Kipp Sunshine Peak Academy	2417 W 29th Av, DNVR, 80211	2112	A2
Knapp Elementary School	500 S Utica St, DNVR, 80219	2195	C2
Knight Fundamental Academy	3245 E Exposition Av, DNVR, 80209	2197	D3
Kohl Elementary School	1000 W 10th Av, BMFD, 80020	1774	D7
Kullerstrand Elementary School	12225 W 38th Av, WTRG, 80033	2109	D1
Kunsmiller Middle School	2250 S Quitman Wy, DNVR, 80219	2195	D7
Kyffin Elementary School	205 Flora Wy, JfnC, 80401	2193	A1
Lafayette Elementary School	101 N Bermont Av, LAFT, 80026	1690	C4
Lake Middle School	1820 Lowell Blvd, DNVR, 80204	2111	E4
Lakewood High School	9700 W 8th Av, LKWD, 80215	2110	B7
Lansing Elementary School	551 Lansing St, AURA, 80010	2115	C7
Laredo Elementary School	1350 N Laredo St, AURA, 80011	2116	E5
Laredo Middle School	5000 S Laredo St, AURA, 80015	2284	D7
Larkspur Elementary School	1103 W Perry Park Av, DgsC, 80118	2954	D5
Lasley Elementary School	1401 S Kendall St, LKWD, 80232	2195	A5
Lawrence Elementary School	5611 Zephyr St, ARVD, 80002	2026	D4
Leawood Elementary School	6155 W Leawood Dr, JfnC, 80123	2363	B2
Legacy High School	2701 W 136th Av, BMFD, 80020	1776	A5
Legacy Point Elementary School	12736 Red Rosa Cir, PARK, 80134	2537	B5
Lena Lovato Archuleta Elementary School	16000 E Maxwell Pl, DNVR, 80239	2032	D4
Leroy Drive Elementary School	1451 Leroy Dr, NHGN, 80233	1861	A5
Lester R Arnold High School	6500 E 72nd Av, CMCY, 80022	1946	C7
Lincoln Charter Academy	6980 Pierce St, ARVD, 80003	2027	A1
Lincoln Elementary School	710 S Pennsylvania St, DNVR, 80209	2196	E3
Little Elementary School	8448 Otis Dr, ARVD, 80003	1943	A3
Littleton Academy	1200 W Mineral Av, LITN, 80120	2364	C7
Littleton High School	199 E Littleton Blvd, LITN, 80121	2364	E1
Littleton Prep Charter School	5151 S Federal Blvd, LITN, 80123	2280	A7
Lochbuie Elementary School	201 Bonanza Blvd, LCHB, 80603	1698	B3
Lois Lenski Elementary School	6350 S Fairfax Wy, CTNL, 80121	2366	A3
Loma Linda Elementary School	333 E Mountain View Av, LGMT, 80501	1356	D7
Longmont Christian School	550 Coffman St, LGMT, 80501	1439	A2
Longmont Estates Elementary School	1601 Northwestern Rd, LGMT, 80503	1355	B7
Longmont High School	1040 Sunset St, LGMT, 80501	1438	E1
Longs Peak Middle School	1500 14th Av, LGMT, 80501	1355	E7
Long View High School	13301 W 2nd Pl, LKWD, 80228	2193	B2

FEATURE NAME Address City ZIP Code	MAP#	GRID
Louisville Elementary School 400 Hutchinson St, LSVL, 80027	1773	C1
Louisville Middle School 1341 Main St, LSVL, 80027	1689	D6
Lowry Elementary School 8001 E Cedar Av, DNVR, 80230	2198	D2
Loyola School 2350 Gaylord St, DNVR, 80205	2113	B3
Lukas Elementary School 9650 W 97th Av, WSTR, 80021	1942	B1
Lumberg Elementary School 6705 W 22nd Av, EDGW, 80214	2111	A4
Lutheran High School 3201 W Arizona Av, DNVR, 80219	2195	E4
Lyn Knoll Elementary School 12445 E 2nd Av, AURA, 80011	2199	E1
Lyons Elementary School 338 High St, LYNS, 80540	1352	D1
Lyons Middle/Senior High School 100 S 2nd Av, LYNS, 80540	1352	D3
Mackintosh Academy 7018 S Prince St, LITN, 80120	2364	B5
Maddox Elementary School 700 W Mansfield Av, EGLD, 80110	2280	D4
Majestic Heights Elementary School 4655 Hanover Av, BLDR, 80305	1687	B7
Malley Drive Elementary School 1300 Malley Dr, NHGN, 80233	1861	A3
Mandalay Middle School 9651 N Pierce St, WSTR, 80021	1942	E1
Manhattan Middle School 290 Manhattan Dr, BLDR, 80303	1687	D5
Manual High School 1700 E 28th Av, DNVR, 80205	2113	B3
Maple Grove Elementary School 3085 N Alkire St, JfnC, 80401	2109	C2
Maranatha Christian Center School 7180 Oak St, ARVD, 80004	1942	A7
Marie L Greenwood Elementary School 5130 Durham Ct, DNVR, 80239	2032	C5
Marrama Elementary School 19100 E 40th Av, DNVR, 80249	2033	C7
Marshdale Elementary School 26663 N Turkey Creek Rd, JfnC, 80439	2358	A5
Martensen Elementary School 6625 W 45th Pl, WTRG, 80033	2027	A7
Martin Luther King Jr Middle School 19535 E 46th Av, DNVR, 80249	2033	D6
Mary E Pennock School 3707 Estrella St, BGTN, 80601	1697	B6
McElwain Elementary School 1020 Dawson Dr, AdmC, 80229	1945	A3
McGlone Elementary School 4500 Crown Blvd, DNVR, 80239	2031	E6
McKinley-Thatcher Elementary School 1230 S Grant St, DNVR, 80210	2196	E4
McLain Community High School 2001 Hoyt St, LKWD, 80215	2110	B4
McMeen Elementary School 1000 S Holly St, DNVR, 80224	2198	B4
Meadow Elementary School 9150 Monroe St, TNTN, 80229	1945	D2
Meadowood Christian School 16051 E Dartmouth Av, AURA, 80013	2284	E2
Meadow Point Elementary School 17901 E Grand Av, AURA, 80015	2285	B6
Meadow View Elementary School 3700 Butterfield Crossing Dr, CSRK, 80109	2702	D1
Meritor Academy 7203 W 120th Av, BMFD, 80020	1858	E2
Meritor Academy-Westminster 8851 Field St, WSTR, 80021	1942	C3
Merrill Middle School 1551 S Monroe St, DNVR, 80210	2197	D5
Mesa Elementary School 9100 Lowell Blvd, AdmC, 80031	1943	D2
Mesa Elementary School 1575 Lehigh St, BLDR, 80305	1770	E1
Mile High Academy 711 E Yale Av, DNVR, 80210	2281	A1
Mission Viejo Elementary School 3855 S Alicia Pkwy, AURA, 80013	2284	D3
Mitchell Elementary School 1350 E 33rd Av, DNVR, 80205	2113	A2
Mitchell Elementary School 201 Rubey Dr, GOLD, 80403	2107	C2
Molholm Elementary School 6000 W 9th Av, LKWD, 80214	2111	B6
Monaco Elementary School 7631 Monaco St, AdmC, 80022	1946	B6
Monarch High School 329 Campus Dr, BldC, 80027	1773	C4
Monarch K-8 School 263 Campus Dr, BldC, 80027	1773	C4
Montbello High School 5000 Crown Blvd, DNVR, 80239	2032	B5
Montclair Academy 212 E 4th Av, DNVR, 80230	2114	D7
Montclair Elementary School 1151 Newport St, DNVR, 80220	2114	C6
Monterey Elementary School 2201 McElwain Blvd, AdmC, 80229	1945	B3
Montessori Academy 1199 N 111th St, LAFT, 80026	1690	C3
Montessori Academy of Bear Creek 9300 W Dartmouth Pl, LKWD, 80227	2278	C2
Montessori Academy of Colorado 1000 Speer Blvd, DNVR, 80204	2112	D6
Montessori Peaks Academy 9904 W Capri Av, JfnC, 80123	2362	B3
Montessori School at Lone Tree 9396 Ermindale Dr, LNTR, 80124	2450	D4
Montessori School of Aurora 18585 E Smoky Hill Rd, CTNL, 80015	2285	C7
Montessori School of Denver 1460 S Holly St, DNVR, 80224	2198	B5
Montview Elementary School 2055 Moline St, AURA, 80010	2115	D4
Moody Elementary School 6390 S Windermere St, LITN, 80120	2364	C3
Moore Middle School 8455 W 88th Av, WSTR, 80021	1942	C3
Morey Middle School 840 E 14th Av, DNVR, 80218	2113	A5
Mortensen Elementary School 8006 S Iris Wy, JfnC, 80128	2362	B7
Most Precious Blood Catholic School 3959 E Iliff Av, DNVR, 80210	2197	E7
Mountain High School 4602 Plettner Ln, JfnC, 80439	2273	D6
Mountain Peak Private School 1833 Sunset Pl, LGMT, 80501	1438	E5
Mountain Ridge Middle School 10590 Mountain Vista Rdg, DgsC, 80126	2449	C7
Mountain Shadows Montessori School 4154 N 63rd St, BldC, 80301	1604	A4
Mountain View Elementary School 12401 N Perry St, BMFD, 80020	1775	D7
Mountain View Elementary School 8502 N Pinery Pkwy, DgsC, 80134	2622	C2
Mountain View Elementary School 1415 14th Av, LGMT, 80501	1355	E7
Mountain Vista High School 10585 Mountain Vista Rdg, DgsC, 80126	2449	B7
Mount Carbon Elementary School 12776 W Cross Av, JfnC, 80127	2361	C1
Mount Zion Lutheran School 1680 Balsam Av, BLDR, 80304	1686	D1
Mrachek Middle School 1955 S Telluride St, AURA, 80013	2201	B6
M Scott Carpenter Middle School 7001 Lipan St, AdmC, 80221	1944	C7
Munroe Elementary School 3440 W Virginia Av, DNVR, 80219	2195	E2
Nederland Elementary School 1 N Sundown Tr, NDLD, 80466	1765	C2
Nederland Middle/Senior High School Eldora Rd, BldC, 80466	1765	B4
Nevin Platt Middle School 6096 Baseline Rd, BldC, 80303	1688	A4
Newlon Elementary School 361 Vrain St, DNVR, 80219	2195	C1
Newton Middle School 4001 E Arapahoe Rd, CTNL, 80121	2365	E4
New Vista High School 700 20th St, BLDR, 80302	1686	D4
Niver Creek Middle School 9450 Pecos St, TNTN, 80260	1944	B1
Niwot Elementary School 8778 Morton Rd, BldC, 80503	1521	B4
Niwot High School 8989 Niwot Rd, BldC, 80503	1521	C4
Normandy Elementary School 6750 S Kendall Blvd, JfnC, 80128	2363	B4
North Arvada Middle School 7285 Pierce St, ARVD, 80003	1942	E7
Northeast Academy Charter School 4895 Peoria St, DNVR, 80239	2031	D5
Northeast Elementary School 1605 Longspeak St, BGTN, 80601	1696	D5
Northeast Elementary School 6598 S Parker Rd, DgsC, 80134	2621	E1
North Elementary School 89 N 6th Av, BGTN, 80601	1696	B5
Northglenn Middle School 1123 Muriel Dr, NHGN, 80233	1861	A4
Northglenn Senior High School 601 W 100th Pl, NHGN, 80260	1860	D7
North High School 2960 N Speer Blvd, DNVR, 80211	2112	A2
North Middle School 12095 Montview Blvd, AURA, 80010	2115	E4
North Mor Elementary School 9580 Damon Dr, TNTN, 80260	1944	D1
Northridge Elementary School 555 Southpark Rd, DgsC, 80126	2448	E3
Northridge Elementary School 1200 19th Av, LGMT, 80501	1356	A5
North Star Elementary School 8740 Northstar Dr, TNTN, 80260	1944	D3
Notre Dame Catholic School 2165 S Zenobia St, DNVR, 80219	2195	C7
Oakland Elementary School 4580 Dearborn St, DNVR, 80239	2032	B6
Oberon Middle School 7300 Quail St, ARVD, 80005	1941	E7
O'Connell Middle School 1275 S Teller St, LKWD, 80232	2194	E4
Odyssey Charter Elementary School 1958 Elm St, DNVR, 80220	2114	A4
Omar D Blair School 4905 Cathay Ct, DNVR, 80249	2033	C5
Options High School 6558 S Acoma St, LITN, 80120	2364	D4
Our Lady Help of Christians Academy 4190 Xavier St, DNVR, 80212	2027	C7
Our Lady of Fatima School 10530 W 20th Av, LKWD, 80215	2110	A4
Our Lady of Lourdes Catholic School 2256 S Logan St, DNVR, 80210	2196	E7
Overland High School 12400 E Jewell Av, AURA, 80014	2199	E6
Overland Trail Middle School 455 N 19th Av, BGTN, 80601	1696	D4
Palmer Elementary School 995 Grape St, DNVR, 80220	2114	A6
Paris Elementary School 1635 Paris St, AURA, 80010	2115	D4
Park Hill Elementary School 5050 E 19th Av, DNVR, 80220	2114	A4
Park Lane Elementary School 13001 E 30th Av, AURA, 80011	2116	A2
Parmalee Elementary School 4460 Parmalee Gulch Rd, JfnC, 80439	2274	E5
Parr Elementary School 5800 W 84th Av, ARVD, 80003	1943	B4
Pathways Middle School 1907 W Powers Av, LITN, 80120	2364	B1
Patterson Elementary School 1263 S Dudley St, LKWD, 80232	2194	C4
Peabody Elementary School 3128 E Maplewood Av, CTNL, 80121	2365	D3
Peace With Christ Christian School 3290 S Tower Rd, AURA, 80013	2285	C2
Peak to Peak Elementary Charter School 800 Merlin Dr, LAFT, 80026	1690	D5
Peak to Peak Middle/High Charter School 800 Merlin Dr, LAFT, 80026	1690	D5
Peakview Elementary School 19451 E Progress Cir, CTNL, 80015	2285	D7
Peck Elementary School 6495 Carr St, ARVD, 80004	2026	C2
Peiffer Elementary School 4997 S Miller Wy, JfnC, 80127	2278	A7
Pennington Elementary School 4645 Independence St, WTRG, 80033	2026	B6
Philips Elementary School 6550 E 21st Av, DNVR, 80207	2114	C4
Pine Grove Elementary School 10450 Stonegate Pkwy, DgsC, 80134	2452	D6
Pine Lane Intermediate School 6475 E Ponderosa Dr, DgsC, 80138	2453	C4
Pioneer Charter School 3230 E 38th Av, DNVR, 80205	2113	D1
Pioneer Elementary School 101 E Baseline Rd, LAFT, 80026	1690	C4
Pioneer Elementary School 10881 Riva Ridge Dr, PARK, 80138	2538	B1
Place Middle School 7125 Cherry Creek North Dr, DNVR, 80224	2198	C5
Platte Canyon High School PrkC, 80456	2689	B1
Platte River Academy 4085 E Lark Sparrow St, DgsC, 80126	2449	E3
Pleasant Hill Academy 421 21st Av, LGMT, 80501	1356	B5
Pleasant View Elementary School 15920 W 10th Av, JfnC, 80401	2108	D6
Polton Community Elementary School 2985 S Oakland St, AURA, 80014	2283	D1
Pomona High School 8101 W Pomona Dr, ARVD, 80005	1942	D4
Ponderosa Elementary School 1885 S Lima St, AURA, 80012	2199	D6
Ponderosa High School 7007 E Bayou Gulch Rd, DgsC, 80134	2621	E5
Powderhorn Elementary School 12109 W Coal Mine Av, JfnC, 80127	2361	D3
Powell Middle School 8000 S Corona Wy, LITN, 80122	2365	A7
Prairie Crossing Elementary School 11605 S Bradbury Ranch Dr, PARK, 80134	2536	E1
Prairie Hills Elementary School 13801 Garfield Pl, TNTN, 80602	1777	D4
Prairie Middle School 12600 E Jewell Av, AURA, 80014	2199	E6
Presentation of Our Lady School 660 Julian St, DNVR, 80204	2111	E7
Prospect Valley Elementary School 3400 Pierson St, WTRG, 80033	2109	E2
Rachel B Noel Middle School 5290 Kittredge St, DNVR, 80239	2032	D5
Ralston Elementary School 25856 Columbine Glen Av, JfnC, 80401	2190	B1
Ralston Valley High School 13355 W 80th Av, ARVD, 80005	1941	B5
Ranch View Middle School 1731 W Wildcat Reserve Pkwy, DgsC, 80129	2448	C6
Rangeview High School 17599 E Iliff Av, AURA, 80013	2201	B7
Redeemer Lutheran School 3400 W Nevada Pl, DNVR, 80219	2195	E2
Red Rocks Elementary School 17199 Bear Creek Av, MRSN, 80465	2276	C3
Regis Jesuit High School 6400 E Weaver Pl, AphC, 80016	2368	E3
Remington Elementary School 4735 Pecos St, DNVR, 80211	2028	B6
Renaissance School 16700 Keystone Blvd, DgsC, 80134	2452	E5
Ridge View Academy 28101 E Quincy Av, AphC, 80137	2287	E4
Rishel Middle School 415 S Tejon St, DNVR, 80223	2196	B2
Riverdale Elementary School 10724 Elm Dr, TNTN, 80233	1862	A5
Riverview Christian Academy 8081 E Orchard Rd, GDVL, 80111	2366	D2
Rock Canyon High School 5810 McArthur Ranch Rd, DgsC, 80124	2450	B7
Rock Ridge Elementary School 400 Heritage Av, CSRK, 80104	2704	D7
Rocky Heights Middle School 11033 Monarch Blvd, DgsC, 80108	2534	B1
Rocky Heights Middle School 11033 Monarch Blvd, DgsC, 80124	2450	B7
Rocky Mountain Elementary School 800 E 5th Av, LGMT, 80501	1439	D2
Rocky Mountain Elementary School 3350 W 99th Av, WSTR, 80031	1859	E7
Rocky Mountain Hebrew Academy 2450 S Wabash St, AphC, 80231	2198	E7
Rocky Mountain School 1700 S Holly St, DNVR, 80224	2198	B5
Rolling Hills Elementary School 5756 S Biscay St, AphC, 80015	2369	D1
Rooney Ranch Elementary School 2200 S Coors St, LKWD, 80228	2193	B7
Rosedale Elementary School 2330 S Sherman St, DNVR, 80210	2196	E7
Rose Hill Elementary School 6900 E 58th Av, CMCY, 80022	2030	C3
Roxborough Elementary School 8000 Village Cir W, DgsC, 80125	2531	A6
Running Creek Elementary School 900 S Elbert St, ELIZ, 80107	2793	B2
Running River School 2650 Table Mesa Dr, BLDR, 80305	1686	E7
Runyon Elementary School 7455 S Elati St, LITN, 80120	2364	D5

Denver Regional Points of Interest Index

FEATURE NAME Address City ZIP Code	MAP#	GRID
Russell Elementary School 5150 Allison St, ARVD, 80002	2026	D5
Ryan Elementary School 1405 Centaur Village Dr, LAFT, 80026	1690	A7
Ryan Elementary School 5851 W 115th Av, WSTR, 80020	1859	B3
Sabin Elementary School 3050 S Vrain St, DNVR, 80236	2279	C2
Sable Elementary School 2601 N Sable Blvd, AURA, 80011	2116	B3
Sacred Heart of Jesus School 1317 Mapleton Av, BLDR, 80304	1686	C1
Saddle Ranch Elementary School 805 W English Sparrow Tr, DgsC, 80129	2448	D6
Sagebrush Elementary School 14700 E Temple Pl, AURA, 80015	2284	C5
Sage Elementary School 5001 Pennsylvania Av, BLDR, 80303	1687	C3
Sagewood Middle School 4725 Fox Sparrow Rd, DgsC, 80134	2622	B5
St. Andrew Lutheran School 12150 Andrews Dr, DNVR, 80239	2031	E5
St. Anne's Episcopal School 2701 York St, DNVR, 80205	2113	C3
St. Bernadette School 1100 Upham St, LKWD, 80214	2110	E6
St. Catherine of Siena School 4200 Federal Blvd, DNVR, 80211	2028	A7
St. Francis de Sales School 235 S Sherman St, DNVR, 80209	2196	E2
St. James School 1250 Newport St, DNVR, 80220	2114	C5
St. John's Lutheran School 700 S Franklin St, DNVR, 80209	2197	B3
St. John the Baptist Catholic School 350 Emery St, LGMT, 80501	1439	B2
St. Joseph's School 604 W 6th Av, DNVR, 80204	2112	D7
St. Louis Catholic School 925 Grant Av, LSVL, 80027	1689	C7
St. Louis School 3301 S Sherman St, EGLD, 80113	2280	E2
St. Mary's Academy 4545 S University Blvd, CHLV, 80113	2281	C6
St. Pius X School 13680 E 14th Pl, AURA, 80011	2116	B5
St. Rose of Lima School 1345 W Dakota Av, DNVR, 80223	2196	C2
Saints Peter & Paul School 3920 Pierce St, WTRG, 80033	2111	A1
St. Therese School 1200 Kenton St, AURA, 80010	2115	C5
St. Thomas More Catholic School 7071 E Otero Av, CTNL, 80112	2366	C7
St. Vincent de Paul School 1164 S Josephine St, DNVR, 80210	2197	C4
Samuels Elementary School 3985 S Vincennes Ct, DNVR, 80237	2282	E4
Sanborn Elementary School 2235 Vivian St, LGMT, 80501	1355	E5
Sanchez Elementary School 655 Sir Galahad Dr, LAFT, 80026	1690	D6
Sandburg Elementary School 6900 S Elizabeth St, CTNL, 80122	2365	C4
Sand Creek Elementary School 8898 S Maplewood Dr, DgsC, 80126	2449	B2
Schenck Elementary School 1300 S Lowell Blvd, DNVR, 80219	2195	E4
Schmitt Elementary School 1820 S Vallejo St, DNVR, 80223	2196	B6
Second Creek Middle School 9950 Laredo Dr, CMCY, 80022	1864	D7
Secrest Elementary School 6875 W 64th Av, ARVD, 80003	2026	E2
Sedalia Elementary School 5449 N Huxtable St, DgsC, 80135	2617	B5
Shadow Ridge Middle School 12551 Holly St, TNTN, 80241	1862	A1
Shaffer Elementary School 7961 S Sangre de Cristo Rd, JfnC, 80127	2362	A7
Shaw Heights Middle School 8780 Circle Dr, AdmC, 80031	1943	D3
Shelterwood High School 12550 Zuni St, WSTR, 80234	1776	A7
Shelton Elementary School 420 Crawford St, GOLD, 80401	2191	E1
Sheperd Valley Waldorf School 6500 W Drycreek Pkwy, BldC, 80503	1520	C6
Shepherd of the Hills Christian School 7691 S University Blvd, CTNL, 80122	2365	C6
Sheridan Green Elementary School 10951 Harlan St, WSTR, 80020	1859	A4
Sheridan High School 3201 W Oxford Av, SRDN, 80110	2279	E4
Sheridan Middle School 4107 S Federal Blvd, SRDN, 80110	2280	A5
Sherrelwood Elementary School 8095 Kalamath St, AdmC, 80221	1944	C5
Shining Mountain Waldorf High School 1179 Union Av, BLDR, 80304	1602	C4
Shining Mountain Waldorf Lower School 999 Violet Av, BLDR, 80304	1602	C4
Shrine of St. Anne School 7320 Grant Pl, ARVD, 80002	2026	E4
Side Creek Elementary School 19191 E Iliff Pl, AURA, 80013	2201	C6
Sierra Elementary School 7751 Oak St, ARVD, 80005	1941	E6
Sierra Middle School 6651 E Pine Ln, DgsC, 80138	2453	D4
Silver Creek Middle/Senior High School 4901 Nelson Rd, BldC, 80503	1436	B4
Silver State Baptist School 875 S Sheridan Blvd, LKWD, 80226	2195	B3
Sinclair Middle School 300 W Chenango Av, EGLD, 80110	2280	D6
Singing Hills Elementary School 41012 Madrid Dr, EbtC, 80138	2540	A7
Sixth Avenue Elementary School 560 N Vaughn St, AURA, 80011	2116	A7
Skinner Middle School 3435 W 40th Av, DNVR, 80211	2111	E1
Skyline High School 600 E Mountain View Av, LGMT, 80501	1356	D7
Skyline Vista Elementary School 7395 Zuni St, WSTR, 80030	1944	A6
Skyview Elementary School 5021 E 123rd Av, TNTN, 80241	1862	A1
Skyview High School 8990 York St, TNTN, 80229	1945	C3
Slater Elementary School 8605 W 23rd Av, LKWD, 80215	2110	C3
Slavens Elementary School 3000 S Clayton St, DNVR, 80210	2281	C2
Smedley Elementary School 4250 Shoshone St, DNVR, 80211	2028	B7
Smiley Middle School 2540 Holly St, DNVR, 80207	2114	B3
Smith Elementary School 3590 Jasmine St, DNVR, 80207	2114	B1
Smoky Hills High School 16100 E Smoky Hill Rd, AURA, 80015	2284	E6
Soar High School 805 Burbank St, BMFD, 80020	1774	C7
Southeast Elementary School 1595 E Southern St, BGTN, 80601	1696	D7
South Elementary School 305 S 5th Av, BGTN, 80601	1696	B6
Southern Hills Middle School 1500 Knox Dr, BLDR, 80305	1771	B1
South High School 1700 E Louisiana Av, DNVR, 80210	2197	B4
South Lakewood Elementary School 8425 W 1st Av, LKWD, 80226	2194	D1
South Middle School 12310 E Parkview Dr, AURA, 80011	2115	E7
Southmoor Elementary School 3755 S Magnolia Wy, DNVR, 80237	2282	C3
South Street Elementary School 1100 South St, CSRK, 80104	2704	A7
Spangler Elementary School 1440 Collyer St, LGMT, 80501	1356	B7
Standley Lake High School 9300 W 104th Av, WSTR, 80021	1858	B6
Stanley British Primary School 350 Quebec St, DNVR, 80230	2198	D1
Stargate School 3951 Cottonwood Lake Blvd, TNTN, 80241	1777	D6
Steck Elementary School 425 Ash St, DNVR, 80220	2113	E7
Stedman Elementary School 2940 Dexter St, DNVR, 80207	2113	E2
Steele Elementary School 320 S Marion Pkwy, DNVR, 80209	2197	A2
Stein Elementary School 80 S Teller St, LKWD, 80226	2194	E1
Stevens Elementary School 4001 Reed St, WTRG, 80033	2110	E1
Stober Elementary School 2300 Urban St, LKWD, 80215	2109	D3
Stony Creek Elementary School 7203 S Everett St, JfnC, 80128	2362	C5
Stott Elementary School 6600 Yank Wy, ARVD, 80004	2025	C1
Stukey Elementary School 11080 Grant Dr, NHGN, 80233	1860	E4
Summit Elementary School 18201 E Quincy Av, AURA, 80013	2285	B5
Summit Middle Charter School 4655 Hanover Av, BLDR, 80305	1687	B7
Summit Ridge Middle School 11809 W Coal Mine Av, JfnC, 80127	2361	D3
Summit View Elementary School 10200 S Piedmont Dr, DgsC, 80126	2449	C6
Sunrise Elementary School 4050 S Genoa Wy, AURA, 80013	2285	D4
Sunset Middle School 1300 S Sunset St, LGMT, 80501	1438	E5
Sunset Ridge Elementary School 9451 N Hooker St, WSTR, 80031	1943	E1
Sunshine Academy 1395 Lowell Blvd, DNVR, 80204	2111	E5
Superior Elementary School 1800 S Indiana St, SUPE, 80027	1773	A6
Swansea Elementary School 4650 Columbine St, DNVR, 80216	2029	C6
Swanson Elementary School 6055 W 68th Av, ARVD, 80003	2027	A1
Tarver Elementary School 3500 Summit Grove Pkwy, TNTN, 80241	1777	D5
Teller Elementary School 1150 Garfield St, DNVR, 80206	2113	D6
Tennyson Knolls Elementary School 6330 Tennyson St, AdmC, 80003	2027	D2
The Living School 5001 Pennsylvania Av, BLDR, 80303	1687	C3
Theodor Herzl Jewish Day School 2450 S Wabash St, AphC, 80231	2198	E7
The Quest Academy 1008 Depot Hill Rd, BMFD, 80020	1774	C7
The Rocky Mtn Sch for the Gifted & Creative 5490 Spine Rd, BLDR, 80301	1604	A1
Thomas Jefferson High School 3950 S Holly St, DNVR, 80237	2282	B4
Thomson Elementary School 7750 Harlan St, WSTR, 80003	1943	B6
Thornton Elementary School 991 E Eppinger Blvd, TNTN, 80229	1945	A2
Thornton High School 9351 Washington St, TNTN, 80229	1944	E2
Thornton Middle School 9451 Hoffman Wy, TNTN, 80229	1945	A1
Thunder Ridge High School 1991 W Wildcat Reserve Pkwy, DgsC, 80129	2448	B5
Thunder Ridge Middle School 5250 S Picadilly St, AphC, 80015	2286	A7
Timberline Elementary School 5500 S Killarney St, CTNL, 80015	2369	E1
Tollgate Elementary School 701 S Kalispell Wy, AURA, 80017	2200	D3
Trailblazer Elementary School 9760 S Hackberry St, DgsC, 80129	2448	A5
Trails West Elementary School 5400 S Waco St, CTNL, 80015	2285	B7
Traylor Fundamental Academy 2900 S Ivan Wy, DNVR, 80227	2279	B2
Triumph High School 10595 Highway 119, GpnC, 80403	1933	B7
Twain Elementary School 6901 S Franklin St, CTNL, 80122	2365	B5
Twin Peaks Charter Academy 820 Main St, LGMT, 80501	1439	B1
University Hill Elementary School 956 16th St, BLDR, 80302	1686	D4
University Hills Lutheran School 4949 E Eastman Av, DNVR, 80222	2282	A2
University of Denver High School 2306 E Evans Av, DNVR, 80210	2197	C6
University Park Elementary School 2300 S St. Paul St, DNVR, 80210	2197	D7
Ute Creek Secondary Academy 1198 Boston Av, LGMT, 80501	1439	A3
Ute Meadows Elementary School 11050 W Meadows Dr, JfnC, 80127	2361	E6
Valdez Elementary School 2525 W 29th Av, DNVR, 80211	2112	A2
Valley View Elementary School 660 W 70th Av, AdmC, 80221	1944	D7
Valverde Elementary School 2030 W Alameda Av, DNVR, 80223	2196	B2
Van Arsdale Elementary School 7535 Alkire St, ARVD, 80005	1941	B6
Van Dellen Christian School 4200 E Warren Av, DNVR, 80222	2197	E7
Vanderhoof Elementary School 5875 Routt Ct, ARVD, 80004	2025	E3
Vassar Elementary School 18101 E Vassar Pl, AURA, 80013	2201	B7
Vaughn Elementary School 1155 N Vaughn St, AURA, 80011	2116	A5
Vikan Middle School 879 Jessup St, BGTN, 80601	1696	C7
Village East Community Elementary School 1433 S Oakland St, AURA, 80012	2199	D5
Virginia Court Elementary School 395 S Troy St, AURA, 80012	2199	E2
Vista Grande Elementary School 8845 Wagner St, AdmC, 80031	1943	C3
Vista Ridge Academy 3100 Ridge View Dr, ERIE, 80516	1692	B4
Vivian Elementary School 10500 W 25th Av, LKWD, 80215	2110	A3
Waldorf School 987 Locust Av, BLDR, 80304	1602	B4
Waldorf School of Denver 735 E Florida Av, DNVR, 80210	2197	A5
Walnut Hills Community Elementary School 8195 E Costilla Blvd, CTNL, 80112	2366	E5
Warder Elementary School 7840 Carr Dr, ARVD, 80005	1942	C6
Weber Elementary School 8725 W 81st Pl, ARVD, 80005	1942	C4
Welchester Elementary School 13000 W 10th Av, JfnC, 80401	2109	C6
Westgate Elementary School 8550 W Vassar Dr, LKWD, 80227	2278	D1
West High School 951 Elati St, DNVR, 80204	2112	D6
West Jefferson Elementary School 26501 Barkley Rd, JfnC, 80433	2442	A5
West Jefferson Middle School 9449 S Barnes Av, JfnC, 80433	2442	A4
Westlake Middle School 2800 W 135th Av, BMFD, 80020	1776	A5
Westland Christian Academy 430 S Kipling St, LKWD, 80226	2194	B3
West Middle School 10100 E 13th Av, AURA, 80010	2115	B5
West Middle School 5151 S Holly St, GDVL, 80121	2282	B7
Westminster Elementary School 7482 N Irving St, WSTR, 80030	1943	E6
Westminster High School 4276 W 68th Av, WSTR, 80030	2027	D1
Westminster Hills Elementary School 4105 W 80th Av, WSTR, 80031	1943	D5
Westridge Elementary School 10785 W Alamo Pl, JfnC, 80127	2362	A2
Westview Elementary School 1300 Roseanna Dr, NHGN, 80234	1860	C5
Westview Middle School 1651 Airport Rd, LGMT, 80503	1355	A7
West Woods Elementary School 16650 W 72nd Av, ARVD, 80007	1940	C7
Wheat Ridge High School 9505 W 32nd Av, WTRG, 80033	2110	B2
Wheat Ridge Middle School 7101 W 38th Av, WTRG, 80033	2110	E1
Wheeling Elementary School 472 S Wheeling St, AURA, 80012	2200	A3
Whiteman Elementary School 451 Newport St, DNVR, 80220	2114	C7
Whitman Elementary School 6557 S Acoma St, LITN, 80120	2364	E3
Whittier Elementary School 2008 Pine St, BLDR, 80302	1686	D1
Whittier Elementary School 2480 Downing St, DNVR, 80205	2113	A3
Wildcat Mountain Elementary School 6585 E Lionshead Pkwy, DgsC, 80124	2450	C6
Wilder Elementary School 4300 W Ponds Cir, AphC, 80123	2363	D3
William Smith Alternative High School 875 Peoria St, AURA, 80010	2115	D6
Willow Creek Elementary School 7855 S Willow Wy, CTNL, 80112	2367	A7
Wilmore-Davis Elementary School 7975 W 41st Av, WTRG, 80033	2026	D7
Wilmot Elementary School 5124 S Hatch Dr, JfnC, 80439	2357	B1

FEATURE NAME Address City ZIP Code	MAP#	GRID
Witt Elementary School 10255 W 104th Dr, WSTR, 80021	1858	A6
WM E Bishop Elementary School 3100 S Elati St, EGLD, 80110	2280	D2
Woodglen Elementary School 11717 Madison St, TNTN, 80233	1861	D3
Woodrow Wilson Academy 8300 W 94th Av, WSTR, 80021	1942	C1
Wyco Drive Elementary School 11551 Wyco Dr, NHGN, 80233	1861	B3
Wyman Elementary School 1690 Williams St, DNVR, 80218	2113	B4
Yale Elementary School 16001 E Yale Av, AURA, 80013	2284	D1
York Junior High School 9200 York St, TNTN, 80229	1945	C2
Zerger Elementary School 9050 Field St, WSTR, 80021	1942	C2
Zion Evangelical Lutheran School 2600 S Wadsworth Blvd, LKWD, 80227	2278	E1
Zion Lutheran School 1400 Skeel St, BGTN, 80601	1696	D6

Shopping Centers

FEATURE NAME Address City ZIP Code	MAP#	GRID
Abilene Street Market S Abilene St, AURA, 80012	2200	B4
Applewood Village Shopping Center Applewood Center Dr, WTRG, 80033	2109	C2
Arapahoe Crossing E Arapahoe Rd, AphC, 80016	2368	E3
Aurora Mall 14200 E Alameda Av, AURA, 80012	2200	B2
Belmar 7200 W Alameda Av, LKWD, 80226	2194	E2
Bowles Crossing 8398 W Long Dr, JfnC, 80123	2362	D1
Broadway Marketplace W Alameda Av, DNVR, 80223	2196	D2
Buckingham Square Shopping Center 1306 S Havana St, AURA, 80012	2199	C4
Cherry Creek Shopping Center 3000 E 1st Av, DNVR, 80206	2197	C1
Colorado Mills 14500 W Colfax Av, LKWD, 80401	2109	A6
Crossroads Mall 1600 Arapahoe Av, BLDR, 80301	1686	E2
East Bank Shopping Center 13701 E Quincy Av, AURA, 80014	2284	B4
Flatacres Market Center E Hilltop Rd, PARK, 80134	2537	D1
Flatiron Marketplace Flatiron Marketplace Dr, BMFD, 80021	1773	E7
FlatIron Crossing 1 W Flatiron Cir, BMFD, 80021	1773	D7
Huron Plaza Shopping Center 700 W 84th Av, TNTN, 80221	1944	C4
Lakeside Center 5801 W 44th Av, LKSD, 80212	2027	B7
Marketplace 3001 S Parker Rd, AURA, 80014	2283	C1
Marketplace at Northglenn 10590 Melody Dr, NHGN, 80234	1860	D5
Parker Pavilions Pavilion Dr, DgsC, 80134	2537	D1
Park Meadows 8401 S Park Meadows Center Dr, LNTR, 80124	2451	B1
Pioneer Hills S Chambers Rd, AURA, 80015	2368	C1
Prime Outlets Castle Rock 5050 Factory Shops Blvd, CSRK, 80108	2703	B1
Quebec Square at Stapleton Quebec St, DNVR, 80216	2030	C7
Southglenn Mall 6911 S University Blvd, CTNL, 80122	2365	B4
Southlands S Quebec St, GDVL, 80111	2366	D1
Southwest Plaza 8501 W Bowles Av, JfnC, 80123	2362	C2
Twin Peaks Mall 1250 S Hover St, LGMT, 80501	1438	D5
Westland Towne Center W Colfax Av, LKWD, 80215	2110	A5
Westminster Mall 5433 W 88th Av, WSTR, 80031	1943	B3

Subdivisions & Neighborhoods

FEATURE NAME	MAP#	GRID
Alcott, DNVR	2111	D1
Arapahoe East, CTNL	2367	B4
Bear Valley, DNVR	2278	E1
Beverly Heights, GOLD	2107	D5
Capitol Hill Annex, DNVR	2113	A5
Cherry Creek, DNVR	2197	C1
Clark Farms, PARK	2453	C5
Eastlake, TNTN	1777	B7
Eastridge, AURA	2199	C7
Edgemont, LKWD	2109	D6
Fort Logan, DNVR	2279	E6
Gateway, AURA	2200	A7
Green Mountain, JfnC	2193	B2
Green Mountain Estates, LKWD	2193	B4
Green Mountain Village, LKWD	2193	D4
Heather Ridge, AURA	2200	A6
Highlands, DNVR	2112	A2
High-Mar, BLDR	1687	C6
Howells, LITN	2364	C2
Loretto Heights, DNVR	2280	A2
Montbello, DNVR	2032	A4
Montclair, DNVR	2114	B5
North Yard, DNVR	2028	C5
Park Hill, DNVR	2114	A1
Sable, AURA	2116	A1
Sandown, DNVR	2030	D7
South Denver, DNVR	2196	D2
Stockyards, DNVR	2029	B6
Union Stock Yards, DNVR	2029	A6
University Park, DNVR	2197	A6
Wellshire, DNVR	2198	B6
Westwood, DNVR	2195	C5
Windsor Gardens, DNVR	2199	A2

Transportation

FEATURE NAME	MAP#	GRID
10th & Osage Station, DNVR	2112	C6
14th & California Station, DNVR	2112	D4
14th & Stout Station, DNVR	2112	D4
16th & California Station, DNVR	2112	D4
16th & Stout Station, DNVR	2112	D4
18th & California Station, DNVR	2112	D4
18th & Stout Station, DNVR	2112	D4
20th & Welton Station, DNVR	2112	E4
25th & Welton Station, DNVR	2112	E3
27th & Welton Station, DNVR	2113	A3
29th & Welton Station, DNVR	2113	A3
30th & Downing Station, DNVR	2113	A2
Alameda Station, DNVR	2196	D2
Amtrak-Denver, DNVR	2112	C3
Auraria West Campus Station, DNVR	2112	B5
Broadway Station, DNVR	2196	E4
Civic Center Station, DNVR	2112	E5
Colfax at Auraria Station, DNVR	2112	C5
Englewood Station, EGLD	2280	D3
Evans Station, DNVR	2196	D6
Greyhound-Aurora, AURA	2116	C5
Greyhound-Boulder, BLDR	1603	A6
Greyhound-Castle Rock, CSRK	2703	D6
Greyhound-Denver, DNVR	2112	D3
Greyhound-Englewood, EGLD	2280	D3
Greyhound-Longmont, LGMT	1439	A2
Invesco Field at Mile High Station, DNVR	2112	B4
Littleton Downtown Station, LITN	2364	B2
Littleton/Mineral Station, LITN	2364	A6
Market Street Station, DNVR	2112	C4
Oxford Station, EGLD	2280	C4
Pepsi Ctr Six Flags Elitch Gardens Station, - DNVR	2112	B4
Union Station, DNVR	2112	C3
University Station, DNVR	2197	B6

Visitor Information

FEATURE NAME Address City ZIP Code	MAP#	GRID
Boulder Convention Visitors Bureau 2440 Pearl St, BLDR, 80302	1686	E1
Denver Metro Convention & Visitors Bureau 1555 California St, DNVR, 80202	2112	D4
Denver Visitors Information Center 918 16th St Mall, DNVR, 80202	2112	D4
Dinosaur Ridge Visitors Center 16831 W Alameda Pkwy, JfnC, 80401	2192	C5
Golden Gate Canyon Visitor Center 3873 Golden Gate Canyon Rd, GpnC, 80403	1935	D7
Visitor Center W Morrison Rd, LKWD, 80465	2276	E4

Note Page

Note Page

Note Page

Note Page

RAND McNALLY

Thank you for purchasing this Rand McNally Street Guide!
We value your comments and suggestions.

Please help us serve you better by completing this postage-paid reply card.
This information is for internal use ONLY and will not be distributed or sold to any external third party.

Missing pages? Maybe not... Please refer to the "Using Your Street Guide" page for further explanation.

Street Guide Title: Denver Regional **ISBN# 0-528-99964-8** **Edition: 2006** **MKT: DEN**

Today's Date: ____________ Gender: ☐M ☐F Age Group: ☐18-24 ☐25-31 ☐32-40 ☐41-50 ☐51-64 ☐65+

1. What type of industry do you work in?
   ☐Real Estate ☐Trucking ☐Delivery ☐Construction ☐Utilities ☐Government
   ☐Retail ☐Sales ☐Transportation ☐Landscape ☐Service & Repair
   ☐Courier ☐Automotive ☐Insurance ☐Medical ☐Police/Fire/First Response
   ☐Other, please specify: ____________
2. What type of job do you have in this industry? ____________
3. Where did you purchase this Street Guide? (store name & city) ____________
4. Why did you purchase this Street Guide? ____________
5. How often do you purchase an updated Street Guide? ☐Annually ☐2 yrs. ☐3-5 yrs. ☐Other: ____________
6. Where do you use it? ☐Primarily in the car ☐Primarily in the office ☐Primarily at home ☐Other: ____________
7. How do you use it? ☐Exclusively for business ☐Primarily for business but also for personal or leisure use
   ☐Both work and personal evenly ☐Primarily for personal use ☐Exclusively for personal use
8. What do you use your Street Guide for?
   ☐Find Addresses ☐In-route navigation ☐Planning routes ☐Other: ____________
   Find points of interest: ☐Schools ☐Parks ☐Buildings ☐Shopping Centers ☐Other: ____________
9. How often do you use it? ☐Daily ☐Weekly ☐Monthly ☐Other: ____________
10. Do you use the internet for maps and/or directions? ☐Yes ☐No
11. How often do you use the internet for directions? ☐Daily ☐Weekly ☐Monthly ☐Other: ____________
12. Do you use any of the following mapping products in addition to your Street Guide?
    ☐Folded paper maps ☐Folded laminated maps ☐Wall maps ☐GPS ☐PDA ☐In-car navigation ☐Phone maps
13. What features, if any, would you like to see added to your Street Guide? ____________
14. What features or information do you find most useful in your Rand McNally Street Guide? (please specify)
15. Please provide any additional comments or suggestions you have. ____________

We strive to provide you with the most current updated information available if you know of a map correction, please notify us here.

Where is the correction? Map Page #: ____________ Grid #: ____________ Index Page #: ____________

Nature of the correction: ☐Street name missing ☐Street name misspelled ☐Street information incorrect
☐Incorrect location for point of interest ☐Index error ☐Other: ____________

Detail: ____________

I would like to receive information about updated editions and special offers from Rand McNally
☐via e-mail E-mail address: ____________
☐via postal mail
Your Name: ____________ Company (if used for work): ____________
Address: ____________ City/State/ZIP: ____________

Thank you for your time and help. We are working to serve you better.
This information is for internal use ONLY and will not be distributed or sold to any external third party.

CUT ALONG DOTTED LINE

CUT ALONG DOTTED LINE

SG-noCD.06

TAPE SHUT TAPE SHUT

get directions at
randmcnally.com

CUT ALONG DOTTED LINE

2ND FOLD LINE

BUSINESS REPLY MAIL

FIRST-CLASS MAIL PERMIT NO. 388 CHICAGO IL

POSTAGE WILL BE PAID BY ADDRESSEE

RAND MCNALLY
CONSUMER AFFAIRS
PO BOX 7600
CHICAGO IL 60680-9915

1ST FOLD LINE

The most trusted name on the map.

You'll never need to ask for directions again with these Rand McNally products!

- EasyFinder® Laminated Maps
- Folded Maps
- Street Guides
- Wall Maps
- CustomView Wall Maps
- Road Atlases
- Motor Carriers' Road Atlases

CUT ALONG DOTTED LINE

SGTG.06